WHO'S WHO IN CALIFORNIA

WHO'S WHO
In California.®

The Twelfth Edition
1979-1980

Published By
WHO'S WHO HISTORICAL SOCIETY

SAN CLEMENTE, CALIFORNIA 92672

TWELFTH EDITION
Sarah Alice Vitale, Editor

Library of Congress Catalog Card Number 56-1715

International Standard Book Number 0-9603166-0-4

Internation Standard Serial Number 0511-8948

PRINTED IN THE UNITED STATES OF AMERICA

Contents

Dedication

The contributions of today's outstanding Californians rest on a foundation built by men and women of achievement whose biographies have graced the pages of past volumes of WHO'S WHO IN CALIFORNIA. This edition is dedicated in memory of those former Californians of distinction, especially

Bing Crosby
A.J. Haagen-Smit
Conrad Hilton
George Moscone
Joseph Quinn
Leopold Stokowski
Frank Tallman
John Wayne

Foreword

This edition of **WHO'S WHO IN CALIFORNIA** is the most comprehensive ever. Its pages record the careers of more notable Californians than any previous volume. Here you will find a wealth of biographical information on outstanding citizens from all fields of endeavor — the arts, business, science, education and government.

First published more than fifty years ago, **WHO'S WHO IN CALIFORNIA** is today recognized as the most reliable biographical reference work on Californians of distinction.

First and foremost, our on-going objective is to make this book the most useful biographical dictionary of its kind for those who turn to it for information — writers, researchers, librarians, historians, students and journalists.

Each biographical profile published in this edition was submitted directly to the Who's Who Historical Society by the biographees themselves, thus insuring data that is accurate and current.

We use two essential criteria in the selection of biographees. Achievement and position. Those individuals who have made significant contributions in their field or to society are eligible for inclusion. Their achievements are the kind often described as "uncommon," deeds that set them apart from their contemporaries.

Others are chosen by virtue of the position they occupy. Though such positions may be as varied as life itself, all are characterized by a high level of responsibility. In any event and in all cases, we insist that each candidate admitted to these pages display a life marked by demonstrated merit, excellence in one's chosen pursuits and service to humankind.

There is another thought worth noting. Society traditionally has been duty-bound to preserve the deeds of its most notable citizens. Such preservation becomes an enduring reminder of the striving for and, in many instances, the attainment of, greatness.

By setting forth the historical record of this state's citizens of achievement, this book serves to achieve that end.

The Publisher

Message From The State Librarian

California is frequently referred to as a nation of twenty-two million people.

So it is, but to one who has criss-crossed its length and breadth many times, the diversity and contrast make it seem more like a great federation of local governments. Differences in geography, climate, industry and business are reflected in the people whose interests are as varied as the land they live on. The underlying uniformity is hard to see and describe but it is there in people's philosophical commitment to their own place, to their local loyalties, and in the responsibility leaders take in order to insure the success and continuity of each locality.

In every community there are dynamic organizations of local leaders whose stake in their area is primary to their thinking. The League of Women Voters in Los Angeles, the Rotary Club in Colusa and the Friends of the Library of Delano are just three of the scores of such organizations. All together it is the public spirited people in diverse localities who make California the strong and vigorous state it is.

The variety of interests and concerns of the entire population is reflected in its elected officials. Thus, California has Democratic Governor Edmund G. Brown, Jr., and Republican Lieutenant Governor Mike Curb as well as legislators who speak for every political, social and economic viewpoint. All are constantly seeking to persuade, compromise, and reach agreement in the law and governance of this huge state.

California bustle and activity began when gold was discovered. Energetic and ambitious people began to pour into the state and many left their mark in history. Their manuscripts, letters, records and stories of exploits are now treasures in the California State Library, established in 1850. The library settled in 1928 in its present location across from the capitol building. One of its specific charges is collection and preservation of California historical documents to be freely available to all.

Letters, manuscripts, books and papers continue to flow into this rich historical and genealogical preserve. At present there are some 24,000 portraits, each identified by name, as well as an index which begins with the first issue of the first newspaper in California, The Californian, dated August 15, 1846. Through this remarkable listing, one may locate thousands of stories of people, places and events.

The concerned residents of California are making today's events happen. From the growers of Tulare County to the transistor makers in the Santa Clara Valley, they are becoming part of the California record. The biographical accounts of many individuals are enriching history. The accounts of their lives and the events of their times can be found in the ever-lengthening history and growing collection of the California State Library.

ETHEL S. CROCKETT
California State Librarian

Guide To Biographies

The biographical profiles in **WHO'S WHO IN CALIFORNIA** are arranged alphabetically according to the surname of the biographee. Where identical surnames occur, the first given name is used. If both surname and first given name are identical, the second given name is used to arrange the names alphabetically.

In the case of compound hyphenated surnames, profiles are arranged according to the first member of the compound.

Some biographees delete part of their full name in ordinary usage. In those instances parentheses are used to indicate that portion of the name which is deleted. For example, SMITH, J(OHN) indicates that the usual form of the name is J. Smith.

Each biographical profile is uniformly composed of the following data, hereby offered in chronological order as a convenient guide:

1. Name
2. Occupation
3. Birthdate and Place
4. Parents
5. Notable Relatives
6. Education
7. Marriage
8. Children
9. Career
10. Career-Related Activities
11. Special Achievements and Awards
12. Military Record
13. Organizations
14. Political Affiliation
15. Religion
16. Hobby and Recreation
17. Home Address
18. Office Address

Abbreviations

A.A. Associate in Arts
AAAS American Association for the Advancement of Science
A. and M. Agricultural and Mechanical
AAU Amateur Athletic Union
AAUP American Association of University Professors
AAUW American Association of University Women
A.B. Arts, Bachelor of
AB Alberta
ABC American Broadcasting Company
AC Air Corps
acad. academy
ACLU American Civil Liberties Union
A.C.P. American College of Physicians
A.C.S. American College of Surgeons.
ADA American Dental Association
adj. adjunct, adjutant
adj. gen. adjutant general
adm. admiral
adminstr. administrator
adminstrn. administration
adminstrv. administrative
adv. advocate
advt. advertising
AEC Atomic Energy Commission
aero. aeronautical, aeronautic
AFB Air Force Base
AFL-CIO American Federation of Labor and Congress of Industrial Organizations
AFTRA American Federation TV and Radio Artists
agri. agricultural, agriculture
AIA American Institute of Architects
AIEE American Institute of Electrical Engineers
AIM American Institute of Management
AK Alaska
AL Alabama
ALA American Library Association
Ala. Alabama
A.M. Arts, Master of
Am. American, America
AMA American Medical Association
A.M.E. African Methodist Episcopal
Amer., America, American
Amtrak National Railroad Passenger Corporation
anat. anatomical, anatomy
ANTA American National Theatre and Academy
anthrop. anthropological
AP Associated Press
APO Army Post Office
apptd. appointed
AR Arkansas
ARC American Red Cross
archeol. archeological
archtl. architectural
Ariz. Arizona
Ark. Arkansas
Arts D. Arts, Doctor of
arty. artillery
ASCAP American Society of Composers, Authors and Publishers
ASCE American Society of Civil Engineers
ASME American Society of Mechanical Engineers
assn. association

assoc., associate, associated
asst. assistant
ASTM American Society for Testing and Materials
astron. astronomical
ATSC Air Technical Service Command
AT&T American Telephone & Telegraph Company
atty. attorney
AUS Army of the United States
aux. Auxiliary
Ave. Avenue
AVMA American Veterinary Medical Association
AZ Arizona

B. Bachelor
b. born
B.A. Bachelor of Arts
B. Agr. Bachelor of Agriculture
Bapt. Baptist
B.Arch. Bachelor of Architecture
B.S.A. Bachelor of Agricultural Science
B.B.A. Bachelor of Business Administration
BBC British Broadcasting Corporation
B.C., British Columbia
B.C.E. Bachelor of Civil Engineering
B.Chir., Bachelor of Surgery
B.C.L. Bachelor of Civil Law
B.C.S. Bachelor of Commercial Science
B.D. Bachelor of Divinity
bd. board
B.E. Bachelor of Education
B.E.E. Bachelor of Electrical Engineering
B.F.A. Bachelor of Fine Arts
bibl. biblical
bibliog. bibliographical
biog. biographical
biol. biological
B.J. Bachelor of Journalism
B.L. Bachelor of Letters
bldg. building
B.L.S. Bachelor of Library Science
Blvd. Boulevard
bn. battalion
bot. botanical
B.P.E. Bachelor of Physical Education
br. branch
B.R.E. Bachelor of Religious Education
brig. gen. brigadier general
Brit. British, Britannica
Bro. Brother
B.S. Bachelor of Science
B.S.A. Bachelor of Agricultural Science
BSA Boy Scouts of America
B.S.D. Bachelor of Didactic Science
B.S.T. Bachelor of Sacred Theology
B.Th. Bachelor of Theology
bur. bureau
bus. business

CA California
CAA Civil Aeronautics Administration
CAB Civil Aeronautics Board
Calif. California
Cal Tech, California Institute of Technology

Can. Canada
CAP Civil Air Patrol
capt. captain
Cath. Catholic
cav. cavalry
CBC Canadian Broadcasting System
CBI China, Burma, India Theatre of Operations
CBS Columbia Broadcasting System
CCC Commodity Credit Corporation
CD Civil Defense
C.E. Corps of Engineers
CEO Chief Executive Officer
ch. church
Ch.D. Doctor of Chemistry
chem. chemical
Chem. E. Chemical Engineer
Chgo. Chicago
chmn. chairman
chpt. chapter
CIA Central Intelligence Agency
CIC Counter Intelligence Corps
clin. clinical
clk. clerk
C.L.U. Chartered Life Underwriter
C.M. Master in Surgery
CO Colorado
CMA, California Medical Association
Co., Company, County
C. of C. Chamber of Commerce
col. colonel
coll. college
Colo. Colorado
com. committee
comd. commanded
comdg. commanding
comdr. commander
commd. commissioned
comml. commercial
commn. commission
commr. commissioner
Conf. Conference
Conn. Connecticut
cons. consultant, consulting
consol. consolidated
constl. constitutional
constn. constitution
constrn. construction
contbd. contributed
contbg. contributing
contbr. contributor
Conv. Convention
coop., co-op. cooperative
CORE Congress of Racial Equality
corp. corporation
corr. correspondent, corresponding
C.P.A. Certified Public Accountant
C.P.H. Certificate of Public Health
cpl. corporal
CSC Civil Service Commission
ct. court
C.Z. Canal Zone

d. daughter
D. Doctor
D.Agr. Doctor of Agriculture
D.A.R. Daughters of the American Revolution
dau. daughter
DAV Disabled American Veterans
D.C., DC District of Columbia
D.C.L. Doctor of Civil Law
D.C.S. Doctor of Commercial Science
D.D. Doctor of Divinity
D.D.S. Doctor of Dental Surgery
DE Delaware
dec. deceased
def. defense

Del. Delaware
del. delegate, delegation
Dem. Democrat., Democratic
D.Eng. Doctor of Engineering
dep. deputy
dept. department
desc. descendant
devel. development
D.F.A. Doctor of Fine Arts
D.F.C. Distinguished Flying Cross
D.H.L. Doctor of Hebrew Literature
dir. director
dist. district
distbg. distributing
distbn. distribution
distbr. distributor
div. division, divinity, divorce
D.Litt. Doctor of Literature
D.M.D. Doctor of Medical Dentistry
D.M.S. Doctor of Medical Science
D.O. Doctor of Osteopathy
Dr. Drive
D.R.E. Doctor of Religious Education
D.S.C. Distinguished Service Cross
D.Sc. Doctor of Science
D.S.M. Distinguished Service Medal
D.S.T. Doctor of Sacred Theology
D.V.M. Doctor of Veterinary Medicine
D.V.S. Doctor of Veterinary Surgery

E. East
Eccles. Ecclesiastical
ecol. ecological
econ., economic, economy
E.D. Doctor of Engineering
ed., educated, editor
Ed.B. Bachelor of Education
Ed.D. Doctor of Education
edit. edition
Ed.M. Master of Education
edn. education
ednl. educational
EDP electronic data processing
E.E. Electrical Engineer
elec. electrical
ency. encyclopedia
Eng. England, English
engr. engineer
engring. engineering
environ. environmental
EPA Environmental Protection Agency
Episc. Episcopalian.
ERDA Energy Research and Development
    Administration
ETO European Theatre of Operations
Evang. Evangelical
exam. examination, examining
exec. executive
exhib., exhibit, exhibition
expt. experiment
exptl. experimental

F.A. Field Artillery
FAA Federal Aviation Administration
FBI Federal Bureau of Investigation
FCA Farm Credit Administration
FCC Federal Communication Commission
FDA Food and Drug Administration
FDIA Federal Deposit Insurance Administration
FDIC Federal Deposit Insurance Corporation
F.E. Forest Engineer
fed. federal
fedn. federation
fgn. foreign
FHA Federal Housing Administration
fin. financial, finance

FL Florida
Fla. Florida
FMC Federal Maritime Commission
found. foundation
FPC Federal Power Commission
FPO Fleet Post Office
frat., fraternity, fraternal
FRS Federal Reserve System
Ft. Fort
FTC Federal Trade Commission, Federal Tariff
    Commission

Ga., GA Georgia
GAO General Accounting Office
gastroent. gastroenterological
gen. general
geneal. genealogical
geod. geodetic
geog. geographic, geographical
geol. geological
geophys. geophysical
gerontol. gerontological
gov. governor
govt. government
govtl. governmental
grad. graduate
GSA General Services Administration
Gt. Great
GU Guam
gynecol. gynecological

hdqrs. headquarters
HEW Department of Health, Education and Welfare
H.H.D. Doctor of Humanities
HHFA Housing and Home Finance Agency
HI Hawaii
hist. historical, historic
H.M. Master of Humanics
hon. honorary, honorable
Ho. of Dels. House of Delegates
Ho. of Reps. House of Representatives
hort. horticultural
hosp. hospital
HUD Department of Housing and Urban Development
Hwy. Highway
H.S., High School

IA Iowa
IAEA International Atomic Energy Agency
IBM International Business Machines Corporation
ICC Interstate Commerce Commission
ID Idaho
IEEE Institute of Electrical and Electronics Engineers
IGY International Geophysical Year
IL Illinois
Ill. Illinois
ILO International Labor Organization
IMF International Monetary Fund
IN Indiana
Inc. Incorporated
incl. include, including
ind. independent
Ind. Indiana
indsl. industrial
inf. infantry
info. information
ins. insurance
insp. inspector
inst. institute
instr. instructor
Internat. international
intro. introduction
I.R.E. Institute of Radio Engineers
IRS Internal Revenue Service
ITT International Telephone & Telegraph Corporation
J.D. Doctor of Jurisprudence

j.g. junior grade
jour. journal.
jr. junior

Kans. Kansas
K.C. Knights of Columbus
KS Kansas
K.T. Knight Templar
Ky., KY Kentucky

L.A. Los Angeles
lab. laboratory
L.A.C.C. Los Angeles City College
lang. language
LB Long Beach
lectr. lecturer
L.D.S. Latter-Day Saints
L.H.D. Doctor of Humane Letters
L.I. Long Island
lit. literary, literature
Litt.B. Bachelor of Letters
Litt.D. Doctor of Letters
LL.B. Bachelor of Laws
LL.D. Doctor of Laws
LL.M. Master of Laws
Ln. Lane
L.S. Library Science (in degree)
lt. lieutenant
Ltd. Limited
Luth. Lutheran

m. married
M. Master
M.A. Master of Arts
MA Massachusetts
mag. magazine
M.Agr. Master of Agriculture
maj. major
M.Arch. Master in Architecture
Mass. Massachusetts
math. mathematical
MATS Military Air Transport Service
M.B. Bachelor of Medicine
M.B.A. Master of Business Administration
MBS Mutual Broadcasting System
M.C. Medical Corps
M.C.E. Master of Civil Engineering
mcht. merchant
M.D. Doctor of Medicine
Md., MD Maryland
mdse. merchandise
M.D.V. Doctor of Veterinary Medicine
M.E. Mechanical Engineer
ME Maine
M.E. Ch. Methodist Episcopal Church
mech. mechanical
M.Ed. Master of Education
med. medical
M.E.E. Master of Electrical Engineering
mem. member, memorial
met. metropolitan
metall. metallurgical
meteorol. meteorological
Meth. Methodist
Mex. Mexico
M.F. Master of Forestry
M.F.A. Master of Fine Arts
mfg. manufacturing
mfr. manufacturer
mgmt. management
mgr. manager
M.I. Military Intelligence
MI Michigan
Mich. Michigan
mil. military

Minn. Minnesota
Miss. Mississippi
M.I.T. Massachusetts Institute of Technology
mktg. marketing
M.L. Master of Laws
M.Litt. Master of Literature
M.L.S. Master of Library Science
M.M.E. Master of Mechanical Engineering
MN Minnesota
mng. managing
Mo., MO Missouri
Mont. Montana
M.P. Member of Parliament
M.P.E. Master of Physical Education
M.P.H. Master of Public Health
M.P.L. Master of Patent Law
M.R.E. Master of Religious Education
M.S. Master of Science
MS Mississippi
M.Sc. Master of Science
M.S.F. Master of Science of Forestry
M.S.T. Master of Sacred Theology
M.S.W. Master of Social Work
MT Montana
Mt. Mount
mus. museum, musical
Mus.B. Bachelor of Music
Mus.D. Doctor of Music
Mus.M. Master of Music

N. North
NAACP National Association for the Advancement of
    Colored People
N.Am. North America
NAM National Association of Manufacturers
NASA National Aeronautics and Space Administration
nat. national
NATO North Atlantic Treaty Organization
nav. navigation
NBC National Boradcasting Company
N.C., NC North Carolina
NCCJ National Conference of Christians and Jews
N.D., ND North Dakota
NE Nebraska
N.E. Northeast
NEA National Education Association
Nebr. Nebraska
neurol. neurological
Nev. Nevada
N.G. National Guard
N.H., NH New Hampshire
NIH National Institutes of Health
NIMH National Institute of Mental Health
N.J., NJ New Jersey
NLRB National Labor Relations Board
NM New Mexico
N.Mex. New Mexico
No. Northern
NORAD North American Air Defense
NOW National Organization for Women
NSC National Security Council
NSF National Science Foundation
NT Northwest Territories
numis. numismatic
NV Nevada
NW Northwest
N.Y., NY New York
N.Y.C. New York City
N.Z. New Zealand

OAS Organization of American States
obs. observatory
O.D. Doctor of Optometry
OEO Office of Economic Opportunity
O.E.S. Order of Eastern Star
ofcl. official

ofcr. officer
OH Ohio
OK Oklahoma
Okla. Oklahoma
ophthal. ophthalmological
ops. operations
OR Oregon
orch. orchestra
Oreg. Oregon
OSS Office of Strategic Services

Pa., PA Pennsylvania
P.C. Professional Corporation
Pasa., Pasadena
P.E.I. Prince Edward Island
PEN Poets, Playwrights, Editors, Essayists and Novelists
    (international association)
P.E.O. women's organization
pfc. private first class
PHA Public Housing Administration
pharm. Pharmaceutical
Pharm.D. Doctor of Pharmacy
Pharm.M. Master of Pharmacy
Ph.B. Bachelor of Philosophy
Ph.D. Doctor of Philosophy
Phila. Philadelphia
philos. philosophical
photog. photographic, photography
phys. physical
Pitts. Pittsburgh
Pl. Place
P.O. Post Office
P.O.B. Post Office Box
polit. political, politics
poly. polytechnic
prep. preparatory
pres. president
Presbyn. Presbyterian
prin. principal
proc. proceedings
prod. produced, producer
prof. professor
profl. professional
propr. proprietor
pro tem pro tempore
psychiat. psychiatric
psychol. psychological
PTA Parent-Teachers Association
pub. publisher, publishing, public
publ. publication
pvt. private

RCA Radio Corporation of America
rec. recreation
recd. received
ref. reference
rehab. rehabilitation
Rel., Religion, Rels.,
Rels., Relations
rep. representative
Repub. Republican
Res. residence
ret. retired
rev. review, revised
Rom. Cath., Roman Catholic
R.I., RI Rhode Island
R.N. Registered Nurse
ROTC Reserve Officers Training Corps
R.R. Railroad
Ry. Railway

s. son
S. South
SAC Strategic Air Command
S.A.G. Screen Actors Guild
SALT Strategic Arms Limitation Talks

S.Am. South America
san. sanitary
SAR Sons of the American Revolution
savs. savings
S.B. Bachelor of Science, Santa Barbara
SBA Small Business Administration
S.C., SC South Carolina
Sc.B. Bachelor of Science
Sc.D. Doctor of Science
sch. school
sci. science, scientific
S.D., San Diego
Sacto., Sacramento
SE Southeast
SEATO Southeast Asia Treaty Organization
secty. secretary
SEC Securities and Exchange Commission
sect. section
S.F. San Francisco
sem. seminary
Sen. Senator
sgt. sergeant
sis. Sister
S.J. Society of Jesus (Jesuit)
S.M. Master of Science
So. Southern
soc. society
sociol. sociological
sor. sorority
spec. special, specialist
splty. specialty
Sq. Square
sr. senior
S.R. Sons of the Revolution
S.S. Steamship
St. Saint, street
sta. station
S.T.B. Bachelor of Sacred Theology
S.T.D. Doctor of Sacred Theology
subs. subsidiary
supr. supervisor
supt. superintendent
surg. surgical, surgery, surgeon
SW Southwest
sym. symphony
syn. syndicate

tchr. teacher
tech. technical, technology
Tel. Telephone
temp. temporary
Tenn. Tennessee
Ter. Territory
Terr. Terrace
Tex. Texas
Th.D., Doctor of Theology
theol. theological, theology
Th.M. Master of Theology
TN Tennessee
tng. training
trans. transaction, transferred
transl. translation, translated
transp. transportation
treas. treasurer
TV television
TVA Tennessee Valley Authority
twp. township
TX Texas

U. University
UAW United Auto Workers
UCI University of California at Irvine
UCLA University of California at Los Angeles
UCSB University of California at Santa Barbara
UCSD University of California at San Diego

U.K. United Kingdom
UN United Nations
UNESCO United Nations Educational, Scientific and Cultural Organization
UNICEF United Nations International Children's Emergency Fund
univ. University
UPI United Press International
U.S. United States
U.S.A. United States of America
USAAF United States Army Air Force
USAF United States Air Force
USAFR United States Air Force Reserve
USAR United States Army Reserve
USC University of Southern California
USCG United States Coast Guard
USCGR United States Coast Guard Reserve
USIA United States Information Agency
USMC United States Marine Corps
USMCR United States Marine Corps Reserve
USN United States Navy
USNR United States Naval Reserve
USO United Service Organizations
USPHS United States Public Health Service
U.S.S. United States Ship
USSR Union of the Soviet Socialist Republics
UT Utah

VA Veterans Administration
Va., VA Virginia
vet. veteran
VFW Veterans of Foreign Wars
vice pres. vice president
vis. visiting
VISTA Volunteers in Service to America
vocat. vocational
vol. volunteer
v.p. vice president
vs versus
Vt., VT Vermont

W. West
WA Washington
WAC Women's Army Corps
Wash. Washington
WAVES Women's Reserve, U.S. Naval Reserve
WHO World Health Organization
WI Wisconsin
Wis. Wisconsin
WV West Virginia
W. Va. West Virginia
WY Wyoming
Wyo. Wyoming

YMCA Young Men's Christian Association
YMHA Young Men's Hebrew Association
YM & YWHA Young Men's and Young Women's Hebrew Association
Y.T., YT Yukon Territory
YWCA Young Women's Christian Association
yr. year

zool. zoological

---, to date

WHO'S WHO IN CALIFORNIA

A

AARONS, THEODORE
Biologist
b. Dec. 12, 1920, Fresno; s. David M. and Tina Aarons; B.S., 1943; postgrad. 1946, 1948; m. Queta Feldman, 1954, Salinas, Calif.; chil.: Daniel A., b. 1954; Siri, b. 1956. Career: research asst., entomology, 1941-42; entomologist, U.S. Army, 1943-46; entomologist, Mosquito Abatement Dists., Calif., 1946-58; dir., Berkeley Pacific Labs, 1959-68; dir., Unilab Research, 1969---; public health entomologist, Vector Control specialist. Publs., Mosquito Biology, 1946-55. Mem.: Soc. for Asian Art, S.F.; regent, John F. Kennedy Univ., Orinda; bd. mem., Univ. of Calif. Art Mus. Home: 104 Vicente Rd., Berkeley, CA 94705; Office: Unilab Research, 2800 Seventh St., Berkeley, CA 94710.

ABBERGER, ROGER ALAN
Interior Designer
b. June 4, 1931, Buffalo, N.Y.; s, William Albert and Ethel Ellen (Kulp) Abberger; B.F.A., Pratt Inst., Brooklyn, N.Y., 1955. Career: designer, Flannery & Assoc., Pittsburgh, 1955-56; designer, Griswold, Heckle & Keiser, 1956-57, N.Y.C.; pres., Roger Alan Abberger ASID, N.Y.C. and L.A., 1957---. Mem.: Am. Inst. Interior Designers, Phi Delta Theta. Hobby: theatre. Office: 1403 N. Laurel Ave., L.A., CA 90046.

ABERNETHY, JOHN LEO
Professor of Chemistry
b. Mar. 6, 1915, San Jose, Calif.; s. Elmer R. and Margaret May (Scott) Abernethy; B.A., UCLA, 1936; M.S., 1938 and Ph.D., 1940, Northwestern Univ.; research assoc., Medical Center, UCLA. Career: asst. prof., Univ. of Texas, 1940-45; research assoc., Northwestern Univ., 1945-47; asst. to full prof., Calif. State Univ. System, 1950-78; vis. assoc. prof. of chem., Claremont Men's College, 1961-62; Fulbright Fellow, San Marcos Univ., Lima, Peru, 1962-63; research assoc., Univ. of Calif., Davis, 1963-64; taught Navy V-22 students, Univ. of Texas, 1942-45. Editorial bd., Jour. of Chemical Education, 1956---; proceedings editor, Calif. Assn. Chem. Teachers. Author: research papers on stereochemistry, enzyme catalysis, papain, Jour. Organic Chem., Jour. Am. Chem. Soc., Tetrahedron, Jour. Chromatography; education papers, Jour. Chem. Educ., 1940---; text: Principles of Organic Chemistry; CACT Proceedings Editor, Calif. Assn. of Chem. Teachers, 1966---. Research grants: National Science Found., Sigma Xi, Research Corp., Radiation Research, Lab. Nuclear Med., UCLA. Mem.: pres., Sigma Xi Club, 1970-71; Alpha Chi Sigma, 1935; Phi Lambda Upsilon, 1938. Republican. Presbyterian. Hobbies: writing, chemical research. Rec.: swimming. Home: 4221 Evart St., No. E, Montclair, CA 91763; Office: Chem. Dept., Calif. State Polytechnic Univ., Pomona, CA 91768.

ABERNETHY, ROBERT GORDON
Correspondent, NBC TODAY Show
b. Nov. 5, 1927, Geneva, Switz.; s. Robert William and Lois May (Jones) Abernethy; ed. A.B. Princeton Univ., 1950; M.P.A., 1952; Woodrow Wilson Sch. of Pub. and Internat. Affairs; m. Jean Clarke Montgomery, Arcadia, Fla., Apr. 30, 1915; dau. Jane Montgomery, b. Feb. 16, 1957. Career: Editor, NBC News, Wash. 1952-55; NBC corr.: London, England, 1955-58; Wash. 1958-66; Los Angeles, 1966---; anchorman, KNBC's "Sixth Hour News," 1966-70; Wash. corr., TODAY Show, 1977---. Wrote and narrated NBC wkly. TV report, "Update," 1961-63. Author: Introduction To Tomorrow, publ. by Harcourt, Brace & World, 1966; A Primer on Communism, Many Shades of Black, TV documentaries, AUS. 1946-48. Trustee, Princeton Univ., 1974-77. Awards: Thomas Alva Edison Mass Media Award, best Am. hist. for youth, 1966; Hon. Mayor of Pac. Palisades, 1971. United Ch. of Christ. Office: 4001 Nebraska Ave., N.W., Wash., D.C. 20016.

ABRAMS, RICHARD M.
Professor of History
b. July 12, 1932, Brooklyn, N.Y.; s. Nathan and Ida (Levine) Abrams; A.B., Columbia Coll., 1953. A.M., 1955, Ph.D., 1962; m. Marcia Ash, Aug. 14, 1960, N.Y.C.; chil.: Laura Susan, b. Apr. 11, 1962; Robert Samuel, b. Jan. 2, 1964; Jennifer Sharon, b. June 2, 1966. Career: instr., lectr. hist., Columbia, 1951-60; instr. hist., Univ. Calif., Berkeley, 1961-62; asst. prof. 1962-66, assoc. prof. 1966-72, prof., 1972---; Fulbright prof. hist., London Sch. Eco. & Polit. Sci., 1968, Univ. London, 1968-69; dir., Nat. Endowment for the Humanities summer seminar for coll. tchrs., 1977, 1979. Author: Conservatism in a Progressive Era, Harvard Press, 1964; The Shaping of Twentieth Century America (w/Lawrence W. Levine), Little, Brown, 1972; The Unfinished Century (s/W.E. Leuchtenburg, et al), Little, Brown, 1973; The Issue of Federal Regulation, Rand McNally, 1963; The Burdens of Progress, Scott, Foresman, 1978. Office: Dept. of History, Univ. of Calif., Berkeley, CA 94720.

ABRAMS, YALE
Marketing Executive
b. Nov. 8, 1940, Phila., Pa.; s. Herman Bernard and Yetta (Magid) Abrams; B.S. Penn. State Univ., 1963; M.B.A., Temple Univ., 1970; m. Terry Lynn Salmon, Sept. 9, 1969, San Francisco; son, Kim Evan, b. Oct. 24, 1974. Buyer, The Boeing Co., Vertol Div., 1966-70; dir. adminstrn., Sta-Power Industries Inc., 1971-72; mgr. of mktg. adminstrn., Mobility Systems Inc., 1972-74; dir. mktg., Transport Pool Inc., 1974-75; mgmt. cons., 1975-76; mgr. of mktg. services, Ecodyne Colling Products, 1976---. Served AUS, 1964-66. Fin. chmn., Bus. & Profl. Advt. Assn. nat. convention, 1978; bd. dir., United Way for No. Bay and vice chmn., Central Sonoma Co., 1978-79. Mem. Sonoma County Press Club. Home: 440 Mayfield Dr., Santa Rosa, CA 95401; Office: P.O.B. 1267, Santa Rosa, CA 95403.

ABRAMSON, MICHELL N., JR.
V.P., Whitaker & Baxter
b. Jan. 14, 1926, S.F.; s. Michell N. and Edna (O'Brien) Abramson; A.B., Univ. of Calif., Berkeley, 1950; m. Mary Allerton Waldo, Feb. 4, 1965, S.F., chil.: Denise, b. 1953; Karen, b. 1955; Colleen, b. 1959; Career: Reporter, Oakland Tribune, 1950-56; account exec., Whitaker & Baxter, 1956-61; v.p., co-principal, Whitaker & Baxter, 1961---. Chmn., trustee, Calif. Wildlife Found. Served U.S. Merchant Marine, 1943-46; deck officer. Mem.: Pub. Rels. Soc. Am.; Calif. Alumni Assn.; Nat. Rifle Assn.; Calif. Rifle & Pistol Assn.; S.F. Press Club; Commonwealth Club of Calif.; Pi Kappa Alpha Frat.; Sigma Delta Chi; E. Clampus Vitus. Office: Whitaker & Baxter, 870 Market St., San Francisco, CA 94102.

ABSHIER, DORCEY GWYNNE
Nuclear Engineer
b. July 16, 1925, Wichita, Kan.; s. Dorcey D. and Leona (Gwynne) Abshier; B.S. (engin. physics), 1948 and M.E., 1950, Univ. of Okla.; m. Gene Eileen Bond, Jan. 12, 1955, Columbus, Oh.; (dec. Aug. 8, 1966); chil.: Holly Gene, b. Oct. 23, 1955; Michelle Gwynne, b. Sept. 21, 1958; Dorcey Bond, b. Dec. 3, 1959; David Edward Ivan, b. Nov. 9, 1961. Career: Applications engr., Ind. Nucleonics Corp., Columbus, 1954; prin. engin. physicist, Battelle Mem. Inst., 1955-56; sr. nuclear engr., Gen. Dynamics, Ft. Worth, Tex., 1956-58; lead design engr., Chance Vought Aircraft, 1958-60; staff engr. Bendix Systems Engrs., 1960; design spec., Gen. Dynamics/Astronautics, 1960-63; spec. research, Space and Information Systems Div., N. Am. Aviation, Downey, Calif., 1963-78; Lockheed Aircraft Co., Burbank, 1978---. Contrib. professional papers, Inst. Elec. and Electronic Engrs. 1961, Conf. 1963. U.S. Army Corps of Engrs. (1944-46), WW II; Army Ord. Corps, 1951-53. Mem.: Am. Inst. of Aerons. and Astronautics Inst. of Elec. and Electronic Engrs., Am. Nuclear Soc., Cryogenic Soc. of Am., Sci. Research Soc. of Am., Am. Phys. Soc., Internat. Platform Assn.; Mason (Blue and York). Deacon, First Christian Ch., Fullerton. Hobby: book collecting. Home: 4910 St. Andrews Circle, Buena Park, CA 90621; Office: Lockheed Calif. Co., Burbank, CA.

ACKERMAN, HARRY S.
TV — Broadcasting Executive
b. Nov. 7, 1912, Albany, N.Y.; s. Harold and Anna (Flannery) Ackerman; ed. B.S., Dartmouth, 1935; m. Elinor Donahur, Apr. 12, 1961; chil.: Brian, Peter, James, Christopher, Stephen, Susan. Career: Free lance actor-writer 1935-36; radio dir. Young and Rubicam, N.Y.C., 1936-42; radio production dir., 1942-45; v.p., dir. radio pgms. 1945; exec. prod. CBS, N.Y.C. 1948; v.p., dir. TV-radio, 1949-51; v.p., dir. TV pgms., Hollywood, 1951-55. exec. dir. spec. prodns., CBS, TV, 1956-57; pres. Ticonderoga Prodns., prod. "Bachelor Father," and "Leave It To Beaver," 1956-57; v.p.-exec. prod., Screen Gems (Columbia Pictures), 1958-73; pres., Harry Ackerman Prodns., Paramount TV, 1974---. Producer: "The Flying Nun," "Mr. Deeds Goes To Town," "Bewitched," TV Shows; feats. "In Name Only" and "Gidget Grows Up." Spec. cons. War Man Power Commission and U.S. Treasury, WW II. Awards: war medal. Mem.: pres. L.A. Acad. of TV Arts and Sci., 1957-60; pres. Natl. Acad. of TV Arts and Scis., 1957-61; (charter) Manuscripts Soc.; bd. dirs., TV Acad. Found.; trustee, Motion Pic. Relief Fund; State Commn., Calif.

Civil War Centennial Commn.; Advis. Council, U.S Civil War Centennial Comm.; U.N. Assn. of L.A.; Am. Arbitration Assn.; TV advisor, Mayor Samuel Yorty, City of L.A.; Dartmouth Club; Navy League of the U.S.; Phi Delta Theta. Hobbies: collecting Am. hist. documents and relics, photog., rare books. Res.: 4525 Lemp Ave., No. Hollywood, CA 91602; Office: 427 N. Canon Dr., Beverly Hills, CA 90210.

ACOSTA, EDGARDO
Art Gallery Director
b. June 13, 1913, Chihuahua, Mex.; s. Dionisio and Concepcion (Calderon) de Acosta; paternal grandfather, lecturer, Smithsonian Inst., was friend of Pres. Harrison, spec. Emmissary of Mex. Govt. sent to France to protest French occupation and became close assoc. French Pres. Sadi Carnot; ed. B.A., UCLA, 1935; Diplome d'Excellence, Conservatoire Musica, Paris, 1937; m. Francesca Hunter, L.A., Calif., Apr. 25, 1941. Career: Pvt. research, art, philosophy and music, Paris, 1947-49, concertized with London String Quartet, 1950, 51; export bus. (exporting modern paintings to Am.), Paris, Fr. 1951-56; est. Edgardo Acosta Gallery of Art (modern paintings), Beverly Hills, 1957, owner-dir., 1957---. Mem.: dir. Beverly Hills Music Assn., 1958-60, pres. 1960. Republican. Catholic. Hobby: reading, sports; collector rare books and modern paintings. Office: 441 N. Bedford Dr., Beverly Hills, CA.

ADAMS, ANSEL EASTON
Photographer — Author
b. Feb. 20, 1902, S.F.; s. Charles Hitchcock and Olive (Bray) Adams; m. Virginia Best, Jan. 2, 1927, Yosemite, Nat. Park; chil.: Michael, b. 1933; Anne (Helms), b. 1936. Career: trained as concert pianist; in 1930 switched to become full-time prof. photog.; helped found Group f/64 with Edward Weston, Imogen Cunningham, etc.; had 1st major exhibit at An American Place, N.Y.C. in 1933; awarded 3 Guggenheim Found. Grants in 1946, 1948 and 1958, to take photographs of the national parks and monuments; helped found first Dept. of Photography at Museum of Modern Art, NYC, 1940; taught at L.A. Art Center School, 1941; helped found Dept. of Photography at S.F. School of Fine Arts, 1946. Bd. Dir., Sierra Club, 1934-71; hon. v.p., Sierra Club, 1977---; chmn. bd. Friends of Photography, Carmel, 1967---. Recipient: hon. degrees from univs. incl. Yale, 1973; Univ. Calif., Berkeley, 1961; John Muir Award 1963; elected fellow of Am. Acad. of Arts and Sci., 1966. Pub. over 30 books over past 50 years, incl. Images, 1974; Photographs of the Southwest, 1976; The Portfolios, 1977; series of tech. books called Basic Photo Series; etc. Home-Office: Route 1, Box 181, Carmel, CA 93923.

ADAMS, ARTHUR R.
Company President
b. Apr. 30, 1909, Hiawatha, Kan.; s. George and Grace (Davis) Adams; Stanford Univ., 1931; m. Lelamae Sutherlin, Laguna Beach, Ca., Mar. 24, 1934 (div. 1962); chil.: Ann Weiler, Carolyn Anderson, Sharon Keith, Peter D. Adams. Career: partner, Rite Hardware Co., 1931-45; president, Adams Rite Mfg. Co., 1946---; chairman & president, Adams Rite Industries, Inc., 1974---. Dir.: Poly Industries; bd. of trustees, Claremont Men's College. Mem.: Oakmont Country Club, Verdugo Club. Republican. Christian Scientist. Rec.: Golf. Home: 495 Madeline Drive, Pasadena, CA 91105; Office: 540 W. Chevy Chase Dr., Glendale, CA 91204.

ADAMS, EARL CLINTON
Attorney at Law
b. May 12, 1892, San Jose, Calif.; s. John F. and Alice (Sinclair) Adams; ed. A.B., Stanford Univ., 1916; J.D. 1920; stu. Harvard Law Sch., 1916-17; m. Ilse Downey, Modesto, Calif., Oct. 14, 1922; chil.: Mrs. Jacquelin Smith (Nancy Camilla) Holliday, II, b. May 6, 1927; Robert Pierce, b. July 28, 1930; Career: admitted to Calif. bar, 1920; practicing lawyer, L.A., 1924---; sr. partner, Adams, Duque & Hazeltine, 1946---. Asst. commr. of corps., Calif. State, 1923-26; dir. L.A. Steel Casting Co.: dir. L.A. By-Products Co.; (past) dir. L.A. Foundry. Pvt., 2nd Lt., 107th Field Artillery, 28th Div., and 346th Field Artillery, 91st Div., U.S. Army, World War I. Mem.: exec. com., L.A. Chap., March of Dimes Natl. Found.; Am. Calif. State Bar Assns.; Am. Legion, Town Hall, Knight Templar, Al Malaikah Shrine, Phi Delta Phi, Delta Tau Delta; clubs: California, Stock Exchange, L.A.; exec. com.-treas., Republican State Central Com., Calif.; United Repub. Finance Com., L.A. Co.; Nixon Fact-Finding Com., 1946. Episcopalian. Hobbies: collector, Western Americana (feat. Russell and Geo. III Silver. Home: 1386 Orlando Rd., San Marino, Calif.; Office: 1000 Pacific Mutual Bldg., 523 W. 6th St., L.A., CA 90014.

ADAMS, PHILLIP ANTHONY
Professor of Biology
b. Jan. 13, 1929, L.A.; s. Edwin Brown and Jeanette (McPherson) Adams; B.S., entomology, Univ. of Calif., Berkeley, 1951; A.M., Ph.D., biology, Harvard, 1958. Career: asst. prof., Univ. of Calif., Santa Barbara, 1958-61; Calif. State Univ., Fullerton, 1963---: professor, 1971---; environmental cons. ---; visiting assoc. prof. of biology, Yale Univ., 1968-69; assoc. prof., marine biology, Chapman Coll., World Campus Afloat, 1967. Contbr. 30 publs. in insect evolution and physiology. Served. USAR, 1952-54; Lt., MSC. Master of topsail ketch Argus, sailing training vessel of Orange Co. Council BSA, 1972-77; mem.: Phi Beta Kappa; Sigma Xi; Phi Mu Alpha Sinfonia (hon.); AAAS; Entomological Soc. of Am.; So. Calif. Acad. of Scis. Hobbies: stringed instrument constrn./playing. Rec.: sail training, scuba, cycling. Office: Dept. of Biology, CSU, Fullerton, CA 92634.

ADAMS, ROBERT CHELL
University Professor
b. Oct. 2, 1931, Wendell, Idaho; s. Alverson Afton and Marguerite Isabelle (Toole) Adams; B.A., edn., soc. sci., Idaho State, 1958; B.A., speech, drama, 1959; M.A., broadcasting, Oregon, 1965; Ph.D., commun., 1971; m. Nora Anita Ross, Feb. 15, 1953, Gulfport, Miss.; chil.: Ross Clayborn, b. Dec. 1, 1953; Diane Richell, b. Nov. 20, 1954; Jonna Katri, b. June 20, 1960; Karen Annette, b. Jul. 25, 1965. Career: Calif. State Univ., Fresno, 1965---: Asst. prof., speech arts dept., 1965; assoc. prof., radio television dept., 1971; dir. computer assisted registration/asst. v.p. for acad. affairs, 1974-77; prof., radio-TV, communication arts and sci. dept., 1978---; coordinator, interdisciplinary grad. Program in Mass communication, 1978---. Baptist, moderator. Home: 4410 N. Laureen Ave., Fresno, CA 93726; Office: Communications Arts & Sciences Dept., CSU, Fresno, CA 93740.

ADAMS, WENDELL EUGENE
President, KINS Radio
b. Apr. 15, 1912, McPherson, Kan.; s. Rev. Oliver M. and Blanche (Vessey) Adams; A.B., Doane Coll., 1934; M.M. (music), Eastman Sch. of Music, 1936; m. Lillian Williamson, Nov. 3, 1933, Omaha, Neb.; chil.: Barbara (Mrs. Hugo Papstein), b. Sept. 9, 1938; Wendy (Mrs. Leonard Anderson), b. Oct. 15, 1942. Career: arranger, copyist CBS Music Lib., 1936-37; arranger, asst. conductor, prod., Mark Warnow: Lucky Strike Hit Parade, Heinz Mag. of the Air, Fels Naptha, We the People, New York on Parade, etc.; dir. popular music, CBS, 1940-41 (prod. shows for Frank Sinatra, Perry Como, Gordon MacRae, Burl Ives, etc.); program mgr., WGBS-FM (CBS), 1941-42; dir. popular music, CBS, 1942-44; sr. prod.-dir., CBS radio network 1945-46; prod., dir.: The Treasure Hour of Song, Symphony orchestra with Metropolitan Stars, 1946-47; prod. dir., Wm. Esty Co., 1947-49; prod. TV & radio programs, supr. of music, Wm. Esty., 1948-53; dir. of radio, also TV film commercials, Wm. Esty. Co., 1953-58 (clients: R.J. Reynolds Tobacco Co., Colgate Palmolive Co., Gen. Mills; National Carbon; Leeming Bros.; Pacquins Inc.; Coca Cola Co.; wrote jingles on co. products); president, gen. mgr., radio station KINS, Eureka, 1958---. Served to Lt. Col., AUS; program mgr. Radio Luxembourg, UN network, 1944. Foreman, Humboldt Co. Grand Jury, 1961; mem. Eureka Harbor Commn., 1959; dir. Calif. Broadcasters' Assn., 1959---, v.p., 1965-69; dir. CBS Radio Affils. 1964-70; dir., v.p. KEET-TV, 1974---; pres. 1975-76; co. chmn. March of Dimes, 1959-66; Mem.: Rotary, pres. 1970-71; Baywood Golf & Country Club; Ingomar Club; Humboldt Lodge No. 79; Redwood Shrine Club; Oakland Scottish Rites; Aahmes Temple (Shrine); Citizens for Realistic Devel. Hobbies: woodworking, golf. Home: 1903 Buhne St., Eureka, CA 95501; Office: KINS, P.O.B. O, Eureka, CA 95501.

ADELL, HIRSCH
Attorney at Law
b. Mar. 11, 1931, Poland; s. Nathan and Nachama Adell; B.A., 1955; LL.B., 1963; m. Judith Fuss, 1963, L.A.; chil.: Jeremiah, b. 1966; Nikolas, b. 1968; Balthasar, b. 1971; Valentine, b. 1973. Career: partner, Warren & Adell, 1963-75; mem., Reich, Adell, Crost & Perry, a profl. law corp., 1975---. Bd. Dir., L.A. Actors Theater Found. Served AUS, 1953-55. Home: 545 S. Norton Ave., L.A., CA 90020; Office: 501 Shatto Pl., L.A., CA 90020.

ADELMAN, BARNETT REUBEN
Corporate Executive
b. Dec. 17, 1925, Helena, Ark.; s. Joseph I and Gerty C.

(Cohen) Adelman; B.S., M.S. (ChE), Columbia Univ., 1948; m. Beverly Chazan, May 27, 1948, New York N.Y.; chil.: Stevan, b. 1948; Susan (Zimmerman), b. 1953; Daniel, b. 1957. Career: Picatinny Arsenal, 1948-49; Jet Propulsion Lab., Calif. Inst. of Tech., 1949-52; Phillips Petroleum Co., 1951-55; Space Technology Lab., 1955-59; president, Chemical Systems Division and United Space Boosters Inc. (div. and subsidiary of United Technologies Corp.), 1959---. Served to Lt. j.g., USNR, 1944-45. Office: 1050 E. Arques, P.O.B. 358, Sunnyvale, CA 94088.

ADKINS, EUGENE ARNOLD
Veterinarian
b. Feb. 5, 1928, Atlanta, Ga.; s. Elmer and Clara L. (Grant) Adkins; A.M., Fullerton Jr. Coll., 1950; D.S., Univ. Calif., Davis, 1956, D.V.M., 1958; m. Helen Jean Brittain, July 2, 1954, Akron, Ohio; chil.: Caryn Leigh, b. June 5, 1959; Christopher Lyle, b. June 13, 1961; Colin Leslie, b. Jan. 9, 1964. Career: Veterinarian, 1958---; Modesto, 1958-59; Grossmont, Calif., 1959; National City, 1959-60; Relief Veterinarian, San Diego Co., 1960, 1963-64; Escondido, 1960---. Dir., San Diego Emergency Animal Clin., 1972-73; dir., Escondido Country Club, 1968-69; area dir., Am. Animal Hosp. Assn. 1973-74; chmn., Small Animal Sect., CVMA, 1973; charter mem. Calif. Acad. of Veterinary Med., 1976; pres., Hidden Valley Community Concert Assn. 1973-74; pres. Sierra Veterinarians Med. Assn., 1974-75; mem. Calif., Am., S.D. Veterinarians Med. Assns.; tournament chmn. Little League, 1977. Served to Capt., USMC 1946-48; USMCR 1950-53. Mem.: Kiwanis, 1962-65; Rotary, 1975-77. Republican. Methodist. Hobby: refinishing furniture. Rec.: skiing, tennis, golf, backpacking. Home: 636 E. 9th Ave., Escondido, CA, Office: Hidden Valley Pet Clinic, 1906 E. Valley Pkwy., Escondido, CA 92027.

ADLER, KURT HERBERT
General Director, San Francisco Opera Company
b. Apr. 2, 1905, Vienna, Austria (U.S. cit. 1941); s. Ernst and Ida (Bauer) Adler; ed. Acad. of Music, Vienna, 1922-26; Univ. of Vienna, 1923-27; (hon.) Mus.D., Coll. of the Pacific, 1956; m. Diantha Warfel, Plainfield, Ill., July 7, 1940 (div. 1963); m. Nancy Miller, Aug. 23, 1965; chil.: Kristin Diantha, b. July 22, 1942; Ronald Huntington, b. Dec. 3, 1943. Career: Cond. Max Reinhardt's Theaters, Vienna, 1925-28; various opera houses and orchs., Germany, Italy, Czechoslovakia, 1928-34; Vienna Volksoper, 1934-36; asst. to Toscanini-instr., Mozarteum, Salzburg, 1936-37; Chicago Opera Co., 1938-43; San Francisco Opera Assn., 1943---; guest cond., Chicago Grant Park Concerts, Ill. Sym., S.F. Midsummer Festival, Univ. of Calif. Orch., Hollywood Bowl, Standard Hour Sym., NBC; cond. Youth Concerts, S.F. Sym., 1949-52; S.F. Art Commn. concerts; asst. to gen. dir., S.F. Opera Co., 1951-53; apptd. artistic dir. 1953-56, gen. dir. 1956---; guest cond., San Carlo Opera, Naples, 1958. Awards: Star of Solidarity, Italy, 1957; Officers Cross, Germany, 1959; Great Medal of Honors by Austrian govt., 1961; Knight of the Order of Merit, Republic of Italy, 1965; Commander's Cross of the Order of Merit, Fed. Republic of Germany, 1969; Bolshoi Theater Medal, USSR (first Am. recipient), 1972; St. Francis of Assisi Award, S.F. 1973. Mem.: founder-v.p., O.P.E.R.A. Am.; Internat. Assn. Opera Dirs.; trustee, Natl. Opera Inst., 1969-70. Lutheran. Rec.: motoring, swimming, tennis, all arts. Home: San Francisco, CA; Office: War Memorial Opera House, S.F., CA 94102.

ADLER, NANCY ELINOR
Psychologist — Educator
b. July 26, 1946, New York, N.Y.; d. Alan and Pauline Adler; B.A., Wellesley Coll., 1968; M.A., Harvard Univ., 1971, Ph.D., 1973; Career: teaching fellow and tutor, Harvard Univ., 1969-72; asst. prof., Univ. of Calif., Santa Cruz, 1972-76; visiting asst. research psychologist, Inst. of Personality Assessment & Research, Univ. of Calif., Berkeley, 1975; assoc. prof., Univ. of Calif., Santa Cruz, 1976-77; assoc. prof., Univ. of Calif., San Francisco, 1977---. Recipient: Phi Beta Kappa, 1968; Sigma Xi, 1968; Woodrow Wilson Fellow, 1968; Nat. Sci. Found. Fellow, 1968-72; Univ. Calif. Regents' Summer Fellowship, 1974. Contbr. articles to psychiat. journs. Pres., div. of population and environmental psychology, Am. Psychological Assn., 1978-79. Office: Univ. of Calif., S.F., 1454-5th Ave., San Francisco, CA 94143.

ADRIAN, DONALD JAMES
Corporate Executive
b. July 10, 1929, Huntington Park, Calif.; s. James A. and Linnie J. (Butcher) Adrian; B.S., Calif. State Poly Univ., 1952; M.A., UCLA, 1964; m. Doris Edmiston, April 11, 1954, Beaumonet, Calif.; chil.: Nanvy (Mrs. Michael

Schroeder), b. June 16, 1959; Thomas, b. Feb. 8, 1968; Steven, b. July 30, 1967. Career: Physicist, Naval Research Lab., Wash. D.C., 1951-52; Nat. Bureau of Standards, Corona, Calif., 1952-53; electronic scientist, Naval Ordnance Lab., Corona, 1953-60; Lab. Dir., Aero-Geo-Astro Corp., 1960-65; lab. dir., Astrophysics Research Corp., Norco, Calif., 1965-72; v.p., dir., Megatek Corp., San Diego, 1972---. Patentee: 20 U.S. patents; publs. in fields of radio propagation, navigation and neuroelectric meas.; sci. meas. edpeditions; Solar eclipse in Brazil 1966, Arctic 1969, 1970, 1973. Mem.: IEEE; Inst. of Navigation; AAAS; Am. Geophysical Union; Neuroelectric Soc.; Optical Soc. of Am. Baptist; deacon 1965-68. Hobby: study of sensory processes and neuroelectric phenomena. Rec.: hiking, camping. Home: 2510 Oak St., Corona, CA 91720; Office: 1055 Shafter St., San Diego, CA.

AGAJANIAN, ESAU TATOS
Real Estate Investor
b. Jan. 25, 1896, Kars, Armenia; s. Tatos and Shogo Agajanian; desc. Bedros Bedrosian, nobleman, Persia; ed. H.S., UCLA, ext. courses in real estate and ins.; m. Virginia Abajian, USSR, June 7, 1920 (dec.); chil.: Lillian Mnoian, b. June 26, 1923; George E., b. Sept. 8, 1924; Violet Hatounian, b. Oct. 29, 1926; Conrad E., b. Sept. 12, 1928. Career: real estate and ins. broker. Author: (book) Agajanian Geneology and poetry, 1971. Russian Tzar Army, 1915-17; Armenian Voluntary Army, 1917-19. Mem.: Master Mason, 1940, Royal Arch, 1945; Master, S. Park Lodge, F&AM, 1961; L.A. Commandery, Knight Templar of Calif., Al Malaikah Temple Shrine; (hon.) USC Faculty 20 club, 1958---; adv. bd. Viewpark Comm. Hosp., L.A., 1960---; exec. com. L.A. Masonic Bd. of Relief, 1962-62; Grand Repr. of Friendship to Masonic Grand Lodge of Parana, Brazil, 1965; bd. dirs. Armenian Edn. Home of L.A. Republican. Immanuel Armenian Congregational Church. Hobbies: prod. hist. motion pics., travel, foreign langs. Home: Los Angeles, CA.

AGRESS, CLARENCE M.
Physician — Educator
b. Mar. 10, 1912, Knoxville, Tenn.; s. Max and Jennie Agress; B.A., Harvard Univ., 1933; M.D., Univ. Texas Medical School, 1937; m. Patricia Patella, Los Angeles, Feb. 13, 1972; chil.: Carol Zaslow, b. Dec. 6, 1945; Edith Schwab, b. Aug. 17, 1948. Career: Internship and residency in med., L.A.Co. Hosp., 1937-41; Tchr., med. instructor, USC, 1941-42; Mag. U.S. Army Med. Corps in China, Burma, India, 1942-45; (learned Chinese language); private practice with Dr. Myron Prinzmetal, 1945-48 (worked on radioactive Iodine as treatment for thyroid disease; extensive investigation on cardiogenic shock, invention of the Agress Catheter); Chief of Medicine, L.A. Co. Harbor Gen. Hosp., 1948-50; Chief, Cardiology, Cedars-Sinai Med. Center, 1962-68; Chief Investigator, Veterans Hospital, Sawtelle, 1946-56; NASA Grantee, Space Program, 1963-68 (developed indirect heart monitoring technique used in moon landing and Man-In-Space Program); Assoc. Clin. Prof., UCLA, 1955---. Author: Energetics, Grossett and Dunlap, 1978; Biochemical Diagnosis of Heart Disease, Chas. Thomas; over 100 published scientific articles. Award of Merit, L.A. Co. Heart Assn.; NASA Award, Contribution to Space Program; citation by Vice-Pres. Hubert Humphrey, 1968; Alpha Omega Alpha Honorary Med. Soc.; Fellow Am. Coll. Physicians; Fellow Am. Coll. Chest Physicians; Fellow Am. Geriatrics Soc.; Fellow: Pan Am. Mec. Assn., L.A. Acad. Med. Mem.: Hillcrest Country Club; California Yacht Club; Racquet Club, Palm Springs. Rec.: Tennis, golf, yachting, writing. Home: 10674 Chalm Rd., L.A.; Office: 2080 Century Park East, L.A., CA 90067.

AHMANSON, WILLIAM H.
Chairman, H.F. Ahmanson & Co.
b. Oct. 12, 1925, Omaha, Nebr.; s. Hayden W. and Aimee (Talbod) Ahmanson; nephew of Howard Fieldstead Ahmanson, noted investments exec. and civic leader; L.A.; bro. Robert H. Ahmanson; ed. B.S., UCLA 1950; m. Gloria June Gamble, July 10, 1964; chil.: Mary Jane, Patricia, Amy, Dorothy, Joanne, Kimberly. Career: H.F. Ahmanson & Co., 1950---; chmn. bd. 1969---; pres. Nat. Am. Ins., Omaha, Calif.; chmn. bd. Home Svgs. and Loan Assn. (L.A.), Ahmanson Bank and Trust Co. (Beverly Hills); dir. Hosp. of Good Samaritan; dir. Dorothy Grannis Sullivan Found.; dir. Bleitz Wildlife Found.; trustee-v.p. Ahmanson Found.; Founders of Music Center. Serv. U.S. Navy (1943-46), WW II. Mem.: L.A., Wilshire Country and Jonathan Clubs. Presbyterian. Hobby: golf, sailing. Office: 3731 Wilshire Blvd., L.A., CA 90010.

AIRD, ROBERT B.
Professor Emeritus of Neurology
b. Nov. 5, 1903; s. John W., M.D. (founding mem.,

Am. Coll. of Surgeons) and Emily M. (state legislator) Aird; student Deep Springs Coll.; A.B., Cornell Univ., 1926; M.D., Harvard Med. Sch. 1930; grad. studies Neurosurgery, Neurology, Neurophysiology, Univ. of Rochester, Univ. Penn., Harvard, Univ. Calif., S.F.; m. Ellinor Collins, Oct. 4, 1935, Bryn Mawr, Pa.; chil.: Katharine (Miller), b. Nov. 5, 1936; Mary (Davis), b. Mar. 6, 1941; John C., b. April 1, 1942; R. Bruce, b. Mar. 29, 1948; Career: with Univ. of Calif. Sch. of Med., S.F., 1939---: asst. prof., 1939; assoc. prof., 1945; prof. of Neurology, 1949-71; Prof. Emeritus, 1971---; chmn., Dept. of Neurology, 1947-66; dir. of Lab. of electroencephalography, 1940-71. Chief author, Management of Epilepsy, Chas C. Thomas, Springfield; author of 230 sci. papers pub. in sci. and med. journs.; guest lectr. USA and abroad; chmn. numerous postgrad. courses; authority on epilepsy, clin. and research, and on electroencephalography. Awards: Royer Award, 1969; William G. Lennox Award, 1970; decorated Comdr. Order of Hipolito Unanue, Peru, 1963; Fullbright Research Scholar in France, 1957-58; Robert B. Aird Visiting Professor of Neurology, endowed and named in his honor, 1973, Univ. Calif. Med. Sch., S.F., 1973; hon. mem.: Assn. of British Neurologists, 1971; S.F. Co. Med. Assn., 1973; Argentine Soc. Neurol., Psychiat. & Neurosurgery, 1963. Dir., Deep Springs Coll., 1960-66, trustee, 1959-71, hon. trustee, 1971---. Mem.: Norwegian Neurolog. Assn.; German Assn. of Neurologists; Peruvian Soc. Neuro. psychiat.; Calif. Acads. of Med. and Sci.; past pres., Am. Electroencephalographic Soc.; past pres., S.F. Neurological Soc.; past mem. editorial bd., Internat. Journ. Electroencephalography & Clinical Neurophysiology. Hobby: musical composition. Rec.: travel. Home: 80 Summit Ave., Mill Valley, CA 94941; Office: Dept. of Neurology, M-794, Univ. of Calif., San Francisco, CA 94143.

ALBERT, SIDNEY PAUL
Professor of Philosophy
b. Apr. 11, 1914, Syracuse, N.Y.; s. Simon and Gertrude (Siskin) Albert; A.B., Syracuse Univ., 1934; Ph.D. (philosophy), Yale Univ., 1939; postdoctoral study (drama) Univ. of Ill., 1953-54, Columbia Univ. 1954-56, Carnegie Inst. of Tech., Northwestern Univ., Stanford Univ., summers 1950-53; m. Lucy Ann Schroeder, Oct. 30, 1955, New York, N.Y.; chil.: Vivian Risa, b. Dec. 27, 1957; Alan Edward, b. July 30, 1959; Laurence David, b. APr. 10, 1964. Career: Instr., philosophy, Univ. of Conn., 1946, and Syracuse Univ. 1946; asst. prof. in charge of philo., Triple Cities Coll. of Syracuse Univ. 1946-50, and at Harpur Coll., State Univ. of N.Y., 1950-53; asst. prof. of philo., L.A. State Coll. (now Cal. State Univ., L.A.), 1956-60, assoc. prof. of philo., 1960-64, prof. of philo., 1964---; chmn., dept. of philosophy, 1960-63; chmn., Assembly, Sch. of Letters and Sci., Calif. State Univ., L.A., 1966-67. Mem.: editorial bd., Shaw Review 1968; contbr. drama and theater publs. Mem.: Am. Assn. of Univ. Profs., Served AUS, 1941-46. Pres. Harpur Coll. chpt., 1950-51, pres. Calif. State Univ., L.A. chpt., 1962-63; Am. Soc. for Aesthetics, pres. Calif. div. 1963-64; pres., So. Calif. Centre, Royal Inst. of Philosophy 1963-64; Am. Philosophical Assn.; Am. and British Societies for Aesthetics; Am. Theatre Assn.; Theatre Library Assn. Democrat; apptd. mem. state central com. 1960-62; elected mem. L.A. Co. Demo central com., 1962-64. Hobby: collecting Shaviana. Rec.: theater. Office: Dept. of Philosophy, Calif. State Univ., L.A., Los Angeles, CA 90032.

ALBERTONI, ALBERT E.
Union Executive
b. Oct. 27, 1908, Sacramento; s. Elvezio J. and Anne (Coutts) Albertoni; student, Univ. Ariz.; m. Kathryne Radovah, Mar. 28, 1937, Oakland. Career: with Oakland Fire Dept. 1939-64, ret. Capt.; v.p. and secty.-treas., Civil Service Employees Ins. Co., S.F., 1957-65; pres.-chmn., exec. bd., legislative rep., Federated Fire Fighters, 1948-60; v.p. (1956-60), secty.-treas. (1964-73), Internat. Assn. of Fire Fighters of Calif., AFL-CIO, 1956-73, secty.-treas. emeritus, 1973---. Contbr. tech. publs. 1956-72. Apptd. by Pres. Nixon to bd. trustees, Wash. Tech. Inst., 1972; Apptd. by Secty. Labor Peter Brennan to Nat. Manpower Advisory Com., 1973. Served to Comdr., USN, 1942-68, So. Pacific theatre WW II; 4 commendations. Mem.: Internat. Assn. Firechiefs; Touch Down Club, Wash. D.C.; Eagles; Moose; Lions Club. Hobbies: hunting, fishing, hiking. Rec.: spectator sports. Home: 941 Terra Calif. Dr. 3, Walnut Creek, CA 94595.

ALBERTSON, CLINTON EDWARD, S.J.
Professor of English
b. Nov. 11, 1918, Los Angeles; s. Clinton Luther and Marie Katherine (Kelly) Albertson; M.A. philosophy, 1943; M.A., Eng. lit., Oxford Univ., 1957. Career: Instr.

in English, Loyola Marymount Univ., L.A., 1943-45, 1954-55, asst. prof. of English, 1954-59, assoc. prof. of English, 1959-70, prof. of English, 1970---. Author: Anglo-Saxon Saints & Heroes, Fordham Univ. Press, 1967. Mem.: Modern Language Assn.; Assn. of Am. Univ. Profs.; Coll. English Assn.; Medieval Assn. of the Pacific. Roman Catholic priest in the Jesuit Order, 1949---. Hobby: art. Rec.: swimming. Address: Loyola Marymount Univ., L.A., CA 90045.

ALBRECHT, ROBERT GLENN
Company President
b. Sept. 18, 1918, Glenn Ellen, Calif.; s. Martin and Gladys (Cramer) Albrecht; student, Denver Univ.; m. Myrtle Evelyn Engebresten, Oct. 24, 1946, Fair Oaks, Calif.; chil.: Sue (Thomas); Bonnie (Bachich); Steven and Kathleen Railsback. Career: constrn. supt., U.S. Forest Service, Calif., 1937-40; constrn. supr., Mercer-Fraser Co., S.F., 1940-43; party chief N.B. Bailiff Land Surveyor, Calif. and Ore., 1946-50; partner, Wismer & Becker Contracting Engrs. Sacto.: v.p., 1955, gen. mgr., 1967, pres., 1972---. Served USAF, 1943-46. Mem.: Am. Arbitration Assn.; Comstock Club; Commonwealth Club; Sacto. Rotary; Northridge Country Club; Cameron Park Country Club; bd. dir., Contractors Mutual Assn.; Calif. C. of C. Hobbies: flying, golf. Home: 3789 Fairway Dr., Shingle Springs, CA 95682; Office: P.O.B. 1168, Sacto., CA 95806.

ALBRECHT, ROBERT GLENN
Engineer — Business Executive
b. Sept. 18, 1918, Glenn Ellen, Calif.; s. Martin George and Gladys (Cramer) Albrecht; ed. I.C.S. (engring.), Denver Univ., 1951; m. Myrtle Evelyn Engebretsen, Fair Oaks, Calif., Oct. 24, 1946; chil.: Sue Thomas, b. Nov. 7, 1941; Bonnie, b. Sept. 18, 1947; Steven, b. Jan. 26, 1952; Kathleen, b. April 28, 1953. Career: Constr. supt., U.S. Forest Serv.; Mercer-Fraser Co., S.F.; party chief, N.B. Bailiff Land Surveyor, Calif.-Ore.; pres.-gen. mgr. Wismer and Becker Contr.-Engrs. 1950---. Served USAF 1943-46. Mem.: bd. dirs.: San Juan Hosp., Contrs. Mutual Assn., Sacto. Met. C. of C., Calif. C. of C.; pres. Fair Oaks Flying Club, 1965-66, 1970-71; Aircraft Owners & Pilots Assn.; Am. Arbitration Assn.; Republican Assn.; Clubs: Rotary, Comstock, Commonwealth, Century, Sutter, North Ridge Country, Cameron Park Country. Presbyterian. Hobby: golf. Home: 3789 Fairway Dr., Shingle Springs, CA 95682; Office: 7820 Folsom Blvd., Sacto., CA 95806.

ALBRECHT, RUTH E.
Professor Emeritus of Sociology
b. Oct. 27, 1910, Wittenberg, Mo.; B.A., Wash. Univ., 1934; M.A., Univ. of Chicago, 1946; Ph.D., 1951; Career: research asst., research assoc. Univ. of Chicago, 1946-49; research prof., Auburn Univ., Auburn, Ala. 1951-57; chmn. Dept. of Family Life, Univ. of Florida, Gainesville, 1957-60, prof. of sociology, 1960-75; currently, writer ---. Author: Older People, Longman's Green, 1954; (w/R.S. Havighurst) Aging in a Changing Society, Univ. of Fla. Press, 1962; Encounter: Love, Marriage and Family, 1972, 1975, Holbrook Press; contbr. articles to sci. journs. Mem.: Council on Aging, State Coll. at S.D, 1975-78; Pi Lambda Theta; Alpha Kappa Delta; Univ. Women's Club of S.D. Protestant. Hobbies: travel, writing, opera. Home: 1399 Ninth Ave., No. 902, San Diego, CA 92101.

ALBRITTON, ROBERT SANFORD
Insurance Executive
b. Feb. 19, 1914, St. Paul, Minn.; s. Elmer Sanford and Mary Eleanor (Bierer) Albritton; ed. B.A., Northwestern Univ. 1935; M.B.A., Wharton Sch. of Finance and Comm., Univ. of Pa. 1937; m. Helen Richards, Minneapolis, Minn., Mar. 14, 1938; chil.: David Richards, b. Nov. 7, 1940; Robert Rapp, b. Feb. 12, 1941. Career: Propr., life insurance brokerage official, prin. assn. with Provident Mutual Life Ins. Co. of Phila., Westwood Village, L.A., 1940---; pres., Albritton, Frank & Page, Inc. Mem.: Million Dollar Round Table of Nat. Assn. of Life Underwriters, 1948---, chmn. 1960; L.A. Country Club. Episcopalian. Home: 2012 Mandeville Canyon Rd., L.A., CA 90024; Honokeana Cove, Maui, Hawaii; Office: 11661 San Vicente Blvd., L.A., CA 90049.

ALDRICH, DANIEL G., JR.
University Chancellor
b. July 12, 1918, Northwood, N.H.; s. Daniel Gaskill and Marian (Farnum) Aldrich; ed. B.S., URI 1939; D.Sc. (hon.) 1960; M.S., Univ. Ariz., 1941; Ph.D, Univ. Wisc., 1943; m. Jean Hamilton, South Dennis, Mass., Aug. 23, 1941; chil.: Daniel G., III; Mrs. Michael (Elizabeth) Toomey; Stuart Hamilton. Career: Research chem. Citrus

Exp. Sta. Univ. Calif., Riverside, 1943-55; prof., soils and plant nutrition, dept. chmn., Univ. Calif., Riverside, Berkeley, 1955-58; univ. dean of agri., 1959-62; chancellor, Univ of Calif., Irvine, 1962---. Dir.: Stanford Research Inst., Fund for Theol. Edn., Morris Plan Co.; trustee, Pac. Sch. of Relig. Maj., U.S. inf., 1943-46; USAR 1946-64; Lt. Col. ret. Mem.: Cosmos Club,, Wash. D.C.; Calif. Club, L.A. Moderator, Congregational-Chr. Chs., So. Calif. and S.W. 1950, 52. Hobbies: athletics, tennis, golf, track and field. Res.: 1392 Galaxy Dr., Newport Beach, CA; Office: Univ. of Calif., Irvine, CA 92664.

ALEXANDER, L. BRUCE
Company President
b. May 5, 1914, Edgar, Clay Co., Nebr.; s. John E. and Mabel (Benjamin) Alexander; ed. Hastings Coll., 1933-34; B.Sc., Univ. of Nebr., 1935-37; M.B.A., Harvard Grad Sch. of Bus., 1938-39; m. Barbara E. Ray, Hastings, Nebr., July 23, 1940; chil.: Suzanne K., b. Sept. 17, 1941; Scott R., b. Oct. 20, 1945. Career: Prodn. mgr., Hoosier-Cardinal Corp., Evansville, Ind. 1939-42; West Coast mgr., Booz-Allen-Hamilton (mgmt. engrs.), 1943-47; pres. Brown Citrus Mach. Corp., 1947---; chmn. bd., Citrus Equip. Corp., 1952---; pres. Florida Citrus, Inc., 1959---. Mem.: San Marino City Club, 1944---; bd. trustees, San Marino Unified Sch. Dist., 1951---; pres. 1957-59; San Gabriel Country Club, 1952---; Young President's Orgn., 1956---; Delta Upsilon. Presbyterian (bd. trustees, San Marino Comm. Ch. 1957-59). Hobby: golf. Home: 2859 Cumberland Rd., San Marino, CA.

ALEXANDER, SANFORD
Newspaper Publisher
b. Nov. 9, 1900, Grenada, West Indies; s. Thomas and Mabel (Mack) Alexander; ed. H.S., St. Marks Coll.; m. Elizabeth Patterson, Reno, Nev. 1943. Career: Founder-pres., S. Alexander Co., Inc.; chmn. bd. dirs. Africa House, Inc.; owner-publ. newspaper chain incl. Herald-Dispatch, L.A. Mem.: People's Temple, L.A. Rec.: tennis, horseback riding. Home: P.O.B. 139, Rosarito Beach, Mexico.

ALFORD, GLORIA K.
Artist
b. Oct. 3, 1928, Chicago, Ill.; d. Isadore L. and Rose (Rice) Kramer; A.B., Univ. Calif., Berkeley; postgrad.: Art Inst. Chicago; Penland Sch. Crafts, N.C.; Columbia Univ.; Pratt Graphics Center; m. Robert Ross Alford, June 18, 1949, Angels Camp, Calif.; chil.: Heidi, b. Apr. 3, 1952; Jonathan, b. Oct. 27, 1953; Elissa, b. Aug. 29, 1960. Awarded: Top honors, Univ. Wis. Art Show, Richland Ctr. 1972; Visiting artist, France-U.S. Cultural Exchange Program, Paris, 1976. Exhibitions: Enviro-Vision, nat. competitive exhib., Everson Mus., Syracuse and N.Y. Cultural Center, N.Y., 1972; New Talent Show, Gimpel and Weitzenhoffer, N.Y.C., 1973; In Her Own Image, Phila. Mus. Art, 1974; 19th Annual Print Exhib., Brooklyn Mus., 1974; Wis. Directions, Milwaukee Art Center, 1975; Reciprocal Influences, Indiana Univ. Art Mus., 1976; Cabrillo Music Festival Art Show, Aptos, Calif., 1977. Current rep. The Richard Mann Gallery, L.A. In permanent collections: Elvehjem Art Center, Univ. of Madison, Wisc.; Prudential Insurance Co., N.Y.; Credit Union Nat. Assn., Madison, Wis. Home: 535 Meder St., Santa Cruz, CA 95060.

ALIBRANDI, JOSEPH FRANCIS
President, Whittaker Corp.
b. Nov. 9, 1928, Boston, Mass.; s. Paul and Anna (Amendola) Alibrandi; B.S., M.E., Mass. Inst. Tech., 1952; m. Lambertha A. Araszkiewicz, May 12, 1957, Boston, Mass.; chil.: Paul J., b. June 25, 1959; Ann-Marie, b. June 7, 1962; Carolyn, b. Nov. 4, 1965. Career: with Fairchild Engring. & Airplane Co., 1951; Raytheon Co., 1952-70; sr., v.p. & gen. mgr., 1968-70; exec. v.p. & dir., Whittaker Corp., 1970, pres., chief exec., dir. 1970---. Chmn. bd., 12th dist. Federal Reserve, 1973---; chmn., French-Am. C. of C., L.A. chpt. 1978; chmn., Bus. Advis. Council and dir. Internat. Student Center, UCLA, 1974---; mem. Corp. Visiting Com., Sloan Sch. of Mgmt. at M.I.T., 1972---; mem. bd. of Councilors, Sch. Bus. Adminstrn., USC, 1977---; life mem.: Am. Ins. Aeronautics & Astronautics, Air Force Assn., Navy League of U.S. Home: 16560 Park Lane Circle, L.A., CA 90049; Office: 10880 Wilshire Blvd., L.A., CA 90024.

ALIOTO, JOSEPH LAWRENCE
Former Mayor of San Francisco
b. Feb. 12, 1916, S.F., Calif.; s. Giuseppe and Domenica (Lazio) Alioto; ed. Garfield Sch., Telegraph Hill; Salesian Boys' Sch.; Sacred Heart H.S. (champion debater); A.B., St. Mary's Coll. 1937, (hon.) LL.D., 1965; LL.B.

(scholarship), Cath. Univ. of Am., Wash. D.C. 1940; m. Angelina Genaro, June 2, 1941, div.; chil.: Laurence E, Joseph M., John I., Thomas R., Angela M., Michael J. m. 2d Kathleen Sullivan. Career: admitted to Calif. bar, 1940; dept. of justice, 1940-41; spec. asst. to Atty. Gen., Bd. Econ. Welfare, S.F., 1940-45; est. pvt. practice law, S.F., 1946-67; elected Mayor of S.F. (thirty-third), 1967-76. Pres. S.F. Bd. of Edn. 1948-54; chmn. S.F. Redevel. Agency, 1955-59; pres. Rice Growers Assn. of Calif. 1959-68; chmn. Calif. Rice Export Assn. 1959-68; chmn. bd. Alioto Enterprises, 1959---; chmn. bd. 1st S.F. Bank, 1964-66. Serv. strategy bds. to pin-point Japanese, Ger. and Italian targets for bombing missions, WW II. Mem.: fellow, Am. Coll. of Trial Lawyers; Am. Bar Assn.; sponsor, Salesian Boys' Club, North Beach; many civic coms. Democrat (campaign leader for former Mayors John Shelley and George Christopher, Sen. Eugene McAteer, others). Home: 34 Presidio Terr., S.F., CA 94118.

ALIOTO, ROBERT FRANKLYN
Superintendent of Schools
b. Nov. 22, 1933, San Francisco, Ca.; S. Michael and Evelyn (Blohm) Alioto; A.A., Hartnell Coll., 1953; B.E., San Jose State Coll., 1958; M.A., 1961; Ed.D., Harvard Univ., 1968; chil.: Deborah Ann Alioto Thompson, Diane A. Alioto, David Russell Alioto, Robert F. Alioto, Jr. Career: Tchr. elementary and jr. high grades, Greenfield, Ca., 1956-60; prin., Carneros Elem. School, Napa, Ca., 1960-62; supt., Shurtleff Elem School, Napa, 1962-65; dir., Inst. for Training Selected Teachers a Liaison Role, Harvard Univ., 1965-67; supt. schs. Pearl River, N.Y., 1967-71; supt. schs. Yonkers, N.Y., 1971-75; supt. schs. San Francisco Unified School Dist., 1975---. Adj. prof., New York Univ., 1973-74; Cons. in sch. dist. admin. reorganization, Warwick, R.Is. and Hudson, Mass.; supt. Student Tchrs., Harvard M.A. Teaching Candidates, 1965-67, Cambridge, Mass.; installation of PPBS, Portland, Maine sch. dist.; Ford Found.-Urban Coalition, Wash., D.C. Publications: co-author Operational PPBS for Education: A Practical Approach to Effective Decision Making, Harper & Rowe, New York, 1971; PPBS at the Polls, Croft School Business Service, April 1970; Using PPBS To Overcome Taxpayers' Resistance, Phi Delta Kappan, Nov. 1969. Contrib. author Accountability in Education, Allyn & Bacon, Inc., Boston, 1972. Author Accelerating the Flow of Communication, IBM Jour., Jul/Aug 1974, Work Processing, Vol. 3, No. 4. Mem: Rotary Club, Ca. and N.Y.; Harvard Grad. Sch. of Ed. Alumni Assn.; pres. Rockland Co. (N.Y.) Sch. Execs. and Public School Athletic League; Napa Co. Elem. Administrators' Assn.; So. Monterey Co. Teachers' Assn.; elected to Supts. Advisory Comm. to N.Y. State Commissioner of Ed.; Exec. Comm., Iota Chap., Phi Delta Kappa, Harvard Univ. Rec.: jogging, golfing, skiing. Home: 210 Lake Merced Hill North, S.F., CA 94132; Office: SFUSD, 135 Van Ness Ave., S.F., CA 94102.

ALJIBURY, FALIH KHIDIR
Agriculturist — Educator
b. Dec. 17, 1934, Iraq; s. Khidir A. and Massouda Aljibury; B.A., Univ. of Baghdad, Iraq, 1955; M.S., Ore. State Univ., 1958, Ph.D., 1960; registered profl. engr., Calif.; m. Antoinette DeSart, Mar. 21, 1959; Corvallis, Ore.; son Haleem, b. 1974. Came to U.S., 1956, naturalized, 1965. Career: Head, Land Use Sect., Iraq Devel. Bd., Baghdad, 1955-56; asst. prof., Univ. of Baghdad, 1960-61; agriculturalist, mem. faculty, Univ. Calif., Berkeley, 1961---; visiting prof. Am. Univ. Beirut, Lebanon, 1967-68; cons. irrigation Govt. Saudi Arabia, 1965---, Lebanon, 1967---, Europe, 1965-68, Comptoire Agricole du Levant, Beirut, 1967---, Calif. Dept. Water Resources, 1970---, Govt. Mexico, 1972---, Libyan Ministry Agri., 1975---. Apptd. to Calif. Water Commn., 1978; awarded Man of the Year 1977, Irrigation Assn. Mem.: Am. Soc. Agri. Engrs.; Internat. Commn. Irrigation and Drainage; Am. Soc. of Agronomy; Western Soc. of Soil Sci.; Soil Sci. Soc. of Am.; Irrigation Assn.; Calif. Irrigation Ist.; AAAS; Toastmasters, pres. 1964; Commonwealth Club of Calif. Home: 1820 Columbia Dr. E., Fresno, CA 93727; Office: 9240 S. Riverbend Ave., Parlier, CA 93648.

ALLAN, ROBERT M., JR.
Business Executive
b. Dec. 8, 1920, Detroit, Mich.; s. Robert M., Sr. and Jane (Christman) Allan; ed. B.S., Stanford Univ. 1941; Stanford Grad. Sch. of Bus.; M.S. (physics, meteorology and astrophysics), UCLA (under A.F. detached duty); Loyola Law Sch.; m. Harriet Spicer, Santa Ana, Calif., Nov. 28, 1942; chil.: Robert M., III; Scott; David; Marilee. Career: Econ. Research Dept., Security First Natl. Bank, 1942; partner, Gen. Ins. Agency, 1946-53; asst. to pres.-work mgr., Zinsco Elec. Prods. 1953-55,

v.p.-dir. 1956-59; asst. to pres., The Times-Mirror Corp. 1959-60, corporate v.p. 1961-64; pres.-dir., Cyprus Mines Corp. 1964-67; pres. Litton Internat. 1967-69; pres. U.S. Naval Postgrad. Sch. Found. 1969---, Prof. Internat. Mgmt. 1969---. Dir.-trustee: U.S. Naval Acad. (Seamanship). Senior Fellow, Monterey Inst. of Foreign Studies. Operations and weather ofcr., USAF 1942-45; retired as Capt., WW II. Awards: Outstanding Businessman of Year in L.A., 1966; Natl. Assn. of Accountants; U.S. Navy Meritorious Service Award, 1976. Helms Athletic Found. Award for services to yachting, serv. to juniors, 1947, 49. Mem.: director, Merchants and Mfgrs. Assn.; regional dir.: Intercollegiate yachting Assn. 1940-55; Olympic Games Yachting Commn. 1964-65; Commodore, 1964; Mason, Phi Gamma Delta, Phi Delta Phi, Trans.-Pac. Yacht, N.Y. Yacht, Monterey Country Club. Hobby: sailing, golf, mag. writing. Home: 2980 Cormorant Rd., Pebble Beach, CA 93953; Office: U.S. Naval Postgrad. Sch., Monterey, CA.

ALLARD, R(OBERT) W(AYNE)
Professor of Genetics
b. Sept. 3, 1919, Los Angeles; s. Glenn A. and Alma (Roose) Allard; B.S., Univ. of Calif., 1941; Ph.D., Univ. of Wis., 1946; m. Ann Wilson, June 16, 1946, Madison, Wis.; chil.: Susan, b. 1949; Thomas, b. 1951; Jane, b. 1954; Gillian, b. 1959; Stacie, b. 1964. Career: asst. prof., Univ. of Calif., Davis, 1946-50; assoc. prof., 1950-54, prof., 1954---; chmn., Acad. Senate, Univ. Calif., Davis, 1976-78. Awards: Crop Sci. Award, Am. Soc. of Agronomy, 1964; Guggenheim Fellow, 1954, 1960; Fulbright Fellow, 1955; elected to Nat. Acad. of Sciences, 1973; pres. Am. Soc. of Naturalists, 1974-75. Served to Lt., USNR, 1943-46. Unitarian. Rec.: skiing, sailing, tennis. Home: 622 Fillmore St., Davis, CA 95616; Office: Dept. of Genetics, UC Davis, Davis, CA.

ALLBEE, LEWIS
School District Superintendent
b. Mar. 11, 1914, E. Hardwick, Vt.; s. Guy Henry and Belle Townsend (Johnson) Allbee; ed. A.B., Middlebury Coll., Vt. 1936; A.M. 1940; Univ. of Paris, 1939; Ph.D., Yale Univ. 1948; UCLA 1955; m. Marjorie Walters, Sudbury, Mass., July 10, 1948; daus.: Allison Walters, b. Dec. 29, 1952; Julia Stroud, b. Oct. 15, 1955. Career: Ger. tchr., Middlebury H.S., Vt. 1936; tchr., So. Ariz. Sch. for Boys, 1936-41; instr. Ecole Normale de Caen, France, 1939-40; St. Johnsbury Acad., Vt. 1940; instr. Norwich Univ. 1945, instr. Yale Univ., New Haven, 1947; prin. E. Grand Rapids H.S., Mich. 1948-49; prin., Los Alamos Schs., N.Mex., 1949-51; asst. supt. 1952-53; supt. 1953-55; instr.: E. N.Mex. Univ., Portales, 1950-56; N. Mex. Univ., State Coll. (summer) 1954; Univ. of N. Mex., N. Mex. Western Coll., Western State Coll. of Edn., Gunnison (summer), 1955; tchr., Culver City Jr. H.S., 1955-56; sutp. Groton Pub. Schs., Conn. 1956-58; asst. supt. Phoenix Union H.S. and Coll. Dist. Ariz., 1958-65; supt. 1960-61; instr. Ariz. State Univ. (summer) 1959; asst. supt. Sr. H.S., S.F. Unified Sch. Dist., Calif. 1965-68, assoc. supt. 1968-69; instr. Stanford Univ. (summer) 1966; evaluated summer progms., Am. Inst. for Foreign Study (Aberdeen, Scot., Univ. of Southhampton, Eng., Univ. of Grenoble, France, Univ. of Salamanca, Spain), 1967; supt. Barstow Unified Sch. Dist., Calif., 1969---. Pub. speaker on subjts. of edn. Author: Edn. as an Implement of U.S. Foreign Policy, publ. 1938-48, many others. Dir., Investigative Br., Naval Censorship, Panama, 1942-43; ch. Area Deck, Officer of Strategic Servs., London, 1943-44, Paris, 1944; exec. officer SPec. Counter Intelligence Units, Sixth Army Group, Fr., Ger., Australia, 1944-45; asst. Capt., Yokosuka Navy Yard, Tokyo Bay, 1945; Naval Missions to China, Malaya, India, Iran, Egupt, Italy, Morocco, 1945-46; Offc. of Naval Intelligence, Wash. D.C. 1951-52; Comdr., USNR 1954. Awards: Spec. Vt. Scholarship, Middlebury Coll., 1932-36. Mem.: fellow, Inst. of Internat. Edn. 1939-40; No. Calif. Ind. Edn. Council; bd. Dirs. S.F. Jr. Achievement; bd. dirs. S.F. Youth Assn.; bd. dirs. So. Ariz. Sch. for Boys, Tucson; bd. academic adv. Am. Inst. Foreign Study; state adv. bd. Calif. PTA; NEA; Calif. Tchrs. Assn.; Am. Assn. Sch. Admrs.; Assn. for Supv. and Curriculum Devel.; bd. dirs. Maricopa Co. Council Retarded Chil.; bd. dirs. Florence Crittenton Home; Rotary Internat., C. of C., Kiwanis, Mason. Page, Vt. House of Reps. 1925-26. Protestant, (Sci. of Mind). Hobby: langs. Rec.: hiking, garden, travel. Home: 28969 Morro St., Barstow, Calif.; Office: 551 S. H St., Barstow, Calif. 92311.

ALLEN, CHESTER W.
Real Estate Developer — Author
b. July 6, 1931, Long Beach, Calif.; s. Chester T. and Gail (Williamson) Allen; (father, pioneer oil tool mfgr.); B.A., Stanford Univ., 1953; chil.: Tami G., b. Apr. 13, 1959;

Mark D., b. Apr. 23, 1961. Career: pres., Allen Coring Ltd., Edmonton, Canada, 1956-58; pres., Allen Industries Ltd., Seward, Alaska, 1958-62; pres., Allen Associates Realtors, 1965-76; pres., Chet Allen, Inc., 1976---. Author & lecturer on Developing, Syndicating and Big Money Brokerage and Analyzing Investment Properties. Pres., Associated Investment and Exchange Counselors, 1970; pres., Bay Area Exchange Counselors, 1976, 1977; gov., National Soc. of Exchange Counselors. 1st Lt., U.S. Marine Corps, 1953-55. Winner, best R.E. exchange in the U.S., 1973; winner, best exchange over $500,000, Calif., 1975, 1977; winner, most outstanding exchange, Calif., 1976. Rec.: flying, tennis, skiing, golf, scuba diving, backpacking. Home: Rte. 1, Box 692, Sutter Creek, CA 95685; Office: Box 610, Jackson, CA 95642.

ALLEN, DONALD EUGENE
Endodontist
b. Sept. 18, 1918, Dodge City, Kan.; s. Charles and Lena (Merk) Allen; D.D.S., Univ. of Mo., Kansas City, 1942; Diplomate Am. Bd. Endodontists, 1965; Fellow Am. Assn. of Endodontists, 1965; m. Elizabeth Jane Allen, Aug. 6, 1943, Coeur d'Alene, Idaho; chil.: Robert Marshall, b. Apr. 14, 1948; Nancy C., b. July 5, 1956; Judith A., b. July 24, 1957. Career: individual practice, 1946---; endodontics, 1958---; tchr., Endodontics Coll. Physicians & Surgeons, 1960-61. Served to Lt. Comdr., 1942-46. Pres., Santa Clara Co. Dental Soc., 1964-65; bd. dir., Salvation Army. Republican; pres., Repub. assem. Santa Clara Co., 1954. Protestant. Hobbies: gardening, building, painting. Rec.: golf, fishing, travel. Home: 1641 University Way, San Jose, CA 95126; Office: 1680-D Westwood Dr., San Jose, CA 95125.

ALLEN, HOWARD PFEIFFER
Utility Company Executive
b. Oct. 7, 1925, Upland, Calif.; s. Howard Clinton and Emma Maude (Pfeiffer) Allen; B.A. cum laude, Pomona Coll., 1948; J.D., Stanford Univ. Law Sch., 1951; m. Dixie Mae Illa, May 14, 1948, Upland; dau. Alisa Cary, b. Mar. 22, 1957. Career: asst. Dean of Law Sch. and asst. prof. of law, Stanford Univ., 1951-54; with So. Calif. Edison Co., 1954---: spec. rep. 1954; asst. to v.p., 1955; spec. counsel, 1959; v.p., 1962; v.p. and asst. to pres., 1969; sr. v.p., 1971; exec. vice pres., 1973---. Dir.: Calif. Fed. Svgs. and Loan Assn.; Republic Corp.; L.A. Co. Fair Assn.; Pacific Coast Electrical Assn.; L.A. area C. of C., 1969---, pres. 1978. Trustee, Pomona Coll.; bd. dir., Friends of Claremont Colleges, Calif. State Univ. and Colleges Found.; v.p., the Chancellor's Assocs.; mem. L.A. Co. Election Commn., chmn, 1971-72; bus. advis. bd., Nat. Alliance of Businessmen; bd. dir., So. Calif. Rapid Transit Dist., 64-67; mem. Mayor's Spec. Com. on Olympics and L.A. Olympic Orgn. Com., 1978---. Mem.: U.S. Supreme Ct. Bar; Calif. State Bar; Am. Calif., L.A. Co., S.F. Bar Assns.; Am. Judicature Soc. Clubs: Calif. Jonathan in L.A.; Bohemian, Pacific Union in S.F. Episcopalian; past vestryman & clerk of vestry. Office: 2244 Walnut Grove Ave., Rosemead, CA 91770.

ALLEN, HOWARD PFEIFFER
Vice President, So. Calif. Edison Co.
b. Oct. 7, 1925, Upland, Calif.; s. Howard Clinton and Emma Maud (Pfeiffer) Allen; ed. B.A. (cum laude), Pomona Coll. 1948; LL.B., Stanford Univ. Law Sch. 1951; m. Dixie Mae Illa, Upland, Calif., May 14, 1948; chil.: Alisa Cary, b. Mar. 22, 1957. Career: Asst. dean-asst. prof. of law, Stanford Univ. Law Sch., Calif. 1951-54; assoc with So. Calif. Edison Co., L.A. 1954---, v.p. 1962-71, sr. v.p. 1971, exec. v.p. 1973---. Dir.: Repub. Corp., Friends of Claremont Coll.; trustee, Pomona Coll.; Calif. Fed. Svgs. & Loan Assn. Mem.: bd. dir., pres., L.A. C. of C.; Masons, Shrine, Scottish Rite, Phi Delta Phi, Phi Beta Kappa, Jonathan Club, Calif. Club, Bohemian Club, Pacific Union Club, S.F. Episcopalian. Home: 2541 Mountain Ave., Claremont, CA; Office: 2244 Walnut Grove Ave., Rosemead, Calif.

ALLEN, JESSE BISHOP
University Dean
b. Nov. 11, 1914, Trixie, Ky.; s. Toulmin G. and Lucy (Bishop) Allen; A.B. economics, Berea Coll., Ky., 1941; M.S. mktg., Indian Univ., Bloomington, Ind., 1942; Ph.D. bus. adm., Univ. of Chicago, 1952; m. Betty Marie Foss, Feb. 4, 1944, Long Beach; Chil.: John, b. Nov. 26, 1944; James, b. Nov. 27, 1946; Barbara (Mrs. Norman Eddy), b. Nov. 23, 1949; Jerry, b. Dec. 26, 1950; Brenda (Mrs. R. THomas Graham), b. Nov. 26, 1953; Thomas, b. Mar. 10, 1955; Bonnie (Mrs. Rick Hrdina), b. Aug. 16, 1958. Career: Instr., DePaul Univ., Chicago, 1946-47; Miami Univ., Oxford, Oh., 1947-48; asst. prof., Washburn Univ., Topeka, Kan., 1948-49; lectr., Kansas State Tchrs. Coll., Pittsburg, Kan., summer 1949; asst. prof., Cal. State Long

Beach, 1952-58; prof. of mktg., Cal. State, L.A., 1958-70; Dean, Bus. and Economics, Humboldt State Univ., Arcata, 1970---. Served Ens. to Lt., USNR, 1942-45; comdr. Armed Guard Units aboard merchant ships. Home: Rt. 1, P.O.B. 419B, Eureka, CA 95501; Office: Siemens Hall, Humboldt State Univ., Arcata, CA 95521.

ALLEN, REX WHITAKER
Architect
b. Dec. 21, 1914, San Francisco; s. Lewis Whitaker and Maude Rex (Allen) Allen; A.B., Harvard Coll., 1936; M.Arch., Harvard Grad. Sch. of Design, 1939; m. Bettie J. Crossfield, Nov. 6, 1971, S.F.; chil.: Alexandra (Fleckles), b. Dec. 25, 1942; Frances Lambert (Dunn), b. Dec. 13, 1946; Mark Batchelor, b. July 8, 1950; Susan Moore, b. Oct. 13, 1951. Career: With Research and Planning Assocs., N.Y.C., 1939-42; Camloc Fastener Corp., N.Y.C., 1942-45; Isadore Rosenfield, architect, N.Y.C., 1945-48; Blanchard and Maher, architects, S.F., 1949-52; Est. pvt. practice, S.F., 1953; pres., Rex Whitaker Allen & Assoc., 1961-71; pres., Architectural Prodns., Inc. and partner, Rex Allen Partnership, 1971-76; pres., Rex Allen-Drever-Lechowski, Architects, 1976---. Author: Hospital Planning Handbook, Wiley & Sons, N.Y., 1976. Prin. works incl. French Hosp., S.F.; Mercy Hosp., Sacto.; Roseville Dist. Hosp.; Highland Hosp., Oakland; St. Francis Hosp., S.F.; Dominican Hosp., Santa Cruz; Alta Bates Hosp., Berkeley; Boston City Hosp. Out-Patient Bldg.; Woodland Memorial Hosp.; Stanislaus Meml. Hosp., Modesto; Madera Community Hosp.; Sacred Heart Hosp., Eugene, Ore.; St. Joseph Hosp., Mt. Clemens, Mich. Fellow, AIA, nat. pres. 1969-70; hon. fellow Royal Archtl. Inst. Can.; mem. Constrn. Specification Inst., pres. S.F. chpt., 1961; bd. dir., S.F. Zool. Soc., 1976---; Mem.: Assn. Western Hosps.; Calif. and Am. Hosp. Assns.; Internat. Hosp. Fedn.; Am. Assn. Hosp. Planning, pres. 1971-72; Pan Am. Fedn. Architecture; S.F. C. of C.; Am. Public Health Assn.; Royal Soc. Health; S.F. Planning and Urban Renewal Assn.; S.F. Museum of Art; S.F. Symphony Found.; Sierra Club; Harvard Club (S.F., NYC). Home: 4718 17th St., S.F., CA 94117; Office: 425 Battery St., S.F., CA 94111.

ALLISON, DONALD ALDEN
Financier — Sportsman
b. Sept. 11, 1907, Los Animas, Colo.; s. Morgan Donaldson and Ada Pearl (Collins) Allison; ed. UCLA 1925-29, ext. elec engr. 1932; navigation, USC 1937-38; navigation certificate, USPS 1940-43; m. Mildred Evelyn Sallee, Los Angeles, Calif., Jan. 1, 1940; chil.: Donald Alden, Jr. (UCLA Grad. Sch.), b. Jan. 28, 1941; Sallie Irene (Sarbonne Sch., Paris, Fr.), b. Sept. 24, 1942. Career: Jr. partner, Brown-Collins Co., 1929-30; vice pres., Don Allison Co. (brokerage-finance bus.), 1932---. Author: mag. articles on Power Boating, Racing, Navigation and Fishing. Navigation instr., Inst. of Navigation, WW II. Mem.: Commodore, Hollywood Yacht Club, 1940---; comdr. U.S. Power Squadron, 1941; pres. Western Region, Am. Power Boat Assn., 1942; dir. Long Beach Yacht Club, 1945---; pres. Tuna Club, 1953; U.S. Sharp Cup Team, 9154-55; (life) Sertoma; Delta Sigma Phi. Republican. Presbyterian. Hobby: reading. Rec.: big game fishing, boating, swimming. Home: 9398 Monte Leon Lane, Beverly Hills, CA; Office: 8271 Beverly Blvd., L.A., CA 90048.

ALLMAN, KATHERINE MIRIAM
College Administrator
b. June 24, 1945, Berkeley, Calif.; d. Ernest Daniel and Zelma Ann (Harding) Allman; A.A. Laney Coll., 1968; B.S. Univ. of Calif., Berkeley, 1971; M.B.A., 1973. Career: mgmt. trainee, Levi Strauss, San Francisco, 1972; acct., Price Waterhouse, Oakland, 1973-74; bus. mgr., Patten Bible Coll., Oakland, Calif., 1974---; treas., Minority Bus. Asst. Student Dev. Found., 1971-75; co-chmn. Black Masters of Bus. Admin. Student Assn., 1971-72; secty., Oakland Local Develop. Corp., 1978---. Mem.: Natl. Assn. of Black Accts.; Western Assn. of Coll. and Univ. Bus. Officers. Christian Evangelical Ch. Home: 3701 Malcolm Ave., Oakland, CA ($/)%; Office: 2433 Coolidge Ave., Oakland, CA 94601.

ALMAGUER, JUAN A.
Physician — Cardiologist
b. Aug. 16, 1940, Monterrey, N.L. Mexico; s. J. Encarnacion and Lydia Guerra De Almaguer; B.A., 1955; M.D., 1964; m. Rita Almaguer, Tampico, Mexico, Dec. 28, 1964; chil.: Rita R., b. Aug. 20, 1965; John A., b. Oct. 6, 1968; Patricia D., b. Apr. 14, 1973. Career: Internship 1965; G.P. residency 1966; GMO, U.S.A.F., 1967-68; int. med. residency, 1969-71; cardiology fellowship, 1971-73; dir., cardiopulmonary dept., Garfield Hosp., 1974; dir., cardiopulmonary dept., Sta. Marta Hosp., 1974---; chief, int. med., Sta. Marta Hosp., 1974---;

1976-77, chief of staff, Sta. Marta Hosp.; 1977-78, chmn., First Hour Pro., Am. Heart Assn., greater L.A. Aff.; dir., ICU-CCU Depts., Sta. Marta Hosp.; rotating dir. CCU, Garfield Med. Center. Captain, U.S.A.F. as GMO, Jan. 1967-Dec. 1968. Mem.: gov. bd., Am. Heart Assn., greater L.A. Aff. Catholic. Hobbies: drawing, painting, traveling. Home: 900 S. El Molino Ave., Pasadena, CA 91106; Office: 500 N. Garfield Ave., Monterey Park, CA 91754.

ALMEIDA, LAURINDO
Guitarist — Composer
b. Sept. 2, 1917, Sao Paulo, Brazil; s. Benjamin and Placedina (Araujo) Almeida; student, Escola Nacional de Musica, Rio de Janeiro, Brazil; m. Deltra Eamon (lyric soprano from Can.), Aug. 3, 1971, Maui, Hawaii; stepchil.: Connie, b. Mar. 21, 1966; Christopher, b. Mar. 10, 1963. Career: performer radio, records, Sao Paulo, Brazil, 1932; soloist with Stan Kenton Orch., 1947-50; composer more than 200 compositions, 1950---; recording artist, Capitol Records, 1952---; guitar underscoring movie music: Star is Born, Godfather, Camelot, Wagon Train, Bonanza, The Agony and The Ecstasy, etc. Winner, 5 Grammy Awards, Acad. of Recording Arts and Sciences (nominated 13 times); awarded Certificate of Appreciation, Am. String Tchrs. Assn., 1977; winner many times, Down Beat, Playboy mags. jazz polls and movie polls, 1947---; credited with Am. debut recordings of Villa-Lobos, Guitar Concerto, Radames Gnatali's, Concerto de Copacabana. Mem. bd. govs., Nat. Acad. of Recording Arts and Sci., 1964---; Mem. ASCAP, N.Y., 1956---; life mem., Am. Fedn. of Musicians; pres., Brazilliance Music Pub.; mem. (incl. Musical group) The L.A.4.; mem. Bohemian Club, S.F. Catholic. Hobbies: plants, woodwork. Rec.: swimming, concert & theatre going. Address: 4104 Witzel Dr., Sherman Oaks, CA 91423.

ALPERIN, MORTON
Company President
b. June 19, 1918, N.Y.C.; s. Simon and Evelyn (Rose) Alperin; ed. B.S., NYU. 1939; M.S., Calif. Inst. of Tech. 1947, Ph.D., 1950; m. Virginia June Harshman, L.A., Calif., 1943, div. 1953; chil.: Terry Michael, b. 1945; James Jeffrey, b. 1948; m. 2d Elaine Patricia Bogen Fisher in 1974, Las Vegas; Career: dir., advanced studies, A.F. office Sci. Research, 1940-57, cons. engr. 1957---; dir. Space Systems and Ind. Automation, Burbank, CA 1959-60; chmn. bd. dirs., Circuitdyne Corp., Pasa.; head, electronic devel. div., Cetron Electronic Corp., Arcadia, CA 1961-62; mgmt. cons., Am. Astrophysics, Monrovia, CA 1962---; pres. TAM Electronics, Pasa; cons. Vehicle Research Corp., Pasa, 1963---; cons. Litton Industries, Beverly Hills, 1963---; cons. Natl. Aeronautics and Space Admn. 1965---; president, Flight Dynamics Res. Corp., Van Nuys, CA 1967---. Editor, Vistas in Astronautics, Vol. I, 1957, Vol. II, 1958. Patentee. Mem.: AAAS, Am. Inst. Aerons. and Astronautics, Brit. Interplanetary Soc., NY Acad. Scis., Sigma Xi. Home: 6000 Lockhurst Dr., Woodland Hills, CA 91367.

ALPERN, HARVEY L.
Physician
b. June 1, 1938, Los Angeles, Calif.; B.A. Pomona Coll., Claremont, 1960; M.D. USC Sch. of Med., 1964. Career: Internship, Cedars of Lebanon Hosp., L.A., 1964-65; Residencies: Med., 1965-67; cardiology, 1967-68, Cedars-Sinai Med. Center; fellowship, St. George's Hosp., London, Eng., 1968-69; pvt. practice, 1969---. Diplomate: Am. Bd. of Internal Med., 1971; Subspec. of Cardiovascular Disease, 1977. Asst. Instr. in Med., UCLA 1970-73. Fellow: Am. Coll. of Cardiology, 1978; Am. Heart Assn. Council on Clin. Cardiology, 1978. Dir: Am. Heart Assn., L.A. Affiliate, 1974-76; PSRO Area XXV, 1978-81. Leo Rigler Award for Outstanding Intern, 1965; Author: Multiple publications on cardiology. Office: 2080 Century Park East, 704, L.A., CA 90067.

ALPHA, TAU RHO
Cartographer
b. Jan. 4, 1939, Lander, Wyo.; s. Andy Gabrial and Fern Mildred Alpha; student, Weber State Coll., 1957-59; B.A., Calif. State Univ., Northridge, 1962; postgrad., Calif. State Univ., Hayward, 1969-71; m. Hazel Ann Marr, Apr. 14, 1962, No. Hollywood; day. Theta, b. June 4, 1967. Career: Cartographer, Office of Marine Geology, U.S. Geol. Survey, Menlo Park, 1962---; author of 60 publ. oblique maps of ocean floor; jr. author on 15 tech. papers of the ocean floor; sr. author: Quantitative Physiographic method of Land Form portrayal: Canadian Cartographer; The Evolution of Icy Bay Alaska: ERTS Final Report, Nat. Tech. Inf. Service; 1978 Regional Geologic and Geophysical Base Maps of Western No. Am. and Adjacent Oceans: U.S. Geol. Survey; A Survey of the properties and uses of selected map projections, U.S. Geol. Survey.

Office: U.S. Dept. of Interior, Pacific Arctic Marine Geology, 345 Middlefield Rd., Menlo Park, CA 94025.

ALTMAN, SHELDON
Veterinarian
b. May 15, 1937, Denver, Colo.; s. Sam B. and Bessie (Radetsky) Altman; B.S. (magna cum laude) Colo. State Univ., 1959; D.V.M., 1961. m. Arlene Barbara, Aug. 23, 1959, Denver, Colo. Chil.: Susan, b. Feb. 4, 1963; Howard, b. Dec. 9, 1964; Eden, b. July 11, 1969. Career: veterinary clin. and surg., Newmark Animal Hosp., Compton, 1961-62; U.S. Army Veterinary Corps, 1962-64; veterinary clin. and surg.: Univ. City Pet Clinic, No. Hollywood, 1965-70; M.S. Animal Hosps., Inc., Burbank, 1970---. Dir.: Shaarey Zedek Cong., 1964---; Emek Hebrew Acad., 1970---. Dir. of Research, Natl. Assn. for Veterinary Acupuncture; cons., veterinary research, UCLA Pain Control Unit; Author: articles on veterinary acupuncture. U.S. Army Capt., 1962-64. Mem.: Am. Veterinary Med. Assn., Calif. Veterinary Med. Assn., So. Calif. Vet-Med. Assn., Am. Vets. for Israel, Am. Animal Hosp. Assn., Center for Chinese Med., Assn. Orthodox Jewish Scientists, Intl. Vet. Acupuncture Soc. Jewish. Office: 2723 W. Olive Ave., Burbank, CA 91505.

ALTUS, GRACE THOMPSON
School Psychologist
b. Jan. 6, 1924, Santa Barbara; d. James Roderick and Mary (Merriman) Thompson; Ph.D., Univ. of Calif., Berkeley, 1949; m. William David Altus, Dec. 24, 1951, Santa Barbara; chil.: Martha Helen, b. 1957; Elizabeth Diane, b. 1958; Deborah Elaine, b. 1959. Career: tchr., Redlands Jr. High Sch., 1944-46; school psychologist, Santa Barbara Co. Schools, 1949-53, dir. of guidance, 1953-56; sch. psychologist, Goleta Union Sch. Dist., 1966---. Fellow, AAAS; fellow, Am. Psychol. Assn., 1956. Pub. articles in profl. journs. Mem., Univ. Calif., Santa Barbara Faculty Women, pres. 1958; mem. Channel City Women's Forum; life mem. Sierra Club. Rec.: Masters swimming, nationally ranked, AAU top ten, 1973---. Home: 767 Las Palmas Dr., Santa Barbara, CA 93110; Office: Goleta Union Sch. Dist., 5689 Hollister Ave., Goleta, CA 93017.

ALTUS, WILLIAM DAVID
Professor Emeritus of Psychology
b. May 28, 1908, Burlington, Kan.; s. Samuel Abraham and Cora Jane (Burch) Altus; A.B., B.S., Kansas State Tchrs. Coll., 1930, M.S., 1932; Ph.D., New York Univ., 1941; m. Grace Merriman Thompson, Dec. 24, 1951, Santa Barbara; chil.: Martha Helen, b. Jan 17, 1957; Elizabeth Diane, b. May 2, 1958; Deborah Elaine, b. Aug. 20, 1959. Career: Clerk, ATSF Railway, 1925-34; principal, Climax High Sch., Kansas, 1934-38; instr., Iola Jr. Coll., 1938-39; instr., Sch. of Edn., N.Y. Univ., 1939-41; instr., Santa Barbara State Coll., 1941-42; asst prof. to prof., Univ. Calif, Santa Barbara, 1946-75; Professor Emeritus of Psychology, 1975---; faculty research lectr., UCSB, 1960-61; chmn., dept. of psychol., 1950-55; contbr. over 60 publ. research articles, 30 research reports to regional and nat. assns. 2d. Lt. to Capt., AUS, 1942-46, psychological officer. Mem.: Channel City Club; Sierra Club; Faculty Club; fellow, AAAS; Fellow, Am. Psychological Assn. (five divs.: teaching, measurement, clin., counseling, mil.) Polit. Independent. Agnostic. Home: 767 Las Palmas Dr., Hope Ranch, Santa Barbara, CA 93110; Office: 6803 Ellison Hall, UCSB, Santa Barbara, CA 93106.

ALVAREZ, ROBERT SMYTH
Library Director
b. June 7, 1912, San Francisco; s. Dr. Walter C. (sr. cons. Mayo Clinic; syndicated newspaper columnist of med. for 24 years) and Harriet (Smyth) Alvarez; brother, Luis W. Alvarez, Nobel Prize winner in physics, 1968; A.B., Univ. of Chicago, 1934; B.S., lib. sci., Univ. of Ill., 1935; Ph.D., Grad. Library Sch. Univ. of Chicago, 1939; m. Janet Crosby, Nov. 4, 1935, Chicago; chil.: David Crosby; Robert S., Jr.; Nancy (Mrs. Eric Wallace). Career: Head, order dept., Enoch Pratt Free Library, Baltimore, 1939-41; dir., Brockton (Mass.) Public Lib., 1941-43; dir., Nashville (Tenn.) Public Lib., 1946-59; dir., Berkeley Public Lib., 1959-61; director, South San Francisco Public Lib., 1966---; tchr. Public Lib. Adminstrn., George Peabody Coll. Library Sch., summers, 1946-59; editor/pub. 3 newsletters: Administrator's Digest, 1965---; Superintendent's Digest, 1977---; Business Information From Your Public Library, 1968---; newspaper columnist on new books, 28 years; many profl. articles; author: Qualifications of Heads of Public Libraries in North-Central States, 1943. Awards: Boss of the Year, Nashville, 1957; Citizen of the Year, So. S.F., 1976. Pres., Tennessee Lib. Assn., 1952-53; pres., So. S.F. Rotary

Club, 19-80; pres., Sequoia Tennis Club, mem. Calif. Golf Club; Nashville, 1954-57; pres., Phi Gamma Delta Alumni Club, Nashville. Episcopalian. vestryman; pres. Men's Club. Rec.: golf. Home: 432 Dorado Way, So. San Francisco, CA 94080; Office: 840 W. Orange Ave., So. San Francisco, CA 94080.

ALVIN, ERNEST E.
Physician -- Plastic Surgeon
b. May 31, 1925, Pittsburgh, Pa.; s. Ernest Eugene (D.D.S.) and Lena (Walling) Alvin; ed. Allegheny Coll. 1941-44; D.D.S., Univ. of Pitts. Dental Sch. 1946; M.D., Hahnemann Med. Coll. 1951; m. Jeanne Elizabeth Gannon, M.D., Pitts., Pa., Oct. 14, 1961; dau. Connie Edith, b. July 14, 1962. Career: Instr., operative dentistry and histology, Univ. of Pa. Sch. of Dentistry, 1946-47; intern, Shadyside Hosp., Pitts., Pa., 1951; res. gen. surg., Bryn Mawr (Pa.) Hosp. 1954; Vets. Adm. Hosp., N.Y. 1955; res. in plastic surg., St. Francis Mem. Hosp., S.F., CA 1956-58; est. pvt. practice, spec. plastic (Maxillo-facial and reconstructive) surg., Santa Ana, Calif. 1962---. Capt., flight surg., USAF 1951-54. Mem.: Am. Soc. of Plastic and Reconstructive Surg., Am. Cleft Palate Assn., Am. Soc. of Maxillo-Facial Surg., Found of Am. Soc. Plastic and Reconstructive Surg., AMA, Calif. Med. Assn. Orange Co. Med. Assn., Psi Omega, Phi Beta Pi. Hobbies: painting, sculpture, photog. Home: 9962 High Cliff Dr., Santa Ana, CA; Office: 801 N. Tustin Ave., Santa Ana, CA.

AMARA, ROY
President, Institute for the Future
b. Apr. 7, 1925, Boston, Mass.; B.S., Mass. Inst. Tech., 1948; M.A., Harvard Univ., 1949; Ph.D., Stanford Univ., 1958; m. Margaret Terestre, July 17, 1949, Boston, Mass.; chil.: Mark Steven, b. June 24, 1950; Dirk Roy, b. Aug. 17, 1952; Christine Margaret, b. Sept. 12, 1956. Career: Stanford Research Insts., 1952-69; sr. research engr., lab. mgr., asst. to the pres., exec. dir., v.p.; president and sr. research fellow, Inst. for the Future, 1970---. USN. 1943-46. Rec.: tennis, swimming, skiing. Home: 491 La Mesa Dr., Portola Valley, CA; Office: 2740 Sand Hill Rd., Menlo Park, CA.

AMES, RICHARD GALYON
Professor of Sociology
b. June 2, 1935, Boston, Mass.; s. Dr. Lawrence M. and Willa Love (Galyon) Ames; desc. one of signers of the Magna Carta in 1215; B.A., George Wash. Univ., 1958; M.A. American Univ., D.C., 1962; Ph.D., sociology, Univ. of No. Carolina, 1970; m. Sue Ann Roedell, June 1971, Castro Valley, Calif.;dau., Andrea Elizabeth, b. Feb. 1974. Career: Analytical statistician, U.S. Bureau of the Census, 1958-60; instr., USC, 1965-67; asst. prof., Syracuse Univ., 1967-69; asst. prof., Cal. State Univ., Hayward, 1969-71; assoc. prof., 1971---; Dean of Acad. Planning, 1975-77. Author: (w/W.P. Richardson, A.C. Higgins) The Handicapped Children of Alamance County: A Medical and Sociological Study, 1965; (w/A.K. Basu, O. Doctorow) Elementary Statistical Theory in Sociology, 1976; research monographs on instructional computing resources for CSU, Hayward; articles for tech. journs. Recipient research grants: Indst. Redel. in Watts (So. Pacific Co.) 1967; Survey of Instructional Computing Usage (Cal. State Univ. and Colleges), 1976; Community Participation in an Urban Forest (U.S. Forest Service) 1978. Mem.: Am. Sociological Assn.; AAAS; Am. Assn. Univ. Adminstrs.; Hayward South Rotary. Hobbies: photog., stained glass. Rec.: camping. Home: 4480 Lawrence Dr., Castro Valley, CA 94546; Office: Calif. State Univ., Hayward, CA 94542.

AMINI, FARIBORZ
Psychiatrist — Educator
b. July 23, 1930, Tehran, Iran; s. Mirz and Farkhondeh (Rezal) Amini; came to U.S. 1949, naturalized 1963; B.S. Math. (highest honors), Univ. Calif., Berkeley, 1953; M.D., Univ. Calif., San Francisco, 1957; m. Elizabeth Ann Cunningham, Feb. 5, 1972; chil.: Ariana Shaheen, Christina Maheen; chil. by previous marriage: Kim Sherren, Lisa, Roshan, Dawn Parveneh. Career: Intern, Detroit Receiving Hosp., 1957-58; research fellow, Cancer Research Inst., Univ. Calif., S.F., 1958-59; resident in psychiatry Neuropsychiat. Inst., Univ. Mich., Children's Psychiat. Hosp. 1959-62; fellow in child psychiatry, UCLA Neuropsychiat. Inst., 1962-63; psychoanalytic training, S.F. Psychoanalytic Inst., 1964-71, mem. faculty, 1973---; mem. faculty, Langley Porter Neuropsychiat. Inst., Univ. Calif., S.F., 1963---; assoc. clin. prof., dir. youth service dept. psychiatry, 1970-77, dir. residency tng. dept.psychiatry, 1976---; dir. out-patient dept. 1977---; visiting lectr. Boalt Hall, Univ. Calif., Berkeley, 1965; also Sch. Criminology; cons. Aid

to Retarded Children, S.F., Family Life Fdn. and Parent Edn. Programs, S.F., Foster Parent Program, S.F., 1975, others. Diplomate Am. Bd. Psychiatry and Neurology. Fellow Am. Psychiat. Assn.; mem. No. Calif. Psychiat. Soc., S.F. Psychoanalytic Inst. and Soc., Phi Beta Kappa, Sigma Xi, Nu Sigma Nu. Contbr. numerous articles to profl. journs. Home: 2027 16th Ave., S.F., CA 94116; Office: 401 Parnassus Ave., S.F., CA 94143.

AMIS, DOUGLAS KEITH
University Administrator
b. Nov. 4, 1948, Valporazio; s. William F. and Victoria B. Amis; A.B., 1971; M.F.A., 1973; M.A., 1975, 1977; D.B.A., 1977; (hon.) B.F.A., 1977; Cert. in Labor-Mgmt. Rels., 1978; Ed.D. (cand.) 1978. Career: instr. for theatre studies, 1971-74; prin., Amis Amis Davis and Liebrenz, 1974---; asst. to Dean, Univ. of S.F., 1974---; prod., KUSF-FM, 1976---; artistic dir., Pleasanton Playhouse, 1971-74; edn. adminstr., Fromm Inst. for Lifelong Learning, 1976-77. Dir., Inst. for Theatre Studies, 1971-74. Mem.: Gerontological Soc., 1976---; Western Gerontological Soc., 1977---; AAUP, 1975---. Democrat. Presbyterian. Hobbies: photog., theatre. Home: 629 Arguello Blvd., No. 103, S.F., CA 94118; Office: Univ. of S.F., San Francisco, CA 94117.

AMOROSO, FRANK
Communications Systems Engineer
b. July 31, 1935, Providence, R.I.; s. Michele, Sr. and Angela Maria Barbara (D'Uva) Amoroso; B.S., M.S. in E.E., Mass. Inst. Tech., 1958; grad. studies: Purdue Univ., 1958-60, Univ. of Turin, Italy (math.), 1964-66 (as guest of Italian govt.). Career: Sr. engr. Edgerton, Germehausen, and Grier, Inc., Boston and Wake Island, 1958; Instr. elec. engrng. Purdue Univ., 1958-59; research engr. Melpar, Inc., Roxbury, Mass., 1959; research engr. Mass. Inst. Tech. Instrumentation Lab., Cambridge, 1960; Litton Systems Advanced Devel. Lab., Waitham, Mass., 1960-61; engr. Melpar Applied Sci. Div., Watertown, Mass., 1961; mem. tech staff RCA Labs. David Sarnoff Research Center, Princeton, N.J., 1962-64; Mitre Corp., Bedford, Mass., 1966-67; sr. applied mathematician Collins Radio Co., Newport Beach, 1967-68; communication systems engr. N.Am. Rockwell Corp., El Segundo, 1968-71, Northrop Electronics div., Palos Verdes Peninsula, 1971-72, Hughes Aircraft Co., Fullerton, 1972---. Contbr. articles profl. journs.; freelance mag. articles (some under pen name) include Biorhythm, the human safety factor, General Aviation Business, Sept. 1975; Model of a middle class commune, The Green Revolution, Spring 1974; Coffee, Tea or the Maharishi, Air California, May 1974; Traffic Safety School with a message, Calif. Highway Patrolman, Nov. 1973. 1st Lt., AUS, Signal Corps., 1961-62. Recipient: RCA Laboratories Award, David Sarnoff Research Center, for research leadinng to improved digital magnetic recording, 1964. Mem.: Calif. and Nat. Socs. Profl. Engrs.; Spellbinders Lit. Guild; IEEE, sr. mem. 1968---; World Plan Exec. Council, exec. gov. of Age of Enlightenment, tchr. Transcendental Mediation Program, 1975---. Hobby: free lance writing. Rec.: tennis, theater, classical music. Home: 271-D W. Alton St., Santa Ana, CA 92707; Office: Hughes Aircraft Co., Box 3310, Fullerton, CA 92634.

ANARGYROS, SPERO DROSOS
Sculptor
b. Jan. 23, 1915, N.Y.C.; s. Drosos and Martha Gustafson (Carlson) Anargyros; ed. scholarships: Art Students Leag., N.U. 1934-35; Master Inst. of United Arts, N.Y. 1936; travel stu., Europe, Africa, Central Am.; Greece, 1970-71; m. Barbara B. Brooks, Boston, Mass, Aug. 26, 1972. Career: Asst. to Mahonri Young, This Is the Place monument, Salt Lake City, 1944-47; exhib. group shows: Natl. Acad. of Design, 1938-40, 53-56, 59; Pac. Acad. Fine Arts, 1940; Calif. State Fair, 1952, 53; deYoung Mus., S.F., 1953, 62, 63; S.F. Art Festivals, 1952, 53, 54, 55; Arch. Leag., N.Y. 1959; Fine Arts Mus., Springfield, Mass. 1959-60; sculpture show, Civic Center, Marin Co. 1965; sculptor works incl. portrait bust of Haile Sellassie, Emperor of Ethiopia, 1943; portrait bust of Athenagoras, A., Patriarch of Greek Orthodox Church 1948: bas-relief portrait of Gen. Simon Bolivar Buckner, Jr., rotunda, State Capitol, Ky. 1949; portrait plaque, Gaetano Merola, S.F. Opera House, 1953; Redwood bas-relief, Pac. Mutual Life Ins. Bldg., S.F., 1955; 17" bronze bas-relief, main ofc. bldg., First Western Bank, S.F., 1957; Hawaii Statehood Medallion, 1959; 15' seal City and Co. of S.F. on Hall of Justice Bldg. 1960; Golden Gate Bridge Medallion commemorating 25th anniversary, 1962; Russell Varian portrait plaque on Physics Lab., Stanford Univ. 1962; Lawrence Mario Gianninni, Bank of Am. Medallion; bas-relief marble portrait, Benjamin Franklin for Franklin Svgs. and Loan Bldg., S.F. 1964; medallion,

Moran Constr. Co Centennial, 1965; sculptures for Chinatown br. Hong-Kong Bank, S.F. 1967; restoring sculpture for Palace of Fine Arts, S.F. 1967---; various portrait busts, medals, incl.: Dr. Jessie Carr, Victor Jules Bergeron (Trader Vic), Charles Buloti, Jr., Raymond Hackett, 1969; His Highness Sheikh Khalid bin Mohammed Al-Oasimi, 1970; 2 busts, Ralph K. Davies, Franklin Hosp., Internat. Bldg.; Commemorative Coin Metal Yellowstone Park Centennial, 1972; 8' bronze of Don Pedro Marinez, K.C.S.S. and medallion, Agana, Guam, April 1973; portrait plaques: Warren A. Bechtel, Bechtel Corp.; Charles J. Berry, Univ. of Alaska, 1973; 12' bronze of Jesus Christ in Resurrection for Memorial Crypt in Agana, Guam, 1974; 7' statue of Hon. P.C. Lujan for Guam, 1974. Project 19, N.E. Africa, 9th A.F., USA, A.F. 1942-44, WW II. Awards: School Art League Medal; St. Gaudens Medal for Fine Draughtmanship, 1934; 1st hon. mention, Natl. Competition for Sculpture, Pomona, Calif. 1938; best Sculpture award, Academic Artists Assn. 1959; Calif. Hist. Soc. Medallion, 1974. Mem.: Natl. Sculpture Soc., 1956, Fellow, 1964; (life) Art Students League., N.Y.; fellow, Internat. Inst. Arts and Letters; Mason (20 years); Bohemian Club. Republican. Christian. Hobbies: fishing, sports cars. Rec.: swimming. Studio: 2503 Clay St., S.F., CA.

ANCKER, CLINTON J(AMES), JR.
Professor of Systems Engineering
b. June 21, 1919, Cedar Falls, Iowa; s. Clinton J. and Fern (Lalan) Ancker; B.S.M.E., Purdue Univ., 1940; M.S., Univ. Calif., Berkeley, 1949; M.E., profl. degree, 1950; Ph.D., Stanford, 1955; m. Margaret Rees, Apr. 11, 1947, Seattle, Wash.; chil.: Clinton J., III, b. June 17, 1948; Evan R., b. Sept. 15, 1950; Megan A. (Bowles), b. June 7, 1953; Scott R., b. Aug. 30, 1957. Career: instr. engring. mechanics, Purdue Univ., 1946-47; asst. prof. engring design, UC, Berkeley, 1947-55; opns. analyst, opns. research office, Johns Hopkins Univ., Md., 1955-56; sr. engr., Booz Allen Applied Research, Inc., 1956-58; mgr., Analco Services Co., 1958-59; head, math and opns. research program, System Development Corp., Santa Monica, 1959-67; dir., Nat. Highway Safety Inst., NHSB, DOT, Wash. D.C., 1967-68; prof. and chmn., Dept. of Indsl. and Systems Engring., USC, 1968---. Contbr. to numerous publs. in engring. and opns. research. 2d Lt. — Capt., AUS, 1941-46, F.A. and tank destroyer units, (Ret.) Col., USAR, 1946---. Mem.: Sigma Xi; Tau Beta Pi; Pi Tau Sigma; Alpha Pi Mu; Omega Rho, nat pres., 1976-78; Soc. of the Cincinnati. Home: 23908 Malibu Knolls Rd., Malibu, CA 90265; Office: Dept. of Indsl. & Syst. Engring., USC, L.A., CA 90007.

ANDERSON, ARNOLD CHARLES
President, Bay Area Rapid Transit
b. Feb. 11, 1913, Oakland, Calif.; s. J.W. and Eulalia Anderson; ed. B.E., Univ. of Calif., Berkeley, 1935; m. Ethel Ann Phillips (dau. of Dr. George W. Phillips, pioneer radio minister, KTAB; bro. Judge George W. Phillips, Jr.), Oakland, Calif.; chil.: Susan Davis, Mrs. Fred (Gail) Remer, Mrs. Lari Remer, Mrs. Neil (Judy) Rasmussen, John W. Career: Real estate broker, 1946---, prof. appraiser, 1950---; Castro Valley Elem Sch. Bd. 1948-51; dir. Township Hosp. Bd. 1950-51; dir.-pres. S.F. Bay Area Rapid Transit Dist. 1957---; Calif. State Inheritance Tax appraiser, 1958---; U.S. Army, 1940-45, WW II; Korea, 1952-54; Col., Inf., USAR (ret.). Mem.: Eucalyptus Lodge No. 243, F&AM. Home: 3566 Jamison Way, Castro Valley; Office: 3335 Castro Valley Blvd., Castro Valley, CA.

ANDERSON, CHARLES ARTHUR
President, Stanford Research Inst.
b. Nov. 14, 1917, Columbus, Oh.; s. Arthur E. and Huldah (Peterson) Anderson; ed. A.B., Univ. of Calif., 1938; M.B.A., Harvard Univ., 1940; m. Elizabeth Rushforth, Reno, Nev., Oct. 27, 1942; chil.: Peter, b. July 18, 1944; Stephen E., b. Apr. 9, 1947; Julia E., b. Apr. 12, 1951. Career: Research asst. Grad. Sch. of Bus. Adm., Harvard Univ., 1940-41, asst. prof., 1945-48; v.p. Magna Power Tool Corp., Menlo Park, 1948-58; assoc. dean-prof. Grad. Sch. of Bus., Stanford Univ., 1958-61; v.p. Kern Co. Land Co., S.F., 1961-64; pres. Walker Mfg. Co., Racine, Wis. 1964-66; pres. J.I. Case Co., Racine, 1966-68; pres.-chief exec. officer, Stanford Research Inst., 1968---. Dir.: Cutler-Hammer, Inc., Milwaukee, 1967---; Natl. Cash Register Co., 1969---; Continental Oil Co., 1970---; Envirotech Corp., Menlo Park, 1973; Owens-Corning Fiberglass Corp., 1973---. Lt. Comdr., U.S. Navy, 1941-45, WW II. Mem.: dir. Calif. State C. of C., 1970---. Rec.: golf, skiing. Home: 2434 Sharon Oaks Dr., Menlo Park, CA 94025; Office: 333 Ravenswood Ave., Menlo Park, CA 94025.

ANDERSON, DORRANCE IVAN
  Dentist
b. Jan. 30, 1917, Blue Earth, Minn.; s. Orville Jay and
Clara Isabelle (Haynen) Anderson; ed. B.S., Ia. State Univ.
1940; D.D.S., Univ. of Minn. 1949 (class pres. 1948-49);
m. Katherine Elizabeth Erickson, Randall, Ia., May 12,
1943; sons: Michael Jon, b. Nov. 10, 1947; Thomas Jay,
b. September 30, 1952. Career: Store mgr., Hap's Ice
Cream Co., Phila. 1936-37; marketing spec., U.S. Dept.
Agri., L.A. 1940-42; Minn. P.O. 1946-49; ofcr. U.S. Pub.
Health Serv. 1949-53; pvt. practice dentistry, Carpinteria,
Calif. 1953---; dir.-cons. World Brotherhood Exch.
1960-63; founder (dental clinics, Madagascar, 1960,
Katmandu, Nepal, Asia, 1961; worked with Dr. ALbert
Schweitzer, Lambarene, Gabon, Africa, 1963; serv. in
jungles of Peru with Wycliffe Bible Translators, Inc. 1964;
serv. on S.S. Hope, Conakry, Guinea, Africa, New Guinea,
Malagasy Repub., Amazonia, Haiti, Sierra Leone,
Sarawak, Korea. Aviator, Capt. USNR, 1942-45, WW II.
Awards: Natl. Dairy Prods. Judging Champion, Conv.
Hall, Atlantic City, N.J. 1940; Alumni Merit Award, Ia.
State Univ. 1969; Mem.: Am., So. Calif. Dental Assns.;
Naval Res. Assn.; Explorer's Club, NYC; Channel City
Club   Santa Barbara; Rotary Club of Montecity, pres.
1969-79; Rotary Internat., World Serv. Com. 1970-73,
Gov. 1973; Navy League, Trinity Luth. Ch., Santa
Barbara. Home: 2251 Camino del Rosario, S.B., CA
93108; Office: 824 Maple Ave., Carpinteria, CA.

ANDERSON, FLORENCE ROSAMOND
  Educator — Consultant
b. San Francisco; d. Gustave Emil and Nellie Elizabeth
(Bengtson) Anderson; B.A., UCLA, 1933; M.A., UCLA,
1938. Career: Instructor, aircraft navigation, USN at
Calif. Poly. Coll., San Luis Obispo, 1943-46; lectr., math.
dept. USC, 1946-50; group leader numerical analysis,
Northrop Aircraft, Hawthorne, 1950-52; instr., math.
dept., El Camino Coll., 1952-53; mem. tch. staff (dir. of
computer programming edn., cons. in numerical analysis),
Rockwell Internat., L.A., 1953-77; Mem.: Am. Math.
Soc.; mathematical assn. of Am.; Assn. for Computing
Machinery, secty. 1970-74, treas. 1964-68; AAUW,
branch secty. 1964-65, branch treas. 1965-66; Pi Mu
Epsilon. Hobbies: travel, photog., music. Rec.: bridge.
Home: 5225 Onaknoll Ave., L.A., CA 90043.

ANDERSON, GUNNAR DONALD
  Artist
b. Mar. 3, 1927, Berkeley; s. Sven and Margaret (Hultien)
Gunnar; student, Calif. Sch. Fine Arts with Clifford Still,
1947-48; B.F.A., Art Center Coll., of Design, with Lorser
Feitelson, 1951; m. Virginia Bullock, Jan. 31, 1953,
Phila., Pa.; chil.: Greta A. (Wagoner), b. Nov. 4, 1955;
Karin, b. Oct. 9, 1960; Paul, b. Feb. 3, 1962. Career: Art.
dir., McCann-Erickson, N.Y.C., 1951-53; Cunningham &
Walsh, 1953-55; Batten, Barton, Durstine & Osborne,
S.F., 1955-63; one man shows: Pantechnicon, S.F.,
1964-71; Gallerie de Tours, L.A., 1964, 65; Norman
Foster Gallery, Corpus Christi, Tex., 1964, 1968, 1970;
Guildhall Gallery, Chicago, 1966, 72; Lord and Taylor
Art Gallery, NYC, 1966-68, 70; Internat. Gallery,
Memphis, 1967, 69, 71; Thor Gallery, Louisville, 1967,
70; Univ. Nebr., Lincoln, 1967; Rosicrucion Egyptian
Mus., San Jose, 1968; Shook Carrington Gallery, San
Antonio, 1968, 72; Shreve & Co., S.F., 1969; Zantman
Art Gallery, Carmel, 1970-73; Frye Mus., Seattle, 1973;
Conacher Galleries, S.F., 1973; Meredith Long Galleries,
Houston, 1970; Dalzell Hatfield Galleries, L.A., 1971;
exhibited in group shows at S.F. Fifth Winter Invitation,
1964; Ft. Worth Art Center, 1966; M.H. de Young Mus.,
S.F., 1968; De Saisset Gallery, Univ. Santa Clara (1st
prize) 1967; rep. in permanent collections at
Brown-Forman Distillers, Louisville; Dalzell Hatfield
Galleriew, L.A.; Guildhall Galleries, Chicago; Conacher
Galleries, S.F.; Meredith Long Galleries, Houston; tchr.
fine art pianting, Acad. of Art Coll., San Francisco.
USCGR, 1945-46. Awards: best figure or portrait, 29th
Ann., Soc. Western Artists, 1971; 3rd prize, Calif. State
Fair, 1971; best in fine art, Soc. Art Center, Alumni,
1972. Illustrator, Oscar Lincoln Busby Stokes, Harcourt,
Brace & World, Inc., 1970. Home: 4583 Belmont Ct.,
Sonoma, CA 95476.

ANDERSON, IVAN DELOS
  Impressionist Artist
b. Feb. 13, 1915, Yankton, S. Dak.; s. Albert and
Elizabeth Anderson; B.A., Yankton Coll., 1937;
cosmetology degree, Polytechnic Coll., L.A., 1939; m.
Bette Stanley (dec.), 1944, San Diego; son, Gregory Ivan
(prominent real estate lawyer, Irvine, Calif.), b. 1951.
Career: designer, Ivan of Hollywood, Beverly Hills,
1938-40; House of Westmore, Hollywood, 1946-47; v.p.,
Nutri-Tonic Corp., Hollywood, 1948-59; profl. fine arts
impressionist artist, painter, 1960---. One man show:

Falco Gallery, Sherman Oaks, 1967; Cagle Galleries,
Lubbock, Tex. 1974; Norton Simon's Hunt-Wesson,
Fullerton, 1974; Huney Gallery, S.D., 1975; The Gallery,
Catalina Island, 1975; Expressions Gallery, Newport
Beach, 1976; Moulton Playhouse, Laguna Beach, 1977;
Chaffey Coll., Cucamonga, 1975; Laguna Beach Mus.,
1974, 75, 76. Rep. in permanent collections: Roy Rogers
Mus., Victorville; Lib. of Congress; L.A. Children's Hosp.;
L.A. Museum; Buffalo Bill Museum, Cody, Wyo.;
numerous pvt. collections; paintings commnd. for posters
include: Hopalong Cassidy, 1976, Catalina Island Casino,
1977, Laguna Beach, Calif., 1977; paintings for
Anderson's Children of the World serigraph series include
Secrets, Mother and Child, Beach Buddies, Boy with
Stick, Baby Brown Eyes and Pinkie. Awarded 45 major
awards including Gold Trophy Grand Nat., 1940, Best
Portrait of Year award, Wilshire Ebel Club, 1967, Grand
prize Meth. Ch. L.A., 1976. Author, illustrator, pub.:
Creative Hairshaping & Hairstyling, 1947 (best litho
textbook of year award, Am. Lithography Soc. 1948);
Hairstyling, 1948. Subject, TV interviews KCET 1978 and
NBC 1979. S/Sgt. AC, AUS, 1941-46. Artist mem.
Laguna Beach Mus., 1970---; exhibitor, Laguna Beach
Festival of Arts, 1974-76; juror Art-a-Fair Festival,
Laguna Beach, 1977-79. Hobbies: fishing, gardening.
Home-Studio: 1060 Flamingo Rd., Laguna Beach, CA
92651.

ANDERSON, JOHN HOWARD
  Veterinarian
b. June 28, 1944, Belleville, Kan.; s. Dean Blair and Laura
Edith (James) Anderson; B.S., 1967, M.S., 1969, D.U.M.,
1975, Kansas State Univ.; postgrad. Univ. of Okla.,
1970-71; Center for Disease Control, Atlanta, 1970; Ph.D.
Med. Mycology, Univ. of Hawaii, 1974. m. Kimberly
Bernhardt, Lake Bluff, Ill., Aug. 16, 1974. dau. Mikaely
Tace, b. Sept. 13, 1978. Career: Grad. teaching asst.,
dept. of botany, Kansas State Univ., 1967-69; grad.
research asst., dept. botany, Univ. Hawaii, 1969-70; grad.
teaching asst., dept. microbiology and botany, Univ. of
Okla., 1970-71; teaching and research asst. dept.
physiology, Sch. Veterinary Medicine, Kansas State Univ.,
1971-75; assoc. veterinarian Lakeshore Animal Hosp.,
Chicago, 1975-76; Valley Veterinary Clinic, Simi Valley,
CA 1976---. Author: The Meliolaceae of Hawaii, 1972;
Cutaneous Asthenia in a Dog, 1978. Mem.: AUMA (pres.
Jr. Kan. chapter 1974); Kan., Ill., Or., So. Calif.
veterinary med. assns.; Medical Mycological Soc. of the
Am.; Human and Animal Mycology; Sigma Xi, Phi Sigma;
Alpha Gamma Rho. Protestant. Rec.: research, literature,
outdoor sports. Office: Valley Veterinary Clinic, 845 Los
Angeles Ave., Simi Valley, CA 93065.

ANDERSON, LEO ELLIS
  Attorney at Law
b. Feb. 20, 1920, Gettysburg, S. Dak.; s. Laurits M. and
Leonora (Ellis) Anderson; ed. pub. schs., grad.
Huntington Park H.S. 1919; Univ. of Redlands, 1920-21;
B.S., B.A., USC, 1924; LL.B. 1927; m. Hollis Norris, Nov.
1, 1933, (dec.); m. Polly Murray, Glendale, Calif., Feb.
12, 1961; son, David H., b. Apr. 23, 1941; stepchil.:
Robert B. Murray, b. Jan. 1, 1940. Career: admitted to
practice law, Calif., 1927; atty. Meserve, Mumper &
Hughes, 1927, partner, 1938---. Dir., Lennox Industries
1950---; pres.-dir., Saybrook Corp., 1967---; trustee, Univ.
of Redlands, 1968-71; trustee, L.A. Philanthropic Found.
Mem. Master, Masonic Lodge, 1938, Grand Master of
Calif. and Hawaii, 1958; potentate, Al Malaikah Temple
of the Shrine, 1968; pres. San Gabriel Country Club
1952-54; Univ. Club of L.A.; Jonathan Club. Republican
(chmn. Repub. Co. Central Com., L.A. 1936-40; State
chmn., Calif. conf. 1946-48, del. Repun. Natl. Conv.,
1936, 40, 44). Protestant. Hobby: gardening. Rec.: golf,
swimming. Home: 1215 S. Orange Grove Blvd., Pasadena,
CA; Office: 333 S. Hope St., 35th Floor, L.A., CA 90071.

ANDERSON, MARTIN CARL
  Economist
b. Aug. 5, 1936, Lowell, Mass.; s. Ralph and Evelyn
Anderson; A.B. summa cum laude, Dartmouth Coll.,
1957; M.S., engrg., bus. ad., Thayer Sch. of Engring. and
Amos Tuck Sch. of Bus. Adminstrn., 1958; Ph.D. indsl.
mgmt., Mass. Inst. Tech., 1962; m. Annelise Graebner,
Sept. 25, 1965. Career: asst. to Dean, Thayer Sch. Engr.,
1959; research fellow, MIT and Harvard Univ., 1961-62;
asst. prof. of finance, Grad. Sch. of Bus., 1965-68; spec.
asst., Pres. of U.S., 1969-70; spec. cons. for Systems
Analysis, U.S. President, 1970-71; mem. Commn. on
Critical Choices for Americans, 1973-75; mem. Council
on Trends and Perspective, U.S. C. of C., 1974-76; mem.,
Defense Manpower Commn., 1975-76; public interest dir.,
Federal Home Loan Bank of S.F., 1972---; mem., Com. on
the Present Danger, 1977---; sr. fellow, Hoover Inst. on
War, Revolution and Peace, Stanford Univ. 1971---. 2nd

Lt. AUS, 1958-59. Author: The Federal Bulldozer: A Critical Analysis of Urban Renewal, 1949-62, MIT Press, 1964; Conscription: A Select and Annotated Bibliography, Hoover Press, 1976; Welfare: The Political Economy of Welfare Reform in the United States, Hoover Press, 1978. Mem. Am. Economic Assn., Phi Beta Kappa. Dir. of Research, Nixon Pres. campaign, 1968; advisor, Reagan pres. campaign, 1976. Home: 565 Arastradero Rd., Palo Alto, CA 94306; Office: Hoover Inst. on War, Revolution and Peace, Stanford, CA 94305.

ANDERSON, MARVIN JOHN
College Dean
b. Jan. 7, 1915, Essex, Iowa; Ph.B. and J.D., Univ. of Wis. 1942; LL.M., N.Y. Univ. Sch. of Law 1964; m. Eda Bach; chil.: Ted Law; Paul Thomas. Career: Law practice in Wis. and Mich.; Gen. Counsel, Secty., v.p. insurance firm; Asst. Dean, Assoc. Prof. of Law, Calif. Western Univ.; Prof. of Law, Registrar, Hastings Coll. of Law, U. of Calif. 1964; Asst. Dean 1965; Assoc. Dean 1966; Vice-Dean 1969; Dean 1971---. Since 1973 has emphasized Hastings Clinical Program. Dir.: Public Advocates, S.F.; No. Calif. Presbyterian Homes, S.F.; S.F. Neighborhood Legal Svc. Found.; Services for Seniors, Inc., S.F.; Alfred and Hamma Fremm Found., S.F.; Trustee: Natl. Jewish Fund (1977 Civic Leader Award); S.F. Theol. Sem.; Whitworth Coll., Spokane, Wash. Mem.: ABA, Assn. Am. Law Schs.; Am. Trial Lawyers; Am. Soc. Legal Hist.; Am. Law Inst.; Am. Soc. Intl. Law; Fellows of the Am. Bar Found.; Order of the Coif; Commonwealth Club; Newcomen Soc.; Oakland Charter Revision Com. Home: 5739 La Salle Ave., Oakland, CA 94611; Office: 198 McAllister St., S.F., CA 94102.

ANDERSON, POUL WILLIAM
Writer
b. Nov. 25, 1926, Bristol, Pa.; s. Anton William and Astrid (Hertz) Anderson; bro., John, prof. of geol., Kent State Univ.; B.S. physics, Univ. of Minn., 1948; m. Karen Kruse, 1953, Berkeley; d. Astrid May (Mrs. Theron Hayes), b. 1954. Career: first published story, 1947; author about 60 books, 200 short stories and essays, etc. ---. Regional v.p., Mystery Writers of Am., 1959-60; Sci. Fiction Writers of Am., 1972-73; mem.: Baker Street Irregulars; Soc. for Creative Anachronism. Hobbies: gardening, carpentry, reading. Rec.: travel, sailing. Home: 3 Las Palomas, Orinda, CA 94563.

ANDERSON, ROBERT NEIL
Research Scientist
b. Nov. 8, 1933, San Jose, Calif.; s. Neil Albert and Millicent (Rosaly) Anderson; ed. B.S. (chem.) Univ. of S.F., 1956; B.S., M.S. (chem. engring.), Univ. of Calif., Berkeley, 1959; Ph.D., Stanford Univ., 1969; m. Drucilla Challberg, Palo Alto, Calif., Feb. 20, 1964. Sons, Todd R. and Scott R. Career: Chem., Arabian Am. Oil Co. 1954-55; research chem., engr.-opns. research analyst, USN Radiological Def. Lab. 1959-69; research assoc. Dept. of Mineral Engring., Stanford Univ., 1969-72; assoc. prof. dept. Applied Earth Sci., Stanford, 1973-74; assoc. prof. 1974-78; prof., 1978---, San Jose State Univ.; v.p. (research), Parlee Anderson Corp. 1971---. Author: approx. 30 sci. publs. High Temperature Sci., 1970. Mem.: Registered Metal. Engr., Calif.; nuclear engr.. Home: 3084 Stelling Dr., Palo Alto, CA 94303; Office: Dept. of Materials Engring., San Jose State Univ., San Jose, CA 95192.

ANDERSON, ROSS F.
Chief Executive Officer, I. Magnin & Co.
b. Mar. 3, 1920, Osceola, Nebr.; s. Frank H. and Edna (Welch) Anderson; ed. A.B., Stanford Univ. 1941; M.B.A., Harvard Grad. Sch. of Bus. Adm. 1943; m. Patricia Garret, S.F., Calif., Oct. 19, 1946; chil.: Ross S., b. Apr. 2, 1951; Bruce G., b. May 23, 1955; Lynn Ann, b. Apr. 30, 1960. Career: R.H. Macy & Co., Inc. 1946-64, v.p. Calif. div. (13 years); Fed. Dept. Stores, Inc., 1964---, group pres.-dir. 1970---; chief exec. ofcr. I Magnin & Co., 1972---; Dir.: Hexcel Corp., 1978---; Congoleum Corp., 1971---; Ampco Foods, Inc., 1974---. Lt., USN 1943-46. Mem.: trustee, Menlo Sch. and Coll.; chmn., Greater S.F. C. of C.; dir. Calif. Retailers Assn., Bay Area Council, S.F. Civic Light Opera Assn., Pacific-Union Club, Bohemian Club. Hobbies: tennis, garden. Home: 98 Stevenson Lane, Atherton, CA 94025; Office: 135 Stockton St., Union Sq., S.F., CA 94108.

ANDERSON, ROY ARNOLD
Chairman of Board, Lockheed Corporation
b. Dec. 15, 1920, Ripon, Calif.; s. Carl Gustav and Esther Marie (Johnson) Anderson; student Humphreys Sch. of Bus.; A.B., Stanford Univ., 1947; M.B.A., 1949, Phi Beta

Kappa; CPA; m. Betty Leona Boehme, June 10, 1948, Stanford; chil.: Ross David, b. 1951; Karyn (Mrs. Paul Meyerhoff, II), b. 1952; Debra Elayne, b. 1953; James Patrick, b. 1967. Career: Westinghouse Elec. Corp., Mgr., factory acctg., 1952-56; Lockheed Missiles & Space Co., mgr., acctg. & finance, and dir., mgmt. controls, 1956-65; Lockheed Georgia Co., dir. of finance, 1965-68; Lockheed Corp., asst. treas., 1968-71; sr. v.p.-finance, 1971-75; vice chmn. bd.-chief financial & admin. officer, 1975-77; chmn. of bd., 1977---. Dir.: Lockheed Corp., 1971---; Avantek, Inc., 1969---; Granite Rock Co., 1969---; United Calif. Bank, 1978---. USNR, 1942-46; 1950-52. Mem.: Stanford Assoc.; Oakmont Country Club, Glendale; Calif. Club; L.A. Club. Republican. Protestant. Rec.: tennis, golf. Home: 4367 Shepherds Lane, La Canada, CA 91011; Office: 2655 N. Hollywood Way, Burbank, CA 91503.

ANDERSON, STUART LeROY
President, Pacific School of Religion
b. Jan. 24, 1912, Elmore, O.; s. George Alfred and Grace Pearl (Longfellow) Anderson; ed. A.B. Albion Coll. 1933, D.D. (honoris causa), 1945; B.D., Chicago Theol. Sem. 1936; M.A., Univ. of Chicago, 1936; Litt. D. (honoris causa), Pacific Univ. 1960; m. Raezella Tom Klepper, Wichita, Kan., Sept. 25, 1935; chil.: Philip Longfellow, b. Apr. 22, 1941; Catherine Raezella, b. Mar. 16, 1948. Career: Ordained to ministry, Congl. Ch. 1936; minister youth, First Ch., L.A., 1936-37; minister, First Ch., Argo, Ill., 1935-36; Glendale, Calif. 1938-43, Long Beach, 1943-50; pres.-prof. homiletics, Pacific Sch. of Relig., Berkeley, 1960---. Moderator, L.A. Assn. Congl-Christian Chs.; U.S. Conf. for World Council Chs. 1961---; asst. moderator, Gen. Synod of United Ch. of Christ, 1961-63. Author: A Faith to Live By, 1959. Mem.: bd. dirs., Rockefeller Bros. Theol. Fellowship Pgm. 1958-64; Tau Kappa Epsilon, Alpha Phi Gamma, Delta Sigma Rho; clubs Rotary, Univ. of Calif. Faculty (Berkeley); Commonwealth (S.F.). Hobby: tennis. Rec.: fishing. Office: 1798 Scenic Ave., Berkeley, CA 94709.

ANDERSON, THEODORE W.
Professor of Statistics and Economics
b. June 5, 1918, Minneapolis, Minn.; A.A. (valedictorian) North Park Coll., 1937; B.S. math, Northwestern Univ., 1939; M.A., math, Princeton Univ., 1942; Ph.D., math, 1945; m. Dorothy Fisher, July 8, 1950; chil.: Robert Lewis; Janet Lynn; Jeanne Elizabeth. Career: asst. in math., Northwestern Univ. 1939-40; instr. in math, Princeton Univ., 1941-43; research assoc., Nat. Defense Research Com., 1943-45; research assoc (Cowles Commn. for research in economics), Univ. of Chicago, 1945-46; Columbia Univ., 1946-63: instr. math. statistics, 1946-47, asst. prof., 1947-50, assoc. prof. 1950-56, prof. 1956-57, chmn. Dept. of Mathematical statistics, 1956-60, 1964-65, acting chmn., 1950-51, 1963; Prof. of Statistics and Economics, Stanford Univ., 1967---; Guggenheim Fellow, Univ. of Stockholm and Cambridge, 1947-48; fellow, Center for Adv. Study in Behavioral Sci. 1957-58; visiting prof.: Univ. of London, Univ. of Moscow, Univ. of Paris, 1967-68; acad. visitor, London Sch. Economics, Polit. Sci., 1974-75; research cons. Cowles Found., 1946-60; cons. Rand Corp., 1949-66; dir.: Naval research proj., math. statistics, Columbia Univ., 1950-68, and Stanford Univ., 1968---; co-prin. investigator, Nat. Sci. Found. Proj., Stanford Univ., 1969---; editor, Annals of Mathematical Statistics, 1950-52. Author: An Introduction to Mutlivariate Statistical Analysis, 1958; The Statistical Analysis of Time Series, 1971; co-author: A Bibliography of Multivariate Statistical Analysis, 1972; Introductory Statistical Analysis, 1974; An Introduction to the Statistical Analysis of Data, 1978; and some 80 articles in statisticaljourns. Mem.: Fellow, AAAS; Am. Statistical Assn.; Econometric Soc.; Inst. of Math. Statistics; Royal Statistical Soc.; Am. Assn. of Univ. Profs.; Am. Math. Soc.; Biometric Soc.; Indian Statistical Inst.; Internat. Statistical Inst.; Phi Beta Kappa; Psychometric Soc.; Sigma Xi; Bernoulli Soc. for Math. Statistics and Probability. Office: Dept. of Statistics, Stanford Univ., Stanford, CA 94305.

ANDERSON, VERNON ELLSWORTH
Professor of Educational Leadership
b. June 15, 1908, Atwater, Minn.; s. Frank Emil and Joanna (Pearson) Anderson; B.S., Univ. of Minn., 1930; M.A., 1936; Ph.D., Univ. of Colo., 1942; m. Alice Parker, Sept. 1, 1931, Wadena, Minn.; dau. Mary Margaret (Mrs. Larry Bayhi), b. Feb. 25, 1933. Career: high sch. prin., Minn. 1930-37; Dean, Worthington Jr. Coll., Minn., 1937-40; Administrv. asst. to Dean, Univ. of Colo., 1940-42; dir. Curriculum Ctr., Assoc. prof. and prof. of Edn., Univ. of Conn., 1946-55; Dean, Coll. of Edn. and prof. of Edn., Univ. of Maryland, 1955-70; ret. Deanship 1970, prof. of Edn., Univ. Md., 1970-73; prof. Emeritus,

1973---; prof. of Edn. Leadership, U.S. Internat. Univ., San Diego, 1974---; dir. of summer sch., Univ. Md., 1955-59. Author: books include Principles and Practices of Secondary Edn. (w/Wm. T. Gruhn) (one of outstanding Edn. books of 1962), 2d 3d., N.Y.: Ronald Press Co.; Principles and Procedures of Curriculum Improvement, 2d ed., N.Y.: Ronald Press, 1965; contbr. monographs, chpts. in books, articles in edn. and nat. journs.: served as speaker, chmn., panel mem. and cons. for confs. in over 20 states, Puerto Rico and Jamaica. Awarded: Distinguished Citizenship, state of Maryland, 1973; emeritus mem., Phi Delta Kappa, 1973; Vernon E. Anderson Lecture series est. by Coll. of Edn., Univ. of Md., 1972; hon. D. of Letters, Susquehanna Univ., Pa., 1972. Editor, School and University, Univ. Colo. 1940-42, Wash. State Curriculum Journ., 1942-44, School Bulletin, Portland Pun. Schs., 1944-46; mem.: Am. Assn. for Higher Edn.; Am. Assn. of Retired Federal Schoolmen's Club; John Dewey Soc.; Md. State Tchrs. Assn.; Nat. Edn. Assn. Lutheran, active in edn. coms. Rec.: travel. Home: 25369 Carmel Knolls Dr., Carmel CA 93923; Office: U.S. Internat. Univ., P.O.B. X26090, San Diego, CA 92126.

ANDERSON, WARREN RONALD
Professor of Electrical Engineering
b. July 31, 1914, Houston, Minn.; s. W. Roy and Helen (Abrahamson) Anderson; nephew of L.A. Weom, pres. Johnston Pump Co., Pasa., Calif. and v.p. Robert Morse and Assocs., Montreal, Can.; ed. A.A., Bethel Coll. 1935; B.S., Univ. of Minn. 1939; B.S. (elec. Engin.), La. State Univ. 1944; m. Dantza Peinovich, Phila., Pa., May 28, 1945; chil.: Richard Godfrey, b. 1946; John Warren, b. 1949; Deborah Annette, b. 1954. Career: Design engr., Automatic Elec. Co., Chicago, 1946; asst. prof., Cal. State Poly. Coll., San Luis Obispo 1946-52; assoc. prof. 1953-58, prof. (elec. engin.), 1958---. Cons. design engr.: Gen. Elec. Co. 1951; edn. cons. 1956; Northrop Aircraft Co. 1952; Western Gear Corp. 1953. U.S. Army Signal Corps, 1942-46, Plant Engin. Agcy. 1944-46, WW II. Awards: Certificate of Appreciation, Am. Inst. of Elec. Engrs. 1963. Mem.: Am. Assn. Univ. Profs.; Cal. State Coll. Profs.; dir. Calif. Soc. Prof. Engrs. 1954-58; pres. Central Coast chpt. 1960-62; dir. Calif. State Employees Assn. 1958-61; senator, Acad. Senate, Calif. State Colls. 1963---, chmn. fiscal affairs com.; various offices, PTA, BSA; (hon.) Poly Phase Club. Republican. Moderator, First Baptist Ch., San Luis Obispo, 1967. Hobby: painting. Home: 573 Jeffrey Dr., San Luis Obispo, CA 93401; Office: Calif. State Polytechnic College, San Luis Obispo, CA 93401.

ANDON, JERAR
Consulting Engineer
b. Feb. 8, 1921, Milford, Mass.; s. Karnid and Zumrout (Khacharian) Andonian; B.M.E., Gen. Motors Inst., 1951; B.S.M.E., Stanford Univ., 1968; m. Nancy Jane Simons, Aug. 29, 1953. Career: Sr. research engr. Gen. Motors Corp., Warren, Mich. and Santa Barbara, 1951-63, 65-69; mech. engr. U.S. Naval Civil Engring. Lab., Port Hueneme, Calif., 1964-65; cons. engr. to mfg. and legal firms in L.A., Washington, D.C. and Santa Barbara, 1969---. U.S. Army, 1942-45, decorated Bronze Star. Registered profl. engr., Calif., Mich. Mem. Soc. of Auto Engrs. (Horning Meml. award 1963), Am. Soc. of Mech. Engrs., Instn. of Mech. Engrs. (Gt. Britain), Tau Beta Pi. Holder patents in field. Home/Office: 98 Loma Media Rd., Santa Barbara, CA 93103.

ANDREWS, CAROL CORDER
Professor of Political Science
b. Wilmington, Del.; d. Kenneth Wilson and Aurelia (Speer) Corder; B.A., Duke Univ., 1960; M.A., Columbia Univ., 1964; Ph.D., 1978; Certificate d'Etudes Politiques: Institut d'Etudes Politiques, Univ. of Paris, France, 1961; certificate, East Asian Inst., Columbia Univ., 1964; Inter-Univ. Program for Chinese Language training, Taipei, Taiwan, 1966-67; son. Frederick Ethan Andrews, b. 1962. Career: researcher, Taiwanese-Mainlander Polit. rels., Brookings Inst., Wash. D.C., 1967; research, Kuomintang Party Archives, Taichung, Taiwan, 1967-68; instr. in Polit. Sci., Holy Names Coll., Oakland, 1970-73; asst. prof. of polit. sci., 1973---; reviewer, articles for Canadian Journ. of Hist., 1977, 1978. Bd. Dir., Alameda Co. chpt., U.N. Assn. USA, 1975-78; bd. dir., World Without War Council of N. Calif., 1979---. Mem.: Phi Beta Kappa; Am. Polit. Sci. Assn.; Women's Caucus for Polit. Sci.; Assn. for Asian Studies; Am. Assn. of Univ. Professors; Commonwealth Club of Calif.; Sierra Club. Democrat. Episcopalian. Hobbies: people, travel. Home: 612 Vicente Ave., Berkeley, CA 94707; Office: 3500 Mountain Blvd., Oakland, CA.

ANDREWS, HAYWARD
Insurance Executive
Apr. 3, 1914, L.A., Calif.; s. Marshall D. and A. Grace (Hayward) Andrews; grandson of Horace Andrews, Cleveland, O.; ed. UCLA 1932-36; m. Elizabeth Jane Easley, L.A., Calif., June 3, 1938. Career: Surety repr., Aetna Casualty & Surety Co., Hartford, Conn. 1937; Ohio, 1937-40, L.A., 1940-42, supt. of agts., L.A. 1946-50; gen. mgr., Aetna Casualty & Surety Co., Portland, Ore. 1950-60; pres. McCollum, Andrews & Assocs. 1960-70; pres. Andrews, Nash & Assoc., 1970---; Pres. Andrews, Nash & Trouville, 1977---; v.p.-dir., Air Servs. and Valley Capital, L.A., 1964-71. Res. Ofcr., 2nd Lt., U.S. Army, 1936-42, active 1942-46, Lt. Col. Inf., WW II. Awards: Army Commendation Medal; Outstanding Achievement Award, Ins. Assn. of L.A. 1964; Pub. Serv. Award, Ins. Brokers Assn. of Calif. 1968; "Mem. of Year," I.I.A.B.A.L.A. 1971. Mem.: chmn., Traffic Safety Comm., Portland, Ore. 1954-58; dir., Ins. Assn. of L.A. 1962-68; pres., 1966; co-founder-chmn., Brush Fire Hazard Abatement, L.A. 1962---; founding mgr.-chmn., Brush Fire Safety Com. 1964---; co-chmn. Casualty & Surety Com., Calif. Assn. of Ins. Agts. 1963-65, 1966-67; Am. Leg., Am. Leg. Luncheon Club; Gov. Com., Calif. Fair Plan Assn. 1969-74; Chancellor's Assoc. of UCLA 1972-76; Waluga Masonic Lodge No. 181, Oswega, Ore.; Scottish Rite, Shrine, Portland, Ore.; Kiwanis Club of L.A.; L.A. Country Club; Kappa Sigma. Republican. Chr. Scbol.: photog. Rec.: swimming, golf. Home: 770 Paseo Miramar St., Pacific Palisades, CA; Office: 2500 Wilshire Blvd., Suite J, L.A., CA 90057.

ANEWALT, ANTHONY
Company President
b. Feb. 4, 1930, San Diego, Calif.; s. H. Philip and Ellen (Cooper) Anewalt; B.A., Stanford Univ., 1951; chil.: John A., b. Dec. 21, 1957; Mary Elizabeth, b. Jan. 31, 1965. Career: Real Estate, insurance salesman, Hotchkiss & Anewalt, Inc., 1952-60; treas., 1961-71; pres. 1972---. Dir.: S.D. Taxpayers Assn., 1972---; Calif. Real Estate Assn., 1966---; S.D. Chpt. ARC 1973---; Calif. Apt. Owners Assn., 1973---; S.D. Apt. & Rental Owners Assn., 1972--- (pres., 1973); Central City Assoc. of S.D., 1972---; S.D.C. of C. Apptd. to S.D. Co. Bd. of Public Welfare. Pres.: S.D. Bd. of Realtors, 1974; S.D. Jr. C. of C., 1960. Honored by Calif. Assn. of Realtors as Hon. Dir. for Life, 1976. U.S.M.C., 1951-53. Mem.: Rotary; Navy League; Am. Arbitration Assn.; Calif. C. of C.; Natl. Assn. of Realtors; Independent Ins. Agents Assn. Clubs: Cuyamaca (founding mem.); La Jolla Beach & Tennis (Life); Who's Who Intl. Hobby: Stamps. Rec.: Tennis, golf. Home: 2484 Azure Coast Dr., La Jolla, CA 92037; Office: 770 B St., No. 202, S.D., CA 92101.

ANGELL, JAMES BROWNE
Professor of Electrical Engineering
b. Dec. 25, 1924, Staten Is., N.Y.; s. Robert Corson and Jessie May (Browne) Angell; ed. S.B. and S.M., MIT 1946, Sc.D. (elec. engin.), 1952; m. Elizabeth Isabelle Rice, Ridgewood, N.J., July 22, 1950; chil.: Charles Lawrence, b. Mar. 14, 1957; Carolyn Corson, b. May 20, 1959. Career: Research asst., MIT, 1946-51; mgr. solid-state circuit research, Philco Corp., Phila, Pa. 1951-60; faculty, Stanford Univ., 1960---; Univ. Carillonneur, 1960---; prof. (elec. engin.), 1962---; Cons., Philco Corp.; cons. Fairchild Semiconductor Div., Dana Labs. Electronics adv. group for Comdg. Gen., U.S. Army Electronics Command, 1964---. Author: 60-pg. sect., handbook of Semiconductor Electronics, 1960; contbr. 20 articles to profl. journs. Mem.: area chmn., Town Incorp. Com. of Portola Valley, Calif. 1963-64; dir. Portola Valley Assn., 1964---; fellow, Inst. of Elec. and Electronics Engrs.; Am. Guild of Organists, Guild of Carillonneurs No. Am.; Am. Assn. Univ. Profs.; AAAS, Tau Beta Phi, Eta Kappa Nu, Sigma Xi, Phi Kappa Sigma. Methodist (dir. Handbell Choir, 1963---). Hobby: music, mt. hiking. Home: 30 Shoshone Pl., Portola Valley, Calif. 94025; Office: Stanford Electronics Labs., Stanford, CA 94305.

ANGELOFF, DANN VALENTINO
President, The Angeloff Company
b. Nov. 15, 1935, Hollywood; s. Dan L. and Spasika Angeloff; B.S., fin., USC, 1958, M.B.A., 1963; m. JoJeanne Ahlstrom, Sept. 26, 1964, San Marino; chil.: Jennifer, b. July 5, 1968; Dann V., Jr., b. July 7, 1971; Julie, b. Oct. 12, 1973. Career: trainee, Dean Witter & Co., Inc., L.A., 1957-60; v.p., Dempsey-Tegeler & Co., L.A., 1960-70; v.p. and dir. of W. coast fin. dept., Reynolds Securities, Inc., 1970-76; pres. and dir., The Angeloff Company, 1976---. Director: Agman, Inc., Fresno; Eskimo Radiator, L.A.; Golden West Homes, Inc., Santa Ana; Margaret Hills, Inc., Newport Beach; Tally Corp., Kent, Wash.; Samco Insurance, Ltd., Hamilton, Bermuda; Sambo's Restaurants, Inc., Santa Barbara.

Served in Calif. Air Nat. Guard. Mem.: The Bond Club, Calif. Club, Jonathan Club, Kappa Beta Phi, Kappa Sigma, USC Assocs., USC Bd. of Governors. Presbyterian. Rec.: tennis; Home: San Marino, CA; Office: 727 W. Seventh St., No. 331, Los Angeles, CA 90017.

ANTON, ROBERT WAYNE
Artist (Magic Realist)
b. July 21, 1946, Glendale, Calif.; s. William G. and Pauline Anton; m. Madelyn Elms, July 22, 1977, Orange Co., Calif. Career: Combat artist and photographer, Vietnam (AUS) 1966-68; comml. artist, graphic artist, photog., Los Angeles, 1969-72; fine arts study work, Oregon, 1972-75; fine arts artist 1976---; extended one-man shows, Portland, Ore. 1974, 75. Best of Show Award, Lake Oswego, Ore. Art Contest, 1974. Paintings on display in MGM Grand Hotel, Las Vegas, Nev. Served AUS, 1965-69, Korea, 1965-66; Vietnam, 1966-68. Hobbies: science, philosophy. Home-Studio: 34021 Golden Lantern, Dana Point, CA 92629.

APPERSON, MARJORIE MAY
Newspaper Publisher
b. San Francisco; d. J. Philip, M.D. and Jessie Earl Sampson; B.A., journalism, Stanford Univ.; chil.: Virginia Lyn, b. June 14, 1952; John Alexander, b. Sept. 22, 1955; April Jean, b. Apr. 23, 1954. Career: co-owner, Mount Shasta Herald, 1950---: editor, 1965---; co-owner and editor, Weed Press, 1970---; co-publisher and editor, Southern Siskiyou Newspapers, 1978---. Dir., Calif. Newspaper Publs. Assn., 1977, 78, pres. and v.p., Mid Valley Unit, 1976, 1975; chmn., Mount Shasta Planning Commn., 1970; mem., Siskiyou Co. Archtl. Advis. Com., 1970---; mem. Siskiyou Co. Overall Economic Devel. Com. 1967-70; v.p., Mt. Shasta Branch, AAUW, 1973. Office: 316 Chestnut St., Mt. Shasta, CA 96067.

APPLEBAUM, ARNOLD NEAL
Company President
b. Apr. 11, 1941, Lynn, Mass.; s. Samuel and Rose Applebaum; grad. Cerritos Coll., 1964; m. Ronnie Harrison, Anaheim, Calif., Oct. 27, 1963; chil.: Robin Lynn, b. Oct. 29, 1965; Edward Blayne, b. Nov. 13, 1957. Career: sole propr. A & A Electronics, Inc., 1965-67; pres., Consolidated Semiconductor Corp., 1965-67; pres. and bd. chmn., Solid State Devices, Inc. 1967---. Devel. of ion implantation systems and processes, 1971---. U.S. patent and trademark — EPION. Mem.: B'Nai Brith, pres. Whittier B'Nai Brith Youth Assn. 1962. Treas. 25th Cong. dist. dem. com. 1963-64. Hobbies: sports car restoration, watch & clock collecting. Rec.: tennis. Home: 525 W. Las Palmas, Fullerton, CA; Office: 14830 Valley View Ave., La Mirada, CA 90638.

ARABIAN, ARMAND
Superior Court Judge
b. Dec. 12, 1934, N.Y.C.; ed. B.S. (bus. adm), Boston Univ. Coll. of Bus. Adm. 1956; LL.B. (class pres.), Sch. of Law, 1961; Distinguished Mil Grad., Qualified Air Borne Sch. 1956; Jump Master Sch., 1956-58; U.S. Army Pathfinder's Sch., 1960; L.L.M., USC 1970; m. Nancy Megurian, Aug. 27, 1962; chil.: Allison Ann, b. Nov. 12, 1965; Robert Armand, b. Nov. 6, 1969. Career: Deputy Dist. Atty., L.A. Co., 1962-63; estab. pvt. practice law, Van Nuys, CA, 1963--- (successfully defended: Glen Roskilly, animal stock dispute, Humane Soc. of Calif., Saugus; Donald Blyth against chgs. by actress Hedy Lamarr). Apptd. Judge, Municipal Ct., L.A. Co. (by Gov. Reagan), 1972-73; Judge, Superior Ct., 1973---. 1st Lt. U.S. Army Inf. Mem.: pres. Sigma Phi Epsilon, 1965; permanent class pres., Boston Univ. Sch. of Law, 1961; INternat. Footprint Assn., Hollywood Masquers Club. Republican. St. Peter's Armenian Apostolic Ch., Van Nuys. Office: Superior Ct., 6230 Sylmar Ave., Van Nuys, CA 91401.

ARBUCKLE, ERNEST COMINGS
Banker
b. Sept. 5, 1912, Lee, N.H.; s. Frank Albert and Ernestine C. (Weeden) Arbuckle; ed. A.B. Stanford Univ. 1933; Stanford Univ. Law Sch. 1933-34; M.B.A., Stanford Univ. Grad. Sch. of Bus. 1936; m. Katherine Norris Hall, Dec. 10, 1942; chil.: Ernest C., Jr., b. Sept. 17. 1944; Joan M., b. Aug. 12, 1946; Katherine H., B. Mar. 15, 1948; Susan H., b. July 11, 1952. Career: Ind. rels.-orgn. analyst, Standard Oil Co., Ltd. 1946-50; exec. v.p., Pac. Coast Div. W.R. Grace & Co., exec. v.p., Foster and Kleiser Div. and v.p. Grace & Co. Central Am. 1950-58; dean, Grad. Sch. of Bus., Stanford Univ., 1958-68; chmn. Wells Fargo Bank, N.A. 1968-77; Chmn.-CEO, Saga Corp., 1978---; chmn. bd., Stanford Research Inst. 1966-70; trustee, Stanford Univ. Dir.: Castle & Cooke, Inc.,

Hewlett-Packard Co., Owens-Illinois, Inc., Safeway Stores, Inc., Utah Internat., Inc.. Lt. Comdr., USN, 1941-45, WW II. Awards: Silver Star, Purple Heart, Freedoms Found. Award. Mem.: California, Pac.-Union, Bohemian Clubs. Hobby: gardening. Rec.: hunting, fishing. Home: 12 Arastradero Rd., Menlo Park, CA; Office: One Saga Lane, Menlo Park, CA 94025.

ARCHER, DOLORES (DEE)
Realtor
b. Mar. 20, 1929, Taft, Calif.; d. Walter and Esther (Kolbe) McWhorter; gr.grandau., Rosa Sepulveda, early Calif. settler; student, Santa Monica City Coll.; licensed real estate broker; div.; chil.: Karen Kelly (Holliday), b. 1948; Patti Kelly, b. 1954. Career: fashion model, 1949-55; real estate agent, 1958; real estate broker, 1960---: opened DK Realty, 1960; pres., treas. Executive Homes, Inc. and Executive Realtors, 1968---. Hobbies: painting, tennis. Office: 17043 Ventura Blvd., Encino, CA 91316.

ARGUE, JOHN CLIFFORD
Attorney at Law
b. Jan. 25, 1932, Glendale, Calif.; s. John Clifford and Catherine Emily (Clements) Argue; A.B., commerce and finance, Occidental Coll., 1953; LL.B., USC, 1956 (Class Pres.); m. Leah Elizabeth Moore, June 29, 1963, La Canada; chil.: Elizabeth Anne, b. Feb. 8, 1967; John Michael, b. Apr. 17, 1968. Career: Admitted to Calif. Bar 1957, since practiced in L.A.: mem. firm Argue & Argue, 1958-59; sr. partner, Flint & MacKay, 1960-72; Argue, Freston & Myers, 1973---. Dir.: Heritage Life Ins. Co., L.A.; pres. So. Calif. Com. for the Olympic Games; bd. of Governors Occidental Alumni Assn., chmn. Alumni Fund campaign 1965. Served AUS, 1956-58. Mem.: Phi Delta Phi, Alpha Tau Omega, Chancery Club. Rec.: golf, skiing. Home: 1314 Descanso Dr., La Canada, CA 91011; Office: 626 Wilshire Blvd., 10th flr., L.A., CA 90017.

ARLT, GUSTAVE O.,
Author — Professor of German Literature
b. May 17, 1895, Lock Haven, Pa.: s. Hans and Helene (Hoffman) Arlt; desc. Dr. Ritter von Arlt, Vienna (the father of modern eye surg.); ed. A.B. Univ. of Chicago, 1915; M.A., 1929; Ph.D., 1931; (hon.) LL.D.: Univ. of Calif., Elmhurst Coll.; Litt.D.: Brown Univ., Univ. of Ife, Nigeria; L.H.D.: Univ. of Nebr., Claremont Univ.; m. Gusti Herrman, Coblenz, Ger., June 25, 1920; chil: Mrs. Fred (Marlene) Sigmund. Career: Asst. prof. De Pauw Univ. 1924-29; assoc. prof. Indiana Univ. 1930-34; prof. Ger. lit., UCLA 1934-61, prof. emeritus, 1961---; govt. off., Wash. D.C., 1961-72; prof. Student and Acad. Affairs Grad. Div., UCLA 1972---. Editor, Modern Language Forum, 1937-42; co-ed., California Folklore Quarterly, 1941-44; assoc. editor, Western Folklore, 1944---. Author (books): German Lit. in the 18th Century, Johann von Eck, Friedrich von Spee: numerous articles, publ. profl. and edn. journs; translator: Franz Werfel's Jacobowsky and the Colonel (adaptation played on Broadway over yr.); (novel) Franz Werfel's Star of the Unborn. U.S. Army, A.E.F. & A.F. in G. (1917-3), WW I. Mem.: bd. dirs., L.A. Faculty Club, 1947-50; v.p. L.A. Chamber Sym. Soc. 1948---; dir. Calif. Lit Centennial, 1949-50; pres. So. Calif. Folklore Soc. 1952; bd. dirs., Hist. Soc. of So. Calif. 1952---; Scabbard & Blade, Phi Mu Alpha. Republican. Rec.: golf. Office: Murphy Hall, UCLA, Los Angeles, CA 90024.

ARMACOST, GEORGE HENRY
Former President, University of Redlands
b. May 6, 1905, Upperco, Md.; s. Joshua Franklin and Mathilda (Nolto) Armacost; ed. grad. Franklin H.S., Reisterstown, Md. 1922; B.A. Dickinson Coll., Carlisle, Penn., 1926; LL.D., 1947; M.A., Columbia Univ., sel. Standard Oil Co., Cleveland, Oh. 1943; NYC 1930, Ph. D. 1940; grad. work, Johns Hopkins Univ., Baltimore, Md. 1926, 27, 30; (hon.) L.H.D., Coll of Osteopathic Physicians and Surgeons, 1945; P.H.D., Denison Univ. 1957; m. Verda G. Hayden, Oberlin, Oh., June 14, 1933; chil.: Peter H., b. July 1935; Michael H., B. Apr. 1937; Samuel H., b. Mar. 1939; Mary Cole, b. Sept42. Career: prin., Kane Hi. Sch., Kane, Pa. 1926-29, 1932-36; instr. Dept. of Secondary Edn., Tchrs. Coll., Columbia Univ. (summers), 1931-37; prof. of edn.-head of dept.-dean of men, Coll. of William and Mary, Williamsburg, Va. 1937-45; pres. Univ. of Redlands, Calif. 1945-70 (ret.); prof. of edn., Alderson-Broaddus Coll., Philippi, W. Va., 1971-73; Mem.: (hon.) Phi Beta Kappa, (hon.) Phi Delta Kappa, (hon.) Kappa Delta Pi, (hon.) Omicron Delta Kappa. Baptist. Rec.: golf. Home: 650 Palo Alto St., Redlands, CA 92373.

ARMSTRONG, ALICE CATT
Editor — Author

b. Feb. 7, Kan.; d. Charles Harmon and Florence Iles (Pakenham) Catt; desc.: Bull, Stout, Welles, Cooper ancestry, Eng.; Sir Edward M. Pakenham, Brit. Gen.; great-grandniece of Carrie Chapman Catt, woman suffrage leader, listed "Twelve Greatest Women," feat. U.S. postage stamp, June 1948, Turkish series, 1950; great-granddau. of Harmon Catt, pioneer bldr. Ft. Scott, founder (donor), Catt Sch., first standard sch., Bourbon Co., Kan.; Catt Rd., Bourbon Co. named in his honor; ed. H.S. and Jr. Coll., Art Inst., Kan.; numerous spec. courses in journalism, writing, English, speech, dramatic arts and bus.; pvt. sch. dramatic arts (3-yr. scholarship); hon.: Dr. of Humane Letters, St. Olav's Acad., Sweden, 1969; LL.D., No. Pontifical Acad., France, 1969; Litt. D., St. Andrew's Univ. of England., 1969; D. Lit., St. Paul's Coll. and Sem., Rome, 1970; Ph.D., Colo. State, 1972; Dr. of Cultural Arts, Bodkin Bible Inst., Va. 1973; Dr. of Arts Philosophy, Great China Arts Coll., Hong Kong, 1974; LL.D., Lagos Coll., by Archbishop of Nigeria, 1976; son, Gary (Natl. All Am. Boy, 1947; ordained minister). Career: State appt.: actress, theatre groups, incl. Pasadena Playhouse, Artists Exchange; teacher, dramatic arts, H.S., adult groups, forum and own studio, Hollywood, 1947-49; founder-pres.-dir., Who's Who Historical Soc.; pub.-author-editor, Who's Who in L.A. Co., 1949---, Who's Who in Calif., 1954---; Who's Who Enterprises, 1961---; Who's Who Executives in Calif., 1963; serv. many civic, park and hist. projects. Author (book): Who's Who — Dining and Lodging on the North Am. Continent, 1958; children's books, poems, stage skits, short stories, radio dialogue, minstrel and spiritual poems; writer, travelogues, Mardi Gras annual Funtour folders, travel brochures, L.A. 1948-49. Civ. def., mgr.-writer-dir., entertainment groups, L.A. area, WWII. Awards: Woman of Achievement by Calif. Women of the Golden West, 1951; Career Girl of Hollywood, 1951; Natl.Travel Guide Award of 1958, by Natl. Writers Club, Denver; citation, Hollywood Mus. Assocs. 1962; acclaimed Most Headlined Calif. Author, news media, 1963; Wisdom Award of Honor, by Wisdom Mag. 1965; Award by Am. Edn. League, 1966; Mem.: Calif. State C. of C., Travel and Rec. Com., 1956-65; L.A. C. of C. (past.) mem. com.-chmn. spec. guests com., Women's Auz., com. L.A. Beautiful (Keep Am. Beautiful, Inc., Western States Conf. 1960, natl. conv., S.F. 1966); orgn. Sigma Delta Chapter, Columbia Univ. (affiliate), L.A. 1954; (hon.) cits. comm., Army and Navy Legion of Valor; (past 1st v.p.-pgm. chmn., So. Calif. Woman's Press Club; Natl. Writers Club, Denver; hist.-membership chmn., natl. pub. rels. dir.-del natl. conv., Natl. Soc. of Arts and Letters; 1st v.p., Calif. Women of the Golden West, Inc. 1954-56; (past.) pgm. chmn., Hollywood Bowl Assn; OES; Natl. Soc. Magna Charta Dames, Phila., Pa.; (life) The Sovereign Colonial Soc. of Ams. of Royal Descent, Phila., Pa.; Bel-Air Fed. Repub. Women's Club. Hobby: research and study relig. truths. Chr. (ordained minister). Home: 1331 Cordell Pl., L.A., CA 90069.

ARMSTRONG, RUTH ANN
Realtor

b. Sioux City, Iowa; d. Harry Morton and Florence Eva (Welch) Armstrong; B.S. (Bus. Ad.) Univ. of Neb. 1945; Career: Spec. in real estate investments & exchanges. Mem.: Menlo Park-Atherton Bd. of Realtors; Calif. Assn. of Realtors; Natl. Assn. of Realtors; Natl. Council of Exchangors. Past pres., Assoc. Investment & Exchange Counselors; past secty., Peninsula Exchangors. State Genealogist, Natl. Soc. of Colonial Dames. Mem.: Gen. Soc. of Mayflower Descendants, D.A.R., Natl. Genealogical Soc., Conn. Soc. of Genealogists, Genealogical Soc. of Vt. Home: 825 Menlo Ave., Menlo Park, VA 94025; Office: Box 1165, Menlo Park, CA 94025.

ARNDT, MICHAEL P.
Electronics Company Executive

b. Aug. 30, 1930, Mt. Vernon, N.Y.; s. Stanley M. and Helen (Wood) Arndt; ed. B.A., magna cum laude, Pomona Coll., 1952; M.B.A. (with distinction), Harvard Grad. Sch. of Bus. Adm. 1954; Career: Analyst, investment dept., N.Y. Life Ins. Co., S.F., 1954-56; v.p. finance, Electronics Group, TRW, Inc., 1956---. Dir.: Club Mar De Cortez, 1963; Harbor Boat Co. 1963-66. Mem.: dir. Phi Delta Alumni Assn. 1964; Phi Beta Kappa, Phi Delta, Friends of Claremont and Pomona Coll. Assocs., Financial Analysts Soc., Repub. Party Assoc. Rec.: sailing, tennis. Home: 251 S. Barrington Ave., L.A., CA 90049; Office: TRW Inv., 10880 Wilshire Blvd., Suite 1700, L.A., CA 90024.

ARNER, SAMUEL DEWALT
Archaeologist — Explorer — Historian

b. June 17, 1900, Vandergrift Hts., Pa.; s. George W. and Elizabeth (DeWalt) Arner; ed. diploma in law, LaSalle Ext. Univ.; stu. Bellvue Coll., Westminster, Colo.;

Zarepath Bible Inst., N.J., stu. (poetry) Univ. of Calif. Ext.; spec. art courses, pre-med., archael.; m. Violet Stewart, Apr. 12, 1935 (div. Oct. 1953); sons: Paul C., b. Jan. 17, 1936; David D., b. Jan. 17, 1939; Jon Peter, b. July 2, 1942; m. 2nd. Irene C. de Lopez de Santa Anna, Palm Springs, Calif., May 30, 1957. Career: Est. Colo., later N. Mex. res. 1926, Palm Springs, CA 1931; owner, Hotel Arner, various bus., enterprises, and large resort acreage holdings, Palm Springs area; trustee, Desert Estate Co., 1946---. Writer, many poems publ. various periodicals incl. The Woodland Ghost, Oteen, When, 1917-66; contrib. theol articles to ch. mags. 1923-27; theol. lectrs., 1926-31; dir. spec. missions to Latin Am. countries; archaeol. research expeditions in Mex., Central Am., S. Am., 1931---; founder-curator, Mus. of Antiquities and Art, Cathedral City, 1960; archeol. research, Middle East (Egypt, Israel, Lebanon, Turkey, Greece), 1969; painter, hist. character portraits; western landscape artist, reprodn. of ancient Maya and Aztec paintings; contrib. numerous sci. reports to profl. journs. Author: 3 books on Hist. of Mex. Featured in numerous publs. on archaeol. expeditions and museum research incl. Riverside Enterprise, Pittsburgh Press, Salt Lake Tribune, S.F. Examiner, Rochester Call-Bulletin, 1966. Guest, various TV-radio interviews on archaeol. expeditions. Candidate for Congress, 1942. Awards: Certificate of Merit for Archeol. Research; many awards incl.: Internat. Poetry Anthology, Eng. 1972; Internat. Art and Antiques, 1973; Achievement Recognition Inst. 1973; Mem.: dir. Palm Springs Repub. Assembly, 1959---; Comdr. Chpt. 66, DAV 1963; Archaeol Inst. of Am., Am. Mus. of Natural Hist., Internat. Oceanographic Found., Western Mus. League, Am. Assn. of Museums, AAAS, Natl. Geographic Soc., Internat. Platform Assn., Am. Inst. of Fine Art; (past) Archaeol. Soc. of N. Mex.; C. of C., Natl. Realty Bd., Lions Club; Calif. Acad. Sci. 1963-66. Presbyterian. Hobby: photog. Address: 68-595 Plumley Pl., Cathedral City, CA 92234.

ARNOLD, DAVID
Owner, Arnold Glass Studios

b. Apr. 6, 1933, Berkeley; s. Arnold and Janet (Sinaiko) Perstein; B.A., Oberlin Coll., 1954; Army Language Sch., 1956; S.F. Art Inst., 1960. Major stained glass commissions: Hilton Hotel commn. 1964, Shalom Nightclub window, 1965, Harrah's Club office panel, 1966, Joseph Magnin display case, 1967, World Trade Club skylight, 1975. Served AUS, security agency, 1956-59. Recipient Louis C. Tiffany Award, 1966. Mem.: Sierra Club, S.F. Folk Music Club. Hobbies: photog., white water rafting, cross country skiing. Address: Arnold Glass Studios, 1331 Kearny St., S.F., CA 94133.

ARNOLD, HON. STANLEY
Superior Court Judge

b. Sept. 22, 1903, Crown Point, Ind.; s. John Dawson and Mary (Weis) Arnold; ed. St. Josephs Coll., Rensselaer, Ind. 1917-21; LL.B., Univ. of Calif., Hastings Coll. of Law, 1948; m. Almeda Lindquist, Susanville, Calif., May 18, 1928; son: Stanley Dawson, b. Oct. 7, 1931 (atty., Arnold and Arnold, Susanville, Calif.). Career: Lawyer, Arnold and Arnold, Susanville, Calif.; dist. atty., Lassen Co., 1948-55; Calif. Senator, 1955-56; judge, Superior Ct., Lassen Co., Calif. 1965-73. Author: Arnold-Kennick Juvenile Court Law, 1962. Mem.: Calif. Council on Criminal Justice; Am. Judicature Soc.; (hon.) Order of the Coif, Hastings Coll. of Law; exalted ruler, BPOE 1935; pres. Rotary Club, 1941; chmn. Lassen Co. Dem. Com. and Calif. State Dem. Exec. Com. 1950-55; bd. govs., Hastings Coll. of Law Alumni Assn. 1965-73. Home: 240 S. Pine St., Susanville, CA.

ARNOLD, RALPH V.
Banker

b. Mar. 26, 1907, Bryant, S. Dak.; s. Oscar and Kathryn (Stoeckel) Arnold; ed. B.A., Pomona Coll. 1928; m. Helen A. Owens, Hollywood, Calif., 1930; chil.: Anthony O. and Barbara Hagan. Career: City Councilman, City of Ontario, 1944-48; pres.-dir. First Natl. Bank of Ontario, 1958---, chmn. bd. 1962---. Dir.: Trans World Svgs. & Loan Assn. 1960---; Fed. Res. Bank of S.F., L.A., Br. 1961---, S.F. 1966; Mem.: past pres., Independent Bankers Assn. of So. Calif.; exec. com., Am. Bankers Assn., 1961---; pres. Calif. Bankers Assn. 1961-62; past pres. Kiwanis Club; Nu Alpha Phi, pres. Red Hill Country Club, 1974. Rec.: fishing, golf, travel. Home: 8430 Country Club Dr., Cucamonga, CA.

ARNST, NORINE M.
Company Executive

b. Oct. 17, 1947, Chicago, Ill.; d. John and Mildred Bortz; B.A. Univ. of Wis., 1969. Career: editor, employee publications, Litton Automated Business Systems,

Athens, Oh. 1969-73; writer/photog. 1973-74; pub. rel. R.I. Hosp. Trust Natl. Bank, 1974-75; personnel dir., Gottschalk's Dept. Store, 1975-78; man., executive devel. training, The Emporium, 1978---. Cited in The Ragan Report, Ideas Unlmtd., & Svc. for editorial excellence, 1969-73. 1978 Young Career Woman of the Month (Business & Industry), Fresno chpt. Bus. & Prof. Womens Club. Mem.: YWCA (gov. member-at-large 1975), West Bay Choral; Chi Omega Alumnae. Rec.: cross country skiing, cycling, racquetball, stained glass. Home: 4727 25th St., S.F., CA 94114; Office: 835 Market St., S.F., CA 94103.

ASCHERMAN, STANFORD WARREN
Surgeon
b. Aug. 18, 1926, Chicago, Ill.; s. Elmer N. (M.D.) and Irma G. (Kapper) Ascherman; ed. A.B., Stanford Univ. 1947; B.S., Univ. of Ill. 1948; M.D., 1950. Career: Intern, Cook Co. Hosp., Chicago, 1950-51; res in surg.: Bellevue Hosp., Columbia Univ.; Mt. Sinai Hosp., N.Y., 1953-54; chief res. surg., Bronx Municipal Hosp. Center, N.Y., 1954-56; pvt. surg. practice, S.F., Calif., 1959---; surg. staff: Peninsula Hosp., Burlingame, Calif.; Sequoia Hosp., Redwood City, Calif. Contrib. to various publs. incl. AMA Archives of Surg. Med. Corps, USAAF, Chanute AFB, Clark AFB, Philippines; Tainan, Taiwan; French Morocco. Mem.: diplomate, Natl. Bd. Med. Examiners, 1950; diplomate, Am. Bd. Surg. 1958; fellow, Internat. Coll. of Surgs.; Pan Pac. Med. Assn.; Phi Lambda Kappa. Jewish. Home: The Comstock, S.F.; Office: Suite 1600-1, 450 Sutter St., S.F., CA.

ASH, ROY LAWRENCE
Chairman-CEO, AM International Inc.
b. Oct. 20, 1918, L.A., Calif.; s. Charles K. and Fay E. (Dickinson) Ash; ed. M.B.A., Harvard Univ. 1947; m. Lila M. Hornbek, L.A., Calif., Nov. 13, 1943; chil.: Loretta, James, Marilyn, Robert, Charles. Career: Bank of Am. 1936-42; 1947-49; chief financial ofcr. Hughes Aircraft Co., 1949-53; co-found. Litton Inds., Inc. 1953, pres.-dir. 1961-72; U.S. Budget Dir. 1972-75; chmn., CEO, AM Internat., 1976---. Dir.: Bank of Am., Bank of Am. Corp., Global Marine, Inc., Pac. Mutual Life Ins. Co.; Western Airlines, 1976---; chmn. Pres. Adv. Council on Exec. Orgn. 1969; co-chmn. Japan-Calif. Assn.; pres.-bd. dirs., L.A. World Affairs Council, 1970-72; trustee, Calif. Inst. of Tech.; trustee, Com. for Econ. Devel. Capt., USAD, WW II. Mem.: Knights of Malta, Harvard Club, Bel-Air Country Club. Home: 655 Funchal Rd., L.A., CA 90024; Office: 1900 Ave. of the Stars, L.A., CA 90067.

ASHBY, JACK LANE
President, Kaiser Steel Corporation
b. Apr. 3, 1911, Berkeley, Calif.; s. Dr. Shirley J. and Lola (McKellips) Ashby; ed. A.B. Stanford Univ. 1933; m. Patricia Robbins, S.F., Calif., June 17, 1936; chil.: Peter, b. Oct. 7, 1937; Robert, b. Sept. 10, 1938; Richard, b. July 28, 1942; Charlotte, b. Mar. 29, 1945; Sarah, b. Sept. 22, 1950. Career: Various positions with financial and investment firms, S.F., 1933-42; E.F. Hutton & Co., S.F. 1933-35; mgr., Brokerage Dept., Eastland & Co., S.F., 1935-38; Irving Lundborg & Co., S.F., 1938-39; No. Calif. Ind. mfg., Commercial Investment Trust Corp., S.F., 1940-41; expediter of materials nad equipment, Kaiser Steel Corp. 1942, sales mgr. 1943, gen. sales mgr. 1944, v.p. and asst. gen. mgr. 1947, v.p.-gen. mgr. 1948, pres. 1959-69; chmn. Kaiser Resources Ltd.; v. chmn.-dir. Kaiser Steel Corp. Dir.: Hamersley Iron Pty. Ltd., Australia; Myers Drum Co. 1954---. Mem.: exec. com.-bd. dirs., Am. Iron & Steel Inst.; bd. dirs., Natl. Ind. Conf. Bd.; Napa Co. Farm Bur., Am. Angus Assn.; Delta Kappa Epsilon; Pac.-Union Club; The Family Club, S.F.; Claremont Country Club, Oakland; Calif. Club. Hobby: gardening. Rec.: golf, fishing, swimming, boating. Home: 2210 Soda Canyon Rd., Napa, CA 94558; Office: Kaiser Center, 300 Lakeside Dr., Oakland, CA.

ASIMUS, DANIEL MARION
Psychiatrist
b. Dec. 8, 1946, Cincinnati, Ohio; s. Fred and Betty Asimus; B.S., Xavier Univ., 1968, M.D., 1972; MSED, USC, 1976, completion of Psychiat. Residency, 1976; m. Chey, 1970, Cincinnati, Ohio; dau. Heide, b. Oct. 19, 1974. Career: completion med. internship 1973; completion psychiatric residency 1976; full-time pres., Physicians National House Staff Assn., 1977; founder and bd. dir., Creative Psychiatric Inst., 1978---: Mem. Natl. Jt. Commn. on Interprofl. Affairs; mem. Secty. Califano's Advis. Com. on Nat. Health Insurance; pres., Calif. Assn. of Day Treatment Programs; chmn., area XVIII PSRO psychiatric com.; med. dir., Day Treatment Program, Glendale Adventist Med. Center; asst. prof. of Psychiatry, Loma Linda Coll. of Med. Contbr. Predicting Interprofl.

Rels. in the '80s, Hospital and Community Psychiatry. Mem.: Am. Psychiat. Assn., Falk Fellow 1973-76; mem. Am. Assn. of Sex Educators Counselors and Therapists; founding mem., Masters and Johnson Found. Rec.: jogging, racquetball, skiing. Office: 50 Bellefontaine St., Suite 102, Pasadena, CA 91105.

ASKIN, WALTER MILLER
Professor of Art
b. Sept. 12, 1929, Pasadena; s. Paul Henry and Dorothy Margaret (Miller) Askin; B.A., Univ. Calif., Berkeley, 1951, M.A., 1952; studies: Ruskin Sch. of Drawing and Fine Art, Oxford Univ.; m. Doris Mae Anderson, Sept. 16, 1950, Berkeley; dau. Nancy Carol (Oudegeest), b. June 27, 1951. Career: tchr.: Calif. State Univ., L.A., 1956---; Legion of Honor Mus., S.F., 1953-54; Univ. Calif., Berkeley, 1954, 1968-69; Univ. of N. Mex., 1972; Pasadena Art Mus., 1959-63, 1974; Calif. State Univ., Long Beach, 1974-75. Exhibited in over 500 museum and univ. art galleries internat.; one man shows include: De Young Mus., S.F., 1954; Paul Rivas Gallery, L.A., 1960; Pasadena Art Mus., 1960; Hollis Gallery, S.F., 1964; Santa Barbara Mus. of Art, 1967; La Jolla Mus. of Art, 1967; Adele Bednarz Galleries, L.A., 1968, 1974; UC, Berkeley, 1968; Hank Baum Gallery, S.F., 1970, 74, 76; Cal Tech, Pasadena, 1973; Hellenic Am. Union, Athens, Greece, 1973; Cal. State Univ., L.B., 1975; Ericson Gallery, N.Y., 1978. Work in permanent public collections include: Calif. State Univs., Long Beach, L.A., San Diego, Stanislaus; Herbert F. Johnson Mus., Cornel Univ.; L.A. Co Mus. of Art; Mus. of Contemporary Art, Chicago; Nat. Trust, England; Norton Simon Mus.; Oxford Mus. of Modern Art, England; S.F. Mus. of Art; State of Calif.; Tate Gallery, London; UC, Berkeley, USC; Univ. of Iowa. Dir.: Pasadena Art Mus., 1963-68; L.A. Inst. of Contemporary Art, 1977-80; L.A. Printmaking Soc., 1963-75-77; Artists for Economic Action, 1973-75; pres., coord. council, So. Calif. Arts Orgns., 1975; Nat. Watercolor Soc.; Pasadena Soc. for Artists. Awards include: Outstanding Artist Award, Pasadena Arts Council, 1970; outstanding prof. award, Cal. State Univ., L.A., 1973. Home: 846 Bank St., So. Pasadena, CA 91030; Office: 26 W. Dayton St., Pasadena, CA 91105.

ASMAR, ALICE
Artist
b. March 31, Flint, Mich.; d. John G. and Helen (Touma) Asmar; B.A. magna cum laude, Lewis & Clark Coll., 1949; M.F.A., Univ. of Wash., 1951; Ecole Nationale Superieure des Beaux-Arts, Paris, France, 1958-59. Solo shows & exhibits, 1960s, Bednarz Galleries; Sabersky Gallery; L.A. Municipal Art Gallery; Samison Gallery, Santa Fe; Roswell Art Mus.; Minneapolis Inst. of Fine Arts; Pasadena Art Museum; Downey Mus. of Art; Bullock's Wilshire; Mary Livingston's Little Gallery; 1970-Dominican Educational Center, Wis.; 1971-Tlaquepaque, Sedona, Ariz.; 1973-Southwest Mus.; 1974-U.S. Embassy, Paris and Brussels; San Marino Library; Framehouse Gallery, Louisville; Toledo Edison Art Center, Oh.; Scottsdale Civic Center; 1975-Bonwit Teller; 1976-Frye Art Museum, Seattle; 1977-Brand Library and Art Center; Office of Secty. of State of Calif.; Senior Eye Gallery in Long Beach; Mus. in Gabrova, Bulgaria; Hatfield Galleries; Poulsen Gallery; 1978-House of Iran in Beverly Hills; 1979-Sutter Buttes Wildlife Gallery, Yuba City; Office of Calif. Gov.; Sedona Art Center, Ariz.; natl. show, Minn. Mus. of Art, West '79-The Law. Awards: 1978, First Prize, Palm Desert Art; 1977, First Prize Hancock Park Arts Council; Mayor of Burbank; 1976, Hon. Mention, Mus. of Science & Industry; 1975, Toluca Lake Art Festival, Second Prize, etching; 1968-69, Ancona, Italy, Biennale Delle Regione; 1967, Wash., D.C., 1st prize, painting; 1958-59, Harriet H. Woolley Grant for study at Beaux-Arts, Paris, France; Work acclaimed in scores of articles. Mem.: Artists Equity, L.A. chpt. bd.; Southwest Mus.; Smithsonian Mus.; League of the Americas; Mu Phi Epsilon, Epsilon Delta chpt. Hobbies: Indian pottery, piano. Rec.: swimming, jogging, walking, travel. Home: 1125 N. Screenland Dr., Burbank, CA 91505.

ASTIN, ALEXANDER WILLIAM
Research Institute President
b. May 30, 1932, Wash. D.C.; s. Allen Varley (dir. Nat. Bureau of Standards 1952-69) and Margaret (Mackenzie) Astin; A.B., Gettysburg Coll., 1953; M.A., Ph.D., Univ. of Maryland, 1958; m. Helen Stavridou, Feb. 11, 1956, Wash. D.C.; chil.: John Alexander, b. Aug. 28, 1959; Paul Allen, b. Mar. 2, 1961. Career: commissioned Officer, Clin. Psychologist, US Pub. Health Service Hosp., Ky., 1957-59; asst. chief, psychol. research unit, VA Hosp., Baltimore, Md., 1959-60; program dir., Nat. Merit Scholarship Corp., 1960-64; dir. research, Am. Council on Edn., Wash. D.C., 1965-73; (tchg. appts.) lectr. Univ. of

Ky. 1958-59; mem. faculty, Univ. of Md., 1959-61; lectr., Northwestern Univ., 1961-63; mem. faculty, Danforth Found. Inst. and Summer Workshop, 1969, 1972, 73; currently: prof. of higher edn., UCLA, 1973---; dir., coop. institutional research prog. of UCLA and Am. Council on Edn., 1966---; pres., Higher Edn. Research Inst., Inc., 1973---; Cons.: Surgeon Gen. advis. com. on smoking and health, 1961-63; Basic Research branch, U.S. Office of Edn. 1971-73; Legal Defense Fund, NAACP, 1976. Awards: Outstanding book award of Choice, 1977 for The Power of Protest; Outstanding book award of Pi Lambda Theta and Am. Lib. Assn. for The College Environment, 1968; award for research, Am. Personnel and Guidance Assn., 1965; contbrn. to Knowledge award, Am. Coll. Personnel Assn., 1978. Chmn., Am. Psychol. Assn. com. on employment and human resources, 1976---; mem. sci. advis. com. Nat. Coalition for Research on Women's Edn. and Devel. 1970---; advis. com., Edn. Policy Center, Inc. 1973---; bd. dir. Am. Assn. for Higher Edn. 1977---; bd. mem. Rutgers Univ., 1978. Mem.: Fellow, AAAS; Am. Edn. Research Assn.; Am. Personnel and Guidance Assn.; Am. Sociological Assn.; Assn. of Institutional Research; Higher Edn. Colloquium; Nat. Council on Measurement in Edn.; Psi Chi; Cosmos Club; Phi Sigma Kappa. Hobbies: music, art. Rec.: travel. Home: 2681 Cordelia Rd., L.A., CA; Office: 924 Westwood Blvd., Suite 850, L.A., CA 90024.

ASTRACHAN, MAX
Educator
b. Mar. 30, 1909, Rochester, N.Y.; s. Israel and Lottie Astrachan; A.B., Univ. of Rochester, 1929; M.A., 1930, Ph.D., 1930, Brown Univ.; m. Fannie Sherman, Rochester, N.Y.; chil.: Gerald, David, Judith. Career: Chmn., dept. of mathematics, Antioch Coll., 1935-49; chmn. Dept. of Statistics, AF Inst. of Technology, 1949-60; with The Rand Corp., Santa Monica, 1960-65; edn. dir., Am. Soc. for Quality Control, 1965-67; chmn. dept. of mgmt. sci., Sch. of Business, Cal. State Univ., Northridge, 1967---. Office: Calif. State Univ., Northridge, Northridge, CA 91330.

ATHAN, PAUL WILLIAM
Manpower Consultant
b. Feb. 24, 1925, Sheboygan, Wis.; s. William Christ and Laura Hedwig (Grupe) Athan; ed. B.S. (hist.), Univ. of Wis. 1949, M.S. (edn.), 1950; postgrad.: Am. Univ., Wash., D.C. 1950-52; San Diego State, 1955-56; Calif. Western Univ. 1961-62; UCLA 1962; USC 1963; m. Sylvia C. Swingle, Sturgeon Bay, Wis., Nov. 24, 1949; chil.: Charles C., b. Feb. 18, 1951; Monava C., b. Jan. 27, 1953; William K., b. Apr. 25, 1955; Nicholas G., b. Feb. 6, 1957; Christy A., b. July 30, 1959. Career: Interviewer-counselor, Wis. Ind. Comm., La Crosse, 1950-51; occupational-orgn. research analyst, U.S. Navy, Wash., D.C. 1951-52; San Diego, Calif., 1952-56; design spec., General Dynamics, S.D., 1956-64; proj. co-ord., Douglas Aircraft, Santa Monica, 1964-65; employment ofcr. 1965-66; training coord.-mem. Univ. Mgmt. Information stu. team, Univ. of Calif., S.D., 1966---. Prod. over 40 research reports for govt.; developer, pgm. mgmt. system, 1962; contrib. articles to Aerospace Mgmt. and Personnel Journ. USNR (1943-46), WW II. Awards: 10 battle stars and 4 ribbons. Mem.: Natl. Security Ind. Assn., Natl. Mgmt. Assn., Am. Personnel and Guidance Assn., Natl. Vocational Guidance Assn., Internat. Soc. for Gen. Semantics, Am. Acad. Polit and Social Sci., Gerontological Soc., Human Factors Soc., Soc. for Information Display, Natl. Geographic Soc., Internat. Platform Assn. Home: 4651 Conrad Ave., S.D., CA 92117; Office: Univ. of Calif., S.D., P.O. Box 109, La Jolla, CA 92037.

ATHERLEY, WILLIAM J.
Controller
b. Dec. 16, 1942, San Francisco; s. Henry J. and Eleanor (Aitken) Atherley; B.A., Stanford Univ., 1964; grad. studies, Univ. Calif., Berkeley, 1976; Univ. of Ore., 1968-70. Career: auditor, Peat, Marwick, Mitchell & Co., CPAs, S.F., 1970-71; auditor, Foremost-McKesson, Inc., S.F., 1971-73; auditor, Coopers & Lybrand, CPAs, S.F., 1973-75; auditor, Kaiser Aluminum & Chemical Corp., Oakland, 1975-76; controller, Chinese Hosp., S.F. 1976---. Army Nat. Guard, 1964. Mem. Stanford Alumni Assn. Republican. Home: 2450 Octavia, No. 2C, S.F., CA 94109; Office: 835 Jackson, S.F., CA 94133.

ATKINS, OLIVER HERBERT
Nurseryman
b. Apr. 7, 1914; Strathmore, Alberta, Can.; s. Herbert William and Hilma Constance Atkins; Oceanside H.S. 1932; agriculture classes. m. Alice Roberta, S.D., July 3, 1959. Career: manager, A.G. Hazzard Nursery, Vista,

1934-50; owner, Oliver H. Atkins Ranches, 1951---; pres., Atkins Nursery, Inc., 1951---. Dir.: S.D. County Farm Bureau, 1965-70; Calif. Avocado Soc., 1968-79 (pres. 1971-72). San Diego County Farmer of Year, 1973; Calif. Avocado Soc. Award of Honor, 1976. 17th Inf., 7th Div., WW II. Mem.: Vista Optimist Club, pres. 1958-59; Lt. Gov. Optimist Intl. 1961-62; Elks Lodge, Natl. Smooth Dancers, Palomar Chpt., pres. 1969, '75, '76. Hobbies: dancing, rare plants. Office: 3129 Reche Rd., Fallbrook, CA 92028.

ATKINSON, NATALIE O.
Educator
b. Aug. 27, 1920, Plainfield, Ind.; d. Orlando and Anna (Imel) Atkinson; B.A., Univ. of Calif., Santa Barbara, 1947; M.A., Stanford Univ., 1952; postgrad. studies. Univ. of Vienna (polit. sci., geography), 1962; S.F. State Univ. (geog.), 1964-67; San Jose State Univ. (Marine Sci.), 1972. Career: instr.: Vienna Dependents Sch., Austria, 1948-50; prin., Trieste Dependents Sch., Italy, 1950-51; American Sch., Sao Paulo, Brazil, 1953-55; Am. Sch., Djakarta, Indonesia, also cons. in edn. to Indonesian Govt., 1956-58; coord. program for mentally gifted minors, Millbrae, Calif., 1959-60; Fulbright Exchange Tchr., Vienna, 1962-63; instr. soc. sci., marine sci., San Bruno Sch. Dist., San Bruno, Calif., 1960---. Author: Marine Sci. Research Handbook, 1978. Mem.: Nat. Assn. of Marine Sci.; Oceanic Soc.; Calif. Sci. Tchr. Assn.; Calif. Acad. of Sci. Rec.: opera; Home: 3374 La Mesa Dr., San Carlos, CA 94070.

ATWOOD, JOHN LELAND
Senior Consultant, Rockwell International Corp.
b. Oct. 26, 1904, Walton, Ky.; s. Elmer Bugg and Mabel (Bagby) Atwood; ed. Wayland Coll., Plainview, Tex.; A.B. Hardin-Simmons, Abilene, Tex. 1926; B.S. (C.E.), Univ. of Tex. 1928; (hon) D.Eng., Stevens Inst. of Tech. 1955; m. Patricia Hall, Oct. 14, 1972; dau.: Marian. Career: Jr. eng., Army Aircraft Br., Wright Field, Dayton, O. 128-30; chief structures engr., Douglas Aircraft Co., Santa Monica, Calif. 1930-34; engr.-v.p. N. Am. Aviation, Inc. 1934, pres. 1948, chmn. bd. 1962 (merged with Rockwell-Std. 1967), pres.-chief exec. N. Am. Rockwell Corp., 1967-70 (ret.), dir.-cons. 1970-79. Dir.: Pac. Indemnity Co. 1959-75; Times Mirror Co. 1965-77; Cyprus Mines Co. 1971---. Awards: Pres. Cert. of Merit, 1948; Comdr. of Merit by Repub. of Italy, 1955; Medal for Advancement of Research, Am. Soc. for Metals, 1959; Distinguished Engin. Grad. Award, Univ. of Tex. 1960; USC Sch. of Bus. Award, 1962. Mem.: Pres.'s Bd. of Pepperdine Univ. 1955---; bd. trustees, So. Calif. Improvement Found. 1955---; trustee, Air Polution Found. 1955-60; adv. council, Jr. Achievement, 1956---; (past) pres. fellow, Inst. of Aeronautic Scis.; Soc. of Automotive Engrs.; dir. Atomic Indusl. Forum; bd. dirs., Am. Mgmt. Assn. 1954-57; dir. L.A. C. of C.; bd. govs., L.A. area Welfare Fed. 1955-56; U.S. C. of C. coms. 1956-60, 1964-70; bd. Aviation Hall of Fame, 1962-70; sponsor, Atlantic Council of U.S., Inc. 1962-69; dir. Calif. State C. of C.; bd. dirs. L.A. World Affairs Council; bd. govs., exec. com.-chmn., Aerospace Inds. Assn. 1964-65; natl. adv. council, Air Force Mus. Found. 1964-70; natl. bd. dirs., Freedoms Found. at Valley Forge, 1964---; (hon.) fellow, Am. Inst. of Aerons. and Astronautics, 1965---; pres.'s Council, Am. Inst. of Mgmt.; adv. com., Independent Colls. of So. Calif., Inc.; cons. com., Natl. Adv. Com. for Aerons.; Tau Beta Pi. Baptist. Office: 2230 E. Imperial Hwy., El Segundo, CA.

AUGUSTUS, CAROL
Company President — Lecturer
b. Oct. 1, 1943, Long Beach, Calif., d. James and Betty (Bailey) Waugh; H.S., 1961. Career: conduct workshops and seminars in communication, relationships, support and personal effectiveness, 1972---; dir., pres. and co-founder of Actualizations, 1975---; lecturer in psychology, education, philosophy. Pres., L'Esprit and Rive Droite (dress boutiques), 1978; pres., CRS Devel. Corp. (real estate devel.), 1978. Mem: Assn. for Humanistic Psychology. Office: 3632 Sacramento St., S.F., CA 94118.

AURNER, ROBERT RAY
Business Consultant
b. Adel, Iowa; s. Clarence Ray and Nellie A. (Slayton) Aurner; B.A., summa cum laude, Univ. of Iowa, 1919, M.A., 1920, Ph.D., 1922; m. Kathryn Dayton, June 16, 1921, Iowa City; son Robert Ray II, b. Mar. 24, 1927. Career: dir. customer rels., The State Bank, Madison, Wis., 1925-28; research dir., The Walker Co., 1925-30; est. Aurner and Assoc. (cons. mgmt. bus. adminstrn.), pres. and exec. dir., 1938---; dir. Carmel Svgs. & Loan Assn., 1960---; v.p., dir., Pacific Futures, Inc., 1962---; dir.,

chmn. bus. advis. com., VNA Corp., 1959-62; Lectr., NBC Station WTMJ, 1929-30; State Commr., Wis. Lib. Certification Bd., 1931-38; v.p., Nat. Assn. of Mktg., 1931; pres. Am. Bus. Communication Assn., 1939-40; mem. faculty, Univ. of Wis., 1925-48; vis. prof. bus. mgmt., Univ. of Pittsburgh, 1934, 36, 39. Adminstrv. cons. Internat. Cellucotton Products Co., Chicago, 1947-52; cons., dir. Communications Div., Fox River Paper Corp., Appleton, Wis., 1947-60; v.p. and gen. cons., Scott, Inc., Milw. and Carmel, 1949---; cons. U.S. Naval Postgrad. Sch. Mgmt., 1957---; Jahn & Ollier Corp., Morris, Schenker, Roth, Inc., First Nat. Bank (chgo.); Allis-Chalmers Corp., Wis. Div. Vital Statistics. Ltd. Partner Salinas-Peninsula Investment Co., 1963---. Dir.: SAE Corp., Evanston, Ill., 1943-53; Carmel Found., 1954---; Hazeltine Fund, 1963---; Monterey Fund for Edn., 1965---; The York School., 1966-69; Am. Auto Assn., Wis. Div., 1936-47; mem. nat. advis. com. Conf. of Am. Small Bus. Orgns., 1947---. Officers Training Command, USNR, 1919; USNR, 1920-24; Attached AUS, Field Grade, Col., 1945-45; Dean, Coll. of Commerce, Biarritz Am. Univ., France, U.S. Army Univ. Center No. 2, European Theater; U.S. State Dept. rep., Dutch-Am. Conf., The Hague, Holland, 1945. Mem.: Phi Beta Kappa; Delta Sigma Rho; Alpha Kappa Psi; Sigma Alpha Epsilon, nat. pres. 1951-53, nat. gov. bd. 1943-53. Office: P.O.B. 3434, Carmel, CA 93921.

AUSTIN, FRED L.
   Aircraft Company Executive
b. Nov. 22, 1914, Los Angeles, Calif., s. Fred L. and Cena M. (Hopkins) Austin; D. Sc., Univ. of Ohio; m. Joyce Joan Richardson, Mexico, Oct. 27, 1959; chil.: Fred L. Austin, III, b. 1944; Judith Gail Henderson, b. 1946; Steven F., b. 1961; Brian R., b. 1963; Christopher F., b. 1965. Career: Airline pilot, Catalina Airlines and TWA, 1937-70; Exec. mgmt., TWA to 1967; founder & pres., Golden West Airlines, 1968-73; pres., Austin & Assoc., 1974-77; aviation cons., pres. and dir., Short Bros. USA, Inc. 1977---. U.S.A.F. Affiliation. Holder of 30 world flight records, incl. fastest time around world over both poles, 1965. Rockwell Jet Comdr. world flight, 8 world records, 1966. Awarded Octavius Chanute Award for Aviation in 1967. Mem.: Explorers Club; Quiet Birdmen; OX5 Club; Wings Club, N.Y.; Natl. Aviation Club, Wash., D.C. Republican. Protestant. Hobbies: flying and prospecting. Home: 30 Drakes Bay Dr., Corona del Mar, CA 92625; Office: 2222 Martin Dr., No. 255, Irvine, CA 92715.

AVERBROOK, BERYL DAVID
   Physician and Surgeon
b. Aug. 17, 1920, Superior, Wis.; s. Abraham B. and Clara (Ziechig) Averbook; ed. Superior State Tchrs. Coll. 1938-39; B.S., Univ. of Wis. 1942; M.D., Univ. Wis. Sch. of Med. 1945; postgrad stu., Univ. of Colo. 1948-50; m. Gloria Sloane, L.A., Calif., Apr. 2, 1955; sons: Bruce Jeffrey, b. July 15, 1956; Allen Wayne, b. Feb. 3, 1960. Career: Intern, Akron City Hosp., Akron, O. 1945-46; surg. res.: Vets. Adm. Hosp., Ft. Logan, Denver, Colo. 1948-50; Rochester Gen. Hosp., Rochester, N.Y. 1950-51; Vets. Adm. Hosp. (Wadsworth) L.A., Calif. 1951-54; chief of surg. serv., Harbor Gen. Hosp. 1954-61; instr. in surg., Univ. Calif. Med. Center, L.A. 1954-58; asst. prof. surg. 1958-61; clin. asst. prof. surg. 1961-65; est. pvt. practice (spec. in tumor and vascular surg.), Torrance, Calif. 1961---. Contrib. to profl. journs. Lt., Capt. (MC), U.S. Army. Mem.: AMA, Calif. Med. Assn.; N.Y. Acad. Sci., Long Beach Surg. Soc., L.A. Acad. Med.; Am. Geriatric Soc., Am. Assn. Med. Colls., Soc. Head and Neck Surgns., Am. Men of Med.; Soc. for Clinical Vascular Surg.; surg. sect., L.A. Co. Med. Assn.; fellow, Am. Coll. of Surgs. Home: 6519 Springpark Ave., L.A., CA 90056; Office: 3640 W. Lomita Blvd., Torrance, CA 90505.

AVERY, ROBERT TOLMAN
   Electro-Mechanical Engineer
b. Feb. 7, 1926, San Luis Obispo; s. Harold Tolman (engr., inventor) and Elizabeth Ella (Murphey) Avery; B.S., Univ. of Minn., 1946; M.S., Stanford Univ., 1948; D. Engr., Univ. of Calif., Berkeley, 1974; m. Beverly Beckman, July 11, 1948, Stockton, Calif.; chil.: Scott Murphey, b. Sept. 7, 1949; Leslie Ann (Ward), b. Oct. 11, 1953. Career: Bridge engr., state of Calif., S.F., 1948-50; design engr., Univ. of Calif. Radiation Lab., Berkeley, 1950-54; research engr., Chromatic TV Labs, Oakland, 1954-55; sr. engr., Varian Assoc., Palo Alto, 1955-61; project mgr., Brobeck Assc., cons. engrs., Berkeley, 1961-66; sr. staff engr., Lawrence Berkeley Lab., Univ. of Calif., 1966---. Reg. Profl. engr. (state of Calif.) in fields of mechanical, electrical and civil engineering; Author, numerous tech. papers; cons., indsl. firms; Holder, more than 15 U.S. and foreign patents related to electron

accelerators, X-ray cancer therapy, magnets and related fields. Mem.: Nat. Soc. Profl. Engrs.; Calif. Soc. of Profl. Engrs.; Am. Soc. of Mech. Engrs. (ASME); IEEE: Internat. Soc. for Rock Mechanics. Home: 1408 Camino Peral, Moraga, CA 94556; Office: Lawrence Berkeley Lab, 1 Cylotron Rd., Berkeley, CA 94720.

AYALA, RUBEN S.
   State Senator
b. Mar. 6, 1922, Chino, Calif.; s. Mauricio R. and Erminia Ayala; student, Pomona Jr. Coll., UCLA Ext. Sch.; grad., Nat. Electronic Sch., L.A.; m. Irene Morales, July 22, 1945; chil.: Buddy, Maurice, Edward, Gary. Career: elected to Chino Sch. Bd., 1955-62; elected city councilman, Chino, 1962, 1st elected mayor of Chino, 1964; elected to San Bernardino Co. Bd. of Suprs., 1966-74, chmn. 1968-72 (also dir. and pres., So. Calif. Regional Assn. of County Suprs., chmn.: San Bernardino Co. Health Com.; Chino Police Commn.; East Valley and West Valley Planning Agencies; Chino Parks and Rec. Commn.; dir. Pomona Freeway Assn.); elected state senator, 32nd senatorial dist., 1974---; (1st Mex. in Senate since 1911); Chmn. Agricultural and Water Resources Com., serves on Local Govt., Natural Resources and Wildlife, Revenue and Taxation Coms. Recipient Outstanding Civic Leaders of Am. Award, 1967; Citizen of the Year awards from Chino C. of C., VFW of San Bernardino Co., Mex. Am. Polit. Assn., Kiwanis Club. USMC, WW II, South Pacific theatre. Mem.: Kiwanis Club; Native Sons of Golden West; Am. Legion; life mem. PTA of Chino. Home: 12941 Rhodes Pl., Chino, CA 91710.

AYDELOTTE, CHARLES W., JR.
   Newspaper Publisher
b. Oct. 9, Kansas City, Mo.; s. Charles W. and Irene (Coleman) Aydelotte; B.A. journalism, USC, 1939; M.S., UCLA, 1959; m. Frances Nyberg, Sept. 15, 1946, Seattle, Wash.; chil.: Jan, Ernest, Lee. Career: pub., Rodgers & McDonald Newspapers, 1961-67; pub., Herald Am. Newspapers, 1967-76; owner and publisher, Beach Cities Newspapers, 1976---. USN, WW II; Capt. (ret.), USNR. Mem.: Calif. Newspapers Publishers Assn., pres. 1974; Kiwanis Club of Angeles Mesa, pres. 1954. Office: 36 14th St., Hermosa Beach, CA 90254.

AYMAR, CATHERINE BEATRICE
   Realtor
b. Nov. 28, 1922, Ferndale, Wash.; d. Morley Victor and Jessie Edna (Fredenburg) Pomeroy; grad. Realtors Inst., 1969; Realtors Certificate Inst., 1975; Certified Residential Spec., 1978; m. Clarence Phillip Aymar, Reno, Nev., July 27, 1955; son, Patrick Mercer, b. Nov. 28, 1946. Career: real estate licensee, 1963-69; real estate broker, 1969---; realtor, founder, Aymar Properties, Inc., 1971---. Pres., Santa Clara Valley Chpt. Women's Council of Realtors, 1976; pres., Calif. State Chpt. Women's Council of Realtors, 1979; dir., San Jose Real Estate Bd. 1978-80; editor, writer, Santa Clara Valley Women's Council of Realtors newsletter, 1975-78. Contrib. author: Communique, Natl. Women's Council of Realtors, Calif. State Chpt. News. Mem.: Feminique Toastmistress (pres., 1972); Santa Clara Toastmistress (pres. 1974); dir., Cupertino Quota Club Intl.; Project Business-affiliate, Jr. Achievement, Inc., 1978; Jr. Achievement Marketing Advisor, 1977-78; Am. Management Assn.; Commonwealth Club of Calif. Methodist. Hobbies: travel, dressmaking. Rec.: walking, bowling, gardening. Home: 917 Kennard Way, Sunnyvale, CA 94087; Office: 3600 Pruneridge Ave., Santa Clara, CA 95051.

AYRES, JAMES MARX
   Mechanical Engineer
b. Nov. 28, 1922, Pomona; s. James Albert and Martha (Oathout) Ayres; B.S. M.E., Univ. Calif., Berkeley, 19 4; M.S., Purdue Univ., 1948; div.; chil.: Denise, b. Mar. 14, 1952; Ronald, b. Dec. 8, 1953; Gary, b. Apr. 20, 1957. Career: chief mech. engr. various engring. firms, 1949-52; Pereira & Luckman, architects and engrs., L.A., 1957-59; pres., Ayres & Kyakawa, L.A., 1959-74; pres., Ayres & Hayakawa Energy Mgmt., L.A., 1974-77; pres., Ayres Assoc., L.A., 1977---. Research fellow radiant heating Purdue Univ., 1947-48; tchg. asst., mech. engring., Univ. Calif., Berkeley, 1948; guest lectr. USC and UCLA Sch. of Architecture, 1965. Mem., L.A. Code advis. bd., 1960-72; Calif. Dept. of Pub. Health Bldg. Safety Bd., 1973-75; Calif. Seismic Safety Commn., 1975---; chmn. L.A. Citizens Community Music Edn. in Schools, 1964-65; trustee, Carthay Circle Assoc., 1965-73. Served to Lt. j.g., USNR, WW II. Contbr. profl. journs.: Outstanding Engineer Merit Award, Inst. Advancement of Engineering, 1975; Registered profl. engr., nat. cert. 8 states; Mem.: Fellow Earthquake Engring. Research Inst., 1973; Am.

Soc. Heating, Refrigerating and Air Cond. Engrs., 1972; Automated Procedures Engring. Cons., pres. 1971; Am. Soc. Mech. Engr.; Nat. Soc. Profl. Engr.; Cons. Engrs. Council; Cons. Engrs. Assn. Calif.; Mech. Engrs. Assn., pres. 1969, Calif. chpt.; Internat. Solar Energy Soc.; Tau Eta Pi, 1976---. Home: 840 N. Larrabee St., No. 207, Bldg. 4, L.A., CA 90069; Office: 1180 S. Beverly Dr., Suite 600, L.A., CA 90035.

AZEVEDO, LAURENCE B.
Mayor of Concord — Merchant
b. Mar. 18, 1936, San Rafael, Calif.; s. Eugene and Helen Azevedo; ed. Diablo Valley Coll. 1959; m. Barbara McCaffrey, Calif. 1953; chil.: Carla, Christine, Matthew, Susan, Linda, Michael. Career: Assoc. with Pac. Tel. Co. 1955-62; pres.-mgr. Diablo Sports Center, Inc. 1962-70; v.p.-dir. Sportsland Corp. (14 retail sporting goods chain), 1970-71. Dir. United Calif. Bank. Prin., Dennis, Coleman, Curtis & Azevedo arch. firm. World Travel Serv. Councilman, City of Concord, 1968, Mayor 1970-72. Rec.: skiing, hunting. Home: 1865 Elkwood Dr., Concord; Office: City Hall and 2193 Concord Blvd., Concord, CA.

B

BACH, MILTON FRANCIS CHRISTIAN (MICKEY)
Syndicated Cartoonist and Artist
b. Sept. 30, Minn., s. Christian and Lucy (Raddee) Bach; B.S. and M.S., Univ. of Wis., 1929-33; m. Virginia Sherwood Fletcher, Los Angeles, 1944. Career: Cartoonist and sports art dir., Minn. Star Journal, 1935-41; Chicago Sun, 1941; editor and publ. army regimental newspaper, Shavetail, 1942; publ. army newspaper in So. Pacific, 1943-45; author Word-A-Day book and daily cartoon feature of same name syndicated and dist. by Field Newspaper Syndicate, appearing in papers worldwide, June, 1946---. U.S. Army Capt., 1942-45. Mem.: Sigma Chi; Natl. Cartoonists Soc.; Newspaper Comics Council; University Club; Greater L.A. Press Club. Hobbies: writing, painting. Rec.: golf, tennis. Home: 2430 Ocean View Ave., Apt. 606-607, L.A., CA 90057.

BACHER, ROSALIE WRIDE
School Administrator
b. May 25, 1925, Los Angeles, Calif.; d. Homer Martin and Reine (Rogers) Wride; m. Archie O. Bacher, Jr., Pasadena, Calif., Mar. 30, 1963. Career: Tchr. English, History, Latin, Jordan H.S., Long Beach, 1949-55; counselor, 1955-65; counselor, Lakewood H.S., 1965-66; research asst., counselor, occupational preparation, Long Beach Unified Sch. Dist.; vice-principal, Washington Jr. H.S.; asst. principal, Lakewood H.S.; vice-principal, Jefferson Jr. H.S., Long Beach, 1970---. Mem.: Phi Beta Kappa; Delta Kappa Gamma, pres., Delta Psi chpt.; area dir., chmn., Calif. State Professional Affairs Comm., Pi Lambda Theta; (pres., Orange County chpt., vice-pres., So. Calif. Council); pres., USC Omicron chpt., Phi Delta Gamma; secty., Long Beach chpt., Phi Delta Kappa. Christian Scientist, first reader. Rec.: music, pets. Home: 265 Rocky Point Rd., Palos Verdes Estates, CA 90274; Office: Jefferson Jr. High Sch., 750 Euclid, Long Beach, CA 90804.

BACKUS, VICTOR J.
Certified Public Accountant
b. May 2, 1919, Lithuania; s. John and Magdalena (Stramaitis) Backus; C.P.A., 1957; m. Sophie Sescila, Lithuania, Feb. 16, 1941; chil.: Mrs. Loretta E. Nelson, b. July 19, 1942; Mrs. Elenor V. O'Neil, b. Oct. 11, 1943; Mrs. Milda M. Gray, b. May 28, 1945. Career: Exec., Farmers' Coop. in Lithuania, 1940-44; employee, Chase Brass & Copper Co., Conn., 1949-53; public accountant, Conn., 1953-59; C.P.A. practice, Calif., 1959---. Mem.: Calif. C.P.A. Soc.; Am. Inst. of C.P.A.s. Rec.: outdoor sports. Home: 5270 Los Franciscos Way, L.A., CA 90027; Office: 1120 So. San Gabriel Blvd., No. 110, San Gabriel, CA 91776.

BADASH, SANDRA BORR
Artist
b. Mar. 2, 1936, Hartford, Conn.; d. Samuel H. and Ann (Olanoff) Borr; B.A. edn., 1958; M.S., art edn., 1964; chil.: Lisa Dale, b. Nov. 1958; Bruce Alan, b. Sept. 1961. Career: tchr. of art, 1960-69; profl. artist, 1970---; art dir., Internat. Art Guild, 1973-74; art gallery dir., 1974-75; fabric designer ---; also State of Calif. Registered rep. for

investment co., insurance, variables, contracts agent. Solo art shows, Europe and U.S., 1970---; TV interviews, 1977. Rec.: tennis, walking. Home: 601 E. Anapamu St., Santa Barbara, CA 93103; Office: Investments, I.D.S., McGrath Ave., Ventura, CA.

BADGLEY, THEODORE McBRIDE
Psychiatrist, Neurologist
b. June 27, 1925, Salem, Ala.; s. Roy Joseph Badgley and Fannie (Limbaugh); M.D., USC Sch. of Med., L.A., 1949; m. Mary Bennett Wells, Dec. 30, 1945, LeGrand, Calif.; Chil.: Justice O'Neil, b. Feb. 7, 1947; Jan Marten (Wolkov), b. Aug. 21, 1950; Mona Jean (Covey), b. Dec. 15, 1954; Jason Wells, b. Feb. 26, 1958; James John, b. July 28, 1960; Mary Rose, b. Oct. 19, 1962. Career: Intern, Letterman Gen. Hosp., S.F., 1949-50; residency in psychiatry, 1950-53; Assoc. clin. prof., psychiat. and neurology, Med. Coll. of Ga., 1954-55; dir. of psychiatric training, Walter Reed Gen. Hosp., 1957-63; chief, dept. psychiat. and neurology, US Army Gen. Hosp., Landstuhl, Germany, 1963-66; chief, psychiat. outpatient svc., Letterman Gen. Hosp., S.F., 1966-67; pvt. practice, tch., research, Bakersfield, 1967---; dir., Kern View Community mental health ctr. and hosp., 1967-69; pres., Sans Dolorosa Inst. Med. Group, Inc., 1969---; contrb. articles psychiat. journs. Served USN, 1943-45; ret. Lt. Col., AUS, 1967. Rec.: chess, skiing, hiking, horse riding. Home: 1733 Crestmont Dr., Bakersfield, CA 93306; Office: 1901 Truxtun Ave., Bakersfield, CA 93301.

BAER, WALTER S., III
Research Physicist
b. July 27, 1937, Chicago, Ill.; s. Walter S., Jr. and Margaret (Mayer) Baer; B.S., Calif. Inst. Tech., 1959; Ph.D. (NSF Fellow), Univ. Wis., 1964; m. Miriam R. Schenker, 1959; chil.: David W. and Alan B. Career: Research physicist, Bell Telephone Labs, Murray Hill, N.J., 1964-66; White House Fellow, Wash., D.C., 1966-67; White House sci. adv. staff, 1967-69; sr. staff, Laird Systems, Inc., L.A., 1969-70; telecommunications cons., The RAND Corp., 1970---; dir. Energy Policy Program, The RAND Corp., 1978---. Cons. to major U.S. corporations, 1970---; dir., Aspen (Colo.) Cable TV Workshop, 1972-73; Mem.: Advis. Council, Aspen Communications Program, 1974---; Computer Sci. and Engring. Bd., Nat. Acad. of Sci., 1969-72; Cable TV Advisory Committee, FCC, 1972-73; Environment and Resource Management Advis. Committee, USC, 1976---. Author: Interactive Television, 1971; Cable Television: A Handbook for Decisionmaking, 1973; also numerous articles; Preceptor award, Broadcast Indus. Conf., 1974; Editor: The Electronic Box Office, 1974; RAND Cable Television Series, 1974; Editorial Bd., Telecommunications Policy. Mem.: Sierra Club. Democrat. Home: 560 Latimer Rd., Santa Monica, CA 90402; Office: 1700 Main St., Santa Monica, CA 90406.

BAILEY, CLYDE GEORGE
NASA Executive
b. Jan. 4, 1916, Huntington, Long Is., N.Y.; s. Clyde Hamilton and Millie (Fasbender) Bailey; ed. A.A., Antelope Valley Coll. 1960; m. Mildred Emolyn Brooks, Wash., D.C., Sept. 29, 1940; chil.: Sandra Lynn (Bailey) Hull, b. Apr. 7, 1944; Heather Brooks, b. Dec. 21, 1951; Berkley Barnett, b. Feb. 7, 1957. Career: Sales-Serv. Automotive Agcy., Hampton, Va.; div. mgr., Natl. Adv. Com. for Aeronautics, Langley Field, Va. 1941-47; supt. aircraft maintenance, High Speed Flight Sta., Edwards, Calif. 1949-58; head, maintenance and mfg. br., Flight Research Center, Natl. Aeronatuics and Space Adm., Edwards AFB 1958---. Mem.: Elks, Alpha Gamma Sigma, Lake Arrowhead Country Club. Republican. Lutheran. Hobby: photog. Rec.: golf, hunting, boating. Home: 1753 W. Ave. J, Lancaster, CA, and Lake Arrowhead, CA.

BAILEY, JANE HORTON
Author — Playwright
b. May 14, 1916, Chicago, Ill.; A.B. (Spanish), Univ. Calif., Berkeley, 1938; m. Donald Ward Bailey, Sept. 29, 1941, Kansas City, Mo.; chil.: David Alan, b. Sept. 11, 1942; Phyllis Wynne (Lochelt), b. May 27, 1945; Christopher Ralph, b. June 25, 1955. Career: caseworker for state relief adminstrn. 1938-40; pub. rels., Padua Hills Inst. and Theatre, 1941; writer, 1959---; publ., El Moro Publications, 1978---; Author: (books) The Sea Otter's Struggle, 1973; Sea Otter, 1979; (drama) When You Leave Don't Say Goodby; numerous mag. publs. Hobbies: travel, golf. Home: 545 Bernardo Ave., Morro Bay, CA 93442.

BAILEY, JOSEPH J.
Physician
b. Mar. 13, 1930, Meridian, Miss.; s. Joe and Evelyn

Bailey; B.S., 1951; M.S., 1952; M.D., 1959; m. Barbara Ann Lindenthal, June 10, 1967, San Diego; chil.: Mark Thomas, b. Oct. 16, 1970; Geoffrey John, b. Apr. 20, 1972; Stephen Joseph, b. Aug. 22, 1975. Career: residency in psychiatry, St. Elizabeth's Hosp., Wash. D.C., 1961-63; psychiat. residency, The Neuropsychiatric Inst., UCLA, 1963-64; acting med. dir., Douglas Young Clinic, San Diego, 1964-65; pvt. practice of psychiatry, 1964---; cons. to Superior Ct., San Diego Co., 1973---; cons., Calif. State Tchrs. Retirement System, 1974---; chief of psychiatry metropolitan correctional center, S.D., 1975---. AUS, 1950-52. Diplomate, Am. Bd. of psychiatry and neurology in psychiatry, 1970. Mem.: Am. Psychiat. Assn., 1965; S.D. Psychiat. Soc., 1965; Am. Acad. of Psychiat. and the Law, 1975; N.Y. Acad. of Sci., 1971. Hobby: gardening. Home: 2427 Romney Rd., S.D., CA 92109; Office: 4655 Cass St., S.D., CA 92109.

BAILEY, NORMAN ARTHUR
Professor of Radiology
b. July 2, 1915, N.Y.C.; s. Louis D. and Ida Bailey; B.S., St. John's Univ., 1941; M.A., N.Y. Univ., 1943; Ph.D., (physics) Columbia Univ., 1952; m. Rose Levine, N.Y.C., 1940; chil.: Philip, b. 1941; Barbara (Black), b. 1948. Career: assoc. in radiology, Med. Sch., 1954-59, and asst. research prof. of biophysics, 1957-59, Univ. Buffalo, N.Y.; Assoc., Clin. Prof. of Radiology, Prof. in residence, radiology, UCLA, 1959-68; dir., radiological sci. div., and prof. of radiology, Emory Univ., Atlanta, Ga., 1967-68; prof. and chief radiological physics, and engring., UC, San Diego, 1968---; also assoc. editor,Medical Physics, 1976---; Cons.: VA Hosp., S.D. 1971---; U.S. Naval Regional Med. Center, S.D., 1968---. Publs: more than 140 pub. articles in field. Certification: Am. Bd. of Radiology, 1956; Am. Bd. of Health Physics, 1960. Active com. mem.: Am. Assn. Physicists in Med., chmn. gen. med. physics; Am. Assn. Physicists in Med., So. Calif. chpt., chmn. tech. seminars com.; Am. Bd. of Radiology; Am. Coll. of Radiology, fellow in physics, chmn. radiation physics com.; Nat. Insts. of Health, mem. radiation study sect.; Natl. Sci. Found.; mem.: AAAS; Am. Physical Soc.; Radiation Research Soc.; Radiological Soc. of No. Am.; Soc. Photo-Optical Instrumentation Engrs. Home: 8656 Cliffridge Ave., La Jolla, CA 92037; Office: Dept. Radiology, M-010, UCSD, La Jolla, CA 92093.

BAILEY, ROBERT LANCE
County Administrator
b. Dec. 12, 1944, Trenton, N.J.; s. Shelvy C. and Sharon Bailey; desc. Abraham Lincoln, 3rd cousin (4 times removed); B.A., geog., Cal. State Univ., Sacto., 1968; M.S., agri., environ. sci., Univ. of Calif., Davis, 1971; M.A. geog., reg. planning, 1970; m. Laura Johnson, June 17, 1967, Sacto.; chil.: Randy L., b. Feb. 8, 1968; Laura J., b. June 27, 1971. Career: assoc. and sr. planner, Sacto. Co. Planning Dept., 1971-77; dir., Sacto. Co. dept. of planning and community devel., 1977---; also Prof. Public Administrn., Cal. State Univ., Sacto., 1978---; dir., Farm Centers Internat., Central Mexico region, 1971. Recipient: Man of the Year award, Am. River Coll., 1966; mem. Phi Kappa Phi, 1968; Alpha Gamma Sigma, 1966; Fed. Research Fellowship, Univ. Calif., Davis, 1968-71. Mem.: Am. Inst. of Planners; Am. Soc. Planning Officials; Assn. Am. Geographers. Spceial interests: cartographic design, statistics. Home: 8394 Mediterranean Way, Sacto., CA 95826; Office: 827 7th St., Sacto., CA 95814.

BAILLIE, JOHN K.
Chairman of the Board, L.A. Federal Savings
b. Mar. 26, 1911, Seattle, Wash.; s. John K. and Gertrude (Mellon) Baillie; ed. B.S. (bus. adm.), USC 1934; m. Phyllis Dooley, Oct. 11, 1957; chil.: Brent K., Paige, Kathy Lyn. Career: chmn., bd.-pres., L.A. Fed. Svgs. Assn., 1950---; dir. King-Stanford Corp., First L.A. Corp., Comdr., USNR. Mem.: commr. L.A. Harbor, 1957-59; del. Soc. Internat. Safety at Sea, 1958---; commr. L.A. Internat. Airport, 1959-60; pres. Conf. of Fed. Svgs. Assns. of U.S. 1968-69; trustee, L.A. City Exhib. Center. Clubs: L.A. Yacht, Transpacific Yacht, L.A.; Newport Harbor Yacht; commodore, Balboa Yacht, Newport Beach. Champion ocean racing fleet (sailing), So. Calif. 1970. Home: 1815 Bayadere Terrace, Corona del Mar, CA 92625; Office: 1 Wilshire Blvd., L.A., CA 90017.

BAILY, RICHARD O.
President, Lexitron Corporation
b. Dec. 14, 1923, Alexandria, S. Dak.; s. Owen R. and Ida Belle (James) Baily; B.S., Univ. of So. Dak., 1947; m. Elizabeth Ann Murry, Dec. 11, 1945, Memphis, Tenn.; chil.: Thomas Owen, b. Aug. 11, 1947; Diette Marie, b. May 10, 1949. Career: various mgmt. positions, Burroughs Corp., 1947-71; pres., Business Machines Div., Singer Co., San Leandro, Calif., 1971-72; vice-pres.,

Singer Co., N.Y., 1972-76; pres. and chief exec. officer, Lexitron Corp., L.A., 1976---. AUS, Infan., 1943-73; USAF, 1943-46; decorated DFC, Air Medal, Presidential Citation. Mem.: U.S. Dept. of Commerce nat. mktg. advisory com., 1970; chmn., Sales Mktg. Exec. Internat., 1970-71, pres. 1969-70; mem. U.S. Council, Internat. C. of C., 1964-65. Home: 2265 Linda Flora Dr., L.A., CA 90024; Office: 9600 De Soto Ave., Chatsworth, CA 91311.

BAIRD, JOSEPH EDWARD
President, Occidental Petroleum Corporation
b. Mar. 18, 1934, Columbus, Ohio; s. Edward Graham and Alice (Hoover) Baird; B.A., Yale Univ., 1959; m. Anne Marie (Breukelman), June 14, 1958, White Plains, N.Y.; chil.: Tracey Anne, b. Jan. 12, 1959; Edward Graham, b. June 19, 1965; Amanda Ruth, b. Nov. 11, 1969. Career: with Chase Manhattan Bank, N.Y.C., 1959-66; Smith, Barney & Co., Inc., N.Y.C., 1966-67; managing dir., Chief Exec. Officer, Western American Bank (Europe) Ltd., London, Eng., 1968-73; pres., Chief Operating Officer, Occidental Petroleum Corp., L.A., 1973---. Dir. Hooker Chem. Corp., Houston, 1974---; trustee, Westlake Sch., L.A. U.S. Army, 1954-56. Mem.: Lloyds of London. Clubs: L.A. Country, Bel Air Bay, Beach Club. Protestant. Rec.: sailing. Office: 10889 Wilshire Blvd., L.A., CA 90024.

BAKER, EUGENE AMES
Artist
b. Jan. 6, 1928, Dyersberg, Tenn.; s. John Franklin and Kalah Rae (Ames) Baker; B.A. art edn., Calif. Coll. of Arts & Crafts, 1951 (with high distinction); m. Mary Ann Rugh, Aug. 27, 1950, Los Gatos, Calif.; chil.: Kim, b. Dec. 10, 1954; Kathleen, b. Mar. 22, 1957. Career: Instr. arts & crafts, Pacific Grove High Sch., 1951-52; instr. in oil painting & drawing, Monterey Peninsula Coll., 1957-62; full time artist, 1962---; four paintings reproduced by Donald Art Company, N.Y. for internat. distbr.; one man shows Zantman Art Galleries, Ltd., 1971, 72, 77; guest artist, Washington State Fair, 1964, 65; rep. in pvt. art collections internat. USN, 1946-48. Owner, Valley Center Art Gallery, 1957-67. Mem.: Carmel Art Assn., past treas. and v.p.; founding bd., Am. Fedn. of Arts, Carmel chpt., 1959. Hobbies: collecting icons, fishing, sailing. Home: 72 Calle de Este, Carmel Valley, CA 93924; Office: P.O.B. 335, Carmel Valley, CA 93924.

BAKER, GERALD LEWIS
Advertising Company Executive
b. Mar. 6, 1943, Evansville, Ind.; s. Lewis Allen and Dorothy Elloise (Woolsey) Baker; B.S., USC, 1966; M.B.A., Cal. State Univ., Long Beach, 1968; m. Sharon Kay Terrill, July 26, 1969, Torrance, Calif.; chil.: Katherine Kimberly, b. Apr. 11, 1975; Matthew Allen, b. June 19, 1976. Career: Dir. of tourism, Colo. Visitors Bureau, 1971-72; deputy dir., Calif. Dept. of Commerce, 1972-75; dir. mktg. & Advt., San Diego Convention & Visitors Bureau, 1975-77; vice pres., Kaufman Landsky Advt., Inc., San Diego, Beverly Hills, 1978---; pres., Destination Marketing, 1978---. V.P., San Diego Civic Light Opera, 1978-79; v.p., Sales and Mktg. Execs, 1978; mem.: Westchester-Madison Masonic Lodge; Colo. Consistory No. 1 Scottish Rite; Al Bahr Shrine; Sigma Chi frat. Methodist, stewardship com. Rec.: tennis, jogging. Home: 6368 Del Paso Ave., S.D., CA 92120; Office: 654 India St., S.D., CA 92120.

BAKER, HARRY S.
President, Producers Cotton Oil Co.
b. Mar. 1, 1904, Dyersburg, Tenn.; s. John Franklin and Lalla Rookh (Sugg) Baker; ed. B.S. (commerce), Ore. State Coll. 1927; m. Tina B. Amick, Ore., Apr. 2, 1927; chil.: David Franklin and Mrs. Fred W. (Jane) Willey. Career: Ginning opns., San Joaquin Cotton Oil Co. 1928-30; gen. mgr., Producers Cotton Oil Co., Helm, Calif. 1930, field mgr. 1933, bd. dirs. 1935---, pres. 1937-67, chmn. bd. 1967---; dir. Bank of Am. NT & SA. Mem.: adv. com., N.Y. Cotton Exch.; past pres., Natl. Cotton Council of Am.; past pres., Natl. Cottonseed Prods. Assn., Inc.; dir. Calif. Mfgrs. Assn.; past pres.-past dir., Fresno City and Co. C. of C.; Cotton and Cottonseed Research and Marketing Adv. Com., Agr. Research Adm., USDA: bd. dirs., Ore. State Coll. Alumni Assn.; Beta Alpha Psi, (hon.) Phi Delta Theta; Alpha Kappa Psi, Scabbard and Blade, Rotary Club of Fresno, Univ.-Sequoia-Sunnyside Club. First Congregational Ch. Rec.: hunting, fishing, golf. Home: 945 S. Clovis Ave., Fresno, CA 93727.

BAKER, HERBERT GEORGE
Professor of Botany
b. Feb. 23, 1920, Brighton, England; s. Herbert Reginald and Alice Emily (Bambridge) Baker; B.Sc., Univ. of London, 1941, Ph.D., 1945; m. Irene Williams, Apr. 4, 1945, Tredegar, Wales; dau. Ruth Elaine (Grimes), b. Mar. 4, 1949. Career: research chemist and plant physiologist, Hosa Research Labs., England, 1940-45; lectr. in Botany, Univ. of Leeds, England, 1945-54; prof. of botany, Univ. Coll. of the Gold Coast, 1954-57; prof. of botany, Univ. Calif., Berkeley, 1957---; dir. of Univ. of Calif. botanical garden, 1957-69; Author: Plants and Civilization, 3 editions, 1965, 1971, 1978, transls. into Spanish, Japanese; one other book on botany; 135 sci. pub. papers. Mil. Civil Defense Force, 1940-45. Pres., Soc. for the Study of Evolution, 1969; pres., botanical soc. of Am., 1979; mem. 13 other sci. societies, Sigma Xi. Hobby: gardening. Rec.: walking. Office: Botany Dept., Univ. Calif., Berkeley, CA 94720.

BAKER, JANE GRIMMER
Public Official
b. June 4, 1923, Hamilton, Ohio; d. Ernest A. and Lillian Grimmer; ed. B.S., Purdue Univ., 1944; m. Harris William Baker, NYC, Mar. 8, 1945; chil.: Cynthia, b. Sept. 18, 1956; Bruce, b. Nov. 10, 1958. Career: Stokeley-Van Camp's Research, 1944-45; Cornell Univ. research, 1945-46; Colo. Univ. dietician, 1946-47; Dairy Council of Indianapolis, 1948-49; TV producer and hostess own show, 1952-56. Councilwoman, San Mateo, 1973-77, dept. mayor, 1974-75; Mayor, City of San Mateo, 1975-76; Mem.: officer: PTA; San Mateo Co. Jr. Museum Aux.; Internat. Orgn. of Women Pilots; Ninety-Nines, Inc.; League of Women Voters of Central San Mateo Co.; pres. AAUW, San Mateo, 1970-71; Presbyterian (Women's Assn. v.p.-asst. deacon). Rec.: flying, sailing, golf. Home: 1464 Woodberry Ave., San Mateo, CA 94403; Office: City Hall, 330 W. 20th Ave., San Mateo, CA 94403.

BAKER, LAURENCE HOLLAND
College Administrator
b. Jan. 23, 1933, Des Moines, Iowa, s. Raymond F. and F. Mildred (Holland) Baker; B.S. Iowa State Univ., 1954; Ph.D., Univ. of Minn., 1961; m. Norma Walters, West Bend, Iowa, August 8, 1953; chil.: Marcia Gallo, b. Aug. 31, 1956; Brian Joseph, b. Aug. 5, 1958. Career: Statistician, Hy-Line Poultry Farms, Des Moines, 1961-63; mgr. computing services, Pioneer Hi-Bred Intl., Des Moines, 1963-69; pres., Pioneer Data Systems, 1969-72; vice-pres., v.p. Cost, Planning and Mgmt., 1972; pres., Evaluation, Systems and Planning, 1972; dir., Information Systems, Calif. State Universities and Colleges, 1973---. Ofcr. U.S. Army 1954-55; Mem.: Assn. Computing Machinery; Assn. for Systems Mgmt.; Am. Mgmt. Assn.; Sigma Xi; Beta Alpha Psi; Gamma Sigma Delta. Clubs: L.A. Athletic, Calabasas Park Country. Presbyterian. Home: 15577 High Knoll Rd., Encino, CA 91436; Office: 5670 Wilshire Blvd., L.A., CA.

BAKER, MARLENE ANN
Insurance Company Executive
b. Nov. 11, 1940, Bridgeport, Conn.; d. James Joseph and Margaret Ann (Manley) O'Boyle; student, Santa Ana Coll.; UCI; Industrial Cons. Mgmt. By Action; Insurance Education Assn.; Risk Mgmt. Principles; prof. mgmt. and insurance seminars; m. Thomas E. Baker, Mariposa, CA; chil.; Suzanne Marie, b. Oct. 17, 1960; Talmadge Elliot, b. Mar. 3, 1963. Career: Firemans Fund, Fresno, 1964-66; Firemans Fund, Santa Ana, 1966; Quinlan & Jennings Insurance, 1967-70; Eric Moore Ins./Russell Moore Ltd., 1970-71; Warmington Insurance, Inc./Calif. Risk Corp., 1971-73; v.p., Quinlan Insurance, Inc., 1973---; worked as rater, underwriter, commercial lines mgr., surplus lines broker, Lloyds of London correspondent, ins. broker. Nom. Boss of the Year 1973; First woman on Agents Advisory Council of Insurance Co. of N. Am. (1978-80 Orange Co.). Mem.: Professional Insurance Agents Assn.; Natl. Assn. Mutual Ins. Agents, Insgroup, Insurosgroup, Orange County Ins. Women's Assn., former Young Republican. Catholic. Hobbies: Ceramics, astrology. Home: 31022 Via Cristal, San Juan Capistrano, CA 92675; Office: 4770 Von Karman, Newport Beach, CA 92660.

BAKER, ORPHA MAE
Artist — Sculptor
b. Apr. 13, 1922, Dinuba, Calif.; d. Philip E. and Beulah (Bartholomew) Phillips; student, Coll. of Sequoias, 1955, 58-59; Fresno State Coll., 1957; m. Raymond A. Morris, Jan. 26, 1941 (div. 1958); m.2d, Jerry D. Baker, Feb. 16, 1960 (div. 1973); chil.: Philip R. Morris; Carol Obegi; Laura Williams; Margaret Morris. Career: Bookkeeper, Morris Roofing Co., 1947-53; various other positions

1960-67; Curator, Desert Caballeros Western Mus., Wickenburg, Ariz., 1967-75; owner, antique shop — The Time Door, Glendora, 1976---. Dir., Desert Caballeros Western Mus., 1967-75. Recipient Outstanding Citizen Achievement Award, Desert Caballeros Orgn., 1970; Citizen of Year, Wickenburg C. of C., 1971; Mem.: Wickenburg Bus. & Profl. Women's Club, pres. 1971-72; Woman of Year 1973; Ariz. Fedn. Bus. & Profl. Women's Clubs, Dist. 7 Dir. 1973-74. Winner of 1st place award Art Show, Hanford, 1953; 8 ribbons — oil, watercolor; creator of dioramas with sculptured figurines. Hobbies: poetry. Rec.: fishing. Office: 216 No. Glendora Ave., Glendora, CA 91740.

BAKER, ROBERT M.L.
Attorney at Law
b. Jan. 10, 1903, Little Rock, Ark.; s. Melle J. and Emma (McDowell) Baker; ed. B.S., Univ. of Claif. 1926; J.D., Sch. of Law, USC, 1932; m. Martha Harlan, L.A., Feb. 14, 1928; chil.: Robert M.L., Jr., b. Sept. 1, 1930. Career: Student editorial bd., So. Calif. Law Review, 1932; admitted to State Bar of Calif. 1932, U.S. Dist. Ct., So. Dist. of Calif. 1933, Tax Ct. of the U.S. 1933, U.S. Ct. of Claims, 1953, Superior Ct. of U.S. 1954. Mem.: L.A. Bar Assn., Am. Bar Assn.; bd. dirs., L.A. Ath. Club, 1946---; bd. mgrs., Univ. YMCA (UCLA), 1950---; bd. dirs., Bel-Air Bay Club, L.A. 1952-54; pres. 1954-55; Calif. Club, L.A.; Phi Kappa Sigma, Phi Delta Phi, Alpha Kappa Psi. Republican. Methodist (bd. of elders, Westwood Community Ch.). Hobby: sports. Home: 10600 Le Conte Ave., L.A., CA 90024; Office: Suite 523, 510 W. 6th St., L.A., CA.

BAKER, ROBERT WARREN
District Attorney
b. Feb. 26, 1930, San Francisco; s. Hiram R. and Myrtle E. Baker; B.A., economics, Univ. Calif, Berkeley, 1952, LL.B., 1957; m. Patty Heinle, July 31, 1976, Viola, Calif., chil.: Grant W., b. Oct. 24, 1956; Stephen H., b. Dec. 29, 1959; Elaine E., b. Dec. 26, 1965. Career: with Calif. Atty. General's Office, Sacto., 1957-58; firm of Downey, Brand, Seymour & Rohwer, Sacto., 1958-61; Deputy Dist. Atty., Redding, 1963-64; Dist. Atty., Shasta Co., 1965---. AUS Corps of Engrs., 1952-54, 1961-62. Mem.: Elks Club, Redding Rotary Club. Democrat, mem. central com. 1966-68. Episcopalian, vestryman, 1966-69. Rec.: skiing, hiking. Home: 613 Terrace Dr., Redding, CA; Office: Drawer A.T., Redding, CA 96001.

BAKER, WILLIAM C.
Lawyer — Business Executive
b. May 14, 1933, Port Arthur, Tex.; s. Harry W. and Martha E. (Newby) Baker; ed. Univ. of Tex. Sch. of Law, 1957; m. Janice Y. Haskin, Dallas, Tex.; chil.: Stacy Allison, b. Oct. 22, 1966, Catherine Suzanne, b. Nov. 19, 1969. Career: U.S. Dept. of Justice (Admiralty-Shipping sect.), 1957-59; trial atty. Zock, Petrie, Sheneman & Reid, N.Y. 1959-62; atty. Wynne, Jaffee & Tinsley, Dallas, 1962-64; atty. Great Southwest Corp., Arlington, Tex. 1964-67, pres.-dir. 1967-69; and affiliates, 1969-70; secty.-gen. counsel, Macco Corp. 1967-69; pres.-dir.-partner, Baker & Caldwell, Newport Beach, 1970-71; partner, Baker-Miller & Assoc., 1973---; pres., Del Taco Corp., Costa Mesa, 1975---. Mem.: State Bar of Tex., N.Y.; Supreme Ct. of U.S.; Phi Gamma Delta; Phi Alpha Delta, The Dallas Club, Balboa Bay Club. Hobbies: coin-stamp collecting. Rec.: horseback riding, hunting. Home: 2242 Mesa Dr., Newport Beach, CA 92660; Office: 345 Baker St., Costa Mesa, CA 92626.

BALDING, GRANT
Ophthalmologist
b. Feb. 27, 1906, Albion, Ill.; s. Grant and Fanny (Bunting) Balding; ed. B.S., Univ. of Ill 1927; M.D., 1930; m. Carolyn George, Crown Point, Ind., Feb. 12, 1927. Career: Cons. ophthal.; No. French Sector, Rheims; cons. in ophthal. and surg. gen. cons. 1948---. Contrib to Eye, Ear, Nose and Throat Monthly Journ.; lectr., Sheffield and Liverpool Univs., Eng. Maj., AUS (1942-46), WW II. Mem.: Acad. of Ophthal. and Otolaryngology, 1946-48; pres. L.A. Ophthal. Journ. Club, 1952-53; Pan.-Am. Ophthal. Congress; Pac. Coast Acad. of Ophthal. and Otolaryngology; diplomate, Am. Bd. of Ophthal.; Oakmont Club, Masonic Lodge, Knights Templar, Shrine, Univ. Club. Nonpartisan. Hobby: oil painting. Rec.: golf. Home: 1125 S. Orange Grove, Pasadena, CA 91105; Office: 101 S. Madison Ave., Pasa., CA.

BALDRIDGE, G. DOUGLAS
Medical Specialist — Educator
b. Nov. 3, 1920, Dallas, Tex.; s. George D. and Dorothy (Betzner) Baldridge; 3rd cousin, Walter Wellman, Am.

explorer set world time and distance records in dirigible (1008 mi. in 72 hrs., attempted to cross N. Pole and Atlantic); ed. A.B., UCLA 1942; M.D., USC, 1948; m. Jane Weiser, Honolulu, Hawaii, Aug. 15, 1969; daus.: Betsy, b. June 22, 1951; Barbara, b. Sept. 15, 1952; Robin, b. Dec. 19, 1956. Career: Intern, L.A. Co. Gen. Hosp. 1946; instr. in dermatology; Univ. Pa. and research fellow, Children's Hosp. of Phila. 1949-51; cons. Oakridge Inst. for Nuclear Stus. 1950; instr. UCLA Med. Sch. 1951-52; asst. prof. of dermatology, USC Sch. of Med., 1951---; courtesy staff, St. John's hosp., cons. VA Hosp., Sawtelle, and cons. Harbor Gen. Hosp., 1951-52; certified spec. Am. bd. of Dermatology, 1952; dir. sect on virus diseases, Am. Acad. of Dermatology, 13-58. Maj., U.S. Army Med. Corps, 1945, Capt. 1946-48. Mem.: AMA, Calif., L.A. Co. Med. Assns.; Soc. for Investigative Dermatology; Phila Electron Microscope Soc.; Westwood Acad. of Med. and Dentistry; N. Am. Clin. Dermatology Soc.; Phi Rho Sigma; Phi Beta Sigma, 1939; Phi Beta Kappa, 1942; Rotary Club of Beverly Hills, 1960; L.A. Co. Club. Hobby: travel. Rec.: golf, tennis, fishing. Home: 10651 Somma Way, L.A., CA 90024; Office: 9201 Sunset Blvd., L.A., CA 90069.

BALES, BRUCE B.
Marin County District Attorney
b. May 12, 1923, L.A., Calif.; s. Homer Robert and Ruby (Reed) Bales; ed. A.B., Univ. of Calif., Berkeley, 1946; Boalt Hall Law Sch., J.D., 1949; m. Jo Ann Onufer, Oakland, Calif., Aug. 9, 1947; chil.: Thomas, Elena, Robert. Career: Pvt. law practice, Harold Jos. Haley & Leonard A. Thomas, San Rafael, 1950-54; Dep. Dist. Atty. of Marin Co., 1954-60; Asst. Dist. Atty., 1960-64; Dist. Atty., 1964---. Lt. (j.g.), USNR, Iwo Jima and Okinawa Campaigns, WW II. Mem.: past pres., of San Rafael Exch. Club; past pres., Marin Co. Centralized Police Servs. Council; past pres. Marin Co. Peace Officers Assn.; Police Sci. Adv. Com., Coll. of Marin; Joint Police Chiefs Assn. of Marin; Marin, Calif. and Am. Bar Assns.; Calif. Dist. Attys. Assn.; Ntl. Dist. Attys. Assn.; Marin Co. B.S.A.; Terra Linda Rotary; Native Sons of Golden West; San Anselmo Post 179, Am. Legion.; BPOE (1108); Elder, First Presbyterian Ch. Hobbies: skiing, duck hunting, tennis. Office: Hall of Justice, Rm. 155, San Rafael, CA 94903.

BALIAN, GERALD E.
Physician
b. June 5, 1939, New York; s. Edward and Sarah Bajakian; B.S., Fordham Coll., 1955; M.D., New Jersey Coll. of Med., 1960; m. Roberta Lynn Huntsinger, Apr. 2, 1977, L.A. Career: medical practice, urology and urological surgery, L.A. ---; Chief of Surgery, Monterey Park Hosp., 1978---; Treas., Monterey Park Hosp., 1976-77; bd. dir., Century Park E. Homeowners Assn., 1977-78; Served to Capt. M.C., AUS, 1961-63. Mem.: Phi Rho Sigma med. frat., life. Rec.: sports. Home: 2170 Century Park E., No. 512, L.A., CA 90067; Office: 2080 Century Park E., No. 1105, L.A. and 5255 E. Pomona Blvd., Suite 11, L.A., CA 90022.

BALL, IRIS GEORGIA
Corporate Executive
b. Oct. 19, 1921, West Union, W. Vir.; d. Cam L. and Oma Ann (Martin) Ball; B.A. in psychology, Calif. State Univ., Northridge, 1973; M.B.A., Pepperdine Univ., 1975. Career: Staff asst., Am. Embassy, Tokyo, Japan, 1952-55; spec. asst., Matson Navigation Co., Honolulu, HI; spec. agent, Prudential Ins. Co., L.A.; mgr., EEO for Women, Dart Industries, Inc., L.A., 1971---. Dir., YWCA of L.A., 1977-78; Author: Characteristics Differentiating the Female Manager from the Female Non-Manager, 1975; in mgmt. training film, Twelve Like You, 1973. Republican. Protestant. Hobbies: Orchid growing, piano. Rec.: Bicycling. Home: 8723 Ramsgate Ave., L.A., CA 90045; Office: 8480 Beverly Blvd., L.A., CA 90048.

BALL, JEAN GAIL
Business Owner
b. Jan. 17, 1927, Elizabeth City, N.C.; d. George Cluster and Dorothy (Tillett) Lyons (Peabody); ed. Temple Univ. Sch. of Fine Arts, 1943-46; diplomas: Spring Garden Inst., Moore Inst. of Design, Phila., Pa.; Real Estate Broker, 1970; m. Comdr. Edwin Lee Ball, USN ret., South Mills, S.C., June 28, 1946; dau. Dianna Lee, b. July 15, 1955. Career: Singer and model, Phila., N.Y., Baltimore, San Diego, 1942-59; real estate bus. 1959---; est. Ball Realty Co., El Cajon, Calif. 1970; Dyana's Beauty Salon; Profl. artist spec. in portraiture. Hons: 9 credits, art shows and 2 exhibits. Little Gallery, Canal Zone and Panama, 1966-69. Mem.: El Cajon Valley Bd. of Realtors; Calif. Real Estate Assn.; Natl. League Am. Pen Women. Hobbies: painting and Little Theatre. Home:

1787 Hillsdale Rd., El Cajon; Office: 790 E. Washington Ave., El Cajon, CA 92020.

BALL, LUCILLE
TV – Film Star
b. Aug, 6, Jamestown, N.Y.; d. Fred (min. engr.) and Desiree (Hunt) Ball (concert pianist); ed. Chautauqua Inst. of Mus.; John Murray Anderson Dramatic Sch., N.Y.; m. Desi Arnaz, Greenwich, Conn., Nov. 30, 1940 (div. 1960); chil.: Lucie Desiree, b. July 17, 1951; Desiderio Alberto, IV, b. Jan. 19, 1953. Career: Appd. Ziegfeld's "Rio Rita," model for wholesale dress co.; model, Hattie Carnegie; feat. model, mags., billboard adv.; first film, Eddie Cantor's "Roman Scandals"; apptd. "Robert," "The Girl from Paris," "Stage Door," "Too Many Girls," "The Big Street"; under contract to M.G.M.; pics. incl.: "DuBarry Was a Lady," "Best Foot Forward," "Meet the People," "Easy to Wed," "Her Husband'd Affairs," "The Long, Long Trailer"; "Forever Darling," Zandra Prodns.; stage plays incl.: "Hey, Diddle Diddle," Broadway, and Elmer Rice's "Dream Girl," on tour; star, "I Love Lucy," CBS-TV, 1960-74; pres. Desilu Prodns., Inc., Desilu Studios. Awards: over 200, incl. 2 TV Emmy Awards. Mem.: S.A.G., Equity. Res.: Beverly Hills, CA.

BALLARD, EATON WALLING
Business Executive
b. June 27, 1911, Seattle, Wash.; s. Roy Page and Olive (Murphy) Ballard; ed., A.B. Stanford Univ. 1932; M.B.A., Harvard Univ. 1937; m. Beverly Holtenhouse, Seattle, Wash., Dec. 28, 1933; chil.: Mrs. Nicholas (Sarah Eaton) Pileggi, b. 1935; Mrs. Donald David (Gretchen Walling) Guard, b. 1937; Jonathan Roy, b. 1942. Career: Marshall Field & Co., Chicago, 1937-38; May Co., L.A., 1939-46; Carter Hawley Hale Stores, Inc., L.A., exec. v.p.-dir. 1947-77; consultant, 1977---; Chmn., Whittaker Corp., L.A.; Dir.: Airborne Freight Corp., Seattle; Am. Mutual Fund., Inc., L.A.; Pacific Am. Income Shares, Inc., L.A.; Music Center Operating Co.; Chmn. trustees, Pacific Oaks Coll.; trustee, Athenian Sch.; Calif. Inst. of the Arts; Lt. USNR (1943-45), WW II. Mem.: Stock Exchange, Calif. Clubs, L.A. Episcopalian. Home: 635 Rockwood Rd., Pasadena, CA 91105; Office: 550 S. Flower St., L.A., CA 90071.

BALLARD, EATON WALLING
Consultant
b. June 27, 1911, Seattle, Wash.; s. Roy P. and Olive Murphy Ballard; A.B., Stanford Univ., 1932; M.B.A., Harvard Univ., 1937; m. Beverly Holtenhouse, Dec. 28, 1933, Seattle, Wash.; chil.: Sarah Eaton (Mrs. Nicholas Pileggi), b. 1935; Mrs. Gretchen Ballard-Guard, b. 1937; Jonathan Roy, b. 1942. Career: with Marshall Field & Co., Chicago, 1937-38; May Co., L.A., 1939-46; Carter Hawley Hale Stores, Inc., L.A., exec. v.p.-dir. 1947-77; consultant, 1977---; chmn., Whittaker Corp., L.A., 1977---. Dir.: Airborne Freight Corp., Seattle; The Christiana Companies, Inc., L.A.; Am. Mutual Fund, Inc., L.A.; Pacific Am. Income Shares, Inc., L.A.; Anchor Growth Fund, Inc., L.A.; Fundamental Investors, Inc., L.A.; Music Center Operating Co., L.A.; chmn. trustees, Pacific Oaks Coll.; Trustee: Calif. Inst. of the Arts; Athenian Sch. Lt., USNR, 1943-45, WW II. Clubs: Stock Exchange, Calif. Episcopal. Home: 635 Rockwood Rd., Pasadena, CA 91105; Office: 550 S. Flower St., L.A., CA 90071.

BALLHAUS, WILLIAM FRANCIS
President, Beckman Instruments
b. Aug. 15, 1918, S.F., Calif.; S. William Frederick and E.R. (O'Connor) Ballhaus; ed. A.B., Stanford Univ. 1940; M.E., 1942; Ph.D. (math.), Calif. Inst. of Tech. 1947; m. Edna Dooley, S.F., Feb. 13, 1944; chil.: William Francis, Jr., b. Jan. 28, 1945; Katherine Louise, b. Apr. 24, 1947; Martin Dennis, b. Mar. 16, 1952; Mary Susan, b. Jan. 19, 1953. Career: Registered civil and mech. engr., State of Calif.; aerodynamacist, structures engr., design spec., proj. engr., Douglas Aircraft, El Segundo, 1942-50; chief, preliminary design, Ft. Worth Div. of Convair, Tex. 1950-52; asst. chief engr., chief engr., v.p.-chief engr., of Norair Div., Northrop Corp. 1953-57; v.p.-gen. mgr. Nortronics Div., 1957-61, exec. v.p., Northrop Corp., 1961-66; pres. Beckman Instruments, Inc. 1966---. Tech. adv. panel on aerons. (research and enging.), Office of Asst. Secty of Def. 1955-59; bd. dirs., Page Communications Engrs., Inc. (subsidiary of Northrop), Wash., D.C., 1959---; bd. dirs., Western Semiconductors, Inc., Santa Ana, Calif., 1961---. Mem.: assoc. fellow, Inst. of Aeron. Scis.; Soc. of Automotive Engrs., Am. Ord. Assn.; Natl. Security Ind. Assn.; adv. Natl. Acad. of Scis. Natl. Research Council; bd. dirs.-mil. systems mgmt. com., Electronic Inds. Assn.; com. on aircraft constr.,

Natl. Adv. Com. on Aerons. 1955-57; adv. Calif. Inst. of Tech. Devel. Pgm.; chmn. Guided Missile Com., Aerospace Inds. Assn. 1957; gen. chmn., SAE Aeronautic Meeting, 1959, A.F. Office of Sci. Research Astronatuic Symposium, 1960; Engr. Fund Com., Stanford Univ. Republican. Catholic. Rec.: tennis, horseback riding, golf, fishing; Home: 21 Portuguese Bend Rd., Rolling Hills, CA; Office: 2500 Harbor Blvd., Fullerton, CA 92634.

BALOCCA, LOUIS A.
Title Insurance Company Executive
b. Sept. 25, 1928, Los Angeles, Calif.; s. Aldo and Teresa Balocca; A.A., L.A. City Coll.; student, Southwestern Univ. of Law, 3 years; UCLA, 2 years; m. Georgina Helen Firth, Tacoma, Wash., Nov. 5, 1956; chil.: Diana Kaylan, Bryan Balocca, Dennis Ward, Donald Ward, Douglas Ward. Career: v.p., Security Title Ins. Co., 1960; v.p. and dir. Calif. Land Title Co., 1961; sr. v.p., Calif. Land Title Co., 1969; sr. v.p., Calif-World Fin. Corp., 1969; dir., exec. v.p., Calif. Land Title Co. and Calif.-World Fin. Corp., 1974---. Pres., Title Records Inc., 1978; Dir.: Calif-World Title Co., S.D.; Universal Title Corp., Santa Clara. U.S. Army Infantry 1954-55 and Courts & Boards Div., Judge Advocate Gen. 1955-56. Mem.: Verdugo Club, Glendale; v.p., Irish Wolfhound Assn. of the West Coast (1977); v.p. and charter mem., Vine Arts Soc., 1967---. Hobby: Coursing hounds. Rec.: swimming, tennis. Home: 3717 El Lado Dr., Glendale, CA 91208; Office: 90 Universal City Plaza, Universal City, CA 91608.

BALTZ, LEWIS
Photographer
b. Sept. 12, 1945, Newport Beach; s. Charles Lewis and Berenice (Anderson) Baltz; B.F.A., S.F. Art Inst., 1969; M.F.A., Claremont Grad. Sch., 1971; m. 2d. Mary Ann Rayner, Dec. 28, 1974, Carmel; dau. Monica Doane, b. Sept. 15, 1966. Career: One man shows: Leo Castelli Gallery, N.Y.C., 1971, 73, 75; Corcoran Gallery Art, Wash., 1974, 76; Internat. Mus. Photography, 1972; Jefferson Place Gallery, 1974; Phila. Coll. of Art, 1975; Univ. N. Mex., 1975; Balt. Mus. Art, 1976; Mus. Fine Arts, Houston, 1976; La Jolla (Calif.) Mus. Contemporary Art, 1976; Gallery December, Dusseldorf, W. Ger., 1976; Univ. Nebr., 1977; Grapestake Gallery, S.F., 1977, 78; Univ. Nevada, 1978; Yarlow-Salzman Gallery, Toronto, Can., 1978; Susan Spiritus Gallery, Newport Beach, 1978; works in permanent public collections: Lib. of Congress, Art Inst. Chicago, Baltimore Mus. Art, Bibliotheque Nationale, Paris, Corcoran Gallery of Art, Wash. D.C., Dallas Art Mus., Internat. Mus. Photog., Rochester, N.Y., La Jolla Mus. Contemporary Art, Mus. of Fine Arts in Boston, Houston and St. Petersburg, Mus. of Modern Art, Nat. Collection Fine Art, Nat. Endowment for the Arts, Oakland Mus., Phila. Mus. of Art, S.F. Mus. Modern Art, Norton Simon Mus., Seagram Collection, N.Y. Lectr., art schs. and univs., U.S. and Can.; guest curator Mus. Fine Arts, Houston, 1977; Mem.: Individual grants panel Nat. Endowment for Arts, 1977; visiting com., Internat. Mus. of Photography, Rochester, N.Y., 1978-81. Nat. Endowment for Arts grantee, 1973, 76; Guggenheim fellow, 1976. Rec.: sailing, handball, tennis. Office: P.O.B. 366, Sausalito, CA.

BALLUFF, JOHN J.
Attorney at Law
b.Oct. 25, 1910, Tooele, Ut.; s. Joseph and Anna M. (Johnston) Balluff; ed. undergrad. St. Mary's Coll., Calif. 1928-29; LL.B., Chicago-Kent Coll. of Law, 1930-33; m. Minette LeClerg, Chicago, Ill., Oct. 3, 1933; sons: John E., b. Dec. 23, 1938; Douglas P., b. Nov. 8, 1941; Robert C., b. Sept. 13, 1947. Career: Gen. and corporate practice law, Chapman & Cutler firm, Chicago, 1935-48; counsel, Douglas Aircraft Co., Ill. 1941-42, spec. labor counsel, Santa Monica, Calif., 1943-44; atty A.T. and S.F. Rly. Co., L.A. 1948-58, asst. gen. atty. 1958-59, gen. atty. 1959-62, gen. atty., Calif. 1962-76. Mem.: Am., Calif. State Bar Assns.; exec. com. Corp. Law Dept., L.A. Co. Bar Assn., 1971---; Calif. Law Revision Comm. (apptd. by Gov. Reagan) 1971-76; com. So. Calif. Golf Assn., 1974-77; Chicago-Kent Soc. of the Round Table, Town Hall. Delta Chi, Palos Verdes Country Club, Calif. Club. Republican. Hobbies: music, bridge. Rec.: golf. Home: 925 Via Panorama, Palos Verdes Estates, CA; Office: same.

BANCROFT, RICHARD A.
Superior Court Judge
b. Aug. 30, 1918, Albany, N.Y.; s. William E. and Anna B. Bancroft; A.B., Howard Univ., 1942, J.D., 1951; LL.M., Univ. Calif. at Boalt Hall, 1952; m. Barbara J. Valim. Career: pvt. law practice, S.F. and bay area, 1952-71; Chief Counsel, Bay View Hunter's Point Found. for Community Improvement, 1971-76; Superior Ct. Judge,

Oakland, 1976---. Author: introductory chpt. to Handling Worker's Compensation Cases, 1963; chpt. 1, Mainstreaming: Controversy and Consensus, entitled Special Education: Legal Aspects, 1976 (edited by O'Donnell & Bradfield); contbr. Calif. Law Review, 1952. USMC, discharged 1946. Polit.: dir., Bay Area Rapid Transit, 1967-70; commr., S.F. Bd. of Permit Appeals, 1962-66. Hobby: gardening. Rec.: fishing, golfing. Office: 1225 Fallon St., Oakland, CA 94612.

BANNAI, PAUL T.
California State Assemblyman
b. July 4, 1920, Delta, Colo.; student, Am. Inst. Banking, 1938-42; Law, UCLA ext.; Licenses: real estate, casualty and life insurance; Nat. Assn. Security Dealers, 1954; m. Hideko; chil.: Kathy, Lorraine, Don. Career: mgr., Star Nurseries, Inc., Montebello, 1946-49; mgr., Golden State Wholesale Florists, 1949-54; owner, Bannai Realty and Insurance Co., 1954---; elected rep., 53rd Assembly Dist., Calif. State Legislature, 1973---. AUS, 1943-46; rep. U.S. Forces at surrender ceremonies in Bali, Java, Timor. Presidential appt. U.S. Commn. to UNESCO, 1976---; mem. Gardena City Planning Commn., 1969-71; chmn. 1971; elected mem., Gardena City Council, 1972; del. Nat. Conf. of Mayors; past pres., Gardena Bd. of Realtors; past v.p., Calif. Real Estate Assn.; charter dist. chmn., BSA, Gardena Valley Dist., awarded Order of Merit; life mem. VFW; past pres. Gardena Valley Lions; mem.: YWCA, Japanese Am. Citizens League, Elks. Office: 1919 W. Redondo Beach Blvd., Suite 107, Gardena, CA 90247; State Capitol, Suite 5150, Sacto., CA 95814.

BANNERMAN, WILLIAM CAMPBELL
Investments Executive
b. Mar. 11, 1900, Chicago, Ill., s. William and Theresa Bannerman; desc. of Sir Henry Campbell Bannerman, former Prime Minister of Eng.; ed. Ind. Univ., Northwestern Univ., Stanford Univ.; m. Elizabeth von KleimSmid, Tijuana, Mex. Santa Barbara, Calif., Aug. 8, 1950; daus.: Mary Louise Frost, b. Jan. 18, 1928; Elizabeth Teresa, b. May 17, 1951. Career: Bldg. bus. 1939---; pres. Calif. Natl., Inc.; property mgmt., So. Calif. 1939---; pres. Natl. Mgmt. Co.; consumer financing 1944---; pres. Columbia Investment Co.; mortgage financing and mortgage banking, 1961---; pres. Investor's Mortgage Serv. Co. Corp., Inf., U.S. Army, WW I. Mem.: L.A. Country Club, Eldorado Country Club, Bel-Air Bay Club, Delta Upsilon. Episcopalian. Hobby: golf. Home: 1145 Calle Vista Dr., Beverly Hills, CA 90210.

BARATI, GEORGE
Music Director
b. Apr. 3, 1913, Gyor, Hungary; s. Miksa B. and Regina (Schreiber) Barati; State Tchrs. diploma, State Artist diploma, Franz Liszt Conservatory, Budapest, Hungary; m. 2d. Ruth Carroll, Oct. 31, 1948, Laguna Beach; chil.: Stephen George, b. Sept. 8, 1940; Lorna (Brun), b. Mar. 7, 1951; Donna, b. Dec. 16, 1956. Career: Solo-Cellist, Budapest Symphony & Municipal Opera 1935-38; Conductor, Princeton String Ensemble & Choral Union, 1940-43; Conductor, Alexandria (La.) Military Symphony, 1944-45; Cellist, S.F. Symphony, 1946-50; Music Dir., Barati Chamber Orchestra of S.F., 1947-52; Music Dir., Honolulu Symphony & Opera, 1950-68; Mus. Dir., Santa Cruz Co. Sym., 1971---. Exec. Dir., Montalvo Assn., 1968---. Composer-Conductor, publishers: Peres Edition, Peer International; Recordings: Decca, Columbia, Lyrichord, CRI. AUS, 1943-46. Home: Villa Montalvo, Saratoga, CA 95070.

BARCOFF, WILLIAM BARTOLOMUCCI
Manufacturing Executive
b. Apr. 27, 1909, Braddock, Pa.; s. Pasquale and Pauline (Santavicci) Barcoff; ed. Columbia Univ.; metallurgist engr., USC; m. Fay Adler, Las Vegas, Nev., July 10, 1951; dau.: April, b. Apr. 1944. Career: Exhib. parachute jumper, 1927-34; test flight inspector, Stout-Ford Tri-Motor Co., Detroit, Mich. 1927-31; radio anncr., Detroit, 1931; mgr. Detroit City Airport, 1931-33; advance publicity dir., Am. Air Aces, 1934; pres. Aviation Facilities, Inc., Floyd Bennett Airport, NYC, 1935-42; mgr. aviation div., MacMillan Oil Co., 1945-51; exec. v.p. aircraft component parts mfg., Prodn. Heat Treating Co. 1952---. USAF (1942-46), WW II. Mem.: (Life) Am. Air Force Assn., Geophysical Research Corp., Lakeside Country Club, Balboa Bay Club. Catholic. Hobby: electronics. Home: 4257 Strohm, Toluca Lake, No. Hollywood, CA.

BAREIS, MILDRED
Market Research Coordinator
b. Montara, Calif.; d. Karl and Johanna (Peppert) Bareis;

B.A., M.A., Univ. Calif., Berkeley; m. Robert Schreiber, June 1976. Career: with Am. Bankers Assn., 1940-41; Federal Reserve Bank of S.F., 1941-44; Henry J. Kaiser Corp., 1944-47; sr. market research coordinator, Crown Zellerbach, 1947---. Mem.: Am. Statistical Assn., S.F. chpt., pres.; Am. Mktg. Assn.; Nat. Assn of Business Economists; S.F. C. of C.; S.F. Acad. of Sci. Hobbies: lapidary, travel. Home: 1935 Funston, S.F., CA 94116; Office: One Bush St., S.F., CA 94119.

BARGER, THOMAS C.
Energy Consultant
b. Aug. 30, 1909, Minneapolis, Minn.; s. Michael T. and Mary Margaret (Donohue) Barger; B.S., mining, metallurgy, Univ. N. Dak., 1931; LL.D. (hon. causa) 1967; DR. Bus. & Commerce, St. Mary's Coll. (Hon. Causa), 1973; m. Kathleen Ray, 1937 (dec. 1971); chil.: Anne E. (Herbert), b. 1941; Michael R., b. 1946; Timothy J., b. 1946; Mary K., b. 1951; Norah M., b. 1953; Teresa C., b. 1955; m. 2d. Kathleen Vachreau, Aug. 14, 1972, Sapphire, N.C. Career: mining engr., Canada, 1931-35; assoc. prof. mining & metallurgy, Univ. N. Dak., 1935-37; with Arabian Am. Oil Co., 1937-69; geologist, govt. rels., v.p., 1958, pres. 1959, chief exec. officer, 1961-69; chmn. bd. 1967-69; cons. on internat. oil and Middle East, 1969---. Dir.: Northrop Corp. 1973; Calif. First Bank, 1973; Offshore Technology 1971; Kratos, Inc. 1972; Wd-40 1977. Author: Energy Policies of the Arab States of the Persian Gulf, Univ. Delaware 1975; distinguished lectr., Soc. Petroleum Engrs. 1976-77; trustee, Univ. San Diego; trustee, Univ. N. Dak. Alumni Assn.; mem. bd. overseers, Univ. Calif., San Diego; Mem.: Explorers Club, N.Y.C., K.C.; Am. Inst. Mining Engrs.; Univ. Club, S.D.; Council of Foreign Rels. Roman Catholic; Knight Comdr. St. Gregory, K. Comdr. with Star Equestrian, Order of Holy Sepulchre. Hobbies: photog., archeology. Rec.: racquetball. Home: 2685 Calle Del Oro, La Jolla, CA 92037.

BARHAM, PATRICIA A.
Columnist
b.Mar. 21, L.A., Calif.; d. Dr. Frank Forrest and Princess Jessica Gorham (Meskhi-Gleboff) Barham; ed. Marlborough Sch. for Girls; Westlake Sch. for Girls, USC; Univ. of Ariz.; D. Litt. (hon.), St. Olav's Acad. 1969. Career: columnist, L.A. Herald-Express; asst in solving L.A. gang murder (M.A. Stager and mob); spec. pictorial feats. (Hearst Pre-date); staff, King Features Syn.; "Right About Fashion" (Hollywood column), syn.; War corr. (Internat. News Serv. and Herald Express, now Herald Examiner): Korean War (only woman in war to make tape recordings of battles on front lines of Korea), 1951; columnist: Hicks Deal Publs., Valley News and Green Sheet, Spotlight, Show Biz, South Tex. Citizen, many other small town newspapers; publr., Soc. West, L.A. 1975; Author: "Pin Up Poems" co-author: (book) "Operation Nightmare," publ. Sequoia Univ. Press, 1952. Awards: reportorial coverage, 1st U.N. Conf., S.F. "best reportorial work of year," by Manuscripters; Journ. Award; Le Grand Prix Humanitaire of the Order of the Crown Thorns, rank of Compagnon, 1971. Mem.: Athena Natl. Lit. Soc., League of Western Writers, Manuscripters, Natl. League of Am. Pen Women. Clubs: Round the World, Las Floristas, Opera Guild of So. Calif., Wilshire Ebell, Newport Harbor Yacht, Waikiki Yacht, Outrigger Canoe (Hawaii); St. Anne's Hosp. Guild, Soc. Serv. Aux., D.A.R., Philharmonic Internat. Com.; L.A. Club, Delta Gamma, Theta Sigma Phi. Episcopalian. Hobby: writing satirical verse. Rec.: horseback riding, swimming. Home: 100 Fremont Pl., L.A., CA 90005.

BARKER, NORMAN, JR.
Chairman of Board, United California Bank
b. July 30, 1922, San Diego, Calif.; s. Norman and Grace (Bolger) Barker; ed. B.A., Univ. Chicago, 1947, M.B.A. 1953; m. Sue Keefe, Chicago, Ill., June 27, 1947; chil.: Peter, Timothy, Michael, Elizabeth. Career: Assoc. with Harris Trust and Svgs. Bank, Chicago, 1947-55; Am. Can Co. 1955-57; United Calif. Bank, L.A., 1957---, chmn.-chief exec. officer and dir.; chmn.-dir. ACSC Mgmt. Servs., Inc., dir. of Automobile Club of So. Calif.; dir.: Western Bancorp., So. Calif. Edison Co., Carter Hawley Hale Stores, Inc., Carnation Co., Lear Siegler, Inc.; trustee: Univ. of Chicago; Occidental Coll., overseer, Henry E. Huntington Lib. and Art Gallery; United Way, Inc. Lt., USNR, 1944-46, 1950-52. Mem.: L.A. Country Club, Pauma Valley Country Club, Bohemian Club, Calif. Club. Catholic. Rec.: golf, tennis. Home: 111 N. June St., L.A., CA 90004; Office: 707 Wilshire Blvd., L.A., CA 90017.

BARKER, WILEY F.
Professor of Surgery
b. Oct. 16, 1919, Santa Fe, New Mex.; s. Charles B. and Bertha M. (Steed) Barker; nephew, Elliott S. Barker, writer and conservationist; nephew, S. Omar Barker, writer; B.S., Harvard, 1941; M.D., 1944; m. Nancy Kerber, June 8, 1943, Santa Fe, N. Mex.; chil.: Robert L., b. May 24, 1951; Jonathan S., b. Dec. 20, 1952; Christina Lee, b. Jan. 15, 1955. Career: medical intern, Peter Brent Brigham Hosp., Boston 1948-49; Wadsworth VA Hosp., 1949-54; Chief, Gen. Surgical Sect. 1952-54; prof. of surgery, UCLA Dept. of Surgery, 1954---, chief., Gen. Surgery Div., UCLA, 1955-77. USN, 1944-46, USNR M.C. 1946-47. Author: 2 books, 110 pub. papers on surgical topics. Pres., Soc. Clin. Surgery, 1973-75; pres., Soc. for Vascular Surgery, 1972; pres., Internat. Cardiovasc. Surg. Soc., 1978. Hobbies: orchid culture, travel, archeology. Rec.: wilderness travel. Office: UCLA Med. Center, L.A., CA 90024.

BARLOW, MELVIN LEWIS
University Professor
b.Mar. 13, 1910, Edmond, Okla.; s. Ralph Rewel and Hazel (Garey) Barlow; ed., A.B. (engin.-physics), USC 1933; M.A. (physics-math), 1934; Ed.D., UCLA; m. Alice Demaree, Altadena, Calif., Oct. 12, 1935; son, Ralph Robert, b. Oct. 7, 1947, Santa Monica, Calif. Career: Research physicist, 1935-39; H.S. instr. (sci.-math), 1939-40; jr. coll. instr. (petroleum tech.-math), 1940-42; supv. (trade-tech, tchr. training), Calif. State Dept. of Edn. 1942-43, 1946-57; dir., Div. Vocational Edn., UCLA, 1953---, prof. (edn.) 1957---. Research staff, Pres. Panel of Cons. on Vocational Edn., U.S. Office of Edn., Wash., D.C., 1962, staff dir., Adv. Council on Vocational Edn. 1967. Author: "History of Indsl. Edn., in the U.S.," publ. Chas. A. Bennett Co. 1967. Vocational training officer, Petroleum engr., USNR (1943-46), WW II. Mem.: pres. Natl. Assn. Ind. Tchr. Educators, 1957; historian, Am. Vocational Assn., 1964---; many others. Non-partisan. Methodist. Hobbies: fishing, writing. Home: 3264 Mountain View Ave., L.A., CA 90066; Office: 405 Hilgard Ave., 131 Moore Hall, L.A., CA 90024.

BARNES, HON. STANLEY N.
U.S. Circuit Court Judge
b. May 1, 1900, Wis.; s. Charles L. and Janet (Rankin) Barnes; ed. A.B., Univ. of Calif. 1922, J.D. 1925 (hon.) LL.D. 1961; Harvard Univ. 1923-24; m. Anne Fisk, L.A., Oct. 18, 1929; chil.: Janet Anne (Mrs. James Hansen), Judith Fisk (Mrs. James H. Reid) and Joyce Rankin (Mrs. David Robinson). Career: Pvt. law practice, S.F., 1925-28, L.A. 1928-46; judge, Superior Ct., L.A. 1947-53; asst. U.S. Atty. Gen. 1953-56; judge, U.S. Ct. of Appeals, Ninth Circuit, 1956---. Lectr., law, USC 1948-49. USN (1918), WW I. Mem.---: pres., L.A. Alumni Chpt., Sigma Chi, 1932, 39, national trustee, 1950-52, natl. pres. 1952-55; dir. L.A. Bar Assn. 1945-47; regent, Univ. of Calif. 1946-48; pres. Alumni Assn. 1946-48; trustee: Southwest Museum, 1947---; David William Cooper Found. 1948---; dir. Calif. Inst. for Cancer Research, 1950-53, 58---; Inst. of Judician Adm.; Am. Judicature Soc.; natl. adv. bd., Am. Law Inst.; natl. council, Fed. Bar Assn., nat. pres. 1954-55; fellow, Am. Coll. of Trial Lawyers; fellow, Am. Acad. of Forensic Scis.; Natl. Football Hall of Fame, 1954; Am. Leg., Phi Delta Phi, S. Pasa Masonic Lodge No. 367; Univ. Club and Calif. Club, L.A.; Bohemian Club, S.F. Republican. Episcopal. Hobby: collecting and lecturing on "masks" ("Masks and Their Use by Primitive Peoples"). Home: 747 S. Orange Grove Ave., Pasa., CA; Office: 1653 U.S. Post Office & Courthouse Bldg., L.A. CA; and 322 U.S. Post Office & Courthouse Bldg., S.F., CA; and U.S. Post Office & Courthouse Blvd., Portland Ore. and Seattle, Wash.

BARRETT, CARLTON LESLIE
Property Management Executive
b. Oct. 22, 1911, Port Huron, Mich.; s. William C. and Elsie (King) Barrett;m. Mary Ellen Kuhn, Detroit, Mich.; chil.: Jack A., b. Sept. 11, 1939; Jayne E. McClelland, b. Nov. 21, 1940; Thomas M., b. Nov. 23, 1941; Patricia A., b. Aug. 8, 1943; Carlton L., II, b. Apr. 18, 1955. Career: property management exec., USN, Grosse Ile, Mich. and John Rogers Naval Base, Hawaii, 1942-46, WW II. Mem.: bd. dirs. Santa Monica Bay Council, 1967-75; Bd. of Dirs., Santa Monica Bay Council Navy League of U.S., 1967-79; Easte;Seal Soc. Aux., L.A.; U.S. Navy League; L.A. World Affairs Council; Leslie Linder's London Club. Rec.: golf, horse racing. Home: 1737 Mandeville Lane, L.A., CA 90049.

BARRETT-CONNOR, ELIZABETH L.
Physician — Professor
b. Apr. 8, 1935, Illinois; d. Willard R. and Florence

(Hershey) Barrett; B.A., Mt. Holyoke Coll., 1956; M.D., Cornell Univ. Med. Coll., 1960; diploma in clin. med. of tropics, London Sch. Hygiene and Tropical Medicine, London, England, 1965; m. James D. Connor, 1965, London, England; chil.: Jonathan, b. 1968; Caroline, b. 1969; Steven, b. 1971. Career: asst. prof. Epidemiology and Med., Univ. Miami Sch. of Med., 1968-70; Asst. Prof. Community Medicine and Med., Univ. Calif., San Diego, 1970-74; assoc. prof. of community medicine and medicine, 1974---; chief, div. of epidemiology, UCSD, 1974---. Contbr. 58 publs. to sci. journs. Home: 6423 Avenida Cresta, La Jolla, CA 92037; Office: Div. Epidemiology, M-007, Univ. Calif., La Jolla, CA 92093.

BARRETT, G. HAROLD
College Professor — Author
b. Mar. 20, 1925, Healdsburg, Calif.; s. Mathew Harold and Gladys (Lutz) Barrett; grandson of Francis Edward Barrett, native S.F. and prominent pioneering rancher, Sonoma Co.; ed. B.A., Univ. of Pac., 1949; M.A., 1952; Ph.D., Univ. of Ore., 1962; m. Carol Joan Bliss, Healdsburg, Mar. 21, 1948; chil.: Joseph George, b. 1949; Patrick John, b. 1950; Edward Paul, b. 1956; Lee Stuart and Jacob Scott (twins), b. 1963. Career: Tchr., Lodi H.S. 1950-54; Compton Coll. 1954-59; instr. Univ. of Ore. 1959-61; asst. prof., So. Ore. Coll. 1961-63; prof. rhetoric and pub. address, Calif. State Univ. at Hayward, 1963---. Author: "Practical Methods in Speech" (widely used coll. textbook), publ. Holt, Rinehart and Winston, 1959; numerous articles in profl. journs., incl. "Scott of the Oregonian vs. William Jennings Bryan.", quarterly Journ. of Speech, Apr. 1962; "John F. Kennedy before Greater Houston Ministerial Assn.," Central States Speech Journ., Nov. 1964. U.S. Navy (1943-46) WW II. Awards: elected Outstanding Faculty Mem. of Yr., So. Ore. Coll. 1963; Mem: bd. dirs., Hayward Festival of Arts, 1967-70; Speech Assn. of Am., Western Speech Assn., Am. Assn. of Univ. Profs., Assn. of Calif. State Coll. Profs., Pi Kappa Delta, Phi Delta Kappa. Democrat. Protestant. Hobby: reading. Rec.: sports, travel. Home: 5126 Crane Ave., Castro Valley, CA 94546; Office: Calif. State Univ., 25800 Hillary St., Hayward, CA 94542.

BARRON, MILTON L.
Professor of Sociology
b. Feb. 25, 1918, Derby, Conn.; B.A., Yale Univ., 1939, M.A., 1942, Ph.D., 1945; m. June 1, 1947; Career: orgns. and propaganda analyst, Dept. of Justice, Wash. D.C., 1943; faculty mem.: St. Lawrence Univ. 1943-44; Syracuse Univ. 1944-48; Cornell Univ. 1948-54; City Coll. of City Univ. of N.Y., 1954-74; visiting prof. and lectr., Wells Coll., Columbia Univ., N.Y. Univ., Stern Coll. of Yeshiva Univ., Fresno State Coll; Fulbright-Hays Lectr., Bar-Ilan Univ., Israel, 1962-63; currently, prof. dept. of sociology, Calif. State Univ., Fresno ---. Author: People Who Intermarry, Syracuse Univ. Press, 1946; The Juvenile in Delinquent Society, N.Y. Knopf, 1954; The Aging Am., N.Y., Crowell, 1961; The Tenth American: Aging in Modern Society (in prep.); co-author: Delinquent Behavior, Nat. Edn. Assn., 1959; editor: American Minorities, 1957 Minorities in a Changing World, 1967, Contemporary Sociology, 1964, The Blending American, 1972; prolific contbr. articles, book reviews to sociological journs., encyclopedias, etc. Mem.: Am. Sociological Assn.; Pacific Sociological Assn.; Sociological Research Assn.; AAUP. Home: 5482 N. Ninth St., Fresno, CA 93710; Office: Calif. State Univ., Fresno, CA 93740.

BARSHAY, MARSHALL E.
Physician
b. Nov. 10, 1938, Brooklyn, N.Y.; s. Murray and Rose Barshay, B.A., 1959; M.D., State Univ. of Buffalo at N.Y., 1963; m. Patricia Gross, Dec. 24, 1973, L.A.; chil.: Adam Dale, b. Jan. 4, 1975; Brigitte Alana, b. July 21, 1977. Career: internship, Phila. Gen. Hosp. 1963-64; med. residency: Ft. Miley VA Hosp., S.F., 1966-67; Wadsworth VA Hosp., L.A., 1967-68; Cedars-Sinai Med. Center, 1967-68; Nephrology Fellowship, Wadsworth VA Hosp., 1971-72; practice internal med., Santa Monica, 1973---; clin. instr., UCLA Med. Sch. Capt., AUS, 1964-66. Mem.: Knights of Pythius, N.Y., 1958-65; Sigma Alpha Mu frat., 1955-59. Hebrew. Hobbies: swim, chess, tennis. Rec.: travel. Office: 1260 15th St., Suite 816, Santa Monica, CA 90404.

BARSHOP, NATHAN
Surgeon
b. Jan. 22, 1913, N.Y.C.; s. Samuel and Esther (Shiffris) Barshop; ed. B.A., Baylor Univ., Tex. 1930, M.D., Coll. of Med. 1934; m. Coe Thelma Fisher, L.A., Apr. 27, 1949; chil.: Deborah Martha, b. Feb. 18, 1950; Melanie Coe, b. Aug. 10, 1951; Mark Nathan, b. May 8, 1953. Career:

Intern: Baylor Univ. Hosp., Dallas, Tex., 1934-35; L.A. Co. Gen. Hosp. 1935-36, res. phys. 1936-40; est. pvt. practice, Beverly Hills and L.A. 1940---. Attending surg., Cedars of Lebanon Hosp., 1947---, bd. of govs. 1961---; attending surg., L.A. Co. Gen. Hosp. 1947---; chief of surg., Mt. Sinai Hosp., L.A. 1948---; dir. and chmn. Tumor Bd. 1953---; chief of staff, 1957-59; bd. govs., Mt. Sinai Med. Center, 1961---. Asst. prof. of surg., USC Coll. of Med. 1948---. Maj., Med. Corps, WW II. Awards: decorated, Pres. Cit. with two oak leaf clusters. Mem.: Beverly Hills Acad. of Med.; diplomate, Am. Bd. of Surg.; fellow, ACS; Soc. of Grad. Surgs., L.A. Surg. Soc., Phi Delta Epsilon (dist. dep., Grand Council, 1957). Jewish (bd. dirs., Leo Baeck Temple, Beverly Hills, 1960---). Hobby: music, literature. Rec.: swimming. Home: 11300 Sunset Blvd., L.A., CA 90049; Office: 405 N. Bedford Dr., Beverly Hills, CA.

BARTLETT, ELIZABETH
Poet
b. N.Y.C.; d. Lewis and Charlotte (Rosefield) Winters; B.S. Tchrs. Coll., N.Y.; grad. study, Columbia Univ.; m. Paul Bartlett, Apr. 19, 1943, Sayula, Mex.; son. Dr. Steven James, b. May 15, 1945. Career: instr., Univ. San Diego, Univ. Calif., Santa Barbara, San Jose State Univ., Southern Methodist Univ.; guest lectr. universities in U.S. and Canada; poetry editor of ETC.: A Review of General Semantics, 1963-76; pub. volumes of poetry: Poems of Yes and No, Poetry Concerto, Behold This Dreamer, It Takes Practice Not To Die, Twelve-Tone Poems, Threads, The Housye of Sleep, Dialogue of Dust, Selected Poems, In Search of Identity, Address in Time, A Zodiac of Poems, Collected Twelve-Tone Poems (in prep.). Dir., Creative Writers Assn., New School for Social Research, 1955. Awarded grants from Nat. Inst. of Arts & Letters, PEN; poetry awards, Nat. Endowment for the Arts, St. Andrews Review; fellowships: Huntington Hartford Fedn., 1959, 60; Montalvo Assn., 1961; Yaddo Fdn., 1970; MacDowell Colony, 1970. Hobby: artwork, occasional exhibits. Rec.: music, travel, theatre. Home: 2875 Cowley Way, 1302, San Diego, CA 92110.

BARTLETT, PAUL ALEXANDER
Writer — Artist
b. July 13, 1909, Moberly, Mo.; s. Rev. Robert A. and Minnie Lou Bartlett; desc. Josiah Bartlett, signer of Declaration of Independence; cousin, Vernon Bartlett, MP, Britain; B.A. Oberlin Coll., 1932; stu., Acad. San Carlos, Mex. City, 1945; Univ. de Guadalajara, 1946; m. Elizabeth Winters, Apr. 19, 1943, Sayula, Jalisco, Mex.; son, Dr. Steven, b. 1945. Career: Most recent job: editor of Publs., Univ. of Calif., Santa Barbara (1965-70). Retired. Mexican historian: first art and historical record of Mexican haciendas: traveled 50,000 m. thru Mex., made 300 pen and ink studies of the rural estates. These 300 ink studies now property of Univ. of Texas, Austin, T. Univ. of Wyo., est. Paul Alexander Bartlett Archives, 1978; published books, short stories, articles, poetry; 400 Mex. drawings, easel paintings; intimate journs., letters of prof. critics, authors, photographs; books and stories in manuscript form also. Publications: (short stories) Accent Review, Kenyon Review, Univ. of Houston Forum, Chicago Review, ETC Magazine, Coastlines, New-Story, North American Review, Literary Review, Accent Anthology, Cross Section Anthology, New Voices 2 Anthology, American Scene '63 Anthology, New Writing 13; (books) When the Oil Cries, Macmillan; Wherehill, Autograph Editions; Spokes for Memory, Icarus Press; Awards: New School for Social Research, 1959; Huntington Hartford Found., 1960; Montalvo Assn., 1961; Carnegie Fund, 1961; Yaddo, 1970. Artistic commendations from Ford Madox Ford, Upton Sinclair, John Dos Passos, Pearl S. Buck. Hobby: outdoor sketching. Rec.: tennis, hiking. Home: 2875 Cowley Way, 1302, San Diego, CA 92110.

BARTLETT, ROBERT HAWES
Professor of Surgery
b. May 8, 1939, Ann Arbor, Mich.; B.A. Albion Coll., Mich., 1960; M.D., cum laude, Univ. of Mich. Med. Sch., 1963. Career: Internship and residency, Peter Bent Brigham Hosp., Boston, 1963-69; NIH trainee fellowship in acad. surgery, 1966-70; research fellow in surgery: Harvard Med. Sch. 1968-70; asst. assoc. and prof. of Surgery, Univ. Calif., Irvine, 1970---; asst. dir. surgical services, Orange Co. Med. Center, 1970-76; dir. Univ. Calif. Irvine Burn Center, 1971---; dir., Student and Resident Training, Dept. of Surgery, UCI; Chief, Gen. Surgery, UCI Med. Center. Spec., applied physiology in surgery. Lectr. hospitals, universities in U.S. and Japan, med. confs.; editorial cons.: Science, 1974; Chest, 1974-77; Journ. of Applied Physiology, 1977; Heart and Lung, 1977; ASAIO Journ. 1978; research cons.: Utah

Biomed. Test Lab., 1974, 75; edit. bd., Artificial Organs, 1977, 78; research grant reviewer: Nat. March Dimes Found., 1974; Nat. Heart and Lung Inst. 1974, 75; Calif. Heart Assn., 1975. Co-author: Mechanical Devices for Cardiopulmonary Assistance Contbr. med. yearbooks, journs., books. Mem.: Beta Beta Beta, Galens Hon. Med. Soc., Alpha Omega Alpha, Am. Fedn. Clin. Research, Am. Trauma Soc., Am. Heart Assn., Am. Coll. Surgeons, Orange Co. and L.A. Surgical Socs., Am. Soc. Artificial Internal Organs, Assn. Adv. Med. Instrumentation, Am. Thoracic Soc., Am. Coll. Chest Physicians, Assn. Acad. Surgery, Am. Burn Assn., Samson Thoracic Surgical Soc., Am. Assn. Thoracic Surgery, Soc. Univ. Surgeons. Research grantee: Donald E. Baxter Found., Hearst Found., Nat. Inst. of Health. Office: UCI Med. Center, 101 City Dr. S., Orange, CA 92668.

BARTLETT, RUHL J.
Professor Emeritus
b. Jan. 24, 1897, Webster, W. Va.; s. Adolphus J. and Mary Amne (Shroyer) Bartlett; A.B., Ohio Univ., 1920; M.A., Univ. Cincinnati, 1924; Ph.D., Ohio State Univ., 1927; LL.D., Tufts Univ., 1974; m. Barbara Ganascia, 1977, Santa Rosa, Calif. Career: Instr., history, Univ. of Iowa, 1924-25, Ohio State Univ. 1926; prof., Tufts Univ., 1927-43; prof., Fletcher Sch. of Law and Diplomacy, 1943-72; Dean, Grad. Sch. Tufts Univ., 1928-29. Author: John C. Fremont, 1930; League to Enforce Peace, 1934; Record of American Diplomacy, 1947; Policy and Power, 1963. USN, 1917-18. Mem.: Phi Beta Kappa, Phi Kappa Tau, Masons. Home: 336 Rockgreen Place, Santa Rosa, CA 95405.

BARTNICKI-GARCIA, SALOMON
Professor of Plant Pathology
b. May 18, 1935, Mexico City; s. Israel and Refugio (Garcia) Bartnicki; bacteriologist-chemist, 1957; Ph.D., microbiology, 1961; m. Ildiko Nagy, Aug. 10, 1975, Las Vegas, Nev.; chil.: Linda Laura, b. Jan. 22, 1969; David Daniel, b. Sept. 10, 1970. Career: asst. prof. of plant pathology, Univ. of Calif., Riverside, 1962-67; assoc. prof., 1968-71, prof. of plant pathology, 1972---. Contbr. 100 articles to sci. journs. Hobby: photog. Rec.: tennis. Home: 1391 Lynridge, Riverside, CA; Office: Univ. of Calif., Riverside, CA 92521.

BARTOL, BARBARA ANN
Lecturer — Author
b. May 23, 1928, Whittier, Calif.; d. Eugene G. and Miriam (Compton) Beddall; B.A., English, Calif. State Univ., Fullerton, 1964; Gen. secondary tch. credential, 1965; postgrad. studies, Pacific Western, Encino, 1978---; m. Robert Paul Bartol, Las Vegas, Nev., April 13, 1969; chil.; Cherryl Ann Grant, b. Sept. 9, 1946; Victoria Lynn Webber, b. Aug. 10, 1947; Kerry Jean Reuvers, b. June 28, 1952; Robin Carole Trask, b. Oct. 24, 1949. Career: tchr., secondary pub. schs., Orange Co., 1965-68; social worker, child welfare, L.A. Co., 1969-71; personnel work, 1973; Durham Bus. Coll. Admissions Rep., Ariz., 1972; founder Bartol Enterprises (imports, gifts), 1975-77; created Diet Recipe of the Month, 1976; founder, Barbara A. Bartol & Assoc. (seminars and workshops on Secrets of Success for Women), 1978---. Lectures: Re-Entry Women Face the Challenge; How to be a Super Success; Exploring You. Author: Stirrings, Natl. Coll. Poetry Anthology, 1960; Secrets of Success for Women, 1979; Women — How to Run a Business from Home, 1977. Delegate & alt., Human Services Comm., Fountain Valley, 1976-77. Mem.: Thomas Jefferson PTA, pres. 1957-58; Epsilon Sigma Alpha, Intl., Eta Epsilon-Anaheim chpt., pres. 1969-70; C. of C., Fountain Valley Women's Div., publicity dir., 1977-78; Women In Mgmt., newsletter editor, 1976---, secty., 1976-79. Rec.: swimming, golf. Home: 7311-1 Toulouse Dr., Huntington Beach, CA 92647.

BARTON, WILLIAM DENNIS
Chairman of Board, Barton Enterprises
b. Sept. 23, 1916, Hot Springs, Ark.; s. William Harvey and Osa Mae (Dennis) Barton; nephew of Bruce Barton; grand-nephew of Clara Barton and William Barton (designer, U.S. Seal); ed. (bus. adm.) Mich. State Univ. 1938; Burroughs Advanced Bus. 1939; Chrysler Mgmt. Sch. 1946; m. Jean Gretchen McGillivray, Oscoda, Mich., June 19, 1939; chil.: Mrs. Harry Bissel (Barbara Jean); Wyeth, b. 1940; William Dennis, Jr., b. 1942; Col. James, b. 1944; Ginger Lei, b. 1951. Career: Foreign and comml. sales mgr., Consolidated Aircraft, San Diego, 1940-46; pres. Consolidated Plastics, 1946-52; dir. Alsynite Corp. 1947-52; chmn. bd., Dumont Corp., San Rafael, 1948-54; chmn. bd. E. & H. Mfg. Co., 1952-56; pres. Gen. Synthetics, Oakland, 1952-58; pres. Barton Enterprises, 1954-62; pres.-chmn. bd., Barton Enterprises, S.A.,

1962---. Patentee, field of missiles. Author: (scenarios) "Flying B-24," 1943; "Birdman" (Glen Ford), 1945; "Sailing Catamarans and Trimarans," 1966. USMC, WW II. Recipient: Serv. Award, Marine Corp. 1945. Mem.: Lambda Chi Alpha, 1934-38; area judge, Natl. Aeron. Assn., 1934-64; Oakland Yacht Club, 1954---. Danville Community Ch. (elder, 1941). Hobby: yachting. Home: 252 La Questa Dr., Danville, CA; Office: Professional Bldg., Danville, CA 94526.

BASCOM, WILLIAM RUSSELL
Director, Lowie Museum of Anthropology
b. May 23, 1912, Princeton, Ill.; s. George Rockwell and Litta Celia (Banschbach) Bascom; B.A., Univ. of Wis., 1933; M.A., 1936; Ph.D., Northwestern Univ., 1939; m. Berta Montero-Sanchez, Nov. 26, 1948, Evanston, Ill. Career: instr.-prof. of anthropology, Northwestern Univ., 1939-42, 1946-57; U.S. Govt. Service: in West Africa, 1942-46, Micronesia, 1946; Prof. and Dir., Lowie Mus. of Anthropology, Univ. of Calif., Berkeley, 1957---. Author: Frontiers of Folklore, 1977; African Dilemma Tales, 1975; African Art in Cultural Perspective, 1973; Shango in the New World, 1972; Ifa Divination: Communication between Gods and Men in West Africa, 1969. Pres., Am. Folklore Soc., 1952-54; exec. bd., Am. Anthropological Assn., 1961-64. Club: Berkeley Yacht. Rec.: gardening, sailing. Home: 624 Beloit Ave., Berkeley, CA 94708; Office: 103 Kroeber Hall, UC Berkeley, Berkeley, CA 94720.

BASKETT, KIRTLEY MORRISON
Journalist
b. Oct. 27, 1905, Mexico, Mo.; s. Cecil Morrison and Martha (Kirtley) Baskett; grandson, James Newton Baskett, author and naturalist, novels: At You-All's House, As the Light Led, Sweetbriar and Thistledown, and others; B.J., Univ. of Mo., 1927; m. Clara Hood Newman, June 19, 1946, Santa Barbara; Chil.: Martha Kirtley (Scully), b. Apr. 26, 1948; Laura Melbourne (Anderegg), b. June 21, 1950. Career: journalist: St. Louis Post-Dispatch, Miami Fla. News, Pasadena Star-News, 1926-30; writer, Universal Studios, 1930-32; staff, Photoplay Mag., 1932-37; freelance mag. writer, 1937---; contbr. Saturday Eve. Post, Liberty, Life, American Mag., Redbook, Good Housekeeping, Reader's Digest, Pageant, Ken, Photoplay, others; writer, first Hollywood star interview radio program, 45 Minutes in Hollywood. Lt. Field Artillery, USAR. Mem.: Sigma Nu frat., Alpha Delta Sigma frat. Hobby: travel. Home: 700 Bradford St., Pasadena, CA 91105.

BASS, ERIC R.
Artist
b. Nov. 6, 1921, N.Y.C.; s. John and Johanna (Redlich) Bass; ed. N.Y.U., USC, Cranbrook Acad., Roosevelt Aeron. Sch., Chouinard Art Inst., Art Center Sch.; m. Betty Zoe Passmore, Chicago, Ill., Oct. 10, 1948. Career: Est. Eric Bass Interior Design and Couture firm, Beverly Hills, Calif. 1949-53; painting exhibs.: Oakland Art Mus., S.D. Fine Arts Mus.; Art Center, La Jolla; L.A. Art Assn.; So. Calif. Exposition; Ringling Mus. of Art, Sarasota, Fla.; Frye Mus., Seattle; William-James Gallery; Adha Artzt Gallery, N.Y.; Southwestern Coll., N.Y.C. Center Gallery, La Jolla Museum of Art, Santa Barbara Museum of Art. Publications: feat. in Arts & Architecture, Architectural Digest, Textiles Suisse, Woman's Day and San Diego Mag. Flight instr., U.S. Army Air Corps, WW II. Mem.: L.A. Mus. Assn.; UCLA Art Council; Center Circle Bd. of La Jolla Museum of Art; World Affairs Council, S.D.; trustee, S.D. Fine Arts Gallery; v.p. Asiatic Arts Com., Fine Arts Society; bd. dirs.: La Jolla Civic Orch. Assn.; S.D. Sym. Assn.; exec. bd. S.D. Art Guild; Univ. Calif., S.D. Chancellor's Club; S.D. Opera Guild; Internat. Inst. of Arts and Letters; Art Center, La Jolla. Home: 1351 Olivet, La Jolla, CA 92037.

BASTIEN, JANE SMISOR
Composer — Music Teacher
b. Jan. 15, 1936, Hutchinson, Kan.; A.A., Stephens Coll., 1955; B.A. Barnard Coll., 1957; M.A., Columbia Univ. Tchrs. Coll., 1958; m. James W. Bastien, Hutchinson, Kan., Mar. 31, 1961; chil.: Lisa Anne, b. Oct. 5, 1964; Lori Jane, b. June 8, 1966. Career: Head of Preparatory Dept. of Music, Tulane Univ., New Orleans, La., 1958-75; pvt. piano tchr., La Jolla, 1975---. Author, Music Through the Piano, series of piano books for children, 1963---; co-author, Bastien Piano Library, with James Bastien, 1976---. Cond. piano tchrs. workshops in U.S.A., Japan, England, Canada, Australia, New Zealand. Mem.: Phi Beta Kappa, 1957; Music Tchrs. Assn. of Calif.; Calif. Profl. Music Tchrs. Assn.; Music Tchrs. Natl. Assn. Presbyterian. Hobbies: needlework, cooking. Rec.: tennis. Home: 2431 Vallecitos, La Jolla, CA 92037.

BASU, BANAJ KAMAL
Project Engineer
b. Aug. 4, 1942, Calcutta, India; s. Balai Lal and Reba (Bose) Basu; B.Sc. physics, 1961; M.S. applied physics, Calcutta Univ., India; m. Anjana Roy, Nov. 20, 1969, Calcutta, India; chil.: Banajyotsna, b. Aug. 20, 1970; Bananjana, b. Mar. 27, 1974. Career: sr. systems engr., Mahindra & Mahindra Ltd., Calcutta, 1964-71; sr. instrumentation and control engr.: Heyward Robinson Co., N.Y. 1971-72; Commonwealth Assoc. Inc., Mich., 1972-74; group project engr., Instrumentation and Control System, C.F. Braun & Co., power div., Alhambra, 1974---. Regis. profl. engr. Calif., 1976. Sr. mem. IEEE; sr. mem. ISA. Hobbies: poetry, films, classical music. Home: 1611 Ave. Entrada, San Dimas, CA 91773; Office: 1000 S. Fremont, Alhambra, CA 91802.

BASYE, PAUL E.
Professor of Law
b. Oct. 2, 1901, Nappanee, Ind.; s. Otto and Carrie C. (Wynekoop) Basye; A.B., Univ. of Mo., 1923; J.D., Univ. of Chicago, 1926; LL.M., Univ. Mich., 1943, S.J.D., 1946; m. Margaret L. deClercq, Evanston, Ill., June 4, 1931; chil.: Charles E., b. Aug. 28, 1934; John P., b. Jan. 30, 1938. Career: practice of law, Kansas City, Mo., 1926-42; Calif., 1944---; present firm: Basye & Prior, Burlingame; prof. of law, Univ. of Mo. at Kansas City, 1938-42; research assoc., Univ. of Mich., 1942-44; prof. of law, Univ. of Calif., Hastings College of Law, 1948---; summer sessions: Stanford Univ., 1950; Univ. of Texas, 1956; USC, 1961, 63. Chmn., sect. of Real Property, Probate and Trust Law, Am. Bar Assn. 1966. Author: Clearing Land Titles, West Pub. Co., 2nd ed. 1970; with Prof. Lewis M. Simes, Problems in Probate Law, Including a Model Probate Code, Univ. of Mich. 1946; articles in various legal journs.; spec. reporter for Nat. Conf. of Commissioners on Uniform State Laws. Mem.: Phi Beta Kappa, 1923; Order of the Coif, 1926. Methodist. Rec.: travel. Office: 330 Primrose Road, Suite 202, Burlingame, CA 94010.

BATISTA, RAMON, JR.
Marriage Counselor
b. Aug. 26, 1927, Tampa, Fla.; s. Ramon and Teresa (Balbontin) Batista; desc. Maximo Gomez, cavalry Gen., Cuba, helped free Cuba from Spain with Jose Marti; B.A., psychology, cum laude, Mexico City Coll., 1955; M.S.W., Ohio State Univ., 1957; LL.B., Blackstone Sch. of Law, Chicago, 1963; m. Laura Mendez Aquirre, May 2, 1954, Mexico City; chil.: Diana, b. May 20, 1957; Rebecca, b. Apr. 26, 1960; Norma, b. Nov. 27, 1962; Ramon IV, b. May 20, 1955; David Joseph, b. Nov. 20, 1967. Career: sr. psychiatric social worker, Juvenile Diagnostic Center, Columbus, Ohio, 1957-58, Fla. Alcoholic rehab. program, Tampa clin. 1958-59, Stockton State Hosp., 1959-65; dir., Catholic Social Service, Community Counseling Center, Modesto, 1965-78; pvt. practice, Modesto, 1978---. Chmn. bd. dirs., Stanislaus Co. Legal Asst. Program, 1970-71. Sgt., AUS M.C., 1946-53, Korean War Vet., Awarded U.N. medal. Roman Catholic, mem. St. Vincent Depaul. Hobbies: piano, swimming, tennis. Home: 604 E. Rumble Rd., Modesto, CA 95350; Office: 913 W. Roseburg Ave., Modesto, CA 95350.

BATZEL, ROGER ELWOOD
Director, Lawrence Livermore Laboratory
b. Dec. 1, 1921, Weiser, Idaho; s. Walter G. and Inez R. (Klinefelter) Batzel; B.S., Univ. of Idaho, Moscow, Idaho, 1947; Ph.D., Univ. Calif., Berkeley, 1951; m. Edwina Lorraine Grindstaff, Aug. 18, 1946, Weiser, Idaho; chil.: Stella Lyne, b. Oct. 27, 1953; Roger Edward, b. Apr. 22, 1955; Stacy Lorraine, b. Nov. 6, 1960. Career: Lawrence Livermore Laboratory, Univ. of Calif., 1953---. assoc. dir., 1961-71; director, 1971---. USAF, 1943-45. Rec.: outdoor sports. Home: 315 Bonanza Way, Danville, CA 94526; Office: P.O.B. 808, Livermore, CA 94550.

BAUER, DONALD de FOREST
Radiologist
b. Dec. 31, 1914, Brooklyn, N.Y.; s. John Leupold and Marie (Jurgens) Bauer; brother, John L.J. Bauer, 1908-1978, 1st Am. Prof. of Art Adminstrn.; A.B., Dartmouth Coll., 1937; M.D., C.M., McGill Univ., 1942; M.Sc., 1943; m. Phyllis Edna Witzel, 1943, Bayport, N.Y.; chil.: Phyllis A.M. (Gual), b. 1945; John L., b. 1947; Rebecca J., b. 1951; Ann V. (Melcon), b. 1954; Donald A., b. 1957. Career: Radiologist, Keizer Mem. Hosp., No. Bend, Ore. 1953-60, Hillside Hosp., Klamath Falls, Ore., 1960-65, Presbyterian Intercommunity Hosp., Klamath Falls, 1965-69, Modoc Med. Center, 1962-69; assoc. radiologist, Queen of Angels Hosp., L.A., 1970-72; Hollywood Presbyterian Hosp., 1972; asst. chief of radiology, Sepulveda VA Hosp., 1973-78; radiologist,

Hawthorne Community Med. Group, 1974---; assoc. professor of radiology, Oregon Inst. of Tech., 1960-70, UCLA, 1973-78. Capt. AUS, 1943-47, physician in Med. Corps. Author: The Practice of Country Radiology, 1963; Family Ark, 1965; A Textbook of Elementary Radiography for Students and Technicians, 1960; Lumbar Discography and Low Back Pain, 1960. Presbyterian, elder and deacon. Hobby: fly fishing. Rec.: boating. Home: Sherman Oaks, CA; Office: Hawthorne Community Medical Group, Inc., 4455 W. 117th St., Hawthorne, CA 90250.

BAUER, HERBERT
University Professor
b. Jan. 21, 1910, Vienna, Austria; s. Fritz and Irma Bauer; M.D., Univ. Vienna, 1936; M.P.H., Univ. Calif., 1948; m. Hanna Goldsmith, 1939, Santa Barbara; chil.: Timothy, b. June 10, 1950; Christopher, b. July 29, 1954. Career: clin. assoc., Vienna, 1936-68; intern, Mt. Zion Hosp., S.F., 1939-40; chief County Physician, San Luis Obispo, 1942-47; dir. TB Control, Orange Co., 1948-49; dir. med. services, Sacto. Health Dept. 1949-52; dir. public health and mental health, Yolo County, 1952-72; fellow, child psychiatry, UC Davis, 1972-74; clin. prof. of Community Health, Univ. Calif., Davis, 1970---. Med. dir. (ret.), U.S. Public Health Service. Past pres.: Calif. Local Health Officers, Calif. Mental Health Directors, Calif. Lung Assn., Yolo County Med. Soc. Awards: Humanitarian Award; Man of the Year; Outstanding Citizen, Davis, Calif.; Liberty Bell Award, Bar Assn.; Gold Medal, Lung Assn. Unitarian. Hobbies: chess, music. Rec.: swimming, reading. Home: 831 Oeste Dr., Davis, CA 95616.

BAUER, WALTER F.
President, Informatics Inc.
b. Mar. 21, 1924, Wyandotte, Mich.; s. Walter Ferdinand and Erna Clara (Schotter) Bauer; B.S., 1946; M.S., 1947; Ph.D., 1951; m. Donna Bothamley, Aug. 27, 1949, Kalamazoo, Mich.; chil.: Thomas, b. 1953; Randall, b. 1957; John, b. 1962. Career: research engr., Univ. of Mich, 1951-54; dir., Computation and data reduction center, TRW, 1954-59; mgr., Information Systems Dept., TRW Corp. 1959-62; pres. and chief exec. officer, Informatics Inc. 1962---. Dir.: Calif. Computer Products, 1968---; Electronic Memories and Magnetics, 1973-77; trustee, Charles Babbage Inst. Contbr. numerous tech. papers various sci. and trade publs. 1st Lt., USAF, 1943-46. Mem.: Phi Kappa Phi, 1948; Phi Eta Sigma, 1942; Assn. for Computing Machinery, 1951---, Nat. Council mem. 1960-62. Rec.: tennis. Office: 21031 Ventura Blvd., Suite 800, Woodland Hills, CA 91364.

BAUMAN, Sister MARY BEATA
Archivist — Professor of Nursing
b. Apr. 14, 1907, Okarche, Okla. (Canadian Co.); d. Joseph and Mary (Ramharter) Bauman; dip. in Nursing, Mercy Sch. of Nursing, S.D., 1928; B.S., Nursing Edn., Lone Mt. Coll., 1936; M.S., nursing sch. adm., St. Louis Univ., 1956; (hon.) Doctor Nursing Sci., Univ. S.F., 1972. Career: nursing supr., 1932-55, also tchr. nursing students; mem. faculty, Univ. S.F. sch. Nursing, 1956-57, Dean, Sch. of Nursing, 1957-71; archivist, Burlingame Community of Sisters of Mercy, Calif. and Ariz. Bd. Dir., St. Mary's Hosp. & Med. Center, S.F., 1970-73; bd. dir., Calif. League for Nursing, 1953-55; appt. by Gov. E. Brown, re-appt. Gov. Reagan to Calif. Bd. Nursing Edn. & Nurse Registration, 1965-69; gov. appt. to Nursing in Nuclear Warfare, 1942 (to tch. nurses in local area following Pearl Harbor); Author: A Way of Mercy: Catherine McAuley's Contribution to Nursing, N.Y., Vantage Press, 1958. Awards: cited by ARC on 50th anniversary of nursing svc. to people of S.F., 1959; Sigma Theta Tau, U.S.F. Beta Gamma chpt. 1970. Republican. Catholic. Home: 2300 Adeline Dr., Burlingame, CA 94010.

BAY, MAX W.
Surgeon
b. Mar. 22, 1904, Russia; s. Yeoshua and Bertha (Kaplan) Bay; gr.nephew, Avraham Shapira, first Shomer of Israel; A.B., USC, 1923; M.D., Univ. Calif., S.F., 1928; m. Fay Reeva, Feb. 23, 1932; son, James Sheldon, b. Aug. 14, 1934; Career: asst. resident in surgery, S.F., 1928-30; resident in surgery Cedars of Lebanon Hosp., L.A., 1930-33; sr. surgeon, 1933-71; chief of surgery, L.A. Co. Gen. Hosp., 1934-59. Pres., So. Calif. chpt., Am. Coll. of Surgeons, 1950-54; pres., Jewish Fedn. Council, 1964-67; pres. Brandeis Inst., 1967-76; chmn., Area Agency on Aging, L.A. Co. 1976. Recipient Maimonides award; diplomate Am. Bd. Surgery. Mem. L.A., Calif. Med. Assn.s, AMA, L.A. Surg. Soc., Alpha Omega Alpha.

Democrat. Jewish. Office: 10535 Wilshire Blvd., L.A., CA 90024.

BAYLESS, JUNE ELIZABETH
City Librarian, Whittier
b. June 8, 1915, Chicago, Ill.; d. Dudley Dean and Lucile (Ladd) Bayless; B.A., Univ. of Tenn. 1937; B.S. (lib. sci.), George Peabody Coll. 1939. Career: librarian: Tyson Jr. H.S., Knoxville, Tenn, 1940-41; Knoxville H.S. 1941-45; Pasadena (Calif.) Pub. Lib. 1945-52; Lamanda Park br. 1948-50, Central (chief, circulation dept.), 1948-50; city librarian, San Marino (Calif.) Pub. Lib. 1952-69; Beverly Hills Pub. Library, 1969-72, Whittier Pub. Lib., 1972---. Contrib. to Calif. Librarian and various profl. journs. Listed, many Am. biog. achievement publs. Mem.: pres. Pasa. Panhellenic Assn., 1952; Am. Lib. Assn. (fed. rels. co-ord. com. 1953-57, council, 1961-65, resolutions com., Natl. Lib. Week, 1965, evaluation com. 1966); Pub. Lib. Assn. bd. 1961-65, pres., 1969-70 (chmn., standards revision, 1965, 67, chmn. nom. com. 1966); Adult Servs. Div. (treas. 1954-56, publs. liaison com. 1961-64, pgm. policy com. 1966-69), Scarecrow Press Awards Jury, 1964-65; Friends of Libs. Com., Lib. Adm. Div. 1964-68; pres. So. Dist., Calif. Lib. Assn. 1956, state pres. 1960, pub. rels. com. 1962-64, const. and by-laws com. 1963, conf. site com. 1963, chmn. 1965; pres. Pasa. Lib. Club, 1957; (hon. life) Calif. Council PTA, dist. adv. bd. 1958-60; Univ. of Calif Statewide Adv. Council on Edn. for Librarianship, 1963-67, chmn. 1965; chmn., Metropolitan Cooperative Lib. System. 1975; advisor, Tri-Hi-Y, San Marino H.S., 1964-65, 67; dir. Altrusa Internat. 1965; pres. Pub. Lib. Execs. Assn. of So. Calif. 1966-67; Pasa. Girl Scout Council, 1966-69; Friends of Henry E. Huntington Lib., Friends of San Marino Pub. Lib., and Whittier Pub. Lib.; League of Women Voters, Alpha Omicron Pi. Republican. Episcopalian. Hobbies: golf, reading. Home: 11846 Floral Dr., Whittier, CA 90601; Office: 7344 S. Washington Ave., Whittier, CA 90602.

BEACH, WARREN
Artist
b. May 21, 1914, Minneapolis, Minn.; s. Joseph Warren and Elizabeth (Northrop) Beach; B.F.A., Yale Univ. 1939; M.A., Univ. Iowa, 1940; M.A., Harvard Univ., 1947; m. Eleanor Denham, Jan. 4, 1941, Waban, Mass.; chil.: David Warren, b. May 11, 1943; Margaret Elizabeth (Ballard), b. June 30, 1946; Richard Denham, b. July 1, 1949. Career: with Walker Art Center, Minneapolis., 1940-41; Addison Gallery of Am. Art, Andover, Mass., 1946-47; asst. dir., Columbus Gallery of Fine Arts, 1947-55; and Dean, Columbus Art Sch., 1947-49; dir. Fine Arts Gallery of S.D. (San Diego Art Mus.), 1955-69; One-man shows: Minn. State Fair, 1941; Grace Horn Gallery, Boston, 1941; Harriet Hanley Gallery, 1941, 42; Little Gallery, Univ. Minn., 1941; Telfair Acad. Arts & Sci., Savannah, Ga., 1975; Trend House Gallery, Tampa, Fla., 1975; publs.: Art Catalogues: The Fine Art Gallery of San Diego, 1960, Master Works from Collection of Fine Arts Gallery of San Diego, 1968, ed. Martin Petersen, curator; Exhibition Catalogues: Modern American Painting 1915, War & Peace Union, Oct. 7-30, 1960; Newspaper in American Art, 1965; Divinely Tall, Divinely Fair, 1967; French Paintings from French Museums, 1967; A Legacy of Spain, 1969; Mexican Colonial Art, 1969. Named Gentleman of distinction, 1970, C. of C., San Diego. Served pvt. to 1st Lt., AUS, Alaskan theater, 1941-45. Pres., Columbus Art League, Ohio, 1954; pres., Western Assn. of Art Museums, 1962; mem. Calif. Arts Commn., 1963-67; mem. C. of C. citizen advis. com. for gen. plan study; mem. S.D. Rotary, 1958-73; Phi Alpha, 1938. Protestant. Hobby: travel. Rec.: tennis. Home: 3740 Pio Pico St., San Diego, CA 92106.

BEACH, WARREN
Director, San Diego Fine Arts Gallery
b. May 21, 1914, Minneapolis, Minn.; s. Joseph Warren (English prof., Univ. of Minn.; noted Am. Eng. lit. critic) and Elizabeth (Northrop) Beach; desc. of Cyrus Northrop (b. Conn. 1834-1922), Am. educator, pres. Univ. of Minn. 1884-1911; ed. B.F.A., Yale Univ. 1939; M.A., State Univ. of Ia., 1941; M.A., Harvard Univ., 1947; m. Eleanor Denham, Mass., Jan. 4, 1941; chil.: David Warren, b. May 11, 1943; Margaret Elizaebeth, b. June 30, 1946; Richard Denajm, b. July 1, 1949. Career: Dir. ext. servs., Walke; Art Center, Minneapolis, Minn. 1940-41; asst. Addison Gallery of Am. Art, Andover, Mass. 1946-47; asst. dir., Columbus Gallery of Fine Arts, Columbus, Oh., 1947-55; dir. The Fine Arts Gallery of San Diego, 1955-69 (ret.). Painter-writer-lectr., 1969---. Contbtd. numerous exhib. catalogues on art. Pvt., U.S. Army, 1941; 1st Lt., Army Ord., hon. disch., 1945, WW II. Mem.: S.D. Rotary Club,

1958-72; pres., Western Assn. of Art Museums, 1961-62; Calif. Arts. Comm. 1964-69; Pi Alpha (Yale Univ.). Protestant. Hobby: tennis, travel. Home: 3740 Pio Pico, San Diego, CA 92106.

BEAGLE, THOMAS A.
Educator
b. Sept. 27, 1931, Genoa, Neb.; s. Arthur Glen (D.V.M.) and Effie Blanche (Goodding) Beagle; B.A. in Radio/T.V., Cascade Coll., Portland, Ore., 1956; M.A. in Drama, Calif. State Univ., San Jose, 1972; postgrad. in T.V., Univ. of Oregon, 1957-58. Career: tchr.: Vale Union H.S., Vale, Ore., 1956-57; Fall River H.S., McArthur, Calif., 1958-66; Antioch H.S., Antioch, Calif., 1966---; Vocational Spec. 1978---. Lighting tech., Oregon Shakespearean Festival, 1963; Drama chmn. Antioch H.S. 1966-74; ORBIT Project, 1974-77; Author: A Theatre Model You Can Handle, Feb. 1973, Dramatics Mag. Editor: Drama/Theatre Framework materials for Basic Course of Study: 22 Calif. Counties; contrib. author: Course Guide, 1976, Am. Theatre Assn.; Secondary Sch. Theatre Journ., Fall 1977. Mem.: Antioch Little Theatre; Calif. Humanities Assn., curriculum chmn.; Antioch Historical Soc.; Secondary Schs. Theatre Assn., dir.; Contra Costa Concert Guild, pres.; U.S. Inst. for Theatre Tech., education comm.; Antioch Community Theatre design advisor; Intl. Thespian Soc., Calif. state dir., 1972-74, Region 2 dir., 1974-78; U.S. Inst. for Theatre Tech.; v.commissioner, ed. comm., 1974-79; Secondary Sch. Theatre Assn., pres., 1976; Phi Delta Kappa, Contra Costa chpt., secty., 1977. Riverview Baptist Ch. moderator. Hobbies: classic cars, photog. Home: 215 Crest St., Antioch, CA 94509; Office: Antioch Unified Sch. Dist., 510 G. St., Antioch, CA 94509.

BEALL, LEWIS LINCOLN
School District Administrator
b. Mar. 27, 1928, Pasadena; s. Horace A. and Helen (Rodman) Beall; B.A., Univ. of Calif., Berkeley, 1949; M.ED., UCLA, 1957; Ed.D., USC, 1963; m. Mary Foard, Dec. 23, 1961, Newport Beach; chil.: Lori Lynn, b. 1963; Scot Lewis, b. 1965. Career: tchr., Monrovia High Sch., 1956-59; principal, Anaheim Hi Sch. Dist., 1959-65; asst. supt., Desert Sands Sch. Dist., 1965-67; asst. supt., Azusa Unified School Dist., 1967-74; supt., 1974---; tchr., Educational Adminstrn: USC, La Verne Coll., Pepperdine Univ., Cal. State, L.B.; writer, travel column, Philadelphia Eve. Bulletin, 1954-56; contbr. to profl. journs. Lt. J.G., U.S. Coast Guard, 1951-53, Deck Officer. Mem.: Assn. Calif. School Administrators, past pres. region XV; bd. dir., Educare, USC; past pres., Azusa Rotary. Office: Azusa Unified Sch. Dist., P.O.B. 500, Azusa, CA 91702.

BEAN, LOWELL JOHN
Professor of Anthropology
b. Apr. 26, 1931, St. James, Minn.; s. Edward John and Agnes (Albertina) Bean; B.A., anthropology, UCLA, 1958; M.A., 1962, Ph.D., 1970. Career: pres., Cultural Systems Research, Inc., 1978---; chmn., Dept. of Anthropology, Cal. State Univ., Hayward, 1974-77, prof., 1967-78; vis. lectr. Univ. Calif., Riverside, 1968; cons. Far West Endl. Lab. Mem. Southwest Indian com. of Am. Friends Service Com., 1962-64; Pres., Southwestern Anthropological Assn., 1975-76; trustee Malki Mus., Inc., 1966---; editor, Ballena Press Anthropological Papers Series, 1972---; assoc. editor, Journ. Calif. Anthropology, 1974---; Fellow, Am. Anthropological Assn.; Curator of Ethnology, Palm Springs Desert Mus., 1962-64; USMC, 1951-53. Awards: Wenner Grenn Postdoctoral Mus. Research fellow, 1971; Am. Philos. Soc. grantee, 1972; Center for Study of Man, Smithsonian Instn. grantee, 1972; fellow, Am. Anthrop. Assn.; Mem.: AAAS, Southwestern Anthrop. Assn., pres. 1975-76. Author: A Reader in Cultural Ecology, 1965; Cahuilla Indian Cultural Ecology, 1970; Mukat's People: The Cahuilla Indians of So. Calif., 1972. Other publs. incl. book reviews, articles and chptrs. in anthrop. journs., books; guest lectr.; universities; museums, confs., 1961---. Hobby: art. Home: 1555 Lakeside Dr. No. 64, Oakland, CA 94612; Office: Dept. Anthropology, Cal. State Univ., Hayward; Cultural Systems Research, Inc., 823 Valparaiso, Menlo Park, CA 94025.

BEARCE, BEULAH MARY
Realtor
b. 1921, West Point, Ill., d. Dr. L.F. and Marie L. Workman; B.S. (High Honors) Univ. of Ill., 1941; M.A., Smith Coll., Northampton, Mass., 1943; m. Wilbur D. Bearce, Laramie, Wyo., 1945; chil.: Gary, b. 1953; Ronald, b. 1954; Mary Sue, b. 1956. Career: tch. asst., Smith Coll;, 1941-43; faculty, Phoenix Coll., Phoenix, Ariz., 1943-47; asst. prof. of Anatomy and Physiology,

Denver Univ., 1948-49; salesperson, Polin Truchan Realty, San Luis Obispo, 1971; broker, Bearce Realty, 1973---. Mem.: Natl. Assn. of Realtors; Calif. Assn. of Realtors; multiple listing bd. of Realtors, 1973---. Author thesis, Medicinal Treatment of Malaria, 1943. Mem.: Biology Club, Univ. of Ill., 1941; AAUW, 1943---; Beta Sigma Phi, 1942---; Kappa Delta Pi (ed. hon.) 1941---. Secty.-Treas., Christian Ch. Hobbies: antiques, local history. Rec.: tennis, riding. Office: 890 Foothill Blvd., San Luis Obispo. CA.

BEARSON, ROBERT
Management Consultant
b. June 13, 1923, Peoria, Ill.; s. Samuel and Sophia (Katz) Bearson; student, Univ. Calif., L.A., 1941-42; B.S., Calif. Inst. Tech., 1947; M.B.A., Harvard, 1949; m. Marilyn Waldman, Mar. 22, 1956 (div.); chil.: Lee Waldman, Matt Edward, Dann Alan. Career: trainee, May Co., L.A., 1949-56, buyer, 1951-54, gen. mgr. Crenshaw, 1954-56, gen. mgr. Lakewood, 1956-61; v.p., dir. ops., merchandising Unimart San Diego, 1961-64; div. merchandising adminstr. Bullocks Dept. Store, L.A., 1964-67; exec. v.p. Shelly's Tall Girl Shops, L.A., 1967; mng. dir. ABM Advisors, Long Beach, 1970---; dir. Golden State Fabrics, San Diego, Mayco Pump Co., L.A., Power Climber, L.A.; sr. instr. UCLA Ext.; instr. Univ. Calif., Irvine. Dist. chmn. Long Beach Area-L.A. Area council Boy Scouts Am.; active Long Beach Community Chest, Am. Cancer Soc.; mem. Planning Commn., City of Lakewood; bd. dirs. Lakewood Community Hemodialysis Center, Doctor's Hosp., Lakewood; Jewish Family Service, pres. Temple Israel, Long Beach; Served USAF, 1943-45. Mem. Greater Lakewood C. of C. (v.p.), Lakewood Center Bus. Men's Assn. (pres.). Democrat. Jewish. Home: 5400 The Toledo No. 311, Long Beach, CA 90803; Office: 3520 Long Beach Blvd., Long Beach, CA 90807.

BEATTY, BARBARA J.
Realtor — Educator
b. July 30, 1935, Champaign, Ill.; d. John M. and Patricia Beatty; B.A., St. Mary of the Woods Coll., Ind., 1960. Career: tchr. music, 1956-59; editor, writer, ednl. pub.: Scott, Foresman and Harper & Row, 1960-67, Chicago; Addison-Wesley Pub. Co., Menlo Park, Calif. 1967-72; real estate agent, 1972-74; real estate broker, investment counselor owner, STF Enterprises, San Jose, 1974---; also instr., real estate courses, Community Colleges, 1974---; developer, mobile home park, Wash. state, 1979---. Hobby: investing. Home: 629 Lisa Way, Campbell, CA; Office: 1150 S. Bascom Ave., No. 7, San Jose, CA 95128.

BEAVER, ROBERT F.
Business — Civic Leader
b. Columbus, Oh.; s. William C. and Elizabeth (Ferguson) Beaver; ed. B.S. (bus. adm.) UCLA, 1932; post-grad. USC; Gen. Secondary Credential 1933; m. Dorothy E. Brent, L.A., Sept. 2, 1933; chil.: Gary E., b. Apr. 17, 1945; Victoria E., b. Jan. 15, 1953. Career: Asst. controller Firestone Tire & Rubber Co., L.A. (20 yrs.), dist. mgr., No. Calif., opns. mgr. Western div.; pres. Willard-Brent Co., Inc. Insp. gen. overseas, WW II (2 yrs.); Maj, Pentagon War Dept. Price Adj. Bd. (2 yrs.). Mem.: (officer) United Fullerton Fund; O.C. Grand Jury, 1964; N. O.C. B.S.A.; O.C. Rapid Transit Com. 1966; Fullerton Comm. for Dev. Commerce and Ind.; Heart Fund of O.C. 1968; Cultural Groups Found.; Chapman Coll. Pres.'s Council; Chil.'s Hosp.; Am. Rev. Bicentennial Comm. of Calif.; Fullerton Joint Powers Lib. Com.; bd. trustees, Calif. State Univ. and Colls.; YMCA; Fullerton Airport Expansion Com.; Pres.'s Assocs. Gold Circle; Calif., L.A. C. of C.s; Merchants & mfgrs., Assn., Assoc. Gen. Contrs. of Am.; Sunny Hills Inv. Club; Delta Sigma Phi; (life) Natl. Rifle Assn., UCLA Alumni Assn.; Chancellor's Assocs., World Affairs Council, Navy League of U.S., U.S. Power Squadron, Equestrian Trails, Inc., Elk, Hacienda Golf Club, Lincoln Club "Man of Year" 1970. Republican (num. state exec. coms.), Del. Natl. Conv. 1968, 72. Presbyterian. Hobby: photog. Rec.: boating, fishing, golf, tennis. Home: 1235 Margarita Dr., Fullerton, CA 92633; Office: 254 E. 27th St., L.A., CA 90011.

BECHTEL, STEPHEN DAVISON
Industrialist
b. 1900; s. Warren A. Bechtel; ed. Univ. of Calif., (hon.) LL.D. 1954; (hon.) LL.D., Loyola Univ. 1958; m. Laura Adaline Peart, 1923; chil.: Stephen Davison, Jr., Mrs. Paul L. (Barbara) Davies, Jr. Career: Registered profl. engr., Calif.; v.p. gen. constr. bus. (with father), 1925-36; 1st v.p.-dir., Six Companies, Inc. (constrs. of Hoover Dam), 1931-35; chmn.-dir., Bechtel Corp. 1936---; co-orgn.-dir., Bechtel-McCone Corp. 1937-46; pres.-dir. Lakeside Corp.;

dir.: Nuclear Power Group, Inc., Continental Can Co., Inc., Ind. Indemnity Co., Morgan Guaranty Trust Co. of N.Y., So. Pac. Co., U.S. Lines Co., Pac. Gas Transmission Co. and Can. Bechtel Ltd. Serv. 20th Engrs., U.S. Army, Fr., WW I; chmn. Calif. Shipbldging Corp., Wilmington, Calif.; and dir., Marinship Corp., Sausalito, Calif. Awards: Alumni Assn. Award, 1951; Achievement Award of Bldg. Ind. Conf. Bd., S.F. 1951; The Moles Award for "outstanding achievement in constr.," 1952; Alumnus of the Yr., Univ. of Calif. 1952; Order of the Cedar (Lebanon), 1956; Knight, Order of St. Sylvester, Pope (Holly See), 1956; Forbes Mag. Award (one of Am's. fifty foremost bus. leaders), 1957; Knight Comdr., Ct. of Hon. 1959; Natl. Def. Transportation Award, 1960; John Fritz Medal and Certificate, 1961; Calif. Industrialist of Yr. 1968, Calif. Mus. of Sci. and Ind. Ind. Mem.: trustee, S.F. Bay Area Council, 1946--, chmn. 1961; dir Stanford Research Inst. 1949---; bus. adv. council, Dept. of Comm., 1950-60, chmn. 1958-59; Pres. Eisenhower's Adv. Com. on Natl. Hwy. Pgm. 1954-55; (sr.) Natl. Ind. Conf. Bd.; trustee, Com. for Econ. Devel., 1956---; bd. trustees, Stanford Univ. 1959---; assoc. USC 1959---; trustee, The Ford Found. 1960---; The Bus. Council, 1961; Cits. Com. for Internat. Devel. 1961; adv. bd., Council for Internat. Progress in Mgmt., Inc., USA; Calif. Inst. Assocs., Am. Soc. of Civ. Engrs., Soc. of Am. Mil. Engrs., Cons. Constructor's Council of Am.; policy bd., Bus. Council for Internat. Understanding; Am. Petroleum Inst., Soc. of Naval Archs. and Marine Engrs., World Affairs Council of No. Calif., The Beavers, The Moles; clubs; The Brook, Links, Pinnacle, River and Fifth Ave., NYC; Blind Brook, Port Chester, NY; Augusta Natl. Golf Club, Ga.; California, L.A.; Claremont Country, Oakland; Cypress Point, Monterey Peninsula, Calif.; Bohemian, Pac.-Union, Stock Exch., Commonwealth, Mason, 32° Shriner, Beta Theta Pi. Republican. Methodist. Home: 244 Lakeside Dr., Oakland, CA; Office: 155 Sansome St., S.F., CA.

BECHTEL, STEPHEN DAVISON, JR.
Chairman, The Bechtel Group of Companies
b. May 10, 1925, Oakland; s. Stephen D. and Laura (Peart) Bechtel; ed. B.S. (C.E.), Purdue Univ., 1946; M.B.A., Stanford Univ. 1948; D. Eng. (Hon.), Purdue Univ. 1972; m. Elizabeth Mead Hogan, Oakland, June 5, 1946; chil.: 5; Career: Engring., and mgmt. positions Bechtel Corp., S.F., 1941-60, pres., 1960-73, chmn. bd. Bechtel Group of Cos., 1973---; Dir. Hanna Mining Co., IBM Co., So. Pacific Co.; Mem. Bus. Council; life councilor, past chmn. Conf. Bd.; mem. Pres.'s Com. on Urban Housing, 1967-69; mem. Nat. Indsl. Pollution Control Council, 1970-73; Nat. Productivity Commn., 1971---; mem. labor-mgmt. com., 1974---, Nat. Adv. Council on Minorities in Engring., 1974---. Trustee Cal. Inst. Tech.. Served with USMC, 1943-46. Registered profl. engr., N.Y., Mich., Alaska, Calif., Md., Hawaii, Ohio, D.C., Va.; Fellow ASCE; mem. Am. Inst. Mettal. Engrs.; Mem. Natl. Acad. of Engring. and NAE Finance Com.; Cal. Acad. Scis. (hon. trustee), Chi Eipslon, Tau Beta Pi. Clubs: Pacific Union (S.F.); Claremont Country (Oakland); Cypress Point (Pebble Beach); Vancouver (B.C.); Ramada (Houston); Bohemian, S.F. Golf (S.F.); Links, Blind Brook (NYC); Augusta (Ga.) Natl. Golf; York (Toronto); Mt. Royal (Montreal). Protestant. Rec.: golf, hunting, fishing, hiking. Office: Fifty Beale St., San Francisco, CA 94105.

BECK, STEPHEN CHARLES
President, Beck Videographics
b. Feb. 7, 1950, Chicago, Ill.; s. Charles and Lorraine (Mandarino) Beck; B.S. EE, Univ. Calif., Berkeley, 1971. Career: inventor: Beck-Direct Video Synthesizer, 1969. Major video tapes and films: Video Synthesis; Cycles; Anima; Union; Video Weavings. Video-artist, Nat. Center for Experiments in television, S.F., 1970-74; pres., Beck Videographics, 1974---; pres., Beck-Tech (electronic game programming), 1978---. Awards: CINE Golden Eagle; Ann Arbor Film Festival; grantee: Nat. Endowment for the Arts, Rockerfeller Found., Am. Film Inst. Video art exhibitions: Whitney Mus., N.Y.C., 1974, 76; Mus. of Art, Caracas, Venezuela; Pompedui Modern Art Mus., Paris, France. National broadcast, PBS TV, 1972. Contbr. publs.: Video Art, 1976, Harcourt, N.Y.; Made in America, 1978; Open Circuits: Future of TV, 1977, MIT Press. Mem.: Phi Beta Kappa, Soc. of Motion Picture & TV Engrs. Office: 1406 Euclid No. 3, Berkeley, CA 94708.

BECKER, JOSEPHINE MOORE (Madge)
Solano County Librarian
b. Sept. 1, 1928, Portland, Ore.; d. Jesse W. and Madge J. (Guthrie) Moore; A.B., Western Coll. for Women, Oxford, Ohio, 1949; M.L.S., Univ. Ill. Sch. Lib. Sci., Urbana, 1952; m. Henry C. Becker, Jr., Jan. 30, 1970, Reno, Nev.; Career: Branch supv./adm. asst., Yakima Valley (Wash.)

Regional Lib., 1954-59; Field libn., U.S. Army Spe. Serv., Germany, 1959-61; Co. Libn. Plumas Co. Quincy, CA, 1961-64; City Libn., Longview, Wash., 1964-70; City Libn., City of Vallejo, CA 1970-74; Acting Co. Libn., Solano Co., Fairfield, 1973-74; Co. Librarian, 1974---. Recipient: Bess Sawhill Robertson Award for excellence in English (Western Coll.), 1949. Secty., Solano Co. Lib. Authority, 1975---; Chmn., North Bay Cooperative Lib. System, 1973-74; Secty., Calif. Inst. of Libraries, 1976-78; Pres. Pub. Lib. Execs. of Central Calif. 1977; v.p./pres.-elect Wash. Lib. Assoc. 1969-70; mem. Soroptimist, pres. 1965-67, 77-78, Fairfield; mem. Delta Kappa Gamma. Hobbies: collect. cat. objects and books. Rec.: travel, photog. Home: 455 Diana Dr., Vallejo, CA 94590; Office: 1150 Kentucky St., Fairfield, CA 94533.

BECKER, LOUISA L. DURET
Writer — Translator
b. Dec. 15, 1922, Antoing (Hainaut), Belgium; d. Francois Bienvenu and Marie Celina (Cocqlet) Duret; Docteur en Philologie Germanique 1944, Liege, Belgium; m. Frederick Howard Becker, Brussels, Belgium, May 20, 1945; 1 son, William Frederick, b. July 4, 1946. Career: Sworn translator, UN relief & rehabilitation administrn. June 1945-July 1945; assignments in France, Netherlands, Germany; translator on displaced persons pro., UN food & agri. administrn. Brussels, Oct. 1946-48; free lance travel writer, 1975---; translator own articles for overseas publs. and fiction writer, 1975---. Mem.: Intl. Platform Assn., 1977---. Translator, Allied Forces, European Theater, 1944-45. Presbyterian. Hobbies: hunting for undiscovered inns and hotels of character worldwide. Home: 6826 Boxford Dr., S.D., CA 92117.

BECKMAN, ARNOLD ORVILLE
Industrialist
b. Apr. 10, 1900, Cullom, Ill.; s. George W. and Elizabeth E. (Jewkes) Beckman; B.S. Univ. of Ill., 1922; M.S., 1923; Ph.D., Calif. Inst. of Tech., 1928; Hon. Degrees: D.sc., Chapman Coll., 1965; LL.D., Univ. of Calif., Riverside, 1966; LL.D. Loyola Univ. of L.A., 1969; D.sc., Whittier Coll., 1971; LL.D., Pepperdine Univ., 1977; m. Mabel S. Meinzer, Bayside, L.I., New York, June 10, 1925; chil.: Gloria Patricia, Arnold Stone. Career: Research Assoc., Bell Tel. Labs., NYC, 1924-26; chem. staff, Calif. Inst. of Tech., 1926-39; v.p., Nat. Tech Labs., Pasadena, 1935-39, pres., 1939-40; pres., Helipot Corp., 1944-58; Arnold O. Beckman, Inc., So. Pasadena, 1946-58; pres. Beckman Instruments, Inc., Fullerton, 1940-65, Chmn. bd., 1965---. Dir.: Security Pac. Nat. Bank 1956-62, Adv. Dir. 1972-75; Continental Airlines 1956-71, Adv. Dir. 1971-73; L.A.C. of C. 1954-58 (pres. 1956); So. Calif. Edison, 1957-72; Calif. C. of C. 1954-72 (pres. 1967-68); Instrument Soc. of Am. (pres. 1952 — hon. life mem. 1959---); Hoag Memorial Hosp. Presbyterian, 1971---; Stanford Research Inst., 1960-70, mem. SRI Council 1970-72; SCM Corp., 1956-63; President's Air Quality Adv. Bd. mem. 1970-74; Calif. State Univ., Fullerton, Adv. Bd., 1962-75; chmn. bd. of trustees, System Develop. Found., 1970---; trustee, Calif. Inst. of Tech., 1953-74, Chmn., 1964-74, Chmn. Emeritus 1974---; Scripps Inst., & Research Found. 1977---. pvt., USMC 1918-19. Mem.: Natl. Acad. of Engring.; Am. Inst. of Chemists (hon.), Am. Chem. Soc., Am. Assn. for Advancement of Sci.; Sigma Xi, Delta Upsilon, Alpha Chi Sigma, Phi Lambda Upsilon. Clubs: Jonathan, California, Newport Harbor Yacht. Home: 107 Shorecliff Rd., Corona del Mar, CA 92625; Office: Box C-19600, Irvine, CA 92713.

BECKMAN, GLEN LEONARD
Consumer and Trade Show Executive
b. July 22, 1930, Los Angeles, Calif.; s. Glenn Leonard and Lillian Nell (Etie) Beckman; m. Karen Marie Nielsen, (dec.) Altadena, Aug. 18, 1956; 1 dau., Tracy Lynn Beckman, b. July 31, 1958. Career: Archtl. Arts, L.A. 1955-60; partner, Continental Exchange Corp., L.A. 1960-63; v.p., Fortune of Calif., L.A., 1963-65; exec. dir., L.A. chpt. Bldg. Contractors Assn. Calif., 1965-67; pres. Industry Productions Am., L.A., 1967---; Shows: Pool, Garden and Patio Living Show; Arts, Crafts and Indoor Plants Show; Gifts and Decorative Accessories Show. USN, 1951-54. Recipient commendations: L.A. Mayor; L.A. Co. Bd. of Suprs.; L.A. City Council. Office: 10992 Ashton Ave., L.A., CA 90024.

BECKMAN, LINDA J.
Research Psychologist
b. Oct. 6, 1941, Detroit, Mich.; d. Max and Bettie (Kozel) Linden; B.A., Univ. Mich., 1963; M.A. (psychol.) UCLA, 1966; Ph.D. (Psychol.) UCLA, 1969; m. Stan Beckman, Jan. 15, 1967, L.A. Career: research asst.: Univ. Mich, 1961-63; Prof. Bertram Ravan, UCLA, 1963-64; Prof.

Harold H. Helley, UCLA, 1964-68; lectr. in psychol., Pierce Coll., Woodland Hills, 1968-70; staff psychologist (social), Camarillo State Hosp., 1968-72; research psychol., Reiss Davis Child Study Center, 1969-71; adjunct assoc. prof. and asst. research psychol., Dept. Psychiat., UCLA Med. Sch., 1971---; spec. interests: women's roles and fertility; alcoholism; attribution theory; profl. career choice. Grantee: U.S. Office of Edn., 1970-71, NIH, 1972-74, 1974-75, 1975-78; cons.: Center for New Directions, L.A., 1976; Calif. Women's Commn. on Alcoholism, L.A., 1977. Contbr. articles, psychol. journs. Mem.: Population Assn. of Am.; Research Soc. on Alcoholism; Am. Ednl. Research Assn.; AAAS; Am. Psychol. Assn.; Western Psychol. Assn. Home: 15045 Encanto Dr., Sherman Oaks, CA 91403; Office: Dept. Psychiatry, UCLA-NPI, 760 Westwood Plaza, L.A., CA 90024.

BECKMAN, MILLARD WARREN
Investment Securities Executive
b. Jan. 8, 1926, Lodi, Calif.; s. Sherwood W. and Christine (Koenig) Beckman; m. Lucille Stark, May 23, 1948, Stockton; chil.: Bruce, b. June 19, 1949; Don, b. Apr. 5, 1951; Joan, b. Mar. 21, 1955. Career: founder Beckman & Co., 1154; pres., chmn. bd., 1961-72, pres., dir., 1972; chmn. bd. and v.p. Beckman Capital Corp. 1972; Chmn. bd. Beckman Development Corp. dba Calif. Celler Masters, Wineries and Wine Tasting Shops, 1973. Home: 135 S. Fairmont Ave., Lodi, CA 95240; Office: 212 W. Pine St., Lodi, CA 95240.

BECKSTOFFER, WILLIAM ANDREW
Vintner
b. Nov. 28, 1939, Richmond, Va.; s. Herman Joseph and Rose Marie (Simonpetri) Beckstoffer; B.S., Virginia Tech., 1961; M.B.A., Amos Tuck-Dartmouth Coll., 1966; m. Elizabeth Kusterer, June 10, 1960, Richmond, Va.; chil.: David Michael, b. July 14, 1961; Dana Marie, b. Oct. 26, 1963; Andrew Tuck, b. Apr. 8, 1966; Kristin Anne, b. June 2, 1967; Stephen John, b. Oct. 4, 1973. Career: Field Engr., C&P Bell Telephone Co., Wash., D.C., 1961-64; Dir., Long Range Planning/Acquisition Analysis, Heublein, Inc., Hartford, Ct., 1966-69; v.p. planning, United Vintners, S.F., 1969-70; Pres., Vinifera Develop. Corp. (subs. of Heublein, Inc.), S.F., 1971-73; Pres., Vinifera Vineyards, Napa Valley Vineyard Co., Mendocino Vineyard Co., 1973-77; Pres., Beckstoffer Vineyards, 1977---. Pres., Napa Valley Grap Growers Assn.; mem. Napa Co. Planning Commn.; bd. dir., North Bay Production Credit Assn. 1st Lt., AUS, 1961-63; Commendation Award. Mem.: World Trade Club, S.F.; S.F. Racquet Club. Roman Catholic. Rec.: tennis. Home: 525 Zinfandel Lane, St. Helena, CA 94574; Office: 1008 Adams St., St. Helena, CA 94574.

BEDDOE, HARRY E(RNEST)
Realtor — Land Developer
b. Nov. 7, 1905, St. Helena, Napa Co., Calif.; s. Benjamin E(rnest) and Anna Mae (Lowe) Beddoe; stepmother, Lou Ellen (Watts) Beddoe; desc. Alfred the Great, King of England; student, Helderberg Coll., Union of S. Africa, 1922; Columbia Union Coll., Takoma Park, Wash., D.C., 1923-26; m. Zelda Elizabeth Nyman, Nov. 28, 1927 (div. 1948), 1 dau. Marilyn Hoyce Lane; m. 2d, Ruth Mae Detwiler, Sept. 29, 1948 (div. 1966); chil.: Barbara Ann Novak, Thomas Weston; m. 3d, Vivian Fa'atasiga Liufau (Queen of Tutuila, Am. Samoa), Aug. 24, 1966 (dec. June 1, 1968), 1 son, David John; m. 4th, Aurora Gozon Corpuz, Feb. 14, 1970; 1 son, Steven Roel Corpuz. Career: secty-treas., Bahamas Mission of Seventh-day Adventists, Nassau, 1927-31; acct., Antillian Union Mission, Havana, Cuba, 1931-35; secty. treas., Leeward Is. Conf., Bridgetown, Barbados, 1935-38; Caribbean Union Conference, Port-of-Spain, Trin., 1938-41; Acct., Gen. Conf. of S.D.A., Wash., D.C., 1941-42; auditor, Lake Union Conf., Berrien Springs, Mich., 1942-43; sr. acct., S.D. Leidesdorf & Co., Chicago, 1943-44; pub. acct. practice, L.A. 1944-47; real estate broker and land develop., Calif. and HI., 1947---. Owner Downey Realty, 1952-65; founder, pres.: Beddoe Investments and Hawaii Lands, Inc.; Golden State HI Corp., 1960-67, chmn. 1967-71; subdivider, Ainaloa, Puna Dist., HI, 1960-67; Computer Matching, 1968; Land Investment Cons., 1970---. Fellow, Assn. of Intl. Accts., London, 1937; Mem.: ARC, chmn. Downey br., 1952-54; Natl. Assn. of Cost Accountants, Natl. Assn. of Realtors; Calif. Assn. of Realtors; Natl. Inst. of Real Estate Brokers; Am. Security Council, 1968---; Led incorporation of City of Downey, 1956. Founder 1st pres., Ainaloa (HI) Comm. Assn., 1966. Elder, Mormon Ch. Hobbies: writing, travel. Home: 2000 Skyline Dr., Fullerton, CA 92631; Beddoe Blvd. at Vanda Dr., Ainaloa, SR Box 100, Pahoa, HI 96778; Office: Box 3243, Fullerton, CA 92631.

BEDROSIAN, EDWARD
Senior Scientist, The Rand Corporation
b. May 22, 1922, Chicago, Ill.; s. Charles and Hazel (Najarian) Bedrosian; B.S.E.E., Northwestern Univ., Evanston, Ill., 1949; M.S., 1950; Ph.D., 1953; m. Patricia Gardner, Apr. 16, 1971, L.A.; chil.: William Charles, b. 1950; Charles Edward, b. 1955; Edward Gardner, b. 1975; Barbara Ann (Patterson), b. 1954. Career: mem. Research staff, Motorola, Inc., Chicago, 1953-55 and Riverside, Calif., 1955-57; sr. scientist, Rand Corp., Santa Monica, 1957---; adjunct prof. Elect. Engring., USC, 1968-71. Awarded Fairbanks-Morse scholarship twice; Airborne Instruments Fellow, Northwestern Univ. Numerous presentations, profl. engring. meetings; pub. articles in tech. journs. Fellow, IEEE; fellow, Inst. for Adv. of Engring.; bd. dir., IEEE WINCON annual conv. 1977-81. Sgt., USMC, 1944-46, Pacific Theater. Mem.: Santa Monica Bay sect., IEEE, chmn. 1975-76; other engring. socs.; Tau Beta Pi; Pi Mu Epsilon; Eta Kappa Nu; Sigma Xi. Hobby: electronics. Rec.: tennis. Home: 3923 Sierks Way, Malibu, CA 90265; Office: The Rand Corp., 1700 Main St., Santa Monica, CA 90406.

BEEBE, GERTRUDE A. (POTTER)
Public Official
b. Aug. 9, 1903, Wheatland, Wyo., d. Fredrick Lyman and Margaret May (Robertson) Potter; student, elem. ed. Univ. of Wyo., 1921-26; m. Joseph E. Travers, L.A., Nov. 9, 1928 (div. 1937); chil.: Joseph E. Travers, Jr., John Travers, Mrs. Constance M. Urquhart, Mrs. Anita M. Hillebrandt; m.2d, James A. Beebe, Dec. 4, 1943 (div. 1949). Career: elem. sch. tchr., Wheatland, Wyo., 1921-27; police matron, 1946-65; city treas., Signal Hill, 1942-68; city clk., 1966-68; city councilman, 1968-76, mayor, 1974-75; clk. in charge, Signal Hill br. Sta. Long Beach P.O. 1956-68. Dir.: L.A. Co. Sanitation Dist. No. 2, No. 29, 1968-76; L.A. Central Basin Water Dist. Mem.: ARC, Signal Hill, 1951-53; Municipal Treasurers Assn. of USA; Municipal Treasurers Assn. of Calif.; Intl. Assn. of Municipal Clks. Mem.: Order Eastern Star, White Shrine of Jerusalem, 1921---. Mormon. Hobby: coin collecting. Home: 1751 E. Hill St., Signal Hill, CA 90806; Office: 2175 Cherry Ave., Signal Hill, CA 90806.

BEEBE, JAMES WARREN
Attorney at Law
b. June 28, 1920, Cambridge, Mass.; s. James Lyndon (noted L.A. Lawyer and civic leader) and Sarah Ruth (Hershey) Beebe; grandson of James Warren Beebe (bus. exec. and pub. off.); ed. S. Pasa.-San Marino H.S., 1936-38; A.B., Stanford Univ., 1939-42; LL.B., USC Law Sch., 1946-49; m. Elza Jeanne Toovey, L.A., May 29, 1964; stepson, William Douglas Wallace. Career: Admitted to State Bar of Calif. 1950; assoc. O'Melveny & Myers law firm, 1949---, partner (spec. pub. law, govt. financing), Jan. 1, 1960---. Author: many articles on subjs. of law, econ., civic and govt. financing, publ. 1954---. Ensign to Lt. USNR (sea serv. Solomon Is., Mariana Is., P.I., Borneo and China) 1942-46. Mem.: dir.-asst. secty. The Music Center Lease Co., asst. secty. Music Center Operating Co., dir.-secty. Theatre and Forum Lease Co.; Am., Calif. State, L.A. Co. Bar Assns. (chmn. many coms.), 1951---; Town Hall (coms.); L.A. Airport Advisors, 1957---; L.A. C. of C. (v. chmn. state and local govt. coms. 1962---); Los Feliz Improvement Assn.; Stanford Alumni Assn.; USC Alumni Assn.; Leg. Lex., Phi Gamma Delta, Phi Alpha Delta, Calif. Club. Republican. (So. Calif. finance chmn.: Watson Amendment, 1958; State Bonds, 1970). First Congregational Ch., L.A. (chmn., bd. trustees, 1967-70). Hobbies: writing, photog., Rec.: travel. Home: 4069 Cromwell Ave., L.A., CA 90027; Office: 611 W. Sixth St., L.A., CA 90017.

BEELER, EDWARD ELI
Editor
b. Aug. 13, 1933, Meeker, Okla.; s. Daniel Ernest and Mary Thelma Beeler; B.A., journalism, Univ. Ore., 1955, grad. work, 1961-62; m. Geraldine Yvonne Mayers, Mar. 9, 1963, Salem, Ore.; chil.: Chad Loring, b. Dec. 25, 1964; Scott Weston, b. Oct. 2, 1966. Career: Reporter, Aberdeen (Wash.) Daily World, 1955; reporter, Wilson (N.C.) Daily Times, 1958-60; Dir., publicity and special activities, Atlantic Christian Coll., Wilson, N.C., 1961; asst. co. editor., Eugene (Ore.) Register-Guard, 1962; co. editor, 1963; mng. editor, El Cajon (Calif.) Daily Californian, 1964-77; editor, Daily Californian, 1977---. Chmn., Calif.-Nev. AP News Execs. Council, 1977-78; dir., Calif. Editors' Conf.; Dir., San Diego Chpt. Soc. of Profl. Journalists, 1974---. Mil. Policeman and Mil. Personnel Spec. 1958-59. Mem.: Rotary Club of El Cajon. Protestant. Rec.: fishing, motorcycle riding. Home: 9340 Fortune Lane, La Mesa, CA 92041; Office: 613 W. Main St., El Cajon, CA 92020.

BEER, REINHARD
Planetary Astronomer
b. Nov. 5, 1935, Berlin, Germany; s. Harry Joseph and Elisabet Maria (Meister) Beer; gr. son, Max Beer, journalist-historian of 19th and 20th century social-polit. conditions in Europe; B.Sc. (honours in physics), Univ. Manchester, U.K., 1956; Ph.D., 1960; m. Margaret Ann Taylor, 1960, Tunstall, Staffordshire, U.K. Career: hon. Turner & Newhall Fellow, Univ. of Manchester, 1960-62; with Jet Propulsion Lab., Calif. Inst. of Tech., Pasadena, 1963---: currently supr., Infrared Astronomy Group, earth & space sci. div. Awarded NASA Exceptional Sci. achievement medal 1974. Discoverer, extraterrestrial deuterium (heavy hydrogen) and carbon monoxide in Jupiter. Pub. 50 papers in profl. journs., 1957---. Mem.: Am. Astronomical Soc.; Optical Soc. of Am.; Internat. Astronomical Union; Sigma Xi. Office: Jet Propulsion Lab., Calif. Inst. of Tech., Pasadena, CA.

BEEVERS, HARRY
Professor of Biology
b. Jan. 10, 1924, Shildon, England; s. Norman and Olive Beevers; B.Sc., Durham Univ., 1944, Ph.D., 1947; m. Jean Sykes, Nov. 19, 1949, Durham, England; son, Michael, b. May 9, 1951. Career: research fellow, Oxford Univ., 1946-50; asst. prof., assoc. prof., prof. of biology, Purdue Univ., 1950-69; prof. of biology, Univ. Calif., Santa Cruz, 1969---. Author: one book, 150 research publs. in plant metabolism. Home: 46 S. Circle Dr., Santa Cruz, CA 95060; Office: Div. of Natural Sciences, Univ. Calif., Santa Cruz, CA 95064.

BEGLARIAN, GRANT
Dean, School of Performing Arts, USC
b. Dec. 1, 1927, Tiflis, Georgia (Soviet Union); s. Boghos and Arax Beglarian; B.M., Univ. of Mich., 1950; M.M., 1952; D.M.A., 1958; m. Joyce Heeney, 1950, Farmington, Mich.; chil.: Eve, b. 1958; Spencer, b. 1960. Career: composer, 1944---; editor, Prentice-Hall Inc., N.J., 1959-60; pres., Music Book Associates, N.Y., 1960-68; dir., Contemporary Music Project, the Ford Found., N.Y., 1963-69; Dean, School of Performing Arts and Prof. of Music, USC, 1969---; mem. faculty: Univ. of Mich.; Interlochen Nat. Music Festival; Merrywood; U.S. Army Music Sch. in Germany. Mem.: Music Panel of Inst. of Internat. Edn., 1972---; Young Musicians Found., 1970---; numerous others. Awarded Gershwin prize, 1958; Ford Found. Award, 1959; ASCAP awards, 1963---. AUS, 1952-54, served in Germany. Christian. Rec.: reading. Home: 333 S. Windsor Blvd., L.A., CA 90020; Office: School of Performing Arts, USC, L.A., CA 90007.

BEHNKE, RUTH ELIZABETH RUE
Real Estate Broker
b. June 27, 1924, Newark, N.J.; d. Harold E. and Ruth E. (Harriott) Rue; B.S., Northwestern Univ., 1946; cert. in Real Estate, Univ. Calif., Berkeley, 1969; m. Albert R. Behnke, Jr., M.D. (Capt. USN, Ret.), July 27, 1957, Orange, N.J.; dau. Alice A., b. Dec. 23, 1958. Career: Parasitologist, Nat. Inst. Health, Bethesda, Md., 1946-50; asst. editor, U.S. Naval Medical newsletter, 1950; adminstrv. asst., Am. Inst. Biological Sciences, 1950-53, Wash. D.C.; Conf. dir., Josiah Macy, Jr., Found., N.Y.C., 1953-57; sales agent, Kay Carriel Real Estate, 1963-66; broker, owner, Ruth Behnke Real Estate, S.F., 1966---; trustee, S.F. Bay Marine Research Center, 1977---; bd. dir., Northwestern Univ. alumni Club of S.F. Bay Area; mem. Delta Zeta, chmn. No. Calif. Coord. Com.; Job's Daughters. Hobby: needlecraft. Home-Office: 2241 Sacramento St., S.F., CA 94115.

BEHRENS, JUNE YORK
Author — Educator
b. Apr. 25, 1925, Maricopa, Calif.; d. Mark Hanna and Aline (Stafford) York; B.A., Univ. Calif., Santa Barbara, 1947; M.A., USC, 1961; postgrad. Univ. Md., (Overseas Program), Munich, Germany; UCLA, Univ. of London; m. Henry William Behrens (sch. prin.), Aug. 23, 1948; chil.: Terry Lynne, Denise Noel. Career: elem. sch. tchr., Calif. 1947-54, 1956-63; overseas schools, 1954-56; vice-prin. L.A., 1966; reading spec., L.A. City Schs., 1966---; Author: Soo Ling Finds a Way (Jr. Literary Guild selection), 1965; A Walk in the Neighborhood, 1968; Who Am I?, 1968; Where Am I?, 1969; Air Cargo, 1970; Look at the Zoo Animals, 1970; Truck Cargo, 1970; Earth is Home: The Pollution Story, 1971; Look at the Farm Animals, 1971; Ship Cargo, 1971; How I Feel, 1973; Look at the Desert Animals, 1973; Look at the Forest Animals, 1974; Train Cargo, 1974; My Brown Bag Book, J. Alden, 1974; Feast of Thanksgiving: The First American Holiday, 1974; True Book of Metric Measurement, 1975; Look at the Sea Animals, 1975; What Do I Hear?, 1976; What Is a Seal?, 1975; Colonial

Farm, 1976; others. Mem.: NEA; AAUW; Calif. Tchrs. Assn. Protestant. Rec.: travels. Home: 230 S. Catalina Ave., No. 402, Redondo Beach, CA 90277.

BEILENSON, ANTHONY CHARLES
U.S. Congressman
b. Oct. 26, 1932, New Rochelle, N.Y.; s. Peter and Edna (Rudolph) Beilenson; grad. Phillips Andover Acad., 1950; A.B., Harvard Coll., 1954; LL.B., Harvard Law Sch., 1957; m. Dolores Martin, 1959, L.A.; chil.: Peter Lowell, b. 1960; Dayna Anne, b. 1961; Adam Laurence, b. 1963. Career: mem., Calif. Assembly, 1963-66; mem., Calif. Senate, 1967-77; mem., U.S. House of Reps., 23rd dist. office, 1977---. Jewish. Office: 1730 Longworth House office bldg., Washington, D.C. 20515.

BEISE, S. CLARK
Banker
b. Oct. 13, 1898, Windom, Minn.; s. Dr. Henry C. and Blanche (Johnson) Beise; ed. B.S., Univ. of Minn. Sch. of Bus. 1922; (hon.) LL.D., St. Mary's Coll., 1960; m. Virginia Carter, Jackson, Mich., Jan. 27, 1934; chil.: Sally Ann, b. Oct. 4, 1938; Carter Clark, b. Sept. 4, 1947. Career: Assoc. with Minn. Trust Co. 1922-24; natl. bank examiner, Minn., 1924-27; Peoples Natl. Bank, Jackson, Mich. 1927-33; natl. bank examiner, S.F., Calif. 1933-36; v.p. Bank of Am. Natl. Trust & Svgs. Assn. 1936-45, exec. v.p. 1945-51, sr. v.p. 1951-54, pres. 1954-63, chmn. exec. com. 1963-69 (pres. ret.); dir.: Bank of Am., N.T. & S.A.; U.S. Army (Fr.), WW I. Awards: Outstanding Achievement Award, Univ. of Minn. 1955; Econ. Statesmanship Award, Univ. of Seattle, 1957; Order of Merit of Italian Republic, 1957; selected by Forbes Mag. survey as one of the Fifty Foremost Businessmen of Am., 1957; Calif. Industrialist of the Yr., 1963. Mem.: (hon.) chmn. Golden Gate Chpt., Am. Red Cross; Bus. Council, Wash., D.C.; past chmn. S.F. Bay Area Council; Natl. Ind. Conf. Bd.; Prudence Lodge No. 97, AF&AM; Delta Chi; clubs: Banker's Club of S.F., Burlingame Country, Pacific Union. Home: 420 El Cerrito Ave., Hillsborough, Calif.; Office: Bank of Am. Center, S.F., CA.

BEKINS, MILO WILLIAM
Chairman of Board, Bekins Van & Storage Co.
b. Dec. 21, 1891, Sioux City, Ia.; s. Martin and Katherine (Cole) Bekins; ed. pub. schs.; m. Dorothy Eloise Watson, L.A., Feb. 24, 1917; chil.: Mrs. Richard H. Daum, Mrs. Charles E. Pettee, June E. and Milo W., Jr. Career: Pres. Bekins Van & Storage Co., chmn bd. (ret. 1959); dir.-officer, Bekins Subsidiary Cos.; dir. Douglas Aircraft Co., Inc.; dir., Citizens Natl. Bank. Mem.: pres.-dir., Calif. Moving & Storage Assn., 1931-32; pres. Beverly Hills C. of C., 1933-34; pres. Natl. Furniture Warehouse Assn., 1937-38; Westlake Masonic Lodge, L.A. Shrine, Al Malaikah Temple; clubs: Calif., L.A. Country, Bel-Air Bay. Baptist. Hobby: boating, fishing. Ref.: golf. Home: 875 Comstock Ave., L.A., CA.

BELDING, HIRAM HURLBURT, III
Physician — Surgeon — Educator
b. Aug. 15, 1918, Riverside, Ill.; s. Hiram H., Jr. and Rose (Merritt) Belding; ed. A.B., Dartmouth Coll. 1940; M.D., Northwestern Univ. Med. Sch. 1943; M.S. (surg.), Univ. of Minn. 1953; m. Barbara Littlefield, Feb. 14, 1973; chil.: Hiram H., IV, b. Oct. 26, 1942; Lindsay (Belding) Heaslet, b. Aug. 4, 1944; David Scott, b. Apr. 23, 1950; Mark Rogers, b. Jan. 20, 1954; Joel Littlefield, b. June 22, 1975. Career: Intern, Henry Ford Hosp., Detroit, 1943, surg.-pediatric res. 1944-45; fellow (gen. surg.), Mayo Clinic, 1947-50, asst. surg. 1950-51; est. pvt. practice (spec. surg.), Riverside, Calif. 1951---; staff: Riverside Comm. Hosp., Riverside Gen. Hosp.; cons. March Field AFB Hosp.; assoc. prof. surg., Loma Linda Univ., 1964-70; pres. bd. dirs., Univ. of Calif. at Riverside, 1962. Contrib. 21 sci. articles, publ. natl. med. journs. 1950---. Capt., U.S. Army Med. Corps, 1945-47, WW II. Mem.: chmn. Air Pollution Com., Riverside C. of C., 1954; United Fund, City of Riverside, 1961; Riverside Bd. Zoning Adjustment, 1963-64; men's adv. bd., League Women Voters, 1964---; Riverside City Planning Comm. 1964-67; Riversity City Council, 1967---. Calif., Riverside Co. Med. Socs.; founding pres., Tricounty Surg. Soc.; Diplomate, Am. Bd. Surg.; L.A. Surg. Soc., L.A. Acad. Med., Am. Coll. Surgs., AMA, Western Surg. Assn., Pacific Coast Surg. Assn., AAAS, Am. Geriatric Soc., Southland Water Assn., Am. Platform Assn., Psi Upsilon, Sigma Xi. Republican. Rec.: fishing, golf. Home: 5484 Apricot Ln., Riverside, CA; Office: 6860 Brockton, Riverside, CA 92506.

BELINN, CLARENCE MAURITZ
Company President
b. Oct. 24, 1903, Lanse, Clearfield Co., Pa.; s. Eric Axel

(dec.) and Hanna Marie Belinn; ed. grad. Air Corps Tech. Sch.; licensed aircraft pilot and engine mechanic (single and multi-engine aircraft); m. Malvina M. Folmar, Wash., D.C., June 5, 1930; chil.: Clarence Edmund, b. June 8, 1931; Elliott R., b. May 8, 1934; Christina M., b. Oct. 27, 1947. Career: U.S. Army Air Corps, 1925-29; Pilot-mech., Wash.-N.Y. Airways, 1929-30; supt. ground opns., maintenance, purchasing and engin., Ludington Lines, 1930-33; co-orig.-dir., maintenance and engin., purchasing agt., chg. airways-airport devel., Boston-Maine Airways, 1933-38; v.p. Kansas City Co. Transport Co. (Kansas City So. Airlines), 1938-40; v.p. Hawaiian Airlines Ltd. 1940-44; dir. air transport div., Matson Navigation Co. and Inter-Is. Steam Navigation Co. 1940-44; founder-pres.-gen. mgr., L.A. Airways, Inc. 1944---; pioneer-founder, world's first helicopter airline. Mem.: Inst. of Aeron. Scis., USA; Soc. of Automotive Engrs.; fellowship, Am. Helicopter Soc., Inc.; Helicopter Inst. of Great Brit.; Am. Inst. of Mgmt.; Alpha Eta Rho; Mason; Protestant. Home: 12312 Viewcrest Rd., No. Hollywood, CA; Office: 5901 W. Imperial Highway, L.A., CA 90045.

BELL, CHARLES GORDON
Professor of Political Science
b. Apr. 8, 1929, L.A.; s. John Alison and Katherine (Titus) Bell; B.A., Pomona Coll., 1952; M.A., USC, 1958; Ph.D., 1966; m. Claudia Myers, Oct. 26, 1965, Santa Ana; chil.: Shannon, b. 1971; Gordon, b. 1974. Career: mem. faculty, Calif. State Univ., Fullerton, 1964---; chmn. Dept. of Political Sci., 1970-73, Prof. of Political Sci., 1972---; dir., Center of Govtl. Studies, 1965-72; assoc. editor, Western Political Quarterly, 1970-73, 1977---; co-author The First Term, Sage Pub. Co., 1975; editor, author, Growth & Change, Dickenson Pub. Co., 1973; co-author, The Legislative Process in California (Am. Polit. Sci. Assn., 1973); editor, Politics in the West (Western Polit. Sci. Assn., 1975); columnist, Fullerton Daily News Tribune, Costa Mesa Daily Pilot; contbr. articles: Western Political Quarterly, Journal of Politics, Social Forces, Am. Journal of Polit. Sci. Mem.: Orange Co. Juvenile Justice Commn., 1975-77; pres., North O.C. Child Center, 1968-69. Rec.: swimming. Home: 18751 De Ville Dr., Yorba Linda, CA 92686; Office: State Univ., Fullerton, CA.

BELL, EVALYN KRUEGER
Landscape Designer
b. July 31, Calif.; d. Louis C. and Jennie (Washburn) Krueger; ed. A.B. (speech), A.B. (art), Univ. of Calif. 1950-51; cert. Rudolph Schaefer Sch. of Design, S.F.; m. Milton R. Bell, Berkeley, Calif. Career: Tchr., Diablo Valley Coll. 1956-61; master judge, Natl. Council State Garden Clubs, 1957, instr. Natl. Council Flower Show Schs., Symposiums, instr. Landscape Design Schs., landscape judge, 1960, instr. 1972, Hon. Roll, 1974; est. study courses for Western States, Dept. Landscape Arch., Univ. of Calif. 1959---; State chmn. Calif. Garden Clubs, 1959-70, chmn. adv. council, bd. trustees, pres. 1968-70 (Natl. Council Spillers Award in Landscape Design, 1966); Panelist: First Gov's. Conf. on Calif. Beauty; Univ. of Ga. Landscape Design Sym. 1964; Calif. Nurserymen's Assn. Conf., Calif. Polytech. Coll; Calif. Anti-Litter League. State Conf.; chmn. Mayor's Conf. 1966, City Council Com., Walnut Creek, 1972, 73, 74; adv. council: Calif. State Parks Found., Atty. Gen's. Com. and City Council, Pleasant Hill; awards chmn. Walnut Creek Action Beauty Council, 1970, pres. 1972-74; adv. com. San Ramon Improvement Assn., and Martinez Scenic Rt. Devel.; landscape design com. Dunsmuir House and Hellman Estate, City of Oakland. Lectr., TV-Radio interviews, writer, Garden Column, Contra Costa Times; many publ. articles. Awards: Woman of Yr., Calif. Garden Clubs, 1967; John J. Lawlor Award, 1971; Environmental Award, 1973; Trophy in Landscape Design; State, Natl. Awards for Radio in garden and landscape subjs.; Community Leader of Am. Award, 1969-70 (nom. 1971-72); AAUW. Protestant. Home: 12 Oak Ct., Walnut Creek, CA 94596.

BELL, JOSEPH N.
Free Lance Journalist
b. Aug. 4, 1921, Bluffton, Ind.; s. Fred D. and Vera (Patterson) Bell; B.A., Univ. of Mo., 1946; m. Janet Patricia Hartman, Oct. 9, 1943, Corpus Christi, Tex.; chil.: David H., b. 1944; Patricia (Dubin), b. 1947; Deborah (Simpson), b. 1951. Career: publicity, St. Louis Cardinals baseball team, 1947; pub. rels. dir., Indiana Service Corp., Ft. Wayne, 1947-49; pub. rels., Portland Cement Assn., Chicago, 1949-55; free-lance writer, 1955---; lectr., non-fiction writing, contemp. Am. film, Univ. Calif., Irvine, 1967---. Movie critic, journalist: National Observer, Christian Sci. Monitor, Good Housekeeping, L.A. Times, others; contbr. articles: Sat.

Eve. Post, Collier's, Saturday Review, Harper's, Reader's Digest, Look, others; Author: Seven Into Space, Hawthorne, 1960 (1st major work on Am. manned space program), series of sports books, etc. Work appears in Best Sat. Eve. Post Short Stories, numerous textbook anthologies. Lt., USN Air Corps, 1942-46, pilot, dive bombers, transports. Mem.: Sigma Delta Chi, Am. Soc. Authors and Journalists. Home: 411 Begonia Ave., Corona del Mar, CA 92625; Office: Univ. Calif., Dept. of English, Irvine, CA 92717.

BELL, ROBERT S.
Electronics Executive
b. May 29, 1915, Milwaukee, Wis.; s. Arthur B. and Nina Louise Zwebell; ed. A.B., UCLA, 1936; J.D., Harvard Law Sch. 1940; (hon.) D.Sc., Heald Coll. of Engin., S.F. 1957; m. Carolyn Crowell, S.F., Jan. 2, 1943; chil.: Robert McKim, b. Dec. 23, 1947. Career: Atty. at law, pvt. practice, 1940-46; admitted to practice, U.S. Supreme Ct.; trial atty., Dept. of Justice; spec. asst. to U.S. Supreme Ct. Justice Clark (head, Anti-Trust Div. for Western States); owner-mgr., Burnham Mfg. Co. 1947-48; asst. to pres., Packard Bell Electronics, 1948, v.p. 1949; exec. v.p. 1951, pres. 1956, chmn. bd. dirs. and pres. 1961-68; merged, Teledyne, Inc., vice pres. 1968---. Dir. Gen. Tel. Co. of Calif. Asst. Judge Advocate, 2nd Air Force; Judge Adv., 20th Air Force; Air Force Judge Adv., Occupational Forces, Japan, WW II. Awards: Space Age award, L.A. Co. Bd. Suprs. Mem.: Calif. and Fed. Bars; dir. Merchants and Mfrs. Assn.; Am. Ord. Assn.; Navy League; Judge Advs. Assn.; Def. Orientation Conf. Assn.; visiting com. UCLA Grad. Sch. of Mgmt.; Atty Gen. Adv. Council; bd. regents, St. John's Hosp., Santa Monica; bd. trustees, City of Hope, Duarte, Calif.; chmn. first Western Space Age Conf.; v.p. Great Western Council, B.S.A.; Confrerie des Chevaliers du Tastevin; (charter) Grand Officer, L.A. chpt., Confrerie de la Chaine des Rotisseurs, and Commanderie de Bordeaux; Newcomen Soc. in N. Am., Radio Pioneers, Town Hall, Phi Kappa Sigma, Harvard Club, Army-Navy Club, Jonathan Club, Bel-Air Bay Club, L.A. Country Club. Catholic. Home: 10428 Sunset Blvd., L.A., CA 90024; Office: 1901 Ave. of the Stars, L.A., CA 90067.

BELLI, MELVIN MOURON
Trial Lawyer — Author
b. July 29, 1907, Sonora, Tuolumne Co., Calif.; s. Caesar A. and Leonie (Mouron) Belli; ed. A.B., Univ. of Calif., Berkeley, 1929; LL.B., Boalt Hall, Berkeley, 1933; m. Betty Ballantine (div.): m. Joy Maybelle Turney, May 3, 1956; chil.: Richard, b. Aug. 18, 1936; Melvin M., Jr., b. June 5, 1939; Susan, b. July 14, 1945; Jean, b. July 22, 1942; Caesar M., b. Mar. 28, 1957; m. Lia Triff, June 2, 1972; dau. Melia, b. Jan. 12, 1973. Career: Sr. partner, Belli, Ashe & Choulos and predecessor firms, S.F. 1940---, L.A., 1958---. Cond. Belli Seminars in Law, 1951---; pres. Belli Found. Lectrs., 1960---; moderator, Annual Belli Seminars, maj. law schs. throughout U.S., incl. Harvard, Yale. Virginia, UCLA, Miss., and many others; cond. law sci. courses: lectr., numerous bar assns. Author: "Modern Trials" (3 vols.); "Modern Damages" (3 vols.); "Ready for the Plaintiff"; "Trial and Tort Trends" (9 vols.). 1951-61; "The Adequate Award," "Demonstrative Evidence and the Adequate Award," "Malpractice," "Life and Law in Japan," Autobiograph. "Belli: My Life on Trial."; numerous law reviews, profl. and non-profl. mag. articles. Mem.: fellow-dir.-(past) dean, Internat. Acad. Trial Lawyers; dir. disability and casualty Inter-Ins. Exch.; Am., Calif., S.F., Fed. and Internat. (patron) Bar Assns.; Hollywood and Beverly Hills Bar Assn.; past pres., Natl. Assn. Claimants Compensation Attys., chmn. torts sect. 1959; chmn. Aviation and Torts Sect., NACCA; Am. Acad. of Forensic Medicine; (past) dir., Barristers Club of S.F.; Lawyers Club of S.F.; pres. Societe Droit; (hon.) La Asociacion Nacional de Abogados, Mex.; Phi Delta Phi, Delta Tau Delta; Mason, Commonwealth Club, S.F.; Press & Union League Club, Olympic Club. Home: 2950 Broadway, S.F., CA; Office: 722 Montgomery St., S.F., CA.

BELLIS, DAVID JAMES
University Professor
b. May 1, 1944, Nashville, Tenn.; s. Carroll J. (M.D., Ph.D., abdominal surgeon, researcher, prof. in So. Calif.) and Helen L. Bellis; B.A., UCLA, 1966; M.A., USC, 1969; Ph.D. (polit. sci.), 1977; m. Ann Seagreaves, 1972, Rolling Hills, Calif. Career: Instr., Polit. Sci., Long Beach City Coll., 1970---; chief, statistics and research, Narcotics Prevention Project, L.A., 1972-73; intake dir., West End Drug Abuse Control, Ontario, Calif., 1973-74; dir. opns., 1974-75; lectr. in pub. adminstrn., USC, 1978---; lectr. in criminology, Cal. State Univ., Long Beach, 1978---; profl. jazz musician, 1960-70; graduate fellow, Town Hall of Calif., 1969-70. Co-author with Kenneth Johnson,

Mexican Democracy: A Critical View, Allyn and Bacon, 1970; author, Heroin Addicts and Politicians: Addiction Treatment Strategies and Their Outcomes (in progress), Johns Hopkins Univ. Press., Pres., L.B. City Coll. faculty assn., 1972. Polit. candidate for city council, Signal Hill, 1978. Hobby: music. Rec.: camping. Home: 2058 Terrace Dr., Signal Hill, CA 90806.

BELLUGI, URSULA
Language Laboratory Director
b. Feb. 21, 1931, Jena, Germany; d. Max and Edith (Kaufman) Herzberger; B.A., Antioch Coll., 1952; Ed. D., Harvard, 1967; came to U.S., 1935; naturalized, 1940; m. Edward S. Klima; chil.: David; Robin. Career: Research fellow, asst. prof. Harvard, 1967-68; vis. asst. prof. Rockefeller Univ., N.Y., 1969; dir. lab. for lang. studies, Salk Inst., 1970---; adj. prof. psychology, UCSD, 1970---; lectr., cons. Office of Edn.; Grantee: Nat. Insts. Mental Health, 1970---; NSF, 1974---. Mem.: Am. Psychol. Assn.; Linguistics Soc. Am.; Internat. Linguistics, Circle. Author with husband E.S. Klima, The Signs of Language, contbr. journs. on language research; editor, Acquisition of Language, 1964. Home: 6649 Michaeljohn Dr., La Jolla, CA 92037; Office: P.O.B. 1809, San Diego, CA 92112.

BELLUOMINI, FRANK STEPHEN
CPA — Partner, Touche Ross & Co.
b. May 19, 1934, Healdsburg, Calif.; s. Francesco and Rose (Giorgi) Belluomini; ed. A.A., Santa Rosa Jr. Coll. 1954; B.A. (with great distinction), San Jose State Univ., 1956; m. Alta Anita Gifford, Santa Clara, Calif., Sept. 16, 1967; dau. Wendy Ann, b. June 8, 1972. Career: Staff acct., Hood Gire & Co., 1956-60; partner, 1960-66; partner, Touche Ross & Co., 1966---. Mem.: treas., San Jose Jaycees, 1958; dir. 1959-60; treas. San Jose Young Republicans, 1960; pres. San Jose chpt., Calif. CPA Soc., 1968-69; state dir., 1968-69, 1972-74; v.p. 1976-77; Am. Inst. of CPAs, Subcom. on State and local Govt. Auditing; dir. Santa Clara Co. Estate Planning Council, 1975-77; Natl. Assn. Accts.; Municipal Finance Officers Assn.; Hosp. Financial Mgmt. Assn.; Natl. Soc. Accts. for Cooperatives; Assn. of Sch. Bus. Officials; Financial Mgrs. Soc. for Savs. Insts. Home: 1782 Wilcox Way, San Jose, CA 95125; Office: 100 Park Center Plaza, San Jose, CA 95113.

BELVILLE, DONALD RAYMOND
Radiologist
b. Jan. 22, 1924, Fairmont, Minn.; s. Harold R. and Olga (Lindell) Belville; desc. Belville, settled, Staten Island, 1670; B.A., Univ. Iowa, 1949, M.D., 1953; m. Ruth Kollin, Nov. 23, 1946; Long Beach; chil.: Mark, b. Dec. 14, 1954; John, b. Apr. 21, 1956; Charles, b. Aug. 21, 1958; Judith, b. Jan. 4, 1961. Career: Radiology: Long Beach Comm. Hosp., Bellwood Gen. Hosp.; dir. radiology, Long Beach Comm. Hosp., 1966---. Capt. AUS Med. Corps., 1955-57, Germany. Mem.: Fillmore Condit. Club; Sigma Nu, 1946. Protestant; trustee; chmn. Christian edn.; chmn. boys brigade. Hobbies: photog., travel. Rec.: gardening. Home: 5051 Crescent Dr., Anaheim, CA; Office: Long Beach Comm. Hosp., 1720 Termino Ave., Long Beach, CA 90804.

BENGYEL, ALAN J.
City Administrator
b. July 11, 1946, Regansburg, Germany; s. Julius and Maria Bengyel; A.A., Yuba Coll., Marysville; B.A., pub. ad., Univ. of Calif., Chico, 1975; M.P.A., 1977; m. Carol C. Angove, Yuba City, Calif., Aug. 22, 1971; stepson: Danny, b. Aug, 16, 1967. Career: administrv. asst. to city administr., Yuba City, 1975-76; dir., Housing & energy programs, Butte Co. Economic Opport. Council, Oroville, 1976-78; city administr., Adelanto, Calif., 1978---. Personnel spec., USAF, 1965-69. Author: Butte Co. E.O.C. Housing Policy Manual, 1977; Do It Yourself Weatherization, 1978; Time Management In Municipal Govt., 1978. Mem.: C. of C.; Rotary Intl. Catholic. Rec.: tennis. Office: P.O.B. 10, Adelanto, CA 92301.

BENHARD, F. GORDON
President, Elpac Electronics, Inc.
b. Oct. 6, 1934, San Francisco; s. Friedrich Hans and Eileen (Lynch) Benhard; B.S.E.E., UCLA, 1956, M.S., 1959; m. Ina Joy Shero, Dec. 22, 1971, Woodland Hills; chil.: Mark, b. May 18, 1965; Heather, b. May 6, 1975; Ryan, b. Aug. 11, 1977. Career: with Hughes Aircraft, Inglewood, 1956-57; corp. v.p. and gen. mgr., Varadyne, Inc., Santa Monica and Van Nuys, 1969-70; Litton Indus.: data systems div., Van Nuys, 1957-69, 1970-71, v.p. and gen. mgr., Litton Office Products Centers, L.A.

and S.F., 1971-72; v.p. and gen. mgr., Elpac Electronics, Inc., Santa Ana, 1972-74; pres., 1974---. Bd. dir., Am. Electronics Assn., 1977, 78; chmn. Orange Co. Council, Am. Electronics Assn., 1977-78; mem. Tau Beta Pi. Hobbies: skiing, music, judo. Home: 2301 Port Carlisle, Newport Beach, CA 92667; Office: 3131 S. Standard, Santa Ana, CA 92705.

BENIRSCHKE, KURT
Research Director, San Diego Zoo
b. May 26, 1924, Glueckstadt, Germany; s. Fritz and Marie Benirschke; M.D., Hamburg, 1948; m. Marion E. Waldhausen, May 17, 1952, Great Falls, Mont.; Chil.: Stephen K., b. Aug. 16, 1953; Rolf J., b. Feb. 7, 1955; Ingrid M., b. Apr. 16, 1956. Career: intern, Teaneck, N.J., 1950; resident in pathology, Boston, 1951-55; pathologist, Boston Lying-In Hosp., 1956-60; Prof. & Chmn. Dept. Pathology, Dartmouth Med. Sch., Hanover, N.H., 1960-70; prof. Reprod. Med., Univ. Calif., San Diego Sch. Med., La Jolla, 1970---; prof. & chmn. Dept. Pathology, UCSD Sch. of Med., 1976-79; dir. of research, San Diego Zoo, 1975---. Author: 15 sci. books; 300 sci. articles. Hobby: photog., writing. Home: 8457 Prestwick Dr., La Jolla, CA 92037; Office: San Diego Zoo, P.O.B. 551, San Diego, CA 92112.

BEN-ISAAC, CLARA
Physician
b. Feb. 13, 1930, Bagdad, Iraq; d. Ezra and Matilda Amit; Pre-med. studies, Royal Coll. of Med., Bagdad, 1947-50; M.D., Jerusalem, 1955; m. Fouad Ben-Isaac, M.D., Jerusalem, March 7, 1955; chil.: Dau. Nava, b. Nov. 11, 1956; son, Eyal, b. Apr. 4, 1964; dau. Gilat, b. Oct. 22, 1966. Career: Intern, Hadassah Hosp., Hebrew Univ., Jerusalem, 1954-55; med. dir., Meggido Med. Health Center, Affula, Israel, 1955-57; Out-patient clinic practice, Sick-Fund Found., Ramat-Gan, Israel, 1957-69; research assoc., Div. of Nephrology, Cedars-Sinai Med. Center, 1970-71, research fellow, 1971-72, adv. research fellow, 1972-74; coordinator, teaching program, 1974-75, dir., teaching program, 1975---; acting dir., Nephrology and Dialysis, 1975---; asst. prof. of Med., Sch. of Med., Dept. of Med., UCLA, 1975---; chmn., Advanced clin. clikship course in Nephrology; Cedars-Sinai, 1975---; administrv. coordinator, Renal Dialysis Unit, 1975---; Chief of Nephrology, Cedars-Sinai Med. Center, 1975---. Com. mem.: Dialysis and Transplantation, Human Subjects. Soc. mem.: Israel Med. Assn.; Natl. Kidney Found.; Am. Soc. of Nephrology; Kidney Found. of So. Calif.; Am. Federation for Clin. Research; Am. Soc. of Internal Med. Co-author: Malignant Neoplasma and Parathyroid Adenoma, Cancer 28: 401-407, 1971; Metabolic Acidosis of Hyperparathyrodism. Arch. Int. Med. 134: 385, 1974; Evidence for Humoral Factor Responsible for the Hypercalciuria (UCaV) of Phosphate Deplation (PD). Spec. fellowship award: Kidney Found. of S. Calif. Mem.: Marina City Club. Jewish. Rec.: Music, nature, swimming. Home: 1200 Shadow Hill Way, Beverly Hills, CA; Office: Cedars-Sinai Med. Center, L.A., CA 90048.

BEN-ISAAC, FOUAD
Physician — Consultant — Pulmonary Disease
b. Dec. 25, 1926, Bagdad, Iraq; s. Ezra and Simcha Ben-Isaac; Pre-Med., Royal Coll. of Med., Bagdad, 1947-51; Hadassah Med. Sch., Hebrew Univ., Jerusalem, 1952-54, intern, Hadassah Hosp., 1954-55, N.D., 1955; ECFMG, 1965; FLEX, 1972; m. Clara Amit, M.D., Jerusalem, Mar. 7, 1955; chil: dau. Nava, b. Nov. 11, 1956; son Eyal, b. Apr. 6, 1964; dau. Gilat, b. Oct. 22, 1966. Career: Asst. B, Dept. of Med., Univ. of Tel-Aviv, 1960-65; Asst. A, Pathology Inst., 1965-66; cons. in Internal med., Israel 1966-69; med. dir.: Harishonim and Assa Hospitals, 1968-69; fellow, div. of pulmonary disease, UCLA, 1969-72; asst. prof. of med. and dir. of fiberoptic bronchoscopy, UCLA, 1972-75; dir., pulmonary care dept.: Metropolitan (1977-78), Parkview (1976-78) and Queen of Angels (1977---) Hospitals, L.A.; pri. practice Jan. 1975---, ltd. to cons. in pulmonary disease, Fiberoptic Bronchoscopy, spec. chest procedures. Pres., owner, California Pulmonary Disease Medical Group, Inc. Queen of Angels Hosp. com. Mem.: ICU com.; Med. com.; Education com.; CPR com., chmn. Captain, Israel Defense Army, 1957-60. Post-Doct. fellowships: Natl. Inst. of Health, Calif. Tuberculosis Assn. Mem.: Israel Med. Assoc. 1956; Israel Soc. of Internal Med. 1966; Local bd. of IMA, Ramat-Gan 1968; Am. Coll. of Chest Physicians 1970; Calif. Thoracic Soc. 1970; L.A. Co. Med. Assn. 1975-76; Am. Coll. of Physicians 1975; Am. Coll. of Chest Physicians, Calif. 1970. Author numerous publ. articles. Inventory of spec. trochar for diagnosis of thoracic diseases. Mem.: Marina City Club, 1977---. Jewish. Rec.: Music, swimming,

outdoors. Home: 1200 Shadow Hill Way, Beverly Hills, CA; Office: 2080 Century Park E., L.A., CA 90067.

BENJAMIN, HERBERT STANLEY
Psychiatrist
b. June 7, 1922, Washington, D.C.; s. Joseph and Katie (Lewin) Benjamin; Ph.B., U. Wis., 1943; postgrad. Columbia U., 1948-49; (Fullbright scholar) Sorbonne, U. Paris, France, 1949-50; M.D., U. Vienna, Austria, 1957, postgrad. Postgrad. Acad. Medicine, 1957-64, certificate in psychosomatic medicine and surgery, 1975; m. Edith Steiner, July 20, 1966; chil.: Oliver, Alice. Career: Resident guest physician in surgery and urology U. Vienna, 1957-60; Intern Cedars of Lebanon Hosp., Los Angeles, 1964-65; resident in psychiatry Cedars-Siani Med. Center, Los Angeles, 1965-68; chief resident in psychiatry, 1967-68; practice medicine specializing in psychiatry and psychosomatic medicine, Beverly Hills, Calif., 1968---; Mem. staffs Cedars-Sinai Med. Center, Los Angeles, Westwood Hosp., Los Angeles, Beverly Glen Hosp., Los Angeles, Encino Hosp., Los Angeles, cons. in psychiatry So. Calif. Permanente Med. group, 1969-70; mem. teaching staff Cedars-Sinai Med. Center, Los Angeles, 1968---; chmn., Internat. seminar in psychosomatic medicine U. Vienna, 1975. Lt. (j.g.), USNR, 1943-48. Mem.: Am., Calif. psychiat. assns.; So. Calif. Psychiat. Soc., Am., So. Calif. Socs. adolescent psychiatry, Am. Med. Soc. Vienna, Pi Gamma Mu. Contbr. numerous articles to encys. Office: 436 N. Roxbury Dr., Suite 220, Beverly Hills, CA 90210.

BENNETT, ALAN HENRY
President, Allied Industrial Distributors
b. Jan. 21, 1943, South Gate, Calif.; s. Vernon E. and Elizabeth A. Bennett; B.B.A., Woodbury Coll., 1964; m. Betty Baskin, L.A., Calif., Oct. 1, 1976; 1 dau. Janean Marie, b. Sept. 24, 1971. Career: Natl. bank examiner, U.S. Treasury Dept., 1964-65; pres., Allied Industrial Distributors, 1970---. USAF 1965-69; Mem. Natl. Industrial Glove Distribrs. Assn., 1978 pres. Mem. W.L.A. Masonic Lodge No. 373. Hobbies: boating, flying, fishing. Home: 30944 Rue de La Pierre, Rancho Palos Verdes, CA 90274; Office: 7800 Compton Ave., L.A., CA 90001.

BENNETT, WILLIAM MORGAN
Member, State Board of Equalization
b. Feb. 20, 1918, San Francisco, Calif.; ed. Univ. of Calif., Hastings Coll. of Law; LL.B., Univ. of S.F. Law Sch. 1946; m. Jane E. Bennett; chil.: William M., Jr., b. July 1, 1946; James P., b. Sept. 26, 1950; Joan P., b. May 24, 1958. Career: Admitted to practice, U.S. Supreme Ct.; U.S. Atty. 1945-48; dep. Atty. Gen., State of Calif., 1949-59; chief counsel, Calif. Pub. Utilities Comm. 1959-62, commr. 1963-68, pres. 1963; elected to Calif. State Bd. of Equalization, 1970---, chmn. 1972, 75, 76, 77. Capt., USAF (B-17 pilot, 50 missions over Europe), WW II. Awards: Distinguished Flying Cross, Air Medal, Pres. Cit., Battle Stars. Mem.: State Bar of Calif. Home: 35 Evergreen Dr., Kentfield, CA 94904; Office: 1020 N. St., Sacto., CA 95814.

BENNETT, WILLIAM PERRY
Attorney at Law
b. Aug. 28, 1938, Inglewood; s. George W. and Lenora Perry Bennett; B.A., Cal. State Univ., Long Beach, 1961; J.D., USC Sch. of Law, 1964; m. Linda Schneider, Aug. 19, 1961, Lynwood; chil.: William Gregory, b. Dec. 19, 1962; Mark Christopher, b. Nov. 29, 1966; Carin Suzanne, b. Nov. 19, 1968. Career: partner, law firm of Powars, Tretheway & Bennett, 1964---; assoc. prof. of bus. and real estate law, Cal. State Univ., Long Beach, 1965---; Judge Pro Tem, Long Beach Municipal Ct., 1978, L.A. Co. Superior Ct., 1975, 76, 77; lectr.: Calif. State Univ., Dominguez Hills, Long Beach City Coll., Calif. Assn. of Licensed Investigators ann. confs., 1976, 78; contbr. articles legal journs. USMCR, 1958-63. Dir., v.p., Long Beach Legal Air Found., 1973; bd. gov., Long Beach Bar Assn., 1970-71, 1973-76; pres., Long Beach Barristers Club, 1971; Mem. Kiwanis Internat., Kiwanian of the Year Award, 1971; bd. dir., March of Dimes, Long Beach chpt. 1973-78; United Crusade, regional campaign, 1973-75; pres., CSULB alumni assn., 1965-67; mem. Order of the Coif; ed. bd., So. Calif. Law Review. Protestant. Hobbies: wine collecting, lecturing. Rec.: skiing, hiking. Home: 1600 Catalina Ave., Seal Beach, CA 90740; Office: 3907 Atlantic Ave., Long Beach, CA 90807.

BENSON, BERGER C.
Company President
b. Mar. 3, 1940; San Mateo, Calif.; B.S., bus. and indus.

mgmt., San Jose State, 1961; m. Carole Anderson, Feb. 1, 1967, Santa Rosa, Calif.; dau. Laura, b. July 19, 1960. Career: assoc. with family paint contracting firm, Berger Benson & Sons, Inc., 1962---; pres., 1972---. Mem.: Mzuri Safari Club of S.F., pres. 1974; pres., Mzuri Safari Found.; pres., Wheeler Is. Land Co. (hunting club). Mem. Calif. Fish and Game Comm., 1974--- (pres. 1978-79); concurrent term as pres., Wildlife Conserv. Bd. Author: local newspaper articles on internat. travel, hunting. Rev.: hunting, fishing. Home: 847 La Mesa Dr., Portola Valley, CA 94025; Office: P.O.B. 5424, San Mateo, CA 94402.

BENSON, GEORGE C. SUMNER
College President Emeritus
b. Jan. 16, 1908, N.Y.C.; s. Eugene Huntington and Helen (Sumner) Benson; ed. A.M. Univ. of Ill. 1929; A.M. Harvard Univ. 1930; Ph.D., 1931; m. Mabel Gibberd, Chicago, Ill., May 10, 1935; chil.: George Charles Sumner and Brien Gibberd. Career: Head tutor, Lowell House, instr. Harvard, 1930-34; lectr., Univ. of Chicago, 1934-36; assoc. prof., Univ. of Mich. 1936-41; personnel dir.-dir. adm. div., OPA, 1940-41; prof. Northwestern Univ. 1941-45; prof. pub. adm., Claremont Men's Coll. 1946---, pres. 1947-69, pres. emeritus, 1969---; dep. asst. Secty. of Def. 1969-72. Memorial Washtenaw Co. Bd. of Suprs., Mich. Author: "Financial Control and Inegration," 1933; "Civil Service in Massachusetts," 1934; "State Administration Board in Michigan," mng. ed., "State Government" mag. 1934-36. Lt. Col., U.S. Army, WW II. Mem.: Pub. Adm. Comm., Soc. Sci. Research Council; Mich. State Planning Comm.; research dir., U.S. Comm. on Intergovernmental Rels.; trustee, Claremont Men's Coll.; Phi Beta Kappa; Univ. Club, L.A. Episcopal. Home: 669 W. 8th St., Claremont, CA; Office: Pitzer Hall, Claremont Men's Coll., Claremont, CA 91711.

BENSON, LYMAN (David)
Professor Emeritus of Botany
b. May 4, 1909, Kelseyville, Calif.; s. Charles A. and Cora I. (West) Benson; A.B., Stanford Univ., 1930; M.A., 1931, Ph.D., 1939; m. Evelyn Berniece Linderholm, Stanford, Aug. 16, 1931; chil.: (Lyman) David, b. Oct. 26, 1938; Robert L., b. Oct. 27, 1941. Career: Instr., Botany & Zoology, Bakersfield Coll., 1931-38; Instr. then asst. prof., Univ. of Ariz., 1938-44; Assoc. prof. & chmn., Dept. of Botany, Pomona Coll., 1944-49; prof. & chmn., Dept. of Botany, Pomona Coll., 1949-74; dir. of the Herbarium, Pomona Coll., 1944-74; Parallel teaching appointments in the Claremont Grad. Sch., 1944-74. Author: 7 books. Pres., Am. Soc. of Plant Taxonomists, 1960; pres. Cactus & Succulent Soc. of Am., 1956, 57, also Fellow; pres., Western Soc. Naturalists, 1955; pres. So. Calif. Botanists, 1949-50. Mem.: Commonwealth Club of Calif. Hobbies: writing, pen-and-ink drawing; photog.; natural hist. Home: 1430 Via Zurita, Claremont, CA 91711; Box 532, Kelseyville, CA 95451; Office: Botany Dept., Pomona Coll., Claremont, CA 91711.

BENTON, HELEN
President, The Thinnery Company
b. Nov. 19, 1928, Boston, Mass.; d. James and Mary Emma; m. William G. Benton, Nov. 16, 1947; No. Hollywood; chil.: Ronald, b. Mar. 17, 1950; Richard, b. Sept. 11, 1951; Patti (Ferguson), b. Feb. 6, 1954. Career: pres and owner: Personalized Parties, 1964-68; Carousel Caterers, 1968-73; The Thinnery Co., (18 retail stores) 1973---. Mem.: Soc. of Nutrition Edn., Inst. Food Technologists, Nutrition Council of Greater L.A.; fourteen C. of C.s. Catholic. Hobby: cooking. Rec.: bicycling, walking, jogging. Home: 11921 Weddington, No. 101, No. Hollywood, CA 91607; Office: 9337 Laurel Canyon Blvd., Pacoima, CA 91331.

BENZING, WALTER CHARLES
Vice President, Applied Materials Inc.
b. Aug. 28, 1924, N.Y.C.; s. Frederick Ludwig and Grace Augusta (Engelhart) Benzing; B.S., Univ. Rochester, 1945; M.S., Mass. Inst. Tech., 1948; Ph.D., Princeton, Univ. 1964; m. Ruth Elinor McBride, Sept. 11, 1948, Milford, N.H.; chil.: Steven M.; David M.; Jeffrey C. Career: to dir. of Chem. Engring. Research & Devel., Merck Sharpe & Dohme Research Labs, 1952-63; to dir. of tech., Union Carbide Corp., electronics div., 1964-68; v.p. and dir. of tech., Applied Materials Inc., 1968---. Patentee (8) in field; contbr. to tech. pbls. Lt. j.g., USN, 1942-48, USNR ret. Mem.: Am. Chem. Soc.; Electrochem. Soc.; Am. Assn. of Crystal Growth; Am. Inst. Chem. Engrs. Rec.: golf, music. Home: 20297 Ljepava Dr., Saratoga, CA 95070; Office: 3050 Bowers Ave., Santa Clara, CA 95051.

BERG, HAROLD EDGAR
Chairman and CEO, Getty Oil Company
b. May 27, 1915, Stilwell, Kan.; s. Rudolph O. and Astrid (Thorud) Berg; A.B., The Colorado Coll., Colo. Springs, 1936; m. Martha Howell, Nov. 9, 1938, Colo. Career: v.p., gen. mgr., Getty Oil Co., mid-continent div., Houston, Tex., 1970-73; pres., Skelly Oil Co., Tulsa, Okla., 1973-74; exec. v.p., chief operating officer, dir., Getty Oil Co., L.A., 1975-76; pres. & dir., 1976---. Dir.: Skelly Oil Co., 1973-74; Baker Internat., Orange, Calif.; advis dir., First Nat. Bank & Trust Co. of Tulsa, Okla.; chmn. bd. trustees, J. Paul Getty Museum; trustee, The Colo. Coll. Mem.: Beta Gamma chpt. of Sigma Chi. Clubs: Los Angeles, Wilshire Country, Petroleum Club of Houston. Presbyterian. Rec.: hunting, fishing, golf. Home: 2011 Cummings Dr., L.A., CA 90027; Office: Getty Oil Co., P.O.B. 54050, L.A., CA 90054.

BERG, HAROLD E.
President, Getty Oil Company
b. May 27, 1915, Stilwell, Kan.; s. Rudolph O. and Astrid (Thorud) Berg; ed. A.B., Colo. Coll., Colo. Springs, 1936; m. Martha Frances Howell, Colo. Springs, Nov. 9, 1938. Career: Dir. Getty Oil Co., v.p.-div. gen. mgr. Mid-Continent E & P Div., Houston, Tex. 1970-73; pres.-dir. Skelly Oil Co., Tulsa, Okla. 1973-74; exec. v.p.-chief opr. officer Getty Oil Co. 1975-76, dir. 1975---, pres. 1976---. Mem.: Beta Gamma chpt., Sigma Chi. Dir., Baker Internat.; Bd. chmn., trustee, J. Paul Getty Museum; trustee, The Colo. Coll. Clubs: Petroleum of Houston, The L.A., Wilshire Country. Presbyterian. Rec.: hunting, golf. Home: 2011 Cummings Dr., L.A., CA 90027; Office: 3810 Wilshire Blvd., L.A., CA 90010.

BERGEN, RICHARD CHENEY
Senior Partner, O'Melveny & Myers
b. Jan. 14, 1914, Frankfort, Ind.; s. Guy Lawrence and Stella (Cheney) Bergen; ed. B.S. (econs.), Northwestern Univ. 1935; LL.B. (cum laude), Harvard Law Sch. 1938; m. Rosemary Hall, L.A., Calif. 1941; daus.: Sandra (Bergen) Strength, b. Aug. 30, 1944; Mary (Bergen) Wright, b. Nov. 24, 1947. Career: Assoc. with O'Melveny and Myers law firm, 1938---, sr. partner. Dir.: Security Pac. Natl. Bank; dir.-v.p.: Drilling & Prodn. Co. Ensign, USNR, Dist. Intelligence Ofc., Eleventh Naval Dist., L.A. 1941-44; staff intelligence ofcr. for Comdr., Amphibious Forces, Seventh Fleet, Pac., Philippine area; Lt. 1946, WW II. Mem.: L.A. Country Club, Calif. Club, Valley Club of Montecito; pres. Men's Garden Club of L.A. Rec.: golf, hunting. Home: 521 N. Cherokee Ave., L.A., CA 90004; Office: 611 W. Sixth St., L.A., CA 90017.

BERGER, JOSEPH
Professor of Sociology
b. Apr. 3, 1924, Brooklyn, N.Y.; s. Harry and Rose (Diner) Berger; A.B. magna cum laude, Brooklyn Coll., 1949; M.A., Harvard Univ., 1952; Ph.D. in Sociology, 1958; m. Margaret Alice Smith, July 9, 1966, Palo Alto; chil.: Adam, b. Nov. 29, 1956; Rachel, b. Dec. 31, 1961; Gideon, b. Dec. 9, 1969. Career: Instr., asst. prof. of sociology, Dartmouth Coll., 1954-59; asst., assoc. prof. of Sociology, Stanford Univ., 1959---; dir. Lab for Soc. Research, 1968-70, 1971-74; vice-chmn. Dept. of Sociology, 1976-77, chmn. 1977---; licensed counselor. Co-author, contbr. books and journs. of sociology, Served to 2nd Lt., AUS, 1943-45, information control div., Mil. Govt. of Greater Hesse, 1946; awarded Bronze Star Medal, Army Commendation Award. Jewish. Hobbies: classical music, baseball. Home: 955 Mears Ct., Stanford, CA 94305; Office: Dept. of Sociology, Stanford, CA 94305.

BERGER, MARTIN
President, Occidental Research Corp.
b. May 23, 1926, N.Y.C.; s. Harry and Elizabeth (Gotthelf) Berger; B.S. physics, Columbia Univ., 1949; m. Helen Cherin, Aug. 31, 1947, N.Y.C.; chil.: Henry, b. July 15, 1949; Susan, b. May 31, 1953; Laura, b. Dec. 31, 1960. Career: research physicist; Uniroyal, Detroit, 1950-54; Chrysler Corp., Detroit, 1954-56; dir., Govt. Research Labs, Exxon Res. & Engring. Co., Linden, N.J., 1956-76; pres., Occidental Research Corp., Irvine, Calif., 1976---; vice pres. R&D, Occidental Petroleum Corp., L.A., 1977---. Contbr. 25 sci. publs. in petroleum and petro-chem. fields 1956-68. U.S. Coast Guard, 1943-46. Hobby: golf. Home: 224 Nata, Newport Beach, CA 92660; Office: 2100 S.E. Main St., Irvine, CA 92714.

BERGER, OTTO
Senior Engineer
b. Feb. 16, 1927, Vienna, Austria; s. Max and Sophie

(Lichtman) Berger; B.E.E., City COII., N.Y., 1950; M.S.E.E., Johns Hopkins Univ., 1956; Engr. degree, Stanford Univ., 1969; m. Joyce Brouillette, Sept. 8, 1951, Crown Point, Ind. Career: electro-mech. engr., The Martin Co., 1950-58: Matador and Vanguard Programs, electro-mech. group head, Vanguard Prog. 1956-58; Lockhood Missiles & Space Co., 1958---: Agena, Ranger, Mariner Programs; mgr. test engring., Cape Canaveral, 1960-64. Patentee: Automatic Autopilot Analyzer, 1956. USN, 1945-46. Fellow, Am. Inst. Aeros and Astronatuics; mem. IEEE, Sigma Xi, Tau Beta Pi, Eta Kappa Nu. Home: 216 Creekside Dr., Palo Alto, CA 94306; Office: P.O.B. 504, Sunnyvale, CA 94088.

BERGERON, LIONEL LEE
Petroleum Company Executive
b. June 9, 1939, Putnam, Conn.; s. Lionel Emile and Anne (Hodgkinson) Bergeron; B.A., Seton Hall Univ., 1964; M.B.A., Univ. of New Haven, 1973; m. Catherine Murphy, Red Bank, N.J., June 12, 1971; chil.: Ellen Ann, b. Aug. 30, 1973; Lionel David, b. Jan. 8, 1976; Damien Lee and Sandra Elaine (twins), b. May 15, 1977. Career: Supervising systems analyst, Travelers Ins. Co., Hartford, Conn., 1972-74; sr. cons. — W. Coast mfg., Office Mgmt. Systems Inc., N.Y.C., 1974; mgr., word processing/administrv. services, Occidental Exploration & Prodn. Co. (subs. Occidental Petroleum Corp.), Bakersfield, Calif., 1974-76, mgr., administrv. systems and security, 1976-78; dir., administrv. systems & security, Occidental Oil and Gas Corp., 1978---. Directs worldwide corporate activities in areas of safety, security; domestically, responsible for develop. & coordination of EEO, AAP & OSHA regulations & programs. USAF, 1957-61. Recipient Pride in Personal Performance award, Western Electric Co., 1965. Mem.: Internat. Word Processing Assn. (dir., 1976); Assn. Systems Mgmt.; Am. Inst. Indsl. Engrs.; Am. Soc. for Indsl. Security. Contrb. articles to profl. publs. Office: Occidental Petroleum Corp., 5000 Stockdale Hwy., Bakersfield, CA 93309.

BERGESON, MARIAN
California Assemblywoman
b. Salt Lake City, Utah; d. Ivan Herbert and Clara Greenwood (Hunter) Crittenden; student, UCLA, 1945-48; B.A., Brigham Young Univ., 1949; m. Garth Stewart Bergeson, 1950; chil.: Nancy (Mrs. Mark Freeman), Garth Jr., Julie Ann, James. Career: mem. Bd. Edn., Newport Beach City Sch. Dist., 1964-65; Newport Mesa Unified Sch. Dist., 1965-77; mem. Juvenile Justice Commn., Orange Co., 1976-78; mem. Calif. State & Orange Co. Republican Central Coms., 1978---; elected Calif. State Assemblywoman, 74th Dist., 1978---. Bd. dir., Orange Co. Sch. Bd. Assn.; pres., Calif. Sch. Bd. Assn.; mem. United Way. Awards: PTA life mem. & cont. service award, 1966, 1975; AAUW Community Service Award, 1973; Newport Harbor C. of C. award, 1967. Latter-day Saints. Home: 1721 Tradewinds Lane, Newport Beach, CA; Office: 833 Dover Dr., Suite 7, Newport Beach, CA 92663.

BERGIN, WILLIAM FRANCIS
Surgeon — University Professor
b. June 2, 1922, Wichita Falls, Tex.; s. Thomas A. and Lillian (Hoffer) Bergin; ed. USC 1947-52; M.D., Harvard Med. Sch. 1952-56; m. Julie Bishop, Denver, Colo., Aug. 2, 1968; chil.: Pamela Susan Shoop, b. June 7, 1947; Steven Allen Shoop, b. Apr. 26, 1950. Career: Commercial pilot, 1945-46; spec. tr. surg. 1956-61; pvt. practice surg. 1961---; asst. clin. prof. surg. Univ. of Calif., Irvine, 1962---. Contrib. to surg. journs. Maj., USAAF 1941-45, WW II. Awards: Distinguished Flying Cross with Oak Leaf Clusters; Air Medal with Oak Leaf Cluster; Order of White Cloud China Burma Campaign with 3 Battle Stars; Little of Commendation (China). Mem.: past pres. Wadsworth Surg. Soc.; Am. Bd. of Surg.; Bay Dist. Surg. Soc.; fellow, Am. Coll. of Surgs.; Internat. Platform Assn.; L.A. World Affairs Council. Hobby: painting. Rec.: flying, hunting, fishing, skiing. Home: 417 Amapola Ln., L.A., CA 90024; Office: 465 N. Roxbury Dr., Beverly Hills, CA 90210.

BERGMAN, ALAN M.
Attorney At Law
b. Jan. 5, 1941, Bayonne, N.J.; s. Leo H. and Gertrude Bergman; A.B., Rutgers Univ., 1962; LL.B., Seton Hall Sch. of Law, J.D., 1965; m. Myrna Friedman, Teaneck. N.J., July 14, 1963; chil.: Scott, b. Aug. 9, 1966; Eric, b. Feb. 27, 1968. Career: asst. & secty. & gen. counsel, Daylin, Inc., 1966-75; v.p. & gen. counsel, First Charter Financial Corp., 1975-77; house counsel, R & B Develop. Co., 1977---. Dir. Kidney Foundation of So. Calif. Mem.: N.J. (1965) and California (1975) Bars. Mem.: Bar Assns. of L.A., Beverly Hills and Am.; Calif. Savs. & Loan

League (attys. com.). Hobbies: tennis, swimming. Office: 2222 Corinth Ave., L.A., CA 90064.

BERGSING, PATRICIA MARGARET
City Librarian
b. Chicago, III.; B.A., Univ. of Montana, 1954; M.L.S., Univ. Calif., Berkeley, 1955; m. Richard M. Bergsing, 1955, San Francisco. Career: Supr. Circulation Dept., Univ. of Montana, 1955-57; branch librarian, Burlingame Public Library, 1958-61; children's librarian, 1961-64; asst. city librarian, 1965-77; city librarian, 1977---. Bd. dir., Coop. Information Network 1975-78; bd. dir., public lib. execs. of No. Calif. 1976-80; past pres., Peninsula Lib. Assn. 1969-70; Mem.: pres., Soroptimist Internat. of Burlingame - San Mateo 1978-79; Burlingame Hist. Soc., Peninsula Press Club; San Mateo Co. Hist. Assn.; San Mateo Co. Arts Council. Rec.: golf, theater. Home: No. 5 Vine St., San Carlos, CA 94070; Office: 480 Primrose Rd., Burlingame, CA 94010.

BERGSTEDT, LINDA STROH
Editor
b. Mar. 26, 1939, Upland, Calif.; d. Conrad Henry and Naoma Elizabeth (Keplinger) Stroh; student, Chaffey Coll., Alta Loma, 1957-59; m. Donald L. Bergstedt, May 27, 1972, Ontario, Calif.; stepchil.: Beverly (Bouma); Barbara (Reed); Carol (Lind). Career: asst. women's editor, Daily Report, Ontario, Calif., 1960-62; women's editor, 1962---; tchr. of creating writing, Chase-King Personal Develop. Center, Upland, 1973. Recipient March of Dimes Press Award, 1970, 71; Am. Cancer Soc. award, 1971; Charter mem. & officer, Press Club of So. Calif., first place award for best news story 1973. Ch. of the New Jerusalem, Swedenborg. Hobbies: gardening, gourmet cooking. Home: 1459 N. First Ave., Upland, CA 91786; Office: 212 E. B St., Ontario, CA 91764.

BERKOVITZ, IRVING H.
Physician
b. July 12, 1924, Boston, Mass.; s. Morris and Frances (Fuxon) Berkovitz; A.B., Harvard Coll., 1945; M.D., Boston Univ. Med. Sch., 1950; m. Anne Marie Stern, Oct. 25, 1953, L.A.; chil.: Karen Dell, b. 1956; Glenn Evan, b. 1958; Joel David, b. 1961. Career: Med. internship, Wadsworth VA Hosp., L.A., 1950-51; psychiatric residency, Brentwood VA Hosp., L.A., 1951-54; psychoanalytic training, 1951-60; pvt. practice med. specializing in psychiatry, 1954---; sr. psychiatric cons. for schs., L.A. Co. Dept. of Mental Health, 1964---. Pvt., AUS M.C., 1943-44. Author: Adolescents Grow in Groups: Experiences in Adolescent Group Psychotherapy, 1972; When Schools Care, Creative Use of Groups in Secondary Schools, 1975; contbr. articles & book chpts. in field. Pres., L.A. Group Psychotherapy Soc., 1966-68; pres., So. Calif. Psychoanalytic Soc., 1975-76. Hobbies: tennis, photog. Office: 11980 San Vicente Blvd., Suite 710, L.A., CA 90049.

BERL, WARREN H.
Chairman of Board, Sutro & Co., Inc.
b. Aug. 24, 1920, San Francisco; s. Edwin D. and Selma (Green) Berl; ed. A.B., Stanford Univ. 1942; m. Aline Meyer, S.F., Jan. 2, 1948; chil.: Douglas A., b. Oct. 7, 1948; Cathryn L., b. May 25, 1951; Susan A., b. Nov. 30, 1953. Career: Partner, Edwin D. Berl & Sons, 1946-57; partner, Sutro & Co., 1957-69; pres. 1970-71; chmn.-pres. 1971-73; chmn. bd. 1973---. Chmn. bd. Pacific Coast Stock Exch. 1961; dir. S.F. C. of C., 1965---; Stanford Athletic Bd. 1967-72; gov. Am. Stock Exch. 1968-71; dir. N.Y. Stock Exch., 1972-75; v. chmn. Securities Ind. Assn. 1972; Jewish Welfare Fed. Finance Com.; v. chmn. United S.F. Repub. Finance Com. 1975-76. USNR Line Officer, 1942-45. Clubs: Stock Exch., S.F. Bond, Pac.-Union, The Family, Spyglass Hill Golf, Lake Merced Golf and Country. Home: 1070 Green St., No. 1501, S.F., CA; Office: 460 Montgomery St., S.F., CA 94104.

BERNACCHI, RICHARD LLOYD
Attorney At Law
b. Dec. 15, 1938, L.A., Calif., s. Bernard and Anne Bernacchi; B.C.S. in Accounting, Univ. of Santa Clara, 1961; LL.B., USC, 1964; m. Shauna Sorensen, Oct. 30, 1964; 1 dau. Vanessa Allison, b. June 26, 1968. Career: joined law firm of Irell & Manella, 1966, partner, 1970---. Officer, U.S. Army in Air Defense Artillery, 1964-66. Awards: Delta Sigma Pi Scholastic Key, Quartermaster Assn. Medal and Scholastic Key; Distinguished Military Grad., Law Sch.; Law Alumni Award. Order of the Coif; editor-in-chief, USC Law Review. Mem.: Am. Bar Assn., Beverly Hills Bar Assn., L.A. Co. Bar, Computer Law Assn. (W. coast v.p. and dir.). Co-author, Data Processing

Contracts and the Law (Little, Brown & Co., 1974). Mem.: Phi Delta Phi legal fraternity (grad. of the Year, 1964). Hobbies: tennis, skiing. Office: 1800 Ave. of the Stars, L.A., CA 90067.

BERNARDI, THEODORE C.
Architect
b. Oct. 3, 1903, Dalmatia, Yugoslavia; s. John A. and Vincenza (Depolo) Bernardi; B.A., Univ. Calif., Berkeley, 1924, postgrad., 1925; m. Beatrice Boot, 1947, Reno; chil.: d. Gene, b. 1928; d. Joan (Breece), b. 1930. Career: draftsman, designer, architect, S.F., 1923-43; partner, Wurster, Bernardi and Emmons, 1944-64; exec. v.p., Wurster, Bernardi and Emmons, Inc., 1964-73; cons., 1974---; lectr., UC Berkeley, 1954-71. Recipient, 1st annual award and award of merit, Nat. AIA, 1956; Archtl. firm award, 1965, Collaborative Achievement Award, Award of Merit, 1966; two awards of merit, No. Calif. chpt., AIA, 1957. Chmn. Archtl. Design Com., S.F. Housing Authority, 1965-69; chmn., Reynolds Award Jury, 1968; chmn., Archtl. Advis. Com., Rte. 17, Marin Co. Plan. Com., 1966-67. Fellow, AIA, 1962; mem. 1944---; bd. dir., 1966; mem. SPUR; mem. Commonwealth Club, 1945---; Tau Beta Pi Hon. Soc., 1927; mem. World Affairs Council. Hobby: foreign travel. Home: 99 Miller Lane, Sausalito, CA 94965; Office: 1620 Montgomery St., S.F., CA 94111.

BERNHARD, HERBERT ASHLEY
Attorney at Law
b. Sept. 24, 1927, Jersey City, N.J.; s. Richard C. and Amalie (Lobl) Bernhard; student, Mexico City Coll., 1938; B.S., N.J. Inst. of Tech., 1949; M.A., Columbia, 1950; J.D. cum laude, Univ. Mich., 1957; m. Nancy Ellen Hirschaut, Aug. 18, 1954; chil.: Linda, b. Jan. 21, 1957; Alison, b. Sept. 3, 1959; Jordan, b. Nov. 24, 1961; Melissa, b. Feb. 15, 1969. Career: Research engr., Curtiss-Wright Co., Caldwell, N.J., 1950-52; research engr., Boeing Aircraft Co., Cape Canaveral, Fla., 1952-55; instr., math, Univ. of Fla., 1952-55; instr. elect. eng., Univ. of Mich. 1955-57; admitted to Calif. Bar 1958; assoc. with O'Melveny & Myers, L.A., 1957-62; partner Greenberg, Bernhard, Weiss & Karma, Inc., 1962---. Recipient Henry M. Bates Award, Univ. of Mich. Law Review, 1957; mem. Am., Calif., L.A. Co. Bar Assns. V.p., So. Calif. Div. Am. Jewish Congress, chmn. advis. com. of Skirball Museum; bd. of Overseers Hebrew Union Coll. USAAF, 1946-47. Mem.: Order of Coif, Tau Beta Pi, Omicron Delta Kappa, Mulholland Tennis Club. Rec.: tennis, skiing. Home: 1105 Tower Rd., Beverly Hills, CA 90210; Office: 1880 Century Park E., No. 1150, L.A., CA 90067.

BERNHEIMER, MARTIN
Music Editor — Critic, Los Angeles Times
b. Sept. 28, 1936, Munich, Germ.; s. Paul and Louise Bernheimer; ed. grad. Norton (Mass.) Center Sch. 1950; Attleboro H.S. 1954; B.A. (hons.), Brown Univ. 1958; Munich Cons. 1959; M.A. (music), NYU 1961; m. Lucinda Pearson, Essex, Conn., Sept. 30, 1961; chil.: Mark Richard, b. June 19, 1964; Nora Nicoll, b. Mar. 17, 1967; Marina and Erika (twins), b. Dec. 16, 1969. Career: Tchr., NYU 1960-62; music staff, N.Y. Herald Tribune, 1959-62; contrib. ed., Musical Courier, 1959-62; mng. ed., Philharmonic Hall Pgm. Mag. 1962-65; asst. music ed., Sat. Review, 1962-65; music critic, N.Y. Post, 1964-65; music ed.-chief critic, L.A. Times, 1965---. Faculty: USC, 1965-71; Calif. UCLA, 1969-75; Calif. Inst. of the Arts, 1975---; Cal State Northridge, 1977---. Contrib. to N.Y. Times, Mus. Quarterly, The Critic, Opera News, Musical Am., Chr. Sci. Monitor, OPERA (Brit.), Abendzeitung (Munich), High Fidelity, Hi-Fi Stereo Review, The Nation, Commonweal, Aufbau (N.Y.), Der Merker (Vienna), Met. Opera Pgm. Mag., State Theater Pgm. Mag. (N.Y.), Music Journ., Pageant; music articles syn. by L.A. Times, other publs., U.S.; writer, liner annotations for RCA Victor, Columbia, London Records. Appd. AM and FM radio, TV interviews and panels. Home: L.A., CA; Office: Times-Mirros Sq., L.A., CA 90053.

BERNSTEIN, ELMER
Composer
b. Apr. 4, 1922, N.Y.C.; s. Edward and Selma (Feinstein) Bernstein; piano scholarship with Henriette Michelson, 1939-49; composition study with Israel Citkowitz, Roger Sessions, Ivan Langstrogh, Stefan Wolpe; grad., Walden Sch., N.Y.C., 1939; studied music edn., N.Y. Univ., 1939-42; m. Pearl Glusman, Dec. 21, 1946; chil.: Peter Matthew, b. Apr. 10, 1951; Gregory Eames, b. July 5, 1955; m. 2d. Eve Adamson, Oct. 25, 1965, Acapulco, Mex.; chil.: Emily Adamson, b. July 22, 1968; Elizabeth Campbell, b. Nov. 14, 1970. Career: concert pianist, 1939-50; (currently mus. dir., San Fernando Valley

Symphony); composed radio scores for USAF radio, Glenn Miller's I Sustain the Wings; U.N. radio scores, 1949; music composer for motion pictures, 1950---: rec. Academy Award for Thoroughly Modern Millie, 1967; nominated for Academy Awards: The Man With the Golden Arm, 1955; The Magnificent Seven, 1960; Summer and Smoke, 1961; Walk On the Wild Side, 1961; To Kill A Mockingbird, 1962; Return of the Seven, 1966; Hawaii, 1966; "My Wishing Doll" from Hawaii, 1966; rec. Emmy award for The Making Of a President, 1960 (1963); rec. Downbeat Award for Toccata for Toy Trains, 1958. Bd. mem., Acad. of Motion Picture Arts and Scis., 1960---; pres. Young Musicians Found., 1960---; Bd. Gov., Performing Arts Council of Music Center, 1967---; bd. gov. Screen Composers Assn., 1959---; pres. Composers & Lyricists Guild of Am., 1970---; mem. Am. Fedn. Musicians; Am. Soc. Music Arrangers; Screen Composers Assn.; Dramatists Guild; Am. Soc. Composers, Authors, and Publishers. Hobby: raising thoroughbred horses. Rec.: boating. Rep., Alvin Bart, Bart/Levy Assoc., Inc., 8601 Wilshire Blvd., Beverly Hills, CA 90211; Address: P.O.B. 25198, L.A., CA 90025.

BERNSTEIN, SOL
Director, L.A. County-USC Medical Center
b. Feb. 3, 1927, West N.Y., N.J.; s. Morris and Rose (Leibowitz) Bernstein; A.B., bacteriology, USC, 1951; M.D., 1956; m. Suzi Maris Sommer, Sept. 15, 1963, L.A.; son, Paul M., b. Nov. 2, 1967. Career: instr. medicine, USC, 1960-63; asst. prof., 1963-67; assoc. prof. of med., 1967---; asst. dir. of Dept. of Med., USC 1965-72; Chief of Profl. Services, Gen. Hosp., L.A. Co.-USC Med. Center, 1972-74; med. dir., LAC-USC Med. Center, 1974---. Bd. Dir., Central Area Tchng. Hosps., L.A., 1974---; acting dir., L.A. Co. Dept. of Health Service, 1978; acting deputy dir., L.A. Co. Central Region, 1977---. PFC, AUS, Infan. 1946-47, Japan; AUS, unassigned, USA, 1952-53. Contbr. articles on cardiac surgery, cardiology and diabetes to med. journs.; participant in films: Two Unusual Open Heart Opns., Diagnosis of Ventricular Septal Defects, Upjohn Pharm. Mem.: L.A. Co. Med. Assn.; L.A. Co. Heart Assn., bd. dir.; Diabetes Assn. of So. Calif., L.A. Soc. Internal Med.; Assn. Physicians, L.A. Co. Hosps.; L.A. Acad. of Med.; Fellow, Am. Coll. of Physicians; Fellow, Am. Coll. of Cardiology; Am. Fedn. Clin. Research; N.Y. Acad. of Sciences; Am. Heart Assn.; AMA; Am. Acad. Med. Directors; Sigma Xi; Phi Kappa Phi; Phi Beta Kappa; Alpha Omega Alpha. Home: 4966 Ambrose Ave., L.A., CA 90027; Office: LAC-USC Medical Center, 1200 N. State St., Rm. 1110, L.A., CA 90033.

BERQUIST, JAMES RICHARD
Actuary
b. June 29, 1928, Tomahawk, Wis., s. Henry Joseph and Francis (Emmerich) Berquist; father — Wis. legislator, co. bd. mem. 20+ years; A.B., Univ. of Mich., 1953; m. Elaine D. Sajna, Rhinelander, Wis., June 10, 1950; chil.: Richard J., Mary J., Thomas J., John C., Terese M. Career: Assoc. actuary, Employers Ins. of Wasau (Wis.), 1953-68; v.p., actuary, Transamerica Ins. Co., L.A., 1968-71; cons. actuary, prin., Milliman & Robertson, Inc., Pasadena, 1971---. USNR, 1946-68, 1950-51. Mem.: Fellow Casualty Actuarial Soc., dir., 1968-70; Am. Academy of Actuaries; Internat. Assn. of Actuaries (ASTIN sect.). Home: 5130 Hayman Ave., La Canada, CA 91011; Office: 251 S. Lake Ave., Suite 400, Pasadena, CA 91101.

BERRISFORD, CHRISTOPHER
Headmaster, The Harvard School
b. Liphook, England; s. Edwin Aris and Susan Helen (Claughton) Berrisford; B.A., Oxford, 1954; M.A., 1957; Ed.M., Harvard, 1962; m. Brenda Houfton, Mar. 23, 1963, London, Engl; chil.: Nicholas, b. Mar. 24, 1964; Sara, b. May 1, 1967. Career: chmn., History Dept., University Sch., Victoria, B.C., Can., 1954-57; Dean, 1957-61, asst. head, 1961-63, Headmaster, St. Mark Sch. of Texas (Dallas), 1963-69; headmaster, Harvard Sch., N. Hollywood, 1969---. Mem., Overseers visiting com., Harvard Grad. Sch. of Edn. 1966-72; vice-chmn., City of Dallas Task Force on Health, 1968-69; trustee; Southwest Outward Bound, Crossroads Sch., Independent Schools Overseas, UCLA Arts Council. Served to 2nd Lt. Royal Artillery, 1948-50. Mem. Headmasters Assn., 1972---; Country Day Sch. Headmasters Assn., 1966---. Home-Office: 3700 Coldwater Canyon Rd., No. Hollywood, CA 91604.

BERRYHILL, JOHN RAY
Attorney at Law
b. Sept. 14, 1914, Tulare, Calif.; s. John Wilbur and Gladys Alma (Ray) Berryhill; A.B., Calif. State Univ. Fresno, 1938; J.D. Hastings Coll. of Law, S.F., 1941; m.

Helen Schorling, Oct. 10, 1941, Fresno; Chil.: John A., b. Mar. 3, 1943; Bruce R., b. May 30, 1947; Keith R., b. Jan. 6, 1952. Career: Spec. Agent FBI, 1941-46; pvt. practice of law, Tulare, Calif., 1946---; City Atty., Tulare, 1950---; asst. secty., J.D. Heiskell & Co., 1976---. Bd. Dir. & Secty., J.D. Heiskell & Co., 1968-76. Pres., Tulare Co. Bar Assn., 1956; pres., Tulare C. of C., 1960; mem. Tulare Elks Lodge, Tulare Rotary Club, pres. 1966. Home: 653 Cherry St., Tulare, CA 93274; Office: 145 N. N St., Tulare, CA 93274.

BERTHOLD, JEANNE SAYLOR
Director of Nursing Education and Research
b. June 4, 1928, Kansas City, Mo.; d. Carl Richard and Anne Elisabeth (Wolfe) Saylor; B.S., Univ. Calif., Berkeley, 1953, M.S. (psychiat. nursing), 1955, Ph.D. (counseling Psychol.), 1961; div. Career: Public Health Staff Nurse, 1945-46; School Nurse, L.A., 1946-47; Sonoma Co. Hosp. staff asst., Santa Rosa, 1947-51; psychiatric nurse, Langley Porter Neuro-Psychiat. Inst., S.F., 1955-61; also instr., lectr., UC Med. Center, S.F., 1955-61; asst. prof. to prof., Case Western Reserve Univ. Sch. of Nursing, Cleveland, Ohio, 1961-71; prof. adjoint., Univ. of Colo. Sch. of Nursing, 1971-73; prof., USC Sch. of Med., 1973---; dir. of nursing research, Rancho Los Amigos Hosp., Downey, 1973-75, dir. Nursing Research and Edn., 1975---. Contbr. articles profl. journs. Mem. Awards Com., Am. Congress Rehabilitation Med., 1976---; mem.: Inst. of Society, Ethics, Life Sci., the Hastings Center; Center for Study Democratic Instns.; AAAS; N.Y. Acad. of Sci.; Nat. Council Measurement in Edn.; Am. Ednl. Research Assn.; AAUP; Am. Psychol. Assn.; Am. Nurses Assn., nat., state, local dist.; Calif. Alumni Assn.; Nat. League for Nursing; Highland Alumnae Assn. Presbyterian. Home: 10330 Downey Ave., No. 8, Downey, CA; Office: Rancho Los Amigos Hosp., 7601 E. Imperial Hwy., Downey, CA 90242.

BERTRAM, JEAN DESALES
Author — Professor of Theatre Arts
b. Sept. 28, Burlington, Ia.; d. Val Randall and Ruth Cecelia (Gustafson) Bertram; great-great-grandau. of Herr Aschler, Burgomeister, Hamburg, Germ., circa 1850-60; great-granddau. of Randall Wright, Phila, Pa.; granddau of George Bertram, Killarney, Ire.; ed. B.A., Univ. of N.V., Greensboro, 1942; M.A., Univ. of Minn. 1951; Ph.D., Stanford Univ. 1963; (div.) son, Larkin, b. June 20, 1961. Career: Actress, radio and little theatre; reporter, Greensboro News-Record Co., N.V., 1942-43; founder, Pub. Rels. Dept., Burlington Indus. (world's largest textile firm), Greensboro, 1943-49; dir. Radio Workshop, Minneapolis Vocational H.S. 1951-52; prof. of theatre arts, S.F. State Univ. Sch. of Creative Arts, 1952---; dir. 60 touring shows, 1968-76. Author: (book) "The Oral Experience of Literature," Chandler Publ. Co. 1967; American Cameos, an original musical commemorating the Bicentennial of the U.S., endorsed by the Am. Revolution Bicentennial Assn., produced & toured in 1976. numerous articles publ. profl. theatre and speech journs. Award: Stanford Wilson fellowship, 1962-63; Mem.: Phi Beta Kappa, 1942; Delta Phi Lambda, 1951; pres. No. Calif. Assn. of Phi Beta Kappa, 1963-65. Charter mem., secty., Omicron chpt., SFSU, 1977---; Republican. Chr. Sci. (chmn. Lecture Com., Finance Co., clerk). Hobby: collecting st. car token from all parts of world. Rec.: golf, hiking, writing poetry. Home: 512 Arballo Dr., S.F., CA; Office: Creative Arts Bldg., S.F. State Univ., 1600 Holloway Ave., S.F., CA 94132.

BETSON, JOHNNIE RICHARD, JR.
Obstetrician — Gynecologist
b. Dec. 6, 1928, Ft. Worth, Tex.; s. Johnnie Richard, Sr. and Prebble (Lewis) Betson; ed. B.S., East Central Okla. State Coll. 1950; M.D., Univ. of Okla. Sch. of Med. 1955; m. Joan Sue Schroeder, Appleton, Wis., June 20, 1955; chil.: Kevin Carey, b. Mar. 31, 1959; Pamela Sue, b. June 2, 1961; Lance Hall, b. Sept. 6, 1964. Career: Intern, Milwaukee (Wis.) Co. Gen. Hosp. 1955-56; res. (spec. obstets. and gynecology), Charity Hosp. of La., New Orleans, 1956-59; staff, Lovelace Clinic and Found. for Med. Research, Albuquerque, N. Mex. 1959-62; est. pvt. practice, Costa Mesa, CA; v-chmn., dept. obstets.-gynecology, Hoag Mem. Hosp., Newport Beach, 1967---; cons. Fairview State Hosp., Costa Mesa; cons. Children's Hosp. of Orange Co.; attending staff, Univ. of Calif., Irvine, Med. Center, Orange, Calif.; chief of staff, Costa Mesa (Calif.) Mem. Hosp., 1968-69. Contrib. 37 med. papers to profl. journs.; 2 surg. mot. pics. Listed various publs. feat. personalities of achievements, U.S.A., London, Eng., USMC, 1946-47. Mem.: bd. dirs., Costa Mesa Rotary Club, 1964, pres. 1968-69; diplomate, Am. Bd. of Obstets. and Gynecology; fellow, Am. Coll. of Obstets. and Gynecologists, 1965; fellow, Am. Med. Writers Assn. 1966; Orange Co. Obstet. and Gynecology

Assn., Am. Soc. Abdominal Surgs., AMA, Flying Surgs. Assn., Phi Chi. Republican. Presbyterian. Hobbies: flying, numismatics. Home: 1311 Galaxy Dr., Newport Beach, CA 92660; Office: 351 Hospital Rd., Suite 618, Newport Beach, CA 92660.

BETTER, NORMAN MICHAEL
Psychologist
b. June 25, 1935, Washington, D.C.; s. Samuel and Betty Better; B.A., American Univ., 1957; M.A., Stanford Univ., 1958; Ed.D., UCLA, 1965; m. Jennifer Reese, Sacto., Dec. 18, 1976; chil.: Jeffrey Kyle, b. Oct. 16, 1960; Kirby Lyle, b. Feb. 1, 1963. Career: European unit mgr., Robert Enders, Inc., M.G.M. Studios, 1956-58; Univ. of Calif., L.A., Berkeley and Riverside campuses, 1958-71, variously as placement counselor, Dean of Men, Dean of Students, Prof. of Counselor Ed., Asso. Dir. of Ed. Relations; Dean of Students, Psychologist, Dir. of Student Assistance, Calif. State Univ., Sacto., 1971---. Mem.: Governor's Com. on Criminal Justice, pres.; three co. com. on Architectural Barriers; cons., state com. of licensing of Sch. Counselors and Psychologist. Contrib. to Puppy Dogtails, univ. lit. mag. European unit mgr. film, Ambassadors with Wings. Papers presented: Discrimination against Women, Calif. Research Assn.; Games People Play, Natl. Affirmative Action Assn. Mem. hon. soc.: Beta Beta Beta, biological sciences; Phi Delta Kappa, ed.; Pi Delta Epsilon, journalism. Home: 1555 Barnett Cir., Carmichael, CA; Office: Calif. State Univ., Sacto., CA.

BETTS, BARBARA LANG
Attorney At Law — Rancher
b. Apr. 28, 1926, Anaheim, Calif.; d. W. Harold and Helen (Thompson) Lang; husband, former Calif. state treas.; B.A., Stanford Univ. (magna cum laude and Phi Beta Kappa), 1948; LL.B., Calif. Western Univ. (formerly Balboa Univ.), 1951; m. Bert A. Betts, S.F., July 11, 1962; chil.: J. Chauncey Hayes IV, b. Aug. 31, 1953; Frederick Prescott Hayes, b. Nov. 2, 1955; Roby F. Hayes II, b. July 11, 1957; Bruce Harold Betts, b. Nov. 14, 1966. Career: admitted to Calif. Bar, 1952; U.S. Dist. Ct., Southern and Northern Districts, Calif., 1952; U.S. Ct. of Appeals, 9th Circuit, 1952; U.S. Supreme Ct., 1978; partner, law firm Barbara Lang Hayes & Roby F. Hayes, 1952-60; city atty., Carlsbad, 1959-63; pvt. law practice, Oceanside, 1952-60, San Diego, 1960---, Sacto., 1962---; rancher 1948-58, 1967---. V.P., W.H. Lang Corp., 1964-70; secty., Internat. Prod. Assoc., 1967-72; v.p., Isle & Oceans Marinas, Inc., 1970---; secty., Margaret M. McCabe, M.D., Inc., 1976---. Mem.: Carlsbad Planning Com., 1959, v.p.; San Diego Co. Planning Congress. Secty., pub. affairs for S.D. and Imperial Co., 1954, pres. of President's Council S.D. and Imperial Co. and Mexico, 1958-59, mem. 1952-62. Mem.: Bar Assns.: Am., S.D. Co., Calif. Trial Lawyers; Am. Judicature Soc., Nat. Inst. of Municipal Officers, 1959-63; U.S. Supreme Ct. Hist. Soc. Co-author with Bert A. Betts, A Citizen Answers, 1972. Mem.: Chambers of C.: Oceanside, S.D., No. S.D. Co. Assn. Mem.: Traveler's Aid, chmn, 1952-54; AAUW; Bus. and Profl. Women's Club, 1953-62; Calif. Scholarship Fed. (life); Soroptimist Internat.; S.D. Hist. Soc.; Fullerton Jr. Asst. League, 1956-66; D.A.R., 1956-64; No. S.D. Co. chpt. for retarded chil., dir. 1957-58. Mem.: Dem. state central com., 1954-62; co-chmn. 28th cong. dist. dem. central com., 1960-62; delegate, dem. nat. convention, 1960. Protestant. Rec.: fishing & hunting. Home: Betts Ranch, Elverta, CA 95626; Office: 8701 E. Levee Rd. Elverta; 3119 Howard Ave., S.D., CA 92104.

BETTS, HON. BERT A.
Former Treasurer, State of California
b. Aug. 16, 1923, San Diego, Calif.; s. Bert A., Sr. and Alma (Jorgenson) Betts; ed. San Diego pub. schs.; S.D. State Coll. 1941; B.A., Calif. Western Univ., San Diego, 1950; CPA Certificate, Nov. 1950; grad. Internat. Acct. Soc.; m. Barbara Lang; chil.: Terry Lou, b. Sept. 24, 1946; Linda Sue, b. Sept. 1, 1947; Sara Ellen, b. Jan. 15, 1949; Bert Alan, b. Oct. 19, 1950; Randy Wayne, b. Nov. 12, 1952; John Chauncey, b. Aug. 31, 1953; Frederick Prescott, b. Nov. 2, 1955; Le Ann, b. Feb. 18, 1956; Roby F., b. Sept. 11, 1957; Bruce Harold, b. Nov. 14, 1966. Career: Partner, CPA firm, 1950, principal, 1951-59; coll. tchr. (acct.-tax.), 1950-58; elected State Treas. of Calif. 1958, re-elected 1962-67 (youngest ever elected to a State Constitutional office; also first exec. officer on state level from San Diego Co. in this century). Propr. Betts Financial, Real Estate and Mgmt. Cons. firm, 1967-77; treas.-chief exec. officer Internat. Prodn. Assocs., 1968-72; trustee, Fidelity Mortgage Investors, 1970-78; dir., Lifetime Communities, Inc., 1978---. B-24 Bomber Pilot, Eighth Air Force, USAAF (30 combat missions over Europe), 1941-45, WW II. Awards: 4 air

medals; Distinguished Flying Cross. Mem.: past 1st v.p., San Diego chpt., Calif. Soc. of CPAs; (past) State Soc. Governmental Acct. Com.; AM. Inst. of CPAs, Natl. Assn. of Accts., Am. Acct. Assn.; past pres., Lemon Grove Sch. Dist. Bd. of Trustees; Past pres., Lemon Grove Men's Club; (past) finance com., S.D. Girl Scouts; citizens adv. coms. to govt. agencies; past treas., S.D. Cerebral Palsy Found.; past v-comdr., Air Force Assn.; past treas., Lemon Grove Lions Club; V.F.W., Am. Leg.; active in B.S.A., treas. Cub Pack 106, Sacto.; Internat. Order of Foresters, (past) Natl. Assn. of State Auditors, Comptrollers, and Treas.; Municipal Forum of N.Y.; (hon.) Calif. Municipal Treasurer's Assn.; pres. Sacto. Co. Am. Cancer Soc. 1967-68; Beta Alpha Psi; Alpha Kappa Psi, Eagles Lodge, Lemon Grove Masonic Lodge. Democrat. (S.D. Co. Dem. Central Com.). Presbyterian. Home: Betts' Ranch, East Levee Road, Elverta, CA; 441 Sandburg Dr., Sacto., CA 95819.

BEUYUKIAN, CHARLES SAM
Aerospace Company Administrator
b. Jan. 10, 1923, Chicago, Ill.; s. Sam and Grace (Garabedian) Beuyukian; student, pub. schs., Chicago; coll. courses: technical, mgmt., academic, fin. m. Mary Panosian, L.A., Apr. 13, 1947; chil.: Linda Marie, b. Nov. 22, 1948; Charles Stephen, b. Aug. 28, 1951. Career: process eng., Northrop Aircraft, Hawthorne, 1950-62; metallurgist, Autonetics Div., No. Am. Aviation, Anaheim, 1962-64; sr. metallurgist, Rockwell Internat., Downey, 1964-75, project mgr. and develop. spec., 1964---. Responsible for technical direction of numerous fabrication programs on Apollo and Shuttle Space Vehicles: aircraft and space vehicle brazing spec. Patents: Tube dimpling tool, 1968; brazing process, 1970. Numerous inventions and NASA tech. briefs, 1966---. Tech. papers publ., 1968, '71, '72, '78. Recipient: NASA—Astronaut's Personal Achievement Award, 1975; Special NASA Technology Award, 1975; NASA-Certificate of Recognition, 1975; Rockwell Internat.-Engr. of the Year, 1978 nominee. Mem.: Am. Soc. for Metals (ASM); Am. Welding Soc. (AWS); Nat. Mgmt. Assn.; welding adv. com., El Camino Coll. Office: Rockwell Internat., Space Systems Group, 12214 Lakewood Blvd., Downey, CA 90241.

BEVERETT, ANDREW JACKSON
Company President
b. Feb. 21, 1917, Midland City, Ala.; s. Andrew J. and Ella L. (Adams) Beverett; B.S., Samford Univ, 1940; M.B.A., Harvard Univ., 1942; m. Martha Sophia Landgrebe, Chicago, Ill., May 26, 1951; chil.: Andrew J. III, James Edmund, Faye A. Career: Exec. positions in corp. planning and mgmt., United Air Lines, Chicago, 1946-66; sr. marketing and econ. cons., Mgmt. & Economics Research, Inc., Palo Alto, 1966-71; sr. econ., Stanford Research Inst., Menlo Park, 1971-72; pres., Edy's on the Peninsula Stores, Palo Alto, 1972---. Active duty, Ensign to Lt., USNR, 1942-46. Mem.: Phi Kappa Phi; Pi Gamma Mu; Am. Marketing Assn.; Toastmasters Club. Home: 19597 Via Monte Dr., Saratoga, CA 95070; Office: 73 Town and Country Village, Palo Alto, CA 94301.

BIAGGINI, BENJAMIN F.
Chairman, President, CEO, Southern Pacific Company
b. Apr. 15, 1916, New Orleans, La.; s. Benjamin F., Sr., and Maggie (Switzer) Biaggini; ed. B.S. (magna cum laude) St. Mary's Univ. of Tex. 1936; Harvard Bus. Sch. (AMP), 1955; m. Anne Payton, San Antonio, Tex., Sept. 9, 1937; daus.: Mrs. James Spencer (Constance Sue) Malott; Mrs. David M. (Marian Anne) Krattebol. Career: Assoc. with So. Pac. Co. 1936---, asst. to chief engr., Houston, 1951-53, exec. asst. 1953-54, asst. to exec. v.p., 1954-55, v.p. 1955-56, v.p., S.F. 1956-63, exec. v.p.-dir. 1963-64, pres. 1964-68, pres.-chief exec. ofcr.-dir. 1968-75, chmn.-pres.-chief exec. ofcr.-dir. 1976---. Director: Tenneco, Inc., Assn. of Am. Railroads, SRI Internat. Mem.: The Business Council, The Conf. Board, The Bus. Roundtable, Transportation Comm., U.S. C. of C., Am. Railway Engring. Assn., Nat. Transp. Policy Study Comm (apptd. by Pres. of U.S.). Co-chmn.: Calif. Roundtable. Trustee: Calif. Inst. of Tech., Natl. Safety Council, Transp. Safety Council, Transp. Council of Calif. Clubs: Pac. Union, Bohemian (S.F.). Hobby: photog. Rec.: golf. Office: So. Pacific Co., SP Bldg., One Market Plaza, S.F., CA 94105.

BIDDLE, WALTER SCOTT
Land Development Executive
b. Apr. 12, 1927, Ogden, Ut.; s. Walter S. and Marjorie (Turner) Biddle; ed. grad. Ogden H.S. 1945; Weber Coll., Ogden, Ut. 1946-47; B.B.A., Univ. of N. Mex. 1950. m. LaVonne Shepherd Wickman, Las Vegas, Nev., Apr. 11, 1964; chil.: J. Gary, b. Jan. 3, 1952; Gregory S., b. June

17, 1953; Cynthia Wickman, b. Apr. 5, 1949; Shelley Jo Wickman, b. Oct. 29, 1951; Bobbette Wickman, b. Nov. 12, 1952. Career: Salesman, Pellissier Dairy Farms, Pico Rivera, 1950, div. sales mgr. 1951, div. mgr. Yami Yogurt Div. 1952-54; mgr. So. Calif. Div., Milk Prods. Assn. of Central Calif., Modesto, 1954-56; gen. purchasing agt., Frank F. Pellissier & Sons, Inc., Pico Rivera, Calif. 1955-57; adm. asst. to pres.-dir. assoc. corps. 1957-61; secty.-gen. mgr., Molecular Engin., Inc., Costa Mesa, Calif. 1961-63; v.p.-gen. mgr., Hercules Constr. Co.-Suburbia Home, Santa Ana, 1963-65; v.p.-gen. mgr., Richard B. Smith, Inc., Broadmoor Homes, Inc., Tustin, 1965; exec. v.p. 1968; pres. Kavanaugh Dev., Inc., 1972---; pres. Biddle Dev. Corp., 1973---; chmn., Biddle/Carter Devel. Corp., San Diego, 1975---; pres., Building Industry Assn. of Calif. 1977-78; Calif. State Gen. Contr. and Real Estate Broker's licenses, Seaman (1/c), USNR (1945-46), WW II. Mem.: dir. Calif. State Jr. C. of C. 1952-61; v.p., 1957-59; pres., 1959-60; pres. Pico Jr. C. of C. 1954; dir. U.S. Jr. C. of C., 1957-61; natl. dir. 1958-59; Aircraft Owners and Pilots Assn.; Santa Ana B.P.O.E., Kappa Sigma, Alpha Kappa Psi, Balboa Bay Club, Big Canyon Country Club. Republican. Hobby: flying. Home: 1907 Yacht Puritan, Newport Beach, CA 92660; Office: 3848 Campus Dr., Newport Beach, CA 92660.

BIDWELL, ROBERT REDDINGTON
Physician — Orthopedic Surgeon
b. Sept. 25, 1913, Akron, O.; s. Carlyle Dickerman and Margaret (Scollins) Bidwell; desc. John Bidwell, founder, settler, Hartford, Conn. 1636; John Bidwell who led first wagon train into Calif. 1841; Shefield Bidwell, English pioneer in telephotography (1848-1909); Gen. Bidwell, Civil War; W.H. Bidwell, ed. Eclectic Mag. 1866; Rt. Rev. Edward J. Bidwell, Bishop of Kingston, 1913; grandson of T.S. Bidwell, surg., Ohio Volunteer Inf. 1863-64; ed. UCLA; M.D., USC 1938; postgrad. Mayo Clinic, 1944; m. Katharine Virginia Kennedy, Beverly Hills, Calif., Oct. 26, 1940; chil.: Mrs. Robert Dunlap (Barbara Hanscom) Hillman, b. June 13, 1942; Robert Reddington, Jr., b. June 20, 1946. Career: Est. Calif. res. 1923; pvt. practice orthopedic surg., L.A. 1945---; orthopedic cons., L.A. div. So. Pac. Co., 1945---; orthopedic staff: Calif., Calif. Baby and Chils., Santa Fe and French Hosps., L.A. Author: articles publ med. journs. Maj. (MC) U.S. Army, 1940-45; WW II. Awards: Cong. Cit. for "meritorious serv. over and above the call of duty." Mem.: Am. Calif., L.A. Co. Med. Assns.; Theta Xi, Nu Sigma Nu. Hobby: carpentry. Rec.: fly-fishing, boating. Home: 24550 Portola Rd., Carmel, CA 93923.

BIDWELL, VIRGINIA E.
Science Researcher — Author — Lecturer
b. Minneapolis, Minn.; d. Dr. Frank W. (noted chem) and Myrtle V. (Thompson) Emmons (violin soloist); desc.: Duke of Antrim, Scot.; Calif. pioneer, John Bidwell; Gen. David Bidwell, Buffalo, N.Y.; John Paul Jones, naval officer; ed. B.A., Univ. of Minn.; Ph.D., Calif.; m. Myron Chapman Bidwell, 1944 (dec.). Career: Radio-TV scripts, Chicago; agt. U.S.N. Intelligence, L.A. 1942-48; sci. research on atmospheric pollution with sci. doctors and mems. House and Senate, 1945---; assoc. with sci. group on radioactive fallout coord. I.G.Y., 1953---; founder, "Atoms for Peace Key" (drew plans for basic idea of Nuclear Non-Breeder Power Reactors, in use since 1954; also "Nose Cone"), 1954. Lectr. Author: "World of Honey, Milk and Fall-Out"; contrib to various sci. journs., periodicals. Mem.: Alpha Xi Delta, Internat. Platform Assn. Hobbies: Interior decorating, sculpturing, reading sci. materials, antiques. Home: P.O.B. 1626, Beverly Hills, CA 90213; P.O.B. 1289, La Jolla, CA 92037.

BIEBER, DAVID J.
President, Loma Linda University
b. Nov. 14, 1910, Tolstoy, S. Dak.; s. John and Kathryn Bieber; ed. M.A., Stanford Univ.; Univ. of Calif., Berkeley, Ed.D. 1971; m. Eva Mae LaFace, Aberdeen, S. Dak., Sept. 5, 1933; son, Donald Oliver, b. July 27, 1938. Career: Tchr., Oak Park Acad. 1936-39; Maplewood Acad. 1939-41; prin. 1941-45; prin. Hawaiian Mission Acad. 1945-49; Monterey Bay Acad. 1949-57; pres. La Sierra Coll., Riverside, Calif. 1964-67; pres. Loma Linda Univ. 1967-74; vice pres. for planning & devel., 1974-76; spec. representative for devel. 1976--- (semi retired). Contrib. articles to profl. journs. Mem.: Rotary Club, 1950---. Seventh-Day Adventists (mem. Gen. conf.; ordained minister). Hobby: gardening. Rec.: golf. Home: 11560 Hillcrest St., Loma Linda, CA 92354; Office: Loma Linda Univ., Loma Linda, CA 92354.

BIERMAN, EDWARD OTTO
Ophthalmologist
b. May 26, 1923, St. Louis, Mo.; s. Max John, M.D. and

Ida (Smolensky) Bierman; M.D., St. Louis Univ., 1947; M.O. (Ophthalmology), 1952; DNP (diplomate of nat. bd.), FAAOO (fellow, Am. Acad. Ophthalmology & Otolaryngology); m. Shirley Fox, Nov. 1947, St. Louis; chil.: Ellen Kessler, b. Aug. 1948; Steven, b. July 1949; Rhonda, b. Feb. 1951; Susan, b. Sept. 1952; James, b. July 1954. Career: med. internship and residency, St. Louis Univ., 1947-50; ophthalmologist, Ross-Loos Med. Group, 1953-58; pvt. practice, Santa Monica, 1953---. Secty. Jt. staffs, St. John's and Santa Monica Hosps., 1953-55. Scientific exhibits, Japan and China, 1978; author: sci. med. articles, pamphlets: The Holy Order, Godtemplation. USN, V-12, 1942-45; Capt. U.S. Army M.C., 1948-52. Mem.: Rotary, asst. secty. Pacific Palisades, dir. 1976---; B'nai Brith, Pac. Pal. pres.; BSA, fund chmn., 1976-77; Mem. bd. edn., Reform Judais, Univ. Synagogue, 1959-60. Hobbies: golf, swimming, research; Rec.: theatre. Home: 17179 Ave. De Santa Ynez, Pacific Palisades, CA 92072; Office: 1304 15th St., Suite 316, Santa Monica, CA 90404.

BIGGERS, JOHN ALVIN
Automotive-Industrial Executive
b. Oct. 27, 1926, Durham, Calif.; s. Alvin C. and Bessie I. (Green) Biggers; ed. pub. schs., Chico, Calif.; grad. Grant Union H.S., Sacto.; m. Esther L. Debler, Sacto., Apr. 20, 1945; chil.: Curtis G., b. Apr. 17, 1950; Merlene A. and Marlene J. (twins), b. Mar. 5, 1951; Calvin B., b. Apr. 26, 1952. Career: With Globe Auto Supply, 1941-44; Gerlinger Motor Parts, Inc., 1944, gen. mgr. 1950, pres. 1968---. Lectr., serv. orgns., colls. Mem.: young exec. forum, Automotive Serv. Ind., 1951-66; chmn. auto sect., United Crusade, 1959-61; dist. finance com., B.S.A. 1960-61; YMCA 1961-65; chmn. Sacto. Parts Jobbers Assn.; bd. dirs. Fairhaven Home; Sacto. Camelia festival, Sacto. Safety Council, ASIA, C. of C., Calif. Automotive Wholesalers Assn.; Trades Adv. Council, Preston sch. of ind.; chmn., All Industries Career Edn., Sacto. Co. Schs.; adv. Council mem., Electrical and Mechanical Tech., Los Rios Jr. Coll Dist.; (hon.) dep. sheriff, 1965---. Republican. Ch. of Nazarene (chmn. bd. stewards, 1951-66, secty., 1951---; choir dir., del. to Internat. Assembly, Portland, Ore. 1964, K.C. 1968; chmn. Laymens Retreat, 1970-72; River Park Community Choir. Hobby: photog. Rec.: swimming, hunting. Home: 5372 Monalee Ave., Sacto., CA 95819; Office: 2020 Kay St., Sacto., CA.

BILBRAY, BRIAN PHILLIP
Mayor of Imperial Beach
b. Jan. 28, 1951, N.A.S. North Is., San Diego, Calif.; s. Hubert Bilbray (dec.) and Mavis Clute (Mrs. George C.). Career: Owner, Clute-Bilbray Tax Service; City Councilman, Imperial Beach, 1976-78, Mayor, 1978---. Mem. Kiwanis, 1976---. Catholic. Hobbies: sailing, surfing, skiing, scuba-diving. Home: 194B Ebony Ave., Imperial Beach, CA; Office: City of Imperial Beach, 825 Coronado Ave., Imperial Beach, 1020 Second St., Imperial Beach, CA.

BILHEIMER, STEPHEN C.
Chairman of the Board, Silverwoods Stores
b. Arkadelphia, Ark.; s. Charles William and Edna (Carpenter) Bilheimer; ed. B.S., Ore. State Coll. 1927; USC; Dr. Bus. Adm. Woodbury Coll.; m. Jeanne Summerfield, S.F., Calif., May 5, 1928; chil.: Mary Flave, b. June 16, 1935; Peter, b. Oct. 4, 1937. Career: Partner-dir., Phelps-Terkel, Inc., L.A. 1925-54; pres. Silverwoods Stores, 1964-67, chmn. bd. 1967--- (21 stores). Awards: USC Sch. of Bus. Adm. "Outstanding Alumnus" Award, 1963; Gen. Alumni Assn. Award for "Outstanding Serv." 1968; Man of Yr. Award, L.A. Realty Bd. 1969; Humanitarian-of-Yr. Award, Aid-United Givers, 1972; Brotherhood Award, Natl. Conf. Chr. and Jews, 1972; Bishop's Award of Merit, Episc. Diocese of L.A. 1972; Mem.: pres. L.A. Airport Comm.; bd. dirs. Calif. Mus. of Sci. and Ind., pres. Calif. Mus. Found.; past pres.: L.A. Stock Exch., So. Calif. Visitors Council, Central City Assn.; Dir. Calif. Fed. Svgs. & Loan Assn., 1945---; dir. Downtown Bus. Men's Assn., 1954; dir. Better Bus. Bur., 1954---; dir. Bel-Air Bay Club, 1954---; pres., L.A. C. of C. 1962-63; dir.-treas. 1963---; past pres.-hon. trustee, Repub. Assocs.; bd. dirs., Hosp. of Good Samaritan Med. Center; pres. All-Year Club So. Calif. 1966-67; past pres. L.A. Rotary Club (No. 5); James A. Garfield Masonic Lodge, L.A. Country Club. St. Albans Episcopal Ch. Hobby: hunting, fishing. Rec.: golf. Home: 142 S. Rockingham Ave., W. L.A., CA; Office: 558 S. Broadway, L.A., CA 90012.

BILLINGTON, RAY ALLEN
Senior Researcher, Huntington Library
b. Sept. 28, 1903, Bay City, Mich.; s. Cecil and Nina

(Allen) Billington; ed. Ph.B. Univ. of Wis. 1926; M.A., Univ. of Mich. 1927; Ph.D. Harvard Univ. 1933; M.A., Oxford Univ. 1953; Litt. D., Bowling Green; LL.D., Park Coll., Redlands Univ., Occidental Coll., Univ. Toledo; L.H.D., Northwestern Univ. 1971; m. Mabel Crotty, Detroit, Mich., Sept. 6, 1928; chil.: Anne B. Bader, Allen. Career: Instr.-asst. prof. Clark Univ., 1931-37; asst. prof., assoc. prof., prof. Smith Coll. 1937-44; Guggenheim Mem. Fellow, 1943-44; prof. (hist.) Northwestern Univ. 1944-63; William Smith Mason prof. hist. 1949-63; Harmsworth prof. Am. hist., Oxford Univ., 1953; Schouler lectr., Johns Hopkins Univ., 1944; Taft lectr., Univ. of Cincinnati, 1954; Blazer lectr., Univ. of Ky. 1960; sr. research assoc., The Henry E. Huntington Library, 1963---. Trustee, Newberry Library, Westerners Found., Occidental Coll.; dir. Social Sci. Research Council. History ed.: Dryden Press, 1949-56; Rinehart & Co. 1956-60; editor: Journ. of Charlotte L. Forten, 1953; The Westward Movement in the U.S. 1959; Frontier and Section, 1961; Histories of Am. Frontiers series, 1962---; "Dear Lady: Letters of F.J. Turner and A.F.P. Hooper," 1970; "America's Frontier Story," 1969; board eds., American Heritage, 1958-62; hist. cons., Encyclopedia Americana, 1962-69; Author: "The Protestant Crusade," 1938; "Westward Expansion," 1949; "United States History, 1865-1950," 1950; "American History Before 1877," 1951; "The Far Western Frontier, 1830, 1860, 1956"; Historians Contribution to Anglo-American Misunderstanding, 1966; "America's Frontier Heritage," 1966; "Genesis of the Frontier Thesis," 1971; "Frederick Jackson Turner," 1973; America's Frontier Culture, 1977; (co-author) "The United States, American Democracy in World Perspective," 1947; "The Making of Am. Democracy," 1950. Mem.: pres. Western Hist. Assn.; chmn. Carnegie Revolving Fund com., Am. Hist. Assn., 1952; pres. Am. Studies Assn. 1959-61; pres., Orgn. of Am. Historians, 1962-63; Calif., So. Calif. Hist. Socs.; Phi Beta Kappa, Phi Beta Kappa Assocs., Sigma Delta Chi. Home: 2375 Lombardy Rd., San Marino, CA; Office: The Henry E. Huntington Library, San Marino, CA 91108.

BILOON, ROBERT FRANCIS (FRANK)
Clinical Engineer
b. Dec. 8, 1920, N.Y.C.; s. Joseph and Amelia (Nichthauser) Biloon; B.E.E. (communications), George Washington Univ., 1949; reg. profl. engr., Calif., Certified Clin. Engr., Cert. Biomedical Technician; m. Lillien Kanousis, Aug. 19, 1964, S.F.; Career: Chief Ionospheric Observatory CRPL Nat. Bur. of Standards 1949-51; Project Engr., Single-Side-Band Design, Crosby Lab., 1951-52; Sr. Research Engr., Aircraft Instrumentation, Republic Aviation, 1952-58; Heavy Radar Field Engring. mgr., RCA Service Co., 1958-64; Head, (med. engring. cons., sales & serv. co.), Frank Biloon Profl. Engring. Co., 1964---. Awards: Cited by USAF BMEWS 1963, US Dir. ARPA Tradex (RCA) 1962. Author: Med. Equip. Service Manual, Prentice-Hall, 1978; numerous inventions med. equipment and components. Mil. enlisted man, officer, AUS 1939-46; CBI theater. Civil Def. Communications Officer, Burlington Co., N.J., 1961-63. Mem.: Am. Radio Relay League WB6MUN; sr. mem. IEEE; Assn. Advancement of Med. Instrumentation. Jewish. Hobbies: amateur radio, philately, old books. Rec.: swimming, skiing, dancing. Address: 425 Park Way, Santa Cruz, CA 95062.

BILOVSKY, PAUL R.
Oral Surgeon
b. Oct. 1, 1942, Los Angeles, B.A., Univ. Calif., Berkeley, 1964; D.D.S., Northwestern Univ. Dental Sch., 1968. Career: Dental internship, Univ. Chicago Hosp., 1968-69; resident in oral and maxillofacial surgery, Valley Med. Center of Fresno (Calif.), 1970-73; pvt. practice of oral and maxillofacial surgery, Hayward, 1973-74; Sherman Oaks, 1975---. Dir. Found. for Advancement of Dental-Oral-Facial Surgery Inc. Contbr. Journ. of Oral Surgery. Mem.: Am. Soc. of Oral Surgeons, So. Calif. Soc. Oral and Maxillofacial Surgeons; Am. and Calif. Dental Assns; San Fernando Valley Dental Soc.; So. Calif. Acad. of Oral Pathology. Home: 15286 Encanto Dr., Sherman Oaks, CA 91403; Office: 4849 Van Nuys Blvd., Sherman Oaks, CA 91403.

BILOW, NORMAN
Scientist
b. Sept. 9, 1928, Chicago, Ill.; s. Phillip L. and Rebecca (Stanislafsky) Bilow; B.S., Roosevelt Univ., 1949; M.S., Univ. Chicago, 1952, Ph.D., 1956; m. Selma H. Rifkin, July 17, 1954, Denver, Colo.; chil.: Steven C., b. July 10, 1960; Sandra R., b. Sept. 24, 1961; Richard K., b. Feb. 18, 1965. Career: Research chemist: Emulsol Corp., 1949-52; Dow Chemical Co. 1956-59; Hughes Aircraft Co., 1959-62; head polymer & physical chem., Hughes Aircraft Co., 1963-73; senior scientist, 1973---. Awards: Indsl. Research Mag. IR-100 award winner, 1970, 74;

Hyland Patent award, 1977, Hughes Aircraft Co. (top inventors award); Author over 25 pub. articles; inventor, 39 issued U.S. patents, many foreign patents; elected Sigma Xi, 1959; guest lectr.: Loyola Univ., L.A.; Univ. Mass.; Univ. Arizona; Calif. Polytechnic Inst.; Cal Tech.; Univ. Ala., Auburn; lectr. sci. soc. nat. meetings. Sgt., AUS M.C., 1952-54. Mem.: Research Soc. of Am., pres. Calif. branch 1973; Am. Chem. Soc.; Am. Inst. of Chemists, 1965-73; N.Y. Acad. of Sci. 1961-66. Rel. pres. Synagogue. Hobbies: gardening, constrn. Home: 16685 Calneva Dr., Encino, CA 91436; Office: Centinela & Teale, Culver City, CA 90230.

BINGHAM, EDWIN S., JR.
President, The Bingham Co.
b. Oct. 15., 1912, St. Paul, Minn.; s. Edwin S. and Amy Belle Bingham; ed. A.B., Univ. of Wis., 1934, J.D., 1936; m. Eleanor Smith, Beverly Hills, CA, Feb. 26, 1977; chil.: Susan B. Romig, Barbara Ann, Rev. John Pratt (Episc.). Career: Dist. mgr. Allstate Ins. Co., No. Calif. 1937-41; Ralph C. Sutro Co., L.A., 1941---; v.p., 1949, dir. 1959---; sr. v.p. 1961-68, pres. 1968---; v.chmn. Sutro Mortgage Investment Trust, 1964---; dir. Western Travelers Ins. Co. 1960-70; dir. Calif. Mortgage Bankers Assn. 1970-71. Mem.: Kappa Sigma; Lambda Alpha, 1971---; L.A. Ath. Club; Riviera Country Club. Republican. All Saints Episcopal Ch., Beverly Hills (vestryman, forman, sr. warden; standing com. Diocese 1969-74; dir. Cathedral Corp. of St. Pauls, 1970---; conv. del. 12 yrs.). Hobby: philately. Rec: golf, garden. Home: 180 N. Las Palmas, L.A., CA 90004; Office: The Bingham Co., 8383 Wilshire Blvd., Beverly Hills, CA 90211.

BINGHAM, STEVEN ANTHONY
Construction Executive
b. Apr. 16, 1941, Union City, Indiana; s. R. Glenn and Hazel V. Bingham; B.S., construction, Ariz State Univ. 1965; m. De-la Hodges, Aug. 4, 1961, Phoenix, Ariz.; chil.: Delane, b. 1965; Brian, b. 1968. Career: with Scripps Inst. of Oceanography, 1959-60; Morrison Knudsen Constrn. Co., 1965; Ameron Pipe Products, 1966; dir. of estimating, Kitchell Contractors, Inc., Newport Beach, 1966---; also instr., Cal. State Univ., Long Beach, 1979---. Named Nat. Estimator of Year, 1977; Ariz. Estimator of the Year, 1975; Diver of the Year, 1971. Mem. Am. Soc. of Profl. Estimators, nat. pres. 1977, Ariz. chpt. pres. 1973; mem. Ariz. Sun Ray Divers, pres. 1972. Hobby: stamps, underwater photog. Rec.: scuba, fishing. Home: 5082 Yearling, Irvine, CA 92714; Office: 1601 Dove St., Suite 155, Newport Beach, CA 92660.

BIRCH, STEPHEN F.
Title Insurance Company Executive
b. Apr. 21, 1923, Los Angeles, Calif.; s. Frank and Lillian Birch; student, pub. schs.; Pasadena Jr. Coll.; m. Margaret Ann Allen, Arcadia, Calif., July 14, 1954; chil.: Terry Ann, b. Mar. 7, 1957; Cynthia Gayle, b. Oct. 22, 1960. Career: Title Ins. and Trust Co., 1940-64; Chief executive officer, Calif. Land Title Co., 1964---. Chmn. of the bd., Calif. Land Title Co.; Dir. Calif.-World Fin. Corp.; Calif.-World Title Co.; Universal Title Corp.; Calif. Land Title Co. of Nev. Co. USN 1942-45. Mem.: past pres., L.A. Downtown Optimist Club; past C.B., Catalina Is. Yacht Club; A.O.P.A.-Bonanza Soc.; Granada Lodge No. 608 L.A. Scottish Rite Al Malaikah Temple; L.A. Athletic Club; Sunset Hills Tennis Club. Congregational Ch. Hobbies: flying, boating. Rec.: skiing, tennis. Home: 15547 Los Altos Dr. Hacienda Heights, CA 91745; Office: 90 Universal City Plaza, Universal City, CA 91608.

BIRD, ROSE ELIZABETH
Chief Justice, California Supreme Court
b. Nov. 2, 1936, Tucson, Ariz.; B.A., magna cum laude, Long Island Univ., 1958; J.D., Univ. Calif., Boalt Hall Sch. of Law, 1965; Career: Clerk to Chief Justice of Nev. Supreme Ct., 1965-66; deputy pub. defender, sr. trial deputy & Chief of Appellate Div., Santa Clara Co., 1966-74; tchr., Stanford Law Sch., 1972-74; Secty. of Agri. & Services Agency & Mem. Governor's Cabinet, 1975-77; Chief Justice, Calif. Supreme Ct., 1977---. Mem. Calif. Acad. of Appellate Lawyers, 1975; mem. Westrn Reg. Selection Panel, Pres. Commn. on White House Fellowships, 1976-77; chmn. Calif. Judicial Council; chmn. Commn. on Judicial Appts.; pres. bd. of directors, Hastings Coll. of Law, Univ. Calif.; mem. USC Law Center bd. of councilors; mem. bd. assocs., San Fernando Valley Youth Found. Democrat, mem. nat. com. 1976-77. Office: State Building, 350 McAllister St., S.F., CA 94102.

BIRDSALL, JOHN EDWIN
Company President
b. June 1, 1937, Los Angeles, Calif.; s. Jack Edwin and Edna Marie (Entner) Birdsall; B.S. in Elec. Engring, 1970, M.S. in Elec. Engring, 1974, Ph.D., 1976, Calif. Christian Univ., L.A.; m. Constance Kelly, L.A., Feb. 10, 1961; chil.: Dean Edwin, b. Mar. 3, 1962; John Phillip, b. Aug. 22, 1963; Yvette Cheyree, b. Mar. 21, 1965. Career: Dir. engring., Spectra-Strip Corp., Garden Grove, 1964-66; div. mgr., Giannini Corp., Whittier, 1966-68; pres., Reo Data Products, Inc., Westminster, 1968-75; pres. Zermatt Corp., Crestline, 1975---. Also prof., Calif. Christian Univ. 1977---. Dir. Reo Data Products, Inc., 1968-75. Awarded Apollo Program Design Participant Certificate from NASA, 1973. Publs.: Counting Systems for Industry, 1975; Printing Technique, 1969; Data Printer in Naval Systems, 1974. Inventions: Spec. printing devices, digital torque instrument. USN, Submarine div., 1955-58. Mem.: IEEE; AAS, Smithsonian Instn.; Rotary Club. Christian. Hobbies: skiing, woodworking. Rec.: hiking, jeeping. Home: P.O.B. 939, Crestline, CA 92325.

BIRKHOFF, WILLIAM N.
Computer Systems Executive — Educator
b. Feb. 2, 1945, Buffalo, N.Y.; s. Pierce and Ruth (Blass) Birkhoff; Gr. Grandfather, David Birkhoff Sr., Consul to the Netherlands; B.S., Clarkson Coll., Potsdam, N.Y., 1968; M.B.A., Univ. of Colo., 1973; m. Anne Lee Trevethan, Stratford, Conn., July 4, 1974. Career: Marketing, IBM, Denver, Colo, 1970-72; computer systems project mgr., Martin Marietta Co., Denver, 1972-74; TRW Systems, L.A., 1975-77; Gen. Dynamics, S.D., 1977---; also tchr., El Camino Coll., 1973-78; tchr., Natl. Univ., 1978---. Pres., Colonial Heritage Consultants, 1978---. Licensed real estate broker. Mem.: Space Park Employees Assn. (treas. 1977); Westwood Club (rules chmn. 1978); Triangle fraternity (advisor 1970); Investment Club (pres. 1970). Home: 17309 Tablero Ct., Rancho Bernardo, CA 92127; Office: P.O.B. 28744, Rancho Bernardo, CA 92128.

BIRON, ROBERT HENRY, JR.
Land Developer
b. Aug. 12, 1912, Minneapolis, Minn.; s. Robert Henry and Alice (Brugger) Biron; ed. Carleton Coll., Northfield, Minn. 1929; B.A., Univ. of Minn. 1963, LL.B. 1935; m. Jean Machamer, Apr. 14, 1951; dau.: Patricia. Career: House Counsel, Minneapolis-Honeywell Regulator Co. 1936-43; v.p. Northrop Aircraft, Inc. 1945-47; v.p. Transcontinental & Western Air, Inc., 1947-48; v.p. Consolidated Vultee Aircraft Corp. (now Gen. Dynamics Corp.), 1947-64; v. chancellor-adm., Univ. of Calif., San Diego, 1964-68. Pres., Rancho La Jolla, Inc. 1968---. Dir. S.D. Gas & Electric Co.; dir., Air Logistics Corp.; trustee, Scripps Clinic & Research Found. Mem.: bd. dirs., San Diego C. of C. 1962-70; bd. Calif. Mfrs. Assn.; bd. dirs., San Diego Soc. for Crippled Chil.; Theta Delta Chi, Phi Delta Phi. Republican. Protestant. Home: P.O.B. 52, Rancho Santa Fe, CA; Office: Interstate 5 at La Jolla Village Dr., La Jolla, CA 92037.

BISHOP, ANNE
Journalist — Public Relations
b. May 1, 1913, Amassya, Turkey; d. Kevork (poet) and Zabel (Isburian) Avakina; ed. Columbia Univ., Oxford Univ., Sorbonne Univ., A.A., LL.B., 1935; m. John Bishop, Crown Point, Ind. 1950; son, John, Jr. (historian and columnist); dau. Elizabeth Maude. Career: Legal Aid Clinic, N.Y.C., 1935; staff, London Daily Mirror and Sun. Pictorial, 1936; dir.-chief, Paris Bureau, 1937; UPI, Time and Life Mags.; combat and foreign correspondent, New York News — Chicago Tribune Syndicate, Supreme Hdqrs., Allied Expeditionary Forces; Pub. rels., L.A., 1975---. Awards: One of the World's Great War Correspondents, 1953. Mem.: Internat. Union of Journalists, 1935---; Screen Writers Guild, 1947; L.A. Co., Calif. Lib. Assns., 1965; The 8-Ball; L.A. Co. Parks and Rec. Assn.; Overseas Press Club; pres. Sr. Citizens Clubs; (life) L.A. Co. Sr. Citizens, 1975; Natl. Hist. Assn., Bicentennial Com., Greater L.A. Press Club, 1970---; Alpha Gamma Sigma, Iota Tau Tau. Republican (chmn. Adv. Com.). Prefet, Sodalist (pres. Cath. Ch. Assn.). Hobbies: aeronautics, literature. Rec.: golf, tennis, swim. Home: 4411 Lockwood Ave., L.A., CA 90029.

BISHOP, JOHN F.
Corporate President
b. Jan. 3, 1924, Yenangyaung, Burma; s. Fay and Florence (Larson) Bishop; ed. B.S. (M.E.) Univ. of Calif., Berkeley, 1945; M.B.A., Harvard Univ. 1948; m. Ann RixW. L.A., Nov. 4, 1945; chil.: Caren Lee, b. July 9, 1949; John Bradford, b. July 21, 1951; Kimberly Ann, b.

Jan. 30, 1956; Suzanne Louise, b. Dec. 3, 1960. Career: Mkt. reserach-distr. Owens-Corning Fiberglass Corp. 1948-51; div. gen. mgr., Beckman Instr., Inc., 1951-59; exec. v.p. Textron Electronics, Inc. 1959-60; pres.-chmn. bd. Jenoa Inc. and predecessor, Bishop-Howlett, Inc. 1960---. Dir.: Systems Devel. Co., Bertea Corp., Electronic Engin. Co. of Calif., Baker Oil Tools, Inc., Mem.: ASME; IEEE; past dir.-exec. com.: Instrument Soc. of Am., Western Electronic Mfrs. Assn.; Young President's Orgn.; Big Canyon Country Club, Calif. Club, Harvard Club, Phi Gamma Delta. Episcopalian. Rec.: golf, tennis, skiing. Home: 20 Linda Isle, Newport Beach, CA; Office: 4500 Campus Dr., Newport Beach, CA 92660.

BIXBY, KATHERINE COSTLOW
Community Organization Executive
b. Feb. 8, 1920, Lusk, Wyo., d. Jesse Patrick and Anna (Thompson) Costlow; B.A., Doane Coll., 1941; m. E. Rew Bixby, Las Vegas, Nev., May 30, 1942; chil.: Patrick William, b. Apr. 14, 1943; Jean Bixby Hennessy, b. Jul. 25, 1944. Career: elementary sch. tchr., 1941-42; tchr., Valley Coll., 1947-77; exec. dir., L.A. Voluntary Action Center, 1971---. Mem. of bd.: Nat. Council of Social Welfare, 1976-79; Elderworks; Nat. Advisory Council, 1978-79; Spec. Services for Groups, 1966-79; Rec. & Youth Services Planning Council, 1976-79; YWCA, 1965-67; United Way, Inc., 1962-69; Calif. United Way, 1970-72. Past pres.: Volunteer Bureau, L.A., 1963-65; Calif. Assn. of Health & Welfare, 1966-67; Camp Fire Girls, L.A., 1954-56; v.p., USO, L.A., 1962-66; V.P., Mental Health Com., 1969-71. Recipient: Koshland Award, 1977; Gold Key, 1965; Agency Leadership Award, 1963; USO Gold Medallion Award, 1966; Armed Forces Rec. Assn. — Outstanding Volunteer Award, 1967; Luther Galick Award, 1957. Home: 920 Crestview Ave., Glendale, CA 91202; Office: 1650 S. Victoria Ave., L.A., CA 90019.

BLACK, ARTHUR L.
Professor of Physiological Chemistry
b. Dec. 1, 1922, Redlands, Calif.; s. Leo M. and Marie A. (Burns) Black; B.S., Univ. Calif., 1948, Ph.D., 1951; m. Trudi McCue, 1945, Boston; chil.: Teresa (Townsend), b. 1946; Janet (Carter), b. 1950; Patti (Black), b. 1952. Career: with Univ. of Calif., Davis, 1952---: asst. prof., 1952, assoc. 1958, prof. of Physiological Chem., 1962---; chmn. Dept. of Physiological Sci., 1967-74; chmn. NIH Nutrition Training Grant Commn. 1972-73. Served to 1st Lt., USAF, 1943-46. Author 97 sci. publs. contbd. profl. journs. Mem.: Phi Beta Kappa, pres. Calif. Kappa 1976; Am. Soc. Biological Chemists; Am. Inst. of Nutrition; Am. Physiological Soc. Hobbies: photog., astronomy, woodworking. Rec.: skiing. Home: 891 Lindin Lane, Davis, CA 95616; Office: Univ. Calif., Davis, CA 95616.

BLACK, JASON
Promotions Executive — Author
b. Dec. 22, 1947, London, U.K.; s. Albert and Genevieve; student, Univ. of London Imperial Coll., 1970; m. Annette (Strawberry) Willis, Apr. 22, 1978, Las Vegas, Nev. Career: internat. v.p., Internat. Concert and Festival Promoters Assn., 1968-72; exec. cons. music div., British Lion Films, 1971-73; owner, pres., J.B. Promotions, 1972---; pres., Securicon, U.K., 1974-77; gen. mgr., Culver City Studios, 1978---; appeared in musical Hair, London, 1972; Zabriskie Point (film by Antonioni & Ponti); writer, articles and short stories, 1963---, pub. in Sci. Fiction Anthologies, Rolling Stone Mag., others. Mem.: Culver City C. of C.; YMCA, Century Club sponsor; exec. bd., D.U.O. Internat. Hobbies: film-making, music, numismatics. Rec.: race-driver, Jai-Alai (amateur status). Office: 9336 W. Washington Blvd., Culver City, CA 90230.

BLACK, MARY ROSE ALLEN
Editor - Lecturer
b. Dec. 2, 1923, Salt Lake City, Utah; d. George H., M.D. (ornithologist & conservationist pioneer, intermountain states) and Ruth (Larson) Allen; m. Dr. Albert Gain Black (dec., Agri. Economics Dean, Iowa State Univ., chief, U.S. Land Banks; chief, Food & Agri. Orgn. of UN; co-chmn. World Bank), Aug. 1954, Rome, Italy. Career: tchr. of Navajo Indians and Salt Lake High Schs., 2 years; chmn. Utah Youth Council, mem. Mayor's Wartime Council on Youth, dir., Utah Assn. for U.N., 1945-49; editor, Land Reborn Mag., jour. for Christian leaders of Am. Christian Palestine Com., 1949-52; free-lance journalist, Middle East, 1952-54; asst. editor, Agricultural Gazette, 1949-54; lived abroad 1954-61, special interest in refugees in newly developing countries, active in clinics and relief rehabilitation; returned to Am., editor, Univ. of Calif., Berkeley, lectr. on Middle East, founder-chmn., California

Christian Com. for Israel, 1961---; founder, mem. exec. com., National Christian Leadership Conf. for Israel, 1978-79. Recipient: Eleanor Roosevelt award for humanitarian service, Hadassah Med. Orgn., 1976; Spec. Award, Lifetime of Christian Service, Zionist Orgn. of Am. Pacific Coast. Pres., Apmin Fine Arts Soc., 1942-44. Unitarian. Hobbies: painting, travel. Home-Office: 3011 College Ave., Berkeley, CA 94705.

BLACK, ROBERT LANGSTON
Executive, Pacific Telephone Co.
b. July 20, 1915, Kansas City, Mo.; s. Sewell W. and Alice M. Black; ed. Univ. of Kan. 1933-35; basic communications pgm., Dartmouth Coll., Hanover, N.H. 1959; m. Patricia McDonald; daus.: Barbara Jean and Mary Joanne. Career: Assoc. with Southwestern Bell Tel. Co., K.C., Mo. 1935-41; various positions, Pac. Tel Co., L.A., S.F. and San Diego, Calif. 1946-54; dist. commercial mgr. 1954-55, div. mgr. 1955-58, gen. commercial mgr., So. Counties area, 1958-70, asst. v.p. 1970---. Dir.: Helix-Imperial Harbor Div. Corp., 1965-67; Pacific Forum, 1969-70. U.S. Army, 1941-46; Command and Gen. Staff Sch., Ft. Leavenworth, WW II; Lt. Col., USAF Res. (ret.). Awards: Bronze Star Medal; Hollzer Award by Jewish Fed. Council, 1974. Mem.: Sigma Chi, 1933---; S.D. Rotary Club, 1954---; S.D. Safety Council, 1955-58; gov. United Success Drive, 1955-57; dir. S.D. Better Business Bureau 1955, adv. bd. 1956-58; dir. S.D. Conv. & Tourist Bur. 1955-59, exec. com. 1958; dir. Econ. Research Bur. 1955---; dir. Fiesta del Pacifico, 1956-60; dir. Invest. in Am. Wk. 1956-58; Tel. Pioneers of Am. 1956---; v.p. S.D. C. of C. 1956, dir. 1956-60, 1960---, exec. com. 1956-58, 59, pres. 1958. The President's Council, 1973---; gov. United Fund Drive, 1954, dir. 1957-62, v.p. 1958-62, exec. com. 1959-62; coms. Am. Red Cross; Dir. Natural Resources Conf. 1957; dir. Armed Servs. UMCA 1958; orgn. com.-exec. com.-dir., United Community Servs. 1962-70; S.D. chpt., Natl. Conf. of Christians and Jews, 1962-64; dir. S.D. Taxpayers Assn. 1965---; S.D. Citizens Com. on Sch. Bldg. 1966-70; Civ. Serv. Comm., Coronado, 1969-70; S.D. Power Squad, 1969-70; Mercy Clinic Adv. Bd. 1971---; Kona-Kai Club, S.D. Town Hall. Home: 710 Balboa, Coronado, CA; Office: 525 B St., San Diego, CA 92112.

BLACKMAN, JOHN CHADWICK
United Airlines Executive
b. May 31, 1933, Hinsdale, Ill.; s. Joseph K. Blackman; ed. Duke Univ. 1951-52; grad. Ill. Coll. of Comm. 1956; m. Mary Bowman, Dec. 28, 1954; sons: Scott, b. Nov. 28, 1955; Marc, b. Aug. 22, 1959. Career: United Airlines acct. 1956, mgmt. tr. 1957, sales repr. 1959, acct. exec. 1961, sales mgr. 1963, asst. to v.p. 1968, v.p. pub. affairs, 1969, v.p. S.E. Region 1971, v.p. Western Region, 1974---. U.S. Army, 1952-54. Mem.: dir.: Greater S.F. C. of C., Downtown Assn. of S.F., S.F. Conv. and Visitors Bureau, Bay Area Urban League and Langley Porter Inst.; Pac. Area Travel Assn.; Chinese Culture Fdn. of S.F.; YMCA of S.C.; Am. Soc. of Travel Agts.; SKAL Club; Olympic Club. Rec.: golf, tennis. Home: 45 Rinconada Circle, Belmont, CA 94002; Office: 400 Post St., S.F., CA 94102.

BLACKMORE, DOROTHY S.
Education Consultant
b. Willows, Calif.; d. Charles LeRoy and Ella (Drew) Smith; Gr.dau., Willis Drew, pioneer in Glenn Co.; A.B. Chico State Coll.; M.S.Ed., Dominican Coll., San Rafael; Ed.D., Univ. Calif., Berkeley; m. Edwin L. Blackmore (dec.), 1935, Willows, Calif.; chil.: Willis Wdwin, b. Aug. 29, 1946; Margaret (Henwood), b. Jan. 9, 1949. Career: classroom and demonstration tchr.: Chico State Coll. Lab. Sch., Calif. Pub. Schs., 1941-51; tchr. educator: Dominican Coll. San Rafael, 1951-66, UC, Davis, 1964-69, Walden Univ. doctoral program, 1974---, The Field Inst., 1975---; staff, cons., program mgr., state facilitator, State Dept. of Edn., 1969---. Bd. dir., Calif. Council on the Edn. of Tchrs., 1969-71; Nat. pres., Assn. for Student Tchg. (AST), 1974-76, Calif. pres. 1962-64. Contbr. edn. journs. and yearbooks. Mem.: Calif. Assn. for Edn. of Young Children; Omicron Theta Epsilon; Kappa Delta Pi; Delta Kappa Gamma; Phi Lambda Theta; Phi Delta Kappa; Internat. Reading Assn.; Calif. Teachers Assn.; NEA; bd. dir., Mental Health Assn., Yolo Co.; League of Women Voters; advis. bd., Sacto. City Coll. Outreach Prog. Episcopalian. Home: 620 Coolidge St., Davis, CA 95616; Office: State Dept. of Edn., 721 Capitol Mall, Sacto., CA 95814.

BLAIR, GEORGE SIMMS
Professor of Social Science
b. May 31, 1924, Homewood, Kan.; s. William H. and Mary (Simms) Blair; son-in-law Jesse L. Barnes, baseball

player; A.B. & B.S. in edn., Kansas State Tchrs. Coll., Emporia, 1948, M.S., 1949; Ph.D., Northwestern Univ., 1951; m. Gloria Jean Barnes, Sept. 10, 1949, El Dorado, Kan.; chil.: David Lawrence, b. May 19, 1952; Rebecca Lynn, b. Feb. 4, 1960. Career: asst. prof. polit. sci., Univ. Tenn., 1951-53; asst. and assoc. prof. polit sci., Univ. Penn., 1953-60; assoc. prof. and prof. of govt., Claremont, 1960-74; Elizabeth Helm Rosecrans Prof. of Govt., Claremont Grad Sch., 1974---. Dir., Capitol Devel. & Control Corp., 1973---. Author: Government at the Grass-Roots, 1977; American Legislatures: Structure & Process, 1967; Legislative Bodies in California, 1966; American Local Government, 1964; Cumulative Voting, 1960; Metropolitan Analysis, 1958; AUS, Amphibious Engrs., 1943-46. Mem.: Pi Gamma Mu, 1948; Pi Sigma Alpha, 1951; Claremont City Planning Commn., 1964-71. Methodist. Hobbies: philately, numismatics. Rec.: tennis. Home: 509 Bowling Green Dr., Claremont, CA 91711; Office: Claremont Grad. School, Claremont, CA 91711.

BLAKE, JOHN RONALD
Physician
b. Aug. 24, 1926, Washington, D.C.; s. John R. and Martha S. Blake; grandson of Wells A. Sherman, mkting spec., U.S. Dept. of Agriculture, grandnephew of Sherman bros.: Prof. Henry C., chemist & nutritionist; Prof. James M., bacteriologist; Prof. Franklin, entomologist; Prof. John H., economist and educator; B.S. in Med., M.D. Duke Univ. Sch. of Med., 1950; m. Wanda Polena, Nev., May 28, 1976; chil.: John R., b. Apr. 10, 1952; Emily W., b. Aug. 4, 1953; Ronald K., b. Feb. 14, 1955; Miriam A., b. Apr. 11, 1956; Andrea S., b. May 9, 1957; Lars D., b. Feb. 16, 1959; Sherman C., b. June 27, 1960. Career: Med. intern, Univ. Hosps. of Cleveland, 1950-51, asst. resident, 1951-52; asst. resident physician, Peter Bent Brigham Hosp. (Harvard Med. Sch.), Boston, 1954-55, asst. in med., 1955-57; research fellow in med., 1955-57; research fellow in med., Children's Med. Center, Boston, 1955-57; res. physician, Stillman Infirmary, Harvard Univ., 1955-57; cons. in cardiology, Children's Med. Center, Boston, 1956-57; instr., postgrad course, Clinical Heart Disease, 1957; pvt. practice of internal med. & cardiology, Sacto., 1957---. Recipient: Diplomate, Nat. Bd. of Med. Examiners, 1951; ; Physician's Recognition Award, AMA, 1974-77; Heart research grantee — 1956-57, 1960-63. Publ. articles in med. journals & lectures on cardiology. Warrant Officer, U.S. Maritime Service and Merchant Marine, 1945-46; Capt., USAF, M.C., 1952-54. Mem.: Nu Sigma Nu Med. frat. 1947; dir., Sacto. Co. Heart Assn., 1958-64; Nat. Assn. on Standard Med. Vocabulary, 1961---; Sacto., Calif. and Am. Soc. of Internal Med., 1958---; the Smithsonian assocs., 1976---; assoc. me. Am. Museum of Natural Hist., 1976---. Founder and pres., the Sacramento Opera, 1979. Presbyterian. Hobbies: cosmology, archaeology. Rec.: opera. Home: 5441 Wildflower Cir., Carmichael, CA 95608; Office: 2740 Fulton Ave., Suite 107, Sacto., CA 95821.

BLAKELY, ROSS MARQUAND
President, Coast Federal Savings & Loan
b. Oct. 2, 1918, Hayes, Kan.; s. Ross John and Nova (Marquand) Blakely; ed. (Sr. Class pres.) Colton H.S. 1936, (Stu. Body pres.) El Centro Jr. Coll 1936-38; B.Sc., UCLA, 1940; grad. Grad. Sch. of Savings & Loans, Ind., Univ. 1966; m. Betty Weymark, Phila., Pa., July 5, 1944; daus.: Sandra B. Jackson, Heather Gilleland, Cynthia Ann. Career: Est. Calif. res. 1928; Coast Fed. Svgs. & Loan Assn., L.A. 1946---, chmn. bd. 1972---, pres. 1974---. USN Comdr. PTO (Marshall Gilbert Is., Coral Sea Battle, Guadalcanal, Tarawa, Iwo Jima, Okinawa), 1941-45; NROTC instr. Univ. of N. Mex. 1945-46; S.F. Group, Pac. Res. Fleet, officer in chg. Ship Activation Sch. 1951-53; Capt., USNR 1960---. Mem.: trustee, Robert and Mary McElhinny Mem. 1949---; Lions Club, L.A., pres. 1965-66; dir. Bill of Rights Commemoration Com. 1962---, chmn. 1970---; past pres. Club No. 1663, Toastmasters Internat.; chmn. L.A. Co. Group, Svgs. & Loan Mgrs., 1963; dir. Merchants & Mfgrs. Assoc., 1974---; Bd. dirs. Fed. Home Loan Bank of S.F., 1976---; L.A. C. of C., Federal Affairs Com., 1975---; Mem.: L.A. Rotary, 1976---; bd. dirs. Navy League, 1964-66; Calif. Svgs. & Loan League, bd. dirs., 1973---; bd. govs. (many coms.) Nat. Svgs. & Loan League; 1966-70, exec. com. 1967-69, pres. 1971-72; bd. govs. Am. Svgs. & Loan Inst., L.A. 1967-70; dir. Conf. of Fed. Svgs. & Loan Assns., v.p. 1970-73; trustee, UCLA Found.; Methodist. Home: San Marino, CA; Office: 855 S. Hill St., L.A., CA 90014.

BLANCHETTE, JAMES EDWARD
Psychiatrist
b. Aug. 28, 1924, Syracuse, N.Y.; s. Joseph Marcel and Margaret Catherine (Vincent) Blanchette; B.A., Syracuse Univ., N.Y., 1950; M.D., State Univ. N.Y., Syracuse Coll.

of Med., 1953; m. Shirley Ruth Brisco, Sept. 1, 1948, Liverpool, N.Y. Career: Intern, St. Vincent's Hosp., N.Y.C., 1953-54; resident Patton State Hosp., Calif., 1954-55. Met. State Hosp., Norwalk, 1957-59; pvt. practice psychiatry, Redlands, 1959---; chief profl. edn. Patton State Hosp., 1960-64, tchg. cons., 1964---; asst. clin. prof. psychiatry Loma Linda Med. Sch.; mem. staffs Loma Linda Med. Center, San Bernardino Community Hosp., St. Bernadine Hosp., Cons. in psychiatry, Redlands Community Hosp. USAAF Band, Washington, D.C., 1945-47; USAAF M.C., 1953-55. Diplomate Am. Bd. Med. Examiners, Am. Bd. Psychiatry and Neurology. Fellow: Am. Psychiat. Assn.; A.A.A.S.; Pan-Am. Med. Assn. Mem.: Am. and Calif. med. assns.; San Bernardino Med. Soc.; So. Calif. Psychiat. Soc. (pres. Inland chpt. 1963-64); Royal Soc. Health; Am. Med. Soc.; Internat. Platform Assn.; Phi Mu Alpha; Arrowhead Allied Arts Council, San Bernardino (past pres.). Mem.: BPOE No. 836; Elk's Navy BPOE No. 1767; U.S. Power Squadron (dist. secty.); U.S. Coast Guard Aux.; Shark Is. Yacht Club; Hollywood Yacht Club. Play string bass, San Bernardino Symphony (past: AF Band, Wash., D.C.; Syracuse Symphony; Univ. of Redlands; Loma Linda Univ.; Riverside Symphonies). Rec.: boating. Home: 972 W. Marshall Blvd., San Bernardino, CA 92405; Office: 236 Cajon St., Redlands, CA 92373.

BLANCHARD, JEAN
Artist
b. Jan. 27, 1913, Chicago, Ill.; d. George W. and Myrtle (Carr) Blanchard (noted artist in Bay area); granddau. of the Hon. James Wellington Carr, at the time of his death in 1959 the oldest active jurist in Am.; Carr family hist. dates back to 1592; student, pub. schs.; grad., Elwood's Sch. of Profl. Writing; art student of Myrtle Kennedy, Edward Runci, Margaret Roach, Barton Menbert; studied watercolor with Charles Fuson, Jake Lee and Rex Brandt in Calif.; with David Burley and Walter Roberts in England. Chil.: J. Robert Hayes II (Repub. nominee, Calif. state Assembly, 39th dist., 1978); Ronald Murray Hayes; Terry Blanchard Raye. Career: motion picture screen cartoonist-artist, Walt Disney Studio, 1935; continued next 43 years at Warner Bros. Studio, MGM, Hanna-Barbera, San Rio Studio, 1935-78. Mem.: Am. Inst. of Fine Art; Valley Artist's Guild, pres. 1974; San Fernando Valley Art Club, 1972-73; Calif. Art Club, pres. (life mem.), 1977---. Mem. Cordon Bleu. Recipient of Outstanding Scouter Award, San Fernando Valley Council, Boy Scouts of Am., 1963. Paintings represented in fine art collections worldwide; numerous one woman shows; many art awards and citations. Hobbies: needle work, raising dogs. Rec.: bowling. Home: 12039 Saticoy St., No. Hollywood, CA 91605.

BLANK, HARRY DAVID
Business Executive
b. May 9, 1924, Pittsburgh, Pa.; s. Samuel and Sarah (Morris) Blank; ed. C.E., Carnegie Inst. of Tech. 1942-43; B.A. (pub. adm.), UCLA 1950; m. Joyce M. Blank, Santa Monica, Calif., Jan. 25, 1959; chil.: Sharon Liane, b. Dec. 17, 1960; Mitchell Conrad, b. Jan. 18, 1964. Career: Soc. Security Adm. 1950-54; L.A. Co. Assessor's office, 1955-61; co-founder, Recon Servs., Inc. 1961, exec. v.p. 1969---. Property tax spec. and real estate cons. to maj. natl. corps. Lectr., many orgns., incl. Soc. of Accts., Bldg. Owners and Mgrs. Assn., Am. Inst. of Real Estate Appraisers. Staff Sgt., U.S. Army Chem. Warfare Serv., 1943-46, WW II. Mem.: v.p. Carthay Circle Homeowners Assn. 1972-73. Judaism. Rec.: sports, chess, travel. Home: 6618 Moore Dr., L.A., CA 90048; Office: 5670 Wilshire Blvd., L.A., CA 90036.

BLANKE, HENRY
Motion Picture Producer
b. Dec. 30, 1901, Berlin, Ger.; s. Wilhelm (noted Ger. painter) and Anna (Graf) Blanke; ed. H.S., Berlin Steglitz; Arbitur, Ger. (2 yrs.); m. Sonja Ruth Kantorowitz, Pomona, Calif., Oct. 24, 1955; dau. Monique Gabrielle, b. Nov. 27, 1957. Career: Personal asst. to Ernst Lubitsch at UFA and EFA, Berlin, Ger. 1919-22; USA 1922; assoc. with United Artists (Pickford, Fairbanks, Chaplin); Warner Bros. (38 yrs.); Paramount Pictures (3 yrs.); prod. over 100 motion pictures, incl.: "Zola," "Juarez," "Pasteur," "We Are Not Alone" (with Paul Muni); "Old Maid," "Old Acquaintance," "Jezebel" with Bette Davis); "Robinhood" (with Errol Flynn); Jack London's "Sea Wolf" with Edw. G. Robinson; "The Maltese Falcon" (with Humphrey Bogart); "The Nun's Story" (with Audrey Hepburn), ret. Awards: Producers of the Champion Pictures, Motion Picture Herold Yearly Issue of Fame. Mem.: Acad. of Arts and Scis., Mot. Pic. Prodns. Assn. Lutheran. Hobby: photog. Rec.: polo, skeet shooting, bowling. Home: 1050 Oakmont Dr., L.A., CA 90049.

BLANKFORT, LOWELL ARNOLD
Newspaper Publisher
b. Apr. 29, 1926, New York, N.Y.; s. Herbert and Gertrude (Goldwater) Blankfort; B.A., hist. and polit. sci., Rutgers, Univ., 1946; m. April Pemberton, Feb. 28, 1974, San Diego; 1 son Jonathan, b. Jan. 13, 1962. Career: Asst. night editor, Long Island (N.Y.) Star-Journal, 1947-49; columnist, London Daily Mail (Paris), 1949; copy editor, Stars & Stripes (Germany), 1949-50; copy editor, Wall St. Journ., 1951; bus. and labor editor, Cowles Mags., 1952-53; pub., Pacifica Tribune, 1954-59; co-publisher and editor, Chula Vista Star-News, 1961---. Awards: Best editorials or series of editorials in non-daily newspapers by Calif. Newspaper Pubs. Assn., 1st Place, 1974, 1976, 1977; 2d Place: 1975; 1978; Best Editorial, nation's suburban newspaper, Suburban Newspapers of Am., 1974; Best Editorials Nationwide, Nat. Newspaper Assn., 1976; spec. award from Am. Bar Assn. for Distinguished contbrn. to pub. understanding of the Am. system of law and justice, 1976. Mem.: Calif. Newspaper Publishers Assn.; Soc. of Profl. Journalists; ACLU, past pres., S.D. chpt.; Chula Vista Girls Club, dir.; Chula Vista C. of C. Hobbies: travel, reading. Rec.: tennis. Home: Old Orchard Lane, Bonita, CA 92002; Office: P.O.B. 1207, Chula Vista, CA 92012.

BLANKS, HERBERT BEVERLY
Company President
b. Oct. 27, 1915, Cleveland, Ohio; s. Anthony Faulkner and Dorothy McGee (Welch) Blanks; Gr.son, Herbert Welch, Methodist Ch. Bishop; B.S., Forestry, Univ. Calif., Berkeley 1937; postgrad., Univ. Chicago, 1944; m. Roxana Holmes, May 26, 1937, Berkeley; chil.: Herbert Elliott, b. Oct. 30, 1942; Donald Allen, b. Sept. 29, 1947. Career: Forest guard, Tahoe Nat. Forest, 1936-38; Ranger, Sequoia Nat. Park, 1938-42; co-partner, Ailing House Pest Control, Inc., Carmel, 1946-74, pres., 1974---. AUS, 1942-46, Inf., Pacific Theatre; ret. Lt. Col., 1975; decorated with Bronze Star, Army Commendation Medal. Charter mem. City of Carmel Forestry Commn., 1955; city planning commnr., 1955-62, chmn. 1960-61; city of Carmel Councilman 1962-70, Mayor 1964-66; mem. Monterey Co. Local agency formation commn. 1967-70; chmn. 1967-68; bd. dir., Assn. of Monterey Bay Area Govts. 1966-70; trustee, Harrison Mem. Library, Carmel, 1971-77; secty.-treas., Monterey Bay Area pest control operators of Calif., 1972---; treas., Monterey Co. Scottish Rite Club, 1972---, pres. 1969; mem. Commonwealth Club; Past Master Carmel Lodge No. 680, F&AM; mem. San Jose Bodies Scottish Rite of Freemasonry (Knight Comdr. of Ct. of Honors, 1975); charter mem. Carmel Hi-12 Club. Community Ch., past pres. bd. of govs. Hobby: stamps. Rec.: travel, fishing. Home: P.O.B. 241, Carmel, CA 93921; Office: P.O.B. 2066, Carmel, CA 93921.

BLOCH, FELIX
Professor Emeritus of Physics
b. Oct. 23, 1905, Zurich, Switzerland; s. Gustav and Agnes (Mayer) Bloch; Ph.D., Univ. of Leipzig, 1928; came to U.S., 1934; naturalized, 1939; m. Lore Misch, Mar. 15, 1941, Las Vegas; chil.: George T., b. 1941; Daniel A., b. 1941; Frank S., b. 1945; Ruth H. (Alexander), b. 1949. Career: lectr. Univ. of Leipzig, 1932-33; prof. of Physics, Stanford Univ., 1934-71; prof. emeritus, 1971---; dir. gen. of CERN, Geneva, 1954-55; Awarded Nobel Prize for Physics, 1952. Mem. Nat. Acad. of Scis.; Royal Soc. of Edinburgh; Royal Dutch Acad.; Am. Physical Soc., pres. 1964-65; Am. Philosophical Soc. Jewish. Hobby: piano. Home: 1551 Emerson St., Palo Alto, CA 94301; Office: Dept. of Physics, Stanford, CA 94305.

BLOCH, HERBERT R., JR.
Civic Leader
b. Oct. 29, 1916, Cincinnati, Ohio; s. Herbert R. and Jean (Kaufman) Bloch; grad., The Taft Sch., Watertown, Conn., 1935; B.A., Yale Univ., 1939; m. Jane Meinrath (dec.); son, Peter M. Bloch, b. July 24, 1948; m. 2d Jean Freiberg Rosenthal, Jan 1, 1969. Career: with Shillito's, div. of Federated Dept. Stores, 1939---; research dir., personnel dir., controller, treas., exec. v.p.; pres., Bullock's, 1973, vice-chmn. 1975, ret. 1976; dir. Judy's. Mil. served in OPA, to 1st Lt. AUS, Quartermaster Corps, and AF, WW II. Vice-chmn., Hebrew Union Coll., Jewish Inst. of Rel., bd. of overseers, Calif. sch.; v.p., Reiss-Davis Child Study Center; secty., Jewish Fedn. Council of Greater L.A.; bd. mem. United Way, Inc.; bd. dir., So. Calif. Philharmonic, Hollywood Bowl Assn.; past dir., Calif. Retailers Assn.; Mem.: Central City Assn., L.A.; So. Calif. Visitors Council; Hillcrest Country Club, L.A.; Stock Exchange Club of L.A.; Queen City Club, Cincinnati; Cincinnati Symphony Orchestra, past bd. dir.; Financial Execs. Inst.; NCCJ, Cincinnati, 1972 Good Citizenship Award; Council of Jewish Fedns. and Welfare

Funds; ARC, Hamilton Co. chpt. exec. com.; Cincinnati Com. for Refugees, past bd. mem. Home: 1705 Angelo Dr., Beverly Hills, CA 90210.

BLOCH, JAMES LOUIS
Realtor — Mayor
b. Apr. 10, 1923, Ritzville, Wash.; s. Jesse L. (M.D.) and Ruth C. (Weil) Bloch; son-in-law of Frank T. Deasy, (dec.) Superior Ct. Judge, S.F.; father was Chief of Staff, San Pedro Gen. Hosp.; B.A. Stanford Univ., 1944; m. Patricia Deasy, S.F., June 24, 1944; chil.: Kathryn P., b. Sept. 28, 1946; Jessica L. Wick, b. Jan. 31, 1949; James D., b. June 28, 1953. Career: Freight forwarder, 1946-47; sales mgr., Blessing Packaging Co., 1947-51; owner, Tri-City Delivery (moving & storage), 1951-77; real estate broker, sales mgr., 1961-72; Realtor, sales mgr., Taylor Properties, Menlo Park, 1972---. Dir., Menlo Park-Atherton Bd. of Realtors, 1969-73, pres. 1974. Lt. USN, Pacific theater (Salvage Officer on an A.P.A.), 1943-46. City councilman, Menlo Park, 1976; Mayor, 1978. Mem.: Menlo Park Host Lions Club, pres. 1967; Suburbans, dir. 1975; Press Club of S.F.; Commonwealth Club. Jewish, 2nd v.p. B'nai Brith. Hobbies: antique cars, stamps. Rec.: sailing. Home: 1185 Trinity Dr., Menlo Park, CA 94025; Office: 807 Santa Cruz, Menlo Park, CA 94025.

BLOOMFIELD, ARTHUR JOHN
Music Critic — Author
b. Jan. 3, 1931, S.F.; s. Arthur Leonard and Julia (Mayer) Bloomfield; B.A., music, Stanford Univ., 1951; m. Anne Elizabeth Buenger, July 14, 1956, S.F.; chil.: John, b. Oct. 8, 1958; Cecily, b. June 23, 1963; Alison, b. May 14, 1965. Career: Music critic: S.F. Call-Bulletin, 1958-59; S.F. News Call-Bulletin, 1962-65; S.F. Examiner, 1965---. Author: Fifty Years of the San Francisco Opera, 1972; The San Francisco Opera, 1978; Arthur Bloomfield s Guide to San Francisco Restaurants, 1975, 77. AUS, 1953-55. Office: 110 Fifth St., S.F., CA 94103.

BLOOMFIELD, WILLIAM EDWARD
Company President
b. May 17, 1913, L.A., Calif.; s. William E. (dec.) and Anna Lorene (Wimmer) Bloomfield (Stockwell); ed. grad. UCLA 1945; m. Margaret Meyer, Escondido, Calif., Apr. 14, 1946; chil.: Mrs. Timothy (Carole) Etzel, Mrs. James (Joanne) Hunter, William Wdward, Jr. Career: assoc. with Pac. Telephone Co. 1936-47; founder-propr. WEB Serv. Co., Inc., 1947; pres. 1953--- (Calif., Ariz., Nev., Ore., Wash., N. Mex.). Mem.: bd. govs. Westside YMCA, 1946---; Santa Monica Bay Power Squad., Santa Monica Bay Council of Navy League, World Affairs Council, Westwood Village Rotary Club, Towl Hall of Calif., Aviation Country Club of Calif., Riviera Country Club. Rec.: flying, tennis. Home: 1262 Corsica Dr., Pacific Palisades, CA 90272; Office: 3690 Freeman Blvd., Redondo Beach, CA 90278.

BLOOMINGDALE, ALFRED S.
Business Executive
b. Apr. 1916, N.Y.C.; s. Hiram C. and Rosalind Bloomingdale; ed. grad. Brown Univ. 1938; m. Betty Lee Newling, Sept. 14, 1946; chil.: Lee Geoffrey, June 26, 1949; Elizabeth Lee, b. Mar. 13, 1951; Robert Russell, b. May 21, 1954. Career: Asst. mdse. mgr. Bloomingdale Bros. 1938-46; motion pic. exec. 1946-50; v.p. Diners Club, 1950-55, pres. 1955-68, chmn. bd. 1964-69, cons. 1970---; chmn. bd.-dir.: Surfside 6 Floating Homes, 1970---; pres., Marina Bay Hotel, 1973---; pres. Alfred S. Bloomingdale Enterprises, Inc., 1970---. Dir.: Lyman G. Realty Co., N.Y.; Beneficial Standard Corp., L.A.; trustee: Loyola-Marymount Coll; bd. regents, St. John's Hosp., Santa Monica; trustee: Brown Univ. Mem.: exec. com. Acad. of Motion Picture Arts and Scis.; Papal Knight Comdr. in the Order of St. Gregory; clubs: Brown Univ. Home: 131 Delfern Dr., L.A., CA 90024; Office: 1888 Century Park E., Suite 1018, L.A., CA 90067.

BLOMQUIST, AGNES
Banker — Business Executive
b. Jan. 2, 1911, Platte, S. Dak.; d. Patrick Richard and Eva (Anderson) Blomquist; ed. grad. Pasa. H.S. 1927; bus. adm., Woodbury Coll. 1927-28; Career: Secty.-treas., P.A. Palmer, Inc. 1928---; exec. v.p.-dir., Newport Balboa Svgs. & Loan Assn. 1936-62, pres.-dir. 1962-69; pres. Lido Isle Properties, Inc. 1948---; pres. Lido Ins. Agcy., Inc. 1953-69. Awards: L.A. Times Woman of the Year, 1962; Woman of Achievement award, Calif. Fed. of Bus. and Profl. Women's Club, 1966. Mem.: pres. Newport Harbor Bus. and Profl. Women's Club, 1939-40 and 1948-49; (hon.) Altrusa Club of Newport Harbor; (assoc.) Assistance League of Newport Beach; Lido Isle Players Club, Inc., Newport Harbor Yacht Club; Irvine Coast

Country Club. Republican. Hobby: little theatre work. Home: 130 Via Xanthe, Lido Isle, Newport Beach, CA.

BLUM, JOAN KURLEY
Fund-Raising Executive
b. July 27, 1926, Palm Beach, Fla.; d. Nenad Daniel and Eva (Milos) Kurley; student, Univ. of Wash., class 1948; m. Robert Cecil Blum, Apr. 15, 1967; chil.: Christopher Alexander, Martha Jane, Louisa Joan, Paul Helmuth, Danna Carolyn. Career: U.S. Dir., Inst. Mediterranean Studies, Berkeley, 1965-67; asst. dir., Univ. of Calif. Alumni Found., Berkeley, 1965-67; pres., Blum Assocs., San Anselmo, 1967---. Mem. faculty Univ. of Calif. Extension (Berkeley, Irvine, L.A., Santa Cruz); Inst. Fund Raising (N.Y.C., Washington, Chgo.); S.W. Inst. Fund Raising of Univ. of Texas; Fund Raising Sch. of Univ. of S.F.; U.K. Voluntary Movement Group (London). Recipient: Golden Addy award, Am. Advt. Fedn., 1972; Silver Mailbox award, Direct Mail Mktg. Assn., 1973; best ann. giving program, Nat. Assn. Hosp. Devel., 1974; Time-Life award, Council Advancement Scholarship in Edn., 1975; Si Seymour award, Nat. Assn. Hosp. Devel. 1976. Mem.: Direct Mktg. Writers Guild; Direct Mail Fund Raisers Assn.; Nat. Soc. Fund Raisers, dir.; Nat. Assn. Hosp. Devel.; Devel. Exec. Roundtable; Women Emerging; San Francisco Advt. Club. Contbr. articles profl. jours. Home: Kentfield, CA; Office: 292 Red Hill, San Anselmo, CA 94960.

BLUROCK, BARBARA STEPHANIE
College Dean
b. Jan. 7, 1927, Brooklyn, N.Y.; d. Walter and Betty Blourock; B.A., speech, Brooklyn Coll., 1950, M.A., edn., 1952; M.A., personnel guidance, N.Y. Univ., 1964; Ph.D., adminstrn., counseling, Union Grad. Sch., 1973. Career: tchr., counselor, high sch., Brooklyn, 1950-68; v.p., editor, prin., pub. house, 1967-68; ednl. cons. and counselor, Puerto Rico, 1968-70; assoc. prof., No. Virginia Community Coll., 1971-72; coord., student affairs, Universidad Boricua, Wash., D.C., 1972-73; asst. prof., San Diego State Univ., 1973-74; asst. Dean of Students, San Diego State Univ., 1974-76; Dean of Counseling and Guidance, Southwestern Coll., Chula Vista, 1976---; v.p., bd. of trustees, Grad. Sch. for Urban Resources and Social Policy; cons., S.D. Unified Schs. Study, 1978; chmn., Assessment Center Task Force, Higher Edn. Assn. of S.D., 1977-78. Contbr. articles to ednl. journs. Chmn., commn. of the Status of Women, 1978-79; Mem.: AAUP; Calif. Women in Higher Edn.; Bus. & Profl. Women's Club; Nat. Women's Polit. Caucus; Calif. Personnel and Guidance Assn.; Am. Personnel and Guidance Assn.; Puerto Rican Forum, Inc., bd. dir. Home: 2843 Eagle St., San Diego, CA 92103; Office: 900 Otay Lakes Rd., Chula Vista, CA 92010.

BLYSTONE, F. LYNN
Pipeline Company Executive
b. Aug. 28, 1935, La Habra, Calif.; s. Frank E. and Reta Lee (Taylor) Blystone; bro., Helen Lee Ann B., nat. mktg. mgr., Walt Disney Studios, Burbank; A.A., Fullerton Comm. Coll., 1955; B.A., Whittier Coll., 1957; postgrad., Geo. Williams Coll., Chicago, 1957-58, Cal. State Univ., L.A., 1963; m. Patricia Baker, Mar. 21, 1964, Bakersfield; chil.: Jon Franklin, b. Apr. 8, 1965; Ryan Taylor, b. June 16, 1969. Career: YMCA Camp Dir., Fullerton, 1953-57; residence asst., Hyde Park branch, YMCA, Chicago, 1958-59; program asst., Pittsburgh YMCA, 1959-60; program and camp dir., Santa Monica YMCA, 1961-62; program dir., YMCA of Kern Co., 1963-65, gen. exec., 1965-70; mgr. special projects & corp. devel., Banister Pipelines Alaska, Inc., 1974-76; chmn. of the bd., pres., chief exec., Bandera Land Co., Inc.; owner, Venture Devel./Bus. Plans, Fairbanks, Ak. 1974-76; owner, Cherry Creek Venture Group, Dencer; Dir.: Aurora Internat., Inc. ---; TriValley Oil & Gas Co., Inc. ---; Western Hemisphere Resources, Inc., 1973-74; Calif. Inland Devel. Corp. 1973-74; v.p. & dir., Kern Co. Economic Opportunity Corp., 1966-70; pres., Mus. Devel. Com., Inc., Bakersfield, 1974; chmn., pres. com., Gr. Bakersfield C. of C., 1971-73; dir., Kern chpt. ARC, 1973-74; dir., YMCA of Kern Co. 1973-74. Named Wm. Sloane House National U.N. Fellow, 1960. AUS, 1958-60, 1961-62. Mem.: Libertas Lodge No. 466 F&AM; Petroleum Club of Bakersfield; Houchin Community Blood Bank. Democrat. Disciples of Christ. Hobbies: backpacking, fund raising, civic work. Home: P.O.B. 1105, Bakersfield, CA 93302; Office: 3333 Quebec St., Suite 8100, Denver, Colo. 80238.

BOARD, ROBERT ROY
University Registrar
b. Sept. 30, 1922, Lewistown, Mont.; s. Wm. Charles and

Irene Anna (Conners) Board; B.S. acctg., Univ. Santa Clara, 1948; m. Mary Lu Bush, Feb. 15, 1948; Stockton; chil.: Gregory Charles, b. June 23, 1950; Bradley Robert, b. Feb. 10, 1953. Career: acctg. systems, Nat. Cash Register, 1948-51; mfgrs. rep., Ames Harris Neville, 1951-56; Systems & Interior Design Cons., Healey & Popovich, 1956-64; reigstrar, Cal. State Univ., Fresno, 1964---. AUS, 1943-45, 112th Cavalry, 1st Cav. Div., wounded P.I. Founder, Tehipite chpt. Sierra Club, 1953, chpt. chmn. 1956-60; cons. U.S. Forest Serv.; mem. Grand Jury, Fresno Co., 1978-79; dir. Three Forests Interpretive Assn.; mem. Sierra Land Use Com.; Masonic; Scottish Rite. Republican. Presbyterian; Elder, Deacon, Synod Rep., Campus Ministry to higher edn. Hobby: photog. Rec.: sailing, travel. Home: 5494 N. Roosevelt, Fresno, CA 93704; Office: CSU, Fresno, CA 93740.

BOARDMAN, DORIS
College Librarian
b. Sulphur Springs, Tex.; d. William F. and Ella Shepherd Glosup; B.A. in lib. sci., Texas Women's Univ.; M.L.S., USC, 1964; m. Willis Boardman, June 19, 1948, L.A.; chil.: John, b. Aug. 9, 1952; Diane, b. Jan. 4, 1956; Cynthia (Hill), b. May 4, 1958. Career: Asst. Lib. (ext. dept.), Texas State Lib., Austin, 1944-45; children's librn. and ref. librn., Mark Twain Br. Lib., Wilshire Br. Lib. and Univ. Br. Lib. of L.A. Pub. Lib., 1945-51; H.S. librn., San Bernardino Co. Free Lib., 1951-54; children's librn., San Bernardino Pub. Lib., 1955; cataloger and ref. librarian, San Bernardino Valley Coll., 1961-72; head librn., Crafton Hills Coll. Lib., Yucaipa, 1972---. Author: Israel, Its Birth and Beginning Years, as Recorded in Government Documents (1978). Mem.: Calif. Lib. Assn.; Calif. Tchrs. Assn.; Faculty Assn. of Calif. Community Colls.; Inland Empire chpt., Calif. Librns.' Assn. Mem. Community Bible Ch., Sun. Sch. secty., ch. clk. Hobby: photog. Rec.: hiking. Home: 139 East 39th St., San Bernardino, CA; Office: Crafton Hills Coll. Lib., 11711 Sand Canyon Rd., Yucaipa, CA 92399.

BOARMAN, PATRICK M.
Professor of International Economics
b. Apr. 23, 1922, Buffalo, N.Y.; s. Marcus Daly and Virginia (Madigan) Boarman; desc. Wm. Boarman, who with Lord Baltimore (Cecil Calvert) helped found the colony of Maryland in 1648; B.A., Fordham Univ., 1943; M.S., Columbia Univ., 1946; Ph.D., Univ. of Geneva, 1965; m. Katrin Schumacher, Dec. 12, 1953; Bad. Godesberg, Germany; chil.: Thomas, b. Sept. 18, 1954; Christopher, b. Jan. 14, 1957; Jesse, b. Feb. 16, 1958; Barbara, b. Mar. 25, 1961. Career: asst. prof. economics, Univ. Wisc., 1956-57; assoc. prof. of Econ., Bucknell Univ., 1962-67; dir. of research, House Republican Conf., House of Reps., U.S. Congress, 1967-68; prof. of Econ., Long Island Univ., 1967-72; dir. of research, center for Internat. Bus., L.A., 1972-75; pres., Patrick M. Boarman, Assoc., Internat. Bus. Consultants, 1975---; prof. Internat. Econ., Monterey Inst. of Foreign Studies, Monterey, 1978---; chief correspondent, CBS, Geneva, Switzerland, 1946-48. Author: Germany's Economic Dilemma, 1964; Union Monopolies and Antitrust Restraints, 1963; The Christian and the Social Market Economy, 1955, others; editor: Balance of Payments Seminar, Foreign Aid and Economic Development; Trade with China; Multinational Corporations and Governments; World Monetary Disorder; Translator: Economics of the Free Society by Wilhelm Roepke, 1963. Decorated D.S.C., Order of Merit, Federal Repub. of Germany, 1956. Mem.: Am. Economics Assn.; Nat. Assn. Bus. Economists; Com. for Monetary Research and Edn.; Royal Economic Soc. Roman Catholic; dir., Office of Cultural Affairs, Nat. Catholic Welfare Conf., Bonn, Germany, 1951-55. Home: 27235 Eastvale Rd., Palos Verdes, CA 90274.

BOAZ, MARTHA T.
Dean, USC School of Library
b. Stuart, Va.; d. James Robert and Kate (Gilley) Boaz; ed. B.S., B.S. in L.S., M.A., in Lib. Sci., Ph.D. Career: Tchr. and librarian, pub. schs., Va., Ky. 1935-40 asst. lib. Madison Coll., Harrisburg, Va. 1940-49; assoc. prof., lib. sci. Univ. Tenn. 1950-51; instr. Univ. of Mich., Ann Arbor, 1951-52; assoc. prof. Sch. of Lib. Sci., USC 1953-55; dean and prof. 1955---. Author: "Fervent and Full Gifts," 1961; ed. Modern Trends in Documentation, 1959; compiler, "Quest for Truth," vol. 1, 1961, vol. II, 1967; contrib. to Library Journ., Am. Libs., Wilson Bulletin, Journ. of Edn. for Librarianship, Calif. Librarian. Mem.: pres. Assn. of Am. Lib. Schs. 1962-63; pres. Calif. Lib. Assn. 1962; pres. Lib. Edn. Div., Am. Lib. Assn. 1969; chmn. Intellectual Freedom Comm. 1965. Office: USC Sch. of Library Science, University Park, L.A., CA 90007.

BOCCARDO, JAMES F.
Attorney at Law
b. July 1, 1911, San Francisco; s. John H. and Erminia (Ferrando) Boccardo; father associated with A.P. Giannini during early days of Bank of Italy, (became Bank of America) B. of A. bank officer for 40 years; A B., San Jose State Univ., 1931; LL.B., J.D., Stanford Univ., 1934; m. Lorraine Dimmett, Stanford, Nov. 19, 1936; chil: Leanne Boccardo Rees, b. June 18, 1938; John H. Boccardo II, b. June 8, 1948. Career: Pvt. law practice, San Jose, Oct. 1934---; sr. partner, law firm of Boccardo, Lull, Niland & Bell, offices in San Jose, S.F., L.A. and Irvine. Founder, chmn. of bd., Community Bank of San Jose, 1965---. Pres.: Samite Claire Corp.; Boccardo Corp.; Boccardo Ranches; Western Gravel Co. Founder and past pres., Inner Circle of Advocates. Fellow of Internat. Acad. of Trial Lawyers.Mem.: Am. Trial Lawyers Assn., Past pres., S.F. chpt. Lecturer, nationwide in legal seminars. Mem.: Masonic Lodge No. 479; Los Gatos Elks; Scottish Rite; San Jose Consistory; Sciots, Islam Temple of the Shrine. Country Clubs: San Jose, La Rinconada, Monterey Penin., Thunderbird, Indian Wells. Rec.: golf, aviation. Home: 14070 Wildway, Los Gatos; 40941 Tonapah Rd., Rancho Mirage, Thunderbird Hts.; Office: 111 W. St. John, San Jose, CA 94113.

BODEEN, DeWITT
Writer
b. July 25, 1908, Fresno, Calif.; s. Gus G. and Ruth (DeWitt) Bodeen; B.A., English, UCLA, 1933. Career: playwright for the theatre (11 plays first presented at Pasadena Playhouse), 1930's-40's.; screenwriter (RKO-Radio Pictures, 1942-48), screenplays include: Cat People, Seventh Victim, Curse of the Cat People, The Yellow Canary, The Enchanted Cottage, Night Song, I Remember Mama, Mrs. Mike, Billy Budd; writer of Live and filmed teleplays, 1950s, for programs incl. Danger!, Cavalcade of America, Somerset Maugham Theatre of the Air, Mr. and Mrs. North, Four Star Playhouse, Schlitz Playhouse of the Air, Climax, Panic!, 20th Century-Fox TV Theatre, Lux Video Theatre, Screen Gems; publs. include "13 Castle Walk, 1975; From Hollywood, 1976, More From Hollywood!, 1977; assoc. editor for Who Wrote the Movie, and What Else Did He Write?, 1969; staff mem., Acad. of Motion Picture Arts & Sci., 1968-70; regular contbr. to film mags., Films in Review, NYC, Focus on Film, London. Charter mem. Writers Guild of Am.; Acad. of Motion Picture Arts & Sciences, 1945-77. Rec.: traveling, walking. Home: Motion Picture Country House, 23450 Calabasas Rd., Woodland Hills, CA 91364.

BODENHEIMER, EDGAR
Professor Emeritus of Law
b. Mar. 14, 1908, Berlin, Germany; s. Siegmund and Rosa (Maass) Bodenheimer; D.J., Univ. Heidelberg, 1933; LL.B., Univ. Wash., 1937; m. Brigitte M. Levy, June 6, 1935, NYC; chil.: Peter H., b. June 29, 1937; Thomas S., b. June 13, 1939; R. Rosemarie, b. Oct. 11, 1946. Career: Atty., U.S. Dept. of Labor, 1940-42; principal atty., Office of Alien Property Custodian, 1942-46; assoc. prof. of Law, Univ. of Utah, 1946-51; prof. of Law, 1951-66; prof. of Law, UC, Davis, 1956-75; prof. emeritus of Law, 1975---; v.p. Am. Soc. of Polit. and Legal Philosophy, 1970-71; mem. editorial bd., Am. Journ. of Comparative Law, 1952-76. Publs.: Treatise on Justice (N.Y., 1967); Power, Law, and Society (N.Y., 1973); Jurisprudence: The Philosophy and Method of the Law, rev. ed. (Cambridge, Mass. 1974). Mem.: Phi Alpha Delta, 1947-75; Phi Kappa Phi Honor Soc., 1970---. Home: 542 Miller Dr., Davis, CA; Office: Sch. of Law, Univ. of Calif., Davis, CA 95616.

BODLE, YVONNE LEE
Author — Educator
b. Dec. 5, 1939, Tucumcari, N. Mex.; d. Joseph M. and Ruby (Bates) Gallegos; ed. B.A., Univ. of Calif., San Jose, 1963; M.A., Columbia Univ., N.Y. 1964; m. Michael E. Bodle, Oxnard, Calif., Dec. 18, 1965; chil.: Robert Jpseh, b. Dec. 3, 1968; Michelle Yvonne, b. Jan. 8, 1971. Career: Secty.-research asst. Safety Research and Edn. Proj., Columbia Univ., N.Y. 1963-64; bus. instr. Hueneme H.S., Oxnard Calif. 1964-65; Ventura Coll., 1965---. Co-author: "The Administrative Secretary: Practicum," 1970; "Retail Selling," "Laboratory Manual for Retail Selling," 1972 (publ. McGraw-Hill Book Co.); "McGrath," 1972; "Villanova Prep Sch. of Ojai," 1974; research stu.-mag. articles, 1964-65. Awards: Award of Merit for Outstanding Achievement, Columbia Univ. Tchrs. Coll. 1964; "Outstanding Career Woman of the Yr.," Bus. and Profl. Women's Club, Oxnard, 1972; feat. Contemporary Authors; Leader in Edn. Mem.: Founder-pres. Ventura Co. Business Educators Assn. 1967-68; Kappa Delta Pi, Pi Lambda Theta, Ventura Co. Forty Leaguers, Oxnard

Hist. Soc. (charter). Catholic. Rec.: horse back and trail riding. Office: 4667 Telegraph Rd., Ventura, CA 93003.

BOEGER, MARY ROSE
Business Owner
b. Aug. 31, 1945, Oregon City, Ore.; d. Ernest and Rose (DeMacon) Steen; B.S., home econ., Chico State Univ., 1967, life tchg. credential, 1970; m. Daniel Edward Boeger, Corvallis, Ore.; chil.: Matthew Wade, b. Oct. 23, 1967; Stephen Andrew, b. Apr. 27, 1970. Career: instr., dept. head, Gridley Union Hi. Sch., 1973-74; prin., The Magic Needle; cert. instr. Kwik Sew Pattern Co., 1978---; dir. Gridley Dist. C. of C., v.p. 1978, pres. elect. 1979; bd. dir., Jr. Womens Club of Gridley, 1968; bd. dir., Tiny Tot Playsch., 1971; mem. secondary advis. com., Gridley Union High Sch., 1977-78; Mem.: Omicron Nu, Alpha Chi Omega; Beta Sigma Phi; Quota Club of Gridley. Hobby: needlecraft. Rec.: tennis, swimming. Office: 893 Hazel St., Gridley, CA 95948.

BOEPPLE, ROLLAND EMERSON
College Librarian
Dec. 25, 1927, Baltimore, Md.; s. John Theuer, and Matie Viola (Flessner) Boepple; A.B., Elizabethtown Coll., Pa., 1949; M.S.L.S., USC, 1962; postgrad. Calif. State Univ., Fullerton and Long Beach; m. Saeko Nakano, Nov. 9, 1958, San Bernardino; chil.: Kathy Elaine, b. Feb. 3, 1960; Leslie Ruth, b. Feb. 24, 1965. Career: Lib. Trainee, then librarian, L.A. Pub. Lib., 1959-62; Libn., Douglas Aircraft Co. Engring. Lib., Long Beach, 1962-64; Libn., Anaheim Pub, Lib., 1964; Libn., Philco-Ford, Aeroneutronic Div., Newport Beach, 1965-67; Dir. of Lib. Services, Santa Ana Coll., Santa Ana, 1967---. Mem.: Assn. of Calif. Community Coll. Adminstrs.; Faculty Assn. of Calif. Community Colls.; Council on Lib. Tech.; Calif. Lib. Assn. Hobbies: piano, pottery. Rec.: sailing, fishing, golf. Home: 17972 Larcrest Cir., Huntington Beach, CA 92647; Office: 17th St. at Bristol, Santa Ana, CA 92706.

BOGDANOVICH, JOSEPH JAMES
President, Star-Kist Foods, Inc.
y 9, 1912, San Pedro, Calif.; s. Martin Joseph (Founder-first pres., French Sardine Co.; dec. 1944) and Antoinette (Simich) Bogdanovich; ed. San Pedro H.S.; USC 1930-34; m. Nancynell Swaffield, Long Beach, Calif., Apr. 3, 1937; chil.: Martin Joseph, b. Mar. 26, 1938; Robert Roland b. Nov. 29, 1940; Joseph James, Jr., b. July 3, 1946; Career: Assoc. cannery prodn. (summers), 1926-30; commerical fisherman, coast of Central Am. 1933; assoc. (apprentice), French Sardine Co., 1937-44; prodn. mgr.-asst. to pres. 1937-44; pres. 1944--- (name changed to Star-Kist Foods, Inc.); est. most modern tuna packing plant in world, 1952, (subsidiary of H.J. Heinz Co. 1963---; dir., H.J. Heinz Co. Viv. Def., WW II. Awards: prodn. mgr. when French Sardine Co. recd. "E" Award. Mem.: Virginia Country Club, Long Beach; Chi Phi. Democrat. Catholic. Rec.: golf, horseback riding, fishing. Home: 31 Saddleback Rd., Rolling Hills, CA; Office: 580 Tuna, Terminal Is., CA.

BOGUE, LUCILE MAXFIELD
Writer
b. Apr. 21, 1911, Salt Lake City; d. Roy and Maude (Callicotte) Maxfield; A.A., Colo Coll., 1932, B.A., Univ. of No. Colo, 1934; M.A., S.F. State Univ., 1972; postgrad. studies France, Japan, Mexico; m. Arthur Bogue, (dec.) Dec. 25, 1935, Aspen, Colo.; chil.: Sharon (Young), b. Jan. 13, 1939; Bonnie, b. May 1, 1941. Career: tchr., Colo. pub. schs., 1934-62; pvt. schs.: Am. Sch., Managua, 1951; Whiteman Sch., Colo., 1957-59; pres. & founder, Yampa Valley Coll., 1962-66 (Colo.) (now br. of U.S. Internat. Univ., S.D.); Dir of Guidance, Am. Sch. in Japan, 1966-68; traveling guidance dir., U.S. State Dept., Japan, 1968. Dean, Anna Head Sch., Oakland, 1968-71; author: plays, poetry, novel, biography, 1972---: works include Westward The Storm, 1978, (Nat. Writers Club winner, novel); Blood of Malinche, 1975 (Grand Prize winner, World of Poetry); A Fresh Moon, 1976 (Gold Medal winner All Nations Poetry Contest); book of poetry, Typhoon! Typhoon!, Tuttle Pub. Co., Tokyo, 1969; Eye of the Condor, pub. by Casa de Cultura, Ecuadorean Govt., 1975. Mem.: East Bay Center for Performing Arts, pres. 1978-79; Calif. Writers Club, pres. 1978-79; Central Bd. of Calif. Writers Clubs of No. Calif., pres. 1978-81. Unitarian, Chmn. nat. hymn & anthem contest, 1978. Hobby: crocheting afghans. Rec.: travel. Home: 2611 Brooks, El Cerrito, CA 94530.

BOHLINGER, JOAN GILLESPIE
Realtor
b. Apr. 21, 1920, Troy, N.Y.; d. Paul and Louise (Young) Gillespie; student, Columbia Univ.; G.R.I. (Graduate Realtors Inst.); m. Thomas A. Bohlinger, June 1943, Mamaroneck, N.Y.; chil.: Thomas Peter, b. Feb. 22, 1951 (capt. USC. football team, Rose Bowl, 1972-73); Peter Young, b. Sept. 21, 1954 (M.B.A., USC, 1978); Linda Joan (Pendlebury), b. Aug. 28, 1949 (M. Pub. Adm., USC). Career: Broadway Showgirl, 1940; designer model in N.Y., 1943; homemaker until 1960; real estate profl., 1960---: co-owner, Tom-Joan Bohlinger Realtors, Santa Ynez. Awarded (with husband), seventeen state and national awards for excellence in mktg., brochures, etc., Real Estate Annual Conventions, 1966-78. Founder, first chairperson, Santa Ynez Valley Div., Santa Barbara Bd. of Realtors; vice-pres., Santa Barbara Bd. of Realtors Women's Council, 1974. Mem. Children's Home Soc., Santa Ynez Valley chpt.; active, Methodist ch., Presbyterian ch.; S.B, Santa Ynez Valley; married couples group. Hobbies: swimming, boating. Home: Oak Valley Ranch, Santa Ynez, CA 93460; Office: 3558 Sagunto St., P.O.B. 416, Santa Ynez, CA 93460.

BOHNSTEDT, JOHN WOLFGANG
Professor of History
b. Feb. 22, 1927, Berlin, Germany; s. Werner A. (Prof. of Humanities, Mich. State Univ. 1946-64) and Bertha Bohnstedt; B.A., soc. sci., Mich. State Univ., 1950; M.A., hist., Univ. Minn., 1952, Ph.D., 1959; m. Frieda Bohnstedt, Sept. 18, 1948, Lansing, Mich.; chil.: Stephen, b. 1957; Mary, b. 1960. Career: tchg. asst. hist., Univ. Minn., 1951-53; instr. European hist., Univ. of S. Dak. (Vermillion), 1955-56; mem. faculty, Cal. State Univ., Fresno, 1956---, Prof. of History, 1968---; Fulbright Fellow, Austria, 1953-54; Author: The Infidel Scourge of God: The Turkish Menace as Seen by German Pamphleteers of the Reformation era (Phila.: Am. Philosophical Soc., 1968); award, Distinguished Tching., CSU Fresno, 1966; chief exec. officer, Grievance Panel, CSU, Fresno, 1976-77; AUS, 1945-47. Mem.: Am. Hist. Assn., Soc. for Hist. Edn., Phi Kappa Phi. Democrat. Hobby: gardening. Rec.: old movies. Home: 5543 N. Bond, Fresno, CA 93710; Office: Dept. of History, CSU Fresno, CA 93740.

BOITANO, JAMES D.
Napa County District Attorney
b. May 21, 1927, Napa; s. David and Teresa Boitano; J.D., Univ. S.F., 1951; student, Napa Jr. Coll., Santa Clara Univ., Univ. Calif.; m. Margaret Mahoney, Aug. 27, 1955, S.F.; chil.: Sarah Marie, b. July 22, 1960; Mary Teresa, b. July 3, 1962. Career: pvt. law practice, Napa, 1952-62; Dist. Atty. of Napa Co., 1963---; Pub. Adminstr. and Guardian of Napa Co., 1969---. U.S. Merchant Marine, WW II. Dir. Imperial S&L Assn. of the North, 1967-74, advis. bd. mem. 1974---; dir., Napa Co. Legal Aid Agency, 1967-76; pres., Napa Co. Mental Health Assn., 1968-69, mem. advis. bd., 1969-75; pres., Queen of the Valley Hosp. Found., 1976-78; dir., No. Bay Reg. Criminal Justice Planning Bd., 1971-74; dir., Napa Boys Club, 1969-72; exec. bd. mem., BSA, Silverado council, 1971---; dir., advis. council, Big Brothers of Napa Co., 1968---; pres., Napa Co. Bar Assn., 1966-67; dir. Univ. of S.F. Law Alumni, 1968-71; dir. Napa C. of C., 1976---; mem.: State Bar Assn., Am. Bar Assn.; ARC, past pres. Napa Toastmasters Club; Elks; Moose; Sons of Italy; K.C.; Calif. Hist. Soc.; Napa Co. Hist. Soc.; Native Sons of Golden West, state pres. 1964-65; Italian Catholic Fedn.; v.p. state Young Republicans 1954-55, chmn. Napa Co. Central Com., 1958-59, no current partisan polit. Roman Catholic. Hobby: native sons. Home: 2876 Pinewood Dr., Napa, CA 94558. Office: Hall of Justice, Napa, CA 94558.

BOLES, JOHN JOSEPH
Economist
b. June 3, 1924, Waterville, Me.; s. Thomas and Mary (Saad) Boles; ed. B.S. (commerce), Univ. of Va. 1947, M.A. (econs.), 1949; Fulbright Fellow, Univ. of Egypt, 1950-51; m. Diane Lindsay Durand, Solvang, Calif., Aug. 27, 1955; chil.: Thomas, b. July 24, 1956; Hilary, b. June 23, 1958; Maria, b. Dec. 1959; Patricia, b. Mar. 12, 1953; Christa, b. Jan. 5, 1965. Career: econs. prof.-asst. prof., Loyola Univ. 1953-57; assoc. prof., Marquette Univ. 1957-60; Middle East and Arab advisor, 1960-63; econ. Occidental Petroleum Corp. 1964---. Dir. St. Jude Hosp.; advisor, St. Thomas Cath. Sch., Ojai, Calif. Author: "Foreign Trade of Soviet Russia," 1954; "Monetary System of Saudi Arabia," 1962; various articles publ. profl. journs. U.S. Marines, WWII. Mem.: Am. Econ. Assn., Am. Polit. Sci. Assn. Home: 804 Country Club Rd., Ojai, CA; Office: Suite 1500, 10889 Wilshire Blvd., L.A., CA 90024.

BOLINGER, DWIGHT LeMERTON
Professor Emeritus of Linguistics
b. Aug. 18, 1907, Topeka, Kan.; s. Arthur Joel and Gertrude Nellie (Ott); A.B. Washburn Coll., 1930; M.A., Univ. Kan., 1932; Ph.D., Univ. Wis., 1936; M.A. (hon.) Harvard, 1963; Litt.D. (hon.) Washburn Univ., 1964; m. Louise Schrynemakers, July 1, 1934, L.A.; chil.: Bruce Clyde, b. Nov. 13, 1936; Ann Celeste (McClure), b. Dec. 28, 1928. Career: Spanish instr., Jr. Coll., Kan. City, Mo., 1937; assoc. prof. of Spanish, Washburn Coll., 1937-44; Sterling Fellow in Linguistics, 1943-44, Yale Univ.; asst. prof., Spanish, USC, 1944-60; chmn. dept. of Spanish and Italian, USC, 1946-59; research fellow in Speech, Haskins Labs., 1956-57; prof. of Spanish, Univ. Colo., 1960-63; prof. of Romance Languages and Literatures, Harvard Univ., 1963-73, visiting prof. emeritus of Linguistics, Stanford Univ., 1977---. Publs.: Interrogative Structures of Am. English, 1957; Forms of English, 1965; Aspects of Language, 1968; Degree Words, 1972; The Phrasal Verb in English, 1971; Meaning and Form, 1977. Mem.: Am. Assn. of Tchrs. of Spanish and Portugese, pres. 1960; Linguistic Soc. of Am., pres. 1972; Linguistic Assn. of Canada and the U.S., pres. 1975-76. Rec.: bicycling. Home: 2718 Ramona St., Palo Alto, CA 94306.

BOLKER, JOSEPH ROBERT
Developer — Builder
b. May 23, 1924, Omaha, Nebr.; B.S., UCLA, 1950; student, Univ. Nebr., Boeing Sch. of Aeronautics, Oakland, Douglas Sch. of Aeronautics, Santa Monica; div.; four daughters. Career: with Biltmore Homes L.A., 1950-55; formed Brighton-Bilt Homes (38 affil. corps.), 1955-71, pres., sole owner, Brighton Internat. Devel. Corp., 1971---; also Rights for Forty Carrots restaurants, 1977---; mem. advis. com., Econ. Devel. Council for Territories of the U.S., 1976---; Recipient: commendations City Councils of L.A., Montebello, Port Hueneme; L.A. Co. Bd. of Suprs., C. of C. and City of Port Hueneme; Congress for Better Living award, McCall's; Gold Nugget Award, Western Bldg. Assn.; First Prize, and Best Builder of Year, Nat. Assn. of Home Builders; Humanitarian Award, L.A.. Served to Lt., USAF, Eng. and France, discharged 1945. Mem.: dir., Bldg. Indus. Assn.; Home Bldrs. Assn. of L.A.; Nat. Assn. Home Bldrs., Wash.; L.A. Beautiful Com., co-founder: Hueneme, Montebello and Oxnard Beautiful; chmn. Eilat, Israel Beautification Com.; active: L.A. to Paris Week, Beverly Hills/Acapulco Sister City, L.A./Eilat Sister City, L.A./Bombay Sister City, L.A. Internat. Visitors program; patron: Leakey Found.; Maude Booth Home; L.A. Music Center; L.A. Co. Art Mus.; Greek Theater and Huntington Hartford Theater; Friends of L.A. Free Clinic; Palm Springs Center Theater of Performing Arts; Modern Mus. of Art, N.Y.; Metropolitan Mus. of Art; Natural Hist. Mus. Alliance; Thalians; dir., Chamber Symphony Soc. of Calif.; dir., Am. Youth Symphony. Mem.: World Bus. Council, Nat. Small Bus. Assn., Am. Jewish Com., World Affairs Council of Desert, Palm Springs Racquet Club; Navy League. Hobbies: theater, opera, ballet, gardening. Rec.: scuba, river rafting, skiing. Home: 187 San Marcos Way, Palm Springs, CA 92262; 2125 Foothill Lane, Santa Barbara, CA 93105; Office: 2220 Ave. of the Stars, Apt. 2402, L.A., CA 90067.

BOLLES, RICHARD NELSON
Clergyman — Author
b. Mar. 19, 1927, Milwaukee, Wis.; s. Donald Clinton and Frances Fethers (Fifield) Bolles; desc. Doty, Mayflower pilgrim, 1620; gr.son., Stephen Bolles, U.S. Congressman, Wis.; B.A., physics, cum laude, Harvard Univ., 1950; S.T.B., Gen. Theol. Seminary, 1953, S.T.M., 1957; m. Janet Lorraine Price, Dec. 30, 1949 (div. 1971), Teaneck, N.J.; chil.: Stephen, b. May 11, 1953; Mark, b. Feb. 15, 1955; Gary, b. Sept. 6, 1957; Sharon, b. Dec. 29, 1958. Career: Fellow and tutor, Gen. Seminary, 1953-55; Vicar, Ch. of the Redeemer, Palisades Park and St. James Ch., Ridgefield, N.J., 1955-58; Rector, St. John's Ch., Passaic, N.J., 1958-66; fellow, Coll. of Preachers, 1964; Canon Pastor, Grace Cathedral, S.F., 1966-68; nat. staff, United Ministries in Higher Edn., 1968---; dir., Nat. Career Devel. Project, 1974---; Author: What Color Is Your Parachute? (best-seller) 1972; co-author (w/John Crystal) Where Do I Go From Here With My Life?, 1974; The Three Boxes of Life and How To Get Out Of Them, 1978. USN 1945-46. Mem. Rotary Club, 1958-66. Episcopal: minister. Hobby: camping. Home: 155 Sharene Lane, No. 217, Walnut Creek, CA 94596; Office: P.O.B., Walnut Creek, CA 94596.

BOLLINGER, ORAN EDWARD
Clergyman
b. Feb. 21, 1914, Fresno; s. Archie Alexander and Edna Millie (Hamilton) Bollinger; A.B. Chapman Coll., 1939;

M. Div., Lexington Theological Seminary, Ky., 1951; Ph.D., Univ. Maryland, 1964; mil. studies, P.I., Paris Univ., France; m. Christina Ruth Cattell, 1961, Gridley, Calif.; chil.: Steve Fred; Lynda Lou (Dunn); David Alan; Laura Lynn. Career: Minister, 1939---; U.S. Army Chaplain (Lt. Col.) Philippines, France, Germany, 1945-54; employment counselor, 1961-64; social worker to welfare dir., Imperial Co., 1964-69; Econ. Opportunity Dir., Kings Co., 1969-71; pastor, First Christian Ch., Turlock, 1971---. Publs.: column, Chaplain's Corner, Stars and Stripes, 1952-54; French Franc Speaks, 1954; Penny-Power Recipes, 1969 (cookbook for low budget); numerous articles. Dir., Mendocino Co. Civil Def., 1955-58; Mem.: Lions Club, pres. 1967; Rotary Club, 1968-71; Mason, 32 degrees. Christian Ch.; state chmn., Men's Commn., 1977-79; chmn. State Evangelism Commn. 1966. Hobbies: stamps, rock cutting, writing. Rec.: fishing, golf, camping. Home: 1010 Edwards Dr., Turlock, CA 95380; Office: 180 S. Denair St., Turlock, CA 95380.

BOND, JAMES GEORGE
University President
b. Apr. 17, 1924, Lorain, Ohio; s. Monroe G. and Coloma R. Bond; ed. B.A., Baldwin Wallace Coll., 1948; LL.D., 1969; M.A., Bowling Green State Univ., 1949; Ph.D., NYU, 1954; D.H., Central New Eng. Colls., 1973; m. Lois Leach, Lorain, Oh., June 24, 1950; chil.: Constance, b. Nov. 1951; Michael, b. June 1954; Timothy, b. Dec. 1958. Career: chief psychol., Toledo State and Receiving Hosp., 1951-72; v.p. Student Affairs-prof. psychol., Bowling Green State Univ., 1967-72; pres. Calif. State Univ., Sacto., 1972---. Spec. Cons. to Am. Assn. of State Colls. and Univs., 1972; chmn. bd. trustees, Meadville Theol. Sch. of Lombard Coll.-Univ. Chicago, 1972-74; chmn. Comm. on Acad. Affairs, Am. Council on Edn., 1973-74; Combat Inf., WW II. Mem.: Bd. trustees, Sacto. area Mental Health Assn. 1973---; gov. bd. Sacto. Area United Way, 1973---; exec. bd. Golden Empire B.S.A. Council, 1973---; bd. trustees, Comstock Club, 1973---; Sutter Club of Sacto.; bd. dir., Am. Justice Inst.; Adv. Bd., Natl. Alliance of Businessmen. Home: 2822 American River Dr., Sacto., CA 95825; Office: 6000 J St., Sacto., CA 95819.

BONINE, VIVIAN WAY SMALL
Film Technician — Poet
b. Sept. 28, 1912, Erath Co., Texas; d. John Mitchell and Lany Virginia (Ellison) Way; desc. of Zachary Taylor, twelfth President of U.S.A.; student, public schs., various universities; hon. Doctor of Arts and Letters, World Univ., Hong Kong, 1970; m. Morris W. Small, Dec. 28, 1931, Clovis, N.M.; chil.: Billy Faye (Mrs. Jerry Paul Jones), b. Mar. 14, 1933; Patricia Ruth (Mrs. F. Jack Webster), b. Sept. 2, 1937; m. 2d Arvel Earl Bonine, Jan. 1, 1959, Portugese Bend, Calif. Career: supr. of practice tchrs., W. Texas State Univ., 1943; civil service clk., Navy Dept., Washington, D.C., 1944-45; film tech., Technicolor Cor., Hollywood, 1946-71; cattle rancher, 1960---; tchr: adult poetry, 1965; children's poetry, 1971. Also writer, mostly poetry, 1955---. Recipient of Woman of the Year, 1975, award — gold laurel leaf crown with title of poet laureate, United Poets Laureate Internat., Manila, P.I. Dir., patrons and sponsors, Anthology on World Brotherhood and Peace, 1978---. Author: two publ. volumes of poetry: Sparks, 1958; Silver Ashes, 1966; Edit., publ. Scriptorium Arboretum; Blue Quail Poems, newspaper poetry column; Ralls Banner, 1967-72; more than 600 poems publ. in 17 states of U.S. and all six continents, incl. many prize winning poems; poetry volumes in progress: California, Land of the Chaparral; Fifty Stars Gleaming. Life mem.: Writers' Club of Pasadena; Poetry Soc. of Tex.; film technician's Local 683, Hollywood, Internat. Alliance of Theatrical and Stage Employees; Ralls Hist. Mus.; Silver Phoenix Club of W. Tex. State Univ. Alumni Assn. Mem.: Calif. State Poetry Soc., Calif. Federation of Chapparal Poets, Nat. Fed. of State Poetry Soc., Inc.; United Poets Laureate Internat. Republican. Protestant. Home: 2556 La Presa Ave., Rosemead, CA 91770.

BONNER, JAMES
Professor of Biology
b. Sept. 1, 1910, Ansley, Nebr.; s. Walter D. and Grace (Gaylord) Bonner; A.B., Univ. of Utah, 1931; Ph'd., Calif. Inst. of Tech., 1934; M.Sc., Oxford Univ. 1963; D.H., Westminster Coll. 1975; m. Ingelore Silverbach; chil.: Joey, b. 1948; Pamela, b. 1950; Jose, b. 1950; Terry, b. 1954. Career: postdoctoral fellow, Holland, Switzerland, 1934-35; Prof. of Biology, Calif. Inst. of Tech., 1935---; Eastman visiting prof., Oxford Univ. 1963-64; author: sci. books, papers. Hobbies: skiing, mountain climbing. Home: 1914 Edgewood Dr., So. Pasadena, CA 91030; Office: Cal Tech, Pasadena, CA 91125.

BONNEY, GEORGE WILLIAM
Judge
b. Aug. 22, 1923, Midwest, Wyo.; s. George William and Bertha Anne (Ormsby); B.A., Univ. Wis., 1950; LL.B., 1952; m. Kerminette Schweers, Aug. 27, 1949, Milwaukee; chil.: Susan Mary, b. 1950; George William III, b. 1954; Michael Kermit, b. 1955. Career: practicing atty., San Jose, 1958-72; judge, Santa Clara Municipal Ct., 1972---. Pilot, USAF, 1942-46. Mem.: Sigma Phi Epsilon; Wis. Alumni Assn.; Calif. Judges Assn.; Train Collectors Assn. Home: 12740 Carniel Ave., Saratoga, CA 95070; Office: 1095 Homestead Rd., Santa Clara, CA 95050.

BOOKMAN, RALPH
Physician
b. Nov. 6, 1914, N.Y.C.; s. Milton R., M.D. and Ernestine Bookman; B.A., Cornell, 1935; M.D., Long Isl. Coll. of Med., 1939; m. Maxine Piness, June 20, 1944, L.A.; chil.: Robert, b. Jan. 29, 1947; Richard, b. Aug. 5, 1950. Career: 2 yrs. residency, Flight Surgeon, USN, 1942-46, 2 yrs. USMC; 2 yrs. residency, L.A. Co. Gen. Hosp.; practice of clin. allergy with George Piness, M.D.; contrbr. articles concerning clinical allergy to med. journs. Dir., United Way of L.A. and United Way Region IV Bd.; dir., L.A. Visiting Nurse Assn.; pres. Salerni Collegium, 1975-76. Mem., v.p., Wilshire Blvd. Temple, L.A. Hobbies: rare books, gardening. Rec.: golf. Home: 374 Comstock Ave., L.A., CA 90024; Office: 240 S. La Cienega, Beverly Hills, CA 90211.

BOONE, DONNA CLAUSEN
Physical Therapist
b. Dec. 12, 1932, Nebr.; d. Otto Ralph and Hallie Rae (Wolfenberger) Clausen; B.A. zoology, Univ. Wyo., 1954; cert., Northwestern Univ. Sch. of Phys. Therapy, 1955; postgrad. studies, UCLA, pathokinesiology, USC; m. Robert W. Boone, Apr. 3, 1965, L.A. Career: chief physical therapist, Ill. Children's Hosp. Sch., 1955-58; sr. physical therapist, Calif. Hosp., L.A., 1959-63; sr. physical therapist, Hemophilia Ctr., Orthopaedic Hosp., L.A., 1963-66, dir. dept of physical therapy, 1966-67, research physical therapist, Hemophilia Ctr., 1967-73, research coordinator, 1973-78. Awards: Dr. Murray Thelin Award of the Nat. Hemophilia Found., 1976; research award, Am. Physical Therapy Assn., Gr. L.A. dist., 1975; guest lectr. Fondazione Carlo Erba, Milan, Italy, 1970; Contbr.: publs. on hemophilia, books and med. journs. Mem.: Am. Physical Therapy Assn., assoc. editor, 1975-81, mem. sects. on research, elect. testing, past pres. So. Calif. chpt., helped design, write & produce all physical therapy recruitment material used in Calif.; chmn., work on nat. subcom. on Socioeconomics; orgn. com. 13th Congress, World Fedn. of Hemophilia, 1978-79; med. advis. bd., Hemo. Found. of So. Calif., 1975. Hobbies: gardening, piano, restoration of classic cars, travel, oenology. Home: 1520 Ontario Ave., Pasadena, CA 91103; Office: 680 Wilshire Pl., L.A., CA.

BOOTH, FRANK E.
Company President
b. Oct. 4, 1910, Long Beach, Calif.; s. Harry W. and Bertha (Bickle) Booth; ed. grad. Stanford Univ. 1932; B.A., Stanford Grad. Sch. of Bus. 1934; m. Arleen Kay King, Glendale, Calif., Dec. 29, 1934; chil.: Karen Kay, b. Apr. 16, 1941; Bonnie Gay, b. Mar. 22, 1943. Career: Standard Oil Co. of Calif. 1934-41; Montgomery Ward, 1941-43; Grayson Heat Control Co. 1943-45; Gen. Tire and Rubber Co. 1945-47; pres.-dir.: Interstate Engring. Corp., 1947---; Interstate Precision Prods. Corp. and Interstate Engring. Corp., de Puerto Rico. Mem.: U.S. Olympic Swimming Team, 1932; Phi Delta Theta; U.S. Olympians, Lincoln Club, Calif. Club. Home: 102 Irvine Cove, Laguna Beach, CA; Office: 522 E. Vermont Ave., Anaheim, CA 92805.

BOQUIST, NORMA FAYE
Journalist
b. Nov. 3, 1922, Wilbur, Wash.; d. Henry T. and Lela D. (Perkins) Martin; Gr.Grandau., Dr. John Nelson Perkins, led wagon train from Iowa to Ore., early 1850s, Oregon's 1st rep. after statehood; student, Holy Names Coll., Spokane, Wash.; Minneapolis Sch. of Art, Minn.; m. Arthur W. Boquist, Feb. 20, 1942, Wilbur, Wash.; chil.: Barry, b. Aug. 6, 1946; Scott, b. Jan. 28, 1949; April (Schromm), b. Apr. 7, 1954; Matt, b. July 21, 1956. Career: secty., 1941-45, women's editor, Sunnyvale Daily Standard, 1961-69; feature reporter, weekend regional editor, Lewiston Morning Tribune, Ida., 1970-72; feature and food editor, Valley Journal, Sunnyvale, 1972-74; staff writer, columnist, San Jose Mercury & News, 1974---; contrbr. California Today, Denver Post, National Tattler, Others. Awards: Vesta award, Am. Meat Inst.,

1966; Sunnyvale Jr. C. of C., 1968; Sunnyvale Parks & Rec. Dept., 1969; Hats Off award, Order DeMolay, Lewiston, Ida., 1971; Santa Clara Citizens Advisroy, 1972; Santa Clara C. of C., 1972; Calif. Parks & Rec. Soc., 1973; Salvation Army awards, 1974, 75; De Anza Expedition Reenactment 1976; Bicentennial Bellringer, Los Gatos, 1976. Mem.: (hon') Beta Sigma Phi, Fed. Women's Club, Altrusa Club Internat. Protestant; pres. women's assoc., Lewiston, Ida., 1952; ch. trustee, Santa Clara, 1963. Hobbies: sketching, music. Rec.: tennis, riding horseback. Home: 909 Rose Blossom Dr., Cupertino, CA; office: 750 Ridder Park Dr., San Jose, CA.

BORCHERDT, WENDY HAWLEY
Civic Leader
b. Apr. 12, 1936, Oakland; d. Stuart Meek and Lois (Weinmann) Hawley; B.A., polit. sci., English, Stanford Univ. (student body v.p.—, 1958; m. Edward Rahr Borcherdt, Jr., July 5, 1958, Palo Alto; chil.: Kimberley, b. May 25, 1959; Edward Rahr III, b. Sept. 20, 1961. Career: assoc., Teren and Co., N.Y. and Virginia Beach, Va., 1976-77; prin., tchr. mgmt. cons., Training for Effective Mgmt., L.A., 1977---; current col.: Overseer (only woman), Hoover Inst. on War, Revolution and Peace, Stanford Univ.; vice-chmn., trustee, Independent Colls. of So. Calif.; vice-chmn., for Legislation Citizens for Law Enforcement Needs; dir., Aman Folk Ensemble (profl. dance orgn.); vice-chmn., Alcohol Information Ctr. Advis. Bd.; vice-chmn., L.A. Philharmonic Orchestra Affils., 1978; v.p., Harvard Sch. Mothers Club, 1978; Mayor's appt., L.A. City Econ., Advis. Council, 1978; past vol.: dir., Good Samaritan Hosp., Aux., 1975-77; mem. budgetary reform com., Episcopal Diocese, L.A., 1975-77; dir. Hancock Park Homeowners Assn., 1974-76; internat. dir., Assn. of Jr. Leagues, Inc., chmn. fin. com. and program planning, 1973-75; pres., Jr. League of L.A., 1972-73; pres. Symphonians to the Jr. Philharmonic, 1966-67; pres. Stanford Women's Club of L.A. Co., 1965-66; founder, pres., First Lutheran Sch. Parents Assn., 1969-71; chmn. Blue Bird Council, Camp Fire Girls, 1969-70; chmn. Hollywood Bowl Season Ticket Com., 1969. Awards include Outstanding Young Woman of Am., 1966; commendations, L.A. Co. Bd. of Suprs., 1967, Philharmonic Affiliates, 1977, 78. Mem.: L.A. Country Club; the Beach Club; Jr. League of L.A.; Jr. Philharmonic Com.; Assistance League of So. Calif.; CARES; The Muses to Mus. of Sci. and Indsty.; Salvation Army Aux. Republican: vol. in Goldwater, Nixon, Reagan campaigns; dir., Republican Assocs.; v.p. Wilshire Republican Club, 1974-77. Mem. All Saints Episcopal Ch., 2nd gr. tchr., women's prayer group com. Hobby: travel. Rec.: paddle tennis, skiing. Home-Office: 401 S. June St., L.A., CA 90020.

BORDA RICHARD JOSEPH
Bank Executive
b. Aug. 1931, San Francisco; s. Joseph Clement and Ethel Cathleen Borda; B.A. econ., Stanford Univ., 1953, M.B.A., Stanford Grad. Sch. of Bus., 1957; m. Judith Maxwell, Aug. 30, 1953, Carmel; chil.: Stephen J., b. Nov. 1957; Michelle, b. Sept. 1955. Career: with Wells Fargo Bank, 1957-70, 1973---: exec. vice pres., So. Calif. exec. office, L.A. ---; Asst. Secty. of the Air Force (Manpower and Reserve Affairs, 1970-73). Dir.: Southern Calif. Building Funds; Greater L.A. Visitors & Convention Bureau; Natl. Life Ins. Co. of Montpelier, Vt.; Scholarships for Children of Am. Mil. Personnel, trustee; Stanford Univ. Athletic Board; Air Force Aid Society. 1st Lt., USMC, 1953-55; Lt. Col., 1955-70 (ret.) Mem.: Phi Gamma Delta; F.A.M.; Army and Navy Club; Univ. Club, S.F. Episcopalian. Rec.: tennis, golf. Home: 8050 Mulholland Dr., L.A., CA 90046; Office: 770 Wilshire Blvd., L.A., CA 90017.

BORKO, HAROLD
University Professor
b. Feb. 4, 1922, New York, N.Y.; s. George and Hilda Borko; A.B., UCLA, 1948; M.A., USC, 1949; Ph.D., 1952; m. Hannah Levin, June 22, 1947, Los Angeles; chil.: Hilda, b. Jan. 22, 1951; Martin, b. Dec. 18, 1952. Career: System Training specialist, RAND Corp., 1956-57; assoc staff head, language processing and retrieval staff, System Devel. Corp., 1958-67; prof., Grad. Sch. of Lib. and Information Sci., UCLA 9168---. Dir., Am. Fedn. of Information Processing Socs., 1966-70, 1974---. Author: Computer Applications in the Behavioral Sciences, 1962; Automated Language Processing, 1967; Computers and the Problems of Soc., 1972; Targets for Reserach in Library Education, 1973; Abstracting Concepts and Methods, 1975; Indexing Concepts and Methods, 1978. Capt., AUS, 1942-46; Med. Corps. Mem.: Am. Soc. for Information Sci., pres. 1966; Fellow, Am. Psychol. Assn.; Assn. for Computing Machinery; Assn. of Am. Lib. Schs.; Am. Soc. of Indexers. Hobby: stamp collecting. Rec.: travel. Home: 11507 National Blvd., L.A., CA 90064; Office: UCLA, 405 Hilgard Ave., L.A., CA 90024.

BORNEMEIER, WALTER CARL
Surgeon — Past President AMA
b. Apr. 22, 1901, Cass County, Nebr.; s. Charles and Lena (Schlueter) Bornemeier; B.A., NorthCentral Coll., 1923; M.D., Northwestern Univ. Med. Sch., 1929; (hon.) Litt.D., NorthCentral Coll., 1970; m. Mabel Kemp, May 29, 1926, Naperville, Ill.; Chil.: Lois (Kertel), b. Sept. 29, 1929; Beatrice (Fiedler), b. June 7, 1932; Walter C. II (J.D.), b. Nov. 16, 1939. Career: began practice of surgery, Chicago, 1929---; instr., Northwestern Univ. Med. Sch. until 1954; editor, Chicago Med. Soc. Bulletin, 1954-55; contbr. publs. on economics of medicine; Speaker of House of Delegates, AMA, 1963-69, past pres., AMA; pres., Chicago Med. Soc., 1954; pres., Chicago Lung Assn., 1950; pres., Niles High Sch. Bd. of Edn. 1953; bd. dir., Tri-Co. Apt. Assn., San Jose, 1974---. Served 1st Lt. to Maj., Med. Corps, WW II, Mediterranean Theatre. Mem.: Masons, 33 degree. Republican. Lutheran. Rec.: gardening. Home: 19273 Harleigh Dr., Saratoga, CA 95070.

BORNSTEIN, JULIE I.
Attorney at Law
b. July 17, 1948, San Diego; d. Leon M. and Pearl (Olensky) Bornstein; B.A. polit. sci., UCLA, 1970; M.A., speech, UCLA, 1971; J.D., USC, 1974; m. Steven J. Gordon, May 19, 1974, San Diego; son, Loren Ryan Gordon, b. Aug. 30, 1978. Career: Law clerk, Hahn & Hahn, 1972-73, Alison Mortgage Investment Trust, 1973-74; lectr., real estate law, 1974; assoc. attorney, firm of Labowe & Ventress, 1974-77; Julie Bornstein, Attorney at Law, 1978; partner, Bornstein & Gurewitz, Attorneys at Law, 1978---. Dir., Women in Business, Inc., 1978---, v.p. 1979---. Mem.: Women Lawyers of L.A., 1974---; L.A. Co. Bar Assn., 1974---; Am. Bar Assn., 1976-78; Nat. Orgn. for Women, 1977---; Nat. Women's Polit. Causes, 1977---. Hobby: cooking. Rec.: tennis, swimming. Home: 13921 Sunset Blvd., Pacific Palisades, CA 90272; Office: 10850 Wilshire Blvd., 11th Floor, L.A., CA 90024.

BORUM, ELIZABETH ANN
Psychologist
b. May 4, 1930, Newman, Calif.; d. John Allen and Helen Eliza (Sheedy) Borum; desc. John Kaar, original settler of Kern Co.; B.A. psychol., Univ. Calif., Berkeley, 1951; M.A., 1953; m. Robert Arthur Arey, Jan. 27, 1951, div. 1960. Career: Research psychologist, Inst. Child Welfare, UC, Berkeley, 1951-53; chief psychometrist and vocational counselor, Vocational Service Center, YMCA, N.Y.C., 1953-57; grad. research psychologist, Inst. of Human Devel., UC Berkeley, 1957-61; research psychometrist, Inst. of Med. Scis., S.F., 1961-67; psychologist, Psychological Clin., probation dept., Contra Costa Co., 1967---; contbr. profl. journs. Recipient: Fremont Poetry Award, 1946, Anchor Poetry Award, 1969. Secty., Counseling Cabinet of YMCAs of N.Y.C., 1957; secty., No. Calif. Council, Psychological Assn., 1975-76; pres., Contra Costa Co. Psychol. Assn.; pres., E. Bay Chpt. of People to People; treas. Alameda Co. U.N. Assn.; trustee, Nike Clubs Inc. 1969-71; pres., Bus. & Profl. Women's Club, Berkeley, 1967-68; mem. Mayor of Berkeley's Bicentennial Com., 1975-76: past pres., Bay Area Fellowship for Ethical Culture. Hobbies: needlework, poetry. Rec.: music, drama, travel. Home: 1830 Lakeshore, No. 304, Oakland, CA 94606; Office: 2525 Stanwell Dr., Concord, CA 94520.

BOSEN, SHIRLEY ELIZABETH ROSE
College Dean
b. Santa Barbara; d. Frank Orton and Elizabeth (Wamsley) Rose; A.B., polit. sci., UCLA, 1948; M.L.S., 1961; m. Evan Lee Bosen, Feb. 7, 1947, Los Angeles; chil.: Robert Craig, b. July 27, 1954; Scott Douglas, b. Nov. 5, 1956. Career: Librarian, Lowell High Sch., 1961-64; librarian, Fullerton Coll., 1964-66; assoc. dean, ednl. resources, Fullerton Coll., 1966---. Mem. bd., Learning Resources Assn., Calif. Comm. Colls., 1973-75, 1977---; mem. bd. San Gabriel Comm. Colls. Lib. Coop., chmn., 1969-71, 1977---; mem. bd., Calif. Comm. Colls. Learning Resources Coop., 1977---; corr. secty., Orange Co. Lib. Assn. 1969-70. Mem.: Beta Phi Mu, Delta Kappa Gamma secty., 1969-71; Pi Sigma Alpha. Episcopalian. Hobby: photog. Office: Fullerton Coll., 321 E. Chapman Ave., Fullerton, CA 92634.

BOSHEAR, WALTON CARR
Company President — Columnist
b. Dec. 5, 1935, Beckville, Tex.; s. Albert Allen and Sarah (Estell) Boshear; Calif. Tchr. credential in Psychol. and Mgmt. 1975; m. Nova Lunn Cox, Apr. 30, 1978; Del Mar, Calif. Career: personnel dir., Albert C. Martin & Assoc., L.A., 1956-66; mgr. info. systems, Holmes & Narver, Inc., Anaheim, 1966-73; pres., Solutions, Rancho Santa Fe, 1973---; pres., LEST, Rancho Santa Fe, 1975---. publ., News Press Publ. Co., 1976-77. Devel. new concept for computer program, Marpho, 1969 and computer use of English lang. in personnel skills inventory, 1970. Author: newspaper and mag. column, Life Enrichment, 1976---; (with Earl Albrect) Understanding People — Models and Concepts, Univ. Assoc., La Jolla, 1977; article for profl. journ., 1976; song, Baby, I'll be OK. Book in progress on mgmt. for Prentice Hall. Pentecostal Ch. Hobbies: reading, woodworking, tennis. Office: P.O.B. 1389, Rancho Santa Fe, CA 92067.

BOSSEN, DORIS STEPHENS
Corporate Executive
b. Oct. 21, 1928, Glendale; d. William Harrison and Esther Alice (Teachworth) Stephens; B.A. polit. sci., Vassar Coll.; Calif. tchr. credential, Occidental Coll.; Cal. State Univ., L.A.; M.A., Ph.D., counseling, psychol., Ohio State Univ.; m. David A. Bossen; chil.: Alison, Amy, July, Laura. Career: mgmt. trainee, Filene's Dept. Store, Boston, Mass., 1950-51; mkt. research, Indsl. Nucleonics Corp., Columbus, Ohio, 1952; tchr., English and Social Studies, L.A. City Schs., 1953; substitute tchr., Columbus, Oh., 1963; asst. to Dean of Women, Ohio State Univ., 1966-67; v.p., Corporate Communications, Measurex Corp., Cupertino. Mem.: Friends Outside advis. bd., Outreach for Women; Beta Gamma Sigma; Public Rels. Soc. of Am.; Am. Personnel & Guidance Assn. Republican. Home: 780 Mountain Home Rd., Woodside, CA 94062; Office: One Results Way, Cupertino, CA 95014.

BOSTON, JEANNE A.
Advertising Company Executive
b. Mar. 13, 1949, Los Angeles; d. Frederick L. and Virginia Boston; student, Cal. State Univ., Northridge, 1967-69; Career: asst. advt. prodn. mgr., Sony/Superscope Inc., Sun Valley, 1969; advt. prodn. mgr., Chiat/Day Inc. Advertising, L.A., 1970; agency controller, prodn. mgr., Holly Flor Inc. Advertising, L.A., 1971-73; agency controller, advt. accounting cons., Abert, Newhoff & Burr, Inc., Century City, 1973---. Mem.: Los Angeles Advt. Softball League. Democrat. Rec.: sailing, skiing. Home: 16643 Valerio St., Van Nuys, CA 91406; Office: 1900 Ave. of Stars, 26th Floor, L.A., CA 90067.

BOTSFORD, HERBERT SIBBET
CPA — Partner, Arthur Young & Co.
b. Dec. 20, 1931, Los Angeles; S. Frederick Laux and Anna May (Sibbet) Botsford; grandson of William Finn Botsford and Herbert Austin Sibbet, early Calif. pioneers; ed. B.S., UCLA, 1955; m. Shirley Woodland, San Marino, Calif., Dec. 19, 1953; sons: Steven Craig, b. Oct. 25, 1955; Brad Sibbet, b. Jan. 5, 1958, Jeffrey Craig, b. May 8, 1959. Career: Licensed CPA, Calif., La., N.C., Va.; tax mgr. Ernst & Ernst CPAs 1955-60; treas.-dir. Azusa Transfer Co. & Transport Systems, Inc. 1960-62; tax partner, Arthur Young & Co., CPAs 1962---. Profl. lectr., U.S. Navy, 1952-54. Mem.: Delta Upsilon, Univ. of Calif, Berkeley, 1949-52; pres. Valley Club, 1961-62; Calif. Soc. of Certified Public Accts.; Am. Inst. of CPAs; Annandale Golf Club, Pasadena; San Joaquin Country Club, Fresno; Mission Hills Country Club, Rancho Mirage; The Downtown Club, Fresno. Episcopalian (treas.-vestryman, St. Edmunds Ch. 1967-71). Rec.: golf, ski, tennis. Home: 2618 W. San Ramon Ave., Fresno, CA 93711; Office: 2030 Fresno St., Fresno, CA 93721.

BOTTICHER, WILHELMINA
Microbiologist
b. Jan. 14, 1916, Pasadena; d. Grosvenor Libeneau and Wilhelmina (Eliot) Wotkyns; B.A., USC, 1944, M.S., 1945; m. Wilhelm Karl Eric Botticher, Jan. 19, 1946. Career: microbiologist: L.A. Co. Health Dept., 1953-56; Solano Co. Health Dept., 1956-62; David Grant Hosp., Travis AFB, 1962-66; Peralta Hosp., Oakland, 1969-70; VA Hosp., Martinez, 1970-74. Publs.: A Simple Identification of Candida and Candia albican, 1964; Alternania as a Possible Human Pathogen, 1965; Serratia Studies, 1969. Mem.: Am. Soc. for Microbiology, 1963-74; Am. Soc. for Med. Tech., 1969-74; APHA, 1955-74. Hobby: raising Cardigan Welsh Corgis. Rec.: gardening. Home: 3151 Mt. Veeder Rd., Napa, CA 94558.

BOUCHER, HAROLD IRVING
Attorney at Law
b. June 27, 1906, Chico; s. Charles A. and Nina E. (Knickerbocker) Boucher; LL.B., J.D., Univ. Calif., Berkeley, 1930; m. Beula Blair Davis, Apr. 11, 1931, San Francisco. Career: law practice, 1930---: partner, law firm of Pillsbury, Madison & Sutro, S.F.; past pres. and regent emeritus, Am. Coll. of Probate Counsel. Mem.: officer, Order of the British Empire; Cercle De l'Union, S.F. Home: 2312 Gough St., San Francisco, CA; Office: 225 Bush St., P.O.B. 7880, S.F., CA 94120.

BOUDART, MICHEL
Professor of Chemistry
b. June 18, 1924, Brussels, Belgium; s. Francois and Marguerite (Swolfs) Boudart; nephew, Gen. Albert Nicaise; Ingenieur Civil Chimiste, Louvain, 1947; Ph.D., Princeton, 1950; m. Paula D'Haese, Dec. 27, 1948, Princeton, N.J.; chil.: Marc and Baudouin, b. Sept. 3, 1949; Vinciane Iris, b. June 6, 1951; Philip, b. Mar. 6, 1953. Career: research assoc., asst. to dir. Project Squid, asst. prof., assoc prof., Princeton Univ., 1950-61; prof., Univ. Calif., Berkeley 1961-64; prof. of chem. engring. and chemistry, Stanford Univ., 1964---. Dir., Catalytica Assoc. Inc., 1974---. Mem.: National Acad. of Sciences, USA. Home: 15 Peak Lane, Portola Valley, CA 94025; Office: Stauffer III, Stanford Univ., Stanford, CA 94305.

BOWER, FAY LOUISE
Professor of Nursing
b. Sept. 10, 1929, San Francisco; d. James Joseph and Emily Clare (Andrews) Saitta; B.S., San Jose State Coll., 1965; M.S.N., Univ. Calif., S.F., 1966; D.N.Sc., 1978; m. Robert Davis Bower, July 2, 1949, Palo Alto; chil.: R. David; Carol (Tomei); Dennis James; Thomas John. Career: office nurse, Palo Alto, 1950-55; staff nurse, Stanford Hosp., 1964-72; mem. Faculty, San Jose State Univ., 1966---: asst. prof. 1966-70, assoc. prof. 1970-74; prof. 1970---; also Coord. Grad. Nursing Program, 1977-78; chmn. Dept. of Nursing, 1978---; visiting prof.: Univ. Miss., Univ. Calif., Harding Coll. Fellow, Am. Acad. of Nursing, 1978. Author: The Process of Planning Nursing Care, 2d ed., 1977; Theoretical Foundations of Nursing I, II, and III, 1972; Nursing Skills I; co-author other nursing texts, publs. on nursing; dir. research and curriculum grants; Mem.: Calif. Nurse's Assn.; Nurse's Assn. of Coll. of Obstet. and Gynecol.; Phi Kappa Phi; Calif. Tchrs. Assn.; AAUP; Internat. Indsl. TV Assn.; Commonwealth Club of S.F.; Health Edn. League for Nursing; Western Gerontological Assn. Catholic, dir. rel. edn. program. Hobbies: writing, reading, movies. Home: 1820 Portola Rd., Woodside, CA; Office: San Jose State Univ., Dept. of Nursing, San Jose, CA.

BOWKER, ALBERT HOSMER
University Chancellor
b. Sept. 8, 1919, Winchendon, Mass.; s. Roy C. and Kathleen (Hosmer) Bowker; B.S., Mass. Inst. Tech. 1941; Ph.D., Columbia Univ., 1949; m. Rosedith Sitgreaves, Easton, Pa., Sept. 26, 1964; chil.: Paul A., b. June 15, 1947; (twins) Caroline Anne and Kathleen, b. Sept. 2, 1950. Career: Research asst. Math. Dept., MIT, 1941-43; assoc., asst. dir. Statistical Research Group, Columbia Univ. 1943-54; asst. prof. math. statistics, Stanford Univ. 1947-50; exec. dir. Dept. of Statistics, 1948-59, assoc. prof. 1950-53; dir. Applied Math-Statistics Labs. 1953-63, dean, grad. div. 1959-63; chancellor, City Univ. of N.Y. 1963-71; chancellor, Univ. of Calif., Berkeley, 1971---. Co-author: "Sampling Inspection by Variables," publ. McGraw-Hill, 1952; "Handbook of Industrial Statistics," 1955, and "Engineering Statistics," 2nd ed. publ. Prentice-Hall, 1972. Mem.: Sloan Commn. on Govt. and Higher Edn.; bd. trustees: Bennington Coll., Univ. of Haifa, (hon.) Inst. Internat. Edn., West Coast bd.; Adv. Council of Pres., Assn. of Gov. Bds. Univs. and Colls.; bd. dirs. S.F. Bay Area Council (1972-76), Natl. Drug Abuse Council; Fellow, Inst. of Math. Statistics, pres. 1961-62; exec. com. Sigma Xi, 1963-66; Phi Beta Kappa; Fellow, Am. Statistical Assn., pres. 1964; Fellow, Am. Soc. of Quality Control; Fellow, AAAS; Opr. Research Soc. of Am.; Biometric Soc. Office: 200 California Hall, University of Calif., Berkeley, CA 94720.

BOYD, WILLIAM CLOUSER
Professor Emeritus of Immunochemistry
b. Mar. 4, 1903, Dearborn, Mo.; s. William O. and Wilmuth (Clouser) Boyd; A.B., Harvard Univ., 1925, M.A., 1926; Ph.D., Boston Univ., 1930; m. Lyle Gifford, June 9, 1931 (div. 1966), Lawrence, Kan.; chil.: Sylvia Lyle, b. Sept. 22, 1934; Cassandra Girard (Crosby), b. May 10, 1967. Career: tchg. fellow, Boston Univ. Med. Sch., 1926-35, asst. prof. 1935-48, Prof. of Immunochemistry, 1948-69, prof. emeritus, 1969---;

visiting prof. 1970-71; research assoc., Univ. of Calif., S.D., 1974---; head, Dept. of Biochem. and Immunochem., US Navy Med. Res. Unit No. 3, Cairo, Egypt, 1949-50. Author: Blood Grouping Technic (with Fritz Schiff) 1942; Fundamentals of Immunology, 1943, 3d ed. 1956; Genetics and the Races of Man, 1950; Biochemistry and Human Metabolism (with B.S. Walker and I. Asimov), 1952, 3d ed. 1957; Races and People (with I. Asimov) 1955; Introduction to Immunochemical Specificity, 1962; 300 papers, 1943-52; 14 sci. fiction stories, 1950-60. Discover (and namegiver) lectins; discovery has had wide application universally. Mem.: Pres., Am. Assn. Imm., 1959; pres., Am. Soc. Human Genetics, 1957; Boston Mycological Club. Hobbies: photog., silversmithing. Rec.: mycophagy, painting. Home: 1241 Prospect St., La Jolla, CA 92037.

BOYER, L. BRUCE
Psychiatrist
b. June 23, 1916, Vernal, Utah; s. Lew and Oral (Fletcher) Boyer; B.A., Stanford Univ., 1937; M.D., Stanford Univ. Med. Sch., 1942; m. Erma Ruth McDonald, June 22, 1939, Salt Lake City; chil.: Sandra Lea (Boyer), b. Jan. 18, 1940; Dewey McDonald, M.D., b. Jan. 4, 1946; Kimberly Bryce, b. Oct. 8, 1947. Career: Clin. Instr., chest med., Stanford Med. Sch., 1943-47; clin. instr., psychiat., Univ. Calif. Med. Sch., 1947-49; research assoc., Anthropology: UC Berkeley, 1957-58, Univ. New Mex., 1958-65; vis. prof., Univ. Ill. Coll. of Med., 1967-70; chmn. Interdisciplinary colloquim on psychoanalytic methods and questions in anthropological fieldwork, Am. Psychoanalytic Assn., 1970-77; cons., Alaska Psychiatric Inst., 1971---; Pvt. practice of psychiat. and psychoanalysis ---; Assoc. Dir. Residency Training, Herrick Mem. Hosp. ---. Author: (with Peter L. Giovacchini) Psychoanalytic Treatment of Schizophrenic and Characterological Disorders, N.Y.: Sci. House Press, 1967; Die Psychoanalytischer Behandlung Schizophrener, Munich: Kindler Verlag, 1976; Childhood and Folklore: A Psychoanalytic Study of Apache Personality, N.Y.: Lib. of Psychol. Anthropology, 1978. Publs.: 45 articles on various psychoanalytic subjects; 53 articles on applied psychoanalysis; contrib. ed., The Psychoanalytic Study fo Soc., 1964-73; assoc. ed. 1973-76, co-ed., 1976---; cons. ed., Revista Argentina de Psiquietria y Psicologia de la Infancia y Adolescencia, Buenos Aires, 1970---; assoc. ed., Tactics and Techniques in Psychoanalytic Therapy, 1972---; mem. advis. bd., Journ. of Psychological Anthropology, 1976---. Capt., AUS M.C., 1944-46. Mem.: Am. Psychiatric Assn., life fellow, 1978; No. Calif. and E. Bay Psychiat. Assns.; Am. and Mexican Psychoanalytic Assocs.; Am. Folklore Soc.; Calif. Acad. of Med.; Sigma Xi; Pi Delta Phi. Office: 3021 Telegraph Ave., Berkeley, CA 94705.

BOYLE-LOPEZ, BARBARA A.
Advertising Company President
b. Mar. 28, 1943, Detroit, Mich.; d. James Joseph and Daisy Irene (Porter) Boyle; m. Pete E. Lopez, Dec. 9, 1967, L.A.; dau. Yvette Emma Lopez, b. Jan. 14, 1969. Career: partner, Navarroli & Lopez Advt., L.A., 1972-74; pres., Cozad & Lopez Advt., L.A., 1974-77; pres., creative dir., Boyle/Lopez Advertising, L.A., 1977---' V.P., L.A. Advt. Women's Assn. (LAAW), bd. dir. Western States Advt. Agencies Assn. (WSAAA). Winner Best Radio Comml., Lulu 1977. Office: 1355 Westwood Blvd., L.A., CA 90024.

BRACE, CLAYTON H.
Broadcast Executive
b. Aug. 8, 1923, Topeka, Kan.; s. Clayton Henry and Gladys (Hawley) Brace; Univ. of Denver, 1941-42; Univ. of Colo., 1942; m. Jeanne Haney, Denver, Colo.; Sept. 10, 1947; chil.: Kimball William, b. Aug. 15, 1951; Dianne, b. Apr. 14, 1954; Lynne, b. May 22, 1955; Kerry, b. Feb. 28, 1961. Career: Page boy, KLZ, Denver, 1941-42; writer, prodn. mgr., 1948; dir. TV research 1950; pgm. dir. KLZ-TV, 1953; asst. secty. Time-Life Broadcast, Colo., KLZ-AM-TV, 1954; asst. to pres. 1958-62; mem. Time Inc. (team to stu. TV in Europe), 1959-60; operations mgr. CLT-TV, Beirut, Lebanon, 1962-63; v.p.-gen. mgr., KGTV, 1963---. AUS Signal Corps, ETO, 1943-45, WW II. Mem.: past pres., Colo. Broadcasters Assn.; past pres. Calif. Broadcasters Assn.; (past) pres. S.D. C. of C.; adv. bd. S.D. State Univ.; San Diegans, Inc.; dir.: Donald N. Sharp Mem. Community Hosp.; bd. overseers, Univ. of Calif., S.D.; campaign chmn., United Way/CHAD campaign, S.D. Co.; v.p., Broadcast Edn. Assn.; World Affairs Council; adv. bd. Automobile Club of So. Calif.; pres. S.D. Rotary Club, 1970; Sigma Delta Chi. Home: 5970 Madra Ave., San Diego, CA 92120; Office: McGraw-Hill Broadcasting Co., Inc., Box 81047, S.D., CA 92138.

BRACEWELL, RONALD N.
Professor of Electrical Engineering
b. July 22, 1921, Sydney, Australia; s. Cecil Charles and Valerie Zitta (McGowan) Bracewell; B.Sc., Univ. of Sydney, 1941, B.E., 1943, M.E., 1948; Ph.D., Cavendish Lab., Cambridge, 1950; m. Helen M.L. Elliott, Mar. 27, 1953, Sydney; chil.: Catherine Wendy (Petrilla), b. Dec. 2, 1953; Mark Cecil, b. Aug. 1, 1957. Career: served with Australian Army Ordnance Corps 1941; devel. microwave radar equip., Radiophysics Lab., Commonwealth Sci. and Indsl. Research Orgn., Sydney, WW II; ionospheric research, Cavendish Lab., Cambridge, Engl., 1946-49; sr. research officer, Radiophysics Lab., Sydney, 1949-54; lectr. radio astronomy, Berkeley Astronomy Dept., Univ. Calif., 1954-55; mem. Elect. Engring. faculty, Stanford Univ., 1955---: apptd. Lewis M. Terman Prof. and Fellow in E.E., 1974---. Awarded Duddell Premium, IEEE, London, 1952, for contrbns. to study of the ionosphere by means of very low frequency waves; elected Fellow, Inst. of Radio Engrs., 1961, for contbns. to radio astronomy; constrd. complex radio telescope at Stanford, which prod. weather maps acknowledged by NASA for support of 1st manned moon landing; pub. 1st explanation of the tumbling of satellites; originated a spaceborne infrared concept that may lead to discovery of planets around stars other than the sun; helped in devel. of computer assisted X-ray tomography; frequent lectr., topics connected with space; Govt. advisor: Nat. Sci. Found. (past chmn. astronomy advis. panel); Naval Research Lab.; Office of Naval Research; Nat. Acad. of Sci.; Nat. Radio Astronomy Observatory; Advanced Research Projects Agency; Cornell Univ. Press. Mem.: ed. advs. bd.: Planetary and Space Sci.; Cosmic Search; Journ. of Computer Assisted Tomography; Reviews of Astronomy and Astrophysics, bd. dir. 1961-68, co-founder, Editor, Paris Symposium on Radio Astronomy, Stanford 1959; co-author, Radio Astronomy, Oxford, 1955; author: The Fourier Transform and Its Applications, McGraw-Hill, 1965, 2d. ed. 1978; The Galactic Club: Intelligent Life in Outer Space, Portable Stanford series, 1974. Contbg. author, 13 sci. books; articles to Encyclopedia of Electronics, Encyclopaedia Britannica; pub. papers in over 30 different sci. journs. Hobby: growing trees. Home: 836 Santa Fe Ave., Stanford, CA 94305; Office: Stanford Univ., Stanford, CA 94305.

BRADBURY, RAY DOUGLAS
Writer
b. Aug. 22, 1920, Waukegan, Ill.; s. Leonard Spaulding and Esther Marie (Moberg) Bradbury; grad. L.A. H.S. 1938; m. Marguerite McClure, L.A., Sept. 27, 1947; chil.: Susan Marguerite, b. Nov. 5, 1949; Ramona Anne, b. May 17, 1951; Bettina Francion, b. July 22, 1955; Alexandria Allison, b. Aug. 13, 1958. Career: Writer, pulp mags., Super-Science Stories, publ. Nov. 1941; first quality mag., Am. Mercury, Aug. 1945; approx. 200 stories publ. such mags. as The New Yorker, Harper's, Charm, Mademoiselle, Collier's, Thrilling Wonder Stories, The Nation, Astounding Science-Fiction, Sat. Eve. Post, Epoch, Cosmopolitan, The Reporter, Startling Stories, others. Author: (books) "Dark Carnival," publ. 1947; "The Martian Chronicles," 1950; "The Illustrated Man," 1951; "The Golden Apples of the Sun," "Fahrenheit 451," 1953; "Switch on the Night," "The October Country," 1955; "Dandelion Wine," 1957; "A Medicine for Melancholy," 1959; (screen play) "Moby Dick" (written for John Huston), publ. 1956; "Something Wicked This Way Comes," 1962; "R Is for Rocket," 1962; "The Anthem Sprinters," 1963. Awards: won Best Am. Short Stories, 1946, 48, 52; appd. in Prize Stories of 1947, also 3d prize winner "Power House," 1948; appd. Best One-Act Plays, 1947-48, edited by Margaret Mayorga (The Meadow); $500 Benjamin Franklin Award for "Sun and Shadow" in Prize Articles of 1954; $1000 Grant awarded by Inst. of Arts and Letters, NYC 1954; Gold Medal Award by Commonwealth Club of Calif. for "Fahrenheit 451," best novel written by Californian in 1953, Sept. 1954. Mem.: pres. pro-tem, Science-Fantasy Writers of Am. 1952-53; v.p. Pac. Arts Found. 1953; bd. dirs., Screen Writer's Guild; Writer's Guild of Am., 1957-61. Hobby: ceramics, oil painting, collecting masks. Rec.: swimming, badminton. Res.: 10265 Cheviot Dr., L.A., CA 90064.

BRADLEY, WILLIAM MARVIN (BILL SILBERT)
Radio Station Executive
b. Jan. 1, 1921, Detroit; s. Louis and Helen (Krause) Silbert; B.S., Univ. Detroit, 1936; postgrad. So. Meth. Univ., 1945; M.S., N.Y. Univ. 1953; son, William N. Silbert. Career: Disc jockey, emcee numerous radio-TV shows, Detroit, 1947-52; panelist Songs for Sales, CBS-TV, 1952; emcee Bill Silbert Show, Let's Go Bowling, WABD-Dumont TV, 1952-53; Bill Silbert Show, WMGM radio; announcer Red Buttons Show, ABC-TV, ;

emcee Nat. Radio Fan Club, NBC Mag. of Air., Mut., KLAC, Hollywood; Bill Bradley Show, KTLA, Hollywood; Crime Story, Greet the People, Ad Lib, Hollywood Diary; Sales mgr. Radio Sta. KLDS-FM (ABC), L.A., 1969---; appeared in motion pictures Bundle of Joy, Thunderjets, Alligator People, Young Jesse James, Lost Missiles, Breakfast at Tiffanys, Return to Peyton Place; appeared on TV shows Bronco, 77 Sunset Strip, Hawaiian Eye, Sugarfoot, Combat, Adventures in Paradise, Police Sta., Michael Shayne, Roaring '20s; numerous commls. Served to 1st Lt. USAAF, 1944-46. Damon Runyon Meml. Fund fellow; Nat. Assn. Mental Health, 1970-74; Mem.: Screen Actors Guild; AFTRA; Variety Clubs Internat., Nat. Acad. TV Arts and Scis.; So. Calif. Broadcasters Assn., VFW (certificate of appreciation, 1958). Home: 13802 Northwest Passage, Marina del Rey, CA 90291; Office: 3321 S. La Cienega, L.A., CA 90016.

BRADSHAW, THORNTON FREDERICK
President, Atlantic Richfield Co.
b. Aug. 4, 1917, Wash., D.C.; s. Frederick and Julia (See) Bradshaw; Phillips Exeter Acad. 1936; A.B., Harvard Coll. 1940; M.B.A., Harvard Bus. Sch. 1942; D.C.S. 1950; (hon.) LL.D., Pepperdine Univ. 1974; (hon.) Dr. Soc. Sci., Villanova Univ. 1975; m. Patricia Salter, N.Y.C., May 11, 1974; Chil.: Mrs. Tom (Nancy) Poor, b. Sept. 3, 1943; Mrs. Richard K. (Priscilla), Page, Jr., b. Oct. 24, 1944; Jonathan, b. Oct. 16, 1953; stepsons: Jeffrey Davenport West, b. Sept. 27, 1948; Nicholas Salter West, b. Feb. 23, 1951; Andrew Philps West, b. May 22, 1953; Eric Raymond West, b. Oct. 26, 1955. Career: Prof., Harvard Bus. Sch. 1942-50; partner, Cresap, McCormick & Paget (mgmt. cons.), N.Y. 1950-56; Atlantic Richfield Co., 1956---, bd. dirs. 1964---. Dir.: Champion Internat., N.Y.; RCA Corp., N.Y.; Security Pac. Natl. Bank, and Security Pac. Corp., L.A.; Am. Petrol. Inst.; The Conf. Bd.; Foreign Policy Assn.; Aspen Inst. for Humanistic Studies; L.A. World Affairs Council; dir., L.A. Philharmonic Assn.; chmn. bd. of Fellows, Claremont Univ. Center; dir., NBC; Conservation Fdn.; Ctr. Edn. in Internat. Mgmt.; visiting com.: UCLA Grad. Sch. of Mgmt.; Div. of Chem. and Chem. Engring. of Calif. Inst. Tech. Lt. (j.g.), USN 1945, PTO, WW II. Awards: Seven Battle Stars. Hobby: reading. Rec.: swim, boating, tennis. Home: 945 Hillcrest Pl., Pasadena, CA 91106; Office: 515 S. Flower St., L.A., CA 90071.

BRADY, GEOFFREY
Consul-General of Australia
b. May 25, 1929, Melbourne, Australia; s. Henry and Kathleen Brady; B.A., Univ. of Melbourne, 1950; M.A., 1962; m. Susanne Buschel, Sept. 21, 1956, Singapore; chil.: Stephen, b. June 11, 1959; Helen, b. Feb. 11, 1965. Career: member, Australian Foreign Service, 1955---; served Dept. of Foreign Affairs in Australian missions in Indonesia, 1956-57; London, 1957-60; Seol, 1963-64; Washington, D.C., 1965-67; N.Y.C., 1971; Kuala Lumpur, 1972-74; Deputy Austral. High Commissioner, Malaysia, 1972-76; Consul-General, S.F., 1977---. Clubs: Bohemian, St. Francis Yacht. Hobbies: lit. and hist. Rec.: golf, jogging. Home: 3580 Jackson St., S.F.; Office: Australian Consulate, 360 Post St., S.F., CA 94108.

BRANDIN, ALF ELVIN
Business Executive
b. July 1, 1912, Newton, Kan.; s. Oscar E. and Agnes (Larsen) Brandin; A.B., Stanford Univ. 1936; m. Marie Eck, Stanford Univ., Calif., June 15, 1936; sons: Alf R., b. Jan. 22, 1938; Jon E., b. Aug. 27, 1940; Erik H., b. Aug. 13, 1946; Mark S. b. Sept. 20, 1950. Career: Assoc. with Standard Group of Detroit, 1936-42; bus. mgr., Stanford Univ. 1946-59; exec. ofc. for land devel., 1951-79; v.p. for bus. affairs, 1959-70; sr. v.p.-dir. Utah Internat. Inc., 1970---. Dir.: Saga Adm. Corp., Hershey Oil Co.; v.p Alameda Dist. 2087; com. VIII Olympic Winter Games; bd. govs., S.F. Bay Area Council; U.S.N. 1942-45, WW II; Comdr. USNR. Mem.: Silverado Country Club, Bohemian Club, Pauma Valley Country Club, Bankers Club, S.F., S.F. Golf Club, Royal Lahaina, Zeta Psi. Republican. Espicopalian. Rec.: golf. Home: 668 Salvatierra St., Stanford, CA; Office: 550 California St., San Francisco, CA 94104.

BRANIN, JEANETTE WELLMAN
Newspaper Editor and Writer
b. May 11, 1909, Sterling, Kan.; d. Edward Chauncey and Jessie Cochrane (Coyle) Wellman; B.A., Univ. Kansas; m. Patrick Willis Irving Branin, May 1, 1947, San Diego; son, Patrick Coyle, b. Feb. 25, 1948. Career: Publicity dir., ARC Blood Donor Service, 1944; dir. publicity, San Diego C. of C. 1945-47; co-owner, mgr., The Branin Advt.

and Pub. Rels. Agency, 1947-53; Women's Editor, Asst. Editor, The San Diego Independent, 1953-68; also producer and hostess, daily TV (Channel 10) program, The Independent Woman, 1955-58; staff writer, The San Diego Union, 1968-76, Food Editor and Staff Writer, 1976---. Recipient of more than 70 awards for excellence in writing, 1953-79. Mem.: Chi Omega Sor., life; Mortar Board, life; Sigma Delta Chi. Home: 4957 Pacifica Dr., San Diego, CA 92109; Office: 350 Camino de la Reina, San Diego, CA 92112.

BRANDOW, GEORGE E.
Consulting Structural Engineer
b. Oct. 27, 1913, Crookston, Minn.; s. Harry W. and Laura (Ramstad) Brandow; ed. B.S.C.E., USC 1936; m. Anita Dunn, L.A., CA July 1, 1938; sons: Peter D., Gregg E. Career: L.A. Co. Bldg. Dept. 1936-38; Arch. Rib Truss Co. 1938-40; John C. Austin Arch. 1940-41; chief engr. Lummus Co., L.A. 1941-43; chief engr. L.A. Refinery, Union Oil Co. 1943-45; est. pvt. practice, Brandow & Johnston Assoc., cons. structural engrs. 1945---. Mem.: chmn. structural engrs. 1945---. Mem.: chmn. Structural Div., Am. Soc. of Civil Engrs., 1955; pres. L.A. Sect. 1956, Natl. dir. 1963-65; pres. Am. Inst. of Cons. Engrs. 1969; pres. USC Alumni Assn. 1970-71; bd. trustees, USC; pres. L.A. Music Center Operating Co.; Town Hall of Calif., San Marino City Councilman; Mem. of Overseers of Huntington Library, Jonathan, Calif. Club. Republican. Methodist. Hobbies: skiing, hiking, tennis. Home: 1490 Virginia Rd., San Marino, CA 91108; Office: 1660 W. Third St., L.A., CA 90017.

BRASTOFF, SASCHA
Designer — Ceramist
b. Oct. 23, 1918, Cleveland, O.; s. Louis and Rebecca (Haimowitz) Brastoff; Cleveland Sch. of Art. Career: Ballet dancer, Cleveland Ballet, 1930-37; sculptor, Sculptor Center, N.Y. 1937-42; designer of costumes, 20th Century-Fox Film Corp. ("Razor's Edge," "Diamond Horseshoe," "If I'm Lucky," and stars Carmen Miranda and Betty Grable), 1946-47; ceramist-designer, Sascha Brastoff Products, Inc. 1947---. Sgt., U.S. Army Air Force (ETO with ATC 1942-46), appd. in "Winged Victory," WW II. Awards: winner, Syracuse Cermic Award, 1946, 48. Hobby: dancing, gradening, dogs. Home: 2522 Military Ave., W. L.A., CA; Studio: 246 - 26th St., Santa Monica, CA 90402.

BRATCHER, TWILA LANGDON
Researcher
b. Wyoming; d. Willis G. and Pearl (Graham) Langdon; desc. John Langdon, signer of U.S. Constitution; m. Ford F. Bratcher, Yuma, Ariz. Career: research assoc., L.A. Co. Mus. Natural Hist.; freelance writer; contbr. to sci. journs., popular mags., travel mags., shell and scuba dive pubs. Mem.: Conchological Club of So. Calif., pres. 1966; Am. Malacological Union; Councilor-at-large, 1972; Pacific Shell Club, chmn. Braille shell project, 1965-72; Western Soc. of Malacologists, pres. 1973; So. Calif. Women's Press Club, pres. 1978, 79. Hobby: shell collecting. Rec.: bridge, scuba diving, travel. Home: 8121 Mulholland Terrace, Hollywood, CA 90046.

BRAUN, THEODORE WILLIAM
Founder-President, Braun & Company
b. Dec. 26, 1901, Newark, N.J.; s. Adam and Elizabeth (Bayles) Braun; spec. stu., Grad. Sch. of Bus., Harvard Univ.; Command and Gen. Staff Sch., Ft. Leavenworth, Kan.; m. Beatrice Banning, St. Paul, Minn., July 3, 1920. Career: Exec. v.p., Calif. Consolidated Water Co. 1926-27; cons. Calif. Consumers Co. and subsidiaries, Arrowhead Springs Corp. and Calif. Date Growers Assn. 1926-32; founder-pres., Braun & Co., L.A., 1936---; ltd. partner, Merrill Lynch, Pierce, Fenner & Smith, Inc. 1955---. Staff, Gordon Gray Report to Pres., U.S. Foreign & Econ. Policy, 1950; spec. com. on reorgn., Natl. Security Council, 1953; asst. to U.S. Secty. of Treas., 1953-54, cons. 1955; adv. com. to secty. of Def., Gen. Mil. Training, 1962. Cons. to Comdg. Gen., 4th Army, Western Def. Command, 1941-43; dir. Tech. Information Div., Army Serv. Forces (1944), WW II. Mem.: v.p. Calif. Inst. for Cancer Research; pres. Town Hall, 1963; bd. dirs., Claremont Colls. 1963-64; bd. dirs., Otis Art Assoc., pres. Hollywood Bowl Assn. 1964; trustee, Harvey Mudd Coll.; Met. Club, Wash., D.C.; So. Cross Club, Bahamas; Men's Garden Club of L.A., Natl. Aviation Club, Confrerie des Chevaliers du Tastevin, Wine & Food Soc. of So. Calif., Wine & Food Soc. of Beverly Hills, North Shore Beach & Yacht Club; Eldorado Country Club, Palm Desert, Calif.; Calif. Club and Bel-Air Country Club, L.A. Home: 537 Perugia Way, Bel-Air, L.A., CA.

BRAY, ABSALOM FRANCIS, JR.
Attorney at Law
b. Nov. 24, 1918, S.F., Calif.; s. A.F., Sr. (presiding Justice, Ct. of Appeal) and Leila (Veale) Bray; grandson of Sheriff R.R. Veale, Contra Costa Co. 1895-1935; ed. A.B. Stanford Univ. 1940; J.D., USC Sch. of Law 1949; m. Lorraine Paule, Oakland, June 25, 1949; chil.: Oliver Whitney, b. Nov. 15, 1954; Brian Keith, b. July 25, 1955; Margot Elizabeth, by Nov. 9, 1957. Career: Legal dept., Iowa Ord. Plant, Burlington, 1940-42; pvt. practice law, 1949---, sr. partner, Bray, Baldwin, Egan and Breitwieser firm, Martinez, Calif. Adv. bd., Bank of Am. 1953-65. Lt., USNR (1942-46), WW II. Awards: Navy Commendation, Navy Unit Citation. Mem.: comdr. Veterans of Foreign Wars, 1962; comdr. Am. Legion, 1955; pres. Contra Costa Co. Devel. Assn. 1959-60; local judge advocate, Navy League, U.S.; chmn. natl. bd. dirs., Camp Fire Girls, 1959-61; 1969-71; Lawyer's Club, Alameda Co.; State Bar of Calif.; pres. Contra Costa Co. Bar Assn. 1964; past pres., Contra Costa Co. Tuberculosis and Pub. Health Assn.; Contra Costa Co. Hist. Soc.; E. Clampus Vitus; Soc. of Calif. Pioneers; chmn., John Muir Dist., B.S.A. 1968; past chmn. Region V, Camp Fire Girls (Calif., Nev., Utah, Ariz., Hawaii); com. Salvation Army; (life) Martinez PTA; pres. Rotary Club, 1969-71; Masons, Elks, Republican. Episcopalian (vestry). Hobbies: photog., ship models. Rec.: hiking. Home: 600 Flora St., Martinez, CA; Office: Ward and Ferry Sts., Martinez, CA 94553.

BRECKNER, ROBERT WILSON
Broadcaster
b. July 15, 1920, Fullerton, Calif.; s. Gary C. and Helen (Wilson) Breckner; A.B., Stanford Univ., 1942; m. Sally Kendrick, June 23, 1945, L.A.; dau. Betsy (Greene). Career: Contact Prod., Network Sales Service, CBS-KNX, Hollywood, 1946-48; film dir., prod.-dir., v.p. & gen. mgr., pres., Times Mirror TV, KTTV, L.A., 1948-63; TV-Radio mgmt. cons., 1963---; pres. and co-owner, Emerald Broadcasting Co., South Lake Tahoe, Calif., KTHO-AM & FM, 1965---; pres., Times-Mirror Communications Co. (Cable TV), L.A., 1970-72; pres., Cinca Communications Co. (Pay-TV), L.A., 1973-75; TV-Radio-Cable broker and cons., L.A., 1975---. Pres., Michael Burke Found., Cardiac Research, St. Johns Hosp., Santa Monica, 1955---; past dir.: Neighborhood Youth Assn., Calif. Cable TV Assn., Radio-TV Charities, Hollywood Ad Club; past pres.: TV Branch, Screen Directors Guild, Hollywood Ad Club; past pres.: TV Branch, Screen Directors Guild, Hollywood. Lt. (S.G.), USNR, 1942-44, Staff, Wm. F. Halsey, 1944-46, Air Combat Intelligence. Mem.: The Beach Club, Santa Monica, past pres.; L.A. Country Club; Alpha Delta Phi. Home: 1014 N. Bundy Dr., L.A., CA 90049; Office: 11755 San Vicente Blvd., L.A., CA 90049.

BREGER, BARBARA CAMILLE
Ophthalmologist
b. May 9, 1938, San Francisco; d. Samuel (M.D.) and Frances Mary (Mordecai) Breger; A.B., Univ. Calif., Berkeley, 1959; M.D., Univ. Calif. Sch. of Med., S.F., 1963; m. Edgar L. Whittingham, Oct. 20, 1973, S.F. Career: Internship, 1963-64; neurology residency, 1964-65; pathology resident, 1965-66; ophthalmology resident, 1966-69; all at the Mount Sinai Hosp., N.Y.C.; practiced in M.Y. for H.I.P., 1969-71; pvt. practice, Beverly Hills, 1971---; contbr. med. articles to profl. journs.; described by L.A. Mag. as "Doctor that doctors go to," June 1978. Finance chmn., physicians div., United Jewish Welfare Fund. Mem.: Braemar Country Club, Tarzana; Jewish. Hobbies: golf, needlepoint. Rec.: swimming. Home: 9905 Stellbar Pl., L.A., CA 90064; Office: 435 N. Bedford Dr., Suite 416, Beverly Hills, CA 90210.

BREINER, SHELDON
Company President
b. Oct. 23, 1936, Milwaukee, Wis.; s. James and Fannie Breiner; B.S., 1959; M.S., 1962; Ph.D., 1967, all in geophysics, Stanford Univ.; m. Phyllis Farrington, Feb. 4, 1962, Los Altos; chil.: David S., b. Jan. 28, 1963; Michelle A., b. Aug. 5, 1968. Career: with Varian Assocs., 1961-68; with geoMetrics, Inc., Sunnyvale, 1969---: chmn., pres., 1972---; cons. prof. and research assoc., Stanford Univ., 1972-75. Dir., Portola Valley Ranch, 1977---; trustee, Peninsula Open Space Trust, 1977---; chmn., geoMetrics Services (Canada) Ltd., 1971---. AUS, 1960; USAR, 1960-66. Conducted archaeological exploration in Mex., Italy, U.S.; author over 20 tech papers and book on geophysical exploration for oil and minerals, archaeol. exploration, earthquake prediction; U.S. Patentee; lectr. worldwide on these subjects; Fellow, The Explorers Club, N.Y. Pres., Foothills Stanford Club, 1971. Hobbies: photog., woodworking. Rec.: backpacking, skiing, long dist. running, soccer. Home: 45

Buckeye, Portola Valley, CA; Office: 395 Java Dr., Sunnyvale, CA 94086.

BREMER, WILLIAM RICHARD
Attorney at Law
b. Jan. 5, 1930, San Francisco; s. Milton and Alice (Herring) Bremer; 2d cousin, Ann Bremer, Calif. artist; B.S., Menlo Coll., 1952; J.D., Univ. of S.F., 1958; m. Margaret Herrington 1959, Norfolk, Va.; chil.: Mark Richard; Karen Elizabeth; William Richard, Jr. Career: pvt. profl. practice of law, 1959---; Arbitrator, Am. Arbitration Assn., 1965---; Arbitrator, Marin Co. and S.F. Co. Superior Cts., 1975---. Col., USMCR; active duty Korean War, 1952-54, USMCR, 1954---. Mem.: Phi Alpha Delta, law frat.; Corinthian Yacht Club; Naval Order; Navy League of The U.S.; pres. S.F. Council, 1978; Navy League U.S., nat. dir., 1978; Montgomery St. Motorcycle Club, past pres. Mayor, City of Tiburon, 1968-69; City Councilman, 1966-70. Home: Tiburon, CA; Office: 300 Montgomery St., Suite 1000, S.F., CA 94104.

BRENDEL, BETTINA
Artist — Lecturer
b. Lueneburg, Germany; d. Dr. Robert (well known poet of German expressionist period, dec. 1947) and Dr. Xenia (Bernstein) Brendel; B.A., Hamburg, Ger., 1940; postgrad. Kunstschule Schmilinsky, Staatl. Hochschule f.Bild.Kunste., 1945-47, USC, 1955-58, New Sch. Social Research, N.Y.; div. 1965; dau. Violet Ann Spitzer (Mrs. Steve Lucas), b. Aug. 1, 1951. Career: Solo exhibitions in West Coast museums, 1958---' Long Beach Mus., La Jolla Art Mus., Pasadena Art Mus., Santa Barbara Mus., Downey Mus. of Art; Rep., Esther Robles Gallery, 1957-62; included in nat. and internat. exhibs.: W. Germany, Italy, Austria, U.K.; included in permanent pub. and pvt. collections, US and Europe; tchr., Landhochschule Marienau, Ger., 1947; mem. faculty, UCLA Ext., 1958-61, 1976. Author vol. poems, Whenever in the World, 1977; contbr. articles, Art Hourn., Leonardo. Mem.: Coll. Art Assn. of Am.; UCLA Art Council; Artists f.Econ.Action.L.A. Co. Mus. of Art. Christian. Rec.: swimming, dancing. Home-studio: 1061 N. Kenter Ave., L.A., CA 90049.

BRENDLER, MERLE ELIZABETH
Savings & Loan Company Executive
b. Nov. 28, 1924, Bloomington, Ind.; d. George B. and Emma (Sidwell) Goode; m. Charles Brendler, Mar. 25, 1967, Houston, Tex.; dau. Cynthia Louise, b. Jan. 17, 1958. Career: with Henry Co. Bldg. & Loan, New Castle, Ind., 1942-46; Valley Bank, Phoenix, Ariz., 1946-50; 1st Nat. Bank of San Jose (Calif.), 1950-55; First Fed. Savings & Loan, 1955-60; El Camino S&L, Sunnyvale, 1960-71, asst. v.p. and mgr., 1969; asst. v.p., branch mgr., Security S&L, Sunnyvale, 1972-77; asst. v.p., mgr., Coast Fed. Svgs., Sunnyvale, 1977---. Mem.: Sunnyvale Bus. & Profl. Women's Club, pres. 1966-67; Soroptimist Internat. of Foothill Cities, pres. 1976-77; United Way of Santa Clara Co., v.p. 1976-77; Sunnyvale C. of C., v.p., 1977-78. Protestant; mem. ch. bd. of trustees 1975-78. Hobbies: crocheting, cooking, organ music. Rec.: golf, bowling, skating, bridge. Home: 1319 Regency Dr., San Jose, CA 95129; Office: 1307 S. Mary Ave., Sunnyvale, CA 94087.

BRENNAN, ROBERT GILBERT
Librarian
b. Mar. 26, 1927, Mt. Vernon, N.Y.; s. Robert G., Sr. and Lydia Gertrude (Jost) Brennan; B.A., Mt. Union Coll., 1951; M.L.S., Pratt Inst., 1952; m. Dawn Hazel Tolson, June 11, 1952, Carroltown, Ohio; chil.: Margaret Lydia, b. Dec. 10, 1958; Thomas Lyle, b. June 24, 1960; Lawrence Andrew, b. Sept. 20, 1962; Amy Elizabeth, b. Mar. 11, 1966. Career: Head, Social sci. and bus. lib., Calif. State Univ., Chico, 1962-66, Dir. of Pub. Servs., lib., 1966---: lib. dir., Harvard Lehi Hemore Mem. Lib., Naugatuck, Ct., 1954-62; Ref. Libn., Dayton Pub. Lib., Dayton, Ohio, 1952-54. Mem.: Appalachian Mt. Club, 1956-62; Rotary, Naugatuck, 1959-62; Am. Philatelic Soc., 1970---. Republican. United Methodist; chmn. administr. bd., 1966. Hobby: philately. Rec.: camping. Home: 11 Woodside Lane, Chico, CA 95926; Office: LARC, Cal. State Univ., Chico, CA 95929.

BRENNEN, STEPHEN ALFRED
Corporate Executive
b. July 7, 1932, New York, N.Y.; s. Theodore and Margaret (Pembroke) Brennen; M.B.A., Univ. Chicago, 1959; A.B. Economics, Univ. of Americas, Mex., 1956; m. Yolanda Alicia Romero, Chicago, Ill., Sept. 20, 1957; chil.: Stephen Roberto, b. Oct. 14, 1958; Richard Patrick, b. May 1, 1961. Career: gen. mgr., Purina Guatemala,

Guatemala City, 1964-66; Ralston Purina Internat., St. Louis, Mo., 1966-67; pres. Purina Colombiana, Bogata, Colombia, 1967-69; pres. Lvg. Marine Resources, Inc., San Diego, 1969-69; man. dir., Ralston Purina Internat. Latin Am., 1970-74; pres., Van Camp Seafood Co., div. Ralston Purina, San Diego, 1974---. Dir. Mex. Am. Bank, San Diego, 1977---. USAF, 1950-54. Author: Successfully yours, 1974. Dir.: S.D. Taxpayers Assn.; S.D. United Way; S.D. Jr. Achievement; S.D. Coalition. Trustee, S.D. Multiple Sclerosis Soc. Mem. Chancellor's Assoc., UCSD. Office: 11555 Sorrento Valley Rd., S.D., CA 92121.

BRESLAW, LEONARD
  Physician
b. Oct. 4, 1924, Denver, Colo.; s. Manuel and Anna Breslaw; A.B., Univ. Denver, 1946; M.D., Univ. Colo. Sch. of Med., 1948; m. Beatrice Bernstein, Dec. 23, 1973, L.A.; chil.: Amy Louise, b. Nov. 13, 1964; Iris Lynn, b. May 18, 1966. Career: Rotating Intern, U.S. Pub. Health Hosp., Staten Is., N.Y., 1948-49; asst. resident, neurology, Bellevue Hosp., N.Y., 1949-50; asst. resident, internal med., Jersey City Med. Center, 1950-51; resident, internal med., Bronx Hosp., 1951-52; resident in gastroenterology and gastrointestinal radiology, Lenox Hill Hosp., 1952-54; med. practice, internal med. and gastroenterology, Century City, Calif. 1955---. Contbr. articles to med. journs. Pub. Health Serv., 1954-56; Fellow, Am. Coll. Physicians, 1963; Am. Coll. of Gastroenterologists, 1974. Currently on staff 23 hosps.: Mem.: Am. Soc. for Gastrointestinal Endoscopy; So. Calif. Gastroenterologic Soc.; L.A. Co. Med. Assn.; Dir. GI Labs., Hawthorne Comm. Hosp.; Dir. GI Labs., Imperial Hosp.; So. Calif. Soc. for Gastrointestinal Endoscopy. Mem.: Phi Beta Kappa, 1946. Office: 2080 Century Park East, Suite 1202, L.A., CA 90067.

BRESLER, BORIS
  Principal, Wiss, Janney, Elstner & Assoc., Inc.
b. Oct. 18, 1918, Harbin, China; s. Samuel and Hena Bresler; B.S.C.E., Univ. Calif., Berkeley, 1941; M.S. Aero. Eng., Calif. Inst. of Tech., Pasadena, 1946; m. Joy Bloom, July 5, 1946, San Francisco; dau. Deborah, b. Feb. 22, 1948. Career: with Univ. Calif., Berkeley, 1946-78: asst. Dean, Coll. of Engring., 1956-59; chmn., Structural Engring. and Structural Mechanics Div., 1963-64; dir., struct. and engr. materials lab., 1963-65; cons., various engring. orgns. incl. Nat. Bureau of Standards, U.S. Naval Civil Eng. Lab., Port Hueneme, Applied Tech. Council, Port of N.Y. Authority (World Trade Ctr.), Bechtel Corp., Skidmore Owings and Merrill, Tudor Engring. Co., Mechanics Research Inc., Portland Gen. Electric Co.; principal, Wiss, Janney, Elstner and Assoc., Inc., Emeryville ---; structural design of shipyard facilities, Kaiser Shipyards, Richmond, 1941-43; stress analyst, design and devel. aircraft structures, Convair Corp., S.D., 1943-45. Awards: Am. Concrete Inst. (ACI) J.W. Kelly Award, 1978; Am. Soc. Civil Engrs. (ASCE), State of the Art of Civil Engring. Award, 1968; Guggenheim Fellowship, 1962; Nat. Sci. Found. Postdoctoral Fellowship, 1961; ACI/Wason Medal for Research, 1959. Mem.: Am. Concrete Inst., fellow; Am. Soc. of Civil Engrs., fellow; Am. Soc. for Testing Materials; Structural Engrs. Assn. of No. Calif.; Reinforced Concrete Research Council; Internat. Assn. of Bridge and Structural Engrs. Home: 570 Vistamont Ave., Berkeley, CA 94708; Office: 5801 Christie Ave., Room 485, Emeryville, CA 94608.

BRESLOW, LESTER
  Dean, UCLA School of Public Health
b. Mar. 17, 1915, Bismarck, N. Dak.; s. Joseph and Mayme (Danziger) Breslow; A.B., Univ. of Minn. 1935, M.D. 1938, M.P.H. 1941; m. Devra Miller, Aug. 20, 1967; sons: Norman E., b. Feb. 21, 1941; Jack W., b. Mar. 25, 1944; Stephen P., b. May 12, 1945. Career: U.S. Pub. Health Serv. Intern, 1938-40; dist. health ofcr., Minn. Dept. of Health, 1941-43; chief, bur. of chronic diseases, Calif. Dept. of Pub. Health, 1946-60; chief, div. of preventive med. servs. 1960-65, dir. of pub. health, 1965-68; chmn. Dept. Preventive Med. and Pub. Health, Sch. of Med., UCLA 1968-72; dean, Sch. of Pub. Health, 1972---. Author: med. publs., ed. cons., Journ. Chronic Diseases. Capt., US Army, 1943-46, WW II. Awards: Lasker Award, Calif. Dept. Public Health. Mem.: Fellow, Am. Pub. Health Assn., 1947---, governing council, 1954-62; dir. Pres. Comm. on Health Needs of the Nation, 1952; pres. Pub. Health Cancer Assn. 1953; Comm. on Chronic Illness, 1954-56; pres. Assn. of State Chronic Disease Pgm. Dirs. 1959-61; chmn. exec. council, Internat. Epidemiological Assn. 1964---; natl. dir.-at-large, Am. Cancer Soc., 1964---; dir. Motor Vehicle Pollution Bd.; dir., State of Calif. Inspection Bd.; diplomate, Am. Bd. Preventive Med. and Pub. Health; fellow, Am. Coll. Preventive Medicine; AMA; AAAS; Public Health Cancer Assn.; Am. Epidemiology Soc.; pres. Am. Pub. Health

Assn. 1968-69. Office: Center for Health Sciences, UCLA, L.A., CA 90024.

BREWER, GERALD BERNIE
  President, Producers Cotton Oil Company
b. Nov. 12, 1929; Fresno; s. Bernie and Emma (Schafer) Brewer; B.S., soc. sci., USC, 1951; m. Lyla Tilston, Dec. 23, 1951, Glendale; chil.: Barbara (Mrs. Tome E. Johnson), b. May 1953; William S., b. July 1959; Nancy, b. April 1956. Career: with Producers Cotton Oil Co., 1953---: gin. mgr. trainee, 1953; personnel mgr., 1954; asst. to pres., 1955; sales mgr., 1958; dir. of sales & oil mill opns., 1961; v.p. and dir. of sales, 1962; exec. v.p., 1969; bd. dir., 1970---; pres. and chief exec. officer, 1972---. Dir., Bangor Punta Corp., 1973, v.p., 1974. Lt., USAF, 1951-52. Mem.: Phi Kappa Psi; Commonwealth Club; Downtown Club; President's Club, Cal. State Univ., Fresno; Sunnyside Country Club. Protestant. Rec.: yachting, tennis. Home: 1465 W. Morris Ave., Fresno, CA 93711; Office: P.O.B. 1832, 2907 S. Maple Ave., Fresno, CA 93725.

BREWER, KARA PRATT
  University Administrator
b. Oct. 29, 1930, Reno, Nev.; d. Kenneth and Kara (Lucas) Pratt; B.A., hist., 1969; M.A., hist., 1972; D.A., English, 1976; m. David P. Brewer, Sept. 10, 1949, Stockton; chil.: Margaret (Eccleston), b. July 21, 1950; Martin S., b. Nov. 26, 1951; Kenneth L., b. May 29, 1953; Paul R., b. Sept. 22, 1954; Elena M., b. June 23, 1957; Clare E., b. Aug. 13, 1959; Sam A., b. Nov. 17, 1961; Matthew A., b. Apr. 5, 1965. Career: Danforth Fellow, 1969-73; grad. study in Ireland, 1969-70; instr., Univ. of the Pacific, Stockton, 1973-74, editorial asst. Pacific Hist., 1974-75, historian in residence, 1976, dir., Alumni-Parent Programs, 1977---. Author: Pioneer or Perish: A History of the University of the Pacific during the Administration of Dr. Robert E. Burns, 1946-71. Mem.: Phi Kappa Phi. Ch. Annunciation Parish, Liturgy Comm. Home: 7922 E. 8 Mile Rd., Stockton, CA 95212; Office: Univ. of the Pacific, Stockton, CA 95211.

BREWER, THALIA BRADFORD
  Historian
b. Frankston, Texas; d. John Powell and Mamie Isabel (Burks) Bradford; desc. (10th gen.) Bradfords of Plymouth Plantation; grad., Mary Hardin-Baylor Coll., Univ. of Texas, pvt. studies; m. Lt. Col. Robert Lee Brewer (Desc. of early Calif. fam., Rail Chief, Alsace-Lorraine Sector, WW II); sons, William Bradford (spec. proj. dir., contemporary design, Hallmark Cards; chosen the Most Outstanding Coll. Cartoonist in Am. by Judges Steve Allen, Groucho Marx and Al Capp); and R. Kent (atty. at law, Walnut Creek). Career: Reporter-feature writer, The Herald, Palestine, Tex.; reporter and columnist, The Statesman, Austin, Tex.; Society ed., The Express, San Antonio, Tex.; spec. assignments, N.Y. Herald-Tribune; press rep., NBC Artists Service, N.Y.C.; secty., Lawrence Radiation Lab., Livermore, Calif.; currently historian, The Eugene O'Neill Found., Tao House, 1976---. Mem.: Mt. Diablo chpt., ARC, pub. chmn.; Las Trampas Council; pres., Eugene O'Neill Nat. Historic Site Assn., 1969-74; v.p., Eugene O'Neill Found., 1974-76. Presbyterian. Hobbies: piano, vis. museums. Rec.: walking. Home: 608 Bradford Pl., Danville, CA 94526.

BRICHANT, COLETTE
  Author — Educator
b. France; d. Henri and Suzanne (Aubourg) Dubois; Ph.D.; m. Andrew Brichant, 1955; Montreal; son, Stephen, b. 1956. Career: Instr.: Peace Corps, Indiana Univ., Russell Sage Coll., Middlebury Coll., Univ. Calif., L.A.; cons., Ednl. Tchg. Service; Author: Tableaux d'histoire; L'Heritage Culturel; La France au travail; Arts de France (all pub. Am. Book Co.); French for the humanities; French for the Social Sciences; French for the Sciences; French Grammar key to reading (pub. Prentice-Hall); DeGaulle artiste de l'action; La France au cours des ages (McGraw-Hill); Premier Guide de France, Prentice-Hall, 1978. Protestant. Hobby: travel. Home: 3232 Glendon Ave., L.A., CA; Office: UCLA, 405 Hilgard Ave., L.A., CA 90024.

BRICKMAN, ROBERT LEE
  School District Superintendent
b. Mar. 8, 1932; B.A. (baccalaureate), Univ. Calif., Santa Barbara, 1957; M.A., Cal. State Univ., L.A., 1960; Ph.D., Claremont Grad. Sch., 1970; postdoct. studies, Univ. of the Pacific, 1970, workshops and seminars annually. Career: dir., Rec. Dept., Santa Barbara, 1955-57; tchr.: Santa Barbara City and Co. Schs., 1956-57, Univ. of

Hawaii, 1957-58, Glendale Unified Schs., 1958-60, DOD Schs., France, 1960-62; dean of students, Garden Grove High Schs., 1962-63; vis. prof., CSU, Fullerton, 1966, Chapman Coll., Orange, 1969-70; principal, Garden Grove Unified Sch. Dist., 1965-73; supt., Encinitas Schs., Encinitas, 1973-77; supt., Vacaville Unified Sch. Dist., 1977---. Mem.: Little League, Pop Warner, Babe Ruth, YMCA, Cub Scouts, past leader, dir., Garden Grove Boys' Club; Western Assn. Year-Round Schs.; Adminstrs. Assn., past pres.; San Dieguito Family Services Assn.; Am. Assn. of Sch. Adminstrs.; Assn. of Calif. Sch. Adminstrs.; AAUP; Solano Co. Taxpayers' Assn.; Vacaville C. of C.; Solano Co. Adminstrs. Assn. Home: Box 980, Vacaville, CA 95688; Office: 751 School St., Vacaville, CA 95688.

BRICKMAN, ROBERT LEE
School District Administrator
b. Mar. 8, 1932, Oshkosh, Wis.; s. Marx W. and Lillian (Struthers) Brickman; B.A., Univ. Calif., Santa Barbara, 1959; M.A., Cal. State Univ., L.A., 1960; Ph.D., Claremont Univ. Career: tchg. asst., Univ. of Hawaii, 1957-58; apec. edn. dept. chmn. 1958-60; teacher, 7-12, 1960-62; Dean, 1962-63; Asst. prin. 1963-65; principal, 1965-70; Supt., Vacaville Unified Sch. Dist., 1970---. Served AUS, 1950-54; airborne infan.; decorated: Purple Heart, Silver Star. Rec.: jogging, biking, surfing. Home: P.O.B. 980, Vacaville, CA 95688; Office: 751 School St., Vacaville, CA 95688.

BRIDGES, ROBERT LYSLE
Attorney at Law
b. May 12, 1909, Altus, Ark.; s. Joseph Manning and Jeffa (Morrison) Bridges; B.A., Univ. Calif., 1930, LL.B., 1933; m. Alice Rodenberger, June 10, 1930, Berkeley; chil.: David Manning, b. May 22, 1936; James Robert, b. Nov. 16, 1938; Linda Lee, b. Aug. 15, 1944. Career: law practice in S.F., 1933---: assoc. firm of Thelen & Marrin, 1933-39; partner, firm, 1939---, firm name Thelen, Marrin, Johnson & Bridges, 1941---. Dir.: Crum & Forster; Indsl. Indemnity Co.; Energy Transportation Services, Inc.; Engring. Mgmt., Inc.; Trans Mt. Pipe Line Co.; Wells Fargo Bank; Wells Fargo & Co.; past dir.: Bechtel Corp.; Calabasas Enterprises, Inc.; Mountain Pacific Pipeline Ltd. Recipient Golden Beaver Award, 1977, heavy constrn. indus. Mem.: Pacific Union Club, Stock Exch. Club, World Trade Club, Commonwealth Club, Claremont Country Club, Oakland, Links, N.Y.C. Home: 3972 Happy Valley Rd., Lafayette, CA; Office: Two Embarcadero Ctr., San Francisco, CA 94111.

BRILL, RICHARD GEORGE
Consultant
b. Dec. 4, 1913, Mystic, Conn.; s. Tobias and Ella A. Brill; A.B., Rutgers Univ., 1935; M.A., Gallaudet Coll., 1936; M.A., Univ. Calif., Berkeley, 1940; Ed.D., Rutgers Univ. 1950; m. Ruth M. Annabil, Dec. 27, 1939, Redlands; chil.: Thomas R., b. Mar. 9, 1943; Jane A., b. May 22, 1946. Career: tchr., Calif. Sch. for the Deaf, Berkeley, 1936-42; prin., Virginia Sch. for the Deaf, Staunton, Va., 1941-46; Bruce St. Sch. for the Deaf, Newark, N.J., 1946-49; asst. prof., Univ. Ill., Urbana, 1949-51; supt., Calif. Sch. for the Deaf, Riverside, 1951-77; holder of hon. endowed Powrie Doctor Chair of Deaf Studies, Gallaudet Coll., Wash., D.C., 1977-78. Author: Education for the Deaf; Administrative and Professional Developments, 1971, 1974; Mainstreaming the Prelingually Deaf Child, 1978; over 40 pub. profl. articles. Ensign to Lt., USNR, 1941-45; commanding officer of a subchaser 2 years. Pres., Am. Instrs. of the Deaf, 1959-61; pres., Council on Edn. of the Deaf, 1966-68; pres., Conf. of Exec. of Am. Schs. for the Deaf, 1974-76; past pres.: Riverside Mental Health Soc., Riverside Comm. Council, Goodwill Industries of the Inland Counties; past bd. mem. Riverside Comm. Hosp. Polit. mem. Riverside Co. Bd. of Freeholders to write a new co. charter. Unitarian-Universalist, past pres. bd. of dir. ch. of Riverside. Home: 116 Ave. Cota, San Clemente, CA 92672.

BRINEY, SUSANNE D.
Realtor
b. Dec. 27, 1924, Chicago, Ill.; d. Keat Bronston and Irene (Webster) Dean; m. Donald Ernest Briney, Aug. 28, 1954, Las Vegas, Nev.; chil.: Patrick R., b. Mar. 17, 1956; Daniel D., b. June 24, 1957; Linda L., b. Sept. 27, 1959. Career: licensed real estate sales person, 1969-72; licensed real estate broker, 1972---; opened own office, Carbon Canyon Realtors, Inc., 1975---. Mem.: N. Orange Co. Bd. of Realtors; Ontario-Upland-Chino Bd. of Realtors; Brea C. of C.; Chino C. of C.; Realtors Marketing Inst. Polit.: San Bernardino Co. Service Area 48, chmn. 1978-79.

Catholic. Rec.: swimming. Home: 16757 Hillside Dr., Chino, CA 91710; Office: 114 Olinda Dr., Brea, CA 92621.

BRINKLEY, ANGELINE ROSE
Community Volunteer
b. Jan. 30, 1924, Mt. Carmel, Pa.; d. Max and Ersilia (Zanella) DeCarli; m. Robert G. Wilkinson, Oklahoma, 1944; chil.: Jean (Crist), b. Apr. 9, 1954; Stephen, b. Feb. 25, 1956; Joan, b. Aug. 21, 1958; John and Paul, b. Apr. 6, 1960; m. 2d. Mardy Brinkley, Mar. 13, 1970, Escondido. Career: volunteer: helped start Vista Coordinating Council; started Poway Coordinating Council, set up master calendar, chmn. 4 years; chmn. Heart Assn., Poway, 1974-78, capt. of 2 areas for 5th yr., mem. Heart Sunday Advis. Com., mem. Fund Raising Advis. Com. for No. Co. Branch, S.D. Co. Heart Assn. 3rd yr., worker on Cyclathons and blood pressure clinics, address envelopes; chmn., co-chmn. for Smas baskets for Poway, Penasquitos, Rancho Bernardo, 1974---; co-chmn., Palomar Family Counseling Service for Poway, steering com.; participant all Radiothons and Telethons for St. Jude Childrens Hosp.; annual projects: Ranchero Days, Vista; Boys Club Carnival, mem. Boys Club Mothers Club; vol., Well Baby Clinics; Opn. Santa, Santas Village, Girls Club, Toys for Tots, Retarded Sch. in Vista, Telecare program, Pow Wow Days Celebration; Kidney Drives, Cancer Drives; Walk for Mankind; fund raiser for 3 orphanages in Mexico, flood victims in Mex. and Idaho; tree recycling program, vol. for Paramedics; started the Emergency Cupboard in Poway, vol., Twin Peaks Retirement home. Mem. Sigma Kappa Pi, held all offices at chpt. and council level; mem. Epsilon Sigma Alpha Internat. sor., 1964---: pres. of 4 chpts., outstanding mem. of chpt., 1968-69; pres. Regional Council level, 1973-74 (Pub. Rels. chmn. for Million Dollar Bike Ride for St. Judes Hosp.); State Council level ESA, Mem., dir. of Calif., voted outstanding mem. Calif. State Council, 1974-75; Internat. Council ESA, 1975 internat. asst. (only 12 out of 33,000 mems. work with world hdqtrs.), 1977-78 Communications Com.; earned highest ESA award, 5th degree of Pallas Athene, 1975. Awards: Tri-City Citizen of the Day, Oceanside, 1971; Vol. of the Year Award for San Diego Co., 1974; award from Heart Assn. every year, 1962---. Catholic. Hobby: crocheting. Rec.: bicycle riding. Home: 13206 Alpine Dr., Poway, CA 92064.

BRISCOE, RALPH O.
Chairman, Republic Corporation
b. Nov. 15, 1927, Trenton, Mich.; B.A., Kenyon Coll., 1950; M.B.A., Harvard, 1952; m. Joan V. Trefry; chil.: Ralph Jr., Donald, Stephen, Linda, Lisa. Career: with Ford Motor Co., 1953-56; Curtiss-Wright Corp., 1956-57; CBS, Inc., 1958-73; chairman of bd. and pres., Republic Corp., Century City, 1973---. Office: 1900 Ave. of the Stars, Suite 2700, Century City, CA 90067.

BROAD, ELI
Chairman of the Board, Kaufman and Broad
b. June 6, 1933, N.Y.C.; s. Leon and Rebecca Broad; B.A. (cum laude), Mich. State Univ., 1954; m. Edythe Lawson, Detroit, Mich., Dec. 19, 1954; sons: Jeffrey Alan, b. Apr. 27, 1956; Gary Steven, b. Mar. 19, 1959. Career: CPA 1954-56; asst. prof. Detroit Inst. Tech. 1956-57; co-founder-president Kaufman and Board, Inc. 1957, chmn. bd. 1968---. Dir.: CMI Investment Corp., Madison, Wis.; Dev. Bd. of Mich. State Univ.; L.A. United Way; Haifa Univ.; YMCA; v.p.-bd. dirs. Windward Sch., Santa Monica; adv. bd. Inst. Internat. Edn.; chmn. bd. trustees, Pitzer Coll., Claremont; trustee, City of Hope; visiting com. Grad. Sch. Mgmt., UCLA. Awards: Man of Year Award, City of Hope, 1965; Golden Plate Award, Am. Acad. Achievement, 1971. Mem.: Natl. Inds. Pollution Control Council; Mayor's Housing Policy COmm., co-founder, Council of Housing Producers, 1974; Bus. Com. for Arts; Hillcrest Country Club, 1975---. Democrat. Natl. Conv. 1968. Hobby: art collecting. Rec.: tennis, skiing. Home: One Oakmont Dr., L.A., CA 90040; Office: 17881 Skypark No., Irvine, CA.

BROCK, JAMES WILSON
Professor Emeritus of Theatre
b. May 23, 1919, Greensfork, Ind.; s. Virgil P. and Blanche (Kerr) Brock; B.A., 1941; M.A., 1942; Ph.D., 1950; m. Marjorie Mellor, 1969, Northside; chil.: Lisa Anne, b. 1956; Tamsen Lee, b. 1958; Julie Michelle, b. 1960. Career: Instr. in speech, Rosary Coll., 1945; assoc. prof. of speech, 1946-55, Albion Coll., asst. prof. of Communication skills, Mich. State Univ., 1955-56, asst. prof. of speech, 1956-57; assoc. prof. of theatre, Florida State Univ., 1957-58; prof. of Theatre, Cal. State Univ., Northridge, 1958-78, prof. emeritus, 1978---; Mgr., dir.,

Plymouth Drama Festival Theatre, Plymouth, Mass. 1956-57; Author: History of Theatre, Mayfield, 1980; playwright: Modern Chancel Dramas, Baker's Plays, 1964. Fellow, Ch. Soc. for College Work, 1964-65. USAF 1942-45, decorated bronze star, 1944. Mem.: Delta Sigma Rho, Tau Kappa Alpha, Theta Alpha Phi. Democrat. Episcopalian. Home: 1-3 Stinson Dr., Grass Valley, CA 95945; Office: Cal. State Univ., Northridge, CA 91324.

BROCK, RICHARD R.
Professor of Engineering
b. Mar. 7, 1938, Sewickley, Pa.; B.S., engineering, Univ. Calif., Berkeley, 1961; M.S., 1962; Ph.D., Calif. Inst. of Tech., 1968; m. Patricia A. Simper, Aug. 29, 1959, Arcadia; chil.: Richard M., b. 1962; Daniel M., b. 1964; Scott C., b. 1966. Career: Civil Engring. Assoc., L.A. Co. Flood Control Dist., 1962-63; asst. prof. of engring., Univ. Calif., Irvine, 1962-73; assoc. prof. and chmn. of civil engring. faculty, Cal. State Univ., Fullerton, 1973-76; prof. and chmn. of civil engring. faculty, 1976---. Contbr. research and publs in hydraulic engring. Mem. Am. Soc. of Civil Engineers and Am. Geophysical Union, mem. Triangle frat., UCLA, 1956-58. Home: 1362 Mauna Loa, Tustin, CA 92680; Office: Dept. of Civil Engring., Cal. State Univ., Fullerton, CA 92634.

BROCKHAUS, WILLIAM LEE
Investment Company Executive
b. Jan. 22, 1943, St. Louis, Mo.; s. Herold August and Leona M. (Stutzke) Brockhaus; B.S., 1966; M.B.A., 1967; D.B.A., 1970. Career: cons., Ernst & Ernst, 1967; research and tch. asst., Indiana Univ., 1968-69; prof. Trinity Univ., 1970-71; principal, Professional Mgmt. Counsel, 1971-75; prof., USC, 1971-76; partner, Brockhaus, Carlisle & Assoc., 1975---; gen. partner, Landmark Investments Ltd., 1978---; Bd. chmn., C.E.O., Edward Human Co., 1976---. Articles on business, mgmt., forecasting in profl. journ. and mags. Grants: Kawneer Co. scholarship; Indiana Univ. and Ford Found. Fellowships; multiple USC Research grants. Recipient: Am. Legion award; Delta Sigma Pi Award; Univ. of Mo. Curators' Award; Beta Gamma Sigma Natl. Bus. Hon.; Inst. of Tech. Hon. Mem.: Acad. of Mgmt.; Am. Finance Assn., Am. Psychol. Assn.; Am. Mgmt. Assn,. Soc. for Advance. of Mgmt.; Am. Soc. for Training and Devel.; Am. Assn. for Advance. of Science; Soc. for Entrepreneur. Research; Nat. Council for Small Bus. Mgmt. Devel. Mem.: Newcomen Soc.; Tau Kappa Epsilon. United Ch. of Christ. Hobbies: acting, writing. Rec.: skiing, water sports. Home: 13802 W. Northwest Passage, Marina del Rey, CA 90291; Office: 3939 Landmark St., Culver City, CA 90230, 1800 Century Park E., L.A., CA 90067.

BRODERICK, LOUISE ANTOINETTE
Community Leader
b. Mar. 29, 1916, Calexico, Calif.; d. Edward Nicholas and Viola (Sick) Drum; ed. pub. schs.; m. Charles M. Broderick, Calexico, June 6, 1937; son, Charles Edward, b. May 11, 1944. Career: employed, S.H. Kress & Co. 1932-36, ofc. mgr. 1934-36; Pac. Tel and Telegraph Co., Calexico, 1936-39, serv. repr., El Centro, 1940-41, serv. repr.-coach-instr., 5 ofcs., San Diego Co. 1942-44; owner-admr. (homes for aged), Broadway Home, San Diego, 1946---; v.p.-treas., Broadway Home, Inc. 1961---; pres.-dir., 1962---. Ed. Bd., Modern Nursing Home Mag. 1964. Awards: Am. Coll. of Nursing Home Admrs. Award; Paul Revere Silver Bowl by Am. Nursing Home Assn.; Region VIII, 1965; Calif. Assn.of Nursing Homes, Sans., Rest Homes and Homes for the Aged, Inc. Cit. for Serv. 1965; The 1965 Leadership Award by Geigy Pharmaceutical Co.; Woman of Achievement for 1966 by President's Council of Women's Serv., Bus. and Profl. Clubs of S.D.; S.D. Woman of the Year, 1966-67. Mem.: adv. com., Insts. for Aged Persons to State Dept. of Soc. Welfare, 1957---, chmn. 1957-60; del. Gov's. Conf. on Aging, Sacto. and L.A., 1960; dir. Sanitarium and Rest Homes Assn. of S.D. Co., 1960-61; v.p. Calif. Assn. of Nursing Homes, Sans., Rest Homes and Homes for the Aged, Inc. 1960-62, pres. 1962-64; gov's. council, Am. Nursing Home Assn., 1961-62, commr. Calif. Comm. on Accreditation of Nursing Homes and Facilities, 1961-66; chmn. Fire Safety Com., 1961, 64, 66; White House Conf. on Aging, 1961; cons. State Dept. Pub. Health Adv. Council, 1962-64; secty-treas., Am. Coll. of Nursing Home Admrs. 1963-67; chmn. Admrs. of Aged Insts. in So. Calif., 1964; chmn. Inter Agency Council, Calif. Coord. Com. for Aged, 1964; del. Surg. Gen's. Conf. on Prevention of Crippling Arthritis, 1965; Govt. Standards Com. of Mentally Impaired Adults in Ret. Homes and Nursing Homes, 1965, chmn. Legislative Com. 1965-66; chmn. Spec. Com. for Inst. Working Group, 1965; Am. Coll. of Nursing Home Admrs. 1965---; Adv. Plan. Com.

of Univ. of Calif. Ext. for Community Edn. and Devel., 1966---; faculty, Spec. Proj. Uniform Acct. Manual, So. Calif. Workshops, 1967; (charter) Outboard Motor Club, 1953---; OES, 1954---; Scottish Rite Woman's Club, 1960-61. Numerous coms. 1957---, pres. 1968. Univ. Chr. Ch. 1942---. Hobby: china painting. Rec.: swimming, water skiing. Home: 2471 E. St., San Diego, CA 92101; Office: 2445 Broadway, San Diego, CA 92102.

BRODY, SIDNEY F.
Investments Executive
b. Nov. 15, 1915, Des Moines, Ia.; s. Abraham and Lena (Freedman) Brody; B.S., Harvard Univ. 1937; m. Frances W. Lasker, Glencoe, Ill., Aug. 14, 1942; chil.: Christopher W., b. Nov. 10, 1944; Susan L., b. Dec. 23, 1947; Career: V.P.-dir., Aeronca Aircraft Co., 1946-48; v.p. Summers Gyroscope Co., 1948-53; pres. Brody Investment Co. 1953---. Dir.: Westland Capital Corp., Am. Electric, Inc., Security Pac. Natl. Bank, Grove Mortgage Corp., Gen. TV, Inc.; and Magnatronics, Inc.; trustee: Unionamerica Mortgage and Equity Trust; EMW Ventures Inc.; (past dir.) Mid-Continent Airlines, Inc. and Marquardt Aircraft Co. Lt. Col. (fighter pilot) USAF, 1941-45, WW II. Mem.: chmn., trustee: L.A. Co. Museum of Art, Thacher Sch., visiting com., Harvard Univ.; L.A. Civic Light Opera, UCLA Art Council, Perf. Art Council; regent, St. John's Hosp.; (past pub) Calif. State Bd. of Arch. Examiners. (past trustee), Leo Baeck Temple. Home: 360 S. Mapleton Dr., L.A., CA 90024; Office: 9477 Brighton Way, Beverly Hills, CA.

BROOKS, BARBARA MERLE MATHEWS
Business Executive
b. Apr. 16, 1925, San Leandro, Calif.; d. William and Merle Mathews; m. John Brooks, Sr. (bd. chmn., Fremont Bank, mem. State Econ. Council), Apr. 16, 1951, Las Vegas, Nev.; chil.: Wm. Mathews, b. June 28, 1952; John, Jr., b. Nov. 26, 1954; Career: worked in family real estate and insurance bus., 1944, mgr., owner, Wm. Mathews, Inc., San Leandro and S.D., 1944---; pres., San Leandro Svgs. & Loan, 1977---. Mem.: San Leandro C. of C.; So. Alameda Co. Bd. of Realtors, Western Assn. of Insurance Brokers; State and Nat. Assns. of Insurance Agents. Hobbies: cooking, antiques, gardening. Office: 2450 Washington Ave., San Leandro, CA 94577.

BROOKS, RICHARD M.
Corporate Executive
b. May 3, 1928, Akron, Ohio; s. Bryant J. and Sophia B. (Mallon) Brooks; B.S., Yale Univ., 1950; M.B.A., Univ. of Calif., Berkeley, 1960; m. Sidney C. Hedin, Dec. 2, 1961, S.F.; chil.: David J., b. June 17, 1963; Scott M., b. June 13, 1965; Susan C., b. May 17, 1968. Career: C.L.U., Mutual of New York, Dallas, Texas., prior to 1957; Calif. and Hawaiian Sugar Co., S.F., 1957---: fin. analyst, 1957-63; raw sugar mgr., 1964-67; v.p.-Finance, 1968-72; Sr., v.p.-finance and adminstrn. 1973---. Officer, Texas Air Nat. Guard, 1951-56. Mem.: Yale Alumni Assn. of No. Calif., pres., 1965-66; Oakland Mus. Assn. dir., 1975---; Golden Gate Scouting, trustee 1978; Piedmont Boy Scout Council, v.p., 1975---; Beta Theta Pi, treas. 1949-50. Hobbies: carpentry, nature. Rec.: camping, tennis. Home: 20 Sierra Ave., Piedmont, CA 94611; Office: One California St., S.F., CA 94106.

BROUGHER, JAMES WHITCOMB, JR.
Baptist Minister
b. June 27, 1902, Chattanooga, Tenn.; s. James Whitcomb, Sr. (noted Bapt. minister) and Cora Morse Brougher (desc. Samuel F.B. Morse); B.A., Univ. of Redlands, 1924, (hon. D.D. 1943); M.Th., Newton Theol. Inst. 1927; m. Helen Ball, Portland, Ore., Sept. 16, 1926; chil.: James Whitcomb III, b. Nov. 16, 1932; Elizabeth Ann Dieudonne, b. Nov. 14, 1934; Linda Louise Phillips, b. Apr. 30, 1939; Rev. Frank Russell, b. Apr. 5, 1940. Career: Stu. pastor: First Bapt. Ch., Ipswich, Mass.; Bethany Bapt. Ch., Roxbury Mass.; First Bapt. Ch., Walleston, Mass.; First Bapt. Ch., Winchester, Mass.; pastor, First Bapt. Ch., Glendale, Calif., 1927---. Moderator, L.A. Bapt. Assn. of Am. Bapt. Chs.; chaplain, L.A. Breakfast Club and radio pgm. 1934---; bd. dirs.: L.A. Bapt. City Mission Soc.; Chil.'s Bapt. Home of So. Calif. (30 yrs.); Am. Bapt. Publ. Soc. of Phila.; Am. Bapt. Edn. Soc. of N.Y.; Green Lake Bapt. Assembly Grounds, Wis.; pres. L.A. Bapt. Ministers Conf. 1930; bd. mgrs. So. Calif. Bapt. Conv., pres. 1942; numerous coms and speaker, Am. Bapt. Conv. (2 yrs.); scholarship dir. Univ. of Redlands, 1941; grand chaplain of Grand Council of Royal and Select Masters, Masons of Calif. 1933---; chaplain, Propeller Club of U.S., L.A.-Long Beach Chpt.; Glendale Kiwanis Club, Glendale C. of C. (life hon. Jr. C. of C.); Meridian Masonic Lodge; chaplain, 1968-76;

Glendale Commandry Knights Templar, Scottish Rite of Pasa.; gen. grand Chaplain of Grand Council Royal and Select Masters Internat. (3 yrs.). Hobbies: fishing, garden. Res.: 321 Lawson Pl., Glendale, CA 91202; Office: 209 N. Louise, Glendale, CA 91206.

BROUGHER, RUSSELL MORSE
Evangelist — Minister
b. May 3, 1896, Paterson, N.J.; s. Dr. James Whitcomb, Sr. (noted minister) and Corinna Sarah (Morse) Brougher; bro. Dr. J. Whitcomb Brougher, Jr. (Bapt. minister); cousin, Brig. Gen. Edward William Brougher; ed. A.B., Occidental Coll., L.A. 1918; Colgate Sem., Rochester, N.Y. 1919-21; TH.G., So. Bapt. Sem., Louisville, Ky. 1921-22; D.D., Linfield Coll., McMinnville, Ore. 1931; m. Laura Celeste Foulkes, Portland, Ore., Aug. 29, 1920. Career: Ordained to ministry, Bapt. Ch., Salt Lake City, Ut. 1922-24; First Bapt. Ch., Paterson, N.J., 1924-27; Bapt. Temple, Brooklyn, N.Y. 1927-37; evangelist, 1937---. Radio lecturer (2 to 4 times per wk.), Paterson, N.J. and Brooklyn, N.Y., 1924-37; Chaplain 1st Lt. (youngest chaplain), 40th Arty. (C.A.C.), WW I. Mem.: Mason, 1920---; Scottish Rite 32°; Commandery Knight Templar; Tau Kappa Alpha; Orators and Debaters Soc.; S.A.R.; (hon.) Kiwanis Club, 1924---; pres. Long Is., N.Y. Bapt. Assn. 1930; pres. Masonic Club, L.B., Calif. 1956; pres. Civic League, L.B. 1958; chaplain Shrine Club, L.B., 1958-59; chaplain, El Bekal Shrine Temple, L.B., 1959---; pres. Property Owners Oil Devel. Assn. 1960---; pres. Pub. Beach Improvement Assn., L.B., 1960; Natl. Chaplain, The Leg. of Hon. Shrine of N. Am. 1960---. Republican. Hobbies: fishing, hunting. Rec.: golf, boating. Home and Office: 800 E. Ocean Blvd., Long Beach, CA.

BROWN, CORRELLA CARMLETTE WRIGHT
Technical Illustrator
b. Dec. 23, 1944, San Diego; d. Dr. Kenneth Lyle (Psychologist) and Corrella Rosalie (Charles) Wright; grandau. of Gladys Charles. author and playwright; cous., Joanne Sayers (Bliss), Broadway actress; student, San Diego Evening Coll.; m. Daniel Lynn Brown (div.), Dec. 18, 1963. Columbus, Ohio; son, Daniel Lynn II, b. Oct. 5, 1964. Career: Inf. opr., Pacific Telephone Co., 1963; transliteration spec., proofreader Battelle Mem. Inst., 1964; exec. secty. Ohio State Dental Assn., 1965-66; Univac (div. Sperry Rand Corp.), 1967-69; Logicon, Inc., 1969-72; Cuyamaca Club (Westgate Corp.), 1972-73; Sr. Tech. Illustrator, Computer Sciences Corp., 1973---. Served USNR, 1976-78. Awards: Gold Bar Exam, Scottish Highland Dancing, Edinburgh, Scotland, 1959. Mem.: So. Calif. Highland Dancing Assn., 1956-62; Jobs Daughters, 1955; Worthington Hist. Soc., 1967; San Diego Track Club, 1978---, newsletter ed., bd. dir.; San Diego Orienteering Club, 1978---. Episcopalian. Hobby: book collecting. Rec.: running, writing, dancing. Office: 2251 San Diego Ave., San Diego, CA 92110.

BROWN, EDMUND G. (PAT)
Former Governor of California
b. Apr. 21, 1905, San Francisco; s. Edmund Joseph and Ida (Schuckman) Brown; ed. grad. Lowell H.S., S.F.; stu. Univ. of Calif. Ext. Div.; grad. S.F. Coll. of Law, 1927; (hon.) LL.D.: Univ. of S.F., 1959; Santa Clara Univ., 1960; m. Bernice Layne, Reno, Nev., 1930; chil.: Barbara (Brown) Casey, b. July 13, 1931; Cynthia (Brown) Kelly, b. Oct. 19, 1933; Edmund Gerald, Jr., b. Apr. 7, 1938; Kathleen (Brown) Rice, b. Sept. 25, 1945. Career: Admitted to Calif. State Bar, 1927; asst. to Milton L. Schmitt (celebrated blind lawyer), S.F.; candidate for Dist. Atty. of S.F., 1939, 43, elected 1943 (serv. 7 yrs.); Dem. nom. for Atty. Gen. of Calif. 1946, 50; elected Atty. Gen. of Calif. 1950, re-elected 1954; Dem. Candidate for Gov. of Calif. 1958 (elected by 1,029,165 votes), inaugurated Jan. 5, 1959, re-elected Nov. 1962 (1959-67); instr. polit. sci., UCLA 1967---; atty. at law Beverly Hills, 1967---. Mem.: Am. Calif. and S.F. Bar Assns.; fellow, Am. Coll. of Trial Lawyers; Native Sons of the Golden West; Comml., Commonwealth Club of Calif.; Comml., Olympic, Bel-Air Country, La Quinta Country, Indian Wells Clubs. Catholic. Hobby reading. Office: 450 N. Roxbury Dr., Beverly Hills, CA 90210.

BROWN, EDMUND G. JR
Governor of California
b. Apr. 7, 1938, S.F.; s. Edmund G (Pat, former gov. of Calif.) and Bernice (Layne) Brown; ed. B.S., Univ. of Calif., Berkeley, 1961; J.D., Yale Law Sch., 1964. Career: Research atty., Calif. Supreme Ct.; assoc. with NATO, Paris, Fr.; atty. Tuttle and Taylor law firm; elected to L.A. Comm. Coll. Bd. of Trustees, 1969; elected, Secty. of State, Calif. 1970-74; elected Governor of Calif., Nov. 1974---. Office: State Capitol, Sacto., CA 95814.

BROWN GARY EUGENE
Police Chief
b. Nov. 2, 1939, Springfield, Mo.; s. Maurice E. and Pauline Z. McLoughlin Brown; A.A. Police sci., Mt. San Antonio Coll., 1960; B.A., govt., Cal. State Univ., Sacto., 1971; M.P.A. USC, 1978; m. Sherrill Stewart, Nov. 20, 1971, Sacto.; chil.: Matthew, b. Sept. 30, 1966; Travis, b. Sept. 14, 1972; Jordan, b. Oct. 1, 1974. Career: training coord., Garden Grove Police Dept., 1960-66; Adminstrv. Sgt., Carpinteria Police Dept., 1966-68; spec. agent, USN Investigative Svc. (ONI), 1968-70; crime studies analyst, Calif. State Dept. of Justice, 1970-71; criminal justice cons., Pub. Systems, Inc., Sunnyvale, 1971-72; Chief of Police: Chowchilla Police Dept., 1972-76, City of South Pasadena, 1976-77, City of San Clemente, 1977---. Contbr. articles to Police Chief, Law and Order publs. Past chmn. Madera Co. Criminal Justice Com., Small City Depts. Com., Calif. Peace Officers Assn.; past mem. exec. bd., Central Calif., Criminal Justice Planning Region. Charter Mem., bd. dir., Kiwanis Club of Carpinteria Valley, 1966-68. Protestant. Hobbies: creative writing, sports cars. Rec.: tennis, horses. Office: San Clemente Police Dept., 100 Ave. Presidio, San Clemente, CA 92672.

BROWN, GILBERT LEHR, JR.
University Administrator
b.Oct. 16, 1917, Pasadena; s. Gilbert Lehr and Ethel (Church) Brown; A.B., 1939; A.M. 1939; Ph.D., 1957; m. Marion Ashton, Aug. 18, 1940, Pasadena; chil.: Joan Candace (Heyenga), b. Dec. 7, 1944; Jill Eileen (Becotte), b. Feb. 23, 1946; Gilbert Douglas, b. Dec. 14, 1949; James Nicholas, b. Dec. 26, 1950. Career: dir. of pub. rels., Univ. of Redlands, 1941-56; asst. to gen. mgr., Forest Lawn Mem. Park, 1957; asst. to pres., Univ. of Redlands, 1958-64; v.p., Univ. rels., Univ. of Redlands, 1956-72; vice-pres., Univ. Rels., Univ. of San Diego, 1972---. Bd. mem., Philip Y. Hahn Found., 1975---; bd. mem., San Felipe del Rio, 1974---. Home: 3235 Harbor View Dr., S.D., CA 92106; Office: Univ. of San Diego, Alcala Park, San Diego, CA 92110.

BROWN, HAROLD
U.S. Secretary of Defense
b. Sept. 19, 1927, New York City; s. Abraham Howard and Gertrude (Cohen); ed. A.B., Columbia Univ. 1945, A.M. 1946, Ph.D. 1949; m. Colene Dunning McDowell, S.F., Oct. 29, 1953; chil.: Deborah R., b. Nov. 5, 1955; Ellen D., b. Dec. 10, 1957. Career: Research scientist, 1945-50; lectr. in physics, Columbia Univ. 1947-48; Stevens Inst. of Tech., Hoboken, N.J., 1949-50; research sci., Radiation Lab., Univ. of Calif., Berkeley, 1950-52; lectr. in physics, 1952-61, group leader, 1952-56, div. leader, 1956-58, assoc. dir. 1958-59, dep. dir. 1959-60, dir. 1960-61; dir. Def. Research and Engring., U.S. Dept. of Def. 1961-69; Secty. of the Air Force, Wash., D.C. 1965-69; pres. Calif. Inst. of Tech. 1969-77; Secty. of Defense, 1977---. Home: Washington, D.C.

BROWN HAROLD ZELIG
Pediatrician
b. Aug. 7, 1924, Brooklyn, N.Y.; s. Nathen and Sylvia (Apeloig) Brown; B.S., Univ. of Chicago, 1943, M.D. 1946; m. Amy Ziegler, May 2, 1948, Chicago, Ill; chil.: Charles, b. 1950; Kenneth, b. 1953; Theodore, b. 1956. Career: Internship & residency in pediatrics, Michael Reese Hosp., Chicago, 1946-47, 1949-52; pvt. practice, Pediatrics, 1952---; mem. faculty, clin. Prof. Pediatrics, USC, 1952---; clin. chief of Peds., Cedars-Sinai Med. Center, 1973-78. Capt., AUS, 1947-49. Pres., Los Angeles Doctors Symphony Orch., 1967-69; Mem.: Am., Calif. and L.A. Co. Med. Assns.; Fellow, Am. Acad. Pediatrics. Jewish. Hobbies: music, violin. Rec.: skiing, tennis. Home: 2669 Hutton Dr., Beverly Hills, CA; Office: 9735 Wilshire Blvd., Beverly Hills, CA 90212.

BROWN, MARGUERITE G.
Bank Executive
b. July 22, 1913, Vinton, Iowa; d. Louis P. and Mabel Gordon; A.A., Iowa State Tchrs. Coll., 1932; m. Myron L. Koenig (dean emeritus, Foreign Services Inst.); m. 2d Walter Brown, Las Vegas, Nev., Oct. 7, 1961; chil.: Anne Koenig, b. July 27, 1940 and twin, Barbara (Mrs. Wm. F. Beekman). Career: tchr., 1932-34; free lance writer, 1946-56; started publ. co., Washington, D.C.; owner, ceramic shop, 1960---; 1956-58; registrar, Woodbury Coll., L.A., 1958-60; started bank vareer, v.p. and asst. mgr., First City Bank, Rosemead, 1972---. Mem.: Am. Inst. of Banking, pres. 1975-77; Rosemead C. of C., pres. 1978-79. Contrib. articles and childrens stories to publ.; writer, Natl. Ceramic Mag.; publ. book on enameling. Mem.: P.E.O. 1935-45; Eastern Star, 1947-56; B.P.W. 1964-65. Republican. Ch. of Divine Sci. Hobbies: painting, writing, dancing. Home: 1531 Cambury,

Arcadia, CA 91006; Office: 9000 E. Valley Blvd., Rosemead, CA 91770.

BROWN, ROBERT ALLEN, JR.
Chairman, Century Financial Corporation
b. Mar. 7, 1921, L.A.; s. Robert Allen, Sr. and Elizabeth (Pattison) Brown; B.S., bus. adminstrn., USC, 1942; C.L.U. 1948; m. Mary Rose Callicott, Nov. 18, 1942, L.A.; chil.: Alyson (Mrs. Donald Schoeny), b. Spet. 18, 1946; Priscilla (Johnson), b. Nov. 26, 1952; Gayle Anne, b. July 22, 1949. Career: partner, R.A. Brown & Son, Pacific Mutual Agents, 1945-68; agency mgr., Pacific Mutual Life Ins. Co., 1964-69; chmn. of bd., Century Financial Corp., 1969---. Dir.: Century Fin. Corp.; The Management Compensation Group. Author: Life and Health Ins. Handbook; co-author: Appraising the Human Asset for Family & Bus. Fin. Planning; contbr., Journ. of Am. Soc. of CLU. Lt. Sr. Grade, 1942-45, Pacific Campaign. Mem.: Million Dollar Roundtable, past pres.; L.A. Life Underwriters Assn.; USC Gen. Alumni Assn., pres. 1978; Skull & Dagger; USC Trojan Club; USC President's Club; Bd. of Trustees, USC; pres. L.A. chpt. CLU; L.A. C. of C.; Stock Exchange Club; Jonathan Club. Methodist ch., chmn. ch. bd. Hobby: painting. Rec.: tennis. Home: 848 Winston Ave., San Marino, CA; Office: 523 W. Sixth St., L.A., CA 90014.

BROWN, STEVE STEWART
Realtor
b.Feb. 12, 1932, Bentonville, Ark.; s. Frank Forrest and Rena Mae (Anglin) Brown; A.A., Long Beach City Coll., 1956; B.S. indsl. Engring., USC, 1958; m. Irene Lucille Posner, June 17, 1955, Long Beach; chil.: Pamela Sue, b. Jan. 18, 1958; Steve Stewart II, b. Nov. 11, 1959; Angela Lynn, b. Apr. 22, 1961; Kelli Jo, b. Nov. 17, 1968; Diana Irene, b. Feb. 10, 1971. Career: Engr., Westinghouse, 1958-63; pres., Steve S. Brown Pub. Co., Inc. 1961-75; ed.-pub. Doberman News, 1961-75; real estate broker, 1975---, Red Carpet Real Estate Franchisee, 1976---. USN, 1950-54. Mem.: Assoc. Bethel Guardian (Mem. of Honor, 1972), Internat. Order of Jobs Daughters, 1973, advis. Redwood Empire Guardian Council Assn., 1974-78; chmn. advis. council, Order of DeMolay, 1974, Dad Advis., 1976; Royal Patron, charter mem., Order of Amaranth, 1976; pres., Kiwanis Club of Northshore, 1977, 78; pres., found., Kiwanis Club of Lakeport, 1978; Worthy Patron, Order of Eastern Star, 1978; Masonic Lodge, Middletown, 1978. Christian. Hobbies: tree growing, chess, etymology. Home: 4684 Terrace Ave., Lakeport, CA 95453; Office: 800 S. Main St., Lakeport, CA 95453.

BROWN, WAYNE RANDOLPH
Company President
b. Dec. 5, 1922, Tacoma, Wash.; s. Avery Galen and Mae (Day) Brown; ed. B.S., Stanfor;Univ. 1948; M.B.A., Stanford Sch. of Bus. 1950; m. Bibbits Strong, Tacoma, Wash., July 10, 1946; chil.: Melinda, b. Feb. 25, 1950; Nathan, b. June 27, 1953; Gordon, b, Sept. 7, 1955; Terrence, b. Dec. 17, 1956. Career: Chmn. bd. Brown & Kauffmann, Inc. 1953-75; pres., bd. chmn., Brown & Kauffmann Properties, 1975---. Dir., Speedspace Corp. 1970. Pilot, USAF 1943-46, 1st Lt., WW II. Awards: Air Medal. Mem.: bd. dirs. Children's Health Council, 1958-68; Sigma Alpha Epsilon; Menlo Country Club, Woodside. Protestant. Rec.: golf, tennis. Home: 161 Tuscaloosa Ave., Atherton, CA; Office: 935 E. Meadow Dr., Palo Alto, CA 94303.

BROWN, WILLIAM REYNOLD
Artist
b. Oct. 18, 1917, L.A.; s. William R. and Ada (Farley) Brown; cous. Marion Talley, opera star; scholarship awards to Pittsburg Art Inst., Otis Art Inst., L.A.; m. Mary Louise Tejeda, Oct. 26, 1946, L.A.; chil.: Marie (Taggert), n. Oct. 27, 1947; W. Reynold, b. Mar. 21, 1949; Franz K., b. Aug. 1, 1950; Elisa (Cipriano), b. Feb. 6, 1952; Cristina (Pahl), b. Dec. 13, 1953; Regina (Ochoa), b. Jan. 31, 1956; Marta, b. May 20, 1957; Marianne, b. Nov. 14, 1959. Career: 40 years free lance illustrator: Artist and asst. to Hal Forrest, drawing nat. syndicated newspaper comic strip, Tailspin Tommy and Four Aces, 1933-39; Illustrator stories & covers, N.Y., 1946-50: incl. Outdoor Life, Boy's Life, Popular Sci., Mech. Illustrated, Motor Trends, Auto, Life, Liberty, True, Argosy; Comml. accts. incl. No. Am. Aviation, Lockheed Republic, Beechcraft, USAF, Goodyear, others; free lance artist for motion pictures, L.A., 1950-70: MGM, Univ. Universal Internat., Allied Artist, Warner Bros., Am. Internat., Disney, Cinerama; important films painted for incl.: Ben Hur, Spartacus, Mutiny on the Bounty, How the West Was Won, The Alamo, (The Alamo is on permanent exhibit at Alamo Mus., San Antonio,

Tex.), Dr. Zhivago, Gran Prix; Instr., head and figure painting, still life and illustration, Art Center Coll. of Design, Pasadena, 1950-76; painter mostly the western scene, 1970---: rep. by Trailside Gallery, Jackson, Wyo. and Scottsdale, Ariz.; Saddleback Inn, Santa Ana; Katchina Gallery, Santa Fe, N. Mex. Participant, USAF Art Program (contbd. 11 oil paintings now hanging in Pentagon and AF Acad.) Awards: Fellowship Am. Inst. of Fine Arts; two 1st awards, Calif. State Fair; Purchase Award, 20th Annual All City Outdoor Art Festival, L.A.; Best of Show: San Gabriel, 1976, Credential Award, 1972, George Phippen Mem. Show, 1976; many others. Home-studio: 4840 N. Live Oak Canyon Rd., La Verne, CA 91750.

BROWNE, TURNER
Photographer — Cinematographer
b. July 6, 1949, Lake Charles, La.; s. Clay and Jessie (Hay) Browne; m. Elaine Partnow (writer, actress), May 6, 1978. Career: Grantee, Sunflower Found., Santa Barbara, 1973, to do a photographic study of the rural Cajun people of La., culminated in the book Louisiana Cajuns/Cajuns De Louisiane, pub. La State Univ. Press, 1977; Cajun collection is permanently housed at La. Arts and Sci. Center, Baton Rouge; dir. of photog. feature motion picture, Only Once In A Lifetime. Mem.: L.A. Center for Photog. Studies. Home: 1175 Hi-Point St., L.A., CA 90035.

BROWNE, WALTER SHAWN
Grandmaster of Chess — Journalist
b. Jan. 10, 1949, Sydney, Australia; s. Walter Francis and Hilda Louis (Leahy) Browne; desc., Sir Bertrand Russell, Lord Chief Justice of England, 1896-1900; m. Racquel Emilse Facal, Mar. 9, 1973, N.Y.C.; stepson, Marcelo. Career: U.S. Closed Junior Champ, 1966; Calif. Champ, 1967-68; Grandmaster title, Oct. 1969; U.S. Closed Chess Champion, 1974, 75, 77; Internat. German Ch., 1975; Pan-Am. Ch., 1974; Nat. Open Champion, 1972, 73; U.S. Open Champion, 1971, 72; distbr.: chess bulletins of strongest chess tourneys, June 1978---. Honors: broke World Record, playing 29 opponents simultaneously winning all games in 45 minutes, Adelaide, Australia, Jan. 1971; played 105 opponents & computer in 7 hrs. 20 min., Jan. 1973, scoring world record: 94 wins, 9 draws, 3 losses; created World record of 50 lectrs. and exhibitions in 2 months with 96% score on 1500 games in U.S. (16,500 miles by car), 1975; chosen by Chess Journalists in top ten players of year, 1974, 75 (only Am. beside Bobby Fischer incld.); winner, U.S. Closed Champ. 3 consecutive times; Only Am. player to win major Internat. Tourney, Rejkavik 1978, since 1972. Hobbies: backgammon, poker, pool, tennis, scrabble, blackjack. Home-office: 8 Parnassus Rd., Berkeley, CA 94708.

BRUN, CHRISTIAN MAGNUS FROM
University Librarian
b. Oct. 3, 1920, Trondheim, Norway; s. Aage and Petra Christine (From) Brun; B.A., Univ. Wash., 1949; B.L.S., Univ. N.C., 1950; M.A., Univ. Mich., 1952; postgrad., Univ. Mich.; m. Jane Carey Fristoe, June 1, 1958, Ann Arbor, Mich.; 1 son: Erik From Brun, b. July 9, 1961. Career: Asst. Curator, Rare Books, Univ. Pa., 1950-51; asst. curator of Maps, William L. Clements Library, Univ. Mich., 1952-58; curator, 1958-63; head, Dept. of Spec. Coll., Univ. of Calif. Library, Santa Barbara, 1963---; also Univ. Archivist, Curator, William Wyles Collection, 1963---. Author (with James C. Wheat), Bibliography of Maps Published in Am. before 1800, Yale Press, 1969; 2nd edition 1978; Guide to the Manuscript Maps in the William C. Clements Library, 1959. Contbr. articles, prof. journ., publs. Served with inf. AUS 1942-45, bronze star. Mem.: Bd. of Editors, Soundings, ex officio bd. Friends of the library, Univ. Calif., Santa Barbara. Mem.: Bibl. Soc. of Am.; Soc. of Calif. Archivists; Am. Scandinavian Found.; Santa Barbara Hist. Soc.; U.C.S.B. Faculty Club, Westerners. Unitarian. Hobbies: book and map collecting. Rec.: camping, hiking. Home: 5663 Via Trento, Goleta, CA 93017; Office: Univ. of Calif. Library, Santa Barbara, CA.

BRUNNER, WILLIAM BARRETT
Author — Lecturer
b. Dec. 29, 1937, Detroit, Mich. Career: tchr. guided missile theory, Point Mugu USN Air Station, 1958-60; realtor since 1962; stock/commoditybroker, Merrill Lynch, 1968-71; advisor, Brunei Oil Consortium, 1971; Chmn. bd., Group One Realty, 1973---; also Mng. Editor Group One Press---. Author: Honk — The Inflation Game, October's Error; co-author Lady Love. Mem. advisory com. L.A. Mayor/City Planning Dept., 1971-75, chmn. sub-com. on transportation. Served in guided missile research, USN, 1956-60. Mem. United Organ. of

Taxpayers Inc. Rec.: Motor home tour of rural Am. Home: 8591 Wonderland Ave., L.A., CA 90046; Office: Group One Press, 7566 Sunset Blvd., L.A., CA 90046.

BRYDON, HAROLD WESLEY
Entomologist
b. Dec. 6, 1923, Hayward, Calif.; s. Thomas Wesley and Hermione (McHenry) Brydon; ed. A.B., San Jose State Coll., 1948; M.A., Stanford Univ. 1950; m. Ruth Bacon Vickery, Berkeley, Mar. 28, 1951; chil.: Carol Ruth, b. July 12, 1953; Marilyn Jeanette, b. July 29, 1955; Kenneth Wesley, b. Oct. 1, 1961. Career: Insecticide sales, Calif. Spray Chem. Corp. 1951-52; entomologist, fieldman, buyer, Beech-Nut Packing Co., San Jose, 1952-53; mgr.-entomologist, Lake Co. Mosquito Abatement Dist., Lakeport, Calif., 1954-58; adv. entomologist agcy. for Internat. Devel., Kathmandu, Nepal, 1958-61; Wash., D.C. 1961-62; Port-au-Prince, Haiti, 1962-63; dir. fly control research, Orange Co. Health Dept., Santa Ana, 1963-66; own bus. and pvt. researcher, 1966---. Author: numerous sci. publs. relating to field of entomology, 1954---. USNR 1943-46, WW II. Mem.: Entomological Soc. of Am., Am. Mosquito Control Assn., Pac. Coast Entomological Soc., Am. Inst. Biological Scis., Am. Leg., Mason, Commonwealth Club of Calif. Republican. Methodist. Hobbies: natural hist., photog. Rec.: fishing, hunting. Home: P.O. Box 312, Westwood, CA 96137; 407 E. Lewelling Blvd., San Lorenzo, CA; Office: 326 Peninsula Dr., Lake Almanor, CA.

BUCHNER, JAMES
Corporate President
b. Aug. 9, 1932, Middletown, Conn.; s. Frank D. and Anna R. (Augeri) Buchner; A.A., Compton Coll., 1956; B.A., Whittier Coll., 1958; B.S.M.E., West Coast Univ. Mech. Engring., 1969; M.S. Mgmt. Finance Sci., 1972; Certificate in Urban Planning, Univ. Calif., Irvine, 1974; m. Dora Guerrero, Pico Rivera; 1 son, Donald J. Career: L.A. Dept. of Water & Power, 1960-72; residential sales rep. 1960-61; comml. lighting spec. 1961-62; gov. cons. 1962-64; power sales cons. 1964-68; pro. planner, 1968; assoc. engr. 1968-69; dir. market research, 1969-72; dir. comml. and indsl. develop., Placentia, 1972-77; pres., Real Estate Consultants and Assoc. 1977; pres., Economic Develop. Corp. of Orange Co., 1977---. USN. 1953-55. Dir., Treas., L.A.D.W.P. Employees Credit Union, 1976-72; dir. Family Services Assn. Orange Co., 1976---, Secty. 1978-79. Community chmn., March of Dimes, 1976-77. Mem.-grower, Fallbrook Citrus Assn.; Certified Indsl. Devel.; Lic. Calif. R.E. Broker. Mem.: Illuminating Engring. Soc.; Am. Indsl. Devel. Council; Exec. com. & bd. dir., So. Calif. Economic & Indsl. Devel. Council; Indshl Devel. Exec. Assn.; So. Calif. Residential Research Council, 1969-72; So. Calif. Research Dir. Council, 1969-72; Am. Soc. of heating, refrig. & air conditioning engrs., 1964-72. Mem.: Elks Lodge 2536; Am. Legion Post 277; L.A. Anchor Club. Rec.: fishing, travel. Office: 403 Bank of Am. Tower, One City Blvd., W., Orange, CA 92668.

BUCKINGHAM, DONALD
President, J.W. Robinson Company
b. Nov. 16, 1905, Washington, D.C.; s. David E. and Roberta R. (Randall) Buckingham; ed. George Wash. Univ., Wash., D.C., 1925-26; m. Eleanor Hodgdon, July 7, 1961; chil.: Joan, b. Jan. 2, 1942; Donald, Jr., b. Sept. 11, 1946. Career: Assoc. with Woodward & Lothrop, Wash., D.C., Oct. 8, 1925; asst. div. mdse mgr., 1930-34; asst. to mdse dir. 1934-35; buyer, men's furnishings, 1935-39; div. mdse mgr., men's div., 1939-42; elected v.p. (chg. pub.-personnel rels.), 1950, v.p. (chg. mdse, adv.-credit div.), 1950, bd. dirs. 1950-53; pres. J.W Robinson Co., L.A. 1953---; v.p. Assoc. Dry Goods Corp. (owns J.W. Robinson Co.), NYC. Loaned by Woodward & Lothrop to War Prodn. Bd. 1942; head, men's furnishings sect., Textile Leather and Clothing Br., U.S. Navy, 1943-45; Lt. Comdr., active duty, Nov. 1945, WW II. Mem.: bd. dirs.-exec. com., Downtown Bus. Men's Assn.; bd. dirs., Calif. Retailers Assn.; bd. dirs., All-Yr. Club of So. Calif.; L.A. Country Club, Calif. Club, L.A. Hobby: golf. Home: 1170 Glenview Rd., Santa Barbara, CA 93103; Office: 600 W. 7th St., L.A., CA 90017; 417 - 5th Ave., New York, NY.

BUCKLER, PHILLIP JAMES
Army Official — University Administrator
b. May 3, 1919, San Diego, Calif.; s. Carl Edward and Lois (Taylor) Buckler; ed. B.A., MPA, USC. Career: Exec. assignments ofcr., health care pgms. and inst. mgmt., US Army, USA and aborad, 1940-66; admr. Health Sciences Center, UCLA 1966-72 (ret.). Mem.: L.A. World Affairs Council, English Speaking Union, Internat. Wine and

Food Soc., Los Amigos del Pueblo, Friends of Huntington Mem. Library, Antiquarian Soc. of So. Calif., UCLA, USC. Home: 452 S. El Molino Ave., Pasadena, CA 91101; Office: P.O.B. 1634, Beverly Hills, CA 90213.

BUCKLEY, ISABELLE PALMS
President, The Buckley School
b. Oct. 3, Detroit, Mich.; d. Charles Louis and Isabelle de Mun (Walsh) Palms; desc., Count Albert de Mun, noted French writer; gr.gr.grandau. to Auguste Chouteau, founder of St. Louis, Mo.; A.B. Manhattanville Coll., N.Y.; pvt. studies: Australia, France, Ireland, Switzerland; m. Col. Harold Buckley (1st American Ace of 95th Squadron), Oct. 20, 1923, Grosse Pointe, Mich.; chil.: Mary Ann; C. Peter; Isabelle de Mun Donnelly (dec.); Sister Ellen Buckley. Career: Founder, president, The Buckley School, 1933---; columnist, New York Herald Tribune syndicate, 1961-66; Author: Guide to a Child's World, 1951; A Child's World (film), 1952; College Begins at Two, 1965. Awarded honorary degrees: L.H.D., Newton Coll., Mass., 1967; L.H.D., Pepperdine Univ., 1975; named Los Angeles Times Woman of the Year, 1969. Mem.: Junior League. Republican. Roman Catholic. Home: 10390 Wilshire Blvd., Apt. 415, L.A., CA 90024; Office: 3900 Stansbury Ave., Sherman Oaks, CA 91423.

BUCKLEY, THOMAS CANNON
Public Relations Executive
b. Mar. 20, 1930, L.A., Calif.; s. Thomas James and Florence Veronica (Cannon) Buckley; B.S., Univ. of Santa Clara, 1952; Advanced Mgmt. Program, Harvard Univ. Grad. Sch. of Business, 1978. m. Adeline Marine Laschiazza, (dec.) Nov. 7, 1959, L.A.; chil: Thomas, b. Nov. 14, 1962; James, b. Dec. 21, 1963; Brian, b. Aug. 26, 1965; Christopher, b. May 23, 1966; Richard, b. Aug. 13, 1967; Timothy, b. June 14, 1970; m. 2d. Judith Ann McKay, June 28, 1974, San Marino. Career: Editor-writer, Am. Cement Corp., L.A., 1957-61; public relations representative, Southern Pacific Co., L.A., 1961-63; asst. pub. rel. mgr., 1963-69, pub. rel. mgr., 1969---. AUS, Europe, 1953-54. Mem.: Public Relations Soc. of Am.; Greater L.A. Press Club; Univ. of Santa Clara Alumni Assn., past nat. dir.; Catholic Press Council of So. Calif., past pres. Club: Los Angeles; Jonathan. Catholic. Home: 3265 Lombardy Rd., Pasadena, CA 91107; Office: 610 S. Main St., L.A., CA 90014.

BUCKS, CHARLES ALAN
Airline Executive
b. Dec. 14, 1927, Lubbock, Tex.; s. Charles Henry and Nell Eleanor (Lattimore) Bucks; student, Texas Tech. Univ., 1946-48; m. Joyce L. Turner, Aug. 19, 1949, Lubbock, Tex.; chil.: Robert, b. Sept. 9, 1959; Dawn, b. May 29, 1961. Career: transportation agent, numerous sales and service positions, Pioneer Airlines, 1948-55 (Pioneer merged w/Continental Airlines, 1955), asst. v.p. sales, 1961; v.p. field sales, 1964; v.p. sales & services, 1966; sr. v.p. mktg., 1970; exec. v.p. mktg., Continental Airlines, 1975---. Dir.: Continental Airlines, 1969---; Carlsberg Capital Corp., 1977---; trustee, Continental Airlines Found., 1965---. USN, 1945-46. Clubs: Lakeside Golf, 1968---; Marina City; Safari Club Internat., past bd. mem. Pres., Calif. Tourism Council, 1975-76. Protestant. Hobbies: gun collection, western art. Rec.: tennis, horseback riding, hunting. Home: 16147 Meadow View Dr., Encino, CA 91436; Office: International Airport, L.A., CA 90009.

BUERGER, EDE MARIE
Clinical Nurse Specialist
b. May 18, 1943, East St. Louis, Ill.; d. Edward A. and Mary G. Buerger; B.S., 1965, M.S., 1974. Career: Head nurse, Eskaton Am. River Hosp., 1966-71; clin. nurse spec., Loma Linda Univ., 1971---. Contbr.: Pepper & Curry, Mental Retardation, 1978; McNall, Current Concepts in Obstetrics & Neonatalogy, 1979; Kowalski, Primary Health Care of Women, 1979 (Vol. I, II); mem. President's Commn. on Prevention of Mental Retardation, 1979. Mem.: chmn., State Nurisng Council, Calif. Nurses Assn., 1968-69; Calif. Jt. Practice Commn., 1971-79; Calif. Nurses Assn., chmn. State Nursing Council, 1968-69; Govt. Advis. Comn., 1975-78; Calif. Jt. Practice Commn., 1971-79; Advis. com., Newborn Screening Prog., State Health Dept., 1978---; advis. com., Genetically Handicapped Person's Prog., Calif. Children's Service, State Health Dept., 1978---. Mem.: Sigma Theta Tau, 1974---. Greek Orthodox Ch. Hobbies: swimming, photog. Home: 238 S. Eureka St., Redlands, CA; Office: Intensive Care Nursery, Loma Linda Univ., Loma Linda, CA 92350.

BUFE, CHARLES GLENN
Research Geophysicist
b. Jan. 2, 1938, Duluth, Minn.; s. Bancroft Washington and Margaret (Lesperance) Bufe; B.S., geophysical engring., Mich. Tech., 1960, M.S., geophysics, 1962; Ph.D., geology, Univ. of Mich., 1969; m. Jacquelyn Abbott, Nov. 18, 1967, Belleville, Mich.; chil.: Glennica Joy, b. June 22, 1969; Sierra Noel, b. Oct. 14, 1973. Career: exploration geophysicist, U.S. Steel, 1962; assoc. research geophysicist, Inst. Sci. & Tech., Univ. Mich., 1967-69; research geophysicist, Earthquake Mechanism Lab., Nat. Oceanic & Atmospheric Adminstrn., S.F., 1969-73; vis. prof., Univ. Wis., 1973; geophysicist, U.S. Geol. Survey, Menlo Park, 1973---; coord., USGS Induces Seismicity Prog., 1978-79, Lt., USAR, 1960-64; Lt., ESSA (now NOAA) Commissioned Corps, No. Pac., 1964-66. Contbr. articles on seismology and tectonophysics sci. journs. Registered Geophysicist, State of Calif. Mem.: Am. Geophysical Union, Seismological Soc. of Am., Soc. of Exploration Geophysicists, Geol. Soc. of Am., Sigma Xi, Am. Assn. for Adv. of Sci. United Methodist ch., trustee, Woodside Rd. Ch. Hobby: fly tying. Rec.: running, skiing, fishing. Home: 2786 Ohio Ave., Redwood City, CA; Office: 345 Middlefield Rd., Menlo Park, CA.

BUFFINGTON, ALBERT LANG
President, Diamond/Sunsweet Inc.
b. July 14, 1924, Birmingham, Ala.; s. A.W. and Ellen (McLean) Buffington; B.A., Stanford, 1947, M.B.A., 1949; m. Ruth Maxwell, Dec. 8, 1945; chil.: Dale Geweke; Lee; Lynn. Career: Line supr., indsl. engr., Proctor & Gamble Mfg. Co., Long Beach, 1949-53; cons., Booz, Allen & Hamilton, L.A., 1953-55; prodn. mgr., asst. gen. mgr., pres. and gen. mgr., Diamond Walnut Growers, Inc., 1955---; pres., Sunsweet Growers, Inc., 1975---; pres., Diamond/Sunsweet Inc., 1975---. Dir., DFA of Calif.; mem., Walnut Mktg. Bd.; mem., Prune Administrv. Com.; mem. Calif. Prune Advis. Bd., 1975---. 1st Lt., USAAF, 1942-45, USAF, 1950-52. Mem.: Consolidated Agri. Industries, Inc., secty.-treas.; Nat. Council of Farmer Coops.; Gr. Stockton C. of C.; Commonwealth Club, S.F.; Rec.: boating. Home: 7221 Alesandria Pl., Stockton, CA 95207; Office: P.O.B. 1727, 1050 S. Diamond St., Stockton, CA 95201.

BULLWINKEL, IRMA NANCY
Realtor
b. Oct. 22, 1920, Lyndhurst, N.J.; d. Henry Edgar and Anna Weidner (Dubuy) Clay; student, Tulsa Univ.; A.A., Napa Coll., 1951; grad., Realtors Inst. of Calif., 1969. m. John Henry Bullwinkel, Nov. 1, 1941, Lyndhurst, N.J.; chil.: John David, b. Oct. 15, 1944; Douglas Kent, b. Sept. 21, 1947. Career: worked for Prudential Insurance Co., Newark, N.J., 1937-41; teller, Chase Nat. Bank, N.Y.C., 1942; real estate agent, Tulsa, Okla., 1950-62; realtor, Napa, Calif., 1962---. Mem.: Napa C. of C., Calif. Real Estate Assn.; Nat. Realtors, Nat. Realtors Marketing Inst.; Napa Co. Bd. of Realtors; Napa Women's Club, pres. 1972-73; Entre Nous; Nat. Notary. Presbyterian. Hobbies: music, reading, crafts. Home: 2636 W. Pueblo Ave., Napa, CA 94558; Office: 1765 Third St., Napa, CA 94558.

BUNZEL, JOHN H.
University President
b. Apr. 15, 1924, N.Y.C.; s. Ernest Everett and Hariett (Harvey) Bunzel; A.B. polit. sci., magna cum laude, Princeton Univ., 1948; M.A. sociology, Columbia Univ., 1949; Ph.D., polit. sci., Univ. Calif., Berkeley, 1954; m. 2d Barbara Bovyer, May 11, 1963; (Hon.) LL.D., Univ. Santa Clara, 1976; chil.: Cameron; Reed. Career: teacher, S.F. State Coll., 1953-56; Mich. State Univ., 1956-57; Stanford Univ., San Jose, 1970-78; sr. research fellow, Hoover Inst., Stanford Univ., 1978---; Author: The American Small Businessman, Knopf, 1962; Issues of American Public Policy, Prentice-Hall, 1964, 2nd ed., 1968; Anti-Politics in America, Knopf, 1967; monograph: The California Democratic Delegation of 1960 (co-author); biweekly columnist, San Jose Mercury-News; contbr. N.Y. Times, Wall Street Jour., scholarly and polit. journs.; conducted wkly. TV program (KPIX S.F.), 1964. Recipient: Presidential Award, No. Calif. Polit. Sci. Assn., 1969; certificate of honor, Bd. of Suprs., city and co. of San Francisco, 1974; Research grants: Ford Found. (Fund for the Republic), 1958-60, (Com. on research in public affairs at Stanford Univ.), 1960-61, (visiting scholar, Center for Adv. Study in Behavioural Sciences), 1969-70; Rabinowitz Found., 1961-62; Rockefeller Found., 1965-66. Dir., No. Calif. Citizenship Clearing House, 1959-61; pres., No. Calif. Polit. Sci. Assn., 1962-63; mem. Am. Polit. Sci. Assn. Democrat; del. to nat. convention, 1968. Home: 1519 Escondido Way,

Belmont, CA 94002; Office: Hoover Inst., Stanford Univ., Stanford, CA 94305.

BURGER, OTHMAR J.
Professor of Plant Science
b. May 23, 1921, Jasper, Ind.; bro., Dr. A.W. Burger, prize-winning tchr. of Crop Sci., Univ. Ill.; B.S., 1943; M.S., 1947; Ph.D., 1950; m. Elizabeth Ann Evans, Aug. 21, 1943, Lafayette, Ind.; chil.: Thomas Glen, b. Mar. 29, 1946; Robert Howard, b. Oct. 15, 1947; David William, b. June 23, 1953. Career: Prof. of Agronomy: W. Va. Univ., 1950-57, 1959-68, Iowa State Univ., 1957-59; asst. dean, Coll. of Agri. and Forestry and Dir. of Resident Instrn., Div. of Agri., W. Va. Univ., 1959-68, asst. to Provost, 1968-69; Dean, Sch. of Agri. nad Home Economics, Cal. State Univ., Fresno, 1969-78; Publs.: 30 articles and booklets on crop physiology and ednl. programs in agri.; elected Fellow, Am. Soc. of Agronomy, 1972. USNR, 1943-46; 1st battalion, 24th Reg., 4th Marine Div., Naval Gunfire Liaison Officer; in invasions of Marshalls, Saipan, Tinian, Leyte Gulf, Iwo Jima; decorated Purple Heart, Bronze Star. Pres., Nat. Assn. of Colls. and Tchrs. of Agri., 1978-79. Mem.: Alpha Gamma Rho, Kiwanis Internat., Alpha Zeta, Sigma Xi, Gamma Sigma Delta, Phi Lambda Upsilon, Alpha Tau Alpha. Catholic. Hobbies: woodworking, stained glass. Rec.: plays organ. Home: 2689 W. San Carlos Ave., Fresno, CA 93711; Office: Dept. of Plant Sci., Sch. of Agri., Cal. State Univ., Fresno, CA 93740.

BURGESS, LARRY E.
Archivist
b. July 18, 1945, Montrose, Colo.; s. Eugene F. and Edyth Burgess; B.A., hist., cum laude, Univ. Redlands, 1967; M.A., Claremont Grad. Sch., 1969, Ph.D., 1972; m. Charlotte Gaylord, Oct. 1973, Redlands, Calif. Career: archivist, A.K. Smiley Public Library, Redlands, 1972---; tchr. (pioneered courses on local hist.), Redlands Adult Edn., San Bernardino Valley Coll., tchr. (Introd. to Archives: Theory and Practice), 1972-78. Editor, (journal) Biblio-Cal Notes; Mem.: So. Calif. Local Hist. Council, editor, journal Biblio-Cal Notes; Alfred, Albert and Damiel Smiley: A Biography, 1969; Co-author, The Lake Mohonk Conferences on the Indian, 1883-1916 (1974); author numerous bibliographies & keepsake pamphlets pub., Lincoln Memorial Shrine, A.K. Smiley Public Lib. Apptd. by Gov. E. Brown, Jr. to Calif. Heritage Preservation Commn., 1977---; pres., Soc. of California Archivist, 1974-76; mem. Alumni bd., Univ. Redlands, 1969-72. Mem.: Chi Sigma Chi; Fortnightly, past pres.; dir., Redlands Rotary Club. Episcopalian; vestryman. Hobbies: gardening, book collecting, travel. Rec.: tennis, running. Home: 923 W. Fern Ave., Redlands, CA; Office: 125 W. Vine St., Redlands, CA, 92373.

BURK, MARGARET BELLE TANTE
Public Relations Counselor
b. Aug. 8, Savannah, Ga., d. James and Belle Alfreda (Dahlgren) Tante; sister of Sup. Ct. Judge James Dahlgren Tante, L.A.; cousin Rev. John Wilder, Chaplain, State of Ga.; Student, Northwestern Univ., Chicago; Art Inst., Chicago; Savings & Loan Inst., L.A.; Licensed real estate broker; m. Harry John Burk, Apr. 7, 1945, L.A.; chil.: Harry John Burk III (Tray), b. May 5, 1046; Linda Margaret, b. Aug. 8, 1947; James Walter, b. June 5, 1950. Career: asst. to plant mgr., Kinney Aluminum to 1945; working v.p., family owned business, Burk Enterprises, 1945-54; personnel counselor, Universal Personnel; Huntington Savings & Loan Assn., 1964-69, as asst. to pres., mgr., Wilshire branch, v.p. and dir. of pub. relations; dir. pub. relations, Ambassador Hotel, 1969-74; partner, Burk/Hudson Public Relations, 1972---; also syndicated columnist, Meredith Newspaper chain. Bd. Mem.: Profl. Women to the Philharmonic; YWCA; L.A. Mayor's Community Advisory Com. (past exec. chmn.). Mem.: Lion's Internat. (1st woman mem.); Wilshire Center C. of C., pres. 1969 (1st woman pres. of a major U.S. C. of C.); Hancock Park Art Council, co-founder, past pres.; Huntington Organ Soc., co-founder; Muses; L.A. Advt. Women; Pub. Relations Soc. of Am.; Radio and Television News Assn.; L.A. area C. of C., Women's Div. Recipient: Hotel/Motel Nat. Gold Key award, 1972; Larchmont Woman of the Year, 1972; Lulu Award, 1972, 73, L.A. Ad Women; Woman of the Year twice from Tehachapi Sing-Out members in state prisons; recognition from many groups incl. city, co., state; L.A. C. of C. Executive of the Month; subject of newspaper & mag. articles. Was candidate for U.S. Treasurer, Nixon Admin. Ch. of Religious Sci. Hobbies: travel, needlepoint. Rec.: swimming, walking. Home: 860 Fifth Ave., L.A., CA 90005; Office: Ambassador Hotel, 3400 Wilshire Blvd., L.A., CA 90010.

BURKE, HALSEY CONANT
President, Burke Industries
b. Nov. 21, 1922, San Jose, Calif.; s. Roscoe E. and Vivian (Halsey) Burke; grad., Kings Point Acad. 1943, Marine Transportation; m. Sharon Rose, Aug. 2, 1969, San Jose; chil.: Carolyn (Makin), b. Feb. 13, 1947; Barbara C., b. Feb. 13, 1947; Dorothy J., b. May 14, 1948; Patricia J., b. Feb. 4, 1951; Michelle Lee, b. Jan. 20, 1971. Career: Chief Officer, Am. Pres. Lines, 1943-46; chmn. and pres., Burke Industries, 1946---. Dir.: Standard Ins. Co., San Jose Water Works, First Nat. Bank, Nat. Jewish Hosp. Mem.: Mason, Rotary, past dist gov., 1972, 73. Office: P.O.B. 190, San Jose, CA 95103.

BURKE, LEO P., JR.
Parks & Recreation Official
b. Sept. 17, 1926, E. St. Louis, Ill.; s. Leo P. and Mary Elizabeth (Spearman) Burke; grandson, Niel Spearman, Maj., Confederate Army; grandson, Richard Burke, Capt., Union Army; student, Community Coll., Burlington, Iowa; m. Ann Coyne Burke, June 7, 1951, Dallas, Tex.; chil.: Mary Jane Burke Firpo, b. Feb. 23, 1952; Sally Burke Wingard, b. Mar. 5, 1953; Leo P., III, b. Mar. 30, 1955; Timothy, b. July 16, 1957; Judy A., b. Mar. 8, 1959; Anne P., b. Oct. 22, 1961; Patrice A., b. June 12, 1965; Tricia M., b. Oct. 4, 1966. Career: Stage Mgr., Aquacade (Water Follies), 1949-57; Ice Arena/Auditorium Supt., Dept. of Parks & Rec., City of Stockton, 1957---. USMC, 1944-46. Mem. exec. council dist. No. 9, Calif. State Theatrical Fed.; Internat. Alliance Theatrical State Employees, local 90, bus. agent for 18 years. Pres., bd. of trustees, San Joaquin Delta Coll. Dir.: Stockton Hall of Fame; proposed Azteca Nat. Bank; San Joaquin Co. Safety Council; United Way Campaign. Chmn.: 1976 Am. Legion dist. convention; Sr. Citizen of the Year Award; various Nat. Am. Legion posts. State pres., Past Comdrs. Club; Comdr., Karl Ross Am. Legion. Mem. Am. Revolution Bicentennial Commn.; Recipient: over 100 nat. and local awards. Mem.: Opportunities Indsln. Center; K.C.; Internat. Assn. of Auditorium Mgrs.; VFW; Stockton Garden Club, hon.; Com. Hon. Mexicana; YMCA Youth Support; Sons of Italy; Ind. Order of Odd Fellows; Nat. Am. Legion Press Club; Univ. of the Pacific Casaba Club; Boy Scouts of Am.; Inst. Regpr. Catholic. Hobbies: bowling, basketball, ice skating. Home: 117 W. Norwich Dr., Stockton, CA; Office: 525 N. Center, Stockton, CA 95202.

BURKE, MARGARET ELIZABETH
President, Focus Personnel Service
b. Jan. 18, 1946, Springfield, Mass.; B.A., indsl. psych., S.F. State Univ., 1975. Student, Mt. Ida Jr. Coll., bus., 1963-65; Career: installment loan analyst, Valley Bank & Trust Co., Springfield, Mass., 1965-67; personnel adminstr., Norton Co., Boston, Mass. 1967-68; adminstrv. asst., Keller & Gannon Engring. firm, S.F., 1968-69; exec. asst. and personnel policy writer, Loomis Armored Car Service, S.F., 1970-72; personnel generalist, Van Waters & Rogers, S.F., 1972-74; founder, pres., Focus Personnel Serv., S.F. (exec. search firm spec. in women and minorities) 1976---. Lectr.: career confs., profl. women's orgns. Mem.: S.F. NOW, jobs chmn.; ERA fundraising chmn., 1976-77; Exec. Women's Forum, charter mem.; S.F. Women in Advt.; Bay Area Big Sisters; Bay Area Profl. Women's Network; Embarcadero Center Forum; No. Calif. Indsl. Rels. Council; Personnel Mgmt. Assn. of Aztlan; Peninsula Profl. Women's Network; Women Enterpreneurs. Rec.: bicycling, swimming, dancing. Office: 41 Sutter St., Suite 406, S.F., CA 94104.

BURKE, YVONNE BRATHWAITE
Country Supervisor
b. Oct. 5, 1932, L.A.; d. James T. Watson; ed. Manual Arts H.S., L.A.; B.A. (polit. sci.), UCLA; J.D., USC Sch. of Law, 1956; m. William Burke, L.A., June 1972; dau. Autumn Roxanne, b. Nov. 23, 1973. Career: Atty. at law, 1956-66; dep. Corp. Commr. Police Comm.; atty. staff. McCone Comm. on Watts riots; elected to Calif. Legislature, 63rd Assembly Dist., L.A. 1966; chmn. Comm. on Urban Devel. and Housing; elected to Congress, 1972-79; apptd. by Gov. to L.A. Co. Bd. of Supvrs., 1979---; v. chmn. Dem. Natl. Conv., Miami Beach, Fla. 1972; Awards: Moot Ct. for Appellate Argument, other compus hons.; Fellow, Harvard Univ. Inst. of Politics, 1972; Chubb Fellow, Yale Univ. 1973; Loren Miller Award by NAACP; Sojourners Truth Award, Negro Bus. and Profl. Women's Clubs; Woman of Ur., by KNX News Radio; one of 100 outstanding women opinion makers in Am. by Harpers Bazaar; hons.: L.A. City Council, L.A. Bd. of Works Com. chmn. John Blatnik (D.Minn.); L.A. Times Woman of the Year, 1975. Home: 5132 Garth Ave., L.A., CA 90056; Office: Hall of Administration, L.A., CA 90012.

BURKETT, WILLIAM ANDREW
Banker
b. July 1, 1913, Herman, Washington Co., Nebr.; s. William H. (dec.) and Mary (Dill) Burkett; desc.: 7th generation desc. of Stuffel Burkett who emigrated to Pa. from Ger. 1700; Maj. Gen. Edward Dodge and Judge John F. Williams, Calif. pioneers, 1849; nephew of late E.J. Burkett, U.S. Senator; ed. Univ. of Nebr., 1931-32; Creighton Law Sch. 1933-34; LL.B., Univ. of Omaha Law Sch. 1938; m. Juliet Johnson, Winnetka, Ill., Oct. 5, 1940; chil.: Juliet Ann (Burkett) Hooker, v. May 21, 1943; Katherine Cleveland, b. June 21, 1947; William Cleveland, b. June 3, 1956. Career: Author: History of America (at age 21 yrs.), selected by Congressional Com. to be carved into Mt. Rushmore Natl. Memorial, Black Hills, S.Dak. 1934; tchr., Am. and European Hist., Calif., 1938; pres. Natl. Hist. Found., 1958---; senior special agent, Intelligence Unit, U.S. Treas. Dept., 1945-50; exec. v.p., Intern-Assn. Unemployment Ins. Com. 1950-53; mem. Calif. Gov.'s Cabinet, 1953-59; apptd. dir of employment, State of Calif., by Gov. Goodwin J. Knight, 1953-55; confirmed by unanimous vote of Senate, 1954; apptd. Supt. of Banks, Calif. State Banking Dept., by Gov. Knight, 1955-58; mem. Calif. Dist. Securities Com. 1955, chmn. Bd. of Investment, State of Calif.; State Liquidator, Yokohama Specie Bank of L.A. and S.F., 1955-59; State Liquidator, The Sumitomo Bank S.F. and Sacto., 1955-59; pres. Burkett & Co., Inc., (mgmt., finance and govt. cons.), L.A. and S.F. 1959-61; cons.: Western Bancorp, 1959-61; United Calif. Bani, 1966-71; pres.-chmn. bd.-dir., Security Natl. Bank of Monterey Co. (brs.: Carmel-By-the-Sea, Monterey, Seaside, Carmel Valley, Pac. Grove and Marina), Calif. 1961-66; pres. and chmn. bd. Security Properties Corp., 1961---; pres.-chmn. bd., Burkett Land Co., Inc., 1961---. Lectr., Commonwealth Club of Calif.; guest, radio-TV pgms. 1952-59; guest speaker, Am. Bankers Assn. Natl. Conv., Chicago, 1958; chief prosecutor of subversives, U.S. Coast Guard, 12th Naval Dist., WW II. Awards: credited by Calif. Crime Com. and U.S. Sen. Crime Investigating Com. U.S. Treas. 1950; credited by Calif. State Leg. Com. for discovery and Dept. of Employment and State Banking Dept. Mem.: Am. Bankers Assn., Calif. Bankers Assn., Independent Bankers Assn.; pres., Natl. Assn. of Supt. of State Banks, 1958-59; bd. trustees, Bishop Kip Sch., Carmel; dir. Pac. Grove C. of C.; State Comdr. Natl. V-Comdr., AMVETS; Rotary Club of Pac. Grove, Commonwealth Club of Calif. (S.F.), Sutter Lawn Tennis Club; v.p.-bd. dirs., Sacto. Town Hall; treas., San Mateo Heart Assn.; Soc. of Calif. Pioneers, Calif. Hist. Soc., Peninsula Golf and Country Club of San Mateo; Monterey Peninsula Country Club; Beach and Tennis Club, Pebble Beach; Carmel Valley Golf and Country Club. Episcopalian. Rec.: swimming, golf. Home: Pebble Beach, CA; Office: P.O. Box 726, Pebble Beach, CA 93953.

BURKHARDT, HANS GUSTAV
Artist – Educator
b. Dec. 20, 1904, Basel, Switz.; s. Gustav and Anna (Schmidt) Burkhardt; ed. Cooper Union, N.Y. 1925-28; Grand Central Sch. of Art, N.Y., 1928-29; pvt. stu., Arshile Gorky Studio, 1929-36; m. Thordi's Olga Haaversen-Westhassel, Las Vegas, Nev., June 18, 1955; dau. Elsa Brown, b. Mar. 31, 1932. Career: Tchr., Long Beach State Coll., USC, UCLA, Calif. Inst. of the Arts; prof. Calif. State Univ., Northridge, Emer. prof. 1974---. One-man exhibs.: Stendahl Gallery, 1939; Circle Gallery, 1940, 41, 42, 54; Instituto Allende, San Miguel Allende, Mex., 1956, 58, 60; Palace of the Leg. of Hon., S.F. 1961; exhibits: L.A. Co. Mus., 1945, 52, 54, 56, 57; Corcoran Gallery of Art, 1947, 51; Chicago Art Inst., 1948, 52; Modern Ins. of Art, Beverly Hills, 1948; Denver Art Mus. 1949, 53; Met. Mus. 1950; Whitney Mus. of Am. Art, 1951, 52, 55; Univ. of Ill. 1951; Pa. Acad. of Fine Arts, 1951, 53; S.F. Mus. 1955, 56; Third Biennial Internat., Sao Paulo Brazil, 1955; Palace of the Leg. of Hon., S.F. 1957; Santa Barbara Mus. of Art, Art USA, Madison Sq. Garden, 1958; The repr. pub. collections, incl.: Art Collection of the State of Calif., Ahmanson Collection, L.A. Co. Mus. of Art, Santa Barbar Mus. of Art, L.B. Mus., La Jolla Art Mus., Pasa Art Mus., Joe Hirshborn; permanent collection fo 150 (paintings, drawings, pastels, prints), OViatt Lib., Calif. State Univ., Northridge; Moderna Museet, Stockholm, Sweden; Kunstmuseum Basel, Switz. (repr. several hundred pvt. collections, USA and Europe). Awards: L.A. Co. Mus. Annual purchase (oil), 1945; Terry Art Inst. Award, Miami, 1951; 2nd prize, L.A. Co. Mus. (modern oils) and 1st prize, Calif. State Fair (modern oils), 1954; Jr. Art Council Prize, L.A. Co Mus., All-City Art Festival purchase prize (oil) and Calif. State Fair Award (pastel), 1957; Santa Barbara Mus. of Art Second Pac. Coast Biennial, Ala Story Purchase Award, 1958; All-City Art Festival First Purchase Award (watercolor); All-City Art Festival First Purchase Award (oil), 1961; Calif. Water Color Society Purchase Award, 1963; numerous minor awards and honorable mention.

Subj. of 2 films by KHJ-TV Studio, 1961, 62; feat. many publs. incl. Art News, Art Digest, Californian, Ariel (Mex.), Art in Am., Art Internat., Art Forum, The Arts, Pictures on Review, Fronteer, L.A. Co. Mus. Annual, Whitney Mus. Annual, Calif. Water Color Soc. Annual, Santa Barbara Mus. of Art, Long Beach Mus. "Arts of So. Calif. Oil Painters," by Arthur Miller, L.A. (Sun.) Times; Prizewinning Painters, 1962; Internat. Directory of Art; The Realm of Contemporary Still Life Painting. U.S. Army, Tex., WW II. Mem.: L.A. Art Assn.; Phi Kappa Phi, 1974; Artist's Equity, Artists for Econ. Action, L.A. Inst. of Contemporary Art, Long Beach Mus. of Art, Laguna Beach Mus. of Art, Kappa Pi. Hobbies: gardening, music. Rec.: camping, friends. Home: 1914 Jewett Dr., L.A., CA 90046.

BURNER, VICTOR JOSEPH
Physician
b. Dec. 3, 1937, Elko, Nev.; s. Carroll Harry and Rose (Hutchinson) Burner; B.A. religion, Yale, 1961, M.D., 1965; postdoctoral, Harvard, USC; m. Mary Herman, M.D. (div.), 1964, Madison, Wis. Career: Mormon missionary, British Isles, 1958-60; Med. internship, Stanford, Palo Alto; med. practice, Mountain View, Calif. 1966-67, La Canada, 1968---: pres., Cosmopolitan Med. Clinic, Inc., La Canada. Staff mem.: Burbank Community Hosp., secty., Monte Sano Hosp. Med. staff; Hollywood West Hosp. Trustee, So Calif. Conservatory of Music; reg. rep., San Diego Opera; trustee, Rome Festival Orch., AUS Med. Corps (reserve) 1956-63. Author: Plasminogen in Human Plasma, 1965; The Burner Family in Europe and America, 1977; David and Jonathan (a libretto), 1979. Mem.: Kiwanis, Elks; Pasadena Athletic Club; Common Cause speaker, 1972-79. Hobbies: violin, chamber music, opera. Rec.: swimming, bicycling, skiing. Home: Alta San Rafael, Pasadena; Office: 927 Foothill Blvd., La Canada, CA 91011.

BURNS, DAN W.
President, Sargent Industries
b. Sept. 10, 1925, Auburn, Calif.; s. William and Edith Lynn (Johnson) Burns; B.S. CE, Univ. of Cape Town, S. Africa; son Dan Burns, Jr., b. July 21, 1962. Career: dir. of materiel, Menasco Mfg. Co., 1951-56; pres. and gen. mgr., Hufford Div., Lear Siegler, Inc. 1956-61; vice pres., Lear Siegler, Inc., 1961-64; pres., chief exec. officer, dir., Sargent Industries, Inc., L.A., 1964---. Served to Capt. AUS, 1941-47; Japanese P.O.W., 1942-43; asst. Mil. Attache to China 1945; Aide-de-camp Gen. George C. Marshall China Mission 1946-47. Mem.: Am. Ordnance Assn.; AF Assn.; Soc. Automotive Engrs.; Am. Inst. Aeros.; L.A. Country Club; Conquistadores del Cielo, pres. 1978-79. Home: 10851 Chalon Rd., Bel Air, CA 90024; Office: 1901 Bldg., Century City, L.A., CA 90067.

BURNS, FRITZ PATRICK
President, F. Patrick Burns Co.
b. May 12, 1925, L.A.; s. Fritz B. and Lucille (Robison) Burns; nephew of Robert S. Burns; ed. Black Foxe Mil. Inst., 1941; Loyola Univ. 1948; USC; Univ. of Wash.: pres. F. Patrick Burns Co., 1955---; v.p., Hilton-Burns Kona Partnership, design cons. Hilton Hawaiian Village Hotel, 1966---. Pres., The Burns Found.; bd. govs., L.A. Music Center; bd. govs. Performing Arts Council; trustee, Loyola Marymount Univ. Bd. govs.; mem., L.A. Bicentennial Cultural Comm. Maude Booth Home for Boys. U.S. Navy, 1943-46, WW II. Awards: Amer. Theater and Asiatic Theater with Bronze Star. Mem.: Res. Research Com. of So. Calif.; Jr. C. of C.; past pres.-dir. Volunteers of Am.; Delta Sigma Phi; The Bachelor's Club. Hobby: art collector. Rec.: swimming. Home: 135 N. Rossmore Ave., L.A., CA 90004; 78-505 52nd Ave., Indio, CA 92201 (Haciendo del Gato); Office: 4950 Wilshire Blvd., L.A., CA 90010.

BURRIS, JOSEPH J.
Attorney at Law
b. Dec. 29, 1913, Aberdeen, S. Dak.; A.B., Stanford Univ., 1936, J.D., 1940; m. Patricia A. (Dirksen); ch: J. Stephen, Susan B. (Dirksen). Career: partner, law firm, Burris, Lagerlof, Swift & Senecal, L.A., ---. Dir.: Stauffer Chem. Co., 1970---; Raffles, Inc., 1962---; trustee, Independent Colls. of So. Calif., 1973---; asst. secty.: Orthopaedic Hosp., 1947---; L.A. Orthopaedic Found., 1947---; L.A. Orthopaedic Med. Ctr., 1947---; Crippled Children's Hosp., 1947---; mem. bd. of govs. Pasadena-Foothill Tennis Patrons Assn., 1961---; mem. bd. of Overseers, Hoover Inst., Stanford Univ., 1971---; mem. L.A. World Affairs Council, 1972---; bd. gov., Town Hall of Calif., 1973---; pres., 1978---; trustee, Pacific Legal Found., 1973---; bd. chmn., 1978---; trustee, Eisenhower Med. Ctr., 1974---; dir. and pres., Stanford Club of L.A.,

1948-50. Lt. Comdr., USNR, WW II. Mem.: L.A. Co. Bar Assn.; Wilshire Bar Assn.; Calif. Bar Assn., Am. Bar Assn.; Phi Delta Theta Frat. Clubs: Annandale Golf, Pasadena, The L.A., Bohemian, S.F. Mem.: Republican Assocs., exec. com. bd. of trustees, 1962---. Home: 827 W. Inverness Dr., Flintridge, CA 91011; Office: 3435 Wilshire Blvd., Suite 2500, L.A., CA 90010.

BURROUGHS, WALTER LAUGHLIN
Journalist — Editor
b. Aug. 21, 1901, Bridgewater, S.D.; s. William S. and Bertha (Laughlin) Burroughs; B.A., Univ. Wash., 1924; postgrad. Univ. Calif. at Berkeley, 1925-28; m. Hazel Georgia Sexsmith, June 1, 1925 (dec. Oct. 1970); dau., Toni (Mrs. Philip Schuyler Doane); m. 2d., Lucy Bell, Feb. 28, 1972. Dir. Publs. Univ. Calif. at Berkeley, 1925-28; gen. mgr. North Pacific Gravure Co., Seattle, 1928-30; gen. mgr. Crocker Union Lithograph and Publ. Co., L.A. 1930-41; co-founder Bantam Books; ind. book pub. with Merle Armitage; Pac. coast rep. H.W. Kaster & Sons, advt. agcy., L.A. 1941-42; exec. v.p. Eldon Industries, L.A. 1946-62; corporate pres., publ. Orange Coast Daily Pilot, Newport Beach, Costa Mesa, Huntington Beach, Calif. 1948-65; chmn., bd., 1965-68; pres. Orion Mgmt. Corp. Trustee, v.p. Children's Hosp. of Orange Co.; trustee Jefferson Trust, Western World Med. Found., Irvine, Calif. Served to col. U.S. Army, 1942-45. Mem.: Soc. Profl. Journalists. Sigma Delta Chi (nat. pres.). Clubs: Bohemian, Jonathan, Newport Harbor Yacht, Rotary, Irvine Coast Country. Home: 511 Cliff Dr., Newport Beach, CA 92663; Office: 1670 Westminster Ave., Costa Mesa, CA 92627.

BUSHNELL, DAVID PEARSALL
Optical Company Founder
b. Mar. 31, St. Paul, Minn.; s. Myron and Mame (Pearsall) Bushnell; desc., David Bushnell, inventor of submarine 1775; desc., Horace Bushnell, famous theologian, Yale 1827; student Cal Tech., 1930-33; B.S., bus. ad., cum laude, USC 1936; m. Nina Gmirkin, Oct. 19, 1947 (div. 1971), L.A.; chil.: David Alan, b. Mar. 21, 1941; Jean (Salfen), b. Oct. 15, 1943; Natasha (Yampolsky), b. Oct. 10, 1950; Steven Ensign, b. Juen 14, 1949; m. 2d. Nanvy Rose, Aug. 27, 1977. Career: founded Bushnell International Inc. 1938 (import/export); asst. fin. mgr., Lockheed Aircraft Corp., 1941-45; founded Bushnell Optical Corp., 1947; merged with Bausch & Lomb, Inc., 1971, vice pres., Bausch & Lomb, 1971-75. Dir.: Balanced Life Ins. Co., 1967-75; Rohe Sci. Corp., 1972-77; Shur-Lok Corp., 1967---; Ernest Homes Center. Mem.: Rotary, Big Canyon Country Club. Trustee, United Ch. of Religious Sci. Hobbies: jogging, tennis, golf. Home: 1089 Marine Dr., Laguna Beach, CA 92651.

BUTLER, DONALD EARNEST
President, SSP Industries
b. Mar. 2, 1927, Coatesville, Pa.; s. John M. and Jane B. (Hanthorne) Butler; B.S., Franklin and Marshall Coll., 1949; m. Laura J. Eaton, Aug. 28, 1948, Lancaster, Pa.; sons, Donald E., b. Sept. 10, 1952; Jeffrey E., b. Jan. 23, 1956. Career: sales mgmt. H.K. Porter Co., Inc., 1952-57; vice pres. and dir., Roylyn, Inc., 1957-60; with SSP Industries (formerly Stainless Steel Products), 1960---: dir. mktg., 1960-64, v.p., mktg., 1964-67, exec. v.p., 1967-68, pres., chief exec. officer, 1968---. Dir.: Mitsubishi Bank of Calif.; Dir. Capital Fund, Inc., Verdugo Hills Hosp., dir. and pres., Verdugo Hills Hosp. Found. U.S.N. aviator, WW II. Regional vice chmn., Nat. Assn. Mfgrs.; dir., Merchants & mfgrs. Assn.; dir., Glendale Symphony Orch. Assn.; Mem.: So. Calif. Com. for Olympic Games; Rotary Club of L.A.; Oakmont Country Club; Sigma K Frat. Past pres. Glendale Bd. of Edn. Episcopalian. Rec.: golf, sailing. Home: 1710 Ivy Bridge Rd., Glendale, CA 91207; Office: 2990 N. San Fernando Blvd., Burbank, CA 91504.

BUTLER, JEFFREY SHERIDAN
Publisher
b. June 19, 1939, Christopher, Ill.; s. Jefferson Macklin and Veneita (Slinger) Butler; B.S. mktg., Univ. Ill.; m. Erin Clarke, Dec. 19, 1976, L.A. Career: with UARCO Bus. Systems Sales, Chicago, 1961-62; dir. pub. rels., Pacific S.W. Airlines, San Diego, 1965-68; founder, pub., East/West Network, Inc., L.A., 1968---: pub. Clipper Mag. (Pan Am Airlines), Mainliner Mag. (United Airlines), Sky Mag. (Delta Air Lines), Flightime (Continental, Ozark, Allegheny and Southern Airlines), Sundancer (Hughes AirWest), PSA Calif. mag. (Pac. Southwest Airlines), ReView (Eastern Airlines). Dir., So. Calif. Visitors Council. Served AUS M.C., 1962-65. Mem.: Sigma Nu. Hobbies: antique collecting, music, art. Rec.: tennis, swimming. Home: Beverly Hills, CA; Office: 5900 Wilshire Blvd., L.A., CA 90036.

C

CAEN, HERB
Newspaper Columnist
b. Apr. 3, 1916, Sacto., Calif.; s. Lucien and Augusta (Gross) Caen; ed. Sacto. Jr. Coll. 1934. Career: Reporter, Sacto. Union, 1932-36; radio ed., S.F. Chronicle, 1936-38; columnist, 1938-50; columnist, S.F. Examiner, 1950-58; columnist, S.F. Chronicle, 1958---; News commentator, NBC, 1939-48. Author: 6 books on S.F. and numerous mag. articles. Pvt., USAAF, June 1942; disch. as Capt., Oct. 1945, WW II. Democratic. Jewish. Rec.: tennis. Office: Fifth and Mission, San Francisco, CA.

CAHILL, JOHN D.
Attorney at Law
b. May 12, 1929, Niagara Falls, N.Y.; s. David J. and Julia C. Cahill; ed. Canisius Coll.; LL.B., State Univ. N.Y. at Buffalo Law Sch. 1953; postgrad., UCLA Law Sch., USC Law Sch.; m. Fae M. Smith, Oct. 20, 1956, Bethesda, Md.; chil.: Kevin Alan, b. May 1, 1958; Tara Anna, b. Apr. 6, 1956; Kennon Dean, b. Apr. 13, 1965. Career: Office of Co. Counsel, L.A., 1957-70; Chief of Tax Sect. and Chief Counsel to Assessment Appeals Bds.; assoc., then partner, law firm of Simon, Sheridan, Murphy, Thornton and Hinerfeld, L.A., 1970-74; partner, Murphy, Thornton, Hinerfeld & Cahill, 1974-79; Apptd. State Inheritance Tax Referee, 1971, 74, 78; apptd. L.A. Retirement Bd. Hearing Officer, 1974-79. Capt., USN, 1953-55; USNR, 1950-79. Mem.: Holy Angels Sch. Bd., 1971-74, pres. 1971-73; Phi Delta Phi; Alpha Kappa Psi, nat. pres. 1968-71; Southwest regional dir., 1962-65; L.A. Co. Central Com., 1967-71. Roman Catholic, past pres., Holy Name Soc. Hobbies: skiing, swimming, travel. Home: 65 La Sierra Dr., Arcadia, CA; Office: 611 W. 6th St., Suite 1610, L.A., CA 90017.

CAHILL, RUSSELL W.
Director, State Dept. of Parks and Recreation
b. July 8, 1938, S.F.; student, Mich. State Univ.; B.A., biology, San Jose State Univ., 1966; married, three children. Career: Deputy Sheriff, Santa Clara Co., 1959-66; U.S. Park Ranger; Yosemite, Glacier Bay, Katmai, Haleakala, 1966-74; staff, President's Council on Environmental Quality, 1970; dir., Calif. Div. of Parks, 1974-77; dir. Calif. Dept. of Parks and Recreation, 1977---. Book in progress on prehistoric Hawaii. Sgt. M.P.C., USAR, 1958-66. Office: 1416 Ninth St., Rm. 1405, Water Resources Bldg., P.O.B. 2390, Sacto., CA 95811.

CAHILL, STARR WILNER
Consulting Engineer
b. Apr. 3, 1917, Merced, Calif.; s. Starr C. and Bernice E. (Bush) Cahill; ed. A.A., Modesto Jr. Coll. 1937; A.B., San Jose State Coll. 1939; grad. courses, UCLA, USC, L.A. State Coll. 1940-63; m. Frances E. Faulds, Santa Cruz, Calif., Aug. 31, 1940; chil.: Gary W., b. Apr. 11, 1944; Sharon A., b. May 13, 1946. Career: Liaison engr., Douglas Aircraft Co. 1940-42; asst. supt., Static Test Lab. 1942-46; proj. engr., Giannini Co., 1946-49; proj. engr., Radioplane Co. 1950-51; proj. engr., Hycon Mfg. Co. 1951-53; chief draftsman, 1953-56, asst. chief engr. 1956-58, dir. engring. operations, 1958-61, v.p. mfg. 1961-63, cons. engr. 1963---. Registered Profl. Engr., Calif. Granted four U.S. Patents, 1956-62. Mem.: Aerospace Design Drafting Adv. Com., Pasa. City Coll., 1956---; The Am. Soc. of Tool and Mfg. Engrs.; Am. Arbitration Assn. Methodist (chmn. commn. on edn.; steward). Hobby: model railroads, photog. Rec.: swimming. Home: 1647 N. Santa Anita Ave., Arcadia, CA 91006.

CAHN, SAMMY
Songwriter
b. June 18, 1913, New York; s. Abraham and Alice (Reiss) Cohen; ed. pub. schs., N.Y.; m. Gloria Delson (actress, Goldwyn Girl); chil.: Steven and Laurie. Career: Violinist, various orchs; est. of ofc. Saul Chaplin, writer, spec. material for such performers as Betty Hutton, Bob Hope, Bing Crosby, Edgar Bergen, Andrews Sisters, Jimmie Lunceford, Frank Sinatra, Vic Damone, Doris Day, Milton Berle, Tony Martin, Lucille Ball, Danny Thomas, Danny Kaye, Martin and Lewis; songwriter (40 songs on Hit Parade): "Rhythm Is Our Business," "Shoe Shine Boy," "Rhythm in My Nursery Rhymes," "Until the Real Thing Comes Along," "Because You're Mine," "Posin'," "Bei Mir Bist Du Schon," "Please Be Kind," "I've Heard That Song Before," "Let It Snow, Let It Snow," "Give Me Five Minutes More," "I Walk Alone," "There Goes That Song Again," "Victory Polka," "It's Been a Long, Long Time," "It's Magic," "Saturday Night Is the Loneliest Night in the Week," "Glad to See You," "Papa, Won't You Dance With Me,." "Jealous," "Be My Love," "The Girl Upstairs," "You're Never Too Young," "Anything Goes," "Meet Me in Las Vegas," "Forever Darling," Recording artist, Decca Records; Warner Bros. Vitaphone Studio, Brooklyn, N.Y.; wrote scores for many mot. pics., incl.: Walt Disney's "Peter Pan," Warner Bros. "Romance on the High Seas," M.G.M.'s "Toast of New Orleans"; invited by city of Phila. to write "Happy Birthday America" to commemorate signing of Declaration of Independence. Prod. "Two Sailors and a Girl," Mario Lanza's "Serenade," Warner Bros.; "Our Town," NBC, others. Awards: (nom. Academy Award 11 times) winner, Acad. Award for "Three Coins in the Fountain," 1954-55; many cits., incl. Time Mag. Mem.: ASCAP, 1936--- (A.A. 1949---). Home: Holmby Hills, CA.

CAHOUET, FRANK V.
Bank Executive
b. May 25, 1932, Cohasset, Mass.; s. Ralph and Mary (Jordan) Cahouet; B.A., Harvard Univ., 1954; M.B.A., Wharton Sch. of Bus., Univ. Penn., 1959; m. Ann P. Walsh, July 14, 1956; chil.: Ann P., b. Sept. 7, 1957; Mary G., b. June 7, 1959; Frank V., Jr., b. May 15, 1964; David R., b. July 8, 1972. Career: With Fidelity Phila. Trust Co., and Mfgrs. Nat. Bank of Detroit, 1956-60; joined Security Pacific Bank, 1960---: comml. loan asst., L.A., 1960; then asst. v.p.; vice pres., Metropolitan Div., 1966; apptd. Sr. Loan Adminstr. European Hdqtrs., London (for Europe, Middle East, Africa), 1969; exec. vice pres., Security Pacific Corp., L.A., 1973---: adminstr. non-banking subs. Dir., Sav-on Drugs, Inc., L.A. 1st Lt., AUS, Field Arty. 105 Howitzer Batt., 1954-56. Mem.: Calif. Bankers Assn.; L.A. World Affairs Council; Harvard Club of So. Calif.; Valley Hunt Club, Pasadena; California Club, L.A.; Wharton Grad Sch.; trustee, Scripps Coll.; trustee, Flintridge Prep. Sch., La Canada. Rec.: tennis, skiing. Home: 1485 Lomita Dr., Pasadena, CA 91106; Office: 333 S. Hope St., L.A., CA 90071.

CAIN, LEO FRANCIS
Educator — University Administrator
b. July 30, 1909, Chico, Calif.; s. Edmund Joseph and Myrtle (Perdue) Cain; ed. A.B., Chico State Coll. 1931; M.A., Stanford Univ. 1935; Ph.D., 1939; m. Margaret Brennan, S.F., Aug. 17, 1940; chil.: Barbara, b. 1942; Nancy, b. 1944; Caroline, b. 1949. Career: tchr., prin. and counselor, Calif. pub. schs. 1930-37; psychol. instr., S.F. City Coll. 1937-39; research assoc., Am. Council on Edn. 1939-40; asst. prof. Univ. of Med. 1940-43; 1944-46; prof. Univ. of Okla. 1946-47; prof.-dean-v.p., S.F. State Coll. 1947-61; pres. Calif. State Coll., Dominguez Hills, 1961-76; pres. emeritus, 1976---; prof., Spec. Edn., S.F. State Univ., 1976---. Spec. cons., Ger. Juvenile delinquency, U.S. Dept. State, 1953; chief, Edn. Survey Team, Liberia, 1961; Pres. Johnson's Com. on Mental Retardation, 1967-73. Classification ofcr., US Maritime Serv. 1943-44; Lt., USNR (1944-46), WW II. Co-author: "Cain Levine Social Competency Scale," "Mentally Retarded Students in Calif. Secondary Schs."; contrib. to profl. publs. encycs. Mem.: adv. edn. policies, N.E.A.; chmn. Am. Found. for Blind; past pres., Internat. Council for Exceptional Chil.; adv. panel, Fed. Ofc. of Vocational Rehabilitation; fellow, Am. Assoc. Mental Deficiency; pres. S.F. Tuberculosis and Health Assn.; Calif. Adv. Com. on Adult Edn.; dir. Internat. Hospitality Center, S.F.; past pres., spec. edn. adv. com., United Cerebral Palsy Assn.; chmn. Mental Retardation Comm., L.A. Welfare Planning Council; Univ.-Coll. Comm. for Tchr. Preparation-Licensing, 1972-77; Handicapped Chil.'s Edn. Task Force, Edn. Comm. of the States, 1972-77; Calif. State Univ.-Coll. Comm. on External Degrees, 1972-76; bd. dirs.-sr. commr., Western Assn. of Schs. and Colls. 1973---; Gov.'s Comm. on Mental Retardation, Rotary Club, Phi Delta Kappa, Kappa Delta Pi. Home: 12 Kenmar Way, Burlingame, CA 94010; Office: S.F. State Univ., 1600 Holloway, S.F., CA 94132.

CALAMIA, WALDON
Food Company President
b. May 1, 1914, Omaha, Nebr.; s. Frank and Florence Calamia; student, pub. schs.; m. Margie, Feb. 7, 1952, Omaha, Nebr. pres., Rod's Food Products, Inc., Industry, Calif., 1950---. Catholic. Hobbies: golf, travel, fishing, hunting. Office: 17380 Railroad St., City of Industry, CA 91748.

CALDWELL, GLADYS L.
Author — Columnist — Lecturer
b. Feb. 25, 1912, Milwaukee, Wis.; d. Charles Lester and

Henrietta (Atkinson) Senn; Univ. student; independent research; m. George H. Caldwell, July 2, 1932, Milwaukee, Wis.; 1 son Dennis James, b. Jan. 3, 1935 (author, Theory of Optical Activity, etc.). Career: Investigative reporter since 1960 on fluoride pollution of air, food and water from indsl. emissions and resultant damage to people and food chain. Gov. Brown apptd. advisor to Calif. Air Resources Bd. on standards for hydrogen fluoride gas. Group advisor internat. re fluoride pollution. Author: Fluoridation and Truth Decay; Fluoride Fallout from Factories Making Us The Endangered Species. Contbr. newspapers, radio, and TV. Republican. Baptist. Hobbies: swimming, hiking, decorating. Home: 3025 Highridge Rd., La Crescenta, CA 91214; Office: Top-Ecol Press, 3025 Highridge Rd., La Crescenta, CA 91214.

CALDWELL, GAYLON LORAY
College Dean
b. Sept. 11, 1920, Hyrum, Utah; s. Morris and Marie (Christensen) Snow; desc. Lorenzo Snow, 5th president, L.D.S. Church; B.S., Utah State Univ., 1947; M.A., Univ. of Nebr., 1948; Ph.D., Stanford Univ., 1952; m. Victoria Mae Bigler, Aug. 1, 1947, Logan, Utah; chil.: Thomas, b. Feb. 19; Camden Stanford, b. Oct. 13; Melissa Marie (Carter), b. Mar. 31; Kim Edith, b. May 10. Asst. Prof. of Polit. Sci., Brigham Young Univ., 1951-53; Assoc. Prof., 1953-60; Dir. Am. Cultural Center, Guatemala City, 1960-62; Dir. Am. Cultural Center, Lima, 1962-63; U.S. Cultural Attache, Lima, 1963-65; U.S. Information Agency, Washington, 1965-68; U.S. Cultural Attache, Mexico City, 1968-70; Dean, Elbert Covell Coll., Univ. of the Pacific, 1970---. Author: Am. Govn't. Today, 1963, revised 1967, transl. into Spanish, 1971. Served Pvt. to Capt., USAF, WW II. Mem.: Stockton Opera Assn.; Sigma Alpha Epsilon, 1938; Commonwealth Club, 1971; Pan Am. Soc. of San Francisco, 1971; World Affairs Council of No. Calif., 1971; Phi Kappa Phi. Hobby: gardening. Rec.: golf, sailing. Home: 2904 Bonnie Lane, Stockton, CA 95204; Office: Univ. of the Pacific, Stockton, CA 95211.

CALDWELL, WILLIAM MACKAY, III
Furniture Company Executive
b. Apr. 6, 1922, L.A.; s. William Mackay II and Edith Ann (Richards) C.; B.S., Univ. So. Calif., 1943; M.B.A., Harvard Univ., 1948; m. Mary Louise Edwards, Jan. 16, 1946; chil.: William Mackay IV, Craig Edwards, Candace Louise. Sec.-treas., dir. Drewry Photocolor Corp., 1957-60; Adcolor Photo Corp., 1957-60; treas., dir. Drewry Bennetts Corp., 1959-60; sr. v.p., chief fin. ofcr. Am. Cement Corp., 1960-67; sr. v.p. corp., 1966-70, pres. cement and concrete group, 1967-70; pres., chmn. bd., chief exec ofcr. Van Vorst Industries, L.A., 1970---; chmn. bd. Van Vorst Corp., Seattle; pres. ELGEA I, 1970---; chmn. bd. So. Cross Industries, Atlanta, chmn. bd. 1967-69, Hawaiian Cement Corp.; v.p., dir. Am. Cement Internat. Corp., Am. Cement Properties; bd. dirs. Am. Cement Found.; dir. Portland de Mallorca Internat. Concrete systems, 1967-69; cons. prof. Univ. So. Calif. Mem.: men's com. L.A. Med. Center, Bd. dirs. Commerce Assocs., Univ. So. Calif. Assocs.; bd. dirs. Pres.'s Circle; Served to lt. USNR, 1943-46. Mem.: Newcomen Soc., Friends Huntington Library, Kappa Alpha (pres. Univ. of So. Calif., 1943-44), Alpha Delta Sigma, Alpha Pi Omega. Presbyterian. Toastmaster pres. San Marino 1956-57. Clubs: Harvard Bus. Sch. of So. Calif. (dir. 1960-63); L.A. Met. Dinner, L.A. Country, Town Hall, Calif. (L.A.); Trojan; Annandale Golf, Calif. Country Club, L.A. Country Club, Big Canyon Country Club (Newport Beach). Home: 1880 Lombardy Rd., San Marino, CA 91108; Office: P.O.B. 927 Pasadena, CA 91102.

CALE, CHARLES GRIFFIN
Attorney at Law
b. Aug. 19, 1940, St. Louis, Mo.; s. Junian Dutro and Judith Hadley (Griffin) Cale; Gr. grandson of W.L.F. Hadley, mem. of Congress (r.-Ill.) 1895-97; desc. Hannah Dustin, Mass. colonial heroine; B.A., Principia Coll. 1961; LL.B., Stanford Univ. 1964; LL.M., USC, 1966. Career: Lawyer, Whyte & Schifferman, 1964-66; partner, Adams, Duque & Hazeltine, 1966---. Asst. Secty., dir. IOF-Florence Hallum Prevention of Child Abuse Fund, 1976---. Mem.: The Bachelors, pres. 1976-77; L.A. C. of C.; California Club; Sigma Alpha Epsilon; Phi Delta Phi legal frat. Rec.: golf, skiing. Home: 2222 Ave. of the Stars, L.A., CA 90067; Office: 523 W. 6th St., L.A., CA 90014.

CALLAWAY, ELY REEVES
Vintner
b. June 3, 1919, La Grange, Ga.; s. Ely R., Sr. and Loula (Walker) Callaway; A.B., Emory Univ., Atlanta, Ga.,

1940; m. Nancy Nita Jacobs, Sept. 1973, Palm Desert, Ca.; chil: Ely Reeves, III; Louise Wiler; Nicholas D. Career: various exec. positions in textile industry, 1964-68; pres. & dir. Burlington Indust., Inc., NYC, 1974---; also Founder and pres., Callaway Vineyard & Winery, Temecula. Served from 2nd Lt. to Maj., AUS, Quartermaster Corp., 1940-45. Dir.: Hampshire Coll., Amherst, Mass.; United Negro Coll. Fund, N.Y.; Boy Scouts of Am. Clubs: University, N.Y.C.; Blind Brook, N.Y.; Pine Valley, N.J.; Eldorado Country, Calif. Baptist. Hobbies: golf, photog., music. Office: 32720 Rancho Calif. Rd., Temecula, CA 92390.

CAMPANIS, ALEXANDER
V.P., General Manager, L.A. Dodgers
b. Nov. 2, 1916, Cos, Dodecanese Island, Greece; s. Guiseppe (Italian Army Gen.) and Tulla Campani; B.S., N.Y. Univ., 1940; m. Bessie Georgiades, Oct. 15, 1940, N.Y.C.; chil.: James Alexander, b. Feb. 9, 1943; George Alexander, b. Sept. 26, 1946. Career: Signed contract with Brooklyn Dodgers orgn., played, Macon, Ga., 1940; Reading, Pa., 1941; Knoxville, Tenn., 1942; Montreal, Canada, 1943, 46, 47; Manager, Nashua, N.H., 1948; Reading, Pa., 1949; Newport News, Va., 1950; Scouting Director, L.A. Dodgers, 1958-68; v.p. and gen. mgr., 1968---. USN, 1943-46, spec. in athletics, 1st class. Greek Orthodox. Hobbies: photog., coin collecting. Rec.: dancing, swimming, golf. Office: Dodger Stadium, 1000 Elysian Park Ave., L.A., CA 90012.

CAMPBELL, GLEN TRAVIS
Singer — Entertainer
b. Apr. 22, 1936, Billstown, Ark.; s. Wesley and Carrie Campbell; m. Sarah Davis, Lake Tahoe, Nev., Sept. 2, 1976; four chil. by previous marriages: Debbie, age 21; Kelli, age 16; Travis, age 12; Kane, age 9. Career: played guitar at age 5 yrs., also banjo, mandolin and bass fiddle; joined Dick Bill band, played rodeos and clubs, Albuquerque, N. Mex.; formed own band, Glen Campbell and his Western Ranglers, 1955; est. Hollywood res. and joined The Champs; orgn. own band, 1961; studio mus. rec. 1963-65; guitarist-vocalist with Beach Boys, 1965; rec. artist, (first hit) "Turn Around, Look at Me," 1965; rec. artist, Capitol Records, 1965---; guest, Joey Bishop Show, 1968; host, Smothers Bros. series, 1969; star, "Glen Campbell Goodtime Hour," CBS-TV, 1969-73; star, mot. pics., "True Grit," 1969; "Norwood," 1970; headlined, London Palladium, 1971; Hilton Hotel. Hotel, Las Vegas, 1972. Awards: 10 Gold Records, Record Ind. Assn. of Am. for: "Wichita Lineman," "Galveston," (3 albums) "Gentle On My Mind," "By the Time I Get to Phoenix," "Hey Little One," others incl. "Glen Campbell Live," "Try a Little Kindness;" Top Male Vocalist, Album of the Yr., Single of the Yr., "Gentle on My Mind" by Acad. of Country Music, 1968; Entertainer of the Yr., Country Mus. Assn.; Best Vocal Perf., Best Contemporary Solo, Best Country Rec., Best Country Perf. by Natl. Acad. of Rec. Arts and Scis. 1968, Album of Yr. 1969; Top Male Vocalist, Top TV Personality, Album of Yr. by Acad. of Country and Western Music, 1969; Jukebox Artist of Yr., Music Operators of Am., 1969; Top Male Vocalist, Billboard, Cash Box, 1969; Top Male Star, Cowboy Hall of Fame, 1969; Top Male Star of the Future, Box Ofc. Mag. 1969; Most Promising New Male Star, Photoplay Mag. 1969; TV Performer of Yr. by U.S. TV eds. 1969; hon. chmn. Natl. Arthritis Found. 1969; hon. chmn. Christmas Seal drive, Ark. 1970; Ky. Col. by Gov. Louie B. Nunn, 1970; hon. Mayor, Studio City, Calif. 1970; headlined command perf. for Queen Elizabeth, Eng., 1971; headlined "Salute to Agr." show, White House for Pres. Nixon, 1971; spec. awards by Houston Livestock Show and Rodeo Assn. 1971; "Merit Who's Who Among Amer. H.S. Students," hons. 1971; hon. chmn. L.A. City Schs. Annual Festival of Music, 1972; runner-up in Pro-Am. 9 yrs. as host of Glen Campbell-L.A. Open golf tournament, PGA tour, 1972, No. 1 Vocalist and No. 1 TV Mus. Show cond. by annual Mot. Pic. Daily-Television Today, 1972. Mem.: Natl. Reading Council (apptd. by Pres. Nixon), 1970; State Com., Natl. Library Week, Ark. 1971. Hobbies: rifle collection, fishing, hunting, golf. Office: 10920 Wilshire Blvd., L.A., CA 90024.

CAMPION, ROBERT THOMAS
Chairman-President, Lear Siegler, Inc.
b. June 23, 1921, Minneapolis, Minn.; s. Leo P. and Naomi (Revord) Campion; ed. Loyola Univ., Chicago, 1939-41; 1946-48; m. Wilhelmina Knapp, June 8, 1946; son, Michael. Career: Partner, Alexander Grant and Co., CPA firm, Chicago, 1946-57; secty. Lear Siegler, Inc., Santa Monica, Calif., 1957---, sr. v.p., 1962-71, chmn. bd., pres.-chief exec. ofcr.-dir. 1971---. U.S. Army Signal Corps (1942-46), WW II. Mem.: Am. Inst. CPAs; Ill Soc. CPAs; Union League, Chicago; Bel Air Country Club.

Republican. Home: 4188 High Valley Rd., Encino, CA 91316; Office: 3171 S. Bundy Dr., Santa Monica, CA 90406.

CANN, WILLIAM HOPSON
Secretary, Cyprus Mines Corporation
b. June 17, 1916, Newark, N.J.; s. Howard W. and Ruth H. (Hopson) Cann; ed. Barringer H.S. 1929-33; A.B., Harvard Coll. 1933-37; LL.B., Harvard Law Sch., 1937-40; m. Mildred Allen, Ridgewood, N.J., Mar. 7, 1942; chil.: William H., Jr., b. July 17, 1943; Sharon L., b. May 10, 1945; John A., b. Mar. 10, 1950; Lawrence E., b. Sept. 21, 1951; Career: Lawyer, Chadbourne, Wallace, Parke & Whiteside, 1940-53; asst. to pres., No. Am. Aviation Inc., 1953-60, v.p.-secty. 1960-75 (merged with Rockwell-Standard Corp. 1967). Coord. for stockholder relations, Cyprus Mines Corp., 1975-77, secty., 1977---. 1st Lt., U.S. Army Air Corps (1942-45), WW II. Mem.: Phi Beta Kappa, Harvard Club of So. Calif. Episcopalian. (former vestryman and jr. warden). Hobby: swimming. Home: 835 Toulon Dr., Pacific Palisades, CA; Office: 555 S. Flower St., L.A., CA 90071.

CANTOR, EDWARD BERNARD
Physician — Inventor
b. June 24, 1913, Norfolk, Va.; s. Louis and Freda (Katz) Cantor; ed. B.S. (hons.), Univ. of Va. 1932; M.D., Univ. of Chicago, 1936; postgrad. Fellowship, Stanford Univ.; (div.) son, Thomas Leslie, b. Oct. 16, 1950. Career: res., Chicago Lying-In Hosp., Woman's Hosp. of Detroit, Mich.; est. pvt. practice, spec. in gynecology, L.A. Co. 1948---; guest surg., Univ. of Rome Clinics. Lectr.: UCLA, Cedars-Sinai Med. Center, Univ. of Rome; Lausanne Univ., Switz.; Paris Obstet and Gynecological Soc.; prod. "Surg. Movie," feat. various natl. med. schs., U.S.A., Europe. Inventor, med. instrument. Author: articles publ. leading med. journs. Mem.: Fellow, Am. Coll. of Obstets. and Gynecology; fellow, Pan-Am. Med. Assn.; diplomate, Am. Bd. of Obstets and Gynecology; past pres., Dina Groman Chpt., pres. Vaginal Surgeons Society; editor of textbook "Female Urinary Stress Incontinence," Cty of Hope, 1956; Phi Delta Epsilon. Democrat. Hebrew. Home: 13900 Panay Way, Marina del Rey, CA 90291; Office: 9735 Wilshire Blvd., Beverly Hills, CA 90212.

CAPLAN, FRIEDA RAPOPORT
Produce Company President
b. Aug. 10, 1923, L.A.; d. Solomon and Rose (Yanova) Rapoport; sister of Paul Steffen R.; B.S., UCLA, 1945; m. Alfred Hale Caplan (labor-rels. cons.), Apr. 28, 1951, Las Vegas, Nev.; chil.: Karen Beth (agri. grad., UC, Davis, in family bus.), b. Oct. 23, 1955; Jacqueline Deborah (Jr., S.D. State Univ., Bus. & mktg. maj.), b. June 10, 1958. Career: started in family owned produce commn. house in accts. payable dept., Guimmara Bros. Fruit Co., L.A., 1956, worked into mushroom sales; pres., owner, operator, Frieda's Finest/Produce Specialities, Inc. (L.A. Produce Mkt.), 1962---; first woman owner of a produce house in West, rep. and spokesman for fresh produce indus. on TV and Radio; credited with developing the market for Asian Pears, Cocktail Avocados, Shelled Blackeyed Peas, bringing back the Blood Orange, Black Radishes, Cherimoya, Hot House Cucumbers, Kiwi, Fresh Ginger, Kumquats, Leeks, Macadamia Nuts in shell, Mushrooms, Pearl Onions, Quince, Passion Fruit, Spaghetti Squash, Sunchokes; pioneered refrigerated air containers to transport perishable items, 1963---. Dir., Terminal Mkt. Div., United Fresh Fruit and Vegetable Assn.; dir., Assoc. Produce Brokers & Dealers of L.A., and treas.; past v.p., 1st woman dir., Produce Mktg. Assn.; past treas., Fresh Produce Council of So. Calif., voted Man of the Year, 1970; weekly appearannce on KABC-TV Eyewitness News for several years. Jewish. Rec.: exercising. Home: 11651 Montecito Rd., Los Alamitos, CA 90720; Office: 732 Market Court, L.A., CA 90021.

CAPOBIANCO, TITO
Gen. Director, San Diego Opera
b. Aug. 28, 1931, La Plata, Argentina; s. Donato and Felicia (Basciano) Capobianco; student, Law, Philos., Univ. of La Plata; m. Elena Antonia Fernandez, Dec. 26, 1955, Buenos Aires, Argentina; chil.: Danilo, b. Jan. 8, 1958; Renato, b. Apr. 1, 1963. Career: Operatic debut, Teatro Argentino, La Plata, 1953; artistic dir. Cincinnati Opera Festival, 1961-65; Tech. Dir., Teatro Colon, 1958-62; Gen. Dir., Chile Opera Co., 1967-70; artistic dir., San Diego Opera, 1975, Gen. dir., San Diego Opera, 1977---; stagy dir. in major opera companies of Argentina, Australia, France, Germany, Holland, Italy, Mexico, Spain and U.S., including NYC, Phila., Houston, S.F., Wash., D.C.; prof. of acting and Interpretation at Acad. of Vocal Arts, Phila., 1962-68; Gen. Dir. and Founder, Juilliard Sch. of Music's Am. Opera Center, 1967-69; Founder of

S.D. Opera Verdi Festival, 1978; Creator and Founder of S.D. Opera Center for young singers, 1977. Awarded the ''Cavaliere dell' Ordine al Merito della Repubblica ¦taliana'' in 1979. Lt. (Res.) Army of Argentina. Mem.: San Diego Rotary Club. Catholic. Rec.: swimming, soccer, racquetball. Home: 5247 Alzeda Dr., La Mesa, CA 92041; Office: P.O. Box 988, San Diego, CA 92112.

CAPPS, ANTHONY T. (CAPOZZOLO)
International Public Relations Executive
b. Apr. 19, Pueblo, Colo.; s. Nicolo and Anna (Solomone) Capozzolo; desc. Antonio Capozzolo, signed Peace Document with King Ferdinand of Spain, 1471; grandson of Domenico Capozzolo, ofcr. in Garabaldi's Army, freed Italy (ancestors early founders of Lucania and Christians of King Solomon's Tribe, migrated to Naples with St. Peter because of Roman persecutions); great-grandson, Mayor of Naples, Italy; ed. L.A. Bus. Coll.; Pueblo, Colo.; pvt. tutor, arts and music stu.; m. Theresa Cecelia Harmon, Hollywood, Calif., Nov. 12, 19. Career: Dance dir., choreographer, prod. mot. pics., TV and radio; feat. Profl. Dance Team, Biltmore Bowl, Cocoanut Grove, L.A.; St. Catherine Hotel, Catalina, 1939-42; dance dir. and prod. NBC, ABC, KCOP-TV, Columbia pics., 20th Century Fox and Calif studios, 1940-60; govt. tours, Puerto Rico, Cuba, Jamaica, Dominican Repub., Haiti, 1954; prod. "Latin Holiday," TV series of Latin Am.; numerous TV interviews on Relig. and Polit. Hist. of Ballet and Opera of last 500 yrs.; exec. dir. Lockheed and Vega Aircraft Co. activities, Burbank, L.A., Glendale, Pomona, Pasa., Bakersfield, Taft, Calif. plants; internat. pub. rels. dir.: Howard Manor, Palm Springs Key Club, Country Club Hotel, Palm Springs Ranch Club; George Cameron Jr., owner, Desert Sun Newspapers, KDES Radio, Palm Springs, Cameron Center and Cameron Enterprises and Oil Co., Burbank radio sta.; Murietta Hot Springs Hotel, Health and Beauty Spa, Palm Springs-Coachella Valley. Founder-pres.-dir. Tony Capps Enterprises (real estate investments, pub. rels., publicity, promotions): chmn.-exec. dir.: golf and tennis tournaments, benefit dinners for civic leaders, govs., senators, congressmen, United Fund for City of Hope (3 times), Natl. Cystic Fibrosis Fund, Palm Springs (Bob Hope) Golf Classic; created adv. "gimmick" for Colgate and Cugat, Coca Cola; founder-pres. Natl. Artists and Art Patrons Soc. of City of Hope, est. Anthony Capps Art Gallery Med. Center; founder-pres. Tri-County Chap., Natl. Football Found. and Hall of Fame, U.S., Jap. and Can. Columnist: The Reporter, 1962-63; and Desert Sun, Palm Springs; L.A. Daily News. Mem.: (charter) Eisenhower Mem. Hosp. Aux.; bd. dirs. Opera Guild of the Desert; bd. dirs. Palm Springs Pathfinders; Desert Art Center of Coachella Valley; Palm Springs Desert Mus.; AFTRA; Desert Press Club; Smithsonian Inst., Wash., D.C.; Advis. bd., Am. Security Council, Wash., D.C.; L.A. Co. Museum of Arts (Patron); The Cousteau Society, New York; founder-pres. Societe Culinaire Philanthropique Internationale, 1973; Natl. Trust for Hist. Preservation, Wash., D.C.; clubs: Balboa Bay. Catholic. Hobby: charities. Home: 2715 Junipero Ave., Palm Springs, CA; Office: P.O. Box 820, Palm Springs, CA 92262.

CARDWELL, HARVEY DEBS
Certified Public Accountant — Author
b. June 18, 1899, Franklin Co., Ky.; s. Charles Plummer and Nannie Ruth (Lanter) Cardwell; ed. acct.-chem. YMCA night sch., Louisville, 1916-20; Walton Sch. of Comm., Chicago, 1921-22; bus. mgmt. La Salle Ext. Univ. 1923; Internat. Corr. Sch., Scranton, Pa.; sons: Kenneth Lanter, Michael Dexter. Career: Tchr., acct.: YMCA Sch. 1931-34; Univ. of Louisville, 1936-37; CPA 1926---. Orgn. first Ky. Relief Adm. under Pres. Herbert Hoover; Author: "The Principles of Audit Surveillance," publ. by D. Van Nostrand Co., Princeton, N.H. 1960, 2d eds., 1975; "Earth Science at Crisis," pub. by Vantage Press, N.Y. 1976. Sgt., U.S. Army, Panama, 1918-19. Mem.: YMCA, Louisville, 1916-50, dir. 1932-50; Ky. Soc. of CPAs, 1926-63, pres. 1934-35; G.W. Pilcher Assocs., Inc. 1931-50; Co-chmn. Mayor's Emg. Personnel Com. 1937; Am. Inst. of CPAs 1937---; budget com. Community Chest, 1946-49; pres. Shawnee Kiwanis Club, 1947; budget com. Co. of Jefferson, 1947-49; Calif. Soc. CPAs, 1951---. Home: 2217 Harbor Blvd., G-8, Costa Mesa, CA 92627; Office: 1651 E. Edinger Ave., Santa Ana, CA.

CARLIN, MAURICE PATRICK
Physician — Surgeon
b. July 3, 1924, Foley, Minn.; s. John F. and Ida (Latterell) Carlin; ed. M.D., Marquette Univ. Med. Sch. 1946; m. Victoria M. Lauer, Buffalo, N.Y., Dec. 22, 1945; chil.: Brian Timothy, b. Dec. 21, 1947; Barry Lawrence, b. June 28, 1949; Tama Denise, b. Mar. 17, 1953; Deirdre Suzanne, b. Feb. 26, 1956; Bonnie Victoria, b. June 14, 1957; Marcianne Therese, b. Nov. 30, 1960. Career:

Intern, Buffalo Gen. Hosp., N.Y. 1947-48; neurology res., Minneapolis, Minn. 1948-50; neuro-surgical res., Univ. of III. 1952-55; est. pvt. practice (spec. neurology-neurological surg.), Santa Rosa, Calif. 1955---. Clin. instr. (neurology - neurosurgery), Univ. of III. 1954-55, Lt., U.S.N., San Diego Naval Hosp., Neurosurgical Dept. 1950-52. Mem.: diplomate, Minn. Neurological Graduates, Am. Bd. Neurological Surg., Am. Bd. Psych. and Neurology; Am. Acad. Neurology, Cong. Neurological Surgs., Harvey Cushing Soc., S.F. Neurological Soc., Calif. Chpt. Assn. of Am. Phys. and Surgs.; Fellow, Am. Coll. of Surgs.; Assn. of Am. Phys. and Surgs.; sect. leader, John Birch Soc., Sonoma Co.; Alpha Kappa Kappa. Hobby: camping, trips. Home: 2424 Osage Ave., Santa Rosa, CA 95405; Office: 1120 Montgomery Dr., Santa Rosa, CA 95405.

CARLSON, JANET MARIE
Advertising Executive

b. Mar. 5, 1935; N.Y.C.; d. Ragnar and Eileen Allanna (O'Donnel) Carlson; student, Hofstra, Adelphi, Cornell; Career: copy dir., J.C. Penneys, N.Y. (1,800 stores), institutional advt., Macy's, N.Y.; creative dir. for May Co. and Broadway Stores, L.A.; v.p. and creative partner, Interpublic Challenge Unit (div. Interpublic Corp.), devel. new products for Gallo Wines, Gulf Tires, the Carnation Co. - "Mighty Dog" dog food; partner, president, copy dir., Carlson/Liebowitz, Inc., L.A. ---. Author: The Shikses' Guide to Jewish Men, 1978. Recipient 84 major awards for creative excellence in print, TV, radio. Mem.: dir., Mus. of Sci. and Industry, L.A.; hon. bd. dir., Univ. Calif., Irvine; L.A. Advt. Women; Am. Assn. of Advertisers; Am. Advt. Fedn. Hobby: writing. Rec.: avid athlete. Home: 1925 S. Beverly Glen Blvd., L.A., CA 90025; Office: 1888 Century Park E., L.A., CA 90067.

CARLSON, RICHARD WARNER
Savings and Loan Association Executive

b. Feb. 10, 1941, Boston, Mass.; s. W.E. and Ruth Carlson; Gr.-gr. grandson, E. Rockwood Hoar, U.S. Atty. Gen.; Univ. of Miss., 1962; m. Patricia Caroline Swanson, Feb. 17, 1979, La Jolla, Calif.; Chil.: Tucker McNear, b. May 16, 1969; Buckley Peck, b. Feb. 3, 1971. Career: journ., L.A. Times, 1962-63; United Press Internat., 1963-65; ABC-TV, S.F.-L.A., 1966-75; free-lance writer & stringer, Time Mag., Look, etc., 1966-70; dir. & producer, documentaries, NBC-TV, Burbank, 1975; anchorman, CBS-TV, San Diego, 1975-76; v.p.-finance, San Diego Fed. Savings & Loan Assn., 1976---. Dir.: Delmar News Press, 1976; Calif. Gen. Mortgage, Inc., 1978; San Diego C. of C., v.p. 1978. Author: A History of Women, San Diego Hist. Soc., 1978 (hard and soft cover eds.). Recipient numerous profl. awards incl. six Assoc. Press TV and Radio awards for investigative reporting, news analysis and commentary; four Golden Mike awards; three Emmy awards; two San Diego Press Club awards; George Foster Peabody award for Excellence, investigative reporting; L.A. Press Club Grand Award; Nat. Headliners Award. Mem.: Financial advisory bd., Jr. League of S.D.; sponsor, La Jolla Soccer League; dir. Muscular Dystrophy Assn., S.D.; chmn., Citizens for Open Space, 1978. Mem.: Actors & Others, L.A., pres. 1972-76; A.J. Liebling Soc. of L.A., co-founder; S.D. Coalition; Calif. C. of C.; Sigma Delta Chi. Republican Bus. & Profl. Club, v.p., 1978; Senate Republican Advisory Comm. mem. 1978. Clubs: La Jolla Beach & Tennis; the City; University of S.D.; Cuyamaca. Episcopalian. Home: 7956 Ave. Alamar, La Jolla, CA 92037; Summer: Howes Is., Machias, Me. 04654; Office: 600 B St., S.D., CA 92183.

CARMICHAEL, DAVID BURTON, JR.
Physician — Educator

b. Sept. 12, 1923, Santa Ana, Calif.; s. David Burton and Phyllis Ann (Adams) Carmichael; B.A., M.D., Univ. Iowa; postgrad., USC, Harvard Univ. 1947-50; m. Ava Louise Smith, Dec. 26, 1944, Sundown, Tex.; chil.: Catherine Ann Xander, b. Aug. 29, 1947; Heather Sue, b. Oct. 16, 1953; Linda Louise, b. Oct. 2, 1955; Ava Lou, b. Nov. 10, 1962. Career: Cardiologist (Fellow), Mass. Gen. Hosp. 1949-50; internist, U.S. Naval Hosps. and Hosp. Ship, U.S.S. Repose in Korean waters, 1950-55; Dir., Heart Center, Donald Sharp Mem. Hosp., San Diego, 1956-57; Cons. cardiologist, Chief of Med. and Chief of Staff, Scripps Mem. Hosp., La Jolla, 1957---. Clin. Prof. of Med., Univ. of Calif., San Diego, Sch. of Med. 1972---. Dir., De Anza Clin. Lab., 1976---. Ret. Rear Admiral, USNR; decorated Legion of Merit, personal and unit commendations. Publs.: book on pvt. aviation, multiple clin. and research papers in cardiovascular disease. Mem.: Gov., So. Calif. Region III, Am. Coll. of Physicians, 1972-76; bd. dir., Am. Coll. of Cardiology; vice chmn., Residency Review Comm., in Internal Med.; chmn. sect. council on CV Disease, AMA, 1977---; Alpha Omega Alpha, Phi Beta Pi; La Jolla Beach and Tennis Club.

Reorganized Ch. of Jesus Christ, Elder. Hobbies: aviation, instrument-rated multi-engine pilot, photog. Home: 8333 Calle del Cielo, La Jolla, CA 92037; Office: 9844 Genesee, Suite 400, La Jolla, CA 92037.

CARMICHAEL, HOAGLUND HOWARD
Composer

b. Nov. 22, 1899, Bloomington, Ind.; s. Howard Clyde and Lida Mary (Robinson) Carmichael; ed. LL.B., Univ. of Ind., Bloomington, 1926; m. Ruth Mary Meinardi, Mar. 14, 1936; chil.: Hoagy Bix, b. Sept. 30, 1938; Randy Bob, b. June 27, 1940. Career: Composer, actor, radio artist, Decca recording artist; writer, Broadway shows and mot. pics.; comps. incl. "Star Dust," "Rockin' Chair," "Lazybones," "Little Old Lady," "Washboard Blues," "Skylark," "Two Sleepy People," "Blue Orchids," "Georgia on My Mind," "Ole Buttermilk Sky," "Lazy River," "Hongkong Blues," "In the Cool Cool of the Evening," (Acad. Award winning song of 1952); star, own TV show, NBC, 1952; feat. actor, "To Have and Have Not," "Johnny Angel," "Canyon Passage," "Best Years of Our Lives," "Night Song," "The Las Vegas Story," "Young Man with a Horn," "Belles on Their Toes." Author: (biog.) "The Star Dust Road." Mem.: ASCAP, Kappa Sigma, Theta Tau Alpha, Theta Nu Epsilon, Bel-Air Country Club. Republican. Chr. Ch. Hobby: painting. Rec.: golf. Home: Highway 111, Rancho Mirage, CA.

CARMICHAEL, JAE
Artist — Instructor — Lecturer

b. Jane Giddings, Aug. 22, 1925, Hollywood, Calif.; d. Paul Hollingsworth and Harriet Caroline (Grant) Giddings; desc.: granddau. of Joshua Reed Giddings, Pasa., Calif. (1874) direct desc. of Edward I of Eng., Joshua R. Giddings, Congressman from Ohio, writer Republican Party's 1st platform; George Giddings from St. Albans, Eng. to Ipswich, Mass. 1635; ed. Mills Coll. 1942-44; B.F.A., USC 1951; Ph.D. (Cinema and Arts), 1969; M.F.A., Claremont 1955. Career: Instr. Pasa. Art Mus. and Pasa. Sch. of Fine Arts, 1953---; owner-dir. Pasa. Sch. of Fine Arts, 1970---; lectr., Otis Co. Art Inst., and Pasa. City Coll., 1969---; gives illustrated lectures statewide; Exhibs. (Mexico, U.S.A., Can., Ger., France, Japan), 1953---: Denver Mus. 1953, 58; Pasa. St. Fair (8 yrs.); Pacific Acad. of Fine Arts, 1958; Butler Inst. Am. Art, Youngstown, Oh. (7 yrs.); Madonna Festival, Adrian, Mich. 1958; Bodely Gallery, N.Y. 1958; Calif. Water Color Soc. 1958---; Am. Water Color Soc. 1958, 59, 60; E.B. Crocker Gallery, 1960; Calif. Natl. Watercolor Soc. Traveling Show, 1971; 1st Titanium Sculpture, Calif. State Coll., Hayward; City Hall Tower Gallery, others. Awards: (prizes) sketch of Pioneer Bridge selected for cover Pasa. Civic Affairs Festival pgm. 1953; Orange Co. Fair, 1953; Pasa. Art Mus. 1954; Pasa. Soc. of Arts, 1955, 60, "Top Honors" 1971; Julia Elizabeth Ford Award, 1956; Art Festival, 1957, 59; won Priz de Paris, famed Raymond Duncan Galleries, Paris, 1959; hon. Laguna Beach Art Festival, 1959; 4 prizes, Pasa. St. Fair, 1959; 1st prize water color, Natl. Art Clun, N.Y.C. 1960; 1st prize oil painting and purchase prize, Pasa. Soc. of Artists, Apr. 1960; many others, 1960---; film, "Cycle of Entelchy," Edinburgh Film Festival, Brussels and 12 foreign countries, 1967; Hons. Leonardo da Vinci Acad., Rome; Gold Plaque, Korean Embassy, 1973; Scroll, Twain Embassy. Mem.: First Century Families, D.A.R., Pasa. Hist. Soc., Pasa. Pioneers, Hunting Mem. Clinic Aux., Pasa. Soc. of Artists, Art Assn., L.A. Art Assn.; Natl. Arts Club, N.Y.; Pasa Art Alliance; dir. Alpha Phi, Delta Kappa Alpha; dir. Pi Lambda Theta, 1951-53; pres. Calif. Water Color Soc. 1978; pres. Pasa. Soc. of Artists, 1970; Valley Hunt Club. Episcopalian. Home: 985 San Pasqual St., Pasadena, CA.

CARR, WILLARD Z., JR.
Partner, Gibson, Dunn & Crutcher

b. Dec. 18, 1927, Richmond, Ind.; s. Willard Z. and Susan (Brownell) Carr; ed., B.S., Purdue Univ. 1948; LL.B., Ind. Univ. Law Sch. 1950; m. Margaret Peterson, Montgomery, Ala., Feb. 15, 1952; sons: Clayton Paterson, b. Nov. 17, 1953; Jeffrey Westcott, b. Feb. 13, 1957. Career: Atty.-partner, Gibson, Dunn & Crutcher law firm (spec. labor rels.), 1952---; admitted to practice U.S. Supreme Ct.; appears before Calif. State Legislature repr. employers on Unemployment and Disability Ins.; speaker, various employer and civic groups, incl. Merchants and Mfrs. Assn., Am. Mgmt. Assn., Adm. Referees Assn., Personnel Ind. Rels. Assn.; mem. Natl. Panel of Arbitrators, Am. Arbitration Assn. Judge Advocate Gen's. Ofc. 1950-52. Ed., Ind. Law Journal. Mem.: Calif. State, L.A. Co. Bar Assns.; chmn. Labor Law Com., Bus. Law Sect., Internat. Bar Assn.; Am. Bar Assn.; chmn. Econ. Controls Com., Corp., Bus. and Banking Sect.; Com. on Development of Law under Natl. Labor Rels. Act, Labor

Law Sect.; bd. dirs. L.A. Area C. of C., chmn. State and Local Govt. Com., chmn. Law and Justice Com., chmn. Personnel Mgrs. Com.; chmn. Men's Adv. Com. L.A. Co.-USC Med. Center Aux. for Recruitment, Edn. Serv.; bd. trustees, vice chmn., Pac. Legal Found.; L.A. World Affairs Council; bd. dirs. L.A. Police Mem. Found.; Natl. Def. Exec. Res.; chmn. bd. dirs. Wilshire Repub. Club; Repub. State Central Com.; Town Hall of Calif. Protestant. Rec.: tennis, bicycling, water skiing. Home: 123 N. McCadden Pl., L.A., CA 90004; Office: 515 Flower St., L.A., CA 90071.

CARRILLO, MICHAEL MYFORD
Oil Company Executive
b. Dec. 11, 1902, Santa Ana, Calif.; s. Clodomiro C. and Francisca Ursula (Preciado) Carrillo; great-grandson of Don Jose Andreas Sepulveda, former owner of Irvine Ranch, Orange Co., Calif.; cousin, Princess Conchita Sepulveda Pignatelli; cousin, Leo Carrillo, noted actor and Calif. leader; bro. Charles C. Carrillo, ret. off. ct. interpreter, Orange Co., Calif.; ed. Santa Ana Jr. Coll.; Orange Co. Bus. Coll.; m. Beatrice Vegley Raney, Santa Ana, Calif.; chil.: James M. (pres. Venterx, Madrid, Spain); Robert El Don (dep. co. clerk, Orange Co., Calif.); Mrs. Donald E. (Marjorie M.) McConnell; Mrs. Glen (Diane Raney) Wigton. Career: Pres., Carrillo Oil Co., L.A., 1938-67; pres. Carrillo Exploronic Co., 1955-67 (ret.). Listed, many books feat. noted leaders, incl. Royal Blue Book, London, Eng. Mem.: L.A. C. of C.; Republican. Roman Catholic. Rec.: music. Home: 335 Lookout Dr., Laguna Beach, CA 92651.

CARSTEN, ARLENE
Director, Institute for Burn Medicine
b. Dec. 5, 1937, Paterson, N.J.; d. Albert F. and Ann (Greutert) Desmet; student, Alfred Univ., N.Y., Univ. Calif. Ext.; m. Alfred J. Carsten, Feb. 11, 1956, Wellsville, N.Y.; chil.: Christopher Dale, b. Dec. 3, 1957; Jonathan Glenn, b. Mar. 10, 1959. Career: music and art dir., Deveraux Sch., Santa Barbara, 1960; piano instr., 1964-71; research cons. for text book on ednl. psychol., 1970; dir., Muskie for Pres. Campaign, S.D., 1972; exec. dir., Inst. for Burn Medicine, 1972---. Bd. dir.: chmn., Pub. Edn. Com., 1978, chmn., Mem. Com., 1979, Mental Health Assn. of San Diego, 1978---; apptd. by Gov. Brown, Jr., to Bd. of Med. Quality Assurrance, 1976---, chmn. 1977; founding mem., dir., trustee, Nat. Burn Found., 1975---; founding mem., dir., Citizens for Paramedics, Inc., 1976; Donated Organ Program, S.D., 1976---; appts. by Co. Supervisors to S.D. Co. Emergency Med. Care Com., 1973-75. U.S. Rep. to 18th Triennial Internat. Congress, Women's Internat. League, New Delhi, India, 1971. Awards: Key to city of Baton Rouge, La., 1976; recognition for service, S.D. Soc. of Clin. Psychologists, 1975; Belles for Mental Health, S.D. Mental Health Assn., 1974; Democrat: mem. co. com., 1972, 74, mem. State Central Com., 1968-74; mem. San Dieguito Demo. Club, 1965-75; campaigner for Unruh, McCarthy, local candidates. Hobbies: bee keeping, stitchery. Rec.: snorkeling, hiking. Home: 1415 Via Alta, Del Mar, CA 92014; Office: 3737 Fifth Ave., Suite 206, San Diego, CA 92103.

CARTER, EDWARD W.
Chairman, Carter Hawley Hale Stores, Inc.
ed. A.B., UCLA, 1932; M.B.A., Harvard Grad. Sch. of Bus. Adm. 1937; LL.D., Occidental Coll. 1962. Career: Merchant; chairman, Carter Hawley Hale Stores, Inc.; dir.: Del Monte Corp., United Calif. Bank, So. Calif. Edison Co., Western Bancorporation, Am. Tel. & Telegraph Co., Pac. Mutual Life Ins. Co., The James Irvine Found.; SRI Internat. Awards: Shuman Award, Harvard Bus. Sch. 1936; Alumnus of the Yr., UCLA 1953; Tobe Award for "distinguished serv. to Am. retailing," 1960; "Calif. Industrialist of the Yr.," 1961; NRMA Gold Medal for "distinguished serv. to retailing," 1971. Mem.: Bus. Council; regent, Univ. of Calif.; visiting com. UCLA Bus. Sch.; The Conf. Bd.; dir. Music Center Opera Assn.; dir. Santa Anita Found.; trustee, Brookings Inst.; Com. for Econ. Devel.; Occidental Coll.; bd. trustees, L.A. Co. Mus. of Art; Dir., chmn., L.A. Philharmonic Assn.; dir. S.F. Opera Assn.; Clubs: Calif., Pac. Union, Bohemian, Burlingame Country, L.A. Country, Harvard, Delta Upsilon. Episcopalian. Home: 626 Siena Way, L.A., CA 90024; Office: 550 S. Flower St., L.A., CA 90071.

CARTER, JACQUELINE R.R.
Aviation Company Executive
b. Apr. 8, 1945, Carmel, Calif.; d. James William and Margaret (de Avila) Sophia Carter; B.A., Long Beach State Univ., 1966; M.A., Stanford, 1968; postgrad. Princeton, 1969, Rutgers, 1968-69, Stanford; m. Ronald Lee Walker, III, Apr. 28, 1972; 1 son, Wayde Christian. Career:

reporter, S.F. Examiner, 1966-67; assoc., Scope Documentary Film Prodns., Washington, 1966---; cons. community relations Long Beach; Office Edn., San Jose, 1970-72; pub. relations — v.p., Walker Aviation, San Carlos, 1972---; pub. relations, Children's Hosp. S.F., 1972-74; dir. film festivals, Rutgers Univ., N.H. with Mus. Modern Art, 1969-70; dir. ednl. fair, Office Edn., San Jose, 1971; founder Nat. Election Activity Team, 1969; officer, Council of Living Theatre, Long Beach, 1964-65; Mem. Women in Communications; Bay Area Soc. Editors; Exptl. Aircraft Assn.; Aircraft Owners and Pilots Assn.; Stanford Alumni Assn.; Phi Beta; Soroptimists Internat., San Mateo, dir. 1977---; advisor, Scouts Exploring Program, 1977---; Peninsula Press Club, 1976---; Editor, Humane Soc. mag., 1976---; speaking & writing assignments on humane movement, 1976---; contbr. feature articles to newspapers and mags. Author: The Newspaper Politician, 1968. Home: 411 Ridge Rd., San Carlos, CA 94070.

CARTER, JAMES M.
United States Circuit Judge
b. Mar. 11, 1904, Santa Barbara, Calif.; s. James Madison and Belle Ann (Hicks) Carter; desc. pioneer families (Hicks and Sawyers) of Ky. and Va. who crossed plains to Calif. in covered wagons; ed. A.B., Pomona Coll. 1924; J.D., USC Law Sch. 1927; Harvard Law Sch.; m. Dorothy Freeland, 1928; chil.: Joan Freeland, b. July 3, 1930, L.A.; m. 2nd, Ruth Doty, Phoenix, Ariz., Sept. 17, 1938; m. 3rd., Bina Ruth Cheney, Dec. 30, 1953. Career: Admitted to Calif. bar, 1928; dir. State Dept. of Motor Vehicles, 1940-43; chief asst. U.S. Atty. 1943-46; U.S. Atty. 1946-49; apptd. U.S. Dist. Judge by Pres. Truman, Sept. 23, 1949, confirmed by Senate, Oct. 15, 1949. Judge, U.S. Circuit Ct., 1968---. Mem.: Ephebian Soc., Sigma Tau, Order of Coif, Phi Alpha Delta, Phi Kappa Phi. Office: U.S. Courthouse, 940 Front St., San Diego, CA 92189.

CARTER, PERRY
Bank President
b. Apr. 27, 1933, Comanche, Tex.; s. Zill and Evelyn (McGlothlin) Carter; Pacific Coast Sch. of Banking, Univ. of Washington, 1971-74; m. Josephine Starlic, Nov. 10, 1957, San Pedro, Calif.; chil.: Michael, Perry, b. Sept. 12, 1957; Richard Zill, b. Sept. 12, 1958; Christine Ann, b. Feb. 11, 1960. Career: v.p., First Nat. Bank of Long Beach, 1959-65; v.p., Newport Nat. Bank, 1965-70; sr. v.p., administrn., Am. Nat. Bank, 1970-74; pres., The Bank of Montecito, 1974-75; pres., Nat. Bank of L.B., 1975---. Sgt., AUS, Korean conflict, 1953-55. Bd. of mgrs., No. Community YMCA, 1977---; Mem. Am. Mgmt. Assn.; Ind. Bankers Assn. of So. Calif. Mem. Elks Lodge No. 888, L.B. Democrat. Catholic. Hobby: citizens band radio. Rec.: trap and skeet shooting, hunting, fishing. Home: 16252 Serenade Lane, Huntington Beach, CA 92647; Office: P.O.B. 7150, L.B., CA 92647.

CARTER, VICTOR M.
Industralist -- Banker — Philanthropist
b. Aug. 21, 1910, Rostov, Russia; s. Mark and Fanya (Rudnick) Carter; ed. pub. schs., L.A., Calif.; m. Adrea Zucker, L.A., Calif., July 15, 1928, dau. Fanya. Career: Est. res., USA 1921; pres. Builder's Emporium, 1949-56; pres. Vimcar Sales Co. 1937-59; past chmn-pres. Republic Pics. Corp. (name-changed to Republic Corp. 1960), 1959-67; dir. United Calif. Bank; past chmn., Hollywood State Bank; dir. So. Calif. Rapid Transit Dist.; past dir. IDB Bankholding Corp.; Hon. chmn., Israel Investment Co.; dir.-hon. life pres. City of Hope; v. chmn. bd. Community TV of So. Calif.; past dir. Harvey Mudd Coll.; admr. Acad. of Mot. Pic. Arts and Scis. Awards: Shield of David, by Foreign Minister of Israel, Abba Eban, 1966; Third Order of Imperial Treas. by Emperor of Japan, 1968. Mem.: bd. govs. Jewish Agcy.-Israel; dir., Cedars-Sinai Med. Center; hon. chmn. bd. govs. Tel-Aviv Univ.; (hon.) Fellow-trustee, Brandeis Univ.; dir. Am. Jewish Joint Dist. Com., Inc.; dir. Am. ORT Fed.; regional exec. com., Anti-Defamation League; v.p.-dir., Greek Theatre Assn.; pres. Japan-Am. Soc. of So. Calif.; dir. B'nai B'rith; Mason; pres. Japanese Philharmonic Orch. of L.A.; pres. Jewish Community Found., 1964-66; pres. Jewish Fed. Council, 1967-68; former dir. L.A. C. of C.; dir. L.A. World Affairs Council; exec. com. Natl. United Jewish Appeal; gen. chmn., United Jewish Welfare Fund Campaign, 1961; pres. United Way, Inc., past pres. 1968-70; chmn. State of Israel Bonds, 1962, 63, 64, 65; gen. chmn. United Crusade, 1967; com-dir., Western Region, Urban League; bd. govs., Welfare Found. of L.A.; dir. Young Musician's Found.; Hobby: civic and philanthropic activities. Home: Penthouse A, 10375 Wilshire Blvd., L.A., CA 90024; Offices: 1900 Ave. of the Stars, Suite 2230, L.A., CA 90067.

CARTY, EDWIN LOUIS
Real Estate Executive

b. Dec. 4, 1897, Santa Barbara, Calif.; s. Cornelius Charles and Emma (Maulhardt) Carty; ed. Univ. of Calif., Davis, 1917-19; m. Doris Corrine McDonell, Old Mission, Ventura, Calif., Dec. 12, 1919; chil.: Mrs. Philip K. (Elizabeth Patricia) Maloney; Robert Charles; Douglas McDonell; Roderick James; Edwin Louis (dec., WW II). Career: Founder-owner, Edwin L. Carty & Sons, Inc., Oxnard, Calif., 1919---. Mayor, City of Oxnard, 1942-48; supv. Ventura Co. 1950-64. Mem.: exec. com., Shoreline Planning Assn. of Calif., Inc.; State Game and Fish Commr. 1939-50; dir. Ventura Co. Camp Fire Girls, 1945-53; U.S. Natl. Forests, 1948; adv. bd., Calif. Centennials Comm. 1950-51; adv. council, Dem. Natl. Com. 1953-54; Dem. State Central Com.; chmn. Ventura Co. Flood Control Bd. 1954-56; Internat. Assn. Game, Fish and Conservation Commrs.; past pres., League Calif. Cities; past pres., Natl. Assn. Municipal Legislators; past dir., Am. Municipal Assn.; past pres., Calif. Safety Council; Pac. Coast Bd. Intergovernmental Rels; past pres., Calif. Mission Trails Assn.; pres. Oxnard Boys Club, 1954; past pres., Oxnard Harbor Realty Bd.; (life) dir.-past regional v.p., Calif. Real Estate Assn.; dir. U.S., Calif., Ventura Co. and Oxnard C. of C.s; past pres., Ventura Prodn. Credit Assn.; Co. Supvs. Assn., Calif.; dir. Quail Prefered, Duck Hunters Assn. of Calif.; Ventura Co. Farm Bur.; (hon.) Point Mugu Game Preserve, So. Calif. Retrievers Club, Inc.; past pres., Ventura Co. Rod and Gun Club; Oxnard Rotary Club; Century Club, L.A.; past pres., Native Sons of Golden West; Izaak Walton League, Elks Club, Sportsmen Club of Am., Rancheros Visitadores; Commonwealth Club, S.F.; Calif. Club, L.A. Roman Catholic. Knights of Columbus. Hobbies: hunting, fishing. Rec.: golf. Home: 338 Roderick Ave., Oxnard; (country home) Ojai, Calif.; (summer) 3032 Solimar Dr., Ventura, Calif.; Office: 747 N. Oxnard Blvd., Oxnard, CA 93030.

CARVER, EUGENE PENDLETON, II
President, Hoffman Properties, Inc.

b. Oct. 15, 1928, Bellingham, Wash.; s. Nathan P. and Mary Louise (Rautenburg) Carver (Gillam); ed. Manlius Mil. Sch., N.Y.; A.B., Dartmouth Coll. 1950; m. Patricia L. Sutherland, Bellingham, Wash., June 6, 1954; daus.: Mary K., b. July 23, 1955; Joan E., b. Dec. 29, 1958; Sara E., b. May 26, 1957. Career: Gen. mgr., Whonnock Lumber Co., Ltd.,Whonnock, B.V., Can. 1953-56; sr. v.p. Western Mortgage Corp., S.F., 1956-69; pres. Hoffman Properties, Inc., L.A., 1969---. Dir., Hoffman Electronics Corp., El Monte, Calif. 1970-78; chmn.-trustee, BankAmerica Realty Investors, S.F. 1973---. Lt., Ordnance Corps, U.S. Army, 1951-53. Mem.: Kappa Kappa Kappa, Hanover, N.Y., 1947---; Merchants Exch. Club, S.F. 1967---; Bellingham Yacht Club, Wash.; King Harbor Yacht Club, Redondo Beach, 1969---; Jonathan Club, 1969---. Episcopalian. Rec.: sailing, skiing. Home: 30032 Avenida Esplendida, Palos Verdes Peninsula, Calif.; Office: 626 Wilshire Blvd., L.A., CA 90017.

CASASSA, REV. CHARLES STEPHEN, S.J.
Chancellor, Loyola Marymount University

b. Sept. 23, 1910, San Francisco, Calif.; s. Charles S. and Margaret G. (Power) Casassa; ed. A.B., Gonzaga Coll., Spokane, Wash. 1934; M.S., 1935; S.T.L., Alma Coll. 1939; Ph.D., Univ. of Toronto, 1946; (hon.) D.D., Univ. of Judaism, 1964; (hon.) S.T.D., USC 1965; (hon.) L.H.D., Calif. Coll. of Med. 1965; LL.D.: St. Mary's Coll. 1967; Univ. of S.F. 1969; L.H.D.: Hebrew Union Coll.-Jewish Inst. Relig. 1967, Univ. of Santa Clara, 1971; D.H.L., Marymount Coll. 1969. Career: Ordained priest, 1938; instr. Loyola Univ. 1939-41; asst. prof., Santa Clara Coll. 1946-49; dean of art 1948-49; pres. Loyola Univ. of L.A. 1949-69; Chancellor, 1969---. Mem.: pres. Independent Colls. of So. Calif., Inc. 1956-58; dir. Knudsen Found.; bd. dirs., L.A. C. of C., 1966-67; bd. dirs., L.A. World Affairs Council; trustee: Univ. of S.F., Loyola Marymount Univ., Ind.-Edn. Council of Calif. 1973---; pres. Friendship Day Camp, Inc.; Knights of Columbus; L.A. Rotary Club. Roman Catholic. Hobby: mystery stories. Home: Loyola Blvd. at W. 80th St., L.A., CA 90045; Office: Loyola Marymount Univ., L.A., CA 90045.

CASE, CLIFFORD E.
Physician — Surgeon

b. Mar. 3, 1901, Little River, Kan.; s. Hiram C. and Lulu (Wood) Case; ed. A.B., Kan. Univ. 1926; M.D., Western Res. Univ. 1929; postgrad. studies: N.Y.U., Cook County Coll., Univ. of Calif. Career: Practicing phys. and surg. 1931---; chief of staff, Sisters Hosp. 1953-56, listed, various biog. publs. 1954---, incl. List of Soc. 1955; Mem.: Santa Barbara Co. Med. Soc., Calif. State Med. Assn., AMA; Internat. Acad. of Med., Obstetrics & Gynecology;

Am. Acad. Gen. Practice; pres. Community Concerts, 1945-55; pres. Santa Maria Concerts Assn., 1955---; Am. Phys. Art Assn., Nu Sigma Nu. Methodist. Hobby: old and rare glass collection (bottles and decanters). Rec.: gardening. Home: 214 E. Camino Colegio St., Santa Maria, Calif.; Office: 218 W. Cypress St., P.O. Box K, Santa Maria, CA 93454.

CASEY, DAVID STODDER
Attorney at Law

b. Sept. 18, 1915, St. Louis, Mo.; s. Charles and Martha Casey; ed. LL.B., St. Louis Univ. 1937; m. Margaret Hackett, San Diego, Calif., Dec. 29, 1968; chil.: David Seabold, Julia Allen. Career: Atty. at law, 1937---: partner, Casey, Gerry, Casey, and Westbrook. Awards: Lawyer of Yr., by S.D. Trial Lawyers, 1974. Mem.: Pres. Cal. State Bar, 1976; past pres. S.D. Trial Lawyers; Calif. Trial Lawyers Assn.; Diplomate, Am. Bd. of Trial Advocates, past pres. S.D. chpt.; gov. State Bar of Calif. Bd. of Governors, 1973-76; fellow, Internat. Acad. of Trial Lawyers; past pres. Friendly Sons of St. Patrick. Catholic. Hobby: gardening. Rec.: golf, tennis. Home: 1550 El Paso Real, La Jolla, CA 92037; Office: 110 Laurel St., San Diego, CA 92101.

CASHMAN, JAMES CHESTER
President, The Homestead Company

b. Jan. 21, 1927, Hartley, Iowa; s. Chester and Kathryn (Fuller) Floyd; B.S., civil engring., Iowa State Univ., 1949; postgrad., U.C. Riverside; m. Ethel Goode Cashman, Sept. 4, 1949, Albia, Iowa; chil.: Susan Marie, b. Mar. 29, 1950; James Martin, b. Aug. 28, 1951; Mary Elizabeth (Usas), b. Aug. 16, 1952; David Michael, b. Nov. 30, 1953; Kevin John, b. July 27, 1962. Career: asst. city engr., Sioux City, Iowa, 1949-52; owner, Cashman Engring. Co., Sioux City, 1954-57; mgr. Jennings Engring. Co., Beverly Hills, 1957-59; vice pres., H&H Constrn. Co., L.A. 1959-61; pres., J & E Constrn. Co., L.A., 1961-67; chief engr., Automated Bldg. Components, Cerritos, 1967-69; pres., Corona Land Co., Corona, 1969-75; pres., The Homestead Co., Riverside, 1975---; vice pres., Living Word, Inc. (retail-wholesale bookstore); treas., Riverside Broadcasting Assn. (proposed TV station). Lt., AUS Corps of Engrs., WW II, So. Pacific Theater. Mem.: Bldg. Inds. Assn. of Calif., pres. 1978, dir. 1974-78; pres., San Bernardino/Riverside chpt. BIA, 3 yrs., state BIA treas., 1978, pres. 1979; chmn. Nat. Assn. of Home Bldgs. Environmental Controls Com., land use com. 7 yrs.; pres. Phi Kappa Tau, Iowa State Coll. 1948-49; Lions Club, Corona, 1970-75; pres. Community Settlement Assn. Riverside, 1976. Trinity Christian Center Ch., Deacon, 1978, chmn. bldg. Com. 1976---. Hobbies: boating, woodworking. Home-Office: 2323 Mary St., Riverside, CA 92506.

CASIDA, JOHN EDWARD
Educator

b. Dec. 22, 1929, Phoenix, Ariz.; s. Lester Earl and Ruth (Barnes) Casida; B.S., Univ. Wis., 1951; M.S., 1952, Ph.D., 1954; m. Katherine Faustine Monson, June 16, 1956; chil.: Mark Earl, Eric Gerhard. Research Asst., Univ. Wis., 1951-53; mem. faculty, 1954-63; prof. entomology, 1959-63; prof. entomology, pesticide chemist and toxicologist, Univ. Calif., Berkeley, 1964---. USAF, 1953. Awarded medal 7th Internat. Congress Plant Protection, Paris, 1970. Haight traveling fellow, 1958-59; Guggenheim fellow, 1970-71; scholar-in-residence, Bellagio Study and Conf. Center, Rockefeller Found., Lake Como, Italy, 1978. Mem. Am. Chem. Soc. (Internat. award research pesticide chem., 1970; Spencer Award in Agri. and Food Chem., 1979), Entomol. Soc. Am. Home: 1570 La Vereda Rd., Berkeley, CA 94708.

CASTY, ALAN
Author — Professor

b. Apr. 6, 1929, Chicago; s. Louis and Gertrude Casty; B.A., Univ. of Calif., Berkeley, 1950; M.A., UCLA, 1956; Ph.D., UCLA, 1973; m. Jill Herman, L.A.; chil.: Lisa, b. Nov. 3, 1958; David, b. Feb. 16, 1962; Erica, b. Nov. 5, 1964. Career: mem. faculty, English Dept., Santa Monica Coll., 1956---; Author: Let's Make It Clear (1977), Development of the Film: An Interpretative History (1973), Building Writing Skills (1971), all pub. Harcourt Brace Jovanovich; The Dramatic Art of the Film (1971), Harper and Row; The Films of Robert Rossen, Mus. of Modern Art, 1969; A Mixed Bag: A Contemporary Collection for Understanding and Response (2d ed. 1975), Staircase to Writing and Reading: A Rhetoric (3rd ed. 1979), The Act of Writing and Reading (2d ed. 1970), The Act of Reading (1962), Writers in Action (1959), all pub. Prentice-Hall; Mass Media and Mass Man (2d ed. 1973), Holt, Rinehart and Winston; The Shape of Fiction, D.C. Heath, 2d ed. 1975. Contbr. articles to other books.

Sgt., AUS, 1951-53. Home: 3646 Mandeville Canyon Rd., L.A., CA 90049; Office: Santa Monica Coll., Santa Monica, CA 90405.

CATES, JO-ANN (JODI)
Editor — Publisher
b. May 10, 1932, Copperhill, Tenn.; d. Jack L. and Willie Wilson; chil.: James Wilson Cates, Jr., b. Sept. 13, 1953; Michael Alan, b. June 26, 1955; William Daniel, b. Sept. 13, 1957; Christopher Thomas, b. Jan. 12, 1962. Career: vocalist, coll. dance band, 1950-53; owner-operator, Jo-Ann Cates Shooting Sch., 1967-69; owner, personal services, tour business, 1969; social and publicity secty. to legal profls., Calif., 1970; placement dir., Bryman Schs., 1971-74; admissions dir., Nat. Inst. of Health Sci. Orange, 1975; owner, Skateboard Co., 1976; salesperson, From the Ground Up (Constrn. inds. newspaper), 1977; owner-editor-pub., 1978---; also tchr. skeet and trap shooting. Contbd. articles, Nashville Scene mag. & newspapers; Author several cookbooks. Recipient: 1st place in region teen-age driving contest, Tenn., 1949; finalist in Mrs. Tenn. contest, 1968; Women's State (Tenn.) Skeet Champion, 1957-69; finalist World Championship Skeet Shooting, husband & wife, 1967-68; only woman mem. on All State Skeet Team, Tenn., 1960-68. Pres.: Altar Guild; Women of the Ch. Hobbies: skeet shooting, writing. Home: 1513 Miramar, Balboa, CA; Office: 3625 W. MacArthur Blvd., Suite 310, Santa Ana, CA 92704.

CATTANI, RAY A.
College President
b. Feb. 18, 1930, San Bernardino; s. August L. and Gertrude (Sommer) Cattani; B.S., Brigham Young Univ., 1957; M.S., Oregon State Univ., 1960; Ph.D., Univ. Arizona, 1963; m. Irene Oates, Feb. 16, 1955, St. George, Utah; chil.: Keith T., b. Sept. 4, 1955; Kent E., b. Sept. 4, 1957; Kyle D., b. June 27, 1960; Kathleen, b. July 31, 1962; Kara I. b, May 7, 1974. Career: mem. chemistry faculty, Phoenix Coll., 1963-66; chmn. chem. dept. and prof. of chem., Mesa Community Coll., Mesa, Arizona, 1966-67, dean of instr., 1967-73; exec. dean Scottsdale Community Coll., Ariz., 1973-76; pres., Reedley College, Reedley, 1976---. Contbr. sci. and tech. journs. Consul., examiner, No. Central Assn., 1970-76, exec. bd., 1976---; pres., Phoenix chpt., Am. Assn. Univ. Profs., 1965; chmn., Central Ariz. sect., Am. Chem. Soc., 1969-71; pres., Ariz. chpt., Am. Inst. of Chemists, 1969-70; bd. dir., Scottsdale C. of C.; mem. Rotary, 1970---. Republican. L.D.S. Ch. Hobby: piano. Rec.: waterskiing, tennis. Home: 8350 S. Frankwood, Reedley, CA 93654; Office: 995 N. Reed Ave., Reedley, CA 93654.

CAVELTI, PHILIP ALFONS
Physician — Specialist
b. Aug. 21, 1914, Gossau, St. Gallen, Switz.; s. Alfons Georg and Margrit (Staerkle) Cavelti; ed. B.A. (gym.), Bern, Switz., 1933; M.D., Univ. of Bern (med. faculty), Bern, Switz., 1939; m. Else Hedwig Etaehlin, Bern, Switz., 1941 (dec. 1961); m. Ursula Swart-Loesch, 1974; chil.: Christine Sylvia, b. May 18, 1946; Thomas Philip, b. Apr. 28, 1948; Nicholas Ernest, b. Dec. 15, 1952. Career: Res. Dept. of Internal Med.-med. faculty, Univ. of Bern, Switz., 1939-41; research assoc.-instr. in med., dept. of med. and George Hooper Found. for Med. Research, Univ. of Calif. Med. Sch., S.F., Calif. 1941-47; Mt. Zion Hosp., S.F., 1947-48; George Piness, M.D. Allergy Group, L.A. 1948-50; pvt. practice med. (spec. allergy), Palo Alto, Calif. 1951---. Author: orig. research in allergic diseases, rheumatic fever, nephritis, auto-antibody mechanisms, etc., numerous sci. publs. Mem.: AMA, Swiss Med. Assn., Am. Assn. of Immunologists, N.Y. Acad. of Scis.; fellow, Am. Acad. of Allergy; Diplomate, Am. Bd. of Allergy and Immunology, 1974; Swiss Allergy Soc. Rec.: skiing, trout fishing. Home: 10696 Mora Dr., Los Altos, CA; Office: Medical Plaza, Welch at Pasteur, Palo Alto, CA 94304.

CAVYN-PEGE, DOROTHY LOUISE
Interior Designer
b. Detroit, Mich.; d. Frederick James and Donalda (MacDonald) Cooke; student journalism, Columbia Univ.; fine arts, UCLA; B.F.A., N.Y. Sch. of Interior Design; m. Trent Cavyn-Pege. Career: interior designer, Valerie Stevens Interiors, Birmingham, Mich. 1953-59; Cannell & Chaffin, La Jolla, 1959-62; Decorator Galleries, Sacto., 1962-69; independent color cons., designer of interiors (projects incl. residential, comml. and pub. interiors; color coord. and space planning), 1969---. Contbr. profl. journs. articles on interior design. Mem.: Am. Soc. of Interior Designers (ASID); Internat. Platform Soc. Hobbies: theatre, travel. Address: P.O.B. 64, Sacto., CA 95801.

CERULLO, MORRIS
Founder, World Evangelism, Inc.
b. Oct. 2, 1931, Passaic, N.J.; s. Joseph and Bertha (Rosenblatt) Cerullo; grad. New England Bible Coll. 1951; m. Vivian Theresa Le Pari, Newburgh, N.Y., July 28, 1951; chil.: Charles David, b. Oct. 23, 1952; Susan Darlene, b. May 24, 1954; Mark Stephen, b. Jan. 1, 1957. Career: Ordained minister, Assembly of God, 1952; pastor, Clairemont Assembly of God Ch., Clairemont, N.H. 1952-53; world crusades, 1953-59; pastor, Calvary Temple, South Bend, Ind. 1959; founder-pres.-minister, World Evangelism, Inc., San Diego (widely known for charismatic healing ministry before audiences ranging up to 200,000, cond. crusades and confs. around world), 1960---. Author: numerous books, produced two TV specials (MASADA: Monument To Freedom Breakthrough) and one 13 week TV series (Breakthrough). Mem.: Natl. Assn. of Evangelicals, Evangelical Press Assn., San Diego C. of C., San Diego Visitors and Conv. Bur. Office: P.O.B. 700, San Diego, CA 92138.

CHADWICK, CATHERINE S.
Library Director
b. Aug. 4, 1907, Spokane, Wash.; d. Howard [nd Edna (Prather) Strahorn; ed. B.A. (cum laude), Puget Sound Univ., Tacoma, Wash. 1928; B.S. (lib. sci.), Univ. Calif., Berkeley, 1934; m. Paul Chadwick, Pasadena, Calif., Apr. 22, 1935; chil.: Mrs. Alan Ungar, William H., Mrs. Richard Langdon. Career: tchr., Wash. H.S. 1928-33; Taft, Calif. 1945-49; librarian, Taft br., Kern Co. Lib. 1949-55; dir. lib. serv. State of Mont. 1955-57; ext. dir. Dept. Lib. and Archives, State of Ariz. 1957-60; dir. lib., Ventura Co. Lib. Servs. Agcy., 1961---. Contrib. to lib. periodicals, 1952---. Mem.: Am., Mont., Ariz., Pac. N.W., S.W., Lib. Assns. (many adv. coms.-bd. dirs.); pres. Calif. Lib. Assn. 1968. Home: 454 Mariposa Dr., Ventura, CA; Office: 651 E. Main St., Ventura, CA 93001.

CHALLIS, RICHARD BRACEBRIDGE
Director, Challis Galleries — Lecturer
b. Aug. 12, 1920, London, Eng.; s. Lionel S. and Eileen C. (Owen) Challis; ed. King's Coll., Wimbledon, 1934-37; Coll. of Aeron. Engring, Chelsea, 1937-39; chil.: Diane Leslie, b. Sept. 3, 1957; David Richard, b. May 7, 1957; Career: Art Dir., L.A. Home Show, 1965-67; Founder-dir. Challis Galleries, Laguna Beach; Lectr. on art, "Mkt. of Fine Art," "Bus. Aspects of the Arts," Univ. of Calif. Sym., Irvine, 1968, 69; auctioneer, many benefits, incl. So. Coast Comm. Hosp., Laguna Mus. of Art, Chil's. Home Soc., KCET, 1969, flood victims, others. Irvine Co. host, series of 18 pgms. on "How to Collect Art," 1973. Capt., Adj., Brit. Army (serv. Europe and Africa), 1939-46. Mem.: Art Dealers Assn. of So. Calif., Beverly Hills. Studio: 1390 S. Coast Hwy., Laguna Beach, CA 92652.

CHAMBERLIN, HUGH ROBERTS
Advertising Executive
b. Jan. 2, 1927, Baton Rouge, La.; s. Hugh and Margaret (Roberts) Chamberlin; ed. B.S. (physics), Principia Coll. 1949; M.B.A., Harvard Grad. Sch. of Bus. Adm. 1952; m. Marilyn Cline, La Jolla, Calif., July 26, 1952; chil.: Douglas Geoffrey, b. July 6, 1960; Candalyn Holly, b. May 10, 1961. Career: Brand mgmt., Drug Prods. Div., Proctor & Gamble, Cincinnati, Oh., 1952-56; assoc. adv. mgr., Carnation Co., L.A., 1956-57, adv. mgr. 1957-61; exec. v.p., Planautics Corp., Encinitas, Calif. 1961-62, pres.-chmn. bd. dirs., 1962-64; gen. adv. mgr., Canadian Div., Carnation Co., L.A. 1964---; dir. San Diego Scientific Corp. Speaker, L.A. Adv. Workshop, 1967. Radar and electronics pgm., U.S.N., 1945-46, WW II; Capt. S.S. Algiers, 1949-50. Awards: Top Promotions of Yr. Award by Food Topics Publs. 1956-57, 1957-58; judge, Adv. Lulu Awards, 1966-67; Mem.: Exec. com., Judge Samuel W. Green Assn., 1959-64, chmn. 1964; pres. Westwood Toastmasters Club, 1959; Principia Assn., Berkeley Hall Patrons Assn., Harvard Club, Encino Tennis Club, Rancho Santa Fe Tennis Club. Republican. Christian Science (chmn. bd. trustees, 38th Ch. Christ, Sci., L.A.). Rec.: tennis, water skiing, surfing. Home: 6324 Tahoe Dr., Hollywood, CA 90028; Office: 5045 Wilshire Blvd., L.A., CA 90036.

CHAMBERS, JACK A.
Psychologist
b. Feb. 26, 1932, Hamilton, Ohio; s. Glen S. and H. Edna Chambers; B.A., Univ. of Miami, 1954; M.A., Univ. Cincinnati, 1955; Ph.D., Mich. State Univ., 1964; m. A. Ruth Coe, Aug. 24, 1957; chil.: Melissa Ann, Wendy Colleen. Career: dir. of personnel, Univ. So. Florida, Tampa, 1960-66, dir. Computer Research Center, asst.

Dean of Adminstrn. 1966-72; prof. of psychology and dir. of Computer Ednl. Center, Mansfield (Pa.) State Coll. 1972-73; prof. of psychology and dir., Center for Information Processing, Cal. State Univ., Fresno, 1974---; also sr. partner, Chambers, Sprecher and Assocs. 1978---. Home: 1637 W. Morris Ave., Fresno, CA 93711; Office: Center for Information Processing, CSU, Fresno, CA 93740.

CHAMPION, JOHN C.
Writer · Director — Producer
b. Oct. 13, 1923, Denver, Colo.; s. Lee R. and Alice (Carr) Champion (nurse with AEF, 1918); desc. Lee R. Champion (dec.), former justice, Colo. Supreme Ct.; ed. Stanford Univ., 1945; m. Madelon F. Green, 1951, Las Vegas; chil.: John Jr., Robert, Gina. Career: Formed Champion Pictures Inc., 1946; wrote and prod. numerous features for Allied Artists, and subsequently for Paramount, Columbia, United Artists and Universal Studios; head writer and prod. of "Laramie," creator of "McHale's Navy," 1961; won National Cowboy Hall of Fame Award for directing and producing "Mustang Country" for Universal, 1976; chmn. of bd., Champion Service Industries; author novel, "The Hawks of Noon," David McKay Co., N.Y., 1965. Mil. pilot, Air Transport Command. Mem.: Directors Guild of Am.; Writers Guild of Am.; Authors League of Am. Office: 680 Wilshire Place, Suite 407, L.A., CA 9000

CHAN, FLORENCE MAY HARN
Librarian
b. Victoria, B.C., Canada; d. Jack Nam and Eva (Lowe) Yipp; B.A., Univ. of British Columbia, 1953; M.L.S., Univ. of Cal., Berkeley, 1956; M.A., San Jose State Univ., 1976; chil.: Jonathan Hoyt Chan, b. 1960; Barry Alan Chan, b. 1963. Career: circulation/reference asst., Victoria (B.C.) Pub. Lib., 1953-54; cataloger, Golden Gate Coll., S.F., 1956-67; catalog/ref. lib., Coll. of San Mateo, 1957-60; head libm., Canada Coll., Redwood City, 1968---. Pub. "Using Library Resources," a worktext, 1976. Mem.: secty., Canada Faculty Senate; secty., Minority Faculty Com.; chmn., San Mateo Comm. Coll. Dist. Lib./Media Caucus; San Mateo Co. Suicide Prevention Center Lib. Com.; San Jose State Univ. Dept. of Instrnl. Tech. Advis. Com.; ALA; Calif. Lib. Assn.; Community Coll. Media Assn.; Calif. Media and Lib. Educators Assn.; Phi Kappa Phi honor soc. Episcopalian, mem. Ch. Women. Hobbies: photog., sewing, piano, travel. Office: Canada Coll., 4200 Farm Hill Blvd., Redwood City, CA 94061.

CHAN, JOHN KEUNG
Physician
b. Dec. 5, 1941, Shanghai, China; s. Joseph C.F. and Kim-Yee W.V. Chan; M.D., Nat. Taiwan Univ. Sch. of Med., 1967; m. Salena Fond, June 27, 1970, Palo Alto; chil.: John K., Jr., b. Aug. 2, 1972; Jerry, b. Apr. 6, 1975; James, b. May 3, 1977. Career: UCLA Med. Center, 1970-72; L.A. City-USC Med. Center, 1972-74; pvt. practice med., 1975---; instr. in pathology, L.A. city-USC Med. Center, 1973. Dir. Calif. Diagnostic Lab., Gardena, 1977---. Rec.: tennis, movies. Home: 1854 Via Del Rey, So. Pasadena, CA 91030; Office: 500 N. Garfield Ave., Suite 210, Monterey Park, CA 91754.

CHAN, LOREN BRIGGS
Professor of History
b. Sept. 10, 1943, Palo Alto; s. Shau Wing and Anna Mae (Chin) Chan; A.B., Stanford Univ., 1965, A.M., 1966; Ph.D., UCLA, 1971; m. Frances Anastasia Chow, Apr. 19, 1975, Palo Alto; dau. Karen Monique, b. Jan. 27, 1976. Career: tchg. asst., UCLA 1968-69; tchg. assoc., UCLA 1969-70; lectr., Cal. State Univ., Northridge, 1970-71; lectr. to assoc. prof., San Jose State Univ., 1971---; adjunct lectr., Univ. Santa Clara, 1977-78. Author: Sagebrush Statesman, 1973; Chinese-American History Reader and Workbook, 1976; New Light on a New Land, 1977. Christian Sci.; treas., v.p. 1978-79, Christian Sci. orgn., univ. Hobbies: philately, amateur radio. Rec.: swimming. Office: 125 S. 7th St., DMH 134, San Jose, CA 95192.

CHANDLER, HARRISON GRAY OTIS
President, Chandis Securities
b. Feb. 12, 1903, L.A., Calif.; s. Harry (L.A. publ. and civic leader) and Marian (Otis) Chandler; grandson of Gen. Harrison Gray Otis; ed. A.B., Stanford Univ., 1926; m. Martha Marsh, Dec. 28, 1957. Career: Times-Mirror Press, 1935, asst. to gen. mgr. 1937, gen. mgr. 1938, v.p. 1941, pres. 1960-68; dir., Times-Mirror Co. 1952---; pres.-chmn. bd. Chandis Securities Co., 1969---. Lt., Lt. Comdr., USNR, 1942-46, armed guard ofcr., merchant tanker to

Australia; Ofc. of Pub. Rels., Navy Dept., Wash., D.C.; tr. film and mot. pic. br. under Dep. Chief of Naval Opns., WW II. Mem.: dir. Lithographers Natl. Assn., 1949; dir. Welfare Fed. of L.A. Area, 1949; dir. Met. Rec. and Youth Serv. Council, 1949; cons. Printing Inds. Assocs., Inc.; YMCA; Repub. Assocs.; Delta Kappa Epsilon; Calif. Club, Sunset Club. Protestant. Hobby: photog., hunting, gardening. Home: 801 Singing Wood Dr., Arcadia, CA 91006; Office: 550 S. Flower St., L.A., CA 90017.

CHANDLER, OTIS
Publisher — CEO, Los Angeles Times
b. Nov. 23, 1927, L.A., Calif.; s. Norman and Dorothy (Buffum) Chandler; grandson of Harry Chandler, founder L.A. Times; ed. B.A., Stanford Univ., 1950; m. Marilyn Brant, L.A., Calif., June 18, 1951; chil.: Norman Brant, b. May 14, 1952; Harry Brant, b. June 5, 1953; Cathleen, b. Aug. 23, 1955; Michael Otis, b. Apr. 21, 1958; Carolyn, b. Aug. 30, 1963. Career: Mgmt. trainee, L.A. Times, 1953-60; publisher, 1960---; v.p. Times-Mirror Co. 1961---; dir. 1962---; pres. Newspapers & Forest Prod. Div., 1965---, Sr. v.p. (Times-Mirror), 1966-68; vice chmn. (Times-Mirror), 1968---; publisher & chief. exec. ofcr., L.A. Times, 1977---. Midshipman, USNR, 1946-48; ofcr. USAF 1951-53. Mem.: Delta Kappa Epsilon (Stanford), 1950. Rec.: surfboarding, fishing, hunting. Home: 1048 Oak Grove Place, San Marino, CA; Office: L.A. Times, T-M Square, L.A., CA 90053.

CHANEY, EARLYNE CANTRELL
Founder — Minister -- Director, Astara
b. Dec. 1, 1916, Dallas, Tex.; d. Edgar Earl and Mae (Wilson) Cantrell; ed. H.S. and bus. coll.; stu. for ministry, 1946-51; m. Dr. Robert Galen Chaney, Eaton Rapids, Mich., Oct. 4, 1947; dau. Sita Earlyne, b. Feb. 11, 1956. Career: Dramatic actress and singer, 1940-46; co-founder-minister-dir., Astara, Inc., L.A., 1951---. Author: relig. and philosophic studies distr. to Astara's students around the world (translated into French), 1953---. Recordings of inspiration meditations for world-wide distr. 1960---. Author: "Remembering, the Autobiography of A Mystic." Mem.: OES, Eaton Rapids, Mich., 1948. Republican. Hobby: writing. Rec.: going to movies. Home: 1534 N. Euclid Ave., Upland, CA 91786; Office: 800 W. Arrow Hwy., Upland, CA 91786.

CHANEY, ROBERT GALEN
Founder — Minister — Director, Astara, Inc.
b. Oct. 27, 1913, La Porte, Ind.; s. Clyde Galen and Maree Frances Chaney; ed. H.S., Greenfield, Oh. 1931; Miami Univ., Oxford, Oh. 1931-33; m. Earlyne Cantrell, Eaton Rapids, Mich., Oct. 4, 1947; dau.: Sita Earlyne, b. Feb. 11, 1956. Career: Sales and adv. 1933-38; ministerial writing and radio activities, 1938---; co-founder Astara, Inc. 1951, minister and dir., 1951---. Created radio pgm. "Quest Eternal," 1959. Author: numerous writings and records on mystic and esoteric philosophy distr. throughout the world. Mem.: Worshipful Master, Masonic Lodge, Eaton Rapids, Mich., 1947; pres. Kiwanis Club, Eaton Rapids, Mich.; 1947; Delta Kappa Epsilon. Republican. Hobby: sports, music. Home: 1534 N. Euclid Ave., Upland, CA 91786; Office: 800 W. Arrow Highway, Upland, CA 91786.

CHANG, PETER A., JR.
District Attorney, Santa Cruz County
b. Feb. 1, 1937, Honolulu, Hawaii; s. Peter A. and Helen Chang; ed. A.B. (U.S. Hist.), Stanford Univ., 1958; LL.B., 1961; m. Maybelle Chang, S.F., 1955. Career: Dep. Dist. Atty., Monterey Co., 1961-64, chief trial atty. 1964-66; elected Dist. Atty. of Santa Cruz Co. 1966, 69 (first Dist. Atty. of Oriental extraction to be elected in Continental U.S.; prosecuted all maj. felonies out of Soledad Prison, 1962-66). Mem.: adv., bd. dirs. numerous law enforcement and charitable orgns. Hobby: musician (trumpet soloist). Office: Courthouse, 701 Ocean St., Santa Cruz, CA 95060.

CHANG, PING-NAN
Consul General of the Republic of China
b. Feb. 2, 1931, China; s. Chin-en and Su-lan (Pai) Chang; B.A., Coll. of Arts, Natl. Taiwan Univ.; M.A., Grad. Sch. of Diplomacy, Natl. Cheng-chi Univ., Taipei; research, Far Eastern Inst., Univ. Wash., Seattle; m. Susan Hsiao, Sept. 6, 1959, Taipei, Taiwan, Republic of China; chil.: Monica, Martina, Malachy, Madeline. Career: Vice Consul and Consul, Chinese Consulate General, Seattle, 1962-69; div. chief, Dept. of East Asian and Pacific Affairs, Ministry of Foreign Affairs, 1969-71; Spec. Asst. to Minister of Foreign Affairs, 1971-74; Consul General, L.A., 1974---. Mil. two years as 2nd Lt., Army of Repub. of China. Mem.: Kiwanis Club of L.A.; World Affairs C

Council of L.A.; Town Hall of L.A.; Marina City Club; L.A. Club; Internatl. Club of L.A. Catholic. Hobby: photog. Home: 434 S. Irving Blvd., L.A., CA 90020; Office: 3660 Wilshire Blvd., No. 1050, L.A., CA 90010.

CHAO, MEI-PA
Choral Conductor — Voice Professor
b. Aug. 29, 1907, Ningpo, Chekiang, China; s. S.S. and S.C. (Yao) Chao; B.A., Univ. of Shanghai, 1929; Laureat du Premier Prix, Conservatoire Royal de Bruxelles, 1933; postgrad studies in Paris, London, Siena; m. Lillian Woo, June 3, 1941, Shanghai, China; chil.: Mei-Wah (1st prize piano competition, Brussels); Winston (Prof., U. of Wis., 4 master degrees); Lydia (M.A., S.D. Univ.); Clara (M.A., USC). Career: Head of National Conservatory of Music, 1936-42; China dir., N.W. Conservatory of Music, 1942-45; dir. of music: Nat. Coll. of Fine Arts, Peking 1948-48; Hong Kong Acad. of Music, 1965-69; St. Stephen's Girls' Coll., Ying Wah Girls' Coll., True Light Girls' Sch., 1948-69. Immigrated, U.S.A. 1969, naturalized, 1976. Prof. of Voice, Conductor, Simpson Coll., S.F., 1969---; voice prof., San Jose City Coll., 1970---. Also choir dir., Los Alton Union Presbyterian Ch. Conductor: Peiping Oratorio Soc. (and pres.), 1947; Peiping Music Assn. (chmn.) 1947; Hangchow Choral Union 1926; Shanghai Choirs' Union 1937; Shanghai Crescendo Chorus 1939; Hong Kong Schs. Music Assn. (chmn.) 1955-69; Hong Kong Crescendo Choral Soc., Melba Girls' Choir, 1962-69; Combined Christian Choir 1963. Author: La Cloche Jaune; The Yellow Bell; Technique and Art of Choral Conducting; Songs Evergreen for Juniors and Seniors, Two Vol. 1966; Art of Singing 1968; A Guide to Chinese Music 1969. Awards: Sino-Am. Cultural, 1935; Outstanding Educator of Am. 1975. Rec.: gardening, travel, reading. Home: 1385 Deroche Ct., Sunnyvale, CA 94087.

CHAPPLE, JOHN LOUIS
Data Products Company Executive
b. July 23, 1943, Daytona Beach, Fla.; s. Wreford and Mary (Cobb) Chapple; B.A., Stanford Univ., 1965; M.B.A., 1969; J.D., 1970; admitted to Calif. Bar, 1971; m. Stephanie Ashby, June 25, 1966, Reno, Nev.; chil.: Michelle, b. Feb. 6, 1967; John B., Nov. 5, 1970. Career: Counsel, Ampex Corp., Redwood City, 1970-72; Gen. Counsel, Itel Corp., 1972-74; also: treasurer, Itel Field Services Corp.; dir., Moran Lanig & Duncan, Inc., pres., F.W.L. Inc.; pres. Indian Pines, Inc., 1972-74; Vice pres., & gen. counsel, Itel Corp., Data Products Group, S.F., 1974---. Profl. football player, San Francisco 49ers, 1964-66; Mem.: Stanford Law Assn.; Stanford Bus. Assn.; Stanford Block "S" Soc.; Underwriting Mem. of Lloyd's of London. Named by UPI to NEA All Am. Team, 1964; Named by UPI to NFL All Am. Rookie Team, 1965; Named by UPI and AP to All Coast Football Team. Republican. Presbyterian. Rec.: Tennis. Home: 120 Glenwood Ave., Atherton, CA; Office: No. 1 Embarcadero Center, S.F., CA 94111.

CHARLEY, PHILIP JAMES
President, Truesdail Laboratories
b. Aug. 18, 1921, Melbourne, Australia; s. Walter George and Constance (Macdonald) Charley; nephew to Sir Philip Charley, Kt., (NSW, Australia); B.S. M.E., Univ. of Wis., 1943; M.S. m.e., USC, 1947; Ph.D., chem., 1960; m. Katherine Truesdail, Jan. 31, 1948, So. Pasadena; chil.: James Alan, Linda Kay, William John. Career: Came to USA 1939, naturalized citizen 1948. Test engineer, General Electric Co., Schenectady, N.Y., 1943-44; lectr. in engring., USC, 1947; project engr., Standard Oil Co. of Calif. (El Segundo, Richmond, San Francisco, Livermore, Oak Ridge, Tenn.), 1948-55; research assoc., USC, 1960-68; vice pres. Truesdail Laboratories, 1955-72, pres. 1972---. Mem.: dir., West. Independent Research Labs., L.A.; chmn. Western Div. Am. Council of Independent Labs. 1945-47; mem. exec. com. 1946---. Mil.: Lt., Royal Canadian Electrical & Mech. Engrs. 1944-46. Recipient, Devel. Award, 1960. Regis. profl. engr. Calif., Ariz., Nev. Mem.: Beta Theta Pi; Sigma Xi; Phi Kappa Phi; Tau Beta Pi; Rotarian (L.A. No. 5). Congregationalist. Hobbies: fishing, gardening. Home: 1906 Calle de los Alamos, San Clemente, CA 92672; Office: 4101 N. Figueroa St., L.A., CA 90065.

CHASE, H. COCHRANE
Advertising Company Executive
b. Feb. 6, 1932, Berwyn, Ill.; s. Henry C. and Roselyn L. (Scott) Chase; B.A., Wesleyan Univ., Conn. 1954, Phi Beta Kappa; m. Janis Kueber, June 19, 1954, Hinsdale, Ill.; chil.: Catherine Ann, b. Dec. 27, 1955; Anthony Scott, b. Nov. 23, 1958; Lisa Marie, b. July 14, 1962. Career: with Steel Warehousing Corp. div. Jessup Steel Co., 1956-63; Ducommun Metals & Supply Co., 1964-65;

Newport Advertising, 1965; founder, chmn. of bd., Cochrane Chase & Co., Inc. (advt., mktg., pub. rels. firm) 1966---. Co-author: The Marketing Problem Solver. USNR, 1954-56. Roman Catholic. Hobby: sailing. Home: 2162 Papaya Dr., La Habra, CA 90631; Office: 660 Newport Center Dr., Newport Beach, CA 92663.

CHATHAM, C. CHARLES
Company President — Educator — Author
b. Feb. 15, 1913, Chippewa Falls, Wis.; s. Meade Storey and Aurilla Maude (Dobbyn) Cheatham; desc.: William Pitt, Lord Adm. Nelson; Henry Clay, Gen. Meade; studied Inst. of Accountancy, Shawnee, Okla., 1931-35; m. Goldie Mae Norton, Mar. 31, 1934, Okemah, Okla.; chil.: Meade Edward, b. Dec. 19, 1937; Sharon Kay Terranova, b. Aug. 23, 1944; Charles Norton, b. Aug. 20, 1946. Career: accounting instr., Insti. of Accountancy, 1931-37, Dean, 1937-39; Dept. head, War Contract Dept., Tech. Products Co., Hollywood and Inglewood, 1940-45; pres., Automotive Wheel Balancer Corp., Burbank, 1945-48; partner, House of Chatham, Realtors, 1944---; Pres., Chatham Educational Corp., Glendale, 1970---. Chmn. bd., Research Inst. for Counselists, Inc., Glendale, 1974---. Author: Winning the Love and Loyalty of your Children, 1979; Educational Seminars (5), 1969---. Radio writer and actor, 1930-33. Mem. Sertoma Club of Glendale, 1952---, pres. 1967, 1968. Home: 1532 Moreno Dr., Glendale, CA; Office: 517 W. Glenoaks Blvd., Glendale, OK 91202.

CHAVEZ, CESAR ESTRADA
President, United Farm Workers of America
b. Mar. 31, 1927, farm near Yuma, Ariz.; s. Librado and Juana (Estrada) Chavez; completed 8th grade; m. Helen Fabela, Oct. 22, 1948, Delano, Calif.; chil.: Fernando, Sylvia Delgado, Linda Rodriguez, Eloise Hernandez, Anna Ybarra, Paul, Elizabeth Villarino, Anthony. Career: organizer, Community Service Orgn., 1952-62; founder, dir., Natl. Farm Workers Assn., 1962-66; dir., United Farm Workers Organizing Com., AFL-CIO, 1966-72; dir., pres. (successor to NFWA) United Farm Workers of Am., AFL-CIO, 1972---. USN, 1945-47, Pacific Theater. Roman Catholic. Home-Office: La Paz, Keene, CA 93531.

CHAVEZ, VICTOR E.
Attorney at Law
b. Aug. 28, 1930; s. Raymond C. and Sarah (Baca) Chavez; B.S., Loyola Univ., L.A., 1953, J.D., Loyola Univ. Law Sch., 1959; chil.: Victoria Marie, Catherine Ann, Stephanie Sue, Christopher Andrew, Robert John, Elizabeth Claire. Career: assoc., Early, Maslach, Foran & Williams, 1960-69; partner, law firm of Pomerantz and Chavez, 1969---. Mem.: Com. of Bar Examiners, State Bar of Calif., 1972-74; vice-chmn., 1974; pres. L.A. chpt. Am. Bd. of Trial Advocates, 1979; pres. Mexican-American Bar Assn., 1971. 1st Lt., USAF, 1953-55. Office: 3700 Wilshire Blvd., Suite 575, L.A., CA 90010.

CHEADLE, VERNON I.
University Chancellor Emeritus
b. Feb. 6, 1910, Salem, S. Dak.; s. Henry Melvin and Inez Eleanor (Engleman) Cheadle; ed. B.A., Miami Univ. 1932; M.A., Harvard Univ., 1934, Ph.D. 1936; LL.D., Miami Univ. 1964; LL.D., Univ. of R.I., 1974; m. Mary Jenkins Low, Pawkatuck, Conn., Dec. 23, 1939; s. William Gerald, b. May 2, 1953. Career: Prof. (botany), dir. grad. studies, R.I. State Coll., 1941-44, 1946-52; prof. (botany), dept. chmn., Univ. of Calif., Davis, 1952-62, acting v-chancellor, 1961-62; Chancellor, Univ. of Calif., Santa Barbara, 1962-77. Contrib. tech. articles to profl. journs. Lt. (s.g.), USNR, 1944-46, WW II. Awards: Outstanding Civilian Serv. Medal, Certificate of Merit from Botanical Soc. of Am. Mem.: Am. Acad. Arts & Scis.; Am. Inst. Biological Soc., Am. Soc. Naturalists; Am. Soc. Plant Taxonomists, Internat. Soc. Plant Morphologists, Soc. for Stu. of Evolution, Soc. for Stu. of Growth and Development, Fellow, Calif. Acad. of Scis. 1970; Torrey Botanical Club; pres. Sigma Xi, Davis, Calif. 1956-57; pres. Botanical Soc. Am., 1961; Phi Delta Theta, Phi Kappa Phi, Phi Beta Kappa, Santa Barbara Club, Commonwealth Club of Calif. Presbyterian.

CHERNY, SAMUEL N.
Physician — Internal Med. — Diabetes — Endocrinology
b. Jan. 14, 1944, Newark, N.J.; s. Morris Ralph and Dorothy (Livingston) Cherny; B.A. in Zoology, Rutgers Univ., N.J., 1966; M.D., Downstate Med. Center, State Univ. of N.Y., 1970; m. Sharon Rosenzweig, June 29, 1969, Huntington, Long Is.; chil.: Dara Michele, b. Aug. 14, 1971; Rachel Lynn, b. July 23, 1975. Career: Med. intern. State Univ.-Kings Co. Hosp. Center, Brooklyn, N.Y., 1970-71; resident, 1971-72; Internist for Navajo Nation, U.S. Pub. Health/Indian Health Service, Gallup,

N. Mex., 1972-74; 2d year resident, Vanderbilt Univ. Hosp., Nashville, Tenn., 1974-75; Fellow in Endocrinology, Albany Med. Center, N.Y., 1977; pvt. practice (solo) in Internal Med., Diabetes and Endocrinology, 1977---; also assoc. attending physician: Cedars-Sinai Med. Center; Midway Hosp. Attend. physician, Century City Hosp. Diplomates: Nat. Bd. of Med. Examiners, 1971; Am. bd. of Internal Med., 1976. Recipient: Physician's Recognition Award, 1977; U.S. Pub. Health Service Summer Fellowship Program: 1967, 68, 69. Contrbr. to med. journs. Mem.: AMA; CMA; L.A. Co. Med. Assn.; Am., Calif., and L.A. Socs. of Internal Med.; Am. Diabetes Assn.; Am. Heart Assn. Mem. Phi Delta Epsilon, grad. club of L.A.; Beta Beta Beta, 1966; Alpha Omega Alpha. Jewish. Hobby: photog. Home: 9627 Beverlywood St., L.A., CA 90034; Office: Century City Med. Plaza, 2080 Century Park E., Suite 1108, L.A., CA 90067.

CHILDS, BARNEY SANFORD
Composer – Professor of Composition
b. feb. 13, 1926, Spokane, Wash.; s. Robert Barney and Alice (Sanford) Childs; grandson of Fernando Sanford, original faculty mem., physics, when Dr. Dr. Jordan began Stanford Univ.; B.A., Univ. Nev., 1949; B.A. (w/honors), Oxford Univ., 1951, M.A., 1955; Ph.D., Stanford Univ., 1959; div.; chil.: Dirje Andres, b. Dec. 10, 1955; Margaret Alice, b. May 2, 1963. Career: faculty mem. Univ. of Ariz., English Dept. 1956-65; Dean, Deep Springs Coll. 1965-69; composer-in-residence, Wisconsin Coll. Conservatory, 1969-71; faculty fellow in music and lit., Johnston Coll., Univ. of Redlands, 1971---; prof. of composition, Sch. of Music, Univ. of Redlands, 1974---; Composer of 140 works, fifty published, ten recorded; co-editor, Contemporary Composers on Contemporary Music, Holt, 1971; co-editor, "The New Orchestration" series, Univ. Calif. Press; contbr. scholarly articles: Perspectives of New Music, Proceedings of the Am. Soc. of Univ. Composers, Source, The Composer, etc. Awards: Rhodes Scholar, 1949; Fellow, The MacDowell Colony, 1963, 68, 70, 74, 78. AUS, 1945-56. Mem.: Nat. Council, Am. Soc. of Univ. Composers, 1968-71, 1974-77, exec. com. 1971-74; nat. advis. bd., Am. Composers Alliance, 1976---; advis. bd., Am. Music. Soc. (England), 1968---. Home: 864 Hartzell, Redlands, CA 92373; Office: Sch. of Music, Univ. Redlands, Redlands, CA 92373.

CHILINGAR, GEORGE V.
Professor of Engineering
b. July 22, 1929, Tbilisi, Ga.; s. Varos and Klavdia (Gorchak) Chilingarian; ed. B.E., USC 1949, M.S. 1950, Ph.D. 1956; m. Yelba M. Salmeron, L.A., June 12, 1953; chil.: Eleanore Elizabeth, b. Mar. 12, 1954; Modesto George, b. Dec. 12, 1956; Mark Steven, b. Jan. 16, 1960. Career: Asst. prof., USC 1956-59, assoc. prof. 1959-70, prof. 1970---; pres. Electroosmotics, Inc., L.A., 1963-66; dir., Archimedes Circle, 1967-72. Author: 300 publs. (books, articles, sci. reviews). Maj., USAFR (active); chief, Petroleum Chem. Lab., USAF 1954-56. Awards: Exec. and Profl. Hall of Fame; listed, various biog. achievement publs. Mem.: Geochem. Soc., Am. Inst. Min. and Metal. Engrs., Am. Geophysical Union, Geol. Soc. Am., Am. Soc. Engring. Edn., So. Calif. and N.Y. Acad. Scis., Am. Assn. Petroleum geol., Skull and Dagger, Phi Kappa Phi, Tau Beta Pi, Sigma Phi Delta, Sigma Gamma Epsilon, Pi Epsilon Tau. Home: 101 S. Windsor Blvd., L.A., CA 90004; Office: Univ. of So. Calif., Univ. Park, L.A., CA 90007.

CHO, ALFRED CHIH-FANG
Scientist -- Engineer
b. Dec. 31, 1921, Shanghai, China; s. Te Chi and Pao-Chen (Wong) Cho; B.Sc., Univ. of Shanghai, 1943; M.A., Univ. Texas, 1950, Ph.D., physics, 1959; m. Louisa Ching, Sept. 14, 1957, Ft. Worth, Tex.; chil.: Christine Seming, b. Apr. 9, 1959; Sharlene Sewah, b. Mar. 20, 1962. Career: Engring. Asst., Shanghai Telephone Co. 1943, 48; spec. instr., dept. of mathematics, Univ. Texas, Austin, 1953-57; sr. structures engr. & sr. physicist, General Dynamics, Ft. Worth, Tex., 1957-62; adjunct prof. of Physics, Texas Christian Univ., Ft. Worth, 1958-62; sr. tech. specialist, supr., mem. tech. staff, Rockwell Internat. Space Div. 1962-69, 1973---; sr. research spec., Lockheed Calif. Co., Burbank, 1969-71; engring. spec., Litton Ship Systems, Culver City, 1971-72; mem. tech. staff, Hughes Aircraft Co., Space & Communication Group, El Segundo, CA 1972-73. Contbr. Journ. of Acoustical Soc., 1958. Mem.: Sigma Pi Sigma, Sigma Xi (research hon. soc.); Acoustical Soc. of Am.; British Acoustical Soc. Hobbies: photog., classical music. Home: 6263 Roundhill Dr., Whittier, CA 90601; Office: Rockwell Internat., Space Div., 12214 Lakewood Blvd., Downey, CA 90241.

CHOW, DAVID T.
Importer-Exporter
b. Jan. 10, 1909, Chefoo, No. China, s. Dr. C.P. and Mu (Shee) Chow; B.A., Peking Univ., 1931; postgrad., Tokyo Comml. Coll., 1935-37; M.S., Univ. of Colo., 1947; hon. Ph.D., The China Academy, Taipei, Taiwan, 1973. Career: estab. Calif. residence 1939; became U.S. citizen 1951; Instr., Oriental Lang. Dept. Univ. of Calif., Berkeley, 1942-44; instr. Army Training Program, Univ. of Chicato, 1944-45; instr., Navy Language Sch., Monterey, 1947-48; owner, David Chow & Company, Inc., (importer-exporter: wholesale home furnishings), L.A., 1948, Pres. 1968---. Awards: Nat. Award of Achievement, U.S. Dept. of Commerce, Minority Bus. Enterprise, 1972; D.A.R. Am. Medal, 1974. Mem.: dir., Fgn. Trade Assn. of So. Calif.; adv. com., Mayor of L.A.; asst. to the pres. Chinese Am. Citizens Alliance; pres., L.A. Chinatown C. of C.; bd. chmn. Chinese Cultural Soc. of L.A.; bd. chmn. Hwa Pei Benevolent Assn.; Bd. chmn. New Kwong Tai Press, L.A.; founder, Gee Tuck Sam Tuck Benevolent Assn. Political Mem.: Republican Nat., State, Central and Co. Coms.; advisor Overseas Chinese Affairs Com., Republic of China; pres., L.A. Co. Republican All Nationalities Council; Chmn., Campaign Coms. for Eisenhower-Nixon 1952, 56; Goodwin Knight for Gov., 1954; Wm. Knowland for Gov. 1958; Richard M. Nixon for Pres. 1960, 68, 72; Thomas Kuchel for Sen. 1962; Barry Goldwater for Pres., 1964; Ronald Reagan for Gov. 1966. Mem. Gov. Reagan's Manpower Policy Task Force. Mem.: 1st Chinese Baptist Ch. Rec.: football, Kung-fu. Home: 520 Bernard St., L.A., CA 90012; Office: 514 Bernard St., L.A., CA 90012.

CHOY, EUGENE KINN
Architect
b. Mar. 5, 1912, Canton, China; s. Kinn Chow and Shee (Wong) Choy; bro. Allan Kinn Choy, noted arch., Bakersfield, Calif.; ed. B.Ar., USC, 1939; m. Lucille Fong, San Diego, June 26, 1941; chil.: Barton, b. Oct. 28, 1943; Reece, b. July 28, 1946. Career: Engr., U.S. Army Corps of Engrs., L.A. 1941-43; test engr., Hughes Aircraft Co., Culver City, 1943-45; chief engr., Marsh, Smith & Powell, archs. 1945-47; pvt. practice arch., L.A. 1947---; Barton Choy, Arch. Partner, 1971---; arch. works incl.: Thompson Ramo Wooldridge, Inc. Research Lab. bldgs. 1956; Brander House, 1959; Visitors Center, U.S. Corps of Engrs., L.A.; Arch. examiner, City of L.A. 1957. Awards: L.A. Beautiful Award for Cathay Bank Bldg., L.A. 1966; 3rd prize award, Natl. Crane Ideas Competition. Mem.: bd. dirs., Lark Ellen Home for Boys; AIA 1947---, chmn. exhib. com. 1962, corporate, 1947---; past dir., Lions Club, 1953---; pres., L.A. Lions Host Club, 1975-76, zone chmn., Dist. 4L-1, Lions Club, 1978-79; Mason. Methodist. Hobby: photog. Rec.: golf. Home: 3027 Castle St., L.A., CA; Office: 2410 Beverly Blvd., L.A., CA 90057.

CHRISTENSEN, DONN WAYNE
Insurance Executive
b. Apr. 9, 1941, Atlantic City, N.J.; s. Donald Frazier and Dorothy (Ewing) Christensen; desc. Sir Walter Scott (Scottish poet, novelist, hist., biographer); ed. B.S., Univ. of Santa Clara, 1964; m. Mei Ling Fill, L.A., June 18, 1976; chil.: Donn Wayne, Jr., b. Feb. 18, 1964; Lisa Shawn, b. Jan. 18, 1965. Career: West Coast div. mgr. Ford Motor Co. 1964-65; Conn. Mutual Life Ins. Co. 1965-68; pres. D. Wayne Christensen & Assocs. 1968---. Bd. dirs.: Hippovideo, Inc., L.A.; Research Devel. Sys., Inc., Pasa.; Duarte Comm. Drug Abuse Council; pres. Woodlyn Property Owners' Assn. 1972-73. Awards: Man of the Yr., L.A. Gen. Agts. and Mgrs. Assn. 1969-72-73-74-75. Mem.: pres. Foothill Comm. Concert Assn. 1970-73; assoc. Soc. of Pension Actuaries; Natl., State Life Underwriters' Assns.; Masters Club of Conn. Mutual Life Ins. Co. 1969---. Hobbies: numismatics, sports, tennis, basketball. Home: 10841 Savona Rd., L.A., CA 90024; Office: 1015 Wilshire Blvd., L.A., CA 90017.

CHRISTY, MYRON M.
Business Executive
b. May 26, 1917, Seattle, Wash.; s. Harold V. and Elsie A. (Jensen) Christy; ed. Univ. of Wash.; B.B.A. (with highest distinction), Univ. of Minn. 1948; A.M.P., Harvard Bus. Sch. 1955; m. Mary J. Deeds, Dec. 28, 1945; chil.: Mrs. Michael (Susan Ellen) Bottles, b. June 24, 1947; John Harold, b. May 4, 1948. Career: Gen. Elec. Supply Corp. 1935-38; Alaska Elec. Light and Power Co. 1938-41; Merchants Motor Freight, 1946-48; Western Pac. Railroad Co., S.F., 1949---: travel acct. 1949, auditor and asst. to gen. auditor, 1950, exec. asst. 1950-54, asst. to pres. 1954-55, asst. to v.p. 1956-57, supt. Western Div. 1958, exec. asst. to pres. 1960-62, exec. v.p.-dir. 1962, exec. v.p.-dir.-gen. mgr. 1964, pres. 1965-73; U.S. Leasing Internat. 1973---: v.p.-dir. subsidiaries and affiliates:

Alameda Belt Line, Central Calif. Traction Co., Delta Finance Co. Ltd., Sacto. No. Ry., Standard Realty and Devel. Co.; pres.-dir.: Oakland Terminal Ry., Salt Lake City Union Depot and R.R. Co., Western Pac. Co.; v.p.-dir.-exec. com. Tidewater So. Ry. Co. Dir.: Bank of Calif., N.A.; Calif. Liquid Gas Corp.; Fruit Growers Express Co.; Golden Gate Chap., Am. Natl. Red. Cross, S.F.; trustee: Golden Gate Coll., S.F.; S.F. Bay Area Council; United Bay Area Crusade. Lt. Col., U.S. Army Transportation Corps, 1941-45, WW II. Mem.: Am. Assn. of R.R. Supts.; Am. Soc. of Traffic and Transportation; Natl. Freight Traffic Assn.; No. Calif. Ind.-Edn. Council; Transportation Assn. of Am. Labor Com.; Statewide Ind. Com., Calif. State C. of C.; v.p.-exec. bd. S.F. Bay Area Council, B.S.A.; Newcomen Soc. in N. Am.; Beta Gamma Sigma; past pres. Pac. Ry. Club; Clubs: Rotary, Bohemian (S.F.); Detroit (Detroit); Sutter (Sacto.). Republican. Home: 36 Via Cheparro, San Rafael, CA 94904; Office: 633 Battery St., S.F., CA 94111.

CHUNG, KYUNG-CHO
Educator — Linguist — Author
b. Nov. 13, 1921, Seoul, Korea; s. Yang Sun and Myong OK (Peng) Chung; B.A., Waseda Univ., Tokyo, 1943; A.B., Seoul Nat. Univ., 1947; postgrad., Columbia Univ., 1948-49; M.A., New York Univ., 1951; LL.D., Pusan Univ., 1965; Litt.D., Sung-Kyun,Kwan Univ., 1968; m. Yosi S. Chung, Oct. 10, 1958; chil.: In Kyung, In Ja. Career: Professor, U.S. Defense Language Inst., Monterey, 1951---; Monterey Inst. Fgn. Studies, 1973-74; Hartnell Coll., Salinas, 1974---. Dir., Korean Research Council; adviser Korean Assn., Monterey, 1974---; Am.-Korean Found.; treas. Korean Research Bull.; So. Carmel Hills Assn., pres. 1962-63. Apptd. hon. prof. of Kunkuk Univ., Seoul. Recipient: Superior Performance Award by U.S. Govt., 1964; Distinguished Service Award by Korean Prime Minister, 1965; Certificate of Achievement, U.S. Def. Lang. Inst., 1976. Mem.: AAUP; Am. Assn. Asian Studies. Contbr. to encyclopaedias and profl. journs., N.Y. Times and others. Author: Korea Tomorrow, 1957; New Korea, 1962; Korea: The Third Republic, 1972; Korean Unification, 1972; Korean, Japanese transls. Korean Ch. Hobby: stamp collecting. Rec.: golf. Home: 25845 S. Carmel Hills Dr., Carmel, CA 93921; Office: P.O.B. 5834, Presidio of Monterey, CA 93940.

CLAIREMONTE, GLENN (Mrs.)
Author — Lecturer
b. May 14, 1896, Staten Island, N.Y.; d. Herman and Nina (Lambert) Gerbaulet; A.B., Univ. of Calif., 1923, postgrad., Columbia Univ., 1929-30; m. Harold Spencer Clairmonte, 1932 (dec.); one son (dec.). Career: Appts. incl. Feature Writer, Carmel Pine Cone, also lectr., Monterey Penin. Coll., 1945-52; freelance copy ed., N.Y.C., 1952-61; lit. tchr., N.Y. Univ., 1958-59; Lit. lectr., Downey Schs., 1959---; English Cons., Elysion Coll., 1960---. Author: Truth To Tell, collection of 20 publ. articles on parapsychology, Unity Books, 1979; Calamity Jane, 1961; Calamity was the Name for Jane, 1959; John Sutter of Calif., 1953; Contours, 1931; Carcassone, 1923; contbr. to profl. journs. and mags. Mem.: Life, Univ. of Calif. Alumni Assn.; Writers Workshop W.; Calif. Council for Adult Edn.; Parapsychology Found. Awards incl.: Cook Poetry Prize, 1923; Kan. Poetry Prize, 1924; gold plaques, Downey, 1972, 74, 76. Hobby: play-going. Home: 8109 Third St., Downey, CA 90241.

CLANCY, JOHN P. (JACK)
Professor of History
b. June 11, 1920, Houston, Tex.; s. E. Earl Sr. and Mary (O'Brien) Clancy; bro.: Edward Earl Jr., ret. criminalist, City of Toledo; Thomas M., ret. Sr. Chief, U.S.N., Virginia Beach; B.A. Univ. of Dayton, 1948; B.E., Univ. of Toledo, 1953; M.Ed., 1956; M.A. Univ. of Detroit, 1965; Ph.D., U.S. Internat. Univ., 1975. Career: tchr. pvt. and publ schs., Ohio, Mich., N.Y. and Calif., 1948-69; Prof. of Philosophy and History, Saddleback Community Coll., Mission Viejo, 1969---; also Adjunct Prof. of Mgmt. Orgn. & Devel., U.S. Internat. Univ., 1978---. S/Sgt., AUS Parachute Troops, 1942-45, Rhineland & Central Europe Campaigns, Combat Inf. Badge. Mem.: Elks, Disabled Am. Vets. Democrat, Vol. for Adlai Stevenson, 1952-60. Hobbies: reading, travel. Rec.: team sports. Office: 28000 Marguerite Pkwy., Mission Viejo, CA 92692.

CLARK, EARNEST HUBERT, JR.
President, Baker International Corp.
b. Sept. 8, 1926, Birmingham, Ala.; s. Earnest Hubert, Sr. and Grace May (Smith) Clark; ed. B.S. (Magna-Cum-Laude), Calif. Inst. of Tech. 1946; M.S., 1947; (hon.) LL.D., Pepperdine Univ. 1975; m. Patricia Margaret Hamilton, Calif., June 22, 1947; chil.: Stephen Donald, b. Apr. 28, 1948; Kenneth Andrew, b. July 12,

1949; Timothy Randolph, b. Sept. 27, 1953; Daniel Scott, b. May 9, 1955; Scott Hubert, b. Oct. 7, 1956; Rebecca Grace, b. July 14, 1960. Career: Joined Baker Oil Tools, Inc. 1947, v.p.-asst. gen. mgr. 1958, dir. 1959, pres.-gen. mgr. 1962, pres.-chief exec. ofcr. 1965, pres.-chmn.-bd. 1969; pres.-chief exec. ofcr. Baker Internat. Corp. 1976---. Dir.: The Bank of Calif., BanCal Tri-State Corp., Beckman Instruments, Inc. 1972---; Calif. State C. of C., Golden State Foods Corp. 1975---. USNR, WW II, 1943-46; Korean War, 1950-52. Mem.: dir. YMCA, Downey, 1957---, dir. Met. L.A. 1968---, Natl. Council YMCA of U.S. 1969---; past pres.-dir. Petroleum Equipment Supplies Assn.; Am. Inst. of Mech. Engrs.; trustee, Harvey Mudd Coll. 1971---; Tau Beta Pi. Catholic. Rec.: tennis, boating, water sports, water-skiing, snow-skiing. Home: 8346 Lexington Rd., Downey, CA 90241; Office: 500 City Parkway West, Orange, CA 92668.

CLARK, GUY STORMAN
Physician
b. May 3, 1938, Griffin, Ga.; s. George Warren, Jr. and Roslyn (Heflin) Clark; B.A., Emery Univ., 1959; M.D., N.W. Univ. Med. Sch., 1963; m. Ramona Ann Richli, Spet. 24, 1972, Tarzana, Calif.; chil.: Laura Lillith, b. Sept. 12, 1973; Warren Richli, b. Jan. 10, 1978. Career: Intern, Wilford Hall, U.S.A.F. Hosp., San Antonio, Tex., 1963-64; flight surgeon, dir. of Aeromed. services, Bergstrom AFB, Tex. Strategic Air Command, PresidentialSupport Lyndon B. Johnson, 1964-66; Chief flight med. 12th tactical fighter wing, Cam Ranh Bay, Repub. So. Vietnam, 1966-67; Resident, internal med., Wadsworth V.A. Hosp., L.A., 1967-7-; Arthritis Found. Fellowship, clin. rheumatology, UCLA, 1970-71; pvt. practice, internal med. and rheumatology, Anchorage, Ak., 1971-75; also: cons. rheumatologist for Ak. Crippled Child. Found.; cons. for Ak. Native Health Service; flight surgeon, Ak. Nat. Guard; pvt. practice, internal med. and rheumatology, Santa Barbara, 1975---. Research activities: Thymus transplantation, immune develop. in induced diseases, 1958-59; Taurine excretion, irradiation, 1960; Pneumoconioses, Am. Thoracic Soc., 1962. Awards: Wm. T. Hornaday, distinguished service to conservation, 1954; Alpha Epsilon Upsilon hon. scholastic soc., 1956; diplomate Nat. Bd. of Med. Examiners, 1956; Ga. rep. gov. conference on conservation, 1954; So. Calif. Rheumatism Assn., 1976. Served in USAF, 1962-67; Ak. Army Nat. Guard as Major: decorations: bronze star, air medal with two oak leaf clusters; Pres. unit citation. Mem.: Santa Barbara Co. and Calif. Med. Assns.; AMA; Am. and Calif. Soc. of internal med. Methodist. Home, Office: Santa Barbara, Calif.

CLARK, LOUISE MILLER
Artist
b. June 28, 1929, Denver, Colo; d. Frank (cartoonist, King Feats. Syn.) and Cathryn (Cooper) Miller; ed. A.A., Modesto Jr. Coll. 1948; Sacto. State Coll., 1949; stu. with profl. artists; m. Richard Carvel Clark, S.F., June 16, 1948; dau. Mrs. Gary (Cathryn Louise) Taylor. Career: Teacher, pvt. art classes; artist, repr. many pvt. collections, numerous exhibs.; 17 One-Man Shows; art dir. Stanislaus Dist. Fair, 1950-65; art dir. Los Banos May Day Fair, 1966-70. Awards: Kingsley Award, Crocker Art Gallery, 1951; Best of Show, Central Calif. Art League, Modesto, 1964; Purchase Award, Delta Art Show, Antioch, Calif., 1966; Camelia Award, Sacto., 1971; Best of Show, Merced, 1974; many 1st, 2nd, 3rd awards at various art shows, Calif. Mem.: pres. Central Calif. Art League 1950-51, div. chmn. 1962; Merced Art League, 1967; v.p. Vacaville Art League, 1973; Oakland Art Assn., S.F. Women Artists, Natl. League Am. Pen Women. Republican. Episcopalian (ch. secty.). Hobbies: bridge, boating, fishing. Studio: 2946 Montana Ave., Merced, CA 95340.

CLARK, RUFUS BRADBURY
Partner, O'Melveny & Myers
b. May 11, 1924, Des Moines, Ia.; s. Rufus Bradbury and Gertrude (Burns) Clark; ed. B.A., Harvard Coll. 1946; LL.B., Harvard Law Sch. 1951; diploma L., Oxford Univ. 1952; m. Polly King, L.A., Sept. 6, 1949; chil.: Cynthia Ann, Rufus Bradbury, John Atherton. Career: Assoc. atty. O'Melveny & Myers, 1952-61, partner, 1962---; Dir.: Automatic Mach. and Electronics, Inc., Govina; Brown Internat. Corp., Covina; Econ. Resources Corp., L.A.; First Charter Financial Corp., L.A.; So. Calif. Water Co.; John Tracy Clinic, L.A.; Prot. Episc. Ch., Chancellor of Diocese, L.A., Mem.: Chancery Club, L.A.; 2nd Lt., AUS, 1943; 1st Lt. 1944, Capt. (APP), 1945, U.S. First Inf. Div., ETO, WW II. Rec.: sailing. Home: 615 Alta Vista Circle, So. Pasadena, CA 91030; Office: 611 W. Sixth St., L.A., CA 90017.

CLARK, STANLEY D.
Attorney at Law
b. May 24, 1925, Long Beach, Calif.; s. John Gee (Superior Ct. Judge, noted tchr.) and Josephine (Hunt) Clark; B.S., Calif. Inst. of Tech., 1945; J.D., Loyola Law Sch., L.A., 1952; m. Doris Donnelly, July 18, 1947, Santa Monica; chil.: Stanley D. II; Kevin Scott; Geoffrey Trent. Career: Admitted to Calif. bar, 1953; atty., Chase, Rotchford, Dowen and Drukker, L.A., 1953-58; partner, Kelley and Clark law firm, San Marino, 1963-67; Clark & Kunert, 1967---; gen. partner: Claremont Tennis Club, Glendora Racquet Club, Lark Ellen Tennis Club. U.S. Naval Reserve, WW II, 1943-45. Tennis tournament Champion: Pacific SW Jr. Singles, 1943; So. Calif. Intercollegiate Singles and Doubles, 1945; etc.; Finalist: Nat. Pub. Parks Doubles, 1952; Nat. Father & Son Hardcourt, 1973. Mem.: San Marino C. of C.; pres. 1960; San Gabriel Valley Bar Assn., pres. 1962; San Marino Rotary Club, pres. 1966; San Marino Tennis Found., pres. 1967-69; Glendora Country Club. San Marino Community Ch., elder and pres. bd. of trustees, 1965. Office: 1777 Padua Ave.. Claremont, CA 91711.

CLARK, STANLEY DIMOCK
Attorney at Law
b. May 24, 1925, Long Beach, Calif.; s. John Gee (noted Superior Ct. judge and L.A. leader) and Josephine (Hunt) Clark; ed. B.S., Calif. Inst. of Tech. 1945; LL.B., Loyola Law Sch., L.A. 1952; m. Doris Donnelly, Santa Monica, July 18, 1947; chil.: Stanley D., II, Kevin Scott, Geoffrey Trent. Career: Admitted to Calif. Bar, 1953; atty. Chase, Rotchford, Dowen and Drukker, L.A. 1953-58; pvt. practice law, San Marino, 1958-63; partner, Kelley and Clark law firm, San Marino, 1963-67; Clark & Kunert, 1967---; dir. Loyd Ford Motors; gen. partner, Claremont Tennis Club; v.p. Lark Ellen Tennis Club, Inc. U.S.N.R. (1943-45), WW II. Mem.: pres. San Marino C. of C. 1960; pres. San Gabriel Valley Bar Assn. 1962; pres. San Marino Rotary Club 1966; pres. San Marino Tennis Found. 1967-69; San Gabriel Country Club. San Marino Community Ch. (pres. bd. trustees, 1965). Rec.: tennis, golf.

CLARK, THOMAS J.
Mayor, City of Long Beach
b. July 13, 1926, San Diego; s. Thomas James, Sr. and Marjorie (Harper) Clark; ed. B.S., Univ. of Calif., Berkeley, 1950, M.S., 1951; m. Lois Clark, Gardena, Calif., Feb. 22, 1952; chil.: Paul, b. Oct. 10, 1954; James, b. Nov. 27, 1956; Carol, b. June 25, 1958. Career: Optometrist, pvt. practice, Long Beach, 1951---. L.B. City Park Comm. 1963-66; L.B. City Council, 1966---; pres. Independent Cities of L.A. Co., 1969-70; League of Calif. Cities State Bd.; Treas., L.A. Co. Div. 1975-76; 2nd vice-pres., 1976-77; 1st vice-pres 1977-78; Mayor, City of Long Beach, 1975-80. U.S. Army 1944-46. Feat. numerous TV-radio interviews. Mem.: pres. L.B. Optometric Soc. 1955-56; pres. E. L.B. Lions Club, 1956-57; bd. dirs. Los Altos United Meth. Ch. Hobby: stamp collecting. Rec.: golf, backpacking. Home: 2267 Albury Ave., Long Beach, CA 90815; Office: 5479 Abbeyfield St., Long Beach and City Hall, 333 W. Ocean Blvd., Long Beach, CA 90802.

CLARKE, EDMUND WILLCOX
Insurance Company Executive
b. Apr. 25, 1918, Bakersfield; s. Dwight L. and Edna (Willcox) Clarke; A.B. (with great distinction), Stanford Univ., 1939, Phi Beta Kappa; m. Mary Patricia Lucas, May 29, 1948, Bakersfield; chil.: Donald A. Garrard; Dwight L. II; Patricia Ann (Annez); Edmund W., Jr.; Gerald Lucas; Marianne P. Career: Branch mgr., E.F. Hutton, Bakersfield, 1947-60; vice-pres., Transamerica Corp. 1960-68, pres., Transamerica Insurance Co., 1962-67; chmn. of bd., 1967-69; with Occidental Life of Calif. (a Transamerica Co.), 1968---: exec. v.p. investments, chmn. finance com. and dir. Transamerica Investment Mgmt. Co., also chmn. of bd. and chief investment officer, 1972---. Dir.: Arbor Life Ins. Co.; Premier Ins. Co.; American Life of N.Y.; Canadian Surety; Countrywide Life Ins.; Olympic Ins. Co.; Transamerica Ins. Group; Transamerica Investment Research; Transamerica Investment Mgmt. Co.; Transamerica Life & Annuity; Occidental Life of Calif. Lt. Col., USMC, WW II, decorated Bronze Star Iwo Jima; Maj., USMCR. Office: 1150 S. Olive St., L.A., CA 90015.

CLAUSEN, ALDEN WINSHIP
President, Bank of America
b. Feb. 17, 1923, Hamilton, Ill.; s. Morton and Elsie (Kroll) Clausen; ed. B.A., Carthage Coll. 1944, LL.D., 1970; LL.B., Univ. of Minn. 1949; A.M.P., Harvard Bus. Sch. 1966; m. Mary Margaret Crassweller, Feb. 11, 1950;

sons: Eric David, Mark Winship. Career: Admitted to Minn. Bar, 1949; Calif. Bar, 1950; assoc. with Bank of Am., N.T. and S.A., 1949---, v.p., 1961-65, sr. v.p., 1965-68, exec. v.p. 1968-69, v. chmn. bd. dirs. 1969, pres.-chief exec. ofcr. 1970---. Mem.: S.F. Bay Area Council; dir. S.F. Opera; dir. Calif. C. of C.; United Way of Am.; The Bus. Council; Japan-Calif. Assn.; SRI Internat., dir.; Business Roundtable; Calif. Roundtable; The S.F. Club; Pac. Union Club; Bohemian Club; Metropolitan Club, Wash.; United Way of Bay Area; Japan-U.S. Adv. Council; Res. City Bankers Assn.; Calif. Bar Assn.; The Conf. Bd.; bd. trustees: Carthage Coll., Harvard Bus. Sch,; bankers Club of S.F., World Trade Club, Burlingame Country Club, Commonwealth Club of Calif.; The Links (N.Y.). Office: Bank of America, P.O. Box 37000, San Francisco, CA 94137.

CLAUSEN, HENRY CHRISTIAN
Lawyer — Masonic Executive
b. June 30, 1905, San Francisco; s. Louis and Lena Clausen; J.D., Univ. of S.F., 1927; postgrad. Univ. Calif. at S.F., 1927-32; Univ. Mich., 1942-43; m. Virginia Palmer, Aug. 17, 1935; chil.: Henry Christian, Florian (Mrs. William Elliott), Donald, Karen Clausen Freeman. Career: Admitted to Calif. bar, 1927, since practiced in S.F.; asst. U.S. atty. for No. Dist. Calif., chief counsel for chief engr. Joseph B. Strauss during constrn. Golden Gate Bridge, 1931-33; law assoc. Judge George E. Crothers, Thomas G. Crothers, Francis V. Keesling and his sons, 1946-67. Pres. San Francisco YMCA; trustee George Washington Univ. Served to Lt. Col., JAG Dept., AUS, 1942-45; conducted under apmt. Sec. War Stimson Army Investigation Pearl Harbor Disaster. Decorated Legion of Merit. Author, Stanford's Judge Crothers, Clausen's Commentaries on Morals and Dogma, Masons Who Helped Shape Our Nation. Mem.: past pres., Calif. Jr. C. of C.; Nat. Lawyers Club Wash. Congregationalist. Mason (K.T., Shriner, sovereign grand comdr. Supreme Council, Ancient and Accepted Scottish Rite of Freemasonry, So. Jurisdiction U.S.A. 1969---, editor in chief of its monthly mag. The New Age). Clubs: Bohemian, S.F. Golf (S.F.); Metropolitan; Columbia Country; Burning Tree (Wash.). Home: 36 San Jacinto Way, S.F., CA 94127; Office: House of the Temple, 1733 16th St. N.W., Wash., D.C. 20009.

CLAWSON, DELWIN M.
Former Congressman
b. Jan. 11, 1914, Thatcher, Ariz.; s. Charles M. and Edna (Allen) Clawson; ancestors were pioneer Mormon settlers in Ariz.; m. Marjorie Anderson, Mesa, Ariz., Oct. 1934; son, James, b. June 2, 1939. Career: Missionary, Ch. of Jesus Christ of L.D.S., Eng. 1931-33; ofc. mgr., U.S. Employment Serv. 1941-42; housing mgmt. adv., Pub. Housing Adm. 1942-47; mgr. Mutual Housing Assn. of Compton, 1947-63; Bishop Compton Second Ward, L.D.S. Ch. 1948-54; Long Beach Stake High Council, 1958---; city councilman, Compton, 1953-57, mayor, 1957-63; elected to Congress, 23rd Dist. of Calif. 1963---. Mem.: Park and Rec. Commn. of Compton, 1949-53; pres., Young Repub. Club of Compton, 1952; pres. Kiwanis Club of Compton, 1954; Lt. Gov., Div. 13, Kiwanis Internat. 1956; L.A. Co. Sanitation Dist. Bds. 1, 2 & 8, 1957---; (charter) dir. Execs. Dinner Club of Compton & Lynwood, 1958---; dist. chmn., Midland Dist., B.S.A., 1960-62, exec. bd. L.A. area, 1962, natl. council repr. 1962; dir. Compton Chap., Am. Red Cross; exec. com., L.A. Co. Com. of Mayors, 1961-62; chmn. Community Chest, Red Cross local campaigns. L.D.S. (sem. teacher, 1955-58; Sun. Sch. tchr.). Hobby: music. Home: 9117 Manzanar Ave., Downey, CA; Office: 2349 Rayburn House Ofc. Bldg., Wash., D.C. 20515.

CLAWSON, RAYMOND W.
Business Executive
b. San Jose, Calif.; s. Benjamin B. and Mae (Names) Clawson; ed. Montezuma Sch., Los Gatos, Calif.; Palo Alto Mil. Acad., Calif.; Pasadena Mil. Acad., Calif.; Am. Univ., L.A.; m. Barbara M. Robbins, 1965; chil. by previous marriages: Russell Miller, Ronald Lewis, Raymond Walden. Career: Independent oil producer; v.p., C.C. Warren & Co. Stock Brokers, Oakland, 1924-27; ind. operator exploration and devel. oil properties, New Mexico, 1936---; publisher Los Angeles Mirror, 1945-47; pres., Ariz. Securities, Inc., Phoenix, 1947-50; Transcontinental Oil Co., Inc., L.A., 1947-49; geophysics cons. in offshore oil drilling operations Gulf of Mexico, 1963---; North Sea, 1970---; Awards: Cert. of Merit for Distinguished Serv. in Petroleum Exploration and Devel., London, Eng. 1973. Clubs: Balboa Bay, Newport Beach; Acapulco Yacht, Mex. Protestant. Hobby: travel. Home: P.O.B. 2102, Newport Beach, CA 92663; Office: P.O.B. 611, L.A., CA 90028.

CLAYTON, MAYME AGNEW
Archivist — Executive
b. Aug. 4, 1923, Van Buren, Ark.; d. Jerry M., Jr. and Mary Dorothy Agnew; B.A., Berkeley, 1974; M.L.S., Goddard Coll., 1975; m. Andrew Clayton (div.); chil.: Avery V. (noted artist); Renai V.; Lloyd L.; Renai Jr. Career: prof. librarian, 1957---: USC Eng. Lib.; UCLA Law Lib.; L.A. Unified Sch.; Councilman Robert Farrell 8th Dist.; cons. to KCOP Channel 13 and Channel 4; cons. to Claremont Coll. Oral Hist. Lib.; founder, archivist, exec. dir. Western States Black Research Center---, (collection of rare and out-of-print materials on Afro-Am. culture and hist.). Featured subject of many articles: Negro Heritage 1974; Sepis 1974; Essence 1975; L.A. Sentinel 1974; L.A. Times 1974; L.A. Woman 1978; Scoop 1978; L.A. Post 1979. Mem.: Iota Phi Lambda; Hollywood Beverly Hills News Media Women; Internat. Black Book Dealers Assn.; L.A. Postal Golf Club; Out Authors Study Club. Ch.: Founders Sci. of Mind. Hobbies: Collecting books, antiques, reading. Rec.: bridge, golf, fishing. Office: 3617 Montclair St., L.A., CA 90018.

CLEARY, JAMES W.
University President
b. Apr. 16, 1927, Milwaukee, Wis.; ed. Ph.B., Marquette Univ. 1950, A.M., 1951; Ph.D., Univ. of Wisc. 1956; m., 3 chil. Career: Dir. of forensics, Notre Dame H.S., Milwaukee, 1949-51; asst. tchr. and coach of debate, Marquette Univ. 1950-51, instr. and head coach, 1951-53; Fellow, Univ. of Wis. 1954-55, tchg. asst. 1955-56, instr. Dept. of Speech, 1956-57, asst. prof. 1957-61, assoc. prof. 1961-63, prof. 1963---, asst. chancellor, 1965-66, v. chancellor, 1966-69; Ellis L. Phillips Fellow in Acad. Adm. (UCLA, Univ. of Southampton, Univ. of Manchester, Cambridge Univ., Univ. of N.Y., Univ. of Essex at Colchester), 1963-65; pres. Calif. State Univ., Northridge (and prof. speech), 1969---. Author: (Books) "Rhetoric and Public Address: A Bibliography," publ. 1964; "John Bulwer's Chirologia...Chironomia, 1644: A Critical Edition," 1974; collab. "Robert's Rules of Order Newly Revised," 1970; many articles, bibliographies, monographs on history. U.S. Army, Inf. ofcr. 1945-47. Awards: Outstanding Teaching Award, Central States Speech Assn. 1959; Alumnus Award for Coll. Teaching, Marquette Univ. 1960; Wm. H. Kiekhofer Mem. Award for Excellence in Teaching ($1,000.00), Univ. Wis. Mem.: Delta Sigma Rho, Alpha Sigma Nu, Phi Kappa Phi. Office: 18111 Nordhoff St., Northridge, CA 91330.

CLEMENTS, ROBERT O., SR.
Architect
b. Jan. 15, 1918, L.A.; s. Stiles Oliver (Architect) and Ida (McAvoy) Clements; B. Arch., USC, 1941; m. Dorothy Francis Ditto, Sept. 13, 1941, Yuma, Ariz.; chil.: Robert O., Jr.; Miriam Goodwin; Stiles M. Career: partner, Stiles & Robert Clements — Architects, 1955-65; pres., Robert Clements and Assoc., 1965---. Recipient numerous archtl. awards. 1st Lt., USMC, Pac. Theater. Mem.: L.A. Opera Guild, past pres.; mem. bd., Marina del Rey Design Control Bd.; AIA; Archtl. Guild USC; Kappa Sigma; Calif. Council AIA; L.A. C. of C.; L.A. Hdqtrs. City Assn. Central City Assn.; Internat. Council of Chopping Centers; Calif. Club; Annandale Golf Club. Presbyterian. Rec.: golf. Home: 1175 Arden Rd., Pasadena, CA 91106; Office: 1201 Huntley Dr., L.A., CA 90026.

CLIFFORD, JOHN CHARLES
Artistic Director, Los Angeles Ballet
b. June 12, 1947, L.A.; s. Robert and Leslie Clifford; grad. Hollywood High Sch. Career: joined N.Y.C. Ballet, 1966: (at 20 years of age, youngest choreographer ever attached to major ballet co.), principal dancer & choreographer, (1st choreography, 1968), eight ballets for N.Y.C. Ballet; two ballets for Deustche Opera, Berlin; one for S.F. Ballet; forty for L.A. Ballet; founder, first profl., L.A. Ballet Co., 1974---; first Am. male to guest with Paris Opera Ballet, 1974. Rec.: all music, theatre of all kinds. Home: 1131 Alta Loma Rd.; Office: 1320 S. Figueroa St., L.A., CA 90015.

CLINTON, JOHN HART
Publisher — Lawyer
b. Apr. 3, 1905, Quincy, Mass.; s. John Francis and Catherine Veronica (Hart) Clinton; 1st cousin to Alexander Francis Hart Morrison, noted S.F. Lawyer; A.B., Boston Coll., 1926; LL.B., Harvard Law Sch., 1929, J.D., 1969; m. Helen Amphlett, Jan. 1933 (dec. 1965); chil.: Mary Jane (Mrs. Raymond Zirkel); Mary Ann (Mrs. Christopher Gardner); John Hart, Jr.; m. 2nd Mathilda (Schoorel) van Dillen; stepchil.: Paul van Dillen; Erik van Dillen. Career: Law practice with firm of Morrison & Foerster (formerly Morrison, Foerster, Holloway, Clinton

& Clark) as associate, 1929-40, partner 1940-72, of Counsel 1972---; newspaper activities: dir. Amphlett Printing Co. (San Mateo Times), 1937---, pres. 1940---; pub. San Mateo Times, 1943---; also pub. San Bruno Herald, Recorder-Progress, Coastside Chronicle, Daly City Herald and San Mateo Post. Dir. and pres., Hotel Leamington, Oakland, 1933-47. Admitted to practice law: U.S. Supreme Court, all Calif. & Mass. cts.; Fed. Communications Commn. Mem. Am. Law Inst.; Am. Judicature Soc.; Harvard Club of S.F.; Bar Assns. of Calif., Am.; S.F.; San Mateo Co. Mem. Indsl. Relations Research Assn. Mem. and past pres.: Calif. Press Assn.; Calif. Newspaper Pubs. Assn; Calif.-Nev. Associated Press; Calif. Newspaperboy Found.; San Mateo. Co. Publishers Assn. Mem.: pres., Calif. Jockey Club Found. Bd. of Regents; San Mateo Co. Devel. Assn.; Co. Hist. Soc.; Rotary; Elks; exec. council Boy Scouts; A⸱⸱S Civilian Advis. Com.; US Naval Inst.; Holland-Am. Soc.; Nat. Rifle Assn.; Peninsula Humane Soc.; Smithsonian Inst.; S.F. Symphony Found.; Wine and Food Soc. of S.F.; Calif. Academy of Sci.; Calif. Hist. Soc.; Internat. Platform Assn.; Newcomen Soc. of N. Am. Hon. Mem., dir. S.F. chpt. multiple sclerosis soc. Clubs: Beach and Tennis, Pebble Beach; Bohemian; Commonwealth Club of Calif.; S.F. Comml. Club; East Bay Holland Club. Roman Catholic. Decorated Knight of the Holy Sepulchre of Jerusalem. Hobbies: photog., beekeeping. Home: 131 Sycamore, San Mateo, CA 94402; Office: 1080 So. Amphlett Blvd., San Mateo, CA 94402.

CLUNIE, ROBERT
Artist
b. June 29, 1895, Scotland; s. Robert and Isabella (Young) Clunie; m. Myrtle Isabel Ireland, Santa Paula, Calif., June 22, 1920; son, Robert Kent. Career: China painting, N.Y.C., 1914; painter, A.T. Ferrell and Co., Saginaw, Mich. 1914-20, foreman, 1917-20; scenic artist, Metro Studios, Hollywood, 1918-19; contract painting, signs, interior decorating, dioramas, fair exhibs., 1920-41; own bus. 1922-29, assoc. 1929-45; painter-exclusive commissions, 1940---. Camouflage artist, U.S.N., WW II; U.S.O. certificate for service, WW II. Awards: (oil painting) 1st and 2nd prizes, Ventura Co. Fair, 1922; 1st Eisttedford, Oxnard, 1924; 1st Gold Medal, Oxnard, 1925; Gardena H.S. purchase 1936; 3rd hon. mention, Acad. of Western Painters, L.A. Co. Mus. 1936, 1st award 1937; hon. mention, Calif. Art Club Annual, L.A. Co. Mus. 1936; 3rd prize, Calif. State Fair, Sacto., 1938; purchase award, Heyburn Schs., Heyburn, Ida. 1938; purchase award, Granite H.S., Ogden, Ut. 1946; purchase, Isbell Sch. Annual, Santa Paula, Calif. 1946; purchase, C. of C. Annual, Santa Paula, 1948; 2 purchase prizes, Santa Paula H.S. Annuals, 1951, 55; popular prize and hon. mention, Calif. State Fair, Sacto., 1955; 2nd popular vote, 1st hon. mention, popular awards, Santa Paula Annuals, 1940--- (won 13 consecutive years), Mem.: (hon. mem.) Alpine Assn. 1975; Internat. Platform Assn., 1975---; past grand master, I.O.O.F. 314, Santa Paula, 1922---; Painter and Sculptors Club, L.A. 1929-59; Art Club, L.A.; bd. govs. Acad. of Western Painters, 1938-41; Spectrum Club, Long Beach; (hon.) China Lake Art League. Protestant. Hobby: chess. Rec.: hiking, fly-fishing, fishing. Home: 2399 N. Sierra Hwy., Bishop, CA 93514.

COBB, JOHN BOSWELL, JR.
Professor of Theology
b. Feb. 9, 1925, Kobe, Japan; s. John Boswell and Theodora (Atkinson) Cobb; M.A., 1949, Ph.D., 1952, Univ. of Chicago Divinity Sch.; m. Jean Loftin, June 18, 1947, Newnan, Ga.; chil.: Theodore, b. Apr. 18, 1948; Clifford, b. Oct. 7, 1951; Andrew and Richard, b. June 21, 1955. Career: tchr., Young Harris Coll., 1950-53; instr. and asst. prof., Emory Univ., 1953-58; asst. prof., assoc. prof., Ingraham Professor of Theology, Sch. of Theology at Claremont, 1958---; also Avery Prof. of Religion, Claremont Grad. Sch. ---; Fulbright Prof., Univ. of Mainz, 1955-56; Fellow, Woodrow Wilson Internat. Center for Scholars, 1976. Dir., Center for Process Studies, 1973---; pub. of journal, Process Studies, 1970---. Author: ten books incl. A Christian Natural Theology, 1965; The Structure of Christian Existence, 1969; Christ in a Pluralistic Age, 1975. Capt., AUS, 1943-46. United Methodist Ch., mem. Pacific and Southwest Conf. Home: 1257 Harvard Ave., No. 1, Claremont, CA 91711; Office: Sch. of Theology at Claremont, Claremont, CA 91711.

COBBLE, JAMES WIKLE
University Dean and Professor
b. Mar. 15, 1926, Kansas City, Mo.; s. Ray and Crystal Edith (Wikle) Cobble; B.A., No. Ariz. Univ., 1946; M.S., USC, 1949; Ph.D., Univ. of Tenn. and the Oak Ridge Inst. of Nuclear Studies, 1952; m. Margaret Ann Zumwalt, July 9, 1949, San Diego; chil.: Catherine Ann, b. Aug. 9, 1952;

Richard James, b. Aug. 20, 1955. Career: Chemist., Oak Ridge Nat. Lab., 1949-52; Postdoctoral Research Assoc., Univ. of Calif., Berkeley, 1952-55; Instr., 1954; Asst., Assoc. and Prof. of Chemistry, Purdue Univ., W. Lafayette, Ind., 1955-73; Prof. of Chem. and Dean of the Grad. Div. and Research, San Diego State Univ., 1973; vice pres., San Diego State Univ. Found. 1975---. Awards: Guggenheim Fellow, 1966; E.O. Lawrence Award, U.S.A.E.C., 1970; Welch Found. Lectr., 1971. Lt. j.g., USN, 1945-46. Mem.: chmn., Geothermal Energy ad hoc com., Nat. Acad. of Scis./Nat. Research Council, 1977-78; mem., Corrosion Advis. Com., Electric Power Research Inst.; exec. com. bd. mem., Assn. of Western Univs., Inc. 1977-80; chmn. accrediting com., W. Assn. of Graduate Schls., 1977-78; mem. jt. grad. bd. of Univ. of Calif. and Calif. State Univ. and Colleges, 1978---; Calif. Postsecondary Commn. jt. grad. bd., 1978---; fellow, Am. Physical Soc.; Am. Chem. Soc.; Sigma Xi; Phi Kappa Phi; Alpha Chi Sigma; Phi Lambda Upsilon. Hobbies: swimming, jogging, music. Home: 1380 Park Row, La Jolla, CA 92037; Office: Dept. of Chemistry, San Diego State Univ., San Diego, CA 92182.

COE, NANCY PATRICIA
Artist
b. Apr. 4, 1934, San Jose, Calif.; d. Henry Sutcliffe and Pearle (Hersey) Coe; Cousin, Mrs. Willard (Minna) Coe; ed. B.A., Stanford Univ., 1956; Career: Reno Little Theatre, Nev. 1960, Villa Montalvo, Saratoga, Calif. 1964, 68; One-Man Shows: Rotating exhib. Carson City State Lib., Washoe Med. Clinic, Reno, Nev. 1962; Triton Mus. of Art, Santa Clara, Calif. 1966, 71, 72; Des Saisset Gallery, Santa Clara Univ. 1967; San Jose City Coll. 1969. Tchr., The Art Gallery, pvt. studio, San Jose, and prof. lectr., S.F. Bay area on Painting and Prayer, 1966-72. Various awards and TV interviews, 1961---. Mem.: Soc. of Western Artists, 1961-74; corr. secty. Santa Clara Co., Natl. League of Am. Pen Women, 1965. Seventh-day Adventist. Hobbies: Crocheting, knit, photog. Rec.: swim, horseback riding. Home: Rancho San Felipe, Rt. 3, Box 440-C, San Jose, CA 95121.

COGGIN, C. JOAN
Cardiologist — Educator
b. Aug. 6, 1928, Washington, D.C.; d. Charles Benjamin Coggin, M.D. and Nanette (McDonald) Coggin; B.A., Columbia Union Coll., Maryland, 1948; M.D., Loma Linda Univ., Calif., 1952. Career: Intern, L.A. Co. Gen. Hosp., 1952-53; resident, 1953-55; Fellow in cardiology, Chil. Hosp. of L.A. 1955-56; research assoc. in cardiology and House Physician, Hammersmith Hosp., London, England, 1956-57; resident in pediatrics and pediatric cardiology, Hosp. for Sick Chil., Toronto, Canada, 1965-67. Am. Bd. of Pediatrics certification, 1968. Apptd.: Asst. prof. of med., Loma Linda Univ. Sch. of Med., 1961-69, assoc. prof. of med. 1973---, asst. dean, scho. of med., internat. programs, 1973-75, assoc. dean, 1975---. Apptd. cons., pediatric cardiology, Glendale Adventist Hosp., 1967-71; coordinator, Calif. Regional Med. Programs, Area VI, 1972-74. Honored by spec. recognition audiences with: Pres. Lyndon B. Johnson; Pakistan Pres. Ayub Khan; King Constantine and Queen Ann Marie of Greece; Queen Fredericka of Greece; Premier Papadopalous; Pres. Richard M. Nixon; Prince Turki bin Abdul-Aviz, Defense Minister of Saudi Arabia. Awards: for service to the people of Pakistan (1963), service to the Greek people (1967), the Republic of South Vietnam (1974); Outstanding Woman of the Year in Sci., Calif. Mus. of Sci. and Industry, 1969; Golden Eagle Cine Award and 1st prize in Venice Film Festival for motion picture Atrial Septal Defects, 1964; Charles Elliott Weniger Award of Excellence, 1976. Mem.: Am. Coll. of Cardiology, Am. Academy of Pediatrics, AMA, Am. Heart Assn., Am. Assn. of Univ. Profs., Calif. Med. Assn., Med. Research Assn. of Calif., AAUW, San Bernardino Co. Med. Assn. Mem.: World Affairs Council, Internat. Platform Assn., MUSES-Calif. Mus. of Sci. and Industry, Am. Women in Radio and TV. Ch. Gen. Conference of 7th Day Adventists: mem. Bd. of Higher Education; named to Outstanding Women of the Year, 1975. Hobbies: travel, photog. Home: 11262 Bellaire St., Loma Linda, CA 92354; Office: Loma Linda Univ. Med. Center, Loma Linda, CA 92354.

COHEN, ANITA JAYNE
Employment Counselor
b. Sept. 27, L.A.; d. David Robert and Delphine (Silberman) Cohen; Jr. Cert., UCLA, 1936; student, Univ. of Minn., 1937-38; A.B., Univ. Calif., Berkeley, 1939; M.S. edn., USC, 1939. Career: with Calif. Employment Devel. Dept. (formerly dept. of employment, later dept. of Human Resources Devel.), 1941---; Sr. interviewer, 1944-47; employment security officer II, supr. various offices, L.A., 1947-63; supr. Terminal Student Sch.

Program, L.A. Central Youth Opportunity Center, 1963-67; supervising employment counselor, L.A. Youth Opportunity Center, 1967-69; supr. Youth Services and Training, L.A. center 1970-73; occupational info. cons. for Office of Edn./Training Liaison and Labor Mkt. Info. Spec., L.A. Central Employment Service Center 1973-77; regional testing program supr. and test release agreement spec., L.A. Co. Regional Office, 1977---. State awards for Merit, 1959, 25-Year Service, 1966. Mem.: pres., Nat. Vocational Guidance Assn., L.A. branch 1964-65; exec. bd., Nat. Rehabilitation Assn. So. Calif. branch 1965-69; UCLA Alumni Scholarship Com., Hollywood-Wilshire area, 1969---; Secretarial Sci. Advis. Com., L.A. Trade Tech Coll. 1974-77. Home: 535 S. Curson Ave. W., Apt. 1-D, L.A., CA 90036; Office: 1525 S. Broadway, L.A., CA 90015.

COHN, NATHAN
Attorney at Law
b. Jan. 20, 1918, Charleston, S.C.; s. Samuel and Rose (Baron) Cohn; ed. LL.B., S.F. Law Sch.; son, Norman I., b. Dec. 5, 1940 (atty. at law). Career: Writer, 1936-40; shipbldr. 1940-44; ins. investigator, 1945-47; admitted to Calif. Bar, 1947, U.S. Supreme Ct. 1957; atty. at law, pvt. practive, 1947---; gen. counsel: S.F.-Oakland Press Photogs. Assn.; S.F. Chap., Showfolks of Am.; Author: (Book) Cohn's Criminal Law Seminar, I, II, III, publ. by Central Book Co., N.Y., 1961, 62, 63; 1st Lt., USAF Reserve, J.A.G. 1948-53. Mem.: (hon.) Ancient Order of Hibernians in Am. 1961---; (hon.) Municipal Motorcycle Ofcrs. of Calif.; S.F. Press Club; Natl. Assn. of Def. Lawyers in Criminal Cases; Criminal Trial Lawyers Assn., No. Calif.; Am. Judicature Soc.; fellow, Internat. Acad. of Law and Sci.; pres. Am. bd. of Criminal Lawyers; fellow, Am. Acad. of Matrimonial Lawyers; diplomate, Am. Bd. of Trial Advocates; Fed., Am., Calif., S.F. Bar Assns.; Lawyers Club of S.F., (past) pres. S.F. chpt., Am. Trial Lawyers Assn.; S.F. Law Sch. Alumni Assn.; Cits. Polit. Adv. Bd.; bd. dirs., No. Calif. Serv. League; co-pres., Irish-Israeli-Italian Soc.; Police Athletic League; Nonpartisan Assocs., B'nai B'rith, Jewish Heritage Found., Vets. Dem. Club, S.F. Chpt. Internat. Foot Printers Assn., Freyers Club, Saints and Sinners, F. & A.M., Scottish rite, Shrine, Moose, Eagles Lodges; Showfolks of Am., S. of Market Boys, Laborites, St. Vincent Godfathers, Calamari Clubs. Hebrew. Office: 1255 Post St., Suite 711, San Francisco, CA 94109.

COLBY, MARY E.
Antique Dealer
b. July 31, 1914, Scottsburg, Ind.; d. Clifford Lawson and Bess Myrtle (Weir) Reid; sister of Dr. Robert Reid, pres. of Medi-Tech and founder of computerized med. technique; A.B., Humanities, Indiana Univ., 1936 and 40 years individual research in fine antiques; m. Dr. Rudolf Myers (dec.); m. 2d Edward Pendleton Colby, Apr. 6, 1954, Pasadena; 1 dau. Dr. Cheryl Colby Davis, tchr. Chico State Univ. & author. Career: Interior decorating dept., L.S. Ayres, Indianapolis; asst. buyer, later buyer, Bullock's Downtown store; buyer, Carson Pirie Scott, Chicago, 3 years; head buyer: gifts, lamps, mirrors, pictures, Robinson's stores, L.A., buyer of antiques abroad, 1947-54; founded with husband corporation, Port O' Call Pasadena, 1955, grew in 18 years to include stores in Brentwood, La Jolla, Newport Beach, 2 in Pasadena; opened two fine antiques shops in San Clemente, 1974; consolidated into 7600 sq. ft. new quarters with various galleries for fine antiques from all over the world, 1978---. Lectures widely on antiques. Authority on antiques appraisals. Mem. Phi Beta Kappa; Alpha Chi Omega; Valley Hunt Club, Pasadena 1955; Town Club, Pasa. 1970; Laguna Philharmonic Com., 1975. Hobbies: antiques, visiting Hawaii. Rec.: daily swim. Home: 1710 Los Alamos, San Clemente, CA 92672; Office: 510 N. El Camino Real, San Clemente, CA 92672.

COLE, WENDELL GORDON
Professor of Drama
b. May 15, 1914, Chicago; s. Herbert and Susan (Richards) Cole; A.B., Albion Coll., 1936; A.M., Univ. of Mich., 1937; Ph.D., Stanford Univ., 1951; m. Charlotte Klein, Dec. 14, 1948, Syracuse, N.Y. Career: mem. faculty, Stanford Univ., 1945---; prof. of dramatic lit., theatre history and design, 1963---; exec. head of dept. 1958-59, 1967-69, chmn. of dept. 1972-73. Author: The Story of the Meininger, 1962; Kyoto in the Momo Yama Period, 1967; film scripts on theatre architecture and design, approx. 45 pub. articles. Home: 853 Esplanada Way, Stanford, CA 94305; Office: Dept. of Drama, Stanford Univ., Stanford, CA 94305.

COLEBERD, FRANCES AGATHA
Writer — Photographer
b. S. San Francisco; d. John W. (city atty. for various

San Mateo Co. townships) and Ada M. Coleberd; A.B., Univ. Calif., Berkeley, postgrad., Stanford Univ. in journalism. Career: Lt. j.g., USNR (W), 1944-46; pub. rels. work with 12th Naval Dist., San Francisco, and Grad. Naval Sch., Del Monte, 1947-50; travel news editor, Sunset Mag., Menlo Park, 1952-68; freelance travel writer-editor-photog., 1968---. Author: Islands of the South Pacific, 1972, Japan, 1973, co-author, Australia, 1974, pub. Sunset Books; Adventures in California, A Recreation Guide to the Golden State, 1976, Hidden Country Village of California, 1977, pub. Chronicle Books. Contbr. articles and photos to numerous travel and geologic books, magazines and Sunday Supplements, 1968---. Awards: photography 1st place, Natl. Presswomen's competition, 1963; 2nd place, Christian Sci. Monitor worldwide photog. competition, 1977. Life mem., Sierra Club; mem. Theta Sigma Phi; mem. Am. Soc. of Mag. Photogs., 1968---. Rec.: hiking, swimming. Home-Office: 1273 Mills St., Menlo Park, CA 94025.

COLEFAX, PETER
Business Executive — Banker
b. Mar. 22, 1903, London, Eng. (naturalized cit.); s. Sir Arthur and Sibyl (Halsey) Colefax; ed. Eaton Coll.; M.A., Oxford Univ.; m. Elda Garbe, 1957; son, Michael; (stepdaus.) Penny Gemar, Barbara Cook. Career: N.Y. Times, 1924-25; Edward B. Smith & Co. (now Smith, Barney & Co.), N.Y. 1925-29; Am. repr., Guinness, Mahon & Co., London, 1930-32; with Cyrus L. Lawrence & Sons, N.Y. 1932-34; Am. Potash & Chem. Corp., N.Y. 1934-45, L.A. 1945---, dir. 1935---, secty.-treas., 1935-41; v.p.-secty. treas. 1941-44, v.p.-secty. 1944-45; exec. v.p.-secty. 1945-46; exec. v.p. 1946-47; pres. 1947-59, chmn. bd. pres. 1959-63; hon. chmn.-dir. Security Pacific Nat. Bank, 1968, adv. bd., 1968-77; dir.: investment Co. of Am., L.A., New Perspective Eval. Inc., dir. emeritus Kerr, McGee Corp.; pres., Santa Barbara Mus. of Art. Mem.: Calif. Club, L.A. Home: 1636 Moore Rd., Montecito, CA 93108.

COLEMAN, WILLIAM ROBERT
Optometrist
b. Aug. 29, 1916, Newport, Rhode Island; s. Frank and Mae Coleman; B.S., and Dr., So. Calif. Coll. of Optometry, 1947, 1948; m. Monique Rundberg, June 1956, San Bernardino; chil.: Philippe Charles, b. Jan. 26, 1958; Kevin Charles, b. Apr. 12, 1960; Tinalse, b. July 6, 1961. Career: Optometrist, 1948---; owner, Coleman Graphics, San Bernardino, 1970---; pres., San Bernardino and Riverside Counties Investment Corp., 1957-58; vice pres., Graphic Art Galleries, 1970. 1st Lt., Med. Corps, WW II. Commr., San Bernardino Co. Mus., 1962-67; bd. dir. of So. Calif. Jewish Hist. Soc.; bd. dir., Friends Touro Synagogue, Nat. Hist. shrine; chmn. San Bernardino Bicentennial Com.; bd. dir. Manuscript Soc., 1978; pres. So. Calif. chpt. 1971; pres. Orange Belt Optometric Soc., 1976. Mem.: Elks, Masons, Shrine. Hobby: collector, original manuscripts of Am. Hist. Home: 3151 Valencia Ave., San Bernardino, CA 92404; Office: 274 Central City, San Bernardino, CA 92401.

COLLIER, RANDOLPH CLAYTON
Investments Executive
b. July 26, 1902, Etna, Calif.; s. Buckner Killibrew and Tamahine (Hecht) Collier; ed. Univ. of Calif.; m. Barbara Ferris, Winnemucca, Nev., May 23, 1971; chil.: John, b. Mar. 27, 1931; Suzanne Young, b, Mar. 16, 1935; Camille Sadler, b. July 19, 1947; Natalie, b. May 4, 1973. Career: Police judge, 1925-38; state senator, 1st Dist., Calif. Legislature, 1939-76; pres. Siskiyou Co. Title Co. Mem.: Odd Fellows, Eagles, Grange, O.E.S., Rebekahs; York rite br., Masonic Lodge; Ben Ali Temple of the Shrine. Episcopalian. Home: Yreka, CA; Office: 206 Fourth St., Yreka, CA 96097.

COLLINS, DANIEL ANDREW
Publishing Company Executive — Dentist
b. Jan. 11, 1916, Darlington, S.C.; s. Andrew Sumner and Lucy (Western) C.; A.B., Paine Coll., 1936; D.D.S., Meharry Med. Coll., 1941; certificate children's dentistry Guggenheim Dental Clinic, N.Y.C.; M.S. in Dentistry, U. Calif. at San Francisco, 1944; m. DeReath Curtis James, Aug. 28, 1941; chil.: Daniel Andrew, Edward J., Charles M., Craig S. Pvt. practice dentistry specializing in oral pathology, S.F., 1941---; exec. dir. Harcourt Brace Jovanovich, Inc., S.F., 1971---, also pres. div. urban edn., 1971---, also corp. dir., founder, secty. Beneficial Savs. & Loan Assn., S.F., 1962---; dir., Natomas Co. 1978; dir. Radio Free Europe, 1977; mem. faculty U. Calif. at S.F., 1942-60, founder Oral-Facial Consultative Service, 1959; clinician, lectr. Howard U., 1956-57; Georgetown U., 1956-57; Stanford Med. Coll., 1958---; co-dir. Comprehensive Health Care project Mt. Zion Hosp., S.F.,

1976---, also mem. staff; cons. Negro Scholarship fund Ford Found., U.S. Office Edn., Surgeon Gen. Army. Mem.: Calif. Gov.'s Com. Study Med. Aid and Health, 1960; Calif. Bd. Pub. Health, 1962---; Calif. Bd. Pub. Edn., 1962-68; mem. Nat. Health Resources Adv. Com., 1964---; nat. adv. com. selection SSS, 1962; mem. Nat. Com. Support Pub. Schs., 1968-76; co-chmn. No. Calif. United Negro Coll. Fund.; chmn. budget study com. S.F. Community Chest; mem. S.F. Mayor's Com. on Youth. Founder, bd. dirs. S.F. chpt. Urban League, v.p. bd. trustees Nat. Urban League; bd. dirs. S.F. Found. Aged Colored People, PACT (Plan of Action for Changing Times), Youth Service, United Bay Area Crusade, Booker T. Washington Community Center, S.F. br. N.A.A.C.P.; trustee: Meharry Med. Coll., Nashville; Paine Coll., Augusta; Golden Gate U., S.F. Served with AUS, 1956-58. Recipient Distinguished Alumni award Negro Coll. Fund., 1950; citation merit Paine Coll., 1957. Diplomate Am. Bd. Oral Pathology, Fedn. Dentaire Internat., S.F. Dental Soc. (dir.), Internat. Assn. Pathology, U. Calif. Dental Coll. Alumni Assn., Alpha Phi Alpha, Sigma Pi Phi. Author: Your Teeth: A Handbook of Dental Care for the Whole Family, 1965. Contbr. articles to profl. jours. Hobby: Hydroponic gardening. Rec.: golf, skiing, fishing. Home: 700 Summit Ave., Mill Valley, CA 94941; Office: 1001 Polk St., S.F., CA 94109.

COLLINS, DOROTHY DELORES SMITH
Librarian
b. July 25, 1934, Nacogdoches, Texas; d. A.V. and Betty (Yarborough) Smith; B.S., sociology, Prairie View A & M Coll., Texas, 1954; M.Ed. elem. Edn., Texas So. Univ., 1957; certificate in Media (NDEA Fellow), Purdue Univ., 1967; M.L.S., USC, 1972; m. Julius A. Collins (dec.) Aug. 14, 1954, Houston, Texas. Career: tchr. pub. schs.: Houston, Texas, 1955-57; Cleveland, Oh., 1958-62; U.S. Army Dependent Schs., Germany, 1963-66; Lancaster, Calif., 1969-74; librarian pub. schs.: Cleveland, 1966-67; Palmdale, 1969-74; field resource librarian, secondary, Dept. of Edn., San Diego Co., 1974-75, coordinator, instructional resources services, secondary, 1975---. Publ. Sch. Lib. Media Programs: A Position Based on the Intermediate and Secondary Edn. Act, Supt. of Schs., Dept. of Edn., S.D. Co., 1976. Mem.: ALA; Am. Sch. Lib. Assn.; Assn. Claif. Sch. Adminstrs.; Assn. of Supervision and Curriculum Devel.; Nat. Edn. Assn.; Calif. Teachers Assn.; Calif. Media and Lib. Educators Assn.; Nat. Council of Women in Adminstrn.; Phi Delta Kappa; Delta Kappa Gamma; AAUW; Delta Sigma Theta. Democrat. Roman Catholic. Home: 6267 Rockhurst Dr., S.D., CA 92120; Office: 6401 Linda Vista Rd., S.D., CA 92111.

COLLINS, NANCY WHISNANT
University Executive
Dec. 20, 1933, Charlotte, N.C.; d. Ward William and Marjorie (Blackburn) Whisnant; ed. Queens Coll. 1951-53; A.B., Univ. of N.C., Chapel Hill, 1955, M.S. 1967; Cornell Univ. 1955-56; m. James Quincy Collins, Jr., Weisbaden, Ger., Apr. 25, 1959; sons: James Quincy, III, b. May 28, 1961; Charles Lowell, b. Dec. 17, 1962; William Robey, b. Jan. 29, 1965. Career: Personnel asst. R.H. Macy & Co., Inc., Corp. personnel ofcr., N.Y. 1955; jr. exec. placement dir. Scofield Placement Agcy., San Francisco, 1956-57; freelance journalist, London, Paris, Frankfort, Europe, 1957-59; pgm. dir. GSA, Hampton, Va. 1959-60; asst. dir. Stanford Univ. and Sloan Exec. Devel. Pgm. 1968-78; Corp. Devl. Ofcr., 1979---. Author: A Socio-Psychological Evaluation of Twelve Ind. Engrs. as Related to Creative and Managerial Effectiveness. Award: Research Grant award, Richardson Found., Greensboro, 1966; feat. Outstanding Young Women of Am. 1967. Mem.: chmn. Woman's Honor Council, Univ. N.C. 1955 Marshall, Dean's List; com. chmn. Kappa Delta; dir., Coro Fdn., 1979---; v.p. YMCA; secty.-treas. Charlotte Carolina Club; Am. Mgmt. Assn.; Overseas Press Club; AAUW; v.p. A.F. Ofcrs. Wives Club, Japan, 1965; v.p. Young Dem. Club, 1965; fund raising comm., Trinity Episcopal Ch.; founding mem., Peninsula Profl. Women's Network. Episcopalian. Hobbies: writing, photog. Rec.: horseback riding, tennis. Home: 1850 Oak Ave., Menlo Park, CA 94025; Office: Dev. Off., Grad. School of Business, Stanford Univ., Stanford, CA 94305.

COLLINS, PATRICK WILLIAM
President, Ralphs Grocery Co.
b. Feb. 5, 1929, Aurora, Ill.; s. Alvin H. and Evelyn D. (Shoger) Collins; ed. B.A., Beloit Coll., Beloit, Wis. 1951; m. Elizabeth D. Hanson, Scott AFB, Ill., May 31, 1953; chil.: Colleen Martha, b. Dec. 27, 1956; Quinn Patrick, b. June 13, 1960. Career: Dist. mgr. Red Owl Stores, Minneapolis, Minn., 1956-61; propr.-pres. Collins Super Valu, Green Bay, Wis., 1961-69; Staff Position Fed. Dept. Stores, Cincinnati, Oh. 1969-70; mdse. mgr. Kroger Co., St. Louis, Mo. 1970-72; v.p. Northern Division, 1972,

exec. v.p. 1975, pres. Ralphs Grocery Co., L.A. 1976. Dir. Western Assn. of Food Chains, 1975. First Lt., Squad Adj., Air Def., USAF, 1951-53. Mem.: treas., Beta Theta Pi, 1947-51; Minnekahda Country Club; pres. Oneida Golf and Riding Club, Green Bay, Wisc. (3 yrs.), Santa Ana Country Club. Catholic. Rec.: golf, skiing. Home: 18831 Smoketree Circle, Villa Park, CA 92667; Office: P.O.B. 54143, L.A., CA 90054.

COLLYER, GILBERT A.
President Emeritus, Shasta College
ed. A.B. (hist.), Coll. of Pac.; M.A., Univ. of Calif., Berkeley; Ed.D., Stanford Univ. Career: Bookkeeper, salesman misc.; tchr., Lincoln Union H.S. Calif.; Long Beach State Coll.; tchr.-v. prin.-dist. supt., Lassen Union H.S. and Jr. Coll., Susanville; pres. asst. supt. Shasta Union H.S. Dist. 1949-63, dist supt.-pres. Shasta Coll. 1963-73 (ret.). Author: A History of El Dorado County from 1800-1859, other publs. Mem.: State Council, pres. State H.S. Adm. (3 yrs.); past chmn. State Accrediting Comm.; orgn.-bd. dirs.-past pres. Calif. Jr. Coll. Assn.; Western Coll. Assn. Exec. Com.; pres Shasta Co. YMCA, bd. dirs. (17 yrs.); bd. dirs. Campfire Girls; Rotary Club; Phi Delta Kappa; Phi Kappa Phi; Redding C. of C. Home: 835 Overhill Dr., Redding, CA 96001.

COLWELL, BUNDY
Chairman of the Board, The Colwell Co.
b. Aug. 24, 1912, Ely, Nev.; s. Alfred B. and Pearl (O'Brien) Colwell; ed. B.S. (bus. adm.) USC Coll. of Comm. 1934; J.D., Sch. of Law, USC, 1936; m. Anne Foster Jackson, Shreveport, La., Aug. 28, 1940; chil.: Stephen B., Penny A. Beard. Career: Atty. at Law; v.p.-gen. counsel, Calif. Fed. Svg. and Loan Assn.; dir. Belmont Svg. and Loan Assn.; dir. Great Western Svg. of So. Calif.; pres.-chief exec. ofcr., The Colwell Co., chmn. bd. Mortgage Bankers, chmn. bd. trustees, Colwell Mortgage Trust. Flight instr. USAF; commercial pilot and instr. Mem.: bd. govs. Mortgage Bankers Assn. of Am., reg. v.p., exec. com., other coms.; Calif. Mortgage Bankers Assn.; So. Calif. Mortgage Bankers Assn.; U.S., Calif. State, L.A. C. of C.; Natl. Assn. Real Estate Bds.; Natl. Inst. of Real Estate Bds.; Natl. Home Bldrs. Inst.; trustee, Flintridge Prep. Sch. for Boys; Am., L.A., Calif. State Bar Assns.; Mont., Calif., Western Hist. Assns.; Natl. Geographic Soc., Audubon Soc., Am. Forestry Assn., Natl. Wildlife Assn., Izaak Walton League of Am., Natl. Model R.R. Assn., Las Flores Hunting Ranch, Club de Caza y Pesca de Las Cruces; Commerce Assocs., Town Hall, Cal Farley's Boy's Ranch, YMCA, (life) Jos. A. Garfield Masonic Lodge, Al Malaikah Shrine Temple, Phi Kappa Tau, Gen. Alumni Assn., Trojan Club, Jonathan Club, Alpha Kappa Psi, Phi Alpha Delta, Lambda Alpha, Legion Lex. Ch. of the Lighted Window (moderator, chmn. bd. trustees, coms.). Home: 4312 Vineta Ave., La Canada, CA 91011; Office: 3223 W. Sixth St., L.A., CA 90020.

COMPTON, RUSSELL F.
Orthopaedic Surgeon
b. Mar. 26, 1921, Chicago, Ill; s. Russell F. and Kathryn A. (Fitzpatrick) Compton; rel. to Arthur Compton, 1892-1962, U.S. physicist; B.S., 1948; Ph.B., 1942; M.D., Univ. of Ill., 1951; m. Ruth E. O'Dea, Aug. 8, 1953, Denver, Colo.; chil.: Dianne M. (Mrs. Robert Royce Hicks), b. Dec. 5, 1954; Russell F., b. Dec. 10, 1955; Joan C., b. Aug. 18, 1958; Robert A., b. July 18, 1961. Career: completion fellowship, orthopaedic surgery, Mayo Clinic, 1956; pvt. practice orthopaedic surgery, Pasadena, 1957---; also asst. prof. of surgery, USC, 1963---. AUS Signal Corps, 1942-46. Mem.: Pres., Pasadena Med. Soc., 1969; v.p., Huntington Mem. Hosp., Pasadena, 1975; councilor, L.A. Co. Med. Soc., 1977-80; del., CMA, 1978-79; chmn. BSA com. 1968; Phi Rho Sigma, 1947---; Univ. Club of Pasadena, 1958---; Mission Lakes Country Club. Roman Catholic. Hobby: photog. Rec.: skiing, tennis, swimming. Home: 3924 Alta Vista Dr., Flintridge, CA 91011; Office: 46 Congress St., Pasadena, CA 91105.

CONANT, RICHARD D.
College Professor
b. May 19, 1932, Hollywood, Calif.; s. Russell Weaver and Marion (Dibble) Conant; desc. John Alden, Mayflower settler, 1620; Roger Conant, founder of Salem, 1626, and first Gov. of Mass. Bay Colony; Wm. Brett, Settler, Bridgewater, Mass. 1645; Timothy Conant, Rev. War Hero; ed. A.B., Occidental Coll. 1955; M.S., UCLA 1956; Ph.D., Univ. of Ore. 1969; m. Sandra Mock, Hollywood, Calif., Sept. 1, 1955; chil.: Cathleen Ann, b. July 26, 1957; James Robert, b. Sept. 7, 1959. Career: Asst. gym coach, Occidental Coll. 1954; tchr. in Lassen Jr. H.S., Hollywood, 1955-56; asst. Varsity gym coach, U.S. A.F. Acad. 1958-60, head ski coach, 1960-62; tchg.

asst., Univ. of Ore. 1967-69; prof. Calif. State Coll. Stanislaus, 1969---, head cross country coach, 1969-70; head track coach, 1970-74, dir. Dept. of Aths. and chmn. Dept. Phys. Edn. and Health, 1970-72. Capt., USAF, jet instr.-pilot and instr. flight exam., Wright Patterson AFB, Dayton, Oh., 1957-58; opr. ofcr., Rome Flight Serv., Ciampino Airport, Rome, It. 1962-65; asst. prof. aerospace stus. Univ. of Puget Sound, Tacoma, Wash. 1965-67. Distinguished Serv. Award, 1966. Mem.: Am. Alliance for Health, Phys. Edn. and Rec.; Am. Coll. of Sports Med.; Am. Corrective Therapy Assn.; asst. dir. Accreditation Council; pres. Stanislaus unit, Calif. Assn. for Health, Phys. Edn. and Rec. 1973-74; Natl. Coll. Phys. Edn. Assn. for Men; Western Coll. Men's Phys. Edn. Soc.; Tau Omega, Arnold Air Soc. Deacon, First United Presbyterian Ch., Turlock. Hobbies: photog., sports, garden. Office: Calif. State Coll., Stanislaus, Turlock, CA 95380.

CONGER, HARRY M., III
President, Homestake Mining Company
b. July 22, 1931, Seattle, Wash.; s. Harry M., Jr. and Caroline (Gunnell) Conger; E.M. Colorado Sch. of Mines, 1955; m. Phyllis Nadine Shepherd, Aug. 14, 1949, Yakima, Wash.; chil.: Harry M., IV, b. Dec. 5, 1955; Preston, b. Jan. 31, 1958. Career: with ASARCO, Silver Bell, Ariz., 1955-56, 1957-63; Kaiser Steel Corp., Eagle Mt. Mine, Calif., 1964-69, Fernie, B.C., Canada, 1970-72; Consolidation Coal Co., Carbondale, Ill., 1972-75; Career: Jr. mining engr., ASARCO, Silver Bell, Ariz., 1955-56, shift boss, mine foreman, 1957-63; mine foreman, mine supt., gen. mine supt., asst. mgr., mgr., Kaiser Steel Corp., Eagle Mt. Mine, Eagle Mt., Calif., 1964-69; vice pres. and gen. mgr. Kaiser Resources, Ltd., Fernie, B.C., Canada, 1970-72; vice pres. and gen. mgr., Midwestern Div. Consolidation Coal Co., Carbondale, Ill., 1972-75; vice pres. and gen. mgr., Base Metals Div., Homestake Mining Co., S.F., 1976, president, 1977---. Dir., Homestake Mining Co., plus subsidiaries of company, 1977---. 2nd Lt., U.S. Corps of Engrs., 1956. Contbr. articles in mining journs. Mem.: Eagle Mt. Sch. Bd. Mem.: Sigma Gamma, earth sciences hon.; World Trade Club; Commonwealth Club. Rec.: tennis, golf. Home: 1879 Piedras Cir., Danville, CA 94526; Office: 650 California St., S.F., CA 94108.

CONIGLIO, PETER JAMES
Attorney at Law
b. May 6, 1929, Monterey, Calif.; s. Horace and Mary E. (Ferrante) Coniglio; B.S., cum laude, Univ. Santa Clara, 1951; LL.B., Univ. San Francisco Sch. of Law, 1956; m. Catherine F. Russo (dec. 1967), June 28, 1952; chil.: Mary Sue (Murray), b. Apr. 19, 1953; Regina F. (Kolhede), b. Oct. 28, 1955; Kimberly A., b. Aug. 11, 1957; Michele K., b. Apr. 18, 1961; Juliana, b. Oct. 8, 1964; m. 2d. Patricia Ann Gregor, Feb. 27, 1971, Monterey; dau. Alyson C., b. Mar. 1, 1973. Career: practicing lawyer, 1956---: mem. firm, Hudson, Martin, Ferrante & Street, Monterey, 1958---, partner 1960---; chmn. bd. and founding dir., Monterey County Bank, 1975---; chmn. bd. of trustees Monterey Hosp., 1976---; Bd. trustee Bing Crosby Youth Fund, 1973---. 1st Lt., USAF, 1951-53, distinguished grad. officer candidate sch. 1953. Chmn. Art Commn., City of Monterey, 1976---; chmn., Monterey Planning Commn., 1966-73; chmn. lay bd., Junipero H.S., 1964-70; Monterey City Councilman, 1973-76; Mayor of Monterey, 1972-76. Mem.: Elks Lodge; K.C., 3rd Degree. Hobby: gardening. Rec.: golf, swimming. Home: 750 Via Mirada St., Monterey, CA; Office: 490 Calle Principal St., Monterey, CA 93940.

CONKLIN, GLADYS
Writer
b. May 30, 1903, Harpster, Idaho; B.S. in lib. sci., Univ. of Wash., 1926; m. Irving Conklin. Career: Children's libn., Ventura, Calif. pub. lib. 1926-28, N.Y.C. pub. lib. 1929-31; Los Angeles pub. lib. 1934-42; supr. children's work, Hayward Pub. Lib., 1950-65; writer of children's books, 1958---: 25 pub. books incl.: I Like Caterpillars, 1958; If I Were A Bird, 1964; Little Apes, 1970; Tarantula, 1970; Llamas, 1975; Cheetahs, 1976; I Watch Flies, 1977; Praying Mantis, 1978. Mem.: Calif. Lib. Assn. Children's Librarians, 1953, pres. children's sect. 1963; Woman's Nat. Book Assn., pres. Ohlone Audubon Hayward, 1965. Rec.: walking, studying nature. Home: 16582 Kent Ave., San Lorenzo, CA 94580.

CONNICK, C(HARLES) MILO
Professor of Religion
b. Mar. 23, 1917, Conneaut Lake Park, Pa.; s. Walter and Iola Belle (Wintermute) Connick; nephew of Charles J. Connick, late Boston stained glass artist, credited with rediscovery of stained glass art of 12th & 13th century,

windows: St. Patrick's, St. John's, N.Y.C., Princeton Univ., Grace Cathedral, Forest Lawn; A.B. with hons., Allegheny Coll., 1939; S.T.B., magna cum laude, Boston Univ., 1942, Ph.D., 1944; postgrad. Harvard Univ., Episcopal Theological Sch., Cambridge, 1942-44; D.D., Allegheny Coll., 1960; m. Genevieve Shaul, June 7, 1941, Boston, Mass.; chil.: Joy (Mrs. J. Bruce Parker), b. Apr. 30, 1945; Christopher Milo, b. Nov. 23, 1947; Nancy (Mrs. David F. Jankowski), b. Nov. 23, 1949. Career: Assoc. minister, St. Paul's Methodist Ch., Lowell, Mass., 1941-42; Copley Methodist Ch., Boston, 1942-43; sr. instr., Curry Coll., Boston, 1942-44; dir., Wesley Found., Harvard Univ., summers 1942-44; head, Bible Dept., The Northfield Sch., E. Northfield, Mass., 1944-46; prof. religion and chmn., dept. Philosophy and Religion, Whittier Coll., 1946---; Danforth Found. Assoc., 1959---; dir., Whittier Coll. Study Tours to Europe, Middle East, Far East, 1955-69. Mem.: Am. Acad. of Religion, pres., W. region, 1953-54; Soc. of Biblical Lit.; Calif. Christian Com. for Israel; pres., Faculty Senate Whittier Coll., 1970-71; pres., AAUP, Whittier Coll. chpt. 1970-72. Author: Build on the Rock, You and the Sermon on the Mount, 1960; Jesus, the Man, the Mission, and the Message, 2d ed. 1974; The Message and Meaning of the Bible, 1965; The New Testament, An Intro. to Its Hist., Lit. and Thought, 2d ed., 1978. Ordained Elder, United Methodist Ch., 1942---. Hobbies: travel, photog., writing. Office: Whittier College, Whittier, CA 90608.

CONVERY, SUSANNAH JOHNSON
Attorney at Law
b. Aug. 25, 1926, Brooklyn, N.Y.; d. F. Willard and Katherine (Dow) Johnson; desc. Elihu Root, U.S. Secty. State, 1905-09; B.A., Connecticut Coll. for Women, 1947; J.D., Hastings Coll. of Law, Univ. Calif., 1960; m. John H. Convery, Apr. 4, 1964, Nev.; chil.: David M.T, Walters, b. Sept. 26, 1947; Katherine Byrd Walnters, b. May 12, 1949; Susannah Scott Muscheid, b. Apr. 27, 1951. Career: research atty., Calif. Supreme Ct., 1960-62; Deputy Dist. Atty., Santa Clara Co., 1962-74; pvt. law practice, Walnut Creek, 1974---. Certified Spec., Criminal law, State Bar of Calif. Editor: lead articles, Hastings Law Review. Mem.: chmn. organizing com., Orinda chpt. AAUW, 1956; mem. bd. govs., Hastings Alumnae Assn., 1977---; mem. AAUW, Alamo-Danville chpt.; Mt. Diablo Bus. Profl. Women, Walnut Creek Bus. Profl. Women; Am. Bar Assn.; Contra Costa Bar Assn.; Santa Clara Co. Bar Assn. Hobbies: bridge, sewing, theater. Home: 36 Waverley Ct., Alamo, CA 94507; Office: 1200 Mt. Diablo Blvd., Walnut Creek, CA 94596.

COOK, ARLENE ETHEL
Writer
b. July 1, 1936, Escondido, Calif.; d. Oscar E. and Leona L. (Wells) Knappe; ed. Palomar Coll., 1955; San Diego State Univ., 1956; m. Richard H. Cook, La Mesa; chil.: Alan J., b. Sept. 28, 1956; Alyse J., b. Oct. 7, 1958; Jon A., b. Jan. 25, 1960. Career: elem. sch. tchr., 1961-67; freelance writer, 1966---; also instr., adult edn. course, Writing for the Marketplace, Poway, 1978-79; stringer for The National Enquirer, 1978---; author: The World of Long Ago, 1971, From the Ashes of Hell, 1973; contbr. to nat mags. more than 200 articles, poems, stories. Mem. Mayor of Escondido 1st Blue Ribbon Commn. 1973; br. pres. Nat. League of Am. Pen Women, 1970-72; v.p. San Diego chpt., Nat. Assn. Investment Clubs, 1970-73; pres., Scribblers, 1972-74. Republican. Lutheran, v.p., Lutheran Women's Missionary League 1974. Hobbies: stained glass, gardening. Rec.: camping. Address: P.O.B. 184, Escondido, CA 92025.

COOLEY, LELAND FREDERICK
Author
b. June 8, 1909, Oakland; s. Arthur Montague and Anita (Lewis) Cooley; 5th generation Californian, desc. Robles family of Burgos Spain to Mexico in 1600s, to Monterey and Santa Cruz 1770; desc. Brig. Gen. E.J. Lewis, Calif. State Militia; ed. Berkeley H.S., Wesley Sch., Calif. Sch. of Fine Arts, cadet, U.S. Merchant Marine; daus.: Pamela Lee, Allison Smith; m. 2d. Lee Morrison, 1957, Okanogan, Wash. Career: Radio journalist, 1930-37; overseas correspondent, Trans-radio Press, 1937; entered TV as one of a half dozen pioneer prods., W6XAO — Don Lee Exptl. Station, L.A., 1937---: in or close to TV since as writer, producer, director (Emmy award winning shows incl. Perry Como Show, Andre Kostelanetz Show); Author 16 pub. books, 1958--- (five are non-fiction works on sociology), (hist. novel, "California" Avon, 1973, required reading in many colls., won Univ. Friends of Lib. Hist. Fiction Award, 1974, The Americana Award, 1977); lectr., state coll. system, others on Calif. hist. and writing; mem. Program Advis. Com., PBS Station KOCE-TV, Golden West Coll. Mil.: C.M.T.C. 6th Coast Arty., S.F., 1928; Calif. Nat. Guard 159th Inf. 1929---;

U.S. Coast Guard Reserve, 1941-45. Mem.: Friends of UC, Irvine lib., pres.; Western Center of Internat. P.E.N., pres.; Authors League; Screen Writers Guild; Radio-TV Directors Guild, founding mem. N.Y.C. 1941; pres., Town of Fire Island Pines. Ch. of England. Rec.: skiing, running. Home: 541 Alta Vista Way, Laguna Beach, CA 92651.

COOMBS, WALTER PAUL
University Professor
b. Aug. 20, 1920, Missoula, Mont.; s. Walter O. and Mina Elizabeth (Gerlach) Coombs; ed. A.B. Mont. State Univ. 1939, LL.B. 1941. Career: Secty., Gov. of Mont. 1941-43; pub. repr., Natl. War Agcys., S.F., Calif. 1943-45; spec. atty., U.S. Dept. of Justice, 1945-46; mgmt. cons., firm of Fisher, Rudge and Neblett, 1946-54; adv. to Govt. of Philippines, 1952; and Govt. of Ecuador, 1958; exec. dir., L.A. World Affairs Council, 1954-67; dir. Internat. Affairs, Calif. State Colls. 1967-73; prof. Soc. Scis., chmn. Am. Stus., Calif. State Polytech. Univ., Pomona, 1973---. Cons. to Mayor, Sister Cities, Internat. Pgms., L.A. Arbitrator and impartial chmn., Fed. Meditation Serv. Dir.: Summer Sch. of World Affairs, S.F. Awards: (decorated) Thailand, 1957, West Germany, 1958, Belgium, 1963, Italy, 1964, Great Britain (OBE, 1970), Finland, 1972. Mem.: dir. Modern Forum of Beverly Hills; dir. Pan Pac. Center, Santa Monica; dir. Japan Am. Soc.; Natl. Acad. of Arbitrators; Univ. Club, L.A. 32nd degree Mason. Republican. Lutheran. Home: 23519 Silver Spring Lane, Diamond Bar, CA 91765; Office: 3801 W. Temple Ave., Pomona, CA 91768.

COOPER, GRANT BURR
Attorney at Law
b. Apr. 1, 1903, New York City; s. Louis Baxter and Josephine (Christiansen) Cooper; ed. LL.B., Southwestern Univ.; m. Phyllis Norton, Tijuana, Mex., Apr. 3, 1935; chil.: Mrs. Rollin David (Natalie) Wallace, b. Sept. 20, 1930; Judith Ann, b. Sept. 26, 1934; Meredith Jane, b. July 17, 1940; Grant Burr, Jr., b. Dec. 20, 1941; John Norton, b. Aug. 3, 1946. Career: Dep. dist. atty., L.A. Co. 1929-35, chief dep. 1940-42; dep. city atty., L.A. 1935-38; chief asst. ins. commr., State of Calif.; atty. at law, pvt. practice, 1944---. Mem.: Health Comm., City of L.A. 1943, pres. 1944; bd. of regents, Am. Coll. of Trial Lawyers; chmn. Criminal Law and Procedure Com., L.A. Bar Assn. 1948-49, bd. of trustees, 1952---; chmn. Criminal Law and Procedure Com., State Bar of Calif., 1950---; Am. Bar Assn.; Larchmont Lodge No. 614, F. & A.M.; Melrose Chap. No. 140, R.A.M.; Al Malaikah Temple. Rec.: fishing. Home: 3447 Wrightview Dr., Studio City, CA 91604; Office: 1880 Century Park E., Suite 1150, L.A., CA 90067.

COOPER, OREN C.
Artist
b. Dec. 5, 1920, Orlando, Fla.; s. Carl J. and Margaret L. Cooper; ed. Art Inst. of Buffalo, 1938-40; Pratt Inst. 1941-42; B.F.A., Yale Univ. 1950; m. Norma Rix, Warsaw, N.Y., June 9, 1954; son, Eric Lee, b. Sept. 25, 1956. Career: Prodn. mgr.: Eastern Illus. and Publ. Co. 1951; Rogers and Porter Adv. 1952-53; instr. Rochester Inst. of Tech. Eve. Sch. 1956; Case Hoyt Art Dept. 1954-56; IBM Corp. 1956---. Exhibits: N.Y. State Bldg., N.Y. World's Fair, 1939-40; Albright Art Gallery, Buffalo; Mem. Art Gallery, Rochester; Robertson Mem. Center, Binghamton, N.Y.; Glendale Fed., Avco, Calif. Fed. Svg. and Loan Assns.; Ebell Theater, Fri. Morning Club. Topographic draftsman, Hdqrs., 38th Inf., No. Ire., Wales, France, Belgium, Czechoslovakia, Germany, 1942-45; Awarded Gold Medal, 1st prize (Marine watercolor), Valley Artists Guild, 1977. Mem.: (Hon.) pres. Valley Artists' Guild, 1972-75; Calif. Art Club, San Fernando Valley Art Club. Presbyterian. Hobbies: music, Spanish, paddle tennis. Home: 19419 Merridy St., Northridge, CA 91324; Office: 3424 Wilshire Blvd., L.A., CA.

COOPER, PHYLLIS NORTON
Attorney At Law
b. May 26, 1915, Coalinga, Calif.; d. Hugh Russell Norton and Albine (Power) Norton Bowron; B.A., magna cum laude, USC, 1925, J.D., 1938; m. Grant B. Cooper (past pres. L.A. Co. Bar Assn., past pres. Am. Coll. of Trial Lawyers, past v.p., Calif. State Bar Assn.), Apr. 3, 1935, Calif.; chil.: Natalie Caroline (Mrs. Rollin D. Wallace), b. 1930; Judy (Hunt), b. 1935; Meredith (Mrs. Robert K. Worrell), b. 1939; Grant B., Jr., b. 1942; John Norton, b. 1946. Career: admitted to Calif. bar 1938, Supreme Ct. of U.S.; pvt. law practice, L.A., 1938-56; mem. firm Cooper & Nelsen, 1956-71; practice with Grant B. Cooper, 1971---. Mem.: USC Law Alumni Assn., pres. 1962, pres. Univ. Assoc. bd. of trustees, 1976---, nat. chmn annual giving, 1966-67; Lawyers Wives of L.A., 1950---; coord. Assistance League Jrs. 1951; pres. bd. dir., Las Benevolas

of Assistance League, 1950; bd. mem. Mun. Art Commn. of L.A. 1944-53; Women's div., C. of C., 1949-54; bd. YWCA, 1947-52; bd. Assistance League So. Calif., 1946---; Phi Beta Kappa; Alpha Chi Omega; Zeta Phi Eta; Phi Delta Delta; Delta Sigma Rho; Trojan League. Home: 3447 Wrightview Dr., Studio City, CA 91604; Office: 1880 Century Park E., No. 1150, L.A., CA 90067.

COOPER, ROGER L.
Industrial Relations Executive
b. Nov. 5, 1927, Edon, Oh.; s. Raymond and Ina Cooper; ed. B.S., Univ. of Denver, Colo.; m. Bonnie Stamm, Mishawaka, Ind., Nov. 1948; chil.: Colleen, b. Oct. 16, 1956; Craig, b. Dec. 1, 1961; Chris, b. Aug. 16, 1963. Career: sr. ind. rels. repr. U.S. Steel Corp., Maywood, Calif. 1952-55; dept. mgr. Giannini Controls Corp., L.A. 1955-58; sr. labor negotiator, Distrs. Assocs. of S.F. 1958-60; mgr. employee rels. Beckman Instruments, Inc. 1960-65; pres. Calif. Processors, Inc. 1970; v.p. Ind. Rels., Calif. Canners and Growers; secty. Personnel Rels. Group, Natl. Council of Farmer Cooperatives; personnel com. Natl. Canners Assn., Wash., D.C. Serv. U.S. Army, Korea. Mem.: Calif. Ind. Rels. Research Assoc.; bd. dirs. No. Calif. Ind. Rels. Council; trustee, various state-wide health plans under labor agreements with Teamsters and Internat. Assn. of Machinists Unions. Home: 23 Darlene Ct., Alamo, CA; Office: 3100 Ferry Bldg., San Francisco, CA 94106.

COOPER, THEODORE W.
Company President
b. Apr. 27, 1923, Hillman, Mich.; s. Clayton T. and Vila M. (Spencer) Cooper; sister, Harriet C. McCawley, exec. v.p., Western Women's Bank, S.F.; ed. B.S. (M.E.), Mich. Tech. Univ. 1952, M.S. 1953; (hon.) Sc.D., Colo. State Chr. Coll. 1973; m. Gwendolyn Anne Gleeson (Melbourne, Australia), Irvine, Calif., May 16, 1970; chil.: Jeannie (Cooper) DeVore, b. June 20, 1943; Gary Arthur, b. Aug. 18, 1946. Career: toolmaker, Chrysler Corp. 1941-47; R.R. Seeber Research Scholarship and instr. M.E. 1952-53; exec. staff: Hughes Semiconductor, 1953-60; Electro-Optical Systems, 1960-63; dept. mgr. Globe Union Inc., 1963-66; chief exec. Technicon Assocs., Inc. 1966-69; pres. Gen. Technicon Co., 1969---. Author: By Popular Choice, Why Not Vocalize the Silent Majority, 1975; Functionality: A Revelation for Science, 1978. U.S. Patents issued on 8 semiconductor devices and processing, 1957-66; Cooper Anti-Pollution (CAPSICE), 1974. U.S. Army, 1942-45, WW II. Mem.: pres. Beta Chpt., Tau Beta Pi, Mich. 1951-52; Mich. Tech. Alumni Assn.; diplomate, Am. Mgmt. Assn., L.A. 1959; IEEE, AAAS, Internat. Platform Assn.; Natl. Voter Adv. Bd., Am. Security Council; Fed. of Am. Scis.; Lake Elizabeth Ranch Club, 1960-70. Hobbies: woodworking, garden. Rec.: fishing, hunting. Home: 1269 Parkwood Dr., Novato, CA 94947; Office: P.O.B. 1413, Novato, CA 94947.

COOPERMAN, STEVEN G.
Ophthalmic Surgeon — Physician
b. Mar. 3, 1942; B.S., Univ. of Calif., Berkeley, 1962; M.D., Northwestern Univ. Med. Sch., Chicago, 1966; two dau.: Jacki, b. Aug. 18, 1969; Kelly, b. Dec. 16, 1972. Career: Internship, UCLA, 1966-67; U.S. Pub. Health Service, FDA, Washington, D.C., 1967-69; resident in ophthalmology, 1969-72; chief resident, Jules Stein Eye Inst., 1972; pvt. practice of ophthalmology, Beverly Hills, 1972---; also mem. teaching faculty, Jules Stein Eye Inst., 1972---; Attending staff: UCLA Med. Center and St. Johns Hosp. & Med. Center, 1972---. Diplomate, Am. Bd. of Ophthalmology, 1972---; Fellow: Am. Bd. of Ophthalmology, 1972---, Royal Soc. of Health, 1969---. Dir. Med. Testing Systems, Inc., L.A., 1974---. Sci. Cons., McGhan Leus Implants. Founder and 1st chmn., Am. Intraocular Implant Soc. 1974, Sci. Advisory Bd. 1974-76. Mem.: exec. com. and dir., W. L.A. Acad. of Med., 1972-75. Mem: AMA; Phi Delta Epsilon; Am. Assn. of Ophthalmology; Fight for Sight Found. Editor, Journ. of the Am. Intraocular Implant Soc., 1974-76. Hobbies: skiing, tennis, auto racing — collector of antique autos, Ferraris; musician, pianist, singer. Office: 435 N. Roxbury Dr., Beverly Hills, CA 90210.

COPLEY, HELEN KINNEY
Chairman — CEO, The Copley Press, Inc.
b. Nov. 28, Cedar Rapids, Ia.; d. Fred Everett and Margaret (Casey) Kinney; m. James S. Copley, La Jolla, Calif., Aug. 16, 1965 (dec. 1973); son, David Casey, b. Jan. 31, 1952. Career: chmn. bd. Copley News Serv., San Diego, 1973---; publ. San Diego Union and Eve. Tribune, 1973---; chmn. bd.-dir. Exec. Com. Communications Hawaii, Inc. 1973---; chmn. bd. James S. Copley Found.,

1974---. Dir.: Wells Fargo Bank, 1974---; Newspaper Adv. Bureau, Inc.; Putnam Found. Mem.: trustee-dir. Freedoms Found. at Valley Forge, 1973---; trustee, Univ. of San Diego, 1973---; trustee, Scripps Clinic and Research Found., La Jolla, 1973---; dir. Calif. C. of C., 1974---; La Jolla Mus. of Contemporary Art; (life) S.D. Hall of Sci.; Natl. Press Club, Wash. D.C.; S.D. Press Club; San Francisco Press Club; Greater L.A. Press Club; S.D. Co. Women's Council, Navy League of U.S.; S.D. Opera Guild; Wash. Crossing Found. (hon. chmn-dir.); dir. Fine Arts Soc. of S.D.; dir. exec. comm., Inter Am. Press Assn.; dir. ANPA; trustee, ANPA Found.; Am. Soc. Newspaper Eds.; Am. Press Inst.; Calif. Newpaper Publ. Assn.; Calif. Press Assn.; Natl. Newspaper Assn.; Western Newspaper Found.; B.S.A.; S.D. Council; Boys' Club of Am.; U.S.C. of C.; S.D. C. of C.; Calif. Hist. Soc.; S.D. Hist. Soc.; La Jolla Town Council, Inc.; Scripps Mem. Hosp. Aux.; U.N. Assn. of Am.; YMCA; YWCA; (life) Zoological Soc. of S.D.; (life) Star of India Aux.; Soc. Serv. League of La Jolla, Inc.; S.D. Soc. of Natural Hist.; Pan Am. League; Natl. Trust for Hist. Preservation; S.D. Charger Backer; Maritime Mus. Assn. of S.D.; (life) Patroness, Makua Aux.; Friends of Internat. Center, La Jolla; Com. for Econ. Devel.; Chil.'s Health Center; Angelitos del Campo; S.D. Sym. Assn.; Republican Assocs. So. Calif.; Repub. Central Com., S.D.; Sigma Delta Chi; Clubs: Aurora Country, Ill.; Univ. of S.D. Pres.; Univ., S.D.; De Anza Country, Borrego Springs; La Costa Country, Carlsbad; La Jolla Beach and Tennis, La Jolla Country, Stadium, Cuyamaca, San Diego Yacht. Roman Catholic. Home: 7007 Country Club Dr., La Jolla, CA; Office: 7776 Ivanhoe Ave., La Jolla, CA 92037.

CORBIN, EVE
Lecturer — Author
b. June 23, Onaway, Mich.; d. James Seward and Selina (Thomas) Yakes; ed. B.M., Albion Coll., Mich. 1922; m. Floyd H. Corbin, San Diego, Calif., Sept. 8, 1956; sons: Russell F. Kenaga, Jr., b. Mar. 28, 1923; James Colborne Kenaga, b. Dec. 21, 1927. Career: Profl. piano accompanist, ch. organist, choir; (charter) founder, Monday Morning Musicale of Royal Oak, Mich.; lectr. (with husband), nationwide conventions, women's groups, sales and civic groups. Co-Author: (with husband, Floyd H. Corbin), How to Relax in a Busy World (book), publ. Prentice-Hall; contrib. various articles to mags. Feat. guest, natl. radio and TV interview pgms., incl. Viewpoint, N.Y.C. and Don McNeill's Breakfast Club, Chicago. Mem.: pres. So. Calif. Women's Press Club, 1969-71; Delta Gamma. Republican. Religious Science. Hobbies: travel, music. Rec.: golf. Home: P.O.B. 75657, L.A., CA 90005.

CORBIN, FLOYD H.
Lecturer — Author
b. Sept. 12, 1907, Afton, Ia.; s. Lory and Doris Corbin; ed. grad. Boyles Coll., Omaha, Nebr. 1924; stu. law, Univ. of Wyo. (2 yrs.); Bachelor of Relig. Sci., Inst. Relig. Sci., L.A. 1948, M.S. 1949; stu. Seabury Sch. of Psychol. 1950-51; (hon.) Ph.D., Tahoe Coll. 1952; m. Eva Yakes, San Diego, Calif., Sept. 8, 1956; sons: James G., b. Nov. 19, 1930; Bruce H., b. Jan. 3, 1933; Career: City agt.; R.R. Dept. of Tours, Chicago; Sun Valley repr.-city passenger agt., N.Y.C. (10 yrs.), various positions (19 yrs.); lost sight in 1944. Lectr. (over 3000 convs., sales, mgmt., colls., civic groups), U.S., Can., Author: 5 books; co-author (with wife), How to Relax in a Busy World, publ. by Prentice-Hall (translated into Japanese, publ. Japan). Appd. many TV-radio interviews, incl. Don McNeill's Breakfast Club, Chicago; Viewpoint, N.Y.C.; Joe Pyne Interviews, KLAC; The One O'Clock Show, Cleveland; Panorama Pacific, KNXT, L.A.; News of the Day, WFAA, Dallas; Sunip pgm., KOTV, Tulsa. Mem.: pres. Internat. Toastmaster Club No. 48, 1947-48; pres. Seabury Sch. of Psychol. Student Body, 1950-51. Ch. of Relig. Sci. Hobbies: lectures, music. Rec.: reading, travel. Home: 2845½ Sunset Pl., L.A., CA 90005.

CORMAN, JAMES CHARLES
United States Congressman
b. Oct. 20, 1920, Galena, Kan.; s. Ranford and Edna (Love) Corman; B.A., UCLA, 1942; LL.B., USC Law Sch., 1948; chil.: Mary Anne, b. Jan. 16, 1948; James Charles, Jr., b. Apr. 3, 1953; m. Nancy Malone, 1978. Career: pvt. law practice, Van Nuys, 1949-57; L.A. City Council, 1957-60; elected to U.S. House of Rep., 87th Congress, 21st Dist. of Calif., 1960---; re-elected to each succeeding Congress. Mem. House Com. on Ways and Means, chmn. subcom. on Pub. Assistance and Unemployment Compensation; Chmn., House Welfare Reform Subcom. 1977; mem. Ad Hoc Energy Com., 1977; mem. Small Bus. Com.; elected chmn. Demo Nat. Congressional Com., 1976; mem. Nat. Advis. Commn. on Civil Disorders, 1967. USMC, 1942-46, 1950-52; Col.

USMCR. Mem.: Am. Legion Post 193; VFW Post 2323; Lions Internat. Methodist. Office: 14545 Friar St., Van Nuys, CA 91411; 2252 Rayburn House Ofc. Bldg., Wash., D.C. 20515.

CORONA, PETER
Superintendent of Schools
b. Dec. 22, 1928, San Diego; s. Joseph and Mary Corona; A.B., Univ. of Calif., Berkeley, 1953; M.A., S.F. State Univ., 1957; Ph.D., U.S. Internat. Univ., S.D., 1969; m. Yolanda Della Zoppa, June 20, 1954, El Cerrito, Calif.; chil.: Joel David, b. June 6, 1959; Marree Ann, b. Mar. 26, 1964. Career: principal, vice prin., tchr., Walnut Creek, 1955-60; supt., Sunol Glen, 1960-70; supt., Benicia Unified, 1970-73; asst. supt., Montebello Unified, 1973-77; Supt. of Schs., Mt. Pleasant Sch. Dist., San Jose, 1977---. Author: The Role of the Superintendent As Perceived by School Administrators and Community Leaders; chmn. of TV program, How to Evaluate Community Concerns, Atlanta, Ga. 1978. Mem.: Calif. State Coms. of School Administrators: Polit. Action, Urban Affairs, Curriculum, Equal Edn. Opportunities; Am. Assn. of Sch. Administrs.; Rotary Club; Amador LIvermore Valley Hist. Soc.; Pleasanton C. of C.; pres. Walnut Creek Park & Rec. Commn. 1967-74; Roman CatholIc, pres. Newman Club, UC, Berkeley. Hobbies: travel, lectr., fishing. Home: 98 Las Lomas Way, Walnut Creek, CA 94598.

CORRIERE, RICHARD JOSEPH
Psychologist
b. June 23, 1947, Chicago; s. Joseph and Loretta (Albanese) Corriere; B.A., Univ. Calif., Irvine, 1969, Ph.D., 1974; m. Konni Pederson, Sept. 12, 1976, L.A.; dau. Signe, b. Dec. 7, 1968. Career: Research asst., UC, Irvine, 1966-69; Research Coord., Psych. Services Center, USC, 1968-69; Research Coord., Dept. of Psych., UCI, 1969-74; Clin. & Research Assoc., Primal Inst., L.A., 1970-71; Tchg. Asst., UCI, 1970-74; Staff Psychologist, Center for Feeling Therapy, L.A., 1972---; co-dir. of Research, The Center Found., L.A., 1973---; dir. of Training, Center for Feeling Therapy, L.A., 1947---; co-dir. and dir. of Training, The Clinic for Functional Counseling and Psychotherapy, L.A., 1978---. Co-Author: Going Sane: An Introduction to Feeling Therapy, Aronson, 1975, Dell, 1976; The Dream Makers: Discovering Your Breakthrough Dreams, Funk & Wagnalls, 1977, Bantam, 1978; Dreaming and Walking: The Functional Approach to Using Dreams, Harcourt Brace Jovanovich, in press; Psychological Fitness, Harcourt Brace Jovanovich, 1979; co-author research articles on work for profl. journs. Mem.: Am. Psychol. Assn.; Assn. for Psychophysiological Study of Sleep; Soc. for Psychophysiological Research; Assn. for Humanistic Psychology; Am. Acad. of Psychotherapists; L.A. Co. Psychol. Assn.; Calif. State Psychol. Assn. Rec.: basketball, soccer, skiing. Home: 1643 N. Gardner, L.A., CA 90046; Office: 7165 Sunset Blvd., L.A., CA 90046.

CORTESE, DOMINIC LAWRENCE
Santa Clara County Supervisor
b. Sept. 27, 1932, San Jose, Calif.; s. Vincent and Rose Cortese; grad., Bellarmine Coll. Prep., 1950; B.S., Univ. Santa Clara, 1954; m. Suzanne Donovan, Monterey; Chil.: David, b. June 3, 1956; Roseanne, b. Dec. 18, 1957; Mary Elizabeth, b. Apr. 9, 1959; Thomas, b. Sept. 15, 1960; James, b. Oct. 29, 1962. Career: rancher-businessman, 1956---; Supervisor, Santa Clara Co., 1968---: chmn., bd. of suprvs., 1971, 75, 79---; chmn. Santa Clara Co. Transit Dist., 1976; chmn., Regional Criminal Justice Planning Bd., 1972; mem. Calif. Criminal Justice Admin. Com., 1976; Mem., Bay Area Air Quality Mgmt. Dist. 1978-79; mem., Job Corps Citizen Advis. Bd., 1979. Instrumental in formation of: regional criminal justice planning bd.; alcoholism and drug abuse commns.; Human Rels. and Consumer Affairs Commns.; Status of Women Commn.; Mobile Home Task Force. 1st Lt., AUS, 1954-56. Mem.: Italian-Am. Heritage Found.; Am. Legion Post 250; Elks; Civic Club of San Jose; BSA exec. bd.; Calif. Canners and Growers; Mex.-Am. C. of C.; Assn. of Bay Area Govts. Catholic. Hobby: winemaking. Rec.: hunting. Home: 1400 San Felipe Rd., San Jose, CA 95121; Office: 70 W. Hedding St., San Jose, CA 95110.

CORWIN, THEODORE B.
Plastic Surgeon
b. Apr. 2, 1944, St. Louis, Mo.; s. David R. and Estelle Corwin; B.A., Knox Coll.; M.D., Univ. of Mo., 1969; m. Sally Balthis, June 25, 1967, St. Louis, Mo.; chil.: Jennifer, b. Mar. 5, 1970; Theodore Ross, Jr., b. Feb. 16, 1971. Career: Fellow, Univ. of Fla., 1973-75; resident surgery, 1970-73; Kaiser Found., pvt. practice, 1975-78; Plastic Surgery Assocs., 1978---; Pub. articles in field.

Mem.: Alpha Delta Epsilon, 1962-65; Am. Bd. of Plastic Surgery, 1975; L.A. Co. Med. Assn. Rec.: skiing, racquetball, sailing. Office: 1250 La Venta Dr., Westlake Village, CA 91361.

COSTA, GUSTAVO
Professor of Italian
b. Mar. 21, 1930, Rome, Italy; s. Paolo and Ida (Antonangelo) Costa; Maturita Classica, 1948; Ph.D., 1954; m. Natalia Zalessow, June 8, 1963, S.F.; dau. Dora Luisa, b. 1964. Career: Instr. of philosophy, Univ. Rome, 1957-60; lectr. of Italian, Univ. de Lyon, 1960-61; instr. of Italian, Univ. Calif., Berkeley, 1961-63; asst. to assoc. to full prof., 1963---; chmn., Dept. of Italian, 1973-76. Author: three books. Mem. Faculty Club. Home: 605 Colusa Ave., Berkeley, CA 94707; Office: Dept. of Italian, UC, Berkeley, CA 94720.

COTTON, RICHARD GRANT
Corporate Executive
b. Feb. 26, 1925, Detroit, Mich.; s. Paul R. and Marjorie Frances (Weiler) Cotton; A.B., Mich. State Univ., 1948; m. Evelyn Phillips, Sept. 14, 1946, Port Huron, Mich.; chil.: Nancy (Mrs. Frank P. Latino), b. Oct. 12, 1947; Mark, b. June 25, 1952; Guy, b. Nov. 7, 1955; Debra, b. June 18, 1957; Karen, b. June 6, 1960. Career: gen. sales mgr., yellow pages, Mich. Bell Telephone Co., 1948-50; div. comml. mgr., 1950-64; sr. vice pres., Wickes Corp., San Diego, 1964---. Dir., Family Svgs. & Loan, Saginaw, Mich., 1952-62. AUS, 1943-45; decorated purple heart and bronze star. Pres., Mich. United Fund, 1969; mem. exec. com., bd. of dir., United Way, S.D. Co., 1976---; mem. bus. advis. bd., San Diego State Univ., 1978. Clubs: La Jolla Country, Cuyamaca. Republican. Pres., Mich. Baptist conv., 1969. Rec.: golf. Home: 6875 Paseo Laredo, La Jolla, CA 92037; Office: 1010 Second Ave., San Diego, CA.

COURTNEY, EUGENE WHITMAL
President, Digital Scientific Corporation
b. E. St. Louis, Ill.; s. Eugene and Goldie Genell (Mitchell) Courtney; B.S., Princeton Univ., 1957; m. Barbara Beckwith, Aug. 1, 1959, La Jolla; chil.: Kevin Eugene, b. Jan. 13, 1966; Kyle Patrick, b. Oct. 27, 1967. Career: engr., Magnavox Co., 1957-59; Systems mgr., Control Data Corp., 1959-66; sys. engr., Castle & Cooke, 1966-67; sales mgr., Data Pathing Inc., 1967-69; v.p., Digital Scientific Corp., 1969-74; pres., 1975---. Dir.: Data Processing Power Corp.; Computer & Communications Industry Assn.; Am. Electronics Assn.; San Diego Hall of Sci., also v.p., engring. Contbr. publ. in tech. journs. Address: P.O.B. 1503, Rancho Santa Fe, CA 92067.

COURTRIGHT, HERNANDO
Proprietor, Beverly Wilshire Hotel
b. July 10, 1904, Coeur d'Alene, Id.; s. George and Margarita (DeVigne) Courtright; ed. USC; chil.: Mrs. Edward LaCava; Mrs. John A. Sisto; Rosellen C.; Hernando, Jr.; DeVigne; Carina Kelley; m. 2d. Florence Falzone, Aug. 1978, L.A. Career: with Bank of America, coll. to 1943; Beverly Hills Hotel, 1943-58; Century City Corp., 1959-61; prop., Beverly Wilshire Hotel, 1962---: (Courtright Corp.). Dir., United Fin. Corp. Clubs: Calif., L.A. Country, G & P Club of L.A., Bohemian, S.F., Rancheros Visitadores. Catholic: Knight of Malta, St. Brigitte, Holly Sepulchre St. Hubert, St. Lazarus of Jerusalem. Address: Beverly Wilshire Hotel, 9500 Wilshire Blvd., Beverly Hills, CA 90212.

COUVILLION, GLYNNE CHARLES
Physician
b. Dec. 17, 1933, Baton Rouge, La.; s. Claude C. (dir. of adult edn. for state of La.) and Nell Marie (Heydel) Couvillion; grad., La. State Univ. and Virginia Mil. Inst. Undergrad. Sch.; M.D., La. State Univ. Sch. of Med., 1958; m. Gilliam Batham, May 25, 1962, British West Indies; chil.: John, b. Nov. 25, 1963; Sarah, b. Oct. 23, 1965; Stephen, b. Dec. 9, 1973. Career: Intern, Charity Hosp., New Orleans, 1958-59; 6 mos. residency in Pathology, 1959-60; Resident physician, Knut Hansen Med. Mem. Hosp., St. Thomas, Virgin Islands, 1960-62; U.S.N. Submarine Med. Ofcr., Underwater Demolition Team Unit, Coronado, Calif., 1962-64; Ophthalmological Residency, Tulane Med. Sch., New Orleans, 1964-67; Retina Fellowship, Retina Found., Mass. Eye & Ear Infirmary, Boston, 1967-69; pvt. practice of med. specializing in Diseases & Surgery of the Retina and Vitreous, 1969---. Mem.: Orleans Parish Med. Soc.; Santa Barbara Co. Med. Soc.; Santa Barbara Ophthalmological Soc.; Retina Soc.; Tulane Med. Ophthalmol. Alumni Assn.; Mass. Eye & Ear Infirmary Ophthalmol. Alumnia Assn.; Eastern Yacht Club, Marblehead, Mass.; Knollwood

Club, Santa Barbara; Univ. Club, Santa Barbara; Olympic Club, S.F. Catholic. Hobbies: horticulture, painting. Rec.: skiing, racquetball. Home: 690 Lilac Dr., Santa Barbara, CA 9310ᴿ· Office: 515 E. Micheltorena St., Santa Barbara, C.ᾳ 93103.

COX, JAMES LOGAN
Public Relations — Advertising Executive
b. July 16, 1916, Hinton, W. Va.; s. J. Logan and Mabel (Williams) Cox; desc. James Cox, author of W.Va. State Constitution; desc. Indian Chief Logan, reputedly only Indian Chief to address both houses of Congress; student, Berea Coll., Ky. 1935; Univ. of Ky. and Univ. of Cincinnati; m. Beverly Jean Finnegan, Dec. 9, 1964, Las Vegas, Nev. Career: Columnist, Hinton Daily News, Hinton, W.Va., 1930; gen. mgr. radio station WJLS, Beckley, W. Va., 1937; program dir. W. Va. Network, 1939; gen. mgr. Radio WISR, Butler, Penn. 1942; asst. to gen. mgr. Radio Div., AP, N.Y., 1943; area dir., station relations, Broadcast Music, Inc., N.Y., 1946; v.p., Glasser-Gailey Advertising, L.A., 1958; founder, pres., owner, the Jim Cox Co., Inc. (advertising and pub. relations), Northridge, 1962---; also owner, Jim Cox Outdoor Advertising. Editorial Asst. to Dir. of Psychol. Warfare, Office of War Information, WW II, N.Y.; named Hon. Col., Calif. Nat. Guard, 1954; named Hon. Citizen, State of Wash., 1953; Awarded Hon. Lifetime Mem.: 21 state broadcasters assns., 1951-55. Was Profl. newspaper columnist at age of 13 (1930). Mem.: Radio Execs. Club of N.Y., program dir., 1949-50; Elks Lodge No. 1497, Burbank, 22 yrs---. Mem. and Sun. Sch. Supt., First Christian Ch., Hinton, W.Va., 1929. Hobbies: writing one liners, poetry & prose. Rec.: swimming, horseshoes, archery. Home: 1239 E. Rose, Orange, CA 92667; Office: P.O. Drawer 5250, Orange, CA 92667.

CRAIG, ELLIS EDWARD
Chairman, Craig & Co.
b. Apr. 18, 1915, Pima, Ariz.; s. William Edward and Diantha (Smith) Craig; Gr.son, James Mormon Craig and Lot Smith, Mormon pioneers; student Gila Jr. Coll., Ariz. State Univ.; m. Jan Boyd, Salt Lake City; chil.: Diana (Mrs. Alexander Uhrich); Michael; Janeth; Gery; Ellis Boyd; Jon Russell; Lynda. Career: drama asst., Ariz. State Univ., 1935; radio announcer, KOY Ariz. network, 1937-39; program dir., Lockheed, 1940-44; founder pres., Craig & Co. (formerly Craig & Reid, Inc.), 1946---; Langford & Craig Oil & Gas Prod.; Park & Craig Restaurants, 1967-78; Primal Power Corp., 1969-78. Lt., AUS, 1944-46. Mem.: Rotary; Sertoma, treas., L.B. Johnson for President clubs, national 1959-60; pres., Theo-Sci. Found., 1965---. High Priest, L.D.S. ch. Hobby: electricity research. Rec.: tennis, horseback riding. Home: 1176 OakHills Way, Salt Lake City, Utah 84108; Office: 4667 MacArthur Blvd., Newport Beach, CA 92660.

CRAIG, GLENDON BROOKS
Commissioner, California Highway Patrol
b. Jan. 8, 1933, Lindsay, Calif.; s. Alton Brooks and Henrietta (Shamblee) Craig; grad. Exeter Union H.S.; student, Cal. State Univ., Sacto. & L.A.; Police Sci. Degree, Coll. of Sequoias, Visalia; m. Dorothy Jackson, Mar. 29, 1952, Reno, Nev.; chil.: Kevin M., b. Mar. 9, 1959; Deborah A., b. Dec. 15, 1962. Career: Calif. Highway Patrol (CHP) traffic officer, 1956-61, Sergeant, 1961-65, Lt., 1965-67, Capt., 1967-70, Inspector, 1971-72, Supr. Inspector, 1972-75, CHP Commissioner, 1975---; with Visalia Police Dept. 1955-56. AUS, 1953-55. Contbr.: The Police Chief Mag., Jan. 1978. Apptd. to Nat. Highway Safety Advis. Com. by Pres. Ford, 1976; Recipient: Award for Pub. Serv., Nat. Hiway Traffic Safety Adminstrn., Internat. Communication and Leadership Award, Toastmasters, Award of Merit, Ida Mayer Cummings Aux., L.A.; Pres., Am. Assn. of Motor Vehicle Adminstrs. 1977-78. Methodist Ch., officer, chmn. Administrv. Bd. of the Florin, 1970-72. Home: 8702 Santa Ridge Cir., Elk Grove, CA 95624; Office: 2555 First Ave., Sacto., CA 95818.

CRAIG, JOHN DAVID
Lieutenant Colonel, USAF (ret.)
b. Apr. 28, 1903, Cincinnati; s. John and Marie Johanna (Leuchsenring) Craig; Petroleum Engr., U.T.C.O., Torrance, 1923; scholar, Univ. Calcutta, India; m. Mildred Euna Das, Aug. 12, 1939, Chicago; chil.: Sharon Day (Daetwyler), b. July 28, 1940; Kathleen Jane (Keefe), b. May 28, 1946. Career: petroleum engr., 1920-24; world travel, 1924-28; motion picture cameraman, India, 1926, Ham. Adams. Expedition 1931; Panama, 1932; dir. Caribbean Exped., 1933; Dominican Republic, 1934-35; Philippines, 1938-39; active duty, USAF, 1941-47; Officer in charge U.S. Air Forces, Bikini Atom Tests

Photos, 1946-47; pres., Crayne TV Prods., various other TV prod. units, 1949---; pres., Morrison-Craig Prods., 1950---. Author: Danger Is My Business, Simon & Schuster, N.Y., London, 1938; mag. articles in Cosmopolitan, Esquire, Popular Mechanics, Coronet, Program, etc. Mem.: Adventurers Club of Chicago, 1935---; Savages Club, London; life mem. Kiwanis Internat., 1939---. Protestant. Rec.: scuba diving. Home: 31532 Crystal Sands Dr., So. Laguna, CA 92677.

CRAIG, THEODORE WARREN
Food Company Executive
b. May 21, 1940, San Francisco; s. Leo Franklin and Gertrude (Benner) Craig; B.S. Chem., Univ. Calif., Berkeley, 1962; Ph.D. org. chem., MIT, Cambridge, 1965; M.B.A. gen. mgmt., Univ. Calif., Berkeley, 1975; m. La Vaughn Elaine Austin, July 15, 1967, Minneapolis; chil.: Daniel Lucian, b. Feb. 26, 1970; Sara Elizabeth, b. June 12, 1972. Career: Sr. Res. Chem./Group Leader, General Mills, Inc., 1965-68; project leader indsl. foods, 1968-71; with Foremost Foods Co., 1968---: group leader indsl. foods, 1971-74; mgr. Product/Process Devel., 1974-76; dir., Research & Devel., 1976---. Holder of twelve U.S. and foreign patents; author of six sci. articles. Bd. dir., Lafayette Hist. Soc. 1976-79. Hobbies: book collecting, Am. hist. Office: 6363 Clark St., Dublin, CA 94566.

CRAMER, JAMES M.
District Attorney, San Bernardino Co.
b. Oct. 14, 1931, Sullivan, Ind.; s. Ralph and Mina Cramer; B.A., Univ. of Redlands, 1956; J.D., Univ. of Calif., Berkeley, 1960; m. Elizabeth Cramer, El Segundo, Calif., Jan. 31, 1959; chil.: Claire, David. Career: Dep. Dist. Atty. 1961-64, chief. dep. 1964-73, Asst. Dist. Atty. 1973-75, Dist. Atty. of San Bernardino Co., 1975---. U.S. Army, Signal Corps, 7th Army Hdqrs., Stuttgart, Ger. Mem.: dir. San Bernardino Co. Bar, past pres. Western div.; dir. Rotary Club; Am. Legion, Elks. Democrat. Methodist (chmn. bd. trustees). Hobby: model bldg. Rec.: hiking. Office: Courthouse, Rm. 200, 351 N. Arrowhead Ave., San Bernardino, CA 92415.

CRANE, HEWITT DAVID
Scientist
b. Apr. 27, 1927, Jersey City, N.J.; B.S. (E.E.), Columbia Univ. 1947; Ph.D., Stanford Univ., 1960; m. Suzanne Gorlin, June 20, 1954, N.Y.C.; chil.: Russell Philip, b. June 10, 1958; Douglas Mitchell, b. Aug. 18, 1959; Daniel Bruce, b. Sept. 13, 1961. Career: with Internat. Bus. Machines, N.Y.C., 1949-51; Inst. for Adv. Study, Princeton, N.J., 1952-55; RCA Labs., Princeton, N.J., 1955-56; staff scientist, SRI Internat., Menlo Park, 1956---. Dir.: Ridge Vineyards, Cupertino, 1967---; Energy Fair, Inc., Pacific Palisades, 1977---. Holder 57 U.S. patents; contbr. 40 tech. publ.; Fellow IEEE; Awards: NASA award for sci. achievement, 1970; Indsl. Research IR-100 awards, 1974, 76. USN, 1945-46. Home: 25 Cordova Ct., Portola Valley, CA 94025; Office: SRI International, Menlo Park, CA 94025.

CRANSTON, ALAN
U.S. Senator
b. June 19, 1914, Palo Alto, Calif.; s. William and Carol (Dixon) Cranston; B.A., Stanford Univ., 1936; m. Geneva McMath, Glendale, Calif., Nov. 6, 1940 (div. 1977); sons: Robin MacGregor, b. Nov. 1, 1947; Kim Christopher, b. Sept. 26, 1951. Career: Foreign corr., Internat. News Serv., Europe and Africa, 1936-38; investment, property mgmt. and real estate bus., Palo Alto, Calif., 1947-58; elected State Controller of Calif. 1959-67; elected U.S. Senator; Nov. 1968. Author: (book) The Killing of the Peace, 1945; (co-author) The Big Story (play), 1940. Chief, Foreign Lang. Div., Ofc. of War Information, Wash., D.C., 1942-44; Pvt. U.S. Army, 1944; Sgt. 1945, WW II. Mem.: pres. Calif. Dem. Council, 1953-57; exec. com. Calif. Central Com. 1954-60; Overseas Press Club of Am. Protestant. Hobby: sports. Rec.: swimming, running. Office: Senate Office Bldg., Wash., D.C. 20510.

CRESTON, PAUL
Composer
b. Oct. 10, 1906, N.Y.C.; s. Gaspare Guttoveggio and Carmela (Collura) Creston; ed. N.Y.C. pub. schs.; m. Louise Gotto, July 1, 1927, Paterson, N.J.; chil.: Joel Anthony, b. Nov. 24, 1938; Timothy William, b. Jan. 18, 1942. Career: organist, St. Malachy's Ch., N.Y.C., 1934-67; faculty mem., N.Y. Coll. of Music, 1934-67; distinguished vis. prof., Central Wash. State Coll., 1967; Composer-in-residence and Prof. of Music, Central Wash. State Coll., 1968-75; concert tour as pianist and accompanist, 1936; music dir., The Hour of Faith, Am. Broadcasting Co., 1944-50; Guggenheim Fellow, 1938-39;

Grantee, State Dept., Am. Spec. in Israel, Turkey, 1960. Author: Creative Harmony, Principles of Rhythm, Rational Metric Notation. Awards: Christopher, for original score to TV film, "Revolt in Hungary"; music award, Nat. Inst. of Arts & Letters, 1943; Music Critics Circle award for Symphony No. 1, 1943; Alice M. Ditson award for POEM for Harp and Orchestra, 1945; Nat. Fedn. of Music Clubs award for Symphony No. 2, 1947; Music. Lib. Assn. award for Two Choric Dances, 1948; 1st prize for Symphony No. 1, Paris Referendum Concert, 1952; gold medal, Nat. Arts Club, 1963; citation of merit, Nat. Assn. of Composers & Conductors, 1941, 43 (pres. 1956-60). Mem.: The Bohemians, gov.; Am. Soc. of Composers, Authors and Publishers (ASCAP), dir. 1960-68, nat. music council exec. com., 1950-68. Rel. Vedanta. Hobbies: linguistics, naturopathy, bowling. Rec.: scrabble, pinochle. Address: Box 28511, San Diego, CA 92128.

CROCKETT, ETHEL STACY
  California State Librarian
b. Jan. 19, 1915, Mt. Vernon, N.Y.; d. Henry Pomeroy and Marian (Putnam) Stacy; B.A., Vassar College, 1936; M.A., San Jose State Univ., 1962; m. Clement Wirt Crockett, Aug. 17, 1936, Dearborn, Mich. (div. 1969); chil.: Patricia (Johnson), b. Nov. 2, 1938; Richard Wirt, b. Sept. 14, 1944; m. 2d. Jack Howard Aldridge, June 22, 1973, Las Vegas, Nev. Career: librarian, Corning, N.Y. Memorial Lib., 1958; Sequoia Union High Sch. Lib., Redwood City, 1960-61; San Jose City Coll. Lib., 1962-68; dir. of Library services, City Coll. of San Francisco, 1968-72; State Librarian, State of California, Sacramento, 1972---; Pres., Calif. Inst. of Librarians, 1973-74; pres., Chief Officers of State Library Agencies, 1974-76; mem., Nat. Advis. Com. on State Statistics, 1975-78; chmn., Calif. Bd. of Library Examiners; v.p., Calif. Sir Francis Drake Commn., 1973---. Named Hon. Col., State of Kentucky; Hon. Lt. Col., State of Alabama; Hon. Citizen of Texas. Mem.: Am. Lib. Assn.; Calif. Lib. Assm.; Book Club of Calif. Unitarian. Hobbies: gardening, book collecting. Rec.: swimming. Home: 1500 7th St., Apt. 14-E, Sacramento, CA 95814; Office: Calif. State Lib., Sacramento, CA 95809.

CROMMELIN, ROBERT WILCOX
  Transportation Engineer
b. May 10, 1928, S.F.; s. Harold H. and Harriet E. (Green) Crommelin; A.A., Modesto Jr. Coll., 1947; B.S., Univ. Calif., Berkeley, 1949; M. Engr., 1955; m. Barbara Darby, Apr. 6, 1956, S.F.; chil.: Stanley R., b. July 6, 1947; Randy S., b. July 23, 1948; Janis E. (Peffley), b. Mar. 15, 1951; Lee Ann, b. Sept. 25, 1957. Career: Traffic engr.: Calif. Div. of Highways, 1949-50, 1953-54; Richmond, Calif. 1955-56; San Leandro, 1956-59; Hayward, 1959-65; Wilbur Smith and Assoc., 1965-68; pres., Robert Crommelin and Assocs., Inc., 1968---. AUS, 1950-53, Korea; currently Col., USAR Corps of Engrs., Registered Profl. Engr., Alaska, Ariz., Calif., Nev., N. Mex., Ore. Pres., Western Dist. Inst. of Transportation Engrs., 1975; vice commodore, Santa Monica Yacht Club, 1979. Hobby: sailing. Home: 5477-25 Nestle Ave., Tarzana, CA; Office: 17071 Ventura Blvd., Encino, CA 91316.

CROWELL, JAMES BENJAMIN
  Bank President
b. June 13, 1933, Orange, Calif.; s. Archie Fred, Jr. and Ruth Rebecca Crowell; B.S., Sch. of Commerce, USC, 1955; m. Barbara Lynn Jeffries, June 29, 1957, Abilene, Tex.; chil.: David Jeffrey, b. Jan. 23, 1960; John Frederick, b. Dec. 20, 1962; Michael Scott, b. Mar. 7, 1971; James Robert, b. July 20, 1972. Career: Capt., USAF, 1955-57; v.p. First California Bank, 1958-71; pres., Eldorado Bank, 1971---. Mil.: USAF R.O.T.C., USC, 1951-55; Navigator, USAF, 1955-57; USAF Reserve, 1957-65; USAF Ret., 1965---. Dir., Independent Bankers of So. Calif., 1957---; Mem.: Western Ind. Bankers, 1957---; Calif. Bankers Assn., 1957---; Am. Bankers Assn. 1957---; Bank Administrn. Inst., 1957---. Past Pres. Santa Ana Young Republicans, 1958-60. Mem.: Santa Ana Elks Club; Santa Ana Rotary Club (past treas.); Tustin C. of C. (past v.p.); Beta Theta Pi Alumni Assn. (treas.), 1955---. Mem. Santa Ana 20-30 Club (past pres.), 1960-69; Garden Grove C. of C. (dir.) 1965-67; Garden Grove Rotary (treas) 1965-67; Mem. 1st Presbyterian Ch., Santa Ana (past Deacon). Rec.: swimming, tennis, fishing and travel. Home: 1371 Treasure Lane, Santa Ana, CA 92705; Office: Eldorado Bank, 17th St. at Prospect, Tustin, CA 92680.

CRUIKSHANK, WILLIAM ADELBERT, JR.
  Attorney at Law
b. Sept. 10, 1923, Seattle, Wash.; s. William Adelbert and Elsie (Cummings) Cruikshank; student L.A. City Coll.,

1942042; J.D., USC, 1949; m. Rita J. Rayburn, Oct. 2, 1954; chil.: William Adelbert III and John Charles. Career: Admitted to Calif. bar, 1949, since practiced in L.A., Beverly Hills; mem. faculty Law Sch., USC, 1950-56. Secty., dir. Four Star Prodns., 1952-55, pres., 1955-57; sectry., dir. First Surety Corp., Burbank, 1953-69; pres., dir. Volkswagen Santa Monica, Inc., 1970---, Volkswagen Fresno, Inc., 1975---, v.p., dir. Trans-World Motors, Inc., Santa Barbara, 1974---. Served to 1st lt. USAAF, 1942-45. Mem.: Am., Los Angeles and Beverly Hills Bar Assns.; Chancery Club, Order of Coif; Phi Kappa Phi; Phi Alpha Delta. Clubs: California (L.A.); Newport Harbor Yacht; Balboa Bay. Home: 708 N. Arden Dr., Beverly Hills, CA 90210; Office: 8383 Wilshire Blvd., Suite 1040, Beverly Hills, CA 90211.

CRUM, JEAN FREDERICK
  General and Thoracic Surgeon
b. Feb. 3, 1920, Lodi, Oh.; s. Clarence Crum; ed. B.S., Baldwin Wallace Coll., Berea, Oh. 1942; M.D., Coll. of Med., Univ. of Cincinnati, Oh. 1945; m. Gloria E. Bell; chil.: Frederick Lee, b. Sept. 22, 1956; Kristina Louise, b. Aug. 9, 1961. Career: gen.-thoracic surg. tr., Cleveland City Hosp., Cleveland, Oh., 1948-54; est. surg. practice, Downey, Calif., 1954---; past chief of staff-chmn. Surg. Sect.: Downey Comm. Hosp., Studebaker Comm. Hosp., Norwalk; past chmn. Surg. Sect., St. Francis Hosp., Lynwood; asst. clin. prof. of surg. USC; attending staff, L.A. Co.-USC Med. Center; asst. clin. prof. of surg. Loma Linda Univ. Lt. (j.g.), USNR, 1946-48. Mem.: diplomate, Am. Bd. of Surg.; fellow, Am. Coll. of Surgs.; Med. Symposium Soc. of L.A.; Am. Cancer Soc., L.A. Co. Br., 1955---, bd. dirs. and coms., pres. 1969; bd. dirs. Health Planning Assn. of So. Calif.; Calif. Hosps. and Related Health Facilities and Planning Servs. Com.; bd. trustees, L.A. Co. Med. Assn., numerous coms. chmn., councilor, 1969-72; pres. 1972-73; del. AMA 1972; bd. trustees, Calif. Blue Shield, 1969-72; L.A. Acad. of Med.; L.A. Surg. Soc.; Rotary Club. Hobbies: gun collecting, hunting, ammunition handloading, camping, skiing. Home: 7123 Rio Flora Place, Downey, CA 90241; Office: 11411 S. Brookshire Ave., Downey, CA 90241.

CSENDES, ERNEST
  Business Executive
b. March 2, 1926, Satu-Mare, Rumania (U.S. Cit. 1955); s. Edward O. and Sidonia (von Littman) Csendes; ed. B.A., Prot. Coll., Hungary, 1944; B.S., Univ. of Heidelberg, W. Ger. 1948; M.S., 1950, Ph.D., 1951; m. Catharine Vera von Tolnai, N.Y.C., Feb. 7, 1953; chil.: Audrey Carol, b. June 1, 1957; Robert Alexander Edward, b. Apr. 14, 1962. Career: Research asst. (chem), Univ. of Heidelberg, 1950-51; came to U.S. 1951; research assoc. (biochem), Tulane Univ., New Orleans, 1951-52; Fellow, Harvard Univ. 1952-53; research chem., E.I. Du Pont de Nemours and Co., Wilmington, Del. 1953-61, organic chems div., Armour & Co., Atlanta, 1961-63; v.p. corporate devel. div., Occidental Petroleum Corp., 1963-64, exec. v.p.-research engr. & devel. 1964-68, exec. v.p.-chief opr. ofcr.-dir., Occidental Research Corp. 1963-68; dir. Occidental Research and Engring. Ltd. of United Kingdom, 1964-68; pres.-chief exec. ofcr. Tex. Republic Inds. 1968---; TRI Ltd., and chmn. TRI Internat. Ltd., Bermuda, 1971; mgr.-dir. TRI Holdings S.A., Luxembourg, 1971; TRI Capitol, Netherlands; Internat. research projects into exploitation of natural resources and regional industrial and agricultural devel., commodity trading, areas of Africa, Europe, USSR, The Middle East, Asia, Far East, Australia, S. Am. (acq. merger, internat. finance, banking, ins. related to securities, leasing, petroleum and minerals). Contbr. approx. 40 articles in sci., Pollution Control, Min., Petroleum, tech. and mgmt. to profl. journs. Patentee: many sci research patents (elastomers, rubber chems., dyes and intermediates, organometallics, organic and biochem., high polymers, plant nutrients, pesticides, process engring. and design of fertilizer plants). Mem.: fellow, AAAS; fellow, Am. Inst. Chems., Am. Chem. Soc., N.Y. Acad. Scis., Am. Defense Preproducers Assn.; London Chem. Soc., Faraday Soc., Ger. Chem. Soc., Am. Mgmt. Assn., Am. Inst. of Mgmt., Soc. of Plastics Engrs., Am. Inst. of Aeronautics and Astronautics, Acad. of Polit. Scis., Columbia Univ., Am. Acad. Polit. and Soc. Sci., Research Soc. of Am., Sigma Xi, Am. Marketing Assn. Hobby: art collector - decorative arts of 18th century France, photog. Rec.: fishing, playing violin, chamber music. Home: 1601 Cassle Rd., Pacific Palisades, CA 90272.

CUADRA, CARLOS ALBERT
  Company President
b. Dec. 21, 1925, S.F.; s. Gregorio and Amanda (Mendoza) Cuadra; A.B., psychol., w/highest hons., Univ. Calif., Berkeley, 1949, Ph.D., 1953; m. Gloria Adams,

May 3, 1947, San Anselmo; chil.: Mary Susan (Nielsen), b. Dec. 21, 1942; Neil Gregory, b. Aug. 3, 1953; Dean Arthur, b. Apr. 27, 1956. Career: staff psychologist, VA Hosp., Downey, Ill., 1953-56; with System Devel. Corp., Santa Monica, 1957-78, as Mgr. of Lib. and Documentation Systems Dept., 1968-70, Mgr. of Edn. & Lib. Systems Dept. 1971,73, Gen. Mgr. of SDC Search Service, 1974-78; pres., founder, Cuadra Assoc., Inc. (specialists in computer-based online info. systems), 1978---; estab. & ed., Annual Review of Information Sci. & Tech., 1964-75. Publs. in fields of psychol. and information sci. Recipient of Merit Award, Am. Assn. for Information Sci. (ASIS), 1968, Best Information Sci. Book Award, ASIS, 1969, named distin. lectr. of Year, ASIS, 1970. USNR, 1944-46. Mem.: Nat. Commn. on Libraries & Info. Sci., 1971---; mem. bd. dir., Info. Indus. Assn.; Phi Beta Kappa, 1949. Hobbies: playing Jazz Piano, bridge. Rec.: skiing. Office: 1523-6th St., Suite 12, Santa Monica, CA 90401.

CUBALESKI, VASA
Yogurt Manufacturer
b. Jan. 6, 1916, Galichnik, Macedonia; s. Mircha and Nasta (Andejevic) Cubaleski; mat. grandfather, Jakov, noted Macedonia fresco artist; pat. grandfather, Ognavov, pres. of Hipotekarna Bank, Yugoslavia; grad., Gymnasium in Business and Food Industry (prodn.), 1931. Trained in family bus. in mgmt., processing and quality control. Career: worked in family food factory 1930-41, processing, researching and lab. testing of cultured foods, working with secret formulas devel. by family; cultured food spec. for nine centuries; this factory prod. food products for the King and palace staff; food mfg. advisor to Food Co-op., Europe, 1945-54; arrived in N.Y. (with $5.00 in pocket) 1954; laborer to quality controller, packing house, Milwaukee, 1954-55; quality control tech., vitamin factory, L.A., 1956-60; founder, owner, pres., Am. Yogurt Co. which became Continental Culture Specialists, 1961---. He was first to use a natural culture from Europe, now has 32 types of yogurt products. Mil.: Active in Resistance Movement, WW II. Recipient: Spec. award from King Peter II of Yugoslavia for personal and bus. high standards and achievements, 1940; Newspaper award for business achievement (youngest recipient in history of Yugos'avia), 1936. Mem. Glendale Kiwanis Club. Chmn., Young Men's Political Club, Belgrade, 1934-41. Eastern Orthodox ch. Hobbies: spec. cooking, health food studies, dog training, assisting immigrants to U.S.A. Rec.: folk dancing, music, walking, travel, soccer. Office: P.O.B. 9285, 1354 E. Colorado St., Glendale, CA 91206.

CUMMINGS, JACK BLAIR
University Administrator
b. Sept. 28, 1928, Pasadena; s. Lawrence B. and Margaret L. (Lawson) Cummings; Ed. B.A., Univ. of Redlands, 1950, A.M., 1965; grad. Calif. Coll. of Mortuary Sci. 1951; L.A. State Coll. 1953; m. Lillian Schaefer, Pasa., Calif., June 23, 1950; chil.: Pamela Dee, b. Oct. 5, 1951; Marc Blair, b. May 14, 1953; Cynthia Lee, b. May 17, 1957; Todd Prescott, b. Dec. 25, 1960; Career: Edwards & Cummings Cortuary, Pasa. 1951-53; Travelers Ins. Co. 1954; Univ. of Redlands, 1954---, dir. Alumni Rels. and Placement, 1954-63; vice pres., 1976; Univ. Rels. 1963-76; Councilman, City of Redlands, 1964-76, Mayor, 1970-76; chmn. Redlands Redevel. Agcy., chmn. Parking Authority, 1970-76; Orgn. of Urban Coalition, 1970-71; pres. Citrus Belt Div., Calif. League of Cities, 1971-72; exec. com. San Bernardino Assoc.; chmn. Advis. Bd., Bank of Redlands, 1976---; Govts. 1973-76; Contrib. to many publs. Awards: 10 achievement awards, Am. Alumni Council, 1958-67; Freedoms Found. Award, 1961; Distinguished Serv. Award, Univ. of Redlands Alumni Assn. 1962; Young Man of Yr., Redlands Jr. C. of C. 1962; AAC Editorial Comment and Opinion Award, 1967; Presidential Award, Reg. Econ. Devel. Corp., 1969. Mem.: Jr. C. of C., Pasa., 1951-54; bd. dirs. Inland Personnel Assn. 1956-61, pres. 1960; bd. dirs. Redlands Kiwanis Club, 1957-63; pres. 1962; natl. bd. dirs. Am. Alumni Council, dist. chmn. Calif., Ariz., Nev., Hawaii, 1963-65; (charter) bd. dirs. Reg. Econ. Devel. Corp., pres. 1968. Pres. Am. Bapt. Youth Fellowship, Western Area, 1948; pres. Pasa. Youth Council of Chs. 1951-52; bd. deacons, First Bapt. Ch., Pasa. 1954; bd. Chr. Edn., First Bapt. Ch., Redlands, 1955-57, b.d trustees, 1968-71; v.p. Redlands Day Nursery, 1978---; Bd. of Deacons, 1978---. Hobbies: bldg., tennis, boating, fishing, water skiing, photog. Home: 1308 Fairview Lane, Redlands, CA 92373; Office: Univ. of Redlands, Redlands, CA.

CUNNINGHAM, CATHARINE JULIE, SISTER
College President
b. Oct. 22, 1910, San Francisco; d. John Francis and Mary Cecilia (McCarthy) Cunningham; B.A., Univ. Calif.,

Berkeley, 1932; M.A., Catholic Univ. of America, Wash., D.C., 1954; D.H.L., h.c., Univ. San Francisco, 1978. Career: Joined Sisters of Notre Dame de Namur, 1932; high school principal, 1942-56; pres., College of Notre Dame, 1956---. Roman Catholic. Office: College of Notre Dame, Belmont, CA 94002.

CURRAN, FRANK EARL
Former Mayor, City of San Diego
b. Dec. 19, 1912, Cleveland, Oh.; s. William E. and Anna (Hayer) Curran; grad. Oceanside-Carlsbad H.S. 1931; stu. (acct., law, gen. admr., ind. mgmt., psychol., night sch. 10 yrs.) San Diego Jr. Coll., Balboa Law Sch., S.D. State Coll., Univ. of Calif. Ext.; m. Florence McKenney. Career: Laborer, stevedore, partner, wholesale-retail prod. market, painting and decorating contr., San Diego Co., dep. Co. Assessor, 1935-41; Oceanside's first City storekeeper, 1937-38; supv. procurement for critical materials, USN 1940-49; secty-mgr. Fraternal Order of Eagles (dir. bldg. new club house), 1949-60; assoc. Shoreline Ins. Co. 1960-63. Elected City Councilman, S.D. 1955-63, V. Mayor, 1957-58, 1961-62, Mayor of San Diego, Nov. 1963-71. Mem.: gen. chmn., S.D. Host City, Inter-Am. Municipal Orgn. Congress, 1960, Cong. presiding ofcr., Punta del Esta, Uruguay, 1962, exec. com. 1967---, bd. dirs. 1970---; bd. dirs League Com. on Internat. Municipal Cooperation, 1961; policy com. S.D. Border Area Pgm., Municipal Alliance for Planning and Devel., coord. with Mex's. Natl. Border Pgm.; bd. dirs. Palm City Sanitation Dist.; gov's. spec. repr. Comm. of the Californias; Calif. Gov's. Adv. Com. on Aviation; Community Rels. Com. U.S. Conf. of Mayors; apptd. chmn. Com. on Internat. Municipal Cooperation, Natl. League of Cities, Cong. of Cities, Detroit, Mich., July 1965; bd. dirs. Natl. League of Cities, 1966--- (steering com. Sister City Pgm., 1967), v.p. 1969-70, pres. 1970; ex. off. S.D. Com., Cooperative Area Manpower Planning System. Home: 4901 Randall St., San Diego, CA 92109; Office; Downtown Assn., 631 Home Tower, San Diego, CA 92101.

CURRAN, JAMES ALBERT
Construction Company Executive
b. Apr. 28, 1917, Boston, Mass.; s. Sylvester Michael and Anne (Coyne) Curran; bro of John J. Curran, chmn., pres., Bay State Bank, Worcester, Mass., and bro. of S. Robert, sr. editor, Buffalo Evening News; B.S., U.S. Naval Acad., 1941; M.B.A., USC, 1956; m. Jane Harvey, July 11, 1942, Pasadena; chil.: Jane Ann (Mrs. Marshall C. Turner, Jr.), b. Aug. 12, 1943; Michael Harvey, b. Mar. 5, 1948. Career: mil. service, USC, 1941-46; with C.F. Braun & Co., Alhambra, 1946---: Head of Estimating and head of scheduling, 1946-53; project mgr., 1953-67; contract mgr., 1967-71; v.p. and secty., 1971---. Mil.: Commd. ensign, USC, 1941, advanced to lt. comdr., 1945, gunnery officer U.S.S. Strong (DD467), damage control officer U.S.S. North Carolina, 1945-46; tchr. tactics U.S. Naval Postgrad. Sch., Annapolis, 1943-44; ret., 1946. Decorated Bronze Star medal with combat V and Letter of Commendation. Contbr. tech. articles in hydrocarbon processing and automation progress, Engineering & Mining Journ., 1957. Mem.: Valley Hunt Club, Pasadena, 1946-71; Annandale Golf Club, 1971---, Chmn., 42nd Assem. Dist., United Republicans of Calif., 1962-63. Roman Catholic. Hobbies: golf, photog., music. Home: 710 Pinehurst Dr., Pasadena, CA 91106; Office: C.F. Braun & Co., Alhambra, CA 91802.

CURTIS, DON McCAULEY
Orthopedic Surgeon
b. Mar. 30, 1911, Salt Lake City, Utah; s. Foster J. and Leah (Nicholson) Curtis; B.A., Univ. of Utah, 1933; Spec. Certificate of Med., 1935; M.D., Rush Med. Coll., 1937; m. Carol Cartwright, June 11, 1964, Las Vegas, Nev.; chil.: Brian K., b. Feb. 26, 1943; Sue Williams, b. June 20, 1945; Wendy Kraft, b. Feb. 3, 1948. Career: intern & resident physician, L.A. Co. Hosp., 1937-41; practice of med. in L.A., 1941-43; Served Lt. to Maj., AUS, 1943-46; practice in Pasadena, 1946---. Clin. instr. of Orthopedics, L.A. Co. Gen. Hosp., 1946-51. Diplomate of Am. Bd. of Orthopedic Surgery. Mem.: AMA and Western Orthopedic Soc. Mil. served: Halloran Gen. Hosp., N.Y.; Rhodes Gen. Hosp., Utica, N.Y.; Tinian; Iwo Jima. Mem.: Phi Delta Theta coll. frat., Phi Beta Pi med. frat. Hobby: automobiles new & old. Rec.: working on automobiles. Home: 501 E. Sandra, Arcadia, CA 91006; Office: 90 N. Madison, Pasadena, CA 91101.

CURTIS, MARK HUBERT
President, Scripps College
b. July 7, 1920, Medford, Minn.; s. James Hubert and Lydia (Krueger) Curtis; B.A., Yale Univ. 1942; M.A. 1947; Ph.D., 1953; m. Maria Isabel Bird y Zalduondo, New Haven, Conn., Nov. 7, 1945; chil.: Mary Katherine,

b. Nov. 17, 1950; Thomas Mark, b. July 21, 1955. Career: Instr. (hist.), Williams Coll. Williamstown, Mass. 1950-53; asst. prof. hist., UCLA, 1953-59; assoc. prof. 1959-64; assoc. dean of grad. div. 1962-64; research prof.-cons., Folger Shakespeare Lib., Wash., D.C. (summer), 1964; pres. Scripps Coll., Claremont, 1964---; Lectr., Danforth Summer Seminar. Pac. Sch. of Relig., Berkeley, 1957; Author: Oxford and Cambridge in Transition (1588-1642), publ. Oxford, Clarendon Press 1959; Hampton Court Conf. and Its Aftermath (hist.) 1961; The Alienated Intellectuals of Early Stuart England (past and present), 1962; Education and Apprenticeship (Shakespeare in his own age), Cambridge, Eng. 1964; William Jones: Puritan Printer and Propagandist, Library, Vol. XIX, 1964, London. Awards: Social Sci. Research Council Fellowship, 1948-49; Guggenheim Fellowship, 1959-60; Fellow, Folger Shakespeare Lib. 1962; Robert Livingston Schuyler Prize by Am. Hist. Assn. 1961; Danforth Found. Short-Term Leave Grant, 1970. Ensign, Lt. Comdr., USNR (1942-46) WW II. Mem.: trustee, Hawaii Loa Coll., Honolulu; Westridge Sch., Pasa.; Loyola Univ., L.A.; Regents' Council of Mt. St. Mary's Coll., L.A.; trustee, Conf. on Brit. Studies; bd. govs. Claremont Pastoral Counseling Center; bd. dirs. Southwest Museum; Phi Beta Kappa; Am. Hist. Assn.; Renaissance Soc. of Am.; treas. Renaissance Conf. of So. Calif. 1956-59, pres. 1963-64; pres. Western Assn. of Colls. 1970-72; pres. Independent Colls. of So. Calif. 1970-72; Assn. of Am. Colls. Comm. on Liberal Learning; fellow, Royal Hist. Soc. Presbyterian. Rec.: fishing, hiking. Home: President's House, Scripps Coll., Claremont, CA; Office: Scripps Coll., Claremont, CA.

CURTIS, WILLIAM DEDENROTH
Monterey County District Attorney
b. July 4, 1930, Monterey, Calif.; s. Guy S. and Kerstine (Larsen) Curtis; Monterey Peninsula Coll. 1949-52; San Jose State Coll. 1952-54; Hastings Coll. of Law; Natl. Coll. of Dist. Attys.; m. Adriana De Groot, Monterey, June 14, 1969; dau. Kerstine L., b. Aug. 19, 1973. Career: Fireman's Fund-Bond Co., 1956-58; partner, Kennedy, Dormody & Curtis law firm, 1958-63; Kennedy, Dormody, Dewar, Romig & Curtis 1963-65, Dewar, Romig & Curits, 1966-70; City Councilman, Monterey, 1965-70; elected, Dist. Atty. of Monterey Co. 1970---. Admitted to practice: Calif. Supreme Ct., U.S. Ct. of Appeals, Fed. Dist. Ct. No. Dist. of Calif., U.S. Supreme Ct. Awards: Outstanding Young Man of Yr., 1960. Mem.: Calif. State, Monterey Co. Bar Assns.; Calif. Dist Attys. Assn. Legislative Adv. Comm.; Calif., Natl. Dist. Attys. Assns.; Monterey Co. Peace Ofcrs. Assn.; Monterey Co. Criminal Justice Planning Com. of Calif. Council on Criminal Justice, past chmn. Reg. M. Coms.; Calif. Trial Lawyers Assn.; dir. Central Mission Trails Heart Assn.; state bd. dirs. Am. Heart Assn.; chmn. Monterey Red Cross, chmn. reg. bd. dirs.; chmn. Assn. Monterey Co. Govts.; bd. dirs. Sports Car Racing Assn. (Laguna Seca track), Monterey Peninsula; bd. dirs. Monterey History and Art Assn.; (life) Delta Hastings Alumni Assn.; Phil Alpha. Hobbies: sports cars, automotive engring., photog. Home: P.O.B. 1369, Salinas, CA 93901.

CUSHMAN, ELLIOTT LOUIS
Publisher
b. Jan. 22, 1915, L.A.; s. Phillip R. and Sara L. Cushman; ed. Glendale Jr. Coll. 1932-33; State Coll. 1933-37; A.A., City Coll.; m. Helen Newbauer, S.F., Jan. 27, 1940; sons: Stephen P., b. Jan. 2, 1941; Lawrence M., b. Mar. 24, 1943. Career: Dist. mgr., Circulation Dept., Glendale News Press, 1927-33; circulation mgr., San Diego Independent (Southwest Color Press), 1933-35, asst. mgr. 1935-39, publ. 1939---. Consultant, Heftel Broadcasting, Hawaii; Stock-holder, KUAM, Guam. Dir. Verified Audit Circulation Corp. Awards: Anti-Defamation League Award, 1961; Salvation Army Award. Mem.: past pres., Better Bus. Bur.; past chmn. bd., Salvation Army; State Scholarship Comm.; Calif. State Heart Assn.; bd. dirs.: San Diego Urban League, Navy League, S.D. Conv. & Tourist Bur., Big Brothers of Am., Calif. Newspaper Publs. Assn., Community Chest, Community Welfare Council, Jewish Community Center, Joint Def. Appeal, Jr. Achievement, Am. Red Cross, S.D. Hosp. Assn., Donald N. Sharp Mem. Hosp., Tri-Hosp. Bldg. Fund, United Fund and United Jewish Fed.; B'nai B'rith; pres. Friends of Library, Univ. of Calif. at S.D.; bd. dirs. Thanks to Scandinavia; Sigma Delta Chi. Republican (co-chmn. Repub. orgn., San Diego Co. 1952). Jewish (bd. dirs., Temple Beth Israel; v.p.-bd. dirs., Temple Solel) Office: 2901 Fifth Ave., San Diego, CA 92103.

CUTLER, MAX
Physician
b. May 9, 1899, Russia; s. Sam and Esther (Tchudnowski)

Cutler; B.S., Univ. of Georgia, 1918; M.D., Johns Hopkins Univ. 1922; grad. studies, Curie Inst., Paris, Radiumhemet, Stockholm; m. Bertie Burger, Apr. 12, 1946, Chicago; chil.: Nina (Miller), b. Mar. 24, 1947; Nancy (Billingsley), b. Oct. 23, 1948; Susie (Baker), b. Feb. 10, 1952. Career: resident surgeon, Johns Hopkins Hosp., 1922-23; asst. in surgery, Michael Reese Hosp., 1923-24; instr. in pathology, Cornell Med. Sch., 1924-26; Rockefeller Fellow in cancer research, Mem. Hosp., N.Y., 1926-30; dir., N.Y.C. Cancer Inst., 1930-31; founder, dir., Tumor Clin., Michael Reese Hosp., 1931-37; cons. & dir. cancer research, U.S. Vet Adminstrn., 1931-46; vis. prof. of surgery under Rockefeller Found., Peking Union Med. Coll., China, 1936-37; founder, med. dir., Chicago Tumor Inst., 1938-52; assoc. prof. of surgery, Northwestern Univ. Med. Sch., 1932-40; surgical staff, St. Johns Hosp., L.A., 1952-58; med. dir., Beverly Hills Cancer Research Found., 1966---; surgical staff mem., Cedars-Sinai, Century City Hosps.; lectr., UCLA Dept. of Mammography. Mil.: Officers Training Sch., Plattsburg, N.Y., 1918. Author: Tumors of the Breast, with Sir George Lenthal Cheatle, 1931 (won Walker Prize given every 5th yr., Royal Coll. of Surgeons of England for outstanding cancer research contbrn.); Cancer, Its Diagnosis and Treatment, 1938; Tumors of the Breast, 1962; more than 100 contrbrns. to med. journs. on cancer. 1st pres., Am. Assn. for Study of Neoplastic Diseases, 1933-34; Mem. Nat. Advis. Cancer Council, 1939-42; N.Y. Acad. of Med.; Am. Radium Soc.; Am. Assn. of Cancer Research; Internat. Coll. of Surgeons; Am. Bd. of Radiology. Jewish. Home: 1840 Fairburn Ave., Apt. 407, L.A., CA 90025; Office: 9641 Sunset Blvd., Beverly Hills, CA 90210.

D

DAAR, DAVID
Attorney at Law
b. May 23, 1931, Chicago, Ill.; s. Julius and May Daar (Scheps); ed. A.B., Sacto. State Coll. 1955; J.D., Loyola Sch. of Law, L.A., 1956; m. Thelma G. Schwartz, L.A., Calif., 1953; chil.: Jeffery Jay, Eric Steven, Karen Lynn. Career: Admitted to practice, State Bar of Calif. 1956, U.S. Dist Ct. 1957, Supreme Ct. of U.S. 1960, Tax Ct. of U.S. 1969. Adv. Com. to State Supt. of Pub. Instrn., Calif. 1965-66; Natl. Panel of Arbitrators, Am. Arbitration Assn. 1966---; faculty, First Natl. Coll. of Advocacy, 1971; Local Bd. Selective Serv. Sys., 1971---. Co-author: Course of Study High Schools Business Law ("Moot Ct." stu. pgm. L.A. City Schs.); (book) Lawyer-Client Employment Agreement, 1965; author numerous articles, Aviation Litigation. USAF, 1950-53. Lectr., Class Action Lawsuits, Trial Strategy Securities litigation; Legal editor, Rotor & Wing Internat., 1974---. Mem.: L.A. Co. Bar Assn., Com. on Fed. Cts. and Practice; State Bar of Calif., Adm. Com. 1970---; chmn. Fed. Cts. Com., 1972; Calif. Trial Lawyers Assn., Amici Curiae Com., 1971. Office: Miller & Daar, 9100 Wilshire Blvd., Beverly Hills, CA 90212.

DAGGETT, ROBERT HALE
Company Executive
b. July 25, 1937, Los Angeles, Calif.; s. Rodney Roosevelt, Sr., and Mary Norma (Falls) Daggett; A.A., Fullerton Jr. Coll., 1956; A.A. San Jose State Coll., 1956. Children: David, b. Nov. 27, 1958; Todd, b. Apr. 14, 1962. Career: Planning dept., Carter Hawley Hale, 1959-63; Chaix & Johnson Associates, 1963---: Assoc., 1968; v.p., 1971; exec. v.p. and mem. bd. of dir., 1974---. Mem.: AIA and Inst. of Store Planners; Nat. Council of Architectural Registration Bds. (NCARB), Archtl. Guild of USC. Clubs: Mission Hills Country, Jonathan. Republican. Methodist. Hobby: Cooking. Rec.: golf. Home: 469 Stanford Dr., Arcadia, CA 91006; Office: 7060 Hollywood Blvd., L.A., CA 90028.

DAHL LOREN SILVESTER
Attorney at Law · Civic Leader
b. Mar. 1, 1921, E. Fairview, N. Dak.; s. William T. and Maud (Silvester) Dahl; 2nd cousin, Knute Rockne, coach, Notre Dame football team fame; ed. A.A., Coll. of Pac. 1940; LL.B., J.D., Univ. of Calif., S.F. 1949; m. Luana Siler, Corning, Calif., Apr. 5, 1942; chil.: Candy, b. Oct. 25, 1954; Walter Ray, b. Nov. 21, 1956. Career: Partner, Dahl, Hefner, Stark & Marois law firm, Sacto., Sept. 1950---; admitted to practice before U.S. Supreme Ct. and Calif. Supreme Ct. Distinguished Serv. Award, Young Man of Yr., City of Sacto., 1956; Mr. Philharmonic, Sacto. Philharmonic Assn. (now Sacto. Sym. Assn.), 1956. Mem.: pres. Univ. of Pac. Quarterback Club, Sacto., 1952; pres. Univ. of Pac. Alumni Assn. 1974-78; bus. dir., Sacto.

United Crusade, 1956; Safety Council, 1957-59; Sacto. Sym. Assn. 1958-59; Comstock Club, Sacto., 1965; Am., Calif. and Sacto. Co. Bar Assns., Am. Judicature Soc., Am. Arbitration Assn., Masons, Scottish Rite, Shrine, Phi Delta Phi, Sutter Club, Del Paso Country Club, Commonwealth Club of Calif. Hobbies: organ, flying. Rec.: golf. Home: 1957 Rockwood Dr., Sacto., CA 95825; Office: 555 Capitol Mall, Suite 1425, Sacto., CA 95814.

DAILEY, MAE HILEMAN
Business Executive -- Community Leader
b. Oct. 19, 1907, Mable, Ore.; d. Richard and Martha J. (Trotter) Hileman; B.A., Univ. of Ore., 1929; Univ. of Chicago, Chicago Theol. Sem. 1934-36; m. Earl Charles Dailey, San Jose, Calif., Nov. 8, 1944; Career: H.S. tchr., 1930-34; soc. serv. 1938-39; asst. dir. Children's Home, 1939-44, exec. dir. 1944-56; co-owner-mgr. Mobile Home Park, 1956-64; co-owner, Royal Pines Pvt. Family Camp, 1964---; pres., exec. dir. Child Care, 1949-52; pres., Community Soc. Workers, 1952-53; sect. chmn. Community Welfare Council, 1952-53; pres. Council of Child Care Agencies, 1952-54; reg. v.p. Calif. Conf. of Soc. Workers, 1952-54; Mothers' March dir., March of Dimes Natl. Found. 1956-67; pres. YWCA, 1970-73; License and Permits Appeals Bd., San Jose, 1972, 1974-75; Quota Club of San Jose, 1948---; pres. 1951-53, gov. 12th Dist. 1968-69; Coord. Council of Women and Clubs, pres. 1952-53, 1966-68, 1973-74; Am. Bus. Women's Assn., pres. 1964-66; Willow Glen Bus. and Profl. Women's Club, pres. 1971-72; Children's Home League, pres. 1972. Congregationalist. Hobbies: lapidary, reading, hiking, camping. Home: 1127 De Lynn Way, San Jose, CA 95125

DALES, E. SCOTT
Appellate Court Judge
b. Jan. 7, 1923, Riverside; s. E.V. and Florence (Wright) Dales; A.A., New Mex. Mil. Inst., 1942; LL.B., USC Sch. of Law, 1950; m. Dorothy Hylton, Feb. 5, 1944, Waco, Tex.; chil.: Denise A., b. May 6, 1949; Craig S., b. July 19, 1951. Career: Admitted Calif. Bar, 1951; dep. dist. atty. to chief trial dep., Riverside Co., 1951-54; pvt. practice of law, 1954-56; Pub. Def., Riverside Co. 1956-61; Judge of Municipal Ct., Riverside Judicial Dist., 1961-66, Judge of the Superior Ct., 1966---; mem. Judicial Council of Calif., 1962-66; Presiding Judge, Sup. Ct., Riverside Co., 1970, 1976-77; Presiding Judge Appellate Dept., Riverside Co. Sup. Ct., 1971-73; Justice pro tempore, 2d div., 4th Appellate Dist., Ct. of Appeal, 1978; mem. Calif. Judges Assn., 1961---. Awards: two for traffic ct. procedures, Am. Bar Assn., 1962, 63; trial judge award, Calif. Trial Lawyers Assn., 1973-74. Served pvt. to capt., U.S. Army Air Corps, 1943-46; pilot in troop carrier squadron, So. Pacific. Mem.: bd. dir. Riverside Community Settlement House, 1966-67; Evergreen Lodge, Free & Accepted Masons, Master 1962; Uptown Kiwanis Club, treas. 1960-61. Hobby: model railroading. Rec.: golf, boating. Office: 4050 Main St., Rm. 142, Riverside, CA 92501.

DALESSI, WILLIAM TUNNELL
Attorney at Law
b. Dec. 11, 1922, Santa Maria, Calif.; s. Alexander A. and Veda Lillian (Tunnell) Dalessi; ed. J.D., Univ. of So. Calif., 1948; m. Margo E. Dalessi, May 21, 1961; chil.: Pamela Ann, b. Dec. 19, 1948; William Brent, b. Jan. 12, 1959; Theodore Alexander, b. Sept. 22, 1966. Career: Sci. staff, Columbia Univ. 1944; atty. at law, Long Beach, 1948---; admitted to practice, Supreme Ct. of U.S. 1957. Mem.: City Council, City of Long Beach, 1957-60. Pilot, B-17, 8th Air Force, WW II. Mem.: bd. dirs., Los Altos YMCA; Charter Revisions Com., City of L.B., 1961-63; pres., Estate Planning & Trust Council, L.B. 1965; Marina Adv. Com. of L.B., 1966; bd. govs., L.B. Bar Assn. 1966; Commodore, L.B. Yacht Club, 1966; Calif., L.A. and Long Beach Bar Assns.; L.B. Mounted Police, 1961---; U.S. Power Squadron; Inter Club Match Race Championship Com. N. Am. Yacht Racing Union, 1965-74; Phi Alpha Delta, N.Y. Yacht, Transpacific Yacht Clubs. Mason, Shrine, Trojan Club. Republican (Central Com. of L.A. Co. 1961; Calif. State Central Com. 1964). St. Gregory's Episcopal Ch. (Bishop's Warden, 1955-57). Hobby: sailing. Home: 16385 Ardsley Circ., Huntington Harbour, CA 92649; Office: 444 W. Ocean Blvd., Long Beach, CA 90802.

DALO, CHARLOTTE OWENS
Attorney at Law
b. Feb. 8, 1922, Pippapass, Ken., d. Elisha and Frances (Reynolds) Owens; B.S., 1942; LL.B., 1945; m. Michael Dalo, Feb. 1960, Tijuana, Mex.; chil.: Denise Ann, b. Feb. 22, 1961; Michael Owen, b. Mar. 3, 1962. Career: pvt. law practice since Jan. 7, 1948. Past pres., So. Calif. Women

Lawyers. Office: 14411 Vanowen St., Van Nuys, CA 91405.

DALTON, JAMES WILLIAM
Physician
b. May 18, 1907, Pasadena, Calif.; s. John Simpson and Alice (Burleigh) Dalton; desc. Philemon and Hannah Dalton, among first Boston settlers who landed on the New England coast Apr. 15, 1635; desc. Issac Dalton, Revolutionary War patriot and New Hampshire pioneer; desc. Capt. William Dalton, Union Army soldier during Civil War; grandson, John Calvin Dalton, M.D., Pasadena resident, 1890; premed student, Univ. of Calif., So. Branch (later known as UCLA); M.D., U.C. Med. Sch. at Berkeley and S.F., 1934, postgrad training in internal med., 1934-37; asst. resident, Univ. of Calif. Hosp. 1934-35; resident, U.C. Service City and Co. Hosp., S.F., 1935-36; resident physician, Univ. of Calif. Hosp., 1936-37; m. Anna Josephine Dickison, Sept. 18, 1937, Pasadena; chil.: Jo Ann, b. Oct. 9, 1938; John Frederick, b. Jan. 7, 1943; James Scott, b. Apr. 17, 1946. Career: pvt. med. pract. with Franklin R. Nuzum, Santa Barbara, 1937---; joined by med. assoc. Theodore Togstad, M.D., 1953; and William Ure, M.D., 1967. Research findings in many publ. articles on hypertension in med. journs., 1937-63. Author, Santa Barbara Co. Pilot Plan for the Med. Care of the Indigent and Aged, pub. Group Practice, 1963. Plan was devel. by Community Health Services Com. (Dr. Dalton, chmn.) of Santa Barbara Co. Med. Soc. in early 1960s, and implemented in S.B. Co. for one year by state. Did Research leading to formation of The Memorial Rehabilitation MRF, a nonprofit corp. providing care for the severely crippled, Feb. 1967 (bd. dir., 1967---). Co-founder, dir., Santa Barbara Heart Assn., 1947---; mem. S.B. Tuberculosis and Health Assn., 1942---; Elected Chief of Staff, S.B. Cottage Hosp., 1955-56; pres., S.B. Co. Med. Soc., 1959-60; Mem. S.B. Regional Health Program Planning Com., 1969-70; mem. exec. com. S.B. Comprehensive Health Planning Assn., 1969; mem. S.B. Co. Mental Health Advisory Bd., 1970-73. Helped to determine the incidence of Rheumatic Fever and Heart Disease, S.B. Co., 1947-48. Mem.: Phi Chi Med. Frat., 1928; Alpha Omega Alpha, 1932; SAR, 1978; mem. 1st Presbyterian Ch. of S.B., 1938---, ordained ruling elder, 1942,79. Rec.: photog., historical sites, musical concerts, walking. Home: 610 Sierra St., Santa Barbara, CA 93103; Office: (Retired) 2301 Castillo St., Santa Barbara, CA 93105.

DALTON, PHYLLIS IRENE
Librarian
b. Sept. 25, 1909, Marietta, Kan.; d. Benjamin R. and Pearl (Travelute) Bull; B.S., Univ. of Nebr., Lincoln, 1931, M.A., 1941; Washburn Coll., Topeka, Kan., 1932; B.S. (lib. sci.), Univ. of Denver, Colo., 1942; m. Jack M. Dalton, Reno, Nev., Feb. 13, 1950; Career: English instr., Jr. H.S., Marysville, Kan. 1931-33; English instr., Sr. H.S., Marysville, 1934-40; circulation libn., Lincoln Pub. Lib., Nebr., 1940-42; asst. reference librarian, Univ. of Nebr. Lib., Lincoln, 1942-45; divisional libn. in the humanities, 1945-48; jr. libn., Calif. State Lib., Sacto. 1948-49; lib. cons. for state employees and agencies, 1949-53; prin. libn., reader servs., Calif. State Lib., Sacto., 1953-57, asst. state libn. 1957---. Mem.: Am. Lib. Assn., Calif. Lib. Assn.; pres. Golden Empire Dist., Calif. Lib. Assn., 1955; pres. Am. Assn. of State Libs. 1964-65; pres. Calif. Lib. Assn. 1969; chmn. survey and standards com., Assn. of State Libs.; chmn. research div., Natl. Legislative Conf. 1966-67. Hobby: gardening. Rec.: reading. Home: 2589 Garden Hwy., Sacto, CA 95833; Office: Library-Courts Bldg., Sacto., CA 95809.

DALY, MAUREEN (McGIVERN)
Novelist — Journalist
b. Mar. 15, 1927, Castlecaulfield, Co. Tyrone, N. Ireland; sister, Maggie Daly, columnist Chicago Tribune; sister, Sheila Daly, v.p., Norman, Craig and Kummell Advt.; sister, Kay Daly (dec.), v.p., Revlon, Inc.; grad., St. Mary's Springs Acad., Fond du Lac, Wis., 1944; Rosary Coll., River Forest, Ill., 1948; m. William P. McGivern, Dec. 28, 1950, Chicago, Ill.; chil.: Megan (Shaw); Patrick. Career: Reporter, columnist, Chicago Tribune and Syndicate 1948-50; assoc. editor, reporter and foreign corres., Ladies Home Hournal, Phila. 1948-54; spl. editor, cons. Saturday Evening Post, Phila, 1958-62; writer for TV-films. Recipient Freedom Foundation Award, 1952, Author: Seventeenth Summer, Spanish Roundabout, Moroccan Roundabout, Twelve Around the World and (with William P. McGivern), Mention My Name in Mombasa. Hobby: mirror collection. Rec.: theatre, travel. Home: 73-305 Ironwood St., Palm Desert, CA 92260.

DANDOY, MAXIMA ANTONIO
Professor of Education
b. Ilocos Sur, Philippines; d. Manuel M. and Isidra

(Mendoza) Antonio; A.B., Nat. Tchrs. Coll., Manila, 1947; M.A., Arellano Univ., Manila, P.I., 1949; Ed.D., Stanford Univ., 1952. Career: elem. sch. tchr., Philippines, 1927-37; Lab. tchr., Philippine Normal Coll., Manila, 1938-49; instr., Arellano Univ., 1947-49; writer and supr., Dept. of Edn., Manila, 1944-45; Lab. Sch. Principal, then assoc. prof. of edn., Univ. of East, Manila, 1953-55; vis. prof., UCLA, 1956; prof. of Edn., Cal. State Univ. Fresno, 1956---. Awards: Scholarship awards, Bus. & Profl. Women's Clubs, Fresno, 1957; Philippines, 1952; Bicentennial award, Kappa Delta Pi, 1976. Apptd. Gov. com. on Juvenile Delinquency, 1958, Gov. Conf. on Traffic Safety, 1959; 1st Floro Crisologo Mem. Lectr., Univ. No. Philippines, 1977. Mem.: Calif. Fedn. Bus. & Profl. Women's Clubs; AAUW; Nat. Council for Soc. Studies; Pi Lambda Theta; Kappa Delta Pi; Phi Delta Kappa; Filipino-Am. Women's Club of Fresno; State Filipino-Am. Coord. Council. Home: 1419 W. Bullard Ave., Fresno, CA 93711; Office: Cal. State Univ., Fresno, Fresno, CA 93740.

DANIELS, IRWIN
Business Executive
b. Dec. 2, 1923, Brooklyn, N.Y.; s. Jacob B. and Jane Lillian (Rader) Cohen; A.B., USC, 1944; m. Estelle May Simon, L.A., Oct. 5, 1947; daus.: Shelley Marcia, b. June 19,1950; Kay Ilene, b. Nov. 6, 1953. Career: Chemist, United Piece Dye Works, 1946-52; partner, Security Builders, 1952---. Grad. Naval ROTC, USC, Ensign, USNR; grad. Naval Mine Warfare Sch.; PTO aboard mine sweepers, participating in 7 invasions, comdg. USS YMS 408 and USS Pioneer (AM 105), 2 yrs. Rec.: tennis, sailing. Home: 1223 Coldwater Canyon, Beverly Hills, CA; Office: 1880 Century Park East, Suite 1200, L.A., CA 90067.

DARBY, JOHN LESLIE
Health Agency Executive
b. Dec. 5, 1926, Vancouver, B.C.; s. Leslie and Ida Mae (Mallory) Darby; A.B., Stanford Univ., 1950, postgrad., 1951-53. Career: Clin. Audiologist, S.F. Hearing & Speech Center, 1953-56; Grad. Research Audiologist, Univ. Calif. Med. Center, S.F., 1956-64; exec. dir., Hearing Society for the Bay Area, Inc. (voluntary health agency), 1956---. AUS Med. Corps., 1945-46, psychological asst., 1950-51. Awards: NAHSA certification in adminstrn., 1974; Fellow, Am. Speech & Hearing Assn., 1978. Editor, Univ. survey reports, 1968, 73. Active positions in: Am. Speech & Hearing Assn., 1968---; Calif. Assn. of Parents of Deaf Children advis. bd., 1966-75; Calif. State Dept. of Health Care Servs., 1972; Calif. Coalition Independ. Health Professions, 1978; S.F. Mayors com. for employment of Handicapped, 1971---; Mem.: Commonwealth Club of Calif., Press Club of S.F. Home: No. 54 Hazel Ave., Mill Valley, CA 94941; Office: 1428 Bush St., S.F., CA 94109.

DARKE, CHARLES B.
Dentist
b. Sept. 22, 1937, Chicago; s. Paul O. and Annie W. Darke; A.A., 1960; D.D.S., 1964, M.P.H., 1972; m. Annetta McRae, Aug. 28, 1965, N.Y.C.; son, Charles B., II, b. Mar. 31, 1971. Career: dir. of dental services, S.F. Gen. Hosp., 1973---; bd. dir., Diamond Heights Neighborhood Assoc., 1973-75; bd. dir., Calif. Children's Lobby, 1973---; mem. examining com., Calif. State Bd. of Dental Examiners, 1976---. USAF, 1965-67; oral surgeon. Hobby: photog. Rec.: scuba diving. Office: 2175 Hayes St., S.F., CA 94117.

DART, JUSTIN WHITLOCK
Chairman of the Board, Dart Industries
b. Aug. 17, 1907, Evanston, Ill; s. Guy Justin and Laura (Whitlock) Dart; B.A., Northwestern Univ. 1929; Mercersberg Acad; m. Ruth Walgreen, Oct. 9, 1929 (div. 1930); chil.: Justin Whitlock, Jr., Peter Walgreen; m. 2d, Jane O'Brien, Dec. 31, 1939; chil.: Guy Michael, Jane. Stephen. Career: Dir. Walgreen Co. 1934-41, gen. mgr. 1939-41; dir.-v.p., United Drug Co., 1942; pres. Liggett Drug. Co., Apr. 1942-46; pres. Rexall Drug and Chem. Co. 1943-67; CEO, 1968---; dir. United Air Lines. Mem.: bd. of councilors, USC Sch. of Med.; bd. trustees, USC; dir. Am. Heart Assn.; exec. bd., BSA; dir. L.A. World Affairs Council; past pres., United Fund, L.A.; Beta Theta Pi; clubs: Calif., Bel-Air Country, L.A. Country, Racquet (N.Y.C.). Rec.: golf, swimming. Office: 8480 Beverly Blvd., L.A., CA 90046.

DARWIN, ROBERT
Airline Executive
b. Nov. 16, 1926, Elizabeth, N.J.; s. Anthony Horochowsky and Olga (Panzl) Darwin; B.S., Rutgers

Univ., 1952. Career: Founder, pres. Robert Darwin Enterprises, Inc., Austin, Tex. 1962---; founder, Robert Darwin Prodns., Paris, France, 1962-64; founder, pres. Transjet Exec. Airways, Inc., Austin, 1965---, chmn. bd., 1966---; pres., Golden Pacific Airlines, Inc., San Francisco, 1971-73; founder, Transjet Exec. Airways, Monterey Peninsula Airport, 1977---. USNR, 1945-46. Mem.: Aircraft Owners & Pilots Assn., 1960---; Sigma Phi Epsilon. Home: Rancho Fiesta Rd., Carmel Valley, CA 93924; Office: P.O.B. 585, Carmel Valley, CA 93924.

DAU, GARY J.
Nuclear Engineer
b. Sept. 3, 1938, Lewiston, Id.; s. George J. and Marjory K. Dau; B.S., mech. engr., 1961; Ph.D., nuclear engr., 1965; m. Brenda Brown, June 23, 1961, Creston, B.C.; sons: Brent George, b. Sept. 20, 1962; Fredric Gary, b. May 26, 1966. Career: Research sci. Battelle Northwest, Richland, Wash., 1964-66; sect. mgr., electronics measurements research 1966-68; dept. mgr. nondestructive testing applied physics, 1968-74, assoc. dept. mgr. nuclear waste tech., 1974-75, staff scientist 1976-77; nondestructive exam. program mgr. Electric Power Research Inst. Palo Alto, Calif., 1975-76, 1977---; tchr., nuclear engring., Joint Center for Grad. Study, 1967-68; pres. Richland Friends of Lib. 1972-74. NDEA fellow, 1961-64; Wash. Water Power Co. scholar, 1957; Standard Oil scholar, 1956; recipient certificate of appreciation, Calif. Soc. Profl. Engrs., 1976; named Outstanding Graduating Mech. Engr., Univ. Idaho, 1961; registered profl. engr., Calif. Mem. Am. Nuclear Soc., Am. Soc. for Nondestructive Testing, N.Y. Acad. Scis. Shalom Unity Ch.; trustee, property administr. Hobbies: photog., woodworking, boating, camping. Home: 3958 Duncan Pl., Palo Alto, CA 94306; Office: 3412 Hillview Ave., Palo Alto, CA 94303.

DAUER, WILLIAM E.
Executive, Greater S.F. Chamber Commerce
b. July 26, 1925, Lincoln, Nebr.; s. William and Elsie Dauer; ed. B.A., Nebr. Wesleyan Univ. 1950; m. Edna Pearson, Lincoln, Neb., Aug. 1, 1948; chil.: Lori, b. Dec. 23, 1953; Brad, b. Mar. 11, 1955. Career: Asst. mgr. Grand Is. C. of C., Nebr., 1950-51, mgr. 1952-56; mgr. Lexington C. of C., Nebr. 1951-52; mgr. Springfield C. of C., Mo. 1956-59; exec. v.p. Kansas City C. of C. 1959-64; exec. v.p., Greater S.F. C. of C. 1964---. Est. Exec. Hdqrs. for Civic Pgms.: created city mag., San Francisco Business, publ. 1967---; Instr., Univs. of Colo. and Houston for U.S. C. of C. Inst. USMC Res., PTO 1942-46, WW II. Awards: Distinguished Serv. Award, Jr. C. of C. 1956; Rotary Internat. Award 1959. Mem.: pres. Nebr. C. of C. Mgrs. Assn. 1954; dir. Mo. C. of C. Execs. 1957-59; pres. Am. C. of C. Execs; pres., Calif. C. of C. Execs.; dir., Calif. Blue Shield; dir., U.S. C. of C.; dir., Nat. Litigation Center; Civic Affairs Coms: state prison, ch. pgms., BSA, Boys Club, YMCA, United Bay Area Crusade, Calif. League for Handicapped; com. Small Bus. Adm.; Export Expansion Council, U.S. Commerce Dept.; Mason, Shrine, Methodist. Rec.: golf, all sports. Home: 2766 Greenwich St., S.F., CA; Office: 465 California St., S.F., CA 94104.

DAVENPORT, CALVIN A.
Professor of Microbiology
b. Jan. 15, 1928, Gloucester, Va.; s. James Robert and Carrie (Brooks) Davenport; B.S., animal sci., Va. State Coll., 1949; M.S., bacteriology, Mich. State Univ. 1950, Ph.D., microbiology & pub. health, 1963; UC, Berkeley Inst. of Protozoology for Coll. Tchrs., 1966; m. Beverly Wills, Aug. 25, 1963, Lansing, Mich.; chil.: Lynn Angela, b. 1967; Dean Darnell, b. 1970. Career: AUS, 1953-55; dir., Serology Lab., Letterman Gen. Hosp., S.F.; Bacteriologist I, Mich. Dept. of Health, 1952-53, 1955-56; med. technologist, St. Lawrence Hosp., Mich., 1958-63; assoc. prof., prof. & chmn. dept. of microbiology, Va. State Coll., 1963-69; assoc. prof., then prof. of microbiology, Cal. State Univ., Fullerton, 1969---; Danforth Found Assoc., 1978; Nat. Research Council Panelist, 1978; cons., Biomed. Unit. Nat. Inst. of Health, 1972---; mem. sr. commn. of Western Assn. of Schs. and Colls., 1976---; dir., Med. Tech. Pgm., CSU, Fullerton, 1969-76; mem. & chmn., Health Sci./Ednl. Activities Council of Orange and So. L.A. Counties, 1971-74. Mem.: Kappa Alpha Psi frat., 1951---. Rec.: tennis, chess. Address: Dept. of Biology, CSU, Fullerton, CA 92634.

DAVIDSON, DAVID BECK
General Surgeon
b. Apr. 8, 1937, Pittsburgh, Pa.; s. James and Elizabeth (Beck) Davidson; B.A., Harvard, 1959; M.D., Columbia Coll. of Physicians & Surgeons, 1963; Am. Bd. of Surgery Certification 1973; Fellow, Am. Coll. of Surgeons, 1975; m. Karen Sarnoff, June 3, 1972, Roslyn Hts., Long

Island, N.Y.; chil.: Christopher James, b. June 1, 1973; Alexandra Elizabeth Nell, b. May 29, 1975; Vanessa Katherine, b. Nov. 16, 1976. Career: Internship, Hosp. of Univ. of Penn. 1963-64; pub. health serv. assigned to Peace Corp on Ivory Coast, West Africa 1964-66; residency in gen. surgery, Columbia Presbyterian Hosp., N.Y.C. 1966-71; fellow in vascular surgery Presbyterian Hosp., N.Y.C. 1971; fellow in pediatric surgery, Baby's Hosp. 1972; pvt. practice associated w/Albert Medwid, M.D., Santa Barbara, 1972---. Hobbies: woodworking, gardening, tennis; Home: 4536 Via Vistosa, Santa Barbara, CA 93110; Office: 2416-C Castillo St., Santa Barbara, CA 93105.

DAVIDSON, EDNA LILLICH
Literary Critic -- Lecturer
b. Philadelphia, Pa.; d. Louis Edward and Jennie Josephine (Glading) Lillich; Quaker ancestors arrived in Phila. on the ship Welcome with Wm. Penn; grad., Emilie Krider Norris Sch. of Dramatic Art, Phila.; student, Univ. of Penn.; Speech with Christine Brooks, N.Y.; singing with Wm. A. Brady, N.Y.; Theory and Harmony courses (Trinity Coll., London) under Dr. H. Alexander Matthews, Phila.; student of Stuart Ross, N.Y.; m. Clifford D. Davidson; Career: U.S.A. tours, N.Y. Concert Mgmt.; speech tchr. and play director, schs. on the Main Line, Phila.; author, three pageants pub. (scores by noted liturgical composer, Dr. H. Alexander Matthews); founder-dir., Celebrity Salons (books, plays, music luncheons at The Beverly Hilton, Beverly Hills), 1955---. Mem.: Assistance League of So. Calif., 1952---; Affiliates of UCLA, 1967---; Smithsonian Inst., 1978---. Episcopalian. Home: 1634 Malcolm Ave., L.A., CA 90024.

DAVIDSON, ROGER H.
University Dean — Professor
b. July 31, 1936, Washington, D.C.; s. Ross Wallace and Mildred (Younger) Davidson; A.B., magna cum laude, Univ. Colo., 1958; Ph.D., Columbia Univ., 1963; m. Nancy Elizabeth Dixon, Sept. 29, 1961, Ft. Collins, Colo.; sons: Douglas Ross, b. Mar. 8, 1966; Christopher Reed, b. Apr. 5, 1969. Career: Asst. Prof. of Govt., Dartmouth Coll., 1962-68; Assoc. Prof. of Polit. Sci., Univ. Calif., Santa Barbara, 1968-71, Prof., 1971---, chmn., Dept. of Polit. Sci., 1976-78, Assoc. Dean, Coll. of Letters & Sci., 1978---. Profl. staff mem., U.S. House of Repr. 1973-74; Spec. Research Cons., U.S. Senate, 1976-77; cons., Nat. Commn. on Causes & Prevention of Violence, 1969; cons., Nat. Commn. on Population & Am. Future, 1972; White House Cons. 1970-71; cons., Calif. Legislature, 1975-76. Author: Congress in Crisis, 1966; On Capitol Hill, 1967, 1972; The Role of the Congressman, 1969; The Politics of Comprehensive Manpower Programs, 1972; Congress Against Itself, 1977; A More Perfect Union, 1978; numerous articles and reviews. Mem.: Phi Beta Kappa; UCSB Faculty Club; UCSB Faculty Assn., exec. com. 1977-78. American Baptist. Hobbies: music, astronomy. Rec.: bicycling. Home: 1029 Randolph Rd., Santa Barbara, CA 93111; Office: 2117 Administration, UC Santa Barbara, CA 93106.

DAVIS, ALEXANDER SCHENCK
Architect
b. Jan. 3, 1930, San Francisco, Calif.; s. William Schenck and Amelia (Francisco) Davis; grandson of Maj. Gen. Wm. Church Davis, AUS (dec.); A.A., Univ. of Calif., Berkeley, 1951, B.A. with honors in Architecture, 1953; M.A. in Architecture, 1957; m. Nancy Barry, Oct. 21, 1953, Berkeley; chil.: Arthur Barry, b. July 19, 1954; Laurel Margaret (Mrs. Bowden), b. Dec. 10, 1956; Pamela Alexander, b. Aug. 11, 1959. Career: Draftsman, Hammarberg and Herman, Architects, El Cerrito, 1956-61; Associate of the firm, 1961-62; project architect, Bonelli, Young and Wong, Architects and Engineers, S.F., 1962-67; Chief Architect, Earl and Wright, cons. engrs., S.F., Anchorage, London, 1967-73; project architect, Keller and Gannon, cons. engrs., S.F., 1974-77; pvt. archtl. practice, 1977--- doing design, constrn. documents, adminstrn. and inspection of constrn. of projects, also solar energy studies & projects. U.S. Coast Guard: Reserve, 1951-56; Active Duty, 1953-55; served as Engring Draftsman, also Art Dir., Armed Forces TV show, March On; awarded Nat. Defense Service Medal. Recipient: D. Zelinsky & Sons Found. grad. scholarship, 1955-56; apptd. a Fellow, Soc. of Am. Registered Architects, 1979. Registered architect: Calif., 1960---; Alaska, 1970---; United Kingdom, 1972---; Nat. Council of Archtl. Registration Bds., 1971---. Mem.: AIA; S.F. Archtl. Club; Soc. of Am. Registered Architects; Soc. of Am. Mil. Engrs.; Constrn. Specifications Inst. Creative works have included Albany Square comml. bldg., Albany; residence on El Toyonal, Orinda; residential, comml. and shopping centers; high-rise bldgs.; food

processing plants; radio station and mil. installations. Mem. Rotary Club, Eagle Scout, com. chmn. Cub Scout Pack 83, 1963-64; Calif. Alumni Assn., Assn. of Coll. Schs. of Architecture; Albany C. of C. Protestant. Hobby: summer cottage at Guernewood Park. Home: 928 Contra Costa Dr., El Cerrito, CA 94530; Office: 1057 Solano Ave., Suite 100, Albany, CA 94706.

DAVIS, BETTE
Film Star
b. Ruth Elizabeth Davis, Apr. 5, 1908, Lowell, Mass.; d. Harlow Morrell and Ruth (Favor) Davis; ed. Cushing Acad., Ashburnham, Mass.; m. Gary Merrill, July 28, 1950; chil.: Barbara Davis Sherry, b. May 1, 1947; (adopted) Margot and Michael. Career: Actress, motion pics. 1931---; leading roles incl.: Of Human Bondage, Bordertown, Dangerous, Jezebel, The Petrified Forest, Dark Victory, Juarez, The Old Maid, The Private Lives of Elizabeth and Essex, The Great Lie, The Bride Came C.O.D., Now Voyager, June Bride, The Story of a Divorce, All About Eve, others; Awards: recd. Mot. Pic. Acad. of Arts and Scis. Awards, Best Woman Actress of the Yr. for Dangerous, 1935 and Jezebel, 1938. Res.: Hollywood, CA.

DAVIS, DONALD ADAMS, JR.
Architect
b. Mar. 27, 1919, L.A.; s. Donald Adams and Grace (Stodart) Davis; ed. A.A. (bldg. constr.), Fullerton Jr. Coll. 1939; naval aviator, Univ. of the Air., Corpus Christi, Tex. 1941; B.Sc. (constr. engring), L.A.U. 1947; B.Ar., USC, 1952; m. Genevieve Rose Krukenberg, Whittier, Calif., May 13, 1945; dau. Dianne Annette, b. July 26, 1948. Career: Constr. ind.-tool designer, Douglas Aircraft Co., Santa Monica, 1939; constr. ind. 1948-51; est. pvt. arch. practice, Calif. 1952---. Long Beach, 1955---, Hawaii, 1959---, Ariz. 1966---. Registered arch.: Calif., Ariz., Hawaii; landscape arch., Calif. Patent: car stacking principals, 4 cars in double-car garage. Naval aviator, S. Pac. (3 yrs.), WW II; Comdr., USNR 1940-47. Awards: Distinguished Flying Cross, 3 Air Medals, Presidential Unit Cit. Mem.: bd. dirs. Exec. Assn. of Long Beach; Am. Inst. of Archs. Hobby: sailing. Rec.: surfing, soaring (Diamond Badge-Lenny Pen); comml. pilot (airplane single and multi-engine, land and sea, instrument and glider instr. rating by Fed. Aviation Agcy.). Home and Office: 39 Nieto Ave., Long Beach, CA 90803.

DAVIS, GRACE MONTANEZ
City Official
b. L.A.; d. Alfredo and Belen (Mendoza) Montanez; B.A., chm., Immaculate Heart Coll., L.A., 1949; M.A., microbiology, UCLA, 1955; chil.: Deirdra Mae, b. 1956; Alison Ann, b. 1957; Alfred Montanez, b. 1960. Career: research chemist, 1950-56; Congressional Adminstrv. asst. (to George E. Brown, Jr.), 1963-64; Poverty Program Spec., 1964-65; Manpower Devel. Spec., U.S. Dept. of Labor, L.A. and San Diego, 1965-75; Deputy Mayor, City of L.A., 1975---. Awards incl.: commendations from Calif. State Senate Rules Com., 1977; Fed. Exec. Bd., 1976; Calif. Fedn. Bus. & Profl. Women's Clubs, 1977; L.A. Boxing Program, 1976; Queen of Angels Hosp. Mother of Year, 1976; Mex.-Am. Woman of Year, 1971; Am. GI Forum award (1st Mex.-Am. to be so honored), 1961; Mex.-Am. Bar Assn. LEX, 1977. Chmn.: Housing and Community Devel. Com., L.A.; mem.: Mayor's Policy Com.; Nat. Advis. Com. on Immigration and Naturalization; Me. Am. Legal Defense Ednl. Fund; Fed. Advis. Council on Social Security; Affirmative Action Assn. for Women; GSA; Calif. Women in Govt. Rec.: tennis, theater, music. Home: 1609 N. Ave. 55, L.A.; Office: 200 N. Spring St., L.A., CA 90012.

DAVIS, GUILLETT GERVAISE, III
Attorney at Law
b. Nov. 18, 1932, Marshalltown, Ia.; s. G.G., Jr. and Alice V. (Denison) Davis; B.S., Georgetown Univ., 1954, J.D., 1958; m. Kathleen Anderson, June 22, 1955, Hanau, Ger.; chil.: Virginia K., b. Mar. 11, 1957; Cynthia E., b. Mar. 17, 1959; Sysan E., b. Mar. 21, 1962; Shauna L., b. Mar. 21, 1965. Career: Admitted to D.C. bar, 1958, Calif. bar, 1959, U.S. Supreme Ct. bar, 1966; law clerk to Judge Stanley Barnes, 9th Circuit U.S. Ct. of Appeals, L.A., 1958-59; Practiced law in S.F., 1959-60; Partner, firm Walker, Shcroeder, Davis & Brehmer, Monterey and Carmel, CA 1960-78; Pres., Schroeder & Davis Inc., Monterey, CA. Dir. numerous corps. Pres., Monterey Peninsula Unified Sch. Bd., 1963-78. Contbr. numerous law articles to tech. journs. Mil.: AUS, 1955-56 (Germany). Mem.: Delta Sigma Pi; Delta Theta Pi. Hobbies: photog., computer software. Rec.: racquetball. Home: 1150 Alta Mesa Rd., Monterey, CA 93940; Office: P.O.B. 3080, 215 W. Franklin St., Monterey, CA 93940.

DAVIS, LANCE EDWIN
Professor of Economics
b. Nov. 3, 1928, Seattle, Wash.; s. Maurice L. and Majorie (Seibert) Davis; B.A., Univ. Wash., 1950; Ph.D., Johns Hopkins Univ., 1956; m. Susan Gray, Dec. 3, 1971, L.A.; dau. Maili (Jennen). Career: Instr. to prof., Purdue Univ., 1955-68; Prof. of Economics, Calif. Inst. of Tech., Pasadena, 1968---; vis. Fellow, Nuffield Coll., Oxford Univ., 1963-64. USN, 1946-48, 1950-52. Pres., Am. Economic Hist. Assn. Home: 1746 Grevelia, St. Pasa, CA; Office: Div. of Humanities & Social Scis., Cal Tech., Pasadena, CA 91125.

DAVIS, PRISCILLA SANFORD
Artist -- Teacher
b. July 27, 1919, Terre Haute, Ind.; d. John M. and Lucille (Wolf) Sanford; great-great-grandniece of James Buchanan, 15th U.S. President; ed. B.A., Ind. State Univ. 1941; stu. art, The Art Center, 1953-55, and UCLA 1961-64; pvt. stu. with Rex Brandt, Arnold Schiffrin, George Post, Jake Lee, 1964---; m. Lon R. Davis, Terre Haute, Ind., July 11, 1941; daus.: Dianne Failla, b. Apr. 7, 1942; Nancy Reddick, b. Apr. 19, 1946; Linda Franco, b. May 19, 1948. Career: Art-Sci. tchr., Eunice Knight Saunders Sch., Calif. 1952-56; art dir., Isabelle Buckley Sch., Sherman Oaks, 1956---. Publ. cover design, Design Mag., May 1934. Artist-painter, exhibs: Calif. Art Club Goldmedal Show, won 2nd award, and 1st Gold Medal award, 1970, 1st prize Watercolor, 1972; 1st prize, Valley Artists Guild, 1974; 1st prize Watercolor, Wilshire Ebell Club, 1974; 1st prize Watercolor, 1975, others. Mem.: AAUW, 1950---; Pac. Palisades Art Assn. 1960; UCLA Med. Center Volunteer Serv. 1963-65; Calif. Art Club, 1968---; Valley Artist Guild, 1972---, pres. 1975---. Republican. Protestant. Home: 12137 Cantura St., Studio City, CA 91604; Office: 3900 Stansbury, Sherman Oaks, CA.

DAVIS, RICHARD L.
Neuropathologist
b. May 20, 1932, Minneapolis, Minn.; B.A., Univ. Minn., 1953, B.S. and M.D., Univ. of Minn. Med. Sch., 1956; Internship, Third Med. Div. (N.Y. Univ.), Bellevue Hosp., 1956-57; m. Anita Brinckmann, May 10, 1964, Wash. D.C.; chil.: Steven, b. Sept. 29, 1965; Pamela, b. Feb. 23, 1967; Lara, b. Oct. 22, 1968. Career: Residency, Univ. Minn. Med. Sch., Dept. of Pathology, 1957-60; Cancer Training Fellow, 1958-60; Spec. Fellow, NINDB, Neuropathology Branch, Armed Forces Inst. of Pathology, Wash., D.C., 1960-61; Asst. chief, Neuropathology, USN Hosp., San Diego, 1965-69; Assoc. Prof. Pathology and Chief, Neuropathology, L.A. Co.-USC Med. Center, 1969---. Served Lt. to Comdr., USN Med. Corps., 1961-69; Army Commendation Medal, 1965. Mem. Phi Beta Kappa, 1953. Home: 2125 Adair, San Marino, CA; Office: LAC-USC Med. Center, 1200 N. State St., L.A., CA 90033.

DAVIS, STUART
Chairman, Great Western Financial Corp.
b. Mar. 29, 1916, Santa Monica; s. William Arthur and Ida (Hansen) Davis; ed. B.S. (bus. adm.), St. Mary's Coll.; chil.: Elenor Lynn (Mrs. Arthur L. Alarcon), Richard Edward; m. Mary Young, Mar. 3, 1978. Career: Dir., First Svgs. and Loan Assn., 1938, pres. 1955-61; chmn. bd., Great Western Svgs. and Loan Assn., L.A.; chmn. bd., Great Western Financial Corp., and chief exec. ofcr. 1964---. Pres., U.S. League of Svgs. Assns., 1978, v.p. 1977. Officer, USNR, WW II. Mem.: dir. Calif. State C. of C.; Regent, St. Mary's Coll.; St. Francis Yacht Club, Calif. Club, L.A.; The Family, S.F.; L.A. Tennis Club, L.A. Country Club. Protestant. Hobbies: Tennis, swimming. Home: 703 N. Canon Dr., Beverly Hills, CA 90210; Office: 8484 Wilshire Blvd., Beverly Hills, CA 90211.

DAVIS, TERRY SERFASS
Clinical Psychologist
b. Nov. 6, 1942, L.A.; d. George Donald and Miriam (Baisden) Serfass; B.A. with distinction, Univ. Redlands, 1966; Ph.D. clin. psychol., USC, 1973; chil.: Sheryl Ann Barak, b. Nov. 24, 1960; Janet Lee Barak, b. May 111 1963. Career: Field Placement Coord., UCLA Psychol. Dept. 1973-75; Lectr., Calif. State Univ., 1975---; cons., Century Inst. for Living, 1975---; dir., Family Rehabilitation Coord. Proj., UCLA Ext., 1975---; v.p. 1976-78, acting pres. 1978---, Rehabilitation Developers, Inc.; also consul., training, edn., various orgns., 1975---. Publs.: VA Newsletter for Research, 1973; Marriage & Family Counselors Quarterly, 1977; Journ. of Studies on Alcohol, 1979. Mem.: dir., past pres., treas., West Area Women's Recovery Home, Inc. (Felicity House); pres., CLARE Found., 1977---; dir., So. Calif. Women's Substance Abuse Task Force, Inc.; Calif. Assn. of Alcoholic Recovery Homes; Valley Women's Center.

Office: 3975 Landmark St., Culver City, CA 90230.

DAVIS, WILLIAM WOODROW
Supervising Engineer
b. Dec. 25, 1913, Floyds, S.C.; s. Henry Vance and Ruth (Jones) Davis; B.S., Univ. of S.C., Sch. of Engring. 1937; m. Cara Belle Chitty, Denmark, S.C., Feb. 13, 1937; chil.: Richard C., Alix, David C. Career: Constr. mgr., Sears, Roebuck and Co., Phila. 1945-55; partner, Patterson and Davis, cons. engrs., Phila. 1955-56; chief civil engr., Gen. Mills, Inc., Minneapolis, 1956-62; v.p. Ken R. White Co., cons. engrs., Denver, 1962-63; supv. engr., Bechtel Corp., S.F. 1963---. Lt. Comdr., C.E. Corps, U.S. Naval Res. (1940-45), WW II. Mem.: chmn. Minn. Student Guidance Com., Engring. Council for Profl. Devel., 1960-62; pres. Minn. Soc. of Profl. Engrs. 1960-61, state dir. 1961-62; Natl. Soc. of Profl. Engrs., Soc. of Am. Mil. Engrs., Am. Concrete Inst., Minn. Acad. of Serv., Franklin Inst., Engrs. Club of Denver, Am. Soc. of Civil Engrs., AAAS, Fellow, Commonwealth Club of Calif. Trustee, Calvary Pres. Ch., Riverton, N.J. 1950-56; trustee, Congl. Ch. of Excelsior, Minn. 1961-62. Home: 5859 Margarido Dr., Oakland, Calif. 94618. Office: 50 Beale St., S.F., CA 94105.

DAWSON, EUGENE ELLSWORTH
President Emeritus, University of Redlands
b. Jan. 23, 1917, Kansas City, Kan.; s. Harold L. and Bessie D. (Ross) Dawson; A.B., Pittsburgh State Univ., 1940; S.T.B. (Williams Scholar), Harvard Univ. 1944; Ph.D., Boston Univ. 1949; postgrad. Univ. Chicago, 1953; L.H.D., Regis Coll., Univ. Colo.; Litt. D., Keuka Coll. 1968; D.D., Univ. Redlands, 1978; m. Arlene Clark, Kans., June 6, 1935; chil.: Eugene F., Jr., b. June 1, 1937; Mrs. Raylond (Lolita) Pfeiffer, b. May 13, 1945; Edward, b. May 6, 1948; Brent, b. July 30, 1952; Deborah, b. Aug. 12, 1957. Career: Asst. prof. psych-dean of men, Kans. State Coll. 1946-49, dean of Adm. and Students-prof. psych. 1949-57; pres. Colo. Women's Coll. 1957-70; pres. Univ. of Redlands, 1970-78; pres. emeritus, Univ. of Redlands, 1978---. Sr. Minister, First Bapt. Ch., Lynn, Mass. 1942-48; pres. Greater Lynn Council Chs. 1944-46; natl. coord. Tchr. Edn.-Relig. Proj. by Am. Assn. of Coll. for Tchr. Edn., 1954-56; past pres. United Ch. Men of Denver. Mem.: pres. Denver Rotary Club, 1964, dist. gov. 1967-68; v.p. Denver Execs. Club, 1965-70. Rec.: tennis, hiking, bicycling. Home: 1361 Willow Lane, Estes Park, Colo. 80517.

DAWSON, JOHN W.
Investment Executive
b. Dec. 20, 1902, Chicago, Ill.; s. John and Martha (Ella) Abbott; ed. Wheaton H.S. 1918; Acad. of Fine Arts, Myer-Booth Art Sch., Lakeview Art Sch., Chicago Art Inst. 1918-1921; m. Mary Elizabeth Hendrickson, Dec. 20, 1969. Career: Golf promotion for pres. of A.C. Spalding & Bros. 1921-42: investment real estate bus, 1942-49; developer: Mission Valley Golf Proj., Thunderbird Country Club and Estates, Palm Springs; Silverado Country Club and Estates, Napa, Calif. 1949-61; pres., Camino Del Rio Properties, Inc., San Diego. Mem.: (past) pres. State Golf Assn.; (past) pres. So. Calif. Golf Assn.; (past) pres.-pres. emeritus, Thunderbird Country Club, Palm Springs; Eldorado Country Club; Marrakesh, Seven Lakes Country Clubs. Sci. of Mind. Home: 47-328 Marrakesh Dr., Palm Desert, CA 92260.

DAWSON, WILLIAM JAMES
Orthodontist — Educator
b. May 16, 1930, San Francisco, Calif.; s. William James and Augusta R. Dawson; B.A., Univ. of Calif., Berkeley, 1952; D.D.S., Univ. of Calif., S.F., 1958; m. Judith Riede, Aug. 11, 1962, San Rafael, Calif.; Chil.: William James, Wendy, Nancy Garms, Sarah Rankin, Evelyn Elizabeth. Career: pvt. practice of orthodontics, 1958---; clin. instr., oral histology, Univ. of Calif. Med. Center, 1958-61; clin. instr., orofacial anomolies, 1964---; asst. research dentist, 1968---. Diplomate, Am. Bd. of Orthodontics; Fellow, Royal Soc. of Health; Life Member, Federation of Dentaire Internationale. Co-author articles in profl. journs., 1970. Served in USAF, 1951-54. Pres., Lagunitas Country Club, 1973-75; chmn., Dominican Coll. Citizen's Advisory Com., 1974-76; advisory bd., Marin Council Boy Scouts, 1975---; dir., Marin Co. of C., 1976---; v.p., Marin Co. Property Owners Assn., 1978---. Mem.: Chi Phi (U.C. Berkeley), Xi Psi Phi (U.C. Dental Sch.), Omicron Kappa Upsilon. Mem.: Elks; Rotary, pres. 1978-79; Bohemian Club, S.F. Polit.: mem., Republican State Central Com., 1971-73; Councilman, Town of Ross, 1967-69; mem., Pub. Employees Retirement System Bd. of Adminstrn., State of Calif., 1969-76. Episcopalian. Hobbies: trout fishing, duck hunting. Rec.: tennis, golf.

Home: P.O.B. 977, Ross, CA 94957; Office: 11 Greenfield Ave. San Rafael, CA 94901.

DEADRICH, LOUIS REX
Attorney at Law
b. Apr. 19, 1900, Johnson City, Tex.; s. John A. and Emma (Washburn) Deadrich; B.A., Univ. of Calif. 1924, J.D. 1926; m. Mildred Stegman, Oakland, Calif., June 24, 1923; son: Don L. Career: Admitted to practice in all cts., State of Calif. 1926; sr. partner: Deadrich & Peters, 1928-29; Deadrich & Spencer, 1941-43; Deadrich, Buckley & Ehlers, 1944-47; Deadrich, Gill, Bates & Stewart, 1949-55; Deadrich & Bates, 1955--- (legal counsel for Pac. Coast Tire and Rubber Co., Gene Reid Drilling Inc., Occidental Petroleum Corp., Valley Ofc. & Sch. Equipment Co.); sr. partner, Deadrich, Bates & Lund, Bakersfield. Instr. in law, Oakland Coll. of Law, 1930-42; pres. Wofford Heights Rec. Co. Serv. Tank Corps, WW I. Mem.: Phi Alpha Delta, 1924---; Sequoia Lodge F. & A.M. 1941---; Oakland Scottish rite bodies, 1942-44; Bakersfield Scottish rite bodies, 1948---; pres. Bakersfield Kiwanis Club, pres. Bakersfield Estates Planning Council, 1959---. Republican (Calif. State Repub. Central Com.; Kern Co. Repub. Central Com.; pres. electorate, 18th Cong. Dist. 1952; assoc. State Repub. Central Com. 1968). Hobby: golf, gardening. Home: 2908 La Cresta Dr., Bakersfield, CA; Office: 1122 Truxtun Ave., Suite 101, Bakersfield, CA 93301.

DE A'MORELLI, RICHARD C.
Author — Parapsychologist
b. Feb. 1, 1952, Kansas City, Mo.; adopted s. Claude and Rowena Hale; B.A., Pacifica Coll., 1972; M.Litt., 1974; Ph.D., Majaanian Inst. Nat. Sci., 1976 (parapsychol., journalism); m. Catherine Mercedes Schmidt, June 17, 1971, Las Vegas, Nev. Career: Correspondent, STAR, 1974---; Articles Editor, Globe News Service, 1974---; editor in chief, Probe the Unknown mag., 1976-77; founder, dir., Moonridge Sanctuary & Retreat, 1978---; Author nine books on psychic and paranormal subjects, with over 1 million copies in print, 1972---: books incl.: Numerology: The Key to Your Inner Self, 1972; Psychic Power: How to Develop Your ESP, 1973; How to Survive the Future, 1976; Psychic Tests for Everyone, 1976. Mem.: World Council on Human Understanding; Internat. Acad. of Biophysical Sciences; Bureau of Psychical Ethics; Project SUM (Canadian UFO research); the Majaanian Order (rel.). Hobbies: stamps, hiking, natural sci. Address: P.O.B. 1609, Anderson, CA 96007.

DEAN, RUTH D.
Associate Publisher — Community Leader
b. Mar. 8, 1909, Elburn, Ill.; d. Harry A. and Eva (Riplets) Dean; B.S., Ia. State Univ. 1930; m. Edwin Wendell Dean, Crystal Lake, Ill., June 9, 1931; chil.: Edwin Wendell, Jr., b. Apr. 4, 1936; Dennis Richard, b. May 29, 1938. Career: Tchr., home econons. and chem., Barrington (Ill.) H.S., 1930-32; assoc. publ-ed., Marengo Repub.-News, 1934-46; Inglewood Daily News, 1946---. Secty.-treas.: Modern Housing, Inc. 1969---; Pen and Sword, Inc., v.p. 1969---; Dean Newspapers, Inc. 1970; Mem.: Delta Zeta; Bd. of Edn., Marengo, Ill., 1937-46; Worthy Matron, Haven Chpt., OES, Ill. 1940-41; pres. Marengo Woman's Club, Ill. 1942-45; treas. McHenry Co. Fed. of Women's Clubs, Ill. 1945; press chmn., Inglewood Council PTA 1949-50; pres. Inglewood Woman's Club, 1951-52; bd. govs., L.A. Art Inst. 1954; Centinela Valley Community Hosp. Aux. to Centinela Mus. Assn. 1955; pres., Chpt. AZ, PEO, 1958-59; Hist. Soc. of Centinela Valley, 1965---; Centinela Hosp., Med. Center, adv. bd., 1976---; Centinela Hosp., Med. Center Bd., 1977---; pres. Kiwanee Club of Inglewood, 1955; chmn. adv. bd. Salvation Army, 1972. Presbyterian. Hobby: community activities. Rec.: travel, oil painting. Home: 3500-412 W. Manchester Blvd., Inglewood, CA 90305; Office: 4043 Irving Pl., Culver City, CA 90230.

DECKER, GEORGE NIXON
Corporate Executive
b. Sept. 27, 1914, Springfield, Mass.; s. George Henry and Mary (Nixon) D.; student Rochester (N.Y.) Sch. Commerce, 1932-33; Ohio Univ., 1934-35; Niagara Univ., 1935-37; m. Rosemary Agnes Charlotte Morgan, Apr. 8, 1939; chil. Sharon Lee (Mrs. James Williams), Robert Charles. Career: Acct., Van Vechten Milling Co., Rochester, N.Y., 1937-38; self employed grain broker Decker Grain Co., Rochester, 1938-40; supr. gen. accounting IBM Corp., Rochester, 1940-43; successively asst. comptroller, comptroller, v.p., first v.p. Kellogg div. Abex Corp., Rochester, 1943-59; pres. Kellogg div. Oxnard, Calif., 1959-62, pres. aerospace group of cos., Oxnard, 1962-71; pres., chief exec. officer Ventura Internat., Inc., Oxnard, 1971---. Vice pres., dir. Coastal

Pipco Co., Oxnard; dir. Flying Flags Recreation Co., Buellton, Travel City, Inc., Sherman Oaks; chmn. bd., Athletic Supply of Hawaii Ltd., Honolulu; dir., B.F. Schoen, Inc., Honolulu. Acting co. Repub. club. Mem.: Financial Execs. Inst. Club: Las Posas Country. Home: 123 Vientos Rd., Camarillo, CA 93010; Office: 500 Esplanade Dr., Oxnard, CA 93030.

DEE, CYNTHIA J.
Library Director
b. June 3, 1941, Somerville, Mass.; d. Stanley and Cecelia Clechon; A.B.. Notre Dame Coll., 1964; M.L.S., Catholic Univ. of America, 1963; m. Jeremiah Dee, July 23, 1970, Annapolis, Md. Career: administrv. asst., St. Anselmo Coll. Lib., 1964-69; director, Park Ridge Public Library, 1969-77; director Public Library, Corona, Calif. ---. Mem.: Soroptimist Internat. of Corona, 1978; Bus. & Profl. Womens Club of Corona, 1978; Calif. Library Assn. 1978; N.J. Library Assn., 1968-77. Hobbies: needlework, gardening. Rec.: bowling, tennis. Home: 1361 Camelot Dr., Corona, CA; Office: 650 S. Main St., Corona, CA.

DEE, JOHN RICHARD
Composer — Educator
b. June 13, 1936, Knoxville, Tenn.; s. Antonio and Hazel Dee; B.A. and M.A., San Jose State Univ.; pvt. studies in Japanese, Chinese, Korean, Indonesian music; composition study with Lou Harrison. Career: Lectr. in music, San Jose State Univ., 1971---; tchr., Center for World Music, Univ. Calif., Berkeley, 1975---; pvt. tchr. ---; Composer many works for Asian instruments (performed often): Praises for Voices and Instruments, 1966-67; Concerto for Flute and Percussion, 1970; composer many theater works: Suite for Violin and Am. Gamelan (composed as a "double music" with Lou Harrison), commissioned by S.F. Chamber Mus. Soc. and pub. by Southern Music; many concerts of Chinese music for Young Audiences, Inc.; TV appearances; concerts of Oriental music performed from L.A. Mark Taper Forum to N.Y. Univ.; contbr. music reviews, short articles to Art Journ. Rel.: Humanist. Hobbies: antiques, art. Home: 35 N. 11th St., Apt. 1, San Jose, CA 95712; Office: Music Dept., San Jose State Univ., San Jose, CA.

DE FAZIO, LYNETTE STEVENS
Dancer — Choreographer — Educator
b. Sept. 29, Berkeley, Calif.; d. Honore and Mabel J. (Estavan) Stevens; student U. Calif., Berkeley, 1950-55; San Francisco State Coll., 1950-51; m. Scott DeFazio, Apr. 16, 1972; children: Joey Panganiban, Joanna Pang. Career: Contract child dancer Monogram Movie Studio, Hollywood, 1938-40; dancer, instr. San Francisco Ballet, 1953-64; performer San Francisco Opera Ring, 1960-67; performer, choreographer Oakland Civic Light Opera, 1963-70; owner, dir. Ballet Arts Studio, Oakland, 1960---; also instr. Peralta Community Coll. Dist., Laney Campus, Grove St. Campus, 1971---; teaching specialist Oakland Unified Sch. Dist., Children's Center, 1968---; fgn. exchange dance dir. Academia de Danses, Paris, France, 1966; cons., instr. U. Calif. at Los Angeles Edn. Extension, Fresno State Coll.; Calif. Childrens Centers Dirs. and Suprs. Assn., Fed. Projects Office Pittsburg Unified Sch. Dist., Tulare City Sch. Dist., 1971-73; researcher HEW Ednl. Testing Service, Berkeley, 1974; choreographer San Francisco Childrens Opera, Toy Oriental Dance Co.; asst. choreographer Chinatown Pageant, S.F.; ballet mistress Dimensions Dance Theaer, Oakland, 1977---; cons. Glenchetta Sch. of Dance, S.F. and Concord, Calif., Robicheau Boston Ballet, TV series Patchwork Family, CBS, N.Y.C. Recipient credential of eminence in dance edn., life credential Calif. Community Colls., standard services credential, children's centers credential all from Calif. Dept. Edn.; Notable Ams. Award, 1976-77. Mem. Profl. Dance Tchrs. Assn. Am. Author: Basic Music Outlines for Dance Classes, 1960, rev., 1968; Teaching Techniques and Choreography for Advanced Dancers, 1965; Basic Music Outlines for Dance Classes, 1965; A Teacher's Guide for Ballet Techniques, 1970; Principle Procedures in Basic Curriculum, 1974; Objectives and Standards of Performance for Physical Developments, 1975. Asso. music composer, lyricist The Ballet of Mother Goose, 1968. Asso. music arranger Le Ballet du Cirque, 1964; Techniques of a Ballet School, 1970, rev. edit., 1974. Choreographer, Ravel's "Valses Nobles Et Sentimentales," 1976. Home-Office: 4923 Harbord Dr., Oakland, CA 94618.

DeFOREST, EDGAR L.
College Educator
b. Aug. 19, 1916, Hull, Mass.; s. Edgar and Ellen (Huntington) De Forest; Diploma in Theatre Arts, Leland Powers Sch. of Theatre, Radio and TV, Boston, 1937; stu. Edinburg, Cambridge and London, 1939; B.S., Boston

Univ. 1940; M.A., USC, 1941; Ed.D., Columbia Univ. 1955; Kellog Grant, UCLA Jr. Coll. Adm. 1962; postgrad Anglo-Irish Lit., Univ. Coll., Galway, Ire. 1972; poetry of W.B. Yeats, Queen's Coll., Belfast; stus. Yeats Tower, Gort, Ire. 1972; New Zealand Lit., 1973; m. Beulah Mary Ingalls, L.A., 1940; sons: Peter Rupert (Dr. and prof., John Jay Coll., Criminal Justice, City Univ. of N.Y.); Edgar Stephen, David Frederick, Richard Erlend. Career: Reading clinician, Boston Univ. Edn. Clinic, 1938-39; speech, Hill-Young Sch. of Speech and Orthopaedic Hosp. 1940-41; tchr. soc. studies, Ontario, 1942-45; Eng. instr. Mich. State Coll. 1945-46; asst. prof.-dir. Reading Clinic, Stutterers Clinic, 1946; dir. Reading Clinic, stu. activities, Suffolk Univ., Boston, 1948-51; dir. reading servs. Mich. State Univ. 1954, asst. dir. Summer Sch. 1955-57; Eng. instr. Ventura Jr. Coll., Calif. 1957, Dir. Reading Clinic, 1958; prof. Eng. speech, Coll. of Desert, 1962---. Author: You Can Aid the Stammering Child, publ. 1946; Communication in the Family, 1958; The Japanese Haiku, 1962. Awards: Ecumenical Council Silver Medal from Pope Paul VI in Rome, 1964; Internat. Edn. Award, Univ. of Seven Seas, 1965; Mem.: New Eng. chmn. Natl. Assn. of Remedial Tchg., 1948-52; founder-pres. Mich. Reading Assn. 1954; Lambda Chi Alpha, Phi Delta Kappa, Delta Kappa Pi, Pi Gamma Mu. Home: Box 220, Pinyon Crest, Mountain Center, CA; Office: College of the Desert, 43-500 Monterey Ave., Palm Desert, CA 92260.

DeGROOT, WILLARD GERALD
Investment Banker
b. Aug. 19, 1917, Holland, Mich.; s. John and Anna (Nyboer) DeGroot; B.A., Hope Coll., Holland, Mich. 1939; M.B.A., Northwestern Univ., Evanston, Ill, 1940; m. Barbara Riley, L.A.; dau.: Mrs. William W. (Wendy) Drewry, Ill; son, John Sheldon. Career: Assoc. with Bateman, Eichler & Co., 1946---, v.p. 1952, exec. v.p. 1957, pres. 1960 (merged with Bingham Walter & Hurry, Inc. 1964), chmn. bd.-chief exec. ofcr. Bateman Eichler, Hill Richards, Inc. 1966---. Dir.: Applied Magnetics Corp., Farr Co., So. Calif. Bldg. Funds; bd. trustees, L.A. Orthopaedic Found. and Orthopaedic Hosp.; bd. fellows, Claremont Univ. Center; bd. councilors, Sch. of Bus. Adm., USC; Reg. Adv. Group Spec. Com., N.Y. Stock Exch. 1967-69; natl. bd. govs., 1970---. U.S. Navy (5 yrs.), Lt. Comdr., WW II. Mem.: pres. Bond Club, L.A., 1954; Dist. Com., Natl. Assn. of Securities Dealers, Inc. 1955-57; Investment Bankers Assn. of Am., chmn. Calif. div. 1961-62; natl. bd. govs. 1962-64; Clubs: The Valley (Montecito), Annandale Golf (Pasa.), Pauma Valley Country, L.A. Stock Exch., Calif. Club. Episcopalian. Home: 3 Oak Knoll Terrace, Pasadena, CA 91106; 2020 S. Pacific Ave., Oceanside, CA 92054; Office: 460 S. Spring St., L.A., CA 90013.

de GUIGNE, CHRISTIAN III
Chairman Emeritus, Stauffer Chemical Co.
b. Aug. 26, 1912, San Mateo, Calif.; s. Christian and Marie Louise (Elkins) de Guigne; Hillsborough pub. schs.; Gunnery Sch., Wash., Conn., 1925-30; The Hun Sch., Princeton, N.H., 1930-32; Harvard Univ., Cambridge, Mass., 1932-33; m. Eleanor Christenson, San Mateo, July 27, 1935; chil.: Christian IV, b. Mar. 13, 1937; Charles, b. Apr. 23, 1939. Career: Assoc. with Stauffer Chem. Co. 1934---, v.p., dir. 1942, pres. 1946, chmn. bd. dirs. 1953---. Dir.: Bank of Calif.; dir. Pac. Telephone and Telegraph Co.; 2nd Lt., air combat intelligence ofcr., Marine Corps, S. Pac. (1942-45), WW II; Capt.-Maj., USMCR (inactive), 1951---. Clubs: Pac.-Union, Bohemian, S.F.; Burlingame Country, Burlingame; The Brook, Racquet and Tennis, N.Y.; The Travelers, Paris, Fr. Home: 891 Crystal Springs Rd., Hillsborough, CA; Office: 636 California St., S.F., CA 94108.

deKIRBY, IVOR
Business Executive
b. July 30, 1915, Winnipeg, Can.; s. George and Florence deKirby; B.A., Univ. of Calif., Berkeley, 1940; m. Edele Lewarton, Berkeley, Calif., Aug. 18, 1940; dau.: Diane, b. July 7, 1942. Career: Adm. mgr., Western region, Ford Motor Co., 1946-49, asst. dist. sales mgr., L.A. 1949; pres., Pearson Ford Co., San Diego, 1950---; secty.-treas., San Diego Auto Lease, 1955---. Councilman and Dep. mayor, City of San Diego, Maj., U.S. Army Ord., (1945) WW II. Mem.: v.p., S.D. C. of C.; v.p. S.D. Conv. & Tourist Bur.; pres. S.D. Co. Motor Car Dealers Assn., Congl. Hobby: fishing, snow-skiing. Home: 3966 Bandini, San Diego, CA; Office: 4300 El Cajon Blvd., San Diego, CA 92105.

DeLAUER, RICHARD DANIEL
Company Executive
b. Sept. 23, 1918, Oakland; s. Michael and Matilda (Giambruno) DeLauer; A.B., Stanford Univ. 1940; B.S., USN Postgard. Sch. 1949; A.E., Calif. Inst. of Tech.,

1950, Ph.D. 1953; m. Ann Carmichael, Baltimore, Md., Dec. 6, 1940; son, Richard Daniel, Jr. Career: Structural designer, Glenn L. Martin Co. 1940; design engr., Northrop Co. 1942; dir. Vehicle Devel. Lab., Space Tech. Labs. 1958, Titan pgm. dir. 1960, v.p.-dir. Ballistic Missile pgm. mgmt. 1962; v.p.-gen. mgr. Systems Engring. and Integration Div., TRW Systems Group, 1966; v.p. TRW Inc. and gen. mgr. TRW Systems Group, 1968---. Co-author: Nuclear Rocket Propulsion, 1958; Fundamentals of Nuclear Flight, 1965 (publ. McGraw-Hill). USN aeron. engring. ofcr. 1943-58. Mem.: bd. dirs. Johnston Coll., Univ. of Redlands; fellow, Am. Inst. of Aerons. and Astronautics, chmn. Spacecraft Tech. Com. 1967-68; Natl. Acad. of Engring.; AAAS; N.Y. Acad. of Scis.; Aerospace Tech. Council of Aerospace Inds. Assn. Home: 222 Ave. of the Stars, L.A., CA 90067; Office: One Space Park, Redondo Beach, CA 90078.

DE LA VEGA, AURELIO
Composer — Educator — Music Critic
b. Nov. 28, 1925; La Habana, Cuba (U.S. cit. 1965); s. Aurelio and Berta (Palacio) de la Vega; Ph.D. (diplomatic and internat. law), Univ. of Havana, 1946; Ph.D. (mus. comp.), Ada Inglesias Inst., Havana, 1956; m. Sara Lequerica, La Habana, Cuba, Jan. 26, 1947. Career: mus. critic, "Alerta" newspaper, 1950-57; prof. of mus. hist. and analysis-dean, Sch. of Mus., Univ. of Oriente, Santiago de Cuba, 1953-59; mus. advisor, Natl. Inst. of Culture, Cuba, 1955-58; guest prof. mus., Central Univ., Las Villas, Cuba, 1956; Asst. prof. mus., Calif. State Univ., Northridge, 1959-62; assoc prof. 1963-66; prof. 1967---. Awards: Va. Colliers Chamber Mus. Award, Wash. 1954; elected to Academic Chair, Sociedad Economica de Amigos del Pais, La Habana, 1956; ofcr. Order of Eloy Alfaro, Panama, 1960; Grand Cross, Order of the Sun, Peru, 1961; recipient: Andrew Mellon Fellowship, Univ. of Pittsburgh, 1964; Mem.: Chmn., West Coast Br., U.S. sect., Internat. Soc. for Contemporary Mus. 1964; (hon.) Phi Mu Alpha 1964; pres. L.A. Chpt., Natl. Assn. Am. comps and conds. 1965-67; Hobby: painting. Home: 18800 Stare St., Northridge, CA 91324; Office: Calif. State Univ., Northridge, 18111 Nordoff St., Northridge, CA 91324.

DELBRUCK, MAX LUDWIG HENNING
Scientist
b. Sept. 4, 1906, Berlin, Germ., (U.S. cit. 1945); s. Hans G.L. (ed. and Berlin Univ. prof.) and Caroline (Thiersch) Delbruck; noted ancestors incl.: Rudolf von Delbruck, Prussian and Ger. Minister of State; Berthold Delbruck, prof. and comparative syntax of Indo-European langs.; Heinrich Delbruck, Prasident des Reichsgerichts; Clemons von Delbruck, Minister of State. Adolf von Harnack, Berlin Univ. prof. and co-founder-pres. Kaiser-Wilhelm-Gesellschaft; ed. Tubingen Univ. 1924; Berlin Univ. 1924-26; Bonn Univ. 1925; Ph.D., Gottingen Univ., 1930; m. Mary Adeline Bruce, Pasa, Calif., Aug. 2, 1941; chil.: Jonathan, Nicola, Tobias, Ludina. Career: Researcher: Physics Dept., Bristol Univ. 1929-31, 1932; Rockefeller Fellowship, Copenhagen Univ. and Zurich Univ. 1931-32; Berlin, Kaiser Wilhelm Inst. 1932-37; est. U.S.A. res. 1937; Rockefeller Fellowship in biol., Calif. Inst. of Tech. 1937-39; prof. 1947---; instr., asst. prof., assoc. prof. of physics, Physics Dept., Vanderbilt Univ., Nashville, Tenn. 1940-47; guest prof.-dir. Univ. of Cologne, 1961-63; hon. prof. 1965---; guest prof. Univ. of Constance, 1966---. Author: many profl. papers on mutagenesis, physics and biol., publ. 1930---. Awards: (hon.) Univ. of Copenhagen, 1962, Univ. of Chicago, 1967, Univ. of Heidelberg, 1968; Fellowships: U.S. Natl. Acad. of Sci. 1949; Royal Danish Acad. 1960; Deutsche Akademie der Naturforscher Leopoldina, 1963; Royal Soc. of London for Improving Natural Knowledge, 1967; Am. Acad. of Arts and Scis.; Kimber Medal for Genetics, U.S. Natl. Acad. of Sci. 1964; Mendel Medal (Leopoldina) 1967; Louisa Gross of Month Prize, Columbia Univ., 1969; Nobel Prize, physiology and med. 1969. Home: 1510 Oakdale St., Pasadena, CA; Office: Dept. of Biology, Calif. Inst. of Tech., Pasadena, CA 91109.

DELFINO, ANDREW
Interior Designer
b. June 20, 1920, San Francisco; Interior Design major, Calif. Sch. of Fine Arts, S.F., 1938-41; Parsons Sch. of Design, N.Y., 1945. Career: Associated with Karl Lengfeld Interior Design, 1948-55; estàb. own firm, Andrew Delfino, Interior Design, 1955---, incorporated 1977, Andrew Delfino, Inc. USAF, 1942-45. Office: 407 Jackson St., S.F., CA 94111.

DELLAVALLE, MABEL CAROLINE
Realtor
b. Feb. 15, Tulare, Calif.; d. Battista (Lt. WW I) and

Domenica (Borzi) Raviscioni; liberal arts student: Fresno City Coll.; Univ. of Calif., Fresno; Univ. of Calif., Santa Cruz; bus. admin. student, Coll. of Commerce, Stockton; real estate, Anthony schs., Fresno; m. Eugene Angelo Dellavalle, July 31, 1949; chil.: Robert, b. Nov. 12, 1963; Eugene, b. Sept. 5, 1951. Career: secty., 1944-49; real estate salesperson, 1971-73; established real estate firm, owner, Mabel Caroline Dellavalle, Realtor, Madera, 1974---. Mem.: Fresno Bd. of Realtors; Madera Bd. of Realtors, Calif. Assn. of Realtors and Nat. Assn. of Realtors. Mem. C. of C. (Gov. Affairs Com. 1979), Madera; pres., Young Ladies Inst. No. 118, pres., St. Joachims Altar Soc., Madera. Hobbies: art, painting, gardening. Rec.: bridge, dancing, bicycling. Office: 110 North D St., Suite 102, Madera, CA 93637.

DELLUMS, RONALD VERNIE
United States Congressman
b. Nov. 24, 1935, Oakland; s. Vernie and Willa Dellums; nephew of C.L. Dellums, dir. Fair Employment Practices Comm.; ed. A.A., Oakland City Coll. 1958; B.A., S.F. State Coll. 1960; M.S.W., Univ. of Calif., Berkeley, 1962; m. Leola (Roscoe) Higgs, Oakland, Jan. 20, 1961; chil.: Ronald Brandon, b. Sept. 7, 1962; Eric Todd, b. Feb. 23, 1964; Piper Monique, b. Nov. 23, 1965. Career: Psych. soc. serv. Dept. of Hygiene, 1962-64; pgm. dir. Bayview Community Center, 1964-65; assoc. dir.-dir. Hunters Point Youth Opportunity Center, 1965-66; cons. Bay Area Soc. Planning Council, 1966-67; Dir. Concentrated Employment Pgm., S.F. Econ. Opportunity Council, 1967-68; Berkeley City Council, 1967-71; sr. cons. Soc. Dynamics, Inc. 1968-70; lectr., S.F. State Coll., Univ. of Calif., Berkeley, Grad. Sch. of Soc. Welfare; elected to Congress, 8th Calif. Dist. 1970--- (chmn. Sub. Com. on Edn.; Armed Serv. Com.). Serv. Marine Corps (2 yrs.). Dellums War Crimes Hearings, publ. 1973. Mem.: Alpha Phi Alpha. Protestant. Hobbies: chess, basketball, music. Home: 53 Fairlawn Dr., Berkeley, CA 94708; Office: 2490 Channing Way, Berkeley, CA; 201 13th St., Oakland, CA; 1417 Longworth Ofc. Bldg., Wash., D.C. 20515.

DEMATTEIS, HON. LOUIS B.
Superior Court Judge — Civic Leader
b. Sept. 6, 1911, Redwood City, Calif.; s. Frank and Ermida (Gamba) Dematteis; LL.B., Lincoln Univ., S.F., 1931; LL.D., 1953; LL.M., Univ. of S.F., 1933; m. Lillian M. Valente, Oakland, May 29, 1938; chil.: Marilyn L., b. Feb. 21, 1940; Lillian M., b. Dec. 30, 1941; Dolores A., b. Feb. 24, 1943; Louis F., b. Apr. 2, 1948; Robert J., b. Mar. 4, 1950. Career: Admitted to Calif. Bar 1932; pvt. law practice, Morrissey & Dematteis law firm, 1932-35; dep. dist. atty., San Mateo Co., 1935-44; pvt. law practice, firm of Currie and Dematteis, 1945-48; asst. dist. atty., San Mateo, Co. 1948-49; dist. atty. 1949-53; judge, Superior Ct., San Mateo Ct., Oct. 1953---. Serv. USN, 1944-45 (hon. disch.), WW II. Mem.: Redwood City Post No. 105, Am. Legion; Univ. of S.F. Alumni Assn. 1929-44; secty., Redwood City Nest No. 1484, Order of Owls, 1929-44; pres. Redwood City br. No. 6 Italian Cath. Fed. 1933-34; state pres. 1938; pres. Redwood City Community Chest, 1937; pres. Redwood City Toastmaster's Club, 1938; dir. San Mateo Co. Area Council, Boy Scouts of Am. 1939---, v.p., 1950---; dir. San Mateo Co. Community Chest, 1941-44; Redwood City War Council, 1942-44; chmn. Sequoia Chpt., Am. Red Cross, 1947-48; secty. San Mateo Co. Law Enforcement Assn., 1949-53; dir. San Mateo Co. Tuberculosis and Health Assn., 1950---; chmn. San Mateo Co. Coord. Com. on Youth, 1950-55; dir. San Mateo Co. Community Council, 1954---; pres. Sequoia Kiwanis Club of Redwood City, 1955---; Redwood Parlor No. 66, Native Sons of the Golden West; Fra Catala Council No. 4595, Knights of Columbus; Vioture No. 393, Forty and Eight Soc.; Galileo Galilie Lodge, Order Sons of Italy in Am. Democrat. Catholic. Hobby: fishing. Rec.: gardening. Home: 823 Blandford Blvd., Redwood City, CA; Office: Courthouse, Redwood City, San Mateo Co., CA.

DEMPSTER, CATHERINE C. (KAY)
Artist
b. June 13, 1914, Great Falls, Mont.; d. Dr. Robert Clayton and Anna (Cajori) Hull; art stu. Univ. of Wash. 1933-35; Art Center Coll. of Design, L.A., 1936-37; pvt. stu. watercolor with Robert E. Wood, Barse Miller, Virginia Jackman; m. Albert T. Dempster (noted artist for Walt Disney), L.A., Nov. 24, 1938; chil.: Joan Fielding, Anthony J., John J., Michael, Teresa M.; Career: Fashion illus. for Arthur and Sydney Arkin, Fashion Clothing Co., 1937; art dept. Broadway Hollywood; feat. in collections: Gene Autry, Don Tatum, Robert Sherman, many others; artist exhib.: Burbank, Monterey Park Lib.; White's Art Gallery, Montrose; Robert Pyle Gallery, Morro Bay; The Gallery, Camarillo; Emerson Gallery, Santa Paula Mem.

Lib.; Cezanne Gallery, Laguna Beach; Calif. Art Club; Art Collectibles, Ventura, London Exch. 1976. Won many awards in Juried Art Shows. Mem.: San Fernando Valley Art Club, Calif. Art Club Gallery, Valley Artists Guild. Catholic. Studio: 5253 Shirley Ave., Tarzana, CA 91356.

DENNEY, CORWIN D.
Company President
b. July 31, 1921, Jeffersonville, Oh.; s. Clark E. and Edith M. Denney; B.S., (aeron. engr.), Univ. of Mich. 1943; m. Nanci M. McCahill, L.A.; chil.: Carolyn J., b. Mar. 9, 1945; Thomas, b. Jan. 2, 1951; Mary C., b. Jan. 20, 1951; Peter, b. Aug. 30, 1952; Anne E., b. Oct. 6, 1953; Des Cygne, b. Mar. 30, 1961. Career: Chief helicopter engr., Marquardt Aircraft Corp., Venice, Calif. 1946-48; pres. Am. Helicopter, Manhattan Beach, Calif. 1948-54; pres. Automation Industries, Inc. 1954---. 1st Lt., U.S. Army Air Corps, Rotary Wing Br., Propeller Lab., Wright-Patterson Air Base, Oh. (1943-46), WW II. Mem.: Sigma Phi Epsilon. Protestant. Hobby: pvt. flying. Home: Century Towers West, Century City, CA 90067; Office: 1901 Ave. of the Stars, L.A., CA.

DENNISON, KEITH ELKINS
Museum Director
b. Sept. 20, 1939; Oakland; s. Keith E. and Safa S. (Lauffer) Dennison; B.A. art hist., S.F. State Univ., 1969; grad. studies with Dr. Ernst Mundt; languages and art hist. Lausanne Switz.; m. Theresa Dennison, June 5, 1971, Sea Ranch, Calif. Career: Asst. Curator of Edn., Mh. de Young Mem. Museum, S.F., 1968-70; visual arts adviser, Calif. Arts Commn., 1970; dir./curator of Art, Pioneer Museum and Haggin Galleries, Stockton, 1972---; also Adjunct Prof. Museology, Univ. of the Pacific. Publs.: Horizons A Century of Calif. Landscape Painting; Manual of the Modular Touring System of the Calif. Arts Commn. Served USAF. Hobbies: art hist., collecting. Rec.: tennis, sailing. Home: 3627 N. Monitor Circ., Stockton, CA; Office: 1201 N. Pershing Ave., Stockton, CA 95203.

DENSON, GAIL
Certified Public Accountant
b. Mar. 26, 1939, Ogden, Utah; son John M. and Ruby Mae (Bartholomew) Denson; A.A., 1961; B.A., Univ. of Redlands, 1963; C.P.A. certificate, 1966; m. Onie Lee Stringer, Feb. 23, 1978, Arcadia, Calif.; chil.: Martin Eugene Miller, b. Sept. 25, 1960; Michael Dean Miller, b. Dec. 11, 1961; Monte Wayne Miller, b. Dec. 9, 1962; William Stern Denson, b. Oct. 18, 1968; Christina Yarnell Denson, b. Aug. 21, 1971. Career: pvt. accounting practice, 1972---. Pres., Sierra Care, Inc., 1978---. Dir.: Gail Denson, an accountancy corp.; Nat. Nurse, Inc. Mem.: Am. Inst. of C.P.A.s; Calif. Soc. of C.P.A.s. Mormon, Sun. Sch. pres., exec. secty., ward clerk. Hobby: stamp and coin collecting. Home: 165 W. Arthur, Arcadia, CA 91006; Office: 2540 Huntington Dr., San Marino, CA 91108.

DENTON, HON. N. EDWARD
District Attorney of Mono County
b. Apr. 24, 1926, Randsburg, Calif.; s. William L. and Vivian (Webster) Denton; A.B. 1949; LL.B. 1952; m. Grace Patricia Crocker, Bridgeport, Calif., Aug. 12, 1950; daus.: Kathleen Patricia, b. Dec. 1951; Maureen Elaine, b. June 13, 1953; Aileen Louise, b. Oct. 15, 1954. Career: Atty. at law, 1952-55; dist. atty., Mono Co., Calif. 1955---. Home: Bridgeport, CA; Office: Courthouse, Bridgeport, CA.

DE ROSE, MARILYN LOUISE
Business Executive — Civic Leader
b. Nov. 28, 1934, Long Is., N.Y.; d. James and Ethel (Newell) De Rose; A.A. (bus. adm.), Fullerton Coll.; postgrad. Calif. State Coll., Fullerton; B.S.L., Western State Univ., Coll. Law, Anaheim; USC. Career: Bookkeeper, Fullerton Publ. Co. 1952-60; acct.-secty. Larry's Bookkeeper Serv., Fullerton, 1960-62; partner, M & M Bus. Serv., Fullerton, 1962-66; formed corp., pres.-gen. mgr. 1966---; owner-mgr. M & M Travel Agcy. Mem.: pres., Fullerton Bus. and Profl. Women's Clubs, 1961-62; (charter) secty., Women's Mgmt. Council, USC 1964; secty-treas., Youthpower USA Found., Inc. 1964---; pres. San Orco Dist., Calif. Fed. of Bus. and Profl. Women's Clubs, 1965-66, pres. 1974-75, treas. Calif. Fed. 1969-71; trustee So. Calif. Youth Leadership Found., and Bus. Edn. Found.; Am. Coll. of Accredited Tax Accts.; Calif. Comm. on Status of Women, 1972; chmn. Interstate Assn. 1973-74, cons. Natl. Research-Edn. 1973-75; edn. comm. Fullerton C. of C.; (charter) Assn. of Profl. Secty. Servs. in Orange Co. Hobby: travel (plan, coord., cond. annual coll. tours). Home: 411 N. Adams

Ave., Fullerton, CA 92632; Office: 400 N. Euclid Ave., Fullerton, CA 92632.

DESPOL, JOHN ANTON
Labor Relations Official
b. July 22, 1913, S.F.; s. Anton and Bertha (Balzer) Despol; grad. Manual Arts H.S. 1929; USC; m. Jeri Kay Steep, L.A., Dec. 7, 1937; sons: Christopher Paul, b. June 26, 1943; Anthony John, b. Aug. 22, 1944. Career: Internat. repr.-admr., United Steel Workers of Am., L.A. 1937-58 and 1960-68; repr. Dempsey-Tegler and Co. 1968-70; Bache & Co. (NYSE), 1970-72; commr. Fed. Mediation Serv. 1973---; cons. Owl Investment Serv. 1973---; Calif. Dep. Labor Commr. II, 1976---; Calif. Def. Council, 1939-41; 10th Regional War Manpower Comm. 1942-45; Natl. Steel Panel, Natl. War Labor Bd. 1944; chmn. trustees, Union Mgmt. Ins. Trust Fund, L.A. 1948-66; secty.-treas., Calif. CIO Council, L.A. 1950-58; gen. v.p., Calif. Labor Fed. AFL-CIO, S.F. 1958-60. Lectr., before univs., clubs, indus. govt. and civic groups of U.S. 1930---. Mem.: pres. Local 2018, United Steel Workers of Am. 1938-40; bd. govs., Town Hall, 1941-44, 1967-70; L.A. Co. Dem. Com. 1942-44; del Natl. Dem. Conv. 1948, 52, 56, 58, 60; exec. com., Dem. State Central Com. 1952-56, chmn. Calif. Cong. Dist. 1954-56, Calif. Leg. Adv. Comm. to State Legislature, 1956-59; tech. adv. com., Econ. Devel. Agcy., State of Calif.; (pub.) Calif. Job Training and Placement council; Calif. adv. com., U.S. Civ. Rights Comm.; bd. dirs., L.A. Community Chest; dir. L.A. World Affairs Council, 1953---; exec. bd., So. Calif. Chpt.-dir., Natl. Conf. Chris. and Jews, 1961-77; dir. Braille Inst. of Am.; dir. Crenshaw YMCA. Democrat 1934-66; Repub. 1966---; Del. Repub. Natl. Conv. 1968. Protestant. Hobbies: photog., writing. Rec.: golf, tennis, sports. Address: 4717 Willis Ave., Suite 7, Sherman Oaks, CA 91403.

DESSEL, NORMAN FRANK
Professor of Natural Sciences
b. July 9, 1932, Ida Grove, Ia.; s. Joseph Albert and Lelah (Bright) Dessel; B.A. physics, 1957; M.A. physics, 1958; Ph.D., physics & Sci. edn., 1961, Univ. of Ia.; m. Marydale Merrill, Sept. 3, 1955; Ida Grove, Ia.; chil.: Diana Elizabeth, b. June 27, 1957; Dirk Norman, b. June 29, 1960; Jennifer Leigh, b. Sept. 24, 1965. Career: with San Diego State Univ., 1961---: asst. prof., assoc. prof. and prof. of physics, 1961-68; prof. of natural scis., 1968---; head, dept. of natural sci. 1968-74; adminstr. grad. fellowships and traineeships, Nat. Sci. Found. 1976-77; dir. physics inst. for Columbia Univ. at Patna Univ., Bihar, India, 1965. Air cadet, USAF, 1953-55, flying officer; Capt., USAF Ret., 1955-61. Author: Atomic Light: Laser, Sterling, N.Y., 1958; Science and Human Destiny, McGraw-Hill, N.Y. 1973; papers on laser optics and sci edn. in journs. and tech. publs. Mem.: Sigma Pi Sigma; Phi Delta Kappa; Phi Mu Alpha. United Methodist Ch., turstee. Rec.: camping, music. Office: San Diego State Univ., San Diego, CA 92182.

DEUKMEJIAN, GEORGE
State Attorney General
b. June 6, 1928, Menands (Albany) N.Y.; s. George and Alice (Gairden) Deukmejian; B.A., Siena Coll., 1949; J.D., St. John's Univ. Sch. of Law, 1952; m. Gloria M. Saatjian, Long Beach, Calif., Feb. 16, 1957; chil.: Leslie Ann, b. Sept. 22, 1964; George Krikor, b. Apr. 26, 1966; Andrea Diane, b. Feb. 5, 1969. Career: Dep. Co. Counsel, L.A.; partner, Riedman, Dalessi, Deukmejian & Woods law firm, Long Beach; elected Assemblyman, Calif. Legislature, 1963-67, Senator, 1967---, Senate Majority Leader, 1969-71; Senate Minority Leader, 1974; Elected Attorney General, 1978. U.S. Army 1953-55. Mem.: C. of C.; Lions Club, Elks Club, Long Beach. Episcopalian. Rec.: golf. Office: 555 Capitol Mall, Sacto., CA 95814.

DEWITT, JOHN BELTON
Conservation Association Executive
b. Jan. 13, 1937, Oakland, Calif.; B.A., Wildlife Conservation, Univ. of Calif., 1959; m. Karma S. Dewitt, 1960, Tacoma, Wash.; chil.: Jeffery C.; Katherine L.; Alexander B.; Charles D. Career: U.S. Forest Service, 1955-56; Nat. Park Service, 1959-61; Bureau of Land Mgmt., 1961-64; Asst. Secty., Save the Redwoods League, 1964-71, exec. dir. and secty., 1971---. Dir., The Nature Conservancy, No. Calif. chpt., 1976-77; mem. advisory council, Trust for Pub. Land, 1975---. Mem.: Sierra Club, Nat. Parks Assn. Hobbies: hiking, climbing, fishing. Office: Save-The-Redwoods League, 114 Sansome St., Rm. 605, San Francisco, CA 94104.

DEXHEIMER, HENRY PHILLIP II
President, The Dexheimer Company
b. Sept. 16, 1925, Dayton, Oh.; s. Henry Phillip (noted

Am. Pioneer photographer and owner chain studios, Oh., Ind.; recd. acclaim as leading U.S., Oh., and Ind. photog.; personal photog. to U.S. Senators, Pres. Harding and Pres. Roosevelt) and Helene (Francis) Dexheimer; B.S., USC 1952; C.L.U. 1971; chil.: James Phillip, b. Aug. 19, 1950; Jana Helene, b. Apr. 23, 1953. Career: Acct. exec., adv. firms, 1946-52; broadcasting sales exec. KBIG, KFXM, KTLA-TV, 1952-58; pres. KFXM Radio Sta. 1956-57; pres.-propr. The Dexheimer Co., ins. agcy. spec. 1958---. Gen. Hdqrs., Armed Forces; Adj. Gen. Dept. 1943-46, WW II. Awards: Sammy by Sales Exec. Club of L.A. 1955; Radio Adv. Bur's. Natl. Salesman Trophy 1955; Natl. Rookie of Yr., Travelers Ins. Co. 1959; (life) Million Dollar Round Table, 1972. Mem.: Phi Kappa Tau, 1948; Alumni pres., Alpha Delta Sigma, 1955; Mason (32º), Shriner, Al Malaikah Temple, L.A., 1956---; pres. Travelers Ins. Co. Men's Club, 1963; bd. dirs. L.A. Life Underwriters Assn. 1963-65; v.p. 1967-69; Life Ins. and Trust Council, L.A. 1969---; Town Hall of Calif., 1969---; natl. bd. dirs. Travelers Chpt., Am. Soc. of C.L.U. 1972-73; L.A. World Affairs Council, 1973---. Republican. Bel Air Presbyterian Ch.; Santa Monica Shrine Club; Marina del Rey Shrine Club. Rec.: bicycling, swimming, reading. Office: 3600 Wilshire Blvd., L.A., CA 90010.

DIAS, FRANCES JEAN
Government Official
b. June 15, 1923, Two Rivers, Wis.; s. Frank and Rosalie (Beale) Kracha; B.A., Univ. Colo., 1944; Calif. Sec. Tchg. Credential, Univ. of Calif., 1947; studies, Stanford Univ.; chil.: Maryanne Dias, b. Oct. 27, 1949; Teresa F. Dias, b. June 8. 1051; Patricia J. Dias, b. Oct. 11, 1953. Career: elected to City Council of Palo Alto, 1961-71, Mayor, 1966-68, vice mayor, 1969; field rep. for Congressman Charles S. Gubser, 1969-71; regional dir., Defense Civil Preparedness Agcy., Santa Rosa, 1971---. USMC Women's Reserve, 1945-46. Served multiple committees: League of Calif. Cities, Natl. League of Cities, Assn. of Bay Area Govt.; pres., S.F. Fed. Exec. Bd., 1976-77; Santa Rosa Planning Commn. 1973-77. Mem.: Commonwealth Club of S.F.; Alpha Omicron Pi; Stanford Convalescent Hosp. Aux. Catholic. Hobbies: Sewing, sports, travel. Office: P.O.B. 7287, Santa Rosa, CA.

DICKASON, JAMES F.
President, Newhall Land & Farming Co.
b. July 5, 1922, S.F.; s. James F. and Jean H. Dickason; B.A., Harvard Univ. 1944; M.B.A., Stanford, Univ. 1951; m. Linda Stewart, S.F., Dec. 9, 1961; chil.: James B., b. Aug. 26, 1952; Thomas H., b. Mar. 28, 1954; Margaret J., b. Apr. 13, 1963; Bradford S., b. Oct. 16, 1965. Career: Asst. secty., secty., v.p., exec. v.p.-dir. White Investment Co. 1951-63; v.p., dir., pres. The Newhall Land and Farming Co., 1963---; pres.-chief. exec. ofcr.-dir. 1975---. Dir.: Knudsen Corp., Calif. C. of C., United Way, Inc.; dir. Wells Fargo Bank; trustee, Southwest Museum, Henry Mayo Newhall Mem. Hosp. Mem.: Lambda Alpha; Calif. Club; Zamorano Club, L.A.; Pac. Union Club, S.F. Rec.: boating. Home: 930 Rosalind Rd., San Marino, CA 91108; Office: 23823 Valencia Blvd., Valencia, CA 91355.

DIEMER, EMMA LOU
Composer -- Educator
b. Nov. 24, 1927, Kansas City, Mo.; d. George Willis (pres., Central Mo. State Coll., 1937-56) and Myrtle (Casebolt) Diemer; B. Mus., Yale Sch. of Music, 1949; M. Mus., 1950; Ph.D., Eastman Sch. of Music, 1960. Career: theory and organ tchr., Park Coll., Parkville, Mo., and Wm. Jewell Coll., Liberty, Mo. 1955-57; piano tchr., Kansas City Conservatory of Music, 1955-57; composer-in-residence under Ford Found. Young Composers Project, Arlington, Va. schs., 1959-61; composer-consultant under MENC Contemporary Music Project, Arlington, Va., 1962-63; prof. of theory & composition, Univ. of Md., 1965-70; prof. of theory & composition, Univ. of Calif., Santa Barbara, 1971---; organist in various churches, 1940-79. Pub. over 100 choral and instrumental works, 1956-79; numerous commissions and awards for compositions, 1955---. Protestant, ch. organist, 1940---. Rec.: biking. Home: 77-A N. San Marcos Rd., Santa Barbara, CA 93111; Office: Dept. of Music, UC, Santa Barbara, CA 93106.

DIETZ, DOROTHY BRILL
Artist — Designer — Teacher
daughter, Henry Edward and Anna Mae (Parfitt) Brill; student, Mills Coll., USC, Ore. State Univ., Julian Art Acad., Sorbonne, Rudolph Schaefer's Sch. Design, Japanese Art Center, Inst. San Miguel de Allende, Art Acad. of Honolulu, Wash. Sch. of Art, L'Ecole de Cordon Bleu, Unity Sch. of Christianity. Career: court reporter, Justice and Superior Cts., San Bernardino Co., 6 yrs.;

owner, operator, interior design studio and art gallery, 20 yrs.; artist; licensed tchr and counselor for Unity Sch. of Christianity. Paintings in solo and group exhibs. in Calif. abd abroad. Awards: 1st and 5th prizes for paintings Nat. Contest of Natl. League of Am. Penwomen; 2 first prizes, Natl. Date Festival, Indio; 2nd prize, Shadow Mountain Palette Club; awarded seal with name, Taka Mizu Dietz by Japanese Govt. Mem.: Alpha Chi Omega; Villages Art Assn.; Villages Golf and Country Club; Internat. 700 Club. Republican. Unity. Rec.: tennis, golf, bicycling. Address: Unit 72, Del Mesa Carmel, Carmel, CA 93921.

DIGANGE, JOSEPH JAMES
  Bank President
b. Feb. 8, 1927, Chicago, Ill.; s. Giuseppi and Jennie (Lio) Di Gangi; student, UCLA Extension Courses; m. Helen Ferra, Dec. 14, 1946, Chicago, Ill.; chil.: Nancy (Mrs. Dennis Cypher), b. Oct. 4, 1947; Cathleen (Mrs. Joel Everitt), b. Apr. 16, 1961. Career: asst. cashier & loan officer, Union Nat. Bank of Chicago, 1949-59; adminstrv. asst., asst. branch mgr., branch mgr., Security Pacific Bank, L.A., 1959-63; v.p.-chief lending officer, exec. v.p. & dir., Am. City Bank, L.A., 1963-72; pres., chief exec. officer & dir., Los Angeles Bank, 1972---. Dir.: Big Brothers of Greater L.A., 1976-78; Palm Springs Bank, 1978; Villa Scalabrini, 1976-78. USN. Hobbies: gardening, horses, music. Rec.: golf. Home: 2586 Casiano Rd., Bel-Air, CA 90024; Office: 1950 Ave. of the Stars, L.A., CA 90067.

DIGBY, JAMES F.
  Research Engineer
b. Aug. 11, 1921, Farmerville, La.; s. Sebe L. and Maud M. Digby; B.S., 1941; M.A., 1942; m. Mary Jane Bruck, Dec. 5, 1959, Pacific Palisades; chil.: Ward McLees, b. 1961; James Andrew, b. 1962; Leslie Jane, b. 1964. Career: Program Mgr. and Project Leader, Rand Corp., 1949---; exec. dir., Calif. Seminar on Arms Control and Foreign Policy, 1976---; dir., European-Am. Inst. for Security Research, 1977---; Cons. to White House, 1959-62; Fed. Aviation Agency, 1961-62; U.S. State Dept. 1975-76. Contbr.: articles to Beyond Nuclear Deterrence, 1977; The Other Arms Race, 1975; others. 1st Lt., AUS and USAF, 1942-46. Home: 20773 Big Rock Dr., Malibu, CA 90265; Office: 1700 Main St., Santa Monica, CA 90406.

DI GIACOMO-GEFFERS, ELIZABETH
  Nursing Administrator
b. Nov. 8, 1939, Mt. Vernon, N.Y.; B.A. nursing, Jersey City State Coll., 1961; graduate nurse, 1960, Jersey City Med. Center (registered in: N.J., Calif., Md.); M. pub. health, Johns Hopkins Univ., 1966, Fellow, Environmental Med. div. of hearing & speech, 1967; married. Career: tchr. of health edn., No. Bergen H.S., N.J., 1961-62; relief hd. nurse, N.J., 1960-62; asst. mgr., Long Beach Mem. Hosp., 1962-63; occupational health nurse, Walt Disney Prodns., Anaheim, 1964-65; sch. nurse, Huntington Beach H.S., 1963-65; spec. nurse, Johns Hopkins Med. Insts., 1966-67; Instr., Univ. of Md. Sch. of Dentistry, 1967, and assoc. dir. Nursing, Johns Hopkins Univ., 1967-68; head nurse, No. Hudson Hosp., N.J., 1968-70; asst. dir. of nursing, Cedars-Sinai Med. Center, 1970---. Editor and author: many studies and research papers used as in-house tchg. presentations as well as publs. in tech. journs. Mem.: AAUW; Fellow, Am. Sch. Health Assn.; Fellow, Am. Pub. Health Assn.; Am. Nurses Assn.; assoc., Am. Heart Assn.; Johns Hopkins Univ. Alumni; Jersey City State Coll. and Med. Center alumni; Nat. Critical Care Inst.; The Royal Soc. of Health. Address: 1301 S. Atlantic Blvd., Monterey Park, CA 91754.

DI GIORGIO, ROBERT JOSEPH
  Chairman, Di Giorgio Corp.
b. Dec. 2, 1911, N.Y.C.; s. Salvatore and Marie Di Giorgio; nephew of Joseph Di Giorgio, founder, Di Giorgio Fruit Corp.; ed. B.A., Yale Univ. 1933; LL.B., Fordham Law Sch. 1936; m. Eleanor Vollmann, Stockton, Calif., 1940 (div.); m. 2nd, Patricia Kuhrts Sharman, 1964; chil.: Ann, b. Nov. 19, 1941; Barbara, b. Sept. 4, 1944; Christine, b. June 29, 1946; Dorothy, b. July 8, 1958. Career: exec. v.p-dir., Di Giorgio Corp. 1938-62, pres. 1962-71, chmn. bd. 1971---. Dir.: Newhall Land Co.; Pac. Tel. and Telegraph Co., Bank of Am., Union Oil Co. of Calif., Carter Hawley Hale Stores, Inc.; Mem.: S.F. Comml. Club, S.F. Commonwealth Club, Pac.-Union Club, Bohemian Club, S.F. Golf CLub, Yale Club (N.Y.C.), Calif. Club. Office: One Maritime Plaza, S.F., CA 94111.

DI GIROLAMO, RUDOLPH GERARD
  Professor of Biology
b. Jan. 26, 1934, Brooklyn, N.Y.; s. Carmine Di Girolamo and Carmella MaResca Di Girolamo; B.S., biology, Mt. St. Mary's Coll., Md.; M.S., St. John's Univ., N.Y.; PH.D., Univ. of Wash., 1969; m. Celina Sau Lin Ing; son, Christopher Robert, b. Aug. 1978. Career: with Univ. of Wash., Seattle, 1964-69: trainee, shellfish sanitation, 1964-69, lectr. Marine Microbiology, 1967-69, research assoc. Prof., Dept. of Sanitary Engring., 1969; prof. and chmn., dept. of biological sciences, Coll. of Notre Dame, Belmont, 1970---, also dir. Marine Resources Center, 1973---. Pfiter research fellow, St. John's Univ., N.Y. 1955-56. Awarded recognition from UN: food virology, World Health Orgn.; marine pollution, Food and Agri. Orgn. Contbr. articles to Skin Divers Mag. and profl. journs. Special interest: planning and coordinating new marine life programs. Mem.: AAAS; Am. Soc. for Microbiology; Am. Fish Soc.; Am. Soc. of Malacologists; Internat. Ocean Found.; N.Y. Acad of Sci. Hobby: marine tropical fish. Rec.: shooting, camping, scuba, fencing. Office: 1500 Ralston Ave., Belmont, CA 94002.

DIKE, PHILIP LATIMER
  Professor Emeritus of Art
b. Apr. 6, 1906, Redlands; s. Andrew Noble and Jennie Eliz. (Twigg) Dike; stu., Chouinard Art Inst., 1924, 28; Art Students League, N.Y., 1928; w/Geo. Luks, 1928,29; Am. Acad., Fountainbleau, France, 1930-31; m. Betty Love Woodward, June 17, 1933, Phoenix, Ariz.; son, Philip Woodward. Career: Instr. drawing, painting, Chouinard Art Inst., L.A., 1931-34; 1945-50; training instr.: drawing composition, color coordination, story design, Walt Disney Prodns., 1933-35, and color coordinator, 1935-45 (Snow White, Fantasia, etc.); Rex Brandt-Phil Dike Summer Sch. of Watercolor, Corona del Mar, 1949-70; prof. of Art Scripps Coll., Claremont Grad. Sch., 1949-70; Prof. Emeritus, 1971---; active exhibiting painter, 1920s---. Contbr. articles to art mags. and books on watercolor painting; rep. in many pub. and pvt. collections incl.: Calif. Water Color Soc., L.A. Co. Mus. of Art, Metropolitan Mus. of Art (NYC), Lib. of Congress (Wash. D.C.), Butler Inst. of Am. Art (Oh.), Wood Mus. (Vt.), Pasadena Mus. of Modern Art, Nat. Acad. of Design (NY); recipient of more than 80 awards. Mem.: Calif. Water Color Soc., pres. 1939; Am. Watercolor Soc., past v.p.; West Coast Watercolor Soc.; Nat. Acad. of Design. Rec.: fishing. Home: 2272 N. Forbes Ave., Claremont, CA 91711.

DILLON, RICHARD H.
  Librarian
b. Jan. 16, 1924, Sausalito, Calif.; s. William T. and Alice Mabel (Burke) Dillon; A.A., Univ. of Calif., Berkeley, 1943; A.B. 1948; M.A., 1949; B.L.S., 1950; m. Barbara A. Sutherland, Berkeley, June 1950; sons: Brian, David, Ross. Career: Sutro Lib. 1950---; Sutro Librarian, 1953---. Author: (Books) Embarcadero, The Gila Trail, Calif. Trail Herd, Shanghaiing Days, The Hatchet Men, J. Ross Browne, Meriwether Lewis, The Legend of Grizzly Adams. Pvt., U.S. Inf., E.T.O., WW II. Awards: Purple Heart, 1944; James D. Phelan Award for best non-fiction book by a Calif. author, for Meriwether Lewis, Commonwealth Club; Award of Merit, Calif. Hist. Soc.; Award of Merit for J. Ross Browne, Am. Assn. for State and Local Hist. Mem.: Calif. Hist. Comm. 1967---; Western Hist. Assn.; Calif. Lib. Assn.; Roxburghe Club of S.F.; Phi Beta Kappa, Phi Alpha Theta. Hobbies: writing, reading, hiking. Rec.: travel. Office: Sutro Library, 2495 Golden Gate Ave., S.F., CA 94118.

DILWORTH, ROBERT PALMER
  Professor of Mathematics
b. Dec. 2, 1914, Hemet, Calif.; s. J. Norman and Myrtle (Palmer) Dilworth; B.S., Calif. Inst. of Tech. 1936, Ph.D. 1939; m. Miriam White, Hamden, Conn., Dec. 23, 1940; chil.: Robert Palmer, Jr., b. Sept. 26, 1941; Gregory Lee, b. Apr. 26, 1947. Career: Sterling research fellow, Yale Univ. 1939-40; instr. in math. 1940-43; asst. prof. of math, Calif. Inst. of Tech., 1943-45; assoc. prof. 1945-51, prof. 1951---. Operations Analyst, USAAF (1944-45), WW II. Home: 3121 Doyne Rd., Pasadena, CA; Office: Calif. Inst. of Tech., Pasa, CA.

DIMMITT, RICHARD BERTRAND
  Author — Librarian
b. Aug. 22, 1925, Huntington Park, Calif.; s. Ralph Bertrand (contr-bldr., Balboa Is.) and Jennie Elizabeth (Lambert) Dimmitt; grandson of Robert Cassell Dimmitt and Xelis Gephart, subdividers of Bell Gardens, Calif.; B.A. (elem. edn.), Long Beach State Coll. 1952; spec. lib. sci. credentials, San Jose State Coll. and Immaculate Heart Coll. (L.A.), 1954. Career: Children's libn., Buena

Park Lib. Dist. 1954-57; head cataloger, Marquardt Engring. Lib., Van Nuys, 1957-58; ref. and film lib, Norwalk br., L.A. Co. Lib., 1958-60; chmn. exhibs. com., Friend of the Lib., Univ. of Calif., Irvine. Author: The Title Guide to the Talkers, 1965; The Actor Guide to the Talkies, 1967; The Red and the Green, 1967. U.S. Army (1944-46), WW II; Korean Conflict, 1950. Awards: Purple Heart, 1945. Mem.: Orange Co. Lib. Assn.; Sliema Creek Yacht Marine, Sliema, Malta, 1964---; The Landfall Club. Republican. Episcopalian. Rec.: horseback riding, sailing. Home: 223 Via Nice, Lido Is., Newport Beach, CA; and 178 The Birkirka Rd., St. Julians, Malta.

DI MUCCIO, MARY-JO
Administrative Librarian
b. June 16, 1930, Hanford, Calif.; d. Vincent and Teresa (Jovino) Di Muccio; B.A., Immaculate Heart Coll., L.A., 1953, M.L.S., 1960; Ph.D., U.S. Internat. Univ., San Diego, 1970. Career: tchr. elem. schs., 1947-62; asst. to head librarian, Immaculate Heart Coll., 1962-72; adminstrv. librarian, city of Sunnyvale, 1972---. Author: Freedom and Responsibility of the Individual in Democratic Society, 1970; Library Informational Handbook for Elementary Schools, 1961; Children's Choices & Parent's Choices in Selecting Children's Literature, 1960. Mem.: Catholic Library Assn., pres., 1973-76; Peninsula Library Assn., secty.-treas., 1976-78; Sunnyvale Community Services, v.p. of exec. bd., 1978-79; Brookline Homeowners' Assn., pres., 1972-73; exec. bd. 1973-76, secty. 1976-78. Mem.: ALA, Special Library Assn.; Calif. Lib. Assn.; Pub. Lib. Exec. of Central Calif.; Continuing Lim. Education Network & Exchange. Mem.: Soroptimist Club, pres. 1977-78; Sunnyvale Bus. & Profl. Women, v.p. 1978-79. Honored by Lib. of Human Resources of the Am. Bicentennial Research Inst. Catholic. Hobbies: tennis, traveling. Rec.: reading. Office: 720-C Blair Ct., Sunnyvale, CA 94087.

DITTMAR, RICHARD FRANK
Construction Industry Executive
b. Nov. 25, 1935, Philadelphia, Pa.; s. John and Helen (Morris) Dittmar; B.S., Sacramento State Coll., 1968; M.B.A., Cal. State Univ., 1971; m. Wiltrud Pabst, July 27, 1963, Sacramento; chil.: Gordon, Steven, Alexander. Career: Pub. Relations dir., Sacramento C. of C., 1962-64; legislative asst., Calif. Legislature, 1964-66; exec. v.p., Calif. State Builders' Exchange, 1967-78; pres., Construction Industry Adminstrs. Corp., 1978---; also pres., R.F. Dittmar & Assoc.; secty-treas., Western Construction Insurance Services Corp. V.P., Constrn. Industry Legislative Council; Dir., Constrn. Force Account Council. Mil.: USAF, 1953-57. Author: numerous articles for trade journs. Apptd. delegation leader, goodwill people-to-people Mission to USSR, 1977. Elected mem., Nat. Honor Soc. for Bus., 1971. Mem.: Sacto. Breakfast Optimist Club; Beta Gamma Sigma; Am. Soc. of Assn. Executives. Polit. candidate, State Assembly, 1978. Catholic. Rec.: Karate, golf. Home: 6359 Perrin Way, Carmichael, CA 95608; Office: 650 University Ave., Sacto., CA 95813.

DIXON, GAIL S.
Savings & Loan Association Executive
b. Jan. 3, 1943, Northampton, Mass.; d. Walter and Mary Jane Hargesheimer; student, Western Wash. State Univ., Bellingham, Wash.; m. Dean O. Dixon, May 8, 1965, Fullerton, Calif.; 1 son, Todd, b. Aug. 15, 1968. Career: variety of positions, including self-employment, reprographics industry, 1964-70; with Great Western Savings & Loan Assn., 1970---; dept. supr. 1972; training representative, 1973; Buena Park Branch mgr., 1974; elected v.p., 1975---. Mem.: Pres., Buena Park C. of C, 1978-79 (first woman elected pres. in 51 year hist. of Chamber), dir. 1975---; bd. dir. Girls Club of N. Orange Co., 1974---; secty. 1977---; secty.-treas., Buena Park Coordinating Council, 1976---; Buena Park Silverado Days Com., 1974---; advis. bd., Beach Community Hosp., Buena Park, 1976---; assoc. bd. mem., Buena Park Boys Club, 1974---; mem. Am. Found. for the Sci. of Creative Intelligence, 1974---. Methodist, mem. workshop commn. Hobby: sewing. Rec.: bicycling. Home: Buena Park Office, 8101 Stanton Ave., Buena Park, CA 90620.

DIXON, KEITH ALAN
Professor of Anthropology
b. San Francisco; B.A., Univ. Ariz., 1950, M.A. 1952; Ph.D., UCLA, 1956. Career: Archaeologist with New World Archaeological Found., Chiapas, Mex. 1956-58; archaeologist in summer seasons for Univ. Museum, Univ. of Penn., Tikal, Guatemala, 1959, 60; asst. prof. to full prof. of anthropology, Cal. State Univ., Long Beach, 1958---; Commnr., Orange Co. Hist. Commn., 1977---. Publs.: monographs, reviews, articles on archaeology in

profl. journs. and sci. series. Home: 2902 Angler Lane, Los Alamitos, CA 90720; Office: Dept. of Anthropology, Cal. State Univ., Long Beach, CA 90840.

DLUGATCH, IRVING
University Research Director
b. Jan. 20, 1910, Brooklyn, N.Y.; s. Louis and Lena (Seigle) Dlugatch; B.S.E.E., Cooper Union, 1936; B.S.E.E., West Coast Univ., 1963; M.S. syst. engring., 1964; Ph.D. math, L.A. Univ., 1977; m. Helen Rosenberg, Dec. 22, 1935, Brooklyn; chil.: Dr. Harvey E., b. July 7, 1945; Norman J., b. Nov. 21, 1939. Career: Section Head, Space Tech. Labs., 1959-61; sr. scientist, Systems Dev. Co., 1966-68; sr. scientist, Operations Research Inc., Silver Springs, Md., 1968-69; program mgr., Hughes Aircraft Co., 1969-74; dir., Graduate Research, Calif. Western Univ., 1977---; pres., IDL Industries, 1971-76. Author: Dynamic Cost Reduction, Wiley-Interscience, 1979; contbr. to Graphics Handbook, McGraw-Hill, 1979; $75 Billion Ripoff, Brasch & Brasch, 1979. Fellow, Inst. for Adv. of Engring.; assoc. fellow, Am. Inst. Aeros. and Astronautics; mem., Sigma Xi-RESA. Hobbies: painting, guitar, bridge. Home: 100 S. Doheny Dr., L.A., CA 90048; Office: 700 S. Main St., Santa Ana, CA 92701.

DOAN, ELEANOR LLOYD
Publicist -- Writer
b. June 4, 1914, Nampa, Id.; d. Fred and Gladys (Werth) Doan; desc. the Doan/Doane families of Doan Family Assn. Inc. of Am.: pres. Dow Chem., Wm. Howard Doane, indslt. and hymn writer; B.A., Univ. Nev.; postgrad. studies in edn., Wheaton Coll., mktg., UCLA. Career: Reporter, Nev. State Journ., 3 yrs; H.S. Tchr., Austin, Nev., 1 yr.; merchandising mgr., writer, Christian Publs. Inc., N.Y., 4½ yrs.; editor, writer, publicist, Gospel Light Publs., Glendale, 32 yrs. Publs. incl.: 157 More Fun to Do Crafts, 1972; Mothers Treasury of Inspiration, 1973; Children's Treasury of Inspiration, 1977; contbr. to journs. and textbooks. Mem.: Gamma Phi Beta; Chi Delta Phi; Kappa Tau Alpha; trustee, The Mustard Seed; trustee, Glint. Presbyterian; leadership training dir., supt., jr. hi. div. Hobby: desert lore, travel. Home: 1240 Moncado Dr., Glendale, CA 91207.

DOBIESKI, ALEXANDER W.
Engineer
b. July 31, 1939, Bridgeport, Conn.; s. Alexander and Jeanette (Sobalewski) Dobieski; B.S.E.E., Univ. Conn., 1961; M.S.E.E., Univ. of Utah, 1965; Ph.D. in Engring., UCLA, 1972; m. Patrica Colby, June 1963, Preston, Id.; chil.: Robyn (Scheid), b. Aug. 14, 1957; Heather, b. Feb. 1972; Kevin, b. Oct. 1964. Career: Research Engr., RCA, N.J., 1961-62; research engr. 1963-68; section head, TRW, 1968-72; Dept. Mgr., 1972-75; project mgr., TRW Defense and Space Syst. Group, 1975---. 1st Lt., AUS Ordnance Corp., Capt. USAR. Contbr. research papers to Mil. Ops. Research Soc. symposiums, others. L.D.S. Ch., various positions. Hobbies: gardening, skiing, karate. Rec.: fishing. Home: 16533 Sequoia St., Fountain Valley, CA; Office: TRW Systems, One Space Park, Redondo Beach, CA 90278.

DOCKSON, ROBERT RAY
Chairman, California Federal Savings & Loan Assn.
b. Oct. 6, 1917, Quincy, Ill.; s. Marshal R. and Letah L. (Edmundson) Dockson; A.A., Springfield Jr. Coll. 1937; B.S., Univ. of Ill. 1939; M.F.S., USC, 1940, Ph.D. 1946; m. Katheryn V. Allison, S.F., Mar. 4, 1944; chil.: Kathy Kimberlee, b. Dec. 14, 1948. Career: Asst. prof.-dir., Bur. of Econ. and Bus. Research, Rutgers Univ. 1946-48; economist, Western home ofc., Prudential Ins. Co. 1948-51; economist, Bank of America, S.F., 1951-53; prof.-head, Dept. of Mktg., Sch. of Comm., USC 1953-59; dean-prof. bus. econs., Sch. of Bus. Adm. 1959-69; dir. Calif. Fed. Svgs. & Loan Assn. 1969---, pres. 1970---, chief exec. ofcr. 1973---; chmn. bd. ---. Am. Specialist for U.S. Dept. of State. Dir.: Pacific Lighting Corp., 1966---; The Bekins Co. 1968---; U.S. Navy (1942-45), WW II. Awards: Asa V. Call Achievement Award; the Star of Solidarity (Italian Govt.). Mem.: Orthopaedic Hosp., John Randolph Haynes and Dora Haynes Found.; bd. govs. Goodwill Inds. of So. Calif.; pres. Greater L.A. C. of C. 1975; bd. Councilors, Grad. Sch. Bus. Adm. USC; Phi Kappa Phi; Beta Gamma Sigma, pres., Town Hall, 1961-62, bd. govs., 1962-65, hon. bd. govs. 1965---; Clubs: Western Internat. Trade Assn.; Newcomen Soc. of N. Am.; L.A. Rotary Club; L.A. Country, L.A. Club, Lincoln, Silver Dollar, Commonwealth, Bohemian, Birnam Wood Golf, The One Hundred Club of L.A. Home: 505 S. Hudson Ave., L.A., CA 90020; Office: 5670 Wilshire Blvd., L.A., CA 90036.

DOCKWEILER, FREDERICK C.
Attorney at Law
b. Jan. 4, 1909, L.A.; s. Isidore Bernard and Gertrude (Reeve) Dockweiler; bros.: Hon. John F. Dockweiler (dec.), Congressman and dist. atty., L.A. Co.; Hon. George A. Dockweiler, judge, Superior Ct., L.A. Co.; Rear Adm. Edward V. Dockweiler, USN (ret.); Thomas A.J. Dockweiler and H.I. Dockweiler; Univ. of Notre Dame, 1928-30; A.B. Stanford Univ., 1930-32; LL.B., Georgetown Law Sch.; m. Helen Rose Scully, L.A., Dec. 14, 1948; chil.: Barbara Helen, b. 1953. Career: Admitted to bar, 1935; atty.-counselor at law, Dockweiler & Dockweiler law firm, 1935---. U.S. Army (1943-45), WW II. Mem.: Am., Calif., L.A. Bar Assns.; B.P.O.E. No. 99; Ramona Parlor 109, N.S.G.W. Democrat. Catholic. Hobby: philately. Home: 626 N. McCadden Pl., L.A., CA; Office: Suite 1035, Van Nuys Bldg., L.A., CA 90014.

DODGE, HENRY WILLIAM Jr.
Physician — Neurological Surgeon
b. Jan. 29, 1918, Houston, Tex.; s. Henry William and Katherine (Dunn) Dodge; ed. Phillips Exeter Acad., N.H. 1934-36; Sheffield Sci. Sch.; B.S., Yale Univ., New Haven, Conn. 1936-40; M.D., Columbia Univ. Coll. of Phys. and Surgs., N.Y.C. 1940-43; M.S. (neurological surg.), Univ. of Minn. Grad. Sch. of Med. 1951; m. Lady Rachel Peeler; chil.: Nina, b. Nov. 28, 1947; Henry, b. Feb. 12, 1949; James, b. Sept. 9, 1950; Debora, b. Aug. 1954. Career: Intern in surgery: John Hopkins Hosp., Baltimore, 1944; Presbyterian Hosp., Columbia Univ. Med. Center, N.Y. 1947-48; fellow (neurosurg.), Mayo Clinic, Rochester, Minn. 1948-51, asst. staff, 1951-52, staff neurological surg. 1952; asst. prof. (neurological surg.), Univ. of Minn. Grad. Sch. of Med. 1956; est. pvt. practice, L.A., 1959---. Capt., U.S. Army Med. Corps, Pac. Theater (1944-47), WW II; Comdr. (neurological surg.), USNR. Mem.: Mayo Found. Alumni Assn.; Am. Bd. of Neurological Surg., Am., Calif., Pan Am., and L.A. Co. Med. Assns., Natl. Bd. of Med. Examiners, Clubs: Bel-Air Golf and Country; Jonathan; Met., N.Y.C.; White Water Country, Racquet, Palm Springs; L.A. Episcopalian. Home: 223 Strada Corta Rd., Bel-Air, L.A., CA 90024; Office: Suite 809, 9201 Sunset Blvd., L.A., CA 90069.

DOERR, CHARLES DAVIDSON
Business Consultant
b. Jan. 9, 1910, Minneapolis, Minn.; s. George Valentine and Eleanor (Davidson) Doerr; ed. A.B., Dartsmouth Coll. 1928-32; m. Virginia Klein, St. Paul, Minn., Apr. 18, 1936; chil.: Georgiana Haynor, b. Mar. 2, 1941; John Davidson (D.D.S.), b. Oct. 11, 1944. Career: Div. mgr. McKesson & Robbins, Inc., St. Paul, Milwaukee, San Diego, 1936-42, v.p. N.Y. 1946-61, sr. v.p.-dir.-treas. 1961-67; bus. cons., San Diego, 1967---. USNR gunnery ofcr. 1942-44; Lt., Mil. Govt. Ofcr. at SHAEF, 1944-45, Bronze Star Medal, 1945. Mem.: pres. Natl. Wholesale Druggists Assn. 1950-51; pres. Bd. of Edn., Bronxville, N.Y. 1958; pres. Am. Found. for Pharmaceutical Edn. 1962-64; trustee: Scripps Clinic and Research Found., La Jolla, 1968-73; Chil's. Hosp. and Health Center, San Diego, 1968---, pres. 1973-74; Calif. Hosp. Assn. 1974; dir.: Univ. Indus., S.D. 1970---; S.D. C. of C., 1972-75; Calbiochem, Inc., S.D. 1974---; Casque and Gauntlet, Delta Kappa Epsilon. Deacon, Reformed Ch., Bronxville. Home: 1796 Soledad Ave., La Jolla, CA; Office: 7734 Herschel Ave., La Jolla, CA 92037.

D'OLIVEIRA, JOSEPH G.
Honorary Consul, Republic of Guyana
b. July 14, 1942, Georgetown, Guyana; s. Carlos and Stella D'Oliveira; brother, Claude Worrell, Minister, Embassy of the Republic of Guyana, Washington, D.C.; cousin, John Carter, Ambassador of Guyana to the Peoples Republic of China; A.A., East Los Angeles Coll., 1972; B.S. with honors in Accounting, Calif. State Polytechnic Univ., Pomona, 1973; m. Yolanda O., Jan. 5, 1974, L.A., Calif. Career: C.P.A., 1975---; Honorary Consul of the Republic of Guyana, Feb. 1976---. Bus. Mgr., Kedren Community Mental Health Center, L.A., 1975-78. AUS, 1966-69, Rank E-6, served in U.S., Germany, Vietnam. Decorated with Bronze Star medal, Vietnamese Service medal, Vietnamese Campaign medal, Good Conduct medal. Bd. Dir., Guyana-Am. Social Club, 1970-77, pres. 1976-77. Catholic. Hobbies: ice hockey, cricket, boxing, track and field. Rec.: tennis, ping pong. Home: 3916 Carnavon Way, L.A., CA 90027; Office: 2040 Ave. of the Stars, Suite 400, L.A., CA 90067.

DONAHUE, KENNETH
Director Emeritus, L.A. County Museum of Art
b. Jan. 31, 1915, Louisville, Ky.; ed. A.B., Univ. of Louisville, Ky. 1936; A.M., Inst. of Fine Arts, N.Y.U.

1947; m. Daisy Cain; chil.: Mrs. John Adams Barker, Craig. Career: Dept. asst.-art librn., Univ. of Louisville, 1936-38; lectr., Mus. of Modern Art, N.Y.C. 1938-43; research fellow, Am. Council of Learned Socs. for Stu. of Italian Baroque painting, Italy, France, Eng., 1947-49; lectr.-curatorial asst., Frick Collection, N.Y.C. 1949-53; curator, The John and Mable Ringling Museum of Art, 1953-57; dir. The Ringling Museums, 1957-64; asst. dir., L.A. Co. Mus. of Art, 1964-66, dir. 1966-79. Author: articles in profl. journs. and exhib. catalogs; contrib to Dizionario Biografico degli Italiani. U.S. Army (1943-45), WW II. Mem.: Coll. Art Assn. Bd. Dirs. 1967-71; Am. Assoc. Mus. V.p., 1970-72, Exec. comm., 1970-74, Council. 1968-78. Am. Assn. Mus. 1969---; IRS Commr's. Art Adv. Panel, Wash., D.C. 1970-74; Art Mus. Dirs. Assn. Home: 245 S. Westgate Ave., L.A., CA 90049; Office: 5905 Wilshire Blvd., L.A., CA 90036.

DONALDSON, JOHN R.
Fresno County Supervisor
b. Nov. 24, 1925, Dallas, Tex.; s. John R. and Marguerette Hoover (Atkinson) Donaldson; B.S., Rice Univ., 1945, M.A., 1947; M.S., Yale Univ., 1949, Ph.D., 1951; m. Shirley Jean Brown, June 30, 1951, Chathan, N.J.; chil.: Nancy Eva (Hughes), b. May 12, 1955; Dorothy Atkinson, b. May 27, 1957; Jane Margaret and John Edward, b. July 16, 1960. Career: Physicist, Calif. Research and Devel. Co., 1950-53; assoc. prof. of Physics, Univ. of Ariz. 1953-54; Physicist and Pvt. through Sp-3, U.S. Army Biological Warfare Lab., 1954-56; asst. prof., assoc. prof., prof. of physics, Cal. State Univ., Fresno, 1956---; physicist at Swiss Fed. Inst. of Tech., Zurich, 1967; elected to Fresno County Bd. Supvs., 1973---, chmn. of bd. of supvs., 1977, 1978. Mem.: Calif. Employment & Training Council, 1977---; chmn. Fresno Employment & Training Commn. 1977; exec. com. mem., Calif. Supvs. Assn., 1978---; exec. com. mem., Calif. Assn. of LAFCOS, 1978---; pres., Fresno Community Chorus. Moderator and choir dir., Coll. Comm. Congregational Ch. Hobby: music. Rec.: backpacking, volleyball. Nat. AAU Champion, Discus 1945; Nat. AAU Volleyball All-American, 1951. Home: 4559 N. DeWitt, Fresno, CA 93727; Office: Bd. of Supervisors, 2281 Tulare St., Fresno, CA 93721.

DONG, RICHARD GENE
Engineer
b. Mar. 16, 1935, Sacto.; s. Chester Q. and May W. Dong; B.S., mech. Engring., Univ. Calif., Berkeley, 1957, M.S., 1959, Ph.D., civil engring., 1964; m. Mae Fong, May 19, 1968, Sacto.; chil.: Michael K., b. Nov. 3, 1970; Catherine E., b. Aug. 15, 1972. Career: Dynamic analyst, Aerojet-General Corp., 1959-61; researcher, Univ. of Calif., 1958-59; with Lawrence Livermore Lab., 1963---: material sci. research 1963-72; group leader 1966-72; soils material researcher 1972-74; structural analyst and seismic studies, 1974-78; project engr. 1978---. Publs: approx. 30 tech. papers, mostly in sci. and tech. journs. and proceedings of tech. confs. Mem.: Sigma Xi, Tau Beta Phi, Pi Tau Sigma, Chi Epsilon. Hobbies: painting, gardening, house designing. Rec.: camping, swimming, skiing. Home: 38 Hornet Ct., Danville, CA 94526; Office: Lawrence Livermore Lab., Livermore, CA 94550.

DOOLITTLE, JAMES HAROLD
American Aviator — Aerospace Executive
b. Dec. 14, 1896, Alameda, Calif.; s. Frank H. and Rosa C. (Shephard) Doolittle; A.B., Univ. of Calif. 1922, (hon.) LL.D.; M.S., Mass. Inst. of Tech. 1924, D.Sc. 1925 (hon.) D.Sc.: Clarkson Coll. of Tech., Univ. of Alaska, Pa. Mil. Coll.; E.D.: Univ. of Mich., Brooklyn Polytech Inst.; Dr. Mil. Sci., Waynesburg, Coll.; LL.D., Northland Coll., Wis.; m. Josephine Daniels, L.A., Dec. 24, 1917; sons: James H., John P. Career: U.S. Army Air Corps, 1917-30, Maj. Reserves and mgr. Aviation Dept., Shell Petrol. Corp. 1930-40; Maj., Army Air Corps, 1940, Lt. Col. 1941, Brig. Gen., Maj. Gen. 1942, Lt. Gen. 1944; led first flight on Tokyo, 1942; Comdg. Gen.: Twelfth A.F. in N. Africa, 1942, Fifteenth A.F. in Italy, 1944, Eighth A.F. in Okinawa, 1945; v.p. 1946-59, dir. 1946-67, Shell Oil Co.; chmn. bd. Space Tech. Labs, Inc. 1959-62; dir. 1959-63. Dir.: Thompson Ramo Wooldridge, Inc. 1961-69; Mutual of Omaha Ins. Co. 1961---; United Benefit Life Ins. Co., 1964---; Tele-Trip Co., Inc. 1966---; Companion Life Ins. Co. 1968---; Mutual of Omaha Growth and Income Funds, 1968---; cons. TRW Systems, 1962-66; trustee, Aero Corp. 1963-69, v. chmn. bd. trustees, chmn. exec. com. 1965-69. Mem.: Army Air Corps Investigating Com. 1934; chmn. Secty. of War's Bd. on Ofcr.-Enlisted Men, 1946; Joint Cong. Aviation Policy Bd. 1948; Natl. Adv. Com. for Aerons. 1948-58, chmn. 1956-58; A.F. Sci. Adv. Bd. 1951-58, chmn. 1955-58; 1959---. Airport Comm. 1952; chmn., Pres's. Task Force Group on Air Inspection — Stassen Disarmament Com. 1955;

President's Foreign Intelligence Adv. Bd. 1955-56; Adv. Bd. Natl. Air Mus.-Smithsonian Inst. 1956-65; Def. Sci. Bd., Pres's. Sci. Adv. Com. 1957-58; Engring. Adv. Council, Univ. of Calif. 1957-66; Natl. Aerons. and Space Council, 1958; Plowshare Com. on Atomic Energy Comm. 1959-71; Natl. Inst. of Health Study, 1963-65; A.F. Space and Missile Systems Orgn. Adv. Bd. 1963---; regent, Chaminade Prep. Sch. 1967-71; (life) Mass. Inst. of Tech. Corp. Awards: Record winner flight across U.S. (21 hrs., 19 minutes), 1922, and first to fly outside loop, 1928; winner Schneider Trophy Race, 1925; awarded Mackay Trophy, 1926; first pioneer in sci. of blind flying, 1929; Spirit of St. Louis Award, 1929; Harmon Trophy of Ligue Internat. des.Aviateurs Award, 1930 and 1950; winner Bendix Trophy Race (Burbank, Calif. to Cleveland, Oh.), 1931, est. new transcontinental record (11 hrs., 15 minutes), 1931; winner Thompson Trophy Race (258.68 mi per hr.), 1932; World's land plane speed record, 1932; Internat. Harmon Trophy, 1940, 49; Guggenheim Trophy, 1942; Wright Bros. Trophy, 1953; F.A.I. Gold Medal, 1954; Silver Quill Award, 1959; Thomas D. White Natl. Def. Award, 1967; Cong. Medal of Hon., Distinguished Flying Cross with two Oak Leaf Clusters, Distinguished Serv. Medal, many others (Bolivian, Chinese, Belgium, French, Polish, Equadorian) incl. Knight Comdr., Order of the Bath (Brit.). Mem.: Fellow, Am. Aeron. Soc., Royal Aeron. Soc.; ASME; pres. Inst. of Aeron Scis. 1940; (hon.) Fellow Am. Inst. of Aerons and Astronautics, others; Clubs: Natl. Aviation Club, Wash. D.C.; Explorers, Boone and Crockett, Wings (pres. 1955), N.Y.; Bohemian, S.F. Home: 233 Marguerita Ave., Santa Monica, CA 90402; Office: 5225 Wilshire Blvd., L.A., CA 90036.

DORFMAN, RALPH ISADORE
Consulting Professor
b. June 30, 1911, Chicago; s. Aron and Anna (Schwartzman) Dorfman; B.S., chem., Univ. Ill., 1932; Ph.D., physiological chem. & pharmacology, Univ. Chicago, 1934; m.2d. Margaret Cameron, Feb. 11, 1965; chil.: Gerald Allen, b. June 19, 1959; Ronald Arthur, b. Jan. 3, 1943. Career: Instr. in Pharmacology, La. State Univ., 1935-36, instr. in physiological chem. 1936-39; asst. prof., Yale Univ., 1939-41, asst. prof. biochemistry, 1941-50, and assoc. prof. 1950-51, Case Western Reserve Univ.; research prof. of biochemistry, Boston Univ., 1951-67; prof. of chem. (affiliate), Clark Univ., 1956-64; assoc. Dir. of Labs., Worcester Found. for Exptl. Biol., 1951-56; Dir. of Labs, 1956-64; pres., Syntex Research, 1973-76 (ret. 1976); visiting Prof. of Pharmacology, Stanford Univ., 1967-73, Consulting Prof., 1973---. Dir. Inst. of Hormone Biology, Syntex Research, 1965-69, exec. v.p., Syntex Research, 1972-73. Bd. Dir.: Syntex Corp.; Delmed, Inc.; Medi-Physics, S.F. Symphony; S.F. Chamber Music Soc.; Geron-X, Inc., pres. bd. Author and/or editor: 15 books, more than 650 sci. papers. Mem.: Nat. Acad. of Sciences, 1978; Am. Acad. of Arts & Scis.; AAAS; N.Y. Acad. of Scis.; Am. Chem. Soc.; Soc. for Exptl. Biol. & Med.; The Endocrine Soc.; Sigma Xi; Phi Lambda Epsilon; Am. Soc. for Biological Chemists; Am. Statistical Soc.; Mex. Endocrine Soc.; Am. Assn. for Cancer Research; Danish Soc. for Endocrinology; Internat. Soc. for Research in the Biology of Reproduction. Hobbies: music, travel. Home: 10465 Berkshire Dr., Los Altos Hills, CA 94022.

DORMAN, ALBERT A.
President, Daniel, Mann, Johnson & Mendenhall
b. Apr. 30, 1926, Philadelphia; s. William and Edith (Kleiman) Dorman; B.S., mech. engring, Newark Coll. Engring., 1945; M.S. civil engring., USC, 1962; m. Joan Heiten, July 29, 1950; chil.: Laura Jane, b. June 26, 1953; Kenneth Joseph, b. May 4, 1955; Richard Coleman, b. Oct. 9, 1957. Career: Instr., U.S. Army Corps of Engrs., Ft. Belvoir, Va., 1945-47; sales engr., Sojean Internat. Corp., Phila., 1947-48; jr. civil engr., Calif. Div. of Hwys., L.A., 1948-49; Assoc. Structural Engr., Dept. of Bldg. & Safety, L.A., 1949-51; Office Engr. and Chief Civil Engr., Bowen, Rule & Bowen, L.A., 1951-54; City engr., mem. City Planning Commn., Lemoore, Calif. 1954-67, Corcoran, Calif., 1955-65; prin. firm Albert A. Dorman, Consult. Engr., Hanford, Calif. 1954-66; with Daniel, Mann, Johnson & Mendenhall, 1966---; vice pres., 1967-73; dir., 1970---; exec. v.p. and chief operating officer, 1973-74; pres., chief operating officer, 1974-77; Pres. and Chief Exec. Officer, 1977---. Dir., Golden West Fin. Corp., Oakland, 1972-75; Dir., Real Estate Resources, Inc., 1970-77; pres., chmn. bd. dirs., Hanford S&L Assn., 1963-72; pres., Hanford Service Co., Inc.; v.p., dir., Tristao Towers, Inc., 1958-62; bd. of trustees, City of Hope, 1973---; dir., CHB Foods, Inc., 1977---. Publs.: papers on urbanization and freeway planning, profl. journs. Awards: Civil Engring. Alumnus award, USC, 1976; Harland Bartholomew Award, Am. Soc. Civil Engrs. 1976. Registered Profl. Engr.: Calif., N.Y.; Ill.; Ore.; Ariz.; Hawaii; Nev.; Penn. Registered Architect in Calif.,

Ore. Home: 727 Brooktree Rd., Pacific Palisades, CA 90272; Office: 3250 Wilshire Blvd., L.A., CA 90010.

DORNAN, ROBERT KENNETH
U.S. Congressman
b. Apr. 3, 1933, N.Y.C.; ed. Loyola H.S., L.A.; Loyola Univ., L.A., 1950-53; m. Sallie Hansen of Santa Monica, Apr. 16, 1955; chil.: Robin Marie, Robert Kenneth II, Theresa Ann, Mark Douglas, Kathleen Regina. Career: Fighter pilot (world's 1st supersonic wing), USAF, 1953-58, Capt. AF Reserve, 1958---; broadcaster-journalist, Southeast Asia; comml. pilot with helicopter, amphibian, jet ratings; TV prod. (won 2 Emmys, 1968-69); prod./host Robert K. Dornan Show, KTLA-TV, 1969-73; elected to 95th Congress, 27th Congressional Dist., 1976, re-elected 1978---. Mem.: House Coms.: Merchant Marine and Fisheries; Sci.; Tech.; subcoms.: Panama Canal; Fisheries, Wildlife, Conservation and the Environment; Sci. Research and Tech.; Adv. Energy Techs. and Energy Conservation Research, Devel. and Demonstration; Fossil and Nuclear Energy Research, Devel. and Demonstration. Active in civil rights; POW/MIA activities. Mem.: AFTRA, VFW, Am. Legion, AF Assn., Navy League, KC. Office: U.S. House of Representatives, 419 Cannon Office Bldg., Wash., D.C. 20515.

DORNBACH, MARY GIST
Executive, Council of California Indians
b. Nov. 16, 1893, Martins Ferry (Camp Klamath), Calif.; d. John Clay (b. Kans., Justice of Peace, Martin's ferry; built first ferryboat at Weitchpec, only means of crossing river at junction of Trinity and Klamath; built first pub. sch. at Weitchpec; built first wagon rd. from Weitchpec to Orleans; owner, farm and gold mine) and Caroline (Tuley) Gist (dau. of Anama Pekwan, Yurok Indian; family owned only Indian ceremonial house between Weitchpec and Requa at Pekwan; long line of Indian med. practitioners); 9th desc. of Christopher Gist of Md. (1706-59); Am. frontiersman, accompanied George Washington on trip to Ft. Duquesne, 1753-54; guide in Braddock's expedition, 1755; ed. pub. schs., Weitchpec, Calif.; pvt. schs., pvt. tutors, Junction City, Kans. and Denver, Colo. 1907-1912, m. George W. Dornbach (grandson of Charles Frank "Dutchie" Dornbach, founder, town of Dutch Flat in Placer Co., Calif. 1851; State Registered Landmark No. 397 dedicated July 22, 1950), Arcata Calif., Oct. 23, 1913; chil.: Mrs. Richard (Florence) Catone, b. July 29, 1914; Mrs. Arthur (Mary Christine) Heath, b. Dec. 13, 1915; Mrs. Charles Thompson (Esther) Forest, b. Apr. 23, 1917. Career: Pres., Am. Indian Found., 1920-36; exec. secty., Council Calif. Indians, Inc. (repr. Indians of Calif. Appellants when U.S. Ct. of Claims awarded Calif. Indians $29,100,000 for natural resources and lands of Calif.), S.F., 1948---. Author: Bulletins on Calif. Indians Claims Cases, 1948-64. Mem.: Am. Mus. of Natural Hist.; Save-the-Redwoods League; S.F. chpt., U.N. Assn. of U.S.; Am. Forestry Assn., Wash. D.C.; regional secty., Natl. Cong. Am. Indians, 1955-58; Assn. on Am. Indian Affairs, N.Y.; Indian Affairs Com., Am. Friends Serv. Com. 1958-59; com. on legislation, Calif. League Am. Indians; steering com., Comm. on Indian Affairs, No. Calif. 1960-62; Internat. Platform Assn. Hobbies: assembling authentic Indian hist. and data on natural resources; landscape gardening. Home and Office: 764 35th Ave., S.F., CA 94121.

DORR, MARY WRIGHT
Public Relations Director, American Bible Society
b. Megargel, Tex.; d. William Odie and Harper Ethel (Dennis) Wright; desc. of Pres. U.S. Grant and Alexander Hamilton, statesman and first U.S. Secty. of Treas.; ed. B.A., Univ. of Calif., Berkeley, 1939; grad. drama, Elizabeth Mack Sch. of Dramatic Art; m. John W. Dorr, L.B., Calif., June 25, 1939 (dec.); chil.: chil.: Diana Jeanne, b. July 14, 1945; John W., Jr., b. Sept. 25, 1948; Robert Denman, b. Sept. 15, 1951 (dec.); Kenneth William and Donald James, (twins), b. Sept. 3, 1957. Career: freelance lecturing and TV-radio commercials, 1959---; Spiritual Life series, KCOP, 1969; Am. Bible Soc. Natl. Dir. Pub. Rels. and volunteer services, 1969---. Interviewer on KNXT, KABC-TV, KTTV, KHJ, KFI, 1976---; exec. dir., Religion in Media Assn., 1974---. Awards: Family of the Yr. award, 1963; won Eastman Award as most outstanding woman in broadcasting in western U.S.A., 1965; Calif. Mother of the Year, 1977. Mem.: Soroptimist, Hollywood Women's Press Club; pres. S.F. chpt., Am. Women in Radio and TV, pres. So. Calif. chpt., natl. v.p. 1964-67, natl. pres. elect, 1967-68, natl. pres. 1968-70; natl. treas., AWARE Internat. (Assn. for Women's Active Return to Edn.), internat. pres. 1969-70; Berkeley Women's City Club; Province pres., Alpha Xi Delta; PEO Sisterhood, 99's Internat.; Women's Div. L.A.

C. of C.; pres. Miracle Mile Chapter Bus. and Profl. Women; World Affairs Counci?; ANTANS; L.A. Ath. Club; elder, Malibu Presbyterian Ch. Hobby: private pilot. Rec.: skiing, swimming. Home: 2700 Neilson Way, Apt. 736, Santa Monica, CA 90405; Office: 1220 W. 4th St., L.A., CA.

DOUGHERTY, CHARLES JOSEPH
Physician
b. Feb. 19, 1913, Wilmington, Del.; s. Charles J. and Anna Frances (Mullen) Dougherty; desc. Sir Cahir O'Dougherty, Lord of Ulster, Chief of Inishowen, 17th Century Ireland; B.S., Catholic Univ., Washington, D.C., 1934; M.D., Jefferson Med. Coll., Philadelphia, 1938; F.I.C.S., 1956; Diplomate Am. Bd. Surgery, 1954; m. Elizabeth Jane Holtzlander, June 11, 1949, Wilmington, Del.; 1 son Charles Magoffin, b. Apr. 9, 1954. Career: Intern, Phila. Gen. Hosp., 1938-40; gen. practice, Wilmington, Del., 1940-42; fellow in surgery, Mayo Clinic, 1942-43 and 1946-68; flight surgeon, USAAF, 1943-46; surgical practice of med., L.A. and Highland, Calif., 1958-59; Wilmington, Del., 1948-48; physician and surgeon, Yucaipa, 1969---. Contrbr. med. papers to journs. and AMA abstracts. Staff surgeon: all hosps., Wilmington, Del., 1948-58; Loma Linda Univ. Hosp., 1958---; Redlands Community Hosp., 1958-74. Chief of Surgical Service, VA Hosp., Altoona, Pa. 1956; Chief Civilian Surgeon, US Naval Hosp., Phila., 1955-57. Mem.: Town Hall of Calif. (com. mem. 1967---); mem. Republican State Central Com., 1967---. Clubs: Los Coyotes Country, Buena Park, 1958-64; Redlands Country Club, 1969---. Roman Catholic. Hobbies: world travel, repub. politics, literature. Rec.: golf, hiking. Home: 756 Cajon St., Redlands, CA 92373; Office: 13391 California St., Yucaipa, CA.

DOUGHERTY, HOWARD WILLIAM
Oil & Gas Producer
b. Jan. 5, 1915, Kansas City, Mo.; s. Frank C. and Elsie (Braecklein) Dougherty; Stanford Univ., Earth Sciences, 1938; m. Louise Olmsted, Aug. 3, 1940, Los Angeles; chil.: William, b. Feb. 15, 1943; Robert, b. April 18, 1945; Patrick, b. Sept. 20, 1947; Michael, b. July 15, 1950; Mary, b. Nov. 15, 1954; Peter, b. Oct. 18, 1952. Career: Oil and gas producer since 1947---. Dir., Santa Anita Consol., Inc.; pres. Pioneer Kettleman Co.; pres., Book Cliffs Oil & Gas Co., Dir., Independent Petroleum Assn., of Am.; form. dir., Hollywood Turf Club; Regent emeritus, Loyola Marymount Univ.; mem. at large, Conservation Com. of Calif; Trustee, Neuro Sciences Inst. Mem. Beta Theta Pi. Clubs: L.A. Country, California, Bohemian, S.F. Relig. Order of Malta, Acting Comdr., Mil. Order of St. Lazarus. Hobbies: hunting & travel. Rec.: Tennis, golf. Home: 535 S. Orange Grove Blvd., No. 7, Pasadena, CA 91105; Office: 900 Wilshire Blvd., No. 1024, L.A., CA 90017.

DOUGHERTY, JOHN F.
Business Executive
b. Aug. 10, 1912, Monterey, Calif.; s. P.J. (mayor and postmaster of Monterey) and Nora (O'Donnell) Dougherty; ed. B.C.E., Santa Clara Univ., 1934; m. Virginia L. Haynes, 1973; chil.: Margaret Mary, b. Oct. 20, 1937; Kathleen Whilden, b. June 20, 1940; Mary Patricia, b. Dec. 7, 1944; Thomas Michael, b. June 3, 1947. Career: Civil engr. 1934-42; owner-mgr., Casa Munras Garden Hotel, Monterey, 1942-65; operator, Carmel Travel Agency, 1970---. Dir.: First Natl. Bank of Monterey, 1948-54; Mem.: v.p.-dir., Monterey Peninsular Assocs., 1945---; dist. chmn. BSA 1951; pres. Calif. Mission Trails Assn. 1957---; Monterey Planning Comm., 1958-61; pres. Acad. of Achievement, Monterey, 1961---; pres. dir., Master Hosts Hotel Assn. 1962; chmn., Monterey Bicentennial year, 1970; Tau Beta Pi, Rotary, Elks Club, pres. 1971 Monterey Peninsular Country Club. Catholic. Democrat (chmn. Monterey Co. Dem. Central Com. 1951). Hobby: travel. Rec.: golf. Home: 163 Mar Vista, Monterey, CA 93940.

DOUGHTY, DONALD LEE
Chairman, Lafayette Federal Savings & Loan
b. Feb. 4, 1929, S.F.; s. Byron Shover and Mildred (Lane) Doughty; B.S., Univ. Calif., Berkeley, 1950, M.S., 1951, Ph.D., 1954 (all in engring.); m. Margaret Bacon, 1952; chil.: Christine, b. 1956; Curtis, b. 1958; Matthew, b. 1960; m. 2d. Phyllis Blamey, Mar. 20, 1977, Orinda, Calif. Career: Research Engr. and tchg. asst., Univ. Calif., Berkeley, 1950-54; with Shell Devel. Co., Emeryville, 1954-57; pres., Orinda Pools, Inc., 1957---; chmn. of bd., Lafayette Fed. Savings and Loan 1961---; also real estate devel. and investor, 1966---. Publs.: papers in Trans ASME; numerous articles on swim pool indus. Past pres., Univ. of Calif. Engring. Alumni, 1968-69; mem.: ASME, F. and A.M., Yerba Buena Lodge No. 403, 1951---; Orinda

Country Club. Chmn., Contra Costa Co. Airport Land Use Com. Protestant. Hobbies: flying, ham radio. Rec.: skiing. Home: 222 The Knoll, Orinda, CA 94563; Office: 3614 Mt. Diablo Blvd., Lafayette, CA 94549.

DOUGLAS, DONALD WILLS, JR.
Business Consultant
b. July 3, 1917, Wash., D.C.; s. Donald Wills and Charlotte (Ogg) Douglas; Stanford Univ.; Calif. Inst. of Tech. 1939; m. 2nd, Jean Ashton, Santa Barbara, Aug. 17, 1950; chil.: Victoria, b. June 27, 1940; Holly, b. June 25, 1947. Career: Engring. strength group, Douglas Aircraft Co., Inc., DC-3 power plant installation, asst. leader of DC-4 power plant group and dir., test stand operations on DC-4, in chg. engin. installation and supv. of tests on C-74, 1939-43; dir., testing div., 1943-51; v.p. in chg. Mil. Rels. 1951-57; dir. 1953---; pres. Douglas Aircraft Co., Inc., Oct. 1957-67, v.p.-dir. McDonnell Douglas Corp. 1967-68, v.p., adm., St. Louis, Mo. 1968-72; pres., Douglas Devel. Corp., component of McDonnell Douglas Corp., 1972-74; chmn., Capistrano Natl. Bank, 1974---; pres., Biphase Energy Systems, Inc. (formerly Biphase Engines, Inc.), 1976---; dir., Hilton Hotels Corp., 1966---; dir., McDonnell Douglas Corp., 1967---; dir., Stanford Research Inst. Mem.: dir. Natl. Ind. Conf. Bd.; v.p. Natl. Def. Transportation Assn.; bd. of govs., Aerospace Industries Assn.; past pres.-dir., Crescent Bay Council; L.A. Country Club, L.A. Yacht Club; Transpacific Yacht Club, L.A. Press Club, Phi Gamma Delta, Conquistadores del Cielo, Rancheros Visitadores. Awards: Gold Knight of Mgmt. Award by Natl. Mgmt. Assn., So. Calif. area. Home: 707 Brooktree Rd., Pacific Palisades, CA 90272; Office: 2907 Ocean Park Blvd., Santa Monica, CA 90405.

DOUGLAS (FINLAYSON), ROBERT
Actor — Director — Producer
b. Nov. 9, 1909, Bletchley, England; s. Robert and Marcia Finlayson; ed. Bickley Hall, 1919-1926; Royal Acad. Dramatic Art, London, 1927-29; m. Suzanne Hopkinson, Aug. 23, 1976, London; chil.: Lucinda Gail (Gabri), b. Jan. 25, 1947; Giles Robert, b. Feb. 28, 1951. Career: Actor and Prod., London, 1930-40; under contract, Warner Bros., Hollywood, 1947-49; freelance actor, Hollywood, 1949-60; dir., prod., New York, 1960-65; TV dir., prod., 1962---: prod., dir. of Hitchcock TV series; dir.: Medical Center, Baretta, Colombo, Quincy plus many top hour TV shows. Lt. Comdr., British Royal Navy, 1940-45; naval pilot. Episcopalian. Hobbies: painting, sculpture. Rec.: golf, tennis, riding. Home: 2619 Eden Pl., Beverly Hills, CA.

DOUGLASS, ENID HART
Historian
b. Oct. 23, 1926, L.A.; d. Frank Roland and Enid (Lewis) Hart; niece Edwin G. Hart, a founder of city of San Marino, early avocado indus. pioneer, La Habra and Whittier; B.A., magna cum laude, Phi Beta Kappa, Pomona Coll., 1948; M.A., Claremont Grad. Sch., 1959; m. Malcolm Paul Douglass, Aug. 28, 1948, San Gabriel; chil.: Malcolm Paul, Jr., b. June 1, 1951; John Aubrey, b. Sept. 10, 1955; Susan Enid, b. July 18, 1960. Career: research asst., Social Sciences, World Book Ency., 1953-54; exec. secty., Oral Hist. Prog., Claremont Grad. Sch., 1963-69; asst. dir., 1969-71, dir., 1971---; also lectr. in history, Claremont Grad. Sch., 1977---. Contbr. profl. articles on oral hist. Apptd. by Gov. Brown to Calif. State Heritage Preservation Commn., 1977---: subcom. mem. State Hist. Records Advis. Bd.; mem. State Planning Advis. and Asst. Council, Gov's Office of Planning and Research, 1977---; charter mem. nat. Oral Hist. Assn.; pres. 1978-79; founding mem. Claremont Heritage Inc. (city hist. soc.), 1977---; mem. Claremont Motion Picture Council, 1965-68; mem. state bd. AAUW, 1952-53. Elected to Claremont City Council, 1978---; mem. Claremont Planning Commn. 1970---, chmn. 1973-76; mem. standing coms. of League of Calif. Cities: Municipal Govt. and Adminstrn, 1971-76; Environmental Quality, 1976---. Rec.: tennis. Home: 1195 Berkeley Ave., Claremont, CA 91711; Office: Harper 154, Claremont Grad. Sch., Claremont, CA 91711.

DOW, EARL ROSS
President, Jurgensen's Grocery Co.
b. Dec. 28, 1904, N.Y.C.; s. Earl R. Dow; ed. Northwestern Univ.; m. Helen Grace Pikas, Chicago, Ill., June 20, 1932. Career: West Coast credit mgr., Swift & Co. until 1943; partner, Jurgensen's Grocery Co. 1944, secty-treas. 1946, v.p.-treas. 1956, exec. v.p.-treas. 1958, pres. 1963---. Mem.: Annandale Country Club, Pasa.; Overland Club, Pasa. Congl. (ch. sch. supt.). Hobby: sports. Rec.: golf. Home: 1540 Kenmore Rd., Pasadena, CA; Office: 601 S. Lake Ave., Pasadena, CA.

DOW, ELLEN ALBERTINI
 Theatre Director — Choreographer — Mime
b. Nov. 26, 1916, Mt. Carmel, Pa.; d. Oliver and Ellen (Stanker) Albertini; B.A. theatre arts, Cornel Univ., Ithaca, N.Y., 1936, M.A. theatre prods. and dramatic lit., 1938; m. Eugene F. Dow, June 27, 1951, Eaglesmere, Pa. Career: profl. dancer, mime, actress: Broadway musical comedy, Second Ave. Theatre, Little Carnegie Hall, stock companies, 1940-51, also dance concerts (Hanya Holm), solo mime concerts, Claretree major theatre for children; N.Y.C. and U.S.A. tours, 1944-45; director-choreographer-tchr.: light opera, opera, musical theatre, mime, L.A. City Coll., 1951-68; also dir., choreographer, educator, Cal State Univ., Northridge, 1959-65; dir., choreographer, educator, L.A. Pierce Coll., 1968---; also summer drama workshops, musical theatre for children; founder-dir., Albertini Mime Players, 1973---. Author: On Mime (tchr's manual); Recipient: N.Y. Times Book Award for Theatre for Children, 1949; creator L.A. Junior Programs, 1970, 1971. Mem.: L.A. Mime Guild; Equity and AGUA (NYC), 1944-51; Internat. Mimes and Pantomimists, 1977-79; Am. Theatre Assn., 1975---; Kappa Delta, secrety., 1934, treas., 1935, pres., 1936; Kappa Delta Epsilon. Catholic. Hobbies: piano, clothing design. Rec.: travel. Home: 20327 Oxnard St., Woodland Hills, CA 91367; Office: L.A. Pierce Coll., 6201 Winnetka Ave., Woodland Hills, CA 91367.

DOWD, LAURENCE PHILLIPS
 University Professor
b. Oct. 21, 1914, Ft. Monroe, Va.; s. Wm. Stuart and Julia M. (Phillips) Dowd; B.A., econ. & bus., Univ. Wash., 1938 (magna cum laude); M.A., oriental studies, Univ. Hawaii, 1940; Ph.D., econ., Univ. Mich., 1954; m. Juliet Rudolph, Sept. 7, 1938, Seattle, Wash.; chil.: William L., b. Nov. 5, 1940 (dec.); Richard S., b. May 26, 1942; Judith I. (Mrs. Stewart Rush), b. June 25, 1944. Career: Purchasing Agent: Lewers & Cooke, Ltd., Honolulu 1939-40, The Austin Co., Seattle, 1941; Instr. to Assoc. Prof., Univ. of Wash., 1940-55; instr. and lectr., Univ. of Mich., 1946-60; prof. of world business, S.F. State Univ., 1960---; dir., Center for World Bus., S.F. State Univ., 1960-68; Trade Repr. in Far East, Port of Seattle, 1954, 1955-57; Fulbright Lectr., Kobe Univ., Japan, 1955-57. Author: Principles of World Business, Allyn & Bacon, Inc., Boston, 1965; Introduction to Export Mgmt., Eljay Press, Burlingame, Calif., 1977. Served 2nd Lt. to Maj., AUS, 1941-45; Adj. and Dir. of Intelligence, M.I.S. Language Sch. Mem.: pres., World Trade Club of Seattle, 1954; pres., World Trade Club of Seattle, 1954; pres., Internat. Managers' Assn. of S.F., 1979; Phi Beta Kappa; Beta Gamma Sigma; Fellow, Acad. of Internat. Bus., 1977. Republican. Protestant. Rec.: gardening, golf, camping. Home: 3047 Hillside Dr., Burlingame, CA 94010; Office: Rm. 325, BSS Bldg.,S S.F. State Univ., 1600 Holloway Ave., S.F., CA 94132.

DOWELL, DOUGLAS CHARLES
 Professor of Mechanical Engineering
b. May 31, 1924, Tacoma, Wash.; s. Malcolm Haskins and Edna Blanche (McConnell) Dowell; B.S., civil engring., 1949; M.S., nuclear engring., 1954; Ph.D., engring., 1964; m. Peggy Egner, May 25, 1975, Las Vegas, Nev.; chil.: Douglas, Jr., b. 1949; Sonja, b. 1954; Regina, b. 1958; Millicent, b. 1960. Career: Tenure Assoc. Prof., USAF Acad., Colo., 1960-68; dir. of ednl. services, assoc. dean of engring., dir. of internat. programs, Calif. State Polytechnic Univ., Pomona, 1968---; also Assoc. Dir., Cal State Univ. Statewide Energy Consortium. Served to Lt. Col., USAF, 1942-68. Mem.: Tau Beta Pi, Chi Epsilon. Home: 627 Greendale Lane, Pomona, CA 91767; Office: Cal Poly, Pomona, 3801 W. Temple, Pomona, CA 91768.

DOWNEY, JOHN F.
 Attorney at Law
b. Dec. 31, 1914, Sacto.; s. Stephen W. and Persis M. Downey; nephew of the late Sheridan Downey, noted U.S. Senator from Calif.; ed. A.B., Stanford Univ. 1936; LL.B., USC 1938; m. Betty Werner, Camp McCoy, Wis., Oct. 16, 1943; chil.: Barbara, b. Sept. 4, 1944; Michael, b. May 30, 1946; Cynthia, b. Apr. 23, 1948; David, b. June 25, 1949; Kathrun, b. July 7, 1951; Eve and Steve (twins), b. Aug. 23, 1952; John F. Jr., b. June 13, 1955; Richard, b. Mar. 24, 1958; Thomas, b. Sept. 3, 1962; Dennis, b. Feb. 26, 1965. Career: Conciliation commr., Tulare Co. 1939-40; atty. at law, Downey, Brand, Seymour & Rohwer law firm, 1946---. Pvt., U.S. Army, Alaska, 1940-41; attended Engr. O.T.S. 1941; combat engr. ofcr., 76th Inf. Div., Europe, 1944-45 (wounded in Ger.); disch. as Maj. (1945), WW II. Awards: Bronze Star Medal with Oak Leaf Cluster; Purple Heart. Mem.: pres. Sacto. Legal Aid Soc. 1956; pres. Sacto. Co. Bar Assn. 1958; fellow, Am. Coll. of Trial Lawyers, 1960; v.-chmn., State Capitol Bldg. and Planning Comm. 1962-67; Sacto.

Human Rels. Comm.; dir.-v. chmn., Sacto. State Coll. Found.; chmn. adv. bd., Sacto. State Coll.; Chancellor's adv. council, Calif. State Univ. & Colls., chmn. 1974-76; past pres., Sacto. Rotary Club; past pres., Sacto. Univ. Club. Protestant. Hobby: snow and water skiing, golf. Home: 3850 W. Land Park Dr., Sacto., Calif.; Office: 555 Capitol Mall, Sacto., CA 95814.

DOYLE, EDMOND T.
 President, Alexian Brothers Hospital
b. Jan. 4, 1938, Cincinnati, Oh.; s. Edmund and Regina (Roan) Doyle; B.S., psychol., 1960; M.S., hosp. & health care adminstrn., 1971. Career: with Bethesda Gen. Hosp., 1968-70; resident, Good Samaritan Hosp., Cin., 1970-71; dir. Para Med. Services, John C. Lincoln Hosp., Phoenix, 1971-73; vice. pres., asst. adminstr., Alexian Brothers Hosp., 1973-75, pres., adminstr., 1975---. USAF Med. Corps Admin., 1960-68. Catholic. Home: 554 Toyon No. 4, San Jose, CA; Office: 225 N. Jackson Ave., San Jose, CA 95116.

DOYLE, JOHN JUSTIN
 Marketing Executive
b. July 20, 1922, Valley Falls, Kans.; s. Morgan J. and Frances L. (Janda) Doyle; ed., A.B., Washburn Univ. 1943; Naval Comm. (Ensign), Notre Dame Univ. 1943; engring. courses, USN, N.C. State Univ. and Gen. Motors Inst. of Tech. 1943-44; m. Elizabeth Jeanne Barker, S.F., Oct. 28, 1950; chil.: Mary Elizabeth, b. May 1, 1952; Anne Marie, b. Sept. 28, 1953; William Morgan, b. July 30, 1956; John J., Jr., b. Sept. 24, 1958. Career: Propr.-mgr., Citizens State Bank, Valley Falls, Kans. 1947-48; propr.-mgr., ins. and real estate agcy., Valley Falls, 1947-48; marketing repr., IBM Corp., 1949-56; mktg. exec. 1957---. Lt. (j.g.), USN (1943-46), WW II. Awards: 8 medals, incl. Pac. Theater Medal, Am. Def. Medal; Mem.: Phi Delta Theta, 1941---; Pi Gamma Mu, 1942---; co-founder-dir., Spokane Symp. Orch. 1961-65; bd. dirs., St. Anne's Infants Home and Home for Unwed Mothers, Spokane; bd. trustees, Cath. Charities, Spokane Diocese, 1961-65; bd. dirs.-v.p. membership, Spokane Junipero Serra Club, 1963-64; div. gen. chmn., YMCA, United Crusade and hosp. drives, Sacto., Seattle, Spokane; chmn. bd. dirs. Civic Interest League of Atherton; Sharon Heights Golf & Country Club, 1971---; Palo Alto Rotary Club, 1972---; Ath. Round Table, Elks Club, Spokane Golf and Country Club, Manito Golf and Country Club. Hobbies: civic activities, stereo Hi-Fi. Rec.: power boating, fishing, golf. Home: 63 Rebecca Lane, Atherton, CA 94025; Office: 525 University Ave., Palo Alto, CA 94301.

DREES, THOMAS CLAYTON
 Corporate Executive
b. Feb. 2, 1929, Detroit, Mich.; s. Clayton H. and Mildred J. (Stevenson) Drees; B.A., Holy Cross Coll., 1951; m. Elaine Hnath, Feb. 9, 1952, East Orange, N.J.; chil.: Danette, Clayton, Barry, Nancy; Career: Sales Engr., Spaulding Fibre Co., N.Y.C., 1953-56, Canada, 1956-58; with Spaulding Fibre Co., 1953-70: sales engr., N.Y.C., 1953-56; sales mgr., Canada, 1956-58; vice pres., gen. mgr., Canada, 1958-60; asst. to pres., Buffalo, N.Y., 1960-63; corp. secty. 1962-70; vice pres., Internat., mng. dir., chmn., Europe, London, 1963-66; exec. v.p., mem. Bd. Dirs., 1966-70; Group v.p., Ipco Hosp. Supply Corp., 1970-72; pres., bd. dir., Ivac Corp., 1972-73; vice pres., gen. mgr., Abbott Labs., 1973-78; pres., chief exec. officer, vice chmn. bd., Alpha Therapeutic Corp., So. Pasadena ---. Publs.: Plasma Supply and Demand — Worldwide, Proceedings of Am. Blood Resources Assn., 1978. Mem.: Govs. Tax Council, N.H., 1969-70; fellow, Inst. of Directors, 1965---; chmn., sch. bd., N.H., 1970; pres., Council, Holy Cross Coll., 1964---; AIEE, 1960---. Rec.: golf, art, theatre. Home: 784 St. Katherine Dr., Flintridge, CA 91011; Office: 820 Mission St., So. Pasadena, CA 91030.

DRELL, WILLIAM
 President, Calbiochem-Behring Corporation
b. Jan. 26, 1922, Chicago; s. Hyman and Ida (Korey) Drell; B.A., UCLA, 1943, M.A., 1946, Ph.D., 1949; m. Ethel Hershenson, Feb. 7, 1943, L.A.; chil.: Elizabeth (Chambers); Eric; Eliot. Career: Research Fellow, Am. Heart Assn., Nutrition Found. with U.S. Pub. Health Serv., post-doctoral fellow, Cal Tech., all prior to 1959; also cons. in basic research related to hypertension, UCLA; treas., vice pres., dir. of research, Calbiochem., 1959-63, pres., 1963-77; pres., Calbiochem-Behring Corp., 1977---. Co-author with Max Dunn, Experiments in Biochemistry, McGraw-Hill, 1951; holder two patents; 25+ profl. publs. Chmn., San Diego chpt., Am. Chem Soc. 1977; trustee, Calif. Found. for Biochem. Research, 1952-78; mem. La Jolla Cancer Research Found., 1977---;

dir., Economic Devel. Corp., 1973-76; bd. dir., San Diego C. of C. Mem.: Chem Soc. of London; Biochem. Soc., London; Am. Soc. of Biological Chemists; Soc. for Exptl. Biol. and Med.; Sigma Xi. Home: 4566 Sherlock Ct., San Diego, CA 92122; Office: 10933 N. Torrey Pines Rd., La Jolla, CA 92037.

DRYDEN, ROBERT E.
   Attorney at Law
b. Aug. 20, 1927, Chanute, Kans.; s. Calvin and Mary (Foley) Dryden; A.A., City Coll. of San Francisco, 1947; B.S., Univ. of S.F., 1951; LL.B., J.D., Univ. of S.F., 1954; m. Jetta Rae Burger, Dec. 19, 1953, Carmel, Calif.; chil.: Lynn Marie (Van Etten) b. Nov. 5, 1955; Thomas Calvin, b. Aug. 13, 1957. Career: Admitted to Calif. Bar, 1955; assoc. atty., Barfield & Barfield, 1955-65; gen. partner, Barfield, Barfield & Dryden, 1965-73; v.p., Barfield, Barfield, Dryden & Ruane, 1973---; mem. faculty, Hastings Nat. Coll. of Advocacy; mem., Lawyer to Lawyer Cons. panel; lectr., Continuing Edn. of Bar; arbitrator, Am. Arbitration Assn.; S.F. Pro-tem Judges panel. Diplomate Am. Bd. of Trial Advocates (nat. exec. com., 1978); Fellow, Am. Coll. of Trial Lawyers; mem. Assn. of Defense Counsel (dir. 1968-69), and Defense Research Inst.; mem. Calif. and S.F. Bar Assns.; Lawyers Club of S.F. 1971---; Mil.: U.S.M.C., 1945-46. Mem.: Justice Matt Sullivan chpt. Phi Alpha Delta; exec. com., Univ. S.F. Law Soc., 1973-74; bd. of govs., U.S.F. Alumni Assn., 1977---. Catholic. Rec.: tennis, skiing, golf. Office: One California St., Suite 2125, S.F., CA 94111.

DU BAIN, MYRON
   Chairman, President, Fireman's Fund Insurance Co.
b. June 3, 1923, Cleveland, Oh.; s. Edward Donald and Elaine Louise (Byrne) Du Bain; B.A., Univ. of Calif., Berkeley, 1943; Stanford Univ. Grad Sch. Bus. Exec. Pgm. 1967; m. Alice Elaine Hilliker, S.F., Sept. 30, 1944; chil.: Cynthia Lynn, b. Nov. 23, 1949; Donald Aldous, b. Oct. 12, 1954. Career: Fireman's Fund. Ins. Cos. 1946---, Marine Dept., mgr., v.p., sr. exec. 1946-68, sr. v.p. 1968, exec. v.p. 1973, pres.-chief exec. ofcr.-dir. 1974; chmn. bd. 1975---. Dir.: Am. Express Co.; United Calif. Bank; Crusader Ins. Co., Eng.; Intercontinental Reinsurance Co. of Hamilton, Bermuda; Pac. Gas & Elec.; AMFAC, Inc.; v-chmn. Bay Area Council; Calif. C. of C.; Greater S.F. C. of C.; trustee: AFIA World Wide Ins.; Ins. Inst. of Am., Inc.; Am. Inst. for Property and Liability Underwriters, Inc.; mem. Property Casualty Ins. Council; SRI Internat., advis. council; Stanford Univ. Grad. Sch. Bus., Advis. Council; Cal. Roundtable. Dir., St. Luke's Hosp. Bldg. Co., S.F. Ofcr. USN 1943-46. Clubs: Pacific Union, Bohemian, Claif. Tennis, S.F.; Links, N.Y.; Lagunitas Country, Marin Co. Episcopalian. Hobby: travel. Home: 36 Evergreen Dr., Kentfield, CA 94904; Office: 3333 California St., San Francisco, CA 94121.

DUBRIDGE, LEE ALVIN
   President Emeritus, Cal Tech.
b. Sept. 21, 1901, Terre Haute, Ind.; s. Frederick Alvin and Elizabeth Rebecca (Browne) DuBridge; A.B. Cornell Coll. 1922; A.M. Univ. of Wis. 1924, Ph.D. 1926; (Hon.) Sc.D., Cornell Coll. 1940; Brooklyn Poly Inst. 1946; Wesleyan Univ. 1946; Univ. of B.C., Can. 1947; Wash. Univ., St. Louis, Mo. 1948; LL.D., UCLA 1948; (hon.) Sc.D. Occidental Coll., L.A., 1962; Univ. of Md., 1955; Columbia Univ., Ind. Univ. and Univ. of Wis. 1957; (hon.) LL.D.: Univ. of Rochester, N.Y. 1953; USC 1957; Northwestern Univ., Evanston, Ill., 1958; Loyola Univ. of L.A. 1963; (hon) L.H.D.: Univ. of Redlands (calif.) and Univ. Judaism, L.A. 1958; (hon.) D.C.L., Union Coll., Schenectady, N.Y. 1961; Sc.D., Pa. Military Coll., Chester, Pa. 1962; Sc.D., DePauw Univ., Greencastle, Inc. 1962; (hon.) Sc.D., Pomona Coll., Calif., Rockefeller Univ., N.Y. and Carnegie Inst. of Tech. 1965; m. Doris May Koht, Ia., 1925 (dec. Nov. 18, 1973); chil.: Barbara Lee, Richard Alvin; m. 2d. Arrola Bush Cole, Mass. 1974. Career: Instr. in physics, Univ. of Wis. 1925-26; fellow, Natl. Research Council, Calif. Inst. of Tech. 1926-28; asst. prof. physics, 1928-33; assoc. prof. physics, Wash. Univ., St. Louis, Mo. 1933-34; prof. physics-dept. chmn., Univ. of Rochester, N.Y. 1934-46; dean of faculty (arts and sciences), 1938-42; pres. Calif. Inst. of Tech. 1946-69, pres. emeritus, 1969---. Sci. adv. to Pres. Nixon, 1969-70. Gen. Advis. com. Atomic Energy Comm. 1947-52; bd. trustees, Rand Corp., Santa Monica, Calif. 1948-61. Author: (with A.L. Hughes) Photoelectric Phenomena, 1932; New Theories of the Photoelectric Effect, 1935; Introduction to Space, 1960; numerous articles, publ. sci. and other journs. Dir. radiation lab., Mass. Inst. of Tech., Natl. Def. Research Com. (1940-45), WW II. Awards: King's Medal for service in cause of freedom, 1946; Research Corp. Award, 1947; Medal for Merit, U.S. Govt. 1948; Golden Key Award, Am. Assn. of Sch. Admrs. 1959; Leif Erikson Award, 1959. Mem.: fellow, AAAS,

1929---, v.p. Sect. B, 1946; Optical Soc. of Am. 1934-48; Inst. of Radio Engrs. 1934-49, fellow, 1941; Am. Philosophical Soc. 1940---; bd. govs., Am. Inst. of Physics, 1940-46; Natl. Acad. of Sci. 1942; fellow, Am. Acad. of Arts and Sci. 1944-55; v.p. Am. Physical Soc. 1946, pres. 1947; Natl. Sci. Bd., Wash., D.C. 1950-54, 1958-64; Am. Assn. of Physics Tchrs., 1955; bd. dirs., L.A. World Affairs Council, 1955-69; trustee, Rockefeller Found. N.Y. 1956-59; bd. trustees, Mellon Inst., Pittsburgh, Pa. 1958-67; bd. dirs., L.A. C. of C. 1959-61; natl. adv. health council, U.S. Pub. Health Serv. 1960-61; chmn. bd. dirs., Community Television of So Calif. 1962-69; bd. trustees, Huntington Library and Art Gallery, 1962-69; pres. Assn. of Independent Calif. Colls. and Univs. 1962-63; Phi Beta Kappa, Sigma Xi; clubs' Bohemian (S.F.), Sunset. Home: 5309 Cantante, Laguna Hills, CA 92653.

DU CHEMIN, AUDREY MAY
   Writer — Editor - Lecturer
b. June 7, 1908, Ardmore, Okla.; d. Robert L. and Josephine (Kearney) Brown; B.A., 1926; M.A., 1933; m. William E. du Chemin (dec.), Denver, Colo. (div. 1930); i dau. Elisabeth Anne Frey. Career: news editor, El Monte Herald, 1942-44; reporter, L.A. Times, 1942-44; publs. editor, Thompson Products, Inc. (TRW) 1944-54; Dir. of Edn. Projects, United Way, 1956-59; Editor, Alumni Journ., Loma Linda Univ. Sch. of Med., 1959-76. Awards: Top-Ten Alumni Editor award, 1959; four Freedoms Found. awards, 1951-54; Pan-Am. Good Neighbor Essay, 1952; Indsl. Editor of the Year 1952. Author: Red Letter Day, 1933. Mem.: Nat. Writers Club; Internat. Platform Assn. Seventh-day Adventist: treas., tchr.; edn. secty.; exec. bd. Lynwood SDA Academy. Hobby: travel. Home: 6721 Rugby Ave., Huntington Park, CA 90255.

DUCKWORTH, DIANE McKENNEY
   College Administrator
b. July 31, 1947, Bend, Ore.; s. Morris Burgett and Emma (Howard) McKenney; B.A. and B.Mus., Willamette Univ., 1970; M.S., S.F. State Univ., 1974; m. Kenneth Edwin Duckworth, div. 1976. Career: Librarian, research asst., Center for Research and Devel. in Teaching, Stanford Univ., 1971, 73; instr., counselor, Spec. Edn., Foothill Coll., Los Altos Hills, 1975-77, assoc. prog. coord., Spec. Edn., 1977-78, Program Administr. Spec. Edn., Foothill Coll., 1978---. Mem.: Mu Phi Epsilon, nat. award 1971; Pi Kappa Lambda, Mortar Board; mem. bd. dirs., Dann Services Rehab agency; Natl. Rehabilitation Assn.; Am. Personnel and Guidance Assn.; Calif. Postsecondary Educators of Disabled. Democrat. Hobbies: cooking, gardening. Rec.: racquetball. Home: 320 Duluth Cir., Palo Alto, CA 94306; Office: 12345 El Monte Rd., Los Altos Hills, CA 94022.

DUCOMMUN, ALAN NORWOOD
   Business Executive
b. Mar. 20, 1916, Alhambra, Calif.; s. Edmond Frederick and Lulu Gladys Ducommun; ed. B.A., Stanford Univ. 1940; chil.: Ann Michelle and Davis Alan (twins), b. Oct. 6, 1959. Career: Assoc. Ducommun Metals & Supply Co. 1936-42, 1946---, dir. 1947---, secty. 1950---; exec. v.p., Ducommun Realty Co.; pres. Am. Metal Bearing Co.; dir. Spacelabs, Inc.; dir. Spring Street Capital Co., Lt., USAAF (1942-46), WW II. Mem.: v.p.-dir. Am. Soc. of Corporate Sectys., Inc.; pres. L.A. Co. Assn for Mental Health; dir. Chil's. Bur. of L.A.; chmn. L.A. Community Chest Budget Review Com. No. 5; bd. govs. Town Hall; Stanford Assocs., Univ. Club of L.A., Sigma Chi. Home: 3 Packsaddle Rd. East, Rolling Hills, CA; Office: 612 S. Flower St., L.A., CA 90017.

DUGGAN, DANIEL LAWRENCE
   Attorney at Law
b. Oct. 11, 1913, Alberta, Can.; s. William George and Margaret (Scanlan) Duggan; A.B., UCLA, 1937; J.D., USC 1940; m. Jean Druffel, Santa Barbara, Dec. 6, 1941; chil.: William Dennis, b. July 15, 1944; Richard Ryan, b. Mar. 9, 1946; Kathleen Joan, b. Oct. 15, 1948. Career: Assoc. with Coldwell, Banker & Co., real estate brokerage firm with ofcs. in Calif., Ariz., Tex., Wash. 1940---, gen. partner, 1952-63, dir.-sr. v.p.-v. chmn. bd. 1963-73 (ret.). Real Estate investments-atty. at law, 1973. Award: William May Garland Realtor Trophy for outstanding serv. to real estate profession, 1967. Mem.: pres. L.A. Realty Bd. 1957; pres.-dir., The Beach Club, Santa Monica, 1957-58; president's real estate adv. com., Univ. of Calif. 1955-65; exec. bd. L.A. Area B.S.A.; dir. L.A. C. of C.; dir. YMCA, L.A.; bd. govs. Town Hall; exec. bd., L.A. Invest in Am. Com.; L.A. Co. Bar Assn., State Bar of Calif., Kappa Alpha, Phi Phi, Phi Alpha Delta, Blue Key, Blue Shield, Skull & Scales, L.A. Club, L.A. Country

Club, Calif. Club. Catholic. Rec.: boating, fishing, hunting. Home: 12751 Evanston St., L.A., CA 90049; Office: 11661 San Vicente Blvd., Suite 101, L.A., CA 90049.

DUIGNAN, PETER JAMES
University Curator
b. Aug. 6, 1926, S.F.; s. Peter James and Delia (Conway) Duignan; B.S., cum laude, Univ. of S.F., 1951; M.A. and Ph.D., Stanford Univ., 1951-60; m. Frances Sharpe, Aug. 13, 1949, S.F.; chil.: Kathleen Patricia, Peter, Frances, Sheila Marie, Rose Marie. Career: with Stanford Univ., 1955---: instr. 1955-57, 1959-60; Curator, African Collection, Hoover Inst., 1960---; Research Assoc., Hoover Inst., 1960-66, exec. secty. 1963-66, Dir. African Program, 1965---; Curator of Africana, Stanford Univ., 1966---; Stella W. and Ira S. Lillick Endowed Curatorship, 1968---, Sr. Fellow, Hoover Inst., 1968---, Curator of Middle East Collection, 1977---, Dir. of Middle East Research Program, 1977---. Co-author w/L.H. Gann several books on colonialism in Africa, 1962-78; Editor: United States and Canadian Publs. on Africa, annual, Hoover Inst., 1961-65; Africana Newsletter, quarterly, Hoover Inst., 1962-64; African Studies Bulletin of the African Studies Assn. of the U.S., thrice yearly, 1965-66; contbr. articles in journs., monographs, book chpts. AUS. So. Pacific Theater, 1944-46. Catholic. Hobby: gardening. Rec.: tennis; Home: 939 Casanueva Pl., Stanford, CA 94305; Office: Africa Collection, Hoover Institution, Stanford, CA 94305.

DUMKE, DOROTHY ROBISON
Civic Leader
b. Lemoore, Calif.; d. Ira Baker and Ina Lee (Freer) Robison; ed. B.A., UCLA 1940; m. Dr. Glenn S. Dumke, Glendale, Calif., Feb. 3, 1945. Career: Edn. and civic leader, L.A. Co., 1949---; bd. dirs., Children's Bur of L.A., 1963-71; bd. dirs., Pasa. Opera Co. 1964-67; Women's Council, KCET, 1964---. Mem.: pres. Women's Faculty Club, Occidental Coll. 1949-50; pgm. chmn. AAUW, Glendale, 1956-57; YWCA, S.F.; Chil's. Bur. of L.A. 1963-71; The Muses of Calif. Mus. of Sci. and Ind., L.A. 1962-71; chmn. 1965-67; com. L.A. Beautiful, 1968-71; Travelers Aid Soc., L.A. 1968---; Natl. Travelers Aid Soc., L.A. 1968---; Natl. Art Assn. 1969---; Friends of L.A. YWCA, 1970---; Les Dames de Champagne, 1972---. Home: 620 Stone Canyon Rd., L.A., CA 90024; Lido Isle, Newport Beach, CA.

DUMKE, GLENN S.
University Chancellor
b. May 5, 1917, Green Bay, Wis.; m. History. A.B., Occidental Coll. 1938, A.M., 1939, LL.D., 1960; Ph.D., UCLA, 1942; H.L.D., Univ. Redlands, 1962; Hebrew Union Coll., 1968; Windham Coll., 1969; LL.D., Univ. of Bridgeport, 1963, Transylvania Coll. 1968, Pepperdine Coll. 1969; Our Lady of the Lake Univ., 1977; tchg. asst. UCLA, 1940-41; instr. history Occidental Coll., 1940-43, asst. prof. 1943-46, assoc. prof. 1947-50, prof. history, 1950, Norman Bridge prof. Hispanic Am. history, 1954, dean faculty, 1950-57; pres. S.F. State Coll., 1957-61; vice chancellor Calif. State Colls., L.A., 1961-62; chancellor Calif. State Univ. and Colls., 1962---. Mem.: exec. com., chmn. Western Interstate Commn. for Higher Edn.; mem. Founding Board of Civilian/Military Inst.; nat. com. for edn. center USAF Acad. Found.; Bd. of Dirs. and Exec. Com. Council on Postsecondary Accreditation. Bd. dirs. Community TV So. Calif.; exec. com. Calif. Council for Humanities in Pub. Policy, 1974-77; chmn. Calif. Selection Com. for Rhodes Scholarships, 1966; mem. com. on State Rels. nat. service Am. Assn. State Colls. and Univs.; bd. visitors USAF Air Univ.; former bd. visitors USAF Acad.; bd. commrs. Nat. Commn. on Accrediting, 1959-65, 70-74; bd. mem. Am. Council Edn., 1967-68; mem. bd. trustees Calif. Industry-Edn. Council Alt. del. Republican Nat. Conv.; 13th Dist. Calif.; 1948, 24th Dist. Calif., 1952. Trustee Univ. Redlands, 1970---. Research fellow, Huntington Library, 1943-45; Haynes Found. grantee, 1943. Mem. bd. of dirs. L.A. Area C. of C. (dir., L.A. World Affairs Council (dir.), Am., Calif. hist. Soc.; Am. (Pac. Coast. Com. on humanities), Calif. (1st chmn. 1968---) council for econ. edn., Assn. Higher Edn., Joint Council Econ. Edn. (bd. mem.), Western Coll. Assn. (past chmn. membership and standards com.), Bd. of Dirs., Am. Mgmt. Assn. (dir. 1970-73, 74-77), Dir., Barclays Bank of Calif., Dir., The Olga Co., Trustee, Natl. Exec. Service Corps., Virginia Country Club, Univ. Club (S.F.), Inst. Internat. Edn. (So. Calif. Advisory Bd. 1972---) Phi Beta Kappa (Hon. Councilor alumni assn.). Methodist. Clubs: California; Bohemian; Commonwealth, Town Hall, Calif. Conservation Council, Long Beach Rotary. Author: The Boom of the Eighties in So. Calif., 1944; Mexican Gold Trail, 1945; (with Dr. Osgood Hardy) A History of the Pacific Area in Modern Times, 1949; (under name Glenn

Pierce) The Tyrant of Bagdad, 1955. Co-author, editor: From Wilderness to Empire: A History of Calif., 1959. Contbr. articles to profl. and popular pubs. Address: Office of the Chancellor, Calif. State Univ. & Colls., 400 Golden Shore, Long Beach, CA 90802.

DUMMETT, CLIFTON O.
Professor of Dentistry
b. May 20, 1919, Georgetown, Guyana; s. Alexander A. and Eglantine (Johnson) Dummett: came to U.S., 1936, naturalized 1946; B.S., Roosevelt Univ., 1941; D.D.S., Northwestern Univ., 1941; M.Sc.D., 1942; M.P.H., Univ. Mich., 1947; D.Sc., 1976; Sc.D., 1978; m. Lois M. Doyle, Mar. 6, 1943, Chicago; son, Clifton O. Jr., b. 1944. Career: Prof., Dean, Sch. of Dentistry, Meharry Med. Coll., 1942-49; Chief Dental Serv., VA Hosp., Tuskegee, Ala. 1949-65; Chief Dental Service, VA Research Hosp., Chicago, 1965-66; Dental Dir., USC Neighborhood Health Center, 1966-67, Health Center Director, 1967, Assoc. Dean and Chmn., Dept. Community Dentistry, USC Sch. of Dentistry, 1967-75, Prof. of Dentistry, 1975---. Pres., Internat. Assn. Dental Research, 1969-70; pres., Am. Assn. Dental Editors, 1975-76; Editor, Nat. Dental Assn., 1952-75; Editor, Am. Assn. Dental Editors, 1964-73; chmn. Dental Sect., AAAS, 1975-76. Mem.: Omicron Kappa Upsilon, chpt. pres. 1946; Alpha Phi Alpha, pres. 1940; Sigma Pi Phi, pres. 1970; Sigma Xi; Delta Omega. Democrat. Episcopalian. Hobbies: music, athletics. Home: 5344 Highlight Pl., L.A., CA 90016; Office: P.O.B. 77006, L.A., CA 90007.

DUNCAN, GERTRUDE INEZ
Educator
b. Dec. 4, 1896, Algona, Iowa; d. Burke Hamilton and Ariadne (Hartley) Samuels; piano diploma, Highland Park Coll. of Music, 1914; studied Chicago Univ., 1924; B.A., Univ. of No. Iowa, 1925; M.A., Columbia Univ., N.Y., 1926; Ed.D., Temple Univ., Philadelphia, 1942; m. Mr. Duncan, Sept. 10, 1927; chil.: Jean Eleanor (Hollingsead), b. July 13, 1933; Robert Barclay, b. Aug. 25, 1936. Career: tchr. rural schs. of Iowa, 1915-18; tchr., Phillips Elem Sch., Des Moines, 1920-22; instr., State Tchrs. Coll., St. Cloud, Minn., 1922-25; instr. supr., Phys. & Health Edn., State Tchrs. Coll., Kutztown, Pa., 1926-28; asst. prof. Women's Activities, Temple Univ., Phila., 1928-48; Tchr., edn. adv., Penn State Dept. of Edn., Harrisburg, 1960-70; tchr. edn. cons. 1970. Devel. and helped implement Approved Program approach to tchr. certification in Penn., 1963-70. Representative of Penn. Dept. of Edn. for accreditation of univs., colls., secondary schs. 1960-70. Originated and devel. TV series on edn. for AAUW in Harrisburg, 1960. Author books, papers on tchr. edn.; contbr. to journs. Recipient: Recognition for 17½ years of Penn. State Service, 1976; Community Leaders of Am. Award, 1971; Honored by Placentia-Yorba Linda AAUW, 1977; Founder's Certificate, the Center for Internat. Security Studies of Am. Sec. Council Edn. Found., 1977. Mem.: AAUW, Harrisburg, Pa., 1928-73, Placentia/Yorba Linda, 1973--- (area rep. 1973-77); E. Assn. of Phys. Edn. for Coll. Women, 1938 (mem. exec. bd.); League of Women Voters, 1946-47; active in Red Cross and Girl Scouts. Presbyterian. Mem. Garden Grove Community Ch. Hobbies: travel, theater, community projects. Home: 1018 E. La Habra Blvd., No. 137, La Habra, CA 90631.

DUNCAN, IRA L.
Former State Official
b. June 7, 1910, Bayard, Nebr.; s. Earl C. and Emma M. (Casper) Duncan; B.S., Golden Gate Coll., S.F. 1957; m. (div. 1951); sons: Thomas Lynn and David L. Career: Mgr., Hagstroms Food Stores, 1937-41; real estate salesman, 1941-43; dept. store supv. 1946-55; real estate broker, casualty ins. broker, 1955-60; sr. clerk, Div. of Hwys., State of Calif. Dept. Pub. Works, S.F., 1960-75 (ret.). Pvt., U.S. Army (1943-45), WW II. Listed, various biog. achievement publs. Mem.: secty-bus. mgr., Am. Soc. of Mil. Insignia Collectors; chmn. Japanese Sword Soc. of U.S., Inc.; Oakland Lodge No. 188, A.F. & A.M., Scottish Rite (32⁰), Aahmes Shrine. Home: 744 Warfield Ave., Oakland, CA 94610.

DUNLAP, CLYDE HILLIARD, JR.
President, C.H. Dunlap Co.
b. Feb. 10, 1920, Muskogee, Okla.; s. Clyde Hilliard, Sr. (dec. Dec. 1958) and Marie (Martin) Dunlap; nephew of Retha R. Martin, cnmn. bd., Dunlap Co. of Texas; ed. P.A., Pasa. Jr. Coll.; m. Jean Harris, Lubbock, Tex., Jan. 12, 1944; chil.: Diane Marie, b. Mar. 20, 1947; Thomas Allan, b. Nov. 25, 1949; Clyde H., III b. Dec. 4, 1953. Career: Assoc. Dunlap Co. of Calif., June 1938---; partner, Jan. 1, 1941---, pres. Oct. 1947---; v.p.-dir., Dunlap Co. of Tex.; pres. C.H. Dunlap Co. of Calif. 1st Sgt., 557th Field Artillery, 1942-44; European Theater of Operations

(1944-45), WW II. Mem.: Modesto City Council; Rotary Club. Presbyterian. Hobby: music. Rec.: travel. Home: 318 Brookway, Modesto, CA; Office: 1700 McHenry, Modesto, CA 95352.

DUNN, GEORGE WILLIAM
Mechanical Engineer
b. Feb. 20, 1918, Coalinga, Calif.; s. Roy S. and Marie Guinn; ed. B.S. (elec. engring.), Univ. of Calif., Berkeley, 1940; m. Marion Walton, Santa Cruz, Calif., Aug. 9, 1939; dau. Mrs. Douglas Morgan, b. Apr. 9, 1942 (grandau. Cheryle Anne, b. Dec. 21, 1966; grandau. Kari Lea, b. Nov. 25, 1969); sons: Michael Oliver, b. June 21, 1946 (grandau. Kathleen Renee, b. Nov. 16, 1970); George William III, b. Apr. 5, 1949. Career: Mech. Contr., 1945-51; cons. mech. engr., 1952---; v.p. (engring.) Frank L. Hope & Assocs., arch. and engrs. 1955-67; owner, George W. Dunn & Assocs., profl. engrs. 1967-69; pres. Dun-Lee-Smith-Klein and Assocs. engrs. 1969---. Contrib. tech. papers to natl. conventions, profl. journs. 1957---. Lt., Maj., U.S. Army Signal Corps (1940-45), WW II. Mem.: dir., Jr. Achievement of San Diego, 1952-57; trustee, Natl. Sch. Dist. 1958-68; San Diego Co. Com. on Dist. Organ. 1965-68; v.p. S.D. Co. Sch. Bds. Assn. 1966-67; S.D. Co. Sch. Bd. 1969-79; pres. S.D. Co. Sch. Bd. 1972-73 & 1977-78; Delegate Assembly, Calif. Sch. Bds. Assocs. 1970-79; Reg. Dir. Calif. Sch. Bds. Assoc. 1972-79; Bd. of Dir. Calif. Sch. Bds. Assoc. 1972-79; Bd. Dir. Calif. Co. Bds. of Edn. 1972-79; Finance Committee Calif. Sch. Bds. Assoc. 1972-79; Fellow, ASHRAE, 1977. Sec. Calif. Co. Bds. of Edn. 1976-77; Natl. City br., Am. Field Serv.; Mason, Univ. Club. Episcopalian (St. Matthews Vestry, jr. and sr. warden). Hobby: model boat bldr. Rec.: fishing, golf. Home: 3251 Holly Way, Chula Vista, CA 92010; Office: Suite 206, 1003 Plaza Blvd., National City, CA 92050.

DUNNE, PHILIP
Writer — Director
b. Feb. 11, 1908, N.Y.C.; s. Finley Peter (humorist and creator of "Mr. Dooley") and Margaret Ives (Abbott) Dunne; student, Harvard Coll., 1929; m. Amanda Duff, July 15, 1939, Virginia City, Nev.; chil.: Miranda, b. 1947; Philippa (Mrs. David Nelson), b. 1951; Jessica, b. 1952. Career: Writer since 1930---; short stories for New Yorker, other mags; many screen plays, incl. How Green Was My Valley, Stanley and Livingstone, The Rains Came, The Late George Apley, The Ghost and Mrs. Muir, Pinky, Ten North Frederick; directed (among others) Ten North Frederick, Prince of Players, The View from Pompey's Head; Author book: Mr. Dooley Remembers, Atlantic-Little Brown, 1962. Awarded Writers Guild of Am. Laurel Award for lifetime achievement; Valentine Davies Award for pub. serv.; Acad. nominations for How Green Was My Valley and David and Bathsheba. Mil Chief of Motion Picture Prod., U.S. Office of War Information, Overseas, 1942-45. Mem.: past v.p., Screen Writers Guild; past gov., Motion Picture Acad. Democrat, vice chmn. State Central Com. of Calif., 1938-40. Hobbies: pvt. pilot, amateur flutist. Rec.: surfing, gardening, fishing. Address: Malibu, CA.

DUNNING, VERA VON HUECK
Citrus Rancher — Club Leader
b. Apr. 5, 1896, Chernigov, Russia; d. Victor V. and Vera A. (Romanova) Gavrilov; desc. of Russian ambassadors, statesmen and warriors, Russian Tzar ancestry printed in Bible in 1637 dates back to 1120; family killed in Russian Rev.; ed. B.A., Princess St. Olga Sch., Russia; grad. work, UCLA and USC; m. William Alfred Dunning, San Bernardino, Dec. 30, 1932 (dec. 1950); son, George Alfred Victor, b. June 24, 1939. Career: Propr.-mgr., 200-acre citrus enterprise (packing plant, transporting and selling prods.). Mem.: v.p. Internat. Sect., Women's Univ. Club, L.A., chmn. 1935-37; dir. Citrus Sect., L.A. Co. Farm Bur., 1951-59; L.A. World Affairs Council, Friends of the Claremont Colls. Soc. Serv. Aux.; Jonathan Club; Hobbies: antiques, archeology, hist. Home and Office: Las Colinas, P.O.B. 272, San Dimas, CA 91773.

DURANT, ARIEL
Author — Historian
b. May 10, 1898, Proskurov, Russia; d. Joseph and Ethel (Appel) Kaufman; m. William J. Durant, Oct. 13, 1913, N.Y.C.; dau. Ethel Benvenuta, b. 1919. Career: Researcher and collab. with husband Will Durant on the first six volumes in The Story of Civilization; Co-author: The Age of Reason Begins, 1961; The Age of Louis XIV, 1963; The Age of Voltaire, 1965; Rosseau and Revolution, 1967; The Age of Napoleon, 1975; A Dual Autobiography, 1977. Awarded Presidential Medal of Freedom with Husband, 1977. Home: 5608 Briarcliff Rd., L.A., CA 90028.

DURANT, WILLIAM JAMES
Author — Historian
b. Nov. 5, 1885, North Adams, Mass.; s. Joseph and Marie (Allors) Durant; B.A., St. Peter's Coll., Jersey City, 1907; M.A., 1908; Ph.D., Columbia Univ., 1917; LL.D., 1927; m. Ida Kaufman, New York City, Oct. 31, 1913; chil.: Ethel Benvenuta. Career: Reporter, N.Y. Evening Journal, 1907; prof. of Latin, Greek, and French, Seton Hall Coll. 1907-11; dir. labor, Temple Sch., N.Y. 1914-27; Author: Philosophy and the Social Problem, 1917; The Story of Philosophy, 1926; Transition, 1927; The Mansions of Philosophy, 1929; 11 vol. Story of Civilization, publ. by Simon and Schuster: Our Oriental Heritage, 1935; The Life of Greece, 1939; Caesar and Christ, 1944; The Age of Faith, 1950; The Renaissance, 1953; The Reformation, 1958; The Age of Reason Begins, 1960; The Age of Louix XIV, 1963; The Age of Voltaire, 1965; Rousseau and Revolution, 1967; The Lessons of History, 1968; Interpretation of Life, 1970 (collab. Ariel Durant); The Age of Napoleon, 1975; A dual Autobiography, 1977. Awards: Pulitzer Prize, 1969. Presidential Medal of Freedom, with wife, 1977. Home: 5608 Briarcliff Rd., L.A., CA 90028.

DURHAM, ALVIN FRANKLIN, SR.
Clergyman
b. Oct. 25, 1915, Roseburg, Ore.; S. Daniel Omer and Roxie Leota (Pringle) Durham; A.B. Kentucky Christian Coll., 1942; student, Northwest Christian Coll., 1933-38; Southeast Missouri State Coll., 1949-50; Platte Valley Bible Coll., 1957-58; L.A. Valley Coll., 1970-72; San Fernando Adult Sch., 1969-70; m. Mavis Resnick, May 29, 1942, Grayson, Ken.; chil.: Deana (Mrs. Fred Dyer), b. Nov. 26, 1943; Alvin Franklin, b. Aug. 24, 1946; Mary (Mrs. Walter Purdy), b. Aug. 7, 1952. Career: columnist, Eugene (Ore.) Register Guard, 1936-37; Ordained Minister, 1939; Minister, Christian chs.: South Portsmouth, Ky., 1941-42; Springfield, Ky., 1942-43; Hickman, Ky., 1943-45; Pine Grove, W. Va., 1945-47; Fredericktown, Mo., 1947-50; Rockwell City, Iowa, 1952-55; Lewistown, Mont., 1955-57; Minatare, Neb., 1957-59; Amity, Ore., 1959-61; Elsinore, Calif., 1961-63; Farmington, N. Mex., 1963-65; Los Osos, Calif., 1965-66; San Fernando, Calif., 1966---. Principal and tchr., Mine La Motte, Mo., 1948-51; Chaplain, State Reformatory for Women, Rockwell City, Iowa, 1952-55; Civil Defense Dir., Lewistown, Mont., 1956-57; lctr. Alberta Bible Coll., Calgary, 1955; Chaplain (maj.) Civil Air Patrol, 1955-76. Bd. dir., Atascadero, Calif., Christian Home, 1966---; pres. 3 years; mem. faculty, Platte Valley Bible Coll., Scottsbluff, Neb., 9158-59. Mem. ministerial assns.; Lions Club, Young Men's Bus. Club, Smithsonian Assoc. (charter mem.). Royal Arch Masons, chaplain, degree team 1943-45. Republican. Hobby: Photog. Rec.: baseball, camping. Home/Office: 1065 Newton St., San Fernando, CA 91340.

DUTTER, VERA ELINOR
Artist — Lecturer
b. Apr. 30, 1904, Hollywood, Calif.; d. Jay (writer-lectr. on nutrition) and Cordelia (Hoovens) Dutter; desc. Wilcox pioneers and co-founders of Hollywood; ed. pub. schs., Hollywood H.S., maj. art, 1922. Career: Painter, portraits on ivory; specialty, miniatures; one of leading exponents in world of foredge painting (disappearing pictures on edges of rare books); exhib. and lectr. on fore-edge art, and many clubs and art exhibs.; works in permanent collections: Mrs. Paul Ecke (wife of Poinsettia King) and world famous collector Mrs. Edward L. Doheny (dec.); feat. mot. pic. short, Unusual Occupations (world-wide) Jerry Fairbanks Studio, 1948; appd. as guest artist, various TV programs; featured in various publications regarding revival of fore-edge painting (hist. goes back to 10th century; first used for identification of valuable books by royalty and dignitaries). Author: Fiction in various publs. Awards: Award of Merit, Am. Inst. of Fine Arts. Hobbies: Fellowship with friends, theatre, traveling. Home: 13681 Cedar Crest Lane, No. 93F, Leisure World, Seal Beach, CA 90740.

DUVALL, ALBERT ING
Medical Orgonomist
b. Dec. 11, 1908, Paris, Tenn.; s. William Sprigg and Maude (Mitchum) Duvall; B.A., Vanderbilt Univ., 1926; M.D., Univ. Tenn., 1933; m. Jeanette Hart, July 5, 1947, Colts Neck, N.J.; chil.: Albert Lowerre, b. Aug. 19, 1948; Cheryl Ann, b. Feb. 19, 1953. Career: Internist, Highland Park Hosp. 1933-35; Monmouth Mem. Hosp. 1935-36; Jr. and Sr. Resident Physician, N.J. State Hosp. for the Insane, 1936-38; Dir., Mental Hygiene Out Clinics for Central N.J., 1938; pvt. practice, psychiatry, L.A., 1948---; studied with Dr. Wilhelm Reich, 1946-57; Ct. Cons. Monmouth Counties, 1938-48; Clin. Staff, Mehlenberg Hosp., Monmouth Mem. Hosp., Gen. Hosp.,

New Brunswick, N.J., Atkin Mem. Hosp., 1941-48; Dir. of Orgonomic Children's Clib. 1950-52. Founding fellow of Am. Coll. of Orgonomy, 1968, v.p., Diplomate, Am. Bd. of Orgonomy, 1973; Life Mem. of Am. Psychiatric Assn.; pres., Am. Assn. of Med. Orgonomists. Mem. Kappa Alpha Phi Chi. Home: 232 San Vicente Blvd. No. 17, Santa Monica, CA; Office: 1100 Glendon, Suite 1543, L.A., CA 90024.

DWYER, R. JEREMY
Poet — Artist
b. July 23, 1932, Syracuse, N.Y.; s. William Joseph and Jerri Dee Van Coy (Montgomery) Dwyer; ed. Central City Bus. Inst. 1949; Dodd-Harris Sch., N.Y., 1949; U.S.A.F. Inst., 1950; Univ. Coll., Chicago-La Salle, 1951-52; (widower); chil': Kirth Aryl, b. Dec. 17, 1960; Debra Ann Goodnight, b. Sept. 3, 1963. Career: founder-dir. Braeloch Inst. 1955-75; tchr., Keyism, 25 yrs.; founder-dir., Cotterstone. Artist, 40 paintings in pvt. collections and maj. galleries, U.S.A. incl. White House portrait, Pres. Lyndon Johnson; Dominican Coll.; Brussels World's Fair, Seattle World's Fair. Author: 500 publ. poems; art critic and columnist, San Rafael Pointer (1 yr.) USN, 1949-50. Awards: numerous hons. and commendations incl. B.S.A., Marin Co. Council and San Rafael Police Dept. 1972; San Rafael City Schs., San Rafael Elks Lodge, City Council, Family Service Agcy. 1973; youngest Poet Laureate in U.S. Democrat. Roman Catholic. Hobbies: travel, college football, camping, fishing. Home: 1456 Lincoln Ave., San Rafael; Office: P.O. Box 913, Mission Br., San Rafael, CA 94902.

DYKEMAN, FRANK CHARLES
Partner, Price Waterhouse & Co.
b. Mar. 21, 1919, N.Y.C.; s. Robert Charles and Emma Pickett (Shaw) Dykeman; B.B.A., N.Y.C. Coll. 1939; LL.B., Fordham Univ., N.Y. 1943; m. Marie E. Clifford, Mass., Nov. 24, 1945. Career: Jr. acct., Price Waterhouse & Co. 1942, various positions, 1942-57, partner 1957---; CPA: Calif., N.Y., Mich., others; atty. at law, N.Y.; lectr., Mgmt. Acct. and Data Processing, Univs. of Mich. and Detroit. Contrib. ed. to Calif. CPA Quarterly; articles publ. in Price Waterhouse Review, Financial Exec. Mag., Savings & Loan Journ.; contrib. chpt. to Accts. Ency. Chief Warrant Ofcr., U.S. Army (1943-45), WW II. Mem.: chmn. mgmt. servs. com., Calif. CPA Soc. 1963-64; gen. budget com.-chmn. gen. relief com., L.A. AID; v.p.-dir., Pasa. Opera Co.; bd. govs. Cath. Acct. Guild; Task Force, Immaculate Heart Coll.; Town Hall, Jonathan Club, Glendora Country Club, Annandale Golf Club. Hobby: travel. Rec.: golf. Home: 246 Arbolada Dr., Arcadia, CA 91006; Office: 606 S. Olive St., L.A., CA 90014.

DYKSTRA, ORVILLE LINDEN
Attorney at Law
b. Sept. 4, 1912, Keosauqua, Ia.; s. Charles Frank and Artie (Vander Linden) Dykstra; B.A., Central Coll., Pella, Ia. 1933, LL.D. 1960; J.D. (with distinction), Univ. of Ia. 1936; m. Ermina Dunn, Central City, Ia., Oct. 11, 1936; chil.: Linda Louise (Dykstra) Johnson, b. Apr. 15, 1940; David Charles, b. July 10, 1941; Judith Anne, b. Dec. 6, 1943. Career: Head, tax dept., Wolf & Co., CPAs, Des Moines, Ia. 1936-40; treas. Globe Hoist Co. 1940-42; partner, Allen, Dykstra, Swift and Austin, 1942-48; exec. com., Brenton Cos. 1948-57; pvt. law practice, 1948-51; partner, Dykstra, Swift and Brown, 1951-57; pres. New Monarch Mach. and Stamping Co., Des Moines, 1955-57; treas. Utah Constr. & Mining Co., San Francisco, 1957-61; v.p.-treas. 1961-71. Ed. staff, Ia. Law Review, 1935-36; lectr., Drake Univ. 1938-40; Ia. State Bar Assn. Tax Sch. 1940-55. Mem.: Am. and Ia. Bar Assns.; (charter) Des Moines Estate Planning Council; Mason, Shrine, 1945-58. Hobby: golf. Home: 186 Westgate Dr., Napa, CA 94558.

DYMOND, HENRY
Insurance Executive
b. Apr. 8, 1922, Covington, Ky.; s. Henry J. and Virginia (Arlinghaus) Dymond; Ph.B., Univ. of Detroit, 1944; C.L.U. Am. Coll. 1957; Mgmt. Diploma, 1958; m. Catharine Stimson, Detroit, Mich., Dec. 30, 1942; chil.: Michael, b. Nov. 1943; Carol Nemecek, b. June 1945 (son, Jason); Damian, b. Dec. 1946; Patrick, b. May 1948 (son, Nicholas); Sheila, b. Dec. 1950; Mark, b. Dec. 1951; Kevin, b. Nov. 1957; Megan, b. July 1960. Career: Underwriter, Equitable Life Assurance Soc. 1947, dist. mgr. 1948-54, dir. Henry Dymond Agcy., 1954-72 founder-pres., Hendy Co., ins. advisors, 1972-74; pres. Henry Dymond & Assocs. 1974---. Awards: won many ins. hons.; L.A. City Council Cit., 1968. Mem.: ASCAP, pres. Cleveland Gen. Agcy. Mgrs. Assn. 1958-59; dir. B.S.A. Council, 1959-62; C. of C.; pres. Century City Rotary Club, 1966-68; chmn. bd. Lake Encino Racquet Club, 1967-69; Cellar Club of L.A.; Rolls Royce Owners

Club. Catholic. Hobbies: tennis, golf. Office: 9363 Wilshire Blvd., Beverly Hills, CA.

E

EAGEN, I. BRENT
Clergyman
b. Dec. 14, 1929, Upland, Calif.; s. James O. and Stella E. (Powell) Eagen; grad., Immaculate Heart Seminary, 1956; M.A., Loyola Univ., L.A., 1960; postgrad., UCLA, 1964; ordained priest Roman Catholic Ch., 1956. Career: Asst. Prof., Univ. of San Diego, 1960-65; dir., Sch. Relations, 1965-67; Chancellor, Diocese of San Diego, 1968---; Pastor, Mission Basilica San Diego de Alcala, 1971---; Prof. Mercy Coll. of Nursing, 1962-64. Secty., bd. of dirs., Edn. and Welfare Corp., 1968---; Secty., bd. of trustees, Univ. of San Diego, 1968---; mem. Nat. Bd. of Dirs., NCCJ, 1974---; pres., Cathedral Plaza Corp., 1972---. Pres., Community Welfare Council, 1970-72. Author: Released Time a Necessary Adjunct to Secondary Education, 1960; San Diego de Alcala, San Diego Journal of History, 1978. Mem.: Catholic Alumni Clubs, nat. chaplain 1967; Canon Law Soc. Am., regional pres. 1968-69; Phi Kappa Theta; Kona Kai Club; Scholia Club. Rec.: tennis; Home: 10818 San Diego Mission Road, San Diego, CA 92108; Office: P.O.B. 80428, San Diego, CA 92138.

EAMES, ALFRED WARNER, JR.
Chairman Board, Del Monte Corp.
b. June 20, 1914, Honolulu; s. Alfred Warner and Carrie Godfrey (McLean) Eames; Univ. of Ore. 1932-35; m. Antoinette Lucas, S.F., Feb. 1938; chil.: Alfred W., IV, b. Jan. 15, 1939; Anthony L., b. July 3, 1941; Peter M., b. Mar. 12, 1948; A. Christopher, b. Oct. 18, 1950. Career: Del Monte Corp., San Francisco, 1935---; dir., 1954, v.p. 1957, exec. v.p. prodn. 1965, pres. 1968, chmn. bd.-chief exec. ofcr. 1969---. Dir.: Ban Cal Tri-State Corp.; Bank of Calif. NA; Calif. State C. of C.; Pac. Gas and Elec. Co.; Fireman's Fund Am. Ins. Cos.; trustee: Com. for Econ. Devel.; Council of Americas. Mem.: The Conf. Bd.; Blyth Zellerbach Com.; Natl. Corps. Com. for United Negro Coll. Fund; Chi Psi. Clubs: Stock Exch., Newcomen Soc. in No. Am., Pac. Union, St. Francis Yacht, Mento Country. Hobbies: hunting, fishing, garden. Office: One Market Plaza, S.F., CA 94119.

EARLY, JAMES MICHAEL
Electronics Company Executive
b. July 25, 1922, Syracuse, N.Y.; s. Frank J. and Rhoda (Gray) Early; B.S., N.Y. Coll. of Forestry, Syracuse, N.Y. 1943; M.S., Ohio State Univ., 1948; Ph.D., 1951; m. Mary Agnes Valentine, Dec. 28, 1948, Logan, W. Va.; chil.: Mary Elizabeth, b. Oct. 7, 1949; Kathleen Regina, b. Dec. 20, 1950; Joan Therese Farrell, b. Dec. 20, 1951; Rhoda Ann Alexander, b. July 25, 1953; Maureen Michele, b. July 20, 1954; Rosemary, b. Mar. 3, 1956; James Michael, Jr., b. Jan. 29, 1959; Margaret Mary (Margo), b. June 6, 1964. Career: Research Assoc., Oh. State Univ. Research Found., Columbus, 1951; dir., Semiconductor Device Lab., Bell Telephone Labs., Allentown, Pa., 1951-69; Div. v.p. of Research and Devel., Fairchild Camera and Instrument Corp., Palo Alto, 1969---. AUS, 1943-45; 1st spec. engr. detachment, Oak Ridge, Tenn. Fellow, IEEE, 1959; Awarded Texnicoi, outstanding alumnus award, Annual Conf. Engrs., Oh. State Univ., 1967. Roman Catholic. Rec.: sailing, skiing. Home: 740 Center Dr., Palo Alto, CA 94301; Office: 4001 Miranda Ave., Palo Alto, CA 94304.

EASTON, ROBERT OLNEY
Author — Environmentalist
b. July 4, 1915, San Francisco; s. Robert Eastman and Ethel (Olney) Easton; grandson, Warren Olney (1841-1921), S.F. attorney, mayor of Oakland, cofounder and first v.p., Sierra Club; S.B., Harvard, 1938; M.A., UCSB, 1960; m. Jane Faust, Sept. 24, 1940, Berkeley, Calif.; chil.: Joan (Mrs. Gilbert W. Lentz); Katherine (Mrs. Armand J. Renga); Ellen (Mrs. Gregory W. Brumfiel); Jane. Career: assoc. editor Coast Mag., 1939-40; free-lance writer 1940---; soldier AUS, 1942-46; co-founder, editor Dispatch, Lampasas, Tex., 1946-50; co-owner, mgr. radio station KHIT (now KCYL) Lampasas, 1948-50; instr. in English, Santa Barbara City Coll., 1960-65; cons. writing and publishing, U.S. Naval Civil Engring Lab., Port Hueneme, 1961-69. Pres., S.B. Citizens for Environmental Defense, 1974---; trustee: S.B. Mus. of Natural Hist., 1972-75, S.B. Community Environmental Council, 1973---; co-chmn. Com. for Santa Barbara, 1972-76;

headed citizens com. establishment San Rafael Wilderness Area, Los Padres Nat. Forest, 1964-68. Author: The Happy Man, 1943, new ed. 1977; (with Mackenzie Brown) Lord of Beasts, 1961; (with Jay Monaghan, others) The Book of the Am. West, 1963; (with Dick Smith) California Condor, 1964; The Hearing, 1964; Max Brand: The Big Westerner, 1970; Black Tide: The Santa Barbara Oil Spill and its Consequences, 1972; Guns, Gold and Caravans, 1978. Editor: Max Brand's Best Stories, 1967; Bullying the Moqui, 1968. Contbr. numerous articles to popular mags. and tech journs.; numerous stories to fiction and nonfiction anthologies. Enlisted pvt. AUS to 1st Lt., 1942-46; decorated, Combat Infantryman's Badge. Home: 2222 Las Canoas Rd., Santa Barbara, CA 93105.

EATON, LEWIS S.
President, Guarantee Savings & Loan
b. Aug. 10, 1919, S.F.; s. Edwin M. and Gertrude (Swift) Eaton; A.B., Stanford Univ. 1942; m. Virginia Stammer, M.D., Fresno, Calif., Apr. 21, 1950; chil.: William L., b. Oct. 10, 1951; Joan E., b. June 13, 1953; John W., b. May 23, 1956. Career: Pres., Fresno Guarantee Savings & Loan Assn. 1946---; pres. Fresno City Bd. of Edn. 1958---; bd. Fed. Home Loan Bank, S.F., 1964-69; pres. U.S. Svgs. & Loan League, 1971; Natl. Parks Bd. 1972---. Pvt.-Capt., U.S. Army Inf. 1942-46; instr. Spec. Serv. Sch., Wash. & Lee Univ., Lexington, Va., WW II. Mem.: treas. Fresno Art Center, 1949-54; pres. Fresno Zoological Soc. 1958; trustee, Valley Childrens Hosp. 1958-59; pres. Calif. Svgs. & Loan League, 1959-60; trustee, Fresno Community Hosp. 1965---; pres. Fresno Co.-City C. of C. 1968-68. Clubs: Rotary, Univ., Sequoia. Episcopalian. Hobby and Rec.: photog., sailing, golf. Home: 4115 N. Van Ness Blvd., Fresno, CA 93704; Office: 1177 Fulton St., Fresno, CA 93721.

EATON, BARRY DAVID
City Planner
b. Dec. 1, 1937, Oakland; s. Joseph Lloyd and Dorothy (Stockton) Eaton; A.B., Univ. Calif., Berkeley, 1960; postgrad., USC 1960-62; div., chil.: Colleen Ann, Cathleen Anissa. Career: Planning asst., city of L.A., 1960-62; city planner and planning dir., city of Azusa, 1962-64; planning dir., Stanton, 1964-66, Thousand Oaks, 1966-70; chief planner, Boise-Cascade Bldg. Co., L.A., 1970-71; community devel. dir., city of Escondido, 1971-72; dir. planning, VTN Corp., Irvine, 1972-74; dir. gen. planning Raub, Bein, Frost & Assocs., Newport Beach, 1974; city planner, Fullerton, 1974---. Recipient special ecology awards from local environmental groups, Thousand Oaks, 1960, and Escondido, 1961. Mem.: Mensa Soc., Calif. Tomorrow, Calif. Roadside Council, Am. Inst. Planners, Am. Soc. Planning Ofcls., Calif. Planning and Conservation League, Regional Plan Assn. So. Calif., Sierra Club, Commonwealth Club. Home: P.O.B. 802, Corona del Mar, CA 92625; Office: City Hall, Fullerton, CA 92632.

EATON, MONROE DAVIS, JR.
Professor Emeritus of Bacteriology
b. Dec. 2, 1904, Stockton, Calif.; s. Monroe Davis, Sr. and Ida Virginia (Petty) Eaton; bro. Ralph M., Prof. of Physiology, Harvard Univ.; M.A., Stanford Univ. 1928; M.D., Harvard Med. Sch., 1930; m. Laura Mitchell, Aug. 9, 1933, Palo Alto; chil.: John Monroe, M.D.; Emily (Lyon); Katherine (Fripp); Lydia. Career: Instr., Yale Med. Sch. 1933-36; asst. prof. bacteriology, Wash. Univ. Med. Sch., St. Louis, 1936-37; staff mem. Internat. Health Div. Rockefeller Found. 1937-47; assoc. prof. bacteriology & immunology, Harvard Med. Sch. 1947-68, prof., 1968-71; Prof. Emeritus, 1971---; adjunct prof., Stanford Univ., Med. Microbiology, 1971-78; dir., Virus Lab., Calif. State Dept. of Pub. Health, 1939-47. Contbr. profl. sci. papers, chpts. in med. books. Mem. Editorial Bd., Annual Review Microbiology, Stanford, 1946-56. Mil.: Mem. U.S. Army Commn. on Influenza, 1941-59; cons. Yellow Fever Vaccination for Jaundice, Surgeon Gen., AUS 1942-44. Home: 1965 Byron St., Palo Alto, CA 94301.

EATON, HON. RICHARD B.
Former Superior Court Judge
b. Dec. 22, 1914, Albany, Ore.; s. Walter McCrum and Edna (Behrens) Eaton (treas. Shasta Co. 1923-29); desc.: grandson of Charles Behrens, Sheriff, Shasta Co., Calif. 1899-1903; nephew of Earl C. Behrens, polit. ed., S.F. Chronicle, 1922-74; ed. A.B., Stanford Univ. 1934, J.D., 1938. Career: Pvt. legal practice, Redding, Calif. 1938-40, 1946-51; U.S. Commr. 1948-51; city judge and justice of the peace, Redding, 1950-51; judge, Superior Ct., Shasta Co., 1951-76 (ret.). Lectr. local colls. and H.S. Author: Court of Sessions, Shasta County, 1947; Life of Chief

Justice Sprague, 1952; Courthouse of Shasta County, 1956; Commissioned ofcr., USAR 1936-74 (ret.); U.S. Army, 1940-46; Lt. Col., Foreign Serv. (Africa, Sicily, Italy), 1942-46, WW II. Awards: Army Commendation Ribbon, 1946; Eagles Civic Awards, 1952; Silver Bearer of Boy Scouts, 1956; Freedoms Found. Award, 1956. DeMolay Legion of Honor, 1968. P.T.A. Distinguished Service Award, 1976; Shasta H.S. Distinguished Community Serv. Award, 1977; Mem.: VFW; State Sch. Commr., Am. Leg. 1952-53; F. & A.M., Master Mason; Jurisprudence Com., Grand Chpt., R.A.M., 1954, 55; exec. bd. Mt. Lassen Council, B.S.A., 1958-76; (hon.) Rotary Club. Republican (mem. Co. Central Com. 1940). Episcopalian. (lay reader, 1946---). Hobby: historical research. Home: 1520 West St., Redding, CA 91974.

EBAUGH, FRANKLIN G., JR.
Physician — Educator
b. Dec. 25, 1921, Phila.; s. Franklin G. and Dorothy (Reese) Ebaugh; A.D., magna cum laude, Dartmouth Coll., 1944; M.D., Cornell Med. Coll., 1946; chil.: Sandra, b. Dec. 15, 1946; Patricia Susan, b. Nov. 18, 1948; Jeanette Helen, b. Oct. 1, 1956. Career: Dean, Boston Univ. Sch. of Med., 1964-69; Dean, Univ. of Utah Sch. Med., 1969-71; Assoc. Dean for VA Affairs, Stanford Univ. Sch. of Med., 1972---; also Chief of Staff, VA Hosp., Palo Alto, 1972---. Contbr. 70 articles on various med. subjects profl. pubs., 1948-79. Pvt., AUS, WW II; Surgeon, U.S. Pub. Health Service, 1953-55; Capt., USNRMC, 1973-78; Col., USAR-MC, 1978---. Chmn., Blood Club, 1962; pres., Nat. Assn. of VA Chiefs of Staff, 1976; mem. Field Advis. Group to the Asst. Chief Med. Dir. for Profl. Services, VA Central Office, 1975---; mem. exec. com. of Am. Soc. of Hematology, 1964-68. Episcopalian. Rec.: skiing, squash. Home: 420 Gerona Rd., Stanford, CA 94305; Office: 3801 Miranda Ave., Palo Alto, CA 94304.

EBLEN, JAMES HAMILTON
Realtor
b. Oct. 2, 1929, Henderson, Ky.; s. Oscar Hamilton and Janet (Reid) Eblen; A.A., Orange Coast Coll., 1971; student, Lumbleau Real Estate Sch., 1968-71; m. Velma Rawlings, Dec. 13, 1951; son Paul Hamilton. Career: real estate agent, Tarbell Realtors, Fountain Valley, 1968-70; sales mgr., Tarbell Realtors, Garden Grove, 1971; Owner, Eblen Real Estate, Fountain Valley, 1972; sales mgr., Percy Goodwin Co., Fountain Valley, 1973; owner, Leadership Real Estate, Huntington Beach, 1973-74; mgr., Tobin Realty, Huntington Beach, 1975-76; gen. partner, E&E Devel. Co., Santa Clara, 1976---. Co-chmn., Citizens Against New Taxes, 1975; Am. Security Council; Calif. Assn. Realtors, 23 Dist. chmn. legislative com.; rep. nat. com., U.S. Senatorial Club; v.p. bd. of Realtors Huntington Beach-Fountain Valley, 1975, named Realtor of the Year, 1975; Graduate Realtors Inst. Certificate, 1978. Hobbies: golf, chess. Office: 712 Charcot Ave., San Jose, CA 95131.

EBOREIME, BABATUNDE ALOOKNAI
Physician
b. Afuze-Emai, Nigeria; A.B. cum laude, Princeton, 1967; M.D. (Albert Einstein), 1971. Bd. certified Obstetrics and Gynecology, Nov. 1977. Career: med. practice in Pasadena. Office: Tunde Airo Eboreime, M.D., 1403 N. Fair Oaks Ave., Suite 3, Pasadena, CA 91103.

ECKE, ROLLIN EVANS
Insurance Company Executive
b. Mar. 19, 1900, Fond du Lac, Wis.; s. Oscar Henry and Edith Mabel (Evans) Ecke; ed. A.B., Univ. of Wis. 1922; J.D., USC 1932; m. Eleanor M. Humphris, L.A., Calif., Nov. 18, 1933; daus.: Suzanne McColl, b. May 21, 1937; Marilyn Dianne, b. Mar. 15, 1941. Career: Wilshire Oil Co. 1923-36, controller, 1927-36; v.p.-controller, Farmers Underwriters Assn. 1936-42, v.p.-treas. 1942-59, financial v.p. 1959-65; dir. Farmers New World Life, 1953---, pres. 1956-65. S.A.T.C. (1918), WW I. Mem.: F. & A.M. 1921---; Phi Beta Kappa, 1922---; Phi Kappa Phi, 1922---; Beta Gamma Sigma, 1922---; Delta Sigma Pi (Wis.), 1922---; Order of the Coif, 1932---; pres. Petroleum Accts. Soc. 1932-33; L.A. Country Club, 1943---; pres. L.A. Control, Financial Execs. Inst. 1947-48; Calif. Club, 1951---; chmn. Council of Profit Sharing Industries, 1963, 64. Hobby: golf, hunting, sailing. Home: 9646 Lawlen Way, Beverly Hills, CA 90210. Office: 4680 Wilshire Blvd., L.A., CA 90005.

ECKEL, JAMES R., JR.
Electrical Engineer — Real Estate Broker
b. Nov. 3, 1927, Morley, Tenn.; s. James R. and Jane Scott (Seymour) Eckel; grandson, Charles Milne Seymour.

prominent lawyer of Knoxville, Tenn., (listed in Who Was Who, 1958), and Flora Nell Gloster Seymour, active in DAR, Magna Charter Dames, Episc. ch.; B.S. magna cum laude, Univ. of Tennessee, 1953, M.S., 1957; J.D., Univ. of W. Los Angeles, 1974. Career: Instr. elec. engring., Univ. Tenn., 1953-57, Univ. Wis., 1957-62; sr. engr. Northrop Corp., L.A., 1962-66; staff engr. TRW Systems, L.A., 1966-69; sr. project engr. Hughes Aircraft Co., L.A., 1969---; also Calif. licensed real estate broker. Mil. USN, 1946-49. Mem.: I.E.E.E.; Am. Inst. Aeros. and Astronautics; Am. Soc. for Engring. Edn. Mem.: Kappa Sigma; Nat. honor socs.: Sigma Xi, Omicron Delta Kappa, Phi Kappa Phi, Tau Beta Pi, Eta Kappa Nu, Phi Eta Sigma. Episcopalian. Home: 5104 Copperfield Lane, Culver City, CA 90230; Office: Hughes Aircraft Co., Centinela Ave. & Teale St., Culver City, CA 90203.

ECKERSLEY, NORMAN C.
Bank Executive
b. June 18, 1921, Great Britain; s. James Norman and Chadwick Eckersley; m. Catherine Bell Harris, July 22, 1950; Bombay, India; 1 d. Mrs. Catherine Anne Robins, b. Dec. 29, 1951. Career: with Chartered Bank: London and Manchester, England, 1947-48; accountant, Bombay, 1948-52; Calcutta, 1958-59; Hong Kong, 1959-60; asst. mgr., Hamburg, 1960-62; mgr., Calcutta, 1962-67; Thailand, 1967-69; pres., The Chartered Bank of London, San Francisco, 1969-74; chmn. and chief exec. officer, 1974---. Chmn., Calcutta Exchange Banks Assn., 1964-66, 67; chmn. Foreign Exchange Dealers Assn., Calcutta, 1964, 66, 67; chmn. Indsl. Finance Corp., Thailand, 1969; chmn. Diners Club (Thailand) Ltd., 1969; chmn. Overseas Banks Assn. in Calif., 1972-74; deputy leader, Thai Trade Mission to W. Germany and U.K., 1969; dir. India C. of C. 1964, 66, 67; dir. Calif. Council for Internat. Trade; mem. exec. com., S.F. Chamber and World Trade Assn.; Dir. Stock Exchange Club, 1977-78. Mil. Served with R.A.F. 1940-46; decorated D.F.C. plus other decorations; C.B.E. Office: 465 California St., San Francisco, CA 94104.

ECKIS, ROLLIN POLLARD
Oil Company Executive
b. June 26, 1905, Oakland, Calif.; s. Rollin Garfield and Daisy (Pollard) Eckis; ed. B.A., Pomona Coll. 1927; M.S., Calif. Inst. of Tech. 1929; m. Caroline Comstock,Pasadena, July 10, 1937; chil.: Rollin Charles, b. June 17, 1939; Nancy May, b. Aug. 14, 1941; Ellen Mott, b. Oct. 10, 1947. Career: Assoc. with Met. Water Dist. 1930; engr.-geol., Calif. State Div. of Water Resources, 1930-34; geol. The Texas Co. 1934-37; dist. geol., Richfield Oil Corp. 1937-46, chief geol. 1946-54, mgr. exploration-v.p. 1954-56, exec. v.p. Atlantic Richfield Co., 1966---. v. chmn. bd. 1969-75, dir. The Chubb Corp., dir. Pacific Indemnity Company. Mem.: trustee, Pomona Coll.; fellow, Geol. Soc. of Am., Am. Assn. of Petroleum Geologists; dir. Am. Petroleum Inst.; Sigma Xi; L.A. Petroleum Club. Pac. Union Club, Calif. Club. Protestant. Rec.: fishing, hunting. Home: P.O.B. 597, Pauma Valley, CA 92061.

EDELSTEIN, IRVIN LEE
Newspaper Publisher
b. Nov. 14, 1915, Toledo, Oh.; s. Joseph and Pauline (Benjamin) Edelstein; B.S. (journ.), Oh. State Univ. 1938; m. Jeanette Levine, Toledo, Dec. 14, 1941; chil.: Susan Dee, b. May 16, 1948; Ronald Alan, b. Apr. 28, 1952. Career: Ed. staff, Toledo Times and Blade, 1945-48; pres. Irvin L. Edelstein Assocs. Adv. Agcy., L.A., 1948---. Pub., L.A. Canyon Crier News, 1975---. Lt., U.S. Army Inf., Pac. area combat, Bougainville (1942-45), WW II. Staff ofcr., U.S. Coast Guard Aux. Mem.: Mayor's Adv. Council of L.A.; advisor, L.A. Labor-Mgmt.-Citizens Com. 1961---; Sigma Delta, L.A. C. of C., Western States Adv. Agencies Assn., Pub. Rels. Soc. of Am., L.A. Press Club, The L.A. Club, Del Rey Yacht Club, Riviera Country Club. Jewish. Hobby: yachting. Rec.: tennis. Home: 14069 Marquessas Way, Marina del Rey, CA; Office: 521 N. La Cienega Blvd., L.A., CA 90048.

EDEN, RAYMOND L.
Association Executive
b. July 19, 1925, Lee, Ill.; s. Bennie and Hannah Eden; ed. B.Sc. (hons.) No. Ill. Univ. 1950; Northwestern Univ. 1950; N.Y.U. 1955; m. Ellen Meace Waterman, Ill., Aug. 17, 1945; son, Steve, b. July 27, 1958. Career: Staff Ill. Assn. for Crippled, 1950-53; exec. dir. Crippled Chil's. Center, Peoria, Ill. 1953-59; exec. dir. Milwaukee Easter Seal Soc. 1959-62; exec. dir. Ill. Heart Assn. 1962-66; exec. dir. Calif. Heart Assn. 1966-69; admr. San Mateo Med. Clinic, Calif. 1969-71; exec. dir. Am. Heart Assn., Greater L.A. Affil., Inc., 1971---; Treas., Neighborhood Church, Palos Verdes Estates; Treas., Little Company of

Mary Hosp., Torrance; Pres., L.A. Council of Nat. Voluntary Health Agencies, L.A. Corp., E.T.O. (wounded at Remagen, Germ., Mar. 1945), WW II. Awards: trustees-Ch. Council, 1969-71. Recipient: Bronze Star, Purple Heart. Mem.: Natl. Assn. of Soc. Workers, Acad. of Certified Soc. Workers, Ansan Shrine, Springfield Consistory. First Congl. Ch. of San Mateo, chmn. bd. Rec.: tennis, golf, skiing. Home: 30317 Via Cambron, Palos Verdes Estates, CA 90274; Office: 2405 W. 8th St., L.A., CA 90057.

EDLUND, DONALD G.
Business Owner
b. Feb. 6, 1935, Detroit, Mich.; s. Gustaf and Ethel (Crompe) Edlund; grandson, Gus Edlund, patentee drill press and typewriter assembly; A.A., Cerritos Coll., 1961; B.S., elec. engr., Univ. Calif., Berkeley, 1964; m. Frances Mays, Dec. 12, 1954, Norwalk; chil.: Terry, b. July 18, 1962; Larene (Schuster), b. Dec. 28, 1957; Laura (Ferraro), b. May 28, 1956. Career: with Autonetics, 1966; owner, Setterberg Jewelry, currently. Award for sci. paper, solid state design, Motorola 1965. Publ.: Radar Principles – Parameters, 1966. USAF, 1958, radio maint. & instr. Radio Sch., Biloxi, Miss. Pres., Paddison Sq. Merchants Assn., 1974; pres., Norwalk C. of C., 1978; Mem.: BPOE; IEEE assoc. mem. 1965; pres., G.T. Sports Car Club, 1968; Old Timers MX Assoc., 1976; Imperial Golf Assn., 1977. Ch. of Christ. Hobby: amateur radio (K6PJL). Rec.: golf, motorcycles. Home: 1357 Walnut 3550, Anaheim, CA; Office: 12407 Norwalk Blvd., Norwalk, CA 90650.

EDWARDS, MARIE BABARE
Psychologist — Lecturer
b. Tacoma, Wash.; d. Nick and Mary (Mardesich) Barbare; ed. N.Y. Univ., Reed Coll., Portland, Ore., B.A., psychol., Stanford Univ., 1948---; M.A., 1949; Ph.D. program, clin. psychol., UCLA, 1958-60; div.; son, Tilden Hampton Edwards III. Career: pvt. practice, consul., sensitivity and human rels. training for orgns., 1950---; counselor, USC Guidance Center, 1950-52; proj. coord., So. Calif. Soc. for Mental Hygiene, 1952-54; pub. speaker for Welfare Fedn. of L.A., 1953-57; field repr., L.A. Co. Assn. for Mental Health, 1957-58; originator, Challenge of Being Single workshops at USC, various univs. in US and Canada, 1970---. Author (w/Eleanor Hoover) The Challenge of Being Single, Tarcher/Hawthorn, Paperback Signet 1975. Mem.: Am., Western, Calif. State, and L.A. Co. Psychological Assns.; Soc. for Humanistic Psychol.; S. Calif. Soc. of Clin. Hypnosis; AAAS; Nat. Acad. of Religion and Mental Health; Soc. for Adv. for Mgmt. Office: 6100 Buckingham Pkwy., Culver City, CA 90230.

EDWARDS, RICHARD "DICK"
Basketball Coach
b. June 21, 1930, Hannibal, Mo.; s. Floyd Logan and Madelin (Truitt) Edwards; ed. B.S., Culver-Stockton Coll., Canton, Mo. 1952; M.A., Claremont Grad. Sch. 1959; m. Marian Fischer, Salina, Kan., Oct. 25, 1952; sons: Michael Richard, b. July 6, 1958; Jon Logan, b. Nov. 30, 1959. Career: Basketball coach: Yreka (Calif.) H.S. 1957-60; El Camino H.S., Sacto., 1960-63; Univ. of Pac., Stockton, 1963-72; Univ. of Calif., Berkeley, 1972---. Coaching record: 76 wins, 33 losses, incl. 2 W. Coast Ath. Conf. Championships, 1965-66, 1966-67, and W. Coast Ath. Conf. Tournament Championship, 1966-67; 6 yr. H.S. coaching record: 134 wins, 21 losses, incl. 4 Conf. Championships and 9 Tournament Championships (210 wins, 54 losses in 10 yrs.) USAF, 1952-56. Mem.: Natl. Assn. of Basketball Coaches, Lambda Chi Alpha, Pi Kappa Delta, Phi Delta Kappa. Lutheran. Rec.: fly-fishing, hunting, golf. Home: 29 Kazar Ct., Moraga, CA; Office: Dept. of Intercollegiate Aths., Univ. of Calif., Berkeley, CA 94720.

EDWARDS, WARD DENNIS
University Professor — Administrator
b. Apr. 5, 1927, Morristown, N.J.; s. Corwin D. and Janet W. (Ferriss) Edwards; B.A., psychology, Swarthmore Coll., 1947; M.A., psychol., Harvard Univ., 1950, Ph.D., psychol., 1952; m. Silvia Callegari, Dec. 12, 1970, Burbank; son, Page, b. May 11, 1960. Career: faculty mem., Brooklyn Coll., 1947-48, Boston Univ., 1948-49, Harvard Univ., 1949-51, Johns Hopkins Univ., 1951-54; research psychologist, Maintenance Lab. and Operator Lab., Personnel and Training Research Center, USAF, 1954-58; with Univ. of Mich. 1958-73: as research psychologist, Engring. Psychol. Lab.; also lectr.; assoc. prof. and prof. of Psychology; head, Engring. Psychol. Lab.; assoc. dir., Highway Safety Research Inst.; with USC, 1973---: as prof. of psychology and prof., indsl. and systems engring., Sch. of Engring. ---; dir., Social Sci. Research Inst. ---. Research interests

mostly concerned with decision analysis and with behavioral decision theory. Cons.: RAND Corp., 1964---; Am. Coll. of Radiology, 1972---; Decisions and Designs, Inc., 1972---; mem. Panel on Earthquake Prediction, Nat. Research Council, 1973---; FDA, Bureau of Drugs, 1976---; Contbr. 120+ publs., profl. journs. and symposiums. Diplomate in Indsl. / Orgnl. Psychology, Am. Bd. of Profl. Psychol., 1971. Seaman 1st class to Yeoman 3rd Class, USN, 1945-46. Hobby: flying, pvt. license. Home: 11466 Laurelcrest Rd., Studio City, CA 91604; Office: Social Sci. Research Inst., USC, 950 W. Jefferson Blvd., L.A., CA 90007.

EFRON, ROBERT
Professor of Neurology
b. Dec. 22, 1927, N.Y.C.; s. Alexander and Rose Efron; B.A., Columbia Coll., N.Y., 1948; M.D., cumlaude, Harvard Med. Sch., 1952; m. Barbara Klein, Dec. 30, 1967, N.Y.; chil.: Carol (Peyser), b. 1952; Paul S., b. 1954; Lucy A., b. 1959. Career: Med. Hous. Officer, Peter Bent Brigham Hosp., Boston, 1952-53; Moseley Traveling Fellow, Harvard, 1953-54; chief, Neurology Div., Dept. Neurology & Psychiat., St. Albans Naval Hosp., 1954-56; research assoc., Nat. Hosp., Queen Sq., London, 1956-60; chief, Neurophysiology-Biophysics Research Unit, VA Hosp., Boston, 1960-70; assoc. chief. of staff for R&D, VA Hosp., Martinez, Calif., also prof. of Neurology, Univ. Calif. Med. Center, Davis, 1970---. Contbr. more than 50 sci. publs. in area of brain function. Lt. j.g., U.S. Maritime Service, 1945-47; Lt., Med. Corps. USNR, 1954-56. Mem.: Bd. Govs., Acad. of Aphasia, 1975-79; advis. bd., Amyotropic Lateral Sclerosis Found., 1972---; advis. bd., Internat. Soc. for Study of Time, 1974-76; others. Mem.: Phi Beta Kappa (Columbia Univ.), Alpha Omega Alpha (Harvard Univ.). Hobbies: music, photog. Rec.: travel, skiing. Home: 2955 Pierce St., S.F., CA 94123; Office: VA Hosp., Martinez, CA 94553.

EHLERS, KENNETH WARREN
Physicist — Inventor
b. b. Aug. 3, 1922, Dix, Nebr.; s. Walter Richard and Clara (Sievers) Ehlers; ed., B.S., Univ. of Colo. 1943; postgrad. Okla. A. & M. Coll. 1943-44; M.I.T. 1945; m. Marion Catherine Ward, Fullerton, Calif., Mar. 4, 1947; son, Gary Walter, b. Nov. 10, 1955. Career: Head, Electronic Aids Dept., Landing Aids Exp. Sta., Arcata, Calif., 1946-50; staff physicist, Lawrence Radiation Lab., Univ. of Calif., Berkeley, 1950---; cons.: Brobeck Inds., Berkeley, 1961---; AVCO Corp., Tulsa, Okla. 1962-65; Applied Radiation Corp., 1962-65; Cyclotron Corp., Berkeley, 1965---. Invesntor, Author, many articles publ. profl. journs. Chief Petty Ofcr. (Aviation electronics), USNR, 1942-46, WW II. Mem.: Am. Physical Soc., Am. Vacuum Soc., AAAS. Republican. Methodist. Hobby: gardening, woodworking. Rec.: hunting, fishing. Home: 3129 Via Larga, Alamo, CA 94507; Office: Lawrence Radiation Lab., Bldg. 16, Berkeley, CA.

EHLERT, ARNOLD DOUGLAS
Librarian
b. Apr. 22, 1909, Mondovi, Wis.; s. Richard Joseph and Cora Edna (Hakes) Ehlert; A.B., John Fletcher Coll., 1932; Th.M., 1942, Th.D., 1945, Dallas Theological Seminary; M.S. in Lib. Sci., USC. 1953; m. Thelma A. Adolphs, Dec. 25, 1933, Rockford, Ill.; chil.: A. Benjamin, b. Aug. 5, 1937; Susan Elizabeth (Bissonette), b. July 6, 1943; Eunice Yvonne (Castle), b. Aug. 19, 1948. Career: Librarian, Dallas Theol. Seminary, 1942-48, Fuller Theol. Seminary, 1948-55; Librn., also Prof. of Librarianship, Biola Coll., 1955-69; Grad. Studies Librn., Talbot Theol. Seminary, 1969-74; Dir. of Librs., Christian Heritage Coll. and The Inst. for Creation Research, 1974---. Author: The Biblical Novel, 1960; Bibliographic Hist. of Dispensationalism, 1965; Brethren Writers, A Checklist, 1969. Editor: The Bible Collector, 1965---. Founder, pres., Internat. Soc. of Bible Collectors, 1964---. Mem.: Phi Beta Mu, Evangelical Theol. Soc., Christian Brethren/Research Fellowship, Am. Theol. Lib. Assn., Christian Librarians Assn. Ordained minister, Evangelical Free Ch. of Am. Hobby: bibliography. Home: 1262 Camillo Way, El Cajon, CA 92021; Office: 2100 Greenfield Dr., El Cajon, CA 92021.

EHRENHALT, MELVIN S.
Physician — Sex Therapist
b. June 5, 1928, Longbranch, N.J.; s. Eli and Frances (Hollander) Ehrenhalt; B.A., Syracuse Univ., 1950; M.D., Albany Med. Coll., 1954; m. Janice Leiter (div.); chil.: Gayle, b. July 26, 1956; Lori, b. Mar. 15, 1958; Kathi, b. Mar. 15, 1961; Donna, b. Sept. 20, 1963; m. 2d Laura

(Shifman) Smith; chil.: (prior marriage) Stacy Smith-Ehrenhalt, b. Jan. 13, 1960; Scott Smith, b. July 4, 1961. Career: intern, Mt. Sinai Hosp., N.Y.C. 1954-55; clin. instr. UCLA Med. Center, 1965-70; Certified Am. Assn. of Sex Educators and Counselors, 1977; chief of staff, OB-GYN, L.A. New Hosp., 1978-79. Diplomate Am. Bd. of AB-GYN, 1964. Fellow, Am. Coll. of OB-GYN. Mil.: Capt. USAF, 1956-58. Mem. Alpha Omega Alpha. Rec.: skiing, sailing, fishing. Home: 3072 Deep Canyon Dr., Beverly Hills, CA 90210; Office: 9201 Sunset Blvd., L.A., CA 90069.

EISENBERG, RICHARD SAMUEL
Optometrist
b. Apr. 29, 1948, Los Angeles; s. Frank and Anne Eisenberg; nephew of Dr. Walter Ellwood, cardiologist; A.A., L.A. Valley Coll., 1968; B.A. in biology, Cal. State Univ., Northridge, 1970; B.S. So. Calif. Coll. of Optometry, 1972, O.D., 1974; Certification spec. in subnormal vision care, 1974; Calif. cert. for use of diagnostic pharmaceutical agents, 1978; m. Deborah Zalinger, Dec. 28, 1969, Sherman Oaks, Calif.; chil.: David Frank, b. Jan. 22, 1976; Rachel Lynne, b. Aug. 21, 1977. Career: pvt. practice in optometry, 1974---. Asst. instr., clin. optometry, S.C.C.O., 1975; optometric cons., Internat. Ladies Garment Workers Union, L.A., 1975-76. Organizer, dir., Health & Safety Fair which served over 3000 people in San Fernando Valley, 1976. Co-chmn. KNBC TV Feeling Fine televised health fair, 1978. Contbr. tech. journ. Recipient: Mayor Tom Bradley's cert. of appreciation award, L.A., 1976; Optometric Speakers Award, 1978. Bd. dir., San Fernando Valley Optometric Soc., 1976---; Optometric Care Council of So. Calif. 1978-79. Mem.: Nat. Eye Research Found., Am. Optometric Assn., Calif. Optometric Assn., S.F. Valley Optometric Soc., Optometric Care Council of So. Calif.; Coll. of Optometrist in vision develop. Mem.: Jaycees, Woodland Hills C. of C., Omega Epsilon Phi Optometry (pres. 1972-73); alumni assns.: Calif. State Univ., Northridge and S.C.C.O. Hobbies: model railroading, running. Home: 23025 Hamlin St., Canoga Park, CA 91307; Office: 21835 Ventura Blvd., Woodland Hills, CA 91364.

ELCONIN, KENNETH B.
Orthopedic Surgeon
b. Nov. 16, 1931, L.A.; s. Benjamin and Abba Elconin; A.A., pre-med., UCLA, 1952; B.A., Univ. Calif., S.F., 1954; M.D., 1956; m. Merle Ensler, June 1957, S.F.; chil.: Elyse, b. Jan. 23, 1959; Steven, b. Apr. 27, 1962. Career: pvt. practive orthopedic surgery, Beverly Hills, 1962---; clin. instr., Orthopedics, UCLA Med. Sch. Contbr.: Clin. Orthopaedics and Related Research journ., med. assn. meetings. Capt., AUS-M.C., 1959-61. Pres., Gr. L.A. Cystic Fibrosis Chpt., 1968-70; mem. Phi Delta Epsilon med. grad. frat. Jewish. Rec.: tennis, skiing, backpacking. Home: 500 Homewood Rd., L.A., CA 90049; Office: 9735 Wilshire Blvd., Suite 238, Beverly Hills, CA 90212.

ELDRIDGE, WILLIAM CAMERON
Partner, William Eldridge Co.
b. Jan. 13, 1912, Omaha, Nebr.; s. Oliver William and Hazel Clee (Smith) Eldridge; B.A., Amos Tuck Sch. of Bus. and Finance, Dartmouth Coll. 1934; chil.: Joan, b. Oct. 1, 1941; Lynn, b. Feb. 13, 1944; Beth, b. Mar. 18, 1947. Career: Merchandising, Montgomery Ward, Chicago, 1934-38; mgr. commercial research, Crane Co. 1938-42; commercial research supv., Radio Corp. of Am. 1942-44; assoc. cons., Chicago, 1944, supv.-mgr.-partner in chg., L.A. ofc. 1948-59; partner, William Eldridge Co., 1959---. Mem.: bd. trustees, Harvey Mudd Coll., Economic Round Table, Pasadena Rotary Club. Hobby: gardening, horses. Rec.: riding, skiing, swimming. Office: 420 South Hill Ave., Pasadena, CA 91106.

ELEY, CHARLES NEILL, JR.
Architect
b. Oct. 5, 1945, Cookeville, Tenn.; s. Charles Neill and Anna (Lipton) Eley; B. Arch., Univ. of Tenn., 1969; Master of City Planning, Univ. Calif., Berkely, 1973; m. Miriam Olsen Phillips, Mar. 26, 1977, S.F. Career: Design Architect, Tenn. Valley Authority, Knoxville, 1969-71, 1972; tchg. asst., Univ. Calif., 1972-73; asst. to Planning Dir., City of Burlingame, Calif., 1973; sr. planner/arch., HKS Assocs., S.F., 1973-76; prin., Charles Eley Assocs., S.F., 1976---. Mem., nat. AIA Energy Com., 1978-79; contbr. numerous articles on energy and arch., Daily Pacific Builder, AIA publs., 1978; designer of unpub. passive solar bldgs. under constrn., 1978-79. Energy cons. to Calif. Council, AIA, 1978---. Address: 342 Green St., S.F., CA 94133.

ELKE, SHIRLEY FRANCES MORGAN
Cartographer
b. Oct. 26, 1927, San Francisco; d. Lt. Comdr. John Francis and Shirley Marie (Wright) Morgan; ed. Acad. of Notre Dame, Wash., D.C., 1945; student cartographic drafting, Columbia Tech. Inst., (D.C.), 1946; UCLA, USC, 1950-54; art studies, Modesto Jr. Coll., 1962-75; m. Richard Louis Elke, Dec. 30, 1960, Oakland, Calif. Career: cartographer, Army Map Service, 1946-48; cartographer, Auto Club of So. California, 1948-50; cartographer to chief cartographer, Texaco Oil Co., exploration dept., 1950-56; chief cartographer Southern Pacific Railroad, Land Dept., Mineral Survey, 1956-60; founder, co-owner, chief cartographer, Compass Maps, 1963---. Awards: Best of Show in fine arts, Stanislaus Co. Fair, 1969; Best of Show in fine arts, Valley Art Show, 1972. Dir. Modesto Chamber of C., 1978---; civic affairs council chmn., 1979; tourism chmn., 1974---; pres., Central Calif. Art League, 1971-72; editor of CCAL Club Bulletin, 1967---; pres., Nat. League of Am. Penwomen, Modesto branch, 1978-80; Nat. Art Board mem. 1978-80; mem. Am. Congress on Surveying & Mapping. Republican. Hobby: painting, enamels. Home: 2501 Edgebrook Dr., Modesto, CA; Office: 1172 Kansas Ave., Modesto (P.O.B. 4369), CA 95352.

ELLENBERG, ALEXANDER H.
Plastic Surgeon
b. Oct. 13, 1933, Stockton; s. Morris and Gertrude (Barron) Ellenberg; A.B., Univ. Calif., Berkeley, 1955; M.D., Univ. Calif., S.F., 1958; m. Maureen Aronow, 1954, L.A.; chil.: Steven, b. Apr. 25, 13; Gary, b. Feb. 19, 1965; residencies in general and plastic surg., Univ. of Calif., 1959-65; pvt. practice in plastic surg., San Jose, 1965---; mem. faculty of plastic surg., Stanford Univ.; lectr. in plastic surg. in France and Israel, 1977---; staff plastic surgeon: San Jose Hosp., O'Connor Hosp., Good Samaritan Hosp., Los Gatos Hosp. Dir.: San Jose Jewish Fedn., San Jose Museum of Art. Mem.: Calif. and Am. Societies of Plastic Surg.; Am. Soc. of Esthetic Plastic Sueg.; Am. Clin. Soc. of Plastic Surg.; San Jose Surgical Soc.; Santa Clara Med. Soc.; AMA; CMA; Israel Med. Fellowship; Fellow, Am. Coll. of Surgeons. Office: 2577 Samaritan Dr., Suite 720, San Jose, CA 95124.

ELLENBOGEN, ERIC
Public Relations Executive
b. Mar. 9, L.A., s. Albert and Lorraine Ellenbogen; A.B., govt., Harvard Univ. Career: Registered Legislative Advocate in State of Calif., 1973-75; statewide field coord., U.S. Senator John V. Tunney, 1976; sr. partner, Ellenbogen, Castro & Assocs., Wash., D.C., 1976-78; vice pres., Resource for Communications, Inc., 1978---; vice pres., Corp. Planning & Devel., ICPR Pub. Rels., L.A., N.Y. 1978---. Pres., Bel Air Mgmt. and Invest. Corp., L.A., 1979---. Awards: Presidential Commendation, 1972; Freedoms Found. George Wash. Honor Medal; Westinghouse Broadcasters Good Mike Award. Mem.: Harvard Club; Signet Soc.; Hasty Pudding Inst. of 1770; Am. polit. Sci. Assn., AAAS. Democrat, mem. State Central Com., 1976-78; mem. Mayor of L.A.s Environmental Advis. Com., 1973. Office: 9255 Sunset Blvd., 8th Flr., L.A., CA 90069.

ELLENBOGEN, RICHARD
Plastic Surgeon
b. Feb. 14, 1944, Port Jeruis, N.Y.; s. Morton and Julia Ellenbogen; related to Karl Marx, Felix Mendelson, Helena Rubinstein, David Halberstam; A.A., Univ. of Florida, 1963; M.D., Univ. of Miami, 1968. Career: Gen. surgery training completed Beth Israel Hosp., N.Y.C., 1971; plastic surgeon, Hague, Netherlands, 1972; hand surgery training, Hosp. for Joint Diseases, N.Y.C., 1972; plastic surgery, State Univ. of N.Y., 1973-75; pvt. practice plastic surgery, L.A. ---. Diplomate Am. bd. of Plastic Surgery. Contbr. numerous plastic surgical scl. papers to tech. publs. Office: 9201 Sunset Blvd., Suite 202, L.A., CA 90069.

ELLERBROCK, GERALDINE BYRNE
Professor of Management
b. May 11, 1920, Shawnee, Oh.; d. Gerald J. and Margaret Winifred (O'Donnell) Byrne; B.S. in edn., Oh. State Univ., 1941, M.S. in indsl. rels., 1967, Ph.D. in mgmt. scis.; m. Dr. Vincent J. Ellerbrock (dec. 1965), Aug. 7, 1943, Shawnee, Oh.; chil.: Timm J., CPA; Tedd V., M.D.; Donn G., J.D.; Vann C.; Kirk B.; Mona Lea. Career: Consultant inds. rels., Columbus and Dayton Oh., 1950-65, 1940-73, Venezuela, 1974; asst. prof. Indsl. Rels., Univ. Dayton, 1970-73; assoc. prof. Indsl. Rels., Cal. Poly State Univ., San Luis Obispo, 1978---. Mem.: Labor Panel of Am. Arbitration Assn.: Accredited Personnel Specialist. Author: People Problems, Knoll Kakery, 1975, 77; Cases-Harvard Case

Clearing House, Knoll Kakery, 1974; Jerome Company, 1976; Vann Engineering-Unionization, 1975; Dave Douglas Co., 1977; Contbr. author: The Personnel Management Process: Cases in Human Resource Administration. Mem.: Beta Gamma Sigma; Pi Omega Pi; Indsl. Rels. Research Assn., Central Coast, secty., treas., 1978---; Nat. Acad. of Mgmt.; Indsl. Mgmt. Soc.; Am. Acad. of Mgmt. (W. div.); pres., AAUW at Cal Poly, 1978---; San Luis Obispo Art Assn.; San Luis Obispo Golf and Country Club; League of Women Voters; Monday Club; Sierra Club. Roman Catholic. Hobbies: people, golf, profl. reading. Home: Four Los Palos Dr., San Luis Obispo, CA 93401; Office: Mgmt. Dept., Sch. of Business, Calif. Polytechnic State Univ., San Luis Obispo, CA 93407.

ELLICK, THOMAS COLEMAN
Corporate Executive
b. Feb. 10, 1932, Omaha, Nebr.; s. Robert P. and Marian Ellick (Herman); B.A., Stanford Univ., 1954; m. Claire Burress, July 23, 1976, No. Hollywood; chil.: Thomas Michael, b. Nov. 14, 1974; Craig Dennis, b. Mar. 12, 1960; Jason Earl, b. June 15, 1972. Career: with Speer & Mays Advt., 1956-61; Council of Calif. Growers, 1961-66; Ellick & Assocs. Advt. & Pub. Rels. 1966-68; asst. to Gov. of Calif. 1968-71; Dir., Corporate Affairs, Fluor Corp. 1971-73, mgr., corp. relations, 1973-77, vice pres., corporate relations, 1977---; treas., Calif. Council for Environmental & Econ. Balance; trustee: Found. for Am. Communications, The Heritage Found., United for Calif.; dir.: Found. for Econ. Freedom, Nat. Assn. of Mfgrs., U.S. Indsl. Council, Lincoln Club of Orange Co. Mem.: Sigma Alpha Epsilon. Rec.: golf. Home: 24342 Donner Ct., Laguna Niguel, CA 92677; Office: 3333 Michelson Dr., Irvine, CA.

ELLINGBOE, JULES K.
Engineer — Administrator
b. Mar. 18, 1927, Tucson, Ariz.; s. Arthur G. and Jessie Lucille (Preston) Ellingboe; B.S. elect. engring., Univ. Ariz., 1950; m. Melinda O'Neil, Oct. 20, 1973, Rolling Hills, Calif.; chil.: Kay (Langbord), b. July 30, 1952; Carol, b. Jan. 19, 1955, Lori O'Neil, b. Apr. 11, 1962; Lynn O'Neil, b. Apr. 11, 1962; Craig O'Neil, b. July 7, 1963, Career: with TRW Corp., 1963---: asst. mgr., Support Systems Lab., 1961-66; proj. mgr., PM7, 1966-71; asst. proj. mgr., Defense Satellite Prog., 1971-74; asst. mgr. of material, 1974-77; proj. mgr., TDRSS Ground Station, TRW Defense and Space Systems, 1977---. Patentee in field, USNR, 1944-46, Pacific Theater. Mem.: Tau Beta Pi, Theta Tau, IEEE. Hobbies: woodwork, fishing. Rec.: soaring, boating. Home: 1420 E. Sycamore Ave., El Segundo, CA 90245; Office: One Space Park, Redondo Beach, CA 90278.

ELLIOTT, VIRGIL L.
City Official
b. Jan. 20, 1918, Barnard, Mo.; s. Edgar D. and Mary (Hill) Elliott; family notables incl. Alva C. Hill, city councilman, Prescott, Ariz.; ed. B.S. (edn.), Northwest Mo. State Coll. 1940; certificate in pun. adm., Univ. of Calif. 1962; m. Helen Cranfill, S.F., Dec. 19, 1953; chil.: Susan, b. Dec. 5, 1956; Edgar, b. Aug. 24, 1960; Ina, b. Aug. 29, 1968. Career: Principal, Burlington Elem. Sch., Longmont, Colo., 1941-42; rewrite, Denver Rocky Mt. News, 1942-43; loftsman, Douglas Aircraft, 1943-46; farm ed., Bakersfield Californian, 1946-47; City Hall reporter-rewrite, S.F. Call-Bulletin, 1947-53; conf. secty. to Mayor of S.F. 1953-55; dir. of pub. serv., S.F. Pub. Utilities Comm. 1955-58; dir. of finance and records, City and Co. of S.F. 1958---. Monthly contrib. to S.F. City-Co. Record mag. U.S.A.R., P.I.O. sect.; regular inf. (1945-46), WW II. Mem.: v.p.-treas., S.F.-Oakland Newspaper Guild, 1950-53; bd. dirs., S.F. Council of Camp Fire Girls, 1958-59; panelist, Governmental Inst., S.F. 1961; pres., S.F. Municipal Exec. Employees Assn. 1964-65, Am. Soc. for Pub. Adm., panel participant, annual conf., Detroit, Apr. 12-15, 1962; Western Gov. Research Assn.; clubs: S.F. Press & Union League, Commonwealth of Calif. Democrat. Presbyterian (elder, deacon, Sun. Sch. supt.). Hobby: photog., home movies, gardening, pro-football fan '49ers. Home: 3134 Jackson St., S.F., CA 94115; Office: 170 City Hall, S.F., CA 94102.

ELLIOTT, WARD EDWARD YANDELL
University Professor
b. b. Aug. 6, 1937, Cambridge, Mass.; s. William Y. and Louise (Ward) Elliott; desc. William Penn, Julia Ward Howe, Philip Lord Wharton, Oliver Cromwell, Charlemagne, Pocahontas; A.B., Harvard Univ., 1959, A.M., Ph.D., 1968; LL.B., Univ. of Va., 1964; m. Myrna

Krahn, June 7, 1969, Claremont; sons: William Yandell, b. July 8, 1971; Christopher David, b. July 8, 1973. Career: Eighth Army Order of Battle Officer, 1960-61; Law Assoc., Covington & Burling, Wash., D.C., 1964; asst. then Assoc. Prof. Polit. Sci., Claremont Men's Coll., 1973---. Author: The Rise of Guardian Democracy, 1974; nominated for Pulitzer, Woodrow Wilson Prizes. Lt., USAR, 1959-61; decorated, Dist. Civilian Serv. Medal, 1973. Chmn., Group Against Smog Pollution; mem. 4th Regional Acad. Advis. Symposium; dir., Planning & Conservation League. Mem.: Fox Club, 1956-59; Hasty Pudding Inst. of 1770, 1956-59; EUSA Compound No. 1 NCO Club, 1960-61; Flat Earth Party, 1968---. Teddy Roosevelt Republican. Christian. Hobbies: singing, writing, creating. Rec.: hiking, gardening. Home: 875 N. College Ave., Claremont, CA 91711; Office: Claremont Men's College, Pitzer Hall, Claremont, CA 91711.

ELLIS, HAROLD ANDRUS, JR.
Chairman, Grubb and Ellis Company
b. Aug. 4, 1931, Portland, Ore.; s. Harold Andrus and Bertha (Fancher) Ellis; B.S., Univ. Calif., Berkeley, 1953; M.B.A., Stanford Grad. Sch. of Bus., 1955; m. Virginia Roach, 1954, Berkeley; chil.: Melinda G., b. Aug. 24, 1961; Stephen Fancher, b. Jan. 8, 1963; James Andrus, b. July 24, 1966. Career: Founder, president and chairman, Grubb Ellis Co., Oakland, 1958---. Trustee, Realty and Mortgage Investors of the Pacific, 1972---; trustee, Nat. Urban Coalition. 1st Lt., USAF, 1955-57. Mem.: Phi Delta Theta, Rotary. Office: 1333 Broadway, Suite 900, Oakland, CA 94612.

ELLIS, HARRIETTE SHIRLEY
Editor
b. Feb. 29, 1924, Memphis, Tenn.; d. Samuel and Edith (Brodsky) Rothstein; student, Memphis Art Acad., 1940-43; undergrad, Memphis State Univ., 1941-42; B.A., Univ. of Alabama, 1944; postgrad., UCLA, 1949-50; Chouinard Inst., 1948; m. Dr. Manuel Kaplan, June 1, 1944, Memphis, Tenn. (div. 1970); chil.: Deborah Elise, b. Feb. 11, 1952; Claire Naomi, b. July 6, 1954; Amelia Stephanie, b. Aug. 10, 1963; m. 2d Theodore J. Ellis, Aug. 22, 1971, Long Beach. Career: Advertising artist and copywriter, New Orleans and Los Angeles, 1944-49; mag. and newspaper copy, Albuquerque, and L.A., 1951-53; free-lance writer, 1969---; editor, Jewish Federation News, Long Beach, 1969---. Dress designer, 1950-52; arts and crafts instr. 1964-60. Recipient: spec. citation for social service in Honduras from Medico, a service of Care, Inc., 1968; Woman of the Year award, Temple Israel, L.B. Mem.: AAUW, L.A. chpt.; League of Women Voters, L.B. Dental Assn. Aux., secty., v.p.; Nat. Council of Jewish Women, Albuquerque chpt. Jewish; bd. dir. Temple Israel; Sisterhood, v.p., western area and nat. bds. dir. Hobbies: reading, archaeology, travel. Rec.: hiking, camping, swimming, ballet. Home: 3210 Val Verde Ave., L.B., CA 90808; Office: 3801 E. Willow St., L.B., CA 90815.

EMBLETON, TOM WILLIAM
Professor of Horticultural Science
b. Jan. 1918, Guthrie, Okla; s. Harry (head, poultry dept., Univ. Ariz., 1923-53) and Katherine (Smith) Embleton: B.S., horticulture, Univ. Ariz., 1941; Ph.D., Pomology, Cornell Univ., 1949; m. Lorraine Davidson, Jan. 22, 1943, Junction City, Kan.; chil.: Harry Raymond, 1944-67; Gary Thomas, b. Jan. 9, 1947; Wayne Allen, b. Dec. 30, 1954; Terry Scott, b. June 8, 1959; Paul Henry, b. Oct. 21, 1960. Career: Scientific aide to Horticultural Sci., Horticulturist, Wash. State Coll., Prosser, Wash., 1949-50; asst. horticulturist to Prof. of Horticultural Sci., Horticulturalist, Univ. Calif., Riverside, Citrus Research Center, 1950---. Publs., 190 profl. papers and articles. Fellow, Am. Assn. Adv. of Sci.; Fellow, Am. Soc. for Horticultural Sci.; recipient Citrograph Reserach Awards; Sigma Xi hon. frat. Capt., AUS, 1942-46; Maj. USAR; decorated Purple Heart and Bronze Star. Mem. Sigma Chi.; pres., Faculty Club., Univ. Calif., Riverside, 1958. Home: 796 W. Spruce St., Riverside, CA 92507; Office: Dept. Botany and Plant Scis., UC Riverside, CA 92521.

EMERY, STEWART JAMES
Human Potential Lecturer — Executive
b. Jan. 30, 1941, Sydney, Australia; s. James (noted Australian photog. and water color painter) and Dorothy (Bailey) Emery; grad. High Sch., 1958; 1 son, Paul, b. Aug. 27, 1965. Career: began in advertising photog., 1959, became a top photog. in Australia; creative dir., J. Walter Thompson, Australia, 1967-68; founded a successful TV and film prod. co., 1969; leader, tchr., seminars and training sessions in human potential, Calif., 1971-75; Bd. chmn., secty., co-founder of Actualizations,

1975---. (Actualizations conducts workshops in communications, relationships, support and personal effectiveness.) Also lectr. internat., TV and radio in psychol., edn. and philosophy. V.P., CRS Develop. Corp. (real estate), 1978---. Author: Actualizations: You Don't Have to Rehearse to Be Yourself, Doubleday & Co., Inc., 1978; contbr. copyrighted articles to New Age Journal and New Woman Mag. Mem.: Assn. for Humanistic Psychol. Office: 3632 Sacramento St., S.F., CA 94118.

EMETT, ROBERT LYNN
Insurance Executive
b. Aug. 9, 1927, Oxnard, Calif.; s. Edward L. and Isabel Louise (Vaughan) Emett (dec.); desc. Dr. Edward H. Emett (minister) and Rowland Emett, noted English artist; ed. H.S., Webb Sch. of Calif.; B.A., Claremont Men's Coll. 1950; m. Carole P. Hopkins; chil.: Michael Scott, Sherry Lynn, Robert Charles, Lindy Louise and James Stewart. Career: Underwriter, Swett & Crawford, 1950; acct. exec., Emett & Chandler (ins. brokers), 1951, ofc. mgr. 1954, S.F. mgr. 1957, L.A. dir. 1960, v.p.-gen. mgr. 1961-62, pres. 1962-68; pres. Pinehurst Corp. 1968-73, chmn. bd. 1973---. S. Pac., USNR (1945-46), WW II; 1st Lt., USAF Res. 1951-59; Mem.: dir. Calif. Cong. Recognition Proj. 1962; pres. Claremont Men's Coll. Alumni Assn. 1963; dir. L.A. Co. Heart Assn. 1964-69; dir. John Tracy Clinic, 1965-70; bd. govs. Mental Health Assn., L.A.; trustee, Claremont Men's Coll. Affiliates; Honnold Lib. Soc.; Eldorado Country Club; L.A. Country Club; Bohemian Club, S.F.; Newport Harbor Yacht Club; Republican (state finance chmn., Young Repubs. 1956-57; L.A. Co. Budget and Expenditures Com. 1962---). Presbyterian. Rec.: golf. Home: 2170 Century Park E., No. 1812, L.A., CA 90067; Office: 1800 Ave. of the Stars, Century City, L.A., CA 90067.

EMMONS, DONN
Architect
b. Oct. 4, 19190, Olean, N.Y.; s. Frederick Earl and Mary (Fogarty) Emmons; bro. Frederick Emmons, Architect; bro. Richard (dec.); stu., Cornell Univ., arch., 1929-33; USC, 1934; m. Nancy Pierson, Apr. 4, 1942, div. 1960; chil.: Zette, b. Oct. 30, 1946; Luli, b. Aug. 10, 1949; Andrew, b. Aug. 12, 1953; m. 2d., Audrey Durland, Oct. 29, 1960, Sausalito. Career: with office of William Wilson Wurster, 1938-42; partner, Wurster, Bernardi and Emmons, 1945-63; prin., Wurster, Bernardi and Emmons, Inc., 1963-69; pres., 1969---; Cons. Arch., UC, Berkeley, 1968-74; cons. arch. Univ. of Victoria, B.C., 1962-66, 1972---; chief cons., arch., Bay Area Rapid Transit System, 1964-67; pres., S.F. Plan. Assn., 1947-49; mem., Potomac River Task Force for U.S. Secty. of Interior, 1966-68; vis. Design Critic, Cornell Univ., 1959-65. Trustee, Heitman Mortgage Investment Trust (Mass. Corp.), 1970---. Lt. Comdr., USNR, Atlantic and Pacific Theater and Office of Naval Research/Special Devices, 1942-45. Recipient of over 30 awards for Excellence in Design; winner of Albert J. Evers Environmental Award, 1976. Certified by Nat. Council of Archtl. Registration Bds., 1965. Mem.: Lambda Alpha Hon. Nat. Planning Frat.; Fellow, AIA (for Outstanding Achievement in Design, 1961); AIA, pres. No. Calif. chpt. 1956; dir., Calif. Council of Architects, 1956. Hobbies: photog., traveling. Rec.: sailing. Home: 15 Girard, Sausalito, CA 94965; Office: 1620 Montgomery St., S.F., CA 94111.

EMPEY, DONALD WARNE
School District Executive
b. Feb. 8, 1932, McMinville, Ore.; s. E. Warne and Anna May (Alsman) Empey; B.A., hist., Willamette Univ., 1954; M.A., edn., Stanford Univ., 1955; Ed.D., instrn. & adminstrn., Univ. Ore., 1964; m. Mary Catherine Reeh, July 14, 1956, Portland, Ore.; chil.: Elizabeth, b. Nov. 1, 1958; Margaret, b. June 17, 1963; Jennifer, b. May 9, 1967. Career: hist. tchr., So. Salem H.S., Salem, Ore., 1955-58; adminstr., Bend Sr. H.S., Ore. 1958-63; dir. of instrn., Arcadia Unif. Sch. Dist., 1964-68; vis. lectr., Claremont Grad. Sch., 1966-68; Dep. Supt., Lake Wash. Sch. Dist., Wash., 1968-69; Asst. Supt., 1969-76; Dep. Supt., Instrn., Glendale Unif. Sch. Dist., 1976---. Contbr. to profl. journs. of edn. Honors: Danforth Found. Fellow, 1976; Phi Gamma Phi; Soc. Sci. hon. Phi Delta Kappa Edn. hon.; named one of outstanding young men in Am., 1966. Bd. dir.: Glendale Camp Fire Girls, 1978; Glendale Law & Order Soc., 1977---; C. of C., Kirkland, Wash., 1973-76; Willamette Univ. Alumni Assn. 1972-76; Coop. Wash. Edn. Centers, 1972-75. USNR, 1950-54. Mem.: Gateway/Glendale Kiwanis Club; Masonic Lodge; Phi Delta Theta,hpt. pres. 1954. Republican precinct committeeman, 1957. Protestant Lay Leader, Ch. Sch. Supt. Rec.: jogging, fishing. Home: 5334 Ramsdell, La Crescenta, CA 91214; Office: 223 N. Jackson, Glendale, CA 91206.

ENDICOTT, JOHN P.
Corporate President
b. Mar. 27, 1918, Pomona, Calif.; s. Paul (former mem. Fed. Home Loan Bank Bd., former pres., U.S. Savings & Loan League) and Marie (Roe) Endicott; B.A., Pomona Coll., 1939; M.B.A., Harvard Bus. Sch., 1941; m. Jean Helmick, 1941, Claremont, Calif.; 1 son Stephen S., b. 1949. Career: Schedules mgr., Douglas Aircraft Co., L.B., 1941-46; exec. v.p./dir., Swedlow Plastics Co., 1946-61; principal, Arthur Young & Co., L.A., 1961-63; exec. v.p./dir., Babcock Electronics Corp., 1963-69; pres., chief exec., dir., Sierracin Corp., 1969---. Dir.: Home Builders Savings & Loan Assn., W. Coast chpt. 1965-68, 1978---; WEMA, 1966-69, chmn. L.A. Council 1968-69; Costa Mesa C. of C., 1965-68; Harvard Bus. Sch. Assn. of S. Calif. 1965-67, 1975-77. Mem. Listed Co. Advis. Com., Am. Stock Exchange, 1978---. Pres., Pomona Coll. Alumni Assn., 1961; v.p. Nat. Security Indsl. Assn., 1978---. Mem. Am. Mgmt. Assn. 1955---. Clubs: Hacienda Golf, 1963-70; Woodland Hills Country, 1970---; L.A. Athletic, 1948-51; Jonathan, 1961-63. Rec.: golf, travel. Home: 4505 Haskell Ave., Encino, CA 91436; Office: 12780 San Fernando Rd., Sylmar, CA 91342.

ENDLER, HARVEY M.
Aircraft Company Executive
b. Feb. 11, 1935, Chicago; s. Joseph and Sadie Endler; bro., James A. Endler, pharmaceutical atty., Chicago; B.S., Univ. Ill., 1956; M.S., Calif. Inst. of Tech., 1958; m. Nancy Lee Kane, Aug. 27, 1965, L.A. Career: with Hughes Aircraft Co., Culver City, 1956-59; microwave proj. mgr., Micromega Corp., Venice, 1960-69; mgr., microwave dept., Guide Industries, Sun Valley, 1969-73; sect. head, Space and Communications Group, Hughes Aircraft Co., 1973---. Mem. IEEE Profl. and tech. group on Microwave Theory and Techniques. Rec.: skiing, jogging. Home: 7236 W. 90th St., L.A., CA 90045; Office: P.O.B. 92919, L.A., CA 90009.

ENGEL, A. RICHARD
Cosmetic Company Owner
b. Dec. 10, 1915, Detroit, Mich.; s. Albert Frederick and Edna (Peppler) Engel; B.A., Principia Coll. 1938; m. Gail L. Lund, Chicago, Ill., Aug. 30, 1941 (div. Feb. 22, 1974); m. Frances Rainsford, L.A., Mar. 1, 1974; son, Eric Richard, b. Mar. 1, 1950. Career: Salesman, 1945-47; est. Gail Richard, Inc. (cosmetic wholesale bus.), propr.-pres.-exec. dir. 1947---. Spec. Training Unit, U.S. Army (1943-45), WW II. Mem.: L.A. Philanthropic Found.; N.Y. Philatelic Found.; L.A. World Affairs Council; Commonwealth Club of Calif.; Philatelic Club, L.A.; Collectors Club, N.Y. Am. Philatelic Soc. Chr. Sci. Hobby: stamp and coin collecting. Rec.: swimming, badminton, piano. Home: 125 S. Carmelina Ave., W.L.A., CA 90049; Office: 161 S. Western Ave., L.A., CA 90004.

ENGEL, MARVIN L.
Dermatologist -- Professor
b. May 12, 1936, Kansas City, Mo.; s. David and Sadye (Shafter) Engel; B.A., Stanford Univ., 1956, M.E., 1959; m. Sara Mizrachi, July 24, 1967, Jerusalem, Israel; daughters, Renat, b. May 25, 1969; Shoshana, b. Nov. 1, 1973; Tamar, b. Nov. 20, 1975; son, Dan, b. Oct. 13, 1970. Career: Internship, Phila. Gen. Hosp., 1959-60; postdoctoral fellow, genetics, Stanford Univ., 1960-61, residency in dermatology, 1960-63; sr. investigator, Nat. Cancer Inst., 1963-65; guest prof., Dermatology Dept., 1965; guest physician, Hosp. St. Louis, Paris, France, 1966; attending physician, Kupat Holim Clin., Jerusalem, 1966-67; clin. asst. prof. of dermatology, Univ. Calif., S.F., 1967---. Mil.: U.S. Pub. Health Serv., N.I.H., Bethesda, Md., 1963-65. Jewish. Home 169 Requa Rd., Piedmont, CA 94611; Office: 1515 Ygnacio Valley Rd., Walnut Creek, CA 94598.

ENGELSEN, EDWARD GEORGE
International Economist
b. Oct. 29, 1922, Portland, Ore.; s. Olaf J. and Jennie (Johnson) Engelsen; B.S., Linfield Coll., 1944; USNR Midshipman Sch., Northwestern Univ., 1944; B. Internat. Mgmt., Am. Graduate Sch. of Internat. Mgmt, 1947; m. Celeste Hidalgo, Nov. 7, 1948, Los Gatos, Calif. Career: International Div., Bank of California, 1947---. Editor/author, Internat. Div.'s quarterly economic review, 1967-76. Publ. work includes: The Euro-Dollar Market, 1967; International Liquidity — Adequacy & Stability, 1967; The Once & Future Europe, 1971; Petrodollars Proliferating, 1975; Dimensions of the Developing North-South Dialogue — The New World Economic Order, 1976. Lt. JG, USNR, active duty, 1943-46, Pacific and Atlantic theatres, anti-submarine warfare. Mem.: Theta Chi, Am. Economic Assn., Nat. Foreign Trade Council, World Affairs Council of No. Calif., AGSIM Alumni Assn. Office: P.O.B. 45000, San Francisco, CA 94145.

ENGLE, RAPHAEL
Graphic Designer
b. June 6, 1934, Calgary, Alberta, Can.; s. Ely and Lilian Engle; cousin, Monica Engle, concert pianist; cousin, Marylin Engle, concert pianist; B.P.A., Art Center Coll. of Design, 1959; M.A., UCLA, 1973; m. Anne Jiry, 1960, L.A.; chil.: Elysa, b. 1963; Shaena, b. 1965. Career: designer with Porter and Goodman, 1959-60; cons. to McCann-Erickson Advt., 1960-63; pres., Ray Engle & Assocs., 1963---; also mem. faculty, Art Center Coll. of Design, 1960---. Mem.: Advis. bd., Noland Paper Co.; advis., L.A. Trade Tech. Coll.; advis. city of L.A. Employment Review Bd. Awards: Cannes Film Festival, 1961; N.Y. Art Directors Club, 1965, 68; Am. Inst. of Graphic Arts, 1960, 62, 63, 68; CA Magazine, 1963, 65, 68; Internat. Center for Typographic Arts, 1964, 69; U.S. Dept. of Commerce, 1967; Type Directors Club, 1965; Trademarks of the World, 1969. Mem.: Soc. of Art Center Alumni, pres. 1967; UCLA Alumni; Marina City Club; Oceanic Soc.; Pac. Mariners Yacht Club; Am. Inst. of Graphic Arts. Hobbies: music, photog. Rec.: yachting, scuba diving, tennis. Home: 2937 Nichols Canyon Rd., L.A., CA 90046; Office: 626 S. Kenmore Ave., L.A., CA 90005.

ENGLERT, ROBERT DIXON
Executive, Dresser Industries, Inc.
b. Feb. 11, 1920, Portland, Ore.; s. Robert Lincoln and Blanche May (Dixon) Englert; B.S., chem., Univ. of Portland, 1942; M.S., chem., Ore. State Univ., 1944, B.S. chem. engring., 1944; Ph.D., chem., Univ. Colo., 1949; m. Patricia Dubb, Feb. 12, 1954, Palo Alto, Calif.; chil.: Janice (Cannon), b. 1945; Jolene (Murphy), b. 1948; Nancy Jane, b. Oct. 15, 1957. Career: Organic chemist, Stanford Research Inst., Menlo Park, 1949-55; Stanford Research Inst., Exec. Dir., Co. Calif. Labs., Irvine, 1955-70; vice pres. and gen. mgr., Environmental Tech. Div., Dresser Industries, Inc., 1970-76; vice pres. & gen. mgr., Advanced Technology Center, Dresser Industries, Inc., 1976---. Holder 12 patents; contbr. 12 profl. publs. USNR, 1942-44. Mem.: Air Pollution Control Assn., Am. Chem. Soc.; AAAS; Sigma Xi; Am. Oil Chem. Soc.; Calif. Acad. of Sci.; N.Y. Acad. of Sci.; Phi Lambda Upsilon; Am. Inst. Chem.; Balboa Bay Club. Protestant. Hobbies: electronics, ham radio. Rec.: tennis. Home: 1312 Sandcastle Dr., Corona del Mar, CA 92625; Office: 1702 McGaw (P.O.B. 19566), Irvine, CA 92713.

ENGLISH, WILLIAM DAVID
Scientist
b. July 11, 1925, Toronto, Can.; s. William D.F. and Frances Mary (Clark) English; B.Sc., Univ. of Manitoba, 1946; M.Sc., McGill Univ. 1950; Ph.D., Pa. State Univ., 1955; Registered Profl. Chem.: Province of Quebec, (accredited) Am. Inst. of Chem.; m. Madeline Mary Zunic, Winnipeg, Can., Sept. 21, 1946; chil.: Patricia Ann, b. Aug. 31, 1956; Robert David, b. Dec. 19, 1958; Randall James, b. Mar. 3, 1961. Career: Sci. ofcr., Def. Research Chem. Labs., Ottawa, Can. 1950-52; research chem., U.S. Borax Research, Anaheim, Calif. 1957-62; research scientist, Astropower Lab., Douglas Aircraft, Anaheim, 1962-64; sr. research sci., 1964-66; group leader, 1966---. Patentee: 30 chem. patents in 7 countries. Contrib. approx. 25 profl. articles on various chem. researches, publ. sci. journs; ed. Cryogenic Tech. 1964---. Dir., at Large, Cryogenic Soc. of Am. (serv. many coms.), 1966---; fellow, Am. Chem. Soc., So. Calif. Acad. Scis., Chem. Inst. of Can., Sociedad Quimica de Mexico, Corp. of Profl. Chems. of Quebec, Soc. of Aerospace Materials and Process Engrs., Research Soc. of Am., Phi Kappa Phi, Phi Lambda Upsilon, Sigma Xi. Evangelical. United Brethren. Hobbies: model railroading, philately. Home: 852 S. Oakwood St., Orange, CA 92667; Office: 23800 Santa Ana Canyon, Anaheim, CA.

ENSSLIN, THEODORE G.
Mayor of Porterville
b. June 24, 1927, Porterville; s. Theodore G. and Lula P. (Penning) Ensslin; desc. Johann Ensslin, 1st mayor of Ruetlingen, Germ.; desc. Andrew Jackson; A.A., 1947; B.A., 1949; M.A., 1976; Ed.D., 1978; m. Dorothy E. Campbell; chil.: Marti, Steven, Lisa, Jeri, Mia, David (8 grandchildren); Career: Coach-Educator, 1949-50, also pub. rels. in secondary schs., 1950; Agriculture Fin. Mgr., 1950---; agent, N.Y. Life Ins. Co., 1958-78, Life Mem. Million Dollar Round Table; Mayor, City of Porterville, 1977-79. Mem.: Sigma Delta Psi, 1949 (nat.

Athletic frat.); Nat. Decathlon Chmn. 1971, 73; author: History of Organiz. of Nat. Decathlon, 1978; Tulare Kings Counties Underwriters Assn. pres. 1960; Exchange Club, pres. 1959; dist. chmn. BSA; bd. dir., Univ. of Nev. Alumni Assn. of Porterville; Coll. Patrons Assn.; life mem. U.S. Nat. Track & Field Team; Alpha Tau Omega, 1949. L.D.S. Ch., Bishop 1951-58. Hobby: genealogy. Rec.: track and field. Home: 143 Carmelita, Porterville, CA 93257; Office: 11 E. Putnam, Porterville, CA 93257.

ENTREKIN, GUY BATTIN, JR.
Chairman of the Board, Bourns, Inc.
b. Dec. 6, 1918, West Chester, Pa.; s. Battin and Flora Delma (Swayne) Entrekin; B.S.E.E., Drexel Univ., 1941, postgrad. Stevens Inst. of Tech., 1945-48; grad., Command & Gen. Staff Sch., AUS, 1943; m. Louanna Hanby, June 16, 1941, Wilmington, Del.; chil.: Sharon (Loge), b. June 18, 1947; Susan (Griffin), b. Feb. 16, 1949; David, b. Dec. 6, 1953. Career: Engr., Western Electric Co., 1945-48; Internat. Resistor Co., Phila., 1949-51, chief. prod. engr. 1951-55, div. gen. mgr. 1955-58; pres. Communications Accessories Co., Lee's Summit, Mo., 1959-62; div. gen. mgr., Bourns, Inc., Riverside, 1963-68, president's staff, 1969-74, exec. v.p., 1975-76, pres., 1976, chmn. bd. and chief exec. ofcr., 1977---; also chmn. bd., Precision Monolithics, Inc.; pres. & dir., Bourns Internat. Ltd.; dir. Bourns NV/SA, Bourns DISC, Bourns Puerto Rico, Inc., BMS Data Handling, Ohmic S.A., AIM, Inc., Murata-Bourns Y.K. Maj., Army Signal Corps, AUS, 1941-45. Mem.: IEEE, 1941---; Am. Mgmt. Assn., 1963---; Am. Electronics Assn. (formerly WEMA), 1963---, dir. 1976-77. Rec.: boating. Office: Bourns, Inc., 1200 Columbia Ave., Riverside, CA 92507.

ENZLER, ELLEN ROCHELLE
Investment Company Executive
b. Jan. 13, 1943, New York; d. Milton Harold and Lillian Bernice (Arbeit) Enzler; B.A., N.Y. Univ.; grad. studies, fin. & investments, City Coll., Baruch Grad. Sch. of Bus. Career: Security analyst: Smith Barney & Co., 1964; Bache & Co., 1965-68; Venture Capital Consulting, 1968-69; H. Hentz and Co., 1970-71; asst. v.p. research, E.F. Hutton & Co., 1972---. Lectr. on investments to numerous orgns. Mem.: L.A. Soc. of Fin. Analysts, pres. of Seminar Com.; past pres. and mem., L.A. Soc. Technological Analysts; past mem. N.Y. Soc. Security Analysts; mem. Ducks Unltd.; Nat. Rifle Assn. Hobbies: big game hunting, book collecting. Office: 888 W. Sixth St., L.A., CA 90017.

EPSTEIN, LOIS BARTH
Physician — Professor
b. Dec. 29, 1933, Cambridge, Mass.; d. Benjamin and Mary Frances (Perlmutter) Barth; A.B., Radcliffe (cum laude), 1955; M.D., Harvard Med. Sch., 1959; m. Dr. Charles Epstein, June 10, 1956, Brookline, Mass.; chil.: David Alexander, b. Sept. 18, 1961; Jonathan Akiba, b. Dec. 8, 1963; Paul Michael, b. Sept. 17, 1967; Joanna Marguerite, b. May 21, 1975. Career: Resident in Pathology, Peter Bent Brigham Hosp., Boston, 1959-60; intern in med., New England Center Hosp., 1960-61; research med. ofcr., Nat. Inst. of Health, 1962-63, 1966-67; NIH Post doctoran and NIH Spec. Fellow, 1963-64, 1964-65; asst., then assoc. research physician, Cancer Research Inst., Univ. Calif., S.F., 1969-74, assoc. dir., 1974-77, Research Assoc., 1977---; Assoc. Prof. of Pediatrics, Univ. Calif. Sch. of Med., 1974---. Contbr. 35+ sci. papers to med. journs. and books. Mem.: NIH Study Sect. on Immunological Scis., 1977---; past mem. NIAID Immunology Training Grants Com., 1972-74; Allergy & Immunology Com. 1974-76. Mem.: Am. Soc. Clin. Investigation, 1977---; Am. Assn. Immunologists, 1972---; Soc. for Pediatric Research, 1977---; Am. Soc. Hematology, 1972---; Am. Assn. Cancer Edn., 1975---; Am. Soc. Cancer Research, 1977---; AMA; CMA. Jewish. Hobbies: working with glass, sewing. Home: 19 Noche Vista Lane, Tiburon, CA 94920; Office: Cancer Research Inst., Univ. Calif., San Francisco, CA 94143.

EPSTEIN, ROBERT STANLEY
Attorney at Law
b. Oct. 24, 1941, Omaha, Nebr.; s. Sidney L. and Gertrude Epstein; B.S., Northwestern Univ., 1963; J.D., Stanford Law Sch., 1966; m. Catherine Aubale, Jan. 15, 1978, San Francisco. Career: clerk to Justice Raymond Sullivan, Calif. Supreme Ct., 1966; assoc. atty., Heller, Ehrman, White & McAuliffe, S.F., 1967-71; partner, Williams, Van Hoesen, Brigham & Epstein, Attorneys at Law, S.F., 1972---. Bd. of Editors, Stanford Law Review, 1964-66. Dir. The Guardsmen, 1976-79; bd. of govs., AIESEC, U.S. Alumni Bd. Mem.: Univ. Club; Phi

Epsilon Pi frat. Hobby: sailing. Office: 235 Montgomery St., Suite 450, S.F., CA 94104.

EPSTEIN, WILLIAM LOUIS
Professor of Dermatology
b. Sept. 6, 1925, Cleveland, Oh.; s. Norman N. and Gertrude E. (Hirsch) Epstein; A.B., Univ. Calif., Berkeley; M.D., Univ. Calif., S.F.; m. Joan Goldman, Jan. 29, 1954; chil.: Wendy, Steven. Career: Instr., Univ. of Penn., 1956-57; asst. prof., Dept. of Dermatology, Univ. Calif., S.F., 1957-63, assoc. prof., 1963-69, prof., 1969---; acting chmn. of dept. 1966-69, chmn., Dept. of Dermatology, 1970---. Research assoc., Francis I. Proctor Found., 1966---; Cancer Research Inst., 1968---; Cons. in Dermatology, Laguna Honda Hosp., Napa State Hosp., San Quentin Prison; Calif. Med. Facility; Stanford Research Inst.; VA Medical Center, S.F.; U.S. Dept. HEW; U.S. Navy Bureau of Med. & Surgery. AUS, 1944-46. Contbr. numerous articles to sci. journs and books. Diplomate Am. Bd. of Dermatology. Mem.: Am. Acad. of Derm.; CMA; Soc. of Investigative Derm.; Pac. Derm. Soc.; Assn. of Profs. of Derm.; Dermatological Soc. of Poland. Democrat. Address: Dept. of Dermatology, U.C., S.F., S.F., CA 94143.

ERBURU, ROBERT F.
President, Times Mirror Co.
b. Sept. 27, 1930, Ventura, Calif.; B.A. (journalism), USC; LL.B., Harvard Law Sch.; m. Lois Stone, 1954; daus.: Susan Kit, b. Sept. 23, 1956; Lisa Ann, b. Feb. 22, 1960. Career: Atty., Gibson, Dunn & Crutcher firm, L.A., 1955-61; gen. counsel-secty. Times Mirror Co. 1961, v.p. 1965-69, bd. dirs. 1968, sr. v.p. 1969-73, pres. 1973---; secty.-dir. Times Mirror Found.; secty. Pfaffinger Found. Mem.: dir. Am. Soc. Corporate Secretaries; So. Calif. Com., Harvard Law Sch. Fund; L.A. Com. on Foreign Rels.; Am., Calif., L.A. Co. Bar Assns.; Sigma Delta Chi. Home: 1518 Blue Jay Way, L.A., CA 90069; Office: Times Mirror Sq., L.A., CA.

ERLICH, ELEANOR EWING
Mathematician — Political Worker
b. Jan. 18, 1918, Pontiac, Ill.; d. William McCord and Sarah (Lovelock) Ewing; desc. Robert Creswell, Am. Revolutionary War patriot; B.A., 1941, and M.A., 1943, Univ. of Ill.; postgard., Harvard Alumni Coll., 1971-75; Cornell Alumni Coll., 1975; m. Richard Erlich, July 7, 1945, Los Alamos, N. Mex.; chil.: Prof. Paul Ewing, b. Aug. 8, 1948; Joan Ewing, b. July 10, 1950. Career: Math. Tchr., Engring. Aid Pgm., Pratt-Whitney Aircraft, E. Hartford, Conn., 1943-44; supr., IBM Machineoperators, Theoretical Div., Los Alamos Scientific Lab., 1944-46; Math. Asst., Cornell Univ., Ithaca, N.Y., 1946; Alternate Del. Democratic Nat. Convetion, 1968; internal affiars chmn., N.Y. state legislaive forum, 1969; bd. mem., Upper Mohawk Hudson; Phi Beta Kappa, 1975-76; bd. mem. Newcomer's Club, 1976. Award: appreciation of service, War Dept., 1945. Mem.: Phi Beta Kappa, 1940, Pi Mu Epsilon, 1940; Friends of the Saratoga Lib., photog. 1978-79; Radcliff Club; S.F. Opera Guild; Founders 100, Univ. Ill. Democratic Niskayuna Town Com., secty. treas. 1968. Presbyterian. Hobbies: photog., bird watching. Home: 14664 Wildberry Lane, Saratoga, CA 95070.

ERLICH, MARTIN
Library Director
b. June 20, 1924, Phila., Pa.; s. Louis and Tema Erlich; B.A. (hist.), Temple Univ., Phila. 1947; B.S. (lib. sci.), Drexel Inst., Phila. 1948; M.A., Wayne State Univ., Detroit, 1954; m. Florrie Hancock, Arlington, Va., Sept. 15, 1951; chil.: Daniel Tim, Brenda Ann, Robert Edward, Philip Alexander. Career: Lib., Dearborn and Detroit, Mich.; head librn., U.S. Coast Guard, Search & Rescue Agcy., Wash., D.C. 1953-56; dir. Mineola Mem. Lib., N.Y. 1956-64; head librn., Stanislaus Co. Free Lib., Modesto, Calif. 1965-66; lib. dir. Orange Pub. Lib., Calif. 1966---. Contrib. approx 20 articles publ. profl. journs. Pfc, AUS, 3rd Army, 1943-45, WW II. Mem.: Am., Calif. Lib. Assns.; Orange Co. Pub. Lib. Admrs.; Pub, Lib. Execs. of So. Calif.; (charter) Natl. Hist. Soc. Hobby: chess. Rec.: bird watching. Home: 1995 Namuria, Orange, CA 92665; Office: Orange Public Library, 101 N. Center St., Orange, CA 92666.

ERTESZEK, JAN J.
Company President
b. Dec. 26, 1913, Krakow, Poland; s. Mer and Rosalia Erteszek; M.L. (magister juris), Univ. of Krakow, 1936, LL.D. 1938; postgrad London, Eng. 1937-38; m. Olga

Bertram, Lvov, Russia, Dec. 6, 1939; chil.: Victoria R., b. May 15, 1944; Mary J., b. Oct. 4, 1945; Christine S., b. Oct. 3, 1949. Career: Export-import bus., N.Y. 1939; pres. Olga Co., Inc., L.A., 1941---. Awards: Freedom Found. Award for Counter Offensive Against Communism in U.S. News. Mem.: dir. Laymen's Movement, 1957---; dir. Goodwill Industries, 1958---. Presbyterian. Home: 631 Bonhill Rd., L.A., CA 90049; Office: 7915 Haskell Ave., Van Nuys, CA 91409.

ERVIN, JOHN WESLEY,
Lawyer — Educator — Minister
b. June 22, 1917, L.A.; s. Frank Earl and Lillian Pearl (Gray) E.; student UCLA, 1935-39, J.D., 1944; LL.M. (research fellow 1945-47), Harvard, 1945, S.J.D., 1955; m. Patricia Connelly, May 24, 1958; chil.: (by previous marriage) Nancy Gray, Shelley Hutchinson, John Chipman Gray. Career: Admitted to Calif. bar, 1944; research asst. justice Calif. Supreme Ct., 1943-44; prof. law, dir. and editor annual Insts. on Fed. Taxation, USC 1947-70; sr. mem. firm Ervin, Cohen & Jessup, Beverly Hills, 1953---; advis. to secty. treasury on fed. tax legislation, 1955. Author: Federal Taxation and the Family, 1955. Founder, Found. for Estab. Internat. Criminal Ct. sec., dir. Philos. Research Soc., Internat. Communications Found.; bd. dirs. So. Calif. Family Counseling Center. Distinguished Internat. Criminal Lawyer certificate 1972. Mem.: Am. (chmn., publs. com. taxation sect. 1954-55), Calif., Beverly Hills bar assns.; Am. Law Inst.; Am. Judicature Soc.; UN Assn. L.A. (pres. 1973---, bd. dirs.); Order of Coif; Phi Delta Phi; Ordained to ministry Ch. of People, local pastor United Methodist Ch. Office: 9401 Wilshire Blvd., Beverly Hills, CA 90212.

ERWIN, DONALD CARROLL
University Professor
b. Nov. 24, 1920, Concord, Nebr.; s. Robert and Carol (Saxson) Erwin; B.S., Univ. of Nebr., 1949, M.A., 1950; Ph.D., Univ. Calif., Davis, 1953; m. Veora Endres, Aug. 15, 1948, Lincoln, Nebr.; chil.: J. Daniel, b. Dec. 29, 1958; Myriam, b. Apr. 4, 1961. Career: Prof., Dept. of Plant Pathology, Univ. of Calif., Riverside, 1953---. Guggenheim Fellow, 1959-60; contrb. 76 research papers in plant pathology to profl. journs. and books. AUS M.C., 1942-46. Mem.: Am. Phytopathological Soc.; Am. Inst. of Biological Scis.; Mycological Soc. of Am.; Sigma Xi (research frat.). Catholic. Home: 3376 Sunnyside Dr., Riverside, CA 92521; Office: Univ. Calif., Dept. of Plant Pathology, Riverside, CA 92521.

ESSEX, ROBERT WM., III
Educator
b. New Orleans, La.; s. Robert Wm., Jr. and Jessie (Stewart) Essex; B.S., 1960; M.P.A., 1970; M.L.S., 1971; Ph.D., 1976; m. Jean Howard (div.), Mar. 20, 1961, Boston, Mass. Career: Serologist, L.A. Harbor Gen. Hosp. 1963-66; vice principal, counselor, librarian, instr. L.A. Unified Sch. Dist., 1966-74; coordinator of instruction, L.A. Southwest Coll., 1974-77; acting asst. dean of instruction (learning resources), L.A. City Coll., 1977-78; acting asst. dean of instrn., West Los Angeles Coll., 1978; coordinator of instruction, 1978---. Mem. Pi Sigma Alpha, 1970, Catholic, Knight of Columbus, Knight of St. Peter Claver. Hobbies: jazz, creole cooking. Rec.: travel, jogging, tennis. Home: 4516 Don Rodolfo Pl., L.A., CA 90008.

ETHERIDGE, RICHARD EMMET
Zoologist
b. Sept. 16, 1929, Houston, Texas; s. Jerry and Ethel Etheridge; B.S., Tulane Univ., 1951; M.S., Univ. Mich., 1952, Ph.D., 1959. Career: Postdoctoral Fellow, Natl. Sci. Found., USC, 1960; mem. faculty, Dept. of Zoology, San Diego State Univ., 1961---; also Research Assoc., L.A. Co. Museum, 1960---; Curator of Herpetology, San Diego Natural Hist. Mus., 1962-72; bd. dir., So. Calif. Acad. of Scis., 1963-69; bd. of govs., Am. Soc. of Ichthyologists and Herpetologists, 1959-61, 1967-70; exec. council Herpetologist's League, 1965-68; bd. dir., Soc. for the Study of Amphibians and Reptiles, 1969-72; Editorial bd., Herpetologica, 1963-77; contrb. 30+ articles in herpetology and paleontology to sci. journs., 1950---. USN, 1952-56. Home: 4865 Lucille Pl., S.D., CA 92115; Office: Dept. Zoology, San Diego State Univ., San Diego, CA 92115.

ETLIN, EVE
Psychodramatist
b. Dec. 28, 1932, Brooklyn, N.Y.; d. Harry and Lilly Rosman; credential in psychodrama, Moreno Inst., N.Y.; student behavioral scis., Brooklyn Coll. and N.Y. Univ.;

student with Dr. Lewis Yablonsky of Inst. of Psychodrama, L.A. and Dr. Ernest Fantel, VA Hosp., W. L.A. M. Jack Etlin (internat. real estate broker-financier, lectr. on motivation), May 28, 1977, L.A.; chil.: Harlan Seth Baum, b. Feb. 28, 1957; Tracy Scott Baum, b. Jan. 4, 1959. Career: with Gateways Hosp. and Mental Health Center, L.A.; Camarillo State Hosp. and Metropolitan State Hosp., Norwalk (became interested in psychodrama, 1966, while working with suicidal patients in a pilot program); pres., Achievement Assocs., Century City, L.A. ---; v.p., Jack Etlin Realty Co., Inc. Mem.: ORT, 1970---; Inst. of Psychodrama, 1968---; Acad. of Psychodrama; Sociometry and Group Psychotherapy. Jewish. Hobbies: dancing, bicycling, acting. Home: 848 S. Holt Ave., L.A., CA 90035; Office: 10100 Santa Monica Blvd., Suite 870, Century City No., L.A., CA 90067.

EU, MARCH FONG
California Secretary of State
b. March 29, 1927, Oakdale, Calif.; d. Yuen and Shin (Shee) Kong; ed. B.S., Univ. of Calif., Berkeley; M. Ed., Mills Coll.; Ed.D., Stanford Univ.; postgrad. Columbia Univ., Calif. State Coll., Hayward; Calif. State Tchg. Credentials, Jr. Coll., adm.-supv.; chil.: Mathew Kipling, Marsha Suyin. Career: Div. chmn. Univ. Calif. Med. Center, S.F., dental Hygienist, Oakland Public Schs.; div. supv. Alameda Co. Schs.; lectr., Mills Coll., Oakland; mem. Alameda Co. Bd. Edn. 1956-66; pres. 1961-62; v.p. Alameda Co. Sch. Bds. Assn. 1963-65, pres. 1965; spec. cons. Calif. State Dept. Edn.; edn.-legislative cons. Santa Clara Co. Ofc. of Edn. Elected to Calif. State Legislature, 15th Assembly Dist., chmn. Assembly Com. on Environmental Quality, other coms.; elected Calif. Secty. of State, Nov. 1974. Awards: Annual Award for Outstanding Achievement, Eastbay Intercultural Fellowship, 1959; Phoebe Apperson Hearst Distinguished Bay Area Woman of Yr. award, 1968; Woman of Yr. Calif. Retail Liquor Dealers Inst. 1969; Loyalty Day Award, VFW 1970; Merit Cit., Calif. Assn. of Adult Edn. Admrs. 1970. Mem.: Oakland Econ. Dev. Council; v. chmn. adv. com. Youth Stu. Centers-Ford Found. Proj. 1962-63; com. Council of Soc. Planning; judge, Mayor's Com. on Excellence of Youth, 1964; bd. dirs. Oakland YWCA 1965; (hon.) So. Calif. Dental Assn.; (charter) pres. Chinese Young Ladies Soc. of Oakland; CTA; (hon, life, charter) pres. Elm PTA; AAUW; Delta Kappa Gamma; dir. Key Women for Kennedy, 1963; dir. Key Women of Alameda Co. 1964; del Dem. Natl. Conv. 1968; exec. com. Calif. State Dem. Central Com., many others. Office: 1320 J St., Sacto., CA 95814.

EVANS, BRYN BENNETT
CPA — Civic Leader
b. July 21, 1919, Amsterdam, Oh.; s. Daniel and Margaret (Bennett) Evans; B.S. (cum laude), Miami Univ. 1941; postgrad. U.S. Naval Acad. 1944-45; m. Lynn R. Peddicord, Sebring, Oh., Sept. 7, 1941; chil.: Bryn, Jr., b. June 7, 1943; Lawrence, b. Oct. 1, 1945; Richard, b. Oct. 23, 1947; Patricia, b. Dec. 2, 1951. Career: Assoc. with Peat, Marwick, Mitchel & Co.; CPA firm, Detroit, 1941-42; Prof. Univ. of N. Mex., 1945-46; Charles M. Ross & Co., CPAs, Riverside, Calif., 1946-47; staff acct., Diehl and Co., Riverside, 1947; CPA, Calif. 1948---; partner Batzle and Evans (formerly Diehl and Co.), Riverside, 1948-54; sr. partner, Diehl, Evans and Co., Santa Ana, 1954---; partner Diehl, Evans and Co., Santa Maria and Lompoc, 1963---; treas.-dir., S.A. Lincoln Corp 1959---; dir. Larry Armour Co. 1959---; dir. V.B. Anderson Co. 1968---. Lt. (s.g.), USN, Pac. Theatre, Aircraft Carriers USS Nassau, USS Breton (1942-44) WW II. Awards: 2 Battle Stars; Mem.: Phi Eta Sigma, 1938---; Delta Sigma Pi, 1939---; Omicron Delta Kappa, 1941---; Phi Beta Kappa, 1941---; Calif. Soc. of CPAs, 1948---; Am. pres.-dir.-treas., Red Hill Tennis Club, 1958-62; Natl. Assn. of Accts. 1960---; Orange Co. Estate Planning Council, 1960---; Santa Ana Country Club, pres.-treas.-dir, Santa Ana C. of C. 1967---; Repub. Assocs. of Orange Co.; (past) chmn. bd. trustees. Home: 1111 S.E. El Camino Lane, Santa Ana, CA; Office: 1910 N. Bush, Santa Ana, CA.

EVANS, CAROL ELIZABETH
Editor -- Researcher
b. Dec. 19, 1905, Ohio, Ill.; d. Arthur T. and Mary (Waterman) Evans; student, Univ. Chicago, 1938-41. Career: Personal secty., Gov. Adlai E. Stevenson of Ill., 1948-61; Research Assoc., Dept. of History, Univ. of Hawaii, Honolulu, 1966-72; asst. editor, "The Papers of Adlai E. Stevenson," 1966-72, 8 Vols. Mem.: L.A. World Affairs Council; Internat. Student Center, UCLA. Democrat. Presbyterian. Hobbies: sewing, needlework. Rec.: swimming. Home: 11650 National Blvd., Apt. 12,

L.A., CA 90064; Office: 1023 Hilgard Ave., L.A., CA 90024.

EVANS, GEORGE ROBERT, JR.
Corporate Executive
b. June 24, 1931, San Antonio, Tex.; s. George Robert and Maude Ellen (Davis) Evans; B.S., Wagner Coll., 1953; postgrad. Northwestern Univ., 1960-61; Wharton Sch. of Bus., 1963; m. Alma Behling, Feb. 23, 1952, White Plains, N.Y.; chil.: Sandra (Livingston), b. Nov. 1952; G. Robert III; Terri (Tavrmond); John; James Patrick; Michelle. Career: Prod. Engr., U.S. Gypsum Co., 1953-69; with U.S. Gypsum Co., 1953-69; Prodn. engr., works mgr., corp. dir. of mktg., v.p. and gen. mgr. Western Div., pres., U.S. Gypsum Export Co.; pres. and chief exec. officer, Kingsport Press Inc., 1969-71; pres. and chief exec. officer, Arcata Graphics Corp., 1971-73; exec. v.p. and chief operating ofcr., Arcata Corp., Menlo Park, 1973---. Dir.: Real Estate Data Inc. 1973---; Graphic Arts Technical Found., 1974---; Environmental Conservation Bd. of Graphics Industries, 1970-75; Book Manufacturers Inst., 1969-73; YMCA, 1971-73; Trustee, Wagner Coll., Staten Island, N.Y. ---; advis. com., Rochester Inst. of Tech., 1974---; Conf. Bd., 1973---. Mem.: Rotary, Lions, Commonwealth Club of Calif.; Newcomen Soc. of No. Am., 1970---. Lutheran. Rec.: hunt, fish, tennis, golf. Home: 47 Ralston Rd., Atherton, CA 94025; Office: 2750 Sand Hill Rd., Menlo Park, CA 94025.

EVANS, JOHN ALEXANDER
Civic Leader -- Merchant
b. Aug. 17, 1906, Colorado Springs., Colo.; s. John P. (merchant) and Mary Grace (Combe) Evans; B.S, Univ. of Calif., Berkeley, 1929; m. Barbara Lee Matthews; chil.: Norman Clark, b. Jan. 8, 1935; Mary Barbara, b. July 14, 1950; Katherine Lee, b. Jan. 28, 1955. Career: President, John P. Evans Co. 1937---. Lt. Comdr., USNR, naval aviation, continental U.S. and Asiatic-Pac. Theater (1942-46), WW II; Comdr., USNR. Awards: Jr. C. of C. Distinguished Serv. Award (key), 39. Mem.: internat. pres., Theta Delta Chi, 1963-64; Commonwealth Club of S.F.; pres. Toastmasters Club, 1936; bd. dirs., Pomona Community Chest, 1937-39, v.p. 1938-39, gen. campaign chmn. 1938; dir. Pomona C. of C. 1938-41; and 1946-49, v.p. 1940-41; bd. dirs., Rotary Club, 1939---, pres. 1941-42; bd. dirs., Natl. Assn. of Retail Clothiers and Furnishers, 1946---, v.p. 1951---, regional v.p. (West Coast); Elks Lodge, Balboa Yacht Club. Republican. Presbyterian. Hobby: horses (breeding, racing, exhib.). Rec.: sailing, horseback riding. Home: 2519 N. Mountain Ave., Claremont, CA; Office: 269 Pomona Mall West, Pomona, CA 91769.

EVANS, LOUISE
Clinical Psychologist
b. San Antonio, Tex.; d. Henry Daniel and Adela (Pariser) Evans; B.S., Northwestern Univ., 1949; M.Sc. in Psychology, Purdue Univ., 1952; Ph.D. in clin. psychol., 1955; Diplomate in Clin. Psychology, Am. Bd. of Examiners in Profl. Psychol., 1966; m. Tom R. Gambrell, M.D., Feb. 23, 1960, Fullerton, Calif. Career: tch. asst., Purdue Univ., 1950-51; intern, Menninger Found. Topeka State Hosp., 1952-53; staff psychol., Kankakee State Hosp., 1954-55; post-doctoral fellow in child clin. psychol., U.S. Pub. Health Service, Menninger Found., 1955-56; staff psychol., Kings Co. Hosp., Brooklyn, 1957-78; dir. of psychol. clin. and instr., Barnes Hosp., Washington Univ. Sch. of med., St. Louis, Mo., 1959; pvt. practice, Fullerton, 1960---; also psychol. cons., Fullerton Community Hosp., 1960---; staff cons., Martin Luther Hosp., Anaheim, 1963---. Fellowships: Internat. Council of Psychologists Inc.; Royal Soc. of Health; Am. Assn. Advancement of Sci.; Am. Orthopsych. Assn.; Am. Psychol. Assn. Recipient: first Purdue Alumni Assn. Citizenship award, 1975; Service Award, Yuma, Ariz. Head Start Program, 1972; first PTA scholarship Evansville, Ind., 1945; Northwestern Univ. scholarship, 1945. Keynote speaker on programs sponsored by civic, edn., cultural, religious and collegiate organizations, 1950---. Delegate: U.S. and Calif. Traffic Safety Conferences, 1964. Mem. Calif., Orange Co., and L.A. Co. Psychological Assns.; L.A. Soc. of Clin. Psychol.; Am. Acad. of Polit. and Social Sci.; Am. Judicature Soc.; Alumni Assns.; Pi Sigma frat.; Center for the Study of the Presidency; fellow, World Wide Acad. of Scholars. Hobby: antiques. Office: 127 W. Commonwealth Ave., Fullerton, CA 92632.

EVANS, MARJORIE WOODARD
Attorney — Scientist
b. Mar. 15, 1921, Denver, Colo.; d. Raymond George and Mary Adelia (Garvin) Woodard; A.B., Univ. of

Colo., 1942; Ph.D., physical chem., Univ. Calif., Berkeley, 1945; J.D., Stanford Univ Sch. of Law, 1972; m. George W. Evans II (dec.), Jan. 30, 1943, Berkeley; chil.: George, b. Apr. 3, 1949; Anne Garvin, b. Nov. 21, 1956. Career: Scientist: Univ. Calif., Berkeley, Calif. Research Corp., N.Y. Univ., Princeton Univ., Stanford Research Inst., 1942-64; dir., Poulter Lab., Stanford Research Inst., 1964-68; Exec. dit., Physical Scis. Div., Stanford Reserach Inst., 1968-69; prin., Evans Assocs., 1969-75; attorney at law, 1972---; also bd. mem., State of Calif. Air Resources Bd., 1976---. Dir.: Rainier Bancorp. 1976---; The Combustion Inst., 1968---; Regent, Univ. of Santa Clara, 1978---. Awards: George Norlin award, Univ. of Colo.; Centennial Alumnus, Univ. of Colo.; Fellow, Am. Inst. of Aeronautics and Astronautics; Phoebe Hearst Distinguished Woman Award. Contbr. to sci. publs. Mem.: Am. Bar Assn.; Am. Chem. Soc.; Am. Physical Soc.; Am. Inst. of Aeronautics and Astronautics; Phi Beta Kappa; Sigma Xi; Delta Delta Delta. Home: 14511 De Bell Dr., Los Altos Hills, CA 94025; Office: 2600 El Camino Real, Suite 506, Palo Alto, CA 94306.

EWING, EDGAR
Artist — Professor of Fine Arts
b. Jan. 17, 1913, Hartington, Nebr.; s. David E. and Laura (Buckendorf) Ewing; grad. Art Inst. of Chicago, 1931-35; European stu., Edward L. Ryerson Fellowship, 1935-37; m. Suzanne P. Giovan, Chicago, Feb. 12, 1941; Career: Faculty, Art Inst. of Chicago, 1937-43; prof. of fine arts, USC 1946---; Artist, maj. exhibs. (natl. and internat., invitational and jury): Art Inst. of Chicago, Butler Inst. of Am. Art (Youngstown, Oh.), Carnegie Mus. (Pittsburgh), Cincinnati Art Mus., Crocker Mus. (Sacto.), Corcoran Gallery of Art (Wash., D.C.), Dallas Mus. of Fine Arts, Detroit Mus. of Art, Denver Art Mus., deYoung Mem. Mus. (S.F.), Natl. Acad. Design (NYC), Oakland Art Gallery, Otis Art Inst. (LA), Pasa. Art Mus., Smithsonian Inst. Mus. (Wash., D.C.); maj. one-man exhibs.: Syracuse Univ. Gallery, Exeter Acad. Gallery, USC 1946; Pepsi-Cola Gallery, NYC 1947; Stanford Univ. Mus. 1948; deYoung Mus., S.F., 1948 (41 paintings), 1955; many others; repr. in over 300 collections incl.: USC Sch. of Med., Dr. William Calentiner, Leonard Firestone, Harold Ramser, Samuel F.B. Morse (Pebble Beach), Stanley Barbee (Hawaii), Abbott Labs. Collection (N. Chicago). AUS Corps of Engrs.; CPIC, RAF, India; CBI Theatre, 8th Army Hdqrs., Philippines, Japan (1943-46), WW II. Mem.: USC Faculty Club; pres. Calif. Water Color Soc. 1954-55. Home: 4222 Sea View Lane, L.A., CA 90065; Office: Univ. Park, L.A., CA 90007.

F

FABER, DONALD ANDREWS
Hospital Administrator
b. Aug. 8, 1925, Mitchell, S. Dak.; s. George G. and Elizabeth (Andrews) Faber; B.A., Univ. of S. Dak. 1949; M.P.H., Univ. of Calif., Berkeley, 1951; m. Charlene V. Woods, Aug. 12, 1950; chil.: Kimberly Rae, Kelly Ann. Career: Adm. res. Peralta Hosp., Oakland, 1951-52; asst. admr. Weld Co. Gen. Hosp., Greeley, Colo. 1952-54; assoc. admr. Virginia Mason Hosp., Seattle, Wash. 1954-55; exec. v.p. Hollywood Presby. Hosp., L.A., 1965---. Mem.: bd. dirs. Comm. on Adm. Servs. in hosps., 1966---; bd. Adv. Com. for UCLA Reg. Med. Pgms. 1966-68; bd. dirs. Hosp. Council of So. Calif. 1967-69, 1972---, exec. com. 1972---; Cits. Adv. Com., City of L.A. Planning Dept. 1968---; bd. dirs. Comprehensive Health Planning Assn. of L.A. Co., 1968---; bd. dirs. Calif. Hosp. Assn. 1969---; bd. dirs. Cobe Labs., Denver, Colo. 1972; Am. Coll. of Hosp. Admrs., Assn. of Western Hosps., Am. Hosp. Assn., Am. Prot. Hosp. Assn., L.A. C. of C., Hollywood YMCA, Century Club, Town Hall of Calif., Rotary Club. Presbyterian. Home: 19014 Minnehaha St., Northridge, CA 91324; Office: 1322 N. Vermont Ave., L.A., CA 90027.

FACTOR, TED H.
Advertising Agency Executive
b. June 15, 1914, St. Louis, Mo.; s. Nathan and Rose Heiman; student, UCLA, 1931-33; USC, 1933-34; m. Barbara Currey Wood, July 11, 1965, L.A. Career: Foreign publicity dir. Max Factor & Co., 1934-36; pres. Ted H. Factor Agency, 1936-54, name changed to Factor-Breyer, Inc. 1951, merged with Doyle Dane Bernbach, Inc., 1954, sr. v.p. charge West Coast oprns., 1954, exec. v.p. West Coast oprns., 1969-74, chmn. & chief exec. Doyle Dane Bernbach/West and v. chmn.

Doyle Dane Bernbach Internat., 1974---; also dir., mem. exec. com. Econ. Resources Corp. Mem. exec. bd., Art Center Coll. of Design; founding mem. Center Study Democratic Instns. Named Man of Year, western states Advt. Agcy., 1970. Mem.: 4 As; Tau Delta Phi; Beverly Hills Tennis Club, past v.p.; Palm Springs Racquet; World Trade. Home: 1374 Laurel Way, Beverly Hills, CA 90210; Office: 5900 Wilshire Blvd., L.A., CA 90036.

FADIMAN, CLIFTON
Author — Editor
b. May 15, 1904, N.Y.C.; N.Y. Pub. Schs.; B.A., Columbia Univ. 1925; m. Annalee Whitmore (coauthor, "Thunder Out of China," former film and TV writer, Time-Life war corr. in China and Far East); chil.: Jonathan, Kim, Anne. Career: assoc. ed., editor-in-chief, Simon and Schuster book publs.; book ed. The New Yorker, 1933-34; master of ceremonies, Information Please, Quiz Kids, radio pgms. 1938-48; essayist and book critic, columnist, contrib to various mags.; bd. editors-contrib., Ency. Brit. 1959---; cons. ed.-contrib.: Brit. Jr. Encyc., Young Child's Ency.; bd. cons. Ency. Brit. Edn. Corp., Inc.; regents lectr., UCLA 1964-65; cons. Univ. of Calif. Med. Center. Author: Party of One, Any Number Can Play, The American Treasury, 1955; (textbooks) Five American Adventures, and Adventures in American Literature; Fifty Years, 1965; Awards: Clarence Day Award, Am. Lib. Assn. 1969. Mem.: bd. of judges, Book-of-the-Month Club; Calif. Cits. for Better Libraries; Writers War Bd.; bd. dirs. Council for Basic Edn. Home: 4668 Vio Roblada, Santa Barbara, CA 93110.

FAIRBANK, JANE DAVENPORT
Editor
b. Aug. 21, 1918, Seattle, Wash.; d. Harold Edwin and Mildred (Foster) Davenport; A.B. magna cum laude, Whitman Coll., Walla Walla, Wash., 1939; postgrad, Univ. of Washington, Seattle, 1940-42; m. William Martin Fairbank, Aug. 16, 1941, Seattle, Wash.; chil.: William Martin, Jr., b. Jan. 7, 1946; Robert Harold, b. Mar. 4, 1948; Richard Dana, b. Sept. 18, 1950. Career: tch. asst., Physics Dept., Univ. of Washington, Seattle, 1940-42; sci. editor, and sci. staff mem., Radiation Lab., Mass. Inst. of Tech., Cambridge, 1942-45; chmn (editor, conference organizer), Second Careers For Women, Stanford, CA 1970---. Editor: Radar Maintenance Manual (2 vols.) 1945; Second Careers for Women, A View from the San Francisco Peninsula, 1971; Second Careers for Women, Vol. II: A View of Seven Fields from the San Francisco Bay Area, 1975. Found mem. Bay Area Consortium on the Edn. Needs of Women, 1971. Mem. Canada Coll. Citizens Advis. Com., 1968. Pres., Woodside High Sch. P.T.A. 1967-68, editor 1962-63, 64-65. Pres., Stanford Faculty Women's Club, 1975-76, editor 1965-67, 1971-72. Mem.: Phi Beta Kappa; Mortar Bd. (pres. 1938-39); hon. life, Calif. Congress of Parents and Teachers. United Ch. of Christ. Hobby: travel. Home: 141 E. Floresta Way, Menlo Park, CA 94025; Office: Second Careers for Women, P.O.B. 9660, Stanford, CA 94305.

FAIRBANK, WILLIAM MARTIN
Professor of Physics
b. Feb. 24, 1917, Minneapolis, Minn.; s. Samuel Ballentine and Helen Leslie (Martin) Fairbank; A.B. Whitman Coll., 1939; D.Sc. (hon.) 1965; Postgrad. fellow, Univ. of Washington, 1940-42; M.S., Yale, 1947; Ph.D. 1948; D.Sc. (hon.), Duke Univ., 1969; D.Sc. (hon.), Amherst Coll., 1972; m. Jane Davenport, Aug. 16, 1941, Seattle, Wash.; chil.: William Martin, Jr., b. Jan. 7, 1946; Robert Harold, b. Mar. 4, 1948; Richard Dana, b. Sept. 18, 1950; Career: Mem. staff, Radiation Lab., Mass. Inst. of Tech. 1942-45; Asst. Prof. of Physics, Amherst Coll., 1947-52; Assoc. Prof., Duke Univ., 1952-58; prof., 1958-59; prof. of physics, Stanford Univ., 1959---. Mem. bd. of overseers, Whitman Coll., 1966---; physics chmn.-elect, Am. Assn. for Advancement of Sci., 1979. Publ. research in the field of low temperature physics, liquid helium, super-conductivity, quantized flux, quarks, gravitation, superconducting accelerators, med. physics. Named Calif. Scientist of the Year by Mus. of Sci. and Industry, 1961. Recipient: Fritz London Award, 1968; Wilbur Lucius Cross Medal, Yale Univ., 1968; Oliver E. Buckley solid State Physics Prize by Am. Physical Soc., 1963; Research corporation Award, 1965; Mem.: Nat. Acad. of Sciences; Am. Acad. of Arts and Sciences; Am. Philosophical Soc.; fellow, Am. Physical Soc.; Tau Kappa Epsilon (pres. coll. chpt. 1938-39). United Ch. of Christ, moderator, Ladera Community Ch. Home: 141 E. Floresta Way, Menlo Park, CA 94025; Office: Physics Dept., Stanford Univ., Stanford, CA 94305.

FAIRFIELD, THEODORE (TED) CORBIN
Consulting Civil Engineer
b. June 20, 1935, Modesto, Calif.; s. Corbin F. and Meta C. (Johansen) Fairfield; student, Modesto Jr. Coll., 1952-54; B.S. in civil engring., San Jose State Univ., 1959; m. Gail Ewin, Aug. 13, 1971, Reno, Nev.; chil.: Terri L. (Anderson), b. Feb. 13, 1956; Connie L., b. Feb. 16, 1959. Career: Eng. in pub. works, city of San Jose, 1957-58; asst. engr., town of Los Gatos, 1959; principal, Mackay & Somps Civil Engrs., San Jose and Pleasanton, 1960-78; cons. civil eng., Ted C. Fairfield, Pleasanton, 1978---. Dir. (past chmn.), Valley Memorial Hosp., Livermore. Served AUS, corps of engrs., 1954-56. Mem. Calif. Council of Civil Engrs. & Land Surveyors, 1977 pres. Registered civil engineer in Calif., Ore., Nev. and Wash. states. Fellow, Am. Soc. of Civil Engrs. Mem. Pleasanton Park & Recreation Commn. 1966-68. Mem. Masons; Pleasanton Rotary Club, pres. 1967-68. Rec.: fishing. Home: 2333 Woodthrush Way, Pleasanton, CA 94566; Office: P.O.B. 1148, Pleasanton, CA 94566.

FALICOV, LEOPOLDO MAXIMO
Professor of Physics
b. June 24, 1933, Buenos Aires, Argentina; s. Isaias Felix and Dora (Samoilovich) Falicov; Liceniado in Chem., Buenos Aires Univ., 1957; Ph.D., Cuyo Univ. Inst. J. Balseiro, Argentina, 1958; Ph.D. in Physics, Cambridge Univ., 1950, Sc.D., 1977; m. Marta A. Puebla, Aug. 13, 1959, Cambridge, Eng.; twin sons, Alexis and Ian, b. Feb. 11, 1968. Career: Prof. of Physics, Univ. of Chicago, 1960-69; Univ. of Calif., Berkeley, 1969---; also vis. staff mem.: Bell Telephone Labs., N.J., 1961; Western Electric Grad. Training Center, 1962-64; No. Am. Rockwell Sci. Center, Thousand Oaks, 1968; IBM Thomas J. Watson Research Center, N.Y. ,1975; also vis. Prof., Cavendish Lab., Cambridge Univ., 1966; Louisiana State Univ., 1967; Univ. of Cuyo, Argentina (apptd. by Orgn. of Am. States), 1970; NATO Summer Sch. on New Develop. in Semiconductors, McGill Univ., Canada, 1971; Univ. of Copenhagen, 1971-72; Winter School, on Electrons in Crystalline Solids, Internat. Centre for Theoretical Physics, Italy; Univs. of Madrid, Toronto and Paris, 1975-77. Fellowships: Am. Physical Soc., Inst. of Physics, Gr. Br.; Alfred P. Sloan Found.; Fitzwilliam Coll., Cambridge; Fulbright; Guggenheim. Author: Group Theory and Its Physical Applications; Estructura Electronica de los Solidos: contrbr. to profl. journs. Fellow: Am. Physical Soc., Cambridge Philosophical Soc., British Inst. of Physics. Home: 90 Avenida Dr., Berkeley, CA 94708; Office: Dept. of Physics, U.C. Berkeley, CA 94720.

FALK, JOYCE DUNCAN
Reference Center Director
b. July 26, 1938, Pecos, Texas; d. Duane Vernon and Edna Mae (Mathis) Duncan; B.A., Univ. of New Mex., 1960; Ph.D., USC, 1969; M.L.S., UCLA, 1972; m. Heinrich Richard Falk, Aug. 14, 1965, Thousand Oaks. Career: Instr., Mt. St. Mary's Coll., L.A., 1965-68; Lectr., Cal. State Univ., Fullerton, 1972-74; dir., Am. Bibliographical Center, ABC-Clio, Inc., Santa Barbara, 1974---. Editor, Proceedings of the Western Soc. for French History, 1976; exec. editor, Historical Abstracts, 1974---; exec. editor, America: History and Life, 1974---; Author: The Theatre Institute Library of Barcelona (Spec. Libraries, Mar. 1978); Research Opportunities at the Theatre Inst. Lib., Barcelona (Performing Arts Resources, 1978). Mem.: bd. dirs., Am. Soc. of Indexers, 1977-78; Bibliography & Indexes Com., Hist. Sect., ALA, 1975-79; Lib. Tech. Advis. Com., Santa Barbara City Coll., 1974---; Phi Kappa Phi; Phi Alpha Theta; Phi Sigma Tau; Am. Hist. Assn.; ALA; Am. Soc. for 18th Century Studies; Soc. for French Historical Studies; Western Soc. for French Hist. Home: 2726 Cuesta Rd., Santa Barbara, CA 93105; Office: 2040 Alameda Padre Serra, Santa Barbara, CA 93103.

FAMILIAN, GARY R.
Investment Company President
b. Feb. 28, 1942, Beverly Hills, Calif.; s. Isadore and Sunny Familian; B.S., indsl. mgmt., USC, 1963; grad. study, Grad. Sch. Bus. Adminstrn., UCLA; m. Elisabeth Adler, chil: Gregory Adam, b. Mar. 3, 1967; Anthony David, b. Jan. 3, 1969; Cara Michele, b. Apr. 9, 1970. Career: v.p. marketing and new products, Price Pfister Brass Mfg. Co., 1962-69; pres. and chief operating officer, Pacific American Industries, L.A., 1969-72; pres. and chief exec., Familian Realty and Investment Corp., 1972---. Active involvement in community; formed Com. for Responsible Utility Rates, 1974. Mem.: bd. govs., v. chmn., L.A. Music Center, chmn. Music Center Unified Fund Campaign, 1978-79; L.A. Pub. Library Commn.; bd., Calif. Partnership of the Arts; Mayor Bradley's Advis.

Com. on Cultural Affairs; collectors com., Nat. Gallery of Art, Smithsonian Inst.; trustee, City of Hope; advis. council, UCLA Hosp. and Clinic; v.p., Constitutional Rights Found.; bd. ACLU of So. Calif.; dir., Calif. Conservation Project; bd., Univ. of Judaism; exec. bd., Am. Jewish Com.; Jewish Fed. Council of L.A. Democrat. Mem. Democratic State Central Com.; L.A. Co. Demo. Com. Active campaigner and fund-raiser. Home: 215 S. Bristol Ave., L.A., CA 90049; Office: 9595 Wilshire Blvd., Beverly Hills, CA 90212.

FARMER, MALCOLM FRENCH
Anthropologist
b. Aug. 6, 1915, L.A.; s. Ollef O. and Nellie (Brennen) Farmer; B.A., Univ. of Ariz., 1940; postgrad., Univ. Wash., 1951-53, 1956-57; m. Ann Dahlstrom, Oct. 25, 1963, Monterey Park. Career: curator, San Diego Mus. of Man, 1940-50, dir., 1946-50; researcher, Navajo Tribe, N. Mex., 1950-51; asst. dir., Mus. of N. Ariz., 1953-56; asst. prof. Am. Anthropology, Whittier Coll. 1959---. Author: Amerindian Interlude A.D. 1400-1600, 1965. USAF, 1943-45; U.S. Infan. 1945. Bd. mem., Verde Valley Sch. 1946---; mem. AAAS. Home: 6146 Southwind Dr., Whittier, CA 90601; Office: Whittier Coll., Whittier, CA 90608.

FARMER, PENELOPE B.
Realtor
b. May 6, 1945, San Diego, Calif.; d. A. Earle and Ruth A. Brown; A.A., Stephens Coll., 1965; B.A., S.D. State Univ., 1968; m. Rudolph D. Farmer, Sr., Sept. 28, 1974, Lakeside, Calif. Career: coll. intern program, U.S. AVSCOM, 1969; real estate salesperson, 1971-74; licensed real estate broker, 1974---; owner with husband, Gold Star Properties, real estate co., 1976---. Mem.: S.D. Bd. of Realtors Profl. Standards Panel; Red Carpet Treasurer, 1979. Hobbies: disco, reading. Rec.: Charger football fan. Office: 6975 Navajo Rd., San Diego, CA 92119.

FARRAHER, JOSEPH JAMES
Educator — Clergyman
b. Oct. 6, 1916, Bakersfield, Calif.; s. James (former pres., Calif. State Bar) and Eva (Scott) Farraher; grandson of Elmon Scott, former justice, Supreme Ct., State of Wash.; A.B., Gonzaga Univ., Spokane, Wash. 1940; M.A., 1941; S.T.L., Alma Coll., Los Gatos, Calif. 1948; S.T.D., Gregorian Univ., Rome, Italy, 1952. Career: Entered Soc. of Jesus, Sept. 7, 1935; instr. Univ. of S.F., 1941-44; ordained Jesuit priest, S.F., June 16, 1947; assoc. prof. (moral theol.), Alma Coll., Los Gatos 1951-56, prof. 1956-68, pres. 1961-67; Jesuit Sch. of Theol. Berkeley, prof. Grad. Theol Union, 1968-73; Acad. Dean, St. Patrick's Sem. 1973-75; visiting prof. of tehol., Univ. of S.F., Univ. of Santa Clara, Coll. of Holy Names (Oakland), Coll. of Notre Dame (Belmont). Advocate (ch. lawyer), Archdiocesan Tribunal, Archdiocese of S.F. 1963-75; mem. Archdiocesan Comm. on Soc. Justice, 1964-77; Author: profl. papers, articles on topics of morality, race rels., theol., publ. Hastings Law Journ., Gregorian Univ. (Rome), Alma Coll., The Cath. Ency. for Sch. and Home, New Cath. Ency. 1952---. Mem.: Cath. Theol. Soc. of Am., Fellowship of Cath. Scholars, 1977---. Roman Catholic. Home and Office: Univ. of Santa Clara, Santa Clara, CA 95053.

FARRELL, HARRY GUY
Newspaper Columnist
B.A., Journalism, San Jose State Univ., 1948; m. Betty M. Regan, Sept. 30, 1948, San Jose. Career: joined staff of San Jose Mercury and News, 1942---: copy boy, 1942-43; military leave, AUS, 1943-46, reporter, 1946-54, political writer, 1954-69, polit. editor, 1969-74, columnist, 1975---; part-time correspondent: Oakland Tribune, 1949-52, Fairchild Publs. 1953-56, Long Beach Independent Press Telegram, 1959. Awards: Calif. Taxpayers' Assn., 1968, 74; Nat. Headliners Club, 1966; Calif. Newspaper Pubs. Assn., 1965, 73; Calif.-Nev. AP Writing Contest, 1st prize, 1973,74; San Jose Newspaper Guild, 1964, 72, 74; Am. Polit. Sci. Assn., 1964; nat. Thomas L. Stokes, 1961. Mem.: San Jose Local 98, Newspaper Guild, AFL-CIO, pres. 1951; Soc. Profl. Journalists; Sigma Delta Chi; Nat. Headliners Club. Protestant. Home: 5366 Cribari Crest, San Jose, CA 95135; Office: San Jose Mercury News, 750 Ridder Park Dr., San Jose, CA 95190.

FAUCHER, DARLENE
Advertising — Public Relations Executive
b. June 3, 1944, Bell, Calif.; d. Duane Orr and Maxine Brady (Schmidt) Taylor; student, San Diego State Univ., 1962-65; m. Michael Joseph Faucher, Mar. 14, 1970,

S.D., Calif. Career: Stewardess, Pacific SW Airlines, 1965-66, saleswoman, 1966-70; bd. chmn. and pres., Faucher & Meenan Advt. and Pub. Relations, S.D., 1970---; partner, Super Production Co., S.D., 1977---. Awards: Graphics Achievement; Graphic Excellence; La Jolla Town Council Beautification; S.D. Community Leadership Develop. Program. Mem.: S.D. Assn. of Advt. Agencies; Pub. Rel. Soc. of Am.; Am. Mktg. Assn.; Small Businesswomen Owners Assn., pres., Mem.: Univ. of Calif. Chancellors Assocs.; S.D. State Univ. Sch. of Bus., Advisory com.; dir., Bayside Settlement House; S.D. C. of C.; La Jolla Town Council. Republican. Mem. Nat. and State Central Coms. Home: 8155 Pasadena Ave., La Mesa, CA 92041; Office: 1276 Cave St., La Jolla, CA 92037.

FAUSSET, RICHARD LYNNE
Investment Banker
b. Aug. 6, 1940, Hollywood; s. Arthur Ray and Mary Margaret Fausset; A.A., bus. adminstrn., Ventura Coll., 1962; m. Marcia Emard, Aug. 28, 1960, Ventura; chil.: Richard, b. 1961; Christa, b. 1962; Matthew, b. 1964; Amy, b. 1968. Career: Sales Rep., Gerber Products Co., Ventura, Santa Barbara, 1961-69; real estate salesman, Edward J. Carr Land Investment, Ventura, 1968-71; asst. to pres., Norris Oil Co., Ventura, 1969-72; pres., Century Beverage Co., Saticoy, 1970-72; partner, Fausset and Beguelin Partners (investment banking and real estate sales & devel.), 1974-76, prin., Fausset and Assocs., 1976---; pres., Coastline Properties, 1972---; princ., Western Securities, 1971---; partner, Courts, Etc.(handball/racquetball/tennis facilities, Tex. and Calif.), 1977---. Pres., Ventura Co. Econ. Devel. Assn., 1978; appointee to Regional Econ. Devel. Pgm. Mem.: Gr. Ventura C. of C.; Ventura Visitors and Conventiona Bureau, chmn. 1972, 74; Ventura Co. Forum of the Arts, dir. 1975; Ventura Marina Assn. Steering Com.; Jonathan Club, L.A.; Ondulando Club; R&A Club. Rec.: racquetball. Home: 163 Nob Hill Lane, Ventura, CA 93003; Office: 405 S. B St., Oxnard, CA 93030.

FEDDERSON, DON JOY
Chairman Board, Don Fedderson Productions
b. Apr. 16, 1913, Beresford, S. Dak.; s. Anthony and Hanna M. (Lewis) Fedderson; Central H.S., Kansas City, Mo.; Kan. City Sch. of Law; m. Yvonne Lime, L.A., Mar. 15, 1969; dau. Dionne Joy, b. Mar. 1, 1970. Career: Creator: Hollywood Bowl Charity Show, 1951; exec. prod.: Life With Elizabeth, 1951; Betty White Show, NBC, 1953; ABC 1958; creator-prod.: The Millionaire, 1953; Do You Trust Your Wife?, 1955; TV cons., Lawrence Welk, 1955; creator-prod.: Date with the Angels, 1957; Who Do You Trust?, ABC, N.Y. 1960; My Three Sons, 1960; co-creator-exec.-prod. To Rome With Love, 1969; Smith Family, 1970; creator-syndicator, Lawrence Welk Network-The Lawrence Welk Show, 1971. Mem.: bd. Trojanaires, USC; pres. Calif. TV Soc. 1951-52; bd. dirs., Ernest Holmes Research Found.; Wilshire Country Club, Bel-Air Country Club; Canyon Country Club, Palm Springs. Hobby: golf. Home: 16071 Royal Oak Rd., Encino, CA 91436; Office: 4024 Radford Ave., Studio City, CA 91604.

FEDDERSON, YVONNE LIME
President, International Orphans
b. Apr. 7, 1935, Glendale, Calif.; d. Fred and Glee Lime; Glendale Pub. Schs.; Glendale Jr. Coll.; Pasadena Playhouse, 1954; m. Don Fedderson, L.A., Mar. 15, 1969; chil.: Brian Richard Schmidt, b. Jan. 18, 1964; Dionne Joy, b. Mar. 1, 1970. Career: motion picture-TV actress, 1955-69; 9 mot. pics. incl.: The Rainmaker, Loving You, The Last Man, and various TV shows. Co-founder-natl. pres. Internat. Orphans, Inc., 1959---. Cross of Merit, The Knightly Order of St. Brigitte; commendation by L.A. Co. Bd. of Supvs.; cit. by Japanese Consul Gen. for Japan and U.S.; Scroll, Mayor Kihachiro Goto, Tokyo, Japan for support of House of Hope Orphanage; Certs of Appreciation, U.S.M.C. Res., Vietnam, 1966; Victor M. Carter Diamond Award, Japan Am. Soc. 1970. Mem.: Mayor's Adv. Bd. for Sister Cities; Bordeaux, France and Nagoya, Japan; Assistance League. Protestant. Hobby: painting. Rec.: tennis, swimming. Home: 16071 Royal Oak Rd., Encino, CA 91316; 2431 Yosemite, 92262; Palm Springs, CA; Office: 18670 Ventura Blvd., Tarzana, CA 91356.

FEHRENBACHER, DON EDWARD
Historian — Educator — Author
b. Aug. 21, 1920, Sterling, Ill.; s. Joseph Henry and Mary (Barton) Fehrenbacher; B.A., Cornell Coll., 1946; M.A. and Ph.D., Univ. Chicago, 1948, 1951; M.A., Oxford, Univ., 1967; D.H.L., Cornell Coll., 1970; m. Virginia Swaney, Feb. 9, 1944, Chicago; chil.: Ruth

(Mrs. Laurence Gleason), b. 1945; Susan (Mrs. Ralph Koprince), b. 1946; David C., b. 1947. Career: Lectr. Roosevelt Coll. (now Roosevelt Univ.), 1947-49; asst. prof., Coe Coll., 1949-53; mem. faculty, Stanford Univ., 1953---: now William Robertson Coe Prof. of History and Am. Studies, 1966---; Guggenheim Fellow, 1959-60; Harmsworth Prof. of Am. His., Oxford Univ., 1967-68; Harrison Prof. of Hist., Coll. of William and Mar, 1973-74; Nat. Endowment for Humanities Fellow, 1975-76; Commonwealth Fund Lectr. in So. Hist., La State Univ., 1978. Author: Chicago Giant: A Biography of "Long John" Wentworth, 1957; Prelude to Greatness: Lincoln in the 1850s, 1962; A Basic History of California, 1964; The Changing Image of Lincoln in American Histiography, 1968; The Era of Expansion, 1800-1848 (1969); The Dred Scott Case: Its Significance in American Law and Politics, 1978. Co-Author: California, an Illustrated History, 1968. Completed and edited: David M. Potter, "The Impending Crisis, 1848-1861" (N.Y., 1976), awarded the Pulitzer Prize in Hist., 1977. Editor and compiler 6 other books; essays in 6 books; articles and book reviews in profl. journs.; contrbr.: Encyclopedia Britannica, Encyc. Americana, ref. works. 1st Lt., Army AF, 1943-45; navigator, 30 missions in heavy bombardment, 8th AF, 1944, decorated Air Medal with clusters and D.F.C. Home: 625 Salvatierra, Stanford, CA 94305; Office: Stanford Univ., Stanford, CA 94305.

FEIN, WILLIAM
Ophthalmic Plastic Surgeon
b. Nov. 27, 1933, New York City, N.Y.; s. Samuel and Beatrice (Lipshutz) Fein; B.S., Coll. of the City of N.Y., 1954; M.D., UCI Coll. of Med., 1962; m. Bonnie Fern Aaronson, Dec. 15, 1963, Beverly Hills; chil.: Stephanie Paula, b. Feb. 3, 1968; Adam Irving, b. May 1, 1969; Gregory Andrew, b. Feb. 7, 1972. Career: Ophthalmology resident, L.A. Co. Gen. Hosp., 1963-66; instr. in ophthalmology, UCI, 1966-69; inst. in ophthalmology, USC, 1969-79; assoc. clin. prof. of ophthalmology, USC Med. Sch., 1978---. Also attending physician in ophthalmology: Cedars-Sinai Med. Center and L.A. Co.-USC Med. Center. Chmn., Dept. of Ophthalmology, Midway Hosp., 1975-78. Contbr. sci. publs. describing new ophthalmic surgeries. Mem.: Am. Soc. of Ophthalmic Plastic and Reconstructive Surgery: Am. and Calif. Assns. of Ophthalmology; Am. Acad. of Ophthalmology; Am. Bd. of Ophthalmology; AMA; Calif. Med. Assn.; L.A. Co. Med. Assn. Home: 718 N. Camden Dr., Beverly Hills, CA 90210; Office: 465 N. Roxbury Dr., Beverly Hills, CA 90210.

FELDMAN, WILLIAM D.
Industrial Realtor
b. Apr. 1, 1932, Chicago, Ill.; s. Newton and Evelyn Feldman, B.S., UCLA, 1954; m. Patricia Mollman, July 21, 1964, Los Angeles; chil.: Dale, b. Apr. 27, 1956; Michelle, b. July 14, 1966; Laurie, b. Jan. 17, 1968; Alisa, b. Sept. 24, 1969. Career: sales, 1957-60; indsl. real estate, Jules Altemus Co., assoc., Stuart Klabin & Co., Inc., (indsl. and office real estate), 1960-64; co-owner, 1964---. 1st Lt. AUS, Field Artillery, 1955-56. Apptd., L.A. City Traffic Commn. 1974, pres. 1976,77,78. 1st v.p., So. Calif. chpt. Soc. of Indsl. Realtors. Jewish. Rec.: running. Home: 11400 Ayrshire Rd., L.A., CA 90049; Office: 701 W. Manchester Blvd., Inglewood, CA 90301.

FELTON, GARY SPENCER
Clinical Psychologist — Educator
b. Mar. 8, 1940, S.F.; s. Jean Spencer, M.D. and Janet (Birnbaum) Felton; B.A., gen. sci., Grinnell Coll., 1961; M.S., clin. psychol., S.F. State Univ., 1966; Ph.D., clin. psychol., USC, 1970; m. Lynn Ellen Sandell, Mar. 21, 1970, L.A.; son, Colin Spencer, b. Mar. 12, 1974; dau., Megan Ariana, b. Mar. 31, 1977. Career: Coordinator of counseling and co-dir. of research programs, Mt. St. Mary's Coll., 1969-71; coord., Human Services Worker Tng. Program, Brentwood VA Hosp., L.A., 1971-72; dir. of Allied Health and coord. of Child Health Care Worker Tng. Program, Children's Hosp., L.A., 1972-75; pvt. practice clin. psychology as Dir., Center of Interpersonal Studies, L.A. ---; also Dir. of Special Edn. Programs and Assoc. Prof. of Psychol., L.A. City Coll., 1971---; cons. psychol.: adult back clinic of Orthopaedic Hosp., L.A., 1967-69; Am. Heart Assn. program, at Cal. State Univ., S.F., 1965-66; several mental health and human services coms., L.A. area, currently. Author: Up from Underachievement, 1977; one monograph and 70+ profl. articles in field of psychol. Mem.: Am., Western and Calif. State Psychological Assns.; So. Calif. Group Osychotherpay Assn.; L.A. Co. Psychol. Assn., L.A. Soc. of Clin. Psychologists; Soc. of Pediatric Psychol.; Assn. for Humanistic Psychol.; Am. Humanistic Assn.; Am. Name Soc.; Am. Fedn. of Tchrs. Hobbies: photog.,

music. Rec.: travel, running, swimming. Office: 11941 Wilshire Blvd., Suite 22, L.A., CA 90025.

FERDERBER, JOSEPH
Aircraft Company Executive
b. Oct. 23, 1919, Cleveland, Oh.; s. Andrew and Anna Ferderber; ed. B.S. (E.E.); Case Inst. Tech., Cleveland, 1942; chil.: Lawrence Joseph, b. Mar. 27, 1946; Julie Ann, b. Sept. 12, 1949; Michael James, b. Sept. 24, 1952. Career: Assoc. Gen. Elec. Co., Schenectady and Ft. Wayne, 1942-43, Syracuse, 1943-49; v.p. Hughes Aircraft Co., 1949---. v.p.-dir. Sheltered Workshop, Santa Monica, 1956. Mem.: dir. Western Electronics Mfgrs. Assn. 1963; Eta Kappa Nu, Tau Beta Pi, Sigma Xi. Unitarian (treas. Pac. Unitarian Ch., dir. 1958-61); Hobby: gardening. Rec.: golf. Home: 27553 Sunnyridge Rd., Palos Verdes Peninsula, CA 90274; Office: Hughes Aircraft Co., Culver City, CA.

FERGUSON, DONALD CONRAD
Police Chief
b. Jan. 12, 1930, Spokane, Wash.; s. David Conrad and Ethel Laura (Green) Ferguson; B.S., adminstrn. criminal justice, San Jose State Univ., 1974; m. Norma Whittier, Apr. 4, 1953, San Jose; chil.: Sheryle Lynn (York), b. May 28, 1955; Sheryn Lee, b. Nov. 14, 1957; Jon Michael, b. Feb. 21, 1963. Career: patrolman with police dept., City of Santa Clara, 1953---: patrolman 1953-56, sergeant, 1956-65, lieutenant 1965-75, elected Police Chief, 1975---. USAF, 1948-49. Mem.: Rotary Club. Home: 2165 Laurel Dr., Santa Clara, CA 95050; Office: 1541 Civic Center Dr., Santa Clara, CA 95050.

FERGUSON, JACK L.
Attorney at Law
b. Sept. 24, 1931, Richmond, Kan.; s. Oliver L. and Mary Marjorie Knittles; student, Napa Coll., 1949-50; Fresno State Univ., 1950-52; LL.B., La Salle Ext. Univ., 1957; m. Madeleine Cash, May 19, 1976, Honolulu, Hawaii; chil.: (previous marraige), Seana D. (Dixon), b. June 21, 1952; Robin L. (Beebe), b. Sept. 4, 1953; Valerie L. (Cullen), b. July 25, 1954; Scott W., b. Mar. 15, 1966; Grant J., b. Mar. 24, 1961. Career: U.S. Postal Clerk, 1953-54; Ins. investigator, Retail Credit Co., 1954-59; right of way agent, Calif. Div. of Highways, 1959-62; atty. at law, 1961---: now Ferguson & Schotte, Attorneys at Law, Napa; asst. dist. atty., Co. of Napa, 1962-63; mem. Napa Co. Bd. of Supvs., 1965-69. Dir., 25th Dist. Agri. Assn., 1973---, pres. 1977, 78; v.-chmn. Napa Co. Bd. of Edn., 1956-59. USMCR, 1949-52. Dir., Napa Boys Club, 1964---. Mem.: Young Lodge No. 12 F&AM; Oakland Lodge of Perfection Scottish Rite Masons; Napa Jaycees; Sons of Italy of Am.; S.F. Mus. Soc.; Napa Co. Bar Assn., pres. 1965; C. of C., dir. 1965; Napa Toastmasters Club, pres. 1973. Catholic. Hobby: coin collecting. Rec.: golf, fishing, hunting. Home: 667 Costa Dr., Napa, CA; Office: 585 Coombs St., Napa, CA 94558.

FERGUSON, LLOYD N.
Professor of Chemistry — International Lecturer
b. Feb. 9, 1918, Oakland; s. Noel S. and Gwendolyn (Johnson) B.S., 1940; Ph.D., 1943, Univ. Calif., Berkeley; m. Charlotte Welch, Jan. 2, 1944, Berkeley; chil.: Lloyd Noel, Stephen Bruce, Lisa Annette. Career: asst. prof., A&T Coll., N.C., 1944-45; mem. faculty, Howard Univ., Wash., D.C., 1945-65, head chem. dept. 1958-65; prof. of chem., Cal. State Univ., L.A., 1965---: chmn. chem. dept., 1968-71; research: Guggenheim Fellow, Cytochem. Dept., Carlsberg Lab., Copenhagen, 1953-54, NSF Faculty Fellow, Swiss Fed. Inst. of Tech., Zurich, 1961-62; (research interests: physical organic chem., sense of taste, cancer chemotherapy). Author: chem. textbooks, journ. publs.; helped devel. collaboration program between U.S. and USSR on cancer chemotherapy, Nat. Cancer Inst., 1973, 74. Awards incl.: Am. Chem. Soc. Award, 1978; Am. Found. for Negro Affairs dist. Am. Medallion, 1976; outstanding prof. award, Cal. State Univ., L.A., 1974; Mfg. Chemists Assn. nat. tchg. award, 1974; Oakland Mus. Assn., 1973; hon. D.Sc., Howard Univ., 1970. Mem.: advisory bds.: Internat. Union of Pure and Applied Chem.; Nat. Acad. of Sciences, nat. research council; Nat. Cancer Inst., chemotherapy; NIH Med. and Organic Chem. Review Com.; FDA com. on research; Dept. of Commerce Sea Grant Review panel. Chmn., Am. Chem. Soc., div. of chem. edn., 1979. Home: 4221 Cloverdale Ave., L.A., CA 90008; Office: 5151 State University Dr., L.A., CA 90032.

FERICANO, PAUL FRANCIS
Poet
b. Jan. 16, 1951, S.F.; s. Frank and Josephine (Anello)

Fericano; ed. 20 different colls., 1969-76; m. Katherine Judeen Daly, Oct. 14, 1972, San Bruno. Career: various jobs while traveling and studying (Poets in the Schls. program, Calif. --- poetry readings and lectrs. every grade level), 1969-76; Coord., Creative Response Outlet for Writers, 1974-77; Editor: The West Conscious Review, 1973-77; Crow's Nest, 1974-78; Contbr. Small Press Racks in Libraries Proj., 1976-78; Author: 4 vols. of poems: Beneath the Smoke Rings (Dithyramb Poetry Series), Cancer Quiz (Scarecrow Books), Loading the Revolver With Real Bullets (Second Coming Press), Stoogism Anthology (Scarecrow Books); pub. poetry, prose and fiction in 200+ literary mags.; Founder, Stoogism Movement (Lit.). Chmn., Millbrae Arts Commn., 1976-77; Small Press Workshop, Canada Coll., 1978. Mem.: Western Independent Pubs. Christian. Hobby: antiques. Rec.: exploring. Address: 1050 Magnolia No. 2, Millbrae, CA 94030.

FERRARO, RICHARD E.
School Board Member
b. July 27, 1924, L.A.; s. Peter Paul and Josephine L. (Civerolo) Ferraro; A.A., L.A. City COll., 1948; B.A., Cal. State Coll., L.A., 1950; M.S., USC, 1957; hon. LL.D., Pepperdine Univ., 1976; m. Erna W. Hoppe, June 20, 1946, Reno, Nev.; Chil.: Richard E., Jr., b. Apr. 15, 1948; Kathleen Robin, b. Apr. 6, 1950. Career: high sch. tchr., 1953-69; instr. and coord. of tchr. tng., USC, 1969-76; polit. sci. instr., L.A. Trade-Tech. Coll., 1969-77; program dir. and asst. prof., Julian A. Virtue Center for Edn. in Am. Economics, Sch. of Edn., Pepperdine Univ., 1977-78; asst. Supt., Ednl. Services, Anaheim Union H.S. Dist., 1978; elected mem. L.A. City Bd. of Edn., 1969---. AUS Air Corps, 1943-46; USAF, 1951-52. Mem. Calif. State Tchrs. Retirement Bd., 1967-75; various offices, Affiliated Tchrs. Orgn. of L.A., 1962-68. Mem.: Native Sons of the Golden West, Parlor 45, past pres.; Secondary Tchrs. Orgn. of L.A., past pres.; Phi Delta Kappa; Calif. Sch. Bds. Assn. Catholic. Home: 4351 Eagle Rock Blvd., L.A., CA 90041; Office: 450 N. Grand Ave., L.A., CA 90012.

FERRIN, WILLIAM JOSEPH
Attorney at Law
b. Jan. 29, 1930, Chicago; s. John William and Ruth (McGurren) Ferrin; B.S., Northwestern Univ., 1951; J.D., USC, 1959; m. Lucy Dolores Leuzzi, June 2, 1956, Inglewood; Chil.: Patricia Mary, b. Dec. 29, 1956; Kathleen Betty, b. Dec. 14, 1958; William Joseph, b. Feb. 6, 1960; Colleen Ann, b. June 18, 1969. Career: Staff Acct., Bauman, Finney & Co., Chgo., 1950-51; Haskins & Sells, L.A., 1954-55; dep. gen. controller, Capitol Records, Inc., Hollywood, 1956-58, secty., controller, dir., Kaufman & Broad (and subsid. corps.), L.A., 1958-62; v.p. finance, Harlan Lee-Byron Lasky Co., Sherman Oaks, 1962-64; admitted to Calif. Bar 1960, pvt. practice of law, Sherman Oaks, 1967---: Judge Pro Tem, L.A. Municipal Ct., 1971---. Dir. Hartford Devel. Co. Capt., USMCR, 1951-54. Mem.: dir., Little League; Am, L.A. Co., San Fernando Valley bar assns.; State Bar of Calif.; Assn. Bus. Trial Lawyers; Am. Arbitration Assn. (arbitrator); Am. Inst. CPAs; L.A. World Affairs Council; Legion Lex; Phi Alpha Delta. Clubs: Jonathan, Town Hall. Republican. Roman Catholic. Home: 4829 Ellenita Ave., Tarzana, CA 91356; Office: 15233 Ventura Blvd., Sherman Oaks, CA 91403.

FIELD, CHARLES DAVISON
Attorney at Law
b. Aug. 2, 1936, S.F.; s. John II (assoc. dean emeritus, UCLA Sch. of Med.) and Sally (Miller) Field; grandson, Austin Miller, M.D., early X-ray researcher; B.A., Univ. Calif., Riverside, 1958; J.D., UCLA, 1963; m. Judy Anderson (artist and mem. Riverside City Planning Commn.), July 6, 1963, Riverside; chil.: Robert D., b. Mar. 27, 1964; John D., b. Apr. 2, 1966. Career: joined law firm, Best, Best & Krieger, Riverside, 1963---: gen. trial practice, 1963-70; gen. labor law practice, 1970---. Grantee, Ford Found., attended Urban Coalition-Law Enforcement Task Force Program, N.Y.; bd. dir., legal advisor, Meditrans, Inc. (non-profit transportation for handicapped), 1973---; Judge Pro Tem, Riverside Superior Ct.; Riverside Municipal Ct.; San Bernardino Arbitration Panel; Am. Arbitration Assn. Panel. Mem.: Calif. State Bar Assn., Commn. on Specialization in Labor Law, 1977; Riverside Urban Coalition; Riverside Co. Barristers, pres. 1970; Riverside Co. Bar Assn., exec. com. 1969-70; Univ. Calif. Bd. of Regents, 1975-77, various Univ. Calif. Coms.; pres. UC, Riverside Found., 1977---, pres. UCR Alumni Assn. 1970-72, 1976-77. Home: 4415 Fifth St., Riverside, CA; Office: 4200 Orange St., Riverside, CA 92502.

FIELD, JOHN LOUIS
Architect
b. Jan. 18, 1930, Minneapolis; s. Harold D. and Gladys (Jacobs) Field; B.A., Yale Coll., 1952; M. Arch., Yale Univ., 1955; m. Carol Hart, July 23, 1961, Berkeley; chil.: Matthew Hart, b. Dec. 18, 1962; Allison Ellen, b. Aug. 8, 1966. Career: Individual archtl. practice, San Francisco, 1959-68; v.p., firm of Bull Field Volkmann Stockwell, Architects and Urban Planners, 1968---. Awards: Albert J. Evers award, 1974; Nat. Endowment for Humanities grantee, 1972; Nat. Endowment for Arts Fellow, 1975; Fellow AIA, mem. Nat. Council Archtl. Registration Bd. Works incl.: Alaska State Capital Master Plan, Stanford Shopping Center Renewal & Sacto. State Coll. Edn. Co-author, producer, dir., film "Cities for People" (Broadcast Media award 1975, Golden Gate award S.F. Internat. Film Festival 1975, Ohio State award 1976). Chmn. archtl. council S.F. Mus. Art, 1969-71; mem. activities bd., 1969-72; Chmn. ed. bd., S.F. Bay Architects' Review. Home: 2561 Washington St., S.F., CA 94115; Office: 350 Pacific Ave., S.F., CA 94111.

FIELD, RUSSELL
Business Executive
b. Oct. 18, 1913, Kansas City, Mo.; s. Russell and Gertrude (Brown) Field; Univ. of Kan., Sch. of Engring., Dept. Arch. 1932-35; exec. tr. pgm., Alexander Hamilton Inst.; Urban design, Europe, 1954; m. Grayce R. Arnold, San Marino, Oct. 6, 1956; chil.: Ann Turner Ford, b. Mar. 22, 1934; Park Turner, b. Sept. 8, 1939; David McLucas Field, b. Apr. 22, 1944; Lindsley McGow Field, b. Jan. 16, 1949. Career: Wight & Wight, Archs., Kan. City, Mo. 1935-37; Eckel & Aldrich, Archs., St. Joseph, Mo. 1938-39; Payne & Field, arch. bldrs., K.C., Mo. 1939-43; N. Am. Aviation Inc., K.C., 1943-45; TWA, K.C., 1945-48; U.S. Atomic Energy Comm., Oak Ridge, Tenn. 1948-53; Holmes and Narver, Inc., engring. constr., L.A. 1954-62; Allison & Rible Archs., L.A. 1962-65; sr. exec. mgmt. staff, Daniel Mann, Johnson & Mendenhall, planning, arch., engring., sys., economics, 1965---. Dir., Wally Findlay Galleries Inc. (Chicago, Palm Beach, N.Y., Paris, Beverly Hills, Tokyo). Mem.: Pres.'s Council, Am. Inst. of Mgmt.; assoc. So. Calif. Chpt. Am. Inst. of Archs.; Beta Theta Pi, Scarab, Abydos Temple of Univ. of Kan.; Bel-Air Bay Club. Episcopalian. Hobbies: drawing, swim. Home: The El Royale, Suite 202, 450 N. Rossmore Ave., L.A., CA 90004; Office: One Park Plaza, 3250 Wilshire Blvd., L.A., CA 90010.

FIELDS, VERNA HELLMAN
Film Editor
b. Mar. 21, 1918, St. Louis, Mo.; d. Samuel (screenwriter) and Selma (Schwartz) Hellman; B.A., USC, 1938; m. Samuel Fields, May 1, 1946, Riverside; sons, Kenneth Hellman, b. Mar. 15, 1949; Richard Hellman, b. June 13, 1951. Career: Tchr. of Film, USC; sound editor, film ed., prod./dir. of documentaries, currently v.p., Feature Prodn., Universal Studios. Films include: Medium Cool, What's Up Doc (1972), American Graffiti, co ed. (1973); Paper Moon (1973), The Sugarland Express, co-editor (1974), Daisy Miller (1974), Jaws (1975). Recipient: Acad. Award, Best Editor for "Jaws." Mem. Bd. Govs., Motion Picture Arts and Scis.; mem. Delta Kappa Alpha, cinema frat. Hobby: archeology. Rec.: bicycling. Home: 5812 Costello Ave., Van Nuys, CA 91401; Office: Universal Studios, Universal City, CA 91608.

FILES, HON. GORDON L.
Appellate Court Judge
b. Mar. 5, 1912, Fort Dodge, Ia.; s. James Ray and Anna (Louis) Files; A.B., Univ. of Calif., L.A. 1934; LL.B., Yale Law Sch., 1937; m. Kathryn Thrift, S.F., Oct. 24, 1942; chil.: Kathryn A., b. Nov. 23, 1944; James G., b. May 23, 1948. Career: Admitted to State Bar of Calif. 1937; practicing atty., Freston and Files law firm, L.A. 1938-59; apptd. judge, Superior Ct. of L.A., 1959-62, Dist. Ct. of Appeal, Div. 4, 1962---. Lt. USNR, WW II. Mem.: bd. trustees, L.A. Bar Assn. 1950-53; bd. govs., State Bar of Calif. 1957-59; pres. Yale Law Sch. Assn. of So. Calif. 1956-60; Yale Law Sch. Grad. Bd. 1957-59; Chancery Club, Order of the Coif, Phi Kappa Sigma, Phi Delta Phi, Phi Beta Kappa. Protestant. Home: 154 S. Arroyo Blvd., Pasadena, CA; Office: 3580 Wilshire Blvd., L.A., CA 90010.

FINCH, ROBERT HUTCHISON
Attorney at Law
b. Oct. 9, 1925, Tempe, Ariz.; Inglewood H.S. (stu. body pres., ed. H.S. newspaper, letterman in track and football); A.B. (stu. body pres.), Occidental Coll. (hon.)

LL'D. 1967; LL.B., stu. body pres., USC; Hon. LL.D.: Occidental Coll. 1967; Lincoln Univ. 1968; UCLA, USC, 1969; Oh. State Univ. 1970; Univ. of Pac., Wash. and Jefferson Coll. 1971; Westminster Coll., Western State Univ., Univ. of San Fernando Valley, 1972; Rockford Univ., Pepperdine Univ. Sch. of Law, 1973; m. Carol Crothers, Feb. 14, 1946; chil.: Maureen, Kevin, Priscilla, Cathleen. Career: Est. Calif. res. 1932---; atty. at law-sr. partner, Finch, Bell, Duitsman & Margulis firm, L.A. 1952-66; Pres., Fed. S&L Assn., Adm. asst., U.S. V.P. Richard Nixon, 1958-60. Instr. polit. sci. counsel-trustee, sci., adv. bd., Marymount Coll. 1960-63; bd. regents, Univ. of Calif. (aud. and edn. policy coms.); bd. trustees, Calif. State Colls.; bd. trustees, Occidental Coll. Elected, 38th Lt. Gov. of Calif., Nov. 1966-69; pres. State Senate; chmn., Comm. of the Californias; exec. com., Natl. Conf. of Lt. Govs.; chmn. John Training and Placement Council; chmn. Bicentennial Comm.; exec. com., Intergovernmental Council on Urban Growth; Gov's. Cabinet, Calif. Toll Bridge Authority; apptd. Secty., Health, Edn., and Welfare (by Pres. Richard M. Nixon), 1970-72; Cabinet coms. and Council; partner, McKenna, Fitting & Finch law firm, 1972-74; pvt. practice, 1974---. USMC 1943-45, WW II; 1st Lt., Korean War, 1951-52. Awards: Natl. Collegiate Oratorical Champion; Eagle Scout Award, B.S.A.; Mem.: bd. dirs., Inglewood C of C. 1952-54; L.A. Co. Com. on Long Term Bldg. Needs, 1953-54; adv. bd., CORO Found.; bd. dirs., Centinela Valley UMCA, 1954-58; statewide com., YMCA Youth and Govt. 1967; L.A. Co. Dist. Atty's Adv. Com.; mgr. Little League, 1962-65; Interdepartmental Com. on Status of Women; bd. govs. Am. Red Cross; turstee, John F. Kennedy Center for Perf. Arts; Econ. Opportunity Council; Council for Urban Affairs; Kappa Sigma, Phi Alpha Delta, Legion Lex., Am. Legion, Town Hall, L.A. Ath. Club, Jonathan Club, Commonwealth Club, Calif. Club. Republican (State Central Com. 1948-74; Calif. Del. Repub. Natl. Conv. 1948, 56, 60, 68; Repub. nom., 17th Cong. Dist. 1952, 54; exec. dir. Repub. Assocs. of L.A. Co. 1955-56; chmn. L.A. Co. Repub. Central Com. 1956-58; natl. dir., Richard Nixon Presidential Campaign, 1960; chmn. exec. com., Repub. Assocs. 1964-65; Calif. mgr. George Murphy Senatorial Campaign, 1964). Presbyterian.

FINE, JERRY
Attorney at Law
b. Feb. 8, 1923, L.A.; s. Nathan and Augusta (Kaufman) Fine; stu. Stanford, 1941-43; B.A., UCLA, 1947; J.D., Loyola Univ., L.A. 1950; m. Gwen Nicholson, Dec. 25, 1956; chil.: Carolyn, Rex, Gary, Gregory. Career: Admitted to Calif. bar, 1951, since practiced in L.A.; partner, firm Fine, Armstrong, Perzik & Friedman, 1956---; lectr., cons. in field; dir. World Team Tennis, 1973-74. Pres. L.A. Strings Tennis Team, 1974. Mem.: nat. council YMCA, 1956-58; adv. council Calif. State Univ. L.A., 1974---; mem. bd. edn. Inglewood Unified Sch. Dist., 1963-71, pres., 1965-66, 69-71; chmn. bd. dirs. Westchester YMCA, 1955-58; bd. dirs. Nat. Athletic Health Inst., 1972---, mem. Calif. Commn. for Econ. Devel., 1972-77. AUS, 1953-56; decorated Purple Heart. Mem. Inglewood Dist. (pres. 1955), L.A., Calif., Am. Bar assns.; Mem., Financial Institutions Comm., State Bar, 1978---; Fellow, Am. Coll. of Mortgage Attys. 1978---; Calif. Sch. Bd. Assn. (dir. 1967-71). Contbg. author: New Dimensions In School Board Leadership, 1969; the Integration of Am. Schools, 1975. Home: 5515 Pacific Ave., Venice, CA 90291; Office: Suite 1900, 10906 Wilshire Blvd., L.A., CA 90024.

FINKEN, MARJORIE MORISSE
Columnist — Editor
b. June 29, 1918, St. Louis, Mo.; d. William J. (dec.) and Alice (Seidler) Morisse (O'Hern); great-grandau. of Ferdinand Diehm (1842-1916), Imperial and Royal Consul of Austria-Hungary in St. Louis, Mo., 1882-1915; grandniece of Albert Diehm, apptd. food admr. for 2 cos., Ill. by Pres. Herbert Hoover, 1914-18; bro. Richard Diehm Morisse (dec. Sept. 1968), aud. of USC, L.A. (20yrs.); ed. grad. L.A. H.S. 1936; stu. (dress design), Chouinard Inst. of Art, 1937-38; art maj., L.A. City Coll., 1938-40; m. John W. Finken, L.A., Apr. 26, 1940 (div. 1957); son, Richard Dale, b. May 8, 1943. Career: Profl. photog.; freelance photog. and rep., South Bay Daily Breeze, May 2, 1956, restaurant ed., 1956---, columnist, "Munchin with Marge," and "Marge to Midnight," 1956---. Awards: recd. first "Rose & Scroll" award for outstanding civic contrib. by Manhattan Beach C. of C. 1954. Mem.: secty-treas., L.A. chpt., Phi Epsilon Phi, 1942-43, 1944-45; pub. chmn., S. Bay Sym. Assn. 1954-55; pub. chmn., S. Bay Comm. Arts Assn., 1954-56; apptd. Calif. Rec. Commr. by Manhattan City Sch. Adm. 1954-60; secty-pub.

chmn.-dir., Inter-City Hwy. Comm. 1956-57; pub. chmn.-corr. secty., Women of Moose Lodge No. 323, Manhattan Beach, 1957-59, (charter) secty.-dir., S. Bay Hosp. Aux., 1959-61; Greater L.A. Press Club; bd. L.A. Chpt. Calif. Press Women; secty. Restaurant Writers Assn., L.A. Co. 1967-70; Pres., L.A. Restaurant Writers Assn., 1977-79; L.A. Mus. of Art; Altrusa Club Internat. Hobbies: theater, concerts, art. Home: 223 Avenue F., Redondo Beach, CA 90277; Office: South Bay Daily Breeze, 5215 Torrance Blvd., Torrance, CA 90509.

FIORE, EDITH ANNE
Clinical Psychologist
b. Sept. 13, 1930, Scarsdale, N.Y.; d. Frank (portrait painter) and Lillian Edith (Holbert) Fiore (owner, mgr. Gallery Bay Surf Club, Antigua, W.I.); B.S., Goucher Coll., Md., 1960; M.S., Univ. Md., 1965; Ph.D., Univ. Miami; m. Greg LeMons (filmmaker — "Skateboard Film Festival"), June 5, 1976, Los Gatos; chil.: Gail Irwin de Nava, b. Oct. 8, 1952; Leslie Luxenberg, b. Nov. 6, 1962; Dana Irwin Plays, b. July 2, 1978. Career: Staff psychologist, Children's Psychiatric Center, Miami, Fla., 1969-70; pvt. practice psychol., Miami, 1970-73; pvt. practice, Saratoga, Calif., 1973---. Author: You Have Been Here Before: A Psychologist Looks At Past Lives, Coward, McCann & Geoghegan, N.Y. 1977; presented paper, Am. Soc. of Clin. Hypnosis, St. Louis, 1978; Mem.: Solar Cross Found. Hobby: UFO Research. Office: 20688 Fourth St., Saratoga, CA 95070.

FIRESTONE, ANTHONY BROOKS
Vintner
b. June 18, 1936, Akron, Ohio; s. Leonard K. and Polly (Curtis) Firestone; B.A., Columbia Coll.; m. Catherine Boulton, Guildford, England, 1958. Career: with Firestone Tire & Rubber Co., 1960-72; vintner, The Firestone Vineyard, Los Olivos, Calif., 1972---. Dir. Firestone Tyre & Rubber Co., Great Britain; pres., the Firestone Vineyard; dir., the Tejon Ranch. Enlisted Corpsman, AUS, 1957-59. Clubs: Cypress Point, California, Rancheros Visitadores. Episcopal Ch., lay reader. Hobby: horses. Home: P.O.B. 36, Los Olivos, CA 93441; Office: P.O.B. 244, Los Olivos, CA 93441.

FIRESTONE, WILLIAM L.
Corporate Executive
b. June 20, 1921, Chicago; s. Samuel and Ida Firestone; B.S., Univ. Colo., 1949; M.S.E.E., Ill. Inst. Tech., 1949; Ph.D., E.E., Northwestern Univ., 1952; Cert. Bus. Adminstrn., Univ. Chicago, 1955; m. Roberta J. Roth, Feb. 1, 1953; Evanston; chil.: Randall S., b. Oct. 1953; Jeffrey I., b. Jan. 155; Gary A., b. June 1959. Career: dir. of engring., asst. gen. mgr., chief engring., Motorola, Inc., 1939-65; v.p., Hallicrafters Corp., 1965-66; group vice pres., Whittaker Corp., 1966-70; v.p., Gen. Instrument Corp., 1970-75; div. v.p., RCA, 1975---. Holder 9 patents; 20 papers publ. profl. journs., 1951-65, two papers awarded 1st prizes by Vehicular Communications Group of IEEE. Registered Profl. Engr. 1st Class Petty Officer, USN, instr. USN Navy Trng. Sch., Treasure Island, Calif. Mem.: Fellow, IEEE; AIM; chmn. engring. com., EIA, 1961; gen. chmn. Globecome, 1961; dir. Chgo. area R&D Council. Hobby: working with hands. Rec.: tennis, flying; Home: 16741 Rayen St., Sepulveda, CA 91343; Office: 8500 N. Balboa Blvd., Van Nuys, CA 91409.

FISCH, ARLINE M.
Professor of Art
b. Aug. 21, 1931, Brooklyn, N.Y.; d. Nicholas H. and Elizabeth (Fischer) Fisch; B.S., Skidmore Coll., 1952; M.A., Univ. Ill., 1954; Sch. of Arts and Crafts (Fulbright Scholar), Copenhagen, Denmark., 1956-57. Career: Instr. in Art, Skidmore Coll., 1957-61; Prof. of Art, San Diego State Univ., 1961---; Fulbright Research Grantee to Denmark (creative work in metal), 1967-68; sabbatical studies and work in London, Copenhagen, 1970-71; NEA Craftsman Grantee, 1974, Apprentice Grantee, 1977. First solo exhibition, Pasa. Mus. of Art, 1962; nat. and internat. exhibitions of Jewelry, 1962---. Author: Textile Techniques in Metal, Van Nostrand Reinhold, 1975; contbr. Calif. Design. v.p., World Crafts Council, 1976---; trustee, Am. Crafts Council, 1972-75; trustee, Haystack Sch. of Crafts, 1975---; founding mem., Soc. of No. Am. Goldsmiths;. Commnr., U.S. Commn. to UNESCO, 1977---. Rec.: tennis; Office: Art Dept., SDSU, San Diego, CA 92182.

FISHER, HON. HUGO MARK
Superior Court Judge
b. Apr. 30, 1921, San Diego; s. Mark and Sicily B. Fisher; S.D. City Schs., S.D. State Coll.; LL.B., Balboa

Univ., 1950; m. Lucia Sloane, Las Vegas, Nev., May 20, 1942; chil.: Anne Marie, b. Aug. 16, 1943; Girard, b. Nov. 6, 1945. Career: Partner, law firm Procopio, Price, Cory & Fisher, S.D., Jan. 1951---. Elected State Senator, 40th Calif. Dist., San Diego Co. 1958-62; admr. Resources Agcy., State of Calif., 1962-66; apptd. judge, Superior Ct. of Calif., S.D. Co. 1966. Mem.: Am., Calif. State and S.D. Co. Bar Assns.; Cabrillo Hist. Assn., S.D. Hist. Soc., Univ. Club of S.D., Elks Club. Democrat (exec. com., Calif. Dem. State Central Com., 1952-54; del. Dem. Natl. Conv. 1952, 56, 60). Unitarian. Office: 220 W. Broadway, Superior Ct., San Diego, CA.

FISHER, LEON HAROLD
Scientist — University Dean
b. July 11, 1918, Montreal, Canada.; s. Jacob and Rachel (Haimowitz) Fisher; B.S., chem., Univ. Calif., Berkeley, M.S., chem., 1940, Ph.D., physics, 1943; m. Phyllis Kahn, Dec. 21, 1941, S.F.; chil.: Robert Alan, b. Apr. 19, 1943; Lawrence Edgar, b. Jan. 13, 1946; Carol Lee Slotnick, b. May 13, 1951; David Bruce, b. May 19, 1953. Career: mem. faculty, Physics Dept., UC, Berkeley, 1943, Univ. N. Mex., 1944, N.Y. Univ., 1946-61; head, research group, Los Alamos Sci. Lab. Los Alamos, 1944-46; asst. mgr., Electronic Scis. Lab., Lockheed Palo Alto Research Lab., Sr. Cons. Sci. and Sr. Mem., 1963-69; prof. of Elect. Engring. and Head, Dept. Info. Engring., Univ. Ill., Chcgo Circle, 1971; prof. of physics and Dean, Sch. of Sci., Cal. State Univ., Hayward, 1971---. Mem.: AAAS, Am. Assn. of Physics Tchrs., Fellow, Am. Physical Soc. Contbr. to profl. journs.; assoc. ed., Physical Review, 1955-58. Jewish. Home: 102 Encinal Ave., Atherton, CA 94025; Office: Sch. of Sci., Cal. State Univ., Hayward, CA 94542.

FISHER, RAYMOND CORLEY
Attorney at Law
b. July 12, 1939, Oakland; s. Raymond H. and Mary (Corley) Fisher; B.A., polit. sci., Univ. Calif., Santa Barbara, 1961; LL.B., Stanford Law Sch., 1966; m. Nancy Fairchilds, Jan. 22, 1961, Rancho Santa Fe; chil.: Jeffrey Scott, b. July 28, 1961; Amy Elizabeth, b. July 21, 1966. Career: Law clerk to Judge J. Skelly Wright, U.S. Ct. of Appeals, 1966-67; Law clerk to Justice William J. Brennan, Jr., U.S. Supreme Court, 1967-68; Atty., officer and mem. of law firm of Tuttle & Taylor Inc., 1968---; special asst. to Gov. Brown on pub. employee collective bargaining legislation and state employee relations matters, 1975. Pres., Stanford Law Revise 1966; Order of the Coif 1966; Rec.: swimming, tennis. Home: 13841 Valley Vista Blvd., Sherman Oaks, CA 91423; Office: 609 S. Grand Ave., L.A., CA 90017.

FLANAGAN, JOHN DILLON
Mortuary Executive
b. Dec. 25, 1916, Ojai, Calif.; s. John and Grace (De War) Flanagan; grad. Anaheim Union H.S.; Long Beach Jr. Coll. 1936; Calif. Coll. of Mortuary Sci. 1936; m. Honorine T. Mansur, Honolulu, Hawaii, Mar. 12, 1969; chil.: John Michael, b. Dec. 30, 1941; Carol Jean, b. June 4, 1946; Deborah Darcelle, b. Feb. 23, 1952; Terri Ann, b. Aug. 14, 1959. Career: Pres. Flanagan & Rodger Mortuary, Fullerton, 1938-45; est. Inglewood res. 1945; propr.-pres., Hardin & Flanagan Mortuary, 1945-62; former propr.-pres.: Halverson-Leavell and Stone & Myers Mortuaries, Torrance; Mottell's Mortuary, L.B.; McNerney's Morturaries, Wilmington, Lomita; Evans-Brown Mortuaries, Sun City, Perris and Elsinore; pres. Custer Christiansen Mortuaries, Covina and W. Covina. Secty. bd. trustees, Meth. Hosp. 1946-60; v.p. bd. trustees, Daniel Freeman Mem. Hosp. 1952; pres. Inglewood Bd. Edn. 1957; pres. bd. trustees, Hawthorne Comm. Hosp. 1958. Chem. Warfare Serv., U.S. Army, WW II. Mem.: charter pres. Fullerton Jr. C. of C. 1938; pres. Inglewood C. of C. 1959; comdr. Inglewood Am. Legion, 1962; Rotary Internat., Elks, IOOF, pres. Young Republs. of N. Orange Co. 1938. St. Martin of Tours Cath. Ch. Hobby: tennis, fishing. Office: 124 S. Citrus Ave., Covina, CA 91722.

FLANNERY, ROBERT GENE
Railroad Company President
b. Sept. 14, 1924, Washington, Ind.; s. Allen H. and Nellie Jane (White) Flannery; B.S.C.E., Purdue Univ. 1948; AMP, Harvard Bus. Ach. 1965; Sys. Mgmt. Course, MIT, 1967; m. Barbara Ann Angell, Feb. 23, 1952; daus. Julia Ann, Jennifer Ann, Amy Lynn. Career: N.Y. Central R.R.: Engring. dept., asst. trainmaster, 1948-56; terminal trainmaster, Bellefontaine, Oh. 1956, dept. div. supt., Buffalo, N.Y. 1957-59; dir. transportation supt. Indianapolis, Ind. 1959; gen. mgr.: No. Dist., Detroit, 1961, Western Dist.,

Cleveland 1963; Eastern Dist., Syracuse, 1965; asst. v.p. N.Y. 1965; v.p. Sys. Devel., 1967; Penn Central Transportation Co.: dept. v.p. 1968-70, exec. v.p., v.p. oprns. 1970; Western Pac. R.R. Co.: exec. v.p., S.F., 1971; pres.-dir. 1973---; subsidiaries: v.p.-dir. Western Pac. Transport Co.; dir.: Sacto. No. Ry., Salt Lake City Union Depot and Ry. Co., Standard Realty and Dev. Co., Tidewater So. Ry. Co.; dir. Fruit Growers Express Co. Radar tech., USN 1943-45, WW II. Mem.: Natl. Def. Exec. Res.; Harvard Bus. Sch. Club, N.C.; F&AM; Pi Kappa Alpha; Newcomen Soc. of N. Am., World Trade Club, Pac. Ry. Club, Commonwealth Club of Calif., S.F. Home: 515 Pullman Rd., Hillsborough, CA 94010; Office: 526 Mission St., S.F., CA 94105.

FLEGAL, ARTHUR RUSSELL
Civic Leader — Antique Dealer
b. Apr. 29, 1919, S.F.; s. Frank Porter (Meth. minister; co-founder, Goodwill Inds., No. Calif.) and Edith (Davis) Flegal (listed, Prominent Personalities in Am. Methodism); ed. B.A., Univ. Calif. 1942; m. Barbara Warren, Oakland, Sept. 24, 1943; chil.: Arthur R., Jr., Leslie Jean, Warren Davis, Stephen Peter. Career: Sales merchandising, Am. Seating Co., others, 1945-68; br. mgr. Educators Mfg. Co., So. Calif. 1965-66; No. Calif. 1967-68; owner-mgr. investment properties, 1968---; Owner, Return Engagement Antiques; Councilman, City of Piedmont, 1968-76, Mayor 1970-72; Local Agcy. Formation Comm.; Alameda Co., 1970-76; chmn. 1975-76. USNR, So. Pac., WW II; Lt. (ret.). Awards: won natl. sales contest (repr. Am. Seating Co.). Mem.: pres. Valley Bear Backers, 1953; pres. Piedmont Council, B.S.A. 1964-65; v.p. Rotary Club, Piedmont, 1978; pres. bd. dirs. Goodwill Inds. Greater E. Bay, 1971-73, dir. 1973---; adv. bd. E. Bay Psychol. Center; Reg. Plan. Com., Assn. of Bay Area Govts., 1975-76, exec. com. 1970-74; past dir. Piedmont Beautification Found.; dir. Lake Merritt Breakfast Club; (life) Univ. Calif. Alumni Assn.; Aahmes Temple of Shrine, Scottish Rite, Oakland. Repub. State Central Com. First United Methodist Ch. (past pres., bd. trustees). Pres., Calif. Conf., Credit Union; pres., Oakland-So. Alameda Co. Chptr. Am. Natl. Red Cross. Home: 215 Pacific Ave., Piedmont, CA 94611.

FLEISCHMANN, ERNEST MARTIN
Executive Director, So. California Symphony
b. Dec. 7, 1924, Frankfurt, Ger.; ed. Chartered Accts., S.A. 1946; B.Mus., Capetown Univ. 1954; m. Elsa Leviseur, Simonstown, S. Africa, 1953; chil.: Stephanie, Martin, Jessica. Career: Cond. Labia Grand Opera Co. and guest cond. maj. S. African orchs. 1950-55; mus. dir. S. African Tercentenary, 1952; mgmt. dir. Sound & Film Servs., Capetown 1954-59; dir. music-drama, Johannesburg Festival, 1956; gen. mgr. London Sym. Orch. 1959-67; Europe dir., CBS Records (classics), 1967-69; exec. dir. L.A. Philharmonic Orch.-So. Calif. Sym.-Hollywood Bowl Assn. 1969---. Cond. music for films, incl.: Last of the Few, 1959; Interlude, 1967. Office: 135 N. Grand Ave., L.A., CA 90012.

FLEISHMAN, MAURICE H.
Architect
b. Aug. 19, 1909, New Brighton, Eng.; s. Harry A. and Ettie (Haft) Fleishman; B.Arch., McGill Univ., Can., 1936; m. Susanne Miller, Apr. 2, 1941, U.S.A.; sons, Allen H. and Harry D. Career: Arch., L.A., 1937-45; Beverly Hills, 1945---; pres., Maurice H. Fleishman and Assoc. Bldgs. incl.: E. San Gabriel Valley Regional Lib., 1961; Santa Monica Co. Courts, 1966; E. Dist. Superior Cts. (Pomona), 1968; Baldwin Park Lib., 1969; W. San Gabriel Regional Lib., 1969; Beverly Hills Municipal Cts., 1970; Malibu Adminstrv. Center, 1970; Whittier Municipal Cts. Bldg., 1972; Criminal Cts. Bldg. (Assoc. Arch.), 1973; Citrus Dist. Superior Cts. and Health Bldg. (West Covina), 1973; Lomita City Hall, 1973; L.A. Co. Adminstrv. Center (Lomita), 1973; Cerritos Lib., 1973; Engring. Scis. Bldg., 1976; Cerritos City Hall, 1978; Rio Hondo Municipal Cts. (El Monte), 1978; Baldwin Park City Hall, 1978; Edwards Air Force Base Lib., 1978. Chmn., Design Control Bd.; Dept. of Small Crafts Harbors, L.A. Co., 1945---. Mem.: McGill Grads. Soc. So. Calif., pres. 1962; Zeta Beta Tau; Profl. Men's Club, pres. 1963; AIA; NCARB. Rec.: sailing. Office: 333 S. Beverly Dr., No. 105, Beverly Hills, CA 90212.

FLEMING, JUNE D.
Library Director
b. June 24, 1931, Little Rock, Ark.; d. Herman and Ethel Dwellingham; ed. B.A. (psychol.), 1953; M.L.S. (lib. sci.), 1954; cert. Stanford Univ. Grad. Sch. Bus., 1973; m. Little Rock, Ark., Mar. 11, 1966; dau. Ethel Lucille Fleming; Career: Brooklyn Pub. Lib. 1954-55;

Little Rock Pub. Sch. Sys. 1955-56; chief librn., Philander Smith COll., Little Rock, 1960-67; lib. Mt. View, Calif. 1967-68; dir. of librs., Palo Alto, 1968---. Mem.: Delta Sigma Theta, Soroptimist Club; (past) bd. dirs. Mid. Peninsula YWCA. Methodist. Hobbies: walking, swimming. Home: 27975 Roble Blanco, Los Altos Hills, CA 94022; Office: 250 Hamilton Ave., Civic Center, Palo Alto, CA 94301.

FLEMING, MARY MADONNA KATZER
Accountant — Educator
b. July 4, 1936, Portsmouth, Ia.; d. John and Alma Katzer; B.S., UCLA, 1964; M.B.A., 1965; D.B.A, USC, 1979; m. Joseph Fleming, May 29, 1965, L.A.; chil.: Cynthia Patricia, b. July 17, 1966; John Michael, b. Jan. 3, 1970. Career: acct. and auditor, Adamson, Warren & Co., CPAs, L.A., 1959-63; supr. auditor, Defense Contract Audit Agcy., L.A. and E. Hartford, Ct., 1965-70; lectr. of Acctg., Central Conn. State Coll., 1965-70; Calif. State Univ., Fullerton, 1974. Contbr. articles on acctg. to profl. journs. Secty., Doctoral Student Assn., 1976-77; chmn. finance com., Pi Lambda Theta, 1978---. Office: CSU, Fullerton, CA 92634.

FLESHER, ARLIE MAE
Realtor and General Contractor
b. July 31, 1926, Devils Lake, N. Dak.; d. Herbert Levi and Mabel Carolyne (Iverson) Sorenson; (Grandfather S. assisted Danish families to emigrate and settle in midwest.); student, Auburn Acad., Wash.; Humboldt State Univ., Arcata; Redwood Jr. Coll., Eureka; m. Mr. Flesher (div.) Jan. 22, 1945, San Francisco; chil.: Lorna Jean (Watkins), b. Oct. 31, 1945; Larry James, b. May 19, 1949 (dec.). Career: design, build, market custom homes for family owned constrn. co., Bayside, Calif., 1948-72; Calif. real estate license, 1969; Calif. real estate brokers license, 1972; B. Gen. Bldg. Contractors Lic. No. 287750, 1973; partner, Sellers Realty Co., Arcata, McKinleyville and Eureka area, 1971-74; owner (Flesher Real Estate) now Mad River Realty, Valley West, Arcata, 1973---. Also broker and cons. on Planned Unit Devel. Exec. v.p., Ja-Pa Petroleum Corp., Oklahoma City, 1969. Mem.: Am. Business Womens Assn., Eureka, 1972-74; Soroptimist Internat. of Arcata; CAI Community Assns. Inst.; Humboldt Co. bd. of Realtors, Inc.; Calif. and Nat. Assns. of Realtors. Hobbies: photog., machine embroidery. Rec.: travel, skin diving. Home: 4530 Valley West Ct., Arcata, CA 95524; Office: 1551 Giuntoli Lane, Arcata, CA 95524.

FLETCHER, DOUGLAS BADEN
Securities Executive
b. Mar. 25, 1925, Pleasant Ridge, Mich.; s. Ernest H. and Gladys M. (Marthan) Fletcher; ed. Roosevelt Sch., Pleasant Ridge, Mich., 1931-37; Cranbrook Sch. for Boys, Bloomfield Hills, Mich., 1937-43; B.A., Princeton Univ. 1946-49; m. Sally Wittenberg, Minneapolis, Minn., Spet. 9, 1950; chil.: David Baden, b. Apr. 10, 1952; Christopher Keech, b. Mar. 13, 1953; James Peter, b. Mar. 1, 1955; Jonathan, b. Oct. 5, 1962. Career: Security Analyst, Walston & Co., N.Y. 1949-53; underwriting dept., Blyth & Co., Inc., L.A. 1953-62; chairman-pres.-dir.: First Pac. Advisors, Inc. (formerly Shareholders Mgmt. Co.), 1962---; Comstock Fund., Inc.; Enterprise Fund., Inc.; Fletcher Fund, Inc.; Harbor Fund, Inc.; Legal List Investments, Inc.; Pace Fund, Inc. 1962-78; chmn.-dir.-CEO Angeles Corp. (formerly Shareholders Capital Corp.) 1968---; exec. com.-bd. govs. Investment Co. Inst. U.S. Army, 1943-46, WW II. Mem.: pres. L.A. Soc. of Financial Analysts, 1960-61; Inst. of Chartered Financial Analysts; pres. Princeton Club of So. Calif. 1962-64. Office: 1888 Century Park E., L.A., CA 90067.

FLETCHER, JOHN GEORGE
Physicist
b. Oct. 28, 1934, Aberdeen, S. Dak.; s. Howard Balle and Linda (Sorgenfrey) Fletcher; A.A., 1953, B.S., George Washington Univ., 1955; M.A., 1957; Ph.D., 1959 (physics), Princeton Univ.; m. Margaret Ellen (Jill) Thompson, Aug. 18, 1956, College Park, Md.; chil.: Linda Joanne, 1958-65; twins, Barbara Ellen and David Howard, b. Sept. 11, 1959. Career: Instr. in physics, Princeton Univ., 1959-60; Fellow of Miller Inst., Univ. Calif., Berkeley, 1960-62; physicist, Lawrence Livermore Lab. (Computer Communications Group Leader), 1962---; lectr. in Applied Sci., Univ. Calif., Davis, 1965---. Contbr. approx. 25 sci. papers in physics and computing sci. profl. publs. Mem.: Phi Beta Kappa, Sigma Xi, Sigma Nu, Am. Physical Soc., Assn. for Computing Machinery. Hobby: photog. Rec.: hiking, bicycling. Office: Lawrence Livermore Lab., P.O.B. 808, Livermore, CA 94550.

FLICK, JOHN EDMOND
General Counsel, Times Mirror Co.
b. Mar. 14, 1922, Franklin, Pa.; s. E.L. and Mary M. Flick; Univ. of Pa. and Northwestern Univ. 1941-44, 45, LL.B., 1948; grad. Legal Judge Adv. Gen's. Sch., Univ. of Va., 1960-61; m. Lois A. Lange, Andalusia, Pa., Apr. 20, 1946; chil.: Gregory A., b. Sept. 18, 1947; Scott E., b. Jan. 15, 1952; Lynn E., b. Sept. 14, 1956; Ann E., b. Oct. 10, 1960. Career: Admitted to Bar of Calif., Ill., Fed. Dist. Ct.; atty at law and faculty, Calif. Western Univ. Law Sch., 1948-50; faculty, U.S. Mil. Acad., West Point, N.Y., 1954-57; counsel-dir. contracts, Litton Inds., Inc. 1963-67; sr. v.p.-gen. counsel-secty. dir. Bangor Punta Corp. 1967-69; bd. dirs. Piper Aircraft Corp. 1969; sr. v.p.-secty.-bd. dirs. The Cosmodyne Corp. 1969-70; v.p.-gen counsel-secty. Times Mirror Co. 1970---; dir. Tejon Ranch Co., 1975---; dir. The Sporting News Co., 1977---. Author: State Tax Liability of Servicemen and Their Dependents, punl. Wash. and Lee Law Review, 1964. Ofcr. Judge Advocate Gen's. Corps, 1950-63; Lt. Col., USAR (ret.). Awards: Acad. Awards by Lawyers Cooperative Co., Judge Adv. Assn., Am. Bar Assn. 1961. Mem.: Am., Fed., L.A. Co., Calif., Ill. Bar Assns.; Judge Adv. Alumni Assn.; Northwestern Univ. Alumni Assn.; Am. Soc. of Corp. Sectys.; Jonathan Club. Methodist ch. (trustee, 1965-67). Hobbies: reading, art, photog. Rec.: swim, bowling. Home: 23680 Park Sevilla, Calabasas Park, CA 91302; Office: Times-Mirror Square, L.A., CA 90053.

FLOOD, JOHN ETCHELLS, JR.
Title Company President
b. Oct. 16, 1929, Sanford, Me.; s. John Etchells, Sr. and Bertha (Goodrich) Flood; A.B., Univ. of N.C., 1952; M.B.A., Harvard Univ., 1957; m. Dorothy Haight, Nov. 27, 1954; chil.: Elizabeth Ann, b. May 13, 1957; John Brian, b. Mar. 28, 1959. Career: Mktg. cons., Litton Industries, 1957-59; mktg. cons. Mobil Chem. Co., 1959-69; gen. mgr., Films Dept. Plastics Div., Chelsea Industries, 1969-71; group v.p., Title Ins. and Trust Co./Pioneer Nat. Title Ins. Co., 1971, pres. and chef exec. officer, 1971---. Club: Los Angeles. Unitarian. Home: 533 Via Media, Palos Verdes Estates, CA 90274; Office: 6300 Wilshire Blvd., L.A., CA 90048.

FLOURNOY, HOUSTON I.
University Dean
b. Oct. 7, 1929, N.Y.C.; s. William R. and Helen (Horner) Flournoy; ed. N.Y. and New England pub. schs.; B.A. (govt.), Cornell Univ. 1950; M.A., Princeton Univ., 1952; Ph.D. (govt.) 1956; m. Marjorie Westerkamp, Denver, Colo., July 11, 1954; chil.: David Houston, b. July 31, 1960; Jean Douglas, b. Feb. 10, 1962; Ann Horner, b. Jan. 26, 1971. Career: Researcher, Div. of Law Revision and Legislature Information, N.J. State Legislature, 1955; legislative asst. to U.S. Sen. H. Alexander Smith of N.J., Wash., D.C. 1955-57; elected Calif. Assemblyman, 49th Dist. (serv. finance ins., edn., election, reapportionment coms.), 1960-66; elected State Controller, State of Calif. Nov. 1966-75; Repub. Candidate for Gov. 1974. Assoc. prof. (govt.) Pomona Coll. and Claremont Grad. Sch. 1957-66; prof. USC 1975---; Dean, Center for Pub. Affairs, 1975---. Mem.: dir. Lockheed Aircraft Corp., 1976---; dir., Gibraltar Financial Corp., 1975---; pub. gov., Pac. Coast Stock Exch. Bd. of Govs., 1975---. Co-author: Legislative Bodies in Calif.; USAF Intelligence ofcr., Korea, 1952-54; Lt. Col., Calif. Air Natl. Guard. Republican. Congregationalist. Rec.: skiing, golf. Office: USC, University Park, L.A., CA 90007.

FLUOR, JOHN ROBERT
Chairman-CEO, Fluor Corp.
b. Dec. 18, 1921, Santa Ana; s. Peter E. and Margaret (Fischer) Fluor; ed. USC 1939-42; and 1945-46; m. Lillian Marie Breaux, Anaheim, May 17, 1944; chil.: John Robert II, b. July 25, 1945; Peter James, b. June 27, 1947. Career: Mfg. cost acct., The Fluor Corp., Ltd., 1946-47, mgr. of mfg. 1947, v.p.-asst. gen. mgr., 1947-49, v.p.-gen. mgr., 1949-52; exec. v.p. 1952-65; pres. 1962-68; chmn.-chief exec. ofcr. 1968---; v.p. (hon.) NAM; dir. Calif. Canadia Bank; dir. Crown Zellerbach Corp.; dir., Texas Commerce Bancshares, Inc.; dir., Pac. Mutual Life Ins. Co.; dir., Santa Anita Consolidated, Inc.; Central Pacific Theater pilot, Army Air Force, WW II. Awards: won Distinguished Flying Cross and the Air Medal for service AAF, WW II; Mem.: Sky Club, N.Y.; Club De Caza y Pesca Las Cruces; chmn. bd. trustees, USC; Eldorado Country Club, Palm Desert, L.A. Club; San Gabriel Country Club; Calif. Club, L.A. Catholic. Hobby: thoroughbred horse racing. Rec.: golf. Home: P.O.B. 2387, Newport Beach, CA 92663; Office: 3333 Michelson Dr., Irvine, CA 92730.

FOLLETT, BARBARA LEE
Writer
b. Mar. 4, 1911, S.F.; d. Ralph C. and Violette (Morris) Lee; ed. Principia Sch., St. Louis; Scripps Coll., 1932; misc. classes: decorating, art, writing; m. Benjamin N. Follett, 1933, Hillsborough, Calif.; chil.: Alan Lee, b. 1936; Teris, b. 1939. Career: Author: Check List For A Perfect Wedding, Doubleday Dolphine Series (750,000 copies sold); Check List for Entertaining, Doubleday Dolphin Series; contbr. articles: Reader's Digest, The Christian Science Monitor, newspapers; question and answer column. Volunteer orgns.: treas., Stanford Children's Convalescent Aux.; treas., Assistance League of San Mateo Co.; pres., De Young Mus. Aux. of S.F. (in charge of introducing Audio Guides to mus.); Burlingame Writer's Club, past pres., 1965---. Hobbies: collecting and fabricating miniatures, golf, bridge. Home: 80 De Sabla Rd., Hillsborough, CA 94010.

FONTENROSE, JOSEPH
Professor Emeritus of Classics
b. June 17, 1903, Sutter Creek; s. Antone and Alice Laura (Eddy) Fontenrose; nephew, Louis Fontenrose, Co. Clerk of Amador Co., 1880-1906; A.B., Univ. Calif., Berkeley, 1925, M.A., 1928, Ph.D., 1933; m. Marie Holmes, June 22, 1942, Reno, Nev.; chil.: Jane (Mrs. Cajina), b. Nov. 15, 1942; Robert, b. Dec. 10, 1944; Anne (m. Azia Mujadedy), b. July 10, 1949. Career: Instr. in the Classics, Cornell Univ., 1931-33; asst. prof. of Greek and Latin, Univ. of Ore., 1934 (Jan.-June); Instr. in Greek, Univ. of Calif., Berkeley, 1934-35; Instr. in Latin, 1937-41; asst. prof. of Classics, 1941-47; Assoc. Prof. of Classics, 1947-55; Prof. of Classics, 1955-70; Emeritus, 1970---; Vis. prof., Brandeis Univ., 1971. Author: Python: A Study of Delphic Myth and Its Origins (1959); The Ritual Theory of Myth (1966); John Steinbeck: An Introduction and Interpretation (1963); The Delphic Oracle: Its Responses and Operations (1978); The Cult and Myth of Pyrros at Delphi (1960); contbr. articles and reviews to lit. journs. Mem.: UC Faculty Club. Socialist. Hobby: books. Home: 823 San Luis Rd., Berkeley, CA 94707; Office: 241 Moses Hall, UCB, Berkeley, CA 94720.

FORBES, EDWARD WHEELER
Industrialist
b. Jan. 26, 1925, L.A.; s. Clarence H. and Bernice (Wheeler) Forbes; B.S., USC 1949; chil.: Wendy Lee, b. Apr. 3, 1951; Edward Dennis, b. Dec. 31, 1952; Sheri Jacqueline, b. Aug. 29, 1964. Career: v.p., pres. Western Engring. and Mfg. Co. 1950---. Founding bd. dirs. Wilshire Natl. Bank, 1962---. USN Elec. Warfare, 1943-46, WW II. Mem.: bd. dirs. Bel-Air Bay Club, 1973-74; Young President's Orgn., Chaparral Club, Trojan Club, Diadons, Delta Tau Delta. Hobbies: amateur radio, licensed scuba diver. Office: 4114 Glencoe Ave., Marina del Rey, CA 90291.

FORD, CORNELIUS WILLIAM
Consultant
b. Oct. 16, 1918, Bingham Canyon, Ut.; s. John William and Esther May Ford; grad. Bingham H.S. 1935; m. Anne Ford, Pueblo Colo., July 18, 1945; chil.: Leanna Jo, b. Apr. 1, 1948; William Douglas, b. June 27, 1951; John Christopher, b. June 18, 1958. Career: Asst. controller, Mill Mutuals Ins. Co., L.A. 1937-39; La Brea Securities Co., L.A. 1939-43; La Brea Securities Co. & Affiliates, 1945-47; exec. v.p., Santa Maria Svgs. & Loan Assn. 1947-56; exec. v.p., pres. Central Svgs. & Loan Assn. 1956-60; exec. v.p. First Svgs. & Loan, Oakland, 1960-61, pres.-dir. 1961, dir. 1969---; pres.-dir. Great Western Financial Corp., and Great Western Svgs. & Loan, 1964-75; cons. 1975---. Pvt., U.S. Air Corps, 1942; 2nd Lt., 8th Air Force, Eng.; P.O.W., Ger. (9 mos.), WW II. Mem.: chmn. City Planning Commn., Santa Maria; Knights of Columbus. Catholic. Hobby: stamps, music. Rec.: golf. Office: 8484 Wilshire Blvd., Beverly Hills, CA.

FORD, GERALD R.
38th President of United States
b. July 14, 1913, Omaha, Nebr.; B.A., Univ. Mich., 1935; LL.B., Yale Univ. Law Sch., 1941; m. Elizabeth Bloomer, Oct. 15, 1948; chil.: Michael Gerald, b. Mar. 14, 1950; John Gardner, b. Mar. 16, 1952; Steven Meigs, b. May 19, 1956; Susan Elizabeth, b. July 6, 1957. Career: Admitted to Mich. bar, 1941; law practice, Grand Rapids, 1941-49, mem. law firm Buchen and Ford; elected from 5th Mich dist. to U.S. House of Reps., 81st-93rd Congresses, 1948-1973; elected chmn. of Repub. Conf., 1963, Minority Leader, 1965, permanent chmn. Repub. Natl. Conventions, 1968, 72; named Vice Pres., U.S., 1973-74, succeeded to U.S.

Presidency, Aug. 9, 1974-Jan. 20, 1977; apptd. mem. of Presidential Commn. to investigate assassination of Pres. J.F. Kennedy, 1963, author (w/John R. Stiles) Portrait of the Assassin, 1965. Awards incl.: Distinguished Congressional Service Award, Am. Polit. Sci. Assn. 1961; George Washington Award, Am. Good Govt. Soc., 1966; Golden Plate Award, Am. Acad of Achievement, 1971; Silver Helmet Award, AMVETS, 1971; Silver Buffalo Award, BSA, 1975; all-city and all-state football honors, Grand Rapids H.S.; named most valuable player, Univ. of Mich., 1934. Lt. Comdr., USN, 1942-46; aircraft carrier USS Monterey. Mem.: Am., Mich. State, Grand Rapids bar assns., Delta Kappa Epsilon, Phi Delta Phi. Republican. Episcopalian. Clubs: Masons, Univ., Peninsular (Kent. Co.). Home: Rancho Mirage, CA 92270.

FORD, HARRY X.
College President
b. Jan. 12, 1921, Seymour, Ind.; s. John William and Emma (Gibo) Ford; stu. John Herron Art Inst., Indianapolis, 1940-41; B.A., UCLA 1949; Tchg. Credential, 1950; M.A., Sacto. State Coll. 1953; m. Celeste de Vaca; sons: John, Anthony. Career: Art tchr., Placer Union H.S., Auburn, 1950-53; Stuttgart Am. H.S., Germ. (designed art pgm. Am. Dependent Schs., Germ; travel research, Western Europe), 1953-58; chmn. Dept. Tchr. Edn., Calif. Coll. of Arts and Crafts, Oakland, 1958-59, pres., 1959---; pres. Union of Independent Colls. of Art, 1972, 73. Aviation cadet tr. 1941-42; 2nd Lt., cadet, USAF, Eng., 1943; prisoner, Ger. Luftwaffe, 1943-45; Capt., WW II; edn. spec., 12th A.F. Res. Pgm., Maj. 1957. Awards: Bronze Star and Air Medal; Hon. Doctorate of Fine Arts, Kansas City Art Institute, 1974. Mem.: Calif. Tchrs. Assn.; Oakland C. of C. 1959-78; treas., Natl. Assn. Schs. of Art, 1976-78; Alameda Co. Art Comm., 1965---, chmn. 1968-69; bd. dirs. Oakland Mus. 1965-66; bd. dirs. Oakland Repertory Theater Assn.; Oakland-Piedmont Arts Council; adv. bd. Paramount Theater of Arts, Oakland, 1972-73; treas. World Print Council; (hon.) trustee Osaka Univ. of Arts, Japan, 1973-74; Bohemian Club. Office: Broadway at College Ave., Oakland, CA 94618.

FORD, WILLIAM F.
Economist
b. Aug. 14, 1936, Huntington, N.Y.; B.A., economics, Univ. of Tex., 1961 (Phi Beta Kappa, Summa Cum Laude); M.A., Univ. Mich., 1962, Ph.D., economics, 1966; m. Diane McDonald, June 11, 1960, Tulia, Tex.; chil.: Eric W., b. Dec. 13, 1964; Kristin E., b. Sept. 19, 1968. Career: Economist, RAND Corp., 1966; asst. prof., Univ. Va., 1967-69; assoc. prof., Texas Tech. Univ., 1969-70; prof. of economics & Dean, Transylvania Coll., 1970-71; exec. dir. and chief economist, Research & Planning Group, Am. Bankers Assn., 1971-75; sr. v.p., chief economist, Wells Fargo Bank (supr. 3 hdwtrs. staff depts.: Corporate Planning, Economics, Govt. Rels.), 1975---. Author: Mexico's Foreign Trade and Development, Frederick A. Praeger, 1966; 30 articles and reviews in economics, banking and finance pub. in profl. journs. USN, 1954-62, submarine service, 1954-57. Home: 153 Riviera Dr., San Rafael, CA 94901; Office: 475 Sansome St., S.F., CA 94111.

FORMHALS, ROBERT WILLARD YATES
Educational Corporation Executive
b. June 14, 1919, L.A.; s. Carl Wright and Muriel (Yates) Formhals; grandson of Carl M. Formhals, automobile mfr. and great-grandson of Prince Janus Sanguszko; 4th great uncle, Michael Yates, M.D.; and 5th great-grandson of Rev. Bartholomew Yates; ed. LL.B., Welch Coll. 1943; D.C.I. Sheffield Coll. 1964; m. Elaine Mary Peters, North Hollywood, Apr. 4, 1947; son, Robert Arthur Clinton, b. Oct. 22, 1953. Career: Personnel mgr., Warman Steel Casting Co., 1942-43, 1944-47; dept. state labor commr. Calif. 1948; adm. asst., State Arch. of Calif. 1948-59; chancellor, Pac. Maritime Acad. 1950-52; exec. secty.-treas., Calif. Sch. Bds. Assn. 1961-67; pres. Assoc. Mgmt. Servs. 1967-70; staff San Jose City Manager, 1970-74. Dir. Hawaiian West Coast Lines, Inc. 1949-51; chmn. Gov. of Calif.'s Adv. Com. on Disaster Preparedness, 1961-67; commr. Calif. Comm. on Sch. Dist. Orgn. 1961-64; cons. to bd. dirs., Calif. Council on Edn. of Tchrs., 1963-67; Author: Handbook of Armed Forces of the World, 1948; Manual of Precedence, 1967; contrib. to ency., Our Wonderful World, publ. 1966-71, others. ERC, U.S. Army, 1940-41, 1943-44, WW II; Calif. Natl. Guard Res. 1950-66; Maj., Inf., Ofc. of Adj. Gen. of Calif. 1960. Awards: Natl. Patriotic Council Award; Grand Master, Order of St. John of Jerusalem, 1963; Knight Comdr. of St. Brigit of Sweden, 1964; Knight Grand Ofcr., of the

White Eagle Crown of Yugoslavia, by King Peter II, 1969. Mem.: Knights of Pyhtias, 1938; Eagles, 1939; State Comm., Young Demo. of Calif., 1940-43, state v.-chmn., 1941-43, natl. com., Dems. for Dewey, 1944, state chmn., Dems. for Knowland, 1956, v.-chmn., Sacto. Co. Repub. Precinct Orgn. 1960; Am. Legion, 1945; Am. Soc. of Safety Engrs. 1955, natl. exec. bd. 1959-60; Am. Soc. of Assn. Execs., 1962; Grupo Americo, 1964; Natl. Com. for Support of Pub. Schs., 1964; Severance Club, 1966; exec. secty., Calif. Soc., Sons of the Am. Revolution. Chr. Sci. Hobby: hist. Rec.: writing. Home: 5609 E. Willow View Dr., Camarillo, CA 93010.

FORTGANG, MARTIN JAY
Psychotherapist
b. June 1, 1947, N.Y.C.; s. Louis and Sylvia (Deutsch) Fortgang; B.A., City Coll. of N.Y., 1968; M.A., clin. psychol., Clark Univ., 1971; Career: research asst. and psychotherapist trainee, Clark Univ., 1969-71, instr., 1969-71; research writer, Research Unlimited of S.F., 1972-74; instr., Calif. Inst. of Asian Studies, 1974---; Psychotherapist for City and Co. of San Francisco, 1974---. Founder and dir., Maitreya Counseling Ark. Co-author: Mindwandering and Cognitive Structure, pub. Transactions of the N.Y. Acad. of Sci., Feb. 1970. Awards: U.S. Pub. Health Service Traineeship, 1968-71; N.Y. State Regents Tchg. Fellowship and Scholarship, 1968; Calif. Profl. Licenses in Marriage, Family and Child Counseling. Mem.: Assn. for Transpersonal Psychology, Phi Beta Kappa, Assn. for Humanistic Psychol., Am. Personnel and Guidance Assn., AAUP; Assn. for Counselor Edn. and Supervision. Rec.: meditation, musical improvisation, camping. Home: 6108 Hillegass St., Oakland, CA 94618.

FOSTER, HELEN LAURA
Geologist
b. Dec. 15, 1919; d. Stanley Allen and Alice Mary (Osborn) Foster; B.S., Univ. Mich., 1941, M.S., 1943, Ph.D., 1946. Career: Tchr. of Sci. and social sci., Blissfield Pub. H.S., Mich., 1941-42; instr. in geology, Wellesley Coll., Mass., 1946-48; Univ. of Mich. Summer Field Camp, Jackson, Wyo., 1947; Mil. Geology Branch, U.S. Geological Surveys, 1948-65; Chief, Geol. Research Sect. Pac. Geol. Surveys, 1949-51; Chief, Far East Intelligence Program, 1951-55; Chief, Ishigaki Field Party, 1955-57; project chief, Yukon-Tanana, Ak., branch of Alaskan Geol., U.S. Geol. Survey, 1965---: past project chief: Tanacross, Big Delta, and Circle Alaska Mineral Resources Appraisal projects. Publs.: over 100 pub. articles on geological subjects, 1946---. Mem.: Potomac Applachian Trail Club, 1960-70; Wanderbirds, 1960-65; Sigma Xi; Phi Beta Kappa; numerous sci. and geol. socs.; v.p., Peninsula Geological Soc., 1978. Hobbies: philately, music. Rec.: skiing, backpacking. Home: 270 O'Keefe St., Palo Alto, CA 94303; Office: 345 Middlefield Rd., Menlo Park, CA.

FRANCIS, DETRA LEE SOPINSKI
Real Estate Broker
b. July 8, 1944, Indianapolis, Ind.; d. Zygmunt J. and Mary A. Sopinski; grad., Laverne College, Calif. Life Secondary Teaching Credential; m. Michael Hoyer Francis, Dec. 24, 1975, Laguna Beach; son, Luke S., b. July 20, 1978. Career: Licensed Real Estate agent, 1972; sales agent, McCormack Real Estate, 1972-75; prin., Dolphin Real Estate, Laguna Beach, 1975---; tchr., biology and physical edn., 1966-72. Participant (pottery) Laguna Beach Festival of the Arts. Home: 731 Manzanita Dr., Laguna Beach, CA 92651; Office: 998 S. Coast Hwy., Laguna Beach, CA 92651.

FRANK, ANTHONY M.
President, Citizens Savings & Loan Association
b. May 21, 1931, Berlin, Germ.; s. Lothar and Elizabeth Frank; A.B., Dartmouth, 1953; M.B.A., Tuck Sch.; m. Gay Palmer, chil.: Tracy Felicia, b. Feb. 15, 1961; Randall Palmer, b. July 6, 1962. Career: asst. to pres., Glendale Fed. S&L, 1958-61; vice pres.-treas., Far West Fin. Corp., 1962; adminstrv. v.p., First Charter Fin. Corp., 1962-66; pres., State Mutual Svgs., 1966-68; pres., Titan Group, 1968-70; pres., INA Properties, 1970-71; pres., Citizens Svgs., 1971---; vice chmn. and chief exec. officer, 1973---, chmn., pres. & chief exec. ofcr., Citizens Svgs. & United Fin. Corp. (holding Co. of CS&L). Chmn., Fed. Home Loan Bank of S.F., 1970-71; pres., Calif. Svgs. & Loan League, 1976; chmn., Calif. Housing Finance Agcy., 1976---. Cpl., AUS, Div. of Intelligence. Hobbies: skiing, hiking. Home: 10 Windward Rd., Belvedere, CA; Office: 700 Market St., S.F., CA 94102.

FRANKEL, JACOB PORTER
College President
b. Sept. 7, 1923, Philadelphia, Pa.; s. Harold Aaron and Ceil (Porter) Frankel; M.S., Univ. of Calif., Berkeley, 1947; Ph.D., UCLA, 1951; m. Helen Bruce, Jan. 27, 1946; chil.: Martha Jean; Molly; David Alan; Deborah; Robert Aaron. Career: Instr., then asst. prof., engring., UCLA, 1948-52; lead metallurgist Cal. Research and Devel. Co., 1952-54; assoc. prof. Northwestern Univ., 1954-56; assoc. prof., then prof., UCLA, 1957-66; assoc. dean, prof. Thayer Sch. Engring, Dartmouth, 1966-68; dean of faculty, Harvey Mudd Coll. Sci. and Engring., 1968-74; president, Calif. State Coll., Bakersfield, 1974---. Dir., Nuclear Division of Systems Laboratories Corp., Sherman Oaks (1957). Author: The Principles of the Properties of Materials, 1957. Mem.: Petroleum Club, Rio Bravo Tennis Club, Phi Beta Kappa, Sigma Xi. Home: 2424 Spruce Street, Bakersfield, CA 93301; Office: 9001 Stockdale Hwy., Bakersfield, CA 93309.

FRANKLYN, AUDREY P(OZEN)
Public Relations Consultant
b. Dec. 8, 1930, Detroit, Mich.; d. Sidney and Rachel Pozen; A.A., L.A. City Coll., 1952; student, UCLA, 1952-55; Career: started Franklyn Agency, 1959---: as impresario promoting Ella Fitzgerald; Mahalia Jackson; Tom Lehrer; Pearl Bailey; became Ella Fitzgerald's exclusive promoter, 1966---; promoter concerts, U.S. and Canada; promoter for Pablo Records, Beverly Hills (one of few women heads of record company's promotion dept.) and Norman Granz; also active in med. arts pub. rels. field; literary promoter (The Happy Hustler by Grant Tracy Saxon, Warner Books; Great L.A. Blizzard, by Thom Racina, Putnam's.; others); has been tagged Picasso of Promotion, on radio and TV show appearances in So. Calif. Mem.: L.A. Press Club; the Pirates; Women in Communication. Hobbies: record collecting, having parties. Office: 1010 Hammond St., No. 312, L.A., CA 90069.

FRANKLYN, ROBERT ALAN
Plastic Surgeon
b. Apr. 30, 1918; s. Joseph and Theresa Franklyn; B.S., New York Univ., 1937, M.D., 1941; m. Wilma Lynne, Jan. 10, 1942, L.A.; Career: Chief Surgeon, Bel Air Hosp., L.A., 1960; chmn., Bd. of Trustees, Metropolitan State Hosp., Norwalk, 1967; Chief plastic surg., The Beauty Pavilion, L.A., 1967; med. practice, Hollywood ---; Author: Supercharge Yourself, 1979; Beauty Surgeon, 1960. Democrat, mem. finance com. 1960-62. Office: 8760 Sunset Blvd., Hollywood, CA 90069.

FRANZBLAU, MICHAEL
Psychiatrist
b. June 24, 1935, Manhattan, N.Y.; s. Abraham (prominent psychiatrist N.Y.C., mem. faculty Mt. Sinai Sch. of Med.) and Rose (Doctor of Psychology, Ph.D., columnist for New York Post 25 yrs., art patron and mem. selection com. for Tony Awards) Franzblau; grad. Bronx H.S. of Sci.; B.S., Bard Coll. 1956; M.D., Einstein Med. Sch., 1961; m. Kathryn Weiser, M.D., 1974, L.A.; chil.: Susan, b. 1961; John, b. 1964. Career: tng. in psychoanalysis, L.A. Psychoanalytic Inst.; practice of psychiatry, Beverly Hills ---; Staff Psychiat. Fed. Correctional Inst., Lomoc, 1965-67; (lifework: study of human mind); Mil.: U.S. Pub. Health Serv., 1965-67. Chmn. Ethics Com., L.A. Psychoanalytic Soc.; mem. Am. Psychiatric Assn.; mem. Am. Psychoanalytic Assn. Hobbies: art, furniture building. Rec.: tennis, skiing. Home: 171 Ashdale Ave., L.A., CA 90049; Office: 450 N. Bedford Dr., Beverly Hills, CA 90210.

FRATIANNE, LINDA SUE
Ice Skater
b. Aug. 2, 1960, Northridge, Calif.; d. Robert D. (attorney at law) and Virginia L. Fratianne. Career: mem. U.S. World & Olympic Team, Innsbruck, Austria, 1976. Awards: gold medal, VII Grand Prix Internat., St. Gervais, France and silver medal, Nebelhorn Trophy, Oberstdorf, Germ., 1973; in 1976: bronze medal, Richmond Trophy, Richmond, England; Silver Medal, U.S. Senior Ladies, Colo. Springs, Colo.; bronze medal, world championships — free style, Goetenberg, Sweden; in 1977: gold medal, U.S. Sr. Championships, Hartford, Conn.; gold medal, Skate Canada, Moncton, New Brunswick; gold medal, World Championships, Tokyo, Japan; in 1978: gold medal, U.S. Sr. Championships, Portland, Ore.; silver medal, World Championships, Ottawa, Quebec, Ont. Home: 18214 Septo St., Northridge, CA 91324.

FRAWLEY, PATRICK JOSEPH, JR.
Company President
b. May 26, 1923, Leon, Nicaragua; s. Patrick Joseph, Sr. and Marie (Peugnet) Frawley; ed. St. Cecilia's Parochial Sch., S.F.; St. Joseph's Mil. Acad., Belmont, Calif.; St. Ignatius H.S., S.F.; m. Gerardine Ann Clancy, Vancouver, B.C., Sept. 12, 1944; chil.: Frances, b. June 25, 1945; Joseph, b. May 15, 1948; Mary Louise, b. Sept. 12, 1949; Eileen, b. Nov. 27, 1951; Michael, b. Jan. 24, 1954; Joan, b. Mar. 30, 1955; Barbara, b. July 29, 1956; Ann, b. Dec. 27, 1957. Career: import-export bus. Nicaragua, 1942; pres. Frawley Corp. (import-export bus.), S.F., 1945-59; founder-owner, Paper Mate Co. 1949-55; investments exec. 1955-58; pres. Eversharp, Inc., 1958-66; chmn. bd. dirs. 1961-66, chmn.-exec. com.-dir., 1967---; chmn. bd.-dir., Technicolor, Inc. 1961-69; chmn. exec. com. Schick Inc. 1971---; chmn. bd. Schick's Shadel Hosp. 1964---; pres. Frawley Enterprises, Inc.; Freedoms Found. at Valley Forge. Royal Canadian A.F. (1942-44), WW II. Roman Catholic. Hobby: chess. Rec.: tennis, swimming, yachting. Home: 618 Club View Dr., L.A., CA 90024; Office: 1901 Ave. of the Stars, Suite 1500, L.A., CA 90067.

FRAZER, EDMUND JAMES
Public Relations Counselor
b. Oct. 3, 1916, Evanston, Ill.; s. George Enfield (atty. and CPA, ret.) and Helen Dixon (James) Frazer; grandson of Dr. Edmund J. James, founder, Wharton Sch. of Finance and pres. of Northwestern Univ., Ill.; ed. B.A., Univ. Wis., 1937; law stu. (4 yrs.) Harvard Univ., Northwestern Univ.; m. Helen Clark, Pasadena, Nov. 24, 1967; son: George Enfield, III, b. Aug. 17, 1950. Career: Radio sports anncr., Wis. 1935-37; sports columnist, Chicago, Ill. 1938-41; Wash. repr. Gas Appliance and Equip. Mfrs. 1940; pres. Natl. Transitads Inc., N.Y.C. 1945-55; propr.-dir. Edmund J. Frazer and Assocs. (internat. pub. rels.), 1955-71; propr. Communications Frazer Internat. 1971---. Ofcr., USNR. Awards: 8 medals and 18 battle stars, Mem.: VFW, Am. Legion, SAR, Alpha Delta Phi, Phi Delta Phi; pres. L.A. Council BSA; clubs: Chancery, Army-Navy, Chicago Press, Annandale Golf; Univ., Chicago and N.Y.C.; Nautico of Palma de Mallorca, Spain; Royal Tennis, Palma de Mallorca, SKOL Travel Paris, Fr. Episcopalian (warden, vestryman). Hobbies: U.S.N., S.F. Giants Baseball. Home: 715 Prospect Ave., South Pasadena, CA 91030; Office: 850 Colorado Blvd., L.A., CA 90041.

FREDERIKSEN, HAROLD DIXEN
Company President
b. Nov. 2, 1930, Askov, Minn.; s. Chris W. and Thora (Dixen) Frederiksen; B.S., civil engring., Utah State Univ., 1953; M.S., civil engring., Univ. Minn., 1957; chil.: Lisa Marie, b. Sept. 9, 1953; Lee Ernest, b. July 31, 1955; Brian Spencer, b. Jan. 13, 1959. Career: Suprv. Engr., Calif. Dept. of Water Resources, 1959-67; Dept. dir. engring., Devel. and Resources Corp., Sacto., 1967-70, v.p., 1970-73, exec. v.p. and gen. mgr., 1973-75; pres., Frederiksen Kamine and Assoc., Inc. (consultants, internat. devel.) Sacto., 1976---. Mem.: U.S. Com. Irrigation, Drainage and Flood Control; mem. U.S. Com. on Large Dams; Fellow, Am. Soc. of Civil Engrs., contbr. profl. articles to ASCE; Patent holder for breakwater (ocean). Lt., USAF, 1953-55, Constrn. Engrs. Home: 1570 Response Rd., Apt. 3078, Sacto., CA 95815; Office: 1900 Pt. West Way, Sacto., CA 95815.

FREE, LEDGER DANIEL
CEO, The Burke Company
b. Dec. 24, 1921, Casper, Wyo.; s. Ledger Daniel and Clara Belle (Williams) Free; A.B., Harvard Univ., 1947; L.D., Stanford Univ., 1950; m. Carole B. Fox, June 18, 1948 (dec. 1962); chil.: Karen P., b. Aug. 18, 1951; Douglas L., b. July 14, 1954; Kenneth B., b. Jan. 27, 1956; m. 2d. Dorothy Ann Clark, Nov. 12, 1966, S.F.; Career: Admitted to Calif. bar, 1951; law clerk, Calif. Dist. Ct. Appeals, S.F., 1951; assoc. Landels & Weigel, S.F., 1953-54; with Bank of America, S.F., 1954-65, v.p., 1964-65; with The Burke Co., San Francisco 1954-65, became pres. and chief exec. ofcr., 1972---; also dir. Instr. S.F. Law Sch., 1954-60. Served Pvt. to Capt., AUS, 1941-45; decorated with Bronze Star, Korean Conflict 1951-53. Mem.: Univ. Club, S.F.; Harvard Club, S.F., pres. 1978---; Bd. of Trustees, United Bay Area Crusade, 1964-66, chmn. Budget Com. 1963-65; Trustee Bay Area Hosp. Planning Com., 1957-60; Foothills Tennis and Swim Club, Palo Alto; Harvard Club N.Y. Republican, assoc. mem. San Mateo Co. Repub. Central Com. 1959-61. Rec.: tennis. Home: 970 Monte Rosa Dr., Menlo Park, CA 94025; Office: 2655 Campus Dr., P.O.B. 5818, San Mateo, CA 94403.

FREED, NANCY LEE
Public Relations Executive
b. Dec. 11, 1923, New York; d. S.A. and Dorothy (Kahn) Wurzburger; cousin, George S. Kaufman; student economics and advt., Columbia Univ., 1940-43; m. Bert Freed (actor, pres. SAG-AFTRA Credit Union), Feb. 12, 1956, N.Y.; chil.: Andrew Charles Sutton, B. Apr. 8, 1952; Carl Robert, b. Dec. 30, 1956; Jennifer, b. Jan. 29, 1958. Career: copywriter, Jasper Lynch & Fishel, 1945-47; asst. advt. mgr./pub. rels. dir., Jay Thorpe, 1947-48; acct. exec., Allen Meltzer Inc. Pub. Rels., 1948-50; asst. prod., NBC TV Vacation Wonderlands 1952; owner pub. rels. firm, Nancy Lee Waring, 1948-52; acct. supr., Carl Ruff Assoc., 1952-59; cons., 1959-64; acct. supr., Harshe, Rotman & Druck, Pub. Rels. 1964-69; Pub. Rels. Dir. Art Center Coll. of Design, Pasadena, 1969-71; own firm, Nancy Lee Freed Pub. Rels., 1971-79; Dir. of Communications, Ruthton Corp., L.A., 1979---; appearances on TV interview shows throughout U.S. 1964---; columnist, West L.A. Independent: Footloose and Nancy Freed, 1960-64. Mem.: L.A. Advt. Women, vice pres., edn. chmn.; chmn. Advis. Bd. of Children's Hosp. Hotline 1968---; Hobbies: painting, sports. Home: 418 N. Bowling Green Way, L.A., CA 90049; Office: 2245 Pontius Ave., L.A., CA 90064.

FREIMARK, ROBERT
Artist
b. Jan. 27, 1922, Doster, Mich.; s. Alvin Otto and Nora Esther (Shinaver) Freimark; B.Ed., Univ. of Toledo, 1950; M.F.A., Cranbrook Acad. of Art, 1951; m. Lillian Tihlarik, Ind.; chil.: Christine Gay, b. 1954; Matisse Jon, b. 1949. Career: Artist in Residence, Des Moines Art Center, 1959-63; San Jose State Univ., 1964---; Santa Reparata Graphic Centre, Firenze, 1974; Columbia Univ., 1963; Cal. State Univ., Fullerton, 1964; Parkersburg (W.Va.) Art Center, 1967; Joslyn Mus., 1962. Completed 200 tapestries (1978) with exhibitions worldwide, Munich, N.Y., Chicago, L.A., Dusseldorf, S.F., etc.; works in over 200 pub. collections, such as Boston Mus. of Fine Arts, Natl. Gallery (Prague), British Mus., Smithsonian Inst., Lib. of Congress, Fogg Mus., L.A. Co. Mus., etc. Mem.: Am. Fedn. of Arts, Am. Craftsmen Soc. Hobbies: hunting, fishing, music. Home: Rt. 2, Box 539A, Morgan Hills, CA 95037; Office: Art Dept., San Jose State Univ., San Jose, CA 95192.

FRESHWATER, DONALD B.
Surgeon
b. Nov. 11, 1916, Olympia, Wash.; s. Eagle and Olivia (Barksdale) Freshwater; Ed. Ohio Wesleyan Univ.; B.S., Univ. of Wash. 1938; M.D., Univ. of Pa. Med. Sch., 1942; certified, Am. Bd. of Neurological Surg. 1952; m. Jean Soltow; dau. Kimberly, b. Oct. 25, 1948. Career: Instr. (neurosurgery), Univ. of Ill. Neuropsychiatric Inst., 1948, 49; staff Lahay Clinic, 1950-53; phys.-surg., Pasadena, Calif.; assoc. clin. prof. of surg., USC 1964---. Author, numerous profl. publs. Med. ofcr., USN, Pac. Theater (1943-47), WW II. Mem.: Phi Gamma Delta, 1934; Phi Beta Kappa, 1938; Phi Chi, 1938; La Canada Country Club, Annandale Golf Club. Republican. Episcopalian. Hobby: yachting, travel. Rec.: travel. Home: Pasadena, CA; Office: 744 Fairmount St., Pasadena, CA.

FRETTER, WILLIAM BACHE
University Administrator
b. Sept. 28, 1916, Pasadena; s. William Albert and Dorothy (Bach) Fretter; A.B., Univ. Calif., Berkeley, 1937, Ph.D., 1946; m. Grace Powles, Jan. 1, 1939, Pasadena; chil.: Travis D., b. May 8, 1940; Gretchen (Sperber), b. Apr. 14, 1943; Richard Brian, b. May 10, 1947. Career: Research engr. radar countermeasures, Westinghouse Electric Co., 1941-45; faculty of Univ. of Calif., Berkeley, 1946---; prof. physics, 1955---; dean Coll. Letters and Sci., 1962-67; spl. research cosmic rays, high-energy particle physics. Fulbright scholar, France, 1952-53, 1960-61; Guggenheim Fellow, 1960-61; decorated chevalier Legion of Honor (France), 1964; Fellow Am. Phys. Soc.; V.P., Univ. of Cal., 1978---. Home: 1120 Cragmont Ave., Berkeley, CA 94708; Office: Office of the Vice President of the Univ. of Calif., 714 University Hall, 2200 Univ. Ave., Berkeley, CA 94720.

FRETZ, DONALD R.
Superior Court Judge
b. June 25, 1922, DeKalb Co., Ind.; s. Harold H. Fretz and Mrs. Kenneth Petersen; B.A., DePauw Univ., 1947; student, Stanford Univ. Law Sch.; J.D., Univ. of S.F. Law Sch., 1950; m. Elizabeth W., Dec. 27, 1948, Columbia, Mo.; chil.: Ann, Elinor, Holly. Career: pvt.

law practice, 1950-62; elected to Superior Ct., Merced, 1962---; Dean, Calif. Coll. of State Trial Judges, 1967, 68, pres., Conf. of Calif. Judges, 1970-71; v.chmn., Nat. Conf. of State Trial Judges, 1978-79; mem. faculty, Natl. Coll., 1967---; mem. faculty: Calif. Coll. of Trial Judges (Ethics) 1969---; Inst. of Judicial Adminstrn., Aspen. Contbr. legal journs. Mem.: Conf. of Calif. Judges; Nat. Conf. of State Trial Judges; Nat. Council of Juvenile Ct. Judges; Am. Bar Assn.; Am. Judicature Soc. Capt., JAG, AUS, 1942-46; USAR, 1946-48. Office: Merced Co. Courts Bldg., Merced, CA 95340.

FREY, CHARLES FREDERICK
Surgeon — Educator
b. Nov. 15, 1929, N.Y.C.; s. Charles and Julia Frey; B.A., Amherst Coll., 1951; M.D., Cornell Univ. Med. Sch., 1955; m. Jane Louise Tower, July 20, 1957, Harrison, N.Y.; chil.: Jane Elizabeth, b. Aug. 25, 1958; Susan Ann, b. Sept. 2, 1959; Charles Frederick, b. Oct. 11, 1962; Robert Tower, b. Sept. 2, 1964; Nancy Louise, b. Oct. 21, 1968. Career: graduate tng., Intern to Chief Resident, Cornell Med. Center, N.Y. Hosp., 1955-63; mem. faculty Univ. Mich., Dept. of Surgery, 1964-76; Chief, Surgical Serv., VA Hosp., Martinez, Calif., 1976---; Prof. and v.chmn. Dept of Surgery, Univ. of Calif., Davis, 1976---. Capt., USAF, 1957-59, Chief of Surgery, Homestead AFB, Fla. Contbr. 92+ profl. articles to med. journs. Founding mem., Am. Trauma Soc., 1972---; chmn., Pancreas Club, 1975---; Chief., Region IX in Am. Coll. of Surgeons com. on Trauma, 1976---; mem. acad. senate, UC, Davis, 1976---. Mem.: Phi Gamma Delta; Nu Sigma Nu. Home: 52 Charles Hill Rd., Orinda, CA 94563; Office: VA Med. Center, 150 Muir Rd., Martinez, CA 94553.

FRICKER, PETER RACINE
Composer
b. Sept. 5, 1920, London, Eng.; s. Edward Racine and Deborah Alice (Parr) Fricker; ed. St. Paul's Sch., London; Royal Coll. of Music, London; hon. D.Mus., 1958; m. Helen Clench, Apr. 17, 1943, London. Career: Dir. of Music, Morley Coll., London, 1952-64; Prof. Royal Coll. of Music, 1955-64; prof., Univ. of Calif., Santa Barbara, 1964---; compositions incl. five symphonies, concertos for piano-violin (2), viola, and organ; chamber music, incl. three string quartets; oratorio, The Vision of Judgment; works for voice, organ, piano, etc. Royal Air Force, 1941-46. Rec.: travel. Office: Dept. of Music., Univ. of Calif., Santa Barbara, CA 93106.

FRIEDMAN, KENNETH SCOTT
Artist
b. New London, Conn.; s. Abraham Morris and Ruth (Shifreen) Friedman; student, Calif. Western Univ., 1965, Shimer Coll., 1965-66; B.A., S.F. State Univ., 1971, M.A., 1971; Ph.D., U.S. Internat. Univ., 1976. Career: Dir., Fluxus West, S.F., San Diego, Exeter, Engl., 1966-75, chmn. bd., 1975; Gen. mgr., Something Else Press, N.Y., Valencia, Berlin, 1971; Exec. dir., Inst. for Advanced Studies in Contemporary Art, San Diego, 1975---; artist and writer: solo and group exhibs. in museums and art galleries throughout No. and So. America and Europe; founder, Contemporary Art/Southeast, Inc., Atlanta, Ga., 1975---; chmn., Assoc. Art Pubs., S.F. and N.Y., 1977---; visiting prof., vis. artist, l?etr., critic to various univs. Awards incl.: F.G. Fischer Awards, 1966; Nebr. State Council on the Arts and Xerox Corp. for Omaha Flow Systems, 1973; Gov's. Award, Idaho, 1975; Tenn. Arts Commn. for Sightings Proj., 1975; E. Tenn. State Univ. Found., 1975; Natl. Endowment for the Arts, 1975; and for Services to the Field, 1978. Mem.: Am. Anthropological Assn., fellow; Coll. Art Assn.; Soc. for the Anthropology and Sociology of Art, v.p., 1976---; W. Assn. of Art Museums, fellow; Am. Assn. of Museums; Am. Sociological Assn.; Am. Soc. for Aesthetics. Home-Office: 6361 Elmhurst Dr., San Diego, CA 92120.

FRIES, IRWIN MELVIN
Magazine Executive
b. July 2, 1932, Brooklyn, N.Y.; s. Louis and Sadye Fries; B.S., USC, 1954;m. Phyllis Ailin, Feb. 16, 1957, L.A.; chil.: Gayle, b. May 19, 1960; Joseph, b. Feb. 24, 1962. Career: Advt. salesman, Fairchild Publs. 1954-57; advt. mgr., John F. Huber Pub. Co., 1957-67; exec. v.p., advt. dir., Performing Arts Magazine, 1967---. AUS, 1954-56. Mem.: Sigma Alpha Mu; Alpha Delta Sigma; L.A. Advt. Club. Home: 4871 Bluebell Ave., No. Hollywood, CA 91607; Office: 9348 Santa Monica Blvd., Beverly Hills, CA 90210.

FRISCH, DAVID MARK
Cardiologist
b. Jan. 30, 1947, Chicago, Ill.; s. Dr. Arnold and Roslyn (Greene) Frisch; B.A. cum laude, Washington Univ., St. Louis, 1968; M.D., Med. Coll. of Wis., 1972; m. Janis Kopps, Dec. 21, 1973, Alexandria, Va.; 1 son Michael Aaron, b. July 1, 1976. Career: intern, USC Med. Center, 1972-73; resident, Georgetown Med. Service, Wash., D.C. Gen. Hosp., 1973-75; cardiology fellowship, Wadsworth VA Hosp.—UCLA Center for the Health Sciences, 1975-77; clin. instr., UCLA Sch. of Med., 1977---; also: Co-dir. CCu, ICU, and dir.: Echocardiography and COU, L.A. Hew Hosp.; dir., Non-Invasive Lab and co-dir.: CCU, ICU, Century City Hosp. (all 1977---). Diplomates: Am. Bd. of Internal Med., 1975; Am. Bd. of Cardiovascular Disease, 1977. Fellow, Am. Coll. of Cardiology, 1979. Fellow, Am. Coll. of Chest Physicians, 1979. Contbg. author: Reciprocity and the Giving of Help, Proceedings Am. Psychol. Assn., 1968; Absence of Morbidity and Mortality in Patients with Bifascicular and Trifascicular Disease during Surgical Procedures, Clinical Research, Feb. 77. Hobby: profl. jazz pianist. Rec.: tennis, racquetball, jogging. Home: 1376 San Ysidro Dr., Beverly Hills, CA 90210; Office: 465 N. Roxbury, Suite 911, Beverly Hills, CA 90210.

FRISCH, ROBERT A.
Financial Planning Executive
b. July 22, 1922, Schenectady, N.Y.; s. Harry and Ann (Hirschman) Frisch; B.S., Western Mich. Univ., 1947; postgrad. Wharton Sch. of Bus., 1956-57; m. Leona A. Abbey, Sept. 9, 1951; chil.: Dana R., Randi. Career: Founder, chief exec. ofcr., the ESOT Group, Inc., L.A.; financial cons.; lectr. on corporate finance and devel., fringe benefits, exec. benefit planning. Active Boy Scouts Am. USAF, WW II; CBI. Mem.: Am. Mgmt. Assn., chmn. employee stock ownership plan seminars; Am. Soc. Chartered Life Underwriters, past pres. Phila. chpt.; Nat. Assn. Security Dealers (prin.). Author: The Magic of ESOT: The Fabulous New Instrument of Corporate Finance. Home: 17146 Margate St., Encino, CA 91316; Office: 3325 Wilshire Blvd., L.A., CA 90010.

FRUCHTHENDLER, SAUL I.
Writer
b. Tucson, Ariz.; s. Jacob F. (father named Tuscon Man of the Year, 1963, has sch. named in his honor) and Jean Fruchthendler; student: Univ. of Arizona and New York Univ. Career: asst. press secty., Sen. Carl Hayden, 1967; entered advt. in 1969 with agencies including McCann Erickson; Young & Rubicam; Foote, Cone & Belding; Daniel & Charles. Motion picture and TV writer, 1974---. Authored over 25 scripts including Five Little Piggies; Nobody Loves Me; and Who Killed the Pied Piper. Recipient: more than 100 advt. awards including Clio, Golden Lion at Cannes Festival, N.Y. Art Directors Club, Copy Club of N.Y. and L.A. Advt. Club's Belding Award. Named mem. of Ad Day USA's top 100 creative people in the U.S. 5 years, 1974---. Author: The Debates of Clarence Darrow, HMS Press, 1972; A New Yorker's Guide to Los Angeles, 1979; in progress, Even a Blind Herring will Occasionally Find an Onion. Home: L.A. Office: The Wordsmith Co., Century City, CA.

FRYER, THOMAS WAITT, JR.
College District Administrator
b. Oct. 6, 1936, Martinsville, Va.; s. Thomas Waitt and Pauline Fryer; B.A., English, Wayland Coll., 1958; M.A., Vanderbilt Univ., 1959; Ph.D., Univ. Calif., Berkeley, 1968; visiting scholar (Urban Social Policy), Harvard Univ., 1971. Chil.: Elizabeth, b. Aug. 18, 1962; Matthew, b. Aug. 31, 1964; John, b. May 23, 1966. Career: instr. of English, Daytona Beach Jr. Coll., Fla., 1959-61; doctoral study & related assignments, 1961-65; assoc. dean of instr., Chabot Coll., Hayward, 1965-67; v.p., Miami-Dade Community Coll. and chief adminstrv. officer, downtown campus, Miami, Fla., 1967-73; chancellor and dist. supt., Peralta Community Coll. Dist., Oakland, 1973-78; chancellor and supt., Foothill/De Anza Community Coll. Dist., 1978---. Contbr. scholarly journs. Awards: Woodrow Wilson Fellowship, UC, Berkeley; Ford Found. Fellow, Vanderbilt Univ.; Kellogg Found. Fellow, Univ. of Florida, Gainesville, and UC, Berkeley; Communication and Leadership Award, Toastmasters Internat., 1977. Dir.: Am. Council on Edn.; Am. Assn. for Higher Edn.; League for Innovation in Community' Coll.; Regional Assn. of East Bay Colleges and Universities, 1974-78; Advisory Com.: Jt. Council on Economic Edn.; Calif. Community Colleges; steering com., Am. Assn. of Community and Jr. Colleges, 1976-77; mem. Nat. Soc. for Study of Edn.; Mem.: Phi Delta Kappa; Oakland Council for Economic Devel., 1977-78; New Oakland Com., 1975-78; Commonwealth Club; World Affairs Council; exec. com., dir., YMCA of Alameda Co.; NAACP;

Oakland-Africa Sister City Com.; E. Bay Mgmt. Group, Oakland, Alameda Co. Home: 10255 Parkwood Dr., No. 8, Cupertino, CA 95014; Office: 12345 El Monte Rd., Los Altos Hills, CA 94022.

FUCIK, WILLIAM J.
Theatre Coach — Director
b. Nov. 19, 1919, Waukegan, Ill.; s. George C. and Gertrude C. Fucik; student, Bach Theatre Arts, 1947; M.T.A., Pasadena Playhouse, Sch. of the Theatre, 1948. Career: Prod., dir., Laguna Beach, Hollywood — Stock, 1948-50; dialogue & dance dir., coach, Hollywood Studios and freelance, 1950-56; workshop dir., theatre dir. and coach, So. Calif. and Mid-West; prod. adminstrv. dir., community theatres, 1956---; also artist, specialist in physique portraits in watercolor, nat. and internat. commns.; photog. Maj., AUS, WWII; commanded a separate Ambulance Co. (1st to cross Rhine River); Presidential Commendation. Mem.: ANTA; SAE frat. Rec.: All forms of dance. Address: 1503 Clay St., Newport Beach, CA 92663.

FUHRMAN, ROBERT A.
Corporate President
b. Feb. 23, 1925, Detroit, Mich.; s. Alexander A. and Elva Brown Fuhrman; B.S., Aeronautical Engring., Univ. Mich., 1945; M.S.E., Fluid Mechanics and Dynamics, Univ. Maryland, 1952; m. Nan McCormick; chil.: Lee Ann Kahl; Richard; William. Career: Project Engr., USN Air Test Center, 1946-53; chief, tech. engring., Ryan Aeronautical Co., 1953-58; v.p. and gen. mgr., Missile Systems Div., Lockheed Missiles & Space Co., 1958-70; pres., Lockheed-Georgia Co., 1970-71; pres., Lockheed-California Co., 1971-73; pres., Lockheed Missiles & Space Co., Inc., Sunnyvale, 1973---. Sr. v.p., Lockheed Corp.; bd. dir., Santa Clara Co. Mfg. Group, 1978---. Contbr. numerous tech. papers to profl. publs. Mem.: Nat. Acad. of Engring., 1976; bd. mem., Aero. & Space Eng., 1977---; AIAA, 1956, fellow, 1978---; United Way of Santa Clara Co., 1976, gen. chmn., 1978---; AIAA Von Karman Lectureship, 1978; Am. Defense Preparedness Assn., 1974, exec. com. 1977---. Office: P.O.B. 504, Sunnyvale, CA 94087.

FULLER, MELVIN L.
President, Inventors Workshop International
b. Mar. 30, 1921, Olmsted Co., Minn.; s. Leroy and Lettie Lee (Campbell) Fuller; desc. Timothy Fuller, Mayflower; Gr.grandson, Lord (James) Durham, Eng.; ed. engr., in mil. sci.; m. Louisa A. Fuccillo, Apr. 26, 1961, Wash., D.C.; chil.: Melvin, Jr., b. May 3, 1946; Tonya, b. Feb. 25, 1952; Deborah, b. Sept. 1, 1954. Career: served in USN and AUS; tchr., Naval Ordnance & Gunnery Sch., Wash., D.C.; tch., Army Ordnance; Fire Control Sch., Aberdeen, Md.; NIKE proof test ofcr., White Sands Proving Grounds, N. Mex.; worke;with Chinese in Army Ordnance, Taiwan; founder-pres., Inventors Workshop Internat., 1971---; (31 chpts. from Hawaii to Alaska). Scientologist. Home: 121 N. Fir St., Ventura, CA 93001.

FULLER, WINSTON ROSELLE
Business Executive – Civic Leader
b. Sept. 12, 1910, Bakersfield, Calif.; s. Clarence Mark and Hazel Beebee (Grandy) Fuller; grad. L.A.H.S. 1928; L.A.S., USC, 1932; m. Frances LaRue Johnson, San Gabriel, Sept. 19, 1934; chil.: (twins) Winston Roselle, Jr. and Mrs. David Stanley (Marilyn La Rue) Atha, b. Feb. 3, 1937. Career: Pres.-owner, Engine Life Prods., Corp., 1948-63; chmn. bd. Johnson Western Gunite Co., 1955-76; pres. Victoria Investment Co., 1962---. Trustee, Rose Hills Mem. Park Assn., 1956---; bd. trustees, USC 1965-68, 77---. pres. Alumni Assn., USC 1966-67; chmn. Calif. Hwy. Comm. 1970-77. Advis. bd., Automobile Club of So. Calif., 1976---. pres., Tournament chmn., Desert Charities (Bob Hope Desert Classic), and Dagger, USC; Clubs: Calif., Newport Harbor Yacht; Eldorado Country; Valley Hunt; San Gabriel Country; Valley Club of Montecito. Congregationalist. Home: 211 S. Orange Grove Blvd., Pasadena, CA 91105.

FULLERTON, GAIL
University President
b. Apr. 29, 1927, Lincoln, Nebr.; d. Earl Warren and Gladys Marshall Jackson; A.B. Univ. of Nebr., 1949, A.M., Sociology, 1950; Ph.D., Univ. of Ore., 1954; m. Stanley James Fullerton, Mar. 27, 1967, Mexico; chil.: (by prev. marriage) Gregory S. Putney, b. Mar. 13, 1951; Cynde G. Putney, b. Mar. 27, 1958. Career: lectr., in Sociology and Anthropology, Drake Univ., Des Moines, Ia., 1955-57; asst. prof. of Sociology, Florida State Univ., 1957-60; asst. prof. of Sociology, San Jose State Univ., 1963-68; assoc. prof., SJSU 1968-72; prof.

of Sociology, San Jose State Univ., 1972---; Dean, Graduate Studies & Research, SJSU, 1972-76; Exec. v.p., SJSU 1977-78; pres., San Jose State Univ., 1978---. Author: Survival in Marriage, Holt, Rinehart & Winston; Co-Author: The Adjusted American, Harper & Row. Mem.: Chi Omega; Phi Beta Kappa; Phi Kappa Phi. Hobby: writing. Address: Office of the President, San Jose State Univ., San Jose, CA 95192.

FULLILOVE, CECIL WOODROW
Investment Co. President
b. Feb. 19, 1919, Yuma Co., Ariz.; s. Robert Lee and Elizabeth Jennie Fullilove; ed. grad. Yuma Union H.S. 1936; m. Mary Ann Swing (Dau. of Lt. Gen. Joseph M. Swing, comdr. 11th airborne, 6th U.S. Army, ret.), Reno, Nev., June 28, 1964; dau., Marjorie Lou Hoefer, b. Jan. 30, 1944. Career: U.S. Immigration and Naturalization Serv., S.F., border patrol, 1941-49, investigator, 1949-58, asst. dist. dir. 1958-60; dept. dist. dir. 1960-63, dist. dir. 1963-70 (ret.); pres. Beverly Plaza Investment Co. 1970---. Aviation cadet, 1943; 2nd Lt., navigator, 313th Bomb Wing 20th A.F., Tinian Is., 1945-46; returned active duty wtih Mil. Air Transport Serv., Kelly Field, 1950-52; 60th Troop Carrier Squadron, Rhine Main, Ger. 1953. Mem.: Order of St. Hubertus, VFW, Am. Leg., A.F. Assn., Res. Ofcrs. Assn., Fed. Postal Employees Assn. Baptist. Rec.: hunting, fishing, golf. Home: 1 La Cuesta, Greenbrae, CA 94904; Office: 2151 Jackson St., S.F., CA 94115.

FULTON, LEN
Novelist — Publisher
b. May 15, 1934, Lowell, Mass.; A.A., Univ. Maine, 1957; B.A., Univ. Wyo., 1961; postgrad., Univ. Calif., Berkeley, 1961-63; son Timothy Clause, b. Oct. 28, 1960. Career: Publisher, Fulton-Fay Pub. Co., Freeport and Kennebunkport, Me., 1957-59; bio-statistician, Calif. State Dept. of Pub. Health, 1962-68; ed./pub., Dustbooks, 1963---. Author: (novels) The Grassman, 1974; Dark Other Adam Dreaming, 1975; travelogue: American Odyssey (w/Ellen Ferber); Editor., Small Press Review (monthly). Chmn., Com. of Small Mag. Editors and Pubs. 1968-71, 1973; Mem., Literature Advis. Panel, Nat. Endowment for the Arts, 1976-68; Panelist, Calif. Arts Commn., 1975; Panelist, Coordinating Council of Lit. Mags., 1970, 71, 72, 74. Home: 5218 Scottwood Rd., Paradise, CA 95969.

FURNAS, DAVID WILLIAM
Plastic-Surgeon — Educator
b. Apr. 1, 1931, Caldwell, Id.; s. John Doan and Esther (Hare) Furnas; A.B., Univ. Calif., Berkeley, 1952, M.D., 1955, M.S., pharmacology, 1957; m. Mary Lou Heatherly, Feb. 11, 1956, S.F.; chil.: Heather Jean, b. Sept. 15, 1957; Brent David, b. Apr. 23, 1959; Craig Jonathan, b. Mar. 4, 1963. Career: Tng. in spclty., Univ. Calif., S.F., 1955-57, 1959-60; Corgas Hosp., Canal Zone, 1960-61; Cornell-New York Hosp., 1961-63; Glasgow Royal Infirmary, 1963-64. Assoc. Prof. Surgery, Univ. of Ia., 1964-68; plastic surg., Proj. HOPE Nicaragua, 1964, Ceylon, 1968; surg., East Africa Flying Doctors Serv., 1972-73; prof. and chief., Div. of Plastic Surg., Univ. of Calif., Irvine, ---. Capt., USAF M.C. and chief of Surg. 6580th USAF Hosp., 1957-59. Publs. in field of plastic and reconstrv. surg., hand surg., tropical surg., microsrugery, craniofacial surg. Mem.: Bd. dirs., Am. Bd. of Plastic Surg., 1979---. Mem. Phi Beta Kappa. Home: 2501 Blue Water Dr., Corona del Mar, CA 92625; Office: 1201 W. LaVeta Ave., No. 506, Orange, CA 92668.

FURTH, GEORGE
Writer — Actor
b. Dec. 14, 1932, Chicago; s. George and Evelyn Furth; B.S., Northwestern Univ. Sch. of Speech; M.F.A., Columbia Univ. Sch. of Dramatic Art. Career: Actor in approx. 25 feature films and 5 TV series; author of COMPANY, TWIGS, THE ACT on Broadway; faculty mem., Drama Dept., USC, L.A. ---. Awards: Tony Award, NY Drama Critics Circle Award, Outer Circle Award, Evening Standard Award, London. Mem.: Phi Gamma Delta, NU. Home: 3030 Durand Dr., Hollywood, CA 90068.

G

GABRIEL, PHILIP LOUIS
Industrialist — Author
b. Fort Fairfield, Me.; s. Samuel and Amelia Gabriel; ed. Wash. State Univ., Southwestern Law Sch.; chil.: Ronald S., M.D., b. 1937; Dennis Jon, LL.B., 1939-78; Phyllis Mary, b. 1949; Robert Philip, M.D., b. 1950. Career: Pres., Crystal Ice Mfg. Co., 1935-64; pres., Gabriel Bros. Dept. Stores, 1947-56; dir. and v.p., Del Mar Turf Club, Del Mar, 1947-54; pres., Smithy Muffler Mfg. Co., 1948-56; pres., Tri-State (Calif.-Ariz.-Nev.) Ice and Cold Storage Assn., 1947-49; bd. of trustees, Gen. Serv. Studios, Hollywood, 1949-55; Mem. of O.P.A. Bd., WW II. Author: I Found America, Vantage, 1950; Citizen from Lebanon, Citadel, 1957; The Executive (best seller), Citadel, 1959; Tomorrow, Tomorrow, Whitmore, 1971; In the Ashes, Whitmore, 1978. Awarded Medal of Honor, Repub. of Lebanon. Mem.: K.C., Whittier, Grand Knight, 1946-47; Dist. Dep., 1947-48; Rotary Club, Whittier, pres. 1946. Republican. Catholic. Rec.: fishing, hunting. Address: P.O.B. 718, Whittier, CA 90608.

GABRIEL, RONALD SAMUEL
Pediatric Neurologist — Lecturer
b. Mar. 19, 1937, Calif.; s. Philip Louis (Industrialist and Author) and Theresa (Shaheen) Gabriel; B.A. in philosophy with honors, Yale Univ., 1959; M.D., Boston Univ. Sch. of Med., 1963; m. Idalia Ortiz, 1962, Concord, Mass.; chil.: Philip Louis, II, b. Aug. 19, 1963; Paula, b. Jan. 16, 1965. Career: internship and pediatric residency, L.A. Co. Gen. Hosp. (USC), 1963-66; neurology residency, UCLA, 1966-68; spec. fellowship, Nat. Insts. of Health Pediatric Neurology, UCLA, 1970-71; supr. and dir., pediatric neurology clinic, UCLA, 1979---; also cons. Reg. Center and crippled Childrens Service, State of Calif., 1979---. Visiting prof., Children's Hosps., Australia, 1978. Recipient: Clin. Faculty Teaching Award Pediatrics, UCLA, 1971-72, 1974-75. Co-author, Textbook of Child Neurology, 2nd edit. 1979, pub. Lea and Febiger. Maj. AUS Med. Corps, 1968-70, pediatric neurology, DeWitt and Walter Reed Army Hosps. Diplomate Am. Bd. of Pediatrics; Fellow, Am. Acad. of Pediatrics; Diplomate and Examiner, Am. Bd. of Psychiatry and Neurology; Fellow, Am. Acad. of Neurology; Mem. Child Neurology Soc. Catholic. Hobbies: conservation and aviation. Rec.: GFA Cattle and Farm Co., mgr. and gen. partner. Office: 2080 Century Park East, Suite 203, L.A., CA 90067.

GAGOSIAN, EARL
Business Executive
b. Oct. 30, 1923, Price, Ut.; s. F.H. and Lillie Gagosian; ed. pub. schs.; m. Mary Catherine Spieler, Santa Monica, June 3, 1950; chil.: Janice, b. July 15, 1951; Wayne, b. July 10, 1954. Career: Assoc. with Travel Lodge Corp., 1946-65, v.p.-dir., 1952-65, v.p.-dir. 5 affiliate corps.; pres.-dir., Royal Inns of Am. (57 hotels) incl.: Santa Barbara, Palm Springs, Needles, Point Loma, Barstow, Yuma, El Monte, San Diego, Bishop, 1965; 39 Royal Inns: N.Y., Calif., Ariz., Colo., Nev., N. Mex., Ore., Tex., Ut., Wash., Mex. 1970. Serv. USN (1942-45), WW II. Latter-day Saint. Hobby: hunting. Home: P.O.B. 719, La Jolla, CA, Office: 4855 N. Harbor Dr., San Diego, CA 92106.

GALBRIATH, JOHN S.
University Professor
b. Nov. 10, 1916, Glasgow, Scotland; s. James M. and Mary (Marshall) Galbraith; ed. B.A., Miami Univ., Oh., 1938; M.A., Univ. of Ia., 1939, Ph.D. 1943; m. Laura Huddleston, Aug. 20, 1940; chil.: James M., John H., Mary P. Career: asst. prof., Oh. Univ., Athens, Oh. 1947-48; chmn. Academic Senate, chmn. Dept. of Hist., prof. UCLA 1948-64; v. chancellor, Univ. of Calif., San Diego, La Jolla, 1964; chancellor 1964-68; prof. hist. UCLA 1968---. Hist. ofcr., 3rd A.F., U.S.Army (1943-46), WW II. Mem.: pres. Pac. Coast br., Am. Hist. Assn. Democrat. Presbyterian. Home: 654 Thayer Ave., L.A., CA 90024; Office: Univ. of Calif., Dept. of History, L.A., CA 90024.

GALINSON, MURRAY L.
Professor of Law
b. May 8, 1937, Minneapolis, Minn.; s. Louis and Kay (Lifson) Galinson; B.A. cum laude, Univ. of Minnesota, 1958, J.D. cum laude, 1961; Ph.D., United States Internat. Univ., 1976; m. Elaine Glickman, Dec. 22, 1959, Minneapolis; chil.: Laura, b. Apr. 29, 1963; Jeffrey, b. May 21, 1965; Richard, b. July 9, 1967. Career: Asst. U.S. Atty., Dept. of Justice, 1961-63; assoc., Erickson, Popham, etc. law firm. Minn., 1963-64; partner, law firm of Mullin, Galinson, Swirnoff & Weinberg, 1965-71; prof. of law, Calif. Western Sch. of Law, S.D., 1972---. Asst. State Pub. Defender, Minn., 1968-71. Dir., Investment Corp. of America, 1968---; bd. chmn., Galent Corp., 1978---. Contbr. articles to legal journs. Author: Laws regulating Calif. marriage, family and child counselors, 1976. Mem.: Masons, Shriners, Sigma Alpha Mu, Phi Delta Phi. Polit. Mem.: Calif. State Democratic com. central com.; S.D. Com. to retain Rose Bird; S.D. com. to elect Yvonne Burke; com. reelect Supr. Jim Bates; S.D. Carter-Mondale campaign; La Jolla Democratic Club, treas., 1973; City Councilman, St. Louis Park, Minn., 1968-71; chmn., Minn. Com. on gun control, 1968. Jewish; v.p., Temple Beth Israel of S.D., 1977---. Hobby: jogging. Home: 1555 El Camino del Teatro, La Jolla, CA 92037; Office: 350 Cedar St., S.D., CA 92101.

GALLISON, JANET FRAZIER
Publishing Company Executive
b. Aug. 16, 1931, Omaha, Neb.; d. Claude and Rosemond (Kinkenon) Frazier; student, Duchesne Coll., 1948-50; B.A., San Diego State Univ., 1970; m. Harold Bailey Gallison, June 23, 1951, Omaha, Neb.; chil: Claudia, b. Dec. 10, 1954; Harold B. II, b. Nov. 13, 1957. Career: Administrv. mgr., San Diego Magazine, 1971; gen. mgr., San Diego Mag. Publishing Co., 1973---. Dir.: S.D. Com. for L.A. Philharmonic, 1966-78; Jewel Ball chmn. 1963; Candlelight Ball chmn. 1961. Mem.: Las Patronas, pres. 1968; La Jolla Beach & Tennis Club, charter 100. Republican. Episcopalian. Home: 7940 Avenida Alamar; Office: 3254 Rosecrans St., San Diego, CA 92110.

GARFIN, LOUIS
Insurance Company Executive
b. June 7, 1917, Mason City, Ia.; s. Sam and Etta Rose (Larner) Garfin; B.A., State Univ. of Ia., 1938, M.S., 1939, Ph.D., 1942; m. Clarice Fagen, Apr. 11, 1943, Minneapolis; chil.: Eugene Arthur, b. June 14, 1947; Erica, b. Apr. 22, 1950; Career: instr., USAAF, Scott Field, Ill., 1942-43; instr. mathmataics, Ill. Inst. of Tech., 1943; instr. math, Univ. of Minn., 1943-44; Actuary, Ore. Ins. Dept., Salem, 1946-52; assoc. actuary, Pac. Mutual Life Ins. Co., L.A., 1952-62; Actuary, 1962-64, v.p. and chief Actuary, 1964---. Dir.: Computer Communications Ins., 1968-73; So. Coast Communities Jewish Center, 1977---; No. Laguna Community Assn., 1975, pres. 1975-78. Ensign to Lt. j.g., USNR, 1944-46; Mem.: Fellow, Soc. of Actuaries; v.p., Am. Acad. of Actuaries, 1976-78; dir., Internat. Actuarial Assn. 1976-80; Actuarial Club of the Pac. States, pres. 1967-68; L.A. Actuarial Club, past pres.; Am. Mathematical Soc.; Am. Risk & Ins. Assn. Phi Beta Kappa; Sigma X. Home: 371 Dartmoor St., Laguna Beach, CA 92651; Office: 700 Newport Center Dr., Newport Beach, CA 92660.

GARRETT, STEPHEN
Director, J. Paul Getty Museum
b. Dec. 26, 1922, Ashtead, Engl.; s. Howard and Ida (King-Harman) Garrett; student, Charterhouse, Engl., 1936-41; M.A., Trinity Coll., Cambridge, 1950; Assoc. Royal Inst. of British Architects; m. Jean Mackintosh, London; chil.: Carey, Georgia, Rebecca, Jason. Career: Architect, London, 1950-73; dir., J. Paul Getty Museum, Malibu, 1973---. Lt., Royal Navy, Britain. Office: J. Paul Getty Mus., 17985 Pacific Coast Hwy., Malibu, CA 90265.

GARRY, FREDERICK W.
Chairman — CEO, Rohr Industries
b. July 12, 1921, Stratford, Conn.; s. Frederick T. and Nellie M. (Flint) Garry; B.S.M.E., Rose-Hulman Inst. of Tech. 1951; (hon.) E.D. 1968; m. Mary Elizabeth Griswold, Milford, Conn., June 28, 1946; chil.: Diana Elizabeth, b. Dec. 15, 1954; Kenneth Griswold, b. Nov. 19, 1957. Career: Exec., Gen. Elec. Co. (22 yrs.): v.p.-gen. mgr. Mil. Engring. Div.; mgr. Mil. Jet Engr. Sales, Engin. pgm; c.p. Tech. Plans, Aircraft Engring. Group; pres. Rohr Industries, Inc. 1974, chmn. bd.-chief exec., ofcr.-pres., 1976, bd. chmn.-CEO, 1978. Bd. mgrs. Rose-Hulman Inst. of Tech. Flight instr., fighter pilot, USMC. Mem.: USAF Assn., Assn. of U.S. Army; Navy League; Am. Helicopter Soc., Soc. of Automotive Engrs., Aircraft Owners and Pilots Assn., C. of C.; Aerospace Inds. Assn. Presbyterian. Hobbies: flying, soaring, boating, photog. Home: 9 Blue Anchor Cay Road, Coronado, CA 92118; Office: P.O.B. 878, Chula Vista, CA 92012.

GARWOOD, JOHN LESLIE
President, Garwood Company
b. June 16, 1917, Toledo, Oh.; s. Carey Virgil and Marie Evelyn (Thrun) Garwood; bro., Charles C. Garwood, pres., Garwood Labs., Inc.; B.S.M.E., Univ. of Toledo, 1939; m. Marjorie Wright Lindecker (dec. 1975), June 28, 1940, Toledo; chil.: Dr. Richard Lee, b. Jan. 15, 1944; William Alan, b. Sept. 2, 1946; Ruth Ellen (Mrs. Jeffery C. Lineberry), b. Nov. 1, 1954; m. 2d Shirley A. Patrick, Nov. 12, 1977, San Clemente; stepson, Daniel James Patrick, b. May 20, 1972. Career: Mech. engr., France Stone Co., Toledo, 1938-41; mech. engr. (R&D) B.F. Goodrich Co., Akron, 1941-47 (research & devel. of De-Icers for Lockheed Constellation Aircraft for TWA Airlines); prodn. engr., Stauffer Chem. Co., L.A., 1947-50; research & devel. engr., No. Am. Aviation (now Rockwell), 1951-54 (totally responsible for Redstone Missile Component Reliability); founder, 1st pres., Garwood Laboratories, Inc., 1954-74; founder-pres., Garwood Co., Bryan, Oh., 1975--- (engring. on practical uses of Solar Energy). Owner, Postal Instant Press, Walnut Creek. U.S. Patentee, automatic false eyelash machine, 1970. Author: What Driving Your Automobile Costs, 1945; co-author: Evaluation of Heart and Lung Machines, with Dr. Henry Lee; fin. sponsor 3 hr. TV special, med. show, The Family, with Dr. James Rue, 1970. Mem.: F&AM Masonic Order, 1949---. Methodist, bd. mem. Hobbies: flying, soaring. Home: 1347-A Locust St., Walnut Creek, CA 94596; 116 S. Lynn St., Bryan, Oh. 43506; Office: 708 S. Vail Ave., Montebello, CA 90640.

GASPARINI, RICHARD JOHN
Industrialist
b. July 17, 1932, Richmond, Calif.; s. John Joseph and Mary (Bertone) Gasparini; A.A., Contra Costa Coll., 1952; student, St. Mary's Coll., Univ. of San Francisco, 1954; Armstrong Sch. of Law, 1969; m. Joan Lora Wiegmann, Aug. 28, 1954, El Cerrito, Calif.; chil.: Debra JoAnn, b. July 29, 1955; Lisa Marie, b. Sept. 24, 1957; Sheryl Jean, b. Oct. 29, 1959; Anna Cecile, b. Aug. 16, 1962; Richard John, Jr., b. Mar. 24, 1964. Career: Sales, operations supt., El Cerrito, 1954-56; sales, service, dist. operations supt., Pacific Cement & Aggregates, S.F., 1956-66; v.p., adminstrn. and mktg., Wiegmann & Rose Machine Works, 1972-75; pres. and dir., 1975-76; pres., chief exec. officer, 1976---. Also pres. & dir., Richmond Steel Products Co., 1972---, (chief exec. officer, treas., dir., pres. 1972-76). Mem.: U.S. C. of C.; Calif. C. of C.; Calif. Mfgrs. Assn.; Council Richmond Industries; Western Gas Processors Oil Refiners Assn. Relig. Catacombs Youth Club, pres, 1950-52. Hobbies: golf, skiing. Home: 1345 Rimer Dr., Moraga, CA 94556; Office: 1430 Potrero Ave., Richmond, CA 94804.

GASTIL, RUSSELL GORDON
Geologist — Educator
b. June 25, 1928, San Diego; s. Russell Chester (Soc. Sci., Freedom House, N.Y.C.) and Frances (Duncan) Gastil; A.B., Univ. Calif., Berkeley, 1950, Ph.D., 1953; m. Janet Manly, Sept. 13, 1959, Alpine, Calif.; chil.: Garth Manly, b. Oct. 11, 1960; Mary Margaret, b. Jan. 14, 1962; George Christopher, b. Aug. 23, 1963; John Webster, b. Feb. 7, 1966. Career: with Shell Oil Co., early 1954; Canadian Javelin, 1956-57; lectr., UCLA, 1958-59; mem. faculty, San Diego State Univ., 1959---; chmn. Dept. of Geological Scis., 1970-72, prof. of Geological scis. ---. Author: We Can Save San Diego, 1975, profl. publs.; work centered on Precambrian rocks of Ariz. and Quebec-Labrador, the geology of Baja Calif. and areas around Gulf of Calif., the plate tectonic evolution of Peninsular Calif. and adjacent W. Mexico. U.S. Army Corps of Engrs., 1954-56. Mem.: Geol. Soc. of Am., v-chmn. Codilleran Sect. 1965; coord. 41st Cong. Dist. Common Cause, 1977; chmn. com. to study potential impact of off-shore drilling for city of S.D.; S.D. Co. com. on seismic safety element for the general plan; Air Pollution Hearing Bd.; chmn. Study Group for Internat. Geodymic Decade; pres., Grossmont-Mount Helix Improvement Assn. Relig. Soc. of Friends, trustee San Diego Meeting. Rec.: tennis; Home: 9435 Alto Dr., La Mesa, CA 92041; Office: San Diego State Univ.

GAYLORD, WILLIAM G.
Interior Designer — Columnist
b. Aug. 5, 1945, Mesquite, Tex.; s. Charles Cyrus and Nellie Ellen (Berryman) Gaylord; student, North Texas State Univ. Career: interior decorator, Gump's, S.F., 1969; pres., William Gaylord & Associates, 1969--- (Design firm of both archtl. and interior areas, residential and commercial clients, including the S.F. Opera House, offices of S.F. mayor, apartments in N.Y.C., Paris and an

all-rubber room for B.F. Goodrich Co.); author, nat. syndicated newspaper column, The Gaylord Touch, distbd. Chronicle Features Syndicate. Guest lectr. for design schools; frequent speaker at conventions, on TV. Awards: Young Designer of the Year, Burlington Industries, 1972; Most Outstanding Designer of the Year, S.M. Hexter Awards, 1975. Mem.: Am. Soc. of Interior Designers; S.F. Jaycees (founding mem.); Olympic Club. Baptist. Home: 1210 Lombard St., S.F., CA 94109; Office: 1555 Pacific Ave., San Francisco, CA 94109.

GAWZNER, WILLIAM PAUL
Hotel Proprietor
b. Sept. 15, 1916, Lake Geneva, Wis.; s. Paul and Irene Catherine (Frey) Gawzner; Cornell Univ., Ithaca, N.Y. 1933-34; m. Jeanne Pinkham, Santa Barbara, Aug. 23, 1969; chil.: James Palmer, b. Aug. 22, 1940; William Paul, Jr., b. Dec. 13, 1947. Career: Br. mgr., Howarth & Howarth, pub. accts., S.F., 1942; comptroller, El Rancho Vegas, Las Vegas, Nev., 1943-45; asst. comptroller, Hilton Hotels Corp., Chicago, Ill. 1946; propr.-gen. mgr., Miramar Hotel, Santa Barbara, 1950-60, owner 1960---. U.S. Army A.F. (1945), WW II. Mem.: pres., Greater Santa Barbara Hotel and Motel Assn., 1974, 75, 76; bd. dirs., Santa Barbara Conv. Bur., 1953---; secty., Mission Trails Assn. 1954-55; bd. dirs., Santa Barbara C. of C. 1955. bd. dirs., Montecito Protective and Improvement Assn. 1955-56 bd. dirs., Montecito Sanitation Dist.; 1955-56; Dir., Cal. State Rest. Assn., 1976---; dir., Cal. State Hotel & Motel Assn., 1974---; Santa Barbara Yacht Club, Montecito Country Club, Phi Epsilon Pi. Episcopalian. Hobby: boating, model RRing, pre-war toy train collecting, photog. Home: Miramar Hotel, P.O.B. M, Santa Barbara, CA 93102.

GAZZANIGA, DONALD ALAN
Film Producer — Writer
b. Jan. 3, 1934, L.A.; s. Dante Achilles, M.D. and Alice Marie (Griffith) Gazzaniga; grandson, Robert Blake Griffith, M.D.; bro., Alan B. Gazzaniga, M.D.; bro. Dr. Michael S. Gazzaniga, Ph.D., Bio Physics; B.A., USC, 1956; m. Maureen A. McCarthy, Aug. 6, 1960, Pomona; chil.: Jeanne Marie, b. June 29; Dan, b. Jan. 26; Suzanne, b. June 7; Kathleen, b. Apr. 15; Maria, b. Oct. 26. Career: Publ. FOCUS Mag., 1961-63; Pub., ed., TOPICS mag., 1963-64; advt. dir., PFF Svgs. & Loan, 1963-64; promotional dir , Cable Flying Serv./Commuter 64 Single Engine Sales Mgr./LTF Dir./Photog., Cessna Aircraft, 1964-66; researcher, writer, photog., 1966-68; founder, Concept Films, Inc., 1968; pres., Airline Flight Evaluators, 1968-70; legislative rep., various clients, 1968-73; motion picture prod., writer, 1970---: pres.: Breakaway Prodns., Concept Films, Inc.; DAG Music; writer, dir. and prod. BREAKAWAY series (starring Wm. Shatner); writer, dir. and prod., TV special, The Spirit of Nuku Hiva (longest Polynesian voyage in modern hist.). 1st Lt. USMC. Mem.: Theta Xi, USC; U.S. Jr. C. of C., 1952-56; pres. Pomona Jr. C. of C., 1964; nat. U.S. Jr. Chamber Opn. Airpark Chmn. Rec.: skiing, hunting, flying. Home: 9403 Whiskey Bar Rd., Loomis, CA 95650.

GEHRING, GEORGE JOSEPH, JR.
Dentist
b. May 24, 1931, Kenosha, Wis.; s. George J. and Lucille (Martin) Gehring; D.D.S., Marquette Univ., 1955; m. Joan Dehmlow, June 25, 1955, Kenosha, Wis.; chil.: G. Michael, b. Sept. 23, 1958; Scott L., b. Dec. 19, 1960. Career: Lt. Comdr., U.S. Navy Dental Corps, 1955-58, U.S.S. Kermit Roosevelt; practice gen. dentistry, Long Beach, 1958---. Past pres., Kiwanis, uptown L.B.; past chmn., L.B. Heart Assn.; dir., Am. Heart Assn.; v.p. Rotary Club; mem.: Com. of 300; Delta Sigma Delta. Rec.: tennis, gardening, boats. Home: 4001 Pine Ave., L.B., CA 90807; Office: 532 E. 29th St., Long Beach, CA 90806.

GEISE, HARRY FREMONT
Meterologist
b. Jan. 8, 1920, Oak Park, Ill.; s. Clarence Kammermann (stepfather) and Roslyn (Muser) Kammermann; ed. Univ. of Chicago, 1938-39; Meterologist Serv. Sch., Lakehurst, N.J. 1943-44; daus.: Marian (Apgar), b. Mar. 27, 1965; Gloria Peterson, b. Mar. 31, 1943; triplet sons, Barry, Gary, Harry, b. Jan 7, 1976. Career: Pvt. weather bur. serv., Chicago, 1937---; chief meterologist, Kingsbury Ord. 1943; meterol., radio sta. WLS and Prairie Farmer newspaper, 1941, 42, 46; assoc. Dr. Irving P. Krick, meterol. cons. 1947-49, media dir.-dir.

Pac. div. 1955-59; Army Air Corps research, developed new temperature forecasting technique, Calif. Inst. of Tech. and Am. Inst. of Aerological Research, 1948-49; cond. weather and travel shows, WBKB-TV, Chicago, radio sta. WOPA, Oak Park, Ill. 1950-51; pvt. weather serv. 1954; staff meteorl., San Jose Mercury and News, radio, KSJO, KNTV, San Jose Calif. KHUB, Watsonville, KGO-TV, S.F.; cond. "The Weather and You" series, Columbia Pac. radio network, 1956-58; Panorama Pac. Weather Show, KNXT-TV, CBS, L.A. 1957-58; prod. over 70 radio pgms. daily, U.S. 1959. est. Weather Center for CBS, N.Y. (demonstrated forecasts 2 yr. in advance), WCBS-TV, 1966-67; pvt. weather servs., incl. Commercial accts. and radio stas. 1962---. Natl. Defense Exec. Reservist, 1968-75; instr., meterol., Santa Rosa, Jr. Coll., 1964-66; Sonoma State Coll., 1967-68. Issued first week in advance forecasts to pub.; recognized relationship between specified solar emissions and maj. changes in earth weather pattern, 1956; initiated thunderstorm warning system, using radio static which became model for U.S. Ord. plants, 1942; Calif.s first tchg. credential based on outstanding eminence in meterol., 1964; discovered a relationship between a particular weather type and rash type tornado outbreaks in Midwest, U.S. 1965; orign. transatlantic weather radio programs from Geneva and London to Calif. and Paris to S.F., Dec. 1965, 77. Author: several TV films, articles publ. in newspapers, mags., trade and profl. journs., numerous radio and TV stas. U.S.A.; Voice of Am., 1968. Speaker on environmental problems, Rotary, C. of C., AAUW, Commonwealth Cluboof Calif., CBS Stations. Aerologist, USMC (1943-45), WW II. Mem.: Am. Meterol. Soc., Fgn. Royal Meterological Soc. Hobbies: travel, writing, reading. Home: 1780 Ave. Del Mundo, Penthouse, Coronado, CA 92118.

GELL-MANN, MURRAY
Physicist
b. Sept. 15, 1929, N.Y.C.; s. Arthur and Pauline Gell-Mann; ed. B.S. (physics), Yale Univ., 1948, (hon.) Sc.D., 1959; Ph.D., MIT, 1951; (hon.) Sc.D., Univ. of Chicago, 1967; Univ. of Ill. 1968; Wesleyan Univ. 1968; Hon. Doctorate, Univ. of Turin, Italy, 1969; m. J. Margaret Dow, Princeton, N.J., Apr. 19, 1955; chil.: Elizabeth Sarah; Nicholas Webster. Career: Research assoc. Univ. of Ill., 1951, 53; Inst. for Advanced Stu. 1951, 55; asst. prof., assoc. prof. Univ. of Chicago, 1952-55; assoc. prof. Calif. Inst. of Tech. 1955-56; Robert A. Millikan prof. of theoretical physics, 1956---; visiting prof., MIT 1963. Developed strangeness theory, theory of neutral K mesons, other sci. contribs. Co-author: The Eightfold Way, publ. 1964; Awards: Dannie Heineman Prize of Am. Phys. Soc. 1959; Ernest O. Lawrence Award, 1966; Franklin Medal, Franklin Inst. of Phila. 1967; John C. Carty Medal, Natl. Acad. of Scis. 1968; Research Corp. Award, 1969; Nobel Prize in physics, 1969. Mem.: Natl. Acad. of Scis. 1960---; Am. Acad. of Arts and Scis., 1964---; Am. Phys. Soc. Hobby: hist. linguistics. Rec.: Wilderness trips. Home: 1024 Armada Dr., Pasadena, CA; Office: Physics Dept., Calif. Inst. of Tech., Pasadena, CA 91109.

GENSLEY, JULIANA TOWNSEND
University Professor Emeritus
b. Feb. 2, 1910, Los Angeles, Calif.; d. James Robert and Mary Beulah (Peauchette) Townsend; A.B., UCLA, 1930; M.A., L.A. State Coll., 1962; m. John Frederick Gensley, Jr., Sept. 23, 1978, Lake Arrowhead, Calif.; chil.: Ruth Robin (Mitchell), b. Nov. 30, 1933; James Richard, b. Jan. 24, 1941. Career: Elem. tchr.: Riverside, 1931-33; San Marino, 1937-40; Wiseburn Sch. Dist., 1942-51; Redondo Beach, 1951-62; professor, Calif. State Univ., Long Beach, 1962-77 (Dept. of Elem. Edn., spltys.: Edn. of young chil., edn. of gifted, language arts, social studies): writer of featured column, Parent Perspective, Gifted Child Quarterly, 1972---. 1st v.p., Nat. Assn. for Gifted Children, 1978-80; 2nd v.p., 1976-78; dir., 1972-76. Contbr. many pubs. Mem. Hon. Socs.: Kappa Delta Pi, Phi Delta Kappa, Chi Delta Phi. Mem.: Sierra Club (nature walk leader); Nature Conservancy; Audubon; Leonis Adobe Assn. (docent). Lutheran Sun. sch. tchr. Rec.: Cold Creek Canyon Preserve, Malibu Creek State Park. Home: 24466 Mulholland Hwy., Calabasas, CA 91302; Office: Dept. of Elem. Edn., Cal State, L.B., CA.

GENTRY, ROBERT W.
Surgeon
b. Apr. 11, 1916, Springfield, Mo.; s. Charles B. and Kathleene M. Gentry; B.S., Cornell Univ. 1934-36; Univ. of Conn. 1937; M.D., Harvard Med. Sch. 1942; M.S. (surg.), Univ. of Minn. 1947; m. Priscilla Moerdyke, Pasadena, 1942; chil.: Perry Charles, b. Mar. 27, 1951; Priscilla Josephine, b. Mar. 1, 1952. Career: Phys.-surg., pvt. practive, L.A.; chmn.-med. dir., radio-TV prodn.

com., Medics (NBC-TV), L.A. Co. Med. Assn. 1953---; med. dir., Ask the Doctor, 1953---. Author: (mot. pic.) Am. Coll. of Surgs., 1936; Mem. FACS; Am. Bd. of Surg.; Pan Am. Med. Soc.; Pan Pac. Surg. Soc.; bd. govs., Harvard Club. of So. Calif., 1962---, pres. 1969; bd. govs., Mayo Clinic Alumni Assn., 1965---; pres. Harvard Med. Soc. of So. Calif. 1966---; Valley Hunt Club and Univ. Club, Pasa.; Shadow Mt. Club, Palm Desert; Psi Upsilon, Gamma Chi Upsilon. Hobby: colored photog. Rec.: summary. Home: 1215 St. Albans Rd., San Marino, CA; Office: 65 N. Madison Ave., Pasadena, CA.

GERBODE, FRANK LEVEN ALBERT
Cardiovascular Surgeon
b. Feb. 3, 1907, Placerville; s. Frank Albert and Anna (Leven) Gerbode; B.A., Physiology (cum laude), Stanford Univ., 1932, M.D., Stanford Med. Sch., 1936; m. Martha Alexander (dec.), Dec. 24, 1931, Piedmont; chil.: Maryanna (Shaw), b. May 27, 1938; Frank Albert, b. Apr. 23, 1940; Penelope Ann (Hopper), b. Oct. 24, 1946; John Philip, b. Nov. 26, 1948. Career: residency in surg. and surgical research, Stanford Univ. Hosps., 1937-40; Prof. of Surg., Stanford Med. Sch. 1940-42, 1945-71; clin. prof. of Surg., Emeritus, 1971-76, clin. prof. of cardiovascular surg., emeritus, 1976---; clin. prof. of surg., Univ. Calif. Med. Sch., S.F., 1964-76; chmn. of Dept. of Cardiovascular Surg., Pac. Med. Center, S.F., 1959---; pres., The Institutes of Med. Scis., Pac. Med. Center, 1959---; Cons.: US Naval Hosp., Oakland, 1948-60, Letterman Army Hosp., S.F., 1949---; Nat. Heart-Lung Inst., Bethesda, Md., 1955-72. Lt. Col., AUS M.C. Mem.: editorial bds.: Annals of Surgery, Review of Surgery, Journ. of Cardiovascular Surgery. Mem. Calif., Am., internat. med. assns. and societies; council mem. at large, S.F. BSA, 1971---; Clubs: Bohemian, Chit Chat, Commonwealth, Pac.-Union, Stanford Assocs., Stanford Club of S.F., Stanford Med. Alumni Assn., Univ. Club, N.Y., St. Francis Yacht. Hobby: painting. Rec.: sailing, hunting, skiing. Home: 2560 Divisadero St., S.F., CA 94115; Office: Pac. Med. Center, P.O.B. 7999, S.F., CA 94120.

GERE, JAMES MONROE
Professor of Civil Engineering
b. June 14, 1925, Syracuse, N.Y.; s. William Stanton and Carol Hixson Gere; B. Civil Engrng., Rensselaer Polytech. Inst., 1949, M.C.E., 1951; Ph.D., applied mechs., Stanford Univ., 1954; m. Janice Macauley Platt, June 1, 1946, Syracuse; chil.: Susan Munro, b. 1955; William Platt, b. 1957; David Stanton, b. 1958. Career: prof. of civil engring., Stanford Univ., 1962---; chmn. Dept. of Civil Engring., 1967-72, assoc. Dean, Sch. of Engring., 1960-70. Nat. Sci. Found. Grad. Fellow, 1952-54. Spec.: earthquake engring., structural engring., applied mechanics. Regis. Civil Engr., Calif., N.Y. Author: Moment Distribution, 1963, trans. Japanese, Spanish; co-author six engring. textbooks; contbr. engring. journs., tech reports. USAAF, 1943-46, bombsight mech. ETO. Mem.: Fellow, Am. Soc. of Civil Engineers; Earthquake Engring. Research Inst.; Am. Soc. for Engring. Edn.; Column Research Council, mem. at large; Sigma Xi, Tau Beta Pi, Chi Epsilon; Rensselaer Soc. of Engrs. Rec.: backpacking. Home: 932 Valdez Pl., Stanford, CA 94305; Office: Dept. of Civil Engring., Stanford Univ., Stanford, CA 94305.

GERKEN, WALTER B.
Chairman-CEO, Pacific Mutual Life Insurance Co.
b. Aug. 14, 1922, N.Y.C.; s. Walter A. and Virginia (Bland) Gerken; B.A., Wesleyan Univ. 1948; M.P.A., Maxwell Sch. of Citizenship-Pub. Affairs, Syracuse Univ., 1958; m. Darlene Stolt, Madison, Wis., Sept. 6, 1952; chil.: Walter C., b. July 10, 1953; Ellen, b. June 10, 1955; Beth, b. Nov. 2, 1956; Daniel, b. July 24, 1958; Andrew, b. Dec. 18, 1961; David, b. May 11, 1964. Career: Supv., Budget & Adm. Analysis, State of Wis. 1950-56; investment spec. Northwestern Mutual Life Ins. Co., 1954-56, investment research ofcr. 1956-59, investments mgr., 1959-67; financial v.p.-Pac. Mutual Life Ins. Co., 1967-69, exec. v.p. 1969-72, pres.-bd. dirs., 1972---. Dir.: Automobile Club, of So. Calif.; Times-Mirror Co.; Whittaker Corp.; L.A. World Affairs Council; trustee: Occidental Coll., Wesleyan Univ.; bd. dirs. Milwaukee Schs., 1965-67. Navigator, USAF, 1942-46; Capt., WW II. Awards: Distinguished Flying Cross, Air Medal, Brit. Coastal Command Cit. Mem.: Stock Exch. Club, Balboa Bay Club, Pac. Union Club, S.F., Calif. Club. Home: 1 Point Loma Dr., Corona del Mar, CA 92625; Office: 700 Newport Center Dr., Newport Beach, CA 92660.

GERLACH, CLINTON G.
Electronics Company Founder
b. June 18, 1926, Rosemont, Nebr.; s. Herman F. and Lena (Knigge) Gerlach; B.S., bus. ad., Univ. Denver, 1949; CPA; m. Juanita R. (Billie) Sowers, Aug. 29, 1953; chil.: Kimberlee Ann, b. Aug. 24, 1955; Clinton G. II (Curt), b. Oct. 28, 1957. Career: with Arthur Andersen & Co., Chicago, 1949-52; controller, Penn-Union Electric Corp., Erie, Pa., 1952-58, pres., 1958-67 (Penn Union sold to Teledyne, 1967), Group exec., Teledyne, 1972; founder and chmn bd., Tannetics, Inc. 1969--- (brought it to sales of $60 million in 1978). Dir.: Zero Corp. (an AMEX Co.), 1973---; Security Peoples Trust Co. (State Bank, Erie, Pa.), 1968---; Hawthorne Fin. Corp., 1978---; Graphidyne Corp., L.A., 1969---. Mem.: Beta Gamma Sigma, Shrine Club, Al Malaikah Temple. Presbyterian. Home: 1551 Sorrento Dr., Pacific Palisades, CA 90272; Office: 4676 Admiralty Way, Suite 534, Marina del Rey, CA 90291.

GERSTELL, A. FREDERICK
Cement Company Executive
b. Feb. 6, 1938, N.Y.C.; s. Robert S. and Alice (Roeth) Gerstell; A.B., Princeton, Univ., 1960; m. Barbara Kroner, Aug. 29, 1959, Easton, Pa.; chil.: Alison Davis, b. Jan. 29, 1962; Andrea Roeth, b. Sept. 14, 1964; Daphne Ford, b. Sept. 12, 1966. Career: v.p., mktg., Alpha Portland Cement Co., 1965-75, dir. 1969-75, v.p., Cement Div., Calif. Opns., Calif. Portland Cement Co., 1975---. Trustee: Westridge Sch., Pasadena, 1976; Lawrenceville Sch., N.J., 1977; United for Calif. 1978. AUS, 1960-66; Mem.: Calif. Club, L.A.; Annandale Golf Club, Pasadena; Metropolitan Club, N.Y.C.; L.A. Athletic Club. Home: 2075 Lombardy Rd., San Marino, CA 91108; Office: 800 Wilshire Blvd., L.A., CA 90017.

GERSTER, ROBERT GIBSON
Composer — Educator
b. Oct. 13, 1945; Chicago; s. Robert Heer and Betty Lou (Gibson) Gerster; nephew, Jack Allen Gerster, chem. engr.; B.Mus., Oh. State Univ., 1967, M.Mus. (Fellow), 1968, Doc. Mus. Arts, Univ. Wash., 1976; m. Pamela Daneal Ward, Aug. 24, 1968, Cuyahoga Falls, Oh.; chil.: David Ward, b. Sept. 20, 1972; James William, b. Oct. 31, 1975; Sara Jeanne, b. Sept. 8, 1977. Career: Lectr., Cal. State Univ., Fresno 1974---; lectr., Northwest Sch. of Fine Arts, Fres., 1977; tchg. asst., Univ. of Wash., 1968, 71-73; Organist-dir., M.C.A.V. Annex Chapel, Saigon, Vietnam, 1970; Carillonneur, The Oh. State Univ., 1964-67; Dir. of Music, United Christian Chapel, Columbus, Oh., 1966-67; Asst. Organist, Trinity Episcopal Ch., Columbus, Oh., 1964-66. Awards: Charles Ives Scholar, Nat. Inst. of Arts and Letters, 1973; Pi Kappa Lambda, 1967; numerous performances of musical compositions in U.S., Europe, East Asia and Central Am.; Recording: Crystal. AUS, 1969-70. Mem.: Am. Soc. of Univ. Composers, coord. W. Regional Conf. IV, 1975; Nat. Assn. of Composers USA; Soc. for Music Theory; Coll. Music. Soc., life mem.; Soc. for Ethnomusicology; Am. Musicological Soc.; Am. Guild of Organists; Broadcast Music, Inc. Organist, dir., Good Shepherd Lutheran Ch., Fresno. Office: CUS, Fresno, CA 93740.

GERTH, DONALD R.
University President
b. Dec. 4, 1928, Chicago, Ill.; s. George C. and Madeleine (Canavan) Gerth; B.A., Univ. of Chicago, 1947; M.A., 1951; Ph.D., polit. Sci., 1963; m. Beverly J. Hollman, Oct. 15, 1955, Scott AFB, Ill.; chil.: Annette C., b. Mar. 26, 1957; Deborah A., b. July 23, 1959. Career: field rep. in S.E. Asia, World Univ. Serv., 1950; asst. to Pres., Shimer Coll., 1951 lectr. in hist. (part-time) Univ. of Philippines, 1953-54; admissions counselor, Univ. of Chicago, 1956-58; assoc. dean of students, admissions and records and mem. dept. polit. sci., Cal State Univ., S.F., 1958-63; assoc. dean institutional rels., Cal. State Univ. and Colleges, 1963-64; dean of students, Cal State Univ., Chico, 1964-68; co-dir., Danforth Found. Research Project, improvement of undergrad. tchg., 1968-69; coordinator, Inst. for Local Govt. and Public Service, 1968-70; assoc. v.p., acad. affairs and dir., internat. programs, CSU, Chico, v.p., academic affairs and prof. polit. 1970-76; president and prof. polit. sci. and public adminstrn., Cal. State Univ., Dominguez Hills, Carson, 1976---. Frequent lectr., moderator, writer on higher edn. in Calif. Served to Capt., USAF, 1952-56. Mem.: Soc. College and Univ. Planning; Town Hall of L.A.; Commonwealth Club of Calif.; Am. Polit. Sci. Assn.; Am. Soc. for Public Adminstrn.; Western Governmental Research Assn.; Calif. Assn. for Public Adminstrn., chmn. 1973-64; Nat. Assn. of Schools of Public Affairs and Adminstrn.; personnel commn., Chico Unified Sch. Dist., chmn., 1971-74; advis. com. on Justice Programs, Butte

Col., 1970-76. Home: 404 Palos Verdes Blvd., Redondo Beach, CA 90277; Office: Cal. State Univ., Dominguez Hills, Carson, CA 90747.

GHERARDI, GINGER
City Official
b. Apr. 11, 1943, Bronx, N.Y.; d. John and Eleanor Apuzzo; B.S., Pratt Inst., 1964, M.S., 1965; postgrad. studies, UCLA, Cal. State Univ., Northridge; chil.: Andy, b. Jan. 21, 1967; John, b. Dec. 31, 1968. Career: tchr. of art, Rothschild Jr. H.S., Brooklyn, 1964-66, Valley State Coll., 1969-70, Moorpark Coll., 1971-73; art tchr., Moorpark H.S., 1973---; elected councilwoman, city of Simi Valley, 1972---; Mayor, 1978. Collab. & illustrator textbook, Arts & Craft Activities Desk Book, Parker Pub. Co.; named Teacher of Year, 1976. Mem.: Ventura Co. Assn. of Govts., 1972---; Transportation, Policy Com. & Exec. Bd.; League of Calif. Cities, 1972---; Transportation Com. rep. Channel Islands Div.; Simi Valley Co. Sanitation Bd. of Dirs., 1972---; Ventura Region Criminal Justice Plan. Bd., 1976-78; Ventura Co. Waterworks Dist. No. 8, chmn. 1977-78; AAUW, 1976---; Community Observer; Horizon Players Community Theater Group, 1968---; Las Manitas; Children's Home Soc., 1973---; Planning Commn., 1968-72, chmn. 1970-71; elected del., State of Calif., Nat. Conf. on Women, Houston, Tex., 1977; Calif. Elected Women's Assn. for Edn. & Research, bd. dir., 1975---. Home: 2410 N. Justin Ave., Simi Valley, CA 93065; Office: 3200 Cochran St., Simi Valley, CA 93065; 280 Casey Rd., Moorpark, CA.

GHORMLEY, BETTY
Realtor
b. Jan. 8, 1925, Greenville, Ill.; d. Glen Erwin and Emma Ghormley; student, USC, 1943; Univ. of Calif., 1963; 1 son, Edmund Glen Anderson, b. Sept. 18, 1944. Career: real estate broker, 1952---. V.P., realty board Traders Club, 1976; Realty bd. Com. chmn., 1976, 1977; treas., Am. Businesswomens Assn., 1963. Founder, Money Anonymous Seminars, 1977. Home: 446 Bonito Ave., L.B., CA 90804; Office: Real Estate B.C., 3132 E. 7th St., Long Beach, CA 90804.

GIANNINI, PETER EUGENE
Judge, L.A. County Superior Court
b. June 8, 1921, Kingsburg, Calif.; s. Peter E. and Lena (Biaggini) Giannini; Reedley Jr. Coll. and Univ. of Santa Clara, 1943; B.S. (cum laude), Univ. of Calif., Berkeley, 1944, LL.B. 1945; m. Mercedes Lowell, Berkeley, Apr. 15, 1944; chil.: Peter Eugene, III, b. Apr. 16, 1945; Paul Lorin, b. Jan. 30, 1947; Christine Ann, b. Dec. 25, 1948; Regina Marie, b. Feb. 14, 1957; Sharon Rae and Joyce Mae (twins), b. Feb. 16, 1960. Career: Admitted to Calif. bar, 1945, pvt. practice law, L.A., 1946-70; Judge, L.A. Judicial Dist. 1970-72; Judge, Superior Ct., 1972---. Mem.: L.A., Am., and Wilshire Bar Assns.; chmn. adm. com., State Bar of Calif., 1955; pres. Brentwood C. of C. 1950; pres. Wilshire C. of C. 1961; pres. L.A. hdqrs., City Devel. Assn. 1965-66; United Way Budget Com. No. 6, So. Calif.; v.p.-bd. dirs., Junipero Serra Boys Club; co-founder-(hon.) dir., Hollywood-Wilshire Sym. Orch.; bd. dirs., Wilshire Town Club; Order of Coif, Phi Beta Kappa, Alpha Sigma Nu. Catholic. Hobby: music. Rec.: hunting, mountaineering. Home: 635 Moreno Ave., L.A., CA 90048; Office: L.A. Co. Courthouse, L.A., CA 90012.

GIANTURCO, ADRIANA
Director, California Dept. of Transportation
b. June 5, 1939, Berkeley; d. Elio and Valentine (McGillicuddy) Gianturco; B.A., magna cum laude and Phi Beta Kappa, Smith Coll. 1960; M.A., Univ. Calif., Berkeley, 1962; m. John L. Saltonstall, Jr., Boston, Mass. Career: Economist, The Planning Servs. Group, 1966-68; dir. of planning, Action for Boston Comm. Devel. 1968-73; dir. of planning, Office of State Planning & Mgmt., Calif.; asst. secty., Business & Transportation Agency, 1975-76; dir., Calif. Dept. of Transportation, 1976---. Office: P.O.B. 1139, Sacto., CA 95805.

GIBSON, ROBERT DANIEL
University Dean — Pharmacist
b. July 2, 1925, Tacoma, Wash.; s. Ray and Madelyn Alice Gibson; cousin, D. Parke Gibson, B.A., 1949; B.S., 1954; Pharm.D., 1958; m. Helen Sigismund, 1951 (div. 1973), Berkeley; chil.: Dana Alice, b. Dec. 24, 1955; Barton Ray, b. Mar. 31, 1957; Todd David, b. May 15, 1959. Career: Univ. of Calif., S.F.: sr. pharmacist, 1962-70; pr. pharmacist, 1970-71; lectr./Pharmacy, 1967---; clinical instr./Pharmacy, 1962-67; dir.,

Pharmaceutical Tech. Lab., 1970---; Asst. Dean, 1972-74; Assoc. Dean, 1975---. Vis. Prof. Fulbright grantee, Univ. of Cairo, 1965-66; Cons., DHEW, SSA, 1969-70. AUS, 1944-46. Publs.: contbr. 16 articles profl. pubs., 1963---; Research: Solid Dosage Form Design, Drug Utilization Review; Devel. & Delivery of Health Care to the Poor & to Minorities; Ethnic Related Diseases. V.P., Edn. Devel., Nat. Pharmaceutical Found.; chmn. Foreign Pharmacy Grads., 1977---; chmn., CPhA Task Force, 1977---; chmn. CPha Task Force of Profl. Servs. for the Underserved, 1975---; chmn. AACP Profl. Affairs Com., 1975-78; Rec.: hiking, camping, flying. Home: 49 Diamond Head Passage, Corte Madera, CA 94927; Office: Univ. of Calif., Sch. of Pharmacy, S.F., CA 94142.

GIBSON, ROBERT LEE
President, California Canners and Growers
b. Feb. 14, 1919, Anaheim, CA; s. Robert Lee and Dorothy (Morrison) Gibson; ed. B.S., Univ. of Calif., Berkeley, 1940; M.S., Mass. Inst. of Tech. 1955; m. Charlotte Lowe, June 1, 1940; chil.: Anne Steiner, Carol Timmerman, Ellen, Robert, Thomas. Career: With Libby, McNeill & Libby, 1940-67 (food tech., foreman, plant supt. prodn. mgr. div. ofc., adm. asst. to v.p., S.F.; adm. asst. to v.p. mktg. Chicago; asst. gen. mgr. West Coast Div., S.F. 1940-58; v.p. gen. mgr. 1958-62; pres.-chief exec., Chicago, 1962-67); pres.-chief exec. ofcr. Calif. Canners & Growers, 1967---. Dir. Ampex Corp., Redwood City, 1973---. 2nd Lt., C.I.C., AUS, WW II. Mem.: Soc. Sloan Fellows, Theta Delta Chi. Home: 428 El Centro Rd., Hillsborough, CA 94010; Office: 3100 Ferry Bldg., S.F., CA 94106.

GIBSON, THOMAS HALL, JR.
Real Estate Developer
b. Mar. 22, 1930, Cleveland, Oh.; s. Thomas H. and Silvia Gibson; B.Sc., Stetson Univ., Fla. 1953; m. Billie Lee Lohman (dec.), Morristown, N.J., June 20, 1953; daus.: Linda Lee, b. July 24, 1954; Donna Jeanne, b. Dec. 31, 1956; m. Paulette Lollar, Aug. 17, 1974; son, Thomas Ryan, b. Oct. 17, 1977. Career: Sales repr. Burroughs Corp. 1957-60; Johnson & Johnson div. mgr. 1960-64; reg. mgr. Xerox Corp., 1964-69; v.p. mktg. Quantor Corp. 1969-71; v.p. mktg. Fox & Carelsador Fin. Corp. 1971-73; owner, Brown, Gibson and Co. real estate devel., 1973-78. Owner, Gibson Development Co., Inc. 1978---. First Lt., USMPC, U.S.Army, 1953-55. Mem.: (charter) Stetson Univ. Circle; Phi Kappa Alpha (pres.-v.p.-secty.-treas.); Omicron Delta Kappa; La Jolla Beach and Tennis Clubs. Home: 7765 Via Capri, La Jolla, CA 92037; Office: 8535 Commerce St., San Diego, CA 92121.

GIBSON, VICTORIA
Lawyer — Educator
b. Los Angeles, Calif.; B.A., Stanford, 1945; LL.B., Stanford Law Sch., 1947; m. Phil S. Gibson (Chief Justice of Calif., ret.), Aug. 3, 1954; 1 son Blaine Alan, b. Apr. 21, 1957. Career: Admitted to Calif. Bar, 1947; research atty., Supreme Ct. of Calif., 1947-53; tching. asst., Stanford Law Sch., 1963-64; appted. by Speaker of the Assembly to be pub. mem., Central Coast Regional Coastal Commn., 1973-76; appted. by Gov. Brown to be mem., State Parks and Recreation Commn., 1976---, chmn., 1978---. Bd. Dir.: Monterey Inst. of Foreign Studies, 1971-72; Monterey Coll. of Law, 1976---. Home: 4130 Segundo Dr., Carmel, CA 93923.

GIBSON, WELDON BAILEY
Executive Vice President, SRI International
b. Apr. 23, 1917, Eldorado, Tex.; s. Oscar and Susie (Bailey) Gibson; B.A., 1938; M.B.A., Stanford Univ., 1940, Ph.D., 1950; m. Helen Mears, Mar. 1, 1941; son, David M., b. Jan. 28, 1937. Career: asst. dir. (new) USAF Inst. of Tech., Dayton, Oh., 1946; joined SRI known then as Stanford Research Inst., 1947---: dir. of economics research, 1947; assoc. dir., 1955; v.p., 1959; exec. v.p., 1960---; creator, SRI International Assocs. Plan incl. 650 companies in 60 nations; originator and co-dir., Internat. Indsl. Conf. (major meeting of world bus. leaders held every 4 yrs., S.F.). Dir.: Plantronics, Inc., Calif.; The Vendo Co., Mo.; Valley Nat. Bank, Ariz.; Tech. Equities Corp., Inc., Calif. Mem. exec. com. Japan-Calif. Assn. co-chmn. Profl. Com.; Internat. Dir.-gen., Pacific Basin Economic Council; co-dir., Internat. Indsl. Conv.; mem. Pac.-Indonesian Bus. Assn. Cons.: Bureau of the Budget (U.S.), 1949-53; U.S. Nat. Security Resources Bd., 1949-53; White House Conf. on the Indsl. World Ahead, 1972. Awarded Medal of Legion of Merit, U.S. 1946; Comdr. of the British Empire, 1947. Col., USAF, 1941-46, dir. of materiel requirements. Hon. Trustee, Soodo Women's Tchrs.

Coll., Korea; Internat. Assoc., Hoover Inst., Stanford Univ.; Mem.: Beta Theta Pi, Alpha Kappa Psi, Phi Kappa Phi, Shrine, Masonic Order, Newcomen Soc. in No. Am., Stanford Assocs. Home: 593 Gerona Rd., Stanford, CA 94305; Office: SRI International, 333 Ravenswood Ave., Menlo Park, CA 94025.

GIEDT, WARREN H.
University Dean
b. Nov. 1, 1920, Leola, S. Dak.; s. William J.P. and Julia E. (Klauss) Giedt; B.A.S., Univ. Calif., Berkeley, 1944, M.S., 1946, Ph.D., 1950; m. Leta McCarty, June 24, 1950, S.F. Career: Prof. of mech. engring., Univ. Calif., Berkeley, 1947-65; chmn., Dept. of Mech. Engring., Univ. Calif., Davis, 1965-69, assoc dean, Grad. Study, 1972---; Fulbright Prof., Univ. of Tokyo, 1963; Editor, ASME Journ. of Heat Transfer, 1967-72; Author: Principles of Engring. Heat Transfer, Van Nostrand, 1957; Thermophysics, Van Nostrand, Reinhold, 1971. Awards: ASEE Western Electric Award, 1968; ASM Jennings Award, 1971; ASEE Burks Award, 1974; ASME Heat Transfer Div. Mem. Award, 1976. Cadet, USAAF, 1943-44, Pilot, 2nd Lt., to Capt., 1944-47. Mem.: Am. Soc. of Mech. Engring., Fellow, ASME, 1971; Am. Soc. of Engring. Edn. Hobby: golf. Home: 2945 Garden Ct., El Macero, CA 95618; Office: Coll. Engring., Univ. Calif., Davis, CA 95616.

GIELICZ, KATHERINE PAMELA
Aerospace Company Executive
b. Dec. 29, 1947, L.A.; d. Felix Arthur and Edna Elizabeth (Pedersen) Gielicz; B.A., Math., USC, 1969, M.S., Computer Sci., 1970, M.S., Elec. Engring., 1974, M.B.A., 1979. Career: Diagnostic Programmer, Nat. Cash Register, 1970-72; mem. of the Tech. Staff., TRW Systems Group, 1972-75; Section Head, Advanced Digital Processor Dept., TRW Defense and Space Systems Group, 1975---. (Currently the only woman engring. sect. hd. in TRW's Electronic Systems Div.). Awards: Soroptimist Achievement, 1976; YWCA Certificate of Achievement 1977; Outstanding Young Woman of Am. 1978; Mem.: IEEE, 1970---; Assn. for Computing Machinery, 1970---; Soc. of Women Engrs., 1968---; Counselor to USC Student Sect., 1974---; Rep. to L.A. Council of Engrs. and Scis., 1976-77; Alpha Delta Pi Sor., Standards chmn. 1968-69; USC Archimedes Circle, bd. dir., 1977--- (Sch. of Engring. Support Group); USC Intergreek Soc., 1977---; Trojan Jr. Aux. 1970-75. Mem. Redondo Beach Harbor Review Bd., 1977---, chmn. 1978-79; Town Hall of Calif. 1978---; mem. U.S. Coast Guard Aux., Flotilla Communications Ofcr., 1973-75. Roman Catholic. Hobbies: crocheting, piano. Rec.: tennis, swimming. Home: 340 The Village No. 304, Redondo Beach, CA 90277; Office: TRW DSSG, One Space Park R6/1176, Redondo Beach, CA 90278.

GIFFORD, BROOKS
Attorney at Law
b. Apr. 22, 1910, Chicago; s. Robert Ladd (noted inventor, educator, financier, philanthropist, listed Who's Who in America, 1926-62) and Evelyn (Brooks) Gifford; A.B., Occidental Coll.; J.D., USC; chil.: Brooks, Jr., Barbara, Robert Brooks, William Charles. Career: Admitted to practice law, 1926---; sr. partner, Brooks Gifford law firm. Dir.: Nu-Way Indus., The Philanthropic and Edn. Found., Ill.; The Principia Corp., Mo. Guest, numerous TV interviews. Lt. Comdr., USNR, 1941; Naval ofcr. procurement, Adm. Halsey's staff, 1942-44; dist. legal asst. ofc., 3rd Naval Dist. 1944; asst. chief of staff, Long Beach Naval Command, 1944-45, Capt., USNR 1963 (ret.). Awards: Silver Beaver Award, B.S.A. 1972; Mem.: Corona Lodge, 32 degree, F. & A.M.; Pasa. Scottish Rite Consistory; Pasa. Humane Soc.; dir. B.S.A. Council (20 yrs.); 4th Ch. of Christ Sci., San Diego, La Jolla; Pres. B.S.A. Assocs; Clubs: Trans-Pac. Yacht; Hobby: Coin collecting. Rec.: flying, tennis, soaring, bridge, dancing. Home: 939 Coast Blvd., La Jolla, 92037; Office: Suite 303, 151 S. El Molino Ave., Pasadena, CA 91101; 939 Coast Blvd., Suite LC, La Jolla, CA 92037.

GILBERT, ROBERT WOLFE
Attorney at Law
b. Nov. 12, 1920 N.Y.C.; s. L. Wolfe and Kate (Oestreicher) Gilbert; A.B. (hon. Polit. Sci.), UCLA, 1941; LL.B. (Univ. prescholarship), 1941-43; State Legislators' scholarship, 1942), Univ. of Calif., Berkeley, 1943; m. Beatrice Fruitman, Las Vegas, Nev., Dec. 25, 1946; sons: Frank Richard, b. Nov. 22, 1952; Jack Alfred, b. July 28, 1954. Career: Exec. asst., Natl. War Labor Bd., Region 10, 1943-44; pvt. legal practice, 1945---; sr. partner, Giblert and Nissen law firm,

1949-74; pres. Robert W. Gilbert, law corp. 1974---. Editor in chief., Calif. Law Review, 1940; commr. Housing Authority, L.A. 1953-60; dir. Calif. Housing Council, 1955-63. Mem.: Order of the Coif, 1944; Inter-Am., Calif. State, Am. Bar, Am. Judicature Assns.; U.S. Supreme Ct. Bar; L.A. Co. Dem. Central Com. 1948-53; pres. Hollywood Dem. Club, 1949-52, 1964-73; Pi Sigma Alpha. Hobby: spectator sports. Rec.: music, theatre, books. Home: 7981 Hollywood Blvd., L.A., CA 90036; Office: 400 S. Beverly Dr., Suite 305, Beverly Hills, CA 90212.

GILLETTE, ALPHEUS JAY, JR.
Aerospace Executive
b. Mar. 7, 1929, Columbia, Mo.; s. Alpheus Jay and Esther (Emmel) Gillette; stu. Wesleyan Univ., 1947-49; UCLA 1949-51; B.A., San Diego State Coll. 1957, M.S., 1960; m. Carole Corkhill, Aug. 5, 1956. Career: Test engr., Gen.-Dynamics Corp. 1951-56, group engr. Convair Div. 1956-58, supv. advanced planning, Astronautics Div. 1958-62, chief of engring., planning and estimating, 1962-65, chief, engring., planning and control, Convair Div. 1965-68, div. mgr. Stromberg DatagraphiX Inc. 1968---. Lectr., Univ. Calif. Ext. 1965---. Mem.: Delta Tau Delta, 1947---; Inst. of Elec. and Electronics Engrs. 1954---; Am. Mgmt. Assn. 1956---. Office: General Dynamics, P.O.B. 2449, San Diego, CA 92112.

GILLMOR, GARY GEORGE
Mayor of Santa Clara
b. Aug. 3, 1936, S.F.; s. Rose Gillmor; B.A., Univ. of Santa Clara; M.S. (edn. adm., tchg. fellow), San Jose State Coll.; m. Dorothy Gillmor (dec.); m. Linda Gillmor, Sept. 1970; chil.: Michelle, Lisa, David, Renee; (stepchil.) Deborah, Kimberly, Matthew, Scott, Jamie. Career: H.S. tchr., Santa Clara Unif. Sch. Dist. (10 yrs.); instr. polit. sci.-hist, West Valley Community Coll.; owner-opr. Gary Gillmor and Assocs., Real Estate, 1967---; City Councilman, 1965---; Mayor, 1969---. Home: 120 Serena Way, Santa Clara; Office: City Hall, 1500 Warburton Ave., Santa Clara, CA.

GILMAN, RICHARD CARLETON
President, Occidental College
b. July 28, 1923, Cambridge, Mass.; s. George Phillips Brooks and Karen (Theller) Gilman; B.A., Dartmouth Coll. 1944; Ph.D., Boston Univ. 1952; (hon.) LL.D.: Pomona Coll. 1966, USC and Coll. of Idaho, 1968; L.H.D., Boston Univ., 1969; m. Lucille Young, Aug. 28, 1948; chil.: Marsha, b. 1950; Bradley Morris, b. 1952; Brian Potter, b. 1955; Blair Tucker, b. 1960. Career: tchg. fellow (relig.), Dartmouth Coll. 1948; faculty, Colby Coll. 1950-56, assoc. prof. of philosophy, 1955-56; exec. dir., Natl. Council on Relig. in Higher Edn. 1950-60; dean-prof. of philosophy, Carleton Coll. 1960-65; pres. Occidental Coll. 1965---. Lt. (j.g.) USNR(1944-46), WW II. Mem.: bd. dirs. Am. Council on Edn.; bd. dirs. Council for Financial Aid to Edn.; bd. dirs. L.A. World Affairs Council; dir. Calif. State C. of C.; bd. dirs. Assn. of Independent Calif. Colls. and Univs.; Independent Colls. of So. Calif.; bd. dirs. Natl. Assn. of Independent Colleges and Univs.; Newcomen Soc.; Twilight Club; 100 Club; Univ. Club, N.Y.; Calif. Club. Home: 1852 Campus Rd., L.A., CA 90041; Office: 1600 Campus Rd., L.A., CA 90041.

GIRAUD, LISE
University Librarian
b. Mar. 27, 1924, Vienna, Austria; d. Friedrich and Stella (Fritz) Kurzmann; ed., B.A., Simmons Coll. 1946; m. Raymond Giraud, Chicago, Feb. 1, 1948. Career: Med. librn., Michael Reese Hosp., Chicago, 1946-48; librn., Yale Univ. 1950-51; librn., Stanford Univ., 1958---. Home: 2200 Byron St., Palo Alto, CA 94301; Office: Stanford Univ. Libraries, Stanford, CA.

GILIAM, EVERETT JOHN
Insurance Company Executive
b. Apr. 11, 1938, L.A.; s. E.J. and Florence L. Giliam; B.S., Calif. Western Univ., 1964; m. Jennie Schoppert, July 14, 1966, Las Vegas, Nev.; chil.: E. John III, b. Aug. 6, 1968; Tiffany L., b. Oct. 19, 1971. Career: Field Suprv., Travelers Ins. Co., 1964-66, Agency Mgr. 1966-69, Mgr., 1969-71, West Coast Regional Mgr. 1971-75; v.p., Natl. Am. Ins. Companies, 1975-77, Sr. v.p., 1977---; chmn. Pub. Rels., 1976---; Recipient Speakers Bureau Award 1971. AUS, 1956-59. Coach, AYSO 1975-78. Mem. United Ch., sr. youth advisor. Rec.: golf, tennis; Home: 8618 Chucker Cir., Fountain Valley, CA 92708; Office: 4909 Lakewood Blvd., Lakewood, CA 90712.

GILLIES, PATRICIA ANN MYERS
Biologist
b. Sept. 23, 1929, Berkeley; d. William W. and Barbara (Weddle) Myers; A.B. biology, Fresno State Coll., 1954, M.A., entomology, 1961; m. Robert W. Gillies (div. 1967), Sept. 17, 1948, Albany; chil.: Catherine Irene (Barton), b. July 2, 1949; Coila Louise, b. June 18, 1960. Career: Tchr. of Biology, Parlier, Calif. 1955-56; USDA Processed Product Inspection, Fresno, 1956-58; sr. Pub. Health Biologist, Vector Biology and Control Sect., Dept. of Health Servs, State of Calif., 1959---. Mem.: Bd. of Trustees, Consolidated Mosquito Abatement Dist., Selma, Calif., 1975---. Contrbr. articles in various profl. journs. related to vector control. Mem.: Calif. Mosquito Control Assn.; Am. Registry of Profl. Entomologists; Soc. of Vector Ecologists; Entomological Soc. of Am.; Am. Mosquito Control Assn.; San Joaquin Entomology Assn. Episcopalian. Hobbies: raising sheep, handcrafts. Home: 9360 E. Clinton Ave., Fresno, CA 93727; Office: 5545 E. Shields Ave., Fresno, CA 93727.

GINZTON, EDWARD LEONARD
Corporate Executive
b. Dec. 27, 1915, Dnepropetrovsk, Ukraine; s. Leonard Louis and Natalia (Philipova) Ginzton; B.S. in electrical engring., Univ. of Calif., 1936, M.S., 1937; Ph.D., Stanford Univ., 1940; m. Artemas A. McCann, July 12, 1939; chil.: Leonard; Nancy; David; Anne (Cotrell). Career: research engr., Sperry Gyroscope Co., N.Y.C., 1940-46; asst. prof. of applied physics, Stanford Univ., 1946-47, assoc. prof., 1947-50, prof., 1951-68; dir., Microwave Lab., Stanford, 1949-59; Stanford Univ. Project M. (SLAC), 1957-60; dir., Varian Associates, 1948---; chmn. of the bd., 1959---, chief exec. officer, 1959-72, pres., 1964-68. Dir. Stanford Bank, 1967-71; bd. mem. Mid-Peninsula Housing Develop. Corp. 1970---; bd. of trustees, Stanford Univ., 1977---; bd. mem. Stanford Univ. Hosp., 1975---; advisory bd., Mid-Peninsula Region of the Union Bank 1971-73, No. Calif. adv. bd., 1973---; Lawrence Berkeley Lab. Sci. and Edn. adv. com. 1972---; adv. bd. chmn., Sch. of Engring, Stanford Univ., 1968-70; adv. com., Sch. of Bus. Adminstrn., Univ. of Calif., 1972-74; co-chmn., Stanford Mid-Peninsula Urban Coalition 1968-72; exec. com. 1968-74. Fellow, IEEE, (bd. dir. 1971-72, awards bd. chmn. 1971-72). Mem., Nat. Acad. of Sciences (Com. on Motor Vehicle Emissions, 1971-74, chmn. 1971-72; Com. on Nuclear and Alternative Energy Systems, co-chmn. 1975---). Mem. del. to USSR, 1973, 1975; to Hungary, 1966; to Bulgaria, 1972. Mem.: Am. Acad. of Arts and Sci.; Nat. Acad. of Engring., council mem. 1974---. Recipient Morris Liebman Memorial Prize, 1958; IEEE Medal of Honor, 1969; Calif. Mfgr. of the Year Award, 1974. Author: Microwave Measurements, 1957. Hon. Socs.: Sigma Xi, Eta Kappa Nu, Tau Beta Pi. Hobbies: skiing, photog., rebuilding Model-A Fords. Home: 28014 Natoma Rd., Los Altos Hills, CA 94022; Office: Varian Associates, Inc., 611 Hansen Way, Palo Alto, CA 94303.

GLADMAN, MAURICE
Chairman of Board, American State Bank
b. Mar. 19, 1919, Winnipeg, Canada; m. Rosabelle St. Clair, Oct. 22, 1943, Dallas, Texas; chil.: Dennis S., b. Dec. 11, 1945; Patricia A. (Hartman), b. Aug. 7, 1947. Career: Business Owner, 1954-73; Chmn. of Bd., Am. State Bank, Newport Harbor, 1973---; exec., Kiwanis Internat., 1973---, pres., 1978-79; pres. Nat. Tire Dealers & Retreaders Assn., 1965; pres., Santa Ana C. of C., 1963; chmn. bd. Salvation Army, Santa Ana, 1969-71; past chmn. of St. Joseph Hosp. Found. 1974-75; past commnr., Orange Co. Civic Center Commn.; mem. Chapman Coll. Bd. of Govs., 1979---; pres. Santa Ana-Tustin YMCA, 1961-62. Col., AUS, 1942-WW II and Korea; decorated Bronze Star Medal, Legion of Merit. Presbyterian, elder, past chmn. trustees. Hobby: photog. Rec.: golf. Home: 12331 Alray Pl., Tustin, CA 92680; Office: 905 N. Euclid, Anaheim, CA 92801.

GLOSSON, VIRGINIA LOUISE
Librarian
b. May 31, 1919, Iowa Park, Texas; d. Andrew and Winifred Lee Gregory; degree, Library Sci., 1948; m. Harold Courtney Glosson, Oct. 29, 1938, Olney, Tex.; dau. Courtney Lynn (Larash), b. Nov. 12, 1943. Career: tchr., 1938-44; library assistant, 1956-62; head librarian, King City Public Library, 1962---. Mem.: Salvation Army, welfare secty., 1954---; Rebekah Lodge, Chaplain 1961-79; Order of Eastern Star, Star Point, 1978-79; pres., P.T.A., 1954; Girl Scout Council, 1950-60. Protestant, community ch., Sun. Sch. tchr., ch. clerk, historian, deaconess. Hobbies: gardening, needlework. Rec.: swimming, walking. Home: 513 Ellis St., King City, CA 93930; Office: 212 S. Vanderhurst Ave., King City, CA.

GLUSHA, LAURA (B. EVELYN LAURA GLUSHAK)
Wildlife Painter — Art Teacher — Lecturer
b. Oct. 15, 1921, Washington, D.C.; d. David Adolph and Ida Lillian (Rosenson) Glushak; rel. Dr. Leopold Glushak, noted surgeon; student N.Y. pub. schs.; Brooklyn Coll.; studied anatomy, N.Y. Med. Coll. (in exchange for med. illustrations); 15 yrs. art training; m. David Miller, Oct. 23, 1959. Career: Med. artist, 1941; free-lance illustrator, 1943; illustrator, Dan C. Miller Orgn., 1943-59; illustrator for ad agencies and film industry, 1959---. Also since 1972--- vol. involvement in the L.A. Zoo with a battered baby monkey, Suck-a-toe. Give lectures and drawing lessons on him in So. Calif. elem. schs. to more than 18,000 children. Devel. unique psychol. drawing system, equally successful with normal, Aphasic, mentally retarded and physically handicapped. Pub. Laura Glusha's Drawing Books of the Endangered Species at the request of tchrs. 12 paintings of endangered species, belonging to the L.A. Zoo, were exhibited at the zoo, 1975. Mem.: Nat. Speaker's Assn., bd. mem. Artist's Equity; Women's Nat. Book Assn.; Bus. and Profl. Women. Hobbies: psychology, animal behavior, music. Rec.: horseback riding, yoga. Home: L.A., CA.

GLYNN, REV. JOHN F.
Headmaster
b. Feb. 26, 1913, Lawrence, Mass.; s. Michael and Margaret (Flatley) Glynn; B.A., philosophy, 1936; M.A., Latin, Greek, 1940; B.A., Spanish, 1972. Career: teacher, Saint Augustine High Sch., San Diego, 1940---; athletic dir., 1940-42; vice principal, 1942-59; headmaster, Villanova Prep. Sch., Ojai, 1960-54, 76---; principal, Central Catholic High Sch., Modesto, 1966-71. Mem. Rotary Club, 1960---; chmn. educational grants, Ojai Rotary, 1977---. Catholic Priest; Prior, Villanova Monastery, Ojai, 1960-65, 1973---. Hobby: music. Rec.: walking. Office: Villanova Prep. Sch., 12096 Ventura Ave., Ojai, CA 93023.

GOBLE, FRANK GORDON
Research Center Founder
b. Mar. 3, 1917, White Plains, N.Y.; s. Frank N. and Nora (Sale) Goble; B.S., highest scholastic honors, Univ. Calif., Berkeley; m. Margaret Hensel, Nov. 26, 1941, Las Vegas, Nev. Career: exec. v.p. and pres., D.B. Milliken Co., 1941-63; founder and pres., Thomas Jefferson Research Center, Pasa., 1963---; Author: The Third Force: The Psychology of Abraham Maslow, 1970; Excellence in Leadership, 1972; Beyond Failure: How to Cure a Neurotic Society, 1977; numerous research reports and mag. articles. Dir.: Coast Fed. Savings & Loan Assn.; Inst. for Contemporary Studies. Mem. Sierra Club, v.p., mem. of bd. of trustees, Santa Anita Ch. Rec.: skiing, fishing, backpacking, badminton. Home: 1496 E. Orange Grove Blvd., Pasa., CA 91104; Office: 1143 N. Lake Ave., Pasa., CA 91104.

GODDARD, JOHN MELVIN
Explorer
b. July 29, 1924, Salt Lake City; s. P.L. "Jack" (v.p. Pierce Bros. Mortuary) and Lettie S. Goddard; ed. L.A. H.S.; B.A. (phys. and anthropology), USC; ethnological stu. with natives of French Morocco, Algeria and Tunisia; m. Susan Diane Stewart, June 19, 1965; chil.: Stewart Randolph, b. May 16, 1967; Lisa Lyn, b. Sept. 4, 1955; Jonelle, b. Jan. 12, 1958; Jeffrey John, b. June 3, 1959. Career: Wrote List of Aspirations and Goals to Accomplish in Life (127) at age 15 yrs.; anthropologist, explorer (over 1,000,000 mi. in 117 countries); pilot, 17 different types of jet fighters, bombers, and broke sound barrier 10 times. Achievements: climbed Equatorial Africa's highest (19,540 ft.) snow-capped Mt. Kilimanjaro; Mt. Vesuvius, Italy; Matterhorn Mt., Switz.; scaled Teewinot in Grand Tetons; climbed Mexico's 17,880 ft. volcano, Popocatepetl; Fujiyama in Japan and Huascaran in Peru; French expedition (sponsored by French Geographical Soc., French Museum of Natural History and French Explorer's Club), history making 10-month expedition in a kayak down entire 4,160 mi. Nile River (conquered world's longest and most important river, never before accomplished in hist. of man); completed length (1500 mi.) Colo. River from Rocky Mts. to Gulf of Calif. in Mex. (approx. 400 rapids and prod. 3500 botanical specimens, many new to sci.; 6-mo. expedition, survey of river Congo (Zaire) in Africa; (first to explore entire length of Congo); collected over 3,000 insects, Congo River, many new to sci. (several now named in hon. of discoverer). Film lectrs. incl.: (top adventure, all-color full-length mot. pics.) Kayaks Down the Congo, Congo Conquest, Kayaks Down the Nile, moderator-guest, 125 TV pgms., Bold Journey, I Search For Adventure and True Adventure. Author: (book) Kayaks Down the Nile. Combat flier, U.S. Army, 15th Air Force, Italy (33 combat bombing missions over Ger., Austria, Hungary,

Yugoslavia, Czechoslovakia), 1942-45 (hon. disch.), WW II; serv. U.S. Merchant Marines. Awards: many Air Force decorations, incl. Air Medal with 4 Oak Leaf Clusters, 4 Battle Stars and Pres. Unit Cit.; acclaimed Am.'s No. 1 Explorer by news critics; hon. by U.S. Jr. C. of C. as one of Calif's 5 outstanding young men, Liotard Medal for spectacular achievement in exploration, by Pres. of France, 1955; Fastest Flying Civ. of Yr. at 1500 m.p.h., 1972. Mem.: (hon. life) Sigma Chi; Adventurers Club of L.A. and Chicago, Explorers Club of N.Y., Savage Club of London, French Explorers Soc. (only Am. mem.), elected Fellow of Royal Geographical Soc.; Ch. of Jesus Christ of L.D.S. (serv. as missionary, Can. and N.W. U.S.). Hobby: oceanography, underwater diving, collecting classical recs. for stereo, collecting primitive carvings (wood and ivory). Rec.: flying, water skiing, horseback riding. Res. and Office: 4224 Beulah, La Canada, CA 91011.

GOLD, CAROL SAPIN
Management Consultant
b. June 28, 1932, New York, N.Y.; d. Cerf Saul and Muriel Louise (Fudin) Rosenberg; B.A., Univ. of Calif., Berkeley, 1955; m. Joseph Bernard Weinstein, Dec. 26, 1976, Marina del Rey, Calif.; chil.: Kevin Bart Sapin, Craig Paul Sapin, Courtney Byrens Sapin. Career: Fashion model, San Francisco, 1951; fashion coordinator, S.F., 1952-55; asst. credit mgr., Union Oil Co., S.F. and L.A., 1956; pub. relations, Braun & Co., L.A., 1966-68; corp. dir. personnel training, Great Western Fin. Corp., L.A., 1968-71; pres., Carol Sapin Gold & Associates, 1971---. Frequent guest appearances on radio and TV talk shows. Author: film: Instant Replay; book: Success Secrets; three library series of audio cassette tapes on Leadership in Supervision and Customer Relations; articles pub. trade journs. and nat. publs. Pres., Sisterhood Temple Emmanuel, La Crescenta, 1964-65; v.p., Jr. League, 1966. Mem.: Sales & Mktg. Execs.; World Affairs Council; Women in Business; Am. Soc. Training & Devel. Home: 25 Northstar, Marina del Rey, CA 90291; Office: 4121 Redwood Ave., Suite 210, L.A., CA 90066.

GOLDEN, CHARLES FRANKLIN
Clergyman
b. Aug. 24, 1912, Holly Springs, Miss.; s. J.W. and Mary P. (Tyson) Golden; B.A., Clark Coll., 1936; B.D., Gammon Theol. Sem. 1937; S.T.M., Boston Univ. 1938; Hon. D.D., Gammon Theol. Sem., 1958; Hon. LL.D., W. Va. Wesleyan Coll.; m. Ida Elizabeth Smith, May 24, 1937. Career: Ordained in 1938; asst. pastor: Birmingham, Ala. and Atlanta, Ga., 1935-36, summer pastor, Cooksville, Tenn. 1937; pastor: Clarksdale, Miss. 1938, Little Rock, Ark., 1938-42; Prof. Religion and Philosophy, Philander Smith Coll. 1938-41; Chaplain, AUS, 1942-46; Board of Missions, 1947-56, dir., div. of Nat. Missions, 1956-60; elected by Central Jurisdictional Conf., bishop, 1960: Bishop, Nashville-Birmingham area, 1960-68; Bishop, S.F. area, 1968-72; Bishop, L.A. area, 1972---; pres., Council of Bishops, 1973-74. Contbr. to ch. periodicals. Mem.: Bd. of Christian Social Concerns, 1964-72, pres. 1968-72; pres. bd. of trustees, Gammon Theol. Sem., 1966---; trustee, Interdenominational Theol. Center, Atlanta, Ga., 1968---; Bd. of Higher Education and Ministry, 1972---; gen. bd., Nat. Council of Churches, 1972; Omega Psi Phi, Sigma Phi Pi. Home: 5885 Clinton St., L.A., CA 90024; Office: 5250 Santa Monica Blvd., L.A., CA 90029.

GOLDINGER, SHIRLEY
Consumer Affairs Director
b. June 27, 1925, Newark, N.J.; B.S., Home Economics, Nutrition & Inst. Mgmt., New York Univ. 1946; M.S., UCLA, 1951; 2 children, Jay, b. Nov. 14, 1953; Sharon, b. Sept. 28, 1957. Career: Home economist, Gen. Electric Co., L.A., 1946; home economics instr., L.A. City High Schs., 1949-51; vol. consumer activist and leader, 1969-75; dir., (new) Dept. of Consumer Affairs, L.A. Co., 1975---. Lecturer on consumer affairs and consumer protection, UCLA, USC, UCI, UCLB, other instns. and groups; consumer rep. at all levels of govt.; radio & TV panelist and interviews; participant in nat. consumer symposiums, incl. Nat. Warranty Update Conference, Wash., D.C., 1977. Pres., Consumer Fed. of Calif., L.A. and Orange Co., 1969-75; dir.: Consumer Fed. of Am., 1972-75; Nat. Assn. Consumer Agency Adminstrs., 1977-78. Pub. mem.: Calif. State Bureau of Automotive Repair, 1972-73 (helped set up initial regulations to implement Calif. Auto Repair Act); Calif. Adv. Com. on Marriage and Family Counseling, 1966-68. Mem.: Calif. and L.A. City Atty's. Adv. com. on Consumer Protection, 1973; L.A. adv. com. for Rapid Transit, 1974; Advt. Review Council of So. Calif., 1971; Calif. Consumer Affairs Assn., 1976-78; U.S. Dept. of Agriculture Adv. Bd. on Meat Labeling, 1975. Awards: Public Affairs

Achievement 1978; U.W.C.A.; 1st annual Consumer Advocate Award, L.A., 1973. Commended by the California Assembly and the L.A. City Council, 1971. Bd. Dir. nominee, Consumers Union, 1978. Democrat: chmn. State Central Com. 1973-75. Home: 535 Ocean Ave., Santa Monica, CA 90402; Office: 500 W. Temple St., Rm. B-96, L.A., CA 90012.

GOLDMAN, CHARLES REMINGTON
Professor of Limnology
b. Nov. 9, 1930, Urbana, Ill.; s. Marcus Selden and Olive (Remington) Goldman; B.A., Univ. of Ill., 1952, M.S., 1955; Ph.D., Univ. of Mich., 1959; m. Evelyn de Amezaga, May 12, 1977, Urbana, Ill.; Christopher Selden, 1955-70; Margaret Blanche, b. June 6, 1957; Olivia Remington, b. June 29, 1959; Ann Aldous, b. Oct. 12, 1960. Career: Asst. aquatic biologist, Ill. State Natural Hist. Survey, 1954-55; Tchg. Fellow, Dept. of Fisheries, Univ. of Mich., 1955-58; Fishery Research Biologist, U.S. Fish & Wildlife Serv., Alaska, 1957-58; Univ. of Calif., Davis: instr., 1958-60; asst. prof. 1960-63; assoc. prof., 1964-66; prof. of zoology, 1966-71; dir., Inst. of Ecology, 1966-69; Prof. of Limnology 1971---. Guggenheim Fellow 1965; NSF Sr. Fellow, 1964; Calif. Acad. of Scis., Fellow. Editor: two books, contrb., 157 sci. articles profl. publs. Pres., West. Sect., Am. Soc. of Limnology and Oceanography, Pres., Natl., 1967-68; v.p., Ecological Soc. of Am., 1973-74. Capt. USAF, 1952-54. Mem.: Explorers Club, 1978---. Episcopalian. Rec.: skiing, fishing. Home: 2094 Alta Loma, Davis, CA; Office: Div. of Environmental Studies, UC, Davis, CA 95616.

GOLDMAN, MARIANNE
Public Relations Consultant
b. Dec. 25, 1923, S.F.; d. Richard Samuel and Alice (Wertheim) Goldman; B.A., Stanford Univ., 1944. Career: Copy girl/reporter, S.F. Chronicle, 1945-46; vol. coord., ARC, S.F., 1946-48; promotion asst., KCBS Radio, 1950-54; dir. pub. rels., KQED-TV, S.F., 1954-63; cons., Stanford Univ., 1965; dir., Symposium on Asian Art, Asian Art Mus., S.F., 1967-68; cons. communications, Assoc. Council of the Arts, N.Y.C., 1969-70; S.F. Mus. of Art, 1970-72; cons. for Wilson Riles, State Supt. of Edn., S.F., 1973; v.p. devel. and pub. rels., Calif. Coll. of Podiatric Med., S.F., 1975-77; cons., Soc. for Asian Art, S.F., 1978. Dir., Conrad House and Telegraph Hill Neighborhood Assn., past pres., mem. United Jewish Community Centers, S.F., past v.p., 1968-72; past secty., and mem., Public Interest Com., S.F. Symphony Assn.; Secty., Lombard Hill Improvement Assn.; regional chmn., Cardinal Club, Stanford Univ.; bd. dir., S.F. Boys Chorus. Clubs: Calif. Tennis and Town & Country. Hobbies: tennis, swimming; Home: 1025 Lombard St., S.F., CA 94109.

GOLDWATER, BARRY MORRIS JR.
United States Congressman
b. July 15, 1938, L.A.; s. Barry Morris (U.S. Senator from Ariz., and Repub. candidate for Pres. of U.S. 1964) and Margaret (Johnson) Goldwater; grad. Ariz. State Univ., 1962; m. Susan Lee Gherman, Mar. 30, 1972; son, Barry Morris Goldwater, III. Career: Engaged in corporate finance and inst. brokerage; partner, Noble Cooke, Div. of Gregory and Sons stock brokerage firm until 1969; elected to U.S. House of Reps., 27th and subsequently the 20th Congressional Dist. Mem.: Calif. State chmn. Friends of Free China, Inc. 1974---; SAR. Episcopalian. Home: L.A., CA; Office: 2240 Rayburn House Ofc. Bldg., Wash., D.C. 20515.

GOLSH, GENEVIEVE
Artist — Lecturer — Writer
b. Apr. 5, 1900, Okla. (Am. Indian heritage); ed. St. Joseph's Acad., Sacto., Univ. of Calif., Berkeley; stu. clay modeling under De Meterio, Royal Acad. of Rome, It. m. Marcus Golsh, Yuma, Ariz., Jan. 18, 1941. Career: Ceramics artist, 1949---; varied art works. Exhibs incl.: Intertribal Indian Ceremonial, Gallup, N.M., 1951, 54; Calif. State Fair, 1954; So. West Museum, L.A.; Bowers Mus., Santa Ana, 1964; Saddleback Art Gallery, Santa Ana, 1964---; designer, Golsh dishes (distrib. world-wide as a collector's item and usage). Lectr. on Indian lore, Indian culture and arts. Awards: 4 Awards of Merit for books and prose by Palomar Dist. Woman's Clubs; Woman of Yr., Natl. League Am. Pen Women, Escondido, 1973; Freddie award in ceramics by Popular Ceramics Mag.; Mem.: Friends of Pala Mission, IPA, Natl. League Am. Pen Women; Ft. Sutter Chpt., OES; Escondido Woman's Club, Dos' Valley Garden Club, Valley Center; Pauma Valley Woman's Club; Gen. Fed. of Woman's Clubs, Wash., D.C.; Casa De 'Cuna, Chil's.

Home Soc. Hobby: garden. Home: P.O.B. 288, Valley Center, CA 92082.

GOOD, MELVIN FRANCIS
Company President
b. Jan. 24, 1931, Hanover, Penn.; s. Melvin Jacob and Francis Mae (Shorb) Good; Bachelor of Mechanical Engring.; M.B.A.; Registered Profl. Engr., Nat. Council of Engring. Examiners Certification; m. Maria Inez Navarro, June 13, 1952, Austin, Tex.; chil.: Mark Richard, b. 1954; Stephanie Lynn, b. 1956; Carla Anne, b. 1960; Valerie Marie, b. 1962. Career: project engr., Natkin & Co., 1955-61; sr. design engr., Gen. Dynamics Corp., 1961-64; mgr., Melvin Good Assoc., 1965---; pres., Alega Corp., 1970---. Panel mem. Am. Arbitration Assn. 1972---; mem. govt. liaison and mayors com. for energy conservation, city of San Diego, 1974-76. Mem.: Calif. and Nat. Socs. of Profl. Engrs. (CSPE, NSPE); Am. Soc. of mech. engrs. (ASME); Soc. of Naval Architects and Marine Engrs. (SNAME), chmn. S.D. chpt. 1974; Am. Soc. of Heating, Refrig. and Air Conditioning Engrs. (ASHRAE), chmn., energy conserv. com., S.D. chpt., 1975. Mil. USAF, 1951-54, 8th Air Force, SAC. Protestant. Home: 6521 Cascade St., S.D., CA; Office: 8977-A Complex Dr., San Diego, CA 92123.

GOODER, GLENN GORDON
College President
b. Jan. 20, 1922, Orient, S.D.; s. Harold Glenn and Helen (Oliver) Gooder; B.A., Fresno State Coll. 1942; M.A., USC 1947; Ph.D. 1952; m. Virginia Spencer, Fresno, Dec. 29, 1942; dau. Elizabeth Ann, b. Oct. 28, 1951. Career: Instr., Pepperdine Coll. 1949-55; L.A. City Coll. 1955-60; dean (Student personnel), L.A. Harbor Coll. 1960-66; acting pres., L.A. Met. Coll. 1966; pres. L.A. City Coll. 1966-70; supt.-pres. Santa Barbara City Coll. 1970---. Bd. dirs., Harbor Area Welfare Planning Council, 1964-66; pres. 1965-66; bd. dirs., Welfare Planning Council, L.A. 1966-68; bd. dirs., Visiting Nurse Assn., L.A. 1967-70; bd. dir. Channel Cos. Comprehensive Health Planning Council, 1972---, pres. 1973-74; Co-Author: Improving Your Speech, publ. 1960. Watch and div. ofcr., USS Chester (1943-46), WW II; Lt. Comdr., USNR (ret.). Mem.: San Pedro Rotary Club, 1960-66; Santa Barbara Rotary Club. Republican. Methodist. Hobby: fishing. Home: 3950 Via Real, Carpinteria, CA 93013; Office: 721 Cliff Dr., Santa Barbara, CA 93105.

GOODKIN, SANFORD RONALD
President of Real Estate Research Company
b. Feb. 8, 1929, Passaic, N.J.; s. Robert and Lillian (Ellman) Goodkin; m. Frances Aist, Bel-Air, Ca., July 9, 1950; chil.: Steven Charles, b. July 17, 1952; Mark Howard, b. Sept. 5, 1957; Debra Ileen, b. July 7, 1961. Career: Est. Calif. res., L.A. 1947, Del Mar 1971; asst. to the pres.; Grandview Bldg. Co. 1957; real estate adv. and mktg. co. 1958; founder-chmn. bd. Sanford R. Goodkin Research Corp., Calif. 1958, est. ofcs. in Ft. Lauderdale, Fla. 1975. Spec. repr. to Pres. John F. Kennedy's White House Conf. on Equal Opportunities in Housing, 1962; cons. Natl. Assn. of Homebuilders, 1962; created first conf., town devels. and churches, Westlake, 1966; spec. Delegate to Prime Minister's Econ. Conf., State of Israel, 1973. Lectr., Harvard Univ. 1969; lectr.-tchr., 7 campuses, Univ. of Calif. Ext. on real estate econs. Internat. cons. to real estate developers, investors. Awards: 2 commendations, by Pres. Franklin Delano Roosevelt, 1943; one of Sunset Mag's. Distinguished Westerners, 75th Anniversary issue, 1972; Max C. Tipton Mem. Award, 1974; State of Israel's Medal of Valor, 1975; Author: (book) The Goodkin Guide To Winning In Real Estate (4th printing), David McKay Publs.; The Goodkin Report, 1965---; Real Estate Dynamics, monthly syndicated column, publ. Profl. Builder Mag. 1970---. (contrib. ed. 1970---). contrib. approx. 100 mag. and news articles to various publs. Mem.: Univ. of Judaism Patron Soc. 1963-68; bd. trustees, 1967-69; bd. trustees, Brandeis Inst., 1967-69; bd. dirs. Interracial Council on Business Opportunities, 1971. Pres., Temple Ramat Zion, Northridge, 1965-66. Hobbies: reading books, history, swim. Office: 1125 Camino del Mar, Suite F, Del Mar, CA 92014; 2881 E. Oakland Park Blvd., No. 301, Ft. Lauderdale, FL 33306; 999 N. Doheny Dr., No. 103, L.A., CA 90069; 25 E. University Blvd., Tucson, AZ 85703.

GOODLETT, CARLTON B.
Newspaper Publisher
b. July 23, 1914, Chipley, Fla.; B.S., Howard Univ., Wash., D.C., 1935; Ph.D., Psych., Univ. Calif., 1938; M.D., Meharry Med. Coll., 1944; son Carry b. 1950. Career: Med. Practice, S.F., 1945; Ed. and Pub., the

Sun-Reporter, 1948---; lectr., S.F. State Coll. (Group Conflict in Urban Am.), 1967-68; acquired Metro-Reporter group newspapers serving 7 S.F. Bay Area locales and cities, 1972; added The Calif. Voice to the Reporter Publ. Co. publications, 1976; chmn., bd., Norfolk Journ. & Guide, Norfolk, Va.; chmn. of bd., Beneficial Devel. Group. Pres., Nat. Newspaper Pubs. Assn., 1973--- (re-elected 3 times); past pres., S.F. NAACP; pres., S.F. Found. to Study our Schs.; past dir., S.F. Council BSA; Chmn., Calif. Black Leadership Conf.; pres., Nat. Black United Fund; mem. Presidium, World Peace Council; mem. Soc. of Sigma Xi.; U.S. Presidential Cons. on civil rights and the role of minority newspapers in Am. Life. Democrat; gubernatorial candidate, primary elections, 1966. Baptist, trustee of Third Baptist Ch., S.F.; past v.p., S.F. Council of Chs. Office: Nat. Newspaper Pubs. Assn., 1366 Turk St., S.F., CA 94115.

GOODMAN, MURRAY
Professor of Chemistry
b. July 6, 1928, N.Y.C.; s. Louis and Frieda (Barcun) Goodman; B.S., magna cum laude, Brooklyn Coll., 1949; Ph.D., Univ. Calif., Berkeley, 1952; m. Zelda Silverman, Aug. 25, 1951; N.Y.C.; chil.: Andrew A., b. Feb. 6, 1954; Joshua S., b. Dec. 5, 1957; David, b. Mar. 28, 1963. Career: Postdoctoral Fellow, MIT, 1952-55; research fellow, Univ. of Cambridge, Engl., 1955-56; mem. faculty, Polytechnic Inst. of Brooklyn, 1956-71; dir., Polymer Research Inst., 1967-71; Prof. of Chem., UCSD, 1976---. Mem., Study Sect. Med. Chem., Nat. Institutes of Health, 1971-74; numerous consultative and advisory positions, pvt. industry, 1959---; Ed., Biopolymers, 1959---; mem. Editorial Bd., Internat. Journ. of Peptide and Protein Res., 1978---; Macromolecular Revs. Contbr. more than 170 papers in the fields of polymer, organic, and biological chemistry to sci. journs.; mem. World Health Orgn. Steering Com. on Fertility Regulation, 1974---; Program Chmn. Fifth Am. Peptide Symposium, 1977. Awarded Distinguished Alumnus Medal, Brooklyn Coll., 1965. Mem.: Am. Chem. Soc., 1949---; AAAS, 1960---; Am. Soc. of Biological Chemists, 1971---; The Chemical Soc., Engl., 1963---; Biophysical Soc., 1971---; Home: 9760 Blackgold Rd., La Jolla, CA 92037; Office: Dept. of Chem., UCSD, La Jolla, CA 92093.

GORDON, BEVERLY RUBENS
Professor of Law
b. May 27, Rockford, Ill.; d. George A. and Rose V. Rubens; J.D. magna cum laude, Southwestern Univ. Sch. of Law, L.A., 1954; m. James B. Gordon, July 4, 1958, Los Angeles. Career: mem. faculty, Southwestern Univ., 1955-64; Dean and faculty mem., Orange Univ. Sch. of Law (now Pepperdine Law Sch.), Santa Ana, 1964-66; founder and assoc. dean, Beverly Law Sch., L.A., 1966-75; dean of adminstrn. and prof., Whittier Coll. Sch. of Law, L.A., 1975, prof. of law, 1976---. Founder and chief staff mem., Beverly G. Rubens Writing Method Class (a Bar Examination prep. class), 1957-74. Author of Rubens Law Summaries. Mem. Iota Tau Tau. Hobbies: reading, travel. Home: 24878 Eldorado Meadow Rd., Hidden Hills, CA 91302; Office: 5353 W. Third St., L.A., CA 90020.

GORMLY, MARY
Librarian
b. S.F.; B.A., anthropology, Univ. of Wash., Seattle, 1947; M.A., anthropology, Univ. of the Ams., Mexico, 1948; M.S., librarianship, Univ. Wash., Seattle, 1959. Career: Instr. in Anthropology, Mexico City Coll., 1948; research tchg. asst., Univ. of Wash., 1949-52; instr. in Engl., Coronet Hall, Mexico City, and archival research, Archivo General de la Nacion, Mex., 1953-55; Librarian & asst. curator, The Amerind Found., Dragoon, Ariz., 1959-61; Librn. (Anthropology and Latin Am. spec.), Cal. State Univ., L.A., 1962---; also instr., primitive and Latin Am. Art, 1973; Anthropological Archivist, Pac. Northwest Archaeological Archives, Univ. Idaho, Moscow, 1976. Contbr. articles in field to profl. journs.; 80 book reviews, Library Journ.; contbr. reviews, Am. West mag. on books pertaining to the Am. Indian. U.S. Naval Reserve, (WR) WAVES, 1943-46. Mem.: AAUP, past secty. and treas. local chpt.; bd. of govs., Pac. Coast Council on Latin Am. Studies, 1971-75; pres., Pasadena Chpt. of AF Assn., 1978---; mem. USAF Aux.; Women's Univ. Club, Seattle; Am. Anthro. Assn.; Am. Ethnological Soc.; Soc. for Am. Enthnohistory; Latin Am. Studies Assn.; Western Hist. Assn.; Calif. Assn. for Aerospace Edn. Roman Catholic. Hobbies: teach Am. Indian Art, Mexican Folk Art; Rec.: collecting Indian artifacts, tch aerospace edn. and survival as mem. of the Civil Air Patrol. Home: 714 W. Washington St.,

Alhambra, CA 91801; Office: Library, CSU, L.A., L.A., CA 90032.

GOTT, FRANK STOREY
Physician
b. Oct. 15, 1919; Erie, Pa.; s. John Shepardson and Mary Ella (Stebbins) Gott; B.A., Western Res. Univ., 1958, M.D., 1962; m. Phillicent Norseen, Dec. 21, 1962; son, Frank Storey. Career: Research assoc. Western Res. Sch. Med., Cleveland, 1955-62; research fellow biol. scis. Okla. Univ. Sch. Med., 1965-68; asst. prof. psychiatry, 1969-70; practice med. specializing in psychiatry and med. hypnosis, Santa Barbara, 1970---. Served with USNR, 1944-46. Mem. Am. Psychiat. Assn., Am. Inst. Hypnosis, AMA, Calif., Santa Barbara med. assns. Contbr. articles to profl. journs. Home: 970 Monte Dr., Santa Barbara, CA 93110; Office: 601 W. Junipero St., Santa Barbara, CA 93105.

GOTTFRIED, IRA SIDNEY
Management Consultants Executive
b. Jan. 4, 1932, Bronx, N.Y.; s. Louis and Augusta (Champagne) Gottfried; B.B.A., City Coll., of N.Y. 1953; M.B.A., USC 1959; m. Judith Claire Rosenberg, Bronx, N.Y., Sept. 19, 1954; sons: Richard Alan, b. Dec. 6, 1956; Glenn Steven, b. Apr. 17, 1959; David Aaron, b. May 28, 1960. Career: Sales mgr., Kleerpak Plastics, 1956-57; dir. Champ Realty Corp., 1956---; head, systems and procedures div., Hughes Aircraft Co. 1957-60; mgr. corp. bus. systems, Aerospace Corp. 1960-61; dir. adm., Eldon Industries, 1962; mgr. bus. data processing, Litton Industries, 1963-64; exec. v.p.-dir., Norris & Gottfried, Inc., 1964-69; chmn. bd.-pres. Gottfried Consultants, Inc., 1970---; dir. Blue Cross of So. Calif. 1968-77, adv. council, Orthopaedic Hosp., L.A., 1978---. Instr. UCLA Ext. Sch. 1965-66, Automation Training Center, 1967; Ind. Edn. Inst. 1967-73. Author-lectr.: many articles and lectures on data processing, systems, time mgmt., civil defense, adminstrn. techs. Lt., USNR 1953-56. Mem.: (life) Alpha Phi Omega; (charter) Assn. Mgmt. Inf. Sys., (founding) Inst. of Mgmt. Cons.; Systems and Procedures Assn. Internat. dir., 1963; (life) Certified Mgmt. Consultant; Data Processing Mgmt. Assn.; Natl. Panel, Am. Arbitration Assn.; Brentwood Country Club, Rotarian (L.A. 5), Jewish. Hobby: comm'l pilot. Rec.: golf, swim., skiing. Home: 12118 La Casa Lane, L.A., CA 90049; Office: 3435 Wilshire Blvd., L.A., CA 90010.

GOTTFRIED, JONAS
Company President
b. Nov. 7, 1929, Buffalo, N.Y.; s. Jacob and Mirl (Roth) Gottfried; B.A., Univ. Buffalo, 1952; M.Ed., City Coll. N.Y., 1958. Career: pres., Sound City, Inc., 1969---; v.p., Carman Prod., Inc., 1969---; treas., Conf. Pers. Mgrs., 1974-78; Mgr.: Teresa Brewer, Jane P. Morgan, Mark Richardson, Ernestine Anderson, Rick Springfield, 5 Man Electrical Band ---. AUS, 1953-55, Army Vocalist. Mem.: bd. dirs., L.A. Symphony Orch.; NARAS; Jr. C. of C.; BSR Frat. Jewish. Hobbies: photog., building. Rec.: fishing; Home: 3552 Alginet Dr., Encino, CA 91316; Office: 15456 Cabrito Rd., Van Nuys, CA 91406.

GOULD, CHARLES LESSINGTON
Publisher, San Francisco Examiner
b. Aug. 17, 1909, Youngstown, Oh.; s. Fred Jay and Kathleen (Murphy) Gould; ed. spec. courses, Cleveland Coll., Northwestern Univ., Hunters Coll., Natl. War Coll.; (hon.) LL.D., Golden Gate Coll. S.F.; hon. LL.D., Western States Law Sch., Fullerton, Calif.; m. Peggy Shannon, Tenafly, N.J., Mar. 30, 1951; sons: Charles L. Jr., b. July 9, 1955; Michael E., b. Aug. 16, 1956; Career: Reporter-writer-promotion mgr., Cleveland News, 1930-34; writer-radio anncr.-promotion dir., Chicago American, 1934-41; plans dir., N.Y. Journ.-American, 1946-50; asst. publ. 1951-61; publ. S.F. Examiner, 1961-74, exec. dir. and v.p. Hearst Found., 1975---. Lt., USN 1942-46, WW II; Korea, 1950-51; Vietnam, 1967; Capt. USNR (ret.); cons.: U.N. and U.S. Naval Def. Awards: Navy's Distinguished Serv. Award, Bronze Star, Air Medal, Commendation Medal; Hon. Certificate for pub. address by Freedoms Found., Valley Forge, Pa. 1964; George Washington Hon. Medal Award for editorial, 1965, and George Washington Hon. Medal Award for public address, 1966, Natl. Recognition Award, 1970. Mem.: dir. Kaiser Alum. & Chem. Corp., Fine Arts Mus., S.F., B.S.A.; dir. Am. Red. Cross Assn.; bd. regents: Univ. of S.F., St. Mary's Coll.; trustee, Golden Gate Coll.; dir. Better Bus. Bur.; dir., Navy League, U.S.; bd. govs.: Adv. Club, Bay Area Council, Bay Area Crusade, Natl. Conf. Chrs. and Jews,

S.F. Sym. Assn., S.F.; dir.: S.F. Conv. Center-Visitors Bur., Boys' Club, Inc.; Ft. Point Mus. Assn.; trustee: Calif. Council Econ. Edn., Am. Adv. Fed.; trustee, No. Calif. World Affairs Council; mem.: Press Club of S.F., N.Y. Ath. Club, Bohemian Club of S.F., Commonwealth of Calif. Catholic. Home: 336 Poett Rd., Hillsborough, Calif.; Office: 690 Market St., S.F., CA 94104.

GOULD, NORMAN LYNN
Tax Consultant — Accountant
b. Jan. 3, 1933, Rogers, Ark.; s. William Elon and Alice (Smith) Gould; ed. Riverside City Coll. 1959-60; Univ. of Pac.; Stockton Coll. 1962-63; B.S., Sacto. State Coll. 1963-65; m. Josephine Ann Gould, Dec. 15, 1961; sons: John Stephen, Mark Elon. Career: Group supv. Stockton-San Joaquin Probation Dept. 1962-65; acct. own firm, 1965---; controller, Yoder Co., Cottonwood, CA 1972-73; acct.-tax cons., Norman L. Gould Co., 1973---. U.S.Army, Japan, 1948-50; Staff Sergeant USAF, Africa-Alaska, 1951-60. Awards: Medal, Korean Conflict; Merit Award, United Crusade, 1969, 70, 71, cit. 1972; cit. Manteca Planning Commn. 1972. Mem.: Rotary Club, City Plan. Comm. 1967-72; treas. Manteca Rental Assn. 1971---; dir. San Joaquin Taxpayers Assn. 1971; treas. Manteca Drug Abuse, 1971-73; co. dir. United Crusade, 1970-72; dir. C. of C., 1969-70; Home: 1234 Slayton Dr., Manteca, CA; Office: 309 E. Yosemite Ave., Manteca, CA 95336.

GOULD, WILLIAM R.
President, Southern California Edison Company
b. Oct. 31, 1919, Provo, Ut.; B.S., Mech. Engring., 1942; grad. course, Naval Arch., MIT, 1942; m. Erlyn Arvilla Johnson, 1943, Ut.; chil.: Mrs. Duane L. Madsen, b. 1944; William R., Jr., b. 1946; Gilbert J., b. 1950; Wayner R., b. 1953. Career: with So. Calif. Edison Co., 1948---: asst. supt. of stm. generation, 1949; supt. of stm. gen., 1954; gen. supt. of oper. dept., 1958; asst. mgr. engring. dept., 1959; mgr. of engring. dept. 1962; v.p., 1963; sr. v.p., 1967; exec. v.p., 1973; pres., 1978---. Dir.: So. Calif. Edison Co.; Assoc. So. Investment Co.; Mono Power Co.; Electric Systems Co.; Energy Services, Inc. (subsidiaries of Edison Co.). Contbr. tech. papers pub. in the nuclear and power generation field. Dir.: Kaiser Steel Corp.; Atomic Indsl. Forum (hon.); pres., WEST Assocs.; pres., U.S. Nat. Com. of CIGRE (internat. Conf. on High Voltage Power Systesm); Breeder Reactor Corp.; Proj. Mgmt. Corp.; Pac. Coast Elec. Assn.; Edison Electric Inst., Policy Com. on Nuclear Power; Electric Power Research Inst.; Eyring Research Inst.; Energy Advis. Bd., Cal. Tech. Trustee, Cal Tech.; mem. Nat. Advis. Bd., Univ. Utah; chmn. of bd., Inst. for Adv. of Engring., Inc.; mem. L.A. Council of Engrs. and Scientists Advis. Com. USN 1942-48. Mem.: Calif. Club; L.A. C. of C.; Electric Club of L.A.; Pacific Coast Elect. Assn.; Lincoln Club. L.D.S. Ch., Bishop. Hobby: photog. Home: 6441 Shire Way, Long Beach, CA; Office: 2244 Walnut Grove Ave., Rosemead, CA 91770.

GOURLEY, ELAINE AUDREY
School Administrator
b. Oct. 3, 1937, Norwalk, Conn.; d. William and Lydia (Szilagyi) Pinces; B.A., 1959; M.S., 1964; m. Elvin Eugene Fourley, Oct. 2, 1955, Inglewood, Calif. Career: Elem. sch. tchr., L.A., 1959-66; Acad. Cons., 1964-66; Asst. principal, 1966-72; principal, 1972---; also tng. tchr. and demonstration tchr., coord. of Headstart Programs, guest lectr. USC and UCLA, speaker at confs. and workshops. Contbr. author: Child Wants To Learn, Little, Brown & Co., 1977. Mem.: Bd. of Govs., USC; pres., Educare, 1978; bd. of dir., Edn. Alumni Assn.; mem. President's Circle; Delta Kappa Gamma, pres. 1972-74; bd. of dirs., Kappa Delta Pi. Hobbies: oil painting, crafts. Rec.: travels — Europe, Gr. Br., Spain, Canada, Mex., Hawaii. Home: 4233 Paseo de las Tortugas, Torrance, CA 90505; Office: 3140 Hyde Park Blvd., L.A., CA.

GRABILL, ARDELLE B.
Real Estate Executive
b. Mar. 26, 1944, Los Angeles, Calif.; d. Espy N. and Betty Hall; student, USC, UCLA; B.A. in English, Cal. State Univ. of Fullerton, 1971; elem. edn. credential, A & I Univ., Texas, 1972; m. James Grabill, Aug. 28, 1964, Nevada. Career: tchr. 4th-7th grades, 1972-74; realtor assoc., Walker & Lee Real Estate, 1975-76; mem. of Winner's Circle Elite Club, 1976-77; also mem. president's council (top 20 in co.) 1976-77; office mgr., Mission Viejo and Lake Forest office, Walke;& Lee Real Estate, 1978---. Ranked 15th in company of 1400 sales associates, 1976; ranked 5th, 1977. Hobby: interior decorating. Rec.: water skiing, running. Home: 23751 Via

Astorga, Mission Viejo, CA 92690; Office: 23862 Bridger Rd., El Toro, CA.

GRADOW, GEORGE S.
Company President
b. May 11, 1943, San Francisco, Calif.; d. Alexander and Betty Gradow; B.A., Washington Univ., 1962; J.D., New York Univ., 1966, LL.M., 1967. Career: Attorney at law, 1966-69; v.p., Galaxie Industries, 1969-71; pres., The Satellite Group, 1971-74; pres., Churchill Group, 1975---. Office: P.O.B. 3999, Pasadena, CA 91103.

GRADY, STAFFORD R.
Board Chairman, Lloyds Bank California
b. Apr. 9, 1921, Grand Rapids, Mich.; s. Stafford R. and Josephine M. (Cusick) Grady; A.B., Geo. Wash. Univ. 1943, LL.B., Law Sch. 1945; m. Roberta Patterson, Wash., D.C., Aug. 26, 1950; chil.: Stafford R., Jr., b. June 26, 1951; Maureen H., b. Jan. 30, 1957; Shaun P., b. Aug. 7, 1960. Career: Law clerk to Chief Judge of U.S. Ct. of Appeals, 1945-47; asst. U.S. Atty., Wash., D.C. 1947-51; spec. atty. Bur. of Internal Revenue, Wash., D.C. 1951-52; partner, Mackay, McGregor & Bennion, L.A. 1952-63; Ins. Commr. State of Calif. 1963-66; Lloyds Bank of Calif. 1966---, pres. 1968-74, chmn. bd.-pres. 1974--- (formerly First Western Bank & Trust Co.); Pres., Lloyds First Western Corp.; bd. dirs.: Lloyds Bank Internat. Ltd.; Purex Corp.; INA Corp.; Charles R. Drew Postgrad. Med. Sch.; Comm. TV of So. Calif; bd. trustees: Occidental Coll.; chmn. Legis. 50-Center for Legislative Improvement; adv. com. The Coldwell Banker Fund. Hons.: repr. U.S. Govt. as guest of Ger. Govt. Nov. 1967; repr. U.S. Govt. at World Conf. on Traffic Safety under auspices of U.N., Geneva, Switz. 1967; invested as Knight of Malta, St. Patrick's Cathedral, N.Y.C., 1975. Mem.: Am., Calif. State, L.A. Co., Mich. State and Dist. of Columbia Bar Assns.; L.A. Clearing House Assn.; Assn. of Res. City Bankers; Bd. of Visitors, Loyola Law Sch., Dir., Ear Research Inst.; dir., L.A. Area C. of C.; Sigma Nu, Phi Delta Phi; Club: Univ., Lincoln, One Hundred Club of L.A., Newport Harbor Yacht, Valley Hunt, Eldorado Country, Calif., L.A. Country, Chevaliers du Tastevin. Roman Catholic. Hobbies: golf, sailing. Office: 612 S. Flower St.,L.A., CA 90017.

GRAFE, PAUL JOHN
Construction Company Chairman
b. Apr. 19, 1895, Clay City, Ind.; s. John Henry and Margaret (Edmonds) Grafe; grad. in civil engring., Rose-Hulman Inst. of Tech., Terre Haute, Ind., 1920, hon. D. Eng., 1950; m. Helen Louise Thickstun, Dec. 11, 1917, Terre Haute, Inc.; chil.: Helen (Nussbaum), b. June 12, 1926; Louise (Nesbitt) b. July 12, 1929; Paula (Gavin) b. July 31, 1931. Career: Engr., Pa. R.R. 1919; timekeeper, supt., C.R. Cummins Co., constructing belt line for PA. R.R. in Detroit and substructure for Marysville Power Plant for Detroit Edison Co.; with Grafe-Callahan Constrn. Co., L.A. and Dallas, 1922---, in charge of constrn. work, v.p., pres., now chmn. bd. Supervised: River levee work in Ill., Ark. and Mo.; Bagnell Dam found., Mo.; All-Am. Canal and San Diego Aqueduct, Calif.; Madden Dam, C.Z.; Shasta Dam, Redding; Prado Dam, Orange Co. Flood Control, Calif.; Delaware Aqueduct for N.Y.C.; Caddoa, Granby, Horsetooth and Soldiers Canyon Dams, Colo.; Hungry Horse Dam, Mont.; Davis Dam, Ariz.; Duchesne Tunnel, Utah; tunnels for city of Chicago. Exec. dir. on secret war work in Pacific, NW Can. and Great Britain. Mil. Engring. dept., Motor Transport Corps, 1917-19, in France and Scotland. Dir., Carrie Estelle Doheny Found. Bd. mgrs., Rose-Hulman Inst. of Tech., Ind. Pres., The Beavers (constrn. orgn.) 1961, awarded Golden Beaver for Mgmt., 1973. Decorated Knight Equestrian Order of Holy Sepulchre of Jerusalem. Mem.: Sigma Nu; Acad. of Polit. Sci., L.A. World Affairs Council. Clubs: California, L.A. Country, Valley Club of Montecity, Saticoy Country. Roman Catholic. Hobbies: golf, Beefmaster cattle breeder (form. breeder of thoroughbred and quarter horses and Aberdeen-Angus cattle). Home: Ferndale Ranch, Santa Paula, CA 93060; Office: P.O.B. 628, Santa Paula, CA 93060.

GRAFF, LEONARD D.
Consultant — Corporation Executive
b. Feb. 21, 1928, La Crosse, Wis.; s. Fred and Ruth Graff; B.S. (ind. engring.) USC 1951; m. Georgia Lewis, Nev., 1948 (div. 1969). Career: Founder, Arlee Foam Rubber Prods., Inc. 1951, pres.-chmn. bd. dirs. 1951-61; pres.-chmn. bd. dirs., Pacific Foam Industries, Inc. 1956; founder, Urethane Machinery Co. (merged with United Foam Co. 1965), pres.-chmn. bd. (Compton, Oakland,

Calif. and Portland, Ore. Plants); pres. Graff Enterprises (considered ony of foremost cons. in polyurethane foam in U.S.; has traveled extensively throughout Europe and Asia as cons.); est. Pac. Foam Industry, Hawaii (largest operation of its kind in Hawaii). U.S. Army Signal Corps, 1946-48. Hobby: Scottish Bagpipes, gun collection. Rec.: golf, skin diving. Home: 32 Chuckwagon Rd., Rolling Hills, CA; Office: 19201 E. Reyes, Compton, Calif.

GRAHAM, ROBERT KLARK
Optical Company Founder
b. June 9, 1906, Harbor Springs, Mich.; s. Frank A. (D.D.S.) and Ellen Fern (Klark) Graham; nephew of Ernest Robert Graham, noted architect; A.B., Mich. State Univ., 1934; B.S. optics, Ohio State Univ., 1937; m. Marta Everton, M.D., Oct. 15, 1960, Houston, Tex.; Chil.: Gregory, Robin, Janis (Butler), Leslie (Fox), Robert Jr., G. Wesley, Marcia, Christie. Career: Instruments, Bausch & Lomb Optical Co., 1937-40; sales mgr., Univis Lens Co., 1940-46; Dir. research, Plastic Optics Co. of Am., 1946-47; founder., Armorlite Lens Co., Inc., pres. 1947-75, chmn. bd., 1947-78; cons., 3M, 1978---. Trustee, Found. for Advancement of Man, 1964---; dir., Intra-Science Research Found., 1972---; dir.: Inst. for Research on Morality, 1972---; Am. Acad. of Optometry, 1948---; Am. Assn. of Physics Profs., 1950---. Lecturer on Optics, Loma Linda Univ., 1948---. Mem.: Mensa, 1964---; Rotary, 1974---; Optical Soc. of Am.; Phi Mu Alpha (profl.); Omega Beta Sigma (hon.); Life fellow, Am. Assn. for Advancement of Sci. Awarded Frederick Wm. Herschel Gold Medal (Germany), 1957. Cited as Man Who Made it Safe to Wear Glasses by Nat. Eye Research Found. 1963. Inventor: variable focus lens, 1937; colorless ultraviolet absorbing lenses, 1952; Hybrid corneal lens, 1977. Co-founder (with Hermann J. Muller) Germinal Repository, 1962. Author: The Evolution of Corneal Contact Lenses, 1959; The Future of Man, 1970. Protestant. Hobby: Eugenics. Rec.: Farming. Home: Sycamore Lane, Escondido, CA 92025; Office: 130 N. Bingham Dr., San Marcos, CA 92069.

GRAHAM, WALTER CHENEY
Orthopedic Surgeon
s. John Thomas and Mattie (Goodwin) Graham; M.D., Univ. of Nebr., 1934; Bd. Certified, Orthopedic Surgery, 1945; m. Lucile Reader, Dec. 7, 1937, Omaha, Nebr. Career: Postgrad. orthopedic surgery, Boston and N.Y. Lt. Col., U.S. Army, WW II; organized first hand surgery unit at Valley Forge Gen. Hosp. as Chief of Orthopedic and Hand Surgery (during WW II). Founding mem., Am. Soc. for Surgery of the Hand, pres. 1948-49. Protestant. Hobbies: golf, dry-fly fishing. Home: 1646 Franceschi Rd., Santa Barbara, CA; Office: P.O.B. 1200, Santa Barbara, CA 93102.

GRAINGER, WILLIAM KEITH
College Librarian
b. Dec. 17, 1922, Paso Robles, Calif.; s. Rolla and Alice Liberty (Jensen) Grainger; B.A., Univ. Calif., Berkeley, 1946; B.L.S., 1947; M.S., USC, 1958; m. Loa Louise Starrh, June 9, 1946, Shafter, Calif.; chil.: William Ketih, b. Apr. 29, 1948; Michael Edwin, b. Jan. 14, 1951; David Lawrence, b. Apr. 21, 1953; Loa Louise, b. Jan. 4, 1957. Career: Asst. Librn., Compton Coll., 1947-54, Bakersfield Coll., 1954-59; Coll. Librn., Pasadena City Coll., 1959---, chmn. dept., 1959---, prof. lib. servs., 1973---. Lt.j.g., USNR, 1942-46. Mem.: ALA; Calif. Lib. Assn.; Calif. Tchrs. Assn., NEA; Phi Delta Kappa; Beta Phi Mu. Republican. Presbyterian, Elder-Trustee, Deacon. Home: 9231 E. Wedgewood St., Temple City, CA 91780; Office: 1570 E. Colorado Blvd., Pasadena, CA 91106.

GRANDE, FRANK A.
Judge
b. June 30, 1937, Akron, Oh.; s. Victor A. and Julia M. (Battestelli) Grande; A.B., Stockton Coll., 1960; B.S., Sacto. State Univ., 1962; LL.B. & J.D., Univ. Calif., Hastings Law Coll., 1965; m. Bette A. Ryan, Feb. 5, 1956, Washoe, Nev.; son, Frank A., b. 1957. Career: Atty. assoc. with law firm, Chargin & Briscoe, Stockton, 1966-67; partner law firm, Chadeayne, Wilkinson, Talley & Grande, Tracy, Calif., 1967-73; sole practitioner, Tracy, 1973; Municipal Ct. Judge, 1974---. Chmn., City of Tracy Planning Commn. 1969-73. Mem.: Pres., Tracy Dist. C. of C., 1978-79; Elks; Rotary Club; Italian Athletic Club, Stockton. Hobby: boating. Rec.: jogging. Home: 1444 Franklin Ave., Tracy, CA 91376; Office: 475 E. 10th St., Tracy, CA 95376.

GRANT, JAMES H., JR.
Sheriff — Coroner
b. Feb. 24, 1942, Kannapolis, N.C.; s. James H., Sr. and Aurora Grant; A.A., Exec. Peace Ofcr. Standards And Trn. Cert. Career: Dep. Sheriff, County of Yuba, Marysville, 1965-72; dir. Olivehurst Pub. Utilities Dist., Olivehurst, 1971-74; sub. teacher, 1971; police sci. instr. Yuba Coll., Marysville and coll. police chief, 1971-74; sheriff-coroner, Yuba Co., 1974---. Cryptographic spec., U.S. Army Europe, 1962-65. Mem.: Linda-Olivehurst Civic Assn., Loyal Order of Moose, 20-30 Club, Rotary Club. Baptist. Hobbies: golf, diving, fishing. Home: 1903 Glenmore Dr., Olivehurst, CA; Office: P.O.B. 1389, Yuba Co. Sheriff's Ofc., Marysville, CA 95901.

GRANT, PETER HENDRICKS
Psychologist — Author
b. May 5, 1935, Saginaw, Mich.; s. Leo B. and Lucille Grant; desc. Ulysses Simpson Grant, 1822-85; B.A., Univ. Mich., 1959, M.A., 1962; Ph.D., clin., psychol., U.S. Internat. Univ., 1969; chil.: Peter H., II, b. Feb. 18, 1961; Kari A. Grant, b. Mar. 31, 1963. Career: Practice of psychology, Peter H. Grant, Ph.D. & Assocs., 1970---; vis. prof., Univ. Calif., San Diego, 1972---; Author: Holistic Therapy: The Risks & Payoffs of Being Alive, 1978, Citadel Press, N.Y. Mem.: pres., La Jolla Optimist Club, 1978; Delta Sigma Phi. Hobbies: bridge, tennis. Home: 2037 Camino Capa, La Jolla, CA 92037.

GRASHAM, JOHN ARTHUR
College District Administrator
b. Sept. 6, 1920, Phoenix, Ariz.; s. John George and Olive Emma (Cage) Grasham; grad., Phoenix Jr. Coll., 1940; A.B. Ariz. State Coll., Tempe, 1942; M.A., USC, 1947; Ph.D., 1950; m. Elizabeth Neale, June 6, 1946, Seattle, Wash.; chil.: James Arthur, b. Jul. 1948; John Elliott, b. Oct. 1950; Neale Alan, b. Dec. 1952; Margaret Anne, b. Apr. 1955; Mary Elizabeth, b. Apr. 1955. Career: with Los Angeles Community Coll. Dist., 1948-70; instructor, dept. chmn., asst. dean, dean, coll. pres.; with Marin Community College Dist., 1970---: college pres., currently district supt. ---; also Fulbright Grant visiting prof., Univ. of Trieste, Italy, 1962-63. Co-author, Improving Your Speech, Harcourt-Brace, 1960. Served USNR, 1942-46. Past pres.: Rotary Club of Dominguez-Carson; Calif. Community & Jr. College Assn., SW region. Methodist, bd. mem. Hobbies: photog., golf, conjuring. Office: Marin Community College District, Kentfield, CA 94904.

GRAY, JAMES H.
Banker
b. Sept. 27, 1937, Long Beach; s. Brewster and Hester (Niswonger) Gray; B.S., mktg., Cal. State Univ., Long Beach; m. Joann Bruse, 1956, Long Beach; chil.: Debra Jo, b. July 4, 1957; Diane Elaine, b. Apr. 15, 1960. Career: Automobile dealer, pres. Jim Gray Volvo, 1961---; pres., dir. and chief operating ofcr., Harbor Bank, Long Beach. Treas., Big 5 Sch. Dists. in Calif. 1972-74; v.p., Bd. of Edn., Long Beach Unified Sch. Dist., 1973; v.p., Long Beach City Coll. Dist., 1973; trustee and dir., Long Beach Comm. Hosp.; commnr., Long Beach Harbor Dept., 1976---; commnr., Calif. Advis. Council for Vocational Edn. & Tech. Tng., 1973-74; commnr., Calif. State Commn. for Ednl. Mgmt. & Evaluation, 1973-75; community bd. mem., United Way; exec. bd., L.B. Council, BSA. Recipient Time Magazine Quality Dealer Award, 1970, 1975 (the only auto dealer in U.S. to win the award twice). Mem.: Long Beach Motor Car Dealers Assn., pres. 1970; Long Beach Kiwanis Club, pres. 1970; Long Beach C. of C., pres. 1976-77; Sigma Alpha Epsilon, pres. 1963. Protestant. Rec.: golf. Home: 6270 Bridle Cir., Long Beach; Office: 6265 E. Second St., Long Beach, CA 90801.

GRAY, RICHARD MOSS
College President and Founder
b. Jan. 25, 1924, Washington, D.C.; s. Wilbur L. and Betty Marie (Grey) Gray; B.A. (Phi Beta Kappa), Bucknell Univ., 1942; M. Divinity summa cum laude, San Francisco Theological Seminary, 1961; Ph.D., Univ. of Calif., Berkeley, 1972; m. Catherine Hammond, Oct. 17, 1943, Berkeley, Calif.; chil.: Janice Lynn (Armstrong), b. May 5, 1948; Nancy Hammond, b. July 8, 1952. Career: advt. exec., N.W. Ayer & Son, Inc., Phila. Pa., 1942-58: bus. prod. dept., copy writer, assoc. copy dir., Detroit Creative Dir. (creation & suprn. of nat. advt. for accounts such as Bell Telephone System, Plymouth Div. of Chrysler Corp., Armco Steel Corp.); univ. pastor, Portland State Univ., 1961-68; chief adminstv. officer, World College West, San Rafael, 1972---. Trustee, Lewis & Clark Coll., 1972-76; trustee, S.F. Theological Sem., 1968---; dir. S.F. United

Nations Assn. USN, 1943-46; Communications Officer on Destroyer U.S.S. Somers (DD381); resigned as Lt. USNR. Mem. Exec. com., Nat. Campus Ministry Assn., 1965-68; assoc. spokesman, div. of higher edn., Univ. of Calif., 1969-70. Ruling Elder, United Presbyterian Ch. U.S.A. Moderator, Portland Presbytery (57 ch. in W. Ore.), United Presby. ch. Home: P.O.B. 1015, Ross, CA 94957; Office: P.O.B. 3060, San Rafael, CA 94902.

GRAY, VIRGINIA M.
Real Estate Executive
b. Mar. 19, 1923, Columbus, Ohio; d. Charles W. and Lucille D. (Smith) Ginn; grad. Realtors Inst. of Calif.; m. Lloyd A. Gray, Aug. 26, 1960, Temple City, Calif.; 1 son Victor J. Dezzani, b. Mar. 11, 1953. Career: Real estate salesperson, 1972-74; real estate broker, 1974---; pres., Oro Pacific Properties, Inc. Mem.: Internat. Real Estate Federation; Nat. Assn. Realtors; Oroville Bd. of Realtors, v.p., 1978; Calif. Assn. Realtors, dist. rep. edn. 1977, 1978, steering com. Edn., 1978. Hobby: silver work (jewelry). Home: 2720 Oro Garden Ranch Rd., Oroville, CA; Office: 3022 Olive Hwy., Oroville, CA 95965.

GRAYSON, HELEN LEE
Designer — Manufacturer
b. July 1, 1913, Galveston, Texas; d. Wade Lee M.D. and Justine Helen (Finch) Hoecker; stu., Tex. Woman's Univ.; m. John Gail Grayson (dec. Jan. 3, 1977), Galveston, Tex. Career: tchr. and performer, organ and piano, 1931-46 (organ soloist in Galveston Musical Club and Central Methodist Ch.); buyer and mgr. of gift dept. of furniture store; moved to Calif. in 1946 and began creating "one of a kind" hand decorated ceramic pieces for boudoir, living room and bath; founder-partner with husband, Grayson Arts, Altadena, 1947---: grew into one of So. Calif's. outstanding suppliers of bath and boutique items sold internationally. Congregationalist, Deaconess. Home-Studio: 570 Sunset Dr., Altadena, CA 91001.

GREASER, CONSTANCE U.
Publications Specialist
b. Jan. 18, 1938, San Diego; d. Lloyd E. and Udean (Rohr) Greaser; B.A., journalism, San Diego State Univ., 1959; M.A., Internat. Rels., USC. 1968; postgrad.: Georgetown Univ. Sch. of Foreign Serv., Univ. of Copenhagen Grad. Sch. for Foreign Students. Career: Supr., engring. support servs., Arcata Data Graphics, 1965-68; mgr. computerized typesetting, Continental Graphics, 1968-70; v.p. and edit. dir., Sage Publs., 1970-74; head of publs., The Rand Corp., 1974---. Contbr. articles on alternatives to traditional forms of publishing to various scholarly journs. Mem.: Soc. of Tech. Communications; So. Calif. Bookbuilders; Women in Communication, Inc.; Orgn. of Women Execs.; Women in Business, pres. 1977, 78. Office: 1700 Main St., Santa Monica, CA 90406.

GREEN, AARON G.
Architect
b. May. 4, 1917, Corinth, Miss.; s. Abraham and Rose (Blunker) Green; stu. Chicago Acad. Fine Arts, 1931-32, Ala. State Univ. 1934-36, Cooper Union, NYC, 1936-40, Taliesin Fellowship, 1940-43; m. Mary Davey Green, Dodgeville, Wis., 1975; chil.: Allan Wright, b. May 24, 1950; Frank Haber, b. 1953. Career: Staff, Frank Lloyd Wright, 1940-43; planner, Raymond Loewy Assoc., 1946-48; West Coast rep., Frank Lloyd Wright, 1951-60; West Coast rep., F.L.W. Found., 1960-74; lectr., Dept. Architecture, Stanford Univ., 1959-70; cons. Archt., San Jose State Univ., 1968-72; mem. Jt. Com. Am. Bar Assn. and Am. Inst. of Archts. Court Facilities, dir. No. Calif. AIA, 1964-66. Awards: 1st Honor Award, U.S. Housing and Home Fin. Agcy. 1964; H.U.D. 1st Honor Award for Urban Design, 1974. Major works: Marin City Housing Proj. (Fed.); assoc. archt. with Frank Lloyd Wright, Marin Co. Civic Center; Master Plan New Community of Hunters Point; Union City Civic Center; St. Stephens Catholic Ch., Walnut Creek; St. Monica's Catholic Ch., Moraga; Adminstrn. Center, Nat. Forest Serv., Stanislaus Nat. Forest and Klamath Nat. Forest; Merced Co. Municipal Cts. Bldg.; San Bernardino Energy Tech. Center. Fellow, for Design, AIA, 1968. 1st Lt., USAF; decorated Air Medal with 3 oak leaf clusters. Hobbies: photog., calligraphy. Home: 2200 Sacramento St., S.F., CA; Office: 319 Grant Ave., S.F., CA 94108.

GREEN, DIANE SEXTON
Artist
b. Dec. 1, 1937, Alhambra, Calif.; d. Carter and Charlotte Sexton; B.A., USC, 1959; studied Otis Art Inst. early

Sixties; L.A. Art League, mid-Sixties; m. Neil H. Green, 1966, Calif.; 1 dau. Kelly, b. Oct. 23, 1970. Career: several one woman shows; recipient: scores of ribbons and awards including L.A. All City Purchase Award, 1970; Best of Show, San Fernando Valley Art Club, 1975 and 1976; Best of Show, Valley Artist Guild, 1976; 3 gold medals, 1976. Several paintings put into line of prints; work represented in galleries nationally. Mem.: Calif. Art Club; Hors De Concour; San Fernando Valley Art Club; Valley Artist Guild. Home: 18202 Rancho St., Tarzana, CA; Office: 5308 Laurel Canyon, No. Hollywood, CA.

GREEN, EARLE MILTON
Author — Educator
b. East Liberty, Oh.; s. Milton Morton and Sylvia (Creviston) Green; B.Sc., Oh. State Univ. 1923; M.A., USC; postgrad. Redlands Univ., Claremont Grad. Sch., UCLA; m. Peggy Luh, W. Palm Beach, Fla. 1925; m. 2nd., Inez Case Anger, Pomona, Calif. 1966; m. 3rd., Julie Simmons Moore, Riverside, Calif., 1976. Career: tchr., soc. studies dept. head, Calif. 1927-67 (ret.). Author: Getting Acquainted with Riverside City History and Govt. 1953; Know Your Calif. Govt., 1962; Getting Acquainted With Riverside County History and Govt., 1965. Serv. WW I, II; Maj., Korean War, USAF, Ret. Awards: Outstanding Tchr. Award, 1958. Mem.: State Council, Calif. Tchrs. Assn. (9 yrs.), v.p. So. Sect. 1939, pres. 1940, chmn. supv. com. Credit Union, 1951-57; bd. dirs., 1957---; pres. 1960, 61, 68, 69; pres. Riverside Div., CRTA, 1974-76; pres. Calif. World Friendship Club, 1938-41; Mason, Al Malaikah Shrine. Hobbies: genealogy, philately. Home: 1480 Bellefontaine Dr., Riverside, CA 92506.

GREEN, WILLIAM PORTER
Attorney at Law
b. Mar. 19, 1920, Jacksonville, Ill.; s. Hugh (Speaker, Ill. House of Representatives, 1945-48) and Clara Belle (Hopper) Green; B.A., Illinois Coll., 1941; J.D., Northwestern Univ. Sch. of Law, 1947; m. Rose Marie Hall, Oct. 1, 1944, Key West, Fla.; chil.: Hugh Michael, b. Feb. 19, 1948; Robert Allan, b. July 24, 1949; Richard William, b. Apr. 2, 1954. Career: Attorney at Law, Los Angeles, 1947---; specializing in Patents, trademarks, copyrights and related matters; mem. of Wills, Green & Mueth Law Corp., L.A. Admitted to Ill. Bar 1947, Calif. Bar 1948. Admitted to practice before U.S. Dist. Ct., Central Dist. of Calif., 5th & 9th Circuit Cts. of Appeal., Ct. of Customs & Patent Appeals, U.S. Patent & Trademark Office, and U.S. Supreme Ct. Mil. activy duty, USNR, 1942-46, Lt. Sr. Grade, Engring Officer, Chief Engr. of Destroyer Escort. Mem. bd. of editors of Illinois Law Review 1946. Mem.: L.A. World Affairs Council; American and L.A. Co. Bar Assns.; L.A. Patent Law Assn. (past secty., treas., bd. of govs.); Lawyers Club of L.A.; Am. Legion (past commdr.); Phi Beta Kappa, Phi Delta Phi; Phi Alpha, Big Ten Club of So. Calif.; Northwestern Univ. Alumni Club of So. Calif.; Phi Beta Kappa Alumni of So. Calif. Republican. Presbyterian, deacon. Hobby: golf. Home: 3570 E. Lombardy Rd., Pasadena, CA 91107; Office: Wills, Green & Mueth Law Corp., 700 S. Flower St., Suite 1120, L.A., CA 90017.

GREENBURG, RUBIN
Company Executive
b. Aug. 5, 1926, Los Angeles, Calif.; s. Isaac M. and Minnie Greenberg; B.S., USC, 1949; (hon.) Ph.D., London Inst., 1963; m. Takako Taguchi, Nov. 4, 1966, L.A., Calif.; chil.: Ilene, b. 1950; Judith, b. 1952; Carol, b. 1956; Derek, b. 1964. Career: Treas., Calif. Duplicating, L.A., 1949-1956; v.p. finance, Internat. Computer Inc., L.A., 1956-1963; comptroller, Electro Optical, Pasadena, 1963-66; v.p., finance, Jacobs Systems Corp., L.A., 1966-71; v.p. finance, Land Dynamics, Fresno, 1971-73; v.p. finance, H.S. Watson Co., Emeryville, 1973---. Dir.: H.S. Watson, Co.; Land Dynamics; Internat. Computer, Inc.; assoc. dir. Nat. Assn. of Accountants, 1977. Counselor, Jr. Achievement. Mil. U.S. Air Corp., 1944-46, North Africa & Europe. Mem.: Masons, Nat. Assn. of Accountants, Calif. Soc. of Pub. Accountants. Democrat. Jewish. Hobby: chess collections. Rec.: skiing, bicycling, travel. Home: 1080 Country Club Dr., Moraga, CA 94556; Office: 1316 67th St., Emeryville, CA 94608.

GREENWELL, JAMES O., JR.
Physician
b. Feb. 5, 1911, S.F.; s. James O. (b. S.F. 1883) and Edith (Snell) (b. San Jose 1884) Greenwell; 4th cousin to Wm. Cullen Bryan, poet and editor; Gr.grandson, Maj. John H. Settle, in Gen. John C. Fremont's party exploring West in 1840s; A.B., Stanford Univ., 1932; M.D., 1936; m. Lily Wilde, Sept. 20, 1953, Menlo Park.

Career: Resident in Chest Disease and Tuberculosis, S.F. Gen. Hosp., Santa Clara Co. Hosp., San Joaquin Gen. Hosp., Bret Harte Sanitorium, 1936-41; at Canyon Hosp. (div. of the San Mateo Co. Dept. of Pub. Health and Welfare), Redwood City, 1941-72; mem. Hon. Staff, Sequoia Dist. Hosp., Redwood City ---; cons. in Chronic Disease Care and Adminstrn., Cons. in Tuberculosis ---. Fellow, Am. Coll. of Chest Physicians; Fellow, Royal Soc. of Health. Awarded 50th Anniversary Medal, Nat. Tuberculosis Assn. 1954. Past pres.: Laenec Soc. of No. Calif.; Calif. Sanitorium Assn.; Calif. Thoracic Soc.; San Mateo Co. Tuberculosis and Health Assn. Mem.: Am. and Calif. Med. Assns.; San Mateo Co. Med. Soc.; Am. Thoracic Soc.; Sierra Club; Bay Area Social Planning Council, 1958-68; Peninsula Sym. Assn.; Phi Chi Med. frat; Calif. Hist. Soc.; Redwood City Rotary Club, charter. Republican. Episcopalian, Vestryman, choir dir., Jr. Warden. Hobbies: vintners art; classic pipe organ; piano (studied piano w/Mischa Lhevinne, 1922-28), classic music. Home: 2107 Edgewood Rd., Redwood City, CA 94062.

GREGG, ALICE ELIZABETH
University Librarian and Administrator
b. Feb. 20, 1920, Lambert, Montana; d. Cyrus Sidney and Mary McCulloch Gregg; desc. Rob Roy MacGregor; B.A., Walla Walla Coll., 1945; M.L.S., USC, 1962. Career: Tchr. English and Spanish, Upper Columbia Acad., Spangle, Wash., 1945-49; secty., Loma Linda Univ., 1949-62; librarian, Loma Linda Univ., 1962---, chmn., acquisitions dept., 1963-65, chmn., Dept. of Tech. Services, 1965---, assoc. dir., 1971---. Mem.: Loma Linda Univ. Faculty Women's Club, pres. 1970-71; adv. of Loma Linda Book Club, 1975-77, co-pres., 1977-78. Contbr. various periodicals. Home: 24414 University Ave., No. 170, Loma Linda, CA 92354; Office: Loma Linda Univ. Library, Loma Linda, CA 92354.

GREGORY, CARL C.
Real Estate Executive
b. Dec. 28, 1918, Birmingham, Ala.; s. Carl C. and Emma (Collins) Gregory; B.S., So. Meth. Univ.; m. Barbara Troster, L.A., Aug. 22, 1942; chil.: Carl C., III, b. Aug. 20, 1944; John Kirk, b. Dec. 16, 1946; Martha May, b. July 3, 1951. Career: Chmn. bd.-pres. Am. Western Properties Corp.; pres. Am. Western Realty Co. Pilot, USAF. Mem.: Sky Club (NYC), Calif. Club, L.A. Country Club. Methodist (trustee, Claremont Sch. of Theol.). Home: 1670 N. Doheny Dr., L.A., CA 90069; Office: 523 W. Sixth St., L.A., CA 90014.

GRENCH, HERBERT ALLAN
Nuclear Physicist
b. Oct. 4, 1932, Elmwood Park, Ill.; s. John and Viola (Freiwald) Grench; A.B., Kalamazoo Coll., 1954; M.S., Univ. Iowa, 1957, Ph.D., 1960; m. Norma Lee Durham, Sept. 4, 1954, Knoxville, Ia.; sons, Paul, b. Oct. 30, 1957; Bruce, b. Sept. 22, 1960. Career: Nuclear Physicist, Lockheed Palo Alto Research Lab., 1960-73; gen. mgr., Mid-peninsula Regional Open Space Dist., Los Altos, 1973---. Mem. Palo Alto Planning Commn., 1965-69; Santa Clara Co. Parks & Rec. Commn., 1972-73. Contbr. 50 articles in physics to tech. journs. Named Citizen of Year, 1970. Rec.: backpacking. Home: 2828 So. Court, Palo Alto, CA 94306; Office: 375 Distel Cir., Los Altos, CA 94022.

GRENCIK, JUDITH MILBURN
Psychologist — Educator
b. Feb. 29, 1936, Denison, Tex.; d. Henry Lynn and Edith Lorili (Lynch) Milburn; student, Tex. Tech. Coll., 1954-57; B.A., Baylor Univ., 1958; M.Ed., La. State Univ., 1960; Ph.D., Univ. Md., 1971; m. Josep Robert, June 26, 1970, Lubbock, Tex.; stepchil.: Bonnie Barkley, b. 1949; Susan Bergeron, b. 1951; Richard, b. 1953. Career: tchr., pub. schs., Tex., 1960-65; research psychologist, L.A. Co. Sheriffs Dept. and Dept. Personnel, 1970-73; instr. psychol., Univ. Calif., Irvine, Est., 1971; counseling psychol. and counseling coord. in Counseling and Human Devel. Servs., 1973-78; instr., Center for Criminal Justice, 1974---; cons., Police Found., 1973-74; Nat. Inst. Occ. Health and Safety, 1973-75; Spec. Cons. Am. Phys. Standards Research Found., Ia. City; psychol. Cons., 200 Company, Tidma Co., 1976---; New Faculty Research grantee, Cal. State Univ., Long Beach, assoc. prof., Dept. of Criminal Justice, 1973---; licensed psychologist, 1978---. Mem.: Am. Psychol. Assn., 1971---; Western Psychol. Assn., 1971---; Am. Assn. Correctional Psychol., 1976---. Unitarian. Hobbies: gardening, camping, music. Special Interest: stress reduction. Home: 20221 Crown Reef Lane, Huntington Beach, CA 92646; Office: Dept. Criminal Justice, Cal. State Univ., Long Beach, CA.

GREW, PRISCILLA CROSWELL PERKINS
State Official
b. Oct. 26, 1940, Glens Falls, N.Y.; d. James Croswell and Evangeline (Beougher) Perkins; B.A., geology, Magna Cum Laude, Bryn Mawr Coll., Ph.D., geol., Univ. Calif. Berkeley; m. Edward Sturgis Grew, June 14, 1975, Groveland, Mass. Career: Asst. prof. Geology, Boston Coll., 1968-72; asst. research geologist, Inst. of Geophysics, UCLA, 1972-77; Adj. Prof., Environmental Sci. and Engring., UCLA, 1976-76; vis. asst. prof., Dept. of Geology, Univ. Calif., Davis, 1973-74; exec. secty., Lake Powell Research Project, 1971-77; dir., Calif. Dept. of Conservation, 1977---. Chmn., State Mining and Geology Bd., 1976-77; chmn., Geothermal Resources Task Force, 1977; chmn., Geothermal Resources Bd., 1978---; Cons. and vis. staff mem., Los Alamos Sci. Lab., 1971-75; secty., Geosciences Advisory Panel, Los Alamos, 1971-75. Contbr. articles to profl. journs. Democrat. Congregationalist. Office: 1416 Ninth St., Sacto., CA 95814.

GRIBBEN, VIRGINIA G.
Bank Executive
b. Mar. 8, 1947, Ind.; d. Thomas H. and Evelyn R. (Witter) Gaddis; B.S. Purdue Univ., 1969; m. Garry Gribben, Sept. 9, 1977, Oakland. Career: Opns. Analyst, Opns., Continental Ill. Nat. Bank, Chicago, 1969-70; 2nd v.p. and mgr., Corporate Cash Mgmt., Banking, The Northern Trust Co., Chicago, 1970-77; v.p. and mgr., Corp. Services Mktg., The Bank of Calif., S.F., 1977---. Hobbies: skiing, sailing, bridge. Home: 70 St. James Pl., Piedmont, CA 94611; Office: 400 California St., S.F., CA 94145.

GRIFFIN, ELINOR REMICK WARREN
Music Composer — Pianist
b. Feb. 23, 1906, L.A.; d. James G. and Maude (Remick) Warren; grad. Westlake Sch. for Girls, L.A.; mus. stu., N.Y.; (hon.) D.Mus., Occidental Coll., June 1954; m. Z. Wayne Griffin; chil.: James Warren, Wayne, Jr., and Elayne Techentin. Career: Extensive concert tours, U.S.; composer numerous compositions; approx. 150 publ. mus. compositions, incl. The Passing of King Arthur, one hour choral sym. poem, Abram in Egypt and Requiem for orch., chorus, soloists; maj. orchestral works perf. widely in U.S., Canada, Europe incl. Sym. in One Movement, Suite for Orchestra; The Crystal Lake. Mem.: (hon.) Sigma Alpha Iota, Delta Kappa Gamma; ASCAP. Republican. Methodist. Hobby: horseback riding, poetry collection. Home: 154 S. Hudson Ave., L.A., CA.

GRIFFIN, Z. WAYNE
Business Executive — Civic Leader
b. June 13, 1907, Hartford, Ky.; s. Z. Wayne and Beatrice (Austin) Griffin; desc. early Ky. settlers; ed. Manual Arts and Pasa. H.S., Pasa., Calif. 1927; B.A., Ore. State Univ. 1931; postgrad. (mus.) USC 1932; m. Elinor Remick Warren (Composer-pianist), Riverside, Dec. 12, 1936; chil.: James, b. Apr. 4, 1927; Z. Wayne, Jr., b. Feb. 2, 1938; Elayne Remick, b. Nov. 22, 1941. Career: Pasa. Comm. Playhouse, 1931; actor-mus. dir., USC 1932-33 (mem. Natl. Collegiate Players); writer-dir., NBC, S.F., 1933; S.F. Examiner radio sta. KYA, 1934; writer-prod., CBS, KHJ, L.A. 1934-37; radio dir.: (Batten, Barton, Durstine and Osborne Adv. Agcy.) Cavalcade of America, The Burns and Allen Show, The Frank Morgan Show, Maxwell House Coffee Time, freelance mot. pic. prod. 1947; founder, Griffin Prodns. 1948; motn. pics. incl.: (1st mot. pic.) Family Honeymoon, 1949; Key to the City (MGM release), Genius in the House, The Big Moose, The Iron Butterfly, 1950; Lone Star (MGM), 1951; Pres., Figureoa Hotel; dir.: Blue Chip Stamps, United Financial of Calif., Lyon Fireproof Storage Co. Mem.: Mayor's Cabinet; chmn. Redevelopment Comm., Bunker Hill-Watts; dir. L.A. Sym-Hollywood Bowl Assn.; Civic Light Opera Assn.; Music Center Perf. Arts Council; pres. So. Calif. Choral Mus. Assn., Young Musicians Found.; Beta Theta Pi; Calif. and L.A. Tennis, Bel-Air Country Clubs. Methodist. Rec.: golf, tennis, hunting. Home: L.A., CA; Office: Union Bank Square, L.A., CA 90017.

GRIFFITH, BEN PERRY
President, Griffith Company
b. Apr. 2, 1905, Moscow, Id.; s. Stephen M. and Della (Brown) Griffith; A.B., Princeton Univ. 1928; Harvard Law Sch. 1928-31; m. Katherine Seaver, L.A., Mar. 28, 1933; chil.: Stephen E., b. Feb. 9, 1934; Mrs. Thomas W. (Gertrude O'Dell) Purkiss, b. Apr. 19, 1935. Career: Atty. at law, Gibson, Dunn and Crutcher, L.A. 1933-36; exec. v.p., Griffith Co. 1937-56; pres. 1956---. Dir.: Am.

Air Lines, Inc., Pac. Mutual Life Ins. Co., Pac. Indemnity Ins. Co. USNR 1942-45; Lt. Comdr.-Chief Intelligence Ofcr., Fleet Air Wing One, WW II. Mem.: pres. So. Calif. Chpt., Assoc. Gen. Contractors, 1951; Eldorado Country Club, Palm Desert; pres. L.A. Country Club, 1967---; Calif. Club. Episcopalian. Hobby: fishing. Rec.: golf. Home: 1001 Linda Flora Dr., L.A., CA 90049.

GRIFFITHS, CADVAN OWEN, JR.
Plastic and Reconstructive Surgeon
b. Aug. 21, 1927, Weehawken, N.J.; s. Cadvan Owen (engr.-nuclear physicist, devel. nuclear propulsion sys. for atomic submarines, aircraft, cars, buses, steamships) and Florence (Raymond) Griffiths; nephew of Frank Riesenberger, chmn. bd. Van Raalte and pres.-first corp. mgr. to inst. profit sharing plan with employees in U.S.; grandson of John Raymond, pres.-chmn. bd. Raymond Corp.; great grandson of Adam Riesenberger, Edn., prof. math., dean, Steven Inst. Tech., founder, Stevens Acad.; A.B. Columbia Coll. 1948; M.D., Coll. of Phys. and Surg. 1951; LL.B., LaSalle Univ., 1978; m. Barbara Williams, Lucedale, Miss., Oct. 22, 1954; chil.: Barbara Gayle, b. Dec. 30, 1955; Cadvan Owen, III, b. May 3, 1957; David Wesley, b. Oct. 20, 1959; Chester Frank, b. Sept. 27, 1962. Career: Plastic and reconstructive surg.-scientist; prof. surg. Columbia Univ. UCLA and Univ. Calif., Irvine 1964-71; dir. research and edn. Research Found. for Plastic Surg. 1969---. Chmn. bd. Dolly Varden Mines, Inc.; chmn. bd.-pres. G. Vest Internat., Ltd.; bd. dirs. Plastic Surgical Council, United Surgical Schs., Great Am. Image Co., BFG Realty & Investments Ltd.; Lt. Comdr., USN to 1959; serv. Third Marine Div. USMC, Japan, Korea, Taiwan; instr. Sch. Aviation Med.; flight surg.-chief med. ofcr., USNAS, Willow Grove, Pa. Tech. dir., screen writer, author; research publs. (20 publs. field of cancer immunology, tissue transplantation, advances in plastic surg.). Mem.: Screen Writers Guild, Phi Beta Kappa; Bel-Air Bay, Columbia Univ. Faculty, L.A., L.A. Athletic, Calif. Yacht., Huntington Valley Country Clubs. Hobbies: music, coin collecting, Early Am. art. Rec.: tennis, golf, fishing. Home: 127 N. Doheny Dr., Beverly Hills, CA 90211; Office: 11600 Wilshire Blvd., L.A., CA 90025.

GRIGGS, H. WARNER
Bank Executive
b. July 23, 1918, Duluth, Minn.; s. Richard L. and Neva (Warner) Griggs; stu., Dartmouth Coll., 1938-39; B.A., Univ. of Minn., 1942; m. Barbara Ware, Mar. 31, 1943, NYC; chil.: H. Warner, Jr., b. Feb. 11, 1944; Capt. Richard W., b. Apr. 2, 1947; Betsy H., b. Feb. 20, 1954. Career: Asst. v.p., Duluth Natl. Bank, 1946-48; v.p., No. City Nat. Bank of Duluth, 1948-61; dir. First Nat. Bank in Hibbing, Va. and Gilbert, Minn.; v.p. in Correspondent Bank Sect. of Bus. Devel. Dept., Union Bank, L.A., 1961---; Regional V.P., Pasadena-San Gabriel Valley Regional Hd. Office, 1963---; Sr. V.P. of Pub. Affairs, 1970---. Dir., treas., William Parker Mem. Scholarship Found.; mem. L.A. Pub. Affairs Ofcrs. Assn.; mem. Council of Ten, United Indian Devel. Assn.; mem. Citizens Advis. Com. on Student Integration, L.A.; mem. L.A. Advis. Council, Nat. Jewish Hosp. & Research Center; mem., L.A. C. of C.; dir. and exec. com. mem., L.A. chpt. ARC; pres., dir., Voluntary Action Center of L.A.; dir., treas., Boys' Clubs Found. of So. Calif., bd. dir., L.A. Police Mem. Found.; dir. and past pres., Caltech Assocs. Tournament of Roses; mem. Altadena Town and Country Club. Lt., USN, 1942-45; gunnery ofcr. on destroyer escort in Pac. Presbyterian. Home: 2085 Fox Ridge Dr., Pasadena, CA 91107; Office: Union Bank, 445 S. Figueroa St., L.A., CA 90071.

GRISSOM, LEE A.
Chamber of Commerce Executive
b. Sept. 7, 1942, Pensacola, Fla.; s. Levi Aaron and Virginia (Olinger) Grissom; B.A., San Diego State Univ., 1965; M. City Planning, San Diego State Univ., 1971; m. Sharon Hasty, May 14, 1966, San Diego; sons, David, Jonathan, Matthew. Career: comm. liaison and research assoc. to sr. research assoc., Western Behavioral Scis. Inst. of La Jolla, 1965-73; mgr., Planning Div., San Diego C. of C., 1973-74, gen. mgr., 1974-75, exec. v.p. and gen. mgr., San Diego C. of C., 1975---. Program Cons. KPBS-TV, Pub. TV ---; prod.-writer and host of program, The City Game, focusing on city planning issues facing S.D. region, 1972-75; contbr. 50+ articles on urban problems to profl. journs. and gen. interest mags. Awards: One of 10 Outstanding Young Men in Am., U.S. Jaycees, 1978; One of 5 Outstanding Young Men in Calif., Calif. Jaycees, 1977; Outstanding Young Citizen, San Diego, S.D. Jaycees, 1976; Pub. Information award, Calif. Council, AIA, 1973; special

award, S.D. Sect., Am. Inst. of Planners, 1973; Merit Award, S.D. chpt., AIA, 1972. Mem.: president's advis. bd., S.D. State Univ., 1976---; bd. trustee, Western Behavioral Scis. Inst., 1977---; bd. trustee, Combined Arts and Ednl. Council of S.D. Co., 1975---; advis. bd. mem., Nat. Alliance of Businessmen, 1976---; Calif. Planning and Advis. Asst. Council, 1977---; bd. trustees, S.D. Council, BSA, 1978; advis. bd. NCCJ, 1974---; S.D. Rotary Club. Rec.: jogging. Office: 233 A St., Suite 300, San Diego, CA 92101.

GROJEAN, THOMAS FRANCIS
Air Freight Company President
b. July 25, 1938, Chicago; s. Francis Thomas and Veronica Mary (Brown) Grojean; B.A.A., Univ. of Notre Dame, 1960; m. Therese Frystak, May 6, 1961, Chicago; chil.: Thomas, Jr., b. Feb. 21, 1962; William, b. Mar. 18, 1963; Janet, b. Mar. 16, 1964; Elizabeth, b. Dec. 15, 1965. Career: Sr. acct., Price Waterhouse, 1961-63; Chief Fin. Ofcr., Southern Airways, 1964-67; Vice pres., finance, Flying Tiger Line, 1968-71, pres., No. Am. Car Corp. (div. Tiger Internat.), 1971-78; also exec. vice pres., Tiger Internat., 1975-78, pres., 1978---. Dir., Tiger Internat., 1970---; dir., Flying Tiger Line, No. Am. Car, Natl. Equipment Rental, 1971---; dir., Stepan Chemical, 1977. Mem.: Am. Inst. CPAs; Nat. Freight Transportation Assn.; Young President's Orgn.; Economic Club of Chicago; Traffic Club of Chicago; Mid-Am. Club; Notre Dame Club; L.A. Country Club; mem. advis. council for Coll. of Bus. Adminstrn., Univ. of Notre Dame. Rec.: tennis, golf. Home: 200 N. Bristol Ave., L.A., CA 90049; Office: 1888 Century Park E., L.A., CA 90067.

GROSS, RITA BERRO
Cosmetics Company President
b. Los Angeles, Calif.; d. Leon and Rachelle (Israel) Berro; student UCLA continuing edn.; div.; chil.: Barbara Gross-Davis; Karen Gross-Andrus. Career: v.p. of sales, Con-Stan Industries, 1962-71; pres., Concept Now Cosmetics by Rita Berro Gross, 1971---. Bd. dir., Direct Selling Assn. contbg. author: Success Secrets, Royal CBS Pub., 1979. Lay Counselor in local L.A. counseling center. Rec.: reading, jogging. Office: 14000 Anson St., Santa Fe Springs, CA 90670.

GROSSMAN, JOHN W., JR.
Artist — Painter
b. July 20, 1932, Des Moines, Ia.; s. John W. and Ruth Grossman; m. Margaret Andrea Clausen, Pac. Palisades, Apr. 11, 1959; chil.: Jason, b. Feb. 16, 1964. Career: Lettering designer, 1950-52, 1964-56, 1959-62; lettering and design instr., S.F. Art Inst., 1960-66; graphic designer, 1962-70; painter, 1965---; graphic design exhibs.: (annual) Artists and Art Dir. Club, S.F. 1963, 64, 65, 67, 68, 69; Adv. and Editorial Art in West, 1966, 68; Internat. Poster Annual, 1968, 70; one-man shows, paintings, Pantechnicon Gallery, S.F. 1967, 69, 72; Pioneer Mus. & Haggin Galleries, Stockton, 1972, 78; Exhibited: Pomeroy Galleries, S.F.; Maxwell Galleries, S.F., Gallery de Silva, Santa Barbara; Shreve's, S.F.; Zantman Art Galleries, Carmel; E.B. Crocker Art Gallery, Sacto.; Louis Newman Galleries, L.A.; Painting presented by Gov. Reagan to Emperor Hirohito, Japan, 1971; Pres. Escheverria, Mex., 1972. Mem.: Calif. Arts Commn., 1967-73; v.-chmn. 1969, chmn. 1969-71. U.S. Army, 1952-54. Rec.: stu. artists, art history, theory of govt., relig. and metaphysics; museums, music, travel. Home and Studios: 71 Oak Grove Ave., Woodacre, CA 94973.

GROSSMAN, MARSHALL BRUCE
Attorney at Law
b. Mar. 24, 1939, Omaha, Nebr.; s. Lee and Elsie (Stalmaster) Grossman; stu., UCLA, 1957-59; B.S.L. and LL.B., USC, 1964; m. Marlene Belle Delson, Aug. 19, 1962, L.A.; chil.: Rodger Seth, b. Sept. 12, 1966; Leslie Erin, b. Oct. 25, 1971. Career: Admitted to Calif. Bar, 1965; assoc., law firm of Schwartz & Alschuler, 1965-67; partner, Schwartz, Alschuler & Grossman, 1967---. Mem.: Comm. Rels. Com. of United Jewish Fedn., 1972---, v.p., 1973-74; chmn., Commn. on Law & Legislation, L.A. Jewish Fedn., 1973-74; co-chmn., L.A. Com. of Concerned Lawyers for Soviet Jews, 1978; chmn., Atty's. div. of L.A. United Jewish Welfare Fund, 1977-78. Mem.: L.A., Beverly Hills & Calif. Bar assns.; Beverly Hills Bar Assn., bd. govs., 1971-76; Beverly Hills Bar Assn. Barristers, pres. 1972-73; Assn. of Bus. Trial Lawyers, bd. of govs., 1974-75; Bd. of Dirs., Pub. Counsel, 1973---; Legion Lex., bd. dir., 1974-76. Mem.: Order of Coif, prodn. editor, USC Law Review, 1964; Tau Delta Phi; Phi Alpha Delta; Mason; Shriner. Jewish.

Office: 1880 Century Park E., Suite 1212, L.A., CA 90067.

GROSSMAN, MORTON IRVIN
Physician — Educator
b. May 4, 1919, Massillon, Oh.; s. David and Jeanette (Feingold) Grossman; B.A. cum laude, Oh. State Univ., 1939; M.D., Northwestern Univ., 1944, Ph.D., physiology, 1944; m. Dorothy Armstrong, Nov. 26, 1957, Ventura; son, David Armstrong, b. Mar. 8, 1960. Career: Assoc. and prof. Physiology, Univ. Ill. Coll. of Med., 1948-53; assoc. and prof. Med. & Physiology, UCLA, 1955---; Chief Gastroenterology, VA Wadsworth Hosp. Center, 1955-62, sr. Med. Investigator and Dir., Center for Ulcer Research and Edn. (CURE), 1962---. Contbr. more than 300 articles to sci. journs.; Editor: Gastroenterology, 1960-65; Cons.: U.S. Food and Drug Adminstrn., Nat. Inst. of Arthritis, Metabolism, and Digestive Diseases; Nat. Commn. on Digestive Diseases; recognized as an authority on: peptic ulcer, gastrointenstinal physiology with emphasis on neurohormonal control of digestive function. Awards: Medal of Swedish Med. Soc., 1970; Mayo H. Soley award for outstanding research, Western Soc. for Clin. Research, 1973; Modern Med. Award, 1976; Friedenwald Medal, Am. Gastroenterological Assn., pres. 1967; Am. Assn. of Physicians; W. Soc. for Clin. Research, pres. 1964; Am. Soc. for Clin. Investigation; W. Assn. of Physicians; Am. Physiological Soc.; Soc. for Exptl. Biology and Med.; So. Calif. Soc. for Gastroenterology, pres. 1966. Home: 420 S. Westgate Ave., L.A., CA 90049; Office: VA Wadsworth Hosp. Center, L.A., CA 90073.

GROTJAHN, MARTIN
Psychiatrist
b. July 8, 1904, Berlin, Germ.; s. Alfred (prof. of Soc. Hygiene) and Charlotte Grotjahn; M.D., Kaiser Friedrich Univ., Berlin, 1929; came to U.S. 1936, naturalized 1942; m. Etelka Grosz, Aug. 18, 1927, Berlin; son, Michael G., M.D., b. July 6, 1935. Career: head physician dept. psychiatry and neurology, Berlin Univ., 1933-36; Menninger Clin., Topeka, Kan. 1936-38; mem. staff, Psychoanalysis Inst., Chicago, 1938-42; Major., Med. Corps., U.S. Army, 1942-45; prof., USC, 1946---: now Prof. Emeritus; practice psychiatry, Beverly Hills ---. Author: 7 books: Beyond Laughter, 3d printing 1970; Psychoanalysis and the Family Neurosis, 1960; Psychoanalytic Pioneers, 1966; A Celebration of Laughter, 1970; The Voice of the Symbol, 1972; The Art and The Technique of Analytic Group Therapy, 1977; 350 sci. publs. Office: 416 N. Bedford Dr., Suite 209, BeverlyHills, CA 90210.

GRUHN, CARL V.
Educator
b. Feb. 20, 1903, Jeannette, Pa.; s. Rev. Carl A. and Louisa A. Gruhn; B.S. in edn., Northern State Coll., 1927; postgrad., Univ. Minn., 1931-33; M.S. in edn., USC, 1941; postgrad., UCLA; Claremont Grad. Sch., workshop of sci. edn. under the Carnegie Found., 1953; Stanford Univ., as a Shell Fellow (Shell Found.), 1958; m. Hannah E. Dystee, Aug. 21, 1941, Salt Lake City, Utah; chil.: Hannah (Towle), b. Aug. 4, 1943; Diana Elizabeth (Guthery), b. Dec. 25, 1944; Carl Dyste, b. July 20, 1946. Career: tchr., sci. and math, Ipswich, S. Dak., 1927-28, Aberdeen, S. Dak., 1928-31, 1933-39; asst. v.p., tchr., counselor, Polytechnic H.S., Riverside, Calif., 1939-42; tchr., S. Pasadena H.S., 1942-68; tchr. of chem., Flintridge Prep Sch. 1968---. Discussion leader on Problems of Space Chem. at jr. colls. in So. Calif. as a mem. of the Internat. Geophysical Year. Tchr., Inst. of Sci. Tching., for teachers of sci. in L.A. Co. Directed lab work for chem. study programs sponsored by Nat. Sci. Found. at Univ. of Utah, Colo. Coll., Central Coll., Pella, Iowa. Recipient: certificate of merit, Industry Edn. Council of San Bernardino, 1963; Engring. 1968, Inst. for Advancement of Engring., L.A., 1968. Mem.: Nat. Sci. Tchrs. Assn., past pres. So. Calif. section; Calif. Tchrs. Assn., life mem. (ret.); Phi Kappa Phi; Phi Delta Kappa; Pi Delta Kappa. Contbr. author: Chemistry an Experimental Science, W.H. Freeman & Co. Mem. Masons. Republican. Baptist ch.: tchr., Sun. Sch. supt., choir dir. 13 yrs., broadcasting quartet mem.; v. chmn. bd. of deacons. Home: 210 South 6th St., Apt. 210, Alhambra, CA 91801.

GRYP, FIRMIN A., JR.
Savings and Loan Association President
b. July 30, 1927, Monterey; s. Firmin A. and Virginia Gryp; A.A., Hartnell Coll. 1950; m. Janice Lund, Salinas, Apr. 16, 1950; daus.: Melinda A., Marsha L.,

Lisa M. Career: Tynan Lumber Co. (bkpr.) 1948-50; teller, Salinas Valley Svgs.-Ln. Assn., 1951-52, appraiser, loan ofcr. 1952-57, secty-mgr. 1957-60, exec. v.p.-mgr. ofcr. 1960-69 (merged, name chg. to Palo Alto-Salinas Svgs. & Loan Assn., chg. to No. Calif. Svgs. & Loan Assn. 1972), pres., mgr. ofcr., 1969---. Pres.-dir. Calif. Svgs. & Loan League 1974-75. USN 1946, 51. Mem.: dir. Rotary Club, pres. 1968-69; Elk. Office: 300 Hamilton Ave., Palo Alto, CA 94301.

GRYTING, HAROLD JULIAN
Research Chemist
b. Dec. 31, 1919, Belview, Minn.; s. Reier Elling and Julia Mathilda (Olsen) Gryting; B.A. cum laude, St. Olaf Coll., 1941; postgrad N. Dak. State Univ., 1941-42; Ph.D., Purdue Univ., 1947; m. Barbara Ruggles, June 25, 1954, Las Vegas, Nev.; Chil.: Corrine Suzanne, b. Aug. 7, 1960; Paul Julian, b. June 25, 1962. Career: Chemist, Naval Weapons Center, China Lake, 1947-52, head explosives research branch, 1952-65, tech. asst. for explosives, 1965-72, assoc. head Applied Research and Processing Div., 1972-74; safety and tech. coordinator, 1974-75, sr. research chemist, 1975---. Chmn., Joint Army, NASA, Air Force, Navy Safety and Environmental Working Group, 1973-77, & Steering Com., 1973---; chmn., initiators com. Joint Tech. Coordinating Group Air Launched Non-nuclear Ordnance Working Party for Fuzes, 1975---, & Qualification Manuals Com. Working Party for Explosives, 1971---. Mem.: AAAS; Am. Chem. Soc. (chmn. Mojave Desert Sect. 1974); Research Soc. of Am.; Am. Defense Preparedness Assn.; Fellow, Am. Inst. of Chemists; N.Y. Acad. of Sci.; Sigma Xi; Phi Lambda Upsilon. Contbr. articles to profl. journs. Patentee temperature-resistant explosives and dispersion methods for ordnance materials. Scoutmaster, Troop 848, BSA, 1975---. Lutheran. Hobbies: Hunting, fishing. Home: 1900 Linda Vista, Ridgecrest, CA 93555; Office: Ordnance Systems Dept., Naval Weapons Center, China Lake, CA 93555.

GUARD, DONALD DAVID
Musician — Author
b. Oct. 19, 1934, Honolulu, Hawaii; s. Carl Jackson and Marjorie Elizabeth (Kent) Guard; B.A. Economics, Stanford, 1956; m. Gretchen Ballard, Nov. 4, 1957, Pasadena; chil.: Catherine Kent, b. 1958; Thomas Jonathan, b. 1957; Sarah Shannon, b. 1963. Career: Leader, Kingston Trio, 1957-61, leader, Whiskeyhill Singers, 1962; studio musician, Sydney, Australia, 1963-66; folk music advisor "Jazz Meets Folk" TV series for Australian Broadcasting Co. 1964; host TV series Dave's Place, Australia, 1965-66; Kalimba soloist for Jim Buckley, 1967. Author: Colour Guitar, 1967; mem. of Hassilev, Settle & Guard singing group, 1974; performer with Modern Folk Quartet, 1977; studio musician with "Manhattan Transfer," 1977; correspondent for Peninsula Magazine, 1977; Author: "Deirdre: A Celtic Legend," Celestial Arts, 1977; leader, The Expanding Band, 1978---; Judge, American Song Festival, 1978; vocalist and main titlist on John Stewart Album, "Bombs Away Dream Babies" R.S.O. Records, 1979. Awards: 6 gold albums, 2 gold singles, 2 Grammies, with Kingston Trio, 1958-61; performed on Acad. Award winning soundtrack "How the West Was Won" 1962; Australian Grammy album, "The Bold Bushrangers," EMI 1963. Mem.: Beta Chi chpt., Sigma Nu, 1954-56. Rel. Kashmir Shaivism. Hobby: creating geometric art effects. Rec.: writing poetry. Home: 1023 Mercedes Ave., Los Altos, CA 94022.

GUERIN, JOHN JOSEPH
Attorney at Law
b. Mar. 24, 1926, L.A.; s. Joseph Paul (National Champion Gymnast, 1920s) and Margaret E. (Jones) Guerin; nephew, Daniel H. Guerin, City Counsel, Montebello, 1940s; J.D., Loyola Univ., L.A. 1949; m. Nadine Martinez, Nov. 1, 1964, Santa Ana; chil.: Josephine, b. July 12, 1965; Michael, b. May 29, 1968; Thomas, b. Oct. 18, 1969; Regis, b. Dec. 17, 1970; Alfred; Teresa Cahl; Yvonne; Edward, Arthur; and Nadine P. Career: Assoc. in law firm, Guerin, McKay & Tendler, 1949-50; assoc., Robinson, Guerin & Powers, Law Firm, 1950-51; partner in law firm, Guerin & Guerin, 1951-67; sole practice, John Guerin, Atty. at Law, 1962---. Pres. and dir., Realty Title, Realty Title Escrow Co.; secty. and dir., Clary Corp.; secty., Addmaster Corp. Appears as attorney in 40 pub. opinions by appellate cts. of Calif. USNR, 1944-46, Ofcr's Tng.; USAR, 1949; Capt., USAFR, 1952-62. Catholic. Rec.: sports. Home: 20431 Kenworth Cir., Huntington Beach, CA 92626; Office: 1118-A Pacific Coast Hwy., Huntington Beach, CA 92648.

GUERRERO, ROBERT RAYMOND
Medical Research Company Executive
b. June 25, 1939, Covina, Calif.; s. Rosendo and Lucille Mascorro; B.A., Cal. State Univ., L.B., 1968; M.A., 1971; Ph. D., N. Ariz. Univ., 1974; post doc., Pasadena Found. for Med. Research, 1976; chil.: Cynthia Loren, b. Sept. 14, 1959; Julie Lynn, b. Nov. 2, 1960. Career: Chem. Lab. dir., Hughes Aircraft, 1965; chem. lab. dir., Tera Pharmaceuticals, 1968-69; botany instr., Cal. State Univ., L.B., 1969-71; ecological cons., Salt River Project environ. impact study, 1972-75; cell biology cons., Huntington Inst. of applied med. research, 1976; research assoc. Atherosclerosis Research, Pasadena Found. for Med. Research, 1976, research assoc. and lab. dir., carcinogenesis research, 1976-78; v.p. and dir. of carcinogenesis research, Vanguard Research Labs., Inc., 1978---. Contbd. 12 research papers and abstracts in invertebrate ecology, platn ecology and in environ. med., Salt River Project Fellowship 1972-75. Mem.: TriBeta biology hon. soc. 1972-74; Tissue Culture Assn. of Am. 1976-78; Calif. Tissue Culture Assn. 1976-78. Hobbies: photog., horticulture, entomology. Rec.: films, insect collecting, bird watching, horticulture displays. Home: 814 S. Euclid Ave., Pasadena, CA 91106; Office: 99 N. El Molino, Pasadena Found. for Med. Research, Pasadena, CA 91101.

GUGAS, CHRIS
Polygraphist — Author
b. Aug. 12, 1921, Omaha, Neb.; s. Nicholas and Vera (Henas) Gugas; B.A., pub. adm., 1970; M.A., USC, 1977; postgrad. Univ. Beverly Hills, Cal. State, 1971; m. Anne Claudia Setaro, June 27, 1942, Oakland; chil.: Chris, Jr., b. July 18, 1943; Steven E., b. Aug. 31, 1946; Carol (Mrs. Giovan), b. June 19, 1951. Career: Asst. Director, L.A. School Security, Los Angeles Bd. of Edn., 1949-50; CIA agent, U.S. Govt., 1950-54; L.A. Bd. of Edn., 1955-57; dir. Central Bureau of Investigation, L.A. 1962; public safety director, Omaha, Nebr. 1963-65; director, Professional Security Consultants, Hollywood, 1966---; security consultant: business, television, motion picture industries; author: The Silent Witness: A Polygraphist's Casebook, Prentice-Hall, 1979; columnist: Los Angeles Daily Journal, Security World Magazine; contbr. over 150 articles on criminology: newspapers, mags., trade journs. Served USMC, 1940-49; decorated: Presidential Unit Citations, four battle stars; 3 Navy Unit Citations. Founder, Nat. Bd. of Polygraph Examiners; pres. Am. Polygraph Assn. 1971-72; pres., Special Agent's Assn. 1960; pres. Marine Corps League, 1945; pres. Combat Correspondents Assn. 1970; pres., Red Cross Council 1939; mem. Calif. Peace Officers, Assn., L.A. Peace Officers Assn.; Am. Criminological Assn.; Silver Dollar Club. Greek Orthodox. Hobbies: electronics, writing. Rec.: sports. Home: 4018 Dixie Canyon Ave., Sherman Oaks, CA 91423; Office: 1680 N. Vine St., Suite 400, Hollywood, CA 90028.

GUNDERSON, THEODORE LEE
Senior Special Agent, FBI
b. Nov. 7, 1928, Colorado Springs, Colo.; s. Jerome A. and Betty (Schell) Gunderson, Univ. of Neb., 1950; grad., Internat. Terrorism, Calif. Specialized Training Inst.; grad. Internat. Symposium on Terrorism, FBI Acad., Vir.; chil.: Gregory Todd, b. Jan. 29, 1956; Lorie Ann, b. Oct. 26, 1957; Theodore Lee, Jr., b. May 16, 1959; Michael Scott, b. July 16, 1963. Career: Spec. agent, FBI, 1952-60, assignments: Phenix City, Ala., Knoxville, Tenn., New York, N.Y., Albuquerque, N. Mex.; supv. spec. agent, FBI Hdqrs., Wash., D.C., 1960-65; asst. spec. agent in charge, New Haven, Conn., 1965-70; Phila., Pa., 1970-73; inspector, FBI Hdqrs., Wash., D.C., 1973; spec. agent in charge, Memphis, Tenn., 1973-75; Dallas, Tex., 1975-77; spec. agent in charge, L.A., Calif., 1977---. (During assignment to FBI Hdqrs. Washington, D.C., handled Organized Crime and Racketeering Investigations under Atty. Gen. Robert Kennedy and spec. investigations for the White House, Lyndon B. Johnson, President). Bd. dir., BSA, L.A. Area Council; bd. dir. SMU Mustang Club, Dallas, Tex. Mem.: Rotary, Sigma Alpha Epsilon. Presbyterian ch., former elder. Hobbies: pub. speaking, athletics. Rec.: golf, racquetball, reading, jogging. Office: Federal Bureau of Investigation, 11000 Wilshire Blvd., L.A., CA 90024.

GUNDLACH, HEINZ L.
Corporate Executive
b. July 6, 1937, Duesseldorf, Germany; s. Heinrich and Ilse (Schuster) Gundlach; LL.M., 1961; J.D., 1962; chil.: Andrew, b. Jan. 6, 1971; Annabelle, b. Nov. 6, 1973. Career: Partner and v.p., Loeb, Rhoades & Co. investment bankers, 1967-75; dir. and mem. exec. com., The Fedmart Corporation, 1975, vice chmn. of bd., 1976---. Protestant. Office: 8001 Othello St., San Diego, CA 92111.

GURASH, JOHN THOMAS
Chairman, Executive Committee, INA Corporation
b. Nov. 25, 1910, Oakland; s. Nicholas and Katherine (Restovic) Gurash; L.A.H.S.; Loyola Univ. Sch. of Law, 1936, 1938-39; m. Katherine Mills, L.A., Feb. 4, 1934; chi..: John N., b. Feb. 8, 1939. Career: Am. Surety Co. of N.Y., underwriting mgr.-asst. mgr. 1930-44; v.p.-dir. Pac. Employers Ins. Co. 1944-53; exec. v.p.-dir. 1959-60. pres.-dir. 1960-68, chmn. bd.-dir. 1968---; pres.-orgn.-dir. Meritplan Ins. Co., 1953-59; v.p. Ins. Co. of No. Am., 1966-70; dir. 1970---; exec. v.p.-dir. INA Corp. 1968-69, chmn.-pres.-chief exec. ofcr.-dir. 1969-74; chmn.-chief exec., ofcr., dir. 1974---. Dir.: Compagnie Financiere de Suez; chmn. bd., Certain-Teed Corp., INA Reinsurance Co.; Bd. trustees, Occidental Coll., Bd. of Dir.: Lockheed Corp., Purex Corp., Household Finance Corp., Mortgage Guaranty Ins. Corp. (MGIC), Lloyds Bank Calif.; Awards: Man of Yr., Pac. Chap., Chartered Property and Casualty Underwriters, 1965; Gold Medal Award, The Netherlands Soc. of Phila., Am. Jewish Com. Award, 1971; John Wanamaker Award, 1972; (hon.) Dr. of Soc. Sci., Villanova Univ., 1972; Gold Medal Award, Poor Richard Club, 1973; Sourin Award, Cath. Philopatrian Lit. Inst. 1973; Natl. Human Rels. Award, Natl. Conf. of Chrs. and Jews, 1973, Citizen of Yr., Delaware Valley Council, 1973. Mem.: dir.: Orthopaedic Hosp., L.A.; Founders of the Music Center of L.A.; Clubs.: mem. Pine Valley Golf, N.J.; L.A. Country Club; Calif., L.A.; Home: 1141 S. Orange Grove Blvd., Pasadena, CA 91105; Office: 1600 Arch St., Philadelphia, PA 19101; 4050 Wilshire Blvd., L.A., CA 90010.

GURDIN, MICHAEL M
Plastic Surgeon
b. Sept. 15, 1910, Pine Bluff, Ark.; s. Nathan and Millie (Nichols) Gurdin; stu., Univ. of Ark., 1927-29; M.D., Tulane Univ., New Orleans, 1933; m. Marlene Seghetti, 1962, Las Vegas; chil.: Mrs. Julie Caput, b. 1941; Dr. Jonathan Gurdin, b. 1945. Career: Intern and House Surgeon, Cedars of Lebanon Hosp., 1933-36; pvt. practice, plastic surg., Beverly Hills, 1946---. Cmdr., M.C. USN, 1940-46. Rec.: skiing, fishing, sailing. Office: 436 N. Roxbury Dr., Suite 207, Beverly Hills, CA 90210.

GUSTAFSON, ROBERT HARMON
Statistician
b. Oct. 28, 1927, Cosmopolis, Wash.; s. Lawrence Elmer and Marion (Overmire) Gustafson; B.A., Math., Sacto. State Coll., 1952, M.A., Math. Statistics, 1953; m. Gloria Elnora Pille, Aug. 1, 1952, Piedmont; dau. Janus Ann, b. Feb. 1, 1963. Career: Meterologist, USAF, 1946-49; lectr., Statistics & Math., Sacto. State Coll., 1951-67; Chief, Statistical Research and Consulting Div., Calif. State Bd. of Equalization, 1952---; also lectr., Statistics and Computers in assessment procedures, 1968---; Cons. in statistics & computers in the appraisal process, other states and foreign govts., 1966---. Contbr. Numerous articles in field, profl. journs.; co-author: Statistics and Computers in the Appraisal Process, Internat. Assn. of Assessing Ofcrs., 1977. Pres., Muscular Dystrophy Assn., Sacto., 1965; pres., Tuberculosis Assn., Sacto., 1968; pres., Altua, Inc. (Alcoholic Recovery Ranch), 1968---; pres. 20-30 Club of Sacto., 1964. Hobby: stamps. Rec.: fishing; Home: 5941 Annrud Way, Sacto., CA 95822; Office: P.O.B. 1799, Sacto., CA 95808.

GUTHRIE, SALLY R.
Editor
b. Jan. 10, 1929, Elmira, N.Y.; d. Harry Evans and Marian (Looney) Record; B.A., Elmira Coll., 1950, M.S., 1969; m. Donald G. Guthrie, 1950, Elmira; chil.: J. Ben, Daniel M., Donald L., Jr., Mary Scott. Career: former editor of Publs. for Homelite, a div. of Textron; ed.; Jonathan (publ. of The Jonathan Club), 1973---. Corporate secty. and edn. ofcr., So. Calif. Business Communicators. Home: 902-A California Ave., Santa Monica, CA 90403; Office: 545 S. Figueroa St., L.A., CA 90071.

GUYOL, JOHN TODD
Company President
b. Aug. 21, 1925, St. Louis, Mo.; s. Matthew M. and Hayden Mary (Todd) Guyol; B.S., chem., Carnegie Inst. of Tech., 1948. Chil.: Anne, b. Jan. 7, 1959; Elizabeth (Meinrath), b. Apr. 13, 1953; Sara, b. Mar. 1, 1952. Career: with Koppers Co., 1948-65; v.p., mfg, U.S. Plywood, and gen. mgr., Diversified Products Div., U.S. Plywood-Champion Papers, Inc., 1966-71; Corp. v.p., Bendix Corp., 1973---; pres. and chief operating ofcr., Am. Forest Products Corp., 1972---. AUS, 1943-46, Pacific Theater; decorated Bronze Star, Purple Heart.

Clubs: Olympic, S.F.; S.F. Yacht; Belvedere. Hobby: painting. Rec.: sailing, tennis. Office: 2740 Hyde St., S.F., CA 94109.

H

HAAS, PETER E.
President, Levi Strauss & Co.
b. Dec. 20, 1918, S.F.; s. Walter A., Sr. and Elise (Stern) Haas; A.B., Univ. Calif., Berkeley, 1940; grad. cum laude, Harvard Grad. Sch. of Bus. Adminstrn., 1943; m. Josephine Baum, 1945; chil.: Peter E., Jr.; Michael; Margaret. Career: Joined Levi Strauss & Co. (LS&Co.), 1945---: exec. v.p., 1958-70, pres., 1970---, chief exec. ofcr. and pres., 1976---. Dir.: Am. Telephone & Telegraph Co., Crocker Nat. Bank; Trustee: Stanford Univ., Calif. Alumni Found.; treas.: Rosenberg Found.; pres., Jewish Welfare Found. Recipient Bay Area Award for Oustanding Contbrn. to Welfare of Youth, Big Brothers of S.F., 1963. Mem.: The Family; Pac.-Union Club. Home: 313 Maple St., S.F., CA 94106; Office: Two Embarcadero Center, S.F., CA 94106.

HAAS, WALTER A., JR.
Bd. Chairman, Levi Strauss & Co.
b. Jan. 24, 1916, S.F.; s. Walter A. and Elise (Stern) Haas; grandson of the noted Mrs. Sigmund Stern; A.B., Univ. of Calif. 1937; M.B.A., Harvard Grad. Sch. of Bus. Adm. 1939; m. Evelyn Danzig, N.Y.C., Mar. 16, 1940; chil.: Robert Douglas, b. Apr. 3, 1942; Elizabeth Jane, b. Dec. 12, 1944; Walter Jerome, b. Nov. 15, 1949. Career: Personnel mgr., Levi Strauss & Co., 1946-51, v.p. 1952-58, pres. 1958-76, chmn. bd., 1976---. Dir.: Pac. Tel. & Telegraph Co., Bank of Am., Mt. Zion Hosp. (1957-59), Maj., QMC (52 mos. active duty), WW II. Awards: "outstanding man of the yr.," S.F. Jr. C. of C., 1951. Mem.: pres. Mfrs. & Wholesalers Assn. 1951; commnr. S.F. Parking Authority, 1953; Alpha Delta Phi; clubs: The Family, Menlo Circus, Presidio Club. Republican. Jewish. Hobby and rec.: golf, fishing, tennis. Home: 2666 Broadway, S.F., CA; Office: 98 Battery St., S.F., CA.

HABERLIN, WILLIAM EARL
Bank Executive
b. Mar. 26, 1925, Honolulu, Hawaii; s. Earl William and Mary Constance (Ferriera) Haberlin; A.A., Univ. Calif., 1944; M.B.A., Harvard Bus. Sch., 1956; m. Mildred Copley, July 3, 1946, San Diego; chil.: James William, b. July 28, 1957; Laura Joyce, b. Oct. 11, 1955; Judith Ann, b. June 18, 1958; Brian, b. Aug. 19, 1963. Career: asst. v.p., United Calif. Bank, 1963-65; sr. Economist, Stanford Research Inst., 1966-67; sr. Planning Asst., Union Bank, L.A., 1967, asst. v.p., 1968, v.p., 1969, sr. v.p., 1974. Contbr. articles, various banking mags, 1968---. Served to Comdr., USN, 1943-63. Mem.: Jonathan Club; La Canada Flintridge Country Club; Lions Club of L.A.; Nat. Assn. of Bus. Economists; Corp. Planners Assn. of So. Calif.; Am. Arbitration Assn. Rec.: golf, tennis. Home: 5660 Bramblewood Rd., La Canada, CA 91011; Office: P.O.B. 3100 Terminal Annex, L.A., CA 90051.

HABERMAN, CHARLES M.
University Professor
b. Dec. 10, 1927, Bakersfield, Calif.; s. Carl and Rose Marie (Braun) Haberman; B.S. in engring., UCLA, 1951; M.S. mech. engring. USC, 1954; Engineer in M.D., 1957; M.S. in A.E., 1961. Career: Northrop Aircraft, 1951-59: lead eng. in charge of fuel systems group, 1953; group eng. in charge of aerodynamics computer-solution group, 1955-59. Cal. State Univ. at L.A., 1959---: assoc. prof., 1963-67, prof. 1967---. Also cons., Northrop Aircraft, 1959-61; cons. Royal McBee, 1960; research spec., No. American Aviation, Lockheed Aircraft, Aerospace Corp., summers of 1962, 1963, 1966, 1978. AUS, 1946-47. Author of engring. textbooks including: Engineering Systems Analysis, 1965; Use of Digital Computers for Engineering Applications, 1966; Vibration Analysis, 1968; Basic Aerodynamics, 1971. Mem.: Am. Soc. for Engring. Edn.; Am. Inst. of Aeronautics and Astronautics; Am. Acad. of Mechanics; Catholic Alumni Club Internat. Democrat. Roman Catholic. Rec.: volleyball, skiing. Office: Cal State Univ. at L.A.

HACKBARTH, RAYMOND WILLIAM, JR.
Investment Company Executive
b. Sept. 24, 1947, Syracuse, N.Y.; s. Raymond William

and Jane Elizabeth Hackbarth; B.A., Allegheny Coll., Meadville, Pa., 1969; J.D., Syracuse Univ. Coll. of Law, N.Y., 1975; m. Barbara Windsor, 1973, Syracuse. Career: St. research cons., New York Jt. Legislative Com. on Crime; criminal justice planner, Central N.Y. Regional Planning & Devel. Bd.; Atty., MacKenzie, Smith, Lewis, Mitchell & Hughes; acct. ofcr., The UMET Trust; dir. of ins. servs., Ticor Mortgage Ins. Co.; gen. counsel and v.p. of investments, Monarch Properties, Inc., Newport Beach ---. AUS, Mil. Police Corps, correctional servs.; Mem.: Phi Gamma Delta. Rec.: skiing, jogging. Office: 1000 Quail St., Suite 160, Newport Beach, CA 92660.

HAFTER, RUTH ANNE
Library Director
b. Apr. 18, 1935, Brooklyn, N.Y.; d. Samuel and Yetta (Treinkman) Goldstein; B.A., Brandeis Univ., Waltham, Mass.; M.L.S., Columbia Univ., N.Y.C., 1963; m. Ronald Saul Hafter, June 13, 1959; N.Y.; dau. Samantha, b. Jan. 22, 1971. Career: with Compton Advt. Co., 1959-61; asst. edn. librarian, Harvard Univ., Cambridge, Mass., 1967-68; univ. librarian, St. Mary's Univ., 1969-75; library director., Sonoma State Univ., Rohnert Park, 1978---. Pres., Halifax Library Assn., 1970-71. Hobbies: collecting chess sets. Rec.: sailing. Home: 1019 San Francisco Way, Rohnert Park, CA 94928; Office: Sonoma State Univ. Library, Rohnert Park, CA.

HAHN, KENNETH
County Supervisor
b. Aug. 19, 1920, L.A.; s. John Henry (former mayor of Kindersley, Saskatchewan, Can.) and Hattie (Wiggins) Hahn; bros.: Henry B., John D., Allen W., Louis A., Rev. George E., Gordon R.; ed. grad. Fremont H.S., L.A. 1938; B.A., Pepperdine Coll. 1942; M.A., USC 1951; LL.D., Pepperdine, 1971; m. Ramona Fox (d. Rev. Harry R. Fox), chi.: James Kenneth, b. July 3, 1950; Janice K., b. Apr. 1952; Career: instr. polit. sci., Pepperdine Coll. Elected City Councilman of L.A., 1947, re-elected, 1949, 51; chmn. Govt. Efficiency Com.; elected Supvr., Co. of L.A., Nov. 1952---. Mem. L.A. Memorial Coliseum Commn., 1952---, pres. 1955, 67 (known as Father of the L.A. Sports Arena); chmn. Military and Veterans Affairs, Parks, Co. Schs., Auditor Controller, Co. Clerk, other key depts. Comdr. APC 9, 7th Fleet, New Guinea Campaign, 1942-46, WW II. Mem.: AMVETS, Am. Legion, Vets. of Foreign Wars. Democrat. Church of Christ. Rec.: golf, public service. Office: 866 Hall of Administration, L.A., CA 90012.

HAHN, LORENA GRACE
Head Nurse — Educator
b. Apr. 16, 1914, Kalvesta, Kan.; d. Albert Hicks and Myrtle May (Bingham) Barnes; Registered Profl. Nurse Degree, Teachers Training, Kansas State Normal; Wesleyan Ministerial training courses & pub. speaking, 1935-44; Certified Critical Care Nurse, 1979; m. Rev. Robert Elwyn Hahn, May 2, 1935, Kansas. Career: L.A. Co.-USC Sch. of Nursing, 1944-47, staff nurse, 1947-50, head nurse, 1950---; also health care provider and critical care nurse, White Memorial Med. Center, 1967---; tchr. - lecturer, particularly in field of Social Psychiatry. Recipient: 32 year perfect attendance award, L.A. Co.-USC Med. Center; 10 year dedicated service award, White Memorial Med. Center. Life mem. L.A. Co.-USC Nurses Alumni Assn. Mem.: Am. Nurse Assn.; Calif. Nurse Assn. (region 6); Nat. Critical Care Inst. of Edn.; O.M.S. Internat. Inc. Wesleyan Ch. Hobby: travel. Rec.: swimming, hiking, spectator sports. Home: 2431 Sichel St., No. 207, L.A., CA 90031.

HAIEK, JOSEPH R.
Publisher
b. Dec. 28, 1932, Jerusalem; s. Rizek and Rebecca Haiek; student, marketing, L.A. City Coll.; journalism, Cal State Univ.; m. Teresa Keklikian, Dec. 1957, Jerusalem; chil.: Alexander, b. Sept. 1958; Cahtrine, b. Mar. 1960; Laila, b. Sept. 1961; Louis b. June 1966. Career: tchr. elem. schs.; self-employed in business; advt. agency assoc.; currently editor and pub. periodicals and reference books on ethnic Arab Am. community and Middle East economic affairs including: The News Circle, The Arab Americans Almanac, Mideast Business Exchange, Mideast Business Guide, Arabic Directory on American Business. Mem.: Catholic Press Council; L.A. Press Club; Nat. Assn. of Arab Americans; Wm. Neima Republican Club; Arab American Soc.; K.C. Republican. Catholic Melkite rite. Hobbies: oil painting, collect Arabic arts. Rec.: swimming, tennis, backgammon. Home: 626 N. Beachwood Dr., L.A., CA 90004; Office: The News Circle Publishing Co., 2007 Wilshire, No. 900, L.A., CA 90057.

HALBERT, HON. SHERRILL
Senior Judge, U.S. District Court
b. Oct. 17, 1901, Terra Bella, Calif.; s. Edward D. and Ellen (Rhodes) Halbert; A.B., Univ. Calif., Berkeley, 1924, J.D. 1927; m. Verna Dyer, Santa Rosa, June 7, 1927; chil.: Mrs. Herbert M. (Shirley Ellen) Hanson, b. Sept. 29, 1929; Douglas James, b. June 28, 1932. Career: admitted to Calif. Bar, 1927; est. law practice, Porterville, 1927, pvt. practive, 1927-41; dep. dist. atty., Tulare Co., 1927-36; dep. atty. gen., Calif. 1942-44; assoc. with McCutchen, Thomas, Matthew, Griffiths & Greene law firm, S.F., 1942-44; pvt. practice law, Modesto, 1944-49; asst. dist. atty., Stanislaus Co., 1944-49; dist. atty. 1949; judge, Superior Ct., Stanislaus Co. 1949-54, apptd. U.S. Dist. Judge, No. Calif. Sept. 16, 1954-69, sr. judge, 1969---. Mem.: Am. Bar Assn., Am. Judicature Soc.; (past) internat. pres., 20-30 Club; Modesto Parlor No. 11, Native Sons of the Golden West; Modesto Lodge No. 272, Elks; Modesto Lodge No. 675, F&AM; Alpha Chi Rho, Phi Delta Phi, Lincoln Fellowship of So. Calif.; Book Club of Calif.; Rotary Club, Sutter Club, Sacto.; Commonwealth Club of S.F. Pres. Calif. Repub. Assembly, 1934-36; v.-chmn., Young Repun. Natl. Fed. 1938-42. Hobby: book collector. Rec.: gardening, Camellia hort. Home: 4120 Los Coches Way, Sacto., CA 95821; Office: 2008 U.S. Courthouse, 650 Capitol Ave., Sacto, CA 95814.

HALL, ADRIENNE A.
Advertising Agency Executive
b. L.A.; d. Arthur E. and Adelina Kosches; B.A., UCLA; m. Maurice Arthur Hall, Princeton, N.J.; chil.: Adam, Todd, Stefanie, Victoria. Career: Founding Partner, exec. v.p., Hall & Levine Advertising, Inc., L.A., 1965---. Dir.: Calif. Life Corp. ---; Calif. Life Ins. Co. ---; Hollywood Radio and TV Soc. ---. Awards: named Women of the Year, Am. Advt. Fedn. 1970; Leadership Award, Man of the Year, Western States Advt. Agencies Assn., 1976; Silver Medal of Distinction, Am. Advt. Fedn., 1978. Chmn. bd., Advt. Club of L.A., 1978-79; v. chmn. bd of govs., Am. Assn. of Adv. Agencies, 1978-79; pres., Western States Advt. Agencies Assn., 1975. Mem.: Blue Ribbon 400 of the Music Center; Art Museum Council, L.A. Co. Museum of Art. Hobby: collecting primitive art. Rec.: tennis, skiing, world travel. Home: Beverly Hills, CA; Office: 2029 Century Park E., Suite 560, L.A., CA 90067.

HALL, JOHN HARRIS
Attorney at Law
b. June 20, 1929, N.Y.C.; s. Harris Tremaine and Dorothy (Harris) Hall; A.B., Princeton Univ., 1949; LL.B., Harvard Univ., 1957; m. Cynthia Holcomb, June 6, 1970, Beverly Hills; chil.: Jonathan David, b. June 18, 1957; Nathaniel Foote, b. Feb. 17, 1960; Andrew Eric, b. May 28, 1961; Mary Karen, b. Mar. 22, 1963; Harris Holcomb, b. Sept. 1, 1971. Career: Assoc. law firm, Latham & Watkins, L.A., 1957-66, partner, 1966-72, 1974---; Dep. Asst. Secty. of Treasury for Tax Policy, 1972-74. Dir. Carson Estate Co. Contbr. articles in legal journs. USAF, 1951-54; decorated, air medal with cluster, D.F.C., Soldier's Medal. Mem.: Bd. of Councillors, USC Law Sch.; Am. Bar Assn., chmn. com. on sales, exchanges and basis, tax sect. 1969-71; L.A. Co. Bar Assn., chmn. tax sect. 1970-71; State Bar of Calif.; chmn. Com. on Tax. 9171-72. Clubs: Calif., Metropolitan, Wash.; Princeton Club of N.Y.; Sky Roamers. Republican. Episcopalian. Jr. and Sr. Warden. Home: 2820 E. Calif. Blvd., Pasadena, CA 91107; Office: 555 S. Flower St., L.A., CA 90071.

HALL, MARC EARL
College District Administrator
b. Nov. 4, 1939, Driggs, Idaho; s. Hyrum Earl and Myrtle Naomi (Marcum) Hall; B.S., Brigham Young Univ., 1964; M.A., Univ. of Calif., Berkeley, 1967; Ph.D., 1972; m. Cherylee Green, Aug. 24, 1962, Idaho Falls, Idaho; chil.: Rebecca Ann, b. 1963; Monica and Marily, b. 1965; Marc Elliott, b. 1968; Deborah, b. 1972; Pamela, b. 1973. Career: Accountant, John Inglis Frozen Food Co., 1964-66; adminstrv. analyst, State Center Community Coll. Dist., 1970-71; adminstrv. asst., Los Rios Community Coll. Dist., 1971-76; dir. mgmt. and planning services, 1976-77; asst. chancellor, 1977---. Vice chmn., bd. dir., Independent Data Processing Center; vice chmn., bd. dir., Los Rios Found. Contbd. articles to edn. journs. Mem.: Calif. Assn. of Inst. Research; Nat. Center Higher Edn. Mgmt. Systems Advis. Council; Calif. Assn. of Sch. Bus. Officials, chmn. Risk Mgmt. Com. Mem.: Phi Delta Kappa, 1975---; Lion's Internat. 1977---. Ch. Jesus Christ L.D.S., regional repr. of mission pres., mission pres., state exec. secty. Office: 1919 Spanos Ct., Sacto., CA 95825.

HALL, MONTY
Television Producer, Emcee
b. Aug. 25, 1925, Winnipeg, Canada; s. Maurice and Rose (Rusen) Hall (outstanding in charitable work in Canada, also distinguished performer); B.S., Univ. Manitoba; m. Marilyn Plottel, 1947, Winnipeg; chil.: Joanna Gleason (actress, Broadway star); Richard; Sharon. Career: Performer, Canadian Army Shows, early career in Canadian radio and TV; performer, U.S.A., 1955---: all networks, variety, game, comedy, most notable: Let's Make A Deal, 1964-77; musical comedy, Sahara Hotel, Las Vegas; variety specials, ABC-TV, others; producer sit. coms., NBC-TV. Author: M.C. Monty Hall, numerous magazine articles, special material. Bd. mem.: Cedars Sinai Hosp., NCCJ, Variety Club, Chmn. of bd., United Jewish Welfare Fund. Hobbies: theatre, music. Rec.: golf, tennis, relaxing at home. Home: Beverly Hills, CA; Office: 7833 Sunset Blvd., L.A., CA 90046.

HALL, RICHARD HANLEY
Orthopedic Surgeon
b. Apr. 19, 1914, Denver, Colo.; s. Asa Z. and Mabel E. Hall; B.A., Univ. Colo., 1937; M.D., Univ. Colo. Sch. of Med., 1940; m. Kathryn Andrews, Nov. 30, 1939, Denver, Colo.; chil.: J. Ronald, b. May 4, 1946; Cheryl A., b. Oct. 30, 1948; Gary W., M.D. (Olympic Medalist, Swimming, 1968, 72, 76), b. Aug. 7, 1951. Career: Rotating internship, Kansas City Gen. Hosp., 1940-41; residencies: Morris Mem. Hosp. for Crippled Children, W. Va., 1941-42; Lahey Clinic, Boston, 1942, 46 (one yr. interrupted by mil. serv.); VA Hosp., W. Roxbury, Mass. 1947-48; Chief, Orthopaedics, VA Hosp., Fayetteville, N.C., 1948-51; and VA Hosp., Long Beach, 1951-57; pvt. practice, specializing in Orthopaedic Surg., Long Beach, 1957---; also instr. in Orthopaedic Surg., USc, 1955---; Chief, Orthopaedic Surgical Sect., VA Hosp., Long Beach, 1951-57; Chief, Orthopaedic Sect., Long Beach Com. Hosp., 1963-64. Contbr. profl. articles to med. journs. and Long Beach Bar Bulletin. Active Duty, USN, 1942-45, ret. Comdr., USNR, 1974. Hobbies: woodworking, singing. Rec.: golf. Home: 9951 Beverly Lane, Garden Grove, CA 92641; Office: 2700 Bellflower Blvd., Suite 312, Long Beach, CA 90815.

HALLET, RAYMON W., JR.
Aerospace Company Executive
b. Nov. 21, 1920, Chicago; s. Raymon W. and Florence (Todd) Hallet; B.S., Mech. Engr., Purdue Univ., 1942; M.S., Engring., UCLA; m. Mary Ellen Zried, Feb. 23, 1944; Westwood; chil.: Julianna Robbins, b. Feb. 20, 1945; Raymon W. III, b. June 14, 1946; Christine, b. July 23, 1947. Career: with Douglas Aircraft Co., 1942-66; Douglas United Nuclear, 1966-70; McDonnell Douglas Corp., 1970---: chief engr. Adv. Space Tech., 1962-64; dir. Research & Devel., 1964-66; v.p., dept. gen. mgr., 1966-70; dir. Adv. Space & Launch Sys., 1970-73; Dir. Energy Systems, 1973-75; pgm. mgr. Solar Energy, 1975---. Cons., Natl. Sci. Found., 1973, mem. Solar Energy Review Bd., NSF, 1973-75; chmn. of bd. Merit Employment Council, 1967; chmn of Univ. Planning Com., 1967-69; chmn. of Atomic Ind. Forum Nuclear Rocket ad hoc sub com., 1964-66. Contbr. publs.: Japanese Rocket Soc., 1960; Internat. Astro. Congress, 1962, 64, 66; German Rocket Soc., 1964; Atomic Ind. Forum, 1965. Protestant. Rec.: swimming. Home: 1906 Holiday Rd., Newport Beach, CA 92660; Office: 5301 Bolsa Ave., Huntington Beach, CA.

HALLOCK, WILES
Director, Pacific-10 Conference
b. Feb. 17, 1918, Denver, Colo.; s. C. Wiles, Sr. and Mary (Bassler) Hallock; A.B., Univ. of Denver, 1939; m. Marjorie Eldred, Mar. 23, 1944; Corpus Christi, Tex.; chil.: Lucinda Eldred (Mrs. James Rinne), b. Mar. 20, 1945; Michael Eldred, b. Feb. 17, 1946. Career: sportswriter, Denver Rocky Mountain News, 1939-41; announcer, WLEU Radio, Erie, Pa., 1945-46; chief announcer, sportscaster, KOWB radio, Laramie, Wyo. 1948-49; sports info. dir., track coach, Univ. of Wyo., 1949-60; sports info. dir., Univ. Calif., Berkeley, 1960-63; pub. rels. dir. Natl. Collegiate Athletic Assn., 1963-67; Dir. Nat. Collegiate Sports Services, 1967-68; Commnr. Western Athletic Conf., 1968-71; exec. dir. Pacific-10 Conference, 1971---. Lt. Comdr., USNR, 1941-44; air navigator and instr., So. Pac.; decorated VPB-54 Air Medal. Mem.: F&AM; Jesters; Rotary; Lambda Chi Alpha. Presbyterian. Rec.: golf, hiking. Home: 1333 Corte Madera, Walnut Creek, CA 94598; Office: 800 S. Broadway, Suite 400, Walnut Creek, CA 94596.

HALLUM, ROSEMARY N.
Educator — Author
b. Oct. 2, Oakland, Calif.; d. Fred F. and Edna B. Hallum; B.A., Univ. of Calif., Berkeley, Gen. elem. and gen. secondary tching. credentials; M.A., Cal. State Univ., San Jose; Ph.D., Walden Univ. Career: tchr., Oakland Unified Sch. Dist.; edn. writer for American Book Co., Educational Activities, Teacher Mag.; early childhood cons.; west coast cons., Educational Activities, Inc.; tchr. workshop leader; disco dance instr. Author: Kindergarten component, new social studies series, N.Y.: American Book Co. 1978-79; contbr. author, New Dimensions in Music series, Am. Book Co., 1970, 1976; articles in Teacher mag.; 8 books, pub. Educational Activities, (EA) N.Y.; 6 filmstrips, EA; 14 records EA, one multimedia kit, EA. Mem.: ASCP; Phi Beta Kappa; Delta Kappa Gamma; Phi Delta Kappa; Calif. Profl. Writers Club; Incaders Desert Racing Motorcycle Club (hon.). Catholic. Hobby: piano. Rec.: dancing, music, jogging. Home: 1021 Otis Dr., Alameda, CA 94501; Office: 746 Grand Ave., Oakland, CA 94610.

HALPRIN, ANNA SCHUMAN
Dancers' Workshop Director
b. July 1920, Winnetka, Ill.; d. Isadore and Ida (Schiff) Schuman; stu. Bennington Summer Sch. Dance, 1938-39; B.S. in Dance, Univ. of Wis., 1943; m. Lawrence Halprin, environmental planner and architect, Sept. 1940; chil.: Daria, Rana (Vassau). Career: Joint studio with Welland Lathrop, S.F., 1948-55; founder, choreographer, artistic dir., performer, S.F. Dancer's Workshop, 1955---; also Master tchr. at Esalen Inst., Univ. of Calif., Berkeley, UCLA, Univ. Ill., Reed Coll., Harvard Sch. of Design; dir. commissioned workshops nationwide, Canada and Israel, 1972---; choreographed The Prophetess, The Lonely Ones, Visions, Birds of Am. or Gardens Without Walls, Esposizione, Visage, Parades and Changes, others; Awarded Guggenheim Fellow Grant, 1970, Choreographer Fellowship, Nat. Endowment for the Arts, 1976-77; Publs.: Collected Writings I and II, Exit to Enter, Movement Ritual I, When a School Comes Home, Citydance 1977, Dance as a Self Healing Art; Films: Parades and Changes, Right On, Anna: A Portrait, The Bust, How Sweet It Is. Office: 321 Divisadero St., S.F., CA 94117.

HALPRIN, LYRA
Editor
b. June 3, 1951, L.A.; d.Leahn Joshua and Saralee (Konigsberg) Halprin; niece, Raphael Konigsberg, distinguished lawyer, first amendment test case, U.S. Supreme Ct., 1956, 1961; B.A., sociology, Univ. Calif., Davis, 1973; M.Journalism, Univ. Calif., Berkeley, 1975; m. Alan T. Jackson, Sept. 23, 1978, Santa Monica. Career: People editor, Gardena Valley News, 1973-75; farm writer, Calif. Farm Observer, 1975; People editor, Woodland Daily Democrat, 1976---; also Yolo Co. correspondent, KFBK radio news, Sacto. One of first three women grantees, Agri. Ednl. Found. for Agri. Leadership Program incl. trips to USSR, Eastern Europe and Wash., D.C., 1976-78; Young Careerist award winner, Capital Dist. Bus. and Profl. Women's Club, 1978. Mem.: Women in the Media. Rec.: water skiing. Home: 2416 Bucklebury Rd., Davis, CA 95616; Office: 702 Court St., Woodland, CA 95695.

HALSTED, ABEL STEVENS, JR.
Attorney at Law
b. Nov. 22, 1907, Pasadena; s. Abel Stevens and Eleanor (Hall) Halsted; A.B., Stanford Univ., 1929; LL.B., Harvard Univ., 1932; m. Anne Croftan, July 8, 1931 (dec. May 1975); chil.: Croftan H. (Mrs. Willis R. Brown), A. Stevens III; m. 2d., Virginia Voorhis, Feb. 14, 1976. Career: Admitted to Calif. bar, 1932, since practiced in L.A.; of counsel Macdonald, Haisted & Laybourne, 1973---; lectr. USC Law Sch., 1952-57. Pres., Town Hall, 1953. Trustee Scripps Coll., Hollenbeck Home; former trustee Poly Sch., Westridge Sch. (both Pasa.). Served to Lt. (s.g.) USNR, 1943-45. Mem. State Bar Calif. (bd. govs. 1964-67, pres. 1966-67), Am., L.A. Co. (trustee 1955-62, pres. 1961-62) bar assns.; Harvard Law Sch. Assn. of So. Calif. (chmn. 1958-60), Am. Judicature Soc. (dir. 1969-71); Phi Beta Kappa. Republican. Episcopalian. Clubs: Calif., Chancery, Sunset, Twilight, Westerners (L.A.); Valley Hunt (Pasa.). Home: 360 W. Bellevue Dr., Pasadena, CA 91105; Office: 1200 Wilshire Blvd., L.A., CA 90017.

HAMER, LOIS V.
Gerontologist
b. Mar. 10, 1916, Ia.; d. Oroville and Lydia (Shafford) Hamer; B.A., Univ. No. Ia., 1937; M.A., Northwestern

Univ., 1941; postgrad. studies, Gerontology, USC, 1973-76. Career: tchr., 1937-43; Defense Dept. 1943-45; pgm. dir. KODL, 1945; dir. and exec. dir., Christian Edn. 1945-62; Peace Corps vol. 1962-65; exec., field of aging, 1965---: now dir., Sr. Adult Pgm., L.A. Valley Coll. Mem.: Women's Internat. League for Peace and Freedom, pres. local chpt., nat. bd., internat. exec. com.; Fellowship of Reconciliation, pres.; active various coms. and councils on aging. Protestant, Deaconess. Hobbies: gardening, stamps. Rec.: drama, travel. Home: 3755 Glenfeliz Blvd., L.A., CA 90039; Office: 5800 Fulton Ave., Van Nuys, CA 91401.

HAMERMESH, CHARLES LUTHER
Aerospace Company Executive
b. May 28, 1925, Brooklyn; s. Isadore and Rose (Kornhauser) Hamermesh; bro., Morton H., staff Physics Dept., Univ. of Minn., bro., Bernard H., chmn. Physics Dept., Cleveland State Univ.; B.S., Chem., Coll. of City of N.Y., 1948; M.S., 1950, Univ. of Tex.; Ph.D., Chem., N.Y. Univ., 1954; m. Ruth Silver, Dec. 29, 1969, L.A.; chil.: Gale, b. Aug. 4, 1951; Eric, b. June 7, 1955; Mark, b. Sept. 8, 1956; Susan, b. July 24, 1958; Scott, b. Sept. 27, 1958; Steven, b. Aug. 2, 1960. Career: Group leader, Interchemical Corp., 1953-59; with Rockwell Internat. (No. Am. Aviation), 1959---: principal sci., 1960-68, group leader, 1978---. AUS, 1943-46. Mem. Bd. and newsletter ed., So. Calif. Polymer Group, Am. Chem. Soc. Hebrew. Rec.: bridge, tennis. Home: 1162-C Westlake Blvd., Westlake Village, CA; Office: Sci. Center, Rockwell Internat., 1049 Camino Dos Rios, Thousand Oaks, CA 91360.

HAMILTON, CAROLINE A.
Realtor
b. Jan. 13, 1928, Reynoldsburg, Ohio; d. Herbert S. and Mabel (Tussing) Erwin; m. Mr. Hamilton, July 1, 1947, Columbus, Ohio; chil.: Kimberly (Turner), b. Apr. 22, 1948; Mark Jay, b. May 19, 1956; Karolyn (Landon), b. Mar. 19, 1951. Career: Real estate sales license, 1966; real estate broker license, 1968; owner, Hamilton Realty. Bd. Dir. Barstow Bd. of Realtors, 1970---: pres. 1970; state dir. 1970, 71, 72, 78; v.p. 1978. Bd. dir. Barstow C. of C., 2nd v.p. 1978, 1st v.p. 1979. Chmn. United Fund 1978. Republican. Pres., Barstow Repub. Womens Club, 1966-67; apptd. by Cong. Jerry L. Pettis to State Central Com. 1970; apptd. by Cong. Jerry Lewis to State Central Com. 1979. Hobby: fine arts china collection. Rec.: camping. Home: 109 College Ct., Barstow, CA 92311; Office: 225 S. Barstow Rd., Barstow, CA 92311.

HAMILTON, THOMAS M.
Attorney at Law
b. June 26, 1915, Winfield, Kans.; s. Calvin Blythe and Pearl (Heinecken) Hamilton; A.B., Southwestern Coll., Winfield, Kans., 1934; J.D., Stanford Law Sch., 1937; m. Charlotte Kuhrts, Feb. 25, 1955; chil.: Robert M.; Valerie (Bowlby); Timothy; Scott; Bruce. Career: Admitted to Calif. bar 1937, since practiced in San Diego; Sr. Partner, Luce, Forward, Hamilton & Scripps, 1959---. Chmn. bd. and chief exec. ofcr., Del Mar Thoroughbred Club; bd. dir., Pac. Legal Found.; bd. trustee, Scripps Clin., and Research Found.; bd. dir., Calif. C. of C., 1978. Lt. Comdr., USNR, WW II; decorated five major combat stars, Presidential Citation, three Bronze Star Medals with Combat Vs; Aide and Flag Secty. to the Comdr. of Western Task Force on D-Day; Aide and Flag Secty. to Comdr. of Amphibious Group 7 which landed Gen. MacArthur at Lingayen Gulf, P.I. Mem.: Am. and San Diego Co. (pres. 1949) bar assns. Home: P.O.B. 296, Hagerman, ID 83332; Office: 110 W. A Street, San Diego, CA 92101.

HAMILTON, THOMAS W.
Physician
b. June 29, 1938, Evansville, Ind.; s. Thomas William and Thelma Catherine Hamilton; B.A., Univ. of Evansville, 1961; M.D., Univ. of Indiana, 1970; Scandinavian Med. Seminar, 1972 and Hong Kong Med. Seminar, 1974; m. Judith Gayle, Feb. 1959; chil.: Michael Alan and Angela Michelle. Career: Athletic dir., Boys' Club, Evansville, Ind., 1959-60; head basketball & track coach, Catholic High Sch., Owensboro, Ky., 1961-62; head track coach, Mater Dei High Sch., Evansville, Ind., 1962-64; med. intern., Santa Barbara Cottage Hosp., 1970-71; co-dir., Goleta Valley Hosp. Emergency Dept. 1972; family physician, S.B., 1971---. Co-founder, Emergency Med. Technician Program, S.B. 1973. Instr. S.B. Paramedic Training Program, 1974---; Instr. S.B. City Coll., 1973---; Advisory bd. mem., Health Occupations, S.B. City Coll., 1973---. Awards: Outstanding Citizen Award, Evansville C. of C., 1959; Distinguished Service Award, Evansville,

1959. Mem. NCAA Nat. Basketball Championship team, Evansville Coll., 1959-60, 1960-61; AMA student repr., Sci. Convention, 1968. Diplomate, Am. Acad. of Family Physicians 1977; Fellow, Am. Acad. of Family Physicians 1978. Pres., S.B. chpt., Am. Acad. of Family Physicians, 1976. Mem.: Calif. and Am. Med. Assns.; S.B. Co. Med. Soc.; Am. Coll. of Emergency Physicians; Calif. Acad. of Family Physicians; Goleta Valley Hosp. Emergency Com., chmn. 1973; S.B. Co. Emergency Services Com. 1973---. Mem.: Neighborhood Youth Corps program, counselor 1965-66; vol. basketball coach, Monte Vista Grade Sch., 1971-72; med. cons., South Coast Youth Football League, 1972-74; mem. S.B. Journal Club, 1973---. Home: 1060 Colleen Way, S.B., CA 93111; Office: 5333 Hollister, Santa Barbara, CA 93111.

HAMMEL, HAROLD THEODORE
Professor of Physiology
b. May 8, 1921, Huntington, Ind.; s. Audry Harold and Ferne Jane (Wiles) Hammel; B.S. in physics, Purdue Univ., 1943; M.S. in physics, Cornell Univ., 1950; Ph.D. in zoology, Cornell Univ., 1953. m. Dorothy King, Dec. 29, 1948, N.Y.C.; chil.: Nannette (Stump—, b. Mar. 18, 1950; Heidi, b. Sept. 17, 1952. Career: Jr. Physicist, Manhattan District's Los Alamos Laboratory, 1944-46; Staff physicist, Los Alamos Sci. Lab., 1948-49; instr., Dept. of Physiology, Univ. of Pa. Sch. of Med., 1953-55; associate 1955-56; asst. prof. 1956-61; Fellow John B. Pierce Found. Lab. 1961-67; assoc. prof. in physiology dept., Yale Univ. Sch. of Med., 1961-67; prof. of Physiology, Scripps Institution of Oceanography, UCSD, 1967---; also assoc. dir. Physiological Research Lab., Scripps Inst. Oceanogr. 1968---; panelist, Regulatory Biology Program, Nat. Sci. Found., 1968-71. As a graduate student in physics worked under Dr. Kerst on critical mass determinations of enriched U^{235} reactors and under O. Frisch on critical mass determination of metal $Plutonium^{239}$. Was member of pit team of bomb assembly group for the Able and Baker tests at Bikini Atoll, 1946. Research from 1967 to present on: direct measurement of phloem sap pressury in oak trees; freezing of oxlem sap without cavitation in winter hardened evergreen trees; substances nucleating freezing in beetles; brain temp. thresholds and sensitivities for thermal regulatory responses in harbor seals, ground squirrels, running dogs, polar and tropical fish and Adelie penguin; body fluids which influence nasal salt gland secretion in marine birds. Contbr. of more than 150 publ. in sci. journs.; two patent applications pending. Mem.: Am. Physical Soc.; Am. Physiological Soc. (Editorial Bd. 1976---; Am. Soc. of Mammalogy; Am. Soc. of Plant Physiology; Am. Assn. for Advancement of Sci. Hobby: Natural Hist. Rec.: Bicycling. Home: 2475 Mango Way, Del Mar, CA 92014; Office: Physiological Research Lab., A-004, Scripps Inst. of Oceanography, La Jolla, CA 92093.

HAMMER, ARMAND
Chairman-CEO, Occidental Petroleum Corp.
b. May 21, 1898, N.Y.C.; s. Julius and Rose (Robinson) Hammer; B.S., Columbia, 1919, M.D., 1921; m.; 1 son, Julian A.; m. 2d. Frances Barrett, Jan. 26, 1956; Pres. Allied Am. Corp., NYC, 1923-25, A. Hammer Pencil Co., NYC and London, Eng., 1925-30; Hammer Galleries, NYC, 1930---; United Distillers of Am., Inc. NY, J.W. Dant Distilling Co., NYC and Dant, Ky., 1943-54; chmn. bd. dirs., pres., chief exec. ofcr. Occidental Petroleum Corp., L.A., 1957---; pres., chmn. bd. MBS; dir. First Bank & Trust Co., Perth Amboy, N.J., City Nat. Bank, Beverly Hills, Calif., Canadian Occidental Petroleum Ltd., Calgary, Alta., Can., Belgische Petroleum Raffinaderij N.V. (RBP), Antwerp, Belgium; Pub. Adv. Com. on U.S. Trade Policy by Pres. Johnson 1968---, Nat. Petroleum Council, 1968---; mem. econ. devel. bd., exec. com. City of L.A., 1968---; mem. adv. com. Com. for Greater Cal., 1969---; mem. L.A. Bd. Municipal Art Commrs.; mem. adv. bd. L.A. Beautiful, Inc., 1969---; mem. pub. adv. com. on U.S. Trade Policy, 1968-69. trustee, chmn. exec. com. Salk Inst. Biol. Studies, 1969; trustee, exec. com., acquisitions com. L.A. Co. Mus. Art; bd. dirs. L.A. World Affairs Council. Decorated comdr. Order of Crown (Belgium), 1969, Decorated by Pres. of Venezuela, Commander of the Order of Andres Bellos, 1975; City commendation, Mayor L.A., 1968; Mem. Calif. Gas Producers Assn. (pres. 1961---), UN Assn. L.A. (exec. bd. dirs. 1969---), AMA, N.Y. County Med. Assn., Alpha Omega Alpha, Mu Sigma, Phi Sigma Delta. Club: L.A. Petroleum. Author: Quest of the Romanoff Treasure. Office: 10889 Wilshire Blvd., L.A., CA.

HAMMON, H. GEORGE
Chemical Research Director
b. Jan. 30, 1918, Rochester, N.Y.; s. H. George (dec.)

and Marian Lee Hammon Albre; A.B., chem., Oberlin Coll., 1940; Ph.D., organic chem., Oh. State Univ., 1949; m. Mary Patton, Apr. 18, 1942, Rochester; chil.: Carol (Lilygren), b. Jan. 17, 1944; H. George, III, b. Aug. 18, 1947; Robert William, b. Jan. 25, 1950; Rex Gordon, b. Aug. 1, 1951; Terry Lee, b. Apr. 1, 1953. Career: Chemist, Ironsides Co., Columbus, Oh., 1940-43; research chem., Warren-Teed Prod. Co., Columbus, 1943-44; research chem., Ivano, Inc., Benton Harbor, Mich., 1949-53; asst. research dir., Hudson Foam Plastics Corp., Yonkers, N.Y., 1953-56; asst. div. chief, Battelle Mem. Inst., Columbus, Oh., 1956-65; Group leader, Polymeric Materials, Lawrence Livermore Lab., Livermore, Calif. 1965---. Patentee and contbr. publs. in field. Chmn., Gordon Research Conf. on Chem. and Physics of Cellular Materials, 1972. Tech. Sgt., AUS, 1945-46; research on toxicology of Cyanide. Mem.: Am. Chem. Soc.; AAAS; Sigma Xi. Hobbies: photog., rug making. Rec.: backpacking, fishing. Home: 701 Glen Rd., Danville, CA 94526; Office: P.O.B. 808, Livermore, CA 94550.

HANCHETT, BONNY JEAN
Editor - - Publisher
b. July 26, 1920, Muskegon, Mich.; d. Val Mott and Dorothy Louise (Mitchell) Howland; B.A., Wash. State Univ. (first woman ed. Univ. newspaper, 1941-42), 1942; m. Ross Allen Hanchett, Lewiston, Ida., Jan. 4, 1943; chil.: Val Howland, b. May 8, 1945; Mary E. Waterman, b. May 15, 1948; Robert L. Hanchett, b. Apr. 27, 1951; Jon A., b. Sept. 23, 1954; Kathryn A., by Apr. 29, 1958. Career: Wire ed. L.A. Times, 1942-43; soc. ed., Everett Daily Herald, 1943-44; reporter, Burbank Herald, 1944; dress shop propr. Everett, Wash. 1950-53; ed.-publ. Lewis River News, Woodland, Wash., 1953-55; ed.-publ. Clear Lake Observer-Am. Lower Lake, Calif. 1955---; Lake Co. corr. Sacto. Bee. Trustees, Lower Lake Elem. Sch. Dist. 1961-62. Mem.: pres. Soroptimist Club of Clear Lake, 1969-70, dir. 1970-71; dir. Clear Lake and Lake Co. Cs. of C. 1970-71, pres. 1974; past pres.-dir. Clear Lake Water Quality Council, Inc.; dir. Miss Lake Co. Pageant; secty. adv. com. Lake Co. Improvement Dist., chmn. exec. coms.; Emblem Club, Clear Lake Highlands Club, Clear Lake Bus. and Profl. Women's Club. Christian Scientist (com. on publ.). Home: Pt. Lakeview, Calif.; Office: P.O.B. 6328, Clearlake Highlands, CA 95422.

HANDSCHUMACHER, ALBERT GUSTAVE
Industrialist
b. Oct. 20, 1918, Phila.; s. Gustave H. and Emma (Streck) Handschumacher; B.S., Drexel Inst. Tech. 1940; Univ. of Pittsburg, 1941; Alexander Hamilton Inst. 1948; m. Inger Jensen, L.A., Apr. 11, 1970; chil.: Albert G., Jr., b. Dec. 1, 1942; David, b. Apr. 8, 1944; Karin Beske and Megan McRae, b. Mar. 7, 1950; Melissa, b. Apr. 25, 1964. Career: Sales mgr. Westinghouse Electric Co., Pittsburgh, Pa. 1941-42; various mgmt.-sr. v.p. Lear Inc., Grand Rapids, Mich. 1945-56; v.p.-gen. mgr. Rheem Mfg. Co., 1956-59; chmn.-pres. Lear, Inc., Santa Monica, 1959-62; bd. dirs.-exec. com.: Gilco Inc., Pasadena, Assoc. Mfrs. Corp., Inc., Monrovia, and Trans-World Financial Co., L.A. 1962---; bd. dirs-coms.-exec. com. Lear Siegler, Inc., Santa Monica, 1962---; pres. 1962-65; chmn. bd.-pres.-chief exec. ofcr. Aeronca Inc., Torrance, 1965---; chmn. bd.: Subsidiaries of Aeronca, Inc., Aeronca Internat., Ltd., Aeronca-Winslow Filters Ltd., dir. Microtron Patritions of Calif., Inc 1967---; bd. dirs-coms.-exec. com. Pac. Am. Industries, Inc., Beverly Hills, 1969---. Maj., USAAF, Wright Field Prodn., procurement specialist 1942-45, WW II. Awards: Outstanding Alumni, Drexel Inst. of Tech. 1951; Testimonial Dinner Honoree, Children's Asthma Research Inst. 1969; Man of Our Times, Aerospace Ind., City of Hope, 1969; Outstanding Alumni Award, Drexel Univ., 1971. Mem.: past reg. dir. Natl. Assn. of Mfrs.; bd. govs. Aerospace Inds. Assn.; Am. Soc. of Heating, Refrig. and Air Cond. Engrs., Inc.; Am. Mgmt. Assoc.; President's Assn.; Soc. of Automotive Engrs.; bd. trustees, Drexel Univ., Pa. 1963---; bd. trustees-coms.-exec. com. City of Hope, 1968---; bd. dirs.-coms.-adv. L.A. Co. Heart Assn. 1970; bd. dirs.-chmn. Nom. Com., United Way, 1972; underwriter, Lloyd's of London, 1973---; Clubs: Met., Wings (NYC), Jonathan, Confrerie de la Chaine des Rotisseurs (charter), Caves des Roy, Town Hall of Calif., Union League (Chicago), Bel-Air Country. Presbyterian. Rec.: golf, boating. Home: 1100 Stone Canyon Rd., Bel-Air, L.A., CA 90024; Office: 24751 S. Crenshaw Blvd., Torrance, CA 90505.

HANNA, THOMAS LOUIS
Author
b. Nov. 21, 1928, Waco, Tex.; s. John Dwight and

Winifred (Beaumier) Hanna; B.A., Tex. Christian Univ., 1949; B.D., Univ. of Chicago, 1955, Ph.d., 1958; m. Eleanor Camp; chil.: Mary Alice, b. Aug. 4, 1953; Michael John, b. Apr. 24, 1958; Wendell France, b. Jan. 11, 1960. Career: Dir., Jean de Beauvais Refugee Club, Univ. of Paris, 1951-52; asst. dir., Norte Maison Orphanage, Brussels, Belgium, 1952-53; chmn. Dept. of Philosophy, Hollins Coll., Va., 1958-64; Univ. of Fla., 1964-71; dir., Humanistic Psychology Inst., 1973-76; fir., Novato Inst. for Somatic Research and Tng., Novato, Calif., 1975---; also ed., Somatics: Magazine-Journal of the Bodily Arts and Scis., 1976---; Writer-in-Residence, Duke Univ. and Univ. of N. Carolina, 1964-65; Fellow, Am. Council of Learned Societies, 1969-70; first pres. Faculty Senate, Univ. of Fla., 1971-72. Author: The Thought and Art of Albert Camus, 1958; The Bergsonian Heritage, 1963; The Lyrical Existentialists, 1963; Bodies in Revolt, 1970; The End of Tyranny, 1976. Office: 1516 Grant Ave., Suite 220, Novato, CA 94947.

HANNAFORD, MARK WARREN
  United States Congressman
b. Feb. 7, 1925, Woodrow, Colo.; s. William Townsend and Ina (Owen) Hannaford; B.A., Ball State Univ. 1950, M.A. 1956; John Hay Fellowship, Yale Univ., 1961-62; m. Sara Lemaster, Ind. 1948; chil.: Mark, b. Aug. 17, 1949; Kim, b. June 27, 1952; Robert, b. July 13, 1954. Career: Est. Calif. res. 1953; tchr., Marshall Jr. H.S. 1953-57; soc. stus. dept. chmn. Lakewood H.S. 1957; prof. polit. sci.,Long Beach City Coll. 1966-74; Serv. Lakewood Planning Commn.; elected to Lakewood City Council, 1966-74; Mayor of Lakewood (2 terms); elected to House of Reps. 1974--- (Com. on Banking, Currency and Housing; Com. on Vets. Affairs; subcoms. on Monetary Policy, Historic Preservation, coins). Del. to Dem. Natl. Conv. 1968. Serv. bomber crew, 5th A.F., S. Pac. 1943-46. Home: 4944 Stevely Ave., Lakewood, CA 90713; Office: 5175 Pacific Coast Hwy., Long Beach, CA 90804; 415 Cannon H.O.B., Wash., D.C. 20515;

HANO, ARNOLD
  Author — Educator
b. Mar. 2, 1922, NYC; s. Alfred and Clara (Millhauser) Hano; B.A., Long Island Univ., 1941; M.A., Cal. State Univ., Fullerton, 1978; m. Marjorie Mosheim, Oct. 4, 1942; chil.: Stephen Arnold, b. Feb. 18, 1944; Susan Carol, b. June 14, 1946; m. 2d. Bonnie Abraham, June 30, 1951, Greenwich, Conn.; dau. Laurel Clare, b. Feb. 7, 1954. Career: Jr. Reporter, N.Y. Daily News, 1941; mng. ed., Bantam Books, 1948-50; editor-in-chief, Lion Books, 1950-54; freelance writer, 1954---; 1st novel pub., 1951, 24 other publ. books since, most recently a biography of Muhammad Ali, 1977; 400+ mag. articles; mem. Faculty (Writing), Univ. Calif., Irvine, 1966---; Named Mag. Sportswriter of the Year, 1964; winner Sidney Hillman Found. Award for mag. writing, 1964. 2nd Lt., AUS, 1942-46, Infan. and Mil. Intelligence, Combat duty in Aleutians and Marshall Islands. Founding chmn., Village Laguna, 1970---; mem. bd. of Adjustment and Design Review, Laguna Beach, 1971-73; mem. Am. Soc. of Journalists and Authors, 1960---. Rec.: running, swimming. Home: 1565 Bluebird Canyon Dr., Laguna Beach, CA 92651.

HANSON, L. THAXTON
  Justice, California Court of Appeals
b. Aug. 24, 1920, Bloomington, Ill.; s. E.E. and Edna (Zae) Hanson; B.S., Sch. of Commerce, Univ. of Ill. 1942; B.S. Coll. of Engring. 1947; J.D., Sch. of Law, Univ. of Mich., Ann Arbor, 1950; grad. Calif. Coll. of Trial Judges, Berkeley, 1968; Natl. Coll. of State Trial Judges, Univ. of Nev., Reno, 1970, grad. course, 1972; (hon.) LL.D., Pepperdine Univ. Sch. of Law, June 8, 1974; m. Evelynne Marie Rasmussen, Mandarin, Fla., Oct. 17, 1942. Career: Trial lawyer, sr. partner, Schell and Delamer law firm; apptd. Superior Court Judge, L.A. Co. by Gov. Ronald Reagan, July 3, 1968; elected to Exec. Com., Superior Ct. of L.A. Co., Jan. 1, 1972, re-elected 1973; Justice, Ct. of Appeal State of Calif. by Gov. Reagan, July 25, 1973---; Capt. Troop Comdr., Sixth U.S. Cavalry, Third Army Hdqrs. E.T.O. (N. France, Normandy, Central Europe, Rhineland, Ardennes) under General Patton; Maj., Opr.-Tr. Staff Ofcr., Ofc. Chief of Field Forces, Ft. Monroe, Va.; Staff of Gen. Mark Clark, Korean Conflict; grad. Command and Gen. Staff Coll. 1959; Natl. Security Mgmt. Course, Ind. Coll. of Armed Forces, 1970; Def. Strategy Serv., Natl. War Coll. 1971; dir. Higher Edn., So. Calif. USAR, Sch., Ft. MacArthur, San Pedro, Calif.; Col., Armor, USAR ret. 1972. Mem.: Res. Ofcrs. Assn. of U.S., U.S. Armor Assn., Vets. Assn. of Sixth U.S. Cavalry, Am. Legion, Am. Legion Luncheon Club of L.A.; Comdr., San Fernando Valley Chpt., Mil. Order of World Wars; Chpt. v.p. Assn. of U.S. Army, L.A., gen. chmn. 1970, 71, 73 Army Ball; bd. trustees, Am. Edn. League Internat., San Fernando Valley, L.A. Co., Am. Bar Assns.; exec. com. Am. Bd. of Trial Advocates; Am. Judicature Soc.; Conf. of Calif. Judges; Univ. of Ill., Univ. of Mich. Alumni assns.; Lambda Chi Alpha Alumni Assn.; Delta Theta Phi. Office: Court of Appeal, State of Calif., State Bldg., 3580 Wilshire Blvd., L.A., CA 90005.

HARE, NORMA QUARLES
  School Administrator
b. July 10, 1924, Dadeville, Mo.; d. James Norman and Mary Delia (Blakemore) Quarles; B.A. and M.A., edn., Fresno State Coll.; m. John Daniel Hare II, June 27, 1944, Ash Grove, Mo.; sons, John Daniel III, b. Jan. 30, 1948; Thomas Christopher, b. Feb. 8, 1950. Career: sch. tchr., 1956-67; elem. sch. principal, So. S.F. Unified Sch. Dist., 1967---. Publs.: Who Is Root Beer?, Garrard Pub. Co., 1977; Happy Radishes, 1978; The Vanishing Woman Principal, The National Elem. Principal, 1966. Mem.: Delta Zeta; AAUW, PTA; Soc. of Children's Book Writers. Res.: P.O.B. 161, Millbrae, CA 94030; Office: 400 Hillside Blvd., So. S.F., CA 94080.

HARGRAVE, MARIAN
  City Official
b. July 1, 1923, L.A.; d. Palmer W. and Anna M. Hargrave; desc. William Bradford, Gov. Plymouth Colony, 1623; cousin, Homer P. Hargrave, Pres. Chicago Bd. of Trade; B.A., UCLA, 1944; M.A., NY Univ., 1958; postgrad. UCLA, Univ. of Mich.; lab. tng., Natl. Training Labs., Inc. Wash., D.C., 1963, 64. Career: Field Dir., Assoc. Dir., 1960-64, Dir., Panel of Americans, Inc., NYC, 1964-66; asst. dir., 1962-66, and dir., Intergroup Rels. Dept. of NYC Housing Authority, 1966-68; dir. of Personnel Mgmt., Comm. Redevel. Agency, City of L.A., 1969---. Trustee, C.G. Jung Found., NYC, 1966-67; Founder, Trustee & V.P., Carnegie Hill Neighborhood Assn., NYC, 1960-62; mem. bd., NYC Metropolitan Chpt., Natl. Assn. of Intergroup Rels. Ofcls., 1962-63; mem. Women's City Club, 1966-69; mem., Nat. Assn. Housing, Redevel. Ofcls., 1967---; v.p., UCLA Student body, 1943-44. Originator and host, weekly KFI Radio program Book of Books, L.A., 1943-44. Mem.: Am. Soc. for Tng., Devel.; Am. Soc. for Personnel Adminstrn.; Personnel & Indsl. Rels. Assn.; Kappa Alpha Theta, Beta Xi chpt., treas. UCLA, 1941-44; Mortar Bd. Hon. Assn., 1943-44; Calif. Club, 1943-44. Hobbies: painting, property investment. Home: 628 Acanto, L.A., CA 90049; Office: 727 W. 7th St., 4th Flr., L.A., CA 90017.

HARKEY, VERNA RAE
  Pianist — Educator
b. Nov. 20, 1928, Fort Worth, Tex.; d. Verne and Rachel I. (Beam) Morrill; B.A., George Pepperdine Coll., 1950; m. Kenneth L. Harkey, Sept. 21, 1951, Long Beach, Calif.; chil.: Karl M., b. Oct. 26, 1956; Kevin L., b. June 29, 1958. Career: tchr. of piano, Long Beach, 1950---. Mem.: Nat. Guild of Piano Teachers; Music Tchrs. Assn. of Calif.; Nat. Music Tchrs. Assn.; Southwestern Youth Music Festival; Epsilon Eta; Mu Phi Epsilon (founder, L.B. chpt.); Ebell of L.B.; Musical Arts, L.B. Ch. of Christ. Home and Studio: 5836 Rogene St., L.B., CA 90815.

HARLAN, RIDGE L.
  Business Executive
b. Feb. 25, 1917, Pilot Grove, Mo.; s. George B. and Dale (Latimer) Harlan; B.J., Univ. of Mo., 1939; postgrad. studies, Harvard Univ., Univ. of Colo., Stanford Univ.; m. Marjory Folinsbee, M.D., June 4, 1976, Canada; chil.: Robert Ridge, b. Sept. 15, 1953; Holly (Molinari), b. July 7, 1947; Brooke Leonheart, b. Nov. 7, 1940. Career: with Batten, Barton, Durstine & Osborn, 1947-57; prin., Harris-Harlan-Wood, 1958-63; asst. dean, Stanford Univ. Grad. Sch. of Bus., 1963-68; prin., Harlan & Clucas, Inc., 1968---; pres. and chief exec ofcr., Barnes-Hind Pharmaceuticals, Inc., 1972-76. Dir.: Am. Microsystems, Inc., Velo-Bind, Inc., Tech. Equities, Inc. Clubs: The Family, Olympic, Commonwealth. Hobbies: flying own aircraft, gardening, cooking, acting, writing. Home: 839 Seabury Rd., Hillsborough, CA 94010; Office: 155 Montgomery St., S.F., CA 94104.

HARMER, RUTH MULVEY
  Author — Educator
b. June 18, 1919, NYC; d. Charles Watt and Mary E.

(Gierloff) Mulvey); A.B., Barnard Coll., 1941; M.A., Columbia Univ., 1942; Ph.D., USC; m. Lowell Harmer, 1950, Tlalmanalco, Mex.; dau. Felicia, b. 1952. Career: Writer, Hartford Courant, 1942-44; Wash. Times-Herald, 1944-47, Modern Mex. Mag., 1947-50, Novedades, 1948-51, Mex. City News, 1950-51; Prof., USC, 1954-59, Cal. State Poly., Pomona, 1960---; Consumer rep.: Calif. State Bd. of Optometry, Calif. State Health Care Servs. Advis. Com. Author: Am. Med. Avarice, 1976; Unfit for Human Consumption, 1971; The High Cost of Dying, 1963; Good Food from Mex., 1951 & 1963; contrb. articles in: Atlantic, Reader's Digest, Modern Drama, Environmental Quality, Progressive, Pageant, Coronet, Frontier, New West, and others. Named Outstanding Prof., Cal. State Coll. and Univ. System, 1978; Outstanding Prof., Cal. State Poly. Univ., 1977, 78. Mem.: Wash. Press Club; PEN; Nat. Council of Tchrs. of Engl.; Modern Language Assn. of Am.; Calif. Assn. of Tchrs. of English. Hobby: photog. Home: 437 Crane Blvd., L.A., CA 90065; Office: Cal. State Polytechnic Univ., Pomona, CA 91768.

HARNEY, DAVID MORAN
Attorney at Law
b. June 30, 1924, Marysville, Calif.; s. George Richard and Eileen (Daly) Harney; J.D., USC, 1948; m. Evelyn Turner, Quantico, Va., Mar. 17, 1945; sons: Brian Patrick, b. July 24, 1949; David Turner, b. Mar. 30, 1954. Career: Research atty., Dist. Ct. of Appeal, 1948-49; admitted to Calif. bar, 1949; assoc. Wright & Garrett law firm, L.A. 1949-51; partner, Harney and Moore law firm, L.A., 1951---. 1st Lt., U.S.M.C. (1942-45), WW II. Mem.: bd. dirs., Internat. Acad. of Trial Lawyers; Am. Bar Assn.; Century Club, Loyola Univ.; USC Law Review, 1948; Hobby: golf. Home: 2222 Nottingham Ave., L.A., CA 90027; Office: 650 S. Grand Ave., L.A., CA 90017.

HARRAH, ROBERT EUGENE
Manufacturing Company President
b. May 31, 1916, Riverside, Wash.; s. William Franklin and Virginia (Clark) Harrah; stu., Taft Jr. Coll., 1934-36; m. Jayne Ann Knoblock, Aug. 10, 1937, Huntington Park, daus.: Margie Lee (Handley), b. Sept. 29, 1939; Bonnie Jean (Rutler), b. Oct. 16, 1941. Career: app. machinist, Baash Ross Tool Co., 1936-41; with Mare Island Navy Yard, 1941-42, owner-opr. machine shop, 1943-52; owner of sawmill, 1952-68; founder, Pres., Remco Hydraulics, Willits, Calif., 1957-68; owner, pres., Harrah Industries, Willits, 1968---; owner, chmn. bd., Microphor, Inc., Willits, 1972---; chmn., chief exec. officer, Stanray Corp., Chicago, 1975-77, dir. 1969-77; asst. to pres. and mem. bd. dirs., Abex Corp., N.Y., 1977---; mem. bd. govs., Railway Progress Inst., Wash., D.C., 1977---; U.S. Corps of Engrs., Panama Canal, 1943. Inventor non-metallic cylinders, two-qt. low flush toilet; pres. bd. of trustees, Howard Hosp., 1968---; trustee, Willits H.S., 1949-59; mem. Willits Planning Comm.; mem. Willits City Council. Mem.: Rotary, 1950-70, past pres.; Shriners, 1946---; Masons. Res.: 451 E. Hill Rd., Willits, CA 95490; Office: P.O.B. 490, Willits, CA 95490.

HARRIS, HON. GEORGE B.
Senior United States District Judge
b. Aug. 16, 1901, S.F.; s. Bernard Dugan and Gertrude (Howard) Harris; ed. Sacred Heart Coll. 1919; LL.B., Univ. of S.F., 1926; m. Aileen Duffy, July 22, 1930; chil.: Gail Sheridan, b. June 2, 1934. Career: Admitted to Calif. State Bar, 1926; apptd. Judge, Municipal Ct., Calif., July 1941; apptd. Fed. Judge, U.S. Dist. Ct., 1946, Chief Judge, 1962---. Mem.: Calif. Pioneers, The Family Club, Bohemian Club. Knight of Malta, Knight St. Gregory. Catholic. Home: 1812 Broadway, S.F., CA; Office: Fed. Bldg., 450 Golden Gate Ave., S.F., CA 94102.

HARRIS, JIMMIE
General Counsel, Daylin Inc.
b. July 27, 1945, Winona, Miss., s. James Edward and Rebecca (Bennett) Harris; BSEE, Univ. Ill., 1967; J.D., Univ. of Calif. (Boalt Hall), 1972. Career: Attorney, Irell & Manella, 1972-76; Secty. and Gen. Counsel, Daylin, Inc., L.A., 1976---. Mem.: Kappa Alpha Psi, Am. Bar Assn., Beverly Hills Bar Assn., L.A. Co. Bar Assn., State Bar of Calif. Rec.: snow skiing. Home: 10990 Rochester Ave., No. 211, L.A., CA 90024; Office: 10960 Wilshire Blvd., L.A., CA 90024.

HARRIS, MICHAEL GENE
Professor — Optometrist
b. Sept. 20, 1942, S.F.; s. Morry and Gertrude (Epstein)

Harris); B.S., Univ. Calif., Berkeley, 1964, M. Optometry, 1965, O.D., 1966, M.S., 1968; D.D., U.L.C., 1974; m. Andrea Elaine Berman, Bov. 29, 1969, Euclid, Oh.; son, Matthew Benjamin, b. Nov. 19, 1976. Career: Instr., Oh. State Univ., 1968-69; Asst. and Assoc. Clin. Prof., Univ. of Calif., Berkeley, 1969-76, Lectr., 1976---; dir., Contact Lens Extended Care Clinic, 1969---; Assoc. chief, Contact Lens Serv., 1974---. Contbr. chptrs. to 3 books, 50+ sci. papers, 2 syllabuses. Democrat, mem. Young Democrats, President's Club, Leadership Club. Rec.: chess, racquetball. Home: 43 Corte Royal, Moraga, CA 94556; Office. Univ. of Calif., Sch. of Optometry, Berkeley, CA 94720.

HARRIS, MICHAEL R.
Historian
b. Aug. 23, 1936, Boise, Id.; s. Sydney and Merle Harris; B.A., Stanford Univ., 1958, M.A., 1962, Ph.D., 1966; Career: Administrator, Instr., and asst. prof. of History, Pomona Coll., 1964-69; Claremont Grad. Sch., 1969-72; dir. Inst. for Study of Change in Higher Edn., 1969-70, asst. dean, 1970-72, asst. prof. of Hist., 1969-72; bd. of editors, Dialogue Magazine, 1966-76; bd. of dirs., Mormon History Assn., 1973-76. Author: Five Counter-Revolutionists in Higher Education, 1970; various articles. Mem. Town Hall of Calif. Home: 462 Landfair Ave., L.A., CA 90024.

HARRIS, NANCY TOLL
Association Executive
b. Feb. 14, 1929, L.A.; d. Gerald Sidney and Maisie Helen (Maxfield) Toll; B.A., Stanford Univ., 1950; m. Dan Edward Harris, Mar. 22, 1952, L.A.; chil.: Anne Joy b. Jan. 28, 1953; Sally Marie, b. Dec. 11, 1954; Peter Toll, b. Nov. 16, 1956. Career: with Mental Health Assn. of Orange Co., 1971---: dir. of Volunteers, 1971-72, assoc. dir., 1972-78, Exec. Dir., 1978---; mem., chmn. and edn. chmn., Orange Co. Dirs. of Volunteers in Agencies, 1972-76; mem. Assn. for Adminstrn. of Vol. Servs., 1974-77; mem. Orange Co. Assn. of Human Resource Adminstrs., 1974---; mem. advis. com., State of Calif. Health Tng. Center, 1974---; profl. mem. United Way of Orange Co., North/South, 1977-78; Vol. Activities: United Way, 1966---; United Crusade, 1964-70; Nat. ARC, Grey Lady, 1952, fund raising, 1956; PTA, 1958-71; Resthaven Comm. Mental Health Center, 1965-75; Vol. Bureau, L.A. Region, Voluntary Action Center, 1965-72; Stanford Club of San Fernando Valley, 1963---. Home: 109 Via Ravenna, Newport Beach, CA 92663; Office: 2110 E. First St., Suite 101, Santa Ana, CA 92705.

HARRIS, WILLIAM T.J.
Insurance Executive — Civic Leader
b. Oct. 28, 1910, Howe, Okla.; s. Henry J. and Susan Frances (Wise) Harris; L.B. City Coll. 1931-33; m. Norma G. Matthews, Long Beach, Nov. 23, 1934. Career: Clerk, L.B. Pub. Lib. 1929-33; underwriter, N.Y. Life Ins. Co., L.B. 1933---, agcy. (N.Y. Life Ins.) orgn., L.A. 1939-40, mem. agts. adv. council, 1950-52, 1957, v.p. (2nd term); life ins. courses, Bus. and Tech. Div., L.B. City Coll. 1947---; apptd. L.B. Civil Serv. Comm., 1951, chmn. 5 yrs. Pub. Speaker on ins. and subjs. of comm. interest. Sgt., U.S.Army Inf. (1942-45), WW II. Awards: Chartered Life Underwriter (highest edn. hon. in life ins.) by Am. Coll. of Life Underwriters, 1948; Mem.: Civil Serv. Commr., City of L.B., 1951-74; L.B. Kiwanis Club, bd. of dirs., 1947-49, 1951-55, 1960, pres. 1954, secty. 1960; N.Y. Life Ins. hon. clubs (continuous qualification); 1936---; pres. L.B. City Coll. Alumni Assn. 1936; pres. 20-30 Club of L.B. 1938 (hon. 1941---; pres. L.B. chpt., Natl. Assn. of Life Underwriters, 1941, bd. dirs., various coms., chmn. L.B. Rec. Comm. 1941-43; bd. dirs., L.B. chpt., Am. Red Cross, 1941-42, 1946; bd. dirs., L.B. Kiwanis Club 1947-49, 1951-55, pres. 1954, 60; Am. Soc. of C.L.U. 1948---; campaign chmn., L.B. Comm. Chest, 1951, exec. com.-treas. 1952; bd. dirs., YMCA 1952-58; (charter) Long Beach-Orange Chpt. C.L.U. 1956---; bd. dirs., L.B. Comm. Hosp., 1956-65, v.p. 1957-59, pres. 1960-65. Methodist. Hobby: pub. speaking, community activities. Rec.: fishing. Home: 640 Santiago Ave., Long Beach, CA 90814.

HARSH, J. RICHARD
Educational Testing Company Executive
b. July 14, 1918, L.A.; s. Charles E. and Bertha M. Harsh; B.S., Occidental Coll., M.A., 1948; m. Barbara Nobles, Oct. 15, 1942, L.A.; chil.: Sandra (Soutar), b. 1943; Patricia (Jenkins), b. 1947; Lanita (Berg), b. 1949; Janet (Hames), b. 1953; Mary, b. 1957; Richard, b. 1960. Career: Instr. Occidental Coll., 1940-42; lectr., Occidental Coll., 1947-53; Cons. and asst. dir., Research

& Guidance, Office of L.A. Co. Supt. of Schs., 1947-63; dir., L.A. Office, Ednl. Testing Serv., 1963---; lectr. in Psychology, USC, 1955-57, Cal. State Univ., L.A., 1957-59, Claremont Grad. Sch., 1962-75. Contbr. articles in edn., psychology, evaluation to profl. journs.; pub. Standardized Reading, Math and Language Tests. Pres., Calif. Assn. Sch. Psychologists; pres., Calif. Ednl. Data Processing; exec. bd. mem., Calif. Edn. Research Assocs. Served to 2d. Lt., USAAF, 1942-45; U.S. Serv. Forces, 1945-46. Protestant. Rec.: High Sierra trips, tennis. Home: 5254 Dahlia Dr., L.A., CA 90041; Office: 2200 Merton Ave., L.A., CA 90041.

HARTH, LENORA FUSON
Community Leader
m. Hampton Addison, Jr.; 1 dau. Deborah Leah. Career: Community service, Southern Calif. Mem.: So. Calif. Symphony Women's Com.; Town & Gown of USC; Nat. Charity League, Coronets Jr. Charity League; Ebell Club; Capitol Hill of Wash., D.C.; Hon. Order Kentucky Colonels. Clubs: La Jolla Beach & Tennis Club, Santa Anita Turf Club, Santa Fe Hunt Club, Wilshire Country Club. Homes: 112 Fremont Pl., L.A., CA 90005 and 8110 El Paseo Grande, La Jolla, CA 92037.

HARTNACK, CARL EDWARD
Chairman, Security Pacific National Bank
b. Apr. 9, 1916, L.A.; s. Johannes C. and Kate (Schoneman) Hartnack; ed. Pac. Coast Banking Sch., Univ. Wash.; grad. (hons.) Am. Inst. of Banking; m. Roberta De Luce, L.A., Sept. 6, 1939; chil.: Richard, b. Nov. 17, 1945; Robert, b. May 5, 1950; Gretchen, b. June 26, 1951. Career: Security Pac. Natl. Bank, L.A., 1934---, supv. 1934-56, v.p. 1956-61, sr. v.p. 1961-69, pres.-dir. 1969-78, chmn. 1978---. Dir.: Pac. Indemnity Co., Superior Farming Co., Whittaker Corp. Mem.: Stock Exch., F&AM, La Jolla Country Club, L.A. Country Club, Calif. Club. Hobbies: garden, boating, photog. Office: 333 S. Hope St., L.A., CA 90051.

HASSOUNA, FRED
Architect — Planner — Professor
b. Mar. 26, 1918, Cairo, Egypt; naturalized U.S. Citizen 1953; s. Amin Sami and Dawlat (Mansour) Hassouna; diploma in architecture with 1st class honors, Higher Sch. of Fine Arts, Cairo, 1940; diploma in Egyptology with 1st class honors, Univ. of Cairo, 1944; diploma in civic design, Univ. of Liverpool, Engl., 1946; M.Arch., USC, 1950, M.S. in pub. adminstrn., 1950; Licensed architect in Calif., 1956---, in Texas 1955---; m. Verna Arlene Dotter, Mar. 9, 1950, L.A. Career: Arch., Curator & Dir. of excavations, Cairo Mus., Egypt, 1940-44; lectr. in Egyptology & Arch., Univ. of Alexandria, Egypt, 1944-45, 1947-48; dir. of Planning, Huyton-With-Roby Urban Dist. Council, Huyton, England, 1946-47; lectr. in City and Regional Planning, USC, 1950-55; Arch. with Kistner, Wright and Wright, Architects and Engrs., L.A., 1952-53; Proj. Arch., Albert C. Martin and Assocs., Architects and Engrs., L.A., 1956-58; Prof. and Head, Dept. of Arch., E. L.A. Coll., 1958-75; Prof. and Head, Dept. of Arch., Saddleback Coll., Mission Viejo, 1975---. Named Fellow, Internat. Inst. of Arts and Letters, 1961---. Pres., Calif. Council of Archtl. Edn., 1977, v.p. 1976, dir. 1973---. Mem.: AIA, past chmn. of Edn. Com. and Students Affairs Com. in Pasadena and Foothill chpt.; Am. Inst. of Planners; Indsl. Tech. Advisory Bd., Cal. State Univ., Long Beach, 1963---; Archtl. Advisory Com., Rio Hondo Coll., 1967---; Advis. Com. on Environmental & Interior Design, Univ. Calif., Irvine, 1976---; Liaison Com. on Arch., Landscape Arch. & Urban and Regional Planning in Higher Edn. in Calif. Hobbies: travel, photog. Rec.: tennis. Home: 31242 Flying Cloud Dr., Laguna Niguel, CA 92677; Office: Saddleback Coll., 28000 Marguerite Pkwy., Mission Viejo, CA 92692.

HATCH, SCOTT ALAN
Editor
b. Apr. 26, 1952, Milwaukee, Wis.; s. Edgar Jerome and Charlotte Dorothy Hatch; B.A. in polit. sci. and hist., Univ. of Colo., 1975; M.A., polit. sci., Marquette Univ., 1977; candidate for J.D., Southwestern Univ., 1980; m. Caren E. Smith, May 1, 1972, Colorado Springs, Colo.; 1 dau. Alison Eileen, b. Mar. 9, 1977. Career: Apptd. news editor, The Commentator (legal journal, Southwestern Univ. Sch. of Law), 1977; editor, 1978; also apptd. assoc. editor, Freedom of Information Com. Bulletin, 1978. Recipient: academic scholarship, Marquette Univ. Grad. Sch. of Political Sci., 1976-77. Profl. publ.: Carter's Human Rights Hypocrisy, L.A. Press, 1978. Pres., St. Eugene's Christian Youth Orgn., 1969-70. Mem.: Phi Alpha Theta, Phi Alpha Delta. Rec.: writing. Home: 2302

N. Catalina, Burbank, CA 91504; Office: 675 S. Westmoreland Ave., L.A., CA.

HATLER, MARGARET ISABELLE
Lumber Company Executive
b. Aug. 16, 1936, Algerine (Tuolumne Co.), Calif.; d. James M. and Dollie E. Wilkie; 4th generation Tuolumne Co. family; student, Shasta Jr. Coll., Redding, 1954; m. Sidney "Bud" Hatler (Supr. 2nd Dist., Tuolumne Co.), Apr. 24, 1955, Sonora, Calif.; chil.: Rocky Ria (Hoheisel), b. Jan. 14, 1956; James Daniel, b. May 27, 1957; Wade Douglas, b. Dec. 13, 1958; Cindy Lou, b. Aug. 5, 1960; Arleen Marine, b. Feb. 18, 1962. Career: Worked in family owned Hatler Lumber Co., 1959---: gang saw operator, off bearer, forklift driver, log scaler, lumber tallier, bookkeeper, secty., office mgr. Apptd. trustee, Sonora Union High Sch. 1978---. Pres., Sonora Union H.S. PTSA 1975-77, auditor, Tuolumne Co. PTA Council, 1975-76, 1st v.p., 1976-77, District 8 PTA Secty., 1976-77. Vol. Belleview Parent Club mem. 1960-75; vol. tchrs. aid, Belleview Grammar Sch. 1972. Vol. chaperone, High sch. hist. students trip to east coast: Washington, D.C., Boston and New York, 1976, 1977, 1978; drama students chaperone to Ashland, Ore. Shakespeare Festival, 1978. Temporary Housemother to many children in need. Mem.: Tuolumne Co. Taxpayers Assn., 1969---; Golden ERA Parlor 99 Native Daughters of Golden West. Hobby: Young people. Rec.: reading, jewelry. Home: Rt. 3, Box 552, Sonora, CA 95370; Office: 13700 Big Hill Rd., Sonora, CA 95370.

HAUK, A. ANDREW
United States District Judge
b. Dec. 29, 1912, Denver, Colo.; s. Al A. and Pearl M. A. (Woods) Hauk; ed. A.B., Regis Coll., Denver, Colo. 1935; LL.B., Cath. Univ. of Am., Sch. of Law, Wash. D.C., 1938; J.S.D., Yale Law Sch., New Haven, Conn. 1942; m. Jean Nicolay, Carmel, Calif., Aug. 30, 1941; chil.: Susan, b. June 20, 1946. Career: Spec. asst. to atty. gen. and counsel for govt., Antitrust Div., U.S. Dept. of Justice (L.A., Pac. Coast, Denver, Wash.), 1939-41; asst. U.S. Dist. Atty., L.A. 1941-42; pvt. law practice with firm Adams, Duque and Hazeltine, 1946-52; pvt. law practice-asst. counsel, Union Oil Co., L.A. 1952-64; judge, Superior Ct., L.A. Co. 1964-66; U.S. Dist. Judge, Central Dist. of Calif. 1966---. Lt., Lt. Comdr., USNR Naval Intelligence (1942-46), WW II. Mem.: L.A. C. of C.; World Affairs Council; L.A. Co., Calif. State, Am. and Fed. Bar Assns.; Lawyers Club of L.A., Am. Judiciary Soc., Am. Legion, Navy League, Far West Ski Assn., Knights of Columbus; bd., Yale Law Sch. Assoc. of So. Calif.; Clubs: Yale of So. Calif., Newman, Shadow Mt. (Palm Desert), Valley Hunt, Jonathan. Hobby: piano, accordion. Rec.: skiing, tennis. Home: 1408 Ridge Way, Pasa., CA 91106; Office: U.S. Courthouse, 312 N. Spring St., L.A., CA 90012.

HAUN, MARVIN GENE
Attorney at Law
b. Dec. 11, 1928, Dinuba, Calif.; s. Oscar Franklyn and Kathryn Reide (Warford) Haun; A.A., Stockton Jr. Coll., 1948; A.B., Coll. of Pacific, 1950; LL.D., Hastings Coll. of Law, 1958; m. Elizabeth A. Quist, Dec. 9, 1961, Hayward; chil.: Catherine, b. June 25, 1963; Steven, b. Apr. 28, 1966. Career: Deputy Co. Counsel, Santa Clara Co., San Jose, 1960-65; partner, law firm of Quaresma, Avera, Benya, Hall & Haun, Fremont, Calif., 1966--- (spec. in hosp., sanitation, condemnation, planning and real estate); Hearing officer, Alameda Co. Civil Serv. Commn., 1973---; bd. dir., Wash. Township Counseling Serv. and Wash. Township Legal Assis. Center, Fremont; Panel mem., Am. Arbitration Assn., S.F., 1963---; atty. for Wash. Township Hosp. Dist., 1966---; atty. for Union Sanitary Dist., 1968---; atty. for New Haven Unified Sch. Dist., 1976---; atty. for Livermore Valley Jt. Unified Sch. Dist. Ednl. Facilities Corp., 1976---. USAF, 1951-55, Korea; decorated Korean and UN Medal. Mem.: Calif. Bar Assn., Am. Soc. Hosp. Attys.; Calif. Assn. of Sanitation Agencies; Assn. of Calif. Hosp. Dist.; Alameda Co. Bar Assn.; Fremont C. of C., pres. 1972, bd. dir. 1970-76; Fremont Rotary, pres. 1976, bd. dir. 1974-77; Protestant. Rec.: sailing, camping. Home: 41539 Fordham Ct., Fremont, CA 94538; Office: 37323 Fremont Blvd., Fremont, CA 94536.

HAWKINS, JOSEPH KEY
Corporate President
b. Aug. 13, 1926, Pomona, Calif.; s. Joseph K. and Helen E. (Hourigan) Hawkins; student, Lignan Univ., Canton, China, 1948-49; Venares Univ., Benares, India, 1949-50; B.Sc., Stanford Univ., 1951; M.S., 1952; m. 1953; div.

1977; chil.: Ann Patrick, b. Mar. 17, 1954; Torrey Sue, b. Oct. 23, 1955; Gale Britta, b. Apr. 1, 1957. Career: Research engr., Douglas Aircraft, El Segundo, 1952-54; dir. of engring., Alwac Corp., Hawthorne, 1954-58; dept. mgr., Philco-Ford, Newport Beach, 1959-68; pres., Robot Research, Inc., San Diego, 1969---. Author: Circuit Design of Digital Computers, Wiley, 1968; co-author, Advances in Information Sciences III, Plenum, 1970; editor, Pattern Recognition, Spartan, 1970; contbd. 25 articles profl. journs. AUS, 1946-48. Mem.: IEEE; Phi Beta Kappa. Hobby: study of law. Home: 3873 Ingraham St., D-104, San Diego, CA 92109; Office: 7591 Convoy Ct., San Diego, CA 92111.

HAWKINS, MYRTLE HELEN
Artist
b. June 17, 1923, Merritt, B.C., Canada; d. Fred and Lydia Petznick; Student Hartnell Coll., San Jose State Univ., A.A., West Valley Coll., 1970; Univ. of Calif.; art student with Maynard Stewart, 1961; Thomas Leighton, 1963; m. William Edwin Hawkins, Mar. 29, 1952, San Jose, Calif.; chil.: Debra Ann, b. Feb. 3, 1954; Bruce Alan, b. Dec. 20, 1956. Career: Tchr. painting to handicapped, Calif. State Dept. of Vocational Rehabilitation, 1969-71, privately---; give lectures and judge art shows; writer, Lansford Pub. Co., free-lance writer; painter in all media in own studio. Commissioned portraits and works in public collections in U.S., Canada, England & Spain. Since 1960 has won over 45 awards in art including 1st place in nat. art competition, Easter Soc., 1965; 1st oil conservative, Cherry Chase Festival; popular vote, Santa Clara Library annual, 1977; Best of Show in S.F. Zellerbach Show; Le Foli Award, 1972. Named Woman of Achievement by San Jose Mercury News, 1973 and 1974. Author: Art as Therapy, Recreation, and Rehabilitation for the Handicapped, Lansford Pub. Co. Organizer, Santa Clara Art Assn. Originator, annual bus tours of art studios to benefit Triton Museum of Art. Pres. Allied Artists of Santa Clara Co., 1972-73; v.p., Santa Clara Assn., 1967, 1969. Mem.: Gualala Arts; Fellow mem., Am. Artists Profl. League of N.Y.; Soc. of Western Artists; charter mem., Santa Clara Art Assn.; co-founder, Calif. Writer's Assn. 1st Congressional Ch., Retreat leader, Mission Springs, 1972. Hobbies: cooking, playing mandolin. Rec.: reading, swimming. Home and studio: 646 Bucher Ave., Santa Clara, CA 95051.

HAWKINS, WILLIS M.
President, Lockheed-California Company
b. Dec. 1, 1913, Kansas City, Mo.; s. Willis M., Sr. and Elizabeth (Daniels) Hawkins Walter; nephew, Charles Daniels, music composer; B.S., Aero. Engr., Univ. Mich., 1937; hon. D.Eng., Univ. of Mich., 1965; hon. D.Sc., Ill. Coll., 1966; m. Anita Ellen Stanfill, June 22, 1940, Van Nuys; chil.: Nancy Gay (Bostick), b. Mar. 2, 1943; Willis M. III, b. June 28, 1945; James Walter, b. Aug. 2, 1956. Career: with Lockheed Aircraft Corp.: designer, 1937-44; Dept. Mgr., 1944; chief of prelim. design, 1949; Lockheed Missiles & Space Co. Chief Engr., 1953; Asst. Gen. Mgr. 1959; Vice Pres. of Parent Corp., 1960; Vice Pres. & Gen. Mgr. Space Div., 1961; Corp. V.P. Sci. and Engr., 1962, 1966; Sr. V.P., 1969; Bd. Dirs., Lockheed Corp., 1970---; pres., Lockheed-California Co., 1976---. Dir. Riverside Res. Inst.; R&D Assocs.; Wackenhut Corp. Asst. Secty. (R&D), U.S. Army, 1963-66. Contbr. to numerous tech. publs. Awarded Distinguished Civilian Serv. Medals by USN, AUS, and NASA. Mem.: Tau Beta Pi; Nat. Acad. of Engrs.; Fellow, Am. Inst. of Aeron. & Aerospace; Fellow, Royal Aero. Soc. Protestant. Hobby: flying, antique airplanes and cars: Home: 4249 Empress Ave., Encino, CA 94136; Office: P.O.B. 551, Burbank, CA 91520.

HAWLEY, PHILIP M.
President, Carter Hawley Hale Stores
b. July 29, 1925, Portland, Ore.; s. Willard P., Jr. and Dorothy E. (Metschan) Hawley; undergrad. Reed Coll., Ore. and Stanford Univ.; B.S., Univ. of Calif., Berkeley, 1946; Harvard Univ. Grad Sch. of Bus. Adm. (mgmt. pgm.) 1967; m. Mary Follen, L.A., May 31, 1947; chil.: Diane (Mrs. Robert Bruce Johnson), b. Dec. 17, 1948; Willard, b. July 29, 1950; Philip, Jr., b. Aug. 7, 1952; John b. Nov. 23, 1954; Victor, b. Aug, 23, 1959; Edward, b. July 15, 1963; Erin, b. Mar. 19, 1965; George, b. Jan. 12, 1968. Career: Merrill, Lynch, Pierce, Fenner and Smith, 1946-48; dept. store and specialty stores, Portland and Salem, Ore., 1948-58; Carter Hawley Hale Stores, Inc. 1958---, pres.-dir. Dir.: Bank of Am., Pac. Telephone and Telegraph Co., Walt Disney Prodns., Atlantic Richfield Co.; v.p. Natl. Retail Merchants Assn.; trustee, Calif. Inst. of Tech. and the Huntington Lib. Ensign, USN, 1944-46, WW II. Awards: Award of Merit, L.A. Jr. C. of C. 1974; Calif.

Industrialist of Yr. by Calif. Mus. Sci. and Ind. 1975; Hon. Comdr. of Most Excellent Order of Brit. Empire, Great Britain; Coro Pub. Affairs Award, 1978; Knight Comdr. of Star of Solidarity of Repub. of Italy. Mem.: chmn. L.A. Energy Conservation Com. 1973-74; Phi Beta Kappa, Beta Alpha Psi, Beta Gamma Sigma. Clubs: Calif., Jonathan, Newport Harbor Yacht; Pac.-Union, S.F.; Multnomah, Portland. Episcopalian. Hobby: book collecting. Rec.: boating. Office: 500 S. Flower St., L.A., CA 90071.

HAY, JOHN THOMAS
Executive Vice President, State Chamber of Commerce
b. Jan. 30, 1921, Lincoln, Nebr.; s. Ronald Harding and Luella (Sands) Hay; bro. Richard Sands Hay, D.D.S., ed. B.S., Univ. Nebr. 1942; Harvard Grad. Sch. of Bus. 1943; m. Mable Secund, Lincoln, May 26, 1942; chil.: Susan, Sally, John T., Jr. Career: Secty., Colby Ch. of C., Kan. 1946-47; mgr. Columbus C. of C., Nebr., 1947-51; asst. mgr. Greater Muskegon C. of C., Mich. 1959-67; mgr. 1952-59; exec. v.p. St. Paul Area C. of C., Minn. 1959-67; exec. v.p. Calif. C. of C. 1967---. Co-founder, Mich. State C. of C. 1958, 59; bd. dirs. Jaycee, Nebr., Mich. (10 yrs); v.p. Great Lakes States Ind. Devel. Council, Mich. 1958-59; 5-man Citizens Adv. Com., Mich. Senate; chmn. Minn. C. of C. Execs. Bus. Climate Com. 1960-63; chmn. Inst. for C. of C. Execs., Univ. of Colo. 1965, bd. of regents (6 yrs.), inst. grad. and instr.; first group of 32 Chamber Execs. to receive Certified Chamber Exec. title, Houston, Tex. 1965; pres. Minn. C. of C. Execs. (4 yrs); co-orgn. State C. of C., Minn. 1966; chmn. Gov's. Blue Ribbon Com., Summer Youth Job Campaign, 1968, 69, Gov's. Com. 1970. Capt., QMC, ETO, U.S. Army (4 yrs.). Award: 4 Battle Stars; Distinguished Serv. Award, Greater Muskegon's Outstanding Young Man of Yr., 1954; FOYM Award (one of 5 outstanding young men, Mich. 1955; mgr. Chamber programs, Muskegon, St. Paul, Calif., recd. 19 Freedoms Found Awards, Outstanding U.S. Chamber Pgm. Work Award, Muskegon, 1958, St. Paul 1969, 62; St. Paul Chamber one of first 7 to receive Accreditation Award. Mem.: Clubs: Sutter, Comstock, Sacto., Presbyterian. Home: 1316 San Augustine Way, Sacto., CA; Office: 455 Capitol Mall, Sacto., CA 95814.

HAYAKAWA, SAMUEL (SAM) ICHIYE
U.S. Senator
b. July 18, 1906, Vancouver, B.C., Canada, Naturalized U.S. Cit.; B.A., Engl., Univ. of Manitoba, 1927; M.A., Engl., McGill Univ., 1928; Ph.D., English, Am. Lit., Univ. of Wisc., 1935; m. Margedant Peters, May 29, 1937 (Mrs. Hayakawa is editor of "Fremontia," Journ. of the Calif. Native Plant Soc.); sons, Alan Romer, b. July 16, 1956; Mark, b. Feb. 6, 1949; dau., Wynne, b. May 17, 1951. Career: mem. faculty, Univ. of Wisc., 1936-39; Ill. Inst. of Tech., 1939-47; Univ. of Chicago, 1950-55; prof. of Engl., S.F. State Coll., 1955-68; acting pres., 1968, pres., 1968-73, apptd. Pres. Emeritus, S.F. State Univ., 1973---; elected to U.S. Senate for 6-yr. term beginning Jan. 3, 1977---. Internationally renowned semanticist; Author: Oliver Wendell Holmes: Selected Poetry and Prose, with Critical Introduction, 1939; Language in Action, 1941 (Book of the Month Club selection); Language in Thought and Action, 1949, 4th ed., 1978, trans. 10 langs.; Language, Meaning and Maturity, 1954; Our Language and Our World, 1959; The Use and Misuse of Language, 1962; Symbol, Status and Personality, 1963. Editor: Funk and Wagnalls' Modern Guide to Synonyms, 1968; ETC., A Review of General Semantics, 1943-70. Columnist: Chicago Defender, 1942-47; Ill. Register and Tribune Syndicate, 1970-76. Certified psychologist, State of Calif. Fellow, Am. Psychological Assn., Am. Sociological Assn., AAAS, Royal Soc. of Arts. Mem. Senate Committees: Agri., Nutrition and Forestry; Budget; Human Resources; also Republican Policy Com. and Nat. Republican Senatorial Com. Hobbies: Collector of African Sculpture, Chinese ceramics, old jazz records. Rec.: tap-dancing, fishing, scuba diving. Home: Mill Valley, Marin Co., CA; Office: 6217 Dirksen Senate Ofc. Bldg., Wash. D.C. 20510.

HAYES, ALBERT E., JR.
Consulting Engineer
b. Dec. 30, 1920, S.F.; s. Albert E. and Virginia (Clark) Hayes; B.S., MIT, 1942; M.S., Calif. Western Univ., 1976, Ph.D., 1976; m. Mollie Milliken, July 4, 1976, Nevada; sons, Douglas Wallace, b. 1957; Robert Clark, b. 1947. Career: Electrical Engr., 1942---; pres. Albert Hayes and Assoc., Registered Profl. Engrs., 1978---. Holder of five issued U.S. Patents. Contbr. numerous articles, tech. journs. Served as civilian sci., Natl. Defense Research Com. sponsored opns., WW II; cited for Effective Serv. in radar research, 1946. Mem.: Order

of Quiet Birdmen, 1970---; Conn. Wireless Assn., 1948---; MIT Club of So. Calif., 1976---. Atheist. Rec.: pvt. pilot. Home: 2512 Monterey Pl., Fullerton, CA 92633; Office: P.O.B. 2946, Fullerton CA 92633.

HAYES, THOMAS JAY, III
Engineering Company President
b. Aug. 26, 1914, Omaha, Nebr.; s. Maj.Gen. Thos. J. and Mary Clarkson (Ringwalt) Hayes; B.S., U.S. Mil. Acad., West Point, 1936; Grad., Indsl. Coll. of Armed Forces, 1957-58; M.S., MIT, 1939; m. Jean Pedley (dau., Col. T.A. Pedley Jr.), Nov. 20, 1942, Nassau, Bahamas; chil.: Capt. Thomas J., IV (dec.); Mary (m. Roy R.B. Attride); Barbara (m. Capt. David J. Basham). Career: 2d Lt. to Maj. Gen., U.S. Army Corps of Engrs., 1936-69 (during WW II, Korean War, Vietnam Opns.); Maj. Gen., 1960-69; Maj. Gen., USA ret. 1969; pres. and chief exec. ofcr., IECO (Internat. Engr. Co., Inc.) hdqtrs. S.F., 1969---. Mem.: bd. of engrs. for Rivers & Harbors, 1967-69; Coastal Engring. Research Bd. 1967-69; Fed. Exec. Bd. 1967-69. Pres., Cia. Internacional de Ingenieria S.A., 1969---; pres., IECO-Afrique Centrale, 1972---; v.p., Morrison Knudsen Co., Inc., 1971-76; dir., Internat. Road Fedn., 1978---. Fellow: Am. Soc. of Civil Engrs., Soc. of Am. Mil. Engrs. Elected to Nat. Acad. of Engring., 1975. Mil. Awards incl.: 2 Distinguished Service Medals (Army), 3 Legion of Merit Medals (Army), AF Commendation Medal, Navy Antarctic Serv. Medal. Hon. Citizen: Wash., D.C., Little Rock, Mobile. Clubs: Press Club, Bankers Club, Engrs. Club, Presidio Army Golf Club, Belvedere Tennis Club. Episcopalian. Hobbies: hist., genealogy, philately. Rec.: fencing. Home: 2646 Chestnut St., S.F., CA 94123; Office: 220 Montgomery St., S.F., CA 94104.

HAYTIN, HAROLD A.
President, Telecor, Inc.
b. Aug. 17, 1918, Denver, Colo.; s. Alexander and Bessie Haytin; B.A., UCLA 1940; UCLA Grad. Sch. of Mgmt.; m. Lois Lasker, St. Paul, Minn., Sept. 4, 1940; son, Dr. Daniel L., b. Apr. 11, 1943; dau. Jane Andrea Hache, b. Nov. 9, 1946. Career: lectr., UCLA Ext., Grad. Sch. of Mgmt.; v.p Hall Distr. Co. 1952-58; exec. v.p Corwin-Hall, 1958-69; pres Newcraft Inc., 1969-72; pres. Telecor Inc. 1972, and chief exec. 1974---; bd. dirs., Louis Roth Co. Mem.: Riviera Country Club. Rec.: golf. Home: 667 Ledo Way, Bel Air, CA 90024; Office: Wilshire-San Vicente Plaza, 8383 Wilshire Blvd., Beverly Hills, CA 90211.

HAYWARD, DAVID KENNETH
Insurance Executive -- City Official
b. Sept. 22, 1929, Midland, Ontario, Can.; s. David P. and Georgina E. Hayward; ed. pub. schs. Can., El Camino Coll., Calif.; B.A. pub. Admin.; B.A. Bus. Admin., La Verne Coll.; m. Margaret Heber, Toronto, Can., June 5, 1950; chil.: Daniel Arthur, b. June 6, 1960; Cheryl Ann, b. Dec. 10, 1960. Career: Est. res. Redondo Beach, 1952; with United Airlines, 1952-57; Auto Club of So. Calif., 1957-62; founder-pres. David K. Hayward Ins. Agcy. 1962---. Elected councilman, City of Redondo Beach, 1961-73; mem. Inter City Hwy. Com. 1961-69, pres. 1965-67; bd. dirs. So. Calif. Rapid Transit Dist. 1965-73; elected Mayor, City of Redondo Beach, 1977---; elected bd. dirs., So. Calif. Rapid Transit Dist., 1977---; Sgt., U.S. Army, Korea, 1953-55. Mem.: L.A. Co. Comm. on Youth, 1971-73; (charter) Palos Verdes Peninsula Council, Navy League of U.S. 1962---, pres. 1968-69; 46th Assembly Dist. Dem. Co. Central Com. 1966-68. Protestant. Hobbies: politics, travel, coins. Home: 2118 Huntington Lane, Redondo Beach, CA 90278; Office: 1926 S. Pacific Coast Hwy., Redondo Beach, CA 90277.

HAYWARD, HOMER M.
Civic Leader — Lumber Company Owner
b. Apr. 11, 1921, Salinas; s. Arthur C. and Nellie (Milhon) Hayward; great-grandson, noted Dias C. Hagle, Sr.; ed. B.S., (bus. adm.) Univ. of Calif. 1943; m. Nancy Eccles, Ogden, Ut.; chil.: Robin Gail, b. June 15, 1956; William Eccles, b. Jan. 30, 1963; Christina Hope, b. Oct. 16, 1965; Wendy Ann, b. Jan. 9, 1968. Career: Pres., Homer T. Hayward Lumber Co., 1946---. Salinas City Councilman, 1949-53; chmn. Monterey Co. Housing Authority, Sept. 1954-69. U.S. Army, Jan. 1943-Nov. 1945, WW II. Mem.: Commonwealth Club of Calif.; Salinas Jr. C. of C.; past pres., N. Calif. Lumbermen's Assn.; Salinas Rotary Club, Sigma Alpha Epsilon, BPOE; past dir. York Sch.; past pres. Calif. Rodeo; past pres. Corral de Tierra Country Club, trustee, Santa Catalina Sch. Found. Rec.: fishing, skiing, hunting, tennis, golf. Home: 10175 Sun Star Road, Monterey, CA 93940; Office: 680 East Romie Lane, Salinas, CA 93901.

HAZARD, JAMES LOCKWOOD
Public Official
b. Apr. 12, 1943, Oakland, Calif.; s. Ellison and Helen Hazard; A.B., Dartmouth Coll., 1966; J.D., Hastings Coll. of Law, Univ. of Calif.; m. Georgia Fowler, June 17, 1967, Darien, Conn.; chil.: Jeffrey, b. Nov. 30, 1971; Kristin, b. Oct. 16, 1973. Career: assoc. law firm, Sellar, Engleking, Hartman & Hazard, 1973-75, partner, 1975---; asst. U.S. Atty., No. Dist. of Calif., 1970-73; elected councilman, City of Walnut Creek, 1974-78; Mayor, 1977. Office: 2815 Mitchell Dr., Walnut Creek, CA 94598.

HAZELTINE, HERBERT S., JR.
Attorney at Law
b. Dec. 12, 1908, Orange Co., Calif.; s. Herbert S. and Emma (Phelps) Hazeltine; A.B., Stanford Univ. 1931; LL.B., Harvard Law Sch. 1934; m. Frances Sue Coffin, L.A., Aug. 5, 1936; chil.: Susan Leith, b. July 11, 1940; Ann Coffin, b. Mar. 14, 1947; Lynn Phelps, b. Aug. 9, 1952. Career: Assoc., Evans and Boyle law firm, 1935-42; sr. partner, Adams, Duque & Hazeltine, 1945---. Dir., Norris Industries, Inc.; pres.-dir., La Bolsa Tile Co.; dir. Prepared Prods. Co.; dir. Metropolitan Life Ins. Co.; Lt. Comdr., USNR (1942-45), WW II. Mem.: secty-dir. Boys Club Found. of So. Calif.; Univ. of So. Calif.; bd. dirs., L.A. chpt., Am. Natl. Red Cross; trustee, The Valley Club of Montecito; The L.A. Cypress Point Golf, Annandale Golf, Calif. Club. Home: 495 Orange Grove Circle, Pasadena, CA; Office: 523 W. 6th St., L.A., CA 90014.

HEADLEE, ROLLAND D.
Executive Director, Town Hall of California
b. Aug. 27, 1916, L.A.; s. Jesse W. and Cleora (Dockeray) Headlee; stu., UCLA; m. Alzora Burgett, May 13, 1939, L.A.; dau. Linda Ann (Pohl). Career: asst. mgr., Finance Assoc., 1946-59; fin. cons., R.D. Headlee & Assocs., 1959-62; acct. exec. and cons., Walter E. Heller & Co., 1962-65; exec. v.p., Genrus Engring. Corp., 1965-67; exec. dir., Town Hall, 1967---: moderator, nat. syndicated weekly radio pgm. "Town Hall on the Air;" moderator, various seminars; 1st Lt., AUS, 1943-46, Gen. Staff Ofcr., Adj. Gen. Dept.; awarded U.S. Army Commendation Medal. Mem.: Town Hall (life), Detroit Economic Club, Mensa, Internat., World Affairs Council, Oceanic Soc., Commonwealth Club, Newcomen Soc., Com. on Foreign Rels., BSA, U.S. Coast Guard Reserve, USAR, Pac. Coast Club. Methodist. Home: 8064 El Manor Ave., L.A., CA 90045; Office: 523 W. 6th St., Suite 232, L.A. CA 90014.

HEARST, DAVID WHITMIRE
Vice President, Hearst Corporation
b. Dec. 2, 1915, NYC; s. William Randolph and Millicent (Willson) Hearst; ed. St. Bernard's Acad., NYC, 1927-30; St. George's Acad., Newport, R.I., 1931-33; Princeton Univ. 1933-36; m. Hope Chandler, NYC, Mar. 23, 1938; chil.: Millicent Phoebe, b. Mar. 24, 1939; David W., Jr., b. Oct. 18, 1944. Career: reporter, N.Y. Journ-Am.; asst. adv. dir., city ed., Baltimore News-Post; classified and display adv., L.A. Evening Herald-Express 1938-44, bus. mgr. 1944-45, gen. mgr. 1945-47, exec. publ. 1947-50, publ. 1950-60; v.p.-dir, Hearst Consolidated Publications, Inc. and Hearst Publ. Co., Inc.; v.p. Hearst Corp.; exec. dir., Hearst Found. Mem.: dir. L.A. Co. Museum; dir. L.A. Community Chest; Maryland Club, Baltimore; Jonathan Club, L.A.; Lakeside Country Club; Calif. Club, L.A. Hobby: flying, photog. Rec.: tennis, swimming, hunting, travel. Office: Hearst Corp., 404 N. Roxbury Dr., Beverly Hills, CA.

HEARST, RANDOLPH APPERSON
Newspaper Publisher
b. Dec. 2, 1915, NYC; s. William Randolph (noted publ., mem. 58th and 59th Congresses, N.Y. State, 1903-07; dec. 1951) and Millicent (Willson) Hearst; grandson of Sen. George Hearst, Calif.; ed. Harvard Univ. 1933-34; Lawrenceville Sch., N.J. 1934; m. Catherine Campbell, Atlanta, Ga., Jan. 12, 1938; chil.: Catherine Millicent, b. Oct. 29, 1939; Virginia Ann, b. Sept. 8, 1949; Patricia Campbell, b. Feb. 20, 1954; Anne Randolph, b. July 29, 1955; Victoria Veronica, b. Dec. 25, 1956. Career: Asst. to Publ. S.F. Call-Bulletin, 1940-44, exec. ed. 1947-49, assoc. publ. 1950, publ. 1950-53; assoc. publ. Oakland Post-Enquirer, 1946-47; pres.-dir. Hearst Publ. Co., Inc., S.F., L.A. 1951-60; pres.-dir. Hearst Consolidated Publs., Inc. 1960-61; pres.-dir.-chief exec. ofcr. 1961-64; dir.-chmn. Hearst Corp., 1965---; dir., Hearst Found.; trustee: William Randolph Hearst Found., 1950---. Capt. Air Transport Command, USAAF (1942-45), WW II. Mem.: S.F. Press

Club, Pac. Union Club, Calif. Hist. Soc.; S.F. Chpt., bd. dirs., Natl Conf. of Chrs. and Jews, Inc.; Piedmont Driving Club, Atlanta, Ga.; Burlingame Country Club. Roman Catholic. Rec.: golf, hunting, fishing. Office: Suite 214, Hearst Bldg., S.F., CA 94103.

HEDLUND, ROBERT L.
Supervisor, Santa Barbara County
b. Oct. 9, 1932, Steilacoom, Wash.; s. Axel and Henny Hedlund; B.A., Alaska Methodist Univ., Anchorage, 1962; M.Ed., Cal. Poly. State Univ., San Luis Obispo, 1969; Ph.D., Univ. of Ut., 1975; m. Erica L. Schalk, June 22, 1956, Am. Lake, Wash.; chil.: Heidi L., b. July 30, 1959; Karen M., b. Nov. 22, 1962. Career: supr., Customer Serv. and Opns., Northwest Airlines 1955-61; instr., secondary sch. and jr. coll., 1962-70; adminstrv. asst., Univ. of Ut., 1970-71; research asst., Ut. State Bd. of Higher Edn., 1971; dissertation research (Addis Ababa Ethiopia), 1971-72; adminstr., Santa Clara Co. Dept. of Edn., 1973-74; elected Supr., 4th Dist., Santa Barbara cO., 1976---. Pres., Lompoc Edn. Assn., 1969-70. Mem. Phi Delta Theta. Hobby: rebuilding and flying antique aircraft. Home: 1301 W. Guava, Lompoc, CA 93436; Office: 401 E. Cypress, Lompoc, CA.

HEFNER, ELIZABETH JOHNSON
Realtor — Investment Counselor
b. June 22, 1936, Oakland, Calif.; d. Willard L. and Alice (Rupp) Johnson; father, past pres., Nat. and Calif. Assns. of Realtors; niece of James G. Fair, gold rush figure and western mining and railroad pioneer; grad. Sarah Dix Hamlin Sch., S.F., 1954; B.A. architecture & design, Univ. of Mich., 1957; B.S. bus. adminstrn., Univ. of Calif., Berkeley, 1959; m. Robert D. Hefner, Aug. 20, 1966, Incline, Nev.; chil.: Richard E., b. 1960; Elizabeth Louise, b. 1963. Career: Owner, broker-realtor, Hefner Associates, Realtors, Sacramento, 1969-76; broker-realtor, investment counselor and developer, Harold Hewit Associates, Inc., Realtors, 1976---. Dir., Lendelof Investment Corp., 1961; pres., Hefner Mgmt. Trust, 1978-79. G.R.I., Grad./Realtors Inst., 1973; CRS, Certified Residential Specialist, 1978; mem. million dollar club. Mem.: D.A.R.; Little Jim Club of S.F. Children's Hosp.; Zeta Tau Alpha frat.; Knights of the Vine of Calif.; U.C. Alumnae Assn.; Sacramento Symyhony League; M.H. de Young Memorial Mus. Soc.; B.S.A. Republican Presbyterian ch., Fleet Commander Mariner's Club, 1956. Hobby: oil & acrylic landscape painting. Rec.: flying. Home: 1321 Grant Lane; Office: 601 University Ave., Suite 130, Sacramento, CA 95825.

HEIDT, JOHN M.
Bank President
b. Dec. 25, 1931; Oceanside, N.Y.; s. Horace and Adaline (Sohns) Heidt; A.B., Stanford Univ., 1954; stu., Pac. Coast Banking Sch., 1965; M.B.A., USC Grad. Sch. of Bus. Adminstrn., 1969; m. Mary Ann Kerans, June 18, 1953, Glendale; chil.: John, b. Sept. 24, 1955; Ann, b. June 24, 1959. Career: Co-owner, mgr., Long Palm Hotel, Palm Springs, 1957-59; with Union Bank, 1959---: exec. v.p., 1971, pres. 1975---. Dir.: Union Bank, Union Bancorp, Union Venture Corp., USC Assocs. Bd. of trustees: St. John's Hosp., Marlborough Sch. Mem. bd. of Councilors of USC. Mem. Am. Bankers Assn., Gov. Council, State V.P. for Calif. Spec. Agent, USAF, 1954-57, Office of Spec. Investigations. Mem.: Phi Gamma Delta; USC Quill and Dagger. Clubs: Metropolitan, Chicago; Calif.; L.A. Country. Rec.: golf. Office: 445 S. Figueroa St., L.A., CA 90071.

HEILBRON, ROBERT FREDERICK
Foundation Executive
b. Dec. 10, 1905, San Diego; s. Carl H. and Katherine (Biewener) Heilbron; B.S., Calif. Inst. of Tech. 1927; B.A., Oxford Univ. 1930, M.A. 1940; m. Beulah Menerey, San Diego, Feb. 10, 1960; son, Robert F., Jr., b. Aug. 10, 1942. Career: Dean, San Diego Jr. Coll. 1946-49; prin. La Jolla H.S. and Point Loma H.S. 1949-56; dir. secondary instruction, S.D. City Schs. 1956-61, asst. supt., Secondary Schs. 1961-62; pres. S.D. Mesa Coll. 1962-68; chmn. bd. Vista Hill Found. 1968---. Mem.: S.D. Rotary Club; dir. Goodwill Inds.; dir. United Way; dir. past pres. San Diego Soc. of Natural Hist.; dir. Hall of Science, First Presbyterian Ch. (elder). Home: 10006 Country View Rd., La Mesa, CA 92041.

HEINDL, CLIFFORD JOSEPH
Physicist — Executive Researcher
b. Feb. 4, 1926, Chicago, Ill.; s. Anton T. and Louise (Fiala) Heindl; B.S., Northwestern Univ. 1947. M.A.

1948; M.A., Columbia Univ. 1950, Ph.D., 1959; stu. Oak Ridge Sch. of Reactor Tech. 1954-55. Career: Sr. physicist, Bendix Aviation Corp. Research Labs., Detroit, 1953-54; asst. sect. chief, atomic energy div., Babcock & Wilson Co., Lynchburg, Va. 1956-58; supv. nuclear and reactor physics group, Jet Propulsion Lab., Pasa., 1959-65; tech. mgr., research and advanced devel., Jet Propulsion Lab., Calif. Inst. of Tech. 1965---. Author: various sci. and tech. papers. Sgt., U.S. Army Med. Corp. (1944-46), WW II. Mem.: Am. Inst. of Aeronautics and Astronautics, Health Physics Soc. Home: 179 Mockingbird Lane, So. Pasa., CA; Office: 4800 Oak Grove Dr., Pasadena, CA 91103.

HEINEMANN, EDWARD HENRY
Consulting Engineer
b. Mar. 14, 1908, Saginaw, Mich.; s. Gustave Christian and Margaret (Schust) Heinemann; stu. pub. schs., Mich. and Calif.; D.Sc. (hon.), Northrop Univ., 1976; m. Zell Shewey, 1959; 1 dau. by previous marriage, Joan (Mrs. William Coffee). Career: engaged as designer and proj. engr., also chief engr. Moreland Aircraft Corp., Internat. Aircraft Corp., Northrop Aircraft Corp., 1931-36; chief engr., El Segundo div. Douglas Aircraft Co., Inc., 1936-58; corp. v.p. in charge combat aircraft engring., 1958-60; in charge design, devel. Navy BT, SBD Dauntless Dive Bombers, Navy R3D transport, A-20 Air Force Havoc attack bomber, DB-7 Boston attack bomber for Brit. and French, A-26 Air Force Invader attack bomber, Navy AD Skyraider attack bomber series, A2D Skyshark attack bomber, F3D land 2 Skyknight night fighters, F3D-3 night fighters, F4D Skyray Interceptor, D-558 Skystreak, D-558-2 Skyrocket, D-558-3 research airplanes, A3D attack bomber, A4D Skyhawk attack bomber; v.p. European sales Douglas Aircraft Co., 1960; exec. v.p. Summers Gyroscope Co., 1960-62; v.p. engring. and pgm. devel. Gen. Dynamics Corp., NYC, from 1962, ret., 1973. Cons. to numerous govt. coms. Recipient Sylvanus Albert Reed award, 1952; Collier Trophy, 1953; So. Calif. Aviation Man of Yr. award, 1954; Paul Tissandier diploma Fedn. Aeronautique Internationale, 1955. Fellow, Am. Inst. Aeros. and Astronautics, Soc. Aero. Weight Engrs. (hon); Inst. Aero Scis. (hon.); Royal Aero. Soc.; Am. Astronautic Soc.; mem. Soc. Naval Architects and Marine Engrs.; Am. Soc. Naval Engrs.; Nat. Acad. Engring.; Soc. Automotive Engrs.; Tau Beta Pi (hon.). Address: P.O.B. 1795, Rancho Santa Fe, CA 92067.

HEMPHILL, JOHN M., JR.
University Professor
b. Nov. 25, 1943, Pratt, Kan.; s. John Sr. and Alma E. Hemphill; B.S., Bus. & Econ., Kans. State Univ., 1965; M.A., Econ., Univ. of Nebr., 1967; D.B.A., Ariz. State Univ., 1972; m. Virginia Scheibler, July 27, 1970, Manhattan, Kan.; sons, Jeffrey John, b. Nov. 25, 1972; Daniel John, b. Aug. 12, 1975. Career: asst. prof., Univ. of Nebr., Lincoln, Coll. of Bus. Adminstrn., 1970-71; asst. prof., Cal. State Univ., L.A., Sch. of Bus. & Economics, 1971-73; assoc. prof., 1973-78, prof., and assoc. dean, 1978---. Dir., Inst. for Govern. Mgmt., 1975---; mem. Editorial Bd., L.A. Bus. and Econ. Mag., 1975---; mem. Acad. of Mgmt.; apptd. to Advis. Council on Public Sector Productivity Improvement Programs, Nat Center for Productivity & Quality of Working Life, 1975---. Author: How to Start Your Own Business...And Succeed, 1978; recipient, regional award for best planning research project for city mgmt., Am. Inst. Planning, 1977; Lectr. on productivity improvement in W. Europe, USIA and U.S. State Dept., 1977. Mem.: Beta Gamma Sigma, 1966; Omicron Delta Epsilon, 1967; Mu Kappa Tau, 1969; Alpha Kappa Psi, 1972; Sigma Phi Epsilon. Hobby: photog. Home: 2880 Barrymore Dr., Malibu, CA 90265; Office: 5151 State Univ. Dr., L.A., CA 90032.

HENDERSON, DOUGLAS JAMES
Research Scientist
b. July 28, 1934, Calgary, Alberta, Canada; s. Donald R. and Evelyn L. Henderson; B.A., Univ. of British Columbia, 1956; Ph.D., Univ. of Ut., 1961; m. Rose-Marie Steen-Nielssen, Jan. 21, 1960, Salt Lake City; daughters, Barbara, b. Apr. 11, 1961; Dianne, b. Feb. 3, 1963; Sharon, b. Dec. 18, 1965. Career: asst. to assoc. prof. of Physics, Univ. of Id., 1961-62; Ariz. State Univ., 1962-64; Univ. of Waterloo, 1964-67; prof. of applied math and Physics, Univ. of Waterloo, Can., 1967-69; research scientist, IBM Research Lab., San Jose, 1969---; assoc. ed., Journ. of Chem. Physics, 1974-76; Co-author: Statistical Mechanics and Dynamics; Co-editor: Physical Chemistry: An Advanced Treatise; co-editor: Theoretical Chemistry: Advances and

Perspectives. Awarded fellowships: Corning Glass Found., Alfred P. Sloan Found., Ian Potter Found., CSIRO Research. Elected Fellow: Am. Inst. of Chemists, 1971; Am. Physical Soc., 1963; Inst. of Physics of Gr. Br., 1965. Mem.: Am. Chem. Soc., Canadian Assn. of Physicists, N.Y. Acad. of Sci., Math. Assn. of Am., Sigma Xi, Phi Kappa Phi, Sigma Pi Sigma. Democrat. L.D.S. Ch. Home: 23454 Skyview Terrace, Los Gatos, CA 95030; Office: IBM Research Lab., San Jose, CA 95193.

HENDRICKS, WILLIAM O.
Research Executive — Historian
b. July 23, 1927, Terre Haute, Ind.; s. William A. and Doris (Hopkins) Hendricks; A.B., Calif. State Coll., L.A., 1954; Ph.D. (hist.), USC 1967; m. Gay Gold; dau. Cathy Jo, b. Mar. 15, 1949. Career: tchg. asst., USC 1956-58; instr.: Calif. Inst. of the Arts, 1958-62; Calif. State Coll., L.A. 1962-63; USC 1963-64; Haynes Found. Fellow, 1964-65; dir. Sherman Found. Library, 1965---. Mem.: Hist. Soc. of So. Calif., Calif. Hist. Soc., Western Hist. Assn. Office: 614 Dahlia Ave., Corona del Mar, CA 92625.

HENIKA, RICHARD GRANT
Food Company Executive
b. Sept. 19, 1921, Wauwatosa, Wis.; s. Elisha Ray and Goldie (Grant) Henika; B.A., chem., Lawrence Univ., 1943; M.B.A., mktg., St. Mary's, 1977; m. Beatrice Kath, Aug. 16, 1941, Wauwatosa; chil.: Barbara Kathleen, b. Oct. 3, 1943; Philip Richard, b. Nov. 27, 1946; James Grant, b. Mar. 25, 1950; Betty Jean (Dresen), b. Dec. 13, 1952. Career: chemist, microbiologist, Western Condensing Co., 1942; head foods sect. 1953; sr. chemist, Foremost Foods Company, 1956, group leader, Ind. Food Products, 1962; assoc. dir. R&D, 1967; mgr. adminstr. Tech. Services, 1974; mgr. Tech. Services, Mgr. Dairy Internat. Divs., patent coordinator, 1977---. Inventor or co-inventor on 12 U.S. patents and 50 patents in 15 foreign countries (bakery and food processing). Staff Sgt., AUS, 1944-46. Mem.: Am. Inst. Chemists, Fellow; Am. Chem. Soc.; Am. Assn. Inst. of Food Technologists. Ch. Vestryman, and sr. warden. Hobbies: bowling, stained glass, riding. Home: 90 Stephanie Lane, Alamo, CA; Office: P.O.B. 2277, Dublin, CA 94566.

HENJYOJI, EDWARD Y.
Plastic Suegeon
b. Dec. 15, 1940, Portland, Ore.; s. Bishop D.Y. and Kazuko W. Henjyoji; B.A., Johns Hopkins, 1961, M.D., 1965; M.S. neuro-physiology, Linfield Coll., Ore., 1964; m. Patricia Honma, 1964, Portland, Ore.; chil.: Kathy, b. 1966; Diane, b. 1968; Marci, b. 1975. Career: Internship, surg. residency, New York Hosp., N.Y.C., 1965-67; surg. residency, Univ. of Tex., San Antonio, 1969-71; plastic surgery residency, Stanford Univ. Med. Center, 1971-73; pvt. practice and staff appt., UCLA, 1974---; dir., hand clinic, UCLA, 1974-76; clin. instr. in surgery, UCLA, 1974---; instr., plastic surgery, Sepulveda Vet. Hosp., 1975---; co-dir. U.S. Army Far East Burn Center, 1967-69. AUS Capt., 1967-69; decorated: Army Commendation Medal. Contbr. profl. pubs. and med. journs.; sci. presentations in field of neurophysiology and plastic surgery. Certification: Am. bd. of Plastic Surgery. Licensure: Maryland 1965; Texas 1969; Calif. 1971. Hon. Soc.: Alpha Epsilon Delta, Delta Phi Alpha; Nat. Merit Scholar. Mem.: Am. Coll. of Surgeons, Fellow; Am. Burn Assn.; Calif. Med. Assn.; L.A. Co. Med. Assn.; Calif. Soc. of Plastic Surgery. Mem.: Beta Theta Pi, secty. treas. 1960-61. Buddhist. Rec.: skiing, tennis, racquetball. Office: 1250 La Venta Dr., Westlake Village, CA 91361.

HENSELMAN, FRANCES WOOD
City Librarian
b. Sept. 2, 1916, Emmett, Ida.; d. Cartee and Dorothy (Selby) Wood; granddau. of Judge Fremont Wood; B.A., UCLA 1939; M.P.A. 1966; B.S., USC 1942; m. Edward Roddy Henselman, Yuma, Ariz., July 2, 1939. Career: Jr. asst. Boise Carnegie Lib., Ida., 1935-36; Long Beach Pub. Lib., Calif. 1937---, gen. lib. 1943-48, dir. Pub. Rels. Dept. 1949-51; adm. 1951-53; asst. city lib. 1953-69, City Librn., 1969---. Mem.: pres. L.B. Pub. Lib. Staff Assn. 1941; pres. USC Sch. of Lib. Sci. Alumni Assn. 1947, 69; chmn. Pub. Rels Sect., Am. Lib. Assn. 1966, sect. chmn., council, 1972-75; pres. So. Dist. Calif. Lib. Assn. 1969; Adult Info. Assn. of USA; U.N. Assn. of USA; L.B. C. of C.; L.B. Covic League, Libraria Sodalitas, Pi Sigma Alpha. Home: 270 Roswell Ave., Long Beach, CA 90803; Office: Long Beach Public Library, Long Beach, CA 90802.

HENSHAW, BETTY RUNALS
Public Relations — Civic Leader
b. Feb. 12, 1916, Ripon, Wis.; d. Guy Warner and Laura (Cunningham) Runals; ed. Scripps Coll. 1933-34; A.B., UCLA 1937; m. Paul Carrington Henshaw, Pomona, May 25, 1939; chil.: Mrs. Paul W. (Sydney Parker) Nordt, III, b. June 30, 1942; Guy Runals, b. Sept. 27, 1946; Paul Carrington, Jr., b. Nov. 1, 1947. Career: reporter, coord. ofc. pub. rels., Am. Embassy, Lima, Peru, and reporter-feat. writer, Peruvian Times and Andean Airmail, 1943-45. Mem.: chmn. pub. rels. Alta Bates Comm. Hisp. Volunteer Assoc., 1954-67; v.p. 1959, pres. 1960; v. chmn. Women's Aux. Am. Min., Metal. and Petroleum Engrs. 1956, chmn. 1957, secty. 1967, gen. chmn. Natl. Conv., 1972; chmn. Round Table, Natl. Conv. 1967, Nat. Dir., 1975, V.P. conv., 1976-77; co-chmn. Women Am. Min. Cong., S.F. Conv. 1958; Eta Chpt., Gamma Phi Beta, pres. Mother's Club, 1963-65; Guild and bd. dirs. Alameda Co. TB and Health Assn. 1960-66; chmn. Christmas Seal Campaign, 1964, 65; ed. adv. com. Alta Bates Comm. Hosp., 1964---, dir., fdn. assoc., 1976, pr. chmn., 1978; chmn. Red and White Ball, 1968; Save S.F. Bay Assn.; World Affairs Council of No. Calif.; Univ. Art Mus. Council, Univ. of Calif., Berkeley; De Young Mus. Assn. Republican. Episcopalian. Hobby: photog. Rec.: Travel. Home: 875 Arlington Ave., Berkeley, CA 94707.

HENSHAW, PAUL CARRINGTON
President, Homestake Mining Co.
b. Nov. 15, 1913, Rye, N.Y.; s. R. Townsend and Clara Ambler (Venable) Henshaw; A.B. (magna cum laude), Harvard Univ. 1936; M.S., Calif. Inst. of Tech. 1938, Ph.D. 1940; m. Helen Elizabeth Runals, Pomona, May 25, 1939; chil.: Sydney Nordt, b. June 30, 1942; Guy Runals, b. Sept. 27, 1946; Paul Carrington, Jr., b. Nov. 1, 1947. Career: head geologist, Morococha Div., Cerro Corp., Peru, 1940-43; geol. Consorcio Minero del Peru, S.A., Mina Calpa, 1943-45; cons. geol. Compania Peruana de Cemento Portland, Lima, Peru, 1945; geol. Day Mines, Inc., Wallace, Ida., 1945-46; assoc. prof., acting head geol. dept., Univ. of Ida. 1946-47; chief geol., San Luis Min. Co., Tayoltita Durango, Mex. 1947-53; chief geol. Homestake Min. Co. 1953-60, v.p. 1961-69, pres. dir. 1970---; Calif. State Min. and Geol. Bd., 1968-69, chmn. 1970---. Adv. trustee, Alta Bates Comm. Hosp., Berkeley, 1960---. Mem.: Am. Inst. Min. and Metallurgical Engrs., Geol. Soc. of Am., Geol.-Chem. Soc., Min. and Metallurgical Soc., No. Calif. World Affairs Council, Soc. of Econ. Geol., Harvard Varsity, Harvard Club of S.F., World Trade Club, Engrs. Club, Stock Exch. Club, Bankers Club, Commonwealth Club, S.F. Hobby: philately. Rec.: travel. Home: 875 Arlington Ave., Berkeley, CA 94707; Office: 650 California St., S.F., CA 94108.

HERNDON, HON. ROY L.
Justice, District Court of Appeal
b. Feb. 21, 1907, Walla Walla, Wash.; s. D.B. and Bertha M. (Eiffert) Herndon; desc. William A. Herndon, law partner and biographer of Abraham Lincoln; ed. B.A., Univ. of Ore. 1929, J.D., Coll. of Law, 1932; m. Mary Lou Beville, Mesa, Ariz., Mar. 11, 1934; chil.: Roy Lee, b. Mar. 3, 1935; Mary Alice, b. Jan. 27, 1940; Thomas Michal, b. July 30, 1941. Career: Admitted to Ore. bar, 1932, Ariz. bar, 1933, Calif. bar, 1936; pvt. practice law, L.A. 1936-49; partner, law firm, Meserve, Mumper & Hughes, 1938-49, and 1973---; apptd. judge, Superior Ct. of L.A. Co. 1949-58; apptd. justice, Dist. Ct. of Appeal, Div. 2, Second Appellate Dist. of Calif. 1958-73. Mem.: trustee, L.A. Bar Assn., 1947-49; San Marino Masonic Lodge No. 685, Scottish rite 32°; Univ. Club of L.A., Phi Kappa Psi, Phi Beta Kappa, Phi Delta Phi. Democrat. Congregational Ch. Rec.: golf, fishing, hunting. Office: 333 S. Hope St., L.A., CA 90071.

HERRICK, MARIAN CLIFFE
Textbook Author — Educator
b. Jan. 24, 1908, Portland, Ore.; d. Thomas and Sarah Ann (Bushell) Cliffe; bro. Thomas Clement Cliffe; ed. B.A., UCLA 1929, M.A., USC 1938. Ed.D. 1950; m. Albert William Herrick, Burbank, 1950. Career: Tchr., L.A. City Schs. 1936-50, coord. 1950-53, supv. math. 1953-67, ext. instr. 1952-72, cons.-lectr., 1965---. Author: math. texts, 1962---, publ. Houghton Mifflin Co., 1967---. Mem.: So. Sect. pres.-treas. Calif. Math. Council, 1953-57, State pres. 1957-59; Delta Epsilon, pres.-v.p.-secty.-treas. 1957-61; Pi Mu Epsilon, Pi Lambda Theta, Delta Kappa Gamma. Presbyterian (choir sect. leader). Hobbies: travel, photog., spectator sports, swimming. Home: 2193 W. Visalia Rd., Exeter, CA 93221.

HERRICK, WILLIAM JAMES
  President, Western 6 Motels
b. Jan. 29, 1927, Carthage, S. Dak.; s. William C. and Ellen L. Herrick; A.A., L.A. City Coll., 1950; student, L.A. State Coll.; m. Donna M. Crawford, June 6, 1953, Pomona, Calif.; chil.: Kathleen, Joan (Cunningham), Leann, William C., Susan, Joseph. Career: Employed, Crocker Bank, 1948-69, v.p. and branch mgr. of banks in Whittier, Maywood, La Puente; founder, partner, pres., Western 6 Motels (aka Calif. 6 Motels). Dir., co-founder, Landmark Bank, La Habra. S/Sgt., USAF, 1945-46. Mem.: Rotary Club, E. Whittier, past pres. 1964-65; Rotary Club of La Habra. Active in polit. fund raising. Catholic. Rec.: horseback riding, golf. Home: 2020 Canyon Ct., La Habra, CA; Office: 1156 S. 7th Ave., Hacienda Heights, CA.

HERRILL, GENEVIEVE WAITE
  C.P.A. — Corporate Officer
b. Feb. 20, 1915, Arizona; d. David C. and Lynette (Hughes) Waite; B.S., Univ. of Calif., Berkeley, 1948; C.P.A. License, Calif., 1950; m. Walter Neff Herrill (dec.), Calif. Career: C.P.A. practice, 1950---: specialized practice in natural resource industries, particularly oil and gas. Pres., Ancora Corp., 1979---; Secty.-treas., Ancora-Verde Corp., 1968---; pres., Eleven-Ninety Sacramento Corp., a community assn. 1977---. Mem.: Metropolitan Club, S.F., 1977---; Am. Inst. of C.P.A.s, 1950---; Calif. Soc. of C.P.A.s, 1950---. Republican. Episcopal. Rec.: travel, opera, ballet, symphony. Home: 1190 Sacramento St., S.F., CA 94108; Office: 24 California St., Suite 408, San Francisco, CA 94111.

HERTWECK, E. ROMAYNE
  Educator
b. July 24, 1928, Springfield, Mo.; s. Garnett P. and Gladys (Chowning) Hertweck; B.A., Psychology, Augustana Coll., Ill., 1962; M.A. psychology, Pepperdine Coll., L.A., 1963; Ed.D. counseling psychol., Ariz. State Univ., 1966; Ph.D., psychol., U.S. Internat. Univ., S.D., 1978; m. Alma Louise Street, Dec. 16, 1955, Moline, Ill.; 1 son William Scott, b. Oct. 24, 1970. Career: Night editor, Rock Island Argus Newspaper, Rock Island, Ill., 1961-62; graduate tching. asst., Pepperdine Coll., L.A., 1963; counselor, VA., Ariz. State Univ., Tempe, Ariz., 1964; assoc. dir. conciliation ct., Miracopa Co. superior ct., Phoenix, Ariz., 1965; instr., Phoenix Coll., 1966; prof. psychol., Mira Costa Coll., Oceanside, 1967---; chmn., Psychology Counseling Dept., Mira Costa Coll., 1973-75; chmn., Behavioral Sci. Dept., 1976---; prof. psychol., World Campus Afloat, spring semester, 1970, S.S. Ryndam; psychol. instr. Chapman Coll. Residence Center, Camp Pendleton, 1969---. Bd. dir. Christian Counseling Center, Oceanside, 1970---. Mem.: Kiwanis; charter mem. Carlsbad club, dir. 1975-78; Am. Psychol. Assn.; Am. Personnel and Guidance Assn.; Western Psychol. Assn.; No. San Diego Co. Psychol. Assn.; Phi Delta Kappa; Kappa Delta Pi; Psi Chi. Republican. Protestant. Hobbies: travel, golf, photog. Home: 2024 Oceanview Rd., Oceanside, CA; Office: Mira Costa Coll., Oceanside, CA.

HESS, EDWARD JORGEN
  University Librarian
b. Feb. 18, 1925, Hamburg, Iowa; s. Edward A. and Luella (Nelson) Hess; B.A., soc. sci. and secondary edn., Peru State Coll., Neb., 1949; M.A., polit. sci., USC, 1954; M.S. lib. sci., 1957; Ph.D. lib. sci., 1970. Career: Tchr. Jr. High and High Schs., Mo. and Calif., 1950-56; lib. cataloger, San Diego State Univ., 1957-58, serials lib., 1958-59, lib. supr. tech. services, 1961-63; lib. dir., Lompoc Pub. Lic., 1965-66; asst. lib. and chief of tech. services, Cal. State Univ., Northridge, 1966-67; asst. lib. and chief of pub. services, 1967-69; lecturer, sch. of lib. sci., USC, part-time 1967-69, full-time 1969-70, asst. prof. 1970-76, asst. univ. lib. for pub. services, USC, 1976---. Calif. Community Coll. Lib. Credential, valid for life. Contbg. author, California Librarian, other publs. Editor, California Librarian, 1969. Served AUS, 1943-46. Mem.: Calif. Lib. Assn., chmn. bylaws com. 1968-69, parliamentarian, 1968, councilor, 1975-77; Am. Lib. Assn., Calif. correspondent for ALA Yearbook, 1976; Am. Soc. for Information Sci.; Calif. Soc. of Librarians, CLA; So. Calif. Tech. Processes Group; Beta Phi Mu; Kappa Delta Pi. Mem.: Sierra Club, 1967---; Nat. Trust for Historic Preservation, 1972---; Western Photog. Collectors Assn., 1974---; Friends of the Chinatown Lib., 1977---. Hobby: photog. Rec.: travel. Home: 517 N. Vista Bonita Ave., Glendora, CA 91740; Office: Univ. Lib., USC, L.A., CA 90007.

HETLAND, JOHN ROBERT
  Lawyer — University Professor
b. Mar. 12, 1930, Minneapolis, Minn.; s. James L. and Evelyn (Lundgren) Hetland; B.S. (law), Univ. Minn. 1952, J.D. 1956; m. Anne Turner Kneeland, Dec. 24, 1972; chil.: Lynda, b. July 8, 1952; Robert, b. Jan. 8, 1954; Debra, b. Apr. 8, 1958. Career: admitted to Minn. State Bar, 1956; pvt. practice of law, Minneapolis, 1956-60; prof. of law, Univ. of Calif., Berkeley, 1959---; law cons. to attys., Berkeley, 1959---; pvt. practice. Visit. Prof. of law, Stanford Univ. 1971; Univ. of Singapore, Repub. of Singapore, 1972. Author: (books) California Real Property Security, 1967; Calif. Real Estate Secured Transactions, 1970; Commercial Real Estate Transactions, 1974; Secured Real Property Transactions, 1977. Articles publ. in profl. journs. 1952---. Contracting ofcr., USN (1953-55), Korean War. Mem.: Minn., Calif., Am. Bar Assns.; Order of the Coif; Delta Kappa Epsilon, Phi Delta Phi. Republican. Home: Orinda, CA; Office: 366 Boalt Hall, Univ. of Calif., Berkeley, CA 94720.

HEYLER, DAVID BALDWIN, JR.
  Attorney at Law
b. May 23, 1926, L.A.; s. David Baldwin and Andree L. (Buchwalter) Heyler; A.B., Stanford Univ. 1948; LL.B. 1951; m. Joan Elizabeth Dekker, Carmel, Aug. 31, 1949; chil.: Mary Andree, b. Apr. 24, 1951; Elizabeth Baldwin, b. Dec. 27, 1953; Katherine Dekker, b. Aug. 5, 1965. Career: Admitted to Calif. bar, 1952; law practice, 1952---; partner Ward and Heyler law firm, L.A. USN Air Corps (1944-45), WW II. Awards: Outstanding Young Man of Yr. 1962, Beverly Hills Jr. C. of C. Mem.; bd. dirs., Beverly Hills Jr. C. of C. 1953-57; bd. dirs., Beverly Hills Men's Club, 1953-58; bd. govs., Beverly Hills Bar Assn., 1954-63; pres. 1962; pres. Beverly Hills Jr. Bar Assn., 1956; legislative com., State Bar of Calif., resolutions com., conf. of dels., 1958, com. state bar journ. 1961-64, chmn. 1962-63, chmn. disciplinary com. 1965, com. bar examiners, 1965-70, chmn. 1968-69; bd. trustees-v.p. John Thomas Dye Sch.; pres. bd. dirs. Bel-Air Assocs. 1972-74; Stanford Assocs.; bd. trustees, L.A. Co. Bar Assn. 1964-65; v.p., pres.-exec. bd. Stanford Alumni Assn.; Clubs: L.A. Country, Calif., Bohemian, San Francisco; Rotary Club of Beverly Hills. Episcopalian. Office: 1901 Ave. of the Stars, Suite 1475, L.A., CA 90067.

HILKER, WALTER R., JR.
  Attorney at Law
b. Apr. 18, 1921, Los Angeles; s. Walter R. and Alice L. (Cox) Hilker; B.S., USC, 1942, LL.B., 1948; m. Ruth Hibbard, Sept. 7, 1943, Evanston, Ill.; chil.: Anne K., b. June 17, 1953; Walter R., III, b. May 13, 1956. Career: Attorney at law, 1948---. Served to Lt., U.S. Naval Reserve, 1942-46; decorated Bronze Star, Navy Unit Commendation Award. Mem.: Beach Club, Santa Monica; Twin Lakes Club, Wrightwood; Balboa Bay Club, Newport Beach; Spring Valley Lake Country Club, Apple Valley, bd. govs., dir., Tennis Assn. Republican. Home: P.O.B. 863, 981 Finch, Wrightwood, CA 92397.

HILLER, ARTHUR GARFIN
  Film Director
b. Nov. 22, 1923, Edmonton, Canada; s. Harry and Rose Hiller; M.A., psychology, Univ. of Toronto; hon. degrees: F.V.Ch.C., Victoria Coll., Glasgow, 1967; Dr. Laureate, Imperial Order of Constantine, Brussells, 1972; Litt.D., London Inst. of Applied Research, 1973; Comdr. Sursam Corda, Belgium, 1972; m. Gwen Pechet, Feb. 14, 1978, Vancouver, Canada; chil.: Henryk, b. Oct. 22, 1958; Erica, b. Mar. 31, 1960. Career: dir., radio, Canadian Broadcasting Corp., 1949-50, dir. TV, 1951-54; dir. TV, Hollywood, 1954-62; dir. mot. pics., Hollywood, 1962---. Films: Americanization of Emily, 1964; Poppi, 1969; Love Story, 1970; Hospital, 1971; Man of La Mancha, 1973; Man In The Glass Booth, 1974; Silver Streak, 1977. Flying Officer, Royal Canadian Airforce, 1942-45. Mem. Dir. Am. Q., Council; bd. mem., Acad. of Mot. Pic. Arts & Scis. Jewish. Rec.: tennis, travel. Home: 1218 Benedict Canyon Dr., Beverly Hills, CA 90210.

HILTON, WILLIAM BARRON
  President, Hilton Hotels
b. Oct. 23, 1927, Dallas, Tex.; s. Conrad Nicholson and Mary Barron (Saxon) Hilton; m. Marilyn Jane Hawley, Chicago, June 20, 1947; chil.: William Barron, Jr., b. 1948; Hawley Anne, b. 1949; Stephen Michael, b. 1950; David Alan, b. 1952; Sharon Constance, b. 1953; Richard Howard, b. 1955; Daniel Kevin, b. 1962; Ronald Jeffrey, b. 1963. Career: founder-gen. partner,

Vita-Pakt Citrus Prods. Co. 1948---; dir. Hilton Hotels Corp. 1954---, v.p. 1954-66, pres.-chief exec. ofcr. 1966---. Pres., San Diego Chargers Ltd., 1961-66; pres. Am. Football League, 1965; dir. Mfrs. Hanover Trust Co. 1970; dir. Conrad N. Hilton Found.; trustee, City of Hope; trustee, advis. bd. Dir. Sports, Inc.; Natl. Exec. Adv. Com. of Natl. Council on Crime and Delinquency; dir., Calif. C. of C.; dir. Realty Com. on Taxation; sponsor, Photographer's Mate (3rd class), USN (hon. disch. 1946). Awards: Hotel Man of Yr., Penn State, 1969. Mem.: L.A. World Affairs Council; Chevalier of Confrerie de la Chaine des Rotisseurs; Bel-Air Country Club, 1951---; Bel-air Bay Club, 1968---; Magestral Knights Sovereign Mil. Order of Malta. Hobbies: hunting, fishing, photog. Home: 1060 Brooklawn Dr., Holmby Hills, CA 90024; Office: 9990 Santa Monica Blvd., Beverly Hills, CA 90212.

HINDERAKER, IVAN
  University Chancellor
b. Apr. 29, 1916, Hendricks, Minn.; s. Theodore and Clara (Hanson) Hinderaker; B.A., St. Olaf Coll. 1938; M.A., Univ. Minn. 1942, Ph.D. 1949; (hon.) LL.D., Pepperdine Coll. 1970; m. Evelyn Birkholz, Minneapolis, Minn., June 7, 1941; son, Mark, b. Dec. 10, 1946. Career: Research asst. Minn. League of Municipalities, Minn. 1939-40; repr. State House of Reps., St. Paul, Minn. 1942-43; asst. prof., prof. (polit. sci.), UCLA, 1948-62; v. chancellor, Univ. of Calif., Irvine, 1962-64; chancellor, Univ. of Calif., Riverside, 1964---. Assoc. budget examiner, U.S. Bureau of Budget, Wash., D.C., 1942-43; assoc. dir. Citizenship Clearing House, Law Center, NYU 1956-57; asst. to secty. U.S. Dept. of Interior, Wash. D.C. 1959-60. 1st Lt., USAAF. Mem.: Am. Polit. Sci. Assn., Rotary Club. Lutheran. Home: 4171 Watkins Dr., Riverside, CA; Office: Univ. of Calif., Riverside, Calif. 92502.

HINDIN, MAURICE J.
  Attorney at Law
b. Oct. 10, 1910, L.A.; s. Theodore J. and Ida Hindin; B.S., USC 1933; LL.B., 1935; LL.D., Calif. Assoc. Colls. 1940; m. Dorothy Sweet, Salt Lake City, Aug. 11, 1938; chil.: Arthur T., b. 1943; Carol, b. 1950. Career: Admitted to practice law, Calif. 1935; admitted to practice before U.S. Supreme Ct. 1942; partner, Hindin & Hindin law firm, Beverly Hills. Mem.: Am. and L.A. Co. Bar Assns.; assoc. IEEE, Am. Trial Lawyers Assn., Friars Club. Hobby: owner-operator, amateur radio sta. W6EUV. Home: 10471 Le Conte Ave., L.A., CA 90024; Office: 8920 Wilshire Blvd., Beverly Hills, CA.

HIRSCH, CLEMENT LANG
  Company President
b. Apr. 26, 1914, St. Louis, Mo.; s. Urban S. and Florence (Hellman) Hirsch; chil.: Lynne, Jan, Christopher, Casey, Clement, Jr., Gregory. Career: Buyer-merchandise mgr., Famous Department Stores; est. pet food mfg. bus. (largest vol. in west), 1937-68; pres. Kal Kan Foods, Inc.; pres 18 other corps., incl. Stagg Foods, Inc. and bldg. corps. USMC WW II. Mem.: pres. Oak Tree Racing Assn.; dir., v.p., Del Mar Thoroughbred Club; trustee, Chapman Coll., Orange; Clubs: Irvine Country, Big Canyon Country, L.A. Turf. Hobby: breeding and racing thoroughbreds (owner, several stake horses). Home: 200 Evening Star Lane, Newport Beach, CA 92660.

HIRT, CHARLES C.
  Conductor — Lecturer
b. Nov. 4, 1911, L.A.; s. Adolph and Della Belle (Mills) Hirt; A.B. Occidental Coll., 1934, (hon.) Mus. D., 1970; M.S., USC, 1940, Ph.D., 1946; (hon.) D.F.A., Westminster Coll., 1971; (hon.) D.H.L., Pacific Univ.; m. Lucy A. Thompson, June 28, 1935, L.A.; chil.: Janice Lynne (Young); Ronald Allen. Career: Music Educator, pub. schs. 1936-41; prof. of Music, USC, 1941---: founder-chm. of Choral and Ch. Music Depts.; appearances here and abroad as choral specialist, conductor, lectr.; conductor of annual Christmas Candlelight Ceremony at Disneyland or Walt Disney World, 1956---. Choral Publs. by Carl Fischer, Inc.; Warner Bros. Music.; Hinshaw Music Pub. Founder, life mem., nat. pres., Am. Choral Dirs. Assn., 1970-72; founder, life mem. (hon.), So. Calif. Vocal Assn.; past pres., hon. life mem., Choral Conductors Guild of Calif. Mem.: ASCAP; Phi Beta Kappa; Phi Kappa Phi; Sigma Alpha Epsilon; Pi Kappa Lambda; Phi Mu Alpha Sinphonia; life mem. Musicians Union, Local 47; La Federation France-Californienne. Elder, 1st Presbyterian Ch. of Hollywood. Home: 1318 Cordova Ave., Glendale, CA 91207; Office: USC Sch. of Music, L.A., CA 90007.

HOADLEY, WALTER EVANS
  Chief Economist, Bank of America
b. Aug. 16, 1916, San Francisco; s. Walter Evans and Marie Howland (Preece) Hoadley; B.A., Univ. of Calif., Berkeley, 1938; M.A., 1940; Ph.D., 1946; (hon.) D.C.S., Franklin & Marshall, 1963; LL.D., Golden Gate Univ. 1968; m. Virginia Alm, May 20, 1939, San Francisco; chil.: Richard A., b. Mar. 11, 1943; Jean (Price), b. May 20, 1946. Career: Sr. economist, Federal Reserve Bank of Chicago, 1942-49; economist, Armstrong Cork Co., 1949-54, treas.-economist, 1954-60, v.p. and treas. 1960-66; director, Federal Reserve Bank of Phila., 1958-66, chmn., 1962-66; chmn., Conference of Chairmen of the Federal Reserve, 1966; sr. v.p. and chief economist, Bank of America NT&SA, 1966-68; exec. v.p. and chief economist, 1968---. Am. Statistical Assn., pres. 1958; Am. Finance Assn., pres. 1969; Conference of Bus. Economists, chmn. 1962; Bus. Council Tech. Cons. to the Comm. on Domestic Economy, chmn. 1963-66; Am. Bankers Assn., Bankers Comm. on Urban Affairs, chmn. 1972-73; Conservation Found., Trustee 1974---. Mil. Econ. adviser, Civil Affairs Officer Training Program, 1943-45. Fellow, Am. Statistical Assn., 1955; Fellow, Nat. Assn. of Bus. Economists, 1968. Mem.: Phi Beta Kappa, 1937. Clubs: Commonwealth Club, Bankers Club of S.F., St. Francis Yacht Club, Silverado Country Club. Polit.: Served on spec. task forces on U.S. Foreign Economic Policy, U.S. Economic Growth for Pres. Nixon, 1969-70; mem. White House Review Com. on Balance of Payments, 1963-65. Methodist; chmn. adminstrv. bd.; mem. bd. Calif. Nev. United Methodist Found., 1976-78. Hobbies: coins, stamps, gardening. Rec.: swimming. Home: S.F., CA; Office: Bank of America NT&SA, P.O.B., 37000, S.F., CA 94137.

HOAG, RICHARD JOHN
  Company President
b. Sept. 9, 1946, Bronxville, N.Y.; s. George Jackson and Virginia Smith Hoag; B.A., Cal. State Univ., Northridge, 1967; J.S.D., USC, 1970; m. Carolyn Bozeman, June 17, 1967, Houston; chil.: Richard John, Jr., b. Mar. 2, 1972; Juliette Dawn, b. Apr. 19, 1976. Career: Corporate Counsel, Property Research Corp., L.A., 1969-71; World Leisure Time Corp., Beverly Hills, 1971-72; v.p. and dir., Fortune Fund. Inc., San Diego, 1972-73; dir. of mktg. and acquisitions, Rossco Inc., L.A., 1973-74; pres. and gen. counsel, Cal-American Group, L.A., 1974---. Dir. and sr. v.p. in charge of Acquisitions for Cal-Am. Mgmt. Lectr., real estate syndication, Univ. Calif., Irvine. Mem.: Calif. Bar Assn., Jonathan Club, Delta Sigma Phi. Rec.: tennis, skiing, racquetball. Home: 17422 Camino de Yatasto, Pacific Palisades, CA 90272; Office: 2029 Century Park E., Suite 960, L.A., CA 90067.

HOCH, ORION LINDEL
  President, Intersil, Inc.
b. Dec. 21, 1928, Cannonsburg, Pa.; s. Orion L.F. and Anna M. Hoch; B.S., Carnegie Mellon Univ., 1952; M.S., UCLA, 1954; Ph.D., Stanford Univ., 1957; m. Jane L. Hoch (dec.), 1952, Pa.; chil.: Andrea, b. May 1, 1959; Brenda, b. Nov. 25, 1960; John, b. June 13, 1962. Career: with Litton Industries, 1961-74: mgr., Crossed Field Dept., Litton Electron Tube Div., 1961-63, v.p., asst. gen. mgr., 1963-65; pres. & gen. mgr., 1965-68; v.p., Litton Components Group, 1968-70; v.p., Litton Industries Inc., 1970-71, sr. v.p. 1971-74; pres., Advanced Memory Systems, Inc., 1974-76; pres., Intersil, Inc., 1976---. AUS, 1946-48. Mem.: IEEE, 1952---. Rec.: tennis. Home: 37 Deodora Dr., Atherton, CA 95025; Office: 10710 N. Tantau Ave., Cupertino, CA 95014.

HOCHBERG, FREDERICK GEORGE
  Business Consultant — Accountant
b. July 4, 1913, L.A.; s. Frederick Joseph and Lottie A. (LeGendre) Hochberg; B.A., UCLA 1937; chil.: Frederick George, b. Oct. 19, 1941; Ann Lawrence, b. May 12, 1943. Career: Chief acct-auditor, Pan Am. Hwy., Swinerton, McClure and Vinnell, Managua, Nicaragua, 1942-44; acct. practice, Avalon, 1946-66; designer-mgr., Descanso Beach Club, Avalon, Calif. 1966; treas. Catalina Airlines, 1967; v.p. Air Catalina, 1967; pres. Aero Commuter, 1967; v.p.-treas.-dir. bus. affairs, Wm. L. Pereira Assocs., planners, archs., engrs. 1967-72; v.p.-gen. mgr. Missouri Hickory Corp. 1972-74; mgmr. consultant, 1974---. v.p., gen. mgr., Solar Engring. Co., 1977---; Treas., Catalina Island, 1954-62; Councilman, 1962-64; Mayor, 1964-66. Author: Los Toros, 1958. Ensign, USN, S. Pac. (1944-46), WW II. Awards: Man of Yr. Catalina Is., 1956. Mem.: Fur C., 1935-37; pres. Blue Key, 1936-37; pres. Phi Phi, 1937; Golden Bruin, 1937; Rotarian, 1946---, pres. 1955-56;

chmn. Avalon Transportation Com. 1952; pres. Avalon C. of C. 1954; secty. Avalon Planning Comm. 1956-58; secty. Santa Catalina Is. Festival of the Arts, 1960; chmn. Avalon Harbor Comm. 1961; pres. Catalina Mariachi Assn. 1961-66; Soc. Calif. Accts.; Mensa; Am. Arbitration Assn. Panel; L.A. C. of C.; dir., Town Hall West; pres. Avalon Music Bowl Assn. 1961; chmn. Avalon Airport Comm. 1964-66; Mensa, 1964; treas. Catalina Is. Museum Soc., 1964-68; chmn. Avalon Harbor Devel. Com. 1965; chmn. Friends of Avalon Found. 1965-67; chmn. Avalon Harbor Devel. Com. 1965; treas., L.A. Child Guidance Clinic. Roman Catholic. Hobbies: tape recording, photog. Rec.: bullfights. Home: 6760 Hillpark Dr., L.A., CA 90068.

HOFER, DAVID LESTER
Radio Station Owner
b. July 6, 1917, Dinuba, Calif.; s. David P. and Margaret D. Hofer; grad., Bible Inst., Los Angeles, 1936; A.A., Reedley Coll., 1938; m. Sylvia Kliewer, Nov. 23, 1938, Reedley, Calif.; Chil.: Donna, b. Mar. 30; Nadine (Klassen), b. June 21. Career: Owner, pres. mgr. Radio Sta. KRDU, Dinuba, 1946---; Radio Sta. KLTA, Dinuba, 1975---, Co-founder, dir., Hume Lake Christian Camps, 1955-70; co-founder, v.p., Fellowship Book Stores, 1968-70. Mem.: Western Religious Broadcasters Assn., pres. 1967-68; Nat. Religious Broadcasters Assn., v.p., 1970-71; Dinuba C. of C., dir., 1960-62; pres., Gideons Internat. 1974-77; chmn. Gideons Internat. Extension Com. for 115 countries, 1977---; Rotary Club, 1952. Mennonite Brethren ch. Hobbies: travel, photog. Rec.: tennis, swimming, golf. Home: 695 Bates Ave., Dinuba, CA; Office: 597 N. Alta, Dinuba, CA 93618.

HOFFBERG, JUDITH A.
Art Information Specialist
b. May 19, 1934, Hartford, Conn., d. George and Miriam Hoffberg; B.A. cum laude, 1956, M.A., 1960, M.L.S., 1964. Career: Acquisitions Librn., John Hopkins Univ., Bologna, Italy 1964-65; Lib. of Congress, Cataloger, 1965-67; Fine Arts Librn., Univ. of Penn., Phila. 1967-69; Bibliographer, Univ. of Calif., San Diego, 1969-71; Brand Art Center Librn., Glendale, 1971-73; Exec. secty., Art Libraries Soc. of N. Am., 1973-77; dir., Umbrella Assocs., 1977---; ed. & pub. Umbrella (a newsletter on contemporary art), 1978---; exec. dir. Assoc. Art Publishers Network, 1978---; bd. dirs. College Art Assn., 1975-79; dir., Franklin Furnace Archive, Adv. Council, Women's Caucus for Art, 1977---. Contbr. Several articles on art librarianship and visual resource collections profl. journs.; co-editor of Director of Art Libraries & Visual Resource Collections in No. Am., 1978. Mem.: ALA; Soc. of Archl. Historians; College Art Assn., bd. dir. Hobbies: collect books, buttons. Home: P.O.B. 3692, Glendale, CA 91201.

HOFFMAN, ARLENE FAUN
Podiatrist — Physiologist — Educator
b. Nov. 23, 1941, NYC; d. Abraham S. and Pearl (Weiss) Hoffman; B.S., Queens Coll., 1962; Ph.D. (USPHS fellow), State Univ., NY Downstate Med. Center at Brooklyn, 1967; postgrad., Stanford Univ., 1966-67; D.P.M., Calif. Coll. Podiatric Med., 1976. Career: Assoc. prof. to prof., dept. basic sciences, Calif. Coll. Podiatric Med.,S.F., 1967---, dir. dept., 1970-75, assoc. dean for curricular affairs, 1972-75, asst. prof. dept. podiatric med., 1978---; Licensed to practice podiatry, N.Y., Ga., Calif. Contbg. author: The Podiatry Curriculum, 1970; ed. adv. bd. Journ Podiatric Med. Edn., 1971-75; sci. ed., Basic Med. Scis., Journ. Am. Podiatry Soc., 1972---; podiatric med. ed. Healing Professions Edn. Exch. Research, newsletter Am. Ednl. Research Assn., 1973---; assoc. ed., Podiatry Yearbook, 1977---. Mem.: Ednl. Research Assn., Am. Assn. Univ. Adminstrs., Am. Pub. Health Assn.; Assn. Women in Sci.; Am. Podiatry Assn.; Nat. Assn. Research in Sci. Teaching. Home: 4 Saint Jude Rd., Mill Valley, CA 94941; Office: 1770 Eddy St., S.F., CA 94115.

HOGOBOOM, WILLIAM PERRY
Superior Court Judge
b. Oct. 31, 1918, Pasadena; s. William Corywell and Grace (Wise) Hogsett; B.A., Occidental Coll., 1939; M.S. in pub. admin., USC, 1941; J.D., USC Law Sch., 1949; Hon. LL.D., South Bay Univ. Coll. of Law, 1978; Hon. LL.D., Mid-Valley Coll. of Law, 1978; m. Betty Cornwall, May 30, 1944, Woodland; chil.: William C., b. Apr. 21, 1945; Peter T., b. May 28 1946; Christian, b. Dec. 14, 1950; Katherine, b. Dec. 19, 1952; Lisa, b. July 5, 1954. Career: Sr. Partner, law firm Iverson & Hogoboom, 1949-68; Judge of Superior Ct., L.A. Co., 1969---, Presiding Judge, 1978---. Lt., USN, Atlantic

1944-45, Pacific 1945-46. Trustee, Occidental Coll; dir., BSA; pres., Rotary Club of L.A., 1972-73. Mem.: Phi Beta Kappa, Phi Kappa Psi, Order of Coif. Episcopalian, Vestryman, St. Edmunds, San Marino. Home: 234 S. El Molino Ave., Pasadena; Office: 111 N. Hill St., L.A., CA 90012.

HOLCOMBE, WILLIAM JONES
Chairman, Teton, Inc.
b. Sept. 7, 1925, Piedmont, S.C.; s. Hovey W. and Hattie Leona (Jones) Holcombe; B.S. Rutgers Univ., postgrad. studies, Rutgers Sch. of Finance; m. Judith Gene Boyce, June 7, 1945, NYC; chil.: Cheryl L. (Gates), b. June 4, 1954; Judith M. (Pettit), b. Dec. 27, 1946. Career: with Hewitt Robins, Inc., 1946-56; v.p., Adsco Industries, Inc., 1956-58; v.p., Yuba Consolidated Industries, 1958-60; chief exec. and chmn., Delaval Turbine Inc., 1960-75; chief exec. ofcr., owner, chmn. bd., Teton, Inc., 1975---; dir.: Occidental Life; United Artists; Transamerica Fin.; Delaval Turbine; Wilbur Ellis Co.; Merchants & Mfrs. Orgn., L.A. USN. 1943-46, destroyer fleet. Mem.: F&AM Masonic Club, 1946---; Engrs. Club, Trenton, N.J.; Presbyterian. Rec.: gardening, outdoor activities. Home: 5642 Mountain View, Yorba Linda, CA 92686; Office: 14111 Freeway Dr., Santa Fe Springs, CA 90670.

HOLGATE, GEORGE JACKSON
President, Riverside University
b. Feb. 19, 1933, Lakewood, Oh.; s. George Curtis and Melba (Klein) Holgate; B.M., Baldwin-Wallace Coll. 1953; M.Sc., USC, 1955, Ed.D. 1962, LL.D. Career: exec. vice pres., Sierra Found., 1953-56; tchr., Oxnard H.S. and Ventura Coll., 1956-62; campus direct. Congo Polytech. Inst. 1962-64; pres. Riverside Univ. 1965---. Music cond.: Ojai Festival, 1956; Ventura Co. Concert Chorale and Chamber Singers, 1956-60; Ventura Bach Festival, 1958; Columbia Orch. 1960. Awards: U.S. Jr. C. of C. Distinguished Service Award, 1962. Mem.: bd. dirs.: Riverside Sym. Orch., Riverside Opera Assn., Calif. Assn. for Pvt. Edn.; Calif. Council of Business Schs.; Phi Mu Alpha Sinfonia; Phi Delta Kappa; Democratic State Central Com. of Calif. 1962; Dem. nominee for Congress, 1962. Hobby: mus. Rec.: fishing, sailing, flying. Office: P.O.B. 1609, Riverside, CA.

HOLL, ROSE ELIZABETH
Company President
b. Aug. 25, 1920, Richardton, N.D.; d. John and Rose (Raskop) Holl; m. Frank Matarazzi. Career: Acct., Benner & Nawman, Inc., Oakland, 1942-44; co-founder-ofc. mgr., Atlas Pac. Engring. Co. 1944-46, secty.-treas. 1947-52, exec. v.p. 1952-64. pres. 1964---; dir.-ofcr., Pioneer Electric Co., Richmond, 1948-57. Mem.: dir. Jr. Achievement, Oakland; Calif. State and Oakland Cs. of C.; clubs: Round Hill Country (Alamo, Calif.), Bermuda Dunes Country (Palm Springs). Roman Catholic. Hobby: gardening, photog. Rec.: photog., art work. Home: 41 Gran Via, Alamo, CA; Office: 67th and Hollis Sts., Emeryville, CA.

HOLLEMAN, JOHN J.
President, Vista College
b. Oct. 25, 1932, Oakland; s. Joseph W. and Grace K. (Greenlee) Holleman; B.A., 1956, and M.A., 1958, zoology, Univ. Calif., Berkeley, 1956; m. Nancy Bracken, Mar. 1956, Berkeley; chil.: Jennifer L., b. Feb. 1960; Linda S., b. Dec. 1962; John G., b. July 1964. Career: staff, Merritt Coll., Oakland, 1957-77; instr., 1957-74, chmn. Dept. Biological Sci., 1966-70, 1971-74, coord. of instr., 1967-74, Div. chmn., and asst. Dean, Sci. and Math. Div., 1974-77; pres., Vista Coll., 1977---; Cons.: Dames and Moore, Soil Engrs. and Geologists, 1971---, Am. Inst. Biol. Scis., 1974-75; dir., Urban Chem. Tech. Intern Proj. HEW, 1973-75; dir., Human Beeings and Their Environment, NSF, 1977---. Contbr. to profl. journs. AUS, 1950-52. Mem.: Ecological Soc. of Am.; Nat. Assn. Biology Tchrs.; Am. Inst. Biol. Scis.; Biol. Soc. of Wash.; Calif. Malacozoological Soc.; W. Soc. of Naturalists; W. Soc. of Malacologists; Calif. Acad. of Scis.; S. Calif. Acad. of Scis. Home: 164 Greenbrook Dr., Danville, CA 94526; Office: 2020 Milvia St., Berkeley, CA 94704.

HOLLEY, ROBERT WILLIAM
Molecular Biologist
b. Jan. 28, 1922, Urbana, Ill.; s. Charles E. and Viola E. (Wolfe) Holley; A.B., Univ. Ill., Urbana, Ill., 1942; Ph.D., Cornell Univ., 1947; studies, Coll. of Wash., Pullman, Wash., 1947-48; m. Ann Dworkin, Mar. 3, 1945; son, Frederick, b. Sept. 30, 1952. Career: Research biochemist, Cornell Univ. Med. Sch., 1944-46;

instr., State Coll. of Wash., 1947-48; asst. prof. & assoc.
prof. of Organic Chem., N.Y. State Agri. Exptl. Sta.,
Cornell, 1948-57; Assoc. prof. & prof. of Biochem.
(part-time), Cornell, 1957-64; Research Chemist,
U.S. Plant, Soil & Nutrition Lab., ARS, USDA, N.Y.,
1957-64; prof. of Biochem. & Molecular Biology,
Cornell, 1964-69, chmn. of dept., 1965-66; Resident
Fellow, Am. Cancer Soc. Prof. of Molecular Biology,
The Salk Inst., 1968---. Awarded: Nobel Prize in
Physiology or Med., 1968; Illini Achievement Award,
Univ. of Ill., 1974; Albert Lasker Award, 1965;
Distinguished Service Award, USDA, 1965; Nat. Acad.
of Scis., 1967. Mem.: Councilor, Am. Chem. Soc.,
1971-74; Am. Cancer Soc. (Calif. Div., Inc.), Fellowship
Screening Com., 1975-77. Hobbies: sculpture, photog.
Home: 7381 Rue Michael, La Jolla, CA 92037; Office:
The Salk Inst., Box 1809, San Diego, CA 92112.

HOLYER, ERNA MARIA
Author — Artist — Educator
b. Mar. 15, 1925, Weilheim, Upper Bavaria, Germany; d.
Mathias and Anna Schretter; A.A., San Jose Evening Coll.,
1964; student, journalism, edn., San Mateo Coll. and San
Jose State Univ., 1964-69; m. Gene Wallace Holyer, Aug.
24, 1957, Unter-Eglfing, Germany. Career: tchr., creative
and nonfiction writing, San Jose Metropolitan Adult Edn.
Program, 1968---; freelance writer, 1960---; freelance
artist, 1958---. Author: 200 plus articles and short stories
publ. variety of mags., contbd. 20 stories, Encyclopaedia
Britannica Edn. Div., Beacon Press, Advent Verlag
Zuerich and Reader's Digest Edn. Div., 1970---; 10 books
pub. 1965---: Rescue at Sunrise, Steve's Night of Silence,
A Cow for Hansel, At the Forest's Edge, Song of Courage,
Lone Brown Gull, Shoes for Daniel, Sigi's Fire Helmet,
The Southern Sea Otter, Hansel, 1979. Art: several
one-woman exhibits; exhibitor, IBC Art Gallery, S.F.,
1973; Portrait Award, annual juried exhibit, 1965, Los
Gatos Art Assn.; paintings in pvt. collections. Recipient:
Woman of Achievement honor certificate, 1973, 1974,
1975, San Jose Mercury-News; Lefoli Award for
Excellence in adult edn. instr., Metro. Adult
Edn. Senate. Erna Holyer Collection, Stanford Univ.
Lib. is open to researchers all over world. Charter mem.,
Calif. Writer's Club, Peninsula br. Hobbies: Calif. hist.,
studies. Rec.: walking, cycling, swimming. Home and
studio: 1314 Rimrock Dr., San Jose, CA 95120.

HOM, BEN L.
Chairman, United Federal Savings & Loan Assn.
b. Sept. 11, 1940, San Francisco; s. J.H. Hom; student,
S.F. State Coll., Anthony Real Estate Sch., S.F.; m. Pat L.
Lee, San Francisco; chil.: May, b. May 6, 1962; Jane, b.
Oct. 16, 1963; Shirley, b. Sept. 28, 1966; Ben Jr., b. Sept.
14, 1972. Career: pres. and mgr., G.S.R. Inc. (Golden
State Realty), S.F., 1964-74; founder, pres., chmn. bd.,
United Federal Savings & Loan Assn., 1974---. (G.S.R.
Inc., pioneer Chinese-Am. real estate agency in Richmond
dist. helped more than 1000 Chinese-Am. families settle
as well as oriental business of all kinds.) (United Federal is
first and presently the only Federal capital stock assn.
managed by Chinese-Am. in U.S.A., objective: to provide
spec. services to Asian residents in S.F. Bay Area.) Dir.
and v.p., Am. Savings & Loan League; dir., Calif. Savings
& Loan League; mem. Chinese Am. Citizen Alliance; dir.
Tom Family Benevolent Assn.; dir.-secty., Chew Lun Nat.
Benevolent Assn. & S.F. Charter; pres. New Chinatown
Improvement Assn.; com. mem. Real Estate Edn.
Advisory Com., Calif. Community Coll.; v.p. Optimist
Club; mem. Commonwealth Club. Home: 2555 Chestnut
St., S.F., CA 94123; Office: 498 Clement St., San
Francisco, CA 94118.

HONIG, NANCY CATLIN
Company President
b. Jan. 2, 1943, Oakland, Calif.; d. Milton and Betty
(Street) Marquard; student, Diablo Valley Coll., 1961-63;
Univ. of Calif., 1976-76; Golden Gate Univ., 1976-77; m.
Louis Honig, June 2, 1973, San Francisco; chil.: Michael,
b. Jan. 14, 1962; Jonathan, b. Mar. 4, 1975. Career:
management cons., 1968-75; pres., Nanvy Honig &
Associates, Inc., 1976--- med. mgmt. and constrn. co. that
has devel. and managed more than 500 med. practices and
clinics in West and Midwest; also, 1976---, designer of and
lectr. in continuing edn. programs of med. socs., colls.
bds., hosps. and assns. Mem.: Advisory bd., Pruett Coll.,
1976---; co-founder, v.p., bd. dir., Profl. Women's
Alliance, 1977; assoc. mem., Physicians' Review Team,
Republic of China, 1978; advisory bd. mem. Women
Entrepreneurs, 1977. Subject of mag. and newspaper
articles, S.F. Chronicle, Health Care Week, Oakland
Tribune, Prep for Practice, L.A. Times, Free Enterprise.
Mem. Democratic Alternative Caucus, 1977---. Home:
2701 Claremont Blvd., Berkeley, CA 94704.

HOOVER, NANCY HOLM
Securities Company Executive — City Official
b. Oct. 29, 1938, San Diego, Calif.; d. Olaf Furnald and
Virginia (Pinney) Holm; m. George Hoover, Apr. 11,
1959, San Diego; chil.: George, b. Dec. 26, 1962, Lisbon,
Portugal; Nina, b. May 1, 1964, Lisbon. Career: Exec.
asst., Psychology Today, 1971-75; acct. exec., Bache
Halsey Stuart Shields Inc., 1976---; also Councilperson,
city of Del Mar, 1974---. Dir.: Del Mar News Press; San
Diego City Club; Concern for Off-Shore Drilling, COOL.
Chmn., S.D. Co. Commn. on Status of Women, 1976---;
co-chmn., Coalition for Responsible Planning. Mayor, Del
Mar, 1976-77. Hobby: photog. Rec.: jogging, tennis.
Home: 367 Pine Needles Dr., Del Mar, CA; Office: 1200
Prospect, La Jolla, CA 92037.

HOPE, FRANK LEWIS, JR.
President, Frank L. Hope & Assocs.
b. Apr. 10, 1930, San Diego; s. Frank Lewis and Marion
(Bullock) Hope; B.A. (arch.), Univ. of Calif., Berkeley,
1953; m. Barbara Pritchard, Berkeley, Dec. 21, 1952;
chil.: Gretchen, b. May 31, 1955, Gail, b. Aug. 5, 1956,
Carolyn, b. Feb. 26, 1960; Leland, b. Nov. 7, 1961;
Jacqueline, b. July 3, 1964. Career: Licensed arch.,
Colo., Nev., Calif., Ga., Wash. D.C., Md.; assoc. with
Frank L. Hope & Assocs., archs. and engrs. 1953, asst.
secty-treas. 1957, secty. 1959, pres. 1964---. 1st Lt.,
U.S. Army, 2nd Armored Div., U.S. Forces in Ger.,
1953-55. Mem.: bd. dirs. First Fed. Svgs. & Loan Assn.,
S.D., 1967-77; pres.-exec. com. Econ. Devel. Corp., S.D.
1968-72; Chancellors Club and trustee, Univ. of Calif.,
S.D. 1968-72; pres. San Diego Chpt. AIA 1971; Fellow,
AIA, 1972; dir., Security Pac. Natl. Bank Bd., 1978---;
pres.-bd. dirs., Jr. Achievement of S.D., Inc., 1964-66;
bd. dirs., Univ. Club of S.D. 1965---; bd. dirs., S.D.
Yacht Club, 1963-72; past pres., S.D. 20-30 Club; pres.
Calif. Council AIA 1971; exec. com. San Diegans, Inc.;
Ambassadors; bd. dirs.-exec. com. S.D. C. of C., S.D.
Rotary Club. Roman Catholic. Rec.: sailing, skiing.
Home: 3430 Bangor Pl., San Diego, CA; Office: 1475
Sixth Ave., San Diego, CA 92101.

HOPKINS, CECILIA ANN
College Administrator
b. Feb. 17, 1922, Havre, Mont.; d. Kost L. and Mary
(Manaras) Sofos; B.S., Mont. State Coll. 1944; M.A.,
S.F. State Coll. 1958; M.A.,(2), 1967; Ph.D., Calif.
Western Univ., 1977; m. Henry E. Hopkins, San Mateo,
Sept. 7, 1944. Career: Bus. tchr., Harve H.S. 1942-44;
secty. George P. Gorham Real Estate, 1944-45; escrow
secty. Fox & Carskadon, Realtors, 1945-50; escrow ofcr.
Calif. Pac. Title Ins. Co., 1950-57; bus. tchr., Westmoor
H.S. 1957-58; instr. Coll. of San Mateo, 1958---, Real
Estate Dept. chmn., 1963-76; dir., Div. of Business,
1976---; Cons., Dept. Real Estate, Sacto.; Comm. Coll.
Adv. Com., chmn. 1971-72; adv. Real Estate Commr.,
Dept. of Real Estate, State of Calif. 1970-71;
Chancellor's Comm. Coll. Adv. Com., 1976---; Comm.
Coll. Real Estate Edn. Endowment Fund Advis. Comm.,
1977 (both State Dept. Comms.), Proj. dir., Career
Awareness Consortium Comm. (State Dept.), 1976---.
Mem.: natl. dir. Inter-Chpt. rels. Delta Pi Epsilon,
1962-65; natl. hist. 1966-67; natl. secty. 1968-69; state
pres. Calif. Assn. of Real Estate Tchrs., 1964-65, (hon.)
dir. 1965---; Real Estate Certificate Inst; S.F. State Coll.
Counseling and Guidance Alumni Assn.; Calif. Bus.
Tchrs. Assn.; Alpha Gamma Delta, Theta Alpha Delta,
Pi Lambda Theta, AAUW. Hobbies: travel, collecting
antiques. Rec.: hiking, swim. Home: 504 Colgate
Way, San Mateo; Office: Coll. of San Mateo, 1700 W.
Hilldale Blvd., San Mateo, CA 94402.

HOPKINS, WILLIAM P., JR.
Anaheim City Attorney
b. Oct. 4, 1921, Chicago; s. William P., Sr. and Genevra
D. Hopkins; B.Sc., De Paul Univ., 1949; M.B.A., Univ.
of Chicago Grad. Sch. of Bus., 1953; J.D., USC Law
Center, 1967; m. Virginia Lyons, June 4, 1950, Chicago;
chil.: Raymond, b. May 4, 1950; Richard, b. May 4,
1950; John, b. June 25, 1952; Mark, b. Apr. 25, 1956;
Jeanne, b. Jan. 10, 1949. Career: Depty. City Atty.,
1968-73; Asst. City Atty., 1974-76; City Atty., City of
Anaheim, 1976---. Mem.: Bar of Supreme Ct. of U.S.,
Am. Bar Assn., Orange and L.A. Co. Bar Assns. Capt.,
AUS, 1942-46, WW II, Europe; 1951-52, Korea. Mem.
Phi Alpha Delta legal frat., Am. Legion. Rec.: golf,
swimming, baseball. Home: 1181 S. Sunkist, Anaheim,
CA 92806; Office: 106 N. Claudina St., Suite 607,
Anaheim, CA 92805.

HOPPER, CHRYSTLE F.
Realtor
b. Nov. 12, 1923, Mo.; d. Albert and Fern (Earles) Farley;

student Jr. Coll. 1943; grad., Real Estate Inst., 1978. Career: employee, Pacific Telephone Co., 1945-60; realtor, Corona del Mar, 1961---. Named Woman of Year, Realtors 1973; named Woman of Year, C. of C. Dolphins, 1976. Bd. dir. Youth Employment Service, 1973-78; Fine Arts Patron, Newport Harbor Art Mus., 1971---; mem. Hist. Soc. of Newport Beach, 1973---; mem. Children's Hear-More Inst., 1975-76; pres., Dolphin Club, 1973-74; v.p. Newport-Harbor C. of C., 1976-78; pres., Calif. Women in Chambers of Commerce, 1977; pres., Orange Co. Council C's. of C., 1977. Democrat. Lutheran, fin. trustee. Hobbies: reading, writing. Rec.: travel. Home: 308 Jasmine Ave., Corona del Mar, CA; Office: 2435 E. Coast Hwy., Corona del Mar, CA.

HOPPING, RICHARD L.
President, Southern California College of Optometry
b. July 26, 1928, Dayton, Oh.; s. Lavon and Dorothy (Anderson) Hopping; ed. B.Sc., Dr. of Optometry, 1952; (hon.) Dr. of Ocular Sci. 1972; m. Patricia Vance, Dayton, 1951; chil.: Ronald, n. Apr. 12, 1952; Debra, b. Mar. 21, 1954; Jerrold, b. Apr. 27, 1956. Career: Optometrist, pvt. practice, 1952-73; cons. Soc. for Visual Care, 1973---; trustee, Assn. Independent Calif. Coll. and Univs. 1973---. Contrib. to profl. publs. 1968---. Mem.: bd. trustees, Am. Optometric Assn. 1966-73; pres. 1971-72; chmn. Judicial Council and speaker, House of Dels. 1972-73; Fullerton C. of C. 1974; Am. Acad. of Optometry, Sigma Alpha Sigma, Beta Sigma Kappa. Bd. Deacons, Westminster Prebyterian. Ch. Hobby: B.S.A., golf. Home: 2741 Anacapa, Fullerton, CA 92653; Office: 2001 Associated Rd., Fullerton, CA 92631.

HORN, JOHN STEPHEN
University President
b. May 31, 1931, Gilroy; s. John Stephen and Isabelle (McCaffrey) Horn; A.B. (with great distinction in polit. sci.), Stanford Univ. 1953, Ph.D. 1958; M.P.A., Harvard Univ. 1955; m. Nini Moore, Concord, Calif., Sept. 4, 1954; chil.: Marcia Karen, b. Nov. 26, 1955; John Stephen, b. Apr. 4, 1960. Career: Adm. asst. Secty. of Labor James P. Mitchell, 1959-60; legislative asst. Sen. Thomas H. Kuchel, 1960-66; sr. fellow, The Brookings Inst., Wash., D.C. 1966-69; dean grad. stus. and research, Am. Universit., Wash., D.C. 1969-70; pres. Calif. State Univ., Long Beach, 1970---. Cong. Fellow, Am. Polit. Sci. Assn. 1958-59; fellow, Inst. of Politics, John F. Kennedy Sch. of Govt., Harvard Univ. 1966-67; Pres. Nixon's Transition Task Force on Orgn. of Exec. Br. 1968-69; v. chmn. U.S. Comm. on Civil Rights, Wash., D.C. 1969---; chmn. 1969, and Urban Stus. Fellowship Adv. Bd., Dept. of Housing and Urban Devel., 1970; natl. adv. com. Law Enforcement Edn. Pgm., Dept. of Justice, 1969---. Sr. cons.-host-narrator: Westinghouse Broadcasting Co. "The Government Story" series (40-30 min. TV shows on exec., legislative, judicial brs. of Fed. Govt.), 1967-69; "The Election Game" series (8-30 min. radio shows on electoral coll. and pres. campaigns), 1970; publs.: The Cabinet and Congress, Columbia Univ. Press, 1960; Unused Power: The Work of the Senate Com. on Appropriations, The Brookings Inst. 1970; (co-author) Congressional Ethics: The View from the House, The Brookings Inst., 1975. Mem.: pres. Hollister chapt., Calif. Scholarship Fed. 1949; exec. bd. Stanford Chpt., Phi Beta Kappa, 1955-58; exec. bd. Stanford Alumni Assn. (pres. 1976-77); Pi Sigma Alpha; Am., Western Polit. Sci. Assns.; Calif. Hist. Soc. Republican. Home: 3944 Pine Ave., Long Beach, CA 90807; Office: 6101 Seventh St., Long Beach, CA 90801.

HORNADY, WILLIAM H.D.
Minister, Founder's Church of Religious Science
b. Apr. 26, 1910, Carson City, Nev.; s. Rev. William H.D., Sr. (Meth. minister) and Mary (Leaming) Hornady; desc. 7 generations of ministers; ed. pub. schs., S.F.; grad. H.S., Santa Cruz, Calif.; Master of Human., Cal. State, L.A.; Fellow, Cal. Lutheran Coll.; D.D., Whittier Coll.; stu. relig., Whittier Coll. (debate team, partner, former pres. Richard Nixon); Dr. Relig. Sci. (relig. sci. and philosophy) under Dr. Ernest Holmes (dean-founder, relig. sci.); attended Jungian Inst., pers. student of Dr. Carl Jung; m. Louise Clara Wright; chil.: William H.D., III. Career: Meth. minister (father's ch.); 2 extensive stu. tours of Orient and Central Am.; assoc. with Dr. Ernest Holmes, Ch. of Relig. Sci., L.A. Radio pgm, This Thing Called Life, KIEV. Author: Prayer for Universal Peace, printed in all langs. throughout world; Success Unlimited, 1955; Life Everlasting, 1957; co-author (with Dr. Ernest Holmes), Help for Today, publ. by Dodd, Mead & Co. 1958; co-author (Harlan Ware) The Inner Light, 1964. Speaker, Armed Forces Radio Serv. broadcasts (extended behind Iron Curtain); world tour, consulted with Dr. Albert Schweitzer,

Lambarene, Africa, 1962. Awards: many citations for youth activities and efforts in behalf of alcoholic and narcotic pgms.; Humanitarians Award, Albert Schweitzer Coll., Switz., 1956; Terra Sancta, State Medal of Israel, 1965; Paul Harris Fellow, Rotary Club Internat., 1974; Freedoms Found. Award, 1963; decorated, Kim Khanh of Vietnam (highest civ. award), 1970. Mem.: past-chmn. bd. trustees, So. Calif. Chpt., Multiple Sclerosis Soc.; served 3 Pres., Comm. on Civil Rights and White House Conf. on Health; bd. dirs., Cancer Prevention Soc.; L.A. Consistory, Adv. bd., Internat. Orphans; Dir., Friendly House, Beatitude Center; Pac. Pioneer Broadcasters, U.S. Yacht Racing Union; Jonathan Club. Scottish Rite, Al Malaikah Shrine; (guest chaplain, U.S. Senate). Office: Church of Religious Science, 3281 W. 6th St., L.A., CA 90020.

HORNBY, ROBERT A.
Utility Executive — Civic Leader
b. Oct. 2, 1900, Topeka, Kan.; s. Alfred Joseph and Louise E. (McJilton) Hornby; ed., Engring., Univ. of Calif.; C.E. certificate, Calif.; m. Mary Louise Duffy, Jan. 16, 1925; dau. Janis Elliott. Career: Assoc. with cons. engr. 1922; rate and appraisal, Calif. Pub. Utilities Commn. 1924; valuation engr., So. Calif. Gas Co., 1925, comptroller, 1930; exec. engr., Pac. Lighting Corp. 1930; v.p. 1934; v.p.-dir. 1945; exec. v.p.-dir. 1950, pres.-dir. 1956-68, dir.-exec. com. 1968-72, v.p.-dir., Pac. Lighting Gas Supply Co. 1950, exec. v.p. 1952, pres. 1957, chmn. bd. 1960-68 (ret.). Dir.: Barclays Bank of Calif., 1968-76; (hon.) Broadway-Hale Stores, Inc.; trustee, Calif. State Colls., 1970-78; Cons.-prof.-lectr., USC Sch. of Bus. USMC (1918-19), WW I; staff ofcr., USAF (1942-45), WW II. Awards: Legion of Merit. Mem.: dir. Am. Gas Assn. 1952-60, chmn. spec. com., Execs on Regulatory Affairs and other coms.; trustee USC, adv. council, Grad. Sch. of Bus.; trustee, No. Calif. Council on Econ. Edn.; Postsecondary Edn. Comm., 1974-78; Dept. of Edn., past pres., Pac. Coast Gas Assn.; former trustee, Inst. of Gas. Tech.; pres. Calif. State C. of C., 1960-62; former trustee, St. Francis Mem. Hosp. (S.F.) and Am. Enterprise Inst. (Wash., D.C.); co-founder, S.F. Volunteers for Better Govt.; Governor's Bus. Adv. Council; clubs: The Family, L.A. Club. Republican. Congregationalist. Home: 435 S. Curson Ave., L.A., CA 90036; Office: 810 S. Flower St., L.A., CA 90017.

HORNER, LARRY DEAN
Accounting Company Executive
b. Apr. 8, 1934, Marquette, Kan.; s. Marion F. and Harriett E. (Ostrom) Horner; B.B.A., Univ. of Kansas, 1956; m. Ingeborg E. Peters, Apr. 22, 1974, Frankfurt, Germany; chil.: Basin; Brian; Adeline; Hal; Adele. Career: joined Kansas City office, Peat, Marwick, Mitchell & Co.-CPA's, 1956, admitted to partnership, 1964---; Sr. Partner of firm's four offices in Germany and mem. of Continental European firm's advisory com., 1970-74; managing partner, Miami, Fla., 1974; transferred to Los Angeles office as managing partner, 1977---. Mem., Operating Com., Peat, Marwick, Mitchell & Co. Mem.: Bd. dir., Central City Assn.; Internat. Trade Com., L.A. C. of C.; chmn. budget com., United Way of Central L.A. Civic involvements including B.S.A., C. of C., United Way, in Miami, Fla.; Kansas City, Mo.; Frankfurt, Germany. Clubs: L.A. Country; California. Hobbies: performing and visual arts. Rec.: golf, tennis. Home: 516 S. Rimpau Blvd., L.A., CA 90020; Office: 555 S. Flower St., L.A., CA 90071.

HORNSTEIN, WILLIAM
Neurologist
b. July 7, 1946, Bronx, New York; s. Irving (former exec. v.p. & dir., Schenley Industries, Inc.) and Dorothy (Davis) Hornstein; B.A., State Univ. of N.Y., Buffalo, 1970; M.D., Chicago Med. Sch., 1975; training completed, Univ. of Minn., Dept. of Neurology, 1978; m. Deborah Badler (grad. Smith Coll., Sch. for Social Work), Sept. 6, 1970, New York, N.Y.; son: Adam Lee, b. Oct. 24, 1976. Career: med. practice, Neurology, Long Beach. Mem.: Am. Acad. of Neurology, L.A. Co. Med. Assn.; L.A. Co. Neurology Soc. Office: 1045 Atlantic Ave., Suite 608, Long Beach, CA 90813.

HOROWITZ, DAVID CHARLES
Consumer Ombudsman, TV News
b. June 30, 1937, N.Y.C.; s. Max Leo and Dorothy (Lippman) Horowitz; B.A. (hons. jour.), Bradley Univ., 1959; M.S.J., Northwestern Univ. 1960; CBS Fellow, Columbia Univ., NY 1962-63; m. Judith Ann Rosenthal, July 13, 1964 (div. 1969); dau. Victoria Ann; m. 2nd., Suzanne E. McCambridge, 1973. Career: Editor-in-chief, Tazewell Co. Newspaper, Ill. 1956; reporter, Peoria

Journ. Star, Ill. 1957-60; reporter-columnist, Lerner Newspapers and Chicago City News Bur. 1959-60; newscaster, KRNT Radio-TV, Des Moines, 1960-62; news writer-prod., ABC Radio Network, NYC 1963; Far East corr. NBC News, 1963-64; pub. affairs dir. WMCA, NYC, 1964-66; corr.-edn. editor, Consumer Ombudsman, KNBC News-Action 4, L.A. 1966---, spec. feats.; Consumer Guideline; Of Consumer Interest, nationally syndicated program David Horowitz Consumer Buyline; worldwide Apollo 15 splashdown, 1971; Calif. earthquake, Feb. 9, 1971; Dem. Conv. 1972. Adv. UCLA publs.; writer, numerous publ. articles. Awards: Natl. Radio-TV Daily Award for Krebiozen — Hope or Hoax for Cancer, 1963; won Emmy for consumer ombudsman, KNBC Newsservice; also winner Emmy, 1975, 1977 for consumer reporting. Guest, The Tonight Show, the Dinah! Show, the Phil Donahue Show, others. Serv. USNR 1954-62. Mem.: bd. dirs. Natl. Broadcast Ed. Conf., Am. Cancer Soc., and Calif. Div.; bd. dirs. L.A. Jewish Home for Aged; patron, L.A. Co. Art Museum; Acad. TV Arts and Scis.; Internat. Radio-TV Soc.; Radio-TV News Dirs. Assn.; Natl. Edn. Writers Assn.; The Guardians; Sigma Delta Chi, Phi Delta Kappa; Overseas Press Club of Am., NYC; Friars Club. Office: 3000 W. Alameda Ave., Burbank, CA 91523.

HORWIN, LEONARD
Attorney at Law
b. Jan. 2, 1913, Chicago, Ill., c. Joseph and Jeanette Horwin; ed. B.A. (hons), UCLA June 1933; LL.B. (cum laude), Yale Law Sch., June 1936; m. Ursula Helene Donig, Beverly Hills, Oct. 15, 1939; chil.: Noel S., b. Sept. 18, 1940; Leonora Marie, b. Nov. 11, 1947. Career: Assoc. with pioneer law firm, Lawler, Felix and Hall, 1936-39; partner (Jack W.) Hardy and Horwin (attys. for L.A. Examiner, Sterling Elec. Motors, others), 1939-42; partner, Witkin-Horwin Review Course on Calif. Law, 1939-42; lectr. on labor law, USC Law Sch. 1941; counsel, Bd. of Econ. Warfare and mem. requirements com., War Prodn Bd. 1942-43; attache, U.S. Embassy, Madrid, Spain, 1943-47; Am. repr. in Spain, Allied Control Council for Ger. 1945-47; lectr. (Spanish lang.) on Am. Constitutional Law, Am. Cultural Inst., Madrid, 1945; lectr., foreign affairs, Town Hall, others, 1949; pvt. law practice, 1950---. Elected to Beverly Hills City Council, 1962, Mayor Pro Tempore, 1963, Mayor of Beverly Hills, 1964; chmn. com. on municipal ct. reorgn., League of Calif. Cities, 1963-65; dir. So. Calif. Rapid Transit Dist, 1964-66; del. L.A. Regional Transportation Study, 1964-66; pres. Friends of Santa Monica Mts. State Park, 1964-66; com. chmn., Transportation Comm., L.A. Goals Council, 1966-70. Author: numerous articles on legal subjs.; editor, Yale Law Journ. 1934-35; Awards: winner, Yale Univ. Israel H. Peres Prize for legal writing, 1934-35; winner, Yale Univ. Edward D. Robbins Mem. Prize, 1935-36. Judaism. Hobby: community projs. and activities. Rec.: hunting, riding, skiing. Home: 434 El Camino Dr., Beverly Hills, CA; Office: 121 S. Beverly Dr., Beverly Hills, CA 90212.

HOSMER, CRAIG
Energy Consultant
b. May 6, 1915, Brea; s. Chester C. and Jane (Craig) Hosmer; ed. A.B. 1937, LL.B. 1940; m. Marian Swanson, 1946; chil.: Susan Jane, b. 1947; Larkin, b. 1950. Career: Atty. at law, atty. for Atomic Energy Comm. 1948; spec. asst. U.S. Dist. Atty. 1948; Congressman, 32nd Dist. of Calif. 1953-75; pres. Am. Nuclear Energy Council, 1975-78; Energy Consultant, 1978---. Rear Admiral, USNR (Ret.); all theatres, WW II. Republican. Office: 1750 K St. N.W., No. 300, Wash., D.C. 20006.

HOSTLER, CHARLES W.
President, Hostler Investment Co.
b. Dec. 12, 1919, Chicago; s. Sidney Marvin and Catherine (Marshall) Hostler; ed. U.S. mil schs., U.S., British, Turkish, Lebanese; B.A., UCLA; law student, 2 yrs., Univ. Bucharest, Rumania; M.A. (USAF Commendation for outstanding acad. achievement), Georgetown Univ.; M.A., Am. Univ. of Beirut, Lebanon; Ph.D. (Gold Key Soc.), Georgetown Univ.; div.; son, Charles W. Jr., b. Nov. 28, 1952; Career: Permanent Col. in Regular AF, 1942-63 (assignments incl.: mem. Policy Planning Staff, Secty. of Def./Internat. Affairs; Asst. to Dir. of Disarmament, Def. Dept.; Sr. Dept. of Def. Rep. on U.S. Del. to Nuclear Test Ban Conf., Geneva; U.S. Air Attache to Lebanon, Jordan, Cyprus and personal rep. of Secty. of AF and Chief of Staff, USAF, and advis. to U.S. Ambassadors in above countries; mem. Jt. Strategic Plans Group, Jt. Chiefs of Staff, Wash. D.C.); also Adjunct Prof., Sch. of Internat.

Serv., Am. Univ., Wash. D.C., 1955-63; Author of books and articles incl.: Turkism and the Soviets, trans. and pub. 4 countries; The Challenge of Sci. Edn., NY 1959; articles in economic, sci. and mil. journs.; dir. Internat. Opns., McDonnell Douglas Corp., 1963-69; chmn. bd., Irvine Nat. Bank, 1969-74; pres., Hostler Investment Co., 1969---; vice chmn., Calif. Contractors State License Bd., 1969-74, chmn., 1977---; Dep. Asst. Secty. for Internat. Commerce, U.S. Dept. of Commerce, 1974-76; regional v.p. Middle East and Africa, E-Systems, Inc., Dallas, 1976-77; mem. bd. of govs., Middle East Inst., Wash. D.C., 1977; mem. Advis. Bd., Hubbs/Sea World Research Inst., San Diego, 1977---; bd. dirs., Wynn's Internat. Inc., 1969-74; Awards: U.S. Legion of Merit; Greek Order of the Phoenix; Order of Holy Sepulchre; Order of Saints Peter and Paul; Lebanese Order of the Cedars; Haitian Order of Honor and Merit; Repub. of China Order of Cloud and Banner, with Cravat; Hon. Citizen of Cyclades Is. of Greece. Home: on board yacht "Charlie's Angel"; Office: P.O.B. 9976, San Diego, CA 92109.

HOTCHKIS, PRESTON
Insurance Executive — Civic Leader
b. June 19, 1893, L.A.; s. Finlay Montgomery and Flora Cornelia (Preston) Hotchkis; desc.: Sir Mathews Duncan (phys.-surg. to Queen Victoria; co-discoverer of chloroform); Lt. Preston (Am. Rev.); ed. A.B., Univ. of Calif. 1961, grad. law (1 yr.); m. Katharine Bixby, Long Beach, Dec. 11, 1923; chil.: Katharine, b. Nov. 23, 1924; Joan, b. Sept. 21, 1927; Preston Bixby, b. May 27, 1929; John Finlay, b. Aug. 3, 1931. Career: Asst. secty., secty., Calif. Delta Farms; admitted to Calif. bar, 1920; assoc. founder, Pac. Finance Corp. 1920, Pac. Indemnity Co. 1926, Consolidated Steel Co. 1929; exec. com., Yosemite Park and Curry Co., 1935---; exec. com., Pac. Mutual Life Ins. Co., dir. Pac. Tel. and Telegraph Co.; pres.-dir., Fred H. Bixby Ranch Co.; v.-chmn. bd., Founders' Ins. Co. 1946-64; regent, Univ. of Calif. 1933-36; dir. Met. Water Dist. So. Calif., 1978. Mem.: San Marino City Council, 1940-55. Ensign, USN, WW I; War Finance Com. 1942-45; L.A. area (1945) WW II. Awards: (citations) War Bond Campaign (from Secty. of Treas.); Navy Relief Campaign (from Secty. of Navy), 1942; Training Within Ind. (from War Man Power Bd.), 1945. Mem.: pres. Calif. Alumni Assn. 1935-36; dir. Calif. State C. of C., pres. 1942-43; trsutee, Southwest Museum; trustee, Good Hope Med. Found.; The Business Council; trustee, U.S. Com., Dag Hammarskjold Found.; natl. adv. council, Girl Scouts of U.S.; Am. Bar Assn.; L.A. and Calif. Bar Assns; pres.-dir. L.A. World Affairs Council; Calif. and Univ. Clubs (L.A.), Bohemian and Pac. Union Clubs (S.F.), Valley Hunt Club (Pasa.); Sigma Nu, Phi Delta Phi. Republican. (chmn. Repub. Natl. Conv., Chicago, 1952). Presbyterian. Home: 1415 Circle Dr., San Marino, CA.

HOUDE, GLENN ROLAND
School Administrator
b. Apr. 2, 1927, Flint, Mich.; s. Roland A. and Mary Houde; B.A., Mich. State Univ., 1950; M.A., 1956; Ed.D., Stanford Univ., 1971; m. Ramona Joyce Dolsen, Mar. 25, 1950, Flint, Mich.; chil.: Denise D., b. 1952; Blair G., b. 1953; Kevin L., b. 1960; Cynthia A., b. 1962. Career: teache; of English, Portland, Ore., 1950-56; supr. vice prin., Portland, Ore., 1956-60; principal, Fremont, Calif. 1960-62; asst. to Supt., Fremont, 1962-65; director secondary edn., Fremont, 1964-65; asst. supt., instruction, Fremont, 1965-70; Supt. of Schools, Elk Grove, Calif., 1970---; shoe salesman, 1942-48; factory worker, Buick Motor Co., 1948-49; salesman, Miller's Dept. Store, Portland, 1952-55. Recipient: Ford Found. Fellowship, Study of Leadership Research and Implications for Teaching, 1974-75; contbr.: Why Teach, L. Sharpe, 1957. Served USN, WW II, hosp. corps., electrocardiograph tech. Bd. dir., Elk Grove C. of C., 1974, pres. 1975; mem. Elk Grove Community Planning Council, 1973-74; Elk Grove Incorporation Com., 1974; Mem.: Elk Grove Rotary Club, pres., dir., 1973-74; Assn. Calif. Sch. Adminstrs.; State Political Action Com., 1975---. Hobbies: bridge, piano. Rec.: golf. Home: 9452 S. Wales Way, Elk Grove, CA 95624; Office: Elk Grove Unified Sch. Dist., Elk Grove Blvd., Elk Grove, CA 95624.

HOUGH, GORDON LETTS
Chairman, Pacific Telephone and Telegraph Co.
b. Jan. 22, 1919, Denver Colo.; s. Peyton Royce and Florence (Letts) Hough; B.A., Stanford Univ. 1942, MBA, Stanford Sch. of Bus.; m. Doris MacDougall, Oct. 24, 1942; chil.: S. Lacklan, b. Dec. 21, 1948; A. Lowry Ewig, b. Apr. 24, 1951. Career: Salesman, Ameron, Inc. 1947-48; Pac. Telephone Co. 1948---, asst. v.p. gen. mgr.

1962, v.p.-gen. mgr. 1964, v.p. So. Calif. 1966; dir.-pub. rels. Pac. Telephone & Telegraph Co., NY 1969, v.p. adm., S.F. 1971, exec. v.p. 1972, pres., S.F. 1975-77; chmn., 1978---. Dir.: Pac. Tel. and Teleg. Co. and Bell Tel. Co. of Nev., Amercon, Inc.; United Calif. Bank; Pac. Am. Income Shares, Inc.; Govt. Research Council; Resources Exch.; Mills Hosp.; trustee: USC, Harvey Mudd Coll.; pres. Ind.-Edn. Council; pres. United Way of Bay Area. Lt. Comdr., USN 1942-45. Mem.: Sigma Alpha Epsilon, The Walnut Elephant, Town Hall. Clubs: Banker's Pac. Union, Sutter, S.F. Golf, The Calif., Burlingame Country. Rec.: golf, gardening. Home: 2030 Forest View Ave., Hillsborough, CA 94010; Office: 140 New Montgomery St., S.F., CA 94105.

HOUK, GARETH WESLEY
Attorney at Law
b. Dec. 12, 1903, Visalia, Calif.; s. Wesley F. and Edith J. (Eliot) Houk (dec.); ed. Visalia Pub. Schs.; grad. H.S. 1922; LL.B., Southwestern Univ.,L.A., CA 1930; m. Martha D. Harder, Carson City, Nev., June 6, 1936; chil.: Gareth W., Jr., b. Dec. 27, 1937; Judith Ann, b. Dec. 25, 1940; James Larry, b. Feb. 29, 1944. Career: Assoc. with Security First Natl. Bank of L.A.; law firm, Woodruff, Musick & Hartke, L.A.; est. pvt. practice (spec. probate and corp. law), Visalia, 1932---; police judge, City of Visalia, and Justice of the Peace, Visalia Township, 1934-48; serv. as referee in bankruptcy-concillation commr. Mem.: past chmn., Visalia Parks Playgrounds and Rec. Commn.; (past) Calif. State Recreation Comm.; (past) pres. Tulare Co. Bar Assn.; Am. and Calif. State Bar Assns.; Legion of Hon., Order of DeMolay, Dist. Gov., Dist. No. 16; (past) pres.-bd. dirs., Tulare Co. YMCA (past) natl. council; Chmn., Tulare Co. Comm. on Aging; (past) pres. Visalia Sportsmen Assn.; (past) pres. Visalia Rotary Club. Hobby: hunting, fishing. Home: 318 Fairway Ave., Visalia; Office: 115 S. Church St., Visalia, CA 93277.

HOUSEL, JAMES ROBERT, JR.
Librarian
b. Feb. 16, 1917, Cripple Creek, Colo.; s. James R. Sr. and Emma (Winters) Housel; bro. Jerry Winters Housel; B.A., Univ. of Wyo. 1941; B.S. (lib. sci.), Univ. of Calif., Berkeley, 1948; M.S.L.S., USC 1971; m. Virginia Marian Elbert, Reno, Nev., June 20, 1947; chil.: Lucille Elaine Burke, Thomas Jerry, Marian Elizabeth. Career: Jr. librn., Richmond Pub. Lib., Richmond, 1948-50; head lib., Ellensburg Pub. Lib., Ellensburg, Wash. 1950-52; dir. 1st Regional Lib. of Miss., Hernando, Miss. 1952-56; head lib., Monterey Park Pub. Lib., Monterey Park, Calif. 1956-59; head librn. Ontario Pub. Lib., 1959---. 1st Lt., U.S. Army, ETO (1942-46), WW II. Mem.: Am., Calif. Lib. Assns.; v.p. Pomona Valley Writer's Club, 1960-63; pres. West End Sym. 1961-62; bd. dirs., Chaffey Comm. Cultural Council, 1966-71; Lib. Assn., Eng.; adv. council, Chaffey H.S. and Chaffey Community Colls.; Inland Lib. Sys.; founder-pres. Calif. Inst. of Parapsychology, 1969---; Valley Comm. Theatre, 1973---; bd. dirs. W. End Sym. 1974---; Friends of Ontario City Pib.; Calif. Hist. Soc., San Bernardino Mus. Assn., Elks, Mason, Sigma Nu. Episcopalian. (treas.-vestryman-sch. bd.). Hobbies: reading, music, camping. Rec.: travel, bowling. Home: 312 N. San Antonio, Apt. 7, Ontario, 91762; Office: Ontario City Library, 215 E. C. St., Ontario, CA 91761.

HOUSTON, IVAN JAMES
Insurance Company President
b. June 15, 1925, L.A.; s. Norman O. and Doris T. (Young) Houston; B.S., Univ. of Calif. 1948, CLU 1973; m. Philippa E. Jones, Santa Ana, Calif., July 15, 1946; chil.: Pamela B., Kathleen Y., Ivan A. Career: Acct. 1948; actuary, 1956; v.p.-actuary 1962; pres.-chief exec. ofcr. Golden State Mutual Ins. Co., 1970-76; chmn. bd., 1976. Sgt. Maj., 370th Inf. Reg., 92nd Div., Italy 1944-45. Awards: Purple Heart, Apr. 1945; Combat Inf. Badge. Mem.: Fellow, Life Mgmt. Inst. 1958---; Am. Acad. Actuaries, 1967---; bd. dirs.: Calif. C. of C., L.A. C. of C., L.A. Urban League; corp. bd. United Way; Kappa Alpha Psi; Sigma Pi Phi. Roman Catholic. Office: 1999 W. Adams Blvd., L.A., CA 90018.

HOUTS, MARSHALL WILSON
Lawyer — Publisher — Author
b. June 28, 1919, Chattanooga, Tenn.; s. Thomas Jefferson and Mary (Alexander) Houts; A.A., Brevard Jr. Coll., 1937; B.S.L., J.D., Univ. of Minn. 1941; m. Mary O. Dealy, Apr. 27, 1946, Pipestone, Minn.; chil.: Virginia, b. 1947; Kathy (Miller) b, 1948; Marsha (Jacobs), b. 1950; Patty, b. 1952; Thomas, b. 1955; Cindy, b. 1957; Timothy, b. 1960. Career: Special Agent, FBI, 1941-44; OSS Agent, 1944-46; pvt. practice

of law, Pipestone, Minn., 1946-51; spec. Municipal Judge, Pipestone, 1947-51; Gen. Counsel, Erle Stanley Gardner's Ct. of Last Resort, 1953-60; Prof. of Law: UCLA Law Sch., 1973---; Prof. of Forensic Pathology, Med. Sch. Univ. Calif., Irvine---; Criminal Justice Cons. to police depts., medical Examiner and Coroners---; creator of TRAUMA (bi-monthly, medico-legal pub.), 1957---; Author (books): King's X: Common Law and the Death of Sir Harry Oakes; They Asked for Death; Proving Medical Diagnosis and Prognosis (11 vols.); Cyclopedia of Sudden, Violent and Unexplained Death; Where Death Delights; Lawyer's Guide to Medical Proof (3 vols.); Photographic Misrepresentation; Courtroom MEdicine: Death (3 vols.); Courtroom Medicine; The Rules of Evidence; From Arrest to Release; From Evidence to Proof; From Gun to Gavel. Mil.: Office of Strategic Services (OSS), 1944-46, China-India-Burma theatre; decorated Bronze Arrowhead, Distinguished Unit Citation. Mem.: Rotary; Gamma Eta Gamma; Am. Acad. of Forensic Scis. Republican Co. Chmn., Pipestone Co., Minn., 1948-51. Home: 313 Emerald Bay, Laguna Beach, CA 92651.

HOWARD, MURRAY
Manufacturing Executive — Realtor
b. July 25, 1914, L.A.; s. Goerge A.J. and Mabel (Murray) Howard; B.S., UCLA 1939; Career: Mgr., Budget Control Dept., Lockheed Aircraft, 1939-45; pres.-chmn. bd., Stanley Foundries, Inc. 1945-59; pres.-chmn. bd., Howard Mach. Prods., Inc., 1959-63; chmn. bd., Murray Howard Realty, Inc. 1961-62; pres.-chmn. bd. 1962---; pres.-chmn. bd. Murray Howard Investment Corp. 1963---; pres. Howard Oceanography, Inc. 1967---; pres. Ranch Sales, Inc., 1968---; pres.-chmn. bd. Murray Howard Development, Inc. 1969---; bd. dirs. Shur-Lok Corp. 1969---; Licensed pub. acct. Dir. Airshippers Pub. Corp., La Brea Realty & Develop. Co. Mem.: Gov. Warren's Calif. Minority Com.; past v.p.-dir., Natl. Assn. Cost Accts: dir. Natl. Assn. of Mfrs.; Delta Tau Delta. Home: 3771 Lockland Dr., L.A., CA 90008; Office: 3440 Wilshire Blvd., L.A., CA 90010.

HOWELL, RITA ARLENE
Court Reporting Company Owner
b. June 5, 1937, Merced, Calif.; d. Joseph A. and Rita (Love) Ferrero; A.A., Armstrong Coll., Berkeley, 1957; m. Donald Lewis Howell, Sept. 7, 1958, Merced, Calif.; chil.: Beverly Jean. b. Sept. 27, 1961; Steven Donald, b. Apr. 9, 1964. Career: Secty., dep. dir. Calif. Dept. Pub. Health, Berkeley, 1959-67; supr. clerical staff, hearing reporter: Gov. Calif. councils on comprehensive planning, pub. health, hosp. council, hosp. adv. bd., Berkeley and Sacramento, 1967-70; owner, mgr., Arlene Howell Court Reporting, San Francisco, 1970---; partner, tchr., Bay Area Inst. of Reporting Sciences, S.F., 1973---. Pres., Exchangettes of Albany-El Cerrito, 1967, of Richmond, 1971. Mem.: Nat. Shorthand Reporters; Calif. Ct. Reporters Assn.; Am. Bus. Women (chpt. pres. 1969). Named Woman of Year, 1968, Am. Bus. Women. Republican. Roman Catholic. Home: 5737 Olinda Rd., El Sobrante, CA 94803; Office: 655 Sutter St., S.F., CA 94102.

HOWELL, WARREN R.
Publisher — Rare Book Dealer
b. Nov. 13, 1912, Berkeley, Calif.; s. John G. and Rebecca R. Howell; Stanford Univ. 1930-32; m. Antoinette Oostermayr, Carson City, Nev., Dec. 31, 1953. Career: Assoc. with John Howell Books, 1932---, partner-mgr. 1945-56; owner, 1956---. Publ.: Filings from an Old Saw (Downey), S.F., 1956; The Journ. of Marius Duvall (Duvall), S.F., 1957; Montgomery and the Portsmouth (Rogers), S.F., 1958; The San Saba Papers, (ed. by Lesley Simpson, translated by Paul Nathan), S.F., 1959. USN, USS Essex, 1943, staff, Adm. R.K. Turner, Comdr. Amphibious Forces, U.S. Pac. Fleet (1944-45), WW II. Lt. USNR. Mem.: dir. Calif. Hist. Soc. 1941-61, fellow, 1961-72; trustee, 1972---; dir. Book Club of Calif. 1956-73; pres. 1973---; dir. Univ. Club, 1948-49; Roxburghe Club, S.F., Master of the Press, 1973---; dir. Univ. Club, 1948-49; Grolier Club, N.Y.; Fellow of the Morgan Lib.; NSGW, Bohemian Club, Pac.-Union Club, Alpha Delta Phi. Republican. Protestant. Home: 1052 Chestnut St., S.F., CA; Office: 434 Post St., San Francisco, CA 94102.

HRACHOVEC, JOSEF P.
Physician — Geriatrician — Educator
b. Aug. 10, 1918, Lazniky, Czechoslovakia; s. Karel and Marie (Drexlerova) Hrachovec, M.D., Charles Univ., Prague, 1948; M.S., 1949; Lic.es Sci., Sorbonne Univ., Paris, 1952, D.Sc., 1955; m. Mary Wade Newton, Dec. 16, 1961, West Palm Beach, Fla.; chil.: Eva Grace-Maria. b.

Sept. 20, 1962; Anna Boydstun, b. June 5, 1966; Ian Wade, b. June 28, 1970. Came to U.S. 1956, naturalized, 1962. Career: Intern Univ. Hosp., Prague, 1948-49; resident, 1949-50; postdoctoral research fellow Sorbonne Univ., 1950-52; research assoc., Inst. de Biologie Physico-Chimique, Paris, 1952-55; researcher, dept. physiology Sch. Med., Paris, 1955-56; research assoc., Coll. Physicians and Surgeons, Columbia, 1956-57; researcher, Center of Gerontology Sch. Med., Paris, 1957-58, dept. physiology N.Y. Univ. Sch. Med., 1958-63; sr. researcher UCLA, 1963-70, assoc. prof. pub. health, Sch. Pub. Health, 1967-70; prof. biology of aging, research assoc. Gerontology Center, USC, 1970-74; program dir. research grant, Nat. Cancer Inst., NIH, Bethesda, Md., 1963-74. Mem. bd. sci. advisers, Rom-Am. Pharm. Am. Co., 1971---; mem. bd. sci. advisers, Center for Life Extension and Control of Aging, Sacramento, 1972---; attache de recherches, French Nat. Center Sci. Research, Paris, 1953-61. Author: Keeping Young & Living Longer — How to Stay Healthy & Active Past 100, Sherbourne Press, L.A., 1972. Fellow Gerontol. Soc. Mem.: Assn. for Advancement Aging Research, mem. council advisers 1969---; Calif. Aging Assn., pres. 1972---; Am. Physiol. Soc.; N.Y. Acad. Sciences; A.A. AAAS; Am. Pub. Health Assn.; Fedn. Am. Socs. for Exptl. Biology. Presbyterian, ch. deacon. Hobbies: biomed. research on aging, life extension. Home: 3480 Federal Ave., L.A., CA 90066; Office: 300 S. Beverly Dr., Suite 105, Beverly Hills, CA 90212.

HUBBARD, DAVID ALLAN
President, Fuller Theological Seminary
b. Apr. 8, 1928, Stockton; s. John King and Helena (White) Hubbard; B.A., Westmont Coll., Santa Barbara, 1949; B.D., Fuller Theol. Sem., Pasa. 1952; Th.M. 1954; Ph.D., St. Andrews Univ., Scotland, 1957; m. Ruth Doyal, Oakland, Aug. 12, 1949; dau. Mary Ruth, b. Mar. 6, 1955. Career: Ordained minister, Conservative Baptist Assn. 1952; lectr. in Old Testament, St. Andrews Univ., Scotland, 1955-56; asst. prof. Biblical stus., Westmont Coll. 1957, dept. chmn. 1958-63; interim pastor, Montecito Community Ch. 1960-62; pres.-prof. Old Testament, Fuller Theol. Sem. 1963---, exec. v.p. Gospel Broadcasting Assn. 1969---, speaker, The Joyful Sound (internat. radio braodcast), 1969---; Tundale Old Testament lectr., Cambridge, Eng. 1965; chmn. Pasa. Urban Coalition, 1968-71; Soc. of Old Testament Stus. lectr., London, Eng., 1971. Author: With Bands of Love, 1968; Does the Bible Really Work?, and Psalms for All Seasons, 1971; Is the Family Here to Stay?, 1972; contrib. to: Baker's Dictionary of Theol., 1960; The New Bible Dictionary, 1962; Higley Commentary, 1967; Is God Dead? (symposium with Bernard Ramm, Vernon Grounds, Billy Graham); numerous articles: World Vision, Chr. Herald, Eternity, Christianity Today, others. Mem.: Am. Coll. of Relig.; Soc. of Biblical Lit. and Exegesis; Univ. Club, Rotary Club, Pasa. Hobby: travel (Europe, Middle East, Eng., Scotland, Far East, Costa Rica, Panama, Mex. 1957---). Office: 135 N. Oakland Ave., Pasa., CA (1101.

HUBBARD, JOHN RANDOLPH
President, University of Southern California
b. Dec. 3, 1918, Belton, Tex.; s. Louis Herman and Bertha (Altiyer) Hubbard; No. Tex. State Univ. 1934-36; A.B., Univ. Tex. 1936, A.M. 1939, Ph.D., 1949; Am. Univ. 1939-41; L.H.D., Westminster Coll., Mo. 1977; m. Lucille Luckett, Jan. 29, 1947; chil.: Elisa, Melisse, Kristin. Career: Pvt. secty. to ICC commr. 1939-41; tchg. fellow, Univ. Tex. 1946-48; visiting prof. La. State Univ. 1948; asst. prof. Tulane Univ., 1953-58; prof. 1958-65; dean, Newcomb Coll. 1953-65; USAID, India, 1966-69; provost, USC, 1969-70; pres. 1970---. Contrib to Journ. Modern Hist., other edn. journs. Aviator, USN, flight instr., patrol plane comdr., Atlantic and Pac. Fleets, 1941-46, WW II. Awards: Distinguished Flying Cross, 4 air medals. Mem.: Royal Aero, Round Table, dir., El Paso Co., Houston; dir., S.C. Comm. TV; trustee, Scholarships for Chil. of Mil. Personnel; Phi Delta Kappa, Delta Kappa Epsilon, Omicron Delta Kappa, Jonathan Club. Hobby: golf. Home: 1085 Virginia Rd., San Marino, CA 91108; Office: USC, Univ. Park, L.A., CA 90007.

HUEMER, RICHARD PETER
Physician
b. June 16, 1933, Hollywood; s. Richard Martin and Mariette (Prevosto) Huemer; B.A., Pomona Coll., 1954; M.D., UCLA, 1958; Postdoct. Fellow, Cal. Inst. of Tech., 1962-65; m. Gloria Wong, Dec. 17, 1964, Studio City; chil.: Peter Eric, b. June 17, 1967; Ariana Mei-Hua, b. Aug. 12, 1968; Michael Brent, b. Dec. 27, 1969. Career: Chief of Research Projects in cancer immunology and exptl. gerontology, Sepulveda VA

Hosp., 1965-71; founder & dir., Molecular Disease Inst., Inc., 1971---; Med. Assoc. of Joseph D. Walters, M.D., 1974-76; pvt. practice of Metabolic Nutrition, 1976---; assoc. ed., Journ. of the Internat. Acad. of Preventive Med., 1977---. Publs.: Elucidated Genetic Basis of Mixed-Leukocyte Reaction, 1968; Genetics of Anti-Cancer Immunity, 1969; Unified Theory of Diagnosis for Orthomolecular Medicine, 1977. Capt., M.C., AUS and Def. Atomic Support Agency, 1959-61; Mem.: Internat. Acad. of Preventive Med.; N.Y. Acad. of Scis.; Sigma Xi Sci. Soc.; Orthomolecular Med. Soc.; others. Office: 32144 Agoura Rd., Suite 116, Westlake Village, CA 91361.

HUFSTEDLER, SETH MARTIN
Attorney at Law
b. Sept. 20, 1922, Dewar, Okla.; s. Seth Martin and Myrtle (Younts) Hufstedler; B.A., USC, 1944; LL.B., Stanford Law Sch. 1949; m. Shirley A. Mount (U.S. Circuit Judge, Ninth Circuit), Albuquerque, Aug. 16, 1949; son, Steven, b. Feb. 20, 1953; Career: Assoc.: Lillick, Geary & McHose, 1950-51; Charles E. Beardsley, 1951-53; partner, Beardsley, Hufstedler & Kemble Law firm, 1953---. Lt. (j.g.) USN, WW II. Mem.: bd. trustees, L.A. Co. Bar Assn. 1964-66, 1967-71; pres. 1969-70; bd. govs. State Bar of Calif. 1971-74; pres. 1973-74; chmn. bd. visitors, Stanford Law Sch. 1972-73; co-chmn. bd. visitors, Stanford Law Sch. 1972-73; co-chmn. Pub. Comm. on Co. Givt. L.A., 1974---; bd. trustees, Am. Bar Found.; Am. Law Inst.; Fellow, Am. Coll. of Trial Lawyers; Chancery Club, pres. 1974-75. Recipient, Shattuck-Price Award, L.A. Co. Bar Assn. 1976. Home: 720 Inverness Dr., Pasa., CA 91103; Office: 611 W. Sixth St., Suite 2220, L.A., CA 90017.

HUFSTEDLER, SHIRLEY M.
U.S. Circuit Court Judge
b. Aug. 24, 1925, Denver, Colo., B.B.A., Univ. N. Mex., 1945; LL.B., Stanford Univ., 1949: article and book rev. ed. Stanford Law Review 1948-49; m. Seth M. Hufstedler, past pres. State Bar of Calif. and L.A. Co. Bar Assn., Aug. 16, 1949; son, Steven, b. Feb. 20, 1953. Career: assoc. with law firm Beardsley, Hufstedler, and Kemble, 1950-60; spec. legal cons. Atty. Gen. of Calif., Colo. River litigation, 1960-61; apptd. Judge, Superior Ct., L.A. Co., 1961, elected 1962-66; apptd. Assoc. Justice, Calif. Ct. of Appeal, 1966; apptd. Circuit Judge, U.S. Ct. of Appeals for Ninth Circuit, 1968. Publs.: New Blocks for Old Pyramids: Reshaping the Judicial System (Charles Evans Hughes Address 1917); The Directions and Misdirections of A Constitutional Right of Privacy (Benjamin N. Cardozo Lectr. 1971), Comity and the Constitution: The Changing Role of the Federal Judiciary (James Madison Address, N.Y. Univ. 1972); articles contbd. to profl. journs. Trustee: Aspen Inst. for Humanistic Studies; CalTech; Occidental Coll.; Colonial Williamsburg Found. Mem. Advis. Council, Jet Propulsion Lab.; Councilor, USC Law Center; vis. com., Harvard Law Sch. Awards incl.: 10 hon. LL.D. degrees; Order of the Coif; L.A. Times Woman of the Year; Herbert O. Harley Award; Golden Plate Award; Ladies Home Journ. Woman of the Yr. in Govt. and Diplomacy. Mem.: Am. Bar Assn., Am. Bar Found.; Am. Judicature Soc.; Inst. for Judicial Adminstrn.; Internat. Assn. of Women's Lawyers; Women Lawyers Assn.; Profl. Women's Symphony Assn.; Supreme Ct. Hist. Soc.; Law Soc.; Town Hall; Address: U.S. Courthouse, L.A. CA 90012.

HUGHES, PETER J.
Attorney at Law
b. Nov. 6, 1928, L.A.; s. Aloysius Peter and Euldene Frances (Frediana) Hughes; A.B., Stanford Univ., 1951, J.D., Stanford Sch. of Law, 1953; m. Doris Sackhoff, Jan. 21, 1956, Ft. Meyer, Va.; chil.: Lyn Frances, b. Nov. 10, 1956; Peter Michael, b. May 23, 1969; Lee Michele, b. July 16, 1960; Dana Kathleen, b. Sept. 4, 1962. Career: Asst. U.S. Atty., So. Dist. of Calif., 1957, San Diego Office, 1958-59; pvt. practice law, 1959---. AUS, 1953-57; JAGC 1954-57. Trustee, Univ. of San Diego, 1973---; mem. bd. of vis., Univ. S.D. Law Sch., 1974---. Mem.: Phi Delta Phi, pres. 1953; Alpha Tau Omega, pres. 1950; Rotary Internat. of S.D., 1974---. Roman Catholic, past pres. Parish Council. Hobby: Indian art. Rec.: skiing. Home: 1524 Buckingham Dr., La Jolla, CA 92037; Office: 110 West A St., Suite 1100, San Diego, CA 92101.

HUILLADE, JOANN
Realtor
b. Sept. 18, 1934, San Antonio, Tex.; d. Kinnie A. and Ressie M. Harper; div.; sons, Jim Blackburn, b. Feb. 20, 1951; Joey Blackburn, b. Aug. 21, 1953; dau.

Cherie Huillade, b. Dec. 11, 1960. Career: Interior decorator, owner, JoAnn's Interiors, 1960---; licensed real estate agent in 1960; sales mgr. and pub. rels. Security Owners Corp. (residential devel.), 1960-69, broker sales mgr., 1969---; founder, Huillade Realty, 1973---, opened Huillade Realty resale office, 1978---. Dir., Security Owners Corp., 1964---. Mem. Contra Costa Bd. of Realtors, 1960---. Affiliated with Easter Seal, 1975---, participant in Telethon 2 yrs. Rec.: dancing, swimming, tennis, horses. Home: 1895 Carriage Dr., Walnut Creek, CA; Office: 127 Aspen Dr., Pacheco, CA 94553.

HULET, E(RVIN) KENNETH
Nuclear Scientist
b. May 7, 1926, Baker, Ore.; s. Frank E. and Marjorie (Suiter) Hulet; B.S., Stanford Univ., 1949; Ph.D., Univ. Calif., Berkeley, 1953; m. Betty Gardner, Sept. 10, 1949, Pasadena; chil.: Carri (Gicker), b. July 28, 1950; Randall Gardner, b. Apr. 27, 1956. Career: AEC Grad. Fellow, Lawrence Berkeley Lab, 1950-53; nuclear chemist and group leader, Lawrence Livermore Lab., 1953---; Fulbright Scholar, Norway, 1962-63. Co-discoverer of element 106. Contbr. over 100 articles in basic nuclear sci., profl. publs. USN, 1944-46. Mem.: Am. Physical Soc.; Am. Chem. Soc.; Am. Inst. of Chemists; AAAS. Rec.: skiing, backpacking. Home: P.O.B. 411, Diablo, CA 94528; Office: P.O.B. 808, Livermore, CA.

HULL, JEROME WEBSTER
Chairman, Pacific Telephone Co.
b. May 7, 1912, Aberdeen, Wash.; s. Jerome W. and Caroline N. (Berry) Hull; ed. Stanford Univ. 1934; B.A., Occidental Coll., L.A. 1935; m. Lucille Spelts, Riverside, Jan. 31, 1941; daus.: Mrs. George (Patricia Ann) Cavender, b. Sept. 17, 1942; Mrs. Paul (Victoria) Hazelrig, b. Nov. 18, 1943; Mrs. Larry (Carolyn Marie) Herrara, b. Oct. 19, 1945. Career: So. Calif. Tel. Co. 1935; Pac. Tel. & Tel. Co. 1936-42, 1946-51, 1954-58, v.p.-gen. mgr. 1960-61, v.p. 1962, dir. 1962---, exec. v.p. 1966-68; pres. 1968-74, chairman, 1975---; Am. Tel. Co. 1951-54, 1958-59, asst. v.p. 1959-60. Dir.: Bell Tel. Co. of Nev. 1962---; Crocker Natl. Bank, 1967---; Pac. Southwest Airlines, 1967---; N.Y. Life Ins. Co. 1967---; Del Monte Corp., 1975---; Di Giorgio Corp., 1970---; trustee, Occidental Coll. Industrialist of the Year, by Calif. Mus. of Sci. and Ind. 1974. Lt. USN, 1942-46, WW II. Mem. Exec. bd. B.S.A., S.F. Bay Area Council; Mgmt. Council Bay Area Employment Opportunity, 1970---; Calif. State C. of C. 1970---; S.F. Opera Assoc. 1971---. Clubs: Pac.-Union, Bohemian, World Trade Club, Commonwealth, Calif., Burlingame. Presbyterian Ch. Hobby: golf. Home: 5 Lupine Way, Hillsborough, CA 94010; Office: 140 New Montgomery St., S.F., CA 94105.

HULL, VIRGINIA TRACY
Travel Agency President
b. Chicago, Ill.; d. Joseph Platt and Ada (Morris) Tracy; B.A., Occidental Coll., L.A.; m. Joseph William Hull, Ojai, Calif., Nov. 26, 1938 (dec. Apr. 1953). Career: Exec. secty., Alphonzo E. Bell Corp., L.A. 1929-38; founder-pres.-owner, Bel-Air Travel, Inc., L.A., 1953---; certified travel counselor, 1966---. Listed, various biog. achievement publs., USA 1965---. Mem.: pres. Soroptimist Club of L.A. W. 1957; secty., Westwood C. of C. 1959-72; v.p. 1973-76, pres. 1976-77; pres. L.A. Travellarians, 1960; secty. So. Calif. Chpt., Am. Soc. of Travel Agts. 1960-62; pres. Natl. Bus. and Profl. Women's Club, L.A. 1965-66, chmn. L.A. Sunset Dist. 1966-67, v.p. 1967-68; pres. 1969-70; world affairs chmn. Calif. State Fed. 1970-71; founder, Inst. of Certified Travel Agents, 1966; chmn. Advance gifts com., United Crusade, Westwood, 1966-67; dir. Am. Red Cross (L.A. chpt., W.), 1966-70, 1973-78; dir.-pres. chmn., Univ. Affiliates, UCLA, 1966-70; Regent, Temescal chpt. DAR, State v.p. adv., 1972-74; Town Hall of Calif.; Mayflower Descendants in Calif. 1969---; Faculty Women's Club, UCLA; Natl. Assn. of Parliamentarians, Alpha Theta Unit; PEO Sisterhood, Internat. Platform Assn., So. Calif. Sym. Assn., Hollywood Bowl Assn. Pres. Margaret Stewart Fellowship, Beverly Vista Presbyterian Ch., Beverly Hills, 1964-65. Hobbies: music, travel. Home: 850 Moraga Dr., Bel-Air, L.A., CA 90049; Office: 612 N. Sepulveda, L.A., CA 90049.

HUMPHREYS, ALEXANDER J., S.J.
Sociologist — Author
b. July 15, 1913, San Francisco, Calif.; s. Milton W. and Hannah M. (O'Riordan) Humphreys; grandnephew Gen.

Robert E. Lee; A.B. in Philosophy, Gonzaga Univ., Spokane, Wash., 1937, M.A. Philos., 1938; M.A. Sociology, Fordham Univ., N.Y., 1942; Licentiate in Sacred Theology, Alma Coll., Los Gatos, Calif., affiliate, Gregorian Univ., Rome, 1946; Ph.D. Sociology, Harvard Univ., Cambridge, Mass., 1953; acad. specs.: anthropology, psychol., philos. and sociology, polit. philos., Classics. Career: instr. philosophy, Univ. S.F. 1939, Univ. Santa Clara, 1938-40; asst./assoc. prof. sociology, Loyola Univ., L.A., 1953---; chmn., Sociology Dept. 1960-69; tchr. Sociology of Law, Loyola Univ., L.A., Law Sch., 1971-75. Author: New Dubliners, pub. Routledge and Kegan Paul, London 1965; The Family in Ireland, Houghton Mifflin Co., Boston 1965; article Evolving Irishmen, 1954; numerous articles publ. edn. and pub. newspapers and mags. Frequent lectr., family and personal counseling. Initiated discussions leading to devel. Honors Program, Loyola Univ., mem. Honors Com., 1954---. Mem. L.A. Police Dept. com. on human relations, 1956-59; mem. spec. com. subsequent to Watts Riots, 1964-66; mem. L.A. Co. Human Relations Com.-extensive relations with Am. Jewish Com. 1954-60; mem. Palos Verdes Human Rel. Council; bd. dir., L.A. chpt., Catholic League for Religious and Civil Rights; bd. dir. Nat. Alcoholic Council, South Bay chpt.; Western Coll. Assn., accrediting com.: Claremont Coll. (1969), UCSD (1965), Fresno State (1956); Am. Catholic Sociological Soc., chmn. local arrangements, 1963. Mem.: Am. Com. for Irish Studies, 1965---; Pacific Sociological Soc., 1954---; Am. Sociological Assn., 1940---; Catholic Soc. for the Study of Religion, 1940---; Nat. Council on Family Relations; Am. Assn. of Univ. Professors; Pi Gamma Mu. Office: Loyola Marymount University, 7101 W. 80th St., L.A., CA 90045.

HUMPHREYS, ROBERT LEE
President, Grey Advertising (West Div.)
b. Dec. 30, 1924, Burbank; s. Robert E. and Nancy Lucille (Gum) Humphreys; ed., B.S., UCLA 1947; m. Marie Wilkinson, Laguna; chil.: Dina Lizette, b. July 11, 1962; Gia Monigue, b. Jan. 7, 1967. Career: Merchandising repr., Life mag., L.A.; promotion mgr., Fortune Mag., NYC; Time, Inc. 1947-50; copywriter, Batten, Barton, Durstine & Osborne, Inc., 1950-51; v.p.-acct., mgmt. repr. supv., Foote, Cone & Belding, L.A., 1951-62; exec. v.p.-dir.; pres. Western Div.-dir., Grey Adv. Inc., 1962---; Bd. trustees, UCLA Found. Lt. (j.g.), USN, USS Calosahatchee (1943-46), WW II. Mem.: v.p., Phi Gamma Delta, 1946; dir., Hollywood Radio & TV Soc.; Far Eastern Art Council of the L.A. Co. Museum of Art; Bankers Club, S.F.; L.A. World Affairs Council; Town Hall, Bel-Air Country Club, Calif. Club. Home: 12830 Parkyns St., L.A., CA 90049; Office: 3435 Wilshire Blvd., L.A., CA 90010.

HURT, ROBERT GLENN
Investment Securities Company Executive
b. Jan. 31, 1919, Pasadena, Calif.; s. Dr. Leslie M. (past pres., AVMA) and Effie Mae (McKim) Hurt; A.B., USC, 1940; postgrad. Harvard Bus. Sch., 1941. Career: trainee, Calvin Bullock, Ltd., N.Y.C., 1946; asst. to west coast head, L.A., 1946-49; northern div. head, 1949-53; resident and sr. v.p., Calvin Bullock, Ltd., San Francisco 1954---. Mil. Pvt. to Lt. Col., AUS Infantry 1941-46. Commander, Military Order of World Wars. Mem.: Alpha Delta Sigma, Phi Kappa Psi; Andreas Canyon Club; Stock Exchange Club; Harvard Club; President's Circle, USC; Am. Legion; Reserve Officers; Assn. Roman Catholic. Home: 937 Ashbury St., S.F., CA 94117; Office: 931 The Mills Bldg., 220 Montgomery St., S.F., CA 94104.

HUTCHINSON, WILLIAM N.L., JR.
Investment Banker
b. Nov. 3, 1922, S.F.; s. William N.L., Sr. and Doris (Seymour) Hutchinson; ed. B.S., Stanford Univ. 1946; M.B.A., Grad. Sch. of Bus. Adm. 1948; m. Bona Comel di Socebran, Livorno, It., Feb. 11, 1961; chil.: Cristiana Isabella, William N.L. III; Career: Sales Engr. Crown Zellerbach Corp., L.A. 1948-51; repr. Mitchum, Jones & Templeton, Inc., S.F. 1952-62, exec. v.p. 1962-67; pres. William Hutchinson & Co., Inc. (mem. N.Y., Pac. Coast, Am., Stock Exchs.), S.F. 1967-72, dir.; V.P. Davis, Skaggs & Co., Inc.; trustee Katherine Delmar Burke Sch. Capt., AUS, 1943-46, WW II. Awards: Bronze Star Medal; Comdr. Crown of Italy. Mem.: Calif. Hist. Soc.; Zeta Psi; clubs: Pac. Union, Bohemian, S.F. Golf, Merchants Exch., Stock Exch., S.F. Bond, Olympic, Repub. Episcopalian. Rec.: hunting, riding, skiing, golf. Home: 2520 Divisadero St., S.F., CA; Office: Davis, Skaggs & Co., Inc., 160 Sansome St., S.F., CA 94104.

HUTTON, CHARLES WARREN
Aerospace Executive
b. Jan. 16, 1919, Washington Co., Va.; s. Charles Arthur and Stella Victoria (Hutton) (Hanneman); B.S. (Metallurgical engr.), Va. Polytech. Inst., 1940; m. Carol Brooks; daus.: Carol Adelaide Sm th, Jennifer Mary Douglas. Career: gen. mgr., govt.-ind. sales, Reynolds Metals Co. 1953, div. sales mgr. 1956; dir. marketing dept., McDonnell Douglas Astronautics Co. (Component of McDonnell Douglas Corp.) 1962, v.p. 1963---. Lt. Col. U.S. Army Artillery (1940-45), WW II. Mem. pres, L.A. chpt., Assn. of U.S. Army, 1967-68; v.p. Natl. Security Ind. Assn. 1167-68; Clubs: L.A. Country, Bel-Air Bay; Rec.: tennis, skiing, boating. Home: 177 N. Saltair Ave., L.A., CA; Office: 5301 Bolsa Ave., Huntington Beach, CA 92647.

HWANG, HENRY Y.
Banker
b. Nov. 28, 1939, Shanghai, China; s. Jim Yu and Edith (Chow) Hwang; B.A., Linfield Coll., 1951; postgrad. for M.B.A., USC; m. Dorothy Huang, June 11, 1955, Los Angeles; chil.: David Henry, Grace Elizabeth, Margery Ann. Career: President, Hwang and Chuang Accountancy Corp. (C.P.A.s) 1960-77; chmn. and pres., Far East National Bank, 1974---. Dir.: Azusa Pacific Coll.; L.A. Chinese C. of C. Mem.: Town Hall, Rotary Club, Wong's Family Assn. Chinese ch., chmn. bd. of trustees, 1970, founding dir., nationalists council. Hobby: singing. Rec.: golf. Home: 1101 W. Alhambra Rd., San Gabriel, CA 91775; Office: 300 Sunset Blvd., L.A., CA 90012.

I

IBBETSON, EDWIN THORNTON
Real Estate — Business Executive
b. Apr. 17, 1923, L.A., CA; s. Robert E. and Ann E. (Thornton) Ibbetson; ed. grad. Woodrow Wilson H.S.; Long Beach Jr. Coll. 1941-42; Calif. Inst. of Tech. 1942-43; m. Harriett A. Hudson, Long Beach, Dec. 28, 1947; chil.: Elizabeth Ann, b. Jan. 19, 1949; Douglas Hudson, b. Jan. 16, 1950; Gregory Bruce, b. Nov. 7, 1951; Timothy Edwin, b. July 21, 1953; Julia Katherine, b. Jan. 31, 1955; Erika Alice, b. Jan. 26, 1963. Career: Est. real estate bus. 1947; pres. Union Devel. Co. Inc., 1961---; pres. Union Farms Inc.; chmn. bd., Dutch Village Bowling Center, Inc.; v.p. Valley Properties, Inc.; dir. Met. Water Dist. of So. Calif. USN 1942-46, WW II. Awards: Bellflower Jr. C. of C. Young Man of Yr., 1959; Realtor of Yr., 1962, 67, 71; mem.: pres. Y's Men's Club, 1952; pres. Bellflower YMCA, 1958-59; pres. Bellflower Kiwanis Club, 1958; Bellflower United Way, 1960; dir. Natl. Assn. of Real Estate Bds. 1966-71; past pres., Bellflower Dist. Bd. of Realtors; chmn-dir., Garden State Bank, 1977-78; dir., 1974---; L.A. Cty. Real Estate Adv. Bd., 1973, chmn. 1976; v.-chmn., Bellflower Svgs. & Loan, 1975. Calif. Real Estate Assn., treas., 1972-78; dir. chmn. Better Bus. Bur., L.B. 1968; adv. bd. Calif. Water Resources Assn.; L.B. Elks Club, So. Calif. Tuna Club. Catholic. Hobbies: stamp and coin collecting. Rec.: golf, dee-sea fishing. Home: 4160 Locust St., Long Beach, CA; Office 8555 Artesia Blvd., Bellflower, CA 90706.

IDE, CHANDLER
Chairman, Natomas Company
b. May 8, 1909, Mt. Vernon, N.Y.; s. Herbert C. and Harriet (McDonald) Ide; B.A., magna cum laude, Pomona Coll.; m. Helen Evans, Oct. 13, 1944, L.A.; chil.: Susan (Junta), b. Mar. 27, 1938; Deborah (Palmer), b. Sept. 11, 1944; Career: Asst. to v.p., Standard Oil Co. of Calif., 1935-41; exec. asst. to Deputy Petroleum Adminstr., PAW, 1941-46; secty-treas., Am. Independent Oil Co., 1947-58; Secty.-treas., Natomas Co., 1956-66, pres. 1966-71; chairman of bd., 1974---; Dir., Bank of Calif., 1968---. Mem. Phi Beta Kappa. Rec.: tennis; Home: Three Swanston Rd., St. Helena; Office: 601 California St., S.F., CA.

IGL, RICHARD FRANKLIN
Attorney at Law
b. Feb. 15, 1923, Klamath Falls, Ore.; s. Englebert Matthew and Rose Ann (Haas) Igl; B.A., Univ. Ore., 1947; M.A. with hons., 1948; J.D., Yale Univ., 1950. Career: admitted to Calif. bar, 1951; law clk. to Judge Thomas Swan, U.S. Ct. Appeals, N.Y. Circuit, Ct. Appeals, N.Y. Circuit, 1950-51; assoc. firm O'Melveny & Myers, L.A., 1951-60; partner 1960-63; pvt. practice,

Beverly Hills, 1963---; Instr. Polit. Sci., Yale Univ., 1949-50; Lectr., Entertainment Law Inst., USC, 1961; lectr., Estate and Tax Planning Course, UCLA, 1963-64. Judge Pro Tem, Beverly Hills Municipal Ct., 1966. Dir.: Crosby Investment Corp., 1960---; Seven Up Bottling Co. of L.A., Inc., 1967-68; W. Inst. for Cancer and Leukemia Research, 1963-68; Beverly Hills C. of C., 1977---; Copyright Soc. of L.A., 1964-66. mem. 1958---. Capt., AUS, 1942-46. Mem.: Am. (del., 1969-72), Calif., L.A. (trustee, 1970-71), Beverly Hills (bd. of govs. 1960-71, pres. 1968) bar assns.; Phi Beta Kappa; Calif. Yacht. Club. Home: 9800 Yoakum Dr., Beverly Hills, CA 90210; Office: 9720 Wilshire Blvd., Bevelry Hills, CA 90212.

ILFELD, FREDERICK W.
Professor of Orthopedic Surgery
b. Jan. 16, 1907, Las Vegas, N.M.; s. Ludwig William and M. (Schutzberger) Ilfeld; A.B., Harvard Coll., 1928, M.D., Harvard Med. Sch., 1932; m. Jane Mandelbaum, Jan. 26, 1938, Santa Fe, N.M.; sons (two are M.D.s) Fred Jr., b. 1940; Thomas, b. 1942; David, b. 1952. Career: Residencies: pathology, Peter Bent Brigham Hosp., Boston, 1932-33; surgery, Univ. Hosp., Cleveland, 1933-35; orthopedic surgery, Children's Hosp. and Mass. Gen. Hosp.; Adj. L.A. Co. Gen. Children's Hosp., Shriners Hosp. Assoc. Prof. of Orthopedic Surgery, USC. Lt. Col. AUS, M.C., 1941-46; Chief Orthopedic Service, 5th (Harvard) Gen. Hosp. Contbr. 37 articles to med. journs. Mem.: Sierra Club; Rocky Mt. Traumatological Assn.; Am. Acad. Orthopedic Assn., Western Orthopedic Assn.; Am. Med. Assn. Jewish. Hobbies: research, tennis, skiing. Office: 436 No. Roxbury Dr., Beverly Hills, CA 90210.

ILLING, HANS A.
Sociologist
b. Aug. 15, 1913, Berlin, Germany, naturalized U.S. Citizen, 1944; s. Leopold and Lisel (Beermann) Illing; Ph.D., Friedrich Wilhelm Univ., 1936; B.A., Univ. Univ. 1944; M.S.W. Tulane Univ., 1948; m. Lillian E. Ulrich, Apr. 19, 1962, L.A. Career: Sr. Psychiatric social worker, Parole Outpatient Clinic, State Dept. of Corrections, L.A., 1960---; staff, Hacker Clinic, Beverly Hills & Lynwood, 1962-70; pvt. practice, Inglewood, 1970---. Contbg. author profl. journs. and books; cons. edit.: Internat. Journ. Psychiatry, 1965---; book rev. ed.: Modern Austrian Lit.; contbg. ed.: Dynamische Psychiatrie, Berlin. Dir.: USO, Salt Lake City, Ut. 1941-45, Riverside, Calif. 1945-46; Calif. Home for the Aged, Reseda, 1960-62. Pres., Westport Hts. Democratic Club, 1962-66. Home: 6112 W. 77th St., L.A., CA 90045; Office: 656 Aerick St., Inglewood, CA 90301.

ING, CELINA SAU LIN
College Dean
b. Sept. 21, 1947, Honolulu, Hawaii; d. Albert Sau Yee and Nancy Ngan (Cheu) Ing; B.A., Maxima Cum Laude, Coll. of Notre Dame, 1972; M.A., Univ. S.F., 1973; Ed.D candidate; m. Rudolph G. DiGirolamo, Ph.D., Nov. 18, 1978, Sacto. Career: City of San Jose, Lib. Dept., 1965-66; secty., Rehabilitation Workshop Adminstrn., Univ. S.F., 1966-68; pgm. asst. ERIC Clearinghouse on Tchr. Edn., Wash. D.C. 1968-69; media estimator, Batten, Barton, Durstine, and Osborn, Inc., S.F., 1970-73; instr., St. Charles Sch., 1973-74; instr., Coll. of Notre Dame, 1975-77; asst. dir. of grad studies & health scis. advis., 1974-77; div. Dean of Social Sciences, Sacto. City Coll., 1977---. Recipient, Regents' Fellowship, Univ. Calif., S.F., 1974-75. Mem.: Calif. Assn. Women Deans and Counselors; Am. Classical League; Am. Hist. Assn.; Am. Assn. for Hist. of Med.; Delta Epsilon Sigma; Alpha Mu Gamma; Acad. Com., West Bay Health Services Agcy.; Los Rios Mgmt. Assn., Secty.-treas., 1978---. Home: 5900 Gloria Dr., Sacto., CA 95822; Office: 3835 Freeport Blvd., Sacto., CA 95822.

INGHRAM, DOROTHY ELLA
School Administrator (Ret.)
b. Nov. 9, 1905, San Bernardino, Calif.; d. Henry Douglas and Mary Ella Inghram; Bachelor of Music, 1936; M.A. in edn., 1958. Career: elem. sch. principal, 1951; dist. superintendent, Mill Elem. Sch. Dist., 1958. Author: Dear Meg (edn. book) 1973; Improving the Services of Substitute Teachers, 1976; Children Live What They Learn, Allyn & Bacon, Inc. Articles: I Can't Sleep, Unity Mag, 1978; Social Studies News, 1959. Honored by San Bernardino Pub. Lib. System & Friends, 1977: Dorothy Inghram Branch Library named in her honor. Recipient: Pacesetters Award, 1978, Inland Area Urban League; award and scholarship to Stanford Univ., NCCJ. Named Woman of Achievemnt, San Orco Dist. Bus. and Profl.

Women, 1974-75. Honored by St. Paul A.M.E. ch. by Dorothy Inghram Scholarship Assn. Mem.: Nat. Council Negro Women (Woman of Distinction Lady in the Bethune Manner, 1970); Delta Kappa Gamma Soc. (spec. recognition); Delta Sigma Theta Sorority (spec. recognition for outstanding service 1966); Cosmos Club Womens Club, pres., 1941---; AAUW; Retired Tchrs. Assn., Friends of Dorothy Inghram Br. Lib.; Kathryn K. Murray Scholarship Assn. St. Paul A.M.E. ch., former organist. Hobbies: crochet, writing. Rec.: bowling. Home: 1424 Trenton St., San Bernardino, CA 92411.

INGWERSON, DONALD WAYNE
School District Administrator
b. Mar. 24, 1933, Pawnee City, Nebr.; s. William and Pearl Ingwerson; B.S., Kansas State Teachers Coll., 1954; M.S., 1957; Ed.D., Univ. of Wyoming, 1970; studied sch. adminstrn.: Claremont Grad. Coll. 1960-61; USC, 1957-66; m. Lona Belle McNutt, Dec. 1954, Iowa City, Iowa; chil.: Marshall, b. Dec. 1957; Tanya, b. May 1959; Heidi, b. Apr. 1971. Career: teacher, counselor, vice principal, Temple City Schools, 1959-62, dist. director of secondary edn., 1962-66; with Jefferson Co. Schools, 1966-72: dir. of Jr. Hi Schs., 1966-67, asst. supt. personnel, 1967-68, asst. supt. curriculum, 1968-69, depty. supt., 1970-72; supt., Orange Unified School Dist. (over 30,500 students enrolled), 1972---. Served AUS. Mem.: Alpha Kappa Lambda, pres.; Xi Phi; Kappa Delta Pi; Phi Delta Kappa; Am. Assn. School Adminstrs.; Colorado Assn. of Sch. Execs.; Assn. of Calif. Administrs. (ACSA): pres., Orange Co. Supts. Com., Calif. State Supts. Com., Blue Ribbon Com., Orange Charter, ACSA, Dir. 1st Ch. of Christ Scientist, Orange; bd. pres.; Sun. Sch. tchr. Hobby: home restoration, renovation. Home: 9505 Center Dr., Villa Park, CA 92667; Office: 370 N. Glassell, Orange, CA 92666.

INKELES, ALEX
Professor of Sociology
b. Mar. 4, 1920, NYC; s. Meyer and Ray (Gewer) Inkeles; B.A., Cornell Univ., 1941, M.A., 1946; Ph.D., Columbia Univ., 1949; studies, Wash. Sch. of Psychiatry, 1956-56, Boston Psychoanalytic Inst., 1957-59; m. Bernadette Mary Kane, Jan. 31, 1942, Ithaca, N.Y.; dau., Ann Elizabeth, b. Jan. 5, 1948. Career: Social sci. research analyst, Dept. State and OSS, 1942-46; cons. program evaluation br., Internat. broadcasting div., Dept. of State, 1949-51; Instr. social rels., Harvard, 1948, lectr., 1948-57, prof. sociology, 1957-71, dir. studies on social aspects econ. devel. Center Internat. Affairs, 1963-71; Margaret Jacks prof. of Edn., prof. of sociology, Stanford Univ., 1971-78; prof. sociology and sr. Fellow, Hoover Inst. on War, Revolution and Peace, Stanford Univ., 1978---. Fellowships: Center Advanced Study Behavioral Sciences, 1955; Foundations Fund Res., Psychiatry, 1957-60; Soc. Sci. Res. Council, 1959; Russell Sage Fdn., 1966; Fulbright, 1977; Guggenheim 1978. Author: six books latest: Becoming Modern, Harvard Univ. Press, 1974, and some 80 articles in profl. publs.; Advis. ed., Little, Brown & Co.; editor: Annual Review of Sociology. Mem. Exec. Com. Behavioral Sci. Div., NRC, 1968-75; Fellow Am. Acad. of Arts and Scis., Am. Philosop. Soc., Am. Psychol. Assn., Secty.-treas., Sociological Research Assn., 1979-80, pres. 1980-81. Sgt., AUS, 1943-46; assigned as research analyst in Div. of USSR Intelligence, OSS, 1943-45, Dept. of State, 1945. Mem.: Eastern Sociological Soc., pres. 1960-61; Am. Assn. for Advancement of Slavic Studies, exec. com. 1961-63; Am. Sociological Assn., pres. sect. on social psychol. 1961; Hobby: collecting Asian bronzes. Home: 1001 Hamilton Ave., Palo Alto, CA 94301; Office: Herbert Hoover Mem. Bldg., Hoover Inst., Stanford Univ., Stanford, CA 94305.

INNES, WILLIAM BEVERIDGE
Company President
b. Mar. 8, 1913, Cambria, Calif.; s. Murray and Katherine (Dorsch) Innes; Ph.D., phys. chem. Univ. of Ia., 1941; m. Dorothy Vida Rundle, Aug. 7, 1938, S.F.; sons, Robert Alexander, b. Nov. 4, 1941; Walter Rundle, b. Dec. 28, 1945; Gordon, b. Jan. 20, 1954; Roger William, b. July 20, 1959. Career: Research chem., Champion Paper and Fiber, 1941-43; research chem., Am. Cyanamid Co., 1943-44, Manhattan Project-Columbia Univ., 1943-45; group leader and research assoc., Am. Cyanamid Co., 1945-64; pres., Purad Inc., Upland, 1964---. Patents and Publs. in the fields of catalysts, air pollution and instrumentation. Mem.: Am. Chem. Soc.; Alpha Chi Sigma; Sigma Xi. Rec.: tennis. Address: 724 Kilbourne Dr., Upland, CA 91786.

IRELL, LAWRENCE E.
Attorney at Law
b. Mar. 23, 1912, Boston, Mass.; s. Hyman and Bessie (Shain) Irell; ed. B.A., UCLA 1932; LL.B., USC Law Sch. 1935; LL.M., Harvard Law Sch. 1936; m. Elaine Smith, Mar. 26, 1939; chil.: Stephen Charles, b. June 26, 1942; Eugene Harvey, b. Feb. 7, 1945; Lauren Catherine, b. Dec. 30, 1946; m. Erin Edwards, L.A., Jan. 18, 1972. Career: Admitted to Calif. Bar, 1936; partner: Berger & Irell law firm, 1941-49; sr. partner, Irell & Manella, L.A. 1949---. Lectr., USC Tax Inst. 1950, 55, 59, 61, 64; instr. Income Taxation of Trusts and Estates, USC 1951-54. Awards: Alumni Award Scholastic Honors, USC Law Sch. 1935; Profl. Achievement Award by UCLA Alumni Assn. 1971. Mem.: pres. Zeta Beta Tau, UCLA 1931-32; ed. bd. Law Review, USC 1933-35, secty-treas. Law Sch. Student Body, 1934-35, Order of the Coif 1935; West Gate Lodge, F&AM, 1937---; dir. Jewish Fed. Council of Greater L.A. 1938-41, 1948-53, 1958-66, 1968-73, v.p. 1965-67, 1971-73, 1977---, trustee, Jewish Comm. Found. 1964---, pres. 1967-69; dir. Jewish Centers Assn., L.A. 1943---, pres. 1956-59; dir. Met. Rec. and Youth Servs. Planning Council, 1950-68, pres. 1963-66; dir. Reiss-Davis Child Study Center, 1951-58, v.p. 1955-58; dir. Natl. Jewish Welfare Bd., 1953-64; pres. Western Reg. 1953-55; Beverly Hills Bar Assn., com. chmn. 1954-60, del. Annual Conf. State Bar Dels. 1960-72, bd. govs. 1963-72, pres. 1969; trustee, Hope For Hearing Research Found. 1959---, bd. dirs. Council of Jewish Fed. and Welfare Funds, Inc. 1960---; chmn. Western Reg. 1966---; chmn. Resolutions Comm. 1969, mem. Overseas Serv. Comm. 1961---; natl. v.p. 1967-70; United Jewish Welfare Fund gen. chmn., 1977 Campaign; Am. Bar Assn., Internat. Law, Tax and other Sects. 1961---; Natl. Council Harvard Law Sch. Assn. 1964-65; trustee, exec. com. UCLA Found. 1967---, gen. counsel, 1967-71, pres. June 1971-75; chmn. bd. 1975---, Bd. of Trustees, UCLA Alum. Assn. 1972-75; com. Town Hall of Calif. 1968-69; dir. Constitutional Rights Found. 1969-73; exec. com. 1970-73, Lawyer's Advis. Council Exec. Comm. 1974---; v. chmn. exec. bd. So. Calif. Chpt., Am. Jewish Com., Natl. Exec. Council, 1970-72; chmn., Foreign Affairs Comm. 1972---; com. chmn. Natl. bd. trustees, 1973---; UCLA Soc. Order of Blue Shield, 1971---; bd. trustees, L.A. Co. Bar Assn. 1971-72; Fed. Bar Assn. 1973---; Alpha Delta Sigma, Hillcrest Country Club. Home: 965 N. Alpine Dr., Beverly Hills, CA 90210; Office: 1800 Ave. of the Stars, Suite 900, L.A., CA 90067.

IRSHAY, PHYLLIS CAROLINE
Library Director
b. July 29, 1924, Danville, Ill.; d. Rev. Zoltan and Emily (Cardiff) Irshay; B.S., home econ., Wayne State Univ., Detroit, 1945, M.L.S., 1953. Career: clerical asst., Doubleday & Co., Detroit, Mich., 1945-47; editorial asst., Ginn & Co., Boston, summer 1958; school librarian, Detroit, Mich., 1948-61; principal librarian, children's services, Anaheim Public Library, 1961-63, asst. director, 1963-66; lib. director, A.K. Smiley Public Library, Redlands, 1967---; writer, bi-monthly column on books for local newspaper. Pres., Film Circuit Council Commn., 1979; chmn., publs. com., Calif. Lib. Assn., 1968; pres., Public Library Execs. Assn. of So. Calif., 1962; v.p., 1973; editor of Biblio-Cal Notes 1968-72, 1978--- of So. Calif. Local Hist. Council. Presbyterian. Deacon, elder. Hobbies: gardening, painting, travel. Home: 621 Lido, Redlands, CA 92373; Office: 125 W. Vine, Redlands, CA 92373.

IRWIN, PAUL
Food Company Executive
b. July 6, 1925, Phila.; s. Samuel B. and Margaret (Regler) Irwin; B.A., econ., Univ. Virginia, 1949; m. Anne Timon, Aug. 6, 1978, Watsonville; chil.: Gail Nava, b. Oct. 8, 1951; Dana Plays, b. July 2, 1953; Carolin, b. Dec. 17, 1961; Laura, b. Dec. 22, 1963; Doug, b. Jan. 11, 1968. Career: with Morgan Guaranty Bank, N.Y., 1949-51; Standard Brands Inc., N.Y., 1951-54; with McCormick & Co., Inc., 1954---: pres. McCormick Foods, 1967-68, pres., Club House Foods, Canada, 1968-73, currently pres. Golden West Foods, Inc. ---. Dir.: Groc. Prod. Mfgrs. Assn., Canada, 1949-73; Container Service Corp., 1975---; Chesepeake Food Brokers, 1976---; pres., Onion Ring Packers Assn., 1978-79. Staff Sgt., U.S. Infan., 1945-46, European theater. Mem.: Phi Kappa Psi, 1947; L'Hirondelle Club, 1965---; The Family, 1978---. Episcopalian. Rec: tennis, skiing. Home: 2661 Beach Rd., Watsonville, CA; Office: Golden West Foods, 1350 Pacheco Pass Hwy., Gilroy, CA 95020.

ISEMAN, CARYL
Realtor
b. Apr. 5, 1942, Brooklyn, N.Y.; d. Jack and Sally Iseman. Career: Office mgr., Budge-it Home Remodeling, Inc., 1969-72; real estate sales agent, Tierra del Mol Realtors, 1972-73; pres., real estate broker, Mission Profl. Properties, San Diego, 1973---. Awards: Woman of Achievement, S.D. Co., Bus. & Profl. Women's Club, 1977; Grad. Realtors Inst. award; 1st woman named to exec. com., S.D. Bd. of Realtors, 1977---. Mem.: Calif. Assn. of Realtors, chmn. equal opportunity in Housing, Dist. 24 Rep. for local govtl. rels., dir. for 2nd 2-yr. term, 1979; S.D. Bd. of Realtors, chmn. Budget and Fin. Com., dir. for 2nd term, 1979; Dept. of Real Estate Realtor/Realist Com.; v.p., Women's Council of Realtors, 1976. Rec.: sailing, racquetball. Home: 342 W. Laurel St., S.D., CA 92101; Office: 480 Camino del Rio St., No. 209, San Diego, CA 92108.

ISENBERG, JON IRWIN
Gastroenterologist
b. Mar. 21, 1937, Chicago, Ill.; s. Lucien and Roselle (Moss) Isenberg; B.S., chem., 1959; M.D., 1963; m. Laury Lipman, Dec. 16, 1962, Chicago; chil.: Nancy, b. May 2, 1964; Noah, b. June 28, 1967; Rebecca, b. Sept. 15, 1971. Career: Intern, Jackson Mem. Hosp., 1963-64; med. resident, Ill. Res. and Ed. Hosp., 1964-66; Gastroenterology Fellow, Wadsworth VA Hosp., 1966-68; Assoc. Chief, GI Wm. Beaumont Army Hosp., 1968-70; V.A. Clinical Investigator, Wadsworth VA Host., 1970-71; Chief, Gastroenterology, Wadsworth VA Hosp., 1971---; Prof. of Med., UCLA, 1978---. Ed., Viewpoints of Digestive Diseases; editorial bd., Gastroenterology. Jewish. Hobby: photog. Home: 367 21st St., Santa Monica, CA 90502; Office: Wadsworth VA Hosp., L.A., CA 90073.

J

JACKSON, CLAYTON RANDALL
Attorney at Law
b. Feb. 19, 1943, L.A.; s. Leonard and Isabelle Jackson; B.S., USC, 1965; J.D., Univ. Calif. Hastings Coll. of the Law, 1968. Career: Assoc. firm of Parker, Milliken, Kohlmeier, Clark & O'Hara, L.A., 1969; partner, McFarland, Kuchins & Jackson, S.F., 1970-75; partner Dunne, Phelps, Mills & Burns, S.F., 1975---. Bd. dir., S.F. Law Sch., 1975---. Mem.: Bankers Club of S.F., 1974---; Commonwealth Club of Calif., 1973---; Sutter Club of Sacto., 1971---; St. Francis Yacht Club, 1977---. Home: 96 Cazneau Ave., Sausalito, CA 94965; Office: 601 California St., No. 1900, S.F., CA 94108.

JACKSON, EILEEN
Former Newspaper Columnist
b. Apr. 15, 1906, San Diego; d. Edward and Vera (Morse) Dwyer; ed. San Diego State Coll., 1923-24; Univ. of Ariz. 1926; m. Everett Gee Jackson (prof. emeritus, noted artist, illustrator fine books), El Paso, Tex., July 21, 1926; dau.: Mrs. Thomas Thole (Jerry) Williamson of San Diego. Career: Ed. staff., S.D. Sun, 1921-25; S.D. Journ. (2 yrs.; both absorbed by Union Tribune Publ. Co.); staff, San Diego Union, 1929---, society editor, 1929-48, society columnist, 1948-76, feat. writer, 1953---; columnist, Straws in the Wind, 1953---. Awards: named Woman of Valor, 1959; Woman of Elegance, 1968; Galley Slave award by Theta Sigma Phi, 1969. Mem.: Alpha Epsilon chpt., Gamma Phi Beta, 1926---; Devel. Comm., San Diego Zoo; natl. bd., Press Women. Hobbies: travel to pre-Columbian sites, Central Am. Rec.: camping in Baja, Calif. Home: 1234 Franciscan Way, San Diego, CA.

JACKSON, GAIL PATRICK
Television Producer
b. June 20, Birmingham, Ala.; d. Lawrence C. and La Valle (Smith) Fitzpatrick; A.B. (hons.), Samford Univ., Birmingham; m. Cornwell Jackson, L.A., July 25, 1947 (div. 1970); chil.: Jennifer Stanley, b. 1951; Thomas Cornwell, b. 1953. Career: Actress, 61 films incl.: Stage Door, My Man Godfrey, My Favorite Wife, Love Crazy, Up In Mabel's Room, Claudia and David, 1932-47; TV producer, Perry Mason series, 1957---. Awards: L.A. Times Woman of Yr., 1961. Mem.: natl. trustee-bd. govs. Acad. of TV Arts and Scis. 1959-63; natl. v.p. and Hollywood chpt. pres., 1960-62; bd. trustees, Columbia Coll. 1963---; regent, Immaculate Heart Coll., L.A.; 1st v.p. The Muses, Mus. of Sci. and Industry, L.A.,

1967-68; natl. hon. chmn. Christmas Seal Campaign, Natl. Tuberculosis and Respiratory Disease Assn. 1970. Home: 2003 La Brea Terrace, Hollywood, CA 90046.

JACKSON, MICHAEL
Broadcaster — Commentator
b. Apr. 16, 1934, London, Engl.; ed. in Great Britain and Repub. So. Africa; m. Alana Ladd (dau. Alan Ladd), Oct. 16, 1965, L.A. Career: Commentator and Interviewer: SABC, Johannesburg, 1952-56; BBC, London, 1956-58; KYA and KEWB, S.F., 1960-62; KABC Radio, 1966---; KABC-TV, 1974-77; KCET TV, 1978---: Lectr. on current events, frequent guest columnist, L.A. Times and L.A. Magazine. Awards: five Emmy Awards for TV, 8 Emmy nominations; Radio-Acad. of Achievement Golden Plate Award; voted "one of the 20 people most influencing the way Californians think," New West Mag.; named Radio Personality of the Year, 3 times, L.A. Times. Hobbies: photog., travel. Rec.: running. Office: KABC, 3321 S. La Cienega Blvd., L.A., CA.

JACOBS, JOSEPH JOHN
Chairman, Jacobs Engineering Group Inc.
b. June 13, 1916, Brooklyn, N.Y.; B.S., Chem. Eng., 1937, M.S., 1939, Ph.D., Polytechnic Inst. of Brooklyn (now Polytech. Inst. of N.Y.); m. Violet Jabara, July 14, 1942; chil.: Margaret, b. Mar. 20, 1945; Linda, b. May 10, 1947; Valerie, b. Dec. 21, 1950. Career: Chem. engr., Autoxygen Inc., N.Y., 1939-42; sr. chem. engr., Merck & Co., N.J., 1942-44; v.p. & tech. dir., Chemurgic Corp., Richmond, CA, 1944-47; pres., Jacobs Engring. Co., 1947-74, chmn. of bd. and chief exec. ofcr., Jacobs Engring. Group Inc., 1974---. Dir., Del E. Webb Corp.; trustee, Harvey Mudd Coll., chmn. bd. of trustees, Polytech. Inst. of N.Y.; advis. bd., St. Luke Hosp. Patents and publs. in various fields of chem. engring.; contbr. author: Kirk & Other's Encyclopedia of Chem. Tech. Fellow: Am. Inst. of Chem. Engrs.; Am. Inst. of Chemists; Inst. for Adv. of Engring. Mem.: Am. Chem. Soc.; AAAS; Phi Lambda Upsilon and Sigma Xi. Office: 251 S. Lake Ave., Pasadena, CA 91101.

JACOBSON, JAMES B.
Insurance Company Executive
b. S.F.; ed. B.S. (magna cum laude), UCLA 1947; Wharton Grad. Sch. of Finance, Univ. of Pa. 1947-48; M.B.A., USC 1954. m. Janice Meilstrip; chil.: Steven B., Karen C., Richard B. Career: CLU Am. Coll. of Life Underwriters; joined Prudential Ins. Co. of Am. 1948---, sales, adm., exec., S.F., L.A., Newark; sr. v.p. in chg. group ins. oprns. 1970-73; sr. v.p. in chg. Western Oprns., L.A. 1973---. Author, (book) An Analysis of Group Creditors Insurance. U.S. Army, 13th Armored Div., E.T.O., 1943-46. Mem.: bd. dirs. Calif. C. of C.; bd. dirs., Assoc. of Calif. Life Ins. Cos.; bd. dirs Chil's. Hosp. of L.A.; dir., Philharmonic Assn., 1977-78; exec. bd. L.A. Council B.S.A.; Orthopaedic Hosp. Adv. Council; bd. dirs. Independent Colls. of So. Calif.; bd. of Councilors, Sch. of Bus., Univ. of So. Calif.; Brigham Young Univ. Coll. of Bus. Natl. Adv. Council; chmn. bd. dirs. L.A. Ballet; bd. dirs. and v.p., L.A. Philharmonic Assn.; adv. bd. Radio Stations KBIG/KBRT; pres. Lambda Delta Sigma, 1942; Sigma Nu; Clubs: Calif., L.A. Country, 100 Club of L.A. Office: P.O.B. 2314, Terminal Annex, L.A., CA 90051.

JACOBY, ROBERT MATTHIAS
Ophthalmologist
b. July 26, 1939, Cincinnati, Oh.; s. Robert Bird and Alice Helen Matthias; grandson, Edward S. Matthias, Judge, Oh. State Supreme Ct.; nephew, John Matthias, Judge, Oh. State Supreme Ct.; B.A., Cornell Univ., 1961; M.D., Baylor Univ. Coll. of Med., 1965; m. Christina Louise Van Esselstyn, Aug. 18, 1967, Palos Verdes; chil.: Robyn Diane, b. Sept. 28, 1971; Alyson Christina, b. Dec. 23, 1975. Career: Internship, Harbor Gen. Hosp., 1965-66; Gen. Med. Office, USN, 1966-68; residency in ophthalmology, Baylor Univ. Coll. of Med., 1968-71; staff ophthalmologist, Santa Barbara Med. Found Clin., 1971---. Lt., USN, 1966-68, Service Vietnam, 1966-67. Mem.: Delta Tau Delta, Alpha Omega Alpha med. frat. Methodist. Home: 4119 Marina Dr., Santa Barbara, CA 93110; Office: 215 Pesetas Lane, Santa Barbara, CA 93110.

JACQUES, KENNETH B.
Orthopaedic Surgeon
b. Dec. 27, 1911, St. Johnsbury, Vermont; s. Frank B. and Laura (Fessenden) Jacques; B.A., Dartmouth Coll., 1933; M.D., C.M., McGill Med. Sch., 1937; m. Elizabeth Matheson, June 15, 1940, Wollaston, Mass.; daus.:

Elizabeth Anne (Fredenberg), b. Nov. 28, 1942; Heather J. (Brown), b. Aug. 8, 1944. Career: Chief of Orthopaedics, U.S. Army Air Corps Rehabilitation Center, 1943-46; practice of orthopaedic surgery, L.A., 1946---. Pres. Med. Staff, Hollywood Presbyterian Hosp., 1978, 79. Maj., AUS, 1943-46. Mem.: Hollywood Rotary Club, Masonic Order. Elder, Ch. of Open Door, 1954-64. Hobbies: photog., Bible study, skiing. Home: 2214 Talmadge St., L.A., CA; Office: 7080 Hollywood Blvd., L.A., CA 90028.

JAGELS, GEORGE DANIEL
Business Executive
b. Aug. 8, 1908, Mountain View, Calif.; s. Henry Richard and Jeanette (Hoffman) Jagels; A.B., Stanford Univ. 1929; LL.B., Harvard, 1932; LL.D., MacMurray Coll., 1969; LL.D., Claremont Grad. Sch. 1971; m. Margaret Melissa Foley, San Marino, Dec. 7, 1946; chil.: Edward Richard, b. Mar. 26, 1949; George Daniel, b. Nov. 14, 1950; Jeffrey Foley, b. Apr. 19, 1954; Jean Elise, b. Apr. 8, 1957. Career: Admitted to Calif. bar, 1932; assoc. Gibson, Dunn & Crutcher, L.A. 1932-37; gen. partner, Woodland Farms, Ltd., Pasa., 1947---; pres. Investment Operating Corp. 1947---; bd. dir. Santa Anita Consolidated. Served from Lt. to Comdr., USNR (1942-46), WW II. Mem.: Am., Calif. Bar Assns.; Fellow, Claremont Univ. Center, 1959---, v.-chmn. Claremont Univ. Center; Pres., Caltech. Assocs., pres., Friends of Huntington Library; bd. chmn., L.S.B. Leakey Found. Am. Law Inst.; Judicature Soc.; Rancheros Visitadores, Santa Barbara; Bohemian Club, S.F.; Calif. Club, L.A.; Republican. Episcopalian. Rec.: tennis, riding. Home: 1285 Oak Grove Ave., San Marino, CA; Office: 202 S. Lake Ave., Suite 330, Pasadena, CA 91101.

JAHNKE, FRED RICHARD
Company President
b. June 20, 1930, Pomona; B.S. bus. admin., USC, 1952, M.B.A. indsl. mgmt., 1960; m. Janet Hodgkinson, 1952, Pasa.; chil.: Steven A. (News Anchorman, KTVQ Montana, CBS affil.), b. 1955; Andrea L., b. 1957; Melanie M., b. 1959. Career: dir. of Internat. Mktg., Consolidated Electrodynamics Corp., 1945-68; dir. of mktg., Astrodata, Inc., 1968-69; v.p., Internat. Group, Bell and Howell Co., 1970-73; pres. Gemini Internat. Corp., 1973---. Mem., Western Internat. Trade Group (advis. to U.S. Dept. of Commerce), 1969-71. USN, 1953-56, Dist. Intelligence Office, Honolulu; Capt., USNR (Ret.). Mem.: Phi Sigma Kappa frat., Commerce Assocs., USC. Rec.: tennis, swimming. Address: 11 Hacienda Dr., Arcadia, CA 91006.

JALLOW, RAY
Chief Economist, United California Bank
b. Oct. 10, 1929, Najaf, Iraq; s. Jawad M. and Maima (Hussain) Jallow; B.A., Univ. of Baghdad, Iraq, 1951; M.A., USC 1956; Ph.D., UCLA, 1966; m. Marcia Benjamin, L.A.; Jan. 30, 1958. Career: Auditor, Internal Revenue, Iraqi Rys., Baghdad, 1947-52; acct. Arab Ins. Co., Baghdad, 1952; est. U.S. res. 1953; pub. auditor, Robert Young, CPA, Pasa, 1956-57; economist, Calif. Bank, 1959-61; dir. econ. research-planning, United Calif. Bank, L.A. 1962-66, sr. v.p.-chief economist, 1970---. Faculty, UCLA Ext. 1963---. Chmn. bd. dirs., U.S. Orgn. for Med. and Edn. Needs. Author: 7 publs. on econ. banking incl.: The Calif. Banking Industry-Trends and Outlook, 1964; The Growth and Structure of Banks Deposits in Calif., 1966; Interest Rates Direction in the U.S.; Recession or Boom, 1967; Economic and Monetary Forecast, 1967. Awards: Merit Awards, Internat. Student Council, USC, 1956, Lions Club, 1958, Optimist Club, 1960. Mem.: Real Estate Research Adv. Council; chmn. bd.-past pres., Moslem Assn. of Am., Am., Western, So. Calif. Econ. Assns.; Natl. Assn. Bus Economists; Am. Finance Assn.; Am. Statistics Assn., Am. Marketing Assn., Blue Key, Beta Gamma Sigma. Hobby: internat. affairs. Rec.: travel, sports. Res.: 2530 Park Oak Ct., Hollywood, CA; Office: United Calif. Bank, 600 S. Spring St., L.A., CA 90054.

JAMES, DOUGLAS BOYNTON
Sheriff-Coroner, Santa Cruz County
b. June 18, 1925, Pasadena; s. Floyd Rigg and Elgiva (Kegler) James; ed. Monterey Peninsula Coll.; St. Mary's Coll.; FBI Natl. Acad.; USC; m. Elizabeth Travers, Monterey, June 7, 1946; chil.: Michael Alan, b. Jan. 6, 1949; Stacy Ann, b. Oct. 28, 1960. Career: Santa Cruz Police Dept. 1952-58; Sheriff and Coroner of Santa Cruz Co., 1959---. USN, WW II, and Korean Conflict. Mem.: pres. Native Sons of Golden West, Parlor No. 90, 1955; pres. Calif. State Coroners' Assn. 1965; Atty. Gen's. Police-Comm. Rel. Comm.; v.p. Calif. State

Sheriff's Assn. 1971; Elk's Lodge, No. 824, Santa Cruz. Catholic. Rec.: golf, swim. Res.: 3430 Merrill Rd., Aptos, CA 95003; Office: Sheriff-Coroner, P.O.B. 623, Santa Cruz, CA 95060.

JAMES, GEORGE BARKER II
Publishing Company Executive
b. May 25, 1937, Haverhill, Mass.; s. Paul Withington and Ruth (Burns) James; desc. Peregine White, first Pilgrim child born in New England; A.B. Harvard Univ., 1959; M.B.A., Stanford Univ., 1962; m. Beverly Alma Burch, Sept. 22, 1962, Stanford, Calif.; chil.: Alexander, b. Sept. 14, 1963; Christopher, b. Oct. 29, 1964; Geoffrey, b. May 11, 1966; Matthew, b. June 17, 1978. Career: Fiscal dir. EG/G, Inc., Bedford, Mass., 1963-67; fin. exec., Am. Brands, Inc., N.Y.C., 1967-69; v.p., Pepsico, Inc., N.Y.C., 1969-72; sr. v.p., Arcata Corp., Menlo Park, 1972---. Chmn. bd., Towle Trust Fund, 1965-67; v.p. and trustee, San Francisco Ballet Assn.; dir., Real Estate Data, Inc.; advisory bd., Stanford Bs. Sch. Alumni Assn. Officer, AUS, 1960-61. Author: Industrial Development in the Ohio Valley, 1962, OVIA. Mem.: Menlo Circus Club (Atherton); Stock Exchange Club (S.F.); Commonwealth Club (S.F.); Harvard Club (Boston and N.Y.); Harvard Varsity Club (Cambridge). Polit. mem. Andover (Mass.) Town Com., 1965-67. Home: 215 Coleridge Ave., Palo Alto, CA 94301; Office: 2750 Sand Hill Rd., Menlo Park, CA 94025.

JAMES, ROBERT CLARKE
Professor of Mathematics
b. July 30, 1918, Bloomington, Ind.; s. Glenn James and Inez (Clarke) James; B.A., UCLA, 1940; Ph.D., Calif. Inst. of Tech., 1947; m. Edith Peterson, Oct. 28, 1945, New Haven, Conn.; chil.: Judith Marie (Grounds), b. Mar. 22, 1947; Linda Inez (Anooshian), b. June 2, 1948; David Vernon James, b. Dec. 4, 1949; Robert Glenn James, b. Apr. 11, 1952. Career: Benjamin Pierce Instr. math., Harvard Univ., 1946-47; instr. math., asst. prof., Univ. Calif., Berkeley, 1947-51; assoc. prof. math., Haverford (Pa.) Coll., 1951-57; prof. math., chmn. dept., Harvey Mudd Coll., Claremont, 1957-67; prof. math., State Univ. N.Y., Albany, 1967-68; prof. math, Claremont Grad. Sch., 1968---; mem. Inst. for Advanced Study, Princeton, 1962-63; fellow, Inst. for Adv. Studies, Jerusalem, 1966-67. Author: Mathematics Dictionary, 1942, revised 1949, 59, 68, 76; University Mathematics, 1963; Advanced Calculus, 1966; numerous articles in profl. research journs. Mem.: Am. Math Soc.; Math. Assn. of Am.; Soc. Indsl. and Applied Math.; AAAS, fellow; Fedn. of Am. Scientists; Phi Beta Kappa; Sigma Xi. Mem. Society of Friends. Home: 1121 Oxford Ave., Claremont, CA 91711; Office: Claremont Grad. Sch., Claremont, CA 91711.

JAMES, WRIGHT ELWOOD
Lawyer -- Government Official
b. Jan. 16, 1900, Compton; s. Edward M. and Lillie (Edwards) James; A.B., Stanford Univ. 1924, LL.B. 1934; m. Josephine Rush, Glenwood Springs, Colo., Sept. 28, 1927; son: William Edward, b. July 5, 1928. Career: Geologist, Gen. Petroleum Corp. 1924-31; lawyer, Bakersfield, 1934---, secty. Laymac Corp.; secty.-dir. Silicz Enterprises. Mem.: Assembly, Calif. Legislature, 1947-48. Lt. Comdr., USNR, Naval Air Combat Intelligence Ofcr., USS Coos Bay; Comdr., Air Pac. and 11th Naval Dist. (1942-45), WW II. Awards: 2 Presidential Unit Cits. Mem.: Phi Gamma Delta, 1920---; Stockdale Country Club, 1939---; chmn. Kern Co. Repun. Central Com. 1955-56; Bakersfield Petroleum Club, 1958---; L.A. Ath. Club, 1960---; L.A. Country Club, 1963---. Hobby: travel. Rec.: golf, fishing, hunting. Res.: 2418 Spruce St., Bakersfield, CA; Office: 1717 28th St., Bakersfield, CA 93301.

JAMIESON, JAMES BRADSHAW
College President
b. June 10, 1931, Los Angeles; s. Charles Cameron and Ruth Jane (Bradshaw) Jamieson; B.A., Claremont Men's Coll., 1955; M.A., Claremont Grad. Sch., 1958; Ph.D., Brown Univ., 1966; m. Perry Ann McNaughton, Dec. 27, 1959, San Berbardino, Calif.; chil.: Jeffrey, b. Dec. 14, 1961; Dalton, b. July 25, 1966. Career: Research political scientist, UCLA, Govt., 1965-65; asst. to pres. for budget & finance, Pitzer, 1965-66; asst. to pres. for devel., 1966-68; v.p. and prof. of polit. studies, Pitzer Coll., 1968-78; Acting Pres., 1978---; pres., Creative Capers, Inc., 1958-60; cons., Inst. of Govt. & Public. Affairs, UCLA. Contbr. articles: Flightime (Continental Airlines inflight mag.), College & University Bus., Mar. 1974; Calif. Dept. of Interior, 1974. Served USAF, airman 2nd class, 1950-52. Awarded: Fellowship, Brown Univ., 1960,

1963, teaching fellow, 1963; Resources for the Future doctoral dissertation fellowship, 1964, Research Grant, Dept. of Interior, 1971. V.P., Claremont Civic Assn.; vice chmn., Claremont Capital Improvement Com.; mem. Am. Polit. Sci. Assn. Club: Claremont Tennis. Home: 367 Blaisdell, Claremont, CA 91711; Office: 1050 N. Mills Ave., Claremont, CA 91711.

JAMISON, MARY KATHRYN
Civic Leader
b. Aug. 6, 1919, Butte, Mont.; d. Robert McLean and Kathryn Mildred (Frey) Thurman; B.A., UCLA, 1940; m. Max Killian Jamison; sons: Max Killian Jamison, Jr., b. 1954; Michael Thurman Jamison, b. 1955; Matthew Robert Jamison, b. 1956. Career: v.p., pres., trustee, Greater L.A. Zoo Assn., 1963---; life mem. and awarded title of Benefactor, 1975; African Exec. Com., Mayor's Council for Internat. Visitors and Sister Cities, 1967---; pres., Toluca Guild of Children's Hosp., 1964; Den Mother, Cub Scout Pack 35, 1964-68; Life mem., Women's Aux. Good Samaritan Hosp.; bd. mem., L.A. Lawyer's Wives, 1956-60. Outstanding Serv. Citation, L.A. Legal Aid Soc., 1960; Founding mem. and 1st v.p., pres., and hon. life mem., San Fernando Valley Lawyer's Wives, 1955---; area chmn. No. Hollywood, United Way; Area chmn. for No. Hollywood and Studio City, Hollywood Bowl Family Night; mem., Altar Guild, St. Savior's Chapel, Harvard Prep. Sch. 1967---; Advis. Com., Science Centers, L.A. Unified Sch. Dist., 1974---; Recipient of Hour Glass Award, 1973, Assistance League; trustee, exec. com., chmn., Nat. Fellows Programs, Founder chmn., Assocs., L.S.B. Leakey Found., 1974---; v. chmn., Pub. Edn. Com., Am. Assn. Zoological Parks and Aquariums, 1972-75; received, Maggie Savor Comm. Communications Award, L.A. Profl. Journalists chpt., Theta Sigma Phi, 1972; trustee, L.A. Co. Mus. of Natural Hist. Found., 1978---. Guest speaker on wildlife conservation. Order of St. Lazerus of Jerusalem, CLJ, CMLJ, 1976. Hobbies: Wildlife edn.; golf; cooking; needlework. Res.: 10074 Valley Spring Ln., Toluca Lake, CA 91602.

JANES, CLAIR W.
Professor of Business
b. Oct. 24, 1925, Marysville, Oh.; s. Glen L. and Effie June (Gamble) Janes; B.S., bus. admin., (cum laude) Oh. State Univ., 1950, M.B.A., 1953; m. Patricia E. McCracken, Nov. 12, 1965, San Jose. Career: mem. audit staff, Price Waterhouse & Co., S.F., 1954-58; mem. faculty, San Jose State Univ., 1958---; Faculty Fellow, Arthur Andersen & Co., Chicago, 1967-68; asst. exec. v.p., San Jose State Univ., 1969-74; Served to Lt. j.g., USN, 1943-46, 1951-53. Mem.: Calif. Soc. of CPAs, pres. San Jose chpt., 1964-65; Inst. of Internal Auditors, pres. San Jose chpt., 1978-79; Am. Inst. of CPAs, 1959---; Am. Accounting Assn., 1977---; Beta Gamma Sigma; Beta Alpha Psi. Republican. Episcopalian; Parish Controller. Rec.: hiking. Res.: 1503 Wendy Way, San Jose, CA 95115; Office: Sch. of Bus., San Jose State Univ., San Jose, CA 95192.

JANOFSKY, LEONARD S.
Attorney at Law
b. Oct. 13, 1909, L.A.; A.B., Occidental Coll., 1931; LL.B., Harvard Univ., 1934; m. Nancy Nielson, Dec. 29, 1948, L.A.; chil.: Irene (Hartzell), b. Oct. 21, 1938; John Stephen, b. Dec. 27, 1951. Career: Assoc. atty. with firm of Faries & McDowell, 1934-42; Sr. Regional Atty., Nat. Labor Rels. Bd., So. Calif. and Ariz., 1935-36; assoc. with Bodkin, Breslin & Luddy, 1945-51; Spec. Trial Counsel, eminent domain proceedings, Housing Authority for City of L.A., 1950-54; partner firm of Paul, Hastings, Janofsky & Walker, L.A., 1951---. Lt. Comdr., USNR, with U.S. Naval Mission to Brazil. Apptd. Del. to Internat. Labour Orgn. Conf., Geneva by U.S. State Dept., 1969-70; chmn. bd. of trustees, Occidental Coll. 1969-72; mem. Overseers' Com., Harvard Law Sch. 1969-74; mem. bd. of vis., Stanford Law Sch. 1972-75. Awards: Medallion for outstanding contbrn. to evolution of legal principles consistent with justice, equity and rule of law, St. Thomas More Law Soc., Loyola Univ., 1977; Shattuck-Price Award for dedication to improvement of legal profn. and adminstrn. of justice, L.A. Co. Bar Assn., 1977; Fellow, Am. Coll. of Trial Lawyers; Fellow, AM. Bar Found. Pres., Am. Bar Assn, 1978-79; Nat. Conf. of Bar Presidents, 1974-75; chmn. sect. of Labor Rels. Law, Am. Bar Assn. 1975-76; pres., State Bar of Calif. 1972-73; pres., L.A. Co. Bar Assn. 1968-69; mem. Am Law Inst. Mem. Rotary. Rec.: swimming, hiking. Home: 661 Thayer Ave., L.A., CA 90024; Office: 555 S. Flower St., 22 Flr., L.A., CA 90071.

JAYNES, MARVIN BERNARD
Chartered Life Underwriter
b. July 10, 1928, Preston, Ia.; s. Bernard and Amanda (Westphal) Jaynes; B.A., Drake Univ., Des Moines, Ia. 1954; m. Marian Freyermuth, July 5, 1949, West Liberty, Ia.; chil.: Jeffrey Philip, b. July 25, 1954; Marvie Lynn, b. Aug. 1, 1956; Douglas Charles, b. July 3, 1959; Carolyn Amanda, b. Feb. 8, 1966. Career: Agent, Conn. Mutual Life, 1958---: sales staff mgmt., 1962, asst. gen. agent 1962; gen. agent, Fresno Agency, 1967; gen. agent, Oakland Agency, 1970---. Acct., General Mills, Inc., S.F., 1954-56; asst. treas., Walnut Creek Canning, 1956-58. Mil. grad., AF ROTC, to Capt. Mem.: Oakland-East Bay Life Underwriters, Gen. Agents and Mgrs. Assn., past dir., treas., v.p., pres.; area chmn.; Gen. Agents Advis. Com., Conn. Mutual, 1976-77; Project 70 bldg. pgm. ($8,000,000), Samuel Merritt Hosp., Oakland, 1966; dir. Young Life, Moraga-Lafayette-Orinda area four years; dir., Walnut Creek Jr. Ice Hockey League, past dir.; S.F. Bay Area Drake Alumni; Commerce Club, v.p.; Delta Sigma Pi, pres.; Accounting Club; Arnold Ari Soc., exec. officer, publs. bd.; Omicron Delta Kappa. Lutheran; service on ch. councils 19 yrs., pres. 7 yrs. Hobbies: family, church. Rec.: tennis, golf. Res.: 1927 Joseph Dr., Moraga, CA 94556; Office: 428 13th St., Suite 100, Oakland, CA 94612.

JENSEN, ARTHUR M.
College President
b. Aug. 22, 1921, Chicago, Ill.; s. Hobart O. and Marie (Severson) Jensen; B.S., Univ. Western Mich. 1949, M.A. 1953; Ed.D., UCLA 1965; m. Marion McBride, Grand Rapids, Mich., May 26, 1945; chil.: Mary Ann, Arthur Ray, Patricia Lynn. Career: Tchr.-counselor, Comstock H.S., Mich. 1949-55; instr. San Diego City Coll., Calif. 1955-59, dir. placement, 1959-63; adm. dean. S.D. Eve. Coll. 1963-66; chief, Bur. of Jr. Coll., Calif. State Dept. of Edn. 1966-67; pres. San Bernardino Valley Coll. 1967---. Author: Adm. of Multicampus Jr. Coll. Dists., publ. UCLA 1965; contrib. edn. journs., incl.: Am. Assn. of Jr. Coll., Calif. Edn. 1961---. USN, WW II, Korean War; Capt. USNR (28 yrs). Mem.: Phi Delta Kappa, 1949---; dir. Calif. Jr. Coll. Assn. 1966-67; Am. Assn. Jr. Colls.; Calif. Tchrs. Assn., NEA, Rotary Club, Navy League, BSA, Salvation Army; pres. San Bernardino Sym. Assn. 1972-74. Protestant. Hobbies: building, reading, photog. Rec.: golf, camping, swim. Res.: 1349 Pine Knoll Crest, Redlands, CA 92373; Office: 701 S. Mt. Vernon Ave., San Bernardino, CA 92403.

JENSEN, D. LOWELL
District Attorney, Alameda County
b. June 3, 1928, Brigham, Ut.; s. Wendell and Elnora Jensen; A.B. (econs.), Univ. of Calif., Berkeley, 1949, LL.B., 1952; m. Barbara Cowin, Alameda, 1951; chil.: Peter, b. Sept. 3, 1955; Marcia, b. Nov. 2, 1956; Thomas, b. July 22, 1960. Career: Admitted to Calif. bar, 1952; dep. Dist. Atty., Alameda Co. 1955, asst. Dist. Atty. 1966, Dist. Atty., July 1, 1969---. Adv. com. Calif. Penal Code Rev. Comm.; bd. dirs. Calif. Crime Tech. Research Found. Cryptographer, U.S. Army, 1952-54. Mem.: Commonwealth Club of Calif. L.D.S. Res.: 5590 Greenridge Rd., Castro Valley, CA; Office: 900 Courthouse, 1225 Fallon St., Oakland, CA 94612.

JENSEN, ROBERT D.
College President
b. July 20, 1940, Oakland, Calif.; Bachelor of Bus. Adminstrn. and Accounting; Master of English/Literature; Doctor of Community Coll. Administrn./Curriculum; m. Ruthanne Jensen; chil.: Marjorie, b. Mar. 13, 1966; Becky, b. June 21, 1968; Shelly, b. Jan. 25, 1971; Megan, b. Jan. 19, 1973. Career: Intern as dean of coll. of edn., Wash. State Univ., 1967-69; asst. dean, instruction, evening & extension edn., Mt. Hood Community Coll., Oregon, 1969-70; asst. dean of instruction, humanities/creative arts, 1970-71, dean of students, 1971-75, dean of college, 1975-76; president, American River Coll., Sacto., 1978---. Hobby: antique autos. Rec.: racquetball, sailing. Home: 2691 Creekside Lane, Sacto., CA 95821; Office: 4700 College Oak Dr., Sacramento, CA 95841.

JESSUP, WARREN T.
Attorney at Law
b. Aug. 1, 1916, Eureka; s. Thurman W. and Amelia (Johnson) Jessup; B.S.E.E., USC 1937; J.D., George Wash. Univ., 1942; m. Evelyn Via, Sept. 13, 1941, Falls Church, Va.; chil.: Thurman W., b. May 30, 1943; Paul H., b. Dec. 1, 1947; Stephen T., b. Feb. 15, 1950;

Marilyn R. (Huffman), b. Oct. 31, 1952. Career: Engr., General Electric Co., 1937-42; Patent Counsel 11th Naval Dist., 1946-50; pvt. patent law practice Huebner, Beehler, Worrel & Herzig, 1950-56; partner, firm of Herzig & Jessup, 1957-59; sole practice, 1959-57; partner, firm of Jessup & Beecher, Sherman Oaks, 1967---; also mem. faculty: USC Sch. of Law and UCLA Sch. of Engring. Ensign to Lt. Comdr., USN, 1942-46, WW II; Comdr., USNR, ret. Registered profl. engr., State of Calif. Admitted to U.S. Supreme Ct., Calif., Dist. of Columbia. Contbr. articles, Journ. of the Patent Office. Soc.; contbr. author, Ency. Patent Practice and Invention Mgmt. Chmn., bd. dirs., Hidden Valley Municipal Water Dist. Mem.: Pi, Phi Delta Phi, Order of Coif, Eta Kappa Nu, dir. Conejo Valley Hist. Soc. Hobby: cartography. Rec.: horseback riding. Office: 15233 Ventura Blvd., Suite 716, Sherman Oaks, CA 91403.

JEWELL, FOSTER R.
Sculptor — Painter — Poet
b. Grand Rapids, Mich.; stu., Chicago Art Inst., pvt. instr. with Matthias Alton, painter; m. Rhoda de Long, ed. and pub. of poetry (JANUS-SCTH); dau. Ramona Braley. Career: His oil painting, "Black Bottom" chosen by N.Y. Arts Council as one of the hundred important paintings of the decade of 1920s; paintings and sculpture rep. in permanent collections; pub. eleven books of poetry, 1958-78, received 26 awards for haiku since 1966; awarded silver medal for sculpture, "Blades of Grass," Oakland, 1948; recipient (w/Rhoda de Lidewell) the first Foster Jewell Creative Inspiration Award, the Very Venice Co., 1977. Mil.: served for duration, WW I, WW II. Address: 1325 Cabrillo Ave., Venice, CA 90291.

JEWELL, JAMES EARL
Lighting Designer
b. July 26, 1929, L.A.; s. Earl Claggett and Frances Estelle (Roe) Jewell; grandnephew, Edwin Markham, 1852-1940, U.S. poet; B.A., Coll. of the Pacific, 1951; M.G.A., Sch. of Drama, Yale Univ., 1957. Career: Head, Engring. Div., Holzmueller Corp., S.F., 1957-67; Sr. Cons., Bolt, Beranek, and Neuman, S.F. and N.Y., 1967-68; with Pac. Gas and Electric Co., S.F., 1968---: illuminating engr., sr. illuminating engr., sr. energy servs. engr. Creator: lighting designer, Magnin Room, Asian Art Mus., 1968; lighting designer, Boy Scout World Jamboree, Farragut State Pk., Idaho, 1965. AUS, 1953-55. Club: Bohemian. Republican. Episcopalian, Gen. Convention Deputy, 1965. Hobby: history. Res.: 749 Rhode Island St., S.F., CA; Office: 77 Beale St., S.F., CA 94106.

JOHNSON, BARBARA JEAN
Judge
b. Apr. 9, 1932, Detroit, Mich.; d. Clifford and Orma (Boring) Barnhouse; B.S., USC, 1953; J.D. USC Law Sch., 1970; m. Ronald M. Johnson, June 24, 1965, Portuguese Bend, Calif.; dau. Belinda (Etezad), b. May 11, 1955. Career: Partner in law firm, Anglea, Burford, Johnson & Tookey, 1971-77; Judge, L.A. Municipal Ct. 1977---; adj. prof. of law, Southwestern Univ. Law Sch., 1975-77; instr., USC Law Sch., 1977---. Mem.: Calif. Women Lawyers, pres. 1976-77; L.A. Women Lawyers Assn., pres. 1975-76; L.A. Co. Bar Assn., trustee, 1975-77; bd. mem. Legion Lex, 1974---; bd. mem., Pasadena Planned Parenthood, 1975-77; bd. mem. Pasadena Ednl. Found. 1976-77. Address: L.A. Municipal Ct., 110 N. Grand Ave., L.A., CA 90012.

JOHNSON, EDWARD LENNART
Chairman, Financial Federation Inc.
b. May 6, 1910, Chicago; s. Carl J. and Hilma S. Johnson; B.S., real estate & land economics, 1932; m. Dorothy Joyce Matschke, Apr. 20, 1940; chil.: Calvin, Gloria Ryan, Janice, Patti Kent. Career: v.p., dir., Bell Fed. Svgs. & Loan, Chicago, 1933-53; exec. v.p., dir., Standard Fed. Svgs. & Loan, L.A., 1953-58; exec. v.p., dir., Am. Svgs. & Loan, Whittier, 1958-59; currently pres., chmn. of bd., Financial Fedn., Inc., ---; instr. real estate financing, Northwestern Univ. v.-chmn., bd. trustee, City of Hope; mem. Am. Acad. of Achievement, recipient The Golden Plate Award, 1964. Clubs: Calif., Jonathan. Polit.: Golden Circle Republic Assocs. Dir. Christianity Today; bd. dir., Campus Crusade for Christ Internat.; trustee, Moody Bible Inst.; trustee & chmn. Advis. Com., Moody Inst. of Sci.; bd. dir., World Wide Pictures; mem. Nelson Bible Award Selection Com. Hobby: photog. Office: 615 S. Flower St., L.A., CA 90017.

JOHNSON, FORDYCE A.H.
M.D. -- Otorhinolaryngology
b. Dec. 6, 1904, Fargo, N.D.; s. Johan and Mary (Bentson) Johnson; B.S., Univ. of Ore., 1927, M.D., 1930; m. Astrid Erickson, May 25, 1933, Portland, Ore.; chil.: Karen (Root), b. Apr. 24, 1939; Kirsten (Rindal), b. June 3, 1941; Gragory Johnson, D.D.S., b. Apr. 26, 1946. Career: Rotating Internship, Emanuel Hosp., Portland, Ore., 1941; residency in surg., Pierce Hosp., Tacoma, Wash., 1932; E.N.T., Episcopal Hosp., Wash. D.C., 1933; med. practice E.N.T., Tacoma, Wash., 1934-42, Pasadena, 1946---; also Att. Staff, USC, E.N.T., 1946---. Maj., AUS Med. Corps., 1942-46. Ed., Journ., Am. Soc. Ophthalmologic and Otolaryngologic Allergy, 1977, 78, 79. Bd. Certified, Am. Bd. of O&O, 1944. Fellow: Am. Laryngological, Rhinolotical and Otological Soc.; Am. Acad. Ophthalmology and Otolaryngology; Am. Soc. of Facial Plastic Surg. Mem.: Am. Soc. Ophthalmologic and Otolaryngologic Allery; Pacific Coast Opthal. and Otolaryng. Soc.; Research Study Club, EENT; Am. Med. Soc.; Calif. Med. Soc.; L.A. Co. Med. Soc.; V.P., Pasadena C. of C., 1964. Clubs: Univ., Pasadena Masonic Lodge, Kiwanis. Republican, honor guest, Congressman John Rousselot, 1978. Congregational Ch. Deacon & Moderator. Hobby: lapidary. Rec.: golf. Res.: 1131 Rodeo Rd., Arcadia, CA; Office: 98 N. Madison Ave., Pasadena, CA 91101.

JOHNSON, GORDON FLOYD
Educator — Administrator
b. Dec. 4, 1924, Mavre, Mont.; s. Gust H. and Estelle Rose Zabel; B.Sc., edn., 1950; M.S., edn., 1955; Ednl. Spec. 1960; Ed.D., exceptional chil., 1966; m. Frances Moser, Aug. 12, 1956, Portland, Ore.; chil.: Kent, b. May 22, 1957; Scott, b. Sept. 9, 1960; Sherri, b. Feb. 6, 1963; Krist, b. Dec. 16, 1965. Career: Elem. Tchr., Ore., 1950-52; Jr. H.S. tchr., 1952-54; special edn. tchr., 1956-58; rec. dir., Stanford Children's Convalescent Hosp. 1958-60; dir., Spec. Instrnl. Pgms., Lebanon (Ore.) Pub. Schs., 1960-64; Clinic Supr., Univ. of Ore., 1964-66; Asst. Assoc., Full Prof. of Spec. Edn., Cal State Univ., Fresno, 1966---, chmn. dept. of advanced studies, 1975-76, coord., spec. edn., 1976---. Cons. on career/vocational edn. for the handicapped, State Agencies, local sch. dists. Contbr. 20+ articles on spec. edn. profl. journs. Pres., Calif. Assn. Profs. of Spec. Edn., 1977-78; coord., Council for Exceptional Chil., Career Edn. for Disabled in Comm. Coll. 1978-79; student chpt. adv., Council for Exceptional Childrenm 1970-75; mem. profl. advis. bd., United Cerebral Palsy, 1977---. AUS, 1943-45, Africa, Italy; USAFR, 1950-66, edn. Hobbies: music & movies of late 20s & 30s. Rec.: camping. Home: 4778 N. Orchard, Fresno, CA 93726; Office: Cal. State Univ., Fresno, Fresno, CA 93740.

JOHNSON, HERMAN DOWELL
University Chancellor
b. Sept. 11, 1925, Rillito, Ariz.; s. Robert Ralph and Ora Mae (Curtis) Johnson; ed. Colo. Coll. 1943-44; Univ. Okla. 1944-46; B.S., Univ. Calif. 1947-48; Armstrong Coll. 1948-49; Ind. Coll. of Armed Forces, 1966-68; m. Janet Joslin, Norman, Okla., May 7, 1946; daus.: Christine Grace Thomas, b. Dec. 1, 1948; Laura Evelyn, b. Aug. 31, 1952. Career: Acct., Univ. of Calif., Berkeley, 1948-49, sr. acct. 1952-55; asst. to chief acct., Lawrence Radiation Lab., Univ. of Calif. 1949-50; acct. ofcr. Univ. of Calif., San Diego, 1955-59; budget and acct. ofcr. 1959-66, acting asst. V. Chancellor (Bus. and Finance), 1966; asst. to V. Chancellor, 1966-67; asst. V. Chancellor (adm.) 1967-68; acting V. Chancellor, 1958-69; V. Chancellor (Bus. and Finance), 1969---. Univ. of Calif. Retirement System Gov. Bd. 1970-73; 2nd Lt., Inf. USMCR 1946-47; 12th Marine Inf. 1947-50; 1st Lt. 1950-52; Maj., USMCR 1952---. Mem.: dir. Torrey Pines chpt., Rotary Club, 1970-71. Hobby: furniture refinishing. Rec.: golf, sailing. Res.: 1625 Malden St., San Diego, CA 92109; Office: University of Calif., P.O.B. 92093, La Jolla, CA 92037.

JOHNSON, JOHN EDWARD
President, Santa Ana College
b. May 9, 1916, L.A.; s. John Cherry and Helen (Hackett) Johnson; B.A. (chem.), Occidental Coll. 1938); M.S., USC, 1948; Ed.D. (adm.), 1955; m. Annalee Thompson, Sept. 5, 1942; daus.: Barbara Ann, b. Nov. 18, 1946; Patricia Louise, b. Nov. 8, 1950. Career: Instr., Santa Ana Sr. H.S. 1939-42, v. prin. 1946-52; dean of men, Santa Ana Coll. 1952-56, dean of Coll. 1956-57, pres. 1957---. USN 1943-46; Comdr., USNR, WW II. Mem.: bd. dirs. CCJCA, Orange Co. Ind. Ed. Council, Am. Assn. Jr. Colls., Comm. H.E. Adm., Phi Delta Kappa, Phi Gamma Delta, Delta Epsilon, Santa Ana Kiwanis Club. Presbyterian. Hobbies: gardening, photog. Res.: 1010 River Lane, Santa Ana;

Office: Santa Ana Coll., 1530 W. 17th St., Santa Ana, CA 92706.

JOHNSON, JUDITH SALTER
Energy Company Executive
b. Aug. 17, 1937, Modesto; d. John West and Agnes Mayes (Zimmerman) Salter; stu., Univ. Calif., Berkeley, 1955-58, Harvard Bus. Sch., 1975-77. Career: with Buttes Gas & Oil Co., Oakland, 1964---: corp. secty., 1966, v.p., adminstrn. and corp. secty., 1976---; with Calif. Farm Bureau Fedn., Berkeley, 1959-63. Dir.: Calif. Taxpayers Assn., 1975---; Oakland City Center Hotel Corp., 1978---. V.P. and dir., Women's Forum-West, 1978---; trustee, Easter Seal Found., 1977---; mem. East Oakland Youth Devel. Center Found., 1978---; mem. Indsl. Retention Task Force, Oakland Com. for Econ. Devel., 1977---. Clubs: Stock Exch. Club of S.F., Commonwealth Club. Home: 6155 Westover Dr., Oakland, CA 94611; Office: 1221 Broadway, Oakland, CA 94612.

JOHNSON, M. MARVIN
Newspaper Publisher
b. Sept. 25, 1929, Quincy, Fla.; s. Phillip M. and Katie G. (Fletcher) Johnson; m. June Yvonne Dearinger, Bainbridge, Ga., June 23, 1950; chil.: Cathi Yvonne Emerzien, b. Nov. 20, 1951; David Marvin, b. Sept. 3, 1954. Career: Mailroom foreman, Fla. Times Union, Jacksonville, 1948-50; Fresno Bee, 1950-51; foreman, prodn. mgr., sales mgr.-bus. mgr., Fresno Guide, 1951-71; pres.-publ. Marshall News Messenger, Marshall, Tex. 1971-74; pres.-publ. S.F. Progress, 1974---. Numerous publs., newspaper awards. Mem.: pres. Sequoia Chpt. Credit Union; v.p. S.F. Press Club; v.p. Greater S.F. C. of C.; bd. dirs. St. Vincent Sch. for Boys, v.p. Godfathers Club; chmn. Urban Renewal Comm., Marshall, Tex.; Fresno Lodge 247, F&AM. Tehran Temple Shriners, Fresno; Moraga Country Club. First Presbyterian. Hobbies: golf, tennis. Res.: 1601 St. Andrews Dr., Moraga, CA 94556; Office: 851 Howard St., S.F., CA 94103.

JOHNSON, M. MARVIN
Newspaper Publisher
b. Sept. 25, 1929, Quincy, Fla.; s. Phillip M. and Katie G. Johnson; student 12 yrs., Univ. of Fla.; m. June Yvonne Dearinger, June 23, 1950; chil.: David M., b. Sept. 3, 1954; Cathi Y., b. Nov. 20, 1952. Career: Gen. mgr., Fresno Guide, Fresno, 1951-70; pres. and publisher, Marshall News Messenger, Marshall, Tex., 1970-73; pres. and pub., San Francisco Progress, 1973-78; pres. and pub., SUN Group (San Diego Urban Newspaper Group) 1978---. Honoree, Nat. Jewish Fund, 1978. V.P., San Francisco C. of C. Rec.: golf, tennis. Office: 2724 Garnet Ave., San Diego, CA 92109.

JOHNSON, MARY LEE CLARE
Realtor
b. Feb. 21, 1932, Wann, Neb.; d. Harry P. and Clara A. (Heldt) Schlesiger; student, Cabrillo Coll., 1962; grad. Realtors Inst., 1977; m. Ralph Allen Johnson, Sept. 2, 1950, Yutan, Neb.; chil.: Christopher Allen, b. Mar. 21, 1952; Christine Ann (Mrs. Michael Grassl), b. Feb. 8, 1954; Curtiss Allen, b. July 28, 1957; Candace Ann, b. Sept. 26, 1967. Career: music tchr., Omaha, Neb., 1948-52; office mgr., Baugh Trucking, 1957-60; secty. legal offices, 1960-64; secty., Meidl Realty, 1965-70; office mgr., Hansen Real Estate, 1970-78; licensed real estate broker, 1971---; owner, Johnson Christensen Realtors, 1978---. Named Soroptimist Woman of Achievement, 1978; Realtor of Year, 1976, Watsonville Bd. of Realtors, Most Submitted Listings, 1976, Largest Dollar Volume, 1974. Pres., Watsonville Bd. of Realtors, 1976, dir., 1971-77; dir., Calif. Assn. Realtors, 1974-77; pres. P.T.A., H.A. Hyde Sch. 1967, E.A. Hall Jr. Hi Sch. 1966. Mem.: Order of Eastern Star, Soroptimist Internat. Polit. CREPAC mem. Lutheran. Hobbies: music, golf. Home: 947 Tuttle Ave., Watsonville, CA; Office: 585-A Arthur Rd., Watsonville, CA 95076.

JOHNSON, RICHARD DORIUS
CPA — Management Executive
b. Aug. 31, 1912, Salt Lake City, Ut.; s. Soren J. and Anna Sophia (Dorius) Johnson; C.P.A., Ore. Univ. 1942; Ph.D. (econs.), USC 1953; m. Verna Swan, Salt Lake City, Apr. 5, 1939; chil.: Dagny J. Merrill, b. June 24, 1940; Merrily Ann, b. Apr. 11, 1942; D'Anne Avon, b. June 26, 1945; Dickulyn Dawn, b. Mar. 17, 1948. Career: Missionary, L.D.S. (Mormon) Ch., Denmark; CPA 1942---; faculty USC 1942-44; est. Richard D. Johnson & Co., CPA firm, Oakland; Johnson, Hankins, MacDonald, Kimball & Co., mgmt. cons.; extensive

property devel. and investments; founder-pres. Foster Found. (The People Speak); pioneer in buffalo ind. devel., No. Australia, 1967---; various bus. and ch. leadership positions. Author: Significance and Measurement of Short Term Liquidity in Going Business Enterprise, 1953; In-Totality, aa philosophic approach to truth and knowledge, 1978. Mem.: CPA assns., Sociology socs. L.D.S. Ch. (mem. 2 bishoprics, serv. many positions). Hobbies: Music, singing, choral directing. Office: 1342 Creekside Dr., Walnut Creek, CA 94596.

JOHNSON, RICHARD GREENE
Physician — Medical Director
b. June 3, 1921, Louisville, Ky.; s. Greene L., M.D. and Anne (Wood) Johnson; B.A., Univ. of La. 1943, M.D. 1946; m. Agnes Campbell, Louisville, Nov. 2, 1946; chil.: Mrs. James (Carole) Bultema, b. July 21, 1948; Richard G., Jr., b. Nov. 2, 1950; Craig, b. June 15, 1953; Holly, b. May 25, 1955; Career: Postgrad, med. tr., NYC, Atlanta, Wash. Reed Hosp., psychoanalytic tr. So. Calif. Psychoanalytic Inst., L.A.; med. dir. Westwood Psych. Hosp.; faculty, UCLA Sch. of Med.; bd. trustees, Centre Coll. of Ky. Med. ofcr., U.S. Army (5½ yrs.). Mem.: Phi Delta Theta, Phi Chi; Clubs: Riviera Tennis, Los Tablos Hunting, Paso Robles. Hobbies: tennis, golf. Res.: 183 Tigertail Rd., L.A.; Office: 825 S. Barrington Ave., Suite 208, L.A., CA 90049.

JOHNSON, RITA B.
Educator
b. July 19, 1933, NYC; d. William and Anna (Kasten) Blaustein; B.A., UCLA, 1956, M.A., 1963; Ed.D., 1966; m. Stuart R. Johnson, Ed.D., Dec. 7, 1964, Calif. Career: Assoc. Prof. of Edn., Cal. State Univ., L.A., 1966-69; Coord. of Edn. Improvement, Nat. Lab. for Higher Edn., 1969-71; Assoc. Dir., Health Scis. Consortium and Assoc. Prof. Family Med., Univ. No. Caro. Med. Sch., 1970-76; Dir., Health Instrn. Exchange League for Innovation in Comm. Coll., 1976-78; Curriculum Dir., Assoc. Prof., Community Med., Charles R. Drew Postgraduate Med. Sch., 1978---; cons. to ten countries, 1964-79; invited U.S. Del. to People's Repub. of China, So. Am., Gr. Br.; Hon. Bd. Mem., Am. Soc. for Preventive Dentistry; Peace Corps Instr., UCLA; Vis. Instr., Duke Univ. and Univ. Calif., Berkeley. Publs.: 80+ incl. books, articles, instructional texts, audio-visual presentations. Mem.: Am. Ednl. Research Assn.; Am. Women for Internat. Understanding; Phi Beta Kappa; Am. Assn. of Med. Colls.; Pan Am. Fedn. of Assoc. Med. Schs. Hobbies: guitar, golf, organ, rug weaving. Rec.: salmon fishing, bird taming. Home: 12408 Deerbrook Lane, L.A., CA 90049; Office: 1621 E. 120th St., L.A., CA 90059.

JOHNSON, THEODORA LUCIA
City Librarian
b. Apr. 27, 1918, Wash., D.C.; d. Lusius Warren and Margaret Crosby Cranston (Brooks) Johnson; A.B., English Lit., Geo. Wash. Univ., 1941; Librarianship Cert., San Jose State Coll., 1953. Career: Reporter: Bethesda (Md.) Journ., 1939-41, Sunnyvale (Calif.) Standard, 1944-45, San Jose Mercury News, 1945-46; ed.: Campbell Press, Saratoga Observer, 1946-51; Lib. Asst., Palo Alto Pub. Lib., 1951-52; Asst. Cataloger, Ref. Librn., 1953-54, Order Librn., 1954-59, Adult Servs. Coord., 1959-60; City Librn.: Lompoc, 1960-62, Azusa 1962-70; Regional Supr., Sacto. City Lib. 1970-71; City Librn., Richmond, 1971---. Mem.: Pub. Lib. Execs. So. Calif., pres. 1970; Pub. Lib. Execs. Central Calif. Pres., 1973; Richmond Dept. Heads Assn., pres. 1974-75; Assn. Mgmt. Personnel; chmn., East Bay Coop. Lib. System, 1974-78, East Bay Info. Serv., 1974, 78; League of Calif. Cities Leisure Servs. Com. Republican. Episcopalian. Home: 755 Western Dr., Richmond, CA 94801; Office: Civic Center Plaza, Richmond, CA 94804.

JOHNSON, THORES G.
Business Executive (Ret.)
b. May 14, 1906, Minnewaukan, N.D.; s. Louis H. and Elizabeth Johnson; ed. Valley City State Tchrs. Coll., N.D., 1927; m. Dorothy Kirk, Sacto., Calif., Mar. 27, 1932 (dec. 1971); m. 2d. Helene T., 1973. chil.: Howard H. Hill and Patricia Hill; chil.: Barbara Winn, Thores K. and Sondra Salazar. Career: Sch. tchr., 1926-28; clerk, Pac. Tel. & Tel. Co., 1928-30; bookkeeper, Made Rite Sausage Co., Sacto., 1930, co-owner 1941, gen. mgr. 1946-66, chmn. bd. 1966-72; dir.-pres., Zephyr Cone Water Co., 1946---; dir., Zephyr Heights Subdiv. 1953---. Mem.: chm. Sacto. C. of C., 1932, chmn. aviation com. 1954-56; Natl. Assn. of Mfrs.

1946---, com. on conservation of natural resources, 1957---; Sacto. Co. Sheriff's Aero Squadron, 1948---, comdr. 1954; dir. Western States Meat Packers Assn. 1955-68, chmn. sausage com. 1957-60; dir. Sacto. Valley Employers Council, 1957-66; dir. Sacto. Safety Council, 1957-67; pres. Sacto. Chpt., Soc. for Advancement of Mgmt. 1957, natl. dir. 1958; group chmn., maj. employees div., United Crusade, 1957-59; dir. Gold Rush Park, 1959; dir. Sacto. Conv. Bur. 1959-66; dir. Sacto. Camellia Soc., 1961; Mason, Shriner, Lions Club, Northridge Country Club. St. John's Lutheran Ch. (pres. Pleasant Ridge Home; council, choir, welfare com. of No. Calif.). Hobby: flying, hunting, fishing. Rec.: golf. Res.: 4884 Kipling Dr., Carmichael, CA 95608; Office: 3353 2nd Ave., Sacto., CA.

JONES, CARLTON BENTON
Commander, Pacific Fleet, U.S. Navy
b. May 12, 1909, Pueblo, Colo.; s. Samuel T. and Carolyn (Berbower) Jones; ed. B.S., Naval Acad.. Annapolis, Md. 1929-33; m. Corinne Regina Bekins, W. L.A., Sept. 3, 1936; chil.: daus.: Carol Diane (Jones) Grover, b. Sept. 15, 1938; Patricia Regina (Jones) Field, b. Jan. 25, 1940; Career: Comm. Ensign, USN, 1933; promoted through ranks to Rear Adm. 1961; sea duty in surface Navy destroyers, battleships, cruisers, mine layers, amphibious ships, 1933-65; Mine Force, U.S. Pac. Fleet and Naval Base, Long Beach, 1965-67; Comdr. Naval Forces Marianas, 1967-68 (ret.). Exec. v.p. Guam C. of C. Shore duty, spec. in Congressional and Legislative liaison between Congress and Navy Dept., Wash. D.C. Convoy Escort Comdr's staff, Atlantic Fleet, escorting convoys to Iceland and Eng. 1940-42; Navy Dept. 1942-44; Comdr. USS Owens, Pac. with Third, Fifth Fleets, 1944-45, WW II. Mem.: Army-Navy Country Club, Arlington, Va. Presbyterian. Rec.: golf, fishing. Office: P.O. Box 283, Agana, Guam.

JONES, CHARLES E.
Business Executive
b. Dec. 4, 1904, L.A.; s. William H. and Delfina (Gallardo) Jones; great-grandson of one of the first Rigadors (councilmen) of L.A., settled in L.A. 1830; Gallardo Street named in his hon.; ed. L.A. pub. H.S.; m. Rose Wade, L.A., Apr. 29, 1922; daus. Betty Loraine Benedict, b. May 7, 1923; Elinor Francis Taylor, b. Sept. 23, 1924; Charlene Lenore Rhinehart, b. Sept. 24, 1931; m. Gooly Hopelian, Feb. 15, 1973. Career: Owner, Jones Auto Express, L.A. 1924-26; partner, Jones Brokerage Co., L.A. 1926-44; pres. Western Package Prod. Co., Pasa. 1942-63; pres. Comml. Commodities Co., 1944-74; pres. Tamarisk Country Club Ranch, Inc., Rancho Mirage (ret.) 1974. Mem.: pres. San Gabriel Shrine Club, 1950-51; F&AM (51 yrs.); Shrine, Knight Templar, Royal Arch Mason (40 yrs.); Delta Phi Epsilon; pres. Western Packaging Assn. 1955; Jesters L.A. Ct., Cave des Roys. Republican. Episcopalian. Hobbies: fishing, gardening. Home: P.O.B. GG, Cathedral City, CA 92234.

JONES, JIMMIE JOE
Newspaper Editor
b. Apr. 23, 1938, Portales, N.M.; s. Luther Frank and Lorene (Veneble) Jones; A.A., Vallejo Jr. Coll., 1958; B.A., journalism, Sacto. State Coll., 1960; m. Thelma Jean McDowell, Nov. 18, 1956, Reno, Nev.; chil.: Victor Paul, b. Mar. 18, 1958; Deborah Lynn (Turner), b. Apr. 20, 1960. Career: Copyboy, Vallejo Times-Herald, 1956-58; reporter, 1960-69; Sunday Editor, 1968-77; mgr. editor, 1977; editor, 1978---; newswriter KCRA-TC, 1959-60. Mem.: Vallejo C. of C., chmn., Cultural Affairs Com. 1976-78; Vallejo Group Theatre, past pres., mem. bd. dirs. Ch. of Christ, former deacon. Hobbies: piano repiar, skiing, flying, Home: 319 Howard Ave., Vallejo, CA; Office: 500 Maryland St., Vallejo, CA 94590.

JONES, THOMAS McREYNOLDS
Lawyer — Corporate Executive
b. Sept. 3, 1941, Pasadena, Calif.; s. Paul McReynolds and Dora (Dixon) Jones; nephew, Wesley M. Dixon (dec.) former chmn. and pres. Container Corp. of Am.; B.S., Univ. of Calif., Berkeley, 1962; J.D., UCLA Sch. of Law, 1965; m. Rita Griffin, Aug. 29, 1970, Newport Beach, Calif.; dau. Felicia Anne, b. Sept. 14, 1974. Career: Admitted to Calif. Bar, 1966; gen. practice of law, 1966-70; asst. apptments. secty. office of former Gov. Ronald Reagon, 1970-73; Chief Deputy Commissioner, Calif. Dept. of Corporations, 1974-75; Asst. Secty. and Asst. Gen. Counsel, Wynn's International, Inc., 1975---. Mem.: State bd. of governors, Calif. Community Colleges (apptd. by Gov.), 1974---, chmn. 1977-78; bd. dir. UCLA

Law Alumni, 1974-77; v.p., Deerfield Community Assn., 1976-77; chmn., Wynn's Internat., Inc. Pension and Profit Sharing Com., 1978; pres., Theta Delta Chi, 1961-62; Phi Delta Phi, 1963---. Sr. class pres., U.C. Berkeley, 1961-62. Clubs: Jonathan, L.A., 1966-68; Balboa Bay, 1969-71; 20-30 Club of Sacramento, 1971-73; Racquet Club of Irvine, 1976-78. Congregational ch. Rec.: tennis. Home: 16 Fox Hill, Irvine, CA 92714; Office: P.O.B. 4370, Fullerton, CA 92634.

JONES, THOMAS VICTOR
Chairman Board-CEO, Northrop Corporation
b. July 21, 1920, Pomona; s. Victor March and Elizabeth (Bretelle) Jones; ed. Pomona Jr. Coll. 1938-40; B.A. (with great distinction), Stanford Univ. 1942; (hon.) LL.D., Geo. Wash. Univ., Wash., D.C. 1967; m. Ruth Nagel, L.A., Aug. 10, 1946; chil.: Ruth Marilyn and Peter Thomas. Career: Engr., El Segundo Div., Douglas Aircraft Co., 1941-47; tech. adv., Brazilian Air Ministry, 1947-51; prof. (head dept.), Brazilian Inst. Tech. 1947-51; staff cons., Air Staff of USAF, Rand Corp., 1951-53; asst. to chief engr., Northrop Corp. 1953, dep. chief engr., 1954-56, dir. devel. planning, 1956-58, corporate v.p. 1958, sr. v.p. 1958-59, pres. 1959, chief exec. ofcr. Apr. 1960-62, chmn. bd. 1963---. Author: Capabilities and Operating Costs of Possible Future Transport Airplanes, 1953. Mem.: L.A. C' of C.; United Way; L.A. World Affairs Council, 1972-73; Fellow, Am. Aerons. and Astrons.; USC Assocs.; adv. com. County-USC Med. Center; Town Hall, Calif. Yacht Club, Georgetown Club, Kappa Sigma, The Beach, and Calif. Club. Res.: 1050 Moraga Dr., L.A., CA 90049; Office: Northrop Bldg., 1800 Century Park E., Century City, L.A., CA 90067.

JONES, WYMAN H.
City Librarian
b. Dec. 17, 1929, St. Louis, Mo.; s. Jay Hugh and Nina Marie (Dallas) Jones; B.A., Adams State Coll., Alamosa, Colo. 1956; M.L.S., Univ. Tex. 1958; m. Janet Grigsby, Bryan A.F. Base, Tex., Jan. 17, 1953; chil.: Gregory Foster, b. Apr. 21, 1954; Mark Jay, b. Apr. 18, 1955; Mansen Matthew, b. Oct. 10, 1960; Ross Christopher, b. June 24, 1962. Career: Sci.-ind. div. Dallas Pub. Lib. 1958-59, chief of branches, 1959-64; dir. Ft. Worth Pub. Lib., Tex. 1964-70; dir. L.A. Pub. Lib., 1970---. Cons. 23 lib. bldgs.; Tex. Gov's. Adv. Bd. on Libs., 1970. Author: monthly column, Lib. Journ., 1964; (ao-author) The Library Reaches Out, 1964; articles to various profl. publs. USAF 1951-55. Mem.: dist. chmn. Tex. Lib. Assn. 1961-62; chmn. State Legislative Com. 1963-64; chmn. Pub. Lib. Div. 1965-66; Am. Lib. Assn., Inter-lib. Coop. Com., 1969, Pre-Conf. Evaluation Comm. 1970-71, Conf. Planning Com. 1971-74. Hobbies: magic, piano, Res.: 1433 Via Cataluna, Palos Verdes Estates, CA 90274; Office: 630 W. 5th St., L.A., CA 90017.

JORDAN, LAN
Psychotherapist
b. Apr. 20, 1923, Detroit, Mich.; d. Charles Paul and Ora Lee (Whatley) Jackson; B.S., Ill. Inst. Tech. (formerly Lewis Inst.), 1940; A.M. in Med. & Psychiat. Adminstrn., Univ. Chicago, 1944; certificate, William Alanson White Inst. Psychiatry, N.Y.C. 1952; Ph.D. in Social Psychol., USC, 1956, postgrad. in marriage counseling 1961-62; dau. Loriel Dawn Jordan. Career: Clinic Mgr. Provident Hosp., Chicago, 1938-40; social worker, Dallas City Co. Dept. Pub. Welfare, 1941; Cook Co. (Ill.) Dept. Pub. Welfare, 1942-44; med. social worker neuropsychiat. dept., L.A. Co. Hosp., 1944-45; L.A. City Health Dept., 1945-57; VA Regional Office, L.A., 1947-49; psychiat. social worker, Bronx (N.Y.) VA Hosp., 1949-52; pvt. practice as psychotherapist, L.A. 1952-62, Beverly Hills, 1962---; founder-dir. Lan Jordan Inst. Counseling and Psychotherapy, Beverly Hills, 1968-74; cons., marriage and family counseling, 1974---. Speaker, lectr. CBS-TV, L.A., 1969; Mt. Sinai Hosp., L.A., 1967; L.A. City Health Dept. 1945-49; child therapist LaFarge Clinic, N.Y.C. 1949-52; founder nurses aide program, L.A. City Health Dept., 1945-47; social service record systems 1945. Named Fellow mem. Menninger Found. 1978. Mem.: Calif. Assn. Marriage and Family Counselors, (Award 1971, Trustee 1970-71, Chmn. Ethics Com. 1971); Am. Assn. Marriage and Family Counselors; L.A. Group Psychotherapy Assn.; USC Alumni Assn.; Alpha Kappa Alpha; Alpha Kappa Delta. Hobbies: dress design, interior decorating, sewing, art work, Thearns. Rec.: guitar. Office: 291 S. La Cienega Blvd., Suite 205, Beverly Hills, CA 90211.

JORDAN, J. ROBERT
Business Owner
b. May 10, 1894, Lincoln, Nebr.; s. George Walter and Mary Elizabeth (Watson) Walter; ed. pub. schs., Boston; widower; chil.: Geoffrey Camile (Mrs. John Evans Schott); John R., Jr. Career: co-owner, sales mgr., Wade Mfg. Co., Charlotte, N.C., 1919-1932; owner, Ray Pressure Snubber Co., Charlotte, N.C. and NYC, 1932-44; name changed to Operating & Maintenance Specialties, 1945---; founder, owner Jordan Industries, Beverly Hills, 1958---. Served pvt. to capt., AUS, 1913-1919, WW I, recipient several citations. Emeritus Mem. Internat. Supreme Council, Order of DeMolay. Res.: 1221 San Vicente Blvd., Santa Monica, CA 90402.

JORGENSON, JOSEPH GILBERT
Professor -- Author
b. Apr. 15, 1934, Salt Lake City, Ut.; s. Joseph Norman and Clela (Bailey) Jorgensen; B.S., Univ. of Ut., ethnology, linguistics, 1956, Ph.D., Ind. Univ., 1964; m. Katherine Will, Aug. 31, 1964, Urbana, Ill.; chil.: Brigham Will, b. July 9, 1970; Sarah Katherine, b. Dec. 11, 1973. Career: worked for and with an Indian tribe, other jobs, 1956-61; asst. prof.: Antioch Coll., 1964-65, Univ. of Ore., 1965-68; assoc. prof., Univ. of Mich., 1968-71, prof., 1971-74; prof. and dir., Program in Comparative Culture, Univ. Calif., Irvine, 1974-78. Dir.: Human Rels. Area Files, Internat., New Haven, 1970---; Anthropology Resource Center, Inc., Cambridge, 1975---; Native Struggles Support Group, Toronto, 1970---. Mem.: Edward L. Bernays Found. nominating com., Boston. Assoc. ed.: Behavior Sci. Research, The Indian Historian, Zetetic Scholar, Southwest Econ. and Soc., Environmental Ethics, Social Sci. Journ. (variously), 1974---. John Simon Guggenheim Fellow, 1974-75; Horace H. Rackham Senior Fellow, 1973; Nat. Sci. Found. Fellow, 1964, 1965, grantee 1970-74, 1978-79; Natl. Inst. of Health Research Grantee, 1966; Am. Philosophical Soc. Grantee 1967, 69. Author: Salish Language and Culture (1969); The Sun Dance Religion (1972) recipient of a C. Wright Mills Book Award, 1973 anda Pulitzer nomination; Western Indians (1979); and others; contbr. to N.Y. Review of Books, Current Anthropology, other journs. Home: 1517 Highland Dr., Newport Beach, CA 92660; Office: UCI, Program in Comparative Culture, Irvine, CA 92717.

JOY, HELANE EKDAHL
Realtor — Executive
b. Dec. 11, 1919, Kansas City, Mo.; d. Vincent James and Irene Theresa (Stockstill) Murphy; m. Dean Alden Ekdahl, Mar. 29, 1941 (dec. June 4, 1954); chil.: Vickie Ekdahl Bisho, b. Oct. 8, 1942; Dean Alden Ekdahl Jr., b. Jul. 29, 1945; m. 2d. Richard Dale Joy, Sept. 17, 1967, Nevada. Career: Owner, mgr., Dean's Dress Shop, 1941-45; office mgr., Calif. Ink Co., Phoenix, Ariz., 1953-54; owner, mgr., Helane's Dress Shop, 1954-63; Licensed real estate salesman, 1964; mgr., Bay & Beach Rental dept., Newport Beach, 1964-67; Mgr., B. White Realtors, 1967-70; pres., Associated Realty Service of Newport Beach, Inc., 1971---. Active in real estate orgns. primarily in edn., polit. affairs, consumer protection and ethics, arbitration coms. Mem.: Orange Co. Council of Real Estate Bds., chmn, 1979; Newport Harbor-Costa Mesa Bd. of Realtors, 1976; Realtor of the Year 1975, polit. action com. 1970-78; Women's Council of Realtors, Newport Harbor-Costa Mesa chpt. pres., v.p., secty. 1971, 1972, 1973; Nat. Assn. of Realtors, 1964-78; Calif. Assn. of Realtors, 1964-78. Mem.: Newport Harbor Area C. of C., dir. 1975-78; Am. Legion Aux., 1977-78. Episcopalian, choir mother. Home: 2052 Tustin Ave., Newport Beach, CA 92663; Office: 2025 W. Balboa Blvd., Newport Beach, CA 92663.

JOSEPH, MARJORY L.
Educator
b. Oct. 8, 1917, Milan, Oh.; s. Ernest J. and Bertha A. Lockwood; B.S., Oh. State Univ., 1939; M.S., 1952; Ph.D., textile chem., Penn. State Univ., 1962; m. William D. Joseph, Aug. 11, 1941, Milan, Oh.; day. Nancy-Joyce David, b. Oct. 19, 1942. Career: costume design and constrn., 1941-44; supr. of workrooms, custom design shop, Ruth Harris, Inc., NYC, 1944-46; co-owner, mgr., Mar Jay Dress Shop, Milan, Oh., 1946-48; tchr. home economics, Birmingham J.S. and Berlin Hts. H.S., Oh., 1948-51; tch. asst., Oh. State Univ., 1951-52; instr. in clothing and textiles research, Penn. State Univ., 1957-62; Instr., prof., dept. head, home econ., Juniata Coll., Pa., 1952-62; prof. and chmn. Home Econ. Dept., Cal. State Univ., Northridge, 1962---. Mem.: Nat. Assn. Coll. Profs. of Textiles and Clothing, pres. elect. 1979; Am. Assn. of Textile Chemists and Colorists; Am. Home Econ. Assn.; Am. Soc. for Testing and Materials (ASTM); Assn. of

Dyers and Colourists; Calif. Home Econ. Assn., L.A. pres. 1968-70; Fellow, Am. Inst. of Chemists; Natl. Council of Adminstrs. in Home Econ.; Assn. of Adminstrs. of Home Econ. in Land Grant and State Univs. Methodist. Hobby: art needleowrk; Res.. 10612 Collett Ave., Granada Hills, CA 91344; Office: Cal. State Univ., Northridge, CA 91330.

K

KAHAN, STANLEY
University Professor
b. Apr. 21, 1931, NYC; s. Jacob and Annette (Zeikin) Kahan; B.A., Coll. City of N.Y. 1953; M.A., Univ. of Wis. 1954, Ph.D. 1959; m. Charlene Frances Owen, Ames, Ia., June 8, 1957; chil.: Amy Sue, b. Feb. 8, 1958; Geoffrey Owen Spencer, b. Sept. 26, 1964. Career: Instr. in speech, Ia. State Univ. 1955-58; instr. Bowling Green State Univ. 1958-61; assoc. prof. drama, Calif. State Univ. Long Beach, 1961---. Dir., Ames Community Theatre, Ia. 1956-57; assoc. dir., Huron Playhouse, Oh. 1958-59; adv. bd. Am. Edn. Theatre Assn., So. Calif. 1963-67; bus. mgr., Edn. Theatre News, 1965-66, adv. bd., So. Calif. Lyric Opera Assn., 1965-67. Author: (books publ. Harcourt, Brace and World) Introduction to Acting, 1962; An Actor's Workbook, 1967. Mem.: Natl. Collegiate Players, Wis. Res.: 1815 Nipomo Ave., Long Beach, CA 90815; Office: Calif. State Univ., Long Beach, CA.

KAHN, DORIS WOODHOUSE
Public Welfare Administrator
b. Dec. 18, 1921, NYC; d. Ira and Valentine (McClatchy) Woodhouse; Granddau., Valentine S. McClatchy, 1st sheriff of Sacto.; M.A., soc. welfare, Univ. Calif., Berkeley, 1947; m. Jacob P. Kahn, M.D., May 9, 1947, S.F.; chil.: Philip, b. Jan. 12, 1949; Victoria, b. Jan. 12, 1952; Elizabeth (Davenport), b. Dec. 19, 1954; Madeleine, b. Aug. 8, 1955. Career: Pub. Welfare Adminstr., Dept. of Soc. Servs. 1968---. Co-author: The Psychiatric Day Hospital; Social Casework, 1963. Mem. French Honor Soc., Berkeley. Chmn. Voters Registration, Gov. Edmund Brown campaign, 1966; fin. chmn. Morrison supervisorial (S.F.) campiagn, 1967-69; co-founder Neighborhood Arts Alliance, 1967; chmn. Com. to save Ft. Mason, 1970; mem. Women's Bd., Presbyterian Med. Center, S.F., 1961-71; mem. Mayor George Moscone select Com. on Yerba Buena Redevel. site, 1976-78; dir., ARC, Salinas, 1943-46; co-chmn. Voters Registration Campaign, 1975; bd. mem. S.F. Chamber Music Soc., 1972---; bd. mem.-founder, Performing Arts Servs., 1975---; bd. mem. Jewish Comm. Center, S.F., chmn. Arts. & Music. Com., 1964-68; Mayoral Appt. to Metropolitan Transportation Com., 1977. Hobby: music. Res.: 3259 Clay St., S.F., CA 94115; Office: P.O.B. 7988, S.F., CA 94120.

KAHN, JACOB PHILIP
Psychiatrist
b. May 16, 1914, Melitopol, Russia; s. Philip and Elizabeth (Kahn) Kahn; M.D., Univ. Calif. at S.F., 1941; m. Doris Woodhouse, May 9, 1947, S.F.; chil.: Philip, b. Jan. 12, 1949; Victoria, b. 12, 1952; Elizabeth (Mrs. Steven Davenport), b. Dec. 19, 1953; Madeleine, b. Aug. 12, 1955. Career: Rotating intern, Franklin Hosp., S.F., 1940-41; asst. resident med., 1941-42; resident psychiatry Langley-Porter Clinic, S.F., 1946-49; research fellow child psychiatry, James Jackson Putnam Children's Center, Boston, 1949-50; fellow child psychiatry, 1950-51; fellow child psychiatry, Judge Baker Guidance Center, Boston, 1950-51; faculty Stanford Sch. Med., 1952---; assoc. clin. prof. psychiatry, 1959---; chief psychiatry Presbyterian Hosp., Pac. Med. Center, S.F., 1959-71; cons., 1971---. Capt., M.C., AUS, 1942-46. Diplomate in Psychiatry and child psychiatry Am. Bd. Psychiatry and Neurology. Fellow Am. Psychiat. Assn., Am. Acad. Child Psychiatry, Royal Soc. Med., Cal. Acad. Med.; mem. Royal Coll. Psychiatrists (founding mem.). Co-author: The Psychiatric Day Hospital; Social Casework, 1963. Contbr. articles to profl. journs. and textbooks. Home: 3259 Clay St., S.F., CA 94115; Office: 3261 Clay St., S.F., CA 94115.

KAHN, ROY M.
Clinical Psychologist
b. June 14, 1926, NYC; s. Morris H. M.D. and Muriel (Frumes) Kahn; A.B., Cornell Univ., 1949; A.M., Boston Univ., 1951, Ph.D., 1961; m. Arlene Miller, 1968, Reno;

dau. Jennifer M., b. 1970. Career: Psychologist and Mental Health Coord., Dept. Mental Health, Mass., 1953-60; dir. psychol. research, 1960-68; also Dept. Chmn. Dept. Psychol. Gaebler Children's Unit, Mass., 1960-68; Supr., psychotherapy, Phillip Brooks House, Mental Health Pgm., Harvard Univ., 1965-68; lectr.: Tufts Univ., Harvard Univ. Med. Sch. Psychiat. Tng. Pgm., 1963-68; Sr. Psychol., Couns. Cntr., Univ. Calif., Berkeley, 1968-70; Profl. lectr. Cal. State Univ., S.F., 1968-75; Univ. Calif., Berkeley Ext., 1969-75; pvt. practice and cons. to Richmond Unified Sch. Dist. Educ. Svcs., 1970---. Spec. Agent, Counter Intelligence Corps., USA, ETO, 1944-46; M.I., USAR, 1946-50. Contbr. articles in books, profl. journs. Fellow, Am. Orthopsychiat. Assn.; Fellow, Mass. Psyhcol. Assn.; Mem.: Am., Psychol. Assn.; Western Psychol. Assn.; Mass. Soc. State Psychologists, treas. 1956-57. Hobbies: art, mus. Office: 21 Ave. Drive, Berkeley, CA 94708.

KAISER, EDGAR FOSBURGH
Industrialist
b. July 29, 1908, Spokane, Wash.; s. Henry J. and Bessie (Fosburgh) Kaiser; Univ. of Calif. Berkeley, 1927-30; (hon.) LL.D., Univ. of Portland, Ore., Pepperdine Coll., Mills Coll., Golden Gate Univ., Univ. of the Pac.; m. Sue Mead, 1932 (dec. 1974), m. 2d. Nina McCormick, 1975; chil.: Carlyn, Becky, Gretchen, Edgar, Henry Mead, Kim John. Career: Constr. Supt., natural gas line, Kan. to Tex. 1930-32; shift supt., Boulder Dam Nev. 1932-33; adm. mgr., Columbia Constr. Co., Bonneville Dam, Ore., 1934-38; adm. mgr., Consolidated Bldrs., Inc., Grand Coulee Dam, Wash., 1938-41; gen. mgr. Kasier shipyards, Portland, 1942-45; gen. mgr. Kaiser-Frazer Corp. plant, Willow Run, Mich., 1945-49; pres., Kaiser Frazer Corp., 1949-56; pres., Kaiser Industries Corp. 1956-67; chmn. bd. of Kaiser Industries Corp.; Kaiser Steel Corp.; Kaiser Aluminum & Chem. Cor.; Kaiser Cement & Gypsum Corp.; 1967---. Also chmn. bd. Kaiser Found. Health Plan and Kaiser Found. Hosps.; dir. BankAmerica Corp.; chmn. bd., Stanford Research Institute; mem. The Business Council; US-USSR Trade and Econ. Council; dir.-v.p., Oakland-Alameda Co. Coliseum; trustee, Eaglebrook Sch., Deerfield, Mass. Awards: Brotherhood Award and Cit., Natl. Conf. Chris. and Jews, 1961; The Moles Annual Award 1962; Gov's Award, S.F. World Trade Center, 1963; Bishop's Plaque for Ind. Statemanship, 1963; Hon. Award, Calif. Israel C. of C. 1965; Comdr. of Natl. Order of So. Cross, Repub. of Brazil, 1965; (hon.) Spec. Com., Family of Man Award Dinner 1966; Industrialist of the Yr., Calif. Mus. of Sci. and Ind., 1966; Hon. Natl. Chmn., U.N. Day, 1966; Construction Man of the Year, Engineers News Record, 1968. Alumnus of the Yr., Univ. of Calif., 1969; Hoover Medal, 1969, Presidential Medal of Freedom, 1969; First Annual Internat. Key Award, Opportunities Industrializations Centers of Am., 1970; Business Statesman of the Yr., Harvard Bus. Sch. of N. Calif., 1971, Grand Officer of Repub. of Ivory Coast, 1972; Golden Beaver Award, The Beavers, 1975; Internat. Achievement Award, World Trade Club, S.F., 1975; New Oakland Comm. Award, 1976. Mem.: Am. Soc. of Civil Engrs.; Assn. AUS; chmn. bd., Oakland Sym. Orch. Assn.; Chi Psi; clubs: Marco Polo, 1925 "F" St., Pac. Union, Bohemian, Arlington, Claremont Country, Commonwealth of Calif., Seattle Yacht, Internat. Club of Wash. D.C. Office: Kaiser Center, 300 Lakeside Dr., Oakland, CA 94666.

KAKITA, LENORE SETSUKO
Dermatologist
b. Aug. 27, 1940, Oakland; d. Hajime M.D. and Grace (Chiyo) Uyeyama; B.S., Univ. of Calif., Berkeley, 1963, M.D., Univ. Calif. Med. Sch., S.F., 1967; m. Edward Yuiti Kakita Aug. 17, 1968, Beverly Hills; chil.: Neil Y., b. Apr. 27, 1971; Garrett T. and Grant N., twins, b. Feb. 15, 1974. Career: Internship, Children's Hosp. of L.A., 1967-68; residency, UCLA, 1968-71; pvt. practice dermatology, La Canada, 1971---; clin. instr., UCLA, 1971-76; asst. clib prof. of med., Dept. of Dermatology, 1976---. Mem.: Am., Calif., L.A. Co. Med. Assns.; L.A. Dermatological Soc.; Am. Acad. of Dermatology; Pacific Dermatological Assn.; Soc. for Investigative Dermatology, Soc. for Tropical Dermatology; Am. Coll. of Physicians. Rec.: concerts, museums, picnics. Res.: 2700 Catherwood Dr., La Canada, CA; Office: 1346 Foothill Blvd., La Canada, CA 91011.

KAKKIS, ALBERT
Physician
b. Sept. 21, 1927, Drama, Greece; s. Emil and Elvira (Benmayor) Kakkis; m. Julia Metaxas, Sept. 5, 1954, Greece; dau. Joyce Ann (Fotinakes). Career: Intern, Morrisania City Hosp., NYC, 1956-57; resident, St.

Luke's Hosp., S.F., 1957-59; resident neurology, VA Hosp., UCLA' 1964-67; practice med., L.A., 1959-61; pvt. practice med. specializing in neurology and neurodiagnostics, Long Beach, 1967---; physician in charge, So. Calif. Permanente Clin., E. L.A., 1961-64; assoc. clin. prof. neurology, UCLA, 1967---; dir. neurology, St. Mary's Hosp., Long Beach, 1967---; mem., dir. Clinic Movement and Paroxysmal Disorders, Long Beach, 1971---; mem. att. staff neurology, Harbor Gen. Hosp., Torrance, ---; cons. neurology, L.A. Co. ---. Med. Ofcr., Greek Army, 1954-56. Councilor, L.A. Soc. Neurology and Psychiat., 1971-74. Hobbies: Musical instruments. Res: 6398 Rochelle Ln., L.B., CA 90815; Office: 1045 Atlantic Ave., Suite 608, Long Beach, CA 90813.

KALLENBERG, JOHN KENNETH
County Librarian
b. June 10, 1942, Anderson, Ind.; s. Herbert A. and Helen S. Kallenberg; A.B., Ind. Univ., 1964, M.L.S., 1969; m. Ruth Barrett, Aug. 19, 1965, San Jose, Calif.; chil.: Jennifer Anne, b. May 16, 1967; Gregory John, b. Sept. 17, 1969. Career: Readers Advis. (Fresno Co.) Librn., 1965-68; Fig Garden Br. (Fresno Co.) Librn., 1968-70; Asst. lib. dir., Santa Barbara, 1970-76; Fresno Co. Librn., 1976---. Councilor, Calif. Lib. Assn., 1975-77, mem. various CLA coms.; chmn. Authority Advis. Council, Calif. Lib. Authority for Systems & Servs., 1978-80; chmn., Calif. Co. Librn's. Assn., 1978-79; pres. 1977. Mem. Fresno Kiwanis Club, dir. 1977-78; No. Santa Barbara Kiwanis Club, v.p. 1975-76. Presbyterian, Elder. Rec.: swimming, gardening. Res: 6521 N. Sixth, Fresno, CA; Office: Fresno Co. Lib., 2420 Mariposa, Fresno, CA 93721.

KALVINSKAS, JOHN JOSEPH
Chemical Engineer
b. Jan. 14, 1927, Phila.; s. Anthony and Anna (Slezute) Kalvinskas; B.S. chem. engr., Mass. Inst. Tech., 1951, M.S. 1952; Ph.D., chem. eng., Cal Inst. Tech., 1959; m. Louanne Adams, Sept. 3, 1955, Little Valley, N.Y.; son, Adrian John, b. Nov. 9, 1965. Career: chem. engr., Explosives Dept., E.I. duPont deNemours & Co., 1959-60, 1952-55; research spec. Heat Transfer Nuclionics, 1960-61, supr. Advanced Proj., 1961-64, mgr.-Propellant Engr., 1964-67; mgr., Env. Mgmt. Syst., 1967-68, Rockwell Internat., dir., Environmental Health Systems, 1968-70; pres., Resource Dynamics Corp., 1970-74; corp. research dir., Monogram Industries, Inc., 1972; proj. mgr., Holmes & Narver, 1974; project mgr. & group supr., Jet Propulsion Lab., 1974---. Holder three U.S. Patents in field. Awards: NASA Certificates of Recognition, 1976, 78; Stauffer Found. Tchg. Fellowship, 1957-58. Contbr. articles profl. journs. USN, 1944-46, electronic tch. Mate 2/C. Mem.: Town Hall of Calif., MIT Club of So. Calif., Sigma Xi; Kappa Kappa Sigma; Catholic. Rec.: golf, hiking, fishing. Res: 316 Pasadena Ave., So. Pasa., CA 91030; Office: 4800 Oak Grove Dr., Pasa., CA 91103.

KAMAR, ASTRID ELAINE
Executive Vice President, Kamar International, Inc.
b. Nov. 29, 1934, L.A.; d. Ernest and Emmy (Kraus) Wennermark; grad., Sawyer's Bus. Sch., 1953; m. Pascal M. Kamar, Feb. 14, 1958, L.A.; chil.: Christopher, b. June 15, 1960; Jenny, b. Feb. 27, 1963; Laurie, b. June 17, 1969. Career: co-founder, with husband, Kamar Imports (inc. in 1961), 1958; co-founder, exec. v.p., Kamar Internat., Inc., 1961---; (note: Kamar Inc. and Kamar Internat. Inc. merged in 1978); co-founder, Blunsdon Co., Ltd., Hong Kong, 1978---; Foreign Serv., State Dept., Wash. D.C. and Kingston, Jamaica, 1956-57; Dir.: Kamar Internat., Inc.; Blunsdon Co., Ltd., Hong Kong; Scan Sea Kamar Products PTE. Ltd., Singapore; Wennermark Investment. Former dir.: Universal Motor Cars; Moon Imports; Sun Imports; Jolimar Briquedese Brindes Ltd., Lisbon, Portugal. Named Internat. Woman of Yr., 1971. Lutheran. Hobby: gourmet cooking. Rec.: tennis, skeet shooting. Office: 23639 Hawthorne Blvd., Torrance, CA 90505.

KAMIN, JOHN V.
Economist — Editor
b. July 4, 1937, Chicago, Ill.; s. John August and Josephine Kamin; B.A. economics, Catholic Univ. of Am., 1959; postgrad. studies, Univ. of Chicago, Grad. Sch. of Bus., Universidad Nacional de Mexico; m. Irene Krol, Dec. 30, 1972; dau. Maria Linda, b. May 3, 1975. Career: pvt. cons., economics, sales, acquisitions, manufacturing, 1960-65; chief economist, editor, The Forecaster Economic Newsletter, 1966---. Author: How to Make Money in Coins, 1976; The Detroit Insider — How to Buy 3-4 Year Old Cars at $200 and Less — How to Buy a New

Car at Lowest Prices — Classic Cars for Fun & Profit, 4th printing 1977; How to Make Money Fast Speculating in Distressed Property, 3rd printing 1977; Power Secrets to Fast Money, 1975; The IMF — Engine of Inflation — How You Can Profit, 1977; Best Hope for the Young Investor to Become Financially Independent and Wealthy, 1975; Hyperinflation — How You Can Come Out Ahead and Your Personal Financial Success Program, 1976. Contbr., columnist, and subject articles in numismatic journs., mags. and L.A. Herald Examiner. TV and radio interviews, 1968---. Lectr.: Nat. Com. for Monetary Reform, 1972-77; 1978 Neb. Dental Assn.; economic seminars. Dir. Adelphi Univ. INP Program — dir. Inst. of Planned Giving, Catholic Univ. of Am. Charter mem. Numismatic Literary Guild; secty., Internat. Assn. of Investment Newsletters; mem. Retail Coin Dealers Assn.; mem.: Pi Gamma Mu, Toastmasters, Sigma Pi Delta. Home-Office: 19623 Ventura Blvd., Tarzana, CA 91356.

KAMINS, BERNARD FRANCIS
Public Relations Counselor
b. Jan. 2, 1915, Cambridge, Mass.; s. Louis and Bella Sarah (Rubin) Kamins; A.B., Harvard Univ. 1938; m. Loretta Cooper, Canton, Mass., June 26, 1938; chil.: Bernard John b. Sept. 9, 1942; Wendie Lou, b. Jan. 16, 1946. Career: publicist, Paramount Pictures, Inc. 1941; dir. of pub., Harry Sherman Prodns. 1942; exec. dir. pub.-adv., Jesse Lasky Prodns. 1945; est. own pub. agency, B.F. Kamins Co., 1948---; pub. chmn., United Repub. Finance Com. of L.A. Co., 1961-63; pub. chmn., Calif. State Repub. Central Finance Com. 1965; pub. rels chmn., 1965; exec. secty. Am. Consumers Council, 1966; tchr., P.R., UCLA Ext. 1971---; L.A. Co. Comm. Improvements Comm. 1972-77; Commendation for Distinguished Serv., 1972-76; Youth Commn. of L.A. Co., 1976-77; Special Study, Dept. of Trans. FAA, Office of Systems R&D Servs., 1977; gen. adv. bd. Santa Monica Coll., 1972; Calif. Arts Comm. (apptd. by Gov.) 1973-76; Author: Basic Propaganda, publ. Houlgate House, 1951. Mem.: counselor sect., Pub. Rels. Soc. of Am.; pub. rels. Com., L.A. Co. Heart Assn.; bd. dirs., Bev. Hills YMCA; L.A. State Mental Hygiene Adv. Bd.; pub. rels chmn., Harvard Club of So. Calif.; Greater L.A. Press Club. Hobby: reading. Rec.: gym, swimming. Res.: 11236 Cashmere St., L.A., CA 90049; Office: P.O.B. 24206, L.A., CA 90024.

KANAGAWA, ROBERT K.
President, Kanagawa Citrus Company
b. Sept. 10, 1917, Sanger, Calif.; s. Yasoichi T. and Jitsuyo Kanagawa; B.A., bus. adm., 1938; m. Yukiye Nakamura, Feb. 12, 1944, Poston, Ariz.; chil.: Rodney, Floyd, Dallas. Career: v.p., treas., Kanagawa Citrus Co., 1938-65, pres. 1965---. Dir.: Valley Children's Hosp., 1969-72; St. Agnes Hosp., 1972, v.p. 1978; 21st Dist. Agri. Assn., 1970---, pres. 1977; Sanger Citrus Assn., 1973---, v.p. 1977-78; Sanger Dist C. of C., Man of Yr., 1968; chmn., Sanger Grapebowl Festival, 1964-73; Trustee: Fairmont Elem. Sch. 1954-58, Sanger Union H.S., 1958-65, Sanger Unified Sch. Dist. 1965-69; mem. Sanger Parks & Rec. Commn. 1963-73; mem. Sanger Sr. Citizens Commn., 1975---; mem. exec. bd., Sequoia Council BSA, 1971---; mem. com., Calif. Council for the Humanities in Pub. Policy, 1977---; chmn. Nation's Christmas Tree Festival, 1959; chrtr. pres., Sanger Japanese-Am Citizens League, 1960-61, 1965, 1975; dist. gov., Central Calif. Dist. Council JACL 1977-78. Methodist, trustee. Rec.: fishing. Res.: 16156 E. McKinley Ave., Sanger, CA 93657; Office: 2720 Jensen Ave., Sanger, CA 93657.

KANG, KI DONG
Electronics Company President
b. Dec. 9, 1934, Seoul, Korea; s. Chong Moo and Byung Soon (Ham) Kang; B.S. elec. engring., Seoul Nat. Univ., 1958; M.Sc., E.E., Ohio State Univ., 1960, Ph.D., E.E., 1962; m. Soonho Kim, Sept. 6, 1959, Columbus, Ohio; chil.: James, b. Jan. 11, 1965; Nancy, b. Mar. 14, 1966. Career: Research assoc., faculty, Ohio State Univ., Columbus, Ohio, 1959-62; sr. engr. to dept. mgr., Motorola Semiconductor Products Div., Phoenix, Ariz., 1962-69; tech. dir., Stewart Warner Corp., Sunnyvale, 1969-73; founder and pres., Korea Semiconductor Inc., Seoul, Korea, 1973-76; founder and v. pres., Integrated Circuits International, Inc., Sunnyvale, 1973-76; founder and pres., KDK Electronics Inc., Sunnyvale, 1976---; founder and pres., KDK Electronics International Sales Corp., Sunnyvale, 1977---. Patents: Holder of several on semiconductor device structures. Awarded Export Promotion Award, Republic of Korea, 1975. Mem.: IEEE; Electromechanical Soc. Baptist. Hobby: radio amateur. Rec.: skiing, mountain climbing. Home: 633 Harrow Way, Sunnyvale, CA 94087; Office: 783 E. Evelyn Ave., Sunnyvale, CA 94086.

KAPLAN, HENRY SEYMOUR
Radiologist
b. Apr. 24, 1918, Chicago; s. Nathan M. and Sarah (Brilliant) Kaplan; B.S., Univ. Chicago, 1938; M.D., Rush Med. Coll., 1940; M.S., Radiology, Univ. Minn., 1944; m. Leah Hope Lebeson, June 21, 1942, Chicago; Chil.: Ann Sharon (Spears), b. Dec. 26, 1951; Paul Allen, b. May 5, 1953. Career: intern, Michael Reese Hosp., Chicago, 1940-41, resident, 1941-43; Fellow, Nat. Cancer Inst., Univ. Minn., 1943-44; Instr. & asst. prof., Dept. of Radiology, Yale Univ. Sch. of Med., 1945-46; radiologist, Nat. Cancer Inst., Bethesda, Md., 1947-48; prof. & chmn. Dept. of Radiology, Stanford Univ. Sch. of Med., 1948-72, dir. Biophysics Lab. 1957-62; Maureen Lyles D'Ambrogio Prof. of Radiology, 1972---, dir. Cancer Biology Research Lab., 1975---; Fellow, Commonwealth Fund & Vis. Sci., NIH, Bethesda, Md., 1954-55. Pres., Internat. Assn. Radiation Research, 1973-79; pres. Am. Assn. Cancer Research, 1965-66; pres., Radiation Research Soc., 1956-57; pres. Assn. Univ. Radiologists, 1954-57; mem. bd. gov., Am. Coll. of Radiology, 1970-72. Mem. Cosmos Club, Wash. D.C. Hobbies: art, photog. Home: 631 Cabrillo Ave., Stanford, CA; Office: Dept. of Radiology, Stanford Univ. 94305.

KAPLAN, JOSEPH M.
Association Executive
b. May 29, 1914, Cleveland, Oh.; s. Edward and Mamie (Krislove) Kaplan; B.A., UCLA, 1935; M.A., Harvard Univ., 1938; Inst. for Orgn. Mgmt., 1960-78; m. Henriette Lurie, Mar. 30, 1941, L.A.; sons, Paul Dana, Drew Alan. Career: exec. v.p., Greater L.A. chpt. Natl. Safety Council, 1939---; Staff Sgt., AUS, 1943-45. Mem.: Rotary Club; Am. Soc. of Safety Engrs.; Am. Soc. Assn. Execs., recipient Kay Award as outstanding local Assoc. Exec. in nation, 1974; Internat. Veterans of Safety, pres. 1976; Radio and TV News Assn.; Inst. of Traffic Engrs. Hobbies: travel, music. Rec.: swimming. Res.: 8871 St. Ives Dr., L.A., CA 90069; Office: 3388 W. 8th St., L.A., CA 90005.

KAPRIELIAN, ZOHRAB ARAKEL
University Dean
b. Sept. 23, 1923, Aleppo, Syria; s. Arakel and Vartouhi (Lusigian) Kaprielian; B.A., Am. Univ. of Beirut, Lebanon, 1942; M.A., 1943; Ph.D., UC Berkeley, 1954. Career: Research fellow, instr., CalTech, 1954-57; asst., assoc., prof. of engring., USC, 1957---; acting Dean, Sch. of Engring, 1969-70, Dean, 1970---; Acad. Adminstrn. and Research, 1970-75, exec. v.p. 1975---. Mem. vis. com., Jet Propulsion Lab., 1969---; mem. advis. com., Inst. for Adv. of Engring., 1974---. Hobbies: gardening, music. Res.: 2396 Roscomare Rd., L.A., CA 90024; Office: USC, L.A., CA 90007.

KARABIAN, WALTER
Attorney at Law
b. Mar. 14, 1938, Fresno; s. John and Gladys Karabian; B.A., USC, 1960, M.S., 1964, grad., Sch. of Pub. Adminstrn., J.D., USC Sch. of Law; m. Carole Wells Doheny, 1977. Career: Dep. Dist. Atty., L.A. Co., 1965-66; elected Assemblyman, 45th Dist., Calif. Legislature, 1966; reelected 1968, 70, 72. ret. 1975; partner in L.A. law firm, Karns & Karabian ---. In the Legislature: mem., Rules Com.; apptd. by Speaker as Maj. Floor Leader, 1971. Contbr. to Loyola Law Review, Pac. Law Journ., UCLA Law Journ., Univ. S.F. Law Review. Democrat. Rec.: tennis, theater. Office: Karns & Karabian, 900 Wilshire Blvd., Suite 530, L.A., CA 90017.

KARALIS, GEORGE DEMETRIUS
Physician
b. Nov. 1, 1945, Chicago, Ill.; s. Demetrius Nicholas and Pauline (Gianakopulos) Karalis; M.D., Univ. of Calif., Irvine, 1970; currently student, Golden Gate Univ. Law Sch. Career: practice of psychiatry and medical hypnosis, 1973---; also hypnosis cons. various legal agencies and law-enforcement agencies. One of first full-time med. hypnoanalysts, pioneering psychoanalysis with hypnotism, religious therapy. Mem.: Am. Soc. of Clin. Hypnosis; Soc. of Med. Hypnoanalysts; Soc. of Clin. and Exptl. Hypnosis; Internat. Soc. of Hypnosis; dir., Am. Soc. of Legal and Edn. Hypnosis. Greek Orthodox. Hobbies: archaeology, religion. Rec.: boating. Home: 233 El Camino Del Mar, San Francisco, CA 94121; Office: P.O.B. 664, S.F., CA 94101.

KARP, JACK RUSSELL
Industrial Realtor
b. July 15, 1938, Pittsburgh, Pa.; s. Samuel and Jean

Karp; B.S., USC; m. Lois Lindell, Apr. 10, 1960, L.A.; sons, Timothy Andrew, b. Aug. 26, 1969; Adam Matthew, b. Jan. 17, 1971. Career: Inds. real estate broker, Jonas, Goodglick & Assocs., 1962-66; Stuart Klabin & Co., 1966-74; founder-pres., Natl. Indsl. Properties (N.I.P.), 1974---. Mem.: lectr. team, Indsl. Real Estate Investment, USC Ext. Sch.; guest lectr. Grad Sch. of Bus. Admin., USC, Stanford Univ., Cal. State Univ. of Dominguez. Calif. Air Nat. Guard, 1961-67. Mem.: Am. Indsl. Real Estate Assn., pres. 1976, 77; L.A. C. of C., editor of Survey of Indsl. Land Values in the L.A. Five Co. Area; mem. So. Calif. Econ. Job Devel. Council; Hawthorne C. of C., past chmn. Indsl. Com., Inglewood Blue Ribbon Com. for Redevel. 1967; chmn. Inglewood Advis. Com., 1968; pres., Sch. of Commerce, USC, 1959-60; Soc. Indsl. Realtors. Rec.: bicycling, tennis. Res.: 31115 Ganado Dr., Palos Verdes Penin, CA; Office: 22122 S. Vermont Ave., Torrance, CA 90502.

KASHA, LAWRENCE NATHAN
Producer — Director
b. Dec. 3, 1934, Brooklyn, N.Y.; s. Irving and Rose I. (Katz) Kasha; B.A., N.Y.Univ., 1954; M.A., 1955. Career: Prod.&Dir. works incl.: nat. company Lil Abner, 1958; nat. tour Camelot, 1963-64; Anything Goes off-Broadway Co., 1962; Broadway co. Bajour, 1964; nat. co. Funny Girl, 1965, London Co., 1966; Show Boat revival, 1966; nat. co. Cactus Flower, 1968; nat. co. Star Spangled Girl, 1968; London co. Mame, 1969; Broadway co. Lovely Ladies Kind Gentlemen, 1970; prod. off-Broadway prodn. Parade, 1960; Broadway prodn. She Loves Me, 1963; Hadrian VII, 1969; Applause, 1970; Father's Day, 1971; Inner City, 1972; Seesaw, 1973; No Hard Feelins, 1973; Heavy Sent, L.A., 1978; Seven Brides for Seven Brothers, 1978; prod. CBS-TV specials Applause, 1973; Another April, 1974; Rosenthal and Jones, 1975; prod. TV series Busting Loose, 1977; Komedy Tonite, NBC, 1978. Playwright (with Hayden Griffin) The Pirate, 1968; (with Lionel Wilson) Where Have You Been, Billy Boy?, 1969; (with David S. Landay) Heaven Sent, 1978); (with David S. Linday) Seven Brides for Seven Brothers, 1978. Awards: Tony Award, 1970; Outer Critics Circle Award, 1973. Mem.: Dir. Guild of Am.; Actors Equity Assn.; Writers Guild West. Address: William Morris, 151 El Camino, Beverly Hills, CA 90212.

KASHIN, NICOLAI NICOLAEVICH
Tax Consultant
b. Feb. 26, 1896, Imperial, Russia; s. Nicolai Vasilievich and Maria Ivanovna (Voronova) Kashin; desc. Vasily Kashin Boyar Voivoda, with Tsar Ivan the Terrible in 1552 conquered the Mongol golden horde; Baccalaureate degree classical gymnasium, Heisingfors, Finland, 1914; honorable degree Artillery Acad., Petrograd, 1915; Comml. Inst., Moscow, 1922; m. Katherine Pastukhova, Feb. 2, 1920, Orenburg, Russia; chil.: George, b. Mar. 11, 1923. Career: Commodities expert, Custom House, 1922-24; tech. accountant and interpreter (Russian, Persian, German, Swedish, Czechoslovakian), Iran, 1925-43; accountant, Public Accounting Firm, L.A., 1946-47; accountant interpreter, Am. Express Co., 1947-62; tax cons., 1963-79. Served as Lt. Col., W.W.I, Russian Artillery in Poland, Austria, Rumania; mil. reserve, 1918-24. Author: studies to promote world peace and understanding of Soviet peoples. Mem.: Persian, Czechoslovakian Clubs, 1925-43. Russian Orthodox ch. Hobby: painting. Rec.: travel. Home: 3235 Barnes Circle, Glendale, CA 91208; Office: 3030 Sawtelle Blvd., Suite 2, L.A., CA 90066.

KASLOW, ARTHUR LOUIS
Physician
b. Jan. 15, 1913, Omaha, Neb.; s. Hyman Y. and Hannah Rebecca (Cutler) Kazlowsky; B.S., Creighton Univ., 1934; M.D., 1935; post doctoral training: Cook Co. Hosp., Chicago, 1948; USC, L.A.; post Doctoral scholar in residence, Inst. Religion, Tex. Med. Center, 1966-67; m. Sally Powers; chil.: Harvey, Art, David, Jeremy, Harmon, Daniel. Career: Intern, Hollywood Presbyn. Hosp., L.A., 1935-36; resident, San Mateo Co. Hosp., 1936-37; instr. student health physician Stanford, 1938-41; practice med. spec. in gastro-enterology, 1950-65, specializing in family med. and counseling, Solvang, 1966---; founder, Kaslow Medical Self-Care Centers, Inc., response point therapy (modified acupuncture) 1971---. Founder of clinic for Dialogue in Human Concerns, Hermann Hosp., 1966-67. Served as M.C. Maj. A.A.F., Flight Surgeon, WWII, 1941-46; Base Surgeon in Azores Islands, Gander, Newfoundland. Inventions: Kaslow stomach tube; Kaslow gastro-intestinal tube; Kaslow stomach irrigation tube; Kaslow Oxygen mast; Kasocidin bacteriacidal solution; non-processed carbohydrate test meal. Present med.

research develops.: nutrigenic diseases; metabolic rejectivity syndrome; smoke & appetite deaddiction; respoint therapy. Pub. papers: multiple sclerosis, neuro sensory deafness, metabolic rejectivity syndrome. Jewish; pres. B'nai Brith Temple, S.B. Hobby: photog. Home: P.O.B. 438, Solvang, CA 93463; Office: Med.-Found. Bldg., 2235 Castillo St., Santa Barbara, CA 93105.

KASMAR, JOYCE VIELHAUER
Psychologist — Educator
b. Nov. 26, 1935, Oak Park, Ill.; d. Otto and Gladys (Carlson) Vielhauer; B.A., Northwestern Univ., 1968; M.A., La. State Univ., 1962, Ph.D., 1965; m. Edward Gaddis Kasmar, July 17, 1965, Riverside, Ill.; dau. Anne Gaelyn, b. Jan. 22, 1973. Career: asst. prof., UCLA Neuropsychiatric Inst., 1965-68; asst. prof., W. Conn. State Coll., Danbury, 1969-70; research assoc., City Univ. N.Y. Grad. Center, 1970-71; postdoctoral scholar, UCLA Sch. Arch. and Urban Planning, 1971-72; prof., Art Center Coll. of Design, 1977---. Mem.: Friends of the Brentwood Lib., pub. chmn. 1972---; Am. Psychol. Assn.; Environmental Design Research Assn.; AAUP; Assistance League of So. Calif. Res.: 503 S. Westgate Ave., L.A. CA 90049.

KATZ, ALFRED D.
Surgeon
b. Nov. 22, 1925, Long Branch, N.J.; s. Samuel and Rose Katz; B.A., Univ. of Wis., 1947; M.D., Yale Sch. of Med., 1950; m. Cecelia Rubnitz, July 1, 1952, Wis.; chil.: Dr. Vern K., b. July 1, 1953; Debre, b. May 12, 1955; Maureen, b. Oct. 12, 1956; Michelle, b. Apr. 18, 1959; Career: Surgical intern, Strong Mem. Hosp., Rochester, N.Y., 1951-52, surg. residency, Cedars of Lebanon Hosp., L.A., 1952-55; oncology residency, Roswell Park Mem. Inst., Buffalo, N.Y., 1955-57; mem. hosp. staffs: Mt. Sinai, Cedars of Lebanon Hosp., Midway Hosp., pvt. practice Head & Neck Surg., 1958---; vis. cons., City of Hope, 1958-63; chmn. Com. on Cancer, L.A. Co. Med. Assn. 1967-74; exec. com. mem. L.A. Co. Chpt. Am. Cancer Soc. 1968---; profl. edn. com., Calif. Div. of Am. Cancer Soc., 1972---; chmn. Dept. of Surg., Cedars-Sinai Med. Center. Served in AUS, WW II European theatre. Mem.: Soc. of Head and Neck Surgeons, Am. Soc. of Clin. Oncology, Soc. of Surgical Oncology, Inc. Jewish, mem. Jewish Fedn. Council, L.A. Hobby: landscaping. Office: 8733 Beverly Blvd., L.A., CA 90048.

KATZ, PAUL WILLIAM
Psychiatrist
b. May 25, 1944, Omaha, Neb.; s. Harold E. and Lucille (Bleiweiss) Katz; B.A., Vanderbilt Univ., 1966; M.D., Univ. of Alabama Sch. of Med., 1970; m. Mary Killingsworth, June 21, 1971, Birmingham, Ala.; chil.: Sara Victoria, b. Feb. 2, 1973; Lisa Rebecca, b. Sept. 29, 1974; Leah Michelle, b. Feb. 22, 1977. Career: Intern, Cedars-Sinai Med. Center, L.A., 1970-71; resident in Psychiatry, 1971-74, Chief Resident in Psych., 1973-74; Lt. Comdr. USN, Chief of Psychiatric Services, U.S. Naval Hosp., Taipei, Taiwan, Republic of China, 1974-76; assoc. attending staff, Cedars-Sinai Med. Center, 1976---; also cons. specialist, Health Services Dept., Co. of L.A., cons. to Juvenile Probation Dept. Psychiat. cons., Family Advisory Center, Taiwan, 1974-76. Mem.: So. Calif. Psychiat. Soc., 1974---; Am. Psychiat. Assn., 1974---; Zeta Beta Tau. Rec.: travel. Office: 116 N. Robertson Blvd., Suite 807, L.A., CA 90048.

KATZOWITZ, COLLEEN
Music Conservatory Administrator
b. Aug. 16, 1939, Wenatchee, Wash.; d. Kenneth and Sara (Austin) Carmody; B.A., econ., Vassar Coll., 1961; m. Saul Katzowitz, Poughkeepsie, N.Y., 1962; chil.: Deboran, b. May 17, 1964; Andrea, b. Nov. 23, 1965. Career: membership secty., ACLU, N.Y., 1961-64; asst. dir. of fin. aid, Vassar Coll., 1967-68; dir. of stu. servs., S.F. Conservatory of Music, 1969---. Mem. bd., Poughkeepsie League of Women Voters, 1966-67; mem. bd., Poughkeepsie ACLU, 1965-67. Res.: 333 Caselli Ave., S.F.; Office: 1201 Ortega St., S.F., CA 94122.

KAUFFMANN, SAMUEL H., III
Business Executive
b. Jan. 17, 1924, Wash., D.C.; s. Samuel H., II (chmn. bd., Wash. Eve. Star) and Miriam (Hoy) Kauffmann; bro. pres., Wash. Eve. Star; ed. Princeton Univ. 1946; Stanford Univ.; m. Gayle E. Somer, Carmel, Jan. 1962; chil.: Eric, b. Oct. 8, 1946; Ingrid Juliana, b. Oct. 18, 1947; Michael Ralstin, b. Dec. 24, 1949; Kathleen Wertz, b. Sept. 9, 1951; Corina, b. Sept. 21, 1951; Larry Ralstin, b. Apr. 20, 1952; Dana, b. Aug. 5, 1953;

David Ralstin, b. Mar. 11, 1954; Sheryl Ralstin, b. Aug. 17, 1955; Michael Lee, b. Dec. 8, 1957; Wayne, b. Sept. 18, 1963. Career: pres., Brown & Kauffmann, Inc. 1953---. U.S. Army Med. Corps, 1943-45, WW II. Mem.: Los Altos Golf and Country Club. Office: 935 E. Meadow Dr., Palo Alto, CA 94303.

KAWANA, KOICHI
Artist — Designer — Educator
b. Mar. 16, 1930, Asahikawa, Hokkaido, Japan; s. Kiichi and Toki (Takeda) Kawana; B.S., Yokohama Municipal Univ., 1951; B.A., UCLA 1955, M.A., 1959, M.F.A. 1964. Career: Tchg. asst. UCLA Art Dept. 1960-63, tchg. fellow, 1963-64, Univ. research artist, 1964-66, lectr., 1966, asst. rpof. art in res. 1966; design cons.-sr. artist, UCLA Campus Archs.-engrs. 1966-69, design cons.-arch. assoc. 1970-73; prin. archit. assoc. 1973---; prof. Adachi-Shiki Sch. of Floral Design, 1961---; UCLA Ext. lectr. in Japanese art, arch. and landscape design, 1962---; pres. Environmental Design Assocs., 1966---; Landscape designs incl.: Seiwa-en, Mo. Botanical Garden, St. Louis; Chicago Horticultural Soc. Botanic Garden, Japanese garden, Glencoe, Ill.; (Japanese garden, Denver Botanic Gardens, and gardens mentioned in Dorothy Loa McFadden's Oriental Gardens in Am., 1976). sect. Bel-Air Country Club; paintings in many collections incl. the White House, Wash. D.C.; tech. advisor, Mike Todd's Around the World in 80 Days, 1955; Universal's Joe Butterlfy, Hal Wallis's A Girl Called Tomiko, 1956, 62. Contrib. articles to profl. journs., Tokyo, U.S. 1959---; Papers delivered before ASPAC Conf., Oaxtepec, Mex., 1970; Asilomar, 1972, 76; Vancouver, B.C., 1973; San Diego, 1974; Honolulu, 1975; Eugene, Ore. 1977; Fullerton, 1978. Awards: natl. 2nd place design competition, Natl. Soc. of Interior Designers, 1961; design competitions, Am. Inst. Interior Designers; Distinguished Serv. Award, Japan Am. Soc. 1965; Design Ball Award, 1970; Cited by Progressive Architecture for garden design for Sepulveda Water Reclamation Plan, L.A., 1972. Order of Merit (ofcr. grade) of the Military and Hospitaller Order of St. Lazarus of Jerusalem, Edinburgh, 1974. Mem.: sec.-treas., Calif. Epsilon Chpt. Phi Sigma Alpha, 1957; Am. Soc. of Interior Designers, 1964---; council, Japanese Am. Soc. of So. Calif. 1965---, chmn. Cultural Com. 1968-71; So. Calif. Hort. Inst.; Calif. Art Edn. Assn.; Far Eastern Art Council, L.A. Co. Mus. of Art; secty. Calif. Delta Chpt. Pi Gamma Mu, 1969---. Zen Buddhist. Hobby: sumi painting. Rec.: travel. Res.: 633 24th St., Santa Monica, CA 90402; Office: Dept. of Archit. & Engrs., USC, L.A., CA 90024.

KAY, JEROME HAROLD
Thoracic Surgeon
b. Mar. 17, 1921, St. Cloud, Minn.; s. Louis and Frances (Kerlan) Kay; A.A., 1941; B.A., 1943, M.D., 1945; m. Adrienne Levin; chil.: Stephen Paul, b. Aug. 15, 1954; Karen Lynne, b. Dec. 22, 1955; Gregory Louis, b. Jan. 13, 1953; Cathy Ann, b. June 27, 1960; Robert Michael, b. Apr. 25, 1964; Richard Keith, b. June 28, 1965. Career: instr. anatomy, Southwestern Med. Coll., Dallas, 1946; instr. surgery, Johns Hopkins Sch. of Med., 1953-54; instr. in surg., asst. clin. prof. surg., USC Sch. of Med., 1956-58, assoc. prof. thoracic surg., 1958---; head physician, thoracic & cardiac surg., LAC/USC Med. Center, 1958---; chief, thoracic & cardiovascular surg., St. Vincent Med. Center, 1958---. Dir., Med. Research Assn. of Calif., 1973; basic sci. examiner in surg. for Cardiovascular Subspec. Bd. of Am. Bd. of Internal Med., 1970, L.A.; Mem. Council on Thrombosis, Am. Heart Assn., 1971; guest examiner, Am. Bd. of Thoracic Surg., Inc., L.A. 1972. Maj., USPub. Health Serv., Nat. Heart Inst., NIH, 1954-56. Fellow, Am. Coll. of Cardiology; fellow, Am. Coll of Surgs.; Mem. Am. Assn. for Thoracic Surg.; Am. Coll. of Chest Physicians; Am. Heart Assn.; Soc. of Thoracic Surgeons; John Paul North Surgical Soc., pres. 1970-73; Office: 123 S. Alvarado St., L.A., CA 90057.

KAYE, NORA
Dancer
b. NYC; d. Mr. and Mrs. Gregory Koreff; m. Herbert Ross, Aug. 21, 1959, Mallorca, Spain. Career: joined Am. Ballet Theatre, 1940: prima ballerina, 1942-50, 1955-60; with N.Y. City Ballet, 1950-55; asst. to Herbert Ross in films, 1960---; exec. prod., Turning Point, 1977. Address: Hera Prodns., Columbia Pictures, 4000 Warner Blvd., Burbank, CA 91522.

KAZANJIAN, JAMES MEHRAN
Gemologist
b. Jan. 26, 1899, Turkey; s. Garabed and Anna (Yakligian) Kazanjian; grammar sch. edn.; m. Euphrates Pashgian, Sept. 2, 1933, Pasadena; chil.: Michael James, b. Oct. 31, 1937; Stanley Myron, b. Jan. 11, 1939. Owner, Kazanjian Bros., Inc., Beverly Hills; internat. gem merchant, gemologist, appraiser. Founder, Kazanjian Found. of Pasadena (scholarships to foreign students at Occidental Coll., USC). Creator, four sapphire heads of U.S. presidents, representing George Washington, Abraham Lincoln, Thomas Jefferson, Dwight Eisenhower; these heads and Star of Queensland were created from five largest sapphires in world, presented through Kazanjian Found. to people of U.S., on view in Smithsonian Inst. Creator, the Ruby Liberty Bell, also in Smithsonian Inst. Hobby: collecting fine gems. Rec.: tennis, jogging, beach. Home: 150 Fern Dr., Pasadena, CA; Office: 332 N. Rodeo Dr., Beverly Hills, CA 90210.

KAZANJIAN, MICHAEL JAMES
Executive Director, Jazanjian Foundation
b. Oct. 31, 1937, Pasadena, Calif.; s. James M. and Euphrates (Pashgian) Kazanjian; B.S., USC, 1960; m. Virginia, 1967, Pasadena, Calif.; son Douglas Michael. Career: exec. dir., Kazanjian Found. — Mil.: Lt., USN. Mem.: Sigma Chi Frat., pres., Alpha Upsilon chpt., 1959; Am. Soc. Appraisers; Rotary Internat. Office: Kazanjian Bros., Inc., 332 N. Rodeo Dr., Beverly Hills, CA 90210.

KEARNS, HENRY
President, Kearns International
b. Apr. 30, 1911, Salt Lake City; s. Henry A. and Mary Orilla (Robbins) Kearns; Univ. of Ut., 1929-32; bus. adm., Internat. Correspondence Sch.; (hon.) Doctor of Bus. Adm., Woodbury Coll., L.A.; m. Marjorie Prescott, L.A., Oct. 30, 1938 (5th generation Californian); chil.: Mrs. Edward Lee (Patricia Helen) Clabaugh, b. Dec. 10, 1940; Henry Timothy, b. May 10, 1943; Mrs. David (Mary) Rohe and and Michael David Prescott (twins), b. Apr. 20, 1949. Career: Automobile business, Hermons & Kearns, 1933; salesman, Upton Chev. Co., Pasa. 1935, sales mgr. 1937, gen. mgr., 1939; partner, Lane Chev. Co., S. Pasa. 1940; pres.-gen. mgr., Victory Mfg. Co. 1942; orgn. Plastics Research Lab. 1944; pres. San Gabriel Valley Motors, 1946-47; pres. Mercury Park, Inc., 1947-52; pres. Rio Hondo Devel. Co.; pres. Policy Holder's Ins. Agcy.; pres., Henry Kearns, Inc. (real estate devel.) 1960-66; bd. dirs., Charter Securities Mgmt. Corp. 1967; pres. Kearns Internat. Co. of Thailand, Ltd. 1967; est. Kearns Internat., Pasa., 1967; pres. Natl. Engring. Sci. Co.; v.p. Pike Corp. of Am.; pres. Am. Capital Corp.; dir. Firestone Tire & Rubber Co., Thailand; adv. to bd. dirs., Mitsui & Co., Tokyo; apptd. pres.-chmn. Export-Import Bank of U.S. (by Pres. Nixon), 1969-73; pres. Kearns Internat. 1973---. Dir.: FMC Corp., Am. Internat. Group, Inc.; Awards: Grand Officier de L'Ordre Nat., Repub. Ivory Coast; Order of the Brilliant Star, Repub. China; Order of Diplomatic Serv. Merit, Repub. Korea; Merit of Honor award, Univ. Ut.; Econ. D., Chuny Ang. Univ., Seoul, Korea; Experienced Internat. Exec., Am. Soc. Internat. Execs.; Outstanding Young Man of Pasa.; Most Useful Young Man of Calif.; Grand Knight, Royal Order of the White Elephant, Govt. of Thailand. Mem.: pres. Pasa. Jr. C. of C. 1942-43; pres. Calif. Jr. C. of C. 1943-44; pres. U.S. Jr. C. of C. 1945-46; dir., U.S. C. of C. 1949; past dir., Citizens Com. for Hoover Reports; natl. assoc., Pasa. Area, Boys Clubs of Am.; pres. Pasa. Tournament of Roses Assn.; exec. com., Friends of Occidental Coll; trustee: Woodbury Univ., L.A.; U.S. Chamber Internat. Com.; Am. C. of C., Eng., Thailand, Japan, P.I.; dir. Export Control Bur.; admr. China Trade Act; chmn. Orig. Export Expansion Com.; chmn. Internat. Trade Fair Com.; alternate chmn., Trade Police Com.; Hoover Comm. Task Force on Intelligence Activities; Natl. Council, chmn. Dels to Internat. Confs. on Finance, Trade, Travel; Comm. Chest; United Fund; Pasa. Civic Music Assn.; Am. Club of Tokyo; Lotus Club of N.Y.; F&AM Community Lodge, 32° Consistory Mason, Shrine, Al Malaikah Temple; Clubs: Annandale Golf Club, Pasadena; 1925 F Street Club, Wash., D.C.; St. Francis Yacht Club, S.F.; Stock Exch. Club, S.F.; World Trade Club, S.F.; Exch. (Pasa.), Rotary (So. Pasa.), Kiwanis (San Gabriel); Burning Tree, Lotus Club of N.Y., Georgetown. Republican (pres. Assembly and Co. Central Com., Pasa.). Episcopalian. Hobby: politics. Rec.: golf. Office: 155 Sansome St., S.F., CA 94104.

KEENE, DONALD L.
President, Bailey and Rhodes
b. Aug. 4, 1933, Orland, Calif.; s. Donald H. and Marjorie L. Keene; B.S. (Bus. Adm.) Univ. of Calif., Berkeley, 1955; Chartered Financial Analyst, 1966; m. Linda Bailey, L.A., Sept. 22, 1956; chil.: Donna, b. June 25, 1961; Bruce Bailey, b. Apr. 3, 1963; Michael Lane, b. Jan. 16, 1965. Career: Portfolio mgr.-research asst., Bailey and Rhodes, 1957, corp. secty-treas.-dir.

1959, v.p. 1967, exec. v.p. 1969, pres. 1971---; Dir., Far Western Life Ins. Co., 1967-69; U.S. Navy Line Ofcr., Pac. Fleet, 1955-57. Mem.: pres. Methodist Youth Fellowship, 1950-51; pres. Larchmont Young Repub. Club, 1964-65; adv. bd. Calif. Mus. of Sci. and Ind. 1967---; pres. L.A. Alumni Chpt., Sigma Chi, 1968; bd. govs. L.A. Soc. Financial Analysts, 1968---; treas. 1969-70; secty. 1970-71; v.p. 1971-72; pres. 1972-73; L.A. Bond Club, Western Pension Conf., Calif. Vintage Wine Soc., Town Hall of Calif.; Beta Gamma Sigma, L.A. Country Club, Calif. Club, Bel-Air Bay Club. Hobby: sports. Rec.: golf, paddle tennis. Res.: 122 S. McCadden Pl., L.A., CA 90004; Office: 611 W. Sixth St., L.A., CA 90017.

KEENEY, EDMUND LUDLOW
President Emeritus, Scripps Clinic and Research Foundation
b. Aug. 11, 1908, Shelbyville, Ind.; s. Bayard G. and Ethel (Adams) Keeney; A.B., Ind. Univ. 1930; M.D., Johns Hopkins Univ. 1934; m. Esther Cox Loney Wight, La Jolla, Mar. 14, 1950; chil.: Edmund Ludlow, Jr.; Mrs. Cameron Leroy (Eleanor Seymour) Smith. Career: intern, Johns Hopkins Hosp., 1934-35; res. 1935-36; instr. in med. 1940-48; est. med. practice, spec. in allergy, San Diego, 1948-55; pres.-dir. Scripps Clinic and Research Found., La Jolla, 1955-77; pres. Emer. 1977---. bd. trustees, Univ. of San Diego, 1974---; dir. Allergy Found. of Am. Author: Practical Medical Mycology, publ. Charles C. Thomas, 1955; contrib. articles, papers in allergy, immunology, mycology to profl. journs.; ed. bd. Journ. of Allergy. Dir. research on fungus infections. Ofc. of Sci. Research and Devel., USN (1942-46), WW II. Mem.: A'A. 1938---; secty. sect. on allery, 1964-65; fellow, Am. Acad. of Allery, 1940---, pres. 1962-64; Am. Soc. for Clin Investigation, 1945---; fellow, Am. Coll. of Phys. 1946---; diplomate, Am. Bd. of Internal Med. (subspecialty allergy), 1946---; Western Soc. for Clin. Research, 1948---; Western Assn. of Phys. 1955---; sci. bd. dirs., Calif. Med. Assn. 1963---; Rotary Club, S.D.; Eldorado Country Club; bd. govs. Cuyamaca Club, Phi Beta Kappa, Alpha Omega Alpha, Beta Theta Pi. Republican. Presbyterian. Rec.: golf, fishing, swimming. Res.: 338 Via del Norte, La Jolla, CA; Office: 10666 N. Torrey Pines Rd., La Jolla, CA 92037.

KELLEHER ROBERT J.
United States District Judge
b. Mar. 5, 1913, NYC; s. Frank and Mary (Donovan) Kelleher; A.B., Williams Coll. 1935; J.D. Harvard Univ. 1938; m. Gracyn N. Wheeler, Stamford, Conn., Aug. 14, 1940; chil.: R. Jeffrey, b. Sept. 28, 1945; Karen Kathleen, b. Apr. 24, 1951. Career: Asst., assoc. atty., War Dept., L.A. Ord. Reg. 1941-42; pvt. practice law, Santa Monica, 1945-48; Asst. U.S. Atty., So. (Central) Dist. of Calif. 1948-51; pvt. practice law, Beverly Hills, 1951-70; U.S. Dist. Judge, Dec. 21, 1970---. Ensign, Lt., USNR, Am., European, African and Pac. Theatres, 1943-45, WW II. Capt., U.S. Davis Cup Team, 1962-63; pres. U.S. Lawn Tennis Assn. 1967-68. Mem.: Am., Fed., State of Calif., L.A. Co. Bar Assns.; Am. Judicature Soc.; clubs: Harvard, So. Calif.; Williams, NYC; Lawyers, La Jolla Beach and Tennis. Res.: 1672 Waynecrest Dr., Beverly Hills, CA 90210; Office: United States Courthouse, 312 N. Spring St., L.A., CA 90012.

KELLER, RAY WARREN
Corporate Executive
b. Mar. 31, 1919, Long Beach; s. Frederick and Adeline (Morrison) Keller; ed. pub. shcs., USA; stu. Natl. Radio Inst.; m. Mary Margaret Whalen, L.A., June 22, 1938; chil.: Mrs. James Roth (Diane) Klein, b. Dec. 17, 1939; Joan M., b. May 23, 1943; Ray M., b. June 10, 1947. Career: Foreman-asst. supt., Hodgeson Shipyard, Long Beach, 1939-44; asst. chief pvt. investigator, Carmona Detectives Agcy., L.A., 1946-51; sales engr., Carver Cotton Gin Co., Dallas, Tex. 1951-53, chief field engr., Atlanta, Ga. 1953-55, br. mgr. Brownsville, Tex. 1955-58, br. mgr., Fresno, Calif. 1962-73; Western Sales Mgr., Rockwell Internat. 1973-77; Western Branch Mgr., Murray-Carver, Inc., 1977---; tech. dir. Empresas Associadas, Mex. 1958-62; cons. engr., Cottonseed Oil Mills. Sgt., U.S. Spec. Forces (1944-46) WW II. Mem. Internat. Oil Mil. Supt's. Assn.; Mason 33rd degree. Republican. Presbyterian. Hobby: electronics. Rec.: swimming, hunting, fishing. Res.: 12123 Hallwood Dr., El Monte, CA 91732; Office: P.O.B. 5930, El Monte, CA 91734.

KELLOGG, MARIAN BACON
Realtor
b. Glove, Ariz.; d. John Alec and Gladys Lillian (Paul) Bacon; grandniece, Gen. George Custer; A.A., Merced Coll.; Certified Commercial & Investment Member (CCIM), Nat. Marketing Inst., Nat. Assn. of Realtors; m. Mark Kellogg, Jr. (div.), June 7, 1945, Phoenix, Ariz.; chil.: Kim John, b. Apr. 3, 1946; Luxon Clark, b. May 25, 1948; Diana Lynn (Fudula), b. Feb. 15, 1951. Career: co-founder, co-owner, Kellogg Surplus Supply, Merced, 1946; pres., MK Real Estate Associates, Inc. ---. Pres., Merced Coll. Found. (blt. athletic stadium, is establishing merit scholarships for agri. students). Contbd. articles, Merced Sun Star & Livingston Chronicle, 1958-63. Mem.: Merced City C. of C.; Calif. Farm Bureau; Eastern Star; Emblem Club; Merced Redevelop. Citizen's Com. 1957-60. Active in March of Dimes; Cancer Crusade; Heart Fund; Campfire Girls, troop leader; PTA, former pres. Weaver Union, Le Conte Sch. Mem.: Beta Sigma Phi; Daughters of Nile; Jaycettes. Mem.: Republican Women, Merced Co. Republican Central Com.; Repub. State Central Com. Hobbies: painting, archaeology. Rec.: horseback riding, travel. Home: 2240 Yosemite Parkway, No. 52, Merced, CA; Office: 760 W. 20th St., Merced, CA 95340.

KELLY, J(OHN) NORMAN
County Administrator (Ret.)
b. Jan. 14, 1907, Douglas, Ariz.; s. John H. and Charlotte (Foley) Kelly; student, L.A. City Coll., USC Sch. of Govt.; m. Catherine M. Goble (div.), Sept. 11, 1943, Ft. Sheridan, Ill.; chil.: Kathleen M. (Thurin), b. June 30, 1944; Colleen E. (DeLand), b. Apr. 13, 1953. Career: advisor, Samuel French, Inc., 1930-35; pub. relations, 1935-39; deputy to L.A. Co. Supervisor, 1939-49; dir., L.A. Co. Dept. of Mil. and Veterans Affairs, 1949-72. Radio announcer, Wayne King All-Army Show, former TV and Radio Panelist. Mil.: grad. The Infantry Sch.; grad., Command & General Staff Coll., U.S. Army; served as dir. of Training and Commander of Hq. & Hq. Co., Ft. Sheridan; ret. Lt. Col., AUS. Mem.: Nat. Advisory Council of Americanism Edn. League, 1972---, past bd. of trustees and exec. com.; founding bd. dir. L.A. chpt. Assn. of U.S. Army; Sonoma Co. Museum Found.; Sonoma Co. Bincentennial Commn., past pres.; v. chmn. Armed Forces Com., L.A. C. of C.; advisor to Mil. Affairs Com., Torrance C. of C. and Armed Forced Com., San Pedro C. of C.; curriculum advisory council, Sonoma Sch. Dist.; Speechcrafters, past pres.; Am. Legion, past comdr. L.A. Co. Post 810; AmVets, L.A. Chpt. 1, past comdr.; Am. Legion Luncheon Club; Seattle Art Museum. Rec.: hiking, travel. Home: 5314 24th Ave. NW, Gig Harbor, Wa. 98335.

KELLY, PAUL BRENDAN
Honorary Director, Crocker National Bank
b. Feb. 18, 1898, Brooklyn, N.Y.; s. Francis and Mary Josephine (Connelly) Kelly; B.A., M.A., Univ. of Calif., Berkeley, 1920; m. Margaret Griffiths, S.F., Apr. 18, 1960; chil.: Paul B., Jr., b. May 2, 1935; Ann S. Livingston, b. June 4, 1937; John Michael, b. Apr. 26, 1939. Career: employee, Anglo London Paris Co., affiliate of the Anglo & London Paris Natl Bank, 1923-33; v.p. Anglo Calif. Natl. Bank, 1933-39; dir. Crocker-Anglo Natl. Bank, 1945, 1st v.p. 1951, v-chmn. bd. 1962---. Dir., Crocker Natl. Bank and Crocker Natl. Corp. Clubs: Pac. Union, Bohemian. Hobby: golf. Res.: 1400 Geary Blvd., S.F., CA; Office: 111 Sutter St., Suite 529, S.F., CA 94109.

KEMPER, DORLA EATON (Deanie)
Realtor
b. Sept. 10, 1929, Calhoun, Mo.; d. Paul M. and Jessie Lee Eaton; student, William Woods Coll., Fulton, Mo., 1947-48; Central Missouri State Univ., Warrensburg, Mo., 1949-52; m. Charles K. Kemper, Mar. 1, 1951, Twin Falls, Idaho; chil.: Kevin Keil, b. Aug. 10, 1957; Kara Lee, b. June 6, 1960. Career: school tchr. Twin Falls, Idaho, 1950-51; tchr. Mission, Kan., 1952-53; tchr., Burbank, Calif. 1953-57; substitute tchr., 1957-66; real estate salesperson, St. Paul, Minn., 1966-68, Calif. 1971-74; real estate broker, 1974-79; pres., Deanie Kemper Inc., realtor, 1976---. Mem.: Graduate Realtors Inst. 1973; Certified Residential Specialist 1978; life mem., Million Dollar Club, Sacramento Bd. of Realtors, 1978; life mem. and secty. Placer Co. Bd. of Realtors, Profl. Standards Com. 1st pres. Battle Creek PTA, St. Paul, Minn. 1965-67; v.p. Hidden Valley Women's Club, 1970-71; Auburn Travel Study Club, pres. 1978-79. Mem. Nat. Soc. DAR, Dist. II Dir. Calif. State Soc. 1978-80; v. chmn., Nat. Defense Com. 1978-80; organizing regent, Gold Trail Chpt. NSDAR 1977-78; regent, Emigrant Trail Chpt. 1972-74. Christian. Home-Office: 8165 Morningside Dr., Loomis, CA 95650.

KENDALL, DOROTHY STEVENS
School Administrator
b. Aug. 21, 1916, Crump, Mich.; d. Elmer E. and Lottie (Boyer) Stevens; ed. San Bernardino Valley Coll. 1940; stu. (physiotherapy), Redlands and Monrovia, Calif.; psych. tech. 1969; m. George Kendall, Glendale, July 24, 1948. Career: Violin tchr., Brush Cons. Music, San Bernardino, 1941-45; tchr., retarded chil., Glendale, 1945-48; phys. therapist, 1948-70; admr-owner, Kendall Manor Sch. (res. sch. for retarded), 1948---. Mem. Calif. Phys. Therapy Assn.; Assn. Res. for Retarded; Internat. Platform Assn. 1970---. Choir dir. Colton Methodist Ch. 1939-44. Hobbies: ceramics, music. Rec.: golf. Office: 680 Jackson St., Colton, CA 92324.

KENNEDY, ROBERT EDWIN
University President Emeritus
b. Oct. 31, 1915, Portland, Ore.; s. Hazel (Bronson) Kennedy; A.B., San Diego State Coll. 1938; M.A., Stanford Univ. 1950; Ph.D., Claremont Grad. Sch. and Univ. Center, 1966; m. Mary Paxton, San Diego, June 12, 1938; Chil.: Robert E., Jr., b. 1940; Mrs. John (Maridel) Salisbury, b. 1943; Stephen, b. 1945; Mrs. Robert (Susan) Lattanzio, b. 1947. Career: reporter, San Diego Sun, 1937-38; exec. secty., Civic Affairs Conf., S.D. 1938-39; adv. mgr., Hamilton's Ltd., S.D. 1939-40; pub. rels.-head journalism dept., Calif. State Poly Coll. 1940-48; dir. pub. rels. 1949-54; asst. to pres. 1954-57; dean, arts and scis. 1957-59; v.p. 1959-66, pres. 1967-79. Author numerous profl. articles publ. natl. and tech. mags. Civ. instr., Naval Flight Prep. Sch., Calif. State Poly. Coll. 1943-46, WW II. Mem.: Sigma Delta Chi 1949---; dir. Calif. Central Profl. Chpt., 1966; natl. bd. dirs., Am. Coll. Pub. Rels. Assn. 1950-52, pres. 12th Dist. 1950-51; dir. San Luis Obispo C. of C. 1950-57; dir. Santa Lucia Council, BSA 1966---; bd. dirs. Am. Assn. of State Colls. and Univs. 1970-74. Methodist (bd. trustees). Hobby: photog. Res.: 251 San Luis St., Avila Beach, CA 93424; Office: Office of Pres. Emeritus, Calif. Polytechnic State Univ., San Luis Obispo, CA 93407.

KERR, JOHN F.
English Professor — Poet
b. May 28, 1930, Monette, Ark.; s. Felix W. and Mary Florence (Fay) Kerr; B.A., Ark. State Univ. 1953; M.A., Univ. Mich. 1956; Ph.D., Univ. Tex. 1965; m. Joanne Thorner, Dec. 21, 1975. Career: tchr.speech, journalism Kennett (Mo.) H.S., 1954-55; asst. prof. Am. lit., fiction writing Westminster Coll., Fulton, Mo. 1956-57; instr. Eng., Univ. Mo., Columbia, 1957-58; Univ. Tex. at Austin, 1958-63; asst. prof. Am. lit. and fiction writing La. State Univ., San Luis Obispo, 1967-69; assoc. prof., 1969-74; prof., 1974---, dir. grad. studies English, 1973-76; lectr. reader poetry, Calif. Served with USMC, 1946-49. Recipient: excellence in teaching award, Univ. Tex. at Austin, 1961; award humorous poetry Calif. Fedn. Chaparral Poets, 1973. Mem. Calif. State Poetry Soc. (pres. 1975-76), AAUP, Modern Lang. Assn., United Profs. Calif., Calif. Fedn. Chaparral Poets. Democrat. Contbr. poetry to mags. and anthologies. Res.: 1694 Newport Ave., Grover City, CA 93433; Office: Dept. of Eng., Calif. Poly State Univ., San Luis Obispo, CA 93407.

KIDD, REUBEN P.
Business Owner — Industrial Engineer
b. Feb. 18, 1913, Bedford, Va.; s. Oscar K. and Estelle (Johnson) Kidd; B.S., Va. Poly. Inst., 1936; m. Margaret Jerome, June 21, 1952 (div. 1961), Van Nuys, Calif. Career: Ranch owner and operator, 1953-56; Calif. registered profl. eng., 1959---; indsl. eng. USAF; plant repr. officer, Aerojet-General Corp., Sacramento, 1956-73; owner Auto Service Shop, 1974---. Bd. Chmn., United States Divorce Reform, Inc., 1962-69; pres., MEN Internat., USA, 1977---. Mil.: Co. Comdr., Civilian Conservation Corps, 1939-42. Battery Comdr., Maj. AUS, 1942-46; Korea, 1950-51; decorated, Silver Star Medal, Italy, 1943. Hobby: coin collection. Rec.: camping, trail bike riding. Home: 5809 Northgrove Way, Citrus Hts., CA; Office: Foothill Precision Tune-Up, 6241 Spruce Ave., Sacramento, CA.

KIEVE, ROBERT S.
Broadcasting Executive
b. Dec. 9, 1921, Jersey City, N.J.; s. Caesar and Lenoir (Steiner) Kieve; B.S., Harvard Coll. 1943; dau. Lenoir S., b. Feb. 4, 1964. Career: Inf. ofcr. Am. Embassy, Madrid, Spain, 1943-47; pgm. dir. Radio WGVA, Geneva, N.Y. 1947-50; promotion writer, CBS, NYC 1950-53; spec. ofc. asst. in White House, 1953-55, 56; spec. asst. to dep. dir. of U.S. Inf. Agcy, 1955-56; v.p.-gen. mgr. WBBF-AM-FM, Rochester, N.Y. 1957-66;

pres., Empire Broadcasting Corp., and gen. mgr. Radio KLIV, San Jose and KARA, Santa Clara, 1967---. Author: El Arte Radiofonico (book), publ. in Spain, 1945. Mem.: v.p. San Jose Sym. Assn. 1970---; dir. San Jose Music Theatre, 1970---; dir.: Chil's. Home Soc., San Jose Citizens Civic Improvement Comm., San Jose Central YMCA. Res.: 999 W. Hamilton Ave., Campbell, CA; Office: P.O.B. 995, San Jose, CA 95108.

KIMBERLING, JOHN FARRELL
Attorney at Law
b. Nov. 15, 1926, Shelbyville, Ind.; s. James F. and Phyllis (Cassidy) Kimberling; student Purdue Univ. BNST, 1946; A.B., Indiana Univ., 1947; J.D., Ind. Univ. Sch. of Law, 1950. Career: Associate, law firm of Bracken, Grey, Defur and Voran, 1950-51; assoc. law firm of Lillick McHose & Charles and predecessor firms, 1953-63, partner, 1963---. Dir.: Mitsui Bank of Calif.; L.A. C. of C.; past pres. and dir., L.A. Jr. C. of C. Mil. Served from Ensign to Lt. J.G. USNR, 1951-53. Fellow, Am. Coll. of Trial Lawyers, 1974. Mem.: Chancery Club of L.A. Mem.: Beta Theta Pi, pres. 1947-48; Phi Delta Phi legal frat., pres. 1950. Mem. L.A. Co. Republican Central Com. Rec.: fishing, backpacking. Home: 2101 Castilian Dr., L.A., CA 90068; Office: Lillick, McHose & Charles, 707 Wilshire Blvd., 45th Flr., L.A., CA 90017.

KING, CLIFTON W.
Clergyman
b. June 9, No. Carolina; s. Samuel Walton Sparks and Anne Elizabeth King; Doctor of Humane Letters; ordained in the Internat. Federation of Divine Sci. Churches; m. Loriene Chase, Ph.D., May 24, 1974, Beverly Hills. Career: Chaplain, AUS; pres., Chase-King Personal Development Centers ---; minister, Santa Anita Ch., Arcadia; minister, Divine Sci. Ch., Beverly Hills; Minister, Encino Community Ch., Tarzana, 1977---. Also lectures on stress; workshops on motivation, successful living; pvt. counseling; former staff mem. USC stress Center; spec. in dream analysis and meditation as healing aids. Mil.: USC, W.W. II; AUS, Chaplain Corps Korean conflict. Author: Two-Way Prayer; Happiness Through the Beatitudes; co-author with Dr. L. Chase-King, The Human Miracle. Mem.: Divine Sci. Fedn. Internat.; Internat. Assn. Ch. Bus. Adminstrs.; Order of St. Luke the Physician; Internat. Platform Assn.; Navy League (Bel Air Council), life mem.; Confrerie de la Chaine des Rotisseurs; the London Club; Lakeside Country Club; Beverly Hills C. of C. Home: 4925 Tarzana Woods Dr., Tarzana, CA 91356; Office: 5955 Lindley Ave., Tarzana, CA 91356.

KING, GEORGE EDWARD BURNS
Chairman of the Board, Burns International
b. Aug. 11, 1921, Ossining, N.Y.; s. Cyrus H. and Kathleen (Burns) King; B.A., Univ. of Detroit, 1942; m. Beryl Clavere, Nov. 11, 1945; chil.: Carolyn (Thomas); Geroge Jr.; Brian; Randal; Garrett; Kelley; Kevin; Lynne; Lisa; Kenneth. Career: Staff announcer, WSPB-Radio, Sarasota, Fla., 1942; WJBK-Radio, Detroit, Mich., 1943; Burns International Security Services, N.Y. and San Francisco, 1945---: started as Trainee; then mgr.; div. mgr.; v.p.; dir.; sr. v.p.; chief exec. and chmn. of bd., 1978---. V.P., Justin Siena Hi Sch. Found.; bd. dir. Justin Siena Hi Sch. Mil. Lt. J.G., USNR, fighter director; decorated with commendation ribbon. Mem.: Elks Club, Rotary Club, Olympic Club, Silverado Country Club, World Trade Club. Home: 1080 La Londe Lane, Napa, CA; Office: 8001 Capwell Dr., Oakland, CA 94603.

KINGSLEY, ELEANOR NEVIN VEALE
Designer — Manufacturer
b. Sept. 12, 1905, Valencia, Kan.; d. Walter Johnson and Mima Anna (Wilson) Veale; desc. James Wilson, signer of Declaration of Independence; B.S. cum laude, USC. 1927; m. William Jackson Kingsley, Aug. 29, 1934, L.A., Calif.; chil.: Sherwood Clark, b. July 5, 1939; Sterling Wilson, b. Mar. 31, 1941; Career: English tchr., Bancroft Jr. Hi Sch., Hollywood, 1928-32; house exec., 1933-63; designer, innovator, mfgr., pres., owner: Jackson Co. Mfgrs.; Kingsley Lib. Equip.; Kingsley Depository Co.; Drop-in-Anytime (lib. equip. street furniture, curb-side depositories for payment of utility bills). Designer and mfgr.: lib. equip. including a computer output communicator, curb-side book returns, drive up/walk up lib. service center; litter receptacles, 7 designs chosen by Am. Pub. Works Assn. Streetscape, Best of the best of street equip. Mem.: Phi Kappa Phi, Delta Sigma Rho, Pi Lambda Theta, Alpha Chi Omega. Episcopal ch. Home: 510 No. Towne Ave., Claremont, CA 91711; Office: 1879 Mt. Vernon Ave., Pomona, CA 91768.

KINGSLEY, ROBERT
Justice, District Court of Appeal
b. Oct. 8, 1903, Cedar Falls, Ia.; s. Frank Amos and Angeline (Van Niman) Kingsley; A.B., A.M., Univ. of Minn. 1923; LL.B., 1926; S.J.D., Harvard Univ. 1928; m. Doris Field Forbes-Manson, Long Beach, June 12, 1937; m. Ninon M. Hogan, July 3, 1976. Career: instr. in law, Univ. of Minn. 1926-27; Thayer Fellow, Harvard Law Sch. 1927-28; asst. prof. of law, USC. 1928-30; prof. 1930; v.-dean, Sch. of Law, 1947-51; assoc. dean, 1951-52; dean, 1952-63; justice, Dist. Ct. of Appeal, 1963---. Mem.: (past) pres., Jr. C. of C., Music Found.; (past) pres., L.A. Music Guild; secty. L.A. Civic Light Opera Assn., 1948---; trustee, L.A. Co. Bar Assn. 1963; Delta Theta Phi frat., University Club, L.A. Congregationalist. Hobby: music. Res.: 231 S. Citrus Ave., L.A., CA; Office: 3580 Wilshire Blvd., L.A., CA 90010.

KINNEY, GILBERT FORD
Professor Emeritus
b. Dec. 29, 1907, Judsonia, Ark.; s. Gilbert Earle and Mabel (Ford) Kinney; desc. Jeremiah Kinne, mem. of Boston Tea Party, 1775; A.B., Ark. Coll., 1928; M.S., Univ. Tenn., 1930; Ph.D., N.Y. Univ., 1935; postgrad., MIT, 1938; m. Martha Stinson, Sept. 6, 1934, Dermott, Ark.; chil.: Abbott Hart K. (Hall), b. Jan. 24, 1936; Gilbert Ford, Jr., b. June 2, 1941. Career: head instr. chem., Pratt Inst., N.Y., 1935-42; civilian scientist Opn. Crossroads, Biking, 1946; Prof. of Chem. Engring, Chmn. dept. of Metallurgy and Chem., Naval Postgrad. Sch., Monterey, 1946-71; now Distinguished Prof. Emeritus; indsl. cons. on explosions and Materials processing. Author three tech. books: on Engring. thermodynamics, on plastics, on explosions. Active duty, USN, 1942-46; active Reserve, USNR, 1946-67; now Capt., USN, Ret. Mem.: Alpha Lambda Tau, Alpha Chi Sigma; Sigma Xi. Presbyterian. Hobby: photog. Res.: 1116 Sylvan Rd., Monterey, CA 93940.

KIRBY, BARBARA LYNN
City Librarian
b. Aug. 3, 1933, Troy, N.Y.; d. Leland Mace and Clara (Darby) Bashford; B.S.L.S., Genesco State Tchrs. Coll., N.Y., 1954; M.L.S., State Univ. of New York, Albany, 1963; m. Maj. Henry Kirby, Jr., July 5, 1953, Troy, N.Y.; chil.: Scott Henry, b. Nov. 5, 1956; Reed Thomas, b. Mar. 29, 1961; Allison Ruth, b. Apr. 15, 1963. Career: Children's librarian, L.A. Public Library, San Pedro, 1954; Jr. High librarian, Schenectady, N.Y. Public Schools, 1954-56; librarian, Troy, N.Y. Hi. Sch., 1958-59; librarian, Culver City Unified Schools, 1966, 1969; librarian, Wilmette, Ill. Sch. Dist., 1967-68; reference librarian 1970-74, asst. city librarian 1974-78, city librarian, El Segundo, 1978---. Mem.: v.p., El Segundo Quota Club, 1977-79; Order of the Eastern Star, Palms chpt. No. 491; Am. Lib. Assn.; Calif. Lib. Assn. Methodist. Hobbies: needlework, genealogy. Rec.: camping. Home: 5133 Pickford Way, Culver City, CA 90230; Office: 111 W. Mariposa Ave., El Segundo, CA 90245.

KIRK, HENRY PORT, III
College Dean
b. Dec. 20, Clearfield, Pa.; s. Henry Jr. and Ann Kirk; B.A., Geneva Coll., 1958; M.A., Univ. of Denver, 1963; Ed.D., USC, 1973; m. Mattie F. Capponi, Feb. 11, 1956, Clairton, Pa.; chil.: Timothy Scott, b. 1957; Mary Ann, b. 1959; Rebecca Alice, b. 1962. Career: Admissions ofcr., Columbia Coll., 1963-65; Dean of Stu., Huron Coll., 1965-66; Assoc. Dean of Students, Cal. State Univ., L.A., 1966-70; Dean of Student Affairs, El Camino Coll., 1970---; Adj. Asst. Prof., USC, 1974-76. Contbr. articles, profl. journs. Mem.: South Bay YMCA, bd. mgrs., Torrance Rotary Club, pres. 1977-78; chmn. Human resources Commn., Torrance, 1977---. Presbyterian, Elder, Deacon, Youth Advisor. Hobby: antique automobiles. Home: 416 Malaga, Redondo Beach, CA 90277; Office: El Camino Coll., 16007 Crenshaw Blvd., Torrance, CA 90506.

KIRKLAND, BERTHA THERESA
Business Executive
b. May 16, 1916, S.F.; d. Lawrence and Theresa (Kanzler) Schmelzer; ed. pub. schs., USA; m. Thornton Crowns Kirkland, Jr., Dec. 27, 1937 (dec. July 22, 1971); chil.: Kathryn Elizabeth, Francis Charles. Career: Ofc. mgr., T.C. Kirkland, Electrical contr., 1954-58; secty.-treas.-dir. T.C. Kirkland, Inc., 1958-74; design and build. elect. estimator, Add-M Electric, Inc. 1972---, v.p. 1974---. Mem.: Arrowhead Country Club. Espicopalisn. Res.: 526 E. Sonora St., San Bernardino, CA 92404;

Office: 387 S. Arrowhead Ave., San Bernardino, CA 92408.

KIRKORIAN, DONALD GEORGE
College Administrator
b. Nov. 30, 1938, San Mateo; s. George and Alice (Sergius) Kirkorian; B.A., Stanford Univ., 1961; M.A., USC, 1966; Ph.D., Northwestern Univ., 1972. Career: Bus. Edn. Tchr., L.A. City Unified Sch. Dist., 1963; tchr., Fremont Union H.S. Dist., 1963-64; lectr., San Jose State Univ., 1964-68; Ext. faculty, 1968-69; Cons., Nat. Assn. of Ednl. Broadcasters, Wash. D.C., 1966-68; Center for the Tchg. Professions, Northwestern Univ., 1970-71; Instrnl. TV Coord., Fremont H.S. Dist., 1964-73; mem. Ext. faculty, UC, Davis, 1974-77; Assoc. Dean of Instrn., Solano Comm. Coll., Suisun City, 1973---. Mem. Advis. Com., Learning Resources and Centers, 1976---; mem. Governing Bd., Bay Area Comm. Coll. TV Consortium 1974---; Site Selection Coord., W. Ednl. Soc. for Telecommunications, 1977---, pres. 1976-77; exec. ofcr., Learning Resources Assn. of Calif. Comm. Colls., 1975---. Contbr. articles to profl. publs. Mem.: Assn. for Ednl. Communications and Tech.; Assn.; Comm. Coll. Assn. for Instrn. and Tech.; Nat. Assn. of Ednl. Broadcasters; Phi Delta Kappa; W. Ednl. Soc. for Telecommunications. Res.: 3850 Rockville Rd., Suisun City, CA 94585; Office: Solano Comm. Coll., P.O.B. 246, Suisun City, CA 94585.

KLAPSTEIN, EARL
Chancellor, Los Rios Community College District
b. Mar. 8, 1922, Lodi, Calif.; s. Emil and Sadie Klapstein; B.A., Univ. of Pacific, 1943; M.A., 1953; Ph.D., USC, 1963; m. Viola C. Wiederich, May 7, 1944, Carson City, Nev.; chil.: Sue, b. Dec. 13, 1946 (tchr.); Tom, b. July 5, 1949 (agri-bus.); Janet, b. July 16, 1951 (lawyer). Career: Dean of students, Cerritos Coll., 1956-66; pres., Yakima Valley Coll., 1962-66; pres., Mt. Hood Coll., 1966-76; Chancellor and Superintendent, Los Rios Community Coll. Dist., 1976---. (Dist. has three colleges: Am. River Coll., Sosumnes River Coll., Sacramento City Coll., br. campus at Placerville); univ. lectr.; community coll. cons. Past pres.: Northwest Assn. of Community Colls.; Oregon Coll. President's Council; Calif. Dean's of Men's Assn.; Artesia Rotary Club, 1961-62. Bd. Mem. Am. Assn. of Community and Jr. Colls., 1959-62; YMCA. Mil. USN, 1943-45. Played football, Pittsburgh Steelers. Participant in TV and radio shows, job-related. Mem.: Delta Lodge No. 471, Stockton, 1950---; Rho Lambda Phi, 1939-43. Methodist ch., trustee. Rec.: fishing, swimming. Home: 1508 Del Dayo Dr., Carmichael, CA 95608; Office: 1919 Spanos Ct., Sacramento, CA 94825.

KLECKNER, JAMES FRANKLYN
Ophthalmic Surgeon
b. Oct. 22, 1924, Pittsburgh, Pa.; s. Ellis H. and Martha (Loux) Kleckner; B.A., Lehigh Univ., 1945; M.D., Jefferson Med. Coll., 1948; Grad. Course in ophthalmology, Wash. Univ., 1949-50; Diplomate, Nat. Bd. of Examiners, Am. Bd. of Ophthalmology; m. Janet Edelman, Sept. 10, 1949, Bethlehem, Pa.; chil.: Nancy (d'Jamily), b. July 15, 1950; James E., b. Nov. 28, 1953. Career: Resident physician, St. Louis City Hosp., 1950; staff ophthalmologist, U.S. Naval Hosp., San Diego, 1950-51; Clin. instr., Wash. Univ. Grad. Sch. of Med., 1952-53; pvt. practice ophthalmic surg., L.A., 1953---; also asst. clin. prof. ophthalmol., Jules Stein Eye Inst., UCLA; pres., Crenshaw Acad. of Med., v.-chief of staff, Century City Hosp., USN 1950-51; Batallion Surgeon, Regimental Surgeon, C.O. "D" Med. Co., 1st Marine Div., Korea, 1951. Mem.: Am. Acad. Ophthalmology; Sigma Chi; Masonic Lodge No. 625 F&AM; Scottish Rite, 32d; Alpha Epsilon Delta; Alpha Omega Alpha. Presbyterian. Hobby: photog. Res.: 6 Oakmont Dr., L.A., CA 90049; Office: 2080 Century Park E., L.A., CA 90067.

KLEIMAN, JOSEPH
Sr. Vice President Whittaker Corp.
b. Oct. 1, 1919, Grand Rapids, Mich.; s. Jacob and Bessie (Targowitch) Kleiman; B.S., Engring., Univ. Mich., 1941; M.S., 1942; m. Shirley Ruth Present, Aug. 30, 1942, Pontiac, Mich.; chil.: Richard Nell, b. June 13, 1944; Robert, b. Mar. 18, 1947; William, b. June 13, 1945. Career: Engr., Reeves Instrument Corp., NYC, 1946-51; v.p., gen. mgr. Belock Instrument Corp., College Point, N.Y., 1951-58; v.p., gen. mgr. Whittaker Gyro div. Telecomputing Corp., L.A., 1958-59; exec. v.p. corp., 1959-64; v.p. corp. devel. Whittaker Corp., 1964-67; sr. v.p., 1967---, also dir. of Yardney Electric and Morbern Industries; v.p. Am. Soc. for Technion-Israeli Inst. Tech.; v. chmn., Union Am.

Hebrew Congregations. Mem. Calif. Soc. Profl. Engrs., Sigma Xi, Phi Lambda Upsilon, Iota Alpha. Jewish. Res.: 11240 Chalon Rd., L.A., CA 90049; Office: 10880 Wilshire Blvd., L.A., CA 90024.

KLEINGARTNER, ARCHIE
University of California Administrator
b. Aug. 10, 1936, Gackle, N. Dak.; s. Emanuel and Otille (Kuhn) Kleingartner; B.A., Univ. of Minn., 1959; M.S., Univ. of Oregon, 1962; Ph.D., Univ. of Wisconsin, 1965; m. Dorothy Hanselmann, Sept. 21, 1957, Minneapolis, Minn.; chil.: Elizabeth Marie, b. Jan. 5, 1960; Thomas David, b. July 9, 1965. Career: Acting asst. prof., 1964-65; asst. prof., 1965-69; assoc. prof., 1969-73; professor, 1973---; v.p. for academic and staff personnel relations, Univ. of Calif. systemwide adminstrn., 1975---; chmn. and assoc. dean, Grad. Sch. of Mgmt., UCLA, 1969-71; exec. assoc. dir., Inst. of Indsl. Rels., UCLA, 1973-75. Dir.: Industry Edn. Council, 1977---; Legal Aid Found. of Calif., 1974---; chmn., Staff Personnel Bd., Univ. of Calif. 1973-74. Served, AUS Finance Conf. UCLA. Rec.: tennis. Home: 500 Grizzly Peak Blvd., Berkeley, CA; Office: 2200 University Ave., 750 University Hall, Berkeley 94720.

KLINE, FRED W.
News Service Executive
b. May 17, 1918, Oakland; s. Walter E. and Jean (Mathews) Kline; student, Univ. Calif., Berkeley, 1938-39; m. Verna Marie Taylor (active press woman), Dec. 27, 1952, L.A. Career: pub. rels., Walter E. Kline & Assoc., 1937-54, v.p. 1945-54; pres. and chmn. of bd., Kline Communications Corp., 1954---; pres., Capitol News Service, 1971---; Capitol Radio News Service, The Fred Kline Agency, Inc., The VM Agency, offices in L.A., Sacto., NYC, Chicago, London. Chmn., L.A. Co. Fire Services Commn. 1977---; mem. Fire Commn., L.A., 1961-65; pres., L.A. City Fire & Police Pension Commn. 1965-67; White House Aide to FCDA, Wash. D.C. 1951-57. Writer daily Affairs of State column (calif.); weekly Motor Talk Column (nat.). Worked with CBS on first use of computer in election results coverage, 1952; helped create and implement statewide paramedic rescue pgm.; helped devel. high-rise fire legislation; saved two lives and helped rescue others during Baldwin Hills Dam disaster, 1963. Awarded hon. and official badges and commendations, fire depts. worldwide. AUS. 1940-45. Bd. dirs., Am. Cancer Soc.; Mem.: Am. Mil. Govt. Assn., pres. 1964-65; Am. Pub. Rels. Assn.; Calif. State Peace Officers Assn.; Catholic Inst. Press; Catholic Press Council; Hollywood Advt. Club; Hollywood C. of C.; Internat. Assn. of Fire Chiefs; Internat. Assn. of Police Chiefs; Internat. Footprinters; L.A. Co. Peace Officers Assn.; Nat. Fin. Publicists; Navy League, dir. 1965-66; Pub. Rels. Soc. Am.; Southland Water Commn.; Writers Guild Am.; Am. Legion; Gr. L.A. Press Club; Athletic Club; Publicity Club; Sacto. Press Club, others. Hobby: fire departments; Res.: 6340 Bryn Mawr Dr., L.A., CA 90068; Office: 1741 N. Ivar Ave., Suite 204, L.A., CA 90028.

KLINENBERG, JAMES R.
Physician — Professor
b. June 17, 1934, Chicago; s. Charles and Bernice Klinenberg; A.B., Johns Hopkins Univ., 1955, A.M., Biochem, 1955; M.D., George Wash. Univ. Sch. of Med., 1959; m. Lynn Potash, Oct. 18, 1959, Wash., D.C.; chil.: Susan Beth, b. Sept. 22, 1961; Ellen Debra, b. Apr. 5, 1963; Richard Alan, b. May 4, 1965; Steven Bruce, b. Oct. 22, 1968. Career: Clin. Tng., Johns Hopkins Hosp., 1959-66; staff physician, UCLA Med. Center Hosp., 1966---, also (asst., assoc.) now Prof. of Med., UCLA Sch. of Med., 1966---; attending physician, Wadsworth Hosp., VA Center, L.A., 1966---; assoc. dir., Inst. for Rehabilitation and Chronic Diseases, UCLA, 1970-72. Postdoctoral Fellow, Arthritis Found. 1966-70, Clin. Scholar Awardee, 1970-75. Pres., So. Calif. chpt., Arthritis Found., 1978---. Surgeon, Commissioned Ofcr., U.S. Pub. Health Svc., 1962-64. Reviewer: JCI, Metabolism, Arthritis & Rheumatism, Archives of Internal Med., Am. Journ. of Physiology, Journ. of Lab. and Clin. Med. Diplomates: Nat. Bd. of Med. Examiners, Am. Bd. of Internal Med., Subspec. in Rheumatology. Mem.: Am. Rheumatism Assn.; Am. Fedn. for Clin. Research; So. Calif. Rheumatism Soc.; Western Soc. for Clin. Research; So. Calif. chpt., Arthritis Found.; L.A. Soc. for Internal Med.; Am. Coll. of Physicians; W. Assn. of Physicians; hon. mem. Am. Osteopathic Coll. of Rheumatology. Res.: 709 Sierra Dr., Beverly Hills, CA 90210; Office: Cedars-Sinai Med. Center, 8700 Beverly Blvd., L.A., CA 90048.

KNEETER, GRETCHEN ADAH
Artist
b. Oct. 5, 1915, Indianapolis, Ind.; d. Emil (pianist, composer, conductor) and Helen (Thomas) Seidel; grandau. Ada Willard (Soubrete Black Crook), Oscar Thomas (Thomas, McIntyre & Heath, minstrels); student, Greenbriar Jr. Coll.; Univ. of Syracuse; B.A., Columbia Univ., 1936; Art Students League of N.Y., 1946; m. Herbert L. Kneeter, July 17, 1947; N.Y.C.; chil.: Charles Emil, b. Oct. 3, 1951; Gretchen Helen, Jr., b. Apr. 6, 1959. Career: played vaudeville at 6 years, at 12 played vaudeville with Harry Fox (I'm Just Wild About Harry, theme song); at 14, ballet with Chester Hale in Capital Theatre, N.Y.; stock at Barter Theatre, Abingdon, Va. and Provincetown, Theatre, Cape Cod; 22 pictures in Hollywood under name of Joy Kendall, 1936-43; operated (with husband) Norwich Summer Theatre, Conn., 1947-53; seriously resumed painting as continuing career, 1968---. Recognized as an outstanding primitive painter, in all mediums; art on permanent display at Haggenmacher Galleries, Marina del Rey and Laguna Beach; one woman showings at Westwood Art Center, 1976 and Kirkeby Center, 1978; illustrator of book to benefit the John Tracy Clinic, 1975; paintings chosen as covers for nat. art mags.; award winner, Beverly Hills Art League, 1976, 77, and 78. Served as Nurses Aide in Mil. and Gen. Hosps. during WW II. PTA pres., 1958; Boy Scout and Girl Scout troop leader, 1960-63 and 1967-69; v.p., Brentwood Guild, John Tracy Clin., 1966; v.p., Calif. Art Club, 1977-78. Mem.: Internat. Soc. of Artists; L.A. Art Assn.; Beverly Hills Art League; Calif. Art Club; Westwood Center of the Arts; Alpha Epsilon Phi. Republican, precinct chmn., 1968-69. Rel. Theosophical Soc. Hobbies: gardening, arts & crafts, needlecraft. Home: 400 N. Bowling Green Way, L.A., CA 90049.

KNIGHT, GRANVILLE FRANK
Physician
b. Oct. 12, 1904, NYC; s. Frank Henry and Belle (Brown) Knight; A.B., Dartmouth Coll. 1926; M.D., Columbia Univ. 1930; m. Dorothy Van De Water, 1928 (div.); chil.: Peter Granville, Sara; m. Eileen Hillyer Bonner, Chicago, Nov. 1, 1947; stepson, William H. Clemons. Career: Intern, Presbyterian Hosp., NYC 1930-32; Bellevue Hosp., NYC, 1933-35; pvt. practice med.: (spec. in allergy and ENT) White Plains, N.Y. 1935-48; (spec. in allergy-nutrition), Santa Barbara, Calif. 1948-63; Santa Monica, Calif. 1963---. Staff: Santa Monica Hosp., Bel-Air Mem. Hosp., med. ofcr. U.S. Naval Sea Corps. 1967-69; pres. Price-Pottenger Nutrition Found. 1967---; commr. L.A. Co. Med. Milk Commn. 1968---. Lectr.; ed.-in-chief, Journ. of Applied Nutrition, 1964-67, assoc. ed. 1967-74; Author: articles publ. profl. journs. and lay mags. Mem.: pres. Am. Acad. of Applied Nutrition, 1954-56, 1972-78; fellow, L.A. Soc. of Allergy and Immunology, West Coast Allergy Soc.; Calif. Soc. of Allergists & Immunologists; Calif. Med. Assn.; LACMA; Am. Med. Writers Assn.; N.Y. Acad. of Scis.; Soc. for Clin. Ecology; AMA; Fellow, Am. Coll. of Allergists; Internat. Assn. of Allergists; (hon.) Internat. Coll. of Applied Nutrition; Am. Geriatrics Soc.; Assn. of Am. Phys. and Surgs.: past speaker, House of Dels., del 1956-70; dir. 1960-67; Am. Soc. of Ophthal. and Otolaryngologic Allergy; faculty of Instrs., dir. Inst. of Nutritional Research; pres. Pure Water Assn. of Am. 1960---; fellow, San Diego Research Inst.; diplomate, Am. Bd. of Clin. Immunology and Allergy; Am. Bd. Otolaryngology; chmn. Dist. Food and Nutrition Com. L.A. Co. Med. Assn. 1965-69; Soc. Mayflower Descendants; S.R.; Gen. Soc. Colonial Wars; dir. Navy League of U.S. 1966-68; S.M. Bay Council; Dragon Sr. Soc., Nu Sigma Nu, Phi Kappa Psi. Republican (coms.) Congregationalist. Hobbies: writing, garden, chess. Res.: 810 20th St., No. 3, Santa Monica, CA 90403; Office: 2901 Wilshire Blvd., Suite 345, Santa Monica, CA 90403.

KNOWLES, JAMES ARTHUR
Inventor — Consulting Engineer
b. May 25, 1924, Los Angeles; s. Samuel and Olive Francis (McKnight) Knowles; desc. Nicholas McKnight, Dean of Men, Columbia Univ.; B.S. mech. engring., USC, 1949; m. Nedra Lee Vance, Aug. 29, 1948, Los Angeles; chil.: James Arthur II, b. July 19, 1949; Kathleen Elizabeth (Altieri), b. July 13, 1951; Richard Michael, b. Nov. 18, 1952; Allison Drew, b. Feb. 20, 1957. Career: Powers Regulator Co., 1949-52; Air Conditioning Co., Inc., 1952-56; United Air Conditioning Corp., 1956-66; James A. Knowles & Associates, Inc., 1969---; President, United Air Conditioning Corp., 1966-69; pres., Sheet Metal and Air Conditioning Contractors Nat. Assn., Inc. of So. Calif., 1963-64; trustee, Automated Procedures for Engring. Cons.; dir., Trojan Club, USC, 1965. Holder, several U.S. Patents, frequent lectr. profl. socs. Lt. j.g.,

USNR. Clubs: Jonathan Club, L.A.; University Club, L.A. Presbyterian. Rec.: pvt. pilot; racquetball, squash. Home: 1215 Rodeo Rd., Arcadia, CA 91006; Office: 3303 Wilshire Blvd., L.A., CA 90010.

KNUDSEN, LARRY STEPHEN
Executive Vice President, Independent Colleges
b. May 11, 1936, Ft. Madison, Ia.; s. Orlando S. and Zora (White) Knudsen; A.B. (Sr. class pres. 1957-58), USC 1958; Harvard Univ. Inst. for Edn. Mgmt. 1974; m. Patricia Jean McCallum, L.A., Jan. 27, 1967; chil.: Thomas H., b. Dec. 28, 1968; Lauren J., b. Sept. 9, 1970. Career: Dir. of Support Orgns. 1961-64; dir. Annual Giving, USC, L.A., 1964-66; dir. Spec. Gifts pgm., Calif. Inst. of Tech., Pasa. 1966-68; devel. ofcr. Rand Corp., Santa Monica, 1968-69; exec. v.p. Independent Colls. of So. Calif. 1969---. Secty., Independent Coll. Funds of Am., 1976---. "On Campus" Pgm. adv., KNBC, 1970---. Ensign, Lt. (j.g.) U.S. Pac. Amphibious Force, USN, 1958-61. Awards: 12 Direct Mail Awards, Am. Alumni Council, 1966-67; first prize, IBM Incentive Awards Pgm., Independent Coll. Funds of Am., 1970. Mem.: Acacia, Blue Key, Alpha Kappa Delta, Rotary Club, Jonathan Club. Rec.: skiing, tennis. Res.: 4937 Oakwood Ave., La Canada, CA 91011; Office: 523 W. Sixth St., L.A., CA 90014.

KNUTH, ELDON LUVERNE
University Professor
b. May 10, 1925, Luana, Ia.; s. Alvin W. and Amanda M. (Becker) Knuth; B.S. (with highest distinction), Purdue Univ. 1949; M.S. 1950; Guggenheim Fellow, 1950-52; Ph.D. (cum laude), Calif. Inst. of Tech., 1954; m. Marie O. Parrat, Portuguese Bend, Calif., Sept. 10, 1954 (div.); m. Margaret I. Nicholson, Envino, Dec. 30, 1973; chil.: Stephen B., Dale L., Margot O., Lynette M. Career: Research engr., Jet Propulsion Lab., 1950-53; Aerothermodynamics group leader, Aerophysics Devel. Corp. 1953-56; assoc. research engr., Dept. of Engring., UCLA 1956-58, assoc. prof. 1959-65, prof. 1965---, head. Molecular-Beam Lab. 1961---, head, Chem., Nuclear, Thermal Div. 1963-65; chmn. Energy and Kinetics Dept., 1969-75; cons. to several serospace cos.; gen. chmn. Heat Transfer and Fluid Mechanics Inst. 1959. Patentee. Author: Introduction to Statistical Thermodynamics, publ. McGraw-Hill, N.Y. 1966; contrib. approx. 70 articles to profl. publs. U.S. Army, E.T.O. (1944-45), WW II. Awards: ARS Student Award, von Humboldt Fellow, 1975-76. Mem.: assoc. fellow, Am. Inst. of Aeronautics and Astronautics; Am. Inst. of Chem. Engrs.; Am. Phys. Soc., Combustion Inst., Soc. of Engring. Sci.; Am. Soc. Soc. for Engring. Edn.; AAAS; Sigma Xi; Tau Beta Pi; Gamma Alpha Rho; Pi Tau Sigma; Sigma Delta Chi; Gimlet Club. Res.: 18085 Boris Dr., Encino, CA 91316; Office: Univ. of Calif., Sch. of Engring. and Applied Sci., L.A., CA 90024.

KOH, KEE SENG
Obstetrician --- Gynecologist
b. May 10, 1946, Singapore; s. Cheng Kwang and Swee Huan (Koo) Koh; M.B., B.S. honours, Monash Med. Sch., Melbourne, Aus., 1971; M.R.C.O.G. mem., Royal Coll. of Obstetricians and Gynecologists, U.K., 1976; F.R.C.S. (C) Fellow, Royal Coll. of Surgeons of Canada, 1976; Diplomate, Am. Bd. Obstetrics & Gynecology, 1978; m. Wai Mei Chan (accountant), Aug. 26, 1970, Melbourne; chil.: Karen Leanne, b. Jul. 9, 1974; Jason Robert, b. Oct. 14, 1976. Career: Intern, Kuala Lumpur Gen. Hosp., Malaysia, 1972-73; Resident (ob.-gyn.) Univ. of Manitoba, Winnipeg, Can., 1973-76; Fellowship (perinatology), USC, 1977-78. Teaching fellow, Univ. of Manitoba, 1974-76; clin. instr., USC, 1977-78. Contbr. Am. and British Med. journs.; med. presentations internationally. Rec.: sports, fishing. Home: 2610 Gardi St., Duarte, CA 91010; Office: 1108 S. Baldwin Ave., Arcadia, CA 91006.

KOLAWOLE, LAWRENCE COMPTON
Painter — Sculptor
b. Aug. 20, 1931, Beaumont, Tex.; s. Sam and Marie (Savannah) Compton; art student, Calif. Sch. of Fine Arts (now S.F. Art Inst.); m. Annie R. Daniels, May 2, 1975; chil.: 1st m., T'schad Bonis, Darius Straughter; 2nd m. William Lawrence Compton II. Career: series of travels from New York, 1954, to Munich, 1965, to Nigeria (was given Nigerian surname), 1966-67, Paris residence 1968-74, return to S.F., 1975; exhibited widely in Calif., N.Y. and U.S. traveling shows, 1950-65; exhibited in Munich, Nurenberg, Stuttgart, Kassel, Cologne, Dusseldorf, Amsterdam and Paris, 1965-75; 46 exhibitions including 21 one-man shows; also Master Guilder, antique furniture restorer, wallpaper designer, exhibit arranger. Represented in permanent collections: Leinbach Mus.-Gallery, Munich; Stadt Witten Mus., Insel Film Gmb, Munich; Nigerian Art Assn., Lagos; represented in art publs. and dictionaries and his pub. biography, The Blue Moor by Gisela Frankenburg. Mil.: USAF, 1951-54. Home and Studio: 357-B Scott St., San Francisco, CA 94117.

KOLENDER, WILLIAM BARNETT
Police Chief
b. May 23, 1935, Chicago; s. David Solomon and Esther (Dickman) Kolender; A.A., San Diego City Coll., 1963; B.A. pub. admin., S.D. State Univ., 1964; m. Marilyn Meyer, June 17, 1973, S.D.; chil.: Michael, Myrna, Joy, Randie, Dennis. Career: Police Ofcr., San Diego Police Dept., 1956---; served in all ranks of dept., apptd. Chief of Police, 1976---. Chmn., Integration Task Force, S.D. City Schs.; bd. mem., NCCJ; v.p., Boys' Clubs of S.D., Inc.; v.p., BSA, S.D. Co. Council v.p.; pres., Police Chiefs Div., League of Calif. Cities; mem. Commn. on Peace Ofcr. Standards and Tng.; exec. com., Calif. Police Chiefs; mem. Police Exec. Research Forum; mem. Internat. Assn. of Chiefs of Police. Awards: San Diego's Outstanding Young Man of the Year, 1970; Mayor's Award, 1972; S.D. State Univ. Alumnus of Yr., 1973; Human Rels. Award, Am. Jewish Com., 1975; Good Guy Award, Leukemia Soc., 1977. Mem. Rotary Club. Jewish. Res.: 4035 Tambor Rd., S.D., CA 92124; Office: 801 W. Market St., San Diego, CA 92101.

KOSITCHEK, ROBERT J.
Physician
b. May 30, 1913, Lansing, Mich.; s. Louis M. and Rena Styer Kositchek; father and bro., Richard, both former presidents, National Clothing Assn.; B.A., Univ. Mich., 1935, M.D., 1939; m. Annabelle Israel, 1940, Lansing, Mich.; children: Ellen Lou (Pressman), b. July 5, 1943; Robert Jr., Jr., cinematographer, b. Nov. 30, 1953. Career: Practice of medicine, 1942---; assoc. for 3 years with Dr. Myron Prinzmetal, noted cardiologist; so practice Internal Med., 1946---; research in devel. of atherosclerosis and the influence of lipo proteins prevention of coronary artery disease, 1958---; developed lipo protein analyses for atherosclerosis and the alpha-beta lipoprotein ratio as indicator of advancing atherosclerosis; Asst. Clib. Prof. of Med., UCLA; Pres., Beverly Hills Acad. of Med., 1953-68. Pres., Beverly Hills Br., Los Angeles Med. Assn., 1979-80. Contbg. author four books, contbr. sci. articles in profl. journs. 1st Lt., AUS M.C., 1939-41. Mem.: Phi Delta Epsilon med. frat., Pi Lambda Phi, Hillcrest Country Club, 1943---. Jewish, past pres. Men's Club, Wilshire Blvd. Temple. Hobbies: research, sports. Rec.: golf, swimming, travel. Res.: 117 S. Burlingame Ave., Los Angeles, CA 90049; Office: 9201 Sunset Blvd., Los Angeles, CA 90069.

KOTCHIAN, A. CARL
Former President, Lockheed Aircraft Corp.
b. July 17, 1914, Kermit, N.D.; s. Adolphus C. and Mamie (Bonzer) Kotchian; A.B., Stanford Univ. 1935, M.B.A. 1938; m. Lucy Carr, Long Beach, Calif., Nov. 8, 1940; son, Robert Lawrence, b. Feb. 8, 1947. Career: Acct., Price Waterhouse & Co., L.A., 1936-40; budget mgr., Vega Airplane Co., Burbank, 1941-43; successively budget mgr., chief cost acct., dir. financial operations, Lockheed Aircraft Corp., Burbank, 1943-51; adir. adm., asst. mfg. mgr., v.p.-gen. mgr., Lockheed-Georgia Co., Marietta, Ga. 1951-59; group v.p., Lockheed Aircraft Corp., 1965-67; pres.-dir. 1967-76. Dir., Rich's, Inc., Atlanta, Ga.; dir. Security Pac. Natl. Bank, L.A.; past pres., Assoc. Inds. of Ga. Mem.: Capital City Club, Atlanta, Ga.; L.A. Country Club, Calif. Club. Westwood Presbyterian Ch., L.A. (past trustee). Rec.: tennis. Res.: 283 Bel-Air Rd., L.A., CA 90024.

KOTTKE, FREDERICK E.
Educator -- Economic Consultant
b. Sept. 6, 1926, Menominee, Mich.; s. Edward F. and Minnie Marie Kottke; B.S., Pepperdine Univ., 1951; Ph.D., economics, USC, 1960; m. Lillian Larson, Aug. 25, 1950, Sturgeon Bay, Wis.; chil.: Karin Lee, b. Feb. 27,

1962; Kurt Edward, b. Sept. 22, 1963. Career: Lectr., bus. adminstrn. Pepperdine Univ., 1951-54; asst. prof. economics, USC, 1955-62; prof./dept. Chmn. economics, Calif. State Coll., Stanislaus, 1963---; economic cons., pres., K K Economic Consultants, Turlock ---. Pres., Calif. State Coll. Found., Stanislaus, 1968-70; bd. dir. Emmanuel Med. Center, Turlock, 1973---. Mil.: USNR, 1944-46. Speaker, General Faculty, Calif. State Coll., 1965-66; 1976-77; Haynes Found. Fellow, USC, 1958-60; pres., Omicron Delta Epsilon, USC, 1956-58; Pollogrammatic Soc., Pepperdine Univ., 1951. Contbd. articles for pub. in Highway Finance and General Economics. Mem. Kiwanis Internat. Lutheran, dir. of parish edn. 1957-63. Hobby: fishing. Rec.: boating. Home: 1890 N. Denair Ave., Turlock, CA; Office: California State Coll., Turlock, CA.

KOVALEVSKY, LEONID
    Senior Research Specialist
b. Apr. 16, 1916, Kiev, Russia (U.S. cit. 1955); s. Georg and Sophie (Doroginsky) Kovalevsky; C.E. (structural engring.), Univ. Belgrade, Yugoslavia, 1935-42; Dr.-Ing. Technische Hochschule, Munich, Germ. 1950; m. Danica Kosutich, Munich, Nov. 6, 1952. Career: Design engr., Ger. 1941-50; employee-council, U.S. Post, Dachau, Ger. 1947-50; est. U.S. res. 1950---; design engr., Corbett Thinghir and Assocs., NYC, 1950-53; sr. engr., Erdman Hosley & Co., Syracuse, N.Y. 1953-56; engr. Daniel, Man, Johnson & Mendenhall & Assocs., L.A., 1958-60; sr. engr.-structure research spec., No. Am. Rockwell Corp., Space Div., Downey, 1957-58; sr. research spec. 1961-69, tech. staff, 1969-70; Rockwell Internat. B-1 Div. 1970-77, L.A. Div., 1977. Author: Shell Analysis Manual (900 pgs.), Field Beams Subj. to Lateral Pressure Loadings, Structural Behavior of Inflated Fabric Cylinders Under Various Loading Conditions, 1968; Structural Analysis of Shells, publ. McGraw-Hill; Structural Interaction with Transportation and Handling Systems, and Discontinuity Stresses in Metallic Pressure Vessels, 1971, NASA publs.; contrib. numerous profl. publs. Awards: 4 Tech. Awards, 1967---. Mem.: Am. Soc. C.E., Calif. Eastern Orthodox Greek. Hobbies: collecting sea shells, fishing. Res.: 1024 Via Nogales, Palos Verdes Estates, CA 90274; Office: 1700 E. Imperial Hwy., El Segundo, CA.

KRANZ, THOMAS FRANCIS
    Attorney at Law
b. Mar. 18, 1939, L.A.; s. Frank G. and Eileen (Savage) Kranz; A.B., Stanford Univ., 1959; LL.D., Univ. Calif., Berkeley, 1964; M.A., hist. UCLA, 1973; m. Travis Barton, Dec. 12, 1975, L.A. Career: L.A. Co. Dep. Pub. Defender, 1965-67; assoc., law firm Alexander, Inman & Fine, 1968-70; staff asst., U.S. Sen. John Tunney, 1970-71; mem. law firm, Alexander, Inman, Kravetz, Tanzer, 1971-75, 1976---; L.A. Co. Dep. Dist. Atty. 1975-76; spec. counsel to the Dist. Atty., apptd. by the L.A. Co. Bd. of Supervisors to re-investigate the assassination of Sen. Robt. Kennedy, 1975-76. Lt., j.g., USN, 1959-61; USNR, 1961-69. Admitted to practice before U.S. Supreme Ct. 1971. Mem.: State Bar of Calif., L.A. Co. Bar Assn., mem. Municipal Cts. Com.; v.p., L.A. Master Chorale Assn.; bd. dir., Internat. Forum of World Affairs Council of L.A.; bd. dir., Florence Crittenton Servs.; mem. Kennedy Assocs., St. Johns Hosp., Santa Monica. Catholic. Home: 101 Ocean Ave., Santa Monica, CA 90402; Office: 9720 Wilshire Suite 300, Beverly Hills, CA 90212.

KRASNER, OSCAR JAY
    Professor of Management
b. Dec. 3, 1922, St. Louis, Mo.; s. Ben and Rose (Persov) Krasner; cousin, Dr. Sol Krasner, Univ. of Chcgo. dean of students; B.S. pub. adminstrn., Wash. Univ., St. Louis, 1943; M.A., Univ. of Chicago, 1950; M.S., USC, 1965; Dr. Bus. Admin., USC, 1969; m. Bonnie Kidder, June 4, 1944, St. Louis, Mo.; chil.: Bruce Howard, b. Oct. 30, 1951; Glenn Evan, b. Sept. 25, 1954; Scott Allen, b. Mar. 29, 1956; Steve Leland, b. Nov. 1, 1958; Michael Shawn, b. Jan. 15, 1960; Bettina Jeanine, b. Sept. 14, 1962. Career: mem. staff. exec. office of Secty., U.S. Navy Dept., 1944-56; supv. consult. eng., Bus. Research Corp., 1956-57; flight propulsion div., General Electric Co., 1957-61; space div., North Am. Aviation, 1962-63; corp. dir., Tech. Resources Analysis, No. Am. Rockwell, 1964-70; pres., Solid State Tech. Corp. of Calif., 1968-71; prof. of mgmt., Pepperdine Univ., 1970---; pres., Rensark Associates Associates (consulting firm), 1976---; co-director, Center for Strategic Mgmt., 1978---. Dir., Cincinnati chpt., Soc. for Advancement of Mgmt. Mem.: Acad. of Mgmt.; World Future Soc. Mil.: AUS, 1942-44. Contbr. articles, profl. mags; speaker, profl. socs. on mgmt. Bd. dir., Long Beach Jewish Community Center, 1969. Hobby: writing. Rec.: jogging. Home: 4709 Autry

Ave., Long Beach, CA 90808; Office: Pepperdine Univ., 8035 S. Vermont Ave., L.A., CA.

KREIDER, FRANK B.
    President, Boysen Paint Company
b. May 2, 1917, Fairview, Pa.; s. George and Frances (Bixler) Kreider; B.S., Carnegie Mellon Univ., 1938; M.S., Univ. of Pittsburgh, 1940; m. Helen Hartzel; daus.: Mrs. Gardnar Stevens, Mrs. Kenneth Radler. Career: with De Soto, Inc., 1960-64; Millar Supply, Inc. 1964=72; pres., Boysen Paint Co., 1973---. Lt. Col., AUS Corps of Engrs., 1940-46. Mem.: F&AM, Islam Temple AAONMS. Rec.: golf. Res.: 571 Old Farm Rd., Danville, CA 94526; Office: P.O.B. 23543, Oakland, CA 94623.

KREISSMAN, BERNARD
    University Librarian
b. Jan. 17, 1919, New York, N.Y.; s. Nathan and Sonia Kreissman; B.S.S., Eng. Lit., City Coll. of N.Y., 1948; M.A. Eng. Lit., Columbia Univ., 1949; M.L.S., 1954; Ph.D., Eng. Lit., Univ. of Nebr., 1962; m. Shirley Relis, New York; chil.: Jane; Judith (Bacigalupi); Gregory. Career: trainee, U.S. Army Signal Corps, 1940-43; library tech. asst., New York Public Library, 1948-54; asst. dir. of libraries for humanities, Univ. of Nebraska, Lincoln, 1954-62; chief librarian, City Coll. of N.Y., 1962-74; university librarian, Univ. of Calif., Davis, 1974---. Served USAF and Signal Corps, 1943-46. Author: Pamela-Shamela: A Study of the Criticism, Burlesques, Parodies and Adaptations of Richardson's ''Pamela'', Univ. of Nebr. Press, 1960; Sir Walter Scott's Life of John Dryden, Univ. of Nebr Press, 1963. Hobby: book collecting. Rec.: climbing, hiking. Home: 926 Plum Lane, Davis, CA 95616; Office: 108 Shields Library, Univ. of Calif., Davis, CA 95616.

KREITZER, DAVID MARTIN
    Artist
b. Oct. 23, 1942, Nebr.; s. David and Norma (Buls) Kreitzer; B.S., 1965; M.A., 1967. Career: Profl. painter: rep. by: Maxwell Galleries, S.F., 1967-72; Wortsman Stewart, S.F., 1973-77; Ankrum Gallery, L.A., 1970---; Gryphon Gallery, Denver, 1976-78; Painting Instr., San Jose State Univ., 1968, drawing and painting instr., Acad. of Art Coll., S.F., 1970. Represented in pub. collections incl.: Hirshhorn Found., Wash. D.C.; Santa Barbara Mus.; S.D. Mus.; Barnes-Hind Corp., Calif.; Sheldon Gallery, Univ. of Nebr. Commissions incl.: covers for: Atlantic Mag., Mar. 1970, Woman's Place; Atlantic Mag., Apr. 1970, Dam Outrage; Motorland Mag., Nov. 1970, Calif. and the War. Res.: 1442 Twelfth St., Los Osos, CA 93402.

KREMAR, JANET
    Librarian
b. June 9, 1936, Moorehead, Minn.; d. Minet Lafayne and Anabel (Lee) Dixon; B.A., L.A. State Coll. 1957; D.Litt. (hon.) Hamilton State Univ. (Ariz.), 1973; m. 2nd, Ludwig Leopold Kremar, IV, Calif., Dec. 27, 1964; chil.: Kirk, b. June 12, 1955; Corey, b. June 21, 1957; Kim, b. Mar. 12, 1962; Nancie, b. July 20, 1963. Career: Dir., Tanglewood Sch. for Girls, 1956-58; librn., Riker Labs. 1958-62; lib. Thompson-Ramo-Wooldridge, 1962-64; supr. of Documentation, The Bunker-Ramo Corp., 1964---. Contrib. numerous articles to Spec. Lib. Journ.; ed. OASIS. Mem.: Jeff Corey Players, 1955; Circle Theatre Group, 1956. Awards: Order of Great Green Angel (Girl Scouts), 1975; YWCA L.A. Leadership Award, 1976; Human Resource of U.S. by Am. Bicentennial Research Inst., 1976; Calif. State Figure Skating Championship, 1955; Most Outstanding Drama Student Award, Valley Coll. 1956; Univ. Women's Scholarship, 1955-56; L.A. chpt., Am. Soc. for Inf. Sci. Award, 1970. Mem.: Am. Lib. Assn. 1963---; Calif. Lib. Assn.; Assn. of Computing Mach., 1964---; Nat. Councilor-at-large Am. Soc. for Inf. Sci., 1978---; L.A. City Schs. Career Guidance Bd., 1964---; (trade tech.) L.A. Colls. Adv. Bd.; ofcr. Spec. Libs. Assn. 1965---, pres. 1977-78; pres. Calif. Ind.-Edn. Council, 1968---; bd. dir., 1976---; Am. Fed. of Mineralogists; pres. Simi Valley Art Assn., 1976; Women's Internat. Bowling Congress; Amateur Ath. Union; Pi Delta Pi, Alpha Psi Omega, Alpha Mu Gamma, Sierra Club. Episcopalian. Hobbies: art, mineralogy. Rec.: skating, skiing, sailing, travel. Res.: 1529 Kane Ave., Simi Valley, CA; Office: 31717 La Tienda Dr., Westlake Village, CA 91359.

KRING, CHARLES UDELL
Business Owner
b. Aug. 31, 1910, Belle Rive, Ill.; s. Charles Harvey and Carolyn (Schoenmetzler) Kring; B.S. (C.E.), Univ. of Ill., 1932; M.S., 1939, Ph.D., 1948; m. Marguerite F. Kay, Wash. D.C., Aug. 25, 1945; chil.: Meredith Kay, b. July 3, 1946; Judith Leslie, b. Sept. 15, 1947; Gary Kevin, b. Aug. 4, 1949. Career: Field engr., S.F.-Oakland Bay Bridge, 1934-35; engr. Golden Gate Bridge, 1936-37; supt. Ben Hur Constr. Co., St. Louis and Indianapolis, 1937-38; bridge engr., Parsons, Brinkerhoff, Hall & Macdonald, cons. engrs., N.Y., 1941-42; chief structural engr., Bermuda Architect-Engrs., Bermuda, 1942-43; cons. engr., Charles U. Kring Assocs., S.F.-San Jose, 1946---; pres. Kring Constr. Co., Inc. 1948---: owner-mgr., Foxworthy Shopping Center, San Jose, 1957---; owner, Kaydell Angus Farm, Los Gatos, 1959---. Author: Selection of Weapons & Estimation of Force Requirements for Aerial Bombardment, 1947. Lectr., Air Univ., Maxwell Field. Scientific cons. (Col.) Hdqrs., 8th Air Force, Eng. 1943-45; sons U.S. Strategic Bombing Survey, London, Tokyo, 1945-46, WW II. Awards: Medal of Freedom, 1945; Mem.: Am. Soc. Civil Engrs., Tau Beta Pi, Alpha Kappa Lambda; Clubs: Commonwelath, San Jose Country. Hobby: photog. Rec.: golf, skiing, riding. Res.: 17101 Hicks Rd., Los Gatos, CA; Office: 1425 Foxworthy Ave., San Jose, CA 95118.

KROES, ROBERT J.
University Administrator
b. Dec. 3, 1935, Racine, Wis.; s. Stephen and Ann (Dolata) Kroes; B.Sc., ELE1, Marquette Univ., 1960; M.A., econ., Univ. of Santa Clara, 1965; m. Katherine Zukowski, Jan. 25, 1958; Milwaukee, Wis.; chil.: Elizabeth, b. Jan. 25, 1959; R. Christopher, b. Feb. 18, 1960; Lisa, b. Aug. 17, 1962; Andrew, b. Aug. 17, 1962; Mark, b. Aug. 11, 1963; Kevin, b. Dec. 25, 1964; Amy,b. Aug. 6, 1969; Michael, b. Dec. 8, 1971. Career: Engr., 1960-69: field of space satellite and inertial guidance tech., computer systems, also Mgmt., Econ. Cons.: Univ. Adminstr., 1969---: now assoc. vice chancellor, UC, Santa Barbara; lectr. on computer information systems profl. orgns. Mem.: Am. Econ. Assn.; dir. C. of C.; Los Ninos, dir. 1975; dir. Girls Club, 1975-78; mem. Airport Advis. com. Home: 994 St. Mary's Lane, Santa Barbara, CA 93111; Office: Univ. of Calif., Santa Barbara, CA 93106.

KRUEGER, ROBERT BLAIR
Attorney at Law
b. Dec. 9, 1928, Minot, N.D.; A.B., Univ. Kans.; 1949; J.D., Univ. Mich., 1952; postgrad. Univ. So. Calif., 1960-65. Career: admitted to Kans. bar, 1952, Calif. bar, 1955; practiced in L.A., 1955---; assoc. firm O'Melveny & Myers, 1955-59; partner firm Blair & Krueger, 1959-61; partner firm, Nossaman, Krueger & Marsh and predecessors, 1961---; adj. prof., nat. res. law, USC; lectr. in field. Fellow, USC, Inst. Marine and Coastal Studies; mem. Calif. Gov's. Adv. Commn. on Ocean Resources, 1966-68; adv. council, Inst. Marine Resources, Univ. Calif., 1966-74; Calif. Adv. Com. on Marine and Coastal Resources, 1968-73; chmn., 1970-73; mem. Nat. Security Council Adv. Com. on Law of Sea, 1972---; chmn. subcom. internat. law and relations, 1972---; mem. U.S. Del. to UN Seabeds Com., 1973; U.S. Del. to 3d UN Law of Sea Conf., 1974---; mem. com. visitors Univ. Mich. Law Sch. Fellow Am. Bar Found.; Mem. Am. (Spec. Com. on Energy Law), Internat., L.A. Co. (chmn. real property sect. 1961-65, trustee, 1972-74) bar assns.; Am. Soc. Internat. Law; Internat. Law Assn.; Law of the Sea Com., 1972---; World Assn. Lawyers, Barristers Club, Tau Kappa Epsilon, Phi Alpha Delta. Asst. editor Mich. Law Rev., 1951-52; ed., L.A. Bar Bull., 1961-63; bd. editors Calif. Bar Journ., 1963-66, 69-74; project dir., Study Outer Continental Shelf Lands of the U.S., 1968, for the Public Land Law Review Comm.; U.S. Options in International Petroleum Affairs, 1975, Fed. Energy Advis.; contbr. numerous articles on offshore and natural subjects to profl. publs. Res.: 501 Vallombrosa Dr., Pasadena, CA 91107; 9828 La Jolla Farms Rd., La Jolla, CA 92037; Office: 445 S. Figueroa St., 30th Flr., L.A., CA 90071.

KRUPP, EDWIN C.
Director, Griffith Observatory
b. Nov. 18, 1944, Chicago; s. Edwin F. and Florence Ann (Olander) Krupp; B.A., Pomona Coll., 1966; M.A., UCLA, 1968, Ph.D., 1972; m. Robin Rector, Dec. 31, 1968, Claremont; son, Ethan Hembree, b. Apr. 12, 1975. Career: Instr. astronomy, El Camino Coll., 1969-74; USC, 1974; Univ. of Calif. Ext., 1975---, mem. bd. dirs., Summer Sci. Pgm., 1977---; Curator, Griffith

Observatory, 1972-74; acting dir., 1974-76; dir., 1976---; ed.-in-chief., Griffith Observer, monthly mag.; lectr., cons. on archaeoastronomy and pseudosci. fads and notions; cons. for ednl. TV, L.A. Co. Supt. of Schs. 1973---; on-camera host, Project Universe, public TV series on astronomy; mem. faculty of Sci. at Sea, TSS Fairsea "Voyage to Darkness" to great eclipse in no. Pacific, Oct. 12, 1977; extensive internat. travels to 150 ancient and prehistoric sites. Author: In Search of Ancient Astronomies, Doubleday, 1978. Office: Griffith Observatory, 2800 E. Observatory Rd., L.A., CA 90027.

KUBLY, DONALD RAYMOND
President, Art Center College of Design
b. Nov. 14, 1917, L.A.; s. Fred and Edna May (Stoner) Kubly; B.F.A., 1964; m. Sara Francis Eager, Sept. 13, 1947, Pasadena; sons, Jon Frederick, b. Apr. 8, 1953; David Scott, b. Dec. 2, 1954; Rod Robert, b. July 2, 1961. Career: Sr. art dir., N.W. Ayer & Son Advt. Agency, Phila., 1948-63; dir., Art Center Coll. of Design, 1963-69, pres. and dir., 1969---. Dir., Am. Inst. of Graphic Arts; bd. mem., L.A. Music Center. Served to Maj., USAF, WW II; fighter/bomber pilot, 82 missions. Res.: 215 La Vereda Rd., Pasadena, CA 91105; Office: 1700 Lida St., Pasadena, CA 91103.

KUCHEL, THOMAS H.
Attorney at Law
b. Aug. 15, 1910, Anaheim; s. Mr. and Mrs. Henry Kuchel; father was pioneer newspaper publ., owner-ed., Anaheim Gazette (48 yrs.); grandson of Conrad Kuchel from Ger. 1830s, one of orig. settlers who founded City of Anaheim, 1859; ed. pub. schs. Anaheim; grad. USC 1932. LL.D., 1935; (hon.) LL.D.: Chapman Coll., Tufts Univ., Boston, USC 1963; Univ. of Santa Clara, Univ. of Pac. 1964; Univ. of Judaism, 1965; Univ. of Calif., 1969; m. Betty Mellenthin; dau.: Karen. Career: admitted to Calif. State Bar, 1935; pvt. practice law, Orange Co. 1935; elected to State Assembly from Orange Co. 1936, re-elected 1938; elected to State Senate 1940, 44 (in absentia); apptd. State Controller by Gov. Earl Warren, Feb. 11, 1946; elected Nov. 1946, re-elected 1950; apptd. U.S. Senator from Calif., by Gov. Earl Warren, Dec. 22, 1952, elected, 1954, re-elected (sr. Senator, Calif.), Nov. 1956-69; U.S. Senate delegate to the Paris Internat. Parliamentary Conf. of Nations comprising NATO; leader, civ. rights; sponsor, Alaska and Hawaii Statehood; asst. Repub. Leader, "Whip," 86th, 87th, 88th 89th Congresses; Partner, Wyman, Bautzer, Rothman & Kuchel law firm, 1969---. Officer, USNR, 1942-45, WW II. Mem.: Am. Legion, Scottish Rite Mason, Elks, Phi Kappa Phi, Phi Delta Phi, Phi Kappa Psi, Native Sons of the Golden West; chmn. Repub. State Central Com. 1940. Episcopalian. Res.: 520 Vick Pl., Beverly Hills, CA 90210; Offices: Two Century Plaza, 14th Flr., L.A., CA 90067; also 600 New Hampshire Ave., N.W., Wash., D.C. 20037; also 31 Quai Anatole-France, 75007, Paris, France.

KUKLIN, JEROME
Manufacturing Company Executive
b. Aug. 3, 1933, Chicago; s. Jacob and Rose Kuklin; B.S., Bus. Admin., Roosevelt Univ., 1956; m. Barbara Kuklin, Feb. 9, 1958; chil.: Steven H., Perry C., Adam L. Career: Mgr. mktg., Universal Screw Co., Chicago, 1962-65; asst. to pres. Champion Screw Co., Chicago, 1965-66; v.p. Ken Industries, Santa Fe Springs, Calif., 1966-67; chmn. bd., pres. Alvo Fasteners, Inc., L.A. 1967-72; pres., chmn. bd. Amalgamated Fasteners, Inc., Los Angeles, 1972---. Mem.: Chicago Bolt, Nut and Screw Assn.; Nat. Sales Mgrs. Assn.; Nat. Office Mgrs. Assn.; L.A. Fastener Assn. (founder, pres. 1967-69). Office: 3250 Union Pacific Ave., L.A., CA 90023.

KURTZ, FRANK ALLEN, JR.
Real Estate Executive
b. Sept. 9, 1911, Davenport, Ia.; s. Dr. Frank Allen, Sr. and Dora (Fenton) Kurtz; grandson of Daniel Webster Boone Kurtz, Greek and Latin scholar, pres. and rebuilder, Univ. of Mo.; founder, Montgomery Coll., Mo.; pres. Stephens Coll.; ed. B.S., B.A., USC 1937; USAF Primary and Advanced Flying Schs., Randolph and Kelly, Tex. 1938; grad. Armed Forces Staff Coll., Norfolk, Va. 1947; m. Grace Margaret (Margo) Rogers (noted author, My Rival The Sky, Cosmopolitan series, publ. 1945), Omaha, Nebr., May 20, 1939; dau. Swoosie (one of nations most highly publicized babies at birth; actress, only Am. Stu. London Acad. repertory theater, USA), b. Sept. 6, 1944. Career: Comm. 2nd Lt., USAF, 1939; comdr. Kirtland A.F. B-29 Bomber Base, Albuquerque, N.M., aide-de-camp, personal pilot to Comdg. Gen., S.W. Pac.; dir. opns. 1st Bomber, 2nd

A.F.; spec. asst. to Comdg. Gen., Air Transport Command; chief. Civil Air Plans-Policy Div., Hdqrs., USAF, Pentagon; chief, Korean Plans-Policy Div., Hdqrs., Far East Command; comdr. Strategic Air Command's No. 1 Jet Bomber Wing, ret. 1959. V.p., W.M. Garland & Co., L.A., 1959-70. Author: (collab.) Queens Die Proudly (best seller, Book-of-the-Month in unprecedented 2 successive issues, Readers Digest), publ. 1943. Awards: Named All-American Citizen; named Most decorated A.F. pilot of WW II; 25 decorations incl. 3 Silver Stars, 3 Distinguished Flying Crosses, 6 Pres. Unit Cits.; pilot of historic B-17 bomber, The Swoose, now in Smithsonian Inst.; credit with saving Pres. Lyndon B. Johnson's life as Congressman on wartime mission aboard The Swoose; Pres. Cit. for Radar Bombing Record, No. 1 Jet Bomber Wing; est. World's Jr. Land-plane Speed Record and 3 Flag Can.-Mex. Horsepower Record (flew record breaking flight carrying good will documents from Calif. Gov. to Pres. of Mex. to White House); Distinguished Serv. Medal by U.S. Jr. C. of C. as "one of America's outstanding young men"; winner, Am. Natl.-Internat. Diving Championships, Paris, Melbourne, London, Bombay, Chiacgo, Honolulu; U.S. Olympic Games; Asa V. Call Achievement Trophy (awarded annually to alumnus of USC who has brought greatest hon. to his Alma Mater). Mem.: (Charter) co-founder, L.A. Club; Silver Dollar Club; (hon. life) L.A. Ath. Club; Quiet Birdman; Daedalians, Blue Key, Skull and Dagger, Sigma Chi, Alpha Eta Rho. Republican. Protestant. Res.: 4404 Placidia, Toluca Lake, No. Hollywood, CA.

L

LA CLAUSTRA, VERA BERNEICIA
Poet — Author
b. Apr. 2, Baker, Ore.; d. Edmon Treseia and Nellie Ann (Vessey) Derrick (desc. Ore. Trail Dickerson, Derrick and Harrow pioneers); ed. grad. H.S. and Sch. of Cosmetology; m. Dr. Gunnar Benson, San Jose; m. 2d. Seraphin La Claustra, Oakland, Apr. 15, 1933; son, William Hugh Benson; stepdau. Mrs. David (Eleanor) Baird. Career: Writer, numerous poems publ.: Wash. Eve. Star, Denver Post, Carmel Pine Cone-Cymbol, Hartford Times, Oakland Tribune, S.F. Examiner, Hartford Courant, Shasta Chronicle, Desert Mag. Anthologies, Rubert Publ. Anthologies, Brit. and Am. Authors and Bouquets of Poems, Rome, Italy; poem group publ. The Am. Mosaic Anthology, and The Spring Anthology, Mitre Pres., Eng. 1971. Author: (3 books) By the Cool Waters, 1953; The Purple Wheel, 1954; collected poems 1971; 8 poems publ. Poet, India; poem publ. in Masters of Modern Poetry, Italy, 1975. Awards: Certificates of Merit: poem, Not I (publ. in Poet, India); Who's Who in Poetry, London; and World Poetry Society, others. Mem.: Ladies Aux. of VFA; Avalon World Arts Academy; Calif. Fedn. of Chaparral Poets; Am. Poetry League; World Poetry Soc. Intercontinental; Centro Studie Scambi Internozional, Rome. Hobby: watercolors and oil paintings. Res.: Mar Monte Apts., 3840 Howe St., Oakland, CA 94611.

LACY, PETER DEMPSEY
Electronics Company Founder
b. Dec. 6, 1920, Jacksonville, Fla.; s. Francis P. and Nina E. (Wray) Lacy; B.S.E.E., Univ. of Fla., 1942, M.S., 1947, Ph.D., Stanford Univ., 1952; chil.: Eamon, b. Dec. 25, 1948; Bridget Minty, b. May 20, 1951. Career: Instr., Univ. of Fla., 1942; research asst. and Sperry Fellow (1949), Stanford Univ., 1946-48; cons. Varian Assocs., 1949; Prof. Engr., Hewlett Packard, 1950-58, cons., 1959; founder, bd. chmn., Wiltron Co. 1960---. Contbr. to Ency. of Electronics, 1962, holder 10 patents. Fellow, IEEE, 1967, chmn. S.F. sect. 1961-62; dir., S.F. Bay sect., Am. Astronautical Soc. 1956-64. Served Ensign thru Lt., USNR. Mem.: Phi Kaypa Pi, Sigma Xi, Sierra Club. Republican. Unitarian. Hobbies: anthropology, nat. hist. Res.: 111 N. Rengstorff Ave., No. 24, Mtn. View, CA 94043; Office: 325 E. Middlefield Rd., Mtn. View, CA 94043.

LADD, ALAN WALBRIDGE, JR.
President, Twentieth Century-Fox Pictures
b. Oct. 22, 1937, L.A.; s. Alan Walbridge and Marjorie (Harrold) Ladd; m. Patricia Ann Beazley, Aug. 30, 1959, L.A.; chil.: Kelli Ann, b. Sept. 29, 1961; Tracy, b. Oct. 13, 1963; Amanda, b. Nov. 14, 1972. Career: Entered motion picture indus as agent for CMA; entered film prodn. 1968: films prod. 1969-70: Walking Stick; A Severed Head; Tam Lin; 1970-71: Villian Zee & Co.;

exec. prod. of Nightcomers; 1972-73: prod. Fear Is The Key; with Twentieth Century-Fox Film Corp., L.A., 1973---: Sr. V.P. Worldwide Prodn., 1974, Pres., Twentieth Century—Fox Pictures, 1976---. USAF, 1961-63. Res.: 706 N. Elm Dr., Beverly Hills, CA; Office: 10201 W. Pico Blvd., L.A., CA 90035.

LADECK, FLORENCE M.
City Official
b. Mar. 11, 1929, Laverne, Okla.; d. Sidney and Margaret (Elder) Johnston; m. Carl M. Ladeck, Feb. 14, 1958, Auburn, Calif.; chil.: Susan Elaine (Larkins); Lynette Kay (Merrill); Stephen Richard. Career: Secty., Placer Co. Assessor, Auburn, 1947-52, 1956-58; clerk, City of Auburn, 1961-64; elected City Clerk, City of Auburn, 1964---. Mem.: Soroptimist Internat., pres. 1972-73. Presbyterian. Hobbies: crocheting, cake decorating. Res.: 145 Orrin Dr., Auburn, CA; Office: 1103 High St., Auburn, CA 95603.

LaFOND, EUGENE CECIL
Oceanography Consultant
b. Dec. 4, 1909, Bridgeport, Wash.; s. William and Bessie (Imes) LaFond; A.B., S.D. State Univ.; D.Sc., Andhra Univ.; m. Katherine Gehring, Sept. 4, 1935, Steamboat Springs, Colo.; chil.: William G., b. Oct. 26, 1941; Robert E., b. Sept. 8, 1944. Career: oceanographer, Scripps Inst. of Oceanography, 1933-41; supr. oceanographer, Navy Labs. in S.D., 1941-68; Prof. of Oceanography, Andhra Univ., 1952-56; cons., Naval Undersea Center, 1968-80; gen. mgr., LaFond Oceanic Consultants, 1968---; secty., gen., Internat. Assn. for the Physical Scis. of the Ocean, 1970---; Dep. Dir. Office of Oceanography UNESCO Paris, 1963-64; Sr. Sci. on USS SKATE to North Pole, 1958; Sr. Sci. on NAGA Expedition to Gulf of Thailand and South China Sea, 1960; Chief Sci. on Internat. Indian Ocean Exped., 1962-63. Author two books and 200+ sci. articles on various phases of oceanography, 1948---. Res.: 4505 Santa Cruz Ave., S.D., CA 92107; Office: P.O.B. 7325, San Diego, CA 92107.

LA FORCE, JAMES CLAYBURN, JR.
University Dean
b. Dec. 28, 1928, San Diego; s. J.C., Sr. and Beatrice La Force; A.B., San Diego State, 1951; M.A., UCLA, 1958; Ph.D. (economics), 1962; (Hon.) Ph.D., Social Sci., Universidad Francisco Marroquin, Guatemala, 1976; m. Barbara Lea Latham, Sept. 30, 1952, Alpine, Calif.; chil.: Jessica, b. 1961; Allison, b. 1963; Joseph, b. 1969. Career: Asst. Prof. of Economics, San Fernando Valley State Coll., 1960-62; asst. prof. of economics, UCLA, 1962-67; assoc. prof. of economics, 1967-71; Professor of Economics, 1971-78; Chmn., Dept. of Economics, 1969-78; Dean, Grad. Sch. of Mgmt., UCLA, 1978---; chmn. and chief exec. officer, The Found. for Research in Economics and Education, 1971---. Office: Grad. Sch. of Mgmt., UCLA, Los Angeles, CA 90024.

LAHANIER, WILLIAM A.
Attorney at Law
b. Feb. 2, 1906, S.F.; s. Camille and Esther (Werner) Lahanier; ed. grad. Pasa. H.S. 1926; LL.B., S.F. Law Sch. 1930; m. June Massoni. Career: gen. law practice, 1930---, spec. trial lawyer, 1945---. Bd. dirs.-exec. v.p., Woodlawn Memorial Park; bd. dirs. Calif. Interment Assn., State pres. 1973; pres., House of Fans, S.F.; State Cemetery Bd. (14 yrs.), v.p. 1974; farmer. Naval Ofcr.-comdr., 1940-45; WW II. Mem.: Masonic Lodge, Shrine; Grand Chancellor of Calif., Knights of Pythias, 1939-40; Order of DeMolay; Calif., S.F. Bar Assns.; S.F. Civil Serv. Comm. (pres. several terms), 1948-58; Calif. Rice Growers Assn.; pres Civic League 1974; Clubs: Comml., Exch., Metropolitan, Pres of S.F., Presidio Ofcr's. and Naval Ofcrs'. Clubs. Secty. Young Republicans (1930s); S.F. sponsor, Mayor Elmer E. Ribonson, Supvs., many others incl. Governor's campaigns. Christian. Hobbies: amateur radio, aquatic, golf. Res.: 1310 Jones St., S.F., 94109; Office: 982 Post St., S.F., CA 94109.

LAKE, ALBERT CHARLES
Library Director
b. July 21, 1912, Vancouver, B.C., Can.; s. Albert James and Daisy (Ryder) Lake; ed. B.A. (1st class hons. Eng. lang., lit.), Univ. Brit. Columbia, 1938; Certificate in Librarianship, Univ. Calif.; m. Dorothea Olive Mackintosh, L.A., Nov. 4, 1939; sons: Albert Keith, b. Aug. 10, 1941; Donald Sydney, b. Feb. 12, 1944; Michael Edward, b. Feb. 13, 1948. Career: Librarian, Kern Co. Free Lib. 1939-41; co. lib. Trinity Co. Free Lib., 1941-43; co. lib. Sacto. Co. Free Lib. 1943-47; lib.

dir., Riverside Pub. Lib. and Riverside Co. Free Lib., 1947---. Contrib. articles to profl. literature. Mem.: pres. Pub. Lib. Sect. Calif. Lib. Assn.; pres. Pub. Lib. Execs. Assn. of So. Calif.; Rotary Club, 1941---; Riverside Breakfast Forum, 1950---; Town and Gown. Republican. Sr. warden, All Saints Episcopal Ch. Hobby: book collecting. Rec.: camping. Res.: 4265 Houghton Ave., Riverside, 92501; Office: Riverside Public Library, Riverside, CA 92502.

LAKOFF, SANFORD ALLAN
Professor of Political Science
b. Bayonne, N.J.; s. Herman and Gertrude (Robins) Lakoff; B.A., Brandeis Univ., 1953; M.A., Harvard Univ., 1955; Ph.D., Polit. Sci., 1959; m. Evelyn Schleifer, June 4, 1961, Mohegan Lake, N.Y. Career: instr., asst. prof. of Gov., Harvard Univ., 1958-65; assoc. prof., prof. of polit. sci. N.Y. State Univ., Stony Brook, 1965-67; prof. of polit. sch., Univ. of Toronto, 1967-74; prof. of polit. sci. and dept. chmn. Univ. of Calif., San Diego, 1974---. Dir., Holobeam, Inc., 1967-78; mem. Calif. Policy Seminar, 1977---; chmn. Advis. Panel, KPBS-TV series on sci. and pub. policy, 1977---; elected to Council of Am. Polit. Sci. Assn. 1977-80. Author of scholarly books, contbr. articles to profl. journs. and newspapers. Hobby: collecting popular sheet music. Res.: 3510 Dove Ct., San Diego, CA 92103; Office: Dept. of Polit. Sci., UCSD, La Jolla, CA 92093.

LA LIBERTE, JOSEPH E.
Mortgage Company Executive
b. Dec. 5, 1922, Chicago; s. Joseph W. and Elizabeth (Lamarre) La Liberte; stu., No. Park Jr. Coll., Chicago, real estate ext. studies, Univ. Calif., Riverside; m. Jeanne T. Miller, Sept. 18, 1948, Hollywood; chil.: Mary Janine, b. June 27, 1949; Dennis R., b. June 21, 1952; Lawrence M., b. Jan. 26, 1955; David E., b. Sept. 30, 1957. Career: service, USN and USAF, 1942-62; sales mgr., Brinkerhoff Realty, Riverside, 1961-63; asst. mgr., Advance Mortgage Corp., Riverside, 1963-65; Orange Co. Area Mgr., 1965-68; with Calif. Mortgage Service, 1968---, now Sr. V.P. ---. Conducts FHA/VA seminars throughout state, guest speaker on real estate financing for Real Estate Bds. Past pres., Orange Co. Mortgage Bankers, mem. So. Calif. and Calif. Mortgage Bankers; chrtr. pres., Toastmasters Internat., Island of Bermuda, 1958. Catholic. Res.: 74-487 Candlewood, Palm Desert, CA 92260; Office: 73-255 El Paseo, Palm Desert, CO 92260.

LAMB, WILLIAM ARTHUR SHERMAN
Physicist
b. Oct. 2, 1921, Fredericktown, Mo.; s. Arthur Earl and Beulah (Sherman) Lamb; A.B., Univ. of Calif., Berkeley, 1947; m. Barbara Freeman Bailey, Del Monte, Calif.; Aug. 10, 1941; chil.: Diana Mae (Lamb) Barkley, b. Mar. 27, 1943; Ann Marie, b. Feb. 24, 1948; W.A. Sherman, b. Apr. 11, 1950. Career: Physicist Naval Radiological Def. Lab., S.F., 1947-50; physicist Calif. Research and Devel. Corp., Livermore, 1950-54; physicist, Lawrence Radiation Lab., Univ. of Calif., Livermore, 1954---; cons. Stanford Research Inst.; cons. F.W. Dodge Corp.; tech. adv., U.S. Del., 2nd Atoms for Peace Conf., Geneva, Switz. 1958. Engring. ofcr., U.S. Maritime Serv. (1942-46), WW II. Mem.: Am. Physical Soc. 1948---. Hobby: photog. Res.: 1683 Cervato Circle, Alamo, CA 94507; Office: P.O.B. 808, Livermore, CA 94550.

LAMBOURNE, RICHARD W.
Financial Analyst
b. June 13, 1910, Salt Lake City; s. Ernest A. and Belle (Weiler) Lambourne; B.A., Univ. of Ut., 1931; M.B.A., Harvard Univ., 1933; m. Laura McGhie, 1933, Salt Lake City; chil.: David E., b. 1936; Kenneth R., b. 1939; Catherine (Engel), b. 1943. Career: Partner, Dodge & Cox, Investment Mgrs., S.F., 1936-56; treas. The Ford Found., N.Y. 1956-61; V.P., I.S.I. Corp., S.F., 1961-69; sr. v.p., Crocker Nat. Bank, S.F., 1969-77; pres. Crocker Investment Mgmt. Corp., S.F., 1974-77; sr. v.p., McMorgan & Co., Palo Alto, 1977---. Dir. FRS Assocs., Menlo Park, 1977---; raw materials procurement spec. 1942-46. Mem.: Chartered Fin. Analyst, 1963---, council of Examiners, 1970---; Security Analysts of S.F., pres. 1950; N.Y. Soc. of Security Analysts; Bond Club of S.F.; Fin. Analysts Fedn., pres. 1952, dir. 1950-56. chmn. Investment Analysis Standards Bd. 1974-78, assoc. ed., Fin. Analysts Journ. 1965-70; recipient: distinguished serv. award, 1976; and Graham & Dodd Award, 1962; Sigma Chi; Alpha Kappa Psi; Phi Kappa Phi. Clubs' Spyglass Hill Golf, Pebble Beach; Stanford Golf, Menlo Country, Woodside. L.D.S. ch. Hobby:

gardening. Rec.: golf. Res.: 385 Westridge Dr., Portola Valley, CA; Office: 100 Welch Rd., Palo Alto, CA 94304.

LANCASTER, PEGGY WILSON
Advertising Executive
b. Reading, Pa.; d. Ray L. and Ella F. Wilson; B.A., Univ. of Pa.; m. William W. Lancaster, Ardmore, Pa. (dec.). Career: writer, radio-TV special events, news dept., writer-prod. syndicated dramatic series, WCAU, WCAU-TV, Phila. 1954-56; copywriter, Arndt, Preston, Chapin, Lamb & Keen, Inc., Phila 1956; head radio-TV Dept. 1957-58; sr. copywriter, Henry J. Kaufman & Assocs., Wash. D.C., 1958-60; newscaster, World-Wide English Dept., U.S. Inf. Agcy. 1958-60; copywriter, MacManus, John & Adams, L.A. 1963-66; sr. copywriter, Gumpertz, Bentley, Fried, Scott, L.A. 1966, assoc. creative dir. 1969, v.p. 1971-76. Principal, Scott Lancaster Mills Atha, 1976---. Awards: Radio Adv. Bur., one of Ten Best Radio Campaigns, 1955; first woman newscaster, World-Wide Dept. of Voice of Am., 1958-60; 11 Lulus (1st place awards in 13 Western States, Alaska, Hawaii, Western Can.) by L.A. Adv. Women, 1965-73; 1st place, Assn. Ind. Advs. 1968, 74; Internat. Broadcast Awards, 1st place, 1969; 2nd place, 1970; Inst. of Outdoor Adv., 71 Best of 71; 6 certs. of Merit, Art Dirs. of L.A. 1971, 72, 73, 74; Belding Award, 1973; Am. Adv. Fed.: Best in the West, 2nd place and 3 Cits. of Excellence, 1973, Natl. Addy Awards and 2 Cits of Excellence, 1973, Best in the West sweepstakes runner-up 1974, Best in the West Cit. of Excellence, 1974; Natl. Addy Award, 2 Certs of Excellence, 1974; Adv. Woman of Yr., (one of 7), by Am. Adv. Fed. 1973; listed Foremost Women in Communications. Mem.: Phila Adv. Women, 1950-56; AFTRA, 1954-58; L.A. Adv. Women, 1963---; com. chmn. 1972; bd. dirs. 1973; Women in Communications, 1972---; com. Profl. Women, So. Calif.-Hollywood Bowl Assn. 1972---. Presbyterian. Hobbies: reading, painting, collecting antique furniture, antique dolls. Office: Scott Lancaster Mills Atha, 2049 Century Park East, L.A., CA 90067.

LANDE, JAMES A.
Research Institute Executive
b. Oct. 2, 1930, Chicago, Ill.; s. S. Theodore and Helen C. Lande; B.A., Swarthmore Coll., Pa., 1952; J.D., Columbia Univ. Law Sch., N.Y., 1955; chil.: Sylvia D., b. June 8, 1962; Rebecca Susanne, b. Mar. 13, 1961. Career: Attorney, office of Chief Counsel, NASA-Ames Research Center, Mountain View, 1967-70; house counsel, Syntex Corp., Palo Alto, 1970-73; mgr., Contracts Dept., Electric Power Research Inst., Palo Alto, 1973---; also lectr., Univ. of Santa Clara Sch. of Law (courses in Govt. Contracts, Adminstrv. Law, Fed. Jurisdiction), 1968---. Defense Counsel, AUS, 1955-57; awarded certificate of achievement, Judge Advocate Gen., Hdqtrs. AUS, Europe. Adj. prof., Univ. of S.F. Sch. of Law, 1972-73; legal editor & research atty., Matthew Bender and Co., 1967. Publs.: Uncle Sam's Right to Damages for Delay in the Wonderland of Govt. Contracting, Santa Clara Lawyer; book review, Basic Techniques of Pub. Contracts Practice, S.C. Law Review. Pres., Syntex Fed. Credit Union, 1971-72. Mem.: Calif. Bar, N.Y. Bar, Fed. district and appellate cts. Hobbies: piano playing, tennis. Home: 1330 33rd Ave., San Francisco, CA 94122; Office: 3412 Hillview Ave., Palo Alto, CA 94303.

LANDE, ROBERT FRANCIS
Orthodontist — Civic Leader
b. Feb. 2, 1921, St. Paul, Minn.; s. Isaac and Nell Lande; ed. grad. San Pedro H.S. 1939; Compton Jr. Coll. 1941; D.D.S., Univ. of Calif. 1945; D.D.Sc., Univ. of Wash. 1950; m. Regina Johnson, San Pedro, Calif., Aug. 13, 1945; chil.: Regina L., b. June 15, 1946; Charles R., b. June 11, 1951; Kristine M., b. May 11, 1953. Career: gen. practice, dentistry, San Pedro, 1947-49, orthodontia, 1950---; instr. USC, Sch. of Orthodontia, 1952---; founder, dental staff, San Pedro Community Hosp., 1960. Speaker before numerous profl. groups on Orthodontic Treatments, Orthodontic Retainer (developed spec. type retainers). Contrib. articles to profl. journs. Presidio, S.F.; Maj. U.S. Army Hosp., Dental Dept., Salsburg, Austria, WW II. Mem.: past pres., Edward H. Angle Soc. of Orthodontists; dir.-edn. chmn., Pac. Coast Soc. of Orthodontists; Am. Bd. of Orthodontists; Am. Assn. of Orthodontists; (charter) chmn., Ill.-Wash. Orthodontic Stu. Group, 1951---; (charter) chmn. Wash. Alumni Orthodontic Stu. Group 1951---; stu. edn. chmn., San Pedro C. of C.; dir. San Pedro YMCA, 1952-60; pres. Comm. Concerts Assn. 1958-59; pres. bd. dirs., Palos Verdes Bay Club, 1965; Antique Auto Club; Town Hall, L.A.; Century Club, USC; UCLA Alumni Assn.; bd. dirs., Univ. of Wash.

Alumni Assn. Masonic Lodge, Elks Club. Hobby: antique autos. Rec.: tennis, boating. water skiing. Res.: 6437 Via Colinita, Miraleste, CA 90732; Office: 1243 S. Meyler St., San Pedro, CA 90731.

LANDERS, NEWLIN J.
Contractor — Business Executive
b. July 10, 1906, N. Salem, Ind.; s. De Loy and Pearl (Paige) Landers; ed. Bus. Contractors Sch.; courses: Personnel Mgmt.; m. Margaret Richart (dec.); chil.: Larry and Marlin; m. Vernette Trosper, Las Vegas, Nev., May 2, 1959. Career: Former owner-mgr.: Landers Mach. Co., Bell Gardens and E. L.A.; Havasu Landing, Calif.; partner, Selwyn-Landers Valve Co., E. L.A.; owner-mgr. Navajo Tract, Apple Valley; propr.; Landers Air Strip, Gas Sta. and Water Delivery Co.; founder, Landers, Calif. (donated land for fire sta. and Homestead Valley Women's Club). Awards: Bus. Man of Week, KJST Radio Sta., Joshua Tree, Calif. 1969; Mem.: Sheriff Rangers, Yucca Valley; (hon.) Landers Volunteer Fire Dept.; bd. dirs. Landers Moose Lodge; dir. Am. League; (life) Intercontinental Biographical Assn.; Comm. Leaders of Am., 1972; Natl. Wildlife Fed. Nararene (former supt. Sun.-Sch. Tchr.). Hobbies: flying (pvt. license), animals. Rec.: radio (mem. Citizens Band). Res.: 905 Landers Lane, Landers; Office: 1105 Landers Lane, Landers, CA 92284.

LANDERS, VERNETTE
Author — School District Counselor (Ret.)
b. May 3, 1912, Lawton, Okla.; d. Fred and La Verne Trosper; ed. A.B. (hons.), UCLA 1933; M.A., 1935; Ed.D. 1953; tchg. life diploma, 1940, gen. life diploma, 1970; m. Maj. Paul A. Lum, M.D. (dec. 1955); son, William Tappan Lum; m. Newlin Landers, Las Vegas, Nev., May 2, 1959; chil.: Larry, Marlin. Career: tchr., Montebello schs., Calif. 1935-45, 1948-50, 1951-59; prof. Long Beach City Coll. 1946-47. L.A. State Coll. 1950; dean of girls 29 Palms H.S. 1960-65; dist. counselor, Morongo Unified Sch. Dist. 1965-72; coord. Adult Edn. 1965-67. dir. Guidance Proj. 1967. Chg. clerk (Volunteer), Landers Post Ofc. 1962---; Landers Volunteer Fire Dept.; v.p. Landers Assn., Inc. 1969-71; dir. Desert Ears (emg. radio serv.), 1970-73. Contrib. articles to profl. mags., journs. 1944---. Awards: Soroptimist of Yr., 29 Palms, 1967; Creativity Award, Internat. Personnel Research Assn. 1972; Hons. for Comm. Serv. Author: Impy, 1974; Talkie, 1975; Impy's Children, 1975; Nineteen O Four, 1976; Little Brown Bat, 1976; Slo Go, 1977. Mem.: Am., Calif. Personnel and Guidance Assns.; San Bernardino Mental Health Assn.; NEA; Calif. Tchrs. Assn.; PTA; Am. Mus. of Natural Hist.; Natl. Wildlife Fedn.; Natl. Hist. Soc.; Intercontinental Biog. Assn.; Internat. Platform Assn.; pres. Bus. and Profl. Women's Club, Montebello, 1940; pres. Hablamos Toastmistress Club, Whittier, 1957; Soroptimist Club, 29 Palms; (life) Desert Mem. Hosp. Guild; (life) Hi Desert Playhouse Guild; (life) Homestead Valley Women's Club; Phi Beta Kappa, Pi Lambda Theta, Sigma Delta Pi, Pi Delta Phi, Mortar Bd. Prytanean Spurs; Landers Garden Club. Landers Comm. Ch. (Bible Sch. lectr., 4 yrs.). Hobby: wild animals. Rec.: flying, garden. Res.: 905 Landers Lane, Landers, CA 92284.

LANDGARTEN, HELEN BARBAR
Art Psychotherapist
b. Mar. 4, 1921, Detroit, Mich.; d. Samuel and Lena (Lindenbaum) Tapper; B.F.A., UCLA, 1963; M.A., Goddard Coll., 1973; m. Nathan Landgarten, Oct. 10, 1942, Detroit, Mich.; chil.: Aleda Carol (Sicardi), b. Dec. 11, 1946; Marc Stuart, b. Apr. 10, 1949. Career: Art psychotherapist, Family Child Dept. of Psychiat. Cedar Sinai Med. Center, Thalians Comm. Mental Health Center, 1967---; Dir. Masters Degree prog. in Art Therapy and prof., Immaculate Heart Coll., L.A., 1973---; licensed Marriage Family Child Counselor, 1975---; mem. faculty, Wright Inst. 1974-77; interviewer radio prog. KPFK Perspectives of Therapy, 1971-73; instr., Calif. Sch. of Profl. Psychol., 1970-72. Mem.: exec. bd., (hon. life mem.) Am. Art Therapy Assn. 1969-75; chmn. Edn. and Tng. bd., 1973-74; (hon. life mem.) So. Calif. Art Therapy Assn., pres. 1972-73, legislative chmn. 1975-76; Am. Orthopsychiat. Assn.; Fellow, Am. Soc. of Psychopathology of Expression; Assn. for Care of Children in Hosps.; chrtr. mem., L.A. Co. Art Mus.; UCLA Alumni Assn. Contbr. profl. publs., TV guest appearances on subject: art therapy. Address: 2021 N. Western Ave., L.A., CA 90027.

LANDRUS, WILFRED MASON
Correspondence School President
b. July 7, 1918, Limon, Colo.; s. Harry O. and E. Detta (Hockersmith) Landrus; B.A., No. Ida. Coll. of Edn.,

1948; M.A., Stanford Univ., 1949; Ed.D., Wash. State Univ., 1956; postdoctoral stu., USC, 1970; m. Clara E. Grant, 1943, Clarkston, Wash.; son, Stephen Grant, b. 1952. Career: Elem. tchr., 1940-42; Counselor, Wash. State Univ., 1949-55; with Chapman Coll. 1955-77; Dean of Students, 1955-58, hd. dept. of edn., 1958-63, dir. Eve. Coll., 1963-66, coord. statewide NDEA proj. 1965-66, chmn. Div. of Edn., 1966-70, acad. coord., Counselor Edn. Prog., 1970-77, prof. Psychol. & Edn., 1963-77; pres., Robert Schuller Correspondence Center for Possibility Thinkers, 1977---; USAAF, 1942-46. Mem.: Calif. State Psy. Assn.; Calif. Personnel & Guidance Assn.; Phi Delta Kappa. Community Ch. Res.: 1446 Greenview Rd., Orange, CA 92666; Office: 4201 W. Chapman Ave., CA 92668.

LANDY, EUGENE E.
Clinical Psychologist
b. Nov. 26, 1934, Pittsburgh, Pa.; s. Jules C. (M.D.) and Frieda Mae (Gordon) (prof. & dir. of psychodrama) Landy; B.A., Cal. State Univ., L.A., 1964; M.S., Univ. of Okla., 1967; Ph.D. psychology, 1968; div.; son Evan Gordon, b. June 22, 1963. Career: Psychological cons.: Cal. State Univ., Fullerton, 1968-69; asst. prof. of Sociology, Cal. State Univ., Northridge, 1968-69; sr. lectr. in psychology, USC, 1968-76; cons. drug abuse, UCLA, 1972-76; pvt. practice, 1968---; marathon group psychotherapy, 1968-76; founder and pres., Found. for Rechanneling of Emotions and Edn. (F.R.E.), 1972---; dir., F.R.E.E. Clinic and Training Center, 1972---; psychological cons. to NBC, CBS, and ABC with on the air interviews on current affairs, 1976---; cons. on numerous TV series and specials, movies, radio: Bob Newhart Show, Love and Marriage Show, AM America, AM Los Angeles, Gibbsville, The Beach Boys' Special, King of the Silver Screen, etc., 1966---; developed 24 hour intensive psychotherapy, training therapists in modality, 1976---. Psychotherapeutic program dir.: L.A. Polyclinic, Topper House, L.A.; clin. staff, Gateways Hosp., 1968-69; staff privileges, Edgemont Hosp., Calabasas Hosp.; dir. Center for Adjunctive Therapeutic Activity, Beverly Hills, 1970-71; dir. of youth culture and drug culture seminars; lectr. profl. groups. Author: The Underground Dictionary, Simon & Schuster, 1971 (Book of the Month Club, Oct. 1971); contbr. The Future of the University, Univ. of Okla. Press, 1969; manuscripts: Marathon, Simon and Schuster, 1979; Life Game; pub. articles in profl. journs. Mem.: Psi Chi; capt. of chess team, Cal. State Univ., L.A.; student body pres., L.A. City Coll., 1955. Office: 303 S. Robertson Blvd., Beverly Hills, CA 90211.

LANDYSHEV, ALEXANDER N.
Professor Emeritus
b. Apr. 29, 1906, Kansk, Siberia, Russia; s. Nicholas A. and Anna I. (Kuskov) Landyshev; profl, E.E. degree, Univ. of Vladivostok, 1927; postgrad studies, Univ. of Leningrad, 1935, Univ. of Moscow, 1940; Univ. of Calif., Berkeley, 1954-56; m. Soja Zoe Bulgakov, Sept. 22, 1931, Kursk, Russia; chil.: Eugene, b. Aug. 12, 1932; Igor, b. Apr. 23, 1934. Career: Elect. Engr.: R&D, Donetz Basin Power System, 1927-42; Energiebauost, Germ., 1942-44; Brown-Boveri & Co., Heidelberg, 1944-45; U.S. Army Engrs., Heidelberg, 1945-49; Prodn. Engr., Precision Mfg. Co., S.F., 1950-54; assoc. in elect. engring., Univ. of Calif. 1954-56; prof. of elect. engring., Cal. Poly State Univ., San Luis Obispo, 1956-72, Prof. Emeritus, 1972---. Contbd. articles to: General Electric Tempo; Am. Inst. of E.E. Journ.; Asilomar Conf., IEEE; Inst. Soc. of Am. Journ. Mem.: IEEE; Inst. Soc. of Am.; Calif. Poly Phase Club; Commonwealth Club of Calif. Hobbies: photog., hist., coin collection, horse riding. Address: 87 Devon Ct., Larkfield, Santa Rosa, CA 95401.

LANE, ELIZABETH L.
Librarian
b. Feb. 15, 1916, Grayville, La., St. John Parish; d. Alcide and Anna (Laurent) Lambert; M.L.S., 1967; children: Eric; Carson; Mark; Ruth (Vanderford). Career: Librarian, St. James Parish, Lutcher, La., 1968-70; librarian, U.S. Navy, Aleutian Islands, 1973-75; Adak, Ak.; administrv. librarian, U.S. Navy, Alameda, Calif., 1975---; editorial asst., Louisiana Historical Assn., Louisiana History index compiled, 1964-68; vol. library work since hi sch. Mem.: Federally Employed Women, regional rep., 1976-79; Toastmasters Internat., dist. treas., 1978-79. Office: NAS Library, Bldg. 2, Wing 3, Alameda, CA 94501.

LANE, HOWARD RAYMOND
Architect
b. Oct. 13, 1922, Chicago, Ill.; s. Mose and Libbie (Sax) Lane; stu., Carnegie Inst. of Tech., 1943-44; Archtl. Assn. Sch., London, 1946; B.S. in Arch., Ill. Inst. of

Tech., 1947; m. Shirley RObbins, June 14, 1947, Chicago; chil.: Rod, b. Feb. 23, 1949; Laura, b. Mar. 30, 1951; Barbara, b. Oct. 19, 1955. Career: Assoc. with Skidmore-Owings & Merrill, Chicago, 1947; Allison & Rible Architects, L.A., 1948; A.C. Martin & Assoc. 1949; Robert Alexander, 1949; Pereira & Luckman, 1950-53; pvt. practice, Encino, 1953---. Dir. Encino Svgs. & Loan. Fellow, AIA. AUS, 1943-47, ETO. Mem.: Encino C. of C., pres. 1966; Assn. C. of C., SFV, pres. 1968; Gr. L.A. Zoo Assn.; L.A. Co. Mus. of Art; chmn. SFV Convention Center, Commn. 1968-69; founder, co-chmn. Valley Round Table Council, 1968-69; Soc. of Am. Mil. Engrs.; Calif. Council AIA pres. 1977; So. Calif. chpt. AIA pres. 1974; Tau Epsilon Phi. Hobbies: steam locomotive model collecting. Res.: 22649 Town Crier Rd., Woodland Hills, CA 91364; Office: 16633 Ventura Blvd., Encino, CA 91436.

LANE, LAURENCE WILLIAM, JR.
Publisher
b. Nov. 7, 1919, Des Moines; s. Laurence William and Ruth (Bell) Lane; stu. Pomona Coll. 1938-40; LL.D. (hon.); B.J., Stanford Univ., 1942; m. Donna Jean Gimbel, Apr. 16, 1955; chil.: Sharon Louise, Robert Laurence, Brenda Ruth. Career: with Lane Pub. Co., publ. Sunset Mag. and books, also prod. Sunset Films, Menlo Park, 1930---; chmn. bd., 1974---; dir. Calif. Water Serv. Co., Crown Zellerbach Corp. Mem.: Adv. bd. Sec. Interior's Bd. Nat. Parks, Historic Sites and Monuments; adv. council Grad. Sch. Bus, Stanford Univ.; former ambassador U.S. Dept. State; mem. Pac. Basin Econ. Council; trustee Colonial Williamsburg Found. Served to Lt. USNR, WW II; PTO. Recipient Conservation Serv. award Secty. Interior. Fellow Coll. of Notre Dame; mem. Newcomen Soc. N.Am., Alaska Bus. Council, Pacific Area Travel Assn. (life), Japan-Calif. Assn., Los Rancheros Vistadores, Advt. Club S.F., No. Calif. Alumni Assn., Alpha Delta Sigma. Republican. Presbyterian. Clubs: Bohemian, Pacific Union (S.F.); Men's Garden (L.A.). Res.: 880 Westridge Dr., Portola Valley, CA 94025; Office: Middlefield and Willow Rds., Menlo Park, CA 94025.

LANE, MARY FRANCES KERNELL
Professor of Psychology
b. Haileyville, Okla.; d. Homer Seiber and Myrtle L. (Jones) Kernell; B.F.A. and M.S., Okla. State Univ., doctoral studies, UCLA, Okla. State Univ. Career: secondary sch. tchr.; Federal shorthand reporter; dir. of recreation, Vance Air Force Base, Okla.; head counselor, Okla. State Univ.; instr. psychology and music, Cooke Co. Jr. Coll.; sr. psychometrist on research project, UC, Riverside; probation officer, L.A. Co.; prof. of psychology, East L.A. Coll. ---; licensed Marriage, Family and Child Counselor ---; hypnotechnician; supr. part-time tchrs. of psychology; pvt. practice control of drugs and smoking. Lectr. on travel and edn. Mem.: Am. Inst. of Parliamentarians, past secty., v.p., pres., Golden Bear chpt.; Internat. Platform Assn., past secty., western region; Sigma Alpha Iota, Life mem.; Am. Psychological Asns.; Am. Humanistic Psychology; Am. Fedn. of Musicians; Am. Fedn. of Tchrs.; L.A. Coll. Tchrs. Assn.; Nat. Edn. Assn.; AAUW; Soc. for Preservation of Variety Arts; L.A. Co. Mus. of Art; L.A. Natural Hist. Mus. Alliance; Nat. Trust for Historic Preservation; Cousteau Soc.; World Wildlife Assn.; Olmstead Circle of Hollywood Presby. Hosp.; Addictive Drugs Edn. Found.; hon. nat. advis. bd., L.A. World Council; patron, Pac.-Asian Culture Mus. Maj., Civil Air Patrol. Office: 1301 Brooklyn, Monterey Park, CA 91754.

LANE, SYLVIA
Professor of Agricultural Economics
b. May 26, 1916, N.Y.C.; A.B., econ., Univ. of Calif., 1934, M.A., 1936, Ph.D., econ., USC, 1957; m. Benjamin Lane, Sept. 2, 1939, L.A.; chil.: Leonard, b. Aug. 3, 1942; Reese, b. Jan. 2, 1952; Nancy, b. Apr. 19, 1953. Career: Lectr., asst. prof., USC, 1946-60, vis. prof. 1967; assoc. prof. Economics, Fin., San Diego State Univ., 1961-65; assoc. prof. finance and assoc. dir., Center for Econ. Edn., Cal. State Univ., Fullerton, 1965-69; prof. agri. economics, Univ. Calif., Davis. Contbr. Am. Journ. of Agri. Economics and others. Mem.: Omicron Delta Epsilon; Am. Agri. Econ. Assn., dir.; Am. Council on Consumer Interests, former dir., mem. Res.: 3028 N. El Macero Dr., Davis, CA 95616; Office: Univ. of Calif., Davis, CA 95616.

LANGE, DONALD E.
Financial Company Executive
b. June 9, 1945, Beaver Dam, Wisc.; s. Eugene and Sylvia (organizer of Independent Dealers Orgn., IDO, midwestern buying coop., 1st in field, 1960) and Sylvia Lange; B.S., Univ. of Wis., 1967; m. Patricia Straub,

Feb. 24, 1968, Madison, Wis.; chil.: Steven, b. Oct. 24, 1974; Nicole, b. Aug. 5, 1976. Career: with Mo. Lake Devel. Proj. 1970-71; with Weyerhaeuser Co., 1971---: br. mgr., then v.p., Weyerhaeuser Mortgage Co., 1971-78, now sr. v.p., Weyerhaeuser Venture Co., 1978---. Lt. j.g., USN, 1967-70. Mem.: So. Calif. Mortgage Bankers Assn., chmn. programs 1978; So. Bay Area Mortgage Bankers Assn., pres. 1972; Delta Tau Delta; "W" Club, Univ. of Wisc. Mem.: Univ. of Wis. Crew Team, winner Natl. Regatta, 1964, 66; rowed in Royal Henley Regatta, 1967. Congregationalist. Hobbies: pvt. pilot, skiing. Home: 17256 Millard Pl., Northridge, CA; Office: 1900 Ave. of the Stars, L.A., CA.

LANGE, KELLY
Television Anchorperson
b. Flushing, Long Is., N.Y.; d. Edmund V. and Alice (Reason) Scafard; B.A. (Eng.), Merrimack Coll., N. Andover, Mass.; dau. Kelly Snyder. Career: Est. Calif. res. 1966; Ladybird reporter from helicopter, KABC Radio, L.A. 1967-72; news reporter and co-host Sunday show, KNBC-TV, L.A. 1971---; weather caster, KNBC News, 1971-76; Anchorperson, 1976---; host, Take My Advice, 1975-76; Kelly's L.A.; interviews: film stars, politicians, govt. leaders; host, NBC Network Rose Parade telecast, 1976, 76, 77, 78, 79. Vacation anchor, NBC's Nightly News, 1976---; Vacation Host, Today Show, 1976---; Tomorrow Show, 1976---; Speaker before clubs and orgns. Hobbies: reading, foreign travel; restores antiques, cars. Rec.: skiing, scuba diving, sailing. Office: 3000 W. Alameda Ave., Burbank, CA 91523.

LANGSDORF, WILLIAM B.
Retired University Executive
b. Oct. 24, 1909, Denver, Colo.; s. William Bell and Julia (Tappan) Langsdorf; desc.: Edwin M. Stanton, atty., Am. Statesman; David Stanton Tappan; ed. Pasa. Jr. Coll.; A.B., Occidental Coll. 1931, M.A. 1932; Ph.D. (hist.), Univ. of Calif., Berkeley, 1936; Stanford Univ., Claremont Coll., Univ. of Chicago; m. Eileen Johnson, San Marino, Calif., June 12, 1938; chil.: Sharon, b. Spet. 24, 1943; William, Jr., b. Oct. 31, 1956. Career: Instr.-asst. prof., Occidental Coll. 1934-39; chmn. Soc. Sci. Dept., Pasa. City Coll. 1939-46; asst. prin. 1946-49; assoc. prin. 1949-50, prin., 1950-54, pres., 1954-59; Pres. Calif. (Orange Co.) State Coll., Fullerton, 1959-70; v. chancellor, Acad. Affairs, Calif. State Univ. and Colls. 1970-73 (Emeritus); assoc. dir., Accrediting Commn. for Sr. Colls. and Univs., Western Region; visiting instr.: UCLA (summer) 1938; Calif. Inst. of Tech. (spring and summer) 1945; Harvard Univ. (summer) 1948. Lectr. on Internat. Rels. 1935-48; Moderator, wkly. radio forum, Pasadena Speaks, KWKW, 1947-48. Co-Atuhor: Issues and Aims of the War; (univ. textbook) Modern World Politics, punl. Crowell Co. 1945; Fighting for Freedom, publ Winston Co. 1947; miscellaneous mag. articles, 1947. Awards: Man of Yr. in Edn., Orange Co. Press CLub, 1964. Mem.: dir. Tues. Eve. Forum, 1943-45; pres. Knights of the Round Table, Pasa. 1947-48, v.p. (2 yrs.); pres. So. Calif. Jr. Coll. Assn. 1948-49, bd. dirs. 1949-50; bd. dirs., Calif. State Jr. Coll. Assn. 1948-49, 1955-59, pres. 1955-56; pres., New Century Club, Pasadena, 1948-49, v.p. (1 yr.); bd. dirs., Pasa. Citizens Council for Planning, 1948-50, pres. 1950-51; pres. Pasa. Breakfast Forum, 1951-52; pres. Dist. 18, Calif. Assn. of Secondary Sch. Admrs. 1952-53; Pac. Coast Com. Am. Council on Edn. 1957---; Natl. Comm. on Accrediting, 1958-59; bd. dirs., So. Calif. Industry-Edn. Council; edn. TV Adv. Com., L.A. Met. Area; Calif. State Colls. repr. on CASSA Accreditation Comm.; bd. dirs., YMCA, North Orange Co.; Phi Alpha Theta, Phi Beta Kappa, Phi Delta Kappa, Sigma Alpha Epsilon. Republican Presbyterian. Res.: 301 Cameo Shores Rd., Corona del Mar, CA 92625..

LANGSTON, BRIAN EVAN
Energy Management Executive
b. Jan. 31, 1949, Altadena; s. Paul Van Cleve and Mildred (Mayne) Langston; B.A. in relig., cum laude, Princeton Univ., 1971. Career: Prod. Moebius Films (internat. documentary film co.), 1971-74; with I.T.Z. Izumi Corp. of Am. (internat. trading firm), 1974-75; co-founder, v.p., Southwest Energy Mgmt., Inc., San Diego, 1975---. Host of weekly TV pgm., Phoenix, 1967-68. Mem. Princeton Club of S.D. Rec.: tennis, swimming. Res.: 503 S. Sierra, No. 162, Solana Beach, CA 92075; Office: 7283 Engineer Rd., San Diego, CA 92111.

LANNI, JOHN MICHAEL
President of Land Development Firm
b. Mar. 14, 1943, Los Angeles; s. Anthony Warren and

Mary Lucille (Leahy) Lanni; desc. Gen. Israel Putnam; ed. Chaminade Prep. Sch.; B.S., mktg., USC; M.B.A., USC; m. Margaret Ellen Hodge, July 31, 1976, Newport Beach. Career: Asst. Commercial Credit Supr., L.A. main office, United Calif. Bank, 1965-68; dir. bus. develop., Great Western Fin. Corp., 1968-71; dir. mktg., Computer Credit Corp., 1971-72; dir. mktg., Kaiser-Aetna, 1972-77; pres., Associated Realty Land and Development Corp., 1977---. Dir., Commerce Associates, 1975---; trustee, Boys Republic, 1976-77; pres., Solteros, 1976, v.p., 1975. Recipient: Andy Mosich Award, USC, 1976. Mem.: Alpha Tau Omega, 1960; L.A. Bachelors, 1972-76; L.A. Jr. C. of C., 1968-73; Soltero's, 1968-76; L.A. Civic Light Opera Assn., 1976---. Home: 1907 Yacht Truant, Newport Beach, CA; Office: 41919 Moreno Rd., Rancho California, Temecula, CA.

LAPHAM, DUDLEY NELSON
Public Official
b. Mar. 13, 1921, Stockett, Mont.; s. Ray Lloyd and Pearl Beatrice (Mann) Lapham; stu. Reed Coll., Portland, Ore.; B.A., Pomona Coll., 1947; m. Constance Sumner, Apr. 19, 1943, Portland, Ore.; chil.: Rosemary (Mrs. Kevin Murphy), b. Dec. 10, 1950; Roger Sumner, b. Apr. 2, 1956. Career: Prodn. control supr., Cal Tech rocket plant, 1944-45; personnel tech., City of Pasadena, 1947-49; personnel dir. and adminstrv. asst. to City Mgr., Alhambra, 1949-51, and Long Beach, 1952-57; City Mgr., La Mesa, 1957-61, Garden Grove, 1961-72; Seaside, 1972-76; Mgr., Monterey Peninsula Water Pollution Control Agency and Monterey Regional Co. Sanitation Dist., 1976---. Vis. lectr. in pub. admin., San Diego State Univ., Fullerton State Univ. First recipient, Distinguished Pub. Adminstr. Award, Fullerton State Coll., 1971. Served to 2nd Lt., AUS, 1942-44. Pres., San Diego chpt., Am. Soc. for Pub. Adminstrs. 1960, pres. Orange Co. chpt. 1970; chmn. Labor Rels. Com., League of Calif. Cities, 1970-74. Mem. Internat. City Mgmt. Assn. 1955-76. Protestant. Rec.: camping, fishing. Res.: 1061 Lorenzo Ct., Seaside, CA 93955; Office: 23845 Holman Hwy., Carmel, CA 93921.

LARK, RAYMOND
Artist
b. June 16, 1939, Phila.; s. Thomas Crawford and Bertha Lark; ed. Phila. Mus. Sch. of Art; Dobbins Vocational Sch.; Temple Univ., Phila., Pa.; L.A. Tech. Coll. Career: Exec. secty. Phys. Drug and Supply Co., Phila. 1958; traffic supv. div. Lockheed Aircraft Corp.; pub. rels. dir. Western States Serv. Co., L.A.; cons. Gen. Employment Enterprises, Inc. L.A.; propr. Raymond Lark's House of Fine Foods, L.A., 1961; art work for mot. pic. studios, Movieland Wax Musuem, Palace of Living Arts, Blue Cross Ins. Co., others; Calif. artist (pencil drawings and oil painter): repr. U.S. in Internat. Art Event of the Yr. 1966; pres. Art West Assoc., Inc. 1968-71 (tour exhibs.: USSR, Moscow, Leningrad, Alma Ata, Baku, European Capitols and USA); exhibs. incl.: Exec. Mansion of Gov. Nelson A. Rockefeller, N.Y. 1967; Cape Cod Art Assn. Gallery, Hyannis, Mass.; Phillip E. Freed Gallery, of Fine Art, Chicago; Charles W. Bowers Mem. Museum, Santa Ana, Calif.; Santa Barbara Museum of Art; Dalzell Hatfield Galleries, Ambassador Hotel, L.A.; Diplomat Hotel, Emerald Gallery, Hollywood Beach, Fla.; Lyzon Galleries, Nashville, Tenn.; Stanford Univ. Fine Arts Gallery; Nador's Art Gallery, Haiti; Fine Arts Gallery, San Diego; Western Wash. State Coll.; L.A. City Hall Municipal Tower Gallery; Hollywood Bowl; Smith-Mason Gallery, Wash. D.C., others. Lectr. on Art: Compton Coll., First Unitarian Ch., L.A. 1969; Natl. Sectys. Assn., Hollywood 1970. Awards: Achievement Award (cost reduction and punctuality, 2 yrs. record), Lockheed Aircraft Corp., Burbank, 1960; First Prize Cash Awards: Immanuel's Art Exhib., L.A., 1967, 68 (2 additional awards, 1968); First Prize Cash Award, Florenz's Art Exhib., Hollywood, 1969; Outstanding Young Men in Am., 1972; feat. Headliner: over 300 artists at South Bay Art Fair, 1965; 200 at The La Cienega Art Festival, 1966; feat.: L.A. Times, 1966, 67, 68; Symbol Mag. 1967; Westways Mag., Nov. 1968; Miami Herald, 1969; Black Artists, 1969; Coast FM and Fine Arts Mag., Internat. Graphic Art Masters, 1970, many others. Hobby: collects art and silver. Rec.: boxing, swim. Res.: P.O. Box 8990, L.A., CA 90008.

LARKIN, FREDERICK G., JR.
Former Bank Official
b. Dec. 28, 1913, Seattle, Wash.; s. Frederick G. and Virginia (Manny) Larkin; B.S., Univ. of Wash. 1934; M.B.A., Stanford Univ. 1936; m. Frances Drayton Williams, L.A., Dec. 17, 1938; dau.: Lucretia Stephenson, b. Feb. 18, 1941. Career: Security Pac.

Natl. Bank, 1936---, v.p. 1949, sr. v.p. 1960, pres. 1961, chief exec. ofcr. 1967---, chmn. bd. 1969---. Dir.: Carnation Co., Getty Oil Co., Rockwell Internat. Corp.; Bank of Canton, Ltd., Hong Kong; Security Pac. Interamerica Bank, S.A., Panama; Tricontinental Corp. Ltd., Australia; Cons. Council, Banco Denasa de Investimento S.A., Brazil; Automobile Club of So. Calif.; Calif. State C. of C.; Fed. Reserve Bank of S.F.; Greater L.A. chpt., Natl. Safety Council; Hwy. Users Fed. for Safety and Mobility; v.p. Hosp. of Good Samaritan; L.A. World Affairs Council; So. Calif. Bldg. Funds; former chmn. bd. L.A. Philharmonic Assn.; trustee: Calif. Inst. of Tech.; John Randolph Haynes and Dora Haynes Found.; bd. of trustees, Occidental Coll. Mem.: Univ. of Wash. Adv. Bd. of Grad. Sch. of Bus.; Assn. of Reserve City Bankers, dir. 1968-71; Am. Automobile Assn. Natl. Adv. Council; dir. Am. Natl. Red Cross, L.A. chpt. 1961-67, 1970-74, chmn. 1964-67; Am. Bankers Assn's. Govt. Borrowing Com., U.S. Treasury, 1964-70; bd. govs. Town Hall, 1965-68; Stanford Univ. Grad. Sch. of Bus. Adv. Council, 1965-71; dir. Merchants & Mfrs. Assn. 1966-67; dir. L.A. C. of C. 1966-67; Fed. Adv. Council, 1967-69; bd. govs. Perf. Arts Council of Music Center, 1969-71; dir. Pac. Mutual Life Ins. Co. 1969-76; Marac Holdings Ltd., New Zealand, 1972-75; Pvt. Export Fund. Corp. 1972-76; v. chmn.-dir. Investment and Underwriting Corp. of P.I. 1974-76. U.S. Coast Guard, 1942-45. Clubs: The Links, N.Y.; Pac.-Union S.F.; Valley of Montecito; Sunset, Stock Exch., Men's Garden, Calif., L.A. Country, L.A.; Phi Kappa Sigma. Episcopalian. Hobbies: golf, garden. Res.: 771 S. Windsor Blvd., L.A., CA 90005; Office: 333 S. Hope St., L.A., CA 90071.

LASEMAN, PAUL
Librarian
b. Dec. 1, 1920, Roff, Okla.; s. Raymond and Mary (Hammock) Laseman; Gr.nephew, Gen. Edmund P. Gaines; B.S., Okla. State Univ., 1946; M.S., 1954; m. Connie B. Young, Oct. 21, 1950, Stillwater, Okla.; chil.: Thomas Gene, b. Feb. 16, 1942; Rachel Mary (Howlett), b. July 14, 1954. Career: tchr., Ponca City (Okla.) H.S., 1948-58; Kern Co. Union H.S. Dist., Bakersfield, 1959-61; Employment ofcr., Calif. State Employment Serv., 1962-63; librn. trainee, L.A. City Lib., San Pedro, 1963-65; ref. librn., L.A. Co., Norwalk, 1965; librn. in charge, Bellflower, 1966, Norwalk, 1967-70, South Gate, 1971---. V.P., Democrat Club, La Mirada, 1967-69; bd. dirs. Calif. Dem. Council, 1967; dir. Norwalk Boys Club, 1970-71; dir. Norwalk C. of C., 1969-70, v.p. 1970; mem. L.A. Co. Dem. Central Com. 1968-69; 1st Lt., USMC, 1943-46; ret. Capt. USMCR. Mem. Westerners L.A. Corral, 1978---; Rotary, 1968---; Lambda Chi Alpha, 1940-46. Unitarian. Hobbies: stamps, gardening, books. Rec.: golf. Res.: 11621 Lisburn Pl., La Mirada, CA 90638; Office: 4035 Tweedy Blvd., South Gate, CA 90280.

LASKY, ROYLE G.
Chairwoman of the Board, Revell, Inc.
b. June 14, 1930, Milwaukee, Wis.; m. Lewis H. Glaser, 1950; chil.: Kim Glaser Selbert and Leslie Glaser Kenner; m. 2d. Gilbert P. Lasky, 1972. Career: v.p., New Products, Revell, Inc., 1958, v.p., product devel., 1962, exec. v.p. 1969, pres. and chief exec. ofcr., 1970, chwn. of bd., 1972---. Speaker, Sales & Mktg. Execs. of L.A., 1975, USC Grad. Sch. of Mgmt., 1975, UCLA Grad. Sch. of Mgmt., 1975, profl. confs. Named Industrialist of the Yr., Soc. of Mfg. Engrs., L.A. Chpt. 1972, San Fernando Valley chpt., 1971; one of four women elected to mem. in Young President's Orgn. Mem.: dir. Toy Mfrs. Assn., 1975, 76; dir., Hobby Industry Assn. of Am., 1974, 75. Featured interviewee: London Fin. Times, 1975; L.A. Times, 1972, 74; Toys Mag., 1974; Success Unlimited Mag., 1975; AP Wire Serv., 1974, 76; Business Week Mag., 1976; others. Hobbies: gourmet cooking, antique Japanese wood block prints. Address: 4223 Glencoe Ave., Venice, CA 90291.

LARSON, JOHN W.
Attorney at Law
b. June 24, 1935, Detroit, Mich.; s. William and Sara Eleanor (Yeatman) Larson; B.S., honors in Econs., Stanford Univ., 1957, LL.B., 1962; m. Pamela Jane Wren, Sept. 16, 1959, Okla. City; dau. Jennifer Wren, b. Sept. 9, 1963. Career: assoc., Brobeck, Phleger & Harrison, S.F., 1962-68, partner, 1968-71, 1973---; asst. secty. Dept. Interior, Wash., D.C., 1971-73; exec. dir. Natural Resources Com., Wash. D.C., 1973; counselor to chmn. Cost of Living Council, Wash. D.C., 1973. Dir. Measurex Corp.; mem. Practising Law Inst.; mem. US-USSR Jt. Com. on Environment; mem. Bd. of Visitors Stanford Law Sch., 1974-77; trustee, Katherine

Branson Sch./Mt. Tamalpais Sch. Mem.: Am. and Calif. Bar Assn.; Order of Coif; Burlingame Country Club, S.F.; Pac. Union Club, S.F.; Univ. Club, S.F.; Univ. Club, Wash.; Chevy Chase Club, Wash. Res.: P.O.B. 349, Ross, CA 94957; Office: One Market Plaza, Spear St. Twr., S.F., CA 94105.

LA SOR, WILLIAM SANFORD
Professor
b. Oct. 25, 1911, Phila.; s. William Allan and Sara Lewis LaSor; A.B., Univ. of Penn., 1931; TH.B., Princeton Theol. Sem., 1934; Th.M., 1943; M.A., Princeton Univ., 1934; Ph.D., Dropsie Univ., 1949; Th.D., USC, 1956; m. Elizabeth Vaughan, June 16, 1934, Mt. Kisco, N.Y.; chil.: William Sanford Jr., b. Dec. 2, 1935; Elizabeth Ann (Mrs. David Kirkpatrick), b. Dec. 26, 1936; Frederick Eugene Vaughan, b. Jan. 25, 1943; Susanne Marie (Mrs. Robert E. Whyte Jr.), b. Jan. 15, 1949. Career: Pastor, 1st Presbyterian Ch., Ocean City, N.J., 1934-38; pastor, Green Ridge Presby. Ch., Scranton, Pa., 1938-43; Chaplain, USN, 1943-46, Ret. Comdr., USNR, 1946-70; assoc. prof. and chmn. Dept. of Relig., Lafayette Coll., Easton, Pa., 1946-49; prof. of Old Testament, Fuller Theol. Sem., Pasadena, 1949-77; sr. prof., 1977---. Pres., Bd. of Tokyo Evangelistic Center, 1957---; CO, Naval Res. Chaplains Co., 1968-70. Author of numerous books, articles in scholarly journs.; prod. of films and film-strips, slide lectrs. on biblical, archaeological and missionary subjects. Mem.: Alpha Sigma Phi, Mil. Chaplains Assn., pres. So. Calif. chpt. 1968-70. Presbyterian. Hobby: photog. Res.: 1790 E. Loma Alta Dr., Altadena, CA 91001; Office: 135 N. Oakland Ave., Pasadena, CA 91101.

LASSWELL, THOMAS ELY
Sociologist — Educator
b. Oct. 29, 1919, Kennett, Mo.; s. Gus and Miriam (Ely) Lasswell; ed. Westminster Coll. 1936-38; A.B., Ark. Coll. 1940; M.S., USC, 1947, Ph.D. 1953; m. Marcia Lee Eck, Oakland, May 29, 1950; chil.: Marcia Jane, b. Mar. 3, 1951; Thomas Ely, Jr., b. Apr. 28, 1952; Julia Lee, b. Apr. 22, 1957. Career: Minute clerk, Mo. Housyof Reps., 1941; prin. Highland Inst., Guerrant, Ky. 1941-42; asst. prof., George Pepperdine Coll., L.A., 1950-54; prof. (sociology) Grinnell Coll., Ia. 1954-59; assoc. prof., USC, 1959-63, dir. res. hons. pgm. 1961---, prof. 1963---, chmn. Dept. Sociology and Anthropology, 1965-66. Visiting prof.: Stephen F. Austin State Coll. Nacogdoches, Tex. 1950, 56, 68; Whittier Coll., Calif. 1957; Northwestern Univ., Evanston, Ill. 1960; cons. Inst. of Human Rels. 1957; v.p. Ia. Council of Family Rels. 1957; spec. cons., L.A. Co. Schs. 1960; cons. in soc. psychol. 1966---. Author: (co-author) Sociology: An Introduction, 1953, 63; Life in Society, 1965; Class and Stratum, 1965; assoc. ed., Sociology and Social Research, 1959---. Lt., USNR (1942-46), WW II. Mem.: fellow, Am. Sociological Assn.; Pac. Sociology Assn., Alpha Kappa Delta, Phi Kappa Phi, Yorke House Club. Presbyterian. Res.: 875 Hillcrest Dr., Pomona, CA 91766; Office: Univ. of So. Calif., Univ. Park, L.A., CA 90007.

LATHROP, MITCHELL LEE
Attorney at Law
b. Dec. 15, 1937, L.A.; s. Alfred Lee and Barbara Isabella (Mitchell) Lathrop; related, Gen. William L. "Billy" Mitchell, Leland Stanford, Alfred the Great, Eng.; ed. The Thatcher Sch.; B.S., U.S. Naval Acad.; J.D., USC; m. Joyce Keen, Glendale, Calif. 1959 (div. 1976); chil.: Christin Lorraine, b. Dec. 21, 1964; Alexander Mitchell, b. Jan. 21, 1967; Timothy Trewin Mitchell, b. Feb. 4, 1971. Career: Dep. Co. Counsel, L.A., 1966-68; atty. assoc. with Brill, Hunt, DeBuys & Burby, L.A. 1968-70; partner, Macdonald, Halsted & Laybourne law firm, 1970---; admitted to practice, U.S. Supreme Ct. Contrib. numerous profl. publs. on Fed. and State Securities law. Ofcr., USN, Vietna,. 1959-63; 2nd command, USS Inflict (MSO), 1961-63. Mem.: L.A. Co., Calif., Dist. of Columbia, Am. Bar Assns.; dir. Opera Assocs. of Music Center, L.A. 1969-74; pres. 1970-72; gov. Soc. Colonial Wars, Calif. 1970-72, councillor, 1974---; Soc. Ams. of Royal Descent; The Plantagent Soc.; trustee, Honnold Lib. of Colls. at Claremont, Calif., 1971---; dir. Music Center Opera Assn., L.A., 1971---, v.p. 1974---; dir. exec. com. chmn. Western Reg. Met. Opera Natl. Council, Lincoln Center, N.Y. 1972---; trustee, The Thacher Sch., Ojai, 1972-76; dir. Calif. Soc. S.R., 1974---, pres. 1976---; Mil. and Hospitaller Order of St. Lazarus of Jerusalem, Knight v-chancellor, Grand Priory of Am., Companion of Merit; secty. Brit. United Servs. Club, L.A. 1974; Judge Advocates Assn., L.A. 1974-76, pres. 1977; dir., Friends of the Claremont Colls., 1975---. Clubs: Met., N.Y.; Calif., Los Angeles, L.A.; Valley Hunt, Pasadena;

Republican. Anglican (former vestryman, St. Mark's Ch., Glendale). Hobby: classical music. Res.: 681 S. Orange Grove Blvd., Pasadena, CA 91105; Office: Sixth Floor, 1200 Wilshire Blvd., L.A., CA 90017.

LAUER, ROBERT LOUIS
Appraisal Company President
b. July 1, 1922, Payette, Ida.; s. Edwin M. and Eva L. (Gish) Lauer; Univ. of Ida. 1942; C.E., Ida. State Univ. 1942-43; C.E., Univ. of Wash. 1944; m. Dorothy M. Sorenson, Seattle, Wash., Feb. 8, 1946; chil.: David Robert, b. Oct. 13, 1947; Barbara Jean, b. Feb. 13, 1949; John Richard, b. Sept. 17, 1956. Career: Assoc. with Gen. Appraisal Co., Seattle and L.A., 1944---, profl. ind. appraiser, 1944---, mgr. Appraisal Research Dept. 1946-55, treas.-dir. 1955-70, exec. v.p. 1970-71; pres.-chief exec. ofcr. 1971---. Dir.: Am. Appraisal Co., Milwaukee; Gen. Appraisal of Can. Ltd., Toronto; Gen. Appraisal Co., L.A. Registered profl. valuation engr. Awards: Paul Harris Fellow Award, Rotary Internat. 1972. Mem.: internat. pres., Am. Soc. of Tech. Appraisers, 1951-62; Fellow, Am. Soc. of Appraisers, 1961---; pres. Rotary Club, Pasa. 1972-73; Pasa. Univ. Club; Pasa. Tournament of Roses Assn. Res.: 1000 Fairview Ave., No. 5, Arcadia, CA 91006; Office: 301 E. Colorado Blvd., Pasa., CA 91101.

LAURIE, EDWARD JAMES
University Dean
b. Nov. 21, 1925, Sparks, Nev.; s. Albert E. and Margaret (Fraser) Laurie; B.S., UCLA, 1946; M.C.A., 1950; Ed.D., 1959; m. Patricia Jean Johnson, Mar. 31, 1962, Reno, Nev.; chil.: Katherine Louise, b. Jan. 23, 1963; Margaret Dee, b. July 3, 1964; Elizabeth Ann, May 7, 1969. Career: Chmn., Dept. Mktg., San Jose State Univ., 1972-76, Prof. of Mktg. and Assoc. Dean, Academic, Sch. of Bus., 1977---. Author: Computing Systems in the U.S., 1960; Computers and How They Work, 1963; Computers and Computer Languages, 1966; Modern Computer Concepts, 1970; Computers, Automation, and Soc., 1979. IBM Nat. Faculty Fellow, 1962. Ensign, USNR, V-12 pgm., WW II; Lt. j.g., Korean War. Mem.: AAUP; Am. Mktg. Assn.; Am. Acad. Polit. and Soc. Scis.; Beta Gamma Sigma; Phi Kappa Phi; Phi Delta Phi; Pi Omega Pi; Tau Delta Pi. Hobbies: Egyptology, Hist. of Sci., Hobbies: gardening. Res.: 1287 Pampas Dr., San Jose, CA 95192; Office: San Jose State Univ., San Jose, CA 95192.

LAUTHER, S. EDGAR
Banker
b. Oct. 13, 1913, Ft. Madison, Ia.; s. Irwin S. and Grace (Liddle) Lauther; ed. Mo. Valley Coll., Marshall, Mo. 1931-34; Duke Univ., Durham, N.C. 1941; m. DeLora L. Whisnant, Decatur, Ill., June 22, 1941; son, Richard C., b. Feb. 2, 1952. Career: Asst. cashier, State Bank of Nauvoo, Ill. 1934-39; asst. cashier, First Natl. Bank, Gibson City, Ill. 1940; asst. natl. bank examiner, Ofc. of Controller of Currency, Chicago, 1940-41; v.p., exec. v.p., pres., Irwin Union Bank and Trust Co., Columbus, Ind. 1946-64; dir. 1947-64; sr. v.p. exec. v.p.-dir.-exec. com.-ofcr. in chg. So. Div., Crocker Natl. Bank, 1964-68; chmn. bd. Am. Fletcher Natl. Bank and Am. Fletcher Corp. Ind. 1968-74; hon. chmn. bd. 1974---. Author: numerous banking articles; contrib. to Commercial Bankers Handbook, 1966. Pvt., Maj., Fin. Dept., U.S. Army (1942-46), WW II. Mem.: treas., Sigma Nu 1932-33; Master, Masonic Lodge, Nauvoo, Ill. 1936-37; pres. Ind. Bankers Assn. 1954-55; pres. Rotary Club, Columbus, Ind. 1957-58; pres. Columbus C. of C. 1958-59; pres. Svgs. Div., Am. Bankers Assn. 1960-61; Stock Exch. Club, 1965-68; L.A. Rotary Club, 1965; Calif. Club, 1965; L.A. Country Club, 1966. Republican (fund raiser, G.O.P. dist. chmn., precinct-poll activities leader). Presbyterian (ch. deacon, elder, trustee). Rec.: golf, reading. Res.: 452 S. Orange Grove Blvd., Pasa., CA 91105.

LAVENSON, JAMES H.
President, San Ysidro Ranch
b. June 8, 1919, Phila.; s. Jay and Caroline (Wolf) Lavenson; B.A., Williams Coll., 1941; Capsule M.B.A., Harvard Univ., 1955; Mgmt. Course, Am. Mgmt. Assn., 1952-53; m. Susan Barker, June 5, 1973, New Rochelle, N.Y.; chil.: Joel, b. July 29, 1946; Michael, b. Apr. 10, 1950; Gary, b. July 24, 1953; Peter, b. Sept. 29, 1956; Ellen, b. Dec. 4, 1965. Career: Exec. trainee, Sears, Roebuck & Co., 1941-42; pres., Lavenson Bur. of Advt., Phila. 1946-64; pres., HCA & Western Hotels (mktg. co.), 1964-65; pres., Premier Corp. of Am., 1965-66; pres., internat. div. of Sonesta Internat. Hotels (then Hotel Corp. of Am.), 1967-69; pres., Doxsee Food Corp. (sub. of Sonesta Internat. Hotels), 1969-75; pres., Plaza Hotel, N.Y.C., 1972-75; pres., SYR Corp.,

Montecito, 1976---. Cons.: Biltmore Hotel, L.A., Princeton Univ., Lincoln Bank, Treadway Inns, Diamondhead Corp., others. Profl. lectr. (Leigh Bur.); Author: The Sensuous Animal, Dell, 1972; Selling Made Simple, 1972; column on salesmanship Jaundiced Eye for Sales & Mktg. Mag., 1971---. Dir.: Sonesta Internat. Hotels Corp., Doxsee Food Corp., Plaza Hotel, Hartman Luggage Co., Precision Plastics Corp., Premier Corp. of Am., Templeton-Damroth Security Mgrs., Inc., Allerton, Berman & Dean, Zebra Assocs., Young Presidents Orgn., Albert Schweitzer Found., Am. Field Serv. Served pvt. to Capt. USAAF, 1942-46. Mem.: Chief Execs. Forum; Metropolitan Presidents Orgn.; World Bus. Council; Internat. Exec. Service Corps; U.S. Power Squadron; NYC Aux. Police; Hotel Sales Mgmt. Assn.; Santa Barbara Co. Dep. Sheriff. Hobbies: sailing, horsemanship. Address: 900 San Ysidro Lane, Santa Barbara, CA 93108.

LAWHERN, RICHARD A.
R&D Manager, U.S. Air Force
b. June 29, 1944, Palo Alto; s. Elmer Bradley and Ollie Mae (Pearson) Lawhern; B.S.E.E. with honors, Cal. State Polytechnic Coll., 1966; M.S.E.E., Univ. of Wash., 1969; Ph.D. Engr. Systems, UCLA, 1976. Career: Research Engr., Varian Assoc., Palo Alto, 1967; entered USAF 1967: grad. edn. under AF grants; proj. engr., Rome Air Devel. Center, 1969-73; systems engr., AF Space & Missiles System Orgn. 1976-78; R&D Mgr., USAF Europe, 1978---. Distinguished Grad., AF Squadron Officers' Sch. 1971; decorated Commendation Medal and two Oak Leaf Clusters, 1970, 72, 78. Mem. Tau Sigma frat., 1976. Hobbies: photog. Rec.: theater, music, hiking.

LAWLER, OSCAR T.
Banker — Civic Leader
b. Nov. 23, 1914, L.A.; s. Oscar and Hilda (Brode) Lawler; B.A., Yale Univ. 1936; m. Joan Day Pattinson, Greenwich, Conn., July 27, 1937; chil.: Daniel Day, b. July 31, 1940; Charles Frederick, b. Jan. 19, 1944; Joan Day, b. Nov. 5, 1946. Career: Pres., Farmers and Merchants Natl. Bank, L.A. 1953-56 (merged with Security First Natl. Bank), chmn. exec. com.-dir. Security Pac. Natl. Bank, L.A. 1956---. Dir., Union Pac. Railroad Co. and subsidiary lines; dir. Security Pac. Corp. 1971---; dir. Assoc. In-Group Donors; trustee: Union Pac. Found., Hollenbeck Home, Rancho Santa Ana Botanic Garden, Dan Murphy Found.; chmn. bd. Barlow San. Assn.; dir. L.A. Chpt. Am. Ord. Assn.; chmn. bd. L.A. Civic Light Opera Assn.; Mem.: Assn. of Res. City Bankers; dir. L.A. C. of C. 1954-56, 1962-66, pres. 1964; pres. Soc. of Friendly Sons of St. Patrick of L.A. 1962-63; Founders of the Music Center; Center; Am., Calif. Bankers Assns.; L.A. World Affairs Council; (assoc.) Beavers; Friends of the Claremont Colls.; Friends of Huntington Lib.; Honnold Lib. Soc.; Calif. Hist. Soc.; Hist. Soc. of So. Calif.; F&AM; Navy League of U.S.; Travelers Aid Soc. of L.A.; Newcomen Soc. in N. Am.; Los Amigos del Pueblo de Los Angeles; Clubs: Men's Garden, L.A.; dir. L.A. Stock Exch.; Petroleum, India House, N.Y.C.; pres. Lincoln Club, 1967-69; Yale, N.Y.C. and So. Calif.; Birnam Wood Golf, Santa Barbara; The L.A., The 100, Sunset, Beach, and Cal. Club. Hobbies: garden, sailing. Res.: 5224 W. 2nd St., L.A., CA 90004; Office: 561 S. Spring St., L.A., CA 90013.

LAWRENCE, DEAN GRAYSON
Attorney at Law
b. Oakland, Calif.; d. Henry Conrad (State Controller, Nev.) and Myrtle (Grayson) Schmidt (Williams); bros.: Lt. Col. Grayson Schmidt, prof. math, U.S. Mil. Acad., and Mills Coll.; William H. Schmidt, admr. State of Nev. Tax Commn.; ed. B.A., Univ. Calif., Berkeley, 1934; J.D., Sch. of Law, 1939; Career: Admitted to Calif. bar, 1943, U.S. Dist. Ct. and U.S. Ct. of Appeals, 1944; Tax Ct. of U.S., 1945, Supreme Ct. of U.S., 1967; assoc. Pillsbury, Madison & Sutro law firm, S.F., 1944-46; gen. practice, Oakland, 1946-50; San Jose, 1952-60; Grass Valley, 1960-63, 1966---; co. counsel, Nev. Co. 1964-66; supv. 2nd Dist., Nev. Co. Bd. of Supvs. 1969---. Mem.: pres.-dir. Nev. Co. Humane Soc. 1966---; secty., Nev. Co. Humane Shelter Bd. 1966---; Humane Soc. of U.S.; State Bar of Calif.; Bus. and Profl. Women's Club; AAUW, Phi Beta Kappa, Sigma Xi, Pi Mu Epsilon, Pi Lambda Theta, Kappa Beta Pi. Episcopalian. Office: 110 Alta Vista Dr., Grass Valley, CA 95945.

LAWRENCE, JEROME
Playwright
b. July 14, 1915, Cleveland, Oh.; s. Samuel and Sarah (Rogen) Lawrence; B.A., Oh. State Univ., 1937, D.H.L.,

1963; D.Litt. Fairleigh Dickinson Univ., 1969; D.F.A., Villanova Univ., 1970. Career: Newspaper ed., Oh. dailies; continuity editor, Radio Station KMPC, Beverly Hills, 1938-39; sr. staff writer, CBS, Hollywood and N.Y., 1939-41; partner Lawrence and Lee as playwright, dir., author of radio, TV, films, stage plays, 1942---: Co-author of 19 plays (trans. into 31 languages) incl.: Inherit the Wind; Auntie Mame; Mame; The Night Thoreau Spent in Jail; The Gang's All Here; Look, Ma, I'm Dancin'; Dear World; Jabberwock; First Monday In October; author numerous radio and TV prodns.; overseas correspondent and co-founder Armed Forces Radio Service. Author: Actor: The Life and Times of Paul Muni. Master playwright, Margo Jones Award Prof. at N.Y. Univ., Oh. State Univ., Baylor Univ., Salzburg Seminar in Am. Studies. Nat. pres., Radio Writers Guild; pres., co-founder Am. Playwrights Theatre; bd. mem.: Dramatists Guild, Authors League, Writers Guild of Am. W., Am. Conservatory Theatre, S.F. Awards incl.: critics, Donaldson and Tony awards for Broadway plays; two Peabody Awards in Broadcasting; two Ohioana Awards; Emmy nomination. Tech. Sgt., AUS, WW II; expert cons. to Secty. of War, served in N. Africa, Italy. Mem.: Phi Beta Kappa, Sigma Delta Chi, Zeta Beta Tau (Man of the Yr.); Players Club, N.Y. Rec.: backgammon, swimming. Res.: 21056 Las Flores Mesa Dr., Malibu, CA 90265.

LAWRENCE, M. LARRY
Chairman of the Board, Hotel del Coronado
b. Aug. 16, 1926, Chicago, Ill.; s. Sidney Arthur and Till Pearl (Astor) Lawrence; student, Univ. of Ariz.; m. Michala Lee, Dec. 25, 1976, Coronado, Calif.; chil.: Lesli (Mrs. Shlomo Caspi), b. Mar. 29, 1951; Andrea, b. Feb. 15, 1955; Robert, b. Aug. 15, 1958. Career: partner-advt., pub. rels., Century, Inc., Chicago, 1947-49; licensed real estate broker, gen. contractor, insurance broker, casualty & life, U.S. Homes, Inc. (FHA and VA projects) Ill., Ind., 1949-53; broker, contractor, officer and partner: Tri-W Bldrs., Fireside Realty, affiliates: residential, comml., Govt. constrn., airports, missile bases and tracking stations, Calif., 1953-61; develop. programs, M. Larry Lawrence & Associates, M.L. Lawrence Develop. Co., etc., 1961-76; chmn. of bd., Hotel del Coronado Corp. 1963---; also pres., Woodglen Vista, Inc.; managing partner, D.G. & Associates, HDC Properties; Coronado Properties Lmtd., M. Larry Lawrence & Assoc.; pres., U.S. Oceanics, Inc. Mil.: U.S. Maritime Service. Mem.: Calif. Hotel/Motel Assn.; San Diego Convention & Visitors Bureau; Coronado Residential Assn.; past: Calif. State Commn. on Tourism & Visitor Services; Young Home Bldrs. of Am., past pres. Chmn., Israel Bonds, 1967---; past chmn., United Jewish Appeal, and United Crusade, past v.p., United Jewish Fedn.; sustaining mem., YMCA; past dir.: Neighborhood House, Tri-Hosp. Drive, Citizens United, Community Service Orgn.; dir.: World Affairs Council; Greater S.D. Sports Assn. Mem.: Coronado Rotary; The Guardians; S.D. Hist. Soc.; Coronado Hist. Assn.; The City Center; S.D. State Univ. Hist. Research Club; Navy League; assoc. U.S. Naval Inst.; Chancellor's Club, UCSD; B'Nai B'rith; S.D. and Coronado C.'s of C.; United Negro Coll. Fund, Inc. Rest & Aspiration Nat. Com., 1978; fin. chmn. Bob Wilson for Senate, co-chmn., Calif. Presidential Inaugural Com., 1977; county and state central coms., 1952-60; chmn., temporary rules com., 1972 nat. convention, Miami; mem. electoral coll., Calif. Democratic Delegation, 1972. Office: Hotel del Coronado, Coronado, CA 92118.

LAWSON, FLOYD MELVYN
Educator — Civic Leader
b. June 5, 1907, Sacramento; s. Gray and Lena (Dunkeson) Lawson; ed. Roseville Pub. Schs., USC, Univ. of Calif., Coll. of Pac. 1928; A.B., Coll. of Pac. 1928; M.A. 1936 Ped.D. 1950; m. Verna M. Kopka, Sacto., 1932. Career: Tchr., Sacto. Sr. H.S. 1929-31, counselor, 1931-36, v.-prin. 1936-40, prin. 1940-43, asst. supt., Sacto. City Unified Sch. Dist., 1946-48, dep. supt. 1948-60, supt., 1961-68; lectr., Sacto. State Coll., 1968-71. Author: (with Verna Kopka Lawson), publ. by D.C. Health and Co.: Our Am.: Today and Yesterday (textbook), 1938; Teachers Guide Book, 1938; Study Guide to Our Am.: Today and Yesterday, 1940; author, numerous articles on tchg. methods, social sci. and sch. adm. Lt. (s.g.), USNR; inst. V-5 Pgm. 1943-44; asst. to academic dir., USN Pre-Flight Sch., St. Mary's Coll., Calif. 1944-45; asst. flag secty.-Comdr. S. Pac. Area and Force (1945), WW II. Awards: Distinguished Serv. Medal, Sacto. Jr. C. of C. 1939. Mem.: pres. Coll. of Pac. Aiumni Assn. 1936-37; Stanford Soc. Edn. Investigation, 1939; pres. Sacto. Town Hall, 1941-43; pres. Xi Chpt., Phi Delta Kappa, 1942-43; dir. Sacto. Child Guidance Clinic, 1946-49; Mil. Order of World Wars, 1946-53; dir., Calif. Mus. Assn., 1947-56; v.p., 1952-56; pres. Rotary Club of Sacto., 1948-49; Prot. Welfare Bd., Sacto., 1950-51;

bd. trustees, Sacto. Comm. Hosps. 1952---; v.-chmn. bd. trustees, Sutter Comm. Hosps. 1953---: Citizens Com. on Redevel., 1954; Univ. Club of Sacto., bd. dirs. 1954-55; Mayor's Youth Com. on Youth Problems, 1954-56; bd. trustees, Scottish Rite Temple, Sacto., 1956---; Royal Order of Jesters; Ben Ali Temple, AAONMS (potentate, 1961); Am. Legion, Block Letter Soc., Scottish rite boddies, 33º Mason, York rite bodies, Knights Templar, Rho Lambda Phi, Theta Alpha Phi, Pi Gamma Mu, Phi Kappa Phi. Republican. Lutheran (ch. council, St. John's Luth. Ch. 1952-57). Res.: 2700 22nd St., Sacto., CA 95818.

LAWSON, JOHN BELLETT
Business Executive
b. Feb. 3, 1908, Phila.; s. Harold and Lucy F. Lawson; ed. Pierce Sch. of Bus. Adm. 1926-29; Univ. Pa., Wharton Sch. Ext. Courses, 1929-40; m. Doris M. Westlake, Detroit, Mich., May 6, 1961. Career: Acct., Price, Waterhouse and Co., Phila. 1930-31; asst. reg. controller, Warner Bros. Theatres, Inc., Phila. 1931-32, 1933-38; asst. treas. Seashore Theatres, Inc., Atlantic City, N.J. 1932-33; controller-bus. mgr., Villanova Coll., 1938-41; controller, Ferracute Mach. Co., Bridgeton, N.J. 1941-43; exec. v.p. 1943-48; bus. cons. Ebasco Servs., Inc., NYC 1948-49; gen. mgr. positions, Ford Motor Co., Detroit, 1949-63; v.p.-gen. mgr. Aeron. Div., Philco-Ford Corp., Newport Beach, 1963-70, exec. v.p. Aerospace and Def. Systems Operations, 1970---. Awards: Orange Co. Mgr. of Yr., 1965; Orange Co. Press Club Man of Yr. 1967. Mem.: natl. bd. dirs. Am. Ord. Assn.; bd. dirs. L.A. chpt., Assn. U.S. Army; Am. Mgmt. Assn.; Financial Execs. Inst.; (hon.) bd. dirs. Newport Beach C. of C.; adv. bd. Orange Coast YMCA; bd. dirs. Orange Empire Council B.S.A., Santa Ana, 1962---; pres.-bd. dirs. Proj. 21, Orange Co. 1964---; bd. dirs. Big Brothers of Orange Co., Santa Ana, 1966---, v.p. 1967-69; bd. govs. Aerospace Inds. Assn. 1970-71; pres. Univ. of Calif., Irvine, Found. 1970-71, bd. dirs. Friends of Univ., and adv. bd. Friends of Lib. Catholic. Rec.: golf, swim. Res.: 32621 Sea Island Dr., Laguna Niguel, CA 92677; Office: Ford Rd., Newport Beach, CA 92663.

LAWSON, ROBERT MACKAY
Business Consultant
b. May 12, 1897, Scotland; s. John Ramsay and Jeanie (Strang) Lawson; m. Amy Bates, Spokane, Wash., June 12, 1919; chil.: Donald Ramsay and Mrs. Vern A. (Doreen) Edwards. Career: Assoc. with Peat, Marwick, Mitchell & Co., L.A. 1920-24; city mgr., S. Pasadena, 1925; CPA firms, Pasa., L.A. and Alhambra, 1925---; cons. State of Calif., L.A. Co., various municipalities and sch. dists. Pres. Caledonia Investment CO.; v.p. Albion Properties, Inc.; pres. Braemar Investment Co. Mem.: Calif. Soc. of CPAs, Am. Inst. of Accts., Tournament of Roses Assn., Overland Club; past pres. Kiwanis Club; past pres., New Century Club; past pres., Univ. Club of Pasadena. Res.: 3210 East California St., Pasadena, CA; Office: First Western Bank Bldg., Pasadena, CA.

LAZAR, RUBIN M.
Attorney at Law
b. Nov. 21, 1928, Montreal, Can.; s. Isaac and Celia Lazar; ed. UCLA 1945-46 and 1948; LL.B. (cum laude), Loyola Univ. Sch. of Law, 1951; m. Serene Sperling, L.A., Dec. 24, 1950; chil.: Mark B., b. Mar. 23, 1954; David J., b. June 18, 1957; Robin, b. Mar. 11, 1960. Career: Law clerk (Hon. Ben Harrison), U.S. Dist. Ct., L.A., 1951-52; est. pvt. practice law, 1952---; partner, Silver and Lazar, 1956---. Lectr. (domestic rels.), Continuing Edn. Series, Calif. State Bar, 1962. U.S. Army, 1946-48. Awards: recipient, Aggeler and Bur. of Natl. Affairs awards, Loyola Univ. Sch. of Law, 1951. Mem.: Am. Judicature Soc.; Am., L.A., Beverly Hills Bar Assns.; chmn. local adm. com., Calif. State Bar Assn. 1959-65; dir. Am. Acad. of Matrimonial Lawyers; arbitrator, Am. Arbitration Assn.; pres. L.A. Lodge, dir. B'nai B'rith, 1959; v.-chmn. atty's. div. United Jewish Welfare Fund, 1962-63; del L.A. Jewish Fed. Council, 1967-74; pres. Adat Ari El (Valley Jewish Comm. Center and Temple), 1969-70; v.p. L.A. Hebrew H.S. 1972-76; Phi Delta Phi, Pi Kappa Delta. Democrat. Res.: 3920 Longridge Ave., Sherman Oaks, CA; Office: 9595 Wilshire Blvd., Beverly Hills, CA 90212.

LEACH, J. FRANK
President, Arcata National Corporation
b. Mar. 11, 1921, New Ross, Co. Wexford, Ire.; s. John Reginald and Evelyn Muriel (Ard) Leach; B.S. (ind. mgmt.), Wayne Univ.; m. Lee Marie Serre, Detroit, Mich., Dec. 1, 1945; chil.: J. Michael, b. Aug. 28, 1947;

Suzanne Lee, b. Oct. 7, 1951. Career: Ford Motor Co. (prodn.-mgr. Cleveland Engring. plant), 1934-54; dir. mfg. Studebaker Packard Corp. 1954-56; v.p. mfg., div. pres., v.p. group exec., exec. v.p. and chief opr. ofcr. Amphenol Electronics Corp. and successor, Bunker Ramo Corp. 1956-72; pres.-chief exec. ofcr. Arcata Natl. 1972---. Dir.: Arcata Natl. Corp.; Consolidated Freight Ways; Sola-Basic Inds.; Henry Pratt Co.; Real Estate Data, Inc.; Bay Area Council; Calif. Roundtable. Clubs: S.F. Stock Exch., Menlo Country, Desert Forest golf, Sunset Ridge Country. Vestryman, Christ Espicopalian Ch. Hobbies: boating, skiing, swim, tennis. Res.: 121 Sheridan Way, Woodside, CA 94062; Office: 2750 Sand Hill Rd., Menlo Park, CA 94025.

LEARN, ELMER W.
University Administrator
b. Jan. 19, 1929, Sayre, Pa.; s. John Walter and Ruth (Warner) Learn; B.S., Pa. State Univ., 1950, M.S., 1951, Ph.D., 1957; m. Arlene Green, Sept. 22, 1956, Tannersville, Pa.; daus.: Diane Marie, b. Aug. 1, 1957; Linda Jean, b. Mar. 29, 1960. Career: Asst. prof. to prof., Dept. of Agri. Econ., Univ. of Minn., 1956-69, head dept. 1963-64, asst. to pres., 1964-65, exec. asst. to pres. and dir. of Planning, 1965-69; exec. vice chancellor, also prof., Univ. Calif., Davis, 1969---. Cons.: 9th Fed. Reserve Bank, 1962, U.S. Dept. of Agri. 1962-65. AUS, 1951-53. Contbr. to numerous publs. on agri. policy, price analysis and foreign trade. Res.: 1702 Sycamore Lane, Davis, CA; Office: Univ. of Calif., Davis, Davis, CA 95616.

LEARS, MARYON PATRICIA
Business Executive
b. Oct. 8, 1919, Portland, Ore.; d. Benjamin Franklin and Iris (Florentine) Lears; ed. U.S.C. Career: Campus repr. to buyer, J.W. Robinson Co. 1936-44; buyer, mdse. mgr. Silverwoods, 1944-45; mdse mgr. 1949---, and West Coast supv. Women's Depts., Hart Schaffner and Marx stores, 1970-72, v.p. (23 stores) 1972---; dir. TV fashion shows. Mem.: L.A. C. of C.; L.A. Adv. Club; Fashion Group; L.A. Museum; World Affairs Council; Republican. Catholic. Hobbies: painting, reading, music. Rec.: golf, sun worshiping, travel. Res.: 10501 Wilshire Blvd., L.A., CA 90024; Office: 225 W. 6th St., L.A., CA 90014.

LEARY, GARY L.
Attorney at Law
b. Apr. 12, 1935, Oakland; s. Frank J. and Evelyn M. Leary; ed. A.A., UCLA, 1955, B.A., 1957; LL.B. 1960; m. Sandra F. Leary, No. Hollywood, Nov. 23, 1956; chil.: Linda Susan, b. July 1, 1958; Thomas John, b. May 24, 1963; Kathleen Ann, b. Apr. 23, 1965. Career: Atty. at law, gen. practice, Clarke, Swink, Thatcher & Leary firm, 1961-72, partner, Clark & Leary firm, 1972---; Contrib. author: Legal articles publ. UCLA Law Review, 1959, 60; Continuing Edn. of the Bar, 1971. Artillery ofcr. U.S. Army, 2nd Lt. 1957; Capt., Calif. Army Natl. Guard, 1965. Mem.: bd. dirs. E. Valley YMCA; pres. No. Hollywood C. of C.; dir. No. Hollywood Rotary Club; Phi Delta Phi, Sigma Alpha Epsilon. Ofcr., Emmanuel Lutheran Ch., No. Hollywood. Hobby: athletics. Res.: 14623 Weddington St., Van Nuys, CA 91401; Office: 4605 Lankershim Blvd., Suite 721, No. Hollywood, CA 91602.

LEASK, BARBARA GLENN WALLACE
Educator
b. Oct. 7, 1925, Fresno, Calif.; d. Joel Glenn and Doris P. Wallace; A.A., Bakersfield Coll., 1945; B.A., San Jose State Coll., 1949; M.A., Pepperdine Univ., 1976; Ph.D. in edn., Pacific Univ., 1978; m. Richard H. Leask, Feb. 14, 1948, Bakersfield; chil.: d. Jerelyn Leask (Harrington), b. Mar. 29, 1951; Larry Richard, b. Mar. 13, 1954; Wally Kent, b. Apr. 14, 1956. Career: tchr. Kindergarten (wartime emergency credential), 1945-47; tchr. dance, 1947-48; 3rd grade tchr., Standard Sch., 1948-49; substitute tchr. city and co. schs., 1957-65; tchr. grades 5 and 6, 1965-67; tchr. third grade, Wingland Sch., 1967---. Recipient: Golden Apple Award, 1974; Outstanding Elem. Tchr. of Am. Award, 1974; Freedoms Found. Valley Forge Tchrs. Medal, 1975; Service Award, Compton Jr. Hi Sch. PTA. Pres., Standard Sch. Dist. Tchrs. Assn., 1978-79; AAUW, pres. 1977-78; chmn. for Standard Sch. Dist. Christmas program; Past Pres.: Delta Theta Tau, Gamma Xi chpt.; First Nighters, Bakersfield Community Theater; Col. Nichols PTA; Bakersfield Council PTA (34 schs); Bakersfield Jr. Womens Club; Kern Co. Matron's Assn. of Bakersfield; Kern Co. Line Officers Assn. Founder, Bakersfield Coll. Alumni Assn., 1945---. Mem.: Eastern Star; Assistance League; Calif. Tchrs. Assn.; Nat. Edn. Assn.; Womens Club of

Bakersfield; Internat. Reading Assn.; Symphony Assocs. of Kern Philharmonic Pol. Campaigner for Evelle Younger for Gov. Presbyterian. Hobbies: ceramics, reading, traveling. Home: 2907 Christmas Tree Lane, Bakersfield, CA 93306; Office: Wingland Sch., 2000 Diane St., Oildale, CA 93308.

LEAVEY, T.E.
Chairman of the Board, Farmers Insurance Group
b. Sept. 1, 1897, Ferndale, Calif.; s. Michael and Rose (Carolan) Leavey; ed. Arcata H.S., Calif.; Univ. of Santa Clara, Calif; LL.B., Georgetown Univ. 1923, LL.D., 1950; m. Dorothy E. Risley; chil.: Kathleen and Terry. Career: admitted to Bar, 1923; Fed. Land Bank Bd., Wash., D.C.; Fed. Land Bank, Berkeley; Natl. Farm Loan Assn., L.A.; co-founder-dir., Farmers Ins. Exch. 1927-48, pres. 1948-59, chmn. bd. 1959---; pres.-dir.: Farmers Truck Exch., Farmers Underwriters Assn., Fire Underwriters Assn., Truck Underwriters Assn.; dir. Farmers New World Life Ins. Co. (known as Farmers Ins. Group, operating in all states west of the Miss.); owner-mgr., Pala Rey Ranch, San Diego Co., Lt. (attended O.T.S.), U.S. Army, WW I. Mem.: agr. com., L.A. C. of C.; trustee, Council of Profit Sharing Inds.; Wilshire Country Club; past pres., Georgetown Alumni Assn.; Delta Theta Phi. Hobby: photography, raising purebred livestock. Rec.: golf, hunting. Res.: 633 Alta Dr., Beverly Hills, CA.

LE COCQ, RHODA P.
Author — Professor
b. Lyndon, Wash.; d. R.B. and Nellie (Straks) LeCocq; ed. B.A., Wash. State Univ., 1942; M.A., Stanford Univ. 1950; stu. Univ. of Hawaii, 1960; M.A., Univ. of Calif., Santa Barbara, 1967; Ph.D., Calif. Inst. of Asian Stus. 1970; stu. The Sarbonne, Paris. Career: Mag.-Book Sect., Ofc. of Information (Pac. Coast Waves), USN, Wash., DC 1942-46; Lt. USNR; mag. writer-owner Le Cocq-Luray, NYC, 1946-48; literary scout, Farrar-Strauss, 1949-53; promotion dept. adv. Safeway Stores, S.F., 1955-57; pub. rel. counsel own firm, Honolulu, 1957-59; pub. rels. dir. Honolulu Acad. of Arts, 1959-61; inf. ofcr. Civil Def., City-Co. of Honolulu, 1961-63; ed. State Dept. of Edn. publs. 1968; pub. inf. and legislative off., Sacto. Co. Welfare Dept. 1969---. Visiting prof.: Ext., Univ. of Calif., Davis, 1970-71; Assoc. prof., Calif. Inst. of Asian Studies, S.F. 1973-79; Author: contrib. to natl. mags.: Red Book, Liberty, Dance, Cosmopolitan, 1942-46; The Shadow Outside, TV, 1957; Behold a Pale Horse, publ. Twenty Best Short Stories, 1966; The Radical Thinkers, 1972; Vision of Suprahumanity, 1973. Mem.: Ret. Ofcrs. Assn., Sacto. Pub. Rel. Round Table, Sacto. Press Club, Internat. Platform Assn., Mensa, Pub. Rels. Soc. of Am., Am. Soc. of Writers, Armed Forces Writers League, Smithsonian Assoc.. Hobbies: travel, tennis, swimming, photog. Res.: 555 Douglas St., No. 107, Broderick, CA 95605; Office: 1725 28th St., Sacto., CA 95816.

LECOQUE
Artist Painter — Sculptor — Writer
b. Mar. 21, 1891, Prague (U.S. Cit. 1960); s. Alois and Francisca Lecoque; ed. Acad. de Beaux Arts (under Prof. Crnic), Zagreb; Acad. Julian (prof. Baschett, Emile Bernard), Paris. Career: est. studio at La Ruche des Artists, painted with distinguished artists such as Auguste Renoir, The Entrance to La Ruche, Paris; other res. and studios: Rome, Naples, Venice, Capri, Flornce, Yugoslavia; USA res. Chicago and Los Angeles 1951---; exhibs. incl.: Gallery Charpentier, Paris, 1912; Glass Palace, London, 1913; Gallery Andre, Paris, 1925; Biennale of Venice, 1926, 28; Gallery Jurecek, Moravska-Ostrava, 1926; Galleries of Bergen, Oslo, 1935; Exposition at Mostara, Yugoslavia, 1941---; Gallery San Marco, Rome, 1945; Gallery Nationale d' Art Moderne, Rome, 1949, 50; Exposition, Florence, 1952; Bohemian Art Club, Chicago, 1952; Exposition, Laguna Beach Art Gallery, Calif. 1955; Camelback Gallery, Scottsdale, Ariz. 1957; Municipal Tower Gallery, L.A. 1958; Gering Galleries of Art, Beverly Hills, 1960; Gallery Benezit, Paris, and San Diego Art Center, Calif. 1961; Gallery Cowie, L.A. and Gallery Bernheim, Paris, 1962; Arcade Gallery, Santa Barbara, 1967; Lilienfeld Gallery, N.Y. 1968; Juarez Gallery, Palm Beach, Fla. 1969; museums: Mus. of Old Montmartre, Paris; Collection des Beaux-Arts Ville de Paris; Mus. of Prague, L.A. Mus., Mus. of Davenport, Ia.; Okla. Art Center, Okla. City; others in Bruno, Milan, Copenhagen, Colo. Springs, Nev., San Francisco, Palm Springs; pvt. collections: pres. Dwight D. Eisenhower, Pres. John Kennedy, and Pres. Richard M. Nixon, Wash. D.C.; Villi Grifaine, Paris; Prince Dado Ruspoli, Marquise Gaby Bianchi, and Curzio Malaparte, Rome; Baron

Mario Cottrau, and J. Panacker, Capri; Arch. Jerome Robert Cerny, Lake Forest, Ill.; Alfred Loeb, Paris; F. Bonino, Buenos Aires; Pauline Todt, Foreign Minister, London; Prince Francois Schwarzenberg, and B. Kryl, Chicago. Awards: 1st Prize, Architect Turek, Prague, 1914; Gold Medal, Societe des Arts, Scis., Lettres, Paris, 1966; feat. TV shows. Author and Poet: many books publ. many langs., incl. Renoir My Friend, Girl with the Wooden Leg, Tragic Weekend. Sculptor (with Rodin and Bourdelle). Mem.: Amer. Inst. of Fine Arts. Hobby: film prod. Studio: 8079 Selma Ave., Los Angeles, CA 90046; Office: 900 N. La Cienega Blvd., Los Angeles, CA 90069.

LEE, HENRY LAWRENCE, JR.
Pharmaceutical Company President
b. Dec. 23, 1926, Wilkes-Barre, Pa.; s. Henry Lawrence, II and May (Robbins) Lee; desc.: Capt. Andrew Lee, Paxtang ranger, Rev. War hero; James Stewart Lee, first to mine and market Pa. anthracite, 1813; Emily Lee Post, social arbiter; Ed. H.S.; Wyo. Sem. 1944; B.S., MIT 1947; Ph.D., Commonwealth Univ. 1955; m. Ria C. Gerhardt, Bayreuth, Ger., May 22, 1948; chil.: Diana T., b. Feb. 4, 1949; Ronald G., b. May 11, 1952. Careers: Tech. writer, Union Carbide, BYC, 1948-51; research spec.-engr., Rocketdyne Div., No. Am. Aviation, Inc., L.A. 1951-55; tech. dir.-exec. v.p., The Epoxylite Corp., El Monte, 1955-71; pres. Lee Pharmaceuticals, 1971---. Author: (textbook) Epoxy Resins — Their Applications and Technology, 1967; Handbook of Epoxy Resins, publ. 1967; New Linear Polymers, 1967; numerous articles publ. profl. journs. Patentee, high temperature resins. Research assoc., chemist, U.S. Army Chem. Warfare Lab., Mass., 1946, WW II. Mem.: Am. Chem. Soc., Am. Soc. for Testing Materials, Soc. Applied Spectroscopy, Soc. Plastics Engrs., Soc. Plastics Ind., AAAS, San Marino C. of C., L.A. C. of C., Mason. Presbyterian. Hobbies: photog., linguistics. Rec.: hunting, golf. Res.: 3543 E. Calif. Blvd., Pasadena, CA 91107; Office: 1444 Santa Anita Ave., S. El Monte, CA 91733.

LEE, PHILIP R.
Former University Chancellor
b. Apr. 17, 1924, S.F.; s. Russell V., M.D. and Dorothy (Womack) Lee; A.B., Stanford Univ., 1945; M.D. 1948; M.S., Univ. of Minn. 1955; Sc.D. (hon.), MacMurray Coll. 1967; m. Catherine Lockridge, Menlo Park, June 13, 1953; chil.: Dorothy Rusk, Paul Barnett, Amy Winton, Margaret Eloesser, Theodore William. Career: Faculty, NYC Sch. of Med. 1955-56; faculty, Stanford Univ. Sch. of Med. 1956-58 (on leave, 1963-68); staff: Palo Alto Med. Clinic, Palo Alto, 1956-65; dir. Health Servs. Ofc. of Tech. Cooperation and Research, AID 1963-65; dep. asst. secty. Health and Sci. Affairs, U.S. Dept. of Health, Edn. and Welfare, 1965, asst. secty. HEW, Wash., D.C. 1965-69; chancellor, Univ. of Calif., S.F., prof. Soc. Med. 1969-72. Lt. (j.g.), MC, USNR, 1949-51. Episcopalian. Res.: 149 Sixth Ave., S.F., CA 94118; Office: 126 Med. Scis. Bldg., Univ. of Calif., S.F., CA 94143.

LEE, ROBERT
Professor of Social Ethics
b. Apr. 28, 1929, S.F.; s. Frank and Fong (Shee) Lee; Gr.grandfather worked on Union Pac. RR in 1850s; B.A., Univ. Calif., Berkeley, 1951; M.A., Pac. Sch. of Religion, 1953; stu., Union Theol. Sem., M.Div., 1955; Ph.D., Columbia Univ., 1958; m. May Gong, Feb. 4, 1951, Burlingame, Calif.; chil.: Mellanie Lynn, Marcus Arthur, Matthew John, Wendy Gale, Michelle Miko. Career: Mem. faculty Union Theol. Sem., NYC, 1955-61; vis. prof.: Mills Coll. of Edn.; Inst. of Relig. & Soc. Studies, Jewish Theol. Sem.; Internat. Christian Univ., Tokyo, Japan; Assn. of S.E. Asian Seminaries, Chung Chi Coll., Hong Kong; Univ. Calif. Ext.; Ch. Divinity Sch. of the Pac.; Pac. Sch. of Rel.; Sr. Fellow, East-West Center, Honolulu, 1972-73; vis. scholar, Stanford Univ. Grad. Sch. of Bus.; co-opted staff, World Council of Chs.; now dir., Inst. of Ethics and Soc., also Margaret S. Dollar Prof. of Soc. Ethics, S.F. Theol. Sem., 1961---. Dir., ISI Trust Fund; ISI Income Fund; Family Service Agency of Marin; Trustee, Found. for Theol. Edn. in S.E. Asia; mem. Interdisciplinary Task Force, Calif. State Dept. of Edn. Fellow, Soc. for Study of Values; Order of the Golden Bear. Ordained minister, United Presbyterian Ch. Author: 12 books incl.: The Spouse Gap; Religion & Leisure in Am.; Stranger in the Land; Soc. Sources of Church Unity (selected for the Kennedy White House Lib.); The Promise of Bennett, others; contrib. to Journs., e.g., National Observer, NY Herald Tribune, others. Office: 2 Kensington Rd., San Anselmo, CA 94960.

LEE-OWENS, LYNDA JOAN
Beauty College Owner
b. Nov. 24, 1940, Orangevale, Calif.; d. Elgin Merrille and Pattie May (Brewer) Lee; 4th cousin, Gen. Robert E. Lee; 3-year diploma, Bethany Bible Coll., Santa Cruz, 1961; cosmetology, Citrus Hts. Beauty Coll., 1970; license, 1970; instr. training, Jerrylee Beauty Coll., Sacramento, 1974; licensed, 1974; m. Walter Richard Compton Lee-Owens (C.P.A.); June 24, 1978, Sacramento; chil.: Lori, b. July 8, 1974; John Thomas, b. Feb. 4, 1976; Cary William, b. Oct. 12, 1969; Laureen Estelle, b. July 29, 1967. Career: piano tchr., 1961-74; owner, Bride's Elite Weddings, profl. photog., 1967-74; dir. and pres., Parries Beauty Coll., Inc., 1970--- (DBA: Jerrylee Beauty Coll., Woodland, Calif. 1972-78); pres. and dir., Vallejo Beauty Acad., Inc. (DBA: Jerrylee Beauty Coll., Vallejo, Calif.), 1974---; pres. and dir., Metropolitan Beauty Schs., Inc. DBA: Jerrylee Beauty Coll. in Sacramento, Calif.; pres. and dir. Roseville Jerrylee Beauty Coll., 1975---; new school to be founded in Auburn, 1979. Editor, Bethany Bible Coll. newspaper, 1960-61; mem. Bethanaires, singers, 1960-61; choir director, organist, youth dir. Citrus Hts. Assembly of God ch., 1961-67. Hobbies: photog., piano, organ, cosmetology. Rec.: skiing, swimming. Home: 7496 Evening Way, Citrus Heights, CA 95610; Office: 5522 Garfield Ave., Sacramento, CA 95841.

LEFEBVRE d'ARGENCE, RENE-YVON
Museum Director -- Curator
b. Aug. 21, 1928, Plouescat, France; stu. Coll. St. Aspais in Fontainebleau; Lyce Albert Sarraut, Hanoi; Ecole Libre des Sci. Politiques, Sorbonne; Pembroke Coll., Cambridge, Eng.; Litt.D., 1952; languages: Chinese 1950, Japanese 1951, Finnish 1952; m. Ritva Anneli Pelanne, Sept. 7, 1955, Hanoi, Vietnam; chil.: Chantal, Yann, Luc. Career: Curator, Mus. Cernuschi, Paris, 1953; mem. Ecole Francaise d.Extreme-Orient, 1954; curator, Blanchard de la Brosse Mus., Saigon and Louis Finot Mus., Hanoi, 1954-58; Quai d'Orsay Grant, Taiwan, 1959; Prof. of Art Hist., Univ. of Calif., Berkeley, 1962-65; curator, Asiatic Collections, M.H. de Young Mem. Mus., S.F., 1964; dir., Avery Brundage Collection, 1965-68; dir. and chief curator, Asian Art Mus. of S.F., 1969---. Trustee: Asian Art Found., Beaudry Found.; bd. mem. Alliance Francaise, S.F.; pres., French-Am. Bilingual Sch., S.F.; founder (1967), bd. mem. Ecole Francaise of S.F.; advis. com. mem., Soc. for Asian Art, S.F. Served with Free French Forces, WW II. Roman Catholic. Hobby: flute. Rec.: bicycling, camping, tennis. Res.: 16 Midhill, Mill Valley, CA 94941; Office: Asian Art Mus. of S.F., Golden Gate Park, S.F., CA 94118.

LEFTWICH, JAMES ADOLF
Writer -- Publisher
b. July 23, 1902, Newport News, Va.; s. David and Eugenia (Mihalovics) Leftwich; stu., August Mil. Acad., 1920; arch., lit., Univ. of Va., 1921-25; m. Ilka Renwick, Sept. 2, 1947; dau.: Jeanne Renwick, b. June 25, 1949, Lambertville, N.J.; m. 2d. Merry Ann Ottosen, Mar. 12, 1963. Career: Newspaperman, feature writer, The New York Sun, 1926-30; N.Y. Am., 1930-33; feature ed., Nat. Radio Press Syndicate, 1932-35; Newport News Times Herald, 1934-36; feature writer and contbr. to various newspapers, publs., 1936---; dir. art pub. rels. Art Assocs., NYC, 1939-42; pub. rels. assoc. Com. Internat. Econ. Policy, Reciprocal Trade Agreements Act, 1944, pub. rels. counsel, N.Y. Bd. Trade, 1943-50; pub. rels. cons., NYC, 1951-56; pub. rels. Ryan Aero Co., 1957; pub. rels. counsel La Jolla Fed. Svgs. & Loan Assn., La Jolla Town Council, La Jolla Decent Lit. Com., 1959-60; estab. La Jolla Press, 1968---. Author: Biog. Henry William Herbert (wrote under name of Frank Forester); O'Malley Loves Josephine (short stories); La Jolla's House of Many Legends; Duel of the Ironclads, Time-Life Books; numerous feature stories on Civil War Naval Hist. Ed.: The Bulletin, for Am. Soc. of Swedish Engrs. Mem.: U.S. Olympic Boxing Team, Paris, France, 1924; intercollegiate and nat. Amateur Athletic Union Middleweight (160 lbs.) Champion. Mil.: Athletic Dir., 111th Field Arty., 1926. Mem.: Nat. Press Club, Wash., D.C., 1934---; Sigma Delta Chi. Episcopalian. Hobby: gun collection. Res.: 2056 Torrey Pines Rd., La Jolla, CA 92038.

LEIGH, CARMA RUSSELL
California State Librarian, Retired
b. Nov. 15, 1904, McLoud, Okla.; d. William Luther and Ida (Jenkins) Russell; A.B., Okla. Coll. for Women, 1925; certificate in librarianship, Univ. of Calif., Berkeley, 1930, M.A., 1932; (hon.) L.H.D. Univ. of Pac., Stockton, 1965; m. Dr. Robert D. Leigh, Oct. 22,

1960 (dec. 1961); dau.: Mrs. Boyd D. (Rita Alice) Collier, b. Apr. 16, 1937. Career: Asst. pub. librn., Berkeley, 1930-31; head librn., Watsonville, 1931-35; Co. librn., Orange Co., Santa Ana, 1938-42; Co. Librn., San Bernardino Co. Lib. 1942-45; Wash. State Librn., 1945-51; Calif. State Librn., 1951-72. Contrib. articles to various lib. publs.; ed. Wash. State Lib. News, 1945-51; A.L.A. repr. on stu. tour. pub. libs. of W. Ger. and W. Berlin, 1952; natl. bd. Natl. Book Com., 1954-72; adv. bd. USC Grad. Sch. Lib. Sci. 1956-67; pub. adm. adv. com. Sacto. State Coll. 1955-57; adv. com. book sect. stu. Univ. Calif., Berkeley, 1956-58; adv. com. Univ. Ext. in Lib. 1963-69. Mem.: (life) pres., Pac. Northwest Lib. Assn., 1950-51; (life) pres. Calif. Lib. Assn., 1955; (life) Am. Lib. Assn., v.p. 1958; pres. Am. Assn. of State Libraries, 1958; adv. com. Women in Mil. Serv., 1953-56; bd. mgrs. Calif. Cong. PTA 9156-60; com. Natl. Plan Lib. Edn. 1963-67; v.p., 1967; chmn. coms. 1968-69; (hon. life) Wash. Lib. Assn.; Calif. Coord. Council on Higher Edn. 1966-68 (many other lib. coms.); mem., Bd. of Friends of Malcolm A. Love Lib., San Diego State Univ. 1977---; mem., Fine Arts Gallery of San Diego. Congregational Ch. Rec.: theater. Res.: 6927 Amherst St., San Diego, CA 92115.

LEIGHTON, JACQUELYN LEA
Designer -- Inventor
b. Utah; dau. Ward Andrew and Eunice Helen Lea (Brenan) Rasmussen; desc. Gen. Robert E. Lee; stu., Otis Art Inst., L.A. Trade Tech. Coll., S.F. Sch. of Design, UCLA; son, Rex Lea Bassett. Career: Asst. to designer IRENE (wardrobe to the stars dept.), M.G.M. Studios; designer (costume uniforms for all theme restaurants), Disneyland; designer ladies uniforms (intro. high fashion), Barco Fashions of Calif.; designer, supr. nat. high fashion lines, Maxwell Shieff Couturier, Beverly Hills; designer, inventor, soft toy specialist, Mattel Toy Co., L.A.; presently owner-operator, The Fashion Salon, Van Nuys, ---; also cons. in fashion design, costume design and product (toys) design for mot. pic. indus., Viking Prodns., Mattel Toy Co., Shindana Toy Co., Western Air Lines, others. Soft toy credits incl. (TV series and mot. pics.): Henrietta Hippo, "New Zoo Review"; Mrs. Beasley, "Family Affair"; Gentle Ben Bear, "Gentle Ben"; Puff, "To Rome with Love"; Capt. Kangaroo; Mt. Potts, "Chitty Chitty Bang Bang"; Dr. Doolittle and Pushmi-Pullyu, "Dr. Doolittle"; Flip Wilson/Geraldine; (TV Commercial Products): Rodney Allen Rippy, Frito Bandito, Charlie Tuna, Ronald McDonald, Pillsbury's Doughboy; (Story Book Dolls): Dr. Seuss characters, Yertle the Turtle, Cat in the Hat, Horton; Cartoon characters: Mickey Mouse, Donald Duck, Woody Woodpecker, Goofy, others; Original Dolls: Teachy Keen (1st teaching doll), Paula Polar Bear, Lovey Lamb, Linus the Lion, Patootie the Clown, Lamby Pie, Bernie Bernard, Lambie Lovelight, T-Bone, and others. Mem. Calif. Apparel Designers Assn., past pub. chmn.; Mattel Mgmt. Assn. Special interests: organic gardening, wholistic health. Address: 13603 Leadwell St., Van Nuys, CA 91405.

LEIMERT, WALTER H., JR.
Real Estate Broker
b. Aug. 2, 1921, Oakland; s. Walter H. and Lucille (Cavanaugh) Leimert; ed. UCLA 1942; sons: Walter H., III, b. Mar. 6, 1955; Norman Timothy, b. May 29, 1956. Career: CBS news commentator, 1943-46; pres. Walter H. Leimert Co., real estate brokers and devels., 1946---. CBS war corr. (1944-45), WW II. Mem.: pres. L.A. Realty Bd. 1961; v.p. Calif. Real Estate Assn. 1962; Phi Gamma Delta; pres. Southwest Republican Club. Catholic. Hobby: UCLA sports broadcasting. Rec.: flying, golf. Office: 606 N. Larchmont Blvd., L.A., CA 90004.

LEISHMAN, LATHROP KING
Business Owner
b. Jan. 5, 1904, Terminal Island, Calif.; s. William Lathrop and Maud Olivia (King) Leishman; B.S., Ore. State Univ., 1926; m. Marie Koiner, Sept. 8, 1926, Pasadena; chil.: Robert Koiner, b. June 27, 1929; William Lathrop, b. Feb. 26, 1933; Linda Marie (Palmer), b. Dec. 3, 1940. Career: partner, Crown City Lumber & Mill Co., Pasadena, 1926-63; partner, Leishman Mgmt. Co., Pasadena, 1963---. Dir., Annandale Golf Club. Mem.: Pasadena Advis. Bd., Lloyds Bank, Calif., 1950---; Merchants & Mfrs. Assn. of L.A.; So. Calif. Retail Lumber Dealers Assn., pres. 1948-49; Grand Marshal, 90th Pasadena Tournament of Roses, mem. 1929---, pres. 1938-39, mem. Football Com., 1938---; bd. dir. Pasadena YMCA; advis. bd., Pasadena Salvation Army; dir. Pasadena C. of C., 1978---; pres. Pasadena Flower Show Assn.; dir. Pasadena Beautiful, 1961---; dir. Children's Home Soc. of Calif. 1935-45.

Recipient L.A. Times' Nat. Sports Award 1956; Nat. Football Found. and Hall of Fame, Distinguished Citizen Award, 1974; Big Ten Conf. Participation Award, 1977; NCAA Spec. Award for Comm. and Collegiate Serv. 1977. Presbyterian, Elder. Hobbies: growing roses, golf. Home: 1329 Cambridge Rd., San Marino, CA 91108; Office: 77 W. Del Mar, Pasadena, CA 91105.

LeMAILE-WILLIAMS, ROBERT L.
Physician
b. June 25, 1940; s. Florence Williams Johnson; B.A. cum laude, Dillard Univ., New Orleans, 1961; certification, Oak Ridge Training Lab. nuclear med. radioisotope, 1960; M.A. microbiology, immunology, Univ. of Texas, Austin, 1967; M.D., Univ. of Mich., 1973; Internship & Residency, 1973-75; m. Florence Robinson, Dec. 27, 1965, Alexandria, La.; chil.: Terrilyn Rene, b. Sept. 22, 1966; Mysheika Robin, b. Apr. 4, 1970. Career: research scientist, Univ. of Mich. Sch. of Pub. Health, 1971-73; housestaff, internal med., 1973-75; cons. on epidemiology, Clinica Los Campesino, Lamont, Calif., 1975; asst. prof., Charles R. Drew Med. Sch., 1976-77; pvt. practice, internal med.: cardiopulmonary, hypertension and infectious diseases, 1977---. Exec. secty. com. on acad. affairs and student rep., Dean's Coms. for 1980s, Univ. of Mich. Med. Sch., 1969-73; contbr. to lecture series on: New Roles for the Black Male, pub. 1970; initiated lecture series on Care & Spec. Health Needs of Black Patients, Mich., 1972. Pub. articles med. journs. Editor, textbook, The Black Patient. Cons. and developer, Focus on Health radio program, KJLH, Compton. Awards: outstanding student award and scholarship: New Orleans Womens Aux. to Dental Soc. 1959; Louisiana Cancer Soc., 1958-59; Nat. Med. Fellowship Inc., 1969-73; Nominee: Woodrow Wilson Fellowship, 1961, Delta Omega Pub. Health Honor Soc., 1969; Beta Kappa Chi, 1959-61. Mem.: Assoc., Am. Coll. Physicians; Assoc. Am. Soc. Internal Med.; Am. Pub. Health Assn.; Mich. and Tex. Publ. Health Assns.; Am. Soc. Microbiology; Alpha Phi Alpha Victor Vaughn Med. Soc. of Mich.; Galens Hon. Med. Soc. of Mich.; Nat. Med. Assn.; Student NMA; Student AMA; AMA. Office: 1127 Wilshire Blvd., Suite 811, L.A., CA 90017.

LeMONS, GREG
Filmmaker
b. July 17, 1940, Fresno, Calif.; s. Dewey and Ilah LeMoss; B.S., Calif. State Univ., San Jose, 1963, M.S., 1964; M.A., Cal. State Univ., S.F., 1974; m. Edith Fiore, June 5, 1976, Los Gatos; chil.: Erik, b. July 8, 1967; Christian, b. Sept. 11, 1969. Career: Filmmaker, 1968---: Ski The Gentle Giant, 1969; Ski Alta, 1970; Ski Fever, 1972. Address: P.O.B. 1050, Los Gatos, CA 95030.

LEMUS, GEORGE
College Professor
b. Apr. 14, 1928, Del Rio, Tex.; s. Leopoldo (M.D.) and Ines (Suarez) Lemus; ed. stu. Universidad Nacional Autonoma de Mexico, 1946-48; B.A., Univ. of Tex., 1952, M.A. 1956, Ph.D. (Latin Am. stus.), 1963; m. Carmen Garcia, Madrid, Spain, Aug. 6, 1957; chil.: Agnes Marie, b. Dec. 23, 1958; Sarita Ann, b. June 15, 1960; Henry Edward, b. Sept. 4, 1961; Robert Leopold, b. Mar. 24, 1963; William Anthony, b. Apr. 20, 1971. Career: Tchr., pub. H.S., Aberdeen, Ida., 1953-54; tchg. fellow, Univ. of Tex., Austin, 1955-57; instr. USAF Lang. Sch., Lackland AFB, Tex. 1957-58; Spanish instr., Loyola Univ., L.A. 1958-60; instr. Santa Monica City Coll., 1959-60; asst. prof., S.D. State Coll. 1960-65; assoc. prof., Spanish, 1965-68; prof. 1968---, chmn. Latin Am. Stus. Com. 1963-66; instr. Grossmont Coll. 1963-69; dir. San Diego State-Mex. City (summer pgms.) Universidad Iberoamericana, 1964, 65; grad. adv. to Latin Am. Studies Pgm., 1967-70; visiting prof., Spanish, Univ. of Colo., Boulder (summer), 1968. Author: Pedagogia Mexicana y Norteamericana Comparada, Hispania, 1962; Francisco Bulnes: su vida y sus obras, Coleccion Studium No. 62, Mex., D.F., Ediciones De Andrea, 1965. Awards: Spanish Govt. Scholar, Direccion Gen. de Relaciones Culturales, Madrid, 1957; Del Amo Sociedad Bascongada de los Amigos del Pais, Bilbao, Spain; listed: Directory of Am. Scholars, Vol. III; Natl. Directory of Latin Americanists, 1965, others. Mem.: Am. Assoc. Tchrs. of Spanish and Portuguese; Philological Assn. of the Pac. Coast; Assn. for Latin Am. Studies; secty.-treas., Pac. Coast Council on Latin Am. Studies, 1964; Ex-Students Assn., Univ. of Tex.; Calif. State Employees Assn.; Sigma Delta Pi, 1952---; Alpha Mu Gamma, 1960---. Democrat. Roman Catholic. Hobby: Frontenis. Rec.: swimming, tennis. Res.: 5730 Lance St., San Diego, 92120; Office: San Diego State Univ., Spanish Dept., San Diego, CA 92115.

LENKEY, SUSAN V.
Art Historian
b. Budapest, Hungary; Baccalaureate degree, 1928; Tch. Diploma in French and German Philology, Pazmany Univ., Budapest, 1934; Ph.D. (summa cum laude) in art hist. and class. archaeology, 1946; dau. Maryll Lenkey-Telegdy. Career: asst. prof. Art Hist., Pazmany Univ., 1945-50; lectr. in Museology Eotvos Univ., Budapest and research asst. Municipal Mus., 1950-56; catalogue asst. Yale Univ. Lib., 1957-60; prof. of art hist., Chapman Coll. World Campus Afloat (4 tchg. trips around world, 2 around Mediterranean), 1969-77; mem. faculty, undergrad., grad. and honor courses, Stanford Univ. on Renaissance Books, 1964---: Art Historian, Rare Book Librn. Emerita; tchr., Univ. Calif. Ext., 1962-75. Hon. v.p. of Archaeol. Inst. of Am., Stanford Chpt.; acad. adv., Inst. for Shipboard Edn. Mem. Royal Commonwealth Soc., London, Contbr. 60+ articles in field of art hist., museology, bibliography; several monographs, Stanford Univ. Press. Roman Catholic. Hobbies: photog., music, travel. Res.: 274 San Luis Dr., Menlo Park, CA 94025.

LEONHARD, WILLIAM EDWARD
President, Ralph M. Parsons Company
b. Dec. 9, 1914, Middletown, Pa.; s. C. Frank and Ruth (Wagner) Leonhard; B.S. elect. engr., Penn. State Univ.; M.S., elect./civil engr., Mass. Inst. Tech.; War Coll.; m. Wyllis Rocker, Feb. 8, 1940, New Hampshire; chil.: William E., Jr., b. Nov. 2, 1941; Richard W., b. May 18, 1944; Donna Jeanne, b. Aug. 25, 1946. Career: USAF, 1936-64: Chief of Staff, Hdqtrs. Systems Command; Dep. Comdr.; Dir. of Constrn., UWAF, Wash. D.C.; dir., Titan III Pgm., United Tech. Center, 1964-66; with the Ralph M. Parsons Co. 1966---: as sr. v.p. and asst. gen. mgr., 1966; exec. v.p., 1971; pres. and gen. mgr., 1974; pres. and chief exec. ofcr., 1975---. Dir.: The Ralph M. Parsons Co.; Blue Cross of So. Calif.; Basic Resources Internat. S.A.; Am. Cancer Soc.; ARC. Awards: Newman Award, ASME; Engr. of the Year, 1961; MIT Corporate Leadership Award, 1977. Brig. Gen., USAF' 1936-64; decorated Legion of Merit (3); Bronze Star. Clubs: Calif., Annandale Golf, Marrakesh Country, Breakfast Forum, The Twilight Club. Lutheran. Rec.: golf. Res.: 309 Patrician Way, Pasadena, CA 91105; Office: 100 W. Walnut St., Pasadena, CA 91124.

LEPIRE, RAY J.
Hospital Administrator
b. Jan. 22, 1923, New Bedford, Mass.; s. John and Marie Lepire. Career: Div. of purchasing, Pomona Valley Comm. Hosp., Pomona; currently dir. purchasing, St. John's Hosp., Oxnard. USN, 1943-45, Naval Air Gunner. Mayor of Pomona, 1973-77: pres. Pomona Planning Commn. 1972; pres., East Gabriel Valley Planning 1971; mem. Purchasing Agents Assn. of A.H.; So. Calif. Hosp. Pur. Agents Assn. Res.: 4548 La Brea St., Oxnard, CA 93030; Office: 333 No. F St., Oxnard, CA 93030.

LERNER, STUART A.
Psychiatrist
b. Feb. 14, 1946, N.Y.C.; s. Nathan and Betty Lerner, M.D., Tulare Med. Sch., 1969; med. internship, USC Med. Center, 1970; Psychiatry residency, UCLA, 1973. Career: Asst. clin. prof. of psychiatry, UCLA, 1973---; clin. dir., partial hospitalization program, Resthaven Community Mental Health Center, 1973-74; clin. dir., West Hollywood Methadone Maintenance Program, 1974-79; Chief Narcotics Expert, L.A. Co. Municipal Ct., 1975---; pvt. practice psychiatry, Beverly Hills, 1973---. Host KCET-TV Sessions on Drugs and Alcohol, 1978. Author: Infective Endocarditis in Narcotics Addicts, Annals if Internal. Med. Dec. 1968. Mil.: ret. capt., USAF Reserves. Mem.: So. Calif. Psychiatric Soc., 1973---; Am. Psychiatric Assn., 1973---. Hobbies: music, cinema. Rec.: swimming. Office: 450 N. Bedford Dr., Suite 203, Beverly Hills, CA 90210.

LESHER, DEAN STANLEY
Newspaper Publisher
b. Aug. 4, 1902, Williamsport, Md.; s. Dr. David T. and Margaret E. (Prosser) Lesher; B.A. (magna cum laude), Univ. of Md. 1924; LL.B., Harvard Law Sch., 1926; m. Kathryn E. Crowder, St. Charles, Mo., Nov. 23, 1929 (dec. Mar. 7, 1971); m. Margaret L. Ryan, Apr. 2, 1973; chil.: Dean Stanley, II, b. June 23, 1934; Melinda Kay, b. Feb. 4, 1946; Cynthia Ann Rice, b. Dec. 30, 1947. Career: Est. law practice, Kansas City, Mo. 1926-40; admitted to practice, Mo., Kan., Nebr. and Calif., U.S. Fed. Cts. and Treas. Dept.; pvt. law practice, Merced, Calif. 1942-46; co-owner and publ. newspapers, 1938---; pres. Lesher Newspapers; co-owner, publ., Merced

Sun-Star, Valley Bomber, Madera Daily Tribune, West Co. Times, Pittsburg Pres., Valley Times, Livermore; Valley Pioneer, Danville; Pleasanton Times, Moraga Sun, Lafayette Sun, Orinda Sun, Contra Costa Times of Walnut Creek, Antioch Daily Ledger and Pittsburgh Press, Calif. Contrib. articles to trade journs. Lectr., speaker and panel mem. before numerous local, regional and state civic, tchrs., trade, serv. and other groups at conventions and meetings. Mem.: Dir., Calif. Newspaper Publs. Assn. (16 yrs.), v.-chmn. Merced Co. Housing Authority 1945-56; Calif. Adv. Com. on Mental Health, 1953-59, chmn. 1956-58; City Planning Comm. (9 yrs.); past dir.: Calif. Comm. on Delinquency and Crime, Calif. Safety Council; Oakland Sym., Oakland Museum; pres. Merced City and Walnut Creek C.s of C.; trustee, Calif. State Univ. and Colls.; dir.: Chil's. Hosp. of E. Bay; Better Bus. Bur.; Bay Area Council; Suburban Newspapers of Am. (7 yrs.); Concord Century Club; pres., Merced Execs. Club; pres., Merced Rotary, dist. gov. 1958-59; S.F. Press, Commonwealth of S.F., Trade, Harvard Club, Mason, Phi Delta Theta, Phi Kappa Phi, Sigma Delta Chi. Republican. Protestant. Hobby: travel, pub. speaking. Office: 2640 Shadelands Dr., Walnut Creek, CA 94598.

LESSER, SOL
Motion Picture Producer
b. Feb. 17, 1890, Spokane, Wash.; s. Lester and Julia (Levy) Lesser; ed. S.F. pub. schs.; m. Fay Grunauer, S.F., Mar. 26, 1913; chil.: Julian, b. Jan. 18, 1915; Mrs. Michael (Marjorie) Fasman, b. Dec. 1, 1917. Career: Founder, Golden Gate Film Exch., 1913, pres.-dir. 1913---; founder, All Star Feat. Distributors, 1915, pres.-dir. 1915---; founder, West Coast Theatres, L.A., 1920, pres.-dir. 1920---; founder, Principal Theatres Corp. 1921, pres.-dir. 1921---; orgn. Principal Theatres Corp. of Am. 1927, pres.-dir. 1927---; est. Sol Lesser Pordns., Inc., 1944, pres.-dir. 1944-62; mot. pic. prod.: Our Town, Stage Door Canteen, Oliver Twist, Tarzan series, many others; pres. Sol Lesser Prin. Mgmt. Corp., 1962---; Awards: Acad. Award Oscar for Kon Tiki as best documentary of yr., 1952; also Oscar Jean Hersholt Humanitarian Award presented by the Acad. in 1960. Mem.: Mot. Pic. Pioneers; Hillcrest Country, Variety and Tamarisk Country Clubs. Jewish (Wilshire Blvd. Temple). Hobby: golf, bridge. Res.: 10375 Wilshire Blvd., L.A., CA; Office: 333 S. Beverly Dr., Suite 210, Beverly Hills, CA 90212.

LEVENSON, HAROLD ALTMAN
President, Harold Levenson Assocs.
b. May 2, 1919, Boston, Mass.; s. Samuel Robert and Sadie D. (Altman) Levenson; chil.: Linda Ann, Lisa Lyn and (stepson) Carl Rossi. Career: exec. v.p., Spring-Time Camps, Colo. 1956---; v.p. Romer Zane Grey Prodns., Inc.; Hollywood theatrical prodns. incl. The Pleasure of His Company (starring Alan Mowbray), Born Yesterday and Abie's Irish Rose; ins. agt., Occidental Life Ins. Co. of Pasa., Calif. 1950; gen. agt., Guaranty Union Life Ins. Co., Beverly Hills, 1951---; gen. agt., United Life and Accident Ins. Co. of N.H., 1958---; pres. Harold Levenson Prodns. (prod. Tom Jones, 1970); pres. Harold Levenson Assocs. Pvt., Maj., U.S. Army, 1941-44, WW II. Awards: winner, numerous life ins. awards, 1950---. Mem.: Lake-Colo. Bus. Men's Assn. (past pub. chmn.); past treas., Natl. Assn. Bldg. Contractors; treas.-chmn. finance com., Masquers Club, Hollywood, 1961-68, v.p. 1968-78; Greater L.A. Press Club; The Vikings; (life) Million Dollar Round Table; Pasa.-San Gabriel Valley Life Underwriters Assn. (past pub. chmn.); bus. chmn., United Crusade, La Canada, 1965, 66; Navy League. Office: 7080 Hollywood Blvd., Suite 422, Hollywood, CA 90028.

LEVIN, ALVIN IRVING
Educator
b. Dec. 22, 1921, N.Y.C.; s. David and Frances Levin; B.M. in edn., Univ. of Miami, 1941; M.A., Calif. State Univ., L.A., 1955; Ed.D. with honors, UCLA, 1968; m. Beatrice Van Loon, June 5, 1976, North Hollywood. Career: composer-arranger for motion pictures, TV, theater: Allied Artists and Eagle-Lion Studios, 1945-65; supr. tchr., L.A. Unified Sch. Dist., 1957-65; adult edn. instr., 1962-63; research spec., office of the superintendent, 1965-67; asst. prof. edn. research, Cal. State Univ., L.A., 1968-69; asst. prof. elem. edn., Cal. State Univ., Northridge, 1969-73; founder and pres., The Levin Found., 1973---; founder and pres., Meet Your New Personality (mind expansion program), 1975---; founder and pres., Divine Love Ch. (internat. meta-phys. ch,), 1977---; founder and pres., The Happy Land Complex (Internat. theme park), 1978---. Ordained Minister, 1975. Author: Symposium: Values in Kaleidoscope (monograph), Cal. State Univ. Press, 1973; Happy Land

(music-drama), 1975; My Ivory Tower, House Warven, 1950. Productions: videotape recordings 1970-71; edn. films, 1963-65; contbd. research reports and review, U.S. Dept. of Edn., 1966-67; Cited for outstanding achievement by Calif. State Senate, 1977, and by No. Hollywood C. of C., 1976, 1977. Mem.: Am. Assn. of Univ. Profs.; Am. Statistical Assn.; Calif. Sch. of Profl. Psychology; Bd. of Overseers: Internat. Council on Edn. for Tching.; Internat. Platform Assn.; L.A. World Affairs Council; Nat. Soc. Study of Edn.; dir., No. Hollywood C. of C.; Phi Delta Kappa. Hobbies: piano, recordings. Rec.: jogging, gym. Home and Office: 12416 Magnolia Blvd., No. Hollywood, CA 91607.

LEVINE, SID BERNARD
Attorney at Law
b. May 10, 1912, L.A.; s. Hyman and Emma Levine; A.B. 1933; LL.B. 1935; m. Shirley Blum, Los Altos, Oct. 13, 1940; chil.: Meldon E. (pres. ASUC), June 7, 1943; Dena A., b. June 15, 1945. Career: Pres., Santa Fe Tank & Tower Co., 1935-56; v.p.-dir. of sales, H. Levine Cooperage, 1935-58; cons.-specialist, tech. wood constr. (followed engring. field 20 yrs.); spec. practice law and investments, 1958---; partner, Royal Investment Co.; dir. City Natl. Bank of Beverly Hills; pres. Sherman Oaks Comm. Hosp.; v.p. Cedars-Sinai Hosp.; v.p. Human Levine Family Found. War Prodn. Bd. (on loan to govt.), WW II. Mem.: (past) Probation Commn., L.A. Co.; v.-chmn., Small Crafts Harbor Comm., L.A. Co.; Westgate Masonic Lodge, No. 335, Al Malaikah Shrine, B'nai B'rith, Tau Epsilon, Am. Soc. of Mil. Engrs., Leg. Lex, Calif. State Bar; comm. rels. com., Jewish Fed. Council; Hillcrest Country Club. Jewish. Hobby: sculpture, politics. Rec.: golf. Res.: 1201 Laurel Way, Beverly Hills, CA; Office: 404 N. Roxbury Dr., Beverly Hills, CA.

LEVY, MILTON LEON
Broadcasting Executive
b. May 21, 1917, La Grande, Ore.; s. G.S. and Gertrude (Fuchs) Levy; ed. B.S., Univ. of Ore., Eugene, 1941; stu. Okla. State Coll. 1942; Univ. of Ariz.; Master of Journ., Univ. of Calif., Berkeley, 1959; m. Dorothy Jean Cameron, Corpus Christi, Tex., Jan. 18, 1943; sons: David, b. July 24, 1944; Charles, b. Dec. 3, 1948. Career: News ed., KBKR, Baker, Ore. 1945-47; adv. mgr., KBKR and Ore. Trail Network, 1947-52; adv. mgr., KLX and KLX-FM, Oakland, 1952, gen. mgr., 1952-54; gen. mgr., Calif. Serv. Agcy. 1954-68, exec. v.p., 1968---; gen. mgr., Calif. Farm Network, Berkeley, 1954---. Prod., TV pgm., Voice of Agri.; exec. v.p. Apricot Prods. of Calif.; exec. secty. Calif. Christmas Tree Growers; (past) adv. commn. San Ramon Valley. Editor and publ.: Contest and Awards Handbook; Honor Awards Handbook, revised eds. 1960, 64; Calif. Cooperative Directory; Media Awards Handbook, 1968; Calif. Agri. Directory. Comdr., Naval A.F., Pac.; staff, Naval Air Base, Guam (1942-45), WW II; Comdr.-pub. affairs ofcr.-staff.-dir. recruiting, Naval Air Res. Awards: Naval Res. Medal, Armed Forces Res. Medal, Am. Campaign Medal, Asiatic-Pac. Campaign Medal, WW II Victory Medal, Natl. Def. Serv. Medal, Vietnam Serv. Medal; commendation, Calif. State Legislature for Calif. Agri. Directory, 1967; radio adv. and promotion awards. Mem.: dir. Baker Co. Community Chest, 1946-52; (past) bd. dirs. Baker Golf and Country Club, Ore.; bd. dirs., Baker Knife and Fork Club, 1947-52; (past) S.F. Press and Union League Club; pres. Golden Gate Chpt., Res. Ofcrs. Assn.; bd. dirs., Danville Homeowners; No. Calif. Council, Meals for Millions Found.; bd. governors-coms. Commonwealth Club of Calif.; Sigma Delta Chi.; pres. Kappa Tau Alpha, 1955-57; BPOE. Hobby: photog. Res.: 621 Sheri Lane, Danville, CA 94526; Office: 2855 Telegraph Ave., Berkeley, CA 94705.

LEVY, SALOMON
Energy Consulting Firm President
b. Apr. 4, 1926, Jerusalem; s. Abraham I. and Sultane (Elyachar) Levy; B.S., Mech. Engring., Univ. Calif., Berkeley, 1949, M.S., 1951, Ph.D., 1953; m. Eileen D. Jaques, Oct. 14, 1951, Oakland; stepson, Marshall D. Smith; dau., Linda Levy Smith. Career: with General Electric Nuclear Energy Business, as gen. mgr., Fuel Dept., 1971-73; gen. mgr., Boiling Water Reactor Systems Dept., 1973-75; gen. mgr., Boiling Water Reactor Opns., 1975-77 (positions from devel. to design to mgmt. up to responsibility for all engring. and mfg. of G.E. nuclear bus.); now pres., S. Levy Inc. (energy cons. firm), Campbell, 1977---. Vice-chmn., CBIN Mgmt. Com., 1973-77; dir., Internat. Power Tech., 1978---. Mem. Nat. Acad. of Engring.; fellow, Am. Soc. of Mech. Engrs.; contbr. tech. articles to profl. publs. Unitarian Ch. Rec.: racquetball, golf. Res.: 1346 Robsheal Dr.,

San Jose, CA; Office: 1999 S. Bascom Ave., Campbell, CA 95008.

LEWINE, ROBERT FISHER
Chairman, Riverside Broadcasting Co.
b. Apr. 16, 1913, NYC; cousin, Richard Rodgers, composer of musicals; B.A., Swarthmore Coll., 1934; H.H.D., Columbia Coll., L.A. 1974; m. Lucille Litwin, May 14, 1938, NYC; son, Robert William, b. Oct. 18, 1945. Career: Vice pres., Opns. Cine-Television Studios, Inc., 1946; v.p., radio & TV dept., Hirshon-Garfield (advt.) Agency, N,Y.; Eastern Pgm. Dir., V.P. Program Dept., V.P. Programming & Talent, ABC-TV, 1952-56; V.P.., TV Network Pgms., Nat. NBC-TV, 1956-59; V.P., Pgms., CBS Films, 1959-62; V.P. Pgms., Hollywood, CBS-TV, 1962-64; exec. v.p., SMA, Ltd. 1964-65; v.p. TV, Warner Bros. Pictures, 1965-68; pres., TeleMedia Systems, Inc., 1968-70; pres., Nat. Acad. of TV Arts & Scis., 1970-76; exec. prod., NBC 1977-78, now chmn. Riverside Broadcasting Co. Lt., USNR, 1942-45. Editorial Bd. mem., TV Quarterly; trustee, Columbia Coll., L.A.; chmn., PAW Soc.; pres., Acad. of TV Arts & Scis. Found., 1964---; pres., Film and TV Study Center; trustee, Am. Women in Radio & TV Found. Recipient Citizen's Award, Atty. Gen. of U.S. Rec.: golf, squash. Res.: 9360 Readcrest Dr., Beverly Hills, CA.

LEWIS, BEN H.
City Official
b. Nov. 27, 1902, Riverside, Calif.; s. David W. and Edith (Binks) Lewis; ed. pub. schs., H.S., jr. coll.; m. Catherine Wasilchen, Riverside, Nov. 13, 1926; daus.: Jacqueline Cramer, b. 1933; Patricia Harnage, b. 1935. Career: Animating cartoonist, 1930-41; title ins. bus. 1941---; pres. Land Title Co. of Riverside, 1941-58; chmn. bd., First Am. Title Co., 1958---. Play dir., Riverside Comm. Players, 1953-65; Mayor, City of Riverside, Apr. 1965---. Mem.: pres. Riverside C, of C., 1955-56; 32⁰ Mason, Knights of Pythias, Odd Fellows Lodge, Lions Club. Ch. of Relig. Sci. Hobby: golf. Res.: 788 University Pl., Riverside, CA 92507; Office: City Hall, 7th and Orange St., Riverside, CA 92501.

LEWIS, JERRY
Comedian
b. Joseph Levitch, Mar. 16, 1926, Newark, N.J.; s. Danny (night club singer, spec. in nostalgic songs of 1920s; master of ceremonies, hotels, clubs) and Rae Lewis (pianist, radio sta. WOR, N.Y.: mus. arranger); ed. pub. schs. H.S. (cheerleader), Irvington, N.J.; m. Patti Palmer, Oct. 3, 1944; sons: Gary, b. July 31, 1945 (m. Sara Jane Suzara, Mar. 21, 1967); Ronnie, b. Dec. 29, 1949; Scott, b. Feb. 22, 1956; Chris, b. Oct. 9, 1957; Anthony, b. Oct. 14, 1959; Joseph, b. Jan. 1, 1964. Career: Debut, N.Y. Hotel (age 5 yrs), singing, Brother, Can You Spare A Dime?, Sept. 7, 1931; entertainer, comedy record routine, N.Y. 1942; night club tours, 1942-46; appd. 500 Club, Atlantic City, July 1946 (Dean Martin singer); formed comedy team with Dean Martin, 1946 (appd. night clubs, theaters, radio and TV pgms. 1946-56, under contact to Paramount Pics. Corp. 1948-56) mot. pics. incl.: My Friend Irma, 1949; At War with the Army, That's My Boy, 1951; Sailor Beware, Jumping Jacks, 1952; The Stooge, Scared Stiff, The Caddy, 1953; Three Ring Circus, 1954; You're Never Too Young, Artists and Models, 1955; Pardners, Hollywood or Bust, Visit to a Small Planet, 1956; (dissolved partnership 1956) under contract to Paramount Studios, 1956-65) pics. incl.: Delicate Delinquent, 1957; The Sad Sack, Rock-a-Bye Baby, The Geisha Boy, 1958; Don't Give Up the Ship, 1959; formed Jerry Lewis Prodns. comedian, prod., dir., writer, pics. incl.: The Bell Boy, Cinder Fella, 1960; (under contract Paramount-York Corp. 1959-65) pics. incl.: The Ladies Man, 1961; The Disorderly Orderly, 1964; The Big Mouth, 1967; Don't Raise the Bridge, Lower the River, Eng. 1968. Pres., Jerry Lewis Prodns., Jerry Lewis Enterprises, Gar-Ron Prodns., Patti Enterprises. Star., Jerry Lewis Show, NBC-TV, 1967; rec. artist-singer: Rock-a-Bye Your Baby (Decca Records, sold 2 million copies), Jerry Lewis Just Sings, More Jerry Lewis, Big Songs for Little People, Dormi-Dormi-Dormi, The Lord Loves a Laughing Man. Master of Ceremonices, Mot. Pic. Acad. Awards, 1955, Inst. for Muscle Disease, NYC (cond. first million dollar telethon, Labor Day, 1966; built inst. named The House That Jerry Build); chmn. Permanent Charities annual fund dr., L.A. 1957---; toastmaster, Screen Prods. Guild, Natl. Conf. of Chrs. and Jews; emcee, annual Baseball Writers dinners, Bonds for Israel, others. Awards: Star of the Yr. by Theatre Owners of Am., 1957; won Internat. Award for Boystown of Italy, 1962; Golden Light Award for tech. achievements in mot. pic. ind. (in recognition of his devel. of closed circuit videotape system that works in conjunction with film camera),

1966. Mem.: SAG, Screen Dirs. Guild, Screen Writers Guild. Res.: Bel-Air, CA; Office: Jerry Lewis Films, Inc., 1888 Century Park E., L.A., CA 90067.

LEWIS, WILLIAM EMIL
Corporate Executive
b. June 29, 1927, Omaha, Nebr.; s. Emil W. and Kathryn M. Lewis; ed. B.S. (M.E.), Nebr. Univ. 1945; Am. Inst. Banking and Finance; m. Dorothy Elizabeth Forsythe, Las Vegas, Nev., June 29, 1963. Career: Asst. controller, Live Stock Natl. Bank, Omaha, 1942-43; spec. agt. U.S. Treas. Dept., Kansas City, Mo. 1947-48; acct.-auditor, R.F. Hassman CPAs, Omaha, 1948-49; West Coast gen. mgr. Kelsey-Hayes Co., L.A. 1949-63; prodn. mgr. Norris-Thermador Corp., L.A. 1963-64; gen. mgr. Star Div. Divco Wayne Inds., Santa Fe Springs, Calif. 1964-65; corporate v.p. Kit Mfg. Co., Long Beach, 1965-70, sr. v.p.-gen. mgr.-dir. 1971 (14 plants, USA), exec. v.p. 1972-73; pres. Viking Homes Div., Ludlow Corp., Anaheim, 1974---. Serv. U.S. Army, WW II. Mem.: Soc. Mfg. Engrs., Certified Mfg. Engr. Christian. Hobby: audiophile. Rec.: golf, sports. Res.: 2275 W. 25th St., San Pedro, CA 90732; Office: 7045 Marcelle St., Paramount, CA 90723.

LEWIS, WILLIAM HENRY, JR.
State Official
b. Nov. 12, 1942, Durham, N.C.; s. W.H., Sr. and Phyllis R. Lewis; A.B., Univ. of N.C., 1965, J.D. 1969; m. Jo Ann Whitsett, Apr. 16, 1965, Gibsonville, N.C.; dau. Kimberly Nanette. Career: various mgmt. positions with First Union Nat. Bank, Charlotte, N.C., 1965-66; lawyer, firm of Latham & Watkins, L.A., 1969-75; spec. asst. to Gov. of Calif., 1975; exec. ofcr., Calif. Air Resources Bd., 1975---. Mem. bd. dirs., Mercury Gen. Corp. and subs., 1972---; mem. Federal Civil Penalties Policy Panel, 1978---. Res.: 2694 Shannon Rd., L.A., CA 90027; Office: 1102 Q St., Sacto., CA 95814; 9528 Telstar Ave., El Monte, CA.

LIBBEY, WILLIAM H.
Vice President, Diamond/Sunsweet Inc.
b. Mar. 18, 1926, Honolulu, Hawaii; s. Valentine B. and Lucile (Hoogs) Libbey; B.S., Calif. Inst. of Tech., 1946; M.B.A., Stanford Grad. Sch. of Bus., 1949; m. Mary Ann Smylie, Nov. 30, 1946, Pasadena; chil.: Susan (Emigh), b. May 3, 1949; Nancy (Mills), b. Aug. 17, 1951. Career: Proj. Engr., Western Contracting Corp. 1949-52; Indsul. Engr., Proctor & Gamble, 1954-55; chief engr., Diamond Walnut Growers, 1955-58; prod. mgr., 1958-74, v.p. prodn., 1974-77, sr. v.p. opns. Diamond/Sunsweet, Inc., 1977---. Trustee, pres., Lincoln Unified Sch. Dist., 1963-76. USN, 1952-54. Hobbies: gardening, golf. Res.: 7410 Alexandria Pl., Stockton, CA; Office: 1050 S. Diamond St., Stockton, CA 95201.

LIBBY, WILLARD FRANK
Nuclear Scientist
b. Dec. 17, 1908, Grand Valley, Colo.; s. Ora Edward and Eva May (Rivers) Libby; B.S., Univ. of Calif., Berkeley, 1931, Ph.D., 1933; Sc.D., Wesleyan Univ. 1955; Syracuse Univ. 1957; (honoris causa) Trinity Coll. of Univ. of Dublin. 1957; Carnegie Inst. of Tech. 1959; (honoris causa) Georgetown Univ. 1962; Sc.D., Manhattan Coll. 1963, Newcastle Univ. Tyne, 1965; Sc.D., Gustavus Coll., 1970; m. Leonor Hickey, Santa Barbara, Aug. 9, 1940 (div.); daus.: Janet Eva and Susan Charlotte (twins), b. July 3, 1945; m. Dr. Leona Woods Marshall, 1966. Career: Instr., Dept. of Chem., Univ. of Calif., Berkeley, 1933-38, asst. prof, 1945; prof. of chem., Dept. of Chem. and Inst. for Nuclear Studies (now Enrico Fermi Inst. for Nuclear Studies), Univ. of Chicago, 1945-49; sr. reviewer, U.S. Atomic Energy Comm. 1945-52, gen. adv. com. 1950-54, mem. 1954-59, Plowshare Adv. Com. 1959-72; research assoc., Carnegie Inst. of Wash. Geophysical Lab. 1954-59; prof. (chem) UCLA 1959---; dir. W.F. Libby Labs., 1972---; cons. to Ofc. of Civ. Def. Mobilization, 1959-61; adv. bd., Guggenheim Mem. Found., 1957-59; dir. Inst. of Geophysics and Planetary Physics, 1962---. Author: (book) Radiocarbon Dating, publ. Univ. of Chicago Press, 1952, 2nd edit. 1955; numerous articles publ. sci. journs.; ed. bd., Science, 1962-70; ed. bd. Ind. Research, 1967-73; Lectr. Our Atomic Future, L.A. World Affairs Council, others. War work, Manhattan Dist. Proj., Columbia Univ. (1941-45), WW II. Awards: Research Corp. award for radiocarbon dating tech. 1951; Chandler Medal by Columbia Univ. for outstanding achievement in field of chem. 1954; Remsen Mem. Lectr. Award, 1955; N.Y. City Coll. Bicentellial Lecture Award, 1956; Am. Chem. Soc. Award for nuclear applications in chem. 1956; Elliott Cresson Medal, Franklin Inst. 1957; Willard Gibbs Medal Award by Am.

Chem. Soc. 1958; Priestley Mem. Award, Dickinson Coll. 1959; Albert Einstein Medal Awards, 1959; Nobel Prize in Chem. 1960; Optimists Club Man of Yr. Award, 1961. Day Medal, Geological Soc. of Am. 1961; Calif. Alumnus of Yr. Award, 1963; Gold Medal by Am. Inst. of Chems. 1970; Lehman Award, N.Y. Acad. Scis. 1971; Mem. Medallion, Guedel Assn., Inc. 1971; Golden Key of City-Hon. Cit., by Mayor Dumas, Baton Rouge, La. 1973. Mem.: AAAS; Am. Inst. of Aerons. and Astronautics, Am. Philosophical Soc., Natl. Acad. of Scis., Am. Acad. of Arts and Scis., Am. Chem. Soc.; Am. Phys. Soc., Heidelberg Acad. of Scis., Bolivian Soc. of Anthropology, Geochem. Soc., Am. Geophys. Union; (foreign) Royal Swedish Acad. of Sci. 1960---; Corr. Fellow, British Acad., 1969; Am. Nuclear Soc., So. Calif. Acad. of Scis., Pi Mu Epsilon, Sigma Xi, Phi Beta Kappa, Alpha Chi Sigma, Phi Lambda Upsilon, Explorers Club, Cosmos Club (Wash. D.C.). Rec.: golf, swimming, bridge, chess. Office: Dept. of Chem., Univ. of Calif., L.A., CA 90024.

LIBERACE
Concert Pianist
b. May 16, 1920, Milwaukee, Wis.; (only Am. Cit. with one legal name); s. Salvatore (profl. musician, French horn) and Frances (Zuchofski) Liberace; bro. George Liberace, violinist-mus. dir.; cousin, Harry Liberace, chief surg, Fitzgerald Hosp., Darby Pa.; ed. Milwaukee pub. schs.; Wis. Coll. Sch. of Music (17-yr. scholarship beginning at age of 4½ yrs.). Career: Register-Pajaronian, 1937---; reporter-city Piano debut as soloist with Chicago Sym. Orch. under Frederick Stock at age 16 yrs.; headliner theatres and clubs, incl. Roxy (N.Y.), Chicago Theatre, Waldorf Astoria, Palmer House (Chicago), Ciro's (Hollywood); concert appearances throughout U.S. and Can., incl. L.A. Philharmonic Orch., Hollywood Bowl. Rus. Aud. (San Diego), Orch. Hall (Chicago); 2 command perfs. for Pres. Harry S. Truman; 1 command perf. for Queen Juliana of Holland; mot. pics., Universal-Internat., RKO and Warner Bros. Studios; star, Sincerely Yours, Warner Bros. Studios, 1955; star Liberace TV Show; guest star, numerous natl. TV and radio shows; Columbia rec. artist. Democrat. Catholic. Hobby: painting, writing, cooking, collecting miniature pianos. Rec.: swimming, mot. pics. Res.: W. Hollywood, CA.

LIDOW, ERIC
Chairman — President, International Rectifier Corp.
b. Dec. 1912, Vilnius, Lithuania; s. Leon and Rachel (Szwarc), M.E.E., Berlin Technical Univ. 1937; m. Elizabeth Hay, Reno, Nevada; chil.: Alan, b. July 22, 1942; Derek Balfour, b. June 12, 1953; Alexander, b. Dec. 4, 1954. Career: Came to U.S.A. from Germany Oct. 1937; co-founder, Selenium Corp. of Am., 1940, company acquired by Sperry Corp. 1945, v.p. engring., 1945-46; founder, pres. and chmn. bd., International Rectifier Corp., 1946---. Sci. achievement: several patents in the field of semiconductors. Trustee: L.A. County Mus. of Art; City of Hope; v.p., Am. Technion Soc. Democrat: delegate, 1956 pres. convention. Hobby: art collector. Office: 9220 Sunset Blvd., L.A., CA 90069.

LIGHTFOOT, CLIFFORD STANLEY
Management Consultant
b. May 19, 1938, L.A.; s. Clifford W. and Theda (Watts) Lightfoot; desc. Francis Lightfoot Lee, signer, Declaration of Independence; ed. B.S., M.P.A., USC; (acct.) UCLA; m. Gloria De Lallo, San Marino, May 20, 1967. Career: City Adm. of L.A. 1959-66; TRW Sys. Group, TRW, Inc. 1966-68; mgmt. cons. Ernst & Ernst, 1968-74; sr. assoc. Natl. Center for State Courts, 1974-78; mgr. Seidman & Seidman, 1978---; guest lectr., Court Insts., Calif. State Univ., San Jose. Contrib. to Journ. of Spacecraft and Rockets, 1968. U.S. Army Security Agcy. 1960-66, USAR, 1966. Mem.: (life) Gen. Alumni Assn., USC; v.p. Sch. of Pub. Admin., USC, 1959-60; SCAPA Praetors, 1969---, bd. dirs., 1971-72, v.p. 1972-73, pres. 1973-74; Western Governmental Research Assn., 1966, exec. comm., 1977, pres., 1977, 78; Westside USC Alumni Club; L.A. Westside Stanford Club; Town Hall of Calif., secty. 1969, chmn. 1970-74, mem., adv. comm., 1978---; The Commonwealth Club, 1974---; L.A. Area C. of C., res. com. 1971-72; Univ. Club, L.A., 1974---. Hobby: photog. Rec.: tennis, swimming, bicycling. Res.: L.A., CA; Office: 9100 Wilshire Blvd., Beverly Hills, CA 90212.

LILLIE, MILDRED L.
Justice, District Court of Appeal
b. Jan. 25, 1915, Ida Grove, Ia.; Calif. resident since 1917; d. Ottmar A. and Florence E. (Martin) Kluckhohn; A.B., Univ. of Calif., Berkeley, 1935, J.D.,

Univ. Calif. Boalt Hall of Law, 1938; m. A.V. Falcone, Aug. 27, 1966, L.A.; Career: admitted to State Bar of Calif., 1938, Fed. Ct., 1942, U.S. Supreme Ct., 1961. With City Atty's. Ofc., Alameda, 1938-39, Fresno, 1939-42; Asst. U.S. Atty., U.S. Atty's Ofc., So. Dist. 1942-46; pvt. law practice, L.A., 1946-47; Judge, Municipal Ct., City of L.A., 1947-49; Judge, Superior Ct., Co. of L.A., 1949-58; Justice, Ct. of Appeal, State of Calif., 1958---; Assoc. Justice Pro Tem, Calif. Supreme Ct., 1960, 1977. Mem.: L.A. Area C. of C., bd. dir. 1975---; L.A. Athletic Club; exec. and admissions bd., Western State Univ. Coll. of Law; Ebell Club of L.A.; L.A. Ballet Guild; Am. Heart Assn.; Civic Light Opera Assn.; Les Dames de Champagne; L.A. Co. Bar Assn.; Am. Bar Assn.; Federal Bar Assn.; Calif. Judges Assn.; Am. Judicature Soc. Roman Catholic. Hobbies: painting, cooking, writing. Res.: 510 S. Burnside Ave., L.A., CA 90036; Office: 3580 Wilshire Blvd., L.A., CA 90010.

LINDHEIMER, JACK H.
Psychiatrist
b. Feb. 29, 1932, Frankfurt, Germany; s. F.S. (M.D.) and Ruth Lindheimer; nephew, Charlotte Selver, leader in field of body awareness; M.D., USC, 1957; m. Cheryl Bellue, Dec. 1, 1978, Lacy Park, San Marino, Calif.; chil.: Mark, b. July 9, 1961; Donna, b. May 30, 1965; Paul, b. Jan. 27, 1967. Career: Completed training in Psychiatry and Neurology, 1963; med. dir., Alhambra Psychiatric Hosp., 1969---; assoc. prof., clin. psychiatry, USC Med. Sch., 1975---. Capt. USAF Reserves, 1960-63. Mem.: Phi Rho Sigma, pres. 1955-56. Rec.: running, bicycling. Office: 4519 N. Rosemead Blvd., Rosemead, CA 91770.

LINDLEY, FRANCIS HAYNES
Attorney at Law
b. May 25, 1899, L.A.; s. Walter and Florence (Haynes) Lindley; ed. Harvard Sch. 1913-16; Williams Coll. 1916-17; A.B., Harvard Univ. 1919-22; USC Sch. of Law, 1923-26; m. Grace N. McCanne, San Diego, Sept. 6, 1930; chil.: Francis Haynes, Jr., b. Oct. 15, 1945; Walter, b. July 17, 1947. Career: Dep. city atty., L.A., 1927-36, asst. city atty., 1936-42, 1945-46; partner, Chapman, Frazer and Lindley, attys. at law, 1953-64; Dir. (past): Bolsa Corps.; Great Basins Petroleum Co.; Rancho Santa Elena, S.A., Mex.; past Safeco Corp.; The O.T. Johnson Corp. 1950-53; Seaman, USN (1917-19), WW I; Maj., USAAC, serv. Tunisia and Sicily, Italy (1942-45), WW II. Mem.: trustee, Whittier Coll.; U.S. Regional (Twelfth) Loyalty Bd. 1947-53; pres. Friends of the Claremont Colls.; trustee Claremont Univ. Center; v.p.-trustee, Hosp. of the Good Samaritan; dir. Hosp. Council of So. Calif.; past dir. Christmas Seal Fund; trustee, Honnold Lib. Soc. 1972---; chmn., The Haynes Found. 1977---, pres. 1937-77; chmn Sect. of Municipal Law, Am. Bar Assn. 1951-52; L.A. Bar Assn.; pres. Town Hall of L.A. 1952; dir. Children's Bureau of L.A. 1961-66; Bd. of Water and Power Commrs., City of L.A., 1966-67; Phi Delta Phi; clubs: Calif., L.A. Country, Lincoln of L.A., Harvard of So. Calif., and The Beach Club. Res.: 639 S. June St., L.A., CA 90005; Office: 310 Douglas Oil Bldg., 530 W. 6th St., L.A., CA 90014.

LINDSEY, JACK B.
Investment Company Executive
b. Nov. 20, 1925, Taft, Calif.; B. Applied Sci. in E.E., Univ. of Calif., Berkeley, 1946; M.B.A., Stanford Bus. Sch., 1950; m. Jean O'Brien, Jan. 24, 1948, Berkeley, Calif.; chil.: Daniel Lee, b. Sept. 28, 1953; David Allan, b. Jan. 6, 1956. Career: Mktg. Mgr., Carnation Co., L.A., 1950-59; asst. to pres., Microdot, So. Pasadena, 1959-61; pres., Lindsey-Westwood Assoc., 1961-64; dir. and pres., Early Calif. Industries, L.A., 1964-74; pres. and pub., Clarke Pub. Co., Portland, 1964-74; pres. and chief exec., Sun Harbor Industries, San Diego, 1974-77; chmn. of bd.; Lindsey-Westwood Assoc., Lindsey Investment Corp., Am. Overseas Trade and Finance Corp., Ltd., 1977---. USN to Lt.j.g.sc, USNR: So. Pacific, China, Korea, 1943-47; Mem.: Order of Golden Bear; IEEE; Mason; Phi Gamma Delta; President's Assn.; President's Round Table; Navy League; Stanford Alumni Assn. Republican: legislative secty. to Gov. Ronald Reagan. Christian Sci. Office: 1594 Hacienda Dr., El Cajon, CA 92020.

LINK, GEORGE H.
Attorney at Law
b. Mar. 26, 1939, Sacramento, Calif.; s. Hoyle and Corrie Elizabeth (Evans) Link; A.B., cum laude, Univ. of Calif., Berkeley, 1961; LL.B., Harvard Law Sch., 1964; m. Betsy Leland, San Francisco; chil.: Thomas Hamilton and Christopher Leland, b. Dec. 26, 1968. Career: lawyer,

Brobeck, Phleger & Harrison, L.A., 1964---: partner, 1969---; managing partner, L.A. office, 1976---. Regent, Univ. of Calif., 1972-75; pres., Calif. Alumni Assn., 1972-75; v.p., Calif. Alumni Found.; pres., Univ. of Calif. Alumni (statewide); chmn., advisory com. to gov., Regents Selection; bd. dir., Internat. House; bd. trustees, S.F. Heart Assn.; mem. bar assns. Clubs: Bohemian, S.F.; Jonathan, L.A. Hobbies: racquetball, travel, reading, gardening. Home: 315 N. Carmelina Ave., L.A., CA 90049; Office: 770 Wilshire Blvd., L.A., CA 90017 and One Market Plaza, San Francisco, CA.

LINKLETTER, ARTHUR GORDON
  TV-Radio Emcee
b. July 17, 1912, Moose Jaw, Saskatchewan; s. Fulton J. and Mary (Metzler) Linkletter; ed. H.S., San Diego, Calif.; S.D. State Coll. (winner, So. Calif. 50-yd. backstroke swimming title; capt., championship basketball team; mem. team, AAU Natl. Handball Championships), 1934; (hon.) Ph.D., Springfield Coll., Springfield, Mass., 1960; m. Lois Foerster, San Diego, Nov. 25, 1935; chil.: Arthur Jack, b. Nov. 20, 1937; Mrs. John (Dawn) Zweyer, b. Dec. 1, 1939; Robert, b. Oct. 15, 1944; Sharon, b. Aug. 8, 1946; Diane, b. Oct. 31, 1948; grandchil.: Michael Arthur, b. Oct. 6, 1958; Dennis Jack, b. June 10, 1960; Kevin Andrew and James Arthur Zweyer (twins), b. July 22, 1960. Career: Came to U.S., age 2 yrs.; worked as bus boy, Chicago; harvest fields, N.D.; forest fire fighter, Wash.; stevedore, New Orleans; theater usher and meat packer, St. Paul, Minn.; coupon clerk, Wall St. 1929; worked on ship, N.Y. to Buenos Aires; radio anncr., KGB, San Diego, 1933, chief anncr. 1934; radio pgm. mgr., San Diego Exposition, 1935, Tex. Centennial Exposition, 1936, S.F. World's Fair, 1937; freelance radio anncr., Hollywood, 1938---; assoc. prod., Cavalcade of Golden West, S.F. World's Fair, 1939-40; partner (with John Guedel), 1942---: People Are Funny, NBC; House Party (CBS-TV; mot. pic., Champagne for Caesar, 1949. Author: (books) People Are Funny, Cavalcade of Golden West, Kids Say the Darndest Things; The Secret World of Kids, publ. Geiss&Assocs., 1959; Kids Still Say the Darndest Things, 1961. State Dept. short wave overseas broadcaster, WW II. Awards: Father of Yr., by Hollywood C. of C., 1950; Foresighter of the Yr. 1959; Grandfather of the Yr. by Natl. Father's Day Comn, N.Y. 1960; Grand Marshall, L.A. Co. Sheriff's Rodeo, Aug. 21, 1960; Heart of Gold Award, Mt. Sinai Men's Club, Mt. Sinai Hosp., L.A. 1960; Mem.: bd. dirs, YMCA; Sun. chmn., Natl. Heart Fund, 1960; chmn. VIIIth Winter Olympics Entertainment Com., Fell. 1961; natl. Easter Seal Campaign chmn., Natl. Soc. for Crippled Chil. and Adults, 1961; Chaine de la Rotissere, Friars, Bohemian, Masquers, Chevaliers du Tastevin, (hon.) Phi Beta Kappa. Protestant. Hobby: writing. Rec.: handball, swimming, outdoor sports. Res.: 1100 Bel-Air Rd., L.A., CA 90024.

LINTON, FREDERICK M.
  Business Owner
b. Aug. 6, 1932, Stanton, Mich.; s. Clarence E. and Clelia J. (Tow) Linton; B.A., Mich. State Univ., 1959, M.A., 1960; m. Peggy R. Jensen, May 27, 1954, Stanton, Mich.; chil.: Michael F., b. May 3, 1955; Melinda Ann, b. Sept. 8, 1958; Margaret Ann, b. Mar. 17, 1967. Career: Tchr., San Diego Pub. Sch. Dist., 1960-66; exec. asst. to pres., Amcord, 1966-69; cons., Peat Marwick & Mitchell, 1969; sr. v.p., Shareholders Capital Corp., 1970-71; pres. & chief exec., Worldwide Boyden Assocs., Inc., 1972-74; founder-owner, Delta Group, Inc. Trustee, Calif. Pediatric Center, 1973-76; dir. & pres., Univ. Calif. Indsl. Assocs., 1975-78; dir., Gr. Irvine Indsl. League; trustee, pres., Calif. Council for Econ. Edn.; mem. Young President's Orgn., 1972-75; Lt. Pilot, USAF, 1951-57 (ret.). Honoree for bus. achievement, Calif. Mus. of Sci. and Industry and Calif. Assembly, 1974; subject of bus. articles in Calif. Bus., Orange Co. Exec. Mag. Mem.: Newport Beach Tennis Club; Internat. Club of L.A. Episcopalian, vestryman. Home: 2706 Vista Umbrosa, Newport Beach, CA 92660; Office: 369 San Miguel Tr., Suite 180, Newport Beach, CA 92660.

LIPMAN, HILLIARD L.
  Real Estate Appraiser
b. Oct. 4, 1939, Boston, Mass.; s. Harold E. and Irene Lipman; B.A., Bethany Coll., Bethany, W. Va., 1961; m. Karen Walker, Aug. 1975, San Diego. Career: partner, Philip E. Klein & Assoc., Baltimore, Md., 1966-72; asst. v.p. and mgr., Coldwell Banker Appraisal Div., San Diego, 1972---. USN, 1962-66, underwater demolition team, lt. USNR; Mem.: Am. Inst. of Real Estate Appraiser, pres., S.D. chpt. 1979, v.p., 1978; San Diego C. of C., advisory planning com. 1973-77. Rec.: jogging, tennis, swimming.

Home: 331 Belvedere St., La Jolla, CA 92037; Office: 1365 Fourth Ave., San Diego, CA 92104.

LIPPITT, ELIZABETH CHARLOTTE
  Writer — Performer — Singer
b. S.F.; d. Sidney Grant and Stella Lippitt; ed. Univ. of Calif., Mills Coll. Career: Writer, perf. own satirical monologues; popular singer; writer, 100 papers including: Chicago American, Shreveport Journ., Miami Herald, St. Louis Globe-Democrat, Jackson News, Union Leader, N.H. Orlando Sentinel, Phoenix Republican, Tampa Tribune, Birmingham Post Herald, St. Petersberg Independent, Houston Chronicle. Awards: 8 Cong. of Freedom Awards. Mem.: Wilderness Soc., Children's Village, Council for World Freedom; Korean Found., AMVETS, Com. for a Free China; Internat. Rescue Com.; Friends of FBI; Freedoms Found.; Am. Conservative Union, Am. Security Council, Natl. Trust for Hist. Preservation, IPA; Metropolitan Club, Olympic Club, Commonwealth Club. Old St. Mary's Catholic Ch. Hobbies: swim (50 mi. swim for Red Cross). Res.: 2414 Pacific Ave., S.F., CA 94116.

LITFIN, RICHARD ALBERT
  News Service Executive
b. Sept. 9, 1918, The Dalles, Ore.; s. Bernard R. and Alberta (Knappenberger) Litfil; B.J., Univ. of Mo.; m. Marie Foley, The Dalles, Ore., June 28, 1944; chil.: Maria (Mrs. Barry Eschen), b. 1945; Tom, b. 1946; Mercedes (Mrs. Robert Zingmark), b. 1949; Regina (Mrs. Dwight Cochran, Jr.), b. 1952; Anthony, b. 1952; Angela, b. 1956. Career: with United Press International: Bureau Mgr., Olympia, Wash., 1946-47; bus. mgr., Pacific Northwest, 1946-52; bus. mgr. Pacific Div., 1953-56; Div. Mgr., 1956-75; v.p., Western Zone, 1975---. Mem. Bd. of Fellows, Univ. of Santa Clara. Ensign, USNR, 1941-43: Battleship Idaho, Pearl Harbor, 1941; assigned Fighting 12, USS Saratoga 1943; decorated D.F.C., Air Medal with Stars. Mem.: Sigma Alpha Epsilon; Sigma Delta Chi; Alpha Delta Sigma; Press, Commonwealth. Republican. Roman Catholic. Hobbies: Naval hist., antiques. Res.: 1790 Oak Ave., Menlo Park, CA; Office: UPI, Fox Plaza, S.F., CA 94102.

LITTLEFIELD, EDMUND WATTIS,
  Mining Company Executive
b. Apr. 16, 1914, Ogden, Ut.; s. Edmond Arthur and Marguerite (Wattis) Littlefield; B.A. with great distinction, Stanford, 1936, M.B.A., 1938; m. Jeannik Mequet, June 14, 1945, Wash. D.C.; chil.: Edmund Wattis, b. Nov. 8, 1948; Jacques Mequet, b. Nov. 21, 1949; Denise Renee, b. Aug. 10, 1953. Career: with Standard Oil Co. of Calif., 1938-41; Golden State Co., Ltd., 1946-50; v.p., treas. Utah Internat. Inc. (formerly Utah Constrn. & Mining Co.), S.F., 1951-56; exec. com., dir. 1951---; exec. v.p., 1956, gen. mgr. 1958---; pres. 1961---; chmn. bd., 1971---; chief exec. ofcr., 1971-78; ofcr., dir. various subsidiaries. Chmn. SRI Internat.; dir.: Wells Fargo & Co., Federated Dept. Stores, So. Pacific Co., Del Monte Corp., Indsl. Indemnity Co., Gen. Electric Co. Mem.: Internat. adv. bd. Pan Am. Mem. Bus. Council. Trustee S.F. Bay Area Council; bd. dirs Center for Advanced Study in Behavioral Scis. Served as Lt. (j.g.) USNR, 1941-43; spl. asst. to adminstr. Petroleum Adminstrn. for Way, 1943-45. Recipient Ernest C. Arbuckle award Stanford Bus. Sch. Assn., 1970, Golden Beaver award, 1970, Bldg. Industry Achievement award, 1972, Harvard Bus. Statesman award, 1974. Mem. S.F. C. of C. (pres. 1956), Am. Inst. Mining, Metall. and Petroleum Engrs., Conf. Bd., Phi Beta Kappa, Chi Psi. Clubs: Burlingame Country; Pacific Union, Stock Exch. (dir.), S.F. Golf; Augusta Natl. Golf; The Links; Pauma Valley Country, Eldorado Country; Bohemian, Cypress Point. Res.: 405 Chapin Lane, Burlingame, CA 94010; Office: 550 Calif. St., S.F., CA 94104.

LLEWELLYN, FREDERICK E.
  General Manager, Forest Lawn Memorial Parks
b. Mar. 28, 1917, Mexico, Mo.; s. Frederick William and Mabel (Eaton) Llewellyn; nephew of Dr. Hubert Eaton, founder of Forest Lawn Mem. Parks; gr.-gr.-grandson of George Washington Eaton, pres. Colgate Univ.; ed. B.S., Calif. Inst. Tech. 1938; M.B.A. (Howard Baker Scholar), Harvard Grad. Sch. of Bus. Adm. 1940; MIT; m. Jane E. Althouse, Glendale, Aug. 15, 1940; chil.: Richard E., b. Jan. 18, 1946; John F., b. Nov. 16, 1947; Ann M., b. Oct. 28, 1952. Career: Dir.-secty., Forest Lawn Life Ins. Co. 1940, pres. 1959; exec. v.p., Forest Lawn Mem. Park Assn. 1946, gen. mgr. 1966---. Author: Endowment Care, Cemeteries in a Major Disaster, 1950; Endowment Care Funds Under the Prudent Man Rule, Perpetual and

Cemetery Care, 1951; Pagan or Religious?, 1952; Endowment Care Funds, a Gimmick or a Trust?, 1958; Pub. Rels. Manual for Cemeteries, 1961; Psychological Attitude Towards Death and Cemeteries, 1963; Investment of Endowment Care Funds, 1964. Lt., USN, Pac. and Am. Theaters (1942-45), WW II. Mem.: dir. L.A. Jr. C. of C. 1947, pres. 1950; area chmn. L.A. Comm. Chest, 1950; Little Hoover Task Force, 1951; chmn. Bus. Exec. Research Com. for Econ. Devel., 1952; dir. Natl. Assn. Cemeteries, 1955, pres. 1956; pres. Harvard Bus. Sch. of So. Calif. 1956; San Marino Masonic Lodge, 1960---; pres. bd. of trustees, San Marino Comm. Ch. 1963; trustee, Univ. of Redlands, 1966-77, chmn. bd. 1969; president's bd. Pepperdine Coll., L.A. 1967; dir. Pasadena Found. for Med. Research, 1967; dir. Mus. of Natural Hist., 1968; dir. L.A. C. of C. 1969, v.p. 1971, pres. 1973, chmn. bd. 1974; trustee, Orthopaedic Hosp., 1976; pres. So. Calif. Visitors Council, 1976-77; dir., So. Calif. Bldg. Funds, 1976; chmn., Univ. Bd., Pepperdine Univ. & mem., bd. of Regents, 1976; chmn., Mayor Bradley's Blue Ribbon Water Conservation Comm., 1977; dir., IT Corp., 1977; dir. Calif. C. Of C., 1977; secty., Greater L.A. Visitors & Convention Bureau, 1977; trustee, Calif. Mus. Found., 1978; Tau Beta Pi, Phi Beta Kappa. Hobby: camping. Rec.: hunting, fishing, baseball. Res.: 1521 Virginia Rd., San Marino, CA; Office: 1712 S. Glendale Ave., Glendale, CA 91209.

LO BUE, PHILIP J.
Senior Vice President, Pacific Stock Exchange, Inc.
b. Aug. 3, 1937, N.Y.C.; B.B.A., St. John's Univ., 1963; N.Y. state certified pub. acct., 1969; Calif. CPA, 1975; m. Bridget, Aug. 21, 1964, N.Y.C.; chil.: Karen Ann, Mar. 24, 1966; Lisa Monica, b. Aug. 23, 1967. Career: with Peat, Marwick, Mitchell & Co., 1962-66; with New York Stock Exchange, 1966-70; with Hornblower-Weeks, Hemphill & Noyes, 1970-71; sr. v.p., Pacific Stock Exchange, Inc., 1971---. U.S. Govt. Advisory Coms.: Protection of pub. funds & securities, Securities and Exchange Commn., 1972-73; Sec. Report Coordinating Group (advisory), 1973-74, U.S. Marine Corps, 1954-57. Mem.: Omicron Delta Epsilon; Delta Mu Delta; Sigma Chi Upsilon; N.Y. State Soc. of CPAs; Calif. State Soc. of CPAs; Am. Inst. of CPAs. Rec.: tennis, handball, trap shooting, hunting, boating. Home: 15415 Los Molinos St., Hacienda Hts., CA 91745; Office: 618 S. Spring St., L.A., CA 90014.

LOEBBECKE, ERNEST JAMES
Retired Chairman of the Board, TICOR
b. Jan. 31, 1911, Chico, Calif.; s. John Frederick Ernst and Mary E. (Kratzer) Loebbecke; ed. S.F. pub. schs.; Univ. of S.F.; (maj. bus. adm.) Southwestern Univ., L.A.; m. Anna E. Davis, Reno, Nev., Aug, 27, 1932; chil.: Mary Ann, b. Feb. 10, 1937; Robert Ernest, b. Feb. 16, 1939. Career: Ofc. mgr., Craig Strachan Co., 1930-33; acct.-chief acct.-treas., Title Guarantee and Trust Co., 1934-42; pvt. practice, CPA, 1943-47; treas.-v.p., Title Ins. and Trust Co., 1947-52, exec. v.p. 1952-55, pres. 1955-63; chmn. bd. and chief exec. ofcr. 1963-69; pres. The TI Corp. 1968-71, chmn. bd.-chief exec. ofcr., 1971-75; dir.: Am. Express and Am. Express Internat. Banking Corp., N.Y.; Fireman's Fund Ins. Co. (S.F.); Knudsen Corp.; pres.-dir. Calif. Ins. Fed. Inc.; Transmix Corp., L.A.; I.T. Corp., Wilmington; TICOR. Awards: (hon.) J.D., Loyola Univ., L.A.; (hon.) Dr. of Bus. Adm., Univ. of S.F.; L.A. Realty Bd. Serv. Watch, 1963; Town Hall Outstanding Cit. Award, 1963; Man of Hope Award, 1968; YWCA Diamond Jubilee Award, 1969; Pub. Rels. Soc. of Am's. Distinguished Citizen's Award, 1969; Calif. Industrialist of Yr. 1972. Mem.: trustee, Harvey Mudd Coll.; Hollywood Turf Club Assoc. Charities, Inc.; co-chmn. Calif. Bicentennial Comm.; Gov.'s Man Power Policy Task Force; Calif. Comm. for Econ. Devel.; regent, Univ. of S.F.; pres. Am. Title Assn.; 1959; past pres., Calif. Land Title Assn.; trustee, Calif. Mus. of Sci. and Ind.; pres., Calif. Mus. Found.; past pres.-dir. So. Calif. Visitor's Council; Adv. Council USC Grad. Sch. of Bus. Adm.; Friends of Claremont Colls.; found.-hon. pres.-dir. United Way; past v.p.-dir, L.A. C. of C.; dir. U.S.C. of C.; past pres.-dir., Calif. State C. of C.; v.p. Hown Hall, 1962; L.A. Club, Sunset, Walker Lake Club, Inaja Club of Calif.; past pres.-dir., All-Year Club of So. Calif.; Pac.-Union Club, S.F.; Twilight Club, Pasa.; Bohemian Club, S.F.; pres. L.A. Kiwanis Club Found., Inc.; Masonic Lodge F&AM No. 678, Calif. Club. Hobby: cabinetmaking, fly tying. Rec.: hunting, fishing, golf. Res.: 3472 Yorkshire Rd., Pasadena, CA 91107; Office: 700 W. Wilshire Blvd., L.A., CA 90017.

LOEFFLER, DAN(IEL THEODORE)
Company President
b. Jan. 21, 1952, Paterson, N.J.; s. Ted and Mary

Loeffler; Grad., Univac Edn. Inst.; m. Linda Eccles, July 24, 1971, San Diego; chil.: Jonathan D., b. Mar. 14, 1972; Mark W., b. May 5, 1974; Laura L., b. July 31, 1976; Suzanne R., b. Feb. 5, 1978. Career: Pres., Prodn. House Corp., 1972---; Pub., The Church News, 1975---; Dir. of Prodn. and Data Processing, Computer Caging Corp., 1977---. Exec. Dir. campaign com., Sen. H.L. Richardson, 1976-77; pub., Christian Bus. Directory, 1975-78; prodn. and ofc. mgr., Morris Cerullo World Evangelism Inc., 1971-74. Mem. Kiwanis. Rec.: backpacking, skiing. Res.: 7049 Pebblebrook Way, Citrus Hts., CA 95610; Office: 6060 Sunrise Vista Dr., Suite 100, Citrus Hts., CA 95610; 4307 Euclid Ave., San Diego, CA 92115.

LOKEY, HULSEY S.
Board Chairman, Host International
b. Apr. 10, 1910, Decatur, Ill.; s. Robert R. and Myrtys (Sawtell) Lokey; ed. Univ. of Fla. 1929-31; m. Edith C. Swarth, 1940 (dec.); m. Rosemary Kraemer, Palm Springs, Feb. 5, 1966; chil.: Sally Teresa, b. Oct. 4, 1949; Linda Myrtys, b. Jan. 26, 1953; Robert Hulsey, b. Mar. 14, 1955. Career: Host Internat., Inc. (formerly Interstate Co., Chicago), 1931, gen. mgr. 1938-41, pres. 1951-69, chmn. bd.-chief exec. ofcr.-exec. com.-dir. Santa Monica, Calif., 1969---; div. dir. Lockheed Aviation Co., 1947-48; v.p. Liggett Drug Co., N.Y., 1948-50. Dir.: Union Bank, Union Am., Inc.; Interstate Brands Corp., K.C.; chmn. bd. Pepperdine Univ.; bd. dirs. L.A. Conv. Bur., Inc.; dir. So. Calif. Visitors Council; dir. City of Hope; dir. Blind Chil's. Center; bd. dirs. Crippled Chil's. Soc. Lt. Col., USAAF 1942-46, CBI, WW II. Awards; Bronze Star Medal, Pres. Cit. Mem.: dir.-v.p. Calif. State C. of C.; dir. Rancheros Visitadores, Santa Barbara; past pres. So. Calif. Bus. Men's Assn.; exec. com. Crescent Bay Area B.S.A.; com. USC Assocs.; Chicago Ath. Assn.; Natl., So. Calif. Restaurant Assns.; Alpha Tau Omega; Outrigger, Honolulu; L.A. Club, L.A. Country Club. Republican. Presbyterian. Res.: 1164 Napoli Dr., Pacific Palisades, CA; Office: Pico at 34th St., Santa Monica, CA 90406.

LOMBARDI, JOHN
College Administrator
b. Feb. 18, 1904, Brooklyn, N.Y.; s. John and Maria Grace (De Petrillo) Lombardi; ed. B.S. (soc. sci.), City Coll., N.Y. 1929; M.A. 1935; Ph.D., Columbia Univ., 1942; m. Janice Pidduck, L.A.; chil.: Mary E., b. June 21, 1940; John V., b. Aug. 19, 1942. Career: Instr. eve. div., City Coll., N.Y. 1930-34; instr. Pasa. Adult Sch., Calif. 1935; proj. supt., Survey of Natl. Archives, 1935-36; instr. L.A. City Coll. 1936, counselor, 1939-41, dean, eve. div. 1946-48; dir. (summer session), L.A. State Coll. 1948; dean of instrn., L.A. City Coll. 1948-55, pres., 1955-66, asst. supt. colls., L.A. Jr. Coll. Dist., L.A. 1966-69; research edn. UCLA 1969---. Author: The Lost Records of the Surveyor General's Office, publ. Pac. Hist. Review, Dec. 1937; Labor's Voice in the Cabinet, publ. Columbia Univ. Press, 1942; The All-Year School, publ. L.A. City Schs. 1954. Capt., USAAF, Western Flying Training Command; inspector, Ground Training, Pilot Training Sch. (1942-46), WW II. Mem.: pres. L.A. City Coll. Faculty Assn. 1940-41; NEA, Calif. Tchrs. Assn.; chmn. com. on adm., Am. Assn. of Jr. Colls. 1961-66; Braille Inst., L.A. Co. Museum Assn. Roman Catholic. Hobby: philately, gardening. Rec.: swimming, travel. Res.: 381 S. Burnside Ave., L.A., CA 90036.

LONERGAN, KENNETH LAURENCE
School Superintendent
b. July 5, 1927, Sacto., Calif.; s. Laurence E. and Rose (Hansen) Lonergan; ed. A.A. Sierra Coll. 1947; B.A., Univ. of Pac. 1950; M.A., Sacto. State Coll., 1958; m. Elvera Isola, Las Vegas, Nev. 1952; sons: Mark, Brian. Career: Tchr., N. Sacto. Schs. 1951-53; Roseville City Schs. 1953-54; prin.: Woodbridge Sch. 1954-56, Cirby Sch. 1956-62, Eich Intermediate, 1962-67, supt. Placer Co. Schs., 1967---. USN, 1945-46, WW II. Mem.: pres., Placer Co. Admrs. Assn. 1959; Calif. Chpt. Sch. Admrs. Assn. 1959; Calif. Chpt. Sch. Admrs. Natl. Assn.; Am. Edn. Assn.; Calif. Tchrs. Assn.; Roseville C. of C.; com. chmn. BSA, 1959-66; bd. dirs. Lions Club, 1964-67; pres. Am. Field Serv. 1965; (hon. life) PTA 1967; bd. dirs.: Pace Center, 1967; Calif. Council for Chil. and Youth, 1967-69; bd. dirs. Calif. Assn. Co. Supt. of Schs. 1968---; Roseville Lodge F&AM; Auburn Knights Templar; Ben Ali Shrine, Sacto. Lutheran (ch. council, 1965-68). Hobbies: fishing, hunting. Res.: 614 Juanita Way, Roseville, CA 95678; Office: 1230 High St., Auburn, CA 95603.

LONG, GEORGE O.
Acupuncturist
b. Aug. 12, 1931, N.Y., N.Y.; s. Mock and Wong (Shee) Long; student, hi sch., China; (hon.) LL.D., 1977; m. Sandra Long; dau. Deborah. Career: acupuncturist-owner, George Long's Acupuncture Clinic. Author: Rejuvenation Through Acupuncture. Kung fu Master, mem. White Crane kung fe club. Democrat, co-chmn. Democrats, S.F., 1974. Office: 1865 Post St., San Francisco, CA 94115.

LOOMIS, DERWARD PRESCOTT
Bank President
b. Mar. 27, 1910, Lindsey, Nebr.; s. Gene and Grace (Young) Loomis; ed. pub. schs., Nebr. 1915-27; LaSalle Ext. Univ. 1936-40; Am. Inst. of Banking, 1938-43; m. Thora Foster, Las Vegas, Nev., May 7, 1938; dau. Mrs. James Ward (Eleanor Ann) Wilmot, b. Apr. 15, 1939. Career: Banker, Ft. Kearney State Bank, Kearney, Nebr., 1934-37; Bank of Am. NT&SA, San Fernando, 1938-43; est. pub. acct. practice, San Fernando 1943-53; pres. San Fernando Valley Bank, Pacoima, 1953-61; pres. Guaranty Bank, Torrance, 1961-62; pres. Boulevard Bank, Sepulveda, 1962---. San Fernanco City Councilman, 1948-56, Mayor 1952-54; Dir.-v.p., Rapid Transit Devel. Found.; dir. Fernando Award, Inc. 1966---; dir. Pacoima Mem. Luth. Hosp., Inc. 1967. Mem.: BPOE No. 1539, San Fernando, 1943---; San Fernando Lions Club, 1943-61, pres. 1947-48; treas. St. Simon's Episc. Ch., 1944-47; Bishop's com. 1945-48; treas. San Fernando Civic Assn. 1946-51, pres. 1960; treas. March of Dimes, Pacoima, 1954-58; alternate del., Dem. Natl. Conv. 1956; chmn. City Traffic and Off-St. Parking Com., San Fernando, 1956-60; treas. San Fernando C. of C. 1956-59, dir. 1956-61, pres. 1960; bd. dirs., San Fernando Valley Council, BSA, 1957---, chmn. Mission Dist. 1957-59, chmn. Mulholland Dist. nom. com. 1964, Mission Dist. 1966-67, council advancement com. 1965---; advance gifts chmn., Comm. Chest, San Fernando, 1958; dir. Sepulveda C. of C. 1963---, pres. 1965, del. to West Valley Assoc. C. of C. and N. and E. Valley Assoc. C. of C., 1964---; dir. Sepulveda Bus. Men's Assn. 1964---, chmn. 1964, 67; Valleywide Com. on Sts., Hwys. and Transportation, 1964---, treas. 1966---; cits. adv. com., San Fernando Valley Area Planning Com., San Fernando Valley Area Planning Stu. (apptd. by Mayor Samuel W. Yorty) 1966---. Hobby: hiking. Res.: 621 Fermoore St., San Fernando, CA 91340; Office: 9154 Sepulveda Blvd., Sepulveda, CA.

LOPER, JAMES LEADERS
President, Community TV of So. California
b. Sept. 4, 1931, Phoenix, Ariz.; s. John D. (pioneer Ariz. educator) and Ellen Helen Loper; B.A., Ariz. State Univ., 1953; M.A., Univ. of Denver, 1957; Ph.D., USC 1966; m. Mary Louise Brion, Sept. 1, 1955, Phoenix, Ariz.; chil.: Elizabeth Margaret, b. Oct. 8, 1964; James Leaders, Jr., b. May 21, 1966. Career: Asst. Acting Dir., Bureau of Broadcasting, Ariz. State Univ. 1953-59; dir. Bur. of Broadcasting Servs., Cal. State Coll., L.A., 1960-64; asst. to the pres., Comm. TV of So. Calif., 1963-64, dir., Ednl. Servs., KCET, L.A. 1964-65, asst. gen. mgr., KCET, 1965-66, v.p. gen. mgr., 1967-71, pres., gen. mgr., 1971-76, pres., chief exec. ofcr., 1977---. Dir.: Comm. TV of So. Calif.; exec. v.p. Assoc. of Otis Art Inst.; Chmn., Bd. of Visitors, Annenberg Sch. of Communications, USC; v.p. and dir., L.A. Civic Light Opera Co.; v.p. and dir., TV Acad. Found.; v.p. and dir. The Performing Tree, L.A.; trustee, Sears-Roebuck Found., Chicago; trustee, Polytechnic Sch., Pasadena; dir., Calif. Confedn. of the Arts; d. Pac. Pioneer Broadcasters; chmn. Mgmt. Edn. Program for Pub. Broadcasters, Harvard Bus. Sch.; chmn. of bd. and dir., Pub. Broadcasting Servs. 1969-72. Past pres.: W. Ednl. Soc. for Telecommunications; Assn. of Calif. Pub. TV Stations; W. Ednl. Network. Mem. advisory bd.: Arts Mgmt. Prog., UCLA; Ednl./Instrnl. Broadcasting; KUSC-FM, USC; Alcoholism Council of Gr. L.A. Mem.: Young Presidents' Orgn.; L.A. C. of C.; L.A. Town Hall; Phi Sigma Kappa, Alpha Delta Sigma, Pi Delta Epsilon, Alpha Epsilon Rho, Bel-Air Bay Club, Valley Club of San Marino, Sunset Club of L.A., L.A. 100 Club. Presbyterian. Hobby: railroad history. Res.: 735 Holladay Rd., Pasadena, CA 91106; Office: KCET, 4401 Sunset Blvd., L.A., CA.

LORING, CHARLES A.
Former Judge
b. June 27, 1915, San Bernardino; s. George W. and Frances (Addleman) Loring; ed. Univ. of Redlands, 1933-35; LL.B., J.D., Univ. of Calif., Hastings Coll. of Law, 1938; (hon.) LL.D., Univ. of Redlands, 1962; m. Ruth Jenkins, Sausalito, June 15, 1937; chil.: David, b. Mar. 29, 1942; Jonathan, b. Dec. 16, 1946; Timothy, b.

Aug. 9, 1948; Linda, b. Sept. 14, 1951; Andrew, b. May 24, 1955. Career: Admitted to Calif. State Bar, 1938, U.S. Dist. Ct., No. and So. Dists. of Calif. 1938; Ariz. 1946, Ninth Circuit Ct. of Appeal, 1938, Supreme Ct. of U.S. 1953; judge, Superior Ct., L.A. Co., 1959---; asst. presiding judge, 1969-71, presiding judge, 1971-73. U.S. Army, WW II. Mem.: Am., L.A. Bar Assns.; F&AM Signet Chptr., No. 57, Royal Arch; L.A. Council No. 11; L.A. Commandry No. 9, Knights Templar; Scottish rite, L.A.; wise master, Chpt. Rose Croix, coroneted 33°, 1975; (hon. life) Hughes Mgmt. Club. Non-Partisan. Res.: 4133 Meadowlark Dr., Calabasas, CA.

LOSCHER, JEAN
Escrow Company Owner
b. July 10, 1928, Chicago, Ill.; d. James and Georgia Mae Maxwell; student, Univ. of Miami, Univ. of Maryland, Ohio Northern Univ., Salisbury State Tchrs. Coll., 1946-53; lifetime tching. credential; certified sr. escrow officer; m. William J. Loscher, Jr., Sept. 6, 1958, San Diego; step-chil.: Michael William, Mark Jon, Jeffry. Career: Escrow officer, Security Title Ins. Co. (now Safeco Title Insurance Co.); div. mgr., First Centennial Title Co.; Instr. escrow courses, Mesa Coll., 1972-76; owner-pres., La Valle Escrow, Inc., 1977---; also speaker and instr. at seminars. Escrow Advis. Bd., San Diego County Community Coll. Dist., 1972---. Mem.: San Diego County Escrow Assn., pres. 1972; Calif. Escrow Assn., pres. 1979---; past chmn. state edn. sub-com. (developed CEA's Brokers Escrow Seminars); helped compile Student Workbook for State Coll. use; panelist, Broker's Escrow Seminars. Flutist with symphony orchestra, Miami, Fla.; saxophone with dance band; active in little theatre work, Fla., Ohio, Calif. Hobbies: creative work with clay, flute, organ. Rec.: swimming. Home: 6359-3 Rancho Mission Rd., S.D., CA 92108; Office: 3717 Camino Del Rio So., S.D., CA 92108.

LOUIE, RUBY LING
Children's Librarian-Educator
b. Apr. 11, 1931, Chicago, Ill.; d. Tsin Nan and Poo (Tsui) Ling; B.A., elem. edn., UCLA, 1956; M.L.S., Carnegie Inst. of Tech., 1957; Ph.D., USC, 1976; m. Hoover J. Louie, Jan. 8, 1961, L.A.; chil.: Leigh-Ellen, b. May 15, 1962; John, b. May 15, 1962. Career: pub. librarian, Greenwich Pub. Library, 1957-59; sr. children's librarian, N.Y. Pub. Lib., 1959-60; regional children's librarian, L.A. County Pub. Lib., 1961-62; elem. sch. librarian, Long Beach Unified Sch. Dist., 1963-70. Children's book reviewer, Library Journal, 1957-60; selection com. for Aurianne Book Award of ALA, 1960-63; guest lectr., storyteller, cons. and workshop leader, 1958-77; for: Assn. of Childhood Edn.; Internat. Reading Assn.; Pre-Sch. Assn. of Calif.; Children's Librarians Award Workshops; Early Childhood Edn. tchrs.; Long Beach Unified Sch. Dist.; L.A. Unified Sch. Dist.; USC and UCLA Schools of Lib. Sci., Edn., Information; Cal. State Univ., L.A. sch. of Edn. Recipient: hon. scholarship, Carnegie Lib. Sch., 1956; doctoral fellowship, USC, 1970-72. Mem.: Ad Hoc Com. for lib. in Chinatown, 1973-76; Friends of the Chinatown Lib., 1976---, pres. 1977; Chinese Community Council, L.A., 1972---; Chinese Hist. Soc. of So. Calif.; Calif. Assn. of Sch. Librarians; Am. and Calif. Lib. Assns.; Pi Lambda Theta; Phi Kappa Phi; Beta Phi Mu; Brownie Scout Leader, 1955-56; Scout camp counselor and storyteller, 1958; advisor, Central City Optimists' Youth Oratorical Contest, 1977. Home: 636 Alpine St., L.A., CA 90012.

LOVE, MALCOLM ANDREWS
University President Emeritus
b. Mar. 10, 1904, Des Moines, Ia.; s. F.A. and Leona M. (McGavran) Love; A.B., Simpson Coll. 1927; LL.D., 1952; M.A., Univ. of Ia., 1933, Ph.D., 1937; L.H.D., Colo. State Coll. 1965; LL.D., Univ. of Nev. 1965; LL.D., Univ. of San Diego, 1968; m. Maude Hale; chil.: Joan (Love) Maher. Career: Supt. pub. schs., Ia.; tchr.-dir., Jr. Coll., Univ. of Toledo, Oh. 1938; dean of adm., Coll. of Liberal Arts, Ill.; Wesleyan Univ. 1938-48; dean, Coll. of Arts and Scis., Univ. of Denver, Colo. 1948-50; pres. Univ. of Nev. 1950-52; pres. San Diego State Coll., 1952-72. Exec. ofc., Naval Training Schs., Oh. State Univ., Columbus, Oh. and Gulfport, Miss., USN (1942-45), WW II. Mem.: Lambda Chi Alpha, Phi Delta Kappa, Phi Kappa Phi, Rotary Internat. Res.: 3200 6th Ave., Apt. C, San Diego, CA 92103.

LOVE, RUTH B.
School District Administrator
b. Apr. 22, 1932, Lawton, Okla.; B.A., elem. edn., San Jose State Univ.; M.A., guidance, S.F. State Univ.; Ph.D., human behavior, United States Internat. Univ., S.D.

Career: tchr., Oakland Unified Sch. Dist., 1954-59; counselor and consultant, 1960-62 (Ford Found. Project, great cities); Instr., adult edn., Oakland Unified Sch. Dist., 1961-65; Consultant, Pupil Personnel Service, Calif. State Dept. of Edn., 1963-65; project dir., Opn. Crossroads, Ghana, W. Africa, summer 1962, established, first Chief, Bureau of Compensatory Edn. Program Devel., State Dept. of Edn., Sacramento, 1965-71; director, Right to Read Effort, U.S. Office of Edn., HEW, Wash., D.C., 1971-75; Supt., Oakland Unified School Dist., Oakland, 1975---; Fulbright Exchange tchr., Cheshire, England, 1960; project coordinator, Girls Correctional Inst., Am. Friends Service Com., Albuquerque, N.M., 1958. Author: Hello World (eight books on career edn.), Field Publs., 1973; contbr. articles, pamphlets, scholarly journs.; lectrs. internat.; Consultant. Awards include: citations from Calif. State Legis., Calif. State Dept. of Edn. (Ruth Love Scholarship Fund), State Bd. of Edn., Mayor of Oakland, Oakland Peace Officers, Dept. of HEW, Edn. Div.; Sacramento Woman of the Year Award, 1967; 3rd Annual Martin Luther King, Jr. Humanitarian Award, 1976; President's and Life Membership awards, Assn. Calif. Adminstrn. in Compensatory Edn. and Assn. of Sch. Adminstrs.; Ruth Love Scholarship award, Univ. of San Francisco, 1977; life mem.; Oakland branch, NAACP; outstanding service award, Nat. Urban League, 1978. Mem.: Center for Edn. Leadership, nat. advis. council; Assn. for Supervision and Curriculum Devel.; Guidance and Counseling Assn.; Assn. for Childhood Edn. Internat.; World Council of Teachers; Internat. Reading Assn.; Am. Personnel and Guidance Assn.; Nat. Edn. Assn.; Delta Kappa Gamma Hon. Soc.; Calif. Tchrs. Assn.; Afro-Negro Internat. Travel Club; People to People Program; Am. and Calif. Assns. of Sch. Adminstrs.; Alpha Kappa Alpha. Rec.: tennis. Office: Oakland Unified Sch. Dist., 1025 2nd Ave., Oakland, CA 94606.

LOVIK, HUGH DOUGLAS
School District Administrator
b. June 17, 1924, Regina, Saskatchewan, Can.; s. Ole John and Anna F. Lovik; brother: former Supt. of Schs., Palmdale, Calif.; B.S., Whittier Coll., 1949; M.S., USC, 1953; Ph.D., 1960; m. Barbara McKinley, Nov. 7, 1947, Alhambra; chil.: Melinda (Ray), b. May 22, 1951; David L., b. July 19, 1954; Karen Ann, b. June 27, 1962. Career: tchr., Rosemead Sch. Dist., 1949-50; tchr., El Monte Union Hi Sch. Dist., 1950-52; Principal-Superintendent, Mineral Union Sch. Dist., 1952-56; Dir. Admin. Services, Riverside Co. Schs. 1956-59; Superintendent of Sch., Reedley, CA, 1959-61; Dist. Superintendent of Schs., Visalia Unified Sch. Dist., 1961---. Advisor to Bd. of Edn., Central Calif. Advisory Com., Calif. State Supt. of Pub. Instr. Bd. dir., Am. Baptist Seminary of the West; dir., Visalia C. of C., 1967-68; dir. YMCA 1961-68; Bd. of Govs., Calif. Assn. of Supt. 1969-72; exec. bd. of Calif. Sch. Adminstrs., 1972-75; pres., Calif. City Sch. Supt., 1977-78. Served, USNR (active) 1942-45, commissioned officer 1945-46. Mem.: Reedley Rotary Club, pres. 1959; Phi Delta Kappa, 1951---. Baptist; Gov. Council, bd. of edn., bd. of deacons. Hobby: antique autos. Rec.: fishing, tennis. Home: 134 W. Green Oaks Dr., Visalia, CA 93277.

LOW, WARREN HARVARD
Optometrist — Tennis Champion
b. Dec. 10, 1923, S.F.; s. Alvin Grant and Annette Violet (Woll) Low; B.S., Stanford Univ. 1948, M.A. 1949; O.D., USC 1952; m. Marlene Mary Pretz Low, 1973. Career: Optometry practice, Lomita, Calif. 1954---; adv. bd., Harbor Coll. 1957-58; pres. Bapico Investment Corp., Torrance, 1959, 1966-67; Natl. Eye Research Found.; chmn. adv. bd., Lomita Gateway Natl. Bank, 1965-67. Author: Eye Problems in the Navy, publ. 1953; Research in Devel. of Bifocal Contact Lens, publ. 1953; The Effect of Smog on Eyes, 1957. Tournament tennis player, Lt. Comdr., USNR, serv. USS Coral Sea, USS Calvert, Sasebo, Kyushu, So. Japan (1953-54), Korean War. Awards: Asiatic-Pac. Ribbon with 9 battle stars, Philippine Invasion Ribbon, China Serv. Medal, Japanese Occupation Ribbon, European Serv. Ribbon, Korean Serv. Medal; winner, over 1000 trophies for tennis tournaments; named Outstanding Leader of the Yr., Lomita, 1959; Individual Speaking Award, Calif. Optometric Assn. 1965-67. Mem.: pres. Stanford Alumni of So. Japan, 1953; adv. bd., Stanford Alumni Assn. 1958; pres. Torrance Toastmasters Club, 1957-58; v.p. Harbor City-Lomita Lions Club, 1957-58; Stanford Club of So. Calif.; bd. dirs.-gen. chmn., March of Dimes, 1968-78, Harbor City-Lomita; gen. chmn., Palos Verdes-Rolling Hills Peninsula Racquet Roundup Tennis Tournament, for benefit of Harbor Found. for Mentally Retarded Chil., 1965-78; Del Amo Kiwanis Club, 1973-78; bd. trustees, So. Calif. Coll. of Optometry, 1970-78; chmn., Bd. of Trustees, 1978; bd. dirs. Com. on Orthoptrics and Eye Training, Natl. Assn.

of Optometrists, 1958; pres. Lomita C. of C. 1958; pres. Torrance Coord. Council, 1958; pres. Torrance-Lomita Br., Am. Red Cross, 1958; adv. bd., Torrance BSA 1958; adv. bd., San Pedro Boys Club, 1959; area gov., Toastmasters Internat. 1965; Calif. and Am. Optometric Assns.; bd. dirs., Jack Kramer Tennis Club, Rolling Hills, 1966; Palos Verdes Tennis Found., Lomita Forum, Torrance Am. Legion, Lomita Toastmasters Club, Execs. Dinner Club of Torrance, Lomita Masonic Lodge, Redondo Beach Elks Lodge, Palos Verdes Tennis Club, Oratory and Forensics; adv. bd., Palos Verdes, Rolling Hills Tennis Tournament. Methodist. Res.: 91 Cypress Way, Rolling Hills Estates, CA 90274; Office: 25332 Narbonne Ave., Lomita, CA 90717.

LOWENGRUB, ILANA GOOR
Sculptor
b. July 10, 1936, Tiberias, Israel; d. Prof. Andre and Dr. Rachel (Sapir) Goor; bro. Dr. Andre Goor, Bezalel Art Sch., Jerusalem, 1955-57; m. Leonard Lowengrub, Israel, Aug. 16, 1957; sons: Kenneth, b. July 10, 1959; Ashley, b. Aug. 25, 1967. Career: Sculptor artist; exhibs. incl. "Ilana's People," Calif. Mus. of Sci. and Industry, L.A., Feb. 6, to Mar. 14, 1971, others. Awards: Resolution Scroll, L.A. City Council, Feb. 1971; Citation Mayor Samuel W. Yorty, Mar. 1971. Res.: 1661 Roscomare Rd., Bel Air, L.A., CA 90024.

LOWTHER, THOMAS J., JR.
Corporation Executive
b. Oct. 7, 1908, Pittsburgh, Pa.; s. Thomas J. and Anna (Lynch) Lowther; descs. settled in Eng. from continent, early 13th Century, and est. Am. res. before Rev. War from Ire.; ed. St. Vincent's Coll., Duquesne Univ.; m. Muriel Johnston, Phila., Pa., July 13, 1934; chil.: Michael C., b. Apr. 6, 1942; Patricia Ann, b. Feb. 14, 1944. Career: Customer engr., IBM, Dayton Scale Corp., Oh., 1928, Tabulating Mach. Co. (eastern Pa., N.J. and Del.), Phila. 1928-31, (western Pa., W. Va. and Oh.) Pittsburgh, 1931-35; est. Calif. res., L.A. 1935; field mgr. of customer engring., IBM (So. Calif., Ariz., N.M., and Tex.), L.A. 1937-43, mgr. 1943-45; spec. rep., Airframe ind. (IBM), 9145-51; asst. br. mgr., 1951-58, br. mgr., L.A. 1958---. Pioneer in electronic computing methods and components. Dir.: Protective Security Corp., Protective Security Life Ins. Co.; exec. com., Security Title Ins. Co. 1963---; exec. com. Financial Corp. of Am. 1963---. Mem.: Calif., State and L.A. C.s of C.; L.A. Downtown Businessmen's Assn.; L.A. Ath. Club; Pac. Coast Club. Res.: 3290 Tareco Dr., L.A., CA 90028.

LUBARSKY, MARTIN
Insurance Executive
b. Mar. 9, 1929, Chicago, Ill.; ed. B.S. (bus. adm.), UCLA 1951; UCLA and Stanford Grad. Sch. of Bus. 1952; m. Lorna Lavine, Beverly Hills, Jan. 1961; chil.: David Alan, Donna Susan. Career: v.p. and dir., Woodside Capital Corp.; assoc. with Doctors Econ. Cons., Ltd. and Woods Agcy., So. Calif.; pres. Oxford Assocs.; pres.-dir. Natpro Corp.; v.p. Natpro Enterprises, Inc.; bd. dirs. Haifa Univ. Found.; (past) bd. dirs. Life Underwriters Assn. of L.A., Inc.; CLU. Mem.: (life) Million Dollar Round Table; Phi Epsilon Pi. Res.: Woodland Hills, CA; Office: 21424 Ventura Blvd., Woodland Hills, CA 91364.

LUCE, GORDON COPPARD
President-CEO, San Diego Federal Savings-Loan Assn.
b. Nov. 21, 1925, San Diego, Calif.; s. Edgar Arthur (Superior Ct. Judge and State Senator) and Carma (Coppard) Luce; grad. S.D. H.S. 1944; B.A., Stanford Univ. 1950; M.B.A., Stanford Sch. of Bus. 1952; grad. Ind. Univ. Sch. of Svgs. & Loan, 1959; m. Karon Ruth Turnbow, San Diego, Sept. 3, 1955; chil.: Kelly Karon, b. Nov. 2, 1956; Randall Coppard, b. Sept. 25, 1959; Andrew Turnbow, b. May 23, 1966. Career: Carnation Co., S.D. 1952-55; mgmt. dir.-sr. v.p. Home Fed. S&L Assn., S.D., 1955-67; secty. Bus. and Transportation Dept. Gov. Reagan's Cabinet, 1967-70; pres.-chief exec. ofcr. S.D. Fed. S&L Assn. 1970---. Bd. Dirs.: Pac. Southwest Airlines; Westmor Corp., Intermark; bd. chmn., Financial Scene. Author: No Passbook Savings," Grad. Sch. of S&L, Ind., publ. 1961. U.S. Inf. 1944-46, WW II. Awards: Bronze Star, 2 Battle Stars, Combat Inf. Badge. Mem.: Calif. State C. of C., Calif. Safety Found., S.D. Rotary Club, Ind.-Edn. Council of Calif., Chancellor's Assocs., pres., Cal. S&L League; chmn. Econ. Devel. Corp. of S.D.; S.D. Hist. Soc.; Eldorado Country Club, Food and Wine Soc. of La Jolla, S.D. Yacht Club, Univ. Club of S.D., Cuyamaca Club of S.D.; past pres.: S.D. Downtown Assn., Stanford Club of S.D., Am. S&L Inst., S.D. C. of C., S.D. Conv. and

Tourist Bur., S.D. Symphony. Chmn. Republican State Central Com. of Calif. 1973-75 (served numerous coms. and ofcs.). Episcopalian. Hobbies: tennis, travel. Res.: 369 Silvergate Ave., S.D., CA 92106; Office: 600 B Street, S.D., CA 92183.

LUCHSINGER, PATRICIA KATHERINE
Artist
b. Dec. 20, 1923, Iola, Kan.; d. John D. and Thelma (Morrison) Olberding; student, Wichita State Univ.; B.A., Colorado Coll., 1945; student, Fine Arts Center, Colo. Springs; tchrs. credential, UCLA; m. Donald Charles Luchsinger, Aug. 8, 1948, No. Hollywood, Calif.; chil.: Michele, b. May 29, 1949; Jordan, b. Nov. 28, 1951; Candice, b. Apr. 23, 1953, (all three have art degrees). Career: cartoons, Walt Disney Studios and Warner Bros., book illustrator for Dennisons Pub. Co., Minneapolis; free-lance, stage scenery, brochures, advt.; posters; water color paintings, ink drawings, egg tempera, gouache, 1945---; also pvt. art tchr. and judge. Several one-woman shows; awarded Best of Show, Royal Exchange Show, London, 1975-78; TV guest appearance, Woman's Touch, 1974. Mem.: Calif. Art Club; Laguna Beach Art Mus.; L.A. Art Assn.; Artists of Southwest; Burbank Fine Arts Fedn.; Valley Artists Guild; San Fernando Valley Art Club, secty. 1968, v.p. 1972. Catholic. Hobbies: antiques, traveling. Rec.: golf, swimming. Home: 7847 Mammoth Ave., Panorama City, CA 91402.

LUCKMAN, CHARLES
Architect
b. May 16, 1909, Kansas City, Mo.; s. Albert and Dora Luckman; Univ. of Ill. Sch. of Arch. (magna cum laude), 1931; (hon.) LL.D., Univ. of Miami, 1950; (hon.) A.F.D., Calif. Coll. of Arts & Crafts, 1958; m. Harriet McElroy, Kansas City, May 28, 1931; sons: Charles, b. Oct. 7; James McElroy, b. June 17; Stephen Albert, b. Oct. 15. Career: Licensed arch. 1931--- now licensed 48 states and Wash., D.C.; engnr., draftsman, Chicago; draftsman, Adv. Dept., Colgate Palmolive-Peet Co. 1931; Chicago sales supv. 1933, mgr. Wis. dist. 1934; div. mgr., Cincinnati hdqrs. 1935; with Pepsodent Co. (later Pepsodent Div., Lever Bros.), 1935-50, sales and adv. 1937, v.p.-gen. mgr. 1938, exec. v.p. 1942-43, pres. 1943-46; exec. v.p., Lever Bros. 1946, pres. 1946-50; pres.-partner, Pereira & Luckman, L.A., 1950-58; pres.-dir., Charles Luckman Assocs., 1958-77; partner The Luckman Partnership, Inc., 1977---. Cons. and coord. arch.: Univ. of Calif., Calif. Inst. of Tech., So. Calif. Sch. of Theol.; master plan and arch. engr. projs. incl.: Strategic A.F. and Naval Bases in Spain, Hilton Hotel (Berlin, Ger.), (counsel) S. Am. hosp. designs, Cape Canaveral and Patrick A.F.B. (Fla.), Prudential Center (Boston), Bunker Hill Urban Redevel. Proj. (L.A.), Union Oil Center, Disneyland Hotel, CBS-TV City, Marineland, Valley Presb. Hosp., Convair-Astronautics Missile and Space Facility, Gen. Atomic Nuclear Research Center (Calif.); The Forum, Inglewood, Calif.; Madison Square Garden, NYC; Aloha Stadium, Hawaii; United Calif. Bank Corp. Hdqrs., L.A.; Phoenix Civic Center; Broadway Plaza, L.A.; chmn. policy bd. for joint venture of archs. transforming L.A. Internat. Airport into nation's finest jet-age terminal. Author: numerous articles and speeches publ. profl. journs. 1946---. Awards: Outstanding H.S. grad. in state, Mo. (awarded 4-yr. scholarship to Univ. of Mo.); voted boy most likely to succeed, Kansas City H.S. classmates; one of ten outstanding young men in U.S., Natl. Jr. C. of C.; named one of fifty foremost industrialists in country, by Forbes mag. poll; firm has won 90 awards in design; Cross of Chevalier by French Legion of Hon.; Star of Solidarity award by Italian Repub. (highest hon. bestowed on an Am.). Mem.: chmn. Beverly Hills Civic Center Devel. Com. 1951-54; dir. Hollywood Bowl Assn. 1957-61; L.A. World Affairs Council, 1957---; bd. trustees, 15 Calif. State Colls. (largest coll. system in world), 1960---; gen. chmn., Jr. Achievement, 1960; Fellow, AIA 1963; bd. Northwestern Univ., Loyola Univ. (L.A.), Univ. of Ill. Found.; adv. com., Ind. Rels. Inst., Univ. of Calif.; dir. Natl. Acad. of Contrs. and Engrs., Santa Monica C. of C., Bostonian Soc., (hon.) Gargoyle, (hon.) Tau Beta Pi, Theta Tau; clubs: Cloud, Barrington Hills Country, Union League of Chicago, Weston Country of Boston, L.A. Tennis, Greater L.A. Press, Town Hall (L.A.), Commonwealth of Calif. (S.F.), Chevaliers Du Tastevin. Methodist. Hobby: rare books, antique pipes, antique apothecary jars. Rec.: swimming, ranching. Res.: 10730 Bellagio Rd., L.A., CA 90024; Office: 9220 Sunset Blvd., L.A., CA 90069.

LUCIUS, WILLIAM RANDOLPH
Mayor of Healdsburg
b. May 1, 1914, Mascoutah, Ill.; s. Alfred E. and Mollie

O. (Schmidt) Lucius; ed. Naval War Coll. 1950; B.S., Univ. Chicago, 1951; George Wash. Univ. 1952; Ind. Coll. of Armed Forces, 1953; postgrad. MIT 1954; m. May Levora, Oak Park, Ill., Sept. 17, 1938; dau. Alexis Michelle Rosa. Career: Pvt. to Col., USMC 1932-56; 1st Marine Aircraft Wing, def. Pearl Harbor, Dec. 7, 1941; Battle of Midway 1942; occupation, Solomon Is. 1944; P.I. 1944, Okinawa 1945; surrender, Teinstein, China, 1945; WW II; dir. Food Serv., USMC, 1951-55; spec. asst. Cong. Liaison, apptd. numerous coms. of Congress, House of Reps and Senate; Marine Corps rep. Hoover Comm. 1951-56 (ret.), Exec., Gen. Foods Corp. 1956-58; dir. (11 Western states), Francois L. Schwarz, Inc., NYC, 1958-64, cons.-bd. dirs., 1964---; exec. secty. Dehydrated Foods Ind. Council; cons.: Gen. Foods Corp., Coca-Cola USA, Am. Potato Co.; bd. govs. Internat. Order of Mil. Wine Tasters, Councilman, Healdsburg, 1966, 70-78; Mayor 1970-72, 1974-76-78; Joint Adv. Com. Bay Area Reg. Orgn.; Met. Transportation Comm., Calif. 1970---; dir. Golden Gate Bridge, Hwy.-Transportation Dist., com. chmn. 1971-78; former chmn. Mayors and Councilmans Assn., Sonoma Co.; Sonoma Co. former del. exec. bd. Assn. Bay Area Govts.; dep. sheriff, Sonoma Co.; chmn. Cal State Transportation Bd., 1973-78; commr. State Hwy. Users Tax Commn., 1975-77. Awards: M.C. Expeditionary Medal (China 1932-35); Yangtze Serv. Medal, Shanghai, 1932; Am. Def. Medal with star, 1941; China Serv. Medal, 1945; Bronze Star with combat "V"; Secty. of Navy Commendation Medal with "V", Air Medal with star; Navy Pres. Cit. with star; Army Pres. Cit.; Am. Campaign, Air Natl. Def., P.I. Pres. Cit., P.I. Liberation Medals; Asiatic Pac. M.C. Theater Campaign Medal with 4 stars, WW II Occupation and Victory Medals; Good Conduct Medal with 3 stars; Healdsburg Citizen of Yr.; U.S. Jaycees, 1969. Catholic. Hobbies: rifle-pistol shooting, wine tasting. Res.: SUnset Hills, Healdsburg; Office: City Hall, 126 Matheson St., Healdsburg, CA 95448.

LUDLUM, JOHN PLUMER
Painter
b. Sept. 12, 1906, Hempstead, L.I., N.Y.; s. Herbert A. and Sara (Schell) Ludlum; desc. of William Ludlum, est. first comml. flour mill at Watermill, L.I., N.Y. 1630; ed. N.Y. pub. schs.; Chicago Art Inst.; Natl. Acad. of Design, N.Y.; m. Shirley Grote (portrait painter and originator, Possibility Thinkers Art Course, serving 2500 students), Oct. 10, 1954. Career: Portrait artist (oils and pastels), many internat. prize winning works; est. new Fluorescent Painting of portraits, murals, nature (only basically new approach to art; spiritual in quality and highly Am. in theme and technique) incl. Nativity (7 ft.; sold for two and one half million dollars, 1974; highest price ever paid for a single painting by a living artist), Holy Night, Holy Family, Madonna del Vetro, Rose Window, The Tower of Hope; freelance painter, murals, portraits; exhibs. incl.: All Ill. Art Soc., Chicago, 1926; Chicago Art Inst.; Natl. Acad. of Design, N.Y.; Art Students League. Awards: Foremost Artist in Fluorescent Painting and Portraiture, by 9th Annual Madonna Festival, L.A. 1954; Nativity won Jury Award and Popular Award, Madonna Art Festival, L.A., 1957; 4 first awards in international competition in fluorescent fine art. Contrib. various articles on The Art of Fluorescent Painting; many TV interviews on art and possibility thinking, 1978. His illustr. biography in Smithsonian. Mem.: founder-1st pres., Greenwich Village Artists, N.Y.; (charter) All Ill. Art Assn.; (Hon.) Westchester Inst. of Fine Arts, N.Y.; Art Students League, N.Y.; Chicago Art Inst. Presbyterian. Hobby: music and home. Studio: Ludlum Art Center, 439 El Camino Real, Tustin, CA 92680.

LUECHAUER, HELYN
Dentist — Educator
b. Aug. 13, 1921, Oakland; d. Virgil Vinson and Lillian H. (Hickox) Anderson; student, Pac. Union Coll. 1939-43; Fresno State Coll. 1960-62; D.D.S., Univ. Calif. S.F. Sch. of Dentistry, 1966; postgrad. Sch. Pub. Health, UCLA, 1974---; m. Jarvis H. Luechauer, D.D.S., Feb. 26, 1944, Berkeley. Career: Pvt. practice of dentistry with husband, Hollywood, 1966---; Asst. clin. prof., UCLA Sch. of Dentistry, 1967---. Lectr. in Nutrition and disease prevention; mem. Calif. state Bd. of Dental Examiners, 1977---; Calif. Advis. Com. on Dental Aux. 1977---; Assn. of Am. Women Dentists, pres. 1976-77, editor, 1977---; Test Constructer, Ednl. Testing Service; Recruiter for Women in dentistry. Trustee, Hollywood H.S. Advis. Council; active in ERA campaign; bd. dir., Safe Food Inst. Mem.: Am., Calif., L.A. Dental Assns.; Am. Coll. of Dentists; Acad. of Gen. Dentistry; Am. Soc. Preventive Dentistry; Newport Harbor Acad. of Dentistry; Am. Pub. Health

Assn.; Far West Med. Assn.; Internat. Acad. of
Metabology; Internat. Acad. of Microendocrinology;
Internat. Coll. of Applied Nutrition; So. Calif. Nutrition
Study Club; Univ. Calif. Assn. Acad. Women; United
European Am. Club; Am. Women in Sci.; Upsilon
Alpha; Soroptimist, L.A. Athletic Club. Republican.
Congregationalist. Res.: 3347 Charleston Way,
Hollywood, CA 90068; Office: 3169 Barbara Ct.,
Hollywood, CA 90068.

LUNA, BARBARA CAROLE
Management Consultant
b. July 23, 1950, NYC; d. Edwin A. and Irma S.
Schlang; B.A., Wellesley Coll., 1971; M.S., applied
math., Harvard Univ., 1973, Ph.D., 1975; m. Dennis R.
Luna, Sept. 1, 1974, NYC. Career: Sr. Fin. Analyst,
Atlantic Richfield Co., 1975; investment banker,
Warburg Paribas Becker, Inc., 1975-77; mgmt. cons.,
Price Waterhouse & Co., 1977---. Mem.: Women in
Business; Harvard Club of So. Calif.; L.A. Athletic Club;
L.A. Jr. C. of C. Hobbies: golf, sailing. Res.: 3945
Westfall Dr., Encino, CA 91436; Office: Price
Waterhouse & Co., 606 S. Olive St., L.A., CA 90014.

LUNA, DENNIS R.
Attorney at Law
b. Aug. 21, 1946, Los Angeles; B.S. (petroleum engring.)
USC, 1968; M.S., 1969; M.B.A., 1979; J.D., Harvard
Univ., 1974; m. Barbara Schlang, Sept. 1, 1974, New
York, N.Y. Career: Profl. petroleum engineer, State of
Calif., 1971---; attorney, firm of McCutchen, Black,
Verleger & Shea, Los Angeles, 1974---. Office:
McCutchen, Black, Verleger & Shea, 3435 Wilshire Blvd.,
L.A., CA 90010.

LUNDEEN, BARBARA B.
Food Science Researcher
b. Oct. 16, 1922, Vienna, Austria; d. Victor C. and Erna
Redlick; B.S., 1944, M.S., 1948; m. Dr. Glen A.
Lundeen, 1948, Corvalis, Ore.; chil.: Marie Aline, b.
Sept. 7, 1961; James Robert, b. June 25, 1957; Elaine
Susan, b. Jan. 7, 1956; Jean Marie, b. Aug. 12, 1953;
Richard Charles, b. Mar. 3, 1952; Glen Richard, b. Nov.
17, 1950. Career: Analytical chem., Albers Milling Co.,
1968-69; nutritionist, Fresno Co. Head Start Prog.,
1970-72; Lectr., Univ. of Calif. Ext., Santa Cruz, 1971;
nutrition cons., Am. Acad. of Pediatrics, 1974; health
coord., Retired Tchrs. Edn. Center, Inc., 1973-78;
Lectr., Calif. Sch. of Profl. Psychology, 1975-78; Dir.,
Food Sci. Research Center, 1968---. Pub. World Food
Problems Bibliography, 1969. Lutheran, mem. ch.
council. Hobbies: nature, skiing, research. Res.: 3451 E.
Bellaire Way, Fresno, CA 93726; Office: 3930 E.
Saginaw Way, Fresno, CA 93726.

LUNDEN, SAMUEL EUGENE
Architect
b. July 14, 1897, Chicago; s. Albert Axel and Christina
Eugenia (Erickson) Lunden; ed. grad. Pasa. (Calif.) H.S.
1915; Calif. Inst. of Tech., Pasa. 1918; B.S. (arch.) MIT,
1921; m. Leila Burton Allen, Mass., Mar. 13, 1925;
chil.: Alice Marie, Robert Allen, Ardelle Leila. Career:
Proj. arch., Cram & Ferguson, Boston, 1921-27; proj.
arch., Gordon B. Kaufman, L.A. 1927-28; ofc. mgr.,
L.A. ofc., Schultz & Weaver, archs., NY 1928; est.
Samuel Lunden arch. firm, 1928-49; partner, Lunden,
Hayward & O'Connor, archs. 1949-57; prin. Samuel E.
Lunden & Assocs. 1957-60; partner, Samuel E. Lunden,
FAIA, and Joseph L. Johnson, AIA, archs.-planners,
1960-78; prin. Samuel E. Lunden, FAIA, Arch., 1978---;
Arch. for: Pac. Coast Stock Exch. 1929; Doheny Mem.
Lib. and Hancock Sci. Research Found., USC; Health
Adm. Bldg., City of L.A.; Las Palmas Sch. for Girls, Co.
of L.A.; Western Fed. Bldg. Modernization 1965; Hosp.
of the Good Samaritan Med. Center, L.A. Inventor,
conductive system for hosp. operating rm. floors for
discharging static charges. Author: Community Devel.
through an Exposition for L.A., publ. Haynes Found.,
1944. Awards: 1st prize, Am. Hosp. Assn. competition
for design of small community hosp. 1945; recipient,
Town Hall Award, 1978; MIT Alumni Assn. Beaver
Award; Hon. Secty. of MIT Kemper Award, AIA, 1963.
Mem.: dir.-treas.-v.p.-pres., So. Calif. Chpt., Am. Inst. of
Archs. 1936-43, natl. v.p. 1945-46, fellow 1945, L.A. C.
of C.; planning commr., Manhattan Beach, 1942-43;
secty. S. Bay Beach and Hwy. Assn. 1943-45; chmn.
Town Hall Regional Planning and Devel. Sect. 1954-56,
bd. govs. 1955-60, 1962-64, 1966-68, pres. Town Hall
1965, pres. MIT Club of So. Calif. 1955; USC Assoc.;
Mem. of Natl. Panel of Arbitrators of Am. Arbitration
Assn.; MIT Corp. Dev. Com. 1965---; L.A. Athletic Club,
Calif. Club, Commonwealth Club of Calif. Protestant.

Hobby: photog. Rec.: fishing. Res.: 6205 Via Colinita,
Rancho Palos Verdes, CA 90274; Office: 453 S. Spring
St., Suite 910, L.A., CA 90013.

LUSKIN, BERNARD JAY
Community College President
b. June 3, 1937, Pittsburgh, Pa.; s. Morris and Esther
Luskin; A.A., Long Beach City Coll., 1959; B.A., Calif.
State Univ., L.A., 1961; M.A., Calif. State Univ., L.B.,
1964; Ed.D., UCLA, 1970; m. Judith Olson; son Ryan.
Career: Bus. Instr.: Roosevelt Hi. Sch., L.A., 1959-60 and
Costa Mesa Hi. Sch., 1960-63; professor, Coast
Community Coll. Dist., 1963---: bus. & computer sci.,
Orange Coast Coll., 1963-65; Assoc. Dean, Admissions &
records; Dean, Fed. Projects; Assoc. Dir. of Vocational
Edn., 1965-69; Vice Chancellor, educational planning and
devel., 1969-76; pres., Coastline Community Coll. and
v.p., devel., KOCE-TV, Channel 50, 1976---. Author: Data
Processing for Decision Making: An Introduction to Third
Generation Information Systems, MacMillan Co., 1968,
2d ed. 1971 (nominated by Acad. of Mgmt. Sci. for
McKensie Award as outstanding bus. book of 1968);
Introduction to Economics, W.B. Saunders Co., 1977;
Everything You Always Wanted To Know About CAI But
Were Afraid to Ask, Computer Uses in Edn., 1972;
Problems in Data Processing, MacMillan Co., 1971; Data
Processing: A Practice Set, Litton Indus., 1965 (1st h.s.
data processing text); Contemporary California Issues
(both Study Guide and Text), Little, Brown and Co.,
1975; many articles and monographs; consulting editor,
Computerworld, Technological Horizons in Education,
Prentice-Hall, MacMillan Co., McGraw-Hill, Inc., other
publs. Served USN, 1956-58. Dir.: Am. Assn. of
Community and Junior Coll.; chmn., Calif. Ednl.
Computing Consortium; Nat. Council for Resource
Devel., pres.; Presidential appt. Nat. Sci. Found. Advisory
Com. for Sci. Edn.; facilitator and researcher, Corp. for
Public Broadcasting, long range planning; mem. Calif.
Assn. Marriage, Family, Child Counselors; steering com.
to Chancellor, Calif. Com. Coll.; Trade Advis. Com., Calif.
Inst. for Men, Chino; Alpha Gamma Sigma; Alpha Kappa
Psi; Calif. Bus. Edn. Assn.; Orange Coast Coll. Faculty
Assn.; Revelers (So. Coast Child Guidance Clin. support);
bd. dir., Laguna Beach Civic League; mem. Assn. for Ednl.
Data Systems; Nat. Soc. for Programmed Instr.; Calif.
Ednl. Data Processing Assn. Home: 16621 Melville Circle,
Huntington Beach, CA 92649; Office: 10321 Slater Ave.,
Fountain Valley, CA 92708.

LUSTIG, JOHN
Librarian
b. Aug. 13, 1931, Vienna, Austria; s. Emil and Elsa
Lustig; B.A., Columbia, 1953, M.A. in lib. sci., 1956; m.
Anne Baumann, Dec. 26, 1954; chil.: Judith, Janes,
Lawrence, Jill, Joyce. Career: Reference Librn.,
Queensborough (NY) Pub. Lib., 1954-56; ref. br. librn.,
San Diego Pub. Lib., 1957-63; librn., No. Bay Coop.
Lib. System, Santa Rosa, 1963-65; audio-visual cons.,
Olympia (Wash.) State Lib., 1966; administrv. asst.,
Redondo Beach Pub. Lib., 1967; chief librn., Monrovia
Pub. Lib., 1967---. Home: 515 Bradbury, Monrovia, CA
91016; Office: 321 S. Myrtle Ave., Monrovia, CA
91016.

LUTHER, FLORENCE JOAN
Lawyer — Educator
b. June 28, 1928, N.Y. state; d. John Philip and
Catherine (Duffy) Thomas; J.D., Univ. of Pacific, 1963;
m. Charles W. Luther (Prof. of Law, Univ. of Pac., legal
writer: Survey of Torts, Survey of Criminal law; lectr.
on Torts), Sacto.; sons, Kevin P. Regan (lawyer), b. Apr.
21, 1950; Brian T. Regan (lawyer), b. June 22, 1952.
Career: Pvt. law practice, firm of Luther, Luther,
O'Connor and Louie, 1964-66; mem. faculty Univ. of
the Pacific-McGeorge Sch. of Law, 1967---; research asst.
to Justices Leonard Friedman, Pierce, Regan 1964-65;
pvt. practice, Fair Oaks ---. Mem.: Am. and Calif. Bar
Assns.; Iota Tau Legal Soc.; Bd. of Advis. and Case Ed.
for Calif. of Community Property Journ., 1972-79;
Mem.: Sierra Club, Friends of Animals. Address: P.O.B.
2151, Fair Oaks, CA 95628.

LYMAN, RICHARD W.
University President
b. Oct. 18, 1923, Phila., Pa.; ed. B.A. (hons.),
Swathmore Coll. 1947; M.A. (hist.), Harvard Univ.
1948, Ph.D., 1954; (hon.) LL.D.: Wash. Univ., St.
Louis, 1971, Mills Coll., 1972; m. Elizabeth Schauffler,
1947; chil.: Jennifer, Holly, Christopher, Timothy.
Career: Tchg. fellow, hist., Harvard Univ. 1949-51;
Fulbright fellow, London Sch. of Econs. 1951-52; instr.
hist.: Swarthmore Coll. 1952-53; Wash. Univ. St. Louis,
1953-54, asst. prof. 1954-58; spec. corr. The Economist,

London, 1953---; assoc. prof. hist. Stanford Univ. 1958-62, prof. 1962---; assoc. dean, Sch. of Humanities and Scis. 1964-67, v.p.-prcvost, 1967-70, acting pres., pres. Stanford Univ. 1970---. Visiting hons. examiner, Swarthmore Coll. 1958, 62, chmn. Hist. Examiners, 1962; policyholders nom. com. TIAACREF, 1967=69; Author: The First Labour Government, 1924 (London), 1957; reviews publ. profl. journs.; bd. eds., Journ. Modern History, publ. Univ. Chicago, 1958-61; co-ed. Major Crises in Western Civilization (2 vols., N.Y., Harcourt, Brace and World, Inc.), 1965. USAD 1943-46, WW II. Awards: Hannah Leedom Fellowship, Swarthmore Coll. 1947-48; Guggenheim Fellowship, 1959-60. Mem.: Am. Hist. Assn.; Conf. on Brit. Studies, N.Y.; Assn. of Contemporary Historians; Soc. for Study of Labour Hist., London; Am. Acad. of Arts and Scis.; Am. Assn. of Univ. Profs.; Fellow, Royal Hist. Soc.; Phi Beta Kappa. Res.: Stanford, CA; Office: Stanford University, Stanford, CA.

LYNCH, ROBERT BERGER
Attorney at Law
b. June 10, 1931, La Crosse, Wis.; s. Jan Potter and Eva (Berger) Lynch; desc. Thomas Lynch, Jr., N.C., signer of the Declaration of Independence; B.S. Marine Engring., U.S. Merchant Marine Acad. 1955; J.D., Univ. of the Pacific Law Sch., 1967; m. Joan Schmidt, Dec. 3, 1955, Kings Pt., Long Island, N.Y.; dau. Jan Frederick, b. Sept. 13, 1956. Career: with Aerojet-General Corp., Sacto. 1955-70; sr. engr. overall design combustion chambers for Titan and advanced rocket engine systems, 1955-61; proposal mgr., Liquid Rocket Operations, 1961-63; asst. contract adminstrn. mgr. on M-1 contract, contract adminstrn. mgr., Phoebus Nuclear Rocket Nozzle Devel. Program, 1966-70; pvt. law practice: contracts, leases, bankruptcy, family law, 1969---; also evening instr. bus. law, Solano Community Coll., and San Joaquin Delta Coll., 1969---. Elected 2 terms to bd. trustees, Los Rios Community Coll. Dist., current pres. Apptd. midshipman, USNR, 1951; Ensign, 1955; now Lt. Comdr., USNR-R; apptd. comdg. officer, Naval Research Unit NRRC 12-9, 1967. Co-author: 16 Years of Rocket Safety RRI, delivered in Paris IAF 1965. Mem.: Fed. Bar Assn., past pres. Sacramento chpt.; Am. Bar Assn.; IEEE; Sacramento Co. Bar Assn. Bar Council; Calif. Trial Lawyers Assn.; Fellow, British Interplanetary Soc. Apptd. loaned exec. from Aerojet to United Crusade, 1968-69; volunteer legal counsel civic groups; charity fund-raising. Episcopalian; chmn. every member canvass. Hobbies: readings in modern hist., coin collecting. Rec.: cycling. Home: 11085 Erla Ct., Rancho Cordova, CA 95670; Office: 2640 Cordova Lane, Rancho Cordova, CA 95670.

LYNCH, WILLIAM C.
County Assessor
b. Feb. 23, 1924, Utica, N.Y.; s. Charles J. and Hazel (Dilworth) Lynch; student, Univ. of Niagara, 1940-41; B.A. bus. admin., Pepperdine Coll., 1948; m. Frances Slater, Apr. 5, 1946, Utica, N.Y.; chil.: David Christopher; Wendy Ann. Career: Business analyst, Dun & Bradstreet, 1948-55; real property appraiser, Contra Costa Co., 1955-57; auditor-appraiser, Sacto. Co., 1957-60; chief auditor-appraiser, 1960-70, elected to Co. Assessor, Sacto. Co., 1971---. Secty.-treas., No. Calif. Assessor's Assn. 1977, v.p. 1978; chmn. Calif. Assessors' Assn. Legislative Com. 1977-78. Sgt., AUS Paratroopers, 3½ yrs. Mem., past pres.: Calif. Fly Fishermen, Calif. Sportsmen's Assn.; past v.p., Internat. Fedn. of Fly Fishermen; Mem.: Soc. of Auditor/Appraisers, State Assn. of Co. Assessors; Elk's Lodge No. 6; founder, Com. of 2,000,000, conservation orgn. Catholic. Hobby: fly-tying. Res.: 1201 Markham Way, Sacto., CA 95818; Office: 827 Seventh St., Rm. 202, Sacto., CA 95814.

LYON, E. WILSON
College President Emeritus
b. June 6, 1904, Heidelberg, Miss.; s. Rufus and Willia (Wilson) Lyon; ed. B.A., Univ. of Miss. 1925; Rhodes Scholar, St. John's Coll., Univ. of Oxford, Eng. 1925-28, B.A., 1927, B.Litt. 1928; Ph.D., Univ. of Chicago, 1932; LL.D., Colgate Univ. 1945; D.Litt., Occidental Coll. 1947; L.H.D. Trinity Coll. 1955; LL.D., Univ. of Calif. 1958; LL.D., Grinnell Coll. 1966; Claremont Men's Coll. 1967, Coll. of Ida. 1967; L.H.D., Claremont Grad Sch. 1968; D.Litt., Univ. of Redlands, 1968; L.H.D., Hamilton Coll. 1974; L.H.D., Pomona Coll., 1974; m. Carolyn Bartel, Richmond, Ind., Aug. 26, 1933; chil.: Elizabeth B., b. July 15, 1936; John W., b. Aug. 16, 1939. Career: Asst. prof. hist., La. Polytechnic Inst. 1928-29; Colgate Univ. 1929-34, prof. of hist. 1934-41; Syracuse Univ. (summers) 1935, 36: Univ. of Rochester, 1940; Univ. of Mo. 1941; pres. Pomona Coll. 1941-69; trustee, Haynes Found., L.A.; dir., the Knudsen Found., L.A.; chmn. bd., Adam H.

Bartel Co., Richmond, Ind. Author: Louisiana in French Diplomacy, 1759-1804, publ. 1934; The Man Who Sold Louisiana, and The Life of Francois Barbe-Marbois, 1942; The History of Pomona College 1887-1969, publ. 1977; ed., The History of Louisiana by Francois Barbe-Marbois, 1977; essay, John Holland Rose, Historians of Modern Europe, Univ. of Chicago Press, 1941; (articles) The Closing of the Port of New Orleans, Am. Hist. Review, 1938; The Franco-American Convention of 1800, Journ. of Modern Hist., 1940; The Western Scholar, Pacific Spectator, 1947; contrib.: Miss. Valley Hist. Review, Journ. of So. Hist., Can. Hist. Review, Am. Scholar, The Dictionary of Am. Hist.; bd. of eds., Journ. of Modern Hist., 1943-46; ed. The Am. Oxoxian, 1956-62. Awards: Hon. Comdr. Most Excellent Order of Brit. Empire, 1964; Hon. Alumnus, Jones Co. (Miss.) Jr. Coll. 1966; Alumni Medal, Univ. of Chicago, 1967; Am. Acad. of Achievement Award, 1968; Alumni Hall of Fame, Univ. of Miss., 1975. Mem.: pres. Western Coll. of Learned Socs.; Pac. Coast Com. on Humanities; Calif. Spec. Comm. on Orgn. Crime, 1951-52; Natl. Com. on Accrediting, 1957-60; Pac. Com., Marshall Scholarship, 1960-66; Ford Motor Co. Scholarships, 1960-66; adv. council, Danforth Grad. Fellowship Pgm. 1964-66; Am., So. Historical Assns.; Orgn. of Am. Historians; La. Hist. Soc.; Univ. Club, Pasa.; Town Hall, L.A.; Univ. Club, L.A.; Calif. Club; Theta Pi, Phi Beta Kappa. Congregationalist. Hobby: gardening. Res.: 534 W. 12th St., Claremont, CA 91711.

M

MABRY, HARRY COOPER
Attorney at Law
b. Feb. 16, 1895, Carlisle Co. (Ky.); s. Jesse J. and Onie (Nance) Mabry; grad. summa cum laude, Southwestern Coll., 1916; LL.B., Yale, 1923, J.D., 1971; m. LaVerne Dages, June 30, 1930; chil.: Dorothy (Mrs. Frank W. Chambers), Marjorie (Mrs. James R. Howard), Elizabeth (Mrs. Russell F. Northrop). Career: Admitted to Calif. Bar, 1924, also Supreme Ct. bar; since practiced in L.A.; former counsel Boulder Dam proj., Boulder Dam power line, Mono Basin Water Devel.; local counsel Mfrs. Trust Co., NYC; spl. counsel Supt. Banks of Calif.; atty. for heirs of Lady Mendl, Don Lee, Jacob H. Wood, Lupe Velez, Jesse D. Anderson, Theodore Kosloff, William Cornell Greene, Mary Greene Wiswall, others. Supt. Moorewood pub. schs., 1913-15; regional rep. Yale Law Sch., 1928-36; chmn. Yale Class Reunion, 1938, 63, 68, 73; mem. Yale Univ. Alumni Bd. 1968---, Yale Law Sch. Grad. Bd., 1957---; Yale class secty. 1962---; bd. govs. Yale Publ. Assn., 1933-38. Served as 1st Lt., U.S. Army, WW I; aviator. Mem. Bar United States Supreme Ct., Am. (mem. resolutions com. 21 yrs., chmn. 1963-64), Calif. State Bar, L.A. Co. bar assns; Am. Judicature Soc.; Chancery Club Am. (pres. 1929-30), Am. Legion (post comdr. 1938-39), SAR (pres. L.A. chpt., 1942-50), Calif. J. C. of C. (pres. 1929-30), ASCAP, Soc. Authors and Composers Mex., L.A. World Affairs Council, Book and Gavel, Pi Alpha Delta, Pi Kappa Delta, Tau Kappa Epsilon. Mason, Scottish Rite, Shriner. Clubs: Yale of So. Calif. (pres. 1934-36); L.A. Athletic, Greater L.A. Press. Author: Road to Yale; Romance and Results in the Devel. of Water and Power Resources of L.A.; Americanism and the Great American, Will Rogers; The Spirit and the Sword; Decision; Just Barely; Will Contests; Oral Agreements to Provide By Will; Impossibilities in Estate Litigation, Apparent or Real; Disputing Indisputable Presumptions, Revoking Irrevocable Trusts, Breaking Unbreakable Wills and Enforcing Unenforceable Agreements; others. Lyricist-Composer: Rainbow of Hawaii; Dear Old Western Home; A Smile Is Worth a Million; I Could Cry Over You; White Christmas Snow; Alleluia; Back to Mexico; Calypso and Limbo; Yosemite, Catalina Isle, Hail Southwestern, Hail, others. Res.: 2226 N. New Hampshire Ave., L.A., CA 90027.

MacBRIDE, THOMAS J.
Chief Judge, U.S. District Court
b. Mar. 25, 1914, Sacto.; s. Frank and Lotta Kirtley (Little) MacBride; ed. grad. Sacto. H.S. 1932; A.B., Univ. of Calif., Berkeley, 1936; J.D. Boalt Hall, Univ. of Calif. 1940; admitted to Calif. bar, 1940; m. Martha Harrold, Sacto., Nov. 7, 1947; chil.: Peter, b. Sept. 30, 1948; Thomas, Jr., b. Nov. 9, 1949; David, b. Aug. 18, 1951; Laurie, b. Dec. 12, 1952. Career: Dep. Atty. Gen. State of Calif. 1941-42; pvt. practice law, Sacto., 1946-61; assemblyman, 8th Dist., Calif. State Legislature, 1955-60; U.S. Dist. Judge, Eastern Dist. Calif. 1961-67; Chief Judge, 1967---; mem. Nat. Comm. on Reform Fed. Criminal Laws, 1967-71; mem. U.S.

Jud. Conf., 1975-78; Operational Intelligence Ofcr. USNR, S.W. Pac. 1942-46, Lt., WW II. Awards: Unit Cit. (destroyer squadron). Mem.: pres. Sacto. Town Hall, 1952, N.E. area YMCA, Sacto., 1960; Univ. Club, Sacto. 1953; Comstock Club, Sacto. 1975; bd. dirs., Sacto YMCA; mem. Am. Bar Assn., v.p. Univ. of Calif. Alumni Assn., 1955, 60; Kappa Sigma; Phi Delta Phi; Scottish Rite Temple: F&AM, Shrine; KCCH; Rotary Club pres. 1966; Senator Outing Club. Chr. Sci. Hobby: gardening, duck hunting, trout fishing. Res.: 1800 Rockwood Dr., Sacto., CA; Office: U.S. Dist. Ct., Federal Bldg., Sacto., CA 95814.

MAC DONALD, MILA JOY
Realtor
b. June 22, 1933, Peekskill, N.Y.; d. Meredith and Mildred (Hadden) Powell; desc. Methodist minister Powell, Beth Page, N.Y., 1636; Gen. Storme, N.Y., 1600s; Abraham Polhemus, pvt., Revolutionary Army, USA, 1774; student; Latin Am. Inst., 1950; N.Y. Univ., 1952; grad., Realtors Inst., 1974; m. Carlos Ramirez Ladewig, 1952, (div. 1958); son Carlos, b. Jan. 19, 1957; m. 2d. Rodney Ian MacDonald, M.D., Sept. 18, 1960, Las Vegas, Nev.; chil.: Meredith Joy, b. Dec. 20, 1961; Kimberly Lynne, b. May 8, 1963. Career: Spanish-English translator, 1952-58; Ted Bate Advt. Agency, 1959-61; translator, 1968-69; Spanish instr., 1973-74; real estate salesperson, 1973---; real estate broker, 1975---; realtor-prin., 1976---. Pres. 1977-78, S.D. Co. Women's Council, Navy League (only women's council in U.S. voted outstanding, 1978): dir., 2d. v.p., editor, mem. com., Wives of Navy Doctors; Mem.: DAR; Colonial Dames; Navy League of the U.S., pres. 1977-78, nat. dir. 1978, 11th Naval Region Recruiting Com., Nat. Com. for Recruiting; E. San Diego Co. Bd. of Realtors, program com.; La Jolla Mus. of Modern Art, mem. com.; U.S.O. bd. dir. 1977---; S.D. Med. Aux.; Globe Guilders; S.D. Symphony women's assn.; Helix So. Tennis Club; Pan Am. League, tennis patrons; Republican Women of Calif. Catholic. Hobbies: tennis, bridge, art, edn., seminars, reading. Home-Office: 4101 S. Tropico Dr., La Mesa, CA 92041.

MACHADO, MARIO J.
TV Host — Announcer — Producer
b. Apr. 22, 1935, Shanghai, China; s. Carlos Jacinto Machado; ed. British pub. sch., Shanghai (multilingual: Portugese, 2 dialects of Chinese); St. John's Mil. Acad., L.A.; St. Francis Xavier's Coll.; bus. mgmt. degree, Univ. of Hong Kong; Univ. of Washington. Career: with IBM five years; controller, nat. company; creator/co-pub., Soccer Corner (1st Am. soccer mag.); founder/pres.: Specials' Ink, Sports Inc., Primo and Trident Publs.; producer, The Hawaiian Entertainer of the Year; profl. broadcaster/communicator, 1967---. Host, nat.-syndicated series (6th season) MEDIX (winner of Emmy awards); co-host KNXT's NOONTIME, 4½ years; Analyst for sporting events, KHJ-TV (L.A.) 1967---: broadcast World Cup Soccer Championships in Mex., 1970, Germany, 1974, Argentina, 1978; voice of soccer for CBS TV Network, 1968, 1974, 1976; host of STAR SOCCER, English PBS network; broadcast Football League Cup Final, Wembley, 1977; Host, The Best of the World Cup, Spanish Internat. Network; host weekly series IT TAKES ALL KINDS, KNXT (Emmy nominee); host for Asian community, SUNSET series; in-flight narrator-interviewer, TWA's EXECUTIVE REPORT, 4 years; narrator, indsl. film/video tapes for major corps.; appeared in movies: KING KONG, BRIAN'S SONG, OH GOD; celebrity guest appearances; voice of Virginia Slims Championships, L.A., 2 years; co-producer with Doron Kauper documentary on Irving Stone; producer, International Stars in Concert and Una Serata Italiana (for Internat. Student Center, UCLA). Recipient: Interceptor Award for best documentary, S.F., 1975; Asian of the Year, L.A. City Asian-Am. Assn., 1978; Seven Emmy and Emmy nominations, 1971-77. Founder, youth soccer league, San Fernando Valley; hon. dir., Am. Youth Soccer Orgn. (AYSO); host, benefit tennis tournament; dir., John Rossi Youth Found. Mem.: Friends of Pala Indian Reservation; Com. to Conserve Chinese Culture, Campfire Girls; U.S.O., L.A. area; hon. mayor, Granada Hills, 7 years. Roman Catholic. Hobby: record collection. Rec.: tennis, soccer. Home: 5750 Briarcliff Rd., L.A., CA.

MACKBY, MAXELL JUDSON
Surgeon
b. Jan. 15, 1914, NYC; s. Jules C. and Selma R. (Marbe) Mackby; nephew of Torquild Rieber, former chmn. bd., Tex. Corp.; ed. B.A., Columbia Univ. N.Y. 1934; M.D., N.Y. State Univ., Coll. of Med., 1938; F.A.C.S. 1963; m. Jo Anne Jicka, S.F., Oct. 10, 1965; chil.: Peter Judson, b. Jan. 3, 1944; Jenifer, b. Nov. 19, 1947; Jo Ellen, b. Nov. 7, 1970. Career: Intern,

Brooklyn Hosp., 1938-40; res. Univ. Hosp. and Mt. Sinai Hosp., NYC, 1940-46; est. med. practice, spec. in surg., S.F., 1956---; clin. surg. faculty, Univ. of Calif. Sch. of Med.; attending surg.: Children's Hosp., Presbyterian Hosp., Univ. of Calif. Hosp., S.F. General Hospital, French Hospital; Author: 2 books and many surg. subjs. publ. profl. journs. Lt. Comdr. (MC), USN; Naval Flight Surg., ETO and Pac. Theatre (1941-46), WW II. Mem.: Pan-Pac. Surg. Soc.; Soc. for Surg. 1948; fellow, ACS 1963; Internat. Coll. of Surgs. Hobby: music. Rec.: skiing, tennis. Res.: 17 Tanfield Rd., Tiburon, CA 94920; Office: 595 Buckingham Way, S.F., CA 94132.

MAGGAL, MOSHE MORRIS
Rabbi — Author
b. Mar. 16, 1908, Nagyecsed, Hungary; stu., Nat. Rabbinical Sem., Budapest, Hungary, 1933, Rabbinical degree, 1934; postgrad., Universitat Zurich, Switz., 1935; Hebrew Univ., Jerusalem, Israel, 1936; m. Rachel Delia Diamond, July 8, 1951, NYC; chil.: Davida Elizabeth (DeMonte), b. Jan. 5, 1954; Michelle Judith, b. Feb. 22, 1957; Elana Ilene, b. May 16, 1963. Career: Rabbi: Temple Meyer David, Claremont, N.H. 1951-52; Temple Beth Aaron, Billings, Mont., 1952-54; Alhambra (Calif.) Jewish Center, 1955-57; Temple Beth Kodesh, Canoga Park, 1959-61; Congregation Ahaveth Israel, Hollywood, 1966-73. Lectr.: Coast Fed. S&L Free Enterprise Speakers Bur., 1971---. Ed.: Hebrew weekly Iton Meyuhad, Tel Aviv, Israel, 1940-47; assoc. ed.: Heritage Newspaper, L.A., 1958-60; Pub. and Ed.: Voice of Judaism, 1960---; Founder, pres., Nat. Jewish Information Serv., 1960---; pres., Beverly Hills Zionist Dist., 1973-76; exec. v.p., So. Pacific Region, Zionist Orgn., 1973---. Israel Defense Army, 1948-49; civilian Chaplain, Great Falls (Mont.) USAAF, 1952-54. Author: Acres of Happiness, 1968. Awards incl. many citations from civic, religious and ednl. orgns.; Spiritual Mobilization Nat. Sermon Contest Award, 1952; Crusade for Freedom Citation, 1952; Hon. Sheriff, Yellowstone Co., Mont., 1954; Hon. Lt.Col., Spirit of '76 Found., 1976. Mem.: Gr. L.A. Press Club; Town Hall of Calif.; L.A. World Affairs Council & Internat. Visitors Prog.; assoc., Smithsonian Instn. Democrat. Jewish. Address: 5174 West 8th St., L.A., CA 90036.

MAGLEBY, KAY BROSSARD
Electronics Company President
b. May 2, 1935, Rigby, Idaho; s. Herbert and Blanche Magleby; gr.grandson, Pony Express Rider, Fisher; B.S.E.E., Univ. of Utah, 1957; M.S.E.E., Stanford Univ., 1960; Ph.D., 1963; m. Barbara Huot, Sept. 1, 1957, Priest Lake, Idaho; chil.: Debbie, b. Jan. 2, 1959; Lowell, b. June 22, 1960; Annie, b. Aug. 5, 1962; David, b. Jul. 23, 1971; Beatrice, b. Dec. 28, 1972. Career: devel. engr., Hewlett-Packard Sampling Oscilloscope (directed computer devel. program); engring. mgr., Palo Alto Div., Hewlett-Packard; currently: pres., Cushman Electronics, Inc. ---. Dir. of Communications, Hewlett-Packard, 1971-73, dir. Data Systems Group, 1969-70; v.p. of engring., Sycor, 1969-70; dir. Coastcom, Inc.; dir., Dicom. Co-author textbook, Introduction to Computer Architecture; numerous articles on instrumentation, computer tech. Mem. Young Presidents' Orgn. Polit.: planning commn., Los Altos Hills, 1968-69. Episcopal. Hobby: woodwork. Rec.: golf. Office: 2450 N. First St., San Jose, CA 95131.

MAGNIN, CYRIL I.
Board Chairman, Joseph Magnin Co., Inc.
b. July 6, 1899, S.F.; s. Joseph (founder, Joseph Magnin, Inc.) and Charlotte (Davis) Magnin; grandson of I. Magnin, founder I. Magnin Co.; B.A., Univ. of Calif. Berkeley, 1922; (hon.) LL.D., Univ. of Pac. 1967; chil.: Donald, Jerry, Mrs. Walter (Ellen) Newman. Career: Jos. Magnin Co., Inc., S.F., 1926---, pres. 1952-67, (sold to AMFAC, Inc. 1967), chmn. bd. 1967---. Gen. partner, Cyril Magnin Investments, Ltd. Chief of Protocol, City of S.F., 1963---. Awards: Calif. Maritime Award, 1959; NCCJ Man of Yr. award, 1962; S.F. Designers Scholarship Com. Award, 1964; Distinguished Citizen Award, City-Co. of L.A. 1965; Hon. Award, Natl. Jewish Hosp., Denver, 1965; Am. Jewish Com. Human Rels. Award, 1967; Gold Star of Solidarity, It. Govt.; French Order Legion of Hon. 1968; San Franciscan Award, S.F. Jr. C. of C., 1969; Golden Plate Award, Am. Acad. of Achievement, 1970; Tribute to Esteem, West Coast Salesmen's Assn. 1970; Pub. Serv. Award, Multi-Culture Inst.; Basil O'Connor Mem. Award, Natl. Assn. March of Dimes; Comdr., Brit. Empire Award, 1972; Off. Cross Order of Merit, Fed. Repub. of Germ. 1972; Order of Phoenix, Greece 1973; St. Francis of Assisi Award, City of S.F. 1975; SPUR Award, 1975; Distinguished Cultural Serv. Award,

Knights of Columbus, S.F., 1975; Comdr., Royal Order of No. Star, 1976. Art patron, sponsor, Exhib. of Archael. Finds of People's Repub. of China (family, guests of govt., Oct. 1975). Mem.: pres.-dir. Calif. Assn. for A.C.T.; bd. govs. S.F. Heart Assn.; treas. Exec. Council, Comm. Emg. Care, Inc.; chmn. emer. March of Dimes; dir. S.F. Internat. Film Festival; trustee-exec. com. Fine Arts Museum of S.F.; former pres.-chmn (life) dir. Greater S.F. C. of C.; trustee: Am. Cancer Soc., S.F. Opera Assn., Boys Town of Italy, Coast Guard Acad. Found., Calif. Mus. of Sea Found.; v.p. Calif. Mus. Found.; Asian Art Comm. of S.F.; dir. Columbia Park Boys Club; bd. govs. Am. Acad. of Achievement; dir. U.N. Assn. of S.F.; dir. Heritage Council; U.S. Dept. State Spec. Fine Arts Com.; (hon.) U.S. Merchant Marine Alumni Assn., S.F.; Blyth-Zellerbach Com.; bd. advs. Natl. Conf. Chrs. and Jews; Clubs: Villa Taverna, World Trade, St. Francis Yacht. Hobby: hiking with Cairn Terrier "Tippy." Res.: Hotel Mark Hopkins, S.F., CA 94106; Office: 59 Harrison St., S.F., CA 94105.

MAGNIN, EDGAR FOGEL
Rabbi, Wilshire Temple
b. July 1, 1890, S.F.; s. Sam and Lilly (Fogel) Magnin; grandson of I. Magnin, founder, I. Magnin & Co.; A.B., Univ. of Cincinnati, 1913; B.H. and Rabbi, Hebrew Union Coll. 1914, D.D. 1945; Dr. Human Letters, Calif. Coll. Med.; S.T.D., USC 1956; m. Evelyn Rosenthal, June 15, 1916; m. Evelyn Rosenthal, June 15, 1916; chil.: Henry David, b. 1920; Mae (Magnin) Brussell, b. 1922. Career: Rabbi, Temple Israel, Stockton, 1914; Wilshire Blvd., Temple, L.A. 1915---. Lectr.: hist., USC 1934---; radio, CBS, KHJ, KFWB. Contrib.: Ency. of Jewish Knowledge, 1938; King Feats. Syn., Inc., Repr. Jewish Welfare Bd., So. Calif., WW I. Awards: Judge Harry A. Hollzer Mem. Award of Jewish Fed. Council of Greater L.A.; Distinguished Alumnus Award by Rabbinic Alumni Assn., Hebrew Union Coll.-Jewish Inst. of Relig. Mem.: v.p. Cedars of Lebanon Hosp.; Central Conf., Am. Rabbi's Arbitration Com.; adv. bd., Natl. Acad. Am. Lit.; pres. L.A. Rabbinical Assn.; dir. Am. Red Cross, exec. com., L.A. chpt.; adv. com., L.A. Philharmonic Orch. Assn.; chmn. Jewish Welfare Bd.; adv. bd.-spec. citizen's com., L.A. Bd. of Edn.; adv. com.-conv. com., L.A. C. of C.; Natl. Council, Natl. Econ. League; adv. bd., Assn. Advancement Home Bldrs.; bd. govs., Menorah Assn.; adv. com., Occidental Coll. Edn. Film Research Inst.; bd. govs., Hebrew Union Coll.; pres. L.A. Coll. of Jewish Studies; (Life) founder-state adv. com., Calif. Zoological Soc. for Control of Cancer; adv. com., Pan-Am. Fellowship; adv. com. U.S. Flag Assn.; Natl. Council, Am. Joint Distr. Commr.; Protective Order Police of Calif.; adv. bd., So. Calif. Safety Council; sponsor, Whittier Inst. Internat. Rels.; Chil's. Civic Repertory Group; L.A. Art Assn.; bd. sponsors, Forty Plus Assn.; adv. bd., Calif. Cong. of Parents and Tchrs.; adv. com., L.A. Visiting Nurses Assn.; adv. bd. Hazel Hurst Found. for Blind; Calif. and L.A. coms. for Sesquicentennial Celebration of Const. of U.S.; (hon.) chaplain, Am. Guild of Organists; v.p. Univ. of Relig. Conf.; exec. com., Natl. Council of Jews and Christians; Natl. Council for Palestine; ed. bd., B'nai B'rith Messenger, Jewish Comm. Press; chmn. U.N. Welfare Fund campaign; campaign com., War Relief; bd. trustees, Inst. Jewish Affairs; Crippled Chil's. Soc. of L.A. Co.; adv. com., Ofc. State Adm. of So. Calif. for sale of war savings bonds and stamps; cits. com., Conf. of Childhood and Youth in War Time; exec. com., Bill of Rights Com.; bd. dirs., Americanism Edn. League; v.p. L.A. chpt., Am. Friends of Hebrew Univ.; L.A. Council, Boy Scouts of Am.; campaign council, L.A. Comm. Chest; bd. dirs., L.A. Co. TB and Health Assn.; L.A. Jewish Comm. Council; adv. bd., L.A. Florence Crittenton Home Assn.; adv. council, Southwestern Univ.; (hon.) com. L.A. Landmarks Restoration Assn.; (charter) Hollywood Bowl; State Reconstr. Employment Com.; Relig. Activities Com.; com. Beverly Hills Council Civil Unity; bd. dirs., Calif. War Chest, Inc.; L.A. com., Golden Gate Internat. Exposition; adv. com., Am. Internat. Family Rels.; relig. com., State Centennial Celebrations; adv. com., Natl. Jewish Hosp., Denver; (hon.) L.A. Dist. 4, B'nai B'rith, (life) gen. com.; Famine Relief Com.; (past) grand pres., Pi Lambda Pi, Theta Phi, 33° Mason, Shriner; clubs: (chaplain) Variety of So. Calif., (dir.) All-Yr. of So. Calif., (bd. govs.) Marine Corps, Faculty (USC), (hon. life) Rotary, Hollywood Press, Men's Club of Beverly Hills, Twenty, Breakfast, Hillcrest Country (L.A.). Republican (del. Inaugural Prayer for Pres. Richard M. Nixon, Jan. 20, 1969). Res.: 615 N. Walden Dr., Beverly Hills, CA; Office: 3663 Wilshire Blvd., L.A., CA 90010.

MAGNIN, JERRY
Merchant — Civic Leader
b. July 30, 1938, S.F.; s. Cyril Isaac and Anna (Smithline) Magnin; ed. B.S. (econs.) Univ. of Pa. 1960; m. Dana deGraaf; chil.: Randolph Allan, Ronald Isaac, Timothy William. Career: v.p., Joseph Magnin Co., Inc. 1960-70; cons. 1970-73, pres. 1973---; chmn. bd. Spectrum Foods, Inc. 1973---; Hobbies: art and music. Rec.: tennis, water skiing. Office: 323 N. Rodeo Dr., Beverly Hills, CA 90210.

MAHER, LEO THOMAS
Bishop of San Diego
b. July 1, 1915, Mt. Union, Ia.; s. Thomas and Mary (Teberg) Maher; ed. St. Joseph's Coll., Mt. View, Calif.; St. Patrick's Sem., Menlo Park. Career: Ordained Priest, Roman Catholic Ch., Dec. 18, 1943; asst. pastor, Holy Name Ch., S.F., 1943-44; asst. pastor, St. Mary's Cathedral, S.F. 1944-47; secty. Archbishop of S.F. 1947-56; Chancellor of Archdiocese of S.F. 1956-62; Archdiocesan consultor, 1959-62; apptd. first Bishop of Santa Rosa by Pope John XXIII, 1962-69, Bishop of San Diego, 1969---. Delegate to Ecumenical Council, Rome, 1962; Grand Prior of the Western Lieutenancy of the Equestrian Order of the Holy Sepulchre. Mem.: bd. dirs., Soc. Propagation of Faith; chmn. bd. trustees, Univ. of S.D. Office: Diocesan Ofc., Alcala Park, San Diego, CA 92110.

MAHONEY, DAVID J., JR.
Board Chairman, Norton Simon, Inc.
b. May 17, 1923, NYC; s. David J. and Laurette (Cahill) Mahoney; stu., LaSalle Acad., 1941; B.S., Univ. of Penn., 1945; stu. Columbia Univ., 1946-47; m. Hildegarde Ercklentz Merrill, June 24, 1978, Port-Au-Prince, Haiti; chil.: David Joseph, III; Barbara Ann. Career: Advt. v.p., Ruthrauff & Ryan, NYC, 1949-51; founder & pres., David J. Mahoney Inc., NYC, 1951-56; also dir.; pres. & dir., Good Humor Corp., Brooklyn, 1956-61; exec. v.p. & dir., Colgate-Palmolive Co., 1961-66; pres. & chief exec. ofcr., Canada Dry Corp., 1966-68; pres., Norton Simon Inc., 1968---; chief exec. ofcr., 1969---; chmn. of the bd., 1970---. Dir.: New York Telephone Co.; Chris Craft Ind.; Adv. bd., Continental Airlines. Trustee: NYU, Univ. of Pa. Mem.: Visitors Com., UCLA; United Coll. Fund; chmn. bd. Phoenix House; The Charles A. Dana Found.; Am. Health Found. Awards: Horatio Alger Award 1977; Corporate Leadership Award, Girl Scouts of Am., 1976; Col. I. Robert Kriendler Leatherneck Award 1976; Patriots Award 1972; Torch of Liberty Award 1970. Res.: 740 Park Ave., N.Y., N.Y. 10021; Office: 277 Park Ave., N.Y., N.Y. 10017.

MAHONEY, JEANNE H.
Title Insurance Company Executive
b. Jan. 6, 1925, Midway, Utah; d. Earl M. and Myrtle (Watkins) Hardy; desc. U.S. Sen. Arthur V. Watkins of Utah; student, Univ. of Utah, 1944; Univ. of Ill., 1960; Santa Monica City Coll., 1968; m. Daryl L. Mahoney, Dec. 15, 1943, Salt Lake City, Utah; chil.: Steven D., b. Aug. 2, 1949; Shauna (Mrs. David Tolbert), b. Sept. 11, 1950. Career: Secty., Richard L. Evans, 1943; U.S. War Dept., 1944-48; escrow officer, loan officer, First Security Bank, 1956-59; mgr., Village Mkt. Shopping Center, LaGrange, Ill., 1959-61; nat. accounts mgr., Lawyers Title Insurance, 1968-72; J. Penner (Post Office devel.), 1972-74; Trust, real properties counsel, Continental Ill. Nat. Bank, 1974-76; v.p., nat. title sales, TICOR, 1976---. City treas., Gallup, N. Mex., 1957-58; Cincinnati Sch. Bd. mem., 1959. Mem.: Gen. Fedn. of Women's Clubs, New Mex. pres., 1958; L.A. C. of C., constr. indus. com.; Women in Bus.; Ticor President's Club, 1978. L.D.S. ch. youth leader 27 years. Home: 11574 Iowa, No. 103, W. Los Angeles, CA 90025; Office: 3540 Wilshire Blvd., L.A., CA 90010.

MAIWANDI, HISSAMUDDIN
Physician
b. Sept. 4, 1941, Kabul, Afghanistan; s. Mohd Ali (prof., Kabul Univ., author) and Shahkoko Maiwandi; grad. Hi Sch., 1957; M.D., 1966; m. Nafissa, Feb. 24, 1966, Kabul, Afghanistan; chil.: Yosuf, b. June 11, 1967; Nadia, b. Aug. 31, 1969. Career: Gen. Surgical training five years; plastic surgical training two years; surgery of hand fellowship one year, all at N.Y. Bellvue and N.Y. Univ. Hosp.; pvt. practice, plastic surgery and hand surgery, 1976---. Active staff: Arcadia Methodist Hosp., San Gabriel Community Hosp., Santa Teresita; tchr., White Memorial Hosp. Mem.: AMA, FACE (applied). Rel.: Islam. Office: 65 N. First Ave., Suite 201, Arcadia, CA 91006.

MALTZ, BERTRAM
Physician and Surgeon

b. Nov. 20, 1940, Johannesburg, S. Africa; ed. Kingswood Coll., Grahamstown, S. Africa, 1956-60; M.B., Ch.B., Univ. of Liverpool, Engl. 1960-66; Med. Licensure: United Kingdom, 1966; S. Africa, 1966, E.C.F.M.G. 1967; M.D., Calif. 1970. Career: Intern, Liverpool Royal Inf., Eng., 1966-67; pathology res. Wadsworth Hosp., VA Center, L.A', 1968-69; res. in rheumatology, 1969-70, internal med. res. 1970-71; asst. clin. prof. of med., UCLA Sch. of Health Scis., L.A.; bd. dirs. Clin. Faculty Assn. and chmn. Tchg. Com.; clin. researcher (drugs), UCLA; Natl. Vets Adm. Studies Group. Visiting cons.: London Hosp., 1969, 75; Univ. of Liverpool, Eng. 1969; Rheumatology Clin. of Gen. Hosp., Johannesburg, S. Africa, 1969, 71; Hammersmith Hosp., London, 1975; Witwatersrand Univ., Johannesburg, 1975; cons. adv. Ed. Bd. of Chronic Disease, UCLA. Sci. Exhibs.: AMA, Am. Acad. of Gen. Practice, Internstate Med. Soc., Chicago Med. Soc. Contrib. to 14 profl. publs 1969---. Lectr. (presentation profl. papers): London Hosp., Univ. of Liverpool, 1969; Univ. of Witwatersrand, S. Africa, 1969; Am. Coll. of Phys., San Diego; N.Y. Acad. of Gen. Pract., N.Y.; AMA Annual Conf., Chicago, 1970; Orthopedic Assn., Johannesburg, 1971; Calif. Acad. Gen. Practice, L.A., and Am. Orthopedic Assn. Annual Conf., Wash., D.C., 1972; New Orleans, 1976; XIII World Congress of Rheumatology, Kyoto, Japan, 1973; VIII European Congress of Ehrumatology, Helsinki, Finland, 1975; Orthopedic Soc., Johannesburg, So. Africa, June, July 1975; VII Pan-Am. Congress of Rheumatology, Bogota, Columbia, 1978. Awards: J. Hill Abram Award, Univ. of Liverpool, 1964; Surg. Presentation Award, Univ. of Liverpool, 1966; Research Award, So. Calif. Rheumatism Soc. 1970. Mem.: AMA; L.A. Co., Calif., Brit. Med. Assns.; Am. Rheumatism Assn.; So. Calif. Rheumatism Soc.; Liverpool Med. Inst.; Royal Coll. of Surgs.; Licentiate, Royal Coll. of Phys.; Fellow, Royal Soc. of Health. Res.: 10433 Wilshire Blvd., L.A., CA; Office: 10921 Wilshire Blvd., Suite 1004, L.A., CA 90024.

MANATT, CHARLES TAYLOR
Attorney at Law

b. June 9, 1936, Chicago; s. William Price and Lucille (Taylor) Manatt; B.S., Iowa State Univ., 1958; J.D., George Wash. Univ. Law Sch., 1962; m. Margaret Kathleen Klinkefus, Dec. 29, 1957; chil.: Michele Anne, b. Nov. 24, 1961; Timothy Taylor, b. May 24, 1965; Daniel Charles, b. May 11, 1969. Career: Partner in law firm of Manatt, Phelps, Rothenberg, Manley & Tunney, L.A. --- (spec. in rep. banking instns.); owner, operator Manatt Land Co. (farming opn.), 1969---; chmn. bd. of dirs., First L.A. Bank, LA, 1973---. Bd. dir. Calif. Bankers Assn., 1976---, 1st v.p. 1977---; mem. govt. rels. council, Am. Bankers Assn., 1976---. Democratic Party Exec. Natl. Committeeman, 1976---, chmn. Nat. Fin. Council, 1978---; chmn., Western States Conf., 1972-76; chmn., Calif. Demo. Party, 1971-73, 1975-77, So. Chmn. 1973-75. Methodist. Res.: 10485 Charing Cross Rd., L.A., CA 90024; Office: 1888 Century Park E., 21st flr., L.A., CA 90067.

MANCINI, JOSEPH ALBERT
Business Owner

b. Dec. 29, 1910, Memphis, Tenn.; s. Albert Joseph and Catherine (Brann) Mancini; aeronautical engring., Univ. of Cincinnati, 1935; m. Monique Guest, June 8, 1976, Paris, France; chil.: Brooks Thomas, b. Apr. 18, 1940; Joseph Coleman, b. Dec. 1944; Phillip Woodson, b. Mar. 9, 1949. Career: pres., Brookman Co., Inc., 1946---; pres., Mancini Enterprises, 1946---; chmn. bd., Varner Ward Lease Co., 1967---. Pres., Sigma Alpha Epsilon Leadership Found.; bd. dir., San Francisco Boy's Club. 1st Lt. Army Coast Artillery. Past pres., Sigma Alpha Epsilon. Clubs: Bohemian, St. Francis Yacht, Olympic, Lakeside Golf. Hobbies: reading, painting. Rec.: golf, hunting, fishing. Home: 999 Green St., S.F., CA 94133; Office: 322 E. Grand Ave., So. San Francisco 94080.

MANKIN, ROXANNE
Business Executive — Educator

b. Nov. 26, 1943, Berkeley, Calif.; d. Henry, M.D. and Gertrude (Schwartz) Mankin; B.A. humanities, Univ. Calif., Berkeley, 1966; M.B.A., Pepperdine Univ. Key Exec. Program, 1979. Career: partner, Mankin, Briles & O'Shea, 1972--- (design, mkt. and present fin. awareness courses to women at more than 15 community colleges, universities, assns., businesses); instr., Women and Money series, Univ. Calif., 1972---; gen. partner, Roxanne Mankin & Co., 1974--- (investment syndicate); assoc., Marcus &

Millichap, Investment Real Estate, 1977---. Dir., Western Women's Bank, 1978; bd. dir., Professional Women's Alliance, 1977-78, co-founder 1st chpt. Devel. prototype, women's fin. awareness series for major Calif. univs. Office: 8 Bret Harte Way, Berkeley, CA 94708.

MANN, BETTY R.
Realtor — Inventor — Author

b. Jan. 13, 1937; Missouri; d. G.F. and Mary P. Miles; ed. pub. schs., Bus. Coll., licensed real estate broker, police sci. Career: real estate agent; real estate broker, Walker & Lee Realty. Recipient: Million Dollar Club life membership, 1975---; eighteen top sales awards in real estate, past 2 years with Walker & Lee Realty. Inventor: patented inventions. Author: TV, short stories. Hobbies: photog., fiction writing. Home, Office: Newport Beach, CA.

MANN, DELBERT
Film, TV and Stage Director

b. Jan. 30, 1920, Lawrence, Kan.; s. Delbert, Sr. and Ora (Patton) Mann; A.B., Vanderbilt Univ. 1941; M.F.A., Uale Univ. Sch. of Drama, 1945-47; (Hon.) LL.D., Northland Coll. 1959; m. Anne Caroline Gillespie, Nashville, Tenn., Jan. 13, 1942; chil.: David, b. 1946; Frederick, b. 1950; Steven, b. 1957. Career: Gen. Shoe Corp., Nashville, Tenn. 1941-42; dir. Town Theatre, Columbia, S.C. 1947-49; stage mgr., Wellesley Summer Theatre, 1947-48; asst. dir., NBC-TV, 1949; dir.: Philco Playhouse, Playhouse 90, Omnibus, Lights Out, Playwright's 56, 1949-55; dir. (films): Marty, Bachelor Party, Desire Under the Elms, Middle of the Night, Separate Tables, The Dark at the Top of the Stairs, The Outsider, Lover Come Back, That Touch of Mink, A Gathering of Eagles, Dear Heart, Quick Before It Melts, Mister Buddwing, Fitzwilly, Kidnapped, Bitch Interval; TV specs.: Heidi, David Copperfield, Jane Eyre, A Man Without A Country, Breaking Up, Tell Me My Name, Home To Stay; directed (plays) A Quiet Place, Speaking of Murder, Zelda; directed (opera) Wuthering Heights, NYC Center. Trustee: Vanderbilt Univ.; prof. lectr. in Film Art, Claremont Men's Coll. 1st Lt. U.S. Army Air Corps; B-24 pilot, 8th A.F. Squadron Intelligence Ofcr. (1942-45), WW II. Awards: Distinguished Flying Cross, Air Medal with 5 Oak Leaf Clusters; Acad. Award and Director's Guild Award as dir. of Marty, 1955. Mem.: past pres. Director's Guild of Am.; Kappa Alpha. Beverly Hills Community Presbyterian Ch. Rec.: sports. Res.: 401 S. Burnside Ave., Apt. 11-D, L.A., CA 90036.

MANN, GORDON L., JR.
Insurance Executive

b. May 5, 1921, Taylor, Tex.; s. Gordon L., Sr. and Ruth (Kirkpatrick) Mann (noted writer, lectr., clubwoman); cousin, Gerald Mann, chmn. bd. Diversa, Inc. and former Atty. Gen., Tex.; ed. UCLA; Loyola Univ. Sch. of Law; Career: exec., Argonaut Ins. Co.; Casualty Claims Mgrs'. Council of L.A.; Chartered Property Casualty Underwriter by Am. Inst. For Property and Liability Underwriters, Inc., Natl. Conv. St. Louis, Mo., 1966, pres. L.A. chpt., and gen. chmn. Natl. Conv., L.A., Oct. 1970; Lectr. on subjs. of ins. and patriotic affairs. Author: article series on ins., pub. Underwriter's Report, other profl. and trade journs. Ensign, USN, aviator, 1941-45; Lt., USNR, WW II. Awards: Am. Legion Award, Fairfax H.S.; Meritorious Pub. Serv. Cit., Dept. USN by Secty. of Navy Paul Nitze, 1965; Natl. Scroll of Honor Award, Navy League; Boss of Yr. by Ins. Women's Assn. 1968. Mem.: Naval Order U.S.; Res. Ofcrs. Assn.; past comdr. Sons of Confederate Vets; post comdr. Am. Legion; natl. com. ROTC; Mil. Order of World Wars; gov. Calif. Div., dep. gov. gen. Soc. of Colonial Wars; bd. Calif. Soc. S.R.; sr. state chmn.-past natl. chmn. Chil. Am. Rev. and S.R. 1776; adv. State Bd. Dirs. Calif. Soc. D.A.R.; past chmn. Masonic Homes Endowment Fund, Garfield Lodge, F&AM; dir. and chmn. awards com.-pres. Christians and Jews for Law and Morality; natl. dir. Navy League of U.S.; past state pres. and past pres., L.A. Council, chmn. Navy League Ball, L.A. 1967; L.A. Co. Mus. of Art Assn. Vestryman, All Saints' Episcopal Ch., Beverly Hills (pres. Men of All Saints' Soc.; alternate, Episc. Diocesan Conv.). Hobbies: reading, writing, pilot (holds comml. license). Res.: 435 S. Curson Ave., L.A., CA 90036; Office: 425 Shatto Pl., L.A., CA 90020.

MANN, HELEN C.
Board of Realtors Executive

b. Mar. 28, 1914, Weld Co., Colo.; d. John G. and Christina (Wolfe) Polzen; student, Colorado State Coll. of Edn., Cabrillo Community Coll. Div. Career: office mgr.,

Watsonville Community Hosp., 1945-58; exec. officer, Watsonville Bd. of Realtors, Inc., 1970---. Certified Profl. Secty. designation. Mem. Internat. Soroptimist of Watsonville. Office: 21 Brennan St., Rm. 14, Watsonville, CA 95076.

MANN, MAURICE
Investment Banker
b. Feb. 22, 1929, Peabody, Mass.; s. Abram S. and Jennie Mann; B.A., Northeastern Univ., 1951; M.A., Boston Univ., 1952; Ph.D., Syracuse Univ., 1955; (hon.) LL.D., Northeastern Univ., 1977; m. Betty M. Melnick of Brookline, Mass.; chil.: Deborah Ellen, b. 1955; Pamela Sue, b. 1957. Career: instr. economics, Syracuse Univ.; asst. prof., Ohio Wesleyan Univ., 1955-58; Ford Found. fellowship, 1956; economist, Bureau of Old Age and Survivors Insurance, Baltimore, Md., 1958-60; economist, Fed. Reserve Bank of Cleveland, 1960-69; sr. asst. dir. of Office of Mgmt. and Budget, Exec. Office of the President, 1969-70; exec. v.p., Western Penn. Nat. Bank (now Equibank), 1970-72; pres. and chief exec. officer, Fed. Home Loan Bank of S.F., 1973-78; v. chmn. and dir., Warburg Paribas Becker Inc., 1978---. Bd. Dir., The Bekins Co.; Apptd. Distinguished Lectr., Claremont Men's Coll., 1978; participant, economic summit conference of Pres. Ford, 1974. Contbd. articles profl. publs. Awarded Chancellor's Medal, Syracuse Univ., 1977; alumni citation, Northeastern Univ., 1973. Mem.: Nat. Assn. Bus. Economists; Am. Economic Assn.; Am. Finance Assn.; Nat. Economists Club; Nat. Alumni Council Northeastern Univ. and Internat. Frat. Lambda Alpha; bd. advisor, Applied Fin. Economics Center, Claremont Men's Coll. Clubs: Commonwealth, Bankers Club of S.F., Concordia-Argonaut. Home: 3255 Jackson St., S.F., CA 94118; Office: 555 California St., San Francisco, CA 94104.

(COUNT) MANOLESCO, JOHN
Researcher — Author
b. Dec. 3, 1918, Timsoara, Roumania; s. Count Emil and Karla von (Kramer) Manolesco; B.Lit., Roumania, 1938; B.A., Loyola Univ., 1965; M.A., McGill Univ., Montreal, 1967; Ph.D., Sussex, 1970; D.D., Indiana, 1970; D.Sc., Sussex, 1972; m. (Countess) Celia Parker, Aug. 15, 1977, Tlaxcala, Mex. Career: 1940-41, British Aux. Navy; B.B.C., Foreign Service, London, U.K., 1942-48; chief advisor, H.H. Maharaja of Ramgarh, co-founder of India's Janata Party, 1948-58; Bus. cons., 1958-62; leading TV host and radio broadcaster, Canada, 1962-72; instr., Coll. Mont-Lasalle and McGill Univ., 1968-71 philosophy and edn., 1968-71; radio host numerous stations, U.S., 1972-76; cons., writer, 1976---. Author: 15 pub. works incl. Guide to Hypnotism; Guide to the Occult, Simon & Schuster; Scientific Astrology, Pinnacle; Meet the Colonel (musical comedy), London, 1948; Permitted to Land. Awards: Albert Schweitzer Gold Medal for lit. achievements, Italy, 1972; Knight of St. John (Danea) 1970; Grand Knight of the Crown, Italy, 1971. Gold card mem. Am. Fedn. of Astrologers, 1968---. Bishop, Christian Life Sci. Ch. Hobbies: Astrology, psychic phenomena. Home-Office: 4393 Lemp Ave., Studio City, CA 91604.

MANSOUR, TAG ELDIN
Professor of Pharmacology
b. Nov. 6, 1924, Belkar, Egypt; s. M. Elsayed and Roukaya Mansour; rel., Gamal Eldin Mansour, Supreme Ct. Justice of Egypt; B.V.Sc. (D.V.M.), Univ. of Cairo, Egypt, 1946; Ph.D., Pharmacology, Univ. of Birmingham, Eng., D.Sc., Biochemistry, 1974; m. Joan MacKinnon, Aug. 1955, Cleveland, Oh.; chil.: Suzanne Laura, b. 1957; Jeanne Roukaya, b. 1960; Dean Andrew, b. 1963. Career: research fellow, Dept. of Pharmacology, Birmingham Univ., 1949-50; lectr. in Pharmacology, Univ. of Cairo, 1950-61; Fulbright Fellow and instr.: Physiology, Howard Univ., Wash., D.C., 1951-52; Sr. instr. and Research Assoc., Dept. of Pharmacology, Case Western Reserve Univ., 1952-54; asst. to assoc. prof., La. State Univ. Med. Sch., 1955-61; assoc. to full prof., now Donald E. Baxter Prof. and chmn. Dept. of Pharmacology, Stanford Med. Sch., 1961---. Commonwealth Fund Awardee for Research in Naples, Italy, 1965; vis. prof., Dept. of Genetics, Univ. of Wis. Contbr. profl. journs. in field of Pharmacology, Biochemistry, Chemotherapy. Mem. edit bds. Biochemical Pharmacology and Arch. Int. de Pharmac. & Therap. Hobby: oil painting. Res.: 867 Mayfield Ave., Stanford, CA 94305; Office: Stanford Med. Sch., Stanford, CA 94305.

MANUEL, WILEY WILLIAM
Justice, California Supreme Court
b. Aug. 27, 1927, Oakland; s. Curtis and Crenella Manuel; A.A., 1949; B.A., 1951; LL.B., 1953; LL.D., 1978; m. Eleanor Mary Williams, June 20, 1948, Berkeley; chil.: Yvonne Temple, b. May 9, 1949; Gary, b. Sept. 27, 1956. Career: Dep. Atty. Gen., 1953-70; asst. atty. gen., 1970-71; chief asst. atty. gen., 1971-76; Judge of the Superior Ct., 1976-77; Assoc. Justice, Calif. Supreme Ct., 1977---. AUS, 1946-47. Pres., Chas. H. Houston Bar Assn., 1962; mem.: Calif. Conf. of Judges; Grand Knight, KC, Berkeley council No. 1499; Serra Assembly; Sigma Pu Rho Boule. Catholic; lay minister of communion; Lector. Hobby: photog. Res.: 4107 Sequoyah Rd., Oakland, CA 94605; Office: 350 McAllister St., S.F., CA 94102.

MAPES, WILLIAM EDWARD
Food Industry Executive
b. Sept. 19. 1934, Kendallville, Ind.; s. William Albert and Garnet Beatrice Mapes; desc. Sarah Bingham, first white woman settler, Ind.; Arthur Mapes, Poet Laureate, Inc.; B.S. edn., Defiance Coll., 1956; M.S. edn., Bowling Green State Univ., 1962; candidate Ph.D., Wharton Bus. Sch., Univ. Pa.; m. Marilyn Ann Salerno, Nov. 24, 1956, Garrett, Ind.; chil.: Sherri Ann; Patti Lynn; William Frederick. Career: with Campbell Soup Co., 1949-63; hourly employee, foreman, gen. foreman, night supt., gen. supt., (V-8 Plant, Napoleon, Ohio), dir., quality assurance, Processed Foods Group, area mgr., Processed Foods; Gen. Supt., John Sexton Co. div. Beatrice Foods, 1963-66; v.p., gen., mgr., asst. to chmn., Kraftco Corp., 1967-70; chmn., chief exec., Am. Consumer Products Corp., Cinn., Ohio, 1970-72; group v.p., Collins Foods Internat., Inc.: v.p., div. mgr., Collins Foodservice Div.; pres., Quick Chef Mfg. Co., 1972-75; v.p., div. mgr., Sizzler Family Steak Houses, 1973-74; pres., chief exec. office: J. Hungerford Smith Co., Inc.; J. Hungerford Smith Co. Ltd. (Canada); and Pacific Aromatics Flavors and Fragrances Co., 1975---. Functioned as a turnaround expert, guiding 7 firms from heavy losses into profits. Worked full-time nights for Campbell Soup Co. while earning his B.S., Phi Beta Kappa, and playing 1st string football all 4 years. Named to Little All America Team, 1957; played one year with Chicago Cardinals. Author 2 novels: To Love and To Die, 1963; Another Place, Another Time, 1969. Mem.: Alpha Tau Omega, Alpha Gamma Upsilon. Republican. Methodist. Hobbies: painting, writing. Rec.: golf, tennis. Home: 1317 Thunderbird Dr., Modesto, CA 95350; Office: 1905 Coffee Rd., Modesto, CA 95355.

MARCHUS, FLOYD I.
Superintendent of Schools
b. Jan. 12, 1911, Rolette, N.D.; s. Gust and Julia (Anfinson) Marchus; B.A., Jamestown Coll., N.D., 1932; M.E., Univ. Mont., 1940; Ed.D., Univ. Calif., Berkeley, 1947; m. Helen Elizabeth Bennett, May 13, 1938, Judd, N.D.; chil.: Diane (Larson), b. Jan. 15, 1940; Darlene (Crockett), b. Feb. 10, 1941; Val, b. Feb. 14, 1942; Jay, b. Mar. 7, 1950. Career: Tchr., One-Room Co. Sch., N.D., 1932; Prin., Edgeley H.S., N.D., 1933-47; Supt., Jud.d Sch. Dist., N.D., 1937-39; Dean of Boys, Thompson Falls, Mont., 1939-41; Supt. 1941-43; Manhattan Proj., U.C. Berkeley, 1943-45; tchr. an; counselor, Oakland Tech. H.S., Oakland, 1945-49; dir. of research, Contra Costa Co. Dept. of Edn., 1949-59; Co. Supt. of Schs., Contra Costa Co., 1959-78. Awards: Hon. Mex.-Am. Award, United Council of Spanish Speaking Orgns. of Contra Costa Co., 1974; Nat. PTA Hon. Life Mem., 1973; State Hon. Life Mem., 32nd Dist. PTA, 1966. Mem.: Contra Costa Co. Heart Assn. chmn. fund drive; March of Dimes, chmn.; United Crusade, chmn. for edn.; YMCA, div. mgr. capital fund drive; Comm. Workshop, Inc. for Handicapped, fund raiser; Easter Seal chmn., 1970-72. Mem. Masonic Lodge, Phi Delta Kappa. Methodist. Hobby: voluntary work with assns. Res.: 1271 Juanita Dr., Walnut Creek, CA 94595; Office: 75 Santa Barbara Rd., Pleasant Hill, CA 94523.

MARCHUS, FLOYD I.
County School Administrator
b. Jan. 12, 1911, Rolette, N. Dak.; s. Gust (County Supervisor, Pierce Co., N. Dak.) and Julia (Anfinson) Marchus; B.A. math, sci., Jamestown Coll., N. Dak., 1932; M.D., Public Sch. Adminstrn., Univ. of Montana, 1940; Ed.D., Pub. Sch. Adm., Univ. of Calif., Berkeley, 1947; m. Helen Elizabeth Bennett, April 1939, Judd, N. Dak.; chil.: Diane (Larson); Darlene (Crockett); Val; Jay. Career: tchr., one-rm. sch., N. Dak., 1932; principal, Edgeley H.S., 1933-37; Supt., Jud Sch. Dist., N. Dak., 1937-39; Dean of Boys, Thompson Falls, Mont., 1939-41; Supt., 1941-43; Manhatten Proj., UC, Berkeley, 1943-45;

tchr. (Math., sci.) and Counselor, Oakland Tech. H.S., Oakland, Calif., 1945-49; dir. of research, Contra Costa Co. Dept. of Edn., Pleasant Hill, Calif., 1949-59; county supt. of schs., Contra Costa Co., 1959---; Instr., pub. sch. adminstrn. (summers): Univ. of Mont. 1950-54, 1965; Univ. of Idaho, 1955-57; Univ. of Colo. 1964, 1966. Author: The Resources of Education, County/Regional, 1971; contbr.: Mr. Superintendent, How Do You Do; Mr. Principal, How Do You Do? Recipient: Hon. Mexican Am. Award, 1974; Nat. PTA hon. life mem., 1973; State PTA hon. life mem., 1966. Past pres., Calif. Edn. Research Orgn.; chmn research council, Calif. Assn. Sch. Adminstrs., 1961-67; chmn., Congressman's Mil. Advisory Com. for selection of apptmts. to U.S. Service Academies, 1966-67; mem., Am. Assn. Sch. Adminstrs.-Nat. Edn. Assn., Dept. of Rural Edn. Jt. Commn. on Regional Service Agencies, 1967-70; study project mission to Russia, European countries, 1965; chmn. fund drives: Heart Assn., March of Dimes, United Crusade, YMCA, Contra Costa Co. Community Workshop, Inc. for Hanidcapped, Easter Seal, 1970-72; bd. dir., Calif. Advisory Council on Edn. Research; mem.: Phi Delta Kappa; Calif. Educational Research Assn.; Calif. Tchrs. Assn.; Nat. Edn. Assn.; No. Calif. Indus.-Edn. Council; No. Calif. Council on Economic Edn.; Assn. Calif. Sch. Adminstrs.; bd., Calif. Advis. Council on Educational Research. Methodist. Rec.: walking, swimming. Home: 1271 Juanita Dr., Walnut Creek, CA 94595; Office: 75 Santa Barbara Rd., Pleasant Hills, CA 94523.

MARCUS, ELIAS GEORGE
Physician
b. Apr. 17, 1900, Lansing, Mich.; s. John George (Missionary to the Arabs in Syria, 1902-08) and Nellie Marcus; ed. B.A., Coll. of Med. Evangs. 1923, M.D. 1925; Univ. Zeugnis certificate, Univ. of Vienna, 1927; Licentiate, Royal Coll. Of Phys. and Royal Coll. of Surgs., Edinburgh, Scotland, 2937; m. Dorothy Jones Fresno, Aug. 30, 1923; chil.: Helen Paloma McLaughlin, b. Apr. 27, 1926; Shirley Louise Corbett, b. July 28, 1928; John Richard, b. Apr. 28, 1930. Career: Intern, Loma Linda Univ. 1925-26; med. missionary work, Africa, 1927-43; est. Mwami Mission and Hosp. and first colony for lepers in No. Rhodesia, 1927 (taught lepers to build individuals dwellings and work as part of treatment, and paid them for their work; over 500 under care at one time); returned to Africa for 51st year Jubilee celebration of the mission & leper colony, Aug. 1978; assoc. founder, Coll. of Phys. and Surgs., S. Africa; dir. Malamulo Mission Hosp., Malamulo, Nyasaland, Africa, 1930-36; administered first blood transfusion in Nyasaland for treatment of blackwater fever (malaria), 1930; saved many lives as a result of this method of treatment; hosp. dir., Bechuanaland Protectorate, 1936-40 (apptd. med. ofcr. by King George V 1939); dir. Nokuphila Mission Hosp., Johannesburg, S. Africa, 1940-43; pvt. practice, USA 1943---; Glendale, Calif. 1944---. Author: (book) Fighting Africa's Black Magic (witchcraft among natives), publ. 1936. Pvt. WW I. Mem.: Calif. and L.A. Co. Med. Assns. Republican. Seventh-Day Adventist (elder-ordained minister). Hobby: carpentry, gardening. Rec.: horseshoes, croquet, hiking, tennis. Res.: 915 Green Lane, La Canada, CA; Office: 125 E. Glenoaks Blvd., Glendale, CA 91207.

MAREE, ANDREW MORGAN, III
President, A. Morgan Maree and Assocs.
b. Mar. 9, 1927, Detroit, Mich.; s. Andrew Morgan, Jr. and Elizabeth Lathrop (Cady) Maree; ed. B.A., Claremont Men's Coll. 1949; M.B.A., Univ. of Chicago, 1950; son, Andrew Morgan, IV, b. Dec. 20, 1954. Career: Assoc. with Hanover Bank, 1950; pres. A. Morgan Maree Jr. and Assocs. (bus. mgmt.), 1951---. Dir. Carson Estate Co.; dir. Four Star TV, 1955-65. USNR (1944-46), WW II. Mem.: Delta Kappa Epsilon, Delta Delta Chpt. 1950-51. Hobby: coin collecting. Rec.: skiing, hunting, horseback riding. Res.: Beverly Hills, CA; Office: 6363 Wilshire Blvd., L.A., CA 90048.

MARIA, NARENDRA LAL
Professor of Mathematics
b. Apr. 22, 1928, Chamba, India; s. Jagmohan and Laj Wanti Maria; B.A. honors, Panjab Univ., 1948; M.A., 1949; Ph.D., Univ. Calif., Berkeley, 1968; m. Krishan Bhambri, July 17, 1957, Ambala City, India; chil.: Geeta, b. May 31, 1958; Rajeev, b. Aug. 27, 1970. Career: Asst. prof., Panjab Univ. Colls., 1950-65; Tchg. Assoc., Univ. Calif., 1965-67; Prof. and Chmn. Dept. of Mathematics, Cal. State Coll., Stanislaus, 1967---. Publs. incl. ten books, numerous research papers and revs. Res.: 3608 Fern Ct., Modesto, CA 95350; Office: Math Dept., Cal. State, Stanislaus, Turlock, CA 95380.

MARIANA, PAUL A., JR.
President, Paul A. Mariana Co.
b. July 8, 1919, San Jose; s. Paul A., Sr. and Victoria (Svilich) Mariana; ed. Fremont Union H.S., 1933-36; (hon., frat. house mgr.) Univ. of Calif., Davis, 1936-37, 1938-40; Univ. of Santa Clara, 1937-38; postgard. Univ. of Calif., Berkeley, 1940-42; m. Mary Frances Guilbert, San Jose, Calif., Aug. 9, 1942; chil.: Mrs. Michael Pratt (Linda Jane), b. Mar. 29, 1943; Paul A., III, b. Feb. 16, 1945; John Guilbert, b. Sept. 11, 1947; David William, b. Sept. 22, 1948; Mark Allen, b. Apr. 11, 1952; Richard Michael, b. June 27, 1954; Marialisa, b. Oct. 24, 1960. Career: Asst. to founder, Paul A. Mariani Co. 1940-44, sales mgr. 1944-45, gen. mgr. 1945-61, pres. 1961---; orgn. onion dehydrating plant, Dehydro Foods, Inc. for Port of Embarkation (WW II), Seattle, 1942-43; est. Mariana Frozen Foods and Freeze-Dry Dept. (fruits and vegetables), 1961; pioneer in spec. packaging dried fruit, moist pack, ready-to-eat dried fruits; created research labs. experiments for U.S. Dept. Agri.; goodwill agri. industry tour of Iran, Afghanistan, 1966 (feat. in Internat. Commerce Mag. by U.S. Dept. of Commerce, May 1966). Mem.: Serra Internat.; Knights of Malta. ; Alpha Zeta. Rec.: sports, boxing, baseball. Res.: 10401 Loyola Dr., Los Altos, CA 94022; Office: 10930 N. Sunnyvale-Saratoga Rd., P.O.B. 428, Cupertino, CA 95014.

MARKOWITZ, SAMUEL S.
Professor of Chemistry
b. Oct. 31, 1931, Brooklyn, N.Y.; s. Max and Florence E. Markowitz; B.S., Rensselaer Polytech. Inst., Troy, N.Y., 1953; M.A., 1955; Ph.D., Princeton Univ., 1957; research stu., Brookhaven Nat. Lab., 1955-57; m. Aondra Diamond, July 4, 1958, Albany, N.Y.; chil.: Michael Dana, b. Mar. 4, 1960; Daniel Raphael, b. May 13, 1963; Jonah Elliott, b. Feb. 23, 1965. Career: U.S. Nat. Sci. Found. fellow: Univ. of Birmingham, Eng., 1957-58, Faculte Des Sciences de L'Universite de Paris, Orsay, France 1964-65; asst. prof. to prof. of chem., Univ. of Calif., Berkeley, 1958---; staff scientist to faculty sr. sci., Lawrence Berkeley Lab, 1958---; vis. prof. Weizmann Inst. of Sci., Rehovot, Israel, 1973-74. Pub. research in sci. journs. on nuclear reactions at high energies, nuclear studies for chem. analysis, "hot-atom" chem., nuclear activation applied to atmospheric air pollution studies, helium-3 and pion-induced reactions, radioactive studies. Mem. Rensselaer Soc. Engrs., 1949-53; vice chmn. UC Summer Softball League, 1964-76. Pres., Berkeley Bd. of Edn. 1971-72, dir. 1969-73; mem. Berkeley Rec. Commn. 1969-72. Jewish, pres. congregation. Rec.: athletics. Res.: 1674 Capistrano Ave., Berkeley, CA 94707; Office: Dept. of Chemistry, UC Berkeley, CA 94720.

MARLAIS, JOHN P.
Attorney at Law
b. Feb. 24, 1918, Campbell, Calif.; B.A., San Jose State Coll. 1940; LL.B. (cum laude), Univ. of S.F., 1949; m. Beatrice J. Hebert, Pac. Grove, Calif., Feb. 15, 1947; son, John P., Jr., b. Jan. 28, 1949. Career: admitted to practice law, Calif., Jan. 1950; Fed. Dist. Cts., U.S. Circuit Ct. of Appeals, U.S. Mil. Ct. of Appeals; est. pvt. practice, San Jose, 1953---; mem. Rankin, O'Neal, Center, Luckhardt, Marlais, Lund & Hinshaw law firm. Co-owner-v.p. Evergreen Water Co. 1958-62. USN 1942-46; staff, Judge Adv., Wash. D.C., 1950-53; Lt. Comdr., USN R. Mem.: Pres.'s Council, San Jose State Univ.; dir. Metro A. Assn. 1965-68; bd. dirs. San Jose C. of C.; Clubs: past dir. West S.J. Rotary; past pres. San Jose Country; past pres. La Rinconada Country; Sainte Claire Club. Res.: 5490 Greenside Dr., San Jose; Office: 315 First Natl. Bank Bldg., San Jose, CA 95113.

MARLOW, MIRAM JESS
TV News Anchorman
b. Nov. 29, 1929, Salem, Ill.; s. Rola and Blanche (Mulvaney) Marlow; B.S. (journ.), Univ. of Ill. 1958; m. Phyllis Puckett, Norfolk, Va., Mar. 12, 1949; dau. Susan Lynn, b. Dec. 17, 1949. Career: Newscaster-news editor, WHBF AM-FM-TV, Rock Is., Ill. 1958-61; reporter-news dir. KNTV, San Jose, 1961-66; reporter, NBC-News, 1966---; anchorman, KNBC News, 1970---; USN 1948-50. Awards: Assoc. Press Award of Merit for TV Commentary, 1965; USC Journalism Award, 1976. Rec.: skiing. Res.: 1006 Alcalde Way, Glendale, CA; Office: 3000 W. Alameda Ave., Burbank, CA 91503.

MARMOR, JUDD
Professor of Medicine
b. May 1, 1910, London, Eng. (U.S. Cit. 1916); s. Clement K. and Sarah (Levene) Marmor; A.B. (hons), Columbia Coll. 1930; M.D., Columbia Coll. of Phys. and

Surgs. 1933; m. Katherine Stern, Ft. Lee, M.J., May 1, 1938; son, Michael Franklin, b. Aug. 10, 1941; Career: U.S. res. 1911---; lectr. in psych., N.Y. Med. Coll. 1943-46; visiting assoc. prof. psychol., USC 1947-50; sr. cons. in neuropsych., US VA, LA 1947-50; clin. prof. psych., UCLA 1952---; past pres.-training analyst, Psychoanalytic Inst. dir. psych. Sinai Med. Center, 1966-72; Franz Alexander Prof. of Psych., USC Sch. of Med., 1972---. Dir.-v.p. Psychosomatic Research Found.; dir. Behavioral Sci. Research Found.; dir. Neumeyer Found.; dir. Human Interaction Research Inst.; dir. L.A. Center Theatre Group; chmn. Contemporary Art Council of L.A.; Co. Museum of Art; past chmn. Com. on Social Issues, bd. dirs. Group for Advancement of Psych.; bd. dirs. Am. Orthopsych. Assn.; past pres., Am. Acad. of Psychoanalysis. Author: approx. 100 profl. publs.; ed. Sexual Inversion: The Multiple Roots of Homosexuality, publ. N.Y. Basic Books, 1965; ed. contrib. Modern Psychoanalysis: New Directions and Perspectives, 1968. U.S. Pub. Health Serv., USN (1944-45), WW II. Mem.: Phi Beta Kappa, Alpha Omega Alpha, Phi Delta Epsilon. Res.: 655 Sarbonne Rd., L.A., CA 90024; Office: 2025 Zonal Ave., L.A., CA 90033.

MARR, LUTHER REESE
Film Studio Executive
b. June 23, 1925, Kansas City, Mo.; s. Luther Dow and Aileen (Shimfessel) Marr; grandson of Luther D. Marr, noted lawyer and banker, one of three authors of Okla's. first state const., Okla's. first Secty. of Edn. and founder, several banks, Okla.; B.A., UCLA 1946; J.D., USC 1950; m. Christelle Taylor, Glendale, July 12, 1956; chil.: Michelle Lois, b. Apr. 7, 1959; Stephen Luther, b. Mar. 15, 1961; Christelle Elizabeth, b. Sept. 24, 1970. Career: Admitted to Calif. bar, Jan. 1951; def. atty., E. Broox Randall & Sons, 1951; def. atty., Employers Mutual Ins. Co., of Wis., LA. 1951-52; assoc. atty., pvt. practice, Hasbrouch & Melby law firm, 1951-54; atty. Walt Disney Prodns., 1954---, corp. secty. 1957-78, v.p., corp. and stockholder affairs, 1978---; corp. secty., Disney Found., Buena Vista Internat., Inc., other subsidiaries; gen. counsel and corp. secty., Calif. Inst. of the Arts, 1965-77. Naval ROTC, UCLA 1944-46; Ensign, USNR, Supply Corps, 1946-47; Lt., Naval Res., resigned, 1957. Mem.: Phi Beta Kappa (UCLA), 1946; Phi Alpha Delta, USC Law Sch., 1950; bd. dirs.-v.p., Glendale Jr. C. of C. 1952-54; Gateway Kiwanis, Glendale, 1959-65. Republican. Chmn., bd. of trustees, First United Methodist Ch., Glendale, 1977-78. Hobby: photog., phonograph rec. collection. Rec.: travel, gardening, woodworking, painting. Res.: 2323 Via Saldivar, Glendale, CA; Office: 500 S. Buena Vista St., Burbank, CA.

MARRIOTT, RICHARD HAROLD
Civic Official
b. Feb. 7, 1918, Ely, Nev.; s. Joseph Edmund and Anna (Bernard) Marriott; B.S., Univ. of S.F., 1940; Univ. Calif. Grad. Sch.; m. Geraldine Thane, S.F., July 17, 1943; chil.: Richard, b. Nov. 2, 1946; James, b. Apr. 4, 1949; Anna Marie, b. Aug. 1, 1951; Mary Beth, b. Oct. 16, 1953; Martin, b. Sept. 23, 1956; Christina, b. Apr. 11, 1959. Career: Assoc. with Alameda Times Star, 1946; Oroville Mercury, 1947; Sacto. Union, 1948-50; Cath. Herald, 1950-52; editor-mgr. Sacto. Valley Union Labor Bulletin, 1952-75. Elected councilman, City of Sacto., 1959---, mayor 1967-75. USMC 1941-42, WW II. Mem.: Univ. of S.F. Alumni Assn.; Univ. of Calif. Alumni Assn.; Sacto. State Coll. Found.; pres. Calif. Labor Press Assn.; past chmn. Sacto chpt., Am. Red Cross; past pres., Sacto. Serra Club. Rec.: fishing. Res.: 2716 10th Ave., Sacto., CA 95818; Office: City Hall, Sacto., CA 95814.

MARSEE, STUART E.
College President
b. Sept. 30, 1917, Gardiner, Ore.; s. William B. (dec.) and Clare Earl (Grimes) Marsee; B.S., Univ. of Ore. 1939, M.S. 1943; Ed.D., USC 1947; m. Audrey Belfield, Portland, Ore., June 1, 1940. Career: Counselor, Pasadena City Coll., 1946-49; asst. supt. for bus. serv., Pasa. City Schs., 1949-57; acting supt.-asst. supt. 1957-58; supt.-pres., El Camino Coll., El Camino Jr. Coll. Dist. 1958---. Ensign, USNR, WW II. Mem.: past pres. Am. Assn. of Jr. Colls. Presbyterian. Res.: 358 Camino de las Colinas, Torrance, CA; Office: El Camino Coll., Torrance, CA 90506.

MARTEN, JOHN FRANCIS, JR.
Investment Banker
b. July 28, 1914, San Jose; s. John Francis and Mary (Twohy) Marten; B.S., Univ. Santa Clara, 1936; m. Patricia Boyle, Nov. 9, 1946; chil.: Maureen, John

Francis III. Career: Title examiner, escrow ofcr. Cal. Pacific. Title Ins. Co. 1936-41; v.p. Inglewood Fed. S&L Assn., 1946-50; exec. v.p. Whittier S&L Assn., 1951-55; pres. Gt. Western S&L Assn., L.A., 1955-64; Gt. Western Financial Corp., 1955-64; investment banker, securities broker, 1963---. Bd. dirs. adv. bd. Daniel Freeman Mem. Hosp., Inglewood, pres. 1962-63; bd. dirs. Cal. Mus. Sci. and Industry, pres. 1970-71; exec. comm., St. John's Hosp. & Health Center, Santa Monica, 1977---; regent Univ. Santa Clara. Served from pvt. to Lt. Col., AUS, 1941-46. Decorated Bronze Star. Mem. Cal. S&L League (pres. 1962-63); Sovereign Mil. Order Malta. Roman Catholic. Clubs: L.A. Country, Calif. (L.A.); Beach (Santa Monica). Res.: 250 N. Cliffwood Ave., L.A., CA 90049.

MARTIN, JOSEPH, JR.
United States Ambassador
b. May 21, 1915, S.F.; s. Joseph and Helen (Jackson) Martin; A.B., Yale Univ. 1936; LL.B., 1939; m. Ellen Chamberlain, Santa Monica, July 5, 1946. Career: Admitted to N.Y. bar 1939, Calif. bar, 1946; assoc. Cadwalader, Wickersham & Taft law firm, NYC 1939-41; lawyer, Williamson & Wallace (later Wallace, Garrison, Norton & Ray), S.F., 1946-50; partner, 1950-55; partner, Miller, Groezinger, Pettit, Evers & Martin, S.F., 1955-70; gen counsel, Fed. Trade Commn., Wash., D.C. 1970-71; Ambassador, U.S. Rep. to Geneva Disarmament Conf. 1971-77; spec. asst. to dir. U.S. Arms Control and Disarmament Agcy., Wash., D.C. 1971-73; partner Pettit & Martin law firm, 1973---. Dir.: (past) Commonwealth Natl. Bank of S.F.; Air West, Inc.; Morris Plan of Calif.; pres. S.F. Pub. Utilities Commn. 1956-60; co-chmn. Com. for Trade and Transportation Develop. of Bay Area, 1958-59; adv. com. Golden Gateway Authority Commn. 1959-61; dir.-chmn. Patrons of Art and Music, Calif. Palace Legion of Honor, 1959-63; dir. Mt. Zion Hosp. 1968-70. Ensign to Lt. Comdr., USN 1941-46; served Guam (Japanese prisoner, 3 yrs.), WW II. Mem.: Calif. State, Am., S.F. Bar Assns.; Pac. Union Club, Natl. Lawyers Club, Burlingame Country Club, Yale Club of NYC. Res.: 2580 Broadway, S.F., CA 94115; Office: 600 Montgomery St., S.F., CA 94111.

MARTINEZ, FRANK R.
College President
b. Dec. 28, 1921, L.A.; s. Frank and Caroline (Bassett) Martinez; B.A. polit. sci., Univ. Redlands, 1947; M.A. hist., USC, 1953, Ed.D., 1963; m. Lois M. Martinez, Mar. 16, 1951, Glendora; chil.: Larry F., b. July 16, 1953; Jay, b. Feb. 6, 1955; Mark, b. Mar. 6, 1956; Barbara, b. July 23, 1960. Career: Instr. and counselor, Citrus Coll., 1947-52, adminstrv. Dean, 1962-64; asst. supt., Endl. Servs., Cuesta Coll., 1964-77, pres.-supt., 1977---. Mem. San Luis Obispo Co. Civil Serv. Commn., 1974-78. USMC, 1942-46, So. Pacific. Mem. Rotary Club, pres. 1959-60. Presbyterian, Elder. Hobby: bullfighting. Res.: 2383 Sunset Dr., San Luis Obispo, CA 93401; Office: P.O.B. J, San Luis Obispo, CA 93406.

MARTINO, ANTONIO PIETRO
Artist
b. Apr. 13, 1902, Phila., Pa.; s. Carmen and Clementina (Baranello) Martino; stu., Pa. Mus. Coll. of Art, Spring Garden Art Inst., Graphic Sketch Club, La France Art Inst., Phila.; m. Mary J. Hoffstetter, June 22, 1927, Phila.; chil.: Anthony C., b. Apr. 9, 1928; Marie (Manos), b. July 14, 1931. Career: Art Inst., Graphic Sketch Club, 1929, West Chester State Tchrs. Coll., 1970. Elected: Nat. Academician, Nat. Acad. Design, 1942; Life Mem. Nat. Arts Club, 1959; Mem. Am. Watercolor Soc., 1945. Awards incl. Bronze Medal, Sesquicentennial Internat. Exposition, Phila., 1926; 1st Hallgarten Prize, Natl. Acad. of Design, N.Y., 1927, 37; Jennie Sesman Gold Medal, Pa. Acad. of Fine Arts, Phila., 1938; 1st Benjamin Altman Award, Nat. Acad. of Design, N.Y., 1943; Gold Medal of Honor, Nat. Arts Club, N.Y., 1958; 1st Prize, Chautauque Art Assn., N.Y., 1960; 1st Prize Watercolor Purchase, Butler Inst. Am. Art, Oh., 1962; Saltus Gold Medal of Merit, Nat. Acad. of Design, NY, 1964; Dana Gold Medal, Phila. Watercolor Club, 1965; 1st Prize, Calif. State Exposition, Sacto. 1973; 1st Prize, 11th Traditional Artists Annual, San Bernardino Mus. 1977; many others. In permanent collections: Nat. Acad. of Design, Springville Mus. of Art, Ut.; Hickory Mus. of Art, N.C.; Univ. Delaware, others. Address: 1864 Rutgers Dr., Thousand Oaks, CA 91360.

MARUGG, JANICE GLOTFELTY
Civic Leader
b. July 1, 1924; Los Angeles; d. Lloyd, Sr. and Rachel

(Neff) Glotfelty; B.A., Occidental Coll., 1947; postgrad., Am. Inst. of Foreign Trade, Phoenix; Pacific Oaks Coll., Pasadena; m. Gerald (Jerry) G. Marugg Jr., Feb. 1, 1948; chil.: Gerald G. III; Lloyd K. Bd. Dir.: Foothill Center YWCA; Job Resources Center; C. of C.; Nat. Friends Com., ALA; P.E.O., chpt. M. Founder and past pres., Monrovia League; past pres.: Santa Anita Family Service, Sierra Madre Community Nursery Sch., Monrovia Guild of Childrens Hosp., Friends of Monrovia Pub. Lib., Friends of Calif. Libs.; past v.p. Monrovia League of Women Voters; current pres., Monrovia Lib. Bd. of Trustees. Espiocal ch., sr. warden St. Luke's. Home: 416 N. Primrose Ave., Monrovia, CA 91016.

MATNEY, JERRY ALVUS
Former Mayor, Huntington Beach
b. Oct. 19, 1932, Decatur, Tex.; s. Clyde Alvus and Audrey Faye (Minor, Olsen) Matney, A.A., Santa Ana Coll., 1956-58; B.A., Cal. State Univ., Long Beach, 1958-60; Grad. work, Chapman Coll., 1961-67; m. Nedra Doreen Files, Anaheim, Feb. 18, 1956; chil.: Dee Ann, b. Dec. 16, 1956; Brett Alvu, b. Nov. 7, 1959. Career: Correctional counselor, Orange Co. Juvenile Hall, 1959-61, Juvenile Hall (Otto Fischer Sch.) tchr., 1961-63, v. prin., 1963-70, prin. 1970-73, Chief Admin. Juv. Ct. Schs. of Orange Co., 1973---; co-owner, Huntington Valley Press, 1966-68; pres.-clerk, Fountain Valley Sch. Bd., 1965-68; Huntington Beach City Council, mayor-Mayor protempore, councilman 1968-76. Sgt., USMC 1953-56. Awards: Distinguished Serv. Award, H.B. Jaycees, 1968; N.E.A. Thom McAn Award as outstanding sch. bd. mem. 1968; Mem.: secty. Santa Ana Coll. Vets. Club 1956-57; pres. Hunt. Cont. Townhouse Assn., 1964-66; v.p. Home Council of H.B., 1966-67; dir. Fountain Valley Boys Club, 1967-68; v.p. Huntington Beach Lion's Club, 1971-72; dir.-pres. Juvenile Ct. Schs. Admin. of Calif., 1972---; Republican State Central Com., 1973-75; Phi Delta Kappa, 1965---; dir. West Orange Co. Red Cross Campaign, 1975; bd. of dirs.-bldg. com. chmn. Methodist Ch. of F.V., 1965-66. Rec.: golf, camping, traveling, writing. Res.: 17951 Scotia Circle, Huntington Beach, CA 92647; Office: 1300 S. Grand, P.O.B. 11846, Santa Ana, CA 92711.

MATTHEW, JOHN BRITTON
Artist — Educator
b. Sept. 16, 1896, Berkeley, Calif.; s. Rev. W.S. Matthew, D.D. (Dean of USC, 1888-90, editor, Calif. Christian Advocate, 1894-1900) and Marion L. (Pomeroy) M. (12 children, all prominent); bro. Allan P., lawyer S.F., 1910-60; sis. Margaret (Mrs. Geo. de Ille), w/ARC in Russia and Siberia, 1917-18; bro. Raymond, Engr., Calif. Div. Water Resources, 1924-60, chief engr. Colo. River Dist.; bro. Theodore, Col. USAF, 1940-45; sis. Gertrude (Mrs. Gerald Van Berger) dir. Red Cross, Palo Alto, 1940-65; A.B. (honors), Univ. of Calif., 1921; grad. Art Inst. Chicago, 1921-24; m. Marjorie La Verne Hubbell, June 15, 1926, Berkeley, Calif.; chil.: Stanley R., b. July 31, 1927; Diane L., b. Aug. 28, 1930. Career: Instr., Lowell Hi Sch., S.F., 1924-26; instr., Sacramento City Coll., 1926-60; (chmn. Art Dept.; organized art students league which produced Art Ball, created scholarships 1926-48; student of Hans Hofmann, 1930, Leon Kroll Henry Lee McFer, Millard Sheets; painted 10 murals for ARC, Ft. Ord, 1945-47; exhibited State Fair, Crocker Art Gallery, one-man shows Sutter's Fort, 1946, Barrios Gallery, 1973); Restorer, 1960-75. (Total of 475 works of art, primarily paintings incl. self-portrait of Sir Joshua Reynolds, pvt. col. La Jolla; painting attributed to Rembrandt, pvt. col. L.A.; 30 works of art in Cathedral of Holy Sacrament, Sacto.; 10 paintings, Sutter Club). Exec. secty., Fed. art proj. for 1st art center in Calif., 1938-41; directed, Crocker Art Gallery, 1950, bd. of trustees, 1950-71, pres. 1957-60. Awarded silver medal, hon. mem., Tomasso Campanella Int. Acad. of Arts & Sci., 1970. Devel. pilot course for ed. TV; TV lectrs., 1957. Sgt. U.S. Engrs. 13th Div. — 213th, 1918-19. Mem.: Alpha K. Lambda, pres. 1920; big "C" Soc.; chmn. Nat. Art Week, Sacto. 1941. Republican. First United Methodist Ch., bd. trustee, 1926---. Hobby: collector, original cartoons. Rec.: hunting, sketching. Home-studio: 1550 12th Ave., Sacramento, CA 95818.

MATTHEWS, AL
Attorney at Law
b. Jan. 14, 1907, Dubuque, Ia.; s. Matthew Clement (judge, Dist. Ct., Ia.) and Emilie Matthews; nephew of Dr. Washington Matthews, asst. surg., U.S. Army, authority on Navajo Indian; grandson of N.B. Matthews, M.D., L.A. in 1870s; 6 lawyers in family; LL.B., McGeorge Coll. of Law, Sacto. Career: Practicing lawyer, L.A.; dep. pub. defender, L.A. Co. 1947-50; responsible for Ct. of Last Resort, founded on Lindley

Case (brought to attention of Earle Stanley Gardner). Awards: Jerry Giesler Award by The Criminal Ct. Bar Assn. 1974. Mem.: pres. Criminal Courts Bar Assn. 1960-61. Jeffersonian Repub. Catholic. Hobby: people. Rec.: chess. Res.: L.A., CA; Office: Box 8264, Universal City, CA 91608.

MATTOON, PAUL FRANKLIN
Attorney at Law
b. June 28, 1903, Ia.; s. Frank E. and Gertrude (Boothy) Mattoon; desc. Philip Mattoon, noted hero in Battle of Falls Fight, 1676; B.S., USC 1925; LL.B., Harvard Univ. 1928; So. Calif. Liberal Arts, Harvard Law; m. Evelyn Wilson, Mass., Oct. 12, 1927; chil.: Paul, II, b. Feb. 23, 1931; Frank, II, b. Aug. 3, 1932; George Douglas, b. Nov. 2, 1936; Sandra G., b. Jan. 12, 1955; Lloyd W., b. Sept. 1, 1958. Career: Atty. at law, pvt. practice, 1928---. Mem.: gen. pres., Gen. Soc. Sons of Revolution, 1958-61; Founders and Patriots; past comdr., L.A. Commandery Knights Templar; master, Masonic Lodge; Harvard Club of So. Calif. Presb. Res.: 400 N. McCadden Pl., L.A., CA 90004; Office: Suite 1, 249 N. Larchmont Blvd., L.A., CA 90004.

MAUDLIN, W. THOMAS, JR.
Real Estate Executive
b. July 28, 1936, Hollywood; s. Warren Thomas and Elizabeth (Rowe) Maudlin; grandson of Dr. J.P. Rowe, noted author, geologist and lectr., Univ. of Mont.; nephew of Dr. Tom Rowe, dean of pharmacy, Univ. of Mich.; cousin, Tom Rowe, Jr., Yale Univ. (highest hons), Rhodes Scholar, Harvard Law Sch.; clerk for Potter Stewart, U.S. Supreme Ct.; ed. A.A., Menlo Coll. 1957; B.S., USC 1959; m. Linda Dean, Las Vegas, Nev., Dec. 28, 1960; sons: Dean, b. May 7, 1962; Scott, b. Mar. 15, 1964. Career: Profl. football, Toronto, Ontario, Can. 1962-63; v.p. Warren Maudlin Co. Real Estate, 1964-66; est. Tom Maudlin Real Estate and Prado Land Co. 1967---; pres. Descolin Inc. 1973---; Ofcr., USMC 1959-61, Capt., retired. Awards: numerous awards incl.: Total Quarterback (12 yrs.); H.S., Menlo, USC, Marine Corps pro-ball, 1952-64. Mem.: San Fernando Valley Bd. Realtors, 1968-71; Phi Delta Theta, USC; Jonathan Club, L.A. Methodist. Rec.: tennis, golf, skiing, volleyball. Res.: 22521 Styles St., Woodland Hills, CA; Office: 21241 Ventura Blvd., Woodland Hills, CA 91364.

MAULLIN, RICHARD
State Official
b. Sept. 1, 1940, L.A.; s. Leonard and Esther Maullin; B.A., polit. sci., UCLA, 1962, M.A., 1964, Ph.D., 1972; m. Michele Clary, Apr. 23, 1967, L.A.; daus.: Nathalie, b. Apr. 19, 1971; Celine, b. June 14, 1977. Career: Soc. Sci., Rand Corp., 1965-71; Dep. Secty. of State, 1971-74; Chmn. Calif. Energy Comn., 1975---. Address: 1111 Howe Ave., Sacto., CA 95825.

MAUNULA, MARCIA LEA
Realtor — Business Owner
b. June 13, 1936, Austin, Minn.; d. Hank and Leota E. Wibben; div.; chil.: Steven D. Holets, b. Dec. 15, 1954; Diane S. Torellie, b. Oct. 2, 1956; Sherrie J. Presley, b. Sept. 27, 1958; Jeannie K. Holets, b. June 13, 1962; Regeana M. Maunula, b. Oct. 3, 1969. Career: real estate, 1970---: salesperson, 1970-71, mgr., real estate office, 1971, investment real estate, 1972, founder-prin., MLM Realtor Investments, 1973---; owner, Jan Howard's Dress Shop, Juanita's Intimate Apparel, 1975---. Bd. dir., Grossmont Center, 1978---. Mem.: Soroptimists of La Mesa; Rosicrusians A.M.O.R.C.; Am. Bus. Women's Assn. Hobby: oil painting. Rec.: family. Home: 7700 Parkway Dr., No. 56, La Mesa, CA 92041; Office: 5500 Grossmont Center Dr., La Mesa, CA 92041.

MAXWELL, EDWARD CREIGHTON
Attorney at Law
b. Mar. 25, 1904, Lincoln, Ill.; s. William K. and Eva (Blinn) Maxwell; LL.B., Univ. of Ill., 1926; m. Mary Muldoon McLoughlin, Yuma, Ariz., Mar. 19, 1931; dau. Maureen (Maxwell) Younkin; step-chil.: James and Thomas McLoughlin, Mrs. S. (Beverly McLoughlin) Thomas. Career: Lawyer, pvt. practice, 1926---. Mgr., Rancho La Colonia, Rancho San Miguel; dir. Santa Clara River Game Preserve. Mem.: Ventura Co. Planning Comm.; past pres., Ventura Co. Bar Assn.; Am. Bar Assn.; v.p. 31st Dist. Agr. Assn.; Rancheros de los Adobes; Sigma Pi, Alpha Alpha Alpha, Phi Delta Phi; clubs: dir. Ventura Co. Rod and Gun; dir. Rancheros Visitadores; Ventura Co. Roping; Elks, Ojai Country, Saticoy Country, L.A. Country and Calif. Rec.: hunting, fishing, horseback riding. Res.: Rancho O'la Colonia, W.

Gonzales Rd., Oxnard; Office: 2419 W. Gonzales Rd., Oxnard, CA 93030.

MAY, ALAN M.
Attorney at Law
b. Dec. 25, 1940, San Francisco; s. Dr. Angelo M. and Alice Grace (Snyder) May; B.A., in govt., George Washington Univ., 1965; J.D., George Washington Univ. Law Sch., 1968; m. Barbara Ann Morgret (div.); son Angelo M., III, b. Oct. 30, 1968, S.F. (5th gen. San Franciscan); Career: field dir., No. Calif. presidential campaign com., Nixon/Agnew, 1968; pres., inaugural com., Nov. 1968-Jan. 1969; asst. to secty., U.S. Dept. HEW, Wash. D.C., 1969-70; asst. to dir. of Cabinet Com. on Edn., Exec. office of Pres., Wash. D.C., 1970; spec. asst. to Asst. Attorney Gen. of U.S., 1970-71; asst. dir., ACTION (Peace Corps, Vista, etc.), Wash, D.C., 1971-73; White House staff cons., 1972-73; pvt. law practice in S.F. and L.A. (criminal law, corporate law, personal injury, domestic rel.), 1973---. Served to 1st Lt., AUS; 11th spec. forces (airborne) Green Berets; intelligence NCO and helicopter gunner, 119th aviation co., So. Vietnam; President's Honor Guard, 3d Infan. (the Old Guard), Va. Mil. awards incl. Air Medal w/2 oak leaf clusters; Vietnam Campaign Medal w/combat star; Combat Aviation Wings; Airborne Wings. Admitted to practice: Supreme Ct. of Calif.; U.S. Dist. Cts., Claims Ct., Appeals Ct. Mem.: State Bar of Calif.; Calif. Trial Lawyers Assn.; Am. Bar Assn.; Fed. Bar Assn.; BSA (Eagle Scout Order of the Arrow); Commonwealth Club; Veterans Pol. Council of S.F., chmn. exec. bd.; VFW; Concordia-Argonaut Club; co-chmn., 1st anniversary presidential inaugural ball, Wash., D.C.; com. (several yrs.) Thanksgiving Day Ball and Debutante Cotillion, Wash., D.C. Offices: 690 Market St., No. 1400, S.F., CA 94104; 1800 N. Highland Ave., No. 315, L.A., CA 90028.

MAY, ANGELO M.
Surgeon
b. Feb. 18, 1913, S.F.; s. Angelo (mfr., financier and philanthropist) and Lucy (Greenfield) May; A.B., Stanford Univ., 1933; M.D. George Wash. Univ. 1937; m. Alice Grace Snyder, Oct. 30, 1937; chil.: Carol Ann Falberg, Marilyn Langer, Alan, David, Daniel. Career: Intern, Mt. Zion Hosp. 1937-38; pvt. practice surg. 1940---; staff: Mt. Zion Hosp., French Hosp., Sequoia Hosp. Med. Corps, Ed., Vascular Surg., U.S. Army, WW II. Awards: Alumni Serv. Award, Geo. Wash. Univ.; Hons. Achievement Award, Angiology Research Found. Mem.: past pres., Vets. Polit. Council, S.F.; Am. Legion; Calif. Thoracic Soc.; pres. Am. Coll. of Angiology, 1969-70; pres. Internat. Coll. of Angiology; Regent, Natl. Lib. of Med.; regent, Angiology Research Found.; coms. Am. Med. Writers Assn.; bd. past pres. Leanec Soc.; bd. govs., Geo. Wash. Univ. Alumni, Wash. D.C.; pres. Geo. Wash. Alumni Club, No. Calif.; S.F., Am. Med. Assns.; Calif. Med. Soc.; S.F., Calif. Heart Assns.; fellow, Am. Coll. of Chest Phys., pres. Calif. chpt.; Calif. Hist. Soc., Med. Friends of Wine, S.F. Bible Club, Mason, Fidelity Lodge of B'nai B'rith Concordia-Argonaut, Phi Delta Epsilon, Commonwealth Club. Hobbies: ancient hist., chess, photog. Rec.: handball, swimming. Res.: 50 Sea Cliff Ave., S.F., CA; Office: 450 Sutter St., S.F., CA 94108.

MAY, CLIFF
Designer — Builder — Subdivider
b. Aug. 29, 1908, San Diego; s. Charles Clifford and Beatrice (Magee) May; ed. San Diego State Coll.; m. Lisa V. Hunter, 1967. Career: Designer-bldr., early Calif. ranch-type homes, San Diego, 1932; est. bus. (designer-subdivider-bldg.), L.A. Staff cons. for House Beautiful (5 yrs.). Author: Western Ranch Houses, Lane Publ. Co. Trustee, Ojai Valley Sch. Mem.: (life) Mag. Round Table on Housing; past dir., N.A.H.B.; pres. L.A. chpt., Bldg. Contractors Assn. 1945-46, bd. dirs. (8 yrs); Sonoma Co. Trail Blazers, Quiet Birdman, clubs: Aviation Country, Rancheros Vistadores. Catholic. Hobby: flying, Rec.: horseback riding, flying, reading. Res.: 2200 Old Ranch Rd., L.A., CA 90049; Office: 13151 Sunset Blvd., L.A., CA 90049.

MAY, JAMES HARVEY
University Librarian
b. Aug. 30, 1937, Trenton, Mo.; s. Rhoudy and Ruby Mae (Chandler) May; B.S., Stanford Univ., 1958; M.B.A., Harvard Univ., 1964; D.L.S., Columbia Univ., 1978; m. Margit Roder, June 10, 1967, Bamberg, Germany; chil.: James, b. Mar. 25, 1968; Tanja, b. Jan. 17, 1970; Anika, b. Oct. 8, 1974. Career: Economic Engr., Gilbert Assoc., Inc., N.Y. and Japan, 1964-67; co-founder, dir., treas., vice pres., Pandex, Inc. (subs. of Macmillan Pub. Co. after 1968), 1967-72; dir., Center

for Communication and Information Research and Asst. Prof., Univ. of Denver, 1972-74; acting lib. dir., assoc. lib. dir., and vis. lectr., Sonoma State Univ., 1974---. Del. White House pre-conf. on lib. svc. to Indians, 1978; reviewer, Nat. Endowment for the Humanities, 1978; profl. cons. Contbr. Satellite Lib. Info. Network, 1974. Mem.: Am. Soc. for Info. Sci., past chmn. Bay Area chpt.; advis. com., Ofc. of Lib. Svc. to Disadvantaged, ALA. Ofcr., USNR, active duty, 1959-62. Mem. Cherokee Nation of Oklahoma, chmn. mem. living in Calif. Hobbies: computer programming, linguistics. Home: 7179 Circle Dr., Rohnert Pk., CA 94928; Office: Sonoma State Univ. Library, Rohnert Park, CA 94928.

MAY, ROLLO
Psychoanalyst — Teacher
b. Apr. 21, 1909, Oh.; A.B., Oberlin Coll., 1930; grad. cum laude, M.Div., Union Theol. Sem., 1938; Ph.D., summa cum laude, Columbia Univ., 1949; chil.: Robert, Carolyn, Allegra. Career: Tchr., Am. Coll., Salonika, Greece, 1930-33; Prof., Harvard, 1964; Princeton, 1967, Yale, 1972; Brooklyn Coll., 1974-75; Regent's Prof., Univ. Calif., Santa Cruz, 1973. Psychoanalyst, NYC, 1950-75, and Supervisory and Tng. Analyst, William Alanson White Inst. of Psychiatry, Psychology and Psychoanalysis. Fellow, Am. Psychol. Assn.; Fellow, Natl. Council of Religion in Higher Edn. Author: The Meaning of Anxiety, 1950, revision 1977; Love and Will, 1969; Power and Innocence, 1953. 1972; The Courage to Create, 1975; Man's Search For Himself, 1953. Awards: Ralph Waldo Emerson Award for Love And Will, given by Phi Beta Kappa, 1970; Dr. Martin Luther King, Jr. Award for Power and Innocence, N.Y. Soc. of Clin. Psychologists. Past pres., N.Y. State Psychological Assn.; past pres., William Alanson White Psychoanalytic Soc. Res.: Tiburon, CA.

McALLISTER, CYRUS RAY
Research Scientist — Consultant
b. Apr. 22, 1922, Portland, Ore.; s. Cyrus Ray, Sr. and Edna Marion (Parkes) McAllister; ed. B.A. (magna cum laude), Univ. of Minn. 1948; M.A., Univ. of Ore. 1951; m. Mary Carter; chil.: Sharon Louise, Cyrus Ray, III, Mark Ross. Career. Tchg. Asst., Univ. of Minn. 1948; instr. Univ. of Ida. 1948-50; analyst, Dept. of Def., Wash. D.C. 1952; staff, Sandia Corp., Albuquerque, N.M. 1952-57; cons. 1957; sr. research scientist, Nuclear Div., Kaman Aircraft Corp., Albuquerque, 1957-59, cons. 1959-60; chmn. bd. McAllister and Assoc., Inc., Albuquerque, 1959-66, pres.-tech. dir. 1960-63; research dir., Booz-Allen Applied Research, Inc., L.A., 1963-66; Aerospace Corp. 1968-72; cons. 1966---. Ed. bd.: IEEE, Am. Soc. of Quality Control, Joint Task Force on Systems Rel., 1960---; Electronic Div. Am. Soc. of Quality Control journ., 1965-66. Contrib. articles to profl. journs. U.S. Army Air Corps., ETO (1940-45), WW II. Listed: Am. Men of Sci., Leaders in Am. Sci., Dictionary of Internat. Biog., London, Eng.; Community Leaders of Am.; Dir. of Environmental Cons. Mem.: Fellow, AAAS, IEEE, Am. Mathematical Soc., Am. Meterological Soc., Society Ind. and Applied Math., Math. Assn. of Am., Am. Statistical Assn., Soc. of Engring.-Sci., Am. Inst. Mgmt., Phi Beta Kappa, Pi Mu Epsilon, Sigma Xi. Res.: 4729 Libbit Ave., Encino, CA 91436; Office: 2350 E. El Segundo Blvd., El Segundo, CA.

McANALLY, DON
Editor — Publisher
b. Oct. 27, 1913, Sewell, N.J.; s. James C. and Ina M. McAnally; ed. pub. sch.; John Wanamaker Cadet Inst., Phila.; Sales Analysis Inst., Chicago; m. Edith McKinney, Dec. 11, 1934, Pitman, N.J.; dau. Shirley M. (English), b. Aug. 29, 1940. Career: reporter-editor, Daily Times, Woodbury, N.J., 1933-43; editor, Owens-Illinois, in N.J., Ohio, 1943-47; publicist, Owens-Illinois, 1948; asst. advt. mgr., LOF Glass Co., Toledo, 1948-53; sales mgmt., LOF Glass Fibers Co., Toledo, 1953-59; editor, Pacific Oil Marketer, L.A., 1960-65; editor-pub., O & A Mktg. News, La Canada, Calif., 1966---; editor-pub.: Automotive Booster of Calif., 1975---; Calif. Sr. Citizen, 1977---; Calif. Businesswoman, 1978---. Named: Award winning editor, Toledo Club Printing House Craftsmen, 1950; Man of the Year, Pacific Oil Conference, 1977; Good Neighbor Award, Toledo, 1949. Clubs: Gabby, Roorag, Silver Dollar, L.A. Episcopalian. Home: 4409 Indiana Ave., La Canada, CA 91011; Office: P.O.B. 765, La Canada, CA 91011.

McBIRNIE, WILLIAM STEUART
Minister — Author — Broadcaster
b. Feb. 8, 1920, Toronto, Ontario, Can.; s. W.S. and Ethyl (Potter) McBirnie; bro. Rev. Robert S. McBirnie,

Ph.D.; B.A. 1944, B.D. 1945, M.R.E. 1947, D.R.E. 1952, D.D. 1958, O.S.J. 1963; Ph.D. 1972, Th.D. 1974. Career: Ordained Bapt. minister, 1939; pres. Comm. Chs. of Am.; co-found. Calif. Grad. Sch. of Theology; pastor, United Comm. Ch., Glendale, 1961---; founder-exec. dir., Center for Am. Research and Edn. 1966---; daily radio broadcasts, Glendale. Author: 210 books on relig., archaeology, polit. sci., anti-Communism. Hobby: classic cars, Wedgewood, Jasperware. Awards: Knighted, Order of St. John of Jerusalem, 1963, 68; Kentucky Col.; Pilgrim Medal, Jerusalem, Israel; Americanism Medal, D.A.R.; Eisenhower Medal Captive Nation's Com., Order of Lafayette. Res.: Glendale Calif.; Office: 213 S. Kenwood, Glendale, CA.

McCARTHY, JANICE MEISER
Realtor — Business Owner
b. Feb. 1, 1921, Ohio; d. Ray Ellwood and Zora Belle (Armitage) Meiser (active poetess at 85 yrs.); desc. John Smith, Gold Rush 49er from Ohio; ed. Tiffin Univ., 1970; Schuster-Martin Sch. of Drama, 1942; Wittenberg Coll. Sch. of Music, 1941; DeAnza Coll., 1970; m. Arthur Oldham (dec.), Aug. 15, 1946, Chicago; son, Rodnie D., b. Jan. 28, 1947. Career: chorus, San Carlo Opera, Cleveland, 1944; chorus (toured with), Russian Grand Opera, 1944-45; mgr., Olan Mills Portrait Studio, Macon, Ga., 1943; owner, chain, J & J Song & Dance Studios, 1955-62; built nat. direct sales orgn., food supplements & cosmetics, 1961-65; cosmetic mfg. and sales, S.F. area, 1965-68; real estate edn., 1967; real estate broker, 1970---; owner, Civic Investments Corp., Cupertino. Mem.: (seated) Merchants Brokers Exchange, internat. trade; Beta Sigma Phi, 1967---; Ft. Nightly Music Club, Ohio, 1943; Bucyrus, O. Little Theatre, 1955-62; Cupertino C. of C.; Better Bus. Bureau of San Jose. Methodist; Sun. Sch. tchr., choir mem. and soloist. Hobbies: knitting, crocheting. Rec.: fishing, cottage in Santa Cruz. Home: 10311 Parlett Pl., Cupertino, CA 95014; Office: 10271 S. DeAnza Blvd., Cupertino, CA 95014.

McCARTHY, LEO T.
State Assemblyman
b. 1930, Auckland, New Zealand; ed. grad. Univ. of S.F.; J.S., S.F. Law Sch.; m. Jacqueline Burke; chil.: Sharon, Conna, Adam, Niall. Career: Atty. at law, S.F.; adm. asst. State Senator Eugene McAteer, 1959-63; elected to S.F. Bd. of Supvs. 1963; reelected, 1967-68; elected, Assemblyman, Calif. Legislature, 1968---, chmn. Labor Rels. Com. 1971-74; Joint Coms. on Aging; Speaker, Calif. State Assembly, 1974---. Strategic Air Command Intelligence Unit, Korean War. Awards: Legislator of Yr. award by Planning and Conservation League 1971; Outstanding State Legislator in U.S., National Council of Sr. Citizens, Wash. D.C. 1972; Torch of Liberty Award, B'nai B'rith Anti-Defamation League, 1976; Mem.: adv. bd. S.F. Mental Health; S.F. Planning and Urban Renewal Assn.; Calif. Comm. on Aging; Rec. Center for Handicapped; S.F. Co. and State Dem. Central Coms.; White House Conf. on Balanced Natl. Growth and Econ. Devel.; New Coalition & the Nat. Conf. of State Legislatures. Office: State Bldg., 350 McAllister St., S.F., CA 94102; 3164 State Capitol, Sacto., CA 95814.

McCARTY, ROBERT CLARKE
Mathematician — Consultant
b. Apr. 29, 1922, Mountain View, Calif.; s. John E. and Eldora L. McCarty; father pioneer road, dam and bridge engr., Santa Clara Co. and S.F., 1909-1952; B.A., San Jose State Univ., 1950; postgrad. USC, 1950-51; M.S. mathematics, statistics, Univ. of Wash., 1957, Ph.D., 1960; m. 2d. Rita Ransier Schmidt, 1969; chil.: Stephanie A. (Garnett), b. July 19, 1946; Michael W. Schmidt, b. Feb. 20, 1949; Teresa K. Schmidt, b. Nov. 13, 1951; Kathleen G. Schmidt, b. Oct. 26, 1955. Career: res. engr., Boeing Co., Seattle, 1952-59; res. math. statistician, Stanford Research Inst., 1959-70; Geophysical Systems, Inc., Santa Barbara, 1970-71; Cons., 1971---; Johns Hopkins Univ. Applied Physics Labs, Md., 1971-72; Dept. of Army, 1975-78; Nat. Sci. Found., Wash, D.C., 1976---; Dept. of Defense (mat.-statistics), 1976---; Prof. of Math, Santa Clara Univ., 1972-75; pres., McCarty Associates, Inc. (sci. consultants), 1976---. Author applied math articles in profl. journs., 1954---. U.S. Coast Guard, WWII, 1941-46; U.S. Coast Guard Reserve, Korean War, 1951-52; ret. Lt. USCGR 1965. Mem.: Master Mason, 1942; 32° Scottish Rite Mason, 1977; Shriner; Islam Temple, S.F., 1977; Aircraft Owners and Pilots Assn., Wash. D.C. Protestant. Hobbies: amateur radio, gun collection. Rec.: flying-comml. pilot, instrument;

swimming. Home-Office: 9425 Marcella Ave., Gilroy, CA 95020.

McCLOSKEY, MAXINE E.
Conservationist
b. Portland, Ore.; d. Leslie and Lydia K. (Sarajarvi) Mugg; A.A., Univ. Calif., Berkeley, 1948; B.S., Portland State Univ., 1962; M.A., Reed Coll., Portland, 1963; m. J. Michael McCloskey (exec. Sierra Club), June 17, 1965, Eugene, Ore.; chil.: Claire Hadnot, b. 1950; Laura Johnson, b. 1952; James Johnson, b. 1954; Rosemary Johnson, b. 1957. Career: Staff mem., U.S. Sen. Richard Neuberger, 1955-56, 59; Instr. U.S. Hist. and Govt., 1962-76, Merritt Coll., Oakland, 1968-76; What conservationist, 1973---, exec. dir. Whale Center, 1978---. Apptd. adv., U.S. Commnr. to Internat. Whaling Comm., 1977, 78; chmn., Citizen Nongame Advis. Com. to Calif. Dept. Fish & Game; U.S. co-chmn., Mex.-U.S. gray whale com.; mem. advis. bd. on Fish and Wildlife Plan for Calif. Dept. Fish & Game. Organizer, symposium on endangered species sponsored by AAAS, 1974. Ed.: Wilderness and the Quality of Life, 1969; Wilderness, the Edge of Knowledge, 1970, Sierra Club. Secty. Project Jonah, 1973-77, pres. 1977; v.p. Regional Parks Assn., 1973-75; ed., Fedn. of Western Outdoor Clubs, 1973-75; Mem.: Sierra Club, Natl. Audubon Soc., Defenders of Wildlife, Nat. Wildlife Fedn. Democrat; alt. del. to bat. conv., 1964; candidate for Ore. State Rep., 1964. Unitarian. Hobby: wildlife viewing. Res.: 93 Florada Ave., Piedmont, CA 94610; Office: 3929 Piedmont Ave., Oakland, CA 94611.

McCLOSKEY, PAUL NORTON, JR.
United States Congressman
b. Sept. 29, 1927, Loma Linda, Calif.; s. Paul N., Sr. and Vera (McNabb) McCloskey; ed. Occidental Coll., Calif. Inst. of Tech.; grad. Stanford Univ. 1950, LL.B., 1953; m. Caroline Wadsworth, Pasadena, Aug. 6, 1949; chil.: Nancy, b. Feb. 16, 1951; Peter Wadsworth, b. Dec. 24, 1952; John Munday, b. Mar. 25, 1955; Kathleen, b. Sept. 13, 1958. Career: Laborer, ath. coach, semi-profl. baseball player, law librn.; admitted to Calif. bar, 1953; dep. dist. atty. Alameda Co. 1953-54; Costello & Johnson law firm, Palo Alto, 1955-56; founder, McCloskey, Wilson, Mosher & Martin law firm (Stanford Profl. Center), 1956. Lectr. on Legal Ethics, Santa Clara and Stanford Law Schs. 1964-67; spec. counsel, City of Woodside, 1965-67. Elected to Congress, 11th Dist., Dec. 12, 1967---. Author: The United States Constitution, 1964; contrib. legal and govt. articles to various publs. 2nd Lt., USMC, Korean War, Lt. Col., Res.; Seaman, USN. Awards: Navy Cross and Silver Star, Purple Heart; Young Man of Yr., Palo Alto Jr. C. of C. 1961. Mem.: pres. Palo Alto Area Bar Assn. 1960-61; pres. Stanford Area Youth Plan, 1960-66; pres. Conf. of Barristers of State Bar of Calif. 1961-62; dir. Family Serv. Assn. 1961-65; del. White House Conf. on Civil Rights, 1963; Com. for Green Foothills, 1963-67; trustee, Santa Clara Co. Bar Assn. 1965-67 (coms.); Planning and Conservation League for Legislative Action, 1966-67; Sierra Club, 1966-67; arbitrator, Am. Arbitration Assn. 1966-67. Presbyterian. Hobbies: fly fishing, backpacking, camping. Res.: 1344 29th St., N.W., Wash. D.C.; Office: 205 Cannon House Ofc. Bldg., Wash. D.C. 20515.

McCLOSKY, J. MICHAEL
Executive Director, Sierra Club
b. Apr. 26, 1934, Eugene, Ore.; s. John C. and Agnes M. (Studer) McCloskey; B.A., Harvard Univ., 1956; J.D., Univ. Ore., 1961; m. Maxine E. Mugg, June 20, 1965, Eugene, Ore.; stepchil.: Claire, Johnson, Laura Johnson, James Johnson, Rosemary Johnson. Career: Northwest Rep., Sierra Club, 1961-64, Conservation Dir., 1965-69, exec. dir., 1969---. Dr.: League of Conservation Voters; Resolve; Jt. Center for Urban Environmental Studies; Arbor Day Found. Author-Contbr. to: The Patient Earth; Wilderness and the Quality of Life; No Deposit-No Return; Action for Wilderness; ed.: The Proceedings of the Fifth Biennial Conf. on N.W. Wilderness; Some Suggestions for Tchg. About Wilderness and Wildland Parks; contbr. articles to profl. journs. and periodicals incl. Sat. Review of Lit., New Republic, Christian Sci. Monitor, N.Y. Times, L.A. Times. Awarded Calif. Conservation Council award, 1969. Capt., Artillery, USAR; active duty, 1956-58, reserve 1958-62. Mem. Calif. Hist. Soc. 1972---; Explorers Club, 1978---; Sierra Club; Internat. Council on Environ. Law; Harvard Club of S.F.; Am. Soc. of Assn. Execs. Res.: 93 Florada Ave., Piedmont, CA 94610; Office: 530 Bush St., S.F., CA 94108.

McCLOY, WILLIAM MALTBY
Appraisal Company Executive

b. Jan. 18, 1910, Seattle, Wash.; s. Roylance R. and Jane (Maltby) McCloy; B.A., Univ. of Wash. 1933; postgrad study courses, UCLA and Pasa. City Coll.; m. Janice McKenzie, Pasadena, Dec. 22, 1962; daus.: Nancy Jane (McCloy) Frykman, b. June 5, 1937; Linda Ann (McCloy) Harlow, b. Oct. 6, 1939. Career: Assoc. with Gen. Appraisal Co., L.A. 1936, dir. 1952---, chmn. 1971---; dir. Transit Mixed Concrete Co.; Sandwell International, Portland, Ore. Ensign, USNR, 1933; naviagtor-exec. ofcr., USS Aldebaran; C.O., USS Uvalde; Philippine Campaign, Lingayen Gulf Invasion and Okinawa, So. Attack Force (1940-45), WW II; Rear Adm. (ret.) 1961---; apptd. by Secty. of Def. McNamara to Res. Forces Policy Bd. 1962-65. Awards: Am. Theater, Pac. Theater with 2 stars, Philippine Campaign awards. Mem.: pres. Rotary Club of L.A. 1954-55; pres. Serv. Club Council, 1955-56; dir. L.A. C. of C. 1961-67; pres., L.A. chpt., Reserve Ofcrs. Assn., 1964-65; Navy League; fellow-international pres., Am. Soc. of Appraisers (58 chpts.), 1967-68; Big Canyon Country Club. Rec.: golf. Res.: 3 Rue duParc, Newport Beach, CA 92660; Office: 301 E. Colorado Blvd., Pasa., CA 91101.

McCONE, JOHN ALEX
Industrialist

b. Jan. 4, 1902, S.F.; s. Alexander J. and Margaret (Enright) McCone; B.S. (engring., Magna Cum Laude), Univ. of Calif., Berkeley; m. Rosemary Cooper, Ida., June 21, 1938 (dec. Dec. 6, 1961); m. Theiline McGee Pigott, Seattle, Wash., Aug. 29, 1962. Career: Llewellyn Iron Works, L.A. 1922, constr. mgr. 1926 (merged); constr. mgr.-v.p. Consolidated Steel Corp. 1929, exec. v.p.-dir. 1933-37; est. Bechtel-McCone Corp., L.A., pres. 1937-45; co-founder, Seattle-Tacoma Shipbldg. Corp. 1939; pres.-dir. Calif. Shipbldg. Corp. 1941-46; dir.: Marinship Corp., Sausalito, Calif.; Ore. Shipbldg. Corp.; pres. Joshua Hendy Corp. 1945-48; chmn. bd. dirs. 1965-75; formed Pac. Far East Line (Japan, P.I., China), 1945. Dir.: Internat. Tel. & Tel. Corp., Pres.'s Air Policy Comm. 1947-48; spec. dep. Secty. of Def. 1948; Under Secty., USAF, 1950-51; chmn. U.S. Atomic Energy Comm. 1958-60; dir. Central Intelligence Agcy. and chmn. U.S. Intelligence Bd., Wash., D.C. 1961-65; chmn. Gov's. Comm. on L.A. Riots, 1965; Pres.'s Comm. on Selective Serv., Pres.'s Adv. Com., Pres.'s Com. on Urban Housing, Secty. of State Com.; trustee, USC 1965---; Awards: Exceptional Civ. Serv. Award, USAF 1951; Knight of St. Gregory by Pope Pius XII, 1955; Grand Cross, Order of St. Sylvester, 1956; Cardinal Gibbons Award, Cath. Univ. of Am. Alumni Assn. 1964; Hoover Medal, 1964; hon. degrees: Univ. of Calif., Notre Dame Univ., Fordham Univ., Clarkson Coll. of Tech., Cath. Univ. of Am. Mem.: co-founder-1st pres., L.A. World Affairs Council, 1954; Phi Kappa Sigma; Clubs: Calif., L.A. Country, Pac. Union (S.F.); Cypress Point (Pebble Beach); Burning Tree, Met., F. St. (Wash. D.C.); The Links (N.Y.), Blind Brook (NYC). Republican. Res.: 1100 Oak Grove Ave., San Marino, CA 91108; The Highlands, Seattle, Wash. 98177; Office: 612 S. Flower St., L.A., CA 90017.

McCONNELL, J. FRANKLIN
University Administrator

b. Nov. 26, 1937, Pittsburgh, Pa.; s. Earl Franklin and Georgetta (McGinley) McConnell; B.A., English, Parsons Coll., 1961; M.A., Philosophy, Univ. of Buffalo, 1968; D.Bus. Admin., Univ. Ind., 1970; m. Marina Semenob, Apr. 29, 1974, L.A.; chil.: Murphy Lee, b. Dec. 20, 1965; Effie R., b. July 14, 1969; Amanda Marie, b. Dec. 27, 1975. Career: Investigative Reporter, Worcester Telegram & Gazette, Mass., 1961-62; assoc. prof., Univ. Buffalo, philosophy, 1962-64; dir. R&D, Bryant Stratton Bus. Schs., 1964-68, v.p. Academic Affairs, 1968-69; pres., Coll. of The South, 1969-72; mgmt. cons., 1972-74; pres., Calif. Western Univ., 1974-77; co-founder, exec. v.p., Dean, Univ. of Beverly Hills, 1977---. Author: monograph, Case for Proprietory Edn., 1969, two textbooks. Pres. and bd. mem., Calif. Pvt. Sch. Assn., 1978; mem. of Accrediting of Bus. Schls., 1967-68. Hobby: astronomy. Rec.: hiking, soccer. Res.: 8129 Blackburn Ave., L.A., CA 90048; Office: 8500 Wilshire Blvd., Suite 801, Beverly Hills, CA 90211.

McCORKLE, CHESTER O., JR.
University Administrator

b. Jan. 18, 1925, Gilroy, Calif.; s. Chester O., Sr. (dean, Calif. State Polytech. Coll., Pomona, ret.) and Avis Jacqueline (Kickham) McCorkle; ed. Calif. State Polytech. Coll., San Luis Obispo, 1941-43; Univ. Redlands, 1943-44; B.S. Univ. Calif., Berkeley, 1947,

M.S. 1948, Ph.D. 1952; m. Nina Grace Mathews, San Luis Obispo, June 11, 1945; chil.: Mrs. Edward (Sandra Lee) Schiller, b. Apr. 26, 1946; Kenneth Carl, b. Apr. 21, 1949; Timothy Kevin, b. May 4, 1953. Career: Research asst. Univ. Calif., Berkeley, 1947-48; agr. analyst, Bank of Am., S.F. 1948-49; asst. spec. Univ. Calif., Berkeley, 1947-48; agr. econ. Univ. Calif., Davis, 1951---, instr., jr. econ., prof. 1952-70, v. chancellor Acad. Affairs, 1964-69, dean, Coll. of Agr. and Environmental Scis. 1969-70; v.p. Univ. of Calif. (9 campuses), Univ. ofc., Berkeley, 1970---. Bd. dirs. Del Monte Corp., 1972---. Contrb. to profl. journs., USA, Athens, Greece, 1952-72. Pvt., 2nd Lt., USMC, 1943-46, WW II; 1st Lt. 1951-52. Mem.: Commn. on Natural Resources; Natl. Acad. of Scis., 1975---; Am. Agr. Econs. Assn. 1946---; Am. Soc. Farm Mgrs. and Rural Appraisers, 1956---, secty. 1958; Western Agr. Econs. Assn., 1952, v.p. 1964-65; pres. 1965-66; Calif. Scholarship Fed.; AAAS; Am. Assn. Univ. Profs.; Alpha Zeta; Commonwealth Club of Calif.; Bohemian Club; Episcopalian. Hobby: music. Res.: 2821 Claremont Blvd., Berkeley, CA 94705; Office: 714 University Hall, 2200 Univ. Ave., Berkeley, CA 94720.

McCORMACK, FRANCIS X.
Petroleum Company Executive

b. July 9, 1929, NYC; s. Joseph and Blanche (Dengel) McCormack; B.A., cum laude, St. Francis Coll., 1951; J.D., Columbia Univ. Sch. of Law, 1954; m. Margaret Hynes, Apr. 24, 1954, NYC. Career: Assoc., Cravath, Swaine & Moore, 1956-62; Sr. Atty., Ford Motor Co., 1962-63; v.p.-gen. counsel, Philco-Ford Corp., 1964-72; asst. gen. counsel, Ford Motor Co., 1970-72; v.p.-gen. counsel, Atlantic Richfield Co., 1972-73; sr. v.p.-gen. counsel, 1973---. Awarded Commendatone al merito della Republica Italiana, AUS, 1954-56. Mem. Univ. Club, L.A., 1973---. Office: 515 S. Flower St., L.A., CA 90071.

McCOY, VIRL GLENN
Company President

b. Jan. 2, 1936, Wesley, Ark.; s. William Francis and Audie (Neal) McCoy; A.A., Fullerton Jr. Coll.; stu., Abilene Christian Coll., Nat. Christian Univ.; m. B. Janice Tate, Aug. 1, 1958, Las Vegas, Nev.; chil.: Mitchell Glenn, b. Jan. 20, 1960; Mark Scott, b. Oct. 7, 1963; Michele April, b. Apr. 4, 1963; Mara Jan, b. Oct. 20, 1965; Mica Elizaebth, b. May 21, 1970. Career: asst. to sales mgr., Ador Corp., 1957-63; mgr., now dir. and pres., Fleetwood Aluminum Products, Inc., 1963---; dir. and pres., Colorado Fleetwood Aluminum, Inc., 1978---; also Minister, Ch. of Christ, 1963---. Mem.: Jr. C. of C., 1958; Lions Club; Yorba Linda Little League, treas. 1972. Minister, Yorba Linda and Orange Ch. of Christ. Hobbies: photog., hunting. Res.: 6262 Hilltop Pl., Yorba Linda, CA 92686; Office: Fleetwood Aluminum Products, 174 Liberty, Anaheim, CA 92801.

McCRONE, ALISTAIR WILLIAM
University President

b. Oct. 7, 1931, Regina, Saskatchewan, Can.; s. Hugh M. and Kathleen Maude (Forth) McCrone; B.A., Univ. of Sask., 1953; M.Sc., Univ. of Nebr. 1955; Ph.D., Univ. of Kan. 1961; m. Judith Saari, Lawrence, Kan., May 12, 1958; chil.: Bruce, Craig, Mary. Career: Jr. Wellsite Geol., Sask. Dept. of Natural Resources, 1951; Wellsite geol.-asst. to Prof. F.H. Edmunds, cons., geol., Saskatoon, 1952-53; Wellsite geol., Brit. Am. Oil Co., Regina, 1953; jr. field geol. Shell Oil Co., Yukon, N.W. Territories and Brit. Columbia, Can. 1954-55; field chief, Shell Oil Co. exploration-mapping, mts.-plateau and MacKenzie Basin, Yukon, N.W. Territories, B.C., Can. 1956-58; supv. NYU research ship Sea Owl oprns. on L.I. Sound, N.Y. 1959-64, assoc. prof. 1964-69; asst. dir. Univ. pgm. at Sterling Forest, N.Y. 1965-66; res. master, Rubin Internat. Res. Hall, NYU and chmn. Dept. Geol.-assoc. prof. 1966-69; assoc. dean, Grad. Sch. Arts and Scis.-prof. geol. NYU 1969-70; coinvestigator, U.S. Pub. Health Serv. Research Contracts Radioecological Stu. of Hudson River, 1964-66; researcher, pollution in Hudson River Estuary, 1964-68; acad. v.p.-prof. geol. Univ. of Pac., Stockton, Calif. 1970-74; pres.-prof. geol. Humboldt State Univ. 1974---. CBS Sunrise Semester, 48 lectrs. on Geol. and Environ. subjs. (NYU) 1969-70. Mem.: Sigma Xi (ofcr. 1965-69, pres. NYU chpt. 1969); Fellow; Geol. Soc. of Am. 1967, AAAS 1967, Calif. Acad. of Scis. 1974; N.Y. Acad. of Scis., Am. Assn. Petrol. Geols.; Soc. of Econ. Paleontologists and Mineralogists, Rotary Internat., Commonwealth Club of Calif. Pres. Rec.: skiing, sailing, golf. Res.: 15 Robert Court West, Arcata, CA 95521; Office: Humboldt State Univ., Arcata, CA 95521.

McCUBBREY, JAMES BRUCE
Patent Lawyer

b. Feb. 25, 1936, Grosse Pt., Mich.; s. James Letham and Annie (McGarrity) McCubbrey; B.S., Univ. Mich., 1958; J.D., 1961; m. Ruth Dunlap, 1974, Mill Valley; chil. (by previous marriage): Nancy Ann, b. 1961; James Palmer, b. 1964. Career: Assoc., Mueller, Aichele & Rauner, Chicago, 1961-65; assoc., Fitch, Even, Tabin & Luedeka, Chicago, Ill. and S.F., 1965-69; partner, 1970---. Trustee, World Coll. West, 1977-78. Admitted to Ill. Bar 1961, Patent Bar 1962, Calif. Bar 1966. Winner Gold Medals, Sr. Olympic Games, ice hockey, 1976, 78. Mem.: Alpha Sigma Phi, Am. Alpine Club, Himalayan Club. Presbyterian, chmn. Mission Strategy Council. Rec.: mt. climbing, ice hockey. Res.: 929 Greenhill Rd., Mill Valley, CA 94941; Office: 235 Montgomery St., S.F., CA 94104.

McCULLOH, WANDA
Realtor — Business Owner

b. Dec. 22, 1936, Hann, Okla.; d. Clifton and Vera (Hubbard) Ketchum; Life-tching. credential, bus. edn., Humboldt State Coll., 1962; chil.: Lori, b. Dec. 25, 1958; Lanna, b. Jul. 28, 1961; Melanie, b. Jan. 25, 1968. Career: Instr. bus.: Burbank Bus. Coll., Empire Coll., Santa Rosa Jr. Coll, 1962-65; Insurance cons. and sales, Metropolitan Life Ins. Co., 1965-71; real estate brokerage, Sonoma Co., 1971---; owner, Plaza Realty ERA (2 offices: residential, comml.). Recipient: Sonoma Co. MLS Lifetime Million Dollar Club award w/3 diamonds, 1975; sales awards, Security Life of Denver: Yearling, Annuity in Force Award, 1973. Mem.: dir., secty., Sonoma Co. Apt. Owners Assn.; treas., ERA (Electronic Realty Assoc.) Brokers' Council Northbay Counties, 1977---; Judge, achievement awards, 1979; bd. dir., Rohnert Pk. C. of C., 1971---, pres., 1977-78; Sonoma Co. Life Underwriters, 1965-70, dir. 1965; Sonoma Co. MLS; Nat. Assn. of Realtors; Northbay Investment Counsellors; Presbyterian, fin. com. Hobbies: early Calif. art, travel, tennis. Home: 1066 Wikiup Dr., Santa Rosa, CA 95404; Office: 6422 Commerce Blvd., Rohnert Pk., CA 94928.

McCUNE, ELLIS E.
University President

b. July 17, 1921, Houston, Tex.; s. Ellis E. and Ruth E. (Mason) McCune; B.A., UCLA, 1948, Ph.D. 1957; m. Hilda May Whiteman, Feb. 8, 1946; son, James Donald, b. Sept. 15, 1948. Career: tchg. asst. UCLA 1949-51; instr., assoc. prof. (polit. sci.), Occidental Coll., L.A. 1951-59; exec. council, Western Polit. Sci. Assn. 1958-61; asst. prof., prof. San Fernando Valley State Coll., Northridge, 1959-63; dept. chmn. 1960-63, dean, Letters and Sci. 1963; dean (acad. planning), The Calif. State Univ. and Colls. 1963-67; pres. Calif. State Univ., Hayward, 1967---. Mem.: pres. Governmental Adm. Group, L.A. 1959; commr. Calif. State Scholarship and Loan Comm. 1964-68; chmn. 1967-68; dir. Hayward C. of C., 1968-74; Western Coll. Assn., 1970-74; dir. Assoc. Western Univs.; adv. com. Inst. for Coll. and Univ. Admr.; dir. Assoc. Am. Colls. 1972-75; Am. Council on Edn.; natl. adv. com. Exch. Tchrs., Dept. HEW, Wash. D.C.; trustee, Calif. Council on Econ. Edn. Res.: 17577 Parker Rd., Castro Valley, CA 94546; Office: CSU, Hayward, CA 94542.

McDANIEL, GLEN
Attorney — Industrial Executive

b. Mar. 21, 1912, Seymour, Tex.; s. Judge Otho and Mary (Kerr) McDaniel; B.A., SMU, 1932; M.A. 1933, LL.D. 1966; LL.B., Columbia Univ. 1936; m. Marilyn Ballentine, L.A., Apr. 15, 1965; chil.: Laurie Esther, Scott Kerr. Career: Atty., Sullivan and Cromwell firm, N.Y. 1932-42; chmn. Navy Bd. of Contract Appeals, and spec. counsel, Undersecty. of Navy, Wash., D.C. 1942-46; v.p.-gen. atty., RCA Communications, Inc. 1946-48; pres. Electronic Industries Assn., Wash. D.C. 1948-51; partner, Lundgren and McDaniel law firm, N.Y. 1951-57; dir.-chmn.-exec. com., Litton Industries, Inc., Beverly Hills, CA 1957---. Dir., Security First Natl. Bank, L.A.; dir. Air Prods. & Chems., Inc., Allentown, Pa. Lt. Comdr., USNR, spec. servs., Wash. D.C. 1942-46). WW II. Mem.: Lambda Chi Alpha, Phi Beta Kappa, L.A. Country Club. Res.: 780 Linda Flora Dr., Bel-Air, L.A., CA 90049; Office: 360 N. Crescent Dr., Beverly Hills, CA 90210.

McDANIEL, WILLIAM HENRY
Certified Public Accountant

b. Sept. 15, 1916, Michigan Valley, Kan.; s. Charlie E. and Sophia E. (Supple) McDaniel; B.S. accounting, USC,

1955; m. Ruth O. Downing, Aug. 20, 1949, Los Angeles. Career: Accountant: Socony Mobile Oil Co., L.A., 1946-54; Collins, Herzinger, Ray & Porter, Eugene, Ore., 1955-57; C.G. Uhlenberg & Co., Redwood City, Calif., 1958-59; pvt. practice, Redding, Calif., 1960---. Chmn. Selective Service Bd. No. 5, 1971-76; Bd. Dir.: Shasta Co. YMCA, 1960-70; Greater Redding C. of C., 1966-71 (pres. 1970); Shasta Lake Recreational Task Force, 1968-75, chmn. 1972-75; Redding Redevel. Agency, 1971---; North Valley Bank, 1972---; Shasta Co. Devel. Corp., 1973---, pres. 1978-79. USMC, 1937-45. Mem.: Elks, 1963---; Pres. Circle, USC, 1968---; Am. Inst. of CPAs, 1957---; U.S. C. of C., 1970---; U.S. Naval Inst., 1972---; U.S. Marine Corps League, 1975---. Republican. Methodist. Home: 2554 North St., Redding, CA 96001; Office: 1815 Yuba St., Redding, CA 96001.

McDONALD, JACK HENRY
Consultant

b. July 16, 1910, Pratt, Kan.; s. John Dennis and Florence (Krieger) McDonald; A.B., Kan. Univ. 1933; m. Loraine Cameron, July 31, 1974, Honolulu. Career: Partner, Fink Abstract & Title Co., Fredonia, Kan. 1933-41; secty. Home Bldg. and Loan Assn., Fredonia, 1936-41; 1936-41; secty. Investors S&L Assn., Pasadena, Calif. 1946-51, pres. 1951-61, chmn. bd. 1961-63; pres. Imperial Corp., San Diego, 1963-71, chmn. bd. 1971-73; dir. Investors Mortgage Ins. Co., Boston; Lt. Comdr., USNR, 8th Amphibious Fleet. N. African-Mediterranean waters (1941-46), WW II. Awards: Golden Plate, Am. Acad. of Achievement, 1964. Mem.: bd. dirs., Tournament of Roses; dir. Am. Burnham Co., San Diego; dir. Ka'Eo Kai, L.A.; past dir., Calif. S&L League; clubs: Annandale Golf (Pasa.), Overland (Ft. Worth), Univ. (Pasa.), Calif. Club, La Jolla Country; Blue Lodge, Knights Templar, Kappa Sigma. Methodist. Res.: 1001 Genter, La Jolla, CA 92037; Office: P.O.B. 2354, La Jolla, CA 92038.

McDUFFIE, MALCOLM
President, Mohawk Petroleum Corp.

b. Nov. 14, 1915, S.F.; s. William Chester and Mary (Skaife) McDuffie; nephew of Duncan McDuffie (dec.), noted relator and conservationist, Berkeley, Calif.; A.B., Stanford Univ. 1934; m. Mary Sutherland de Surville, Pasadena, Dec. 8, 1951; chil.: Cynthia de Surville, b. Nov. 18, 1952; Malcolm Duncan, b. May 6, 1955. Career: Assoc. with P.C. Field Gasoline Corp. 1941-42; mgr. Bar Z Ranch, Mendocino Co., Calif. 1942-45; prodn. supt., Mohawk Petroleum Corp., Bakersfield, 1945-48, asst. to v.p. L.A. 1948-51; v.p. prodn.-exploration, 1951-69; pres. 1969---, dir. 1963---. Dir.: Reserve Oil and Gas Co. 1973---; Western Crude Oil Co. 1973---; Mendocino Co. Livestock Marketing Assn. 1944-45; v.p. West Coast Chem. & Solvent Corp. 1950---; Lac Chems., Inc. 1951-55; Independent Refiners' Assn. of Calif., Inc. 1955---, secty-treas. 1955-66, v.p. 1966-67, pres. 1967; Pac. Moulded Prods. Co., L.A. 1956---; dir. Santa Barbara Mill and Lumber Co. 1964---. Mem.: Phi Delta Theta, Rancheros Visitadores, Chevaliers du Tastevin; clubs: Calif., Sunset, Bohemian, Petroleum (L.A.), Coral Casino Beach and Cabana, Flintridge Riding. Republican. Episcopalian. Rec.: hunting, skiing. Res.: 501 Bradford St., Pasa.; 588 Picacho Lane, Santa Barbara, CA; Office: 550 S. Flower St., L.A., CA 90017.

McELROY, WILLIAM DAVID
University Chancellor

b. Jan. 22, 1917, Roger, Bell Co., Tex.; s. William D. and Ora (Shipley) McElroy; B.A., Stanford Univ. 1939; M.A., Reed Coll. 1941; Ph.D., Princeton Univ. 1943; m. Nella Winch; m. 2nd Marlene Anderegg De Luca, Towson Md., 1967; chil.: Mary Elizabeth, b. Nov. 7, 1942; Ann Reed, b. Feb. 23, 1946; Thomas Shipley, b. Jan. 19, 1948; William David, Jr., b. Jan. 17, 1950; Eric Gene, b. Oct. 6, 1968. Career: Ofc. of Sci. Research and Devel., 1942-46; instr. in biol., Johns Hopkins Univ. 1946; asst. prof. 1946-48; assoc. prof. 1948-51; prof. 1951-69; chmn. Dept. Biol. 1956-69; dir. U.S. Natl. Sci. Found. 1969-72; chancellor, Univ. of Calif., S.D., 1972---. Chmn., AIBS Microbiology Adv. Com., Ofc. of Naval Research, 1952-57; exec. ed. Archives of Biochem. and Biophysics, 1958-59; ed., Biochem. and Biophysical Research Communications, 1959; Pres's. Sci. Adv. Com. 1962-67; bd. dirs. Planned Parenthood Assn. of Md., Inc.; bd. dirs. Natl. Insts. of Health, 1966---; bd. trustees, Baltimore Comm. Coll. 1969; trustee: Brookhaven Natl. Lab.; Marine Biological Labs., Woods Hole, Mass. Awards: Rumford Award, Am. Acad. of Arts and Scis. Mem.: Kappa Sigma, 1937-39; Sigma Xi, 1942-45; Am. Acad. Arts and Scis. 1960---; Soc. of Biological Chems., pres. 1963-67; Natl. Acad. of Scis. 1963---; Am. Inst. of Biol. Scis., pres. 1968. Rec.:

tennis, golf, sailing. Res.: 9630 La Jolla Farms Rd., La Jolla, CA; Office: Chancellor's Ofc., UCSD, La Jolla, CA 92093.

McGAUGH, JAMES LAFAYETTE
University Chancellor
b. Dec. 17, 1931, Long Beach; s. William Rufus and Daphne (Hermes) McGaugh; B.A., San Jose State Univ., 1953; Ph.D., Univ. Calif., Berkeley, 1959; m. Carol J. Becker, Mar. 15, 1952; chil.: Douglas, b. Nov. 3, 1954; Janice, b. Nov. 27, 1959; Linda, b. Nov. 21, 1967. Career: Asst. Prof. Psychology, San Jose State Univ., 1957-60, assoc. prof., 1960-61; assoc. prof. of psychol., Univ. Ore., 1961-64; assoc. prof., Dept. Psychobiology, Univ. Calif., Irvine, 1964-66, prof. 1966-74, Dept. Chmn. 1964-67, 1971-74, acting dean, Sch. of Biological Scis., 1967-68, Dean, 1968-70, v. Chancellor, Acad. Affairs, 1975-77; exec. v. chancellor, UC, Irvine, 1978---. Cons., VA, 1964---; mem. NIMH Com. on Behavioral Pharmacology, 1965-67; mem. NIMH Biological Sci. Tng. Review Com. 1968-72; chmn. 1971-72; mem. NIMH Preclin. Psychopharmacology Research Com., 1975---. Mem. Ed. Advis. Bds.: Agents and Actions, 1969-73; Brain Research, 1974---; Internat. Journ. of Psycobiology, 1971---; Journ. of Neurobiology, 1969---; Psychopharmacologia, 1966---; Psychopharmacology Communications, 1975---. Co-ed., Advances in Behavioral Biology, 1971---. Ed.: Behavioral Biology, 1972---. Mem. Am. Psychol. Assn. Com. on Research Support, 1978---; mem., Nat. Acad. of Scis. Com. on Aging, 1978-79; Mem.: Soc. of Neurosci., Am. Coll. of Neuropsychopharmacology, UNESCO Internat. Brain Research Orgn., Fellow, AAAS, Fellow Am. Psychol. Assn., Psychonomic Soc., Council of Biology Eds., Sigma Xi, Phi Beta Kappa. Democrat. Rec.: skiing. Res.: 2327 Aralia St., Newport Beach, CA 92660; Office: 509 Adminstration Bldg., Univ. of Calif., Irvine, CA 92717.

McGOWAN, A. CLAY
Land Development Executive — Rancher
b. Nov. 2, 1918, San Francisco; s. Henry William (noted Sacto. Valley lawyer) and Elizabeth McGowan; A.B., Univ. of Santa Clara, 1940; Calif. Gen. Insurance Agent, 1940; m. Faye Thompson, Sept. 25, 1943, S.F.; chil.: Mindy, b. May 3, 1954; Mark William, b. Aug. 20, 1956; Scott Anthony, b. Dec. 14, 1961; Career: pres., Victor Industries Corp. (mfg., collapsible tubes), 1955-53; sr. v.p., co-founder, Chico Svgs. & Ln. Assn., Chico, Paradise, Yuba City, 1962-74; pres., No. Valley Services Corp., Chico, 1962-74; partner, Orchard Lanes Bowling Alley, Chico; Current: owner, Clay McGowan & Assoc., Chico (land, bus. devel., investments); pres., Yuba Plaza Shopping Center, Inc., Yuba City; partner, Village Plaza Shopping Center, Redding; owner, Diversified Farming; Partner: Simmental Assoc. No. 1 (purebred cattle Ark., Tex.); Visucom Prodns., I., S.F. (edn. films); McGowan Bros., Chico; Butte Creek Country Club Estates Subdiv.; 2 comml., indsl. subdivs.; Bd. dir., Host Internat., Inc., L.A. (airport svcs. co.), chmn. Host employee benefits, pension & profit sharing coms. Past pres., radio sta. KBLF, Red Bluff; past bd. mem.: Brown Jordan Furn. Mfg. Co., El Monte; Victor Corp., L.A.; Am. Lantern Corp., Cleveland. Served Pvt. to Maj., USAF, 1941-46, China, Burma and India, decorated with bronze star medal. Mem.: bd., Calif. State C. of C., chmn. small bus. com.; U.S. C. of C., small bus. com.; state and No. dist. bds., Children's Home Soc. of Calif. (awarded No. Dist. Man of the Year, 1964); bd. regents, Univ. of Santa Clara; Chico State Univ. Assocs., Found. bd. govs. 12 years; chmn., Chico C. of C. mem. dir., 1978; Chico Rotary Club, pres., 1967-68; Commonwealth Club, S.F.; Sonoma Co. Trail Blazers, Santa Rosa; bd. dir., Rancheros Vistadores, S.B.; Butte Creek Country Club, founding pres. 1962; Racquet Club, Palm Springs; Family Club, S.F.; Elks Club, Chico. Republican, co. central com., 1950-51. Catholic; advisory bd,, Chico St. Coll. Newman Club, Bishop's advisory com. Rec.: golf, horses, boats. Home: 78 Northwood Commons, Chico, CA; Office: 676 E. 1st Ave., Chico, CA 95926.

McGRATH, CHARLES ROBERT
Superior Court Judge
b. July 6, 1937, Oxnard, Calif.; s. George Dominick and Mary Agnes (Rouer) McGrath; B.S., hist., Loyola Univ., L.A. 1959, J.D., 1963; m. Beverlee Ellen Reed, May 29, 1961, Tacoma, Wash.; chil.: John Charles, b. Jan. 20, 1963; Deborah June, b. Sept. 1, 1964; Daniel Patrick, b. Dec. 7, 1966; Bridget Nellie, b. Apr. 25, 1972. Career: Med. malpractice ins. claims adjuster, Farmers Ins. Group, 1961-64; assoc. atty., firm of Nordman, Cormany, Hair & Compton, Oxnard, 1964-68; jr. partner, 1968-70, sr. partner, 1970-74; Municipal Ct. Judge, Ventura Co., 1974-79, Superior Ct. Judge,

1979---. USMCR, 1959-65. Apptd. pub. mem., State Bd. of Registration for Profl. Engrs., 1971-74; chmn., Enforcement and Legislative Coms. Mem.: Rancheros Visitadores, 1970---; Rancheros Adolfo, dir. 1975---; Ventura Co. Sheriff's Posse, 1968---, pres. 1973-74. Roman Catholic. Rec.: trail riding. Res.: 5011 W. Gonzales Rd., Oxnard, CA 93030; Office: 800 S. Victoria Ave., Ventura, CA 93003.

McGUCKEN, JOSEPH THOMAS
Clergyman
b. Mar. 13, 1902, L.A.; s. Joseph A. and Mary (Flynn) McGucken; S.T.D., No. Am. Coll., Rome, Italy, 1928; LL.D., Loyola Univ., L.A. 1942, Univ. of S.F., Univ. of Santa Clara, 1962. Career: Ordained Roman Catholic Priest, Jan. 15, 1928; admr. Holy Trinity Parish, L.A., Oct. 1928; asst. St. Vibiana's Cathedral, L.A., Oct. 1928; asst. Cathedral Chapel, L.A., Jan. 1929; secty. to Bishop Cantwell, Dec. 1929; Papal Chamberlain, July 1937; chancellor, Archdiocese of L.A., Nov. 1938; Domestic Prelate, 1939; Consecreated Aux. Bishop of L.A., Mar. 19, 1941; pastor, St. Andrews Ch., Pasadena, Feb. 1944; Vicar Gen., Archdiocese of L.A., Mar. 19, 1948-57; Bishop of Sacto., Jan. 14, 1957-62; archbishop, S.F. 1962-77. Retired Feb. 22, 1977. Awards: Comdr., Order of Ysabella, the Cath., Spain. Res.: 29 Rockaway Ave., S.F., CA 94127; Office: 445 Church St., S.F., CA 94114.

McGUIRE, KATIE
Creative Dance Specialist
b. Mar. 28, 1946, Dallas, Tex.; d. Alfred G. and Gladys (Horn) McGuire; desc. Capt. James Cook, 1728-79, explorer; granddau., Judge Jesse O. McGuire; B.F.A., cum laude, 1971; M.F.A., So. Methodist Univ., 1977. Career: Dance movement specialist, Nat. Endowment for the Arts, 1972-79; founder, Creative Dance Theatre, Berkeley, 1976---; dance therapist, 1974-76; lectr., 1973-78; dir., Creative Dance Theatre and Children's Creative Dance Theatre; choreographer: The Metaphysical Circuit, An Electric Concert, 1972; Awakening, 1975-76; hbj, 1974; Gypsy Dusk to Dawn, 1976; Mary Dreams, 1977; Pendulums, 1976; Wings of Paralda, 1979. Collab. with Stephen Beck, Anima, prize-winning video-art tape, 1974. Hobby: costuming. Office: 659 Arlington, Berkeley, CA 94707.

McHOSE, JOHN C.
Attorney at Law
b. Sept. 19, 1902, Springfield, Mass.; s. John Van Nest and Manetta May (Enck) McHose; A.B., Stanford Univ., 1924, J.D. 1926; m. Laurel Rogers, Dec. 12, 1970; chil.: Terry Jon, b. Sept. 7, 1944. Career: Pvt. practice law, S.F., 1927-29, L.A. 1929---; counsel, Lillick, McHose, & Charles law firm. Sports columnist, S.F. Call, 1925-29. Asst. regional rep., U.S. War Shipping Adm., South and S.W. Pac. areas (1942-45), WW II. Mem.: Dir. L.A. C. of C. 1949-57, v.p. 1956-57; pres. Propeller Club, L.A.-Long Beach, 1952-53; pres. Stanford Alumni Assn. 1955-56; pres. So. Calif. Golf Assn., 1957-58; Phi Delta Theta; clubs: pres. Wilshire Country, 1962. Republican. Episcopalian. Rec.: golf, duck hunting. Res.: 32859 Seagate Dr., Rancho Palos Verdes, CA; Office: 707 Wilshire Blvd., L.A., CA 90017.

McINTOSH, RALPH RAYMOND
Tile Contractor
b. May 4, 1929, Wilmar, Calif.; s. Lawrence Ray and Ruth Violet King; ed. L.A. Trade Tech, 1950; East L.A. Jr. Coll.; Pasadena City COll.; Ceramic Tile Cons. degree, 1976; m. Drusilla Anne Wetzel, June 12, 1948, Alhambra, Calif.; chil.: Cheri Lynn (Cahart), b. Feb. 12, 1950; Christy Ann (Williams), b. April 16, 1954. Career: endentured Calif. state apprenticeship, G.N. Lavenberg Tile Co., L.A., 1947-50; tile setter, R.H. Brown Co., Pasadena, 1952-56; contractor/owner, Ralph R. McIntosh Tile Co., 1956---; working with artist Hanns Scharff, restoration of mosaic floors, Calif. state capitol, Sacramento. Recipient: Golden Tile Award of So. Calif., 1978. Trustee, Joint Apprenticeship & Edn. Com., Tile Finishers, 1975---; trustee, Tile Insurance Trust Fund, 1962-74; chmn. several years; mem. Tile Layers Local No. 18, 1948---; mem. Assoc. Tile Contractors of So. Calif., pres., 1970. Hobby: family activities, auto racing and football fan. Rec.: Hiking, backpacking, fishing. Home-Office: 256 W. Naomi Ave., Arcadia, CA 91006.

McINTYRE, JAMES FRANCIS CARDINAL
Clergyman
b. June 25, 1886, NYC; s. James Francis and Mary (Pelley) McIntyre; ed. NYC pub. schs.; N.Y. City Coll.; Columbia Univ.; Cathedral Coll. (Sem.) NYC; St.

Joseph's Sem., Yonkers, N.Y. (recipient, 12 hon. univ. and coll. degrees, U.S.). Career: Ordained priest, Roman Catholic Ch. 1921; apptd. Chancellor of Archdiocese of N.Y. 1934; Titular Bishop of Cyrene and Aux. of N.Y. 1940; Archbishop of Titular See of Paltus and Coadjutor Archbishop of N.y' 1946; apptd. Archbishop of L.A., 1948-70; elevated to Sacred Coll. of Cardinals, 1953---. Res.: 637 S. Kingsley Dr., L.A., CA.

McKEE, LOGAN
Rear Admiral, U.S. Navy — Industrial Consultant
b. Mar. 18, 1898, Lawrenceburg, Ky.; s. Lewis Witherspoon and Eliza Schenck (Irwin) McKee; desc. of John Witherspoon, signer, Declaration of Independence; great-grandson of Rear Adm. James Findlay Schenck, landing force ofcr. who serv. under Commodore Stockton in USS Congress during Mex. War and taking of Calif. by U.S.; ed. B.Sc., Naval Acad. 1921; M.Sc., Columbia Univ. 1929; m. Elizabeth Millard, Shelbyville, Ky., Aug. 14, 1926; dau.: Mrs. J.C. (Jane) Ingram of L.A., b. Oct. 23, 1927. Career: USN (all ranks, Midshipman to Rear Adm.), 1917-59; asst. design dir., design dir., Bur. of Ships, 1943-47, Inspector Gen. 1957-58; shipyard comdr., Norfolk Naval Shipyard, 1954-57; material ofcr., Task Force 24, which cond. escort of convoy operations, N. Atlantic. Lectr. USC 1958-61 (ret.); cons. N. Am. Aviation, 1960-62; cons. Gordon M. Jackson Co., L.A. 1961. Author: Use of Hydrogen Peroxide by Germans During WW II, publ. 1945. Mem.: exec. com.-bd. govs., Army-Navy Country Club, 1943-47; bd. trustees, Naval Acad. Alumni Assn. 1961-62. Hobby: carpentry. Rec.: golf, flying. Res.: 738 Glorietta, Coronado, CA 92118.

McKEE, RAYMOND WALTER
Certified Public Accountant
b. Dec. 24, 1899, Joplin, Mo.; s. Charles Edward and Sarah Ellen (Epperson) McKee; desc. pioneer settlers of Rushville, Ill. and Ky.; armorial achievement confirmed by Patent of Arms by Sir Thomas Innes of Learney, Lord Lyon King of Arms of Scotland, 1960 (notable ancestry incls. Capt. Thomas McKee of McKee's Half Falls); ed. CPA; m. Frances Ida Howe, Huntington Park, Calif., Nov. 1, 1947; chil.: June (McKee) Gibbons, b. Sept. 3, 1916; Michael Raymond, b. Aug. 17, 1948; David Joel, b. Feb. 23, 1951; Judith Frances, b. Feb. 11, 1953; Roderick Hugh O'Neill, b. Dec. 31, 1954; Duncan Heremon MacAoidh, b. Mar. 17, 1957; Edwin Malcolm MacEth, b. Mar. 7, 1960; Brude mac Mailchon Howe, b. Apr. 14, 1962. Career: CPA; former lectr., cost acctg., St. Louis Univ. Comptroller, Western Div., Anchor Hocking; dir.: Finish Kare Prods., Inc., ARC Corp., Cross Water Co., Maywood Mutual Water Co. No. 3. Author: Accounting for the Petroleum Industry, publ. by McGraw-Hill, 1925; Handbook of Petroleum Acctg., publ. by Harper, 1938; Saludos California, 1949; Book of McKee, publ. by Hodges, Figgis & Co., by Dublin, Ireland, 1959. Mem.: Natl. Soc. S.A.R.; Sons of the Revolution; Episcopalian. Hobby: ancient Irish and Scottish hist. Res.: Gort Na Cloca Mora, La Puenta, CA; Office: 504 Bank of Am. Bldg., 13006 E. Philadelphia St., Whittier, CA 90602.

McKELVEY, GEORGE IRWIN, III
College Administrator
b. May 5, 1925, Glen Ridge, N.J.; s. George and Florence McKelvey; A.B., Univ. of Rochester, 1950, M.A. 1958; m. Velma Vegara, So. Pasa, June 28, 1959; son, George Stuart, b. Jan. 11, 1965. Career: Exec. secty. Alumni Assn., Univ. of Rochester, 1950-54, dir. Alumni rels. 1954-56; assoc. dir. Alumni rCouncil, 1956-57; dir. of devel., Harvey Mudd Coll. 1967-58; v.p. devel. and planning, 1968; dir. Bates Found. for Aeron. Edn. Aviation Found. for Aeron. Edn. Aviation Cadet, USNR, 1943-44; Ensign, USMS 1945-46. Mem.: Council for the Advancement and Support of Edn.; Univ. Club, L.A.; Men's Garden Club, L.A.; Psi Upsilon. Presbyterian. Office: Harvey Mudd Coll., Claremont, CA 91711.

McKEUN, ROD
Poet — Composer — Author — Singer
b. Apr. 29, 1933, Oakland, Ca. Appeared in films, TV, concerts, night clubs; composer background music for TV, motion picture scores, modern classical music; pres. Stanyan Records, Discus Records, New Gramophone Soc., Mr. Kelly Prodns., Montcalm Prodns., Stanyan Books, Cheval Books, Biplane Books, Rod McKuen Enterprises; v.p. Tamarack Books. Composer-lyricist: Soldiers Who Want to be Heroes; Seasons in the Sun; Ally Ally Oxen Free; The World I Used to Know; Love's Been Good to Me; The Loner; If You Go Away; The Lovers; A Man Alone; Without a Worry in the World; The Single

Man; Stanyan Street; Jean; We; Natalie; Champion Charlie Brown; I'm Not Afraid; A Boy Named Charlie Brown; Solitude's My Home; Joanna; I'll Catch the Sun; Kaleidoscope; A Cat Named Sloppy; Everybody's Rich But Us; The Ivy That Clings to the Wall; I Think of You; Doesn't Anybody Know My Name; Bend Down and Touch Me; Pastures Green; Listen to the Warm; The Beautiful Strangers; There Goes a Man Who Tried; Amsterdam; Miles to Go; Mr. Kelly; I've been to Town. Major classical works: Concerto for Four Harpsichords; Symphony No. 1; Piano Variations; Concerto for Guitar and Orch.; Seascapes for Piano and Orch.; Adagio for Harp and Strings; Concerto for Cello and Orch.; Concerto for Balloon and Orch.; classical commns.: Concerto No. 3 for Piano and Orch., (ballet), The Plains of My Country, 25th Anniversary London Royal Philharmonic Orch. 1972; The City, Louisville Orch., 1973; The Ballad of Distances, Edmonton Symphony, 1973; Symphony No. 3, 50th Anniversary Menninger Clinic, 1975; Bicentennial Ballet, Pitts. Ballet, 1975. Film scores include The Prime of Miss Jean Brodie, 1969; Me, Natalie, 1969; Joanna, 1968; A Boy Named Charlie Brown, 1970; Come To Your Senses, 1971; Scandalous John, 1971; Wildflowers, 1971; Lisa, Bright and Dark, 1973; The Borrowers, 1973. Author: Stanyan Street and Other Sorrows, 1966; Listen to the Warm, 1967; Twelve Years of Christmas, 1968; In Someone's Shadow, 1969; And Autumn Came, 1954, 1969; Caught in the Quiet, 1970; With Love, 1970; Fields of Wonder, 1971; The Carols of Christmas, 1971; And to Each Season, 1972; Beyond the Boardwalk, 1972; Come to Me in Silence, 1973; America-An Affirmation, 1974; Seasons in the Sun, 1974; Alone, Moment to Moment, 1974; The McKuen Omnibus, 1975; Celebrations of the Heart, 1975; Hand in Hand, 1977; The Sea Around Me, 1977; Coming Close to the Earth, 1977; Touching the Sky, 1978; (prose) Finding My Father, 1976. Bd. dirs. Am. Nat. Theatre Ballet, Animal Concern; adv. bd. Internat. Edn., Fund for Animals. Mem. ASCAP, Writers Guild, AFTRA, AGVA, Nat. Acad. Recording Arts and Scis. (bd. gov.), Bd. dir. Market Theatre, Johannesburg, So. Africa, Modern Poetry Assn. Nominated for Pulitzer prize in classical music for The City, 1973; Acad. award for best song Jean, 1969, Acad. award for best song score A Boy Named Charlie Brown, 1970; recipient Grande Prix du Disc, Paris, 1966; Golden Globe award, 1969, Motion Picture Daily award, 1969, Grammy award for best spoken word album, Lonesome Cities, 1969; Freedoms Found. award, 1975; recipient Man of the Year award from Menninger Foundation, 1975; Entertainer of the year, 1975, Los Angeles, Shriners' Club; Horatio Alger Award, 1976; Emmy award 1970 for Say Goodbye; Emmy award 1977 for Hello Again; Humanitarian award, 1977, First Amendment Society; composer and co-author of 20 hour TV documentary The Unknown War, 1978. Home: P.O. Box G, Beverly Hills, CA 90213; Office: 8440 Santa Monica Blvd., Los Angeles, CA 90069.

McKIG, BILLIE ELOISE OLSON
Dental Hygienist
b. Forest City, Iowa; d. Mark and Hazel (Staley) Olson; ed. Marquette Univ., R.D.H.; m. Maj. Woodland Styron, Jan. 2, 1946; dau. Rev. Monica Styron, b. Oct. 19, 1947; m. 2d. Dr. Robert McKig (dec.), Aug. 30, 1962, Riverside; dau. Susan, b. June 8, 1963. Career: pvt. practice, dental hygienist, 23 years; dental hygienist in husband's office, 1977-78. Mem.: pres., So. Calif. Dental Hygiene Assn., 1955; P.E.O.; PT chpt.; Eastern Star, Palomar chpt.; Chi Omega Soc.; San Diego Co. Dental Soc., women's aux. Presbyterian. Hobby: Collecting hist. of Iowa. Rec.: golf, swimming. Home: 4851 W. Alder Dr., San Diego, CA 92116; Office: 2602 First Ave., San Diego, CA.

McKINNEY, KEITH CLARK
Energy Company President
b. Oct. 1, 1923, Kingman, Ariz.; s. Forrest Menlo and Irma (Patterson) McKinney; B.S., Univ. of Calif., Berkeley, M.S., Indsl. Engr.; m. Thelma McDonald, Nov. 4, 1943, Santa Ana; chil.: Keith Wayne, b. July 13, 1945; Thomas Clark, b. Oct. 14, 1949; Jean Lynn, b. Sept. 17, 1959. Career: Indsl. Engr., Cutter Labs., 1951-52; with Pacific Lighting Corp. and Subs., 1952---: staff asst., Supply Analysis Staff, So. Calif. Gas Co., 1952-58; adminstrv. engr., Pac. Lighting Gas Supply Co., 1958-65; dir. System Planning & Econ. Dept., Pac. Lighting Serv. Co., 1965-72; v.p. and gen. mgr., Pac. Alaska LNG Co., 1972-77, pres. 1977---; v.p., gen. mgr. Pac. Indonesia LNG Co., 1973-77, pres. 1977---; v.p., gen. mgr., Pac. Lighting Marine Co., 1973-77; pres., Pac. Marine Assoc., 1977---; v.p., gen. mgr. Western LNG Terminal Co., 1974-77, pres. 1977---; dir. of Liquefied Natural Gas Projects, So. Calif. Gas Co., 1972---. Tech. 5th Gr., AUS, WW II, European Theater, 1943-46. Registered Profl. Engr., Calif.; mem. Gov. Reagan Com. on Efficiency in Govt., 1967. Mem.: Pac. Coast Gas Assn.; Am. Gas Assn.; regional dir., Cryogenic Soc. of

Am., 1970---; Internat. Group of LNG Importers, 1972---; Sigma Xi; Tau Beta Pi; L.A. Area C. of C.; L.A. Club; Town Hall of Calif.; World Affairs Council; Internat. Club of Wash. Rec.: golf, bridge. Res.: 1651 Ridley Ave., Hacienda Hts., CA 91745; Office: 700 S. Flower St., Suite 3300, L.A., CA 90017.

McKNIGHT, LENORE RAVIN
Physician — Child Psychiatrist
b. May 15, 1943, Denver, Colo.; d. Abe, M.D. and Rose (Steed) Ravin, M.D.; father, past pres. Colo. Heart Assn.; mother, past pres., Colo. Dermatology Soc.; B.A., Univ. of Colo., 1965; M.D., Univ. of Calif., San Francisco Med. Center, 1969; m. Robert Lee McKnight, 1967, Denver, Colo. Career: pediatrics intern, Childrens Hosp., S.F., 1969-70; gen. psychiatry fellowship, 1972-74; Youth Guidance Center, S.F., 1974-75; pvt. practice in child psychiatry, Walnut Creek, Calif., 1974---; asst. clin. prof., UCSF Med. Center, 1975---. Recipient: Fellowship, Internat. Inst. of Edn., Univ. of Edinburgh, 1964; Grant, study childhood nutrition, Nat. Inst. of Health, Sierra Leone, West Africa. Mem.: Am. Psychiatry Assn.; No. Calif. Psychiatric Soc.; Am. Acad. of Child Psychiatry; Am. Med. Women's Assn. Hobby: raise, train, show Arabian horses. Office: 130 La Casa Via, Walnut Creek, CA 94598.

McLAUGHLIN, DONALD H.
Board Chairman, Homestake Mining Company
b. Dec. 15, 1891; B.S., Univ. Calif., Berkeley, 1914, M.A. 1915, LL.D., 1916; Ph.D., Harvard Univ., 1917; D.Eng. (hon.), 4 insts.; m. Sylvia Cranmer, Dec. 29, 1948, Denver, Colo.; chil.: Donald, Jr., b. 1926; Charles (prof. of hist., Am. Univ.), b. 1929; Jean (Boucher), b. 1953; George, b. 1955. Career: Chief geologist, Cerro de Pasco Copper Corp., 1919-1925; prof. & chmn., Dept. of Geology & Geography and Div. of Geological Scis., Harvard Univ., 1925-41; Dean, Coll. of Mining, UC Berkeley 1941-43, Prof. of Mining Engring., 1941-43; cons. geologist, various orgns., 1925-43; pres., Homestake Mining Co., 1944-61, chmn. of bd., chmn., exec. com., 1970---. Dir.: Western Airlines; San Luis Mining Co.; Wells Fargo Bank, others. Regent, Univ. of Calif., 1951-66; mem., Nat. Sec. Bd., NSF, 1950-60; pres., Am. Inst. Mining, Metallurgical and Petroleum Engring. Publs: numerous papers on geology and gold. Mem.: Kappa Sigma; Phi Beta Kappa; Tau Beta Pi; Sigma Xi; others. Office: 650 California St., 9th Flr., S.F., CA 94108.

McLAUGHLIN, GLEN
Business Executive
b. Dec. 21, 1934, Shawnee, Okla.; s. Champe and Mattie Bet (Jenkins) McLaughlin; B.B.A., Univ. of Okla., 1956; M.B.A., Harvard Univ., 1964; m. Ellen Marr Schnake, Aug. 29, 1967; Glen Wallace, b. Feb. 28, 1969. Career: Asst. treas., Foremost-McKesson, Inc., S.F., 1964-69; exec. v.p. and dir., McFarlane's Candies, Oakland, 1969-70; dir. fin. & adminstrn., Memorex Corp., London, Eng., 1970-71; v.p. fin., Four-Phase Systems, Inc., Cupertino, 1971---; pres. and chmn., Four-Phase Finance, Inc., 1977---; chmn. bd., Four-Phase Systems Ltd., Toronto, Ont., Can., 1977---; chmn. bd., Four-Phase Systems Ltd., Marlow, Bucks, England, 1978---; dir., Four-Phase Systems Internat. Inc., 1972---. Served to 1st Lt., USAF, 1956-62; Capt. USAF Reserves, 1964-65. Mem.: pres., Jr. Achievement of Santa Clara Co. 1978; Fin. Execs. Inst.; Planning Execs. Inst.; Nat. Assn. of Accountants; Data Processing Mgrs. Assn.; English-Speaking Union; guarantor, S.F. Light Opera Assn.; Commonwealth Club; Harvard Bus. Sch. Club of No. Calif.; Nat. Genealogical Soc.; Sigma Alpha Epsilon. Hobby: genealogy. Rec.: swimming. Home: 20264 Ljepava Dr., Saratoga, CA 95070; Office: 10700 N. DeAnza Blvd., Cupertino, CA 95014.

McLEMORE, BEVERLY ALICE
Social Worker
b. Sept. 8, Los Angeles; d. James Howard and Alice Lee (Mackey) True; student, L.A. Trade Tech. Coll., 1964; A.A., West L.A. Coll., 1972; UCLA, 1973; Lifetime Cosmetology Tchr. Credential.; div.; chil.: Donna (Curtis); Gregory McLemore; Darryl McLemore. Career: real estate agent, 1962---; bookkeeper, Boys Mkt., 1964-72; cosmetology tchr., Leimert Beauty Coll., 1975; social worker, L.A. Co., 1975---. Former owner, Style Master Beauty Salon. Awarded NAACP Merit Award, 1958. Mem.: L.A. Urban League, womens guild; Alpha Delta chapt., Gamma Phi Delta; Rinkidinks L.A., treas. 1967. Polit. V.I.P. (very involved people) pres., 1977. Guidance Ch. of Religious Sci. Rec.: reading, dancing, bicycling, bowling. Home: 5074 Parkglen Ave., L.A., CA 90043;

Office: J.C. Moore Realty, 3909½ W. Slauson Ave., L.A., CA 90043.

McMAHON, PETER JOSEPH
Economist — Company President
b. Jan. 9, 1931, Bellmore, L.I., New York; s. Peter Joseph and Rose Marie (Homolka) McMahon; B.C.E., Manhattan Coll., N.Y., 1951; M.B.A., USC, 1960; Ph.D. economics, 1972; m. Pamela Lynn Brennan, Nov. 8, 1975, Tarzana, Calif. Career: constr. eng., FAA, 1951-52; pres., PJM Constr. Co., 1955-57; So. Calif. fep., HUD, 1957-61; project mgr., Koebig & Koebig, 1961-64; proj. mgr., Janss Devel. Co., 1964-65; chief economist, Daniel, Mann, Johnson, Mendenhall, 1965-69; dir. economics, Summa Corp., 1972-74; pres., P.J. McMahon & Associates, Inc., Inc. and P.J. McMahon & Assoc. Internat., Inc., 1974---. Active since 1955 in urban land economics, mkt. research, fin. feasibility analysis, transportation economics, resource economics, engring. and constr.; has conducted over 400 economic studies (incl. mkt., fin. & devel. strategy analyses) for projects in USA, Central Am., Europe, So. Africa, incl. Calif. projects in Mission Viejo, Anaheim Hills, Marina City. Other studies incl. Use & Occupancy of Pub. Lands of the U.S.; Outdoor Recreation Plan for state of Ariz. Expert witness before Fed. Power Commn., Calif. Pub. Util. Commn.; Calif. Coastal Commn.; Nevada 8th Judicial Dist. Ct. 1st Lt., USMC, 1952-55, Korean War. Registered Profl. Eng.: Vermont, Me., Mass., Ala., Miss.; gen. contr.: Calif. Hobby: dobermans. Rec.: sport fishing, surfing. Home office: 1151 Dove St., Ste. 112, Newport Beach, CA 92660; PJM Internat. offices: 3 Lambeau, Brussels, Belgium; 30 Hout St., Cape Town, So. Africa.

McMASTER, PAUL E.
Orthopedic Surgeon
b. June 24, 1902, Penca, Nebr.; s. Fred A. and Ruth (Hartwell) McMaster; B.A., Morningside Coll., 1924; M.D., Univ. of Chicago Rush Med. Coll., 1929; fracture training, Univ. of Vienna, 1936: m. Jane Douglas, Oct. 12, 1951, Beverly Hills. Career: intern, Presbyterian Hosp., Chicago, 1928-29; orthopedic resident, Univ. of Chicago Clinics, 1930-33; assoc. clin. prof. orthopedic surgery, 1951--- (acting Head of Dept., 1951-58); Diplomate Am. Bd. Orthopedic Surgeons, 1938. Contbr. numerous papers, orth. lit. Cmdr., USNR Med. Corps, 1941-46. Mem.: Western Orthopedic Assn., pres., 1964; Am. Orthopedic Assn., v.p., 1968; Am. Acad. Orthopedic Surgeons, 1939---; FACS, 1940;;; AMA, 1933---; Frats.: Sigma Nu and Nu Sigma Nu; Clubs: Los Angeles and Eldorado. Hobby: golf. Home: 1021 N. Crescent Dr., Beverly Hills, CA; Office: 435 N. Roxbury Dr., Beverly Hills, CA 90210.

McMILLAN, EDWIN M(ATTISON)
Professor Emeritus of Physics
b. Sept. 18, 1907, Redondo Beach; s. Edwin H. and Anna Marie McMillan; B.S., Calif. Inst. Tech., 1928, M.S., 1929; Ph.D., Princeton Univ., 1932; m. Elsie Walford Blumer, 1941, New Haven, Conn.; chil.: Ann (Nunes), b. 1943; David M., b. 1945; Stephen W., b. 1949; Career: Nat. Research Fellow, Univ. Calif., Berkeley, 1932-34; research assoc., 1934-35, instr. 1935-36, asst. prof. 1936-41, prof., 1946-73, Prof. Emeritus of Physics, 1973---; staff mem., Lawrence Berkeley Lab., 1934---, assoc. dir. 1954-58, dir. 1958-73. Co-Discoverer of Neptunium & Plutonium (chem. elements); Inventor of the Synchrotron (particle accelerator). Awarded Nobel Prize in Chem. (jointly), 1951; Atoms for Peace Award (jointly), 1963. Office: Lawrence Berkeley Lab., Univ. of Calif., Berkeley, CA 94720.

McMILLAN, JOHN ROBERTSON
Petroleum Company Executive
b. Sept. 6, 1909, Burlington, Vt.; s. Trevellick A. and Jeanie Newton (Miller) McMillan; ed. UCLA, 1927-28; B.S. (mech. engring.), Calif. Inst. of Tech. 1931; m. Eleanor Deacon, Sept. 30, 1933; chil.: Laurie Ann, b. Jan. 17, 1941; Linda Joan, b. July 17, 1944. Career: Petroleum engr., Barnsdall Oil Co. 1929-43; mgr. field opns., Fullerton Oil Co. 1943-47, v.p.-dir. (chg. exploration and prodn.), 1947-54; pres.-dir. 1954; dir. Huntington State Co. 1954; exec. v.p.-dir., Monterey Oil Co. 1954-61; dir. Transwestern Pipeline Co. 1957-61, pres. 1957-58; pres. Monterey Div., Humble Oil & Refining Co. 1961; pres.-dir., Monterey Gas Transmission Co. 1961-63; partner, Lacal Petroleum Co., 1963; pres.-dir., Reserve Oil and Gas Co., 1963-73, chem. 1974; chmn. bd. Can. Res. Oil and Gas Ltd. 1969---. Mem.: Am. Inst. of Mining, Metal. and Petroleum Engrs., Am. Assn. of Petroleum Geologists; chmn. petroleum br. AIME 1955; Western Oil & Gas

Assn., dir., pres. 1972-73; Am. Petroleum Inst., dir.; Natl. Petroleum Council mem.; Assocs. of Calif. Inst. of Tech., dir., pres. 1968-70; Theta Xi; clubs: Calif., Petroleum (L.A.), Petroleum (Midland, Tex.), Ramada (Houston, Tex.), Gnome, Annandale Golf (Pasa.). Protestant. Rec.: fishing, golf. Res.: 1025 Hillside Terr., Pasa., CA 91105; Office: 550 S. Flower St., L.A., CA 90371.

McNAMARA, FRANCIS X., JR.
United Way Executive
b. Feb. 19, 1925, Haverhill, Mass.; s. Francis X. and Mary L. (Haley) McNamara; B.S., Coll. of Holy Cross, Mass. 1945; postgrad. Boston Law Sch. 1946-47; M.S., Boston Coll. Grad. Sch. of Soc. Work, 1949; m. Barbara Johnston, Belmont, Mass., Nov. 12, 1949; chil.: Francis X., III, b. Feb. 12, 1953; Kathleen Louise, b. Dec. 17, 1960. Career: Dir., Haverhill Comm. Chest and Comm. Council of Greater Haverhill, 1949-50, 1952-55; exec. dir. Peninsula United Fund, and Welfare Planning Council, 1955-60; exec. dir. United Fund, Inc., R.I. 1960-67; gen. mgr. United Way, Inc., L.A., 1967---; exec. v.p., 1978, United Way, Inc., L.A. USN-ROTC, 1942-45; Line Ofcr. 1943-46, 1950-52. Mem.: bd. dirs. Fund and Council Tr. Scholarships pgm., Fund Raising Adv. United Way of Am.; bd. dirs.: Natl. Health and Welfare Ret. Assn.; L.A. and Wilshire Center C.s of C.; Mayfield Sr. Sch.; chmn., United Way of Am's. Council on Social Work Edn.; mem. United Way of Am's. Natl. Profl. Adv. Council; Natl. Assn. of Soc. Workers; Town Hall, L.A.; Friends of Huntington Library. Roman Catholic. Res.: 3601 E. California St., Pasadena, CA 91107; Office: 621 S. Virgil Ave., L.A., CA 90005.

McNAMARA, JOSEPH DONALD
Police Chief
b. Dec. 16, 1934, NYC; s. Michael and Eleanor McNamara; B.S., John Jay Coll., 1968; Harvard Law Sch. Fellowship, 1970; Dr. Pub. Adm., Harvard Univ., 1973; m. Rochelle McNamara, Jan. 1964, Manhattan; chil.: Donald, b. Jan. 5, 1965; Laura, b. Apr. 15, 1966; Karen, b. Mar. 9, 1968. Career: with NYC Police Dept. 1956-70, Dep. Inspector, Dir, of Crime Analysis, 1972-73; Chief of Police, Kansas City, Mo., 1973-76; Chief of Police, San Jose, 1976---. Dir., Am. Acad. of Profl. Law Enforcement; dir., Police Exec. Research Forum. TV appearances on Meet the Press, The Today Show, The Advocates; Young Am. Leader chosen by Time Mag., 1976; numerous publs. and lectrs. Mem.: Am. Soc. of Crimonology; Major Cities Police Chiefs Assn.; Internat. Assn. of Chiefs of Police; Calif. Police Chiefs Assn.; Nat. Council on Crime and Delinquency; Calif. Peace Ofcrs. Assn.; Am. Soc. of Pub. Adminstrn.; hon. mem., Better Bus. Bur., Santa Clara Valley; mem. Pub. Safety Com. Calif. League of Cities; bd. dir., San Jose Police Activities League. Rec.: tennis; Office: P.O.B. 270, San Jose, CA 95103.

McNEELY, E.L.
Chairman-CEO, Wickes Corporation
b. Oct. 5, 1918, Pattonsburg, Mo.; s. Ralph H. and Viola (Vogel) McNeely; stu., Central Bus. Coll., Kansas City, Mo., 1935-36, Univ. of Mo., 1936-37; A.B., No. Mo. State Univ., Kirksville, 1940; Rockhurst Coll., Kansas City, 1942; m. Alice Elaine Hall, Sept. 18, 1948, Evanston, Ill.; chil.: Sandra (Mrs. Ronald Gessl), Gregory, Mark, Kevin. Career: With Montgomery Ward & Co., 1940-64, Divisional Mdse. Mgr., 1961-64; dir. of mktg. Wickes Corp., Saginaw, Mich. 1964-65, sr. v.p. 1965-69, prs., 1969-74, chief exec. ofcr., chmn. 1974---. Dir.: Dayco Corp.; Fed.-Mogul Corp.; Mich. Nat. Corp.; Mich. Nat. Bank of Detroit; Transamerica Corp.; Wickes Corp. Ofcr., USNR, 1942-46. Clubs: Saginaw, Union League, Metropolitan, Chicago; La Jolla Country, Cuyamaca, San Diego. Republican. Presbyterian. Rec.: golf. Res.: 1020 La Jolla Rancho Rd., La Jolla, CA 92037; Office: 1010 Second Ave., San Diego, CA 92101.

McNEILL, ROY LIZARS
Independent Oil Producer
b. July 30, 1930, Santa Monica; s. Hector Agnon and Jane Adelaide (Graham) McNeill; grandson of D.R. McNeill, founder-orgn. Calif. Baseball League and Pac. Coast Baseball League; bldr-propr. Old Central Theater and Central Park, S.F.; grandnephew of Bro. Agnon, Jesuit, Agnon Field, St. Mary's Coll., Moraga; gr.-gr.-grandnephew of Wm. Home Lizars, painter-engraver, Natl. Gallery of Scot., Edinburg and Dr. John Lizars, surg., Lizars Lines in surg. and noted med. Author: ed. A.A., Santa Monica Coll. 1950; B.S., Univ. of Miss. 1952; m. Barbara Lee Harris, Santa Monica, Mar. 4, 1961; daus.: Andrea Lee, b. June 19,

1964; Diana Jane, b. Mar. 19, 1967. Career: proj. coord. Airesearch Mfg. Corp. 1956-61; assoc. v.p. Coldwell Banker Co. 1961-73; pres. McNeill Bros. Sales, 1968---; Independent oil producer, 1968---; dir. Hilliard Oil and Gas Co. 1970---; v.p. Cabot, Cabot & Forbes, 1973-75; assoc. of Kendall Internat. 1975---. Lt., U.S. Naval Aviation Serv., China Theater, Korean Theater, Attack Squad., Task Force 77, 1951-56. Awards: Pres. Unit Cit. Mem.: Independent Petroleum Assn. of Am., Soc. Ind. Relators, Bel-Air Bay Club. Res.: 200 Homewood Rd., L.A., CA 90049; Office: 11675 Wilshire Blvd., L.A., CA 90025.

McNITT, ROLLIN LEE, JR.
President, Rose Hills Memorial Park
b. Jan. 11, 1916, Eagle Rock, Calif.; s. Rollin Lee and Marjore Elizabeth (Hilton) McNitt; A.B. (cum laude), Stanford Univ. 1937, LL.B. 1940; m. Elizabeth M. Church, So. Pasa., Sept. 4, 1937; chil.: Robert Clyde, b. July 28, 1940; Roger Lee, b. Oct. 1, 1942; Marcia M. Young, b. Jan. 1, 1945; Margaret Elizabeth, b. Mar. 11, 1947; Evelyn Louise, b. May 26, 1948. Career: Admitted to State Bar of Calif. 1941; atty. for Bldg. and Loan Commr., L.A. 1940-41; secty-exec. v.p.-dir. gen. mgr., Whittier S&L Assn. 1945-51; exec. v.p.-trustee-gen. mgr. 1951-59; pres. Rose Hills Mem. Park, Whittier, 1959---. Dir.-v.p., Guarantee S&L Assn. Lt., USNR (1942045), WW II. Mem.: past pres.-dir., Natl. Assn. of Cemeteries; dir. Western Cemetery Alliance; dir.-secty.-treas., Interment Assn. of Calif.; pres.-bd. trustees, Whittier Union H.S. Dist. 1949-55; chmn. Whittier City Planning Comm. 1955-71; Calif. State Cemetery Bd. 1960-71; L.A. Co. Cits. Com., on Efficiency and Econ. 1964-65; Whittier Post, Am. Legion; Stanford Assocs., Kappa Sigma. Hillcrest Congregational Ch. (trustee). Hobby: Stanford Aths. Res.: 6216 S. Stanford Way, Whittier, Calif. 90601; Office: P.O.B. 110, Whittier, CA 90608.

McRAE, DOUGLAS F.
Business Executive
b. June 26, 1940, Elizabeth, N.J.; s. Walter Douglas and Marion V. Hudkins McRae; B.S., La Salle Coll., Phila., 1962; M.A., George Washington Univ., Wash. D.C., 1965; m. Judith Ann Brown, June 2, 1962, Middletown, N.J.; chil.: Douglas B., b. Feb. 18, 1963; Glenn A., b. Feb. 9, 1965; Shawn L., b. May 18, 1968. Career: with The United States Trust Co. of New York, 1965---: acct. exec., section and dept. head, personal trust & investment div., N.Y., 1965-77; mgr., Calif. Regional office, 1977---; apptd. Asst. Secty., 1969; asst. v.p., 1971; apptd. v.p., 1974. Served USMC, 1961-65, Capt. USMCR. Mem.: Investment Assn. of N.Y.; N.Y. Soc. of Security Analysts; L.A. World Affairs Council; Palm Springs Desert Mus.; YMCA of Metro. L.A.; the California Club. Home: 6926 Verde Ridge Rd., Rancho Palos Verdes, CA 90274; Office: 433 N. Camden Dr., Beverly Hills, CA 90210.

McSHANE, EDWARD DANIEL, S.J.
Professor of Church History
b. Oct. 20, 1913, S.F.; s. Edward Goldsmith and Margaret Agnes (Burschinsky) McShane; ed. grad. St. Ignatius H.S. (Gold Seal, Calif. Scholarship Assn., Chpt. 211), S.F. 1931; Jesuit Novitiate, Los Gatos, Calif. 1931; (humanities) Santa Clara Univ.; M.A., Gonzaga Univ., Spokane, Wash. 1939; S.T.L., Alma Coll., Los Gatos, Calif. 1946; Hist. Eccl. D., Pontifical Gregorian Univ., Rome, Italy, 1950. Career: Instr., Univ. of Santa Clara and Loyola Univ., L.A.; ordained priest, Roman Catholic Ch. 1945; prof. chmn. hist. Alma Coll., Los Gatos, 1950-69; Jesuit theologate for Pac. Coast; prof. hist. theol., Grad. Theol. Union, Berkeley, 1967-69. Adv. ed., The Catholic Historical Review, 1957-60; staff ed., The New Catholic Encyclopedia, Renaissance and Reformation History, 1962-66; asst. Provincial of Jesuit Calif. Prov. 1969-72; prof. chmn. hist. Univ. of Santa Clara, 1972---. Author: Monograph, The Anti-mendicantism of John Wyclif, publ. 1950; The Middle Ages, 1959; Hist. of the Church, 1300-1648, 1960; contrib. writing to profl. journs., incl. Thought, The Cath. Hist. Review, Theological Studies. Mem.: Am. Hist. Soc., Am. Cath. Hist. Assn., Renaissance Soc. of Am., Am. Soc. of Ch. Hist. Res. and Office: Univ. of Santa Clara, Santa Clara, CA 95053.

McWALTERS, JAMES G.
Commercial Brokerage Company Executive
b. Oct. 7, 1940, NYC; s. John and Mary McWalters; Midshipman, U.S. Naval Acad., Annapolis, B.S., (top 2% in grad. class) Aeronautical Engr. and Nuclear Sci., 1964; m. Patricia Roeweller, Apr. 19, 1975, San Diego. Career: Precision machinist, Ariz. Gear, Tucson,

1958-60; prodn. supr., No. Am. Aviation, Downey, 1960; founder-pres., Advanced Protective Systems, Inc., San Diego, 1969-71, merged with Sterling Security Svc., S.D., 1971; joined Grubb and Ellis Co., 1972---: investment mktg. 1972-73, mgr. of new tract sales, San Diego, 1973-74, sales mgr. in L.A., 1974-75; mgr. of Investment Bus. Devel. 1975-76; mgr., L.A. Comml. Brokerage Co., 1975-78, v.p., 1975---, bd. of dirs., 1976---; Investment Div. Coordinator, 1974---. USN, 1960-69; conducted first boarding and search opns. aboard minesweeper Excel, Vietnam, 1964-65; 3 yrs. aboard nuclear submarine Snook incl. Vietnam service star. Rec.: flying, skiing, golf, tennis. Res.: 925 Country Club Dr., Burbank, CA 91501; Office: 1126 Wilshire Blvd., L.A., CA 90017.

MEDBERRY, CHAUNCEY JOSEPH, III
Board Chairman, BankAmerica Corporation
b. Oct. 9, 1918, L.A.; s. Chauncey Joseph, Jr. and Geneva (Raymond) Medberry; B.A., UCLA, 1938; postgrad., Univ. of Munich, Germ., 1939; m. Thirza Cole Young, Mar. 14, 1958; chil.: Julie Ann Young (Mrs. G.E. Pendergast); Ralph D. Young III; Debora D. Young; Chauncey Joseph Medberry IV. Career: With Bank of Am., L.A., 1939---; sr. v.p. 1965-68, exec. v.p., S.F. 1968, chmn. of Gen. Fin. Com., 1969; chmn. of bd. 1971; chmn. of bd., BankAmerica Corp. Dir. Getty Oil Co.; dir., Assn. of Reserve City Bankers. Trustee: Calif. Inst. of the Arts; Calif. Inst. of Tech.; Com. for Econ. Devel.; Good Samaritan Hosp.; Pomona Coll. Mem.: Huntington Lib., bd. of overseers; L.A. Clearing House, pres. 1973; Salvation Army, Nat. Adv. Council; chmn. bd. of visitors, Grad. Sch. of Mgmt., UCLA. Clubs: Calif., Links, N.Y., L.A. Country, P-U Club, S.F.; Sky Club, N.Y.; Bohemian, S.F. Office: 555 S. Flower St., L.A., CA 90071.

MEDEARIS, ALLEN MILLER
Attorney at Law
b. Jan. 19, 1921, Liberty, Mo.; s. Dr. Thomas Whittier (noted Coll. admr. and clergyman, Riverside, Calif.) and Mara E. (Miller) Medearis; LL.B., 1948, J.D. 1969; postgrad. engring., psychol.; chil.: Christy Allyn, b. July 4, 1955; Kellee Alana, b. July 1, 1958; Career: admitted to Okla bar, 1948, Calif. bar 1957; candidate for State Rep., Okla. 1948; exec. Mo. Bapt. Found. 1949; claim adjustor, Transit Casualty Co., 1950-58, mgr. Tulsa City Lines and Sacto. City Lines; trial lawyer, Transit Casualty Co. and L.A. Met. Lines, 1957-58; partner, Hagenbaugh, Murphy, Medearis law firm, 1958-69; sr. partner, Medearis and Grimm firm 1969---. USN (1944-45), WW II. Mem.: L.A. Calif. State Bar Assns.; Oneota Club, dev. bd. Calif. Baptist Coll.; Hiking Club, Elks. Pres., Bible Class, First Baptist Ch., Pasa. 1967. Hobby: cars. Rec.: hiking. Res.: 1049 Oak Grove Pl., San Marino, CA; Office: 1331 W. Sunset Blvd., L.A., CA 90026.

MEDLEY, PATRICIA JOAN
Mental Health Administrator (Ret.)
b. June 17, 1928, Pasadena, Calif.; d. Howard A. and Lois Medley; B.S., 1950; M.S.W., Univ. of Calif., Berkeley, Sch. of Social Welfare. Career: chief psychiat. social worker, 1952-72; pvt. practice with incorporated group, 1954-72; Santa Clara Co. Community Mental Health Center, San Jose, 1955-64; spec. cons. Calif. Dept. of Edn., 1960-62; adminstr., Santa Clara Co. Mental Health Services, 1964-72; chief psychiat. social worker, USAF, Park Base, Pleasanton, Calif., 1955-58. Consultant: Conference of Local Mental Health Depts. 1968-72; parents of handicapped chil., Santa Clara Co., 1964-66; Midpeninsula com. on services to chil.; Santa Clara Co. Mental Health Advisory Bd.,; Nat. Inst. of Mental Health; adminstrs. of Local Bay Area Mental Health (founder). Mem.: Nat. Assn. of Social Workers, 1950---; Certified Social Workers, chpt. edn. com.; Santa Clara Co. Social Planning Com., 1968-69. Home: 21491 Burr Way, Hayward, CA 94541.

MEGAHEY, THOMAS J.
University President
b. Mar. 31, 1910, Belfast, N. Ire.; s. John and Eva (Fulton) Megahey; B.A. 1939, B.D. 1941, M.Th. 1942, D.D. 1947, D.Th. 1956; Ph.D. 1973; m. Alberta Buttimer, Phila., Pa., June 11, 1939; daus.: Carole Jean Spenser, b. Apr. 29, 1941; Ruth Anne, b. Oct. 3, 1947. Career: Ordained minister, 1940; chs. serv.: Dubuque, Ia. 1941-45; Chicago, Ill. 1945-46; Eagle Rock, Calif. 1956-67; Beverly Hills, 1967-73; pres. Breed Univ. 1973---. Dir. Neighborhood House, Chicago, 1947-53; Chaplain, Ill. Senate, 1953. Mem.: Masonic Lodge, 1943---, chaplain, Grand Lodge, 1954-55; bd. dirs.

YMCA 1967-72; bd. dirs. Rotary Club, Beverly Hills, Century City; Royal Soc. of Health, 1973; chmn. pub. rels.-L.A. pres., chmn. Stewardship Com., Chicago, L.A. Country Club. Hobby: candle making. Rec.: golf. Res.: 809 S. Bundy Dr., L.A., CA 90049.

MEINERS, HENRY CITO
Oil Company Executive
b. Feb. 11, 1916, Pendleton, Ore.; s. George and Catherine (Schrum) Meiners; B.S., Ore. State Univ. 1938; D.Sc., MIT 1942; m. Marie Franklin, Stevenson, Wash., Sept. 2, 1938; chil.: Carol Ann, b. May 22, 1944; Janice Marie, b. Aug. 12, 1947; Alan Henry, b. Sept. 18, 1950. Career: Assoc. with Union Oil Co. of Calif. 1942---. process supv., asst. mgr., mgr. Oleum Refinery, supt., mgr. L.A. Refinery, 1942-56; process cons., research dept. 1956---. U.S. Patents: 3,063,933 and 3,069,349, 1962. Mem.: Am. Inst. of Chem. Engrs., Am. Chem. Soc., AAAS, Inst. of Mgmt. Sci.; Fellow, Am. Inst. Chemists; N.Y. Acad. Sci.; v.p. Calif. Council of Dad's Clubs, 1952-53; So. Calif. dir. Oregon State Univ. Dad's Club; BSA, Phi Lambda Upsilon, Phi Kappa Phi, Sigma Xi, Beta Theta Pi, Tau Beta Pi, Pi Mu Epsilon, Palos Verdes Breakfast Club, L.A. Ath. Club. Hobby: photog. Rec.: skiing, hiking. Res.: 3909 Via Picaposte, Palos Verdes Estates, CA; Office: Union Oil Center, 461 S. Boylston, L.A., CA.

MEISEL, FREDDA BLECHMAN
Community Leader
b. Feb. 23, 1935, Coatesville, Pa.; d. Harry and Anna (Epstein) Blechman; stu., Antioch Coll., 1953-55; B.S., Drexel Univ. 1957; m. Harris Meisel, M.D., July 7, 1957, Coatesville; chil.: Melody, b. 1960; Alexander Harris, b. 1961; Benjamin Harris, b. 1970. Career: own weekly radio show, Tips for Teens, WCOJ, Chester Co., Pa., 1949-53; Voice of Am. brotherhood broadcasts, radio show at Valley Forge Mil. Hosp., Pa.; own daily television chil's. program, Aunt Mary's Birthday Party, WHP-TV, Harrisburg, Pa., 1959; daily columnist, Phila. Bulletin, Coatesville Record; vol., Am. Field Serv., Mex., 1955; community vol., 1970---. Recipient: Danforth Found. Award, 1953; B'nai B'rith Americanism Award, 1953; mem. Internat. Platform Assn., 1977---; dir.: Santa Barbara Scholarship Found., 1974---; Youth Theatre Prodns. of Santa Barbara, Inc., 1974---; Performing Arts Center Assn. of Santa Barbara, 1974---. Mem.: Jr. League of Santa Barbara; pres., KCET-TV Santa Barbara Affiliates; Comm. TV of Santa Barbara. Office: 992 Cocopah Dr., Santa Barbara, CA 93110.

MEISEL, HARRIS
Physician
b. Mar. 17, 1932, Phila., Pa.; s. Alexander Edmund and Sophia S. (Schor) Meisel; B.F.A., Temple Univ., 1954; student Ursinus Coll., 1955; M.D., Univ. of Pa. Med. Sch., 1959; Fellowship in Rehabilitation Med., Stanford Univ. Med. Center, 1962-65; m. Fredda Blechman, July 7, 1957, Coatesville, Pa.; chil.: Melody, b. Oct. 31, 1960; Alexander Harris, b. Oct. 17, 1961; Benjamin Harris, b. Oct. 31, 1970. Career: Internship, Harrisburg PolyClinic Hosp., Pa. 1959-60; Navajo Indian Serv., U.S. Pub. Health Serv. Hosp., Shiprock, N.M., 1960-62; founder, Med. Dir., Meml. Rehabilitation Found. Center and Clin. Dir., Rehabilitation, Santa Barbara Gen. Hosp., 1965---; contbr. profl. articles to med. journs., poetry to Ariz. Highways, Am. Physicians Poetry Assn. Proceedings, Mother's Manual. Established: fly in medicine clinic for Mavajo Indians, N.M.; Stroke Pgms. in St. Francis and Cottage Hosps.; R&D work with biomed. engrs. on engring solutions to med. problems, projects incl. electrical stimulator for denervated muscles, touch micro switches for alarm system for paralyzed patients, curb climbing motorized wheelchair, voice operated electric wheelchair control system, communication devices for mute patients, others. Mem.: AMA; CMA; Santa Barbara Co. Med. Soc., Am. Congress Rehabilitation Med.; Am., Northwest and Calif. Soc. for Physical Med. & Rehabilitation; Internat. Med. Soc. of Paraplegia; Nat. Paraplegic Found.; Calif. Assn. of Physically Handicapped; Am. Spinal Injury Assn.; Am. Physician's Poetry Assn. Hobbies: painting, sculpture, writing, music. Office: 433 Camino Del Remedio, Santa Barbara, CA 93110.

MENDENHALL, DORIS ANNE
Artist — Civic and Social Leader
b. May 28, Van Nuys, Calif.; d. Dr. Harry Vernon and Rose Catherine (Stachowiak) Hopgood; ed. Ore. Univ., UCLA; m. Ferdinand Mendenhall (newspaper publisher); daus.: Doris Anne, b. Oct. 12, 1956; Laura Lee, b. Dec. 26, 1958; Margo Mia, b. June 30, 1960 (Van Nuys). Career: Propr., pvt. pre-schs., San Fernando Valley, Van

Nuys, Sherman Oaks. Artist, feat. several one-man shows of oil painting incl.: Dept. of Adoptions of L.A. Co., Henry Van Wolf Studios; actress, TV, 1958-59; appd. various TV guest shows, Model, cover girl on Teen Life, Valley Que, Calif. Publs., Mag. and Hobbies, Inc. Adv., Mayor Yorty's Adv. Com.; chmn. L.A. 184th Birthday Anniversary celebrations, 1965; apptd. chmn., Mayor's Council for Internat. Visitors and Sister Cities, 1966-67; chairman, L.A. Co. Dept. of Adoptions. Awards: elected, Miss L.A. Co. Young Republican 1957; Ebell Art Award, 1970, 71; Gold Medal Award of Calif. 1970; The Lincoln Savings Artist Award; Fri. Morning Club Award; L.A. Co. Award for Serv. to Orphaned Chil.; Co. Adoption Award; Dept. of Soc. Servs. Civic Award; Grand Dame, Order of St. Brigitte. Mem.: past pres. Adoptaides; Las Patroncitas Guild, Valley Presbyterian Hosp.; Assis. League of So. Calif. Hilltoppers, dir. 1970---; past pres. Valley Spastic Chil's. League; bd. dirs., Valley YWCA; dir. Child Welfare of Am., Inc.; pres. Women's Div., Calif. Newspaper Publs. Assn. 1962; L.A. Orphanage Guild, The Group, ARCS; bd. govs., Otis Art Inst., 1964; chmn. Speakers Bureau, Freedoms Found., bd. So. Calif. 1965; Philharmonic Assn., L.A.; bd. dirs.: Calif. Assn. of Adoption Agcy's., San Fernando Valley Child Guidance Clinic, Youth Counselor San Frenando Valley, PTA, Natl. Art Assn., Valley Artists Guild Lifelighters, Diadames Inc.; The Ladies of Charity 100, The Blue Ribbon 400, Garden Club; L.A. C. of C. Women's Div.; L.A. World Affairs Council; Les Dames de Champagne; Muses. Republican Women's Club. Res.: 917 Oxford Way, Beverly Hills, CA 90210.

MENDENHALL, FERDINAND
Newspaper Executive
b. June 15, Burlington Jct., Mo.; s. Walter (dean of San Fernando Valley publs.) and Blanche (Carter) Mendenhall; desc. Engl. Mendenhall bros. who settled near Boston prior to Rev. War; ed. Van Nuys pub. Schs., Calif.; Stanford Univ.; LL.D. (hob.) Univ. of San Fernando Valley Coll. of Law; m. Doris Anne Hopgood; daus.: Doris Anne, Laura Lee and Margo Mia. Career: v.p.-ed., exec. ed. The Valley News. Dir. Valley Fed. S&L Assn.; (past) v.p. L.A. Bd. of City Planning Commrs.; dir. Met. Water Dist. of So. Calif.; commr. L.A. Conv. and Exhib. Center Authority; L.A. Co. Econ. and Efficiency Com.; chief of protocol, State of Calif., 1967---. USN, European, African, Am., Pac-Asiatic theaters; Fleet Marine Force, Pac. (134-46), WW II; Capt. USNR. Awards: Americansim Award of Sigma Tau Sigma, 2 certificates for Distinguished Serv., Am. Legion; Walter Mendenhall Man of Yr. 1961, Van Nuys C. of C.; Man of Yr. Testimonial Dinner by Mid-Valley B'nai B'rith; Distinguished Eagle Scout Award; Grand Knight, Order of St. Lazarus; USN Distinguished Serv. Award, 1969; Grand Knight, Order of St. Brigitte, 1969. Mem.: U.S. Naval Inst.; VFW; Am. Legion; past pres. Calif. Newspaper Publs. Assn.; pres. Calif. Press Assn.; past gen. chmn., Calif. Editors' Conf.; Greater L.A. Press Club; (past) lt. gov., Kiwanis Internat.; L.A. World Affairs Coubcil; pres. Van Nuys C. of C. 1961000; chmn. Edn. Com. and dir. L.A. C. of C. (6 terms); Edn. and Water Resources Com.; Calif. State C. of C.; bd. councilors, USC Sch. of Bus. Adm.; pres., L.A. Pub. Facilities Corp.; v.p. Boy Scouts (1st Eagle Scout in San Fernando Valley Council), Salvation Army, San Fernando Valley State Coll.; v.p.-bd. dirs. Valley Presbyterian Hosp.; bd. govs., British United Servs. Club; L.A. Athletic Club; Conferie des Chevaliers du Tastevin; (life) Stanford Alumni Assn.; Stanford Club of L.A.; Masonic orders, Shrine, DeMolay Leg. of Hon.; (life) Phi Sigma Kappa, Sigma Delta Chi, Ram's Head, Beta Phi Gamma, Alpha Phi Omega; 1st pres., San Fernando Valley Young Republicans; Repub. State Central Com.; trustee, Repub. Assoc. Protestant. Res.: 917 Oxford Way, Beverly Hills, CA 90210; Office: 14539 Sylvan Ave., Van Nuys, CA.

MENDENHALL, WILLIAM FRANKLIN
Mayor of Signal Hill
b. Jan. 15, 1914, Greensboro, N.C.; s. Edward E. Sr. and Ida M. (Allred) Mendenhall; desc. of John Mendenhall and Elizabeth Maris who migrated to Concordville, Delaware Co., Pa. with William Penn about 1680, and his grandson Mordecai Mendenhall and Charity Beeson who moved to Guilford Co., N.C. 1751; James V. Allred, Gov. of Tex. 1936-39; ed. George Sch. (pvt.), Bucks Co., Pa.; N.C. State Coll.; m. Mildred Sorenson, Long Beach, chil.: Edwin Gray, b. Sept. 3, 1939; Marianne, b. Oct. 27, 1944. Career: Judge, Magistrate Ct., Guilford Co., N.C. 1946-50; real estate and ins. bus., Indianapolis, Ind.; elected to City Council of Signal Hill, Apr. 1962, elected mayor, Apr. 1963-65; city councilman, 1965-78; v.-mayor, 1967, mayor 1968-74, 1978---; Fire Comm., City of Signal Hill

1962-63; Police Commr. 1962; Safety & Health Commr. 1963; treas.-secty., Independent City of L.A. Co., 1965-67; Commr. of Pub. Safety, 1967; off. L.A. Co. Sanitation Dist. No. 62, chmn. bd. dirs. Sanitation Dist. No. 29, 1962-70. U.S. Army, 1940-45, WW II. Mem.: L.A. Co. and Cities Disaster and Civ. Def. Com.; Calif. Police Ofcrs. Assn.; League Calif. Cities; pres. Calif. Soc. S.A.R., L.A. chpt., 1968-70; Am. Water Works Assn.; Calif. Feather River Proj. Assn., U.S. Conf. of Mayors, Joint Soc. of Engrs., Assn. of the U.S. Army, Independent Bus. Men's Assn. of Greater Long Beach; Am. Legion. Republican. Soc. of Friends Ch. (Quaker). Hobby: amateur radio. Rec.: fishing. Res.: 3309 Falcon Ave., Long Beach, CA 90807; Office: City Hall, 2175 Cherry Ave., Signal Hills, CA 90806.

MENON, VIJAYA BHASKAR
President, Capitol Industries - EMI, Inc.
b. May 29, 1934, Trivandrum, India; s. K.R.K. (ex-fin. secty., Indian Republic) and Saraswathy Menon; uncle, K.P.S. Menon, ex-foreign secty., Indian Republic; B.A. (honors) economics, St. Stephens Coll., Univ. of Delhi, India, 1953; M.A. philosophy, polit. & economics, Christ Ch., Univ. of Oxford, U.K., 1956; m. Sumitra Paniker, Jan. 21, 1972, Madras, India; chil.: Siddhartha, b. Jan. 23, 1973; Vishnu, b. Dec. 5, 1974. Career: mng. dir., chmn. bd., Gramophone Co. of India Ltd., 1957-70; mng. dir., EMI Internat. Services Ltd., London, 1970-71; pres. & chief exec., Capitol Industries — EMI, Inc., 1971---; chmn. & chief exec. Capitol Records, Inc. Dir., EMI Ltd., London. Hindu. Rec.: tennis, reading. Office: 1750 N. Vine St., Hollywood, CA 90028.

MERDINGER, CHARLES JOHN
Civil Engineer — Academic Administrator
b. Apr. 20, 1918, Chicago, Ill; s. Walter F. and Catherine (Phelan) Merdinger; Midshipman, U.S. Naval Acad., Annapolis, 1937-41; postgrad. Stu. (Civil Engr. Corps, USN) Rennselaer Polytech. Inst., 1944-46; Rhodes Scholar (also Ofc. of Naval Attache, London), Oxford Univ., Engl., 1947-49; m. Mary F. McKelleget, Oct. 21, 1944, Cambridge, Mass.; daus.: Anne (Mrs. Fred R. Kern), b. 1946; Joan (Mrs. Edward W. Bough), b. 1948; Susan, b. 1950; Jane, b. 1952. Career: Pvt. 1st class, Wisc. Nat. Guard, 1935-37; Ensign, USS Nevada (sunk at Peark Harbor, Dec. 7, 1941), 1941-42; Lt, j.g., & Lt., USS Alabama, Atlantic (Murmansk Run) and Pacific, 1942-43; LCDR in charge of contrn., Panama Canal Zone, 1946-47; Bureau pf Yards & Docks, Wash. D.C. 1949-51, 1965-67; asst. public works ofcr., Naval Shipyard, Bremerton, Wash. (Korean War), 1951-53; Head of Seabees, Adak, Aleutian Islands, Alaska, 1953-54; Ofcr. in charge of constrn. Naval Air Station Miramar, S.D. (1st Master Jet Air Sta., Navy), 1954-56; CO, Naval Civil Engring. Lab., Port Hueneme, 1956-59; Pub. Works Ofcr., U.S. Fleet Activities, Yokosuka, Japan, 1959-62; Head of English, Hist., Govt. Dept., U.S. Naval Acad., Annapolis, 1962-65; Pub. Works Ofcr. & Head of Seabees, Da Nang, Vietnam (TET Offensive), 1967-68; CO, W. Div., Naval Facilities Engring. Command, San Bruno, Calif. 1968-70; ret. from USN as Capt., 1970; pres., Wash. Coll., Md., 1970-73; v.p., Aspen Inst. for Humanistic Studies, Aspen, Colo., NYC, 1973-74; Dep. Dir., Scripps Inst., La Jolla, 1974---. Awarded All Am. Lacrosse, 1945; Legion of Merit with Conbat "V", 1968; Navy Meritorious Svc. Medal, 1970; Nat. Hist. & Heritage Award, Am. Soc. Civil Engrs., 1972; Scouting Awards. Mem.: Pearl Harbor Survivors Assn.; Sigma Xi, Tau Beta Pi, Chi Epsilon, Phalanx Vincents'; trustee, Found. for Ocean Research; others. Author: Civil Engring. Through the Ages, 1963; contbr. Aqueduct, Ency. Britannica, 1974; numerous articles on constrn., edn., mgmt., personnel. Roman Catholic. Rec.: tennis, skiing. Res.: 5538 Caminito Consuelo, La Jolla, CA 92037; Office: A-010, Scripps Inst. Oceanography, UCSD, La Jolla, CA 92093.

MERRIFIELD, DONALD PAUL, S.J.
President, Loyola Marymount University
b. Nov. 14, 1928, L.A.; s. Arthur S. and Elizabeth (Baker) Merrifield; B.S., Calif. Inst. of Tech. 1950; M.S., Notre Dame Univ. 1951; A.M., Ph.L., St. Louis Univ. 1957; Ph.D., MIT, 1961; S.T.M., Univ. of Santa Clara, 1966; S.T.D., USC, 1969; Career: Mem. of Jesuits, 1951---; physics instr. Loyola Univ. 1961-62; cons. molecular physics, Jet Propulsion Labs., Pasa., 1962-69; lectr., Engring. Sch., Santa Clara, 1965; ordained, June 9, 1965; asst. prof. physics, Univ. of S.F. 1967-69; pres. Loyola Univ. of L.A., June 1969---. Calif. State Assem. Sci. and Tech. Adv. Commn., 1972---; chmn. Western Reg. Planning Counsel of United Way, 1972. Awards: Alumni Distinguished Serv. Award, by Calif. Inst. of Tech. 1971. Mem.: Sigma Xi, Alpha Sigma Nu; Am. Phys. Soc. Res.: 7101 W. 80th St., L.A., CA; Office:

President's Ofc., Loyola Marymount Univ., Loyola Blvd. at W. 80th St., L.A., CA 90045.

MERRITT, SYLVIA STERN
Law Librarian
b. Mar. 24, 1924, Chicago, Ill.; d. Louis A. and Rose (Cooperman) Stern; B.S., Law, Univ. Ill., 1945, LL.B., 1946; M.L.S., Immaculate Heart Coll., L.A. 1965; m. John F. Merritt, Aug. 21, 1955, Beverly Hills; sons: Jon, b. Aug. 17, 1956; Dan, b. June 14, 1959. Career: Ed., Commerce Clearing House, 1947-49, Rules ed., 1949-53; Administrv. Policy Coord., L.A. City Bd. of Edn., 1953-56; ref. librn., UCLA Law Lib., 1965---. Mem.: Westside GASP, 1976---; dir., Calif. GASP, 1977---; Lung Assn. Coastal Regional Council, 1978---; mem. Com. on Index to Legal Periodicals, Am. Assn. of Law Libraries, 1977---. Admitted Ill. Bar, 1947. Res.: 10507 Louisiana Ave., L.A., CA 90025; Office: 405 Hilgard Ave., L.A., CA 90024.

MESSICK, DON JERRY
Newspaper Publisher
b. Mar. 6, 1936, McAlister, Okla.; s. Roy E. and Nilar P. (Kirkpatrick) Messick; m. Janice N., June 24, 1955, Huntington Park, Calif.; chil.: Mark, b. Sept. 2, 1956; Kenneth, b. July 29, 1958; Dane, b. Apr. 29, 1960; Michael, b. Dec. 27, 1963; Christy, b. Sept. 5, 1969. Career: teenage employee, Door Mfg. Co., L.A., 1953-56; indsl. engr. trainee, Revere Copper & Brass, L.A., 1956-60; sr. indsl. engr. and plant mgr., Pioneer Mfg., City of Industry, 1963-66; president and pub., Highlander Community Newspapers, San Gabriel Valley, 1966---: started with one newspaper, 6,800 circulation; now 17 papers with 402,000 circ. in 40 cities. Mem.: La Puente C. of C.; Calif. Dept. of Transp. Com.; Community Planning Com.; Men's Club, Queen of Valley Hosp.; BSA, leadership. Mormon ch.; leader, youth programs. Rec.: tennis, golf. Home: 2048 Avocado Terrace, Hacienda Hts., CA 91745; Office: 1201 S. Hacienda Blvd., Hacienda Hts., CA 91745.

METTLER, RUBEN FREDERICK
Chairman-CEO, TRW
b. Feb. 23, 1924, Shafter, Calif.; s. Henry F. and Lydia Mettler; B.S. (E.E.), Calif. Inst. of Tech. 1944; M.S. (E.E.), 1947, Ph.D. (E.E. and A.E.), 1949; m. Donna Jean Smith, Van Nuys, May 1, 1955; sons: Matthew Frederick, b. Feb. 27, 1958; Daniel Frederick, b. Sept. 3, 1960. Career: Assoc. with Hughes Aircraft Co. 1949-54, assoc. div. dir., Systems Research and Devel., 1953-54; spec. cons. to Ass. Secty. of Def. 1954-55; bd. dirs., The Ramo Wooldridge Corp. Guided Missile Research Div. 1955-58 (name changed to TRW Systems Group, TRW Inc. 1965), exec. v.p. and dir., TRW Inc., 1965-68; asst. pres., TRW Inc., 1968-69; pres., TRW Inc., 1969-77; chmn. of bd. and CEO, TRW Inc., 1977---. Dir., BankAmerica Corp., Goodyear Tire & Rubber Co., and Merck & Co.; formerly v. chmn. of Ind. Adv. Council of DoD; mem. of steering com. reviewing studies of mgmt. of DoD; formerly chmn. of task force on Natl. Sci. Policy apptd. by Pres. Nixon; mem., Caltech. Assocs., 1963---; bd. of trustees, Caltech., 1969---; bd. of adv. Council for Fin. Aid to Ed and Case Western Reserve Univ.; trustee, Natl. Safety Council and Cleveland Clinic Found.; bd. of gov. of Renaissance Club; adv. com. of United Negro College Fund; bd. of trustees of Comm. for Econ. Devel.; aerospace chmn. of U.S. Ind. Payroll Sav. Comm.; mem. of Smithsonian Natl. Assoc. Bd.; Economic Club of N.Y.; Emergency Com. for Am. Trade, Rockefeller Univ. Council, The 50 Club of Cleveland, and James Smith's Smithson Soc.; natl. chmn. of Nat. Alliance of Businessmen, 1978---. Author: several book-length classified reports on airborne electronic systems. Holds joint patent application for maj. interceptor fire control systems. Ofcr., USN (1943-46), WW II. Awards: Eta Kappa Nu Award for nation's most outstanding young elec. engr., 1954; Natl. Jr. C. of C. Award for one of ten outstanding young men of Am., 1955; So. Calif's Engr. of Yr., 1964; So. Calif. Marketing Man of Yr., 1965; Alumni Distinguished Serv. Awards, Calif. Inst. of Tech. 75th Anniversary Celebrations, 1966. Mem.: fellow, IEEE; fellow, Am. Inst. of Aerons. and Astronautics; Natl. Acad. of Engring.; bd. dirs., Calif. Inst. of Tech. Alumni Assn.; Theta Xi, 1942-43; Cosmos Club, Wash. D.C. Res.: 12846 Highwood St., L.A., CA 90049; Office: One Space Park, Redondo Beach, CA 90278.

MEUB, DANIEL WARREN
Neurosurgeon
b. Feb. 2, 1924, Los Angeles; s. Albert Philip and Olga

(Gablowsky); m. Betty May Rinehart, Pasadena; A.B., Univ. of Calif., 1947; M.D. chil.: Karen Robbins Brown, b. Apr. 15, 1948; Kristin Doreen Craig, b. Apr. 12, 1950; Daniel Jay, b. May 28, 1953; Eric Albert, b. Oct. 17, 1958. Career: Res. in neurosurg., Univ. of Calif. Hosp., 1947-53; research neurological surg., Univ. of Calif. 1955; clin. instr., Univ. of Calif. Med. Sch.; est. pvt. practice, neurological surg., Palo Alto, 1955---; cons. in neurosurg., San Mateo Community Hosp., 1955---; staff, Palo Alto, Stanford, Sequoia, El Camino hosps.; assoc. clin. prof., neurological surg., Stanford Univ. Sch. of Med. 1962---; chief of staff, Sequoia Hosp., 1976-78. Capt., U.S. Army, chief, neurological surg., Ft. Campbell Army Hosp. 1953; Letterman Army Hosp. 1954-55. Mem.: Diplomate, Am. Bd. Neurological Surg.; fellow, ACS; Harvey Cushing Soc.; Cong. Neurological Surg.; S.F. Neurological Soc.; Menlo Circus Club, Atherton. Hobby: Cello. Rec.: tennis. Res.: 75 Barry Lane, Atherton, CA; Office: 1101 Welch Rd., Palo Alto, CA.

MEULI, ESTHER ADELLE WEBSTER
Judge
b. Jan. 9, 1918, Oakland; d. John Calvin and Blanch (Hagler) Webster; student, Coll. Pacific, 1937-38; LL.B., Univ. of Calif., Berkeley, 1941; m. Jasper George Meuli, Oct. 19, 1954, Reno, Nev. Career: asst. mgr., Sonora Angles, San Andreas, 1943-53; Clerk, Justice Ct. 1st Jud. Dist., Sonora, 1953-60; Judge, Justice Ct., 1st Judicial Dist., Sonora, 1960-67, 1970-79. Mem.: Soroptimist, treas., 1960-61; Peace Officers, Judges & Marshalls; Emblem Club. Catholic. Hobbies: painting, gardening. Rec.: golf. Home: 173 Bradford Ave., Sonora, CA 95370.

MEYER, RUTH NATHAN
Specialty Store Executive
b. Jan. 17, 1911, Parkersburg, W.Va.; d. Ben and Julia (Newberger) Nathan; B.A., Mills Coll., 1933; m. Fred Stern Meyer, May 29, 1935, L.A.; chil.: Susan (Mrs. Jack Blumenthal), b. May 9, 1938; Bruce, b. Dec. 1, 1941. Career: v.p., Geary's, Beverly Hills; lectr., radio and TV interviews on porcelain and crystal. Bd. Dir.: The Visiting Nurse of L.A.; Julia Ann Singer Psychiatric Center; Mills Coll. Alumnae of L.A.; past pres., past regional gov. of So. Calif.; Hancock Park-Windosr Square Historical Soc.; past pres., Vista Del Mar Assocs.; past pres., Third St. Sch. PTA. Rec.: travel, study-porcelains and crystal. Res.: 414 N. McCadden Pl., L.A., CA 90004; Office: 351 N. Beverly Dr., Beverly Hills, CA 90210.

MICCICHE, JOSEPH JOHN
Public Relations Counselor
b. Apr. 28, 1910, Paterson, N.J.; s. Rosario and Eugenia Micciche; cous., Gen. Nicola Micciche, Italian Army; B.S., bus. admin., USC, M.A., pub. admin.; m. Monica C., Dec. 18, 1965, L.A. Dir. of Pub. Rels., Co. of L.A., 1947-55; gen. mgr., State Bureau of Sci. and Indsutry, 1955; Civil Defense Dir., City of L.A., 1951-53. Mem.: UNICO Natl., largest serv. club of Italian-Americans in U.S., pres. 1978; L.A. Breakfast Club, v.p. pgms., 1977; Publicity Club of L.A., pres. 1954; L.A. Optimist Club, pres. 1953; Commerce Assocs., USC, pres. 1961; Joachim League of St. Anne's Maternity Home, pres. 1970; Radio and TV News Assn. of So. Calif., pres. 1964. Recipient numerous awards; Publicist of the Yr., 1953; Golden Mike Award, 1952. Mem. Liberal Arts Lodge, Masonic Order, 1977; Al Malaikah Shrine, 1973. Hobby: crossword puzzles. Rec.: handball. Res.: 1616 Bluejay Way, L.A., CA 90069; Office: 1320 Biltmore Hotel, L.A., CA 90013.

MICHAELIS, RUTH
Opera Singer — Lecturer — Stage Director
b. Feb. 27, 1909, Posen, Poland; d. Sigismund and Martha (Liebusch) Michaelis; ed. pvt. Lyceum grad.; pvt. mus. stu. (piano), Conservatory of Posen; vocal training with Hans Beltz, Berlin; drama with Jeanne Robert, Berlin. Career: Began at Municipal Theatres, Halberstadt, Cottbus, Augsburg; State Opera, Stuttgart; contract, Bavarian State Opera, munich, 1939-60; tchr., Turkish State Opera Sch., Istanbul (8 mos. annually returning to Munich for Summer Opera Festivals), 1956-60; joined The Salzburg Festivals, 1942, 43, 46, 47, 58; est. res., USA, on invitation of Lotte Lehmann, to conduct her master classes, Music Acad. of the West, Santa Barbara (during Fidelio prodn.), 1961, opera-staging, Santa Barbara Civic Opera, Univ. of Calif. at Santa Barbara and Pasa. Opera Co.; tchr., individual vocal training-faculty, USC 1962-72. Guest perfs. in Lisbon, Athens, London (Covent Garden), Bordeaux, Rome, Venice, Zurich and throughout Ger.; recording artist, Bach Cantatas, Christmas Oratorio, operas, others.

Lectr., series on opera, Opera Guild of So. Calif. 1963-64, others. Author: (book) Turkish folk songs with a record of orig. folk singers (Christian Wegner Verlag Hamburg); The German Lied (Inter Nationes, Bonn); The Church Year in Song (Schirmer, N.Y.). Awards: Kammersaengerin Award, 1955; 1976 Officer's Cross of the Order of Merit of the Fed. Repub. of Germany. Mem.: German-Am. Women's Club, Munich; co-pres. Deutscher Lyceumclub, Munchen (10 yrs). Protestant. Hobby: photog. Rec.: gardening. Res.: 1930 Mission Ridge Rd., Santa Barbara, CA 93103.

MIKALSON, ROY G.
College President
b. July 21, 1921, Eureka, Mont.; s. Lawrence and Barbara Mikalson; B.A., Univ. of Washington, 1947; M.A., 1948; Ph.D., Univ. of Calif., Berkeley, 1964; m. Eva M. Johnson, July 31, 1949, Missoula, Mont.; chil.: Steven A., b. 1950; Barbara G. (Brownstone), b. 1953; Jeffrey R., b. 1959; Thomas L., b. 1960. Career: Instructor, Montana Univ., Missoula, 1948-49; instr., Lower Columbia Coll., Longview, Wash., 1950-62; Dean of evening coll., Coll. of Marin, Kentfield, Calif., 1964-66; pres., Clackemas Community Coll., Oregon City, Ore., 1966-68; pres., Modesto Jr. Coll., 1968-71; Supt.-Pres., Santa Rosa Jr. Coll., 1971---. Served AUS, Infantry, 1940-45, So. Pacific; 7 campaigns, 4 decorations. Mem.: Elks, Rotary International, Commonwealth Club. Hobby: writing. Rec.: hiking, golf, swimming. Home: 4050 Alta Vista, Santa Rosa, CA; Office: 1501 Mendocino Ave., Santa Rosa, CA 95401.

MILES, TICHI WILKERSON
Publisher
b. May 10, 1932, Los Angeles; d. Albert Clarence and Beatrice (Velderrain) Noble; ed. Sacred Heart Convent, Mex., Univ. Mexico; m. William Miles, Nov. 13, 1965; chil.: William Wilkerson, Cynthia Wilkerson. Career: publisher, editor-in-chief, Hollywood Reporter, 1962---; pres. Hollywood Reporter Corp. Mem.: exec. com. L.A. Mayor's Com. Internat. Visitors and Sister Cities, 1966---; founder, Internat. Festival Adv. Council, 1971---; named offcl. hostess, L.A., 1974; bd. dirs. Friends of Univ. So. Calif. Libraries, Inst. Advance Planning, Bd. Edn. for Sr. Adults, L.A. Music Center; exec. bd. dirs. Bilingual Children's TV; sponsor Make It on Your Own, 1976, Hollywood Reporter Key Art awards; active Motion Picture Country Home, Motion Picture and TV Relief Fund, L.A. Orphanage. Recipient award Treas. Dept., 1966; Nat. Theatre Owners award, 1967; certificate Am. Women in Radio and TV, 1968; also award distinguished philanthropic service Nat. Jewish Hosp., Denver; citation Will Rogers Hosp., O'Donnell Meml. Research Labs., Montague Library and Study Center; letter Program, Youth Opportunity Hubert H. Humphrey, 1968; Golden Flame award Calif. Press Women, 1970, Woman of the Yr. award, Girl Fridays of Show Bus., 1972; Personal Mgrs. Industry, 1976; Bronze plaque Mayor of L.A., 1972; citation L.A. City Council; Star on Wall, Hollywood C. of C., 1975; Shofar award United Jewish Appeal, 1976. Mem. Printing Industry Am., Cinema Circulus (dir.), Women of Motion Picture Industry (chmn.) Am. Women in Radio and TV (dir.), Calif. Press Women, Nat. Acad. TV Arts and Scis., UN Assn., Internat. Newspaper Promotion Assn., Western Publs. Assn., Dames des Champagne, Calif. Thoroughbreeders Assn., Hollywood C. of C. (dir. 1972---), Women in Film (founder, pres.), Los Angeles Film Industry Council (dir.), Delta Kappa Alpha. Office: Hollywood Reporter, 6715 Sunset Blvd., Hollywood, CA 90028.

MILES, WILLIAM MAUPIN
Attorney at Law
b. Aug. 11, 1909, Fresno; s. W.O. and Betty (Maupin) Miles; A.B., Univ. Calif., 1930; LL.B., Harvard Univ., 1933; m. Billie Jane Blasingame, Spet. 18, 1937, Fresno; chil.: Jimmie Lee (Whitling), b. Sept. 1941; Betsy Jane (Pavich), b. Apr. 1945; Amanda, b. Mar. 1950. Career: Admitted to Calif. Bar 1933; admitted to practice before Supreme Ct. of U.S., 1958; legal practice in Fresno, 1933-44, 1946---. Lt. USNR, 1944-46. Secty., Kings River Water Dist. Past dir.: Fresno Arts Center, Fresno Co. Tuberculosis Assn. and Heart Assn., The Downtown Club, Bonner Packing Co., Fresno Co. Legal Services, Inc. Mem.: Chi Psi frat.; Univ. of Calif. and Harvard Alumni Assns.; The Downtown Club; Fresno Co., Calif. and Am. Bar Assns.; Fellow Am. Coll. of Probate Counsel. Methodist. Res: 35885 Lodge Rd., Tollhouse, CA; Office: 2844 Fresno St., Fresno, CA 93716.

MILLER, ALEXANDER JOSEPH
Merchant — Civic Leader
b. Sept. 19, 1910, Aurora, Ill.; s. Frank J. and Martha (Lazar) Miller; ed. pub. schs., USA; m. Florence Ellen Crider; chil.: Timothy Orin, b. Jan. 27, 1952; Victoria Ann, b. Nov. 14, 1953. Career: Various banking positions, 1934-39; sales and acct. 1940-42; owner-exec. mgr., several indepenment super mkts., 1945-58; est. Tiny Tim Markets, Inc., Santa Ana, Orange Co., Calif., pres. 1958-70; pres. Mini Mart Food Stores, 1970---. USAF, 332nd S.E. Flying Training Squadron (1942-45), WW II. Awards: Kiwanian of the Yr., 1956; The Knightly Order of St. Brigitte of Sweden, 1963. Mem.: BPOE, No. 794, 1950---; Knights of Columbus, Santa Ana; Am. Legion Post No. 131, Santa Ana; bd. dirs., N. Santa Ana Kiwanis Club, 1955-58; founder-first comdr., Ambassadors Club, Santa Ana C. of C. 1956-57; chmn. membership com., Santa Ana C. of C. 1956-57, dir. 1956-60; bd. dirs., Santa Ana Boys Club, 1956-58; bd. dirs., Orange Empire Boy Scout Council of Orange Co. 1956-60; Santa Ana Planning Comm. 1956-60; trustee, Santa Ana Bd. of Edn. 1957-62; first v.p., So. Calif. Retail Grocers Assn. 1958-63; pres. Americanism Edn. League, USA 1959---; U.S. C. of C. Roman Catholic. Hobby: sculpturing. Rec.: boating, horseback riding. Res.: 2301 N. Flower St., Santa Ana, CA.

MILLER, CARL PATTERSON, SR.
Business Executive — Civic Leader
b. Oct. 30, 1897, Riley, Kan.; s. A.Q., Sr. and Martha (Patterson) Miller; B.S., Kan. State Coll. 1920; m. Marvel Mona Merillat, Sleepy Eye, Minn.; Sept. 24, 1920 (dec. Oct. 23, 1948); m. 2nd Ruth Bohe, June 5, 1950; chil.: Carl Patterson, Jr., b. Jan. 28, 1924; Martha Irene, b. Dec. 4, 1935. Career: Ed.-gen. mgr., Belleville (Kan.) Telescope, 1920-25; asst. financial ed., L.A. Times, 1925-27; mgr. L.A. ofc., N.Y. News Bur. 1927-28; secty.-gen. mgr. L.A. Stock Exch. 1928-29; v.p. Pac. Coast Edition, The Wall Street Journ., 1929-39, publ.-exec. dir. 1939-64; dir. Valencia Heights Water Co., 1942-50; dir. Covina Natl. Bank, 1945-50; pres. San Gabriel Valley Newspapers, Inc. 1945-60; dir. Gen. Telephone Co. of Calif. 1955---; chmn. Fed. Home Loan Bank of S.F. 1956-58; dir. So. Calif. Bldg. & Loan Assn. 1958---; chmn. L.A. Met. Transit Authority, 1958-59. Mem.: Natl. pres., Sigma Delta Chi, 1935, founder-pres., L.A. chpt., 1933; pres. L.A. Rotary Club, 1945-46; dir. Covina Highlands Civic Assn. 1945-50; dir. L.A. C. of C. 1949-57, v.p. 1954, pres. 1955; secty.-treas.-exec. com., Calif. Newspaper Publs. Assn. 1950; trustee, Covina Hosp. and Pomona Coll. Assn.; gov. Dist. 160, Rotary Internat. 1951-52; v.p.-dir. 1957-59, pres. 1963-64; pres. L.A. Trade Fair, Inc. 1955; pres. Ind. Planning Assn., E. San Gabriel and Pomona Valley, 1955-57; dir., L.A. Co. Fair Assn. 1955---; Masonic Lodge No. 334, 32°; Scottish rite, Shrine, Sigma Nu; Clubs: L.A. Country, Eldorado Country, Palm Desert; Balboa Bay, L.A. Press, L.A. Adv. Republican. Presbyterian. (trustee, 1944-49). Rec.: golf, yachting and travel. Res.: 1014 Kaimoku Pl., Kai Nani, Honolulu, Hawaii 96821; 553 Emerald Bay, Laguna Beach, CA.

MILLER, CLIFFORD ALBERT
President, Braun & Co.
b. Aug. 6, 1928, Salt Lake City, Ut.; s. Clifford E. and LaVeryl (Jensen) Miller; ed. Univ. Ut. 1945-49; UCLA, 1956; m. Barbara R. Anderson, June 22, 1951; chil.: Clifford Alexander, Christin Elise, Stephanie Diane. Career: Staff corr., bur. mgr., UPI, Salt Lake City, 1949-55; exec. v.p. Braun & Co., Inc., L.A. 1955-70, pres.-dir., 1970---. Pres., Admail Cons., Inc. (subsidiary), L.A., 1964; pres. Internat. Student Center, 1966-67, chmn. bd., 1968; pres. Family Serv. of L.A. 1968-69; bd. dirs., L.A. Master Chorale, 1968---; past pres., L.A. Jr. C. of C. Art Fedn.; White House Cons., 1969-72. Trustee, Repub. Assocs. 1965-68. Mem.: Skull and Bones, Pi Kappa Alpha, Sigma Delta Chi, Calif. Club. Res.: 2419 Westridge Rd., L.A., CA 90049; Office: 3055 Wilshire Blvd., Ste. 540, L.A., CA 90010.

MILLER, C. EDWARD
Oil Company Executive
b. Dec. 23, 1901, Wasco, Ore.; s. William Edward and Nancy (Pyburn) Miller; grandson of Thomas Jefferson Miller, bldr. first toll bridge in Ore. 1932; B.A., Columbia Univ., 1924; m. Nelda Sharp, Juarez, Mex., Oct. 10, 1942; chil.: C. Edward, Jr. and Diana N. Career: Est. Calif. Res. 1945; chmn. bd., Time Oil Co. 1931---; chmn. bd. Westoil Terminals Co. 1950---; v.-chmn., U.S. Oil and Refining Co., 1955---; Maj., U.S. Army; asst. dir., Foreign Div. War Prodn. Bd., WW II. Mem.: pres. L.A. Grad. Chpt., Phi Gamma Delta, 1959,

60; pres. Arthritic and Rheumatism Found. 1964; Calif. Club, L.A. Country Club. Episcopalian. Hobby: fishing, swimming. Res.: 530 Leslie Lane, Beverly Hills, CA 90210, desert home: Marrakesh Country Club; Office: 5150 Wilshire Blvd., L.A., CA 90036.

MILLER, HARRY O.
Attorney at Law
b. Aug. 26, 1931, Mattoon, Wis.; s. Harry A. and Hilda J. Miller; ed. B.S., Univ. of Wis., 1954, J.D. 1956; m. Sally Ward Culver, Manitowoc, Wis., Apr. 18, 1954; chil.: Ann Marie, b. Mar. 16, 1955; Barbara Ruth, b. Oct. 22, 1956; Sally Elizabeth, b. July 29, 1959; Shoshanna Louise, b. Mar. 22, 1962; Nathan Markham, b. Dec. 6, 1966; Mathew James, b. Aug. 13, 1968. Career: Assoc. with Langer & Cross law firm, Baraboo, Wis. 1956-59; mgr. Pension Dept., Pac. Mutual Life Ins. Co. 1959-63; dir. contracts and research, 1963-66; chief dep ins. commr., State of Calif., 1966-68; partner, Maddox & Miller, law firm, 1972-75; pres., Miller, Dorais & Wheat, 1975-78; chmn. of bd., Mille; & Daar, 1978---. Mem.: Assn. of Life Ins. Counsel, Western Pension Conf.; Bar Assns. of Calif., Wis., Beverly Hills; Town Hall of Calif., Phi Kappa Phi, Gamma Eta Gamma, Sierra Club. Hobbies: chess, gardening. Res.: 439 Beverwil Dr., Beverly Hills, CA; Office: 9100 Wilshire Blvd., Suite 720, Beverly Hills, CA 90212.

MILLER, KENNETH MICHAEL
Electronics — Industrial Executive
b. Nov. 20, 1921, Chicago, Ill.; s. Mathew and O'Tillio (Otto) Miller; ed. Ill. Inst. Tech. 1940-41; UCLA 1961; IBM Exec. Computer Course and Mfg. Exec. Sem.; m. Sally Ballingham, Pacific Palisades, Calif., June 20, 1970; chil.: Barbara Anne Woodcock, b. Jan. 12, 1946; Nancy Jeanne Hathaway, b. Mar. 31, 1951; Kenneth Michael, b. Dec. 15, 1954; Roger Allan, b. Jan. 9, 1958. Career: Gen. mgr. Lear, Inc., Lear Cal. Div., Santa Monica, 1948-60; v.p. gen. mgr. Motorola Aviation Electronics, Inc., Culver City, 1960; v.p.-gen. mgr. Daystrom, Inc., Instrumental Div., L.A. 1961; gen. mgr. The Singer Co., Metrics Div., Bridgeport, Conn., L.A. 1962-65; v.p.-gen. mgr. Lear Jet Inds. Inc., Detroit, Mich., Wichita, Kan., 1965-66; pres.-dir. Infonics, Inc., L.A. 1967-68; v.p.-gen. mgr. Computer Inds. Inc., Van Nuys, Calif. 1968-69; pres.-dir. Wilcox Electric, Inc., Kansas City, Mo. and dir. operations, Tech. Prods. Group, Am. Standard Inc. 1969-73; pres.-dir.-CEO, Penril Corp., Santa Ana, Calif. and Rockville, Md., 1973---. Seminars: IEEE Microelectronics, ICE Integrated Circuits; Stanford Research Inst. Mgmt.; Am. Mgmt. Assn. Mergers and Acquisitions; Direct Cost, Acct. and Gen. Mgmt.; WEMA Merger and Acquisitions. Aircraft pilot. Pub. Speaker. Awards: Jobmakers Award, Mfrs. Assn. of Bridgeport, 1963; feat. Leading Men in USA and Leaders in Am. Sci. Mem.: trustee, Park City Hosp.; bd. Assocs. Univ. of Bridgeport; Bridgeport Reg. Planning Council; Bridgeport Mfrs. Assn.; Detroit Bd. of Commerce; ARRL; Aircraft Owners and Pilots Assn.; Am. Inst. Aeron. and Astronautics; Am. Mgmt. Assn.; Electronics Inds. Assn.; IEEE; Instrument Soc. of Am.; Natl. Aeronautics Assn.; Soc. Non-Destructive Testing; Soc. Automotive Engrs.; A.F. Assn.; dir. Mfrs. Assn., Bridgeport; Bridgeport, Engring. Inst.; pres. Bridgeport C. of C., 1964; Am. Men of Sci. 1968---; Rolling Hills Country Club, Whicita; Algonquin Club, Bridgeport. Hobbies: flying, licensed radio amateur K6IR. Res.: 18819 Vintage St., Northridge, CA 91324; 16904 Geo. Washington Dr., Rockville, MD 20853; Office: 5520 Randolph Rd., Rockville, MD 20852.

MILLER, PAUL A.
Utility Company Executive
b. Nov. 30, 1924, S.F.; s. Robert W. and Elizabeth (Folger) Miller; A.B. Harvard Univ., 1948; sons, Robert L., Charles B., Christian F., Gordon E. Career: Staff Aide, So. Calif. Gas Co., 1948; treas., dir., Pacific Lighting Corp., 1952-58, v.p., treas., 1958-66, exec. v.p., 1966-68, pres. and chief exec. ofcr., 1968-72, chmn. of the bd., chief exec. ofcr., 1972---. Dir., Wells Fargo & Co., Wells Fargo Bank, N.A.; trustee, Mutual Life Ins. Co. of N.Y.; dir., Calif. C. of C., Music Center Opera Assn., L.A. World Affairs Council, United Way, Inc. (L.A.) and mem. bd. of govs., United Way of Am.; pres. and dir. L.A. Civic Light Opera Assn.; trustee, Am. Enterprise Inst., USC, and mem. bd. of visitors, UCLA Grad. Sch. of Mgmt. Clubs: Calif., L.A., L.A.; Pacific Union, Bohemian, S.F.; Brook, Racquet and Tennis, N.Y. Office: 810 So. Flower St., L.A., CA 90017

MILLER, LEWIS J.
Real Estate Appraiser and Consultant
b. Sept. 30, 1922, Valley Junction, Iowa; B.S., engring., UCLA, 1957; Certificate of Real Estate, UCLA Ext., 1954; Certificate of Real Estate Appraisal, 1967. Career: senior real estate appraiser and consultant, Lewis J. Miller & Associates, 1947---. Recipient Award of Merit, Nat. Assn. of Real Estate Bds., 1953. Articles pub. in profl. real estate journs., 1969-78. Mil. AUS Signal Corps and Corps of Engrs., 1943-45. Mem.: Sr. mem., Am. Soc. of Appraisers; Soc. of Am. Mil. Engrs.; Calif. Assn. of Real Estate Tchrs.; charter mem., Real Estate Certificate Inst.; Soc. of Subdiv. Appraisers; charter mem., Nat. Assn. of Review Appraisers; Am. Arbitration Assn. Nat. Panel; Am. Coll. of Real Estate Cons. Office: 8421 Wilshire Blvd., Suite 202, Beverly Hills, CA 90211.

MILLER, ROBERT CUNNINGHAM
Director Emeritus, California Academy of Sciences
b. July 3, 1899, Blairsville, Pa.; s. Coursen Herbert and Alma (Gilmore) Miller; A.B., Greenville Coll. 1920; A.M., Univ. of Calif. 1921, Ph.D., 1923; m. Lea Van Puymbroeck, Ghent, Belgium, Sept. 15, 1937. Career: Asst. prof., assoc. prof., prof. of zoology, Univ. of Wash. 1924-38; visiting prof., Lingnan Univ., Canton, China 1929-31; dir. Calif. Acad. of Scis., 1938-63; Author: The Sea and numerous mag. articles and tech. publs.; mng. ed., Pacific Discovery, 1948-63; Award: Fellows Medal, 1969. Mem.: Fellow, AAAS; secty. Pacific Div., 1944-72, pres. 1973-74; Fellow, Calif. Acad. of Scis.; Central Coast Council-chmn. Salmon Resources Com., Calif. State C. of C. 1944-45, Sardine Industry Com. 1945-46, Natural Resources Com. 1949---; chmn. Tuna Ind. Com., Calif. State Reconstr. and Re-employment Comm. 1945-47; Calif. State Marine Research Com., 1948-56; pres. Calif. Conservation Council, 1959-61; honorary state pres., Izaak Walton League 1961, 62. Hobby: bird watching, gardening. Res.: 3003 Dwight Way, Berkeley, CA 94704; Office: Calif. Acad. of Scis., Golden Gate Park, S.F., CA 94118.

MILLER, RONALD W.
Executive Vice President, Walt Disney Productions
b. Apr. 17, 1933, Los Angeles; s. John W. and Stella Miller; ed. USC; m. Diane Disney, 1954, Santa Barbara, Calif.; chil.: Christopher, b. Dec. 10, 1954; Joanna, b. Apr. 4, 1956; Tamara, b. July 3, 1957; Jennifer, b. May 8, 1960; Walter, b. Nov. 11, 1961; Ronald, Jr., b. Oct. 10, 1963; Patrick, b. Nov. 19, 1967. Career: Los Angeles Rams, 1956; 2nd asst. dir., Walt Disney Productions, 1957, asst. producer, 1960, co-producer, 1964, producer, 1967, v.p. in charge of TV and exec. producer, 1968, exec. v.p. in charge of production and creative affairs, 1976---. Bd. dir., Walt Disney Prodns., 1966---; bd. trustees, Calif. Inst. of the Arts, 1967-73. Mil. AUS, 1954-55. Mem.: Sigma Chi Frat.; Acad. of Motion Picture Arts & Sciences; Nat. Acad. of TV Arts & Sciences; USC Assocs.; Motion Picture Pioneers; Frat. of Friends of the Music Center. Episcopalian. Rec.: tennis, golf, skiing. Office: 500 S. Buena Vista, Burbank, CA 91521.

MILLER, J. RUSSELL
Magazine Publisher
b. Nov. 16, 1944, Coshocton, Oh.; s. James Franklin and Kathleen (Vickers) Millers; GGGG Gr.son, Miles Standish, 1584-1656, mil. leader of Plymouth Colony; B.B.A., Univ. Mich., 1967; MPI, USC, 1973; m. Karen Morgan, July 3, 1978, Palm Beach, Fla.; stepsons, James D. Westwood, Jr., b. Sept. 5, 1962; Joel Warner Westwood, b. Dec. 22, 1965. Career: Advt. sales, San Diego Mag., 1971; owner and pub. Applause Mag., 1976---; owner and pub., Musician's News mag., 1971---. Cons. to Calif. Real Estate Assn., Western League of Cities, Toastmasters Internat. Bd. Dir. & Pres., Western Opera Theatre; Verdi Com., San Diego Opera. Lt. j.g., USN, 1970-71, communications officer, USS Snohomish Co., USS Caroline Co. Mem.: Lambda Chi Alpha; pres. and founder, San Diego Young Execs. Club; Hunger Proj. Polit. exec. com. Wilson for Gov. 1978. Rec.: alpine skiing. Res.: 8034 Linda Vista Rd., No. 2R, San Diego, CA 92111.

MILLER, THORMUND AUBREY
Transportation Company General Counsel
b. July 14, 1919, Pocatello, Id.; s. Roy Edmund and Lillian (Thordarson) Miller; B.A., Reed Coll., 1941; LL.B., Columbia Law Sch., 1948; Advanced Mgmt. Prog., Harvard Grad. Sch. of Bus. 1961; m. Hannah A. Flansburg, Feb. 10, 1946, Portland, Ore.; chil.: Karen Lynette (Van Gerpen), b. Mar. 7, 1948; Christine Alison, b. Sept. 5, 1951. Career: admitted to Calif. Bar,

1949; Dist. of Columbia bar, 1951; U.S. Supreme Ct. bar, 1960; mem. firm McCutchen, Thomas, Matthews, Griffiths & Greene, S.F., 1948-50; with So. Pacific Transportation Co., 1950---: atty. 1950-56, asst. gen. atty. 1956-59, gen. atty. 1959-66 (all in Wash. D.C.); sr. gen. atty. 1966-74, gen. solicitor 1975-79, gen. commerce counsel ---; dir. and gen. counsel, So. Pacific Communications Co., 1973---. Dir., Tops-on-Line Services, Inc., 1970---. Lt., USNR, 1942-46; lost service Destroyer Squadron Staff. Mem.: University Club, Wash. D.C.; Commonwealth Club; San Francisco Commercial; Phi Delta Phi. Presbyterian, trustee. Res.: 228 Polhemus Ave., Atherton, CA 94025; Office: One Market Plaza, S.F., CA 94105.

MILLIGAN, A.A.
Bank President
b. Oct. 29, 1917, Oxnard; s. John Leslie and Julia (Levy) Milligan; B.A., Stanford Univ., 1938; m. Jeanne Welch, Dec. 12, 1942, Chicago, Ill.; sons, Michael Steacy, b. June 29, 1944; Marshall Craig, b. Nov. 9, 1951. Career: with Bank of A. Levy, 1940---; pres. 1955---. Pres.: Independent Bankers Assn., 1957-58; Western Independent Bankers, 1960; Calif. Bankers Assn., 1963-64; American Bankers Assn., 1977-78. Lt., USN, 1942-45. Mem.: Rotary, Oxnard, pres. 1949-50; Sigma Nu frat. Res.: 1444 Irvine Lane, Santa Barbara, CA 93108; Office: 143 W. Fifth St., Oxnard, CA 93032.

MILLIKEN, RALPH MALCOM
Former President, California Medical Association
b. Oct. 11, 1910, Crowley, La.; s. James Samuel and Grace Myrtle (Sawdon) Milliken; A.B., Pomona Coll. 1932, M.D., USC Sch. of Med. 1937; m. Alice Mae Jones, Wash., D.C., Nov. 19, 1971; chil.: Mrs. Wm. (Susan Jane) McConnell; b. Oct. 17, 1942; Ralph Malcom, Jr., b. Oct. 21, 1944. Career: Intern, St. Vincent's Hosp., L.A. 1936-37; res. 1937-38; VA Hosp., L.A. 1946-48; gen. surg., L.A. 1949---. Courtesy staff, Hosp. of Good Samaritan, L.A.; sr. staff surg. St. Vincent's Hosp.; staff surg., Calif. Hosp., chief of surg. 1963-65; attending staff, Surg. Clinic, chmn. 1967-76; staff secty.-treas. 1968, 1971-73, v. chmn. 1974, bd. trustees, 1974. Lt. Comdr. S. Pac., USNR M.C., 1944-46. Mem.: L.A. Co. Med. Assn., dist bd. govs. 1957, secty.-treas. 1968, pres. 1970, bd. trustees, chmn. 1974-75; chmn. House of Delegates, 1971-73; Calif. Med. Assn., councilor, 1969---, del. to House of Delegates, chmn. Ref. Com. 1969, Calif. Med. Polit. Action Com. Bd. Dirs. 1969---, chmn. coms. 1970---, pres. 1976-77; AMA, alternate del. to House of Delegates, 1970-74, del. 1975-76, chmn. coms. 1975; Fellow, Am. Coll. of Surg. 1950---; Cert. Am. Bd. of Surg. 1952; L.A. Surg. Soc.; pres. Med. Symposium Soc. 1958; secty. L.A. Acad. of Med. 1973---; (Civic) Exch. Club of L.A., pres. 1960; pres. Circle Ranch Found., Inc. (Boy Scout Camp), 1965, bd. trustees 1960-70, Award for Serv. to Youth, 1968. Republican. Hollywood Presbyterian Ch. Hobbies: guns, dogs. Rec.: hunting, fishing, tennis, swim. Res.: 2524 Ivanhoe, Los Angeles, CA 90039; Office: 2200 W. Third St., L.A., CA 90057.

MILLS, DON HARPER
Physician — Lawyer
b. July 29, 1927, Peking, China; s. Dr. Clarence A. (M.D., Ph.D., emeritus prof. of exp. med., Univ. of Cincinnati) and Edith C. (Parrott) Mills (Am. Cit.); bro. Russell C. Mills, Ph.D., prof. and assoc. dean, Univ. of Kan., Sch. of Med.; B.S., Univ. of Cin. 1950, M.D. 1953; J.D., USC Sch. of Law, 1958; m. Lillian Snyder, Chilicothe, Oh., June 11, 1949; chil.: Frances Jo., b. July 15, 1957; Jon Snyder, b. Feb. 18, 1962. Career: Intern, L.A. Co. Hosp. 1953-54; fellow in pathology, USC 1954-55; admitting phys., L.A. Co. Hosp. 1954-57, attending staff 1959---; asst. in pathology, Hosp. of the Good Samaritan, L.A. 1956-65, consulting staff (path.), 1962-72; affil. staff. (path.), 1972---; dep. med. examiner, L.A. Co. Coroner, 1957-61; profl. practice, forensic med. 1958---; instr. pathology, USC Sch. of Med., 1958-69; clin. prof. Path., 1969; instr.-assoc. clin. prof. legal med., Loma Linda Univ. Sch. of Med. 1960-66. Contrib. approx. 300 articles to profl. journs. 1956---; ed. bd., So. Calif. Law Reivew, USC, 1956-58; exec. bd., Trauma, 1964---; ed. cons., Journ. of Forensix Scis. 1965---. Hosp. Corps, USN, 1946-47. Awards: Peter T. Kilgore Prize, Univ. of Cinn., 1953; Mem.: Beta Theta Pi, 1944-50; Nu Sigma Nu, 1949-53; Alpha Omega Alpha, 1953---; Delta Theta Phi, 1955-58; Order of the Coif, USC 1958---; L.A., Calif., Am. Bar Assns.; AMA, Assn. of Am. Med. Colls., AAAS, Am. Judicature Soc.; traffic safety com., L.A. Co. Med. Assn. 1962-64; com., L.A. Heart Assn. 1963-65; cons. Calif. Hosp.

Assn. Medicolegal Edn. Com., Joint Calif. Med. Assn. 1963-65; cons. med. review and adv. com., Calif. Med. Assn. 1966-69; fellow, Am. Acad. of Forensic Scis., chmn. jurisprudence sect. 1966-67, gen. pgm. chmn. 1966-67. Republican. Presbyterian-Methodist. Hobby: photog. Rec.: travel. Res.: 1141 Los Altos Ave., Long Beach, CA 90815; Office: 600 S. Commonwealth Ave., L.A., CA 90005.

MILLS, JAMES ROBERT
State Senator
b. June 6, 1927, San Diego; s. William Scott and Beatrice Emily (Wrighton) Mills; B.A., San Diego State Univ., 1950; M.A., 1960; m. Joanna Rowe Rohrbough, Jan. 9, 1959, Santa Ana; chil.: Beatrice Madeleine, b. Aug. 29, 1961; William John, b. Sept. 18, 1964; Eleanor Ann, b. Mar. 4, 1966. Career: Elected to Calif. State Assembly, 1960: chmn. Rules Com., Finance and Ins. Com.; elected to State Senate, 40th Dist., 1966---: Chmn., Rules Com., chmn. Transportation Com., President Pro Tempore, 1971---. Curator, San Diego Historical Soc., 1955-60; contbg. ed., San Diego Mag., 1957-62; Author: Historic Landmarks of San Diego County, 1959; San Diego, Where California Began, 1960; The Gospel According to Pontius Pilate, 1977. Dir., AMTRAK, 1978---. AUS, 1950-53. Mem.: Blackmer Lodge, F&AM; Knights of Pythia; various C.s of C.; Am. Legion; VFW; Sierra Club. Baptist. Rec.: sailing, bicycling. Office: State Capitol, Sacto., CA 95814.

MINTZ, LEIGH WAYNE
University Dean
b. June 12, 1939, Cleveland, Oh.; s. William Michael and Laverne (Bulicek) Mintz; B.S., geology, Univ. of Mich., 1961, M.S., 1962; Ph.D., paleontology, Univ. Calif., Berkeley, 1966; m. Carol Sue Jackson, Aug. 4, 1962, Ionia, Mich.; chil.: Kevin Randall, b. June 14, 1969; Susan Carol, b. Oct. 10, 1972. Career: Asst. Prof. 1966-70, Assoc. Prof. 1970-75, Prof. of Geological Sciences, Cal. State Univ., Hayward, 1975---, Assoc. Dean of Instrn. 1969-70, Assoc. Dean of Sci. 1971-72, Dean of Undergrad. Studies, 1972---; Author: textbook, Historical Geology, 1972, 2d ed. 1977; a lab. manual in paleontology, 1970; two other books; 13 sci. papers, 1960-75. Natl. Sci. Found. Fellow. Mem.: Phi Beta Kappa, Phi Kappa Phi, Phi Eta Sigma, Kappa Sigma, Sigma Xi. Hobby: photog. Res.: 5940 Highwood Rd., Castro Valley, CA 94546; Office: Calif. State Univ., Hayward, CA 94542.

MINUDRI, REGINA URSULA
Library Director
b. May 9, 1937, San Francisco; d. John C. and Molly (Halter) Minudri; B.A., S.F. Coll. for Women, 1958; M.L.S., Univ. of Calif., Berkeley, grad. sch. of library & info. studies, 1959. Career: reference librarian, Menlo Park Pub. Lib., 1959-62; regional librarian, Santa Clara Co. Lib., San Jose, 1962-68, 1972; project coord., Young Adult Project, Mountain View, 1968-71; asst. dir., Alameda Co. Library, 1972-77; director., Berkeley Pub. Lib., 1977---; editor, adult books for young adults column, sch. library journ. 1967-76; lectr., Univ. of S.F., 1970-73; lectr., Univ. of Calif., Berkeley grad. school of Lib. & Info. Studies, 1978---. Bd. Dir., Young Adult Services Div., Am. Lib. Assn., 1972-76; bd. dir., Calif. Soc. of Librarians, 1974-78; mem. Calif. Lib. Assn. Council, 1968-72, 1974-78. Recipient: Grolier Award 1974, for outstanding lib. service to children and young adults. Hobbies: travel, music, ballet. Rec.: spectator sports. Home: 2373 Woolsey St., Berkeley, CA 94705; Office: 2090 Kittredge St., Berkeley, CA 94704.

MIRASSOU, DANIEL
Vintner
b. Jan. 2, 1945, San Jose; s. Edmund A. and Mildred Mirassou; stu., Bellarmine, Andrew Hill and Judson Prep.; studies in enology and viticulture, Fresno State Coll.; m. Mary Adams, June 5, 1972, Las Vegas, Nev.; sons, Marcel, b. Feb. 20, 1966; Maximilian, b. July 8, 1958. Career: worked for father in family vineyards (winery estab. in 1954, operated by 5 generations of Mirassous, America's oldest winemaking family and vineyards) age 6 through 20, (on and off); started a vineyard, Mirassou Properties, 1959; started San Vicente Vineyards (truck farming and vineyards), 1964; began mktg. Mirassou brand of wine nationally, 1966; bought winery, Mirassou Enterprises, 1976; (partner in all above), now v.p. mktg., Mirassou Sales Co. ---. Speaker and panel mem. on trade and consumer events, occasional appearances on TV and radio. Mem. Santa Clara Winegrowers Assn., 1970; dir., Monterey Winegrowers Council, pres. 1975, mem. Wine Inst.,

mem. Grap-Naming Com., Pub. Rels. and Advt. Com. Catholic. Hobbies: sculpture, watercolors, gardening, photog. Rec.: skiing. Res.: 3751 Yerba Buena Ct., San Jose, CA 95121; Office: 3000 Aborn Rd., San Jose, CA 95121.

MIRASSOU, EDMUND A.
President, Mirassou Vineyards
b. May 18, 1918, San Jose, Calif.; s. Peter and Justine Mirassou; m. Mildred Denevan, Feb. 14, 1939, San Jose; chil.: Peter, b. Feb. 11, 1940; Colleen (Wells), b. May 22, 1941; James, b. Mar. 26, 1943; Daniel, b. Jan. 2, 1945. Career: pres. and gen. partner, Mirassou Vineyards. Mem.: bd., Calif. State Wine Advisory Bd., 1938 until dissolution in 1975, chmn. bd., 1953-73; 2nd v.p., Wine Inst.; bd. mem., 1940---; Santa Clara Valley Water Dist., bd. 1972-76; Agri. Blue Ribbon Com.; Wine and Food Soc. of London, S.F. chpt. 1956---; Exec. Bulls, 1974---; Alexian Bros. Hosp., bd. 1968-75; Evergreen Soil Conservation Dist., 1942-55; charter mem. Evergreen Youth Center, 1948---; Serra Center, bd. 1960-65; Apptd. to State Bd. of Food and Agriculture, 72-82, advis., Dir. of Agri. and Gov.; mem. delegation to Pres. Johnson on wine indus., 1967. St. John Vianney Parish, chmn, fund raising, 1950, St. John Vianney grade sch., chmn. fund raising, 1955. Office: 3000 Aborn Rd., San Jose, CA 95121.

MIRISCH, DAVID
Promotion Firm President
b. July 24, 1935, Gettysburg, Pa.; s. Irving and Frances (Lewis) Mirisch; B.A., speech, Ripon Coll., 1958; chil.: Angela, Michael. Career: publicity, United Artists Pictures; publicity, Rogers and Cowan; advt. and publicity, Braverman-Mirisch; pres., publicity and promotion firm, David Mirisch Enterprises. Mem. Theta Chi frat., 1957-58. Rec.: sports. Office: 9911 W. Pico Blvd., No. 650, L.A., CA 90035.

MIRMAN, NORMAN J.
Founder, The Mirman School
b. Oct. 5, 1919, NYC; s. Sol and Jennie Mirman; ed. B.S. 1941, M.Ed. 1953, Ed.D. 1961; m. Beverly Marmour, New Haven, Conn., Apr. 15, 1943; chil.: Leslie Ann, b. Mar. 14, 1948; Alan Michael, b. Mar. 10, 1951. Career: Tchr., L.A. City Schs. 1952-62; relig. sch. prin. 1952-63; founder-dir. The Mirman Sch. for Gifted Chil. 1962---. Exec. bd.: Western States Univ. Coll. of Law, Beverly Coll. of Law. Contrib. articles to Gifted Child Quarterly. First Lt., USAF, 1942-46. Awards: Air Medal. Mem.: pres. Natl. Assn. For Gifted Chil. 1971-72; chmn. Synagogue Bd. of Edn. Hobbies: music, books. Rec.: tennis, travel. Res.: 126 N. Canyon View Dr., L.A.; Office: 16180 Mulholland Dr., L.A., CA 90049.

MITCHELL, HOLLY
Actress -- Show Producer
b. Evanston, Ill.; B.A. magna cum laude, theatre, TV, Univ. of Mich.; m. William (Bill) Cox, Grand Rapids, Mich.; chil.: Kerry Kevin and Mitchell Shawn. Career: spec. events program dir., Wood-TV, Grand Rapids, Mich.; currently: actress, spokeswoman: theatre, radio, TV; fashion coordinator, commentator and show producer; producer-dir., convention industrials and entertainment; owner, Holly Mitchell Presents (prodn. co. spec. in creative programming for conventions, social affairs). Former photog., fashion model. Mem.: AFTRA; Screen Actors Guild; Actor's Equity. Home: 3934 Fairbreeze Cir., Westlake Village Island, CA 91361; Office: 1616 Glendon Ave., L.A., CA 90024.

MITCHELL, JOHN H.
Film Company President
b. Apr. 27, 1918, NYC; s. Ralph and Lillian Mitchell; A.B., Economics, Univ. of Mich., 1939; m. Patricia W., 1969, NYC; dau.: Joan E. (Fletcher), b. Aug. 22, 1948. Career: with Erwin, Wasey Advt. Agency, 1939-41; Mutual Broadcasting System, 1941-46; v.p., then exec. v.p., then pres., Screen Gems, Inc., 1962-69; pres., Columbia Pictures TV, 1969-77; pres., John H. Mitchell Co. Inc., 1977---. Dir., Columbia Pictures. Lt., USN, 1942-45. Mem. Hollywood Radio & TV Soc., pres.; Acad. of TV Arts & Scis., first v.p. Office: 1888 Century Park E., Suite 1820, L.A., CA 90067.

MITCHELL, JOSEPH NATHAN
Insurance Company President
b. Oct. 10, 1922, Winnipeg, Manitoba, Canada; naturalized U.S. Citizen, 1936; s. Edward D. and Anna (Copp) Mitchell; stu., UCLA, 1940-42, Univ. of Wis.,

Univ. of Besancon, 1945; m. Beverly Henigson, Oct. 27, 1946, L.A.; chil.: Jonathan Edward, Jan Ellen, Karin Helene. Career: with Beneficial Standard Life Ins. Co., 1946---: dir. 1946---, now chmn. of bd. Chmn., exec. com., Transit Casualty Co.; chmn. bd., Fidelity Interstate Life Ins. Co.; Dir.: Beneficial Nat. Life Ins. Co.; Beneficial Nat. Corp.; British Pacific Life Ins. Co., Vancouver, B.C.; Beneficial Assurance Co.; Calif. Fed. S&L Assn.; Pacific Lighting Corp.; Beneficial Standard Mortgage Co.; Beneficial Standard Properties, Inc.; dir. and v.p., Ampal American Israel Corp., N.Y.; v.p. & treas., Jackson-Mitchell Pharmaceuticals, Inc., Santa Barbara. Cpl., AUS Signal Corps, 1942-46; European Theatres of Opns., French interpreter. Mem.: Young Presidents Orgn. 1959-72; World Bus. Council; Mayor's Steering Com. on Urban Coalition; Dist. Atty's. Adv. Council; sr. v.p., L.A. Area C. of C.; bd. mem. L.A. Safety Council; exec. com., Invest-In-Am.; 100 Club; Lincoln Club; L.A. 200 Com.; NCCJ, co-chmn. 1976; Jewish Fedn. Council Gr. L.A.; Jewish Community Found.; Cedars-Sinai Med. Center, v. chmn. bd. dirs.; United Jewish Appeal; United Way & United Crusade, bd. mem.; State of Israel Bonds; Am. Technion Soc., bd. govs.; Am. Jewish Jt. Distbn. Com., exec. com. Clubs: Hillcrest CC; Tamarisk CC; Palm Springs Tennis; Los Angeles. Hobbies: photog., golf, bridge. Res.: 1001 N. Roxbury Dr., Beverly Hills, CA 90201; Office: 3700 Wilshire Blvd., 10th flr., L.A., CA 90010.

MITTMAN, CHARLES
Medical Director, City of Hope
b. June 11, 1935, Chicago, Ill.; s. Bernard and Sylvia (Klang) Mittman; A.B., Univ. of Chicago, 1956, B.S., 1957. M.D. 1960; m. Ilene Pavelove, June 23, 1957, Chicago; sons, Scott Harvey, Brian Sheldon, Jeffrey Alan, David Saul. Career: Intern, Univ. of Chicago Clinics, 1960-61, resident, 1961; Surgeon USPHS, Nat. Heart Inst., Baltimore City Hosp., 1961-64; Asst. in Med., Johns Hopkins Univ. Sch. of Med., 1963-64; Asst. in Med., Univ. of Chicago Clinics, 1964-65; USPHS Post-Doc. Fellow, Univ. Chicago, 1965-66; Instr., Dept. of Med., Univ. of Chicago, 1966; dir., Dept. of Respiratory Disease, City of Hope Med. Center, Duarte, 1966-78, asst. med. director, City of Hope, 1977-78, exec. medical dir., 1978---. Asst. Clin. Prof. of Med., UCLA Sch. of Med., 1967-73, assoc. clin. prof. of med., 1973---. Fellow, Am. Coll. of Chest Physicians. Recipient, Distinguished Service Award, Univ. Chicago, 1979. Mem.: L.A. Lung Assn., pres. 1977-78. Jewish, pres. Foothill Temple, 1976. Hobbies: photog., hiking. Office: 1500 E. Duarte Rd., Duarte, CA 91010.

MOCK, RICHARD M.
Engineer — Executive
b. July 28, 1905, NYC; s. Dudley M. and Sadie (Danneberg) Mock; B.S. on M.E., Daniel Guggenheim Sch. of Aerons., Coll. of Engring., NYU, June 1927; m. Claire Gasper, Elkton, Md., Mar. 7, 1938; chil.: Barbara Joan, b. Oct. 21, 1940. Career: Experimental Dept., Ware Radio Corp., NYC 1925; Leoning Aeron. Engring. Corp., NYC, 1926; tech. ed., Aviation Mag. 1927-28; proj. engr.-asst. to pres., Bellanca Aircraft Corp., New Castle, Del. 1928-29; proj. engr., Heinkel Aircraft Co., Ger. 1929-30; tech. repr. (ofc. at Douglas Aircraf Co., Santa Monica), Fokker Aircraft Co., Netherlands, 1931-40; sales mgr. electro-mech. div.-mgr. Calif. div., Lear, Inc. 1940-42, chief engr. 1942-45, mgr. electro-mech. div. 1945-47, exec. v.p. 1947-48, pres. 1948-59, chmn. exec. com. 1957-61; dir. exec. com., chmn. acquisition com. 1961-62 (name changed to Lear Siegler Inc.); bd. dirs.-exec. com. Aeronca Inc. 1965---. Dir.: Astek Instrument Corp., Astrodata, Inc. and Digitronics Corp., 1961-64, mem. bd. & exec. com. Servo-Mechanisms Inc. 1962-64 (now Teledyne), mem. bd. of Astrodata Inc. 1961-66, mem. bd. of Spacerays, Inc. 1965-68, mem. bd. Solany Industries, 1963-67, mem. bd. and chmn. bd.-dir. Stereo Tape Club of The Month, Inc. 1969-70. mem. bd. Dr. Pepper Bottling, So. Calif. 1976-77. Contrib. articles on electronics and bus. mgmt. to various tech. publs.; ed. adv. com. (instruments), Aero/Space Engring. Mag. Mem.: Am. Inst. of Elec. Engrs., Am. Ordnance Assn.; Registered Profl. Engr., State of Oh.; adv. com., Coll. of Engring.; Daniel Guggenheim Sch. of Aerons., NYU; assoc. fellow, Inst. of Aeron. Scis.; Instrument Soc. of Am., Am. Rocket Soc., Def. Orientation Conf. Assn., Assn. of U.S. Army; So. Calif. adv. bd., Liberty Mutual Ins. Co.; dir.-chmn., West L.A. Council, Jr. Achievement of L.A.; trustee-mem. exec. com, City of Hope, L.A.; assoc. Soc. of Automotive Engrs.; Tau Beta Pi; natl. panel, Am. Arbitration Soc.; chmn. L.A. Co. Heart Assn. 1977-78; mem. bd. dir., Am. Heart Assn. (natl.). Hobby: photog., fishing. Res.: 3029 Corda Dr., Bel Air, CA 90049.

MOHR, MILTON E.
President, Quotron Systems, Inc.
b. Apr. 9, 1915, Milwaukee, Wis.; s. Henry O.C. and Agnes (Schellenberg) Mohr; B.S.E.E., Univ. of Nebr., 1938, (hon.) Dr. of English, 1959; chil.: Lawrence H., b. Oct. 8, 1945; Douglas C., b. July 14, 1943. Career: communication research, Bell Telephone Labs., Inc., NYC, 1938-50; dept. head, radar lab., Hughes Aircraft Co., Culver City, 1950-54; v.p., Thompson Ramo Wooldridge, Inc., Canoga Park, gen. mgr. RW div., TRW Computers Co. 1954-65; v.p., gen. mgr., def. systems div., Bunker-Ramo Corp., 1965-66, pres. chief exec. officer corp. 1966-70; pres., chief exec. officer, Quotron Systems, Inc., 1970---. Recipient: hon. mention as outstanding young elec. engr. Eta Kappa Nu, 1948. Fellow IEEE; mem. Am. Inst. Aeros. and Astronautics; Pi Mu Epsilon; Sigma Tau; Eta Kappa Nu. Office: 5454 Beethoven St., L.A., CA 90066.

MOHR, MILTON ERNST
President, Quotron Systems
b. Apr. 9, 1915, Milwaukee, Wis.; s. Henry O.C. and Agnes (Schellenberg) Mohr; B.S., Univ. of Nebr. 1938, (hon.) D.Eng. 1959; m. Vyvian M. Crane, June 7, 1938; sons: Lawrence H., b. Oct. 8, 1945; Douglas C., b. July 14, 1943. Career: Communication research staff, Bell Telephone Labs., NYC 1938-50; dept. head, radar lab., Hughes Aircraft Co., Culver City, 1950-54; v.p.-gen. mgr., TRW Computer Div., Thompson Ramo Wooldridge, Inc. 1954-64; v.p. The Bunker-Ramo Corp. 1964-66, v.p. 1966-70; pres. Quotron Systems, Inc. 1970---. Awards: hon. mention, Outstanding Young Electrical Engr., Eta Kappa Nu, 1949. Mem.: fellow, Inst. of Elec. and Electronics Engrs. 1936---; Sigma Tau, 1937---; Pi Mu Epsilon, 1937---; Eta Kappa Nu, 1949---; N.Y. Acad. of Scis. 1952---; Natl. Aviation Assn.; Am. Inst. of Aerons. and Astronautics, Inc. 1958---. Office: 5454 Beethoven St., L.A., CA 90066.

MONGAN, MARTIN
Public Official
b. Nov. 7, 1908, S.F.; s. Patrick and Sarah Mongan; A.B., Univ. of Calif., Berkeley, 1930; bus. adm., Univ. of S.F. 1945-49; m. Audrey V. Cunningham, S.F., Oct. 22, 1938; chil.: Thomas, b. Nov. 17, 1939; James, b. Apr. 10, 1942; Margaret, b. Aug. 6, 1944. Career: Cashier-chief dep. county tax collector, S.F. 1943-47; S.F. Co. Clerk, 1947---; S.F. Co. Recorder, 1960---. Mem.: pres. S.F. Municipal Execs. Assn. 1952-53; S.F. Bar Assn., Univ. of Calif. Alumni Assn., Commonwealth Club of S.F. Democrat. Catholic. Hobby: gardening, golf. Res.: 2237 17th Ave., S.F.; Office: 312 City Hall, S.F., CA 94102.

MONIHAN, WILLIAM JOSEPH
Library Relations Director
b. Nov. 14, 1914, S.F.; s. William Joseph and Helen May (Hunter) Monihan; M.A. (philosophy), Gonzaga Univ. 1939; Licentiate in Sacred Theol., Alma Coll. 1946. Career: Entered Soc. of Jesus, 1932, ordained to priesthood, Roman Catholic, 1945. Librn., Univ. of S.F., 1947-64, dir. of libs., 1964-66, dir. lib. rels. 1966---. Mem.: Am. and Calif. Lib. Assns.; Roxburghe Club of S.F. 1961; Zamorano Club, L.A. 1965; Grolier Club, N.Y., 1967. Res.: Univ. of S.F., S.F., CA; Office: Xavier Hall, Univ. of S.F., Golden Gate and Parker Ave., S.F., CA 94117.

MONTGOMERY, GEORGE C., II
Attorney at Law — Executive
b. Sept. 17, 1933, Salinas, Calif.; s. George C. and Edith (Parise) Montgomery; B.A., USC, 1956; LL.B., Loyola Law Sch., 1959, J.D.; m. 2d. Christina Di Meglio, Nov. 17, 1978, Los Angeles; chil.: George C. III, b. Oct. 25, 1959; Susan E., b. Sept. 10, 1960; James E., b. Jan. 23, 1962; John M. and Robert E. (twins), b. June 19, 1963. Career: pvt. practice of law, 1960---: founder, sr. mem., Montgomery, Bottum, Regal & McNally, currently pres. and chmn. bd.; pres., chmn. bd.; George C. Montgomery Enterprises; C.G. Regent Investments, Inc.; v.p., Norso Distbrs., 1962-77; v.p., Biota Internat., 1970-77; dir., Trans Pacific Drug Co. Ltd., 1972-78. Mil. Capt. AUS, 115th CIC, 1953-55. Mem.: ABA; Am. Judicature Soc.; Phi Delta Phi, Magister, 1958-59; Riviera Country Club; Rancho Las Palmas Country & Tennis Club. Young Republicans; Republican Nat. Com. Roman Catholic. Hobbies: flying, sailing, writing. Rec.: golf, tennis. Home: 536 N. Rockingham Ave., L.A., CA 90049; Office: 1100 Glendon Ave., L.A., CA 90024.

MONTGOMERY, JAMES FISCHER
President, Great Western Financial Corp.
b. Nov. 30, 1934, Topeka, Kan.; s. James Maurice and Frieda Ellen (Fischer) Montgomery; B.A., UCLA 1957; m. Linda Jane Hicks, Nev., Aug. 25, 1956; chil.: Michael James, b. Nov. 11, 1962; Jeffrey Allen, b. July 19, 1964; Andrew Steven, b. Sept. 2, 1966; John Gregory, b. Nov. 2, 1969. Career: Asst. to the pres. Great Western Financial Corp. 1960-64; pres.-dir. United Financial Corp. and Citizens S&L Assn. 1964-75; pres.-dir.-chief opr. ofcr. Great Western Financial Corp. and Gr. Western S&L Assn. 1975---. Dir.: Savings Assn. Central Corp., Calif. Taxpayers' Assn.; (past) Calif. S&L League, Inner City Housing Corp., Assoc. Bldg. Ind., trustee, UCLA Fdn., Svs. Assns. Mortgage Co., Inc. U.S. Army, 1958-60. Mem.: Los Angeles Country Club, California Club. Rec.: golf, tennis. Office: 8484 Wilshire Blvd., Beverly Hills, CA 90211.

MONTGOMERY, ROBERT BRUCE
Drilling Company President
b. Aug. 21, 1920, Palo Alto; s. Chester A. and Lena (Talboy) Montgomery; A.B., Stanford Univ. 1947; m. Ruth Ann Greene, Calabasas, Calif., June 24, 1950; chil.: Melinda Ann, b. 1952; Marilee Ruth, b. 1953; Robert Bruce, Jr., b. 1954. Career: Nelson Howard Co. 1948-49; Thomas Pike Drilling Co. 1950-53; secty-treas., Casey & Montgomery Drilling, Inc. 1953-58; pres. R.B. Montgomery Drilling, Inc., 1958---; owner: Montgomery Citrus Ranch, Deer Creek Horse Ranch; owner, AMC Drilling, Inc., Calgary, Can. Lt., USN (1942-47), WW II. Mem.: Balboa Bay Club; dir. Stockdale Country Club of Bakersfield, 1958; dir. Bakersfield Country Club, 1958-62, pres. 1960; Rancheros Vistadores, Petroleum Club of Bakersfield, Petroleum Club of L.Aa., Jonathan Club of L.A. Episcopalian. Hobby: golf, hunting. Rec.: boating. Res.: 7211 Meadowbrook Lane, Bakersfield, CA 93309; Office: 3504 Standard Rd., Bakersfield, CA.

MONTGOMERY, RUTH ANN
Educator — Club and Civic Leader
b. May 15, Bisbee, Ariz.; d. Roy T. and Ethel (Bonner) Greene; A.B., Stanford Univ.; USC; Univ. of Mex. Grad. Sch.; m. Robert Bruce Montgomery, Los Angeles, June 24, 1950; chil.: Melinda Ann, b. Feb. 22, 1952; Marilee Ruth, b. Feb. 8, 1953; Robert Bruce, Jr., b. Nov. 6, 1954. Career: Educator-Counselor, L.A. City Schs. 1946-50. Mem.: pres. L.A. Jr. Alumnae Assn. of Alpha Phi, 1946; bd. dirs., League of Crippled Chil., L.A. 1948-50; pres. 1950; founder-pres., Assistance League of Bakersfield, 1956-59; Bakersfield Mem. Hosp. Aux., Mercy Hosp. Aux. 1957---; bd. dirs., Kern Philharmonic Assn. 1959-60; dir. regional council, Natl. Assistance Leag. 1959-61, secty-treas. 1961-63; pres. Alpha Phi Alumnae Assn. 1961-64; past pres.-bd. dirs., Stanford Club of Kern Co.; Repub. Women of Kern Co., Local Aid Bd., Alpha Phi, Pi Lambda Theta; AAUW, Bakersfield Country Club, Stockdale Country Club, Jonathan Club, Balboa Bay Club, Valley Club and Birnum Wood, Santa Barbara; Awards: Kern Panhellenic Woman of Yr., 1957; Unique Serv. Award, Natl. Asst. League, 1960. Episcopalian. Rec.: golf, bridge. Res.: 7211 Meadowbrook Lane, Bakersfield, CA 93309.

MOODY, GEORGE FRANKLIN
Executive V.P., Security Pacific National Bank
b. July 28, 1930, Riverside, Calif.; s. William Clifford and Mildred E. (Scott) Moody; student, Riverside City Coll., 1948-50; grad. (honors), Pacific Coast Banking Sch., 1963; m. Mary Jane Plank, Jan. 19, 1950, Riverside; chil.: Jeffrey George, b. May 21, 1952; Jane Ellen Fowler Moody, b. Mar. 27, 1954; John Franklin, b. Aug. 29, 1956; Joseph William, b. Feb. 6, 1961. Career: bus. office, Univ. of Calif., Riverside, 1950-52; with Security Pacific National Bank, 1953; v.p., personnel director, Los Angeles; sr. v.p., Inland Div. Adminstrn., 1970-71; exec. v.p., 1971-73. Mem. and bd. dir.: Exec. Com., Los Angeles C. of C., v.p. Trade/Transport. Council; M & M Assn., vice chmn. bd.; YMCA; Hollywood Presbyterian Med. Center; Nat. Conference Christians and Jews; Hacienda Golf Club; pres., Colo. River Assn. Presbyterian ch., elder. Home: 1726 Heather Hill Rd., Hacienda Hts., CA 91745; Office: 333 South Hope St., (H54-10), Los Angeles, CA 90071.

MOORE, CHRISTINE ERIKSON
Educator — Executive
b. Mar. 21, 1944, Chicago, Ill.; d. Carl A., Jr. and Suzanne (Calcutt) Erikson; grandau. of Carl A. Erikson, noted architect; B.M. Music, SMU, 1966; tchr. credential, Cal. State Univ. Sacto., 1972; m. Jerry M. Moore, July 19, 1970; Hinsdale, Ill.; dau. Lindsay, b. Aug. 22, 1975.

Career: camp counselor, Minne Wonka Lodge, Three Lakes, Wis., summers, 1963-69; secty. AP, Dallas, 1966-67; music tchr., Rio Linda Union Sch. Dist., 1967-71; partner, mgr., Erikson-Moore Suisun (real estate rental co.) Suisun City, 1971---. Named Outstanding Spiritual Woman, Fairfield Women's Com., 1976; Mem.: Christian Community Resource Vols., 1973-75; AAUW, Calif. Div. Group effectiveness training team, 1974-77; pres. Fairfield chpt. 1975-76; Delta Gamma. Republican. Christian Sci. Rec.: tennis, golf. Office: 25 Country Club Dr., Suisun City, CA 94585.

MOORE, EUDORAH M.
Crafts Coordinator, National Endowment for the Arts
b. June 15, 1918, Denver, Colo.; d. Bradish P. and Anna Reynolds (Garvey) Morse; A.B., Smith Coll., Northampton, Mass.; m. Anson Churchill Moore, July 2, 1940, Denver, Colo.; chil.: William A. II, b. 1942; Anna M. (Valeri), b. 1944; Anson C., Jr., b. 1954; Reynolds M., b. 1958. Career: Curator Design, Pasadena Art Museum 1961-71; director, California Design, 1971-78; crafts coordinator, Nat. Endowment for the Arts, 1978---. Pres. and founder, Pasadena Art Alliance, 1954; pres. bd. of trustees, Pasadena Art Mus., 1956-61. Res.: 1080 Glen Oaks Blvd., Pasadena, CA 91105; Office: NEA Visual Arts, 2401 E Street N.W., Washington, D.C. 20506.

MOORE, GORDON EARLE
President, Intel Corporation
o. Jan. 3, 1929, San Francisco; s. Walter and Florence Moore; B.S., Univ. Calif., Berkeley, 1950; Ph.D., Calif. Inst. of Tech., 1954; m. Betty I. Whittaker, Sept. 9, 1950; chil.: Kenneth G., b. Dec. 8, 1954; Steven E., b. Oct. 28, 1959. Career: Johns Hopkins Univ., 1954-56; Shockley Lab., 1956-57; Fairchild Semiconductor, 1957-68; president and chief exec. officer, Intel Corp., Santa Clara, 1968---. Dir.: Micro Mask, Inc.; Silverking Oceanic Farms, Inc. Hobby: fishing. Office: 3065 Bowers Ave., Santa Clara, CA 95051.

MOORE, PHYLLIS J.C.
City Librarian
b. Jan. 31, 1927, Binghamton, N.Y.; d. John Oscar and Gladys J. (Tilbury) Clark; B.A. honors Eng. lit., Hartwick Coll., 1949; M.S. (L.S.), Syracuse Univ., 1954; M.A. cum laude, Yeshiva Univ., 1968; Ph.D., Colo. State Univ., 1973; m. R. Scott Moore, Sept. 14, 1974, Falls Church, Va. Career: Librarian 1, Free Library of Phila., Pa., 1954-57; main lib., command libn., U.S. Govt., Spec. Services, Lib. Div., Europe, 1957-62; sr. libn. II, Yonkers, N.Y., Pub. Lib. 1962-67; dir., Hastings-on-Hudson, N.Y., Publ. Lib., 1967-68; cons., Westchester Country Lib. System, N.Y., 1968-72; dir., Falls Church (Va.) Pub. Lib., 1972-77; city librarian, Alameda (Ca.) Free Lib., 1978---. Recipient: Elliott Howell Reed Memorial Award (Language & Lit.), 1959; Community Svc. awards; Tournament of Plays, Best Actress, 1958,59,60, Best Orig. Writing. Mem.: Nat. Humane Soc., adv. bd., 1968---; Metropolitan Opera Guild; Am. Film Festival, Juror, 1968-72; Am. Film Inst.; Nat. Commn. of Fine Arts, exec. bd.; Internat. Oceanographic Found.; Am. Lib. Assn., exec. council, 1975-79; Mask and Lute (Nat. honor soc., dramatics), pres., 1974-78-; Bay Area Library System, chmn., 1978---; D.A.R.; Gamma Phi Delta; Sigma Alpha Iota; Alpha Psi Omega; Epsilon Delta Chi; AAUW; League of Women Voters (Council); Defenders of Wildlife, adv. bd. Presbyterian ch., deacon. Hobbies: writing, music, art, theatre. Rec.: gardening, nature walks, sports. Home: 1151-C Park Ave., Alameda, CA 94501; Office: Alameda Free Library, Oak and Clara Ave., Alameda, CA 94501.

MOORE, RUSSELL JAMES
Art Museum Director
b. Jan. 13, 1947, Stockton; s. Robert Bryce and Marjorie Ann (Rinaudo) Moore; rel., John Bauer, composer and conductor; B.A., art hist., Univ. Calif., Davis, 1969; M.A., UCLA, 1972; student, Harvard Univ. Inst. in Arts Administration, 1977; m. Pamela Crossley, Aug. 10, 1974, Lodi, Calif. Career: Gallery Asst., Art Collector's Gallery, Beverly Hills, 1969-71, Multiples Art Gallery, Los Angeles, 1970-71; Asst. Curator, Utah Mus. of Fine Arts, Univ. of Utah, Salt Lake City, 1972-74; Curator, Bowdoin Coll. Mus. of Art, Brunswick, Me., 1974, acting dir. 1976-78; Director, Long Beach Mus. of Art, 1978---. Catholic. Office: Long Beach Museum of Art, 2300 East Ocean Blvd., Long Beach, CA 90803.

MOORE, WILLIAM ESTILL, JR.
Rancher — Business Executive
b. Dec. 19, 1920, Bowling Green, Ky.; s. William E. and Carolyn (Elkin) Moore; B.A. (econs. and chem.), Stanford Univ. 1942; m. Margaret Shanks, N.J. 1951; chil.: Carrol Meteer, b. 1952; William Estill, III, b. 1954; Marilyn Taylor, b. 1956; Thomas Edwin, b. 1959; James Rogers, b. 1964. Career: Asst. to the president, Tejon Ranch Co. 1947-48, v.p. 1948-59, dir., exec.v.p. 1958, pres.-chief exec. ofcr. 1960, exec. cons. 1970---; v.p. Chandler Sherman Corp. 1949-56, pres. 1956-70; dir. Arvin-Edison Water Storage Dist. 1953, secty. 1967-71; dir. Title Ins. & Trust Co. 1956---, exec. com. 1957---, investment com. 1959---; dir. Wheeler Ridge-Maricopa Water Storage Dist. (charter) 1959---, secty. 1968---; (charter) dir. Heritage S&L Assn. 1963---; (charter) dir. Tejon-Castaic Water Dist. 1965---; (charter) dir. Pac. Western Industries, Inc. 1965---; dir. Pioneer Natl. Title Ins. Co. 1966---; dir. Kings Co. Development Co. 1967, exec. cons. 1971---; exec. com. The TI Corp. 1968---; pres.-dir., Rowland Land Company. Lt. Col., USMC (ret.), WW II. Awards: (cits.) Navy Cross, Silver Star, Purple Heart, Letters of Commendation. Mem.: resident adv., Delta Upsilon, 1946-47; dir.-v.p.-exec. com., Water Assn. of Kern Co. 1954---, pres. 1970---; dir. Kern Co. Water Comm. 1955, pres. 1966; Food and Wine Soc. of London, 1955---; dir. California Water Resources Assn. 1956---, secty.-treas. 1962---; dir.-exec. com., So. Calif. Water Coord. Conf. 1958---; Young Pres's. Orgn. 1961; dir.-exec. com.-policy com., Irrigation Dists. Assn. 1961---; dir.-exec. com. United Community Fund, 1963---; trustee, Natl. Devil Pups, Inc. 1967---. Republican (delegate State Central Committee 1958-60). Presbyterian. Hobby: sports, internat. affairs. Rec.: golf, tennis, marksmanship. Res. 2930 22nd St., Bakersfield, CA 93301; Office: 3120 18th St., Bakersfield, CA 93301.

MOORHEAD, CARLOS J.
United States Congressman
b. May 6, 1922, Long Beach; s. Carlos A. and Florence Moorhead; B.A., UCLA, 1943; J.D., USC, 1949; m. Valery Tyler, July 19, 1969. Career: Atty. at law, Glendale, 1949---; elected Assemblyman, 43rd Dist., Calif. Legislature, 1967-72; U.S. Housy of Reps. (Judiciary Com., Claims and Govt. Rels.), 1972---. House Committee on Judiciary, ranking member on Subcommittee of Administrative Law & Government Relations; House Interstate & Foreign Commerce Committee, subcommittee of Energy and Power and Communic ations. Inf. ofcr., U.S. Army, 1943-46; Lt. Col., Res. Judge Advocate Gen. Corp, WW II. Mem.: Past pres. Glendale Bar Assn.; past pres. Glendale Acacia Hi-12 Club; BPOE, Glendale Lodge No. 1289; Meridian Lodge, No. 667, F&AM; Glendale Shrine Club; mem. Calif. Law Review Commn. 1969-73; past pres. 43rd Dist. Calif. Repub. Assn. 1959. Presbyterian. Res.: 1106 N. Louise St., Glendale, CA 91207; Office: 420 N. Brand Blvd., Suite 404, Glendale, CA 91203; Rm. 1208 Longworth House Ofc. Bldg., Wash. D.C. 20515.

MORETTI, ROBERT
Consultant
b. June 3, 1936, Detroit, Mich.; s. Marino and Mary Moretti; ed. grad. (magna cum laude) Notre Dame H.S., Sherman Oaks, Calif. 1954; grad. Univ. Notre Dame (stu. govt. ofcr. 3 yrs.), South Bend, Ind., June 1958; m. Marilyn Ann Stoko; chil.: Michael, Matthew, Marina, Leslie. Career: Mfg. cos., Glendale, 1958-63; elected to Calif. Legislature, 1963-74; Assembly Rules Com. 1965; chmn. Finance and Ins. Com. (1st freshman legislator in hist.), 1966, mem. 1970; chmn. Govt. Orgn. Com.; mem. Revenue and Tax Com., Subcom. on Unemployment Ins. and Govt. Efficiency and Cost Control; speaker, Calif. State Assembly, 1971-74; candidate for Gov. 1974; State Energy Comm. 1975-78; dir. Internat. Cons. firm, 1977---. Lectr.: Univ. Ill., Univ. Calif. at Riverside, Eagleton Inst. of Politics, Rutgers Univ. Awards: Outstanding Freshman Legislator by Capitol Press Corps, 1965; one of 36 state legislators chosen from USA to attend Eagleton Inst. of Politics, Rutgers Univ. (seminar on upgrading state legislatures). Mem.: PTA, C. of C., Moose, OPtimists Club; adv. staff, BSA, Notre Dame Alumni Assn. Democrat. Catholic. Rec. : golf, tennis, basketball. Res.: CA.

MORELLI, ROBERT MICHAEL
Psychiatrist -- Author
b. Sept. 26, 1938, Bell, Calif.; s. Albert and Flora Morelli; B.S., 1960; M.D., 1964; Psychiatry, 1969-72; m. Nomi Borenstein, Sept. 9, 1974, La Habra Hts., Calif.; chil.: Monique Caroline, b. Jan. 8, 1968; Vanessa Paula, b. July 12, 1971. Career: Internship, Santa Clara Co. Hosp.,

1964-65; So. Calif. Permanente Med. Group, Bellflower, 1967-69; staff psychiatrist, Trailback Lodge of Long Beach, 1972-73; pres., More Inst., 1973-75; physician, Hollywood Med. Clinic, 1975; staff psychiatrist, Sunset So. Calif. Permanente Med. Group, 1975; pvt. practice, G.P., Los Angeles, 1975-77; med. dir. of drug abuse program, Metropolitan State Hosp. 1972-73; Morehouse Med. Clinic, Brea, Calif., 1977---; pres., Winners Co., 1978---. Author: Winning, Creating a Successful Lifestyle, 1978; Columnist, L.A. Woman's Magazine; L.A. radio: KOST-FM, KUTE-FM. Mil. USAF, Azores, Portugal, 1605th, USAF Hosp., 1965-67. Hobbies: hist., biography, philosophy, liberal arts. Home: 655 N. Brea, No. 10, Brea, CA 92621; Office: 739 S. Brea Blvd., Brea, CA 92621.

MORGAN, JACOB RICHARD
  Cardiologist
b. Oct. 10, 1925, E. St. Louis, Ill.; s. Clyde A. and Jennie Ella Henrieta (Van Ramshorst) Morgan; B.S. (honors) pharmacy, Univ. of Texas, 1953; M.D. (hon.), 1957; cardiology fellowship, Scripps Clin. & Research Found., La Jolla, 1967-68; m. Alta Eloise Ruthruff, Aug. 1, 1953, Richmond, Calif.; chil.: Elaine Louise (Delovich); Stephen Richard. Career: chief of med., U.S. Naval Hosp., Taipei, 1962-64; staff, internal med., U.S. Naval Hosp., San Diego, 1964-67, chief of cardiology, 1969-73; prof. med. and assoc. chmn., Dept. of Med., Texas Tech Univ. Sch. of Med., 1973-75; dir. cardiology, Paradise Valley Hosp., National City, 1976---. Contbd. 35 articles on heart disease, nat. med. journs., 1970---; 16 presentations, nat. med. meetings. Mil.: Naval line officer, 1943-46, 1950-53, Naval Med. Officer, 1957-53; ret. Capt. USN, 1973. Mem.: Am. Heart Assn.; Fellow: Am. Coll. of Physicians, Am. Coll. of Cardiology, Am. Coll. of Chest Physicians, Council on Clinical Cardiology. Home: 9881 Edgar Pl., La Mesa, CA 92041; Office: 2400 E. 4th St., National City, CA.

MORGENTHALER, HELEN MARIE
  President, The Morgenthaler Co.
b. Apr. 9, Chicago; d. Albert Mitchell and Clara (Mattes) Morgenthaler; gr.-granddau. of Johann Matsch, Prince of Pisein, Austria; desc.: Oliver St. John, aide-de-camp to William the Conqueror; King Henry VII of Eng.; gr.-granddau. of Lord John St. John, 12th Earl of Blendshoe, Ire.; Lord John Somers, High Chancellor, Great Brit., rewriter Anglo-Saxon Code of Laws, others; ed. Miss Orton's Sch. for Girls, Pasa.; USC. Career: designer, flora appliques and secty. Pioneer Wall Paper Co., L.A. 1940-49; pres. Clara Somers Co. (mfrs.-designers resort wear) 1950-59; pres. The Morgenthaler Co. (mgr., designers, importer of Oriental handpainted wall murals, silk wall coverings; factories in Seoul, Korea, Shimizu, Japan, Hong Kong), 1960---. Patents: design on unique belt designs, 1949; invented process to permanently dye fiber woven wall covering, 1957. Mem.: Assistance League of So. Calif., chmn. Gift Shop display; founder, Pasa. Guild of Chil's. Hosp., chmn. Thrift Shop, 1961, chmn. Doll Fair, Chil's. Hosp., L.A.; founder (life) L.A. Orphanage Guild; patroness, Athenaeum of Calif. Inst. Tech., Pasa.; Town Hall of Calif.; L.A. World Affairs Council; San Marino Woman's Club. Hobbies: garden, astrology, cruising, exploring-travel unusual countries. Res.: 1730 West Drive, San Marino, CA 91108.

MORKETTER, ROBERT STANLEY
  Industrial Executive — Engineer
b. Jan. 9, 1924, Whittier; s. George Henry and Ruth Sybyl (Fulbright) Morketter; cousin, Senator William Fulbright, Ark.; B.S. (M.E.), Univ. of Calif., Berkeley, 1948; (adv. bus.) Univ. of Wash. 1953; m. Josephine Crane, Oakland, Calif., Dec. 9, 1949; chil.: Robert Stanley, Jr., b. 1951; Cynthia Ann, b. 1953; Thierry Crane, b. 1959. Career: Assoc. with Proctor and Gamble Mfg. Co., 1948-53; chief ind. engr., Air Material Command, Sacto., Calif. 1954-56; Internat. Atlas Servs., Div. of Atlas Corp. 1957---, plant mgr., Oakland, 1957-58, gen. mgr. 1958, Paris, France, 1958-63, Oakland, 1964---, v.p. 1961-66, pres. 1967---; pres. Global Assocs. (subsidiary of IAS), 1964---; dir.: Serima, France, 1959; Babb Co. Ltd., Great Brit. 1960; Babb Sarl, France, 1960; chmn. Global Assoc., USA 1964. Pac. Theater, U.S. Army (1943-46), WW II. Mem.: pres. Skull and Keys, 1947; Tau Beta Pi, 1947; chpt. pres., Kappa Sigma, 1948; dir. Big C Soc. 1956-58; Chevalier de Tastevin, France, 1963; Oakland C. of C; Commonwealth Club of Calif. Republican. Episcopalian. Hobby: underwater photog. Res.: 124 Waldo Ave., Piedmont, CA 94612; Office: 2010 Webster St., Oakland, CA.

MORRELL, JAMES WILSON
  Corporate Executive
b. Feb. 13, 1931, Kalamazoo, Mich.; s. Wilson and Evelyn Morrell; B.A., Kalamazoo Coll.; m. Marylyn Eck, June 21, 1952; chil.: Martha, b. May 2, 1956; David, b. June 10, 1958. Career: with Saga Corp., 1955---: mgr., Kalamazoo Coll., 1955-58; dist. mgr., Mich. dist. coll. div., 1958-62; regional v.p., Coll. Div. (mid-west region), 1962-66; v.p. administrn., Saga Corp., 1966-68; exec. v.p. of adminstrn., 1968-70; pres., Scope Corp., 1970-71; pres., Saga Enterprises, Inc., 1971-78; exec. v.p. and chief operating officer, Saga Corp., 1978---. Bd. dir., Resource Center for Women. AUS, 1953-55. Mem.: Young President's Orgn.; Am. Mgmt. Assn., former dir. Hobby: photog. Rec.: tennis. Res.: Two Mesa Ct., Atherton, CA 94025; Office: One Saga Lane, Menlo Park, CA 94025.

MORRIS, DE WITT FRANKLIN
  Recording Company Executive
b. June 20, 1918, Grand Mound, Wash.; s. Frank W. and Winifred E. (Dove) Morris; ed. pub. schs.; grad. Radio & Television Inst., Chicago (correspondence); student: Wash. State Coll.; USC; Univ. of Calif.; m. Ethel Rawson, July 11, 1937, Centralia, Wash.; chil.: Roger Alan, b. June 7, 1938; Ronald Scott, b. Mar. 16, 1940. Career: engr., announcer, radio station KELA, Centralia, Chehalis, Wash., 1937-40, chief engr., 1940-42; engr., Associated Broadcasters, San Francisco, 1942-45; chief engr., Universal Recorders of Calif., Hollywood 1945-58; exec. v.p. and dir., United Recording Corp., Hollywood, 1958---. Dir.: United Recording Electronics Industries, Coast Recorders, Inc. Contbr. Audio Engring. Soc. Journ., 1977. Fellow, Audio Engring. Soc., 1975, western v.p., 1974-75; Mem.: Magnolia Park Lodge No. 715, F. & A.M., Jr. deacon, 1977, se. deacon, 1978. jr. warden, 1979. Protestant. Hobbies: flying, photog. Rec.: golf, fishing, gardening. Home: 11916 Salem Dr., Granada Hills, CA 91344; Office: 8480 San Fernando Rd., Sun Valley, CA 91352.

MORRIS, EFFIE LEE
  Editor
b. Apr. 20, Richmond, Va.; d. William H. and Erma (Caskie) Morris; B.A., Case Western Res. Univ., Cleveland, Oh. 1945, B.L.S. 1946, M.S.L.S. 1956; m. Leonard Jones, Honolulu, Hawaii, Aug. 25, 1971. Career: Chil's. librn.: Cleveland Pub. Lib. 1946-55; N.Y. Pub. Lib. 1955-58; chil's. spec., Lib. for Blind, 1958-63; coord. Chil's. Servs. San Francisco Pub. Lib. 1963-78; sr. ed., Harcourt Brace Jovanovich, 1978---; Contrib. to profl. publs. Mem.: pres. Children's Servs. Lib., Calif. Lib. Assn. 1969-71; pres. Pub. Lib. Assn. of Am. Lib. Assn. 1971-72; Women's Natl. Book Assn., Alpha Kappa, Altrusa Club. Hobby: reading. Res.: 66 Cleary Ct., San Francisco, CA 94109; Office: Harcourt, Brace, Jovanovich, Div. Urban Edn., 1001 Polk St., San Francisco, CA 94109.

MORRIS, HENRY MADISON, JR.
  College President
b. Oct. 6, 1918, Dallas, Tex.; s. H.M. and Emily Ida (Hunter) Morris; B.S., Rice Univ., 1939; M.S., Univ. of Minn., 1948; Ph.D., 1950; m. Mary Louise Beach, Jan. 24, 1940, Houston, Tex.; chil.: Henry M. III, b. May 15, 1942; Kathleen Bruce, b. Aug. 10, 1944; John David, b. Dec. 7, 1946; Andrew Hunter, b. Sept. 29, 1949; Mary Ruth (Schmitt), b. Feb. 14, 1951; Rebecca Jean (Barber), b. Dec. 19, 1953. Career: Asst. Hydraulic Engr., Internat. Boundary and Water Commn., El Paso, 1939-42; Instr. in Civil Engring., Rice Univ., 1942-46; Instr. and Asst. Prof. in Civil Engring. and Research Proj. Leader, St. Anthony Falls Hydraulic Lab., Univ. Minn. 1946-51; prof. and head, Dept. of Civil Engring., Univ. of Southwestern Louisiana, 1951-56, acting dean, 1956; prof. of applied sci., So. Illinois Univ., 1957; prof. of hydraulic engring. and chmn. Dept. of Civil Engring., Va. Polytech. Inst. 1957-70; now pres., Christian Heritage Coll.; dir., Inst. for Creation Research, San Diego. Pres., Creation Research Soc., 1967-73; secty.-ed., Civil Engring. Div., Am. Soc. for Engring. Edn., 1967-70; pres., La. Gideons, 1954-56, mem. 1942---. Founder, Calif. Baptist Ch., Blacksburg, Va.; participant NSF Conf. on Fluid Mechanics, 1960, on Water Resources, 1963, Panels for Evaluation of Undergrad. Research, 1965, 66, 76; IBM Seminar on Computer Langs. 1967; prepared Helps in Gideon Hotel and hosp. Bibles; prepared Gideon Scripture Memory Course; lectr. worldwide. Author: 26 books on hydraulics, Biblical, creationist subjects; contbr. encyclopedias, tech. journs., mags. and newspapers. Mem.: Fellow, AAAS; Fellow, Am. Soc. of Civil Engrs.; Fellow, Am. Sci. Affiliation; Am. Geophysical Union;

Geological Soc. of Am; Am. Assn. of Petroleum Geologists; Geochem. Soc.; Soc. for Econ. Paleontologists and Mineralogists, others. Address: 2716 Madison Ave., San Diego, CA 92116.

MORRIS, ROBERT E.
Utility Company President
b. Oct. 24, 1921, Parsons, Kan.; s. Harry A. and Eddie E. Morris; B.S., E.E., Ga. Inst. of Tech., Atlanta; m. Carolyn B. Morris (dec. 1968); m. 2nd. Isabel Blair, La Holla, Calif., Aug. 22, 1970; chil.: Janet Perez, Carolyn W., Kenneth J., Robert S., Martin Blair, Carolyn Blair. Career: gen. sales mgr., Allis-Chalmers, Milwaukee, Wis. 1940-64; dept. dir. Monsanto Co., St. Louis, Mo. 1964-65; mgr. dir. Glengayle Assocs., St. Louis, 1965; mgr. sales div. San Diego Gas & Elec. Co. 1965, v.p. mktg. div. 1969, sr. v.p. adm. 1971, pres.-chief exec. ofcr. 1975---. Commr., Calif. Economic Development Comm. 1974-77. 1st Lt., U.S. Signal Corps, 1942-46. Mem.: Tau Beta Pi, Eta Kappa Nu, Alpha Tau Omega. Hobby: golf. Res.: La Jolla. Office: 101 Ash St., San Diego, CA 92101.

MORSE, LOWELL W.
Investments Executive — Public Official
b. May 1, 1937, West Palm Beach, Fla.; s. Alton M. and Blanche V. (Jones) Morse; B.S., Univ. Santa Clara, 1968, Russian linguist, Def. Lang. Inst. Grad. Sch.; m. Vera Giacalone, Monterey, Calif., June 22, 1958; sons: Lowell W., Jr., Stephen D., Michael S. Career: City Clerk-Dir. of Finance, Pacific Grove, 1961-63, asst. city mgr. 1963-66; city mgr. Los Altos Hills, 1967-69; pres. Westwind Properties, Inc. 1969-72; pres. du Pont, Morse and Co. 1972; pres. Morse and Assocs., Inc. 1974---; pres., Profl. Financial Coordinators, Inc., 1972---. Russian interpreter, U.S. Army Security Agcy. Contrib. articles to Western City Mgr. 1964. Mem.: pres. Monterey Bay chpt., Am. Red Cross, dir. Palo Alto-Stanford Chpt.; dir. United Fund, Los Altos; past pres. Kiwanis Club, Pac. Grove; Rotary Internat., Los Altos. Protestant (pres. Young Marrieds, Bapt. Ch., Monterey, Chr. Ch., Los Gatos). Hobby: hunting. Res.: 14403 Black Walnut Ct., Saratoga, CA 95070; Office: 4040 Moorpark Ave., San Jose, CA 95117.

MOSELEY, JACK MEREDITH
Motion Picture Executive
b. May 31, 1907, Spokane, Wash.; s. Jirah Brown and Mable (Whitney) Moseley; ed. grad. pub. schs.; m. Madlyn Jessie Stearns, Mex., Jan. 3, 1929; day. Diana (Moseley) Handfuss, b. Jan. 20, 1930. Career: Paramount Pics. Lab., Hollywood, 1934-53, and 1955-60; chief sensitometric control, Gen. Film Lab. 1953-55; supv. United Film Lab., Hollywood, 1960---. Dir., Sherman Grinberg Enterprises. Awards: Oscar Dept. Award for The Ten Commandments. Mem.: Soc. Mot. Pic. and TV Engrs. Hobby: electronics. Rec.: travel. Res.: 2006 Overland Ave., West Los Angeles, CA 90025; Office: 1040 N. McCadden Pl., Hollywood, CA.

MOSLEY, JACK MEREDITH
Thoracic and Cardiovascular Surgeon
b. July 20, 1917, Hodge, La.; s. Dr. Charles Hodge and Lucille (Hays) Moseley; ed. B.S., L.A. State Univ., 1939; M.D., La. State Univ. Med. Sch. 1943; m. Eva M. Stanek; chil.: Kathryn Sue, b. Jan. 9, 1955; Jack M., Jr., b. Mar. 4, 1956. Career: Intern, Univ. Hosp., Minneapolis, 1943-44; res. in surg., Univ. Hosp., Syracuse, N.Y. 1946-48; fellow in surg., Lahey Clinic, Boston, 1948-49; instr. in surg., Syracuse Univ. Med. Sch. 1949-50; est. pvt. practice, gen. and thoracic surg., Cleveland, Oh. 1950-52; res. thoracic surg., New Orleans, 1953; instr. thoracic surg., Tulane Univ. 1953. Pvt. practice, gen.-thoracic surg., Moseley Surg. Med. Group, Inc. 1953---; staff: Santa Barbara Cottage Hosp., St. Francis Hosp. and Santa Barbara Gen. Hosp.; past chmn. health sect., Welfare Planning Council, City of Santa Barbara. Certified, Bd. of Thoracic Surgeons, Am. Coll. of Surgeons and Am. Bd. of Surg. Author: sci. papers, articles, publ. Am. Journ. of surg., Journ. of AMA, other profl. publs. Capt., U.S. Army Med. Corps, 52nd Gen. Hosp. (Syracuse Univ. Unit), ETO, Eng. (1944-46), WW II. Mem.: Calif. Med. Soc., AMA, Santa Barbara Co. Med. Soc., Am. Coll. of Chest Phys., Am. Thoracic Soc., S.E. Surg. Cong., Pan Pac. Surg. Assn., AM. Trudeau Soc.; pres. bd. dirs. Wood Glen Hall; diplomate, Am. Bd. of Surg.; diplomate, Am. Bd. Thoracic Surg.; ACS, Valley Club. Res.: Happy Canyon Rd., Santa Ynez, CA; Office: 2420 Fletcher Ave., Santa Barbara, CA 93105.

MOSK, STANLEY
Supreme Court Justice
b. Sept. 4, 1912, San Antonio, Tex.; s. Paul and Minna (Perl) Mosk; Ph.B., Univ. of Chicago, 1933; LL.B., Univ. of Tex. 1935; (hon.) LL.D., Univ. of Pacific, 1970, Univ. of S.D., 1971, Univ. of Santa Clara, 1976; m. Edna Mitchell, Beverly Hills, Sept. 27, 1936; son: Richard Mitchell, b. May 18, 1939. Career: admitted to Calif. bar, 1935; exec. secty. to Gov. Olson of Calif. 1939-42; judge, Superior Ct., L.A. 1943-59; Atty. Gen. of Calif. 1959-64; assoc. Justice of Supreme Ct., Calif. 1964---. Cobtrib. articles to Fortune, S. Atlantic Quarterly, Liberty, Am. Mercury, legal publs. Pvt., U.S. Army, WW II. Mem.: Am. Legion; bd. of regents, Univ. of Calif. 1940; Anglo-Am. Mission, 1961-62; Phi Sigma Delta, Eagles, Elks, Rotary Club, B'nai B'rith, Beverly Hills Tennis Club, Santa Monica. Democrat. Res.: 1200 California St., San Francisco, CA; Office: State Bldg., San Francisco, CA 94102.

MOSS, CAROL E.
Los Angeles County Librarian
b. Apr. 27, 1933, Seattle, Wash.; d. Cecil Charles and Margaret C. Stickle; B.A. (mkt.), 1959; M.A., Library Sci. 1970; dau. Karen J. Moss. Career: Librn., San Jose Pub. Lib. 1954-72 (chil's. lib. 1956-59, br. lib. 1959-61, asst. city lib. 1962-72); asst. city lib. San Francisco Pub. Lib., 1972-73; Los Angeles Co. Librarian, 1973---. Contrib. to profl. journs. Mem.: treas., Assn. of Chil's. Librarians of No. Calif., 1958-60; secty-treas. Public Library Execs. of Central Calif. 1966-68; pres. Peninsula Library Assn. 1968; Am., Calif. Library Assns.; Am. Soc. for Information Sci.; Public Library Execs of So. Calif. Hobbies: reading, wine. Rec.: travel, theater. Res.: 336 S. Occidental Blvd., L.A., CA; Office: 320 W. Temple St., L.A., CA 90012.

MOSS, ERIC OWEN
Architect
b. July 25, 1943, Los Angeles; s. Morton and Ruth Moss; B.A., UCLA, 1965; M.A., arch., Univ. Calif., Berkeley, 1968; M.A., urban design, Harvard Univ., 1972; m. Maureen McGuire, Sept. 1969, Honolulu, Hawaii; chil.: Jessica Anne, b. Jan. 17, 1972; Damon Matthew, b. June 21, 1973. Career: Began own practice architecture, 1976---. Design Awards, Exhibits: Design Award for Plays Del Rey, Duplex, AIA, 1977, Sunset Mag. Spec. Design Award, 1977, AIA Awards Exhibition for Playa Del Rey Duplex at L.A. City Hall and Pacific Design Center, 1977; Progressive Arch. Mag. Design Award for Morgenstern Warehouse, Downtown, L.A., 1978. Publs.: Summary of Recent Work by Eric Moss, Architecture & Urbanism mag., Tokyo, Japan, Apr. 1978; Playa Del Rey Duplex, Domus Mag., Milan, Italy, Jan. 1978; Morgenstern Warehouse, Progressive Architecture mag., awards issue, Jan. 1978; L.A. Architect, July 1977, Nov. 1977; L.A. Times, Real Estate Sect., May 29, 1977. Address: 8760 Holloway Drive, L.A., CA 90069.

MOSS, JAMES EARL
San Diego Historical Society Executive
b. Feb. 2, 1931, Poplar Bluff, Mo.; s. Henry Earl and Mabel Ann (Frescoln) Moss; B.S., bus. & pub. adminstrn., Univ. of Mo., Columbia, 1956; M.A., Am. Hist., 1958; postgrad. studies, 1958-61; m. Tontia Sue Ferm, Sept. 17, 1977, San Diego; chil.: James Mueller, b. Feb. 17, 1963; Amanda Ann, b. Oct. 17, 1960. Career: Instr. Hist., Univ. of Mo., 1957-58; Instr. Am. Hist., Economics, Columbia Coll., Mo., 1958-61; asst. dir., State Historical Soc. of Mo., Columbia, Mo., 1961-66; exec. dir., Harris Co. Heritage and Conservation Soc., Houston, Tex., 1966-69; exec. dir., San Diego Hist. Soc., 1969-70, 1971---; exec. dir., Hawaiian Mission Children's Soc., Honolulu, 1970; editor, contbg. author, Missouri Historical Review, 1961-66. Author: Duelling in Missouri History, The Age of Dirk Drawing and Pistol Snapping, Lowell Press, 1966. USN, 1951-54. Mem.: Am. Assn. for State, Local Hist., chmn. awards com., council; Calif. State Heritage Preservation Commn.; Calif. State Historic Records and Publs. advis. bd.; Am. Assn. of Museums; Nat. Trust for Historic Preservation; Western Hist. Assn.; Calif. Historical Soc.; cons., S.D. Hist. Sites Bd.; bd. dir., S.D. Com. of 100 for preservation of Spanish Colonial Arch.; advis., Jr. League of S.D., Inc.; S.D. Balboa Park House of Hospitality Assn.; Central Area Com., S.D. Park and Recreation Bd.; Rotary Club. Home: 4491 Ampudia St., S.D., CA 92103; Office: Serra Mus., Presidio Pk., P.O.B. 81825, S.D., CA 92138.

MOSS, JAMES EDWARD
Investments Executive
b. Nov. 22, 1926, Cambridge, Oh.; s. Clyde Robert

James and Mabel Hammond (Hall) Moss; grandson of Thomas James Moss, founder, Moss-Rigby Coal Co.; grandnephew of William Charles Moss, pioneer, Wenatchee, Wash.; A.B., USC 1950; m. Nita Scott Borzage, L.A., CA; sons: Stephen Jon, b. Sept. 24, 1960; John Thomas, b. Nov. 24, 1962; William James Edward, b. Sept. 13, 1964. Career: Sales mgr. Obergfel Bros. 1952-56; dist. mgr. Investors Diversified Servs., Inc. 1956-59, div. mgr. 1959---. USN, No. Atlantic, 1944-45, WW II. Mem.: pres., Young Republs. 1952; dr. chmn. Am. Cancer Assn. 1960; bd. dirs. Sales & Market Execs. 1965-70; pres. Toluca Lake C. of C. 1966-67; bd. trustees, St. Paul's Episcopal Ch. Clubs: Wilshire Country, La Quinta Country, Cave des Roys. Rec.: golf, tennis, swim. Res.: 339 N. Palm Dr., Beverly Hills, CA 90210; Office: 4444 Riverside Dr., Toluca Lake, No. Hollywood, CA 91505.

MOSS, JOHN EMERSON
U.S. Congressman
b. Apr. 13, 1915, Carbon Co., Ut.; s. John Emerson and Della Orta (Mower) Moss; ed. Sacto. Jr. Coll. 1931-33; m. Jean Kueny, Reno, Nev., Sept. 15, 1935; chil.: Jennifer Afton, b. Mar. 14, 1946; Allison Effie, b. Oct. 17, 1949. Career: Assoc. Moss & Moss, real estate brokers, Sacto., 1943-48. Elected to Calif. Legislature, 9th Assembly Dist., Nov. 2, 1948, re-elected 1950; asst. Democratic floor leader of Assembly, 1949-52; elected U.S. Rep., Congress, Nov. 4, 1952---; dep. Majority Whip, 1962-70. USN (1943-45) WW II. Mem,: Am. Legion, Disabled Am. Veterans, Sacto. C. of C., Mason, Commonwealth Club of Calif. Protestant. Res.: 3300 19th St., Sacto., CA; Office: 2185 Rayburn House Ofc. Bldg., Wash., D.C. 20515; 8056 Fed. Bldg., 650 Capitol Mall, Sacto., CA 95814.

MOVIUS, WILLIAM ROBERT
Otolaryngologist
b. Oct. 15, 1913, Billings, Mont.; s. Dr. Arthur James (surgeon, founder of the Billings Clinic) and Joanna Marion (Murray) Movius; B.S., Northwestern Univ. 1936, M.B., 1939, M.D., 1940; m. Alice Whitney Burton, Mar. 11, 1944, Minneapolis; chil.: (twins) Edward Crale, M.D. and Alice Burton (Mrs. Dennis Painter), b. 1945; John Robert, b. 1947. Career: Intern, Ancker Hosp., St. Paul, 1939-40; instr. anatomy, Univ. of Minn., 1940-41; teaching fellowship in otolaryngology, 1941-44; mem. Billings Clin., Billings, Mont., 1944-47; pvt. practice of otolaryngology, San Diego and La Jolla, 1947-48; ear, nose, throat cons., Scripps Clinic, 1948-74; clin. prof. of surgery otolaryngology, UCSD; cons., otolaryngology, VA Hosp., S.D.; staff of Children's Hosp., mem. staff mem. Scripps Hosp., 1947-78. Past mem., Scripps Mem. Hosp. exec. com.; surgical supr. com., Scripps Hosp. Mem.: AMA; S.D. Co. Med. Soc.; Calif. Med. Assn.; Fellow, Am. Coll. of Surgeons, 1947; Am. Acad. Ophth. & Otolaryngologists, 1948; Pacific Coast Oto-Ophthalmological Soc., 1949; Sigma Nu Frat.; Phi Chi med. frat.; Mason; Kiwanis, 1952-70; Rotary, 1970-76; Scoutmaster, Troop 565, La Jolla, 1968-70, silver beaver award, 1969; Mission Bay Yacht Club, 1947-78; dir., 1962; Skimmer fleet capt. Presbyterian ch., former elder. Hobbies: sailing, flyfishing, boat racing. Rec.: hiking, swimming. Home: 2345 Paseo Dorado, La Jolla, CA 92037; Office: 7255 Girard Ave., Suite 13, La Jolla, CA 92037.

MRAULE, JIMMY
Executive Secretary
b. June 13, 1937, Price, Utah; d. James and Teresa (Guarascio) Welch; bro. Dominic, treas., Salt Lake Tribune; grad., Carbon Hi Sch., 1955; m. Donald J. Mraule, Dec. 31, 1955, Price, Utah; Chil.: Scott, b. Mar. 7, 1957; Michelle, b. Feb. 20, 1959; Tracy, b. Sept. 15, 1961. Career: Clerk II, Supt. Office, Los Rios Community Coll. Dist. (seventh largest community coll. dist. in U.S.A.), 1965, secty. to dir. of Maintenance, 1965, secty., Asst. to Supt., 1967-69, secty., dir. of research and devel., 1969-72, exec. secty., Chancellor/Supt., 1972---. Exec. recorder, Los Rios Bd. of Trustees; chmn., Los Rios Confidential Employees In-Service Planning Workshop; past pres., Los Rios chpt., Calif. Sch. Employees Assn. Mem.: Los Rios Classified Salary Com.; Los Rios Policies and Procedures Com. Presentation Parish, religious edn. tchr. Hobby: sewing. Home: 3606 Ronk Way, Sacramento, CA 95821; Office: 1919 Spanos Ct., Sacramento, CA 95825.

MUDD, HENRY THOMAS
Chairman of the Board, Cyprus Mines Corporation
b. Dec. 26, 1913, Los Angeles; s. Harvey S. and Mildred (Esterbrook) Mudd; A.B., Stanford Univ. 1935; M.S.,

MIT, 1938; m. Ann N. McCook, Sept. 13, 1968; chil.: Harvey S., II, b. Feb. 28, 1940; Henry T., Jr. and John W. (twins), b. Feb. 6, 1942; Victoria K., b. May 5, 1946; Virginia B., b. Jan. 7, 1949. Career: Chmn. bd.-chief exec. ofcr., Cyprus Mines Corp.; chmn. Pima Min. Co.; v. chmn. bd., Marcona Corp.; dir.: Rockwell Internat. Corp., United Calif. Bank, Western Bancorporation, Union Oil Co. of Calif., So. Pac. Co., Pacific Mutual Life Ins. Co. Author (Fluorspar and Cryolite) Industrial Minerals and Rocks, Vol. II, 1949. Chief, Fluorspar Sect., Way Prodn. Bd., Wash., D.C. 1942-44; Lt., USNR (1944-46), WW II. Mem.: trustee, Thacher Sch., Ojai, Calif.; chmn. bd. trustees, Harvey Mudd Coll.; fellow, Claremont Univ. Center; trustee, The Council of the Americas, Inc.; adv. com., Calif. Community Found.; dir. L.A. Civic Light Opera Assn.; Am. Inst. of Min. and Metal. Engrs., Min. & Metal. Soc. of Am., Delta Tau Delta; clubs: California, Bohemian, Sunset, Town Hall; dir.-treas. Men's Garden of L.A. Republican. Res.: 10433 Wilshire Blvd., L.A., CA 90024; Office: 555 S. Flower St., L.A., CA 90071.

MUELLER, GOERGE EDWIN
Aerospace Company President
b. July 16, 1918, St. Louis, Mo.; s. Edwin and Ella Flora (Bosch) Mueller; B.S.E.E., Mo. Sch. of Mines, 1939; M.S., Purdue Univ. 1940; Ph.D., Ohio State Univ. 1951; (hon.) Ph.D.: Univ. of Mo., N.M. State Univ., Purdue Univ., Wayne State Univ., Oh. State Univ.; m. 1st Maude Elizabeth Rosenbaum, Dec. 1941 (div. 1974); m. 2d Darla Hix Schwartzman, Feb. 1978; daus.: Karen Ann (Mueller) Hyvonen, b. Mar. 17, 1944; Jean Elizabeth (Mueller) Porter, b. Dec. 15, 1946; Career: Bell Tel. Labs. 1940-46; prof. of E.E., Oh. State Univ. 1946-58; Ramo Wooldridge and Space Tech Labs. (TRW, Inc.), 1958-63; Natl. Aeron. & Space Adm., assoc. admr. Manned Space Flight, 1963-69; sr. v.p. Gen. Dynamics Corp. 1969-71; chmn. bd. pres. System Development Corp. 1971---. Awards: NASA Distinguished Serv. Medal, 1966, 68, 69; Natl. Medal of Sci., 1970; Mem.: fellow, Am. Inst. of Aerons. and Astronautics, pres. 1979; fellow Am. Astronautical Soc.; fellow, AAAS; fellow, IEEE; (hon. fellow, Brit. Interplanetary Soc.; Nat. Acad. of Engring.; Am. Geophysical Soc.; Am. Physical Soc.; Inter. Astro. Fed.; Univ. Club (N.Y.), Calif. Yacht Club, Jonathan Club. Res.: L.A., CA; Office: 2500 Colorado Ave., Santa Monica, CA 90406.

MULL, ARCHIBALD MARISON, JR.
Attorney at Law
b. Dec. 27, 1904, Sacto.; s. Archibald M., Sr. and Lillian Claudia (Bottoms) Mull; A.B., Univ. of Calif. 1927, LL.B. 1930; LL.D., Univ. of Redlands, 1957; m. Dorothee Cavitt, Minden, Nev., Jan. 13, 1959; chil.: Barbara Ann, b. Oct. 29, 1932; Archibald Marison, III, b. Aug. 20, 1935; Marison, b. Jan. 29, 1960; George Warren Malcolm, b. July 4, 1961. Career: Atty. at law, 1930---. Mem.: pres. State Bar of Calif., 1949-50. Republican. Baptist. Res.: 1301 45th St., Sacto., CA 95819; Office: 715 Crocker Bank Bldg., 1007 7th St., Sacto., CA 95814.

MULLIN, JOHN STANLEY
Law Firm Partner
b. July 14, 1907, Los Angeles; s. John Francis and Adella (Bishop) Mullin; A.B., Stanford Univ. 1930; LL.B., Harvard Univ. 1933; chil.: Michael, b. 1937; Kathleen, b. 1940; Patricia, b. 1947; John Stanley, Jr., b. 1957. Career: Atty., Mathes & Sheppard, 1933-36, partner, 1936-45; partner, Sheppard, Mullin, Richter & Hampton, 1945---. Dir.: Burbank Lumber Co., McIntosh Lumber Co., Kingman Limber Co., Flagstaff Lumber Co., Mullin, Inc. Lt., USNR 1941-45, WW II. Mem.: U.S. del to Internat. Ski Congress, 1951, 55, 57, 59, 61, 63, 65, v.p. 1961-67; trustee, L.A. Bar Assn. 1955-57; chmn. Am. Bar Assn. (sect. of real property, probate and trust law), 1958-59; House of Dels. 1960-61, 1968-76; commr., Dept. of Water and Power, L.A.; Fellow, Am. Coll. of Probate Counsel; Fellow, Am. Bar Found.; past pres., Chancery Club; past pres., The Beach Club; pres., The California Club, 1977---. Office: 333 S. Hope St., L.A., CA 90071.

MULLIN, WAYNE FRANCIS
Company President
b. Nov. 18, 1900, Los Angeles; s. John Francis and Adella (Bishop) Mullin; ed. L.A. Polytech. H.S. 1917; USC 1917; A.B., Stanford Univ. 1921; m. Charlotte McGrath, L.A., Oct. 25, 1934; son, John Frederick, b. Jan. 25, 1940. Career: Pres., Mullin Lumber Co.; secty.-treas., Burbank Lumber Co., Tarzana Lumber Co., Terry Lumber Co., Flagstaff Lumber Co., Verde Valley

Lumber Co., Kingman Lumber Co.; dir. Western Fed. S&L Assn., 1935-78; Pfc., U.S. Army Inf. 1918, 2nd Lt., Inf. ORC 1921, WW I. Mem.: pres. S.W. Optimist Club, 1930; pres. So. Calif. Retail Lumber Assn. 1957-59; dir. Natl. Retail Lumber Assn., 1957-61; dir. Merchants & Mfrs. Assn. 1957-62; dir. L.A. C. of C. 1957-62; v.p. 1960; Masonic Lodge, Beta Theta Pi, L.A. Rotary Club, L.A. Country Club. All Saints Episcopal (ch. vestry). Rec.: golf, swimming. Res.: 726 N. Elm Dr., Beverly Hills, CA; Office: 1950 W. Slauson Ave., L.A., CA 90047.

MUNZER, RUDOLPH JAMES
Chairman, Petrolane Gas Service
b. Mar. 9, 1918, Minneapolis, Minn.; s. William Warren and Myrtle (Drysdale) Munzer; ed. L.A. H.S.; Stanford Univ. 1940; Naval Training Pgm., Columbia Univ.; m. Daphne Donohue, Beverly Hills, June 1946; chil.: Daniel, b. 1949; Anne, b. 1952; William, b. 1955. Career: v.p. Andrews Butane Co. 1946; v.p. Petrolane Gas Serv. 1954, exec. v.p.-gen. mgr. 1955, pres. 1957-70; chmn., chief exec. ofcr., 1970---; Dir.: Beckman Instruments, Pacific Indemnity Co., Investment Co. of Am., First Am. Title and Ins. Co. Lt. (s.g.), commanded USS Weaver (destroyer escort); hon. disch. (1945), WW II. Mem.: v.p. Natl. LP-Gas Council, 1959-60; pres. Natl. Liquefied Petroleum Gas Assn. 1960-61; clubs: Virginia Country (L.B.), Calif. (L.A.), Republican. Catholic. Hobby: golf. Res.: 4260 Virginia Rd., Long Beach 7, CA; Office: 1600 E. Hill St., Signal Hill, CA.

MURDOCK, DAVID H.
Development Company Owner
b. Apr. 10, 1923, Kansas City, Mo.; s. Merte and McDonald Murdock; m. Gabriele Michael, Calif.; sons, David, Jr., b, Oct. 3, 1969; Justin Michael, b. Oct. 22, 1972. Career: Owner, David H. Murdock Development Co.; chmn. bd.-pres.-dir. Pacific Holding Corp., L.A. Clubs: Phoenix Country, Cloud of Phoenix, Cave des Roys. Res.: Beverly Hills, CA; Office: 10889 Wilshire Blvd., L.A., CA.

MURPHY, FRANKLIN DAVID
Chairman, Times-Mirror Co.
b. Jan. 29, 1916, Kansas City, Mo.; s. Franklin E. and Cordelia A. (Brown) Murphy; A.B., Univ. of Kan. 1932-36; M.D., Univ. of Pa. Sch. of Med. 1937-41; m. Judith Harris, Kansas City, Mo., Dec. 28, 1940; chil.: Judith J., b. Aug. 27, 1942; Martha A., b. Sept. 20, 1943; Carolyn L., b. Mar. 30, 1949; Franklin L., b. June 10, 1950. Career: Med. practice and instr. in med., Univ. of Kan. 1946-48; dean, Sch. of Med.-assoc. prof. of internal med. 1948-51, chancellor 1951-60; chancellor, UCLA 1960-68; chmn. bd., Times-Mirror Co., L.A. 1968---. Dir.: Hallmark Cards, Ford Motor Co., BankAmerica Corp.; Times-Mirror Co. Capt., U.S. Army, 1944-46, WW II. Awards: one of ten outstanding young men by U.S. C. of C., 1949; Samuel Crumbine Award, 1961; Outstanding Civ. Serv. Award, U.S. Army, 1967; Adm. Bldg. of UCLA, dedicated Franklin David Murphy Hall by Bd. of Regents, Oct. 18, 1968; recipient, 1977 Thomas Hart Benton Award. Mem.: Inst. of Internat. Edn.; pres., Samuel H. Bress Found.; Am. Bd. of Internat. Med.; ACP; L.A. CC. of C. 1960---; Calif. Club, Bohemian, Century Club (N.Y.); Bel-Air Country Club, 1960---; Phi Beta Kappa, Sigma Xi, Alpha Omega Alpha, Nu Sigma Nu, Beta Theta Pi. Episcopalian. Res.: 419 Robert Lane, Beverly Hills, CA 90210; Office: Times-Mirror Sq., L.A., CA 90053.

MURRAY, ARTHUR BEACH
County Librarian
b. May 14, 1927, Des Moines, Ia.; s. Marhsall and Alice Murray; A.B., Antioch Coll. 1950; M.L.S., Emory Univ. 1951; M.S., San Diego State Coll. 1964; m. Carol-Faith Platt, Yellow Springs, Oh., July 29, 1950. Career: Ref. librn.: Dayton Pub. Lib. 1951-55; San Diego County Lib. 1955-60, asst. lib, 1960-65, S.D. Co. Librn., 1965---. Pvt., U.S. Army, 1945-46, WW II. Mem.: Pac. Beach Investors, 1960---, pres. 1964; pres. San Diego Co. Execs. Assn. 1969. Hobby: reading. Rec.: walking, travel. Res.: 329 Dunemere Dr., La Jolla, CA 92037; Office: San Diego Co. Library, 5555 Overland Ave., San Diego, CA 92123.

MURRAY, RICHARD GEORGE
Landscape Architect
b. Jan. 2, 1934, Sioux City, Ia.; s. George Kellogg and Pauline Lucille Murray; GG Nephew Gen. Robert E. Lee; B. Landscape Arch., Univ. Calif., Berkeley; m. Marcia Lynn Golden, 1974, Berkeley; chil.: Alison

Elizabeth, b. June 17, 1966; Scott Richard, b. Mar. 13, 1969; Erica Lynn, b. Nov. 28, 1974; Erin Rebecca, b. Apr. 11, 1977. Career: Design cons., Solomone and Hoy, Landscape Design, 1960-61; Monterey Co. Planning Dept., 1961-62; mem. faculty, Monterey Peninsula Adult Sch., 1968-69; landscape arch., Richard Murray Assoc. 1962-77; Murray-Allison Assoc. 1978---. Chmn., bd. of Archtl. Review, City of Seaside, 1978. AUS, 1953-56. Mem.: Am. Soc. of Landscape Architects, v.p. No. Calif. chpt. 1968-69; pres., State Bd. of Landscape Architects, 1973, 1976; Pres. Univ. Calif. Alumni, Monterey Bay chpt. 1977, 78; dir., Monterey Jr. C. of C., 1963. Presbyterian, Deacon. Hobby: woodwork. Res.: Atherton and Mesa Dr., Carmel, CA; Office: P.O.B. 5816, Carmel, CA 93921.

MYERS, JOHN WESCOTT
Chairman, Pacific Airmotive Corp.
b. June 13, 1911, Los Angeles; s. Louis W. and Blanche (Brown) Myers; B.A., Stanford Univ. 1933; LL.B., Harvard Law Sch. 1936; m. Lucia Raymond, Yuma, Ariz., Mar. 21, 1941; chil.: Louis Wescott, II, b. Mar. 21, 1943; Lucia Elizabeth, b. June 9, 1950. Career: Law practice with O'Melveny & Myers law firm, 1936-39; asst. gen. counsel, Lockheed Aircraft, 1939-41, test pilot, 1941-42; chief engring. test pilot, Northrop Aircraft, Inc. 1942-44; v.p.-dir. 1944-55; chmn. bd. Pacific Airmotive Corp. 1956---. Mem.: Inst. of Aeron. Scis., Soc. of Experimental Test Pilots, Calif. and L.A. Bar Assns., Conquistadores del Cielo, Sunset Club, Bohemian Club. Res.: 718 N. Rodeo Dr., Beverly Hills, CA; Office: 2940 N. Hollywood Way, Burbank, CA.

N

NAGLE, ROBERT O.
President, C and H Sugar Company
b. Feb. 10, 1929, Watertown, S.D.; s. John Raymond and Kathleen (McQuillen) Nagle; B.S., Econ., Univ. Wis.; LL.B., Univ. Calif., Berkeley, 1957; m. Louise Emerson H'Doubler, Mar. 14, 1954, chil.: Robert O., Jr., b. July 20, 1957; Charles F., b. Feb. 18, 1959; Margaret L., b. Jan. 12, 1961. Career: Atty., partner, firm of Morrison & Foerster, S.F., 1957-63; gen. atty., Spreckels Sugar Div., Amstar Corp., S.F., 1964-66; v.p. and gen. atty., 1966-68, exec. v.p. and gen. atty., 1968-71, v.p., Amstar Corp., N.Y., 1971-76; pres. and chief exec. ofcr., Calif. and Hawaiian Sugar Co., S.F., 1976---. Lt. j.g., USN, 1951-54; decorated Air Medal, Bronze Star, three Battle Stars and Korean Service Medal. Dir.: The Sugar Assn., Inc., Wash., D.C., 1976---; S.F. C. of C., 1978---; Boalt Hall Alumni Assn., UC Berkeley, 1976---; Legal Aid Soc. of S.F., 1978---. Mem.: Am. and S.F. Bar Assns.; State Bar of Calif.; Order of Coif; Pacific Union Club, Bankers Club, S.F.; Claremont Country Club, Oakland. Res.: 215 Crocker Ave., Piedmont, CA 94610; Office: One California St., San Francisco, CA 94106.

NAJARIAN, MELVIN KENNETH
Attorney at Law
b. Sept. 16, 1939, Fresno; s. Kenneth M. and Elizabeth (Marashian) Najarian; B.A., UCLA, 1961; J.D., Univ. Calif., Berkeley, 1964; m. Barbara Fletcher, Heidelberg, Germany; chil.: David Kenneth, Susan Elizabeth. Career: Hotel Mgr., Yosemite Nat. Park, summers 1961-63; Defense Appellate Atty., U.S. Ct. of Mil. Appeals, Wash. D.C., 1965-66; Atty. for U.S. Army, Europe, Heidelberg, Ger., 1966-69; Gen. Counsel, U.S. Peace Corps, Wash. D.C. and Regional Counsel, ACTION, 1969-72; partner, law firm Haas & Najarian, S.F. 1973---. Chmn. bd., Pacific Coast Containers, Vancouver, Can. Maj., AUS, 1965-69. Cons. to dir., ACTION, Wash. D.C., 1973-77; ed.: Peace Corps Handbook, 1970; contbr. articles profl. journs. Office: 530 Jackson St., S.F., CA 94133.

NAKAMURA, HIROMU
Psychologist
b. Nov. 6, 1926, Los Angeles; s. Genjiro and Misao (Kamura) Nakamura; A.B., Univ. of Redlands, 1948; M.A., UCLA 1951; Ph.D., USC, 1973; m. Tamaye Yumiba, L.A., March 27, 1955; chil.: Glenn Vernon, b. Oct. 19, 1957; Colleen Patricia, b. May 11, 1962. Career: Clin. psychol. intern, Massillon Oh. State Hosp. 1951-52; clin. psychol., Patton (Calif.) State Hosp. 1952-58; clin. psychol. Pac. State Hospital, Pomona, 1958---, pgm. dir. 1971---. Contributed articles to profl. journs. Mem.: Fellow, Royal Soc. of Health; Am., Calif.

State Psychol. Assns.; Am. Assn. on Mental Deficiency, AAAS, Am. Public Health Assn., Psi Chi. Presbyterian. Res.: 3861 Shelter Grove Dr., Claremont, CA 91711; Office: P.O.B. 100, Pomona, CA 91766.

NAMIAS, JEROME
Research Meteorologist
b. Mar. 19, 1910, Bridgeport, Conn.; s. Joseph and Sadie (Jacobs) Namias; stu., Mass. Inst. Tech., 1932-34, 1940-41; M.S., Univ. Mich., 1934-35; (hon.) D.Sc., Univ. Rhode Island, 1972; m. Edith Paipert, Sept. 15, 1938, Boston; dau. Judith Ellen. Career: Meteorologist, TWA, 1934; Blue Hill Meteorological Observatory, Blue Hill, Mass., 1935-36; research assoc., MIT, 1936-41; chief, Extended Forecast Div., U.S. Weather Bureau, 1941-71; Research Meteorologist, Scripps Inst. of Oceanography, UCSD, 1968---; cons. to USN and USAF. Author: An Intro. to the Study of Air Mass and Isentropic Analysis, 1940; Extended Forecasting by Mean Circulation Methods, 1947; 30-Day Forecasting: A Review of a Ten-Year Experiment, 1953; 150+ tech. articles publ. in sci. journs., monographs and encyclopedias, many pub. in Collected Works of J. Namias, 1934-74, Short Period Climatic Variations, Univ. Calif. San Diego, 1973. Awards and citations for Aerological Research, Am. Meteorological Soc. 1938 and 1955; for Weather Forecasts in connection with Invasion of N. Africa, Navy Secty. 1943; Meritorious Serv., 1950 and Gold Medal Award, 1965, U.S. Dept. of Commerce, 1950; Public Service, Rockefeller Found., 1955, 77. Fellow, Am. Meteorological Soc., Councilor: 1940-42, 1950-53, 1960-63, 1973-76; Fellow, Am. Geophysical Union; Fellow, Wash. Acad. of Scis.; Fellow, AAAS; mem. Royal Meterological Soc. of G.B.; Mex. Geophysical Union; Bd. Editors, Geofisica Internat., Mex.; Sigma Xi, Explorers Club Fellow. Rec.: fishing, music. Res.: 240 Coast Blvd., Apt. 2C, La Jolla, CA 92037; Office: Scripps Inst. of Oceanography, La Jolla, CA 92093.

NAPTON, LEWIS KYLE
Professor of Anthropology
b. Nov. 15, 1933, Bozeman, Mont.; s. Lewis Williams and Francis (Kyle) Napton; B.S., Mont. State Univ., 1959; M.A., Anthropology, Univ. Mont., 1965; Ph.D., Anthrop., Univ. Calif., Berkeley, 1970; sons, Lewis Scott, Robert Place. Career: Tchg. Asst., anthropology, Univ. Mont., Missoula, 1964-65; mem. faculty 1966; mem. faculty, Univ. Calif., Berkeley, 1969-73; prof. of anthropology, Cal. State Coll., Stanislaus, 1974---. Dir., Inst. for Archeol. Research, Cal. State Coll. Found., 1973---; dir. of archeol. field projects, Mex., Australia, E. and N. Africa, USA, 1954-56. Awarded A.B. Guthrie Creative Writing Scholarship 1959; publs. in Cultural Resource Mgmt., notably: Archeological Overview of Yosemite National Park, Calif. Mem.: Sigma Psi, Nat. Sci. Hon. 1971; Alpha Kappa Delta. Hobby: oil painting. Res.: 2321 Peace, Turlock, CA 95380; Office: Calif. State Coll., Stanislaus, Turlock, CA 95380.

NASH, MERRILL L.
Company President
b. June 16, 1924, Mangham, La.; s. Martin L. and Mable E. (Watson) Nash; B.S.C.E., La. State Univ. 1949; m. Betty Henderson, Mangham, La., Dec. 13, 1952; chil.: Susan, b. Sept. 1, 1956; Linda, b. Feb. 19, 1962; Brian, b. May 3, 1967. Career: pres., Livingston-Graham Inc. 1959-64; pres. Paul Hardeman, Inc., 1965-68; chmn-pres. Brown Co., 1969---. Ensign, USN Aviator, 1943-45. Clubs: Jonathan, L.A.; Annandale Golf, Pasa.; Balboa Bay, Newport Beach, Office: 251 S. Lake Ave., Suite 606, Pasadena, CA 91101.

NASON, FRED NORTHRUP
President, Beverly Hills Transfer Co.
b. Mar. 18, 1905, Hollywood; s. Malcolm Craig and Jessie (Stevens) Nason; B.S., USC 1927; m. Violette Marie Johnson, Beverly Hills, Oct. 16, 1928; sons: Fred Nason Jr., b. Dec. 2, 1930; Richard Allan, b. Feb. 27, 1934. Career: pres., Beverly Hills Transfer and Storage Co. 1928---. Chmn. bd. trustees, West Coast Univ. 1952---. Mem.: pres. Beverly Hills Rotary Club, 1946-47; pres. Beverly Hills YMCA 1948-50; Sigma Chi, Bel-Air Bay Club, L.A. Country Club, The Beverly Hills Club. Hobbies: hunting, fishing. Rec.: golf. Res.: 721 N. Rexford Dr., Beverly Hills, CA 90210; Office: 221 S. Beverly Dr., Beverly Hills, CA 90212.

NAYLOR, GEORGE LeROY
Lawyer — Railroad Official
b. May 11, 1915, Bountiful, Ut.; s. Joseph F. and Josephine (Wood) Naylor; desc. of Isaac Chase, Daniel Wood, Richard Warren of Mayflower; Hannah Morley

and Samuel Naylor; ed. Univ. of Ut. 1934-36; George Wash. Univ. 1937; J.D., Univ. of S.F., 1952; m. Maxine Lewis, Ogden, Ut., Jan. 17, 1941; chil.: Mrs. Ralph (Georgia Lee) Price, b. Aug. 27, 1944; Mrs. Glenn B. (Rose Maree) Hammer, b. Sept. 29, 1948; George L., b. Jan. 3, 1950. Career: Docket clerk, Ut. State Legislature, 1939; foreman, U.S. Park Serv. 1939-40; owner-operator, Moxum Hotel Cafe, 1941; secty-legislative rep. IUMMSW, 1943-44; examiner, Personnel Dept., So. Pac. Co. 1949-54; chief examiner, 1955, asst. mgr. 1956-61; carrier mem., 3rd Div., Natl. R.R. Adjustment Bd., Chicago, 1961---, chmn. NRAB (1970, 1973---). Author: (books) Underground at Bingham Canyon; Choice Morsels in Tax and Property Law, 1966; Defending Carriers Before the NRAB, publ. 1969; articles on estate planning, U.S. Army (Asiatic-Pac. campaign, secty. to Gen. Davis, Chief of Information & Edn. Sect. AFPAC), WW II. Bishop Ch. of Jesus Christ of L.D.S. (Mormon). Res.: 120 Center St., Barrington, Ill.; Office: One Market St., S.F., CA; 220 S. State St., Chicago, Ill.

NEELY, MARY BELLE KNOX
Corporate Secretary
b. Apr. 14, 1914, Ira, Tex.; d. William P. and Millie Elizabeth Knox; cousin to Pres. James Knox Polk; ed. Sawyer Bus. Coll., Rio Hondo Coll.; m. Robert Frank Neely, June 28, 1939, Pomona; chil.: Robert Micael (asst. Supr. Sch., Norwell, Mass.), b. 1942; William Scott (sales exec., Knoll Internat.), b. 1944. Career: head bookkeeper, So. Service Co., Monrovia and Ontario, Calif., 1935-39; civic and sch. vol. work, 1935-60; office mgr., Peerless Spray Chem. Co., Covina, 1961-69; corp. secty., Abbey-Scherer Co., Costa Mesa, 9169---. Protestant. Hobbies: bridge, reading. Home: 25461 Posada Lane, Mission Viejo, CA 92675; Office: 3130 Airway Ave., Costa Mesa, CA 92626.

NEHER, ROBERT TROSTLE
Professor of Biology
b. Nov. 1, 1930, Mt. Morris, Ill.; s. Oscar Warner and Etha Mae (Trostle) Neher; B.S., 1953; M.A., biol., 1955; M.R.E., rel. edn., 1957; Ph.D., botany, 1963; m. Mary Timmons, June 12, 1954, N. Manchester, Ind.; chil.: Kenneth Edward, b. Apr. 13, 1956; Jon Oscar, b. Nov. 7, 1958; Daniel Allen, b. May 12, 1961. Career: Tchg. Asst., Indiana Univ., 1953-55; Christian Edn., Ch. of the Brethren, Elgin, Ill., 1956; Prof. of Biology, Univ. of LaVerne (formerly LaVerne Coll.), LaVerne, Calif. 1958---, prof. and div. chmn. 1966---; NSF Fellow at Ind. Univ. 1961-62. Mem.: bd. dirs., L.A. Co. Juvenile Diversion; mem. L.A. Co. Watershed Commn. Publs. on Genetic Studies of Tagetes, 1966; acquaculture studies of the Kaupulehu Fish Ponds and Adjacent Areas, Kona Village, No. Mem.: Sigma Xi.; Am. Soc. of Plant Taxonomists, Calif. Botanical Soc. Polit.: elected LaVerne City Councilman, 1976---; mem. LaVerne Planning Commn., 1972-75; mem. LaVerne Commn. on Environmental Quality, 1968-72. Ordained Minister, Ch. of the Brethren. Rec.: stamp collecting, archery. Res.: 2373 Bonita Ave., LaVerne, CA 91750; Office: Univ. of LaVerne, 1950 Third St., LaVerne, CA 91750.

NEIL, JESSIE M.
Civic Worker
b. Oct. 20, 1927, Pasadena; d. Cecil D. and Jessie (Parsons) Pruitt; B.A., Asiatic Studies, USC, 1950; m. Edmund R. Neil, Mar. 24, 1956, Westwood, Calif.; chil.: Edmund R., Jr., b. Jan. 25, 1959; Jessica R., b. Apr. 26, 1963; R. William, b. Feb. 20, 1971. Career: dir. Design, Leland Gardens Bldg. Corp., 1950-56; sales dir., Wash. Square Bldg. Corp. 1950-52; pres., Barrett Devel. Corp., 1951-70; secty., Reliance Bldg. Corp., 1951-68; secty., So. Counties Escrow Corp., 1956-79; pres., Futuramic Homes Inc., 1956-68. Founder: Cardiac League, A Guild of Huntington Mem. Hosp., Pasadena, 1963, pres. 1966-68; pres., Women's Council, Huntington Mem. Hosp. 1967; vice pres., San Marino League, 1968-73; pres. Docent Council, Pasadena Mus. 1971-72. Awards: Graphics Award, Pasadena Arts Council, 1968; Eve Award. Mem.: Costume Council, L.A. Co. Mus.; Assocs. of USC; Founders, Los Angeles Center; life mem., Arcadia Methodist Hosp.; Blue Ribbon 400, L.A. Music Center; World Affairs Council; Internat. Platform Assn.; Fellow, Pasadena Mus. Rec.: flying. Res.: 301 Hermosa St., So. Pasadena, CA 91030.

NEITER, GERALD I.
Attorney at Law
b. Nov. 11, 1933, Los Angeles; s. Harry and Ida Neiter; B.S.L., USC 1957, J.D., USC Sch. of Law, 1957; m. Margaret Rowe, Mar. 5, 1961, Los Angeles; chil.: David, b. Jan. 20, 1958; Karen, b. May 28, 1962; Michael, b.

June 7, 1966. Career: Admitted to state bar of Calif. 1958, U.S. Supreme Ct., 1963; assoc. Dolman, Kaplan, Neiter, Hart, Sheppard, Mullin, Richter, Balthis & Hampton, L.A.; now principal, law firm of Hart, Neiter & Leonard, L.A. ---; Judge Pro Tem, Municipal Cts., Beverly Hills, L.A.; mem. State Bar Discip. Com. Lectr.: State Bar 1976; mem. Bd. of Govs., Century City Bar, 1976-78; contbr. continuing edn. of Bar publs. Jewish. Rec.: skiing, fishing. Res.: Encino; Office: 1888 Century Park East, L.A., CA 90067.

NELSON, DOROTHY WRIGHT
Law Center Dean
b. Sept. 30, 1928, San Pedro, Calif.; d. Harry E. and Lorna Amy Wright; LL.B., UCLA 1950; J.D. 1953; LL.M., USC 1956; m. James F. Nelson (judge, L.A. Municipal Ct.), L.A., Dec. 27, 1950; chil.: Franklin Wright, b. Aug. 22, 1958; Lorna Jean, b. July 21, 1961. Career: pvt. practice law, 1953-60; lectr. in law, USC 1956, instr. 1957, asst. prof. 1959, assoc. prof. 1961, prof.-interim dean, 1967, dean-prof. USC Law Center, 1969---. Co-chmn. panel, President's White House Conf. on Chil. 1970; bd. dirs. Am. Natl. Inst. for Social Advancement; Judicial Process Task Force, Calif. Council on Criminal Justice. Contrib. numerous articles on law to profl. journs.; research surveys on judicial adm. and cts.; book reviews, 1956---; Awards: UCLA Law Alumnus of Yr. 1967; L.A. Times Woman of Yr. 1968; UCLA Alumni Profl. Achievement Award, 1969; Mem.: UCLA Alumni Assn., Law Alumni Assn., Gold Shield; Legion Lex, Alumni Assn., Law Alumni Assn. of USC; State and Fed. Bars; bd. dirs. Am. Judicature Soc.; gov. bd. Continuing Edn. of Bar; coms. Am. Bar Assn.; coms. Calif. State Bar; AAUW; Phi Beta Kappa, Bahai World Faith (treas. Natl. Assembly of U.S.). Hobbies: gardening, cooking. Rec.: tennis, swim, fishing, camping. Res.: 725 Arden Rd., Pasadena, CA; Office: USC Law Center, Univ. Park, L.A., CA 90007.

NELSON, HELEN MARTHA
Library Director
b. Dec. 20, 1929, Anaconda, Mont.; d. Ole Bertin and Caroline Helen (Massey) Nelson; B.A. (hon.), Univ. of Mont., 1951; M.L.S., Univ. of Wash., 1960. Career: Asst. documents & serials librarian, Univ. Mont. 1951-52; tchr., Mont. schs. 1952-59; librarian, U.S. Army, Europe, 1960-68; library dir., Oceanside Pub. Lib., Oceanside, 1968---. Council mem., Serra Coop. Lib. System Admin., 1969---, chmn. 1973-74; bd. dir., exec. council, ARC Oceanside-Carlsbad br. 1970-71; bd. dir., Calif. Inst. of Librarians, 1978---; Calif. Library Assn. Council, 1978---; v.p. Palomar chpt., Calif. Lib. Assn. 1978---. Mem.: Am. Lib. Assn.; Mont. Lib. Assn.; AAUW; Oceanside C. of C.; So. Calif. Local Hist. Council; Pub. Lib. Execs. Assn. of So. Calif.; Phi Alpha Theat; Kappa Tau; League of Women Voters; Fine Arts Soc. of San Diego; Zoological Soc. of S.D.; Am. Assn. for State & Local Hist. Lutheran; Council mem. 1971-77, pres. 1974-77. Hobbies: travel, photog., crewel embroidery. Home: P.O.B. 238, Oceanside, CA 92054; Office: Oceanside Public Library, 615 Fourth St., Oceanside, CA 92054.

NELSON, JEAN E.
City Librarian
b. Feb. 9, Los Angeles; d. Harry Abor and Agnes (Kissane) Olson; B.A., 1965; M.L.S., 1966; M.P.A., 1972; m. William G. Nelson (div.), Los Angeles; sons: William Brent, Lawrence Paul, Carl Douglas, Warren Dale. Career: Young Adult Librn., Pub. Lib., Whittier, 1966-68; Br. Librn., Whittier Br. Lib., 1968-72; City Librn., San Bruno, 1972-74; City Librn., Fullerton, 1974---. Chmn. Pub. Lib. Adminstrs. of Orange Co., 1977; pres. Pub. Lib. Execs. of So. Calif. 1978; pres., So. Calif. Film Circuit 1978-79; chmn., Santiago Lib. Sys. 1979-80; elected rep to CLASS 1978-80. Mem.: U.S. Amateur Ballroom Dancers Assn.; USTTA (Women's Team asst. to World Championship Table Tennis, Korea 1979). Hobbies: ballroom dancing, table tennis, golf. Res.: 9403 S. Klinedale, Downey, CA 90240; Office: Fullerton Pub, Lib., 353 W. Commonwealth, Fullerton, CA 92632.

NESBIN, ESTHER WINTER
Former Librarian
b. Aug. 5, 1910, Denver, Colo; d. Oscar A. and Helen (Schmandt) Winter; B.A., Univ. Buffalo, N.Y. 1931, Certificate in Lib. Sci. 1932; m. Anthony T. Nesbin, L.A., Sept. 21, 1946 (dec.). Career: Lib. ref. asst. Grosvnor Lib., Buffalo, 1931-42; instr. lib. sci. Univ. Buffalo, 1939-42; librn., Temple of the Jewelled Cross, L.A. 1942-46; lib.-instr. in lib. sci. Palomar Coll., San Marcos, Calif. 1947-65; dir. lib. servs. 1965-68, asst. dean lib. servs. 1969-77. Cons.: Palo Verde Jr. Coll.

Lib., Blythe, 1957; Monterey Jr. Coll. Lib., Monterey, 1958; Camp Pendleton Law Lib. 1964. Shaker Lit. publ. Grosvnor Lib. Tech. Manual 1940, 69. Mem.: pres. Palomar Cactus and Succulent Soc. 1958-60; Escondido Historical Soc. hon. mem.; Vista Historical Soc.; Phi Rho Pi, Nat. Jr. Coll. Speech Assn. Hobbies: Calif. cactus and succulents, children's books. Res.: P.O.B. 102, San Marcos, CA 92069.

NESPOR, HELEN M.
Educator
b. Dec. 15, 1939, Czechoslovakia; d. Bohumil and Anezka Nespor; B.A., Univ. of Melbourne, Australia, 1961; M.A., Oh. State Univ., 1964; Ph.D., Univ. of Calif., Berkeley, 1969. Career: Pgm. Planning and Devel. Cons., Calif. State Dept. of Edn., 1972---; Commissioner, Calif. State Commn. on Status of Women, 1972---; supr. tchr. edn., Univ. Calif., Berkeley, 1969-71; contbr. articles profl. journs.; LP record; work with TV & satellites; prod. radio pgms. Pres., bd. dir., Univ. Calif. Edn. Alumni Soc., 1976-77; chmn. Calif. Task Force on Global Perspectives in Edn., 1975-77; pres., Internat. Platform Assn., 1970. Hobbies: orthomolecular med., music, art, literature. Res.: 5811 Mendocino Ave., Oakland, CA 94618; Office: Calif. State Dept. of Education, 721 Capitol Mall, Sacto., CA 95814.

NEUMANN, HARRY GEORGE CHARLES
Research Microbiologist
b. June 15, 1914, Los Angeles; s. Harry Charles, A.S.C. (noted cinematographer) and Eva U. Neumann; student Glendale Coll., 1932-35; B.A. bacteriology, UCLA, 1938; postgrad.: USC, 1940; UCLA, 1949; m. Geraldine Davis (gr.granddau. of Wm. Health Dvais, early Calif. pioneer), Feb. 23, 1944, Highland Park, CA; son Gary Lynn, b. July 20, 1952. Career: Water quality analyst (microbiology), L.A. Dept. Water & Power, 1940---; research microbiologist, 1946-75, head, Microbiological Labs., 1975---. Served Med. Dept. AUS, 1941-42; to Commned. Ofcr., Med. Adminstrv. Corps 1942-45, Hosp. ship John L. Clem, Mediterranean; decorated Am. defense ribbon, 4 bronze stars. Conducted water quality research for largest, most complex water system in USA on varied aspects: reclamation; indsl. microbiology of cooling towers and systems for electric generating stations; membrane filter tech. Contbd. articles, tech. journs., 1950, 51. Mem.: Am. Acad. of Microbiology; Am. Soc. for Microbiology, and So. Calif. br.; Am. Water Works Assn.; Dept. of Water & Power Assn., Inc.; Soc. for Study of Democratic Insts.; UCLA Alumni Assn., life mem.; Glendale 20-30 Club, past secty.-treas.; Theta Xi frat. Democrat. Episcopalian. Hobbies: photog., gardening, travel. Res.: 17051 Los Alimos St., Granada Hills, CA 91344; Office: 111 N. Hope St., L.A., CA 90012.

NEUMANN, MARLEN ELDREDGE
Educator — Civic Leader
b. Dec. 20, 1915, Miraj, India; d. Mark and Mary Helen (Woodsmall) Eldredge; niece of Ruth Frances Woodsmall, gen. secty. of World YWCA (dec. 1963); B.A., Rollins Coll., Fla., 1936; M.A. (internat. rels.), Uale Univ. 1941; Univ. of Grenoble, Fr. 1936-37; m. Dr. Robert G. Neumann (U.S. Ambassador), Bustin's Is., Me., July 27, 1941; chil.: Ronald Eldredge, b. Sept. 30, 1944; Marcia Woodsmall, b. Jan. 24, 1949 (dec.); Gregory Woodsmall, b. Jan. 18, 1952. Career: Pvt. secty. to Ruth Woodsmall, gen. secty. of World YWCA on oft. trip to Orient and India, 1938-39, asst. warden-dir., Summer Conf. Center, Ootacamund, India, 1938; lectr., India and Internat. Problems, 1941-43; instr. (econ.-polit sci.), State Tchrs. Coll., Oshkosh, Wis. 1942-43; information-liaison ofcr., Dept. of State, 1943-45; ext. tchr., Univ. of Wis. 1946-47, UCLA 1949-50, Mem.: Pledge chmn., Chi Omega, 1935, treas. Upsilon Beta Chpt. 1936; co-founder. League of Women Voters, Oshkosh, Wis. 1942, pres. 1942-43, state bd., Calif. dir. state fiscol policy stu. 1947-50, bd. dirs., L.A. div. 1949-50, 52-54, 56-57, 61-62 (asst. to pres., foreign econ. policy, U.N.), del. L.A. Area Council Non-Govt. orgns. accredited to U.N. 1952-54, chmn. 1956-57, pres. L.A. div. 1957-59; cons. on community affairs, 1959-60; state bd.-dir. Natl. U.N. Study, 1962-64, v.p. 1964; L.A. City Civil Serv. Comm. 1958-61; chmn. World affairs com., Women's Div., L.A. C. of C. 1958-62; bd. dirs. U.N. Assn. of L.A. 1959-69, pres. 1965-67; bd. dirs. Met. Hearing Center, L.A. 1963-64; women's plan. com., Japan Internat. Chr. Univ. Found. 1963---; McCone Comm., Gov's. Comm. to Investigate L.A. Riots, 1965-67; hon. pres. Am. Women's Assn., Kabul, 1967-73; Diplomatic Wives Assn., Kabul, 1967-73; secty. 1968, pres. 1969; Afghan Soc. for Rehab. of Phys.

Handicapped, 1969-73; hon. pres. Am. Women's Assn., Rabat, Morocco, 1973-76, treas. Circle Diplomatique de Bienfaisance, Rabat, 1975-76; Bookroom Mgr., AAFSW Bookfair, Wash., D.C. 1978. Republican. Espicopalian. Hobby: hiking. Rec.: deck tennis, ping-pong. Res.: 4986 Sentinel Dr., No. 102, Bethesda, MD 20016; 11865 Lucile St., Culver City, CA 90230.

NEUMANN, ROBERT GERHARD
Diplomat — Educator
b. Jan. 2, 1916, Vienna, Austria; s. Hugo and Stefanie (Tausky) Neumann; ed. Diplome Superieur, Universite de Rennes, Fr. 1936; diploma Consular Acad., Vienna, Austria, 1937; diploma, Geneva Sch. of Internat. Studies, 1937; (law) Univ. of Vienna, 1934-38; M.A., Amherst Coll. 1940; Ph.D. (Shevlin Fellow), Univ. of Minn. 1946; m. Marlen Eldredge, Bustin's Is., Maine, July 27, 1941; chil.: Ronald Eldredge, b. Sept. 30, 1944; Marcia Woodsmall, b. Jan. 24, 1949 (dec. Dec. 16, 1949); Gregory Woodsmall, b. Jan. 18, 1952. Career: Instr., State Tchrs. Coll., Oshkosh, Wis. 1939-42; lectr., Univ. of Wis. 1946-47; asst. prof., UCLA 1947-52; assoc. prof. 1952-58, prof. 1958-69; dir. Inst. Internat. and Foreign Studies, 1959-65, chmn. Atlantic and W. European Pgm. 1965-66; dir. Am. Seminar on Politics, Econ. and Soc. Sci., Nice, Fr. 1957; advisor NATO Ministerial Conf., Paris, 1962; cons. to U.S. Secty. of Def. 1962-66; cons. to Dept of State, Policy Plan Council and Bur. of European Affairs, 1963-66; cons. to Ford Found. 1964-66; sponsor, Atlantic Council of the U.S.; U.S. Ambassador, 1966-76; sr. assoc. for Parliamentary&Congressional Rels., Center for Strategic and Internat. Studies, Wash. D.C., 1976---; dir., Inst. for the Study of Diplomacy, Georgetown Univ., 1977---. Author: European Government, publ. McGraw-Hill (4 eds.), 1950, 55, 60, 68; The Government of the German Federal Republic, publ. Harper and Row, 1966; ed. writer, L.A. Times, 1952-59; bd. eds., Revista di Diritto Europeo, Rome; contrib. numerous articles to journs., newspapers; Toward a More Effective Exec.-Legislative Relationship in the Conduct of America's Foreign Affairs, publ. CSIS, 1977. Pvt., 1st Lt., U.S. Army (1942-46), WW II. Awards: Hon. Medal, Univ. of Brussels, 1955; Knight's Cross, Legion of Hon., Fr. 1957; Ofcr's Cross, Order of Merit, Ger. 1963. Mem.: Calif. Repub. Central Com. 1954-60; adv. bd., Austro-Am. Inst. of Edn.; Inst. for Strategic Stus., London; chmn. internat. rels. sect., Town Hall, L.A. 1956-61; Am. Soc. of Internat. Polit. Sci. Assn., Phi Delta Theta. Roman Catholic. Hobby: hiking. Res.: 4986 Sentinel Dr., No. 102, Bethesda, MD 20016; 11865 Lucile St., Culver City, CA 90230.

NEUTRA, DIONE
Cellist — Singer — Author
b. Apr. 14, 1901, Munich, W. Germany; dau. Alfred Niedermann; granddau., Niedermann, noted Swiss novelist, painter, wood cutter; pvt. studies in cello and voice; m. Richard J. Neutra, architect (dec. 1970), Dec. 23, 1922, Hagen, W. Germ.; sons: Frank, b. Jan. 6, 1924; Dion, architect, b. Oct. 8, 1926; Raymond, physician, b. Mar. 12, 1939. Career: Asst. to Husband, (originator of biorealism, meaning the application of biological and behavioral scis. to knowledge of arc.) in internat. archtl. practice for 48 years; Calif. Council, AIA, 1978; for dedication of much of her life to the advancement of modern architecture; through her writings, lectures and concerts has kept alive the spirit and meaning of the Modern Movement; has made a last contbrn. to minds of all in contact with her. Lifelong musician, cellist, singer; gave program of music, song and readings on tour of 14 European cities, 1976; author of biography: "The Shaping of an Architect." Quotation: "Happiness is to fulfill your own potential." Rec.: concerts, plays. Home: L.A., CA.

NEVINS, RICHARD
Member, State Board of Equalization
b. Apr. 21, 1921, Los Angeles; s. Richard and Katharine Bass (Tilt) Nevins; ed. H.S., Midland Sch., Los Olivos, Calif., 1936-39; B.A., Yale Univ. 1939-43; m. Mary Lois Minton, Garden City, L.I., N.Y., May 17, 1946; chil.: Richard, Jr., b. June 5, 1947; William McCay, b. Aug. 28, 1948; Henry Minton, b. Nov. 29, 1950. Career: Assoc. with Marsh & McLennan and Cosgrove & Co., 1946-58; elected to Calif. State Board of Equalization, 4th Dist., 1958---. Weather Serv. USAAF (1943-46), WW II. Mem.: L.A. Urban League; Pasadena Chpt., NAACP; L.A. Co. Dem. Central Com. 1954; Dem. State Com. 1954; state pres., Calif. Fed. of Young Dems. 1956-58; del. Dem. Natl. Conv. 1956, 60, 64, 72; Western Govt. Research Assn.; Am. Soc. for Pub. Adm. 1959---, pres. L.A. Met. Chpt. 1966-67; Natl. Assn. of Tax Admrs. 1961---; Internat. Assn. Assessing Ofcrs. 1961---. Res.:

561 Bradford St., Pasadena, CA 91105; Office: 333 E. Walnut St., P.O. Bin 77, Pasadena, CA 91109.

NEWBURY, RAY LEON, JR.
Astronomer
b. Jan. 9, 1933, Rock Island, Ill.; s. Ray L. and Gertrude G. Newburn; B.S., Calif. Inst. of Tech., 1954, M.S., 1955; m. Virginia L. Gaskin, May 4, 1968, So. Pasadena; sons: Steven Ray and Kevin Francis, b. Aug. 9, 1972. Career: with Jet Propulsion Lab. 1956---: scientist, sr. sci., group supr., now mem. of tech. staff, 1975---. Contbr. profl. papers in Icarus, Astrophysical Journ., Astronomical Journ., Astron. Soc. of Pacific; space sci. reviews; two books; hobby papers in Western Express, Skinned Knuckles. Mem. numerous antique car clubs. Res.: 3226 Emerald Isle Dr., Glendale, CA 91206; Office: 4800 Oak Grove Dr., Pasadena, CA.

NEWHALL, SCOTT
Newspaper Editor
b. Jan. 21, 1914, San Francisco; s. Almer A. and Anna Nicholson (Scott) Newhall; GG Gr.son, Henry Mayo Newhall, founder of Newhall, Calif.; stu., Univ. of Calif., 1932-35; m. Ruth Waldo, Nov. 20, 1933, Reno, Nev.; sons, Jonathan, Anthony. Career: with the San Francisco Chronicle: 1935-71; photog., editor, This World, Sunday Editor, Opns. Mgr., Exec. Editor, 1953-70; editor, 1970-71, Editor in Chief, San Francisco Magazine, 1971; Publ., The Signall, Newhall ---; Author: Eppleton Hall; served as correspondent in Engl., WW II. Chmn. Bd. Gov., Irrawaddy Steam Nav., Co.; Dir., Newhall Newspapers, Inc.; Newhall Land and Farming Co.; Cypress Lawn Cemetery Assn.; Trustee: Calif. Inst. Arts; Trustee Emeritus, S.F. Maritime Museum Assn.; Palace Arts and Scis.; bd. dir., Calif. Hist. Soc. Mem.: Berkeley Fellows, Univ. of Calif.; Pacific Union Club. Hobbies: Numismatic, sailing. Res.: Mansion House, Park St., Piru, CA; Office: 1050 North Point, S.F., CA 94109.

NEWMAN, FRANK C.
Justice, Supreme Court of California
b. July 17, 1917, Eureka, Calif.; s. Frank J. and Anna (Dunn) Newman; A.B., Dartmouth, 1938; LL.B., Univ. Calif., Berkeley, 1941; LL.M., Columbia Univ., 1947; J.S.D., 1953; LL.D., Univ. Santa Clara, 1978; m. Frances Burks Newman, 1940, Palo Alto; chil.: Robert, Julie, Carol. Career: Atty. OPA, NYC and Wash. D.C., 1942-43; Office Gen. Counsel, Navy Dept. 1943-46; Prof. of Law, Univ. Calif., Berkeley, 1946-77, Jackson H. Ralston Prof. Internat. Law 1974-77, Dean UC Berkeley Law Sch. 1961-66; vis. prof. law schs., Harvard, 1953-54, Univ. Wash., summer 1952, Salzburg Seminar in Am. Studies, Austria Summer 1954, 64, Strasbourg Inst. of Human Rights Summer, 1970, 71, 75, 77, Center Advanced Study in Behav. Scis. 1957=58; law book editorial bd. Little, Brown & Co., 1956-77; Counsel Gov. Calif. Commn. on Unemployment Compensation 1952; Cons. Gen. Acctg. Office, 1959; bd. dir. Fed. Home Loan Bank, S.F. 1962-70. Mem. exec. com., chmn. of drafting com., Calif. Constitn. Revision Commn. 1964-72; mem. nat. adv. council ACLU, Amnesty USA. Served from ensign to Lt., USNR, 1943-46. Mem.: Am. Soc. Internat. Law; v.p. Internat. Inst. Human Rights. Res.: 53 Acacia Dr., Orinda, CA; Office: Calif. Supreme Ct., State Bldg., S.F., CA 94102.

NEWMAN, MELVA J.
Social Worker
b. Mar. 3, 1932, Shreveport, La.; d. William and Minnie Lee Burton-Collins; B.A., psychol., UCLA, 1953; M.S.W., USC, 1957; ,. Joseph Newman, June 25, 1957, L.A.; chil.: Sheri, Toni, Collette. Career: Social worker, La Casa De San Gabriel, 1953-55; Dep. probation ofcr., L.A. Co. Probation Dept., El Rileno Sch. for Girls, 1957-58; Soc. work spec., Neighborhood Youth Assn. 1958-60; Pasa. YWCA 1960-73; Chief of Soc. Serv., Central City Comm. Mental Health Center 1969; Family-Child Therapist, pvt., 1970---; also Asst. prof. Sociology Dept., Cal. State Univ., L.A., 1970-77; social work cons. Pasadena Art Headstart 1975---; Community Housing Service, Elizabeth Fry Center 1977; Turner Sch. for Learning, summer 1978; Inst. for Study of Black Parenting; Assn. of Black Soc. Workers; now Lectr., Child Welfare Grant Prog., Cal. State Polytech. Univ. Mem. State Adv. Council on Child Abuse Prevention, 1977-78; Alpha Kappa Alpha; Recipient Achievers Award for distinguished serv. to disadvantaged children and families, Soc. for Study of Negro Life and Hist., 1960, contbd. Play Therapy-Mother and Chil, IV World Congress of Soc., Honolulu 1977. Res.: 524 E. Loma Alta Dr., Altadena, CA.

NEWMAN, NANCY MARILYN
Neuro-Ophtalmologist
b. Mar. 16, 1941, S.F.; d. Fred and Marion Newman; B.A., magna cum laude, psychol., Stanford Univ., 1962; M.D., Stanford Univ. Med. Sch., 1967. Career: NIH Trainee: in Neuropharmacology, 1961-63, in Devel. Neurology, Pediatrics Dept., 1963-64, Stanford Univ.; in Neurophysiology, Inst. of Visual Scis., S.F., 1964-65; clin. clkship. in Neuroophthalmology Lond., 1966-67; internship, Mt. Auburn Hosp., Cambridge, Mass., 1967-68; NIH Trainee in Neuro-Ophthalmology, Wash. Univ., St. Louis, 1968-71; residency, Ophthalmology, Wash. Univ., St. Louis, 1968-71; Fellowship studies, El Salvador, S.F., 1971-72; cons. in neurophthalmology, VA Hosp., S.F., St. Mary's Hosp., S.F. 1972-74; Prof. of Ophthalmology, Pac. Med. Center, S.F., 1972---; Cons., S.F. Gen. Hosp., 1972---; Prof., Cal. State Univ., S.F., 1974; Assoc. Examiner, Am. Bd. of Ophthalmology, 1975---; apptd. Physician/Cons., Vets. Adminstrn., Martinez, 1978---. Honors incl.: Nat. Merit Scholar, Calif. State Scholar, Soroptimist Fellowship, Fellow, Am. Bd. of Ophthalmology & Otolaryngology, 1974, Am. Bd. of Ophthalmology, 1973; Award, Internat. Eye Found., 1971; NIH Fellow, 1971-72. Mem.: S.F., Calif., Am. Med. Socs.; Assn. for Research in Vision and Ophthal.; Pan Am. Assn. of Ophthal.; Soc. of Heed Fellows; Pacific Coast Oto-Ophthal. Soc.; Lane Med. Soc., v.p. 1975-76; founder, Internat. Congress of Neuro-Ophthal.; Cordes Soc.; chrtr. mem. Am. Soc. of Ultrasound; fellow, Am. Coll. of Surgeons; founder, Orbit Soc. Res.: 819 Spring Dr., Mill Valley, CA 94941; Office: Pacific Medical Center, 2340 Clay, San Francisco, CA 94115.

NEWMARK, MILTON MAXWELL
Attorney at Law
b. Feb. 24, 1916, Oakland, Calif.; s. Milton and Mary (Maxwell) Newmark; A.B., Univ. Calif., Berkeley, 1936, J.D. 1947; m. Marion Irene Johnson, July 31, 1941; daus.: Mari Anderson, Lucy Sammons, Grace M. Career: admitted to Calif. Bar, 1941; partner (with father), law practice, S.F., 1940-56; pvt. practice law, S.F. 1956-62; Lafayette, Calif. 1962---. Lectr. on bankruptcy, State Bar of Calif. Continuing Edn. Pgm. 1962---. U.S. Army (1942-46), WW II. Lt. Col., USAR. Mem.: Am. Legion; Mt. Diablo, S.F., Am. Bar Assns.; Alameda Co. Repub. Central Com. 1940-41, pres. Alameda Repub. Assembly, 1950; Scabbard and Blade; Shriner. Congregationalist. Res.: 609 Terra Calif. Dr., No. 6, Walnut Creek; Office: 986 Moraga Rd., P.O. Box 375, Lafayette, CA 94549.

NICHOLAS, COLLEEN M.
Realtor
b. June 12, 1932, Lafayette, Ind.; d. Maj. Gen. (ret.) Harold A. (dec., was Adj. Gen. of Ind.) and Florence M. Doherty; grandau. of Arthur Doherty, Episc. Bishop of Nebr.; grad. Purdue Univ., 1954; chil.: James G., b. Jan. 2, 1958; Christopher G., b. Feb. 16, 1960. Career: v.p., Nicholas Mgmt. Co., Santa Monica, 1969-72; v.p., Wayman of Fallbrook (realtors), 1973-77; pres., Wyman Co., 1977---. Mem.: bd. dir. and treas., 1977, Fallbrook C. of C.; secty., treas., 1977, Fallbrook Bd. of Realtors; del. 1976-77, Calif. Assn. Realtors; Pi Beta Phi, 1953. Episcopalian; pres. Women of St. Matthews, Pac. Palisades, 1968; Rec.: tennis, racing sailboats. Home: 39295 DeLuz Rd., Fallbrook, CA; Office: 1102 S. Main St., Fallbrook, CA.

NICKEL, KAREN LOUISE
Clinical Chemist
b. Feb. 22, 1939, Trail, B.C., Can.; d. Theodore W. and Marianne G. Sahlstrom; B.S., Oregon State Univ., 1961; M.S., 1966; Ph.D., Kansas State Univ., 1968; m. Phillip A. Nickel, Ph.D., Aug. 30, 1959, Albany, Ore.; chil.: Mark Phillip b. Sept. 29, 1963; Jamie Louise, b. May 22, 1967. Career: research assoc., Sci. Research Inst., 1961-63; grad. research Asst., Kansas State Univ., 1963-68; instr. chemistry, 1969; analytical chemist, Burroughs Corp., 1969-71; clin. chemist trainee, 1972, clin. chem., Westlake Hosp. 1972; mgr., radio assay, Reference Lab., 1973---. Calif. licensed clin. chemist, 1973---; Nat. reg. clin. chemist, 1975; Am. Bd. clin. chemists, 1978; Mem.: Am. Assn. Clin. Chemists; So. Calif. sect. edn. chmn., 1976-78, chmn, 1979; Clin. Radioassay Soc., mem. chmn. So. Calif. sect. 1977---; Am. Chem. Soc., 1966---. Baptist, youth leader. Hobby: stained glass windows. Rec.: skiing. Office: Reference Lab., 1011 Rancho Conejo Blvd., Newbury Park, CA 91320.

NICOLAIDES, JOHN DUDLEY
Aerospace Engineer
b. Feb. 13, 1923, Washington, D.C.; s. Phidias John and Marie (Kelly) Nicolaides; B.A., Lehigh Univ., 1943; postgrad., Rensselaer Poly. Inst., 1943-44; M.S. in Engring., Johns Hopkins Univ., 1953; Ph.D., Catholic Univ. of Am., 1962; m. Virginia Driscoll, June 9, 1945, Albany, N.Y.; dau., Kathleen, b. Dec. 3, 1961. Career: Project Engr., General Electric Co., 1946-48; research sci., Ballistic Research Lab., Aberdeen Proving Ground, Md., 1948-53; asst. Aerodynamics, Hydrodynamics and Ballistics, then Tech. Dir. Astronautics, Bureau Naval Weapons, 1953-61; asst. to assoc. adminstr. Space Scis. & Applications, then dir. Program Review & Resources Mgmt., NASA, 1961-64; chmn. & prof. Dept. Aerospace Engring., Univ. of Notre Dame, 1964-74; pres., A-E-R-O, 1969---; Head, Aerospace Engring. Dept., Cal Poly Univ., San Luis Obispo, 1975---; cons. in field, 1964---. Author: Missile Flight Dynamics, 1957; Advances in Space Sci. and Technology, vol. 5, 1955; Designer: Parafoil Flying Wing, Plus six golf ball, Free Wing Flyer flying machine. Ofcr., USNR, 1943-46. Mem.: Am. Inst. Aeron. and Astron.; Pilots Club; Sigma Xi. Roman Catholic. Hobbies: golf, flying. Res.: 2048 Skylark Lane, San Luis Obispo, CA 93401; Office: Cal Poly, San Luis Obispo, CA.

NIELSEN, HELEN BERNIECE
Author
b. Oct. 23, 1918, Roseville, Ill.; d. Niels Christian and May (Christensen) Nielsen; ed. (scholarships) Chicago Art Inst. 1931-33; journalism ext. course, 1935. Career: Costumier, Old Globe Theatre, Chicago, 1933-35; freelance journalism; draftsman, 1941-45; script writer, Perry Mason and Alfred Hitchcock TV series; many other TV scripts, short stories and novelettes (mystery and Suspense); first publ. novel, The Kind Man, 1951; Gold Coast Nocturne, 1951; Orbit Delayed, 1952; Woman on the Roof, 1954; Borrow the Night, 1955; The Crime is Murder, 1956; False Witness, 1957; The Fifth Caller, 1959; Sing Me a Murder, 1960; Woman Missing and Other Stories (anthology), 1962; Verdict Suspended, 1964; After Midnight, 1966; A Killer in the Street, 1967; The Falling Man, 1968 (15 publ. books 1971). Darkest Hour, Shot on Location, The Severed Key, The Brink of Murder, all since 1971. Awards: (short story hons.) Best Detective Stories of Yr. (David Cooke), 1955, 59; Best of Manhunt, 1957; Alfred Hitchcock Anthologies, 1962, 70; Ellery Queen's Double Dozen, 1964; Best Legal Stories (2, John Welsome, Faber, London), 1970; feat. in Contemporary Writers, and Boston Univ.-Mugar Libraries Memorabilia Collection, others. Mem.: Author's League of Am.; dist. secty. Calif. Dem. Club, Stevenson Dem. Club, 1957, del. Dem. State Conv. First Ch. Chr. Sci., Boston, 17th Ch. L.A. Hobby: raising Norwegian Elkhounds. Rec.: travel. Res.: 2622 Victoria Dr., Laguna Beach, CA 92651.

NIELSEN, THOMAS H.
Vice President, The Irvine Company
b. Nov. 7, 1930, Fullerton, Calif.; s. Harold and Ellen Nielsen; B.S., Engr., summa cum laude, Univ. Wash., 1952; M.B.A., Stanford Univ., 1957; m. Marilyn Oldroyd, Mar. 5, 1955, Utah; chil.: John Thomas, b. Mar. 5, 1956; Peter Martin, b. Aug. 22, 1958; Kirsten Helen, b. July 15, 1962. Career: Asst. Secty. of the Air Force, Fin. Mgmt., 1967-69; Sr. v.p., U.S. Financial 1969-72; pres., Malone Devel. Co., 1972-78; pres., T.H. Nielsen Corp., 1973---; v.p., The Irvine Co., 1978---. Lt., USN, 1952-55. Mem.: Phi Beta Kappa, Tau Beta Pi, Sigma Pi. University Club, City Club, Assoc. Bldrs. & Contrs. Rec.: tennis, jogging. Res.: 2587 Ardath Rd., La Jolla, CA; Office: 610 Newport Center Dr., Newport Beach, CA 92663.

NIEMEROW, RICHARD ALLAN
Business Owner — Executive
b. Nov. 7, 1945, Los Angeles; s. Morris and Dorothy Niemerow; student, Calif. Polytech. Coll., Pomona; B.A. sociology, Cal. State, Northridge; cons. training, Hubbard Coll., L.A.; m. Celia Steinlauf, Dec. 22, 1968, Sherman Oaks, Calif.; chil.: Adena, b. Aug. 23, 1972; Daryl, b. Apr. 19, 1974; Daron, b. June 23, 1978. Career: exec. trainee, Ohrbachs Dept. Store, 1967-68; dept. head, Longs Drugs, 1968-69; mgmt., Better Drugs, 1969-71; computer inventory control, Bergen Brunswig Corp., 1971-73; part owner, Vicente Pharmacy of Calif., Inc., 1973---; pres., Exec. Mgmt. Specialists, Inc., 1976---. Served, U.S. Coast Guard, Disaster Recovery Unit. Pub. speaking tours on mgmt., Rotary Clubs, bus. groups. Mem.: Brentwood Bus. Assn.; W.L.A. Chamber of C.; So. Calif., Am. and Santa Monica Bay Pharmaceutical Assns. Jewish. Hobbies: painting, photog. Rec.: racquetball, tennis, fishing. Home: 4430 Estrondo Dr., Encino, CA 91436; Office: 1758 Taft Ave., Hollywood, CA 90028.

NIENOW, HARVEY CHARLES
Patent Lawyer
b. Dec. 21, 1922, Milwaukee, Wis.; s. Bernhard C. and Alma M. Nienow; B.S., mech. engr., Univ. Wis., 1947; J.D., Marquette Univ., 1950; m. Mary Debney, Oct. 22, 1955, Milwaukee, Wis.; chil.: Mary Elizabeth, b. Dec. 25, 1956; Thomas Harvey, b. Aug. 17, 1958; John Robert, b. May 25, 1960; Paul William, b. Oct. 26, 1965. Career: engring. instr., Marquette Univ. Sch. of Engring.; patent lawyer, Cutler Hammer, Milwaukee, Wis., 1950-53; patent lawyer, BASO, Inc., Milwaukee, 1953-57; patent lawyer, Borg Warner Corp., Santa Ana, 1957-61; patent lawyer, Nienow & Frater (pvt. practice), Santa Ana, 1961---. USNR, 1944-46. Mem.: Orange Co. Bar Assn., 1961---, dir. 1970-74; Patent Law Assn. of Milwaukee, Secty.; Santa Ana-Tustin YMCA, dir. 1966-72; pres. 1967-70; Boys Club of Santa Ana, 1970---, dir. 1970---; B.S.A. Orange Co. Council, 1973---; Las Flores Com. Chmn. 1975---; v.p. Scouting, Orange Council 1978; Santa Ana-Tustin Comm. Chest, 1967-71, pres. 1970-71; Santa Ana Comm. Hosp. Trustee, 1969-74. Clubs: Rotary of Santa Ana, pres. 1966-67; Mason (Shriner), 1958---; Santa Ana Country, mem. House Com. Presbyterian, Elder. Hobbies: woodworking, golf, bridge. Home: 918 River Lane, Santa Ana, CA 92706; Office: 888 N. Main St., Suite 908, Santa Ana, CA 92701.

NIERENBERG, WILLIAM A.
Director, Scripps Institute of Oceanography
b. Feb. 13, 1919, NYC; s. Joseph and Minnie (Drucker) Nierenberg; B.S. (physics), City Coll. of N.Y. 1939; Univ. of Paris; M.A. (physics), Columbia Univ., N.Y. 1942, Ph.D., 1947; m. Edith Meyerson, N.Y. 1941; chil.: Victoria Jean Tschinkel, b. Oct. 31, 1947; Nicolas Clarke Eugene, b. Dec. 15, 1956. Career: Tutor, City Coll. of N.Y. 1939-42; physicist, Manhattan Proj., NYC, 1942-45; instr. Columbia Univ. 1946-48; asst. prof. Univ. of Mich. 1948-50; assoc. prof. Univ. of Calif., Berkeley, 1950-53; dir. Hudson Labs., Columbia, 1953-54; cons. Natl. Research Council, Wash. D.C. 1954-59; prof. Univ. of Calif., Berkeley, and secty. Am. Phys. Soc., NYC 1954-60; cons. Natl. Security Agcy. 1958-60; cons. Ofc. of Sci. and Tech., Wash. D.C. 1958-73; prof. assoc Univ. of Paris, Fr. 1960-62; asst. secty gen. for Sci. Affairs, NATO, Paris, 1960-62; cons. Inst. for Def. Analyses, Washington D.C., 1963-73; dir. Scripps Inst. of Oceanography, Univ. of Calif. at S.D. La Jolla, 1965---, v.-chancellor, Marine Scis. 1969---; cons. Advanced Research Projs. Agcy., Wash., D.C. 1967---; cons. Natl. Council on Marine Resources and Engring. Devel., Wash. 1968---; White House Task Force on Oceanography, 1969-70; Author: 130 profl. publs. incl. NATO Sci. Pgm., Unless Peace Comes (London), Tech. and Polit. Problems of the Ocean Floor, 1969; Awards: William Lowell Putnam Prize Golden Dolphin Award, Townsend Harris Award, CCNY Alumni Assn.; Officer de L.ordre Natl. de Merite by French Govt.; Assn. Artistico Letteraria Internazionale. Mem.: (60 profl. socs.) fellow, Am. Phys. Soc.; bd. dirs. Natl. Oceanography Assn.; internat. Adv. Com. Hebrew Univ. Red Sea Marine Research Sta.; adv. bd. Hebrew Univ. of Jerusalem at Eilat, Israel; Am. Acad. of Arts and Scis.; Navy League of U.S.; AAAS; World Affairs Council of S.D.; Town Hall; Phi Beta Kappa, Sigma Xi; clubs: Explorers, Cosmos. Res.: 9581 La Jolla Farms Rd., La Jolla, CA 92307; Office: Scripps Inst. of Oceanography, La Jolla, CA 92093.

NIGG, CYRIL C.
Food Company President
b. Mar. 12, 1905, Mankato, Minn.; s. Peter J. and Rose (Ulman) Nigg; ed. A.B., Univ. of Calif., L.A. 1927; m. Edith Witkowski, L.A., Feb. 9, 1928; chil.: C. Peter, b. Nov. 3, 1929; Mrs. Leon W. (Nancy) Doty, b. Feb. 28, 1931. Career: Pres., Bell Brand Foods, Ltd.; chmn. bd., Tom Sawyer Foods, Inc.; dir. Calif. Consumers Corp.; dir. Bee Industries, Inc.; dir. Food Employers Council. Awards: recipient, UCLA Alumnus of Yr. Award, 1957; Knight Comdr. of Order of St. Gregory the Great. Mem.: past pres., Natl. Potato Chip Inst.; past pres., Sales Execs. Club; past pres. Food Industries Sales Mgrs. Club; past pres., Illuminators, Inc.; past pres., UCLA Alumni Assn.; regent Immaculate Heart Coll.; trustee, Catholic. Welfare Bur.; dir Archbishop's Fund for Charity; Kappa Sigma, Rotary Club, Newman Club, Calif. Club. Cath. Res.: 875 Comstock Ave., L.A., CA 90024; Office: P.O. Box 2402, Terminal Annex, L.A., CA 90054.

NILAND, WILLIAM PATRICK
College President
b. Dec. 21, 1917, Lowell, Mass.; s. William Francis and Sabina Agnes (Shaughnessy) Niland; A.B., St. Mary's Coll. of Calif. 1939; M.A., Cath. Univ. of Am. 1945;

Ed.D., Univ. of Calif., Berkeley, 1964; m. Elizabeth Janes Tierney, Carmel, Calif., Feb. 14, 1952; chil.: William Francis, b. 1953; Ann Marie, b. 1954; Joseph James, b. 1956; Martha Marie, b. 1957. Career: Tchr., H.S. and Colls. Calif. 1940-45, 1952-54; prin. Armstrong H.S., Sacro., 1945-48; acad. dean, St. Mary's Coll., Calif. 1949-51; dean-instr., Coalinga (Calif.) Coll. 1954-57, pres. 1957-62; lectr. in edn-supv. grad. internship pgm., jr. coll. tchr. edn., Univ. of Calif., Berkeley, 1962-65; pres. Diablo Valley Coll. 1965. Mem.: Calif. Teachers Assn., Natl. Assn. English Tchrs.; Am. Sociology Assn.; chmn. bd. trustees, St. Mary's Coll. 1973-74; Comm. on Instr., Am. Assn. Jr. Colls.; Elk. Democrat. Roman Catholic. Hobbies: lapidary, writing. Rec.: golf, rock hounding. Res.: 417 Candleberry Rd., Walnut Creek, CA; Office: 321 Golf Club Rd., Pleasant Hill, CA 94523.

NIXON, RICHARD MILHOUS
Former President of United States
b. Jan. 9, 1913, Yorba Linda, CA; s. Francis A. and Hannah (Milhous) Nixon; A.B., Whittier Coll. 1934; LL.B. with honors, Duke Univ. Law Sch. 1937; m. Thelma Catherine Patricia Ryan, June 21, 1940; daus.: Mrs. Edward Finch (Patricia) Cox; Mrs. Dwight David (Julie) Eisenhower, II. Career: Gen. law practice, Whittier, Calif., 1937-42; atty. with Office of Emergency Mgmt., Wash., D.C., Jan.-Aug. 1942; elected to 80th Congress, 12th Calif. Dist. 1947-49; mem. House of Reps., Edn. and Labor Com., Un-Am. Activities Com., Congress, 1947-50; elected U.S. Senator, 1950-53; elected v.p., U.S. of Am., Nov. 4, 1952; re-elected 1956 (1952-61); Repub. nom., U.S. Pres. 1960; Repub. nom., Gov. of Calif. 1962; atty. at law, counsel, Adams, Duque & Hazeltine firm, L.A. 1961-63; mem. firm. Mudge, Stern, Baldwin & Todd, NYC 1963-64; partner, Nixon, Mudge, Rose, Gutherie & Alexander, NYC 1964-67; dir. Harsco Corp.; elected 37th President of the U.S.A., Nov. 5, 1968; re-elected, 1972 (resigned Aug. 9, 1974). Author: Six Crises, 1962; The Memoirs of Richard Nixon, 1978. Lt. Comdr., USN (1942-46), WW II. Mem.: bd. of trustees, Whittier Coll.; Order of the Coif, Soc. of Friends Church. Res.: 4026 Calle Ariana, San Clemente, CA 92672.

NOBLE, CHARLES EDWARD
Business Executive
b. Sept. 18, 1930, Boston; s. Charles A., Jr. and Agnes (von Adelung) Noble; A.B., cum laude, Harvard Coll., 1952; stu., Harvard Bus. Sch. 1954. Career: Security analyst, Bank of Calif., 1957-58, with Loomis Sayeles & Co., 1958---: vice pres. and mgr. San Francisco office, dir., 1968---. Pres., San Francisco Boys Club, 1979; Trustee, The Thacher Sch. 1978; Chmn. Wine & Food Soc. of S.F., 1975-77. AUS, 1954-56. Mem.: University Club of S.F., pres. 1961; Pacific Union Club; S.F. Golf Club; Bohemian Club; Villa Taverna; Harvard Club, N.Y.C. Rec.: golf, duck shooting. Res.: 1170 Sacramento St., San Francisco, CA 94108; Office: Two Embarcadero Ctr., San Francisco, CA 94111.

NOLAN, WILLIAM FRANCIS
Author
b. Mar. 6, 1928, Kansas City, Mo.; s. Michael Cahill and Bernadette (Kelly) Nolan; ed. Kansas City Art Inst. 1946-47; San Diego State Coll. 1947-48; L.A. City Coll. 1953. Career: Cartoonist, Hall Bros. Greeting Card Co., Kansas City, 1945; commercial artist, 1948-51; freelance artist, 1951-52; interviewer, Calif. State Dept. of Employment, Inglewood, 1955; freelance writer, 1956---; film actor, 1961---; guest lectr., UCLA; sci. fiction book reviewer, L.A. Times, 1966---. Author: Impact 20 (collection of short fiction), 1963; Men of Thunder, 1964; John Huston, King Rebel, 1965; Sinners and Supermen, 1965; Logan's Run, 1967; editor: Omnibus of Speed, 1958; When Engines Roar, 1964; The Pseudo-People, 1965; Man Against Tomorrow, 1965; 3 to the Highest Power, 1968; A Sea of Space, 1968; contrib. ed. several mags., managing ed., columnist, ed.-publ.: Ray Bradbury Review, 1952; 325 publ. stories, articles, essays to mags. and newspapers, TV writer, screen plays, Columbia Studios, Am. Internat., Triangle Prodns., Mot. Pics. Internat.; writings translated into Spanish, French, Ger., Italian, Swedish by publs. around world. Awards: Adventure on Wheels, cited by Am. Lit. Assn. as one of outstanding books for young adult, 1959, writings selected for 25 anthologies, incl. Years Best S.F., Adventures for Americans (sch. text), A Cavalcade of Life in Writing (coll. text); Hobbies: collecting books, motor racing. Res.: 1337½ S. Roxbury Dr., L.A., CA 90035.

NOORDEWIER, SHARON SPENCER
Business Executive
b. May 2, 1940, Candillac, Mich.; d. Daniel William and Martha (Heinz) Spencer; cousin, Sir Winston Spencer Churchill, 1874-1965, Br. statesman, prime minister; stu., Mich. State Univ.; Cal. State Univ., Fullerton & Hayward; m. Paul William Ronan, 1974, Walnut Creek; chil.: Pamela Noordewier, b. Oct. 31, 1960; Michael Noordewier, b. Sept. 13, 1963; Cynthia Greig, b. Jan. 4, 1951. Career: Dir. of Systems & Devel., Pacific Securities Depository Trust Co. (subs. of Pacific Stock Exch.), 1975, v.p., 1976---. Hobby: writing. Rec.: running. Res.: 284 Los Cerros, Walnut Creek; Office: 301 Pine St., San Francisco, CA 94104.

NORRIS, KENNETH STAFFORD
Professor of Natural History
b. Aug. 11, 1924, Los Angeles; s. Robert DeWitt and Jessie (Matheson) Norris; bro. Robert Norris, Prof. Geology, UC Santa Barbara; B.A., UCLA, 1948; M.A., 1951; Ph.D., Scripps Inst., 1959; m. Phyllis Strout, 1953, Los Angeles; chil.: Susan, b. 1954; Nancy, b. 1956, Barbara, b. 1958; Richard, b. 1959. Career: Past v.p., Marine Park Corp.; Curator, Marineland of the Pacific, 1953-60; dir. Oceanic Inst., Hawaii, 1968-71; Prof. of Natural History, UCLA, 1968-72; dir. Coastal Marine Lab., Univ. Calif., Santa Cruz, 1972-74; chmn., Environmental Studies Bd., UC Santa Cruz, 1977-78. Lt., j.g., USN, 1942-46; deck, gunnery, Pacific and European Theatres, Philippine invasion. Publs. include articles, books on desert biology and zoogeographic hist., physiological ecology, ichthyology, conservation, natural hist. and echonavigation of marine mammals. Awards: Brain Research Inst., UCLA 1966; Mercer Award, Best Research in Am. Ecology, 1963, 64; Stoye Award, Best Research Paper, Ichthyology, 1950; Stoye Award, Herpetology, 1951; Fellow: Calif. Acad. of Scis., L.A. Co. Mus., AAAS, Am. Fisheries Soc.; Man of Yr., Am. Cetean Soc., 1976. Mem.: trustee, Pacific Marine Research Center; adv. council, Hubbs-Sea World Research Inst., 1977---; adv. com., Ocean Research and Edn. Soc. 1976---; adv. com., US Marine Mammal Commn., hd. for tuna-porpoise problem, 1972-75; adv. com. Friends of Sea Otter, 1973---; founder, Hawaii Environmental Simulation Lab.; mem.: World Population Council, Sigma Xi, W. Soc. of Naturalists, Nature Conservancy. Ch. Gospel Ministry, Minister. Res.: 1987 Smith Grade, Santa Cruz, CA; Office: Univ. Calif. Santa Cruz, CA 95064.

NORRIS, WILLIAM A.
Attorney at Law
b. Aug. 20, 1927, Turtle Creek, Pa.; s. George and Florence (Clive) Norris; A.B. Phi Beta Kappa, Princeton Univ., 1951; J.D., Stanford Univ., 1954 (Order of the Coif, exec. editor, Stanford Law Review); m. Merry Wright, Nov. 23, 1974, San Marino, Calif.; chil.: Barbara, b. July 6, 1951; Donald, b. Jan. 20, 1953; Kim, b. Apr. 21, 1955; Alison, b. Jan. 9, 1959. Career: Law clerk, Mr. Justice Wm. O. Douglas, U.S. Supreme Ct., 1955 term; lawyer, Tuttle & Taylor, Los Angeles, 1956---. Spec. council, President's commn. on airlines controversy, 1961; mem. Calif. State Bd. of Edn., 1961-67; mem. bd. of trustees, Calif. State Coll., 1966-71; pres., L.A. Police Commn., 1973-74. Democratic nominee, Atty. Gen. of Calif., 1974. Home: 315 S. June St., Los Angeles, CA 90020; Office: 609 S. Grand Ave., L.A., CA 90017.

NORTHEY, LYAL ELITTA
Realtor
b. Sept. 1, 1913, Greeley, Co., Nebr.; d. Jens Wicheli Kligio and Lydia K. Johansen; B.A., Stanford Univ., 1938; M.A., 1943; m. 2d. 1945, Reno, Nev.; chil.: Colitta Yvonne Gibb-Brown; Verone C. Gibb; Durward E. Gibb; Reavis E. Gibb; Arley T. Kisling. Career: tchr. all grades, one room sch., Nebr., 1930-35; secty., Co. Supt. Edn., 1935-38; Calif. Lic. active real estate broker, 1939: also land and farm broker, International; owner, Lyal E. Northey Realty; active in shopping center and sub-div. activities; Honored by streets named: Lyal Lane in Shasta and Tehama counties: profl. certified G.R.I., 1970; promotional weekly TV show for realtors, Santa Rosa, 1972-76; originator: hist. renovation of town of Los Molinos; chmn., C. of C. beautification com.; rider, Shasta Co. Sheriff Posse, 1960---; Mem. Bus. & Profl. Women. 1944---, pres. 7 times; Eastern Star, 1944---. Baptist ch. Hobby: 12 polled Hereford mini ranch. Office: 9217 Lyal Lane, Los Molinos, CA 96055.

NORWOOD, B.J. SCOTT
Educator
b. June 24, 1926, San Diego; s. Guy Johns and Louise (Trabert) Norwood; B.S., UCLA, 1949; M.B.A., Harvard Univ. Grad. Sch. of Bus., 1951; m. Barbara Brown, Jan. 28, 1956, San Diego; chil.: J. Scott, b. 1958; Beverly L., b. 1960. Career: Asst. Prof., now Prof. of Business, San Jose State Univ., 1955---; Cons. and Bd. Dir., Radiation Detection Co., Sunnyvale, 1960---, chmn. exec. com. 1966-72, chmn. of the bd., 1972---. Served USN, WW II, now USNR. Contbr. to profl. and trade journs. Named Outstanding Prof. of San Jose State Univ., 1976; named an Outstanding Educator of America, 1973. Mem.: Phi Kappa Phi, pres. San Jose State Univ. Chpt. 1976-78; Alpha Tau Omega frat.; Eta Mu Pi frat. Res.: 19561 Moray Ct., Saratoga, CA 95070; Office: Sch. of Business, San Jose State Univ., San Jose, CA 95192.

NOWELL, ELIZABETH CAMERON
Author
b. Berkeley; dau. Alfred George and Edith (Catton) Cameron; desc., William Robert Wheaton, Calif. pioneer, 1849; A.B., San Jose State Coll., 1929; M.A., Stanford Univ., 1937; m. Vice Adm. Arthur Granville Robinson (dec.); m. 2d. Nelson Taplin Nowell (dec.). Career: Mem. Faculty, San Jose State Coll., 1928, 1939; Univ. of Calif., Ext. Div. 1939-42; head elem. div., John C. Winston Co., 1942-43; Silver Burdett 1943-44; D.C. Heath 1944-46; Univ. of Minn. English Dept. 1947; writer, editor, General Mills, 1947-50; freelance writer, 1950---; Assoc. Editor, American Home Mag., California Edition 1965-70; author 24 books for children, numerous teaching manuals, feature articles in nat. mags. Pen names: Elizabeth Clemons, Elizabeth Cameron. Mem.: Community Hosp. Aux. Bd. of Dirs. 1962; Vis. Nurses Bd. of Dirs. 1965; Symphony Guild bd. dir. 1957, 73; Harrison Mem. Lib. 1971-75; pres. Monterey Peninsula Chpt. Embroiderers' Guild of Am. 1977-78; Nat. Bd., Nat. Embroidery Teachers Assn. 1977---; nat. bd., Embroiderers' Guild of Am., 1979---. Episcopalian, Vestry, 1974-77. Hobbies: Canvas embroidery, collecting shells. Address: P.O.B. 686, Carmel, CA 93921.

NOYCE, ROBERT N.
Chairman, Intel Corporation
b. Dec. 12, 1927, Burlington, Ia.; s. Ralph and Harriet Noyce; B.A., Grinnell Coll., 1949; Ph.d., Mass. Inst. Tech., 1953; m. Ann S. Bowers, Nov. 28, 1976, Los Altos, Calif.; chil.: William, b. July 15, 1954; Pendred, b. Oct. 16, 1955; Priscilla, b. June 12, 1957; Margaret, b. Sept. 7, 1960. Career: Tech. staff, Research Div., Philco Corp., 1954-56; tech. staff mem., Shockley Semiconductor Lab., 1956-57; v.p., Fairchild Camera & Instrument, 1957-68; Chmn. of Bd., Intel Corp., Santa Clara, 1968---. Dir., Coherent Radiation Inc.; chmn., Caere Corp., 1977---. Trustee, Grinnell Coll. Awards: IEEE Medal of Honor, 1978; IEEE Cledo Brunetti Award 1978; Harry Goode Award, Am. Fedn. of Information Processing 1978; Stuart Ballantine Medal, 1966. Fellow, IEEE; mem. Nat. Acad. of Engring. Hobby: flying. Office: 3065 Bowers Ave., Santa Clara, CA 95051.

NOYES, PETER R.
TV News Journalist, Editor — Director — Producer
b. July 23, 1930, Los Angeles; s. Philip W. (L.A. civic leader) and Amelia (Stikeleather) Noyes: gr.son of Charles Noyes, Demo. party leader, mem. S.D. bd. of edn.; B.S., Loyola Univ., L.A., 1952; M.S., UCLA, 1957; m. Grace Bohanon, Oct. 3, 1959, L.A.; son John Philip, b. Aug. 17, 1960. Career: asst. city editor, Pacific Stars & Stripes, 1953-54, Wash. correspondent, 1954-55; writer — city editor, L.A. City News Service, 1956-61; writer, producer, KNXT (CBS) TV News, L.A., 1961-65; news dir. KXTV (CBS) Sacramento, 1965-66; exec. producer, KNXT News, L.A., 1966-72; sr. producer, KABC-TV News, L.A., 1972-75; news dir., KFMB-TV News, San Diego, 1975-77; exec. editor, KNBC News, Burbank, 1977-79; head of Unit 4 investigative team, 1979---; also instr. Journalism, USC, 1974---. Recipient: Peabody Award, investigative reporting, 1976; Emmy Awards for 1970, 1971, 1974; Grand Award of L.A. Press Club, 1972, 1974, 1975; Golden Mikes for broadcasting excellence, 1965-68, 69, 70, 75; Author: Legacy of Doubt, pub. 1973. Served USN, journalist, 1953-55. Mem.: Big Brothers, dir., 1968-69; Catholic Press Council of So. Calif., pres., 1974; Kappa Tau Alpha; Delta Sigma Phi. Roman Catholic. Office: KNBC News, 300 W. Alameda Ave., Burbank, CA 91523.

NUNIS, DOYCE BLACKMAN, JR.
Historian
b. May 30, 1924, Cedartown, Ga.; s. Doyce B., Sr. and

Winnie Ethel (Morris) Nunis; B.A., UCLA 1947; M.S. (edn.), USC 1950, M.Ed., 1952; Ph.D. (hist.) 1958. Career: Tchr., Calif. pub. schs. 1948-51; grad. fellowship, USC 1951-53; lectr., Dept. of Am. Civilization & Institutions, USC 1953-56; instr. in hist., El Camino Coll., Calif. 1956-59; UCLA 1959-65; assoc. prof., prof. hist., USC 1965---. Author: (books) Andrew Sublette, Rocky Mountain Prince (1808-53), publ. L.A. 1960; Josiah Belden, 1841 Calif. Overland Pioneer: His Memoir andEarly Letters, publ. Georgetown, Calif. 1962; The Golden Frontier: The Recollections of Herman Francis Rinehart (1851-69), publ. Austin, Tex. 1964; The Calif. Diary of Faxon Dean Atherton (1836-39), publ. San Francisco, 1964; The Gold Rush Letters of Jasper Smith Hill, publ. San Francisco, 1964; The Letters of A Young Miner (1849-52), punl. 1964; Journey of James H. Bull, Baja, Calif. Oct. 1843 to Jan. 1844, publ. 1965; The Trials of Isaac Graham, publ 1967; A Med. Journey in Calif. by Pierre Garnier, M.D., publ. 1967; Hudson's Bay Company's First Fur Brigade to the Sacramento Valley (1829-30), publ. 1967; Past is Prologue: A Centennial Profile of the Pacific Mutual Life Ins. Co., publ. 1968; A Journey on Two Oceans, publ. 1971; The Vigilance Committee of 1856: Three Views, publ. 1971; The Drawings of Ignacio Tirsch, publ. 1972; Los Angeles and Its Environs in the 20th Century (bibliography), publ. 1973; A History of American Political Thought, 2 vols., publ. 1975; The Mexican War in Baja California, publ. 1977; contrib. numerous articles to scholarly hist. mags.; ed. So. Calif. Quarterly, 1962---. Awards: Del Amo Found. Grant for research abroad, 1956; Henry E. Huntington Lib. Grant-in-Aid, 1960; John Simon Guggenheim Mem. Fellowship, 1963-64; Award of Merit, Am. Assn. State and Local Hist., 1965. Mem.: Hist. Soc. of So. Calif. 1962---; L.A. Corral of Westerners, Phi Alpha Theta, Pi Sigma Alpha, Zamorano Club; fellow, Am. Philosophical Soc. 1969; research assoc. L.A. Co. Mus. of Natural Hist. 1972. Office: Dept. of Hist., USC, Los Angeles, CA 90007.

NYLAND, GEORGE
Plant Pathologist
b. Apr. 3, 1919, Eastburg, Alberta, Canada; B.S., Washington State Univ., 1940; M.S., Louisiana State Univ., 1942; Ph.D., Wash. State Univ., Pullman, Wash., 1948; m. Gertrude A. Gunning, May 18, 1941, Baton Rouge, La.; chil.: Thomas G., b. Apr. 5, 1945; Robert J., b. Dec. 26, 1952; Scott A., b. Aug. 22, 1953. Career: Plant pathologist and instr., Wash. State Univ., 1946-47; asst. prof., Univ. Calif., Davis, 1948---, professor, 1962---; Plant Pathologist ---. Lt., USN, 1942-46. Researcher on virus and virus like diseases of fruit trees and ornamentals; thermotherapy of virus diseases. Res.: 656 Sunset Ct., Davis, CA 95616; Office: Univ. Calif., Dept. Plant Pathology, Davis, CA.

NYLES, ROBERT DAVID
Jungian Analyst
b. Mar. 21, 1926, Tientsin, China; B.A., Univ. Calif., Berkeley, 1949; M.A., Univ. of London, 1955, Ph.D., 1956; postgrad. Inst. of Psych., Maudsley Hosp., Univ. of London; Clinique Psych. Ste. Anne, Univ. of Paris; Nat. Inst. Mental Health; Tng. in Analytic Psychology with Prof. C.A. Meier, Clin. & Research Center for Jungian Psychol., Zurich, Switzerland. Career: Jungian Analyst in pvt. practice ---. Res.: P.O.B. 406, Inverness, CA 94937; Office: 1735 Highland Pl., Berkeley, CA 94709.

OAXACA, VIRGINIA C.
Savings and Loan Company Executive
b. Dec. 30, 1940, El Paso, Tex.; d. Angel and Lucinda Nevarez de Oaxaca; B.S. edn., Univ. of Texas, 1962; M.S. counseling & psychology, 1969; grad. Sloan-Merrill Fellow, Grad. Sch. of Bus., Stanford Univ., 1974. Career: personnel mgr., master-charge div., United Calif. Bank. L.A., 1974, a.v.p. for employee realtions, 1975-76; dir. personnel, Rockwell Internat. Space Div., Downey, 1976-77; sr. v.p., Gibraltar Savings and Loan, Beverly Hills, 1977---. Recipient: 1978 Woman of the Year Award for Bus. & Industry, YWCA, L.A.; Stanford-Sloan-Merrill Fellowship, 1973; Nat. Edn. Act. fellowship, 1969. Mem.: Women in Business, pres. bd. dir., 1978; bd. dir., Alumni Assn. of Stanford Univ. Grad. Sch. of Bus.; Orgn. of Women Execs. of L.A.; mem., L.A. Mayor Bradley's Bicentennial Com., 1976. Hobby: real estate; Rec.: tennis, golf. Home: 15480 Antioch, No. 103, Pacific Palisades, CA 90272; Office: 9111 Wilshire Blvd., Beverly Hills, CA 90213.

OBICHERE, BONIFACE IHEWUNWA
Professor of History
b. Nov. 4, 1932, Awaka, Owerri, Nigeria; s. Obichere Ogbuagu Eke and Ibari Ikeri Dikeecha Obichere; B.A. (hon.), Univ. of Minn., 1961; M.A., 1964; postgrad., Univ. of Calif., Berkeley, 1963-64; Ph.D., Oxford Univ., Eng., 1967; m. Armer Gean Brown, Aug. 22, 1964, Berkeley; child: Chikere Ingbolelenwa, b. Apr. 24, 1972, Santa Monica, Calif. Career: hist. master, Mt. St. Mary's Coll., Azaraegbelu, Emekuku, Owerri, 1957-59; tching. asst. Univ. of Calif., Berkeley, 1962-63; tutor, Inst. of Commonwealth Studies, Oxford Univ., 1966-67; Prof. of Hist., UCLA, 1967---; visiting prof., Univ. of Hawaii, Honolulu, 1969-70; visiting prof., Univ. of Ghana, 1970-71; visiting prof., Univ. of Ibadan, Ibadan, Nigeria, 1976-77; dir., African Studies Center, UCLA, 1972-78; lectr. London Services Edn. Com., 1966-67; tutor, African Studies Program, Nations Inc., Berkeley, 1963; instr., Africa Program, St. Paul, Minn., 1963-64; Bd. dir., African Studies Assn., USA, 1971-74; bd. dir., Operation Crossroads Africa Inc., 1975---; bd. dir., L.S.B. Leakey Found., 1973---; founder and editor, The Journal of African Studies, 1974---; editorial bd., Nigerian Behavioural Sci. Journ., Journ. of Black Studies; and Studia Africana, Univ. of Cincinnati, Oh. Author: articles and books incl. West African States and European Expansion, Yale Univ. Press, New Haven, London, 1971; Studies in Southern Nigerian Hist., Frank Cass Ltd., London, 1978; Crisis in Zimbabwe (Rhodesia), Westview Press Inc., Colo., 1979; African States and the Military: Past and Present, Frank Cass Ltd., Lon., 1978; Mem.: Town Hall of Calif.; World Affairs Council of L.A.; Internat. Relations Club; The Inn Club of Am.; Chevron Travel Club; Newmann Club; Am. Hist. Assn.; Hist. Soc. of Nigeria; Hist. Soc. of Ghana; Assn. of Am. Univ. Profs.; Societe Francaise d'Histoire d'Outre-Mer; Internat. Political Sci. Assn.; Economic Hist. Soc.; Royal African Soc. of Britain; Roman Catholic. Hobbies: photog., swimming. Rec.: soccer, tennis. Home: 973 Keniston Ave., L.A., CA 90019; Office: Dept. of Hist., UCLA, 405 Hilgard Ave., L.A., CA 90024.

O'BRIEN, JOHN C.
Professor of Ethics & Economics
b. Hamilton, Scotland; s. Patrick and Mary (Hunt) O'Brien; came to U.S. 1963, naturalized 1968; Diploma Commerce, Univ. Strathclyde, Scotland, 1951; B. Commerce, Univ. London, 1952; A.M., Univ. Notre Dame, 1959; Ph.D., 1961; tchr. certificate, Glasgow Coll., Edn.; m. Jane Estelle Judd, Sept. 1967, Fresno, Calif.; chil.: Kellie Marie, b. 1968; Kerry Patrick, b. 1969; Tracy Anne, b. 1972; Kristen Noel, b. 1976. Career: tchr., Scotland, 1952-56; tching. fellow, Univ. of Notre Dame, 1957-61; mem. faculty: Univ. of British Columbia, Univ. Saskatchewan; Univ. of Pittsburgh; Wilfrid Laurier Univ.; Univ. of Dayton; Cal. State Univ., Fresno, 1965---; visiting prof. Univ. of Pittsburgh, 1970; acad. cons., Catholic Inst. for Social Ethics, London, Eng. Pub. articles and papers in economics, ethics, edn. philosophy, fiction in USA, India, Pakistan, New Zealand, Portugal, Scotland, Tokyo, Japan, Austria, etc. Roman Catholic; soccer coach, St. Anthony's Raiders. Hobbies: art, photog. Rec.: jogging, soccer. Home: 2733 W. Fir Ave., Fresno, CA 93711; Office: CSU Fresno, Cedar and Shaw, Fresno, CA.

O'BRIEN, JOHN JAMES, JR.
Educator
b. Aug. 23, 1923, Hoboken, N.J.; s. John J., Sr. and Bessie (Mount) O'Brien; B.A. Montclair State Coll., 1946; M.A., Columbia Univ., 1949; postgrad. Tchrs. Coll., Columbia Univ., 1950-51; Stanford Univ., 1958; Oregon State Univ., 1959-61; m. Blanche de Puy; chil.: John J. O'Brien III, b. Jan. 13, 1947; Karen (Eversole), b. Jan. 3, 1949. Career: teaching asst. in math, Montclair State Coll., 1946-47; tchr. of math various hi schs., N.J., 1947-53; Jefferson Union Hi. Sch., Daly City, Ca., 1953-54; Roosevelt Jr. H.S., San Jose, Ca., 1954-67; Willow Glen H.S., San Jose, 1967---; instr. math San Jose State Univ. summers 1964-68; instr. extension div. 1961-66; instr. DeAnza Coll. continuing Edn., 1965---; instr. San Jose State Univ. Fall 1972; instr., NSF in-service for hi sch. math tchrs. San Jose State Univ., 1968-69. Author: booklet on math, visual, tching aids, Programmed Remedial Multiplication; co-author: SMSG Programmed First Course in Algebra. Recipient: G.E. Fellowship, 1958; Nat. Sci. Found. Grants, 1959-61. Served with AUS, 1943-45; Decorated Purple Heart, Bronze Star. Mem.: Santa Clara Valley Math Assn., pres. 1967-68; Am. Fedn. of Tchrs., treas. San Jose local 1960-61; bd. dir., Calif. Math Council, 1969-76; CMC

Affiliates' Coordinator, 1969-76; Nat. Council Math Tchrs.; Phi Delta Kappa; Kappa Delta Pi; Math Assn. of Am.; Council Community Coll. Hobbies: reading, travel. Home: 838 S. Baywood Ave., San Jose, CA 95128; Office: Willow Glen Hi Sch., 2001 Cottle Ave., San Jose, CA.

O'BRIEN, RAYMOND F.
President, Consolidated Freightways, Inc.
b. May 31, 1922, Atchison, Kan.; s. James C. and Anna M. (Wagner) O'Brien; B.S., Univ. of Mo. 1948; grad. Advanced Mgmt. Pgm., Harvard Univ. 1966; m. Mary Ann Baugher, Sept. 3, 1947; chil.: William T., b. July 18, 1951; James B., b. Dec. 28, 1949; Kathleen, b. Mar. 5, 1955; Christopher, b. Jan. 12, 1960. Career: Acct. with Peat, Marwick, Mitchell & Co. 1948-52; Riss & Company 1952-58; Consolidated Freightways, Inc. 1958---, controller, 1961, v.p.-treas. 1962, v.p. finance 1967, exec. v.p. 1969, pres. 1975---. 1st Lt., USAF, WW II. Clubs: World Trade, Palo Alto Hills Country, Commonwealth of Calif. Office: 601 California St., San Francisco, CA 94108.

OCKO, FELIX HUGH
Physician
b. Oct. 18, 1912, Brooklyn, N.Y.; s. Samuel E. and Annie (Richman) Ocko; B.S., City Coll., N.Y., 1932; M.S., Emory Univ., 1933; M.D., Rush Med. Coll., Univ. Chicago, 1937; m. Ida Blank, Aug. 4, 1941, Atlanta, Ga.; chil.: Jo Ellen Bazan, b. Dec. 17, 1943; Jonathan Kevin, b. May 29, 1946. Career: Med. Officer, USN, 1937-61 (ret. Capt. M.C., 1961); certified flight surgeon, USN; Chief of Psychiatry, U.S. Naval Hospitals: Gt. Lakes, St. Albans, Oakland. Certified, Am. Bd. of Psychiatry and Neurology 1949; Certified in Psychoanalysis 1961; Dir. of Residency Tng. 1961-71, and Chief of Service, 19688-71, Herrick Mem. Hosp., Berkeley; pres., S.F. Psychoanalytic Inst. and Soc., 1976-77; Asst. Clin. Prof. Psychiat., State Univ. of N.Y. Downstate, 1954-59; Assoc. Clin. Prof. Psychiatry, Med. Sch., Univ. Calif., San Francisco, 1961---. Office: 2006 Dwight Way, Berkeley, CA 94704.

O'CONNOR, DENNIS M.
Hospital Director
b. Apr. 18, 1942, Sioux City, Iowa; s. A.M., D.D.S., and Edna O'Connor; premed. stu., Santa Clara Univ., Monterey Peninsula Coll., San Jose State Univ., M.D., Creighton Univ. Sch. of Med., 1971; m. Paula Imbriana, Monterey, Calif., June 12, 1956; sons, Patrick Michael, b. July 31, 1969; Dennis Alan, b. Aug. 14, 1970. Career: Rotating internship, Herrick Mem. Hosp., Berkeley, 1971-72; residency in Psychiatry, Napa State Hosp., 1972-74 (recipient Outstanding Residents Award); Staff Psychiatrist, Napa State Hosp., 1974-77, Executive Director, 1977---. Mem. Alpha Omega Alpha Honor Med. Soc., 1971---. Diplomate, Nat. Bd. Med. Examiners, 1972. Mem.: Napa Co. Med. Soc.; Calif. Med. Assn.; No. Calif. Psychiatric Soc.; Am. Psychiatric Assn. Address: 3701 Jomar Dr., Napa, CA 94558.

O'CONNOR, GEORGE RICHARD
Research Director
b. Oct. 8, 1928, Cincinnati, Ohio; s. George Leo and Sylvia (Voss) O'Connor; B.A., Harvard Univ., 1950; M.D., Columbia Univ., 1954. Career: Research fellow, Inst. of Biochem., Uppsala, Sweden, 1960-61; State Serum Inst., Copenhagen, Denmark, 1961-62; Asst. Prof. Ophthalmology, Univ. Calif., San Francisco, 1962; assoc. prof. 1968, prof. of Ophthalmology and Dir., Francis I Proctor Found. for Research in Ophthalmology, 1970---. Mem. Visual Sciences Study Sect., NIH, 1965-69; mem. nat. advis. eye council, NIH, 1974-78; Assoc. Editor: Investigative Ophthalmology, 1966-71; Assoc. Editor: Archives of Ophthalmology, and American Journ. Ophthalmology; author 60+ articles on research in eye diseases, mainly toxoplasmosis. Served U.S. Pub. Health Service, Bethesda, Md., 1955-57. Hobbies: archaeology, foreign languages. Res.: 22 Wray Ave., Sausalito, CA 94965; Office: 95 Kirkham St., San Francisco, CA 94122.

ODER, ALBERT LEE
Funeral Director
b. Feb. 25, 1912, Bucyrus, Ohio; s. Clark and Hazel (Lee) Oder; Virginia ancestors, 1774; ed. Cincinnati Coll. of Embalming; S.F. Coll. of Mortuary Sci.; chil.: Julia L., b. Jan. 18, 1948. Career: Funeral director, U.S. Naval Hosp., Bethesda, Md.; Ph.M. 2/c to CPhM (1942-45), WW II; recd. comm. 1960. Mem.: Calif. Funeral Dirs.; pres. Met. Funeral Dirs. Assn. 1950; pres. Berkeley Conv. and Tourist Bur. 1951-52; pres. High 12,

1952; pres. Alameda Co. Vets Comm.; United Crusade; Am. Red Cross Blood Drive of Berkeley; Berkeley Community Welfare; pres. Berkeley C. of C. 1955; dir. Kiwanis Club, 1956; Am. Natl. Assn. Approved Morticians, treas. 1957---; Grand Jury, 1959-60; 1st v-comdr., 10th Dist., Am. Legion 1960 (various ofcs. since 1946); Mason, Elks, Shrine, Eagles, 40 & 8; orgn.-past pres., Trade Club. Republican. Presbyterian. Hobby: coin collection, interior decorating, orgn. work. Res.: 1725 Shattuck Ave., Berkeley, CA 94709; Office: 2414 Grove St., Berkeley, CA 94704.

ODOM, VINCENT LEWIS
Realtor
b. Aug. 30, 1912, Cherryvale, Kan.; s. Clyde W. and Evelyn (Gould) Odom; B.A., Baker Univ. 1933; S.T.B., Boston Univ., 1938; m. Helen Rohrbacher, June 12, 1939, Iowa City, Iowa; Career: Clergyman, Miami, Oakland Park and St. Petersburg, Fla. 1938-43; Chaplain, USN, 1943-46; sales rep. Mission Chem. Co., 1946-51, mgr. 1951-55; co-owner, The Blue Line Co., 1955-57; Mgr., Carter & Higgins Ins. Co., 1957-66; owner, realtor, Odom Realty, La Mesa, 1966000. Attpd. Gov. Spec. Com. on Taxation 1973; dir., United Way, E. San Diego, Co. 1975-76; dir., ARC, 1968---; dir., YMCA bd. mgmt. 1968-75; dir. Grossmont Council BSA 1973-74; mem. Citizens Adv. Council Lemon Ave. Sch. 1973-75; dir. La Mesa C. of C. 1978-79; Mem.: Nat. Assn. of Realtors, mem. Calif. Assn. of Realtors, dir. 1974-78, chmn. Insurance Com., 1978; mem. E. San Diego Co. Bd. of Realtors, pres. 1975; named Realtor of the Year 1975, La Mesa Bd. of Realtors; Hon. Life. Mem. and Service Award 1975, Calif. PTA, Mt. Helix Council; Hon. Svc. Award, Heartland Human Rels. Assn. Mem.: La Mesa Kiwanis Club, 1969---. Methodist. Hobbies: woodwork, gardening. Res.: 4724 Glen St., La Mesa, CA; Office: 4718 Nebo Dr., La Mesa, CA 92041.

O'DONNELL, JOHN D.
Industrial Real Estate Developer
b. Oct. 20, 1932, Lorain, Ohio; s. John and Dorothy (Farquhar) O'Donnell; ed. USC 1959; m. Patricia Dwyer, Sherman Oaks, Calif. 1960; chil.: Leslie-Ann, b. Mar. 23, 1963; John David, b. Jan. 7, 1964; Douglas Dwyer, b. Jan. 18, 1967. Career: Ind. sales, dept. mgr. Coldwell Banker & Co. 1959-70; pres. Butterfield Land Co. 1970---; gen. and mgr. partner, John D. O'Donnell and Partners, Industrial Real Estate Developers, 1970---. USAF, Korean War, 1950-54. Mem.: Beta Theta Pi, 1957-59; Clubs: Balboa Bay, Jonathan, Jack Kramer Tennis. Rec.: flying, fishing, tennis, skiing. Res.: 1906 Galaxy Dr., Newport Beach, CA 92660; Office: 500 Newport Center, Suite 640, Newport Beach, CA 92660.

OELRICH, MARGARET H.
Health Care Administrator
b. Jan. 28, 1927, Chicago, Ill.; d. Paul and Myrtle (Matson) Malmborg; B.S., Occupational Therapy, W. Mich. Univ., 1949; m. Carl M. Oelrich, Oct. 22, 1949, Chicago; son, Paul, b. Aug. 12, 1950. Career: Occupational Therapist: N. Shore Health Resort, Winnetka, Ill., 1949, Kalamazoo State Hosp., 1950-53, Pacific State Hosp., Pomona, CA. 1953-55, also coordinator volunteer servies, 1955-60; with City of Hope Nat. Med. Center, Duarte, 1960---: dir., occupational therapy, 1960-72, coordinator, Home Health Service, 1971-75, dir., Rehabilitation 1972---. Named Outstanding Occupational Therapist-Health Care Adminstr., So. Calif. Occup. Therapy Assn., 1975. Mem.: Am. and Calif. Occupational Therapy Assn.; Nat. Panel of Am. Arbitration Assn.; Calif. Assn. of Rehabilitation Facilities. Lectr., workshops, seminars on Working with the Fatally Ill Patient, and Death and Dying. Hobbies: needlework, indoor plants, gardening. Res.: 800 W. First St., No. 1405, L.A., CA 90012; Office: 1500 E. Duarte Rd., Duarte, CA 91010.

OFFER, CHARLES SAMUEL
Financial Company Executive
b. Jan. 1, 1913, Los Angeles; s. Leland S. and Rebecca (Goldberg) Offer; ed. Univ. of Wash. 1932; Southwestern University Law School, 1931-34; chil.: Arlene Scult, b. Dec. 31, 1935; Charles S., Jr., b. Mar. 18, 1938. Career: Founder, Budget Finance Plan, Inc., Hollywood, 1937---, secty. 1937-45, pres. 1945--- (incl. subsidiaries); pres. Monarch Acceptance Corp., L.A. 1938---; pres. Fire & Casualty Underwriter's Agcy. 1947---; pres. Credit Finance Plan Utah; pres. Credit Industrial Laon Plan, Ut. 1952; pres. Budget Credit Plan, Ohio, Ky., W.Va., Md. 1953---; Budget Finance Plan, Bldg. Corp. 1955-68; chmn. Budget Industries, 1968-78; Chmn., Financial Corp. of America, 1978---; Founding Chairman, Budget Capital Corporation; vice

chairman, State Savings & Loan Association, Stockton; Vice Chairman, Century Bank; Dir. City of Hope, Guardians of Jewish Home for Aged, Vista Del Mar Child Care Center. Mem.: Sigma Tau; Elks Club; Del Rey Yacht; Coronado Yacht; Outrigger Canoe Club, Honolulu; Friars Club. Hobby: fishing, hunting, yachting. Res.: 17 Blue Anchor Cay, Coronado, CA 92118; Office: 6420 Wilshire Blvd., Los Angeles, CA 90048.

OGG, WILSON REID
Attorney at Law
b. Feb. 26, 1928, Alhambra, Calif.; s. James Brooks (Lawyer, L.A. Co., City Atty. of Alhambra, 1932-40) and Mary (Wilson) Ogg; ed. A.B., Univ. of Calif., Berkeley, 1949; J.D., Univ. of Calif. Sch. of Law, 1952. Career: Est. pvt. practice law, Berkeley, Calif. 1955---; Real Estate broker and consultant, 1974---; Calif. Community Coll. Instr. for Law & sociology, 1976. Research atty.-legal ed., Continuing Edn. of the Bar., Univ. of Calif. Ext. 1958-63; editor: Legal Aspects of Doing Business Under Govt. Contracts and Subcontracts, 1958; Basic Calif. Practice Handbook, 1959; U.S. Army, Pusan and Taequ, Korea, 1952-54; English instr., Taequ English Lang. Inst., Korea, 1954; psychol. instr., 25th Sta. Hosp., Taequ, 1954. Awards: Commendation Ribbon with Medal Pendant; Mem.: v.p. Internat. House Assn., Berkeley, 1961-62; pres. California Society for Psychical Study, Inc., 1963-65; Natl. Panel of Arbitrators, Am. Arbitration Assn. 1963---; fellow, Internat. Acad. of Law and Sci. 1964---; Calif. State, S.F., Bar Assn.; Soc. for Psych. Research, London; Center for Stu. Dem. Insts., Santa Barbara; S.F. Opera Guild; S.F. Mus. of Art; S.F. Symphony Association; Fellow, Worldwide Academy of Scholars and The World University; mem. Commonwealth Club of California; Town Hall of California; World Futures Society; Mechanics' Institute; City Commons Club of Berkeley, Internat. Platform Assn.; Faculty Club Univ. of California, AAAS, Press Club of San Francisco, Durant Masonic Lodge, No. 268, BPOE, No. 1002. Democrat (del., Berkeley Caucus, 1967). First Unitarian Ch., Berkeley (trustee-secty., 1957-58). Res.: Pinebrook Place, 1104 Keith Ave., Berkeley, CA 94708.

OGILVIE, LLOYD JOHN
Clergyman
b. Sept. 2, 1930, Kenosha, Wisc.; s. Varde Spenser and Kathryn (Jacobson) Ogilvie; B.A., Lake Forest Coll., 1952; Garrett Theological Seminary, 1955; postgrad., New Coll., Univ. Edinburgh, Scotland, 1956; m. Mary Jane Jenkins, Mar. 25, 1951, Waukegan, Ill.; chil.: Heather (Sholl), b. Mar. 9, 1953; Scott Varde, b. Apr. 26, 1954; Andrew Ghlee, b. Dec. 6, 1959. Career: pastor, Gurnee Community Ch., Gurnee, Ill., 1954-56; pastor, Winnetka Presbyterian ch., Winnetka, Ill., 1956-62; sr. pastor, 1st Presbyterian ch., Bethlehem, Pa., 1962-72; sr. pastor, 1st Prebyterian Ch. of Hollywood, Calif. 1972---; weekly TV sermons, Let God Love You; speaker, world and nat. conferences; author 11 books: A Life Full of Surprises, You've Got Charisma, (Abingdon Press); Let God Love You, Life Without Limits, Crumbeat of Love, When God First Thought of You (Word Books); If I Should Wake Before I Die, Lord of the Ups and Downs, Loved and Forgiven, The Autobiography of God, (Regal Books); Cup of Wonder (Tyndale House Publsrs.). Rec.: golf, fishing, sailing. Home: 3012 Arrowhead Dr., L.A., CA 90068; Office: First Presbyterian Ch. of Hollywood, 1760 N. Gower St., Hollywood, CA 90028.

OGLESBY, CLARKSON HILL
University Professor
b. Nov. 9, 1908, Clarksville, Mo.; s. Edwin Bright and Frances (Thomas) Oglesby; A.B. (Gr. Distinction), Stanford Univ., 1932, Engr. in Civil Engring., Stanford, 1936; m. Ardis Hansen, June 8, 1938, Phoenix, Ariz.; daus.: Virginia Lee (Hancock), b. Feb. 13, 1941; Judith Lynn (Donaghey), b. Apr. 13, 1943; Marjorie Kay (Zellner), b. Dec. 3, 1946. Career: with Arizona Highway Dept., 1928-41; Vinson and Pringle Constrn. Co., 1941-43; Silas Palmer Prof. of Civil Engring., Stanford Univ., 1943-75, Emeritus, 1974---; Vis. Prof. in Columbia, Chile, Austalia, S. Africa; Fulbright Prof., Imperial Coll., London, 1965-66; mem. (numerous posts), Transportation Bd., Nat. Academies of Sci. and Engring. Awardee for Outstanding Achievement in Heavy Engring. Constrn., The Beavers, 1964. Author: Highway Engring., John Wiley and Sons 1954, 1963, 1975; (w/H.W. Parker) Methods Improvement For Construction Managers, McGraw-Hill, 1972; numerous papers pub. by Transportation Research Bd. Mem.: Phi Beta Kappa, Sigma Xi, Tau Beta Pi. Res.: 850 Cedro Way, Stanford, CA 94305; Office: Terman Engring. Center, Civil Engr. Dept., Stanford, CA 94305.

O'GRADY, GERALD P.
Airline Executive
b. Jan. 9, 1914, St. Albans, Vt.; s. James E. and Harriet M. (Coleman) O'Grady; A.B., magna cum laude, Tufts Coll., 1935; LL.B., Georgetown Univ., 1939; m. Mary McDuffie, Nov. 10, 1942; chil.: Gerald Patrick, Kevin E. Career: admitted to D.C. bar, 1938, Cal. bar, 1971; atty. CAB, Washington. 1939-41; aso. Whiteford, Hart, Carmody & Wilson, Washington, 1941-46; practice law, Washington, 1947-67; v.p. Western Air Lines, Inc., Los Angeles, 1967-72; sr. v.p. 1972---; dir. Pacific No. Airlines, Inc. 1947-67; Mem. Am. Fed., Los Angeles County bar assns., State Bar Cal., Phi Beta Kappa, Alpha Sigma Phi. Clubs: Congl Country, Internat. (Washington). Res.: 7722 W. 79th St., Playa del Rey, CA 90291; Office: 6060 Avion Dr., Los Angeles, CA 90009.

O'HALLORAN, LAVERNE M. KATHLEEN
Realtor
b. Nov. 15, 1921, Laurium, Mich.; d. Joseph W. and Della K. (Gervais) Shaffer; m. John R. O'Halloran, Jr., July 15, 1942, Fond du Lac, Wisc.; chil.: Sheila Anne (Stoll); Gregory John; Michael John; Maureen Therese; Sean Thomas; Margaret Eileen. Career: Realtor, Settlers Real Estate, Fresno, ---; pres., C & R Investments, 1973-74. Mem.: charter mem., Infant of Prague Adoption Agency aux. 1954---; secty. 1955; pres., Calif. Citizens for Decent Lit., 1961-63; bd. dir., Nat. Citizens for Decent Lit., 1963-64; pres., Central Calif. CDL, 1959-64; Calif. Arts Soc.; Fresno Art Center. Republican; chmn. Fresno Co. United Republicans, 1962; clean campaign ballot initiative area coordinator, 1966. Catholic; pres., Sacred Heart Mothers Club; secty., Sacred Heart Altar Soc.; Secty., Deanery, Nat. Council Catholic Women; pres., Legion of Mary, Jr. Presidium. Hobbies: gardening, sewing. Rec.: golf, reading. Home: 3503 N. Bond, Fresno, CA 93726; Office: 4747 N. First St., Fresno, CA 93726.

O'HERN, MARY M. BRADY
Professor
b. Oct. 6, 1907, Jacksonville, Ill.; d. William J. and Nancy (Porter) Brady; B.A., Illinois Coll., 1930; M.A., Univ. Iowa, 1945; Ed.D., N.Y. Univ., 1957; m. Leon Lee O'Hern, Aug. 15, 1970, Riverside. Career: tchr., Versaille (Ill.) High Sch., 1931-35, Meredosia (Ill.) High Sch., 1936-37; asst. prof. Shurtleff Coll., 1937-45; Assoc. Prof. James Madison Univ., Harrisonburg, Va., 1945-57; prof. and chmn. Dept. of Bus. Edn., So. Ill. Univ., Alton, Ill., 1957-70; vis. prof., Cal. State Univ. Los Angeles, 1970-76; vis. prof., Univ. N.Dak., summers 1966, 69, 70; research assoc. Center Vocational and Tech. Edn., Ohio State Univ. 1968. Mem. Exec. Bd., Ill. Bus. Edn. Assn., 1965-68, publ. chmn. 1966-69. Author text: Advanced Key-Driven Calculator Manual, 1957; contbr. Nat. Education Assn. Yearbooks, other profl. publs. Awards for Distinguished Pub. Service, Ill. Bus. Edn. Assn., 1965-66, and Illinois Coll. 1971. Mem.: Soroptimist Club of Alton, pres. 1962-63; Delta Kappa Gamma, treas. 1966-69, 1970-78; Delta Pi Epsilon, founder So. Ill. Univ. chpt. 1967; Pi Omega Pi; Nat. Bus. Edn. Assn.; Calif. Bus. Edn. Assn. Presbyterian, v.p. women's assn. 1978---. Hobbies: writing, needlecrafts, gardening. Home: 6523 N. Kauffman Ave., Arcadia, CA 91006.

O'KEEFE, DENNIS ROBERT
Scientist
b. Nov. 15, 1939, Ottawa, Ont., Can.; naturalized U.S. Citizen 1977; s. Dalton S. and Colombe O'Keefe; B.Sc., Univ. Ottawa, 1962; M.Sc., Univ. Toronto, 1964; Ph.D., applied sci. & engr., 1968. m. Gail P. Burns, Oct. 9, 1965, Toronto; chil.: Timothy Robert, b. Apr. 7, 1967; Mary Kathleen, b. Oct. 7, 1970. Career: Staff Scientist, General Atomic Co., San Diego, 1968---. Areas of scientific research: surface physics & chemistry; rarefied gas dynamics; gas-surface interactions; ultra-high vacuum tech.; advanced energy concepts; nyclear reactor engring. Mem. Am. Physical Soc. Address: General Atomic Co., P.O.B. 81608, San Diego, CA 92138.

O'KEEFE, JOHN C.
Bank Executive
b. Aug. 29, 1927, Chicago, Ill.; s. John and Anna (McCullough) O'Keefe; B.A., bus. admin., Claremont Men's Colls.; postgrad. Univ. of San Francisco Sch. of Law; m. Margaret Jones, July 1978, San Francisco; sons, John C., Jr., b. May 25, 1955; Timothy T., b. July 31, 1956; Daniel L., b. Dec. 1, 1966. Career: Asst. to President, Ampex Corp., Redwood City; Field Secty., Council of Profit Sharing Industries, Calif.; Calif. State Inheritance Tax Referee; Pres., Directors Securities Inc., Santa Barbara, 1971---; Chief Exec. Officer, The Bank of

Montecito, Montecito, 1977---. Dir., Music Acad. of the West, Santa Barbara. Club: Birnam Wood Golf, Montecito. Rec.: tennis. Office: 1717 Fernald Point Lane, Santa Barbara, CA 93108.

OLDKNOW, WILLIAM HENRY II
Chairman of the Board, De Anza Land and Leisure Corp.
b. Sept. 3, 1924, Atlanta, Ga.; s. Oscar Stuart and Louise (Scruggs) Oldknow; gr. son. of Wm. H. Oldknow, motion picture pioneer; B.S., USC, 1946; m. Constantina Demetrios Skouras, Jan. 15, 1949, Los Angeles, chil.: Elizabeth L. (Turk), b. 1950; Theodora (Coffey), b. 1952; Constantina W., b. 1955; Theresa Ann, b. 1958. Career: pres., Sero Amusement Co., L.A., 1947---; chmn. bd., De Anza Land and Leisure Corp., L.A., 1973---; v.p., East Point Amusement Co., Atlanta, Ga., 1952---. Trustee, Scripps Coll., Claremont, 1966-70; dir., Nat. Assn. Theatre Owners, 1967-77. Mil. Lt. j.g. (ret.) USNR; USN, 1942-46. Mem.: Bel Air Country Club; Jonathan Club, L.A.; Piedmont Driving Club, Atlanta; Los Angeles (Santa Anita), Hollywood and Del Mar Turf clubs. Greek Orthodox; mem. archdiocesan council, Greek Orthodox Archdiocese of No. and So. America. Hobbies: ancient hist., numismatics. Rec.: breeder of thoroughbred race horses, Calif. and Ken. Home: 1161 Virginia Rd., San Marino, CA 91108; Office: 1615 Cordova St., L.A., CA 90007.

OLIN, SPENCER C., JR.
Historian
b. Feb. 13, 1937, Los Angeles; s. Spencer C. and Mary C. Olin; B.A., Pomona Coll., 1958; M.A., Claremont Grad. Sch., 1961, Ph.D., 1965; m. Patricia Lynn Wood, Sept. 11, 1976, Lake Arrowhead; son, Eric Spencer, b. Oct. 14, 1968. Career: Instr. in History, Pomona Coll., 1964-65; Dept of History, Univ. Calif., Irvine, 1965---: asst. prof., 1965-69, acting vice chancellor for student affairs, 1965-66, assoc. prof., 1969-78, chmn. Dept. of History, 1977---, prof. of hist., 1978---; vis. lectr. in History, Univ. of Stirling, Scotland, 1971-72. Statewide pres., Univ. of Calif.-Am. Fedn. of Tchrs. (UC-AFT); mem., bd. dir., Planned Parenthood Assn. of Orange Co. 2nd Lt., AUS, 1959-60, Armor; Capt., USAR, 1960-67, Infan. Author: California's Prodigal Sons: Hiram Johnson and the Progressives, 1911-1917, Univ. Calif. Press, 1968; Why War? Ideology, Theory and History, co-author Keith L. Nelson, Univ. Calif. Press, 1979; (Reader) Racism in California: A Reader in the History of Oppression, coeditor Roger Daniesl, Macmillan, 1972; contbr. articles Pacific Historical Review, Calif. Historical Soc. Quarterly, Calif. History. Rec.: tennis. Res.: 113 W. Yale Loop, Irvine, CA 92714; Office: Univ. of California, Irvine, CA 92717.

OLIPHANT, CHARLES ROMIG
Physician — Surgeon
b. Sept. 10, 1917, Waukeegan, Ill.; s. Charles L. (M.D.) and Mary Goss (Romig) Oliphant; ed. St. Louis Univ. 1936-40; M.D., St. Louis Univ. Sch. of Med. 1943-; (postgrad. Naval Med. Sch., Md. 1945-46); m. Claire E. Canavan, St. Louis, Mo., Nov. 7, 1942; chil.: James R., Cathering R., Mary G., William D. Career: Intern, U.S. Naval Med. Center, Bethesda, Md. 1943-44; est. pvt. practice med.-surg., San Diego, Calif. 1947---; chief staff, Balboa Hosp., S.D. 1957; chief staff, Doctors Hosp., S.D. 1958, 1971-76; chief surg. 1967-72. Chmn. bd. dirs., S.D. Med. Assocs., Inc. 1957---; chmn. bldg. com., Doctors Hosp. 1957---. U.S. Navy Med. Corps, Pac. Fleet (1943-47), WW II. Mem.: pres. S.D. Chpt., Amer. Acad. Gen. Practice, 1958; bd. dirs., Goodwill Inds. of S.D. 1963-65; chmn. radio-TV com., S.D. Med. Soc. 1966-68; (charter) Fellow: Amer. Geriatric Soc., Am. Acad. of Family Practice; diplomat, Amer. Bd. of Family Practice; Fellow, Amer. Soc. Abdominal Surgs.; SAR, AMA, Calif. Med. Assn., S.D. Med. Soc., Alpha Kappa Kappa. Republican. Episcopalian. Hobbies: woodworking, fishing, hunting. Res.: 4310 Trias, San Diego; Office: Suite 410, Centre City Bldg., 233 A St., San Diego, CA 92101.

OLSON, ALVIN WALTER
College President
b. May 16, 1924, Yakima, Wash.; B.A., Univ. of Wash. 1947, and 1949-50; M.A., Univ. of Puget Sound, 1949; Stanford Univ. 1950-51; Ph.D., Syracuse Univ. 1956; m. Jean McCrea; chil.: Karen Anne, Marc. William, Linda Kristine. Career: Tchr., Menlo Atherton H.S., Menlo Park, 1950-53; teacher-admr. San Francisco State Coll. 1955-61; Phillips Found. Intern. in Acad. Adm. and visiting prof. Univ. of Wis. 1962-63; asst. to pres.-visiting prof. Mills Coll., Oakland, 1964-66; prof.-chmn. Dept.

Geography, San Francisco State Coll., 1966-70; dean, Coll. of Arts & Scis., Western III Univ. 1970-75; pres. Calif. State Coll., Stanislaus, Turlock, 1975---. Researcher. Author: Many professional publs. 1958---, incl (book), Minerals and World Politics, The Historical Geography of River Towns on the Mississippi. Broker, Wilbur Ellis Co., Seattle. Serv. U.S. Navy. Awards' Natl. Sci. Found. Grant, Northwestern Univ. 1961; Ellis L. Phillips Found. Grant, Univ. of Wis. 1962-63; NDEA Grant, Inst. in Geography, 1967. Mem.: American Assn. Univ. Professors; California Council of Geography Teachers, Exec. Com. 1958-62; pres. 1960-61; Assn of Amer. Geographers; Assn. of Pac. Coast Geographers; Ill. Council of Liberal Arts Deans; Amer. Conf. of Acad. Deans; Amer. Assn. for Higher Educ.; Phi Kappa Phi, Phi Delta Kappa, Pi Gamma Mu. Res.: 1891 El Camino Dr., Turlock, CA; Office: 800 Monte Vista Ave., Turlock, CA 95380.

OLSON, DEAN C.
Founder, Olson Bros.
b. Nov. 20, 1907, Fairview, Ut.; s. Peter and Christina (Larson) Olson; B.S., Univ. of Utah (all conf. guard, football team, 1928, 29), 1930; m. Alma May Keysor, Los Angeles, Calif., May 18, 1935; chil.: Deanna Louise, b. Dec. 18, 1936; Linda Maria, b. July 25, 1939; Peter Dean, b. May 1, 1942. Career: Est. Olson Brothers, Inc., L.A. 1932; co-owner, br. plants founded in Calif.; Fontana, 1938; Modesto and Ventura, 1944; Secty. of Agri. 1945---; pres. Pac. Dairy and Poultry Co. 1947---; bd. dirs., Inst. of Amer. Poultry Industries, 1950---. City Councilman of Beverly Hills, Calif. 1948-52; Mayor of Beverly Hills, 1951-52. Mem.: Phi Delta Theta, L.A. Country Club. Ch. of Jesus Christ of Latter-day Saints (Bishop, Beverly Hills Ward). Hobby: hunting, freshwater fishing. Res.: 521 N. Arden Dr., Beverly Hills, CA; Office: 13400 Riverside Dr., Sherman Oaks, CA 91423.

OLSON, HENRY DEXTER
Research Engineer
b. Sept. 21, 1931, San Mateo, Calif.; s. Oscar Henry and Bessie (DeYoung) Olson; B.S., M.S. (elect. eng.), Stanford Univ., 1953, 1954; m. Jane McKenzie, Apr. 12, 1960, Grants Pass, Ore.; dau., Dana DeYoung, b. Mar. 4, 1962. Career: research asst., Electronic Research Lab., Stanford Univ., 1956-58; senior research engr., SRI Internat. (formerly Stanford Research Inst.), 1958---. AUS, 1954-56; elect. engring. asst.; conducted tropospheric radio propagation research in Ariz. desert. Contbr. more than 135 tech. articles various periodicals; contbr. to Radio Handbook, 19th, 20th, 21st eds., ITT Editors and Engrs., Vice Pres., Austin Healey Club, Pacific Centre, 1977-79. Hobby: amateur radio, W6GXN. Rec.: Austin Healey Sports Cars. Res.: 1751 Croner Ave., Menlo Park, CA 94025; Office: 333 Ravenswood Ave., Menlo Park, CA 94025.

OLSON, WILLARD PAUL
Aerospace Company Scientist
b. Aug. 6, 1939, Detroit, Mich.; s. Paul Edwin and Alfhild Ruth (Peterson) Olson; B.S., physics, UCLA, 1962, M.S., 1964, Ph.D., 1968; m. Linda Reddell, Nov. 7, 1964, Hacienda Hts., Calif.; sons, Keith Anders, b. Aug. 29, 1968; Kristian Andrew, b. Jan. 6, 1971. Career: Cons., Rand Corp., 1964-66; McDonnell Douglas Astronautics, Huntington Beach, 1968---: sr. scientist, 1968-74, br. chief, 1974-77, Head of Thermodynamics & Environments Dept., 1977---. Lectr.; author: six dozen+ publs.; editor: one book. Res.: 16285 Mt. Islip Cir., Fountain Valley, CA; Office: 5301 Bolsa, Huntington Beach, CA 92647.

O'MALLEY, JOHN A.
Company President
b. July 6, 1933, Philadelphia, Pa.; s. John and Grace O'Malley; B.S., chem, Rutgers Univ., 1959; Ph.D., physical chem., Univ. of Penna., 1963; m. Mary E. Wright, June 5, 1974, Camden, N.J.; chil.: John Jr., b. Sept. 3, 1955; Robert, b. Feb. 22, 1957; Teresa, b. Jan. 15, 1978; David, b. May 12, 1969. Career: Lab. technician, Socony-Mobile Research Labs., N.J., 1952-54, 56-57; Med. Technician, AUS, 1954-56; Asst. Instr., phys. chem., Univ. of Penna., 1959-63; Instr. Phys. Chem., Rutgers Univ., 1960-62; Asst. Prof., Phys. Chem., Drexel Univ., Phila., 1962-67; Dir. of R&D, Harleco, Phila. 1967-69, V.P., 1969-73; v.p., Chem. Oxford Labs., Inc. Foster City, Calif., 1973-76, pres., 1977---. Mem. Nat. Com. for Clin. Lab. Standards, dir. and secty.-treas., 1972---; Am. Assn. for Clin. Chem., chmn. No. Calif. Sect. 1976; Lions Club, Alpha Chi Sigma; Phi Lambda Upsilon. Contbr. tech. articles to profl. journs. and publs.; speaker, profl. assn. meetings.

Apptd. Research Participant, Oak Ridge Nat. Labs., 1966. Elected Councilman, Merchantville, N.J. 1972-75. Rec.: bridge, sports. Res.: 1105 Hidden Oaks Dr., Menlo Park, CA 94025; Office: Oxford Labs. Inc., Foster City, CA 94404.

O'MEARA, SARA ELIZABETH BUCKNER
Orphanage Founder
b. Sept. 9, 1934, Knoxville, Tenn.; d. Claude Smith and Lillian (O'Dell) Buckner; desc. Maj. Gen. Simon Bolivar Buckner, Civil War hero; Robert E. Buckner, inventor, first wagon brake; ed. Briarcliffe, N.Y.; (drama) the Sorbonne, Paris; Pasa. Playhouse, 1957; m. Robert Emery O'Meara, Clearwater, Fla., Apr. 13, 1973; sons: John Leland Hopkins, Jr., b. Feb. 20, 1961; Charles Stanford Hopkins, b. July 31, 1966. Career: TV actress, 1957-61; Goodwill Tour of Far East, auspices of State Dept. 1959; founder-chmn. bd. International Orphans, Inc. 1959---. Awards: cit. by L.A. County Supvs.; cert. USMC Res. for Serv., Vietnam, 1966; cit. Jap. Govt.; plaque, USMC Marines, Vietnam, 1966; SERTOMA Award, 1st place, L.A., 2nd place natl. 1966; Cross of Merit, Dame, Knightly Order of St. Brigitte, 1967; cit. Repub. of Vietnam, 1968; Marine Award, Vietnam, 1969; scrolls: House of Hope Orphanage, and Mayor K. Goto, Japan; Kiwanis Club, Reseda; Mem.: Mayor Yorty's Community Adv. Com.; adv. bd. Sister Cities; Bordeau, France, Nagoya, Jap.; adv. bd. Educ. Film Co.; Assistance League So. Calif.; past pres. Spastic Chil's. League; World Affairs Council. Presbyterian. Res.: 5425 Shirley Ave., Tarzana, CA.

ONAK, THOMAS PHILIP
Professor of Chemistry
b. July 30, 1932, Omaha, Nebr.; s. Louis A. and Louise (Penner) Onak; B.A., San Diego State Univ., 1954; Ph.D., Univ. Calif., Berkeley, 1958; m. Sharon Neal, June 18, 1954, La Jolla. Career: Research chemist, Olin Mathieson Chem. Corp., 1957-59; California State Univ., Los Angeles, 1959---: asst. prof., assoc. prof., Prof. of Chemistry, 1966---. Fulbright Fellow, Univ. of Cambridge, Eng. 1965-66; NIH Career Devel. Awardee, 1973-77; named Outstanding Prof., CSU, Los Angeles, 1969. Sci. publs. include book "Organoborane Chemistry, Academic Press, N.Y. 1975; contbr. papers and reviews to profl. journs. Mem. Am. Chem. Soc., Chem. Soc., London. Hobby: classical music. Res.: 632 Alta Vista Cir., S. Pasadena, CA 91030; Office: 5151 State University Dr., Los Angeles, CA 90032.

OOSTING, MARY ROBINSON
Tapestry Artist
b. Sept. 6, 1910, Chattanooga, Tenn.; d. James Bright and Gertrude (Weber) Robinson; student, Univ. of Chattanooga, Ecole de Chaumiere, Paris, France, Univ. of New Mex., Sarah Lawrence Coll., 1931-32, B.A., 1963; m. Gerard Barber, 1937 (dec. 1960); chil.: Ann (Nyborg), Helen (Gerget), Gerard M., Bruce A.; m. 2d.; son: Henry Oosting, Jan. 18, 1970, Mill Valley. Career: v.p., prodn. mgr. Robinson & Barber Handprints Inc., Ossining, N.Y., 1937-50; stylist, Richard E. Thibaut Wallpapers Inc., NYC, 1952-53; acct. exec., Selvage Lee & Chase Inc. Public Rels., NYC, 1954-55; ednl. dir. Conn. State Dept. Mental Health, Hartford, Conn., 1956-64; also art therapy instr. Mental Hosp. Hartford, 1956-64; exec. dir. Westchester Children's Assn., N.Y. Solo Art Shows: Honolulu Hale, Honolulu, Hawaii, 1974; Garden Cafe Gallery, Burlingame, Calif., 1975; Arden Wood Gallery, San Francisco, 1976; Renaissance Gallery, Ukiah, Calif., 1978; Juried shows: Octagon Gallery, Daily City, 1976; Corridor Gallery, Redwood City, 1976; Twin Pines Gallery, Belmont, 1977; Sundance Gallery, San Mateo, 1977; Participant 25th International Exhibition, Galerie Internationale, NYC 1978. Awards: Purchase award, Commn. on Culture and The Arts of the City and Co. of Honolulu 1974; permanent art collection, San Mateo Co. Arts Council. Mem.: Nat. Home Fashions League, 1952-53; S.F. Women Artists 1977-78; San Mateo Co. Arts Council, 1976-78; Assn. Honolulu Artists, 1975-78; Historical Keeping Soc., Guilford, Conn., 1950-55. Hobby: travel Europe, USA, Orient. Res.: 857 S. Oak St., No. 7, Ukiah, CA 95482; Agent: Galerie Internationale, NYC.

OPEL, ARTHUR WILLIAM, JR.
Medical Research Administrator
b. May 9, 1943, Pasadena; s. Arthur William and Lois Marie (White) Opel; B.A., Pepperdine Coll.; m. Judy Kopecky, Feb. 5, 1966, Sierra Madre, Calif.; dau. Julianna Marie, b. Sept. 20, 1969. Career: Research in cell biology, Pasadena Found. for Med. Research, 1961-72, administrator, 1972-77, exec. director 1977---; exec. dir., Huntington Inst. of Applied Med. Research,

Huntington Mem. Hosp., Pasadena, 1978---. Prod. numerous film and video programs in cell biology for medical edn. Bd. dir. Sierra Madres Council, Girl Scouts of Am. 1977---; bd. govs., University Club of Pasadena, 1979---. Mem.: Rotary Club of Pasadena. Presbyterian. Hobbies: aviation, amateur radio. Res.: 3353 Villa Knolls Dr., Pasadena, CA 91107; Office: 99 N. El Molino Ave., Pasadena, CA 91101.

ORDIN, ANDREA SHERIDAN
United States Attorney
b. Jan. 4, 1940, Los Angeles; d. Michael and Maria Antonia (Wread) Sheridan; B.A., UCLA, 1962; LL.B., UCLA Law Sch., 1965; m. Robert L. Ordin, Los Angeles; chil.: Allison, Richard, Maria. Career: Dep. Atty. Gen., State of Calif., 1965-72; So. Calif. Legal Counsel, Fair Employment Practice Commn., 1972-73; dir., Los Angeles Co. Bar Assn., 1974-75; asst. Dist. Atty. of Los Angeles County (third position), 1975-77; U.S. Attorney for Central Dist. of Calif., 1977---. Dir. Am. Judicature Soc., 1976---; dir. Legal Aid Found., 1976---. Hobby: sailing. Address: United States Courthouse, 312 N. Spring St., Los Angeles, CA 90012.

O'REILEY, PATRICK
Zoological Society Executive
b. Jan. 31, 1924, Chicago, Ill.; s. Pat and Josephine (Lee) O'Reiley; A.B., Indiana Univ., 1947; M.A., Univ. of Chicago, 1949; m. Anna Popa, Jan. 1, 1949, New Haven, Ind.; chil.: Mikai, b. Dec. 27, 1951; Tim, b. June 13, 1955. Career: personnel analyst, City of San Diego Civil Service Commn., 1954-62; with Zoological Soc. of San Diego; personnel dir., 1962-73, Devel. Dir., 1973---. Dir. Mission Valley Tennis Club, S.F.; pres., Personnel Mgmt. Assn. of San Diego; pres., Consiar Flyers, Inc. Capt., USAFR, active duty, 1943-46, reserve duty, 1946-56. Hobby: gen. aviation pilot. Res.: 3254 Goldfinch St., San Diego, CA 92103; Office: P.O.B. 551, San Diego, CA 92112.

ORLET, HERMANN K.
Television Station Manager
b. Dec. 7, 1936, Fresno, Calif.; s. Dr. Otis Lowe and Lila (Morton) Orme; bro., Dr. Evan M. Orme; B.A., music, Univ. Calif., Berkeley, 1961; M.A., theatre arts, UCLA, 1967, Ph.D., edn., 1978; m. Joan F. King, Apr. 2, 1966, Fresno; daus.: Jennifer Ariana, b. Feb. 6, 1973; Juliana Alair, b. Nov. 1, 1978. Career: Prod., dir., KUCR-TV, Ch. 24, San Bernardino, 1966-68; coordinator and dir., ednl. services, KCET, Ch.28, Los Angeles, 1968-73; Station and Gen. Mgr., KTEH, Ch.54, San Jose, 1973---. Mem. State of Calif. Instructional TV Advis. Com., 1977---; chmn. TV advis. com., Calif. Pub. Broadcast Commn., 1978-79. 1st Lt., AUS, 1961-63; Capt., USAR. Recipient Best of West Award (TV Series), Newsseekers, 1971-72. Mem.: Sigma Pi, pres. 1958; Phi Delta Kappa; Order of Golden Bear; Big C Soc.; Nat. Assn. of Edn. Broadcasters. Hobbies: model trains, filmmaking. Res.: 16360 Belmont Ave., Monte Serena, CA 95030; Office: 100 Skyport Dr., San Jose, CA 95110.

ORPHAN, RICHARD C.
Research Laboratory Administrator
b. Dec. 11, 1921, Pueblo, Colo., s. Joseph W. and Margaret (McAfee) Orphan; B.S., U.S. Mil. Acad., 1940-43; student, Princeton Univ., 1946-48; M.A., Redlands Univ., 1978; m. Jean Barnes, Aug. 31, 1947, NYC; chil.: Pamela (Mrs. Dennis Gardella), b. Oct. 7, 1950; Barbara (Mrs. David Golay), b. July 15, 1956; Richard, Jr., b. Sept. 8, 1953; Margaret L., b. Mar. 15, 1963. Career: officer, U.S. Army, 1943-63: mil. asst. Office Secty. of Defense, 1954-58, Chief, Ammunition Officer, Eighth US Army, Korea 1959-60; dir., Feltman Research Labs., Picatinny Arsenal, N.J. 1960-63; Ret. Lt. Col. 1963; Staff, Lawrence Livermore Lab., 1973---: now Program Mfr. Chmn., Jr. Sci. Symposium, 1961-62; Master, F&AM Lodge No. 724, 1971; mem. Commonwealth Club. Democrat. Presbyterian, Elder, Deacon. Hobbies: stamps, painting. Home: 624 Camino Amigo, Danville, CA 94526; Office: P.O.B. 808, Livermore, CA 94550.

ORR, FRANK F.
Newspaper Editor
b. Nov. 1, 1914, San Diego, Calif.; s. Frank C. and Priscilla (Fletcher) Orr; A.B., Stanford Univ. 1935; m. Zoe Ann Hill, San Jose, Calif., Aug. 30, 1941; Career: Reporter, Santa Paula Chronicle, 1935-36; Santa Ana Journal, 1936-38, managing ed., Watsonville Register-Pajaronian, 1940-48, editor, 1949---. Pvt. to Capt., U.S. Army European Theatre (1942-46), WW II.

Awards: editor of newspaper which won Sigma Delta Chi Award for pub. serv. in newspaper journalism, 1955, and Pulitzer Prize for meritorious pub. serv. 1956. Mem.: American Society of Newspaper Editors; Pulitzer Prize journalisn juror, 1960, 61, 62, 67, 69, 72; Press, Commonwealth Clubs, San Francisco; Rotary Club, Elks Club. Episcopalian. Res.: 332 E. Beach St., Watsonville, CA; Office: 1000 Main St., Watsonville, CA.

ORR, GEORGE VERNON Jr.
State Director of Finance
b. Nov. 12, 1916, Des Moines, Ia.; s. George Vernon and Wilhelmina (Van Niewaal) Orr; B.A., Pomona Coll. 1937; M.B.A. Stanford Univ. 1939; m. Joan Peak, Pasadena, Calif., Mar. 31, 1941; chil.: Carolyn, b. Apr. 19, 1947; Robert Vernon, b. Sept. 12, 1949. Career: Mgmt. tr. Bullocks' Dept. Store, L.A. 1939-42; partner, Verne Orr Motors, 1946-59; partner, Verne Orr Co. 1959-62; pres. Investors Savings & Loan Assn. 1962-66; Calif. Dir. of Motor Vehicles, 1967-69; Calif. Dir. of Finance, 1970---; past pres.: Pasa. Merchants Assn., Family Assistance of Pasa., L.A. Co. United Way, 1963; foreman, L.A. Co. Grand Jury, 1962. Ensign, USNR 1942; supply ofcr., Naval Tr. Sch., Chicago, 1943; Lt. Comdr., USS Mercury, AK-42, S. Pac. 1944-45. Awards: Salvation Army of Pasa. Man of Yr., 1970. Mem.: Pres., Kiwanis Club, Pasa, 1951; Carmelita Lodge F&AM; Phi Beta Kappa, Alpha Delta Mu, Univ. Club, Balboa Yacht Club. Methodist (chmn. bd. stewards-off. bd.). Hobbies: amateur radio, photog. Res.: 1444 Hillcrest Ave., Pasadena, CA 91106; Office: State Capitol, Sacramento, CA 95814.

ORTIZ, MARTIN
Sociologist — Educator
b. Nov. 11, 1919, Wichita, Kan.; s. Tirso and Florence (Espitia) Ortiz; ed. Friends Univ., Wichita, 1941, 46; Santa Barbara Coll., Calif. 1945; B.A., Whittier Coll., Calif. 1948; M.S., George Williams Coll., Chicago, 1950; postgrad. Univ. Chicago, 1951; m. Marcelyn Russell; stepchil.: Nancy, Tom, Linda; Career: Program director East Los Angeles YMCA, 1946-48; exec. dir., Mex.-Amer. Council, Chicago, Inc. 1949-54; spec. repr. TV and Health Assn., L.A. Co. 1955; exec. dir. E. Central Area Welfare Planning Council, 1956-67; instr. Dept. Adult Edn., L.A. City Schs. 1961-65; hearing examiner, Bd. of Police Commrs., City of L.A. 1961---; instr. Whittier Coll. 1961-69; cons. Mex. Amer. Affairs, UCLA, dir. seminars, 1962-67; v.-chmn. Narcotic Addict Evaluation Authority, State of Calif. (apptd. by gov.), 1963---; cons. NDEA Insts., Pasa. Coll. 1966-67; cons. Dept. of Health, Edn. and Welfare, U.S. Govt. 1966-67; cons. Serv. Center Pgm., State of Calif., 1966-68; cons. Volt Tech. Corp., San Francisco, 1967---; cons. Inter-Agcy. Com. on Mex. Amer. Affairs, Wash., D.C. 1968---; dir. Center of Mex. Amer. Studies and Mexican American Affairs, Whittier College 1968---. Author: publs. on Mex. Amer. culture and edn., mags. and seminars, Santa Barbara, S.F., L.A., Pasa. incl. USC 1967, UCLA 1968 and Spanish-Speaking Com. on Urban Affairs, KMEX-TV, L.A. USMC, PTO 1942-45, WW II. Mem.: Natl. Conf. of Soc. Welfare; Amer. Sociological Assn.; Assn. for Stu. of Community Orgns.; L.A. Co. Dist. Atty's. Adv. Council; E. L.A. Serv. Center Adv. Council; Law and Justice Task Force, Greater L.A. Urban Coalition; pres.-dir. Cleland House of Neighborly Serv.; Human Rels Com., City of Pasa.; Co-chmn. So. Calif. Employers' Conf. on Mex. Amer. Employment, Whittier Coll., Jan. 1969; Calif. State Narcotics Ofcrs. Assn.; Atty. Gen's Comm. on Police-Community Rels., State of Calif. 1971---; Amer. Correctional Assn. Soc. of Friends, Quaker. Hobbies: travel, photog. Rec.: hiking, swim. Res.: 440 Prospect Sq., Pasadena, CA 91103; Office: Whittier College, Whittier, CA 90608.

ORTLIEB, ROBERT
Sculptor — Teacher
b. July 4, 1925, San Diego, Calif.; s. William and Ruth (Powers) Ortlieb (noted artist, teacher, painter); ed. B.F.A., USC 1950; M.F.A. 1951. Career: Art survey stu. Europe (1952), Mex., Guatemala (1960), S. Amer. (1967); 80 mus. exhibs. incl.: (stone, wood, terra cotta, bronze) NIY. Creative Galleries, Cincinnati Art Mus., Denver Art Mus., Dallas Mus. of Fine Arts, Ill. State Mus., Oakland Art Mus., Santa Barbara Mus. of Art, Pasa. Art Mus., L.A. Co. Mus., USC Upstairs Gallery, S.F. Mus. of Art, and Maxwell Galleris, San Francisco; Cowie Galleries, Biltmore Hotel, L.A.; Crocker Art Gallery, Sacramento; Bergstrom Mus., Wis.; repr.: Graphic Arts Traveling Exhib. (Paris, Eng., Italy, Yugoslavia, Algiers, Iran, France), 1953; Archivio Storico D'arte Contemporanea Della Biennale Di Venzia, Italy; Contemporary Artists, Met. Mus. NYC; Achenbach Found. for Graphic Arts; Calif. Palace Legion of Hon., S.F.; Awards: 1st sculpture award: Calif. State Fair and Exposition, Sacramento, 1948, 57; hon. mention, 1952, 53, 54, 55, 56; 2nd award, 1964; prints, Laguna Beach Art Gallery, Calif. (6 awards, 1955-57); Annual Juried Exhib., L.B. Art Mus., 1957; 50th Natl. Orange Show, Orange, 1965, 2nd award, 1967; Riverside Art Gallery, Calif. 1967; 2nd sculpture awards: Ariz. State Fair, 1949; S.W. Reg. Art Show, 1961; hon. mention: City of L.A. Art Exhib., 1950; Chaffey Community Art Assn., Ontario, 1954; Bess Gilbert Sculpture Award, San Diego Fine Arts Gallery, 1950; Graphic Arts Show, 1953; American Inst. of Fine Arts, USC 1962; California Art Club Annual Gold Medal Award, 1971. One-man exhibition, Sculpture and drawings, Edward Dean Museum, March 1975; The Apothecaries Base Relief in Bronze, Lobby, USC Pharmaceutical Science Center; Featured publications, London, Los Angeles, France, N.Y., Sacramento, and Twelve Calif. Sculptors, 1968, others. Sculpture instr-lecturer: Riverside Art Center, Calif. 1962---; USC Sch. of Arts, Idyllwild Arts Found. 1964---; Univ. Loma Linda, La Sierra Campus, Riverside, 1970---; Everybody's Village, Art Center, Sch., Palm Springs, 1968---. Hobby: photog. Rec.: golf. Studio: 11111 Jerry Lane, Garden Grove, CA 92640.

OSTERBROCK, DONALD E.
Director, Lick Observatory
b. July 13, 1924, Cincinnati, Oh.; s. William and Elsie (Welllin) Osterbrock; Ph.B. and B.S., Univ. of Chicago, 1948, M.S., 1949, Ph.D., 1952; m. Irene Hansen, Sept. 19, 1952, Williams Bay, Wis.; chil.: Carol, b. June 13, 1954; Willia, b. June 6, 1956; Laura, b. Oct. 17, 1959. Career: Postdoctoral Fellow and Instr. in Astronomy, Princeton Univ., 1952-53; Instr. and Asst. Prof. in Astronomy, Caltech. and Staff Mem., Mount Wilson & Palomar Observatories 1953-58; Asst. Prof., Assoc. Prof. and Professor, Univ. of Wis., 1958-73; Prof., Astronomer and Dir. of Lick Observatory, Univ. Calif., Santa Cruz, 1972---. Guggenheim Fellow, Princeton, 1960-61; NSF Sr. Postdoctoral Fellow, Univ. Coll., London 1968-69; Chmn. Dept. of Astronomy, Univ. of Wisc. 1967-68, 1970-72; Hill Family Vis. Prof., Univ. of Minn. 1977-78. Author: Astrophysics of Gaseous Nebulae, 1974. USAAF, 1943-46. Mem.: Nat. Acad. of Sci.; Am. Acad. of Arts and Sci.; Wis. Acad. of Sci., Arts and Letters; Am. Astronomical Soc., v.p. 1975-77; Royal Astronomical Soc., London, Congregationalist. Rec.: hiking, bird watching. Res.: 120 Woodside Ave., Santa Cruz, CA 95060; Office: Lick Observatory, UCSC, Santa Cruz, CA 95064.

OSTROW, MARTIN M.
Attorney at Law
b. May 31, 1925, Detroit, Mich.; s. Harry and Esther Ostrow; B.S., Northwestern Univ., 1948; J.D., USC, 1951; Grad., Internship in Pyb. Affairs, Coro Found., 1955; Grad., Indsl. Coll. of Armed Forces; m. Leora Seigenberg, Apr. 12, 1953, Los Angeles; chil.: Marlee Gayle, b. Feb. 14, 1956; Bradley Harris, b. Feb. 23, 1957. Career: Admitted to Calif. Bar 1951, U.S. Supreme Ct. 1957. Deputy Atty. Gen., State of Calif. 1953-57; Exec. Dir., California Land Title Assn. 1957-61; pres., World Leasing Corp., 1961---; pres., Applied Mgmt. Control (bus. mgmt.) 1970---; pres., Scholarships for Children of Am. Mil. Personnel, 1972---; pvt. practice of law, Beverly Hills, 1957---. Served USAF, WW II, Korean Conflict; Brig. Gen., USAFR. Nat. Pres., AF Assn. Mem.: Am., L.A. County, Beverly Hills Bar Assns.; Tau Delta Phi, pres.; No. Hollywood Democratic Club, pres.; Nu Beta Epsilon. Contbr. articles to various publs. Res.: 136 S. Fuller Ave., Los Angeles, CA 90036; Office: 212 So. Gale Drive, Suite 200, Beverly Hills, CA 90211.

OSTRUM, MAXINE S.
Physician
b. Aug. 8, 1921, Philadelphia, Pa.; d. Samuel B. and Rose (Shay) Ostrum; niece to Harry Shay, M.D., med. researcher, and Herman Ostrum, M.D., Chief Radiology, Phila. Gen. Hosp.; B.A., Temple Univ., 1942; M.D., H. Hahanerman Med. Coll., 1945; m. Theodore L. Orloff, M.D., Nov. 14, 1948; Phila., Pa.; dau. Judith Carol Orloff, M.D., b. June 25, 1951. Career: med. resident, Woman's Hosp., Phila.; med. staff, Hahanerman Hosp., 1948-57; pvt. practice, Phila., 1948-57; pvt. practice, Beverly Hills, 1958---; clin. instr. Family Practice, UCLA, 1974---; nursing faculty, Woman's Hosp., Phila., 1948-51. Fellow, Am. Acad. Family Practice; Am. Physicians Fellowship; Mem.: AMA; CMA; Pacific Coast Fertility Soc. Jewish.

Rec.: tennis, reading, swimming. Home: 10760 Weyburn Ave., L.A., CA 90024; Office: 435 N. Bedford Dr., Beverly Hills, CA 90210.

OTIS, GEORGE K., II
Publisher — Author
b. 1917, Ohio; s. Dr. J.D. and Mabel (Hollingsworth) Otis; desc. James Otis, Am. Revolution Patriot; Otis Elevator family: ed. Earlham Coll.; m. Virginia Walker, 1953, Santa Barbara; chil.: George Otis III, b. 1954; Don, b. 1957; April, b. 1961; Heather, b. 1965. Career: v.p. and gen. mgr. Lear, Inc. (Learjet); pres., Concertone, Inc.; pres., Astro Sci. Corp.; pub. and bd. chmn., Bible Voice Pub. House ---; pres., High Adventure, Inc. ---; host of nationally syndicated TV show, High Adventure; author: High Adventure; Crisis America; You Shall Receive; The Blueprint; Like a Roaring Lion; Future World; Eldridge Cleaver: Ice and Fire; Terror at Tenerife; God Money and You; The Thunder of His Power; Mach II. Past mem., Young Presidents Orgn. Hobby: pilot. Home: 9450 Vanalden Ave., Northridge, CA; Office: 16233 Lindbergh Ave., Van Nuys, CA.

OTT, DUDLEY E.
Energy Industry Consultant
b. Apr. 22, 1911, Oakland, Calif.; s. Charles F., Sr. and Alice (Alexander) Ott; B.S., elec. engr., Univ. of Calif., 1933; m. Myrtle C. Davis, Aug. 23, 1941, Yuma Ariz.; chil.: Dudley E., Jr., b. Oct. 10, 1942; Diane C., b. Aug. 25, 1944. Design Engr., power plant opr., Fibreboard Prods., Inc., Antioch, 1933-36; Design Engr., Calif. Chem. Co., Newark, Calif., 1936; Assoc., W. Harry Archer & Assocs., San Francisco, 1936-40; Insurance Inspector, Hartford Steam Boiler Insptn. and Insurance Co., S.F. and L.A., 1940-43; Staff Engr., Golden State Co., Ltd., S.F., 1943-48; Sr. Engr., Arabian Am. Oil Co., S.F. and Saudi Arabia, 1948-50; Project Engr. 1950-61, Proj. Dir. 1961-62, Supr. Engr. 1962-65, Proj. Mgr. 1965-72, Power Div. Bechtel Corp., S.F. and L.A.; Prin. Engr., San Francisco Power Div. Bechtel Power Corp., S.F. 1972-76; Power Plant Cons. 1976---. Project Engr. responsible for design: first comml. nuclear power sta., Dresden Nuclear Power Sta., Unit 1; first nuclear plant to use Vapor Suppression containment SM-1a.; first nuclear plant to transfer spent fuel elements in other than vertical position, San Onofre, Unit 1. Mem. UN Internat. Atomic Energy Agency team to study feasibility of nuclear power generation in So. Korea; Leader, Pakistan Atomic Energy Agency team, study feasibility nuclear power generation E. Pakistan; proj. engr. responsible, study of conversion of Savanna River "R" reactor from prodn. of plutonium to generation of power. Mem.: Eta Kappa Nu; Fellow, Am. Soc. Mech. Engrs., chmn. S.F. Sect. 1964-65, v.p. and chmn. Policy Bd. Power Dept. 1971-75; Am. Nuclear Soc. Methodist, chmn. fin. com. Hobby: antique cars. Address: Berkeley, CA.

OTTOMAN, RICHARD E.
Radiologist — Professor
b. Aug. 3, 1910, Guthrie, Okla.; s. Adolph and Fern (Christian) Ottoman; ed. Jackson (Mich. H.S.) 1926-29; Jackson Jr. Coll. 1932-34; Coll. of Lit., Sci. & Arts, Univ. of Mich. 1934-36; M.D., Sch. of Med., Univ. of Mich. 1936-39, 1940-41; m. Mary Elizaebth Merrill, Los Angeles, Calif., Nov. 27, 1943; dau.: Bonnie Ann. Career: Rotating intern, Virginia Mason Hosp., Seattle, Wash. 1941-42; spec. training (internal med), Birmingham V.A. Hosp., Van Nuys, Calif., staff phus. 1946-47; res. (radiology), 1947-50, asst. radiologist 1950; asst. radiologist to chief therapeutic radiologist, Long Beach (Calif.) V.A. Hosp., 1950-52; visiting roentgenologist, L.A. Co. Harbor Gen. Hosp. 1950---; courtesy cons., St. John's Hosp., Santa Monica, Calif., attending staff, 1950---; cons. (radiology and radioisotopes), St. Joseph Hosp., Burbank, Calif. 1950---; instr. (radiology), USC 1950-52; asst. prof. (radiology), Sch. of Med., UCLA 1952, cons. radiobiology AEP, 1952, assoc. prof. (radiology-anatomy), 1954, pvt. practive privileges, 1955---, prof. (radiology and anatomy) and v.-chmn. Dept. of Radiology, 1961---; cons. (radiology), Valley Hosp., Van Nuys, 1956---. Author: approx. 28 med. publs. to professional journs. 1945-63. 1st Lt., Maj., U.S. Army Med. Corps, 1942-46; Comdg. Ofcr., 675 Med. Coll. Co. 1944-45; U.S. and European Theatre of Operations. WW II. Awards: recipient, Unit Meritorious Serv. Cit.; listed: Amer. Men of Sci., Directory of Med. Specialists, Leaders in Amer. Sci., Dictionary of Internat. Biography, others. Mem.: trustee-secty.-treas., James T. Case Radiologic Found.; Natl. Geographic Soc.; The Museum Assn., L.A.; Diplomate, Amer. Bd. of Radiology, 1950; Radiological Soc. of N. Amer.,

Pac. Roentgen Soc., Radiological Soc. of So. Calif., Soc. of Nuclear Med.; Amer., Calif. and L.A. Co. Med. Assns.; Amer Assn. for Advancement of Sci., Amer. Fed. for Clin. Research, Pac. Fertility Soc., So. Calif. Soc. of Gastroenterology, N.Y. Acad. of Scis., Amer. Assn. of Univ. Radiologists, Amer. Assn. of Univ. Profs., Calif. Soc., Med. Soc. of UCLA, Amer. Nuclear Soc.; cons. Planned Parenthood Centers, L.A. 1957, med. adv. com. 1959; fellow, Amer. Coll. of Radiology. Town Hall; Phi Rho Sigma. Res.: 2260 Westridge Rd., Los Angeles, CA 90049; Office: UCLA, Center for the Health Sciences, Los Angeles, CA 90024.

OVERHOLSER, J. HOMER HAROLD
Industrialist
b. June 18, 1914, Springfield, Ohio; s. Alden Earl and Nora Liscilla (Hartman) Overholser; student, Wittenberg Coll., 1933-35; bus. adminstrn., UCLA, 1940, 1954; Registered Calif. Profl. Engr.; m. Marian Lee Whelan, Nov. 10, 1939, Los Angeles; chil.: James Alan, b. 1941; Sharyl Ann (Conlon), b. 1944. Career: design engr., Nat. Supply Co., 1935-56; devel. engr., Chrysler Airtemp Div. 1936-38; project engr., Vultee Aircraft Corp., 1938-39; engring supr., Northrop Aircraft Corp., 1939-43; chief engr., Hydro-Aire, Inc., 1943-46; exec. v.p., 1952-62; asst. gen. mgr., Pacific Div. Bendix Corp., 1953-58; v.p., dir., Woodlake Realty, Inc., 1962---; v.p., dir., S.O.M. Corp., 1964---; pres., Overholser Found., 1968---; secty., dir., chmn. finance com., Varadyne Industries, Inc., 1969---; chmn. bd. and pres., Alphatec Internat. Inc., 1977---; chmn. bd., pres., Nat. Golf Products Inc., 1977---; chmn. bd., exec. v.p., Nat. Golf Media, Inc., 1977---; chmn. bd., chief administrv. officer, Lyricard Corp. of Am., Inc., 1978---. Partner: O.K. Enterprises (farming), 1960-74; Southridge Devel. Co., 1961-70; and Wonder Palms Devel. Co., 1971-74 (real estate); H&O Co., 1964-74 (indsl. R.E.); Fullerton Hilton Inn, 1968-74, and Hotel Devel. Co., 1970-74 (hotels); Ratran Ltd., 1963-67 (underwater communication); Am. Investment Co., 1962-64; Contemporary Films, 1972-75. Past Directorates & Bd. chmnships: Hydrodyne Corp.; Poly Industries, Inc.; Dynamatics; U.S. Systems, Inc.; Solar Systems, Inc.; Buckingham Palace Corp.; Woodland Savings; Casa Electronics Corp.; Corp. Svc., Inc.; Wesco Industries, Inc.; Precision Dipbraze, Inc.; Southwest Bank; Nat. Post-Pak Systems, Inc.; Am. Investment Co.; Am. Hydrocarbon Corp.; Basic Industries, Inc.; Intercontinental Engring. & Mfg. Corp.; Aero Spacelines, Inc.; Independence Bank; Jaco Mgmt. Corp.; E.M.C. Instrumentation, Inc.; Saalfield Aircraft Corp.; Calif. Time Airlines; Interdyne, Inc.; Zolomatics, Inc.; Palm Springs Mobile Country Club; Microwave Sensor Systems, Inc.; United Optical Systems, Inc.; Clerke, Technicopr.; Clerke Rec. Corp.; Aqua Systems, Inc.; Blue Haven Pools, Inc.; Optical Corp.; Sierra Pacific Fin. Corp.; Sierra Western Life Ins. Co.; Electromask, Inc.; J.Y.S. Corp.; Spectran Internat., Ltd.; Royal Catfish Indus., Inc.; Internat. Houseboats and Rec., Inc.; Western-Pacific Resources, Inc.; Royal Pac. Fin. Corp.; World Fin. and Mtg. Corp.; Sierra Pac. Devel. Corp.; Georgetown Assocs., Inc.; Hotel Devel. Corp.; Karr Publs.; Foreign Commerce Corp.; Consolidated Rec. Products, Inc.; Los Cocos Devel. Corp.; Highland Assocs., Inc.; So. Calif. Hotel Corp.; Highland Park Ford, Inc. Patent Holder: hydraulic valves, fuel valves, hydraulic fluid transmission and tire warning device. Designer: 1st self contained room air conditioner; first wing folding method for USN airplanes; pure hydraulic drive for cars; devel.: 1st sonic altimeter for helicopter blind landings; Pregnant Guppy, 1st outsized cargo plane: pioneered Decca Navigation System in Can. Awarded Certificate of Merit for Dist. Serv. in bus. devel. Mem.: Inst. of Aero Sci.; Am. Ordnance Assn.; Am. Soc. Mech. Engrs.; Am. Inst. of Mgmt.; Am. Helicopter Soc.; Air Force Assn.; Assn. U.S. Army; Am. Soc. Air Affairs; SAE Fuel Valve Com.: Internat. Platform Assn.; L.A., No. Hollywood and Hollywood Chambers of C.; Mason, 32nd Degree; Shriners; L.A. Co. Mus. of Art, patron; L.A. World Affairs Council; Am. Security Council, advis. bd.; S.A.R. Republican. Church of God, deacon. Rec.: fishing, travel. Home: 4961 Palomar Dr., Tarzana, CA 91356; Office: 5955 Desoto Ave., Woodland Hills, CA 91367.

OWEN, CHARLES A., III
Real Estate Executive
b. Nov. 15, 1935, Detroit, Mich.; s. Charles A., Jr. and Florence (Buchanan) Owen; ed. Black-Foxe Mil. Inst.; USC; m. Linda S. Brown, July 28, 1973; chil.: Debra Gayle, Stacy Louise, Charles A., IV, Anthony Craig. Career: pres., Owen Properties, Inc. (assoc. 1957---); real estate exec. John Burnham & Co., S.D. Mem.: Mayor's Community Adv. Com.; dir.-corp. secty. Apt. Assn. of L.A. Co.; dir.-v.p. Larchmont Blvd. Assn.; dir. Wilshire Center C. of C.; dir.-adm. v.p. Wilshire YMCA; pres.-dir. Miracle Mile Assn.

1967-69; Wilshire Rotary Club; Repub. Assocs.; (hon.) bd. dirs. Hollywood-Wilshire Sym. Assn.; Wilshire Masonic Lodge; L.A. Consistory (32°), Al Malaikah Temple; dir.-v.p. Wilshire Dinner Club, 1968-69; Clubs: S.D. Rowing, La Jolla Beach and Tennis, Rancho Santa Fe Golf. Episcopalian. Hobby: tennis, water skiing, golf. Res.: 6673 Avenida de las Pescos, La Jolla, CA 92037; Office: 1555 Sixth Ave., San Diego, CA 92112.

OWENS, GARY B.
Radio-TV Performer - Author
b. May 10, Mitchell, So. Dakota; s. Bernard and Vanetta Owens; gr.son of Elizabeth Wilson Clark, cous. of Pres. Woodrow Wilson; scholarship student, Minneapolis Art Inst., 1948; speech scholarship, Dakota Wesleyan Univ., 1956; m. Arleta Markell, June 26, 1956, Plankinton, S.D.; chil.: Scott, b. 1960; Christopher, b. 1963. Career: Radio personality, KOIL, Omaha, 1956, WIL, St. Louis, 1958, Crowell-Collier Broadcasting chain, S.F. and L.A., 1959-62; KMPC, L.A., 1962---; also regular performer, Rowan & Martin's Laugh-In, 1968-72; the Green Hornet, 1965; host, the Gong Show, 1977; host, Letters to Laugh-In, 1968; the Hudson Bros., 1974; the Wacko Show, 1978; narrator & actor on over 500 cartoons; over 500 TV shows; also Columnist: Hollywood Citizen News, 1965-66; Daily Republic, 1955-56; So. Dak. Sports, 1954; Radio & Records, 1977-78; AP, 1953-56; also Performer-Writer: Sesame Street; Children's Television Workshop, 1969---; Electric Company, 1970---; also Writer: Laugh-In; Jim Nabors show; the Radio Show; Jayward Prodns. (the Nuthouse, Bullwinkle) all TV; also Recording Artist: 15 albums; 5 motion pictures; over 4000 TV and Radio commercials; also Author: The Gary Owens What To Do While Holding The Phone Book, 1973, Hawthorne-Tarcher pub. 3rd printing; Elephants, Grapes, Pickles, Price, Stern Sloan, 1965, 13th edition now in print; the Gary Owens Commonplace Book, 1979, Pinnacle Pubs. Named: World's best radio personality, 1977 (Internat. radio forum, Toronto); U.S. top radio personality 10 times, Billboard mag. and Gavin Poll, 1963-78; Outstanding Citizen, L.A., All Cities Employee Assn., 1973. Recipient: Emmy Award, 1968 (Laugh-In); distinguished service award, Hollywood Jaycees, 1966; trophies as one of top TV Announcer, 4 years, Fame, TV Daily; named Humanitarian of the Year, L.A. by Encino B'nai Brith; honored by: L.A. Mayors, Sam Yorty and Tom Bradley; L.A. Co. Bd. of Suprs.; L.A. City Council; Big Bros.; Calif. Hiway Patrol; BSA; U.S. Treas. Dept. Mem.: advisory bd., telecommunications, Pasadena City Coll., 1965---; bd. of govs., NARAS; bd. of govs. NATAS (Grammy & Emmy Awards), 1970-73; chmn. S. Calif. Multiple Sclerosis Drive 1972; grand marshall, So. Calif. Diabetes Assn., 1973-78 (over $2 million raised); hon. mayor, Woodland Hills, 1964-65; Mayor, Encino, 1972. Hobbies: cartooning, antiquarian books. Rec.: Karate, basketball, target shooting. Office: 5858 Sunset Blvd., L.A., CA 90028.

OWYANG, JUDITH FRANCINE
Art Critic
b. Feb. 9, 1940, Sacramento, Calif.; d. Mervyn and Esther (Yen) Owyang; niece of pioneer avitrix, Frances Owyang Lee (dec. 1920); ed. B.A. (art hist.), USC 1969; stu. with Dr. Edward S. Peck, dir. USC Art Galleries, and journ.-newswriting with publisher Jack C. Searles, USC. Career: Exhibs.: Calif. Spring Fair, Calif. State Fair and Exposition, Town and Country Village Gallery, Sacramento, 1964; art ed. Santa Monica Eve. Outlook; column, The Art Scene, publ. Outlook West 1970---. Mem.: Santa Monica Chpt., AAUW; Kappa Pi, 1966---. Hobbies: sculpture, printmaking, surf fishing. Res.: 2030 S. Sherbourne Dr., Los Angeles, CA 90034; Office: 1914 Sawtelle Blvd., W. L.A., CA.

OXX, WILLIAM G. III
Educator — Writer — Illustrator
b. Jan. 19, 1923, Newport, R.I.; s. William G. and Mary Elizabeth (Bjorkman) Oxx; desc.: John Howland of Plymouth Colony; William Arnold, 2nd Gov. of R.I.; King David I of Scot.; lineage incl. Bliss, Gardner, Greene, Lindsay, Munro families of Bristol and Newport, R.I.; A.B. (hist.), University Redlands, 1959; M.A., 1951; postgrad. Institute of Russian Affairs, Columbia Univ., N.Y.; 6 Calif. State adm. and teaching credentials, San Fernando Valley State Coll. 1955-61; m. May Isobel Anderson (La Fleche, Sask., Can.), Calif., Feb. 11, 1956; chil.: William IV, Sheri Lynn, Jonathan James. Career: Fellow, instr. hist., Univ. Redlands, 1948-51; L.A. City Schs., instr. U.S. Govt., Russian Hist., Mil. Naval Science, 1954---; coached numerous Southern California Debate League inter-scholastic varsity and jr. varsity forensic teams

(won 75 1st-2nd-3rd place sweepstakes trophies, incl. 303 gold, silver and bronze, Southern California Debate League medals). Appointed (by California Supt. of Public Instr. Dr. Max Rafferty) Task Force for Studying of Physical Attacks on Calif. Teachers Com. 1969-71; dist. asst. chmn. Mayor's Task Force on Narcotics and Drugs Com. 1970; approx. 250 pub. speaking engagements and many TV-radio appearances, 1951---. Author: contrib. ed. (books) Vanguard of Freedom, 1975; Bible and Christianity (Lakeside Press), 1952; A Hist. of Flight, 1953; Pictorial Hist. of the World (Simon & Schuster), 1956; America (Ency. Brit. Press), 1954; (co-author) Brig. Gen. Francis Hudson Oxx, U.S.A. (Ret.), The Descendants of Samuel Oxx, Bristol, Plymouth Colony; 23 articles incl. The Spanish Navy During the Civil War: 1932-36 (1944); Why Japan Fears the Red Fleet, 1945; The Soviet Naval Service (1948); airbrush illustrator, Warships of the World, 1946; Army-Navy Journal of Recognition (vols. 1-24), 1942-45; dissertation, Perry to Pearl Harbor: Rise of Navalism in Imperial Japan, 1853-1941 (vol. 1), Pearl Harbor to Halsey, 1941-45 (vol. 2); U.S. Naval Intelligency, Navy Dept., 1941-45; USNR 1947-54; mem. naval intelligence team under Commander-in-Chief Adm. Ernest J. King, Pearl Harbor Trial, U.S. Senate, 1945. Awards: 2nd place intercollegiate Western States Championship; James W. Kyle Award for Excellence in Journalism, 1949; 1st and 2nd Diamond Awards, Natl. Forensic League 1966, 71. Mem.: Univ. Redlands Varsity Debate Team, 1948-50; pres. Pi Kappa Delta; Alpha Phi Gamma; founder-pres. L.A. Westlake-Wilshire Toastmasters, 1951 (hon. life pres. 1968); Gen. Soc. Colonial Wars; Calif. Soc. S.R.; S.A.R. (pres. Gen. Patton Chpt.); Soc. Mayflower Descendants; Soc. War of 1812; St. Andrew's Soc., San Francisco; St. George Soc. N.Y.; Hereditary Register of the U.S.A.; (hon. life) PTA 1959. Republican. Protestant. Hobbies: hist. research, marine art, book collecting (pvt. lib. 3000 vols.). Rec.: sailing, music, golf. Res.: 3806 Mainsail Cir., Westlake Village, CA 91361.

P

PACILEO, RICHARD FRANK
Sheriff
b. Aug. 14, 1934, Farrell, Pa.; s. Rocco and Theresa Pacileo; ed. A.A. (police sci.) Amer. River Coll., Placerville, 1972; Lincoln Univ. Law Sch., Sacramento, 1973-75; m. Virginia Evelyn Magnaghi, Placerville, Calif., May 17, 1956; chil.: Kathleen Jean, b. Sept. 4, 1957; David Richard, b. Mar. 12, 1959; Joseph Vincent, b. Sept. 28, 1961. Career: Sgt., El Dorado Co. Sheriff's Dept. 1965-71; Judge, El Dorado Judicial Dist. Ct. 1971-75; sheriff-coroner-public admr., County of El Dorado, 1975---. USAF, Korean War, 1955-56. Mem.: chmn. bd. dirs. El Dorado County Fire Dist.; dist. com. chmn. El Dorado County BSA; law-legislative com. Calif. State Sheriff's Assn.; trustee, El Dorado Council on Alcoholism, 1975; Amer. Legion; Deputy Grand Knight, Knights of Columbus; Elks. Catholic. Hobbies: hunting, fishing, garden. Res.: China Hill Rd., El Dorado, CA; Office: 300 Fair Lane, Placerville, CA 95667.

PACK, (WALTER) FRANK
Clergyman — Educator
b. Mar. 27, 1916, Memphis, Tenn.; s. Joseph Walter and Mary Elizabeth (Gibson) Pack; A.A., David Lipscomb Coll., 1935; B.A., Univ. of Chattanooga; M.A., Vanderbilt Univ.; Ph.D., USC; m. Della Carlton, June 22, 1947, Los Angeles. Career: Instr., David Lipscomb Coll., Nashville, Tenn. 1940-44; Prof., Pepperdine Univ., 1945-49, Chmn. Religion Dept. 1963-75, Dean, Grad. Sch., 1967-78, Distinguished Prof. of Religion, 1978---; Prof. of Bible, Abilene Christian Univ., 1949-63; minister, Churches of Christ, 1932---: at present, minister, Culver Palms Ch. of Christ, Los Angeles. Staff writer, Gospel Advocate, 20th Century Christian; Editor, Our Bible (1951); Author, with Prentice Meador, Preaching to Modern Man, 1969, Living Word Commentary on the Gospel of John, 2 vols., 1975, Tongues and the Holy Spirit, 1973. Mem.: Phi Beta Kappa, Phi Kappa Phi, Pi Gamma Mu, Alpha Chi; Soc. of Biblical Literature; Am. Acad. of Religion; Am. Soc. of Ch. Hist.; Evangelical Theological Soc.; Evangelical Philosophical Soc. Hobbies: antiques, photog. Rec.: swimming, jogging. Res.: 10858 Wagner St., Culver City, CA 90230; Office: Pepperdine Univ., 24255 Pacific Coast Hwy., Malibu, CA 90265.

PACKARD, DAVID
Industrialist
b. Sept. 7, 1912, Pueblo, Colo.; s. Sperry Sidney and Ella Lorner (Graber) Packard; B.A., Stanford Univ. 1934, E.E. 1939 (Block "S," football and basketball); Colo. Univ. 1934, advanced course in engring. 19434-36; m. Lucile Salter, Apr. 8, 1938; chil.: David Woodley, b. Oct. 7, 1940; Nancy Anne, b. Aug. 22, 1943; Susan, b. Sept. 26, 1946; Julie Elizabeth, b. Mar. 20, 1953. Career: Gen. Elec. Co., Vacuum Tube Engring. Dept., Schenectady, N.Y. 1936-38; co-founder-partner, Hewlett-Packard Co., Palo Alto, Calif. 1939-46; pres. 1947-64, chmn. bd.-chief exec. ofcr. 1964-69, chmn. bd. 1972---. Deputy Secretary of Defense, 1969-71. Chmn. bd., Hewlett-Packard Co., 1972---. Director, Palo Alto National Bank, 1945-58; adv. bd., Anglo-Calif. Natl. Bank, 1948-57; Bd. of Edn., Palo Alto, Calif. 1948-56; pres. 1951; dir. Varian Assocs. 1949-59; dir. Palo Alto Mutual Savings & Loan, 1953-66; bd. trustees, Stanford Univ. 1954-69, pres. 1958-60; dir. Granger Assocs. 1957-66; dir. Crocker-Anglo Natl. Bank, 1957-59; bd. dirs., Stanford Research Inst. 1958---, exec. com. 1958---; dir. Pac. Gas and Elec. Co. 1959-59; dir. Systems Development Corp. 1958-63; dir. Natl. Airlines, Inc. 1962-64; dir. Natl. Merit Scholarship Corp. 1963-69; dir. Gen. Dynamics Corp. 1964-69; dir. U.S. Steel Corp. 1964-69; internat. adv. com. Chase Manhattan Bank, 1955-69; dir. Univs. Research Assocs. 1966-69; trustee, Colo. Coll. 1966-69; Dir.: Caterpillar Tractor Co., Standard Oil CO. of Calif., Trans-World Airlines, Atlantic Council, Calif. State C. of C. Author: articles on electronics and measurements. Patents: 4 patents issued, and several pending in field of electronics and measurements. Ind. Adv. Com. on Test Equipment, War Production Bd., 1943-45, WW II. Awards: American Way of Life Award, Pueblo Sertoma Club, 1963; Herbert Hoover Medal, Stanford Univ. Alumni Assn. 1966; 16 awards, 1969--- incl. Man of Yr., Bus. Statesman of Yr., Indus. of Yr., Grand Cross of Merit, Fed. Republic of Ger., Silver Helmet Def. Award; Hon. D.Sc., Colo. Coll. 1964; LL.D., Univ. of Calif. 1966; Cath. Univ. 1970; D. Litt., So. Colo. State Coll. 1973. Mem.: Alpha Delta Phi, pres. 1933-34; Phi Beta Kappa, 1933; Tau Beta Pi, 1934; Sigma Xi, 1939; IEEE; Inst. of Radio Engrs. 1938, chmn. S.F. sect. 1944, fellow, 1948; New York Academy of Scientists; American Management Association, 1956-59, v.p. at large, 1959; adv. bd., Hoover Inst. on War, Rev. and Peace, 1958; bd. trustees, World Affairs Council of No. Calif. 1958-64; The Links N.Y.; Pac. Union, S.F.; dir. Amer. Ord. Assn., S.F. Post 1960-63; Engrs. Club of S.F., Stock Exch. Club, Commonwealth Club of Calif., California Club, Bohemian Club. Office: 1501 Page Mill Rd., Palo Alto, CA 94304.

PAGE, GERALD W.
Insurance Executive
b. Dec. 14, 1905, St. Paul, Minn.; George H. and Minnie A. (Thompson) Page; ed. USC Coll. of Commerce, 1922-24; CLU, Amer. Coll. of Life Underwriters; m. Amy R. McGuigan, Menlo Park, Calif., Feb. 1961; chil.: Donald W., b. Mar. 31, 1936; Geraldine W., b. Oct. 16, 1944; Sarah Ann W., b. June 3, 1951; Theodore E.W., b. Feb. 23, 1953. Career: Life Insurance, Los Angeles, Calif. 1923---; gen. agt., Provident Mutual Life Ins. Co. of Phila., 1949-70; gen. agt. emeritus, 1971---; trustee American Coll. of Life Underwriters, 1952-70. Cons. Editor, Life and Health Ins. Handbook. Awards: Farrell Award by Los Angeles C. of C., 1961; Mem.: Life Underwriters Assn. of L.A., dir. 1945-47, pres. 1948-49; L.A. Chpt., Amer. Soc. of Chartered Life Underwriters, dir. 1945-47, officer, 1947-49, pres. 1949-50; dir. Amer. Soc. of Chartered Life Underwriters, 1947-50, officer, 1950-53, pres. 1953-54; (life) Million Dollar Round Table; chairman, life insurance committee, L.A. C. of C. 1959; pres. Life Ins. Mgrs. Assocs. 1962; Life Ins. & Trust Council; Wilshire Lodge No. 445, F&AM (Master, 1942); Scottish Rite Bodies; Al Malaikah Shrine; Kiwanis Club, L.A.; World Affairs Council; adv. com. Recording for Blind. Inc., L.A.; Town Hall; Jonathan Club; First Presbyterian Church (elder). Hollywood. Hobby: music, photog., gardeninginging. Rec.: golf, travel. Res.: 4339 Mariota Ave., North Hollywood, CA 91602; Office: 615 S. Flower St., Los Angeles, CA 90017.

PAIGE, HENRY REID
Maj. Gen., U.S. Marine Corps (Ret.)
b. Mar. 30, 1904, Ogdensburg, N.Y.; s. Alfred S. and Ella (Reid) Paige; ed. B.S., U.S. Naval Acad. 1927; grad. Natl. War Coll. 1949; (hon.) LL.D., St. Lawrence Univ. 1960; m. Gladys Brundage, Potsdam. N.Y., July 9, 1927; chil.: Mrs. M.D. Donnelson, b. May 27, 1928;

Mrs. H.B. Packard, b. Apr. 17, 1931; Reid B., b. Oct. 11, 1935; Mrs. L.B. (Mary Ellen) Marquand, b. Nov. 18, 1940. Career: USN midshipman, 1923-27; comm. 2nd Lt., USMC, June 2, 1927; comm. 2nd Lt., USMC, June 2, 1927, 1st Lt. 1933, Capt. 1936, Maj. 1941, Lt. Col. 1942, Col. 1942, Brig. Gen. 1953, Maj. Gen. 1955---; serv. Nicaragua, 1929-30; tech. adv., logistics, Ofc. Chief of Naval Operations, 1945-48; pres. tactics and techniques bd., Marine Corps Development Center, 1950-53; Asst. Div. Comdr., 2nd Marine Div. 1953-54; Asst. Div. Comdr., 1st Marine Div., Korea, 1954-55; dir. Marine Corps Edn. Center, 1955-57; Asst. Chief of Staff (logistics), U.S. Marine Corps, 1957-59; Comdg. Gen., 1st Marine Div. (reinforced), 1959-62. Contrib. various articles, publ. mil. professional mags. 1940---. Awards: Nicaraguan Medal of Merit, WW II; Leg. of Merit, 1946; Army Commendation Ribbon, Korean War; Oak Leaf Cluster in lieu of 2nd Leg. of Merit for serv. on U.N. Command Mil. Armistice Comm.; Korean Ulchi Medal by Govt. of Korea. Mem.: Marine Corps Assn.; (life) First Marine Div. Assn.; bd. mgmt., N. Co. YMCA 1962-63; dir. Oceanside C. of C. 1963-65; dir. Rotary Club, 1963-65, pres. 1966-67; dir. Oceanside USO 1963-65. Protestant. Rec.: golf. Res.: 2905 Mesa Dr., Oceanside, CA 92054.

PAINE, ROGER WARDE, JR.
U.S. Naval Officer (Ret.)
b. Aug. 13, 1917, Austin, Texas; s. Roger Warde (Rear Adm., USN) and Corine (Malone) Paine; B.S., U.S. Naval Acad., 1939; M.S., Mass. Inst. of Tech., 1949; m. Isla Vaile, June 1, 1941; Coronado, Calif.; chil.: Roger Warde III, b. Feb. 27, 1942; Isla Rea (Mrs. Richard Warren Moore), b. Sept. 12, 1944; Barbara Jean (Mrs. William B. Cramer), b. July 8, 1946. Career: Commissioned Ensign, USN, 1939---: advanced through grades to Rear Adm. 1967; commanded submarines, 1943-46, destroyers, 1951-58, cruisers 1961-67, attack carrier strike group, 1967, Tng. Command, Pacific Fleet, 1970-72; specialized nuclear weapons and guided missile engring., 1946-61; Staff Physicist, Los Alamos Sci. Lab., 1949-51; retired 1974. Dir. Navy Information Systems, 1968-70; Spec. Asst. to Dir. of Defense Research and Engring. (Dr. Harold Brown), 1963-66. Numerous Pub. works in field of nuclear weapon design and research, most titles classified. Awarded Silver Star Medal, Legion of Merit Medal, Bronze Star Medal (2), Navy Commendation Medal, Jt. Service Commendation Medal. Mem.: U.S. Naval Inst.; Am. Physical Soc.; Am. Inst. of Physics; ARC, vice chmn. San Diego Chpt. 1972-75. Republican. Episcopalian. Rec.: theater, opera, concerts. Res.: 1756 Circo Del Cielo, El Cajon, CA 92020.

PAINE, THOMAS OTTEN
President-CEO, Northrop Corp.
b. Nov. 9, 1921, Berkeley; s. Commodore George Thomas and Ada Louise Otten; A.B., Engring., Brown Univ., 1942; M.S., and Ph.D., physical metallurgy, Stanford Univ., 1947, 1949; m. Barbara Pearse, 1946, Long Beach; chil.: Marguerite Ada, b. Mar. 28, 1950; George Thomas, b. Jan. 19, 1953; Judith Janet, b. Mar. 8, 1954; Frank Taunton, b. Nov. 5, 1957. Career: Research Assoc. Stanford Univ. 1947-49; GE Research Lab., Schenectady, N.Y. 1949-50; Mgr., GE Meter & Instruments Lab., Lynn, Mass. 1951-58, Mgr., Tech. Analysis, GE R&D Center, Schenectady, N.Y. 1959-62; Mgr. TEMPO, GE Center for Advanced Studies, Santa Barbara, 1963-67; Adminstr., NASA, 1968-70 (dir. during first seven manned Apollo Missions, initial moon landings, during devel. of nation's post-Apollo space program); sr. v.p., and group exec. Power Generation Group, GE Co., 1973-76; pres., Chief Operating Officer, Dir., Northrop Corp., 1976---. Lectr.: U.S. Army War Coll., Indsl. Coll. of Armed Forces, Naval War Coll., Am. Mgmt. Assn. Secty. and Editor, E.J.C. Engring., Research Com. on Nation's Engring. Research Needs 1965-85; Coinventor: Fine Particle Iron Magnets; Patentee. Engring. Officer, USN, 1942-46, submarine serv. Pacific area; decorated U.S. Navy Submarine Combat Insignia with stars and Commendation Medal, 1944-45. Awarded the NASA Distinguished Service Medal 1970; the order Al Merito Della Repubblica Italiana, 1971; 1972 Washington Award, W. Soc. of Engineers; 1976 John Fritz Medal, United Engring. Socs.; 1976 Faraday Medal of U.K. Inst. of Elect. Engrs. Fellow, Am. Astronatuical Soc.; mem. Nat. Acad. of Engring. IEEE. Episcopalian. Hobbies: oil painting, photog., book collecting. Rec.: beachcombing, sailing, skin diving. Res.: 765 Bonhill Rd., Los Angeles, CA 90049; Office: 1800 Century Park E., Los Angeles, CA 90067.

PAL, PRATAPADITYA
Art Museum Director
b. Sept. 1, 1935, Bangladesh; s. Gopesh and Bidynt Pal; M.A., 1958; D.Phil., 1962; Ph.D., 1965; m. Chitralekha, 1968, India; chil.: Shalmali, b. 1969; Lopamudra, b. 1976. Career: Keeper of the Indian Collections, Mus. of Fine Arts, Boston, Mass., 1967-69; Adj. Prof. of Fine Arts, USC, 1971---; Curator of Indian and Islamic Art, Los Angeles County Mus. of Art, 1970---, Acting Chief Curator, 1978-79, Acting Director, 1979---. Author: The Classical Tradition in Rajput Painting, 1978; The Ideal Image, 1978; The Sensuous Immortals, 1977; Nepal Where The God Are Young, 1976; The Arts of Nepal I, 1974. Office: 5905 Wilshire Blvd., Los Angeles, CA 90036.

PALEVSKY, MAX
Industrialist
b. July 24, 1924, Chicago, Ill.; s. Isadore and Sara (Greenblatt) Palevsky; B.S., math, Univ. of Chicago, Ph.B., 1948; m. Lynda Edelstein, Nov. 10, 1972, Los Angeles; chil.: Nicholas George, b. Sept. 15, 1956; Madeleine Francois, b. Dec. 18, 1960; Alexander b. Oct. 28, 1973. Career: Research Analyst & mathematician, Bendix Aviation Corp., L.A., 1952-56; gen. mgr., v.p., dir., Packard Bell Computer Corp., L.A., 1957-61; pres., Scientific Data Systems, Inc., Santa Monica, 1961-69; chmn. of bd. and dir., Xerox Data Systems, Inc., El Segundo, 1969-72; chmn. Exec. Com., Dir., Xeron Corporation, 1969-72; Bart-Palevsky Productions, 1974-78. Dir., Intel Corp., 1969---; Alza Corp., 1969-78; American Ballet Theatre, 1977---; Folger Shakespeare Library, 1977---; Trustee, Univ. of Chicago, 1972---. Capt., USAAF, 1942-46. Office: 924 Westwood Blvd., Suite 700, Los Angeles, CA 90024.

PALMER, BEVERLY B.
Psychologist — Public Health Commissioner
b. Nov. 22, 1945, Cleveland, Ohio; d. Lawrence E. Blazey; B.A. Psychol., Univ. Mich.; M.A. and Ph.D., Counseling Psychol., Ohio State Univ.; m. Richard C. Palmer, M.D., June 24, 1967, Cleveland, Ohio; son, Ryan, b. 1975. Career: Tchr., Southwestern City Schools, Grove City, Ohio, 1967-69; Adminstrv. Assoc., Ohio State Univ., 1969-70; Research Psychologist, Health Services Research Center, UCLA, 1971-77; Assoc. Prof. Dept. of Psychology, Cal. State Univ., Dominguez Hills, 1973---; apptd. by Los Angeles Co. Bd. of Supervisors as Commissioner of Public Health, Los Angeles Co., 1978---. Honored by L.A. Co. Bd. of Suprs. for community activities, 1972. Mem. Am. Psychol. Assn. Office: California State University, Dominguez Hills, Carson, CA 90747.

PALMER, JOHN ALFRED
University Administrator
b. May 22, 1926, Spokane, Wash.; s. Cary Alfred and Blanche Leota (Trussell) Palmer; B.A., Univ. of Wash., 1950; M.A., Cornell Univ., 1952, Ph.D., 1962. Career: Instr. of English, Cornell Univ., 1957-62; Asst./Assoc./Full Professor, English, Calif. State Univ., Los Angeles, 1967-69, Dean, Sch. of Letters and Sci., 1969-70, vice pres. for Academic Affairs, 1970---. Author: Joseph Conrad's Fiction, Cornell Univ. Press, 1969; Twentieth-Century Interpretations of The Nigger of the 'Narcissus', Prentice-Hall, 1969. USN, 1943-46. Office: 5151 State University Dr., Los Angeles, CA 90032.

PALMER, JOHN T.
Professor of Counseling
b. Dec. 10, 1921, Mendenhall, Miss.; s. Charles A. and Mary Jane (Gates) Palmer; B.A., Univ. of So. Miss., 1943; M.A., Columbia Univ., 1946; Ph.D., USC, 1957; m. Elizaebth Ann Davis, Aug. 27, 1955, Glendale; sons: Tom, b. Apr. 2, 1960; Scott, b. Mar. 31, 1966. Career: Asst. Prof. Univ. of So. Miss., 1947-53, Dir. of Student Activities & Asst. Dean of Men, 1953-55; Counselor and Dir., USC Guidance Center, 1955-57; Asst. Prof. of Psychol. and Coordinator of Academic Advisement, S.F. State Univ. 1957-59; Assoc. Dean of Students, Counseling & Testing, Cal. State Univ., Northridge, 1959-60; Dean of Students, 1960-66; Vis. Prof., Univ. of Hawaii, Summer 1966; Dean of Students and Prof. of Psychol., Sonoma State Univ., 1966-72; Dept. Chmn. and Prof. of Counseling, 1972-77; vis. prof. USC Overseas Program (Europe) 1976-77; Prof. of Counseling, Sonoma State Univ. 1976---. AUS, 34th Infan. Div., Africa and Italy; decorated Bronze Star. Cited for Outstanding Community Service (1966) by L.A. City Council, L.A. County Bd. of Suprs., Mayor Sam Yorty. Mem.: Calif. Coll. Personnel Assn., pres. 1971-72; Northridge

Rotary Club, pres. 1963-64; dir. Van Nuys Salvation Army, 1961-67; Calif. Personnel & Guidance Assn., pres. 1971-72; dir. Am. Personnel & Guidance Assn. 1976-79; Rotary Internat., Masonic Lodge, Alpha Tau Omega, Phi Delta Kappa, Omicron Delta Kappa, Alpha Phi Omega, Blue Key. Presbyterian. Hobbies: boating, gardening. Res.: 878 Wildwood Trail, Santa Rosa, CA 95405; Office: Sonoma State Univ., Rohnert Park, CA 94928.

PALMER, RICHARD CLETUS
Psychiatrist
b. May 5, 1944, Cincinnati, Ohio; s. Cletus T. and Mary Louise Palmer; B.S., Univ. Mich. 1966; M.D., Ohio State Univ., 1970; m. Beverly Blazey, June 24, 1967, Cleveland, Ohio; son, Ryan, b. 1975. Career: Internship, Good Samaritan Hosp., 1970-71; Psychiatry residency, Harbor Gen. Hosp., 1970-71; Psychiatry residency, Harbor Gen. Hosp., Torrance, 1971-74; Fellowship, community psychiatry, UCLA 1973-74; pvt. practice psychiatry, Torrance, 1976---; asst. clin. prof., UCLA, 1976---. Contbd. Alert Allies of Adolescents, Ohio State Med. Journ. 1969; recipient Dept. of Psychiat. Award, Ohio State Univ. Med. Coll. 1970. Lt. Comdr., M.C., USN, Long Beach Naval Med. Center, 1974-76. Mem.: Am. Psychiatric Assn. So. Calif. and South Bay (treas. 1978---) Psychiat. Socs. Beta Theta Pi. Rec.: tennis, skiing. Res.: 29978 Knoll View Dr., Rancho Palos Verdes, CA 90274; Office: 3250 Lomita Blvd., Torrance, CA 90505.

PALMITER, LEO A.
Superintendent of Schools
b. Aug. 13, 1919, Long Beach, Calif.; s. Paul and Eunice Palmiter; A.B. Chico State Coll.; M.A., Sacramento State Coll.; m. Elizabeth Elwood Foord, Yerington, Nev. 1940; chil.: Larry R., b. Feb. 6, 1942; Lanette Silva, b. May 20, 1944; Leonard W., b. Mar. 10, 1946; Lizabeth K. Atcheson, b. Apr. 10, 1948; Leo A., b. Feb. 7, 1952. Career: Elem. teacher: Churn Town Sch. Dist., Shasta, 1941-42; Colusa Elem. Sch., Colusa Co. 1942-45; elem v.-prin., prin. 1944-45; elem. dist. supt.-prin. Del Paso Heights Sch. Dist. 1946-50; dir. edn. research-asst. county supt. Sacramento, 1950-69, Sacramento County Supt. of Schs., Jan. 1, 1969---. Mem.: (hon. life) PTA; KVIE bd. dirs.; Pub. Sch. Instr. TV Com.; coach-mgr.-treas.-pres. N. Sacramento Little League 1949-65; committeeman troup 51 BSA 1958-67; Methodist. Hobbies: hunting, fishing, gardening. Res.: 602 Garden St., Sacramento, CA 95815; Office: 6011 Folsom Blvd., Sacramento, CA 95819.

PANAGOPOULOS, EPAMINONDAS P.
Professor of History
b. Feb. 26, 1915, Athens, Greece (U.S. cit. 1955); s. Peter and Vassiliki (Papathanasiou) Panagopoulos; ed. LL.B., Univ. of Athens, 1941, M.A. (polit. sci.), 1946; Ph.D. (hist.), Univ. of Chicago, 1952; m. Beata Maria Kitsikis, Tarpon Springs, Fla., Dec. 26, 1949; chil.: Peter, b. Oct. 2, 1950; Beata Domenica, b. Dec. 10, 1953. Career: Atty. at law, 1941-44; U.S. Information Serv., Athens, Greece, 1944-46; est. U.S. res. 1946; prof. of hist., Wayne State Univ., Detroit, Mich. 1952-56; prof. of hist., San Jose (Calif.) State Coll. 1956. Author: Alexander Hamilton's Pay Book, publ. Wayne State Univ. Press, 1961; New Smyrna: An Eighteenth Century Greek Odyssey, publ. Univ. of Fla. Press, 1966; contrib. to hist. quarterlies. Maj., Greek Army, WW II. Awards: Golden Cross of Gallantry, Silver Cross with Swords. Mem.: Amer. Hist. Assn., St. Augustine Hist. Soc., Fla. Hist. Soc. Greek Orthodox. Res.: 12386 Priscilla Lane, Los Altos Hills, CA; Office: San Jose State Univ., San Jose, CA 95114.

PANIC, MILAN
Company President
b. Dec. 20, 1929, Belgrade, Yugoslavia (U.S. cit. 1963); s. Spasdie and Zorka (Krunich) Panic; ed. 7th Real Gym., Belgrade, 1941-48; B.S., Univ. of Belgrade, 1955; Univ. of Heidelberg, 1955-56; USC 1957–59; m. Jelica Narandic, Belgrade, Yugoslavia, June 12, 1950; chil.: Nick, b. July 18, 1951; Dawn, b. July 29, 1957; Milan, Jr., b. June 5, 1958; Vivian, b. June 8, 1962. Career: Est. U.S. res. 1956; Kaiser Steel Corp. 1956-57; chem. Cyclo-Chem. Corp., L.A. 1957-58; research asst., dept. chem., USC 1958-59; research chem., Calif. Corp. for Biochem Research, 1959-61; pres. Internat. Chem. and Nuclear Corp. 1961--- (chmn. bd.-dir. 10 cos., Switz., Mex. USA). Mem.: trustee Pasadena Art Museum; Amer. Nuclear Soc., Amer. Chem. Soc., Swiss Chem. Soc., Internat. Soc. Chemotherapy; Verdugo Club, Glendale, Republican.

Orthodox Serbian. Hobbies: skiing, flying. Res.: 1050 Arden Rd., Pasadena, CA 91106.

PANOFSKY, WOLFGANG KURT HERMANN
Physicist
b. Apr. 24, 1919, Berlin, Ger. (U.S. cit. 1942); s. Erwin (prof. art-art critic, Inst. for Advanced Stu., Princeton, N.J.) and Dorothea (Mosse) Panofsky; ed. A.B., Princeton Univ. 1938; Ph.D., Calif. Inst. of Tech. 1942; (hon.) D.Sc.: Case Inst. of Tech. 1963, Univ. of Saskatchewan, 1964; m. Adele DuMond, Pasadena, Calif., July 21, 1942; chil.: Richard Jacob and Margaret Anne Miller (twins), b. Oct. 13, 1943; Edward Frank, b. Apr. 19, 1947; Carol Eleanor, b. Jan. 12, 1951; Steven Thomas, b. Dec. 13, 1952. Career: Est. U.S. res. 1934; dir. Ofc. of Sci. Research and Dev. Proj., Calif. Inst. of Tech., Pasa. 1942-43; cons. Manhattan Dist., Los Alamos, N.Mex. 1943-45; physicist, Radiation Lab., Univ. Univ. of Calif. Berkeley, 1945-46, 1951---, asst. prof. 1946-48, prof. physics, Stanford Univ. 1951-63, dir. High-Energy Physics Lab. 1953-61; dir.-prof., Stanford Linera Accelerator Center, Stanford Univ. 1961---. Mem.: U.S. Atmoic Energy Comm. 1945-60; physics panel, Natl. Sci. Found. 1954-58; USAF Sci. Adv. Bd. 1955-57; Stanford Research Inst. 1958; High-Energy Phys. Div., Argonne Natl. Lab. 1958-60, 1963---; Advanced Research Projs. Agcy. 1958-62; Ofc. of Dir. Def. Research and Engring., Ad Hoc. Group, 1959; WAE Foreign Serv. Ofcr., Dept. of State, chmn. U.S. Del., Geneva, v.-chmn. U.S. Del. Group 2, 1959; Pres.'s Sci. Adv. Com. 1960-64; adv. com. Lawrence Radiation Lab., Berkeley, 1964; cons. Ofc. of Sci. and Tech., Exec. Ofc. of the Pres. 1965---; steering com. JASON div., Inst. for Def. Analyses, 1965---; High-Energy Physics Adv. Panel to Atomic Energy Comm. 1968---; adv. com.: Brookhaven Natl. Lab., and Cambridge Electron Accelerator Lab. 1968---; Caltech for Physics, Math. and Astronomy, 1969---; co-chmn. Stanford Mid-Peninsula Urban Coalition, 1969---. Apptd. to President's General Advisory Council (ACDA), 1978; Member DOE Nonproliferation Alternative Systems Assessment Program, 1978. Co-author: Classical Electricity and Magnetism, 1955, 2nd edit. 1962; numerous sci. papers in professional journs. Awards: Guggenheim Fellowship, 1959; Ernest Orlando Lawrence Mem. Award, 1961; Richtmyer Lecture, 1963; Calif. Inst. of Tech. Alumni Distinguished Serv. Award, 1966; Calif. Scientist of Yr. Award, 1967; Natl. Medal of Sci. 1969. Award, Officer, French Legion of Honor, 1977; Hon. Doctorate, Columbia Univ. 1977. Mem.: Natl. Acad. of Scis.; Amer. Acad. of Arts and Scis.; fellow, Amer. Phys. Soc., council, 1956-60; Phi Beta Kappa, Sigma Xi, Sierra Club. Rec.: hiking, mus. Res.: 25671 Chapin Ave., Los Altos Hills, CA 94022; Office: Stanford Linear Accelerator Center, P.O.B. 4349, Stanford, CA 94305.

PAPIANO, NEIL LEO
Attorney at Law
b. Nov. 25, 1933, Salt Lake City, Utah; s. Leo and Ruth (Cotten) Papiano; A.B. Stanford Univ., 1956, M.A., 1957; LL.B., Vanderbilt Sch. of Law, 1961. Career: attorney, Trippet, Yoakum & Ballantyne, 1961-66; partner: Trippet, Yoakum & Papiano, 1966-70; Partner: Iverson, Yoakum, Papiano & Hatch 1970---; Dir.: Pacific United Services, 1969-73; SCOA Industries, Inc., 1972---; Ocean Tech., Inc., 1961---; King Nutronics Corp., 1961---; Stanford Univ. Athletic bd., 1978. Recipient: Nathan Burkan Nat. Copyright Law Award, 1961. Mem.: pres., L.A. Jr. C. of C., 1966; Greater L.A. C. of C., 1966, 1973-76; v.p. dir., L.A. County Welfare Planning Council, 1966-71; bd. of gov., USO, 1967-71; bd. gov., Orthopaedic Hosp., 1974-75. Home: 2390 Montecito Dr., San Marino, CA 91108; Office: 611 W. Sixth St., Suite 1900, L.A., CA 90017.

PAPPAGIANIS, DEMOSTHENES
Medical Microbiologist
b. Mar. 31, 1928, San Diego; s. George John and Mary (Jerzakis) Pappagianis; A.B., Univ. of Calif. Berkeley, 1949, M.A. 1951, Ph.D. 1956; M.D., Stanford Sch. of Med., 1962; m. Alice Ertel, Jan. 28, 1956, Reno, Nev.; daughters, Michele, b. Oct. 10, 1956; Marika, b. Feb. 17, 1961. Career: Asst. Research Bacteriologist, Univ. Calif., Berkeley, 1955-58; 2d. Lt. to Capt., Med. Service Corps, USAR; (Capt. M.C., AUS) Intern, Walter Reed Gen. Hosp., Wash., D.C., 1962-63; Assoc. Prof., Sch. of Pub. Health, UC, Berkeley, 1963-67; Prof. and Chmn. (1968), Dept. of Med. Microbiology, Sch. of Medicine, UC, Davis, 1967---. Physician/Surgeon Certificate Calif.

1963---; Fellow, Am. Acad. Microbiology, 1978; contbr. numerous sci. publs.; research in Coccidioidomyeosis or "San Joaquin" or "Valley Fever." Assoc. mem., Armed Forces Epidemiological Bd., Commn. on Acute Respiratory Disease, 1965-72. Mem. Alpha Omega Alpha, 1961---. Res.: 1523 Orange Lane, Davis, CA 95616; Office: University of California, Davis, CA 95616.

PARCHER, CARROLL WILMOT
Newspaper Publisher
b. Sept. 13, 1903, Glendale, Calif.; s. Wilmot and Nannie (McBryde) Parcher; ed. Pub. Sch., Glendale, Calif.; m. Frances Morgan, Tujunga, Calif., Nov. 8, 1924; chil.: Mrs. A.R. (Margaret Ann) Faulkner, Jr., b. Aug. 24, 1926; Stuart Michael, b. Dec. 2, 1930; Janice Mary, b. Oct. 10, 1943. Career: Founder, Crescenta Valley Ledger (wkly. newspaper), Montrose, Calif. 1922; co-publ. Tujunga Record Ledger, 1922-38; field investigator-chmn. bd., Los Angeles Co. Supvs. 1931-32; field secty., Los Angeles City Council, 1933-36; columnist-feat. writer, Glendale News-Press, 1939-42; assoc. ed. 1942-44, editor-publ. 1947-73 (ret.) chmn. bd. dirs., Verdugo Savings & Loan Assn. 1955---. Councilman, City of Glendale, 1975---. Mem.: Lt. Gov., Calif.-Nevada Dist., Kwanis Internat. 1930; v.p.-dir., So. Calif. Assoc. Newspapers, 1948-73; pres. L.A. Chpt., Sigma Delta Chi, 1950; pres. Verdugo Club, Glendale, 1954; pres. Calif. Newspapers Publs. Assn. 1959; pres. Calif. Press Assn. 1971-72; Native Sons of the Golden West. Clubs: Oakmont Country, Republican. Protestant. Res.: 1401 Valley View Rd., Glendale, CA 91202.

PARDUE, ANDREW MICHAEL
Plastic Surgeon
b. June 23, 1931, Nashville, Tenn.; s. Andrew Peyton and Rubye Pardue; B.S., Univ. of the South, Sewanee, 1953; M.D., Univ. Tenn., 1957. Career: Internship, U.S. Naval Hosp., St. Albans, N.Y. 1957-58; Sch. of Aviation Med., USN, 1958; Flight Surgeon, USN, 1959-62, on board USS Wasp, USS Lake Champlain, USS Antarctica; resident in gen. surgery, Pittsfield Affil. Hosps., 1962-66; resident in plastic surg., Cornell Med. Center, NYC, 1966-68; pvt. practice of plastic, reconstructive, cosmetic surg., Thousand Oaks, 1968---; Instr. anatomy, fellow exptl. surgery, Albany Med. Coll., 1966-68. USN, 1956-62. Fellow, Am. Coll. Surgeons, Internat. Coll. of Surgeons; Diplomate of Am. Bd. of Plastic Surg.; mem. Am. Soc. Aesthetic Plastic Surg., Am. Burn Assn., Am. Cleft Palate Soc. Episcopalian. Hobby: early Am. Hist. Rec.: hunting, fly fishing. Res.: Hidden Oaks Ranch, 1993 W. Potrero Rd., Thousand Oaks, CA; Office: 327 S. Moorpark Rd., Thousand Oaks, CA 91360.

PARISH, H. CARROLL
Educator
b. Feb. 13, 1920, Pasadena, Calif.; s. Hayward Carroll and Gertrude I. (Riggs) Parish; desc.: Edward Riggs (1614-71), founder of Milford, CT, and Newark, N.J.; Capt. John Rolfe, Va. pioneer; Joseph Hamilton (1819-84), honored Ore. pioneer and legislator (Old Oregon Trail, 1947); ed. B.A. (internat. rels.), UCLA 1949, M.A. 1950, Ph.D. 1958. Career: Secty. CIVIC, 1938; L.A. Co. Youth Commr. 1938-42, pres. 1938; exec. bd., L.A. Co. Coord. Councils, 1939-41; assoc. prof. naval sci., UCLA 1946-47, 1952-54, asst. dean, 1957-62, assoc. dean of students, 1962-71; dean, financial aids, 1966-71; assoc. dean, acad. servs., 1971; adjunct professor of political science, University of LaVerne; Provost-trustee, Miller Community Coll. 1972---; attache, California State Legislature, 1947; property management exec.; v.p.-treas. Environmental Design Assocs. 1966---; partner, Claremont Co., Riverside-Illinois Co., and Manhattan Co. Fulbright Fellow to Japan and lectr., Waseda Univ., Tokyo, 1958-59; comdg. ofcr., Naval Res. Ofcrs' Sch. 1965-68; lecturer, Asiatic Studies, USC 1961. Author: Thailand Bibliography and numerous articles on Asian and international affairs. Capt., USNR; decorated for combat service, Pacific area (for valor at Okinawa when ship was hit by Kamikaze plane); meritorious serv. as flag secty. to comdr., assault transport div., WW II; serv. as Flag Lt. and aide to comdr., Destroyer Flotilla, Korean conflict. Mem.: Jonathan Club, 1942---; Amer. Leg., chmn. Naval Affairs Comm., Natl. Conv. 1949, 50, 52; Natl. Security Comm. 1950-53; Soc. of Colonial Wars, Amer. Polit. Sci. Assn.; (life) Navy Leag.; gov.-gen. Order Founders and Patriots of Amer.; fellow, AAAS; pres. Natl. Assn. Student Financial Aid Admrs. 1971; Asian Studies on Pac. Coast, chmn.-permanent secretariat; Order of Golden

Merit, Japanese Red Cross; Knight Grand Ofcr. Order of St. John the Bapt. of Amer.; Knight-Grand Prioral ofcr., Order of St. Lazarus of Jerusalem; Knight of Honour, Venerable Order of the Rose of Lippe; Amer. Coll. Personnel Assn.; past pres., Council of Internat. Students; pres. Amer. Siam Soc.; chmn. Council, Japan-Amer. Soc.; Fellow, Internat. Inst. of Arts and Letters; Internat. Inst. of Arts and Letters; Internat. Polit. Sci. Assn., Assn. for Asian Studies, Asia Soc. Chancellor, Western Region Pi Gamma Mu; Pi Sigma Alpha, Alpha Mu Gamma, Phi Eta Sigma. Episcopalian. Hobby: philately. Rec.: travel. Res.: 633 24th St., Santa Monica, CA 90402.

PARK, EDWARD CAHILL, JR.
Scientist
b. Nov. 26, 1923, Wollaston, Mass.; s. Edward Cahill and Fentress (Kerlin) Park; grandson of Robert Ezra Park, sociologist; ed. grad. Milton (Mass.) Acad. 1941; A.B., Harvard Univ. 1947; postgrad. Amherst Coll. 1947-49; Ph.D., Univ. of Birmingham, Eng., 1956; m. Helen T. O'Boyle, Scarsdale, N.Y., July 28, 1951. Career: Instr. in physics (Ford Found interne), Amherst Coll., Mass. 1954-55; staff, Lincoln Lab., MIT 1955-57; dir. Jefferson Investment Corp., Boston, 1956-60; staff, Arthur D. Little, Inc., Cambridge, Mass. 1957-60, electronics systems group leader, Santa Monica, CA 1961-64; sr. staff engr., Hughes Aircraft Co., Culver City, Calif. 1964-68; Litton Systems, Inc. 1968-70; phys. sci. sr. Rand Corp. 1970-72; sr. scientist R&D Assocs. 1972---. Holder of 2 patents on superconductive circuits. Author: tech. articles on nuclear physics, instrumentation, Laser radar, space communications systems. 1st Lieutenant, USAAF communications ofcr., Army Airways Communications System (1943-46), WW II. Mem.: Inst. of Elec. and Electronic Engrs., Optical Society of America, Cum Laude Society, Sigma Xi, 20-Ghost Club, Eng.; Fellow, Explorers Club. Hobbies: music, art, automobiles. Rec.: swimming; Res.: 932 Ocean Front, Santa Monica, CA 90403; Office: R&D Assocs., Marina del Rey, CA 90291.

PARKER, MAURICE WESLEY III
Athlete — Actor
b. Nov. 13, 1943, Chicago, Illinois; s. M.W., Jr. and Mary (Joslyn) Parker; desc. Capt. David Parker of Rev. War, Shot Heard 'Round the World; B.A., hist., humanities, USC. Career: with Los Angeles Dodgers, 1964-72; announcer, actor, 1973---. Awards include 1st Brian Piccolo Award, 1972; Lou Gehrig Award, 1972; Hobbies: sports, bridge, chess. Office: 2140 Colorado Ave., Santa Monica, CA 90404.

PARKER, RACHEL RUDMOSE
Corporate Executive
b. May 29, 1945, Boston, Mass.; d. Dr. Wayne (devel. automatic audiometer, John Tyndall Scholar, Harvard Univ.) and Christelle (Simmons) Rudmose; student, liberal arts, Univ. of Colo.; m. 2d. Charles Lee Parker, Feb. 2, 1974, Palos Verdes Estates; chil.: Erik Stephan Olson, b. Oct. 21, 1964; Kristophen Wayne Olson, b. Mar. 16, 1967. Career: Dir., sales support, John Roberts, Inc., Austin, Tex., 1969-72; asst. to gen. mgr., Albert C. Martin and Assocs., L.A., 1972-76; v.p., Grieger's, Inc., Pasadena, 1976---. Bd. dir. and corp. secty., Grieger's, Inc. Mem.: Pi Beta Phi Sorority, social v.p., Univ. of Colo. Hobby: harpsichord. Home: 615 Alegria Place., San Marino, CA 91108; Office: 900 S. Arroyo Pkwy., Pasadena, CA 91109.

PARKHURST, DONALD BURTON
Illustrator — Historian
b. Jan. 15, 1928, Webster, Mass.; s. Alden B. and Helen Irene (Sturges) Parkhurst; B.A., religion & philosophy, Pacific Union Coll., Angwin, Calif., 1954; grad. studies, hist., Cal. State Univ., Hayward; chil.: Martin, b. Mar. 26, 1952; Helen (Teruel), b. Apr. 25, 1953; Daniel, b. Aug. 26, 1955; Gordon, b. Aug. 1, 1959. Career: clinical lab. technologist; tchr., Jr. and Sr. High Sch., 3 years. Served AUS, 1946-49 to staff sgt., acting 1st sgt., 27th Malaria Survey Detachment, 20th Inf. Reg. Copyrighted research on early motion picture indus., Niles, Calif., 1912-1916; excerpts pub. in Fremont newspaper, The Argus, Dec. 1977; creator: cartoon strip, The Yolk's On Us, 1977--- (appears in Vallejo Independent Press and The Independent, Livermore, etc.); polit. & editorial cartoons in Tri-Valley Herald and The Times, Livermore, 1977-78; forthcoming cartoon strip entitled Eagle of the Republic. Hobbies: cartooning, creative writing. Rec.: motorcycling, sailing. Res.: 3082 San Fernando Way, Union City, CA.

PARKINSON, ARIEL
Painter — Designer
b. July 12, 1926, Oakland; d. Dr. T. Eric and Laurel Reynolds; B.A. 1946; M.A. 1947; m. Thomas Parkinson, 1948, Piedmont; daughters: Katherine Laurel, b. 1950; Chrysa, b. 1964. Career: Painter, designer: Major exhibitions; San Francisco Mus. of Art 1962, 64, Lincoln Center, N.Y., 1975; major commns.: University of California, 1961-71, San Francisco Opera 1971, San Francisco Ballet 1976, EPA film, "Use It, Use It Up." Citizen adv.: pres., Berkeley Solid Waste Mgmt. Commn., 1972-73, 1976-77, now Mem. State Solid Waste Mgmt. Board. Res.: 1001 Cragmont, Berkeley, CA.

PARKS, D(ALE) GENE
Gynecologist
b. Mar. 12, 1946, Vinita, Okla.; s. Norman F. and Esther (Spurlock) Parks; B.S., zoology, Okla. State Univ., 1968; M.D., Oklahoma Univ., 1972. Career: rotating intern, San Bernardino Co. Hosp., 1972-73; obstetrics-gynecology residency, Kaiser Found. Hosp., L.A., 1973-76, chief resident, Obstetrics-gynecology, 1976; co-dir., Marina Women's Med. Group, Marina Del Rey, 1976---; med. dir., Venice Family Planning Clin., 1976---; med. dir., Calif. Union of Primary Health Care Providers, 1978---; staff gynecologist, Women's Clin. of L.A.; chmn., Infection Tissue Transfusion Com., Marina Mercy Hosp., 1976---; Clin. Instr., UCLA Dept. Obstetrics-Gynecology, 1978---. Research studies on: water intoxication; macrosomia; low dose estrogen contraception presented, med. symposiums; ongoing research: Danazol, oral contraveptive. Recipient: Lew Wentz Service Scholarship 1967; 2d place resident research award, L.A. Obstetrical-Gynecological Soc., 1974. Mem.: Phi Kappa Phi, 1968; Alpha Omega Alpha, 1971; Am. Bd. Obstetrics and Gynecology Bd.; Am. Coll. Obstetrics and Gynecology, Jr. Fellow; L.A. Obstetrical and Gynecological Soc.; L.A. Co. Med. Assn.; CMA. Hobbies: tennis, long distance running. Home: 5515 Pacific Ave., No. 1, Marina Del Rey, CA 90291; Office: 4560 Admiralty Way, Marina Del Rey, CA 90291.

PARKS, D.C.
Philanthropist — Author — Lecturer
b. Oct. 17, 1913, Taft, Calif.; s. Travis Winn (farmer and professional baseball player) and Ruby Clara Parks; bro. C.W. Parks, trap shooter, Calif. Pita State Singles Champion and State All-Around Champion, 1959; ed. H.S., Calif.; m. Olivia Lauderdale, Bakersfield, Calif., Dec. 22, 1942; chil.: (adopted) Roberta Carol, b. Aor. 26, 1939; Clifford Wayne, b. Apr. 26, 1939; Clifford Wayne, b. Apr. 28, 1946. Career: Rancher-farmer, Bakersfield (own champion FLC Royal Mixer $30,000 Great Register of Merit bull); est. one of the most outstanding Hereford ranches in the world, 1954-59 (ret.); Hereford livestock awards incl.: Champion Hereford and top bull hons., Natl. Hereford Show, Cow Palace, S.F., Nov. 1955; champion bull, Natl. Hereford Show, Cow Palace, S.F., July 1956; Royal winner and various prizes to 49 calves, Nov. 1956; winner, Portland, Ore. Hereford Show, 1956; 21 prizes, Kern Co. Fair, Oct. 1957; won Gold Spike Champ, Golden Spike Natl. Livestock Show, Ogden, Ut., Nov. 1957; won Grand Champion Prize, California State Fair, Sacramento 1958. Partner, Parks Bros. and Parks Bros. Invesments, 1959---. Founder-pres. Addictive Drugs Edn. Found. 1969---. Lecturer: guest speaker, Diamond Head School, Honolulu, Hawaii, 1959; Freedom Forum, Free Enterprise; Harding Coll. Acad., Searcy, Ark. 1961; How to Be Successful with a Physical Handicap, Pepperdine Coll. 1962; Kern Co. Stu. Council Govt. Conv. 1962; Bible and biblical hist. Author: Narcotics and Narcotics Addiction (used schs and legal depts. edn. pgm). Awards: Outstanding Farmer of the Year, who despite lack of eyesight (loss of sight handicap at age 29 yrs.), by Kiwanis Club, 1957; Kern Co. Man of the Yr. Award for youth achievement, 1959; recd. Pres. Mem. Award from Parlor No. 42, Native Sons of Golden West, 1959; 8 membership awards and citizenship award from the Grand President, est. D.C. Parks Scholarship Found. and chmn. bd. dirs.-pres 1959 (achievement scholarship to be awarded to youth exhib. at Kern Co. Fair); gavel from Senator Oren E. Long, Hawaii; Founder's Award, Pepperdine Coll. 1960; certificate, Californians for Pepperdine, 1960; Citizens Award, Calif. Freedom Forum, 1961; many cits. and awards, incl. Lion of Yr., S. Bakersfield Lions Club, 1964, 66; Amer. Edn. Leag. cit. for outstanding serv. 1966; Bob Elias Hall of Fame, 1967; Cong. of Freedom Liberty Award, 1970. Mem.: pres. Old River Harvest Club, 1940-42; pres. Lakeview Rec. Center, Amer., Kern Co. Farm Bur. Assns.; board directors, Kern Co. Free Enterprise Assn. 1961-62;

Kern Co. Centennial Com. 1961-62; Amer. Security Council, Kern County Historical Society, Americanism, Educational League, California State Chamber of Commerce; PTA (philanthropist, PTA colls.). Church of Christ. Hobby: gardening, fishing. Res.: 2639 Belle Terr., Bakersfield, CA.

PARMA, HAROLD ARTHUR
Civic Leader
b. July 2, 1902, Santa Barbara, Calif.; s. G.B. and Catherine (Pendola) Parma; A.B., Univ. of Calif., Berkeley, 1925, J.D. 1927; m. Mary-Margaret Ambrose, Yuma, Ariz., Oct. 17, 1930. Career: Admitted to Calif. State Bar, Oct. 7, 1927; asspc. with Orrick, Palmer and Dahlquist law firm, San Francisco, 1927-29; with Heaney, Price & Postel, Santa Barbara, 1929; partner, Heaney, Price, Postel & Parma, Santa Barbara, 1935-53; Price, Postel & Parma, Santa Barbara, Calif. 1953---; exec. com., Irrigation Dists. Assn. of Calif., chmn. Water Dists. Sect. 1950-57; Govt. Appeal Agt., Local Bd. No. 80, 1940-51; dir.: Parma Co., Citizens Savings & Loan Assn. 1937-71; adv. com. Security Pac. Natl. Bank, Santa Barbara, 1965-72; (past) chmn.-pres-dir. Great Western Savings and Loan of Santa Barbara. Mem.: Santa Barbara Found.; pres. Jr. Chamber of Comm., Santa Barbara, 1933; Bd. Library Trustees, Santa Barbara, 1933-39; Santa Barbara Co. Emergency Relif Com., SERA 1934; Amer., Santa Barbara Co. and Calif. State Bar Assns.; Pi Kappa Phi, Order of the Coif, Phi Delta Phi, Santa Barbara Club, Valley Club of Montecito. Hobby: gardening, hunting, fishing, golf. Res.: 1574 Green Lane, Santa Barbara, 93108; Office: 200 E. Carrillo St., Santa Barbara, CA 93102.

PARNELL, DALE
College District President
b. July 16, 1928, Monmouth, Ore.; s. Archie and Hattie Parnell; B.A., Williamette Univ., 1951; M.A., Univ. of Oregon, 1956, D.Ed., 1964; m. Beverly M. Lush, May 24, 1947, Pasadena; chil.: Sue (Shields), b. 1948; Paul, b. 1949; Teresa (Autrey), b. 1951; Steve, b. 1954; Tim, b. 1956. Career: Tchr. secondary schs., Salem and Springfield, Ore., 1950-54; Vice Principal and Prin., Springfield High Sch. 1954-60; Supt., Lane Co. Schs., Ore. 1960-64; Oregon Supt. of Pub. Instr., 1968-74; Chancellor, San Diego Community COll. System, 1974-76; Pres. and Supt., San Joaquin Delta Community Coll. Dist., 1976---. Chmn., Nat. Council of Equal Edn. Opportunities, 1971-74. Mil.: Edn. and Tng. Command, Navy Advis. Com. Author: The Case for Competency-Based Education, Phi Delta Kappa, 1978; many pub. articles; nat. speaker. Mem. Phi Delta Kappa. Democrat. Protestant. Rec.: racquetball. Home: 1544 Griffin Pt., Stockton, CA 95207; Office: 5151 Pacific Ave., Stockton, CA 95207.

PARODE, ANN
Bank Executive
b. Mar. 3, 1947, Los Angeles; dau. Lowell C. and Sabine (Phelps) Parode; B.A., Pomona Coll., 1968; J.D., UCLA, 1971; m. Thomas M. Murray, Aug. 12, 1978, La Jolla. Career: Admitted to Calif. Bar 1972; assoc., law firm of Luce, Forward, Hamilton & Scripps, 1972-75; Legal Counsel, San Diego Trust & Savings Bank, 1975---, now Vice Pres. and Legal Counsel. Mem.: San Diego County Bar Assn., 1977---, v.p., 1977-78; Lawyers Club of San Diego, dir. 1974-78; pres. 1977-78; dir., UCLA Law Alumni, 1977---; Legal Affairs Com. Calif. Bankers Assn., 1977---; Calif. State Bar, Bus. Law Sect., 1977---; Disciplinary Examiner, 1976; Order of the Coif. Office: 540 Broadway, Suite 650, San Diego, CA 92101.

PARRY, EDWARD P.
Scientist
b. Nov. 5, 1922, Ogden, Utah; s. Walter and Jeanette (Patterson) Parry; B.S., Univ. Utah, 1945; Ph.D., Univ. Minn., 1950; m. Noreen Eilts, Aug. 29, 1951, Austin, Minn.; children: Barbara, (Davis), b. 1955; Bruce Edward, b. 1956; Claudia Diane, b. 1961. Career: Mem. Faculty, Univ. Minn. 1945-51; Instr. Chem., Union Conn., 1951-54; Asst. Prof. Chem., Wash. State Coll., 1954-56; Research Assoc., Union Oil CO. of Calif., 1956-62; Group Leader, North Am. Aviation, North Am. Rockwell, Rockwell Internat. Sci. Center, 1962-71, Dir. Environmental Monitoring and Services Center, Rockwell Internat. Corp., 1971---. Mem. Am. Chem. Soc., N.Y. Acad. Sci., AAAS, Sigma Xi. Office: 2421 West Hillcrest Dr., Newbury Park, CA 91320.

PARRY, ROBERT T.
Economist
b. May 16, 1939, Harrisburg, Pa.; s. Anthony C. and Margaret R. Parry; B.A., magna cum laude, Phi Beta Kappa, Gettysburg Coll., 1960; M.A., Univ. of Pa., 1961; Ph.D., 1967; m. Brenda L. Grumbine, 1956, Harrisburg, Pa.; chil.: Robert R., b. June 26, 1957; Lisa L., b. June 9, 1962. Career: asst. prof. economics, Phila. Coll. of Textiles and Sci., 1963-65; economist, Fed. Reserve Bd. of Govs., 1965-70; lectr. money and banking, Georgetown Univ., 1969; sr. v.p. & chief economist, Security Pac. Nat. Bank, 1970-76; v.p., Bunker Hill Fixed Income Securities, Inc. (close; end bond fund), 1978---. Author: numerous articles on bus., economics. Awarded fellowship, Univ. of Pa., Nat. Defense Edn. Act, 1960-63. Mem.: Nat. Assn. Bus. Economists, pres. L.A. chpt. 1975. Rec.: swimming, tennis. Office: Security Pacific Nat. Bank, P.O.B. 2097, Terminal Annex, L.A., CA 90051.

PARSONS, STUART OVERTON, JR.
Engineer
b. Aug. 11, 1926, Denver, Colo.; s. Stuart Sr. and Gladys (East) Parsons; dir. desc. Cornet Joseph Parsons, co-founded Springfield and Northampton, Mass. in 1635; B.A., Univ. Colo., 1948; M.A., 1950; Ph.D., indsl. psych., USC; m. Harriet Jaggard, July 9, 1955, Denver, Colo.; daughters: Carol Lee (Tousley), b. 1957; Cynthia Anne, b. 1960; Pamela Clare, b. 1963. Career: with Colo. Merit System Council, Denver, 1947-48; city & county of Denver, 1950-51; Psychological Research In., L.A., 1951-53; Lockheed Aircraft Corp., 1954-57; with Lockheed Missiles & Space Co., 1957---: now group engr., Human Factors, Maintainability & Logistics Engring. Contbr. articles profl. publs. USN, 1944-46, aviation electronics tech.; Col., USAFR, 1950--- HQ Logistics Command. Mem.: Human Factors Soc., nat. secty.-treas. 1965-66; exec. council 1974; Soc. of Logistics Engring.; Am. Inst. Aero. & Astro., assoc. fellow. Registered Profl. Engr.; Calif. State Certified Psychologist. Episcopalian. Rec.: Nat. Ski Patrol. Res.: 19740 Via Escuela Dr., Saratoga, CA 95070; Office: Lockheed Missiles & Space Co., Sunnyvale, CA 94088.

PARTNOW, ELAINE
Actress
b. Oct. 28, 1941, Los Angeles; dau. Al and Jeanette (Bernstein) Partnow; student UCLA, 1962; HB Studio, New York, 1965; m. Turner Browne, photog. and cinematographer, May 6, 1978, Broussard, La. Achievements: Performed in over thirty state prodns. nationally; starred in Whiskey Flats, film honored at San Francisco, Edinburgh & Venice film festivals, 1968-69; Awarded Best Actress, Pasadena Playhouse, 1959; Best Actress, UCLA, 1961; Editor, compiler; The Quotable Woman: 1800-1975, Corwin Books, 1977. Mem.: Screen Actors Guild, Actors Equity Assn., Am. Fedn. of Television and Radio Artists. Res.: 1175 Hi Point St., Los Angeles, CA 90035.

PASCOE, WILLIAM THOMAS, III
Chairman-CEO, Amcord, Inc.
b. June 23, 1916, Wilkensburg, Pa.; s. William Thomas, Sr. and Harriet (Gozzard) Pascoe; Grad., Engr., Univ. of Ill., 1940; m. Sarah Lee Martin, Sept. 15, 1972, Aspen, Colo.; sons: William Thomas, IV, b. Mar. 7, 1958; Michael Steven, b. Oct. 12, 1959; Marc Jonathan, b. June 26, 1962. Career: With Livingston Shipbldg. Co. 1940-41; California Shipbldg. Co. 1941-42; Old World Food Co., 1946-47; Chmn. bd., Pascoe Steel Corp. (acquired by Am. Cement Corp.) 1968, Pres. and Chief Exec. Officer, 1969---, Chairman of the Board and CEO 1975---. Dir.: Hollywood Park, Inc.; Brown Co.; Oak Tree Racing Assn.; Roessler-Chadwick Found.; Calif. Thoroughbred Breeders Assn. Maj., AUS, 1942-46. Mem. Sigma Phi Epsilon. Hobbies: Thoroughbred racing & breeding. Rec.: ocean racing, skiing. Address: 610 Newport Center Dr., Newport Beach, CA 92663.

PASTERNAK, ALFRED
Physician
b. Sept. 28, 1930, Hungary; s. Simon and Anna (Liebman) Pasternak; M.D., Budapest Univ. Med. Sch., 1955. Career: asst. clin. prof., UCLA Sch. of Med.; attending physician, Cedars-Sinai Med. Center, L.A. Diplomate: Am. Bd. Obstetrics-Gynecology; fellow, Am. Coll. Obstetricians and Gynecologists; fellow, Pan-Am. Obstetrical and Gynecological Soc.; fellow, Am. Assn. Gyn. Laparoscopists. Articles pub. sci. journs. Citations: city of Los Angeles, 1978; Calif. State Assem. 1978; congressional records, U.S. House of Representatives,

1976. Recipient: Flame of Truth award, fund for higher edn., 1976; 1st prize, nat. essay contest, med. sch., 1955; 1st prize, nat. study contest and high sch. valedictorian, 1949. Mem.: Phi Delta Epsilon med. frat. Hobby: collection of manuscripts. Rec.: theatre, tennis, skiing. Office: 2080 Century Park E., L.A., CA.

PATON, NEIL E.
Metallurgist
b. Mar. 12, 1938, Auckland, New Zealand; s. Eric and Dulcie (Hutchinson) Paton; B.E., Univ. of Auckland, 1961, M.E., 1962; Ph.D., Mass. Inst. of Tech., 1969; m. Louise Lachance, Oct. 15, 1964; chil.: Sonya, b. 1970; Eric, b. 1972. Career: Research Metallurgist, Atlas Steels, Canada, 1962-65; Group Leader, Structural Materials Dept. Rockwell Internat. Sci. Center, 1966-77, Dir. Materials Synthesis & Processing Dept., 1977---. Awarded Titanium Metals Corp. Am. Fellowship 1965-68; named Rockwell Internat. Engr. of the Year 1976. Mem.: Sigma Xi; Nat. Acad. of Sciences, Solid State Sciences Com. 1974-79; AIME. Hobbies: mountaineering, sailing. Res.: 297 Upper Lake Rd., Thousand Oaks, CA 91360; Office: 1049 Camino Dos Rios, Thousand Oaks, CA 91360.

PATRICHI, MIHAI D.
Electronics Company President
b. Oct. 28, 1911, Rumania; s. Dimitrie and Lucretzia (Negru) Patrichi; ed. M.E. (electro-mech., aeron.), Poly. University, Bucharest, Rumania, 1936-43; chil.: Michael Philip, Ileana Maria, Alexander Christopher. Career: Technical advisor to King Michael of the Royal Court of Rumania, 1944-47 (abdication and left country with Royal household to Switz.); cons. engr., Missile Research Mfg. Co., Van Nuys, Calif. 1951-55; pres.-chmn. bd., Networks Electronic Corp., Chatsworth, Calif. 1955---. Prof. (thermodynamics), University of Bucharest. Author: articles publ. Electrical Design News, 1961-62. Maj., Rumanian Air Force, WW II. Mem.: Amer. Rocket Soc. Greek Orthodox. Rec.: flying (pilot). Res.: 10779 Bellagio Rd., Bel Air, Los Angeles, CA 90024; Office: 9750 DeSoto Ave., Chatsworth, CA 91311.

PATRICK, DONALD ALLEN
Corporate Executive
b. Apr. 17, 1925, Clifford, Mich.; s. Stanley A. and Glenadine L. Patrick; B.S., C.E., Univ. of Mich. 1944; M.S. C.E., Univ. of Calif., Berkeley, 1952; M.E.A., George Washington Univ. 1969; m. Nori Sato, Tokyo, Japan, Mar. 5, 1973. Career: Repr. dir. K.J. Halifax Assocs., Tokyo, 1970---; dir.-exec. v.p. Pacific Architects and Engineers (parent co. PAE Internat.); v.p. PAE Internat., Tokyo, 1970-73; pres., L.A. 1973---. Author: tech. articles publ. Civil Engr., 1970; Mil. Engr. 1970; Japan Econ. Journal, 1972; Amer. Chamber of Comm. in Japan Journal, 1975. U.S. Navy, Civil Engineer Corps (serv. Vietnam, P.I., Japan, Guam, Va., Calif., Pa., Wash., D.C.), PTO, ATO (1943-70); Asiatic-Pac. Theater, 1945, WW II; Legion of Merit with Combat "V", ret. Capt. 1970. Mem.: Fellow, Amer. Soc. of Civil Engrs.; Natl. Soc. Professional Engrs.; Soc. of Amer. Mil. Engrs., pres. Yokouska, Japan and Saigon, Vietnam posts; Rotary Internat.; Petroleum Club, L.A. Protestant. Rec.: golf. Res.: 9983 Sunland Blvd., Sunland, CA 91040; Office: 600 S. Harvard Blvd., Los Angeles, CA 90005.

PATT, JACK MICHAEL
Professor
b. Mar. 20, 1918, Detroit, Mich.; s. Rev. Jacob E. (Seventh-day Adventist minister, 40 yrs.) and Johanna (Hoehne) Patzkowski; bro. Dr. A.J. Patt, head, ENT Dept., Chr., Med. Coll., Vellore, India 1954-66; bro.-in-law, Dr. Donald H. Abbott, pres. Calif. Bd. Med. Examiners, 1964=65; B.A., Andrews Univ., Berrien Springs, Mich. 1941; M.A., Pac. Union Coll., Angwin, 1953; Ph.D., Stanford Univ. 1958; m. Vonda Muriel Kantz, San Diego, Calif., Mar. 26, 1950; sons: Dennis Cornell, b. Feb. 19, 1952; Leslie Alan, b. Dec. 19, 1953. Career: Teacher-coach, Pentwater Mich.) H.S. 1941-42; Lakeview H.S., St. Clair Shores, Mich. 1946-67; teacher, Ray Lyman Wilbur Jr. H.S., Palo Alto, Calif. 1953-55, head, Soc. Sci. Dept. 1955; Prof. hist. and edn., Calif. State Univ., San Jose, 1955---. Fulbright grant to Vietnam, Univ of Dalat, Vietnamese-Amer. Assn., Saigon, 1966-67; Mt. View Acad. Bd., Calif. 1957-65; Alta Vista Sch. Bd., San Jose, 1958---, chmn. 1961-63, treas. 1963-66; dir. Doctor's Hosp., San Jose, 1959-69; v.p. 1963-65; dir. Spotswood Hosp., Los Gatos, 1960-65; pres. 1962-65. U.S. Army ETO (1942-46), WW II. Awards: decorated, Belgian Fourregeure. Mem.: Amer. Hist.

Assn., Natl. Council for the Soc. Studies, Assn. of State Coll. Instrs., Amer. Assn. of Univ. Profs., Natl. Council for Stu. of Edn. Chmn., Bd. of Elders, San Jose Seventh-Day Adventist Ch. 1960-65. Hobbies: stamp collecting, travel. Rec.: baseball, basketball. Res.: 2436 Cottle Ave., San Jose, CA; Office: Calif. State Univ., San Jose, CA 95125.

PATTEN, BEBE
Educator — Minister
b. Sept. 3, 1913, Waverly, Tenn.; d. Newton Felix and Mattie Priscilla (Whitson) Harrison; grad. Life Coll., 1933; D.D., McKinley-Roosevelt Coll., 1941; D.Litt., Temple Hall Coll. and Sem., 1943; m. Carl Thomas Patten (dec.), Oct. 23, 1935, Tennessee; chil.: Bebe Rebecca, Ph.D., Priscilla Carla, Ph.D., b. Jan. 30, 1950; Tom, B.A. in religion. Career: ordained to ministry, Ministerial Assn. of Evangelism, Kansas City, Mo.; Kan. City Christian Ch., 1935; founder, nat. daily radio program, The Shepherd Hour, 1934---; TV, weekly broadcast, 1976---; nat. evangelist, 1933-50; pastor, Christian Cathedral, Oakland, 1950---; founder-pres., Patten Bible Coll., Oakland, 1945---; founder-pres. Acad. of Christian Edn. (grades k-12), Oakland, 1944---. Invited to Israel's 30th anniversary breakfast with Prime Minister Menachem Begin, 1978, presented commendation from Calif. Senate Rules Com. Recipient: medallion, Israeli Foreign Ministry for Religious Affairs, 1969; medal by Govt. Press Office, Jerusalem, 1971; pvt. interview w/David Ben-Gurion, 1973; Gentile Honoree, Jewish Nat. Fund., 1975; Hidden heroine, S.F. Bay Girl Scout Council, 1976. Author: Give Me Back My Soul, pub.: Japanese, Chinese, Spanish, English, 1973; editor The Trumpet Call, 1953---; composer, 20 pub. gospel songs, 1945. Mem.: exec. bd. Bar-Ilan Univ. Assn., Israel, Zionist Orgn. of Am.; Religious Edn. Assn.; Am. Assn. for Higher Edn.; Am. Acad. Religion; Soc. of Biblical Litl.; Am. Jewish Hist. Soc. Rec.: swimming, tennis. Home-Office: 2433 Coolidge Ave., Oakland, CA 94601.

PATTEN, BEBE REBECCA
College Dean
b. Jan. 30, 1950, Berkeley, Calif.; d. C. Thomas and Dr. Bebe (Harrison) Patten; B.S. summa cum laude, Patten Bible Coll., 1969; B.A., philosophy, Coll. of Holy Names, 1971; M.A., Wheaton Coll., 1972; Ph.D., Drew Univ., 1976. Career: tching. fellow prof., Drew Univ., 1974-75; asst. prof. of New Testament, Patten Bible Coll., 1975---; academic dean, 1977; co-pastor Christian Cathedral, 1964---. V.P., Christian Evangelical Ch. of Am., 1964---. Contbr. articles, religious publs.; presented paper, W. coast div., Soc. of Biblical Lit., 1977; instr. violin; exec. dir. summer music camps, 1975---; violinist, symphony mem.: Wheaton Coll., 1971-72; Drew Ensemble, 1972-75; Young Artists Symphony, N.J., 1972-75; Somerset Hill Symphony, 1973-74; Peninsula Symphony, 1977---; Madison Chamber Trio, N.J., 1973-75; TV performances, Chan. 38 KVOF TV, 1976---; founder. 45-mem. Youth Orchestra, Christian Cathedral, 1969-71; founder-conductor 45-mem. orchestra, Patten Christian Schs., 1975---; violinist, harpist: Christian Cathedral, Holy Names Coll., 1966-71; Berkeley Symphony Youth Orchestra, 1968. Mem.: Am. Acad. of Religion, 1975---; Soc. of Biblical Lit., 1975---; Am. Assn. of Univ. Profs., 1975---. Christian Evangelical Ch. Rec.: tennis, skiing, sailing. Home-Office: 2433 Coolidge Ave., Oakland, CA 94601.

PATTEN, PRISCILLA CARLA
Educator
b. Jan. 30, 1950, Berkeley; d. Carl Thomas and Bebe (Harrison) Patten; B.S., summa cum laude, Patten Bible Coll., 1969; B.A., psychology, Coll. of Holy Names, 1971; M.A. N. Testament, Wheaton Coll., 1972; Ph.D., New Testament, Drew Univ., 1976. Career: teachng. fellow, Drew Univ., 1974-75; asst. prof. New Testament, Patten Bible Coll., 1975---; chmn. Dept. Biblical Studies, 1977---; also co-pastor, Christian Cathedral, 1964---; v.p., Christian Evangelical Ch. of Am., 1964---. Contbr.: the Trumpet Call, Christian newspaper; performer, KVOF TV, 1976---; founder, dir. 60 mem. chorale, Christian Cathedral; dir. 50-mem. Youth choir, Patten Christian Schs., 1976---; violinist, harpist: Christian Cathedral; Holy Names Coll., 1966-71; Berkeley Symphony Youth Orchestra, 1968; Wheaton Coll. Symphony, N.J., 1971-72; Drew Univ. Ensemble, 1972-75; Young Artists Symphony, N.J., 1972-75; Somerset Hill Symphony, N.J., 1973-74; Peninsula Symphony, 1977---; Madison Chamber Trio, N.J., 1973-75; instr. violin: exec. dir. summer music camps, 1975---. Mem.: Am. Acad. of Religion, 1975---; Am. Assn. of Univ. Profs., 1975---; Soc. of Biblical Lit., 1975--- (presented paper on Parables in Gospel of Mark before Pacific W. Coast div., 1977). Christian Evangelical Ch. of Am. Rec.: tennis, skiing, sailing. Home-Office: 2433 Coolidge Ave., Oakland, CA 94601.

PATTERSON, GEORGE ELLIOTT, III
Radio Station Executive
b. Nov. 18, 1920, Baltimore, Md.; s. George E., Jr.
and Helen (Medford) Patterson; desc. Elizabeth
Patterson of Baltimore (1785-1879), married, Jerome
Bonaparte, bro. of Napoleon Bonaparte, 1803; B.S.
(electronics), Pac. Internat. Coll.; m. Emma Lue
Askew, Las Vegas, Nev. 1964 (dec.); chil.: Mrs.
William R. (Virginia Patricia) Burch, b. 1937; George
E., IV, b. 1942. Career: Actor, 1943-50; radio
announcer, 1950---; chief engr., KBVM, Lancaster,
Calif. 1957-60; engring. dir., KITN-KITI, Olympia and
Chehalis, Wash. 1960-61; engr. KJTV, 1961---; news
dir., KLYD Radio Sta., Bakersfield, 1966-68; engring.
dir. KMPC, 1968---. Mem.: AAAS, IEEE; Amer., Kern
Societies for Psych. Research; Kern Press Club; Engrs.
Club of L.A. Unity. Hobbies: research in radiation and
high voltage, parapsychology research, collect antique
weapons. Res.: Bakersfield, CA; Office: 307 E. 21st
St., Bakersfield, CA 93303.

PATTERSON, JERRY M.
U.S. Congressman
b. Oct. 25, 1934, El Paso, Tex.; s. Levin M. and Ella
M. Patterson; desc.: Sir Christopher Wren, noted arch.;
Lewis Mumford, Amer. author; B.A., Calif. State
Univ., L.B. 1960; postgrad. USC; J.D., UCLA Sch. of
Law; m. Mary Jane Crisman, Yuma, Ariz., Feb. 8,
1955; chil.: Patrick Alan, b. Feb. 13, 1960; Jane
Michelle, b. June 10, 1965. Career: Adm. asst. to City
Administrator, Garden Grove, Calif. 1960-63; attorney
at law, pvt. practice, 1967---; Councilman, Santa Ana,
1969-74; Mayor 1973-74; City Atty., Placentia,
1973-75; Congress, elected to 38th District, 1976---;
exec. com., SCAG, 1971-74; v.p. Orange Co. League
of Cities, 1971; president, Orange Co. Chpt., Amer.
Soc. for Pub. Adm. 1973-74; U.S. Coast Guard, Hosp.
Corp. 1953-57. Awards: Natl. Defense Medal. Mem.:
Sigma Chi, Phi Delta Phi; pres. Toastmasters Club.
Deacon, Congregational Ch. Rec.: camping, tennis,
skiing. Office: 123 Cannon House Office
Building, Washington, D.C. 20515.

PATTERSON, LUCILE LAURA
Business Owner
b. Aug. 8, 1912, Brea, Calif.; d. Frank and Esther
Hambleton; grad. Riverside Bus. Coll., 1947; m. Mr.
Hambleton, May 30, 1958, Winter Haven, Calif.
Career: owner, opr., restaurant, 1950-61; owner, Fire
& Casualty Insurance Agency, San Bernardino, 1962---.
USN, 1945-46, Bureau of Ships, Wash. D.C. Mem.:
Grange; VFW Aux. Chaplain. Res.: 2160 First Ave.,
San Bernardino, CA 92405.

PATTISON, WILLIAM J.
Corporate Executive
b. July 18, 1914, Chicago, Ill.; s. William Lawrence
and Bonnie Edwina (Abbott) Pattison; ed. Francis W.
Parker Sch. 1920-32; Rensaeler Poly. Inst. 1932-33;
MIT 1933-37; m. Margaret Taylor, May 2, 1942; chil.:
Margaret Watson, Jr., b. Feb. 27, 1944; Pamela
Williams, b. Oct. 18, 1946; Polly Abbott, b. Dec. 8,
1950; Priscilla Dudley, b. Nov. 30, 1956. Career:
Diesel Engine field serv. mgr., Fairbanks Morse & Co.
1937, installation engr., Buda engine; power plant
engr., Grumman Aircraft Engring. 1937-48; Wash.
Repr., The Garrett Corp. 1948; asst. to the pres.
1950, dir. mil. rels. and foreign operations, 1952, dir.
sales and servs. for AiResearch Mfg. Div. 1953, v.p.
1963---, dir. The Garrett Corp. 1963---. Naval Aviator,
Combat Squadron, N. Atlantic and S. Pac., Fleet Air
Wing engring. ofcr., BuAer Power Plant Div., WW II.
Awards: Silver Star, Air Medal, Pres. Cit. Rec.: sailing.
Res.: 12928 Evanston St., Los Angeles, CA 90049;
Office: 9851 Sepulveda Blvd., Los Angeles, CA 90009.

PAUL, BRIAN L.
Architect
b. Aug. 24, 1939, New Orleans, La.; s. John A. and
Elise May (Chamberlin) Paul; B.Arch., USC, 1964;
chil.: Elise, b. 1963; Marisa, b. 1965; David, b. 1966.
Career: Designer, firm of John Carl Warnecke & Assoc.
1964-65; Architect, Richard George Wheeler & Assoc.,
1965-69; Pvt. Practice, Brian Paul & Associates,
Architects & Planners, San Diego, 1969---. Awards:
Honor Award, S.D. Chpt. AIA 1972; Award of
Excellence, Sales & Mktg. Council, 1976, 77; Gold
Nugget Award, Pacific Coast Bldrs. Conf. 1977; Orchid
Award, S.D. chpt. AIA 1977. Mem. AIA, Pres. San
Diego Chpt. AIA 1976; Dir. Calif. Council AIA 1975, 76.
Club: Stardust Country. Rec.: golf, racquetball. Office:
1250 Sixth Ave., Suite 1200, San Diego, CA 92101.

PAUL, JAN S.
Author
b. Apr. 2, Iowa City, Iowa; dau. Joseph and Ruth
(Figgins) Smith; Degrees: A.A., B.A., B.S., M.S., Ph.D.,
D.Sc.; m. Gerald W. Paul, Sept. 8, 1948, State Center,
Iowa; children: Jennifer Laure, Del Derek, Gabrielle
Julianne. Career: Research & devel., U.S. Govt., AEC
and NASA, 1960-77. Mil.: RCAF, 1944; WAF,
1945-60. Author 3 books: Knotted String; Lintens;
Twilight of Honor. Awarded 5 Pulitzer nominations;
named Kern County Woman of Year, 1976; Merit
Award, STC. Mem. past pres., Altrusa Club of Gr.
Bakersfield; Address: P.O.B. 6488, Bakersfield, CA
93306.

PAUL, M. DAVID
Real Estate Developer
b. Mar. 26, 1937, Twin Falls, Idaho; s. Melvin V. and
Marie E. Paul; B.A., Long Beach State Coll., 1959; m.
Phyllis Wilson, Apr. 19, 1964, Bel Air, Calif.;
daughters Kristin Suzanne b. Nov. 11, 1966; Marcy
Lynelle, b. Oct. 2, 1971. Career: Founder, partner,
Wilshire Center Devel. Co., 1967---; name changed to
M. David Paul & Assoc., 1974---; Mng. Gen. Partner,
1974---; founder-Mng. Gen. Partner, Center Constrn.
Co., 1971; founder, dir., pres., Krismar Constrn Co.,
Inc. 1974---. Guest Lectr., UCLA Graduate Sch., 1977.
Hobbies: drawing, painting. Res.: Bel Air; Office: 233
Wilshire Blvd., Suite 990, Santa Monica, CA 90401.

PAUL, RICHARD DORSEL
Corporate Executive
b. Mar. 26, 1927, Rexburg, Idaho; s. Alfred Henry
and Jennie (Jensen) Paul; student Riverside Coll.,
1949-50; Woodbury Coll., 1950-51; B.A., Econ.,
Pomona Coll., 1955; M.B.A., mgmt., USC, 1963; m.
Florence Phillian, Aug. 6, 1950, Monterey; chil.:
Adrienne (Mrs. Horst W. Meyer); Robin S. Career:
Chief accountant, Sun Gold, Inc., Riverside, 1955-57;
partner, R.D. Paul, Anaheim, 1957-59; supr. internal
audit, ITT Cannon Electric, Los Angeles, 1959-61;
controller, Universal Ecso Corp., Downey, 1961-62;
mgr. accounting, Ramph M. Parsons Co., Los Angeles,
1962-68; asst. controller, Fluor Corp., Los Angeles,
1968-70, controller Los Angeles Div., 1970-72,
Controller Fluor Engrs. and Constructors, Inc., L.A.,
1972-74, vice pres. Finance, 1974-76, controller, Fluor
Corp. 1976-78, v.p. and controller, 1978---. Served
with U.S. Merchant Marine, 1944-45; USN, 1945-49.
Mem.: Nat. Assn. of Accounts; Financial Exec. Inst.;
AMA Fin. Council. Hobby: sailing. Res.: 209 Santa
Ana Ave., Newport Beach, CA 92663; Office: 3333
Michelson Dr., Irvine, CA 92730.

PAULEY, EDWIN WENDELL
Industrialist
b. Jan. 7, 1903, Indianapolis, Ind.; s. Elbert L. and
Ellen (Van Petten) Pauley; ed. grad. Georgia Mil.
Acad. 1918; Occidental Coll. 1919-20; B.S. (comm.
and bus. adm.), Univ. of Calif. 1922, M.S. 1923; m.
Barbara Jean McHenry, Oct. 23, 1937; chil.: Edwin
Wendell, Jr., Susan Jean, Stephen McHenry, Robert
Van Petten. Career: Independent oil prod., Calif., Tex.,
N.Mex. and Okla. 1923---; founder-pres. The Petrol
Corp., L.A. 1929---; Fortuna Petroleum Corp. 1933;
pres. Independent Petroleum Assn. 1934-38; Seaboard
Royalty Co. 1935---; orgn. People's Bank, Lakewood
City, Calif.; dir. Griffith & Legg Constr. Co.; partner,
John S. Griffith, bldrs. and developers, Lakewood
City, Calif.; propr. constr. and real estate bus.; spec.
repr. Calif. Govt., Natural Resources Comm. 1939;
Interstate Oil and Compact Comm. 1940; spec.
repr.-liaison officer, U.S. Govt., and Brit. agcys. to
secure 100 tankers, 1940-41, and to formulate plans
for coord. of petroleum ind. 1941; petroleum coord.
for European War on petroleum lend-lease supplies for
Russia and Eng. 1941; U.S. ind. and commercial adv.,
Tri-Parte Potsdam Conf.; rep. between oil ind. and
Brit. Govt. on enemy petroleum supplies, 1941; orgn.
State of Calif. Def. Council, 1941; U.S. repr., Alliance
Comm. on Reparations (rank of Ambassador),
1945-46; spec. adv. on reparations to Secty. of State,
1947-48; spec. assit. to Secty. of the Army, 1947.
Mem.: repr. independent oil men, planning and coord.
com., NRA 1933; v.-chmn., Community Chest Drive,
L.A. 1938; repr. Gov. of Calif. on Pan Amer. Highway
Conf. 1939; regent, University of California, 1939-72;
mem. Big C Soc.; finance chmn., China Relief, L.A.
1941; Phi Kappa Psi; Mason; clubs: Univ., Calif.
Yacht, Catalina Yacht, (v.-commodore) Transpacific
Yacht (winner, Class A, Transpacific Yacht Race, San
Francisco to Honolulu, 1939). Democrat (treas. Dem.
Natl. Committee, secty. 1941-43). Protestant. Res.:

9521 Sunset Blvd., Beverly Hills, CA; Office: 10,000 Santa Monica Blvd., Los Angeles, CA.

PAULSEN, GEORGE ARTHUR
Thoracic Surgeon
b. Apr. 17, 1922, Cascade, N.H.; s. Levi and Marie (Nelsen) Paulsen; ed. B.S., Univ. of N.H. 1943; M.D., Tufts Univ. 1946; m. Virginia Pearson, Los Angeles, Calif., Jan. 25, 1946; sons: Mark Steven, b. July 23, 1949; Theodore Alan, b. Oct. 18, 1951; Thomas Craig, b. July 3, 1955; Donald Scott, b. Jan. 6, 1958. Career: Intern, Mass. Mem. Hosp., Boston, 1946-47; res. in surg. 1946-48, 1950-52; thoracic surg. training, L.A., 1952-55; est. pvt. practice, thoracic surg., Bakersfield, Calif. 1955---; chief surg. Kern Co. Gen. Hosp. 1960-63; chmn. staff 1964; staff, thoracic surg. serv., Mercy Hosp., Mem. Hosp., San Joaquin Hosp., Kern Co. Gen. Hosp., Bakersfield; cons. (thoracic surg.): La Vina Hosp. and San., Alta Dena; Sierra View Hosp., Porterville, Antelope Valley Hosp., Lancaster. Author: 14 professional publs., incl. Amer. Journ. of Surg., Ariz. Med., Journ. of Thoracic Surg., Western Journ.of Surg. Obstets. and Gynecology, Calif. Med., Diseases of the Chest, The Amer. Surg. 1955---. 1st Lt., Capt., USAF Med. Dept., Alaskan Theater, 1948-50. Mem.: fellow, ACS; diplomate, Amer. Bd. of Surgs.; Amer. Coll. Chest Phys.; Amer. Acad. Thoracic Phys.; diplomate, Pan Amer. Med. Assn.; Amer. Thoracic Soc; co-founder, Soc. Thoracic Surgs.; pres. TB and Health Assn. of Kern Co. 1959; pres. Amer. Cancer Soc. of Kern Co. 1962-63; So. Sierra Council, BSA, 1963-70; reg. exec. bd. 1970---, pres. 1970-71; director, Southern California Tennis Association; president, Bakersfield Tennis Patrons Association, 1964-65; pres. Bakersfield Surg. Soc. 1965; pres. Heart Assn. of Kern Co. 1965; Alpha Chi Sigma, Phi Chi. Presbyterian. Hobbies: photog., Boy Scouts activities. Rec.: tennis, hiking. Res.: 120 Westbluff Ct., Bakersfield 93305; Office: 1730 D St., Bakersfield, CA 93301.

PAYNE, GLEESON LESLIE
Insurance Company Executive
b. July 29, 1918, Fossil, Ore.; s. Leslie and Pearl (Brown) Payne; B.A., Univ. of Ore., 1941; m. Constance Walbridge, Paso Robles, Calif., Feb. 7, 1943; chil.: Leslie Ann, b. June 20, 1946; Nancy Lee, b. Aug. 20, 1949. Career: Ins. broker, Aetna Casualty & Surety Co. 1941-43; partner, Ingham, Coates & Payne Ins. firm., 1946---; pres. Founder's Life Ins. Co.; Ins. Commr. State of Calif. (apptd. by Gov. Reagan), 1972-75; mgr. L.A. Life Ins. Co. 1973-75; pres. Natl. Amer. Life Insurance Co., 1975---; pres., Stuyvesant Life Insurance Co., 1978---; v. chmn., exec. v.p., Nat. Amer. Insurance Co. of N.Y., 1978---. Captain, U.S. Army Infantry (1943-45), WW II. Awards: decorations incl. Bronze Star, French Croix de Guerre; Pasadena's Outstanding Young Man, 1950, Mem.: student body pres., Univ. of Ore. 1941; pres. Breakfast Panel, L.A. 1948; pres. Pasa. Safety Council, 1948-49; dir. Pasa. Community Chest, 1948-51; com. chmn., Pasa. C. of C. 1949-51; pres. Pasa. Quarterback's Club, 1950; dir. Pasa. Tournament of Roses; pres. Pasa. Rotary Club, 1951; secty. Pasa. YMCA 1951---; pres. University Club of Pasa. 1952; (hon.) dir. Pasa. Huntington Aux. Clinic, 1953-54; dir. Calif. Ins. Agts. Assn. 1953-55; (hon.) dir. Pasa. Jr. League Finance Com. 1954-55; v.p. United Community Servs. 1955, pres. 1956; dist. gov. Rotary Internat. 160-C, 1955-56; Presbyterian. Hobby: golf. Rec.: golf, sports spectator. Res.: 815 Plymouth Rd., San Marino, CA 91108; Office: 3731 Wilshire Blvd., L.A., CA 90010.

PAYNE, J. HOWARD
Surgeon
b. Oct. 17, 1916, Los Angeles, Calif.; s. Warren E. and Cynthia (Pell) Payne; ed. grad. Van Nuys H.S. 1934; A.B. (cum laude), USC 1938; M.D., USC School of Medicine, 1942; m. Jeannine Ann Poole, Sept. 23, 1961; chil.: John Howard, Jr., b. Oct. 13, 1944; Patricia Ann, b. May 2, 1947; William Dudley, b. July 29, 1950. Career: Intern, L.A. Co. Hosp. 1941-42. res. pathology, 1942-43, res. surg. 1943-46, jr. attending surg., 1946-60, sr. attending surg. 1960---; asst. in surg., USC School of Medicine, 1942-45; instr. in surg. 1945-52, asst. clin. prof. surgery, 1952-58, clinical professor surgery, 1967---; staff: surgeon, Good Hope Hosp. Assn. 1946; Good Samaritan Hosp. 1948---. Contrib. to surg. clinics of N. Amer. and med. journs. Mem.: fellow, ACS; pres. Soc. of Grad. Surgs. 1955; Pac. Coast Surg. Assn.; Amer. Bd. of Surgs.; N. Amer. Chpt., Internat. Angiology; L.A. Surg. Soc.; L.A. Acad. of Med.; Amer., Calif. and L.A. Co. Med. Assns.; American Surgical Association; Western Surgical

Association; Society for Vascular Surgery; Societe Internationale de Chirurgie; chmn. bd. dirs., Found for Surg. Research; bd. dirs., Found. for Heart Research; pres. USC Med. Alumni Assn. 1952; Master Mason; pres. Phi Rho Sigma; pres. So. Calif. Chpt., Phi Rho Sigma Alumni Assn.; Alpha Omega Alpha, Kappa Zeta, Kappa Alpha; bd. dirs., Trojan Club. Republican. Protestant. Hobby: photog. Rec.: golf, swimming, sports spectator. Res.: 621 N. Cherokee Ave., Los Angeles, CA 90004; Office: 1127 Wilshire Blvd., Los Angeles, CA 90017.

PEARSON, DONALD E.
Bank President
b. Mar. 17, 1930, Pasadena, Calif.; s. John L. and Elma M. Pearson; B.A., Swarthmore Coll., Pa. 1952; J.D., Harvard Law Sch., Cambridge, Mass. 1955; m. Carol Brunner, Scotch Plains, N.J., June 13, 1953; daughter, Kathryn Elizabeth, b. Apr. 14, 1960. Career: Atty., Adams, Duque & Hazeltine law firm, L.A., 1957-70, partner 1964-70; pres. Calif. Friends Homes, 1965-70; Calif. Supt. of Banks, 1970-77; pres., Ahmanson Bank & Trust Co., 1978---; pres. Conf. of State Bank Supvs. 1973-74. Mem.: Amer., Calif., L.A. Co. Bar Assns.; Town Hall of Calif.; Pasa. Tournament of Roses Assn.; City Club, San Marino. Alhambra Friends Community Ch. (bd. adm. 1965-70; trustee). Res.: 665 Winthrop Road, San Marino, CA 91108; Office: 3701 Wilshire Blvd., L.A., CA 90010.

PECHE, DALE C.
Painter
b. Nov. 28, 1928, Long Beach, Calif.; s. George F. and Mildred G. Peachy; desc. George Washington Peache, co-founder, City of Los Angeles and S.R.; James W. Marshall discovered gold in Calif. 1849, repr. Smithsonian Inst., Wash., D.C., monument in Coloma; ed. Long Beach City College; B.P.A., Art Center Coll of Design. 1951; spec. stu.: Reckless, Tyler, Legakes, Feitelson, Polifka, Williamaoski, Kramer; m. Marilyn Wise, Monterey Co., Aug. 30, 1968. Career: Design, N. Amer. Aviation, 1955-60; owner-designer, Graphic Directions, 1960-68; art dir., Publs. Serv. 1968-71; Design Vista, 1971-72. Exhibs.: Ind. Graphics Inst. 1956-71; N.Y. Art Dirs. Show, 1958-71; L.A. Art Dirs. Show, 1962-72; Orange Co. Ad Club, 1962-72; Natl. Acad. of Design, N.Y. 1974; Royal Acad. of Art, London, Eng. 1974; Palos Verdes Art Mus. 1974; Butle; Inst. Art 1974; one-man shows, Challis Galleries, 1971; Calif. Natl. Watercolor Soc., L.A. 1972; West Coast Amer. Realists, Inland Exhibition, San Bernardino, 1972; Galleries Choice, Chaffey Coll. Mus. 1973; comms.: painting by The Vatican, 1972; 3 paintings, Amer. Fine Arts Calendar, Cleveland, 1972, 73; 2 paintings, Artists of Amer. calendars, 1974; Duncan McIntosh Christmas Cards, others. U.S. Army artist, Gen. McArthur's Hdqrs. Staff, 1945-48. Awards: 25 awards, Ind. Graphic Inst. 1958-71; 13 awards, N.Y. Art Dirs. Show; 2 awards, L.A. Art Dir. Show, 1963-72; 20 awards, Orange Co. Art Dirs. Hobbies: research collecting art, skiing. Office: Challis Galleries, Laguna Beach, CA 92652.

PECK, JEAN MARIE
University Librarian
b. Nov. 15, 1925, Buffalo, N.Y.; dau. Charles and Irene Peck; B.S., Nursing Admin., Univ. of Buffalo, 1956; M.S. in Lib. Sci., Syracuse Univ., 1961. Career: Staff Nurse, N.Y. Hosp., 1946-47; Millard Fillmore Hosp., 1948; Cedars of Lebanon Hosp., 1948-49; Dartmouth Coll. Infirmary, 1949-50; VA Hosp., Buffalo, 1951-54; Nursing Service Supr., Buffalo Gen. Hosp., 1956-60; Librarian, Adminstr. Lin., Mich. State Univ., 1961-66; now Librarian, Head of Catalog Dept., Gen. Library, Univ. of Calif., Berkeley ---. Mem.: Beta Pi Mu, 1960---; ALA, 1961---; Sierra Club; Nat. Audubon Soc.; Point Reyes Bird Observatory. Office: 212 Doe Library, Univ. of California, Berkeley, CA 94720.

PEED, GARLAND POWELL, III
Community College District Chancellor
b. July 30, 1930, Freeport, Long Island, N.Y.; s. Garland Powell, II and Florence Patricia (Kelley) Peed; B.S., UCLA, 1952; M.A., Los Angeles State Univ., 1960; postgrad. for Ed.D., USC; m. Stephanie Anne Dahlstet, Mar. 12, 1976, San Diego. Career: tchr. and coach, Calif. High Schs., 1953-56; asst. bus. mgr., Temple City Unified Sch. Dist., 1956-60; Dean, Business Edn. and Asst. Bus. Mgr., San Bernardino Valley Coll., 1960-64; asst. supt., business, State Center Community Coll. Dist., Fresno, 1964-73; asst. chancellor, San Diego Community Coll.

Dist., 1973-76; Chancellor, 1976---: (serves more than 80,000 students through four 2-year colleges, 6 adult edn. centers, Educational Cultural Complex). Pres., San Diego & Imperial Counties Community Coll. Assn., 1977-78; pres., Community Coll. Urban Dist. Assn., 1978-79; v.p., Higher Edn. Assn. of S.D., 1976-79; Mem. Fresno Co. Grand Jury, 1968; Economic Opportunity Commn., Fresno Co. 1968-72; speaker, nat. and internat. seminars, workshops, conferences: Parent-Teacher Founders Day Award recipient 1964; participant in: YMCA, Boys' Clubs, Girl Scouts, United Way, Athletic Booster Clubs. Home: 5451 Mt. Burnham Dr., S.D., CA 92111; Office: 3375 Camino del Rio South, San Diego, CA 92108.

PEEK, PAUL
Associate Justice, California Supreme Court
b. June 5, 1904, West Union, Ia.; s. William Mason and Mary Ellen (Widdows) Peek; ed. pub. schs., Long Beach, Calif.; Univ. of Ore.; LL.B., Southwestern Univ. Law Sch. 1930; m. Elizabeth Goodrich Nash, Pasadena, Calif. 1930; chil.: Diane Elaine, b. Aug. 10, 1936; Philip Michael, b. July 7, 1943. Career: Pvt. law practice, Long Beach and Los Angeles, 1930-40; elected to State Assembly, 1936, re-elected, 1938, speaker of assembly, 1939, resigned, 1940; Secty. of State, 1940; apptd. to Third Dist. Ct. of Appeal, 1942, presiding justice, 1960; apptd. to Supreme Ct. of Calif. 1962-67 (ret.). Mem.: bd. of regents, Univ. of Calif. 1939-40; Calif. Judicial Council, 1946; Amer. Bar Assn. Methodist. Res.: 4501 Parkridge Rd., Sacramento, CA.

PEELER, STUART THORNE
Corporate Executive
b. Oct. 28, 1929, Los Angeles, Calif.; s. Joseph D. and Elizabeth (Boggess) Peeler; ed. A.B., Stanford Univ. 1950, J.D. 1953; m. Lenore June Thorp, Mar. 31, 1973; dau.: Heather Lynn, b. Aug. 3, 1960. Career: Atty. at law with Musick, Peeler & Garrett, 1953-73, partner, 1958, v.p.-secty. Santa Fe Internat. Corp. 1973-74; sr. v.p., gen. counsel & dir., 1975---; dir. Supron Energy Company; dir. California Portland Cement Company; trustee, J. Paul Getty Museum. Serv. 11th Airborne Division, U.S. Army. Awards: Commendation Medal. Mem.: U.S. Tuna Team, Internat. Tuna Cup Match (1956, 57, 58, 65, capt. 1966). Clubs: California, Petroleum. Republican. Congregationalist. Hobby and Rec.: hunting, deep-sea fishing. Res.: 17665 Sequoia Tree Lane, Irvine, CA 92664; Office: 505 S. Main St., Orange, CA 92668.

PEET, RAYMOND EDWARD
Aerospace Company Executive
b. Jan. 27, 1921, Oneonta, N.Y.; s. Ursil L. and Hanna (Thomas) Peet; B.S., U.S. Naval Acad., 1942; M.S., in Elec. Engring., Mass. Inst. Tech., 1948; Grad., Nat. War Coll., 1965; m. Dian Hutchinson, July 13, 1945, Union, Ore.; son, Gary Raymond, b. June 23, 1950. Career: Commd. Ensign, USN, 1942, advanced through grades to Vice Adm., 1970; assigned to Little Beaver Squadron, WW II; aide to chief naval opns., 1958; with naval reactor bd. AEC, 1959; commdg. officer in USS Bainbridge, 1961; with COMPHIBTRALANT, 1967-69; dir. Office Program Appraisal, Office Secty. Navy, 1969-70; Comdr. 1st Fleet, U.S. Pacific Fleet, 1970-72; dir. Def. Security assistance Agcy., dep. asst. secty. def., 1972-74; ret. 1974; V.P., International Teledyne Ryan Aeronautical, div. of Teledyne Inc., San Diego, 1974---; now Asst. to the Pres. Cons.: Ketron Inc.; Solar Internat. Turbines. Contbd. articles, U.S. Naval Inst. PROCEEDINGS 1977-78; decorated Dept. of Defense and Navy Dept. Distinguished Service Medals. Mem. Sigma Xi. Chmn., San Diego Fiscal Bd. of Overseers, 1978---; past v.p. San Diego Symphony Orchestra Assn.; past pres. World Affairs Council, San Diego; mem. bd. Visitors, Univ. San Diego Law Sch. 1976; Bd. Mgrs. San Diego YMCA, 1977; Rotary, San Diego, 1970; Dir., S.D. Council Navy League, 1974. Club: La Jolla Country. Rec.: golf, squash, racquetball. Res.: 7433 Fairway Rd., La Jolla, CA 92037; Office: Teledyne Ryan Aeronautical, 2701 Harbor Dr., San Diego, CA 92116.

PEEVER, ARTHUR JAY
Food Products Company Executive
b. Jan. 23, 1933, Toledo, Oh.; s. Raymond A. and Doris (Goodremont) Peever; B.S. with honors in Accounting, Cal. State Univ., Los Angeles, 1958; m. Barbara M. Davis, Jan. 2, 1953; chil.: Gary, Alan, Linda. Career: Mgr. Haskins & Sells, Los Angeles, 1958-68; controller Coca-Cola Bottling Co., Los Angeles, 1968-72, v.p., treas., controller, 1972-75, sr.

v.p. fin., 1975---. USAF, 1950-54. CPA, Calif. Mem.: Am. Inst. CPAs, Financial Execs. Inst. (dir. Los Angeles chpt.), Calif. Soc. CPAs, World Affairs Council. Clubs: Jonathan; Town Hall, Los Angeles. Res.: 327 S. Reese Place., Burbank, CA 91506; Office: 1334 S. Central Ave., Los Angeles, CA 90021.

PEGRAM, HELEN
Philanthropist
b. Oct. 25, Bismarck, N. Dak.; d. Albin and Linnie Lee (Slaughter) Hedstrom (listed, First and Important Families in America); ed. pub. schs., USA; m. Max West Pegram, M.D., Tupelo, Miss., Aug. 24, 1945; chil.: Candice Lynn, b. Nov. 6, 1947; Casandra, b. Jan. 7, 1949; Robert Max, b. Apr. 2, 1954. Career: Active in community, civic, philanthropic and social groups. Mem.: Natl. Charity League, Pasa. Spastic Children's League; D.A.R., St. Vincent's Hosp. Aux., USC Med. Faculty Wives, Friends of Huntington Library, Pasa. Philharmonic Com., Flintridge Riding Club, Balboa Bay Club. Presbyterian. Rec.: tennis. Res.: 1530 Charlton Rd., San Marino, CA.

PEGRAM, MAX WEST
Plastic Surgeon
b. Aug. 5, 1920, Potts Camp, Miss.; s. Robert Hugh and Pearl (West) Pegram; ed. B.A., Univ. of Miss. 1940; M.D., Northwestern Univ. 1943; m. Helen Hedstrom, Tupelo, Miss., Aug. 25, 1946; chil.: Candice, b. Nov. 6, 1947; Sandra, b. Jan. 7, 1949; Robert, b. Apr. 2, 1954. Career: Clin. assoc. prof. of surg., USC Med. Sch.; pvt. practice, spec. plastic surg., Los Angeles, Calif. Contrib. sci. articles to med. journs. Lt. Col., U.S. Army Med. Corps; chief of plastic surg. serv., Letterman Army Hosp., S.F., Calif., WW II. Mem.: Amer., Calif. and L.A. Co. Med. Assns., Calif. Soc. of Plastic Surgs., Amer. Soc. of Plastic and Reconstructive Surgs., Amer. Bd. of Plastic Surg., Phi Delta Theta, Phi Chi; clubs: Valley Hunt, Balboa Bay, Flintridge Riding, The Los Angeles. Republican. Protestant. Hobby: tennis, horses. Res.: 1530 Charlton Rd., San Marino, CA; Office: 201 S. Alvarado St., L.A., CA 90057.

PENDELL, THOMAS ROY
Clergyman
b. May 28, 1912, Los Angeles; s. G. Roy and Gayle (Crego) Pendell; A.B., UCLA, 1934; M.Th., USC, 1938; M.Div., Garrett-Evangelical Theol. Sem., 1941; m. Carol Embree, June 15, 1943, Pasadena; sons: David, b. 1944; Dale, b. 1947; Howard, b. 1950. Career: Exec. Secty., Nat. Council of Methodist Youth, 1938-40; pastor, Arizona, 1941-44, San Diego 1944-48, 1954-61, Newport Beach, 1948-54, San Gabriel, 1961-64, Anaheim, 1964-68, Sherman Oaks, 1968-71, Wesley United Methodist Ch. of Riverside, 1971---. Pres., Nat. Council of Methodist Youth, 1937-38; pres., So. Calif. Ministers Convocation, 1955; chmn., Methodist Conf. Div. of World Peace, 1964-71; mem. Nat. Council, Am. Fellowship of Reconciliation, 1966-69, 1974---. Contbr. articles in Motive, Christian Century, ch. press. United Methodist. Hobby: photog. Res.: 6951 Malibu Dr., Riverside, CA 92504; Office: P.O.B. 4185, Riverside, CA 92514.

PENDLETON, MORRIS BLANCHARD
Manufacturer
b. Feb. 4, 1901, Saratoga, Calif.; s. John Louis and Jessie (Larimore) Pendleton; ed. Pomona Coll. 1922; m. Gladys Shepard, Claremont, Calif., Aug. 30, 1924; chil.: John Morris, b. May 10, 1929, Pasa., Calif.; Mrs. Carl. H. (Barbara) Wittenberg, Jr., b. Mar. 14, 1936, Pasa. Calif.; Career: student employee, Plomb Tool Co. 1918-22; gen. mgr. 1922-28, v.p.-dir. 1928-36, pres.-dir. 1937--- (name changed to Pendleton Tool Inds., Inc.); secty.-treas., Shepard-Pendleton, Ltd. 1930---; secty-treas., Shepard-Pendleton Oil Co. 1934---; dir. Penens Corp. 1942, secty. 1944-45, v.p. 1945---; v.p. dor., P&C Hand Forged Tool Co. 1942---; bd. govs., Smaller War Plants Corp. 1943-45; dir. Moisture Register Co. 1943---, secty. 1945; gen. partner, All Amer. Mfg. Co. 1943---; gen. partner, All Amer. Fabricators, 1945---; gen. partner, Eagle Mfg. Co. 1945---; dir.-secty., Sierra Drawn Steel Corp. 1946---; dir. Drayer-Hanson, Inc. 1947---; secty.-treas., Brown Citrus Mach. Corp. 1947-59, secty.-dir. 1959---; dir. Ind. Tools Mfg. Corp.; dir. Pico Precision Prods. Co. Adv. com. dist. chief, U.S. Army Ord., WW II; Flotilla 22, USCG Aux. Mem.: bd. dirs., L.A. C. of C. 1943---, chmn. mil. affairs com. 1943; c.-chmn., Cits. Manpower Comm., L.A. Co. 1944-45; natl. trustee, Com. Econ. Development; dir. Army Ord. Assn.; dir.

S. Calif. Council of Inter-Amer. Affairs, 1944-45; natl. trustee, Com. Econ. Development; dir. Army Ord. Assn.; dir. So. Calif. Council of Inter-Amer. Affairs, 1944-47; adv. bd., ind. rels. pgm. com., NAM, 1945---; v.p.-repr., Inauguration Philippine Commonwealth, 1946; Masonic Lodge No. 367, S. Pasa. Chpt. Knights Templar, 1946---; adv. com. of 7, Civ. Prodn. of So. Calif. 1946-47; dir. Westlands Bank; regent, Pepperdine University; trustee, Pomona Coll., 1946---, pres. Alumni Assn. 1946-47; dir. Pomona Coll. Assocs. 1947---; adv. bd. Calif. Casualty & Indemnity Exch. 1947---; Calif. State-wide Ind. Com.; v.-chmn., state adv. council, Calif. Dist. of Employment; trustee, San Marino Sch. Bd.; Pasa. Tournament of Roses Assn.; dir. All Yr. Club of So. Calif.; Shrine, Al Malaikah Temple; clubs: L.A. Rotary, Jonathan, San Marino City, Balboa Bay, San Gabriel Country. Republican Res.: 467 Taylor Drive, Claremont, CA 91711; Office: 2833 Leonis Blvd., Suite 309, Vernon, CA 90058.

PENZL, HERBERT
Linguist — Educator
b. Sept. 2, 1910, Neufelden, Austria; s. Dr. Johann and Hedwig (Schmidt) Penzl; grad., Gymnasium XVI, Vienna, Austria, 1929; Hon. Fellow, Brown Univ., 1932-34; Ph.D., Univ. Vienna, 1935; m. Vera Rothmuller, Aug. 21, 1950, Murau, Austria. Career: Prof. of German, Rockford (Ill.) Coll., 1936-38, Univ. Ill. 1938-50, Univ. Mich 1950-63; prof. Germanic philology, Univ. Calif., Berkeley, 1963---. Smith-Mundt Prof. of Gen. Linguistics, Kabul (Afghanistan) Univ., 1958-59; Guggenheim fellow, 1967. Author: six books, numerous articles, profl. journs. AUS, 1943-45. Res.: 1125 Grizzly Peak Blvd., Berkeley, CA 94708; Office: 5333 Dwinelle Hall, Univ. of California, Berkeley, CA 94720.

PEREIRA, WILLIAM LEONARD
Architect
b. Apr. 25, 1909, Chicago, Ill.; s. Saul and Leah Pereira; ed. Univ. of Ill. 1926-30; m. Margaret I. McConnell, Crownpoint, Ind., June 24, 1934; chil.: William L., Jr. and Monica I. Career: Arch. 1930---; assoc. with Holabird & Root, Chicago, 1930-32; pvt. practice, Chicago, 1932-39; designing mot. pic. prodns., Hollywood, Calif. 1939-46; cons. arch.; William H. Block Dept. Store, Indianapolis; Lake Co. (Ill.) Tuberculosis San.; N.Y. World's Fair, San Francisco World's Fair; designed Pan Pac. Theatre and Rec. Center, Los Angeles, and Motion Picture Relief Fund Housing Proj., L.A.; professor of architecture, USC 1947-58; partner-chmn. bd., Pereira & Luckman, planners, archs. and engrs. 1950-58 (registered arch. in 25 states of U.S.); designed: CBS TV City, Marineland of Pac., J.W. Robinson's stores in Beverly Hills, Pasa. and Palm Springs, Bullock's Fashion Sq., Convair Astronautics and Gen. Atomic (San Diego, Union Oil Center and IBM Bldg. (L.A.); master-planning, Cape Canaveral and Patrick Air Force Base, Fla.; Univ.f of Calif. Santa Barbara campus, U.S. Naval and Air Force bases (Spain), Bunker Hill redevelopment in L.A., L.A. Internat. Airport (in assn. with Welton Becket and Paul Williams); independent Practice, 1958---; projs. incl.: Locheed Research Center, Saugus, Calif.; Hoffman Sci. Center, Santa Barbara; Gen. Tel. Research and Development Center, Palo Alto; Astopower Research Center, Newport Beach; Los Angeles County Museum of Art, Met. Water Dist and Occidental Center, L.A.; master plan for: Bishop Ranch, Goleta; Irvine Ranch, Orange Co.; Univ. of Calif., Irvine; Santa Catalina Is.; Mt. Park, USC and Occidental Coll., L.A. Masterplan for Houston Center, Tex. Adv. com. to directors, Crocker Bank; Natl. Council of Arts (appts. by Pres. Johnson), 1965; Govs. Action Adv. Com. on Calif. Beauty; bd. trustees, Cath. Welfare Bur.; bd. dirs. Urban Amer., Inc. Awards: recd. Natl. Council Registration Bds. Certificate, 1938; recd. Scarab Gold Medal Recognition Award, 1940; Humanitarian Medal from Motion Picture Industry, 1942; rec.d Oscar award as dir. spec. photog. in Reap the Wild Wind from the Acad. of Mot. Pic. Arts and Scis. 1942; distinguished hon. award from AIA for Mot. Pic. Relief Fund Housing Proj. 1946; Phila. Art Alliance Medal; 21 awards from AIA; L.A. C. of C. Award for creative achievemnt, 1957; hon. doctorate, Otis Art Inst. 1964; many cits. for progressive and modern arch. Mem.: fellow, AIA; Gargoyle Soc., Soc. of Amer. Mil. Engrs., Acad. of Mot. Pic. Arts and Scis. Res.: 135 N. Rossmore Ave., Los Angeles, CA; Office: 5657 Wilshire Blvd., Los Angeles, CA.

PERERA, MICHAEL GERARD
Physician
b. Oct. 18, 1941, Colombo, Ceylon; s. Abdon Ingatius and Lilian Grace Perera; M.D. 1967; m. Bernadette LaFever, June 13, 1970, Indiana; dau. Drishani Maria; Career: Internship, Penna. Hosp., 1968-69; med. resident, Metropolitan Hosp., N.Y. 1969-72; bd. certified Internal Med. 1972; Fellow, Allergy & Immunology, Univ. Cincinnati, 1972-74; pvt. practice Arcadia ---. Elected fellow, Royal Coll. of Physicians, 1973, Fellow, Am. Acad. of Allergy, 1977, Fellow, Am. Coll of Allergy, 1977; Bd. Certified Allergy & Immunology, 1975. Hobby: photog. Res.: 2178 Highland Oaks Dr., Arcadia, CA; Office: 612 W. Duarte Rd., Suite 702, Arcadia, CA 91006.

PEREZ, EDWARD J.
Deputy City Attorney
b. June 8, 1944, E. Chicago, Indiana; s. Margarito and Julia Cortez; B.S., mktg., 1967; J.D., 1975. Univ. San Diego Sch. of Law. Career: Deputy City Atty., City of Los Angeles, 1975---; exec. trainee, The Emporium; sr. engr., Traffic Operating Sales Mgr., Pacific Telephone Co., 1968-71; sales rep., Xerox Corp., 1971-72; Criminal prosecution, Pub. Utilities Reg., Deputy City Atty., City of Los Angeles, 1975---. Trustee, CORO Found. 1977-78; Pres., CORO Assoc. of So. Cliaf. 1978---, v.p. 1976-77, bd. of govs., 1976; vice chmn. Advis. Bd. for Centro Legal de Santa Monica, 1978---; treas., Assn. of Deputy City Attys., 1978---. Mem.: Oceotol hon. frat.; Sigma Alpha Epsilon, pres. 1966-67. Rec.: racquetball. Res.: 8351 Dunbarton Ave., L.A., CA 90045; Office: City Attorney, 1800 City Hall East, Los Angeles, CA 90012.

PERRINE, RICHARD LEROY
Scientist
b. May 15, 1924, Mountain View, Calif.; s. George Alexander and Marie (Axelson) Perrine; A.B., chem., San Jose State Coll., 1949; M.S., 1950; Ph.D., chem., Stanford Univ., 1953; m. Barbara Jean Gale, Apr. 12, 1945, Swindon, Wilts, England; children: Cynthia Gale (McCarthy), b. 1954; Jeffrey Richard, b. 1957. Career: Research chemist, Calif. Research Corp., La Habra, 1953-59; Lectr., USC 1957-59; assoc. prof. 1959-63; prof. of engring. & Applied Sci. 1963---, chmn. Environmental Sci. & Engring. 1971---; cons.: environmental sci. & engring., energy resources, flow in porous media. Dir., Aspendell Mutual Water Co., 1973-77; mem. L.A. County Engery Commn., 1973---; mem. Research Screening Com., Air Resources Bd., 1976-78; mem. Advisory Council & Chmn. Tech. Com., South Coast Air Quality Mgmt. Dist. 1977---; mem. Air Conservation Com., Lung Assn. Recipient, Outstanding Engr. Merit Award in environmental engring., Inst. for Advance Engring., 1975. Contbr. articles profl. journs. AUS, 1943-46. Mem.: Am. Chem. Soc., Am. Inst. of Chem. Engrs., Soc. of Petroleum Engrs., AAAS, Canadian Inst. Mining & Metallurgy, Nat. Assn. for Environ. Edn., Air Pollution Control Assn., Am. Water Resources Assn., N.Y. Acad. of Sci., California Tomorrow, Sierra Club, Wilderness Soc., Audubon Soc, Mem. Explorer's Club, Tau Delta Phi, Phi Lambda Upsilon, Tau Beta Pi, Sigma Xi. Rec.: wilderness, mountains. Res.: 22611 Kittridge St., Canoga Park, CA 91307; Office: 405 Hilgard Ave., Los Angeles, CA 90024.

PERRY, DAWN
School Administrator
b. Dec. 8, 1925, California; B.A., UCLA, 1947; M.A., Cal. State Northridge, 1963; m. Chester A. Perry, 1950, Indiana; chil.: Valera (Memmer), b. Feb. 10, 1952; Madeline, b. Oct. 6, 1954. Career: Spanish tchr., Marlborough Sch., 1947-49; Spanish-English tchr., Winchester Hi Sch., Indiana, 1949-50; elem. sch. tchr., Danville Sch., Calif., 1950-51; elem. tchr., L.A. Unified Sch. Dist., 1956-68; elem. sch. principal, L.A. Unified Schs., 1968---. Dir., Santa Rosa Scholarship Assn., 1969-73; Mem.: Kappa Delta Pi pres. So. Calif. Alumni chpt., 1972-74; Encino C. of C., dir. 1973-75. Home: 16638 Knollwood Dr., Granada Hills, CA 91344; Office: Hesby Elementary Sch., 15530 Hesby St., Encino, CA.

PERKINS, JOHN ALANSON
University Administrator
b. June 29, 1914, Owosso, Mich.; s. Glenn E. and Clara M. (Reed) Perkins; A.B., Univ. of Mich., 1938, A.M., 1939, Ph.D., 1941; L.H.D., Waynesbury Coll., 1968; LL.D. (hon.) USC 1960, Univ. Penna. 1963, Univ. Del. 1968, Wilkes Coll. 1969; m. Margaret

Hiscock, Sept. 3, 1937, Ann Arbor, Mich.; chil.: John James, b. Mar. 8, 1942; Margaret Carey, b. May 7, 1948. Career: Secty. to Sen. Arthur H. Vandenberg of Mich. 1936-37; Teaching Fellow, Dept. Polit. Sci., Univ. Mich., 1939-41, Instr. 1941-43, asst. prof. 1945-46, prof. polit. sci. 1949-50, asst. provost 1949-50, secty. Inst. for Public Adminstrn., 1945-46; Budget Dir. State of Michigan, 1946-48, Controller 1948-49; Pres., Univ. Dir. State of Michigan, 1946-48, Controller, 1948-49; pres., Univ. of Delaware 1950-67; UnderSecty. HEW, 1957-58; Pres., Dun and Bradstreet, 1967-68, chmn. of bd. 1968-69; pres. and CEO Wilmington (Del.) Med. Center, 1969-70; Prof. of Pub. Mgmt., Northwestern Univ., Evanston, Ill., 1971-72; Prof. Polit Sci., Univ. Calif., Berkeley, 1972-77, Prof. Emeritus, 1977---; Vice Pres., Adminstrn., Univ. of Calif. Systemwide, 1971-77, V.P. Administrn., Emeritus, 1977---. Dir. Alfred P. Sloan Found., 1968---; Trustee, Inst. for the Future, 1978---, Calif. Coll. of Arts and Crafts, 1977---, Pacific Sch. of Religion, 1978---; Dir.: Wilmington Trust Co. 1969-70, Bank of Del. 1966-67, Diamond State Telephone 1962-67, Atlas Chem. Industries 1963-67, Dun and Bradstreet 1967-71; exec. bd. mem. UNESCO 1953-55; Trustee, Ednl. Testing Service, 1971-75. Vestryman, Sr. Warden, St. Clement's Ch., Berkeley. Hobby: oil painting; one man shows in San Francisco, Berkeley, resort country of Harbor Springs, Mich. Rec.: golf, riding. Res.: 769 Spruce St., Berkeley, CA 94707.

PERKINS, RALPH E.
Business Owner
b. 1907, Jacksonville, Ind.; s. John and Nora Perkins; m. Laura Askew, June 14, 1930, Glendale; chil.: Virginia L. (Addis), b. 1934; Neale A., b. 1938. Career: Circulation Mgr., Alhambra Post Advocate, 1925-30; Pub., East Pasadena Herald and Alhambra Messenger, 1930-44; also owner, Moonlight Rollerway, Pasadena; Pres., Alhambra Finance Co., Pasadena Investment Co., Pasadena Associates Group, United Calif. Discount Corp. (Safariland Ltd. Inc.), Safariland Ballistics Inc. (v.p. and bd. chmn.), Pasadena Factor Co. (owner) Ralph Perkins & Assoc. Inc. (bd. chmn. & pres.), 1943---. Mil.: Coast Guard Reserve. Mem.: Masons; Elks; alumni assn. BSA; Alhambra Hist. Soc.; life mem. Alhambra Hosp., past trustee, Safari Club Internat.; Hunters Hall of Fame; Las Flores Shooting Club; Nat. Rifle Assn.; Quail Hunters Assn.; Ducks Unlmtd.; life mem. Soc. for Preservation Big Horn Sheep; patron mem. BSA, Maui, Hawaii. Christian Church. Res.: Four Bradbury Hills Rd., Bradbury, CA; Office: 1940 S. Walker, Monrovia, CA 91016.

PERKINS, ROY FRANK
Medical Research Director
b. Aug. 31, 1918, Rock Island, Illinois; s. Frank and Jennie Perkins; B.S., 1939, M.D. 1941; M.S. in Pathology, 1949; m. Marian Mazursky, Mar. 13, 1942, Los Angeles; chil.: Marc, b. 1944; Nancy, b. 1947; Frank b. 1949; John, b. 1950; James, b. 1954. Career: INternship 1941-43, Fellow and Staff mem., Mayo Clin. 1943-49; partner and co-founder Alhambra Med. Clin. 1951-79; Assoc. Clin. Prof. of Med., Loma Linda Univ., 1949-79; Clin. Prof. of Med., USC, 1964-79; Sr. Assoc., Booz, Allen & Hamilton, 1967-79; Dir. Dept. of Health Care Services, AMA 1966-67; vis. prof. of Med., Univ. of Trujillo, Peru, 1963, Cayetano Heredia Univ., Peru, 1970; Dir. Div. of Community and Satellite Med., Scripps Clin. & Research Found. 1979---. Pres. Diabetes Assn. of So. Calif. 1959-60; Gov. of So. Calif. and American Diabetes Assn. 1960-63. Capt., USMC, 1944-46. Res.: 1847 Caminito Velasco, La Jolla, CA 92037; Office: 10666 N. Torrey Pines Rd., La Jolla, CA 92037.

PERLMAN, ALFRED EDWARD
Transportation Company Executive
b. Nov. 22, 1902, St. Paul, Minn.; s. Louis and Leah (Levin) Perlman; ed. B.S.C.E., MIT 1923; Harvard Sch. of Bus. Adm. 1931; D.Sc., Clarkson Inst. of Tech., LL.B. (hon.) DePauw Univ.; m. Adele Sylvia Emrich, June 15, 1937; chil.: Michael Lewis, Lee Alfred, Mrs. Stephen (Constance Gene) Spahn. Career: Draftsman, asst. to pres. No. Pac. Ry. 1923-24; cons. Ry. Div., Reconstruction Finance Corp. 1934-35; asst. engr., Chicago, Burlington & Quincy R.R. 1935-36; engr. Denver & Rio Grande Western R.R. 1936-41, chief engr. 1941-47, gen. mgr. 1947-52, exec. v.p. 1952-54; cons. U.S. Dept. of State on Korean R.R. 1949; cons. Govt. of Israel R.R. 1950; pres.-dir. N.Y. Central Sys. 1954-68; pres.-dir.-chief adm. ofcr. Penn Central Co. 1968-69; v. chmn. Penn Central Transportation Co. 1969-70; pres. The Western Pac. R.R. Co. 1970-72,

chmn. bd. dirs.-chief exec. ofcr. 1973---; Western Pac. Subsidiaries; v.p.-dir.: Alameda Belt Line, Delta Finance Co., Ltd., Sacramento No. Ry., Salt Lake City Union Depot and R.R. Co., Standard Realty and Dev. Co., Tidewater So. Ry. Co.; pres.-dir. Oakland Terminal Ry.; dir. Western Pac. Inds., Inc.; chmn. bd. Western Pac. Transport Co. Trustee: Amer. Mus. of Immigration, Elmira Coll., Denver Univ. Awards: Man of Yr. award, N.Y. Foreign Forwarders and Brokers Assn. 1966; Gold Medal Award. West Side Assn. of Commerce, 1967; Syracuse Univ. Salzberg Mem. Medal, 1968; Outstanding Achievement in Mgmt., Amer. Inst. of Ind. Engrs. 1970; Gold Medal Award, Amer. Soc. for Metals; Progressive Railroading's Railroading's Railroader Award, 1972. Mem.: Mil. Airlift Committee, USAF; (hon. life). Transportation Assn. of Amer.; Natl. Freight Traffic Assn.; YMCA Grand Central Br., NYC; Newcomen Soc. of N. Amer. Clubs: Pac. Ry. (hon.), Westchester Country, Sky, Traffic, N.Y.; Olympic, Bankers, S.F. Office: 526 Mission St., San Francisco, CA 94105.

PERUSSE, LYLE FRANCIS
Writer
b. Oct. 6, 1916, Lincoln, Nebr.; s. Francis Joseph and Elva (Liles) Perusse; ed. certificate, Beutel Bus. Coll. 1936; A.B., Oberlin Coll. 1950; M.A., Harvard Univ. 1951; B.L.S., Univ. of Calif., Berkeley, 1952. Career: Statis clerk, Gen. Mills, Inc., Tacoma, Wash. 1936-42; librarian, Sch. of Arch., Univ. Minn. 1952-54; ref. staff, UCLA 1955-57; supv. lib., art and music sect., Pasa. Pub. Lib. 1957-64; librarian, Corona Pub. Lib. 1964-77; freelance writer, 1978---. Secty.-chmn. Exec. Council, Inland Lib. System; Certified Calif. Co. Lib. 1968---; Natl. Trust for Hist. Preservation. Editor, Calibrarian, 1956-58; contrib. professional and other publs.; So. Calif. Com. for Reactivated Hist. Amer. Bldgs. Survey, 1958-64. Pac. Theater Operations, USNR (1942-45), WW II. Mem.: pres. Pasa. Lib. Club, 1961-62; Amer. Lib. Assn.; Calif. Lib. Assn.; Bibliographical Soc. of Amer.; Amer. Guild of Organists; L.A. Chpt. Alliance Francaise de la Riviera Californienne; Society of Arch. Historians; Public Library Executives of Southern California; Kiwanis Club of Corona; YMCA; Phi Beta Kappa. Protestant. Hobbies: gardening, woodworking. Rec.: water sports. Res.: 974 W. Rancho Rd., Corona 91720.

PETERS, KENNETH L.
School District Administrator
b. June 27, 1915, Orange, Calif.; s. C. Rex and Mary E. (Butler) Peters; B.S., USC, 1936, M.S., 1948; m. Mary Ann Peters, 1959, Las Vegas, Nev.; chil.: Stephen C., b. Jan. 1947; Kent W., b. Oct. 27, 1961; Craig R., b. Feb. 22, 1963. Career: Principal, Montebello Sr. High Sch., Montebello, 1946-50; prin., Beverly Hills H.S., 1950-59; asst. supt., Beverly Hills Unified Sch. Dist., 1957-59; Superintendent of Schs., 1959---. Dir.: John Thomas Dye School; Tchrs. Mgmt. and Investment Corp.; Beverly Hills C. of C. Served to Lt. Comdr., USN, 1942-45, active duty, Ret. 1959. Named Man of the Year, 1978, Beverly Hills C. of C.; Man of the Year, Maple Center, Beverly Hills, 1975; Citizen of the Year, B.H. Realty Bd., 1970; Mem.: Suburban Sch. Supts. Assn., pres., 1974, 1965; Calif. City Schs., pres. 1964; Beverly Hills Rotary Club, pres. 1959. Home: 4632 El Caballero Dr., Tarzana, CA 91356; Office: 255 Lasky Dr., Beverly Hills, CA 90212.

PETERSON, NAD ALMA
Corporate Executive
b. May 6, 1926, Mt. Pleasant, Utah; s. Angus Alma and Crystal (Olsen) Peterson; student, Univ. of Utah, Georgetown Univ.; A.B., George Washington Univ., 1950, J.D., with honors George Washington Law Sch., 1953; m. Martha Peterson, Sept. 7, 1948, Salt Lake City, Utah.; chil.: Anne Carrol (Darger, b. Feb. 25, 1953 (Wellesley '74); Christian, b. Oct. 18, 1955 (Harvard '79); E. Elizabeth, Feb. 8, 1960 (Harvard-Radcliffe '81); Robert and Lane (twins), b. Dec. 3, 1962 (Newport Harbor H.S.). Career: Attorney, firm of Pierson, Ball & Dowd, Wash., D.C., 1953-60; Asst. Gen. Counsel and Secty., Dart Industries, Inc., Los Angeles, 1960-67; Chief Counsel, Fluor Corp., Irvine, 1967-73, General Counsel, 1973---. Admitted to practice: District of Columbia 1953, Supreme Ct. of U.S. 1958, State of Calif. 1960. Served USNR, WW II; Pacific Theatre, U.S.S. St. Louis. Mem. George Washington Law Rev. 1952-53; Phi Delta Phi; Am., Calif. (Bus. Law Sect.), Orange County Bar Assns.; Los Angeles Area C. of C. Clubs: Balboa Bay, Big Canyon Country. Res.: 1325 Galaxy Dr., Newport Beach, CA 92660; Office: 3333 Michelson Dr., Irvine, CA 92730.

PETERSON, NORMAN WILLIAM
Naval Captain
b. Aug. 26, 1933, Highland Park, Ill.; s. Jens E. and Marie Petersen; B.S.E.E., Univ. of N. Mex., 1956; M.S. E.E. with distinction, Naval Post Graduate Sch., 1962; m. Ann Nevin, Aug. 24, 1956, Mexico City, Mex.; chil.: Richard, b. June 17, 1957; Robert, b. Aug. 3, 1958; Thomas, b. Nov. 11, 1959 (dec.); Anita, b. Oct. 21, 1961; David, b. Apr. 2, 1963. Career: USN, 1952---: pub. works officer, Naval Station, Key West, Fla., 1956-59; Fleet Anti-Air Warfare Training Center, Damn Neck, Va., 1962-64; Naval Air Station, Miramar, San Diego, 1970-73; Engring. Coordination officer for SW div., Naval Facilities Engring. Command, 1964-66; exec. officer, Amphibious Constrn. Batallion One, 1966-67; Force Civil Engr., Comdr. Naval Air Forces Pacific Fleet, 1967-70; exec. offiver, Pub. Works Center, Great Lakes, Ill., 1973-75; Capt., Civil Engr. Corps, 1976; comdg. officer, Navy Civil Engr. Research Lab., 1975-78; comdg. officer, Navy Pub. Works Center, San Francisco Bay, 1978---. Estab. only mil. indsl. plant, Vietnam, 1967; awarded Navy's 1st Bronze Hammer award for outstanding constrn. 1973; constructed Rayburn Hall Polaris Missile Training Facility, 1964; Decorated Meritorious Service Medal, 1967-68; Navy Commendation Medal, 1967-70; Navy Unit Citation, 1967-68; Meritorious Unit Commendation, 1967, 1973; Vietnam Armed Forces Merit Citation-Gallantry Cross, 1967; Vietnam Merit Citation, Civil Actions, 1st Class, 1967. Bd. Dir. United Way of Ventura Co. Mem.: Lambda Chi Alpha; Zeta Mu, pres. 1955-56; Soc. Am. Mil. Engrs.; Am. Pub. Works Assn.; IEEE; Navy League; Oxnard Gem and Mineral Soc. ways and means, 1977-78; Am. Philatelic Soc., Germany; Philatelic Soc., Mex.; Elmhurst Philatelic Soc. Internat. Hobbies: stamps, astronomy, rock hounding. Rec.: motor biking. Home: 102 San Pedro, Alameda, CA 94501; Office: P.O.B. 24003, Oakland, CA 94623.

PETERSEN, ORVAL LYMAN
Education Consultant
b. Mar. 24, 1924, Seattle, Wash.; George N. and Norvella (Lyman) Petersen; ed. B.S., Univ. Wash. 1950; B.A. 1951; M.Ed. 1956; Ed.D., Stanford Univ. 1958; Ph.D., Met. Univ. 1963; M.I.B.A. 1970. Career: Boeing Airplane Co. 1942-47; teacher Sunnyside Sch. Dist. Wash. 1951-59; instr. Chaffey H.S. Dist., Ontario, Calif. 1959-60; asst. supt. 1965-69; edn. cons. San Bernardino Co. Schs. Edn. Center, 1969---. Contrib. to professional journs.; feat. various publs. Mem.: v.p.-dir. Montclair Rotary Club, 1961-69; bd. dirs. San Bernardino-Riverside Co. Ind. Edn. Council, 1962---; Calif. Assn. for Supv. and Curriculum Development, 1964-67; sci. adv. com. Calif. State Bd. Edn. 1964---; Calif. Edn. Data Processing Assn.; Calif. Acad. of Sci.; Natl. Sci. Teachers Assn.; Calif. Teachers Assn.; coms. NEA; AAAS 1964---; (hon.) Natl. Register Edn. Researchers, 1966; v. chmn. Amer. Red Cross, Ontario; United Fund; bd. dirs. Jr. Chamber of Comm.; counselor, BSA; Internat. Platform Assn. 1970---; (hon.) Intercontinental Biog. Assn., Eng. 1970. Methodist (ch. sch. supt., Sunnyside, 1956-59). Hobby: photog. Rec.: travel, hiking. Res.: 903 W. Bonnie Brae Ct., Ontario, CA 91762.

PETERSEN, ROLAND CONRAD
Painter — Printmaker
b. Mar. 31, 1926, Endelave, Denmark; U.S. Citizen; s. Jul and Eli (Hansen) Petersen; A.B., Univ. of Calif., Berkeley, 1949, M.A., 1950; m. Sharane Havlina, Aug. 12, 1950, Provincetown, Mass.; chil.: Dana Mark, b. Sept. 4, 1953; Maura Brooke, b. Apr. 17, 1956; Julien Conrad, b. Aug. 19, 1959; Karena Caia, b. Mar. 30, 1961. Career: postgard. studies Hans Hofman Sch. of Art, San Francisco Art Inst., Calif. Coll. of Arts and Crafts, Atelier 17, Paris, France, with Stanley W. Hayter, Islington Studio, London, Eng. 1977; Teaching: Instr. of painting, Wash. State Univ. 1952-56; Prof. of painting and printmaking, Univ. Calif., Davis, 1956---; Instr. printmaking, UC Berkeley, 1965. Guggenheim Fellow, 1963; Appointee, Inst. of Creative Arts, Univ. of Calif., 1967, 70; Fulbright travel awardee, 1970; U.C. Recents Fellow, 1977. Commissions: De Beers Mining Co., So. Africa, 1967; Dams of the West, portfolio of 25 color prints, U.S. Dept. of Interior, 1970. Solo Exhibitions include: Oakland Art Mus., 1954; Calif. Palace of Legion of Honor, S.F., 1961; Gump's Gallery, S.F., 1962; Staempfli Gallery, N.Y., 1964, 65, 67; Crocker Art Gallery, Sacto., 1965; Adele Bednarz Gallery, L.A., 1966, 69, 72, 73, 85, 76; M.H. De Young Mem. Mus., S.F., 1968; La Jolla Mus., 1971; Phoenix Art Mus., 1972; Santa Barbara Mus., 1973; Davis Art Center, 1976; Univ. of Reading, England, 1977. Work in many pub. collections. Rep. Dealers: Staempfli Gallery, NYC;

Bednarz Galleries, L.A. Served USN, 27 mos., Iwo Jima. Res.: 858 Linden Lane, Davis, CA 95616; Office: Univ. of Calif., Davis, CA 95616.

PETERSON, RUDOLPH ARVID
Banker
b. Dec. 6, 1904, Svenljunga, Sweden; s. Aaron and Anna (Johansson) Peterson; ed. B.S., Univ. of Calif. Coll. of Comm. 1925; m. Patricia Price, 1927 (dec.); m. Barbara (Welser) Lindsay, Walnut Creek, Calif., Dec. 25, 1962; chil.: Mrs. Stephen W. (L. Linnea) Bennett and Dr. R. Price Peterson; stepchil.: Robert, Lorna, Margaret and Anne Lindsay. Career: Field rep., asst. mgr., Commercial Credit Co., S.F., v.p.-gen. mgr., Mex. City, Mex., div. mgr., Chicago, 1925-36; dist. mgr., Bank of Amer. NT&SA, Fresno, v.p., S.F., supv. state-wide lending div. 1936-46; pres. Allied Bldg. Credits, St. Paul and Los Angeles, 1946-52; v.p. (supv. banking interests, 5 Western states), Transamerica Corp., S.F., 1952-55; pres., Bank of Hawaii, 1955-61; v.-chmn., Bank of Amer. NT&SA, S.F., 1961-63, pres. 1963-70, chmn. exec. com. 1970-76; honorary dir., 1976---; adminstr. & dir. UN Devel. Program, 1972-76; chmn. policy com. The Becker Warburg Paribas Group Inc., 1976---; chmn. S.G. Warburg N. Am. Ltd., 1977---; chmn. Paribas N. Am., 1977---; dir. Alza Corp., Di Giorgio Corp., Schlage Lock Co., Scandinavian Airlines System, Inc., trustee: Calif. Acad. Scis., Calif. Alumni Found., Calif. Inst. Tech., Asia Found., James Irvine Found., Internat. House at the Univ. of Calif., Berkeley. Decorated comdr. Royal Order Vasa (Sweden); Grand Cross of Civil Merit (Spain); Order of Merit (Italy); named Swedish-Am. of Year, Vasa Order, 1965; Man of Yr., Cons. Engrs. Assn. Calif., 1968; Univ. Calif. Alumnus of Year, 1968; Calif. Industrialist of Year, Calif. Mus. Sci. and Industry, 1969; recipient Capt. Robert Dollar Meml. award for contbn. to advancement Am. foreign trade, 1970. Mem.: Swedish C. of C. of USA; past dir., Calif. State C. of C.; Bohemian, Pacific-Union, Villa Taverna (S.F.); Cypress Point (Pebble Beach); The Links Club (NYC). Hobbies: gardening, swimming, reading. Res.: 86 Sea View Ave., Piedmont, CA; Office: Bank of Amer. Center, S.F., CA 94137.

PETREE, NEIL
Civic Leader
b. Mar. 18, 1898, Norborne, Mo.; s. Louis E. and Kittie (Neil) Petree; ed. pub. H.S., San Jose, Calif.; A.B. (econ.), Stanford Univ. 1919; m. Vera Thomas, May 1919. Career: Salesman, buyer, mdse mgr. Weinstock Lubin and Co., Sacramento (dept. store and mail order co.), 1919-24; div. mdse. mgr., sales mgr., gen. mdse. mgr. Hale Bros. Dept. Stores, S.F., 1925-29; v.p. Assoc. Dry Goods Corp., N.Y.; v.p. Lord and Taylor, N.Y., 1929-30; v.p.-gen. mdse mgr., James McCreery & Co., N.Y. 1930; pres. James McCreery & Co. 1931-38; pres.-dir., Barker Bros. Corp., L.A. 1938-60; chmn. Barker Assoc. Cos.; pres.-dir. W.J. Sloane, Inc. 1957-59. Dir.: Bank of Amer., Pac. Mutual Life Ins. Co., Pac. Lighting Co., Investment Co. of Amer. Aviator, French Army; Aviation Lt., American Army, WW I; pres. L.A. Area Community Chest; chmn., Los Angeles Civic Lt. Opera; pres., L.A. Convention Center. Awards: Cavalier Award by furniture industry for merchant doing most for county during yr 1944; L.A. Am. Legion Award, 1962; recd. L.A. Realty Bd. Award as cit who perf. most useful serv. to L.A. 1953; Town Hall Civic Award of L.A.; L.A. Jr. C. of C. Award of Merit, 1957; Western Achievement Award for Furniture Ind. 1958. Mem.: trustee, Stanford Univ.; pres. Greater L.A. Plans, Inc.; pres. Automobile Club of So. Calif.; dir.-(past) pres.: Calif. State C. of C., L.A. Downtown Business Men's Assn.,; Hollywood Bowl Assn., Hollywood Turf Club Assoc. Charities; dir. L.A. Community Welfare Fed.; Delta Tau Delta; clubs: California; L.A. Country. Res.: 65 Fremont Pl., L.A., CA 90005.

PETIT, JOHN TANNER
Electronics Executive
b. Aug. 2, 1923, Salt Lake City, Ut.; s. Dr. William A. and Laura Mildred (Tanner) Petit; ed. A.A., Pasa. Jr. Coll. 1943; Calif. Inst. Tech. (3 yrs.); Columbia Univ. NYC 1944-45; N.A., UCLA 1947, M.S. 1949, Ph.D. 1951; S.M. (Sloan Fellow), MIT 1958; m. Jo Betty Hibbits, Pasa. Calif., Sept. 14, 1946; chil.: Gregory John, b. Aug. 22, 1947; Patricia Eileen, b. Apr. 19, 1950; Brent Jeffrey, b. July 2, 1951; Christopher Wayne, b. Nov. 15, 1952; Career: Research Assoc., UCLA 1946-48, instr. 1948-50; asst research, Inst. Geophysics, 1949-54; pres.' staff, Hughes Tool Co. 1952-58, dept. dir. 1962; co-founder-pres.-chmn. bd. Faim Ice Co., Burbank, Calif. 1955---; staff asst. to

gen. mgr., Hughes Aircraft Co., Culver City, Calif. 1958; dir. Ind. Dynamics, 1958; orgn-pres.-chmn. bd., Dynamic Intelectronics Corp. 1961---; spec. asst. to gen. mgr., gen. mgr., Scientific Industries, Inc. (subsidiary Highes Aircraft Co.) 1962; sr. cons., Hughes Dynamics, Inc. (div. Hughes Tool Co.), 1962, v.p. 1963; founder-pres.-chmn. bd., Information Processing Labs., L.A., 1965---; cons. in computers, physics, math. and bus. orgns. Inventor: ADMA (the automatic drafting machine, Hughes Aircraft Co.); SODAC (source data recording and collection device). Lectr.: civic, ch., edn. and professional groups, incl. A Survey of Operations Research, Calif. Tech. Mgmt. Club, 1963; In Business — A Tech. Dimension, Exec. Lecture Pgm., Brigham Young Univ., Provo, 1966. Author: 27 profl. publs., incl.: A Speedy Solution of the Cubic, Math. Mag. 1947; Earth Tides, Transaction, Amer. Geophysical Union, 1954; Economic Models, MIT 1958; A Case Study of TWA, 1958; A Management Concept for the Defense Industry and A Profit Center Plan for Ind. Dynamics, Hughes Aircraft Co., 1960; Survival of Our Amer. Economic System, 1961; Industrial Dynamics in Practice, AMA Mgmt. Bulletin, 1962; On the Data Processing Functions in Genealogy, 1965. Apprentice seaman, USNR, West Coast Sound Sch., S.D., Pearl Harbor, Guiuan, Samar, P.I. (1944-46), WW II; Lt., USNR, 1946---. Listed, various natl. and internat. biog. publs. Mem.: Natl. Geographical Soc., Seismological Soc., Amer. Mgmt. Association, Amer. Geophysical Union, Operations Research Soc. of Amer., Inst. of Mgmt. Scis., Sci. Research Soc. of Amer., Sigma Xi, Pi Mu Epsilon, Lambda Delta Sigma. Ch. of Jesus Christ of L.D.S. (Mormon, high priest). Hobbies: music (organ, piano), genealogy. Res.: 1145 S. El Molino Ave., Pasadena, CA; Office: 17000 Ventura Blvd., Encino, CA.

PETTIS, SHIRLEY NEIL
   Former U.S. Congresswoman
b. July 12, 1924, Mt. View, Calif.; d. Harold O., Ph.D. and Dorothy McCumber; ed. Andrews Univ., Mich.; Univ. of Calif., Berkeley; m. Congressman Jerry Lyle Pettis, Pasadena, Calif., Mar. 2, 1947 (dec.); chil.: Peter Dwight, b. Aug. 23, 1955; Deborah Neil, b. June 10, 1958. Career: Managing dir. Audio-Digest Found. 1953-54; secty-treas. Pettis Inc. 1953-67; elected to U.S. House of Reps., Apr. 28, 1975---. Author, newspaper column, 1967-61. Mem.: Calif. Elected Women's Assn. for Edn. and Research; Am. Newspaper Women's Club; Natl. Women's Polit. Caucus, Republican Task Force; Environmental Study Conf.; Am. Historical Soc. Seventh-Day Adventist. Rec.: swim, flying, horseback riding. Res.: 24934 Tulip Ave., Loma Linda, CA 92354.

PETTIT, WILLIAM ALFRED, JR.
   Physician
b. Mar. 1922, Salt Lake City, Utah; s. Wm. Alfred and Laura (Tanner) Pettit; grandson, Edwin Pettit, early trailmaster of the West; A.B. cum laude, USC 1945; M.D., Univ. Penna., 1945; m. Barbara Dene Kleinman, July 5, 1950, Saint George, Utah; children: Wm. Alfred III, b. 1955; Robert John, b. 1958; Richard Glen, b. 1961; David Allen, b. 1966. Career: Internship, L.A. Co. Gen. Hosp., 1949-50; Exec. Asst. to Dir. of Research Sci. of Aviation Med., Pensacola, Fla., USN 1950-53; med. resident, Univ. of Penna. Sch. of Med., 1953-54, resident on ophthalmology, 1954-56; pvt. practice, Pasadena, 1956---. Active in Scouting 30+ years; chmn. Rosebowl Dist., San Gabriel Valley Council, 1975-77; bd. dir., 1977---. Mem.: Phi Beta Pi, Alpha Sigma chpt. L.D.S., missionary, Canada 1941-43. Hobbies: philately, orchids, music. Res.: 535 S. Lotus, Pasadena, CA; Office: 595 E. Colorado St., Pasadena, CA 91101.

PETTITE, WILLIAM CLINTON
   Public Affairs Consultant
b. Reno, Nev.; s. Sidney Clinton and Wilma May (Stibal) Pettite; m. Charlotte Fryer, Carmichael, Calif., June 18, 1858; sons: Patrick Keane, b. May 22, 1959; William Ellis b. Jan. 31, 1961; Joseph Clinton, b. June 30, 1962. Career: Legislative cons., clients incl.: Gov. Charles C. Gossett, Ida.; Sen. E.S. Wright, majority leader, Ida. Senate; U.S. Sen. Henry Dworshak and Congressman Hamer Budge, 1959---; publ. Market Lake Citizen-County Enterprise Newspapers, Roberts, Ida. 1959-61; Co. Probate Judge, Ida. 1959-61; acting Co. Coroner, Ida. 1960-61; v.p.-dir. San Juan Community Servs. Dist., Orangevale, Calif. 1962-66, 1968-72; secty.-trustee, Fair Oaks Cemetery Dist. 1963-72; pres.-dir. Fair Oaks Irrigation Dist. 1964-72; dir. Sacramento Co. Assn. of

Dists. 1967-72, pres. 1970-71; publ. Storey Co. Legend (Newspaper), Virginia City, Nev. 1970; pub. rels. dir. Golden Days of World Boxing Champs, Reno, Nev. 1970; cons. Senate-Assembly Joint Audit Com., Calif. Legislature, 1971-73; alternate, Sacramento Co. Grand Jury, 1972-74. Author: (book) Memories of Market Lake (hist. S.E. Ida.); contrib. articles to numerous publs., professional journs. Awards: Ida. Centennial Award for civic serv. (with U.S. Sen. Frank Church), 1968; Ida. Centennial Award (with Ezra Taft Benson, Secty. of Agri.), 1969. Mem.: com. Natl. Council of Juvenile Ct. Judges, 1959-61; St. Patrick's Mummers Guild; Chmn., Repub. Co. Central Com. 1959-61, asst. Sgt. at Arms, Repub. Natl. Conv. 1956, del. Repub. State Conv. 1960. Res.: P.O. Box 2127, Fair Oaks, Calif. 95628; Office: State Capitol Bldg., Suite 5080, Sacto., CA 95814.

PETTY, KEITH
   Attorney at Law
b. June 13, 1920, Swan Lake, Ida.; s. William D. and Emma L. (Johnson) Petty; B.S., Univ. Ida. 1942; J.D., Stanford 1948; m. Gail Wells, Jan. 11, 1943; chil.: Kaye (Mrs. Robert Paugh), Richard Jane, Scott. Admitted to Cal. Bar, 1949; tax accountant Pacific Telephone & Telegraph Co., San Francisco, 1948-50; John F. Forbes Co., S.F. 1950-54; practiced law, S.F. 1954---; mem. Firm Petty, Andrews, Tufts & Jackson, and predecessor firms, S.F. Dir. Lakeview Tahoe, Inc., Plastic Center Inc. Served as Lt. USNR, 1942-46. CPA, Cal. Mem. Cal., Ida. Bar Assns. Mem. Ch. of Jesus Christ of Latter-day Saints (bishop, mem. high council). Office: 650 California St., Suite 3130, S.F., CA 94108.

PEW, LAFAYETTE GLEN
   Electronics Executive and Engineer
b. May 24, 1924, Mesa, Maricopa Co., Ariz.; s. Lafayette and Emma Myrle (Horne) Pew; ed. grad. Mesa Union H.S. 1941; B.S., Ariz. State Univ., Tempe, 1950; m. Ella Louise Alexander, Berkeley, Jan. 11, 1945; chil.: Chearn, Kathleen, Bonnie, Stephen, Patricia, John. Career: owner-mgr., Hobby Shop, Santa Ana, Calif. 1946-47; engr.-anncr., KARV Radio Broadcasting System, Mesa, Ariz., 1947-48; lab. instr. dept. engring., Ariz. State Univ. 1948; engr. KPHO-TV Sta., Phoenix, 1948-50; studio engr., KPIX-TV Sta., S.F., 1950-57; designer-constructed spec. equipment, 1952-54. studio engr. supv., maintenance engr. 1957; video serv. engr., Ampex Corp., Redwood City, 1957, instr. 1957-59, video field engr. (overseas), 1959, video serv. engr. mgr., Ampex Internat. Operations (overseas), 1959-61; dept. mgr., Redwood City, 1961-62; coord. worldwide depots and inventories, 1962-63; propr.-mgr., Electro Acoustic Co., San Carlos, Calif., 1954-70, pres. 1970---; mfrs. rep.: Whittier ofc. 1966; Grason-Stadler Co., Inc., West Concord, Mass.; Aural Research, Temple City, Calif.; others, Minn., Ill., N.Y., Tex.; designed-constructed first comml. TV film recorder in S.F. for Diner Films; spec. equip.: Vets Hosp.; Univ. of Calif. Med. Center, Stanford Univ., instr. 1963-67; S.F. Hearing & Speech Center, cons. 1965---; pres. Hyrum William Pew Family Orgn. 1967---; pres. Medical Measurements, Inc. 1970-71; Co-author: A Method of Controlling Tester Bias in Audiological Evaluations, A Comparison of Auditory Amplifiers in the Classroom in a School for the Deaf, A Comparison of Auditory Amplifiers for the Deaf, publ. Journs. of Speech and Hearing, Audiology, 1955-66. U.S. Navy Radio Material Sch. (installation and repairs submarine radar, radio, sonar, loran 1942-46), WW II. Listed, various biog. publs. USA. Mem.: Blue Key, 1949---; Soc. of Mot. Pic. and TV Engrs., 1952---; Ch. of Jesus Christ of L.D.S. (Mormon, bishop's counselor, 1962-64; Stake High Council, 1964-73). Hobbies: photog., art, electronics. Res.: 1900 Eucalyptus Ave., San Carlos 94070; Office: 1590 Laurel St., San Carlos, CA 94070.

PEW, MARY JEAN
   College Dean
b. June 9, 1930, St. Paul, Minn.; dau. Maurice and Katherine (Dowd) Pew; B.A., Immaculate Heart Coll., L.A., 1957, M.A., 1959; Ph.D., Fordham Univ., 1961; m. Douglas Faigin. Career: with IMmaculate Heart Coll., L.A. 1961---: instr./asst. prof./assoc./full prof. of Govt. 1961---, chmn. dept. Hist., Govt., 1969-75, Academic Dean, 1975---; vis. lectr. on Am. Law and Politics, Univ. of Witwatersrand, Johannesburg, So. Africa. Trustee, Cal. State Univ. and Coll. System, 1975-83, trustee, Coro Found., 1975-76. Contbr. profl. journs. Mem.: Am. Polit. Sci. Assn.; Western Polit. Sci. Assn.; com. on Status of Women; So. Calif. Polit. Sci. Assn., pres. 1971-72. Office: 2021 N. Western Ave., L.A., CA 90027.

PFAU, JOHN MARTIN
College President
b. Apr. 28, 1918; s. Anton and Anna (Mayer) Pfau; A.B. (hist.), Univ. of Chicago, 1947, M.A. 1948, Ph.D. 1951; m. Antreen McDonnell, Chicago, 1942; daus: Madelaine, b. Sept. 16, 1951; Ellen, b. Nov. 29, 1953. Career: Instr. in Am. Hist., N. Central Coll., Naperville, Ill. 1948-50; assoc. prof. hist., N.E. Ill. State Coll 1951-59, adm. asst. to dean, 1955-56, asst. dean 1956-59; prof. hist.-chmn. div. soc. scis.: Chico State Coll. 1959-61, Sonoma State Coll. 1961-62; pres. Calif. State Coll., San Bernardino, 1962---. USN 1942-45, WW II. Mem.: Am. Hist. Assn., Orgn. of Am. Historians; pres San Bernardino Sym. Assn. 1963-69; San Bernardino Sym. Assn. 1963-69; San Bernardino Community Hosp. Corp. 1963---; chmn., Am. Assn. of State Colls. and Univs., Com. for the Humanities, 1975---; Mem., Calif. Council for the Humanities in Pub. Policy, 1977---; (charter 1964) bd. dirs. World Affairs Council of Inland So. Calif.; accreditation com. Calif. State Bd. of Edn. 1967-69; statewide advanced placement com. Calif. State Dept. of Edn. 1969; Rotary Club. Res.: 4370 Golden Ave., San Bernardino, CA 92404; Office: 5500 State College Parkway, San Bernardino, CA 92407.

PFEFFER, J. ALAN
University Professor
b. June 26, 1907, Brooklyn; s. Isaac and Henny (Halpern) Pfeffer; A.B. magna cum laude, Univ. Buffalo, 1935, M.A. 1936; Ph.D., Columbia, 1946; m. Bertha Manoff, M.A., Feb. 27, 1938; children: Robert I., M.D. and JoAnne P. Jares, M.S.W.; Career: Grad. asst., Univ. Buffalo, 1935-36; instr. German, 1939-46; asst. assoc./prof., 1946-62; exec. ofcr. German sect. modern lang. dept., 1952-62; prof. chmn. dept. Germanic langs., lit. Univ. Pitts., 1962-72; chmn. humanities council, 1968-69, dir. Inst. Basic German, 1960---; instr. German, Buffalo Collegiate Center, 1936-37; Columbia extnesion div., 1937-39; consultant FBI, 1943-44; head German Desk, U.S. Army Service Forces, 1944-45; cons. prof. Stanford Univ., 1976---; cons. N.D. Lang. Insts.; lectr. various European univs. Recipient Gold Medal Goethe Inst. Germany, 1972; DAAD faculty fellowship, 1972; Featschrift, Deutsche Weltliteratur, 1972; Mem. AAUP (local pres.), N.Y. State Conf. Univ. Profs. (councilor), Am. Assn. Tchrs. German (pres. Western zone), Modern Lang. Assn. (adv. com. Publ. German Tchrs. Guides), N.Y. Fedn. Fgn. Lang. Tchrs. (pres.), Nat. Fedn. Modern Lang. Tchrs. Assn. (chmn. state survey acad. preparation tchrs. modern lang., exec. council, pres.), Delta Phi Alpha (nat. 1st v.p.), Phi Beta Kappa (local pres.). Author, editor: Civil and Military German, 1943; German-English and English-German Dictionary of Everyday Usage, 1947; The Proverb in Goethe, 1948; Essays on German Language and Literature in Honor of Theodore B. Hewitt 1952; Modern German-Civilization, Composition and Conversation, 1953; German Review Grammar, rev. edit., 1969; Basic Spoken German Series; vol. I, Word List, Level I, 1962; vol. II, Index of English Equivalents, Level I, 1965; vol. III, Idion List, Level I, 1968; vol. IV, Dictionary of Basic (spoken) German, 1970; vol. V, World List, Level II, vol. VI, German-English Glossary of 2000 Utility Words, 1974; Basic Spoken German Grammar, 1974; Grunddeutsch: Erarbeitung und Wertung drei deutscher Korpora, 1975; Kontexta, 1976. Asst. editor Modern Lang. Journ. 1954-59; mng. editor, 1959-62; assoc. editor German Quar., 1958-62; editorial bd. Zielsprache Deutsch, 1970-72. Contbr. articles, revs. to profl. publs. Res.: 685 Cowles Rd., Santa Barbara, CA 93108.

PFEIFER, LUANNE
Writer
b. Nov. 27, Tampa, Fla.; dau. Willard George and Mary (Tierney) Malsie; B.S., Seattle Univ., 1950; Fellowship, Fletcher Sch. of Law and Diplomacy, Tufts Univ., 1978; m. James Wayne Pfeifer, Aug. 13, 1955, Malibu; children: Kathleen, b. 1956; Dianna, b. 1957; Michael, b. 1962. Career: Sports writer, Santa Monica Outlook, 1956-67; columnist, Los Angeles Times, 1968-69; senior editor, World Travel Mag. 1970; Los Angeles correspondent, Times-Mirror Mags. Awards: U.S. Ski writing award, 1969; W.B. Berry Journalism Award, 1967. Mem.: U.S. Ski Writers Assn., secty. 1969-70, v.p. So. Calif. Ski Writers Assn., 1975-76. Mem.: Malibu Hist. Soc., Am. Soc. of Journalists & Authors. Rec.: ice skating, sailing. Res.: 3224 Malibu Canyon Rd., Malibu, CA 90265.

PHELAN, THOMAS PATRICK
Former President, Pacific Stock Exchange
b. Mar. 17, 1906, Los Angeles; s. Daniel J. and Anne (Nolan) Phelan; ed. A.B. (econs.), UCLA, 1929; m. Carleen White, L.A., June 13, 1936; chil.: Marilyn, b. Oct. 28, 1937; Cloanne, b. Aug. 16, 1939; Sharon, b. July 22, 1946 (dec. July 6, 1964). Career: Asst. to secty-dir. of statistics and research, Statistical Dept., L.A. Curb Exch. 1929; mgr. Clearing House, L.A. Stock Exch. 1935, secty. 1938, v.p.-secty. 1947, exec. v.p. 1051, pres. L.A. Div., Pac. Coast Stock Exch. 1959, pres. Pac. Stock Exch., Inc. 1961-74. Mem.: govt. coms., Calif. State and L.A. C. of C.; trustee: Assn. of Independent Colls. and Univs.; Coll. of Holy Names, Oakland; dir.: L.A. Area U.S. Orgns.; Downtown Assn. of S.F.; Central City Assn. of L.A.; chmn. Parks and Rec. Comm., City of San Gabriel; com. Loyola-Marymount Univ.; S.F. C. of C.; Bond Clubs of L.A. and S.F.; Stock Exch. Club, S.F.; Amer. Soc. of Corp. Sectys.; Bankers Club, S.F.; Commonwealth Club of Calif., S.F.; Stock Exch. Club of L.A., Rotary Club of L.A., Phi Delta Theta, Alpha Kappa Psi. Republican. Roman Catholic.

PHELPS, MASON
Industrialist
b. Jan. 18, 1925, Evanston, Ill.; s. Mason and Louise (Lamb) Phelps; B.A., Yale Univ. 1948; m. Margaret Taylor Williamsville, N.Y., July 5, 1947; son, Mason, Jr., b. Sept. 26, 1948; dau., Evans Michelson, b. June 8, 1950; son, Taylor, b. June 27, 1954. Career: Pheoll Mfg. Co. 1948, plant mgr. 1950, pres. 1953 (name chg. Voi-Shan Inds., Inc.), pres-chmn. bd. VSI Corp. 1963---. Dir.: Clow Corp., Ill.; Marshall Inds., San Marino, Calif. USMC 1943-45, WWII. Clubs: Onwentsia (Ill.), Chicago, Calif., Valley Hunt. Protestant. Rec.: tennis, skiing, sailing. Res.: 480 S. Orange Grove Blvd., Pasadena, CA 91105; Office: 600 N. Rosemead Blvd., Pasa., Calif. 91107.

PHILBIN, JOSEPH R. (MICHAEL)
Insurance Agency Executive
b. May 23, 1934, Freeport, N.Y.; s. John and Mary (Rogers) Philbin; B.A., Middlebury Coll., 1956; sons, Kevin, b. 1959; John, b. 1960. Career: Special Agent, INA, 1959-61, American Casualty, 1961-62, Royal Globe, 1962-63; CNA, 1963-71; president, Cal Fed. Insurance Agency, 1971---. Pres. and dir., Calif. Assn. of Affiliated Agencies, 1974---. Res.: 30257 Via Victoria, Rancho Palos Verdes, CA; Office: 5670 Wilshire Blvd., Los Angeles, CA 90036.

PHILLIPS, RANDALL CLINGER
Educator
b. Dec. 3, 1924; Santa Maria, Calif.; s. Glenn Randall (Bishop, Meth. Ch. Rocky Mt. Area) and Ruth Phillips; B.S., USC 1946; M.Th., Sch. of Relig. 1950; D.S.T., USC 1966; m. Dorothy Dean Cooper, Feb. 14, 1968; daus.: Melinda, b. Apr. 14, 1955; Ruth, b. Sept. 28, 1951; Janet, b. Mar. 17, 1953. Career: Minister, Sherman Oaks Meth. Ch. 1949-54, Burbank First Methodist Ch. 1954-59, Wilshire Meth. Ch. 1959-78; vice-pres. United States Internat. Univ., 1978---. Lectr.: Willamette Univ. 1958; Hawaiian Isl. 1959. Supply ofcr., USN, Panama area (1943-46) WW II. Mem.: Cahuenga Masonic Lodge No. 513; Al Malaikah Shrine, 33⁰ Mason, Blue Key, Kappa Alpha. Republican. Hobby: coin collecting. Rec.: golf, swimming. Res.: 110 Solace Ct., Encinitas, CA 92024; Office: 10455 Pomerado Rd., San Diego, CA 92131.

PHILPOT, DELBERT E.
Scientist
b. Sept. 24, 1923, Loyal, Wis.; s. Lacey Delavan and Nettie Amelia Philpott; B.S., Indiana Univ., 1947, M.S., 1948; Ph.D., Boston Univ., 1963; student Oshkosh State Teachers Coll. 1941-42, 45, Syracuse Univ. 1943, Ill. Inst. Tech. 1950-51; div. Career: Research assoc., Univ. Ill. Med. Sch., Chicago, 1949-51; Head Electron Microscope Lab., Inst. Muscle Research & Marine Biol. Lab., Woods Hole, Mass. 1951-63; Prof. Biochemistry, Univ. Colo. Med. Sch., Denver, 1963-66; Head, Ultrastructure Research, Mercy Inst. Biomed. Research and co-dir., 1966; Head, Ultrastructure Lab., NASA, Ames Res. Center, Moffett Field, Calif. 1966---; dir., Mercy Inst. Biomed Research, Denver, 1968-73. Inventor Ultramicrotome, 1952; Publs.: over 140 articles in profl. journs, chpts for sci. books; pictures on covers of Science, Journ. of Applied Physics. AUS, 1942-44; ETO; Decorated Bronze Star, Purple Heart, Two Major Campaign Stars. Awarded NASA Apollo Achievement Award 1969;

Apollo 17 Achievement Award 1974; joint U.S./USSR Bio Mission Award 1976; NASA/USSR Soyuz Space Achievement Award 1978. Biological Dir. Electron Microscope Soc. of Am. 1969-72; exec. secty. 1971-72; Biol. dir., No. Calif. Soc. Electron Microscopy, 1967-70, pres. 1969-70; dir., Certification of Electron Microscopists, 1978---. Mem.: Experimental Aircraft Assn., v.p. 1978---; secty., Falmouth (Mass.) Aviation Com. 1953-59. Presbyterian. Hobbies: flying, ham radio, bldg. own airplane. Rec.: gardening. Res.: 1602 Kamsack Dr., Sunnyvale, CA 94087; Office: NASA, Ames Res. Center, Moffett Field, CA 94035.

PHILLIPS, CHARLES EDWARD
Corporate Executive
b. June 2, 1935, Ft. Smith, Arkansas; s. Mark and Anda (Wood) Phillips; B.A., 1956; m. Sue M. Whiteley, Jan. 27, 1956, Inglewood, Calif.; sons: Mark C., b. 1957; Todd H., b. 1958; Kent M., b. 1963. Career: Vice Pres., Mktg., Califone Roberts Div. Rheem Mfg. Co., 1967-68, president, 1969-72, v.p., Califone International, 1972-74; exec. v.p., Akai America Ltd., 1974---. Dir.: J.M. Nelson Co., Vancouver, B.C., Canada; Aka America Ltd. Rec.: baseball, skiing. Office: 2139 E. Del Amo Blvd., Compton, CA 90224.

PHILLIPS, EDWIN ALLEN
Professor of Botany
b. Mar. 18, 1915, Lowell, Fla.; s. William Henry and Jane (Goodman) Phillips; A.B., Colgate Univ., 1937; M.A., Univ. Mich., 1940, Ph.D., 1948; m. Margaret Ellen Knight, Jan. 16, 1942; chil.: Ellen Knight, Nancy Jane. Instr. botany Colgate Univ., Hamilton, N.Y., 1946-48; prof. botany Pomona Coll., Claremont, Calif., 1948---, chmn. dept. botany, 1973-77; vis. prof. plant ecology Univ. Mich. Biol. Sta., summers, 1955-56, 58, 70-71; cons., mem. steering com. Univ. Hawaii Fundamental Approach to Sci. Teaching Study, 1969---; sci. cons. Govt. India, AID, summers, 1964-65; mem. research adv. bd. San Dimas Exptl. Forest, 1957---; participant AID Sci. Edn. Survey, State Dept., Indonesia, 1972; researcher Kenya Nat. Parks, 1972. Served with USNR, 1941-45; comdr. Res. Recipient Wig Distinguished Prof. award, Pomona Coll., 1966. NSF Fellow Harvard, summer 1959, St. John's Coll., Oxford Univ. 1961-62. Fellow, AAAS; mem. Am. Inst. Biol. Scis. (steering com. biol. sci. curriculum study, film com., lab. innovation com), Bot. Soc. Am., Am., Brit. bryological socs., Ecol. Soc. Am., Soc. Am. Naturalists, Phi Beta Kappa (pres. local chpt. 1958, 65), Sigma Xi (pres. local chpt. 1966). Author: Methods of Vegetation Study, 1959; Field Ecology, 1964; Basic Ideas in Biology, 1971; Co-author: Basic Demonstrations in Biology, 1971; The Environment and Organisms; an Ecosystem Approach, 1971-74; revision plant sects. 4th edit. Biological Science, An Inquiry into Life, 1977. Editorial bd., Vegetatio, 1955-74. Res.: 1201 N. College Ave., Claremont, CA 91711; Office: Pomona Coll., Claremont, CA 91711.

PHILLIPS, ELEANORE ROBERTS
West Coast Editor, Vogue Magazine
b. June 26, 1910, Los Angeles; d. Wesley and Ivy (Gardner) Roberts; grad., Mt. Vernon Jr. Coll., 1930; div.; chil.: Ellie Phillips Valianos, b. Apr. 17, 1943; Franklyn Phillips, Jr., b. Nov. 7, 1945. Career: writer weekly articles for Los Angeles Times from England, 1938; writer Hollywood news for Hedda Hopper, 1940; fashion publicity, Margaret Ettinger pub. rel. office, 1940-43; fashion publicity, Paramount Pictures, 1943-44; West Coast fashion editor, Look Mag., 1944-47; West Coast editor, Jr. BAZAAR, 1947-48; GLAMOUR Mag. 1948-54; VOGUE Mag., 1954---; HOUSE & GARDEN, 1971---. Mem.: program chmn. Costume Council, L.A. County Mus., 1957-61; Colleagues, v.p. 1960-61, pres. 1969-70; fashion group, Hollywood Women's Press Club; Fashion Circle West, program chmn. 1969-71. Hobbies: reading, art. Rec.: gardening. Office: Vogue, 3921 Wilshire Blvd., L.A., CA 90010.

PHILLIPS, JOHN RICHARD
Professor of Engineering
b. Jan. 30, 1934, Albany, Calif.; s. Eric and Adele (Rengel) Phillips; B.S., Univ. Calif., Berkeley, 1956; M.Engring., Yale Univ., 1958; D.Engring., 1960; m. Joan Soyster, Mar. 23, 1957, Pasadena; daughters: Elizabeth Huntley, b. 1962; Sarah Rengel, b. 1963; Katie Hale, b. 1966. Career: Assoc. Prof. of Math., Jacksonville State Coll., Ala., 1961-62; Asst. Prof. of Engring., Harvey Mudd Coll., Claremont, 1966-68, Assoc. Prof./Prof. of Engring., and C.F. Braun Fellow

in Engring., 1968---. Dir., Engring., Clinic, 1977---; Lectr. in Chem. Engring., Cal. State Poly., Pomona, 1971; Vis. Prof., Chem. Engring., Univ. Edinburgh, 1975; Cons. Engr., Claremont Engineering Co., 1973; Research Engr., Chevron Research Co., Richmond, 1962-66; Chem. Engr., Stanford Research Inst., 1960. Cons.: Occidental Research Corp., La Verne; Occidental Oil Shale, Inc., Grand Junction, Colo.; R.J. Schoofs and Assoc., Moraga; Cyprus Mines Corp., L.A.; Lockheed Aircraft Service Co., Ontario, Calif. 1st Lt., AUS, 1960-62; Chem. Corps, CBR Combat Devel. Agcy. Registered Chemical Engr., State of Calif. Patentee: Hot Ball Desalination, 1974; Contbr. articles profl. journs. & Confs. Mem. Alpha Delta Phi, Am. Inst. of Chem. Engrs., Tau Beta Pi, Sigma Xi. Office: Harvey Mudd College, Claremont, CA 91711.

PICKERING, WILLIAM HAYWARD
Research Director
b. Dec. 24, 1910, Wellington, New Zealand; s. Albert William and Elizaebth Ann (Hayward) Pickering; ed. B.S., Calif. Inst. of Tech. 1932, M.S. (E.E.), 1933, Ph.D. (physics), 1936; m. Muriel Bowler, Pasa., Dec. 30, 1932; chil.: William Balfour, b. May 1, 1939; Mrs. Wayne (Anne Elizabeth) Mezitt, b. Mar. 27, 1943. Career: Instr., Calif. Inst. of Tech. 1936, asst. prof., assoc. prof., prof. (E.E.), 1947---; div. chief, Jet Propulsion Lab. 1951-54; dir. 1954-76; dir., Research Inst., Univ. of Petroleum and Minerals, Dhahran, Saudi Arabia, 1976---; dir. U.S. lunar and planetary missions: Ranger (first close-up pics of moon); Mariner to Venus and to Mars (first pics. Martian surface); Surveyor (first U.S. lunar soft-lander). A.F. Sci. Adv. Bd. 1945-48; chmn. IGY Working Group on Tracking and Computation, U.S. 1957-58; Army Sci. Adv. Panel, 1963-65; Author: many tech. publs. Advisor, U.S. Army and A.F.; cond. stus. Japanese balloon warfare for USAF, WW II. Awards: James Wyld Mem. Award by Amer. Rocket Soc.; Robert H. Goddard Mem. Trophy by Natl. Space Club; Crozier Gold Medal by Amer. Ord. Assn.; Spirit of St. Louis Medal by Amer. Soc. of Mech. Engrs.; Procter Prize, Sci. Research Soc. of Amer.; Magellanic Premium by Amer. Philosophical Soc.; Columbus Gold Medal, Geneva, Italy; Prix Galabert, Paris, France; Order of Merit, Italy; Distinguished Civ. Serv. Award, U.S. Army; Distinguished Serv. Medal, Natl Aeron. and Space Adm.; Natl. Medal of Sci., awarded by the President of the United States, 1975; many others. Mem.: Pres. Amer. nst. Aeron. and Astronautics, 1965-66; pres. Internat. Astronautical Fed. 1965-66; Natl. Acad. of Scis.; Natl. Acad. of Engring.; Internat. Astronautics Acad.; Amer. Assn. of Univ. Profs.; Amer. Geophysical Union; AAAS; Amer. Acad. of Arts and Scis. Unitarian. Rec.: swimming, fishing, hiking. Res.: 292 St. Katherine Dr., Pasadena, CA 91103.

PIERCE, JACK WILLIAM
Marketing Executive
b. Aug. 23, 1921, Reno, Nev.; s. Michael William and Alice (Walgren) Pierce; B.S., 1943; M.S., 1947; Engr., 1948; m. Nina Nesbit, July 19, 1949, Ontario, Calif.; sons: John Gordon, b. 1953; Peter Woodford, b. 1960. Career: Deputy Gen. Mgr., Asst. chief engr., Eastern Municipal Water Dist., 1953-58; Supr. Engring. Standards, Southern Calif. Gas Co., 1958-70; Vice Pres., Energy, Toups Corp., 1970-75; project dir., Daniel, Mann, Johnson & Mendenhall, 1975-77; dir., corporate devel., Lowry & Associates, Irvine, 1977-79, v.p. mktg., 1979---. Mem.: Visiting com., Dean Sch. of Engring., Cal. State Univ., L.A., 1965---. Contbr. tech. articles profl. journals. Lt. j.g., USNR, 1943-46; Civil Engr. Corps, Hawaii, Iwo Jima, Japan, China. Elected Fellow, Inst. for Advance Engrs. 1971. Clubs: Red Hill Country; Kiwanis, dir. 1972-75; Republican. Catholic. Rec.: golf, swimming. Res.: 622 Vista Valinda, San Clemente, CA 92672; Office: 17748 Sky Park Blvd., Irvine, CA 92714.

PIERCE, JOHN ROBINSON
Professor of Engineering
b. Mar. 27, 1910, Des Moines, Iowa; s. John Starr and Harriet (Robinson) Pierce; B.S., Calif. Inst. of Tech. 1933, M.S. 1934, Ph.D., 1936; D.Eng., Neward Coll. of Engring., 1961; D.Sc., Northwestern Univ. 1961, Yale Univ. 1963, Polytech. Inst. Brooklyn 1963, Columbia Univ. 1965, Univ. Nevada 1970, USC 1970; and others; m. Ellen Richter, Apr. 1, 1964; chil.: (previous marriage): John Jeremy, Elizabeth Anne. Career: with Bell Tel. Labs., 1936-71: as exec. dir., research, communications scis. div. (1965-71), chief work in electron devices, espec. traveling-wave tubes, microwaves, various aspects of communication;

proposed unmanned passive and active communication satellites, 1954; initiated Echo I satellite, Echo program, Telstar; Presently, prof. of Engring., Calif. Inst. of Tech., Pasa. ---: research interests concerned with energy consumption in personal transportation, auditory perception, satellite systems, synthetic aperture radar, communication. Author: 12 sci. books, numerous tech. papers, articles on popular sci. and short stores. Awarded Founders Award, Nat. Acad. of Engring., 1977; Medal of Honor, IEEE, 1975; Marconi Award, 1974; John Scott Award 1974, and S. Ballantine Medal, 1960, Franklin Inst.; H.T. Cedergren Medal, 1964; Valdemar Poulsen Gold Medal, 1963; Edison Medal, IEEE, 1963; Nat. Medal of Sci., 1963; Gen. H.S. Vanderberg Trophy, 1963; Golden Plate Award, 1962; Aerospace Man of the Yr., AF Assn. 1962; IRE Morris Liebmann Mem. Prize, 1947. Fellow: IEEE, Am. Physical Soc., Acoustical Soc. of Am.; mem.: Nat. Acad. of Engring., Am. Acad. of Arts and Sci., AF Assn., Sci. Fiction Writers of Am., Nat. Acad. of Scis., chmn engring. sect. 1975-78; Am. Philosophical Soc.; Swedish Royal Acad. of Sci. Res.: 931 Canon Dr., Pasadena, CA 91125; Office: Dept. of Electrical Engring., Calif. Inst. of Tech., Pasa., CA 91125.

PIKE, JOHN JACOB
  Business Executive
b. Mar. 18, 1912, Bakersfield; s. Percy M. and Elizabeth (Potter) Pike; bro. Thomas P. Pike; ed. (valedictorian) Harvard Mil. Sch. 1929; A.B., Stanford Univ. 1933; (div.) chil.: Mrs. Jeffie (Pike) Wesson, b. Aug. 6, 1940; John J., Jr., b. Oct. 12, 1942; Tyrone Farrar, b. Aug. 8, 1954. Career: Republic Supply Co. of Calif. 1933-61; pres. dir. J.J. Pike Corp. 1961-73; pres.-dir. Calif. Med. Centers, 1970-73; pres.-owner J.J. Pike Co. 1973---. Trustee, Claremont Men's Coll. 1948-62; dir. Security First Natl. Bank 1948-61; pres.-dir.: L.A. Municipal Art Patrons, 1954-64; dir. 1964---; pres.-dir. So. Calif. Building Funds, 1954---; dir. So. Counties Gas Co. 1962-70; Mem.: Alpha Delta Phi; Clubs: California, L.A. Country, Bohemian. Episcopalian. Hobby: photog. Rec.: golf, tennis, swim. Res.: 800 W. First St., L.A., CA; Office: 555 S. Flower St., Suite 2565, L.A., CA 90071.

PIKE, THOMAS POTTER
  Industrialist
b. Aug. 12, 1909, L.A.; s. Percy M. and Elizabeth M. (Potter) Pike; ed. Harvard Sch. 1927; A.B. (econ.), Stanford Univ. 1931; m. Katherine M. Keho, Stanford Univ., June 15, 1931; chil.: John Keho, b. July 31, 1934; Mrs. Craig S. (Josephine) Barnes, b. Apr. 22, 1937; Mrs. David (Mary Katherine) Coquillard, b. Feb. 20, 1940. Career: Republic Supply Co. of Calif. 1931-38, v.-chmn. 1958-61, chmn. 1961-65 (now Pike Corp. of Am.), chmn. 1965-69; founder, Thomas P. Pike Drilling Co. 1938, pres. 1938-53; Asst. Secty. of Def. Supply and Logistics, Wash., D.C. 1953-54; spec. asst. to Pres. Dwight D. Eisenhower, 1953-58; v.-chmn. Fluor Corp. 1969---. Dir.: Hewlett-Packard Co., Palo Alto, 1958---; Stanford Research Inst. 1961---; KCET Comm. TV 1967---; Independent Colls. of So. Calif., 1969---; Rand Corp. 1970. Mem.: chmn. Repub. Finance Com. of L.A. Co., 1949-52; chmn. Calif. Repub. Finance Com. 1953; Calif. mgr. Nixon's Presidential Campaign, 1960; pres. bd. trustees, Stanford Univ. 1961-62; pres. Master Calendar of L.A. 1964-68; pres. Alcoholism Council of L.A. 1964-68; dir. Natl. Council on Alcoholism and Alcoholism Council of Greater L.A. 1965---; pres. Recovery House for Women, 1965---; v.-chmn. bd. regents, Loyola Univ. 1967-69; chmn. Secty. of HEW's Natl. Adv. Com. on Alcoholism, 1969---; L.A. C. of C.; Merchants and Mfrs. Assn.; Alpha Delta Phi; clubs: Valley Hunt, Pasa.; Bohemian, Eldorado Country, Univ. Calif. Roman Catholic. Hobbies: music, politics. Rec.: tennis, swimming. Res.: 1475 Circle Dr., San Marino, CA 91108; Office: 611 W. 6th St., L.A., CA 90017.

PINCKNEY, EDWARD ROBERT
  Physician — Author
b. Nov. 16, 1924, Boston, Mass.; B.S., Univ. of Del. 1946; M.D., Syracuse Univ. 1948; M.P.H., Univ. of Calif., Berkeley, 1954; LL.B., 1965; m. Catherine Larkum, NYC, Sept. 1944; dau. Cathey Lee, b. July 21, 1950. Career: Intern, chief res. in internal med., United Hosp., Port Chester, N.Y. 1948-49; phys., pvt. practice internal med., Rye, N.Y. 1949; Beverly Hills, Calif. 1953---; med. ofcr., Panama Canal Health Dept. 1949-53; dir. pub. health, Napa Co., 1954-56; lectr., Sch. of Pun. Health, Univ. of Calif., Berkeley, 1955-56; assoc. prof. med-dir. med. clinic, Northwestern Univ., 1956-59; assoc. clin. prof., Loma

Linda Coll. of Med. 1959-64; attending phys., Cedars of Lebanon Hosp., L.A. Author: (books publ. by maj. publs). You Can Prevent Illness, 1960; Atlas of Common Foot Diseases of Chil. and Prevention, 1961; How to Make the Most of Your Doctor and Medicine, 1964; contrib. med. articles to Grolier Internat. Encyc. 1964; screen plays, TV shows, numerous sci. and lay articles; 3 mot. pics., incl. The Interns, The New Interns, The Handcuffed Hands; regular mag. column, Blue Print for Health; weekly book reviewer, King Feats. Syndicate, Parade of Books (throughout U.S. and foreign newspapers); co-author: (with Cathey Pinckney; Mirror of Your Mind (daily and Sun. feat. in 100 U.S. and newspapers); TV stories and scripts for Ben Casey Show; newspapers and mag. articles, incl. Saturday Review; Med. Ency. of Common Illness, 1962; The Fallacy of Freud and Psychoanalysis, 1965; Black guard Charlie (hist. biog. of Charles Pinckney, Jr., of S.C., signer, U.S. Const.), 1968; sr. ed., Journ. of AMA, 1956-59; ed. The New Physician, 1957-64; exec. dir.-chief med., ed., Audio Postgrad. courses in med., publ. Ency. Brit. Films, 1959-62; exec. ed., Trauma (med. journ. for attys.); 1962-65); assoc. ed., Phys. Mgmt. U.S. Army (1943-46), WW II; USNR Med. Corps, 1950-53; Awards: Hon. Award in Med. Journalism, Amer. Med. Writers' Assn. 1960. Mem.: Writers Guild of Amer., West (screen and TV brs.); Authors' Guild of Amer.; Natl. Assn. of Sci. Writers; L.A. Co., Calif. Med. Assn.s; dir. Am. Med. Writers Assn. 1960-65; gov.-v.p., Amer. Med. Authors, 1961---; diplomate, Amer. Bd. of Preventive Med.; Council Med. TV, Inst. Advancement Med. Communication; fellow, ACP; U.S. com., World Med. Assn.; (charter) Amer. Assn. Pub. Health Phys.; Assn. Amer. Med. Colls.; Amer. Soc. Tropical Med. and Hygiene; Amer. Pub. Health Assn.; Soc. Clib. and Exp. Hypnosis; AAAS; Authors League; AMA. Republican. Presbyterian. Office: P.O.B. P, Beverly Hills, CA 90213.

PIPER, MARVIN ANDREW
  Physician — President, Piper Medical Center
Feb. 2, 1938, New Plymouth, Idaho; s. Andrew and Zelma (Wells) Piper; gr. nephew of Jay J. Nethery (dec. 1970), v.p. Gen. Conference Seventh-Day Adventist Ch., Md.; B.A. chem., theology, Walla Walla Coll., 1960; M.D., Loma Linda Univ., 1964; med. studies, Internat. Med. Edn. Corp., 1977; m. Priscilla Gerry Kempton, June 26, 1960, Portland, Ore.; chil.: Jonathan Andrew, b. Apr. 29, 1962; Christopher James, b. July 22, 1966. Career: Rotating internship, Glendale Sanitarium and Hosp., 1965; residency in neurosurgery: Rancho Los Amigos Hisp., 1965; White Memorial Med. Center, 1966; resident physician in gen. surgery, White Memorial Med. Center, 1968-69; practicing neurosurgeon and gen. surgeon, 1969---; specialist, heart disease, 1977; bd. chmn., Piper Enterprises, 1971---; owner, pres., Piper Med. Center, 1976---. Mil.: Capt. and sr. med. officer, AUS, 1966-68; Capt., USAFR, 1969; Maj., Calif. Air Nat. Guard, USAF, 1971---(apptd. by gov.); decorated for Distinguished services, 5th Army. Recipient: AMA Physician's recognition award, cont. med. edn. 1969; diplomate: Nat. Bd. Med. Examiners, 1965; TV speaker on physical fitness with Muhammad Ali, 1977; lectrs.: sickle-cell anemia, 1977; columnist: Helping Health Get Better, Altadenian and Pasadenian, 1977. Mem.: Golden Baton Soc., Pasadena Symphony; Pasadena Arts Council; Coleman Concerts, Caltech; sponsor, Bach Festival, 1st Congregational Ch., L.A. Seventh-Day Adventist ch., ordained Deacon; choir and youth leader; assoc. pastor, Wash., 1960. Hobbies: art, music, art, antique & classic cars, ancient Roman coins. Rec.: horseback riding. Home: 598 Arbor St., Pasadena, CA; Office: 2052 N. Lake Ave., Altadena, CA.

PIQUE, Z.W.
  Corporate Executive — Engineer
b. Jan. 29, 1912, Water Valley, Ky.; s. George H. and Pearl (Weaks) Pique; B.S., Univ. of Ky. 1932; B.A. (humanities), Transylvania Coll. 1933; E.E., Univ. of Ky. Grad. Sch. 1938; grad. Sales Engring. Course, Carnegie Inst. of Tech. 1946; grad. Sales Analysis Inst. 1947; grad. Ind. Coll. of Armed Forces, 1950; grad. U.S. Army Command and Gen. Staff Coll. 1954; grad. Marketing Course, Colgate Univ. 1956; grad. Mgmt. Course, Am. Mgmt. Assn. Acad. 1957; grad. Inst. for Mgmt., Northwestern Univ. Grad. Sch. 1950; grad. U.S. Army Spec. Warfare Sch. 1967; Doctor of Humanities, London Univ., 1973; m. Constance Edith Elias, Kansas City, Mo., Dec. 26, 1946; chil.: Margaret Edith, b. Dec. 17, 1948 (dec.); Robert Lee, b. Nov. 25, 1950; William Hunter, b. Sept. 13, 1952; Bruce Alan, b. Apr. 24, 1955. Career: Ky. Utilities Co. (lighting engr., Paducah, comml. serv. engr., Maysville,

mgr. power sales, Lexington), 1934-39; lamp and lighting spec., Gen. Elec. Supply Co., Louisville, Ky. 1939-40; mgr., Westinghouse Elec. Supply Co., Johnstown, Pa., Wash., D.C., dist. mgr., Dallas, Tex. 1946-55; corp. training dir. gen. sales mgr., gen. mgr. capacitor div. Tex. Instruments Inc., Dallas, 1955-58; dir. marketing, Ind. prod. group, Hughes Aircraft Co., L.A. 1958-60; v.p. mktg., Hoffman Electronics Corp., L.A. 1960-61; v.p. (mktg.), Statham Instruments Corp., L.A. 1961-62; pres. Inter-Rep., Inc., Redondo Beach, Calif. 1962-64; v.p.-dir. Capital for Tech. Inds., Inc., Santa Monica, 1965-68; dir. mgmt. dev. AMERON, 1968-77; Management Cons., 1977---. Dir., Ind. Diversification Inst., L.A.; dir Transport Data Processing, Inc., Montecello, Calif.; dir. Sage Instruments, Inc., White Plains, N.Y.; Task Corp., Anaheim; McKee Automation Corp., North Hollywood; dir. Tasker Inds., Van Nuys; dir. Prod. Techniques Inc., Downey, Calif.; dir. Liskey Aluminum, Inc., Baltimore; Calif. Resistor Corp., Santa Monica. Registered profl. engr., Ky. 1938, Pa. 1946, Wash. D.C., Tex. 1952. Author: Survey of Library Illumination, 1932; The Controlled Materials Plan, 1942; The Produce Manager in Electronics, 1955; Selection, Training, Motivation and Control of a Direct Sales Force, 1967 (others publ. 1932-77). U.S. Army, 1941-46, 2nd Lt., Maj., Ord. Corps; exec. ofcr., Cincinnati Ord. Dist.; comdg. ofcr., Vigo Ord., Terre Haute, ind.; ord. ofcr., Base M., A.F. Western Pac., Batangus, Luzon, P.I., WW II; Col., Ord. Corps, commandant, USAR Sch., Santa Monica. Awards: Amer. Mgmt. Assn. Annual Award, 1961; Hon. Order of Ky. Cols.; listed, various natl. and internat. biog. publs. Mem.: Am. Soc. Mech. Engrs., Am. Mil. Engrs. Soc., Natl. Soc. of Profl. Engrs., Natl. Soc. of Sales Training Executives, Inst. of Elec. and Electronic Engrs., Am. Ord. Assn., Am. Mgmt. Assn., Res. Ofcrs. Assn., Assn. of U.S. Army. Illuminating Engring. Soc. Res.: 261 Rocky Point Rd., Palos Verdes Estates, CA 90274.

PITCHESS, PETER J.
Sheriff
b. Feb. 26, 1912, Salt Lake City, Ut.; s. John P. and Rena (Demos) Pitchess; B.S., Univ. of Ut., 1938; LL.B., 1940; m. Athena Takis, Salt Lake City, Feb. 27, 1938; sons: John, b. Mar. 21, 1942; Andrew, b. Dec. 4, 1943. Career: Spec. agt., FBI 1940-52; chief of security, Richfield Oil Corp., 1952-53; undersheriff, Co. of L.A. 1953-58; sheriff, 1958---. Awards: Citizen of Week, Apr. 10, 1965. Mem.: Soc. of Former Spec. Agts. of FBI; past pres., L.A. Co. Peace Ofcrs. Assn.; Gov's. Adv. Com.; Gov's. Adv. Com. on Juvenile Justice; Atty. Gen's. Adv. Com. on Criminal Statistics; Internat. Assn. of Chiefs of Police; past pres., Calif. Peace Officers' Assn.; (hon.) chmn., Community Chest Campaign, 1959; pres. So. Calif. Chpt., Arthritis & Rheymatism Found. 1959-60; exec. bd., Boy Scouts of Amer. 1960; bd. dirs., Big Bros. of Greater L.A., Inc. 1960; Rancheros Visitadores; Al Malaikah Shrine. St. Sophia Cathedral (bd. trustees). Rec.: golf, riding. Res.: L.A., CA; Office: 265 Hall of Justice, L.A., CA 90012.

PITTS, CHARLES FRANKLIN
Business Executive
b. Jan. 26, 1925, Belton, Mo.; s. P.H. and Mary (Taylor) Pitts; B.S., Central Mo. State Coll. 1949; m. Mary Anna Vest, Belton, June 8, 1947; chil.: Charles Franklin, b. Aug. 27, 1953; Debra Lynn, b. Aug. 7, 1956; Kevin Scott, b. Sept. 6, 1959. Career: Acct., Mo. Gas and Elec. Serv. Co., Lexington, 1949-51; supv. Financial Analysis and Pricing, Ford Motor Co., Aircraft Plant, Claycomo, Mo. 1951-56; controller, Learcal Div., Lear Siegler, Inc., Santa Monica, Calif. 1956-58; asst. gen. mgr. Astronics Div. 1958-65, pres. 1966-67; v.p.: Comml. Prods. Group, 1968-70, Comml. and Ind. Group, 1971-73, Climate Control and Housing Group, 1973---. USN (Am., Asiatic, PTO), 1942-46, WW II. Mem.: Am. Legion, Am. Mgmt. Assn., BPOE, Kappa Sigma Kappa, Bel-Air Country Club. Methodist. Hobby: reading. Rec.: golf, fishing. Res.: 1227 Villa Woods Dr., Pacific Palisades, CA 90272; Office: 3171 S. Bundy Dr., Santa Monica, CA 90406.

PITTS, VERA LEOLA JOHNSON
Community Leader — Professor
b. Jan. 23, 1931, Wichita, Kan.; d. Wade and Maggie (Mills) Johnson; B.A., Univ. Calif., Berkeley, 1953; M.A., Cal. State Univ., Sacto., 1962; Ph.D., Mich. State Univ., 1967; m. Leonard Edward Pitts, Feb. 22, 1952, Oakland. Career: Social worker, San Joaquin Co.

Welfare Dept., 1953-54; tchr., counselor, adminstr., Stockton Unified Sch. Dist., 1954-65; instr. Mich. State Univ., 1966-67; asst. prof., City Coll., N.Y., 1967-69; prof., Dept. Sch. Adminstrn. and Suprn., Cal. State Univ., Hayward, 1969---, acting dept. chmn. 1976, 77. Awarded Outstanding Young Woman of Am., 1966; Mott Fellowship, 1965; Danforth Found. Assoc., 1971; AAUW Travelship to Issues Conf., Kansas City, Mo. 1975; Outstanding Bay Area Woman, 1976; Rockefeller Found. fellowship 1977. Mem. AAUW, 1st v.p. Calif. div. 1978, pres. San Mateo br. 1974-75; dir. Cayote Point Mus., 1976---; UC Alumni Councillor 1973-75; dir., Child Care Coordinating Council of San Mateo Co., 1972---, pres. 1973-74; citizens advis. com. San Mateo H.S. Dist. 1974-75, Elem. Sch. Dist. 1976; AAUP; Calif. Tchrs. Assn.; Assn. for Childhood Edn.; Calif. Profs. of Edn. Adminstrn.; Pi Lambda Theat; Delta Kappa Gamma; Urban League; Foster City Tennis Club; Camaradas Bridge Club. Res.: 600 Sandy Hook Ct., Foster City, CA 94404; Office: Cal. State Univ., Hayward, CA 94542.

PITZER, KENNETH SANBORN
Educator
b. Jan. 6, 1914, Pomona; s. Russell K. and Flora (Sanborn) Pitzer; B.S., Calif. Inst. of Tech., 1935; Ph.D., Univ. Calif., Berkeley, 1937; (hon.): D.Sc., Wesleyan Univ. 1962; LL.D., Univ. Calif., Berkeley, 1963; LL.D., Mills Coll., Oakland, 1969; m. Jean Mosher, July 7, 1935, San Dimas; chil.: Ann Elizaebth, b. Nov. 6, 1936; Russell Mosher, b. May 10, 1938; John Sanborn, b. July 11, 1941. Career: Instr. through prof. of chem., Univ. of Calif., Berkeley, 1937-61, also Dean, Coll. of Chem., 1951-60; tech. dir., Maryland Research Lab., Wash., D.C., 1943-44; dir. of research, AEC, Wash, D.C., 1949-51; pres., Prof. of Chem., Rice Univ., Houston, Tex., 1961-68; pres., Prof. of Chem., Stanford Univ., 1968-71; prof. of chem., UC, Berkeley, 1971---. Trustee, Pitzer Coll., 1966---; dir., Owens-Illinois, 1967---; Nat. Acad. of Sci., chmn. Chem. Sect. 1958-61, counselor, 1964-67, 1973-76; AEC, Gen. Advis. Com. 1958-65; trustee, RAND Corp., 1962072; NASA Sci. and Tech. Advis. Com. 1964-65; dir., Fed. Reserve Bank of Dallas, 1965-68. Author: Selected Values of Physical and Thermodyanmic Properties of Hydrocarbons and Related Compounds, 2d ed. 1953; Quantum Chemistry, Prentice-Hall, Inc. 1953; Thermodynamics, with Leo Brewer, McGraw-Hill, 1961; numerous publs. on physical and theoretical chem., research, and univerity governance. Awarded Guggenheim Fellowship, 1951; Am. Chem. Soc. medals 1943, 1969, 1976; Distinguished Alumnus awards, UC, Berkeley, 1951, and Caltech. 1966; Nat. Medal of Sci., USA, 1975; Gold Medal, Am. Inst. of Chemists, 1976; Clayton Prize, Inst. of Mech. Engrs., London, 1958; Centenary Lectr., Chem. Soc., Gr. Brit. 1978; others. Fellow: Am. Acad. of Arts and Scis., Am. Physical Soc., Am. Nuclear Soc., Am. Inst. of Chemists; Am. Philosophical Soc.; Faraday Soc.; Am. Chem. Soc., Counselor. Clubs: Bohemian, S.F.; Chemists, N.Y.; Cosmos, Wash. D.C. Rec.: Sailing. Res.: 12 Eagle Hill, Berkeley, CA; Office: Univ. of California, Berkeley, CA 94720.

PLANT, DAVID NESFIELD
Hotel Executive
b. Apr. 13, 1922, Sausalito, Calif.; s. Thomas G. and Helen (Nesfield) Plant; ed. Bellarmine Coll. Prep., Calif. State Poly. Coll.; m. Nora Pomeroy, Oct. 5, 1943; chil.: Peter Nelson, b. Aug. 22, 1944; Susan Honey, b. Mar. 15, 1947; Thomas David, b. Dec. 31, 1953. Career: Gen. Mgr., Shelly Creek Mill & Timber Co., Cave Junction, Ore. 1946-48; owner-operator, Deer Creek Ranch, Selma, Ore. 1948-51; secty.-treas., Plant Shipyard Corp., Alameda, Calif. 1951-53; res. mgr., St. Francis Hotel, S.F. 1953-66; gen. mgr., Sir Francis Drake Hotel, S.F., 1966---. Adv. bd., Bayview Fed. S&L Assn. 1967---; Lt., USN Air Corps (1942-45), WW II. Mem.: pres. Louise A. Boyd Natural Sci. Mus., San Rafael, 1954-55, 1962-63; pres. Ross (Calif.) Sch. Bd. 1960-62; pres. S.F. Rotary Club, 1964-65; dir. S.F. Sym. Found. 1964-65; pres. Sales and Mktg. Execs. 1965-66; dir. Am. Red Cross, 1965-66; dir. S.F. Boys Club; pres. Calif. No. Hotel Assn. 1965-66; pres. Better Bus. Bur. 1965-67; dir. Calif. State Hotel Assn. 1966; Downtown Assn., Jr. Achievement, Bonifaces Internat., St. Francis Mem. Hosp. Assn., Drake Navigators Guild, Guardsmen, Skal; Clubs: The Mariners, Elks, Propeller, Commonwealth, Family, Inverness Yacht. Roman Catholic. Hobbies: yachting, photog. Rec.: fishing, boating, gardening. Res.: 2727 Vallejo St., S.F., CA; Office: Sir Francis Drake Hotel, 450 Powell St., S.F., CA 94101.

PLATT, JOSEPH BEAVEN
University President
b. Aug. 12, 1915, Portland, Ore.; s. William Bradbury
and Mary (Beaven) Platt; B.A., Univ. of Rochester,
1937; Ph.D., Cornell Univ. 1942; (hon.) Doctorate,
USC 1969; m. Jean Ferguson Rusk, Lexington, Mass.,
Feb. 9, 1946; chil.: Ann Ferguson, b. Aug. 20, 1947;
Elizabeth Beaven, b. Nov. 8, 1955. Career: Seaman, SS
Atlantic, Argonaut SS Lines (summer), 1933; seaman,
Amer-S. African SS Lines (summer), 1934; salesman,
Hecker Flour Co., Buffalo, N.Y. (summer), 1935;
seaman, SS Black Gull, Black Diamond SS Lines
(summer), 1936; camp pioneer, BSA,, Rochester Area
Council, Rochester, N.Y. (summer), 1937;
teacher-research asst., Physics Dept., Cornell Univ.
1937-41; spectrophotometry, Eastman Kodak Co.
Research Labs., Rochester, N.Y. (summer) 1938,
X-rays (summer), 1939; instr. Univ. of Rochester,
1941-43, asst. prof., assoc. prof., assoc. chmn., Dept.
of Physics, 1946-56 (co-designer-constructor,
240-million volt cyclotron; dir. research team which
produced mesonic atoms from which Xrays were
discovered), professor, 1951-56; staff-section chief
(radar research), Radiation Laboratory, MIT,
Cambridge, Mass. 1943-46; chief of physics br.,
Research Div., U.S. Atomic Energy Comm., Wash.,
D.C. 1949-51; cons. to Natl. Sci. Found. and U.S.
Ofc. of Ord. Research, 1953-56; pres. Harvey Mudd
Coll. 1956-76, pres. Claremont Univ. Center, 1976---;
trustee, Analytic Servs., Inc., chmn. 1962; (USAF);
trustee, Analytic Services, Inc., 1959---; chmn. 1962---,
(USAF) Arlington, Va., 1959---. Consultant to National
Defense Research Com. 1941-45; civ. serv., USAF,
introduced radar devices into combat use in European
and Pac. Theaters of Operation, 1943-46; sci. cons.,
U.S. Army Air Corps., Jan.-Sept. 1944; Mine Adv.
Com., USN (1955-61); WW II. Mem.: Com. on
physics, Natl. Research Council, 1954, com. on tables
of constants, 1956, committee on science, (UNESCO),
1960-62; Amer. Nuclear Soc. 1955-56; fellow, Amer.
Physical Soc.; Amer. Assn. of Physics Teachers; assoc.
Optical Soc. of Amer.; Fed. of Amer. Scientists; So.
Calif. Ind.-Edn. Council, 1957-69; Univ. Club of
Claremont, 1957---; Town Hall 1957---; panel on
special projects in sci. edn. Natl. Sci. Found. 1957-63;
com. chmn. 1974; chairman, Personnel Task Force,
California Com. on Medical Aid and Health, 1959-60;
American Council on Edn. 1967; governing bd., Amer.
Inst. of Physics, 1960; com. on sci., UNESCO, NAS,
1960-62; sci. adv., UNESCO Gen. Conf., Paris, 1960,
alternate del. 1962; panel on internat. sci., President's
Sci. Adv. Com. 1961-64, and 1966; adv. com. stu.
med. edn. needs, CCHE, Calif. 1962-63; trustee,
Thacher Sch., Ojai, 1962-76; bd. dirs. L.A. World
Affairs Council, 1970---; bd. trustees, Aerospace Corp.,
1971--- (vice-chmn. 1975---—; chmn. Master Plan,
Coord. Council of Higher Edn. 1971-73; trustee,
Carnegie Found. for the Adv. of Teaching, 1970-78;
director, Automobile Club of Southern Calif., 1973;
mem., Carnegie Council on Policy Stud. in Higher
Edn., 1975; Director, Bell & Howell, 1978; IEEE;
Cosmos Club, Wash.; Twilight, Bohemian, S.F.; Los
Angeles, Sunset and Calif. Clubs, Los Angeles; (hon.)
Sigma Xi, (hon.) Phi Beta Kappa, (hon.) Phi Kappa
Phi. Res.: President's House, Claremont University
Center, Claremont, CA; Office: 100 Harper Hall,
Claremont University Center, Claremont, CA 91711.

PLESSET, ERNST HAECKEL
Corporate Executive
b. Aug. 17, 1913, Pittsburgh, Pa.; s. Benjamin M. and
Anna (Swartz) Plesset; ed. B.S., Univ. of Pittsburgh,
1933; A.M. Harvard Univ. 1939, Ph.D. 1941; m.
Pauline Riedeburg Mills, Las Vegas, Nev., May 5,
1959; chil.: Mrs. Daniel (Sarah Jean) Quillen; Julius
L., Mark J. Mills, Ann Mills. Career: Physicist,
Manhattan Dist., Berkeley, Calif. 1942-43; physicist to
research mgr., research labs., Douglas Aircraft Co.,
Santa Monica, 1943-47; chief physics div., Rand Corp.
Santa Monica, 1947-56; cons. 1957-61; exec. dir.,
Devel., Westinghouse Elec. Co., Pittsburgh, Pa.
1956-57; pres. E.H. Plesset Assocs., Santa Monica,
1957-64, chmn. bd. 1957-67; pres. Capital for Tech.
Inds. Inc., Santa Monica, 1961-67; chmn.-chief exec.
1961-67; chmn. CapTech. Inc., 1967---. Chmn. bd.
regents, Immaculate Heart Coll., L.A. 1969-71. Cons.
Ofc. of Secty. Def. 1949-52; Technological Capabilities
Panel, Sci. Adv. Com. to the Pres. 1954-55; Nuclear
Task Force Adv. Com. on Disarmament to Hon.
Harold Stassen, 1955-57; Sci. Adv. Bd. to Chief of
Staff and Secty., USAF, 1957-63; chmn. Ad Hoc.
coms., chmn. Nuclear Panel; v.p.-trustee, Isotope
Found, Inc. 1959---; cons. to Dir. of Def. Research
and Engring. 1961-65; energy conversion com., United
Aircraft Corp. 1962-65; Motor Vehicle Pollution
Control Bd., State of Calif. 1962-67. Chmn. 1966-67.

Awards: Dept. of A.F. Decoration for Exceptional Civ.
Serv. to Sci. Adv. Bd. 1964. Mem.: fellow, Am. Phys.
Soc. Res.: 309 Manuella Ave., Woodside, CA 94062.

PLETSCH, MARIE ELEANOR
Plastic Surgeon
b. May 3, 1938, Walkerton, Ont., Canada; d. Ernest
and Olive Pletsch; M.D., Univ. Toronto, 1962; m.
Ludwig Breiling, M.D., Aug. 25, 1967, San Francisco;
children: John, b. 1969; Michael, b. 1973; Anne, b.
1976. Career: Internship, Cook Co. Hosp., 1962-63,
Gen. Surg. Residency, 1963-64; Residency, St. Mary's
Hosp., 1964-66; plastic surg. residency, St. Francis
Hosp. 1966-69; pvt. practice plastic surgery, Santa
Cruz, 1969---. Office: 3003 Salisbury Lane, Santa
Cruz, CA 95065.

POAGE, ROY NORMAN
Company President
b. Sept. 12, 1918, Weaverville, Calif.; s. Levi Price and
Alice Lillian Poage; B.S., mech. engr., Univ. Calif.,
Berkeley, 1940; m. Lilliam Swacina, Dec. 27, 1959,
Porguguese Bend, Calif. Career: Sales engr., Pameco
Aire, San Francisco, 1948-62, v.p. sales, 1962-69,
president, Pameco-Aire, 1969---; pres., chmn. bd.,
Pameco-Aire Asia, Pte., Ltd., Licensed Profl. Engr.,
State of Calif. 1st Sgt., AUS ---1966. Mem. Sales &
Mktg. Execs. Assn., 1964---. Hobbies: gardening, sports.
Res.: 2323 Warner Range Ave., Menlo Park, CA
94022; Office: 700 Dubuque Ave., So. San Francisco,
CA 94080.

POKRAS, SHEILA FRANCES
Judge
b. Aug. 5, 1935, Newark, N.J.; d. Moses J. and
Pauline Gabrelle; B.S., Temple Univ., Philadelphia,
1957; J.D., Pepperdine Coll. of Law, 1969; m.
Norman Martin Pokras, Sept. 11, 1954, Newark, N.J.;
children: Allison Ruth, b. May 25, 1959; Andrea
Ellen, b. May 1, 1961; Laurence Neal, b. Dec. 7,
1964. Career: Tchr., 1957-59; lawyer, 1970;
Councilwoman, City of Lakewood, Calif., 1972-76;
apptd. (Gov. E. Brown, Jr.) Judge of the Municipal
Ct., Long Beach, 1978---. Democrat; mem. State
Central Com.; Calif. del. Demo. Nat. Conv. 1976.
Jewish. Rec.: jogging. Res.: 3960 Boulton Dr.,
Lakewood, CA 90712; Office: 415 W. Ocean Blvd.,
Long Beach, CA 90801.

POLLARD, RUTH M.
Bank Administrator
b. Oct. 27, 1918, Meridian, Idaho; d. Dr. Frank G.
and Marie Josephine (LeGrand) Burkhardt; student,
Oregon State Coll., Phoenix Coll.; Certificate, Am.
Inst. of Banking; m. Herbert R. Pollard, Nov. 7, 1937;
Caldwell, Idaho; children: David L., b. 1940; Pamela
C. (Mrs. Neil E. Vadnais), b. 1944. Career: with U.S.
National Bank of Portland, Ore., 1953-57; Operations
Ofcr., Arizona Bank, Phoenix, 1957-63; Asst. Cashier,
Bank of Yuma, 1963-69; Asst. Mgr. Santa Barbara
Nat. Bank, Montecito, 1969---. Mem.: Nat. Assn. of
Bank Women, Inc., group chmn. 1978; past pres., Bus.
& Profl. Women's Club, Yuma, Ariz.; 1968 Woman of
the Year, Yuma; mem. (first woman) Credit Workers
Internat., Santa Barbara, 1978---. Episcopalian.
Hobbies: antiquing, horseback riding. Res.: 1167
Tunnel Rd., Santa Barbara, CA 93105; Office: 1030
Coast Village Rd., Santa Barbara, CA 93103.

POLLOCK, JOHN P.
Attorney at Law
b. Apr. 28, 1930, Sacramento; s. George and Irma
(Phleger) Pollock; A.B., Stanford Univ., 1942; J.D.
Harvard Law Sch., 1948; m. Juanita Gossman, Oct.
26, 1945, Stanford Univ.; children: Linda P. (Fellows),
b. 1948; Madeline P. (Chiotti), b. 1949; John P., Jr.,
b. 1962; Gordon G., b. 1944. Career: Partner, law
firm Musick, Peeler & Garrett, 1953-60; partner firm
Pollock, Williams & Berwanger (and predecessor firms),
1960---. Trustee, Pitzer Coll., 1968-76, The Jones
Found. 1969---, Good Hope Med. Fdn. 1974---, Los
Angeles Co. Bar Assn. 1961-66. AUS, 1942-45. Pres.,
Los Angeles Area Council, BSA, 1971. Clubs:
California, El Niguel Golf. Protestant. Res.: 1021 Oak
Grove Ave., San Marino, CA; Office: 800 W. 6th St.,
Los Angeles, CA 90017.

POLSKY, RICHARD M.
Management Consultant
b. Jan. 24, 1904, Akron, Oh.; s. Harry O. and
Fannye M. Polsky; ed. grad. Culver Mil. Acad., 1922;

grad. Yale Univ. 1927; m. Margaret Porter, Montgomery, Ala., Oct. 5, 1944; chil.: Sally, Richard M., Jr., Paul and Patty Ann. Career: v.p., The A. Polsky Co., Akron, Oh. 1927-41; pres.-owner, Trenwith's Inc., 1946-66; mgmt. cons., 1966---. Bd. dirs., Santa Barbara Natl. Bank. Capt., USAAF (1942-46), WW II. Awards: Man of the Yr., Santa Barbara, 1954. Mem.: pres. Santa Barbara Retail Merchants Assn. 1949-50; pres. Santa Barbara C. of C. 1954-55; (life) bd. dirs., Salvation Army; bd. dirs., Santa Barbara Mus. of Art; bd. dirs., Community Chest; Better Bus. Bur.; Family Serv. Agcy.; Hillside House (Cerebral Palsy); chmn. Easter Seal Campaign, 1959; bd. dirs.-treas., Univ. of Calif. Affiliates, Santa Barbara; bd. dirs. Univ. Club, Santa Barbara; Mason, Coral Casino, Montecito Country Club. Republican. Hobby: photog. Rec.: fishing, swimming. Res.: 1424 La Vereda Lane, Santa Barbara, CA; Office: 1014 Anacapa St., Santa Barbara, CA 93101.

POMEROY, FRANCES MUIR
   Poet — Civic Leader
b. June 23, 1902, Farmington, Wash.; d. Alexander and Margaret Agnes (Beattie) Muir; ed. Calif. schs.; teachers diploma, UCLA; m. Hugh R. Pomeroy, 1923 (dec. 1961); chil.: Mrs. Denis E. (Helen Margaret) Sullivan; grandchil.: Mary Frances (N.J.); Career: Piano artist, writer and poet; introduced Pathfinder method of character devel. in pun. schs.; dir. Tujunga and N. Hollywood vacation schs.; leader, PTA, pres. Tujunga-Sunland Coord. Council (secured clubhouse and 5-acre addition to Sunland Park); chmn. com.-pioneer (6 yrs.) in est. L.A. City John Steven McGroarty Park and Rec. Center (nstrumental in preserving late Calif. Poet Laureate John Steven McGroarty's home, hist lib. and landmark), Tujunga, Calif. 1954; chmn. com., annual Star of Bethlehem Parade, N. Hollywood, Dec. 1954; chmn. com.-est. Jim Jeffries (world's heavyweight champion; dec. Mar. 3, 1953) Barn as permanent landmark, Knott's Berry Farm Ghost Town, Buena Park, 1955; active, Cahuenga Pass Park (10 yrs.); many other civic and hist. projs., incl. erection of bronze Statues of Gen. Pico and Fremont at Campo de Cahuenga, El Camino Real Bell, 1972, and El Paseo de Cahuenga Park, 1972. Author: (poem) Tujunga, selected and exhibited at New York World's Fair; (stage play of early Calif. Hist.) Sister Elsie in Tujunga; (book) Catholic School Plays, 1941; writer-dir., revival of John Steven McGroarty's Mission Play, 1950; writer, The Nativity and Ten Commandments (dramatized by chil. of First Meth. Ch., N. Hollywood); also Christmas plays, benefit pgm. for Dutch chil. 1949. Mem.: (past) pres. Roosevelt PTA; Landmarks chmn., N. Hollywood Woman's Club; Hollywood Browning Soc.; Chaparral Poets, McGroarty chpt.; (past) chmn. hist. and landmarks, Studio City Civic Club; chmn. Mission Plays-landmarks, chmn., San Fernando Valley Hist. Soc., pres. 1958-63; using live baby as Jesus, produced her Nativity drama at Toluca Lake Methodist Ch., 1976. Donor of Thomas Edison bas-relief to Lankersheim school, No. Hollywood, and bronze bust of Lincoln to Burbank, 1975, both creations of noted sculptor, Henry Van Wolf. 7th yr. as pres., Susanna Wesley Guild, Methodist Ch., No. Hollywood, 30th yr. as Cal. Heritage chmn. No. Hollywood Women's Club; hist. and landmarks com.-publicity chmn., Lankersheim Pioneers of N. Hollywood. Methodist (historian, dir. Jr. Ch., N. Hollywood). Hobby: piano, poetry, philately. Res.: 11332 Otsego St., No. Hollywood, CA 91601.

POMEROY, GARY WARREN
   Marketing Executive
b. June 10, 1938, Pasadena; s. William S. and Gladys A. Pomeroy; B.A., Occidental Coll., 1960; Heritage Found. Fellowship, 1959; m. Melinda Jane Van Ide, Nov. 11, 1960, Los Angeles; chil.: Bradley Warren, b. June 8, 1963; Jennifer Lee, b. Feb. 13, 1966. Career: Sales rep., Spreckles Sugar Co., L.A., 1960-63; McKinley Equip. Corp., L.A. 1963-64; sales mgr. and rep., Skyline Corp., Hemet, 1965-67; gen. mgr. and dir. mktg., Redman Western Corp., City of Industry, 1967-70; v.p. and dir. of sales, Kaufman & Broad Home Systems, L.A. 1970-73; dir. of mktg., v.p. mktg., Golden West Homes, Santa Ana, 1973---. Guest lectr.: Cal. State, Fullerton. Author: How to Successfully Sell New and Resale Manufactured Homes, 1977; columnist, contbr. numerous trade publs., L.A. Times, Orange Co. Register. Awarded J.E. Wells Meml. Award for serv. to Industry, 1977. 1st Lt., Calif. Army Nat. Guard, 1960-66. Dir., Recreation Vehicle Indus. Assn. 1976-77; v. chmn., Western Regional Bd. of Govs. 1976-77; chmn. mktg. com., Western Manufactured Housing Inst., 1976---. Mem.: Kappa

Sigma frat., 1957-60; Delta Upsilon; Inst. of Residential Mktg., Nat. Assn. of Home Bldrs. Rec.: tennis. Res.: 2907 Ebbtide Rd., Corona del Mar, CA 92625; Office: 1308 E. Wakeham St., Santa Ana, CA 92705.

POPE, ALEXANDER H.
   County Assessor
b. June 4, 1929, NYC; s. Clifford H. and Sarah (Davis) Pope; A.B. with honors., Univ. of Chicago, 1948; J.D., Phi Beta Kappa, Coif, 1952; chil.: Virginia, b. July 14, 1959; Stephen, b. Oct. 17, 1957; Daniel, b. Jan. 4, 1963. Career: admitted to practice in Ill. 1952, Repub. of Korea 1963, Calif. 1955, U.S. Supreme Ct. 1970. Assoc. law offices of David Ziskind, L.A., 1955; Partner, firm of Shadle, Kennedy & Pope, L.A., 1956; Partner, Fine & Pope, L.A., 1957-78; legislative secty., Gov. of Calif., 1959-61; L.A. Co. Assessor, 1978---. Contbr. Univ. of Chicago Law Review 1951, 52. Served AUS, 1952-54, Seoul, Korea. Mem. Calif. Highway Commn., 1966-70; mem. L.A. Bd. of Airport Commrs., 1973-78, pres. 1975; pres., Inglewood Dist. Bar Assn., 1967; Westchester Mental Health Clin., 1963; pres., Univ. of Chicago Alumni Club of Gr. L.A. 1970-71. Vice Chmn., L.A. Co. Democratic Central Com., 1958-59; nat. bd. mem. Vols. for Stevenson 1952. Rec. tennis, hiking. Res.: 870 Hilgard Ave., Suite 407, L.A., CA 90024; Office: 500 W. Temple St., Rm. 320, L.A., CA 90012.

POPE, OPAL
   Manufacturing Company Executive
b. Oct. 29, 1918, Morris, Okla.; dau. Jacob and Ethel Schweikhard; student, Tulsa Univ.; m. Thomas Pope (dec.); sons: Thomas Lee, Ronald Berton. Career: Employee Rels., Grayson Heat Control, 1945; secty., treas., Foodcraft Products, 1946-51; controller, secty. treas., Armored Luggage Mfg. Co., Hawthorne, 1951---. Mem.: Soroptimist Club, Inglewood. Rec.: dancing. Res.: 104 Via Sego, Redondo Beach, CA 90277; Office: 12730 Yukon Ave., Hawthorne, CA 90250.

POSLEY, BETTY R.
   Artist — Portrait Painter
b. May 7, 1913, Bottineau, N. Dak.; d. John Clayton (early soil conservationist) and Helen Barbara (Brown) Russell; grad., N. Dak. State Coll., Fargo, 1936; student, Chouinard Art Inst., 1938-40; m. David Robert Posley, Aug. 31, 1941, Madison, Wis.; chil.: Sandra (Cannaday), b. Dec. 2, 1946; David Robert, 2nd., b. July 4, 1949. Career: Comml. art. for Powers, Minneapolis, 1940; on staff: Tiche-Goettinger, Dallas, 1942-43; Brandeis, Omaha, 1945-46; Halliburton's, Okla. City, 1951-53; Rothschild's, Okla. City, 1953-56; freelance comml. artist, 1940---; traditional style, oil paintings, noted for portraits; recipient: many awards incl. gold medal award, Valley Artists' Guild, 1975; 1st awards: Friday Morning Club, 1975-76; Ebell Club, 1975-76. Mem.: Phi Mu Soro.; v.p., Valley Artists' Guild, 1972---; treas., 1974---. Hobby: sewing, travel. Home-Studio: P.O. Box 267, Jamestown, CA 95327.

POSPISIL, RICHARD E.
   Board Chairman, Telecommunications Technology, Inc.
b. Nov. 22, 1931, Cedar Rapids, Iowa; s. Earl and Alma (Pudil) Pospisil; B.S., Iowa State Univ., 1957; m. Barbara Weaverling, 1952, Riverside; chil.: Lisa, b. July 1953; Jane, b. Mar. 1956; Donald, b. June 1957; Sara, b. Jan. 1960. Career: project engr., Lockheed R&D Labs., 1957-61; supr. space communications, Watkins Johnson, 1961-65; Dir. engring., Sierra Philco Ford, 1965-69; co-founder, pres. and chmn. of bd., Telecommunications Technology, Inc., Sunnyvale, 1969---. Original concept, design: digital envelope delay test set 1966; estab. Space Communications sect., Watkins Johnson 1961; patents: modular enclosure for electronic instruments 1971 and Duty cycle gate for PAM System 1962. Recipient: Outstanding citizen award, Ford Motor Co. 1967. Served USMC, 1951-53. Mem.: IEEE, 1955---; Alpha Tau Omega, 1950---; Am. Elec. Assn. (WEMA), 1958---; Jr. C. of C. Los Altos, 1961-65, pres. 1962-63; Eta Kappa Nu, 1956---; Tau Beta Pi, 1967---. Mem. Los Altos Planning session & archtl. review com. 1965-68. Mt. View Presbyterian Ch.; clerk session 1967-68; chmn. bd. deacons, 1965-66. Hobbies: stamps, photog. Rec.: sailing, skiing (snow, water), hiking. Home: 10230 Scenic, Cupertino, CA 95014; Office: 555 Del Rey Ave., Sunnyvale, CA 94086.

POSSONY, STEFAN THOMAS
Writer — Lecturer — Editor
b. Mar. 15, 1913, Vienna, Austria, naturalized U.S. citizen; s. Ernst and Hermine (Siller) POssony; Matura, Vienna, 1931; Ph.D., Univ. of Vienna, 1935; LL.D. (hon.), Lincoln Univ.; hon. Academician of Chunghua Acad., Repub. of China; m. Regina Golbinder, 1961, Wash., D.C.; dau. Andrea Michelle (Ross), b. Feb. 1944. Career: special adviser, USAF, Wash., D.C., 1946-62; prof. internat. rels., grad. sch., Georgetown Univ., Wash., D.C., 1946-61; Sr. Fellow, Hoover Inst. on War, Revolution and Peace, 1969---. Mem. faculty, Nat. War Coll., 1952; CB5, foreign language spec. 1942-43; Psychological Warfare Spec., Office of Naval Intelligence, 1943-46. Awarded Exceptional Civilian Service Decoration, AF, 1959; Bundesverdienstkreuz I. Klasse, 1969; Order of Brilliant Star, Repub. of China, 1972. Assoc., Foreign Policy Research Inst., Phila., 1955---; Cons.: USAF, White House, 1976, Govt. of Japan, 1977. Author: Book (many pub. in 4 languages), Chpts., Articles (too numerous to list). Secty., Am. Conservative Union, 1976---. Roman Catholic. Res.: 1370 Montclaire Way, Los Altos, CA 94022; Office: Hoover Institution, Stanford, CA 94305.

POTOLSKY, ABRAHAM ISAAC
Physician
b. Sept. 1, 1940, Brooklyn, N.Y.; s. Aaron and Celia (Goldberg) Potolsky; B.S., cum laude, Brooklyn Coll., 1961; M.D. summa cum laude, State Univ. of N.Y., 1965; m. Greta Boxer, Nov. 23, 1964, Brooklyn, N.Y.; sons: Matthew David, b. 1966; Adam Steven, b. 1970. Career: Intern and Med. Resident, Peter Bent Brigham Hosp., Boston, 1965-67; Sr. Med. Resident, Stanford Univ., 1969, Hematology fellow 1970-72; Internist and Hematologist, Sansum Med. Clin., Santa Barbara, 1972---; Dir., Clinical Cancer Research, Sansum Med. Research Found. Mil.: Epidemic Intelligence Ofcr. Leukemia Sect., Center for Disease Control, Atlanta, Ga. 1967-69. Contbr. articles to med. journals. Mem.: AMA, CMA, Alpha Epsilon Pi, Alpha Omega Alpha. Rec.: surfing. Res.: 1757 Glen Oaks Dr., Santa Barbara, CA 93108; Office: 317 W. Pueblo, Santa Barbara, CA 93102.

POTTER, GEORGE KENNETH
Artist
b. Feb. 26, 1926, Bakersfield, s. Howard E. and Edythe (Keast) Potter; B.A., sculpture, San Francisco State Univ., 1974; student, Acad. of Art, S.F.; Acad. Frochot, Paris, France; m. Heliodora Carneiro de Mendonca, July 30, 1954, SS. Argentina (at sea); dau. Helen Marcia, b. 1955; m. 2d. Ruth Mary Griffen, Aug. 4, 1962, Sacramento; children: Katherine Werle, b. 1963; Claire Lorraine, b. 1966; Cynthia Ann, b. 1970. Career: Art Director, McCann-Erickson, Rio de Janeiro, Brazil, 1954-55; Johnson & Lewis, San Francisco, 1957; Michelson Advt., Palo Alto, 1959-60; Pres. West Coast Watercolor Soc. 1968-69. USMCR, 1944-46; commended for service with Naval Hdqtrs., Initial Landing Japan. Works: Triptych stained glass, Moffitt Hosp. U.C. San Francisco, 1976; Dome of stained glass and resin, Hale Mem. Gallery of Soc. of Calif. Pioneers, Civic Center, S.F. 1974; Mural for Dept. of Motor Vehicles, Oakland Coliseum Br. 1975; Murals, Moore Bus. Forms, Oakland 1969; Town Hall Mural, Corte Madera, 1968; murals, Macy's of Calif. Sacto. 1963, San Mateo 1964, Stockton 1965; Olympic Club, Foyer of Lakeside CC 1960; Au Vieux Logis, Paris murals 1951; easel paintings in collections worldwide, 1948---. Solo shows: Rotunda Gallery of the City of Paris 1949, Maxwell Galleries 1958, Maxwell Galleries, 1962, Marquoit Galleriew 1973, San Francisco; Palo Alto Cultural Center 1977; Gallerie 8, Rotunda, 1952, Paris; Francis Young Gallery, Ross, 1953; Univ. Santa Clara and Coll. of Marin, 1958; Univ. of Calif. Berkeley, Rosacrucian Mus., San Jose, 1959; Gallery 5, Santa Fe, N.M. 1960; Brazilian-Am. Inst., Brazil, 1955. Rec.: cycling. Res.: 105 Sonora Way, Corte Madera, CA 94925.

POUND, LELAND EARL
Newspaper Editor
b. July 23, 1945, Chico, Calif.; s. Raymond Lyons and Jessie Ruth (Globe) Pound; B.A., Univ. Calif. Riverside, 1967; grad. student, Brigham Young Univ. Career: Asst. mgr., J.J. Newberry Co., Buena Park, 1968-69; Reporter, Daily News-Tribune, Fullerton, 1968-70; editor, News-Times, Placentia, 1970-77; editor, Newport Harbor Ensign, Newport Beach, 1977---. Secty.-treas., Pathfinder Publs., Inc. 1975-77. Mem.: Kiwanis Club of Placentia; YMCA, Placentia Community Chmn. 1976-77; Orange Co. Calif.

Genealogical Soc., ed. 1971-75, 1978---. Republican. Presbyterian. Hobbies: genealogy, stamp collecting. Res.: 110 Orange Grove Ave., Placentia, CA 92670; Office: 2721 E. Coast Hwy., Corona del Mar, CA 92625.

POWER, JOHN B.
Partner, O'Melveny & Myers
b. Nov. 11, 1936, Glendale, Calif.; s. Halbert J. and O' Fyrn (Feaster) Power; A.B. (magna cum laude), Occidental Coll. 1958; J.D., NYU Sch. of Law, 1961; m. Ann M. Durfey, Downey, Calif., June 17, 1961; sons: Grant, b. May 20, 1962; Mark, b. Dec. 2, 1963; Boyd, b. Mar. 1, 1967. Career: Atty. at law, 1961---; partner, O'Melveny & Myers, L.A. Mem.: Sigma Alpha Epsilon, Phi Beta Kappa, L.A. Ath. Club. Res.: 946 S. Madison, Pasadena, CA 91106; Office: 611 W. Sixth St., L.A., CA 90017.

POWER, ROBERT HARBISON
Restaurateur — Historian — Civic Leader
b. Apr. 19, 1926, Woodland, Calif.; s. Edwin Ignatius and Helen (Harbison) Power; ed. Vaca Valley Grammar Sch.; Vacaville Union H.S.; A.A., S.F. City Coll. 1948; m. Margaret Casey, S.F. June 25, 1949; chil.: Diane Marie, b. Oct. 29, 1950; Mark Robert, b. Sept. 24, 1952; Linda Ann, b. Oct. 31, 1955; Julie Ellen, b. Aug. 14, 1959; John Casey, b. Aug. 16, 1962; Brian Edward, b. March 15, 1966. Career: Partner, Nut Tree (world-famous restaurant), Nut Tree, Calif. 1948---; treas. Power Land, Inc. 1954---; Chmn. bd. Buttes Gas & Oil Co. 1961---. Author: Portus Novae Albionis Rediscovered; Pioneer Skiing in Calif., publ. for VIII Winter Olympics in Squaw Valley; Francis Drake and S.F. Bay: A Beginning of the British Empire, UC Davis, 1974; orig.-ed., Solano Co. Hist. Soc. Note Book (mo. publ. 18 yrs.). USAR 1943; Pvt. Inf. 1944-45; Company I, 358th Reg., 90th Div., Ger. (1945), WW II. Awards: Purple Heart, Combat Inf. Badge and European Theater Ribbon and two battle stars; Award of Merit, Am. Assn. for Local and State Hist. Mem.: Solano Co. Planning Comm. (12 yrs.); Press Club of S.F., Calif. Heritage Council, Solano Co. Hist. Soc., Pres., Calif. Hist. Soc., 1976; (7000 mem.) Book Club of Calif., Book Club of Sacto., Commonwealth Club of Calif., Republican (alternate del. to 1956 Repub. Natl. Conv., del. 1960; v.-chmn. No. Calif. Eisenhower-Nixon Campaign; treas. Repub. State Central Com. of Calif.; state pres., Calif. Repub. Assembly). Roman Catholic. Hobby: hist. research. Res.: Nut Tree Rd., Nut Tree, CA; Office: Nut Tree, CA 95688.

POWERS, MALA
Actress
b. Dec. 20, 1931, San Francisco; d. George Evart and M. Dell (Thelen) Powers; stu. Univ. Cal. at L.a.; pupil Michael Chekhov; m. M. Hughes Miller, May 17, 1970; 1 son by previous marriage, Toren Michael Vanton. Motion picture appearances incl. Cyrano de Bergerac, 1950, Outrage, Edge of Doom, Yellow Mountain, Bengazi, Tammy, Daddy's Gona A'Hunting; stage prodns. include Absence of a Cello, 1964-65, Hogan's Goat, Night of the Iguana, Bus Stop, Far Country, The Rivalry; also starred radio and TV prodns. including Lux Radio Theater, This is Your FBI, Cisco Kid, Hazel, Man from Uncle, G.E. Theater, Bonanza, Ironside, Perry Mason, Owen Marshall; co-star with Anthony Quinn in The Man and the City, 1971-72; lectr. in field. Entertainer troops, USO, Korea 1951-52; chmn. So. Calif. Mother's com. March of Dimes, 1972-74. Mem. Acad. Motion Picture Arts and Scis. (mem. fgn. film com.), Nat. Acad. TV Arts and Scis., ANTA (v.p., exec. com. 1974000). Editor The Secret Seven and the Grim Secret; The Secret Seven and the Old Fort Adventure, 1972. Mem. Unity Sch. Christianity. Res.' 4317 Forman Ave., No. Hollywood, CA 91602; Office: 1270 Ave. of Americas, Suite 2212, NYC, NY 10020.

PRAGER, ELLIOT DAVID
Surgeon
b. Sept. 10, 1941, NYC; s. Benjamin and Sadye Prager; A.B., Dartmouth Coll., 1962; M.D., Harvard Univ., 1966; m. Phyllis Warner, July 1, 1967, NYC; children: Rebecca, b. 1969; Sarah, b. 1971; Katherine, b. 1973. Career: Surgical Resident, Roosevelt Hosp., 1966-71; Surgical Fellow, Lahey Clin., 1971-72; Staff Surgeon, USN Hosp., Phila. (Lt. Comdr.) 1972-74; Surgeon, Sansum Med. Clinic, Santa Barbara, CA 9174---. Rec.: tennis, jogging. Res.: 1685 E. Valley Rd., Santa Barbara, CA; Office: 317 W. Pueblo, Santa Barbara, CA 93102.

PRATER, ARTHUR NICKOLAUS
Consultant
b. Oct. 22, 1909, Driscoll, N. Dak.; s. William Julius and Cora Elizabeth (Richards) Prater; A.B., UCLA 1932; M.S., Calif. Inst. of Tech. 1933, Ph.D. 1935; m. Phoebe Thelma MacFarlane, Ventura, Calif., Nov. 7, 1936; son: Nowland Reichardt, b. Nov. 11, 1940. Career: Research assoc., Calif. Inst. of Tech. 1938-41; research chem., Western Regional Research Lab. 1941-45; tech. dir., Gentry Div., Consolidated Foods Corp. 1945-55; bd. dirs.-exec. com. 1950-64, pres. 1956-64; v.p. Consolidated Foods Corp., 1957-64, cons. 1964---. Pres., Research and Devel. Assocs., Food and Container Inst. for Armed Forces, 1953-54; treas. Inst. of Food Technologists, 1958---. Awards: Food Man of the Yr. Award, So. Calif. Sect., Inst. of Food Technologists, 1960. Res.: 17400 Weddington St., Encino, CA.

PRATOR, RALPH
President Emeritus, Cal State University, Northridge
b. Nov. 16, 1907, La Veta, Colo.; s. Charles and Isabella (Duncan) Prator; A.B., Univ. of Colo., 1929, M.A., 1933; Ed.D., Univ. of Calif., Berkeley, 1947; m. Lois Skinner, Denver, Colo., June 17, 1937; chil.: Bruce Bradley, b. Dec. 22, 1944; Lewis Charles, b. Nov. 30, 1946; Roxanna, b. June 7, 1948. Career: Prin.-ath. coach, Flagler (Colo.) H.S., 1929-30, McAlister (N.Mex.) H.S., 1931-33; ath. coach-soc. sci. teacher, Huerfano Co. H.S., Walsenburg, Colo. 1933-34; Del Norte (Colo.) H.S. 1934-36; ath. dir.-dean of men, Mesa Coll., Grand Junction, Colo. 1936-40; dir. of admissions and personnel activities-dir. of summer sessions, Univ. of Colo., Boulder, 1940-50; pres. Bakersfield Coll., Bakersfield, Calif. 1950-58; visiting lectr. Fresno State Coll. (summers) 1952, 53, 54, 55, visiting prof., 1956, 1957; pres. San Fernando Valley State Coll., Northrdige, 1958-68; pres. emeritus-prof. Calif. State Univ., Northridge, 1968. Dir. Valley Fed. S&L Assn. Comdr.-Personnel Rels. Ofcr., USN Air Sta., Quonset Point, R.I. (1942-45), WW II; Capt., USNR. Awards: Man of Yr. in Edn., San Fernando Valley, 1968; Distinguished Alumni Medal, Univ. of Colo. 1973; Distinguished Serv. Cit., Sigma Phi Epsilon. Mem.: pres. L.A. City Dev. Assn. 1970; dir. Valley Council, BSA; dir. Child Guidance Clinic; Rotary Internat.; Sigma Phi Epsilon, Phi Delta Kappa. Hobby: golf, gardening. Res.: 8934 Enfield Ave., Northridge, CA; Office: 18111 Nordhoff St., Northridge, CA.

PREOBRAJENSKA, VERA N.
Composer — Musician
b. Apr. 27, 1926, San Francisco; d. Nicholas A. and Tatiana N. Preobrajensky; student, Mills Coll., Univ. Calif., Berkeley; B.A., 1953, M.A., 1972, Ph.D., 1973; pvt. studies with Darius Milhaud, Ernst Bloch, Roger Sessions, Frederick Jacobi, Ernst von Dohnonyi, Alexander Tcherepnine, Dmitre Shostakovich. Career: Dir. of Musical Artists of America Concert Series, 1959-61; pianist for ballet classes, Women's Physical Edn. Dance Dept., Univ. Calif. Berkeley 1965-68, and Univ. Calif., Santa Cruz, 1977---. Music publications: Russian Liturgical Chorales, 1961-71. Mem. American Soc. of University Composers, American Women Composers, Nat. Composers USA. Rel.: Russian Orthodox. Hobby: creative writing, poetry, short stories, novels. Rec.: gardening. Res.: 935 High St., Santa Cruz, CA 95060.

PRESLEY, PHYLLIS LOUISE
Physician
b. Aug. 4, 1920, De Ruyter, N.Y.; d. Hanserd K. Presley, Atty. (dec.) and Rena Craft Presley Meyers; mother-in-law (dec.) Emma Melendy Meyers, 1st dietician for L.A. Co. Hosp.; M.D., C.M.E. now Loma Linda Univ., 1945; m. 2d Edward T. (Ted) Meyers (radio, TV non-stop 43 years, currently KHJ-TV), Aug. 26, 1951, Montecito, Calif.; chil.: Bonnie Lynn (Mrs. Jimmie Bauer), b. Apr. 28, 1944; Dana Renee (Garrison), b. July 2, 1952; Edward Presley, b. Aug. 9, 1953; Michael Frederick, b. Mar. 23, 1961. Career: gen. practice of med. and obstetrics, 1946---. Hold five patents on designs for hosp. clothing. Mem.: AMA; CMA; L.A. Co. Med. Assn. Hobbies: art, painting, design. Rec.: hiking, fishing. Home: 385 No. San Rafael, Pasadena, CA 91105; Office: 1933 W. Valley Blvd., Alhambra, CA 91803.

PRESTON, FREDERICK WILLARD
Surgeon — Educator
b. June 27, 1912, Chicago, Ill.; s. Frederick Augustus and Margaret (Atwater) Preston; B.A., Yale Univ.,

1935; M.D., Northwestern Univ., 1942, M.S. Physiology; M.S. Surgery, Univ. of Minn., 1947; m. Barbara Gay Hess, July 31, 1961, Chicago; sons, Frederick Willard, Jr., b. Aug. 29, 1943; David Eldred, b. May 10, 1948; William Blackmore, b. Aug. 28, 1952. Career: Fellow in surg., Mayo Clin., 1941-45, 1946-48; asst./assoc./prof. of surg., Northwestern Univ. Med. Sch., 1958-75; chmn., Dept. of Surgery, Santa Barbara Gen. Hosp., 1975-79, dir. of Surgical Edn. 1975---. Attend. Surg., VA Hosp., Hines, Ill., 1950-53, Northwestern Mem. Hosp., Chicago, 1950-75; Staff, VA Research Hosp., Chicago, 1953-72; Chief, Surgical Serv., 1953-67. Past pres. Chicago chpts.: Am. Assn. for Cancer Research and Am. Coll. of Surgs. Served Lt. to Maj., AUS, 1945-48; ETO, 1943-46. Author: Basic Surgical Physiology, with John M. Beal; 8 chpts in textbooks; 124 articles pub. in field of surg., surgical research, onocology, and trauma in surgical journs. Clubs: Univ. Club, Chicago; La Cumbre Golf and Country, Santa Barbara. Republican, Episcopalian. Rec.: mountain climbing, fishing. Res.: 755 Via Airosa, Santa Barbara, CA 93110; Office: 300 San Antonio Rd., Santa Barbara, CA 93110.

PRICE, P. BUFORD
Physicist
b. Nov. 8, 1932, Memphis, Tenn.; s. Paul B. and Eva (Duprey) Price; B.S. Physics, Davidson Coll., 1954; M.S. and Ph.D. in physics, Univ. of Va., 1956, 58; m. Jo Ann Baum, June 28, 1959, Rye, N.H.; chil.: P. Buford III, b. Apr. 27, 1959; Heather, b. Apr. 7, 1961; Pamela, b. Jan. 4, 1964; Alison, b. Dec. 8, 1967; Career: physicist, Gen. Electric Research & Devel. Center, Schenectady, N.Y., 1960-69; prof. of physics, Univ. Calif., Berkeley, 1969---. Holder six patents; author: one book, 200 pub. papers in fields of solid state, nuclear, cosmic ray and elementary particle physics; elected mem. U.S. Nat. Acad. of Scis. 1975, mem. Space Sci. Bd. 1972-75. Chmn., Cosmic Physics Div., Am. Physical Soc., 1974-75. Awarded for Distinguished Service, Am. Nuclear Soc., 1974-75. Awarded for Distinguished Serv., Am. Nuclear Soc. Award 1964; Ernest Orlando Lawrence Award, AEC 1971; NASA Medal for Exceptional Sci. Achievement, 1973; John Simon Guggenheim Fellowship, 1976-77; hin. D.Sc., Davidson Coll., 1973. Rec.: skiing, biking. Res.: 1056 Overlook Rd., Berkeley, CA 94708; Office: Univ. of Calif., Berkeley, CA 94720.

PRICE, FRANK
Film Production Company President
b. May 17. 1930, Decatur, Ill.; s. William F. and Winifred (Moran) Price; student, Mich. State Univ., 1949-51; m. Katherine Huggins, May 15, 1965, Las Vegas, Nev.; sons: Stephen, b. 1955; David, b. 1961; Roy, b. 1967; William F. III, b. 1972. Career: Writer and story editor, CBS, Inc., 1951-53; Screen Gems, Inc., 1953-57; NBC, 1957-59; Exec. Prod., Universal TV, 1959-71, producing such shows as The Virginian, Ironside, It Takes a Thief, also movies for television: Doomsday Flight, Alias Smith and Jones; v.p., Universal TV, 1964, sr. v.p. 1971, exec. v.p. in charge of prodn. 1973, pres., 1974-78; pres., Columbia Pictures Prodns., 1978---. Dir. MCA, Inc., 1977-78, v.p. 1976-78. Mem. Writers Guild of Am., West. 1957---. Res.: 600 Doheny Rd., Beverly Hills, CA; Office: The Burbank Studios, Burbank, CA 91505.

PRICE, HARRISON A.
Engineer — Consultant
b. May 17, 1921, Oregon City, Ore.; s. Harry and Isabel Price; B.S., Caltech, 1942; M.B.A., Stanford Univ., 1951; m. Anne Shaw (Lieder Singer), Apr. 29, 1944, NYC; chil.: Dana Anderson, b. 1949; David, b. 1949; Bret, b. 1950; Holly, b. 1954. Career: Mgr. Economics Research Div., Stanford Research Inst., 1951-55; Gen. Mgr. Defense Plants Div., Harvey Aluminum, 1958; pres., Economics Research Corp., 1958-73; sr. v.p., Planning Research Corp., 1973-77, chmn. of bd., 1978; pres., Harrison Price Co., cons. in engring. & econ., 1978---. Founder, dir., Cal Arts, 1961---; dir. McCulloch Oil, 1977---; dir. Music Center, 1965-78; dir. Sea World, 1971-77; dir. Planning Research Corp. 1973-78. Served in USAF, 1944-46; U.S. Strategic bombing survey. Clubs: Cosmos Club, Internat. Club, Wash. D.C.; L.A. Athletic Club. Hobbies: wine, music. Rec.: skiing, jogging. Address: 542 Lorraine Blvd., L.A., CA 90020.

PRICE, LEONARD ATKINSON
Physician
b. May 31, 1935, Ogdensburg, N.Y.; s. George L. and

Laura (Chapman) Atkinson; B.S., St. Lawrence Univ., 1956; M.D., Queen's Univ., Can., 1962; m. Diane Watters, Aug. 1, 1964, Flint, Mich.; children: Dawn Laura, b. 1966; Geoffrey, b. 1968. Career: Intern, Resident, Hurley Hosp., Flint, Mich. 1962-66; Fellow, Allergy, Immunology, Rheumatology, Scripps Clinic., La Jolla, 1966-67; Long Beach VA Hosp. staff, 1967-69; pvt. practice, Allergy-Immunology, Santa Barbara, 1969---. Bd. Certifications: Internal Med. 1970, Allergy-Immunology, 1971. Pres., Med. Soc. Santa Barbara Co. 1978, chmn. Health Care Services, 1973, 74. Lung Assn. Bd., Tch. Staff mem. Santa Barbara Cottage & Gen. Hosp.; Med. Cons., UC, Santa Barbara Student Health Center. Lt. AUS, Mil. Police, 1957; USAR, 1956-64. Rec.: golf, fishing. Res.: 4586 Via Maria, Santa Barbara, CA 93111; Office: 2320 Bath St., Santa Barbara, CA 93105.

PRIDE, L. FRANCES
  Nursing School Dean
b. Kansas; grad. Sch. of Nursing, Boulder, Colo., 1945; B.S., Union Coll., Lincoln, Nebr., 1950; M.S., Univ. of Colo., 1956; Ph.D., Univ. Md., 1967; Ph.D., Georgetown Univ., 1976; licensed Marriage and Family Counselor, Calif., 1976. Career: Med. Supr., Boulder Mem. Hosp., Colo., 1945-50; instr. in Nursing, Union Coll., Lincoln, Nebr. 1950-56, asst. prof. 1956-60; assoc. prof. of Nursing, Columbia Union Coll., 1960-67, prof., assoc. dean, dir. grad. div. in Nursing, Loma Linda Univ., 1974---. Cons., curriculum, many univs. Contbr. profl. aticles journs. Mem. Calif. Nurses' Assn., Inland Co. HSA, 1977---; Am. Nurses' Assn.; Assn. of Seventh-Day Adventist Nurses (1970 S.D.A. Nurse of the Year); AM. Ednl. Research Assn.; Assn. Adventist Forums; Am. Counseling and Guidance Assn.; Am. Assn. Marriage and Family Counselors. Seventh-Day Adventist Ch. Hobby: antique brass candlestick collection. Res.: 25210 Lawton Ave., Loma Linda, CA 92354; Office: Sch. of Nursing, Grad. Div., Loma Linda Univ., Loma Linda, CA 92354.

PRIM, WAYNE LAVERNE
  Attorney at Law
b. Oct. 22, 1926, Grenora, N. Dak.; s. Frank E. and Christine (May) Prim; B.S., Univ. of Wash., 1950, LL.B., 1951; m. Loretta J. Wesch, Mar. 16, 1974; chil.: Andrea, b. Aug. 12, 1974; Wayne, Jr., b. Mar. 19, 1958. Career: with Ernst & Ernst, CPAs, Seattle, 1950-52; admitted to Washington bar, 1950, Calif. bar, 1953; spec. atty. for IRS, S.F., 1952-54; partner with law firm of Howard, Prim, Rice, Nemerovski, Canady & Pollak, 1954---. Chmn. of bd., dir., Butler Publs., 1965-68; dir., mem. exec. com., Arcata Corp., 1968---; partner, Hambrecht & Quist, Investment abnkers, 1968---; trustee, pres., S.F. Ballet Assn., 1974-75, now chmn. exec. com.; trustee, Menlo Sch. and Coll.; speaker, Western Assn. of Venture Capitalists. Capt., USAAF and USNR, 1944-46. Mem.: Delta Upsilon, Delta Theta Phi, Phi Alpha Delta. Clubs: Menlo Circus, Atherton; Bankers, Villa Taverna, S.F. Rec.: tennis, skiing. Res.: 30 Cowell Lane, Atherton, CA 94025; Office: 650 California St., Suite 2900, S.F., CA 94108.

PRIMUTH, DAVID JAMES
  Retail Company President
b. Aug. 17, 1938, Racine, Wis.; s. Rudolph and Alvina Primuth; B.A., Wheaton Coll.; M.A., Marquette Univ.; m. Carol J. Glittenberg; chil.: Jonathan, b. Sept. 14, 1964; Jill, b. Oct. 5, 1966. Career: v.p. of Finance and Adminstrv. Servs., Symonds, Inc., Chicago; v.p. and controller, The Wickes Corp., San Diego, Feb. 1971, sr. v.p. and chief fin offcr., May 1971, dir. and exec. v.p., 1975, pres. 1978---. Dir., Nat. Corp. for Housing Partnerships, Wash. D.C.; Dep. Dir., Calif. Roundtable; mem. Calif. C. of C., Statewide Econ. Devel. Com., Statewide Agri. Com.; dir., San Diego Hosp. Assn.; dir., Sharp Hosp., Dir. Metro YMCA of San Diego, Co.; regional dir., Young Life Internat.; mem. Advis. bd., San Diego Comm. Coll. and Sch. of Bus. Adminstrn., Univ. of San Diego; trustee, Assn. for Bus. Edn. Hobbies: sailing, golf. Office: 1010 Second Ave., San Diego, CA 92101.

PRINCI, CARL VICTOR
  Radio Commentator — Opera Authority
b. Sept. 27, 1920, Boston, Mass.; s. Joseph M. and Teresa M. (Strati) Princi; studied Italian, French, Spanish, Ger. langs.; assoc. broadcasting, Boston Univ.; m. Althea Giordano, Boston, Mass. Jan. 20, 1946; daus.: Elaine A., b. Dec. 14, 1946; Valerie M., b. May 16, 1949; Carla V., b. Nov. 2, 1955. Career: Actor,

New England Stock 1934-41; anncr.-newscaster, WESX, Boston, 1940; chief anncr.-newscaster, WCHA, Chambersburg, Pa. 1945, pgm. dir. 1947; pgm. dir.-newscaster WLEA Hornell, N.Y. 1948; sta. mgr. WKMO, Kokomo, Ind. 1949; staff, radio stas. KIEV, KMGM and KWKW; opera host-commentator, KFAC World of Opera, 1954---, dir. pgm. and community involvement. Narrator-actor, 35 mot. pics. 1949---; actor-narrator, TV Prodns., narrated 3 LP albums, incl. Walt Disney's Great Operatic Composers; spec. in dramatic readings, poetry and prose; lectr. on The Development of Opera (opera hist. and current prodns.), incl. Bizet and His Carmen, The Inseparable Pair, The Passionate Puccini and Verdi — The Man and Master, L.A., 1960---; cond. opera tours to opera capitals of Europe and U.S. 1963---; cond. weekend tours to S.F. for A Night At The Opera' host and arr., Delta Opera House, World of Opera, the Ambassador Hour, Global Village and GTE Hour (biannually). Teaching credential, L.A. City Sch. Adult Edn. 1965---. (Charter) bd. dirs., L.A. Opera Co.; adv. bds., opera cos. and Sym. Assn. of So. Calif. Contrib. articles on opera to various profl. publs., incl. Opera News, Psychol. Warfare. U.S. Army; prod. radio pgms. for Armed Forces Radio, ETO (1942-46), WW II. Mem.: TV Acad. of Arts and Scis. Hobby: carpentry. Rec.: golf. Res.: 4906 Ledge Ave., No. Hollywood, CA; Office: 5773 Wilshire Blvd., L.A., CA 90036.

PRINTUP, CARTER ALSTON, JR.
  Cardiac Surgeon
b. Jan. 31, 1935, San Diego; s. Carter and Helen Mae (Farmer) Printup, Sr.; B.A., UCLA, 1956; M.D., USC Med. Sch. 1960; m. Lia Jeanne de Beaumont, Oct. 8, 1960, Glendale; children: Carter Alston III, b. 1962; Victoria Jeanne, b. 1963; Katherine Anne, b. 1965. Career: Lt., USN, Med. Ofcr., 1960-64; Surgical Resident, 1964-68; Cardiac Surgery Resident, 1968-70; pvt. practice, cardiac surgery, Pasadena 1970---. Hobby: art. Rec.: tennis, skiing. Res.: 882 Flintridge Ave., Flintridge, CA 91011; Office: 50 Bellefontaine, Pasadena, CA 91105.

PRIVETT, STEPHEN A., S.J.
  Principal, Bellarmine College Preparatory
b. Dec. 8, 1942, San Francisco; s. John A., Jr. and Margaret Frances (Arena) Privett; B.A., Gonzaga, 1967; M. Div., Jesuit School of Theology, 1972. Career: Roman Catholic Priest, 1972---; vice-pres., College of Queen of Peace, 1972-73; principal, Bellarmine College Preparatory, 1975---. Trustee, Univ. of Santa Clara, 1974---; trustee, Hillbrook Sch., 1977---. Home-Office: 850 Elm St., San Jose, CA 95159.

PROCTOR, HARVEY A.
  Utility Company President
b. Mar. 25, 1916, Denver, Colo; s. Harvey T. and Mabel (Eustice) Proctor; B.S., M.E., Univ. of Colo. 1939; m. Virginia Jacobberger, Omaha, Nebr., June 22, 1939; sons: Michael E., b. Dec. 6, 1940; Harvey C., b. Mar. 27, 1945; James T., b. July 31, 1946. Career: So. Calif. Gas. Co. mgmt., v.p.-dir. 1939-64, chmn. 1972---; exec. v.p. Hood Corp., pres. Hood Co. Farms, Boise, Id., 1965; v.p.-controller, So. Calif. Gas. Co. 1966, dir. 1966---, exec. v.p. 1969, pres.-dir., 1971---; sr. v.p. Pac. Lighting Serv. Co. 1968, exec. v.p. 1969, pres. dir. 1971---. Dir., AID, L.A. 1970---; L.A. Central Cabinet, United Crusade Campaign, 1973. Mem.: Psi Kappa Psi, 1937; fellow, Am. Soc. Mech. Engrs.; dir. Pac. Coast Gas. Assn. 1960-64; chmn. Am. Gas Assn. 1973---; chmn. Gas Supply Com. 1971-73; trustee-exec. com. Inst. of Gas. Tech., Chicago, 1972; Town Hall of Calif., L.A. Club, Jonathan Club. Office: 720 W. 8th St., L.A., CA 90017.

PROCTOR, RICHARD JAMES
  Geologist
b. Aug. 2, 1931, L.A.; s. George and Margaret Proctor; B.A., Cal. State Univ., L.A., 1954; M.A., UCLA, 1958; m. Ena McLaren, Feb. 12, 1955, Pasadena; chil.: Mitchell, b. 1959; Jill, b. 1960; Randall, b. 1963. Career: Chief Geologist, Metropolitan Water Dist. of So. Calif., 1962---; also vis. assoc. prof. of geology, Calif. Inst. of Tech., 1975---. Co-author: Engring. Geology in So. Calif., 1966. Recipient, E.B. Burwell Meml. Award of the Geological Soc. of Am., 1972. Fellow, Geological Soc. of Am. Mem. Assn. of Engring. Geologists, pres. 1979; Am. Soc. of Civil Engrs. Underground Technology Research Council; L.A. Co. Geologists Appeals Bd.; Am. Arbitration Assn. AUS, 1954-56, Corps of Engrs. Hobby: wine

making. Res.: 327 Fairview Ave., Arcadia, CA; Office: Box 54153, L.A., CA 90054.

PRONZINI, WILLIAM JOHN
Writer
b. Apr. 13, 1943, Petaluma, Calif.; s. Joseph and Helene (Guder) Pronzini; m. Brunhilde Schier, July 28, 1972, Furstenfeldbruck, W. Germany. Career: Sports reporter, warehouseman, office typist; full-time profl. writer, 1969---: 1st pub. short story, 1966, first pub. novel, 1971; Author: 18 novels, 200 short stories and articles; editor: six anthologies. Mem.: Author's Guild; Writers Guild of America-West; Mystery Writers of America, Inc., chpt. v.p. 1976-77; Western Writers of America, Inc. Hobby: collecting books, mags. Address: P.O.B. 27368, San Francisco, CA 94127.

PROVENZANO, TONY
Artist
b. May 19, 1921, Tampa, Fla.; s. Victor and Annie (La Russa) Provenzano; ed. Chouinard Art Inst. 1949; art, Tampa Univ., Fla.; Jepson Art Sch. (6 yrs.); pvt. stu. with Pratt, Carter, Cross, Jepson, Murphy, Lutz, Crodrey, Huebner, Kramer, Diamond, Haines, Dike; m. Alice Gonzalez, L.A., Dec. 2, 1950; daus.: Debbie A., b. Aug. 8, 1956; Lori A., b. Oct. 27, 1959. Career: Tech. illus.: Tech. Prod. Co. 1954-55; Lockheed Missile Systems Div. 1955-57; Bendix Electrodynamics, 1957-69. Mag. and tech. illustrator. Tchr., art classes in oil and pastels. Exhibs.: L.A. Co. Museum, Burbank Central Lib., Pasa. Lib., Glendale Fed. Svgs., Fri. Morning Club, Ebell Club, Calif. Fed. Svgs., Alhambra City Hall, Naval and Marine Res. Center, Calif. Art Clun; Am. Mag. Youth Forum, 1940-41; Bendix-Pac. Art Exhibit, 1962; San Fernando Valley Art Club; Valley Artists Guild; Latham Found.; judge, many juried shows, incl. Celebration of the Arts, 1976; painted many navy shops of WW II (comm. by ret. naval offcrs.). Winner, many prizes for painting. U.S. Army (Battle Russell Is., New Georgia Is., Asiatic PTO), 1942-45. Qualified marksman, 2 Bronze Stars, others. Mem.: bd. dirs. House Com., Valley Artists Guild; West Valley Art Guild; San Fernando Valley Art Club. Hobby: collecting Western antiques. Rec.: golf. Studio: 11577 Gilmore St., N. Hollywood, Calif. 91606.

PRYDE, PHILIP RUST
University Professor
b. Jan. 8, 1938, Pittsfield, Mass.; s. David and Viola (Rust) Pryde; B.A., Amherst Coll., 1959; Ph.D., Univ. Washington, 1969; m. Lucy Tripp, June 24, 1961, New Haven, Conn. Career: Asst. Prof. of Geography, San Diego State Coll., 1969-75; Prof. of Geography, S.D. State Univ., 1975---. Author: Conservation in the Soviet Union, Cambridge Univ. Press, 1972; Editor: San Diego, An Introduction to the Region, Kendall/Hunt, 1976. AUS, 1960-63; Security Agency. Co-chmn., San Diego County Regional Goals Program, 1971-74. Mem.: Assn. of Am. Geographers, Am. Geographical Soc., Am. Planning Assn. Mem. San Diego Co. Planning Commn., 1977-80; chmn. 1979. Res.: 5377 Redding Rd., San Diego, CA; Office: San Diego State University, San Diego, CA 92182.

PRZYGODA, REV. JACEK
Professor Emeritus
b. Oct. 10, 1910, Poland; s. Jan and Zofia Przygoda; Maturity Exam, Poland, 1928; M.A., Louvain, Belgium, 1947; student, Univ. of Mich., 1949-50; Ph.D., Univ. of Ottawa, Can., 1952; Career: Ordained Roman Catholic priest, 1933; tchr., Poland, 1933-36; editor, Diocesan Weekly, Sandomierz, Poland, 1937-38; Belgium, 1938-48; Chaplain, Rector, Pol. Catholic Mission, Belgium, Netherlands, Luxembourg, 1938-48; instr.: St. Mary's Coll. and Hi. Sch., Orchard Lake, Mich., 1949-50, 54-55; instr. asst., assoc. Prof., Loyola Univ., L.A., 1955-76; OLQA, Seminary, Mission Hills, Calif., 1976---. Author: Life with Poles in Belgium; Jezu, ufam Tobie (prayer book in Polish); Texas Pioneers from Poland, 1971; editor, Polish Americans in Calif., 1928-77; recipient: gold apple, tchr. remembrance day found., 1976; hon. mem.: Polish Am. Congress of Texas. Mil.: Maj., Underground Army, Belgium, 1942-44, sr. chaplain. Mem.: Polish Am. Hist. Assn., founder Calif. chpt. 1972, pres. 1972; N.Y. Am. Catholic Hist. Assn.; Phi Gamma Mu; Omicron Delta Epsilon; Phi Tau Kappa. Hobbies: writer, editor, pub. Home-Office: 15101 S.F. Mission Blvd., Mission Hills, CA 91345.

PUCKETT, ALLEN EMERSON
President, Hughes Aircraft Company
b. July 25, 1919, Springfield, Oh.; s. Roswell C. and Catherine C. (Morrill) Puckett; B.S., Harvard Coll. 1939; M.S., Harvard Univ. 1941; Ph.D. (aeron. engring.), Calif. Inst. of Tech. 1949; m. Marilyn I. McFarland; chil.: Margaret A., James R., Allen W., Nancy L., Susan E. Career: Research cons. (aerodynamics), Calif. Inst. of Tech. 1941-45; lectr. (aerons.)-chief, Wind Tunnell Sect., Jet Propulsion Lab., Caltech., 1945-49; tech, cons., Wind Tunnel Design, Des Moines Steel Co., Pittsburgh, 1943-45; tech. cons. U.S. Army Ord., Aberdeen Proving Ground, Md. 1945---; Hughes Aircraft Co. 1949--- (head, Aerodynamics Dept., Guided Missile Lab. 1949-54; dir. advanced planning, Research and Devel. Labs. 1954-55; dir. opns., Weapon Systems Devel. Labs., 1955-57; assoc. dir., Systems Devel. Labs. 1957-59; v.p.-dir. Aerospace Engring. Div. 1959-61; v.p.-asst group exec., Aerospace Group, 1961---; v.p.-asst. gen. mgr. 1965-77; pres., 1977---. Author: 7 tech. papers on high speed aerodynamics; co-author: (book) Introduction to Aerodynamics of a Compressible Fluid; co-ed. (book) Guided Missile Engineering. Awards: recipient, Inst. of Aeron. Scis. Lawrence Sperry Award, 1949. Mem.: U.S. Mil. Tech. Mission, 1945; U.S. Mil. Intelligence Mission, 1947; guided missile com., Research and Devel. Bd. 1952-54; com. on aerodynamics, NACA 1953-55; past chmn. subcom. on high speed aerodynamics; subcom. on automatic stabilization and control, NASA 1956-59; chmn. research adv. com. on control, guidance and navigation, 1959---; steering group, adv. panel on aerons., Ofc. of the Dir. of Def., Research and Engring. 1956-61; chmn. steering group, mutual weapons devel. pgm. 1956-61; Fellow, Am. Inst. of Aeronautics and Astronautics, 1957---, pres. 1972; science adv. commn., Ballistic Research Labs. U.S. Army Ordnance, Aberdeen Proving Ground, Md., 1958---; cons. President's Sci. Adv. Com. 1960---; cons. Operations Evaluation Group, Chief of Naval Opns., 1960---; member, cons. Def. Sci. Bd. 1962, v.-chmn., July 1962-64, exec. com.-bd. dirs. 1962-66; Army Sci. Adv. Panel, Dept. of Army, 1965-67; NASA Research and Tech. Adv. Comm. 1968---; Am. Rocket Soc., Phi Beta Kappa, Sigma Xi, Balboa Yacht Club, Calif. Yacht Club; Cosmos Club, Jonathan Club. Hobby: sailing. Res.: 935 Corsica Dr., Pacific Palisades, CA 90272; Office: Hughes Aircraft Co., Culver City, CA.

PUTNAM, HELEN
Mayor
b. May 4, 1909, Bakersfield, Calif.; d. John and Winifred (Campbell) Du Mont; ed. Alameda pub. schs.; A.B., Univ. Calif., Berkeley, 1930; m. Rutherford Putnam, Oakland, 1937; chil.: William Rutherford, Mrs. McKenzie (Kate) Oliver. Career: Teacher, elem., jr. H.S., Petaluma, 1931-41; teacher-prin.: Martin Sch. 1958-60, Waugh Sch. 1961-63, Two Rock Sch. 1963--- . Pres., Petaluma Bd. of Edn. 1947-59; pres. Redwood Empire Div., League of Calif. Cities, 1968-69; mem. City Council, 1965; elected Mayor, City of Petaluma, 1969---; dir. League of Calif. Cities, 1970-72; v.p. 1974-75; Radio Pgms. KSRO, 1950-54; Author: children's book in preparation, 1970. Mem.: pres. Calif. Sch. Bds. Assn. 1958-59; pres. Petaluma Dem. Club, 1964-65; chmn. Sonoma Co. Mayors and Councilmen's Assn. 1968-69; chmn. Calif. Assn. of Local Agcy. Formation Comms.; v.p. at lg. Univ. Calif. Alumni Assn.; Delta Kappa Gamma. Res.: 900 B St., Petaluma, CA; Office: City Hall, Petaluma, CA 94952.

PUTNAM, ROBERT SARGENT
Corporate Executive
b. Sept. 29, 1915, Redlands; s. Harold Worthy and Laura (Sargent) Putnam; B.A., Univ. of Redlands, 1937, D.Bus.Admin. (hon.) 1975; m. Virginia Demaree, June 12, 1938, Dinuba; chil.: Janet Rae (Mrs. Charles E. Johnson), b. 1943; Barbara Carol (Mrs. Jark J. Carpenter), b. 1948. Career: Civilian Personnel Ofcr., USN, 1941-53; mgr. indsl. rels. Solar Aircraft Co., San Diego, 1953-59; mgr. admin. Thiokol Chem. Corp., Brigham City, Utah, 1959-61; dir. indsl. rels., TRW Semiconductors, Lawndale, 1961-64; Scientific Data Systems, Santa Monica, 1964-65; v.p. indsl. rels., Norris Industries, Inc., L.A., 1966---. Dir., chmn. Past Pres's. Com., Univ. Redlands Alumni Assn., 1961---, pres. 1958; pres., San Diego Personnel Mgmt. Assn., 1955-56; ASPA nat. dir. 1971-74, chmn. Employee & Labor Rels. Com. 1968-74. ASPA pres's. council, 1975---; mem. Town Hall of Calif., 1966---. Lt. Comdr., USNR, 1942-48. Presbyterian Ruling Elder. Rec.: golf, fishing. Office: One Golden Shore, Long Beach, CA 90802.

PUTTER, IRVING
Professor of French
b. Dec. 3, 1917, NYC; s. Joseph and Anna (Schrank) Putter; B.A., City COll. N.Y., 1938; M.A., Univ. of Iowa, 1941; Ph.D., Yale Univ., 1949; m. Lucie Agnes (Nguyen Kim Xuyen), S.F.; chil.: Paul, b. June 26, 1943; Candace Anne (Newlin), b. July 29, 1948. Career: Lectr. through Prof. of French, Univ. of Calif., Berkeley, 1947---, chmn. Dept. of French, 1968-71. Guggenheim Fellow, 1955-56; Fulbright Research Fellow, 1955-56; awarded Humanities Research Professorship, Univ. of Calif., 1971-72, 1978-79. Publs. incl. numerous articles in Revue d'Histoire Litteraire, Studi Francesi, Romanic Review, Modern Language Quarterly, Cahiers de L'Association Internationale des Etudes Francaises, etc. Res.: 115 St. James Dr., Piedmont, CA 94611; Office: Univ. Calif., Dept. of French, Berkeley, CA.

Q

QUALEN, JOHN MANDT
Actor
b. Dec. 8, 1899, Vancouver, B.C., Can.; s. Olaus P. and Anne (Hegelund) Qualen; B.A., Lyceum Arts Conservatory, 1923; m. Pearle Larson, Sept. 4, 1924; chil.: Meredith (Mrs. David Kilpatrick), Kathleen (Mrs. Tom Roberts), Elizabeth (Mrs. Erle Bacon). Career: Appeared as father of Dionne Quintuplets for 20th Century Fox, 1936-37; appeared in the Grapes of Wrath, American Romance, The High and The Mighty, The Searchers; actor in movies and TV, 1938---; featured parts in Mr. Ed, The Third Man, Liberty Valance, Andy Griffith, Medical Center, The Odd Couple, Danny Thomas shows, FBI; recent movies The Seven Faces of Dr. Lao; The Prize, Those Crazy Calloways, all 1963; Sons of Katie Elder, I'll Take Sweden, Big Hand for a Little Lady, Fire Creek, Hail Hero, Frasier, The Sensuous Lion. Recipient Northwestern Univ. award for oratory, 1920, silver medal Beloit Univ., 1920, Citation from King Haakon of Norway. Mem.. Acad. Motion Picture Arts and Scis., Acad. TV Arts and Scis. Mem.: Authors Club, treas.; Hollywood Masquers, bd. govs., historian. Address: 22903 A Nadine Circle, Torrance, CA 90505.

QUALSET, CALVIN ODELL
Agronomist
b. Apr. 24, 1937, Newman Grove, Nebr.; s. Herman and Adeline (Hanson) Qualset; B.S., agri., Univ. of Nebr., 1958; M.S., agronomy, Univ. of Calif., Davis, 1960, Ph.D., genetics, 1964; m. Kathleen Bogaler, 1957, Lincoln Nebr.; chil.: Douglas Mark, b. 1958; Cheryl Lynn, b. 1960; Gary Allen, b. 1965. Career: Asst. prof. of Agronomy, Univ. of Tenn., Knoxville, 1964-67; asst./assoc./Full Prof. of Agronomy, UC, Davis, 1967---, chmn., Dept. of Agronomy and Range Sci., 1975---; Consl. to Devel. and Resources Corp., 1972; Ford Found., 1974; UN Food and Agri. Orgn. 1978. Elected Fellow, Am. Soc. of Agronomy 1978; Sr. Fulbright Scholar to Australia, 1976-77; Tech. Ed.: Crop Science, 1974-76. Mem.: Alpha Zeta; Sigma Xi; Phi Kappa Phi; Genetics Soc. of Am.; AAAS; Genetics Soc. of Canada; Indian Genetics and Plant Breeding Soc.; Am. Genetics Assn.; Soc. for Advancement of Breeding Research in Asia and Oceania. Christian. Res.: 518 Cleveland Ct., Davis, CA 95616; Office: Univ. of California, Davis, CA 95616.

QUILLEN, ROGER WAYNE
Clinical Psychologist
b. Jan. 6, 1932, Chicago, Ill.; s. Nathanial and Isabel K. (Hodges) Quillen; B.A., Univ. of Colo., 1958; M.A. (USPHS Fellow), Univ. of Utah, 1964, Ph.D., 1970; m. B. Jeanette Chandler, May 24, 1970, Stockton; stepchil.: Lynne Phillips, b. May 5, 1955; David Colby, b. Dec. 22, 1953; Jonathan Sidell, b. Oct. 5, 1960. Career: Clin. psychologist, Stockton State Hosp., 1967-72, Office of Program review, 1972-74, program dir., 1974---; pvt. practice (part-time) psychologist, Stockton, 1973---; cons., Family Service Agency, Modesto, 1969---; adjunct prof., Univ. of the Pacific, 1976---; lectr. psychology, Stanislaus State Coll., 1975-76. Bd. Dir.: Calif. State Psychology Assn., 1974---; Stockton Women's Center, 1977---; San Joaquin Assn. for Retarded, 1969-78. Mil.: USNR; active duty, 1952-55, 3rd class petty officer, aviation electronics. Mem.: Am. Psychology Assn; San Joaquin Co. Psychol. Assn., past pres., v.p.; pres. elect 1978, Psychologists in Pub. Service, div. Calif. State Psychol. Assn.; Assn. for Advancement of Psychology;

Nat. register for Health Service Providers in Psychol. Unitarian. Hobby: repair 1967 Jaguar. Rec.: bridge, skiing. Home: 1025 Seward Way, Stockton, CA 95207; Office: 1036 W. Robinhood Dr., Suite 206, Stockton, CA.

QUIMBY, FREDERICK C., JR.
Attorney at Law
b. Feb. 5, 1926, NYC; s. Frederick C. and Gladys (Thompson) Quimby; (film industry pioneer; head of MGM Short Subject Dept., prod. MGM cartoons, winner 8 Acad. Awards.) B.A., UCLA, 1947; J.D., USC, 1952; m. Dorothy Linn, June 16, 1950, L.A.; chil.: Frederick C. III (Rick), b. Oct. 4, 1962; Carol Louise, b. Nov. 14, 1964. Career: admitted to Calif. Bar, 1952; with law firm Trippet, Newcomer, Yoakum and Thomas, 1952-55; Moss, Lyon and Dunn, 1955-60; pvt. practice of law own office, 1960-62; sr. partner, firm of Veatch, Carlson, Quimby, Nelson and Kohrs, 1962---. Arbitrator: Am. Arbitration Assn. and L.A. Superior Ct. Arbitration program; Lectr. and moderator: Continuing Edn. of the (Calif.) Bar program. USN, 1943-45. Mem.: Am. Bd. of Trial Advocates; So. Calif. Defense Counsel Assn.; Delta Sigma Phi frat, UCLA; The Beach Club. Episcopalian. Rec.: tennis, swimming. Res.: 522 N. Elm Dr., Beverly Hills, CA; Office: 3200 Wilshire Blvd., L.A., CA.

QUINN, A. THOMAS
Chairman, Air Resources Board
b. Mar. 14, 1944, L.A.; s. Joseph (dec.) and Grace Quinn; B.S., Northwestern Univ., Evanston, Ill., 1965; m. Daniela Buia, 1965, Altadena; chil.: Douglas T., b. Oct. 6, 1967; Laura Jean, b. July 4, 1969. Career: pres., Radio News West, Inc., L.A.; Campaign mgr., Brown for Secty. of State, 1969-71; Dep. Secty. of State, Calif., 1971-74; Campaign mgr., Brown for Gov., 1974; Environmental Advisor to the Gov.-elect, 1974-75; Spec. Asst. to Governor for Environmental Protection, 1975; chmn., Air Resources Bd., Calif., 1976---. Office: 1709 11th St., Sacto., CA 95814.

QUINN, THOMAS MICHAEL
College President
b. Aug. 9, 1922, Oakland, Calif.; s. Thomas L. and Helen (Buckley) Quinn; B.A., 1947; M.A. 1960; Ph.D. 1962; LL.D., 1963. Career: Prin., Mont La Salle H.S., Napa, Calif. 1949-54; prof. psychol., St. Mary's Coll. 1960-62, pres. 1962---. De La Salle Bd. 1948-53. Res. and Office: St. Mary's Coll., Moraga, CA 94575.

QUINN, WILLIAM FRANCIS
Surgeon
b. Jan. 3, 1906, Phila., Pa.; s. William Francis and Kathryn Smull (Longacre) Quinn; desc. John Longacre, dir. Phila. Mint; B.S., Wash. Univ. 1926; M.D., Loma Linda Univ., 1931; m. Emma Kittridge, L.A. June 6, 1936; chil.: Margaret Elizabeth, b. Sept. 9, 1938; Robert Russell, b. Sept. 1, 1942. Career: Res. surg., L.A. Co. Hosp. 1932-35; pvt. practice surg., L.A.; asst. prof. surg., Loma Linda Univ. 1949---. Mem.: v.p. L.A. Civic Light Opera Assn., 1947---; pres. Calif. State Bd. of Med. Examiners, 1948-49; fellow, Am. Coll. of Surgs.; L.A. Co. Med. Assn., AMA, Jonathan Club, L.A. Country Club. First Congregational Ch., L.A. 1949--- (bd. of trustees). Hobby: light opera. Rec.: golf, hunting, fishing. Res.: 4880 Glencairn Rd., L.A., CA 90027; Office: Calif. Med. Bldg., 1401 S. Hope St., L.A., CA.

QUINNELLY, JAMES LESLIE
Quality Engineer
b. June 16, 1920, Meridian, Miss.; s. James B. and Maude (Stroud) Quinnelly; B.S. chem. engr., Miss. State Univ., 1941; M.S. engring., Univ. of Mich., 1948; m. Dolores Brinkmann, May 16, 1946, Ft. Bliss, Tex.; chil.: Jane (Orbison), b. Mar. 23, 1947; Fred, b. July 21, 1951. Career: office, chief of research & devel., Army Gen. Staff, 1963-66; operations analyst, Aerojet-General Corp., Downey, 1966-70; cons., military R&D, Anaheim, 1970-74; quality engr., Bechtel Power Corp., L.A., 1974---. Served AUS, 2nd Lt. through Lt. Col., 1942-66; awarded Legion of Merit. Registered Profl. Engr., Calif. Mem.: Nat. Soc. of Profl. Engrs.; Am. Soc. Mech. Engrs.; Soc. Automotive Engrs.; Am. Nuclear Soc. Mason. Lutheran; pres., Stewardship Council 1978. Home: 319 W. Alberta, Anaheim, CA 92805; Office: Bechtel Power Corp., P.O.B. 60860, L.A., CA 90060.

QUIRK, WILLIAM EDWARD
Former Pacific Telephone Co. Executive
b. June 15, 1914, Portland, Ore.; s. Joseph Francis and Mary (McNicholas) Quirk; ed. Holy Rosary Parochial Sch. 1920-28; Columbia Prep. Sch. 1928-32; Portland Univ. 1933; B.S. (E.E.) Ore. State Coll. 1937; m. Josephine Caroline Hulme, Portland, Ore., Oct. 5, 1940; chil.: Nancy Jean, b. Apr. 6, 1944; Patricia Ann Grove, b. Aug. 7, 1941; William Edward, Jr., b. Aug. 26, 1948. Career: Traffic. student, Pac. Telephone Co., Portland, Ore. 1941; traffic chief, Medford, Ore. 1942; traffic asst. 1943, traffic chief, 1945, traffic supt. 1948, dist. traffic supt. 1949, area personnel supv., Adm. Dept. 1950, gen. traffic personnel supv. 1951, labor rels. mgr. 1955, asst. v.p., Adm. Personnel Dept., Seattle 1955, asst. v.p. Adm. Pub. Rels., S.F. 1956; gen. traffic mgr. So. Counties area, San Diego, 1958, v.p. gen. mgr. 1960---. Dir., Central Fed S&L Assn., S.D. 1966---. Distinguished Serv. Award in field of human rels., Natl. Conf. of Chrs. and Jews, 1966; Man of Distinction Award, Women's Guild of Temple Emanu-El, 1966, S.D. Press Club Jeadliner Award, Community Serv. 1973. Mem.: Alpha Sigma Phi, 1935---; Sigma Tau, 1936---; pres. Jr. Achievement, 1961-62; City of S.D. Charter Review Com. 1961-62, 1973-74; dir. Kiwanis Club, 1962-63; dir. Am. Cancer Soc. 1962; dir. Am. Nat. Red Cross, 1962-63; dir. S.D. Soc. for Crippled Chil. 1962-67; pres. S.D. C. of C. 1964-65, dir. 1970; pres. Econ. Devel. Corp., S.D. Co. 1964-65; pres. Navy League of U.S., S.D. Council, 1967, natl. dir. 1968---, chmn. Natl. Conv. Com. 1970; U.S. Naval Inst.; dir. United Comm. Servs.; chmn.-v.p. United Crusade, 1969; chmn. Natl. Security Seminar, 1969; S.D. Com. for Salk Inst.; trustee-v.p. Chil's. Hosp. & Health Center, 1969---; bd. trustees, Calif. Council Econ. Edn. 1970-73; Kona Kai Club; Cuyamaca Club. Catholic (lay chmn., S.D. Diocese of Cath. Com. on Scouting). Hobby: hi-Fi; Rec.: golf, swimming. Res.: P.O.B. 1154, Rancho Santa Fe, CA 92067; Office: 525 B St., San Diego, CA.

R

RADER, STANLEY ROBERT
Treasurer-General Counsel, Worldwide Church of God
b. Aug. 13, 1930, White Plains, N.Y.; s. Nathan and Pearl Janet (Baron) Rader; B.S., UCLA, 1951; J.D., USC Law Sch., 1963; m. Natalie Gartenberg, Jan. 26, 1951, Las Vegas, Nev.; chil.: Janis Anne, b. Jan. 22, 1952; Carol Lee (Little), b. May 16, 1953; Steven Paul, b. Apr. 3, 1955. Career: mem. law firm, Rader, Helge & Gerson, Attorneys; exec. v.p., Ambassador Cultural Found.; exec. editor, Quest/78; past mem. Rader, Cornwall & Kessler, CPAs; prof. of law, USC (law, language & ethics, and Contracts), 1963-65; Bd. Dir.: Worldwide Church of God, treas., gen. counsel, secty. exec. com.; Ambassador Coll. and Ambassador Internat. Cultural Found.; L.A. Ballet; L.A. Chamber Orchestra. Contbr. column, The Plain Truth Mag. Recipient: The Fourth Class of the Order of the Sacred Treas. conferred by Emperor of Japan, 1978; Order of the Coif 1963. Mem.: University Club; Phi Alpha Delta; Annandale Golf Club; Tucson Nat. Golf Club; Pasadena Bar Assn.; L.A. Co. Bar Assn.; Beverly Hills Bar Assn.; CPA Attorneys. Worldwide Ch. of God. Rec.: tennis, golf, riding, skeet shooting. Home: 840 Loma Vista Dr., Beverly Hills, CA; Office: 300 W. Green St., Pasadena, CA.

RAE, MATTHEW SANDERSON, JR.
Attorney at Law
b. Sept. 12, 1922, Pittsburgh, Pa.; s. Matthew S. and Olive (Waite) Rae; ed. A.B., Drake Univ. 1946; LL.B. 1947; postgrad. Stanford Univ. 1951; m. Janet Hettman, S.F., May 2, 1953; daus.: Mary-Anna S., b. Sept. 11, 1959; 'argaret S;. b. Oct. 13, 1961; Janet S., b. Sept. 14, 1962. Career: Asst. to dean, Duke Law Sch. 1947-48; admitted to Md. bar, 1948, Calif. bar, 1951, Supreme Ct. of U.S. 1967; assoc.-Karl F. Steinmann law firm, Baltimore, Md. 1948-49; natl. field rep., Phi Alpha Delta Law Frat. 1949-51; research atty., Calif. Supreme Ct. 1951-52; research atty., Calif. Supreme Ct. 1951-52; partner Darling, Hall, Rae & Gute, 1953---. 2nd Lt., USAAF, WW II. Mem.: A.F. Assn.; Aircraft Owners and Pilots Assn.; v.p. L.A. Co. Repub. Assembly, 1959-64; L.A. Co. Repub. Central Com. 1960-64; 1977---, mem. exec. com., 1977---; chmn. 27th Senatorial Dist. 1977---; v. chmn., 17th Cong. Dist. 1960-62, 28th Cong. Dist. 1962-64, chmn. 46th Assembly Dist. 1962-64; Repub. State Central Com. of Calif. 1966---, exec. com. 1966-67; pres. Calif. Repub. League 1966-67; Comdr. Allied Post, Am. Legion, 1969-70; S. Bay Bar Assn.;

Fellow, Am. Coll. of Probate Counsel; exec. council, Internat. Acad. Estate and Trust Law, 1974---; chmn. probate and trust law com. L.A. Co. Bar Assn. 1964-65; sect. probate, trust and real property law and taxation, Am. Bar Assn.; bulletin chmn., Calif. State Bar 1970-71; chmn. Probate Com. 1974-75, exec. comm., Estate Planning, Trust and Probate Law Sect., 1977---; Lawyers Club of L.A.; Supreme justice, Phi Alpha Delta, 1972-74; pres. Legion Lex, 1969-71; Chancery Club, World Affairs Council, IPA, Rotary Internat., Sigma Nu, Phi Beta Kappa, Omicron Delta Kappa, Commonwealth Club, pres. Town Hall, 1975. United Presbyterian. Hobby: theatre. Rec.: volleyball, swimming. Res.: 600 John St., Manhattan Beach, CA 90266; Office: 523 W. Sixth St., Rm. 400, L.A., CA 90014.

RAFFIN, STEVEN BENNETT
Physician
b. Aug. 22, 1942, S.F.; s. Bennett Lyon and Caroline Meyer; bro., Thomas Alfred Raffin, M.D.; A.B., Stanford Univ., 1964; M.D., Wash. Univ., St. Louis, 1968; m. Sherry Matlof, Dec. 23, 1967, St. Louis; sons: Eric Daniel, b. Dec. 14, 1970; Alec Cary, b. Oct. 28, 1972; Michael Ian, b. Aug. 22, 1975. Career: Internship and Residency, internal med., Jewish Hosp., Wash. Univ., 1968-71; Fellowship in Gastroenterology, Univ. of Calif., S.F., 1971-73, instr. in med., 1973-74; tng. ofcr. and staff Gastroenterologist, Lt. Comdr., Naval Regional Med. Center, Oakland, 1974-76; pvt. practice Internal Med., Gastroenterology, San Bruno, 1976---; also Clin. Asst. Prof. of Med., Univ. Calif., S.F., 1976---. Staff: Peninsula Hosp. and Med. Center, Burlingame; UC Hosps., S.F. Publs.: 4 chpts. on Diseases of the Stomach, Gastrointenstinal Disease, Sleisenger & Fordham, eds., WB Sanders Co. 1973, 78. Fellow, Am. Coll. of Physicians (FACP); Mem.: Am. Gastroenterological Assn.; Am. Soc. for Gastrointestinal Endoscopy; No. Calif. Soc. for Clin. Gastroenterology; AMA; CMA; San Mateo Co. Med. Soc.; Coyote Point Yacht Club. Rec.: sailing, fly fishing. Office: 841 W. San Bruno Ave., San Bruno, CA 94066.

RAGLAND, BARBARA JOANNE
Microbiologist
b. Nov. 12, 1930, Twin Falls, Idaho; d. Howard D. and Thelma R. Leland; B.A. cum laude, Cal. State Coll., Chico, 1971; m. John Alberto Ragland, Apr. 8, 1950, Pocatello, Idaho; chil.: Terry Douglas, Peggy Jeannine, Wendy Colleen. Career: Tng., microbiology, med. technology, Corning Mem. Hosp., Corning, Calif., one year; Med. Technologist, Microbiologist, Student Health Center, Cal. State Univ., Chico, 1972---. Mem.: Calif. Assn. Med. Lab. Technologists; Nat. Registry Microbiologists; Phi Kappa Phi; Corning Bus. Profl. Women, secty. 1978; Toastmistress Club, secty. 1977; Corning Argonauts. Republican. Methodist. Hobby: craftwork. Rec.: camping. Res.: 1126 5th Ave., Corning, CA 96021; Office: Warner & College Dr., Chico, CA 95929.

RAGLAND, JAMES FRANKLIN
Historian — College Professor
b. May 8, 1917, Broken Bow, Nebr.; s. James B. and Ida B. (Busch) Ragland; M.A., USC 1949; postgard. Univ. of Mich. 1949-50; Ph.D., Stanford Univ. 1954; m. Ruth Hines, Wayfarers' Chapel, San Pedro, Calif., July 12, 1963. Career: Teaching fellow, USC 1947-49; teaching fellow, Univ. of Mich. 1949-50; Newell Scholar, Stanford Univ. 1950-51; Univ. fellow, 1951-53; Rosenberg Research fellow, 1953-54; asst. prof. (hist.) Calif. State Univ., Long Beach, 1955-62, assoc. prof. 1963-67, prof. 1967---. Grantee: Am. Philosophical Soc. 1959-60; Rockefeller Found., N.Y. 1960-61; grant, Berle, Berle and Brenner law firm, N.Y. 1962-63; grant, Long Beach State Coll. found. 1964-65. Author: contrib. to various profl. journs. incl. Franklin D. Roosevelt and the Spanish Civil War, Am. Philosophical Soc., Am. Hist. Assn. 1960-65; Skeleton in the Diplomatic Closet, publ. The Churchman, 1964; 2 books publ. W.W. Norton and Houghton Mifflin. Mem.: Am. Hist. Assn., Am. Acad. of Polit and Soc. Sci., Phi Kappa Phi, Phi Alpha Theta, Baptist. Hobby: research writing. Rec.: reading, travel. Res.: 1010 Crestview Ave., Seal Beach, CA 90740; Office: 6101 E. Seventh St., Long Beach, CA 90801.

RAINS, OMER L.
State Senator
b. Sept. 25, 1941, Kansas City, Mo.; s. Roy M. and B. Janice Rains; B.A. & J.D., Univ. Calif., Berkeley; m.

Diana Waldie, Sacto.; chil.: Kelly, b. Apr. 24, 1963; Mark, b. Mar. 30, 1967. Career: with Ventura Co. District Atty's. Office, 1966-69; pvt. law practice, 1969-74; Calif. State Senator, 1974---. Chmn., Ventura Planning Commn. 1970-73; Dir., Regional Plan Assn. of Calif., 1970-74. Named Ventura's Outstanding Citizen 1971. Mem.: Univ. of Calif. Alumni Council, 1972-74; Ventura C. of C., v.p. 1974; State Bar Assn., Chmn. Ethics Com. 1970, Law Day Chmn. 1969; Rotary Internat.; Phi Delta Phi; Planning & Conservation League; Environmental Coalition; Navy League; 4-H; Common Cause. Office: State Capitol, Rm. 5082, Sacto., CA 95814.

RALEIGH, JOHN HENRY
Author — Educator
b. Aug. 30, 1926, Springfield, Mass.; s. John Joseph and Theresa A. (King) Raleigh; B.A., Wesleyan Univ., Conn., 1943; Ph.D., Princeton Univ., 1948; m. Jo Dodson, Aug. 1, 1949, Berkeley; chil.: Kingsley, John, Lydia. Career: Lectr., Univ. of Calif., Berkeley, 1947-49, asst. prof. of English, 1949-54, assoc. prof., 1954-60, prof. of English, 1960---; chmn., English Dept. 1969; v.-chancellor for Academic Affairs, Berkeley campus, 1969-72; Guggenheim Fellow, 1962. Author: Matthew Arnold and Am. Culture, U.C. Press, 1957; The Plays of Eugene O'Neill, Univ. of So. Ill. Press, 1965; Time, Place, and Idea, Univ. So. Ill. Press, 1968; The Chronicle of Leopold and Molly Bloom: Ulysses As Narrative, U.S. Press, 1977. Mem. Modern Language Assn. Rec.: squash. Res.: 1020 Keeler Ave., Berkeley, CA 94708; Office: English Dept., Univ. of Calif., Berkeley, CA 94720.

RALPHS, ZANDRAH KROFT
Foundation President
b. Oct. 17, 1918, Waco, Tex.; dau. Davis Robert and Nell (Whitman) Gurley; B.A. & M.A. Fine Arts, Lit., Humanities, Baylor Univ., 1939; Grad. Nat. Acad. of Metaphysics, 1970; Ordained as Minister and Counselor; m. Albert George Ralphs, Sr., Dec. 16, 1962; dau. Gloynn Alexander Ross. Career: v.p., R.I. Harrell & Co., Houston, Tex., 1945-47, also hosted own radio show; tchr., L.A. Adult Sch., 1953-56; Founding Pres., Zandrah Interiors & Tenure Trends Inc., 1957-63; Head, Barker Bros. decorating Dept., L.A., 1954-57; founding pres. and dir.: Try Foundation, Inc., L.A. 1969---; Bright Future Child Devel. Center, 1971; The Am. Acad. of Arts in Europe, 1972; Campaign for Conscience, 1975. Bd. Dir.: Assitance League of So. Calif.; Am. Indian Scholarship Fund; Carroll Righter Ednl. Found.; St. Paul's Remedial Reading & Learning Center. Dame, The Sovereign Order of the Hosp. of St. John of Jerusalem (Dacia) King Valdemar the Great Priory in Demark. Mem.: Jacques Cousteau Soc., L.A. Symphony, Hollywood Bowl Assn. Rel.: tchr. Metaphysical Philosophy classes 1968---. Hobbies: painting, photog. Office: 1508 Crossroads of the World, Suite 102, L.A., CA 90028.

RAMBO, BEVERLY J.
Professor of Nursing
b. Aug. 18, 1925, Osseo, Wis.; d. Lorrin R. and Alma (Ringhand) Nelson; Diploma, Chicago Wesley Mem. Hosp.; B.S.N., San Diego State Univ., 1961, M.A., 1968; M.Nursing, UCLA, 1971; m. Carl J. Rambo (dec.), 1955, San Diego. Career: Asst. Dir. Nursing, Edgemoor Hosp., Santee, 1961-64, dir. 1964-69; instr., Grossmont Coll., 1971-72; asst. dir. Hollywood Presbyterian Hosp. Sch. of Nursing, 1972-73; asst. prof. of Nursing, Mount St. Mary's Coll., L.A., 1973---. Active Duty, U.S. Navy Nurse Corps, 1952-58; reserve duty, 1958-76, rank Comdr.; Commanding Ofcr., Med. Co., 1976. Co-author with D. Watson, Your Career in Health Care, 1976; Author: Ward Clerk Skills, McGraw-Hill, 1978; co-editor: Nursing Skills for Allied Health Services, W.B. Saunders, Vols. 1, 2, 1977 2nd. ed. Vol. 3, 1979. Mem.: Reserve Ofcr's. Assn. chpt. 57, v.p. for Navy, 1968-69; Calif. Nurses' Assn. bd. dir. 1969-70. Res.: 4606 Maytime Lane, Culver City, CA 90230; Office: 10 Chester Pl., L.A., CA 90007.

RAMO, SIMON
Aerospace Scientist — Company Founder
b. May 7, 1913, Salt Lake City, Ut.; s. Benjamin and Clara (Trestman) Ramo; B.S., Univ. of Utah, 1933; (hon.) D.Sc. 1961; Ph.D., Calif. Inst. of Tech., 1936; D.Eng., Case Inst. of Tech. 1950; D.Sc., Union Coll. 1963; D.Eng., Univ. of Mich. 1966; D.Sc., Worcester Polytech. Inst. 1968; D.Sc., Univ. of Akron, 1969; LL.D., Carnegie-Mellon Univ. 1970; D.Eng., Polytech. Inst. of N.Y. 1971; LL.D., USC 1972; D.Sc., Cleveland

State Univ., 1976; m. Virginia Smith, Beverly Hills, July 25, 1937; chil.: James Brian, b. Spet. 24, 1946; Alan Martin, b. Oct. 26, 1949. Career: Gen. Electric Co., 1936-46; v.p. dir. opns. Hughes Aircraft Co., 1946-53; exec. v.p.-bd. dirs., The Ramo-Wooldridge Corp., L.A. 1953-58; sci. dir., U.S. Intercontinental guided missile program, 1954-58; pres. Space Tech. Labs 1957-58; pres.-dir., The Bunker-Ramo Corp. 1964-66; dir. TRW Inc., 1954---. exec. v.p. 1958-61; v. chmn. bd. 1961-78; chmn. exec. com. 1969-78. Dir.: Union Bank, 1964---; Union Bancorp, Inc. 1973---; Times Mirror Co. 1968---; Visiting Prof. Mgmt. Sci., Calif. Inst. of Tech; chmn. bd. og gov., Perform. Arts Council of L.A. trustee: Calif. Inst. of Tech. 1964---; Natl. Symphony Orch. Assoc.; trustee emeritus, Calif. State Univs. Awards: Eta Kappa Nu, 1941; Electronic Achievement Award, Pac. Reg. I.R.E., 1953; Steinmetz Award, 1959; Schwab Award, Am. Iron and Steel Inst. 1968; Distinguished Serv. Gold Medal, A.F. Communications Electronics Assn. 1970; WEMA Medal of Achievement, 1970; Outstanidng Achievement in Business Mgmt., USC 1971; Kayan Medal, Columbia Univ. 1972. Award of Merit, Am. Cons. Engrs. Council, 1974. Mem.: White House Energy R&D Adv. Council, 1973-75; U.S. Dept. of State Adv. Comm. on Sci. and Foreign Affairs, 1973-75; Secty's. Adv. Council Dept. of Commerce, 1976-77; Roster of Cons. to Admin. ERDA, 1976-77; chmn., President's Com. on Sci. & Tech., 1976-77; Mem.: Fellow, Am. Phys. Soc.; IEEE; Am. Astronautical Soc.; Inst. for Advancement of Engring.; Am. Philosophical Soc.; Am. Acad. of Arts and Scis.; Am. Inst. of Aerons. and Astronautics; AAAS; mem. (charter) Natl. Acad. of Engring.; Natl. Acad. of Scis.; Internat. Acad. Astronautics, Paris, Fr.; Author Sci. and engring. books. Office: One Space Park, Redondo Beach, CA 90278.

RAMO, VIRGINIA MAY (Mrs. Simon Ramo)
University Trustee
b. Yonkers, New York; d. Abraham Harold and Freda (Kasnetz) Smith; B.S. in edn., USC; Doctor of Humane Letters (hon.) USC, 1978; m. Simon Ramo, Beverly Hills; chil.: James Brian; Alan Martin. Career: bd. of trustees, USC, 1971---; vice chmn., 1977---; vice chmn., Bd. of Overseers, Hebrew Union Coll. (Calif. sch.), 1972-75; v.p., Ramo Found., 1959-76. Nat. pres., Achievement Rewards for Coll. Scientists Found., 1975-77; Recipient: Distinguished Achievement award, Am. Heart Assn., 1978; Alpha Epsilon Phi Community Service award, 1975. Nat. co-chmn., annual giving, USC, 1968-70. V.P. & dir., Founders of the Music Center, L.A.; v.p. & dir., Blue Ribbon 400 of Performing Arts Council of the Music Center; v.p. & dir., L.A. Music Center Opera Assn.; secty., corporate bd., United Way; Bd. of Directors: Friends of the Library, USC; President's Circle, USC; L.A. Heart Assn.; Muses, Calif. Mus. of Sci. & Industry; UCLA Affiliates; Med. Aux., UCLA; Les Dames of Los Angeles; Women's Council, L.A. Community Edn. TV; Women's Guild, Cedars of Lebanon Hosp. Bd. of Councillors: USC Sch. of Performing Arts (co-chmn., 1975-76), USC Schools of Med. and Engring. Office: c/o TRW Inc., One Space Park, Redondo Beach, CA 90278.

RAMSDEN, CHARLES H.
Plastic Surgeon
b. June 13, 1927, Ottawa, Canada; s. Claude and Christine Ramsden; M.D., Queen's Univ., 1954; daus.: Jannica, b. June 17, 1968; Laura, b. July 10, 1970. Career: Internship, Vancouver Gen. Hosp., 1954-55; resident in Gen. Surg., Shaughnessy Hosp., Vancouver, B.C., 1955-56; resident in surg., Kaiser Hosp., Oakland, 1956-57, resident in Ophthalmology, 1957-58; Jr. resident in Plastic Surg., L.D.S. Hosp., Salt Lake City, Ut., 1958-60; vis. plastic surg. in Gr. Brit., 1960-61; Fellowship in Plastic Surg. with African Med. and Research Found., Nairobi, Kenya, 1961, 62, and tchg. Fellowship 1967, now Advis., mem. bd. dirs.; tchr. plastic surg. aboars SS HOPE, Guayiguil, Ecuador, 1964; Instr. Plastic Surg., USC, 1965-77; pvt. practice, Burbank, ---. Diplomate Am. Bd. of Plastic Surg. 1965; Fellow, Am. Coll. of Surgeons, FACS, 1967; Cons. in plastic surg., Olive View Co. Hosp. Contbr. articles to med. journs., med. books. Staff mem.: St. Joseph Hosp., L.A. Co. Hosp., Olive View Hosp., Children's Hosp., L.A., Sherman Oaks Hosp., Tarzana Hosp. Mem.: Am. Assn. of Cosmetic Surgeons; Calif. Soc. of Plastic Surgeons; AMA; L.A. Co. Med. Assn.; Am. Soc. of Plastic & Reconstructuve Surgeons, Inc. Clubs: Safari Club Internat., Lakeside Golf. Rec.: skiing, golf, big game hunting. Office: 2625 W. Alameda Ave., Burbank, CA 91505.

RAMSEY, JACK
Library Director
b. June 12, 1922, Kansas City, Kan.; s. Clay and Floy Ramsey; A.B., Univ. of Kansas, 1945; M.S., Univ. Ill., 1946; M.L.S., 1947; m. Sue Worsley, Apr. 4, 1946, Urbana, Ill. Career: Librarian, N.Y. Pub. Lib., 1947-48; Adminstrv. Asst., Lib. of Stockton and San Joaquin Co., 1948-49; Co. Librarian, Solano Co., 1949-52; Lib. Dir., City of Glendale, 1952-59, 1966---; Chief of Customer Rels., H.W. Wilson Co., NYC, 1959-65. AUS, 1944-45. Mem.: Phi Kappa Psi frat.; Beta Phi Mu (hon. lib. sci. frat.), past pres.; N.Y. Library Club, 1947---, past pres. Republican. Episcopalian. Vestryman. Hobby: music. Rec.: travel. Res.: 548 Mesa-Lila Rd., Glendale, CA 91208; Office: 222 E. Harvard St., Glendale, CA 91205.

RAMSEY, PATRICIA SMITH
Lawyer — Hotelier
b. Nov. 17, 1927, Oakland; d. Edward James (Calif. Judge, 1945-61) and Lillian (Hartmeyer) Smith; GGGranddau. James Harvey Thompson, M.D., (Dist. Atty. & Judge, Calif.); m. Robert James Ramsey (Dec.), Sept. 26, 1959, Las Vegas, Nev.; stepchil.: Donna (Mrs. James Treadwell); Robert James Ramsey, Jr. Career: Admitted to Calif. Bar, 1952; asst. Pub. Defender, Alameda Co., 1952-53; Owner, dir., treas., corporate Legal Counsel, Highlands Inn, Carmel, 1963---. Contbr. articles numerous local publications. Hobby: antique collecting. Res.: Carmel Highlands; Office: P.O.B. 1700, Carmel, CA 93921.

RANKIN, PEGE BETTY
Educator
b. July 23, 1919, Twin Falls, Ida.; d. Marion P. and Margaret (Conway) Rankin; desc. Alexander Hamilton, 1757-1804, Am. Statesman; B.A., Univ. Calif., Berkeley, 1941; M.A., Univ. San Francisco, 1976; tchrs. credential, 1967; m. Herbert E. Rankin, June 5, 1941; children: Greg Robert, Todd Conway. Career: Tchr. Contract Bridge San Francisco Bay Area, 1950-69; press officer, Oakland (Cal.) Pub. Schs., 1967---; tchr. journalism Skyline High Sch., Oakland, 1967---. Tchr. guide European coll. tours, summers 1970---. Chmn. div. fund Am. Cancer Soc. 1958; organizer, condr. Mental Health Bridge Charity, 1961; mem. Friends of Herrick Hosp., Friends of Berkeley Library. Wall Street Journ. Newspaper Fund fellow, 1969. Mem. Am. Assn. Univ. Women, Am. Contract Bridge League, Oakland Press Hobor Assn., Women in Communications (scholarship chmn. 1973), Columbia Scholastic Press Assn., Journalism Educators, No. Calif. Dir. 1975-78, v.p. 1978---; Alpha Chi Alpha. Republican. Methodist. Club: Fannie Hill Ski (San Francisco). Office: 12250 Skyline Blvd., Oakland, CA 94619.

RANNEY, HELEN MARGARET
Professor of Medicine
b. Apr. 12, 1920, Summer Hill, N.Y.; A.B. cum laude, Barnard Coll., Columbia Univ., 1941, M.D., Coll. of Physics and Surgeons, Columbia Univ., 1947. Career: Intern in Med. and Asst. Resident, Medicine, Presbyterian Hosp., N.Y., 1947-50; Clin. Fellow in Med., Am. Cancer Soc., Columbia Univ., 1951-53, instr./assoc. in Med., Columbia Univ., 1954-58, asst. prof. of Clin. Med., 1958-60; assoc. prof. of med., Yeshiva Univ., 1960-65; prof. of medicine: Albert Einstein Coll. of Med., N.Y., 1965-70, State Univ. of N.Y., Buffalo, 1970-73, Univ. of Calif., San Diego, 1973---; also chair, Dept. of Med., 1973---. Bd. dir., Squibb Corp. Co-author: Human Hemoglobins, 1977, Hemoglobinopathies, 1977; contbr. numerous articles med. journs., 1951---; Editorial bds.: Am. Journ. of Med., Am. Journ. of Physiology, Journ. of Clinical Investigation. Awarded Joseph Mather Smith Prize, Columbia Univ. 1955; Dr. Martin Luther King, Jr. Med. Achievement Award, 1972; 1978 Gold Medal, Alumni Assn. Columbia Univ., Phi Beta Kappa, Alpha Omega Alpha; Sigma Xi (Faculty). Mem.: Nat. Acad. of Scis., Inst. of Med. mem. com. 1975---; Fellow, Am. Acad. of Arts and Scis.; Assn. of Am. Physicians, Councillor 9178-83; Am. Coll. of Physicians, Awards Com. 1977-79; Assn. of Profs. in Med.; Am. Soc. for Clin. Investigation; Am. Soc. of Biological Chemists; Am. Physiological Soc.; Am. Soc. of Hematology, pres. 1973-74; Central Soc. for Clin. Research; Western Assn. of Physicians, pres. 1976-77; Internat. Soc. of Hematologists. Res.: 6229 La Jolla Mesa Dr., La Jolla, CA 92037; Office: 225 W. Dickinson St., San Diego, CA 92103.

RAPPAPORT, HERMAN H.
Company President
b. Sept. 24, 1916, New Haven, Conn.; s. M. and Rhea (Small) Rappaport; B.C.E., City Coll. of N.Y. 1939; m. Rhoda K. Rappaport, NYC, June 22, 1942; daus.: Mrs. Robert (Donna Jane) Beck, Mrs. Stephen (Susan) Harris. Career: Chem. engr., Standard Oil Co. of N.J. 1940-42; proj. mgr., Gen. Elec.; lan. dir. Manhattan Proj. with Union Carbide, Columbia Univ. and Oak Ridge, Tenn. 1943-46; chem. mfr. 1947-48; dir. process design ind. div., Bechtel Corp. 1949-53; apptd. Urban Transportation Adv. Council (by Secty. of Transportation, Wash. D.C.— 1969; pres., PEG Found.; pres., The Rappaport Co.; orig. devel. air rights and space, City Mall above Beverly Hills Freeway. Writer, articles on econs. of real estate, orgn. and mgmt. Awards: Certificate for work on atomic bomb. Manhattan Proj., by War Dept.; Commendation for urban redevelopment as leading exponent of free enterprise by L.A. Bd. of Supvs.; Distinguished Serv. Award by Natl. Home Improvement Council. Mem.: L.A. Co. Repub. Finance Com.; natl. chmn. Businessmen's Adv. Com., Insts. for Pgms. Abroad; chmn. bd. govs., Beverly Hills Club, 1965-69. Res.: 244 N. Almont Dr., Beverly Hills, CA; Office: 124 S. Lasky Dr., Beverly Hills, CA 90212.

RASMUSSEN, JOHN M.
Company President
b. Mar. 1, 1929, Kimballton, Iowa; s. Jens F. and Altje R. Rasmussen; student, Iowa State Univ.; B.A., Simpson Coll., 1951; m. Lorraine Acker, Aug. 12, 1951, Atlantic, Iowa; chil.: James D., b. Sept. 2, 1955; Joanne R., b. Jan. 2, 1960. Career: self-employed, Iowa, 1953-65; with Puritan Leasing Co., 1965---; gen. mgr., 1970-76, v.p., 1974-76; pres., dir., 1977---; v.p., Blythe Ice Co., 1974-76; v.p., Palo Verde Equipment Co., 1974-76; pres., dir., 1977; pres. and dir.: Puritan Vacuum Pre-cooling Co.; California Lettuce Growers, Inc.; Pepsi Cola Bottling Co. of Ventura, 1977---; secty., dir., Musilog Corp., 1977---. Served as Sgt. AUS, 1951-53, Korean conflict. Dir., Santa Barbara C. of C., 1974---; Mem.: Masonic lodge, past master 1965; Univ. Club of Santa Barbara; Lambda Chi Alpha. Methodist Ch. bds. Hobbies: cards, gardening. Rec.: golf, sports events. Home: 3636 Tierra Bella, Santa Barbara, CA; Office: 1600 Anacapa St., Santa Barbara, CA.

RASZKOWSKI, HARVEY JOSEPH
Surgeon
b. Sept. 28, 1909, Stanley, Wis.; s. Joseph Guy and Marie (Larsen) Raszkowski; ed. B.S., Univ. of Wis. 1934. M;D; 1036; M.S. (surg.), Univ. of Minn. 1944; m. Rosella Anna Franseen, Madison, Wis. July 2, 1938; son: Robert Reed, b. Aug. 21, 1941. Career: Intern, Grad. Hosp., Univ. of Pa. 1936-38; fellow-first asst. in surg., St. Francis Hosp., Lynwood, Calif., 1948---, chief of staff, 1954. Author: contrib. 6 profl. srticles to med. journs., publ. The Journ. of the Am. Med. Assn. (Oct. 1942, Mar. 1957, May 1959), The Am. Journ. of Surg. (Mar. 1959, Oct. 1962), The Am. Journ. of Roentgenology, Radium Therapy and Nuclear Med. (Oct. 1962). U.S. Army Med. Corps, 1944-46; 1st Lt.-Maj., chief of surg., 161st Gen. Hosp., WW II. Mem.: Fellow, ACS; diplomate, Am. Bd. of Surg.; Western Surg. Assn., Pan Pac. Surg. Assn., Internat. Soc. of Surgs., L.A. Surg. Soc., Nu Sigma Nu. Methodist. Hobby: fishing. Res.: 7622 E. Third St., Downey, CA; Office: 3650 E. Imperial Hwy., Lynwood, CA.

RATLIFF, LOUIS JACKSON, JR.
Mathematician
b. Sept. 1, 1931, Cedar Rapids, Iowa; s. Louis Jackson and Ruth Sarah (Sidlinger) Ratliff; B.A., State Univ., Iowa 1953; M.A. 1958, Ph.D. 1961; Career: Lectr., Indiana Univ., 1961-63; mem. faculty, Univ. Calif., Riverside, 1963---, prof. of mathematics, 1969---. 1st Lt., USAF, 1953-57. Mem. Am. Mathematical Soc., Phi Beta Kappa. Seventh-Day Adventist. Res.: 3139 Newell Dr., Riverside, CA 92507; Office: Univ. Calif., Riverside, CA 92521.

RAYMOND, GENE
Film and Television Star — Producer — Director
b. Raymond Guion, Aug. 13, 1908, New York City, N.Y.; s. LeRoy and Mary (Smith) Guion; ed. Profl. Chil's. Sch., NYC; m. Jeanette MacDonald, L.A., June 16, 1937; (dec. Jan. 14, 1964). Career: Stage debut at age 5 yrs.; Broadway shows: Rip Van Winkle, The Crowded Hour, Mrs. Wiggs of the Cabbage Patch, Pied

Piper of Hamlin, The Potters, Cradle Snatchers, Tkae My Advice, Mirrors, The Shotgun Weddings, Say When, Young Sinners; co-star (with Jeanette MacDonald) on tour, The Guardsman, 1951; co-star: Voice of the Turtle, Empress Theatre, St. Louis, Mo. and Baltimore, Md. 1952; Angel Street, Richmond, Va. 1952; The Petrified Forest, Straw Hat Circuit, 1952, St. Louis, 1953; Call Me Madam, Dallas, Tex. and Toronto, Can.; Private Lives (Sombrero Playhouse), Phoenix, Ariz. 1953; The Moon is Blue, Ashbury Park, N.J.; Be Quiet, My Love, Bar Harbor, Me., Newport, R.I., Somerset, Mass., Vancouver, B.C. 1953; Detective Story, Design for Living, 1954-55; mot. pics. incl.: Personal Made, Ladies of the Big House, Forgotten Commandments, If I Had a Million, Red Dust, Sadie McKee, Ex-Lady, Zoo in Budapest, Brief Moment, Ann Carver's Profession, Flying Down to Rio, The House on 56th Street, Transatlantic Merry-Go-Round, Behold My Wife, The Woman in Red, The Bride Walks Out, The Smartest Girl in Town, That Girl From Paris, There Goes My Girl, Life of the Party, She's Got Everything, Transient Lady, Stolen Heaven, Cross Country Romance, Mr. and Mrs. Smoith, Smilin' Through, The Locket, Sofia; orgn. Masque Prodns. (with Matty Kemp), 1948: prod.-dir.-star, Million Dollar Weekend, 1950; composer: Will You?, Alligator Swing, Let Me Always Sing, Please, I Do, It's All Over; star, The Amazing Mr. Malone, ABC series, 1950; appd. Ed Sullivan TV show, 1951 (wrote and presented orig. song, How Do You Do?), later appd. Sullivan's annual Citation Pgm.; guest star, Ken Murray's TV show, 1951; TV shows incl. Robert Montgomery Presents, Tales of Tomorrow, Fireside Theatre (host-narrator for series, 1954-55; guest artist: Lux Video Theatre, Pulitzer Prize Playhouse, Toast of the Town, Broadway TV Theatre, Schlitz Playhouse of Stars, Ethel Barrymore Theatre; (panel shows) Twenty Questions, It's News to Me, Who Said That? Maj., pilot, intelligence officer (Eng.), AAF (1942-45), WW II; Col. USAAF. Mem.: Bel-Air Country Club, L.A. Tennis Club; N.Y. Ath. Club, The Players, N.Y. Hobby: gymnastics, fencing (medalist), collection of Lincolniana. Rec.: tennis, golf, equestrian, hunting. Home: 250 Trino Way, Pacific Palisades, CA 90272.

READING, JOHN HARDEN
City Official
b. Nov. 26, 1917, Glendale, Ariz.; s. Cecil V. and Lillian Mae (Ingram) Reading; B.S. (bus. adm.), Univ. of Calif. 1940; m. Hazel Mary Swortfiguer, San Antonio, Tex., Feb. 21, 1941; chil.: chil.: Joanna Lee, b. Nov. 19, 1948; Ronald James, b. Nov. 13, 1950. Career: Pres. Ingrams Food Prods. Co., Inc. 1952---; pres. Reds Early Calif. Foods, Inc. 1952---; pres. Reading Mach. Co., Inc. 1952---. City Councilman, City of Oakland, 1961-66, mayor, 1966---. USAF 1940-46, disch. as Col., WW II. Hobbies: sailing, fishing. Res.: 4735 Sequoyah Rd., Oakland, CA; Office: City Hall, 14th and Washington St., Oakland, CA 94612.

REAGAN, MICHAEL D.
University Chancellor
b. Mar. 12, 1927, NYC; s. Oliver and Katherine (Wagner) Reagan; A.b., Coll. of the Holy Cross, 1948; Ph.D., Princeton Univ., 1959; m. 2d. Celeste Mellom, 1970; Career: Mem. Faculty: Williams Coll., Princeton Univ., Syracuse Univ.; Prof. of Political Sci., Univ. Calif., Riverside, 1964---, Dean of Soc. Scis., 1973-75, Dean of Humanities and Soc. Scis., 1975-77, The Vice Chancellor, 1978---. Author: The Managed Economy, 1963; Sci. and the Fed. Patron, 1969; The New Federalism, 1972; contbr. many journ. articles in area of Am. Nat. pub. policy. Staff Sgt., USMCR, active duty, 1945-46, 1950-51. Hobbies: photog., working outside. Office: Univ. of Calif., Riverside, CA 92521.

REAGAN, NANCY DAVIS
Former First Lady of California
b. July 6, Chicago, Ill.; d. Dr. Loyal and Edith (Luckett) Davis; ed. Girls Latin Sch., Chicago; Smith Coll., Northampton, Mass.; m. Ronald Reagan (former Gov, of Calif.), L.A., Mar. 4, 1952; chil.: Patricia Ann and Ronald Prescott. Career: Active many philanthropic, social, civic and governmental groups of Calif. Chosen Woman of Year by L.A. Times 1968. Elevated to permanent List of Best Dressed in the country. Active in POW-MIA affairs and in the Foster Grandparent Program. Awards: Calif. Am. Mothers' Com. Govt. Award, 1970. Res.: 1669 San Onofre Dr., Pacific Palisades, CA 90272.

REAGAN, RONALD
Former Governor of California
b. Feb. 6, 1911, Tampico, Ill.; s. John E. and Nellie (Wilson) Reagan; B.A. (sociology and econs.), Eureka Coll., Ill. 1932; m. Jane Wyman, L.A., Jan. 25, 1940 (div. 1948); chil.: Maureen, Michael; m. 2nd., Nancy Davis, Mar. 4, 1952; chil.: Patricia Ann, b. 1952; Ronald Prescott, b. May 20, 1958. Career: Lifeguard, Eureka, Ill.; radio writer-sports anncr. 1932-37; guest artist, many radio shows; actor, mot. pics. 1937-66; pics. incl.: The Voice of the Turtle, The Hasty Heart, King's Row, Night Unto Night, Prisoner of War; pgm. supv., Gen. Electric Theater. Lectr. on government history and politics, USA. Governor of Calif., Nov. 1966-75; chmn. Repub. Governor's Assn., USA 1969. Republican Candidate for President, USA, 1976. Capt., USAAF (1942-45), WW II. Mem.: pres., SAG (6 terms); co-chmn., Motion Picture Industry Council; Tau Kappa Epsilon. Hollywood-Beverly Chr. Ch. Hobby: horses. Rec.: swimming, golf, horseback riding. Res.: Pacific Palisades, CA.

REAL, MANUEL L.
U.S. District Judge
b. Jan. 27, 1924, San Pedro, Calif.; s. Francisco Jose and Maria (Dulcenombro) Real; ed. B.A. 194[; L.A.B., 1951; m. Stella Michalik, L.A., Oct. 15, 1955; chil.: Michael, Melanie Marie, Timothy, John Robert. Career: Asst. U.S. Atty. 1952-55; pvt. practice law, 1955-64; U.S. Atty., L.A. 1964-66; U.S. Dist. Judge, 1966---. Chmn. Model Neighborhood Comm. on Justice, 1970-73. USNR 1943-45, ret. 1945-64. Mem.: Sigma Chi. Roman Catholic. Office: U.S. Dist. Court, 312 N. Spring St., L.A., CA 90012.

RECTOR, MARGARET HAYDEN
Playwright
b. May 23, 1916, Azusa, Calif.; d. Dr. Floyd Smith and Anna Martha (Miller) Hayden; father helped found the junior coll. movement in Calif. bringing it back from Univ. of Chicago and Beloit, founder of Citrus Coll. (Azusa-Glendora) in 1915; A.A., Citrus Coll., 1936; B.A., Pomona Coll., 1938; postgrad.: Stanford Univ., Columbia Univ., UCLA, USC-Idyllwild, St. John's Coll.; m. Dr. Robert Wayman Rector, Aug. 25, 1940, Claremont, Calif. Bridges H. Chil.: Cleone Ann (Grabowski), b. Feb. 14, 1944; Robin Suzanne (Krupp), b. Mar. 29, 1946; Bruce Hayden, b. Jan. 24, 1950; Career: writer of plays, 1938---; also free-lance writer for: House Beautiful, Am. Home mags., 1941-46; nat. and internat. pub. rel., Curt Wagner firm, 1956-66; playwright: 14 theatrical prodns. in Hollywood (Warner Playhouse and Evergreen Stage Company), at UCLA, at San Diego's Old Globe contest, Grossmont Summer Stock Company; producer, Warner Playhouse, 1966; Author: Norton And Gus, Grossmont Press, 1976. Mem.: AAUW; Am. Nat. Theatre and Acad. Aux.; ANTA; Surfwriters; UCLA Faculty Wives and Writers' Workshop (offices held in all assns.); Writers' Guild; UCLA Affiliates; ANTA Westside Playwrights' Unit. Democrat, activities orginzer Md. Dem. Party, 1946-56. Hobby: family hist., albums, scrapbooks. Rec.: swimming. Home-Office: 10700 Stradella Ct., L.A., CA 90024.

RECTOR, ROBERT W.
Data Processing Company Executive
b. Jan. 28, 1916, San Jose; s. Joseph J. and Eva G. (Hembree) Rector; gr.son of Waman C. Hembree, Ore. pioneer; B.A. mathematics, San Jost State Coll., 1937; M.A., math., Stanford Univ., 1939; Ph.D., math, Univ. of Maryland, 1956; m. Margaret Hayden, Aug. 25, 1940, Claremont; chil.: Cleone (Grabowski), b. Feb. 14, 1944; Robin (Krupp), b. Mar. 29, 1946; Bruce Hayden, b. Jan. 24, 1950. Career: assoc. prof. of mathmatics, US Naval Acad., Md., 1946-56; adminstrv. mgr. and staff mathematician, Space Tech. Labs., L.A. (Ramo-Wooldridge Corp.), 1956-61; asst. dir., data processing center, Aerospace Corp., El Segundo, 1961-65; v.p. div., Informatics, Inc., Canoga Park, 1965-70; v.p., corp. ops., Cognitive Systems, Inc., Beverly Hills, 1970-71; assoc. dir., short courses and conferences, UCLA ext., engring. and sci., 1970-73; exec. dir., Am. Fedn. of Information Processing Socs., Inc., N.J., 1973---. Capt. USNR, active duty 1942-46. Pub. articles: The Profl. Aspects of Privacy and Confidentiality, 1974; The Fourth — Another Generation Gap?, 1969; Space Age Computing, 1959. Mem.: Am. Fedn. Information Processing Socs., Inc., exec. com. & treas., 1970-72; Assn. for Computing Machinery, chmn. L.A. chpt. 1962-64; Pac. Journ. of Mathematics, secty., bd. of govs., 1957---; Am. Assn. Advancement of Sci.; Math. Assn. of Am.; Am. Soc. for Engring. Edn.; Am. Soc. of Assn. Execs.; L.A. Mayor's Space Advisory Com. 1964-72. Rel. Disciples of Christ. Hobby: philately. Rec.: music. Home: 10700

Stradella Ct., L.A., CA 90024; Office: American Fedn. Information Processing Societies, 210 Summit Ave., Montvale, N.J. 07645.

REDDICK, BENJAMIN OTIS
Newspaper Publisher
b. Mar. 14, 1915, Huntington Park, Calif.; s. John James and Partheny Josephine (Hance) Reddick; ed. grad. Huntington Park Union H.S. 1934; m. Dorothy Daly, Bell, Calif., Sept. 27, 1935; sons: Richard Daly, James Douglas, Randolph Lee. Career: Photographer-reporter, Huntington Park Signal, 1929-40, Long Beach Press Telegram, 1941-42, L.A. Examiner, 1942-45; propr. Newport Balboa Press, 1945 (purchased The News-Times and merged publs. forming Newport Harbor News-Press), 1949, publ. 1949-62; publ. San Fernando Valley, Valley Times, North Hollywood, 1963-65; propr.-publ., The Daily Press and Journ., Paso Robles, Calif. 1967---. Dir., Orange Co. Coast Assn., 1945-64; dir. Long Beach Fed. S&L Assn., 1947-60; apptd. to Bd. of Supvs., Orange Co. (by Gov. Goodwin J. Knight), 1958. Mem.: dir. Calif. Newspaper Publs. Assn. 1948-62; dir. Americansim Edn. League; dir. Freedom Documents Found.; exalted ruler, Newport Harbor Elks Lodge, 1950. Hobby: photog. Rec.: fishing. Res.: 355 W. Fourth St., Paso Robles. Office: The Daily Press, 1212 Pine St., Paso Robles, CA 93446.

REDFIELD, PETER SCRANTON
President, Itel Corporation
b. Apr. 21, 1931, Cambridge, Mass.; s. Scranton Howard and Marie (Dibell) Redfield; B.A. liberal arts, Colgate Univ., 1953; m. Alice Daukas, June 15, 1957, Cambridge, Mass.; chil.: Charles Scranton, b. Nov. 17, 1959; Anne Marie, b. Apr. 18, 1963; Sarah Chadwick, b. Sept. 4, 1964; Career: mgmt., Varian Assoc., Palo Alto, 1959-61; mgmt. cons. data processing, McKinsey & Co., S.F., 1962-66; dir. adminstrv. services, Transamerica Corp., S.F., 1966-67; formed SSI Computer Corp., now Itel Corp., 1967---. Dir.: Hong Kong Bank of Calif., Inc.; George Lithograph Co.; Systron-Donner Corp.; bd. trustee, Colgate Univ., Hamilton, N.Y. Served to Lt. j.g., USN. Mem.: Menlo Circus Club, Atherton; Burlingame Country Club, Hillsborough; Pacific Union Club; World Trade Club; Bankers Club; Villa Taverna, S.F.; The Links, N.Y. Rec.: tennis, golf. Home: Atherton, CA; Office: One Embarcadero Center, S.F., CA 94111.

REDIGER, ALBERT J.
Burbank Civic Leader
b. Aug. 24, 1904, Milford, Nebr.; s. David A. and Emelia L. (Krenzin) Rediger of No. Hollywood; bro. of Alvin E., Walter W. and Amanda M. Rediger; ed. pub. schs., Nebr. and No. Hollywood, Calif.; Bus. Coll., L.A.; m. Nellie M. Whitaker, Milford, Nebr., Jan. 11, 1929; chil.: Donald E. Career: Propr.-pres., Automotive Serv. Unit, Burbank, 1929---. Pres. Burbank Coord. Council, 1944-45; elected to Burbank City Council, 1943-47, v.-mayor, 1945-47; police and fire commr., chmn. Traffic and Safety Comm.; lib. and park commr., commr. of Streets and Hwys. Awards: recipient, citizen of the yr., awarded by City of Burbank, 1954. Mem.: (life) Burbank Optimist Club, 1937---, pres. 1943-44; Boy Scouts of Amer., Verdugo Hills Council Com. 1940-46, Burbank dist. chmn. 1947-49, council pres. 1950-52; bd. dirs. Burbank YMCA 1944-56; bd. dirs., Optimist Home for Boys, 1945---, v.p. 1949---; Burbank Globe Trotter Series, 1945---, chmn-treas. 1951---; bd. dirs., Burbank C. of C. 1948-50, pres. 1952-54; (hon. life) Calif. Congress of Parents & Teachers, Inc.; div. chmn.-budget com., Community Chest drives; Red Cross drives; March of Dimes, Salvation Army Com. 1951---. First Assembly of God, N. Hollywood (off. bd.-treas. Missions Dept.). Rec.: baseball, fishing. Res.: 730 E. Grinnell Dr., Burbank, CA; Office: First at Magnolia, Burbank, CA.

REED, HENRY CARLYLE
Publisher Emeritus, The Sacramento Union
b. July 9, 1915, Glendale, Ariz.; s. Henry Clay (ed.-publ., Imperial Press, first newspaper in Imperial Valley during pioneering days of W.F. Holt) and Blanche (List) Reed; ed. Ariz. State Coll., Tempe, 1933-34; Woodbury Bus. Coll., 1934; m. Eleanor Pitkin, Ramona, Calif., Mar. 31, 1962; daus.: Carolyn Ione, b. Jan. 29, 1940; Darlene Anne Harden, b. Sept. 10, 1945. Career: Asst. ed., Glendale (Ariz.) News, 1934-36; Central Ariz. Light & Power Co. 1936-38; publ. El Cajon Valley News, 1938-53; co-publ., La Mesa Scout and gen. mgr., Intercity Pres, publs. and

printers, 1938-52; ed. El Cajon Valley News, 1953-54; pub. rels. cons., Carlyle Reed & Assocs. 1954-56; legislative rep., San Diego Union and Tribune, 1956; spec. rep. of dir., Water Resources, State of Calif., July 9, 1956-Sept. 1, 1957; publs. ofc. rep., Union-Tribune Publ. Co., San Diego, and legislative rep., Copley Newspapers, 1957; asst. to the publ., Union Tribune, 1964-66; publ., The Sacramento Union, 1966-74; Disaster Acting Gov. No. 1, 1967---; Mem.: bd. dirs.-exec. com-past pres. Calif. Newspaper Publs. Assn.; (past) bd. dirs.-exec. com., Sacto. Met. C. of C.; exec. com. Golden Empire Council, BSA; adv. com. Calif. State Univ., Sacto.; bd. govs. Mercy Hosp. Found.; (past) State Water Quality Control Panel; Select Com. on Revision of Master Plan for Higher Edn. in Calif.; Commodore, Port of Sacto.; (charter) dir., Sacto. Chpt. Navy League; 1st v.p., Calif. Press Assn.; (past) Sacto. Rotary; Del Paso Country Club; Sutter Club; Sacto. Chpt. Grandfathers Club of Am.; bd. dirs., Sacto. Sym. Assn.; Sacto. Host Com.; charter S.D. and Sacto. Chpts. Sigma Delta Chi. Hobby: photography. Res.: 5094 Keane Dr., Carmichael, CA; Office: 301 Capitol Mall, Sacto., CA 95812.

REED, MARY STEVENS
Educator
b. Crandall, Ind.; d. Albert Thomas and Mabel (Fellmy) Stevens; B.S., M.S., Ind. State Univ., Terre Haute; Ed.D., USC 1965; m. Howard L. Reed; son, Vernon Lawrence (m. Patricia Randolph); granddaus.: Leslie Katherine, Melissa Lee. Career: Demonstration tchr., Terre Haute City Schs., Ind. State Univ.; tchr.-dir. spec. edn.-reading cons (est. first spec. edn. pgm. in No. Ind.); curriculum cons.-dir. summer sch., E. Whittier Sch. Dist., Calif. 1952-54; dir. rezding clinic-cons., Long Beach City Schs., Calif. 1954-57; instr. Calif. State Coll., L.B. 1954-60; dir. curriculum, Funnerton (Calif.) Elem. Schs. 1957-63; instr. Calif. State Coll., Fullerton 1960-63; dir. instructional servs. and curriculum, El Segundo (Calif.) Unified Sch. Dist. 1963-73; Supt. El Segundo Unified Sch. Dist. 1973---. Cons. Calif. State Dept., reading-lang. progms., Orange Co. and Santa Barbara Co. 1964---; instr. UCLA Ext. courses, 1964-65; prof. USC Ext. courses in lang. arts, reading, 1965---; visiting prof., USC, Graduate Overseas Pgm, 1976-78; L.A. Co. Regional TV Adv. Com., pres. Fullerton Elem. and H.S. Dist. Curriculum Council, 1963; apptd. by State Bd. of Edn. to Study Com. for Jr. H.S. Edn.; U.S. Natl. Com. for Childhood Edn. World Conf., Paris, Fr., 1966; com., Calif. State Dept. of Edn. 1966-68; co-chmn. El Segundo Community Leadership Seminars, 1966; chmn. Elem. Sect., State Adv. Com. for Calif.; apptd. to Calif. State Adv. Com. for Child Devel. Centers, 1967. Lectr.: Programmed Learning in Elem. Schs., Natl. Audio-Visual Assn. 1962; Is the Curriculum Realistic?, Dept. of Classroom Tchrs. and PTA Regional Conf.; Changing Role of Curriculum Director, Creativity and Executive Women. Author: Test Items for Calif. Achievement Test, Form WXY, Calif. Testing Bur., L.A.; Reading Clinic and Its Relation to Guidance, Journ. of Natl. Assn. of Women Deans and Counselors, 1956; Book Length Stories, Ginn and Co. 1962; co-author, Our Family of Man, published 1971; consulting ed. (textbooks), Franklin Publ. Co. Awards: Eddy for regional edn. TV, KCOP, L.A. 1960; Calif. rep. to Columbia Univ. Natl. Conf. Curriculum 1963-2000; Hon. Ky. Col. for serv. to community of El Segundo, 1966; nom. Woman of Yr. by El Segundo Bus. and Profl. Women's Club, 1967; Citizen of Mo., El Segundo C. of C., Apr. 1967, Mem.: (life) PTA, Fullerton, 1960; (charter) Educare, USC 1961; pres. Rho Chpt., Delta Kappa Gamma, 1962064; natl. bd. dirs., ASCD, 1963---; exec. bd.-v.p.-pgm. chmn., Calif. Assn. for Supv. and Curriculum Development, 1965-66, conf. com. 1967; Delta Epsilon, 1965---; Assn. of Gifted, Math. Council, L.A. Co. Curriculum Assn., Internat. Reading Assn.; coms. Quota Club, El Segundo; Community Christmas Parade Com., El Segundo C. of C. 1965; edn. adv. com. Calif. Gov's. Comm. on Status of Women; judge, Jr. Miss Contest, El Segundo Jr. C. of C. 1965, 66; dir. So. Sect., Calif. Assn. for Elem. Sch. Admrs., chmn. coms.; chmn. El Segundo res. area Campaign for United Way, 1966; pres. El Segundo Chpt., Bus. and Profl. Women, 1966-67, panelist, Creativity and Exec. Women, Natl. Conf. 1967. Res.: 2359-C Via Mariposa E., Laguna Hills, CA 92653.

REED, SHERRY MARIE LIBRAND
Occupational Therapist
b. Jan. 9, 1947, Mivot, N.Dak.; d. Sam and Doris (Spoonland) Librande. B.S., Colo. State Univ., 1969; m. Stephen Michael Reed, Jan. 4, 1970, Ft. Collins, Colo. Career: Occupational therapist, Four Seasons

Nursing Home, Ft. Collins, 1970; Peace Corps tchr., Med. Tng. Center, Nairobi, Kenya, 1970-73; Occupational Therapist, Denver Sch. System, Summer 1974; Dir. Occ. Therapy, Mills Mem. Hosp., San Mateo, 1974---. Developed Pediatric Occ. therapy clinic, Kenyatta Nat. Hosp. Nairobi, Kenya, E. Africa, 1972; Coordinator for the devel. of criteria for the evaluation & treatment of the CUA patient for the Calif. State Dept. of Health, 1977; Financial mgmt. cons. for Occ. Therapy 1977---. TV and Newspaper Interviews (Kathryn Crosby Show, K60 Perspective) publicizing Occ. Therapy to community, 1976. Mem.: Calif. Occ. Therapy Assn.; Am. Occ. Therapy Assn. (AOTA), co-chmn. publicity com. Nat. Conf. 1976. Hobby: cross-country skiing. Res.: 36001 Spruce St., Newark, CA 94560; Office: 100 S. San Mateo Dr., San Mateo, CA 94401.

REEVES, FRANK EDGAR
Engineering Association Executive
b. Jan. 14, 1902, Boston, Mass.; s. David Victor and Emma Louise (Lindig) Reeves; B.S. and M.S., Mass. Inst. of Technology, 1925; m. Victoria Ollene Clark, Aug. 3, 1970, Los Angeles. Career: supr. elec. testing, Boston Edison Co., 1925-43; control engr., Electrical Apparatus Co., Boston, 1943-48; power plant design engr.: Fay, Spofford & Thorndike, Boston, 1948-49, and Barnard & Burk, Baton Rouge, La., 1949-52; power plant coordinating engr., Ebasco Internat., NYC, 1952-53; dist. mgr., Automatic Switch Co., L.A., 1953-70; exec. mgr., Institute for the Advancement of Engring., L.A. ---; also exec. secty., L.A. Council of Engrs. and Scis. ---; Supr. power plant elect. design for plants in Lafayette, La.; Ladd AFB, Alaska; Hydro-elec. plant, Peixoto, Brazil; Trombay, India; various Central Am. countries, 1948-53; and Chile; also tchr. E.E., Harvard Univ., 1948 and Wentworth Inst. Boston, 1949. Registered E.E., Mass., N.Y., Calif., La.; reg. control systems engr., Calif.; tchr. certificate, Calif. Dept. of Edn., 1967. Author: A Manual of Electrical Control, 1950; 70 articles on E.E. and pub. tech. journs.; editor, SPARKS, bi-weekly publ., Elec. Club of L.A. Awards: Archimedes Engr. Achievement award, Calif. Soc. of Profl. Engrs., 1979; Fellow, Inst. Advance. of Engring. and mem., Coll. of Fellows; Inter-Profl. Achievement Award, Soc. of Mfg. Engrs., 1974; Dist. Contrbrns. to Engring. Profession award, San Fernando Valley Engrs. Council, 1978. Mem.: pres., Baton Rogue Chpt., L.A. Soc. of Profl. Engrs., 1950; pres., Engrs. & Archits. Inst., L.A. (3 terms), 1955-58; pres., Elec. Club of L.A., 1963; pres., L.A. chpt., Calif. Soc. of Profl. Engrs., 1963-65; founder, 1st pres., Inst. for Advance. of Engring., L.A., 1967; Life mem.: Nat. Soc. of Profl. Engrs., Instrument Soc. of Am., Eta Kappa Nu; Soc. Am. Mil. Engrs.; Elect. Maintenance Engrs. Assn.; So. Calif. Meter Assn.; BPOE Elks "99", L.A., 1956---. Hobbies: music, organ playing. Home: 1661 Mokawk St., L.A., CA 90026; Office: 1052 W. 6th St., Suite 334, L.A., CA 90017.

REHFELDT, PHILLIP RICHARD
Musician — Educator
b. Sept. 21, 1939, Burlington, Iowa; s. Romiss and Rachel Rehfeldt; B.M.Ed., Univ. of Ariz., 1961; M.M., clarinet, Mount St. Mary's Coll., L.A., 1962; A Mus.D., clarinet, Univ. of Mich., 1969; m. Sally Webb, Dec. 22, 1961, Tucson, Ariz.; sons: Phillip Andrews, b. 1962; Stephen John, b. 1966; Matthew Charles, b. 1970; Douglas William, b. 1977. Career: Tchr., Tucson Pub. Schs., 1962-65, No. Mich. Univ., 1965-68, San Bernardino Valley Coll., 1969-74; Prof. of Music, Univ. of Redlands, 1969---. Major solo appearances; Internat. Computer Music Conf., UCSD, La Jolla, 1978; Monday Eve. Concerts, L.A., 1978; Internat. Clarinet Symposium, Toronto, 1978 and Denver, 1975; Am. Soc. of Univ. Composers nat. convention, Phoenix, 1975 and Urbana, 1977; concerts of spec. commd. works, Music for Clarinet and Friend, with composer, Barney Childs; Faculty Wind Quintet of Univ. of Redlands; Riverside Symphony Orch., soloist 1975, 78; Redlands Symphony Orch., Redlands Bowl Symp. Orch.; San Bernardino and Palm Springs Orchestras, prin. bassoon, 1971-74; Univ. Mich. Contemporary Directions Ensemble, 1967-69. Author: New Directions for Clarinet, UC Press, 1978; contbr. articles in The Clarinet, Proceedings of Am. Soc. of Univ. Composers, Journ. of Research in Music Edn., others. Latest recording: American Music for Wind Quintet, Advance Recordings, 1979. Mem.: Am. Soc. of Univ. Composers, Internat. Clarinet Soc.; ALA; Orange Belt Musicians Assn., Local 1967; Pi Kappa Lambda. Res.: 610 W. Cypress, Redlands, CA 92373; Office: Univ. of Redlands, Sch. of Music, Redlands, CA 92373.

REIDHAAR, DONALD L.
General Counsel, University of Cal. Regents
b. Sept. 22, 1933; Grangeville, Ida.; s. James Joseph and Lois (Heimark) Reidhaar (Luginbuhl); A.B. (cum laude), Univ. of Wash. 1957; LL.B. Boalt Hall Sch. of Law, Univ. of Calif. 1960; m. Dolores Ferchalk, St. Maries, Ida., Mar. 18, 1956; dau. Lisa Ann, b. Sept. 9, 1962. Career: Law clerk to Justice Kenneth J. O'Connell, Ore. Supreme Ct. 1960-61; assoc. Pillsbury, Madison & Sutro law firm, S.F. 1961-62; asst. counsel, The Regents of Univ. of Calif. 1962-71, assoc. counsel, 1971-73; gen. counsel, 1973---. U.S. Army, Ft. Ord, Calif. 1954-55. Mem.: Ore. State, Calif., U.S. Supreme Ct. Bars; Natl. Assn. Coll. and Univ. Attys. 1973---; City Commons Club of Berkeley, 1973---; Commonwealth Club of Calif., 1973---. Democrat. Our Savior's Lutheran Ch., Lafayette. Hobbies: gardening, fishing, reading, hiking. Res.: 632 Los Palos Dr., Lafayette, CA 94549; Office: 590 Univ. Hall, 220 Univ. Ave., Berkeley, CA 94720.

REINER, IRA
City Controller
b. Feb. 15, 1936, L.A.; s. Max and Helen Reiner; B.S., fin., USC, 1959; J.D., Southwestern Univ. Sch. of Law, 1964; m. Diane Wayne, Municipal Ct. Judge; chil.: Ann, b. Sept. 16, 1975; Tom, b. Nov. 17, 1977. Career: admitted to Calif. Bar, 1964, Supreme Ct. of the U.S., 1969; Dep. L.A. City Atty., 1964-67; Superior Ct. Judge Pro Tem, Juvenile Div., 1974-75; Apptd. (by Mayor Tom Bradley) mem., L.A. City Fire Commn., v.p. 1973-75; elected mem., L.A. Community Coll. Nd. of Trustees, 1973-75, v.p., 1977; elected L.A. City Controller, 1977---. Office: 200 N. Spring St., Rm. 220, City Hall, L.A., CA 90012.

REINES, FREDERICK
Physicist — Educator
b. Mar. 16, 1918, Paterson, N.J.; s. Israel and Gussie (Cohen) Reines; M.E., Stevens Inst. Tech., 1939, M.S. 1941; Ph.D., NYU, 1944; D.Sc. (hon.), Univ. Witwatersrand, 1966; m. Sylvia Samuels, Aug. 30, 1940; chil.: Robert G., Alisa K. Career: Mem. staff Los Alamos Sci. Lab., 1944-59; group leader Theoretical div., 1945-59; dir. AEC expts. on Eniwetok Atoll, 1951; prof. physics, Univ. Calif. at Irvine, 1966---; also dean phys. scis. 1966-74. Mem. Cleve. Symphony Chorus, 1959-62. Guggenheim fellow, 1958-59; Sloan fellow, 1959-63. Fellow Am. Phys. Soc., AAAS; mem. Am. Assn. Physics Tchrs., Argonne Univ. Assn. (trustee 1965-66), Am. Acad. Arts and Scis., Phi Beta Kappa, Sigma Xi (Stevens honor award, 1972), Tau Beta Pi. Contbr. numerous articles to profl. journs. Contbg. author: Effects of Atomic Weapons, 1950; Methods of Experimental Physics, 1961. Co-discoverer elementary nuclear particle, free antineutrino, 1956. Res.: 2655 Basswood St., Newport Beach, CA 92660; Office: Univ. Calif. at Irvine, Irvine, CA 92717.

RENDA, DOMINIC P.
Airline President
b. Dec. 25, 1913, Steubenville, Oh.; s. Joseph J. and Catherine Roberta Renda; B.S., Ohio State Univ. 1938, J.D., Coll. of Law, 1938; m. Patricia Marie Vogts (div.); chil.: Dominique P., b. Dec. 28, 1962; Dominic P., Jr., b. Dec. 17, 1964; Patrick B., b. July 19, 1968. Career: Gen. practice law, Steubenville, Oh. 1939-40; adm. asst. to U.S. Congressman 18th Dist., Oh. 1941-42; sr. v.p.-legal counsel, Western Airlines, 1946-67; sr. v.p. Internat. and Pub. Affairs, Continental Air Lines, pres.-chief exec. ofcr. Air Micronesia, 1968-72; bd. dirs. Western Airlines, 1973---, exec. v.p. 1973-76, pres. 1976---. Dir.: Bank of Montreal, Calif. 1974---; L.A. Area C. of C., 1975---; bd. councilors, Sch. of Internat. Rels., USC; dir., So. Calif. Region-Natl. Conf. of Christians and Jews; trustee, PEACE Found., Ponape, Caroline Isls.; chmn. Devel. Comm., Marymount High School. Bus. Adm. Adv. Council, Coll. of Adm. Sci., Oh. State Univ., and Alumni Adv. Bd. Lt. Comdr., Ofc. of Judge Advocate Gen. and Bureau of Yards and Docks, USN, 1942-46. Clubs: L.A. Ath., Marina City, Riviera Country, Bel-Air Country. Res.: 4314 Marine City Dr., Marina Del Rey, CA 90291; Office: World Way, 6060 Avion Dr., L.A., CA 90009.

RENFREW, CHARLES BYRON
United States District Judge
b. Oct. 31, 1928, Detroit, Mich.; s. Charles W. and Louise (McGuire) Renfrew; A.B., Princeton, 1952; J.D., Mich. Law Sch., 1956; m. Susan Wheelock, June 28, 1952; chil.: Taylor Allison Ingham, b. Feb. 12,

1957; Charles Robin, b. Jan. 5, 1959; Todd Wheelock, b. Oct. 16, 1962; James Bartlett, b. Jan. 22, 1965. Career: Associate, law firm of Pillsbury, Madison & Sutro, S.F., 1956-65, partner, 1965-72; U.S. Dist. Judge, No. Dist. of Calif., 1972---. USN, 1946-48; AUS, 1952-53. Office: 450 Golden Gate Ave., S.F., CA 94102.

RENSCH, JOSEPH ROMAINE
Utility Company Executive
b. Jan. 1, 1923, San Bernardino, Calif.; s. Joseph Romaine and Lucille (Ham) Rensch; B.S., Stanford Univ. 1947; J.D., Golden Gate Coll. 1955; m. June Burley, Pasadena, Mar. 25, 1946; sons: Steven Roger, b. Oct. 1, 1947; Jeffrey Powell, b. July 28, 1950. Career: Mech. engr., Coast Counties Gas & Elec. Co. 1947-54; Pac. Gas & Elec. Co. 1954-56; admitted to Calif. bar. 1955; Dow Chem. Co. 1956; So. Cos. Gas Co. of Calif. 1957-58; asst. v.p.-spec. counsel, Pac. Lighting Serv. Co. 1958-61, v.p. 1962-65, sr. v.p. 1965-67, exec. v.p. 1967-69, pres. 1969-70, chmn. bd, 1971-73; exec. v.p. Pacific Lighting Corp. 1968-71; dir., pres. 1972---. Dir.: Union Bank, 1971---; The Bekins Co. 1972---; Union Bancorp, 1973---; Kaiser Steel Corp. 1973---; Dir.: Foremost-McKesson, Inc. 1975---; The Olga Co., 1976---; Lockheed Corp., 1978---. Mem.: dir. Pac. Gas. Assn. 1964-68; pres. 1967; dir. Interstate Natural Gas Assn. 1968-73; dir. Am. Gas Assn. 1969-73; Alpha Tau Omega; Tau Beta Pi; clubs: dir. L.A., pres. 1971; The Family, S.F.; California, dir. L.A. Country, Pauma Valley Country, Palos Verdes Golf. Hobbies: reading, music. Rec.: golf, tennis. Office: 810 S. Flower St., L.A., CA 90071.

RETTE, JOHN J.
Medical Association Executive
b. Dec. 17, 1942, Phila.; s. Frank and Stella Rette; B.S., LaSalle Univ., 1964; M.B.A., Drexel Univ., 1971; m. Joan Busfield, May 14, 1965, Phila.; Chil.: Alicia, b. 1973; Christopher, b. 1976; Ashley, b. 1978. Career: with Sears Roebuck & Co., 1964-69; Phila. Med. Soc., 1969-73; Exec. dir., Orange Co. Med. Assn., 1973---. Mng. Editor, award winning med. journ. (1st place nat. 1977); chmn., Southeast Orange Civic Assn. Mil.: USAR. Mem.: Am. Soc. of Assn. Execs.; Am. Assn. of Med. Soc. Execs.; So. Calif. chpt. Assn. of Execs. Hobby: oil painting. Rec.: sailing, tennis, skiing. Res.: 705 S. Yorba, Orange, CA; Office: 300 S. Flower, St., Orange, CA 92668.

REYNOLDS, RICHARD H.
Professor of Art
b. May 16, 1913, New York, N.Y.; s. Raymond R. and Alice S. Reynolds; A.A., San Bernardino Valley Coll., 1933; B.A., Univ. of Calif., Berkeley, 1936; Gen. Sec. Tchg. cred., 1939; M.A., Coll. of the Pacific, 1942; D.F.A., Morningside Coll., Sioux City, Iowa, 1976; m. Marjorie Merrihew Sharper (artist), Aug. 10, 1939, Berkeley; dau. Barbara Gwynne (Mrs. George Nagata). Career: advt. art, S.F., 1936-39; instr. art, Stockton Coll. and Coll. of the Pacific (now Univ. of Pac.), 1939-43, Stockton Coll., 1946-48; instr. art, Univ. of Pacific, 1948---: prof. of art and chmn. Dept. of Art, 1948-73; sr. prof. of art, 1973---; also visiting prof., Univ. Idaho, 1954; visiting prof., Alaska Methodist Univ., 1962. Recipient: commns. and awards for painting and sculpture, recent: bronze relief, Bert Swenson, for Swenson Golf Course, Stockton, 1968; metal falcon sculpture for Atwater Hi Sch.; bronze relief for new wing, Stockton Record Bldg.; bronze relief plaque, Quemada, N. Mex. Lib., 1973; drawing, painting awards, San Joaquin Co. Fair & Exposition, 1974; 3 painting awards, Stockton Art League annual exhib., 1974, purchase award, 1975; 1st prize sculpture, San Joaquin Co. Fair, 1976; 2nd prize; Bank of Stockton's Bicentennial art exhibition, 1976; shell grantee, 1960; life fellow, Internat. Inst. of Arts and Letters. Publ.: Arts and Archit., 1947; Pacific Review, 1948; Contbr. articles, book reviews, art mags.; radio, TV interviewee on the arts; honored by city of Stockton, 1978. Served to Lt. j.g., USNR; visual aids artists and ordnance instr., Naval Sch. of Indoctrination, Univ. Arizona, 1943; intelligence and surface controller, Philippine Sea Frontier. Mem.: Pacific Arts Assn., pres. No. Calif. sect. 1952; dir. Stockton Art League, pres. 1952; hon. bd. dir., San Joaquin Concert Ballet Assn.; Phi Sigma Kappa; Phi Kappa Phi, past pres.; Phi Delta Kappa; Nat. Art Edn. Assn., Nat. mem. chmn. 1952; Coll. Art Assn. of Am. Home: 1656 W. Longview Ave., Stockton, CA 95207; Office: Univ. of the Pacific.

REYNOLDS, ROBERT A.
Broadcasting Company Executive
b. May 27, 1922, NYC; s. Wilder R. and Beulah (Allen) Reynolds; A.B., Asbury Coll., 1942; m. Lois Scott, June 14, 1949, Los Angeles; children: Scott Alen, b. Dec. 8, 1954; Robyn Louise, b. July 22, 1956. Career: Instr., Azusa Pacific Coll., 1948-49; Asst. to Pres., Far East Broadcasting Co., Inc., Whittier, 1951-57; dir. for Asia, 1957-60; v.p. for Opns., 1960-77, v.p., treas., 1977---. Lt. j.g., USNR Ret. Res.: 1273 Oakthorn Lane, La Mirada, CA 90638; Office: P.O.B. One, Whittier, CA.

REYNOLDS, ROBERT O'DELL
President, California Angels
b. Mar. 30, 1914, Morris, Okla.; s. Clarence Edward and Cynthia Evelyn (O'Dell) Reynolds; ed. H.S. Okmulgee, Okla., 1932; A.N., Stanford Univ. 1936 (3 Rose Bowl games, Stanford Varsity, 1933, 34, 35); m. Enna Lee McDaniel, Forest Hills, N.Y., June 14, 1941; chil.: Christopher, b. May 4, 1942; Daniel, b. June 20, 1944; Kirkwood, b. June 25, 1952. Career: Tool pusher, Okla. oil fields, 1936-37; profl. football player, Detroit Lions, 1937-38; salesman-sales mgr.-gen. mgr., KMPC, Sta. of the Stars, Hollywood, 1938-52, partner (with Gene Autry), 1952-68; dir. Leisure Enterprises; Regent, Univ. of Calif.; bd. dirs.-exec. com. Major League Promotion Corp.; pres. The Golden West Baseball Co. (Calif. Agenls Baseball Club), 1960---; v.p.-dir., L.A. Rams, 1963---. Awards: elected to Natl. Football Hall of Fame, 1961; Sports Honor Roll and Stanford Hall of Fame; various civic and govt. hon. cits. Mem.: L.A. Jr. League; Zeta Psi; Stanford Ath. Bd.; clubs: Univ., L.A.; Bel-Air Bay, Sunset, Town Hall, Orange Co., Balboa de Mazatlan, One Hundred, Pauma Valley Country, La Grulla Gun, L.A. Country. Republican. Episcopalian. Hobby: cards, reading. Rec.: swimming, golf, hunting. Res.: 12712 Parkyns, L.A., CA 90049.

RHEEM, RICHARD SCOFIELD
Land Company President
b. Dec. 24, 1903, Oakland, Calif.; s. William S. and Helena (Stratton) Rheem; ed. grad. Univ. of Calif. 1925; m. Constance Patterson; chil.: William Sponsler, Robert Scofield, Constance (Rheem) Birley. Career: Pres. Rheem Mfg. Co. 1930-57, chmn. bd. dirs. 1957-60; pres. Rheem Calif. Land Co. Investments and oil devel. Mem.: dir. Calif. State C. of C.; trustee, M.H. deYoung Mem. Museum, S.F.; Pac.-Union, St. Francis Yacht Clubs, S.F.; Transpacific Yacht Club; Burlingame Country Club, Hillsborough; California Club, L.A. Hobby: sailing. Office: P.O.B. 307, Rheem Valley, CA 94570.

RHODUS, LILLIAN BINGHAM
Artist
b. Mo.; d. Elijah and Elizabeth (Evans) Bingham; great-granduncle, George Caleb Bingham, early Am. artist and polit. leader, Mo.; great-grandfather, Elijah Bingham, pioneer, Mo.; ed. Laguna Sch. of Art, 1967-69; pvt. stu. with Leon Franks. m. Camobell W. Rhodus, L.A., Calif., Sept. 15, 1942; son, David, b. July 4, 1945. Career: Freelance artist, illustrator, portrait painter, pvt. teacher; teacher, San Gabriel Fine Arts Gallery, 1970. Awards: 4 gold medals, 100 ribbons; Best of Show and Cash Awards, Fri. Morning Club, L.A. 1971; Immanuel Presb. Ch., L.A. 1970, 71; Gold Medals: San Gabriel Fine Arts Show, 1969; Valley Artists Guild, 1970, 72, 74; Certificates of Merit: L.A. Home Show, 1969; Artists of the South West, 1972, 74, 75. Mem.: Calif. Art Club, Artists of the South West, The Valley Artists Guild (exhib. chmn. 1970-71, rec. secty. 1976). Rec.: camping, fishing. Studio; 21430 Dumetz Rd., Woodland Hills, CA 91364.

RICARDO-CAMPBELL, RITA
Economist — Fellow, Hoover Institution
b. Boston, Mass.; d. David and Elizabeth (Jones) Ricardo; Ph.D., Harvard Univ., 1946; m. Wesley Glenn Campbell (dir. of Hoover Inst., Univ. Caif. Regent), 1946, Boston, Mass.; chil.: Mrs. Barbara Lee Bizewski, b. 1954; Diane Rita, b. 1956; Nancy Elizabeth, 1960. Career: Tchg. Fellow & Tutor, then instr., Harvard Univ., 1946-48; asst. prof., Tufts Coll., 1948-51; Economist, Nat. Wage Stab. Bd., 1951-53; Economist, Ways & Means Com., U.S. House of Rep. 1953; Cons. Econ., 1957-61; archivist and research assoc., Hoover Inst., 1961-68, sr. fellow, 1968---. Mem. Adv. Council of Soc. Sec. 1974-75; mem. Nat. Adv. Drug Com., FDA 1972-75; mem. Nat. Adv. Food & Drug Com., Feb. 1975; mem. Nat. Citizens Adv. Council on the Status of Women, 1969-76; mem. Health Servs. Industry Com. (phase II), 1971-73; mem. Task Force on Taxation, Council on Environmental Qual. 1970-72.

Dir.: Gillette Co., 1978---; Watkins-Johnson Co., 1974---. Mem.: SRI Internat. Adv. Council, 1977---; Simmons Coll. Corp., 1975---; Ind. Coll. of No. Calif. 1971---; commn. chmn., Western Interstate Commn. for Higher Edn. (WICHE) 1970-71; v.-chmn., WICHE 1969-70, Commr. from Calif. 1967-75; Phi Beta Kappa; Mont Pelerin Soc. Pub.: Social Security: Promise and Reality, 1977. Rec.: tennis, swimming. Office: Hoover Inst., Stanford Univ., Stanford, CA 94305.

RICE, DONALD B., JR.
President, The Rand Corporation
b. June 4, 1939, Frederick, Md.; s. Donald B., Sr. and Mary C. Rice; ed. B.S., Univ. Notre Dame, 1961; M.S., Purdue Univ. 1962; Ph.D., 1965; m. Susan Fitzgerald, Evanston, Ill., Aug. 25, 1962; sons: Donald B., III, b. June 11, 1963; Joseph J., b. Feb. 3, 1965; Matthew F., b. Jan. 31, 1969. Career: Purdue Res. Halls head counselor, Purdue Univ. 1961-62, instr.-research assoc. 1963-65; asst. prof. mgmt. U.S. Naval Postgrad. Sch. 1965-66, acting dep. dir. of academics, Navy Mgmt. Systems Center, 1966-67; dir. cost analysis, Ofc. of U.S. Secty. of Def. 1967-69; dep. asst. Secty. of Def. 1969-70; asst. dir. Exec. Ofc. of Pres., Ofc. of Mgmt. and Budget, The Rand Corp., 1970-72, pres. 1972---. Contrib. articles to profl. publs. Army ROTC, Notre Dame Univ., 1961; Capt., Ord. Corps, U.S. Army, 1965-67. Awards: Union Carbide Scholarship in chem. engring., Notre Dame Univ. 1957-61; Ford. Found. Doctoral Fellow in mgmt. and econs., Purdue Univ. 1962-65; Meritorious Civ. Serv. Medal by U.S. Secty. Laird, 1970, Mem.: Am. Econ. Assn., Inst. of Mgmt., Sci. AAAS, Tau Beta Pi, 1961. Rec.: golf. Res.: 518 Georgina Ave., Santa Monica, CA 90402; Office: 1700 Main St., Santa Monica, CA 90406.

RICHARD, DONAT R.
Physician
b. Oct. 17, 1910, St. David, Quebec, Canada; s. Noe and Rosilda Richard; B.A., Univ. of Montreal, 1936; M.D.C.M., McGill Univ., Montreal, M. Mary Martin Wade, Mar. 24, 1952, Charlottesville Univ.; chil.: Robert Ronald, b. 1952; Dennis Raymond, b. 1954; Carol Ann (Burton), b. 1956. Career: Practicing Obstetrician-Gynecologist, Glendale, 1947---; Instr. to Assoc. Clin. Prof., Loma Linda Univ., 1947---; Assoc. Clin. Prof., USC, 1960---; Att. to Sr. Attending Physician, L.A. Co. Hosp., 1947-70. Dir., ICN Pharmaceuticals, 1960---, Exec. Com. Mem. 1969---. Founder-Dir.: Houston Properties, Inc., Glendale, 1961---; Internat. Chem. and Nuclear Corp., City of Industry, 1961---; Franville Fragrances, Inc., Hollywood, 1966---; Dir. CAP Services, Inc., Hollywood; Camden. Fin. Co-developer: First antiviral drug, Virizole, 1960---. Served Lt. to Capt. M.C. AUS, 1941-46, 148th Gen. Hosp. Mem.: Am. Bd. of Obstretrics and Gynecology; Fellow, Am. Coll. of Surgs.; Founding Fellow Am. Coll. of ACOG Obstets. and Gynecologists; AMA; CMA; L.A. Co. Med. Assn.; Am. and Pac. Coast Fertility Socs.; Glendale Toastmastesr Club, past pres.; McGill Graduates Soc., past pres.; Verdugo Club, Glendale, dir. 1961-65, pres. 1963-64; Canadian Club of L.A.; Oakmont Country Club, Glendale. Polit. Fund raiser, local to nat. Episcopalian. Hobby: Observe state of Union. Res.: 1650 Melwood Dr., Glendale, CA 91207; Office: 655 N. Central Ave., Glendale, CA 91203.

RICHARD, OSCAR WILLIAM
Vice Chairman, Bank of Newport
b. Mar. 7, 1906, Gresham, Wis.; s. George F. and Anna L. Richard; ed. grad. Northwestern Mil. Acad. 1925; Northwestern Mil. N.W.C. (2 yrs.); m. Jennie Viola Corbett, Oshkosh, Wis., Sept. 1, 1928; m. 2nd., Linda Lane, Apr. 2, 1966; son, John Charles, b. May 11, 1943. Career: Instr. bus. adm. Oshkosh Bus. Coll. 1927-33; mgr. Newport Public Market, 1934-47; est. Richard's Lido Market, Newport Beach, Calif. 1948-66. Awards: Bos of Yr., Newport Harbor Bus. and Profl. Women's Club, 1951; Man of Yr., Newport Harbor C. of C. 1953; Natl. Retailer of Yr., Brand Names Found. 1954; Citzen of Yr., Newport Harbor C. of C. 1953; Natl. Retailer of Yr., Brand Names Found. 1954; Citizen of Yr., by Orange Coast Coll. 1955. Mem.: past dir. Certified Grocers of Calif.; past dir. Food Employers Council of L.A.; past dir., Super Market Inst.; past dir., Small Bus. Adm. Bd. of Region XIV; past pres., Lido Shop Assn.; past pres., Newport Harbor United Fund; past exec. v.p. Calif. Safety Council; past dir., Newport Beach Lib. Bd.; past pres., Orange Co. Philharmonic Soc.; (hon.) Future Farmers of Am. 1954; (life) PTA 1955; pres. Newport-Harbor

C. of C. 1961; dir.-past pres., Boy Scouts of Am., Orange Co. Christian Scientist. Hobby: youth activities. Rec.: golf, travel. Res.: Fourteen Atoll Dr., Corona del Mar, CA 92625.

RICHARDS, VICTOR
Surgeon
b. June 4, 1918, Ft. Worth, Tex.; s. J.K. and Minnie (Certan) Richards; A.B., Stanford Univ. 1935, M.S. 1939; m. Jennette O'Keefe, San Diego, June 7, 1941; chil.: Lane Jennette, b. Nov. 3, 1944; Victoria M. Burris, b. Nov. 6, 1945; Victor F.W., b. Jan. 12, 1948; Peter C., b. Aug. 2, 1949. Career: Intern to res. in surg., Stanford Hosp. 1938-43; instr. in surg., Stanford Med. Sch. 1943-48; asst. prof. of surg. 1948-53, assoc. prof. 1953-55, prof.-chmn. Dept. of Surg. 1955-59; Commonwealth Research Fellow, Harvard Med. Sch. 1950-51; clin. prof. of surg., Stanford Univ. Sch. of Med. 1960---; clin. prof. of surg., Univ. of Calif.; chief of surg.: Presb. Med. Center, S.F. 1959-68; Children's Hosp., S.F. 1965---. Author:(book) Surgery for General Practice; Cancer: The Wayward Cell, Univ. of Calif. Press, 1972; approx. 150 publs.; ed. b.d Am. Journ. of Surg., Journ. of Family Practice, Continuing Edn. for Family Phys.; ed. ONCOLOGY. Mem.: (hon.) Alpha Omega Alpha, 1938; AMA, Calif. Med. Assn. 1939---; Sigma Xi, 1940; v.p. Pan Pac. Surg. Assn. 1972-75; S.F. Surgical Soc., Pacific Coast Surgical Soc., Am. Surg. Assn., Internat. Soc. of Surgs., Am. Thoracic Assn.; fellow, Am. Coll. of Surgs.; Commonwealth Club of Calif. 1941---; Bohemian Club, 1968---. Episcopalian Hobby: photog., writing. Rec.: tennis, swimming. Res.: 2714 Broadway, S.F., CA; Office: 3838 California St., Suite 612, S.F., CA 94118.

RICHARDSON, DARWIN LLOYD
Physician — Surgeon
b. Jan. 5, 1921, Cisco, Tex.; s. Loyd, and Kathryn (Hebert) Richardson; B.S., Univ. Okla. 1942, M.S. 1947, M.D., Sch. of Med. 1947; m. Wanda Gordon, Stephenville, Tex.; sons: Wayne, James, David, Robert, Mikel, Donald, Troy, Norman. Career: Instr., Nursing Sch., St. Anthony Hosp., Dodge City, Kan.; Okla. Gen. Hosp. Okla. City Univ. 1946-47; intern. Univ. Colo. Med. Center, 1947-48; faculty, Univ. Kan. Sch. of Med. 1952-60; practice med.-surg. Wyo., Minneola, Kan. 1950-60; De Leon, Tex. 1960-65; est. Calif. res. and pvt. practice, Needles, 1965---; dist. surg. Santa Fe Ry.; diplomat, Am. Bd. of Family Practice, 1970; med. examiner, Fed. Aviation Agcy. Elected to City Council, 1968---, Mayor, City of Needles, 1970. Author: Eutopia in the Desert, publ. Colo. 1970; articles publ. profl. journs. USA, Oxford, Eng., Buenos Aires, S.A. 1946---. Enlisted, AUS, 1942, WW II. Feat. in Pioneers of the Prairie. Awards: Outstanding Citizen Award, 1973; Mem.: AMA, Amer. Acad. of Gen. Practice; Fellow, Am. Soc. of Abdominal Surgs. 1966; Diplomate, Am. Bd. of Family Practice, 1970; (life) Fellow, Am. Acad. of Family Phys. 1972; Am. Geriatric Soc.; Western Assn. of Ry. Surg.; San Bernardino Co. Med. Soc.; pres. Kiwanis Club, Minneola 1953-54; pres. De Leon C. of C., Tex. 1961-62; pres. Comanche Cancer Soc. 1962-63; pres. Needles Toastmasters Club, 1967-68; pres. Needles C. of C., 1969-70; Republican. Needles Chr. Ch. (elder, chmn. Ch. Bd. 1969-70). Hobbies: woodwork, photog. Rec.: hunting, fishing, flying, golf. archery, bowling, scuba diving. Res.: 526 Desnok, Needles; Office: Santa Fe Clinic, 834 Front St., Needles, CA 92363.

RICHARDSON, NORVAL R.
Civic Leader
b. Jan. 19, 1907, Chicago, Ill.; s. William A. and Augusta T. Richardson; B.S., M.S.; m. Cynthia Brosnahan, Montgomery, Ala., Nov. 30, 1933; chil.: William Ralph, b. July 7, 1941; George Patton, b. Oct. 22, 1948; Cynthia Anne, b. May 7, 1952; Terri Eden, b. Dec. 22, 1953. Career: Naval aviator, Ensign to Capt., USNR 1931-64 (ret.); chief engr. U.S. Post Ofc. Bldg., Chicago, 1933-37; asst. to v.p.-gen. mgr. Bendix Radio Corp. 1937-41; admr. Vista Hill Hosp., Chula Vista, 1964---. Chmn., San Diego Aerospace Museum, 1961-64; chmn. Inst. Aerospace Scis., S.D. 1962-63; chmn. Am. Inst. Aeron. and Astron. 1964-67; chmn. Balboa Park Comm., S.D. 1964-68; pres. S.D. Hall of Sci. and Planetarium, 1968---; pres. S. Bay Guidance Center, 1968---. Mem.: pres. Lambda Chi Alpha, 1929-30; Rotary Club, 1964---; v.p. Nature Assn. of Pvt. Psych. Hosps. 1970---; v.p. S.D. C. of C. Health Co.; v.p. S.D. Mental Health Assn. 1970---; pres. Chula Vista C. of C. 1970-71. Protestant. Rec.: athletics. Res.: 4541 Cresta Verde Lane, Bonita, CA 92002; Office: 3 N. Second Ave., Chula Vista, CA 92010.

RICHARDSON, REDMOND RODGERS
Labor Union Official

b. Mar. 22, 1909, Koshkonong, Mo.; s. Thomas Jefferson and Mary Madalene (Rodgers) Richardson; m. Avis Isabelle Wilcox, Sept. 2, 1934, Beverly Hills, Calif.; chil.: Ronald Dale, b. Sept. 13, 1936; Marsha Ann (Underhill), b. June 12, 1942; Carolynn Sue (Bryans), b. May 6, 1945; Gordon Lynn, b. Feb. 27, 1948; Sharon Kay (Williams), b. Jan. 8, 1952; Sandi Sue (Davis), b. Mar. 23, 1958. Career: stock boy to store mgr., A & P Tea Co., 1929-38; employee and self-employed, grocery, gas station bus., 1939-46; joined Laborers Local 89, S.D., 1946: brick tender, plaster tender, 1946-50; elected to exec. bd. Local 89: apptd. asst. bus. repr. Oceanside branch, 1950; elected head bus. repr. Local 89, 1951-63; appted. secty-treas., San Diego Co. Labor Council, 1963, elected secty.-treas. for four year terms consecutively, S.D.-Imperial Counties Labor Council, 1964-80; also chmn., bd. trustees, Office Employees Internat. Union Local 139 Pension Plan; pres., v.p., Internat. Labor Affairs Coordinating Com.; AFL-CIO-CTM Border Com.; secty.-treas., Labor Day Ball Scholarship fund; S.D. gen. apprenticeship, chmn. program com.; chmn., S.D.-Imperial Countires Trade Union Council for Histadrut. Apptd. by gov., dir., 22nd dist. Agri. Assn., 1960-68, 1976-80; pres. bd. of dir. 1965-66; Commn. of Californias, 1964; Non-Partisan Voter Registration Com.; Mayor's full employment coordinating com.; selective service appeals bd., dist. No. 1; S.D. Mayor's Com. for Jobs, Inc.; City Charter Revision Com.; Citizens Salary Review Com. Recipient: 1st Murray Goodrich Honor award. Mem.: S.D. Urban League, Inc. advis. bd.; Atty. Gen's. Vol. Advis. Com.; UCSD advis. bd.; United Way, S.D. bd. dir., vice chmn. campaign 13 years; Consumer Fedn. of Calif., policy bd.; NCCJ, bd. dir.; citizens advis. com. on Sch. Finance; S.D. Evening Coll. Found; S.D. Co.'s Human Resources advis. bd.; Community Campership Council, chmn.; Nat. Alliance of Businessmen for Jobs, bd. dir.; United Way. Protestant. Home: 7825 El Paso St., La Mesa, CA 92041; Office: 2232 El Cajon Blvd., S.D., CA 92104.

RICHENS, MURIEL WHITTAKER
Counselor — Educator

b. Prineville, Oregon; d. John Reginald and Victoria Cecilia (Pascale) Whittaker; B.S., Ore. State Univ.; M.A., San Francisco State Univ., 1962; certificate in sch. adminstrn., Univ. of Calif., Berkeley, 1967; postgrad.: Univ. Birmingham, Eng., 1973; Center for Human Communications, Los Gatos, Calif., 1974; Univ. of Puerto Rico, 1977; Guadalajara summer sch., Mex., 1978; m. Kent J. Richens, 1941; chil.: Karen, John, Candice, Stephanie, Rebecca. Career: instr., S.F. State Univ., 1960-61; instr., Burlingame High Sch., 1963---; counselor, 1968---; instr. Coll. San Mateo, 1964; counselor Crestmoor High Sch., San Bruno, 1974-75; pvt. practice marriage, child and family counseling, Sam Mateo, 1975---; Guest W. Germany/European Acad. seminar, W. Berlin, 1975. Mem.: Nat. Alliance for Family Life; NEA; Am. and Calif. assns. marriage and family counselors; San Mateo Union High Sch. Dist. Counselors Assn., pres., 1975-76; No. Calif. Personnel and Guidance Assn.; Mental Health Assn. San Mateo Co.; Calif. Tchrs. Assn.; AAUW; Univ. Calif., Berkeley Alumni; ARC lifeguard; Am. Contract Bridge League (life master, certified bridge instr., tournament bridge dir.); Women in Communications; Pi Lambda Theta; Delta Pi Epsilon, v.p. 1966. Home: 847 N. Humboldt St., San Mateo, CA 94401; Office: 650 N. Delaware St., San Mateo, CA 94401.

RICHMOND, JOHN
Attorney at Law

b. Dec. 10, 1907, Oakland, Calif.; s. Samuel and Sarah Richmond; B.S., Univ. Calif., Berkeley, 1925-28, M.S. 1933-34; LL.B., Oakland Coll. of Law, 1938-42. Career: Pres., Richmond Enterprises, 1928---, atty. 1946---; atty. at law, pvt, practice, S.F., 1946---. USAAF 1942-45, WW II. Mem.: Am. Fed., Calif. State, Alameda Co. Bar Assns.; Am. Judicature Soc.; co-founder, Natl. Lawyers Club, USA; master, Henry Morse Stephens Lodge, F&AM 1958; Scottish Rite, Aahmes Temple Shrine; Masters and Past Masters Assn. (Mason); comdr. VFW, Berkeley, 1962; pres. United Vets. Council, Berkeley, 1963; fellow, Intercontinental Biog. Assn. 1970; Univ. Calif. Alumni Assn.; Pan Xenia. Rec.: golf. Office: 1611 Bonita Ave., Berkeley, CA 94709.

RICHTER, BURTON
Physicist — Educator

b. Mar. 22, 1931, Brooklyn, N.Y.; s. Abraham and Fanny Richter. B.S, Mass Inst. of Tech., 1952, Ph.D., 1956; m. Laurose Becker, 1960, Calif.; chil.: Elizabeth,

b. 1961; Matthew, b. 1963. Career: Research Assoc., Brookhaven Nat. Lab., 1954; High Energy Physics Lab., Stanford Univ., 1956-59; Assoc. Prof., Dept. of Phusics, Stanford Univ., 1959-63; Assoc. Prof., Stanford Linear Accelerator Center, 1963-67; Prof., 1967---. Awarded Nobel Prize in Physics, 1976; E.O. Lawrence Award, U.S. Energy Research and Devel. Adminstrn. 1975. Contbr. over 80 articles in various sci. journs. Office: P.O.B. 4349, Stanford Linear Accelerator Center, Stanford, CA 94305.

RICHTER, WILLIAM B.
College President

b. Aug. 17, 1916, Dickinson, N. Dak.; s. L.W. and Bernice Richter; nephew of Geo. Blanchard, U.S. Rep. Wisconsin; B.A., social sci., 1940; M.A. hist., 1941; Ed.D. adminstrn., 1953; m. Reva Horsley, Mar. 17, 1958, Portland, Ore.; chil.: William Henry, b. 1934; Larry (State Assemblyman, N. Dak.), b. 1936; Jean (Jacobson), b. 1946. Career: 15 years teacher and adminstr., 1940-42 and 1946-59; 18 years, coll. and univ. level, 1959-78; currently Supt./Pres., Ohlone Coll., Fremont-Newark Community Coll. Dist., Fremont, Calif. ---; Instr., high sch., 1954-56; supt. recreation for schs. & city, 1955-56; vice prin. high sch. 1956-63; research asst. 1963-64; prin., San Leandro High Sch. 1964-68; Dir. of Eve. Programs & Community Services 1968-69; dir. Arts & Science, 1969-70; Dean of Instr., 1970-75. Served to Lt. Sr. Grade, USN, 1942-46. Mem.: Am. Assn. of Jr. Coll.; Rotary Club; CGCA; CTA; ACSA; ACCCA. Protestant. Rec.: gardening. Home: 43102 Starr St., Fremont, CA 94538; Office: Ohlone Coll., P.O.B. 3909, Fremont, CA 94538.

RICKARD-RIEGLE, BARBARA KATHERINE
Radio News Bureau Chief

b. May 1, 1931, Los Angeles; d. Thomas and Katherine (Blackburn) Rickard; gr.dau. of Thomas Rickard, Mayor of Berkeley, 1898-1904; grad., Ursuline Acad., Santa Rosa; chil.: Katherine (Pennington); Karen (Dwyer); K. Christopher Riegle; Melissa (Collinsworth); Richard J. Riegle. Career: editor, Phenix City Herald, 1955-57; news dir., editorial writer, Atlanta and Columbus, Ga., 1957-63; polit. writer, columnist, L.A. Herald Examiner, 1963-66; congressional news secty., 1966-67; women's editor, KNX-CBS, 1967-71; bureau chief, Orange Co., KFWB, 1971---. Winner of 40 state and nat. reporting and writing awards: radio, TV, news, documentaries; Author: The Long Hot Summer of 1962 (rise of GOP in Ga.); Thirteen Thoughts; Something is Missing in Broadcasting — The Majority Sex; Dinner for One (cookbook). Mem.: bd., Am. Women in Radio & Television; bd. Calif. Press Women; Sigma Delta Chi; Press Club; I.R.E. (Investigative Reporters & Editors). Hobbies: painting, writing poetry. Home: 2512 Chain Ave., Anaheim, CA 92804; Office: KFWB News 98, 6230 Yucca St., L.A., CA 90028.

RIDDER, DANIEL HICKEY
Publisher

b. May 3, 1922, NYC; s. Bernard H. and Nell (Hickey) Ridder; A.B., Princeton Univ. 1943; m. Frani Ackerman, Long Beach, Calif., Oct. 13, 1971; chil.: Daniel H., Jr., b. July 17, 1949; Randy Helen, b. Aug. 29, 1950; Richard J., b. Nov. 21, 1952. Career: Assoc. with Journ. of Commerce, N.Y. and Grand Forks Herald, publ. St. Paul Dispatch, Pioneer Press, 1952-58; co-publ. Long Beach Independent Press-Telegram, 1958-69; publisher, 1969---; v.p. & mgr. of Operating Committee of Knight-Ridder Newspapers, Inc.; pres. of Twin Coast Newspapers, Inc.; dir. The Associated Press; dir. The L.A. Co. Museum of Art; dir. Partnership for the Arts in Calif., Inc.; gen. bd. United Way of L.A.; bd. trustees: St. Mary's Hosp., L.B.; formerly bd. trustees-past chmn.: Calif. State Colls., Bd. of Dir., Nspr. Adv. Bureau; USN 1942-46; ETO Amphibious Force in Asiatic Pac. Theatre on CVE-USS Prince William; Lt. (j.g.), WW II. Awards: Normandy Invasion Battle Star; Campaign Ribbons, Asiatic and European-African Middle East Theatre. Mem.: Clubs: Virginia Country (L.B.), Eldorado Country (Palm Desert), Somerset Country (St. Paul, Minn.), L.A. Country. Rec.: golf, tennis. Res.: 5531 Bryant Dr., Long Beach 90815. Office: 604 Pine Ave., Long Beach, CA 90844.

RIDDER, JOSEPH BERNARD
Publisher

b. May 3, 1920, NYC; s. Bernard Herman and Nell (Hickey) Ridder; ed. William and Mary Coll., 1943; m. Virginia Dunne, NYC, Dec. 30, 1950. Career: Gen. Mgr., St. Paul Dispatch and Pioneer Press, Minn. 1949-52; publ. San Jose Mercury and News, 1952-77; pres., San Jose Mercury and News, 1977---. Lt., USN,

WW II. Mem.: exec. v.p. Music and Arts Found. of Santa Clara Valley, 1966---; exec. bd. Santa Clara Co. Council, BSA 1969---; bd. trustee, Santa Clara Univ. 1974-80. Res.: Saratoga Hills Rd., Saratoga, CA; Office: 750 Ridder Park Dr., San Jose, CA 95131.

RIDDER, P. ANTHONY
Newspaper Executive
b. Sept. 22, 1940, Duluth, Minn.; s. Bernard H., Jr. and Jane (Delano) Ridder; B.A. (econs.), Univ. of Mich. 1962; m. Constance Meach, Traverse City, Mich., Nov. 6, 1960; chil.: Katherine Lee, b. July 18, 1961; Linda Jane, b. July 24, 1963; Susan Delano, b. May 18, 1965; Paul Anthony, Jr., b. Apr. 27, 1968. Career: Assoc. with Aberdeen S.D. American News, 1962-63; Pasadena Star News, 1963-64; San Jose Mercury-News, 1964, asst. publ. 1966, bus. mgr.-gen. mgr. 1968---; v.p. Northwest Publications, Inc. Mem.: chmn. Santa Clara Co. Sports Arena Com. 1969; chmn. bd. dirs. San Jose C. of C. 1975; gen. chmn. Central Area-Santa Clara Co., United Way; Psi Upsilon; Clubs: San Jose Rotary, Sainte Claire; San Jose Country; Cypress Point, Pebble Beach; La Rinconada Country, Los Gatos. Res.: Saratoga. Office: 750 Ridder Park Dr., San Jose, CA 95131.

RIDGWAY, DAVID WENZEL
Film Producer
b. Dec. 12, 1904, L.A.; s. David Nelson and Marie (Wenzel) Ridgway; A.B., UCLA 1926; M.B.A., Harvard Univ. 1928; m. Rochelle Devine, Wilmette, Ill., June 22, 1955. Career: Prod., Mot. pics., RKO Studios, Hollywood, 1928-42; prodn. mgr.-prod., Ency. Brit. Films, Wilmette, Ill. 1946-60; film prod.-exec. dir., CHEM Study, Natl. Sci. Found., Berkeley, Calif. 1960---. Mot. pic. spec., War Prodn. Bd., Wash., D.C. 1942-43; Lt. Comdr. USN (1943-46), WW II. Awards: 15 natl.-internat. awards for chem. films; Chris awards for 6 films, Film Council of Greater Columbus, 1962, 63; CINE Golden Eagle Awards for 5 films, 1962, 63, 64; Bronze Medal for film Padua, 1963. Mem.: Soc. of Mot. Pic. and TV Engrs.; Trustee, Am. Sci. Film Assn.; Delta Upsilon, Alpha Kappa Psi. Rec.: travel. Res.: 1735 Highland Pl., Berkeley 94709; Office: University of Calif., Lawrence Hall of Science, Berkeley, CA 94720.

RIDGWAY, EDWIN ROWLEY
Business Executive
b. June 15, 1915, Los Angeles; s. Thomas C. and Grace (Rowley) Ridgway; ed. Thacher Sch., Ojai, 1930-33; Deerfield (Mass.) Acad. 1933-34; Stanford Univ. 1934-38; Babson Inst., Babson Park, Mass. 1939-40. Career: Mgr., Rowley-Ridgway Estates, 1938---. Cryptographer with 7th Air Force, AAFPOA and USASTAF, Hickam Field and Guam, WW II. Awards: decorated, Hon. Officer of The Order of the British Empire (O.B.E.), Aug. 1968; Mem.: chmn. L.A. br., English-Speaking Union; dir. natl. bd., English Speaking Union of U.S.; v.p. bd. dirs., Travelers Aid Soc. of L.A.; L.A.-Sister City Com.; Baronial Order of Magna Charta; Huguenot Soc. of Am.; S.R.; The American Club (London); International Club of Los Angeles; Brit. United Services Club; Lincoln Club, The Beach Club, California Club. Republican. Immanuel Presbyterian. Hobby: cabinet making, enameling, swimming, genealogy. Res.: 232 S. Rimpau Blvd., Los Angeles, CA 90004; Office: 3600 Wilshire Blvd,, Suite 1614, L.A., CA 90010.

RIEMENSCHNEIDER, PAUL ARTHUR
Radiologist
b. Apr. 17, 1920, Cleveland, Ohio; s. Albert and Selma (Marting) Riemenschneider; B.S., Baldwin-Wallace Coll., 1941; M.D., Harvard Med. Sch., 1944; m. Mildred McCarthy, May 12, 1945, Manlius, N.Y.; children: Barbara Ann, b. 1946; Nancy Emelia Christensen, b. 1947; David Andrew, b. 1948; Paul Albert, b. 1950; Mary Elizabeth, b. 1952; Sarah Bache, b. 1957. Career: INstr./Prof. and Dept. Chmn., Dept. of Radiology, State Univ. of N.Y., Upstate Med. Center, Syracuse, N.Y. 1950-64; Chief Diagnostic Radiology, Santa Barbara Cottage Hosp., 1964---. Trustee, Am. Bd. of Radiology, 1972---; Pres., Am. Coll. of Radiology, 1964; Pres., Am. Roentgen Ray Soc., 1979; Pres., Assn. of Univ. Radiologists, 1960. Author: numerous sci. articles and books. Lt. j.g., USNR M.C., 1945-47, Lt. Col., USNR, 1954-56. Mem. Lambda Chi Alpha (High Alpha), Alpha Omega Alpha. Republican. Episcopalian, Sr. Warden. Rec.: golf, tennis. Res.: 2740 Sycamore Canyon Rd., Santa Barbara; Office: P.O.B. 689, Santa Barbara, CA 93108.

RIGGS, BEATRICE SMITH
Realtor — Civic Worker
b. Apr. 27, 1906, Lead, S.Dak.; d. Harry and Cora (Brown) Downing; ed. Los Angeles pub. schs.; m. Earl F. Riggs (dec.), Aug. 2, 1947, Los Angeles; son, Harold C. Smith; stepchil.: Mrs. George Schuchard, Park Riggs, Ribert Riggs, Mrs. Virginia Hitter. Career: with Security Bank, 1936-38; cashier, Yellowstone Park Co., 1938-42; Exec. Secty., Nathan Cramer Insurance Counselor, 1942-47; Realtor, 1956---: now Shelley Realtor, Cucamonga. Mem. San Bernardino County Mus. Commn., 6 yrs., past pres.; vol. dir., pres., Chaffey Community Cultural Center, 10 yrs.; Mem. aux., Sons of Union Vets. of the Civil War, nat. pres. 1959-60; Publ.: Historical Analysis, Sphere of Influence of City of Ontario, pub. 1978, Annexation and prezoning. Author, book in progress on volunteer work. Republican, secty. to Congressman Pettis 6 mos. Christian Sci. Ch. Hobbies: needlepoint, knitting. Res.: 1515 W. Arrow Hwy., No. 29, Upland, CA 91786; Office: 9554 Foothill Blvd., Cucamonga, CA 91730.

RIGGS, DURWARD SIDNEY
Executive Director, Commonwealth Club
b. Feb. 4, 1935, Hutchinson, Kan.; s. John Lawrence and Melba (Holmes) Riggs; B.A. (hist.) 1962; grad. stu. (polit. sci. and internat. rels), 1966; m. Barbara Bornet, Ashland, Ore., Dec. 28, 1967; chil.: Dana Lawrence, b. Mar. 11, 1969; Susan Elizabeth, b. June 9, 1971. Career: Ins. investigator, Santa Barbara, 1960-63; sr. research assoc. Johnson Research Associates, Goleta, 1962-64; asst. exec. secty. Commonwealth Club of Calif. 1965-69, exec. dir. 1969---. Editor, many pub. issue publs. incl. Land Use, Open Space and the Govt. Process, 1974. U.S. Army (interpreter: Russian, Far East, Japan, Middle East), 1957-60. Mem.: Govt. Research Assn.; Assn. for Asian Studies; Amer. Polit. Sci. Assn.; Am. Acad. for Polit and Soc. Sci.; Aircrafts, Owners and Pilots Assn.; Exp. Aircraft Assn.; Soaring Soc. of Amer.; Calif. Aviation Council. Hobbies: sailing, flying, archery, writing. Res.: 1327 S. Mayfair, Daly City, CA; Office: 681 Market St., S.F., CA 94105.

RIKER, ALLAN GARY
Engineering Company Executive
b. Oct. 25, 1939, Newark, N.Y.; s. Orville Thorne and Ruth Evelyn Riker; B.S., Elect. Engr., Univ. Ariz., 1961; M.B.A., Ariz. State Univ., 1970; m. Sherry Lynn Ross, June 6, 1978, Tucson, Ariz.; children: Stephen Ross, b. 1961; Heather Lynn, b. 1964. Career: Engr., Salt River Proj., Tempe, Ariz. 1961-63; Motorola, Inc., Phoenix, 1964-72; Mgr. Semiconductor Products Div., Quality Assurance dept., v.p., dir., Aero Metal Products Corp., West Caldwell, N.J., 1963---; plant mgr., Pulse Engineering, San Diego, 1974---. Mem.: Theta Tau, 1957---; United States Power Squadron, exec. ofcr.; Silver Gate Yacht Club; IEEE; ASQC. Republican. Methodist. Rec.: sail racing. Res.: 4350 Morning View, La Mesa, CA 92041; Office: 7250 Convoy Ct., San Diego, CA.

RILES, WILSON CAMANZA
Superintendent of Public Instruction
b. June 27, 1917, Alexandria, La.; s. Wilson Ray and Susie Ana (Jefferson) Riles; B.A., No. Ariz. Univ. 1940, M.A. 1947; (hon.) LL.D.: Pepperdine Coll., L.A. 1965; Claremont Grad. Sch., 1972; USC 1975; Dr. Humane Letters: St. Mary's Coll., Univ. of Pacific, Stockton, 1971; Univ. of Judaism, L.A. 1972; m. Mary Louise Phillips, Nov. 13, 1941; chil.: Michael Leigh, Mrs. Ronald Bostick, Wilson C. Jr., Phillip Gregory. Career: Admr.-tchr., Ariz. pub. Schs. 1940-54; exec. secty. Pacific Coast Reg., Fellowship of Reconciliation, L.A., 1954-58; cons.-chief, Dept. Bur. of Intergroup Rels. Calif. State Dept. of Edn., assoc., dep. supt. of pub. instr. 1958-70; elected Supt. of Pub. Instruction, Calif., 1971---. USAAF, 1943-46, WW II. Awards: Distinguished and Notable Serv. Cit., Univ. of Calif., Berkeley, 1973; Spingarn Medal, NAACP 1973. Mem.: (past) chmn. Task Force on Urban Edn., U.S. Ofc. Edn., Pres. Johnson's Task Force on Urban Edn.; American College Testing Program; National Council on Educational Research; Education Commission of the States; Stanford Center for Research and Dev. Coms.; (ex.-officio): bd. trustees, Calif. State Univ., and Colls.; bd. regents, Univ. of Calif.; bd. trustees: adv. bd. Calif. State PTA; Natl. Acad. of Pub. Adm.; adv. Calif. Conservation Council; trustee, Nutrition Found., Inc.; Cleveland Conf.; Commonwealth Club of Calif. Office: 721 Capitol Mall, Sacramento, CA 95814.

RILEY, ROBERT L.
Scientist
b. Jan. 8, 1935, Iola, Kan.; s. William J. and Frances E. Riley; B.S., Regis Coll., 1956; postgrad in chem., San Diego State Univ., 1959-65; UCLA 1967; m. Zada F. Schwartzman, May 30, 1958, Albuquerque, N.M.; dau. Bridget Ann, b. 1966. Career: Research chemist, Gen. Dynamics Sci. Research Lab., San Diego, 1957-62; staff chemist, General Atomic Co., S.D., 1962-71; guest sci., Max Planck Inst. for Biophysics, Frankfurt Germany, 1971; Mfg. Research & Devel., Gulf Environmental Systems Co., S.D. 1971-74; dir. Basic Development Fluid Systems Div., Universal Oil Products Co., Inc., San Diego, 1974---; V.P., research & dev., Fluid Systems Internat., S.D., 1977. Indsl. Research Awardee, 1972; U.S. Dept. of Interior grantee; U.S. Army grantee. Patentee in field, Contbr. to chpts. in books, articles in profl. journs. Mem.: Am. Chem. Soc.; AAAS; Nat. Water Supply Improvement Assn. Res.: 5803 Cactus Way, La Jolla, CA 92037; Office: 4901 Morena Blvd., Bldg. 806, San Diego, CA.

RILEY, RUSSELL L.
University Administrator
b. Feb. 11, 1911, Mendon, Mo.; s. Fred and Lucille (Daily) Riley; B.S. bus. admin., Univ. of Mo., 1934; m. Betty Thalheimer, 1957, Virginia; chil.: Robert Lee, b. 1958; Kathleen Ann, b. 1959; Fred D., b. 1962; Linda B., b. 1963; Marie L., b. 1963. Career: with Montgomery, Ward and Swift Co., 1934-37; U.S. Govt. service, 1937-69; retired from U.S. Diplomatic Service 1969; asst. to vice chancellor, acad. affairs, Univ. of Calif., Irvine, 1969---; chief cashier, U.S. Railroad Retirement Bd. 1940-41; asst. adminstr., U.S. Internat. Information Adminstrn. and dir., U.S. Internat. Edn. Exchange Service, 1952-58; Consul General of USA in Malta, So. Africa, Liberia (Charge D'Affaires, U.S. embassy 1964-65) and Newfoundland, 1958-68. Contbr. oral hist. archives of Harry S. Truman Library. USAR 1933-61; Lt. Col., Armored Field Artillery, Europe, WWII. Mem.: pres. Acacia frat. 1933; Mason, Royal Arch Mason, Knight Templar, Scottish Rites, Shriner. Protestant. Home: 11771 Carlisle Rd., Santa Ana, CA; Office: UCI, Irvine, CA.

RIORDAN, RICHARD J.
Attorney at Law
b. May 1, 1930, Flushing, N.Y.; s. William O. and Geraldine (Doyle) Riordan; bro. William F. Riordan, gen. chmn. U.S. Lawn Tennis Assn.; ed. Santa Clara Univ. 1950; A.B., Princeton Univ. 1952; J.D. Mich. Univ. Law Sch. 1956; m. Eugenia Warady, Pittston, Pa., Sept. 10, 1955; chil.: William O'Brien, b. Aug. 21, 1956; Mary Beth, b. July 16, 1957; Kathleen Ann, b. May 7, 1959; Patricia Marie, b. Sept. 4, 1960; Carol Ann, b. Dec. 29, 1963. Career: Assoc. with O'Melveny & Myers law firm, 1956-59; partner, Thompson, Waters & Moss, 1962-65; Nossaman, Waters & Moss, 1965; Nossaman, Waters, Scott, Krueger & Riordan law firm, 1965---. Trustee: Immaculate Heart Coll., John Tracy Clinic; trustee-chmn. bd. The R.R. Found.; dir.: Goodwill Inds. of So. Calif., Inc.; treas.-exec. coms. Greater L.A. United Way. U.S. Army Artillery, Korea, 1952-54. Mem.: Order of the Coif, Phi Delta Phi. Hobbies: skiing, tennis. Res.: 1930 Edgewood Dr., South Pasadena, CA 91030; Office: Union Bank Sq., 445 S. Figueroa St., Los Angeles, CA 90017.

RIPPEL, MABEL AMELIA
Educator — Music Consultant
b. Jan. 28, 1914, Philadelphia, Pa.; d. Henry O. and Amelia (Forderer) Rippel; cousin, Robert Forderer, inventor, Vicki kid and congressman at large, Pa.; cousin, U.V. Pres. Eisenhower family; B.S., Univ. Pa. 1935, M.A. 1937; postgrad. fellow, Trinity Coll. of Music, London, Eng. 1938; postgrad. UCLA 1940-41; USC 1954-55. Career: Research asst. in psychol., Univ. of Pa. 1935-37; soc. serv., St. Agens Settlement House, Phila. 1936-48; co-owner, Rippel Sch. of Music, Phila. 1938-49; teacher, Ramsey Mil. Sch., Santa Monica, Calif. 1950-51; Inglewood H.S. 1951-52, Mt. View Sch. Dist., Bakersfield, 1952-53; Arcadia Sch. Dist. 1953-54; concert work, 1954-55; music coord., Midland Sch. Dist., Sunnymead, Calif. 1955---; cond. Midland Sch. Dist. bands and choirs, 1955---; cond.-orgn., Moreno Valley Youth Marching Band, 1964---. Awards: C. of C. Community Award, 1966; Hon. FIBA 1970; Cit. Bd. Dirs. Moreno Valley, 1971. Mem.: IPA; Matinee Mus. Club, Phila.; Phila. Mus. Club, (hon. life) PTA, Psychol. Club, Calif. Teachers Assn., NEA. Lutheran (choir dir.). Res.: 140 N. Sunset Place, Monrovia, CA.

RISCHIN, MOSES
Historian — Educator
b. Oct. 16, 1925, NYC; s. Meer and Rachel (Nelson) Rischin; A.B., Brooklyn Coll., 1947; A.M., Harvard Univ., 1948; Ph.D., 1957; m. Ruth Solomon, Aug. 16, 1959, So. Orange, New Jersey; daughters: Sarah Elisabeth, b. 1963; Abigail Sophia, b. 1964; Rebecca Mira, b. 1967. Career: Faculty mem.: Brandeis Univ., 1953-54, New School for Social Research, 1955-58, UCLA, 1962-64, San Francisco State Univ., 1964---, Prof. History, 1967---. Cons. Nat. Endowment for Humanities, 1974---; mem. Nat. Advisory Bd., Scholars of Immigration Hist. Research Center, Univ. Minn., St. Paul, 1974---; S.F. Bicentennial Commn., Am. Issues Forum, 1974-76; mem. Am. Hist. Assn., Bd. Editors: Pacific Hist. Rev. 1974---; mem. Am. Jewish Historical Soc.; pres. Immigration Hist. Soc. 1976---; mem. orgn. of Am. Historians, Pelzer Award Com., 1971-74; bd. dir., S.F. chpt., Am. Jewish Com., 1973-75. Author: An Inventory of American Jewish History, 1954; Our Own Kind, Voting By Race, Creed Or National Origin, 1960; The Promised City, New York's Jews, 1870-1914 (1962); The American Gospel of Success, 1965; Immigration and the American Tradition, 1976. Ed.: American Minority Hist. Series, 1974---; Advis. Ed.: Modern Jewish Experience Series; Nat. Advis. Council: Harvard Ethnic Encyclopedia, 1974---. Awarded Fellowships: Am. Council Learned Socs. 1966-67; Guggenheim, 1968; Fulbright-Hays, 1969; Nat. Endowment for the Humanities, 1977-78. Rec.: swimming. Res.: 350 Arballo Dr., S.F.; Office: 1600 Holloway Dr., San Francisco, CA 94132.

RISELEY, JERRY BURR, JR.
Attorney — Author
b. Mar. 17, 1920, Stockton, Kansas; s. Jerry Burr and Esta Ella (Scott) Riseley; desc. Vice President Aaron Burr; B.Sc., Univ. of Kansas, 1941; J.D., USC, 1948; M.S., Fort Hays Kan. State Univ., 1969; M.S. lib. sci., USC, 1972; m. Eunice Olive Smith, July 31, 1943, Cairns, Queensland, Aus.; chil.: Valerie Lillian, b. Sept. 6, 1944; Stephanie Ann, b. May 14, 1947; Cheri-Llynn, b. Nov. 12, 1958; Melanie Ann, b. Jul. 20, 1961; Christopher Scott, b. Dec. 28, 1965. Career: writer, columnist, 1948-68; pvt. law practice, L.A. 1948-69; Fellow, div. edn., Psychology & Philosophy, Fort Hays Kan. State Univ., 1969; curator, Black Hist. & Culture Collection, Vermont Sq. Library, 1970; trial lawyer, Sterling, Clifton & Riseley, Beverly Hills, 1971-73; law office, Jerry B. Riseley, L.A. and Encino, 1973-78; cont. as outside litigation staff atty., legal dept. head, L.A.-Encino office of Maryland Casualty Co. Dir., Christopher Park Lib. 1974---. Dept. of Calif. Judge Advocate DAV, 1952-53; Nat. Exec. Com., Disabled Officers Assn.; Judge pro tem, L.A. Municipal Ct., 1978---; Disciplinary Referee Pro Tem, State Bar of Calif., 1975---. Served AUS, Combat Infan., parachutist WWII; decorated with bronze star. Author: Trade Law Book, 1967; Academic Freedom, 1969; Tomorrow the Water, 1969; Complete Bibliography Contemporary Atuhors, Vol. 23-24, papers collected Archive 944, UCLA, research lib. Mem.: Phi Delta Kappa; Bohemian Order of Goats. Polit. candidate, Judge, Superior Ct., 1954. Episcopal, secty., St. Michael's Sch. Bd. 1965. Hobby: photog. Rec.: running. Home: 8856 Lemona Ave., Sepulveda, CA 91343; Office: 16133 Ventura Blvd., No. 935, Encino, CA 91436.

RISPLER, JACOB
Dermatologist
b. Aug. 28, 1948, NYC; s. Samuel and Beula Rispler; B.S., Brooklyn Coll., 1969; M.D., Mt. Sinai Sch. of Med., 1973; Career: Intern, Beth Israel Hosp., N.Y. 1974; Resident/Chief Resident, Dermatology, Temple Univ. Hosps., Phila., 1974-77; Chief of Dermatology, UCLA SFUMP, Adj. Asst. Prof. of Med., Dermatology, UCLA, 1977---; also pvt. practice, West Covina, 1978---. Board Certified Am. Bd. of Dermatology 1977. Mem.: Am. Acad. Dermatology, Soc. Investigative Dermatology, Am. Fedn. Clin. Research. Res.: 11740 Wilshire Blvd., Los Angeles, CA 90025; Office: 1433 West Merced Ave., West Covina, CA 91790.

RISSER, JOSEPH C.
Orthopedic Surgeon
b. Aug. 6, 1892, Des Moines, Iowa; s. William Henry and Amelia (Brotchie) Risser; M.D., Univ. of Iowa, 1923; 2 yr. residency, N.Y. Orthopedic Hosp., Fellowship, 4 yrs.; certified: Am. Bd. of Orthopedic Surgery, 1938; m. Vida Risser (dec.); chil.: Joseph C., Jr., b. Dec. 20, 1925; Katherine Louise (Luque), b. Jan. 10, 1934; m. 2d. Eunice Anderson, Oct. 9, 1965, Pasadena. Career: 4 yr. fellowship, N.Y. Ortho. Hosp.; pvt. practice, New York;

pvt. practice, emphasis on scoliosis, Pasadena ---; staff mem., Orthopedic Hosp., L.A.; St. Luke Hosp. and Huntington Memorial Hosp., Pasadena; instr. in med. courses, annual meetings of Am. Acad. of Orthopedic Surgeons; research in scoliosis, 1932--- (earliest paper pub. co-authored with Dr. Hibbs and Dr. Ferguson); next paper pub., Encyclopedia of Med.; othe;papers publ. incl. Scoliosis, Past and Present, Bone & Joint Journ., 1964; began Risser Orthopedic Research, for edn. foreign doctors in scoliosis. Recipient: Gold Medal Award, 1962, Knight Comdr., 1962, Order of Grand Knight, 1972, Cavaliere di Gran Croce (highest govt. honor), 1973; Republic of Italy; Commended by: L.A. City Mayor and Council, 1962; Argentine hosp., Chiba Univ., Japan; Brazilian Soc. Orthopedics. Mem.: Am. Acad. Orthopedic Surgeons; Am. Orthopaedic Assn.; AMA; CMA; L.A. Co. Med. Assn.; Western Orthopedic Assn.; Price-Pottenger Nutrition Soc. Home: 2097 N. Villa Hts., Pasadena, CA; Office: 2627 E. Washington Blvd., Pasadena, CA 91107.

RITTENHOUSE, FLOYD OLIVER
Former College President
b. Mar. 10, 1906, Bozeman, Mont.; s. Wilton Dana and Hulda Emma (La Fave) Rittenhouse; nephew of Sidney Noble Rittenhouse, noted pioneer radio minister (ret.), Loma Linda, Calif.; B.A., Emmanuel Missionary Coll. 1928; M.A., Ohio State Univ. 1932, Ph.D. 1947; m. Nellie Blair Hubbard, Wash., D.C., Aug. 31, 1937; chil.: Dana C. Dutcher, b. Dec. 14, 1938; Judith Ann, b. Aug. 28, 1948. Career: Teacher, H.S., Sutherlin, Ore. 1924-26; (hist.-Spanish) Mt. Vernon Acad., Mt. Vernon, Oh. 1928-33; prin. Takoma Acad, Takoma Park, Md. 1933-38; hist. instr. So. Jr. Coll., Collegedale, Tenn. 1938-40; dean-assoc. prof. hist. Columbia Union Coll., Takoma Park, 1940-48; dean-prof. hist. So. Miss. Coll., Collegedale, 1948-52; dean, Andrews Univ. Berrien Springs, Mich. 1952-55, pres. 1955-63; pres. Pac. Union Coll., Angwin, Calif. 1963-72 (ret.). Mem.: Phi Alpha Theta, 1932---; Rotarian, Berrien Springs, Mich. and St. Helena, Calif. 1956---. Seventh-Day Adventist. Hobbies: reading, hiking. Res.: 155 Edgewood Lane, Angwin, CA 94508.

RITTER, JAMES HENRY
Surgeon
b. May 27, 1926, Long Beach; s. Ferdinand Theodore and Juanita (Richardson) Ritter; B.A., Stanford Univ., 1947; M.D., Stanford Med. Sch. 1951; m. Estelle Macauley, Mar. 11, 1966, Whittier; children: Stephen James, b. 1952; Alice Marie, b. 1953; Carl Henry, b. 1955; Julie Ann, b. 1960. Career: Pvt. practice surgery, Whittier, 1959-72; Chief Surgical Services, Ft. Defiance Indian Hosp. (USPHS), 1972-75; Clin. Director Surgery, Santa Barbara Gen. Hosp., 1976-78; also Clin. Prof. Surgery, USC. Served USN, 1944-45; USN Med. Officer, 1952-54; USPHS, Med. Dir., 1973-74. Res.: 815 Hot Springs Rd., Santa Barbara, CA 93108; Office: 300 San Antonio Rd., Santa Barbara, CA 93105.

ROBBINS, ALAN
State Senator
b. Feb. 5, 1943, Philadelphia, Pa.; s. Martin and Gladys Robbins; grandnephew, Sholom Aleichem, noted Russian author; ed. B.A., UCLA 1963, J.D., UCLA Sch. of Law, 1966; m. Miriam Elbaum, No. Hollywood, Calif., Sept. 27, 1967; chil.: Jacob, b. Aug. 15, 1970; Leah, b. Nov. 3, 1972. Career: Cons. California Legislature (Const. rev. writer), 1962 65; pvt. practice law, 1966-73; elected to California State Senate, 1973. Chmn.; Subcommittee on Violent Crime; chmn., Select Committee on Public Transportation Problems in Los Angeles. U.S. Army, 1967; Lt., USNR 1968---. Awards: Amer. Jurisprudence Prize in Land-Use Planning. Mem.: Dean's Council, UCLA Sch. of Law, 1971-74; bd. dirs. Vista Del Mar Valley Assocs.; N. Hollywood Lodge B'nai B'rith; adv. bd. Great Western BSA Council; chmn. Real Estate Sect., San Fernando Valley Bar Assn. 1971-72. Rec.: tennis, skiing. Res.: 5475 Katherine Ave., Van Nuys. Office: 5080 State Cpitol, Sacramento, CA 95814.

ROBBINS, JACOB BERNARD
Architect
b. Sept. 2, 1923, Philadelphia; student, Univ. of Penna., 1942; Univ. N. Carolina (Meteorology, USAF), 1944; B.S., Univ. of Chicago, (USAF), 1944, M. Econ., 1949; Fulbright Fellow, Delft Technische Hochschule, Holland, 1954; M.Arch., Harvard Grad. Sch. of Design, 1953; m. Elizabeth King; children: Deborah, Peter, Daniel. Career: Architect: John Lyon Reid and Partners, S.F.; Gerlad M. McCue and Assoc.,

Berkeley, Jacob Robbins and Assoc., Oakland; Dir. of Planning and Community Devel., City of Fremont; now Prin., Robbins and Ream, Inc., San Francisco---. Fellow, AIA; mem. Am. Inst. of Planners; Calif. Council AIA, v.p. environmental affairs; S.F. Bay Conservation and Devel. Commn.; exec. com. Bay Area Planning Dirs.; Chmn., Oakland Planning Commn.; chmn., Oakland Urban Design Advisory Com.; Oakland Citizens Com. for Urban Renewal; Oakland Museums Assn., Council on Arch.; chmn. Environmental Design Exhibs. Com., Oakland; Save S.F. Bay Assn.; Sierra Club. Office: 243 Kearny St., San Francisco, CA 94108.

ROBERTS, BRADLEY HOUSE
Advertising Agency Executive
b. Jan. 23, 1927, New Rochelle, N.Y.; s. Ernest House and Grace (Notton) Roberts; ed. Gov. Dummer Acad., So. Byfield, Mass., 1945; A.B., Hamilton Coll., Clinton, N.Y., 1950; m. Jean Edgertown Hypes (dec. 1971), Oct. 21, 1950, Glencoe, Ill.; chil.: Bradley H., Jr., b. Aug. 2, 1954; Barbara K. (Mrs. David Gainza), b. Apr. 6, 1956; Sarah Hypes, b. May 21, 1959. Career: prod. advt. mgr., Swift & Co., 1950-52; sales & advt. mgr., Earle Chesterfield Mill Co., Asheville, N.C., 1953; comml. mgr., Skyway Broadcasting Co., Asheville, 1953-56; acct. exec., Compton Advt., Inc., 1956-57; acct. exec. and mgmt. supr., Needham, Harper & Steers Advt., Inc., Chicago, 1957---: exec. v.p., 1966, vice chmn., mgr., dir., NH&S/West ---. Dir.: USP Needham Pty., Ltd., Melbourne, Australia; USP Needham, S.E. Asia Pte. Ltd., Singapore. Served with USNR, 1945-56. Chmn., Western region of Am. Assn. of Advt. Agencies, 1978; dir.-at-large, nationally. Office: Needham, Harper & Steers Advt., Inc., 10889 Wilshire Blvd., L.A., CA 90024.

ROBERTS, CHESTER LLEWELLYN
Gynecologist
b. Sept. 21, 1914, Bethany, W.Va.; s. Chester Joseph and Bessie (Bushey); B.A., Lawrence Coll., 1936; M.D., Stanford Univ. Med. Sch. 1941; m. Mary Zierten, Dec. 28, 1941; South Gate; Chil.: Marilyn (Chatem), b. 1946; Kenneth, b. 1948; Nancy (Cowsill), b. 1950; Dean, b. 1953. Career: Founder, Physician, Roberts Medical Group, Glendale, 1942---; Chief of Staff, Behrens Mem. Hosp., 1974. Fellow, Am. Coll. of Obstetricians and Gynecologists, 1951; Fellow, Internat. Coll. of Surgeons, 1952; Life Fellow, L.A. Obstetrical and Gyn. Soc., 1951. Dir.: Chevy Chase CC, 1978-79; Pacific Slope Red Angus Assn. 1972-74; Flying Physicians Assn., 1968-77, pres. 1978-79; Verdugo Hills Hosp., 1974-76, pres. 1972. Mem.: L.A. County Med. Assn., pres. Glendale br. 1953; Camera Cir. of Glendale, pres. 1958; Los Charros Assn, past pres.; Photographic Soc. of Am., 1949---; Sigma Phi Epsilon; past mem.: Aircraft Owners and Pilots Assn.; Civil Air Patrol. Methodist, Sun. Sch. Supt. Contrib. numerous articles med. journs.; award winning photographic salon exhibitor. Hobby: photog. Rec.: golf. Res.: 3271 E. Chevy Chase Dr., Glendale, CA 91206; Office: 1808 Verdugo Blvd., Glendale, CA 91208.

ROBERTS, GEORGE ADAM
President, Teledyne
b. Feb. 18, 1919, Uniontown, Pa.; s. Jacob Earle and Mary M. (Bower) Roberts; student U.S. Naval Acad., 1935-37; B.Sc., Carnegie Tech., 1939; M.Sc., 1941; D.Sc., 1942; m. Betty E. Matthewson, May 31, 1941; chil.: George Thomas, William John, Mary Ellen; m. 2d, Jeanne Marie Polk, Technician Bell Telephone Labs., NYC, 1938; research dir. Vasco Metals Corp. (formerly Vanadium Alloys Steel Co.) Latrobe, Pa., 1940-45; chief mettalurgist, 1945-53; v.p. 1953-61, pres. 1961-66, past chmn. bd., pres., dir. Teledyne, Inc. (merger with Vasco Metals Corp.), L.A., 1966---; hon. lectr. Societe Francaise de Metallurgie, 1960. Chmn.. Spl. Com. Manpower for Metallurgy and Ceramic Profession. Past dir. Latrobe Borough Authority; pres. Am. Soc. Metals Found. Edn. and Research, 1955-56; trustee, 1954-59, 63-64; mem. Greater Latrobe Sch. Bd., 1959-64. Recipient silver medal from Paris, 1955. Fellow Metall. Soc. Am. Inst. Mining, Metall. and Petroleum Engrs., Am. Soc. for Metals (chmn. Pitts. chpt. 1949-50, internat. pres. 1954-55; Gold medal 1977); mem. Metal Powder Industries Fedn. (dir. 1952-55, pres. 1957-61), Am. Iron and Steel Inst., ASTM, Soc. Mfg. Engrs., Tau Beta Pi, hon. life mem. several fgn. socs. Methodist. Author: Tool Steels, 1944, 62. Contbr. articles trade journs. Office: 1901 Ave. of the Stars, Los Angeles, CA 90067.

ROBERTS, GEORGE CHRISTOPHER
Research and Development Executive
b. May 27, 1936, Ridley Park, Pa.; s. George H. and Marion C. (Smullen) Roberts; m. Adriana Toribio, July 19, 1966. Career: Program mgr., Arde Research, 1965-67; space life sci. program mgr. Research div. Gen. Am. Transp. Corp., 1967-69; dir. research and devel. waste mgmt., Monogram Industries, Inc., L.A., 1969-71; pres., Environmental Protection Center, Inc. L.A., 1970---; chmn., chief exec. officer, Inca Corp., Inglewood, 1971---; pres., chief exec. officer, Inca-One Corp., L.A. ---; pres., Inca-Two Corp. and pres., Inca-Three Corp., L.A. ---; v.p., Chimu Assoc., 1978---. Patents: advanced waste treatment systems automotive safety systems; marine and recreational vehicle, portable sanitation equipment and specialty chemicals. Home: 755 Firth Ave., Brentwood, CA 90049; Office: 9625 Bellanca St., L.A., CA 90045.

ROBIE, SUZANNE SPAFFORD
Greeting Card Company President – Artist
b. July 23, 1945, Toledo, Ohio; d. John Lester and Elizabeth (Bradley) Spafford; B.A., San Diego State Coll., 1968; m. Frederick Carleton Robie III, July 12, 1968, San Diego; chil.: Kirsten Marie, b. Apr. 9, 1973; Jennifer Suzanne, b. Dec. 11, 1974. Career: exhibited and sold artwork in San Diego, 1963-67; sole artist and co-partner (with Wm. C. Murr), Suzy's Zoo, Berkeley, 1967; (moved bus. to S.D.) chief exec., 1970---, (incorporated bus. 1976), pres. and sole designer, 1976---; also art tchr., Point Loma High Sch., San Diego, 1968-69. Internat. Distbr. and publication of greeting cards and related products, 1968---; (products range from porcelain and bisque giftware to clothing items, paper tableware). Mem.: Kappa Delta; P.E.O. Sisterhood. Presbyterian. Hobbies: piano, antiques, watercolor painting, fine music. Rec.: skiing, family excursions. Home: 3725 Dupont St., S.D., CA 92106; Office: 10971 S.D. Mission Rd., San Diego, CA 92108.

ROBINSON, ELMER EDWIN
Former Mayor of San Francisco
b. Oct. 3, 1894, San Francisco, Calif.; s. Ralph S. and Edyth (Rahlves) Robinson; ed. grad. Kent Law Sch. 1914; m. Doris Gould, 1916 (dec.); m. Ora Norris Martin, 1944 (dec.), dau.: Elizabeth Jane. b. July. 18, 1919 (6 grandchil., 6 great-grandchil.). Career: admitted to California Bar, 1915; law practice, San Francisco, 1915-35; staff, Dist. Atty. of San Francisco, 1919-23; apptd. judge, Municipal Ct., S.F. 1935; apptd. judge, Superior Ct., Sept. 1935, elected 1936-48 (ret.); presiding judge, Superior Ct. 1936; mem. Judicial Council of Calif. 1938-42; pres. Calif. Conference of Judges, 1940-41; elected Mayor of S.F. 1947, re-elected, 1951-56; pres. U.S. Conf. of Mayors, 1954-55. Awards: (hons.) apptd. Hon. Curator of Americana, Stanford Univ. Libs. 1940---; Hon. Conseil Municipal of Paris, France; Hon. Cit. of Caen, France; Comdr. Royal Order of the Phoenix, Greece; Ofcr. of Leg. of Hon., Fr.; The Star of Solidarity, First Class, Italy; Grand Ofcr., Order of the Star of Ehtiopia; Comdr. Order of Orange-Nassau, Netherlands. Mem.: pres. Woodlawn Mem. Park Assn.; (hon.) bd. dirs. Who's Who in Calif. 1959---; Mason 33°, Scottish, York Rites; Past Potentate Islam Temple, Shrine; Past Grand Chancellor, Knights of Pythias of Calif.; (hon. life) DeMolay Legion of Hon.; clubs: The Family, Saint Francis Yacht, Olympic, (past) S.F. Press. Republican. Episcopalian. Res.: 1200 California St., San Francisco, CA 94109; Office: 703 Flood Bldg., San Francisco, CA 94102.

ROBINSON, W. HARLYN
Hospital Administrator
b. Aug. 26, 1929, Keene, Texas; s. W.C. and Leola Robinson; student Bus. Edn., Pacific Union Coll., 1951; m. Julia K. Babb, Aug. 7, 1949, St. Helena; sons: David, Richard, James. Career: Office Mgr., Stansberry Auto Agency, St. Helena, 1951-53; Administr., Modesto City Hosp., 1953-78. Mem. Governing Body, Health Systems Agency, Modesto, 1977-78; Am. Coll. of Hosp. Adminstrs., 1967---; No. San Joaquin Valley Health Council, pres. 1962, trustee 1967; Vis. Nurse Assn., pres.; Sister City Com. Address: 730 17th St., Modesto, CA 95354.

ROCHE, RICHARD GERALD, JR.
School Superintendent — Civic Leader
b. June 12, 1924, Oakland, Calif.; s. Richard Gerald and Julia (Mahoney) Roche; A.A., Compton Jr. Coll. 1942; A.B., Humboldt State Coll. 1946, M.A. 1952; postgrad. Univ. of Calif., Berkeley, S.F. State Coll.; m. Pearl Ham, Houston, Tex., Sept. 18, 1943; chil.:

Janet Pearl, b. Jan. 19, 1945; Richard Gerald, III, b. Aug. 28, 1947. Career: Teacher, Riverside 1946-47; ath. coach-teacher, South Fork H.S., Miranda, 1947-48; v.prin. Jr.-Sr. H.S. 1948-51; prin. S. Humboldt Unified Sch. Dist. 1952-60, asst. supt. 1959-61; supt. St. Helena Unified Sch. Dist., 1961---. Lecturer, Amer. H.S., edn. subjs. Contrib. articles on conservation and edn. carious publs. USAAF, ETO 1942-45, WW II. Mem.: Amer. Legion, Phi Delta Kappa, Mason, C. of C.; People for Open Space; div. past pres.-dir. Amer. Red Cross; past dir. Redwood Reg. Conservation Council; Bay Area Sch. Bd.; Native Sons of Golden West; dist. pres. Calif. Assn. Secondary Sch. Admrs. 1956-57; pres. Humboldt-Del Norte Chpt. Calif. Inter-Scholastic Fed. 1956-57; Calif. Teachers Assn.; Calif. Assn. Sch. Admrs.; Internat. Platform Assn. Democrat. Episcopalian (vestryman). Hobbies: reading, writing, fishing. Res.: 1800 Spring Mountain Ct., St. Helena; Office: 465 Main St., St. Helena, CA.

ROCHE, SHIRLEY KERN (KANDI)
Business Owner
b. June 22, 1939, Wetzel Co., W. Virginia; d. Delbert Victor and Vareda Roupe Kern; (Kern family contbrs. to Am. Hist. since 1752 and contbrs. to Calif. hist. since early 1800), desc. Lt. Edward R. Kern from Ind., topographer for Capt. John C. Fremont's expedition of 1845, Kern River (named by Capt. Fremont), Kern Lake, Kern County (by legislative act, Apr. 2, 1866) and city of Kernville are named in his honor; desc. William Kern, arrived Calif. mid-1800, started Kern's Farms, Kern's Fruits and Jellies; m. Andrew Stephen Roche (div.); chil.: Desiree June Hall, b. Jan. 1, 1963; Joseph R. Hall, b. Sept. 8, 1961. Career: presently co-founder, pres., Calif. Canadian Beauty Corp. ---; owner, Dana Marina Beauty Supply & Wigs, ---, Dana Point. Columnist, Laguna Hills News Post, Kandi's Kapers, 1977; lectr. on "The Woman Beautiful"; Author: (tapes) I Weigh 120 Lbs.; artist in oils: one-woman show, Security Pac. Bank, Huntington Beach; painting for Huntington Beach Sch. Lib., 1972; researcher in Kirlian photog., 1975---. Co-founder, Women Unlimited in So. Orange Co.; Mem.: C. of C., Dana Point; Dana Point Marina Assn.; Nat. orgn. for Women. Hobby: sketches in pen and ink, oil painting. Home: 33382 Cheltam Way, Dana Point, CA 92629; Office: 25022 Del Prado, Suite F, Dana Point, CA 92629.

ROCKWELL, BURTON LOWE
Architect
b. June 3, 1920, Utica, N.Y.; s. Burton L. and Blanche Louise (Taylor) Rockwell; B.Arch., Mass. Inst. Tech., 1946; M.Arch, 1947; m. Ruth Aldrich, May 19, 1949, San Francisco; chil.: Peter Grant, b. 1952; Abbie (Mrs. Josef Kruger). Career: Project architect John Lyon Reid, San Francisco, 1947-53; partner John Lyon Reid and Partners, S.F., 1953-60; Reid Rockwell Banwell & Tarics, S.F., 1960-62; Rockwell & Banwell, S.F., 1962-70; pvt. practice, San Francisco, 1970---; with Rockwell, Chatham, Marshall Assos., 1977---; cons. internat. health care facilities and project mgmt., 1972---; lectr. Univ. of Calif. at Berkeley, 1962-71; vis. prof. Mass. Ins . Tech., 1969-70; prin. works include Health Sci. and Instrn. Bldg., Univ. of Calif. at San Francisco Med. Center, Santa Cruz County Govt. Center, Lafayette-Orinda United Presbyterian Ch., Dixie and Oakview schs., Dixie Sch. Dist., San Rafael. Mem. S.F. Art Commn., 1961-68; chmn. S.F. Civil Design Com., 1965-68; mem., bd. of Examiners, S.F. Dept. of Public Works, 1977---; adv. com. Bay Area Conservation and Devel. Commn., 1966---; adv. com. Calif. Council Higher Edn., 1968-70; alumni vs. com. MIT, 1968-69; bd. dirs. S.F. Community Music Center, 1972-74; Eastshore Park Project Corp., City and County of San Francisco, 1975---. Research on air movement in and around bldgs., arch. in the fluid environment, 1951---; cons. spec.: ednl. facilities, bell towers, health care facilities, internat. project. mgmt., urban design and rural environment. Capt. AUS, 1942-46, Iceland, Europe. Recipient 21 awards including 2 nat. AIA honor awards for ch., sch. and med. bldgs. Fellow AIA (pres. No. Calif. chpt. 1965, Calif. council 1968), Calif. Conf. Architects and Engrs. (chmn. 1968). Club: Commonwealth of Calif. Res.: 1 Belmont Ave., San Francisco, CA 94117; Office: 888 Post Street, San Francisco, CA 94109.

RODES, JOHN EDWARD
Professor of History
b. May 3, 1923, Frankfurt, Germany; s. Charles A. and Olivia nee Veit (1890-1966, actress) Rosenthal; Grands., Toby E. Rosenthal, 1848-1917, painter in S.F. and Munich; Oxford Sr. Sch. Cert., 1939; B.A., USC, 1943; M.A. 1948; Cert. d'Etudes Superieures,

Sorbonne, 1947; Ph.D., Harvard Univ., 1954; chil.: Elizabeth Ann (Mrs. James Kendall), b. 1958; Jennifer Harriet, b. 1960. Career: French Liaison Interpreter, War Dept., 1946; mem. faculty, USC 1947-48, Simmons Coll. 1948-50; instr./prof. of hist. Occidental Coll., 1950---; chmn. Hist. of Civilization, 1953-62; Guest prof.: USC, Cal State Univ. L.A., Univ. of Hawaii, Univ. of British Columbia; Fulbright Prof., Univ. of Saar, Germany and Univ. of Puget Sound. Author: Germany: A History, 1964; A Short History of the Western World, 1970; The Quest for Unity, 1971. AUS, 1943-46; USAR, 1946-49, mil. intell., civil affairs. Mem.: Phi Beta Kappa, Phi Alpha Theta. Res.: 416 E. Mendocino St., Altadena, CA 91001; Office: Occidental Coll., Los Angeles, CA 90041.

RODGERS, KATHRYN T.
Realtor
b. Feb. 14, 1915, Virginia, Minn.; d. George Andrew Spehar; grad. Realtor Inst., G.R.I.; m. Victor C. Rodgers, Mar. 7, San Diego. Career: employee, family bus. George Spehar Electric Co. 7 years; direct sales, store demonstrn.; blue print reading; time study analyses; bookkeeper; etc.; presently owner, exec., K.T. Rodgers, Realtor, San Diego. Licensed minister, 1964---; ch. lectr. Mem.: S.D. Bd. of Realtors; Anne Rebekka Lodge. Democrat. Universal Ch. of the Masters, minister. Hobbies: organ, astrology, the arts. Office: 4680 Hawley Blvd., San Diego, CA 92116.

RODRIGUEZ, ARMANDO M.
College President
b. Sept. 30, 1921, Gomez Palacio, Durango, Mexico; s. Andres and Petra Rodriguez; B.A., San Diego State Coll., 1949; M.A., 1951; postgrad., UCLA; Ltt.D. (Hon.), John F. Kennedy Coll., Wahoo, Neb., 1970; m. Beatriz Serrano, July 18, 1948, San Diego; chil.: Rodrigo, b. Apr. 16, 1953; Mrs. Christina Blackburn-Rodriguez, b. June 5, 1949. Career: Phys. Ed. Instr., S.D. State Coll., 1947-49; tchr., Memorial Jr. H.S., San Diego, 1949-54; guidance cons., S.D. City Schs., 1954-57; visting tchr., 1957-58; vice prin., Gompers Jr. H.S., 1958-65; prin., Wright Brothers Jr. Sr. H.S. (1st Mexican-American prin. in S.D.), 1965; cons., Calif. State Dept. of Edn. (1st Mex.-Am. cons.), 1965-66, Chief, Bureau of Intergroup Rels., 1966-67; HEW Secty's Com. on easing tension, 1969; dir., office for Spanish speaking Am. Affairs., U.S. Office of Edn., 1967-70, asst. Comm., Regional Office Coord., 1971-73; president, E. L.A. Coll., 1973---; nat. spkr.; contbr. edn. journs.; Served AUS, Signal Corps, 1942-46. Dir., Federal Reserve Bank of S.F. (1st Spanish surnamed dir. of L.A. branch); former chmn.: Bilingual Edn. Com.; William Randolph Hearst, Jr. Found.; Nat. Mex.-Am. Anti-Defamation Com.; mem., Nat. Commn. on Future of State Colleges and Universities; mem. Calif. Reform of Intermediate/Secondary Edn. Commn.; bd. trustee, Redlands Univ.; Nat. Edn. Task Force de la Raza; Nat. Urban Coalition; Calif. Sch. Fin. Reform Commn.; dir., Hispanic Urban Center; Mem.: College Federal Council; World Affairs Council; Am. Ethnic Studies Program; League for Innovation; Calif. Assn. of Secondary Sch. Adminstrs.; L.A. Co. Museum of Art Advisory Bd., 1975; KCET Advisory Bd., 1975. Roman Catholic. Hobbies: fishing, tennis. Home: 10648 Spyglass Hill Road, Whittier, CA 90602; Office: E. Los Angeles Coll., 1301 Brooklyn Ave., Monterey Park, CA 91754.

ROESCHLAUB, RONALD CURTIS
Lawyer — Business Executive
b. Apr. 16, 1913, Denver, Colo.; s. Harry Morris and Roy (Turner) Roeschlaub; B.A., UCLA 1935; M.A. 1937; LL.B., Harvard Univ. (magna cum laude), 1940; m. Jean Clinton Davis, Los Angeles, Calif., Jan 9, 1965; chil.: Ronald William, b. June 16, 1948; David J. Davis, IV, b. Apr. 17, 1948; Diane Jean Davis, b. Mar. 19, 1950; Bruce Clinton Davis, b. May 26, 1952; Career: Private practice law, Los Angeles, 1940---. Pres. Irontite Prods. Co., Inc.; dir. Clinton's Restaurants. Lt., Supply Corps, USNR (1942-45), WW II. Mem.: L.A. Athl. Club, Los Angeles Country Club, Pi Gamma Mu. Rec.: travel. Res.: 5005 Los Feliz Blvd., Los Angeles, CA 90027; Office: 707 Wilshire Blvd., Suite 3636, Los Angeles, CA 90017.

ROEST, ARYAN INGOMAR
Professor of Biological Sciences
b. June 13, 1978, Chicago, Ill.; s. Pieter Kornelis and Neeltje (Bloemendal) Roest; student, Univ. Rochester, B.S., Univ. Va., 1945; B.S., Ore. State Univ., 1947; M.S., Ph.D., 1954; Tng., NSF Summer Insts. in Marine Biol., Ore. 1961, and Desert Biol., Ariz. 1965; m. Colette Pouteau, Mar. 18, 1950, Portland, Ore.;

children: Sandra Lee (Kirkpatrick), b. 1951; Sharon Diane, b. 1955; Lisa Kristine, b. 1957; Michele Louise, b. 1961. Career: Survey crew chief, Ore. State B.d of Forestry, 1949; Fish Census, Ore. State Game Commn. 1953; Mammal Census, Ore. State Bd. of Forestry, 1954; Instr., Inst. of Nature Study, Univ. Calif., ext., Santa Barbara, 1957, 58, 59, 60, Vis. Asst. Prof., 1959; Instr. Central Ore. Community Coll., 1952-55; Prof., Biol. Sci. Dept., Calif. Polytech. State Univ., San Luis Obispo, 1955---; vis. prof., Moss Landing Marine Labs. 1967. Ensign, USNR, 1943-46. Contbr. many sci. articles, profl. publs. Mem.: Morro Bay Mus. Assn., past secty.; Morro Coast Audubon Soc., past pres.; Citizens Advisory Com. on Sea Otter and Abalone, Calif. Dept. Fish & Game, 1967. Hobby: bird study. Res.: 285 Hermosa Way, San Luis Obispo, CA 93401; Office: California Polytechnic State University, San Luis Obispo, CA 93407.

ROETTGER, DORYE
Musician — Author — Lecturer
b. Oct. 22, 1932, Utica, N.Y.; d. Albert Frank and Marion Emma (Farber) Rutger; ed. Natl. Hon. Soc., New Hartford H.S., N.Y. 1949; Ithaca Coll., B.M., Univ. Ext. Cons., Chicago, 1955; Ph.D., Univ. of Eastern Florida, 1972; grad. Utica Sch. of Comm.; Palmer Inst. of Authorship; pvt. stu. music, dance, art. Career: Professional oboist in concert, theatre, film and rec. studios, sym., opera and chamber music, inc. Carnegie Hall, Town Hall, Brooklyn Acad. of Mus., Aeolian Hall, N.Y.; The Music Center, Wilshire Ebell Theatre, Royce Hall, Beckman Aud., Bing Theatre, L.A.; and tours USA 1951---; visiting artist: USC, UCLA, L.A. City Coll., Calif. Inst. Tech., Univ. Nev. (concert pgms.-lecture demonstrations); vocalist (soprano), pianist, accompanist and voice coach; musicologist; write, pgm. notes for L.A. Mus. of Natural Hist. concert series, Orange Co. Philharmonic Orch., Inner City Cultural Center concert series; founder-dir. Festival Players of Calif., Inc. 1957 (creator over 2000 children's pgms., perf. schs. Western U.S., Mex.); Prod. annual "Chamber Music for Children" Featival; prod. edn. films-records; creator, Artistic Apprenticeship, proj. for young musicians; prod. monthly concerts-with-commentary national Pacifica Radio, 1971---; Lectr.: music and fine arts, L.A. City Schs., Teacher workshops; L.A. Co. Div. Spec. Edn.; many clubs and organizations; Inner City Inst. Perf. Arts; originator, "Music and People: A Survey of World Cultures" lecture course; Author: numerous articles, pub. profl. journs., incl. Music Educators Journ., Sounding Board, Overture; cultural ed.-feat. writer, Co. News Bur., L.A. 1966---; nationally syndicated column "Bridging the Culture Gap" 1971---; genl. adm. Festival Players Membership Assoc., training pgm. for children and adults in music and art. Awards: Commendation for meritorious public serv., Calif. State Assembly; Certificate of Appreciation, L.A. City Council; Merit Award, L.A. Co. Bd. Supvs.; cited, Congressional Record, 1971, an inspiration to the Nation; Project Head Start; L.A. City Schools Volunteer Program, California Federation of Music Clubs, L.A. Mayor's Office and Voluntary Action Council, others. Mem.: State chmn., Dept. of Edn., and chmn., Western Region, Music in Schs. and Coll., Natl. Fed. of Music Clubs; Advisory Comm., L.A. Arts for Communities, Inc.; Steering Comm., Community Resource Unit, L.A. City Schs. Vol. and Tutorial Pgm.; Legislative Comm. chmn., Calif. Music Council; President's Comm. on Cult. Affairs, Local 48 AFM; Fine Arts chmn., L.A. Explorer's Division, Boy Scouts of America; Internat. Platform Assoc.; Am. Musicological Soc.; Calif. Mus. Educs. Assn.; Natl. Assn. Mus. Therapy; OES, Christian Sci. Hobbies: history, fine arts. Rec.: travel, hiking, swim, animal care and training. Res.: 3809 DeLongpre Ave., L.A. CA 90027.

ROGERS, BONNIE
College Dean of Library Services
b. Apr. 14, 1940, Olive Hill, Kentucky; d. Willis and Ollie D. Rogers; E.A., Morehead (Ken.) State Univ., 1961; M.L.S., Univ. of Maryland, 1967; postgrad., UCSD and USC, Ed.D. candidate. Career: tchr., jr. High Sch., 1961-66; cataloging librarian, U.S. Naval War Coll., Mahan Lib., Newport, R.I., 1967-68; asst. head ref. librarian, U.S. International Univ., Elliot Campus, San Diego, 1968-69; Eve. Dean, Palomar Community Coll., 1976, Dean of Library Services, 1977---; assoc. prof., coord. library pub. services, 1969-77. Author of bibliographies: Afro-American, Native Americans and The Chicano, Internat. distribution; contbr. articles and papers. Mem.: Am. Library Assn.; Calif. Lib. Assn.; Community Coll. Librarians chpt., CLA, secty. treas. 1978, pres. 1979; bd.

dir., San Diego METRO Library Coop.; Calif. Tchrs. Assn.; National Edn. Assn.; Beta Phi Mu; S.D. Area Community Coll. Learning Resources Coop., pres. 1978-79. Home: 751 Hoska Dr., Del Mar, CA 92014; Office: Palomar Community Coll., 1140 W. Mission, San Marcos, CA.

ROHRING, FRANK JOHN
Utility Company Executive
b. Aug. 27, 1913, Los Angeles; s. Frank John and Mildred (Tate) Rohring; ed. So. Calif. pub. schs. and colls.; m. Muriel Head, Los Angeles, Apr. 29, 1937; son, John Gary, b. Dec. 31, 1939. Career: Commercial dept., So. Calif. Edison Co. 1937-45; lighting cons. 1945-50, lighting engr., gen. ofc. 1950-55, ind. development engr. 1955-60, mgr. area development 1960---. Dir., Elec. Ind. Show, L.A. 1950; coord. first So. Calif. Ind. Development Com's. tour of Wash., D.C., N.Y. and New Eng. Registered professional engr., Calif. Assoc. ed., wkly. publ. "Sparks," 1955-57. Listed, various USA and internat. biog. publs. Mem.: Pac. Coast Elec. Assn., L.A. Elec. Club, Amer. Ind. Development Council, Internat. Council of Shopping Center Owners, Kern Co. Econ. Progress Com., Soc. of Ind. Realtors; past pres., Elec. Maintenance Engrs. Assn. 1951-52; co-founder-dir., Progress Assn. of L.A. Co.; chmn. Illuminating Engrs. Soc. S. Pac. Conf. 1955; exec. com., Ind. Development Com., L.A. C. of C. (5 counties of So. Calif.); v. chmn., Econ. Development Exec. Com., Calif. State C. of C.; co-founder, L.A. Ind. Development Breakfast Club; La Brea Lodge 650, F&AM (32º), L.A. Consistory Scottish rite, Shriner, Al Malaikah Temple. Res.: 4057 Marcasel Ave., Los Angeles, CA 90066.

ROLLE, ANDREW F.
Historian — Educator
b. Apr. 12, 1922, Providence; s. John B. and Theresa (Maurizio) Rolle; B.A., Occidental Coll., 1943; M.A., UCLA, 1949; Ph.D. 1953; grad. (Clin. Assoc.), So. Calif. Psychoanalytic Inst., 1976; m. Frances Johanna Squires, Dec. 22, 1945 (separated); chil.: John Warren, Alexander Frederick, Julia Elisabeth. Career: Am. vice consul, Genoa, Italy, 1945-48; vis. prof. UCLA, 1975, 76; editorial assoc. Pacific Hist. Rev., 1952-53; asst. prof. Occidental Coll., 1953-56, assoc. prof., 1957-62, prof., chmn. dept. history, 1962, 65-66, 73-74, Cleland prof. history, 1965---; Served to 1st Lt., M.I., AUS, 1943-45, 51-52. Decorated cavaliere Ordine Merito (Italy); recipient award of merit. Am. Assn. State and Local Hist., 1957; silver medal Italian Ministry Fgn. Affairs, 1963; Commonwealth award for non-fiction, 1969. Huntington Library-Rockefeller Found. fellow, 1954; resident scholar Rockefeller Found. Center, Bellagio, Italy, 1970, 71; Mem. Am. Studies Assn. (past regional sect.-treas., 2d. pres.), Phi Beta Kappa. Author: Riviera Path, 1946; An American in California, 1956; The Road to Virginia City, 1960; (with Allan Nevins, Irving Stone) Lincoln: A Contemporary Portrait, 1961; California: A History, 1963; Occidental College: The First Seventy-Five Years, 1963; The Lost Cause: Confederate Exiles in Mexico, 1965; The Golden State, 1967; California, A Student Guide, 1965; Los Angeles, A Student Guide, 1965. Editor: A Century of Dishonor (Helen Hunt Jackson), 1964; The Immigrant Upraised, 1968. Editor: Life in California (Alfred Robinson), 1971; The American Italians: The History and Culture, 1972; Gli Emigrati Vittoriosi, 1973; (with George Knoles others) Essays and Assays, 1973; (with Francesco Cordasco and others) Studies in Italian American Social History, 1975; (with John Caughey and others) Los Angeles: The Biography of a City, 1976; (with Allan Weinstein and others) Crisis in America, 1977. Contbr. to Ency. Brit., Ency. Americana, also journs. Research interest: application of psychiatric techniques to study of biography and history. Res.: 1244 Glen Oaks, Pasadena, CA 91105; Office: 1600 Campus Rd., Los Angeles, CA 90041.

ROLPH, HENRY R.
Superior Court Judge
b. Jan. 16, 1915, San Francisco; s. Thomas (U.S. Congressman, 1940-44) and Katherine (Renton) Rolph; nephew of Hon. James Rolph Jr., Mayor of S.F. 1912-31, Gov. of Calif. 1931-34; ed. Palo Alto Mil. Acad. 1926-28; Lowell H.S., S.F., 1928-32; A.B., Stanford Univ. 1936; LL.B., Stanford Law Sch. 1940; m. Barbara Sherwood (Kappa Alpha Theta, A.B., Stanford Univ. 1940), Piedmont, Calif., Dec. 27, 1946; chil.: Henry R., Jr., b. May 20, 1948; Barbara Josephine, b. July 17, 1950; Thomas Bates, b. Oct. 22, 1959. Career: Admitted to Supreme Ct. of Calif. and U.S. Fed. Ct., No. Dist., Calif. 1940; Ninth

Circuit Ct. of Appeal, 1946; U.S. Ct. of Customs and Patent Appeals, 1953; U.S. Supreme Ct. 1953; admiralty atty-partner (gen. Fed. and State practice, incl. ins., taxation and corp. law), law firm Graham James & Rolph, ofcs., S.F., Long Beach, Calif., Wash., D.C. and Tokyo, Japan; Superior Ct. Judge, S.F. City and Co. 1967---. Supv. City and Co. of S.F. 1956-61 (ret.), chmn. Edn., Parks and Rec. Comm., Judiciary and Police Coms., acting Mayor, Apr. and Oct. 1957 and July 1958; Enlisted, Marine Corps, 12th Dist. Res. Battalion, S.F. 1936; 2nd. Lt., USMC Res. 1938, active duty, 1941-46; commanded Weapons Co., 28th Marines, Iwo Jima Campaign, participated in taking Mt. Suribachi; Mil. Gov., Yamaguchi Prefecture, Japan (1945), WW II; Col. USMC Res. Awards: Bronze Star, Presidential Unit Cit. Mem.: dir. Marines Mem. Assn. 1954---; pres. Marine Exch. of S.F.; Fed. Rules-Adm. of Justice Coms., S.F. Bar Assn.; State Bar of Calif.; Amer. Bar Assn.; dir. S.F. Bay Area Council; treas. com. for passage of $7,000,000 S.F. Rec. and Park Bonds (Prop. C), 1955; secty. adv. council, Salvation Army; exec. council, Red Shield Youth Assn.; exec. council, Boy Scouts of Amer.; bd. govs., Port of S.F. Propeller Club; dir. No. Calif. Bible Soc.; Chi Psi. Episcopalian. Hobby: stamp collecting, photog. Rec.: gardening, golf. Res.: 2626 Lyon St., San Francisco, CA; Office: 482 City Hall, San Francisco, CA 94102.

ROOD, RODNEY W.
Corporate Executive
b. Oct. 1, 1915, Minneapolis, Minn.; s. Paul W. and Neva (Nystrom) Rood; B.A., UCLA, 1938; m. Margaret Anne Davey, Dec. 20, 1940, Los Angeles; chil.: David, b. Aug. 29, 1945; Brian, b. Aug. 4, 1948. Career: adminstrv. asst. to Mayor Fletcher Bowron, city of L.A. 1948-52; asst to pres., Richfield Oil Corp., 1953-65; with Atlantic Richfield Co., 1966---: pub. affairs mgr., 1966-70; asst. to chmn., 1970-72; elected v.p., asst. to chmn., 1972---. Dir.: Fin. Fedn., 1974---; Hollywood Presbyterian Hosp.; Calif. Mus. Found.; Calif. Hist. Soc.; L.A. Civic Light Opera Assn.; Independent Colleges of So. Calif.; Greater L.A. YMCA; So. Calif. Com. for the Olympic Games. Clubs: California, L.A.; Carlton, Wash., D.C.; Home: 4136 Pembury Pl., Flintridge, CA; Office: 515 S. Flower St., L.A., CA 90071.

ROSE, MASON H., V
Lawyer — City Councilman
b. Mar. 28, 1937, Los Angeles; s. Mason H. IV and Florence (Wright) Rose; B.B.A., Univ. New Mex., 1959; J.D., Loyola Univ. Sch. of Law, L.A., 1970; m. Wynonah Dee Roe, June 7, 1962; chil.: Angela Marie, Scott Mason, Kellie Dee. Career: Admitted to Calif. Bar. 1971; assoc. Kindel & Anderson, L.A., 1971-75; partner firm Nichols and Rose, Beverly Hills, 1975---; elected City Councilman, City of Rolling Hills, 1974---, Mayor, 1975-76. One of 1st lawyers to prosecute cases in federal and state cts. to estab. civil rights of handicapped. Chmn. Nat. Advisory Com. Archtl. and Transportation Barriers Compliance Bd., Wash. D.C., 1976---; mem. Calif. Atty. Gen's. Task Force for Handicapped; Commr., L.A. Co. Commn. for Handicapped, chmn. 1976-77; trustee, Torrance Mem. Hosp.; bd. dir., Calif. State (1977---) and Los Angeles Co. (1974---) Easter Seals Soc.; Co-founder, Calif. Assn. for Physically Handicapped, bd. dir. 1971-73; co-founder, Western Law Center for the Handicapped, L.A., bd. dir., 1976---; bd. dir. Nat. Center for Law and the Handicapped, South Bend, Ind., 1977---; bd. dir. Nat. Rehabilitation Assn., So. Calif. chpt. 1971-75. Mem. Calif., Los Angeles, Beverly Hills Bar Assns. Res.: 37 Crest Rd. W., Rolling Hills, CA 90274; Office: 9952 Santa Monica Blvd., Beverly Hills, CA 90212.

ROSENBERG, RICHARD M.
Bank Executive
b. Apr. 21, 1930, Fall River, Mass.; s. Charles and Betty (Peck) Rosenberg; B.S., Journalism, Suffolk Univ., 1952; M.B.A., Golden Gate Univ., San Francisco, 1963; LL.B., 1966; m. Barbara K. Cohen, Oct. 21, 1956; sons: Michael, b. 1960; Peter, b. 1962. Career: Publicity Asst., Crocker Anglo Bank, San Francisco, 1959-62; Banking Services Officer, Wells Fargo Bank, S.F., 1962-65; Asst. Vice Pres. 1965-68, Vice Pres., Mktg. Dept. 1968, St. V.P., Mktg. and Advt. Div. 1970-75, Sr. V.P. & Deputy Mgr., Trust Div. 1975, Exec. V.P. & Group Head, Corporate Services Group, 1975, Exec. Vice Pres. & Deputy Mgr., Retail Banking Group, 1976---. Comdr., USNR. Res.: 66 Oakdale, San Rafael, CA 94901; Office: 420 Montgomery St., San Francisco, CA 94104.

ROSENDIN, RAYMOND J.
Business Executive
b. Feb. 14, 1929, San Jose; s. Moses L. and Bertha C. (Pinedo) Rosendin; ed. San Jose State Univ. 1948; BSEE, Heald's Engring. Coll. 1950; m. Jeanette Marie Bucher, June 30, 1951 (dec. Feb. 21, 1967); m. Diane Cathryn Perry, Honolulu, Hawaii; Mar. 10, 1972; chil.: Mark R., b. May 29, 1952; Patricia A., b. July 29, 1953; Debra Jeffrey, b. Mar. 24, 1955; Cynthia Claire, b. Oct. 26, 1961; David R., b. Aug. 18, 1966; stepchil.: Michael R., b. July 13, 1961; Kevin W., b. Jan. 23, 1963; Mark D., b. Mar. 6, 1965. Career: Exec. v.p., Rosendin Elec., Inc. 1950---. Mem.: Natl. Elec. Contractors Assn., pres. Santa Clara Co. Chpt. 1956, gov. 1957; dir. Greater San Jose C. of C.; Bd. of Regents-Bd. of Fellows, Univ. of Santa Clara; dir. Santa Clara Valley Youth Village, Community Bank of San Jose, Fr. Schmidt Youth Found.; (past) Santa Clara Co. Grand Jury; dir. United Fund; La Rinconada Country Club, St. Claire Club, Univ. Club of San Jose. Catholic. Res.: 1880 E. Campbell Ave., San Jose, CA 95125; Office: 880 N. Mabury Rd., San Jose, CA 95133.

ROSENE, LEE C.
Corporate Executive
b. Nov. 5, 1912, Chicago, Ill.; s. David and Belle (Baim) Rosene; ed. pub. schs., USA; spec. courses, Amer. Mgmt. Assn.; m. Dorothe Ann Rosen, Dec. 30, 1934; chil.: Sara Lynn Radell, b. Jan. 7, 1945; Alexander, b. Sept. 22, 1946. Career: Sales rep., Max Factor & Co. 1936-46, div. sales mgr., Chicago, 1946-51, regional sales mgr. 1951-57, dir. U.S. Sales, 1957, v.p.-dir. 1960-68, sr. v.p. 1968, pres. Max Factor Dev. Div. 1970---. Mem.: chmn. So. Calif. Cosmetics and Pharmaceutical Div. of United Jewish Welfare, 1965-67; Amer. Mgmt. Assn.; Beverly Hills Club; dir.-v.p. Merchants Club, City of Hope; So. Calif. C. of C.; Town Hall of Calif.; Brentwood Country Club. Hobby: numismatist. Rec.: golf. Res.: 2222 Ave. of the Stars, Los Angeles, CA 90067; Office: 1655 N. McCadden Pl., Hollywood, CA 90028.

ROSENGRANT, BARRY LEE
Real Estate Developer
b. Feb. 1, 1933, Des Moines, Iowa; s. Harry Dean, noted DVM, Iowa, and Pearle Estelle Rosengrant; B.A., cum laude, Tarkio Coll., 1955; postgrad., Univ. of Minn., 1960; m. Charlotte Joan Petersohn, Feb. 5, 1953, Tarkio, Mo.; chil.: Edwin Lee, b. 1954; Teresa, b. 1956. Career: Mkt. Research and div. mgr., Pillsbury Co., Minneapolis, 1955-59; Regional Mgr. Abbot Labs., Chicago, 1959-61; Regional mgr., div. mgr., Knoll Internat., 1961-64; exec. v.p., Architectural Potter, 1965; founder, pres., chmn. Artec., L.A. 1966-78 (mfg. and design of furniture and interior archtl. furnishings); chmn., Greenwood & Co. Real Estate Devel., Los Angeles, 1978---; lectr. various design schs. and colls., 1961-78. Recipient first place design award, Indsl. Design Mag. 1970. Rec.: swimming. Res.: 2705 Krim Dr., L.A., CA 90064; Office: 1888 Century Park E., Los Angeles, CA 90067.

ROSENSTEIN, BETTY LEBELL
Educator — Researcher — Business Executive
b. June 29, 1921, Los Angeles; d. Frank and Adele (Summerfield) Lebell; B.A., UCLA, 1943, M.A. 1951; Ed.D., 1967; m. Allen B. Rosenstein, Taos, N.Mex.; chil.: Jerry, b. May 3, 1944; Lisa, b. Oct. 29, 1952; Adam, b. Mar. 26, 1957. Career: Dept. secty. UCLA 1942-44; UCLA English teacher, and Vets. Adm. 1945, Spanish teacher, 1947-49, instr. ext. classes "Life Styles," 1968; Psychol. inst. Pepperdine Univ. 1972; founder-dir.-instr. social dance and pvt. groups, 1961-63; teacher, relig. sch.; teacher, UCLA Ext. Adult Edn.; edn. cons. UCLA Task Force; Natl. Univ. of Venezuela, S. Amer. (initiate and present seminars on edn. planning); translator, Venezuela, other Latin Amer. countries; lectr., Community Center, Jr. H.S. Venezuela. Radio prod.-anncr.: Betty Rose's Camp Fannin Show, KGKP (30 min. daily), Tyler, Tex. and Hat Time, Trading Post, KGKB, 1943. Developed, mfr., natl. distrib.: University Spanish teaching Records, 1947---; orig. Shower Caddy, 1956---; researcher: Problem Marriages for Redbook mag.; Activity Patterns of Women, Needs of Women; editor in chief, Open Channels (off. publ. Adult Edn. of Greater L.A.; award, 1972). Minerva Award, AWARE, Inc. 1963. Mem.: Am. Edn. Research Assn.; treas. Phila. Phrateres, 1942; secty. Adult Edn. of Greater L.A. 1970; Commissioner, Los Angeles Co. Commission on Status of Women, 1976-79; v. chairperson, 1976; Board member, Calif. Pre-School

Advocacy; pres. Adult Educators of Greater L.A., 1975-77; com. chmn. Natl. Conv. Amer. Educ. Assn., L.A. 1971; Sigma Delta Pi; Alpha Delta chpt., Pi Lambda Theta. Jewish. Hobby: shell collecting. Rec.: music, reading, travel. Res.: 314 S. Rockingham Ave., L.A., CA 90049.

ROSENTHAL, RICHARD J.
Psychiatrist
b. Jan. 12, 1939, NYC; s. Sam and Yvette (Kapelov) Rosenthal; B.A., Cornell Univ., 1960, M.D., Albert Einstein, 1964. Career: Internship, Montefiore Hosp. 1964-65; residency in psychiatry, Mt. Sinai Hosp., N.Y., 1965-68; clin. assoc., Los Angeles Psychoanalytic Inst., 1970---; Asst. Prof., UCLA Sch. of Med., 1971---; Vis. Scholar, Inst. of Religious Studies, UC, Santa Barbara, 1977-78; Dir. of Edn., San Gabriel Valley Mental Health Center, 1970-71. Chief, Neuropsychiat. Unit, USMC Recruit Depot, San Diego, 1968-69; Lt. Comdr., USN, 1970. Contbr. profl. articles Am. Journ. of Psychiatry, others. Office: 435 N. Roxbury Dr., Beverly Hills, CA 90210.

ROSHONG, DEE ANN DANIELS
Guidance Counselor
b. Nov. 22, 1936; Kansas City, Mo.; s. Vernon Edmond and Doradell (Kellogg) Daniels; B.Music Edn., Univ. Kansas, 1958; M.A., Counseling, Guidance, Stanford Univ., 1960. Career: Supr. of Vocal Music, Antioch Dist. Schs., Merriam, Kan., 1959-60; Counselor, Fresno City Coll., 1961-65; Coordinator of Counseling Services, Chabot Coll., 1965---. Writer, coordinator, symposia: I, a Woman, 1974; Feeling Free To Be You And Me, 1975; All For The Family, 1976; I Celebrate Myself, 1977; Person To Person In Love And Work, 1978; The Healthy Person In Body, Mind And Spirit, 1979, all for Chabot Coll. Mem.: Alpha Phi; Calif. Community and Jr. Coll. Assn. Student Personnel Commn.; Calif. Personnel and Guidance Assn. Christian Sci. Hobbies: music, writing. Res.: 808 Comet Dr., Foster City, CA 94404; Office: Chabot Coll., Valley Campus, Livermore, CA.

ROSKY, BURTON SEYMOUR
Lawyer — CPA
b. May 28, 1927, Chicago, Ill.; s. David T. and Mary W. Rosky; B.S., UCLA 1948; J.D., Loyola Univ., L.A.; m. Leatrice J. Darrow, Los Angeles, June 16, 1951; sons: David Scott, b. Nov. 26, 1957; Bruce Alan, b. May 16, 1959. Career: Auditor, City of Los Angeles, 1948-51; sr. acct. Beidner, Temkin & Ziskin, CPA 1951-52; Calif. Certified Pub. Acct. 1952; admitted to Calif. Bar, 1954; supv. Army Audit Agcy. 1952-54; est. pvt. practice law, 1954-72; Duskin, Rosky & Fidler, law firm, 1972---. Contrib. author to profl. journs. Guest lectr., profl. orgns. on Tax and Current Bus. Problems. USNR 1945-46, WW II. Awards: Amer. Theatre Medal, Victory Medal. Mem.: Calif. Soc. of CPA; Calif., Beverly Hills Bar Assns.; arbitrator, Panel Amer. Arbitration Assn.; pres. Calif. Assn. of Atty.-CPA 1963, dir. 1963---; pres. Amer. Assn. Atty.-CPA, 1964, dir. 1964---; B'nai B'rith, Mason, Phi Alpha Delta; pres. Tau Delta Phi, UCLA; Mayor's Adv. Com. of L.A.; L.A. Co. Art Mus., Amer. Mus. of Natural Hist., Smithsonian Inst.; bd. dirs. Temple Beth Hillel Brotherhood. Hobby: photog. Rec.: spectator sports. Res.: 5738 Sunnyslope Ave., Van Nuys, CA 91401; Office: 8383 Wilshire Blvd., Suite 760, Beverly Hills, CA.

ROSS, DICKINSON CROSBY
Insurance Agency President
b. July 5, 1923, Los Angeles; s. Almon Bartlett, M.D. and Nora D. (Dickinson) Ross; ed. L.A. H.S., Univ. of Calif., Berkeley; (bus. adm.) USC 1947; m. Terry Brunton Barker, La Jolla, Calif., Nov. 15, 1947; chil.: Robyn Terry, b. Mar. 23, 1950; Dickinson Crosby, Jr., b. Dec. 18, 1951. Career: Provident Mutual Life Ins. Co. 1946-47; Reinsurance Underwriters, Inc. 1950-53; Johnson & Higgins of Calif. 1953---; asst. v.p. 1958, v.p. 1961, bd. dirs.-exec. v.p. 1965, pres. 1973---. USAAF 1942-46, WW II. Mem.: chmn. L.A. chpt. Multiple Sclerosis; Greater L.A. Zoo Assn.; L.A. Council BSA; bd. trustees, Repub. Assocs.; Phi Kappa Psi; Clubs: California, Lincoln, The Beach, The Los Angeles, Los Angeles Country. All Saints Episcopal., Beverly Hills. Hobbies: golf, skiing, boating. Res.: 13900 Old Harbor Lane, Marina Del Rey, CA 90291; Office: 4201 Wilshire Blvd., Los Angeles, CA 90010.

ROSS, HARVEY M.
Physician
b. June 10, 1929, Denver, Colo.; s. Marion B. and Beatrice L. Ross; Ph.B., Univ. of Chicago, 1949; M.D., Emory Med. Sch., 1954. Career: Staff and Clin. Dir. Gracie Square Hosp., NYC, 1960-68; pvt. practice, Los Angeles, 1968---. Vice Pres., Internat. Coll. of Applied Nutrition, 1975-77; v.p., bd. govs., 1976-79; Acad. of Orthomolecular Psychiatry, 1977-79; editorial bd., Journ. of Orthomolecular Psychiatry, 1977-79; trustee, Huxley Inst., 1976-79. Lt. Comdr. Ret., USN. Author: Fighting Depression, Larchmont Books; lectr.: numerous TV and radio appearances. Office: 9201 Sunset Blvd., L.A., CA 90069.

ROSS, HUCH C.
Engineering Company President
b. Dec. 31, 1923, Turlock; s. Clare W. and Jeanne (Pierson) Ross; grandson, Frank A. Pierson, former Mayor of Turlock; cous., Frank S. Pierson, Judge Superior Ct., Stanislaus Co.; student, Calif. Inst. of Tech., 1942; San Jose State Coll., 1946-47; B.S.E.E., Stanford Univ. 1950; m. Sarah A., Dec. 16, 1950, San Jose; sons: John, b. 1953; James, b. 1955; Robert, b. 1957. Career: Instr., San Benito High Sch. and Jr. Coll., 1950-51; Chief engr., Jennings Radio Mfg. Corp., 1951-62, chief engr., ITT Jennings, 1962-64; owner, Ross Engring. HV (high voltage) Consultants, 1964---; pres., chief engr., prin., Ross Engring. Corp. 1964---. Registered Profl. Electrical Engr. 1954; Fellow, IEEE, 1966; patentee, high voltage devices; publs. in field. USAF, 1943-46. Chmn., Nat. Electric Auto Symposium, 1960-61; mem. Am. Soc. of Metals; Am. Vacuum Soc. Hobbies: electronics, electric auto. Rec.: camping, gardening. Res.: 11915 Shadybrook, Saratoga, CA 95070; Office: 559 Westchester Dr., Campbell, CA 95008.

ROTH, HENRY LOGAN
Insurance Company President
b. Apr. 30, 1917, Kansas City, Mo.; s. Henry Logan and Margaret Roth; ed. Univ. of Nebr., Tex. A and M, Univ. of Pa.; m. Margaret Elaine Quisenberry, Santa Ana, Calif., Sept. 20, 1943; chil.: Donald, b. Apr. 29, 1952; Susan, b. Oct. 16, 1955. Career: Assoc. with Globe Investment Co. 1936-40; pres. Acme Agencies, Inc. 1940; Beneficial Standard Life Ins. Co. 1940---; developed fire and casualty sales div. 1948, v.p. 1954, developed career life div. 1957, sr. v.p. 1966, pres. 1969; v.p. Beneficial Fire Casualty Co., 1952---; v.p. Fidelity Interstate Life Ins. Co. 1960---; v.p. Brit. Pac. Life Ins. Co., 1965---; v.p. Beneficial Standard Corp. 1967---. Lt. (j.g.), USN. Mem.: bd. dirs., Toluca Lake Little League, Inc. 1960-65; bd. dirs., Wally Moon's Baseball Camp; Marina com., Balboa Bay Club, Newport Beach. Catholic. Res.: North Hollywood, CA; Office: Beneficial Plaza, 3700 Wilshire Blvd., Los Angeles, CA 90010.

ROTH, LESTER WILLIAM
Presiding Justice, Court of Appeal
b. Apr. 5, 1895, NYC; s. Herman and Hannah (Kornfeld) Roth; LL.B., USC 1916; m. Gertrude Frances Freedman, Brooklyn, N.Y., July 7, 1926; chil.: Harlan Charles, b. 1928 (dec.); Mrs. Hal (Eleanor Lois) Ross, b. 1933 (dec.). Career: Law practice, 1916-18; law firm, Lissner, Roth & Gunter, L.A. 1920-31; judge, Superior Ct., L.A. Co. 1931-36, justice pro tem, Dist. Ct. of Appeals, 1934-36; law firm, Mitchell, Silberberg, Roth & Knupp, 1936-42; Roth & Brannen, 1942-47; v.p. Columbia Pics. Corp., Hollywood, 1947-52; pvt. practice law, Beverly Hills, Calif. 1952-63; justice, Ct. of Appeal, Nov. 1963; presiding justice, 1954---. Dir.: Standard Cabinet Works, Los Angeles, 1929---; Guaranty Union Life Ins. Co., Beverly Hills, 1940-55; City Natl. Bank of Beverly Hills, 1953---; 2nd Lt., USMC (1918-19), WW I; chmn. Draft Appeal Bd., State of Calif., L.A. Dist. (1942-45), WW II; govt. appeal agt., Selective Serv. System, 1962. Mem.: pres. Big Brothers' Assn., L.A. 1921-25; pres. B'nai B'rith, 1923-25; dir. Fed. Jewish Welfare Orgns. 1924-40; trustee, Cedars of Lebanon Hosp., L.A. 1929-51; pres. City of Hope, 1932-35; chmn. Mayor's Com. on Cleaning and Dyeing, 1937-38; dir. Hillcrest Country Club, L.A. 1948---, pres. 1949-53; dir. L.A. Jewish Community Council, v.p. 1950-52; natl. v.p., Amer. Jewish Com. 1951-52; natl. adv. com. 1952---; chmn. Com. Internal Security Act, Calif. State Bar Assn. 1952-54, chmn. com. on photog. in courtrooms, 1957-59, corps. and corporate securities com. 1959, personal injury claims com. 1959---, com. on free trial and free press, 1959---, com. on adm. agcys. and tribunals, 1962; L.A. Bar Assn.; chmn. adv. com. to lawyers, Beverly Hills Bar Assn., pres. 1959; Amer.

Coll. of Trial Lawyers; co-chmn. Natl. Conf. of Chrs. & Jews, 1957-59; Acad. of Mot. Pic. Arts & Scis.; dir. Tamarisk Country Club, Palm Springs. Hobby: horseback riding, golf. Res.: 1201 Loma Vista Dr., Beverly Hills, CA; Office: Court of Appeal, 3580 Wilshire Blvd., Los Angeles, CA 90010.

ROUGH, JAMES GRAY
Consul-General of Western Samoa
b. Jan. 6, 1892, Scotland; s. Hugh and Jane Rough: ed. Bellahouston Acad., Glasgow, 1904-1907; trainee in foreign languages and acctg. under Sir William Burrell (Consul of Austro-Hungarian Govt.) Glasgow, 1907-1912; m. Gertrude B. Harmon, June 17, 1938, L.A.; dau. Mary Eleanor, b. May 4, 1940. Career: trainee in Consular representation and tramp steamship bus., exporting & importing, 1907-1912, in full charge of Consulate, 1912-1915; East India merchandizing bus. and steamship agency work in Singapore and Bangkok; also repr. Lloyd's, London, Eng.; founded Am. Shellac Co., L.A. 1938-68; apptd. Consul of Western Samoa, July 1969---. Awarded two High Chief Titles in W. Samoa, later the Order of Vailima (O.V.S.). Interview with Pope Paul VI on state visit to Samoa, Aug. 1970. Bd. dir., U.S. Coast Guard Acad. Found., New London, Conn., two 3 year terms. Mil.: fought in Singapore Vol. Rifles, and Marine Police, during the mutiny of two E. Indian regiments stationed in Singapore to protect the colony; mutiny broke out Feb. 15, 1915. Home-Office: 3422 Madera Ave., L.A., CA 90039.

ROUNDS, DONALD EDWIN
Medical Research Investigator
b. Jan. 17, 1926, Maywood, Ill.; s. Howard G. and Dorothy S. Rounds; B.A., Occidental Coll., Los Angeles, 1951; Ph.D., UCLA, 1958; m. Helen L. Cann, Mar. 16, 1951, Pasadena; daughters: Robin Anne, b. 1959; Wendy Jeanne, b. 1962. Career: Dir., Dept. Cell Biology, Pasadena Found. for Med. Research, 1959-64; dir., Dept. Laser Biol., 1964-72 and Research Coordinator, 1965-72, Sr. Research Investigator, 1972---; also pres., Vanguard Research Labs., Inc., Pasadena, 1978---. Adj. Assoc. Prof. Anatomy, USC Sch. Med., 1970---; clin. prof. Pathol., Loma Linda Univ. Sch. Med., 1974---; Reviewing Editor: In Vitro, 1970---. Pres., Calif. Tissue Culture Assn., 1969-71; chmn., Gordon Research Conf. on Lasers in Med. and Biol. 1972. Publs.: 133+ sci. articles, abstracts and book chpts., 1952---. AUS, 1945-47. Am. Baptist. Res.: 1261 Sonoma Dr., Altadena, CA 91001; Office: 99 N. El Molino Ave., Pasadena, CA 91101.

ROURKE, ROBERT ALFRED
Naval Engineer
b. July 1, 1917, San Francisco; s. Alfred Edward and Florence (Moses); B.S. mech. engr., Univ. Calif., Berkeley, 1942; M.S., naval constrn. and engring., Mass. Inst. of Tech., 1948; m. Barbara E. Johnson, Feb. 14, 1943, Portsmouth, Va.; chil.: Kathryn Louise, b. 1944; Thomas Alfred, b. 1946. Career: Naval Engring. Officer (commd. Ensign through Comdr.), 1942-62; Marine cons., General Elect. Co., Syracuse, N.Y. 1962-66; Chief Naval Arch., Litton Industries, Culver City, 1966-67; Dir. of Engring., Harbor Boat Bldg. Co., Terminal Island, 1967-70; Asst. Design Mgr., Litton Ship Systems, Culver City, 1970-72; Naval Arch., Fluor Drilling Svcs., L.A. 1972-73; west coast rep., J.J. Henry Co., Inc., NYC, Naval Architects and Marine Engrs., 1973---; instr. naval arch., UCLA, 1974, Long Beach Naval Shipyard, 1974-78. Chmn., L.A. Metro, Sect., Soc. of Naval Architects and Marine Engrs. 1970-71. Club: el Niguel Country. Protestant. Rec.: golf. Res.: 31303 East Nine Dr., Laguna Niguel, CA 92677.

ROUSE, ALLISON M.
Associate Justice, California Court of Appeal
b. Sept. 22, 1919, Visalia, Calif.; s. Allison and Loretta (Newman) Rouse; J.D., Univ. of S.F. Sch. of Law, 1948; m. Dorothy June Barker, San Francisco, Jan. 12, 1952. Career: Pvt. practice law, S.F. 1949-52; Dep. Dist. Atty., San Mateo Co. 1952-68; sr. trial dep. Criminal Div. 1968; apptd. Superior Ct. Judge, San Mateo Co. (by Gov. Ronald Reagan), 1968; Criminal Div. 1969, Presiding Judge, 1970; Judge, Juvenile Ct., San Mateo Co. 1971; apptd. to Ct. of Appeal, State of Calif., 1971---; Assoc. Justice, Div. 2, First Appellate Dist., S.F. Antiaircraft Artillery, Panama Canal Dept., U.S. Army; Lt. Col., Judge Advocate Gen's. Corps. (USAR), WW II. Mem.: judicial adv. Com. on Criminal Law and Procedure, State Bar of Calif. 1967-71; bd. dirs. Calif. Crime Tech. Research

Found. 1969---; (past) bd. dirs. San Mateo Co. Bar Assn.; Amer. Bar Assn.; Conf. of California Judges; bd. dirs. Bay Area Soc. Planning Council; pres. bd. trustees, Redwood City Library; bd. dirs. Lowell H.S. Alumni Assn.; Amer. Legion, Native Sons of Golden West, Res. Ofcrs. Assn. of U.S., Commonwealth Club of Calif. Republican (County Central Com. 1960s). Protestant. Office: 4020 State Bldg., San Francisco, CA 94102.

ROUSH, GEORGE EDGAR
Patent Lawyer

b. Feb. 29, 1916, Tuolumne, Calif.; s. George Edgar and Ethyl Ruth (Gaskill) Roush; B.S., Univ. of Calif., Berkeley, 1940; J.D., NY Law Sch. 1951; m. Sarah Catherine Kragness, Asbury Park, N.J., Mar. 29, 1944; chil.: Jane Margaret, b. Feb. 26, 1949; George Edgar, III, b. June 20, 1954. Career: Admitted to U.S. Patent Ofc. practice, agt. 1947, atty. 1953; admitted to N.Y. bar 1953, U.S. Ct. of Customs and Patent Appeals, 1954; United States Supreme Court, 1970; patent agent, Philips Labs., Irvington-on-Hudson, N.Y. 1946-48; patent atty.: RCA Labs., Princeton, N.J. 1948-56; Hytron Div. CBS, Danvers, Mass. 1956-57; Marchant Calculators, Inc., Oakland, Calif. 1957-60; IBM, Inc., San Jose, Calif., 1960---. 2nd Lt., Lt. Col., Signal Corps, U.S. Army (1940-46), WW II. Mem.: Pi Tau Sigma, 1938---; fellow, Internat. Acad. of Law and Sci.; (sr.) Inst. of Elec. and Electronics Engrs.; (assoc.) N.Y., S.F., Amer. Patent Law Assns.; (assoc.) Patent Ofc. Soc.; (assoc.) Amer. Radio Relay League; Amer. Bar Assn.; secty. Kiwanis Club of Cambrian Park, San Jose, 1964-65; v.p. 1966, pres. 1967. Episcopalian. Res.: 16250 Jacaranda Way, Los Gatos, CA 95030; Office: Monterey and Cottle Rds., San Jose, CA 95193.

ROUSSELOT, JOHN HARBIN
United States Congressman

b. Nov. 1, 1927, Los Angeles, Calif.; s. Harbin Michon and Mary (Gibson) Rousselot; B.A., Principia Coll., Ill. Chil.: Craig, Robin, Wendy. Career: Life underwriter, Penn Mutual; lease management Foster and Kleiser, administrative assistant, director, public rels. Pac. Finance Corp. 1950-54; pub. rels. cons. John H. Rousselot and Assocs. 1954-58; natl. dir. pub. inf. Fed. Housing Adm. 1958-60; elected, U.S. House of Reps., (Banking and Currency, P.O., Civic Serv. Coms.), 1961-63; natl. dir. pub. rels. The John Birch Soc., 1963-67; mgmt. cons. 1967-70; elected to Congress (spec. election), 1970, reelected, U.S. House of Reps. 24th Cong. Dist. 1972---. Awards: TV Emmy (for Lomax-Rousselot KTTV show); Pas. Jr. C. of C. Man of Yr., 1963. Mem.: (hon.) Yale Polit. Union; Pub. Rels. Soc. of Amer.; v. chmn. L.A. Co. Repub. Central Com.; exec. com. Repub. State Central Com.; bd. dirs. First Ch. Chr. Sci., San Marino; Capitol Hill Club. Res.: 735 W. Duarte Rd., Arcadia, CA 91006; Office: 1706 Longworth Bldg., Wash., D.C. 20515.

ROWE, HARRY MANUELL, JR.
Library Consultant

b. Oct. 15, 1921, Vallejo, Calif.; s. Harry M., Sr. and Josephine (Marshall) Rowe; A.B., Univ. of Calif., Berkely, 1946; M.L.S. 1947; postgrad. 1952-55; m. Mary Lou Haire, Feb. 1, 1975; chil.: Richard S., b. Dec. 17, 1946; Nancy J. and Douglas P. (twins), b. July 23, 1949; Harry M., III, b. Oct. 3, 1953. Career: Circulation ref. librarian, Coalinga Dist. Lib., Calif. 1947-48; head lib., Coalinga H.S. and Jr. Coll. Lib. 1948-49; dist. lib., Coalinga Dist. Lib. 1949-52; county lib., Solano Co. Lib. 1952-57; city librarian, Fullerton Pub. Lib. 1957-68; county lib., Orange County Lib. 1968-79. Instr.: Coalinga Coll. 1949-52; Vallejo Jr. Coll. 1952-57; Fullerton Jr. Coll. 1957-67; USC 1957-73; (lib. sci. and polit. sci.) Calif. State Univ., Fullerton, 1973---; Chapman Coll. PACE, USS Midway, Far East, 1974. Author: California Here We Came, Orange Co. hist. bibliography, publ. 1965; regular contrib. to Calif. Librarian. Staff Sgt., 98th Inf. Div., Pac. Theater, U.S.Army, WW II. Mem.: pres. Yosemite Dist. Calif. Lib. Assn. 1952, pres. Golden Gate Dist. 1954; pres. So. Dist. of Calif. Lib. Assn. 1962; state pres., Calif. Lib. Assn. 1966, chpt. councilor Amer. Lib. Assn. 1972-76; pres. Kiwanis Club of Fairfield, 1957; dist. council ofvr., BSA, 1959-67; Calif. Historical Comm. 1963-64; pres. Kiwanis Club of Fullerton, 1964; adv. com., Calif. Cong., PTA 1967-69; Lt. Gov., Calif.-Nev.-H.I. Dist., Kiwanis, 1970-71, Zone Adm. 1974-75, 76-77; secty. Orange County Hist. Comm. 1973---; Vallejo Lodge No. 487, F&AM; E. Clampus Vitus; Delta Chi. Episcopalian. Hobbies: book collecting, reading. Rec.: sports, golf, singing. Res.: 5009 Woodman Ave., Apt. 112, Sherman Oaks, CA 91423.

ROWE, MARY LOU
Librarian

b. Aug. 12, 1933, Kempner, Tex.; d. Buford and Lenna Fields; A.A., Kilgore Jr. Coll., 1952; B.A., N. Texas State Univ., 1953; M.L.S., USC 1963; m. Harry Manuell Rowe, Jr., former Orange County Librarian, Feb. 1, 1975, Santiago Canyon. Career: Elementary Sch. Librarian, Dallas Independent Sch. Dist., 1953-56; Documents Librarian, Stanford Research Inst., 1956-57; Tech. Librarian, Ampex Corp., 1957-58; Information Spec., Sylvania Electronic Products, 1958-59; Documents Librarian, Hughes Aircraft, 1959-63; Asst. Library Dir., Anaheim Pub. Lib. 1963-77; City Librarian, Beverly Hills Pub. Lib., 1977---. Lectr. in Administrn.: Santa Ana Coll., 1974-75, Cal State Univ., Fullerton 1975, 77. Mem.: Calif. Lib. Assn., Local Arrangements Chmn. 1972, Chmn. Lib. Devel. & Standards Com. 1973; ALA; Am. Soc. for Pub. Adminstrs.; Libraria Sodalitas Bd. 1977-80; Anaheim C. of C., Women's Div. chmn. various com., bd. dir. 1968-77; Episcopalian. Rec.: golf, flying. Res.: 5009 Woodman Ave., Apt. 112, Sherman Oaks, CA 91423; Office: 444 N. Rexford, Beverly Hills, CA 90210.

RUBEN, IRWIN
Psychiatrist

b. Mar. 14, 1946, Chicago, Ill.; s. Sidney (lawyer) and Ethel Ruben; B.S. cum laude, Univ. of Ill., 1967; M.D. cum laude, 1967; m. Linda Jenkins, Dec. 25, 1960, Chicago; chil.: Lisa, b. Feb. 24, 1973; Jessica, b. Sept. 22, 1978. Career: completed pscyhiatric training, USC-L.A. Co. Med. Center, 1975; pvt. practice, 1975---; also clin. instr. in psychiatry, USC, 1976---; asst. clin. prof. of psychiatry, USC, 1979---. Lectr., psychosomatic med., 1979; paper: Patients Attacks Against Psychiatrists, pub. Voted outstanding med. student in psychiat., Univ. of Ill., 1974; awarded Bamberger Scholarship. Mem.: So. Calif. Psychiatric Assn.; West L.A. Bus. and Profl. Assn.; Phi Delta Epsilon; AOA. Office: 435 W. Roxbury Dr., Beverly Hills, CA 90210.

RUBENDALL, DONALD E.
Company President

b. May 28, 1913, Fonda, Ia.; s. Ellis and Mary (Mullins) Rubendall; ed. Fonda H.S. 1929-32; Signal Corps Electronic Sch., West H.S. and Univ. of Minn. 1942-44; m. Inez Christensen, Newell, Ia., Nov. 28, 1935; chil.: Alan, b. Oct. 5, 1939; Robert, b. Aug. 9, 1945; Julie Jo, b. July 13, 1951. Career: Gen. mgr., Good-All Electric Mfg. Co. 1944-51; pres. San Fernando Elec. Mfg. Co. 1951---; pres. Gen. Scientific Corp. 1951---; bd. dirs. Behrens Mem. Hosp. 1969---. Mem.: Leading Knight, BPOE, 1944---; Noble Grand, Odd Fellows, 1946-51; Presbyterian (chmn. financial bd., hosp. bd., elder). Hobby: woodworking, photog., flying, Res.: La Canada, CA; Office: 1501 First St., San Fernando, CA 91341.

RUBENSTEIN, ARTHUR
Pianist

b. Jan. 28, 1889, Warsaw, Poland; s. Ignace and Felicia (Heyman) Rubinstein; ed. Warsaw and Berlin Acad. of Music; stu. violin with Joachim, Berlin; stu. piano with Rozycki and Barth; m. Aniela Mlynarska, July 27, 1932; chil.: Eva, paul, Alina-Anna, John-Arthur. Career: Berlin Sym. Orch. at age 13 yrs.; first U.S. tour, 1906 (debut with Phila. Orch.); tours throughout Europe, Africa, China, Japan, Java, Philippine Is.; numerous other internat. perfs.; annual perf., Hollywood Bowl; recording artist, numerous recs. incl. entire works of Chopin. Awards: decorated, Legion of Honor (France), Cross of Alfonso XII (Spain), Comdr. of the Crown and Officer of Leopold I (Belgium), Polonia Restituta (Poland), Comdr. Chilean Republic. Res.: Beverly Hills, CA.

RUBIN, EDWARD
Attorney at Law

b. Apr. 30, 1912, Brooklyn, N.Y.; s. Goerge and Bella Rubin; A.B., UCLA, 1933; J.D., Duke Univ. Sch. of Law, 1936; m. Nancy Cordner, Oct. 30, 1943, San Francisco; chil.: Laurence D., atty.; Peggy (Ueda), field examiner, Nat. Labor Rels. Bd. Career: Admitted to State Bar of N.Y. 1937, Calif., 1941, U.S. Supreme Ct. Mem. law firm Mitchell, Silberberg & Knupp, 1953---, now sr. partner ---. Lectr. Commercial and preventive law, Cal. State Coll., L.A.; lectr. USC Sch. of Law, Beverly Hills Bar Assn. Entertainment Law Inst., USC Grad. Sch. of Cinematography, L.A. Copyright Soc., San Fernando Valley Univ. Coll. of Law. Pres., State Bar of Calif., 1977-78; pres., Beverly Hills Bar Assn., 1971, past mem. bd. govs., Law

Found. (1st pro bono found. sponsored by bar assn.); mem. L.A. County Bar Assn., exec. com. 1966-67, 1972; mem. Am. Bar Assn., chmn. com. on Entertainment and Sports Industries, mem. Patent, Trademark and Copyright Sect., Fellow, Am. Bar Found.; mem.: Am. Arbitration Assn.; Am. Judicature Soc., L.A. Copyright Soc., Nat. Conf. of Bar Presidents, Nat. Council Juvenile Ct. Judges, Nat. Juvenile Ct. Found., Inc., Women Lawyers Assn. of L.A., World Assn. of Lawyers; bd. govs. UCLA, past pres. Bruin Hoopsters; nat. bd. trustee, City of Hope; World Peace Through Law Center; L.A. Internat. Film Festival, bd. advisor; AFC Internat. Scholarships Found.; Am. Film Inst.; UN Assn. of L.A.; L.A. Co. Art Mus.; NCCJ; Natural Hist. Mus.; YMCA; Guardians of Jewish Home for Aged; Phi Beta Kappa; Order of Coif. Co-author: Preventive Law, 1950; contbr. profl. journals. Res.: 204 Ashdale Pl., L.A., CA; Office: 1800 Century Park E., Suite 800, Los Angeles, CA 90067.

RUBINSTEIN, MICHAEL
Professor of Medicine
b. Nov. 28, 1915, Wilno, Poland; s. Isaac (Senator of Poland) and Esther (Flensberg) Rubinstein; M.A., Univ. of Wilno, 1936; M.D., magna cum laude, 1938; postgrad., Univ. of Vienna, Austria and Univ. of Paris, France (faculty of med.); m. Vera Freudmann, Mar. 31, 1948, NYC, N.Y.; chil.: Alan I (M.D.), b. Sept. 2, 1949; Jonathan S. (M.D.), b. Dec. 28, 1950; Daniel B. (M.D.), b. Mar. 20, 1952. Career: Rotating internship, Maimonides Hosp., Brooklyn, N.Y., 1940-41; med. internship. Columbia Univ. div., N.Y., 1941; resident, hematology, Mt. Sinai Hosp., NYC, 1942-47; Hematologist, Montefiore Hosp., NYC, 1943-54; mem. hematology staff, Mt. Sinai Hosp., NYC, 1943-54; assoc. prof. of med., Loma Linda Univ. ---. Hon. Asst. Etranger, Faculty of Med., Paris, France. Author, over 100 publs., field of physiology, hematology, med.; monographs in English, German, French, Spanish, Polish, Russian, Hebrew, some awarded prizes by AMA, etc. Mem.: AMA, CMA, L.A. Co. Med. Assn.; fellow, Am. Coll. of Physicians; Internat. Soc. of Hematology; AM. Soc. of Hematology; AAAS; sci. and learned socs. USA and abroad. Beth Jacob Congregation, Beverly Hills (founding mem.). Hobbies: literature, hist., music. Home: 803 N. Bedford Dr., Beverly Hills, CA 90210; Office: 435 No. Bedford Dr., Beverly Hills, CA 90210.

RUBKE, WALTER C.
Clergyman
b. Oct. 26, 1923, San Francisco; s. William and Helen Rubke; M.Div., 1948; Ph.D., 1962; m. Gudyun Wadewitz, June 20, 1948, San Francisco; children: Linda Kennell, b. May 14, 1949; Susan, b. Apr. 11, 1953; Jane, b. July 29, 1959. Career: Instr., Concordia Acad., Portland, Ore. 1948-49; Pastor, Grass Valley, Chicago Park, Auburn, Calif. 1949-51; Dean of Students, California Concordia Coll., Oakland, 1951-64; Pres., Concordia Lutheran Coll., Austin, Tex., 1964-69; v.p. for Student Affairs, Valparaiso Univ., Valparaiso, Ind., 1949-75; pastor, First Lutheran Ch., Yuba City, 1975---. Hobby: stamp collecting. Rec.: tennis. Res.: 1220 Railroad Ave., Yuba City, CA 95991; Office: 850 Cooper Ave., Yuba City, CA 95991.

RUBY, CHARLES LEROY
Educator — Civic Leader
b. Dec. 28, 1900, Carthage, Ind.; s. Edgar Valentine and Mary Emma (Butler) Ruby; paternal desc., U.S. Pres. Andrew Jackson; ed. Certificate, Ball State Univ., Muncie, Ind. 1922; A.B., Central Normal Coll., Danville, Ind. 1924, LL.B., 1926, B.S. 1931; M.A., Stanford Univ. 1929; J.D., Pac. Coll. of Law 1931; Ph.D., Olympic Univ. 1933; postgrad. Ind. Univ., Fresno State Coll., UCLA, USC; m. Rachael E. Martindale, Pine Village, Ind., Aug. 30, 1925; chil.: Mrs. Norman (Phyllis Arline) Braskat; Dr. Charles L., Jr.; Martin Dale. Career: Prin., Pine Village H.S. 1923-25; tchr., El Centro pub. schs. 1926-27, Central Union H.S. 1927-29; prof. (law), Fullerton Jr. Coll. 1929-66; prof. Central Normal Coll., Ind. (summers), 1929-33; prof. Armstrong Coll., Berkeley (summer), 1935. Admitted to Ind. Bar, 1926; admitted to U.S. Supreme Ct. 1970; founder-dir., Fullerton Pub. Forum, 1929-39; tour dir., NEA and Calif. Teachers Assn. Mex., Hawaii (2 yrs.); guest, radio-TV pgms. Writer-researcher, contrib. articles to profl. publs., USA Dep. Sheriff, Orange Co. 1958-66. Instr. V5-V12 pgm. (1942-45), WW II. Awards: commendation, Calif. State Senate, 1978; Medal of Merit, ANA 1954; Citation, Calif. State Assembly, 1966. Mem.: dir., No. Orange Co. Mus. Assn. 1975-78; pres., No. Orange Co. Ret. Sr., Vol. Program, 1975-77; rep., Fullerton Sr. Citizen

Com., 1978; dir., No. Orange Co. Vol. Board, 1977---; mem. Fullerton Task Force, 1977---; Elks Lodge; founder, Elk's Natl. Found.; Town Hall of California; president, Fullerton Rotary Club, 1940-41; gov. Amer. Numismatic Assn. 1951-53; (life) pres. and charter mem. Numismatic Assn. of So. Calif.; pres. Coin Clubs in Orange Co., Long Beach, Garden Grove, Indianapolis; (hon. life) Calif. Bus. Educators Assn.; (hon. life) Pac. Southwest Law Teachers Assn.; (life) Calif. Edn. Assn.; (life) NEA; pres. Orange Co. Teachers Assn. 1953-55; dir.-div. chmn., Calif. Teachers Assn. 1958-65, pres. So. Sect. 1962-63, dir. Credit Union, Teachers Ins. Board, Real Estate Trust (9 yrs.); Stanford Univ. Law Soc.; Calif. State Council on Edn.; pres. Fullerton Secondary Teachers Assn.; pres. Fullerton Jr. Coll. Faculty Club; Calif. Assn. Univ. Profs.; parliamentarian, Orange Co. Dem. Central Com. 1962---; U.S. Assay Commn. (apptd. by Lyndon Johnson), 1968; pres. Pac. Southwest Law Assn. 1969-70; IPA Methodist (Sunday School teacher). Hobbies: Indian artifacts, philately, numismatics. Rec.: hunting, fishing, travel. Res.: 308 N. Marwood Ave., Fullerton, CA 92632.

RUDELL, WILLIAM BARNUM
Attorney at Law
b. Nov. 10, 1939, Los Angeles; s. Lloyd Kenneth and Marion Elizabeth (Barnum) Rudell; A.B., cum laude, Princeton Univ., 1961; Grad. Inst. of Internat. Studies, Geneva, Switzerland, 1962-63; LL.B., Yale Law Sch., 1965. Career: Crown Counsel and Dir. of Public Prosecutions, Repub. Botswana, Africa, 1965-67; Corporate secty. and gen. counsel, Rudell Machinery Co., Inc., NYC, 1967-68; of counsel, law firm Halstead & Baher, Los Angeles, 1968---; Consul of the Republic of Botswana in state of Calif., 1970---; pres. and commr., Hollywood Burbank Airport Authority, 1977---. Dir., Burbank YMCA, 1971-76; Verdugo Hills Council BSA, 1972-76; Bridge: A Way Across, Inc., 1974-76. Awards: named Outstanding Young Man in Am. 1972; Africa-Asia Pub. Service Fellowship Program, 1965-67; Summer Research Fellow, OAS, Bogota, Colombia, 1964; Rotary Found. Fellowship for Internat. Understanding, 1962-63. Publs.: The Gospel of Sci. Mgmt., 1961; New Haven's 'Great Leap' Forward: The Role of Community Progress, Inc., 1964; Urban Planning in the Soviet Union, 1964; Concerted Rent-Withholding on the NYC Housing Front: Who Gets What, Why and How?, 1965; Community Development in Ciudad Kennedy: An Examination of Existing Programs of Social Service with Proposals for Their Coordination and Expansion, 1964. Polit.: Councilman, Burbank City Council, 1973-77, Mayor 1975-76; mem. Burbank Planning Bd. 1970-72; chmn. 1972; mem. Burbank Redevel. Agency, 1973-77, chmn. 1975-76; mem. Republican Co. Central Com. 1975-77; Republican State Central Com., assoc. mem. 1974---. Mem.: Burbank Kiwanis Club, pres. 1974-75; Wicket & Cricket, pres. 1973-75; The Bachelors, 1975---; Silver Rats, 1970---; Princeton Club of So. Calif.; Cap & Gown Club of Princeton Univ.; Sierra Club; Explorers Club; L.A. Consular Corps; L.A. Co. Bar Assn.; Burbank Bar Assn.; State Bar of Calif. Episcopalian Rec.: Mountaineering. Res.: 4420 Sarah St., No. 34, Burbank, CA 91505; Office: 615 S. Flower St., Suite 1750, L.A., CA.

RUDOLPH, BERTRAM FREDERICK, JR.
Real Estate — Business Executive
b. Sept. 7, 1928, San Francisco, Calif.; s. Bertram Frederick and Minnie Josephine (Brinan) Rudolph; great-great-grandson of Johann Heinrich Wilhelm Rudolph, Jr., early San Francisco gun mfr., inventor, importer, brewer; ed. Hartnell Coll. 1946-47; Stanford Univ. 1949-50; Univ. of Calif., Berkeley, 1950-51; grad. NBC Inst. 1950; Monterey Peninsula Coll. Sch. of Real Estate, 1967; m. Diana Louise Sawyer, Terr. of Hawaii, Mar. 30, 1957; chil.: Ursula Kirsten, b. Mar. 25, 1958; Stefanie Ingeborg, b. Dec. 6, 1965. Career: Pres., Calmont Radio & TV Co., Inc., Salinas, 1947-49; v.p.-treas. Telemir Prodns., Inc., Monterey 1948-49; gen. agt. Rubak Marine Assocs., Ltd., Auckland, New Zealand, 1951-53; dir. Samoan Airlines, Ltd., Apia, 1952-54; dir. South Pac. Airlines (Aust.) Pty. Ltd., Papeete, Tahiti, 1953; dept. mgr. Cockett Airlines, Ld., Honolulu, 1953-54; pres. Rainbow Tours, Ltd. Waikiki, 1954-58; asst. dept. mgr. Peninsula Daily Publ. Co., Monterey, 1959-67; partner, Rommel, von Kreling & Becker, Pebble Beach, 1967---; dir. Dudley & Grimes Ranch Co., San Ardo, 1971---. Contrib. to Sat. Eve. Post, 1952. Calif. Historian, 1966. Spec. Rep. Sundicat D'Initiative de Tahiti, 1952-56; reg. v.p.-dir. Conf. of Calif. Historical Socs., Univ. of Pac., Stockton, 1965-67, 1970-71; (charter) dir. Old Monterey Bicentennial, Inc. 1967-68;

rider, 1st and 2nd annual Pebble Beach Steeple Chases, 1967-68; ambassador-at-large, City of Monterey, 1967-69. Serv. Korean Airlift with Gen. Claire L. Chennault's Flying Tigers, Mil. Air Transport Command. Mem.: Soc. Calif. Pioneers; San Francisco and Honolulu Sym. Assn.; Polynesian Soc.; Honolulu Acad. of Arts; Papua and New Guinea Soc.; Calif. Rifle and Pistol Assn., Inc.; pres. Monterey County Taxpayers' Assn. 1971---; chmn. Monterey Bay Area Aviation Adv. Bd. 1971---; Monterey Co. Republican Central Com. 1977-78. Lutheran. Hobbies: history, genealogy, cartography. Rec.: flying, tennis, mountaineering, swim. Res.: P.O.B. 2302, Carmel, 93921; Office: P.O.B. 822, Pebble Beach, CA 93953.

RUFF, HOWARD J.
Newsletter Editor — Author
b. Dec. 27, 1930, Berkeley; s. Wilson Rex and Rena (Braley) Ruff; student, Brigham Young Univ., 1951-54; m. Kay Felt, Apr. 19, 1955, Salt Lake City; chil.: Larry, b. Jan. 30, 1956; Eric, b. Apr. 28, 1957; David, b. Feb. 10, 1959; Pamela, b. July 15, 1960; Sharon, b. Mar. 13, 1962; Patricia, b. July 23, 1963; Ivan (dec.), b. Aug. 16, 1966; Timothy, b. Nov. 24, 1970; Deborah, b. Apr. 9, 1972. Career: devel. advt. & mktg. programs for Evelyn Wood Reading Dynamics (earned outstanding franchise award 4 yrs.); co-founder, the Lowry-Nickerson Real Estate Investors course; distbr., the Neolife Co. of Am. (food supplements; recipient the founder's award as top distbr.); soloist on 1,000,000 selling album w/Tabernacle Choir, A Concert of Sacred Music; soloist w/Philadelphia Orch.; soloist, Ed Sullivan Show; editor and pub., The Ruff Times newsletter and fin. advisory service ---; host: nat. TV talk show: Ruff House; author: Famine and Survival in Am.; How to Prosper During the Coming Bad Years, best seller, 1979; sponsor: internat. fin. seminars. Mil.: served USAF, 1955-59; band and singing sgts., soloist. L.D.S. ch.; missionary; councilor to Bishop; choir dir.; Sunday sch. pres. and tchr. Hobbies: singing (musical theatre, concert). Rec.: fishing, flying. Office: Box 172, Alamo, CA 94507.

RUFFO, ALBERT JOHN
Attorney at Law
b. July 1, 1908, Tacoma, Wash.; s. John and Louise (Gallucci) Ruffo; ed. B.S. (Electrical Engineering), 1931, Juris Doctor, 1936; LL.D. (hon.) Univ. of Santa Clara, 1973; Nobili Medal, 1931 (hon. award, Univ. of Santa Clara); Tau Beta Pi (Scholastic Engring. Hon. Soc.); Tower Award, San Jose State Univ., 1974; m. Marianne Gagliardi, Tacoma, Wash., June 30, 1937; chil.: Anne Louise O'Donnell, b. July 29, 1939; James Thomas, b. Dec. 31, 1941; Stephen John, b. Oct. 6, 1944; Patrick Albert, b. Apr. 15, 1948; John Anthony, b. Feb. 24, 1952. Career: Asst. football coach, Univ. of Santa Clara, 1930-43; line coach, Univ. of Calif., Berkeley, 1945; asst. coach, S.F. Forty-Niners, 1946-47. Univ. of Santa Clara, Athletic Hall of Fame. Pierce Co., Wash., Athletic Hall of Fame. Pvt. practice law, Calif., 1937---; Pres., Ruffo, Ferrari & McNeil, Profl. Corp., 1968---. San Jose City Council, 1944-52; Mayor, City of San Jose 1946-48. Trustee, Calif. State Colls. and Univs., 1961-71, chmn. of bd. of trustees, 1964-66; bd. of regents, Univ. of Santa Clara, 1967-71; regent emeriti; v.-chmn., 1969-70; adv. bd., San Jose State Univ., 1972---; chmn. 1977; President's Council, San Jose State Univ., 1972---; President's Council, St. Mary's Coll.; President's Council, Dominican Coll., Dir. of Spartan Found. Mem.: Bd. of govs., State Bar of Calif., 1953-56, v.p., 1955-56; fellow: Amer. Bar Assn.; San Jose Civic Club, past pres.; San Jose Rotary Club, past dir., pres. 1970-71; Serra Club, first pres.; bd. of dirs., O'Connor Hosp. Found.; bd. of dirs., Archbishop Hanna Center for Boys; Am. Judicature Soc.; Eagles, Univ. Club; San Jose County Club; Knights of Malta; National Jewish Hosp., Honoree 1977; San Jose Charter Revision Committee. Roman Catholic. Res.: 1680 Hedding St., San Jose, CA 95126; Office: 101 Park Center Plaza, Suite 1300, San Jose, CA 95113.

RUGE, NEIL MARSHALL
Law Professor
b. Dec. 28, 1913, Wash. D.C.; s. Oscar and Ruth (Jones) Ruge; B.A., Stanford Univ., 1935; J.D., Univ. Calif., Berkeley, 1938; Veteran's Certificate, Harvard Bus. Sch., 1947; m. Helga Kley, July 23, 1949, Palermo, Italy; chil.: Carl S., b. 1951; Madeleine (Walters), b. 1955. Career: Pvt. practice of law, 1939-41; U.S. Foreign Service, 1947-69; Prof., Cal. State Univ., Chico, 1969---; 1st secty. of Am. Embassy, Guatemala, 1968. Served Pvt. to Maj., AUS, 1941-46, ETO, 3 campaigns, Bronze Star; Maj. to Col.,

USAR, 1946-69. Past pres., No. Calif. and Nev. American Bus. Law Assn.; mem. Sierra Club; Phi Beta Kappa; Delta Sigma Pi. Rec.: travel. Res.: 936 Bryant Ave., Chico, CA 95926; Office: Cal. State Univ., Chico, CA 95926.

RUIZ, RAMON EDUARDO
Public Official
b. Sept. 9, 1921, La Jolla; s. Ramon and Dolores (Urueta) Ruiz; Ph.D., History, Univ. Calif., Berkeley, 1954; m. Natalia Marrujo, Oct. 14, 1944, San Diego; daus.: Olivia Teresa, b. 1956; Maura Natalia, b. 1962. Career: Prof. Latin American Hist.: Univ. of Oregon, Eugene, 1955-57; Smith COll., Mass., 1958-69; Univ. Calif., San Diego, 1970---, Dept. Chmn. 1971-76; asst. prof. Latin Am. Lit., So. Methodist Univ., 1957-58; vis. prof., Mexican Hist.: Univ. Texas, Univ. Mass., Mt. Holyoke Coll., Amherst Coll., Univ. de Nuevo Leon, Monterrey, Mex.; Dir., Div. of Public Programs, Nat. Endowment fo; the Humanities, Wash. D.C. 1979---. Lt. USAAF, 1943-46, Pacific Theater. Author: The Great Rebellion: Mexico, 1905-1924, in press; Labor and the Ambivalent Revolutionaries: Mexico, 1911-1923, 1976; La Revolucion Mexicana y el Movimiento Obrero, 1911-1923, 1978; Cuba: The Making of a Revolution, 1968, 1970 (listed among the 21 best hist. books for 1968 by Book World); Mexico: The Challenge of Poverty and Illiteracy, 1963. Editor other books; Co-cauthor two children's books; contbr. articles, editorials, book reviews to profl. mags. and mags., newspapers. Awards: William Harrison Mills Traveling Fellow in Internat. Rels., UC, 1950; John Hay Whitney Found. Fellowship, NYC, 1950; Fulbright Fellowship, Chile, 1962; Fulbright Prof., Mex. 1965-66; Phi Beta Kappa; Sigma Delta Pi. Club: Santa Fe Hunt. Rec.: horseback riding. Res.: Rancho Santa Fe; Office: National Endowment for the Humanities, 806 15th St. N.W., Rm. 1200, Wash., D.C. 20506.

RUMMERFIELD, WALTER GLEN
Church Official
b. Nov. 14, 1911, Protection, Kan.; s. Walter and Clara Zora (Bachman) Rummerfield; student W. Texas State Univ. Cramwell Inst., 1946-56; B.S. bus. adm., 1957; Coll. of Univ. Truth MetaPhys. Sem., D.D., Ph.D., 1961-67; USC, 1961-65; Calif. Christian Univ.; Calif. Univ. Inst.; Sch. of Relig. & Ecumenical Seminary: S.T.D., J.C.D., J.S.D.; m. Grace King, July 1936, Kansas City, Mo.; chil.: Judith Ann, b. Dec. 20, 1942; Michael Ray, b. Mar. 9, 1948. Career: farm worker, 1919-31; grocery work & business, 1931-37; insurance agent, supr., asst. supt., mgr., broker, 1937-49; analyst & consultant, 1949-57; clergyman 1957-66; editor & publisher, founder: Voice in the Wilderness (religious news of church world), 1964---; L.A. World News, 1966-68; president, California Christian Univ. and church archbishop, 1959---. Served USN; Petty Officer in fire control gunnery, survivor, Destroyer sunk 12/44, Ormac Bay; decorated Purple Heart, Unit Citation. Mem.: Masonic, 1945-55; Khiva Temple Shrine, 1951-54; Knighted in Knight's Templar 1951; VFW, 1945; Am. Legion, 1945. Author: Psychology of Religion...Applied to Everyday Living, 1960; Bible Philosophy; 23rd Psalm in Meditation. Republican. Ecumenical ch. Hobbies: research, news, travel. Home: 17865 Adelanto Rd., Adelanto, CA 92301; Office: 18761 No. Bellflower St., Adelanto, CA 92301.

RUSACK, ROBERT CLAFLIN
Clergyman
b. June 16, 1926, Worcester, Mass.; s. Roy Leonard and Dorothy (Claflin) Rusack; B.A., Hobart Coll. 1946, D.D. 1967; Gen. Theol. Sem. 1946-47, 1949-51, S.T.D., 1965; fellow, St. Augustine's Coll. Canterbury, Eng. 1957-58; m. Janice Morrison Overfield, Salt Lake City, Ut., June 26, 1951; chil.: Rebecca Morrison, b. Feb. 4, 1953; Geoffrey Claflin, b. June 11, 1956. Career: Ordained deacon and priest, Episcopal Ch. 1951; vicar, St. James's Chm, Deer Lodge, Mont. 1951-57; chaplain, Mont. State Prison, 1951-55; Gov. of Montana's Chaplaincy Adv. Com. 1954-57; rector, St. Augustine-by-the-Sea Parish, Santa Monica, Calif. 1958-64; consecrated, Suffragan Bishop of Los Angeles, Sept. 29, 1964; Bishop Coadjutor of L.A., Oct. 24, 1972; Bishop of L.A., Jan. 26, 1974. Mem.: bd. dirs., Diocese of L.A. Council, 1961---; dir. Home for the Aged, Alhambra, 1963---; dir. St. Paul's Cathedral Corp. 1963---; dir. Seaman's Ch. Inst., San Pedro, 1964---; dir. Bishop Gooden Home, Pasa. 1964---; dir. Episc. Ch. Home for Chil. 1964---; dir. Neighborhood Youth Assn., L.A. 1964---; v.p. Univ. Relig. Conf., UCLA 1964---; dir. Alcoholism Council of Greater L.A. 1965---; v.p. City Mission Soc. of L.A.

1965---; chmn. Comm. on Ch. Music of Epis. Ch. 1965---; trustee, Gen. Theol. Sem., N.Y. 1971---; L.A. Ath. Club, L.A. Country Club. Res.: 13828 Sunset Blvd., Pacific Palisades, Calif.; Office: The Diocese of Los Angeles, 1220 W. Fourth St., Los Angeles, CA 90051.

RUSH, PAULA GERALDINE
Realtor
b. Mar. 29, 1926, Wilson, Okla,; d. M.D. and Cordia Jennings; m. Leonard R. Rush (Lt. Col., USAF, dec.), Mar. 25, 1946, Tacoma, Wash.; chil.: Sheila (Margetich), b. Dec. 29, 1946; Leonard R., Jr., b. Apr. 26, 1950; Sharon (Tuthill), b. Dec. 15, 1956. Career: real estate agent, 1968-76; real estate broker, co-owner, Red Carpet Realtors, Rancho Cordova, CA 1976---. Secty.-treas., Sacramento Red Carpet Council, 1977-78. Home: 2238 Baywater Lane, Rancho Cordova; Office: 10447 Folsom Blvd., Rancho Cordova, CA 95670.

RUSKIN, ARNOLD MILTON
Engineer — Educator
b. Jan. 4, 1937, Bay City, Mich.; s. Dave Burnard and Florence Shirley Ruskin; B.S. (chem. engr.), Univ. Mich., 1958, B.S.E., Materials Engr., 1958; M.S.E., Engr. Mat'ls., 1959, Ph.D., 1962; M.B.E., Claremont Grad. Sch., 1970; m. Dorothy L. Darrah; dau. Sandra Jean. Career: Instr. in Materials Engr., Univ. of Mich., 1961-62; lectr. in Applied Physics, Rugby Coll. of Engr. Tech. (England), 1962-63; asst./assoc./prof. of Engring., Harvey Mudd Coll., Claremont, 1963-73; Union Oil Co. Fellow in Engring., 1966-73, Asst. Dir./Dir. of the Freshman Div., 1971-73; Assoc. Prof./Prof. of Bus. & Econ., Claremont Grad. Sch. 1970-73; Engr. Mgr., Everett/Charles, Inc., 1973-74; Cont. Edn. Spec., UCLA, 1974---; Lectr. in Engr. Sys. 1975-77, Adj. Prof. of Engr. & Appl. Sci., 1977---; v.p., Claremont Engring. Co., 1973-79; mem. tech. Staff, Jet Propulsion Lab., CalTech, 1978---. Nat. Sci. Pre-Doctoral Fellow, 1958-61. Author: Materials Considerations in Design, 1967; 18 papers and publs. Honors: Tau Beta Pi, Phi Kappa Phi, Phi Lambda Upsilon, Sigma Xi, Omicron Delta Epsilon, Phi Eta Sigma. Mem. Archtl. Commn., City of Claremont, 1974-76, chmn. 1976. Res.: 545 W. Twelfth St., Claremont, CA 91711.

RUSS, EDMOND J.
Mayor
b. Mar. 28, 1928, Torrance; s. Frank Joseph and Elvira Virginia (Novelli) Russ; LL.D., UCLA Law Sch., 1954; m. Irene Cecelia Rudder, July 2, 1950, Redondo Beach; children: Cynthia Marie (Grosh), b. 1952; Ann Louise (Wisecaver), b. 1955; Linda Jean, b. 1957; Janette Michelle, b. 1960; David Frank, b. 1963. Career: Pvt. practice, Attorney at Law, Gardena, 1954---; elected Mayor, City of Gardena, 1969-70, 1974---; Councilman, 1968-72. Mem. U.S. Congress of Mayors, Urban Econ. Standing Com.; vice chmn., South Bay Communication Authority; mem. Policy Bd., So. Bay-Centinela Juvenile Diversion Project; dir. L.A. Co. Sanitation Dist. No. 5, past v.p., South Bay Cities Assn. Mem. KC, Past Grand Knight, 1958; pres. Kiwanis Club, 1964; mem. Elks; C. of C.; Calif., American, South Bay, L.A. County Bar Assns. Catholic, past pres. and judge advocate of St. Anthony Guild Assn. Hobby: golf. Res.: 1142 W. 158th St., Gardena, CA 90247; Office: 1515 W. Redondo Beach Blvd., Gardena, CA 90247.

RUSSELL, CAROL JOANNE
Bank Executive
b. Jan. 2, 1936, Placerville; d. Harold and Esther (Townzen) Willette; gr.granddau. of Francis Edward Fallon, orchestra leader, S.F. Old Opera House; m. Ralph A. Russell, Oct. 1, 1966, Placerville; chil.: David A., b. Mar. 2, 1956; Brent M., b. Mar. 4, 1959; Sheri D., b. Feb. 1, 1961; Gary Job, b. Jan. 26, 1963; Scott T., b. Apr. 10, 1968. Career: opns. supr., Mother Lode Bank, 1969, main office Placerville opns supr. (started dept. of Central Acctg., Mother Lode Bank) 1973; asst. cashier & opns. mgr., River City Bank, 1975---. Mem.: Placerville Emblem Club, past treas.; Bus. & Profl. Womens Club, past treas.; Highway 50 Assn., secty. to bd., 1977-78, bd. dir. 2½ yrs.; Soroptimist Club; Nat. Assn. of Banking Women. Roman Catholic. Rec.: bowling, swimming. Home: Pleasant Valley Rd., El Dorado, CA; Office: 348 Main St., Placerville, CA 95667.

RUSSELL, CHARLES MERVIN, JR.
Religious Organization Executive
b. Dec. 12, 1921, Miami, Fla.; s. C.M., Sr. and Ouida (Capers) Russell; ed. Greenville Coll., Ill.; B.A., Bethany Coll., Lindsborg, Kan. 1958; postgrad. Calif. State Coll. 1964; D.D., Azusa Pac. Coll. 1966; m. Martha Leone Noble, Riceville, Ia., July 13, 1942; chil.: Joyce Landry, b. Sept. 6, 1943; Janice Irvine, b. Feb. 17, 1946; Mervin Dean, b. Oct. 1, 1949. Career: Ordained minister, Free Meth. Ch. 1944; pastor, Minneapolis, 1942-46, McPherson, Kan. 1954-58; regional youth dir., Free Meth. Ch. of N. Amer. 1946-49; conf. supt., No. Ia.-Minn. Conf. 1949-53; gen. dir. youth, Winona Lake, Ind. 1958-62; exec. v.p., World Gospel Crusades, Inc., Los Angeles, 1963-65, pres., Upland, Calif. 1965---. Radio speaker-prod., Heart Melodies, Meditations With The Sky Pilot. Author: Youth Wants to Know, Design For Young Adult Fellowship, Design For Diligent Witness; ed. Youth in Action, 1958-62; ed. Crusades, 1963---. Mem.: regional pres., Natl. Assn. of Evangs. 1956-58; youth dir., Natl. Holiness Assn. 1959-60; chmn., youth comm., Natl. Sun. Sch. Assn. 1962. Hobbies: aviation (pvt. pilot), ham radio. Rec.: golf, swimming. Res.: 1178 N. San Antonio Ave., Upland, CA 91786; Office: P.O.B. 3, Upland, CA 91786.

RUSSELL, DONALD JOSEPH
Railroad Executive
b. Jan. 3, 1900, Denver, Colo.; s. Donald McKay and Josephine (Nunan) Russell; student, Stanford Univ., 1917-20; LL.D. (hon.), Loyola Univ., Los Angeles, 1955; m. Mary Louise Herring, Feb. 8, 1921; daughters: Donna Louise (dec.), Mary Ann (Mrs. Richard Kendall Miller). Career: Engineering, constrn., maintenance and opn. depts., So. Pacific Co., 1920-41, asst. to pres. 1941; vice pres., 1941-51, exec. v.p., 1951, pres. 1952-64, chmn. bd. 1964-72, hon. dir. 1972---. Dir. Emeritus, Tenneco Inc., Hon. Mem. Bus. Council. Founding Director, Stanford Research Inst. (SRI). Served with RAF, 1918-19. Mem.: Delta Tau Delta, Sigma Phi Upsilon. Clubs: Bohemian, Press, Pacific Union (San Francisco); Burlingame CC. Republican. Catholic. Res.: 2298 Pacific Ave., San Francisco, CA 94115; Office: Southern Pacific Bldg., One Market Plaza, San Francisco, CA 94105.

RUSSELL, GEORGE VERNON
Architect
b. July 4, 1905, San Bernardino, Calif.; s. James and Sarah (Culbertson) Russell; ed. B.Ar., Univ. of Wash. 1928; Diplome Ecole Des Beaux Arts Americaines en France, Fontainebleau; m. Mary Adelaide Younie, London, Eng., Dec. 31, 1942; chil.: Kristy Anne, b. 1946; Colin James, b. 1947; Ian Goerge, b. 1949. Career: Work in arch., N.Y. 1929-32; licensed to practice arch., N.Y. 1932, Calif. 1936---; arch. works incl.: Langford Lodge Air Depot, No. Ireland; cons. to 8th Air Force Serv. Command on Warton Air Depot, Warton, Eng.; Mobile Quarters for Gen. Eisenhower; Richfield Oil Corp., Bakersfield and New Cuyana, Santa Barbara County, Calif.; Republic Supply Co., Los Angeles and San Leandro; The Flamingo Hotel Casino, Las Vegas, Nev.; Lockheed Aircraft Serv., Inc., Burbank, Calif.; Joyce, Inc., Pasadena, Calif. and Columbus, Oh.; Harvard, Westridge, many other sch. structures; United Artists Corp., Ciro's, The Trocadero, L.A.; many shops, Beverly Hills; many dwellings. Author: (articles and illus. publ.) Ency. Brit. (current yearbook), Time, Arch. Forum, Arch. Record, Progressive Arch., The Arch. (Great Brit.), Vitrium (Italy), The Journ. of the Amer. Inst. of Archs., The Bulletin of the AIA, Western Industry, others. Participant in numerous western bldg. and panel discussions; moderator of First Annual Symposium on Design, So. Calif. Chpt., AIA; critic of 5th yr. design, Coll. of Arch., USC 1953---. Awards: MIT Prize, 1928; So. Calif. Merit Award for work perf. 1949-54; AIA Natl. Merit Award for ind. arch., Seattle, 1953; Natl. Award of Merit for Res. Arch., Boston, 1954; work exhib. internat. by AIA; exhib. Western Ger. Trade Fair by U.S. State Dept. 1953. Mem.: chmn. pub. works com., AIA, So. Calif. Chpt., del. to Natl. Conv. 1954; Phi Kappa Psi, Sigma Omicron Lambda, Calif. Club, Town Hall, Los Angeles; Valley Hunt Club, Pasadena; Rancheros Visitadores, Santa Barbara. Hobby: mus. (cello), painting. Rec.: riding, fishing, travel (Europe, N. Africa, Cuba, Mex.). Res.: Pasadena, CA; Office: 410 Rosenell Terr., Los Angeles, CA.

RUSSELL, JAMES THOMAS
Sculptor
b. May 30, 1938, Pinebluff, Ark.; s. James Thomas, Sr. and Winnie Lee Russell; B.A., painting, Cal State Univ., Long Beach 1965; M.A., sculpture, 1970, M.F.A., monumental sculpture, 1977; m. Darlene J. Zimmerman, Dec. 19, 1959, Hawthorne; children:

Brady James, b. 1968; Holly Ann, b. 1970. Career: 1970-79: Exhibited sculpture in 50 profl. exhibitions and 20 invitationals; Recipient over one dozen awards, incl. Best of Show All USA, Fine Arts Center, Scottsdale, Ariz., 1978; Grantee, National Endowment for Humanities, 1975; Erected Voyagers a 12 Ft. stainless steel sculpture, Cal. State Univ., Long Beach; Commissioned by State of Calif. to create Angelic Duet four story, stainless steel sculpture for Los Angeles State Bldg., 1979. Sculpture Juror, Southern Calif. Expo., Del Mar, 1978. Solo exhibitions: Cal. State Univ., Long Beach, 1970, 77; Riverside Mus. of Art, 1976; Joyce Hunsaker and Assoc., Beverly Hills, 1976; Palos Verdes Art Assn., 1969, 70. Constrn. and concept of his monumental sculpture is subject of 28-minute documentary film prod., USC Cinema Dept. Res.: Palos Verdes Estates, CA.

RUSSELL, JEFFREY BURTON
University Dean
b. Aug. 1, 1934, Fresno; s. Lewis Henry and Ieda Velma Russell; B.A., Univ. Calif., Berkeley, 1955, M.A., 1957; Ph.D., Emory Univ., 1960; m. Diana Mansfield, June 30, 1956, San Francisco; children: Jennifer, b. 1957; Mark, b. 1960; William, b. 1962; Penelope, b. 1966. Career: Asst. prof., Univ. N. Mex., 1960-61; Fellow of Soc. of Fellows, Harvard Univ., 1961-62; Asst. Prof./Assoc./Prof., Univ. Calif. Riverside, 1962-75; Dir. of Medieval Inst. and Grace Porf. of Medieval Studies, Univ. of Notre Dame, 1975-77; Dean of Grad. Studies, Calif. State Univ., Sacramento, 1977---. Mem. Bd. of Editors, Viator, UCLA, 1970-75. Author: Dissent and Reform In the Early Middle Ages, 1965; Medieval Civilization, 1968; A History of Medieval Christianity: Prophecy and Order, 1968; Medieval Religious Dissent, 1971; Witchcraft In The Middle Ages, 1972; The Devil: Perceptions Of Evil From Antiquity To Primitive Christiantiy, 1977; contbr. articles, scholarly journals. Works in progress: Witchcraft: A History, London: Thames & Hudson, 1979; Medieval Heresy: A Bibliography, with Carl T. Berkhout, Univ. Notre Dame Press; Shadowbearer, a novel. Mem. Sierra Club, 1955---. Hobby: numismatics. Res.: 4245 Dartmouth Dr., Sacto., CA 95819; Office: Cal State Univ., Sacramento, CA 95819.

RUSSELL, T. NEWTON
Attorney at Law
b. Mar. 17, 1918, Diamondville, Wyoming; s. Thomas C. and Cecelia (Sneddon) Russell; B.A., Stanford Univ., 1940, J.D., Stanford Univ. Sch. of Law, 1943; m. Margery Allan, Nov. 10, 1967, Ross, Calif.; sons: (by previous marriage) Thomas G., b. 1948; James N., b. 1951. Career: Practice of law in Fresno, 1943---. Dir., Fresno Auditorium Corp., 1968---; Fresno Art Advisory Com., 1966---; Mem. Bd. of Governors, Fresno Regional Found., 1968---. Sculptor of TRISEM Fulton Mall, Fresno. Hobby: sculpture. Res.: 1585 West San Madele, Fresno, CA; Office: 2220 Tulare St., Fresno, CA 93721.

RUTH, CRAIG MILLER
Developer
b. July 18, 1930, Akron, Pa.; s. Clarence M. and Kathryn (Buch) Ruth; B.A., Muskingum Coll., New Concord, Ohio, 1952; m. Marion Jane Nelson, Apr. 18, 1958, Rye, N.Y.; chil.: Robert Nelson, b. Aug. 18, 1959; Lee Kathryn, b. Sept. 12, 1961; William Walter, b. Feb. 22, 1963; Ann Alva, b. Aug. 1, 1964. Career: tchr., coach, Freeport High Sch., N.Y., 1955-56; asst. dir. of admissions, athletics, Northwestern Univ., Evanston, Ill., 1956-57; partner in constrn. firm, 1957-65; project mgr., So. Calif. for hi-rise bldgs., Murdock Devel. Co., 1965-66; mktg. mgr. for Del Amo Center, Torrance, and The City in Orange, Calif. (2 of So. Calif. largest master planned projects), 1966-68; mktg. & mgmt. dir., Ketchum, Peck & Tooley, 1968-74 (Bonaventure Hotel, 55 story world hdqtrs. for Security Pacific Bank, Avco Bldg. in Newport Beach, 800 Wilshire Blvd., L.A., etc.); joined Wm. Tooley as part owner, exec. v.p., Tooley & Company (hi-rise office bldgs., hotels), 1975---. Lectr. Grad. Sch. of Bus., Stanford and USC, 1977-78. Recipient 1965 Award for Bldg. Constrn. of Yorba Linda Village; named one of Outstanding Young Men of Am., U.S. Chamber of C., 1965; profiles and interviews in profl. and bus. mags. concerning mktg. orgns. and real estate; capt. of undefeated H.S. basketball state championship team, N.Y.; weekly radio broadcasts with own dance band while in coll. Served to Capt., USMC, 1953-55. Dir., Bldg. Owners & Mgrs. Assn., 1977-79; dir., Miraleste Homes Assn.; mem.: Stag Club, Varsity M. Club, Big Ten Club. Covenant Ch., Rolling Hills. Hobbies: boating, trumpet. Rec.: tennis, flying, water skiing. Home: 4045 Miraleste

Dr., Rancho Palos Verdes, CA 90274; Office: 3303 Wilshire Blvd., L.A., CA 90010.

RUTH, MARION NELSON
Realtor
b. Feb. 10, 1935, Rye, N.Y.; d. Alfred Walter and Alva (Schank) Nelson; B.A. philosophy, Northwestern Univ., Evanston, Ill., 1957; m. Craig Ruth, Apr. 18, 1958, Rye, N.Y.; Chil.: Robert Nelson, b. Aug. 18, 1959; Lee Kathryn, b. Sept. 12, 1961; William Walter, b. Feb. 22, 1963; Ann Alva, b. Aug. 1, 1964. Career: v.p., Ruth Developers, 1965; partner, Real & Ruth Interiors, 1968; pres., Ruth Realty, Rancho Palos Verdes, 1974---. Chmn., Miraleste H.S. Pool Found. (raised $125,000), 1967; pres., Miraleste Homes Assn.; Mem.: Palos Verdes Youth Commn.; Rancho Palos Verdes Bicentennial Com.; Palos Verdes Home Assn. Bd. (1st woman mem.); v.p., Miraleste High Sch. P.T.A., 1979; mem. chmn., Nat. Charity League, 1979; Miraleste Booster Club, chmn ways & means, 1979; Delta Gamma, 1954---; Big Ten Club 1979; Mother's Club Kappa Sigma of USC, 1979. Covenant Ch. Hobbies: pvt. pilot; tennis; arts. Rec.: swimming, water & snow skiing. Home: 4045 Miraleste Dr., Rancho Palos Verdes, CA 90274; Office: 15 Miraleste Plaza, Rancho Palos Verdes, CA 90274.

RUTTER, WILLIAM J.
Scientist — Educator
b. Aug. 28, 1928, Malad City, Idaho; s. William H. and Cecelia (Dredge) Rutter; B.A., Harvard, 1949; M.A., Univ. Utah, 1950; Ph.D., Univ. of Ill., 1952; m. Jacqueline Waddoups, Aug. 31, 1950 (div. Nov. 1969); chil.: William Henry II, Cynthia Susan; m. 2d, Virginia Alice Bourke, Oct. 3, 1971. Career: USPHS postdoctoral fellow Univ. of Wis., 1952-54; Nobel Inst., 1954-55; from asst. prof. to prof. biochemistry, dept. chemistry Univ. Ill., 1955-65; prof. biochemistry Univ. Wash., 1965-69; Hertzstein prof. biochemistry, chmn. dept. biochemistry and biophysics Univ. Calif. at San Francisco, 1969---; biochem. cons. Abbott Labs., 1958-75; USPHS Biochemistry and Nutrition Fellowship Panel, 1963-66; Cons. physiol. chemistry study sect. NIH, 1967-71; mem. basic sci. adv. exec. com. Nat. Cystic Fibrosis Research Found., 1969-74; chmn., 1972-74, pres's. adv. council, 1974-75; exec. com. div. biology and agr. NRC, 1969072; mem. developmental biology panel NSF, 1971-73; mem. biomed. adv. com. Los Alamos Sci. Lab., 1972-75; pres. Pacific Slope Biochem. Conf., 1972-73; mem. bd. sci. counselors Nat. Inst. Environ. Health Scis., 1976---; mem. adv. com. biology div. Oak Ridge Nat. Lab., 1976---; basic research adv. com. Nat. Found., 1976---; bd. dirs. Keystone Life Sci. Study Center, 1976---. Served with USNR, 1945. Guggenheim fellow, 1962-63. Mem. Am. Soc. Biol. Chemists (treas. 1970-76, mem. editorial bd. journ. 1970-75), Am. Soc. Cell Biology, Am. Chem. Soc. (Pfizer award enzyme chemistry 1967), Am. Soc. Developmental Biology (pres. 1975-76). Assoc. editor Journ. Exptl. Zoology, 1968-72; editor PAABS Revista, 1971-76; editor, J. Cell Biology; Editor, Archives of Biochemistry & Biophysics, 1978---; editorial bd. various journs. Res.: 80 Everson St., San Francisco, CA 94131.

RYAN, HAROLD JOY
Agricultural Commissioner (Retired)
b. Feb. 9, 1892, Lincoln, Nebr.; s. Thomas and Ella (Stoddard) Ryan; A.B., entomology, Pomona Coll., 1914; m. Inez Sheets, Dec. 19, 1914, Pomona; children: Nancy (Mrs. W.W. Zabriskie), b. Sept. 21, 1915; David Joy, b. June 11, 1922; John Allen, b. Sept. 19, 1928. Career: County Horticultural Inspector, Agri. Pest Control, Citrus Packing House work, San Diego & Los Angeles Counties, 1914-17; Sci. Asst. in Ext. Entomology Bureau of Ent., USDA, 1917-18; Agricultural Commr. (title until 1929, Horticultural Commr.), 1918-62. Mem./Chmn., Co. Agri. Commr's. Quarantine Com. 1918-62. Pres. State Assn. Calif. County Agri. Commrs. 1921; mem. three-man com. to redraft Horticultural Statutes for Calif. Agricultural Code of 1933; Cons. (on leave from County) USDA Bureau of Entomology and Plant Quarantine, Aug.-Oct. 1935; neutral mem., chmn., Calif. Orange Adminstrv. Com., 1943-50. Publs.: Editor, com. chmn., Plant Quarantines in California, Univ. of Calif., Dept. of Agri. Sciences, 1969; contbd. numerous articles in plant pest control and quarantine (with emphasis on orgn. of programs aimed at detection of newly introduced pests), Agricultural periodicals, profl. journs., meetings of Western States Plant Quarantine Bd.; Annual Reports of County Dept. Action. Awards: Los Angeles C. of C., "...35 years as advisory mem. Agri. Com.," 1955; Los Angeles County Bd. of Suprs., "...outstanding service as Agricultural

Commissioner," 1966; Calif. Citrus Quality Council, 4th Annual Albert J. Salter Memorial Award "...initiation and support of appropriate programs and regulations to protect crops from pests and to provide equitable mktg.," 1979. Emeritus mem. Entomological Soc. of Am. (former Am. Assn. Econ. Ent.), past pres. Pacific Slope Br.; co-founder, emeritus mem. So. Calif. Entomological Club; Advis. mem., L.A.C. of C., 1918-1970; co-founder, Theodore Payne Found. for Wild Flowers and Native Plants, bd. mem. & advis. com. 1962-68; bd. dir., San Jacinto Mountain Conservation League, 1969-71; mem.: Sierra Club, Andreas Canyon Club, Theodore Payne Found., Vice Chmn. Christian Com. for Israel, Kappa Delta Frat. Pomona Coll., Zamorano Club. Protestant. Hobbies: book collecting, fly tying. Rec.: fly fishing, natural life observation. Res.: 1108 Garfield Ave., So. Pasadena, CA 91030.

S

SABETTA, JOSEPH A.
Bank President
b. Dec. 12, 1940, Gustine, Calif.; s. Frank and Melia Sabetta; ed. San Benito Coll. 1958; chil.: Rebecca, b. Sept. 14, 1962; Michael, b. Aug. 14, 1963. Career: Bookkeeper-teller, United Calif. Bank, 1961062; ofcr. Bank of Amer. 1963-64; loan ofcr., asst. mgr., asst. v.p., mgr., v.p.-mgr. Bank Calif. 1964-72; founder-chmn. bd.-pres., First Pacific Bank, 1973---. USN 1958-74. Mem.: pres. C. of C.; dir. Kiwanis Club; dir. Lions Club; chmn.: United Crusade, Downtown Beautification, Heart Fund. Rec.: golf, tennis; Res.: 100 S. Doheny Dr., Los Angeles; Office: 630 N. La Cienega Blvd., Los Angeles, CA 90069.

SAELMAN, BENJAMIN
Aerospace Company Engineer
b. Nov. 15, 1917, Los Angeles; s. Samuel Henry and Ray (Kashtan) Saelman; B.A., honors in math., UCLA, 1939; postgrad. studies in Engring., aeronautics; m. Phyllis Markman, July 28, 1963, Las Vegas, Nev.; children: Raymond, David. Career: Engr., Lockheed Aircraft Corp., Burbank, 1940---, group engr. 1969. Registered Profl. Engr., State of Calif., Contbg. editpr, Design News, 1953-75, contbr. tech. papers numerous sci. journs. Mem.: Am. Inst. of Aero. & Astro., Pi Mu Epsilon. Jewish. Res.: 7762 Melita Ave., No. Hollywood, CA 91605; Office: 2555 N. Hollywood Way, Burbank, CA 91520.

SAHLEIN, DON
Corporate Executive
b. Mar. 7, 1924, Jackson, Mich.; s. David A. and Pauline (Byoir) Sahlein; nephew, Carl Byoir, noted public relations leader; B.S., UCLA, 1948; m. Leona Silver, Mar. 28, 1952, Las Vegas, Nev.; daughters: Gail Laurie, b. 1952; Stacey Anne, b. 1955. Career: Vice Pres., Leo-f & Rose Publicist, Hollywood, 1948-52; Sales Mgr., Los Angeles Wholesale Electric Co., 1952-56; Pres., Hollywood Camera Co., 1956-71; currently chmn., exec. com., Gordon Enterprises, Inc., No. Hollywood ---. Screen appearances: child actor under contract to Paramount Motion Picture Studios; featured player in weekly radio program of Associated Studios. USAAF 1942-45, decorated D.F.C., Air Medal with three clusters; USAAF Reserve, 1945-59. Mem.: Soc. Photog. Instrumentation Engrs.; Am. Soc. Photogrammetry; Def. Orientation Conf.; Les Amis d'Escoffier; Profl. Photogs. Assn.; Photogs. Assn. So. Calif.; Soc. of Photo-Technologists; World Affairs Council; Vikings; No. American Mensa; Founders Guild; Los Angeles Internat. Visitors Com.; L.A. Mayor's Bordeaux Sister Com.; Wine & Food Soc. of Hollywood, secty.-treas.; Les Gastronomes, chmn. Jewish. Hobbies: photog., water skiing, flying. Res: 3455 Caribeth Dr., Encino, CA; Office: 5362 Cahuenga Blvd., No. Hollywood, CA 91609.

SALK, JONAS EDWARD
Director, The Salk Institute
b. Oct. 28, 1914, NYC; s. Daniel B. and Dora (Press) Salk; B.S., Coll. City of N.Y. 1934; LL.D. 1955; M.D., NYU Coll. of Med. 1939; Sc.D. 1955; LL.D., Univ. of Pittsburgh, 1955; Ph.D., Hebrew Univ. 1953; LL.D., Roosevelt Univ. 1955; Sc.D.: Turin Univ. 1957, Univ. Leeds 1959, Franklin and Marshall Coll. 1960; m. Donna Lindsay, June 8, 1939 (div. 1968); m.

Francoise Gilot, June 29, 1970; children: Peter Lindsay, Darrell John, Jonathan Daniel. Career: Certified by American Board of Preventive Medicine and Public Health; fellow in chem. NYU College of Medicine 1935-36; Christian A. Herter fellow in exp. surg. 1937-38, fellow in bacteriology, 1939-40; intern, Mt. Sinai Hosp., NYC, 1940-42; Fellow in med. scis., Sch. of Pub. Health, Univ. of Mich. 1942-43; research fellow, 1943-44, research assoc. 1944-46, asst. prof. 1946-47; dir. of Virus Research Lab., Sch. of Med. Univ. of Pittsburgh, 1947-63; assoc. prof. 1947-49, commonwealth prof. 1955-63, prof. at large, 1963---; dir. The Salk Inst. for Biol. Stus. 1963-75; fellow, 1963---; founding director, 1975---; Cons. to Secty. of War in epidemic diseases, Comm. on Influenza, Army Epidemiological Bd. 1944-47; cons. to Secty. of Army in Epidemic Diseases; Comm. on Influenza, Armed Forces Epidemiological Bd. 1947-54; Expert Adv. Panel on Virus Diseases, World Health Orgn. 1951---. Developed vaccine, preventive of poliomyelitis, 1954. Adj. prof. of Health Sciences, Dept. of Psychiatry, Community Medicine, UCSD, 1970---. Awards: Criss Award, 1955; Lasker Award, 1956. Contrib. sci. articles to professional journs. Mem.: Assn. of Amer. Phys.; Amer. Soc. for Clin. Investigation; Amer. Epidemiological Soc.; Amer. Assn. of Immunologists; Amer. Coll. of Preventive Med.; AMA; Soc. for Exp. Biol. and Med.; Soc. of Amer. Bacteriologists; Fellow: AAAS, Amer. Pub. Health Assn.; Phi Beta Kappa, Alpha Omega Alpha, Sigma Xi, Delta Omega. Res.: 2444 Ellentown Rd., La Jolla, CA; Office: P.O. Box 1809, San Diego, CA 92112.

SALMON, VINCENT
Acoustical Consultant
b. Jan. 21, 1912, Kingston, Jamaica; s. Albert and Etheline (Baruch) Salmon; Ph.D., theoretical physics, Mass. Inst. of Tech., 1938; m. Madeline Giuffra (dec.), June 11, 1937, Millville, N.J.; children: Margaret S. (Goodman), b. 1939; Jean L., b. 1942; Career: With Jensen Mfg. Co., Chicago, 1939-49; Physicist in charge of research & develop., SRI Internat., Menlo Park, Calif., 1949---, Staff Scientist, Indsl. Health, Inc., Palo Alto, Dir. of Acoustical Services, 1971-76. Mem.: Acoustical Soc. of Am.; past pres. (recipient Biennial Award 1946), Acoustical Soc. of Am.; Inst. of Noise Control Engring., Nat. Council of Acoustical Consultants. Unitarian, past pres. Hobby: photog. Res.: 765 Hobart St., Menlo Park, CA 94025.

SALSBURY, GLENNA OSBORN
Lecturer — Educator — Author
b. Sept. 13, 1937, Peoria, Ill.; d. Glenn A. and Helen (Lake) Arnold; B.A., Northwestern Univ., 1959; M.A. Am. Lit., UCLA, 1961; M.A., theology, Fuller Theological Seminary, 1977; m. 2d. James W. Salsbury, Feb. 10, 1979, Laguna Beach; chil.: Monica Osborn, b. July 1, 1964; Melissa Osborn, b. Oct. 31, 1965; Michelle Osborn, b. May 15, 1968. Career: high sch. English tchr., Kern Co. Unified Sch. Dist., 1959-60; 1961-63; instr. Biblical Lit., Cal. State, Bakersfield, 1967-69; pres., Cameo Ministries, 1972---; pres., Cameo Tapes and Books, 1972---; dir. of training, Tarbell Realtors, 1977-79, v.p. of human resources, 1979---; columnist internat. for teenagers, A Visit with Glenna, 1963-68; hosted West Coast TV show, Let's Study the Bible, 2 yrs.; author: The Bible: Fact or Fiction?, Reflections, Have You Considered Job?. Can Humans be Christian?; lectr. on goal-planning, mgmt. skills, real estate sales training. Chmn., Christian Bus. and Profl. Women, 1963-67; advisor, leader, Bible Study Fellowship (internat. study program), 1964-72; mem. Alpha Phi, pres. Beta chpt., 1958-59. Hobbies: reading, writing. Home: 24381 Calle Pequeno, El Toro, CA 92630; Office: 18062 Irvine Blvd., Tustin, CA 92680.

SAMMONS, FRANCIS EDWARD, JR.
Corporate Executive
b. Nov. 16, 1913, Evanston, Ill.; s. Francis and Rose (Stokes) Sammons; student, Univ. of Ill.; m. Catharine Strong, July 17, 1943, Tacoma, Wash.; sons: Thomas Edward, b. 1947; Charles Patrick, b. 1949; Timothy Devitt, b. 1952. Career: v.p., circulation dir. Street & Smith Publs., Inc., NYC 1947-52; dir. S-M News Co., NYC, 1949-52; v.p. sales and advt. Bankers Life & Casualty Co., Chicago, 1952-56; v.p. J. Walter Thompson Co., NYC 1956-60; v.p., dir. publicity and pub. relations Ted Bates & Co., Inc., NYC 1960-61; partner, Fordyce & Dole Assocs., Inc., NYC 1961-64; v.p. mktg. Brown Kauffmann, Inc., Palo Alto, 1965-74; dir. communications Potlatch Corp., San Francisco, 1974---; Dir.: Mental Research Inst., Menlo

Park, 1968-74; mem. Advt. Club, San Francisco (dir.), U.S. Golf Assn. Club; Palo Alto Hills Golf and Country. Res.: 325 Claremont Way, Menlo Park, CA 94025; Office: 2 Embarcadero Center, San Francisco, CA 94111.

SAMPLINER, ROBERT BRUCE
Psychiatrist
b. June 17, 1913, South Pasadena; s. Jerome Mortimer and Charlotte (Jaskulex) Sampliner; B.A., 1934; M.D., 1937; M.P.H., 1965; Career: Pvt. practice Psychiatry, 1945---; formerly Clin. Dir., Edgemont Hosp., L.A.; Chief Psychiatric Clinic County Hosp., UCI Unit; Regional Chief, Co. Dept. of Mental Health; Chief Cons. Alcohol, Co. Dept. of Mental Health. Maj., AUS M.C., 1940-45. Bd. dir., Opera Guild of So. Calif.; mem. UCLA Design for Sharing. Hobbies: garden, music. Rec.: concerts, operas, piano. Res.: 646 S. Hudson Ave., Pasadena, CA 91106; 10 Methuen Park, London, England; Office: 8383 Wilshire Blvd., Beverly Hills, CA 90211.

SAMSON, PAUL CURKEET
Physician
b. June 12, 1905, Emporia, Kan.; s. Paul Bryant and Rena Mae (Curkeet) Samson; B.S., M.D., Univ. of Mich. 1928; M.S. (surg.), 1935; m. Marion Doris Smith, Piedmont, Calif., July 13, 1940; stepchil.: Robert Bruce Atterbury and Arthur Montell Atterbury. Career: Intern, Presbyterian Hosp. 1928-30; James Herrick Fellow in Med.-asst. dean, Rush Med. Coll. 1930-32; asst. res. (pathology), Univ. Hosp., Univ. of Mich. 1932-33, asst. res. (surg.) 1933-34, instr. (surg.) and Mary E. Bissell Fellow (thoracic surg.), 1934-36; instr. (surg.) to assoc. clin. prof. surg., Stanford Univ. Sch. of Med. 1937---; chief of surg., Peralta Hosp., Oakland, Calif. 1947-50; chief of surg., Samuel Merritt Hosp., Oakland, 1950-56; chief of staff 1956---; chief of thoracic and cardiac surg.: Chils' Hosp., East Bay, Oakland; Highland Alameda Co. Hosp., Oakland, 1946-48; cons. 1958---; cons. in thoracic and cardiac surg.: San Joaquin Gen. Hosp., French Camp, Calif.; Travis Air Force Base Hosp., Travis, Calif.; Letterman Army Hosp., S.F.; Cowell Mem. Hosp., Univ. of Calif., Berkeley, Secty. Tree Slough Land Co. 1950-56. Author: approx. 90 sci. publs. in various med. journs. of U.S. 1931---. Active duty, AUS, 1941-46; disch. Lt. Col., Med. Corps, AUS (30 mos. overseas), WW II. Awards: European-African-Middle East Serv. Medal; Amer. Theatre Serv. Medal; Amer. Def. Service Medal; Bronze Serv. Arrowhead for D-Day Landings in So. France, Aug. 1944; Leg. of Merit, Mediterranean Theatre, May, 1945; battle stars for following campaigns: Tunisia, Sicily, Naples-Foggia, So. France, Rhineland, Central Europe, Rome-Arno. Mem.: Phi Kappa Sigma, Alpha Omega Alpha, 1928---; chmn. Tyee Club of Brit. Columbia, 1950-54; secty. Amer. Assn. for Thoracic Surg. 1950-56; chmn. surg. sect., Calif. Med. Assn. 1952-53; pres. Calif. TB and Health Assn. 1952-53; pres. Amer. Trudeau Soc. 1956-57; v.-chmn. bd. govs., A.C.S., 1958-60; ch.m. 1960---. Res.: 15 La Salle Ave., Piedmont, CA; Office: 3115 Webster St., Oakland, CA 94609.

SANCHEZ, SALVATORE, JR.
City Official
b. Dec. 22, 1926, Los Angeles; s. Salvador and Maria Rosario (Aguilar) Sanchez; great-grandson of Delfin Sanchez, ind. Cuba, Mex.; feat. Ency. Espasa of Spain (1850-60); ed. A.S., Ventura Coll. 1950, A.A. 1955; Long Beach State Coll. 1951-52; Mex. City Coll., and Univ. Mex., D.F. 1953-54; B.A., Univ. Calif., Santa Barbara, 1957; postgrad. UCLA 1957-58; credential courses, 1958-65, 1970-71; m. Margaret Orrantia, Tijuana, Baja Calif., Mex., Feb. 13, 1949; chil.: Mary H. Friedrich, b. Mar. 29, 1950; Margaret Ann b. July 12, 1951; Leon E., b. Aug. 4, 1952; Mark A., b. Feb. 19, 1959. Career: Mgmt. tr. Mobil Oil Co., L.A. 1957-58; hist. instr. Haydock Jr. H.S. 1958-63; instr. Camarillo H.S. 1963-64; N.Y. Life Ins. Co. Underwriter, and bldg. constr. 1964-66; instr. Fremont Jr. H.S., Ocean View School, 1966-68; instr.-counselor, Ventura Coll. 1968---. Elected, Oxnard City Councilman, 1966---; Mayor, City of Oxnard, 1970---. Apptd. (by Gov. Brown) Fair Employment Practices Comm. 1962-65; chmn. Ventura Co. Edn. Council, 1963-65; co-chmn. Oxnard Community Rels. Comm. 1963-66; Human Rels. Comm., 1964-66; (charter) Oxnard Citizens' Adv. Com. 1965-66; apptd. (by Gov. Reagan) State Comprehensive Health Planning Comm. 1966-69. Lectr. on Amer.-Mex. Problems, UCLA, Univ. Calif., Santa Barbara, 1969-71. Yeoman, USN 1946-47; USNR 1949-57. Mem.: Latin Amer. Vets. Club; NEA;

Calif. Teachers Assn.; Life Underwriters Assn.; Founder-chmn. Los Amigos Scholarship Club and United Latin Amers., Inc. 1963-70; founder, Los Amigos Club of Oxnard; founder, Guadalupe Ch. Bldg. Fund. Com.; adv. bd. dirs.: Oxnard Boys' Club, Ventura Co. Chpt. Big Brothers of Amer.; USO; Knights of Columbus; pres. Kappa Sigma, 1951-57; Oxnard Elks Lodge; Oxnard Noontime Lions Club, 1969-70; Catholic. Hobby: rock collections, mineral ores. Rec.: reading, travel. Res.: 233 W. Fir Ave., Oxnard, CA; Office: Ventura College, and City Hall, 305 W. Third St., Oxnard, CA 93030.

SANDBERG, NEIL C.
Educator
b. Apr. 25, 1925, NYC; s. Jack and Lena Sandberg; B.A., Columbia Univ., 1949; M.P.L., USC, 1971, Ph.D., 1972; m. Mary Keiser, 1954; NYC; son, Curtis, b. 1956. Career: Regional Director, American Jewish Com. 1950-78; Prof. Sociology, Loyola-Marymount Univ., 1965---; prof. Contemporary Jewish Life, Univ. of Judaism, 1977, 78; prof. Jewish Sociology, Hebrew Union Coll., 1976-78. Author: "New Towns: Why and For Whom," Praeger 1973; "Ethnic Identity and Assimilation: The Polish-American Community," Praeger 1974; "Stairwell 7: Family Life In The Welfare State," Sage 1978. Recipient Award for Literature, Kosciusko Found. 1974. USN, 1943-45. Jewish. Res.: 2001 Sunset Plaza Dr., Los Angeles, CA 90069; Office: 6505 Wilshire Blvd., Los Angeles, CA 90048.

SANDERS, JOSEPH STANLEY
Attorney at Law
b. Aug. 9, 1942, Los Angeles; s. Hays and Eva (Cook) Sanders; B.A., Whittier Coll. 1963; M.A., Magdalen Coll., Oxford Univ., 1965; LL.B., Yale Law Sch., 1968; m. Phyllis Moore, Sept. 2, 1966, Los Angeles; children: Edward Moore, b. 1973; Justin Hays, b. 1976. Career: Staff Atty., Western Center on Law & Poverty, Los Angeles, 1968-69; Exec. Dir., Lawyer's Com. for Civil Rights Under Law, L.A. 1969-70; assoc. law firm of Wyman, Bautzer, Finell, Rothman & Kuchel, Beverly Hills, 1969-71; partner, law firm Rosenfeld, Lederer, Jacobs & Sanders, Beverly Hills, 1971-72; partner, law firm Sanders & Tisdale, L.A. 1972-77; partner, law firm, Sanders & Booker, Beverly Hills, 1978---. Publs.: "Rhodes Scholar Looks at South Africa," 1970; "I'll Never Escape the Ghetto," 1967, Ebony Mag. TV: "The Advocate," Boston, Mass., 1978. Awarded Rhodes Scholarship; 10 Outstanding Young Men of Am. Award, 1971; Distinguished Alumni Award, L.A. City Schs. Bicentennial, 1976; First Team NAIA All-American Football, 1961; Small Coll. NAIA Discus Champion, 1963; All-Blue Discus Champion, 1964-65. Co-founder Watts Summer Festival, 1966; trustee, Whittier Coll. 1974---, c-chmn. Alumni Fund, 1970-71; dir. Black Arts Council; coordinator Calif. Conf. of Black Attys. 1969; trustee, Center for Law in the Pub. Interest, L.A., 1973---; bd. dir. Econ. Resources Corp., 1974---; mem. Mayor's Citizens Com. on Rapid Transit, 1975; bd. dir. Arthritis Found., So. Calif. Chpt. 1976---; mem. Calif. Postsecondary Edn. Commn. 1976---; mem. Mayor's Com. on Cultural Affairs, 1975---; bd. dir. ARC, L.A. 1976---; Mem.: Langston Law Club, L.A. Co. Bar Assn., Am. Bar Assn., 1969---; L.A. World Affairs Council, 1971---; Com. on Foreign Affairs, L.A., 1972---. Democrat; co-chmn. Rules Com., Calif., 1976---. Hobby: photog. Rec.: tennis, marathon jogger. Office: 8484 Wilshire Blvd., Suite 900, Beverly Hills, CA 90211.

SANDS, LEONARD SCHNEIER
Attorney at Law
b. Nov. 20, 1932, Montreal, Quebec, Canada.; s. Nathan Schneier and Zina Sands; A.A., 1953; LL.B., J.D., Loyola Univ. 1957; m. Ada Picaizen, San Diego, June 9, 1951; sons: Michael D., b. Feb. 4, 1960; Howard G., b. Feb. 5, 1962; Andrew I., b. Nov. 26, 1965. Career: Trial counsel, Pollock & Pollock law firm, 1958-59; pvt. practice, 1959-63; founder-sr. partner, Sands, Schaffer, Pachter, Kaplan & Gold, Attys. at Law, 1963-73; Sands, Pachter, Kaplan & Gold law firm, 1973---. Arbitrator, Amer. Arbitration Assn., Judge Pro Tem., Beverly Hills Municipal Ct.; guest lecturer, USC Dept. of Sociology, USAR, Serv. 1957-58. Mem.: Amer., L.A., Beverly Hills Bar Assns.; Trial Lawyers Assn.; Amer. Judicature Assn.; Amer. Arbitration Assn.; Phi Delta Phi, 1953-55; Loyola Univ. Law Alumni Assn. 1956---; B'nai B'rith, Pac. Palisades, 1958---; Anti-Defamation League, 1958---; BPOE, Elks 99, 1958-72. Hobbies: reading, ski, tennis.

Res.: 19324 Pacific Coast Hwy., Malibu, CA 90265; Office: 6420 Wilshire Blvd., Los Angeles, CA 90048.

SANDY, DONALD, JR.
Architect
b. Oct. 20, 1933, Racine, Wis.; s. Donald and Violet Sandy; B.Arch. Univ. of Ill., 1957; m. Carol Gene Cordes, Jan. 26, 1963, Palo Alto; daughters: Heather Leigh, b. 1963; Jill Margaret, b. 1967. Career: Architect, John Flad & Assocs., Madison, Wis., 1957-58; Schram, White & Wong Architects, San Francisco, 1958-60; Donald Sandy, Jr. & Associates, Architects, S.F., 1960---. Sgt., AUS, ---1963. Awards incl.: Award of Excellence, Stockton City Planning Commn. 1974; Award of Excellence for Design, Archtl. Record, 1974; Gold Nugget Award of Merit, Pacific Coast Bldrs. Conf., 1975; two in 1977; Sensible Growth Grand Award and three Merit Awards, Nat. Assn. of Better Bldrs. and Better Homes and Gardens Mag., all in 1976; First, Plywood Design Award, 1977. Award winning projects: University Park, Stockton; Oakbrook; Governor:s Square East; Selby Ranch; Tree Swallow Ct., Stockton; Fong Apts., Sacramento. Mem.: SCARAB, archtl. frat., pres. 1956; Big Brothers of S.F., bd. dir. 1968---; founding mem. Marin Tennis Club; San Francisco Yacht Club; AIA, 1967---; College of Fellows 1978. Presbyterian. Hobby: classic automobiles. Res.: 16 David Ct., San Rafael, CA; Office: 1349 Larking St., San Francisco, CA 94109.

SANKEY, IRIS
State Official
b. Oct. 13, 1928, Oak Park, Ill.; dau. Sam and Jennie (Estes) Lawrence; B.A., San Diego State Coll., 1965; m. Harold G. Sankey, Apr. 20, 1947, Los Angeles; Children: Elyse (Kemper); Jerry. Career: Commissioner, Escondido Parks and Recreation Commn., 1965-73; mem. San Diego County Energy Element of San Diego Gen. Plan, 1973-76; mem. Palomar College Devel. Found., 1975---; mem. California Health Manpower Commn., 1976; mem. State Bd. of Equalization, 1976-79. Res.: 567 S. Sierra, No. 89, Solana Beach, CA 92075; Office: 604 Cedar, San Diego, CA 92101.

SARKAR, ANIL KUMAR
Professor of Philosophy
b. Aug. 1, 1912, Ranchi, India; s. Surendra and Sarojini Sarkar; M.A., 1935; Ph.D., 1946, D.Litt., 1960, Patna Univ., India; m. Aruna Mitra, Nov. 21, 1941, Calcutta, India; dau. Shreela (Goel). Career: Prof. of Philosophy, Rajendra Coll., Chapra, India, 1940-44; Sr. Lectr., Univ. Ceylon, 1944-64; vis. prof. of Philosophy, Univ. of N.M., 1964-65; Prof. of Philosophy, Cal State Univ., Hayward 1965---; Research Prof. and Dir., South Asian Studies, Calif. Inst. of Asian Studies, S.F., 1965---; Research fellow, Indian Inst. of Philosophy, Amalner (India) Research Scholar, Patna Univ.; postdoctoral scholar, London Univ., 1951-52, 1958-59. Mem. Indian Philos. Congress, secty. 1954, sect. Pres., 1956, gen. pres. Plenary Session (vi)1976; Rep. Indian Sci. Congress in Ceylon, 1956-57; mem. Am. Philosophical Assn. 1964---; panelist, Wooster Conf. of Philos. & Rel., 1965; Panelist, Meeting of Minds, Kirtland 2d. annual sci. symposium, Albuquerque, N.M. 1965; panelist, conf. on Vedanta and Whitehead, Sch. of Theol., Claremont, 1978. Author: An Outline of Whitehead's Philosophy, 1940; Changing Phases of Buddhist Thought; Whitehead's Four Principles from West-East Perspectives, 1974. Address: Cal. State University, Hayward, CA.

SARPKAYA, TURGUT
Engineer — Educator
b. May 7, 1928, Istanbul, Turkey; s. Hasip and Huriye Sarpkaya; B.S. and M.S., Mech. Engr., Istanbul Tech. Univ., 1950, 1951; Ph.D., Univ. of Iowa, 1954; m. Gunel Ataissik, 1963, Lincoln, Nebr. Career: Research Engr., Mass. Inst. Tech., 1954-55; Lt. U.S. Army Corps of Engrs., 1955-57; Asst./Assoc. Thomas L. Fawick Distinguished Prof, Univ. of Nebr., 1957-66; Prof., Univ. of Manchester, England, 1966-67; Prof. & Chmn., Naval Postgrad. Sch., Monterey, 1967-71; Distinguished Prof. of Mech. Engring., 1972---; Prof., Univ. of Gottingen, Germany, 1971-72. Publs.: one book, editor two books, approx. 100 tech. papers in mech. engring. and fluid mechanics. Awards: Moody Award, ASME, 1967; Collingwood Prize, ASCE, 1957; Sigma Xi Research Award, 1972. Gen. Chmn., Heat Transfer and Fluid Mechanics Inst., 1971-72; Chmn. Fluids Engring. Div., ASME, 1977. Fellow, ASME; Fellow Royal Instn. of Naval Architects; mem. AIAA, ASEE. Hobbies: chess, swimming. Res.: 25330 Vista

del Pinos, Carmel, CA 93923; Office: Naval Postgraduate School, Monterey, CA 93940.

SATO, IRVING SHIGEO
Educator
b. Sept. 4, 1933, Honolulu, Hawaii; s. Jusaku and Matsuyo Sato; b. Edn. with honors, 1955; M.Sc. in edn., 1962; m. Helen Nakayama, Aug. 18, 1956, Honolulu. Career: Classroom Tchr. Grades 10-12, 1957-66; Tchr. Jr. Coll. Level, 1958-61, Grades 4-6 (gifted), 1963-64; Coordinator, Humanities Team Tching. (research proj. on gifted, gr. 10-12), 1964-66; Instr., Edn. of the Gifted at the Grad. Level, Univ. of Denver, Univ. Colo., 1966-68; Cons., Gifted and Creative Student Programs, Colo. Dept. of Edn., 1966-68; Assoc. Dir. Calif., Curriculum Guides for the Gifted, 1968-70; Dir. Fed. Project on Gifted Child Edn., 1969-70; Adviser to HEW on Gifted Children's Ednl. Assistance Act, 1970-71; Speaker: confs. and workshops for Educators and Parents nationwide, 1966---; Cons. Edn. of Mentally Gifted, Calif. State Dept. of Edn. 1968-72; Assoc. Field Editor, Teaching Exceptional Children, 1973-76; Instr. (part-time) USC, 1970---; Adj. Faculty mem. College of New Rochelle, N.Y. 1978; Cons., Govt. of Iran on Iran's Gifted Project, 1976---; Dir., Nat./State Leadership Tng. Inst. on the Gifted and the Talented, 1972---. 1st Lt., AUS, 1955-57. Awards: Phi Kappa Phi, Phi Delta Kappa; Citation of Merit, Nat. Assn. for Gifted Chil. 1973; Educator of the Year, Calif. Assn. for the Gifted 1976; Recognition, US Office of Edn. 1974. Hobbies: theatre. Res.: 1744 Via Del Rey, So. Pasadena, CA; Office: 316 W. 2nd St., Suite PH-C, Los Angeles, CA.

SAUSMAN, KAREN
Naturalist
b. Nov. 26, 1945, Chicago, Ill.; d. William and Ann (Lofaso) Sausman; B.S., Loyola Univ., Chicago, 1966; grad. studies in wildlife biology, Univ. Redlands, 1967; Calif. Life Tchging. Credential, 1967; m. George Service, Sept. 1, 1975, Royal Carrizo, Calif. Career: animal keeper, Lincoln Park Zoo, 1964-66; Naturalist, led month long field trip for Jr. H.S. students, Western U.S., 1968 summer; tchr., Palm Springs Unified Sch. Dist. Jr. H.S., 1968-70; film crew mem. with wildlife photogs. Jen and Des Bartlett for TV film, "The World of the Beaver," 1969; Seasonal Pk. Ranger, Joshua Tree Nat. Monument, 1969-70; Director-Naturalist, Living Desert Reserve, Palm Desert, 1970---; also freelance wildlife illustrator; instr. Coll. of the Desert, 1975---; part-time instr. dog. tng. classes, 1978---. Artist, Deep Canyon and Desert Wilderness for Science, Univ. of Calif.; illustr. articles for several mags.; Editor: Zoological Parks Fundamentals, 1977---. Dir., Am. Assn. Zoological Parks and Aquariums, 1978-80; past bd. mem., Desert Protective Council; mem. Southern Calif. Chpt. Western Interpretive Assn.; Am. Assn. Museums; Council of Directors of Arboreta and Botanical Gardens; Calif. Native Plant Soc.; Nat. Audubon Soc.; Pres. Coachella Valley Audubon, 1978-79; Kennel Club of Palm Springs; Calif. Sierra Doberman Pinscher Club. Address: P.O.B. 1775, Palm Desert, CA 92260.

SAVAGE, ROENA MUCKELROY
Musician — Educator
b. Oct. 30, 1908, Henderson, Texas; d. Winwright W. and Mary (Holliman) Muckelroy; B.Music, USC, 1927; M.A., Univ. Missouri, 1952; m. W. Sherman Savage, Aug. 25, 1930, Kansas City, Mo.; daughters: Eloise (Logan), b. 1936; Inez (Allen), b. 1938. Career: Faculty mem. Lincoln Univ., 1927-31, 1948-50, 1952-53; chmn. Voice Dept. & Humanities, Jarvis Christian Coll., 1960-64; Chmn. music dept., Thomas Jefferson H.S., Los Angeles Unified Sch. Dist., 1966-70, ret. 1970---; faculty mem. Tenn. A&M Coll., summer 1952, Morgan State (Md.) Univ., 1959-60; tchr., Adult Edn. San Bernardino & Redlands High Schs., 1938-40. Concert Artist: Natl. Tours, L.A. Debut 1944, NYC 1948; Radio Series: Romance and History in Songs of the World: KWOS (Mo.), KFXM, San Bernardino, Calif. Author and exec. dir. "Hearthstones USA," endorsed Bincentennial Prodn. 1976-77. Winner: Calif. Eisteddfod Contests "Grand Finals" 1927; Recipient: Nat. Award of Nat. Assn. Negro Musicians, Inc. for contbn. to music as singer and tchr., 1974; Who's Who in Music, 1951. Mem.: Delta Sigma Theta, founder USC chpt.; Nat. Assn. Tchrs. of Singing, Inc.; Music Tchrs. Assn. of Calif.; Nat. Assn. Negro Musicians, Inc.; Eastern Star; AAUW. Sanctuary Choir, Presbyterian. Democrat. Hobbies: writing, singing groups. Res.: 5063 Onaknoll Ave., Los Angeles, CA 90043.

SAVAGE, W. SHERMAN
Historian
b. Mar. 7, 1890, Wattsville, Accomac County, Va.; s. Adam and Annie Melissa (Godwin) Savage; A.B., Howard Univ., 1921; grad. study, Univ. Kansas, 1922-23; A.M., Univ. Oregon, 1925; Ph.D., Ohio State Univ., 1934; m. Roena Muckelroy, Aug. 25, 1930, Kansas City, Mo.; daughters: Eloise (Logan), b. 1936; Inez (Allen), b. 1939. Career: Prof. of History, Lincoln Univ., 1921-60; Jarvis Christian Coll., 1960-66; Los Angeles State Coll., 1966-70, now Professor Emeritus ---. Cpl., 808th Pioneer Infan. WW I. Contbr. profl. journs. Mem.: Social Sci. Tchrs. in Negro Colls., past pres.; exec. com. Assn. Study Afro-Am. Life & Hist.; Phi Beta Sigma frat., nat. pres.; Am. and Western Historical Socs.; Orgn. Am. Historians. Hobby: athletics. Res.: 5063 Onaknoll Ave., Los Angeles, CA 90043.

SAVITSKY, HELEN
Geneticist
b. Feb. 17, 1901, Poltava, Russia (U.S. cit. 1954); d. Ivan and Anastasia (Degtjareva) Harechko; ed. M. Sch., Highest Qualification Com., Moscow, 1938; Ph.D., Univ. of Leningrad, Russia, 1940; m. Viacheslav F. Savitsky, Harkov, Russia, Jan. 6, 1926. Career: Chief lab. cytology, White Ch. Breeding Sta., Russia, 1927-30; prof. cytogenetics, chief lab. cytology, All Union Research Inst. Sugar Ind., Kiev, Russia, 1930-41; prof. cytogenetics, chief lab. cytology (lab. of oil crops), Ukrainian Plant Breeding Inst., Kiev, Russia, 1941-42; prof. Univ. of Posen, Poland, 1943-45; cytogeneticist, Univ. of Halle, Ger. 1945; sci. collab., Sugar Beet Breeding Firm Schreiber, Nordhausen, Ger. 1945-46; prof. Ukrainian Tech. Inst., Regensburg, Ger. 1946-47; est. U.S. res. 1947---; cytogeneticist, Beet Sugar Development Found., collab, USDA, Salt Lake City, Ut. 1947-60; geneticist, U.S. Dept. of Agr., Salinas, Calif. 1960---. Research on monogerm sugar beets, polyploidy, interspecific bybridization in genus Beta L. Awards: Meritorious Serv. Award. Amer. Soc. Sugar Beet Technologists, 1960; Superior Serv. Award, U.S. Dept. Agr. 1968; Award of Merit, Sugar Industry of Netherlands, 1969. Mem.: American Society of Genetics, American Society Botany, Amer. Soc. Sugar Beet Technologists, Genetics Soc. of Can. Greek Orthodox Ch. Res.: 1003 Baywood Place, Salinas, Calif. 93901; Office: U.S. Dept. Agriculture, P.O.B. 5098, Salinas, CA 93901.

SAWYER, ERNEST WALKER, JR.
Corporate Executive
b. Harrow-on-the-Hill, Hove, Eng.; s. The Hon. Ernest Walker; (exec. asst. Secty. of Interior, Hoover Cabinet, spec. assignment with Winston Churchill and Lord Beaverbrook, Admiralty and Communications, WW I; sent first wireless message across Atlantic) and Florence Victoria (Davies) Sawyer; grandnephew of Albert Finlayson, former Brit. Ambassador to Argentina; ed. Colo. Sch. of Mines, Harvard Univ., UCLA; grad. Univ. of Calif., Berkeley, 1948; m. Miriam Camille Patty (desc. of Capt. James Cook, aide-de-camp to Gen. Robert E. Lee, Gen. Sir Isaac Brock of Guernsey and Ralph Waldo Emerson, Amer. poet), Beverly Hills, Calif., 1949; chil.: Camille Agnes, Christian Emerson. Career: Pres., Sawyer Petroleum Co. 1955-69; bd. dirs. Sawyer Exploration Co.; pres. Ore. Trail Land and Cattle Co.; dir. Sawyer Found.; pres. Natural Resources Co., Inc. (NARCO); Sawyer-Smith Cattle Co.; Frawley Corp., 1978---; bd. dirs. Glendale Community Hosp. of Calif., Capt., U.S. Army Corps of Engrs. 1942-46, WW II. Awards: Distinguished Unit Pres. Cit. (unit comdr.); Meritorious Serv. Unit Plaque; Battle Hon. New Guinea Campaign, Battle Hon. Bismark Archipelago Campaign, Battle Hon. Borneo Campaign; Australian Govt. 1936-45 Campaign Award, Australian Pac. Star. Mem.: Amer. Nuclear Soc.; Amer. Assn. of Petrol. Geol.; Amer. Inst. of Min., Metal., and Petrol. Engrs.; Amer. Inst. Prof. Geols.; Geol. Soc. of P.I.; Calif. Cattleman's Assn. Clubs: Bel Air Bay Club. Bd. trustees, United Found. Ch. Relig. Sci., L.A. Res.: 4239 Oakwood Ave., La Canada, Flintridge, CA 91011; Office: 1901 Ave. of the Stars, Suite 1500, L.A., CA 90067.

SAXON, DAVID STEPHEN
Educator — Physicist
b. Feb. 8, 1920, St. Paul; s. Ivan and Rebecca (Moss) S.; B.S., Mass. Inst. Tech., 1941; Ph.D., 1944; L.H.D., Hebrew Union Coll., L.H.D. Univ. Judaism (hon.), 1977; LL.D., Univ. of S.F. 1978; m. Shirley Goodman, Jan. 6, 1940; children: Margaret Elizabeth, Barbara Susan, Linda Caroline, Catherine Louise, Victoria Jean, Charlotte Mala. Career: Research

physicist, Radiation Lab., Mass. Inst. Tech., 1943-46; Phillips Labs., 1946-47; mem. faculty UCLA, 1947-75; prof. physics, 1958-75, chmn. dept., 1963-66, dean phys. scis., 1966-69, exec. vice chancellor, 1968---, univ. provost, 1974-75; pres. Univ. Calif. at Berkeley, 1975---; vis. scientist Centre d'Etudes Nucleaires, Saclay, France, 1968-69; vis. prof. faculty scis. Univ. Paris, Orsay, France, 1961-62; cons. to research orgns., 1948---; spl. research theoretical physics, nuclear physics, quantum mechanics, electromagnetic theory, scattering theory. Guggenheim fellow, 1956-57, 61-62; Fulbright grantee, 1961-62; Mem.: Am. Phys. Soc., Am. Assn. Physics Tchrs.; Am. Inst. Physics; AAUP; Sigma Xi; Sigma Pi Sigma. Author: Elementary Quantum Mechanics, 1968; The Nuclear Independent Particle Model, 1968; Discontinuities In Wave Guides, 1968; Physics for the Liberal Arts Student, 1971. Res.: 70 Rincon Rd., Kensington, CA 94707; Office: President's Office, 714 University Hall, Univ. Calif., Berkeley, CA 94720.

SCANDLING, WILLIAM F.
Company President
b. June 17, 1922, Rochester, N.Y.; s. Frederic D. and Helen (Moran) Scandling; A.B., Hobart Coll., N.Y. 1949, (hon.) LL.D., 1967; m. Margaret Warner, Rochester, N.Y., Apr. 19, 1949; son: Michael W., b. Jan. 18, 1951. Career: Dir., Empire Broadcasting Corp.; co-founder, ofcr.-dir. Saga Corp., 1948---, now pres.; chmn. bd. trustees, Hobart and William Smith Colleges, Geneva, N.Y. Serv. U.S. Army Air Corps, PTO, 1943-45, Mem.: Kappa Alpha Soc. 1946---; Genesee Valley Club, Rochester, N.Y. 1961---. Hobbies: reading, travel, swim. Res.: 38 Barry Lane, Atherton, CA; Office: One Saga Lane, Menlo Park, CA 94025.

SCHABER, GORDON DUANE
Law School Dean
b. Nov. 22, 1927, Ashley, N.Dak.; s. Ronald and Esther (Schatz) Schaber; B.A., Sacramento State Coll. 1949; LL.B., Univ. of Calif. 1952; LL.D., McGeorge Sch. of Law, 1961. Career: Atty., pvt. practice, 1953-65; prof.-asst. dean, McGeorge Sch. of Law, Univ. of Pac. 1953-56, dean, 1957---; judge, Sacramento Co. Superior Ct. 1965-70. Chmn. Sacramento City Planning Comm. 1959-65; c.chmn., State of Calif., Educational Facilities Authority, 1978---. Awards: Outstanding Young Man of Yr., Sacramento C. of C. 1963. Mem.: Amer. and Calif. State Bar Assns., Amer. Judicature Soc., Sacramento C. of C.; Order of Coif, 1954; Univ. Club of Sacramento, 1960---; Sutter Club of Sacramento; chmn. Sacramento Co. Dem. Central Com. 1960, 62, 64; Calif. State Bd. of Control, 1962-65. Lutheran. Res.: 937 Piedmont Dr., Sacramento, CA; Office: 3282 Fifth Ave., Sacramento, CA.

SCHAEFER, GERSCHEN LION
Physician — University Educator
b. Apr. 24, 1924, Chicago, Ill; s. Henry M. and Brunetta Schaefer; B.S., Univ. Ill. 1946; B.M., Chicago Med. Sch. 1950, M.D. 1951; m. Jacqueline Talmy, Chicago, Ill., June 21, 1946; chil.: Corri Ann, b. Sept. 25, 1953; Gregg Alan, b. Sept. 19, 1954; Stacy Beth, b. Dec. 5, 1956. Career: Intern, Mt. Sinai Hosp., Chicago, 1950-51, res. internal med. 1951-54; asst. med. dir. Winfield Hosp. (TB), Ill. 1954-56; secty.-asst. dir. Chest Dept., Mt. Sinai Hosp., Chicago, 1954-56; act. med. dir. TB unit. San Bernardino Co. Hosp., Calif. 1956-57; secty-dept. chmn. Riverside Community Hospital, 1956-68, chmn. Dept. Med. 1967-69; Riverside Co. Gen. Hosp. 1957---, chief. Dept. Med. 1960-61, Faculty: clin. asst. Dept. Med., Chicago Med. Sch. 1954-56; postgrad. course, Amer. Coll. Chest Phys., L.A. 1959; panel moderator-speaker: Univ. Calif. Ext., Riverside; Calif. State Coll., Fullerton; Cal Poly Coll.; Loma Linda Univ. Med. Sch. Contrib. many articles, papers to medical journs., contbs., convs., incl. Internat. Cong. on Diseases of Chest, Copenhagen, Denmark, Aug. 1966. U.S. Navy, 1942-46; WW II. Mem.: Riverside Co., Calif. Med. Assns.; Fellow, Amer. Coll. of Chest Phys., Calif. Gov's. Com.; bd. dirs. Riverside Co. Tuberculosis and Health Assn. 1957; pres. 1965-66, coms.; bd. dirs. Amer. Cancer Soc., Riverside; adv. com. Riverside Co. Bd. Supvs.; bd. dirs. Riverside. Co. Health Council; adv. com.: Calif. Air Resources Bd., Calif. Dept. of Health, Atty. Gen's. Environmental Task Force, 1972-73; chmn. numerous other med. coms., Calif.; Amer., Calif., Inland Socs. Internal Med.; Amer. Thoracic Soc.; N.Y. Acad. Scis.; assoc. Fellow, Amer. Coll. Cardiology; Fellow, Royal Soc. of Health; AAAS. Jewish. Hobbies: photog.,

tennis. Res.: 5276 Tower Rd., Riverside, CA 92506; Office: 4049 Brockton Ave., Riverside, CA 92501.

SCHAEFFER, CARL GEORGE LEWIS
Public Relations and Advertising Executive
b. Sept. 2, Cleveland, Ohio; s. George S. and Margaret (Fraybarg) Schaefer; A.B., UCLA, 1931; m. Virginia Clark, Sept. 2, 1938; dau., Susan Diane (Mrs. Cedric Francis). Career: Free-lance mag. writer, 1931; reporter Hollywood (Calif.) Citizen-News, 1931-35; with Warner Bros.-Seven Arts, Burbank, Calif., 1935-71, dir., internat. relations, 1962-71; owner Carl Schaefer Enterprises, Hollywood, 1971---. Mem. Internat. com. Acad. Motion Picture Arts and Scis., 1940---; chmn. internat. Hollywood Museum, 1964. Vice chmn. Hollywood-Wilshire council BSA, 1957-58; mem. Mayor L.A. Council Internat. Visitors, 1964---; mem. Interview bd. Los Angeles Police Dept., 1965---; Mng. dir. Internat. Festival Adv. Council, 1971---. Served with AUS, World War II; ETO. Decorated Huesped de Honor (Mex.); Legion of Honor (France); Ordine al Merito (Italy); l'Ordre de la Courrenne (Belgium). Mem.: Am. Soc. French Legion of Honor, Assn. Motion Picture and TV Producers (chmn. internat. co., 1967-68, 69-70), Internat. Press Photo-Journalists (hon.), Fgn. Trade Assn., So. Calif. (past pres., chmn bd.), Brit.-Am. (dor.), L.A. C. of C., Western Publs. Assn., Blue Key, Sigma Alpha Epsilon, Alpha Delta Sigma; Mason (Shriner). Clubs: Pres., Brit. United Services (Los Angeles). Republican. Methodist. Hobbies: photog., still life painting. Rec.: gardening. Address: 3320 Bennett Dr., Hollywood, CA 90068.

SCHARFF, EMIL
Accounting Firm Executive
b. Mar. 11, 1923, Los Angeles; s. Emil and Bee (Wiles) Scharff; B.S., Accounting, USC, 1953; m. Charlotte Scharff, Sept. 21, 1957, Honolulu; dau.: Sharon, b. 1959. Career: Accountant, Arthur Young & Company, L.A. Office, 1953-59, San Diego, 1959, mng. partner, 1963, mng. partner, San Francisco office 1975---. USAAF, 1943-46; weather observer and upper air technician. Mem.: Beta Gamma Sigma; Delta Sigma Pi; San Diego Lions Club, pres. 1970-71; Nat. Assn. Accts., pres. San Diego Chpt., 1970, Nat. v.p. 1971-72, currently mem. Exec. Com. and Chmn. Chpt. Opn. Com.; bd. dir., San Francisco Commerce Assocs.; USC. Hobby: Boating. Res.: 110 Country Club Dr., Hillsborough, CA 94010; Office: Post at Montgomery, San Francisco, CA 94104.

SCHARFFENBERGER, GEORGE T.
Business Executive
b. May 22, 1919, Ridgewood, N.Y.; s. George Ludwig and Martha (Watson) Scharffenberger; B.S., Columbia Univ., N.Y. 1940; CPA, State of N.Y. 1943; m. Marion Nelson, Paterson, N.J., July 17, 1948; chil.: Ann Marie, b. May 4, 1949; George Thomas, Jr., b. Aug. 17, 1950; John Edward, b. Sept. 23, 1951; Thomas James, b. Apr. 2, 1954; James Nelson, b. Aug. 14, 1955; Joan Ellen, b. Sept. 25, 1962. Career: Staff acct., Arthur Andersen, 1943-44; various positions ranging from controller to pres., ITT-Kellogg Div., Internat. Tel. and Telegraph Corp. 1943-59; v.p. Litton Industries and pres., Westrex Div. 1959-61, exec. v.p. Litton Systems, 1961-62, sr. v.p. Litton Industries 1962-66; pres.-chief exec. ofcr.-dir., City Investing Co., 1966---. Dir.: IC Industries, Inc.; Litton Industries, Inc.; U.S. Army (1945-46), WW II. Mem.: dir., Electronic Inds. Assn. 1959---; N.Y. Chpt., Financial Execs. Inst. 1961---; American Arbitration Assn.; director, Georgetown Univ.; trustee, USC. Christian Science. Hobby: bee-keeping. Rec.: trail riding. Res.: 4 Appaloosa Lane, Rolling Hills, CA 90274; Office: 9100 Wilshire Blvd., Beverly Hills, CA 90212.

SCHATZ, ROBERT KEITH
Police Chief
b. May 23, 1927, Pocatello, Idaho; s. John and Irene Schatz; B.A., Adminstrn. of Justice, San Jose State Univ., 1955; m. Diana D. Mast, Apr. 28, 1973, Palo Alto; children: John Robert, b. 1960; Suzanne Irene, b. 1964; Matthew William, b. 1974. Career: with Police Dept., Mountain View, 1950---: Police officer 1950, Sgt. 1963, Lieutenant 1956, Asst. Chief of Police 1960, Chief of Police 1971---, Capt., AUS, 1951-53, Mil. Police. Mem.: Calif. Police Chief Assoc., FBI; Nat. Acad. Grad. Assn. Calif. Peace Officials; Assn. Internat. Assn. of Chiefs of Police. Office: 947 Villa St., Montain View, CA 94041.

SCHAUER, RICHARD
Superior Court Judge
b. Sept. 18, 1929, Los Angeles, s. B. Rey (former Superior Ct. Judge and Justice, Calif. Supreme Ct.) and Eva (Summers) Schauer; B.A., Occidental Coll., 1951; J.D., UCLA, 1955; admitted to Calif. bar, 1955; m. Loretta Choy, Jan. 23, 1963, Carmel; children: Steven, b. 1952; Douglas, b. 1954; Kimberly, b. July 7, 1963; Stacey Lynn, b. July 11, 1965. Career: Pvt. practice of law, 1955-63, spl. bus. and real estate practice; law prof., Loyola Univ. Sch. of Law, Lectr. Calif. Bar Rev. Course, Judge of the Municipal Ct., Los Angeles, 1963-65; apptd. to Superior Ct., L.A., 1965, re-elected in 1966, 72, 78; Justice pro tempore, Ct. of Appeal, 2d. Dist., 1973; Asst. Presiding Judge, L.A. Superior Ct., 1977-78. USNR, 1950-52. Contbr. articles various legal publs. Mem.: Order of the Coif; Editor in Chief, UCLA Law Rev., 1954-55; Phi Delta Phi; Rhodes Scholar nominee; Phi Beta Kappa; Phi Gamma Delta. Republican. Protestant. Rec.: hunting, fishing. Res.: 2534 Canyon Dr., L.A., CA 90028; Office: 111 N. Hill St., Los Angeles, CA 90012.

SCHAUWECKER, HARRY E.
Company President
b. Feb. 4, 1928, Parkersburg, W. Va.; s. Walter and Johanna (Hopf) Schauwecker; B.E.E., Ohio State Univ.; LL.B., La Salle Univ.; m. Donna Bourque, Fullerton, Calif., May 29, 1958; chil.: Chritsian Erich, b. Jan. 25, 1962; Paula Elyse, b. Nov. 2, 1963. Career: Lectr. in enging. UCLA 1956-63; dir.-pres. Valor Instruments, Inc. 1957-60; v.p.-dir. U.S. Sci. Corp., L.A. 1961-63; pres. H.E. Schauwecker & Assocs., L.A. 1963-69; dir. Add Corp. 1968-72; pres.-dir. Thiem-Trans-Rex., Inc. 1968-69; exec. v.p.-gen. mgr.-dir. Thiem Inds., Inc., Torrance, 1969-74; pres. Logicon-Intercomp, Inc., Torrance, 1974---; dir., Logicon Systems of Canada, Montreal, Que.; dir., Nortech, Inc., Antigo, Wis.; editorial bd., On Line Systems. L.A. chmn. Bus. and Ind., March of Dimes, 1970-71, exec. com. 1971---, chmn. 1973-74. USN, 1946-47, WW II. Contrib. 10 publ. papers, 1952---; 2 patents, 1963, 1965. Mem.: (Sr.) IEEE, Eta Kappa Nu, Tau Beta Pi; Town Hall of Calif., Christ Lutheran Ch. (v.p.-trustee, San Pedro, 1966-67). Office: 24225 Garnier St., Torrance, CA.

SCHAWLOW, ARTHUR L(EONARD)
Physicist — Educator
b. May 5, 1921, Mt. Vernon, N.Y.; s. Arthur and Helen (Mason) Schawlow; B.A. 1941; M.A., 1942; Ph.D., 1949; Physics, Univ. of Toronto; Hon. doctorates: Universities of Ghent (Belgium), Toronto (Canada), and Bradord (England); m. Aurelia Townes, May 19, 1951, Greenville, S.C.; children: Arthur Keith, b. 1956; Helen Aurelia, b. 1957; Edith Ellen, b. 1959. Career: Postdoctoral Fellow & Research Assoc., Columbia Univ. 1949-51; vis. assoc. prof., 1960; Research Physicist, Bell Labs., Murray Hills, 1951-61; J.G. Jackson-C.J. Wood Prof. of Physics, Stanford Univ., 1961---, exec. head, 1966-70, acting chmn. 1973-74. Co-inventor optical maser or laser (with C.H. Townes); author: Microwave Spectroscopy (with C.H. Townes), 1955; Introductions to Scientific American Readings on Lasers and Light, 1969; over 140 sci. papers. Awards: California Scientist of the Year, 1973; Frederick Ives Medal, Optical Soc. of Am. 1976; Third Marconi Internat. Fellowship, 1975, presented by King Carl Gustaf of Sweden. TV appearances: 21st Century program with Walter Cronkite, Experiment Series with Don Herbert, films for Canadian and British TV networks. Fellow, American Physical Soc., mem. Council 1966-69; Fellow, Optical Soc. of Am., dir.-at-large 1966-68, pres. 1975; chmn., Physics Sect. AAAS, 1979. Hobby: collecting jazz records. Res.: 849 Esplanada Way, Stanford, CA 94305; Office: Stanford University, Stanford, CA 94305.

SCHEIBEL, ARNOLD B.
Physician
b. Jan. 18, 1923, NYC; s. William and Ethel Scheibel; B.A. 1944, M.D. 1946, Columbia Univ.; M.S. neuroanatomy, Univ. Ill., 1952; m. Madge Ragland (dec.), San Antonio, Tex., Mar. 3, 1950. Career: Asst./Assoc. Prof., Univ. of Tennessee, 1952-55; Asst./Assoc./Prof. of Anatomy and Psychiatry, UCLA Med. Center, 1955---. Board certified psychiatrist, 1953; Guggenheim Fellow, 1953-54, 1959. Mil.: pfc., ASTP, 1943-45; Capt. M.C. AUS, 1948-50. Publs.: 200 on devel., structure and function of the brain. Hobby: painting. Address: Dept. of Anatomy, Sch. of Medicine, UCLA Med. Center, Los Angeles, CA 90024.

SCHERMERHORN, RICHARD A.
Sociologist — Educator
b. Oct. 18, 1903, Evanston, Ill.; s. William David (former Pres., Dakota Wesleyan Univ.) and May Day (Hoffman) Schermerhorn; B.A., 1924; M.A., 1927; Ph.D., 1931; m. Helen Katherine Karban, Sept. 6, 1926, Evanston, Ill. Career: Faculty mem. Kansas Wesleyan Univ. 1932-33, Clark Coll. and Spelman Coll., Atlanta, 1933-38; Prof. of Sociology, Baldwin-Wallace Coll., 1940-47; Univ. of Rhode Island, 1947-48; Case Western Reserve Univ., 1948-72, Prof. Emeritus of Sociology, 1972---. Mem. faculty, Salzburg Seminar in Am. Studies, Summer 1958; chmn., Ohio Conf. of Chpts., AAUP, 1952-53; pres., Soc. for Study of Social Problems, 1958-59; vis. prof. of sociology: Lucknow Univ., India 1959-60, La Trobe Univ., Australia 1972, Fulbright grant; Indian Inst. of Tech., Kanpur, India, USAID Program. Author: These Our People, Minorities in American Culture, D.C. Heath 1949; Society and Power, Random House 1961; Psychiatric Index for Interdisciplinary Research, U.S. Govt. Printing Office 1964; Comparative Ethnic Relations, Random House 1970; Ethnic Plurality in India, Univ. Ariz. Press. 1978. Named Gen. Edn. Bd. Fellow, 1938-39; Yale Fellow 1939-40; Alumnus of the Year, Dakota Wesleyan Univ. 1978. Mem.: Assn. for Asian Studies; Asian Studies on Pacific Caost; American (Sydney Spivak Fellow, 1977) Indian, and Pacific, Internat. Sociol. Assns., (v.p. research com. on Ethnic, Race, Minority Rels. 1970-78); Phi Kappa Phi; Claremont University Club. Unitarian. Hobby: piano playing. Res.: 155 N. Cambridge Ave., Claremont, CA 91711.

SCHIFF, ALICE G.
Pediatrician
b. Mar. 4, 1894, Rees, Germany; d. Jacob and Fanny (Muller) Goldstein; M.D. degree 1920; German license 1920; Public Health Degree, Germany, 1923; Calif. license 1938; AAP license 1944; m. Hans Schiff, M.D. (dec.), Mar. 22, 1922, Dusseldorf, Germany; children: Eva Schindler (Rainman), D.S.W. (orgnl. cons.), b. 1925; Gunther H. (lawyer), b. 1927. Career: Asst. at Children's Hosp., Dusseldorf, 1922-25; pvt. practice in Pediatrics, Cologne, 1925-35; staff physician, Cedars-Sinai MEd. Center, 1938---; pvt. practice, Beverly Hills, 1937---. Rec.: travel. Res.: 403 N. Oakhurst Dr., No. 105, Beverly Hills, CA 90210; Office: 465 N. Roxbury Dr., Beverly Hills, CA 90210.

SCHINE, GERALD DAVID
Entertainment Company Executive
b. Sept. 11, 1927, Gloversville, N.Y.; s. J. Myer and Hildegarde (Feldman) Schine; grad. Fessenden Sch., West Newton, Mass., 1941, Phillips Acad, Andover, Mass., 1945; A.B., Harvard, 1949; m. Anna Kristina Hillevi (Rombin), 1957; children: Anna Vidette Angela, Jonathan Mark, Alexander Kevin, Frederick Berndt, Benjamin Axel, William Lance. Career: Pres., gen. mgr. Schine Hotels, 1950-63; exec. v.p. Schine Enterprises, 1952-57; pres., 1957-63; pres. Ski Dek Corp., 1961-67, David Schine & Co., Inc., Mgmt. Internat., Inc., Auto Inns Am., Inc., 1963-72; Ambassador Hotel Co. Los Angeles, 1960-63, 64-67; exec. producer The French Connection, 1971; writer, producer, dir. That's Action!, 1977; now pres. David Schine & Co., Inc., Schine Music, Myhil Music, Schine Prodns., Los Angeles; Adviser, spl. asst. atty.-gen. U.S. charge subversive activities, 1952; assited Investigation Communist infiltration into UN; chief cons. Senate Permanent Subcom. on Investigations; Com. on Govt. Operations; Jan. to Nov. 1053; directed investigation of Internat. Information Adminstrn., also Voice of America, Dept. State, 1953; mem. Los Angeles Citizens Com. for 1960 Democratic Conv. Trustee Hotel Industry Devel. Fund; past dir. Symphony Club of Miami, Community Concert Assn. Miami Beach, Fla.; past chmn. adv. bd. Conv. Bur. Miami Beach; mem. citizens adv. com. Hotel Employees Med. Plan; past dir. Com. 1000 for Variety Children's Hosp.; past dir. Greater Miami Philharmonic Soc., Inc.; nat. bd. trustees City of Hope; past chmn. Miami Beach Com. Opera Guild; trustee Hope for Hearing Found. Served as Lt. Army Transport Service, 1946-47; pvt. AUS, 1953-55. Mem. Young President's Orgn. Am. (founding mem.), Nat. Bus. Aircraft Assn., Aircraft Owners and Pilots Assn., AIM (pres's. council), So. Fla. Hotel and Motel Assn. (founding pres.), Dade County (Fla.) Devel. Com. Clubs: Lotos; Harvard (NYC). Author articles and pamphlets. Hobby: flying. Res.: 626 S. Hudson Ave., Los Angeles, CA 90005.

SCHLAX, WILLIAM NICHOLAS
Geologist
b. Feb. 1, 1922, Seattle, Wash.; s. Maj. William N. and Lillian Edna (LaFond) Schlax; B.S., Univ. of Wash. 1947; m. Joan Hay, Bakersfield. Calif., Apr. 22, 1948; chil.: Christopher, b. Aug. 18, 1949 (dec. Feb. 17, 1952); Wendy, b. Oct. 11, 1952; Michael, b. July 31, 1954; Krista, b. Mar. 4, 1958. Career: Geologist, U.S. Geol. Survey, Portland, Ore. 1947; sr. geol., Superior Oil Co., Bakersfield, Willows, Los Angeles, Calif. 1948-57; cons. geol., G.H. Roth & Assocs., North Hollywood, Calif. 1957-59; engin. geol., Dames & Moore, L.A. 1959-62; cons. geol., Van Nuys and Santa Rosa, Calif. 1962---; engin. geol., Moore & Taber, Santa Rosa, 1964---. Discoverer, Los Medanos Gas Field, Contra Costa Co., Calif., 1957-58. Author: professional publs. Tech. Sgt., USMC (Battle of Midway, Guadalcanal-Tulagi Landings, capture and def. Guadalcanal, 1941-45), WW II. Mem.: Amer. Assn. of Petroleum Geols., Assn. of Engin. Geols. Catholic. Rec.: tennis, cycling. Res.: 508 Buena Vista Dr., Santa Rosa, CA 95404; Office: 2281 Cleveland Ave., Santa Rosa, CA 95401.

SCHLEGEL, DAVID EDWARD
Plant Pathologist
b. Sept. 3, 1927, Fresno; s. Edward Paul and Lydia (Denny) Schlegel; m. Betty Adkins, Sept. 12, 1948, Portland Ore.; children: Marsha Elaine (Burlingame), b. 1957; Linda Elise (Genge), b. 1957; Mark David, b. 1959; Susan Eilene, b. 1964. Career: Faculty, Dept. of Plant Pathology, Univ. Calif., Berkeley, 1954---: Prof. and Plant Pathologist, 1968---, chmn., Dept., 1970-76, Assoc. Dean for Research, Coll. of Natural Resources, 1976---, Acting Dean, 1977---, also Acting Assoc. Dir. Exp. Station, 1977---. Grants: Miller Prof. 1966-67; NIH, 1959-73; NSF, 1974-78; AID Assoc. Proj. Dir. Pest Mgmt. and Related Environmental Protection. Contbr. tech. papers profl. journs. Research Emphasis: plant virology, physiology of plant virus diseases; virus inhibitors and products of infection; use viruses as biocides; Pest mgmt. and crop protection. Mem.: AAAS; Am. Phytopathological Soc.; Am. Inst. for Biol. Sci.; Soc. for Gen. Microbiology. Office: Univ. California, Berkeley, CA 94720.

SCHLOSSER, ANNE GRIFFIN
Librarian
b. Dec. 28, 1939, N.Y.C., N.Y.; d. C. Russell and Gertrude (Taylor) Griffin; B.A. hist., Wheaton Coll., Norton, Mass.; M.L.S., Simmons Coll., Grad Sch. of Lib. Sci., Boston; certificate, Modern Archives Adminstrn., Am. Univ., Wash., D.C.; m. Gary J. Schlosser, Dec. 28, 1965, Sea Girt, N.J. Career: Head of Theater Arts Library, UCLA, 1964-69; head librarian, Charles K. Feldman Library, Am. Film Inst., 1969---. Project director: Motion Pictures, Television and Radio: A Union Catalogue of Manuscript and Special Collections in The Western United States (Boston, G.K. Hall, 1977). V.P., film and TV study Center, 1973-74; mem. Internat. Fedn. of Film Archives, documentation commn., 1967-74. Rec.: running, sailing. Office: American Film Inst., 501 Doheny Road, Beverly Hills, CA 90210.

SCHMIDT, JAMES CRAIG
Savings and Loan Company Executive
b. Sept. 27, 1927, Peoria, Ill.; s. Walter Henry and Clara (Wolfenberger) Schmidt; student Ill. Wesleyan Univ., 1945, 48-50; Ph.B. in Bus. Adminstrn., 1952; postgrad. Univ. Ill. Coll. Law, 1950-52; J.D., DePaul Univ., 1953; m. Jerrie Louise Bond, Dec. 6, 1958; children: Julie and Sandra, b. 1959, Suzanne, b. 1968. Career: Spl. agt. Fidelity & Deposit Co., Chicago, 1956-58; with Home Fed. Savings & Loan Assn., San Diego, 1958-67; asst. secty. bus. and transp. State of Calif., 1967-69; exec. v.p., mng. officer, dir. San Diego Fed. Savs. & Loan Assn., 1969---; pres. Calif. Gen. Mortgage Co., 1969---; v. chmn., Financial Scene, Inc. 1978---; pres., Conf. Fed. Savs. and Loans of Calif., 1974-75. Mem. Calif. Toll Bridge Authority, 1969-74; mem. Calif. State Transp. Bd., 1972-78; past pres. SEED, Inc. San Diego; past chmn. San Diego Bal. Commn. Task Force. Served with USN, 1945-48. Mem. Calif., Ill. Bar assns., Aztec Athletic Found. (dir.), Sigma Chi, mem. exec. com., San Diego Holiday Bowl; Phi Delta Phi. Clubs: Rancho Las Palmas Country, San Diego Country, San Diego Rotary. Protestant. Office: 600 B. St., San Diego, CA 92183.

SCHMITZ, JOHN G.
State Senator
b. Aug. 12, 1930, Milwaukee, Wis.; s. J.J. and

Wilhelmina (Frueh) Schmitz; B.S., Marquette Univ. 1952; M.A., Calif. State Coll., Long Beach, 1960; m. Mary E. Suehr, Milwaukee, Wis., July 10, 1954; chil.: John P., Joseph E., Jerome T., Mary Kay, Theresa Ann, Elizabeth Louise, Philip. Career: Instr. (philosophy, hist. polit. sci.), Santa Ana Coll. 1960-65. Elected to Calif. State Senate, 34th Dist. (chmn. Calif. Govt. Com.), 1964-70; elected to U.S. House of Reps, June 1970-73. Polit. Sci.-hist. dept., Santa Ana Coll. 1973-78; elected 36th Dist., State Senate, 1978---. Aviator, USMC 1952-60 (jet fighter, helicopter squadrons); Lt. Col., USMCR; instr. anti-Communism course, El Toro M.C. Air Sta. Leadership Sch. 1957-63. Awards: Man of Yr., Sacramento Co. Young Repubs. 1968; United Taxpayers of Calif. Award for meritorious pub. serv. to Taxpayers of Calif. 1969; Cit. for outstanding serv. 6th Dist. Amer. Legion, 1969; We the People Statesman of Yr. Award, 1970. Mem.: Natl. Soc. of State Legislators; Mil. Order World Wars; Amer. Legion; Knights of Columbus, Order of the Alhambra; John Birch Soc.; Calif. Rifle and Pistol Assn.; Natl. Repub. Assn.; Orange Co. chmn. Calif. Repub. Assembly; Calif. Young Repubs.; United Repubs. of Calif. Roman Catholic. Res.: Corona del Mar; Office: 1530 W. 17th St., Santa Ana, CA 92706.

SCHMUNK, DONALD FRED
Physicist
b. Mar. 9, 1937, Portland, Ore.; s. Fred and Arpa (Pfaff) Schmunk; B.S., Portland State Coll., 1959; M.S., Oregon State Coll., 1960; postgrad. USA, 1962, UCLA, 1967; m. Sara May Goldstein, Mar. 3, 1968, Inglewood, Calif.; chil.: Dennis Donald; Sara Lynn; Donna May; Angela Joy. Career: tech. staff mem., Pacific Semiconductors, Inc., Lawndale, 1961-64; tech. staff, TRW Systems (formerly Space Tech Labs), Redondo Beach, 1964-66; group mgr. research, TRW Semiconductors, 1966-67; group scientist, supr. solid state materials studies, Autonetics div., North Am. Rockwell (now Rockwell Internat. Corp.), 1967-71, staff engr., mfg. liaison, Microelectronics Center, 1971-72; mgr. process devel., research and engring., 1972-73. mgr. process engring. Microelectronics Device Div. Rockwell Internat. Corp., 1973-75; mgr. device and process characterization, 1975=77, project engr. electronic systems group, 1977---. Mem.: IEEE; Full Gospel Business Men's Fellowship Internat., v.p. 1977---, dir. chpt. 1967-77; Nat. Rifle Assn.; Calif. State Marksman Precision Air Pistol Champion 1974. Quaker; Rose Dr. Friends Ch. Hobbies: electronics, mini computers, philately, astronomy. Rec.: archery, target shooting, camping. Home: 3245 E. Greenleaf Dr., Brea, CA 92621; Office: 3430 Miraloma, Anaheim, CA 92803.

SCHNEIDER, HERBERT WALLACE
Philosopher — Educator
b. Mar. 16, 1892, Berea, Ohio; s. Frederick W. and Marie (Severinghaus) Schenider; Ph.D., Columbia Univ., 1917, L.H.D., LL.D.; m. Grehafore Wetphal; sons: Edward W., b. 1940; Frederick W., b. 1943; Robert W., b. 1952. Career: Prof. of Philosophy, Columbia Univ. 1926-67, Colorado Coll., 1958-59, Claremont Graduate Sch. 1960-74; Secretariat of UNESO, 1953-56; Dir. Blaisdell Inst. at Claremont, 1960-63; Acting Dean, Claremont Grad. Sch. 1961-62; Vis. Prof. Emory Univ., Oglethorpe Coll., Emory Univ., Atlanta, Ga. Author: The Puritan Mind, 1930; A History of American Philosophy, 1946; Wasy of Being, 1961. AUS, M.C., WW I. Mem. Century Assn., NYC; Res. 245 West 10 St., Claremont, CA.

SCHNEIDERS, EDMUND FRANCIS, JR.
Chairman, American National Group
b. Mar. 12, 1935, Los Angeles; s. Edmund Francis, Sr. (sr. v.p. Sec. Pac. Nat. Bank, L.A.) and Mildred (O'Neill) Schneiders; B.A., Stanford Univ., 1956; m. Martha Sweeney, Nov. 30, 1963, Pasadena; chil.: Edmund Francis, III, b. Nov. 26, 1964; Ann Elizabeth, b. Apr. 30, 1966. Career: bus. training course, Gen. Electric Co., 1956-57; v.p. and dir., 20th Century Underwriters, Inc., 1958-61; v.p. and dir., John D. Lusk and Son, Inc., 1962-65; organizer, pres. and dir., Southern Counties Mgmt. Co., 1965-78; chmn. of the bd., Am. Nat. Group, 1978---. Served to Capt. AUS. Regent, Loyola Marymount Univ., 1978---; mem. Young President's Orgn., 1973---; Alpha Delta Phi, 1953-56. Hobby: boating. Home: 1590 Stone Canyon Rd., L.A., CA; Office: 405 S. Beverly Dr., Beverly Hills, CA 90212.

SCHNIER, BRIAN ROBERT
Physician
b. June 28, 1938, Utica, N.Y.; s. Harry and Eva Schnier; B.A,, Hamilton Coll.; M.D., Univ. Rochester; m. Linda, Nov. 22, 1964, North Carolina; children: Ellen, b. 1967; David, b. 1968. Career: Fellow, Internal Med., Mayo Clin., 1964-65; Chief, Internal Med., USAF, 1965-67; Resident in Diagnostic Radiology, Stanford Univ., 1967-70, Instr. in Diagnostic Radiology, 1970-71; Staff Radiologist, Cottage Hosp., Santa Barbara, 1971---. Contbr. articles to sci. publs. Board Certified Diag. Radiology, 1971; Fellow, Am. Coll. Angiology, 1978. Mem. So. Coast Radiologic Soc., pres. 1978-79. Bd. dir., County Mental Health, 1975-76; bd. dir., Freedom Med. Clinic, 1973-75. Mem. Cold Spring Sch. Bd., 1977---. Pres., Cong. B'nai B'rith, 1978. Hobby: computers. Res.: 710 Knapp Dr., Santa Barbara, CA 93108; Office: P.O.B. 689, Santa Barbara, CA 93102.

SCHOBER, FRANK J., JR.
Commanding General, California National Guard
b. Nov. 17, 1933, Los Angeles, Calif.; s. Frank Jose and Mildred (Lucien) Schober; paternal grandmother, Aurora Arguello of Calif. pioneer family; ed. B.S. (summa cum laude), Univ. of Santa Clara, 1956; Master (pub. adm.), Harvard Univ., 1962; m. Gale Rogers, Glastonbury, Conn., July 14, 1974; chil.: Chris, b. Aug. 15, 1962; Wake, b. Aug. 4, 1963. Career: Platoon leader, U.S. Army, 1956, Co. Comdr. 1960; asst. prof. West Point, 1964-67; advisor, Saudi Arabian Army, 1968-69; Comdr., Vietnam Conflict, 1970-71; speech writer to Army Chief of Staff, 1972-74; Vital Speeches, Apr. 15, 1976; research analyst, Army Strategic Studies Inst., 1974-75; Comdg. Gen., Calif. State Military Forces, 1975---. Mem.: VFW, Assn. of U.S. Army, Newcomen Society of N. Amer., Commonwealth Club of Calif., Anglo-Cath. Hobbies: historiography, jogging. Res.: 8188 Plumeria, Fair Oaks, CA 95610; Office: P.O.B. 214405, Sacramento, CA 95821.

SCHOLANDER, PER FREDRIK
Physiologist
b. Nov. 29, 1905, Orebro, Sweden; s. Torkel and Agnethe Faye (Hansen) Scholander; M.D., Univ. Oslo, 1932, Ph.D., 1934; m. Susan Irving, June 20, 1951, Brookline, Mass. Career: Research Fellow Physiology, Univ. Oslo, 1932-39; Research Assoc., Zoology, Swarthmore Coll., 1939-43; Research Biologist, 1946-49; Research Fellow, Biological Chem., Harvard Med. Sch., 1949-51; Physiologist, Woods Hole Oceanographic Inst., 1952-55; Prof. Physiology, Dir Inst. Zoophysiology, Univ. Oslo, 1955-58; Prof. of Physiology, Scripps Inst. Oceanography, U.C., San Diego, 1958---, Dir. Physiological Research Lab., 1963-70; Research Assoc. Zoology, Univ. Washington, Seattle, 1972---. Co-author: Osmosis and Tensily Solvent 1976; Harvey Lectr. 1962; NIH Lectr. 1972. Awards: Nat. Acad. Sciences; Norwegian Acad. Sci.; Royal Swedish Acad. Sci.; Am. Acad. Arts and Sciences; Am. Philosophical Soc.; Rockefeller Fellow 1939-41; John Simon Guggenheim Fellow 1969; D.Sc., Univ. Alaska, 1973; Univ. of Uppsala 1977, 500 Years Jubilee. Served Capt. to Maj., USAAF, 1943-46; Chief Physiological Aviation Physiologist, Aeromed. Lab., Wright Field. Clubs: Explorers, Cosmos. Hobbies: violin, mushrooms. Res.: 8374 Paseo del Ocaso, La Jolla, CA 92037; Office: Scripps Inst. Oceanography, La Jolla, CA.

SCHORE, ROBERT M.
Physician
b. July 13, 1943, Detroit, Mich.; s. Henry and Sarah Schore; B.S. 1965; M.D. 1969, Univ. Mich.; m. Dee Sauter, May 22, 1977, San Diego; dau. (previous marriage), Heather, b. 1971; stepson Jack Jeter, b. 1963. Career: Intern, Kaiser Found. Hosp., Oakland, 1969-70; pvt. and group family practice, 1970-74; specialty Homeopathic Med., San Diego, 1974---; founder and pres. Homeopathic Med. Clinic and Research Center, Inc., San Diego, 1978---. Served USAF, ---1970. Mem. Phi Delta Epsilon med. frat. Jewish. Hobby: piano. Res.: 1833 Malden St., San Diego, CA 91209; Office: 4747 Mission Blvd., San Diego, CA 92109.

SCHOTTKE, LORRY S.
Industrial Realtor
b. Dec. 26, 1914, Los Angeles, Calif.; s. Ernest A. and Irma E. (Schmidt) Schottke; ed. Pasa. City Coll.

1932-34; Sawyer Sch. of Bus. 1937-38; Alexander Hamilton Inst. 1962-63; John Carey Inst. 1964-66; UCLA 1965; m. Elizabeth Morrow Burke, Las Vegas, Nev., Jan. 31, 1953. Career: Industrial realtor; chmn. bd. Sho-Fel Industries, Inc. (mfr.) 1956-73; pres. 1950-61; chmn. bd. Lorry Schottke Co.; v.p.-treas. Lomalta Corp. (land development-sub. divs.), 1964-67; secty. 1411 Garfield Corp. 1964-67; pres. Schottke & Assocs. 1975---; partner (ltd.): Real Estate Investments Cons.; bd. dirs. Chronometrics, Inc. 1973---; Coachella Valley Assocs., Fairbanks Assocs., Hillcrest Assocs., Eastgate Assocs. Past chmn. Aerons. Comm., State of Calif. Calif. Real Estate Brokers license; participated, edn. seminars, CREA, IRA; mil. writer, Tech. Manuals, USN. USN 1943; Instr. Sch., Plane Comdr. Sch., Electronics Sch.; Sr. Natl. War College, Wash., D.C. 1964; pilot, egnr. tr., naval aviator; comdg. ofcr. Air Transport Squad; Wing Staff Comdr.; operations ofcr., Pac.; Capt., USN 1965. Mem.: L.A. Realty Bd., Los Angeles C. of C.; chmn. coms. Wilshire Rotary Club; Town Hall of Calif.; Order of Daedalians; Quiet Birdman; (charter) dir.-pres. Trojan Shrine Club; past master, James A. Garfield Lodge, F&AM 1966; Al Malaikah Temple, Shrine, asst. dir. Shrine Club; Royal Arch Masons, Calif.; Grand Commandery K.T. of Calif.; past comdr. Aviation Post, Amer. Leg.; chmn. Boy's State, Calif.; Hollywood Council, Navy League; Skull and Dagger, USC; So. Calif. Golf Assn.; Oakmont Country Club. Hobbies: golf, swim, travel (Japan, Hong Kong, Guam, P.I., Her. Fr., Eng., Ire., Iceland, Newfoundland, Azores, S. Africa, Bahamas, Panama, Puerto Rico, Mex., Labrador). Res.: 1315-D N. Central Ave., Glendale, CA 91202; Office: 9808 Wilshire Blvd., Beverly Hills, CA 90212.

SCHROEDER, WILLRICH (BILL)
Athletic Foundation Director
b. Nov. 13, 1904, Beaumont, Tex.; s. Fred and Frances (King) Schroeder; m. Iona Miller, Oct. 16, 1935, Yuma, Ariz.; dau., Jan Ellen. Career: with California Bank, Los Angeles, 1925-36; estab. The Athletic Foundation, 1936---; mng. dir., Helms Athletic Found., 1937-70, United Savings Helms Athletic Found., 1970-73, Citizens Savings Athletic Found., 1973---; vice pres., United Savings, Citizens Savings & Loan Assn., 1970---; The Found. operates: Sports Museum, houses the most complete collection of Olympic Games awards and memorabilia in existence, as well as trophies and artifacts entrusted by athletes, coaches and sportsmen; Sports Library, most complete in world, open for public use; World Trophy Awards, granted annually to top amateur athlete in each of six areas of world, with selections dating to 1896; Halls of Fame, conducted annually for many sports; extensive High Schools Awards program, 1937---. Co-owner and gen. mgr. Hollywood Bears Football Club (Pacific Coast League 1946 champions), 1945-46; Organizer and pres.: Calif. Baseball League, 1941-47, Sunset Baseball League, 1947; Far West Baseball League, 1947; mem. Exec. Com. So. Calif. Com. for Olympic Games, 1940-78, v.p. 1974-78; Editor, Football Digest, 1943-67; Helms Sports Reporter, KECA, L.A., 1937-39; chmn., War Charity Games, 1943 and 1944, 4th Air Force, vs. Coll. of Pacific, Wash. Redskins, 2d. Air Force; Founder, U.S. Olympians, So. Calif. Chpt., 1950; mem. U.S. Olympic Com., 1952---. Recipient awards, City and County of Los Angeles, L.A. Secondary Sch. Adminstrs., U.S. Olympic Com., Japanese Olympic Com., Nat. Football League, Nat. Athletic Trainers Assn., many others. Res.: 1428 Allen Ave., Glendale, CA 91201; Office: 9800 S. Sepulveda Blvd., L.A., CA 90045.

SCHRUT, ALBERT HERMAN
Psychiatrist
b. Feb. 18, 1924, Detroit; s. Samuel and Sadie (Goldwater) Schrut; B.A., Wayne Univ., 1947; M.D., 1951; Ph.D., psychoanalysis, S. Calif. Psychoanalytic Inst., 1977. Career: Intern Highland Park (Mich.) Gen. Hosp., 1951-52; resident VA Hosp., Long Beach, Calif. 1952-54; Clinton Valley Center, Prentice, Mich., 1954-57; pvt. practice adult and child psychiatry and psychoanalysis, Los Angeles, 1956---; attending psychiatrist, sr. teaching staff dept. psychiatry Cedars-Sinai Hosp., L.A. 1958, assoc. dir. parenting research project, 1972---; asst. clin. prof. psychiatry USC Sch. Med. 1961---; training analyst, supr. So. Calif. Psychoanalytic Inst., 1973---. Sgt., AUS, 1943-46, ETO, decorated Bronze Star. Fellow Am. Psychiat. Assn., So. Calif. Psychoanalytic Inst. (Franz Alexander essay prize 1966); mem. AMA, Am. Acad. Psychoanalysis, Am. Psychoanalytic Assn., Internat. Psychoanalytic Assn., Los Angeles Pediatric Soc. Diplomate Am. Bd. Psychiatry and Neurology. Certified by Amer. Psychoanalytic Assn. in Adult and Child Psychiatry and Psychoanalysis. Author articles in field. Office: 2080 Century Park E., Los Angeles, CA 90067.

SCHRUTH, PETER ELLIOTT
Broadcasting Executive
b. Mar. 10, 1917, Fargo, N.D.; s. John and Mary (Elliott) Schruth; B.B.A., Univ. Minn., 1939; Grad. FBI Acad.; m. Anne Killmade, Aug. 3, 1946, St. Louis, Mo.; children: Barbara (Root), b. 1947; Susan, b. 1949; Peter, b. 1951; Mark, b. 1960. Career: Copywriter, Campbell-Mithun, Special Agent, FBI, 1941-45; Western Mgr., Holiday Mag., 1946-53, Mgr. and Pub., 1954-63; v.p., Westinghouse Broadcasting, 1964---. Officer and bd. mem.: San Francisco Urban Renewal Assn.; Convention & Visitors Bureau; Calif. Roundtable; Calif. Broadcasters Assn.; Otis Art Inst. Mem. Chi Psi, exec. council, 1968-72. Clubs: Bohemian, Menlo Country, University (N.Y.) Mem. Bd. of Edn., Greenwich, Conn., 1968-74. Catholic. Rec.: tennis, golf, swimming. Office: 2655 Van Ness Ave., San Francisco, CA 94109.

SCHUETZENDUEBEL, WOLFRAM
Energy Company Manager
b. Feb. 17, 1932, Alt-Landsberg, Germany; s. Gerhard E. and Kaethe S.; B.S. mech. engr., 1956; M.S.M.E., M.S., power engr., 1958; D.Sc., Eng., 1979; m. Ingeborg Lesch, Dec. 15, 1960, Berlin, Germany. Career: Mgr., Boiler Eng. Dept., Riley Stoker Corp., 1958-61; sr. R&D engr., Combustion Engineering Inc., 1961-68; project mgr., Fort St. Vrain Steam Generators, General Atomic Co., 1968---, Mgr., Tech. Services, Steam Generator Program, and Mgr., Steam/Water Systems. Mem.: ASME, chmn. Nuclear Heat Exchanger Com. chmn. 1976-78, program chmn. & exec. com. Nuclear Eng. Div.; Nat. Assn. of Corrosion Eng.; Am. Nuclear Soc.; Assn. of German Profl. Engr.; German Atomic Forum. Foreign correspondent for Energie (German monthly journ.); holder 39 patents; contbr. tech. papers profl. journs. Res.: P.O.B. 1151, Rancho Santa Fe, CA 92067; Office: General Atomic Co., P.O.B. 81608, San Diego, CA 92138.

SCHUILING, ERNA I.
Civic Leader
b. 1919, Minnesota; B.S., Univ. Minn.; m. Walter C. Schuiling, 1941, Minn.; son, William Thys, b. 1954. Career: Tchr., Secondary Schools, 1940-58; dir., Red Cross Youth, San Bernardino, 1961-66; exec. dir., Inland Adolescent Clin., 1966-71; asst. to the Pres., San Bernardino Valley Coll., 1974. Lectr., moderator, tchr. on radio, TV, seminars. Vice-chmn. Desert Advisory Council, U.S. Secty. of Interior; mem. Regional Parks Commn.; Local Agency Formation Commn. of San Bernardino County; mem. Project Review Bd. Inland Counties Health System Agency; pres., San Bernardino Para-Transit Coalition; pres., County Council of Community Services, San Bernardino; Mem. League of Women Voters of Calif., dir. 1967-71; state pres., League of Women Voters of Ga., 1971-73. Address: 3577 Lugo, San Bernardino, CA 92404.

SCHULER, DONNIE S.
Educator
b. Sept. 24, 1942, Cedar Hill, Tenn.; d. Herbert and Rachel Rigsby; B.A., 1964, M.A., 1969. Career: Tchr., secondary schools, Nashville, Tenn., 1964-66, Auburn, Ky., 1967-68; Ednl. Therapist, Dist. of Columbia Dept. of Human Resources, 1969-72; Supr., Tchr., Learning Center, San Diego Community Coll., 1973-76; Counselor, National Univ., San Diego, 1978---. Mem. Am. Sociological Assn. Democrat. Baptist. Hobby: Bridge. Rec.: bike riding, tennis. Res.: 11941 Bajada Rd., San Diego, CA 92128.

SCHULLER, ROBERT HAROLD
Clergyman — Author
b. Sept. 16, 1926, Alton, Iowa; s. Anthony and Jennie (Beltman) Schuller; B.A., Hope Coll., Holland, Mich. 1947; B.D., Western Theol. Sem. 1950; m. Arvella DeHaan, June 15, 1950; children: Sheila, b. 1951; Robert, b. 1954; Jeanne, b. 1958; Carol, b. 1964; Gretchen, b. 1967. Career: pastor, Ivanhoe Reformed Ch., Chicago, 1950-55; founder, sr. pastor, Garden Grove Community Ch., 1955---; founder, pres., Hour of Power TV program, 1970---; founder, dir., Robert H. Schuller Inst. for Successful Ch. Leadership, 1970---; pres., bd. dirs., Chirstian Counseling Services, Inc.; founder, Robert H. Schuller Correspondence

Center for Possibility Thinkers, 1976; bd. dir. Religion in Am. Life, 1975---. Author: God's Way to the Good Life; Your Future Is Your Friend; Move Ahead With Possibility Thinking; Self Love — The Dynamic Force of Success; Power Ideas for a Happy Family; The Greatest Possibility Thinker That Ever Lived; Turn Your Scars Into Stars; You Can Become the Person You Want to Be; Your Church Has Real Possibilities; Love or Loneliness — You Decide; Positive Prayers for Power-Filled Living; Keep On Believing; and Peace of Mind Through Possibility Thinking; Reach Out For New Life; Turning Your Stress Into Strength. Awards: Distinguished Alumnus, Hope College, 1970; Freedoms Foundation of Valley Forge, 1974; Hon. Mem., Relig. Guild of Architects; Headliner of the Year in Rel., Orange Co. Press Club, 1977; Clergyman of the Year, Religious Heritage of America, 1977; LL.D. (hon.) Azusa Pacific College (Calif.), 1970; D.D. (hon.) Hope College (Mich.), 1973; LL.D. (hon.) Pepperdine University (Calif.), 1976; Lit. D. (hon.), Barrington College (RI), 1977. Mem. Rotary Club. Address: Garden Grove Community Ch., 12141 Lewis St., Garden Grove, CA 92640.

SCHUTZ, DAVID N.
Editor
b. Sept. 8, 1917, Reno, Nev.; s. Isaac and Eva (Jacobs) Schutz; A.B., San Francisco State Coll. 1939; Master of Journ., Northwestern Univ. 1940; m. Sibyl Hurning, Chicago, Ill., Sept. 18, 1940; chil.: Jerome H., b. Feb. 7, 1942; Laraine E., b. Aug. 31, 1943; Beverly R., b. Dec. 25, 1949. Career: Reporter, Evanston Daily News-Index, 1940-41; rewrite-reporter, Kewanee Star-Courier, Ill. 1941; dir. publs.-student body mgr., San Francisco State Coll. 1941-44; news ed., Redwood City Tribune, July 1944, managing ed. Nov. 1944-49, ed. 1949---. Dir., Peninsula Newspapers, Inc. 1966---. U.S. Army (1945), WW II. Mem.: Amer. Legion; pres. Jr. C. of C. 1948; pres. Rotary Club, 1950; Freedom of Information Com., Sigma Delta Chi, 1953-55; natl. chmn., Assoc. Press Managing Editors Association, Freedom of Information Committee; president, FOE 1954-55; bd. dirs., Redwood City C. of C. 1954-56; local chmn., Assoc. Press News Execs. Council, numerous coms.; bd. dirs., Calif. Newspaper Publs. Assn. 1954-56; chmn. editors conf. 1955; Amer. Soc. of Newspaper Editors; president Suburbans, Inc. 1955; adv. com. to State Senate Com. on Govt. Adm. Jewish. Hobby: reading, travel. Rec.: golf. Res.: 204 Myrtle St., Redwood City, CA; Office: 901 Marshall St., Redwood City, CA.

SCHWARTZ, ELIZABETH
Educator — Writer
b. Sharon, Wis.; d. Christian and Barbara (Straka) Schwartz; Ph.B., (cum laude), Univ. Chicago, 1927; M.S., Northwestern Univ. 1931. Career: Teacher, Lombard, Ill. pub. schs., 1924-27; Gary, Ind. 1927-29; asst. pub. ofc. Chicago UWCA 1929-30; spec. pub. Ofc. of Pres., Univ. Chicago, 1932-33; teacher, Oak Park Pub. Schs., Ill. 1936-46; Sacramento City Unified Sch. Dist. 1946-66; pgm. asst. lang. arts, 1966-69; chmn. Eng. Dept., Kennedy H.S. 1969---. Founder-dir. Oak Park Chil's. Theater, Ill., 1936-45; Freelance writer; ed. Chi State News, 1959---; co-author, Kaleidoscope Readers, 1969. Mem.: Natl. Council Teachers of English; Calif. Assn. Teachers of Eng.; Internat. Reading Assn.; NEA; Calif. Writers Club; Natl. Audubon Soc.; Delta Kappa Gamma. Res.: 1901 Ninth Ave., Sacramento, CA 95818.

SCHWARTZ, PETER WILLIAM
Association Executive
b. Oct. 23, 1949 Indio, Calif.; s. Nicholas and Erika (Sack) Schwartz; B.A. polit. sci., Cal. State Univ. Fullerton, 1971, Career: with Schwartz Furniture, Corona, 1973; dir. mem. services, Western Home Furnishings Assn., 1975-77; div. sales mgr., Barker Bros., L.A., 1977-78; exec. vice pres., Western Home Furnishings Assn., 1978---. Mem.: Chi Phi chpt., brother master, Alpha Epsilon Pi. Hobby: travel, domestic, foreign. Rec.: theater, sports. Office: 1933 S. Broadway, Suite 244, L.A., CA 90007.

SCHWARZER, WILLIAM W.
U.S. District Judge
b. Apr. 30, 1925, Berlin, Germany, naturalized U.S. cit. 1944; s. John F. and Edith (Daniel) Schwarzer; A.B. cum laude, USC, 1948; LL.B. cum laude, Harvard Law Sch., 1951; m. Anne Halbersleben, Feb. 21, 1951, Cambridge, Mass.; children: Jane Elizabeth, b. 1955; Andrew William, b. 1958. Career: Admitted to

Calif. bar, 1953, U.S Supreme Ct. bar, 1967; teaching fellow, Harvard Law Sch., 1951-52; assoc. and partner, firm McCutchen, Doyle, Brown & Enersen, 1952-76; U.S. Dist. Judge for No. Dist. Calif., San Francisco, 1976---. Counsel Pres.'s Commn. on CIA Activities in U.S., 1975; trustee World Affairs Council No. Calif., 1961---; bd. dirs. William Babcock Meml. Endowment, San Rafael, Calif. 1962---. Served with Intelligence, U.S. Army, 1943-46. Fellow Am. Coll. Trial Lawyers; mem. Am., San Francisco bar assns., State Bar of Calif., Aircraft Owners and Pilots Assn., Far West Ski Assn. Clubs: Bohemian, Mt. Tam Racquet. Contbr. articles to legal and aviation publs. Office: 450 Golden Gate Ave., San Francisco, CA 94102.

SCHWARZOTT, WILHELM
Educator - Concert Pianist
b. Dec. 14, Vienna, Austria; s. Karl and Maria Schwarzott; grad., Royal Music Conservatory, Oslo, Norway, 1939; certificates: Vienna State Acad., Vienna Univ., 1938; M.A. equivalent, Univ. of Denver, 1957; advanced study w/prof. Dagmar Walle-Hansen (Leschetizky's 1st asst.) 8 yrs., pvt. tutoring; m. Eva Hafslund (div.), Feb. 1940, Norway; chil.: Tone, b. 1941 (actress, Nat. Theater, Oslo; poetess, bpu. J.W. Cappelen, Oslo); s. Jan.1944. Career: prof., dir. of Klaverakademiet, Oslo, 1950-55; head, piano dept., Univ. of Denver, 1957-61; and Calif. State Polytech. Univ., San Luis Obispo, 1961-63; faculty, S.F. Conservatory of Music, 1963-67; Lectr. in music, Univ. of Calif. ext., S.F., 1966---; adjudicator and faculty mem., Am. Coll. of Musicians, 1959---; Performer: concert pianist, soloist, chamber music, Europe, 1935---; USA, 1957---; founder, 15-yr. mem., Oslo Chamber Trio; Sibelius String Quartette and other ensembles on Am. Edn. TV and European broadcasts. Mil.: enlisted, Norwegian Army; refugee, Sweden, 1944-45. Mem.: Calif. Music Tchrs. Assn., 1971---, pres. S.F. chpt., 1975-77, dir. 1977---; elected mem. Artist Soc., Norway, 1953; Internat. Platform Assn., 1971. Hobby: philately. Rec.: fishing, skiing. Home: 1882 - 11th Ave., S.F., CA 94122.

SCHWEGMANN, JACK CARL
Environmentalist
b. Nov. 4, 1925, Denver, Colo.; s. Leo B. and Agness (Skene) Schwegmann; B.S., Tulane Univ., 1948; M.S., Univ. Okla., 1950; Ph.D., La. State Univ., 1953; m. Nanette Taylor, Dec. 27, 1948, New Orleans, La.; sons: Gerard Bruce, b. 1949; Michael Carl, b. 1955. Career: with Kaiser Aluminum Chem. Corp., 1953---: dir., Environmental Services, Metals Div., 1967-68; dir. Environmental Services, all corp. divs., 1968---. USAAF, 1944-46. Chmn., Environmental Com., The Aluminum Assn., 1977-78. Mem.: Am. Phytopathological Soc.; Am. Inst. of Biol. Sciences; AAAS; Sci. Research Soc. of Am.; Sigma Xi; N.Y. Acad. of Sci.; Air Pollution Control Assn., dir. 1966-68. Club: Ballena Bay Yacht. Republican. Roman Catholic. Rec.: sail boating. Res.: 2001 Sandcreek Way, Alameda, CA 94501; Office: 300 Lakeside Dr., Oakland, CA 94643.

SCOTT, FRANKLIN D.
Curator
b. July 4, 1901, Cambridge, Mass.; s. George Harvey and Mary Maude (Cole) Scott; Ph.B., Chicago, 1923; Ph.D., Harvard, 1932; 4 hon. doctorates; m. Helen Giddings, May 30, 1925; dau. Mary Karin (Mrs. A.N. Gunn). Career: Tchr., Ill. High Schs., 1921-22, 1923-25; Simpson Coll., Iowa, 1925-28; Wis. State Teachers Coll., 1932-35; Northwestern Univ., 1935-69; now Curator, Honnold Lib., Claremont ---; vis. prof.: USC, summers, 1947, 51; Stanford Univ., 1962-63; Pomona Coll., 1969-70, 78; Univ. Calif., Riverside, 1973. Author: 15 books, several hundred articles in profl. mags. and encycs. Pres., Swedish Pioneer Historical Soc., 1965-67; editor of Quarterly, 1967-74; pres., Lib. of Internat. Rels., Chicago, 1945-47. Mil. OSS, 1942. Mem. University Club of Evanston, pres. 1957, others. Res.: 572 Harrison St., Claremont, CA 91711; Office: Honnold Lib., Claremont, CA.

SCOTT, LOUIS EDWARD
Advertising Agency Executive
b. June 17, 1923, Waterbury, Conn.; s. Louis Arthur and Ellen (Eckert) Scott; B.S., Univ. Calif., Berkeley, 1944; m. Phyllis Corrine Denker, Jan. 27, 1942; children: Susan Louise (Mrs. Paul Revere Hutchinson, Jr.), b. 1945; Eric Richard, b. 1950; Jane Lynn, b. 1955. Career: Acct. Exec., McCarty Co., Los Angeles, 1946-50; with Foote, Cone & Belding, 1950---:

copywriter, 1950-55; account group supr., 1955; vice pres., 1956; gen. mgr., Los Angeles office, 1959; sr. v.p., 1963; now pres., chmn. of Exec. Com., mem. Fin. Com., sr. exec. in charge of western offices, Foote, Cone & Belding Communications, Inc. ---; Dir., Foote, Cone & Belding Advt., Inc. Served U.S. Maritime Serv. and USNR, WW II. Mem.: Am. Assn. of Advt. Agencies, named Western Advt. Man of the Year, 1972; Dir. (past chmn.) Western Region, Los Angeles Advertising Club; Town Hall. Clubs: Jonathan, Balboa Bay, California, Newport Harbor Yacht, Santa Ana Country. Hobbies: golf, yachting. Res.: 2691 Bayshore Dr., Newport Beach, CA 92663; Office: 2727 West 6th St., Los Angeles, CA 90057.

SCOTT, PETER DALE
Author
b. Jan. 11, 1929, Montreal, Quebec, Canada; s. Francis Reginald and Marian Mildred (Dale) Scott; B.A., McGill Univ., 1949, Ph.D., polit. sci., 1955; m. Mary Elizabeth Marshall, June 16, 1956; children: Catherine Dale, b. 1959; Thomas, b. 1961; John Daniel, b. 1964. Career: Lectr. in Polit. Sci., McGill Univ., 1955-56; Canadian Foreign Service, (United Nations, Warsaw, Vienna) 1957-61; Asst. Prof. Speech, Univ. Calif., Berkeley, 1961-66; Asst./Assoc. Prof. of English, 1966---. Guggenheim Fellow, 1969-70. Author: (w/F. Schurmann, R. Zelnik) The Politics of Escalation, 1966; The War Conspiracy, 1972; (w/Paul Hoch, Russell Stetler) The Assassinations, 1976; Crime and Cover-Up, 1977; others. Trustee, Polish Arts and Culture Found., 1970---; Gen. Secty., exec. com. mem., Foisard Soc., 1957---. Hobby: bird-watching. Res.: 2823 Ashby Ave., Berkeley, CA 94705; Office: Univ. of California, Berkeley, CA 94720.

SCOTT, SUSAN REED
Business Consultant
b. 1945, Chicago, Ill.; d. Duane E. and Louise Reed; mem. Soc. of Mayflower Descendents; B.A., polit. sci., Stanford Univ., 1967; M.B.A., Bus., San Jose State Univ., 1978; m. Robert J. Scott, 1971, Livermore. Career: Mgr., KYTE-FM, Peer Broadcasting Co., Livermore, 1968-73; Editorial page ed., editorial writer, columnist, bus. page ed., Tri-Valley Herald, Livermore, 1973-76; columnist, 1977---; licensed real estate sales agent, 1979---; bus. cons., Bay Area firms, 1979---. Awards: Calif. Newspaper Pub. Assn. (CNPA) Award for best editorial series, 1976; Calif. Press Women awards, 1974, 75, 76; Beta Gamma Sigma, 1977. Mem.: Livermore C. of C., dir. 1973-77, v.p. 1977; Calif. Press Women, Bay Dist. Pres. 1975-76. Hobby: politics. Res.: 1590 Foothill Rd., Pleasanton, CA 94566.

SCROGGS, JOYCE F.
Librarian
b. Mar. 6, 1945, San Diego; d. Arden M. and Lucille F. (Scott) Scroggs; B.A., Howard Univ., 1968; M.L.S., Rutgers Sch. of Lib. Service, 1969; m. Raymond F. Balog, 1972, San Francisco. Career: Librarian I, San Francisco Pub. Lib., 1971-72; reference librarian, Sutter Co. Lib., 1972-75; Plumas Co. Librarian, 1975---. Prod., monthly TV show for cable TV, Marysville, 1974-75; pub. article, California Librarian, July 1974. Mem.: Exec. bd., Calif. Co. Librarians' Assn.; 1977 pres., North State chpt., Calif. Librarians Assn.; AAUW; Beta Phi Mu. Hobbies: sewing, 4-H. Rec.: swimming, hiking, fishing. Address: P.O.B. 270, Quincy, CA 95971.

SCUDDER, BARBARA ANTHONY
Civic Beautification
b. Nov. 5, 1914, Alameda, Calif.; d. Edwin Requa, Jr. and Beatrice (Cummings) Anthony; father, E.R. Anthony, supt. coast div., So. Pacific R.R. until 1931; B.A., Univ. Calif., Berkeley, 1935; lifetime elem. tchng. credential; m. Edward Leiter Scudder, Sept. 15, 1936, Berkeley; chil.: Susan (Porter), b. Oct. 4, 1942; Sally (Darran), b. July 7, 1945; Stacy (McCauley). Former owner Anthony House (1630 Central Ave., Alameda), blt. in 1871, Victorian period archit.; promotes preservation and restoration of beautiful Victorians. Mem.: Alumni Assn., Univ. of Calif., life mem. Hobbies: Victorian architecture, piano. Rec.: walking, photog. Home: 22020 Longeway Rd., Sonora, CA 95370.

SCUDERI, SAMUEL A.
Physician
b. Jan. 1, 1902, Italy (est. USA res. 1908); s. Salvatore and Rosa (Vitale) Scuderi; ed. pub. schs.,

Tampa, Fla.; Univ. of Fla. 1921-23; Univ. of Chicago, 1923-25; Univ. of Chicago Med. Sch. 1924-28; M.D. 1928; m. Leah Ciocca, Los Angeles, Calif., Dec. 3, 1932; chil.: Robert, b. Dec. 12, 1937 (m. Carole Ann Monterroso; grandchil.: Jamie Lynn, Philip Michael, Gregory Allen); Thomas, b. Apr. 3, 1942; Richard, b. June 20, 1944. Career: Est. Calif. res. and med. practice, L.A. 1928---; house staff-attending staff, L.A. Co. Hosp., 1928-49; instr. in med. Loma Linda Univ. Med. Sch. 1933-48; L.A. City Phys. (part time), 1937-48; Awards: Hon. by Italian Govt. with Star of Italian Solidarity. Mem.: Sons of Italy, Garibaldina M.B. Soc., Alpha Kappa Kappa; state del., Calif. Med. Assn.; Amer. and L.A. Co. Med. Assns.; BPOE. Catholic. Hobby: golf. Rec.: music, light opera. Res.: 4627 Gainsborough Ave., Los Angeles, CA 90027; Office: 1401 S. Hope St., Suite 419, Los Angeles, CA 90015.

SEABORG, GLENN T.
Scientist — Educator
b. Apr. 19, 1912, Ishpeming, Mich.; s. H. Theodore and Selma (Erickson) Seaborg; A.B. (chem.), UCLA 1934; Ph.D. (chem.), Univ. of Calif., Berkeley, 1937; over 40 hon. D.Sc., Sc.D., LL.D., L.H.D., Lit.D., D.Eng., D.P.A., D.P.S., U.S.A., Can. and Romania, 1951---; m. Helen L. Griggs, June 6, 1942; chil.: Peter Glenn, b. May 31, 1946; Lynne Annette, b. Sept. 6, 1947; David Michael, b. Apr. 22, 1949; Stephen Keith, b. Aug. 14, 1951; John Eric, b. Nov. 18, 1954; Dianne Karole, b. Nov. 2, 1959. Career: Research assoc. (wtih Prof. Gilbert N. Lewis), Coll. of Chem., Univ. of Calif, Berkeley, 1937-39; instr. Dept. of Chem. 1939-41; asst. prof. 1941-45; sect. chief. Metallurgical Lab., Univ. of Chicago, 1942-46; prof. Dept. of Chem., Univ. of Calif., Berkeley, 1945-71; dir. nuclear chem. research, Lawrence Radiation Lab. 1946-58; assoc. dir. 1954-61; chancellor, Univ. of Calif., Berkeley, 1958-61; chmn. U.S. Atomic Energy Commn., Wash., D.C. 1961-71; prof. Univ. of Calif. 1971---; assoc. dir., LBL, 1972---; Apptd. (by Pres. Eisenhower), Pres.'s Sci. Adv. Com., Wash., D.C., 1959-61; bd. trustees Edn. Broadcasting Corp. 1970---; pres. AAAS 1972, chmn. bd. 1973; pres. Am. Chem. Soc., 1976. Researcher: co-discoverer plutonium, americium, curium, berkelium, californium, einsteinium, fermium, mendelevium, nobelium (elements 94-102), and element 106, nuclear energy source isotope (Pu-239) and uranium-233, 1940-58. Author: over 200 papers on gen. subj. of nuclear chem. and nuclear physics, and Ency. articles, publ. 1936---; The Transuranimum Elements: Research Papers, publ, 1949; Prodn. and Separation of U233, U.S. Atomic Energy Comm. 1951; The Actinide Elements, publ. by McGraw-Hill Book Co., Inc., N.Y. 1954; The Transuranium Elements, 1958; Man-made Transuranium Elements, 1963; The Chemistry of the Actinide Elements, publ. London and NYC 1957; Elements of the Universe, 1958; Edn. and the Atom, 1964; Man and Atom, 1971; Nuclear Milestones, 1972. Awards: award in pure chem., Am. Chem. Soc. 1947; named one of America's Ten Outstanding Men of 1947 by U.S. Jr. C. of C. 1948; Wm. H. Nichols Medal by N.Y. Sect., Amer. Chem. Soc. 1948; John Ericsson Gold Medal by Amer. Soc. of Swedish Engrs. 1948; Univ. of Calif. Alumni Award, Alumnus of the Yr., Berkeley, 1948; Nobel Prize for Chem., Stockholm, Sweden, 1951; Dickson Achievement Award, Alumnus of Yr., by UCLA Alumni Assn. 1953; John Scott Award and Medal, City of Philadelphia, Pa. 1953; Perkin Medal by Amer. Sect., Soc. of Chem. Ind. 1957; winner, Fourth Annual Thomas Alva Edison Found. Award for Best Sci. Book for Youth; U.S. Atomic Energy Comm. Enrico Fermi Award, Wash., D.C. 1959; Sci. & Engin. Award of Fed. of Engin. Socs., Drexel Inst. of Tech., Philadelphia, Pa., 1962; Swedish Amer. of Yr. 1962; Distinguished Hon. Award, U.S. State Dept. 1971; Ofcr. Legion of Hon., Repub. of France; Gold Medal Award, American Inst. Chems. 1973; many others. Mem.: Alpha Chi Sigma; Phi Beta Kappa; Sigma Xi; Fellow, Amer. Acad. of Arts and Science; Royal Swedish Acad. of Engin. Scis.; Royal Soc. of Arts (Eng.); Chem. Soc., London, Royal Soc. of Edinburgh. Clubs: Cosmos, Chevychase (Wash., D.C.), Commonwealth, Bohemian. Res.: 1154 Glen Rd., Lafayette, CA 94549; Office: Lawrence Berkeley Lab, Univ. of Calif., Berkeley, CA 94720.

SEARS, DONALD ALBERT
Professor of Linguistics — English
b. May 25, 1923, Portland, Maine; s. Albert J. and Doris (Robinson) Sears; B.A., magna cum laude, Bowdoin COll., 1944; M.A., Harvard Univ., 1949; Ph.D., 1952; m. Oretta

Ferri, Jan. 4, 1964, Arlington, Va.; chil.: Gail (Small), b. Feb. 26, 1946; Jennifer (Talbot), and Jeanne (Prince), b. Dec. 20, 1948; Elizabeth Ellen, b. Nov. 26, 1950; Stephen Donald, M.D., b. Aug. 18, 1952. Career: Instr., Dartmouth Coll., 1948-52; Asst. to Prof., Upsala Coll., 1952-62; Dir. of Freshman English, 1953-60; Assoc. Dir. of Development, 1961-62; Prof. and Chmn of English, Skidmore Coll., 1962-64; Staff Assoc. Am. Council on Edn., Washington, D.C., 1964-65; Prof. of English, Howard Univ., 1965-66. Chair of Languages, Ahmadu Bello Univ., Kano and Zaria, Northern Nigeria, 1966-67; Prof. of English, Calif. State Univ., Fullerton, 1967---, chmn., Faculty Council, 1971-72. Hon. Pos.: Visit. prof., Univ. of Mass., 1957. Exec. Dir., Coll. Eng. Assn., 1962-70; Editor, The CEA Critic, 1960-70; Dir., Book-of-the-Month Club Writing Fellowship Program, 1965-70; Author: The Harbrace Guide to the Library and Research Paper, 1956, 1960, 1973; The Discipline of English, 1963, 74; John Neal, 1978; Co-author (s/Francis X. Connolly) The Sentence in Context, 1960; contbr. literary journs.; poems in reviews and little mags. Recipient: Lindback Found. Award for Distinguished Tchg., 1961; hon. life mem.: Coll. English Assn. of Ind., 1968; Maine Hist. Soc., 1963; Pi Delta Epsilon; Alpha Psi Omega. Served AUS Air Corps, 1943-46; USAF, 1950. Mem.: Coll. English Assn.; Mod. Lang. Assn.; Milton Soc.; Malone Soc.; Linguistic Soc. of Am.; Am. Assn. for Applied Linguistics; Phi Beta Kappa; Lotos Club (NYC); Nat. Lawyers Club (D.C.). Congregational Ch., past sr. deacon. Home: 1448 Sunny Crest Dr., Fullerton, CA 92635; Office: Dept. of Linguistics, Cal. State Univ., Fullerton, CA 92634.

SEARS, HAROLD W.
President, Goodyear Rubber Company
b. Sept. 14, 1920, Decatur, Nebr.; s. Harry A. and Margaret Sears; student, Univ. Nebr. 1939-41, rubber chem., USC, 1948-49; m. Donna Langley, 1946, Calif.; children: Larry, b. 1948; Cathy (Dockery), b. 1949. Career: chemist, plastic and rubber products, 1941-48; owner, pres., Stillman Rubber Co., 1948-60; owner, pres. Bell Metrics, 1960-64; owner, Bettis Rubber Co., 1965-70; owner, pres., Goodyear Rubber Co., 1973. Dir., The Los Angeles Rubber Group. Republican. Catholic. Hobby: pvt. pilot. Res.: 31 August Lane, Newport Beach, CA 92660; Office: 8833 Industrial Lane, Cucamonga, CA 91730.

SEARS, ORETTA FERRI
Superior Court Judge
b. Feb. 1, 1928, Cararra, Italy; d. Angelo Count Ferri and Andreina Countess Baratta F.; desc. Enrico Ferri, founder of Italian Penal system; B.A. summa cum laude, Upsala Coll., 1960; LL.B., J.D., UCLA Law Sch. (mem. Law Review), 1963; m. Donald Albert Sears, Jan. 3, 1965, Arlington, Va.; dau. Gail Aurora (Small), stepchil.: Jennifer (Talbot), Jeanne (Prince), b. Dec. 20, 1948; Elizabeth Sears, b. Nov. 19, 1950; Stephen Donald Sears, M.D., b. Aug. 20, 1952. Career: Trial Attorney, Lands & Natural Resources, Dept. of Justice, Wash., D.C., 1963-66; Lectr. in Law, Ahmadu Bello Univ., N. Nigeria, 1966-67; Depty. Dist. Atty. in charge Writs and appeals sect., 1968--- Orange Co., head of writs and appeals sec., Municipal Court Deputy Dist. Atty., 1968-78; Judge, Superior Ct. of Orange Co., Jan. 1979---. Contbr. legal journs. Awards: Upsala award; Am. Jurisprudence Prize for excellence in Bills and Notes, Sales; Prosecutor of the Month; DA Assn. Award for oustanding case, 1977; performer: radio Florence; stage plays in Italy, 1943-46; Nat. Rollerskating Champion, Italy, 1944-46. Mem.: Advisory com., Atty. Gen., 1974---; appellate com., Dist. Atty's. Assn., 1970---; Calif. Bar, 1963---; Am. and Fed. Bar Assn.s; Orange Co. Bar Assn.; Orange Co. Criminal Bar Assn.; Nat. Lawyers Club (D.C.); Lotos Club (NYC); Coll. English Assn.; (hon.) N.J. Hist. Soc. Republican: sustaining mem., Orange Co. Success Finders. Lutheran. Rec.: breachcombing, rock-hounding. Home: 1448 Sunny Crest Dr., Fullerton, CA 92701; Office: Superior Ct., 800 Civic Center Dr. W., Santa Ana, CA 92701.

SEARS, WILLIAM WHITCOMB
Realtor
b. Mar. 27, 1899, Charlevoix, Mich.; s. Frank C. and Ida (Canfield) Sears; ed. grad. Univ. of Chicago, 1924; m. Martha V. McGavic, Oyster Bay, N.Y., Aug. 8, 1948; chil.: Mrs. H. Hamilton (Maribel) Allport, Jr., b. 1925; (stepson) Philip M. Bethke. Career: Assoc. Gorrell & Co. (Investment securities), 1924-29; mgr. Seneca Securities Corp., Chicago, 1929-37; v.p.-dir., Milbank Corp. of Chicago and Milbank Mgmt. Corp. of NYC 1937-39; Sears Real Estate Co., Winnetka, III. 1939-48; Sears Realty Co., Santa Barbara, Calif.

1949-63; v.p.-treas.-dir., E. Valley Ranch Co., 1964---. Merchant Marine (navigator's papers for any size ship on any ocean, recd. at age 18 yrs.; govt. acclaimed youngest person who ever had or ever will receive such papers); WW I. Mem.: pres. Evanston North Shore Bd. of Realtors, 1947-48; Alpha Delta Phi, Santa Barbara Club, Valley Club of Montecito; v.p.-treas.-dir., Birnam Wood Golf Club, 1967---. Chr. Sci. Rec.: golf. Res.: 2081 China Flat Rd., Santa Barbara, CA 93108; Office: 1941 E. Valley Rd., Santa Barbara, CA.

SEAVER, BLANCHE EBERT
Composer — Civic Worker
b. Sept. 15, 1891, Chicago, III.; d. Theodore and Ann Mathilde (Mathisen) Ebert; ed. grad. Chicago Mus. Coll. 1911; (hon.) Dr. Humane Letters, USC 1966; (hon.) D.F.A., Pepperdine Coll. 1961; LL.D., Pomona Coll. 1970; B.B.A., Woodbury Coll. 1970; L.H.D., Okla. Chr. Coll. 1972; D.F.A., MacMurray Coll., III. 1973; m. Frank Roger Seaver, Sept. 16, 1916. Career: Piano teacher, accompanist coach, Hull House, Chicago, 1909-12; Los Angeles, 1912-16; Composer: spec. arr., Battle Hymn of the Republic, Phila. Sym. Orch. (soloist and chorus Leopold Stokowski cond.), 1919; Calling Me Back To You, 1921; Just For Today, 1926; If God Sent Me You, 1927; The Flower, 1928; Stay With Me, O Lord, 1941; Alone With Thee, 1932; No Llores Yo Volveri, 1934; Morrow Rock, 1937; Remember Me, 1946; Close at Thy Feet, My Lord (I come to kneel), others. Chmn. The Seaver Inst.; (hon.) chmn. Hydril. Co., L.A.; est. Frank R. Seaver Coll. of Liberal Arts, Pepperdine Univ. 1975. Awards: Jane Addams Award for Distinguished Serv. by Rockford Coll. 1963; Woman of the Yr., L.A. Times, 1963; S.A.R. Award for Outstanding Citizenship, 1965; Freedom Club Award, 1966; Grand Dame, Knightly Order of St. Brigitte, L.A. 1966; Grand Cross Dame, Knightly Order of St. Brigitte, Naples, Italy, Oct. 1966; Bd. Trustees Award, Pepperdine Alumni Assn. 1968; Blanche and Frank R. Seaver Chair of Sci., Pomona Coll. 1969; John Wayne Golden Circle of Calif. Award, 1970; Geo. Washington Award, Freedoms Found. at Valley Forge, 1970; Merit Award, Repub. Party of L.A. Co. 1970; County of L.A. Most Hon. Citizen, 1970; Seal of L.A. by Mayor Yorty, 1970; Amer. Patriot Award, American Educational League, 1971; Los Angeles Co. Chpt. Freedoms Found. Hon. Award, 1971; Distinguished Amer. Award, 1971; Mary and Joseph League Hon. 1971; Chr. Freedom Found. Patriot of Yr. Award, 1971; Distinguished Patriot Award, Relig. Heritage of Amer., Wash., D.C. 1973; Council of Trustees Award, Freedoms Found. 1973. Mem.: Nine O'Clock Players; dir. Las Madrinas, 1941-44; trustee, L.A. Sym. Assn. 1949-51; adv. board, 1951-55; chairman (sponsoring opera patronesses) Symphony Orch. Patroness Guild; (charter) chmn., Hollywood Bowl Patroness Com. 1952---; pgm. chmn., Women's Com. Sym. Salons, 1956-60; adv. bds.: St. Elizabeth Day Nursery, Soc. Serv. Aux., St. Anne's Hosp. Guild, L.A.; dir. St. John's Hosp. Guild, L.A. Orphanage Guild and St. Vincent's Hosp. Aux., L.A.; founder-natl. dir., Achievement Rewards for Coll. Scis. 1958---; trustee, USC 1960---; trustee, Pomona Coll., Calif. 1964---; bd. assocs., Children's Hosp., L.A., bd. dirs. 1967---; (hon.) bd. trustees, First Congregational Ch., L.A. 1966. Res.: 20 Chester Place, Los Angeles, CA 90007.

SEAVER, RICHARD CARLTON
President, Hydril Company
b. June 10, 1922, Los Angeles; s. Byron Dick and Mary Louise (Schmidt) Seaver; B.A., Pomona Coll., 1946; J.D., Univ. Calif., Berkeley, 1949; postgard. study, USC Sch. of Law, 1950; m. Sallie Tiernan (div.); children: Richard, Jr., b. 1947; Christopher, b. 1949; Patrick, b. 1950; Victoria, b. 1953; Martha, b. 1955; m. 2d. Joan Tierney Sutherland, Nov. 10, 1971. Career: Admitted to Calif. bar, 1950; assoc., law firm Thelen, Marrin, Johnson and Bridges, Los Angeles, 1950-57; Secty. and Counsel, Hydril Company, Los Angeles, 1957-64; pres. 1964---. Dir.: Episcopal Ch. Found., N.Y.; DeAnza Land and Leisure Corp.; The Seaver Inst., Pres.; Merchants and Mfrs. Assn.; Petroleum Equip. Suppliers Assn.; Estelle Doheny Eye Found.; Republican Assocs.; Trustee: Pomona Coll., Harvard Sch., Hosp. of the Good Samaritan; mem. The Stanford Cabinet, Stanford Univ.; Univ. Bd., Pepperdine Univ.; Council for Marine Sci., USC; Advisory Council, Coll. of Bus. Adm. Found., Univ. Texas at Austin. Awards: The Bishops Award of Merit, Episcopal Diocese of Los Angeles, 1968; LL.D. (hon.), Pepperdine Univ., 1970; Order of the Cross, Empire of Iran, 1977. Served 2d Lt. to Capt., AUS, 1942-46; Infan., Pacific Theatre; decorated Bronze Star Medal

with Oak Leaf Cluster, USAR, 1946-51. Clubs: California, Newport Harbor Yacht (Commodore 1970), Los Angeles Yacht, St. Francis Yacht (S.F.), Los Angeles Country. Episcopalian. Res.: 149 S. Bristol Ave., Los Angeles, CA 90049; 8 Bay Island, Balboa, CA 92661; Office: 714 W. Olympic Blvd., Los Angeles, CA 90015.

SEBRELL, JOHN BARHAM
Business Owner — Author
b. May 21, 1907, Sebrell, Va.; s. Benjamin Wilmer and Annie Barham (Little) Sebrell; ed. Eastman Sch. of Bus., Randolph Macon Coll.; m. Peggy Dick Wallace, El Toro Marine Base, Jan. 12, 1948; (stepdau.) Anne Wallace McKechnie. Career: Pres., Sebrell Pen Co.; pres.-dir., J.B. Sebrell Adv. Agcy., Los Angeles; pres. J.B. Sebrell Corp.; pres. J.B. Sebrell Inds., Inc.; pres. Gypsum Corp.; owner, J.B. Sebrell Co. (mfr. swimpool pumps, heaters, filters, diving bds., 7 hundred swimpool accessories and chem. prods.); owner J.B. Sebrell Printing Co. and Abbey Envelope Mfg. Co.; propr.-publ. Swimpool Advertiser; ed.-publ., Small Bus. Mag. Author: How to Market a New Product, 1947; How to Double Your Sales, 1947; How to Collect Due Accounts and Cut Your Credit Losses, 1947; J.B. Sebrell Offset Scrapbook of Office Forms and Advt. Ideas, 1947; How Not to Prune and How To Prune Fruit and Shade Trees, 1949; How to Keep Your Pool Beautiful and Clean. Mem.: pres. Small Bus. Men of Amer.; Better Bus. Bur.; Direct Mail of L.A. Club, L.A. Ath., Execs. Club, Marathon Club, Phi Kappa Sigma. Temple Meth. Ch. Hobbies: Inventing, investing in new ideas. Rec.: swimming. Res.: 8562 Parrot Ave., Downey, CA 90240; Office: 301 S. San Pedro St., Los Angeles, CA 90013.

SECHLER, ERNEST E.
Professor of Aeronautics, Emeritus
b. Nov. 17, 1905, Pueblo, Colo.; B.S. Engring. Calif. Inst. of Tech., 1928, M.S. mech. engring. 1929, M.S., aeronautics, 1930, Ph.D., aeronautics, 1934; m. Margaret Lorraine Nelson, June 18, 1931; dau. Lorraine Barbara (Emery), b. 1936. Career: Instr., Cal. Inst. of Tech., 1930-37, asst. prof., assoc. prof., prof. of Aeronautics, 1937-76, exec. ofcr. of Aeronautics, 1966-71, Prof. Emeritus, 1976---. Profl. Calif. Engr. Cons.: AF, 1939-40; TRW Systems, 1953---; No. Am. Aviation, 1965-68, 1973; Lockheed Aircraft Co., 1975---(on windmill programs). Mil.: Cons., AF Sci. Advisory Bd., 1945; Nat. Advisory Com. for Aeronautics, subcom. on structures, 1949-58; Vista Project, 1951; NASA, chmn. com. on structural design, 1958-61, chmn. com. on space vehicle structures, 1961-63; mem. SABER (Secty. Navy's Advis. Bd. on Edn. Requirements); USFAA cons. to supersonic transport devel. program 1968. Mem.: Am. Inst. Aeron. & Astron.; AF Assn.; Sigma Xi; Soc. for Exptl. Stress Analysis; Calif. Acad. of Scis.; Nat. Def. Preparedness Assn.; others. Hobbies: gardening, lapidary, jewelry making. Rec.: foreign travel. Res.: 2265 Montecito Dr., San Marino, CA 91008; Office: Cal. Tech., Pasadena, CA 91125.

SEE, CAROLYN
Writer — Educator
b. Jan. 13, 1934, Pasadena; d. George and Kate Louise (Sullivan) Laws; Ph.D., UCLA, 1963; m. Richard See, 1954, Los Angeles; dau. Lisa Lenine, b. 1955; m. 2d. Thomas Sturak, 1964, San Diego; dau. Clara Elizabeth Marya, b. 1965. Career: Instr. of English, UCLA, 1963-65; Assoc. Prof. of English, Loyola Marymount University, 1970---. Author: The Rest is Done With Mirrors, Little, Brown, 1970; Blue Money, David McKay, 1973; Mothers, Daughters, Coward McCann, Geoghegan, 1977; Rhine Maiden (novel in progress). Freelance writer: over 100 magazine pieces, 1967---: in Esquire, Atlantic, Sports Illustrated, McCalls, Today's Health, TV Guide, others; TV scripts: two episodes ABC's Family, 1978. Mem.: Modern Languages Assn., Writers Guild of Am. Democrat. Hobby: serious gardening. Rec.: disco dancing. Res.: 2627 Hodgson Cir., Topanga, CA 90290; Office: 7107 West 80th St., Los Angeles, CA 90045.

SEELEY, T. TALBOT
Psychiatrist — Educator
b. June 17, 1943, Dayton, Ohio; s. Frank Perry and Edith (Alexander) Seeley; rel. Nathanial Steven Seeley, engr. Panama Canal, mem. NY Stock Exchange; grad., Phillips Exeter Acad.; B.A., Oberlin Coll., 1965; M.D. Univ. of Rochester Sch. of Med. and Dentistry, 1969; m. Diane Masters, M.D., Feb. 28, 1976, Ventura, Calif.; chil.:

Louise Talbot, b. Mar. 23, 1969; Stanly, b. Dec. 24, 1972. Career: Residency in pathology, bd. eligible, 1974; residency in psychiatry, bd. eligible, 1978; post doctoral fellow, Nat. Inst. of Health, cancer research, 1972-74; pathologist, Sacramento Co. Coroners (Juan Corona murders), 1972-74; med. dir., Yolo County Health and Family Planning, 1973-74; researcher, UCLA, 1977-79, Asst. Clin. Prof. of Psychiatry ---. Contbr.: Calif. Medicine; Domes; In Vitro; Dir., Seeley Found.; A.S.S.E.C.T., therapist educator; S.S.S. advis. bd. Mem.: Am. Psychiat. Assn.; Internat. Acad. Pathologists; Soc. Sigma Xi. Mem. Young Republicans, 1961-62. Awarded Nathanial Gordon Prize in biblical studies, 1961. Rec.: guitar, swimming. Home: 612 W. Duarte, Arcadia, CA; Office: 9701 Wilshire Blvd., Beverly Hills, CA.

SEEMANN, GERALD ROBERT
Company President
b. Mar. 29, 1937, Melrose Park, Ill.; s. Robert W. and Leona (Klein) Seemann; B.S., mech. engr., Texas Tech. Univ., 1959; MSME, Okla State Univ., 1960; Ph.D., astro sci., Northwestern Univ., 1963; m. Lorraine M. Sayegh, June 14, 1969, Los Angeles; children: Michelle, b. 1973; Scott, b. 1976. Career: Mgr. of Reentry Physics Research, Litton Systems, Inc. 1964-68; v.p., Engineering Flight Dynamics Research Corp., 1968; chief of Thermo Optics, McDonnell Douglas Astro. West, 1968-70; founder, pres., Developmental Sciences, Inc., City of Industry, 1970---. NATO Lectr. in five countries, 1963-64, 1968. Publs.: Over 50 profl. papers and articles, 1161---, contbr. over 75 tech. reports. Hon. Trustee, Nat. Assn. of Remotely Piloted Vehicles. Registered Profl. Engr. Mem.: L.A. C. of C., chmn. Mass Transit Com.; Am. Inst. of Aero. & Astro., Assoc. Fellow; Inst. for Advance. of Engrs., Fellow; Sigma Xi; Tau BetaPi; Phi Delta Theta; Am. Soc. of Mech. Engrs., Small Bus. Com.; Am Mensa Club. Methodist. Res.: 3372 Albedo St., Hacienda Hts., CA 91745; Office: 15757 E. Valley Blvd. (P.O.B. 1264), City of Industry, CA 91749.

SEGIL, CLIVE MELWYN
Orthopedic Surgeon
b. Oct. 24, 1938, Repub. of So. Africa; s. Arnold and Miriam Segil; M.B., B.Ch., Witwatersrand Univ., Johannesburg, 1963; F.R.C.S. (Edin.), 1967; F.A.C.S., 1973; m. Larraine Diane Wolfowitz, Mar. 9, 1969, Johannesburg; son, James Harris, b. 1971. Career: Intern, Johannesburg Gen. Hosp., 1964; Surgical Resident, 1965; Orthopedic Resident, 1967-69; Royal Coll. of Surgeons, Edin., 1966; Hadassah Hosp., Jerusalem, 1966; Clin. Asst., Sir John Charnley, Wrightington, Eng., 1970; Clin. Research Fellow, Toronto East Gen. & Orthopedic Hosp., Univ. of Toronto, 1971-72; Orthopedic Surgeon, pvt. practice, Beverly Hills, 1976---. Attending orth. surgeon, Cedars/Sinai Med. Center, Children's Hosp., L.A. New Hosp., Midway Hosp. Mem.: L.A. County, Calif., Am. Med. Assns.; So. African Med. Assn.; So. African Orthopedic Assn.; So. Calif. Rheumatism and Arthritis Found.; Secty. Cedars/Sinai Alumni Assn. Diplomate Am. Bd. of Orthopedic Surgery. Office: 8920 Wilshire Blvd., No. 335, Beverly Hills, CA 90211.

SEHON, JAMES D.
School District President
b. Sept. 26, 1943, Larksport, Miss.; s. LeRoy and Belle Sehon; nephew of Charles L. Richland, inventor schull boat hulls & mech. bailer; degrees: A.A., B.A., M.A.; m. Karen Seifert, June 21, 1964, St. Helena, Mont.; chil.: Jason, b. Sept. 16, 1968; d. Jamie, b. Dec. 17, 1970; Alice Ann, b. Apr. 16, 1978. Career: sch. tchr., 1965-68; constr. supr., 1968-72; county supr., 1972-76; school supt., Bella Vista Sch. Dist., 1976---. Pres., P.D.K.; lectr. A.P.A. Author: Wildlife of Northern Calif., Prentice-Hall, 1969. Served USN, U.S.S. Midway. Mem.: Elks, Kiwanis, Lions, Rotary East, Grange Hall 1603. No. Valley Baptist ch., elder. Hobbies: hunting, writing. Rec.: foosball, shuffleboard. Home: 3409 Wimbledon, Redding, CA 96001; Office: Box 70, Bella Vista, CA.

SEIN, KOUNG
Physician
b. Jan. 8, 1938, Burma; s. U. Po Aung and Daw Pu Sein; M.D. 1960; Fellow, Am. Coll. of Cardiology, 1978; m. Htay Kyi, Burma; children: William A., Thidor, Ommar. Career: Med. Internship, St. Clare's Hosp., NYC 1971-72; Resident Albert Einstein Coll. of Med. 1972-74; Cardiology Fellow, Western Rescue Med. Sch., 1974-76; Pvt. Practice, cardiovascular diseases, Glendale, 1976---; Chief of Med., No.

Glendale Hosp., 1979---; Chmn., Cardiac Catheterization Com., Glendale Mem. Hosp., 1979---. Diplomate Am. Bd. of Internal Med., Cardiovascular Diseases; mem. Am. Coll of Physicians. Rec.: golf, tennis; Res.: 4020 Hampstead Rd., La Canada-Flintridge, CA 91011; Office: 655 N. Central Ave., Glendale, CA 91203.

SEKELY, STEVE
Motion Picture Director — Writer
b. Feb. 25, 1899, Budapest, Hungary; s. Marcel and Maria (Wechsler) Sekely; ed. Coll. of Hungary; m. Klara (Baba) Majos De Nagyzsennye (step-daughter of Count Balazs Forgach), Rome, Italy, 1954. Career: First short story, publ. Hungary mag. at age 15 yrs.; writer, newspaperman; foreign corr. in Ger., France; prod. one-act plays, Hungary, Ger., Austria, France; writer, many short stories, mot. pic. scripts; dir. Rhapsody der Liebe (silent film), Ger. 1927; dir. Universal Pics. (first talkie, Europe), 1928; dir. Lila Akaz, Budapest, 1934, dir. remake by Hungarofilm M.P. Ind. 1973; dir.-prod. 61 feat. films, 46 TV films (Hungary, Austria, Ger., Fr., Italy, Eng., Mex., Spain, India, Hollywood); Dir. tr. films, USN, WW II; Mem. of the Sovereign Military Order of Malta (Knight of Malta), 1977---. Mem.: Fellow Internat. Inst. of Arts and Letters, France; Mot. Pic. Acad. Arts and Scis.; Natl. Acad. TV Arts and Scis.; Societe des Auteurs, Fr.; Racquet, Century Club, Palm Springs. Catholic. Hobbies: reading, travel. Res.: 248 Vereda Norte, Palm Springs, CA 92262.

SELETZ, EMIL
Neurosurgeon — Sculptor
b. Feb. 12, 1909, Chicago; s. I. Joseph and Esther (Goldberg) Seletz; sisters: Rachelle Seletz, M.D. (noted surgeon and art critic) and Jeanette Seletz, Ph.D. (painter, poet, novelist); M.D., Temple Univ., Sch. of Med., 1932; m. Sylvia Fine, Jan. 2, 1950, Las Vegas, Nev.; chil.: Josepha, M.D. (surgeon), b. Sept. 26, 1950; James Jay, J.D. (pianist, atty.), b. Feb. 28, 1952; Med. Career: Postgrad. work in neurosurg., L.A. Co. Gen. Hosp. 1932-36, Johns Hopkins Hosp., 1936-37; pvt. practice in neurosurg., 1938---; attending in neurosurg. and asst. prof., L.A. Co.-USC Med. Center, 1938-64; author: textbook, Surgery of Peripheral Nerves, 50 sci. papers on brain & spine surgery; inventor: new surgical instruments incl. nonrigid brain canula; lectr. bar. assns. and med. socs. on medicolegal aspects of brain injuries; fellow, Am. Coll. of Surgeons. Mem.: Internat. Coll. of Surgeons, Am. Assn. Neurologic Surgeons, Royal Soc. of Med., London, others. Maj. AUS Med. Corps, 1942-46; Chief of Neurosurg., Wakeman Gen. Hosp., Ind. Art Career: Portrait sculpture commns. incl.: Sir William Osler, Albert Einstein, Verne C. Hunt, Joseph Widney, Walter Dandy, Norman Topping, Robert-Gordon Sproul, Howard C. Naffziger, Ben Gurion, Will Rogers, F.D. Roosevelt; three heroic Lincoln sculptures for L.A. Co. Adminstrn. Bldg.; Orange Co. Court House; Temple Univ. Law Sch., Phila. (Nov. 1978); Heroic Beethoven. Awards: five 1st prizes in West Coast art shows: L.A. Painters and Sculptors Club, 1951, 53; Artists of the S.W., 1951, 53, 55. Mem.: Harvey Cushing Soc.; dir. L.A. Authors Club, 1956-59; dir., Artist of the S.W., 1956-59; Painters and Sculptors Club; Calif. Art Club. Office: 9201 Sunset Blvd., Los Angeles, CA 90069.

SELETZ, JEANETTE
Poet — Novelist
b. Dec. 19, 1912, Chicago; d. I. Joseph and Esther (Goldberg) Seletz; sister Rachelle Seletz, M.D., noted L.A. Proctologist; bro. Emil S., M.D., Neurosurgeon and portrait sculptor; Ph.D., lit., Univ. Chicago, 1935. Career: writer: editor, Poet, 1932-38; contr. Poet's Corner, Calif. Poets, 1932; The Crown Anthology of Verse, 1938; The Poetry House, 1938; Eminent American Poets, 1936; assoc. editor: Poetry, Caravan Fla., 1936-38, Sev. Mags.; editor, Versemaker; contr. newspapers; Author medical novel, Hope Deferred (from which TV Series, Ben Casey derived), transcribed into Braille by Lib. of Congress, 1946; Jone Brent, M.D., Col. of Poetry, pub. Warren H. Green, St. Louis. Painter: seascapes and still life. Mem.: Order of Bookfellows, Womens Poetry League, Writers Guild. Rec.: painting. Home: 4421 Dundee Dr., Hollywood, CA.

SELETZ, RACHELLE
Physician — Proctologist — Teacher
b. Sept. 15, 1906, Chicago; d. I. Joseph and Esther (Goldberg) Seletz; sister, Jeanette Seletz, poet, painter, novelist; brother Emil S., Neurosurgeon and sculptor;

M.D., Univ. of Illinois, 1926. Career: residency in Proctology, L.A. Co. Gen. Hosp., 1927-30; instr. in resident training program, 1930-42; staff mem. & Proctologic clin. service, Queen of Angels Hosp. and Coll. of Med. Evangelists, 1935-45; Chief and sr. attending proctologist, Cedars Sinai Med. Center, 1935-79. Originator new painless technique in proctologic surgery, 1950; contr. numerous sci. papers to prol. journs. Mem.: Am. Proctologic Soc.; AMA; CMA. Avocations: violin, literature, art. Office: 9301 Sunset Blvd., Los Angeles, CA 90069.

SELIG, ROBERT WILLIAM, JR.
Marine Products Company President
b. May 8, 1939, Denver; s. Robert William and Olive S. (Slinde) Selig; B.A., in Econs., Colo. Coll., 1961; diploma in internat. bus. Netherlands Inst. for Representation Abroad, Breukelen, 1960; M.B.A. in Fin., Stanford Univ. 1969; m. Joyce Archer, Dec. 22, 1962; children: Erik Matthew, Wendi Janine, Robin Merewyn. Career: Pres., Davis Instruments Corp., San Leandro, Calif., 1969---, also dir.; dir. Fafco Corp. Fund raiser YMCA, Stanford Univ. Served to capt. Intelligence Corps., U.S. Army, 1962-67. Mem. Colo. Coll. Alumni Assn. (pres. Norcal) Alpha Kappa Psi, Beta Theta Pi. Res.: 3 Cedar Lane, Woodside, CA 94062; Office: 642 143rd St., San Leandro, CA 94578.

SELVIG, JETTIE COLEEN PIERCE
Attorney at Law
b. Dec. 16, 1932, Bee Branch, Van Buren Co., Ark.; d. Jefferson Davis, Sr., and Ruba Ann (Bivens) Pierce; LL.B., Ark. Law Sch., Little Rock, 1954; m. Rolf Stanley Selvig, Sr. (Oslo, Norway); sons: Rolf Stanley, Jr., b. Feb. 25, 1963; Erik Keith, b. Nov. 20, 1965; John Leif, b. Dec. 25, 1966. Career: Admitted to Ark. bar, 1953, Calif. bar, 1961, U.S. Supreme Ct. 1969; pvt. practice law, Belli & Choulos firm. Awards: Certificate of Hon., Bd. of Supvs. City-Co. San Francisco, 1969; Countess of Pulaski, Proclamation by Quorum Ct. of Pulaski Co., Ark. 1969. Mem.: Homestead PTA; Calif. Bar Assn.; S.F. Trial Lawyers Assns.; Calif. Applicant's Attys. Assn.; Amer. Bar Assn. S.F. Bar Assn. (coms.: Law Day, Juvenile Ct., Fed. Ct. Applate); (life) Lawyer's Club of S.F. (coms. and del. State Bar Conv.); Queen's Bench Assn.; of S.F. Bay Area Women Lawyers (exec. bd., chmn. pub., asst. secty.-treas., coms.); (life) pres. Natl. Assn. Women Lawyers (State del., assembly del., bus. mgr., treas., v.p.), 1969-70; Res.: Mill Valley, CA; Office: Belli Bldg., 722 Montgomery St., San Francisco, CA 94111.

SERUTO, JOSEPH GEORGE
Company President
b. Jan. 14, 1912, Tusa, Italy; B.A. chem., Ohio State Univ.; M.S., chem., N.Y. Univ.; m. Mary Elizabeth Reed, Jan. 20, 1940, St. Louis, Mo.; chil.: Anna Dale (Sullivan), b. Dec. 23, 1940; Katherine (Sullivan), b. Dec. 14, 1943; Joseph Vincent, b. June 28, 1945; Barbara (Legacy), b. Mar. 26, 1950; Nanvy, b. July 8, 1956. Career: research chemist, Am. Cyanamid, Bound Brook, N.J., 1940-48; pres., Western Organics, Inc., Norwalk, 1948-61; pres., gen. mgr., Specialty Organics, Inc., Irwindale, 1961---. Patentee: chemical patents on dyestuffs and intermediates. Chem. researcher on war projects. Mem.: Am. Chem. Soc. and Am. Inst. of Chem. Engrs. Rec.: boating. Home: 9743 Val St., Temple City, CA; Office: 5263 N. Fourth St., Irwindale, CA 91706.

SERVOS, KURT
Professor of Geology
b. Dec. 20, 1928, Anrath, W. Germany; s. Albert and Ilse Servos; B.S., Rutgers Univ., 1952; M.S., Yale Univ., 1954; Career: Sr. Curator (geol.), N.Y. State Mus., 1956-57; Asst. Prof. of Mineralogy, Stanford Univ., 1957-60; Asst. Prof. of Geology, Cal. State Univ., Hayward, 1964; Geologist, Stanford Research Inst., 1966-67; Prof. of Geol., Menlo Coll., 1967---. Contbr. articles & revs., sci. journs. Dir., Pippin's Pocket Opera, 1978---. Mem.: Tau Delta Phi, 1948---; Peninsula Geol. Soc., treas. 1976-77; Bay Area Mineralogists, co-found. & treas. 1972---; Geol. Soc. of Am., Minerological Soc. of Am.; Am. Crystallographic Assn.; Mineralogical Assn. of Canada; Geochem. Soc.; Internat. Assn. of Geochem. and Cosmochem.; Deutsche Mineralogische Gesellschaft; Mineralogical Soc. (Gr. Brit.). Jewish. Hobbies: opera. M.C. Escher. Res.: 1281 Mill St., Menlo Park, CA 94025; Office: Dept. of Geol., Menlo Coll., Menlo Park, CA, 94025.

SESSLER, ANDREW M.
Director, Lawrence Berkeley Laboratory

b. Dec. 11, 1928, Brooklyn, N.Y.; s. David and Mary (Baron) Sessler; B.A., math., Harvard Univ., 1949; M.A. 1951, Ph.D., 1953, theoretical physics, Columbia Univ.; m. Gladys Lerner, Sept. 23, 1951, NYC; children: Daniel, b. 1954; Jonathan, b. 1956; Ruth, b. 1957; Lorna, b. 1964; Career: Asst. Prof., Ohio State Univ., 1954-58; Midwestern Universities Research Assn., 1955-56; Sabbatical Leave at Lawrence Berkeley Lab., 1959-60; Assoc. Prof., Ohio State Univ., 1958-61; Lawrence Berkeley Lab., 1961---, now director. Mem. High Energy Physics Advisory Panel, AEC, 1969-72; Argonne Universities Assn. Com. on High Energy Physics, 1971-73; editorial bd., Nuclear Instruments and Methods; Fellow, Am. Physical Soc.; Sigma Xi; AAAS. Jewish. Rec.: bicycling, backpacking, skiing. Res.: 3071 Buena Vista Way, Berkeley, CA 94708; Office: Lawrence Berkeley Laboratory, Univ. of Calif., Berkeley, CA 94720.

SETE, BOLA
Acoustical Guitarist

b. July 16, 1923, Rio de Janeiro, Brazil; s. Acacio and Hilda (Santos) de Andrade; M.Music, Rio de Janeiro Conservatory, 1946; m. Glada Anne Hurd, Feb. 8, 1971, Hollywood. Career: Formed own musical group, 1950, toured South America, 1950-53; toured Europe 1953-58, Puerto Rico 1959; plyaed with Dizzy Gillespie, 1962; solo acoustical guitar concerts, 1971---. Named New Guitarist of the Year, Downbeat Mag., 1965; Recipient European Film Festival Award for best original music in a Documentary, 1967; Cindy Award, 1968. Res.: 66 Buckelew St., Marin City, CA 94965.

SEYMORE, WILLIAM ANDREWARTHA
Life Insurance Company Executive

b. Jan. 16, 1943, Greensburg, Pa.; s. Francis G. and Rosehanna (Andrewartha) Seymore; student, Duff's Business Coll., Pittsburgh, Pa.; m. Elizabeth Waters, Feb. 20, 1971, Las Vegas, Nev.; Children: David Matthew, b. 1965; Mary Elizabeth, b. 1961; Joshua William, b. 1972. Career: with firm of Deeley, Davies, Mulvihill & Rehlin, Pittsburgh, 1962-65; Haskins & Sells, Honolulu, and Los Angeles, 1966-74; with California Life Group, 1974---, now exec. vice pres. USN, 1965-66. Mem. Am. Inst. of CPAs, Jonathan Club. Rec.: basketball, golf. Res.: 2353 E. Burnside, Simi Valley, CA 93065; Office: 3255 Wilshire Blvd., Los Angeles, CA 90010.

SEYMOUR, JOHN
Mayor

b. Dec. 1937, Chicago, Ill.; s. John, Sr. and Helen L. Seymour; B.Sc., UCLA, 1972; grad. Sch. of Mortgage Banking, Stanford Univ.; G.R.I., Realtor's Inst.; m. Judy, Orange County; children: Jack, Lisa, Shad, Jeffrey, Sarena. Career: founder, prin., Seymour Realty and Investment Co., Anaheim, 1965---. Elected City Councilman, 1974, reelected through 1982, served as Mayor Pro Tempore, 1974-77, elected Mayor, 1978-80. Apptd., City Planning Commn., 1970; pres., Anaheim Beautiful, 1973; bd. dir., Anaheim Family YMCA. Mem. C. of C., pres. 1973; mem. Anaheim Bd. of Realtors, pres. 1969; mem. Calif. Real Estate Assn., 1st v.p. 1978, chmn. Make Am. Better Com.; Anaheim Rotary Club. USMC, 1955-59. Mem. Garden Grove Community Ch. Rec.: handball, golf, tennis. Office: 204 E. Lincoln Ave., Anaheim, CA 92805.

SHADE, JAMES WILLIAM BALL
Architect

b. Dec. 7, 1926, Salem, Ore.; s. Hobert Eugene and Gertrude (Hoppe) Shade; B. of Architecture, Univ. of Ore., 1951; m. Patricia I. Southard, June 18, 1953, Eugene, Ore.; chil.: Nancy Ann., b. Oct. 10, 1958; Carol Ann, b. June 8, 1961; Career: prin. James W.B. Shade & Assoc., AIA Architects & Planners, Turlock and Modesto ---. Mil. USNR, 1944-46. Mem.: Coll. Council, Evangel. Coll., Springfield, Mo.; Bethany Bible Coll., Santa Cruz; Century and Arrowhead clibs, Cal. State COll., Stanislaus; Full Gospel Bus.men's bd. dir., past pres.; Turlock Pkg. Commn.; Turlock Beautification Com.; Turlock Planning Commn.; chmn., Turlock Interchurch Fellowship; Modesto-Turlock Campus Life bd. dir.; Rotary Club bd. dir.; bd. dir. The Met (Cal Christian Center); Turlock Golf & Country Club; Turlock Racquet Club; Emanuel Hosp., Turlock, past dir.; Turlock Exchange Club, past pres.; Turlock C. of C., past dir.; AIA, past pres., treas. Sierra Valley chpt.; Turlock Aesthetic Com., past chmn; Safety commn., past chmn. Assemblies of God; deacon, Sun. sch. supt., tchr. Hobbies: photog., flying. Rec.: golf,

racquetball, handball. Home: 1501 La Salle Dr., Turlock, CA; Office: 310 E. Main St., Turlock, CA 95380.

SHAINLINE, JOHN WILLIAM
University Administrator

b. June 20, 1923, Norristown, Pa.; s. Thomas and Mary; A.B., psychology, history, Gettysburg Coll., 1947; M.A., edn./admin., Columbia Univ., 1952; Licensed Family, Child, Marriage Counselor; certified Rehabilitation Counselor, Columbia Univ. 1955; m. Constance Eudora Carter, Aug. 20, 1969; children: Mike, Jan, Leslie, Craig, Dennis. Career: Dean of Students, Gettsburg Coll., 1957-65; Dean of Students, Asst. to Pres., Cumberland County Coll. 19565-66; Asst. Dean of Students, Cal. State Univ., Long Beach, 1966-69, Dean of Students, 1969-70, Vice Pres. for Student Affairs, 1971---. Vocational cons. Social Security Adminstrn.; cons. in drug abuse Title III Project. Bd. Dir.: Cal. State Univ., L.B. Found., Forty-Niner Shops, Forty-Niner Athletic Found.; Long Beach YMCA, 1976---; Nat. Rehabilitation Assn., Harbor Chpt., 1970---(pres. 1971); St. Mary's Med. Center, Long Beach, 1976---. Author: Handbook for Faculty Advisors, The Entering Student (with others), Drug Abuse and You, The Danger of LSD: Do We Have The Answer? (with C. Lee Chandler). Awards: subject of Yearbook dedication, Gettysburg Coll. 1965; Human Rels. Commn. Achievement Award, Student Affairs Div., Cal. State Univ., L.B., 1973; named to Hall of Fame, Eisenhower H.S., Norristown, Pa., 1978. USMC, 1942-45. Mem.: Calif. Marriage Counselors Assn.; Nat. Assn. Student Personnel Adminstrs.; Am. Calif. Personnel and Guidance Assn.; Acad. of Rel. and Mental Health. Lutheran. Res.: 371 Margo Ave., Long Beach, CA 90803; Office: 1250 Bellflower Blvd., Long Beach, CA 90804.

SHALLENBERGER, GARVIN F.
Attorney at Law

b. Jan. 7, 1921, Beloit, Wis.; s. Garvin D. and Grace Shallenberger; B.A., Univ. Mont., 1942; J.D., Univ. Calif., Berkeley, 1949; m. Mary Louise Hillman, May 5, 1945, San Francisco; children: Diane (Brunson), b. 1947; Dennis, b. 1952. Career: Admitted California Bar, 1949; law practice with Steiner Larson, Los Angeles, 1949-50; with Walter Danielson, L.A., 1951; firm of Crider, Tilson & Ruppe', L.A., 1952-59; firm Rutan & Tucker, Santa Ana, 1960---. Judge Pro Tem, Orange Co. Superior and Municipal Cts., as needed. Served to Capt., AUS, 1943-46. President, California State Bar Assn., 1977-78, mem. bd. of govs., 1975-78; pres., Orange County Bar Assn., 1972, bd. dir., 1969-72; V.P., Big Brothers of Orange Co., 1961-68; charter mem., Am. Bd. of Trial Advocates, 1st secty., 1959---; mem. Am. Coll. of Trial Lawyers. Rec.: tennis. Res.: 12292 Browning Ave., Santa Ana, CA 92705; Office: 401 Civic Center Dr., W., Santa Ana, CA 92702.

SHANE, FREDERICK E.
Artist

b. Feb. 2, 1906, Kansas City, Mo.; s. Meyer and Florence (Marks) Shane; student Kansas City Art Inst., 1923-24; Broadmoor Art Acad., 1925-26; pvt. study with Randall Davey, 1924; m. Louise Stutzman (dec.), 1930, dau. Miriam Claire; m. 2d. Dorothy March Henley, 1970. Career: Art Studios in Santa Fe, N.M., 1927, Paris 1928, NYC 1928-29, Kansas City 1929-32; mem. faculty, art dept., Univ. of Mo., 1932-71, chmn. Art Dept. 1958-67, Professor Emeritus of Fine Arts, 1971---; art studio, Beverly Hills, 1972---. Artist correspondent, AUS M.C., 1944. Work in pub. collections: City Art Mus., St. Louis; Nelson Gallery of Art, Kansas City; Springfield Mus. of Art, Univ. of Mo., Jefferson City Jr. Coll., Mural-U.S. Post Office, Eldon, State Hist. Soc., Missouri; IBM Corp. Collection; State Univ. of N.Y., Oswego; Abbott Collection, Paintings of Army Med., War Dept. Wash. D.C.; Delaware Art Center, Wilmington; Colo. Springs Fine Arts Center; Stephens Coll.; Mus. of N.Mex.; Grunwald Fdn. Collection, UCLA. Rep. in pvt. collections coast to coast. Solo exhibitions nationwide; major museum exhibitions incl. Chicago Art Inst., Corcoran Gallery of Art, Wash. D.C.; Pennsylvania Acad. of Fine Arts; Carnegie Inst.; Whitney Mus., N.Y.; Nelson Gallery, Kansas City, Mo.; St. Louis Art Museum; Denver Mus. of Art; N.Y. World Fairs, 1939-40, 1964-65; Watercolor USA Nat. Invitational Exhibition 1976, Springfield (Mo.) Art Mus.; others. Awards incl. Bronze Medal, K.C. Art Inst., 1927; J.M. Wood Portrait Commn. Award, Stephens Coll. 1947; First Byler Award for outstanding achievements as artist and teacher, 1971. Book: Fred Shane Drawings,

Univ. of Mo. Press, 1964, covering 38 years of work, awarded Top Honor, Chicago Book Clinic for Midwestern Books for 1965. The Fred Shane Papers (in microfilm) and Tapes are preserved in the Archives of Am. Art, the Smithsonian Inst., Univ. of Mo., archives of the State Historical Soc. of Mo. Address: 633 N. Foothill Rd., Beverly Hills, CA 90210.

SHANSBY, J. GARY
President, Shaklee Corporation
b. Aug. 25, 1937, Seattle, Wash.; s. John Jay and Jule E. (Boyer) Shansby; B.A., gen. bus., mktg., Univ. Wash., Seattle; m. Joyce Anne Dunsmore, June 21, 1959, Seattle; children: Sheri Lee, b. 1961; Jay Thomas, b. 1965; Kimberly Ann, b. 1963. Career: sr. mktg. and sales, Household Products Div., Colgate-Palmolive Co., N.Y., 1959-67; pres. and gen. mgr., Household Research Inst., subs. Am. Home Products Corp., N.Y., 1968-72; vice pres. & gen. mgr. subs. co., The Clorox Co., Oakland, 1972-73; vice pres., partner, Booz, Allen & Hamilton, Inc., San Francisco, 1973-75; pres., chief exec. officer, Shaklee Corp., Emeryville, 1975---. Mem. Calif. Roundtable; UC, Berkeley Bus. Sch. Bd., founder of J. Gary Shansby Chari on Mktg. Strategy; A.C.T. bd.; S.F. Internat. Film Festival Bd.; Nutrition Found.; Direct Selling Assn.; Alameda Co. United Way Campaign, chmn. maj. employers div. 1977; Olympic Club, Diablo CC, Sigma Nu frat., Univ. Wash. Alumni Assn., Pennask Lake Fishing Club. Hobbies: antique and art collector. Rec.: skiing, tennis. Office: 1900 Powell St., Emeryville, CA 94608.

SHAPELL, NATHAN
Board Chairman, Shapell Industries
b. Mar. 6, 1922, Sosnowitz, Poland, (U.S. cit.); s. Benjamin and Hela Schapelski; ed. pub. schs. Poland; m. Lilly Szenes, Munchberg, Ger., July 17, 1946; dau. Mrs. Paul (Vera) Guerin, b. May 9, 1947; son, Benjamin, b. Nov. 9, 1953. Career: Chmn. bd.-chief exec. ofcr. Shapell Industries, Inc. (listed N.Y. Stock Exch.), home builder-community developer, 1953---. Adv. bd. Union Bank, Beverly Hills; commr., State of Calif. Comm. on Govt. Reorganization and Econ. Author: Witness to the Truth, publ. David McKay & Co. 1974; Prisoner, Auschwitz, Ger., WW II. Awards: Natl. Conference Chrs. and Jews, 1974. Mem.: Dist. Atty's Adv. Council of L.A. Co.; Atty. Gen's. Adv. Council State of Calif.; past bd. dirs.: Vista del Mar Child Care Center, Proj. Hope, Cedars-Sinai Med. Center, Jewish Fed. Council of L.A.; assoc. chmn. State of Israel Bonds; del. Dem. Conv. 1968; L.A. bd. dirs. Amer. Friends of Tel Aviv Univ.; bd. trustees, City of Hope; bd. govs. Res. Publica-Claremont Men's Coll.; Beverly Hills Stock Exch. Club; Georgetown Club, Wash., D.C.; Hillcrest Country Club, L.A. Hebrew (bd. trustees, Temple Beth Am, pres. 1965-67). Hobbies: writing, pub. speaking, horseback riding. Office: 8383 Wilshire Blvd., Beverly Hills, CA 90211.

SHAPIRO, ISADORE
Chemical Consultant — Engineer
b. Apr. 25, 1916, Minneapolis, Minn.; s. Jacob and Bessie (Goldman) Shapiro; B.C.E. (high distinction), Univ. of Minn. 1938, Ph.D. (phys. chem), 1944; post-doctoral research fellowship, 1944-45; m. Mae Hirsch, Minneapolis, Minn., Sept. 4, 1938; chil.: Stanley Harris, b. Apr. 4, 1941; Jerald Steven, b. Dec. 3, 1943. Career: Asst. instr. (chem.), Univ. of Minn., Minneapolis, 1938-41; research fellow, 1944-45; research chem., E.I. du Pont de Nemours and Co., Phila., Pa. 1946; head, chem. lab., U.S. Naval Ord. Test Sta., Pasadena, Calif. 1947-52; rater, U.S. Civil Serv. Bd. Examiners, 1948-52; dir. Research Lab., Olin Mathieson Chem. Corp., Pasa., Calif., 1952-59; head, Chem. Dept., Hughes Tool Co., Aircraft Div., Culver City, Calif. 1959-62; pres. Universal Chem. Systems, Inc., 1962-64; pres. Aerospace Chem. Systems, Inc., 1964-66; dir. contract research, HITCO, 1966-67; prin. scientist, McDonnell Douglas Astronautics Co., Santa Monica, 1967-70; cons. Garrett AirResearch Mfg. Co., Torrance, 1971---. Author: approx. 30 papers presented at tech. soc. meetings, incl. participation in the XVI (Paris), XVII (Munich), and XIX (London), International Congresses for Pure and Applied Chem.; 70 papers publ. sci. journs., incl. Journ. of Amer. Chem. Soc., Journ. of Chem. Physics, Journ. of Phys. Chem., Nature Analytical Chem., Journ of Inorganic and Nuclear Chem., Review Sci. Instruments, others. Holder, 17 patents, others pending (pioneer in research, discoverer of the Carborane Series of compounds; contrib. to catalysis, mass spectrometry, infrared spectroscopy, nuclear magnetic resonance

spectrometry, propellant and missile chem., boron hydrides, organoboranes, reaction kinetics, surface chem., fiber and composites tech. incl. Boron Carbide and carbon filaments). 1st Lt., Anti-Aircraft Artillery, U.S. Army (1941-44), WW II. Listed: Many biog. achievement books, incl.: Amer. Men of Sci., Leaders in Amer. Sci., Internat. Year Book and Statesmen's (London); Men of Achievement, Aviation. Mem.: Fellow, American Institute of Chemists; American Chem. Society, American Physical Society; Natl. Inst. of Ceramic Engrs.; Amer. Ceramic Soc.; AAAS; Amer. Ord. Assn.; Amer. Inst. of Aerons. and Astronautics; Internat. Plansee Soc. for Powder Metal; Amer. Assn. Contamination Control; Amer. Inst. of Physics, Soc. of Rheology, Amer. Inst. of Mgmt., Sigma Xi, Tau Beta Pi, Phi Lambda Upsilon. Rec.: travel (Europe). Res.: 5624 W. Sixty-Second St., Los Angeles, CA 90056.

SHARP, LINDA N.
Communications Company President
b. Feb. 17, 1947, Clayton, N.M.; d. Frank and Ada Sharp; B.S., Math., Oreg. State Univ., 1969. Career: Correspondent, KOAT-TV, N. Mex. Tech. News Bureau, 1966-67; Sci. writer, news bureau, Oreg. Stater Alumni Mag., 1966-67; Pub. Rels. Dir., St. Vincent Hosp. & Med. Center, 1969-71; Pub. Rels., AT&T Long Lines, 1971-73; President, Sharp Communications, Inc., San Mateo, 1974--- (advt., pub. rels., corp. communications). Mem.: San Francisco Peninsula chpt., IABC (awards 1973, 78), past pres.; Calif. Press Women (Awards 1973, 78, 79), founder local chpt.; N. Calif. Advt. Agencies Assn.; Metropolitan Club; S.F. Publicity Club; Women in Advt.; Women in Communications; Soc. Profl. Mgmt. Cons.; Prodn. Women's Club. Office: 1650 Borel Pl., Suite 234, San Mateo, CA 94402.

SHARP, ULYSSES S. GRANT
Admiral, U.S. Navy (Ret.)
b. Apr. 2, 1906, Chinook, Mont.; s. Ulysses S. Grant and Cora (Krauss) Sharp; ed. grad. U.S. Naval Acad. Annapolis, Md. 1927; postgrad. (engrning.), 1934-36; Naval War Coll., Newport, R.I., 1949-50; m. Patricia O'Connor, San Diego, Calif., Aug. 2, 1930; dau. Mrs. Russell F. (Patricia) Milham, Jr., b. June 13, 1931; son, Commander Grant Sharp, b. Jan. 5, 1938. Career: USN, USS N. Mex. (battleship) 1927-28; USS Saratoga, USS Henderson, USS SUmner, USS Buchanan, 1928-32; USS Richmond, USS Winslow, 1936-38; WW II: Bur. of Ships, 1940-42; comdg. ofcr. USS Hogan, USS Boyd, 1942-44; staff, Comdr. Destroyer Force, U.S. Pac. Fleet, 1944-48; comdg. ofcr. Fleet Sonar Sch., San Diego, 1948-49; Comdr., Destroyer Squad. Five, 1950-51; staff, Comdr., U.S. Second Fleet, 1951-53; comdg. ofcr. USS Macon, 1953-54; staff, Comdr.-in-Chief, U.S. Pac. Fleet, 1954-55; Rear Adm.-Comdr., Cruiser Div. Three, 1956-57; dir. Strategic Plans Div., Ofc. of Chief of Naval Operations, 1957-58; Comdr., Cruiser-Destroyer Force, U.S. Pac. Fleet, 1959-60; V. Adm., Comdr., U.S. First Fleet, 1960; Dep. Chief of Naval Operations, 1960-63; apptd. Adm. and Comdr.-in-Chief, U.S. Pac. Fleet, 1963-64; Comdr.-in-Chief, Pacific, 1964-68; (ret.); cons. Teledyne Ryan Aeron. 1968---. Contrib. to Reader's Digest, 1969. Awards: 2 Navy Distinguished Serv. Medals; Army Distinguished Serv. Medal; Silver Star Medal with Gold Star; Bronze Star Medal with Gold Star; Navy Commendation Medal with 2 Gold Stars and Combat "V"; Amer. Def. Serv. Medal with Fleet Clasp; Amer. Campaign Medal; European-African-Middle Eastern Campaign Medal with 1 star; Asiatic Pac. Campaign Medal with 7 stars; WW II Victory Medal; Natl. Def. Serv. Medal; Korean Serv. Medal with 3 stars; U.N. Serv. Medal, and Philippine Liberation Ribbon with 1 star; decorated: Most Exalted Order of the White Elephant, 1st Class, Thailand; Order of the Rising Sun with Grand Cordon, 1st Class, Japan; Order of Cloud and Banner, with Grand Cordon, Repub. of China; Order of Natl. Security Merit, 1st Class, Repub. of Korea; Legion of Hon., Repub. of Philippines; Natl. Order of Vietnam and Gallantry Cross with Palm, Repub. of Vietnam; Order of Naval Merit, Brazil. Mem.: Order of World Wars; Navy League; Rotary Club, S.D.; La Jolla Country Club. Republican. Hobby: golf. Res.: 876 San Antonio Place, San Diego, CA 92106; Office: Teledyne Ryan Aeron., 2701 Harbor Dr., San Diego, CA 92138.

SHARPE, RUSSELL THORNLEY
College President
b. Oct. 9, 1905, East Greenwich, R.I.; s. William Langford and Flora (Thornley) Sharpe; B.S. Harvard College 1928; Sheldon Traveling Fellow, Harvard University 1929; Ph.D., Stanford University 1955; m.

Betty Ward, Piedmont, Calif., Aug. 26, 1946; chil.: William Forsyth, b. June 16, 1934; Saxon Elisabeth, b. Feb. 8, 1954. Career: Dir. Stu. employment-secty. com. on scholarships, Harvard Coll. 1929-40; chief, recruitment and placement, V.A., Br. 12, S.F., 1946-48; v.p. Golden Gate Coll., S.F. 1948-53, pres. 1958-70; pres. emeritus, 1970---; pres. Monticello Coll., Alton, Ill. 1953-58; Contrib. to professional journs. 1934---. Maj., U.S. Army; Col. Awards: Legion of Merit, 1945. Mem.: USAF (1940-46), WW II. Secty. Harvard chpt., Phi Beta Kappa, 1938-40; pres. Eastern Coll. Personnel Ofcrs. Assn. 1938-40; chmn. adm. com., Assn. of Amer. Jr. Coll. 1956-58; Univ. Club of S.F., 1959---; Rotary Club of S.F. 1966-70; Bohemian Club, 1967---; exec. com. Assn. of Independent Calif. Colls. and Univs. 1968-71; trustee: S.F. Consortium, 1968-70; bd. dirs. Oakland Mus. 1969-71. Episcopalian. Res.: 59 Golden Hinde Blvd., San Rafael, CA; Office: Golden Gate College, 536 Mission St., San Francisco, CA 94105.

SHAVER, JESS CARMAN
University Professor — Researcher
b. Oct. 5, 1910, Eufaula, Okla.; s. Sylvester B. and Jane (Parker) Shaver; B.A., Northeastern State Coll., Tahlequah, Okla. 1934; Ed.M., Univ. of Okla., Norman, 1941; Ed.D. 1950; m. Helen Ruth Manning, Quinton, Okla., May 2, 1936; chil.: James Larry, b. 1937; Mary Ruth, b. 1942. Career: Teacher, Dist. 25, Haskell Co., Okla. 1931-32; English teacher, Centralia H.S., Okla. 1934-36; teacher, Keota Pub. schs., Okla. 1936-37; teacher-H.S. prin., McCurtin H.S., Okla. 1937-42; Amer. hist. teacher, Durant Sr. H.S., Okla. 1942-46; asst. prof. edn., Ark. State Teachers Coll., Conway, 1946-47; acting head, dept. edn. 1947-48, assoc. prof. 1950-53; edn. spec. (test constr. sect., prodn. control div., publs.). Ext. Course Inst., Gunter AFB, Montgomery, Ala. 1953-57; assoc. prof. (head dept. edn. and psychol.-dir. teacher training-dir. teacher placement), Georgetown Coll., Ky. 1957-59; asst. prof. edn., Long Beach State University, 1959-62, assoc. prof. 1963-70, professor 1970---; dir. Teacher Edn. Research Survey, Shaver Survey (4 each yr.), Calif. State Coll. at Long Beach, 1961-67. Co-author-ed.: Adolescence: Quest for Relevance (textbook), 1968; Candidates for Maturity, 1970; Tributaries of Learning, 1977; author: Relevant Statistics for the Classroom Teacher, 1970. Mem.: Kiwanis Club, 1947---; Phi Delta Kappa, Kappa Delta Pi, 1949---; edn. 1963---, asst. to div. chmn. 1961---, Assn. for Supv. and Curriculum Development; Amer. Assn. Univ. Profs.; Calif. Coll. and Univ. Faculty Assn.; NEA; Calif. Teachers Assn.; Assn. of Calif. State Coll. Profs.; Amer. Assn. of Sch. Admrs.; Assn. of Higher Edn. Baptist (Sun. Sch. teacher, lay speaker at denominational meetings). Hobby: writing Haiku poetry. Rec.: gardening, walking. Res.: 603 Termino Ave., Long Beach, CA 90814; Office: California State University, 1250 Bellflower Blvd., Long Beach, CA 90840.

SHAW, MILDRED (Mrs.)
Educational Consultant
b. Plymouth, Iowa; d. M. and Lessie H. Sutton; B.A., Ariz. State Univ., 1939; M.A., Claremont Grad. Sch., 1960; lib. credential, Univ. of Ariz., Tucson, 1963; n. Warren C. Shaw, June 25, 1937, Boulder City, Colo. Career: tchr., Dysart Sch., Peoria, Ariz., 1939-45; Pima Co. Sch. librarian, Tucson, 1949-53; art consultant, Duarte Unif. Sch. Dist., 1953-63; audio visual coordinator, 1963-68; instructional services consultant, 1969---. Contbr. School Arts Mag.; Arts & Activities Mag.; Teacher Mag.; The Instructor Mag.; co-author: Puppets for All Grades, 1960; Awarded Schoolmen's Medal, Freedom Found. at Valley Forge, 1977. Mem. Quota Club Internat., 2nd v.p., 1971-73, program chmn., Monrovia, Duarte; Delta Kappa Gamma, pres., 1972-74; Creative Arts Soc. of Sierra Madre, 15 yr. sponsor; Coll. Women's Club of Pasadena, 1975---; Women in Edn. Leadership, L.A. Co., 1972---; Internat. Reading Assn., secty., 1973-75; Duarte Women's Club, art chmn. 1965-71; Duarte Glaaxy of Arts, pres., 1969-74; charter mem. Rancho de Duarte Garden Club, speaker & demonstrator, arts & crafts chmn. 1970-73; High Sch. Garden Club, advisor, 1973-76; AAUW, 1955---. Methodist. Hobbies: painting, writing. Rec.: bridge, cooking. Home: 1635 S. 3rd Ave., Arcadia, CA 91006; Office: 1565 E. Central, Duarte, CA.

SHAW, STANFORD JAY
Historian
b. May 5, 1930, St. Paul, Minn.; s. Albert and Belle (Paymar) Shaw; B.A., Stanford Univ., 1951; M.A.,

1952; M.A., Princeton Univ., 1956; Ph.D., 1958; M.A. (hon.), Harvard Univ., 1962; m. Ezel Kural, 1967, Malibu; dau. Wendy Miriam Kural S., b. 1970. Career: Research Assoc. (1958-60), Asst. Prof. (1960-65), Assoc. Prof. of Turkish History, Harvard Univ., 1965-68; at UCLA: Prof. of Turkish and Near Eastern Hist. 1968---, Editor in Chief, Internat. Journ. of Middle East Studies, 1968---, pres., Turkish Studies Assn., 1975---; Ford Found. Fellow, 1955-58; Guggenheim Fellow, 1966-67; Fellow, Am. Research Inst. in Turkey, 1968, 71. Mem. Nat. Grants Com. for Middle East Awards, Inst. for Internat. Edn., 1973-74; Chmn. Publs. Com., Middle East Studies Assn., 1968---; Studies Assn., 1968; Dir. Harvard Univ. Middle East Summer Inst., 1963-67; bd. dirs., Am. Research Inst., Turkey, 1976---; mem.: AAUP; Middle East Inst.; Internat. Soc. for Oriental Research; corresponding mem. Turkish Historical Soc. (Turk Tarih Kurumu); Am. Hist. Assn. Author: History of the Ottoman Empire and Modern Turkey, 2 vols. (History Book Club Selection, 1976, 77); Between Old and New: The Ottoman Empire Under Sultan Selim III, 1789-1807, Harvard Univ. Press 1971; The Budget of Ottoman Egypt, 1968; Ottoman Egypt in the Age of the French Revolution, 1964; Ottoman Egypt in the Eighteenth Century: The Nizmname-i Misir of Ahmed Cezzar Pasha, 1962; The Financial and Administrative Organization and Development of Ottoman Egypt, 1517-1798 (1962). Jewish. Hobby: collect old radio programs on tape. Office: UCLA, Los Angeles, CA 90024.

SHAWL, STANLEY H.
Financial Consulting Firm Executive
b. July 16, 1936, Visalia; s. Harold and Deltha (Beardsley) Shawl; B.S., Univ. Calif., 1959; student U.C. Grad. Sch. of Bus., 1961-62; C.L.U., Am. Coll. of Life Underwriters, 1966; Grad., Am. Inst. of Banking, 1968, Pacific Coast Banking Sch., 1972; m. William "Billie" Joan (Nelson), July 23, 1961, Mill Valley; children: Scott Nelson, b. 1966; Sara Lynn, b. 1968. Career: Field Underwriter, Fidelity Mutual Life Insurance Co., S.F., 1962-66; V.P., Harold Shawl and Sons, Inc. (farming, investment corp.), 1966---; mng. partner, Stanley H. Shawl, Co., 1967---; Asst. Trust Ofcr., Bank of Calif., N.A., Sacto., 1967-69; Instr. Am. Inst. of Banking, 1967-69; Trust Ofcr., Bank of Calif., 1969-74; V.P., United California Bank, 1975-78; Instr., Am. Coll. Life Underwriters, 1969---, Los Rios Coll. Dist., 1978---; V.P., Assoc. Benefit Consultants, Inc., 1978---. USN, 1959-61; USN Air Reserve, 1962---. Mem.: Sacramento Estate Planning Council, past pres.; Am. Soc. C.L.U.; N. Calif. Trust Ofcrs. Assn.; Calif. Alumni Big C. Soc., past dir.; Sacto. Assn. Life Underwriters; Commonwealth Club of Calif.; Jaycees; Sacto. Metro. C. of C.; Am. Cancer Soc.; YMCA; Kiwanis Club, V.P.; U.S. Naval Inst.; Civil Air Patrol. Presbyterian. Res.: 5181 Finlandia Way, Carmichael, CA 95608; Office: 3426 American River Dr., Suite 1, Sacramento, CA 95825.

SHEA, JOHN MARTIN, JR.
Corporate Executive
b. Nov. 14, 1922, Santa Barbara, Calif.; s. John Martin and Karmel Kathryn (Knox) Shea; B.A., Univ. Wash., 1944; m. Marion Abie; children: Michael Knox, Patrick Campbell, Katherine Martin. Career: Vice pres., gen. mgr. Yaras & Co., Far East, Manila, P.I., Hong Kong, Tokyo, Japan, 1946-52; pres. Shea Oil Co., Pasadena, Calif., 1953-57; v.p., dir. Am. Petrofina Inc.; sr. v.p. mktg., refining, transp., crude oil, dir. Am. Petrofina Co. of Tex., 1957-64; pres. Colonial Oil Products Co., Des Moines, Osmond Oil Co., Waco, Tex., 1958-64; chmn. bd. Freeman, Gossage & Shea, advt. and cons., San Francisco, 1964-65; chmn. bd. CEO, Beacon Bay Enterprises, Inc., Newport Beach, Calif., 1964---; Shea, S.A., Buenos Aires, Argentina, 1968---; dir. Commercebank, Newport Beach. Pres. bd. trustees, Newport Harbor Art Mus., Newport Beach. Trustee, Palm Springs Desert Museum. Served to Lt. (j.g.) USNR, WW II. Office: Beacon Bay Bldg., 260 Newport Center Dr., Newport Beach, CA 92660.

SHEBS, THEODORE LEE
Real Estate Developer
b. Oct. 26, 1919, Minneapolis; s. Simon H. and Edna Leona (Todd) Shebs; student, Univ. Chicago, 1937-38, Univ. Santa Clara, 1943; Univ. Calif., 1965-68; m. Rosemary Latenser, Feb. 27, 1960, San Francisco; children: Stephen Norman, b. 1954; Sharon Ruth, b. 1957; Richard Dennis, b. 1961. Career: Area Sales Mgr., Johns-Manville Sales Corp., 1940-60; partner, Norman O'Connor (Insurance) Agency, 1960-72; owner 1972---; Realtor and Insurance Broker: secty.-treas.,

Shebs & Mohr, Inc., 1971---, D&S Devel. & Sales Co., 1961---; real estate developer in residential subdivisions, apt. bldgs., office bldgs., 1962---. Lectr. on real estate investments and syndications. Mem.: Los Gatos-Saratoga Bd. of Realtors, pres. 1965; Calif. Assn. of Realtors, dir. 1962, 65, 66; West Valley Community Coll., chmn. Real Estate Edn. Advisory Com., 1967. Lt., AUS, 1942-45; 11th Armored Div., Infan., ETO; Calif. Nat. Guard, 1947-54, Capt. of Infan., Commd. unit, winner of Eisenhower Trophy 1952, 53, 54. Mem.: Independent Insurance Agents Assn.; Los Gatos C. of C., dir. 1964; Rotary Club, dir. 1961; La Rinconada Country Club, pres. 1974. Republican. Rec.: golf. Res.: 19520 Farwell Ave., Saratoga, CA 95070; Office: 225 Saratoga Ave., Los Gatos, CA 95030.

SHEETS, FRANK THOMAS, JR.
Cement Company President
b. Feb. 5, 1916, Springfield, Ill.; s. Frank and Naomi Gault (Launder) Sheets; B.S., Civil Engr., Purdue Univ., 1938; m. Frances Converse Deal, Nov. 5, 1938, Springfield, Ill.; children: Joan, b. 1941; Elizabeth Converse, b. 1946; Frank III, b. 1949. Career: Sales & Engr., Southwestern Portland Cement Co., Fairborn, Ohio, 1938-42; Operations & Engr., 1946-51; Dir. of Engr. & Mfg., Los Angeles, 1951-57; V.P. Mfg., 1957-70; Exec. V.P. & Gen. Mgr., 1970-71; dir., pres., Southwestern Portland Cement Co., Los Angeles, 1971---. Dir., Southdown, Inc. Lt., USNR, 1942-46. Clubs: Jonathan, San Gabriel Country, Valley Hunt. Hobbies: tennis, golf. Res.: 2001 Oak Knoll, San Marino, CA 91108; Office: 3055 Wilshire Blvd., Los Angeles, CA 90010.

SHEETS, MILLARD OWEN
Architectural Designer — Artist
b. June 24, 1907, Pomona, Calif.; s. John G. and Millie (Owen) Sheets; ed. pub. schs.; grad. Chouinard Sch. of Art, 1929; m. Mary Baskerville, Los Angeles, Calif. 1930; chil.: Millard Owen, Jr., David, Carolyn, John Anthony. Career: Travel and painter, Europe, 1929-30; teacher-lecturer: Chouinard Sch. of Art, 1929-35 and 1948---; Univ. of Hawaii, 1935-36; Univ. of Calif. 1937-38; Univ. of Ia. 1938; Tulane Univ., Sophie Newcombe Coll. 1939; T.S.C.W., Denton, Tex. 1939; Univ. of N. Mex. 1941; Okla. A&M 1941; dir. Fine Arts Exhib., L.A. Co. Fair, 1931---; asst. prof. of art, Scripps Coll. 1932-38; dir. Art Dept., 1938-53, lecturer on art, Sept. 1955---; apptd. dir., L.A. Co. Art Inst., 1953-58; round the world painting tour, 1967; arch. mosaic design-artist, various bldgs. incl. Howard Ahmanson Bldgs. and Los Angeles County Art Institute; Travis Savings and Loan, San Antonio, Tex. 1967; Home Savings and Loan, Sunset and Vine, Hollywood, 1968; Santa Rosa Savings and Loan, Novato, 1968; interior mosaic design, Shrine of Immaculate Conception Cathedral, Wash., D.C. 1968; Repr. in permanent collections: (museums) Met. Mus. of Art, NYC; Chicago Art Inst.; The White House, Wash., D.C.; Whitney Mus. of Amer. Art, N.Y.; Mus. of Moder. Art, N.Y.; L.A. Mus.; San Francisco Mus.; Brooklyn Mus. of Art; Wood Mem. Gallery, Montpelier, Vt.; Witte Mem. Mus., San Antonio, Tex.; Houston Mus. of Fine Art; San Diego Mus. of Fine Art; Ft. Worth Mus. of Art; M.H. deYoung Mem. Mus., San Francisco; Albany Mus. of Hist. and Art; Ariz. State Fair Collection, Phoenix; L.A. Pub. Lib.; Municipal Art Collection, Phoenix; Poly H.S., L.A.; Gardena (Calif.) H.S.; Horace Mann Sch., L.A.; Univ. of Okla. Art Assn.; R.I. Sch. of Design, Providence; UMCA, Pasa.; s. Pasa. Jr. H.S.; Dayton Art Inst.; Seattle Mus. of Art; Indianapolis Pub. Lib.; Cleveland Mus. of Art; Pomona (Calif.) H.S.; L.A. Women's Ath. Club; San Bernardino Valley Jr. Coll.; Webb Sch. for Boys, Claremont, Calif.; Mills Coll., Oakland, Calif.; Belmont H.S., L.A.; Montclair Art Mus.; Hackley Art Gallery, Muskegon, Mich.; Ontario Art Assn.; Pasa. Art Inst.; Carnegie Inst.; High Mus. of Art, Atlanta, Ga.; (murals) 6 Golden Gate Internat. Exhib., San Francisco, 1939; State Mutual and Loan Bldg., L.A.; J.W. Robinson Co.; So. Pasa. Jr. H.S.; Bullock's Men's Store; Beverly Hills Tennis Club; Ct. of the Flowers and So. Cos. Bldg., State Bldg. of Rec., S.F. World's Fair; Glass Mosaic, Lyman's, L.A.; (4 panels) Dept. of Interior Bldg., Wash., D.C.; Puppet Room, Melody Lane, L.A.; main lobby, Beverly Hills Hotel; (3 panels) Amer. Trust Co., Sacramento. Illus.: Fortune Mag., Life Mag., Ladies' Home Journ., Cole of Calif., Amer. Pres. Lines, Lockheed Aircraft Corp., Sunset Mag., Northrop Aircraft Co., Hawaiian Pineapple Co. War artist, Life Mag., Burma-India front, WW II. Awards: first prize: (landscape) Ariz. State Fair, 1928; L.A. Co. Fair, 1928-30; (watercolor) Ebell Club, L.A. 1930; (watercolor) Santa Cruz Art League 1931, 33; Painters

and Sculptors Club, 1932; (watercolor) L.A. Mus. 1932; (landscape) Calif. State Fair, 1932-33 (watercolor) 1938; Calif. Water Color Soc. Exhib., L.A. Mus. 1945; (oil) San Gabriel Valley Artists Exhibit, Pasa. 1948; $1750 prize, Davis Natl. Competition, San Antonio, 1929; guest of hon., Internat. Water Color Exhib., Art Inst. of Chicago, 1938; Watson F. Blair purchase prize, Chicago Art Inst. 1938; Phila. Water Color Club prize, 1939; Dana Water Color Medal, Pa. Acad. of Fine Arts, 1943; drawing prize, L.A. Mus. 1946; art prize, Orange Co. Fair, 1946; repr. Ency. Brit., Chicago. Mem.: pres. Calif. Water Color Soc. 1946-47. Hobby: horses. Rec.: tennis. Res.: Barking Rocks, Gualala, CA 95445; Office: 661 E. Foothill Blvd., Claremont, CA 91711.

SHEINBAUM, STANLEY K.
Economist
b. June 12, 1920; A.B. Far East Hist., summa cum laude, Stanford Univ., 1949, Doctoral studies in Economics, 1949-56; married, four children, ages 25 to 38. Career: Prof. of Economics, Stanford Univ., 1950-53; Mich. State Univ., 1955-60, Univ. of Calif., Santa Barbara, 1963; Fulbright Economics Fellow, Paris, France, 1953-55; Staff Fellow, Program on Overseas Devel., Hoover Inst., Stanford Univ., 1955; Economist Fellow, Center for Study on Democratic Instns., Santa Barbara, 1960-70; Grantee, 20th Century Fund: Study of Power, Ownership and Property in Modern Capitalism, 1961-64; Regent, Univ. Calif. 1977---. Economics Cons.: Ency. Britannica, 1961-64, Calif. State Commn. on Manpower and Tech., 1963-65; Campus Dir., Tech. Assistance Project in Pub. Adminstrn. and Econ. Devel. in Vietnam, U.S. Foreign Aid Program, Mich. State Univ., 1955-69. Democrat. Address: 240 Bentley Circle, Los Angeles, CA 90049.

SHELDON, JOEL VROMAN, JR.
Company President
b. Aug. 2, 1910, Nome, Alaska; s. Joel Vroman and Vesta (Storey) Sheldon; B.A., Univ. of Wash. 1932; m. Robert Belle Brown, Pasadena, Calif. Jan. 12, 1937; chil.: Joel Vroman, III, Julie (Sheldon) Hopf. Career: Assoc. with A.C. Vroman, Inc., Pasa. 1933--- (now pres.). Defense Serv., Calif. Inst. of Tech. (1942-45), WW II. Mem.: pres. Pasa. C. of C., 1958-59; pres. Pasa. Rotary Club, 1959-60; chmn. Pasa. Chpt., Amer. Red Cross, 1960-62; L.A. Co. United Crusade Com. 1964---; dir. Pasa. Citizens Council on Planning; Tournament of Roses Assn.; past pres., Pasa. Merchants Assn.; past dir., Pasa. Sym. Assn.; Univ. Club of Pasa. Res.: 1898 Homewood Dr., Altadena, Calif.; Office: Vroman's, 2085 E. Foothill Blvd., Pasadena, CA 91009.

SHEPARD, RICHMOND
Mime
b. Apr. 24, 1929, New York City; s. John and Gladys (Marshall) Shephard; B.A., Adelphi Univ., 1951; M.A., Cal State Univ., Los Angeles, 1969; Ph.D., Pacific Western Univ., 1978; children: Armina, b. 1960; Vonda, b. 1963; Rosetta, b. 1964; Luana, b. 1968. Career: Founder 1st Mime Company in America, 1952; founder, The Mime Guild, 1972; performer on The Today Show, Steve Allen, Mort Sahl, Donald O'Connor, Merv Griffin, Dinah Shore Shows, Kojak, The F.B.I., That Girl, I Spy, others; performer in major theaters throughout the U.S. 1952---. Author: Mime: The Technique of Silence, Drama Book Specialists, N.Y., 1971. Awarded 3 N.Y. Theatre Awards, 1955, 62. Res.: 17241 Hatteras St., Encino, CA 91316; Studio: 6472 Santa Monica Blvd., Los Angeles, CA 90038; Theatre: 6314 Santa Monica Blvd., Hollywood, CA 90028.

SHEPARD, ROGER NEWLAND
Psychologist
b. Jan. 30, 1929, Palo Alto, Calif.; s. Orson Cutler (ret. Prof., Stanford Univ.) and Grace Newland Shepard; B.A., Stanford Univ., 1951; M.S., Yale Univ., 1952; Ph.D., 1955; m. Barbaranne Bradley, Aug. 18, 1952, Redfield, S. Dak.; children: Newland Cheneweth, b. 1955; Todd David, b. 1957; Shenna Esther, b. 1961. Career: Postdoctoral research assoc., Nat. Acad. of Sci., Nat. Research Council, Naval Research Lab., Wash. D.C., 1955-56; Research Fellow, Harvard Univ. 1956-58; Tech. Staff, Bell Telephone Labs., N.J., 1958-66, dept. hd. 1963-66; prof., Harvard Univ. and Dir. Psychol. Labs., 1966-68; Prof. of Psychology, Stanford Univ., 1968---; Guggenheim Fellow, 1971-72. Recipient, Distinguished Sci. Contbn. Award, Am. Psychol. Assn. 1976; elected to Nat. Acad. of Sciences 1977. Coeditor: 2-vol. book, trans. & pub. in

Japanese, contbr. sci. papers profl. publs. Mem.: Psychometric Soc., pres. 1973-74. Office: Stanford University, Stanford, CA 94305.

SHEPHERD-LOOK, DEE L.
Psychologist — Educator
b. Dec. 24, 1943, Peoria, Ill.; d. Dee Edgar and Dolores Elaine (Hollister) Shepherd; A.B. cum laude, Immaculate Heart Coll., 1965; Ph.D., UCLA, 1972; m. Launis Allen Look, Sept. 4, 1971, Santa Monica, Calif.; chil.: Launis Allen, Jr., b. June 12, 1973; Jeremy Edgar Look, b. Aug. 11, 1976. Career: cons., Montessori Nursery Sch., Glendale, 1965-70; Research Fellow, Yale Univ., 1968; supr. of trainees, L.A. Free Clin., 1973-75; cons. to profls. and parents: child develop., death and dying, 1971---; clin. practice, Western Psychological Center, 1978---; assoc. prof. of psychology, Cal. State Univ., Northridge, 1971---. Contbr. articles in Encyclopedia of Neurology, Psychiatry, Psychoanalysis and Psychology; profl. journs. Mem.: Am. Psychol. Assn.; Western Psychol. Assn.; Soc. for Psychol. Study of Social Issues. Roman Catholic. Hobbies: model train constr., piano. Rec.: fencing, swimming, backpacking. Home: 6727 Kentland Ave., Canoga Park, CA 91307; Office: 18111 Nordoff Blvd., Northridge, CA 91330.

SHEPPARD, CHARLES ARTHUR
Professor of Theatre Arts
b. Sept. 7, 1943, Burbank; s. Charles Frederick and Elizabeth Sheppard; B.F.A., 1964; M.A., theatre arts, 1970; m. Sherry Lamb, July 1965, Ashtabula, Ohio; children: Charles and Christine, b. Nov. 24, 1972. Career: Asst. Headmaster, Grand River Acad., Ohio, 1964-69; prof. Theatre Arts, Chaffey Coll., Alta Loma, 1971---. Founder, Children's Touring Theatre, 1971. Mem.: Am. Theatre Assn., So. Calif. Ednl. Theatre Assn., Am. Nat. Theatre Assn., Calif. Tchrs. Assn. Hobby: films. Office: Chaffey College, Alta Loma, CA.

SHERWIN, GERALD ANTHONY
Attorney at Law
b. June 4, 1935, Antigo, Wis.; s. Gerald F. and Verna A. Sherwin; B.S., Univ. of Wis., 1959; J.D. Univ. Calif., Berkeley (Boalt Hall), 1962; m. Martha Shaver, Oct. 8, 1976, Tracy, Calif. Career: Deputy county counsel, San Joaquin Co., Stockton, 1962-64; Asst. City Atty., Stockton, 1964-67; Sr. Deputy County Counsel, San Joaquin Co., Stockton, 1967-69; partner, Sherwin, Zuckerman & Sargent, Attorneys at Law, Stockton, 1969-73; County counsel, San Joaquin Co. Stockton, 1973---. Admitted to practice: Calif. Supreme Ct. (1963), U.S. Circuit Ct. (9th Cir.) (1953), U.S. Dist. Courts (Northern & Eastern Dist., Calif.), U.S. Supreme Ct. (1966). Mil.: USN (aviation), 1954-56. Hobby: pvt. flying. Office: 222 E. Weber Ave., Stockton, CA.

SHIELDS, L. DONALD
University President
b. Sept. 18, 1936, San Diego; s. Clifford L. and Malta Shields; B.A., chem., Univ. of Calif., Riverside, 1959; Ph.D., chem., UCLA, 1964; m. Patricia Ann Baldwin, Sept. 1, 1957, San Diego; chil.: Ronald, b. 1958; Steven, b. 1960; Cynthia, b. 1962; Laurie, b. 1968. Career: asst. to Chancellor (sch. rels.), Univ. of Calif., Riverside, 1955-57; v.p. for adminstrn., Calif. State Univ., Fullerton, 1967-70; acting pres., 1970-71; pres., 1971---(apptd. as youngest pres. [age 34] of a pub. state univ.); also chmn., Nat. Sci. Bd. Programs Com., 1978---; prof. of chem., Cal. State Fullerton, 1967---; visiting prof. of chem., UCLA, summers 1964---67; chemist, U.S. Dept. of Agri., summers, 1958, 1959; asst research chemist, Kelco Co., S.D., summer 1955-57; Consultant: Calif. State Sen. Dennis Carpenter, 1973, Calif. State Sen. John Harmer, 1968-69, Nat. Sci. Found., 1970. Author: Modern Methods of Chemical Analysis, 2nd edition 1976; Analytical Methods of Organic and Biochemistry, 1966, John Wiley & Sons, Inc., N.Y.; Contbr. articles to scientific journs. Recipient: Pres. Ford apptd. to Nat. Sci. Bd., 1974; apptd. 1st Western U.S. rep., bd. of Trustees, Nat. Commn. for Coop. Edn., Boston, Mass. 1977; named 1973 Headliner of the Year in Edn., Orange Co. Press Club; Distinguished Am. Award, Nat. Football Found. and Hall of Fame, Orange Co. chpt. 1974; Calif. State Jaycees Award, 1970; Distinguished Tching. Award, State Legislature, 1965. Vice chmn., legislative and pub. affairs com., Chancellors Council of Presidents, 1977---; rep., Library Devel. Advis. Council, Calif. State Univ. and colleges system, 1976---; mem. Finance and Capital Outlay Com. and Exec. Com., Chancellor's Council of Pres.; Mem.: Am. Chem. Soc.; AAAS; Am. Coll. Pub. Rels. Assn.; Am. Inst. of Chemists; Town Hall of Calif.; Orange Co. Economics Devel. Council; World Affairs

Council of Orange Co. trustee; Orange Co. Sports Celebrities bd. dir.; Orange County and Fullerton Chambers of C.; Sigma Xi; Phi Lambda Upsilon. Office of the President, Calif. State Univ., Fullerton, Fullerton, CA 92634.

SHIFFMAN, MAX
Professor of Mathematics
b. Oct. 30, 1914, NYC; s. Nathan and Eva (Krasilchick) Shiffman; B.S., New York City Coll., 1935; M.S., N.Y. Univ., 1936; Ph.D., 1938; m. Bella Manel (div.), June 1938, NYC; chil.: Bernard, b. 1943; David, b. 1945. Career: mathematics research & tchr.: St. John's Univ., 1938-39; N.Y. City Coll., 1928-42; math research for AUS, 1941; for U.S. office of Naval research and U.S. office of Sci. R&D, 1942-48 (at N.Y. Univ.); research tchg. & math research as assoc. prof., N.Y. Univ., 1946-49; prof., Stanford Univ., 1949-66; math. research cons., Rand Corp., 1951; cons. math logistics, George Washington Univ., 1958-60; cons., U.S. Govt. & USN, 1962-64; prof. of math., Cal. State Univ., Hayward, 1967---; founder, owner & mathematician, Mathematico, S.F. and Hayward, 1970---; research in aerodynamics of airplane wings, 1949-53 and currently. Lectr. Princeton Univ., 1946, 200th anniversary of Princeton, 1946, and at 100th anniversary of Riemann's doctoral dissertation, 1951. Mil. Award of Merit (highest civilian honor), USN, 1945; mathematician (civilian) for USAF, 1951, USN and U.S. Army, 1958-60; aided in Cuban crisis, 1962-63; Arab-Isareli dispute, 1969-73; peace in Vietnam, 1973. Contbr. research publs. in math. incl.: The Plateau Problem for Minimal Surfaces of Arbitrary Topological Structure, 1938; Instability for Double Integral Problems in the Calculus of Variations, 1941; Games of Timing, 1953; Measure-Theoretic Properties of Arbitrary Point Sets. Mem.: Am. Mathematical Soc., 1935---; Mathematical Assn. of Am.; Soc. for Indsl. & Applied Math., 1969---. Republican; helped form Peace and Freedom Party, 1966-67. Jewish. Hobbies: painting, photog., gradening, model airplanes. Rec.: dancing, music, theatre. Home-Office: 16913 Meekland Ave., No. 7, Hayward, CA 94541.

SHILLITO, BARRY JAMES
Aerospace Company President
b. Jan. 1, 1921, Dayton, Ohio; s. Lucian W. and Mary Ellen (O'Connor) Shillito; B.S. (bus. adm. econos.), Univ. of Dayton, 1949; postgard. UCLA 1958; m. Eileen Cottman, Dayton, Oh., Dec. 2, 1942; chil.: Barry L., b. July 17, 1944; Elaine A. Tanavage, b. June 20, 1946; Daniel G., b. Nov. 7, 1948; James K., b. Sept. 3, 1952; M. Colleen, b. May 12, 1957. Career: Sect. chief-ofcr. Air Material Command, Wright-Patterson AFB, Ohio. 1949-54; dept. dir. Hughes Aircraft Co. 1954-58; exec. v.p., pres. Houston-Fearless Co., L.A. 1958-62; pres. Logistics Mgmt. Inst., Wash., D.C. 1962-68; Asst. Secty. of Navy (Installations and Logistics), Wash., D.C. 1968-69; pres. Teledyne Ryan Aeron., San Diego, 1973---, v.p. Teledyne, Inc., 1977---. Pilot, USAF 1942-46. Mem.: Amer. Legion, Knights of Columbus; UCLA, and Dayton Univ. Alumni Assns. Rec.: golf, swim. Res.: 555 San Fernando St., San Diego, CA 92106; Office: 2701 Harbor Dr., San Diego, CA 92112.

SHINE, HENRY MARTIN, JR.
Association Executive
b. June 7, 1921, Lincoln, Me.; s. Henry Martin and Mary Ann (Carter) Shine; A.B., Harvard Coll. 1947; LL.B. (cum laude), Univ. Notre Dame, 1951; grad. fellow, Oil and Gas Law, So. Meth. Univ. Sch. of Law, 1951-52; m. Marguerite Ann Timlin, Wash., D.C., Sept. 30, 1961; daus.: Mari Marguerite, Christanna Jeanne. Career: Asst. to Commr. Storey, Hoover Comm. 1953-55; asst. staff dir. Comm. on Civil Rights, 1958-59; legislative dir. and dir. Natl. Housing Center, Natl. Assn. of Homes Bldrs. 1961-66; Brookings Inst. Lecturer, Pub. Affairs Fellowship Pgm. 1965-65; dir. Calif. State Dept. Professional & Vocational Standards, 1967-69; asst. to Secty., Cong. Liaison, Interior Dept., Wash., D.C. 1969; exec. dir. President's Council on Youth Opportunity, 1969-71; dir. Govt. and Ind. Rels., President's Comm. on Financial Structure and Regulations, 1971-72; exec. v.p. Calif. Bankers Assn. 1972---. Naval ofcr. PTO WW II. Comdr. USNR. Mem.: Assembly for Bank Dirs.; S.F. Bay Area Council, BSA Exec. Bd.; Natl. Council, Fed. Bar Assn. 1961-74; Amer. Bar Assn.; Tex., Wash., D.C. Bar Assns.; Clubs: Boundry Oaks Racquet, Marines' Mem., Metropolitan, Wash. D.C. Roman Catholic. Hobby: stamp collector. Rec.: reading, tennis, skiing, swim. Res.: 900 Val Aire Pl., Walnut

Creek, 94596; Office: 650 California St., San Francisco, CA 94108.

SHIPPEY, DAVID B.
Vice President, Saga Corporation
b. Dec. 20, 1927, San Francisco; B.S., Univ. Calif. Berkeley, 1950; m. Roberta E. Long, June 23, 1951, San Anselmo; chil.: Mathew, b. 1952; Ann, b. 1956; Elizabeth, b. 1958. Career: Mng. Accnt., Price Waterhouse & Co., 1950-59; v.p., dir., exec. com., Di Giorgio Corp., San Francisco, 1959-71; v.p. finance, treas., Saga Corp., Menlo Park, 1971---. Dir.: Ross Valley Homes, Inc., Gentran, Inc., Miramonte Mental Health Agency. USN, 1945-46. Mem.: Financial Execs. Inst., Calif. Soc. CPAs, Am. Inst. CPAs. Res.: 557 Cresta Vista Lane, Portola Valley, CA 94025; Office: One Saga Lane, Menlo Park, CA 94025.

SHIPSTAD, EDWIN HAROLD
Co-Founder — Producer, Ice Follies
b. Feb. 16, 1907, St. Paul, Minn.; s. Frank Otto and Hilma Helen (Johnson) Shipstad; ed. St. Paul (Minn.) H.S.; m. Lulu Heim, Forest Lake, Minn., June 9, 1935; chil.: Edwin Joseph, b. June 20, 1936; Robert Harold, b. Feb. 16, 1938; Donald Raymond, b. Dec. 3, 1939. Career: Skating star with bros. Harry and Roy (boy wonder at age 13 yrs.); founder-orig. first ice skating shows with Oscar Johnson and bro. Roy Shipstad, 1936; creator, world's first professional Ice Extravaganza (20th annual edit. 1956, traveling 20,000 miles, 21 cities, 48 wks., USA; 399 perfs. annually; costumes created by Helen Rose). Appd. many Ice Follies radio-TV shows, USA War Bond Drives, spec. War Bond matinees and spec. servicemen's shows throughout USA (1942-46), WW II. Mem.: Encino C. of C.; clubs: (hon.) Optimist, (hon.) Rotary, Bel-Air Country, Olympic (San Francisco). Lutheran. Hobby: photog. and skate collections. Rec.: golf, bowling, fishing. Res.: Encino, CA; Office: 1001 N. La Brea Ave., Los Angeles, CA 90046.

SHMITKA, RICHARD OTTO
Consulting Geologist
b. Minneapolis, Minn.; s. Clarance Fredrick and Lillian Beatrice (Lusian) Shmitka; A.A., math, Pierce Coll., 1965; B.Sc. geology, Cal. State Univ., Northridge, 1968; M.Sc. geology, Univ. Calif., Davis, 1970. Career: cons. geologist, Maurseth, Howe, Lockwood, Ventura, 1972; geologist, Fugro, Inc., Long Beach, 1973-75; geologist, Dames & Moore, L.A., 1975-77; pvt. geologic cons., Instr., 1976---; current research in Mathematical physics of relative motion as applied to cosmology; geol. studies Upper Sespe Creek, Ventura Co., 1969-73; site investigation studies for Puerto Rico Nuclear Power plant, 1973-75; discoverer new species of venerid clam, chione rickyi, 1969; spec. interest in stratigraphy and paleontology as they relate to correlation and dating fault movements; astronomy, mathematical relativity, cosmology. Certified community coll. instr. earth scis., 1976. Publs. incl. Introduction to a field trip along Sespe Creek, Paleogeography Field Guide No. 3, 1978; Evidence for major right-lateral separation of Eocene Rocks Along the Santa Ynez Fault, S.F. and Ventura Counties, Geol. Soc. Am., Feb. 1973. Mem.: Am. Assn. Petroleum Geologists; Geol. Soc. of Am., assoc. mem.; Paleontology Soc.; Sigma Xi; Soc. of Economic Paleontologists and Mineralogists. Hobby: philosophy of sci. Rec.: camping, tennis, swimming. Home-Office: 8554 Lurline Ave., Canoga Park, CA 91306.

SHOCKLEY, WILLIAM BRADFORD
Inventor — Scientist
b. Feb. 13, 1910, London, Eng.; s. William Hillman and Cora May (Bradford) Shockley; B.Sc., Calif. Inst. of Tech. 1932; Ph.D., MIT, 1936; (hon.) Sc.D.: Univ. of Pa. 1955, Rutgers Univ. 1956; Gustavus Adolphus College, 1963; m. Emmy Lanning, Columbus, Oh., Nov. 23, 1955; chil.: Alison (Shockley) Iannelli, b. 1934; William Alden, b. 1942; Richard Condit, b. 1947. Career: Tech. staff, Bell Tel. Labs. 1936-42; research physicist, 1945-64; sci. adv., Policy Council, Joint Research & Development Bd. 1947-49; dir. Transistor Physics Research, 1954-55; dir. Shockley Semiconductor Lab. of Beckman Instruments, Inc. 1955-58; dir. Research Weapons Systems Evaluation Group, Dept. of Def. 1954-55; pres. Shockley Transistor Corp. 1958-60; dir. Shockley Transistor Unit of Clevite Transistor, 1960-63; dir. Stanford Electronics Labs 1963---. Visiting lecturer, lecturer, Stanford Univ. 1958-64; Alexander M. Poniatoff prof. of engin. sci. 1964-76; exec. cons. Bell Tel. Labs., 1965-75. Inventor, junction transistor and holder over

70 U.S. patents. Author: Electrons and Holes in Semiconductors, 1950; Mechanics, 1966, ed. Imperfections of Nearly Perfect Crystals, 1952. Research dir., Anti-Submarine Warfare Operations Group, USN 1942-44, expert cons., Ofc. Secty. of War (1944-45), WW II. Awards: Medal for Merit, Ofc. Secty. of War, 1946; Air Force Assn. Cit. of Hon. 1951; Leibmann Prize, I.R.E. 1952; Army Certificate of Appreciation, 1953; Buckley Prize, Amer. Phys. Soc. 1953; Comstock Award, Natl. Acad. of Scis. 1954; Nobel Prize (physics), 1956; Wilhelm Exner Medal, Austria, 1963; Holley Medal, Amer. Soc. M.E. 1963; Calif. Inst. of Tech. Alumni Distinguished Serv. Award, 1966; Natl. Aerons. and Space Adm. Certificate (Apollo 8), 1969; NASA Pub. Serv. Group Achievement Award, 1969. Mem.: fellow: IEEE, Amer. Acad. Arts and Sciences; Army Science Adv. Panel, 1951-63; Air Force Sci. Adv. Bd. 1959-63; Natl. Acad. of Scis.; fellow, Amer. Physical Soc.; fellow, IRE; Amer. Inst. of Physics, Sigma Xi, Tau Beta Pi, Cosmos Club, Univ. Club, Wash., D.C.; Bohemian Club, S.F. Hobby: sailing; Office: Stanford University, 797 Esplanada Way, Stanford, CA 94305.

SHONK, ALBERT D., JR.
Publishers' Representative
b. May 23, 1932, Los Angeles; s. Albert D., Sr. and Jean (Stannard) Shonk; B.S. bus. admn., USC, 1954. Career: Field representative, Marketing Div., L.A. Examiner, 1954-55; Asst. Mgr., Mktg. Div., L.A. Examiner, 1955-56; Mgr., Mktg. Div., L.A. Examiner, 1956-57; Acct. Exec., Hearst Advertising Service, 1957-59; Acct. Exec., Keith H. Evans & Assoc., 1959-63; San Francisco Mgr., Keith H. Evans & Assoc., 1963-65; Owner & pres., Albert D. Shonk Co., 1965---. Founder & v.p., Inter-Greek Soc., USC, 1976---; dir. Signet Circle Corp., pres., 1977---; dir. Florence Crittenton Services, Secty., 1978---; hon. life mem. Junior Advt. Club of L.A., past dir., treas., v.p.; mem. Phi Sigma Kappa (dist. gov., 1960-62, nat. v.p., 1962-70, grand council 1962-70, 1977---—; Alpha Kappa Psi; Interfrat. Alumni Assn. of So. Calif., secty., v.p., pres., 1957-61. Presbyterian. Home: 3460 W. 7th St. (Wilshire Towers), L.A., CA 90005; Office: 3156 Wilshire Blvd., L.A., CA; 681 Market St., S.F., CA 94105.

SHORE, DINAH
TV Host — Singer
b. Mar. 1, 1920, Winchester, Tenn.; d. S.A. and Anna (Stein) Shore; B.A., Vanderbilt Univ. 1939; m. George Montgomery, Las Vegas, Nev., Dec. 5, 1943 (div. May 1962); chil.: Melissa Ann, b. Jan. 4, 1948; John David, b. Mar. 3, 1954. Career: Singer, Chamber Mus. Soc., Lower Basin St., 1940; singer, Eddie Cantor Show, 1941; mot. pic. star: Thank Your Lucky Stars, 1942; Up In Arms, 1943; others; recording artist, RCA Victor; singing star, radio-TV Dinah Shore Show, NBC, 1942-70, Dinah's Place, NBC-TV, 1970---. Entertained Allied Troops, European Theatre Operations, 1944. Awards: Best Popular Female Vocalist, Mot. Pic. Daily Annual Radio Poll, 1941-54; America's Best Known Female Singer, Gallup Polls, 1950-52; Emmy Award, best TV singer, 1954; TV Woman of the Yr., 7 consecutive yrs., by dirs. of U.S. Pres., 1955-62; one of Most Admired Women in World, annual Gallup Poll. 1957-71. Hobby: painting. Rec.: tennis. Res.: Encino, CA; Address: KTLA, 5800 W. Sunset Blvd., L.A., CA 90028.

SHOSTAK, STANLEY RICHARD
Attorney at Law
b. July 16, 1931, Omaha, Nebr.; s. Max Reubin and Reva R. (Gross) Shostak; A.A., Univ. Calif., Berkeley, 1951; A.B., 1953; J.D., (Boalt Hall), 1956; m. Carole Ruth Blumenthal, San Francisco, Calif., July 4, 1953; chil.: Stuart Robert, b. Nov. 7, 1956; Dennis Alan, b. Mar. 16, 1959; Cynthia Robin, b. Nov. 22, 1965. Career: Assoc. Geary, Spridgen & Moskowitz law firm, Santa Rosa, 1956-57; Dep. Dist. Atty., Sonoma County, 1957-59; partner, Stein and Shostak, L.A. 1959---. Guest instr. Customs and Internat. Trade, UCLA Ext.; panelist, Seminars on U.S. Customs, 1974-76. Admitted to practice: U.S. Supreme Ct., U.S. Citcuit Ct. of Appeals; U.S. Dist. Ct., U.S. Ct. of Customs and Patent Appeals; U.S. Customs Ct. Mem.: Calif., L.A. Co. (Internat. Law Com.), Customs, Amer. (Internat. Law Sect.) Bar Assns.; dir. The Foreign Trade Assn. of So. Calif. 1968, '74, pres. 1973, chmn. bd. 1974; chmn. World Trade Week Com., L.A. Area C. of C. 1976; Amer. Importer Assn., Amer. Judicature Soc., Mexican-American C. of C., Encino B'nai B'rith Lodge, Masonic Lodge, Scottish Rite, Shrine. Jewish. Rec.: golf, gardening. Res.: 4211 Clear Valley Dr., Encino, CA 91436; Office: 3435 Wilshire Blvd., Suite 2004, Los Angeles, CA 90010.

SICILIANO, ROCCO CARMINE
 Chairman of the Board-CEO, Ticor
b. Mar. 4, 1922, Salt Lake City, Ut.; s. Joseph
Vincent and Mary (Arnone) Siciliano; ed.
(valedictorian), Sr. H.S., Salt Lake City, 1940; B.A.
(hons. Beehive, grad. srs.) 1944; LL.B., Georgetown
Univ. Law Sch. 1948; m. Marion Stiebel, Boston,
Mass., Nov. 8, 1947; chil.: Loretta Silverman, b. Jan.
10, 1949; A. Vincent, b. July 19, 1950; Fred R., b.
Oct. 14, 1951; John, b. Aug. 24, 1954; Maria, b.
Sept. 4, 1961. Career: Legal asst., Natl. Labor Rels.
Bd., Wash., D.C. 1948-50; asst. secty.-treas. Procon
Inc., Des Plaines, Ill. 1950-53; asst. Secty. of Labor
(apptd. by Pres. Eisenhower), 1953-57; chmn. U.S.
Del. to Maritime Prep. Conf., Internat. Labor Orgn.,
London, 1956, Geneva, 1957; spec. asst. to the Pres.,
Personnel mgmt., White House, 1957-59; partner,
Wilkinson, Cragun & Barker law firm, Wash., D.C.
1959-69; pres.-chief exec. ofcr., Pac. Maritime Assn.,
San Francisco, 1965-69; Under Secty. of Commerce,
1969-71; pres.-chief exec. ofcr., The TI Corp., of
Calif., L.A. 1971-73; chmn. of bd.-chief exec. ofcr.,
Ticor, L.A., 1973---. Apptd. by Pres. Nixon, mem. Pay
Board, Wash., D.C. 1971; 1st Lt., U.S. Army, 1943-46;
Inf. Platoon Leader, 10th Mt. Div., Italy; personnel
staff ofcr., hdqrs., U.S. Forces, Australia, 1944-45, WW
II. Awards: Combat Inf. Badge, Bronze Star for Valor,
Spec. Commendation Ribbon by Gen. Mark Clark,
1946. Mem.: Amer. Bar Assn.; Natl. Adv. Council,
Univ. of Utah; Bd. of Visitors, UCLA Grad. Sch. of
Mgmt.; Adv. Council of Stanford Univ. Grad Sch. of
Bus.; Vice Chmn. & Trustee, Com. for Econ.
Development; Nat. Acad. of Pub. Admn.; bd. dirs.
Calif. C. of C.; L.A. Area C. of C.; Pres., L.A.
Philharmonic Assn.; Bd. of Dirs., ARA Services, Inc.,
Phil.; Pacific Lighting Corp., L.A. Clubs: Metropolitan
& Federal City, Wash., D.C.; Family, S.F.; The Los
Angeles. Roman Catholic. Res.: 612 N. Rodeo Dr.,
Beverly Hills, CA 90210; Office: 6300 Wilshire Blvd.,
L.A., CA 90048.

SIDJAKOV, NICOLAS
 Graphic Designer — Illustrator
b. Dec. 16, 1924, Riga, Latvia; s. Nicolas and Lydie
(Somac) Sidjakov; ed. Lycee Francaise, Riga; Ecole des
Beaux Arts, Paris, 1946-47; m. Jean McFarland, Paris,
France, Oct. 27, 1954; sons: Nicolas, b. June 24,
1956; Gregory, b. Nov. 16, 1963. Career: Commercial
artist, Paris, 1950-54; est. U.S. res. and bus., freelance
graphic designer-illus., San Francisco, 1955---. Awards:
Illus. among Ten Best Illustrated Children's Books for
Baboushka, N.Y. Times, 1957, 58; recipient many
awards, certificates of merit, S.F., L.A., Chicago,
Detroit, N.Y. Art Directors Shows; N.Y. Soc. of Illus.,
Western Adv. annual award, 1958-61, N.Y. annual,
1960, 61; Amer. Inst. Graphic Arts Award for one of
50 best ads. of yr. 1960; designer-illus. The Friendly
Beasts, Amer. Inst. Graphic Arts Award for one of 50
best children's books, designer-illus. The Three Kings,
Amer. Inst. Graphic Arts and N.Y. Times awards,
1960; The Emperor and the Drummer Boy, N.Y.
Times Award, 1962. Mem.: S.F. Artists and Art Dirs.
Club, Olympic Club, S.F. Hobbies: chess, books. Rec.:
tennis. Res.: 114 San Carlos Ave., Sausalito, CA.

SIEGEL, DANIEL CHARLES
 Physician — Psychiatrist
b. May 10, 1917, Detroit, Mich.; s. William and Yetta
(Apple) Siegel; ed. B.A., Univ. of Mich. 1938, M.D.,
Med. Sch. 1941; M.Sc. (psychiatry), Univ. of Mich.
Grad. Sch. 1948; grad. Inst. for Psychoanalytic Med.
of So. Calif. 1950-58; m. Carol Greenhouse, Detroit,
Mich., July 14, 1946; children: Emily Louise, b. Apr.
20, 1949; Mark William, b. Aug. 7, 1950. Career:
Med. intern, Cincinnati (Ohio) Gen. Hosp. 1941-42;
Neuropsychiatric Inst., Univ. of Mich. Hosp. 1946-49;
instr. (psychiatry), Univ. of Mich. Med. Sch. 1948-49;
pvt. practice-psychoanalysis, 1949---; attending staff,
L.A. Co. Hosp.; asst. prof., Coll. of Med. Evangs.
1949-55; training and supervising analyst, Southern
Calif. Psychoanalytic Institute, 1963---; bd. dirs.,
Hathaway Home. for Chil. 1953-59; cons. (psychiatry),
Calif. Inst. of Tech. 1955---; cons. Pac. Oaks Nursery
Sch. Maj. (MC), U.S. Army (1942-46), WW II. Awards:
recipient, 4 campaign awards, Meritorious Serv. Award,
Silver Star. Mem.: Alpha Omega Alpha, 1940; Phi
Kappa Phi, 1941; Phi Delta Epsilon; bd. govs., Welfare
Fed. of L.A. 1956-58; Community Planning Council,
Pasa. area, 1957-68; life fellow, Amer. Psychiatric
Assn.; fellow, Acad. of Psychoanalysis; fellow, Amer.
Assn. for the Advancement of Sci.; Amer.
Psychoanalytic Assn.; Internat. Psychoanalytic Assn.;
AMA; L.A. Co. Med. Assn., So. Calif. Psychiatric
Assn., So. Calif. Psychoanalytic Soc. and Institute;
N.Y. Acad. of Scis.; diplomate, Amer. Bd. of

Psychiatry and Neurology. Hobby: photog., sculpture.
Office: 181 N. Oak Knoll Ave., Pasadena, CA 91101.

SIEGEL, STUART ELLIOTT
 Physician
b. July 16, 1943, Plainfield, N.J.; B.A., summa cum
laude, Boston Univ., 1967; M.D., magna cum laude,
1967; m. Linda Wertkin; son, Joshua, b. 1971. Career:
Intern and Resident, Dept. of Pediatrics, Univ. Minn.
Hosps., 1967-69; Asst. Prof. of Pediatrics, USC Sch. of
Med., 1972-76, Assoc. Prof., 1976, Coordinator for
Pediatric Oncology, 1976---; Assoc. Hematologist,
Attending Physician and Cons. to Clin. Labs.,
Childrens Hosp. of Los Angeles, 1972-76, Head Div. of
Hematology-Oncology, 1976---. Surgeon, USPHS, NIH
Nat. Cancer Inst., Med. Br., Bethesda, Md., 1969-72.
Pres., So. Calif. Childrens Cancer Services, Inc., Ronald
McDonald House Project; participant, Nat. Leukemia
Radiothon, 1978; mem. advisory bd., Nat. Leukemia
Broadcast Found. Mem.: L.A. County Med. Assn.;
L.A. Pediatric Soc.; Western Soc. for Pediatric
Research; AMA; AAAS; Am. Assn. for Cancer
Research; Am. Soc. of Hematology; Am. Soc. of
Microbiology; Am. Soc. for Clin. Oncology. Res.:
10354 Summer Holly Cir., Los Angeles, CA 90024;
Office: 4650 Sunset Blvd., Los Angeles, CA 90027.

SIEROTY, ALAN G.
 State Senator
b. Dec. 13, 1930, Los Angeles; s. Julian and Jean
Sieroty; A.B., Econ., Stanford Univ., 1952; LL.B.,
USC, 1956. Elected State Assemblyman, 1967-77,
State Senator, 1977---. Mem.: ACLU, Am. Jewish
Com., Western Law Center for the Handicapped. Mem.
B'nai B'rith, Beverly Hills. Hobbies: music, art. Res.:
11340 W. Olympic Blvd., No. 359, Los Angeles, CA
90064; Office: 849 S. Broadway, Los Angeles, CA
90014.

SIGG, ROBERT W.
 Lawyer — State Official
b. Feb. 11, 1922, New Jersey; s. William F. and Jane
Elizabeth Sigg; B.A., Queens Coll., 1946; LL.B.,
Cornell Univ. Sch. of Law, 1949; m. Patricia
Genevieve Davies, Westwood, Calif., June 4, 1949;
sons: Clay Walker, b. Oct. 5, 1950; Eric, Whitman, b.
Oct. 6, 1952. Career: Admitted to Calif. State Bar,
1956; labor-ind. rels., dir. Personnel Servs.,
Consolidated Western Steel Div., U.S. Steel Corp.
1949-65; dir. employee and pub. rels.-mgr. ind. rels.
Amer. Potash and Chem. Corp. 1965-67; L.A. law firm
(Hill, Farrer and Burrill), 1967; apptd. (by Gov.
Reagan) Calif. Unemployment Ins. Appeals Bd.,
1967---, chmn. 1968---. USAAF, Italy, 1943-45, WW II.
Mem.: Phi Alpha Delta, 1947---; Repub. State Central
Com. 1962-65; exec. com. L.A. Co. Res.: 5412
Raimer Way, Carmichael, CA; Office: Calif.
Unemployment Insurance Appeals Bd., 714 P St.,
Sacramento, CA 95814.

SILLS, DAVID G.
 Attorney at Law
b. Mar. 21, 1938, Peoria, Ill.; s. George and Mildred
Sills; B.S., Bradley Univ., 1958; J.D.; m. Susan Lee
Cooey, July 26, 1968, Orange. Career: Counsel, Illinois
Nat. Bank and Trust Co., 1961-62; pvt. practice,
1965---, now partner firm Sills, Dougherty &
Hendrickson, Newport Beach. Capt., USMC, 1960,
1962-65. Mem. Orange Co. Supper Club, 1973---.
Chmn., Republican Assocs. of Orange Co., 1968-69,
City Councilman, City of Irvine, 1976---, Mayor,
1976-77. Congregationalist. Hobby: Long distance
running. Res.: Irvine, CA; Office: 1401 Dove St., Suite
600, Newport Beach, CA 92660.

SILVERMAN, HILLEL E.
 Rabbi, Sinai Temple
b. Feb. 24, 1924, Hartford, Conn.; s. Dr. Morris
(Rabbi, Emanuel Synagogue, Hartford, 50 yrs.) and
Althea (Osber) Silverman; B.A., Yale Univ., 1944;
student, Hebrew Univ., Jerusalem, 1947; ordained
Rabbi, Jewish Theol. Sem. of Am., 1949, Ph.D., 1952;
D.D. (hon.), Univ. of Judaism, 1974; m. Devora
Halaban, Jan. 8, 1950, Cleveland, Ohio; children: Gila,
b. 1951; Sharon, b. 1959; Jonathan, b. 1968. Career:
Staff mem. Seminary, Dir. Camp Ramah, 1949-51;
Chaplain, USN, 1951-53, Comdr., USNR---; Rabbi,
Congregation Shearith Israel, Dallas, Tex., 1954-64;
Rabbi, Sinai Temple, Los Angeles, 1964---. Exec.
Com., United Jewish Appeal, past chmn. Rabbinical
Advisory Council; Bd. dir., Jt. Distbn. Com. and World

Council of Synagogues; Israel Bonds Rabbinic Steering Com.; Zionist Orgn. of Am. Exec.; Commn. on Jewish Chaplaincy; Jewish Community Rights Council; Steering Com., Jewish Theol. Sem.; Dir. Am. Friends of Hebrew Univ., Tel Aviv Univ.; Ben Gurion Univ.; Shaare Zedek Hosp. of Jerusalem; Synagogue Council of Am. Plenum; Nat. Deputy Chaplain, Jewish War Vets. of Am. Dir., L.A. United Jewish Welfare Fund, Jewish Fedn. Council, Community Rels. Council, L.A. Crime Control, ARC, Akiba Acad., Hope for Hearing; V.P., Southern Calif. Bd. of Rabbis. Author: From Week to Week, Judaism Meets the Challenge, Judaism Looks at Life; contbr. religious mags. and journals; contbg. editor, Benenu. Recipient Prime Minister's Medal, Israel, 1974. Address: 10400 Wilshire Blvd., Los Angeles, CA 90024.

SILVERMAN, SOL
Attorney at Law
b. June 25, 1900, San Francisco; s. Jacob and Anna (Cohn) Silverman; A.B., 1923; J.D., Boalt Hall Sch. of Law, Univ. Calif., Berkeley, 1926; m. Carolyn Silverman (dec. 1973); chil.: Jack, b. Nov. 19, 1924; Dr. Sol, Jr., (chmn., dept. of oral biology, UC Med. Center, internat. authority on oral cancer), b. May 12, 1926; m. 2d Blanche Nelson Jaffe, June 26, 1974, San Francisco. Career: admitted to practice law, 1926; U.S. Supreme Ct., 1935; apptd. mem., Court of Last Resort, to aid in the adminstrn of justice, whenever and wherever deemed necessary, 1977; Moot Ct. Judge, Hastings Law Sch., 3 yrs.; apptd. state chmn., Calif. Commn. on Boxing Safe Guards, Gov. Edmund Brown, 1963-66 (after 2 world champions died as result of ring battles); Mem.: Nat. Conference for Uniform State Laws, 1959-66; Nat. Council of State Govts., 1959-66; Calif. Interstate Co-operation Commn., 1959-66; Calif. Commn. for Constitution Revision, 1964-71; Dir.: Boalt Hall Sch. of Law, 1974-76; Junior Achievement, 1964-67; Salvation Army, S.F., 1966-67. Rated highest grade as lawyer, Martindale's rating, 1963. Honored by resolutions of tribute from: Calif. State Senate and State Assembly and S.F. Bd. of Supervisors; Spirit of Life (Man of the Year) Award, City of Hope, 1976; Certificate of Award by presidents of ABA and S.F. Bar Assn., 1961, monthly pub. The Brief Case, May 1963, dedicated to him. Dir., S.F. Bar Assn., 1955-57, chmn.-editor, monthly journ., (The Brief Case) 1951-67; chmn., Calif. State Bar Journ., 1956-59; mem. bd. of editors, 1971-74; chmn. San Mateo County Forums, 1953-55; Pres.: Jewish Nat. Fund., No. Calif., 1956-63; ZOA No. Calif., 1971-73; Univ. Calif. Alumni of Boxers and Wrestlers, 1954-61. Polit. chmn. Helen Gahagan Douglas candidacy for US Senate, San Mateo Co.; active election coms. mem. Mem. Temple Emanu-El, tchr. 1922-26. Hobbies: all sports spectator, writing. Rec.: jogging. Home: 1200 California St., No. 26D, S.F.; Office: 1901 Mills Tower, San Francisco, CA.

SIMMONS, EDWARD BENEDICT, JR.
Headmaster, Dunn School
b. Jan. 30, 1946, Montclair, N.J.; s. Edward B. and Catherine C. Simmons; B.A., Weslyan Univ. 1967; M.S., Univ. of New Hampshire, 1971; Ed.D., Harvard Univ., 1978; m. Priscilla Clifford, June 7, 1968, Mountain Lakes, N.J.; chil.: Michael B., b. Nov. 28, 1969; Patrick E., b. Feb. 20, 1973; Sunithi A., b. July 16, 1977. Career: instr., Lawrenceville Sch., N.J., 1967-71; director, Middle Sch., Am. Internat. Sch., Vienna, Aus., 1971-74; Dean of Students, Harvard Univ. Summer Sch., 1974-76; Headmaster, Dunn Sch., Los Olivos, 1976---. Mem.: Chi Psi Frat., v.p., 1966-67; Skull & Serpent hon. soc., life mem. Hobbies: amateur radio (WA6LUX), antiques. Rec.: mountain climbing, skiing. Home-Office: Dunn School, Los Olivos, CA 93441.

SIMON, BRADLEY ALDEN
City Librarian
b. Mar. 9, 1929, Meriden, Conn.; s. Walter Henry and Rachel (Wetherbee) Simon; B.S., Southern Conn. State Coll., 1951; M.S., Fla. State Univ., 1955; postgrad. studies, Univ. of Miami, 1956-57, Ariz. State Univ. 1965-67. Career: Extension Librarian, Ft. Meade, Md., 1955-56; Base Librarian (SAC), Homestead AFB, Fla., 1956-57; Asst. Dir. of Libraries, Pub. Lib. of Charlotte and Mecklenburg Co., N.C., 1957-61; Dir. of Libraries, Volusia Co. (Daytona Beach), Fla. 1961-64; Lib. Cons., M. Van Buren, Inc., Charlotte, N.C., 1964; Head Librarian, Central Piedmont Community Coll., Charlotte, N.C., 1964-65; Cons., Colo. State Lib. 1965-66; Coordinator, Ariz. Lib. Survey, Ariz. State Univ., 1966; Lib. Dir., Scottsdale Pub. Lib., Ariz., 1966-71; City Librarian, Pomona Pub. Lib., Calif. 1971-77; Newport Beach Pub. Lib. 1977-78; Chula

Vista Pub. Lib. 1978---. Pres., Pub. Libraries Div., Ariz. Lib. Assn., 1967-70; Steering Com. Mem. Lib. Automation Research and Consulting, 1969-71; mem. Adminstrv. Council, Metropolitan Coop. Lib. System, L.A., 1971-74; Dir. Pomona Municipal Mgmt. Club, 1972-73; mem. Pub. Lib. Execs. of So. Calif. (PLEASC), pres. 1975; Bd. Dirs. Pub. Lib. Assn. (PLA), 1974-79; ALA, pres. 1975-76; Pub. Lib. Film Circuit of So. Calif. Awards: Hometown Builder Award 1975, Fraternal Order of Eagles, Pomona; John Cotton Dana Internat. Pub. Rels. Award, 1973, 1974, 1975 (Grand Prize). Contbr. articles, book revs. in various profl. and gen. media publs. USAF Air Intelligence. Mem.: DeMolay, Kappa Delta Phi, Royal Arcanum, Rotary Internat., Scottsdale Fine Arts Commn., 1966-71; Newport Beach City Arts Commn., 1977-78; Pomona Valley Hist. Soc., 1971---; Phoenix Chamber Music Soc., 1968-71; Newport Harbor Art Mus., 1977---. Presbyterian. Hobbies: authorship, antique autos. Rec.: sailing, tennis, camping. Res.: P.O.B. 1843, Chula Vista, CA 92012; Office: 365 F. St., Chula Vista, CA 92010.

SIMON, NORTON
Industrialist
b. Feb. 5, 1907, Portland, Ore.; s. Myer and Lillian (Glickman) Simon; ed. H.S., San Francisco, Calif.; m. Jennifer Jones, Eng., May 30, 1971; sons: Donald Ellis, b. Apr. 6, 1936; Robert Ellis, b. Nov. 23, 1937. Career: Propr., L.A. Steel Prods. Co., 1927-33; pres. Val Vita Food Prods. Co., 1931-43; pres.-chmn. bd. dirs., Hunt Foods, Inc. 1943---; dir.-exec. com.: No. Pacific Railway Co. 1951---; Harbor Plywood Corp., 1954---; investor, widely diversified interests; principal stockholder, Hunt Foods, Inc., The Ohio Match Co., others. Res.: 100 N. Hudson Ave., Los Angeles, CA; Office: The Hunt Center, Fullerton, CA.

SIMONIAN, VAHE HAROLD
Clergyman
b. Mar. 2, 1928, Boston, Mass.; s. T. Haig and Berjouhie (Garabedian) Simonian; B.A., honors, George Pepperdine Coll., 1950; B.D., Princeton Theological Seminary, 1953; Rel.D., Sch. of Theology, Claremont, 1966; Ph.D., 1970; Merrill Fellow, Harvard Divinity Sch., 1969; m. Ani Ketenjian, Feb. 16, 1957, Beirut, Lebanon; chil.: Gary Patrick, b. Mar. 17, 1965; Christopher, b. Oct. 12, 1966; Ian Vahe, b. Apr. 27, 1972. Career: asst. pastor, Santa Barbara Presbyterian Ch., 1953-55; dean and prof., Near East Sch. of Theology, Beirut, 1956-57; visiting prof. & acting pres., Haigazian Coll., Beirut, 1956-57; sr. pastor, Kirk O' The Valley Presbyn. Ch., Reseda, 1957-62; sr. pastor, Pacific Palisades Presbyn. Ch., 1962-70; sr. pastor, Pasadena Presbyn. Ch., 1970---. Bd. Trustee, San Francisco Theol. Semin., 1974---; advisory council, Am. Heart Assn., 1978---; mem.: Chi Alpha, 1971---; Rotary Club of Pacific Palisades, pres. 1969; Rotary Club of Pasadena, 1970---; Tournament of Roses, 1971---. Ch. offices: moderator, presbytery of San Gabriel UPCUSA, 1975; chmn. major mission funding task force, UPCUSA, 1974-75; nat. vice-chmn., major mission fund UPCUSA, 1976---. Rec.: golf, tennis, bridge. Home: 2726 N. Porter Ave., Altadena, CA; Office: 54 N. Oakland Ave., Pasadena, CA 91101.

SIMPSON, JAN ROBIN
Industrial Finishing Company Executive
b. Feb. 1, 1952, Duluth, Minn.; d. Jay David and Dorothy Jean Alleman; student: Univ. Calif., Berkeley; UCSB; Stanford Univ. Sch. of Radiology; m. Richard Joseph Simpson, Aug. 2, 1975, Portola Valley, Calif. Career: founder, Calif. Indsl. Finishing, Inc., 1976--- (spec. in painting and metalizing electronics parts for the computer industry). Hobbies: cooking, piano. Rec.: jogging, swimming. Home: 13741 Quito Rd., Saratoga, CA 95070; Office: 442 Nelo St., Santa Clara, CA 95050.

SINGHER, MARTIAL
Opera Singer
b. Aug. 14, 1904, Oloron Ste. Marie, France; s. Paul Joseph and Marie Jeanne (Dubourg) Singher; Professorate French Lit., Paris 1927; 1st prizes singing opera-comique, opera, Conservatoire National Paris, 1929-30; Dr.Music, Univ. Chicago, 1955; m. Eta Busch (dau. Dr. Fritz Busch, famous orchestra conductor), Jan. 10, 1940, Copenhagen; sons: Charles Michel, b. 1940; John Peter, b. 1943; Philip Thomas, b. 1953. Career: Leading baritone, Paris Opera, 1930-41 and opera-comique, 1938-41; leading baritone, Teatro Colon, Buenos Aires, 1936-43; leading baritone, Metropolitan Opera, N.Y., 1943-59; Soloist with all leading Am. orchestras (N.Y., Boston, Phila., Chicago,

Cleveland, S.F., L.A., Minneapolis, etc.); Recitalist over 3 continents. Prof. of Voice and dir. Opera Depts., Conservatoire Province at Montreal, 1950-54; Curtis Inst., Phila., 1955-68; Peabody Inst., Baltimore, 1960-63; Music Acad. of the West, Santa Barbara, 1962---. Lectr., tchr. master classes; recordings for RCA Victor, Columbia, Vanguard, others; staged and prod. 30 operas. Mil. duty in France. Mem.: Am. Acad. of Tchrs. of Singing, 1964---; Chevalier de la Legion d'Honneur, France, 1959. Roman Catholic. Res.: 840 Deerpath Rd., Santa Barbara, CA 93108; Office: 1070 Fairway Rd., Santa Barbara, CA 93108.

SINHA, YAGYA NAND
Research Scientist
b. Oct. 21, 1936, Rohua, Bihar, India; s. Baidyanath and Rajeshwari Sinha; Ph.D., 1967; m. Savitri, May 28, 1958, Katesar, India; children: Manjula, b. 1959; Anita, b. 1964; Suman, b. 1965; Arun, b. 1967. Career: Science, 1957---: Research Asst., Livestock Research Station, Bihar, Datna, India, 1959-61; grad. asst., Mich. State Univ., 1962-67; research assoc., Cornell Univ., Ithaca, N.Y., 1967-69; assoc., Scripps Clin. and Research Found., 1969---. Contbr. tech. articles profl. publs. Pres., India Assn. of San Diego, 1971-72. Rec.: tennis, badminton. Res.: 8385 Aries Rd., San Diego, CA 92126; Office: 10666 N. Torrey Pines Rd., La Jolla, CA 92037.

SIPPEL, ASTA
Realtor
b. Jan. 10, 1921, Estonia; d. Madis and Helene Parras; Coll., elem. sch. tchr. edn.; m. Thomas W. Sippel, June 16, 1946, Munich, Germany; son, Robert Thomas, b. Oct. 16, 1953. Career: elem. sch. tchr., Estonia, 1943-44; part-time tchr., Germany, 1945; Calif. licensed real estate agent, 1972---; Calif. licensed real estate broker, 1974---; certified Grad. Realtor Inst. (GRI) 1976). Community vol. work for Heart Fund, Cancer Fund, Mothers March of Dimes, schools, etc.; leader in Estonian Youth Group, 1943-44; mem. Vet. of Foreign Wars Aux., 1947-79; Ex-Anima Club, pres. 1961, secty.-treas., 1969-70; Valley Childrens Hosp. Guild, treas., 1971; Kings Co. Bd. of Realtors; Calif. Assn. of Realtors; Nat. Assn. of Realtors, 1973---. Methodist. Hobbies: crafts, knitting, ceramics. Rec.: snow and water skiing. Home: 38 Oleander, Lemoore, CA 93245; Office: 352 West D, Lemoore, CA.

SISSON, JOHN EARL
Attorney at Law
b. Mar. 1, 1904, Red Bluff, Calif.; s. Elmer L. and Margaret (Cullen) Sisson; A.B., Univ. Calif., Berkeley, 1925; M.A., 1927; J.D., 1927; m. Alyce May Elder, Aug. 7, 1927 Martinez; son, John Earl, Jr. (lawyer), b. Feb. 27, 1933. Career: Law practice in Los Angeles, 1927---. Dir., Southern California Tennis Assn., v.p.; dir. and v.p., Youth Tennis Found. Dir.: Interstate Shopping Centers, Inc.; Traveltime, Inc.; Secty., Linde Corp., others. Clubs: Los Angeles Country, California, Los Angeles Stock Exchange, Los Angeles Tennis. Episcopalian. Rec.: tennis, golf. Res.: 1489 Hampton Rd., San Marino, CA 91108; Office: One Wilshire Blvd., Suite 1212, Los Angeles, CA 90017.

SKAALEGAARD, HANS MARTIN
Artist — Gallery Owner — Lecturer
b. Feb. 7, 1924, Faroe Islands, Europe; s. Ole Johannes and Hanna Elisa (Fredriksen) Skaalegaard; painting signature used is Hans Skalagard, old Nordic spelling, dating back to ninth century in the Faroe Isls.; art studies, Royale Acad. of Copenhagen, with noted marine artist Anton Otto Fisher, N.Y.; m. Mignon Diana Haack Haegland, Mar. 31, 1955, Santa Rosa; dau. (adopted), Karen Solvieg Haegland Skaalegaard (Sikes), b. June 2, 1953. Career: Seamans apprentice at age 13 aboard sailing ships; served with Am. Merchant Marine throughout WW II, and after (painting constantly); award winning art exhibits of ship paintings, NYC, 1952-54; moved to S.F., continued sailing and painting, 1954-65; over fifty one-man exhibits, some with lectrs.; opened Skaalegaard Square-Rigger Art Gallery (featuring his ship paintings) 1966---; continued exhibiting and lectring. on ships and the sea. Awarded silver (1970) and gold (1972) medals; title Master Painter from Internat. Acad. of Arts, Letters & Sciences, Tommaso Campanella of Rome, Italy; exhibited in Biarritz, France; eleven of painting pub. by Bernard Picture Co.; currently working on Naval Heritage Series, the most important naval vessels of the USA historically; repr. by Haggenmaker Galleries, Beverly Hills and Laguna Beach, Tilbert Galleries in S.F. and Hawaii; paintings displayed at Naval Post Grad. Sch., Allen Knight Maritime Mus., Salvation Army Bldg., all in Monterey,

and at Robert Louis Stevenson Sch., Pebble Beach; pvt. collections of admirals, generals, etc. worldwide. Bd. dir., Allen Knight Maritime Mus. for Monterey Hist. & Art Assn., 1972---; Dir., Aasgaarden Lodge 112, Sons of Norway, 1974-77; bd. dir., U.S. Navy League; Mem. Assn. of U.S. Army, Stilwell chpt.; Hon. mem., Monterey Civic Club. Republican; supporter for Sen. Burt Talcott. St. Phillips Lutheran Ch., council mem. 1967-68. Hobbies: studying Naval hist. Home: 25197 Canyon Dr., Carmel, CA 93923; Office: Los Cortes Bldg., P.O.B. 6611, Carmel, CA 93921.

SKALNIK, JOHN GORDON
Professor of Engineering
b. May 30, 1923, Medford, Okla.; s. John Robert and Ella Catherine (Semrad) Skalnik; B.S., Okla. State Univ., 1944; M.S., Yale Univ., 1947; Ph.D., 1955; m. Dianne Fleck, May 30, 1947, New Haven, Conn.; sons, John Robert, b. 1949; David Gordon, b. 1957. Career: Asst. Prof., Yale Univ., 1944-55, Assoc. Prof., 1955-65; Professor, Univ. Calif., Santa Barbara, 1965---, Chmn. Dept. of Elect. Engring. 1968-70, Dean, Coll. of Engring., 1970-76. Co-author: Microwave Theory and Techniques, 1953; Microwave Principles, 1957; Theory and Applications of Active Devices, 1966. Mem.: IEEE, Electrochem. Soc., Sigma Xi. Res.: 567 Ronda Dr., Santa Barbara, CA 93111.

SKIRBALL, JACK H.
Film Company President
b. June 23, 1896, Homestead, Pa.; s. Abram and Sarah (Davis) Skirball; ed. Bachelor of Hebrew, Dr. of Humane Letters and Rabbi, Hebrew Union Coll., Cincinnati, Oh., 1921; B.A., Western Res. Univ. 1923; postgrad. work, Univ. of Chicago; LL.D., USC, 1973; m. Audrey Marx, Beverly Hills, California, Apr. 7, 1949; children: Sally, b. Oct. 10, 1950; Agnes, b. Mar. 21, 1952. Career: Asst. Rabbi (to Dr. Louis Wolsey), Cleveland, Oh. 1923-25; Rabbi, Evansville, Ind. 1926-33; mgr. (in chg. prodn.) Edn. Films, 1933-39; pres. (independent mot. pic. prod.) Skirball Prodns. 1939-52; pres. Films for Television of Hollywood, Inc. 1952---; pres. Vacation Village, Inc., San Diego, 1961---; pres. Bowlero Corps; pres. Gen. Internat. Films, Inc. 1975---; Dir. relig. and entertainment, Jewish Welfare Bd. (all camps from Pittsburgh to Denver), Chicago hdqrs., WW I. Mem.: chmn. bd. trustees, Hebrew Union Coll.; Jewish Inst. of Relig. at L.A.; past pres., So. Council-past v.p., Union Amer. Hebrew Congs.; pres. So. Indiana Red Cross Soc.; chmn. Anti-Tuberculosis Soc.; head, Open Forum (founder, inter-racial com.); trustee: UCLA Hope for Hearing; Reiss-Davis Childs Clinic; com. Community Chest; Rotary Club; Res.: 722 N. Elm Dr., Beverly Hills; Office: 1900 Ave. of the Stars, Suite 1850, Los Angeles, CA 90067.

SKLAR, GEORGE
Novelist — Playwright
b. May 31, 1908, Meriden, Conn.; s. Ezak and Bertha (Marshak) Sklar; B.A., Yale Univ., 1929, student, Yale Sch. of Drama, 1929-31; m. Miriam Blecher, Aug. 22, 1935, Manchester, Vt.; children: Judith (Rasminsky), b. 1940; Daniel J., b. 1942; Zachary H., b. 1948. Career: Playwright, 1932-40, 1966---; Screenwriter, 1940-45; Novelist, 1946-65; Plays: Merry Go Round, 1932; Peace on Earth, 1933; Stevedore, 1934; Parade, 1935; Life and Death of an American, 1939; Laura, 1946; And People All Around, 1966; Brown Pelican, 1972; Jigsaw, 1976. Novels: The Two Worlds of Johnny Torero, 1946; The Promising Young Men, 1951; The Housewarming, 1953; The Identity of Dr. Frazier, 1961. Mem. Dramatists Guild, exec. bd. 1936-40; Authors League, 1940-46. Hobby: Collecting New Orleans jazz records. Rec.: listening to records. Res.: 530 N. Fuller Ave., Los Angeles, CA 90036.

SKORNIA, THOMAS ALLAN
Electronics Company Executive
b. Nov. 16, 1934, Elmhurst, Ill.; s. Joseph W. and Frances (Carusiello) Skornia; B.A., Grinnell Coll., 1958; J.D., Harvard Univ., 1961; m. Kirsten Olsen, May 22, 1976, Atherton, Calif. Career: admitted to Calif. Bar, 1962; law clerk, U.S. Circuit Judge, S.F., 1961-62; appellate atty., tax div., U.S. Justice Dept., Washington, D.C., 1962-63; assoc., Cooley, Crowley, S.F., 1963-66; sr. partner, Skornia & Rosenblum, S.F. & Palo Alto, 1970-77; dir. & secty., Advanced Micro Devices, Inc., Sunnyvale, 1969-77; v.p. and gen. counsel, 1977---; coordinator, com. of Calif. Semiconductor Industry, 1973; also regular lectr. on bus. matters, Univ. of Calif. extension program: Starting and Financing Your Own Bus., Mergers and

Acquisitions, Venture Capital, Going Public; contbr. author, 2 chpts. of Winning the Money Game. Trustee,Marin Jr. Coll. Dist., 1966-68; Mem.: Calif. & Fed. Bar Assns., 1962---; Am. Bar Assn., Bay area sect. on taxation, 1965---. Polit. candidate for congress, 12th dist., CA, 1974 primary; Office: 901 Thompson Pl., Sunnyvale, CA 94086. Home: 651 Forest Ave., Palo Alto, CA 94301;

SKOUBO, LEO AXELGAARD
Electronics Engineer
b. Aug. 30, 1931, Hermiston, Ore.; s. Adolf Wilhelm Jensen and Anne (Axelgaard) Skoubo; B.S.E.E., 1959, m. Velma Stoneking, Sept. 28, 1962, Los Angeles; son, Keith Stoneking. Career: Sr. Electrical Engr., AiResearch Mfg. Co., 1959---; founder, owner, Quality Engravers, Lomita. Dir., American Electro Products, Inc. Patentee (U.S., France, Canada, Britain) on SCR Turbine overspeed control. Charter mem. Solar Energy Soc. of Am. Sgt., AUS, 1940-53, Austria. Luterhan, Missouri Synod, Elder. Hobbies: gardening, electronics. Res.: 1850 W. 261st St., Lomita, CA 90717; Office: 2525 W. 190th St., Torrance, CA 90509.

SKOURAS, CHARLES PETER, JR.
Motion Picture Executive
b. Nov. 18, 1925, St. Louis, Mo.; s. Charles Peter and Florence (Souders) Skouras; B.S., U.S. Mil. Acad. 1944-48; m. Diane Marie Mellos, Los Angeles, Calif., Nov. 25, 1953; chil.: Charles Peter, III, b. Aug. 28, 1954; Christiana Florentia, b. Apr. 9, 1956. Career: Mot. pic. ind. 1953---, prod. 20th Century Fox Film Corp. 1958-62; sr. v.p.-treas., Sero Amusement Co. 1962---. Ofcr.-dir.: Valley Drive-In Theatre Corp.; Ambassador Mo. Building Corp.; Charles P. Skouras Found.; dir. L.A. Music Center Founders. Ofcr., USAF, 1948-53; comdg. ofcr., Air Corp-W. Squadron, Korea, 1951-52. Mem.: Bel-Air Country Club, 1948---; Army Ath. Assn. 1948---; Balboa Bay Clyb; Amer. Philatelic Soc. 1965---; Elgin Golf Club, Scotland, 1966---; L.A. County Art Mus. Founders Assn. Greek Orthodox (trustee, St. Sophia Found. 1952-58). Hobby: philately. Rec.: golf, hunting. Res.: 924 Hillcrest Rd., Beverly Hills, CA 90210; Office: 1615 Cordova St., Los Angeles, CA 90007.

SKYLES, GEORGE HARMON
Librarian
b. July 9, 1935, Hill City, Idaho; s. George William and Bertha Lorena (Fielding) Skyles; B.S., Brigham Young Univ., 1960, M.A., 1962, M.L.S., 1968; postgard., Portland State Univ., 1962, USC, 1967-68, Fullerton Coll., 1978-79; m. Mary Beth Anderson, Dec. 12, 1958, Santa Monica; children: Donna LeAnne, b. 1961; Paul Jeffrey, b. 1962; Brian Lee, b. 1964; Kenneth Dean, b. 1966. Career: Tchr., Lyman (Wyo.) High Sch., 1962-63, Whittier (Calif.) Union H.S. 1963-66; Librarian, El Rancho High Sch. & Adult Sch., 1967---. Designer: El Rancho H.S. Library, 1971. Mem.: Calif. Media & Lib. Educators Assn., State Treas., 1977-79; pres., El Rancho chpt., Calif. Council for Adult Edn., 1978-79; El Rancho Edn. Assn., v.p. 1971, bd. dir. 1968-70; El Rancho Fedn. of Tchrs., Calif. Fedn. Tchrs., Am. Fedn. of Tchrs. (AFL-CIO). Republican, precinct treas., Provo, Utah, 1960-62. L.D.S. Ch., missionary, 1955-58. Res.: 1401 Carpenter St., La Habra, CA 90631; Office: 6501 S. Passons Blvd., Pico Rivera, CA 90660.

SLOANE, MARGARET N.
City Librarian
b. Jan. 5, 1914, Dallas, Tex.; d. Bowers Calhoun and Josie (Cox) Newberry; B.S., 1935; M.A., 1936; M.L.S., 1957; m. Paul Sloane (dec.) May 2, 1939, Phoenix, Ariz. Career: post librarian, Ft. Ord, 1957-59; librarian, TRW, 1959-68; mgr., Ford Found., 1968-71; Librarian, Redondo Beach pub., 1971-73; City Librarian, Cerritos, 1973---. Mem.: Am. Lib. Assn.; Am. Soc. for Information Sci.; Special Libraries Assn.; Calif. Lib. Assn. Hobbies: writing, siamese cats. Home: 730 Esplanade, Redondo Beach, CA; Office: 18025 Bloomfield Ave., Cerritos, CA 90701.

SMALL, ALICE JEAN
Painter — Educator
b. Sandpoint, Ida.; d. Edward Hayes and Alice (McNeil) Small; niece of Wakelin McNeil, famous Ranger Mac, Peabody Award, Univ. Wis.; Castle McNeil, Scot., writer, educ., artist; B.A., Univ. of Wash. 1943; M.F.A., Univ. Calif., Berkeley, 1945; San Jose State Coll. 1968; grad. stu. art: Chicago Inst. Design, Cranbrook Acad. Art, Mich.; Ala. Poly Tech. Inst., Monterey Peninsyla Coll., Monterey Inst. Foreign

Stus., N.Y. Sch. of Art; Bauhaus, Moholy-Nogy; Ecole de Beaux Arts, Paris; water color: Russia, Japan, Mex. 1960-70. Career: Dir. painting, Fed. Settlement, NYC, 1943; prof. of art: Univ. Wash. 1945, Univ. W. Va. 1948; dir. Art Dept., Univ. Tampa, Fla. 1950; reg. dir. U.S. Army Crafts, Far East, Jap. 1953; Europe 1957; U.S. Inf. Serv., Mex. 1960-66; research dir. art; Army Edn. Center, Ft. Ord, 1967-72; lecturer in Spanish Art, Calif. 1972-74; Greco, Goya, 1974; Exhibs. of oil-water color: Seattle Art Mus. 1940; Riverside Gallery, Argent Gallery, NYC 1942; Corcoran Gallery, Wash., D.C.; Ringling Mus. of Art, Sarasota Mus., Tampa Univ., Fla. 1945; Fairbanks, Alaska; Vancouver Gallery of Art, Can.; Amer. Cultural Center, Tokyo, Japan 1951; Europe, Far East, 1957; 50 watercolors of The Americas for Pres. Eisenhower and Prince Phillip, People to People, Mex. 1960; murals, Hist. of Calif. Gold Rush, Carmel River Sch., 1970; 500 paintings, pvt.-mus. collections around the world; exhibited watercolors, San Jose, Laguna Beach, Newport Beach, Pebble Beach Schools; murals, Fla., Wash., Calif., Jap. TV interviews-lectures throughout world. Around the World Sketchbook, publ. Internat. Mag. 1969, 73; Adventures of an Artist, Europe, 1974; Calif. Sketch Book, Mex. Sketch Book, U.S. Army Texts.; Illus. Drawings, publ. 1974-75; Mem.: Santa Clara Valley Water Color Society; Monterey Water Color Society. Awards: Outstanding Alumnae, Univ. Wash.; Woman of Yr., Fla.; OWL Award, Natl. League American Pen Women, others. Res.: 17 Mile Dr., Fan Shell Beach, Pebble Beach, CA 93953.

SMILER, DENNIS GENE
Oral Surgeon
b. June 30, 1939; ed. stu. USC 1957-58; La. State Coll. 1958; D.D., Univ. of Pa. 1964; Prosthodontic Tr. Inst., Lanstuhl, Ger. 1964; Postgrad. 1965; Boston Univ. 1966, Grad. Sch. of Dentistry, 1967; M.Sc.D. 1968; Licensed: Calif., Mass. 1966; Postgrad. Walter Reed Army Med. Center, Wash., D.C. 1968; married, 4 children. Career: Lab. tech., Bio-Sci. Labs., L.A. 1960; intern, Roosevelt Hosp., N.Y. 1967, res. 1968-69; staff oral surg., Wac'sworth Hosp., Vets. Adm., L.A. 1969, cons. 1969---; est. own ofc. L.A. 1970---; staff: Chil's. Hosp., L.A.; Kaiser Found., Panorama City; Midway, Encino, Sherman Oaks Hosps.; asst. clin. prof. USC Sch. of Dentistry, 1972---. Pres., Found. Oral and Maxillo-facial Surg. Inc. 1976---. Contrib. many professional publs. on med. research. Lecturer, professional subjs., Ger. 1964-66, USA 1966---. Capt., U.S. Army, 98th Gen. Hosp., Ger. 1964-66. Awards: 3 rd. Prize in Kellogg Essay Contest, June 1968. Mem.: Amer. Soc. of Oral Surgs.; L.A., Amer. Bds. of Oral Surgs.; Bd. Certified Oral Surg.; Fellow, Amer. Dental Soc. of Anesthesia, 1974; Fellow-pres. So. Calif. Acad. of Oral Pathology, 1975. Hobby: teaching basic sailing for YMCA Sailing Club, air pilots license, fishing. Res.: 13433 Galewood, Sherman Oaks, CA; Office: 6200 Wilshire Blvd., Los Angeles; 5644 Van Nuys Blvd., Van Nuys, CA.

SMITH, BERNARD JOSEPH
Consulting Engineer
b. Aug. 29, 1900, Liverpool, Eng. (U.S. Cit. 1930); s. Thomas Joseph and Sarah Anne (Crum) Smith; ed. pvt. tutors, math. 1923-24; St. Edwards Coll.; Blackrock Coll., Dublin; Oxford Univ.; B.E. (hons.), Univ. of Liverpool, 1923, M. Engring. 1926; m. Julia Susan Connolly, Toledo, Ohio, June 4, 1929; chil.: Bernard Joseph Connolly, Mrs. C.E. (Sarah Anne Kathleen) Shcaffer, Mrs. William J. (Maureen Sheila) Gallagher, Jr., Una Eileen, Mrs. William M. (Aislin Therese Crum) Nickey, Thomas Eugene Malachy, Mrs. Edwin (Joan Pauline) McClintoch; Dr. John Philip Michael. Career: Est. U.S. res. 1912; res. engr. Underpinning & Found. Co. NYC, Phila. 1924; inspector and undergroun;conduit engr., N.Y., N.J. Tel. Co. and Ohio Bell Tel. Co. 1924-26; asst. engr. Alexander Potter, cons. engr. 1926-30; pvt. research in hydrology and hydraulics, 1930; design engr. Humble Oil & Refining Co. 1930-32; city engr. Baytown, Tex. 1931-33, city mgr. 1932-33, cons. engr. 1931-34; engring. inspector, PWA, Ft. Worth, 1934-35, engring. examiner, 1935-37; pvt. cons. engr. 1937-38; dir. research and personnel, City of Ft. Worth, 1938-41; lecturer, Tex. Christian Univ. 1940-43; state planning engr. and acting state dir., Tex. Pub. Works Res. 1941-42; asst. reg. rep. and economist, Natl. Housing Agcy., Dallas, 1942-47; lecturer on econs., bus. adm. and engring., So. Meth. Univ. 1947-53; cons. engr., Dallas, 1947---; chief, San Francisco Bay Development, U.S. Corps of Engrs., S.F. dist. 1957-65, mem. Amer. Economic Assn.; mem. Soc. of Evolutionary Economics; mem. History of Economics Soc.; Commr. Santa Cruz County, Calif., Water Advisory Commn.;

spec. cons. S.F. Bay Conservatism and Development Comm., 1966---. Lecturer on professional subjects and radio conf. panelist. Licensed professional engr., Tex., N.J.; registered engr., Calif., N.J., Tex. Author: Town Building 1939; El Paso Housing Market, 1945; The International Scene, 1946; numerous professional papers, bus. digests, 1963---; contrib. articles to U.S. and foreign mags. and journs. Listed: Amer. Men of Sci.; Leaders in Amer. Sci., others. Mem.: fellow, Amer. Soc. of C.E.; pres. S.F. Irish Lit. and History Soc. 1961-63; Amer. Waterworks Assn.; bd. govs. Dallas Fed. Reference Exch.; Gov. Reagan's Task Force on Transportation; Amer. Econ. Assn.; Tex. Soc. Professional Engrs.; County Louth Archaeol. Soc.; Third Order of St. Francis Club; Clogher Hist. Soc.; Commonwelath Club; Serra Club, Dallas. Pres., Holy Name Soc.; Holy Trinity Ch. Hobbies: photog., painting, travel. Office: P.O.B. 663, Aptos, CA 95003.

SMITH, CLAUDE VAULDON
Insurance Underwriter
b. Dec. 12, 1903, Elkhart, Iowa; s. J.A. and Sara Smith; B.S., bus. admin., USC, 1925-29; Lillian Deshner, June 30, 1935, La Jolla. Career: Insurance agent, Los Angeles, 1929-40, San Francisco 1940-44, New Haven (Conn.) 1942-44, L.A. 1945-70, named a correspondent for Lloyd's of London, 1950, elected underwriting mem., Lloyd's, London, 1972--- (mem. 4 Underwriting syndicates at Lloyd's). Trustee, Univ. of La Verne, 1959---. Mem. Delta Phi Epsilon (nat. profl. foreign service frat.), v.p., dir., 1954-58; Wm. D. Stephens Lodge No. 698 Masons; Scottish Rite; Al Malaikah Shrine Temple, L.A., 1954---. Protestant. Hobbies: Leisure World Concert Orchestra, San Clemente barbershop chpt. Res.: 2182-N Via Puerta, Laguna Hills, CA 92653.

SMITH, DOROTHY OTTINGER
Jewelry Designer -- Civic Leader
b. Indianapolis; d. Albert Ellsworth and Leona Aurelia (Waller) Ottinger; desc. George Washington; student Herron Art Sch. of Purdue Univ. and Indiana Univ., 1941-42; m. James Emory Smith, June 25, 1943; children: Michael Ottinger, b. 1944; Sarah Anne, b. 1948; Theodore Arnold, b. 1954; Lisa Marie, b. 1957. Career: Comm. artist, William H. Block Co., Indpls., 1942-43, H.P. Wasson Co., 1943-44; dir. Riverside Art Center, 1963-64; jewelry designer, Riverside, 1970---. Commd. designs for Jr. League of Riverside, Art Alliance (Riverside Art Center), Handweaver's and Spinners Guild of Riverside. Sculpture selection panelist, Riverside City Hall, 1974-75; Juror, Riverside Civic Center Purchase Prize Art Show, 1975-76; mem. Mayor's Commns. on Civic Beauty and Sister City Sendai, 1965-66; mem. pub. bldgs. and grounds subcom., gen. plan citizens com. City of Riverside, 1965-66. Recipient awards: valuable and distinguished serv., City Council, 1977; Outstanding contbrns. to the cultural arts of Riverside, Mayor Ben H. Lewis, 1977. Adviser Riverside chpt. Freedom's Found. of Valley Forge; Founder, Art Alliance of Riverside Art Center and Mus., 1964, pres. 1969-70; bd. dir., chmn. spl. events Children's League of Riverside Community Hosp., 1952-53; bd. dirs. Crippled Children's Soc. of Riverside, spl. events chmn., 1952-53; bd. dirs. Jr. League of Riverside, rec. secty. 1960-61; bd. dirs. Nat. Charity League, pres. Riverside chpt. 1965-66; mem. exec. com. Riverside Arts Found., 1977---, fund dr. chmn. 1978-79, project rev. chmn., 1978-79; bd. dirs. Gemco Charitable and Scholarship Found., 1977---, Juror 1977-79. Mem.: Riverside Art Assn., pres. 1961-63, 1st v.p. 1964-65, 1967-68, trustee 1959-70. Presbyterian, Bd. of Women Deacons. Res.: 3979 Chapman Pl., Riverside, CA 92506.

SMITH, GEORGE ALLEN
Mortgage Banker
b. Apr. 4, 1935, New York City; s. Samuel and Edith (Romanov) Smith; B.S., UCLA Sch. of Engring., 1957; M.B.A., Harvard Grad. Sch. of Bus., 1959; m. Pamela Jean Hastings, Feb. 24, 1974, Los Angeles; Chil.: James Bernard, b. Aug. 15, 1966; Jill Heather, b. Dec. 29, 1968; Rebecca Hastings, b. Feb. 14, 1978. Career: dir. adminstrn., Aerospace Corp., 1959-64; v.p. and treas., College Park Fullerton, 1964-68; with Sonnenblick-Goldman Corp. of Calif. (mortgage bankers and realtors), 1968---, pres., 1975---; active real estate investor. Home: 237 Woodruff Ave., L.A., CA 90024; Office: 1901 Ave. of the Stars, No. 1200, Los Angeles, CA 90067.

SMITH, GORDON PAUL
Economist — State Official
b. Dec. 25, 1916, Salem, Mass.; s. Gordon and May (Vaughn) Smith; ed. grad. Mt. Hermon Prep. Sch. 1940; B.S., Univ. Mass. 1947; M.S., Univ. Denver, 1948; postgrad. NYC; m. Ramona Chamberlain, San Francisco, Calif., Sept. 27, 1969; sons: Randall B., b. Aug. 26, 1946; Rodney F., b. Feb. 25, 1949. Career: Sr. researcher, Tax Found., Inc. 1948-51; v.p. Booz, Allen and Hamilton, mgmt. cons. 1951-67, 1969-70; asst. to pres. Republic Aviation Corp. 1954; advisor, Hoover Comm., Wash., D.C. 1954-55; cons. State of Hawaii, 1960-61; Alaska, 1963; chmn.-pres. Palo Alto-Stanford Univ. Med. Center, 1960-65; founder-pres. Santa Clara Mid-Peninsula Health Planning Council, 1963-65; Calif. State Dir. of Finance, 1967-68; pres. Gordon Paul Smith & Co. 1968-69. Dir., Calif. Intergovt. Council on Urban Growth; v. chmn. Calif. Franchise Tax Bd.; dir. San Francisco Harbor Finance Bd.; dir. Calif. Wildlife Conservation Bd.; dir. S.F. and L.A. World Trade Authority; dir. Calif. Toll Bridge Authority, 1967-68; v. chmn. Calif. State Lands Comm., 1967-68; chmn. Calif. State Bd. of Public Works, 1967-68; chmn.-dir. Empire Resources Internat., Inc. 1968-69; pres.-chief exec. ofcr.-chmn. exec. com.-dir. Golconda Corp. and chmn. bd. Bastian-Blessing, Inc. 1971---; dir. First Calif. Co. 1970-71. Author: numerous articles on govt., finance, mgmt. Lecturer: maj. platforms, incl. Commonwealth Club, S.F.; Town Hall, L.A.; maj. radio-TV pub. affairs pgms. 1st Lt., U.S. Army, Armored Forces, ETO 1943-46, WW II. Awards: Spec. Commendation, Hoover Comm. 1955; Distinguished Alumni Award, Univ. Mass. 1963; nom. Freedom Award, Freedoms Found., Valley Forge, 1970; Mem.: ind. dev. com. Calif. State C. of C. 1961-65; dir. Univ. Mass. Alumni Bd. 1965---; dir. Mt. Hermon Prep. Sch. Alumni Bd. 1965---; Theta Chi; clubs: World Trade, Stock Exch., S.F. Golf, The Family, S.F.; L.A. Country Club. Calif. Repub. State Central Com., platform Com. 1967---, del Natl. Conv. 1968. Episcopalian. Hobby: painting. Rec.: golf, tennis, music. Res.: 1009 Lombard St., San Francisco, 94109; Office: 555 California St., San Francisco, CA 94104.

SMITH, HOWARD RUSSELL
President, Avery International
b. Aug. 15, 1914, Clark Co., Ohio; s. Lewis H. and Eula Smith; A.B., Pomona Coll., Claremont, Calif. 1936; m. Jeanne Rogers, Pasadena, Calif., June 27, 1942; chil.: Stewart Russell, b. Aug. 29, 1946; Douglas Howard, b. Jan. 27, 1949; Jeanne Ellen, b. Feb. 4, 1956. Career: Security analyst, Kidder, Peabody & Co. 1936-37; Internat. Labor Ofc., League of Nations, Switz. 1937-40; asst. to pres., Blue Diamond Corp. 1940-46; v.p.-gen. mgr., Avery Prods. Corp. 1946-56, pres. 1956 and chmn of the bd., 1975---. Dir.: Haug Assocs.; Beckman Instruments, Inc., Fullerton; chmn. bd. Community TV of So. Calif.-KCET; bd. dirs.: chmn. bd. trustees, Pomona College; bd. fellows, Claremont Univ. Center and Grad. Sch.; bd. Los Angeles Philharmonic Assn.; dir., Security Pacific Natl. Bank; dir. Security Pacific Corp.; dir., Southern California Edison Co. Assn. Comm. ofcr., USN (3 yrs), spec. assignment to War Dept., Wash., D.C., WW II. Clubs: Valley Hunt, Big Canyon Country, San Gabriel Country, Calif. Clubs: Eldorado Country Club; Los Angeles Country Club. Hobby: boating, hiking, golf. Res.: 1458 Hillcrest Ave., Pasadena, CA; Office: 415 Huntington Dr., San Marino, CA 91108.

SMITH, JACK
Columnist
b. Aug. 27, Long Beach, Calif.; s. Charles F. and Anna M. Smith; ed. grad. Belmont H.S., L.A. 1934; m. Denise Bresson, Los Angeles, Calif., June 17, 1939; sons: Curtis Bresson, b. Mar. 26, 1945; Douglas Franklin, b. Dec. 4, 1947. Career: Reporter, The Bakersfield Californian, 1938; Honolulu Advertiser, 1941-42; United Press Bur., Sacramento, 1943; L.A. Daily News, 1946-49; L.A. Herald-Express, 1950-53; reporter-columnist, Los Angeles Times, 1953---. Author: Three Coins in the Birdbath, publ. Doubleday, 1965; Spend All Your Kisses, Mr. Smith, 1978. Combat corr., USMC (1944-45), WW II. Res.: 4251 Camino Real, Los Angeles, CA 90065; Office: Los Angeles Times, Times-Mirror Sq., Los Angeles, CA 90053.

SMITH, JAMES MYNATT
Newspaper Editor — Publisher
b. Nov. 15, 1910, Palacios, Tex.; s. Bon Huer and Margaret Mildred (Bradford) Smith; bro. Brooks Smith,

noted concert pianist, and accompanist for Jascha Heifetz, Zino Francescatti, Rise Stevens, others; ed. grad. McAllen (Tex.) H.S., 1928; m. Irabel Parks, McAllen, Tex., June 21, 1936; chil.: Bon Robert, b. Apr. 16, 1938; James Mynatt, Jr., b. June 25, 1938; Joanna Carol, b. May 23, 1944. Career: McAllen Daily Press, Tex. 1928; managing ed., McAllen Monitor, 1936, ed.-gen. mgr. 1947; est. Calif. res. 1952; ed.-assoc. publ., Fontana Herald-News, 1952-54; ed.-assoc. publ., The Daily News, Whittier, 1954-64, ed.-publ. 1964---; v.p.-dir. Owens Whittier Publ. Co. 1954---; dir. Owens Publs., Inc., Richmond, Calif.; pres. Review Publ. Co., East Whittier, Calif. 1961---. Pvt. to Maj., Tex. State Guard, 1940s. Mem.: dir. McAllen Rotary Club, 1948-49; dir. Whittier Community Concert Assn. 1954---, pres. 1961; dir. Whittier C. of C. 1961-69, pres., 1968; dir. Whittier Community Chest, 1956---; Amer. Society of Newspaper Editors, 1958---; pres. Whittier YMCA, 1959-60; treas. Whittier Chpt., Amer. Red Cross, 1960-61, 1963-70; dir. Whittier Coll. Assocs. 1966-67; bd. govs. L.A. County Mus. of Natural Hist. 1967---; trustee, Whittier City Library, 1968---; Sigma Delta Chi. Baptist (deacon Fontana, Calif.). Hobby: photog. Rec.: hunting, fishing. Res.: 5760 S. Citrus Ave., Whittier, Calif.; Office: 7037 S. Comstock Ave., Whittier, CA 90608.

SMITH, JEAN HARCOURT
Psychologist
b. Sept. 3, 1921, Milroy, Ind.; d. James Roy and Ila Mildred (Hite) Harcourt; B.S., bus., music, Ball State Univ.; M.A. elem. edn.; postgrad., Whittier Coll.; L.A. State Univ.; UCLA; Pepperdine Univ.; USC; Calif. Grad. Inst., Orange; m. Robert Leroy Smith (dec. 1974), Oct. 4, 1942; son Robert Stephen. Career: tchr. (grades 7-12): Harrison Township, 1943-44; Yorktown High Sch., 1944-45; tchr.: Muncie City Schs., 1951-60; East Whittier Sch., 1961-67; Psychometrist, Ocean View Sch. Dist. 1967-68; Psychologist, Orange Unified Sch. Dist. 1968-79; also pvt. practice, Tustin and Laguna Beach; licenses: Marriage, Family, Child Counselor; Edn. Psychologist; credentials: Gen. Elem. Life; Gen. Secondary Life; designated services life; Gen. Adminstrv.; honored by Notable Am. Award, DAR, 1976, 1977; Pi Lambda Theta; Delta Kappa Gamma Soc.; Mem.: Calif. & Nat. Assns. of School Psychologists; Am. Psychol. Assn.; Calif. and Am. Assns. of Marriage, Family and Child Counseling; Nat. Alliance for Family Life; Harbor Clin. and Experimental Hypnosis Soc.; L.A. Guidance Counseling Service. Offices: 3125 Alta Laguna Blvd., Laguna Beach, CA 92651; 17842 Irvine Blvd., No. 222, Tustin, CA 92680.

SMITH, JOHN EDWIN
University Librarian
b. Jan. 28, 1917, San Francisco, Calif.; s. Paul and Gertrude (Free) Smith; ed. A.B., UCLA, 1939; library certificate, Univ. of Calif., Berkeley, 1940; m. Lucille Tomlin, Los Angeles, Calif., Nov. 7, 1946; chil.: Michael David, b. Dec. 12, 1947; Diana Dale, b. Jan. 19, 1949; Douglas Paul, b. July 23, 1956. Career: Reference asst., Lib. Assn. of Portland, Ore. 1940-41; lib. asst., U.S. Dept. of Agr. Lib. 1941-42; industrial rels. librarian, UCLA, 1946-47; head acquisitions, 1948-53; Santa Barbara City and County librarian, 1953-61 (on leave, 1958-59); librarian, Inst. for Adm. Affairs, University of Tehran, Iran; lib. adv., USC Pub. Adm., Pakistan Proj. 1961-63; Univ. librarian, Univ. of Calif., Irvine, 1963---. United States Army Medical Department, 1942-45; hon. disch., Tech. Sgt. (1945), WW II. Mem.: com. Amer. Lib. Assn. 1948-53; council, 1955-58; chmn. Com. on Intellectual Freedom; Calif. Lib. Assn. 1948-50; Rotary Club, Santa Barbara, 1954-55. Dem. Rec.: reading. Res.: 1631 Pegasus St., Santa Ana, CA; Office: Univ. of Calif. Library, Irvine, CA 92664.

SMITH, JOHN MICHAEL
Management Consultant
b. Nov. 18, 1940, Jackson, Mich.; s. John Milton and Ruth (Miller) Smith; B.S. chem., Univ. of Mich., 1962; Ph.D., inorganic chem., UCLA, 1966; m. Valerie Chan, Aug. 24, 1968, Los Angeles; son Christopher Morgan, b. Oct. 15, 1969. Career: research asst., Los Alamos Sci. Labs., summers 1962-66; asst. prof. of chem., Cal Tech, 1966-68; pub. rel., exec., Ch. of Scientology, 1968-75; founder, exec. dir. mgmt. cons., Executive Management Specialists, Inc., 1975---; co-founder and mgmt. counselor, Interface Mgmt. Systems, L.A. 1974-75; chem. cons. to Richfield Oil Co. and Eastman Kodak. Recipient: Outstanding Tchg. Asst. Award, UCLA; awards for excellence, training and counseling centers; L. Ron Hubbard counseling course; speaker in U.S., Europe on

organo-metallic chem. and chemical edn.; publs. in Journ. Am. Chem. Physics; Inorganic Chemistry; Journ. Molecular Spectroscopy. Ch. of Scientology. Hobbies: motorcycling, reading, philosophy. Home: 1758 Taft Ave., Hollywood, CA 90028; Office: 1800 Argyle, No. 406, Hollywood, CA 90028.

SMITH, LENORA B.
Business Owner
b. Jan. 9, 1926, Tenn.; d. William and Cleo (Davis) Burnett; student, bus. coll., Shasta Community Coll.; sons, William Gregory Smtih, b. 1953; Michael Glenn Arnold, b. 1960. Career: Program Dir. and traffic mgr., Radio & TV stations, Phoenix, Miami, Union City, Tenn., Santa Monica, Fresno, Redding, 1944-62; owner, opr., House of Steno, Redding, 1962-76, pres. House of Steno, Inc. (franchising House of Steno in 4 states), 1976---. Mem.: Soroptimist Club, past recording secty.; Secty., Bicentennial Com. of Shasta Co. 1975-76. Protestant. Rec.: sailing. Res.: P.O.B. 1243, Redding, CA 96001; Office: 1708 Placer St., Redding, CA 96001.

SMITH, MARY BENTON
Travel Writer — Editor
b. Aug. 19, 1903, Madill, Okla.; d. John Wiley and Mary Jane (Scobee) Benton; ed. UCLA 1924-25; B.S., Univ. of Ore. 1928; m. Thor Merritt Smith, South Pasadena, Apr. 17, 1930; daus.: Mrs. Jay (Deanne) McMurren, b. Aug. 12, 1931; Mrs. Richard P. (Suzanne) Mueller, b. Aug. 10, 1934; Mrs. Henry Hudson (Marianne) Hubbard III, b. Nov. 16, 1937. Career: Reporter, San Pedro News-Pilot, 1921-24; promotion writer, Hollywood Citizen, 1924-25; reporter, News Bur., Univ. of Ore. 1925-28; editor (jr. pg.), Press-Telegram, Long Beach, 1928-32; instr. journ. and English, Univ. of Nev. 1942-43; acting corr.-chief of bur., Assoc. Press, Reno, Nev. 1943-45; travel scout, Sunset Mag., Menlo Park, Calif. 1945-51; owner-contrib., Mag. of the Year, NUC 1947-48; accredited corr., Assoc. Press, to signing Japanese Peace Treaty, S.F., 1951; sr. exec.-publicity div., Macy's, S.F. 1951-52; report ed.-researcher, Nowland and Co., Inc. Greenwich, Conn. 1957-59; asst. ed., ed., Pac. Travel News, S.F. 1962-72. Author: (co-editor) Sunset Travel Books: Australia, New Zealand, Japan, 1964; Sunset Travel Books: Hong Kong, 1965; Islands of the South Pacific, 1966; Taiwan, 1968; Southeast Asia, 1968; (contrib. ed.) The Sea of Cortez, Lane, 1966; San Francisco, Lane, 1969. Mem.: pres. Alpha Chi Omega 1928; Theta Sigma Phi; dir. Peninsula YMCA, Burlingame, Calif. 1952; dir. Broadway Theatre League, Santa Barbara, 1960-61; dir. AAUW, Santa Barbara, 1961-62; Soc. Amer. Travel Writers. Republican. Episcopalian. Res.: 74 La Cumbre Circle, Santa Barbara, CA 93105.

SMITH, MICHAEL HARRISON
Art Gallery Director
b. Aug. 21, 1945, Los Angeles; s. Albert L., Jr. and Geraldine (Ward) Smith; m. Debra Taylor, June 8, 1969, Pasadena; sons, Taylor Albert, b. 1972; Edward Brinton V, b. 1975. Career: currently Director, Baxter Art Gallery, Calif. Inst. of Tech. Office: Caltech, Pasadena, CA 91125.

SMITH, MONROE G.
Corporate Executive
b. Dec. 24, 1910, Camden, N.J.; s. Charles E. and Anna (Githens) Smith; ed. Prep. Sch., Swarthmore, Pa. 1928-29; B.S., Univ. Pa. 1933; m. Lois A. Wade, Springfield, Mass., June 20, 1936; chil.: Charles M., b. Mar. 29, 1941; Judith A., b. June 24, 1945; Wade M., b. Oct. 9, 1944. Career: Spec. agt. F.B.I. 1943-46; asst. comptroller, Standard Brands, Inc., NYC 1946-49; pres.-dir. The Silex Co., Hartford, Conn., and Silex Co., Ltd., Montreal, Can. 1950-53; exec. v.p.-dir. Rockwood and Co., Gobelin Co., Our Mothers, Inc., Brooklyn, N.Y. 1953-55; comptroller-gen. mgr.-group v.p. ESB Co., Phila., Pa. 1955-67; comptroller-dir. ESB, Co., Ltd., Toronto, Can. 1955-65; comptroller-dir. Willard Storage Battery Co., Ltd., Can. 1955-65; dir.-comptroller-group v.p. Atlas Mineral prods. Co., Mertztown, Pa., and Jessall Plastics Co., New Kensington, Conn. 1956-65; pres.-dir. Cleveland Elec. Vehicle Co., Ohio, 1957-63; v.p.-dir. Timely Brands, Inc., Boston, Mass. and Montreal, Can. and Ohline Co., Pasa., Calif. 1961-66; v.p.-dir. Mktg. Servs., Inc., Rancho Santa Fe, Calif. 1962---; v.p.-dir. Battronic Trucks, Inc., Boyertown, Pa. 1963-67; pres.-dir. Diagnostic Data Inc. 1968---; bd. chmn., VOCON, Inc. Mem.: pres. Phila. chpt.-dir. Natl. Security Ind. Assn. 1961-66; dir. Material Handling

Inst. 1963-67; pres. 1965; dir. Ind. Truck Assn. 1965-67; Amer. Ord. Assn.; dir., Alliance Development Corp.; Amer. Mgmt. Assn.; Amer. Soc. Naval Engrs.; Soc. Former F.B.I. Agts.; Financial Execs. Inst.; Natl. Ind. Conf. Bd.; Natl. Football Found.; Newcomen Soc. of Amer.; Sigma Phi Epsilon, Phi Sigma Chi; clubs: Univ. of Pa. Varsity, Merchants and Mfgrs., Mercantile, BYO, Univ. of Pa. Football, Apollo, Ambassadors, Brooklyn, Vesper; Mfrs. Mercantile, BYO, Univ. of Pa. Football, Apollo, Ambassadors, Brooklyn, Vesper; Mfrs. Country and Golf, Phila.; Seaview Country. N.J.; Sharon Heights Country and Golf, Menlo Park. Protestant. Hobbies: sports, garden. Rec.: hunting, fishing, boating, golf. Res.: 201 Family Farm Dr., Woodside, CA; Office: 518 Logue Ave., Mountain View, CA 94043.

SMITH, PATRICIA ANN (Mrs. Harry Lee)
Civic Leader — Choral Conductor
b. Jan. 15, 1919, Patton, Pa.; d. Charles E. and Hilda (Mullin) O'Rourke; father, noted author of engineering textbooks incl. O'Rourke's General Engring. Handbook; B.A., Cornell Univ. 1939; M.A., UCSD, 1972; m. Harry Lee Smith, Sept. 23, 1939, Ithaca, N.Y.; chil.: David Lee, b. 1940; Judith (Misty) (Taylor), b. 1943; Stephen, b. 1948 (dec. 1966); Veronica (Barta), b. 1952. Career: resided in Buenos Aires, Argentina, 1939-65; director, choruses, Buenos Aires, 1955-65; hon. secty. Mozarteum, Buenos Aires, 1958-65; founding conductor, La Jolla Civic Chorus, 1966-72, Univ. Chorus, 1969-71; pres. bd., La Jolla Civic/Univ. Symphony Assn.; pres., San Diego Co. Com. for L.A. Philharmonic, 1971-74; founding bd. mem., UCSD Medical Aux., bd. of Country Friends; v.p., San Diego Opera Assn.; chmn., La Jolla Aux. S.D. Symphony, 1977-80; chmn. La Jolla Guild S.D. Opera, 1977-78; secty., bd. of Social Service of La Jolla, 1975-78. Mem. Delta Delta Delta. Hobbies: golf, tennis, painting. Home: 7710 Revelle Dr., La Jolla, CA 92037.

SMITH, PAUL SAMUEL
Former College President
b. July 3, 1897, Richmond, Ind.; s. Harry J. and Louise (Wolfe) Smith; ed. A.B., Earlham Coll. 1919; A.M., Univ. of Wis. 1922, Ph.D. 1927; m. Lillian E. McMinn, Aug. 28, 1923; chil.: Eleanor Patricia. Career: Fellow, history, Univ. of Wis. 1919-20, teaching asst. 1920-22; prof. Amer. Hist., Whittier Coll., Whittier, Calif. 1923-51, dir. summer session 1939---, pres. 1951-70 (ret.). Lecturer, constitutional govt.; radio lecturer, series discussions on problems of democratic govt. Author: Amer. Political Institutions and Social Idealism, 1928; A. New Approach to Amer. Constitution, 1931; New Approach to the Study of Amer. Constitution (pamphlet), Calif. State Dept. of Edn. 1940. Mem.: Amer. Hist. Assn., Amer. Polit. Sci. Assn., Pi Gamma Mu. Soc. of Friends Ch. Res.: 14314 Bronte Dr., Whittier, CA 90602.

SMITH, PHYLLIS R.
Civic Leader
b. Aug. 30, 1924; d. Earl J. and Ruth (Fisher) Lake; ed. USC; B.A., UCLA 1946, postgrad. stu.; m. Marvin T. Smith, Jr. (pres. Karen Graphic, Inc.), Mar. 29, 1947; dau. Lesley Karen, b. May 11, 1968. Career: Elem. teacher, Beverly Hills Unified Sch. Sys. (5 yrs.); lecturer, L.A. City Coll. (1 yr.); Gov's. Adv. Com. on Mental Health, 1968-73; Citizens Adv. Council to State Dept. of Mental Hygiene, 1969-71, 5 yr. Task Force Plan, 1970-73; Calif. State Health Planning Council, 1969-73; chmn. Adv. Council to Calif. Hosp. Comm. 1972-73; chmn. Calif. Health Facilities Comm. (apptd. by Gov. Reagan), 1973---. Awards: Agency Leadership Award, United Way of L.A. County; First Pres.'s Cup, Calif. Assn. for Mental Health. Author, Survey of Volunteer Opportunities in Museums. Mem.: Women's Adv. Com. for Pay TV; bd. dirs. Friends of Santa Monica Mts. State Park; exec. com. Assistance League of So. Calif.; exec. Volunteer Com., Hollywood Bowl; trustee, exec. bd. L.A. Co. Museum; chmn. Art Museum Council, L.A. Co. Mus. of Art; bd. dirs.-exec. com. Valley Presbyterian Hosp. 1957-65; Chil's. Bur. of L.A. 1958-68, 1970---; pres. Homemaker's Serv. of L.A. 1962-64 (chmn. Pan-Pac. Show); v. chmn. Natl. Conf. Soc. Welfare, 1964; United Way, 1964---, area bd. dirs.-exec. com. 1967-69, L.A. reg. chmn. 1967, bd. dirs. L.A. Planning Council, 1972-73; bd. dirs.-exec. com. L.A. Co. Mental Health Assn. 1965-71, comm. 1969; bd. dirs. L.A. Child Guidance Clinic, 1968-69; bd. dirs. L.A. Chpt. Amer. Natl. Red Cross, chmn. campaigns; L.A. Welfare Planning Council, 1966-70, area chmn.; div. chmn. L.A. Heart Assn.; bd. dirs. Welfare Planning Council, S.F. Valley, 1967-72; exec. com. Calif. Assn. of Mental Health, 1967-71;

Calif. Assn. Health and Welfare, 1967-69; reg. v.p. Child Welfare League of Amer. 1968-70; com. Camarillo State Hosp. 1968-73; L.A. Council Natl. Voluntary Health Agcys. Bd. 1968-69; exec. com. So. Calif. Plays for Living, 1968-69; Natl. Charity League, L.A. 1970-72; Town Hall of Calif. 1970-73; bd. dirs. Alcoholism Council of Greater L.A., S.F. Valley, 1970-73; L.A. Co. Bd. Supvs. Task Force, 1971-73; chmn. Mental Health Task Force, S.F. Valley Health Planning Com. 1971-73; Sierra Club, L.A. Country Club, Bel-Air Presbyterian Ch. Rec.: tennis, golf, gardening. Res.: 4200 Clear Valley Dr., Encino, CA 91436; Office: 555 Capitol Mall, Sacramento, CA 91814.

SMITH, ROBERT EVERETT
Engineer
b. May 12, 1927, Summitville, Ind.; s. Everett M. and Jessie May (Brookshire) Smith; nephew of Rosco George, one of orig. inventors of television; ed. B.S. (aeron. engring.), Purdue Univ. 1950; M.S., Wash. Univ. 1956; m. Mary Elizabeth Merriman, Covina, Calif., Dec. 27, 1952; chil.: Marietta Ann, b. Nov. 5, 1953; Robert Merriman, b. Jan. 28, 1956; Paul Christopher, b. May 11, 1960. Career: Aircraft structures engr., N. Amer. Aviation Corp., L.A. 1950-52; engr. Emerson Elec. Mfg. Co., St. Louis, 1952-56; staff engr., FMC Corp., San Jose, Calif. 1956-57; sr. structures engr. 1957---. Lecturer: San Jose State Coll. 1956---; Univ. of Santa Clara, 1959---; bd. dirs., Purdue Univ. Contrib. articles to sci publs. Radar tech., U.S. Navy (1945-46), WW II. Mem.: pres. Alpha Tau Omega, 1950. Republican (dir. precinct workers). Episcopalian (sr. warden). Hobbies: hunting, fishing. Rec.: swimming, golf. Res.: 15381 Via Caballero, Monte Sereno, CA 95030; Office: FMC Corp., P.O. Box 367, San Jose, CA 95103.

SMITH, ROSE MARIE
Educator — Lecturer
b. Media, Pa.; d. Joseph and Kathrine (Ume) Eberhart; ed. Julia Richman H.S., NYC, 1914-18; grad. Calif. Real Estate Coll. 1941; L.A. Adult H.S. (spec. courses); pub. speaking, Hollywood H.S. and Dale Carnegie (grad.); grad. Ray Anger Inst. of Human Rels. 1953-54; lecturer credential, L.A. Bd. of Edn. 1958; Methods of Teaching, UCLA Ext. Div.; adult teachers' credential, State of Calif. 1960-66; B.A., English Ecclesiastical Found. 1952, M.A. 1957, Ph.D. 1962; (hon.) L.H.D., St. Andrews Episcopal Coll. 1961; Inst., Andrus Gerontology Center, USC 1973; m. Edwin L. Smith, Yonkers, N.Y. 1923 (dec. 1972); son, Robert Borthwick Smith (Attorney at law, Los Angeles). Career: Founder-director, Wayside Village, 1927-38; real estate broker, 1941---. Red Cross Gray Lady Volunteer, Veterans Hosp. 1948-50; instr. (world geography-world affairs), Franklin Adult Sch. 1959-60; gerontology cons. L.A. Bd. of Edn. 1960; instr. L.A. City Schs. Lecturer and world traveler (with husband), approx. 24 extensive tours on 5 continents, visiting 125 countries, 1923---; subjs. incl.: Mission in Iran, Mission in Egypt, Indonesia, New Zealand, Islands of World, Japan-New Zealand-Australia-Hawaii, Land of Midnight Sun, Iron Cutrain Countries (Russia and satellites), South Pacific Is., Across the Nation, People and Problems of Europe, The Deep South, Is. of Rhodes (Greece), Central Amer., Samoan, New Caladonia, The Pulse of the Nation (Wash. D.C.), L.A., Eng., NYC. Appd. on Welcome Travelers radio pgm. 1951; founder, Journey's End Found., USC 1973. Awards: winner, Queen for a Day (for dedicated serv. to shut-ins), ABC-TV, Nov. 28, 1962. Mem.: Traveler's Century Club; So. Calif. Chpt., Soc. of Woman Geographers; Hollywood Soroptimist Club; Beth Toast-mistress Club; O.E.S. Republican. Presbyterian. Hobby: travel, photog. Res.: 5191 Franklin Ave., Los Angeles, CA 90027.

SMITH, THOR MERRITT
Educator
b. Nov. 13, 1906, Reno, Nev.; s. Alfred Merritt and Ivan (Sessions) Smith; ed. B.A., Univ. of Nev. 1927; grad. Air War Coll. 1952; m. Mary Benton, South Pasadena, Calif., Apr. 17, 1930; daus.: Mrs. Jay (Deanne) McMurren, b. 1931; Mrs. Richard (Suzanne) Mueller, b. 1934; Mrs. Henry (Marianne) Hubbard, b. 1937. Career: Exec. assignments, Hearst newspapers, 1930-38; assoc. bus. mgr.-asst. to publ., San Francisco Call-Bulletin, 1939-51; v.p. (chg. pub. servs.), Amer. Wkly., NYC 1952-59; asst. to publ., Santa Barbara News-Press, Calif. 1960-62; exec. v.p.-gen. mgr., S.F. Conv. and Visitors Bur. 1963-64; assoc. dir. dev. Mills Coll. 1965-67, v.p. 1968-72. Author: Wake of Glory, publ. Bobbs-Merrill, 1945. Capt., U.S. Army Air Corps,

intelligence ofcr., 8th A.F., plan ofcr. for Operation Overlord; press aide to Gen. Eisenhower; Col., Gen. Staff Corps, USAF (1942-45), WW II. Awards: Legion of Merit, Medaille de la Reconnaissance Francaise. Mem.: San Francisco Adv. Club, Sigma Nu, Sigma Delta Chi, Alpha Delta Sigma, Commonwealth Club of Calif. Episcopalian. Res.: 74 LaCumbre Circle, Santa Barbara, CA 93105.

SMITH, WALKER, JR.
Company President
b. Apr. 6, 1927, Los Angeles, Calif.; s. Walker and Marguerite B. Smith; great-grandson of T.B. Walker (dec.), founder of T.B. Walker Art Center, Minneapolis, Minn.; ed. B.A., Stanford University, 1950; m. Molly Muntzel, Portland, Ore., Oct. 7, 1955; chil.: Kim, b. Apr. 9, 1956; Walker, III, b. Mar. 15, 1958. Career: Mgr., Hillcrest Forests, Redding, Calif. 1950-58; v.p.-dir., Shasta Forests Co., Redding, 1950---; exec. v.p., Smith & Sons Investment Co., San Bernardino, 1958---; pres. Shasta Savings & Loan Assn., Redding, 1955-58, dir. 1958---; dir. Smith & Sons Sales Co., Santa Ana, 1960---; pres.-dir., Nine Point, Inc., San Bernardino, Calif. 1960---. U.S. Coast Guard (1944-46), WW II. Mem.: Shasta Co. Repub. Central Com. 1954-58; clubs: Redding Rotary, 1956-58; Redlands Golf, Azure Hills Country, Irvine Coast Country, Lido Is. Yacht. Rec.: golf, tennis, sailing. Res.: 901 Zurich Circle, Newport Beach, CA 92660.

SMITH, WILLIAM FRENCH
Attorney at Law
b. Wilton, N.H.; s. William French and Margaret (Dawson) Smith; ed. A.B. (summa cum laude), Univ. Calif. 1939; LL.B., Harvard Law Sch. 1942; m. Jean Webb, Los Angeles, Calif.; chil.: William French, III, Stephanie Oakes, Scott Cameron, Gregory Hale. Career: Admitted to California Bar, 1942; partner, Gibson, Dunn & Crutcher law firm. Director: Legal Aid Found., L.A. 1963-72; Pac. Lighting Corp. 1967---; bd. trustees, Claremont Men's Coll. 1967---; bd. regents, Univ. of Calif. 1958---, chmn. 1970-72, 1974-75, 1976; bd. dir. Independent Colls. of So. Calif., Inc. 1969-74; bd. dirs. Pac. Tel and Telegraph Co. 1969---; bd. dirs. Pac. Mutual Life Ins. Co. 1970---; bd. dirs. World Affairs Council, 1970--- (pres. 1975---; bd. dirs. Center Theatre Group, L.A. Music Center, 1970---. Lt., USNR 1942-46, WW II. Mem.: bd. dirs. Calif. State C. of C. 1963--- (pres. 1974-75); Amer., L.A. Co. Bar Assns.; chmn. Disciplinary Review Bd., State Bar of Calif. 1966-68; Amer. Judicature Soc.; Amer. Law Inst.; fellow, Amer. Bar Found.; U.S. Adv. Comm. on Internat. Edn. and Cultural Affairs, 1971---; bd. dirs. Partnership for the Arts in Calif., Inc. 1971---; mem., bd. of dirs., Crocker Nat. Bank, Crocker Natl. Corp., 1971---; mem., bd. dirs., Jorgensen Steel Corp., 1974---; U.S. Del., The East-West Center for Cultural and Tech. Interchange, Hawaii, 1975---; mem., Panel on Internat. Information, Edn. and Cultural Relations, 1974---; mem. Advis. Council, Harvard Univ. Sch. of Govt., Cambridge, 1977---; mem., Advisory Bd., The Center for Strategic and Internat. Studies, Georgetown Univ., 1978---; Natl. Trustee, Natl. Symphony Orchestra, Wash., D.C. 1975---; mem., Executive Comm., The Calif. Roundtable, 1976---; Mayor's Ad Hoc Com. on City Finances, Los Angeles, 1975---; Mayor's Labor-Mgmt. Advisory Comm., City of Los Angeles, 1974---; mem., Calif. Found. for Commerce and Edn., 1975---; bd. trustees: Henry E. Huntington Lib. and Art Gallery, 1971---; The Cate Sch. 1972---; Phi Beta Kappa, Pi Gamma Mu, Pi Sigma Alpha. Res.: 1256 Oak Grove Ave., San Marino, CA; Office: 515 S. Flower St., Los Angeles, CA 90071.

SMITH, WILLIAM WEBER
Physician
b. Aug. 16, 1914, San Diego; s. Grover E. and Sophia (Weber) Smith; gr.son of W.W.H. Smith, M.D., prof. med., Rush Med. Coll., Chicago, Ill; B.S., Stanford Univ., 1935; M.D., 1939, Stanford Med. Sch.; m. Gertrude Janeway, Los Angeles, 1941; chil.: Antony W., b. Nov. 30, 1941; Gertrude S., b. Nov. 3, 1944; Gregory R., b. Apr. 15, 1946; Diana Hll, b. Sept. 8, 1950; Mark, b. Oct. 22, 1953; Hilary, b. Jan. 30, 1956. Career: medical practice, pres., Wm. W. Smith, M.D., Inc. Pres., Beverly Hills Clinic, 1965. Served med. corps, USNR, 1942-44. Bd. trustee, St. Johns Hosp., Santa Monica, 1977-79; dir.: L.A. Heart Soc., 1941; L.A. Visiting Nurse Soc., 1950; Beverly Hills C. of C., 1960-66; Hathaway Home, 1972-74; Mem.: Phi Delta Theta; L.A. Country Club; Am. Coll. of Physicians; Los Angeles Acad. of Med. Roman Catholic. Hobbies: art, music, gardening. Rec.: hunting, fishing, skiing. Home:

334 Burlingame, W. L.A., CA; Office: 133 Lasky Dr., Beverly Hills, CA.

SMYTH, JEANNINE
Advertising Agency Executive
b. Dec. 26, 1946, Minneapolis, Minn; d. Vernon and Julie (Miller) Sonenstahl; student, Bethel Coll., St. Paul, Minn., 1964-66; Univ. of Minn., 1966-68. Career: High Sch. English tchr., St. Paul, Minn., 1968; cost controller, Litton Industries, Carlisle Graphics Div., S.F., 1968-71; vice-pres., finance and operations, Wilton, Coombs & Colnett, Inc., S.F., 1971---. Home: 2455 Alpine Rd., Menlo Park, CA 94025; Office: 855 Front St., San Francisco, CA 94111.

SNOW, RAYMOND M.
Attorney at Law
b. May 7, 1942, San Francisco; s. Alvah Levern and Ann Katharine Snow; B.S., Univ. of Mo., 1965; J.D., Univ. San Francisco, 1969; m. Suzanne Lee Partridge, Apr. 23, 1966, Palo Alto; children: Lisa Ann, b. 1970; Brian Mitchell, b. 1974; Sara Louise, b. 1977. Career: Project Engr., Bechtel Corp., S.F., 1965-70; admitted to Calif. bar, 1970, U.S. Supreme Ct. bar, 1976; pvt. law practice, Snow, Snow & McMorrow, Fremont, 1970---. Hearing Officer, Alameda Co. Civil Service Commn., 1973-77; mem. Housing Element Study Com., City of Fremont, 1973; Ohlone Coll. Com. to Estab. Philosophy and Goals, 1974; trustee, Newark Community Coll. Dist., 1974---, pres. 1977-78. Mem.: Am., Alameda Co., Washington Township (bd. dir. 1973-74) Bar Assns.; Calif. Trial Lawyers Assn.; Washington Township Men's Club; Fremont Rotary Club; Fremont C. of C., bd. dir. 1978---. Hobbies: duck hunting, fishing, handball. Res.: 4076 Norris Rd., Fremont, CA 94536; Office: 3100 Mowry Ave., Suite 307, Fremont, CA 94538.

SNYDER, JOHN JOSEPH
Optometrist
b. June 30, 1908, Wisc.; s. Burt F. and Alta L. Snyder; A.B. (hon.), UCLA, 1931; B.S., L.A. Coll. of Optometry, 1948; O.D., 1949; postgard., USC, 1945, 1946, 1947. Career: tchr., grades 1-8, La Plata County Schs., Colo., 1927-28; Supr. Pub. schs., Marvel, Colo., 1932-33; tchr. (biology, physics, chem), Durango, Colo High Sch., 1933-41; Optometrist practice, L.A., currently in Torrance. Bd. dir., Francia Boys Club, L.A., 1959-62; pres. Exchange Club of So. L.A., 1958, secty. 1963. Mem.: AAAS, Am. Inst. Biological Sciences; Nat. Eye Research Found.; Calif. and Am. Optometrists Assn.; L.A. County Optometrists Soc. Republican, precinct worker. Protestant. Rec.: fishing. Home: 735 Luring Dr., Glendale, CA 91206; Office: 19800 Hawthorne Blvd., Suite 417, Torrance, CA 90503.

SNYDER, PHYLLIS
Lawyer - Realtor
b. Feb. 26, 1946, Philadelphia, Pa.; d. Benjamin and Shirley Dolfman; B.S., Temple Univ., 1967; M.S. Public Health, UCLA, 1970; Dr. of Pub. Health, UCLA, 1972; J.D., Western State Univ., 1975; m. Lawrence K. Snyder (div.), Dec. 18, 1966, Philadelphia; chil.: Jeff, b. Jan. 29, 1970; Jill, b. Sept. 10, 1971. Career: tchr. pub. schs., Phila., 1967-68; pub. health cons., 1968-72; instr. and tchg. asst., UCLA; law clerk, 1973-74; pvt. practice attorney at law, 1977---; real estate broker, 1976---; Exchangor, 1977---; attorney for Literary License Unlimited (lit. agency), 1977---; pres., Hollywood Experience, 1978---; real estate developer, 1977-79; pub. cons. Bd. Dir., the Hollywood Corporation, 1978---; owner, Bond Realty, 1977---. Mem.: Les Amies, 1978---; Executive Women in Orange Co. Hobby: reading. Rec.: swimming, tennis. Home: 2282 Glenneyre St., Laguna Beach, CA 92651; Office: 27812 Forbes Rd., Laguna Niguel, CA 92677.

SOARES, FRANK JESS
Certified Public Accountant
b. Aug. 15, 1908, Ventura, Calif.; s. Manuel Jacinto and Anna (Macial) Soares; ed. B.S., USC, 1946; m. Marie Kyle, Ventura, Calif., Sept. 4, 1937. Career: CPA, pvt. practice, 1946-56; sr. partner, Soares, Sandall, Bernacchi and Petrovich, CPA firm, Ventura, 1956---. Ventura City Councilman, 1948-50. Staff Sgt. 301 Ord. Regiment, 1942-46, WW II. Mem.: Channel Counties Chpt., Calif. Soc. of CPAs, treas., secty., v.p., pres., dir. 1949-53, dir. State Chpt. 1956-58; Amer. Legion, Lions Club, BPOE, Beta Gamma Sigma, Beta Alpha Psi, Phi Kappa Phi, Los Posas Country Club.

Res.: 4125 Village 4, Camarillo, CA 93010; Office: 5450 Telegraph Rd., Ventura, CA.

SOBOROFF, STEVEN L.
Shopping Center Developer
b. Aug. 31, 1948, Chicago, Ill.; s. Irving E. and Evelyn (Suekoff) Soboroff; B.S., Ins. and Real Estate, 1970; M.S., 1971. Career: Calif. Real Estate Broker, 1971---; assoc. Joseph K. Eichenbaum Assocs. (shopping center dev.), 1971---; Center Leasing Assocs., Inc. (real estate); teacher, Shopping Centers 1975, and 1977, UCLA; est. Irvine E. Soboroff Scholarship, Univ. of Ariz.; publ. essay, Shopping Centers 1975, UCLA, Univ. of Ariz. Mem.: Zeta Beta Tau, 1967; Big Bros. of Amer. 1968---. Jewish. Office: 8447 Wilshire Blvd., Suite 310, Beverly Hills, CA 90211.

SOKOL, ANTHONY EUGENE
Professor Emeritus
b. Mar. 28, 1897, Vienna, Austria; s. Anton and Klara (Kuban) Sokol; student, Univ. of Vienna; A.B., Miss. State Tchrs. Coll.; student, Naval Officers Sch.; M.B., Stanford Univ., 1930, Ph.D., 1932; m. Martha Hille, 1929 (dec. 1938); son, Otto M., b. 1929; m. 2d. Else Mueller, 1939; Career: Lt., Austro-Hungarian Navy, 1915-1919; officer, Royal Steamship Co., Dutch East Indies, 1920-23; secty., Austro-Am. Inst. of Edn. and head, Dept. of Languages, Miss. State Teachers Coll., 1926-28; Prof. of German, Stanford Univ., 1929-42; adminstr., Army Special Tng. Program, Far East, also head Dept. of Asiatic & Slavic Studies, 1942---, Research Assoc., Hoover Inst. of War, Revolution & Peace, Prof. of International Security Affairs, Dept. of Polit. Sci., Stanford Univ., now Prof. Emeritus. Author: Sea Power in the Nuclear Age, 1961, Japanese trans. 1965; several books in German; book chpts. in Geography of the Pacific, Otis W. Freeman, 1951 and American Military Policy, Edgar S. Furniss, Jr., 1957; contbr. numerous articles on cultural and mil. affairs, SE Asia, Germany, Austria to profl. publs.; books to be pub.: Beautiful Women in World Art, Austria-History and Civilization, The Hidden Art Treasures of Austria. Mem.: U.S. Naval Inst., AAUP. Hobbies: writing, ships, photog. Res.: 1641 Portola Ave., Palo Alto, CA 94306.

SOLOMON, RUTH FREEMAN
Novelist
b. Apr. 21, 1908, Kiev, Russia; d. Harry and Jennie (Packard) Freeman; sister to Leonard Freeman (dec.), past pres., Writers Guild and Producers Guild; A.B., summa cum laude, Syracuse Univ., 1929; humanities, Univ. of Vienna, 1930; m. Joseph C. Solomon, M.D., Mar. 21, 1930, Long Island, N.Y.; chil.: George Freeman, M.D., b. Nov. 25, 1932; Daniel Freeman, b. Dec. 11, 1939. Career: author: The Candlesticks and the Cross, publ. 1967 (3rd Am. paperback edition: Signet Pocket Book); The Eagle and the Dove, 1971; The Ultimate Triumph, 1974; Two Lives, Two Lands, 1975; foreign editions in French, German, Swiss, Spanish, Dutch, Austrian, Flemish. Mem. civilian advisory com. to Sixth Army of U.S.; bd. mem. Fromm Inst. of Life Long Learning, Univ. of S.F.; founding mem. Am. Women for Internat. Understanding; women's forum West; mem. Am. Women for Internat. Friendship; Mem.: World Affairs Council; Commonwealth Club; Opera Guild; Symphony Assn.; S.F. Ballet Assn.; Phi Beta Kappa; Delta Sigma Rho; Sigma Delta Chi. Hobbies: travel, study. Rec.: time with gr.children. Home: 1080 Chestnut, San Francisco, CA 94109.

SOMERVILLE, ADDISON W.
Psychologist
b. Aug. 6, 1927, Greensboro, Ala.; s. Earnest and Ellen S.; B.S., Howard Univ., 1948, M.S., 1950; Ph.D., Ill. Inst. of Tech., 1963; m. Carolyn Coffey; children: Laurene, b. 1952; Ernest, b. 1959; Christopher, b. 1969. Career: Clin. & Counseling Psychologist, Ill. Inst. Tech., Chicago, 1954-58; staff psychol., Ill. State Hosp., 1954; asst. dir., Planning Mental Health, VI, 1964-65; prof. psychol., Cal. State Univ., Sacramento, 1965---; Cons., Calif. Hwy. Patrol, 1966---; Tng. Dir., Delinquency Prevention Unit, Sacto. Police Dept., 1971-72; Mgmt. Devel. Inst., State Personnel Bd., 1972---; NIMH Project Dir., Tng. for New Careers in Psychology, 1972---. Mem. Suicide Prevention Service, pres. 1971-72; pres., Sacto. Valley chpt., Calif. State Psychological Assn., 1979, bd. dir. 1968-75. Author: book chpts. in Intergration, The Schools, and Social Change, 1969; Working with Police Agencies, 1974; contbg. editor, School Psychologist journ.; contbr. articles police and psychol. journs. AUS M.C. 1950-52.

Mem.: Calif. Assn. Marriage & Family Counselors; Am., and Western, Calif. State Psychol. Assns.; Council for Exceptional Children; Psi Chi; Sacto. Valley Marriage Counseling Assn.; Am. Assn. of Correctional Psychologists; Calif. Tchrs. Assn.; Nat. Assn. of Sch. Psychols.; Ill. Acad. Criminology; Nat. Alliance Black Educators and Adminstrs.; Nat. Assn. Black Psychols. Rec.: skating. Res.: 61 Grand Rio Cir., Sacto., CA 95826; Office: Cal. State Univ., 6000 J Street, Sacramento, CA 95819.

SOMMER, ROSELLE L.
Realtor
b. Sept. 6, 1921, Chicago, Ill; d. Oscar P. and Isabel I. Lipman; student, Northwestern Univ., 1938-39; grad., Realtors' Inst. (G.R.I.); m. Herbert A. Sommer, Aug. 10, 1941, Chicago, Ill.; chil.: Netta (Roberts), b. Feb. 27, 1947; Helene (Crandall), b. Feb. 23, 1949; Merle E., b. Sept. 17, 1957. Career: real estate broker, 1964---; certified comml. investment mem.; award winner, largest real estate exchange, 1972, 1973; award winner every year since 1968 for over $1 million volume sales. Pres., Long Beach Jewish Community Center, 1973-74; pres. Long Beach Jewish Community Fedn., 1979; chmn., Budget Review Panel, United Way, 1975-76; secty. NCCJ. Jewish. Hobbies: painting, needlework. Home: 4471 Green Ave., Los Alamitos, CA 90720; Office: 11232 Los Alamitos Blvd., Los Alamitos, CA.

SONENSHINE, SHEILA PRELL
Attorney at Law
b. July 9, 1945, Butte, Mont.; d. Milton and Debbie Prell; student, Brandeis Univ.; B.A., econ., UCLA, 1967; J.D., Loyola Univ. Sch. of Law, 1970; postgrad., USC Law Center, 1971; m. Ygal Sonenshine, June 18, 1967; children: Jacob, b. 1970; Daniel, b. 1973; Mandy, b. 1978. Career: Sr. Partner, law firm Sonenshine & Armstrong, Newport Beach, 1971-78; asst. prof. of law, Irvine Univ. Sch. of Law, 1973-74; pvt. practice, Law Offices of Sheila Prell Sonenshine, Newport Beach, 1978---. Dir., Raygal Design Assoc., Inc., 1973---; apptd. by Gov. E.G. Brown, Jr. bd. dirs., 32nd Dist. Agri. Assn., 1976---; mem. advisory bd., American City Bank; bd. dir., Girl Scouts of Orange Co., 1977-78; mem. bd. visitors, Loyola Univ. Sch. of Law, 1978-79, chmn. Orange Co. Alumni chpt. 1978; lectr.; contbr. New Dawn mag., 1977, Orange Co. Bar Journ. Mem.: Orange Co. Bar Assn., founder, chmn. Women and Individual Rights Sect., 1974, del. to Calif. State Bar Convention 1974; mem. Judiciary and Client Rels. Coms. 1976-79; Jewish Fedn. Council of Orange Co., Community Rels. Com. 1977-79; United Jewish Appeal of Orange Co., co-chmn. Atty's. Div. 1973; founding mem., Sisterhood of Temple Bat Yahm. Res.: 2437 Monaco, Laguna Beach, CA 92651; Office: 550 Newport Center Drive, Suite A, Newport Beach, CA 92660.

SOOY, FRANCIS A.
University Chancellor
b. Univ. of Calif. Sch. of Med. 1941. Career: Res. tr. in Otolaryngology, Univ. Calif. and Wash. Univ., St. Louis; bd. cert. Amer. Bd. of Otolaryngology, 1944; faculty, Univ. of Calif., S.F. Sch. of Med. 1946---, chmn. Otolaryngology, 1958-72, chancellor, 1972---. Serv. numerous Sch. of Med. and Univ. Calif. Coms. Researcher-contrib. to publs. in Otolaryngology, problems of deaf. Mem.: pres. Med. Alumni Assn. 1963-64; chmn. Acad. Senate Budget Com. and Acad. Senate Com. on Coms.; chmn. Assembly of Acad. Senate, Calif.; chmn. Acad. Council of Calif.; Natl. Inst. of Health Adv. Neorological Diseases and Blindness Council and subcoms. 1964-69; Collegium, Oto-Rhino-Laryngologicum Amicitae Sacrum, Lyon, France, 1965; pres. Soc. of Univ. Otolaryngologists, 1969-70; pres. Pac. Coast Oto-Ophthalmological Soc. 1973-74. Office: University of Calif., San Francisco, CA 94122.

SOUTH, WILL
Sales Executive
b. July 13, 1925, Los Angeles; s. Rev. Will and Freda E. South; student, Chaffey, Coll., 1946; Calif. Sch. of Insurance, 1952; m. Sara Ann South, Sept. 25, 1976, Dublin, Calif.; chil.: Wayne A., b. 1947; Jan A. (White). Career: employed Alpha Beta mkts., 1946-52; Hostess Cake, 1952-58; Neal Steckman Food Brokers, 1958-65; v.p. sales, Jan-U-Wine Foods, 1965-70; western regional sales mgr., Skinner Macaroni Co., 1971-74; national retail sales mgr., Ghiradelli Chocolate Co., 1974---. USN, 1942-46; WW II, petty officer; USN 1950-51, Visual Communications. Active in Ch.: youth and music dir.;

currently marriage counseling; 15 years on radio in gospel quartets and instrumental music. Hobbies: music, motorcycling. Home: 361 Tahitian Circle, Union City, CA 94587; Office: 1111 - 139th, San Leandro, CA 94578.

SPANGLER, RAYMOND L.
Publishing Executive
b. Jan. 24, 1904, Oakland, Calif.; s. Martin L. and Myra (Raymond) Spangler; A.B., Stanford Univ. 1926; m. Nita Reifschneider, Reno, Nev., Sept. 22, 1946; chil.: Jon Martin, b. Feb. 15, 1952; Mary Raymond, b. May 17, 1953; Thor Raymond, b. Oct. 4, 1956. Career: Editor, South San Francisco Enterprise, 1926-37; adv. mgr., Watsonville Register-Pajaronian, 1937---; reporter-city ed., Redwood City Tribune, 1937-45; ed. and publ. 1945-49; publ. 1949-69; dir. Associated Press 1951-61; v.p. Peninsula Newspapers Inc.; pres. Calif. Freedom of Inf. Com. 1969. Mem.: High Priest, King Solomon Chpt., Royal Arch Masons, 1937; master, Francis Drake Lodge, F&AM No. 376. 1941; patron Ruth Chpt., OES 1942; Sigma Delta Chi, natl. pres. 1966; E. Campus Vitus, Commonwealth Club. Hobby: gardening. Rec.: fishing, golf. Res.: 970 Edgewood Rd., Redwood City, CA; Office: P.O.B. 841, Palo Alto, CA 94301.

SPECTOR, PHILLIP
President, Phil Spector Enterprises
b. Dec. 25, 1940, New York City, N.Y.; s. Benjamin and Bertha (Spektor) Spector; ed. grad. Fairfax H.S., L.A.; sons, Donte Phillip, Gary Phillip, Louis Phillip. Career: Pres., Phil Spector Enterprises (producer, Beatles recordings), London, N.Y., L.A.; record prod. Warner-Spector (feat. Cher Album, others), 1975---. Office: P.O. Box 69529, L.A., CA 90069.

SPELLMAN, HOWARD A., JR.
Engineering Geologist
b. Sept. 17, 1927, Springfield, Mass.; s. Howard and Pauline Spellman; Howard (father) figure skater with Ice Follies, Pauline (mother) concert pianist, Carnegie Hall; B.S., geology, Univ. of Cincinnati, 1953; postgrad, USC; m. Mollie Miller, Sept. 7, 1952; Cincinnati, Ohio; chil.: Trista, b. Nov. 24, 1956; Shauna, b. Jan. 22, 1959. Career: principal engineering geologist, Converse Ward Davis Dixon, Inc., Pasadena, USN, WWII, 1945-48; firecontrolman on light cruise USS Spokane, North Atlantic theatre. Pres., Assn. of Engineering Geologists, 1977-78, pres., Southern Calif. sect., 1972; mem. Phi Delta Theta Frat., Ohio Theta, 1950-53. Episcopal. Hobbies: photog., rock collection. Rec.: tennis, sailing, golf. Home: 1236 Oakglen Ave., Arcadia, CA 91006; Office: Converse Ward Davis Dixon, 126 W. Del Mar Blvd., Pasadena, CA 91105.

SPERO, STANLEY L.
Broadcasting Executive
b. Oct. 17, 1919, Cleveland, Ohio; s. Morris B. and Hermine (Harve) Spero; B.S., cum laude, USC, 1942; postgrad., Cleveland Coll., 1943; m. Frieda Kessler, June 30, 1946, Cleveland, Ohio; children: Laurie, b. 1953; Lisa, b. 1955; Leslie, b. 1958. Career: Acct. Exec.: WHKK Radio, Akron, Ohio, 1946-48, KFAC Radio, Los Angeles, 1948-52, KMPC Radio, Hollywood, 1952-53; vice pres., gen. sales mgr., KMPC Radio, 1953-68, v.p. and gen. mgr. 1968-78; vice pres., sports, Golden West Broadcasters, Los Angeles, 1978---. Served with U.S. Maritime Serv., 1942-43. Named Station Manager of the Year, Gavin Award, 1974. Mem.: Hollywood Advt. Assn., dir. 1972---, pres. 1960-61; pres., Permanent Charities Com. Entertainment Indus., 1972; So. Calif. Broadcasters Assn., chmn. 1972; Am. Advt. Fedn., bd. gov. 1972; Advt. Assn. West; Hollywood C. of C., dir. 1972. Jewish. Res.: 5027 Hayvenhurst St., Encino, CA 91316; Office: 5858 Sunset Blvd., Hollywood, CA 90028.

SPITZER, ARTHUR
Chairman, Digas Company
b. Aug. 3, 1912, Austria; s. Mendel Tokar and Maria Spitzer; (hon.) LL.D., Pepperdine Univ., Malibu, 1975; chil.: Violet, b. Aug. 1, 1951; Travis, b. Apr. 24, 1971. Career: Ministrie of Interior, Munich, Germany, 1947-50; owner, Digas Company, 1953-70; pres. Digas Co., div. Tesoro Petroleum Co., 1971-76; chmn., Digas Co., 1977---; Dir., Tesoro Petroleum Co., San Antonio, Tex., 1978---; dir., com. for Caribbean, Wash., D.C., 1977---; dir., Internat. Student Center, UCLA, 1975---; dir., University Bd., Pepperdine Univ., 1977---. Awarded

golden medal for service to govt. of Austria, Sept. 1977; estab. Chair for Sci. and Mgmt.. Pepperdine Univ., Malibu, 1975; Center for Sci., Dr. Edward Teller, Univ. of Colo., 1973-75; Mem. Comn. Economic Devel., state of Calif. Clubs: Racquet Club, Palm Springs; Beach & Tennis Club, La Jolla. Hobbies: reading, travel. Rec.: tennis, skiing. Home: 1011 N. Crescent Dr., Beverly Hills, CA 90210; Office: 9201 W. Olympic Blvd., Beverly Hills, CA 90212.

SPRAGUE, ROBERT RAYMOND
Banker — Civic Leader
b. July 11, 1915, Los Angeles, Calif.; s. Norman Frederick (regent, Univ. of Calif.; mem. State Bd. of Health) and Frances Edith (Ludeman) Sprague; desc. Los Angeles pioneers, 1880; ed. grad. Beverly Hills H.S.; B.A., USC 1936; Amer. Savings & Loan Inst. night sch. 1936-42; m. Jean Warner, Pasadena, Calif., June 11, 1942; chil.: Robert Raymond, Jr. (m. Karen Peterson, Aug. 20, 1966), William Frederick, Lois May and Jean Warner, Jr. Career: Assoc. with Western Fed. Savings & Loan Assn.; orgn. constr. co., Southwest Homes, Inc. 1940; orgn.-pres.-gen. mgr., Pioneer Savings & Loan Assn. (ofcs. in L.A., Long Beach, Huntington Park, Santa Monica, Burbank), 1943-68; v. chmn.-dir.-exec. com. Gibraltar Savings and Loan Association 1969---; dir.-v.-chmn., Fed. Home Loan Bank, S.F.; apptd. commr., Dept. of Bldg. and Safety, by Mayor Poulson, 1955. Author: You Owe It To Yourself, Your Inheritance, The Pioneer Farmer, A Real Friend; articles, publ. Calif. Savings and Loan League, U.S. Savings and Loan League; Pioneer Savings and Loan Assn., Southwest Homes, Inc. Mem.: past pres.-bd. dirs., Calif. Savings & Loan League; exec. com., U.S. Savings & Loan League; dir.-exec. com., Invest in Amer.; natl. chmn., banks and savings & loan com., Amer. Heritage Found.; trustee, Pomona Coll., Pomona, Calif.; dir. Natl. Conf. of Chrs. and Jews; Rotary Club of Los Angeles, Community Chest, Heart Fund, Red Cross of Amer.; bd. dirs., Big Sister League; bd. dirs., L.A. Orthopaedic Hospital; C. of C.; Stock Exch. of Amer.; pres. Wilshire Town Club; Shark Island Yacht Club, Wilshire Country Club, Irvine Country Club, Town Hall, California Club, Republican Assocs. Baptist. Res.: 376 S. Hudson Ave., Los Angeles, CA; Office: 9111 Wilshire Blvd., Beverly Hills, CA.

SPREITER, JOHN R.
University Professor
b. Oct. 23, 1921, Oak Park, Minn.; s. Walter F. and Agda E. Spreiter; ed. B.E. (aeron.) Univ. of Minn. 1943; M.S., Stanford Univ. 1947; Ph.D. 1954; postgrad. Univ. of Grenoble Les Houches Summer Sch. of Theoretical Physics, 1962; Enrico Fermi Sch. of Theoretical Physics, 1966; m. Brenda Owens, Stanford University, Calif., Aug. 7, 1953; daus.: Terry Anne, b. May 30, 1954; Janet Lynne, b. Sept. 23, 1957; Christine Patricia, b. Jan. 28, 1964; Hilary Maureen, b. Mar. 8, 1968. Career: Research scientist, NASA Ames Aeron. Lab., Moffett Field, Calif. 1943-58, NASA Ames Research Center, 1958-62; chief, Theoretical Studies br., Space Sci. Div. 1962-69. Lecturer, Space Physics and Aerodynamics, Stanford Univ. 1951-69; prof. Stanford Univ. 1968---. Chief Petty Officer, USN 1944-46, WW II. Mem.: treas. Saratoga Tennis Club, 1956-62; Fremont Hills Tennis and Swim Club. Protestant. Rec.: tennis, swim, skiing. Res.: 1250 Sandalwood Lane, Los Altos, CA; Office: Div. of Applied Mechanics, Stanford Univ., Stanford, CA 94305.

SPRING, JOHN WALTON
Geographer — Educator
b. Mar. 19, 1939, Los Angeles; s. Carl Chaffee and Emilie (Temple) Spring; B.A., 1963; M.A., 1975, geography; Gen. Secondary, Standard Elem., Community Coll., Calif. Tchg. Credentials; m. Mary Helen Melendres, Aug. 28, 1960, Los Angeles. Career: Tchr., Ocean View Sch. Dist., Huntington Beach, 1965-79, instr., Golden West and Coastline Colleges, 1976-79. Awards: Appreciation award, services for the Blind, 1968; Judges' Special Award, Costa Mesa Jr. C. of C., for outstanding serv. to the Blind, 1969. Youth Dir. (vol.) Summer Programs, Services for the Blind, Inc., Santa Ana, 1967-68; vol. instr., First Aid and Water Safety, ARC, 1960-73; Asst. Scoutmaster, Orange Co. Council BSA, 1968-70, com. mem. 1969-71. Served US Coast Guard Reserve, opns. div., 1957-65. Mem.: Assn. Am. Geographers; Am. Geog. Soc.; Nat. Assn. Geog. Edn.; Assn. Pacific Coast Geographers; Calif. Council for Geographic Edn.; The Coastal Soc. Republican, cartographer, Orange Co. Central Com. 1965-67. Reformed Ch. Am., Garden

Grove Community Ch. Rec.: snorkeling and SCUBA. Address: P.O.B. 6204, Santa Ana, CA 92706.

SPROUL, JOHN ALLAN
Energy Company Executive
b. Mar. 28, 1924, Oakland; s. Robert G. (pres., Univ. of California, all campuses, 1930-58) and Ida (Wittschen) Sproul; A.B., Univ. of Calif., 1947, LL.B., 1949; m. Marjorie A. Hauck, June 20, 1945, Wash., D.C.; children: John Allan, Jr., b. 1949; Malcolm, b. 1951; Richard, b. 1953; Catherine, b. 1955. Career: Attorney, Pacific Gas and Electric Co., 1949-52, 1956-62, Sr. Atty., 1962-70, Asst. Gen. Counsel, 1970-71, v.p., Gas Supply, 1971-76, sr. v.p., 1976-77, exec. v.p., 1977---; Atty., Johnson and Stanton, 1952-56. 1st Lt., USAF, 1943-46. Dir.: subsidiary companies and LNG subs. companies, Pacific Gas and Electric Co. Mem.: Calif. Constitution Revision Commn.; State Bar of Calif.; Commonwealth Club; Bohemian Club; World Trade Club; Engrs. Club of S.F.; Orinda Country Club; Pacific Coast Gas Assn.; dir. Am. Gas Assn., 1977---; dir. Canadian Am. Soc. of S.F., 1975---; Air Resources Bd., advisory council, 1977---; advisory trustee, Alta Bates Hosp., 1978---; alumni bd., Big C. Soc., 1978---. Rec.: spectator sports, golf, trout fishing. Res.: 8413 Buckingham Dr., El Cerrito, CA 94530; Office: 77 Beale St., San Francisco, CA 94106.

SROUR, RAJA KAIRALLA
Plastic Surgeon
b. Mar. 28, 1945, Lebanon; s. Kairalla and Evelyn Srour; B.S., 1965; M.D., Am. Univ. of Beirut, 1969. Career: Gen. Surgery training, Am. Univ. of Beirut, 1969-73; plastic surgery training, Columbia Presbyterian Hosp., NYC, 1973-76; pvt. practice plastic surgery, Los Angeles, 1977. Certification Am. Bd. of Plastic Surgery, 1978. Pres., resident staff orgn., American University of Beirut, 1971-72. Greek Orthodox. Hobbies: painting, sports. Home: 999 N. Doheny, L.A., CA 90069; Office: 9201 Sunset Blvd., Suite 910, L.A., CA 90069.

STADEL, W.W.
Medical Institutions Director
b. Jan. 31, 1912, Topeka, Kan.; s. Walter S. and Ethel R. (Taylor) Stadel; A.B., M.D., Univ. of Kan. 1936; m. Mary A. Vale, Liberty, Mo., Oct. 8, 1935; chil.: Patricia A., b. Mar. 17, 1939; Bruce V., b. July 3, 1943. Career: Internship-res., Latter-day Saints Hosp., Salt Lake City, Ut. 1936-38; pvt. practice, Mariposa, Calif. 1938-40; res. hosp. adm., Alameda County Institutions, Oakland, Calif. 1940-41, asst. supt. 1941-45, supt. 1945-46; asst. med. dir., Alameda Co. 1946-48; supt. San Diego Co. Gen. Hosp., San Diego, Calif. 1948-55; dir. San Diego Co. Dept. of Med. Institutions, 1955---. Mem.: fellow, Amer. Coll. Hosp. Admrs.; pres. Calif. State Bd. of Vocational Nurse Examiners; bd. of regents, Natl. Lib. of Med., past pres., Calif. State; Council on Professional Practice; Amer. Hosp. Assn.; (past) pres. Hosp. Council of San Diego Co.; San Diego Co. Med. Soc.; Calif. State Med. Assn.; AMA; San Diego Yacht Club. Hobby: sailing. Res.: 350 Dickinson, San Diego 3, CA; Office: Univ. Hospital, 225 W. Dickinson St., San Diego, CA 92103.

ST. AMAND, R. PAUL
Physician — Internal Medicine
b. Feb. 10, 1927, Newburyport, Mass.; s. Aurele and Aurore St. Amand; B.S. Tufts Univ., Medford, Mass., 1948; M.D. Tufts Univ. Med. Sch., Boston, 1952; chil.: Donna, b. May 10, 1949; Dann, b. Nov. 5, 1953; Viveca, b. July 19, 1959; Kytti, b. Jan. 30, 1961. Career: Med. Internship, L.A. Co. Harbor Gen. Hosp., 1952-53; res. internal med. 1953-56; asst. in med. UCLA Sch. of Med., 1956; clin. instr. in med. UCLA 1956-65; asst. clin prog. in med. UCLA, 1965---; Chmn. dept. med., Centinela Valley Community Hosp., 1959. Dir.: Centinela Valley Community Hosp., 1974; Med. Student Program, Univ. Guadalajara Autonoma, Mexico, 1976-77; pres., Marina Svc. Co. 1974-78; pres., Centinela Med. Group 1974. Speaker: AMA 1965-66; Am. Heart Assn. 1963-77; U.S. Maritime Svc. 1945; USN 1945-45. Mem.: Kiwanis Intl. (secty., dir., v.p.); 1966 pres., Am. Field Svc., Inglewood; Interservice Club Council (v.p., pres.) Centinela Days City Inglewood (chmn. 1970); Boy Scouts: v.p. exec. bd. L.A. Area Council 1978-79; Natl. Advisory Bd., BSA 1977-78; Silver Beaver Award 1974. Hobby: cooking. Rec.: golf, tennis, travel. Office: 4560 Admiralty Way, Marina del Rey, CA 90291.

STAPLES, JAMES R.
College President
b. Jan. 5, 1920, Piggott, Ark.; s. Albert J. and Lula Ann (Kerr) Staples; B.A., Ouachita Bapt. Univ., Ark. 1946; B.D., New Orleans Bapt. Theol. Sem. 1949; stu. Southwestern Bapt. Theol. Sem.; Ed.D., Ariz. State Univ. 1970; m. Elaine Mayberry, Holcomb, Mo., Dec. 25, 1941; chil.: Albert James, b. July 7, 1943; Renee Elaine, b. Mar. 29, 1958. Career: Western Elec., New Orleans, 1942; tooling insp. N. Amer. Aircraft, Dallas, 1942-43; est. own bus.; Pastor: Harmony Bapt. Ch., Ark. 1944-46; First Bapt. Ch., Pearl River, La. 1946-48; Joiner Bapt. Ch., Ark. 1948-50; N. Phoenix Bapt. Ch., Ariz. 1950-60; exec. v.p. Grand Canyon Coll., Phoenix, 1962-66; pastor, Royal Palms Bapt. Ch., Phoenix, 1966-70; president Calif. Bapt. College, 1970---. Editor, Ariz. Bapt. Deacon, 1960-62, 1970; wkly. radio pgm. KTAR, Ariz. (9 yrs.). Pres., Ariz. So. Bapt. Conv. (2 yrs.), exec. bd. (5 yrs.), Foreign Mission Bd. 1952-57; Chief of Clergy, Civ. Def., Greater Phoenix, 1953-58. Mem.: Riverside Press Council, 1973-76; v.p. Inland Empire Higher Edn. Council; v.p. Assn. of So. Bapt. Schs. and Colleges, 1975-76. Hobbies: travel, painting, garden. Rec.: tennis, golf. Res.: 5170 Palisade Circle, Riverside, CA 92506; Office: 8432 Magnolia Ave., Riverside, CA 92504.

STARING, GRAYDON S.
Attorney at Law
b. Apr. 9, 1923, Deansboro, N.Y.; s. William Luther and Eleanor Mary (Shaw) Staring; student, Colgate Univ., 1943-44; A.B., Hamilton Coll., 1947; J.D., Univ. Calif., Berkeley. 1951; m. Joyce Lydia Allum-Poon, Sept. 1, 1949, San Francisco; children: Diana Hilary (Mrs. Lawrence A. Hobel), b. 1953; Christopher Paul Norman, b. 1960. Career: Instr. in speech, Hamilton Coll., 1947-48; Attorney, office of Gen. Counsel, Navy Dept., San Francisco, 1952-53; Attorney, Admitalty & Shopping Sect., U.S. Dept. of Justice, S.F., 1953-60; assoc., firm of Lillick McHose & Charles, San Francisco, 1960-64, partner 1965---; lectr. Calif. Cont. Edn. of the Bar; Assoc. editor, American Maritime Cases, 1966---; Contbr. legal articles in U.S. Naval Inst. Proceedings, Calif. and Tulane Law Revs. Admitted to Calif. Bar 1952, U.S. Supreme Ct. 1958. USNR, 1943---, now Comdr. Ret. Mem.: State Bar of Calif., chmn. Fed. Cts. Com. 1975-76, Jt. Com. (with fed. judges) for N. Dist. of Calif. for Standardization of Local Rules; American Bar Assn., chmn. Maritime Insurance Law Com. 1975-77; Federal Bar Assn., pres. S.F. Chpt., 1968; Bar Assn. of San Francisco, dir. 1969-70, secty. 1972, treas. 1973; Maritime Law Assn. of U.S., chmn. Practice and Procedure Com. 1976---, exec. com. 1977---; Legal Aid Soc. of S.F., dir. 1974---, v.p. 1975-77; Propeller Club of U.S.; World Trade Club of S.F.; Lambda Chi Alpha; Phi Alpha Delta. Episcopalian, Vestryman. Res.: 195 San Anselmo Ave., San Francisco, CA 94127; Office: Two Embarcadero Center, 26th Flr., San Francisco, CA 94111.

STARK, FRANKLIN CULVER
Attorney at Law
b. Apr. 16, 1915, Unityville, S. Dak.; s. Fred H. and Catherine (Culver) Stark; A.B., Dak. Wesleyan Univ. 1937; LL.D., 1959; J.D., Northwestern Univ. 1940; m. Alice Catherine Churchill, Miller, S. Dak., Sept. 16, 1941 (dec. May 14, 1975); m. 2d. Carlyn Kaiser Sacton, July 18, 1976; chil.: Margaret C. Stark-Roberts, b. Oct. 10, 1944; Wallace C., b. Feb. 18, 1947; Judith S. Schreiman, b. Jan. 31, 1950; Franklin C., Jr., b. Jan. 12, 1954. Career: admitted to Ill. bar, 1940, Calif. bar, 1946; assoc. Sidley, McPherson, Austin & Burgess law firm, Chicago, 1940-41; Fitzgerald, Abbott & Beardsley firm, Oakland, Calif. 1946-47; sr. partner, Stark, Stewart, Simon & Sparrowe (formerly Stark & Champlin, and Stark, Simon & Sparrowe), 1947---. Staff, Ofc. Gen. Counsel, O.P.A., Wash., D.C. 1941-42; pres. Oakland Council of Chs. 1941-46; Oakland Meth. Found.; Calif.-Nev. United Meth. Found.; chmn. bd. trustees, Calif.-Nev. Meth. Homes, 1966-73; bd. advs. E. Bay Psychol. Center; Bd. dirs. Dak. Wesleyan Univ.; bd. dirs. Fred Finch Youth Center; b. trustees, Sch. of Theol. at Claremont; bd. dirs. Fred Finch Youth Center. Lecturer on law, Univ. of Cal. Berkeley, 1946-66; Editor-in-chief, Ill. Law Review, 1939-40; assoc. ed. NACCA Law Journ. 1950----; USNR 1942-45, Comdr. (ret.), WW II. Mem.: Amer., Calif. State, Alameda Co. Bar Assns.; Amer. Judicature Soc.; Amer. Trial Lawyers Assn.; World Peace Through Law Center; Oakland C. of C.; Amer. Leg., Phi Kappa Phi, Pi Kappa Delta, Phi Alpha Delta, Order of Coif, Mason, Shriner, Elk; clubs: Athenian Nile, Kiwanis,

Commonwealth, S.F. Repub. United Meth. Ch. (del. to annual conf. Calif.-Nev.; Council of Ministeries, Stewardship, Finance; del. to 13th World Methodist Council, Dublin, Ireland 1976). Rec.: travel, hunting, fishing, sailing, camping, skiing. Res.: 333 Wayne Ave., Oakland, CA 94606; Office: Financial Center Bldg., Oakland, CA 94612.

STARK, LAWRENCE
Physician — Educator
b. Feb. 21, 1926, NYC; s. Edwar and Frieda (Blatt) Stark; A.B., Columbia, 1945; M.D., Albany (N.Y.) Med. Coll., 1948; postgrad. Trinity Coll., Oxford (Eng.) Univ., 1949-50, Univ. Coll., Univ. London (Eng.), 1950-51; children: Stefanie, Mathilde, Elizabeth. Career: Intern U.S. Naval Hosp., St. Albans, N.Y., 1948-49; clin. fellow Neurol. Inst., Columbia-Presbyterian Hosp., N.Y.C., 1951-52; instr., then asst. prof. neurology Yale Med. Sch., 1954-60; head neurology sect. Mass. Inst. Tech., 1960-65; prof., chmn. biomed. engring. dept. Presbyterian-St. Luke's Hosp., Univ. Ill. at Chicago Circle, 1965-68; prof. physiol. optics and engring. sci., UC Berkeley, 1968---; prof. neurology UC, San Francisco, 1968---; dir. Biosystems, Inc., Biocontracts, Inc., direct Access Corp. Cons. to industry; adviser NSF, NIH, 1967---; mem. vision com. NRC, 1964---. Served with M.C., USNR, 1952-54. Guggenheim fellow, 1968-70. Diplomate Am. Bd. Psychiatry and Neurology. Fellow, IEEE; recipient Morlock Award in Biomedical Engring., 1977; founding mem. Biophys. Soc., Biomed. Engring. Soc., Am. Soc. Cybernetics, Soc. Neurosci.; mem. Sigma Xi, Eta Kappa Nu. Clubs: Harvard (Boston); Cliffdwellers (Chicago). Author: Neurological Control Systems, 1968; Biomaterials, 1969; Biomedical Engineering, 1971; Hering's Theory of Binocular Vision, 1977. Contbr. articles to profl. journs. Home: 9 W. Parnassus Ct., Berkeley, CA 94708.

STARK, WALTER VICTOR
Gen. Manager, L.A. Jr. Chamber of Commerce
b. Oct. 13, 1920, London, England; s. Carl Victor and Nellie Stark; m. Ruth Cecily Mattock, Oct. 5, 1946, Limpley Stoke, Eng.; chil.: Jane (Idlof); Paul; Peter. Career: London Editorial, Manchester Guardian Newspaper, 1937-47; com. reporter, Poplar Borough Council, 1947-50; photographer and journalist, Nat. Assn. of Local Govt. Officers (NALGO), London, England, 1950-52; editor, Occidental Life Insurance Co., 1952-55; publicity mgr., Forest Lawn Memorial Parks, 1955-60; gen. mgr., Los Angeles Jr. Chamber of Commerce, 1960---. Mil.: Served in Royal Air Force, World War II, 1940-46. Home: 717 Cordova Ave., Glendale, CA 91206; Office: 404 S. Bixel St., L.A., CA 90051.

STARKEY, JOHN PHILLIPS
Mortgage Company President
b. Feb. 13, 1928, San Diego, Calif.; s. Harold B. and Augusta B. Starkey; ed. Chula Vista Grammar and Jr. H.S.; Coll. 1950; m. 2nd, Doris Heillis, Las Vegas, Nevada, July 20, 1958; chil.: Christina, b. Sept. 11, 1950; Janet T., b. June 2, 1960; John P. Jr., b. Aug. 24, 1962. Career: v.p.-secty. So. Mortgage Co. 1950-58; pres. 1958---; propr.-pres., John P. Starkey Co. 1957---. U.S. Army Signal Corps, WW II. Mem.: S.D. Council of Navy League of U.S.; Sigma Alpha Epsilon, 1948; SAE Alumni Club, S.D. Club, S.D. C. of C., Univ. Club of S.D., S.D. Rotary Club; county campaign chmn., Muscular Dystrophy, 1954, exec. com. 1954---, pres. 1955-59; treas. Federal Services campaign for National Health Agencies, San Diego County, 1958---; Aircraft Owners and Pilots Assn.; Natl. Real Estate Fliers Assn.; finance com. chmn.-chmn. exec. com. Mission Bay Assocs.; S.D., Calif., Natl. Mortgage Bankers Assn.; S.D. Aerospace Mus., v.p. 1968-69, pres. 1969---; bd. dirs. Mus. of Man, 1968---; chmn. Aviation Comm. for S.D. 200th Anniversary, 1968-69; chmn. S.D. Co. Air Show, 1969; chmn. St. Louis Air Race, 1969; S.D., Calif., Natl. Rea! Estate Bds.; S.D. Conv.-Tourist Bur.; Stardust Country Club; Cuyamaca Club of San Diego; Young Men in Government; treasurer Young Repubs. of San Diego Co. 1953; regional v.p., Young Repubs. of Calif. 1954, State Conv. chmn., treas. 1955; regional dir., Young Repubs. Natl. Fed. 1955-57, chmn. region 10 council, 1955, 57, 59; So. Counties campaign coord., Eisenhower-Nixon Committee, 1956; San Diego County Repub. Central Com. 1958---; Repub. Associates of S.D. County. All Souls Episcopal Ch. Rec.: flying, golf, water skiing, swimming, handball, volleyball. Res.: 3115 McCall St., San Diego, CA.

STARR, CHAUNCEY
Research Institute Executive
b. Apr. 14, 1912, Newark, N.J.; E.E., Rensselaer Polytech. Inst., Troy, N.Y., 1932, Ph.D., 1935, Research Fellow, 1932-35; Charles A. Coffin Fellow, Harvard Univ., 1935-37. Career: Research Assoc., MIT (properties materials at low temperatures, prodn. of liquid hydrogen), 1938-41; research in electronic devices, Bureau of Ships, Navy Dept. 1941-42; Manhattan Dist., incl. Radiation Lab. of UC Berkeley, Tenn. Eastman Corp., Oak Ridge and Clinton Labs., Oak Ridge, 1942-46; pres. Atomics Internat. Div., L.A. and vice pres. North American Rockwell, Inc., 1946-66; Dean, Sch. of Engring. and Applied Sci., UCLA, 1966-73; pres., Electric Power Research Inst., Palo Alto, 1973-78, vice chmn. 1978---. Publs. sci. books, articles in profl. mags., reviews. Awards: Hon. Dr. Eng., Rensselaer Polytech. Inst. 1964; AEC award for meritorious contbns. to nat. atomic energy program, 1974; Pender Award, Univ. Pa., 1975; French Legion of Honor, 1978. Current mem.: Council of Nat. Acad. of Engineering; Foreign Mem., Royal Swedish Acad. of Engineering Sci.; Am. Nuclear Soc.; Office of Tech. Assessment Energy Advisory Com.; prin. rep. to Internat. Electric Research Exchange; cons. prof. to Sch. of Engineering, Stanford Univ.; U.S. del. to US/USSR Jt. Com. on Cooperation of Peaceful Uses of Atomic Energy; del. to U.S. Nat. Energy Conf. for World Energy; Energy Subcom. of US-Israel Bi-National Advisory Council for Indsl. R&D. Address: 95 Stern Lane, Atherton, CA 94025.

STAUFFER, BEVERLY M.
Civic Leader — Art Patron
b. July 21, Boston, Mass.; d. Frederick and Elizabeth (Flood) Schweppe; ed. Emerson Coll.; m. John Stauffer (dec.). Career: Pres., John and Beverly Stauffer Found.; bd. trustees, Pepperdine Univ., Malibu; est. Beverly M. Stauffer: Clin., Mem. Hosp. of Glendale; Clinic, Hawthorne Community Hosp.; Boys Club of Palm Springs Rec. Lodge, Idlewild; Dormitory, and the Art Center, Whittier College; Sch. of Langs., Pomona College; Chapel, and electronics pianos for Sch. of Music, Pepperdine Univ. Republican. Catholic. Mem.: Los Angeles Country Club, Calif. Club, Jonathan Club, L.A. Club, Thunderbird Country Club, Palm Springs; Alta Club, Salt Lake City. Hobbies: music, art, philanthropy. Rec.: golf. Res.: Talmadge Apts., 3278 Wilshire Blvd., Los Angeles; Office: 3243 Wilshire Blvd., Los Angeles, CA 90010.

STEADMAN, DAVID WILTON
Curator
b. Oct. 24, 1936, Honolulu, Hawaii; s. Alva Edgar and Martha (Cooke) Steadman; B.A., Harvard Univ., 1960; M.A., Univ. Calif., Berkeley, 1966; Ph.D., Princeton, 1974; m. Kathleen Reilly, Aug. 1, 1964, Ross, Calif.; children: Alexander Carroll, b. 1966; Kate Montague, b. 1968. Career: Lectr., The Frick Collection, NYC, 1969-71; Asst., Acting and Assoc. Director, The Art Museum, Princeton Univ., 1971-74; Dir., Galleries of the Claremont Colleges, 1974---; Curator, Norton Simon Museum, 1977---. Publs.: exhibition catalogues: The Graphic Art of Francisco Goya, 1975; 18th Century Drawings from Calif. Collections, 1976; Works on Paper 1900-1960 from Southern California Collections, 1977. Office: Montgomery Gallery, Pomona Coll., Claremont, CA 91711.

STEEL, ROBERT B.
Marketing Executive
b. Feb. 15, 1931, Perth Amboy, N.J.; s. Paul and Viola (Beagle) Steel; grands., Dr. Jesse Warren Beagle, Field Secty., So. Baptist Home Mission Bd.; B.A., Furman Univ., 1952; M.A., Fla. State Univ., 1956; m. Shirley Brandon, Apr. 7, 1957, San Diego; daughters: Nancy Ann, b. 1963; Barbara Lee, b. 1960. Career: Engr., writer, later dir., Audio Visual Tng., Convair-Astronautics (div. of Gen. Dynamics Corp.), San Diego, 1956-60; gen. mgr., Miles-Samuelson Inc., S.D., 1960-61; sales engr., UNIVAC Div., Sperry Rand Corp., S.D., 1961-63; mktg. proposal mgr., Litton Data Systems, L.A., 1964; dir., Advt. and Pub. Rels., Informatics Inc., L.A., 1964---; co-founder, v.p., Marketing Methods, Inc., Los Angeles, 1975---. Prod. of tech. films for IBM Corp., N.Y., NASA, USAF; Co-founder, bd. dir., California Theater Ensemble, 1975-76; founding mem., dir., The Los Angeles Mime Guild, 1978---: Publicity chmn., First U.S.-Japan Computer Conf., Tokyo, 1972; mem. Assn. for Computing Machinery, award for outstanding service to chpt., 1970. Res.: Northridge, CA; Office: 3303 Wilshire Blvd., Suite 500, Los Angeles, CA 90010.

STEELE, ARNOLD E.
Zoologist — Research Biologist
b. June 21, 1925, Estherville, Iowa; s. Joseph and Laurena (Howard) Steele; GGrandson, Capt. Samuel Keller, Union Army, Civil War; B.A. 1953, M.S. 1957, zoology; m. Joan Heckert, Dec. 8, 1954, Marshalltown, Iowa; sons: Ronald, b. 1955; Randal, b. 1958; Rodger, b. 1963. Career: Parasitologist, U.S. Dept. Agri., Coastal Planes Research Sta., Tifton, Ga., 1955, Transferred to Plant Nematology, 1956, trans. to USDA, Salinas, Calif., 1959---: research biology and control of plant parasitic nematodes. Active duty, USN, 1943-49; commd., USAR, 1952-78, Ret. Maj. Assoc. Editor, Journal of Nematology, 1974-76, pub. articles on biology and control of nematodes affecting prodn. of sugarbeet and vegetables. Mem.: Sigma Xi, Am. Phytopatological Soc.; Soc. of Nematologists; European Soc. of Nematologists; Orgn. of Tropical Am. Nematol.; Helminthological Soc. of Wash.; Reserve Officers Assn. Methodist. Hobbies: photog., electronics. Res.: 53 Talbot St., Salinas, CA 93901; Office: U.S. Agr. Research Sta., Salinas, CA.

STEEN, HAROLD KARL
Director, Forest History Society
b. May 12, 1935, Vashon, Wash.; s. Ralph Edward and Stella Isaline (Collings) Steen; B.S. Forestry, 1957, M.F., 1962, Ph.D., 1969; m. Judith Arlene Kippola, June 16, 1962, Silverdale, Wash.; Career: with U.S. Forest Service, 1957-65; asst. dir. and editor, Forest History Society, 1969-72, assoc. dir. for Research and Library Services, 1972-78; exec. dir., 1978---. Author: The U.S. Forest Service: A History, 1976. USNR, 1953-61. Res.: 114 Escalona Dr., Santa Cruz, CA; Office: Forest History Society, 109 Coral St., Santa Cruz, CA 95060.

STEGENGA, PRESTON J.
Advisor — Consultant, International Affairs
b. July 9, 1924, Grand Rapids, Mich.; s. Miner and Dureth (Bouma) Stegenga; B.A., Hope Coll., 1947; M.A., Columbia Univ.; Ph.D., Univ. Mich. 1952; m. Marcia De Young, July 28, 1950, Sparta, Mich.; children: James, b. 1954; Susan, b. 1957. Career: Assoc. Prof. Hist. & Polit. Sci., Berea Coll., Kentucky, 1948-55; pres., Northwestern Coll., Iowa, 1955-66; chief, Cornell Univ. Proj. in Africa, 1966-68; director, Internat. Center, Cal. State Univ., Sacramento, 1968---; Cons.: UN Devel. Program; Am. Assn. State Colls. & Univs.; Advisor, Pres. Republic of Liberia. Pres., v.p., dir., UN Assn.; v.p., dir., World Affairs Council; dir., Calif. Council of UN University. Author: Anchor of Hope; contbr. to various profl. and ednl. journals. AUS, 1944-45, ETO, Counter-intelligence Corps. Recipient: Award for Distinguished Service, UN. Mem.: Phi Kappa Phi; Phi Delta Kappa; hon. Paramount Chief, Kpelle Tribe, W. Africa; pres., Tri-State Coll. Assn. Reformed Ch. in Am. Hobbies: stamp collection, sports. Res.: 545 Mills Rd., Sacramento, CA 95825; Office: Cal. State Univ., Sacramento, CA 95819.

STEGNER, WALLACE EARLE
Author — University Professor
b. Feb. 18, 1909, Lake Mills, Ia.; s. George Henry and Hilda (Paulson) Stegner; B.A., Univ. of Ut. 1930; Univ. of Calif. 1932-33; M.A., State Univ. of Ia. 1932, Ph.D. 1935; m. Mary Stuart Page, Dubuque, Ia., Sept. 1, 1934; son, Stuart Page, b. Jan. 31, 1937. Career: Instr. English, Augustana Coll., Rock Is., Ill. 1933-34; Univ. of Ut. 1934-37; Univ. of Wis. 1937-39; Harvard Univ. 1939-45; prof. English-dir. creative writing, Stanford Univ. 1945---. Writer, short stories, various mags., editor-compiler texts and anthologies, 1934---. Author: (books) Remembering Laughter, 1937; On a Darkling Plain, 1938; Fire and Ice, 1939; Mormon Country, 1941; The Big Rock Candy Mountain, 1942; One Nation (with editors, Look mag.), 1945; Second Growth, 1948; The Preacher and the Slave, 1950; The Women on the Wall, 1950; Beyond the Hundredth Meridian, 1954; The City of the Living, 1956; A Shooting Star, 1961; Wold Willow, 1962; The Gathering of Zion, 1964; All the Little Live Things, 1967; The Sound of Mountain Water, 1969; Angle of Repose, 1971; The Uneasy Chair, 1974. Assistant to Secty. of the Interior, 1961; adv. bd. Natl. Parks (historical sites, bldgs. and monuments), USA 1962-66. Awards: Guggenheim fellowship, 1950, 52, 59; numerous other grants and fellowships, incl. Center for Advanced Studies in Behavior Scis. Europe and Far East, the Wenner-Gren Found. for stu. of village democracy (researched in Demark, New Eng. and Saskatchewan); awarded Little Brown & Co. Novelette Prize for Remembering Laughter, 1937; won O. Henry first prize award for short story, 1950;

Houghton-Mifflin Life in Amer. Award for One Nation, 1945; Literary Guild selections incl. All the Little Live Things, 1967, and Commonwealth Club Gold Medal for Fiction, 1968; Pulitzer Prize in fiction, 1972, for Angle ot Repose. Mem.: (hon. life) Sierra Club; Phi Beta Kappa, 1930. Res.: 13456 S. Fork Lane, Los Altos Hills, CA; Office: Stanford Univeristy.

STEIN, ADRIENNE
Attorney at Law
b. Nov. 15, 1924, NYC; d. Isidore and Lena (Florea) Bakst; B.B.A., 1944; J.D., 1967; m. Jack M. Stein; children: Gilbert, Peggy, Harvey. Career: Admitted to California bar 1967; law practice, Long Beach, 1967---; assoc. firm Gyler & Gottlieb, Inc., 1967-73; partner, firm Gottlieb, Gottlieb & Stein, 1974---; mem. faculty, Pacific Coast Univ., 1968. Bd. dir., pres., Long Beach Jewish Community Center; dir., Long Beach Jewish Comm. Fedn.; mem. Long Beach chpt. ACLU; United Way; Calif., Los Angeles Co. and Long Beach bar assns. Res.: 5850 Empire Grade Rd., Santa Cruz, CA 95060; Office: 675 E. Wardlow Rd., Long Beach, CA 90807.

STEIN, JUSTIN J.
Physician — Surgeon
b. Oct. 18, 1907, Haskell, Tex.; s. Justin John and Annie Minnie (Frederick) Stein; ed. So. Meth. Univ. 1926-29; Baylor Med. Coll. 1929-33; spec. stu., Mayo Clinic and Found. 1933-34; M.D., Univ. of Minn. 1934; m. Lillian May Kolar, Oct. 23, 1936; dau.: Justine Johanna. Career: Intern, Cincinnati Gen. Hosp. 1934-35; tumor surg.-therapist, Edward Hines, Jr. Hosp., Hines, Ill. 1935-41; cons. Elmhurst (Ill.) Community Hosp. and West-Lake Hosp., Melrose Park, 1938-41; tumor surg.-therapist, L.A. Tumor Inst. 1946-52; attending surg.-mem. tumor bd., Malignancy Serv., L.A. Co. Hosp. 1948-59; cons. oncologist, Vets. Adm., West L.A. 1948-75; attending radiologist, L.A. Co. Harbor Hosp. 1952-75; mem. hosp. staffs: Calif. Luth. Hosp. (exec. med. bd. 1950-53), Crenshaw Hosp., Santa Monica Hosp., UCLA Med. Center, Desert Hosp. (Palm Springs); cons. in radiology; Vets. Adm. Regional Ofc., L.A. 1948-75; L.A. Dept. of Health, Edn. and Welfare, 1952---; U.S. Naval Hosp., San Diego, Calif. 1959---. Surg. Gen., USN 1974---. Assistant prof. surgery, Coll. of Med. Evangs., L.A. 1948-52; prof. (radiology), UCLA Sch. of Med. 1952---, acting chmn. Dept. Radiology, 1960; dir. Cancer Reserach Inst. and chmn. com. on cancer edn. and reserach, UCLA Med. Center, 1955-70. Contrib. numerous sci. articles to med. journs. Lt. Comdr. (MC), USNR (1941-46), WW II. Awards: decorated, two Pres. Unit Cits., Amer. Def. Medal, Asiatic Pac. Medal with 4 combat stars, Naval Res. Medal, WW II. Medal. Mem.: Chmn. Gov's. Emg. Medical Adv. Comm. 1950-67; conf. chmn., 12th annual Co. Med. Socs. Civ. Def. Conf. (sponsored by AMA); diplomate, Amer. Bd. of Radiology; fellow, Internat. Coll. of Surgs., pres. So. Calif. Chpt. 1952; v-regent, 1953-60; Calif. State Bd. of Med. Examiners, 1952-70; pres. 1956; dir. Calif. Inst. for Cancer Research, 1955-75; pres. American Cancer Society, Inc. 1974; Fellow, Royal Soc. of Med. (Eng.); Radiological Soc. of N. Amer., Inc., Radiological Soc. of So. Calif., Pac. Roentgen Soc.; v.p. Med.-Dental Vets Assn. 1958; pres. 1959; fellow, ACS, and rep. Amer. Coll. of Radiology to Comm. on Cancer, 1960-68; fellow, Amer. Coll. of Radiology, chmn. Comm. on Cancer, 1961, chancellor, 1965-68; AAAS; Radiation Research Soc., Research Soc. of California, Soc. of Nuclear Med., AMA, Pan Amer. Med. Assn. (councillor for radiotherapy for U.S.); co-founder, Amer. Club of Therapeutic Radiologists; Amer. Radium Soc., secty. 1963-65, pres. 1966; trustee, Amer. Bd. of Radiology, 1965-78; L.A. Radiological Soc., James Ewing Soc., Kappa Sigma, Phi Chi. Res.: 3526-A Bahia Blanca West, Laguna Hills, CA 92653; Office: Veterans Hospital, 5901 E. 7th St., Long Beach, CA 90822.

STEINBERG, HOWARD
Corporate Executive
b. Aug. 23, 1926, Chicago; s. Leo and Hattie Steinberg; B.S., chem., Univ. Ill., 1948; Ph.D., chem. (AEC Fellow), UCLA, 1951; AEC Postdoctoral Fellow, Mass. Inst. Tech., 1951-52; m. Eve Taubman, 1946, Chicago; children: Gary, b. 1949; Erik, b. 1956; Lisa, b. 1956. Career: Research Chemist, Aerojet Gen. Corp., Azusa, 1952; Research assoc., UCLA, 1952-53; collaborator, U.S. Dept. of Agri., Pasadena, 1953-54; mgr. Organic Research, U.S. Borax Research Corp., Anaheim, 1954, asst. dir./assoc. dir./dir. Chem. Research, 1958-63, v.p., U.S. Borax & Chemical Corp., Anaheim, Calif. 1963-69, pres. 1969---; v.p., Tech.

Dept., U.S. Borax & Chemical Corp., 1969---, Dir. 1973---. Dir.: Ireco Chem. Co., 1970-75; No. Orange County Cultural Groups Found., 1970-71. Mem. Sci. & Engring. Advisory Council, Cal. State Univ., Fullerton, 1964---. Atomic Energy Commn. Patentee: numerous U.S. and foreign patents in field of boron chem. Author: Organoboron Chemistry, Vol. 1, 1964, co-author Vol. 2, 1966; Editor: Progress in Boron Chemistry, Vol. 1, 1964, Progress in Boron Chemistry, Vol. 2, 1970; Progress in Boron Chemistry, Vol. 3, 1970; contbr. numerous papers in Journal Am. Chem. Soc., other profl. journs. USAAF, 1945. Mem.: Am. and British Chem. Socs.; Soc. Chem. Industry; Am. Mining Congress; Am. Inst. Mining Engrs.; Indsl. Research Inst.; Assn. for Corporate Growth; Sigma Xi; Pi Mu Epsilon; Phi Lambda Upsilon. Hobby: woodworking. Res.: 1401 Miramar Dr., Fullerton, CA 92631; Office: 3075 Wilshire Blvd., L.A., CA 90010.

STENTZ, CARL EARL
Industrial Executive — Civic Leader
b. Apr. 7, 1904, Cleveland, Oh.; s. Earl Carlton and Mary (Davis) Stentz; B.S., Univ. Okla. 1926; postgrad. Univ. Akron, Oh. 1926-27; m. Lucile Killingsworth, Ardmore, Okla., June 9, 1927; dau. Mrs. Robert (Nancy Carolyn) Williams, b. July 17, 1935. Career: B.F. Goodrich Co., Akron, Oh. 1926-30; chief chem. Pac. Goodrich Co. 1931-32; supt. E.M. Smith Rubber Co. 1932-37; propr.-pres. Latex Seamless Rubber Co. 1937-51; owner-pres. Arrowhead Rubber Co. 1940-44; v.p.-gen. mgr. Golden States Rubber Mills, 1944-46; cons. and rubber researcher, 1951-58; pres. Jeep Min. Co. 1951-56; investments exec. 1954-69 (ret.); owner, Ritz Theater, Escondido, Calif. Pres., Alhambra City Comm. 1946-51; chmn. adv. council, Civil Def.; (charter) L.A. Co. Anti-Smog Com. 1949; tax com.-dir. League of Calif. Cities; Alhambra Park and Rec. Comm.; dir. Sanitation Dists. 2 and 16; dir. Girl Scouts Bldg. Corp.; Mayor, City of Alhambra, 1950-51. Awards: Jr. C. of C. Hon. Roll Award, 1949, 50; Outstanding Citizen of Alhambra Community Servs. Award, 1950; Natl. Trophy for Best Mineral Collection in U.S. by Amer. Fed. of Mineralogical Socs. Natl. Show, Las Vegas, Nev. 1966. Mem.: 1st state pres. DeMolay, Okla. 1924; founder-pres. Oneonta Stamp Club, 1931; dir. Calif. Fed. of Mineral Socs.; Palomar Gem and Mineral Soc.; Mineral Soc. of So. Calif.; Optical Mineralogist; (life) hon. dir. The Flagg Found. for Advancement of Earth Scis.; Arizona Small Mine Operators Assn.; secty. L.A. Rubber Group of Amer. Chem. Soc.; San Gabriel Valley Civic Assn.; Jr. and Alhambra C.s of C.; Amer. Fed. of Mineralogical Soc.; Natl. Register of Sci. and Tech. Personnel; Alhambra Quarterback Club; Hilltoppers and Rancho Amigos, Escondido; (hon. life) founder-pres. Exch. Club of Newport Harbor, 1957; dist. gov. Natl. Exch. of Calif. 1960-61, state dir. 1960-62, past pres. Alhambra Chpt.; asst. secty. Natl. Exch. Clubs, 1964-65; past pres.-dir. Alhambra Community Chest; past pres. Alpha Sigma Phi; Alpha Chi Sigma, past pres. Interfraternity Council; pres. 21 Club; Masonic Lodge; (life) Elks Lodge, gen. chmn. Alhambra Elks Minstrels. Hobby: collector fine mineral specimens. Methodist. Res.: 79 Pinestone (Woodbridge), Irvine, CA 92714.

STEPHENS, ALBERT LEE, JR.
Chief U.S. District Judge
b. Feb. 19, 1913, Los Angeles; son Judge Albert Lee Stephens (dec., U.S. Ct. of Appeals); bro., Assoc. Justice Clarke E. Stephens, Calif. Ct. of Appeal; B.A., cum laude, USC, 1936; LL.B., USC Law Sch., 1938 (L.Rev. staff); m. Barbara McNeil, Sept. 20, 1939; children: Virginia, b. 1943; Marylee, b. 1944. Career: Admitted to Calif. Bar, 1939, U.S. Supreme Ct., 1944; Lectr., UCLA Law Sch., 1954-55, USC Law Sch., 1961-63, mem. Moot Cts., USC Law Sch. 1962-63; apptd. Judge, Superior Ct., Los Angeles Co., 1959-61; nominated (by Pres. John F. Kennedy and confirmed by U.S. Senate), Judge, U.S. Dist. Court, Central Dist. of Calif., 1961-60, Chief Judge, 1970---. Councillor, Sch. of Politics and Internat. Rels., USC, chmn. 1966-67; bd. Advisors, Whittier Coll. Sch. of Law, 1977---; Fellow, Am. Bar Found. Mem.: Am. Judicature Soc.; Am. (chmn. Nat. Conf. of Fed. Trial Judges, 1976---), Federal and L.A. County (trustee, 1955-57, 1959-61) Bar Assns.; Lawyers' Club of L.A., bd. of Govs., 1950, 55-56; USC Alumni Assn., pres. 1974-75; Chancery Club, pres. 1960-61; Town Hall, L.A.; World Affairs Council of L.A.; University Club; Native Sons of Golden West; Am. Legion; Phi Alpha Delta, Phi Kappa Tau, Blackstonian, Pi Sigma Alpha, Skull & Scales, Skull and Dagger. Presbyterian. Chambers: U.S. District Court, Los Angeles, CA 90012.

STEPHENSON, PATRICIA PETERS
Artist — Educator
b. July 6, 1928, Tucson, Ariz.; d. Ivan and Wilma (Croxen) Peters; ed. B.S., Univ. of Ariz. 1951; m. Roger E. Stephenson, Tucson, Ariz., Apr. 8, 1951; chil.: Carol Ann, b. Nov. 7, 1955; Roger Emmett, b. Dec. 12, 1956; Brian Peter, b. Oct. 10, 1958. Career: Teacher, art and home econs., Tucson pub. schs. 1952-55; teacher, Covina-Valley Sch. Dist. 1966-67. Artist, exhib. group show, Tucson Fine Arts Assn., 1949-54; freelance commercial artist, 1955---; exhib. art, L.A. and San Bernardino Cos.; arts and crafts spec., local Campfire Girls, 1962---; instr. Tri-Community Adult Edn. and Charter Oak Sch. Dist. 1972---. Lecturer: Indian crafts and designs; origins of various popular Mex. foods; book reviews: Discovering Mexican Cooking, 40 book clubs, soc. and serv. groups, L.A., Santa Barbara, San Bernardino and Orange Cos. 1959-66. Co-author-illus.: Discovering Tucson (book accepted as approved supplementary text by State of Ariz., Dept. of Edn.), 1954; designer, pgm. books and theme drawing, Sierra Vista Annual Dist. Cruises, Presbyterian Mariners, 1964, 65, 66, 67; designer, numerous pgm. booklets. Awards: Woman of the Yr. by E. San Gabriel Valley Alumni Assn., Delta Delta Delta, 1958; hob. at homecoming as Outstanding Alumnae, Univ. of Ariz., Nov. 1966. Listed, various biog. publs., USA. Mem.: secty. Alpha Rho Tau, 1950-51; pres. Tucson Alumni Assn. of Delta Delta Delta 1953-54 (hist.-chaplain, Phi Beta Chpt.); Amer. Calif. Home Econs. Assns.; Pasa. Art Museum; Panhellenic Club; PEO; DAR Presbyterian (deacon, chaplain, Mariners Club). Res.: 2714 E. Larkwood, West Covina, CA 91791.

STERLING, JOHN EWART WALLACE
Chancellor, Stanford University
b. Aug. 6, 1906, Linwood, Ontario, Can. (naturalized U.S. cit. 1947); s. The Rev. William and Anna (Wallace) Sterling; B.A., Univ. of Toronto, 1927; M.A., Univ. of Alberta, 1930; Ph.D., Stanford Univ. 1938; LL.D. (hon.) Pomona Coll. 1949; LL.D. (hon.), Occidental Coll. 1949; LL.D. (hon.), Univ. of San Francisco 1950; LL.D. (hon.) Univ. of Toronto, Can. 1950; D.C.L. (hon.), Durham Univ., Eng. 1953; LL.D. (hon.) Univ. of Caen, France 1957; LL.D (hon.): Univ. of Brit. Columbia, Northwestern Univ. and Univ. of Calif. 1958; (hon.) Litt.D., USC 1960; (Hon.) LL.D.'s: Univ. of Denver, Loyola Univ. and McGill Univ. (Can.) 1961; Columbia Univ. 1962; St. Mary's Coll. 1962; Univ. of Santa Clara, 1963; McMaster Univ. 1966; m. Ann Marie Shaver, Ancaster, Ontario, Can., Aug. 7, 1930; chil.: William Wallace, b. July 3, 1939; Susan Hardy, b. Sept. 9, 1941; Judith Robinson, b. Dec. 28, 1944. Career: Lecturer in history, Regina Coll., Saskatchewan, 1927-28; instr. in hist.-ath. coach., Univ. of Alberta, 1928-30; research asst., Hoover Lib., Stanford Univ. 1932-37; instr. in hist., Stanford Univ. 1935-37; asst. prof. of hist., Calif. Inst. of Tech., Pasadena, Calif. 1937-40; assoc. E.S. Harkness prof. of hist. and govt. 1945-48; news analyst, CBS, 1942-48; mem. res. civ. faculty, Natl. War Coll., Wash., D.C. 1947; 5th pres., Stanford Univ., 1949-68; chancellor, 1968---, trustee, 1969; chmn. Amer. Rev. Bicentennial Comm., Wash. D.C. 1969-70; chmn. bd. dirs., Stanford Research Inst. 1949-66. Bd. dirs.: Independence Life Ins. Co. of Amer. 1957; Shell Oil Co. 1968---; Dean Witter & Co. 1972---; Tridair Inds. 1972---. Co-editor, vol. series in Hoover Inst., publ. 1932-37. Awards: Hon. Comdr., Civ. Div. of Order of Brit. Empire by Queen Elizabeth, Jan. 1957; Distinguished Cit. Award by Palo Alto C. of C., Feb. 12, 1959; Comdr's Cross of Order of Merit for promoting internat. good will, Fed. Republic of Ger., May 1959; Chevalier de la Legion d'Honneur, France 1960; Second Degree of IMperial Order of Rising Sun, Japan, 1961; Grand Gold Badge of Honor for Merits to the Republic of Austria, 1965. Mem.: fellow, Soc. Sci. Research Council, 1939-40; dir. Huntington Lib. and Art Gallery, San Marino, Calif. 1948-49, bd. trustees, 1954-68; Comm. on Financing Higher Edn. 1949-52; Ford Motor Co. Scholarship Bd. 1951---; bd. dirs., Fireman's Fund Ins. Co., S.F. 1952---; v.p. World Affairs Council of No. Calif. 1953---; bd. trustees, Thacher Sch., Ojai, Calif. 1954-64; adv. com., Spec. Awards to Colls. and Univs., Equitable Life Assurance Soc. of U.S. 1955---; bd. on Health Research Facilities, U.S. Pub. Health Research Facilities, U.S. Pub. Health Service 1956-57; secty.-treas., Assn. of Amer. Universities, 1958-60, 1962-64; trustee, The Asia Found. Comm. on Edn. Exch. 1960---; Council on Foreign Rels.; U.S. Adv. Comm. on Educational Exch. 1960-61; Amer. Edn. and Internat. Affairs, 1960-63; Tulane Univ. Bd. of Visitors, 1960---; adv. com., Foreign Rels. of U.S., Dept. of State, 1965---; fellow, American Geographical Society, Amer. Hist. Assn., Pac.

Coast Hist. Assn., Canadian Inst. Assn., Canadian Polit. Sci. Assn.; Calif. Club, L.A; Pac. Union, Bohemian, The Family, Commonwealth, S.F.; University Club, N.Y.; Sunset, Burlingame Country Clubs. Res.: 2220 Stockbridge Ave., Woodside, CA 94062; Office: Stanford University, Stanford, CA 94305.

STERN, ARTHUR P.
Engineer — Business Executive

b. July 20, 1925, Budapest, Hungary; s. Leon and Bertha (Frankfurter) Stern; ed. Diploma, Swiss Fed. Inst. of Tech. 1948; MSEE, Syracuse Univ. N.Y., 1956; m. Edith Margureite Samuel, Montreaux, Switz., Sept. 17, 1952; chil.: Daniel, b. Feb. 2, 1954; Claude, b. Sept. 18, 1955; Jacqueline, b. May 2, 1958. Career: Research engr. Jaeger Inc., Basel, Switz. 1948-50; instr. Swiss Fed. Inst. of Tech. 1950-51; engr. Gen. Elec. Co. 1951-57; mgr. Electronic Devices Lab. 1957-61; dir. engr. Electronics Div., Martin Marietta Corp. 1961-64; dir. operations, Def. Systems Div., Bunker-Ramo Corp. 1964-66; v.p.-gen. mgr. advanced prod. div., Magnavox Co. 1966---. Author: 20 tech. and sci. articles; co-author, 2 tech. books; 12 U.S. and several foreign patents. Mem.: chmn. engring. div. United Jewish Appeal, Syracuse, N.Y. 1955-57; gen. chmn. Internat. Solid State Circuits Conf. 1960; dir. IEEE 1970---, secty. 1972, treas. 1973, v.p. 1974, pres. 1975 (serv. approx. 20 electronics engring. coms.). Res.: 606 N. Oakhurst Dr., Beverly Hills, CA 90210; Office: 2829 Maricopa St., Torrance, CA 90503.

STERNBERG, HARRY
Artist — Teacher

b. July 19, 1904, NYC; s. Simon and Rose (Brand) Sternberg; student, Art Students League, NYC; m. Mary Elizabeth Gosney, Oct. 9, 1939, Clearwater, Fla.; dau. Leslie Louise, b. 1947. Career: Tchr. graphics and painting: at Art Students League, NYC, 1933-67, Idyllwild Sch. of Music and Art, 1955-67, New Sch. of Social Research, NYC, 1937-39, Museum of Modern Art, Veterans Centre, 1943-45; also USC, San Diego State Univ., Brigham Young Univ. Author: Silk Screen Color Printing, Modern Methods and Materials of Etching (McGraw-Hill), Composition, Abstract-Realistic Drawing, Woodcut (Pitman Publications); Director-prod. art film: The Many Worlds of Art. One man shows (1932---) incl. ACA Gallery, NYC (bienially), Weyhe Gallery, NYC, Garelick Gallery, Chicago, Heritage Gallery, L.A., Walker Art Centre, Mnpls., McKnight Art Centre, Wichita State Univ. Work rep. in many pvt. collections; pub. collections abroad: Victoria and Albert Mus., London, Biblioteque Nationale, Paris, Nat. Mus., Tel Aviv, New Zealand Mus. of Art; permanent collections of Whitney Mus., Mus. of Modern Art, Metropolitan Mus., H.de Young Mem. Mus., Syracuse Univ. Mus., Fogg Mus., Brooklyn Mus. of Art, Addison Gallery of Am. Art, Cleveland Mus. of Art, Univ. Nebr., Art Students League, Thorne Mus. of Keene State Coll., Lib. of Congress, N.Y. Pub. Lib., Univ. of Minn., Hirshorn Mus. Guggenheim Fellow, 1936. Mem. Artists Equity, Fine Arts Guild, Fine Arts Gallery Museum. Hobby: gardening. Res.: 1606 Conway Dr., Escondido, CA; Studio: 1718 E. Valley Pkwy., Escondido, CA 92025.

STERPA, SEBASTIANO
Realtor

b. July 18, 1929, Veiano, Italy; s. Giuseppe and Clementina (Fiori) Sterpa; grad. Giulio Cesare Liceum, Rome, Italy 1948; student, Law Univ. of Rome; Bus. Adminstrn., UCLA; m. Carole Uptegraft, July 29, 1978, Carmel, Calif.; chil.: Patricia (Vitale); Terry S. Career: real estate sales agent, 1955-62; opened Sterpa Realty, 1972, incorporated in 1964, pres., Sterpa Realty Register, 1964--- (9 residential sales offices, 175 sales associates); assoc. mem. of several publications, master instr., Calif. Assn. of Realtors, 1978---. Co-founder and dir.: Burbank Citizens Bank, Realty Register and Lincoln Title Co., 1977-78. Charter mem., Italian American Found., 1974---. Apptd. Knight of the Italian Labor Soc., President of Italian Republic, 1977. Dir., Internat. Inst. of Los Angeles, 1976, 77, 78; Sertoma Internat., 1965---, pres. 1966; Dir., Nat. Assn. of Realtors, 1977, 78, 79; state treas. Calif. Assn. of Realtors, 1978, 79, pres., Burbank Bd. of Realtors, 1967-68; pres., Burbank C. of C., 1972; vice-chmn., Verdugo Hills Heart Assn., 1966; fund raising chmn., 1967; chmn., United Way-Commerce & Industry Div., East, L.A. County 1978; Mem. St. Peter's Ch., L.A.; exec. com. of Villa Scalabrini Retirement project. Rec.: golf, travel. Home: 1530 Greenbriar Rd., Glendale, CA 91206; Office: 303 S. Glenoaks Blvd., Burbank, CA 91502.

STETLER, MARY E.
Realtor

b. Nov. 25, 1927, Los Angeles, Calif.; d. Richard C. and Clara C. Redwood; student, L.A. City Coll., 1947-48; grad., Anthony Real Estate Sch., 1969; G.R.I. Graduate Realtors Inst., 1979; m. Richard L. Stetler, Oct. 11, 1950, Beverly Hills; chil.: Mary Susan (Hampton), b. Oct. 30, 1951; Janet Chrystel (Rountree), b. Apr. 21, 1953; Richard Lowell, Jr., b. Nov. 30, 1954. Career: employee, San Jose Nat. Bank, 1960-66; real estate sales agent, 1969-73; real estate broker, 1973---; opened own office, Stetler Realty (Omega Brokers), 1974---. Recipient: awards for service to Santa Clarita Valley Bd. of Realtors, 1972, 1973. V.P. and secty., Omega Brokers Franchise; mem. Santa Clarita Valley Bd. of Realtors, dir. 1973, chmn. edn. com., 1974, chmn. mem. com., 1975, treas. 1976, chmn. orientation com. 1977; mem. Soroptimist Club of Santa Clarita Valley. Placerita Baptist Ch., Newhall. Rec.: golf, bowling. Home: 19237 Friendly Valley Pkwy., Newhall, CA 91321; Office: Omega Brokers, Stetler Realty, 24309 San Fernando Rd., Newhall, CA 91321.

STEVENSON, WARD BARKER
Bank Executive

b. Jan. 20, 1920, Minneapolis, Minn.; s. William John and Stella (Bain) Stevenson; ed. Univ. of Minn. 1941; m. Barbara Nauman, Los Angeles, 1977; chil.: Ward B. Jr., Mrs. Mark (Pamela) Courtney, Mrs. Walter (Candis) Schuster. Career: Ind. rels. mgr.-dir. pub. rels. Pillsbury Co., Minneapolis 1943-55; v.p. pub. rels. Benton & Bowles Adv. Agcy. 1955-60; v.p. pub. rels. ITT, 1960-62; v.p. pub. and govt. rels. First Natl. City Bank, NYC, 1964-70; sr. v.p. Hill & Knowlton, Inc. 1970-74; sr. v.p. pub. affairs and mktg. Crocker Nat. Bank, San Francisco, 1974. Adv. bd., Air Tr. Command, USAF; USNR 1944-46, WW II. Awards: USAF Award of Merit, 1965; Pub. Rels. Soc. of Amer's. Annual Award for outstanding service, 1968. Mem.: treas. (developed Socs. Code of Ethics), Pub. Rel. Soc. of Amer. 1955-56, v.p. 1962, pres. 1963; Phi Kappa Psi, Silver Spur. Hobby: pilot (holds comml. pilot's license). Res.: 480 S. Orange Grove Blvd., Pasadena, CA 91105; Office: 611 W. 6th St., Los Angeles, CA 91107; One Montgomery Street, San Francisco, CA 94114.

STEVER, RON
Insurance Company Executive

b. July 18, 1904, Los Angeles, Calif.; s. Fred A. (dec.) and Laura M. (Brown) Stever; B.A., Coll. of Comm., USC 1926; m. Alda Mills, Los Angeles, Calif., June 27, 1928; chil.: Richard Lee, b. May 2, 1930; Gary Mills, b. June 29, 1940. Career: Gen. contractor, Pasa. 1926-32; gen. agt., Equitable Life Assurance Soc. L.A. 1932---; CLU 1936; gen. agt. 1941---; chmn. Ron Stever and Co., cons. actuaries; pres. Emett, Chandler & Stever, ins. brokers; chmn. exec. com., Crescent Wharf & Warehouse Co.; adv. bd., Crocker-Citizens Natl. Bank, L.A. 1955---. Mem.: Natl. Assn. of Life Underwriters (mem. Million Dollar Round Table, 1935---, chmn. 1943); dir. Pasa. Chpt., Amer. Red Cross, 1939; pres. Pasa. Community Chest, 1940-42; pres. bd. trustees, Scripps Coll., Claremont; bd. of fellows, Claremont Grad. Sch. and Univ. Center; dir. Braille Inst. of Amer., Inc.; bd. of councilors, USC School of Medicine; Phi Kappa Psi, Alpha Kappa Psi, Mason, Bohemian Club, S.F.; Valley Club of Montecity, Santa Barbara; Annandale Golf Club, Valley Hunt Club, Calif. Club of L.A. Republican. Presbyterian (trustee, Pasa. Ch. 1958--—. Hobby: football. Rec.: golf, travel. Res.: 505 S. Orange Grove Blvd., Pasadena, CA 91105; Office: 2999 W. 6th St., Los Angeles, CA 90005.

STEWART, ARTHUR CHICHESTER
Investments — Petroleum Executive

b. July 22, 1905, Los Angeles, Calif.; s. William Lyman and Margaret Elizabeth (Chichester) Stewart; grandson of Lyman Stewart, founder, Union Oil Co.; ed. B.A., Stanford Univ. 1927; grad. Sch. of Bus. Adm. Harvard Univ. 1928; m. Ruth Nicholson (dec.); m. 2nd Betty Jane Cox, Tulsa, Okla., Apr. 12, 1966; daus.: Ruth (Stewart) Martin, b. Nov. 17, 1931; Barbara (Stewart) Jameson, b. Jan. 21, 1933. Career: Union Oil Co. (summers), 1923-26, sales analyst, 1928, res. mgr. 1929, foreign sales, China-Japan, 1930, sales 1939-41, v.p. 1941-45, corporate dir. 1941---, exec. com. Union Oil Co. of Calif. 1941-65, sr. v.p. 1955-60, sr. v.p. research adm., nat. rels. 1960-65; pres. Union Oil Co. of Calif. Found. 1964---. Dir.: Consolidated Steel Corp. 1940-42; Pac. Airmotive, 1948-64; trustee, Stanford Univ. 1954---; pres. Santa

Anita Found. 1963-64; dir. Community Hosp. of Monterey Peninsula, 1966---. Cons., Secty. of Navy, 1943; reg. ind. cons. Def. Plant Corp. 1943-46, WW II. Mem.: Beta Theta Pi; pres. Lambda Sigma 1926; dir. L.A. C. of C. 1948-57; v.p. 1957; dir. Del Monte Forest Homeowners Assn. 1966-72; dir.-v.p.-secty. Cypress Point Club, 1966-70; Pac. Union Club; Old Capitol Club; California Club. Presbyterian. Hobby: handicrafts. Rec.: bridge, boating, reading, golf. Res.: 17 Mile Dr., Pebble Beach; Office: P.O. Box 767, Pebble Beach, CA 93953.

STEWART, MARY AGNES SIMPSON
Music Critic — Journalist
b. Feb. 25, Battle Creek, Mich.; d. William Ray and Mary Ann (Hays) Simpson; desc. of John Witherspoon, Peter Montague, Hon. Judge Joseph Hays; ed. Roosevelt H.S., Seattle, Wash.; Univ. of Wash.; postgrad course (journ.), San Diego State Coll. 1952-53; grad. 14th Inst. Genealogical Research, U.S. Archives, Amer. Univ., Wash., D.C. 1964; grad. S.E. Univ. of Wash., D.C. 1965; m. William R. Stewart, Oklahoma City, Okla., May 4, 1918; chil.: William R., Jr. (Colonel, USAF, USMA 1943); Ray Simpson (M.S., bus. adm., Stanford Univ. 1951); Stanley Hays (A.B., S.D. State Coll. 1958). Career: Mus. ed., first journ. class of Long Beach H.S., publ. High Life, 1916; mgr. for L.E. Behymer in Hawaii, 1924-28; presented concerts for La Jolla Museum of Art; associate editor, Hotel Life and Ocean Travel Mag., Hawaii, 1925-36; San Diego ed., Pac. Coast Musician, 1944-50; La Jolla news corr., L.A. Times, 1953-59; column, Now Hear This (Calif. and U.S. patent rights). Author: History of Music of San Diego; Josefa, S.D. Mag. 1969; researcher, Time-Life Book, The Spanish West, 1976 (early Carrillo family); ANRC Gray Lady, San Diego, Calif. 1941---. Awards: Hon. cert. 30-yr Red Cross Award, 1972; Agnes Boulevard in North Hollywood named in biographies hob. by Earl White. Mem.: Nat. Soc. Colonial Dames of Am., 1970; Women in Communications, Inc., 1972; First Families of Virginia, 1977; Sigma Alpha Iota; founder-president, Theta Chi Mothers Club; past pres., La Jolla Chptr., Natl. League of Amer. Pen Women; DAR, registrar, La Jolla Chpt. 1966-67; Soc. Serv. League of La Jolla; (charter) historian, S.D. Opera Guild, 1950-55; Women's Com. for Fine Arts, S.D., S.D. Sym. and L.A. Philharmonic; chmn. La Jolla Assocs. of S.D. Philharmonic Com. 1973-76; (life) Library Association of La Jolla; La Jolla Woman's Club; Natl. Genealogical Soc., Wash., D.C.; S.D. Genealogical Soc., Clan Hay, Soc. of Friends of Glasgow Cathedral; Scottish Record Soc., Scotland. Hobbies: archives research, interior decorating (French). Rec.: swimming, travel. Res.: 7118 Olivetas Ave., La Jolla, CA 92037.

STEWART, PATRICIA RHODES
Clinical Psychologist
b. Feb. 11, 1910, Vallejo, Calif.; d. Butler and Sarah Virginia (Ryan) Rhodes; A.B., with great distinction, Stanford Univ., 1930; M.A., San Jose State Univ. 1959; Ph.D., Univ. of London, 1963; m. John Kenneth Stewart (div.), Aug. 15, 1930, Stanford; children: John Kenneth, Jr., Nancy (Bowditch). Career: Asst. Dir. and tchr., Presidio Hill Sch., San Francisco, 1939-42; tchg. asst. in Psychology, San Jose State Univ., 1959-60; clin. psychologist, Napa State Hosp., 1964-77; pvt. practice clinical psychology, Berkeley, 1977---. Publs.: Children in Distress: American and English Perspectives, Sage Publs. 1976; A Manual for the Story Participation Test, SPT Services, 1977. Mem. exec. com., Calif. Region, Am. Friends Service Com., 1956-60, 1965-66, 1970-74. Phi Beta Kappa 1930. Society of Friends, clerk, Berkeley meeting, 1972-74. Res.: 48 Gravatt Dr., Berkeley, CA 94705; Office: 3045 Telegraph Ave., Berkeley, CA 94705.

STEWART, SAMUEL B.
Lawyer — Banker
b. Oct. 5, 1908, Chattanooga, Tenn.; s. Samuel Bradford and Dora (Pryor) Stewart; ed. Chattanooga H.S.; B.A. (hons. in polit. sci.), Univ. of Va. 1927; J.D., Columbia Univ. Sch. of Law, 1930; m. Celeste Dorwin, NYC, Ny, Apr. 2, 1934; chil.: Mrs. James F. (Linda) Dickason, b. Dec. 25, 1935; James D.C., b. Mar. 16, 1939 (dec. Apr. 7, 1962). Career: Atty., assoc. with Cravath, deGersdorff, Swaine & Wood, NYC, 1930-39; partner, Blake, Voorhees & Stewart, NYC 1939-47; v.p.-gen. counsel, Bank of Amer. NT&SA, 1947, exec.v.p.-gen. counsel, 1959-67; chief exec. ofcr. trust activities, 1962-67 (managing com.-chmn. trust investment policy com.), sr.

administrv. ofcr. and sr. v. chmn. bd. 1967-73; also chmn. gen. trust com. 1969---. Spec. counsel on Price Adjustment (apptd. by Pres. Truman); spec. com., U.S. Senate, for investigation of natl. def. pgm. (1943-44), WW II. Editor, The Business Lawyer, 1959-60. Mem.: Phi Beta Kappa, 1923; coms. past pres., S.F. Commercial Club; Bohemian Club; pres. Greater S.F. C. of C. 1969-70; pres. Legal Aid Soc. of S.F. 1963-65; (life) dir.-past pres., United Bay Area Crusade; S.F. Golf Club, Silverado Country Club; Commonwealth Club. Elder, Calvary Presbyterian Ch. Hobby: golf, music, spectator sports. Res.: 2288 Broadway, Apt. 2, S.F., CA 94115; Office: Bank of Amer. Center, San Francisco, CA 94137.

STILLWELL, RAY
Librarian
b. Fort Worth, Texas; s. Charles and Ida E. (Spears) Stillwell; B.A., UCLA, 1929; Certificate in Librarianship, Univ. of Calif., Berkeley, 1930; M.S., Columbia Univ. Sch. of Lib. Serv., NYC, 1943. Career: ref. librarian, Tex. Tech. Coll., Lubbock, 1934; asst. lib. Securities and Exchange Commn., Wash. D.C., 1935-42; Phila., 1942-43; head cataloger, Office of Foreign Relief & Rehabilitation Operations, Wash. D.C., 1943; head cataloger, United Nations Relief & Rehabilitation Adminstrn., Wash. D.C., 1944; lib., Troop Information and Edn. Sect., GHQ, FEC, Tokyo, Japan, 1947-49; asst. attache (Dir. of lib. serv.), USIS Library, Am. Embassy, Lisbon, Portugal, 1950-52; supvr. lib., The Artillery Sch., Anti-Aircraft and Guided Missiles Branch, Fort Bliss, Texas, 1953-54; supvr., Engring. Lib., Temco Aircraft Corp., Dallas, 1955-56; lib., Fourth U.S. Army Language Training Facility, Fort Hood, Tex. 1958-64; lib., Tech. Lib., USN Fleet Computer Programming Center, Pacific, San Diego, CA 9164-69. Home: 570 Tarento Dr., San Diego, CA 92106.

STOCK, WILLIAM JOHN
President, Stang Hydronics Inc.
b. Nov. 9, 1925, Los Angeles; s. William Conrad and Ruth Alberta (Briggs) Stock; B.S. UCLA 1949; M.B.A., USC, 1963; m. Barbara Lee Melvin, Jan. 21, 1949, Los Angeles; children: Eileen Anne (McEwen); Bonnie Jean (Barat); Laurie Ruth. Career: Sr. Underwriter, Prudential Insurance Co., 1948-54, Salary Adminstr., 1954-55, asst. mgr., Data Processing, 1955-60, Comml. Loan Officer, 1960-67 (all in Los Angeles); treas., Hitco, L.A., 1967-70; v.p. fin., Stang Hydronics, 1970-73, exec. v.p. 1973-75, president, 1975---. Dir., Stang Hydronics Inc., 1971--- Contbg. author chptrs. in bus. textbooks. AUS Infan., 1944-46; decorated Purple Heart and Battle Citations. Mem.: Rotary Internat.; Delta Sigma Phi; Beavers; Accounting Soc.; Chem. Engring. Soc., student mem.; The Dewatering Indus. Assn., Inc. Rec.: golf. Res.: 33882 Calle Borrego, San Juan Capistrano, CA 92675; Office: P.O.B. 3217, San Clemente, CA 92672.

STONE, CHARLES ALLEN
University Administrator
b. Nov. 5, 1917, Olathe, Colo.; s. Eugene Marion and Clara Mae (Ballard) Stone; B.A., 1946; M.A., 1947; Ed.D., 1950; m. Joyce Burdette, Aug. 6, 1961, Washington, D.C.; chil.: Robin (Valles), b. Apr. 4, 1944; Sue (Muguruza), b. Sept. 21, 1945; Warren, b. Aug. 9, 1953; Paul, b. Apr. 14, 1961. Career: Chemistry tchr., Los Gatos Hi Sch., 1946-68; math instr., Sacramento Jr. Coll., 1948-50; dir. admissions, Calif. State Univ., Hayward, 1966-68; Dean of Admissions and Records, San Francisco State Univ., 1968---; also mgmt. cons., 1958---; Served USAF, 1940-1966, ret. Col.; Dean, sch. of systems and logistics, Air Force Inst. of Tech., Wright-Patterson AFB, Ohio, 1962-66; decorated: Distinguished Flying Cross; Soldiers Medal of Valor; Air Medal (7 Oak Leaf Clusters); Legion of Merit (2 Oak Leaf Clusters); Navigator, duty in So. Pacific, Central Pacific, Korea and Vietnam. Lectr. on Atomic Weapons; Military Doctrine and Power; Investments. Publ.: Megabuck Managers, 1961; Death of Mops and Buckets, 1966; Maintenance Management, 1966; Status Reporting, 1960; So You Want to Go To College, 1967. Mem.: Phi Delta Kappa; Inst. of Navigation, pres., Dayton, Ohio chpt.; Nat. Security INdustry Assn.; Nat. Aviation Club; Corporation Eleven, pres. Protestant. Hobby: construction. Rec.: fishing, jogging. Home: 198 Arbor Lane, Moss Beach, CA 94038; Office: S.F. State Univ., 1600 Holloway St., San Francisco, CA 94129.

STONE, JAMES RALPH
Financial Consultant
b. June 11, 1910, Sebastopol, Calif.; s. Grover C. and Mercie (Breaks) Stone; B.A., econ., Univ. Calif.,

Berkeley, 1931; m. Lois McMullen, Aug. 18, 1934, Piedmont, Calif.; sons: Robert G., b. 1936; Gary R., b. 1938. Career: Partner, The Stone Co., Santa Rosa, 1931-74; pres. and chmn. of bd., Santa Rosa Savings, 1952-68; exec. v.p., Great Western Savings, Santa Rosa, 1968-77; v.p., Great Western Financial Corp., Beverly Hills, 1968-77, cons., 1977---; pres., Tristo, Ltd., 1975---. Dir., Compu-Com., 1978---. Chmn. bd., Sonoma County Employees Retirement System, 1965-78. Dir., Calif. Savings & Loan League, 1964-67, pres. 1967-68; mem. Legislative Com., U.S. Savings and Loan League, 1962-70; dir., Federal Home Loan Bank of S.F., 1968-74, chmn. FHLB Advis. Com. to Pres., 1975-76. Chmn. Designate, Fed. Home Loan Bank Bd., 1976. Past dir.: Boys' Club, YMCA, Big C Soc.; trustee: Santa Rosa Symphony. Past pres. 20-30 Club, 30-Up Club, Rotary Club, C. of C., Santa Rosa Golf and Country Club. Mem.: U.SOlympic Team, 1932. Hobbies: golf, hunting. Res.: 1925 Alderbrook Ln., Santa Rosa, CA 95405; Office: 835 Fourth St., Santa Rosa, CA 95404.

STONE, MARTIN
Chairman of the Board, Monogram Industries
b. May 5, 1928, St. Louis, Mo.; s. Sam and Dorothy Stone; A.B., UCLA, 1948; LL.B., Loyola Sch. of Law, 1951; LL.M. 1956, (hon.) LL.D., 1973; m. Connie Dickey, Los Angeles, Calif., Dec. 22, 1974; chil.: Eric L., b. June 20, 1952; Nancy Leigh, b. Mar. 10, 1954; Lori, b. Sept. 29, 1966; Sam, b. Nov. 21, 1975. Career: Monogram Industries, Inc. 1951---, chmn. bd.-pres. 1961---; publisher, Calif. Business, Inc. 1976---. Dir.: Natl. Urban Coalition, 1971-77; Common Cause, 1972-77; trustee, Loyola-Marymount Univ. 1972-74. Rec.: tennis, baseball (pitch batting practice for Boston Red Sox). Office: 100 Wilshire Blvd., Santa Monica, CA; Laxfield Rd., Weston, Mass. 02193.

STONE, NELSON
Corporate Executive
b. Jan. 30, 1923, Chicago, Ill.; s. Julius and Clara (Finklestein) Stone; B.A., 1947; J.D., 1948; children: Marla Susan, b. 1960; Julian David, b. 1964. Career: Attorney, U.S. Govt., 1948-52; House Counsel, Gruen Watch Co., 1952-56; Counsel, Fairchild Camera, 1957-68, vice pres., Legal, 1968-69, v.p., Gen. Counsel, Secty., 1970---. Dir., Subs. Cos., Fairchild Camera, 1964---. Served Pvt. to 1st Lt., USAAF, 1943-46. Mem. Federal Bar Assn. Hobbies: antiques, music. Res.: 646 Towle Pl., Palo Alto, CA; Office: 464 Ellis, Mountain View, CA 94040.

STRANGE, WILLIAM JOSEPH
Librarian
b. Sept. 13, 1924, Winchester, Kans.; s. William Carl and Effie Francis (Hull) Strange; B.S., Emporia (Kansas) State Univ., 1950; M.S., 1962, postgrad.: UCLA, Immaculate Heart Coll.; Cal. State Univ., L.A.; div.; chil.: Carol (Jackson), b. Mar. 16, 1953; Joy (Cull) b. Feb. 22, 1954; Shannon, b. Sept. 18, 1957; Eric, b. Jan. 4, 1961. Career: Teacher and/or librarian: Bern (Kan.) High Sch., 1950-52; Lincoln (Kan.) High Sch., 1952-54; Ilwaco (Wash.) High Sch., 1954-55; Delano (Calif.) Jt. Union High Sch., 1955-57; La Puente High Sch., 1957-61; Palos Verdes High Sch., 1961-64; Los Angeles Harbor COll., 1962-64; Dir. of Lib. Serv., Glendale Community Coll., 1964---. Served USN, WW II; Pacific Fleet, Hawaii, Midway, Guam, Japan, Panama. Mem.: Alpha Kappa Lambda. Democrat. Protestant. Rec.: nature, jeeping. Home: 3205 Los Feliz Blvd., No. 13-117, L.A., CA 90039; Office: 1500 N. Verdugo Rd., Glendale, CA 91208.

STRAIN, SIBYL MARJORIA SHIPP
Educator
b. Hiram, Ga.; d. John Seaborn and Nellie Jewel (Barber) Shipp; B.A., summa cum laude, Berry Coll., 1942; M.A., Columbia Univ., 1955; Profl. Dip. Reading Spec., 1956; Ph.D., USC. 1976; postgrad.: UCLA, Loyola Univ., L.A.; Whittier Coll.; m. Numa Alonza Strain (dec. 1969), Aug. 19, 1944, New York, N.Y.; dau. Laura Majoria. Career: Tchr., Possum Trot ELem., Berry Coll., 1940; Hiram, Ga. Hi. Sch., 1942-43; Exec. asst. to research dir., J.M. Mathes, Inc. (adv.) New York, 1947-49. Reading Spec., Pasadena Pub. Schs., 1956-67; asst. supr., H.S. and Coll. Reading Center, Tchrs. Coll., Summer 1959; guest lectr. Pepperdine Coll., Summer 1964; asst. dir. Nat. Charity League — USC Reading Center, 1966-67; prof. psychology and reading, L.A. Southwest Coll., chairperson Psychology Dept., 1967-73, chairperson Behavioral Sci. Dept., 1978---; Mil. Lt., USN, 1943-47; head communications dept., Port Dir. New York, Counselor to WAVES, 1943-47; USNR Korean War,

1947-51; decorated Am. Theater Ribbon, Victory Medal; commendation for recruitment and Ednl. serv. Contbr. National Poetry Anthology, 1960. Mem.: Southwest Coll. Acad. Senate, secty., 1967-68; exec. council, 1967-71, 1978---; coalition for Handgun Control; L.A. Co. Art Mus.; Am. Mus. Natural Hist.; Smithsonian Inst.; founder, Friends of Pasadena Pub. Lib.; friend, USC Lib.; Educare, USC; charter mem. Hon. Assn. Women in Edn., USC; charter mem., Calif. Women in Higher Edn., state steering com., 1975-76, chmn. Panel on Women's Studies, State Conf., 1975; Navy League of USA; NOW; ACLU; AAUW; newsletter editor, Pasadena, 1965-66; League of Women Voters, AAUP; Nat. Council Administrv. Women in Edn.; Nat. Edn. Assn.; Calif. Tchrs. Assn.; L.A. Coll. Tchrs. Assn., pres. Southwest Coll. chpt. 1967=69, 1975-77; Calif. Community Coll. Assn. state bd., 1967-77; Am. Fedn. of Tchrs.; Kappa Delta Pi; Pi Lambda Theta, pres. Pasadena chpt. 1964; Phi Delta Gamma; Berry Coll. Alumni Assn.; USC Alumni Assn. Democrat; com. McGovern for Pres. Presbyterian. Hobbies: writing, gardening, travel. Home: 2236 Las Lunas St., Pasadena, CA 91107; Office: 1600 W. Imperial Hwy., L.A., CA 90047.

STRAUBE, GENE F.
Electronics Company President
b. Aug. 29, 1928, NYC; s. Eugene and Agnes (Kramer) Straube; B.A., Columbia Coll., 1949; B.S.E.E., Columbia Univ., 1950; M.B.A., USC, 1964; children: Christopher, b. 1958; Kimberly, b. 1961; Alison, b. 1962. Career: Applications engr., Hughes Semiconductor Div., Los Angeles, 1953-54; mgr. and product engr., Pacific Semiconductors, Inc., Culver City, 1954-58; dir. mktg., Elgin Nat. Watch Co., Burbank, 1958-60; pres., Straube Assoc. Mt. States, Inc., Westminster, Colo., 1964---; pres., Straube Assoc., Inc., Mountain View, Calif., 1960---. Bd. dir., Miramonte Mental Health Services, Palo Alto, 1965---, chmn. 1975-76. Lt. Comdr. USN, 1950-53. Mem. Phi Beta Kappa, Tau Beta Pi. Res.: 740 Tan Oak, Portola Valley, CA 94025; Office: 2551 Casey Ave., Mountain View, CA 94043.

STRAYER, RICHARD LEE
Company President
b. Sept. 14, 1934, Ocheyedan, Iowa; s. Glayde Watters and Mary Ann (Graves) Strayer; B.S., with highest honors, UCLA, 1961; M.B.A., 1962; D.B.A., USC, 1970; m. Eileen Curtis, July 28, 1956, Gillingham, Dorset, England; children: Susan Rae, b. 1960; Wendy Anne, b. 1962; Richard Curtis, b. 1972. Career: with nat. travel bureau, 1959-61; Instr., accounting, UCLA, 1961; sr. accountant, CPA, Peat, Marwick & Co., L.A., 1962-65; lectr., USC, 1965-68; consultant, 1965---; exec., co-founder, bd. dir., Kronos, Inc., 1969-73; pres. 1971-73; Prof., Cal. State Univ., Northridge, 1968---; co-founder, pres., bd. dir., Maxtek, Inc. (electronic instrument mfg.), 1975---. Contbr. articles, reviews profl. publs. Awards: Award of Merit, Controllers Inst. of Am., Outstanding Prof. Award, Merit award, Soaring Soc. of Am., Haskins & Sells Found. Award. Mem.: Am. Inst. of CPAs, Calif. Soc. of CPAs, Fin. Exec. Inst.; Am. Accounting Assn.; Alpha Gamma Sigma; Beta Gamma Sigma; Beta Alpha Psi. Congregationalist; trustee, treasurer. Res.: 7901 Mary Ellen Ave., No. Hollywood, CA 91605; Office: 2908 Oregon Ct., Torrance, CA 90503; Cal. State University, 18111 Nordhoff St., Northridge, CA 91330.

STRICKLER, GERALD B.
Clergyman — Educator
b. June 30, 1921, Wrightsville, Penna.; s. Francis H.H. and Edna (Brenner) Strickler; desc. Henry Strickler, Swiss immigrant and one of 1st settlers in Eastern Pa. early 1700s; A.B., Gettysburg Coll., 1944; B.D., Lutheran Theol. Sem., 1946; M.A., N.Y. Univ., 1948; S.T.D., Temple Univ., 1955; M.Div., Lutheran Theol. Sem. 1973; Ph.D., Calif. Western Univ., 1978; m. Margaret Gotwalt, Aug. 6, 1945, York, Pa.; children: Susan (DeQuattro), b. 1948; Michael, b. 1951. Career: Pastor, St. Matthew's Lutheran Ch., No. Hollywood, 1946-48; Prof. of Religion and Philosophy, Midland Coll., Fremont, Nebr., 1949-58; Prof. & Dept. Chmn. of Philosophy, Cal State Univ., Long Beach, 1958---. Interim Pastor, Lutheran Chs. in N.Y., Pa., and Calif. Dir.: Martin Luther Hosp., Anaheim; Pacific Lutheran Theol. Sem.; Dean, Long Beach Dist. of Pacific SW Synod of Lutheran Ch. in Am. Hosted several TV programs; contbg. writer on rel., philos. Mem.: Masons; Shriners. Republican, Nat. Com., Calif. Party. Ordained Clergyman, United Lutheran Ch. in Am. Rec.: fishing, bridge. Res.: 11311 Caroleen Lane, Garden Grove, CA; Office: Cal. State Univ., Long Beach, CA 90840.

STRONG, LEONELL C.
   Cancer Researcher
b. Jan. 19, 1894, Renova, Pa.; s. Clarence A. and Ella
M. Strong; B.S., Allegheny Coll., 1917; Ph.D.,
Columbia Univ., 1922; Hon. Sc.D., Allegheny Coll.,
1939; Hon. M.D., Univ. Perugia, Italy, 1957; Medals of
Merit, Univs. of Liege and Louvain; m. Katherine
Bittner, June 27, 1918, Meadville, Pa.; sons: Leonell
C., Jr., Wilson Willard. Career: Assoc. Prof. Biology,
Physics, St. Stephen's Coll. (now Bard), 1921-25;
Research Fellow, Genetics of Cancer, DPH, Harvard
Univ., 1925-27; Assoc. Prof. Genetics, research assoc.
cancer, Univ. Mich., 1927-30; Cancer Research, Roscoe
B. Jackson Mem. Lab., 1930-33, Yale Univ. Sch. of
Med., 1933-53; Dir., Biol. Sta., Springville, N.Y.,
Roswell Pk. Mem. Inst., 1953-64; Prof. Genetics, Grad.
Sch., Univ. Buffalo, 1955-64; vis. Fellow, Salk Inst.
for Biol. Studies, 1964-68; Dir., Leonell C. Strong
Research Found., Inc., 1968---. Guest Lectr. on cancer
research, univs. worldwide; Speaker at internat. med.
confs. and symposia; publ. 315 papers in cancer
research, 1921-78. Major contbns. in research include
estab. of 40 inbred strains of mice, used in cancer and
biol. research. Freemason, Rotarian, pres. Springville,
N.Y. Republican. Presbyterian. Hobby: Elizabethan lit.
Res.: 8533 Sugarman Dr., La Jolla, CA 92037; Office:
11661 Sorrento Valley Rd., San Diego, CA 92121.

STRYCULA, THOMAS FRANCIS
   Educator — City Official
b. Feb. 25, 1911, Wis.; s. John and Antonia
(Rosechek) Strycula; B.A., Univ. of Ala. 1932;
teaching credential, San Jose State Coll. 1967; M.A.
1968; Univ. of Wis., Univ. Wash., Univ. Calif.; m.
Maribel Knowles, San Francisco, Calif., Sept. 17, 1936;
chil.: Mrs. Ronald (Susan Knowles) Lanphere, b. Jan.
14, 1945; Thomas James, b. Sept. 30, 1954. Career:
San Francisco Dept. of Soc. Serv. 1933-40; probation
ofcr., S.F. Juvenile Ct. 1940-47, supv. 1947-55, chief
probation ofcr. 1955-67 (ret.). Educator, Campbell
Union H.S. Dist., Calif. 1967---. Lt., U.S. Army, S.W.
Pac., WW II; Maj., USAR (ret.). Awards: Bronze Star
Medal P.I. Pres. Unit Cit. Mem.: Natl. Council on
Crime and Delinquency; Natl. Council of Soc. Welfare;
Western Probation Parole and Correctional Assn.; Calif.
Teachers Ass.; Red Shield Youth Assn., Salvation
Army, S.F. 1957---; bd. mgrs., Central YMCA, S.F.
1959-67; S.F. Council, BSA 1959-66; S.F. Com. on
Youth, 1960-66; com., S.F. Community Fund,
1960-66; bd. dirs., S.F. Municipal Employees Credit
Union, 1961---; pres. Calif. Probation Parole and
Correctional Assn. 1962-63; probation servs. adv. com.,
United Calif. Youth Authority, 1962-66; gov. bd. Met.
YMCA, S.F. 1962---; pres. Chief Probation Ofcrs. of
Calif. 1965-66; chmn. law enforcement-corrections adv.
com., Co. Supvs. Assn. of Calif. 1965-66; (hon. life)
PTA; S.F. Municipal Execs. Assn., S.F. Presidio Ofcrs.
Club, Golden Gate Breakfast Club, S.F. Rec.: skiing.
Res.: 148 Colton Ave., San Carlos, CA 94070.

STUCHEN, JACOB MANN
   Business Executive
b. Sept. 22, 1900, Russia; s. Samuel and Sara Stuchen;
B.A. (hons.), Univ. of Toronto, Can. 1921; Barrister of
Law, Osgoode Hall, Toronto, Can. 1924; m. Betty
Kasler, Toronto, Can., Dec. 25, 1930; chil.: Mrs. Geoff
(Barbara) Miller, b. July 2, 1933; Robert S., b. Aug.
8, 1936. Career: Career: Chmn. bd. dirs., Maple
Industries, Inc., Los Angeles. Elected to Beverly Hills
City Council, 1964--- (recd. largest no. votes in city's
hist.), Mayor, City of Beverly Hills, 1966-67, 1970-71.
Dir., Cedars-Sinai Hosps., exec. com., Joint Conf.
Com., Med. Center Planning Com.; Dist. Atty's. Adv.
Council; adv. bd., Hebrew Union Coll., L.A.;
President's Council of Brandeis Univ.; (past) Mayor's
Human Rels. Comm., Rockford, Ill.; chmn. Beverly
Hills Planning Comm. 1960. Coll. Ofcrs. Training
Corp., Univ. of Toronto, Can. Awards: Scholarship,
Law Soc. of Upper Can.; Beverly Hills Citizen's Award
for Outstanding Citizenship; Top-Two Award, Beverly
Hills Courier, 1967; Man of Yr. Award, Beverly Hills
C. of C. 1967 (many other awards for civic, soc.
welfare and philanthropic serv.). Mem.: Sigma Alpha
Mu and A.F. and A.M., Palestine Lodge, Toronto (30
yrs.); (past) bd. dirs., Amer. Natl. Red Cross Assn.,
Community Chest, chmn. Jewish Community Council,
chmn. USO Council (4 yrs.), Rockford, Ill.; USC
Assocs; bd. dirs., Amer. Natl. Red Cross Assn., Beverly
Hills; bd. dirs., Jewish-Fed. Council of Greater L.A.
(community rels. and planning coms., chmn. nom.
com.); chmn. Jewish Centers Assn. Friendship Com.;
gen. chmn., United Jewish Welfare Fund Campaign for
Greater L.A. 1960; bd. trustees, Beverly Hills YMCA;
chmn. Community Chest Advance Gifts Com. for

Beverly Hills, Bel-Air, 1962; chmn. United Crusade
Campaign, 1964; treas. United Jewish Welfare Fund
Campaigns, Beverly Hills, 1964, 65. Temple Emanuel
Bd.; bd. trustees, Wilshire Blvd. Temple. Res.: 1114
Wallace Ridge, Beverly Hills, CA; Office: 9763 W. Pico
Blvd., Los Angeles, CA 90035.

STUPPY, LAURENCE JUSTINIAN
   Physician
b. Oct. 5, 1914, St. Joseph, Mo.; s. John Joseph and
Marie Theresa (Eberhart) Stuppy; B.S., Calif. Inst.
Tech.; M.D., Harvard Med. Sch.; m. Mary Dorian
Lissner, June 28, 1941, Los Angeles; children: Henry
Lissner, b. 1942; Laurence II, b. 1944; Mary Laurie
(Mrs. Lowell Martin), b. 1946; Elizabeth Jane (Mrs.
James Pike), b. 1947; William Patrick, b. 1950; John
Joseph, b. 1955. Career: Pvt. practice medicine, Los
Angeles ---. Pres. staff, St. Vincent's Med. Center, L.A.
1978---. Fellow Am. Coll. Physicians; Fellow, Am.
Coll. Cardiology. Bd. Certified Am. Bd. Internal Med.
AUS, 1941-45, Col., M.C. USAR, Ret. Roman
Catholic. Res.: 357 S. Lorraine Blvd., L.A., CA 90020;
Office: 321 N. Larchmont Blvd., Los Angeles, CA
90004.

STYNE, MARILYN MEYERS (Mimi)
   Realtor
b. Dec. 14, 1933, Denver, Colo.; d. Fred and Bertha
(Hirschfield) Meyers; dau.-in-law to Jule Styne,
songwriger; student, Univ. of Mo., Univ. of Colo.; m.
Stanley Styne (div. 1969), Dec. 31, 1955, Beverly Hills;
chil.: Bruce Alan, b. Apr. 28, 1952; Beth Ann, b. June 13,
1957; Julia Faith, b. Nov. 18, 1960; Caroline Patricia, b.
Mar. 14, 1967. Career: started in residential real estate
with Wm. H. Riley, 1970; formed partnership with Larry
Shield and Wm. Riley, 1975; became Shields & Styne,
1976; proprietor, Mimi Styne & Assoc., 1978---; v.p.,
Grubb & Ellis Co. Mem.: Beverly Hills Realty Bd. profl.
com.; Museum of Modern Art, N.Y.; Los Angeles Co.
Museum. Polit. campaign fund raiser, John V. Tunney,
1976. Hobby: interior decorator. Rec.: jogging, jusic,
theatre. Home: 220 S. Swall Dr., Beverly Hills, CA;
Office: 357 N. Camden Dr., Beverly Hills, CA 90210.

SUERSTEDT, HENRY
   Electronics Company Executive
b. Oct. 14, 1920, Berkeley; s. Henry and Cecilia
(Reiter) Suerstedt; A.A., San Francisco City COII.,
1940; USN Post Grad. Sch., 1949; Armed Forces Staff
Coll., 1954; B.S., Univ. Md., 1957; m. Mary Josephine
Bass, Apr. 13, 1946, El Paso, Tex.; children: Candace
Cecilia, b. 1947; Cynthia Marie, b. 1950. Career:
Commd. Ensign USN, 1941, advanced through ranks
to Rear Admiral, 1969; Comdg. Officer, Torpedo
Squadron 100, 1945; Comdr. Escort Carrier Air Group
84, 1964; Comdg. Ofcr. Attack Squadron 213, 1948,
1949; Comdg. Ofcr. Fighter Squadron 54, 1953; Air
Ofcr. Navigation USS Sicily, 1953-54; Head,
Conventional aircraft weapons br., Bureau of Naval
Ordnance, 1955-58; Air Opns. Ofcr. Carrier Div. 5,
1958-59; staff, Comdr. in Chief Pacific, 1959-60; dir.,
Strike Warfare, Initiator, Proj. Mgr. A7A Corsair II
Attack Aircraft, Bureau of Naval Weapons, 1960-63;
Comdg. Ofcr., USS Union, 1964; Comdg. Ofcr., USS
Tripoli, 1965-67; Asst. Comdr. for Logistics/Fleet
support Naval Air Systems Command, 1968-69;
Deputy Comdr., U.S. Naval Forces, Vietnam, 1970;
Comdr. U.S. Jt. Task Force 8, 1970-71; Deputy
Comdr. Plans Programs and Comptroller, Naval Air
Systems Command, 1971-72; Comdr. Naval Weapons
Center, China Lake, Calif. 1972-73. Now Director,
Western Region, Harris Corp., PRD Electronics Div.,
San Diego. Mil. Awards: Silver Star; Legion of Merit
with Combat V and 3 Gold Stars; D.F.C. with Gold
Star; Bronze Star with Combat V; Air Medal with 1
Silver and 4 Gold Stars; Navy Commendation Medal
with Combat V and 1 Gold Star. Mem.: Am. Inst.
Aeronautics and Astronautics (presented papers,
1972-73); Soc. Logistic Engrs.; Navy League; Retired
Officers Assn. Republican. Episcopalian. Rec.: deep sea
fishing. Res.: Two the Inlet, Coronado, CA 92118;
Office: 591 Camino De La Reina, Suite 418, San
Diego, CA.

SUHLER, SAM(UEL) A(ARON)
   Librarian
b. Sept. 18, 1929, Luling, Texas; s. James and Minnie
Mae (Walcowich) Suhler; B.F.A., Univ. Texas, Austin,
1950; M.Edn., Southwest Texas State Coll., 1954;
M.L.S., Univ. Texas, Austin, 1959, Ph.D., 1966.
Career: Asst. Ref. Librarian, Austin Pub. Lib.,
1954-65; research assoc. in Texas Hist., Univ. Texas,

Austin, 1965-66; field cons., Texas State Lib., 1966-67; Local Hist. Librarian, Fresno County Lib. 1967---. Recent Publs.: Local History Collection and Services in a Small Public Library (Small Libraries Project Pamphlet No. 19, 1970); Oral History Interviews of Local Government Officials, News Notes of California Libraries, 72, No. 1, 30-5, 1977. Mem.: ALA, v. chmn. and chmn. Hist. Sect., Ref. and Adult Services Div., 1974-75. Democrat. Judaism. Reform. Hobbies: swimming, fishing. Res.: 221 W. Herndon, Pinedale, CA 93650; Office: 2420 Mariposa, Fresno, CA 93721.

SULLIVAN, MAURICE WILLIAM
   Author
b. July 28, 1925, Meriden, Conn.; s. Maurice Stephen and Marjorie (Doyle) Sullivan; B.A., Yale Univ. 1947; M.A. 1949; B.A., Univ. of Puerto Rico, 1951; M.A., Middlebury Coll. 1952; Ph.D', Univ. of Madrid, Spain, 1952. Career: Master modern langs., Choate Sch., Wallingford, Conn. 1948-49; instr. Ger.-Spanish, Univ. of Puerto Rico, 1949-51; lecturer in linguistics, Univ. of Madrid, 1951-52; instr. in Spanish, Yale Univ. 1952-53; asst. prof. modern langs., Marquette Univ. 1953-54; assoc. prof. modern langs., Hollins Coll. 1954-59, prof.-deptt. dir.-dir. grad. studies, 1958-61, dir. Foreign Lang. Inst., under Natl. Def. Edn. Act (summers), 1959, 60. Pres., Sullivan Assocs., Los Altos, Calif. 1961---. Author: 100 textbooks in fieldds of linguistics, reading, English, psychol., astronomy and chess; 2 mot. pic. scripts, poems, plays and approx. 50 articles publ. professional journs. Sgt., USMC, ETO (1943-46), WW II. Awards: Individual Cit. and Commendation for servs. as bodyguard, Adm. W. Glassford, ETO. Mem.: Phi Beta Kappa. Hobby: stu. med. Office: P.O. Box 693, Los Altos, CA 94022.

SULLIVAN, WILLIAM JOSEPH
   Psychiatrist — Psychoanalyst
b. Mar. 2, 1921, Buffalo, N.Y.; s. William J. and Camille (Nelson) Sullivan; B.A., Univ. Buffalo, 1948; M.A., 1951; M.D., 1955; Ph.D., Southern Calif. Psychoanalytic Inst., Beverly Hills, 1977; m. Caroline Lemke, June 11, 1960, Santa Monica; children: Deidre Ellen, b. 1961; Shawn Michael, b. 1963. Career: Med. Internship, 1955-56; psychiatric residency, 1956-59; psychoanalytic tng. 1958-65; pvt. practice of psychiatry and psychoanalysis, Beverly Hills, 1959---; asst. prof. of psychiatry, USC, 1967---; sr. faculty mem. So. Calif. Psychoanalytic Inst., Beverly Hills, 1967---; Psychiatric cons., L.A. County Dept. of Mental Health, 1963--; chmn. L.A. Dist., Acad. of Mental Health and the Clergy, 1963-68; Med. Dir., Community Counseling Clin. United University Ch., L.A. Psychiatric cons., L.A. Sch. Dist., 1964-67, L.A. County Welfare Planning Council, 1964-66, Pastoral Counseling Clin. of 1st Presbyterian Ch., Asst. Med. Dir. Westwood Community Methodist Ch. Contbr. many publs., articles especially in psychiatric aspects of flying and flying safety. Served to Maj., USAF, 1942-46, mil. pilot. Mem.: AMA, CMA, L.A. County Med. Soc., Am. and So. Calif. Psychiatric Assns.; So. Calif. Psychoanalytic Soc.; So. Calif. Psychoanalytic Inst.; Am. Acad. of Psychoanalysis; Far Western Med. Assn.; Flying Physician Assn. Rec.: tennis, hunting, flying. Res.: 2204 Westridge Rd., L.A., CA 90049; Office: 9950 Santa Monica Blvd., Beverly Hills, CA 90212.

SULSER, JILL M.
   Realtor
b. May 21, 1936, New Jersey; d. Ralph and Josephine (Vicari) Ruggiero; grad., Holy Family Acad., 1958; student Glendale Coll., 1961-63, El Camino Coll. 1974-75; div.; children: Dee Lynn, b. May 15, 1957; Christine, b. July 2, 1961; Ken, b. June 7, 1969. Career: advt. modeling, 1961-65; secty., TRW, 1965-68; real estate agent, 1971---, owner-broker, Avante Realty, Manhattan Beach, 1976---. Vice President, South Bay Board of Realtors, 1976, 77, 78; pub. rels. rep. 21st Dist., 1977-78. Hobby: gardening. Rec.: tennis, skiing, horseback riding. Res.: 1207 5th St., Manhattan Beach, CA 90266; Office: 1020 Manhattan Beach Blvd., Suite 202, Manhattan Beach, CA 90266.

SUMMERS, GENE RUDOLPH
   Business Owner — Architect
b. July 31, 1928, San Antonio, Texas; s. Frank Leslie and Etta (Nelson) Summers; B.Arch., Texas A&M Univ., 1949; M.Sc. in Arch., Ill. Inst. of Architecture, 1951; m. Anne E. O'Bannon, Aug. 17, 1951, Chicago; children: Blake, b. 1958; Karen, b. 1960; Scott, b.

1964. Career: Proj. Arch. with Mies van der Rohe, 1950-66: Seagram's Bldg. 1956, N.Y., Bacardi Bldg. 1958, Mex., Museum of Art 1960, Berlin, U.S. Federal Center, 1960, Toronto Dominion Center 1960, Social Service, Univ. of Chicago, 1961, Museum of Art, 1966; partner in charge of design, C.F. Murphy Associates, 1967-73: Skil Mfg. Center 1968, Malcolm X. Jr. College, Westside College, 1969, McCormick Place (Convention Center 1970, Audi Home/Juvenile Home 1970, Kemper Arena, Kansas City, 1973, Convention Hall, Kansas City, 1973, Rehabilitation Center of Chicago, 1973; President/owner, Ridgway Ltd., 1973---, Canada Business Center, Lake Forest, 1974, Biltmore Hotel, L.A., 1976, Cerritos Indsl. Center, 1978. President, Olive-Hill Owners' Assn.; advisory council, Los Angeles Conservancy; trustee, Newport Harbor Art Mus.; bd. dir., Hathaway Home for Children; bd. dir., L.A. Convention Bureau, 1976-78; dir. Arts Club of Chicago 1965-73. Named Fellow, AIA, 1969. AIA Special Citation, 1978, for Biltmore Hotel Restoration. 1st Lt., U.S. Corps of Engineers, 1953-55. Hobby: horticulture. Res.: 851 Diamond Ave., Laguna Beach, CA 92651; Office: 515 S. Olive St., L.A., CA 90013; 610 Newport Center Dr., Newport Beach, CA 92660.

SUMMERS, GEORGE VERNON
   University Library Director
b. Apr. 21, 1929, Youngstown, Ohio; s. George and Mabel (Ferguson) Summers; B.A., Columbia Union Coll., 1951; M.S. Lib. Sci., Drexel Univ., 1963; grad. studies in English, Univ. of Md., Lehigh Univ.; Ph.D., lib. sci., USC, 1973; m. Roberta Joan Behringer, Aug. 9, 1953, Washington, Pa.; children: Barbara, b. 1955; Linda, b. 1957. Career: Librarian, Mt. Pisgah Acad., N.C., 1951-52; Lib. Asst., Univ. Md., 1952-53; prin., Pittsbuigh Jr. Acad., Pa., 1953-55; Librarian, Blue Mt. Acad., Pa., 1955-64; director, Univ. Libraries, Loma Linda Univ., 1964---, prof., Loma Linda Univ. 1968---; Lectr. in Health Edn., Sch. of Health, Loma Linda Univ., 1973---; vis. asst. prof., Sch. of Lib. Sci., USC 1973---. Publs.: Library Science Syllabus, 1963; contbr. profl. journs.; unpub. regional studies. Lib. Cons. to five So. Calif. hospitals; chmn. Com. on Estab. Regional Med. Lib. for Pacific SW, 1966-68; pres., bd. of dirs. for SIRCULS Network, 1975-76; trustee, Med. Lib. Scholarship Found., 1968-69; chmn. Taskforce to Devel. Network of Academic and Pub. Libraries in Inland Empire of So. Calif. Mem.: ALA; Med. Lib. Assn. (chmn. Com. on Certification 1973); Med. Lib. Group of So. Calif. (pres. 1966-68); Christian Librarians Assn. (pres. 1975-76); Calif. Lib. Assn.; AAUP; Am. Soc. for Information Sci.; Am. Assn. for History of Med.; Beta Phi Mu. Seventh-day Adventist, Elder. Hobbies: piano, trumpet, voice, book collecting: Mark Twain, Norman Rockwell, Saul Bellow. Res.: 25070 Tulip Ave., Loma Linda, CA 92354; Office: University Library, Loma Linda University, Loma Linda, CA 92354.

SUNDBERG, JOHN LAWRENCE
   Hospital Administrator
b. June 2, 1908, Omaha, Nebr.; s. August P. and Jennie E. (Anderson) Sundberg (Swedish Norwegian ancestry); ed. Central H.S., Omaha, 1927; Creighton Coll., Omaha, 1931-32; Certificatye in Acct., Internat. Accts. Soc., Chicago, 1938; Univ. of Ore., Portland Ext. 1939-40; courses in hosp. adm.; Univ. of Chicago 1939; Stanford Univ. 1947; Univ. of Colo. 1950; courses: hotel comdr., Cambridge, Mass, 1953; 1st Western Advanced Hotel Ambassador, L.A. 1957; m. Violette E. Eskelson, Chicago, Ill., Oct. 4, 1933, dau. Suzan E., b. Nov. 15, 1941. Career: Purchasing agt., Emanuel Hosp., Portland, 1938-41; admr. Dallas Gen. Hosp., Ore. 1946-49; orgn. and est.: Caldwell (Ida.) Mem. Hosp. 1950; Pacoima Mem. Luth. Hosp., L.A. Co., Calif. 1960; Dominguez Valley Hosp., Compton, Calif. 1962; adm. Culver City (Calif.) Hosp. 1955-56; adm. Crenshaw Hosp., L.A. 1956-59; adm. Norwalk Hosp., Calif. 1961-62; admr. Dominguez Valley Hosp., Compton, 1962-71; v.p. Natl. Med. Enterprises, Inc. 1971---. Capt., Lt. Col., Med. Adm. Corps; exec. ofcr., S. Pac. Sta. and Evacuation Hosp., P.I. (1941-45), WW II. Col., USAR (ret.). Mem.: v.p.-bd. trustees, Ore. Assn. Hosps. 1948-49, pres. elect, 1949; chmn. small hosp. sect., Assn of Western Hosps. 1951-52, v.p. 1952-53, chmn. accts. sect. 1956-57, chmn. proprietary sect. 1965-66; Ida. del., Amer. Hosp. Assn. 1951, 52, 53; pres. Ida. Hosp. Assn. 1952-53; Hosp. Mgmt. Natl. Adv. Com. on Small Hosps. 1954-55; treas. Crenshaw Rotary Club, 1958-59; exalted ruler, BPOE, No. 906, Santa Monica, 1961-62, dep. grand exalter ruler, S. Central Coast Dist. 1968-69; Fellow, American College of Hosp. Admrs.; pres. Assn. of Community Hosps.

So. Calif. 1964-65; Amer. Legion; Res. Ofcrs. Assn. of U.S.; v.p. Calif. Elks Assn. 1965-66; bd. dirs., Compton C. of C. 1967-69; bd. dirs.: United Hosp. Assn. 1969-70, exec. v.p. 1973-75; bd. dirs. Fed. of Amer. Hosps. 1970-74; pres. Compton Rotary Club, 1970; bd. trustees, Calif. Hawaii Elks Assn. 1974---. Republican. Lutheran (board deacons, Augusta, Portland; board trustees-v.p. Lutheran Church of Our Redeemer, L.A.). Hobby: lodge activities. Rec.: golf. Res.: 9460 Petit Ave., Sepulveda, CA 91343; Office: 11440 San Vicente Blvd., Los Angeles, CA 90049.

SURTEES, ROBERT L.
Cinematographer
b. Aug. 9, 1906, Covington, Ky.; s. James D. and Besse R. Surtees; m. Maydell Powell, 1930, Glendale; children: Nancy (Corby); Bruce; Linda (Lowers); Tom. Career: Director of photography, 1928---: with EFA also UFA Studios, Berlin, Germany, with MGM Studio 20 years. Awards: Film Achievement awards, Look Mag. award: for King Solomon's Mines; Foreign Correspondents' award for Quo Vaids; 3 Academy (Oscars) awards for Bad and the Beautiful, 1952, King Solomon's Mines, 1950, Ben Hur, 1959; Academy Awards nominations: Thirty Seconds Over Tokyo, 1944; Mutiny on the Bounty, 1962; Dr. Doolittle, 1967; The Graduate, 1967; Summer of '42, 1971; The Last Picture Show, 1971; The Sting, 1973; The Hindenburg, 1975; A Star is Born, 1976; The Turning Point, 1977. Hobby: amateur radio. Rec.: golf. Res.: 25535 Hacienda Place, Carmel, CA 93923.

SUTHERLAND, JAMES J.
Electronics Company Executive
b. Nov. 26, 1915, Boston, Mass.; s. Donald B. and Anna F. (Hunter) Sutherland; B.S., Boston Univ. 1937; m. Raymah Wright, Panama City, June 9, 1939 (dec.), m. Esther L. Finch, Jan. 2, 1971. Career: Gen. mgr., electronics div., Sylvania Elec. Prods. 1949-54; exec. v.p.-gen. mgr., Vacuum Tube Prods. Co., Inc. 1955-59; mgr. (vacuum tube prods. div.), Hughes Aircraft Co., Oceanside, 1959-70; asst. group exec. (industrial electronics group), Hughes Aircraft Co., Culver City, 1970-74; v.p., Hughes Aircraft Co., 1975---. Dir., Oceanside Natl. Bank, 1964---; chmn. Carlsbad Planning Comm. 1965, 67. Contrib. numerous articles on econs. and tech. subjs. to professional journs. Patentee in mech. and electronic components. Mem.: dir. Western Electronics Mfrs. Assn. 1957-59, v.p. 1958; dir. Oceanside Boys Club, 1961---, pres. 1966; (sr.) Inst. Elec. and Electronics Engrs.; Amer. Vacuum Soc. Hobbies: art, photog. Rec.: golf. Res.: 28802 Crestridge Road, Rancho Palos Verdes, CA; Office: 23822 Hawthorne Blvd., Torrance, CA 90509.

SUTRO, JOHN ALFRED
Attorney at Law
b. July 3, 1905, San Francisco; s. Alfred and Rose (Newmark) Sutro; A.B., Stanford Univ., 1926; LL.B., Harvard Law Sch., 1929; m. Elizabeth Hiss, Oct. 16, 1931, New Canaan, Ct.; children: Caroline (Mrs. Gerald F. Mohun), b. 1932; Mrs. Elizabeth S. Mackey, b. 1934; John A., Jr., b. 1936; Stephen, 1938-62. Career: Admitted to Calif. bar, 1929; practice law firm of Pillsbury, Madison & Sutro, 1929---, partner 1935---, now advisory partner. Dir. Kaiser Steel Corp., 1972-75. Bd. dir.: Consultants, Inc., 1956---; Bank of Calif., NA, 1966---; BanCal Tri-State Corp., 1972---; Calif. Acad. of Sci., trustee, 1966, vice chmn. 1971---; St. Luke's Hosp., 1975---. Comdr., USNR, 1940-45. Awards: 1957 Navy Distinguished Pub. Serv. Award; 1971 St. Thomas More Soc. Annual Award; 1974 Am. Judicature Soc. Herbert Harley award; 1975 Bar Assn. of San Francisco John A. Sutro Award; 1975 NCCJ Annual Brotherhood Award. Mem. Nat. Advis. Council, Navy League of U.S., 1968---; vice chmn. Nat. Judicial Coll., 1977---; bd. of councilors USC Law Center, 1968---; bd. of visitors Univ. Santa Clara Sch. of Law, 1973---; chmn. exec. com. Friends of Stanford Law Lib., 1962---; trustee Hastings Law Center Found., 1976---; trustee, S.F. Law Lib., 1965, pres. 1976---; San Francisco Airports Commn., v.p. 1970-74; S.F. C. of C., pres. 1973; State Bar of Calif., 1929---, pres. 1965-66; Bar Assn. of S.F., 1933---, pres. 1962; American Bar Assn., 1934---, chmn. Standing Comm. on Judicial Selection, Tenure & Compensation, 1975-78; Am. Judicature Soc., 1961---, exec. com. 1967-70; Fellows of Am. Bar Found., 1965---, chmn. 1973-74. Res.: 3598 Jackson St., San Francisco, CA 94118; Office: 225 Bush St., San Francisco, CA 94104.

SUZUKI, TERRY
Business Executive
b. Feb. 15, 1932, Nagoya, Japan; s. Motoo and Moto Suzuki; ed. Tamagawa Univ. 1958; USC 1962; Buddah Univ.; m. Ryoko Hatashita, Los Angeles, Calif., Apr. 29, 1962. Career: Dos Pueblos Orchid Co. 1959-61; tech.: USC Sch. of Med. 1962-64; UCLA Dept. of Plant Pathology, 1965-68; staff research assoc. UC Riverside, 1968-72; bus. exec. 1972---. Contrib. to professional publs. Awards: Mayor Nachikatsuura, Japan, 1969; Cit.: Sister City Founder's Award, 1969; City Council for community serv. 1969; Internat. People to People Pgm., Wash., D.C., 1971; White House, 1972; Award, Sister City Assn. 1972; State of Calif. Assembly 1974; Cit. by Amer. Legion Post 397 Most Valuable Citizen of Yr. 1974; Cit. Japan American Sr. Citizens, 1975. Mem.: Jaycee secty., 1964; mgr. Jap.-Amer. Choir, 1965; founder-charter pres. bd. Monterey Park Sister City Assn. 1966-75; pres. M.P. Coord. Council, 1971-73; Japanese C. of C. of So. Calif. 1973---; Jap. Community Pioneer Center, 1973-75; adv. Kenjinkai-Kyogikai, 1973---; founder-pres. M.P. Japanese Amer. Sr. Citizens, Inc. 1974; bd. dirs. M.P. Hist. Soc.; v. chmn. City Art and Cultural Comm. 1975---. First Un. Meth. Ch. Hobbies: flowering, travel. Res.: 1045 Aldine Terr., Monterey Park, CA 91754; Office: 10201 E. Valley Blvd., El Monte, CA 91731.

SVEC, PHILLIP E.
Physician
b. May 5, 1913, River Falls, Wis.; s. Dominic and Emma Svec; ed. grad. Ellsworth, Wis. H.S. 1930; B.E., River Falls Teachers Coll., Wis. 1934; B.S., Univ. of Wis. 1935, M.D. 1939; m. Dorothy Irwin, Los Angeles, Calif., Sept. 6, 1941; chil.: Sharon Bockemohle, b. June 26, 1942; Bonnie Dougherty, b. Feb. 28, 1950; Phillip J., b. Mar. 23, 1952; Career: Intern and res., Calif. Hosp., Los Angeles, 1939-41; pvt. practice med., L.A. 1941-42, internal med. 1946---; chief of cardiology, Calif. Hosp. Baby Clinic, 1946---; chief of staff, Calif. Hosp., L.A. 1964-66; chief med. 1967---; pres. Phillip E. Svec, M.D., Inc.; med. dir. Shrine, 1951, 52, 53, 56, 63. TV appearances with Happy Wanderers; auctioneer for Calif. Hosp. philanthropies, May 1966. Maj. Flight Surg., USAF Med. Corp. (1942-46), WW II. Award: Svec Hall (named in his honor) dedicated by Calif. Hosp. 1969; Ky. Col., DeMolay Hon. Legion of Hon., Saint Gabriel Conclave (Mil. Order of Constantine). Mem.: Calif. Hospital dev. com., L.A. Philanthropic Assn., chmn. Diagnostic and Cancer Treatment Center, 1969---; AMA; council, L.A. Co. Med. Assn. 1964-66; L.A. Acad. Med., Calif. Med. Assn., Calif. Soc. of Internal Med., Amer. Soc. Internal Med., L.A. Acad. of Internal Med.; (life) Univ. of Wis. Med. Alumni; (life) Lutheran Hosp. Soc. of So. Calif., Calif. Hosp. Plan. Bd. and Emg. Bd.; Golden Circle, Calif.; (life) bd. trustees, Philanthropic Found.; adv. bd.: L.A. Co. Dist. Atty., Atty. Gen. of Calif.; Silver Dollar Club, Sundowners Club; Masonic Lodge No. 689, Commandry 43, Scottish rite, Al Malaikah Shrine, Los Angeles Royal Jester Ct. 84; Jonathan Club, L.A. Protestant. Hobby: magic and sleight of hand. Rec.: hunting, fishing. Res.: 445 Audraine Dr., Glendale, CA 91202; Office: 1401 S. Hope St., Los Angeles, CA 90015.

SWAIN, DONALD CHRISTIE
University Administrator
b. Oct. 14, 1931, Des Moines, Iowa; s. G. Christie and Irene (Alsop) Swain; B.A., Univ. of Dubuque, 1953; M.A. Hist., Univ. of Calif., Berkeley, 1958; Ph.D., 1961; m. Lavinia Lesh, Mar. 5, 1955, Pasadena; chil.: Alan Christie, b. Feb. 27, 1957; Cynthia Catherine, b. Sept. 29, 1960. Career: Asst. research historian, U.C. Berkeley, 1961-63; asst. prof. of hist., U.C., Davis, 1963-67, assoc. prof., 1957-71, prof. of hist., 1971---; also Academic asst. to Chancellor, U.C. Davis, 1967-68, asst. vice chancellor, academic affairs, 1971-72, vice chancellor, academic affairs, 1972-75; academic vice pres., Univ. of Calif. System, 1975---. Author: Federal Conservation Policy, 1921-1933 (1963); (co-ed) The Politics of American Science 1939 to the Present (1965); Wilderness Defender: Horace M. Albright And Conservation (1970); numerous articles and reviews in scholarly journals. Served USNR, active duty 1953-56. Mem.: Orgn. of Am. Historians; Am. Hist. Assn., Presbyterian. Rec.: tennis, hiking. Home: 561 Woodmont Ave., Berkeley, CA 94708; Office: 2200 University Ave., Berkeley, CA 94720.

SWAN, EVELYN ANNE
Medical Programmer
b. Feb. 17, 1943, Wash. D.C.; d. Charles Frederick and Eleanore (Hobson) Swan; B.S., math., Univ. Okla.,

1964. Career: research engr., Gen. Dynamics Corp., 1964-69; Principal programmer, research cardiology, Univ. Calif. Med. Center, San Diego, 1969---. Contbr. articles in American Journal of Physiology, Circulation, San Diego Biomedical Symposium. Mem.: Assn. for Computing Mach., So. Calif. Regional Rep., 1976---, S.D. chpt. chmn. 1973-74; Kappa Delta Sorority; Nat. Trust for Historic Preservation; San Diego Zoological Soc. Rec.: word games and puzzles. Hobby: needlepoint, So. Calif. Hist. Res.: 2453 Geranium St., San Diego, CA 92109; Office: 225 W. Dickinson St., San Diego, CA 92103.

SWANSON, EDWIN ARCHIE
University Professor — Administrator
b. July 5, 1908, St. Edward, Nebr.; s. Andrew E. and Alma (Nordgren) Swanson; ed. B.S., Nebr. State Teachers Coll., Kearney, 1932; postgrad. George Wash. Univ., Wash., D.C. 1934; M.S., USC 1936, Ed.D. 1949; m. Fern E. Anderson (dau. Dr. and Mrs. J.T. Anderson, Kearney, Nebr.), Aug. 25, 1933; sons: Edwin Burton, John LeRoy. Career: Teacher, Nebr. pub. schs. 1925-35; teaching fellow, Sch. of Edn., USC 1935-36; instr. (English-bus.), Fullerton Jr. Coll., Fullerton, Calif. 1936-37, 1938-39; visiting instr. edn.-com.-acting chmn., dept. of ofc. adm., USC 1937-38, summer sessions, 1937, 39, 42; assoc. prof.-head dept. comm., Ariz State Coll., Tempe, 1939-46; prof. School of Bus., San Jose State Univ., 1946---, chmn. Dept. of Bus. Edn. 1957-68; summer sessions: visiting faculty mem., grad. professional courses in bus. edn., Univ. of Tenn. 1940, 71; Univ. of N.C. Woman's Coll., Greensboro, 1941; Armstrong Coll., Berkeley, 1944, 45; Colo. State Coll. of Edn., Greeley, 1946; Univ. of Fla., Gainesville, 1953. Author: contrib. to (Harl R. Douglass, ed.) The High School Curriculum, Ronald Press, 1947, 56, 64 edits.; articles-editorials, NEA journ.; Bus. Edn. Forum; Bus. Edn. World; N. Mex. Bus. Educator; Natl. Bus. Edn. Quarterly (ed. 1939-41, ed. bd. 1939-48, chmn. 1961-62, others); Education Bulletin of California Bus. Education Assn.; School Review (annual contrib. Selected Bibliography for Business Education, 12 yrs.); Calif. Journ of Secondary Edn. (ed. cons. 1958-60); editor: chmn. matl. edn. and publs. com., Natl. Bus. Edn. Assn. 1960-62, ed. New Media in Teaching the Bus. Subj., 1965 Yearbook; Criteria for Evaluating Bus. and Ofc. Edn., 1969 Yearbook. Mem.: executive board, Natl. (United) Bus. Edn. Assn. 1946-53; natl. pres. 1950-51; pres. Western Bus. Edn. Assn. 1954-55; pres. Western Bus. Edn. Assn. 1954-55; area coord., No. Calif., Nev., Hawaii. Phi Delta Kappa. 1955-66, pres. Alpha Sigma Field Chpt. 1946, pres. Alpha Omega Field Chpt. 1955-56, natl. budget-finance com. chmn.-cons. 1959, 61, 63; chpt. pres., Phi Kappa Phi, 1956-57; Natl. Policies Com., Bus. and Econ. Edn. 1963-64; (life) NEA, Calif. Teachers Assn., Calif. Bus. Edn. Assn., AAAS, Amer. Mgmt. Assn., Amer. Assn. Univ. Profs., (life) Amer. Assn. Higher Edn., Delta Pi Epsilon, Pi Omega Pi, Gamma Rho Tau, Xi Phi, Kappa Delta Pi, Commonwealth Club of Calif., S.F. Res.: 2390 Mazzaglia Ave., San Jose, CA 95125; Office: Calif. State Univ., San Jose, CA 95192.

SWARTZ, MARC J.
Professor of Anthropology
b. Oct. 31, 1931, Omaha, Nebr.; s. Samuel and Esther (Brown) Swartz; B.A., Washington Univ., St. Louis, 1952, M.A., 1953; Ph.D., Harvard Univ., 1958; m. Audrey Rosenbaum, Sept. 16, 1952, Chicago; children: William, b. 1964; Robert and Matthew (twins), b. 1968. Career: Instr., Univ. of Mass., 1957-58; Asst. Prof., Univ. of Mass. 1958-59 and Univ. of Chicago 1960-62; Assoc. Prof., Mich. State Univ., 1962-64, prof., 1964-69; prof. Anthropology, Univ. Calif. San Diego, 1969---, Dept. Chmn. 1972-76. Guggenheim Fellow, 1975-76. Mem. Mombasa Club, Kenya, 1974---. Polit.: campaign advisor to J.F. Kennedy. Res.: 8552 Notingham, La Jolla, CA 92037; Office: UCSD, La Jolla, CA 92093.

SWATEK, FRANK E.
Microbiologist
b. June 4, 1929, Oklahoma City, Okla.; s. Clarence Michael and Bessie (Doubek) Swatek; B.S., San Diego State Coll., 1951; M.A., UCLA, 1955; Ph.D., 1956; m. Mary Frances Over, Jan. 28, 1951, San Diego; children: Frank Edward Jr., Lorraine Beth, Martha Lynn Lyons, Susan Ann, Cheryl Lee. Career: Professor and Chmn., Dept. of Microbiology, Cal. State Univ., Long Beach, 1956---; Lectr., USC Med. Sch., 1961---; cons.: Long Beach VA Hosp., 1956---; Douglas Aircraft Co., 1960---; U.S. Communicable Disease Center, 1962-64; Ogden Tech. Lab., 1968---; Hyland Lab.,

1969---. Author: Microbiology Textbook, 1967; General Microbiology Lab. Manual and Workbook, 1969; numerous papers on Microbiology. Mem.: Soc. Sigma Xi, N.Y. Acad. of Sci., Mycologia, Sabourandia, Am. Soc. for Microbiology, Am. Public Health Assn., Med. Mycological Soc. of the Americas; Fellow of Royal Soc. of Health 1970; Fellow of Am. Acad. of Microbiology, 1977. Catholic. Hobbies: boating, fishing, photog. Office: 1250 Bellflowe;r Blvd., Long Beach, CA 90840.

SWEENY, ALFREDO E.
Pediatrician
b. Jan. 15, 1931, Buenos Aires, Argentina; s. Patrick and Adelaida (Indorado) Sweeny; M.S., 1961; m. Hebe Rosini, D.D.S., Mar. 23, 1962, Argentina; chil.: Roy Patrick, b. Nov. 27, 1963; Valery Sandra, b. Apr. 30, 1965; Alfredo E., Jr., b. June 23, 1970. Career: instr. pediatrics, USC, 1974; asst. clin. prof. of pediatrics, USC, 1977---; asst. dir. outpatient dept., Children's Hosp., L.A., 1972---. Club: Rancho Las Palmas Country Club, Rancho Mirage. Hobbies: tennis, soccer. Home: 248 S. Windsor Blvd., L.A., CA 90004; Office: 321 N. Larchmont Blvd., Suite 1010, L.A., CA. 90004.

SWENSON, DIANNE LEE
Realtor
b. May 30, 1941, Stockton; d. Joseph and Mary (Hoisington) Theiler; student, San Francisco City Coll., 1959; St. Francis Sch. of Nursing, 1962; Fullerton Coll.; Univ. Calif., Irvine, 1977; Grad., Realtors Inst., certified residential broker, Nat. Council Exchangors; m. Lawrence Paul Swenson, Nov. 14, 1972, Ohau, Hawaii. Career: Registered Nurse, 1962-67; Realtor, Investment Counselor and Exchangor, 1967---; owner, Tyler's Gifts 'N Gourmet, 1976---; owner, Photo Finish, 1976---; co-owner, Swenson Realtors and Swenson Constrn., Yorba Linda. Co-author: How to List and Sell Condominiums. Mem.: No. Orange Co. Bd. of Realtors, dir. 1976, 77; Calif. Assn. of Realtors, dir. 1974, 76, 77; chmn. Young Realtors Calif. Assn. of Realtors, 1976---; coordinator, Heritage House Project 1975, 76, 77; pres., Placentia Yorba Linda Soroptimist 1977. Hobby: interior decorating. Res.: 1111 Kenwood Pl., Fullerton, CA 92631; Office: 18452 Yorba Linda Blvd., Yorba Linda, CA 92682; 1750 Kalakaua Blvd., Suite 2504, Honolulu, Hawaii 98628.

SWIG, BENJAMIN H.
Chairman of the Board, Fairmont Hotel Company
b. Nov. 17, 1893, Taunton, Mass.; s. Simon and Fanny (Levy) Swig; ed. Taunton H.S.; m. Mae Aronovitz, Boston, Mass., Dec. 24, 1916 (dec.); chil.: Melvin M., b. Dec. 24, 1917; Betty (Swig) Dinner, b. 1923; Richard L., b. 1925; Career: Engaged in real estate bus., NY and Bostn until 1945; est. Calif. res. and real estate bus., San Francisco, 1945---; chmn. bd., Fairmont Hotel Co., S.F. 1945---; chmn. bd. Lilli Ann Corp.; pres. Fairmont-Roosevelt, Fairmont-Dallas and Fairmont-Mayo Hotel Cos. Awards: Over 100 awards incl. (hon.) LL.D.: Univ. of Santa Clara, 1962; Carroll Coll. 1968; L.H.D., Hebrew Union Coll. 1964; Brandeis Univ. 1966; Norwich Univ. 1967 (1941---—. Mem.: v.p.-dir. Amer. Friends of Hebrew Univ.; natl. exec. bd.-exec. Amer. Jewish Com.; finance and investments com., Amer. Jewish Hist. Soc.; natl. council, Amer. Jewish Joint Distr. Com.; bd. dirs. Amer. ORT Fed.; Legacy development com., Anti-bd. trustees, Beth Sholom Found.; v.p.-dir., Brandeis Camp Inst. of the West; natl. bd., Brandeis Clubs; fellow, Brandeis Univ.; regional v.-chmn., Brandeis Univ. Assocs.; dir. Calif. Safety Council; statewide coms., Calif. State C. of C.; dir. Calif. Taxpayers' Assn.; chmn. Careers Unlimited for Women; Citizens Legislative Adv. Committee; Soc. of Hon. Fellows, City of Hope; bd. govs., Civic League of Improvement Clubs & Assns.; com. Albert Einstein Coll. of Med.; exec. bd., Calif. Sch., Hebrew Union Coll. ---; Jewish Inst. of Relig.; bd. dirs., Israel Development Corp.; bd. dirs., Israel Investors Corp.; natl. adv. bd.-No. Calif. adv. bd., Jewish Natl. Fund; bd. dirs.-v.p., Jewish Heritage Found.; (hon.) pres. bd. overseers-exec. com. of Natl. Planning Com.; (hon.) pres. Northern Calif. Region Friends of the Sem., Jewish Theol. Sem. of Amer.; v-chmn., Jewish Theol. Sem. of Amer. Action Com.; bd. dirs., Jewish Welfare Fed. of S.F., Marin Co., Peninsula; dir. Mt. Zion Hosp. Found.; S.F. Adv. bd.-natl. bd.-natl. exec. com., Natl. Conf. of Chrs. & Jews, Inc.; Bay Area World Fellowship Planning Com., Natl. Jewish Welfare Bd.; bd. dirs., Redwood Empire Assn.; bd. govs., Eleanor Roosevelt Inst. for Cancer Research; exec. com., Salvation Army; bd. govs., State

of Israel Bands; natl. advisor, Synagogue Council of Amer.; natl. bd. dirs., United Synagogue of Amer; bd. govs., W. Coast Univ. of Judaism; (hon. life) bd. trustees-bd. dirs., Union of Amer. Hebrew Congs.; co-chmn. United Press & Union League Club, United Jewish Appeal; Concordia-Argonaut Club of S.F.; Commonwealth Club of S.F. Res. and Office: Fairmont Hotel, San Francisco, CA.

SWINK, JACK W.
Superior Court Judge
b. Oct. 10, 1924, Swink, Colo.; s. Walter and Kathleen (Monkman) Swink; ed. Univ. Redlands; Tex. Tech.; USC; LL.B. (summa cum laude), Southwestern Univ. 1949; m. Doris J. Nelson, No. Hollywood, Calif., Nov. 26, 1950; chil.: Bonnie, Clark and Scott. Career: Pvt. practice law, North Hollywood, Calif., 1950---; partner, Clarke, Swink, Thatcher & Leary law firm. Judge, Superior Court, Los Angeles, 1972---. Author-lecturer on legal topics. Serv. USAF, Fifth AF Div., WW II. Awards: Hon. Mayor, City of Los Angeles, 1942; Outstanding Young Man of Ur., C. of C. 1954; Good Citizen Serv. Award, 1955; YMCA Man of Yr., 1969. Mem.: Pres. No. Hollywood H.S. Alumni Assn. 1948; dir. UMCA 1952---; chairman bd. mgrs., East Valley YMCA, 1966-68; chairman Community Chest, 1954; division chairman, Amer. Red Cross, 1955; pres. San Fernando Valley Bar Assn. 1959; pres. No. Hollywood Rotary Club, 1962; Calif. State, Los Angeles Co. and Amer. Bar Assns.; Town Hall of Calif.; Ephebian Soc.; Century Club; Lakeside Golf Club. Republican. Methodist (chmn. bd. trustees, No. Hollywood, 1964). Rec.: golf, boating. Res.: No. Hollywood, CA; Office: Superior Court, Los Angeles, CA 90012.

SYMONS, IRVING JOSEPH
Investments Executive
b. Nov. 21, 1907, Sonora, Calif.; s. Thomas Frederick and Mary Ellen (Barry) Symons; ed. grad. Sonora Elem. and H.S.; A.B., Univ. of Calif., Berkeley, 1928; m. Jane Thatcher. Career: President of Hales & Symons, Inc. (lumber and building materials), 1928---, president 1945---; pres. of Oakdale Investment Co. 1945---; pres. Sonora Investment Co. 1945---. Serv. USN (1942-45), WW II; Lt. Comdr., USNR (ret.). Mem.: past pres., Tuolumne Co. C. of C.; dir., Calif. State C. of C., 1955---; World Affairs Council of No. Calif.; Commonwealth of Calif. Republican (presidential elector, 1952). Catholic. Rec.: travel, fishing. Res.: 3 Hilltop Acres, Sonora, CA; Office: 730 S. Washington St., Sonora, CA 95370.

SYMONS, WILLIAM, JR.
State Official
b. Oct. 5, 1913, Laws, Inyo Co., Calif.; s. William and Rhoda (Aldridge) Symons; ed. grad. pub. schs., Bishop, Calif.; m. Audrey Hawkins, Bishop, Calif., June 23, 1936 (dec. Nov. 26, 1970); son, John Leslie, b. Feb. 26, 1943. Career: Rancher-cattle bus. ret. 1961. Justice of Peace (2 yrs.); Sch. Bd. Trustee (8 yrs.); County Supv. (14 yrs.); dir., 18th Dist. Agr. Assn. (12 yrs.); State Senator 28th Dist. Calif. 1963-66; commr. (apptd. by Gov. Reagan) State Pub. Utilities Comm. 1967-78, pres. 1968-70; Natl. Assn. of Regulatory Utility Commrs.: Elec. and Nuclear Energy Com. 1967-70; Ad Hoc. Com. on Fed.-State Regulatory Relationshops, 1969; Com. on Communications, and Exec. Com. 1969-78; Fed. FCC-State NARUC Joint Bd. 1970---. Protestant. Res.: 26 Thorndale Place, Moraga, CA 94556; Office: State Bldg., Civic Center, 350 McAllister St., San Francisco, CA 94102.

SZEKELY, DEBORAH
Owner-Founder, The Golden Door
b. May 3, 1922, Brooklyn, N.Y.; d. Harry and Rebecca (Seidman) Shainman; ed. USA, Mex., Tahiti; m. Vincent E. Mazzanti, M.D. psychoanalyst, Calif.; June 17, 1972; chil.: Livia Soledad, b. Apr. 4, 1956; Alexandre Odin, b. Feb. 19, 1958. Career: Founder/operator Rancho La Puerta, Tecate, Baja Calif., Mex. 1940---; Founder/Pres./Dir. The Golden Door, Inc., Escondido, Calif. 1959---. Author: Secrets of the Golden Door, Wm. F. Morrow, 1977. Mem.: Founder-bd. dirs., Globe Guilders, 1956; pres., Amer. Nati. Theatre Acad., San Diego, 1957; Nat. sponsor, Save the Children Federation; Bd. Dirs., Francis Parker Sch., San Diego; Women's Committee Salk Institute; Bd. Dirs., Seniors in Philanthropic Serv., 1961, v.chmn. 1962-65; San Diego C. of C. 1962---; founder/v.p. Combined Arts of S.D. 1964---; bd. dirs., San Diego Ballet 1965-70; bd. dirs. Theatre and Arts Found., 1966---; Advisor to bd. dirs. Old Globe Theatre, 1966---; Pres's. Council on Physical Fitness

and Sports; San Diego Stadium Authority Governing Bd., Chmn. 1976; Bd. trustees, The Menninger Found., Topeka Kansas, 1974---; v-chrperson, bd. of overseers, Univ. of Calif. at San Diego; Bd. dirs., Univ. of Calif. at San Diego Sch. of Med.; Chancellor's Club, Univ. of Calif. at S.D.; advisory bd. for Sch. of Bus. of the Univ. of San Diego; San Diego Council of Boy Scouts of America; Small Bus. Adminstrn., Small Business person of the year award, 1976. Address: P.O. Box 1567, Escondido, CA 92103.

T

TAGAVI, BIJAN
Plastic Surgeon
b. Sept. 4, 1936, Teheran, Iran; s. Taghi and Khanouma Tagavi, both Profs., Tehran Univ.; B.A., Univ. Montpellier, France, 1956; M.D., Medical Sch. of Paris, Sorbonne, 1963; Diplomate, Am. Bd. of Plastic Surgery, 1976. Career: Internship, Staten Island Hosp., Staten Island, N.Y., 1965-66; Residency in gen. surgery, Flower 5th Ave. Hosp., NYC, 1966-68, Hosp. for Jt. Diseases, NYC, 1968-69, New Jersey Hosp., 1970-72; Attending plastic surgeon, N.Y. Infirmary, 1972-76; pvt. practice, Plastic and reconstructive surgery, Teheran, Iran and NYC, 1972-77, Los Angeles, 1977---. Newspaper interviewee Los Angeles Times, Herald-Examiner, Century City News. Mil.: Vol. Physician for Vietnam, 1969. Mem.: Century City Rotary Club, 1978; Am. Soc. of Plastic and Reconstructive Surgeons, 1978. Hobbies: flying, collecting cars. Rec.: hunting, skiing. Res.: 2177 Summitridge Dr., Beverly Hills, CA; Office: 2080 Century Park E., Suite 1110, Los Angeles, CA 90067.

TAIT, ROBERT N.
District Attorney
b. Oct. 5, 1914, Fort Wayne, Ind.; s. Edwin and Mabel Tait; ed. B.A., Kent State Univ., Oh. 1936; LL.B., Hastings Coll of Law, Univ. of Calif. 1957; m. Vira June Theile, Nev., Sept. 19, 1965. Career: Personnel Dept., Hawaiian Comm. Sugar Co., Hawaii 1936-41; chief investigator, War Crimes, Japan, 1945-48; v.p.-gen. mgr. Taiyo Trading Corp., San Francisco, 1948-50; Dep. Dist. Atty., San Luis Obispo County, 1958-63; Asst. Dist. Atty. 1963-69, Dist. Atty. and legal counsel to Bd. of Supvs. 1969---. Admitted to Calif. State Bar, 1958; Cert. Criminal Law Spec. 1973. Spec. Agt., Counterintelligence Corps., U.S. Army, 1941-45, Lt. 1944; Capt. (attached to G-2 and FBI), 1950-53; Mem.: Calif. Council on Criminal Justice; coms. Dist. Atty's. Assn.; exec. com. Dist. Atty's. Uniform Crime Charging Proj.; chmn. Task Force on Criminal Procedure, Calif. Conf. on Judicary, 1974; adv. council of Proj. Star, Calif. Dept. of Justice Comm. on Peace Ofcrs. Standards and Tr.; coms. Calif. State Bar; Fed. Bar, San Luis Obispo Co. and San Francisco Bar Assns.; Natl. Dist. Attys. Assn.; Nat. Counterintelligence Assn.; pres. San Luis Obispo County Chiefs Assn.; SLO C. of C., Amer. Legion, Rotary, Elks, Morse, Nipomo Men's Club. Protestant Rec.: golf, swim. Res.: 177 Paso Robles Dr., San Luis Obispo, 93401; Office: Courthouse Annex, San Luis Obispo, CA.

TAKEUCHI, WAYNE YUSHI
President, Chaix & Johnson Associates
b. Apr. 23, 1932, Sacramento; s. Frank Fujio and Kachi (Yoshinaga) Takeuchi; Gr.Uncle Takeshi Gotoh was Deputy to Manchurian Emperor Puji, 1935-39; Gr. Grandfather Yoshinaga, famous architect bldr. devel. Kumamoto City in late 1800s early 1900s; Warrior family, Samurae Kawasaki, during 1600-1800; grad. with honors, Art Center Coll. of Design, BPA, 1955; m. June Junko Kobayashi, Feb. 4, 1956, Toronto, Ont., Can.; chil.: Robin Keiko, b. Feb. 5, 1960; David Toshio, b. Mar. 4, 1965. Career: awarded full tuition scholarship, General Motors, 1952-55; GM "B" Body Designer, 1955; special Firebird project, Oldsmobile Interior Asst. St. Head; Sundberg Ferar; senior designer, Chaix & Johnson, 1956, associate, 1961, vice pres., 1969, executive v.p., 1976, pres., 1977---. Mem.: Optimist, SACA, IDSA. Hobbies: cabinetry, painting. Rec.: skiing, tennis, biking. Home: 3050 Landa St., L.A., CA 90039; Office: 7060 Hollywood Blvd., L.A., CA 90028.

TALLMAN, JOHANNA E.
University Libraries Director
b. Aug. 18, 1914, Lubeck, Germany; d. Friedrich Franz

and Johanna (Voget) Allerding; A.B., Univ. of Calif., 1936; certificate in Librarianship, 1937; m. Lloyd Anthony Tallman, May 8, 1954, Laguna Beach. Career: San Marino Pub. Lib., 1937-38; L.A. County Pub. Lib., 1938-42; Pacific Aeronautical Lib., 1942-44; Engring. and Math. Sci. Lib., UCLA, 1945-73; Dir. of Lib., Calif. Inst. of Tech., 1973---; lectr., Sch. of Lib. Service, UCLA, 1961-73; Fulbright Lectr., Brazil, 1966-67; over fifty contbrs. profl. journs. Pres., Librarians Assn., Univ. of Calif., 1970-71; chmn., Sci.-Tech. Div., Special Libraries Assn., 1969-70; pres., So. Calif. chpt. 1965-66; chmn., L.A. Regional Group of Catalogers, 1946-47; bd. dir., Pasadena Hist. Soc. Mem. Zonta Internat., pres. Pasadena chpt. 1976-77. Home: 4731 Daleridge Rd., La Canada Flintridge, CA 91011; Office: 1201 E. California Blvd., Pasadena, CA 91125.

TAMKIN, CURTIS SLOANE
Mortgage Banker — Real Estate Developer
b. Sept. 21, 1936, Boston, Mass.; s. Hayward and Etta (Goldfarb) Tamkin; A.B. (econs.), Stanford Univ. 1958; m. Priscilla Ann Martin, Hillsborough, Oct. 1975; Career: V.P., Hayward Tamkin & Co., Inc., treas.-dir. 1963-70; trustee, Prime Mortgage Investors; partner, Property Development Co. 1970---. Author: various technical publs. in mortgage banking field. Lieutenant (j.g.), USNR, Far East, 1960-63. Mem.: corporate secty.-dir., So. Calif. Choral Music Assn. 1965-72, v.p. 1973, pres. 1974-78; dir. L.A. Jr. C. of C. 1968-69; Cabinet, Music Center Unified Fund, 1975---, bd. govs. Perf. Arts Council of L.A. County; Rotary Club; Univ. Club, Los Angeles Club. Finance Com. Brown for Secty. of State, 1970. Hobby: print collecting. Rec.: skiing, tennis, golf. Office: 3600 Wilshire Blvd., Los Angeles, CA 90006.

TAMKIN, S. JEROME
Investor — Consultant
b. Apr. 19, 1926, Los Angeles, Calif.; s. William W. and Thelma Tamkin; ed. B.S., M.A., Ph.D., LL.D.; job instruction training course, War Man Power Comm. 1943; Univ. of Calif. (chem, phisics, math.; active sports, sci. clubs and chem. research) 1944; U.S. Edn. Center (naval engring., electricity), 1944; rubber chem., USC 1944, chem. Engring., ind. engring., sales bus. adm. and mgmt. 1936-52; MIT (advanced electrons), 1945; U.S. Armed Forces Inst. (radio communications, econs., aerology), 1945; Fremont Coll., Santa Fe, N.Mex. (mgmt. and sci. processes), 1949-52; spec. foreign langs., tech. German and Spanish; (hon.) LL.D., St. Andrews Univ., London, Eng.; m. Judith Deborah, March 23, 1963; chil.: Sherry Dawn, Wendy, Gary. Career: Research Staff, Chem. Dept., UCLA, 1943; research chem.-analyst supv., U.S. Rubber Co. 1943-44; cons. engr. (mfg.-chem.-research and design), Econ. Sheet Metal Co., L.A. 1943-50; cons. electro-chem. engr., Elec. Research & Mfg. Co., L.A. 1944-46; cons. engr., Cardox Corp., Chicago, Ill. 1944-46; research engr., USC Coll. of Engring., Navy Research proj. 1946-48; chief cons. engr., Dallons Labs., L.A. 1946-52; pres.-gen. mgr., Majicolor, Inc., L.A. 1947-49; plant mgr., Wilco Co., L.A. 1948-53; v.p. (mfg., ind. sales), 1953-55; gen. mgr. Pan. Pac. Oil Co., Long Beach, Calif. 1948-55; cons. engr.-mgmt. cons., Jensen, Beam & Martin, L.A. 1954-55; v.p.-sales mgr.-stockholder, Unit Chem. Corp., L.A. 1955-56; pres. Jaylis of the Pac., L.A.; pres. Phillips Mfg. Co. 1957-62; pres.-dir. Inst. Food Equipment Corp. 1962-67; v.p.-dir. Dyna Mfg. Co., L.A. 1962-68; dir. Amer. Communication Systems, Inc. 1967-71; exec. v.p.-dir. Amer. Med. Internat., Inc. 1966---; dir. Rosen Oil Co., 1970-72; dir. Corsair Capital Co. 1969-71; pres. TGT Petroleum Corp., Wichita, 1972---; cons. Daylin Inc., 1973-75; Contrib. writer to numerous tech. mags. and journs. 1944---. Patents incl. Electronic Gas Detector, U.S. Patent, No. 587,802; Circuits for Automatic Control of Hazardous Vapors, U.S. Patent No. 587,803. Spec. engring. ofvr. USN 1944-46; Naval Research Labs., Wash. D.C.; USN Engring. Exp. Sta. and USN Acad., Annapolis, Md. (1944-46), WW II; ofcr. USNR. Mem.: U.S. Naval Inst.; Community Warden, W. Adams-Baldwin Hills Community of Civ. Def. (organizer-admr., approx, 4,000 volunteer workers); commr., L.A. bd. Environmental Quality, 1972-73; dep. sheriff, L.A. Co.; dir. Sun Air Found.; Amer. Inst. of Mgmt., Amer. Mgmt. Assn., So. Calif. Suggestion Soc., (tech.) Inst. of Aeron. Scis., Amer. Soc. of Naval Engrs., Soc. of Amer Mil Engrs., Amer. Chem. Soc., (assoc.) Amer. Inst. Of Elec. Engrs., Soc. Mot. Pic.-TV Engrs., Amer. Acad. of Cons., Amer. Inst. of Chem. Engrs., Soc. for the Advancement of Mgmt., (life) Calif. Scholarship Fed., Alpha Eta Rho. Clubs: Sunrise Country Club, Malibu Riding & Tennis. Hobby: photog., flying. Rec.: tennis, swimming. Res.:

The Riviera Estates, Pacific Palisades, CA; Office: Suite 1166, Kirkeby Center, Los Angeles, CA 90024.

TANENBAUM, BARTON
Physician — Urologist
b. Nov. 24, 1941, Brooklyn; s. Oscar and Sara Tanenbaum; B.S., Brooklyn Coll., 1963; M.D., Univ. of Pittsburgh, 1967; m. Arleen Cohen, June 10, 1973, Los Angeles. Career: Internship and Residency, Jewish Hosp. & Med. Center, of Brooklyn, N.Y., 1967-72; Tng. in Urologic Surgery and male infertility; pvt. practice, Los Angeles, 1972---. Exec. Com., Temple Hosp. and French Hosp., Los Angeles. Contbr. articles to med. journs. Mem.: Los Angeles County Med. Assn.; Am. Fertility Soc.; Am. Geriatric Soc.; Am. Venereal Disease Assn. Jewish, v.p., Young Israel of Century City. Hobby: oil painting. Office: 436 N. Roxbury Dr., Suite 107, Beverly Hills, CA 90210.

TANGUAY, MARY GWEN
Realtor
b. Sept. 28, 1948, d. By Norway, Michigan; d. Byron E. and Eileen (Brackett) Tanguay; B.A. (French), Univ. Mich., 1970; student, Santa Monica Coll.; West L.A. Coll.; m. John J. Batsakes, Aug. 23, 1976, Los Angeles; chil.: Elaine Kay; Mary Jane. Career: student-tchr., Univ. Mich., 1966-71, tchr. Psychology, 1967-71; real estate sales agent and office mgr., 1972---; licensed Real Estate Broker, co-owner, Redwood Realty, 1974---; also tchr. real estate, 1973---, give seminars for local bd. of Realtors. Part owner, Alexander's the Greatest (Mediterranean seafood restaurant). Recipient: Regent's Alumni Scholarship; Nat. Merit Scholar; apptd. to tchg. position while still an undergrad., Univ. Mich.; Norway High Sch. Valedictorian, State Finalist Debate. Helped found Drug Abuse Center, Ann Arbor, Mich., drug counseling, 1969-71; dir. Northville Div., Outreach proj. (Univ. Mich.), 1969-71; bd. dir., Venice-Marine del Rey Board of Realtors, 1976-79; mem. Calif. Assn. of Realtors, past Edn. Chmn. 20th Dist.; Mem.: Nat. Assn. Realtors; life mem. Univ. of Mich. Alumni Assn., U. of M. Club of L.A.; Nat. Orgn. of Women. Lutheran. Hobbies: interior decorating, buying real estate. Rec.: water sports, golf. Home: 120 Wavecrest Ave., Venice, CA; Office: 1711 Pacific Ave., Venice, CA 90291.

TANIS, NORMAN EARL
University Librarian
b. Aug. 15, 1929, Grand Rapids, Mich.; s. Aaron and Gertrude (Medendorp) Tanis; A.B. 1951; A.M.L.S. 1962, M.A. 1956, D.H.L. 1975, LL.D. 1976; m. Marion L. Anderson, 1955, Grand Rapids, Mich.; children: Kathy, b. 1963; Laura, b. 1965. Career: Librarian, Henry Ford Community Coll., 1956-66; dir., Kansas State Univ., Pittsburg Lib., 1966-69; Director of Libraries, Cal. State Univ., Northridge, 1969---. Co-author: Academic Library Collection Development, 1974; Native Americans of North America, 1975; Cost Analysis of Library Functions, 1978. Mem. Assn. of Coll. and Research Libraries, pres. 1973-74; Phi Kappa Phi, 1959---, pres. 1975; Phi Beta Mu, 1975---. Hobbies: art collecting, photog. Res.: 18900 Olympia, Northridge, CA; Lib.: 18111 Nordhoff St., Northridge, CA 91330.

TANNENBAUM, PERCY H.
University Professor
b. May 31, 1927, Montreal, Canada; s. Chaim and Ronya Tannenbaum; B.Sc. 1948, M.S. 1951, Ph.D. 1953; m. Brocha Kaplan, Sept. 16, 1948, Montreal, Canada; children: Brian Dov, b. 1950; Nil, b. 1955. Career: Reporter and staff writer, Montreal Herald, 1947-50; asst. prof., Mich. State Univ., 1953-54; research asst., prof., Univ. Ill., 1954-59; prof. of psychology and journalism and dir. of Mass Communication Research Center, Univ. Wis., 1959-67; Prof. of Communications and Psychol., Univ. of Pa., 1967-70; prof. of Pub. Policy and Research Psychol., Univ. Calif., Berkeley, 1970---; cons., Panel Social Psychol., NSF, NIMH, Nat. Acad. of Sci., govt., industry. Co-author: Measurement of Meaning, 1957; co-editor: Series of Cognitive Consistency: A Source Book. Fellow, Center for Advanced Study in Behavioral Sciences, 1965-66; Fellow, Am. Psychol. Assn., AAAS; Mem.: AAIP; Am. Assn. for Pub. Opinion Research; Internat. Assn. of Mass Communication Research. Res.: 962 Cragmont Ave., Berkeley, CA 94708; Office: Grad. Sch. of Pub. Policy, Univ. of Calif., 2607 Hearst, Berkeley, CA 94720.

TAPER, BARRY H.
Investments Executive
Career: Sr. v.p.-dir., First Charter Financial Corp. Dir.: Alliance Savings & Loan Assn., Lancaster, Calif.; Amer. Savings & Loan Assn., Berkeley Savings & Loan Assn., Home Mutual Savings & Loan Assn., Mutual Savings & Loan Assn. of Alhambra, Pioneer Investors Savings & Loan Assn.; pres. Barry Taper Found. Office: 9465 Wilshire Blvd., Beverly Hills, CA.

TARGOW, ABRAM MORRIS
Allergist
b. June 19, 1907, Rochester, N.Y.; s. Morris and Rose (Portyansky) Targow; A.B., Univ. Mich., 1927; Ph.D., Univ. of Chicago (Dept. of Physiol. Chem. & Pharmacology), 1933; M.D., Univ. Chicago, 1934; m. Jeanette Goldfield, Jan. 11, 1935, Chicago; children: Patricia (m. Harry Skinner), b. 1936; Richard, b. 1944. Career: Intern, Mt. Sinai Hosp., Chicago, 1934-35; Splty. tng., office assoc. Dr. S.M. Feinberg, Prof. Med. (Allergy) Northwestern Univ. Med. Sch., 1936-39, also Asst. in Med., Allergy, Northwestern Univ. Med. Sch.; Asst. Assoc. Clin. Prof. Med., Allergy, USC Sch. of Med., 1947-64, Emeritus Clin. Prof. Med., Allergy, 1964---; pvt. practice of Allergy, Beverly Hills, 1947---. Chief, Dept. of Allergy, Cedars-Sinai Med. Center, 1965-78. Mem.: Los Angeles Allergy Soc., pres. 1956; Am. Coll. of Allergists, 2d.v.p. 1955. Res.: 1835 N. Doheny Dr., Los Angeles, CA 90069; Office: 9400 Brighton Way, Beverly Hills, CA 90210.

TARSON, HERBERT HARVEY
University Administrator
b. Aug. 28, 1910, New York, N.Y.; s. Harry and Elizabeth (Miller) Tarson; B.A., UCLA, 1949; Ph.D., U.S. International Univ., 1972; m. Lynne Barnett, June 27, 1941, Los Angeles; son Stephen Glenn, b. Oct. 7, 1944. Career: Career officer AUS and USAF, 1940-64; asst. to Chancellor, Long Island Univ., 1964-69; dean of admissions, Texas State Tech. Inst., 1970-72; vice pres., Academic Affairs, Nat. Univ., San Diego, 1972---. Mil. AUS, exec. officer, Ft. Snelling, Minn., Asst. Adj. Gen., 91st Infan. Div. Club: Cuyamaca, 1975---. Hobbies: hiking, photog. Home: 4611 Denwood Rd., La Mesa, CA 92041; Office: 4141 Camino Del Rio So., San Diego, CA 92108.

TAUTENHAHN, GUNTHER
Composer
b. Dec. 22, 1938, Kowno, Lithuania; s. Otto and Ida (Grigoleit) Tautenhahn; U.S. Citizen, 1956; studied violin, piano and composition, NYC. Pub. works include: Brass Quintet, Concerto for Double Bass and Chamber Orchestra; Double Concerto for French Horn and Timpani with Orchestra; Concerto for Bassoon and Percussion Instruments; Two Symphonic Sounds for Orchestra; Concept 3 for Orchestra; Sonata for Violin; Solo Emotions of a Note No. 3 for Violin and 2 Percussion Instruments; Tone Blocks for Clarinet and Piano; Suite for Double Bass; Dorn Dance for Saxophone; Flute and Saxophone Quartet; Concerto for Saxophone and Orchestra. Awards: Young American Composers, 1963; commission, Internat. Trp. Guild., 1976; Inventor clock face to help tch. musical note values and time; Author: The Importance of One, 1971; Controlled Expressionism, 1976; Fiber Movements, 1978. Name included in ASCAP directory and symphonic catalog, A.M.C. chamber music catalog, Directory of New Music, 1973, 1976. Mem.: ASCAP, Am. Soc. Univ. of Composers; Nat. Assn. Composers; Am. Music Center; Internat. Composers Assn. Home: 1534 Third St., Manhattan Beach, CA 90266.

TAW, RICHARD LLEWELLYN, JR.
Cardiologist
b. June 27, 1944, Los Angeles; s. Richard L., M.D. and Mary (Millard) Taw; B.A., Occidental Coll., 1966; M.D., Johns Hopkins, 1970; Fellow, Amer. Coll. of Cardiology, 1977; children: Richard L., III, b. 1966; Bryan Jr., b. 1970. Career: Intern, Resident, Chief Resident, Cardiology Fellow, Johns Hopkins Hosp., 1970-75; mem. Faculty, UCLA, 1975-77; pvt. practice, 1977---; asst. clin. prof. of med., UCLA ---; asst. dir. of Cardiovascular Dept., St. Johns Hosp. (Echocardiography). Contbr. articles in cardiology and echocardiography to med. journals. Pres., Echocardiography Found. of So. Calif., 1978---. Office: 2001 Santa Monica Blvd., Santa Monica, CA 90404.

TAYLOR, DERMOT BROWNRIGG
Professor
b. Mar. 30, 1915, Dublin, Ireland; s. Roland L. and Sarah (White) Taylor; M.D., Trinity Coll., Ireland, 1938; m. Charlotte Taylor, 1965, Las Vegas; dau. Tina M., b. May 7, 1966. Career: Asst. Prof., Trinity Coll., 1938-39; lectr. in physiology, King's Coll., Univ. London, 1939-45; lectr. pharmacology, 1945-50; assoc. prof. of pharmacology, Univ. Calif., San Francisco, 1950-53; prof. of pharmacology, UCLA, 1953---, dept. chmn., 1953-68. Traveling fellow, Univ. London, 1948. Contbg. author: Essentials of Pharmacology, 1968; A Guide to Molecular Pharmacology-Toxicology, 1973. Mem. Biochemical Soc. Protestant. Rec.: boating. Res.: 6982 Wildlife Rd., Malibu, CA 90265; Office: Dept. of Pharmacology, UCLA, Los Angeles, CA 90024.

TAYLOR, JEAN LANDON
Professor
b. Feb. 24, 1902, Marcellus, Mich; s. William L. and Dora (Smith) Taylor; A.B., Western Mich. Univ., A.M., Columbia Univ.; postgrad., Univ. Chicago; m. Thelma Vogt (dec.), 1923, Benton Harbor, Mich.; dau. Jame T. (Armstrong), b. 1933; m. 2d. Lillian Mary Freer, Oct. 6, 1974, Palos Verdes Estates. Career: Reporter (waterfront), S.F. Examiner, 1921; Kalamazoo Gazette 1923-24; tchr., H.S., Western Mich. Univ., 1926-28; head, English Dept., Morgan Pk. Mil. Acad., Chicago, 1929-45; co-founder, chmn (2 yrs.), English sect., Pvt. schls. Assn. of Central States; Dir. Publs & Photog., Compton Coll., 1945-67; co-founder, W. Coast Div., Nat. Assn. Journ. Dirs.; co-founder Journalism Assn. Jr. Colls., Calif. Contrib. articles on edn. and Biblical subject, local newspapers, profl. journals. USN 1919-21. Past del. to White House Confs. on Edn.; cons. Nat. Edn. Assn. Wash. D.C., 1961-63. Awards: Gold Key, for service to Journ., Columbia Univ., 1957; lifetime hon. mem. Quill & Scroll Soc. (H.S. Journ.); Award for outstanding service to journ., youth edn., Calif. Journ. Assn. for Jr. Colls., 1967; Appreciation, Calif. State Senate, 1967; hon. life mem.: Calif. Tchrs. Assn. and Nat. Photo. Instrs. Assn.; Service Award, United Crusade, 1967, 68, 69. Past pres., Calif. Tchrs. Assn., so. sect.; pres., Calif. Ret. Tchrs. Assn., So. Bay Div., 1978; life mem. F&AM; Kiwanis, Phi Delta Kappa. Methodist. Hobbies: clock bldg., genealogy. Res.: 4917 Rockbluff Dr., Rolling Hills Estates, CA 90274.

TAYLOR, WALLER, II
Attorney at Law
b. Nov. 29, 1925, Los Angeles, Calif.; s. Reese Hale (chmn. board, Union Oil Co.) and Kathryn (Emery) Taylor; grandson of Waller Taylor, pres. Consolidated Steel Corp.; ed. B.A., Univ. of Tex. 1943-45; B.A., Univ. of Calif. 1946-47; LL.B., Stanford Univ. 1947-50; m. Jane Carvey, Ft. Worth, Tex., Oct. 31, 1945; chil.: Stephen Emery, b. July 16, 1948; Grant Carvey, b. May 16, 1950; Waller, III, b. Apr. 25, 1952. Career: Atty. at law, Adams, Duque & Hazeltine law firm, 1951-55, partner, 1955---. Dir.-v.p. Hosp. of Good Samaritan. Ensign, USN (1943-46), WW II. Mem.: Pres.-dir. UMCA of L.A.; Phi Alpha Delta, Delta Kappa Epsilon, Phi Sigma Alpha; Links (New York); Bohemian (S.F.), and Calif. Clubs. Repub. (hon. trustee, Repub. Assocs.; chmn. Gov's. Ball, L.A. 1967; exec. com. Repub. State Central Com.). Rec.: golf, fishing, hunting, sailing. Res.: 2605 Century Towers West, 2220 Ave. of the Stars, Los Angeles, CA 90067; Office: 523 W. 6th St., Los Angeles, CA 90014.

TAYLOR, WALTER WALLACE
Lawyer — Executive
b. Sept. 18, 1925, Newton, Ia.; s. Carroll W. and Eva (Greenly) Taylor; A.A., Yuba Coll. 1948; A.B., Univ. of Calif. 1950; M.A. 1955; J.D., McGeorge Coll. of Law, 1961; m. Mavis Harvey, Oct. 9, 1948; chil.: Joshua M., b. 1952; Kevin E., b. 1955; Kristin L., b. 1956; Jeremy W., b. 1958; Margaret b. 1961; Melissa, b. 1963; Amy, b. 1968. Career: Adm. analyst, USAF, Sacramento, 1951-53; personnel research analyst, Calif. State Personnel Bd., Sacramento, 1954-56; Civil Serv., personnel analyst, sr. chief counsel counsel-gen. mgr. Calif. State Employees' Assn., Sacramento, 1956-75; counsel to Calif. Commission for Teacher Preparation & Licensing, 1977---; Civil Serv., personnel cons. Author: feature column, Know Your Rights. USCG Res. (1943-46), WW II. Mem.: Amer., Calif., Sacramento Co. Bar Assn. Democrat. Protestant. Res.: 4572 Fair Oaks Blvd., Sacramento, CA 95825; Office: 1020 O St., Sacramento, CA 95814.

TEICHER, JOSEPH DAVID
Medical Center Director
b. Aug. 1, 1917, NYC; s. Nathan O. and Jetta (Cramer) Teicher; M.A., Columbia Univ. 1934; M.D., NYU Coll. of Med. 1940; F.A.P.A. 1962; m. Alice Buhrman, NYC, Sept. 19, 1942; chil.: Jon Steven, b. May 13, 1947; David Allen, b. Jan. 24, 1950. Career: Cons. psychiatrist, Bronxville Sch., Bronxville, N.Y. 1946-52; dir. Child Guidance Clinic, St. Luke's Hosp., NYC 1947-52; pvt. practice (psychoanalysis), NYC 146-52; dir. Child Guidance Clinic of L.A., Apr. 1952-60; chief psych. serv., Children's Hosp., L.A. 1953-58; prof. (psych.). USC Sch. of Med. 1960---; dir. Chil's Psych. Servs., L.A. Co. Gen. Hosp. 1960---. Many TV & Radio appearances. Author: (Book) Everyday Problems of Your Child, publ. Little, Brown and Co.; many scientific publications; mental hygiene ed., Social Serv. Digest, 1946-48. Lt. Med. Corps. USNR (1943-46), WW II. Mem.: com. on child psychiatry. Amer. Psychiatric Assn.; diplomate, Amer. Bd. of Psych. and Neurology; Amer. Psychoanalytic Assn., Amer. Orthopsychiatric Assn., Soc. for Child Development, Amer. Group Therapy Assn.; faculty, Inst. Psychoanalytic Med. of USC. Hobby: music. Rec.: tennis. Res.: 1333 S. Beverly Glen Blvd., Los Angeles, 90024; Office: 152 So. Lasky Dr., Beverly Hills, CA 90212; Dept. of Psychiatry, USC, 1934 Hospital Pl., Los Angeles, CA 90033.

TELLER, EDWARD
Nuclear Scientist
b. Jan. 15, 1908, Budapest, Hungary (naturalized Mar. 4, 1941, Wash. D.C.); s. Max (noted lawyer) and Ilona (Deutch) Teller; ed. Karlsruhe Tech. Inst., Ger. 1926-28; Univ. of Munich, 1928-29; Ph.D. (physics), Univ. of Leipzig, 1930; (hon.) D.Sc.; Yale Univ. 1954; Univ. of Alaska, 1959; Fordham Univ., George Wash. Univ., USC and St. Louis Univ. 1960; Rochester Inst. of Tech. 1962; Univ. of Detroit, 1964; (hon.) LL.D.: Boston Coll. 1961; Seattle Univ. and Univ. of Cincinnati, 1962; Univ. of Pittsburgh, 1963; (hon.) Doctor of Humane Letters, Mount Mary College, 1964; m. Augusta Harkanyi, Budapest, Hungary, Feb. 24, 1934; chil.: Paul, b. Feb. 10, 1943; Susan Wendi, b. Aug. 31, 1946; Career: Research assoc., Leipzig, 1929-31; Gottingen, 1931-33; Rockefeller fellow, Copenhagen (with Niels Bohr), 1934; lecturer, Univ. of London, 1934-35; prof. of physics: Goerge Wash. Univ., Wash., D.C. 1935-41; Columbia Univ. 1941-42; Univ. of Chicago, 1946-52; Los Alamos (on leave from Univ. of Chicago), 1949-52; Univ. of Calif. 1953-60; physicist: Univ. of Chicago, 1942-43; Manhattan Engr. Dist. 1942-46; Los Alamos Sci. Lab. 1943-46; cons. Livermore br., Univ. of Calif. Radiation Lab. 1952-53; dir. 1958-60; assoc. dir., Lawrence Radiation Lab., Univ. of Calif. 1954---; prof. of physics-at-large, 1960---; chmn. Dept. of Applied Science, Davis-Livermore, 1963-66. Sci. adv. bd., USAF Pres.' Foreign Intelligence Adv. Bd.; (past) gen. adv. com., Atomic Energy Comm. Research; chem. poluatomic molecules and theory of atomic nucleus; active in development of Sherwood Proj. (controlled thermonuclear pgm); and Proj. Plowshare (peaceful uses of nuclear explosives). Awards: Joseph Priestly Mem. Award, Dickinson Coll., Carlisle, Pa. 1957; Albert Einstein Award and Gen. Donovan Mem. Award, 1959; Midwest Research Inst. Award and Living History Award by Research Inst. of Amer. 1960; Thomas E. White and Enrico Fermi Awards, 1962. Mem.: Natl. Acad. of Scis.; fellow, Amer. Nuclear Soc.; fellow, Amer. Phys. Soc., Amer. Acad. of Arts and Scis., Amer. Ord. Assn. Hobby and Rec.: piano, chess, hiking. Res.: 1573 Hawthorne Terr., Berkeley, CA; Office: Lawrence Livermore Labs., Livermore, CA 94550.

TENNANT, FOREST S., JR.
Health Services Director
b. Jan. 23, 1941, Dodge City, Kan.; s. Forest S., Sr. and Vivian (White) Tennant; B.A., Univ. of Mo. 1962; M.D., Univ. of Kan. 1966; M.P.H., UCLA, 1973, Dr. P.H. 1974; m. Miriam Isaac, Stockton, Kan., Setp. 17, 1966. Career: Res. internal med. Univ. of Tex. Med. Dept. 1967-68; Post-Doctoral Fellow, U.S. Pub. Health Serv., UCLA Sch. of Pub. Health, 1972-74, asst. prof. 1974---; exec. dir. Community Health Projects, Inc., W. Covina, 1974---; prin. investigator, Public Health Found. of L.A. County 1974---. Author, 52 sci. publs. 1968-77. Diplomate, Amer. Bd. of Preventive Med. 1974; Fellow, Amer. College of Preventive Med. 1976. Maj., U.S. Army, Med. Ofcr., 1968-72. Author: numerous articles in med. & scientific journs. Awards: Army Commendation Medal, Meritorious Serv. Medal. Mem. Amer. Public Health Assn.; L.A. County Med. Assn.; West Covina C. of C. (pres. 1978); Rotary

Internat., bd. mem.; W. Covina Repub. Club, bd. mem. Methodist. Hobbies: writing, garden. Rec.: golf, skiing, fishing. Res.: 1744 Aspen Village Way, West Covina, CA 91791; Office: 336½ S. Glendora Ave., West Covina, CA 91790.

TENNEY, PAUL ARTHUR
Banker
b. May 30, 1935, San Diego; s. Harold Arthur and Dorothy (Palmer) Tenney; GGrands., Lot Smith, leader against U.S. Army in Utah War of 1857; grad., San Diego City Coll., 1954, Brigham Young Univ., 1955, Am. Inst. of Banking, 1967; m. Janice White, 1955, Mesa Ariz.; children: Marion, b. 1956; Julia, b. 1959; Norah, b. 1961; Matthew, b. 1965; Tom, b. 1968. Career: v.p. comml. banking, U.S. Nat. Bank, 1955-74; v.p. and mgr., First State Bank of Oregon, 1974-77; pres., chief exec. officer, American Bank & Trust Co., 1977---. Bd. Dir., Am. Inst. of Banking, 1962-65. Contbr. articles in Banking News Letter, 1965. Dir., Rotary Club, Milwaukie, Ore., 1973-74. L.D.S. Ch., Bishop 1970-73, High Council 1969, 73. Hobbies: photog., camping, Res.: 3877 Eastwood Ct., Pleasanton, CA 94566; Office: 1940 Tice Valley Blvd., Walnut Creek, CA 94595.

TEPLITZ, ELLIOT
Founder — Director, Letterology Institute
b. May 26, 1945, Miami Beach, Fla.; s. Louis and Jeanette (Lazaroff) Teplita; A.A. and Assoc. of Sci. (outstanding scholastic achievement award) Miami Dade Jr. Coll., 1967; Univ. of Miami, 1969. Career: Songwriter, 1800 songs, 1962---; personal mgr. several entertainers, 1964-68; owner, Recording Co., 1966; booking agent, 1966-68; recoar; prod., 1969; invented and began research, testing sci. of Leterology, 1970---; invented self-defense technique for women called Rockiaki, taught this at Free Univ., Berkeley, 1970; recording artist, 1972; authored first (1970) and second (1977) books on Letterology, 1970, 1977; host, radio talk show, Letterology Hour, S.F., 1978; creator, Letterology Correspondence Course; presentation of Letterology Seminars, 1978; TV guest appearances on celebrity talk shows, featured in national and internat. media, 1978. Mem. Jr. Exchange Service Club; ARC; Thespian hon. soc. Hobby: movie buff. Offices: 1330 University Ave., Berkeley, CA 94702; 1755 N. Highland Ave., Suite 1401, Hollywood, CA 90028.

TERINO, EDWARD OWEN
Physician
b. July 30, 1937, Teaneck, N.J.; B.A. cum laude, Amherst Coll., 1958; M.D., Union Univ., Albany Med. Coll., 1962; m. Lisa DuBoise, 1976; Los Angeles; children: Tara, Vanessa, Wendy, Laura. Career: Intern, Surgery, Yale New Haven Med. Center, 1962-63, research fellow, Cardiovascular and Transplantation, 1962-64, asst./4th year/chief resident, gen. surgery, 1964-68; res.&chief resident Plastic Surgery, Univ. N.C., 1968-69; Univ. Fla. Coll. of Med. 1969-70; Instr. in Surgery, Yale Univ., 1966-68; Univ. N.C., 1968-69, Univ. Fla., 1969-70; Instr. in Plastic Surgery, UCLA, 1974---, Sepulveda Veterans Hosp., 1974---; pvt. plastic surgery practice, Westlake Village, 1971----. Certification: Am. Bd. of Surgery, 1971, Am. Bd. of Plastic Surgery, 1972. Public service, numerous interplast trips, Hope Ship Service. Publs.: contbr. profl. articles in med. and surg. journals; papers presented on Ednl. TV and Radio programs, med. society meetings. Capt., USAR, 1963-70. Fellow, Am. Acad. of Compensative Med.; Fellow, Am. Coll. of Surgeons; Mem.: Am., Calif. Socs. of Plastic and Reconstructive Surgeons; Cleft Lip and Palate Assn.; Educational Found. Internat. Programs Com.; Internat. Soc. for Burn Injuries; Internat. Coll. Surgeons; Pan Pacific Surgical Assn.; Am. Soc. ofr. Aesthetic Plastic Surgery, candidate. Res.: 474 Potrero Rd., Lake Sherwood, Thousand Oaks, CA 91230; Office: 2660 Townsgate Rd., Westlake Village, CA 91361.

TERRELL, A. JOHN
Telephone Industry Executive
b. Dec. 27, 1927, Pasadena, Calif.; s. Harry E. and Elizabeth (Eaton) Terrell; grandson of Benjamin Harrison Eaton, Gov. of Colo.; ed Chaffey Coll., Ontario, 1947-48; B.B.A., Univ. of New Mex., 1952; m. Elizabeth Schalk, Denver, Colo., June 6, 1949; chil.: Patricia E., b. Sept. 5, 1951; Marilee D., b. Dec. 8, 1953; J. Scott, b. May 28, 1957. Career: Plant oprs., communications cons. Mt. Bell Tel. Co. 1951-56; systems analyst, dept. mgr. ACF Inds., Inc., Albuquerque div. 1956-62; mgr. communications and servs., oprs. planning principal, bus. research,

Hunt-Wesson Foods, Div. Norton Simon Ind., Inc. 1962-68; v.p.-gen. mgr. Wells Fargo Sec. Guard Serv., Div. Baker Inds., Inc. 1968-71; budget admr. Hyland Labs., Div. Baxter Travenol Labs., Inc. 1971---, mgr. adm. 1974-77; American Telephone Management Inst., Inc., Executive vice pres., 1977. Publs.: contrib. to many professional journals, 1966---. U.S. Merchant Marine, So. Pac., Leyte, P.I. 1944-45, WW II; U.S. Army, 82nd Airborne Div. Paratrooper, 1946-47; USAR 1947-50. Awarded Combat Bar. Mem.: dir.-secty.-v.p. Albuquerque Jaycees, 1951-61; dir. N. Mex. Tuberculosis Assn.; dir.-treas.-v.p. Bernalillo Co. T.B. Assn. 1957-61; Repub. div. chmn. Bernalillo Central Com. 1961-62; Orange Co. Com. Sch. Dist. 1964-66; Natl. Assn. of Accts. 1963--- (most valuable mem. 1974-75), dir. 1976-77; pres. Greater Irvine Lions Club, 1975-76. Episcopalian. Rec.: flying, skiing, swim, writing. Res.: 1725 Port Charles Pl., Newport Beach, CA 92660; Office: 2192 Dupont Drive, Suite 214, Irvine, CA 92715.

TERRY, THOMAS D., S.J.
Clergyman
b. May 20, 1922, Pittsburgh, Pa.; s. Charles Dutton and Catherine (McQuade) Terry; A.B. St. Louis Univ. 1945; B.S. (chem.), Ph.L. 1947, S.T.L. 1953; Ph.D., Univ. of Calif., Davis, 1959. Career: Wine chem., Novitiate of Los Gatos, 1959-61; dean, Coll. of Arts & Scis., Univ. of Santa Clara, 1961-66; academic v.p. Loyola Univ. of L.A. 1966-68; pres. Univ. of Santa Clara 1958-76; dir., Planning, Calif. Jesuits 1977---, pres. Noviatiate Wines, 1978---; Mem.: Sigma Xi, Amer. Soc. of Enologists. Roman Catholic. Res. and Office: P.O. Box 519, Los Gatos, CA 95030.

TERZIAN, SHOHIG SHERRY
Medical Information Director
b. Constantinople, Turkey; d. Ardashes Garabed and Ebraxe (Momjian) Terzian (parents both from Erzeroum in historic Armenia, Asia Minor); A.B., cum laude, Eng. Lit., Radcliffe Coll.; M.S., Columbia Univ. Grad. Sch. Lib. Serv.; postgrad., New Sch. of Social Research, UCLA, Univ. Wis. Career: Research Asst., U.S. War Dept., U.S. Office of War Info., U.S. State Dept. Internat. Info. and Cultural Affairs Div., NYC, 1942-43; Research Librarian, Time, Inc., NYC, 1943-46; Librarian, Prudential Insurance Co. of Am., L.A., 1947-48; Librarian, Neuropsychiat. Inst., UCLA, 1961-74, Dir., Mental Health Information Serv. Neuropsychiatric Inst. and faculty mem. Dept. of Psychiatry & Biobehavioral Sciences, UCLA Sch. of Med., 1975---. Contbr. articles to scholarly quarterlies, profl. journs. Mem.: Assn. of Western Hosps., founder, charter chmn. Hosp. Libns. Sect.; Spl. Libraries Assn., pres. Placement & behavioral sci. chmn. So. Calif. chpt.; Calif. Lib. Assn., pres. hosp. and instns.; Inst. for Study of Social Trauma, cons.; L.A. County Commn. on Status of Women, mem. employment and sr. women coms.; L.A. Trade Tech. Coll., mem. advis. com., lib. technician prog,; Columbia Univ. Alumni Assn. So. Calif., dir., assoc.ed.; Assn. for Mental Health Affil. with Israel, hon. mem., chmn. Lib. Com. So. Calif. chpt.; Harvard & Radcliffe Clubs of So. Calif., v.p. and dir.; UCLA Faculty Center, Los Angeles Mental Health Assn. Democrat, mem. Westwood Demo Club. Armenian Orthodox Christian. Hobby: exploring wonders of Calif. Res.: 969 Hilgard Ave., Apt. 907, Los Angeles, CA 90024; Office: Neuropsychiatric Inst., UCLA, L.A., CA 90024.

TESSA, CLEMENT D.
Physician and Surgeon
b. Mar. 1, 1923, Port Chester, NY; s. Nickalous and Faustina (Bianco) Tessa; ed. (premed.) NYU 1941-43, 1946-47; M.D., Coll. of Med. and Surg., Des Moines, Ia. 1951; m. Marie Madello, Port Chester, NY, June 9, 1946; sons: Michael Wayne, b. Jan. 8, 1953; Gary Stephen, b. Mar. 2, 1956 (dec.). Career: Intern, Des Moines Gen. Hosp. 1591-53; est. pvt. practice, med. and surg., North Hollywood, Calif. 1953---; chmn. med. records. com., Community Hosp., N. Hollywood, 1954-57; chief of staff, 1963-65; dep. chief of staff, Victor Hosp., N. Hollywood, 1957-61; chief of staff 1961-63. Contrib. to professional journals; research on theory of cellular expression. expression. U.S. Army Med. Corps, ETO (1942-45), WW II. Mem.: AMA; N. Hollywood, Calif., World Med. Assns.; Amer. Coll. Neuropsychs.; L.A. Heart Assn.; Amer. Cancer Soc.; Quinto Lingo; Catholic. Phys. Guild; Encino Men's Club. Hobby: photog. Rec.: golf, swimming. Res.: 15556 Meadowgate Rd., Royal Oaks Estates, Encino, CA 91316; Office: 6442 Coldwater Canyon Blvd., North Hollywood, CA 91606.

TEUTSCH, WALTER
Music Conductor — Educator
b. Oct. 11, 1909, Rugsburg, Germany; s. Arthur and Clara Teutsch; Abitur 1928; J.V.D., Univs. of Munich, Heidelberg, Bonn, Berlin, Wuerzburg, 1933; Diploma, Leopold Mozart Conservatory of Music, 1936; m. Gertrude Oettinger, Apr. 6, 1941, Salt Lake City; children: Miriam, b. 1950; Karin (Haldeman), b. 1951. Career: Prof., Head Div. Fine Arts, Westminster Coll., 1943-55; prof., Dept. Chmn. and Dir. of Opera, Calif. Western Univ. (now U.S. Internat. Univ.), 1955-75; Instr., Mesa Coll., 1975---; Conductor, Salt Lake Philharmonic Choir, 1949-55; assoc. conductor, Utah Opera Theater, 1952-55; music dir., organist many churches. Episcopal. Res.: 4581 Tivoli St., San Deigo, CA 92107.

TEXIDO, WILLIAM JOSEPH
Corporate President
b. Apr. 4, 1936, New Rochelle, NY; s. Harold Ames and Harriett Texido; B.S., elec. engr., 1957; m. Helen M. Keefe, Feb. 16, 1963, Rochester, Minn.; children: Mary, b. 1964; Michael, b. 1966. Career: Mktg. Rep., IBM, 1965-68; pres. Rail Div., Itel Corp., 1968-77; pres., CEO, dir., Brae Corp., San Francisco, 1977---. Trustee, Sacred Heart Schools. Mil.: Underwater Demolition Team, 1957-60. Club: Menlo Circus. Rec.: tennis. Res.: 69 Almendral Ave., Atherton, CA 94025; Office: Three Embarcadero Center, San Francisco, CA 94111.

THACKER, ERNEST W.
Clergyman — Professor
b. Mar. 29, 1914, Santa Ana; s. Joseph and Ernestine (Wichmann) Thacker; Grad. Orange Union H.S., 1931; A.A., Santa Ana Coll., 1933; A.B., Univ. Redlands, 1935; Emory Univ. M.Div., 1938; Ph.D., USC, 1952; m. Lorelei Ihrig, Jan. 26, 1947, Los Angeles; children: Joel Ernest, b. 1948; Alice Joanna, b. 1955; Elizabeth Lorelei, b. 1957. Career: Methodist Minister, So. Calif. 1938-48; Examiner in American Studies, USC, 1946-51; Pastor, Calvary Methodist Ch., L.A., 1951-53; Lectr. Am. Studies, USC, 1951-53; prof. hist. and polit sci., Los Angeles Valley Coll., 1953---, chmn. Dept. Hist., 1955-66, 1975-77. Guest, TV programs on polit. sci., Community Coll. Dist. Co-author: Politics and Government in California, Harper and Row, 10th ed. 1979; American and California Government, Lucas Bros. 1953. Chmn., Negotiating Council, Los Angeles Community Coll. Dist. 1969-70; pres., L.A. Valley Coll. Faculty Assn., 1958-59; pres. Affil. Coll. Faculty Assn., 1959-60; pres., L.A. Coll. Tchrs. Assn. 1969-71. Democrat, v.p. Adlai Stevenson Demo. Club, 1959-60. United Methodist Ch. Hobby: photog. Res.: 8800 Newcastle Ave., Northridge, CA 91325; Office: 5800 Fulton Ave., Van Nuys, CA 91401.

THALHEIMER, FLORENCE W.
TV Moderator — Civic Leader
b. July 19, 1904, Chicago, Ill.; d. Leo E. and Edith P. Weiss; ed. grad. Germantown H.S.; m. Byron A. Thalheimer, Feb. 9, 1929, Philadelphia, Pa. (dec. 1973); chil.: Judy Gale, b. June 13, 1930; Mrs. Robert (Suzy) Gluck, b. Dec. 6, 1932. Career: Community and edn. leader, Philadelphia, Pa. and Beverly Hills, Calif. 1937---; adult edn. teachers credential, 1951-53; mem. Bd. of Edn., Beverly Hills, Calif. 1951-61, pres. 1954, 60; prod.-coord., Discovery, coll. pgm., KABC-TV, 1957; first dist. TV and radio chmn.-delegate, Gov. Warren's Conf. Edn. TV, 1958-61; prod.-moderator, The Intelligent Parent (open forum TV pgm), KLAC-TV, L.A. 1960-62; panel, World Is in Your Hands, KTTV, L.A.; cons. TV Edn. Channel 28, KTHE (edn. dir. for sch. pgms.; prod.-moderator, Families are First; edn. dir. PTA), 1961---; pub. affairs dir. DCOP-TV: prod.-moderator, Intelligent Parent, 1955---; Essentially Sex, Potentially Potent (career clinic); Fed. Exec. Bd. (taxpayer clinic); World Talk (interviews); Stop: Look: Listen to Florence Thalheimer 1973---; Guest, Billie Burke Show, KTTV, Mayor's Youth Adv. Bd. Awards: presented Key to City by Mayor of Kyoto; Best Woman Broadcaster, Pub. Serv. Pgms. by American Women of Radio-TV, 1973-74; over fifty awards for Community Serv.; forty TV programs awards; Woman of Achievement award by Beverly Hills Bus. and Profl. Women, 1959; Los Damas and Holy Name Adoption Soc. Award, 1967; Golden Mike Award, Amer. Leg. Natl. Award; Los Angeles Mauor's Community Rels. Award; Los Angeles Anti-Drug Commission Award; Variety Boys Club Serv. Award (for TV series), 1968; Federal Executive Award (for TV series on Tax), 1968; Woman of the Year, Town & Country Fine Arts Club; Justicia Award, L.A. Bar Assn. (first woman);

U.S. Consular Award for series World Talk, 1969; L.A. chpt. Calif. Press Women Angie Award, 1970. Mem.: PTA, Phila., Pa. 1937-54, exec. 1939, Adult Edn. Council, 1939-46, pres. Cheltenham H.S. PTA 1939, orgn.-teacher, chils. summer camps, 1946; bd. dirs., Natl. Conf. of Chrs. and Jews, 1946-56; parent edn. chmn., Beverly Hills H.S. 1947, various coms. 1947-53; Community Chest chmn., Beverly Hills Schs. 1948-60; radio-TV chmn., Dist. PTA 1948-67; L.A. Cits. Adoption Com. 1949-56; Calif. Soc. of Crippled Chil.; Hollywood Women's Press Club; PTA, Beverly Hills. Wilshire Blvd. Temple (sch. bd.). Hobby: world travel, entertaining distinguished guests who visit U.S.; Rec.: fishing. Res.: Georgian Hotel, No. 803, 1415 Ocean Ave., Santa Monica, CA 90401.

THARP, LECILE CONFER
Realtor
b. Apr. 29, Jay County, Ind.; d. Lester Raymond and Bertha (Michael) Confer; Bach. of Music Edn. (piano), Am. Conservatory of Music; A.A., bus. adm. & acctg., San Bernardino Valley Coll.; m. William Albert Tharp, Louisville, Ken.; chil.: Twyla, b. 1941, choreographer (movie HAIR), dancer (Guggenheim awards); Stanley W., b. 1944, commodity trader, Mid-America Commod. Exchange; Stanford V., b. 1944, estate planning, Gr. West Assurance Co. (twin sons served in Peace Corps); Twanette T. (Garvey), b. 1945, sculptor-designer, (Arthur Fiedler Medallion), Martha's Vineyard, Mass. Career: spec. piano teaching, Louis Robyn system and DALCROZE Eurythmics for very young students. piano studio, Indiana; automotive acct.; mgr.-owner, movie theatre; real estate broker; Investment and Exchange Counselor, Tharp Realty, San Bernardino, ---; President, three corporations; Dir., San Bernardino Music Tchrs. Assn. of Calif.; Mem.: Nat. and Calif. Assns. of Realtors; San Bernardino Bd. of Realtors; Nat. Council of Exchangors; Internat. Real Estate Fedn. Am. chpt.; Internat. Exchangors Assn.; Inland Empire Real Estate Exchangors; San Gabriel Valley Real Estate Exchangors; Apartment Assn. of Inland Empire Inc.; San Bernardino C. of C., econ. devel. div.; Order of Eastern Star; Altrusa Internat.; Meals on Wheels, secty.-treas.; Toastmasters Internat.; Chicago Sunday Evening Club (choir broadcast under dir. Edgar Nelson. Quaker (Soc. of Friends). Hobby: commodity research. Rec.: contract bridge; ballet, opera, concerts, gourmet food. Office: Tharp Realty, 3272 North E. Street, Suite C, San Bernardino, CA 92412.

THAW, RICHARD FRANKLIN, II
Business Owner
b. Nov. 3, 1943, Corvallis, Ore.; s. Dr. Richard and Lucilla (Rae) Thaw; B.A., San Jose State Univ., 1966, M.A., 1971; Ph.D., Human Behavior, Communications, U.S. Internat. Univ., 1977; m. Kathleen R. Johnson, Nov. 1968, San Jose; son, William Franklin, b. 1975. Career: Educator, elem., secondary schs. and university level, 1966-78; founder, pres., Vandalism Prevention, Inc., 1977---. Publs: Preventable Property Damage: Vandalism and Beyond, in Crime Prevention Rev. Apr. 1978; Uses of Sign Language in the Elementary School Classroom, in Media, Method and Ideas Workshop, Apr. 1970. Mem.: Phi Delta Kappa, Phi Sigma Kappa. Res.: 1010 Creekside Ct., Morgan Hills, CA 95037; Office: 1605 Park Ave., San Jose, CA.

THIMANN, KENNETH V(IVIAN)
Biologist — Educator
b. Aug. 5, 1904, Ashford, Kent, Eng.; s. Phoebus and Muriel (Harding) Thimann; B.Sc., London, 1924; Ph.D., London, 1928; Hon.A.M., Harvard Univ., 1939; Hon. Ph.D., Basel, 1961; m. Ann Bateman, 1929, London; children: Vivianne (Mrs. J. Nachimas), Prof., b. 1931; Karen (Mrs. J. Romer) Dean, b. 1936; Linda (Mrs. J.T. Dewing, Jr.), b. 1943. Career: Instr. in bacteriology, Kings Coll., London, 1927-29; Instr. in biochem., Cal. Inst. of Tech., 1930-35; asst., assoc. and full prof., Harvard Univ., 1935-65; dean of sciences, Univ. Calif., Santa Cruz, 1965-67, provost of Crown Coll. (UCSC), 1965-72, Prof. of Biology, 1972--- (prof. Emeritus of Biology, Recalled). Author: Phytohormones, with F.W. Wenb, 1937; The Life of Bacteria, 1955, 1963; The Natural Plant Hormones, 1972; Hormones In the Life of Plants, 1977. Councillor, Nat. Acad. of Sci., 1968-72; Pres.: Am. Soc. of Plant Physiologists, 1950; Am. Soc. of Naturalists, 1955; Soc. of Gen. Physiologists, 1949; Am. Inst. of Biological Sciences, 1965. Mil.: Opns. Research Analyst, USN, 1942-45, Wash. D.C.; London, Pearl Harbor. Hobbies: music, stamps, gardens. Res.: 36 Pasatiempo Dr., Santa Cruz, CA 95060; Office: The Thimann Labs, Univ. of California, Santa Cruz, CA 95064.

THOMAS, DANNY
Comedian
b. Jan. 6, 1914, Deerfield, Mich.; s. Charles and Margaret (Simon) Jacobs; cousins: Kahlil Gibran, author, The Prophet; Habib Pasha El-Saad, former pres., Republic of Lebanon; H. B. Peter Arida, Patriarch of the Maronites of Lebanon; ed. Woodward H.S., Toledo, Oh.; m. Rosemarie Cassaniti, Detroit, Mich., Jan. 15, 1936; chil.: Margaret Julia, b. Nov. 21, 1937; Theresa Cecilia, b. Nov. 9, 1942; Charles Anthony (Tony), b. Dec. 7, 1948. Career: Debut, 5100 Club, Chicago, Ill., Aug. 12, 1940 (3-yr. contract followed, 1940-43); Oriental Theatre, Chicago, 1943; La Martinique Club, NYC 1943-44; Roxy Theatre, NYC 1948; Ciro's, Hollywood, Calif. 1949; London Palladium, Eng. 1950; Chicago Theatre, Ill. 1952; annual appearances: Chez Paree, Chicago; Chase Hotel, St. Louis; Fairmont Hotel, S.F.; Flamingo Hotel, Las Vegas, Nev.; Riviera, Ft. Lee, N.J.; Copacabana, NYC; Latin Quarter, Boston, Mass.; Town Casino, Copa City, Miami Beach, Fla.; mot. pics.: Unfinished Dance, 1946; The Big City, 1947; Call Me Mister, 1950; star, I'll See You In My Dreams, 1951; Jazz Singer, 1952; radio: Danny Thomas Show, Blue Network, Chicago, 1943; Fanny Brice Show, NBC, Hollywood, 1944; Danny Thomas Show, CBS, Hollywood, 1948; TV: Four-Star Review, NBC-TV, 1950-51; All-Star Review, NBC-TV, 1951-52; Danny Thomas Show (wkly), CBS-TV. Capt., Spec. Servs. Div. (rec.), U.S. Army; entertained troops overseas, Philippine Is. and S. Pac. area, WW II. Awards: Variety and Billboard Award, Best Comic in Radio, 1948; Box Ofc. Blue Ribbon Award for perf. in Big City, 1948, and I'll See You In My Dreams, 1951; Mt. Sinai Heart of Gold Award, Mt. Sinai Men's Club, L.A. 1949; chosen Man of Yr., for charitable deeds (bldr. hosp. for destitute in South as shrine to St. Jude Thaddeus); Look Award for I'll See You In My Dreams, 1951. Maronite Rom. Catholic. Hobby: woodcraft, photog. Rec.: golf, tennis, basketball. Res.: Beverly Hills, CA.

THOMAS, DONALD KIRK, JR.
Manufacturing Company Executive
b. Dec. 7, 1927, Los Angeles; s. Donald Kirk and Leta (Nichols) Thomas; B.S., USC, 1950; m. Jane Moore, June 9, 1956, San Gabriel, Calif.; children: Linda, b. 1957; Pamela, b. 1959; Kirk, b. 1961. Career: Salesman, Mass. Mut. Life Ins. Co., Los Angeles, 1950-52; sales rep. IBM, Los Angeles and Long Beach, Calif., 1954-58; instr. customer exec. and sales tng. programs, San Jose, Calif., 1958-60; sr. product planning rep., Enidcott, N.Y., 1960-62; marketing rep., Los Angeles, 1962-65; treas., gen. mgr. Fibre Containers Co. Mfg. Div., Los Angeles, 1965-71, dir. 1967-71; pres. Southwest Partition Co., Inc., Los Angeles, 1972---. Chmn. bd. mgrs. South Pasadena-San Marino YMCA, 1976-77. Served with USNR, 1946, 52-54; Mem. Delta Tau Delta, Alpha Kappa Psi. Republican. Presbyterian. Clubs: Oneonta. Rec.: golf. Home: 1710 Laurel St., South Pasadena, CA 91030; Office: 2211 N. Hollywood Way, Burbank, CA 91505.

THOMAS, GEORGE J., III
Orthopaedic Surgeon
b. Jan. 22, 1942, Winston-Salem, N.C.; s. George J. Jr. and Thelma (Williams) Thomas; father Geo. J. Thomas Jr., M.D., urologist, civic leader, Louisiana; M.D., Howard, Univ., Wash., D.C. 1968; m. D.C. Fields, Aug. 21, 1965, New Orleans, La.; two daughters, two sons. Career: Internship, Wash. Hosp. Center, 1968-69; gen. surgery residency, VA Hosp., Martinez, Calif., 1969-70; Orthopaedic surgery residency, St. Mary's Hosp., S.F., 1970-73; pvt. practice of medicine, Granada Hills, 1975---. Pres., Geo J. Thomas III, M.D., Inc.; pres. and chmn. bd., T & S Mining Co.; pres., chmn. bd., Parker Wms. Mining & Invest. Co. Lt. Comdr., USNR, 1973-75; chief of orthopaedic surgery, US Naval Hosp., Port Hueneme. Recipient Francis Bundich Scholarship Award, 1967; Fellow, Am. Coll. of Surgeons, 1977; Fellow, Am. Acad. Orthopaedic Surgery, 1978; Diplomate Am. Bd. of Orthopaedic Surgery, 1975; certified CMA, AMA. Mem.: L.A. County and Nat. Med. Assns.; AMA; CMA; Charles Drew Med. Soc.; Golden State Med. Assn.; Nat. Assn. of Mil. Surgeons of U.S.; Bd. dir., San Fernando Red Cross; Shriner Temple No. 95; Prince Hall Mason 32°; Pi Lambda Phi; life mem. NAACP; Africare; Urban League. Republican. Hobbies: metaphysics, photog. Rec.: camping, swimming, sports. Home: Granada Hills, CA; Office: 10339 Balboa Blvd., Suite 307, Granada Hills, CA 91344.

THOMAS, GRACE FERN
Psychiatrist
b. Sept. 23, 1897, Gothenburg, Nebr.; d. George W. (Attorney) and Martha C. (Johnson) Thomas; B.S., Univ. Nebr., 1924; M.A. chem., Creighton Univ., 1926; M.D., USC Sch. of Med., 1935; M.A. Religion, USC, 1968; Internship, L.A. Co. Gen. Hosp., 1935-36; gen. rotating med. residency, Riverside Co. Hosp., 1936-37; residency in psychiatry, L.A. Co. Psychopathic Hosp., 1937-38; spec. training under Dr. J.P. Frostig of Vienna (Aus.) Clinic, Camarillo State Hosp., 1941-42; resident in Psychiatry, Colo. Psychopathic Hosp., 1943-44; staff psychiat. Inst. of Living, Hartford, Conn., 1944-45; Grad. Sch., Coll. of Physicians and Surgeons, Columbia Univ. 1952. Career: instr. chem., biology, Duchesne Coll., Nebr., 1925-27; clin. lab. tech., various hospitals, 1927-32; staff psychiat., Calif. State Hosp. System., 1938-43; pvt. practice, Long Beach, Calif. 1946-51; Capt., Med. Corps, AUS, 1945-46; chief, mental hygiene clin., VA Hosp., Albuquerque, N. Mex., 1951-54; psychiat. dir., Stark County Guidance Center, Canton, Ohio, 1955-58; and Huron Co. Guidance Center, Norwalk, Oh. 1958-62; dir., Arrowhead Mental Health Center, San Bernardino, 1962-64; dir., Mendocino Co. Mental Health Services, Ukiah, 1964-65; chief. profl. edn., Porterville State Hosp., 1965-66; dir. Tuolumne Co. Mental Health Services, Sonora, Calif. 1966-70; psychiat. cons. Emanuel Hosp. Mental Health Clin., Turlock, 1970---; psychiat. cons. Stanislaus Co. Mental Health Clin., Modesto, 1972-74; apptd. expert med. witness to Superior Cts. in Ohio, New Mex. and Calif.; lectr. to lay orgns. on psychiatric and religious subjects. Author: Collaborative Psychotherapy between Psychiatrists and Clergy in Problems of Guilt and Suffering, 1968. Mem.: Phi Beta Kappa, Sigma Xi, Univ. of Nebr. 1924; Phi Kappa Phi (in med.) 1935; pres. Nu Sigma Phi, USC, 1934; Soroptimist Internat. 1970---. United Methodist Ch.; ordained minister, 1963. Hobby: cats. Home: 2001 La Jolla Ct., Modesto, CA 95350; Office: 913 W. Roseburg Ave., Modesto, CA.

THOMAS, JAMES C., III
Land Developer — Business Executive
b. Oct. 12, 1927, Beaver Co., Pa.; s. James C., II and Mabel (Winegar) Thomas; ed. grad. H.S., Long Beach Poly. Jr. Coll. (2 yrs.); m. Maryann Peterson, Arcadia, Calif., Feb. 25, 1962; dau. Tambrey Anne, b. July 1, 1965. Career: Est. small mach. shop, Glendale, Calif. (developed 2000 employee bus.), Utility Metal Prods., Pasa. (sold in 1958); land developer, Desert Shores, Salton Sea, Marina, 1958-64; propr. Hollywood hotel, 1964-65; propr. Hollywood Knickerbocker Hotel, 1965-67. Feat. in Richfield Success Story, TV, 1957. Trustee, City of Hope, 1965---. Mem.: Masonic Lodge, 1950---; Overland Club, Pasa. 1958---; Hollywood C. of C. 1963; Kiwanis Club of Hollywood, 1965---. Presbyterian. Hobby: boating. Rec.: water skiing. Res.: 4311 Meadow View Place, Encino, CA 91316.

THOMAS, KAREN RUTH
Educator
b. Feb. 13, 1943, Denver, Colo.; d. William L. and Ruth S. Nygren; B.A., Univ. of No. Colorado, 1965; postgrad., Temple Buell, Denver; San Diego State Univ., 1970-72; m. Fred P. Thomas III, Sept. 4, 1971, Denver, Colo.; dau., Lisa Ruth, b. June 18, 1976. Career: Tchr.: Sch. dist. No. 1, Denver, Colo., 1965-70; Lemon Grove, Calif., 1970---; (shorthand, typing, Spanish, art, music, bookkeeping, bus. law); also Head Start, summer, 1965. Spec. interest, aiding low achievers and children with learning disabilities; work with bilingual children; music tchr. 1965-69, Denver, Colo. Recipient: 3 awards, Rocky Mountain Accordian contest; performer with accordian group, 1959=61; mem. Rocky Mountain Accordian Soc.; Mem.: Calif. Tchrs. Assn. (lifetime tchg. cred.); Lemon Grove, Calif. Tchrs. Assn.; Nat. Edn. Assn.; Colo. Edn. Assn.; Nat. Bus. Hon. Soc.; Alpha Phi; Univ. of No. Colo. Alumni Assn. Lutheran; youth group leader. Hobbies: music, art. Rec.: nature study, field trips. Home: 7870 Michelle Dr., La Mesa, CA 92041; Office: 7885 Golden Ave., Lemon Grove, CA 92045.

THOMAS, LOWELL
Author — Commentator
b. Apr. 6, 1892, Woodington, Darke Co., Oh.; s. Harry George, M.D. and Harriet (Wagner) Thomas; ed. B.Sc., Univ. of No. Ind., Valparaiso, Ind. 1911; B.A., M.A., Univ. of Denver, 1912; M.A.; Princeton Univ. 1916; LL.D., Albright Coll. 1934; Lafayette Coll. 1937, Wash. and Jefferson Coll. 1942; Litt.D., Grove City Coll., 1933, St. Bonaventure, 1938; Franklin and Marshall Coll. 1942. Rider Coll., N.J.

1948, Ohio Wesleyan, 1949; L.H.D., Clark Univ. 1941; Temple Univ. 1942; Boston Univ. 1943; Union Coll. 1944; Univ. of Tampa, 1949; D.L., Olivet Coll. 1950; m. Frances Ryan, Denver, Colo., Aug. 4, 1917 (div.); son: Lowell Jr., b. Oct. 6, 1923; m. 2d, Mary Ann Mudd, Jan. 1977. Career: Reporter-ed., Cripple Creek, Colo. and Chicago Journ.; prof. of oratory, Chicago Kent Coll of Law, 1912-14; instr. Dept. of Eng., Princeton Univ. 1914-16; discoverer of Lawrence of Arabia; historian, man's first flight around the world, 1924; radio news commentator, 1930---; voice of Fox Movietone News, 1934-49; prod. non-fiction feat.-length films; first TV news commentator, 1940; prod. Cinerama 1952-57; prod. High Adventure TV series, 1957-59; others. Apptd. by Pres. Eisenhower as spec. ambassador to Coronation of King of Nepal, 1958; Author: 46 vols. of biog., travel and adventure. Chief of Civ. Mission sent to Europe by Pres. Wilson to prepare hist. rec. of WW I; broadcaster to Amer., reports from London, Paris, Luxembourg, Rome, from a mobile truck behind the front lines; flew over Berlin Apr. 24, 1945, in a P51 Mustang and described final battle between Germans and Russians, WW II. Mem.: fellow, Amer. Geographical Soc.; Royal Geographical Soc.; (life) Amer. Mus. of Natural Hist.; (hon. life) Eng. Speaking Union; Kappa Sigma, Tau Kappa Alpha, Phi Delta Phi, Sigma Delta Chi, Alpha Epsilon, Mason; clubs: Princeton; (hon.) pres. Explorers; past v.p., Dutch Treat; past v.p. Overseas Press; Assn. of Radio & TV News Analysts; Adventurers; Pine Valley Golf, N.J.; St. Andrew's Golf, Scotland; pres. Marco Polo, NYC; past pres., Circus, Saints and Sinners; Bohemian. Protestant. Hobby: everything concerning the world of exploration. Rec.: skiing, golf. Res.: Bohemian Club, San Francisco, Calif.; Office: Radio Sta. KCBS, San Francisco, CA and Hammersley Hill, Pawling, N.Y.

THOMAS, WILLIAM F.
Newspaper Editor
b. June 11, 1924, Bay City, Mich.; s. William F. and Irene Marie (Billette) Thomas; B.S., Northwestern Univ., Evanston, Ill., 1950; M.S., 1951; m. Patricia Ann Wendland, Dec. 28, 1958; son: Michael William, Peter Matthew, Scott Anthony. Career: Asst. chief copy ed. Buffalo Eve. News, 1950-55; ed. Sierra Madre News, 1955-56; city ed. L.A. Mirror 1957-62, asst. city ed. L.A. Times Met. Editor, 1962-71, exec. editor, 1971, exec. v.p.-ed. 1972---. U.S. Army, 1943-46, WW II. Res.: 16025 Valley Wood Rd., Sherman Oaks, CA 91403; Office: Times Mirror Sq., Los Angeles, CA 90053.

THOMAS-ONDO, FLORENCE
Realtor — General Contractor
b. Aug. 22, 1923, Roxboro, No. Carolina; d. Patrick H. and Omega M. (Clayseat) Clay; cousin to Henry Clay, Ken. statesman; coll. accounting degree; real estate brokerage license, 1976; gen. bldg. contractors license, 1977; m. John A. Thomas (div.), 1959; m. 2d. Joseph Ondo, Sept. 15, 1977, So. Lake Tahoe, Calif.; stepchil.: Joseph; James; Jonathan; Joy (Macari). Career: cost acct., constrn. field, 1955---: worked in all areas of constrn.: tunnel constrn., earthmoving, engring., estimating; real estate agent, 1974---; real estate broker, Omega-West Realty, 1976---; gen. contracting, Ondo-Omega Constrn. Co., 1977---. Mem.: Sutter Buttes regional theatre, 1970---: acting, backstage; Northern Calif. Arts, Inc., 1968---; Soroptimist Internat. of Marysville-Yuba City, pres. 1975-76; past mem., Women in Constrn.; Bus. & Profl. Women. Democrat. Hobbies: oil painting, writing, drama. Rec.: swimming, gardening. Home: 6798 Sutter Ave., Sutter, CA 95982; Office: Omega-West Realty, 2168 Live Oak Blvd., Yuba City, CA 95991; Ondo-Omega Constr. Co., P.O.B. 28, Yuba City, CA 95991.

THOMPSON, JOAN E.V.
Savings and Loan Executive
b. Jan. 17, 1931, Los Angeles; d. Al and Elizabeth Jensen; student, L.A. City Coll.; Savings & Loan Inst.; m. William J. Thompson, Nov. 3, 1951 in Los Angeles; children: Vivian, b. 1953; Valrie, b. 1955; Vickie, b. 1959. Career: with State Savings and Loan Assn., Oakdale, 1949---: as teller, loan clk., opns. officer, asst. br. mgr., mgr., Vice-Pres., 1978---. Mem.: Beta Sigma Phi, pres.; Soroptimist Internat. of Oakdale, pres.; Oakdale Grange; Young Homemakers of Am., pres.; Oakdale C. of C. Hobbies: lead glass, sewing. Rec.: camping. Res.: 1137 S. Stearns Rd., Oakdale, CA 95361; Office: P.O.B. 397, Oakdale, CA 95361.

THOMPSON, PAUL FRANCIS
Library Director
b. Nov. 6, 1926, Mount Etna, Iowa; s. Forist and
Tessie (Florence) Vern; grad., Modesto Jr. Coll., 1947,
San Jose State Coll., 1958; m. Betty Jean Cover, Oct.
9, 1927, Modesto; children: JoAnn (Abbas), b. 1949;
Dennis Paul, b. 1953; Mark David, b. 1954; John
Wayne, b. 1956. Career: Library director, Turlock Pub.
Lib., 1957-68, Lompoc Pub. Lib., 1969---. AUS,
1945-46. Mem.: Turlock Lions Club, pres. 1968; pres.,
Black Gold Cooperative Lib. System. Hobby: fishing.
Rec.: chess, shuffleboard. Res.: 1412 W. Nectarine
Ave., Lompoc, CA 93436; Office: 501 E. North Ave.,
Lompoc, CA 93436.

THOMSON, JUNE ANNA MAE
College Administrator
b. Dec. 9, 1913, Nanking China; d. Rev. William Frederick
(dec.; prof. Univ. Nanking and USC) and Mildred Esther
(Stuart) Hummel (dec.); gr.dau., George Arthur Stuart,
M.D., pres., Univ. of Nanking, founder of Wu Hu Gen.
Hosp.; cous., Arthur Wm. Hummel, Jr., U.S. Ambassador
to Pakistan; sister, Comdr. Robt. Stuart Hummel, USN
(ret.), head U.S. civil defense; student, L.A. City Coll.,
1931-33; UCLA, 1933-34; USC, 1934-35; B. Garden Sc.
(hon.) Cal. Poly. State Univ., 1961; certificate in
Techniques of Teaching, Univ. of Calif. voc. edn. div.; Cal.
State dept. edn. indsl. edn. bureau, 1976; m. John Ansel
Armstrong Thomson (originator, vitamins and
horticulture hormones) June 24, 1938, Los Angeles; chil.:
Sheryl Linn (Clark), b. Feb. 8, 1940; Patricia Diane,
b. Jan. 12, 1943; Robert Royce, b. June 18, 1946;
Career: Placement asst., 1964; placement interviewer,
1966; placement dir., 1966; placement coordinator, Los
Angeles Pierce Coll., 1977---; vice-chmn. U.S. Civil Service
Commn's. Mid-Coast Govt. Coll. Assn. 1975---. Secty.,
Calif. State Employment Dept., S.F. Valley, 1973; chmn.:
In-serv. training conf. and placement workshop, L.A.
Community Colls. 1974; Career Day, L.A. Pierce Coll.
1968-72; co.chmn. 1973-76; co-chmn. Career Week 1977;
mem. com., Employment of Handicapped, L.A. Co. 1972;
25 positions in PTA councils; bd. mem. China Soc. of So.
Calif. 1971-77; mem. advis. com. ADEPT (aid to disabled
with employment, placement, training), 1974---; Girl
Scout and Cub Scout leader; vol.: Travelers Aid, United
Way, ARC; Mem.: Coll. Placement Assn.; UCLA Alumni
Assn.; L.A. World Affairs Council; So. Calif. Horticultural
Assn.; Am. Nutrition Soc.; Friends of the Earth; Nat.
Health Fedn.; Sierra Club; L.A. Co. Mus. of Art;
Mid-Valley Coordinating Council, 1974-75; Costeau Soc.
Republican. United Methodist; Wesley Fellowship pres.;
Sun. Sch. tchr., chmn. Commn. on Missions. Awards:
Outstanding service, Calif. Comm. Coll. Placement Assn.
1970; Service Appreciation Award, L.A. Pierce Coll.,
1968; Calif. Merit Award for civic service, 1948. Rec.:
bridge, tennis, travel, horticulture. Office: L.A. Pierce
Coll., 6201 Winnetka Ave., Woodland Hills, CA 91317.

THOMSON, JOHN ANSEL ARMSTRONG
Manufacturing Chemist — Nutritionist
b. Nov. 23, 1911, Detroit, Mich.; s. John Russell and
Florence (Antisdel) Thomson; student, UCLA, 1934-35;
A.A., Pasadena, Jr. Coll., 1935; A.B. cum laude, USC,
1957; B. Garden Sc. (hon.) Cal. Poly. State Univ., San
Luis Obispo, 1961; m. June Anna Mae Hummel, 1938,
Los Angeles; chil.: Sheryl Linn (Clark), b. Feb. 8, 1940;
Patricia Diane, b. Jan. 12, 1943; Robert Royce, b. Jan.
18, 1946. Career: founder, pres., Vitamin Institute (J.A.
Thomson Bio-organic Chemists 1930-39) 1930---; mfg.,
research & devel.; cons., lectr. writer in biochemistry,
nutrition, sociology; agri. hormones specialty. Originator
over 100 chemical products, over 30 trademarks; incl.
Superthrive, Cutstart, Seedyield, agri. vitamins-hormones
(all 3 classified by govt. for nat. defense, WW II); Aquasol
(1940) and Auzon crystals (1950), vitamin products for
humans. Awards: Sci. and Indus. Gold Medal, S.F. World
Fair 1940; BSA Awards, 1959, 1960, 1964; Calif. State
Seal of Merit, 1948; Ben Franklin essay award, DAR,
1931; essay award, L.A. C. of C., 1934. Youth leader,
active in BSA, PTA, YMCA; Olympic Games Coms.; ARC;
Mem.: Soc. for Nutrition Edn.; Am. Inst. Biological Sci.;
AAAS; Internat. Soc. Horticultural Sci.; Am.
Horticultural Soc.; Nat. Rec. and Park Assn.; Am.
Forestry Assn.; Western Gerontological Assn.; Nat.
Nutritional Foods Assn.; Soc. of Am. Florists,
Ornamental Horticulturists; Am. Assn. of Nurserymen;
Nat. Landscape Assn.; Nat. Health Fedn.; Am. Nutrition
Soc.; Am. Physical Fitness Research Inst.; Calif. Assn. of
Nurserymen; Calif. Landscape Suppliers Assn.; Calif.
Florists Assn.; No., So. Calif. Turfgrass Councils; Am.
Chem. Soc.; Cancer Control Soc.; Huxley Inst. Biosocial
Research. Clubs: L.A. World Affairs Council; Sierra Club;
Soc. Colonial Wars; USC and UCLA Alumni Assn.; Men's

Garden Club, No. Hollywood; Republican; State Central
Com. 1948-50. Methodist; mem. and evangelism commn.
1973-75. Rec.: swimming, tennis. Office: P.O.B. 230,
5411 Satsuma Ave., No. Hollywood, CA 91605.

THOMSON, PAUL HARRIS
Horticulturist — Editor
b. June 29, 1916, Landour-Mussoorie, United Provinces,
India; s. Clinton Harris and Bertha Evelyn (Mangon)
Thomson; ed. Bethany High Sch., Lincoln, Nebr., m.
Helen Adelaide Benleher, Oct. 11, 1941, Yuma, Ariz.
Career: Chicago Burlington and Quincy R.R. (helped
install 1st signal control system 125 mi. Akron-Denver,
1937); horticultural work as nurseryman, plant
propagator, 1958-78; co-founder (w/John M. Riley)
California Rare Fruit Growers, 1968, exec. dir. 1973---,
editor, its newsletter, 1968---; written definitive articles
on rare fruits and nuts; author and publisher (Bonsall
Publs.) Jojoba Handbook. Dir. Calif. Macadamia Soc.
1960-68; dir. No. Am. Fruit Explorers 1975-78. Mil.
Nebr. Nat. Guard, 1934-37; served as 1st Lt., USMC
1938-58. Mem.: Avocado Soc.; No. Nut Growers Assn.
(contbr. on macadamia and jojoba for nut tree manual);
Southern Fruit Council; Palomar Cactus and Succulent
Soc.; Western Australia Nutgrowing Soc. Christian Ch.,
choir dir., 1939-78. Hobby: research on the genus
Dudleya. Rec.: growing, collecting rare plants. Address:
Star Route, Box P, Bonsall, CA 92003.

THOR, ERIC P., JR.
Research Director
b. Feb. 11, 1947, Lincoln, Nebr.; B.S., Univ. of Calif.,
Berkeley, M.S., Ph.D.; m. Janet Wertsch. Career:
Treas., International Resources Assn., 1973; pres.,
chmn. bd., 1973---; dir. of Agri-Bus. MBA Program,
Golden Gate Univ., 1977---; head, Calif. Energy
Research, Bank of Am., 1978---. Res.: 22 Marinero
Cir., No. 50, Tiburon, CA 94920; Office: Bank of
America, 555 California St., San Francisco, CA 94137.

THORPE, JAMES
Director, Huntington Library-Art Gallery
b. Aug. 17, 1915, Aiken, S.C.; s. J. Ernest and Ruby
H. Thorpe; A.B., The Citadel, 1936; M.A., Univ. of
N.C. 1937; Ph.D., Harvard Univ. 1941; Litt.D.,
Occidental Coll. 1968; L.H.D., Claremont Grad. Sch.
1968; Litt.D., The Citadel, 1971; doctor of
Humanities, Univ. of Toledo, 1977; m. Elizabeth
Daniells, Toledo, Oh., July 19, 1941; chil.: James, III,
b. Sept. 10, 1942; John D., b. Oct. 11, 1944; Sarah
M., b. Apr. 20, 1947. Career: Prof. of English,
Princeton Univ. 1946-66, Master, Grad. Coll. 1948-55;
dir. Henry E. Huntington Library and Art Gallery,
1966. Author: (pibl) 6 books and various articles of
literary scholarship. Col. USAF (1941-46), WW II.
Mem.: Fellow, Amer. Acad. of Arts and Scis.; Fellow,
Amer. Antiquarian Soc.; Fellow, Claremont Center;
Grolier Club, Zamorano Club, Twilight Club.
Democrat. Episcopalian. Hobby: horticulture. Res.:
1650 Orlando Rd., San Marino, CA 91108; Office:
Huntington Library and Art Gallery, San Marino, CA
91108.

THORNE, KIP STEPHEN
Physicist — Educator
b. June 1, 1940, Logan, Utah; s. Prof. David Wynne
and Dr. Alison (Comish) Thorne; B.S. in Physics, Calif.
Inst. Tech., 1962; A.M. in Physics (Woodrow Wilson
fellow 1962-63, Danforth Found. fellow 1962-63),
Princeton, 1963, Ph.D., in Physics (Danforth Found.
Fellow 1963-65, NSF Fellow, 1964-65); 1965,
postgrad. (NSF Postdoctoral fellow), 1965-66; m.
Linda Jeanne Peterson, Sept. 12, 1960 (div. 1977);
children: Kares Anne, Bret Carter. Career: Research
fellow Calif. Inst. Tech., 1966-67; assoc. prof.
theoretical physics, 1967-70; prof., 1970---. Fulbright
lectr., France, 1966; vis. assoc. prof. Univ. Chicago,
1968; vis. prof. Moscow Univ., 1969, 75, 78; visiting
sr. research assoc., Cornell Univ. 1977; adj. prof. Univ.
Utah, 1971---. Alfred P. Sloan Found. Research fellow,
1966-68; John Simon Guggenheim fellow, 1967;
recipient Sci. Writing award in physics and astronomy
Am. Inst. Physics-U.S. Steel Found., 1969. Mem. Nat.
Acad. Scis., Am. Acad. Arts and Scis.; Am. Astron.
Soc.; Am. Phys. Soc., Internat. Astron. Union, AAAS,
Internat. Com. on Gen. Relativity and Gravitation,
Committee on US-USSR Cooperation in Physics, Sigma
Xi, Tau Beta Pi. Co-author: Gravitation Theory and
Gravitational Collapse, 1965; Gravitation, 1973.
Research in gravitation theory, relativistic astrophysics,
cosmology. Office: 130-33 Calif. Inst. Tech., Pasadena,
CA 91125.

THORNTON, CHARLES BATES
  Chief Executive Officer, Litton Industries
b. July 22, 1913, Knox Co., Tex.; s. Word Augusta and Sara Alice (Bates) Thornton; ed. Columbus Univ., Wash., D.C.; B.S., George Wash. Univ. 1937; (hon.) LL.D., Tex. Tech. Coll. 1957; D.Sc., Geo Washington Univ., 1964; LL.D., USC, Pepperdine Univ. 1971; m. Flora Laney, Wash., D.C., Apr. 10, 1937; chil.: Charles Bates, Jr., b. May 8, 1942; William Laney, b. Mar. 26, 1945. Career: Dir. of Planning, Ford Motor Co. 1946-48; cons. to Under Secty of State, 1947; v.p. Hughes Tool Co. and v.p.-asst. gen. m,r., Hughes Aircraft Co. 1948-53; chmn. bd.-pres., Litton Industries, Inc. 1953-61; chmn. bd.-chief exec. ofcr. 1961---; bd. dirs. United Calif. Bank, 1959---; bd. dirs., Station KTTV, L.A. 1959-63; dir.-exec. com., First Western Bank Corp. 1960---; dir. Western Bancorp; dir. Union Oil. Co. 1962072; Dir.: Hollywood Turf Club; L.A. World Affairs Council; natl. dir. Jr. Achievement, Inc.; gen. chmn. United Crusade Campaign, 1976; Cyprus Mines Corp.; MCA, Inc.; Harvard Sch. Council; Trans World Airlines. Colonel, Consultant to Commanding General, USAAF (1946), WW II. Awards: decorated, Distinguished Serv. Medal, Leg. of Merit, Commendation with two Oak Leaf Clusters; Salesman of the Yr. Award by Sales Execs. Club of L.A. 1959; Man of Yr., Beverly Hills C. of C., 1964; Horatio Alger Award, Amer. Schs. and Colls. Assn. 1964; Calif. Industrialist of Yr. 1964, 66; USC Bus. Mgmt. Award, 1967; Community Leadership Award, United Way, 1976; many others. Mem.: Bd. dirs., Southern Calif. Ind.-Edn. Council; founds. com. L.A. branch, Amer. Cancer Soc.; bd. dirs., L.A. C. of C. 1956-61; chmn. electronics industry com.; trustee, Natl. Security Ind. Assn.; adv. bd., 13th Internat. Mgmt. Conf.; bd. dirs., All-Yr. Club of So. Calif. 1958---; bd. dirs., Merchants & Mfrs. Assn., L.A. 1958---; bd. govs., Welfare Fed. of L.A. 1958---; Planning Council, Gen. Mgmt. Div., Amer. Mgmt. Assn. 1958---; bd. dirs., YMCA, L.A. 1960---; bd. dirs., Electronic Inds. Assn., pres. adv. council, 1960---; founding friends, Harvey Mudd Coll., Claremont, Calif. 1960---; dir. Sci. and Engring. Dept. 1963---; def. ind. adv. council, Dept. of Def. 1962---; bd. trustees, USC 1963---; Calif. Inst. Assocs. 1963---; finance com.-dir., So. Calif. Sym. Assn.; L.A. Country Club, California Club; Army-Navy Country Club, Wash., D.C.; The Beach Club Santa Monica; Bel-Air Country Club, Sigma Alpha Epsilon, One Hundred Club, L.A. Res.: 320 Carolwood Dr., Los Angeles, CA 90024; Royal Oaks Farm, Hidden Valley, CA; Office: 360 N. Crescent Dr., Beverly Hills, CA 90213.

TIBBITTS, SAMUEL JOHN
  Hospital Administrator
b. Oct. 7, 1924, Chicago, Ill.; s. Samuel J. and Marion (Swanson) Tibbitts; B.S., UCLA, 1949; M.S., Univ. of Calif., Berkeley, 1950; m. Audrey Slottelid, Pasadena, Calif., Aug. 28, 1949; chil.: Scott, b. Sept. 26, 1953; Brett, b. June 29, 1955. Career: Adm. res., Calif. Hosp., L.A. 1950-51; adm. asst. 1951-52, asst. supt. 1954-59, admr. 1959-66; asst. supt., Santa Monica Hosp. 1952-54; pres. Comm. on Adm. Servs. in Hosps. 1964; pres. Luth. Hosp. Soc., So. Calif. 1966---; dir. Martin Luther Hosp., Inc.; dir. Calif. Pediatric Center. Med. Corps, U.S. Army, 1946-47. Awards: Ritz E. Heerman Award, 1960. Mem.: fellow, Amer. Coll. of Hosp. Admrs.; chmn., bd. of trustees, American Hospital Assn., 1978; pres. Hosp. Council of Calif. 1961-62; bd. dirs., Hosp. Council of So. Calif.; dir. Calif. Hosp. Assn.; dir. Amer. Hosp. Assn.; dir. Amer. Prot. Hosp. Assn.; dir. San Diego Hosp. Assn.; dir. San Diego Hosp. Assn.; Delta Omega. Res.: 1224 Adair, San Marino, CA; Office: 1423 S. Grand Ave., Los Angeles, CA 90015.

TILDEN, JOHN(Jno.) LESLIE
  Former Boy Scout Executive
b. June 19, 1897, nr. Beattie, Kan. (on Oregon Trail route); s. William Lincoln and Lisetta (Debo) Tilden-Lipke; gr. grandson, John Phillips Tilden, mgr. of Daniel Webster's horse farm; desc. Nathaniel Tilden, mayor, Tenterden, Eng., Mayflower financier; gr. nephew, Samuel J. Tilden, N.Y. Gov., presidential candidate vs. Rutherford B. Hayes; student Jr. Coll., St. Joseph, Mo. 1916-17; hon. degree, social work, S.F. State Coll., 1944; m. Marie Stratton Arnold, June 16, 1919, Sedalia, Mo.; chil.: John Leslie, Jr., b. Sept. 16, 1920; William Frederick, b. Oct. 7, 1922. Career: credit mgr., Robinson Heavy Hdw. Co., St. Joseph, Mo.; tchr. Social Work, Univ. Minn. extension; asst. bus. mgr., Lowrie Paving Co., S.F.; salesman trainer, Equitable of Iowa Life Ins. Co.; tchr. night class in Bus. Mgmt., Heald Bus. Coll., S.F.; profl. Boy Scout Exec., 1917-62: joined 1st BSA troop in St. Joseph, director, 1st Scout Camp in No. Mo., transferred

to Sedalia, Mo., 1917, (dir. YMCA and head 6 Scout Troops); attended 1st Nat. Exec. Training Program, 1919; dir., Wichita, Kan. Council, organized 14 counties in area, 1923, devel. new branch, Lone Scouts; formed 1st Air Scout Troop (w/Council pres. Sessna, of small airplane fame), presented hon. mem. to Adm. Byrd; Scout Exec., Minneapolis, Minn., 1932, helped devel. Nat. U.S. Cub Scout Program; apptd. chmn. Rural Scout Commn.; exec., S.F. Council, 1938; pres., Council Social Agencies under Community Chest; apptd. by Mayor Rossi to Civilian Defense Bd.; apptd. to Staff for U.N. created by Alger Hiss, 1945; estab. Crippled Children Scout Troops, S.F.; retired in 1962 with 10,000 scouts, 3400 leaders in San Francisco. Mil. Enlisted Signal Corps, 1918-19. Mem.: Masonic Lodges, Scottish Rite; Am. Legion; Rotary; C. of C.; Commonwealth Club; Olympic Club. Lakeside Presbyterian Ch.; founding com., elder. Hobbies: photog., stamp collecting, bonsai, model R.R. Rec.: golf, bowling, camping. Home: 85 Vasquez Ave., S.F., CA 94127.

TILLER, WILLIAM ARTHUR
  University Professor
b. Sept. 18, 1929, Toronto, Canada; s. Arthur and Vera Emma (Pash) Tiller; B.A.Sc., Engring. Physics, Univ. Toronto, 1952, M.A.Sc., Ph.D., Physical Metallurgy, 1955; m. Jean Elizabeth Ackroyd, June 28, 1952, Toronto; children: Andrea Jean, b. Nov. 19, 1957; Jeffrey Earl James, b. July 1, 1960. Career: Advisory physicist, mgr., Westinghouse Elect. Co. Research Lab., Pittsburgh, Pa., 1955-64; Prof., Dept. of Materials Sci. & Engring., (Dept. chmn. 1966-71), Stanford Univ., 1964---. Guggenheim Fellowship, 1970-71. Co-author two books; pub. over 135 sci. articles. Office: Dept. of Mats. Sci. & Engring., Stanford University, Stanford, CA 94305.

TILTON, DAVID LLOYD
  Chairman, Financial Corporation of Santa Barbara
b. Sept. 21, 1926, Santa Barbara; s. Lloyd Irvine and Grace (Hart) Tilton; B.A., Social Sci., Stanford Univ., 1949, M.B.A. Stanford Grad. Sch. of Bus., 1951; m. Mary Caroline Knudtson, June 6, 1953, Minneapolis; children: Peter, b. 1954; Jennifer, b. 1956; Michael, b. 1958; Catharine, b. 1960. Career: With Santa Barbara Savings and Loan Assn., 1951---: apptd. exec. v.p., 1959, pres., dir. 1965, chmn. bd., 1973; also chmn. of bd., pres., dir. Financial Corp. of Santa Barbara (parent co. S.B. Savings and Loan Assn.), 1973---. Dir. Collins Foods Internat. Inc. Pres., The Cancer Found. of Santa Barbara, 1976-78; bd. dir., Calif. Savings and Loan League, 1964-66, 1977-78. USNR, WW II. Mem. Delta Chi. Rec.: tennis, fishing, hunting. Res.: 630 Oak Grove Dr., Santa Barbara, CA 93108; Office: 1035 State St., Santa Barbara, CA 93102.

TOBERMAN, CHARLES EDWARD
  Real Estate and Investments Executive
b. Feb. 23, 1880, Seymour, Tex.; s. Philip and Lucy Ann (Blackburn) Toberman; ed. Tex. A&M Coll.; Met. Bus. Coll., Dallas, Tex.; m. Josephine Bullock, Wichita Falls, Tex., Apr. 25, 1902 (dec. Mar. 3, 1970); chil.: Homer M., Jeannette (Fletcher), Catherine (Torrence). Career: est. own real estate ofc. May 4, 1907, inc. Apr. 24, 1912; pres.-dir., C.E. Toberman Co. 1912---; erected and promoted many bldgs., incl.: Grauman's Egyptian Theatre, 1922; Grauman's Chinese Theatre, Hollywood Roosevelt Hotel, Hollywood Masonic Temple, 1926; pres.-chmn. bd.: Fed. Trust & Savings Bank, 1922; First Fed. Savings & Loan Assn of Hollywood, 1934; chmn. bd.: Hollywood Paper Box Co. 1926; Black-Foxe Mil. Inst. 1932; secty.-treas.-dir., Home & Commercial Bldrs., Inc. 1939; secty.-dir. Hollywood Bd. of Trade. Awards: Hon. Mr. Hollywood by Hollywood C. of C. 1971. Mem.: pres.-dir., Hollywood Bus. Men's Club; Hollywood and L.A. C.s of C.; (charter) Hollywood Bowl Assn. and Pilgrimage Play Found., dir.-pres. 1933-51, pres. emeritus, 1952---; bd. dirs., Who's Who Hist. Soc. of L.A. Co., Inc. 1951---; (hon.) bd. dirs., Who's Who in L.A. Co. 1952---; Hollywood Round Table, L.A. Realty Bd., Hollywood YMCA, Greater Hollywood Taxpayers Assn., Calif. Real Estate Assn., Natl. Assn. of Real Estate Bds.; v.p.-dir., Hollywood Blvd. Assn., So. Calif. Golf Assn., Masonic Lodge, Al Malaikah Temple; Hollywood Chpt. No. 120, RAM of Calif; Hollywood Lodge No. 355, F&AM; L.A. Consistory 32° Lodge of Perfection, Scottish Rite of Freemasonry; Knights of Templar Past Comdrs. Assn. of So. Calif.; Past Masters Assn 233, Masonic Temple Assn.; clubs: Hollywood Soc., Hollywood and L.A. Ath. (pres.-dir.) Lakeside Golf, The Masquers, (v.p.-dir.) Wilshire Country and L.A. Breakfast, Hollywood Shrine and Masonic Clubs. Republican. Episcopalian. Rec.: golf. Res.: 7150 La Presa Dr.,

Hollywood, CA; Office: Suite 201, 1717 N. Highland Ave., Hollywood, Calif. 90028.

TOBIAS, HARRY
  Music Publisher — Song Writer
b. Sept. 11, 1895, NYC; s. Max and Minnie (Kursch) Tobias; cousin, Ida and Eddie Cantor; ed. grammar sch., Worcester, Mass. 1910; m. Sophie Diamond, Jacksonville, Fla., Dec. 23, 1923; chil.: Mrs. Phil (Lucille) Rock, b. Jan. 24, 1935 (granddau. Evelyn Gale Rock, b. June 12, 1954; grandson, Jerry Alan, b. Oct. 9, 1956). Career: Clerk, dept. stores, Worcester, Mass.; first song, National Sport, publ. 1911; est. Hollywood, Calif. res. 1929---; composer, many songs, incl.: At Your Command (written for Bing Crosby), Ernest Are You Earnest With Me, Sweet and Lovely, No Regret, Daughter of Peggy O'Neill, Sail Along Silv'ry Moon, I Remember Mama, In God We Trust, With a Prayer in Your Heart (and a Bible in Your Hand), Moonlight Brings Memories, The Light of the World, Ashes of Roses, There's Only One Love in a Lifetime, Wedding of the Birds, Star of Hope, On the Sunny Side of the Rockies, I'm Sorry Dear, Los and Found, Go to Sleep Little Baby, I'll Have the Last Waltz with Mother, I'll Keep the Lovelight Burning, Pet Your Little Arms Around Me, Moon on My Pillow, Miss You, It's a Lonesome Old Town, Wait for Me Mary, Wild Honey, The Bowling Song (with bros.; off. theme song of Bowling Down Cancer Dr. 1962); Brother (with bro.; adopted by Natl Conf. of Chrs. and Jews, Inter-Faith Movement and B'nai B'rith A.D.L.), others. Sgt., US Army, Camp Joseph E. Johnson, Jacksonville, Fla. (1917-19), WW I. Mem.: ASCAP 1922---; Amer. Leg. Post 43; Jewish War Vets. Post 603; B'nai B'rith Fairfax Lodge; Natl. Conference of Christians and Jews; Valley Jewish Community Center; Friars Club of California. Hobby: baseball, ping-pong, golf. Rec.: swimming. Res. and Studio: 4129 Greenbush Ave., Sherman Oaks, CA.

TOBRINER, MATHEW O.
  Justice, California Supreme Court
b. Apr. 2, 1904, San Francisco, Calif.; s. Oscar and Maud (Lezin /) Tobriner; A.B. (magna cum laude), Stanford Uni . 1924; M.A., 1925; LL.B., Harvard Univ. 1927; S.J.D., Univ. of Calif. 1932; m. Rosabelle Rose, San Francisco, Calif., May 19, 1939; sons: Michael Charles, b. Sept. 23, 1940; Stephen Oscar, b. July 17, 1944. Career: admitted to Calif. bar, 1928, U.S. Supreme Ct. bar, 1941; assoc. David Livingston and Lawrence Livingston, 1928-30; assoc. late Judge Milton D. Sapiro, 1930-32; chief atty., Solicitor's Ofc., U.S. Dept. of Agr. 1932-34; pvt. practice law, Tobriner, Lazarus, Brundage and Neyhart firm (repr. labor unions, coop marketing assns., corps. and gen. practice), 1934-59; apptd. Justice, Dist. Ct. of Appeal, 1st Appellate Dist., Div. 1, S.F., Mar. 30, 1959-62; assoc. justice, Calif. Supreme Ct. 1962---; mem. Judicial Council, 1964-66. Assoc. prof. of law, Hastings Law Sch. 1959. Author: Principles and Practices of Cooperative Marketing (with E.G. Mears), 1926; contrib. articles to legal publs. Seaman first class, Volunteer Port Security Force, U.S. Coast Guard (1943-45), WW II. Mem.: v-chmn., S.F. Legal Aid Soc.; bd. dirs., S.F. Bar Assn.; Lawyers Club of S.F., co-founder, 2nd pres.; Barristers' Club; co-chmn. Com. NLR Act.-Sect. Labor Rels. Law, Amer. Bar Assn.; Calif. State Bar, Com. Adm. Agcys. 1955; Order of Coif, Phi Beta Kappa, Delta Sigma Rho. Democrat (v-chmn. Dem. Campaign Com. 1948; exec. com., Gubernatorial Campaign, 1954). Hobby: painting (watercolors). Res.: 3494 Jackson St., San Francisco, CA; Office: State Bldg., San Francisco, CA.

TODD, MALCOLM CLIFFORD
  Surgeon
b. Apr. 10, 1913, Carlyle, Ill.; s. Malcolm Newton and Grace (Heitmeier) Todd; desc. Mary Todd Lincoln; A.B., Univ. Ill., 1934; M.B., Northwestern Univ., 1934; M.D., 1938; student, Balliol Coll., Oxford, 1945; Hon. Ph.D., Brown Univ., 1975; m. Ruth Schlake, June 12, 1945, London, England; son, Malcolm Douglas, b. Dec. 1, 1951. Career: Internship, St. Luke's Presbyterian Hosp., Chicago, Resident in Surgery, Cook Co. Hosp., 1938-41. Acad. Appts.: Clin. Instr. Surgery, Northwestern Univ. 1939-41, Instr. Cook Co. Grad. Sch. of Med. out-patient Dept. 1938-41; Assoc. Clin. Prof. of Surg., Univ. Calif., 1962-67, Clin. Prof. of Surgery, UC Irvine, 1967---; vis. lectr. numerous univ. med. schs. Hosp. appts.: Sr. Surgeon, Long Beach Mem. Hosp. Med. Center; St. Mary's Med. Center, Long Beach Community Hosp.; Cons. staff: Los Altos, Long Beach VA Hosp., LAC-USC Med. Center. Advisory cons. panel mem. on Manpower, HEW; cons.,

Advanced Health Systems, Inc., USPHS, Korn-Ferry Co., Long Beach Sch. Dist. Mem. Nat. Commn. on Cost of Health Care, 1978. Edit. Bd. med. journs.; contbr. over 125 sci. & socioecon. articles profl. journs. 129th pres., AMA: vis. 50 states and 57 med. schs., chmn. del. to Peoples Repub. of China; apptd. by Pres. Ford to Pres. Com. on Refugees and Econ. Cost Control panel, 1975; apptd. by Pres. Nixon del. to World Health Orgn., 1970, 71, 72. Past pres., Calif. Med. Assn., Internat. Coll. of Surgeons; pres., Karl Myers Surgical Soc. of Chicago; fellow, Assn. for Advancement of Med. Instrumentation. Dir.: Long Beach C. of C., ARC, Community Chest. Maj., AUS, 1942-46, Chief Surg. svcs. Gen. Hosps. ETO. Mem.: Pi Kappa Alpha, pres. 1933; Alpha Kappa Kappa, pres. 1937; Pi Kappa Epsilon, Pi Kappa Alpha, v.p. & sup. council, 1978-80. Republican. Lutheran. Hobbies: photog., golf. Res.: 5330 El Parquest, Long Beach, CA 90815; Office: 2840 Long Beach Blvd., Long Beach, CA 90806.

TOFF, HOWARD DAVID
  Psychiatrist
b. July 21, 1947, Philadelphia; s. Fred and Evelyn Toff; B.S., Pa. State Univ., 1968; M.D., Jefferson Med. Coll., 1970; m. Carol Saturansky, Ph.D., July 4, 1976, Brooklyn, N.Y.; son, Stephen Andrew, b. June 27, 1978. Career: Intern, San Francisco Gen. Hosp., 1970-71; resident, Cedars Sinai Med. Center, 1973-76; Fellow, Family & Child Psychiatry, Cedars Sinai Med. Center, 1975-77; staff psychiat., Ross Loos Med. Group, 1977-78; adminstrv. psychiatrist, Cedars Sinai Med. Center, 1978---. Med. Officer, USPHS, 1971-73. Office: 8631 West Third St., Los Angeles, CA 90048.

TOLIVER, RAYMOND FREDERICK
  Aviator — Author
b. Nov. 16, 1914, Fort Collins, Colo.; s. Francis LeRoy and Hattie Lorena (Lowe) Toliver; student, Colo. State Univ., 1933-37, Air Command & Staff Coll., 1948, Air War Coll., 1951; m. Jennie Sue Miller, Apr. 28, 1935, Longmont, Colo.; children: Suzanne Toliver (Kemp), b. 1936; Nancy Rae (Belknap), b. 1938; Janet Mary (Moskal), b. 1941. Career: Flying Cadet, Randolph & Kelly Fields, Texas, 1937-38; commd. 2nd Lt., active duty 1938-40; pilot, TWA Airline, 1940-41; RAF Ferry Command, 1941-42; serve: to Col., USAF, 1942-65, Comdr. 20th USAF Tactical Fighter Wing, England, 1956-59; with Lockheed Aircraft Corp., 1965-74. Author: Fighter Aces, 1965; Horrido!, 1968; Blond Knight of Germany, 1970; Fighter Aces of the Luftwaffe, 1977; The Interrogator, 1978; Fighter Aces of USA, 1979. Mem.: Am. Fighter Aces Assn., Permanent Historian; Soc. of Exptl. Test Pilots; Quiet Birdmen. Protestant. Rec.: skiing. Res.: 5286 Lindley Ave., Encino, CA 91316.

TOLL, MAYNARD JOY
  Attorney at Law
b. Sept. 11, 1906, Los Angeles, Calif.; s. Charles H. and Eleanor Margaret (Joy) Toll; A.B., Univ. Calif., Berkeley, 1927; LL.B., Harvard Law Sch. 1930; m. Ethel Coleman, Los Angeles, Calif., Aug. 16, 1929; chil.: Arline Joy Kensinger, b. Nov. 1, 1941; Deborah Ann Reynolds, b. Mar. 24, 1934; Janet Suzanne Davidson, b. July 25, 1939; Maynard Joy, Jr., b. Feb. 5, 1942; Roger Coleman, b. Feb. 20, 1945. Career: Assoc. O'Melveny & Myers law firm, 1930-40, partner, 1940---. Dir.: bd. Automobile Club of So. Calif.; Cyprus Mines Corp.; Russell Reynolds Assoc., Inc.; Earle M. Jorgensen Co.; Western Fed. Savings & Loan Assn.; Council on Legal Edn. for Professional Responsibility; pres. Amer. Bar Found. Mem.: chmn.-bd. Amer. Judicature Soc. 1972-74; Natl. Legal Aid and Defender Assn., pres. 1966-70; tax sect.; Amer. Bar Assn.; pres. L.A. Co. Bar Assn. 1963; past pres. Town Hall; trustee: Hosp. of Good Samaritan; Haynes Found.; Fellow: Amer. Coll. of Probate Counsel; Hollywood Turf Club Assoc. Charities, Inc.; Salt Air Club, Calif. Club, L.A. Club. Res.: 414 S. Irving Blvd., Los Angeles, CA 90020; Office: 611 W. Sixth St., Los Angeles, CA 90017.

TOLLENAERE, LAWRENCE R.
  Corporate President
b. Nov. 19, 1922, Berwyn, Ill.; s. Cyrille and Modesta (Van Damme) Tollenaere; B.A. (engring.), Ia. State Univ. 1944, M.A. 1949; M.B.A., USC 1969; Doctor of Laws, (hon.) Claremont University, June 1977; m. Mary Elizabeth Hansen, Los Angeles, Calif., Aug. 14, 1948; chil.: Elizabeth, b. Jan. 24, 1951; Homer, b. June 1, 1952; Stephanie, b. Oct. 16, 1953; Caswell, b.

June 24, 1956; Jennifer Mary, b. Feb. 21, 1964. Career: spec. engr. Aluminum Co. of Amer., Huntington Park, Calif. 1946-47; asst. prof. (ind. engring.) Ia. State Univ., Ames, 1947-50; sales rep. Amer. Pipe and Constr. Co., South Gate, Calif. 1950-53, spec. rep. So. Amer., 1953-54, 2nd v.p.-div. mgr. Colombian div., Bogota, Colombia, 1955-57, div. mgr.-v.p. So. Calif. 1957-63, div. Concrete Pipe Operations, Monterey Park, Calif. 1963-65, pres. Corp. Hdqrs. 1965-67, pres. and chief exec. ofcr., 1967--- (corp. name changed to AMERON, 1969). Dir.: Amer. Pipe and Constr. Co. to 1969; AMERON, 1969---; Avery Prods. Corp., San Marino; Newhall Land and Farming Co., Valencia; bd. Gifford-Hill-American, Inc., Dallas.; Bd. Norris Industries, Long Beach; bd. Pacific Mutual Life Insurance Co., Newport Beach. Ensign to Lt. (j.g.), USNR 1944-46, WW II. Mem.: bd. Fellows, bd. trustees, Claremont Univ. Center; chmn. bd. trustees, Claremont Univ. Center; chmn. bd. trustees, Claremont Grad. Sch.; chmn. bd. overseers, Henry E. Huntington Lib. and Art Galleries, Pasa.; bd. govs. Ia. State Univ. Found.; bd. dirs.-exec. com. Merchants & mfrs. Assn. L.A.; Fellow, Soc. for Advancement of Mgmt.; bd. The Beavers; Amer. Water Works Assn.; mem. Newcomen Soc. in N. Amer; Alpha Tau Omega; clubs: Lincoln, Order of Knoll; California, Jonathan, San Gabriel Country, Pauma Valley Country. Republican. Congl. Hobby: stamp collecting. Rec.: hunting, fishing, horseback riding. Res.: 1400 Milan Ave., South Pasadena, CA 91030; Office: 4700 Ramona Blvd., Monterey Park, CA 91754.

TOMA, KAY
Medical Center President
b. Nov. 10, 1913, Okla.; s. George and Martha Toma; ed. H.S. (pres. Freshman, Sophomore and Jr. classes); M.D., Univ. of Tenn. 1941; m. Ellen Glaviano, June 24, 1966; chil.: Paula K., b. May 14, 1948; Martha Jo, b. Aug. 15, 1949; Michael G., b. Nov. 20, 1950; Patricia Ann. b. Nov. 15, 1952; James J., born Aug. 1, 1955; Michelle Kay, b. June 8, 1969. Career: Chief of Staff, Falfurrias City Hosp., Tex. 1947-48; pres. Bell Med. Center; chief of staff, Mission Hosp., Huntington Park, 1960---, exec. bd.; Calif. State Bd. Med. Examiners, 1970-78; vice pres. & dir., Charter Thrift & Loan, Fullerton, 1978; Mem. bd. dirs., Capital National Bank, Downey 1978; pres. Aladdin Jewels, Las Vegas, Nev. 1978; bd. dirs. Mechanics Natl. Bank. Maj., USAF (serv. 1942-46), WW II; USAF res. 1946---, Chief of Med., Shepard A.F.B., Wichita Falls, Tex., Korean War 1949-51. Awards: Bronze Star and Purple Heart. Mem.: AAGP Masons; charter Fellow, Amer. Acad. of Family Phys.; pres. Bell C. of C. 1973-74, bd. dirs.; Greek Orthodox, Hobby: tennis, sports. Res.: 15970 Carmenia, Whittier, CA 90603; Office: 5101 E. Florence Blvd., Bell, CA 90201.

TOMPKINS, DOROTHY CAMPBELL
Analyst
b. July 9, 1908, St. Paul, Minn.; d. Harry Arthur and Alta (Hayes) Campbell; B.A., Univ. Calif. Berkeley, 1929, M.A., 1937; m. John Barr Tompkins, June 1941. Career: Public Adminstrn. Analyst, Inst. of Governmental Studies (formerly Bureau of Pub. Adminstrn.), Univ. Calif., Berkeley, 1937-74; editor, Calif. Pub. Survey, bimonthly digest, 1949-72; Contbg. ed., Crimonology, 1966-73. Publs. incl.: The Offender: A Bibliography, 1963; Probation since World War II: a Bibliography, 1964; Poverty in the United States During the Sixties: A Bibliography, 1970; Schools: How to Pay For Them?, 1972; Power From the Earth: Geothermal Power, 1972; Strip Mining for Coal, 1973; Court Organization and Administration: A Bibliography, 1973; Furlough From Prison, 1973; Selection of the Vice President, 1974. Awarded: Joseph Andrews Bibliographical Award, Am. Assn. of Law Libraries. Mem.: Mus. Soc. of San Francisco, Internat. Netsuke Collectors Soc. Res.: 909 Regal Rd., Berkeley, CA 94708.

TONELLI, P.R. (Tony)
Dept. of the Navy Civilian
b. Feb. 13, 1922, Cottonwood, Ariz.; s. Peter, Sr. and Julia (Arrigoni) Tonelli-LaSalvia; LL.B., LaSalle Ext. Univ., Chicago, Ill., 1965; m. Michie, Aug. 13, 1965, U.S. Embassy, Tokyo, Japan; dau. Martha Ann. b. Sept. 6, 1951 (dec. 1970). Career: USN, 1939-63, ret. as Aviation Chief Machinist Mate E-8: assigned to USS Saratoga, aircraft carrier, 1939-43; flight training unit, Jacksonville, Fla. 1943, flight inspector, Mil. Aviation Transport Command, 1946-48; instr., Aviation Fundamentals Sch., Memphis, Tenn. 1948-50; tchr. Crash Fire Fighting, all Naval Aviation Bases on W. Coast, Alaska, Pacific area, 1950-52; crash fire, rescue chief, Naval Air Sta., Alameda,

Calif. 1952-53; Air Group Staffs, Pacific Area, 1954-61; security chief and leading chief, Aux. Landing field, Kisarazu, Japan, 1961-63; adminstrv. asst. Spec. Services, Naval Sta., L.B., 1963-74; mgr., Navy Bowling centers, Seal Beach, Fallbrook, 1974---. Made TV comml. for Chrysler Corp. with Joe Garagiola, 1975; editor, mag. for Santa Clara Valley Fleet Reserve Assn. Mem.: VFW; Fleet Reserve Assn.; past pres. 4 different branches, dir. Long Beach Br. 43; Internat. Assn. of Fire Chiefs, 1950-60; past secty.; Nat. Baseball Congress; Calif. Umpires Assn.; Amateur Softball Assn.; Japan Bowling Assn. 1964-69; past pres.; Toastmasters Internat., 1969---, DTM, 1978; Am. Inst. of Parliamentarians, pres. Golden Bear chpt. 10; Acad. Parliamentary Procedure and Law, past pres. Thais M. Plaisted group; secty.-treas. USS Saratogs Reunion Com. (currently 1,350 mems.); Roman Catholic; lay lectr. Hobbies: coins, First day issue envelopes collector. Rec.: hunting, fishing, golfing. Home: 6382 Cantiles Ave., Cypress, CA 90630.

TOPPING, NORMAN HAWKINS
University Chancellor
b. Jan. 12, 1908, Flat River, Mo.; s. Moses H. and Charlotte Amanda (Blue) Topping; A.B., USC, 1933; M.D., 1926; (hon.) LL.D., Occidental College, 1962; LL.D., UCLA, 1962; Sc.D., USC, 1963; L.H.D., Hebrew Union College, 1966; LL.D., Loyola Univ. 1968; m. Helen H. Rummens, Seattle, Wash., Sept. 2, 1930; chil.: Brian B., b. Oct. 3, 1934; Linda Elizabeth (Topping) King, b. Aug. 9, 1938. Career: Intern, U.S. Pub. Health Serv., Marine hosps., S.F. and S.F. and Seattle, staff, Natl. Insts. of Health (br. U.S. Pub. Health Serv.), Bethesda, Md. 1937-52, asst. chief, div. infectious diseases, 1946-48, asst. surg. gen.-assoc. dir. 1948-52; chmn. health committee, Foreign Operations Adm.; v.p. (med. affairs), Univ. of Pa. 1952-58; pres. USC 1958-70, Chancellor, 1970---. Bd. dirs., So. Calif. Rapid Transit Dist. 1964-73, pres. 1971-73. Awards: Typhus Comm. Medal; Bailey K. Ashford Award, Amer. Soc. of Tropical Med.; Award of Wash. Acad. of Sci. Mem.: Assn. of Amer. Phys., Amer. Assn. for Advancement of Sci.; Amer. Epidemiological Soc., Soc. for Experimental Biology and Med.; chmn. com. on virus research and epidemiology, Natl. Found. Infantile Paralysis, 1956-58, chmn. research com. 1958-77; Los Angeles, L.A. Country, Calif. Clubs. Hobby: photog. Rec.: golf. Res.: 100 S. Plymouth Blvd., Los Angeles, 90004; Office: USC, 3810 Wilshire Blvd., Suite 1202, Los Angeles, CA 90010.

TORF, JANE HAMILTON
Antique Dealer
b. Aug. 29, 1916, Marshall, Ill.; d. George and Rosa (Bennett) Beuhler; student, Acad. of Arts, Chicago; m. Allen Britt Hamilton (dec. 1957), Feb. 26, 1940, Terre Haute, Ind.; daughters: Judy (Cappello), b. 1941; Janet (Agajanian), b. 1946; m. 2d. Al Torf, 1965. Career: with Marshall Fields, Chicago, 1935-40; owner, Hamilton House Antiques, Glendora, Calif. 1951---. Lectr. on antiques for Clubs, 1960-65. Vice pres., So. Calif. Antique Dealers Assn., 1966, 1977, 78, co-show chmn., 1969-70. Mehtodist. Rec.: swimming, tennis. Res.: 603 N. Doheny Dr., Beverly Hills, CA; Office: 1030 E. Alosta, Glendora, CA 91740.

TOTH, ROBERT CHARLES
Newspaper Reporter
b. Dec. 24, 1928, Blakely, Pa.; s. John and Tillie Toth; B.S., Chem. Eng., Washington Univ., St. Louis, 1952; M.S., Journ., Columbia Univ., 1955; Pulitzer Traveling Scholar, 1955-56; Nieman Fellow, Harvard Univ., 1960-61; m. Paula Goldberg, Apr. 11, 1954, St. Louis, Mo.; children: Jessica, b. 1963; Jennifer, b. 1967; John, b. 1970. Career: Assoc. Editor, Rubber World, 1953-54; Reporter, Providence Journal, 1955-57, N.Y. Herald Tribune, 1957-62, N.Y. Times, 1962-63, L.A. Times, 63---; London bureau chief, 1966-70, State Dept. correspondent, 1970-72, White House correspondent, 1972-74, Moscow Bureau chief, 1974-77, Washington bureau, 1977---. USMC, 1946-48; Munitions Engr., AUS, 1952-53. Awards from Overseas Press Club, Sigma Delta Chi, Polk Award for Foreign Correspondents, 1978. Rec.: tennis, skiing, swimming. Res.: 21 Primrose St., Chevy Chase, Md. 20015; Office: 1700 Penna. Ave. N.W., Wash., D.C. 20006.

TOWNES, CHARLES HARD
Physicist
b. July 28, 1915, Greenville, S.C.; s. Henry Keith and Ellen (Hard) Townes; B.A. Modern langs., B.S. physics, Furman Univ. 1935; M.A., physics, Duke Univ., 1936; Ph.D., physics, Calif. Inst. of Tech., 1939; hon.

Doctorates from 20 univs. 1960-78; m. Frances H. Brown, May 4, 1941, Berlin, N.H.; children: Linda Lewis (Rosenwein), b. 1943; Ellen Screven (Anderson), b. 1946; Carla Keith (Lumsden), b. 1949; Holly Robinson, b. 1952. Career: Asst. in Physics, Cal Tech., 1937-39; tech. staff, Bell Telephone Labs., 1939-47; assoc./prof. physics, Columbia Univ., 1948-61, dept. chmn. 1952-55, exec. dir. Columbia Radiation Lab., 1950-52; v.p., dir. research, Inst. for Def. Analyses, 1959-61; provost and prof. physics, MIT, 1961-66, Inst. Prof., 1966-67; Univ. prof., Univ. of Calif., 1967---: also Nat. lectr., Sigma Xi, 1950-51, Guggenheim Fellow, 1955-56, Fulbright lectr., Univs. of Paris, Tokyo, 1955-56, dir. Enrico Fermi Internat. Sch. of Physics, 1963. Awards: Stuart Ballantine Medal, Franklin Inst. 1959, 1962; Comstock Prize 1959 and John J. Carty Medal 1962, Nat. Acad. of Scis.; Rumford Premium, Am. Acad. of Arts and Scis., 1961; Thomas Young Medal, Prize, The Inst. of Physics and the Physical Soc., Eng., 1963; Nobel Prize for Physics, Royal Acad. of Scis., Stockholm, 1964; Medal of Honor, IEEE, 1967; C.E.K. Mees Medal, Optical Soc. of Am., 1968; NASA's Distinguished Pub. Service Medal, 1969; Michelson-Morley Award, 1970; Wilhelm Exner Award, Austria, 1970; Plyler Prize, Am. Physical Soc., 1977. Trustee, Carnegie Inst. of Wash., 1965---; bd. dir., The Perkin-Elmer Corp., 1966---; mem. corp., Woods Hole Oceanographic Inst., 1969---; bd. dirs., General Motors, 1973---; Mem. Pub. Policy Com. and Audit Com., Gen. Motors Corp.; trustee, The Internat. Council on the Future of the Univ., Inc., 1974---; mem. Office of Sci. and Tech. Policy, ad hoc Advis. Com. on Space Systems, 1977---; mem. Nat. Sci. Found. Astronomy Advis. Com., 1977---; mem. Nat. Acad. of Scis. Council, 1978-81, NAS Council Com. on Nat. Sci. Policy, 1978-81. Fellow, Am. Physical Soc., pres. 1967, IEEE; Mem.: Nat. Acad. of Scis., Am. Acad. Arts and Scis., Am. Philosophical Soc., Am. Astronomical Soc., Societe Francaise de Physique, AAAS, Soc. Royale des Scis. de Liege, Nat. Inventors Hall of Fame, S.C. Hall of Fame, foreign mem., Royal Soc. of London. Clubs: Bohemian, University Club NYC, Cosmos, Wash. D.C., Explorers. Protestant, Deacon. Hobby: natural hist. Res.: 1988 San Antonio Ave., Berkeley, CA 94707; Office: Dept. of Physics, Univ. of Calif., Berkeley, CA 94720.

TOWNER, GEORGE R.
Business Executive
b. Sept. 15, 1933, NYC; s. Rutherford H. and Marion (Washburn) Towner; B.A., Univ. Calif., Berkeley, 1956; M.A., 1957; Career: Asst. Dir., Kaiser Found., 1958-60; pres., Berkeley Instruments Corp., 1962-67; chmn. bd., Towner Systems Corp., 1968-78; cons., Mars Data Systems, 1979---. AUS, 1955-57. Mem. Mensa, 1964---, pres. San Francisco Region, 1975-77. Res.: 814 Gail Ave., Sunnyvale, CA 94086; Office: 14666 Doolittle Dr., San Leandro, CA 94577.

TRACY, LOUISE TREADWELL
Founder-President, John Tracy Clinic
b. July 31, New Castle, Pa.; d. Alliene Wetmore and Bright (Smith) Treadwell; ed. Lake Erie Coll.; (hon.) D.Sc., Northwestern Univ. 1951; (hon.) Dr. of Humane Letters, USC 1953; (hon.) Dr. of Liberal Arts, Lake Erie Coll. 1955; (hon.) Dr. of Humane Letters, MacMurray Coll., 1956; (hon.) Litt.D., Gallaudet Coll., Wash., D.C. 1966; (hon.) Dr. Humane Letters, Whitworth Coll., Spokane, 1974; (hon.) Dr. of Humane Letters, Ripon Coll., 1966; m. Spencer Tracy (film star), Cincinnati, Oh., Sept. 1923 (dec.); chil.: John, b. June 26, 1924; Milwaukee, Wis.; Louise (Susie), b. July 1, 1932, Los Angeles, Calif. Career: founder-pres.-dir., John Tracy Clinic (in hon. of son); pioneer in edn. of parents of deaf and hard of hearing children. Author: New Avenues to Understanding, Suggestions to the Parents of Deaf and Hard of Hearing Children; Talk, Talk, Talk to Deaf Children (punl. Amer. Edn. 1965); The Education of a Young Deaf Child Begins with His Parents in His Home. Episcopalian. Res.: 700 S. Beverly Glen Blvd., Los Angeles, CA 90024; Office: 806 W. Adams Blvd., Los Angeles, CA 90007.

TRATNER, ALAN ARTHUR
Environmentalist
b. Jan. 21, 1947, Detroit, Mich.; s. Max and Shirley (Tribuck) Tratner; student Art Center Coll. of Design, 1965-66; Woodbury Univ.; Stanford Univ. Career: pres., exec. dir. Environ Edn. Group, Inc., Reseda, 1972---; art dir., tech. cons. Environ. Quality mag., 1970-73; spec. cons. Environ. and energy edn., Los Angeles Unified

Sch. Dist., Laurel Sci and Ecology Center, 1972-75; assoc., Environ. Communications, Inc., Venice, Calif., 1973; conf. leader Energy Conservation Inst., Redwood City, 1975; prof. environment and energy, Pepperdine Univ., continuing edn., L.A. 1973---; Mem.: Mayor's Energy Policy Com., L.A. 1973-74; mem. environ. adv. com., L.A. City Attys. Office, 1974; mem. L.A. Co. Transp. Task Force, 1973; mem. Comprehensive Health Planning Council, L.A., 1973; Adv. Council of Ecology Center So. Calif. 1972; Calif. Citizen Action Group, 1973; bd. dir. Environ. Telethon, 1973; cons. to commr. L.A. Dept. Environ. Quality, 1973---; bd. advisors, Inventor's Workshop Internat. 1972---; L.A. Unified Sch. Dist. Energy Adv. Unit, 1974---; U.S. Energy Research and Devel. Adminstrn. Energy Invention Evaluation Bd. of Inventor's Workshop, Inc., 1976---; Mem. Wind Energy Soc. of Am.; Geothermal Energy Assn. Editor-in-chief Energies mag., 1974-75; mng. publisher, Geothermal World Directory, 1975-76; contbr. articles to profl. journs.; patentee in field. Home: 18014 Sherman Way, Reseda, CA 91335.

TRIPLETT, RAYMOND F.
CLU, New York Life Insurance Company
b. Oct. 14, 1921, Detroit Lakes, Minn.; s. Raymond LeRoy and Barbara A. (Wambach) Triplett; ed. U.S. Maritime Acad. 1943; m. Shirley J. Koenig, Minneapolis, Minn., Feb. 14, 1942; chil.: Mrs. James Allen (Kathleen T.) Hayes, b. Sept. 7, 1944; Mrs. John B. (Barbara K.) Sullivan, b. July 6, 1948; Mrs. Michael Noyes (Joan D.), b. Mar. 5, 1951; Therese M., b. Mar. 30, 1953; Raymond J., b. Apr. 29, 1955. Career: Western sales mgr., Minn. & Ontario Paper Co. 1950-53; CLU-field underwriter, N.Y. Life Ins. Co., San Jose, 1953---. Faculty lectr., 10 univs. 1965-70. Author: numerous articles on estates planning and taxation in natl. publs. Ensign, USMC (1942-44), WW II. Mem.: pres. Santa Clara Co. Estate Planning Council, 1958; pres. San Jose Life Underwriters Assn. 1962; pres. Santa Clara Co. CLU 1964; pres. N.Y. Life Pres'. Council, 1965-66; pres., N.Y. Life Agents Adv. Council, 1966; trustee, Amer. Coll. of Life Underwriters, 1971-73; natl. pres. Amer. Soc. of Chartered Life Underwriters, 1972-73; Santa Clara Co. Personnel Bd., 1965-66; Santa Clara Co. Judicial Selection Adv. Bd. 1967---; (life) Million Dollar Round Table, Natl. Assn. of Life Underwriters; past pres., Catholic Layman's Retreat Assn. Hobbies: sailing, hunting. Res.: 16203 Hillvale, Monte Sereno, CA; Office: Suite 520, 777 N. 1st St., San Jose, CA 95112.

TROKE, MARGARET MARY KLAUSNER
Library Consultant
b. Nov. 21, 1911, Omaha, Nebr.; d. Joseph H. and Mary Jaynes (Keyser) Klausner; A.B., certificate in Lib. Sci., Univ. of Denver, 1939; m. Frank J. Troke, Mar. 5, 1964. Career: Lih. asst., Sacramento City Free Lib. 1929-35; ref. asst. 1935-37; br. librarian, 1937-41, supv. ref. lib. 1941-44, asst. city librarian, 1943-44; sr. asst., documents div. (summer), Denver Pub. Library, Colo. 1939; librarian, Napa County Library, 1944-46; dir. lib. serv., Stockton and San Joaquin County Public Library, 1946---; admr. 1949-69; Cooperative Library System, Stockton, 1967-74 (ret.); library cons.; mem. Calif. Pub. Library Development Bd. 1963-69;, chmn. 1967-69; mem. Lib. Adv. Com. to County Supvs. Assn. of Calif. 1968---. Contrib. articles to professional publs. Mem.: Amer. Soc. for Pub. Adm.; Calif. Library Assn., pres. 1953, pres. Pub. Lib. Sect. 1950-55; secty. Stockton Community Youth & Welfare Council, 1954-55, v.p. 1957, treas. 1958---; Cath. Social Serv. 1954-55; bd. dirs. 1958---; dir. 5th annual Inst. Workshop on Planning Pub. Lib. Bldgs., Sacramento, Mar. 1957; Amer. Library Assn., chmn. Reg. II Membership Com. 1957-58, pres. Lib. Adm. Div. 1959-60; bd. dirs., United Crusade, 1958---; co-dir., 7th annual Inst. on Pub. Lib. Systems, Sacramento, Mar. 1959; San Joaquin-Calaveras Girl Scout Council, Amer. Assn. of Univ. Women, League of Women Voters, Bus. and Professional Women, Sierra Club. Democrat. Catholic. Hobby: reading, music, gardening. Rec.: hiking, skiing. Res.: 825 W. Euclid St., Stockton, CA 95204.

TROTTER, HUGH BERRY
Vice-President, Heidrick & Struggles, Inc.
b.July 17, 1927, Chicago, Ill.; s. Hugh Berry, Sr. and Elizabeth (Ammeter) Trotter; B.S., Northwestern Univ. (highest dist.), 1950; M.B.A., 1951; m. Suzanne Sherman, Dec. 22, 1951, Kenilworth, Ill.; chil.: Melinda Elizabeth, b. June 30, 1954; Katherine Sherman, b. July 4, 1956; Suzanne Whitney, b. June 9, 1960; Hugh Scott, b. Dec.

23, 1963. Career: with Dresser Industries, Inc. 1953-60; corp. fin. analyst, Dallas, Tex., 1953-54; production mgr., Dresser Opns., Inc., Whittier, 1954-57; secty.-treas., Dresser Dynamics, Inc., L.A., 1957-59; asst. to v.p., Internat. opns., Dallas, Texas, 1959-60; mgmt. cons., McKinsey & Co., L.A., 1960-67; v.p. and mgmt. com. mem., Cyprus Mines Corp., 1967-71, L.A.; with Heidrick & Struggles, Inc., L.A., 1971---: assoc. 1971-72, v.p., mgr., 1972---. Served USAF, Asst. Squadron Sgt.-Maj. 1946-47; recruiting sgt. 1951-52; audit officer, 1952-53. Mem.: Alpha Delta Phi, v.p. NW chpt. 1949-50; University Club of L.A., 1960-76; dir., 1964-67; San Marino Tennis Found., dir. 1976-78; California Club; Valley Hunt Club. Hobbies: war games, logic problems, bridge. Rec.: tennis. Home: 2580 Oak Knoll Ave., San Marino, CA 91108; Office: Union Bank Sq., Fifth & Figueroa Sts., L.A., CA 91107.

TROUTMAN, WILLIAM
Business — Investments Executive
b. Apr. 1, 1917, Floreffe, Pa.; s. Michael and Elizabeth (Blakemore) Troutman; B.S., Mt. Union Coll. 1938; postgrad. UCLA, Univ. of Chicago; m. Jane Elizabeth Gillis, Carmel, CA, Nov. 28, 1953; dau. Joyann Elizabeth, b. Jan. 10, 1962. Career: Sales Development, Canton Engraving Co., Ohio, 1938-41; Cruttenden & Co., L.A. 1946-47; John B. Dunbar & Co. 1947-49; v.p. Shearson, Hammill & Co., Inc., L.A. 1949-74; v.p. Loeb, Rhoades & Co., 1974---. Dir.: Magnetiica, Inc.; Trafalgar Assocs.; (past) Automation Inds., Inc. Meteorologist Capt. USAF 1941-46, WW II. Mem.: F&AM Lodge; Com. So. Calif. Golf Assn.; dir.-v.p. La Quinta Country Club; Bel-Air Country Club. Res.: 9581 Lime Orchard Rd., Beverly Hills, CA 90210; Office: 9440 Santa Monica Blvd., Suite 500, Beverly Hills, CA 90212.

TRUESDAIL, ROGER WILLIAMS
Consulting Chemist
b. Feb. 6, 1899, Burlingame, Kan.; s. Ernest Leonard and Ruth (Williams) Truesdail; B.S., U. Redlands, 1921; M.S., U. Oreg., 1922; Ph.D., U. Wash., 1926; m. Dorothy Pinter, June 27, 1923; chil.: Betty Barbara (Mrs. George M. Fielding), Katherine Ann (Mrs. Philip J. Charley), Audrey Mae (Mrs. Ronald H. McClure). Career: Head dept. chemistry and physics, Mt. Angel Coll., Oreg., 1922-23; acting head dept. chemistry, U. Relands, 1923-24; instr. chemistry U. Nev., 1926-27; asst. prof. chemistry Pomona Coll., 1927-31; lectr. chemistry U. of So. Calif., 1935-44; founder, 1931, then pres., now chmn. bd. Truesdail Labs., Inc., Los Angeles. Official chemist Calif. Horse Racing Bd., 1938---; adv. com. Nat. Conf. Adminstrn. Research, 1955-60; mem. Citizens Smog Com. Los Angeles, 1946, Pasadena Tournament Roses, 1952---; Trustee, vice chmn. exec. com., chmn. trustees faculty com. U. Redlands, 1935-74, trustee emeritus, 1974---; trustee Sch. Theol. Claremont, 9155-65; bd. dirs. S. Pasadena YMCA, 1940-48; bd. dirs., bd. govs. So. Calif. Goodwill Industries, 1971---. Fellow AAAS, Am. Inst. Chemists (Councillor 1954-55), Am. Pub. Health Assn. (councillor food and nutrit:on sect. Western br. 1958-59); charter mem. Inst. Food Technologists; mem. Am. Chem. Soc. (chmn. So. Calif. sect. 1939-40); Am. Council Ind. Labs. (pres. 1949-51, secty., 1954-75, charter mem.); Assn. Official Racing Chemists (pres. 1953-54); Am. Air Force Assn., Am. Ordnance Assn., Navy League U.S., Los Angeles C. of C. Sigma Xi. Congregationalist (past moderator). Rotarian (pres. Los Angeles 1946-47). Clubs' Oneonta (pres. 1941-42) (S. Pasadena); University (Los Angeles). Author numerous papers in field. Home: 1199 Arden Rd., Pasadena, CA 91106; Office: 4101 N. Figueroa St., Los Angeles, CA 90065.

TRUHILL, LUCIEN D.
Economic Development Executive
b. Sept. 18, 1914, Flushing, Long Island, N.Y.; s. Henry A. and Anna Truhill; B.A., Rutgers Univ., 1936; grad. studies, Univ. Okla.; Certified Profl. Indsl. Developer, Am. Indsl. Devel. Council, 1972; m. Shirley Miller, Oct. 12, 1940, Elizabeth, N.J. Career: Pres. & Chief Exec. Officer, Orange County C. of C., 1962---; chmn. bd. Orange Co. Economic Devel. Corp., 1976---. Corps. Engrs., AUS, WW II; decorated Bronze Arrowhead Award, 1st Assault Wave, D-Day, Normandy. Orange Co. Metro. Chmn. Nat. Alliance Bus., 1977-78, chmn. executive 1978-79. Mem. Anaheim Rotary Club. Rec.: golf, baseball, swimming. Res.: 31842 Paseo Terraza, San Juan Capistrano, CA 92675; Office: 401 Bank of America Tower, The City, Orange, CA 92668.

TRUMAN, ROLLAND ALBERT
Superior Court Commissioner
b. Apr. 30, 1912, Loma Linda, Calif.; s. Archibald William, M.D. (chief of staff-med. dir., various hosps. USA and China; natl. lecturer and writer) and Daisy Ethel (Nary) Truman; third cousin U.S. Pres. Harry Truman, 1945-52; B.A., USC 1940, J.D. 1942; D.D. (hon.), Universal Life Ch., 1969; LL.D., Univ. of Eastern Fla. 1971; m. Laurel A. Weibel, M.D., Bellflower, Calif., Sept. 15, 1953; chil.: Rolland Gilbert, b. July 7, 1945; Norris Wesley, b. Mar. 24, 1948; Tracy Norton, b. May 31, 1962; Tamara Ann, b. Apr. 30, 1963; Trina Maureen, b. Oct. 3, 1964; Trent Martin, b. Feb. 24, 1966; Tricia Lynn, b. Oct. 24, 1968. Career: Atty., Pac. Elec. Ry. Co. 1942-44; gen. practice law (spec. in bus.-corp. law, contracts, real property, domestic rels., negligence, probate), 1944-63; admitted to practice, U.S. Supreme Ct. 1957; Superior Ct. Commr.-judge pro tem, 1963---. Rancher, citrus and avocado, 1968---; Sunkist Growers, Inc., and Calavo, 1970---. Dir. Anaheim Mem. Hosp., 1961-63. Author: How to Be a Doctor's Husband, Los Angeles Co. Med. Assn. Bulletin, 1954, AMA 1955; Tobacco As Science Sees It, 1955; Lyrics For Fun, 1968. Mem.: Delta Theta Phi, 1941---; Calif. State, L.A. Co. Bar Assns. 1942---; dir. treas., Long Beach Jr. C. of C. 1946-47; pres. Audubon Screen Tours, L.B. 1947-49; chmn. Young Dems. of Calif. 1947-48, state conv. chmn. 1948, Dem. Central Com., L.A. Co. 1949-52; pres. Agassiz Nature Club, L.B. 1948-50; dean, Peon Univ. 1948; pres. Angelus Nature Club, L.A. 1950-51; dir. L.A. Audubon Soc. 1961; chmn. South Gate Community Chest, 1952-53; dir. Kiwanis Club of South Gate, 1954-63 (ed. Kiwanis Star, 1961-62); Amer. Bar Assn. 1957---; bd. trustees, White Mem. Med. Center, L.A.; parliamentarian (council cabinet), L.A. Co. Employees Assn. 1965; chmn. awards com., First Annual Freedom Awards Dinner, Ch. State Council 1965-66, dir. at lg. 1967---; L.B. City Coll. Stage Band, 1965---; L.B. Bar Assn. 1966---; So. Calif. co-chmn., State Bar Art Exhibs. 1966-67; Mile-A-Thon Internat. 1967---; Kiwanis Club, Long Beach, 1967---; Fallbrook Citrus Assn., 1970---; Good Sam Club, 1972---. Seventh-day Adventist (master guide, 1935; dir. Pathfinder Club, 1954-58, chmn. bldg. com. 1957-58). Hobbies: photog., oil painting, amateur radio (license W6QPZ). Rec.: music, camping. Res.: 4522 Greenmeadow Rd., Long Beach, 90808; Office: Superior Ct., 415 W. Ocean Blvd., Long Beach, CA 90802.

TRUSCOTT, GRAHAM BRIAN
Clergyman
b. Feb. 12, 1937, Invercargill, New Zealand; s. Eric George and Vera Christina Truscott; M.S.T., 1972; Ph.D. religion, 1974; m. Pamela, Feb. 8, 1958, Christchurch, New Zealand; chil.: Stephen Graham, b. Dec. 17, 1958; Deborah Lynn, b. Jan. 30, 1961; Ruth Vatsala, b. Jan. 8, 1964; Mark John, b. Dec. 17, 1965. Career: prin. clarinetist, Radio Broadcasting Orchester, Christchurch, N.Z., 1958-59; founder and director, New Life Missions, hdqtrs. Poona, India, 1960-77; founder, Pastor, Restoration Temple, La Jolla, 1978---; Author: You Shall Receive Power (A Fresh Study of the Holy Spirit in the light of the new awakening in historic churches), 1967; Power of His Presence (The Restoration of the Tabernacle of David), 1969; The Only Foundation, 1970; Missionary Training and Discipleship, 1975; Every Christian's Ministry, 1977. Hobby: music. Rec.: swimming. Home: 2138 Balfour Ct., San Diego, CA 92109; Office: 470 Nautilus, Suite 202, La Jolla, CA 92037.

TRUST, SAMUEL S.
Music Company President
b. July 22, 1919, Pittsburgh, Pa.; s. Matthew and Esther Trust; B.M., Cincinnati Conservatory Music, 1955; bus. studies, Rutgers Univ.; m. Joan Van Genderen, June 28, 1959, Brooklyn, N.Y.; children: Jennifer, b. 1960; Benjamin, b. 1963. Career: with Broadcast Music, Inc., 1958-68: dir. of logging, 1964, exec. dir. pub. adminstrn 1966; pres., Beechwood Music Corp., 1969-71; pres., ATV Music Corp., 1973---. Dir., National Music Publishers' Assn., USN, 1955-57; trumpet soloist with 7th Fleet Band, USS Oriskany, Yorktown, Hancock, Lexington. Rec.: golf. Res.: 23955 Park Belmonte, Calabasas Park, CA; Office: 6255 Sunset Blvd., Suite 723, Hollywood, CA 90028.

TRUXAL, FRED STONE
Curator
b. Feb. 20, 1922, Great Bend, Kan.; s. Kenneth E. and Grace M. (Dunsworth) Truxal; A.B., Univ. of Kan.

1947; M.A. 1949; Ph.D. 1952; m. Margaret Osmond, Abilene, Tex., Aug. 14, 1943; chil.: Carol Ann (Truxal) Rice, b. Dec. 2, 1945; Robert A., b. Nov. 7, 1951. Career: Agt., U.S. Dept. Agri., Wash., D.C. 1942; asst. instr. (biol.-entomology), Univ. of Kan. 1947-52; asst. to Kan. State entomologist, Lawrence (summers), 1948-51; asst. prof. biol., Ottawa Univ. 1951-52; curator of entomology, Los Angeles Co. Museum of Natural Hist. 1952-61, chief curator, life scis. div. 1961---; adjunct prof. biol., USC 1957---; cons. Pac. Horizons, 1959---. Contrib. annual tech. articles in field of entomology to professional journs. Pvt., Capt., U.S. Army Med. Corps (1943-46), WW II. Mem.: treas. Lorquin Entomological Soc. 1953---; fellow-v.p., So. Calif. Acad. Scis. 1955-58; dir. 1955-62, pres. 1959-60, adv. bd. 1963---; bd. dirs., Ethnic Art Council of L.A. 1966---; fellow, AAAS; Entomological Soc. of Amer., Kan. Entomological Soc., Soc. of Systematic Zoology, Western Museums League, Sigma Xi, Phi Sigma, Republican. Methodist. Hobby: photog. Rec.: swimming, fishing, hunting. Res.: 8111 Vicksburg Ave., Los Angeles, CA 90045; Office: 900 Exposition Blvd., Los Angeles, CA 90007.

TRZYNA, THADDEUS CHARLES
Public Affairs Director
b. Oct. 26, 1939, Chicago, Ill.; s. Thaddeus Stephen and Irene (Giese) Stephen; B.A., internat. rels., USC; Ph.D., govt., Claremont Grad. Sch.; div.; dau., Jennifer, b. 1964. Career: U.S. Foreign Service Officer, 1962-69; Am. Vice Consul in Katanga, 1962-63; Third Secty., Am. Embassy, Kinshasa, Zaire, 1963-64; Secty., Natl. Mil. Info. Disclosure Policy Com., Dept. of State, Wash. D.C., 1964-67; President, Center for Calif. Public Affairs, affil. Claremont Colleges, 1969---. Editor, The California Handbook; Environment Protection Directory. Author or ed. some 30 books and articles on environmental protection and Calif. current affairs. Regional v.p., Sierra Club, 1975-77, chmn. Sierra Club Internat. Com. 1977---. Democrat. Unitarian. Office: P.O.B. 10, Claremont, CA 91711.

TSCHOEGL, NICHOLAS WILLIAM
Professor of Chemical Engineering
b. June 4, 1918, Zidlochovice, Czechoslovakia; s. Paul John and Harriet (Robert) Tschoegl; B.Sc. (honours) New So. Wales Univ. of Tech., Sydney, Australia, 1954; Ph.D., 1958; m. Sophia Maria Glazmak, Apr. 6, 1946, Budapest, Hungary; sons, Adrian Edward, b. 1947; Christopher Anthony, b. 1954. Career: Sr. Research Ofcr., Bread Research Inst. of Australia, 1958-61, Proj. Assoc., Dept. of Chem., Univ. of Wis., 1961-63; Sr. Physical Chemist, Propulsion Scis. Div., Stanford Univ., 1963-65; Assoc. Prof. Materials Scis. 1965-67 and prof. chem. engring. Calif. Inst. Tech., 1967---. Awarded Humboldt Prize (sr. U.S. Scientist Award) Alexander von Humboldt Found., Bonn. G.F.R. 1976. Res.: 566 W. California Blvd., Pasadena, CA 91106; Office: Caltech., Pasadena, CA 91125.

TSEU, ROSITA H.
Artist
b. Jan. 6, 1916, Peking, China (U.S. Cit. 1956); d. Un-Yuen Hau, Minister of Finance, China, 1915-17; stepmother, Chin Ying; Un Tseng Hsu, uncle Minister of Communications, Repub. of China, 1932-42; ed. Coll. Municipal Francaise, Shanghai, 1940-46; Ecole des Beaux Arts, Paris, Fr.; Soochow Art Acad., Shanghai; Otis Art Inst., L.A.; Brit. Commercial Inst., 1947; legal secty. tr. course, Beverly Hills H.S 1964; m. Joseph K.T. Tseu, Shanghai, China, Mar. 4, 1947; chil.: Regina Hsu Pan, b. Oct. 4, 1936. Career: Secty-adm. asst. J.G. White Engin. Corp. 1950-52; adm. asst. (translate govt. documents: Chinese, Frence, English), Internat. Corp. Adm., Taiwan, 1952-56; est. U.S. res. 1956; teacher, demonstrator, artist; mgr. dir. Sergei Bongart Sch. of Art, 1976; spec. in Oriental art and portraiture; exhibs; numerous one-woman shows; demonstrator: Scandinavian Amer. Art Soc.; Southwest Art Assn.; Burbank Art Assn.; Marina del Rey Art Assn.; San Gabriel Fine Arts Assn.; Valley Artists Guild; High Desert Artists, Inc., Victorville; painted Adm. Jarrett, Madame Chang Hsueh-Liang (wife of Gov. of Manchuria), Rabbi Willner, Anna Chennault (wife of Gen. Chennault), others; winner over 100 awards and numerous gold medals, blue ribbons. Mem.: Calif. Art Club, Valley Artists Guild, Artists of the Southwest, Inc., Amer. Inst. of Fine Arts, San Gabriel Fine Art Assn., Beverly Hills Art League. Catholic. Hobby: stamp collecting. Studio: 6869 Pacific View Dr., Hollywood, CA 90068.

TUCKER, DOROTHY LOUISE McNEILL
Psychologist
b. Sept. 1, 1923, Racine, Wis.; d. Frank J. and Bess (Phillips) McNeill; B.S., Univ. Minn., 1945; M.S., Ill. State Univ., 1949; Ed.D, UCLA, 1959; m. Elbridge A. Tucker, Nov. 26, 1958, West Covina. Career: Rec. dir., Study and Treatment Center for Emotionally Disturbed Children, Mnpls., 1945-46; Head, Girls Phys. Ed. Dept., Washington Pk. H.S., Racine, Wis., 1946; Instr., W. Ill. Univ., 1949-52; tchr., San Bernardino City Schs. 1952-54; instr., counselor, San Bernardino Valley Coll., 1955-57; asst./assoc./prof. Psychol. and tchr. preparation, Cal State Polytech. Univ., Pomona, 1957-65, Coordinator, Secondary Prep. Program, 1963-72, dir., Tchr. Preparation Center, 1972-73, Prof., Psychology and Tchr. Prep., 1973-76, Prof. Emeritus, 1973---. Calif. Licensed Psychologist, 1959---. Mem. Personnel Bd., West Covina, 1975---, chmn. 1977-78, mem. Citizens' Advis. Com. 1974-75; Pi Gamma Mu, Pi Lambda Theta, Eta Sigma Upsilon, Delta Kappa Gamma; Am., Western Psychol. Assns.; Pomona Valley Mental Health Assn.; Edgewood Family Counseling Agency; So. Hills Women's Golf Club. Res.: 2915 Mesa Dr., West Covina, CA 91791.

TUCKER, DUNDAS PREBLE
Rear Admiral, U.S. Navy (Retired)
b. Apr. 20, 1902, NYC; s. Preble and Dewitt Clinton (Willis) Tucker; desc. Edward Preble, Commodore, USN, co-founder, Amer. naval traditional successful leader in Tripolitan War of 1803; Gen. George Clinton, Gov. of NY and 4th v.p. of U.S.; ed. B.Sc., U.S. Naval Acad. 1925; M.Sc., Harvard Univ. 1934. Career: U.S. Navy, Battle Fleet, 1925-28, Asiatic Fleet, 1929-31, Battle Force 1934-41; pgm. dir. electronics, guided missiles and nuclear matters, Navy Bur. of Ord. 1942-46; war plans and navy research facilities, Ofc. of Naval Research, 1947-49; Comdg. Ofcr., Navy Electronics Lab., San Diego, Calif. 1950-53; Comdg. Ofcr., Ofc. Naval Research, Chicago, Ill. and Pasa., Calif. 1954-56, ret. 1956---. Orig. Radar and Guided Missile Sects., Bur. of Ord.; orig. and developed Navy's first serv.-approved guided missile. Mem.: Army and Navy Club, Wash., D.C. Episcopalian. Hobby: shooting, inventing, electronics, writing. Rec.: theatre, gardening, workshop, music. Res.: 1829 Soledad Ave., La Jolla, CA.

TUDBURY, PATRICIA BREED
Physician
b. Mar. 8, 1918, Washington, D.C.; d. Warren Chamberlain and Ethel Putnam (Wheeler) Tudbury; A.B., Mills Coll., 1938; M.A. zoology, Univ. Calif., Berkeley, 1941; M.D., Yale Univ. Sch. of Med. 1947. Career: Internship and residency, Children's Hosp. San Francisco, 1947-49; practice of Internal Med., S.F. 1949-51, Visalia Clin., Visalia, 1951-55, Pomona, 1955---; Chief of Staff, Pomona Valley Community Hosp. Fellow, Am. Coll. of Physicians, 1963. Chief of Staff, Casa Colina Rehabil. Hosp., Pomona, 1971; mem. L.A. Co. Med. Assn., pres. dist. 14, 1967-68; Nat. Corresponding Sect., Am. Med. Women's Assn., 1979, councillor 1975-78; bd. dir., L.A. Co. Br., Am. Cancer Soc. 1956-58; bd. dir. Mt. San Antonic Council Camp Fire Girls 1960-68; bd. dir. YWCA 1972-77; Soroptimist Club, Bus. and Profl. Women's Club, AAUW, Sierra Club. Episcopalian, Vestryman. Office: 142 E. Nemaha St., Pomona, CA 91767.

TUDOR, W. PENDLETON
Publisher
b. Mar. 5, 1930, Oakland; s. J. Dwight and Betty Tudor; B.S., USC, 1951; M.B.A., 1953; m. Mary Alice Ghormley, Oct. 14, 1961, Beverly Hills; chil.: Mary Elizabeth; Bradford Pendleton; Douglas Maclean. Career: executive, Time Inc., 1955-74; management consultant, 1975-78; president MAC Publications, Inc., 1978---. Board mem.: Performing Tree Inc.; National Arthritis Found.; So. Calif. chmn. U.S. Olympic Committee. Served USN. Mem.: Beta Theta Pi. Clubs: Los Angeles Country; Bel Air Bay. Presbyterian. Hobby: community vol. work; Rec.: golf, tennis, family vacations. Home: 1642 Mandeville Canyon, L.A., CA 90049; Office: MAC Publications, Inc., 6565 Sunset Blvd., Los Angeles, CA 90028.

TUNSTALL, VELMA BARRETT
Poet- Author
b. Aug. 11, 1914, Vidette, Ark.; d. Sterling Isam and Cecil Anna (Jack) Barrett; ed. country schs.; m. Earl Archer Tunstall, Oct. 30, 1934, Santa Ana; Chil.: Patricia Gail (Hall); Deanna Mae. Poetic works have appared in literary magazines: El Viento, The Archer; anthologies: Shore, Quality American Poetry, Dawn, Anthology of American

Poetry, Better Thoughts; newspapers: Salem Headlight, West Plains Daily Quill, Springfield Daily News, Golden Poppy Newsletter. Pen name. Shana Barrett Tunstall; publications include two poem patterns, The Shannette, 1974; The Shana, 1975; Shadows on My Soul, a volume of lyrics for kindred souls; Highlander, Christmas, 1978; Poet, pub. in India, 1978. Elected, Hall of Fame, West Plains, Missouri, 1972; Founder fellow, Internat. Academy of Poets; mem. Internat. Platform Assn.; life mem., American Soc. of Distinguished Citizens; mem.: Nat. Fedn. of State Poetry Societies, Inc.; World Poetry Soc.; Calif. State Poetry Society; Jackson County Historical Soc. (Ark.). Hobbies: cooking, gardening. Rec.: music, reading. Home: 928 Third Pl., Upland, CA 91786.

TURNER, CLAUDE C.
School District Superintendent
b. Jan. 6, 1927, Kans.; s. Claude C. and Elsie (Gable) Turner; grandson of C.C. Turner, warden, N.D. State Penitentiary; ed. B.S., So. Ore. Coll. 1951; M.Ed., Univ. Ore. 1954; Ph.D., U.S. Internat. Univ. 1971; m. Janette Turner; children: Gerald C. (Vietnam casualty, age 21); Leila E. Hudak, b. July 15, 1948. Career: Teacher-instr. phys. edn. Ore. City Pub. Schs. 1951-54; asst. prin. Lake Oswego Pub. Schs. 1954-56, prin. 1956-58; prin. Belmont Sch. Dist. 1958-65, supt. 1965---. Contrib. to professional publs. 1966---. U.S. Army Med. Corps., Panama, 1945-46, WW II. Mem.: pres. Clackamas Co. Edn. Assn., Ore.; coms. Ore. State Edn. Assn.; Ore. City Rotary Club, 1952-54; Lake Oswego Jr. C. of C., 1954-57; bd. dirs. Belmont C. of C. 1965---. Presbyterian (supt. Sun. Sch., Ore. 1952). Hobbies: travel, photog. Res.: 9 Paddington Ct., Belmont, CA 94002; Office: 2960 Hallmark Dr., Belmont, CA 94002.

TURNER, JANET E.
Artist — University Professor
b. Apr. 7, 1914, Kansas City, Mo.; d. James Ernest and Hortense (Taylor) Turner; A.B., Stanford Univ. 1936; grad. Kansas City Art Inst. 1941; M.F.A., Claremont Coll. 1947; Ed.D., Columbia Univ. 1960. Career: freelance illus., portraits, 1940-42; asst. prof. Stephen F. Austin State Coll., Tex. 1947-56; asst. Teachers Coll., Columbia Univ., NYC, 1957-58, instr. 1958; asst. prof. Chico State Univ., Calif. 1959, assoc. prof. 1963, prof. 1968---. Exhibs. (prints-paintings incl. approx. 400 group, 90 circuit, 20 overseas, 25 countries; 120 one-woman exhibs., USA): Met. Mus. of Art, NYC; N.Y. World's Fair; 4th Internat. Bordighera Biennale, Italy; NAWA Exch., Stedelyke Mus., Amsterdam; NAWA Graphics for India; SAGA Exchange, London, England; USIS Circuit: Boston Pub. Lib.; Ore. State Coll. exch., Athens, Greece; Meltzer Gallery; 22 cities of Israel and Japan, 1965-66; collections incl.: U.S. Inf. Serv. (70); Benzalei Natl. Mus., Jerusalem; Biblioteque Nationale, Paris; Victoria and Albert Mus., London; Anchorage Mus., Alaska; Library of Congress, Wash., D.C.; Phila. Mus. of Art, Cleveland Mus. of Art, S.F. Mus. of Art, Brooklyn Art Mus., Dallas Mus. of Fine Arts; Feat. in numerous publs. incl.: Time, Ford Times; Biegeleisen (second edit. on serigraphy), Today's Art, 1956; Art Review, La Revue Moderne, Paris; illus. for Yazoo Rineharts, 1956; Books II and IV of Prize Winning Prints, biog. books. Awards: awards for paintings or prints; 25 purchase awards and Cannon Prize, Natl. Acad. of Design; J.S. Guggenheim Found. grant, 1953; Tupperware Art Found. grant, 1956. Co-recipient, Outstanding Prof. Award, Calif. State Univ. and Colls. System, 1975. Mem.: Natl. Acad. of Design; fellow, Internat. Inst. of Arts and Letters, Switz.; Amer. Color Print Soc., Print Club of Phila., Soc. of Amer. Graphic Artists, L.A. Printmakers, Delta Kappa Gamma, Pi Lambda Theta, Kappa Delta Pi. Res.: 567 E. Lassen Ave., Chico, 95926; Office: Chico State Univ., Chico, CA. CA.

TUOHEY, CONRAD GRAVIER
Attorney at Law
b. Dec. 27, 1933, NYC; s. James J. and Rose (Gravier) Tuohey; B.A., George Washington Univ., Wash., D.C. 1957; J.D., Univ. Mich. Law Sch. 1960; m. Judith Octavia Jeeves, Md., July 7, 1956; daus.: Octavia Jeeves, b. Oct. 16, 1961; Heather Gravier, b. Jan. 12, 1963; Meighan Judith, b. Dec. 2, 1969; Caragh Rose, b. Oct. 27, 1971. Career: admitted to Calif. bar, 1962; asst. counsel, Aerojet-Gen. Corp., L.A. 1960-64; atty. at law, Santa Ana, Calif. 1964---; sr. partner, Tuohey, Barton & McDermott firm. Bd. dirs.: Walker & Lee, Inc.; Citizen's adv. bd. Orange Co. Transit Com. 1966-68; adv. bd. Calif. Partners of the Americas, 1966-67, secty-treas. 1967-69, bd. dirs.

1968-73, pres. 1969-72, bd. dirs. Natl. Assn. Partners of the Alliance, Inc., 1971-73; exec. bd. Friends of Calif. State Univ. Fullerton, 1967, pres. 1969-71; AUS, Rifle Squad leader, Korea, 1951-54. Awards: Korea Serv. Medal with 3 battle stars; Combat Inf. Badge; Distinguished Serv. Award, Outstanding Young Man in 1967, Fullerton Jaycees. Mem.: Calif. L.A. Co., Orange Co. ((chmn.) and Amer. Bar Assns.; Calif. Trial Lawyers Assn.; Orange Co. Dem. Central Com. 1966-72; 1972 Dem. Nom., 23rd Cong. Dist. 1972; adv. bd. Family Serv. Assn. of Orange Co. 1967-69; Bldg. Ind. Assn. (orange Co.) chmn., Legal com. 1978---; mem. Nat. Assoc. of Home Bldrs. Legal com., 1978---; bd. dirs. N. Orange Co. YMCA 1969-71; Phi Sigma Kappa, dist. gov. 1971---; Phi Delta Phi. Res.: 24762 Red Lodge Place, Laguna Hills, CA 92653; Office: 1200 N. Main St., Suite 800, Santa Ana, CA 92701.

TUSHINSKY, JOSEPH SANFORD
Chairman of the Board, Superscope, Inc.
b. June 24, 1910, NYC; s. Jacques and Fannie Tushinsky; bro. Irving Tushinsky, co-inventor, Superscope (anamorphic wide screen process); m. Rebecca Del Rio, Los Angeles, Nov. 7, 1958; chil.: Joseph Sanford, Jr., b. June 30, 1967; Robert Joseph, b. Oct. 12, 1967; Joy Rebecca, b. Jan. 8, 1969. Career: Trumpet player with Toscaninni, 1941; producer-mus. dir. Carnegie Hall Light Opera Co. 1942; motion picture producer; assoc. prod. Delightfully Dangerous, star, Jane Powell, 1943; assoc. prod. Charles Rogers United Artists Prodns. 1943-45; pres. Superscope, Inc. 1952---. Co-inventor, Superscope wide screen process; author, screen treatment, My Wild Irish Rose. Inf. WW II. Mem.: bd. trustees, City of Hope; bd. trustees, Art Center Coll. of Design. Hobby: automatic piano (owns 18,000 classical piano rolls and initiated manufacturing and marketing of pianocorder reproducing system). Rec.: golf. Office: 20525 Nordhoff St., Chatsworth, CA 91311.

TUSLER, ROBERT LEON
Musician -- Educator
b. Apr. 1, 1920, Stoughton, Wis.; s. Leon and Elva (Koble) Tusler; A.B. 1946, B.M. 1947, M.A. 1952, Ph.D. cum laude, 1958; m. Adelaide Gest, 1949 (D. 1966), son Mark, b. 1952; m. 2d. Alida Penters, 1972, Utrecht, Netherlands. Career: Organist Choirmaster, St. John's Episcopal Ch., Wichita, Kans., also instr. in piano, Friends Univ., Wichita, 1946-48; tchg. asst. UCLA, 1949-56, prof. of music, 1958---; organist and choirmaster, Grace Lutheran Ch., Culver City, 1950-56; dir. of music, Wilshire Presbyterian Ch., L.A. 1959-77. Author: The Style of J.S. Bach's Chorale Preludes; The Organ Music of Jan Pieterszoon Sweelinck; contbr. articles in scholarly journals. Protestant. Hobbies: rugmaking, gardening. Res.: 19044 Santa Rita, Tarzana, CA 91356; Office: 405 Hilgard Ave., L.A., CA 90024.

TUSTIN, KAREN
Public Defender
b. Dec. 9, 1942, Bremerton, Wash.; d. Ole and Anna Kleiv; B.A., Stanford Univ., 1964, LL.B., 1968; m. Douglas Tustin, 1965, Montana; children: Ole, b. 1968; Jason, b. 1971. Career: Attorney, firm of Hiller & Irwin, San Diego, 1970-73; Deputy Pub. Defender, El Dorado Co., 1974---. Mem.: AAUW, status of women rep. 1973-75; El Dorado Co. Bar Assn.; State Bar of Calif.; Calif. Public Defenders Assn.; League of Calif. Cities. Mem. City Council, Placerville, 1977---; City Planning Commn. 1974-77. Res.: 1769 Country Club Dr., Placerville, CA; Office: 3003 Bedford Ave., Placerville, CA 95167.

TUTTLE, W. GERARD
University Administrator
b. July 25, 1899, Westfield, N.J.; s. William P. and Marie V. (Lathrop) Tuttle; grandson of William Gerard Lathrop, trustee, Columbia Univ., NYC 1894-98; ed. Fessenden Sch., W. Newton, Mass.; Hotchkiss Sch., Lakeville, Conn.; A.B., Princeton Univ. 1922; m. Hattiellen Dean Vestal, Berkeley, Calif., Oct. 18, 1934; dau. Patricia Marie, b. Apr. 7, 1928. Career: dir., inds. rels.: Vultee Aircraft, Downey, Calif. 1936-43; Consolidated Vultee Aircraft, San Diego, 1943-45; Garwood Inds., Inc., Wayne, Mich. 1946-51; Hughes Aircraft Co., Culver City, Calif. 1951-54; v.p. Amer. Bosch Arma Corp., Garden City, N.Y. 1955-65; dir. exec. mgmt. pgms. Pepperdine Univ. 1965---. Chmn. Southern Calif. Aircraft Ind. Com. (consolidated, Douglas, Lockheed, N. Amer., Northrop, Ryan and

Vultee), 1942-46; President's Com. for Employment of the Handicapped; N.Y. Gov's Adv. Council on Youth and Work, 1961-65; SATC, WW I; Calif. Selective Serv. Appeal Bd. No. 15; Spec. War Labor Bd., Aricraft Panel; L.A. area Manpower Comm., WW II. Awards: 3 cits from bd. dirs., Aircraft War Prodn. Council; Job Well Done Award, Natl. Vocational Guidance Assn. 1955. Mem.: Assocs. of Engr. Corps., Co. K, 7th Regiment, N.Y. 1923---; Charter Club, Princeton, N.J.; chairman, industrial relations com., Aircraft Prodn. Council, 1942-44; Univ. Club of L.A. 1945---; chmn. Inds. Rels. Adv. Com., L.A. 1952-54; bd. dirs., Western Coll. Placement and Recruitment Assn. 1952-54; bd. dirs., YMCA, Westchester, 1952-54; bd. dirs., Westchester C. of C., 1952-54; Personnel Ind. Rels. Assn., L.A. 1954---; Amer. Soc. Personnel. Assn. 1955-65. Amer. Mgmt. Assn. 1955-65; (hon. life.) exec. com.-dir. inds. rels. dept., Electronic Inds. Assn. 1961-65; bd. dirs., Amer. Red Cross, Nassau Co., N.Y. 1962-65; L.A. Personnel and Guidance Assn. 1966---; The Soc. of the Cincinnati; Nassau Club, Princeton, N.J. 1967---; Newcommen Soc. of N. Amer.; IPA; Town Hall, 1968---. Res.: 5299 E. Ocean Blvd., Long Beach, CA 90803; Office: 8035 S. Vermont Ave., Los Angeles, CA 90044.

TYRELL, JOHN RIX
Attorney at Law
b. May 6, 1921, Alhambra, Calif.; s. John James and Ruth (Sands) Tyrell; ed. grad. Garfield Grammar Sch., Alhambra; grad. Alhambra H.S. 1939; A.A., Pasadena Jr. Coll., June 1941; A.B. (polit. sci.), USC 1949; J.D., USC Sch. of Law, 1952; m. Marion Mallman, Alhambra, Calif. July 2, 1943; chil.: Sandra Sue, b. July 29, 1959; Jon Sands, b. Oct. 21, 1960; Randy Rix, b. June 6, 1966. Career: Life Guard (summers), City of Alhambra, 1939, 40, 41, 49, 50, 51; serv. U.S. Post Office, Alhambra, 1940, 48, 49, 50; master router, Vega Aircraft Corp., Burbank, Calif., 1941-42; various positions from welder's helper to sales engr., C.E. Howard & Co., L.A. and South Gate, Calif. 1945-48; atty. at law, Alhambra, 1954-56; partner, Davidson, Tyrell & Davidson law firm, Alhambra 1956-70; pvt. practice law, 1970---. Temple City Councilman, 1960-76, Mayor, 1962, 66, 73, 78. Aviation cadet, naval aviator, U.S. Navy, 1942-45; Commissioned Ensign, 1943; Lt. (j.g.), 1944, Lt. 1945; WW II; legal ofcr., Fleet Air Serv. Squadron Seven, and adm. ofcr., Adm. Dept. Head, Composite Squadron Eleven, 1953-54. Mem.: (past) bd. dirs., Alhambra C. of C.; (past) exec. com., Alhambra Coord. Council; (past) bd. of control-chmn. juvenile counselor com., Alhambra Exch. Club; Juvenile div., Alhambra Police Res.; (past) adv. Alhambra Youth Coord. Council; Amer. Leg. Post 139, Alhambra; Arcadia Tennis Club; So. Dist. Fed. Bar of Calif.; Amer., Calif., L.A. and San Gabriel Valley Bar Assns.; Amer., Calif., Los Angeles Trial Lawyers Assn.; trustee, Alhambra Community Hospital; (patron) Pasa. Tournament of Roses Assn.; exec. board, Alhambra Dist., San Gabriel Valley BSA; Temple City C. of C.; U.S. Power Squadron, Pasa.; Alhambra YMCA; secty. Calif. Contracts Cities Assn. 1963-64, v.p. 1965-66, pres. 1966-67; USC Alumni Assn.; bd. trustees, Community Hospital of San Gabriel, 1973---, chmn. 1978-79; Phi Alpha Delta; Alhambra Masonic Lodge No. 322, F&AM; Pasa. Consistory Scottish Rite (32nd deg.); Shrine, Al Malaikah Temple, Alhambra Hi Twelve, Arcadia Tennis Club, Altadena Town and Country Club. Rec.: tennis, swimming, boating, fishing. Res.: 5709 N. Alessandro, Temple City, CA; Office: 1154 S. Garfield Ave., P.O. Box 710, Alhambra, CA 91802.

U

UDALL, JAMES MILLARD
Real Estate Executive
b. Jan. 23, 1906, San Francisco, Calif.; s. Andy Robertson and Sarah (Kell) Udall; ed. grad. (econs.) Univ. of Calif., Berkeley, 1930; m. Helen Thompson, Los Angeles, Calif., Mar. 26, 1930 (div. 1946); m. Lydia Udall; chil.: Laura, b. Dec. 13, 1933; Linda, b. Jan. 25, 1942; James Millard, Jr. b. June 23, 1945. Career: Film ed., Paramount Pics. (3 yrs.); real estate mgmt. 1934---; pres. Udall & Richards, Hollywood mgr., W.I. Hollingsworth & Co. 1946-50; propr.-pres., Econ. Maintenance Co. (painting and maintenance); past pres., Washomobile Co. of So. Calif. USN (3 yrs.; overseas, S. Pac.), WW II; Lt. Comdr., USNR 1946-50, Comdr. 1950. Mem.: Aviators' Post, Amer. Leg.; past

pres., L.A. Chpt., The Inst. of Real Estate Mgmt.; v.p.-dir., Calif. Real Estate Assn. 1948; pres. 1952; Apartment Assn. of L.A. Co., Inc. 1949; dir.-treas., Hollywood Rotary Club, 1949; pres. L.A. Realty Bd. 1950; past pres., Hollywood-Wilshire Div., L.A. Real Estate Bd.; dir. Natl. Real Estate Fliers Assn., pres. 1950; dir. natl. assn., Real Estate Bd., 1950, pres. 1959; Lakeside Golf Club; Bel-Air Country Club; Aviation Country Club; Alpha Delta Phi. Rec.: golf, flying planes. Res.: 4545 White Oak Ave., Encino, CA; Office: 1307 Westwood Blvd., West Los Angeles, CA 90024.

UEBERROTH, PETER VICTOR
Chairman, First Travel Corp.
b. Sept. 2, 1936, Chicago, Ill.; s. Victor C. and Laura (Larson) Ueberroth; student, San Jose State Univ.; m. Virginia Nicolaus, Long Beach; four children. Career: started Transportation Consultants International, 1963; company went public, chairman, chief executive officer, First Travel Corporation, 1967---. Director, Century Bank. Mem.: Delta Upsilon, Bel Air Country Club, Jonathan Club. Christian. Rec.: water sports, golf, tennis. Office: 7833 Haskell Ave., Van Nuys, CA 91406.

UMAN, STEPHEN JONAS
Physician
b. Jan. 26, 1947, Jersey City, N.J.; s. Robert and Mildred (Hoffman) Uman; M.D., 1969; Diplomate: Am. Bd. of Internal Med., 1973, Infectious Diseases, 1976; m. Gwen Cassell, Oct. 24, 1971, Los Angeles; son, Russell Eli, b. Oct. 1, 1973. Career: Fellow, Infectious Diseases, Univ. of Wisconsin, 1973-75; practice of med., Infectious Diseases, Los Angeles, 1975---. Hebrew. Office: 6360 Wilshire Blvd., L.A., CA 90048.

UNRUH, JESSE MARVIN
California State Treasurer
b. Sept. 30, 1922, Newton, Kan.; s. Isaac and Nettie (Kessler) Unruh; ed. B.A., USC 1948, 2 yrs. grad. stu. econ. 1948-50; m. Virginia Lemon, Columbia, Mo., Nov. 2, 1943 (div.); chil.: Bruce, b. Feb. 27, 1947; Bradley, b. Dec. 1, 1948; Robert, b. Feb. 9, 1951; Randall, b. June 17, 1952; Linda, b. Dec. 4, 1955. Career: Asst. dist. supv., U.S. Bur. of the Census, 1950; elected State Assemblyman, Nov. 2, 1954-71; Dem. Candidate for Gov., Nov. 1970; elected speaker, Calif. Assembly, Sept. 30, 1961-68; pres. Natl. Conf. of State Legislative Leaders, 1965; cons. Eagleton Inst. of Politics, Rutgers, 1965---; elected Calif. State Treas., Nov. 1974---. U.S. Naval Air Corps (21 mos. overseas in Aleutian Is.), 1943-45, WW II. Mem.: Amer. Leg., Leimert Park Post; Artus Frat. Democrat. Methodist. Hobby: carpentry. Rec.: camping. Office: 915 Capitol Mall, Rm. 110, Sacramento, CA 95814.

UPRIGHT, PHYLLIS
Bank Executive
b. Sept. 5, 1925, Scottsbluff, Nebr.; d. Carl William and Ivah (Cotton) Lemke; A.A., bus. adm., 1972; m. Alan M. Upright, Mar. 8, 1944, Tulsa, Okla; chil.: Debra S. (Shipman), b. 1946; Ann Marie (Levasseur), b. 1949. Career: with Patton State Hosp. 1951-55; Bank of America, San Bernardino, 1956---: bookkeeper, 1956, escrow ofcr. 1958, asst. mgr. 1973, mgr. 1976---. Mem.: Am. Inst. of Banking, past Women's Com. chmn.; Bus. and Profl. Women's Assn., past Program Chmn.; Escrow Assn. (Calif.); Nat. Assn. of Bank Women, past publicity chmn.; Women's Div. C. of C., secty. Hobbies: stained glass, creative stitchery. Rec.: houseboating. Res.: 26967 Baseline, Highland, CA 92346; Office: Bank of America, 130 West 40th St., San Bernardino, CA 92406.

URBACH, ROY JAMES GUNTHER
Electronics Engineer
b. Sept. 6, 1946, San Mateo; s. Gunther and Rose Urbach; BSEE, Calif. Polytech. State Univ., 1969; m. Virginia LoBue, Aug. 5, 1972, San Luis Obispo; dau. Elizabeth Ann, b. June 6, 1976. Career: Asst. Electronics Engr., GTE Lenkurt, Inc., San Carlos, 1969, electronics engr., 1970, sr. electronics engr., 1975, supr. electronics engr., 1978---. Co-Patentee of pulse-correcting system for a telephone signaling system, 1973. Mem. IEEE. Hobby: music. Res.: 406 Falcato Dr., Milpitas, CA 95035; Office: 1105 County Rd., San Carlos, CA 94070.

URIST, MARSHALL R.
Orthopedic Surgeon — Educator
b. June 11, 1914, Chicago; s. Irwin and Minna Urist; bro., Carl Henry Urist (dec.), Prof. of Jurisprudence, Univ. Mich.; B.S., Univ. Mich., 1936; M.S., Univ. Chicago, 1937; M.D., Johns Hopkins Med. Sch., 1941; Hon. M.D., Univ. of Lund, Sweden, 1977; m. Alice E. Pfund, Aug. 16, 1941, Baltimore, Md.; children: Marshall McLean, b. 1944; Nancy Scott (Miller), b. 1947; John Baxter, b. 1950. Career: Dir., Bone Research Lab., UCLA Med. Center, 1950---; Prof. Dept. of Surgery (Orthopedics), UCLA, 1950---; Chief cons. to Surgeon Gen., Orthopedic Surg. 1945-65; staff, Wadsworth Hosp., U.S. VA Med. Center, Los Angeles, 1948---. Editor-in-chief, Clinical Orthopaedics and Related Research, 1966---; Author: Physiology of Bone, 1955-68, four editions; 243 publs. on subject of bone physiology, biochemistry, orthopedic surgery. AUS M.C., 1943-46, Chief of Orhtopedic Surgery, 22nd Gen. Hosp., England, 1944. Pres., Hip Soc., 1978-79; pres., Soc. of Internat. Research on Orthopedics and Traumatology, 1978-81; pres., Assn. of Bone & Joint Surgeons, 1967-68. Hobby: gardening. Rec.: agri. Res.: 796 Amalfi Dr., Pacific Palisades, CA 90272; Office: 1033 Gayley Ave., Los Angeles, CA 90024.

URREA, PETRONIO DAVID, JR.
Contact Lens Company Executive
b. Nov. 8, 1939, San Francisco; s. Petronio David, Sr. and Martha Herren (Clark) Urrea; student, S.F. City Coll., 1957-60; Univ. of Calif., Berkeley, 1960-62; Doctor of Pharmacy (with honors), Univ. of Calif. Sch. of Pharmacy, 1966; m. Theresa Blanche Keller, Aug. 17, 1963; chil.: Cheryl Lynn; Kimberly Lynn; Deborah Lynn. Career: clinical liaison, Barnes-Hind Pharmaceuticals, Sunnyvale, 1967-68, mgr. clinical liaison 1968-69, director medical affairs, 1970-72, director, medical and tech. affairs, 1972; v.p., med. and tech. affairs, 1972-73, v.p., research and product devel. 1973-76; vice pres. operations, Continuous Curve Contact Lenses, Inc., San Diego, 1976---. Patent applications: (Sibley, Yung & Urrea) cleaning agents for contact lenses, 1976; novel surfactant containing boiling solution, 1976; hypochlorite cleaning of contact lens, 1976. Publ. (w/Szekely, Kirk) Total Hygienic Contact Lens Care, Ophthal. Journ. U.S. Coast Guard Reserve 1958-66; outstanding athletic award, 1958. Catholic. Hobbies: sailing, pvt. pilot. Rec.: water sports. Office: 8006 Engineer Road, San Diego, CA 92111.

UTT, RICHARD HAYS
Writer
b. Apr. 29, 1923, Stoneham, Mass.; d. Charles D. and Miriam (Clark) Utt; B.A., Pacific Union Coll., 1945; M.A., Andrews Univ. (Mich.), 1958; grad. studies, Univ. Calif. Berkeley, 1966; m. Gwendolyn Woodward, July 6, 1947, Angwin, Calif.; children: Charles, b. 1949; Jeannette (Galloway), b. 1950; David, b. 1955; Lynn, b. 1957. Career: Pres., Costa Rica Mission of Seventh-day Adventists, 1953-57; Asst. Editor, Signs of the Times, 1958-61; book editor: Pacific Press Publishing Assn., Mountain View, 1961-76; Freelance writer, editor, 1976---. Author: eleven pub. books incl.: A Century of Miracles, 1963; The Builders, 1970; Uncle Charlie — A Biography of Charles E. Weniger, 1978; The Vision Bold, 1978; 400 pub. articles and stories. Res.: 5545 Riverside Ave., Rialto, CA 92376.

V

VAIL, JAMES HAROLD
Musician — Educator
b. Mar. 15, 1929, Los Angeles; s. Harold Parsons and Harriet Lourene (Perry) Vail; B.Mus., Curtis Inst. of Music, Phila., 1951; M.M., USC, 1956, D.M.A., 1961; m. Barbara Di Iullo, Feb. 2, 1957, Los Angeles; children: Stephen James, b. 1958; Susan Lourene, b. 1959. Career: Organist and Choirmaster, St. Elisabeth's Episcopal Ch., Phila., 1947-49, St. Mary's Episcopal Ch., 1949-51, St. John's Episc. Ch., Los angeles, 1954-59, 1961-69, La Jolla Presbyn. Ch., 1959-61, St. Alban's Episc. Ch., L.A., 1969---; mem. Faculty, Immaculate Heart Coll., Los Angeles, 1957-60, USC Sch. of Music, 1961---. Dean, L.A. chpt., American Guild of Organists, 1964-66; pres., L.A. chpt. Choral Conductors Guild of Calif., 1970-72. AUS, 1970-72. Mem.: Am. Guild of Organists, Am. Choral Directors Assn., Choral Conductors Guild of Calif., Hymn Soc.

of Am. Episcopalian. Rec.: cycling, running. Res.: 3005 Motor Ave., L.A., CA 90064; Office: USC, Los Angeles, CA 90007.

VALE, BARBARA JANE
Painter
b. Apr. 22, 1923, Long Beach, Calif.; d. Lloyd Willard (founder, Sta-Lube, Inc.) and Vella Elizabeth (Bateman) Vale; great-grandau. of Elizabeth Bateman, noted painter; ed. (life scholarship), Otis Art Inst., L.A.; m. Gilbert D. Herrmann, Los Angeles, Calif. 1943 (dec. 1953); m. Martin J. Marx, Minden, Nev. 1953 (div. 1965); chil.: Greg Bruce Herrmann, Martis Jane Marx. Career: Draftsman-prodn. illus., Douglas Aircraft Co. 1942-43; fine arts painter, interior decorator, prodn.-commercial-med. illus., antique appraiser, arch.-landscape designer; owner, Vale Arts Unlimited, 1944---; paintings in many permanent collections, incl. Harvard Sch. of Law; illus. in Butte Remembers, publ. 1973; 24 one-woman shows. Art teacher, USAF, 1952-53; Chico Art Center, 1966-67; Paradise Art Center, 1970-71; chmn. No. Calif. Opened Juried Art Show, 1964, 65, 66, others. Mem.: Soc. Western Artists, 1960-70; Oakland Art Assn. 1960-63; Creative Arts Center, Chico, 1962---; Natl. League Amer. Pen Women, 1965---; Soroptimist Club of Chico, 1972---; Red Cross. Unitarian. Studio: 1228 Downing Ave., Chico, CA 95926.

VALENS, EVANS GLADSTONE, JR.
Author
b. Apr. 17, 1920, State College, Pa.; s. E.G. and Mable (Grazier) Valens; B.A., Amherst Coll. 1941; m. Winifred A. Crary (div.) Oct. 1941, Northport, N.Y.; children: Thomas Crary, b. 1945; Marc John, b. 1949; Jo Anne, b. 1950; Dan Malcolm, b. 1951. Career: Reporter: El Paso Herald-Post, 1942; UPI, 1942-44: in San Francisco, Salt Lake City, Central Pacific theatre (until wounded late in Okinawa campaign); post-war: Nurenberg Trials, Frankfurt, Berlin, 1948 Winter Olympics bureau chief, St. Moritz, Bureau Chief for southern Germany, Munich; freelance author, 1951---; prod., director & writer, KQED (Ednl. TV), San Francisco, 1954; writer-producer, NBC, NYC, 1957; freelance, KQED, 1963. Mil.: 4-F, decorated Purple Heart. Prod.-Dir. filmed series for Nat. Edn. TV (30 to 45 minute shows, 3 to ten in each series): The Atom with Edward Teller; The Elements with Glenn T. Seaborg; Virus with U.C. Berkeley Virus Lab. Staff; The Measure of Man with John Dodds (Stanford). Author TV plays and films: The Silver Lieutenant, 1954; The Red Myth (7 1/2-hr. dramatic docu. scripts), 1957; IGY—The International Geophysical Year (10-part live show, NBC), 1957; Johns Hopkins File (7 1/2-hour shows for ABC), 1957; narration for Moonwalk One (feature-length documentary of Apollo 11). Author books: Me & Frumpet, 1958; (w. Gleen Seaborg) Elements of the Universe, 1958 (Edison award for Best sci. book for youth); w. W.M. Stanley, Viruses and the Nature of Live, 1961; Wingfin and Topple, 1962; Wildfire, 1963; The Number of Things: Pythagoras, Geometry and Humming Strings, 1964; Magnet, 1964; Motion, 1965; A Long Way Up (bio. of Jill Kinmont), 1966; Cybernaut, 1968; The Attractive Universe: Gravity and the Shape of Space, 1969; w. Ernst G. Beier, People-Reading, 1975; The Other Side of the Mountain, 1976; The Other Side of the Mountain, Part II, 1978. Res.: Mill Valley, CA 94941.

VAN BUSKIRK, ROBERT DAVIS
Business Executive — Civic Leader
b. Oct. 5, 1917, Seminole, Okla.; s. Frank J. and Fronia (Brame) van Buskirk; desc. pre-revolutionary ancestry; ed. A.B., USC 1939; J.D. 1941, M.B.A., 1958; m. Phyllis E. Wetherill, Kansas City, Mo., Oct. 12, 1947; chil.: Robert L., b. Apr. 23, 1951; Lynn E., b. Aug. 14, 1953. Career: Assoc. counsel, Bank of Amer. 1947-54; dir.-secty.: trust ofcr., Security Title Ins. Co. 1955-57; LAACO Inc., 1957---; dir. & Sec. 1964---; LAACo Investment Corp. 1963---; Flag Park, Inc., 1970-76; treas. CAAL, Inc., 1971-76; Horton & Converse Labs, Inc., 1972---. Capt., U.S. Army Air Corps (AUS), WW II. Mem.: Amer., Calif. and L.A. Bar Assns.; USC Law Alumni Assn., Beta Gamma Sigma, Phi Kappa Tau, Pi Sigma Alpha, Tau Kappa Alpha, Sigma Sigma, Blackstonian, Blue Key, Trojan Squires, Inter-frat. Council; dir. L.A. Jr. C. of C. 1949-54, treas. 1950, v.p. 1951, pres. 1953, trustee, Charity Found. 1950-53, pres. 1952, trustee, Music and Golf Found. 1952-54; youth div., Met. Welfare Council, 1952-53; dir. L.A. C. of C. 1953; adv. bd., So. Calif. Sym. Assn. 1953-54; adv. bd., L.A. Police Relief Assn. 1953-54; pres. Round Table, 1955-56;

treas. Wine and Food Soc. of So. Calif. 1956-57, gov. 1958---; Town Hall. Clubs: Kiwanis, Rolls-Royce Owners, Riviera Country, Riviera Tennis, San Marino City. Episcopalian. Hobby: books, wines. Res.: 1585 Shenandoah Rd., San Marino, CA 91108; Office: 611 W. Sixth St., Suite 3030, Los Angeles, CA 90017.

VAN BRUNT, BERGEN
Attorney at Law
b. Nov. 27, 1911, Frankfort, Ind.; s. Geddes and Caroline Van Brunt; cous., Barbara Bel Geddes, actress, and Norman Bel Geddes, Houston; student, Univ. Utah, Purdue Univ.; LL.B., Indiana Univ. Sch. of Law, 1936; m. Cecile Saunders, Apr. 24, 1953, San Francisco. Career: Claims Atty., Maryland Casualty, Indpls., 1936-39; claims mgr., Ohio Casualty, Detroit, 1936-42; claims mgr., Ohio Casualty, San Francisco, 1945-46; partner, law firm Jackson & Van Brunt, S.F., 1946-53; law firm of Bergen Van Brunt, S.F., 1953---. Lt., USNR, 1942-45, gunnery ofcr. Pacific. Awards: Gold Medal, 1968, Good Citizenship Medal, 1969, Calif. Soc. of SAR; Patriots' Medal of Nat. Soc. SAR, 1971. Mem.: Barrister's Club of San Francisco, v.p. 1950; S.F. Bar Assn., bd. dir. 1950; Lawyers Club of S.F., pres. 1964, dir. 1954---; del to state conf. of Calif. State Bar Delegates, 1950-75; Am. Bd. of Trial Advocates, pres. 1968; S.F. Trial Lawyers Assn., pres. 1968; Lawyers Club of S.F., bd. govs. 1960---; Calif. Trial Lawyers Assn., 1964---. Mem.: Beta Theta Pi, pres. S.F. chpt. 1958; Big Ten Univ. Club, pres. 1961; Fin. Center Toastmasters, S.F., pres. 1958; SAR, pres. S.F. chpt. 1964, Chancellor of Calif. Soc. 1964-74, chancellor, S.F. chpt. 1974---; Zane Irwin Post of Am. Legion, comdr., 1968; VRW, S.F. Naval Post Capt. 1967; Kentucky Col., 1970---. Republican, San Mateo Co. Central Com., 1957-62. Presbyterian. Hobby: geneology. Res.: 1220 Cardigan Rd., Hillsborough, CA 94010.

VAN DEERLIN, LIONEL
Congressman
b. July 25, 1914, Los Angeles, Calif.; s. Lionel and Gladys Mary (Young) Van Deerlin; B.A., USC 1937; m. Mary Jo Smith, Northfield, Minn., Oct. 8, 1940; chil.: Lionel James, b. July 12, 1942; Lawson John, b. Nov. 2, 1947; Victoria, b. Oct. 11, 1950; Elizabeth Louise, b. Mar. 31, 1953; Mary Susan, b. Apr. 5, 1954; Lawrence Jeffrey, b. May 4, 1955. Career: Newspaperman, San Diego Sun., Minneapolis Tribune and Baltimore Sun., 1937-42; city ed. San Diego Daily Journ. 1946-50; news dir. KFSD (now KOGO radio-TV, and XETV, 1953-61. Dem. Candidate for Cong. 1952-58; elected, House of Reps. 1962, U.S. Congressman, Jan. 1963---, chmn. Subcommittee on Communications; U.S. Army News Serv., staff, Stars & Stripes, Mediterranean Theater, 1941-45, Staff Sgt., WW II. Mem.: Sigma Alpha Epsilon, Sigma Delta Chi. Episcopalian. Rec.: tennis. Res.: 3930 Argyle Terr., N.Y., Wash., D.C. 20011. Office: 2408 Rayburn House Ofc. Bldg., Wash., D.C. 20515.

VAN DE KAMP, JOHN K.
District Attorney
b. Feb. 7, 1936, Pasadena, Calif.; s. Harry and Georgie Van de Kamp; nephew of founders of Van de Kamp Bakery and restaurant business; now owners of Lawry's Foods, Inc.; m. Andrea (Fisher) Van de Kamp, 1977. B.A., Dartmouth, 1956; J.D., Stanford Univ. 1959. Career: Chief Asst. U.S. Atty. (chief of Criminal Div., chief of Complaint Unit), 1960-67; U.S. Atty., Central Dist. of Calif. 1966-67; dep. dir. Exec. Ofc. of U.S. Attys. 1967 (spec. assignments: March on Pentagon, 1967; Chicago riots and Resurrection City, 1968); dir. Exec. Ofc. of U.S. Attys., Wash., D.C. 1968; Fed. Pub. Defender, Central Dist. of Calif. 1971-75; Dist. Atty. of L.A. County, 1975---. Democratic nom. for Congress, 1969; dir. Jesse Unruh's Campaign for Gov. 1970. U.S. Army, 1959-60; Natl. Guard, ret. 1965. Mem.: bd. trustees, L.A. County Bar Assn.; Bd. dirs., Natl. Dist. Atty's. Assn.; bd. dirs., Calif. Dist. Atty's. Assn.; adv. comm., San Gabriel Council of B.S.A.; Bd. Councilors for USC; Calif. State Bar Com on Legal Servs. and Amer. Correctional Assn.; bd. dirs. March of Dimes. St. Andrews Catholic Ch., Pasa. Rec.: golf, tennis. Office: 18-709 Criminal Courts Bldg., Los Angeles, CA 90012.

VANDEMAN, DOROTHY D.
Author — Educator
b. Aug. 12, 1909, Indianapolis; d. Roy Leo and Mary (Montgomery) VanDeman; B.A., Whittier Coll., 1931; M.A., Claremont Coll., 1934; postgrad., USC, Natl. Coll. of Edn., U.C. Santa Barbara. Career: Grad.

Fellow, Scripps Coll., 1932-33; directing tchr., Broadoaks Sch. of Whittier Coll., Pasadena, 1934-40; instr., Santa Barbara State Coll., 1940-44; asst./assoc./prof., Univ. Calif., Santa Barbara, 1944-64, prof. emeritus, 1964---, counselor, 1966--- (based on spiritual philosophy of "Through Faith The Victory," co-authored with Edith M. Leonard), Co-author, Foundations of Learning in Childhood Education; others. Mem.: Assn. for Childhood Edn. Internat.; Delta Phi Upsilon; Delta Kappa Gamma; Internat. Platform Assn. Soc. of Friends, Quaker. Hobbies: poetry, needlecraft. Address: P.O. Drawer JJ, Santa Barbara, CA 93102.

VANDERBILT, FRANCES COLLINS
Writer — Musician
b. Sept. 18, 1910, Columbus, Ga.; d. R. Bernard and Stella (Cantrell) Collins; ed. grad. Atlanta Cons. of Music, 1929; postgrad. Cincinnati Cons. of Music, 1930-31; Juilliard Grad. Sch. of Music, 1934-38; Ger.-Amer. Mus. Students Exch. Scholar, Hochschule fur Musik, Berlin, Germ. 1938; m. Donald B. Vanderbilt, Columbua, Ga., June 1, 1946; dau.: Mrs. Robert Alan (Barbara) Williamson, b. Dec. 29, 1947. Career: Violin soloist, N.Y. Concert Co. 1929-31; faculty, Druid Hills Sch. of Music, Emory Univ., Ga. 1932-34; violin soloist, Natl. Conv. of Mu Phi Epsilon, 1932-34; Beethoven Trio, 1932-38; pvt. teacher, 1934-38; violist, Atlanta Philharmonic Orch. 1941-42; violinist, Jean ten Have Trio 1947-54. Music ed.-critic: Dekalb New Era, Decatur, Ga. 1934-38; Atlanta Constitution, 1941-42; South Coast News, Laguna Beach, Calif. 1954-69. Awards: won Disneyland Community Serv. Award for Laguna Beach Civic Ballet Co. 1965. Mem.: (life) pres. Mu Phi Epsilon Alumnae, Atlanta, 1938; Red Cross, 1943-46; (life) Natl. Soc. Arts and Letters; coord. Orange Co. Philharmonic Soc. 1957-60; bd. dirs. Laguna Beach Community Concert Assn. 1958---, v.p. 1965-67; O.A. Chpt. P.E.O. 1959---; chpt. pres. Natl. Leag. Amer. Pen Women, 1960-62, natl. auditor, 1964-66; (charter) Laguna Beach Chamber Music Soc. 1960---, v.p. 1966-67; (charter) 1st v.p. Woman's Club of Laguna Beach, 1961-62, 1965-66; bd. dirs. First Nighters Assn. 1962---; bd. dirs. Laguna Beach Civic Ballet Co., Inc. 1965-67. Res.: 1025 Canyon View Dr., Laguna Beach, CA 92651.

VAN DEURS, GEORGE
Rear Admiral, U.S. Navy, Retired
b. July 25, 1901, Portland, Ore.; s. Henry Martin and Sallie Forester (Nice) van Deurs; B.S., U.S. Naval Acad., 1920; Naval Aviator 1923; Sr. Course, Naval War Coll., 1947; M.A., San Francisco State Univ., 1953; m. Ann Shepard, Spr. 13, 1924, Pensacola, Fla.; daughters: Sally (Mrs. D.H. Shannon), b. 1925; Kay, b. 1927. Career: Midshipman, USN, 1917, progressed through the grades to Rear Adm., Ret., 1951: (comd. Patrol Squadron 23 at Pearl Harbor, 1939-41; Supt. of Aviation Tng. and Chief of Staff, Corpus Christi, Tex., 1941-43; Plans Ofcr., Chief of Staff to Comdr. Air South Pacific, 1943-44; Comdg. Ofcr. USS Chenango, 1944-45); freelance author, photog., 1951---. Author: Wings For The Fleet, Naval Inst. Press, 1966; Anchors In The Sky, Presidio Press, 1978; contbr. many articles on aviation, Calif., travel to popular mags. Mem.: Army & Navy Clubs, Wash. D.C.; Golden Eagles; Quiet Birdmen; Clear Lake Riviera Golf & Yacht Club. Hobby: cabinet making, trick photog. Res.: 312 Golden Gate Ave., Belvedere, CA 94920.

VAN DYKE, JOHN JOSEPH
Physician — Pulmonologist
b. Jan. 23, 1938, Los Angeles; s. Douglas and Bernadette Van Dyke; B.S., Loyola Univ., 1958; M.D., USC, 1962; m. Suzanne Kolda, Jul. 29, 1961, Pasadena; chil.: Tracy, b. Sept. 2, 1962; Suzie, b. Sept. 4, 1963; Kelly, b. Mar. 30, 1965; Michael, b. Sept. 1, 1967; Jennifer, b. Feb. 8, 1973. Career: Internship, L.A. Co. Hosp. (rotating) 1962-63; residency, USAF Med. Center, Lackland AFB. Texas, 1966-69; fellowship, Fitzsimmons Gen. Hosp., Denver, Colo., 1969-70; certified, Am. Bd. Internal Med., 1970, Diplomate, Pulmonary disease, 1975; med. practice, Lake & Van Dyke Med. Corp., Pasadena ---; also asst. clin. prof. (chest. med.) USC, 1971---; director Inhalation Therapy, Santa Teresita Hosp., Duarte, 1972---; director, Inhalation Therapy, Methodist Hosp. of So. Calif., Arcadia, 1973---. Instr. in med., UC Davis, 1970; chief, Pulmonary Disease Sect. David Grant USAF Med. Center, 1970-71; Inst. research protocols, La Vina Hosp., 1973-75. Served USAF Med. Corps, 1961-70. Contbr. articles to med. journs. Mem.: AMA, CMA; L.A. Co. Med. Assn.; Am. Thoracic Soc.; Am. Coll. Physicians, fellow, 1974---; Am. Coll. of Chest

Physicians, cons. to Pulmonary Rehabilitation Com. 1973; Am. Bd. of Internal Med.; Am. Geriatric Soc.; Calif. Thoracic Soc.; Trudeau Soc.; Ventilation Session of So. Calif. Active mem.: Sierra Madre Environmental Club; YMCA Indian Guide Program, La Canada; St. Bede the Venerable Catholic Ch. Hobby: sports. Home: 937 Vista del Valle, La Canada, CA; Office: 111 Congress St., Suite C, Pasadena, CA 91105.

VAN VELZER, VIRGINIA CLAIRE
Writer
b. Sept. 19, 1927, State College, Pa.; d. Harry L. and Golda L. (Cline) Van Velzer; sis. Verna Van Velzer; ed. B.S. (magna cum laude), Univ. of Ill. 1950; postgrad. Syracuse Univ. 1956. Career: Tech. asst., Ill. State Geol. Survey, 1948; personnel tech. Wright-Patterson AFB, Ohio, 1952-53; librarian, Battelle Mem. Inst., Columbus, 1953-54; statistician, Syracuse Bd. of Edn., N.Y. 1954-55; lib. Gen. Elec. Co., Syracuse, 1955-56; tech. writer-editor, Gen. Elec. Co., Palo Alto, Calif. 1956-61; founder-dir. Tech. Publs.-Library, Microwave Electronics Corp. 1961-64; proj. admr.-sr. tech. writer-bibliographer, GTE Sylvania, Inc., Mt. View, 1964---. Joint Council for Sci. and Math. Edn., Santa Clara Co. 1965-67. Contrib. many articles, tech. series, bulletins to professional publs. 1950---; editor, 4 tech. books, publ. McGraw-Hill, Allied Radio, 1949---. Awards: H.S. Spec. Award and Honors Day; Natl. Hon. Soc. 1945; Undergrad. Scholarship Award, 1945; Grad. Fellowship Award, 1950; Univ. of Ill. Bronze Plaque, 1950; Gen. Elec. Electronettes Valentine Queen, 1957; Merit Award by Soc. of Tech. Writers and Publs. 1966. Mem.: H.S. Mortar Bd. 1945; Univ. of Ill. Alumni Assn.; Alpha Lambda Delta, 1947; Phi Beta Kappa, Chi Kappa Phi, Psi Chi, 1950; Alpha Tetheta Upsilon, 1954---; IEEE, div. bd. dirs. Golden Gate Chpt. 1965-66, natl. coms.; Amer. Bus. Writers Assn. 1965-69; natl. conv. com. 1967; Soc. Tech. Writers and Publs., chpt. bd. dirs. 1965-69; coms. and chmn. Stanford Univ. Seminar, 1966; Spec. Lib. Assn. 1965---; Calif. Lib. Assn. 1969---; Marquis Biog. Lib. Soc. 1969---; Amer. Craftsmen Council; Mineral Lit. Center African Violet Soc. of Amer., Inc. 1972---; Cat Fanciers Assns.; Natural Hist. Socs.; YWCA; Borzoi, Players, Camera, Natl. Travel, Sierra Clubs. Hobbies: lapidary, crafts, travel, hort., reading. Res.: 4048 Laguna Way, Palo Alto, CA 94306; Office: P.O.B. 205, Mt. View, Calif. 94040.

VAN WOLF, HENRY
Sculptor
b. Apr. 14, 1898, Ger. (U.S. cit. 1935); s. Johann Baptist and Maria (Bruendl) Wolf; ed. elem sch., Munich, Ger. 1904-12; Munich Art Sch. 1912-16; stu. sculpture and bronze tech. under Ferdinand von Miller, Munich, 1919-1926; m. Veronica Jaendl, Munich, Ger. 1922; sons: Henry, b. May 5, 1923; Richard Werner, b. Apr. 3, 1941; Joseph John, b. Mar. 3, 1948. Career: Est. U.S. res. 1928; professional sculptor, natl. and internat. exhibs. 1921---; Brooklyn Mus. 1930; Roerich mus., N.Y. 1932; Allied Artists of Amer. 1936-37; Arch. Leag. 1937; Springfield Mus. 1938; Calif. Art Club, 1943-52; Painters and Sculptors Club of L.A. 1948---; Artists of Southwest 1950-55; life-size animal sculptures in foreground, Red Hook Nursery, Brooklyn, N.Y. 1939; U.S. Govt. comm. for sculpture, Fairport, N.Y. P.O. 1939; sculptures, Inglewood Park Cemetery, Calif. 1949, 54; statue, Ben Hogan, Golf House, N.Y. 1955; bronze doors for St. Nicholas Episc. Ch., Encino, Calif. 1956-57; Good Shepherd, sculpture in bronze, Garden Grove Community Ch., Calif. 1964; Indian statue in bronze (Fernando), Van Nuys Mail; numerous portraits famous personalities. Feat. on natl. broadcast, Radio and TV Comm. of So. Bapt. Conv., Ft. Worth, Texas, Feb. 1965. Awards: 36 first prizes for sculpture: Calif. Art Club, 1948, 50, 52; Painters and Sculptors Club, 1948, 50, 51, 52, 53, 55; San Fernando Valley Profl. Artists Guild, 1949, 69; Ebell Club, L.A. 1949, 65, 66, 70; L.A. City Art Exhib. 1949, 66, 70; Artists of Southwest, 1950, 51, 53, 54; Calif. Internat. Flower Show Art Exhib. 1951. Mem.: dir. Council of Traditional Artists Socs.; founder-pres., Valley Artists Guild (San Fernando Valley Professional Artists Guild), 1948-50, 1952-53; Natl. Sculpture Soc.; fellow, Amer. Inst. of Fine Arts; v.p. Painters and Sculptors Club of L.A.; Fed. Internationale of La Medaille, Paris. Catholic. Hobby: painting. Res.-Studio: 5417 Hazeltine Ave., Van Nuys, CA 91401.

VARGAS, ERNEST ARTHUR
Attorney at Law
b. Sept. 7, 1938, Lima, Peru; s. Ernesto J. and Irma Ida (Frank) Vargas; B.A., UCLA, 1961; J.D. Loyola

Law Sch., 1964; son, Robert, b. Dec. 13, 1956. Career: Admitted to Calif. State Bar 1965, U.S. Ct. of Mil. Appeals 1965, U.S. Dist. Ct. 1974, U.S. Ct. of Appeals, 9th Circuit and U.S. Supreme Ct., 1977. Atty., partner, law firm Oliver, Sloan, Vargas, Shaffer & Lindvig, 1965---. Arbitrator, Los Angeles Co. Superior Ct., Am. Arbitration Assn. Lectr., Univ. Calif., 1978. Mem.: L.A. County, Calif. and Am. Bar Assn.; L.A., Calif. and Am. Trial Lawyers Assn. Capt., USAR 1964-65; Mem.: Masonic Order; Nat. Order of Sojourners; Big Brothers; BSA, L.A. El Camino Dist. Chmn. 1968; UCLA Alumni Assn.; Loyola Law Sch. Alumni Assn. Rec.: skiing, scuba diving. Office: 611 W. Sixth St., No. 3300, Los Angeles, CA 90017.

VASQUEZ, SUSAN DOLORES
Purchasing Executive
b. Nov. 20, 1946, Berkeley; d. Robert and Gloria Hughes; Certified Purchasing Mgr. (C.P.M.), 1975; m. Gary Vasquez, Jan. 19, 1974, Berkeley; dau. Tina, b. Oct. 28, 1970. Career: Purchasing agent, Bio-Rad Laboratories, Richmond, 1968, purchasing mgr. 1972, materials mgr. 1978---. Speaker on Women in Purchasing, 1978; pub. articles on purchasing, 1969, 74. Mem.: dir., Purchasing Mgmt. of No. Calif.; Nat. Assn. of Purchasing Mgmt., exec. com. chem. group, 1976, pub. rels. chmn. Dist. I; Phi Alpha Delta, pres. 1975. Rec.: golf, swimming. Res.: 205 Iris Road, Hercules, CA; Office: 2200 Wright Ave., Richmond, CA 94804.

VAUGHAN, EARLE RUSSELL
Military Academy Administrator
b. July 7, 1912, Denver, Colo.; s. Dr. Russell U. and Harriette S. Vaughan; ed. Antioch Coll., Yellow Springs, Ohio, 1929-31; Loyola Univ. Coll. of Law, 1931-34; LL.B., Amer. Univ. Coll. of Law, 1935; m. Edith Gibbs, Los Angeles, Calif., b. Nov. 21, 1938; Charles Julian, b. July 7, 1944; Charaline Page, b. Feb. 7, 1955. Career: Admitted to Calif. State Bar, 1935; pres. Page Mil. Acad. 1938---. Lt. Col., Calif. Army Natl. Guard; Lt. (s.g.), USNR (ret.). Mem.: pres. Norco Lions Club, 1950; pres. United Motor Cts. 1951; pres. L.A. Apt. Assn. 1958; pres. Calif. Apt. Owners Assn. 1959-60; pres. Natl. Apt. Owners Assn. 1960-61; pres. bd. dirs., Bldg. & Safety Commrs., City of L.A. 1961-66; pres. Wilshire C. of C. 1963; bd. dirs., United Cerebral Palsy Found. 1963; post comdr. Amer. Legion, 1968-69; L.A. Ath. Club; Jonathan Club; Mason (32°) Shriner. Episcopalian (vestry, Ch. of Our Saviour, 1952-55). Hobby: bridge. Res.: 276 S. Lorraine Blvd., Los Angeles, CA; Office: 565 N. Larchmont Blvd., Los Angeles, CA 90004.

VAUGHAN, JOSEPH ROBERT
Food Company President
b. Jan. 28, 1916, Los Angeles, Calif.; s. Vincent and Lucile (Eichler) Vaughan; A.B., Loyola Univ. 1937, J.D. 1939; m. Margaret Koetters, Los Angeles, Calif., Jan. 20, 1940; daus.: Barbara, Christine, Judith. Career: Partner, Vaughan, Brandlin, Robinson and Roemer law firm, 1939-65. Dir. Knudsen Creamery Co. of Calif. 1962---, v.p. 1965, exec. v.p. 1965-69, pres. Knudsen Corp. 1969---, pres. and chief exec. ofcr. 1971---. Mem.: Loyola Coll. of Law Alumni Bd. Govs. 1954-57; bd. dirs. Daniel Freeman Hosp. 1955, secty. 1959-60, pres. 1963-65; dir. L.A. Beautiful, Inc. 1957-65; L.A. Co. Bar Assn.; com. chmn. State Bar of Calif. 1959-60; Amer. Arbitration Assn., Natl. Panel of Arbitrators, 1961-65; bd. dirs.: L.A. Area C. of C. 1971-73; Better Bus. Bureau, 1972-73; Natl. Dairy Council, 1972---; Milk Ind. Found. 1973---; Fed. Res. Bank of San Francisco, L.A., 1973---, chmn. 1974---; bd. trustees, Pac. Legal Found. 1973---; bd. regents, Loyola Marymount Univ. 1973---; L.A. adv. bd. Salvation Army, 1973-75; Economic Round Table, 1974---; Rotary Club of L.A.; Los Angeles Club, Roman Catholic. Rec.: tennis. Res.: 404 S. Lorraine Blvd., Los Angeles, 90020; Office: 231 E. 23rd St., Los Angeles, CA 90011.

VAUGHAN, RICHARD PATRICK
Clinical Psychologist
b. May 19, 1919, Los Angeles; s. Vincent B. and Elizabeth Lucille (Eichler) Vaughan; A.B., St. Louis Univ., 1943, M.A., 1945; S.T.L., Alma Coll., Los Gatos, 1951; Ph.D., Fordham Univ., 1956. Career: Prof. and chmn. dept. of psychology, Univ. of San Francisco, 1956-67, Dean of Arts and Sci., 1967-69; vice-provincial for Edn., Calif. Jesuits, 1969-71; Regional Provincial Superior, Calif. Jesuits, 1971-77; adj. prof. of psychology, Loyola Marymount Univ. 1977---; clin. psychologist ---. Bd. dir.: Am. Catholic

Psychological Assn., Conf. of Major Superiors of Men, USA. Roman Catholic; Regional Superior of Calif. Jesuits; Chmn. Region 6, Conf. of Major Superiors. Address: 7101 W. 80th St., Los Angeles, CA 90045.

VAUGHN, JOHN VERNON
Industrialist — Civic Leader
b. June 24, 1909, Grand Junction, Colo.; s. John S. and Alice A. (Baylis) Vaughn; A.B., UCLA 1932; m. Dorothy M. Pickrell, Glendale, Calif., Oct. 12, 1934; chil.: Mrs. Richard H. (Dorothy Dee) Stone, b. 1936; John Spencer, b. 1939. Career: Asst. credit mgr., salesman, br. mgr., Natl. Lead Co. 1932-37; sales mgr., Sillers Paint & Varnish Co. 1937-46, pres.-dir. 1946-60 (merged with Benjamin Moore & Co. 1959); propr-pres.-chmn. Dartell Labs., 1959-70; v. chmn. bd., Crocker National Bank, 1970-74; Cons., Coopers & Lybrand, 1974---. Dir.: Calif. Fed. Savings and Loan Assn. Orthopaedic Hosp. pres. 1973, chmn., 1974---; dir. O.K. Earle Corp. 1968---; dir. Pac. Lighting Corp. 1971---; hon. dir. Crocker Natl. Corp. 1974---; Awards: UCLA Distinguished Serv. Award, 1956, Community Serv. Award, 1969, UCLA Alumnus of Yr. 1971; L.A. Realty Bd. Most Distinguished Citizen, 1972; LAACC Community Serv. Award, 1974, other honors. Mem.: Jonathan Club, 1945-73; dir. 1961-64; pres. 1964; San Marino Lodge, F&AM 1945---; Scottish Rite, 1946---; (charter) Young Presidents' Orgn. 1951-56; dir. L.A. Better Bus. Bur. 1952---, chmn. bd. 1959-61; pres. L.A. Paint, Varnish & Lacquer Assn. 1952; v.p. Natl. Paint, Varnish & Lacquer Assn. 1953; San Gabriel Country Club, 1955---, dir.-v.p. 1965-68; v.p.-chmn. San Marino Rec. Comm. 1956-58; pres. UCLA Alumni Assn. 1957-58; regent, Univ. of Calif. 1958-59; dir. L.A. C. of C. 1961---, v.p. 1964, v.p.-treas., 1966, pres. 1969, chmn. 1970; dir. YMCA, L.A. 1965---; chmn. Cits. Adv. Council on Pub. Transportation, 1965-67; dir. Natl. Conf. of Chrs. and Jews, Inc. 1966---; dir., Chancellor's Assocs., 1966---; trustee, Welfare Planning Council, 1967---; dir. Calif. Mus. of Sci. and Ind. 1968---; Regent, Forest Lawn Mem. Park, 1968---; trustee, Natl. Safety Council, 1968---; dir.-v.p. Mgmt. Council for Merit Employment, Tr. and Research, 1969---; vice chmn., Invest in Amer. 1970---; trustee, Claremont Men's Coll. 1970-71; trustee, Pepperdine Univ. 1972---; World Bus. Council, 1972---; dir. Friends of Claremont Colls. 1973---; pres. Calif. Mus. Found. 1973---; pres. L.A. Clearing House Associates, 1973---; dir. So. Calif. Visitors Council, 1970---; v.p. World Affairs Council, 1970---; Newcomen Soc., Town Hall, Lincoln Club, Calif. Club; pres., Beta Theta Pi and Beta Theta Pi Alumni Assn. of So. Calif. Republican. Hobby: hunting, stream fishing. Rec.: golf. Res.: 1199 Sherwood Rd., San Marino, CA; Office: 1000 W. Sixth St., L.A., CA 90017.

VEITCH, STEPHEN W.
Attorney at Law
b. Aug. 19, 1927, Albuquerque, New Mexico; s. Kenneth E. and Edna M. (Oxnard) Veitch; B.A., Univ. of N. Mex., 1949; J.D., Stanford Law Sch., 1957; m. Nancy Baker, June 28, 1951, Pasadena; chil.: Christopher Oxnard, b. Dec. 16, 1953; Julia Blair, b. Feb. 3, 1958. Career: probate adminstr., Wells Fargo Bank, 1957-59; senior vice president, Van Strum & Towne, Inc., 1959---. Dir., Anza Pacific Corp., 1960-76; Advisory bd. mem., Anza Shareholders' liquidating trust, 1976---. USN, 1945-46; 1st Lt., USAF, 1950-54. Mem.: Pacific Union Club, S.F.; University Club, S.F.; Menlo Circus Club, Atherton; Commonwealth Club, S.F.; Sigma Chi Frat. Episcopal. Home: 33 Spencer Lane, Atherton, CA 94025; Office: One Embarcadero Center, Suite 2109, San Francisco, CA 94111.

VENER, STUART L.
Physician
b. Mar. 14, 1946, Los Angeles; s. Melvin and Uretsky Vener; B.A. 1967, M.D. 1970; m. Bryna Weis, Dec. 27, 1977, Los Angeles; dau. Dvora, b. 1973. Career: Physician, Los Angeles, 1970---; clin. instr./asst. clin. prof., UCLA Sch. of Med., 1975---. Staff, Wadsworth VA and UCLA Hosps. Recipient Distinguished Tchr. Award, UCLA Dept. of Med., 1977. Diplomate: Am. Bd. of Internal Med., 1973; Am. Bd. of Endocrinology & Metabolism, 1975. Mem.: Phi Beta Kappa, 1967---; Alpha Omega Alpha, 1970---; Phi Delta Epsilon, 1975---; Am. Coll. of Physicians, 1975---; Fellow, Endocrinology & Metabolism, 1975. Hobby: choral music. Office: 2080 Century Park East, Suite 707, Los Angeles, CA 90067.

VENUTI, WILLIAM J.
Professor of Civil Engineering
b. Aug. 16, 1924, Philadelphia; s. Emilio and Marni (Scalzi) Venuti; Ph.D., Stanford Univ., 1963; m. Twila Black, 1949, Denver, Colo.; children: David, b. 1951; Paul, b. 1952; Stephen, b. 1954; Thomas, b. 1956; Lisa, b. 1958; Philip, b. 1959. Career: Instr., Univ. of Colo., 1952-55; prof. of Civil Engring., San Jose State Univ., 1955---. Lt., USN, 1943-46. Rec.: jogging. Res.: 16091 Greenwood Rd., Monte Sereno, CA 95030; Office: Dept. of Civil Engring., San Jose State Univ., San Jose, CA.

VERGER, MORRIS DAVID
Architect — Planner
b. Mar. 25, 1915, Fort Worth, Tex.; s. Joseph and Dora (Bunyan) Verger; B.Arch., Univ. Calif., Berkeley, 1943; m. Florence Brown, June 21, 1939, Santa Barbara; children: Paul, b. 1945; Alice (Swanton), b. 1949. Career: Naval Arch., U.S. Nacy Bureau Ships, 1943-45; draftsman various archtil. firms, 1946-50; pvt. practice as architect/planner. Works incl. Hunting Drive Sch., L.A., 1975; Flax Artist Materials Bldg., L.A., 1976; Archtl. Program and Design Frank D. Lanterman High Sch., L.A., 1978. Lectr. Arch., UCLA Ext.; vis. critic, Cal. State Univ., San Luis Obispo; leader seminar on Inter-Active Planning; developed method for computer design of Interstitial Space. Archtl. Program for Terman Engring. Center, Stanford Univ., 1974. Recipient design awards Westwood C. of C. 1974, 75; Presidential Citation 1976. Fellow AIA, pres. So. Calif. chpt. 1975, v.p. Environmental Affairs, Calif. Council 1976, elected Calif. AIA vice pres. 1979, pres. designate 1980. Res.: 1362 Comstock Ave., Los Angeles, CA 90024; Office: 10880 Wilshire Blvd., Suite 903, Los Angeles, CA 90024.

VERHEY, ROBERT S.
Business Executive
b. Mar. 7, 1943, Minnesota; s. Seymour and Jane (Williams) Verhey; B.A., Duke Univ., 1961; M.B.A., Amos Tuck Sch. of Bus. Adm., Dartmouth COll., 1965-67; m. Judith Ann Hilker, Aug. 21, 1965, St. Paul, Minn.; children: Robert Williams, b. 1967; Anne Merrill, b. 1974. Career: Mgr., Fin. Planning, Xerox Corp., Pasadena, 1967-70; mkt. mgr., Memorex Corp., Santa Clara, 1970-71; gen. mgr., Fibreboard Corp., San Francisco, 1972-75; v.p. fin. & treas., 1975---. Mem.: The Guardsmen of San Francisco; Republican Central Com. Presbyterian. Rec.: golf, sailing, rafting. Res.: 150 Hacienda Dr., Tiburon, CA 94920; Office: 55 Francisco St., San Francisco, 94133.

VERMEER, RICHARD DOUGLAS
Corporate Executive
b. July 2, 1938, Bronxville, N.Y.; s. Albert Casey and Helen (Valentine) Vermeer; B.S., Fairleigh Dickinson Univ., 1960; M.B.A., LeHigh Univ., 1967; m. Grace Dorothy Ferguson, May 22, 1960; children: Carin Dawn; Catherine Jeanne; Robert Brooke. Career: Fin. exec. trainee, Gen. Electric Low Voltage Switchgear, 1961-63; Internal Auditor, Campbell Soup Co., 1963-64; Sr. Systems Analyst, Air Products & Chemicals Inc., 1964-67; Mgr., fin. systems, TransWrodl Airlines, 1967-71; Regional Controller, Kaufman & Broad Inc., 1971-76; v.p. and controller, Global Marine Inc., 1976---. AUS, 1960. Mem.: Mensa; Am. Mgmt. Assn.; Jr. C. of C., Allentown, Pa., dir. 1966; Planning Execs. Inst.; Nat. Assn. of Accountants; Fin. Execs. Inst. Res.: 32009 Foxmoor Ct., Westlake Village, CA 91361; Office: 811 W. 7th St., Los Angeles, CA 90017.

VESPER, HOWARD G.
Oil Company Executive
b. June 13, 1902, Pasadena, Calif.; s. Arthur E. and Sadie A. (Gockley) Vesper; B.S. (chem. engring.), Calif. Inst. of Tech. 1922; m. Ruth Cawthorne, Pasadena, Calif., June 17, 1923. Career: Various positions with Standard Oil Co. of Calif., incl. exp. lab.; chem. in research lab.; foreman, exp. lab. of Research and Development Dept.; foreman, mgr., Research and Development Dept., El Segundo refinery, 1922-31; staff asst.-gen. asst., Research and Development Dept., S.F. Calif. 1931-33; tech. salesman, Foreign Trade Dept., N.Y. 1933-37; asst. mgr., Lubricants Div., Marketing Dept., S.F. 1938-40; mgr. 1940-42; mgr. Gasoline & Fuel Oil Div., Marketing Dept. 1942-45; pres. Calif. Research Corp. 1946-54, chmn. bd. dirs., Calif. Research and Development, 1952---; v.p. Standard Oil Co. of Calif. 1952-56, v.p., Western Div., 1954-56, v.p.-dir. Western

Operations, Inc. 1957-58, pres. 1958-65, v.p.-dir. 1965-67 (ret.). Gen. Adv. Com., U.S. Atomic Energy Comm. 1965-75, chmn. 1969-75; dir. Homestake Min. Co. Mem.: Strybing Arboretum Society; bd. trustees, Calif. Inst. of Tech.; bd. govs., Commonwealth Club of Calif., S.F. 1975---; past pres., Ind. Research Inst.; fellow, Calif. Acad. of Scis.; Amer. Chem. Soc., Amer. Inst. of Chem. Engrs., Soc. of Automotive Engrs., Soc. of Chem. Ind., (charter) Pasa. Community Playhouse, Tau Beta Pi, Alpha Chi Sigma; clubs: World Trade and Bohemian, S.F.; Claremont Country Club, Oakland. Protestant. Hobby: gardening, music, golf. Res.: 244 Lakeside Dr., Oakland, CA 94612.

VIAL, DONALD
State Industrial Relations Director
b. Stockton; s. Angelo Francisco and Angela Clair (Pareto) Vial; B.A., polit. sci. and econ.; M.A., econ.; m. Rosemary Soghomonian, Aug. 1, 1948, Pasadena; children: Diane Krista, b. 1950; Katherine Mari (Anderson), b. 1953; Elizabeth Ann, b. 1956; Stephanie Daria, b. 1965. Career: Economist, Calif. State Fedn. of Labor, AFL, 1952-58; dir. of Research and Edn., Calif. Labor Fedn., AFL-CIO, 1958-64; chmn., Center for Labor Research and Edn., Univ. of Calif., Berkeley, 1964-74; (apptd. by gov.) Dir. of Indsl. Rels., State of Calif., 1975---. Bd. dir., Indsl. Rels. Research Assn. AUS, 1943-46. Hobbies: carpentry, gardening. Res.: 40 Mount Lassen Dr., San Rafael, CA 94903; Office: 455 Golden Gate Ave., San Francisco, CA 94101.

VICENCIA, FRANK D.
California Legislator
b. Aug. 23, 1931, Artesia; grad. Excelsior H.S., 1949; m. Alice "Lil" Costa, 1954; children: Steve, Michele (Jondle), David, Michael, Laura. Career: Operated Dairy Supply Bus., 1954-59; gen. mgr., Milk Producers Council, 1959-64; legislative rep. Southern Calif. Rapid Transit Dist. League of Calif. Milk Producers, 1964-74, also Public Rels. bus.; elected to 54th Assembly Dist., Calif. Legislature, 1974, 76, 78---. AUS, ---43; Korea. Catholic. Hobbies: softball, basketball, tennis. Res.: 9860 Crestbrook, Bellflower, CA 90706; Office: 8040 East Alondra Blvd., No. D, Paramount, CA 90723.

VICTOR, JANET MARSHALL
Publisher — Editor
b. Jan. 27, 1914, Wichita, Kans.; d. Clifford Ormand and Claribel (Macomber) Bentley; GGrandniece, Duke of Ormond, Eng.; A.A., Compton Coll., 1934; B.A., Whittier Coll., 1936; M.S. in Lib. Sci., USC, 1938; m. Donald C. Victor, Oct. 22, 1961, Los Angeles. Career: Society editor, reporter, Bell Indsl. Post, 1930-36; asst. librarian, Maywood, 1932-36; head book reviewer, Los Angeles Co. Library, 1936-41; retouch artist, various photographic studios, also instr., L.A. Inst. Photog. Art, 1943-57; founder, publisher, editor, Rangefinder Mag. for Profl. photogs., Los Angeles, 1952---. Exec. Mgr., Profl. Photogs of So. Calif., 1954-61, Indsl. Photogs. of So. Calif., Am. Soc. of Mag. Photogs. Recipient achievement awards: Profl. Photos. of Am., Profl. Photogs. of Calif., Profl. Photogs. West, Western Publs. Assn. Secty., Western Publications Assn., 1958-60. Hobby: vineyardist. Res.: 14231 Cohasset St., Van Nuys, CA 91405; Office: 1312 Lincoln Blvd., Santa Monica, CA 90406.

VIDOR, KING WALLIS
Motion Picture Director
b. Feb. 8, 1895, Galveston, Tex.; s. Charles S. and Kate (Wallis) Vidor; ed. Peacock Mil. Acad., San Antonio, Tex.; Tome Inst., Md.; m. Elizabeth Nicholas, Ariz.; chil.: Suzanne Vidor, Mrs. Egan (Antonia) Merz, Mrs. Dean (Belinda) Jones. Career: Dir.-prod., mot. pics. incl.: The Turn in the Road, 1918; The Jack Knife Man, 1920; Wild Oranges, 1924; The Big Parade, 1925; The Crowd, 1928; Hallelujah, 1929; Street Scene, The Champ, 1931; Our Daily Bread, 1934; Stella Dallas, 1937; The Citadel, 1938; Northwest Passage, 1940; H.M. Pulham, Esq. 1941; Duel in the Sun, 1946; The Fountainhead, 1949; War and Peace, 1956; Solomon and Sheba, 1958. Author: A Tree Is a Tree, publ. by Harcourt, Brace and Co., Inc. Awards: Chevalier of Republic of Italy, Sept. 1970. Hobbies: painting, music. Res.: 1115 La Altura Rd., Beverly Hills, CA 90210.

VIERHELLER, RALPH CHARLES
Veterinarian — Hospital Administrator
b. May 12, 1915, Fresno, Calif.; s. Charles Emil and Clara May (Sloan) Vierheller; ed. Fresno State Coll.

1933-35; D.V.M., Colo. State Univ. 1939; m. Edna Helen Kettlewell, Los Angeles, Calif., Nov. 18, 1940; chil.: Edward Charles, b. Apr. 24, 1942; Denis Kieth, b. Feb. 10, 1944; Janet Lynn, b. Aug. 2, 1954. Career: Small animal veterinarian, L.A. 1939-42; owner-admr., Whittier Dog and Cat Hosp., Whittier, 1946---; pres. Drs. Vierheller-Clark, Inc., Pico Rivera, 1961---; Speaker: many national, state and local veterinary organizations. Author: Author: numerous articles on subject of orthopedic and ophthalmic surg., publ. veterinary journs., others. Lt. Maj. Veterinary Corps., USAAF (1942-46), WW II. Awards: one of 6 veterinarians to receive award of recognition from Collie Club of Amer. for research into eye anomalies of collie dogs; Amer. Veterinary Med. Assn. Practitioner Research Award, 1971. Mem.: Amer. Animal Hosp. Assn.; pres. S.E. Chpt., So. Calif. Veterinary Med. Assn. 1957, pres. 1961; dir. Whittier Rotary Club, 1960-62; dir. Amer. Veterinary Med. Assn. 1961-63; pres. Amer. Soc. Veterinary Ophthal. 1964-65; pres. So. Calif. Veterinary Golfers Assn. 1964-65; pres. Calif. Veterinary Med. Assn. 1968-69; diplomate, Amer. Coll. Veterinary Surgs. 1970; diplomate, Amer. Coll. Veterinary Ophthal., 1970, Regent 1973---; University Club, Whittier. Republican. Protestant. Hobby: flying (pvt. pilot license). Rec.: golf, travel. Res.: 1651 El Portal Dr., La Habra, CA 90631; Office: 1301-F Beach Blvd., La Habra, CA 90631.

VIESSELMAN, JOHN OSCAR
Psychiatrist
b. Sept. 30, 1941, Fairmont, Minn.; s. James and Valerie Viesselman; B.A., Phi Beta Kappa, Univ. of Minn., 1964-67; M.D., UCLA Sch. of Med., 1971; Psychiatric residency, Wash. Univ. Sch. of Med., St. Louis, 1971-73; res. child psychiatry, UCLA Sch. of Med., 1973-75; m. Leonette Thaemert, 1965, Minneapolis; children: Heather, b. 1967; Scott, b. 1969. Career: psychiatrist, Olive View Psychiat. Center, Van Nuys, 1973-75; staff psychiatrist, outpatient dept. Gateways Hosp., L.A., 1973-76; Behavior Therapy Seminar, UCLA Sch. Med., 1974-75; Ward Psychiatrist, Sepulveda VA Hosp., 1975-76; Adj. Asst. Prof. of Psychiatry, UCLA Sch. Med., 1976---, now Asst. Clin. Prof. of Psychiat. Mil. Service, 1959-63. Mem.: Am., So. Calif. Psychiatric Assns., So. Calif. Soc. for Child Psychiatry, AAAS, Assn. for Advance. Behavior Therapy. Lutheran. Hobbies: computers, golf, tennis. Office: 595 E. Colorado Blvd., Suite 405, Pasadena, CA 91101.

VINSON, GLADSTONE ELMORE
Advertising Agency Executive
b. Dec. 19, 1919, Dallas, Texas; s. John and Gordie (High) Vinson; cous., the late Chief Justice, Fred Vinson; B.B.A., Texas A&I Univ., 1939; m. 2d. Jean Marine, Oct. 8, 1966, Las Vegas, Nev.; daughters, Kathleen, b. 1949; Victoria, b. 1953. Career: Account exec., Roger & Smith Advt., Dallas, 1946-47; v.p. Armstrong, Schramm Co. Advt., San Diego, 1947-57; pres. Armstrong, Fenton & Vinson, 1957-59; v.p. D'Arcy Advt. Co., San Diego, 1959-64, Los Angeles, 1965-68; pres. Kaufman, Vinson, Lansky, Inc., San Diego, 1968-72; pres. Barnes-Chase Advt., San Diego, 1972; partner, chmn. Buchanan-Vinson Advt. Inv., 1972---. Bd. dir.: Jr. Achievement, NCCJ 1968-72, Multiple Sclerosis Soc. 1977---. Chn. Greater S.D. Sports Assn. 1977-79; pres. San Diego Holiday Bowl 1978-79; chmn. San Diego Stadium Club 1977-79. Capt. USNR 1942-46. Mem.: Navy League, San Diego Opera Guild, San Diego Symphony Assn., University Club, La Jolla Country Club, Globe Theatre Guild. Republican. Episcopalian. Hobbies: civic work, travel. Res.: 2249 Caminito Preciosa Norte, La Jolla, CA 92037; Office: 1335 Hotel Circle South, San Diego, CA 92108.

VIRTUE, CONSTANCE
Musician
b. Jan. 6, 1905, Cincinnati, Ohio; d. Robert Stewart and Edith (Rankin) Cochnower; Mus.B., College Conservatory of Music, Univ. of Cincinnati, 1927; Master of Sacred Music (S.M.M.), Union Theol. Sem., NYC, 1945; m. Clark W. Virtue, M.D., Capt. (M.C.) USN. Ret. (Navy doctor 30 yrs., 20 yrs. civilian practice), July 3, 1928, Cincinnati, Oh.; children: Christie (Mrs. Henry Gardner); Robert Clark. Career: Piano composer and student. age of ten on; music scholarships, 1919-27; ch. organist, choir dir., Mt. Auburn Presbyterian Ch., Cincinnati, 1927, St. Lukes Evangelical Lutheran, NYC 1945, First Unitarian, San Diego, 1960-65, others; lifelong pvt. tchr. of piano, organ and theory; organ instr. Convent of the Sacred

Heart, El Cajon 1960-68; tchr. music hist., class piano, Grossmont Coll. 1961-63. Originator of Virtue Notagraph (7-line semitone staff notation), 1933---, pres. and editor: Virtue Notagraph Editions, 1973---. Pianist, local artists concerts; toured with opera program for Alaska Music Trails, 1968; live music and lectr. courses Music Speaks for Univ. Calif. Ext., San Diego, 1969,70,72; composer two music dramas: What Gift to the King, and The Queen of Camelot, anthems, instrumental works, songs and orchestra piece, Mystic Sonnet. Awarded 1st place in 5 composition contests, Mu Phi Epsilon Research Award 1938 for original notation system. Mem.: Am. Guild of Organists, Music Teachers Assn. of Calif., Music Educators, Idyllwild Assoc. of USC, Musical Merit Assn. of Gr. San Diego, Calif. Rare Fruit Growers, Mu Phi Epsilon. Hobby: gardening. Res.: 4940 Beaumont Dr., La Mesa, CA 92041.

VITALE, DANIELLE RENEE CARTIER
Educator
b. April 17, 1943, Neuchatel, Switzerland; Cer., Ecole Superieure de Commerce, Neuchate, 1961; Dip., Ecole Benedict, Neuchatel, 1964; grad. work, educ., UCLA, 1970; Dip., Center for Early Edn., L.A., 1973; m. Dr. Simone J. Vitale, 1970. Career: Secty. Acct., Mutuelle Vaudoise Ins., Neuchatel, Switzerland, 1963; Secty., Publicitas, Geneva, Switzerland, 1964-65; co-founder with husband, Montessori-Vita Schls., Inc., 1970-75; vice pres, Penfield Schls., Inc., 1973---; dir., Children's Corner Pre-Sch. 1973---. Awards: Doctorate of Humane Letters (hon.), 1973; dip. honor for community services, 1973; awards community leaders and noteworthy Americans, 1976-77. Pres., Altrusa Internat., Glendale chpt. 1976-77. Hobbies: travel, needlepoint. Home: 918 E. Tujunga Ave., Burbank, CA 91501; Office: 1320 Glenwood Rd., Glendale, CA.

VITALE, DONALD EUGENE
Publisher
b. Feb. 16, 1930, Oak Park, Ill.; s. Sylvester and Anne (Potenza) Vitale; student, Loyola Univ., Los Angeles; Northwestern Univ.; UCLA; m. Sarah Brengle, June 9, 1956, Manhattan Beach; chil.: Mark Francis, b. 1957; John Vincent, b. 1958; Valerie Anne, b. 1959; Paul Keigwin, b. 1962. Career: copyboy, reporter, rewrite, City News Bureau, Chicago, 1950-51; editor, Los Angeles Daily Journal, 1954-59; editor, Southern California Business, L.A. C. of C., 1959-61; Pub. Rels. Dir., Los Angeles C. of C., 1961-65; assoc. dir. of Corp. Communications, Dart Industries (then, Rexall Drug & Chem. Co.), 1965-67; pvt. practice pub. rels., Don Vitale & Assoc., Beverly Hills, 1967-70; PIP (printing) franchisee, 1970-79; rancher, San Diego Co., 1975---; publisher, Who's Who in California, 1978---; sr. lectr., USC Sch. of Journalism, 1966-71; Prod. radio show Big Problems in Small Business, L.A. 1966-67; playwright: The Aquarium, prod. New Playwrights Found., Hollywood, 1973; Bidding and Other Fables, prod. The Evergreen Stage Company, 1976, 78. AUS, 1951-53, Korea, decorated 2 Battle Stars; USAR 1954-60, Psychological Warfare Unit. Apptd. Exec. Secty., Mayor's (Yorty) Small Bus. Council, 1967; mem. Advisory Bd., Mount St. Mary's Coll., 1963-65; pres. Catholic Press Council of So. Calif., 1966-67; mem. Greater L.A. Press Club, 1954-71; Avocado Growers Bargaining Council, 1975---. Hobby: rare books. Rec.: theatre. Res.: 2022 Calle de Los Alamos, San Clemente, CA 92672; Office: P.O.B. 4240, San Clemente, CA 92672.

VITALE, SIMONE JOSEPH
President, Penfield School
b. Mar. 19, 1908, Trappeto, Palermo, Italy; s. Simone and Anna (Amato) Vitale; Ph.D. philosophy and theology, Pontifical Univ. Pius XI, Molfetta; Master's Degree Medieval Hist., summa cum laude, Cal. State Univ., L.A. 1972; M.L.S., summa cum laude, USC, 1958; m. Daniel Renee Cartier, 1970. Career: tchr., Humanities, history and philosophy, Monreale and Corleone, Palermo, Italy; estab. permanent residence, Calif., 1955; profl.librarian, and teacher in Calif. until 1970; lectr., Astara, internat. philosophical and religious organ., 1962-72; co-founder with wife, Montessori-Vita Schools for early childhood edn. 1970---: Merged with Penfield Schools, Glendale, 1973. Publications: monthly contbr. editor of Italian mags.: GLI Arcani of Milan and Il Giornale dei Misteri od Florence; pub. book: Jeane Dixon, Profeta del Nostro Tempo, 1977; former weekly column, Italo-Americano, Italian Community Newspaper in Calif.; works in progress: Encyclopedia of Prophets and Prophecies; History of Prophecy. Mem. Beta Phi Mu; Phi Delta Kappa. Home: 918 East Tujunga Ave., Burbank, CA 91501.

VOEGELIN, HAROLD STANLEY
Attorney at Law
b. Sept. 10, 1919, Summit, N.J.; s. Frederick E. and Aestelle (Dorland) Voegelin; A.B., Univ. of Mich. 1942; J.D., Univ. of Mich. Law Sch. 1948; m. Winifred Nemec, Honolulu, Hawaii, Dec. 24, 1962; son: Frederick P., b. May 10, 1950; stepchil.: Jon F. Martin, b. July 21, 1943; Janis L. Martin, b. Nov. 24, 1946. Career: Teaching asst. in const. law, Univ. of Mich. 1947-48; assoc. McEntee and Willis law firm, Los Angeles, 1948-52; assoc.-partner, Brady and Nossaman, L.A. 1952-57; partner, Wood, Voegelin and Barton law firm, 1957-60; partner, Voegelin, Barton, Harris and Callister, L.A. 1960-70; Voegelin & Barton, 1971---; Dir.: Nesbitt Food Prods., Inc. L.A.; Smith Internat., Inc., Newport Beach; A.J. Bayer Co., Torrance; chmn. bd. dirs. West Coast Commodity Exch., Inc., L.A.; pres. Five-Thirty Investment Corp., L.A.; dir. S. Coast Child Guidance Clinic, Newport Beach. Lecturer, USC Inst. on Fed. Taxation, 58, 62, 64, 68; speaker, Title Ins. and Trust Co. Tax Forum, L.A. 1957; Inst. on Internat. and Comparative Law, So. Methodist Univ., Dallas, Tex. 1969. Contrib. articles to professional journs. USN (1942-46), WW II, Lt. Comdr., USNR. Awards: first prize, Legal Essay Competition, L.A. Co. Bar Assn. 1949. Mem.: pres. L.A. Jr. C. of C., 1955; dir. L.A. Jr. C. of C.; v.p.-dir., United Cerebral Palsy, Inc., L.A.; chmn. com. on continuing edn. of bar, L.A. Co. Bar Assn. 1961-62; trustee: Whittier College, Whittier; Murphey Found.; Nesbitt Found.; South Coast Repertory Theater, Costa Mesa; Calif. State, Inter-Amer., Internat. Bar Assn.; Amer. Judicature Soc.; sect. taxation-sect. internat. and comparative law, Amer. Bar Assn.; adv. bd. Internat. Comparative Law Center, Dallas, Texas 1971---; Theta Delta Chi; Delta Theta Phi; Pres.' Club, Univ. of Mich.; Clubs: Balboa Bay, Newport Harbor Yacht (Newport Beach), Lincoln of Orange Co., California (L.A.), Capitol Hill, Wash. D.C. Presbyterian. Res.: 32 Harbor Island, Newport Beach, CA 92660; 800 W. First St., Los Angeles, CA 90012; Office: 606 S. Olive St., L.A., CA 90014; 4343 Von Karman, Newport Beach, CA 92660.

VOGELBACH, KARL-HEINRICH
Cardiologist
b. Aug. 16, 1944, Magdeburg, Germany; s. Dr. Hans-Heinrich V. and Katinka Vogelbach-Von Menz; M.D., Univ. of Munich, W. Germany, 1971; m. Jana E. Kolarova, Dec. 1974, New Orleans; dau. Alexandra, b. 1962. Career: Spl. Cardiology Tng., 1973-78; dir. of Cardiology, St. Luke Hosp., Pasadena, 1978---; also Clin. Instr., LAC-USC Medical Center. Contbr. articles med. sci. publs. 1969---. Lt. AF, West Germany, 1963-65. Rec.: tennis, skiing. Res.: 1914 Midlothian Dr., Altadena, CA 91101; Office: 2632 E. Washington Blvd., Pasadena, CA 91109.

VOGT, ROCHUS
Physicist
b. Dec. 21, 1929, Neckarelz, Germany; s. Heinrich Otto and Paula (Schaefer) Vogt; T.H. Karlsruhe (Germany) 1950-52; (Cand. Phys. 1952) Universitaet Heidelberg, 1952-53; S.M., Univ. of Chicago, 1957, Ph.D., 1961; m. Micheline Bauduin, 1958, Heidelberg; children: Michele, b. 1963; Nicole, b. 1967. Career: Research assoc., Univ. Chicago 1961-62; asst./assoc./prof. of Physics, Calif. Inst. of Tech., 1962---, chmn. Div. of Physics, Mathematics, Astronomy, 1978---, chmn. of the faculty 1975-76; chief scientist, Jet Propulsion Lab. 1977-78. Reserach Interest: Astrophysics. Address: Calif. Inst. of Tech., Pasadena, CA 91125.

VOHS, JAMES ARTHUR
President, Kaiser Foundation Health Plan
b. Sept. 26, 1928, Idaho Falls, Idaho; s. John Dale and Lucille Vohs; B.A., Univ. of Calif., Berkeley, 1952; m. Janice Hughes, Sept. 19, 1953, Piedmont, Calif.; chil.: Lorraine, b. Nov. 10, 1955; Carol Jan, b. June 10, 1957; Nancy Lynn, b. Apr. 24, 1959; Sharla Jane, b. May 28, 1963. Career: Employed, various Kaiser orgns. 1952---: pres., Kaiser Foundation Health Plan and Kaiser Foundation Hospitals. Mem., secty., HEW's Task Force on Medicade and related programs, 1969-70; vice chmn., Forum on Health Care Delivery, White House Conf. on Children 1970; Regent, Holy Names College 1972---; Bd. Dir., Marcus Foster Institute 1977---; Mem., Inst. of Medicine, 1979. Served U.S. Army, 1946-48. Catholic; pres., Parish Council. Home: 17 Westminster Dr., Oakland, CA 94618; Office: One Kaiser Plaza, Oakland, CA 94612.

VOLK, HARRY J.
Chairman, Union Bank
b. July 20, 1905, Trenton, N.J.; s. Michael T. and Susan (Harkins) Volk; ed. A.B., Rutgers Univ. 1927, LL.B., Law Sch. 1930; chil.: Robert H., b. Nov. 27, 1932; Richard R., b. Jan. 28, 1934; Carolyn E., b. Jan. 3, 1942. Career: v.p., Prudential Ins. Co. 1940-57; pres., Union Bank, 1957-69; chmn.-dir. 1969---; chmn.-dir. Union Bankcorp, 1969---. Dir.: Pac. Lighting Corp., Times Mirror Co. 1952; Western Air Lines, Inc. Div. Chief, P.S. Strategic Bombing Survey (1945), WW II. Mem.: pres. Rutgers Univ. Alumni Assn. 1940-45; trustee, Rutgers Univ. 1942-47; dir. L.A. C. of C. 1949-52; trustee, Calif. Inst. of Tech.; trustee, Hosp. of Good Samaritan; L.A. Clearing House Assn., USC Assocs., L.A. Co. Museum of Art, The Founders, Assocs. of Calif. Inst. of Tech. Found. Benefactor. Res.: 365 N. Rockingham Ave., Los Angeles, CA 90049; Office: 445 S. Figueroa St., Los Angeles, CA 90017.

VOLPERT, RICHARD S.
Attorney at Law
b. Feb. 16, 1935, Cambridge, Mass.; s. Dr. Samuel A. and Julia (Fogel) Volpert; A.B. Amherst Coll., 1956; LL.B., Columbia Law Sch., (Stone Scholar) 1959; m. Marcia Flaster, June 11, 1958, New Rochelle, N.Y.; chil.: Barry S., b. Nov. 25, 1959; Samuel A., b. Dec. 14, 1961; Linda A., b. Apr. 26, 1963; Nancy J., b. Nov. 18, 1966. Career: associate, O'Melveny & Myers, 1959-67; partner, 1967---; author: Creation and Maintenance of Open Spaces in Subdivision: Another Approach, UCLA Law Review, 830; draftsman, Open Space Maintenance Act, Calif. Govt. Code; cons., lectr., Calif. continuing edn. of the Bar: California Zoning Practice, Ground Leases, Gen. Real Property Practice Course; practice consult., Calif. Real Estate Law & Practice, Matthew Bender, 1974. Editor and chmn.: Calif. State Bar Journ. 1972, 73, and Los Angeles Bar Journ., 1965-67; dir. Western Center on Law and Poverty, 1971-75; dir., L.A. Neighborhood Legal Services Soc. 1969-71; exec. com. L.A. Co. Bar Assn., 1968---; v.p. L.A. Co. Natural Hist. Mus. Found., 1977---; trustee, 1974---; pres. Amherst Club of So. Calif. 1972-73; bd. of councilors, USC Law Center, 1976---; bd. dir. Univ. of Judaism, 1973---; chmn., Center on Contemporary Jewish Life; chmn., Community Rel. Com., Jewish Fedn. Council of L.A., 1977---; exec. bd., Am. Jewish Com., L.A. chpt., 1967---; Anti Defamation League, B'nai Brith, regional bd. 1964---; L.A. area C. of C., chmn., Land Use Task Force, 1973---; dir., L.A. County Bar Found., 1977---. Mem.: Am. Bar Assn., Los Angeles Co. Bar Assn.; University Club of L.A.; Am. Soc. of Planning Officials; Urban Land Inst.; Fellow, Am. Bar Found.; Central City Assn.; exec. com. mem. Nat. Jewish Community Relations Advisory Council. V.P., Pacific SW region, United Synagogue of Am. 1963-64; chmn. bd., Valley Beth Shalom, Encino, 1972-75; chmn. bdg. com. 1975-77. Hobbies: photog., wine. Rec.: travel. Home: 4001 Stansbury Ave., Sherman Oaks, CA 91423; Office: 611 W. Sixth St., Los Angeles, CA 90017.

VON BREYMAN, GABY
College Professor
b. Jan. 24, 1911, Davidson, Sask., Can.; d. Robert and Helene (Collin) Wilson; A.B., USC 1934, M.A. 1935; Certificate La Sorbonne, Paris, Fr. 1938; m. George E. von Breyman (prof., Ventura Coll.), Los Angeles, Calif., Oct. 5, 1946; son, Edward G., b. Oct. 14, 1948. Career: Lycees, Belgium and Fr. 1920-27; teaching asst. USC 1934-35; instr. French-Spanish, Thiel Coll., Greenville, Pa. 1936-37; instr. Ventura Coll., Calif. 1937-40, 1946-61; Salinas and Covina H.S.s, 1940-46; asst. prof. Calif. Luth. Coll. 1961-64, assoc. prof. 1964-69, chmn. French Dept. 1966---, prof. 1969---. Contrib. to publs. Mem.: dir. NDEA Inst. in Spanish, 1967, 68; pres. Tri-Counties Foreign Lang. Assn. 1968-70; Calif. Council Teachers of Foreign Langs, 1968-71; State Liaison Com. for Foreign Langs, 1970-72; Calif. Colls. and Univs. Faculty Assn., So. Calif., 1970-71; (hon.) Directory of Amer. Scholars; Phi Beta Kappa, Pi Kappa Phi, Pi Delta Phi, Sigma Delta Pi, Delta Kappa Sigma. Emmanual Presbyterian. Hobbies: travel, reading, photog. Res.: 764 Calle Mandarinas, Thousand Oaks, CA 91360; Office: Calif. Lutheran College, Thousand Oaks, CA.

VON DEWITZ, ARDEN
Artist
b. Mar. 7, 1915, NYC; s. Baron Hrolf and Baroness Valkyrien Von Dewitz; B.A., Stickney Art Sch., Pasadena, 1930; m. Amalie Wyss, Jan. 31, 1941, San Diego; dau. Mrs. Marlene Demontford, b. 1942. Career: Instr. painting, Laguna Beach Sch. of Art, 1963; instr. anatomy and life drawing & painting, Art Dept. Marymount Coll., Palos Verdes Estates, 1965; Art instr. Los Angeles City Schs. TV appearances: Scope, and Guidelines, 1966; eighteen ½-hr. shows, ABC-TV; CBS-TV Steps in Learning. Past pres. Am. Inst. of Fine Arts, Beverly Hills. Life mem. Laguna Beach Mus. of Art; mem. Nat. Gallery Soc. Victoria, Australia. Hobby: boating. Address: P.O.B. 407, Encino, CA 91316.

VON HAFFTEN, ALEXANDER HENRY
Business Executive — Civic Leader
b. Apr. 11, 1914, Minneapolis, Minn.; s. Alexander William and Katherine Vivian (Henry) von Hafften; A.B., Stanford Univ. 1934, M.B.A. 1939; m. Emily Sebelle Harden, Palo Alto, Calif., Dec. 8, 1945; chil.: Katharine Ann, Carolyn Sebelle, Sebelle Hermina, Alexander Henry, Jr., Robert Lathrop. Career: Surety Bond special agent, Hartford Accident and Indemnity Co., San Francisco, 1941-43; community rels. counsel, Calif. Chain Stores Assn., S.F. 1943-47; legislative rep-dept. mgr., S.F. C. of C. 1947-48; mgr. Wash., D.C. ofc., S.F. C. of C. 1948-50; wheat grocer, Kiowa Co., Colo.; exec. dir. No. Calif. Suppliers Assn. 1952---; pres. Bernal Land, 1959. Spec. Asst. War Finance Com., No. Calif. Retail Div., U.S. Treas. Dept. (1943-46), WW II. Mem.: v-chmn. S.F. Emg. Food Fund, 1946; div. chmn., S.F. Red Cross Campaign, 1947; pres. Calif. Soc. of Assn. Execs. 1956-57; dir. S.F. Tuberculosis Assn. 1960-72, pres. 1972-73; pres. Calif. Lung Assn. 1973-74, dir. Amer. Lung Assn. 1974-79; dir. adv. council, Graduate Sch. of Business, 1960; pres. Stanford Business Sch. Alumni Assn., 1960; Amer. Soc. of Assn. Execs.; San Francisco Golf Club; Omylpic, Univ. and Commonwealth Clubs, S.F. Hobby: golf, music. Res.: 3898 Washington St., San Francisco, CA; Office: 369 Pine St., San Francisco, CA 94104.

VON HOFE, HAROLD
Professor
b. Apr. 23, 1912, Plainfield, N.J.; s. Henry and Claire von Hofe; B.S., N.Y. Univ., 1936; Ph.D., Northwestern Univ., 1939; m. Lenore Curtis, Feb. 27, 1947, Ontario, Calif.; sons: Harold, b. 1951; Eric, b. 1954. Career: Instr., asst. prof., assoc. prof., prof. of German, USC, 1939---, dir. USC Program in Vienna, 1963---, interim Dean, Graduate Sch. 1974-77. Director, Feuchtwanger Inst. for Exile Studies, 1978---. Author: A German Sketchbook, 1950; Im Wandel der Jahre, 1955, 6th ed. 1979; Der Anfang, 1958, 3d ed. 1968; Cultural History of the United States of America, 1963, 2d ed. 1972; Faust, 1965; Germany Is Different, 1972; Correspondence of L. Marcuse, 1976; Essays, Polemics, Portraits, 1979. Mng. editor, German Quarterly, 1957-63; advisory editor, Charles Scribner & Sons, 1963---. Mem.: Exec. Com. Philological Assn. of the Pacific Coast; v.p., Am. Assn. of Teachers of German, 1957-60; pres. Delta Phi Alpha, 1964-68. Rec.: tennis, swimming. Res.: 12733 Mulholland Dr., Beverly Hills, CA 90210; Office: USC, Los Angeles, CA 90007.

VON KALINOWSKI, JULIAN ONESIME
Lawyer — Textbook Author
b. May 19, 1916, St. Louis, Mo.; s. Walter E. and Maybelle (Michaud) von Kalinowski; grandson of Baronin Henrietta Pfaeler von Kalinowski of Weisbaden, Germany; B.A. (cum laude), Miss. Coll. 1937; LL.B. (dean's list, hons.), Univ. of Va. Law Sch. 1940; m. Shirley Stone, Pasadena, Calif., Jan. 12, 1946; chil.: Julian O., Jr., b. Dec. 29, 1954; Wendy Jean, b. July 2, 1956. Career: Lawyer/mem. of exec. com., Gibson, Dunn & Crutcher; Author: 15 volume text, and current service, entitled Antitrust Laws and Trade Regulation (Matthew Bender Co.); Editor-in-chief, World Law of Competition (Bender & Co.); numerous articles on antitrust law and frequent speaker on the subj. at bar-related meetings; 1972-73 chmn. of the Sect. of Antitrust Law of the Amer. Bar Assn. Ofcr., USN (1941-46), WW II, Capt., USNR Ret. Mem.: fellow, Amer. Coll. of Trial Lawyers; fellow, Amer. Bar Found.; chmn. Antitrust Sect. Amer. Bar Assn. 1972-73; Lawyer Delegates Com. to Ninth Circuti Judicial Conf.; Internat., Calif. State, Va. State Bar Assn.; U.S. Supreme Ct. Bar; U.S. Ct. of Claims Bar; Natl. Legal Aid and Defender Assn.; Phi Kappa Psi, Phi Alpha Delta; Clubs: L.A. Ath., New York Ath., The Sky (N.Y.), Pac.-Union (S.F.), La Jolla Beach and Tennis, Calif. Episcopalian. Hobbies: legal writing, sports. Rec.: golf. Res.: 800 W. First St., Los Angeles, 90012, and 8166 Paseo del Ocaso, La Jolla, 92037. Office: 515 S. Flower St., Los Angeles, CA 90071.

VOORHIS, H. JERRY
Author — Former Congressman
b. Apr. 6, 1901, Ottawa, Kan.; s. Charles B. and Ella Ward (Smith) Voorhis; B.A., Yale, 1923; M.A., Claremont Grad. Sch. 1928; LL.D. (hon.) St. Francis Xavier Univ., Nova Scotia, 1953; m. Alice Louise Livingston, Nov. 27, 1924, Washington, Iowa; chil.: Alice Nell (Hansen), b. Dec. 20, 1925; Charles Brown II, b. June 28, 1931; Dr. Jerry Livingston, Ph.D., b. July 2, 1938. Career: farm & factory laborer & R.R. freight handler, 1923-25; tchr., Allendale Farm Sch., Ill., 1925-26; headmaster, Wyoming Episcopal Home for Boys, 1926-27; headmaster, Voorhis Sch. for Boys, 1928-38; mem. U.S. House of Representatives, 1937-47; exec. dir., Cooperative League of USA, 1947-67. Author: The Morale of Democracy, Greystone Press, 1941; Out of Debt, Out of Danger, Devin Adair, 1943; Beyond Victory, Farrar & Reinhart 1944; Confessions of a Congressman, Doubleday, 1947; The Christian in Politics, Association Press, 1951; American Cooperatives, Harper & Row, 1961; The Strange Case of Richard Milhaus Nixon, Paul Eriksson Inc., 1972, Popular Lib. (CBS) 1973; Cooperative Enterprise, Interstate Pubs. 1975; The Life and Times of Aurelius Lyman Voorhis, Vantage Press, 1976; Confession of Faith, Vantage Press, 1978. Chmn. bd. trustees, Cooperative Found., St. Paul, Minn., 1965---; bd. mem., Boys Club of San Gabriel Valley, 1970---; bd. mem., Pomona Valley Council of Churches, 1971---; hon. bd., Cooperative League of USA; hon. bd., Group Health Assn. of Am. Mem.: Univ. Club of Claremont; Common Cause; Nat. Catholic Rural Life Conf.; World Federalists USA; Sierra Club; Audubon Soc.; Community Service Orgn. Democrat. Episcopal, past sr. warden, present lay reader. Hobbies: gardening, geog., hist. Rec.: playing pool, birds. Home: 633 W. Bonita Ave., Claremont, CA 91711; Office: 114-A No. Indian Hill Blvd., Claremont, CA 91711.

VORON, DAVID ALAN
Dermatologist
b. Apr. 5, 1945, Philadelphia; s. George Jacob and Bess (Mann) Voron; B.S., cum laude, Muhlenberg Coll., 1966; M.D., Temple Univ. Sch. of Med., 1970. Career: Med. Internship, Cedars-Sinai Med. Center, L.A., 1971-72, dermatology residency, Temple Univ. Sch. of Med., 1972-73; chief resident in Dermatology, Med. Coll. Wis. 1973-74; Certification in Dermatology by Am. Bd. of Dermatology, 1974, in Dermatopathology by Am. Bds. of Pathology and Dermatology, 1977; pvt. practice dermatology and dermatopathology, Arcadia, 1974---; Asst. Clib. Prof. of Med., USC Sch. of Med. Contbr. articles med. journals. Mem.: Am. Acad. of Dermatology, Soc. for Investigative Dermatology, Internat. Soc. of Tropical Derma., Am. Soc. of Dermatopathology, AMA, CMA, L.A. Co. Med. Assn., L.A. Dermatological Soc., Metropolitan Dermatological Soc. of L.A. Office: 612 W. Duarte Rd., Suite 205, Arcadia, CA 91006.

VOSPER, ROBERT GORDON
University Librarian
b. June 21, 1913, Portland, Ore.; s. Chester Vivian and Anna (Stipe) Vosper; B.A., Univ. of Ore. 1937, M.A. 1939; m. Loraine Gjording, Aug. 20, 1940; chil.: Ingrid, Kathryn, Elinor and Stephen. Career: Jr. Librarian, Univ. of Calif., 1940-42; asst. ref. librn., Stanford Univ. 1942-44; head, Acquisitions Dept., Library, Univ. of Calif., Los Angeles, 1944-48; asst. librn., 1948-49, assoc. librn., 1949-52; dir. of libraries, Univ. of Kan. 1952-61; dir. Farmington Plan Survey, 1957-58; annual lib. lecturer, Univ. of Tenn. 1957; Walters Memorial Lecturer, Univ. of Minn. 1959; Guggenheim Fellow, 1959-60; Fulbright Lecturer, Italy, 1960; univ. librn.-prof. of lib. serv., UCLA 1961---. Author: various professional articles and books. Mem.: pres. Assn. of Coll. and Research Libs., 1955-56; council, Amer. Lib. Assn. 1955-56, 1960-64, pres. 1965-66; dir., Assn. of Research Libs. 1962-65, chmn. 1963. Res.: 10447 Wilkins Ave., Los Angeles, CA 90024; Office: University Research Library, University of Calif., Los Angeles, CA 90024.

VREELAND, ROBERT WILDER
Electronics Engineer
b. Mar. 4, 1923, Glen Ridge, N.J.; s. Frederick King and Elizabeth (Wilder) Vreeland; B.S. (E.E.), Univ. of Calif., Berkeley, 1947; m. Jean Fullerton, San Francisco, Calif., Jan. 21, 1967; Robert W., Jr., b. Aug. 15, 1969. Career: Electronics Engr., Litton Inds., San Carlos, 1948-55; electronics engr., Univ. of Calif., S.F. 1955---. Contrib. to med. and electronics journs. Mem.: Inst. of Elec. and Electronics Engrs., Amer. Radio Relay League. Hobbies: amatuer radio, photog. Res.: 45 Maywood Dr., San Francisco, CA 94116; Office: Research and Development Lab., University of Calif. Medical Center, San Francisco, CA 94127.

W

WACHS, JOEL STAHLER
City Councilman
b. Mar. 1, 1939, Scranton, Pa.; s. Archie and Stahler Wachs; B.A., UCLA, 1961; J.D., Harvard Law Sch., 1964; LL.M., taxation, NYU, 1965. Career: Tax Atty., Kadison, Pfaelzer, Woodard & Quinn, 1965-70; Los Angeles City Councilman, 1971---, pres. pro tem., 1978. Mem. UCLA Alumni Assn., Community Service Awardee, 1976, v.p. 1968-70. Lectr., USC Law Center, 1969. Hobby: contemporary art. Rec.: football. Res.: Studio City, CA; Office: City Hall, 200 N. Spring St., L.A., CA 90012.

WADE, GLEN
Professor of Engineering
b. Mar. 19, 1921, Ogden, Utah; s. Lester Andrew (Chief Justice Utah State Supreme Ct.) and Nellie (Vanderwerff) Wade; B.S. in E.E., Univ. Utah, 1949; M.S. in EE, 1949; Ph.D., Stanford Univ., 1954; m. LaRee Bailey, Mar. 20, 1955; Brunswick, Me.; children: Kathleen Ann, b. 1949; Ralee (Hall), b. 1953; Lisa Jean (Bossier), b. 1956; Mary Sue (Clements), b. 1957. Career: Research group leader, assoc. prof., Stanford Univ. 1956-60; Asst. dir. of Research Div., Raytheon, 1960-63; Distinguished Prof. and chmn. Sch. of Engring., Cornell Univ., 1963-66; prof. of Elec. Engring., Univ. Calif. Santa Barbara, 1966---. Awards: Eta Kappa Nu award, Young Elec. Engr. competition 1955; Nat. Electronics conf. award for best paper 1959; Distinguished teaching award 1977, UCSB Acad. Senate. Bd. dir. and exec. com. mem. IEEE, 1970-72; editor: IEEE Transactions on Electron Devices, 1961-71, Proceedings of the IEEE, 1977---. USNR, 1944-46. L.D.S., Sunday Sch. tchr., State Presidency, Bishopric. Hobbies: music, sports, photog. Res.: 1098 Golf Rd., Santa Barbara, CA 93108; Office: EE&CS Dept., Univ. Calif., Santa Barbara, CA 93106.

WADE, PATRICK JOHN
Neurosurgeon
b. Dec. 27, 1941, Glendale; s. William J. and Yvonne P. Wade; B.S., Loyola Univ., L.A., 1963; M.D., USC Sch. of Med., 1967; m. Christina T., Apr. 30, 1966, Montebello; children: Matthew Patrick, b. 1971; Theresa Anne, b. 1975; Thomas Edward, b. 1977. Career: Internship and gen. surgical tng., LAC-USC Med. Center, 1967-68, 1970-71, Neurosurg. Tng. 1971-75; estab. pvt. practice, 1975---. Hosp. appts.: St. Vincent Med. Center, Mem. Hosp. of Glendale, Glendale Adventist Med. Center, Orthopaedic Hosp., L.A., Good Samaritan Hosp., Verdugo Hills Hosp., Queen on Angels Hosp., Glendale Community Hosp. Dir. courses: Micro-Neurosurg. Dissection, Ear Surgery, Evaluation of Neurosurg. Patient, all 1979. Lt. Comdr M.C. USNR, 1968-70. Mem.: Am., Calif., L.A. Co. Med. Assns.; Am. and Calif. Assns. of Neurol. Surgs.; So. Calif. Neurosurg. Soc.; L.A. Soc. of Neurol. and Psychiat.; Assn. Mil. Surgeons. Roman Catholic. Hobby: 18-20th Century sculpture. Res.: 4101 Commonwealth, Flintridge, CA 91011; Office: 655 N. Central, Suite 201, Glendale, CA 91203.

WADE, WILLARD GILBERT
Telephone Company Executive
b. Jan. 8, 1906, Aspen, Colo.; s. Harry Willard and Pauline Alice Wade; B.B.A., Univ. of Colo. 1930; m. Alma L. Schmoker (dec.); m. 2nd, Valeta Vandergrift, Glendale, Calif., Jan. 6, 1962; dau.: Diane Ray (dec.). Career: Assoc. with Calif. Interstate Telephone Co. and predecessor cos. 1930-76, chmn. bd. dirs.-pres. 1954-65, cons.-dir., 1965-76. Councilman, Bishop, Calif., 1951-56, mayor, 1953-55; councilman, Victorville, Calif. 1962-66, Mayor 1962-64; Grand Jury of San Bernardino County, 1966. Mem.: pres., Calif. Independent Tel. Assn. 1955-54; Rotary Club; trustee, Elks Club, 1957-59; exec. bd., Boy Scout Council, 1960-65. Mason. Protestant. Hobby: fresh-water fishing. Res.: 1387 Galaxy Dr., Newport Beach, CA 92660.

WADSWORTH, BURTON WAYNE
College President
b. Mar. 3, 1924, Tacoma, Wash.; s. Delos E. and Manda A. Wadsworth; B.A., Fresno State Coll., 1949; M.A., 1950; m. Margaret Sutphin, Aug. 16, 1945, Fresno; chil.: Time, b. Oct. 14, 1946; Mark, b. Mar. 24, 1949; Jolynn, b. June 4, 1952. Career: Tchr., Indsl. Arts, Antelope Valley Coll.,

1950-55; Dean of students, Antelope Valley Coll., 1955-61; Dean of Students, Victor Valley Coll., 1961-68; Acting dir., 1968-69. President, 1969-71, Supt./Pres. Victor Valley Coll., 1971---. Served USAAF, 1943-46. Mem. Kiwanis, 1962---. Methodist. Hobbies: photog., woodworking. Home: 15362 Apple Valley Rd., Apple Valley, CA 92307; Office: Victor Valley Coll., P.O. Drawer OO, Victorville, CA 92392.

WAGNER, CHARLES ROBERT
Physician and Surgeon
b. Jan. 12, 1913, Philadelphia, Pa.; s. Peter and Anna Wagner; ed. psychosomatic med., USC Sch. of Med. 1930-33; D.O., L.A. Coll. of Osteopathic Phys. and Surgs. 1937 (course in eye, ear, nose and throat, Grad. Sch.); grad. L.A. Coll. of Med. Evangs. Grad. Sch.; M.D., Coll. of Med. and Surg., Met. Univ. 1947; stu. psych., gynecology and steroid therapy, Zurich, Switz. 1951; m. Dorothy Lello, Los Angeles, Calif., June 3, 1940; chil.: George Robert, b. Feb. 28, 1943; Peggy Ann, b. June 14, 1944; Jane Robin b. Dec. 7, 1948. Career: Intern, Coll. of Osteopathic Phys. and Surgs. Clinic, L.A. (2 yrs.), res. Eye, Ear, Nose and Throat (2 yrs.); gen. med. practice, 1939---; Amer. Coll. of Gen. Practitioners in Osteopathic Med. and Surg. (7 yrs.); asst. clin. prof. (gen. med.), L.A. Coll. of Osteopathic Phys. and Surgs. (3 yrs.); chief of staff, La Bra Hosp. 1958-61; Calif. Coll. of Med. 1962; dept. chief, Hollywood Community Hosp. 1963, chief of staff, 1965-66; Amer. Acad. of Family Practice, 1966---. Mem.: bd. dirs., Calif. Soc. of Amer. Coll. of Gen. Practitioners (3 yrs.), pgm, chmn. 1959, pres. 1960; bd. dirs., L.A. Analytical Psych. Club (6 yrs.), treas. (3 yrs); secty. L.A. Analytical Psych. Edn. Fund, Inc. (1 yr.), pres. (1 yr.); L.A. Heart Assn., Med. Research Assn. of Calif., U.S. Com. on World Med. Assn., Calif. and Amer. Osteopathic Assns.; fellow, Amer. Coll. of Gen. Practitioners in Osteopathic Med. and Surg.; fellow, Amer. Coll. of Psychoanalysts; pres. Amer. Soc. of General Practitioners, 1961, fellow, 1962; chmn. D.O. Committee for Pat Brown in Gubernatorial Election, 1958. Jewish. Rec.: tennis, travel. Res.: 2722 Forrester Dr., Los Angeles, CA; Office: 809 S. Hobart Blvd., Los Angeles, CA.

WAGNER, KURT JOSEPH
Plastic and Reconstructive Surgeon
b. Mar. 9, 1934, Vienna, Austria; s. Bernard, M.D. and Sonia (Kaunitz) Wagner; B.A., M.D., State Univ. N.Y. Coll. of Med., N.Y. Center, 1958; m. Cassilda Kathleen Kelly, NYC, Mar. 18, 1967; daus.: Allison, b. Dec. 14, 1960; Stacy Lynn, b. Nov. 2, 1962. Career: Intern, 1958-59, gen. surg. 1959-62; plastic surg. St. Anthony's Hosp., Okla Univ. 1963; N.Y. Hosp., under Dr. Herbert Conway, 1964; chief of plastic surg. USAF Hosp., Wright-Patterson A.F. Base, Dayton, Oh., and N. Central and Northeastern States, 1964-66; est. pvt. practice, spec. in plastic and reconstructive surg., Beverly Hills, Calif. 1966---; Cedars of Lebanon Hosp., L.A. Calif. 1966---; Mem. Hosp. of L.A., Culver City, 1966---; West Hills Doctor's Hosp., Canoga Park, and Beverly Hills Doctor's Hosp. 1967---. Author: 8 sci. publs. on Plastic and Reconstructive Surg. 1962---, incl. N.Y. State Journ. of Med. 1965; Incidence of Cleft Lip and Palate in NYC, Cleft Palate Journ. 1966; Military Med. 1966. Mem.: Phi Beta Kappa, 1954---. Hobbies: sculpting, music, piano. Rec.: tennis, golf, swim. Res.: 8364 Mulholland Dr., Los Angeles, CA 90046; Office: 414 N. Camden Dr., Beverly Hills, CA 90210.

WAGNER, MARJORIE DOWNING
University Administrator
b. Mar. 16, 1917, NYC; d. Charles and Marguerite (Ohland) Coogan; B.A., 1938, M.A., 1939, Ph.D., Yale Univ., 1942; m. John Wagner, June 6, 1974, Claremont; children: Francis Downing, b. 1955; Nicholas Downing, b. 1958; (Mrs.) Margaret Wagner-Harrington, b. 1956. Career: Instr. English, Barnard Coll., NYC, 1942-47; prof. English, Brooklyn Coll., 1947-61; Dean of Coll., Sarah Lawrence Coll., 1961-65; Dean of Faculty, Scripps Coll., Claremont, Calif., 1965-74; President, Sonoma State Univ., 1974-76; Vice Chancellor, Faculty-Staff Affairs, Cal. State Univs. and Colleges, 1977---. Mem. Pi Lambda Theta, Kappa Gamma Pi. Res.: 28411 Lomo Dr., Rancho Palos Verdes, CA 90274; Office: 400 Golden Shore, Long Beach, CA 90802.

WAGNER, ROGER
Musical Director
b. Jan. 16, 1914, Le Puy, France; s. Francis (Noted organist-comp.) and Louise (Colombet) Wagner; B.A., Coll. of Montmorency, France, 1932-36; D.Mus., Univ.

of Montreal, 1949; m. Janice Schmidt, Los Angeles, Calif., Dec. 30, 1939; chil.: Jeannine, b. Jan. 12, 1941; Richard, b. June 8, 1944; Jacqueline, b. Aug. 20, 1945. Career: Mus. dir., St. Joseph's Ch., L.A. 1937---; supv. youth choruses, City of L.A. Bur. of Music, 1945-53; mus. dir., L.A. Municipal Art Comm. 1945---; Christmas radio pgm., L.A. Greetings and the Nation, NBC 1945---; founder-dir., Roger Wagner Chorale, soloists with L.A. Philharmonic and Hollywood Bowl, 1946---; dir. choral music, UCLA, 1949---; faculty 1954---; founder-dir., So. Calif. Choral Music Assn. 1964---, tour of Europe, 1966. Prod. Tapestries of Melody, own Sun. Pgm., CBS, 1951; rec. artist, 2 Bach cantatas and 1st vol. of Monteverdi madrigals, Allegro Records, N.Y.; rec. artist, Pope Marcellus Mass, 18 waltzes of Brahms, 10 folk songs of Brahms, under contract to Capitol Records, 1952---; composer: Mass in Honor of St. Francis; Heritage of Freedom, publ. by Carl Fischer; Cantata, spec. request by Igor Stravinsky, for world premiere perf. (2 solo voices, 5 instruments), Nov. 1952; mot. pics.: Joan of Arc, Sunset Boulevard, Great Sinner, Come to the Stable, Way of a Goucho, Les Miserables, Happy Time, The Egyptian and others; com.-cond. music.: Desiree, We're No Angels, The Sign of the Pagan, Roger Wagner Chorale (20th Century-Fox short subj.); European tour (appd. London, Paris, Amsterdam, The Hague), 1953; invited by London County Council for Command Perf., Coronation of Queen Elizabeth, 1953; dir. TV musical, The Christmas Carol (mus. score by Beranrd Herman, lyrics by Sherwood Anderson), Dec. 1954. Author: Roger Wagner Choral Series, publ. Schirmer, Inc., Lawson-Gould Music Publs., Inc. French Army, 1934-36. Awards: won 2nd place, French Natl. Finals, as outstanding ath., Paris, 1936; (hon.) scroll by Hollywood Bowl Assn. for contrib. to cultural activities, 1951. Mem.: Musicians Union Local 47, AFTRA, AGMA, SAG, Ojai Valley Vlub, Elks Club. Catholic. Hobby: golf. Rec.: sports. Res.: Hollywood, CA; Office: So. Calif. Choral Music Assn., Music Center, Los Angeles, CA.

WAHLQUIST, JOHN T.
University President Emeritus
b. Sept. 10, 1899, Heber, Ut.; s. Charles John (juvenile judge) and Elizabeth (Campbell) Wahlquist; B.S., Univ. of Ut. 1924, M.S. 1926; Ph.D., Univ. of Cincinnati, 1930; m. Grace Dorius, Salt Lake City, Ut., Aug. 30, 1923; chil.: Don D., b. Jan. 27, 1925; Carl D., b. June 14, 1927. Career: Instr., Univ. of Ut. 1924-30, asst. prof. 1930-31, assoc. prof. 1931-35, prof. 1935-52; dir. William M. Stewart Sch., Univ. of Ut. 1932-41; dean, Sch. of Edn. 1941-52, dir. summer session, 1941-48; pres. San Jose State Coll. 1952-64; visiting prof. (summers): Univ. of Cincinnati, 1931, 32; George Washington Univ. 1935; Univ. of Wash. 1937; San Francisco State Coll., 1938, 39; UCLA 1940, 41; USC 1946, 47; Syracuse Univ. 1954; Utah State Univ. and Oregon Coll. of Edn., 1955; Univ. of Calif., Berkeley, 1956; Univ. of Alaska, 1959; Ut. State Univ. 1965; Univ. of Utah. 1966. Author: Status of Jr. College Instructors, United States Office of Edn. 1931; Teaching as the Direction of Activities, 1936 (revised edit. 1936); The Activity School, Univ. of Ut. 1936; Philosophy of American Education, The Ronald Press Co. 1942; An Introduction to American Education, The Ronald Press Co. 1947 (revised printing, 1960); co-author: The American College, The Philosophical Lib. 1949; Lehrenals Anleit-ung zur Tatig Keit, Frankfort, Ger. 1950; (ed.-co-author) The Administration of Public Education, Ronald Press Co. 1952; contrib. to: Edn. Adm. and Supervision, Edn. Forum, The Elem. Sch. Review, Journ. of Edn. Review. Awards: (hon.) listed Leaders in Edn., Internat. Blue Book, Presidents of Amer. Colleges and Universities, various other biog. vols. of noted Amer. leaders. Mem.: Ut. Textbook Com.; Phi Kappa Phi, 1924---; Phi Delta Kappa, 1929---; Alpha Phi Omega, Tau Delta Phi; Salt Lake City Rotary Club, 1936-52, 2nd v.p. 1944-45, pres. 1945; secty. Ut. Edn. Council, 1940-42; Natl. Council of Edn. 1940-48; dir. dir. NEA, 1941; White House Conf. on Rural Edn. 1944; pres. Ut. Conf. on Higher Edn. 1946; fellow, Ut. Acad. of Arts, Sci. and Letters; Natl. Conf. on Edn. of Vets, 1946; Natl. Clinic on Teacher Edn. 1946; Natl. Soc. Coll. Teachers of Edn.; Natl. Soc. for Stu. of Edn.; Ut. Course of Study Com. 1947-52; natl, dir., Horace Mann League, 1948-52; San Jose Rotary Club, 1952---; Commonwealth Club. Rec.: travel (Europe, Can., Mex.). Res.: 420 S. 12th St., San Jose, CA 95112.

WAKEMAN, HAROLD R.
Sculptor
b. Dec. 14, 1901, Bedford, Ia.; s. Frank E. and Elizabeth (Wilson) Wakeman; A.B., UCLA, 1925; m.

Virginia Bunnell, Los Angeles, Calif., Mar. 1, 1935; son, Charles Bunnell, b. Aug. 5, 1944. Career: Corp. and pvt. enterprises, 1926-40; L.A. Dept. Water & Power, 1940-65 (ret.). Orign. Tumblewood, active Rhythm of Nature sculpture, 1951; active manu art orgns. 1965---. Exhibs.: Westwood Center of the Arts, 1963068; Ebell Club Salon of Art, L.A. 1966, 68; Amer. Artists Professional League of N.Y. Inc., Grand Natl. Exhib., Lever House, 1967; Amer. Sav. & Loan Assn., L.A. (cond. series, 18 monthly at 18 brs.), 1967-68; Clyde Zulch originals, Gallery of Fine Arts, Corona del Mar, 1967---; L.A. Home Show, 1969; Kirkeby Center Gallery, 1969---; Madame Wu's Chinese Garden, Santa Monica, 1970---; Showcase 21, 1971---; Pasa. Lib. 1971; San Gabriel Fine Arts Assn. 1972---; Calif. Art Club Annuals, 1973---; Beachbum Burt's First Annual Winter Arts Festival, Redondo Beach, 1975. Guest, Truth or Consequences, KTTV, Describe the Artist series, 1968; feat. articles: L.A. Herald-Examiner, L.A. Times, S. Pasa. Review, Health Mag., Grit Publ. Co. (Pa.), Intake, others, 1965---. Awards: Internat. Art Festival, 1965, 66, 67, 68; Amer. Inst. of Fine Arts Award of Merit, 1966, Fellow, 1968; Fellow, Amer. Artists Professional League of N.Y. Inc. (Jury Exhib.), 1968; Award of Merit, Council of Traditional Artists Societies, 1969; Galleria of Fine Arts, 1971; Third place sculpture, San Gabriel Fine Arts Eighth Annual Show, 1972; Award of Merit, Showcase 21, 1972; spec. recognition award, Ebell Club Salon of Art, L.A. 1974, Sculpture Award, Third Place Award, Gold Medal Show, 1976. Cit. of appreciation for serv., Mayor Yorty, L.A. 1968. Lecture film series, Tumblewood Fine Art Sculpture, Ebell Salon of Art L.A. 1975. Inventor: owner patents on Orthopaedic Shoe-Shaping Device, 1962; Demountable Display Rack, 1974; pending (sci. of color and light), 1976. Mem.: Beta Theta Pi, Gamma Nu Chpt. Republican. Methodist. Hobbies: orchids, photog., travel, beachcombing. Studio: 300 Dalkeith Ave., Los Angeles, CA 90049.

WALCHA, HERBERT G.
Banker — Civic Leader
b. Aug. 29, 1913, Redlands, Calif.; s. George and Margaret Walcha; cousin, Helmut Walcha, eminent blind organist, foremost Bach interpreter, Frankfort, Ger.; ed. Harvard Mil. Sch. 1931; A.B., USC, 1935; m. Lorraine Loewe, San Mateo, Calif., Sept. 4, 1938; Chil.: Mrs. A.D. (Lynne) Cline, Jr., b. Dec. 21, 1940; Thomas L., b. Nov. 20, 1942; Richard S., b. Aug. 23, 1950. Career: Associated with Bank of Amer. 1936-40; partner, Loewe and Zwierlein Dept. Store, 1940-69; mgr.-v.p. Amer. Savings and Loan Assn. 1970---. Dir.: chairman, advisory board, Peninsula Investment Company, San Mateo. Mem.: San Francisco Better Bus. Bur. 1961---; San Mateo Parking Comm.; v.p. San Mateo C. of C.; v.p. San Mateo-Burlingame Credit Assn.; v.p. Greater Downtown San Mateo, Inc.; past dir., San Mateo Rotary Club. Rec.: swimming, travel. Res.: 960 W. Santa Inez Rd., Hillsborough, CA; Office: 480 S. Ellsworth Ave., San Mateo, CA 94401.

WALDORF, LYNN O.
Football Coach (Ret.)
b. Oct. 3, 1902, Clifton Springs, N.Y.; s. Ernest Lynn and Flora (Janpt) Waldorf; A.B., Syracuse Univ., 1925; m. Louise Jane McKay, Aug. 14, 1925, Western Springs, Ill.; daughters: Mary Louise (Osborne), b. 1926; Carolyn Janet (Pickering), b. 1931. Career: Football coach, Okla. City Univ., 1925-27; asst. coach, Univ. of Kansas, 1928; Hd. football coach, Okla State Univ., 1929-33, also Ath. Dir. 1931-33; hd. football coach, Kansas State Univ., 1934; football coach, Northwestern Univ., Evanston, Ill. 1935-46, Univ. of Calif., Berkeley, 1947-56; dir. of personnel, San Francisco 49ers, 1957-72; Scout and Cons. 1972-77. Pres., Am. Football Coaches Assn., 1950; chmn. Selection Com., East-West Shrine Game, 1973-77. Awards: First Coach of the Year (Football) 1935; inducted College Football Hall of Fame, 1966. Mem. Pi Kappa Alpha, Rotary Club, 1931---. Res.: 726 Grizzly Peak Blvd., Berkeley, CA 94708.

WALDO, SALLY
Real Estate Broker
b. Jan. 8, 1903, Seattle, Wash.; d. Hyman & Lena (Kaplan) Rosenstein; ed. Elem. grades, Bisbee, Ariz.; Miss Riley's, 1 yr., Ariz.; Sisters of Loretto Acad., 6 yrs. piano, Bisbee, Ariz.; Zay Rector Bevitt studio, 2 yrs., piano, San Diego, Calif.; San Diego High Sch., San Diego, Calif (1915-19); Modesto Jr. Coll., Modesto; Sawyer Sch. for Secretaries, San Diego (1921); m. Claude A. Waldo (noted Land Surveyor & Civil Engr., 1925-69; career: Exec. secty., Claude A.

Waldo, Land Surveyor, Contra Costa Co., Calif. 1945-69; insurance broker (licensed), 1950---; Business Opp. & Real Estate Broker, 1949---; mem.: Calif. Democratic Campaign Committee, 1936; sponsor mem., 50-50 Bill (equal rep. for women on State Central Comm. 1937; only woman member, Constitution Revision Comm., Natl. Conv., Young Demo. Clubs of Amer., 1937); Member, Stanislaus Co. Calif. Dem. Co. Central Com., 1936-38; mem., advisory bd., Women's Div., Demo. State Central Comm., 1936-38; Natl. Committeewoman, Young Demo. Clubs of Calif. 1937-39, 1st v.p. 1936-37, chmn. Women's Activities 1935; Calif. chmn. Circulation, Natl. Young Dem. newspaper, 1937; organizer, 3 Young Demo. Clubs, Stanislaus Co., 1935; v.p. San Joaquin Dist. Demo. Women's Study Clubs, 1940; Calif. Fedn. of Women's Clubs: publicity chmn., San Joaquin Valley Dist. Conv., Modesto, 1935; Legislation chmn., Stanislaus Co., Modesto, 1935; charter mem., publicity chmn., Women's Progressive Club, 1934; charter mem., 1st pres., Tres Artes Club (Modesto, 1934); charter mem., Toastmistress Club, Modesto, 1937---; charter mem. Modesto Art League, Modesto, 1941---; first woman mem., City Commons Club, Berkeley, Jan. 1972; mem.: Women's City Club (S.F.); Irish-Israeli0Italian Soc. (S.F.); Honorary, S.F. Press Club; Mt. Zion Hosp. Aux. (S.F.); Order of Eastern Star No. 571 (Lafayette, Calif.); Martinez Grange (Martinez, Calif.); Internat. Platform Assn.; Cleveland Heights, Oh.; Town Hall Forum, L.A.; Political Science Club, Berkeley; Civic Arts League, Walnut Creek, Calif.; Sustaining mem., Marquis Library Soc., N.Y.; assoc. mem., Amer. Inst. of Mgmt. Res.: P.O.B. 710, Lafayette, CA 94549.

WALD, ROBERT M.
Management Consultant
b. Oct. 12, 1927, Chicago, Ill.; s. Martin, Jr. and Mabelle (Martin) Wald; A.B., Johns Hopkins Univ., 1948; M.A., 1950; Ph.D., Northwestern Univ., 1953; m. Dolores Klyczek, Dec. 18, 1948, Chicago Heights, Ill.; sons: Robert M., Jr., b. 1952; Jeffrey A., b. 1953. Career: Instr., Northwestern Univ., 1950-52; assoc. Fry Consultants, 1952-59, v.p. 1959-62, sr. v.p. 1962-65, exec. v.p. 1965-72; pres., Robert M. Wald and Assoc., Los Angeles, 1972---. Contbr. profl. publs. on the characteristics of corp. execs. Chmn. Am. Heart Assn., Greater L.A. affil., 1978-79, dir. 1975-77; trustee, Whittier Coll., 1975---. Mem.: Calif. State Personnel Bd., 1969---; dir. Multiple Sclerosis Soc. 1965-75; dir. Better Bus. Bureau of L.A., 1963-75. Hobby: stamp collecting. Res.: 8734 Lindante Dr., Whittier, CA 90603; Office: 3540 Wilshire Blvd., L.A., CA 90010.

WALDIE, JEROME R.
Former U.S. Congressman
b. Feb. 15, 1925, Antioch, Calif.; s. George and Alice (Crosiar) Waldie; A.B., Univ. of Calif. 1950, LL.B. 1953; m. D. Joanne Gregg, Santa Rosa, Calif., June 20, 1948; chil.: Jill, Jonathon, Jeffrey. Career: Atty. at law, Antioch, Calif. 1953-58. Elected, Calif. State Assemblyman, Antioch, 1958-66, Congressman, U.S. House of Reps. 1966-75; Wash. rep.: Natl. Assn. of Letter Carriers, ALC-CIO; Alameda Naval Air Sta's Fed. Emplouees Assn. 1975. Signal Corps (rank of T-5), U.S. Army Inf. (1943-46), WW II. Mem.: Amer. Leg., Elks, Moose, IOOF. Dem. Congl. Ch. (trustee). Hobby: duck hunting. Rec.: swimming. Res.: 8921 Seven Locks Rd., Bethesda, Md., and Antioch, CA.

WALKUP, WILLIAM EDMONDSON
Chairman, The Signal Companies
b. May 31, 1918, Nashville, Tenn.; s. John Pegram and Marion (Edmondson) Walkup; ed. UCLA 1936-38; Spanish lit., Univ. of Mex. 1938; UCLA Ext. 1939; m. Dorothy Sanborn, Phoenix, Ariz., Sept. 2, 1939; chil.: William Sanborn, b. July 30, 1940; Marion Elena Pace, b. Apr. 17, 1945; Frank Sanborn, b. Feb. 24, 1954. Career: Signal Oil and Gas Co. 1939---; adm. asst. to pres. 1948-55, dir.-controller, 1955, financial v.p. 1958, group v.p.-staff, 1962, sr. exec. v.p. 1964; exec. v.p.-v. chmn. The Signal Cos., Inc. 1968, chmn. bd. 1969---. Dir.: Garrett Corp. 1964---; Mack Trucks, Inc. 1967---; UOP Inc. 1975---. Mem.: dir. Men's Garden Club, L.A. 1952---, pres. 1973-75; dir. Los Angeles Country Club, 1975---; Beta Theta Pi. Republican. Protestant. Hobbies: reading, writing, music, garden. Rec.: golf. Res.: 1140 Brooklawn Dr., Los Angeles, CA 90024; Office: 9665 Wilshire Blvd., Beverly Hills, CA 90212.

WALLACE, CLARK
Real Estate Developer
b. May 9, 1933, Oakland; s. Wm. Edwin (pres. CAR, 1949) and Edith D. (Bowring) Wallace; B.S. bus. admin., Univ. Calif. Berkeley, 1955; m. Geraldine Munger, Nov. 13, 1955, Tustin; children: Tia, Marshall, Wendy. Career: realtor, developer, Orinda-Moraga area, 1958--- (with family firm started 1938): opened office in Moraga, 1965; sales & devel. Moraga Ranch properties, 1962---; developer Moraga Med. Center, Villa Moraga (50 unit apt. complex), Bollinger Bluffs (90 lot housing devel.), Moraga Country Club (521 homes), others. Elected pres. (125,000 mem.) Calif. Assn. Realtors (CAR), 1978, 1st v.p. 1978, dir. 1961---, Hon. Dir. for Life 1975; Pres., Contra Costa Bd. of Realtors (Realtor of the Year, 1974), 1964; dir. Nat. Assn. of Realtors; apptd. by Gov. Brown, State of Calif. Real Estate Advisory Commn. 1978. Mem.: Orinda Assn., 1959--- (Orinda Man of the Year 1969), pres. 1968; pres., Orinda C. of C., 1966-68; Orinda Sch. Parents Club, pres. 1965-66; Contra Costa Co. Hwy. Advis. Com., 1966-69; Commonwealth Club of Calif.; Contra Costa U.C. Alumni Club, pres. 1967, U.C. Alumni Council 1969-71; trustee, Orinda Union Sch. Dist., 1969-78, pres. 1972, 1977, pres., Moraga CC Homeowners Assn., 1972-78. Lt., USN, 1955-58. Mem. Theta Xi frat., pres. 1955. Rec.: tennis. Res.: 13 Bel Air Dr., Orinda, CA 94563; Office: 1398 Moraga Way, Moraga, CA.

WALLACE, J. CLIFFORD
U.S. Circuit Judge
b. Dec. 11, 1928, San Diego; s. John Franklin and Lillie I. Wallace-Stephens; B.A., San Diego State Univ., 1952; LL.B., Univ. Calif., Berkeley, 1955; m. Virginia Lee Schlosser, Apr. 8, 1957, Salt Lake City, Utah; children: Paige (Wood), Laurie, Teri (Carpenter), John C., Jr. Career: admitted to Calif. Bar, 1955; atty. 1955-70; U.S. Dist. Judge, So. Dist. of Calif., 1970-72; U.S. Circuit Judge, 1972---. Dir., So. Assn. of Calif. Defense Counsel, 1968-70; v.p., San Diego County Bar Assn., 1967-68, dir. 1966-68. Mem. Am. Board of Trail Advocates. USN, 1946-49, Aviation Electronics Technician, 2d. Class. Vice Pres., Sigma Chi, 1951-52. Assoc. editor Calif. Law Rev., 1954-55. Rel. Stake Pres.; regional rep. Rec.: Sports. Office: U.S. Courthouse, 940 Front St., San Diego, CA 92101.

WALKER, GEORGE R.
Attorney at Law
b. Apr. 9, 1928, Columbus, Oh.; s. B. Earl and Dorothea M. Walker; ed. B.Sc. (bus. adm) Ohio State Univ. 1950; J.D. (cum laude), 1952 (ed. Univ. Law Journ.); grad. Judge Advocate Gen's. Sch., Univ. of Va., 1952; m. Patricia A. King, Columbus, Oh.; June 10, 1953; chil.: Kathleen Cora, b. Mar. 11, 1954; Jeffrey George, b. Feb. 28, 1955; Carolyn Lee, b. Mar. 15, 1956; Rebecca Zoanne, b. Apr. 8, 1957; Career: Atty. at law, Monterey and Carmel, Calif. 1955--- (now mem. Walker, Schroeder & Davis law firm). 1st Lt., Judge Adv. Gen's. Corps, U.S. Army, 1952-54. Awards: Young Man of Yr. by Jr. C. of C., Monterey Peninsula, 1960. Mem.: Amer. Bar Assn.; secty. Monterey Co. Bar Assn. 1957, pres. 1959; com. chmn., Calif. Supreme Ct. session commemorating 110th anniversary of signing of Calif. Constitution, Monterey, 1959; dir. Tri-County Cerebral Palsy Assn. 1959-62; founder-dir., Legal Aid Soc. of Monterey Co. 1960; adm. com., State Bar of Calif. 1960-64; continuing edn. 1962-66; dir. Monterey Peninsula Garbage and Refuse Disposal Dist. 1960-64; dir. Alcoholism Council of Monterey Peninsula, 1962-64; pres. Estate Planning Council for Monterey Co. 1964; dir. Beacon House (alcoholism rehabilitation), 1964-69; general counsel and secty., American Recreation Centers, Inc.; executor, Alexander F. Victor Estate and Found. for Birth Control for Underdeveloped Countries; dir.-treas. Carmel Found. 1967---; gen. partner, Custom House Assocs.; developer, Monterey Urban renewal proj.; Monterey Hist. and Art Assn., Order of Coif, Beta Theta Pi, Phi Delta Phi; Pacheco, 20-40- and Commonwealth Clubs; International Platform Association; secty. Monterey Co. Repub. Central Com. 1963-64; Carmel Presbyterian Ch. (elder-mem. session; deacon, 1961-63, pres. bd. trustees, 1964-69; pres. Carmel Presbyterian Found.-Trust Fund). Hobby: photog., antiques, travel. Rec.: skiing, hiking, camping. Res.: Carmel, Calif.; Office: Professional Bldg., Monterey, Calif.

WALKER, JOSEPH
Research Director
b. Dec. 28, 1922, Rockford, Ill.; s. Joseph and Elizabeth McEachran; B.S., Beloit Coll., 1943; M.S.,

Univ. Wis., 1948, Ph.D., 1950; m. June Enerson, Jan. 22, 1944, Los Angeles; children: Joseph A., b. 1944; Amy (Filice), b. 1948; Richard Hugh, b. 1951; Jeanne Ann, b. 1958. Career: Research Chemist, Pure Oil Co. Research Center, Crystal Lake, Ill., 1950; Project Technologist, Union Oil of Calif., 1952-54, Sect. Supr., 1954-58, Div. Dir., 1958-64, Research Coordinator, 1964, Dir. of Research, 1965, Assoc. Dir. of Research, 1966---. Lt. j.g., USN, 1943-46, in Aerology. Mem.: Sigma Alpha Epsilon, Phi Beta Kappa, Sigma Xi. Pres. of Sch. Bd., Crystal Lake, Ill., 1963-65. Res.: 3010 Anacapa Pl., Fullerton, CA 92635; Office: Valencia & Imperial Hwy., Brea, CA.

WALL, ELLERTON E.
Business Executive
b. May 5, 1913, Honolulu, Hawaii; s. Walter E. and Edith (Dietz) Wall; ed. Punahou Acad., Univ. of Hawaii, Univ. of Ore., USC; m. Virginia Dorr, Honolulu, Hawaii, July 12, 1935; chil.: Anne (Wall) Gaines, b. May 18, 1938; Janet (Wall) Dietz, b. Sept. 9, 1941; Steven S., b. Mar. 19, 1946. Career: Assoc. with Standard Oil Co. & subsidiary cos. 1934---; pres. Calif. Oil Co., N.J. 1958-63; reg. v.p. Standard Oil Co. of Calif., L.A. 1964---. Mem.: dir. L.A. Chamber of Comm. 1964-72, v.p. 1969-71; pres. So. Calif. Visitors Council, 1968; v.p. Merchants and Mfrs. Assn. 1969-72; Phi Kappa Psi. Clubs: Birnam Wood Golf, Jonathan, 100 Club of L.A., L.A. Country, Calif. Club. Presbyterian. Rec.: golf, hunting. Res.: 170 Coronado Cir., Montecito, CA 93108.

WALLACE, LEE
Entertainment Executive
b. Aug. 12, 1926, NYC; s. Alfred Applebaum and Ruth Krissel Thompson. Career: Founder, Teleshows, Inc.; exec. Du Mont Television Network; partner, Affiliated Artists Reps.; prod. CBS Television Network; dir. of casting, 20th Century-Fox Film Corp.; v.p. Celebrity Service, Inc. (Hollywood, N.Y., London, Paris, Rome). Freelance journalist, contrib. L.A. Times, Arch. Digest, Amer. Cultural Review, London Times, Arts in Amer., Paris Match; Assoc. Press corr. for Taxco, Mex.; TV-radio pgms. as internat. authority on travel, celebrities, epicureanism, connoisseur of fine food and wines. Author: The Melting Pot (cookbook); How To Be A Movie Star; How To Be At Home Anywhere In The World (a book based on res. in N.Y., Malibu, Paris, Taxco, Mex., London, Berlin, Taormina, Hollywood). Res.: Apdo. 83, San Miguel de Allende, Gto. Mex.; Office: 8746 Sunset Blvd., Los Angeles, CA 90069.

WALLACE, LEON
Physician — Educator
b. Aug. 12, 1920, NYC; s. Abraham and Rose (Burstein) Wallace; B.A., 1940; M.D., USC Sch. of Med., 1944; m. Fern Witen, Sept. 14, 1945, NYC; children: Daniel, b. 1949; Laura, b. 1951. Career: Internship, Los Angeles Co. Gen. Hosp. 1943-44; Fellow cardiology, Michael Reese Hosp., Chicago, 1944-45, Fellow pathology, 1946-47; Resident in Med., Bellevue Hosp., N.Y. 1945-46; currently Asst. Clin. Prof. of Medicine, USC Sch. of Med. ---; med. practice, Los Angeles ---. Diplomate, Am. Bd. of Internal Med., 1952; Fellow, Am. Coll. of Physicians, F.A.C.P., 1960; Fellow, Am. Coll. of Cardiology, F.A.C.C., 1969. Mil.: Capt. AUS. Hobbies: art, travel. Office: 6200 Wilshire Blvd., Suite 1200, Los Angeles, CA 90048.

WALLACE, PHYLLIS T.
Realtor
b. Oct. 28, 1928, Lynn, Mass.; d. Phillip and Irene DuBois; student, Boston Univ., 1946, Cal. State Univs., Fullerton, Cerritos; m. Jack D. Wallace (pres., Cascade Pump Co.), Dec. 31, 1949, Marblehead, Mass.; children: Joanne Mayo, b. Jan. 17, 1951; Claire Woodburn, b. Jan. 22, 1952; James D., b. Dec. 29, 1954; Theodore L., b. Nov. 17, 1956. Career: Secty., American Bank Note Co., 1947; Real Estate Agent, 1964---; Real Estate Broker, owner, Herbert Hawkins Realtors, Fullerton, 1975---. Mem.: Calif. and Nat. Assns. of Realtors, 1965---; C. of C.; Fullerton Recreational Riders, 1977---. Rec.: horseback riding. Res.: 5360 Burlingame, Buena Park, CA; Office: 2051 N. Euclid, Fullerton, CA 92635.

WALLACH, PAUL
Author — Journalist — Broadcaster
b. May 23, 1926, Los Angeles; s. Dr. E.W. (stepfather) and Carolyn Bak; B.A., UCLA, 1946; m. Christine L.

Badger, Oct. 5, 1971, Orange, Calif.; chil.: Stuart, b. Aug. 2, 1952; Brad, b. Jan. 13, 1954; Ward, b. July 5, 1960. Career: freelance author, 1946---; pres., The Wallach Co., Pub. Rels. and Advertising Mgmt., 1954-70; columnist critic Westways Magazine, 1972---; host, daily talk show, 4 hours a day on KIEV-AM; assoc. prof., Sch. of Journalism, Cal. State, L.B.; guest lectr., Univ. of Calif.; author: Guide to the Restaurants of Southern California, Ward Ritchie Press; Paul Wallach's Treasury of the Great Recipes of the West, Ward Ritchie Press; Guide to the Restaurants of Northern California. Founder-chmn., The Epicurean Soc. of No. America; mem. Chef's de Cuisine; mem. L'Escoffier Soc. Awarded citation of merit, Calif. State Legislature and U.S. Congress. Served USNR, Warrant Officer; Med. Corps, 2nd Marine Div., WW II, decorated: Purple Heart with cluster; bronze star; Presidential citation. Hobbies: collecting art, archeology. Home: 1361 Greenbriar Rd., Glendale, CA 91207; Office: P.O.B. 71217, (Biltmore Hotel), Los Angeles, CA 90071.

WALLIS, HAL B.
  Motion Picture Producer
b. Sept. 14, Chicago, Ill.; s. Jacob and Eva (Blum) Wallis; ed. pub. schhs.; m. Martha Hyer, Palm Springs, Calif., Dec. 31, 1966; chil.: Brent, Jr., b. Apr. 10, 1933. Career: Salesman, electric heating co., Kan., Nebr. and Mo. 1916-22; mgr. Garrick Theatre, 1922; head, publicity dept., Warner Bros. Studios, 1922-24; publicity dept., Pictures Corp. (Sol Lesser, pres.); chg. publicity, dept., Warner Bros. Studios 1925-28; studio mgr. 1928; exec. prod. 1928-31; supv. such pics as The Jazz Singer (first talking picture and Acad. Award winner), Dawn Patrol (Acad. Award winner for screen play), Little Caesar, Five Star Final, Sally (first big technicolor hit); prod. 1931-34: One Way Passage, I Am a Fugitive From a Chain Gang, Gold Diggers of 1933; chief prodn. exec., Warner Bros. 1934-43, winner 25 Acad Awards for such pics as Dangerous (starring Bette Davis); A Midsummer Night's Dream, The Story of Louis Pasteur, Anthony Adverse, The Charge of the Light Brigade, Casablanca, The Maltese Falcon, This Is the Army, Air Foce, Watch on the Rhine, Yankee Doodle Dandy, Kings Row, Sergeant York, One Foot in Heaven, Captains of the Clouds, Dive Bomber, Knute Rockne, All This and Heaven, Too," Virginia City, The Fighting 69th, Dark Victory, Angels With Dirty Faces, Dodge City, Robin Hood, Four Daughters, The Life of Emile Zola; independent prod. (releasing through Paramount Pics, Inc.), 1944---: The Affairs of Susan, You Came Along, Love Letters, The Strange Loce of Martha Ivers, The Searching Wind, The Perfect Marriage, Desert Fury, I Walk Alone, Sorry, Wrong Number, Rope of Sand, So Evil My Love, My Friend Irma; Dart City, September Affair, Quantrell's Raiders, 1950; Red Sky at Morning, 1975. Awards: winner of numerous Academy Awards; won Irvine Thalberg Award, 1938 and 1943. Rec.: horseback riding, deep-sea fishing. Res.: 515 S. Mapleton Dr., Los Angeles, CA 90024; Office: Universal Studios, Universal City, CA.

WALSH, EUGENE B.
  Consultant
b. Dec. 26, 1915, Denver, Colo.; s. Michael and Bertha (Eckstein) Walsh; M.B.A., Pepperdine Univ.; m. Bessie Hearne, Los Angeles, Calif., Jan. 25, 1941; chil.: Glenn, b. Jan. 6, 1947; Carl, b. June 30 1949. Career: Controller-treas. Ben Hur Prods., Inc. 1946-51; controller, Ralphs Grocery Co., 1951, v.p.-gen. mgr. 1961, exec. v.p. 1968, pres. 1970-73, chmn-chief exec. ofcr. 1973-76; v.p. Fed. Dept. Stores, Inc. (parent co. of Ralphs), 1968, bd. dirs. 1969, asst. to chmn. 1976-77, Mgmt. Consultant, E.B. Walsh & Co.; Dir., Foremost McKesson. Dir.: Pres. Food Inds. Circle of City of Hope; dir. Natl. Assn. of Food Chains; dir. L.A. Area C. of C. Instr. USC Food Mkt. and Mgmt. Pgm. 1972-74; resource spec. Continuing Edn. Corp. Licensed PA; author, many punl. articles; natl. pub. speaker. Maj. U.S. Army Inf. Awards: 1967 Man of Yr., by Pi Sigma Epsilon, USC; 1975 Food and Beverage Ind. Humanitarian Award by Natl. Conf. of Chris. and Jews; 1976 Man of Yr., Exec. Pgm. Assn. UCLA. Mem.: Dean's Council, Pepperdine Univ. Sch. of Bus. and Mgmt., and Mgmt. Assoc. Pgm.; bd. govs. Food Employers Council, So. Calif.; NAFC-SMJ Joint Adv. Bd.; Adv. Council Tech. Applied to Food Ind.; food ind. chmn. L.A. County United Crusade; pres. South Hills Country Club, 1959; San Gabriel Co. Club. Hobbies: reading, teaching, golf. Res.: 620 W. Huntington Dr., Arcadia, CA 91006; Office: P.O.B. 5128, Pasadena, CA 91107.

WALSH, MICHAEL H.
  U.S. Attorney
b. July 8, 1942, Binghamton, N.Y.; s. Thomas John and Elizabeth H. Walsh; B.A. Econ., Stanford Univ., 1964; LL.B., Yale Law Sch., 1969; m. Joan Royter, Aug. 26, 1967; children: Kimberly Ann, Jennifer Lynn, Jeffrey Michael. Career: Asst. Dean of Admissions, Stanford Univ., 1964-65; White House Fellow (Spl. Asst. to Secty. of Agri.), 1965-66; Sr. Staff Atty., Defenders, Inc., 1969-72; Atty. in pvt. practice, Sheela, Lightner, Hughes, Castro & Walsh, 1972-77; United States Atty., San Diego, 1978---. Mem.: Common Cause, Nat. Gov. Bd. 1970-77, Chmn. Calif. sect. 1973-76, vice chmn. Nat. Gov. Bd. 1977-78, state chmn. Campaign for Prop. 9 (Polit. Reform Act) 1974; Trustee, Stanford Univ., 1976-81; Commn., White House Fellows, 1977---; Bd. of Overseers, Univ. Calif., 1973---; Bd. of Gov., Public Advocates, Inc., 1973---; San Diego Co. and Calif. State Bar Assns. Res.: 1440 Crest Rd., Del Mar, CA 92014; Office: 940 Front St., San Diego, CA 92189.

WALSH, (PEARL) JERI
  Book Editor
b. Nov. 9, 1914, Los Angeles; d. John H. and Bertha (Frisch) Lane; Pub. Rels. Certificate, UCLA, 1972; m. 2d. John E. Walsh (dec.), Sept. 1951, Las Vegas, Nev.; son, John E., Jr., b. 1955; m. Norman H. Nittinger, 1937, Santa Barbara; son, David L., b. 1943; Career: Writer, editor, publs. asst., Rand Corp., Santa Monica, 1947-51, U.S. Naval Weapons Sta., China Lake, 1941-54; Pres., Or-State Inc., Tarzana, 1957-68; Tech. Editor, Mobil Research, Dallas, also rep. for Youth Edn. Systems, 1967-68; tech. writer, RCA Van Nuys, 1968-71; mgr., Carriage Trade Travel, Century City, 1971-72; sr. writer, UCLA Neuropsychiat. Inst., Research Dept., Camarillo, 1972-74; tech. writer, AUS Corps of Engrs., Los Angeles, 1974---; also book production and math. editor for major books pubs. incl. Wiley, Prentice-Hall, McGraw-Hill (freelance), 1951---. Mem.: Soc. for Tech. Communication, publicity dir. for 26th Internat. Tech. Communication Conf., L.A. May 1979; Publicity Club; Am. Med. Mktg. Assn.; Inst. for Advance. of Engring., Fellow; Inst. of Certified Travel Counselors, holds CTC; So. Calif. Bookbuilders Assn.; SERVAS. Christian. Hobbies: youth, travel. Res.: 8633 Balboa Blvd., Apt. 5, Northridge, CA 91325; Office: P.O.B. 2711, Los Angeles, CA 90053.

WALSH, WILLIAM DESMOND
  Corporate Executive
b. Aug. 4, 1930, New York City; s. William J. and Catherine Grace (Desmond) Walsh; B.A., Fordham Univ., 1951; LL.B., Harvard, 1955; m. Mary Jane Gordon, Apr. 5, 1951, NY; chil.: Deborah, Caroline, Michael, Suzanne, Tara Jane, Peter. Career: Admitted to N.Y. State Bar 1955; asst. U.S. atty. So. Dist. N.Y., N.Y.C., 1955-58; counsel N.Y. commn. Investigation, N.Y.C., 1958-61; mgmt. cons. McKinsey & Co., N.Y.C., 1961-67; sr. v.p. Arcata Corp., Menlo Park, Calif., 1971--- (graphic arts, forest products, specialty food packaging). Dir. DPF, Inc., Hartsdale, N.Y.; bd. dirs. Herbert Hoover Memorial Boys Club; mem.: Am. and N.Y. State Bar Assns.; club: Sharon Heights Golf Country. Home: 279 Park Lane, Atherton, Ca 94025; Office: 2750 Sand Hill Rd., Menlo Park, CA 94025.

WALTER, JOHN, JR.
  Physicist
b. Feb. 16, 1924, Newkirk, Okla.; s. Walter John and Carrie (Hollingsworth) John; B.S., Cal Tech, 1950; Ph.D., Univ. Calif., Berkeley, 1955; m. Carol Salin, Jan. 22, 1954, Berkeley; children: Kenneth Elliot, b. 1956; Laura Ann, b. 1958; Claudia Susan, b. 1961; Leslie Ellen, b. 1962. Career: Instr., Dept. of Physics, Univ. of Illinois, 1955-58; Sr. Physicist, Lawrence Livermore Lab., 1958-71; Prof. and Dept. Chmn., Physical Sciences Dept., Cal. State Coll., Stanislaus, 1971-73; Research Specialist, Air and Indsl. Hygiene Lab., Calif. State Dept. of Health, Berkeley, CA 1973---; also Research Assoc., Univ. Calif., Berkeley, 1976---. Contbr. articles on nuclear physics, X-rays, fission, air pollution and aerosol physics (50+) in sci. journs., 1953---. AUS, 1943-46, ETO. Mem.: Tau Beta Pi, Sigma Xi, Fellow, Am. Physical Soc., Am. Assn. of Physics Tchrs. Hobby: photog. Res.: 195 Grover Lane, Walnut Creek, CA 94596; Office: 2151 Berkeley Way, Berkeley, CA 94704.

WALTER, RUBY L.
Realtor
b. Feb. 16, 1921, Wichita Falls, Tex.; d. Fred H. and Verdie Butcher; student Kansas City Business Coll., 1940; Mt. San Antonio Coll., 1959; Lumbleau Real Estate School, 1973; m. David N. Walter, Aug. 17, 1940, Paola, Kan.; chil.: Carolyn (Mrs. L.W. Wilson), b. Aug. 5, 1942; Frederick J., b. Mar. 12, 1944. Career: exec. secty., West Covina Sch. Dist. 1955-63; real estate agent, co-owner, David Walter REalty, 1964-69; broker, 1969---. Past pres., Calif. State Employees Assn., West Covina chpt. 1962; past pres., Women's Council of Nat. Assn. of Realtors, So. Orange Co. Bd. of Realtors, 1973. Mem.: Calif. and Nat. Assns. of Realtors, 1964---; San Clemente C. of C., 1970---; Women's Club of San Clemente, 1976---. Methodist; ch. secty., choir. Hobby: photog. Rec.: tennis, dancing, travel. Home: 2303 Calle La Serna, San Clemente, CA 92672; Office: 317 N. El Camino Real, San Clemente, CA 92672.

WALTERS, DOROTHY MAE
Marketing Executive — Lecturer
b. Dec. 31, 1924, Los Angeles; grad. Alhambra, H.S.; m. Robert Emmitt Walters, Jan. 27, 1945, Alhambra; children: Michael, Jeanine (King), Lillet (Bossenmeyer). Career: Pres., owner, founder, Hospitality Hostess, Inc., 1958---; co-owner, Double HH Press, Publisher Newsletter and Royal CBS Publishing Co., 1978---; R&D Real Estate, 1958---; Lectr. on Sales to Women all across USA, Canada, England; Seminar speaker; Author: Selling Power of a Woman, 1962; Never Underestimate the Selling Power of a Woman, 1977; Success Secrets, 1978; Pub. newsletter Sharing Ideas for Women, 1978---; Narrator of cassette-album: 7 Secrets of Selling to Men, Selling Power of a Woman, Success Unlimited. Hobbies: Crewel embroidery, gardening. Address: 600 W. Foothill Blvd., Glendora, CA 91740.

WALTRIP, ELIZABETH JANE NEWELL
Educator
b. Feb. 1, 1921, Denver, Colo.; d. Thomas Van Buren and Dora Elizabeth (Hull) Newell; bros.: James W. Newell, noted interior designer (Lance Reventlow home); L.J. Newell, M.D.; T.E. Newell, M.D., Dayton, Oh.; P.A. Newel, regional mgr., Ball Bros. Co., Cincinnati; Dr. Robert F. Newell, Nebr.; B.S., Univ. of Houston, 1945; M.A., Univ. of Tex., El Paso, 1951; Ed.D., Tex. Tech. 1955; m. V. Drexel Waltrip, Hayward, 1948-50; bd. dirs. (Eagle leader, Masonic Lodge, Shrine, First Bapt. Ch.), Las Vegas, Nev., July 21, 1942. Career: Teacher, pub. schs., Houston, 1945, El Paso, Tex. 1946-56; teacher, Mt. Diablo Unified Sch. Dist., Concord, Calif. 1956---; dir., local annual Sch. Bell Awards; dir. edn. pgm. sta. KWUN. Dir., Investments Unlimited, 1956---. Writer, wkly edn. column, Our Schs., Edn. Corner, Contra Costa Times; contrib. to various professional publs. Awards: KABL's Citizen of the Day, Feb. 23, 1967; 6 Arthur Corey Communications Awards, Calif. Teachers' Assn. Mem.: pres. Div. of Mental Retardations, Calif. Council for Exceptional Chil.; bd. dirs., Council Exceptional Chil., Contra Costa Co. 1958-63, pres. 1972; del. Calif. Dem. Council, Fresno, 1963; bd. dirs., Bio-Co. Epilepsy League 1963-65; pres. Bay Area Assn. for Childhood Edn. 1968; exec. bd. Mt. Diablo Unified Dist. Edn. Assn. 1972-73; NEA; treas. Downtown Martinez Homeowners Assn. 1972-73; Contra Costa Mental Health Assn.; California Assn. Neurologically Handicapped Chil.; Calif. Council for Retarded; Internat., Amer. Assn. on Mental Deficiency; (hon.) Alpha Delta Kappa. Baptist. Hobbies: antiques, growing succulents. Residence: 2814 Marion Terr., Martinez, CA 94553; Office: Mt. Diablo Unified Sch. Dist., 1936 Carlotta Dr., Concord, CA.

WANDLING, HAROLD SYLVESTER
Physician and Surgeon
b. Aug. 10, 1922, Alton, Ill.; s. Harold Sylvester and Mildred (Linkogle) Wandling; B.S., Univ. Ill 1942; M.S., 1943; B.S., 1948, M.D. 1950; m. Josephine Cenar, Jan. 27, 1952; chil.: Lance Alan, Sherie Renee. Career: Res. phys. Franklin Hosp., San Francisco, CA 1952-55; VA Hosp., Oakland, 1955-58, asst. and chief, orthopedics-phys. med.-rehab. 1955-58; diplomate, Amer. Bd. Surg. 1958; staff Hollywood Presby. Hosp. 1959---; (courtesy) Good Samaritan Hosp. 1960---; St. Vincent's Hosp. 1965---; surg. teaching staff, Queen of Angels Hosp., and Cedars of Lebanon Hosps. 1960-63; USNR 1944-46, 1950-51. Mem.: Hollywood Acad. of Med.; AMA; Calif. Med Assn.; treas. League of the Americas, L.A. 1959-61; pres. 1963-64; pres. Beverly Hills Acad. of Med. 1963-64; fellow, Amer. Coll. of Surgs.; fellow, Internat. Coll. of Surgs.; fellow, Amer.

Soc. Abdominal Surgs.; bd. govs. Met. Dist., L.A. Co. Med. Assn. 1966---, many coms. incl. chmn. Fee Complaint Com., and Pub. Inf. Com.; Hollywood-Wilshire Dist. v. chmn. BSA; Beverly Hills C. of C. and Civic Assn.; L.A. Tennis Club; Pi Kappa Epsilon, Mason. Republican. Presbyterian. Res.: 223 S. McCadden Pl., Los Angeles, CA 90004; Office: 1930 Wilshire Blvd., Los Angeles, CA 90057.

WANG, GEORGE SHIH-CHANG
Executive — Engineer
b. May 4, 1933, Anking, China; s. C.S. and L.K. Wang; B.S., Civil Engring., Univ. of Mich., 1958; M.S., civil and nuclear engring., 1960; Ph.D. engring., UCLA, 1970; m. Ann Chen, Ann Arbor, Mich.; chil.: David, Julia, Gregory, Tracy. Career: Asst. Research Engineer, Engring. Research Inst., Univ. of Mich., 1959-62; sr. nuclear engr., Bechtel Power Corp., 1962-64, project nuclear engr., 1964-67, asst. chief nuclear engr., 1967-68; chief nuclear & environmental systems engr., 1968-72, engineering manager, 1972-77; gen. mgr., Helium Breeder Associates, San Diego, 1977-78; Engineering manager, Bechtel Power Corp., 1978---. Registered profl. engr., Calif. Pres., Univ. of Mich. Club of Orange Co., 1973---; mem.: Chi Epsilon; Am. Soc. of Civil Engrs.; Am. Nuclear Soc.; Who's Who in Atoms. Office: P.O.B. 60860 Terminal Annex, L.A., CA 90060.

WANGLIN, ANN JEANNETTE
Civic Leader
b. May 10, Spokane, Wash.; d. John James and Maybelle Margaret (Gibson) Georgeson; desc. of Dashiell Hammett, noted Amer. Writer of detective and fiction, author The Thin Man; Adm. Richard E. Byrd, distinguished aviator, explorer and author; dir. Navy-MacMillan Polar Expedition, flew over North Pole 1925 (claims entry to the inner earth, found human life, animal life, and vegetation); also discovered Edsel Ford Mts.; flew over South Pole, 1929; author: Skyward, 1928; Little America, 1930; Discovery, 1935; bro. Harry Flood Byrd, Gov. of Va. 1926-30, U.S. Senator, 1933; ed. B.A., UCLA; (hon.) Ph.D. Hamilton State Univ. 1973; m. Byron Chase Wanglin, Los Angeles, Calif., Apr. 6, 1951; chil.: Ronald Chase, b. Nov. 23, 1952; Valerie Ann, b. Mar. 16, 1954; Michael James, b. Nov. 21, 1955. Career: Civic and social leader, Beverly Hills-Los Angeles, 1952---; pres. Rotary Annes of Westwood Village, 1959-60; (charter) Brentwood-Bel-Air Women's Club, 1960-67; pres. Spastic Children's Leag. 1961-62; Beverly Hills adv. com., Aississtance League, 1964-67; pres. Univ. Affiliates of UCLA 1964-65; bd. dirs., UCLA Alumni Assn. 1965-67, bd. dirs., Gold Shield (hon, alumni), 1967-69; Women's Council of Channel 28 KCET; bd. dirs.-corr. secty., Com. for Performing Fine Arts, 1967---. Mem.: Natl. Charity League 1952---; The Beach Club; Muses of L.A. County Museum; Sigma Kappa. Chr. Ch. Hobbies: travel, art. Res.: 612 N. Roxbury Dr., Beverly Hills, CA.

WANGLIN, BYRON CHASE
Publisher — INsurance Executive
b. Feb. 7, 1903, Webb City, Mo.; s. Byron Chase and Edith (Hampton) Wanglin; desc.: Gen. Wade Hampton and Col. William Wanglin, Civil War heroes; ed. Wash. Univ., St. Louis, Mo., 1920-21; B.S., U.S. Naval Acad. 1925; m. Marjorie Waite (dec.); m. 2nd, Ann Jeannette Georgeson, Apr. 6, 1951; chil.: Ruth Sharon, b. May 4, 1937; Ronald Chase, b. Nov. 23, 1952; Valerie Ann, b. Mar. 16, 1954; Michael James, b. Sept. 21, 1955. Career: Serv. USN fleet, 1925-30; founder-propr.-publ., various newspapers, incl. Westwood Hills Press, Santa Monica Press, Beverly Hills News; assoc with First Fed. Savings & Loan Assn., Westwood, Calif. 1933-39; acquired ins. agcy. interests, 1937; newspaper and ins. bus. 1946---. Comdr., U.S. Navy; prof. naval sci. and tactics, USC 1942-43; comdg. ofcr., Navy V-12 Unit, Occidental Coll., L.A., CA 1943-44; U.S. Navy Oriental Lang Sch., Stillwater, Okla., 1945; USN Intelligence, Secty. of Navy's ofc. (1946), WW II. Mem.: bd. dirs., Westwood Village Bus. Assn. 1930-41, 1946-49, pres. 1948; regional dir., Boy Scouts, 1934-37; adv. council, All-Yr. Club of So. Calif. 1935-49; pres. West L.A. Rotary Club, 1937; secty. Los Rancheros Breakfast Club, 1937-40; bd. dirs., YMCA 1946-49; pres. Westwood Village Bus. Assn., 1948; Exec. Club pf Beverly Hills and Bel-Air, 1958---; U.S. Naval Acad. Alumni Assn., Military Order of World Wars, Masonic Lodge, No. 677, UCLA Young Men's Club, Young Men's Club of Westwood; Clubs: The Beach, L.A. Breakfast. All Saints Episc. Ch., Beverly Hills. Hobby: world travels. Res.: 612 N. Roxbury Dr., Beverly Hills, CA; Office: 10920 Wilshire Blvd., Suite 408, Los Angeles, CA.

WARBURTON, AUSTEN D.
Attorney at Law
b. Nov. 12, 1917, Santa Clara; s. Henry L. and Mary (Den) Warburton; GGG Gr.son, Jose Francisco Ortega, discoverer of San Francisco Bay; GG Gr.son, Luis Antonio Arguello, First Mexican Gov. of Calif.; A.B., San Jose State Univ., 1938; J.D., Univ. of Santa Clara, 1941. Career: Attorney, 1941---; Secty. Com. of Bar Examiners, 1942; Prof. of Law, Univ. of Santa Clara, 1946-66. Mem.: City of Santa Clara Council (Vice-Mayor) 1958-63; Civil Service, Planning, Historic Landmarks, Parks & Recreation Commns. 1950-60; Santa Clara Co. Juvenile Justice Com. 1950---. Bd. Dir.: Santa Clara Youth Village, Valley Village, Alpha Beta. Author: Indian Lore of the North California Coast, 1966. AUS, 1942-46. Chairman, Santa Clara City Bd. of Freeholders, 1949-50. Episcopalian, Vestryman. Hobbies: history, art. Res.: 790 Locust St., Santa Clara, CA 95050; Office: First Nat. Bank Bldg., San Jose, CA.

WARD, GEORGE P.
President, Systron Donner Corp.
b. Apr. 9, 1938, Philadelphia; s. George and Mary (Stinson) Ward; B.S., Aeronautical Engring., Penna. State Univ., 1959; m. Joan Aitken, June 28, 1959, Phila.; sons: George P., Jr., b. 1960; Richard C., b. 1962. Career: Program mgr., Thiokol Chemical Corp., 1962-66; mktg. mgr., General Electric Space Div. 1966-74; mgr. X-Ray Equipment Business GE-MEd. Systems Div. 1974-76; Gen. mgr. Special Health Products Dept., 1976-77; dir., pres., chief exec. ofcr., Systron Donner Corp., 1977---. Capt., USAF Reserve, active duty, 1959-62. Dir. Assn. for Advance of Med. Instrumentation. Mem. Sigma Pi frat., 1957---. Catholic. Rec.: skiing, boating, golf. Res.: 2452 Biltmore Dr., Alamo, CA 94507; Office: One Systron Dr., Concord, CA 94518.

WARD, MURRAY
Business Executive
b. Apr. 7, 1901, Iowa; s. Thomas F. and Maude (Murray) Ward; grandson of Benjamin F. Murray, State Sen. of Ia.; B.A., Stanford Univ. 1924; m. Virginia Ducommun, Indio, Calif., Mar. 28, 1942; chil.: Anthony Converse, b. May 6, 1941. Career: Petroleum engr., Shell Oil Co. 1926-29; statistician, Hill Richards & Co. 1932-37; v.p. 1937-46, pres. 1946-54; sr. v.p. E.F. Hutton Co. 1954-66; sr. cons. 1966---. Dir.: Ducommun Inc. 1946---; Telecomputing Corp. 1951---. Comdr., USN 1941-46, staff Comdr. in Chief, U.S. Pac. Fleet, WW II. Awards: Legion of Merit with Combat V by Secty. of Navy. Mem.: gov. Natl. Assn. Security Dealers, 1951-53; pres. Bond Club of L.A. 1952; v.-chmn.-bd. govs., L.A. Stock Exch. 1952-54; clubs: California, Bel-Air Bay, L.A. Yacht, Trans-Pacific Yacht, L.A. Country, Eldorado Country. Res.: 10464 Bellagio Rd., Los Angeles, CA 90024.

WARD, PETER LANGDON
Geophysicist
b. Aug. 10, 1943, Washington, D.C.; s. John Langdon and Ruth (Page) Ward; B.A., Dartmouth Coll., 1965; M.A., Columbia Univ., 1967; Ph.D., 1970; m. Karen Marlies Olsen Lahr; children: Christopher Langdon W., b. 1969; Tonya Holyoke W., b. 1972; Taya Marlies Lahr, n. 1972; Nils Njorn Lahr, b. 1973. Career: Research Assoc., Lamont Doherty Geol. Obs., 1970-71; Geophysicist, U.S. Geol. Survey, 1971---. Chief, Br. of Seismology, 1975, Chief, Br. of Earthquake Mech. and Prediction, 1975-77, coordinator, Earthquake Prediction Program, 1977-78. Contbr. sci. papers profl. journs. Mem.: AAAS, 1965---; Seismological Soc. of Am., Am. Geophysicial Union, Fellow, Geological Soc. of America. Rec.: camping, hiking. Res.: 380 Nova Lane, Menlo Park, CA 94025; Office: 345 Middlefield Rd., Menlo Park, CA 94025.

WARD, RITCHIE R.
Science Writer
b. Apr. 6, 1906, Medicine Lodge, Kansas; s. Frank C. and Mary (Ritchie) Ward; B.S., chem., Univ. Calif., Berkeley, 1927, M.J. journ., 1966; m. Claire Marshall (dec. 1974), Aug. 23, 1933, Honolulu; son, William A.R., b. 1938. Career: Chemist, Hawaiian Sugar Planters' Assn., 1929-34; chemist & personnel dir., mgr. tech. information servs., Shell Devel. Div., Shell Oil Co., 1934-62; freelance sci. writer, 1962---. Author: Practical Technical Writing, Alfred A Knopf, 1968; The Living Clocks, Knopf, 1971 (now avail. in 8 langs.); Into the Ocean World, Knopf, 1974; contbr. articles in Natural History, Ecolibrium, Current

Biography, Smithsonian, Horizon, Writer's Digest, Dir., Calif. Writers Club, 1976-79. Mem. Alpha Chi Sigma, Sigma Delta Chi. Hobby: music. Res.: 93 El Toyonal Rd., Orinda, CA 94563.

WARD-STEINMAN, DAVID
Music Composer
b. Nov. 6, 1936, Alexandria, La.; s. Irvine and Daisy Ward-Steinman; gr.-nephew, David B. Steinman, bridge designer, e.g. Mackinac Straits bridge; B.Mus. cum laude, Fla. State Univ., 1957; M.Mus., Univ. Ill., 1958, Doctor of Musical Arts, 1961; postdoctoral, Princeton Univ., 1970; m. Susan Lucas, Dec. 28, 1956, Jacksonville, Fla.; children: Jenna, b. 1961; Matthew, b. 1965. Career: asst./assoc./full prof. of Music, San Diego State Univ., 1961---, composer in residence ---; Guest Faculty, Eastman Sch. of Music, summer 1969; Ford Found. Composer-in-residence, Tampa Bay area, Fla. 1970-72 Vis. Composer in Residence, Quincy Coll., Ill., 1968; Outstanding Prof. Award, Cal. State Universities and Colls. 1968; Dir., Comprehensive Musicianship Program, San Diego State Univ., 1967---. Prin. Compositions (pub. by Marks unless noted): Piano Sonata (1956-7, unpub.); Symphony, 1959; Prelude and Toccata for orch., 1962; Fragments from Sappho, for soprano, flute, clarinet, piano, 1962-65; Song of Moses, oratorio voice & orch. (1963-64, S.D. State Coll. Press); Western Orpheus, ballet, choreography by Richard Carter, 1964; Cello Concerto, 1964-66; These Three, 1966; Jazz Tangents, 1966-77; The Tale of Issoubochi, libretto by Susan Lucas from Japanese fairy tale, 1968; Childs Play (1968 Highgate). Mem. Golden State Flying Club. Hobbies: philately, numismatics. Res.: 9403 Broadmoor Pl., La Mesa, CA 92041; Office: San Diego State Univ., San Diego, CA 92182.

WARNE, WILLIAM ELMO
Water Resources Consultant
b. Sept. 2, 1905, Seafield, Ind.; s. William R. and Nettie Jane (Williams) Warne; A.B., Univ. of Calif. 1927; (hon.) LL.D., Seoul Natl. Univ., 1959; (hon.) Dr. of Econs., Yonsie Univ., Korea, 1959; m. Edith M. Peterson, Pasadena, July 9, 1929; chil.: Mrs. David C. (Jane Ingrid) Beeder, b. Dec. 8, 1934; William Robert, b. Nov. 30, 1937; Mrs. John W. (Margaret Edith) Monroe, b. Sept. 1, 1944. Career: Reporter, S.F.Bulletin and Oakland Post-Inquirer, 1925-27; news ed., Brawley News, Calif. 1927; news ed., Calexico Chronicle, Calif. 1928; ed.-staff writer, Assoc. Press, Los Angeles, San Diego, Wash., D.C. 1928-35; dir. of Reclamation, Dept. of Interior, 1935-42, asst. commr. 1943-47; asst. secty., Dept. of Interior, 1947-51; chief of staff, War Prodn. Dr., War Prodn. Bd. 1942; dir. AID, Iran, 1951-55, Brazil, 1956; Korea 1956-59; dir. Calif. Dept. of Fish and Game, 1959-60; Agri. Dept. 1960-61; admr. Calif. Resources Agcy. 1961-63, Water Resources, 1961-66; dir. Development and Resources Corp. 1967-69; distinguished practitioner in residence, USC, Sch. of Pub. Adminstrn., Sacramento Campus, 1976---; water resources cons., 1969---; chmn. President's Com. on San Diego Water Supply, 1944-46, chmn. Fed. Inter-Agency River Basin Com. 1948, Fed. Com. on Alaskan Development, 1948; pres. Group Health Assn., Inc. 1945-52; chmn. U.S. Del, 2nd Inter-Amer. Conf. on Indian Life, CUzco, Peru, 1949---; U.S. Del., 4th World Power Conf., London, Eng. 1950; bd. dirs. Near East Found. 1956-58, 1959-64; Calif. Water Pollution Bd. 1959-66; Comm. on Interstate Cooperation, 1960-66; adv. bd., Fed. Water Pollution Control, 1962-65; mem. Gov's. Cabinet, 1961; U.S. com., Internat. Comm. on Large Dams; dir. Natl. Water Supply Improvement Assn. 1971---; assoc. dir. WATERCARE, 1973-77. Author: Mission for Peace, publ. Bobbs-Merrill, 1956; The Bureau of Reclamation, Praeger Publs. 1973. How the Colorado River was Spent, NWSIA Jrnl. 1975. 2nd Lt., ORC 1927-37. Awards: Distinguished Serv. Award, dept. of Interior, 1951; Distinguished Pub. Serv. Honor Award, Foreign Operations Adm. 1955; Order of Crown, Shah of Iran, 1955; Outstanding Serv. Cit., UN Command, 1959; Achievement Award, Lambda Chi Alpha, 1963. Mem.: Sigma Delta Chi, Lambda Chi Alpha; Natl. Press Club, Wash., D.C. 1935---; Sutter Club, Sacramento, 1965---; Amer. Acad. of Pub. Adm. 1969---; chmn. NAPA Standing Com. on Environ. and Resource Mgmt. 1970---; Explorers Club, N.Y. 1978---. Res.: 2090 8th Ave., Sacramento, CA 95818.

WARNECKE, JOHN CARL
Architect
b. Feb. 24, 1919, Oakland; s. Carl I and Margaret (Esterling) Warnecke; B.A. architecture (cum laude),

Stanford Univ., 1941; M.A. archit., Harvard Sch. of Design, 1942; chil.: John Carl, Jr.; Rodger C.; Margaret E.; Frederick P. Career: Architect, Miller & Warnecke (father's firm), Oakland, Calif., 1945; architect, John Carl Warnecke & Assoc., S.F., Calif., 1946-58; architect, Warnecke & Warnecke, S.F., Calif., 1951-58; and chmn. of bd., Chief Exec. officer, John Carl Warnecke & Assoc., S.F., N.Y.C., Wash., D.C., L.A., 1958---. Awards incl.: Arnold Brunner Prize, Nat. Inst. Arts & Letters, 1957; Assoc., Nat. Acad. of Design, 1958; Fellow, AIA (in design), 1962; mem. Fine Arts Commission, Wash. D.C., 1963-67; guest archt., Com. on Sci. and Tech. USSR tour, 1970; guest archt. of Chinese Soc. of Architects, tour of Peoples Republic of China, 1974; firm awards for Rickover Hall, US Naval Acad. Annapolis, 1976; Hennepin Co. Govt. Center, Minneapolis, 1977; Joseph Mark Lauinger Memorial Lib., Wash. D.C., 1976; the Pasadena Center, 1974; restoration of Renwick Gallery, Wash. D.C., 1974; S.F. Internat. Airport International Rotunda, 1974; S.F. Internat. Airport Elevated Roadways, 1972; 323 Broadway, N.Y. Telephone & Telegraph Equip. Bldg., N.Y., 1972; Hawaii State Capitol, Honolulu, 1970; Michelson-Chauvenet Hall, US Naval Acad., Annapolis, 1970; Kaiser Center for Tech., Pleasanton, Calif., 1970; Lafayette Square Office Bldg., Wash. D.C., 1969; Roscoe Maples Athletic Pavilion, Stanford Univ., 1969; Lutheran Coll. Chapel, Irvine, Calif., 1968; Central Lib., UC, Santa Cruz, 1967; Asilomar Hotel and Conference Grounds, Pacific Grove, Calif., 1966; Herrick Iron Works, Hayward, 1966; Oakland Internat. Airport, 1960; Mark Thomas Inn, Monterey, 1956; landscape archt. awards incl. Blair House Garden, Wash. D.C., Humanities Bldg., Scripps Coll., Claremont; John F. Kennedy Gravesite, Arlington Nat. Cemetary; Asilomar Hotel and Conference Grounds; Ampex Corp., Redwood City. Mem.: Olympic Club, S.F.; Pacific Union Club, S.F.; Transportation Club, S.F.; Doubles Club, N.Y.; N.Y. Athletic Club; Federal City Club, D.C.; Hawaii Canoe Club, Hawaii. Democrat. Episcopalian. Office: 61 New Montgomery St., San Francisco, CA 94105.

WARNER, CARYL ROWLAND
Attorney at Law

b. Jan. 5, 1908, Los Angeles, Calif.; s. Rowland Moseley and Emily Caryl (Clark) Warner (Eng. teacher, L.A. H.S., with Mary Foy); nephew of Frederick H. Clark, L.A. Supt. of Schs., (90s), and George T. Clark, librarian, Stanford Univ. and author, Life of Leland Stanford; and desc. of Puritan leader, Andrew Warner, co-founder with Rev. Thomas Hooker of Hartford, Conn., 1640; Harvard Univ. situated on former Andrew Warner's farm, Cambridge, Mass.; grandson of Col. Robert Clark, N.H. Militia, migrated to San Francisco, 1853, mem. Calif. Legislature, 1861 (slavery opponent); cousin, Frederick Crocker, noted civ. engr. who was awarded Cert. of Merit by Pres. Truman, engr.-dir. salvage of battleship Okla. at Pearl Harbor; asst. in constr. of Pasadena Bridge and the Golden Gate Bridge; ed. J.D., Southwestern Univ.; m. Carol Ann McGinnis; stepdau., Amy; chil.: Rick A., Caryl Christopher, Jack C., James and Carolyn. Career: Surveyor, City of L.A. 1926-29; admitted to law practice, Calif. and fed. cts. 1929; editor, legal column, L.A. Daily Journ., 1932---; dean of legal columnists, USA; instr. Hollywood Ave. H.S. 1932-35; regional property officer, U.S. Ofc. Civ. Defense, 9th Region (Western states), San Francisco, 1942-43; judge, Superior Ct. of L.A. County (pro tem), 1950; pvt. practice law, L.A.; partner, Warner & Tabash; chief counsel, Press Photogs. Assn. Greater L.A. Lt. (j.g.), USNR (1943-45), WW II; Lt. Comdr., USNR (ret.). Awards: Cert. of Merit, Calif. Assembly for Mil. Serv. 1944; cit. by L.A. City Council and Joint Congl. Com. on Atomic Energy as chmn. AMVETS Natl. Civ. Def. Com. Mem.: Calif. and L.A. Co. Bar Assns. (serv. on various coms.); charter organizer, AMVETS, Calif., State Dept., and Natl. Dept. 1945-55; (charter) organ. Criminal Cts. Bar Assn. of L.A., 1948; First Century Families; Calif. Soc. Sons of the Rev.; L.A. Ath. Club; SAR; founder, 100 Yr. Club of Calif., pres. 1953; Phi Alpha Delta; 3rd Deg. Mason; OES. Republican. Hobby: golf. Office: 250 E. First St., Suite 1212, Los Angeles, CA 90012.

WARREN, CHARLES MARQUIS
Film & TV Producer

b. Dec. 16, 1912, Baltimore, Md.; s. Charles and Beatrice (Porter) Warren; great-grandnephew of Pres. Franklin Pierce; desc.: Col. John Porter, Amer. Rev. Forces; F. Scott Fitzgerald, godfather; ed. McDonogh Mil. Sch., McDonogh, Md. 1931; Baltimore City Coll. 1932; m. Anne Crawford Tootle, Baltimore, Md., Oct. 4, 1941; chil.: Anne C., b. Aug. 27, 1945; Jessica Porter, b. Aug. 11, 1946; Victoria Lance, b. Sept. 17,

1947. Career: Playwright, No Sun, No Moon, 1933; author: 3 Sat. Eve. Post serials; (2 textbooks) Wilderness and History of American Dental Surgery, publ. Century Press, 1942; best-selling books: Only the Valiant, publ. Macmillan, 1943; Bugles Are for Soldiers, publ. Doubleday, 1944; Valle y of the Shadow, publ. Doubleday, 1948; Deadhead (mustery), publ. Coward-McCann, 1951; prod.-dir.-writer, Little Big Horn and Hellgate, Commander Films, Inc. and Flight to Tangier, 1953, Paramount Studies; dir.: Seven Angry Men, Allied Artists, 1954; Tension at Table Rock, RKO, The Black Whip and Cattle Empire, 20th Century-Fox and Trooper Hook, United Artists, 1956; screen writer: Streets of Laredo, The Redhead and the Cowboy, Pony Express and Beyong Glory, Paramount Studios; Springfield Rifle and Only the Valiant, Warner Bros.; orig.-prod.-dir., Gunsmoke TV series; pres. Commander Films, Inc.; pres. Charles Marquis Warren Prodns., Inc. 1952---; creater-prod.-dir.-writer, Rawhide TV series. Pvt. through ranks, U.S. Army; Comdr., USN; 5 yrs. with Navy Combat Photographic Unit, participated in 7 major amphibious assaults in S. Pac. (Tarawa, Bougainville, Eniwetok, Kwajalein, Roi, Green Is., Emirau), WW II; comdr. USNR. Awards: recipient, Purple Heart, Bronze Star, 5 Battle Stars; Streets of Laredo recd. Acad. nom. for screen play; Gunsmoke TV series won TV Acad. nom. 1955; listed, various biog. works hon. distinguished Americans, Acad. of Mot. Pic. Arts and Scis., Writers' Guild of Amer., Acad. of TV Arts and Scis. Republican. Episcopalian. Hobby: still and mot. pic. photog. Rec.: fishing, spectator sports. Res.: 1130 Tower Rd., Beverly Hills, CA.

WARREN, STAFFORD LEAK
Professor Emeritus

b. June 19, 1896, Maxwell City, N.Mex.; s. Edwin Stafford and Clara (Avis) Warren; 3rd cousin, Sheriff Eugene W. Biscailuz, L.A.; ed. B.A. Univ. of Calif., Berkeley, 1918. M.A., M.D. 1922; m. Viola Lockhart, Berkeley, Calif., May 22, 1920 (dec.); m. Gertrude Turner Hubberty, M.D. July 18, 1970; chil.: Mrs. Clarence (Jane) Larsen, born June 2, 1922, San Francisco, Calif.; Dean Stafford, b. Apr. 16, 1927, Rochester, N.Y.; Roger Wright, b. June 20, 1928, Rochester, N.Y. Career: Asst. in pathology, Johns Hopkins, 1923; intern, Mass. Gen. Hosp. 1924; asst. in radiology, 1925; res. phys., Huntington Mem. Hosp. 1925; Rockefeller fellowship, med. and radiology, European Clinic, 1925-26; asst. prof. of med., Univ. of Rochester, 1926-30; assoc. prof. of med., prof. of radiology, 1930-43; radiologist in chef, Strong Mem. Hosp. 1926-43; dir. Atomic Energy Prok., Univ. of Rochester, 1943-46; dean-prof. of biophysics-dir. Atomic Energy Proj., UCLA Sch. of Med. 1947-62, v.-chancellor for health scis., 1962-63; v.-chancellor emeritus, 1963---; spec. asst. to the Pres. (apptd. U.S. White House adv. by Pres. Kennedy) 1963-64; Pres. Johnson, 1964-65; UCLA prof. emeritus, 1965---; cons. U.S. Public Health Service, Vets. Administration, Atomic Energy Comm. Author: Publ. over 100 papers in field of research, cancer, arthritis, radio-biology, physics, 1922-49. Col. Med. Corps, AUS; chief, med. sect. and adv. to comdg. gen., Manhattan Proj., 1st tech. serv. detachment in Japan, 1943-46; chief, Radiological Safety Sect. and adv., Joint Task Force I at Bikini, WW II; appted. head, Calif. Civ. Def. Com. by Gov. Earl Warren, 1960. Awards: Awarded Legion of Merit for outstanding serv. at Bikini Atoll (primarily responsible for safety of the 42,000 participants in atom bomb tests at Bikini); Distinguished Serv. Medal for outstanding part in atom bomb development, Nov. 3, 1945. Mem.: Chmn. Roentgen Ray Soc. of Rochester, 1930-40; v.p. Amer. Soc. for Clin. Investigation, 1936; treas.-trustee, Rochester Museum Assn. 1936-47; co-chmn., Rochester Res. Comm. 1940-43; treas. Amer. Venereal Disease Assn. 1940-47, exec. com. 1940-49, v.p. 1948; chmn. State Radiological Safety Adv. Com. 1950---; med. adv. com., Fed. Civ. Def. Adm. 1953---; City of L.A. Def. & Disaster Bd. 1954---; State Adv. Com. on Mental Health, 1954---; fellow, Amer. Soc. of Air Affiars; adv. council, Natl. Soc. for Med. Res.; Amer., Calif. and L.A. Co. Med. Assns.; med. and sci. adv. bd., L.A. Co. br., Amer. Cancer Soc.; adv. council, Med. Res. Soc. of So. Calif.; Amer. Assn. for the Advancement of Sci., Amer. Pub. Health Assn., Gerontological Soc., Amer. Assn. for Cancer Research, Assn. of Mil. Surgs., L.A. Co. Med. Assn. Res. Found., Natl. Multiple Sclerosis Soc., Western Assn. of Ind. Phys. and Surgs., L.A. Acad. of Med., Sigma Xi, Alpha Omega Alpha, Phi Chi. Protestant. Hobby: hunting, fishing, photog. Rec.: gardening. Office: UCLA, Medical Center, Los Angeles, CA 90024.

WASHINGTON, PORTER LOVE
Aeronautical Engineer
b. May 18, 1912, Marietta, Okla.; s. Russell Love and Edna May (Askew) Washington; desc. Samuel Washington, bro. Geo. Washington, first Pres. of U.S.; grandson of Jerre C. Washington, early pioneer developer of Okla. Terr.; great-grandson of Sobe Love, first rep. to Congress from Okla., also repr. Chickasaw nation; m. Lucy Estelle Doheny, Reno, Nev., Aug. 18, 1955; stepchil.: Lawrence Van Cott Niven, b. Apr. 30, 1938; Michael Crombie Niven, b. July 30, 1940; Mrs. Z. Wayne (Cynthia Leigh Niven) Griffin, Jr., b. June 24, 1942. Career: jr. engr. Tex. Power and Light Co., constr. estimator, sys. engr. 1930-38; draftsman, Douglas Aircraft, El Segundo Div. 1938, liaison engr., Tulsa Div. 1943-46; investments exec. 1946-70 (ret.). Pres., Portero Inc., Mem.: Hollywood Lodge No. 355 F&AM; Hollywood Commandery No. 56 Knights Templar, Royal Arch Masons, Al Malaikah Shrine; L.A. Chpt., Chevaliere du Tastevin, Cave des Roys. Repub. All Saint's Episc., Beverly Hills. Hobby: breeding and showing purebred Keeshonden dogs (won 954 Best of Breeds, over 500 variety groups, 200 Best in Show awards, unchallenged record in Amer.). Rec.: hunting, fishing. Res.: 619 Doheny Rd., Beverly Hills, CA 90210; Office: 136 El Camino Dr., Beverly Hills, CA 90212.

WASH, ROBERT M.
County Counsel
b. May 27, 1908, Fresno, Calif.; s. H.M. and Effie (Rutherford) Wash.; grandson of James Rutherford who crossed plains in covered wagon, arriving at Hangtown (now Placerville), August 1850; ed. A.B., University of California, Berkeley, 1930; J.D. Univ. of Calif. Sch. of Jursiprudence, Boalt Hall, 1934; m. Irene Eredia, Santa Barbara, Calif., June 21, 1949 (dec.); chil.: John Philip, b. June 26, 1951; Thomas Rutherford, b. June 26, 1952; (step-dau.) Ellen Lynne Stuart, b. June 7, 1943. Career: Pvt. law practice, 1934-43; dep. dist. atty.m Fresno Co. 1943-50; co. counsel, Fresno Co. 1950-78. Operates ranch, Lone Star Dist., upon which grandfather I.H. Wash settled in 1890. Instr., San Joaquin Valley and local Hist., Univ. of Calif., Santa Cruz Ext. Author: This Is My Valley (publ. poetry of San Joaquin Valley and Sierras), 1966. Mem.: gen. chmn., Fresno Co. Centennial, 1956; Dist. SAR; Calif. Writers and Artists of San Joaquin Valley, Woodman of the World, Fresno Club Rotary International (life); Univ. of Calif. Alumni Assn.; Fresno Co. chmn. State Bicentennial Celebration, 1969-70; chmn. Fresno National Bicentennial Comm. 1976; Amer. Conservative Union; Amer. Judicature Soc.; Fowler Fri. Eve. Club; past pres., Fresno Co. Historical Soc.; Calif. Hist. Soc.; Past Noble Grand Humbug, Jim Savage chpt., Ancient and Hon. Order of E. Clampus Vitus; Commonwealth Club of Calif. Rec.: packing and fishing in the High Sierras, amateur theater. Res.: Lone Star Ranch, 3535 S. Temperance Ave., Fresno, CA 93725; Office: 304 Hall of Records, Fresno, CA 93721.

WASSER, GAIL M.
Communications Consultant
b. Nov. 22, 1941, Success, Ark.; d. Paul A. and Dathel (Boyd) Webber; GGG-niece, Rutherford B. Hayes, 19th U.S. President; B.A. summa cum laude, Cal. State Univ., Fresno, 1976, M.A. with distinction, 1977; m. William Wasser, Aug. 13, 1960, East St. Louis, Ill.; son, Michael, b. July 30, 1961. Career: Pub. Rels. Asst. for Cal. State Univ. Fresno Alumni Assn., 1975; Instr., Fresno City Coll., 1977; Pub. Rels. Coordinator for Women's Reentry Prog. & Women's Forum, CSU, Fresno, 1974-76; Lectr. Journalism Dept., 1974-77; Dir. Enrollment campaign, Fresno City Coll., 1977; cons., Fresno City Coll. 1977; pub. rels. publicity for Summer Festival of Arts, CSU Fresno Child Drama Center, 1978; educator, cons., 1976---. Mem.: Assn. for Edn. in Journalism; BSA; CSU, Fresno Alumni Assn.; Calif. Women in Higher Edn.; Nat. Women's Polit. Caucus; Phi Kappa Phi; Sigma Delta Chi; Soc. of Profl. Journalists; YWCA, bd. dir. 1978---. Res.: 4746 N. Fruit, Fresno, CA 93705.

WASSERMAN, LEW R.
Chairman — Chief Executive, MCA, Inc.
b. Mar. 15, 1913, Cleveland, Oh.; s. Isaac and Minnie (Chernick) Wasserman; m. Edith T. Beckerman, Ripley, N.Y., July 5, 1936; dau. Mrs. Jack (Lynne Kay) Myers, b. Oct. 18, 1940. Career: Natl. dir., adv. and publicity, Music Corp. of Amer., Chicago, 1936-38, v.p. M.C.A., NYC, 1938-39, v.p. chg. motion pic. div. 1940, pres. 1946-73; chmn. bd.-dir.-chief exec. ofcr.-exec. com., MCA, Inc. (subsidiary corps). Mem.:

chmn. bd. emeritus Assn. of Mot. Pic.-TV Producers, Inc.; trustee, John Fitzgerald Kennedy Library; trustee, John F. Kennedy Center for Perf. Arts; trustee, Lyndon Baines Jounson Found.; Calif. Inst. Tech.; treas. Music Center Found.; pres., Research to Prevent Blindness; Natl. Comm. Lyndon Baines Johnson Mem. Grove on the Potomac; Rockefeller Univ. Council; (hon.) chmn. bd. Center Theater Group of L.A. Office: MCA, Inc., Universal City Studios, Universal City, Calif. 91608.

WATERS, DORIS
Advertising Agency Executive
b. Oct. 1, 1947, Prague, Czechoslovakia; d. Otto M. and Hanna Springer; niece, Adolf Adler, noted psychologist; B.A., German, Wagner Coll., N.Y., 1968; m. Thomas R. Waters, May 17, 1969, Saratoga, Calif.; son, Gregory Christopher, b. July 23, 1976. Career: with Continental Airlines, Los Angeles, 1971-72; media buyer, Ogilvie & Mather, Houston, 1972-73; Acct. Exec., Young & Rubicam Advt., Houston, 1973-74; Sr. Acct. Mgr., Dailey & Assoc., San Francisco, 1974---. Mem. Delta Phi Alpha, 1968---. Rec.: backpacking, skiing. Res.: 10 Ardmore, Larkspur, CA 94939; Office: 574 Pacific Ave., San Francisco, CA 94133.

WATERS, LAUGHLIN E.
U.S. District Judge
b. Aug. 16, 1914, Los Angeles; s. Frank Joseph and Ida Pauline (Bauman) Waters; sisters: Mary E. Waters, Judge of Municipal Ct., L.A.; Ethel Waters Vetter, M.D.; A.B., UCLA, 1939; J.D., USC Sch. of Law, 1946; m. Voula Davinis Waters, Aug. 22, 1953, Los Angeles; children: Laughlin, Jr., b. 1954; Maura Kathleen, b. 1955; Deirdre Mary, b. 1958; Megan Ann, b. 1960; Eileen Brigid, b. 1964. Career: Mem. Calif. Legislature 1947-53; United States Atty. for the So. Dist. of Calif. 1953-61; Partner, Nossman, Waters, Krueger and Marsh 1961-76; United States Dist. Judge for the Central Dist. of Calif., 1976---. Infan. Capt., AUS, 1942-46; landed D-Day, Normandy; awarded Bronze Star, Purple Heart with Cluster, Combat Infan. Badge; Order of Golden Cross of Merit with Swords (Poland). Fellow, Am. Coll. of Trial Lawyers; Fellow, Am. Bar Found.; Mem.: USC and UCLA Law Assns.; Am. Judicature Soc. Federal Bar Assn.; USA Legion Lex; Alpha Delta. Clubs: California, Lincoln, Soc. for Friendly Sons of St. Patrick, past pres., Los Angeles, past pres. Republican, chmn. Calif. Central Com. 1952-53. Roman Catholic, pres. Catholic Big Brothers, L.A., Knight of Malta. Res.: 112 North June St., L.A., CA 90004; Office: U.S. Courthouse, 312 N. Spring St., L.A., CA 90012.

WATERS, MAXIME
California Legislator
b. Aug. 15, 1938, St. Louis, Mo.; d. Remus and Velma (Moore) Carr; B.A., sociology; m. Sidney Williams, July 23, 1977, Houston, Tex.; children: Edward, b. 1955; Karen, b. 1958. Career: Head Start Tchr.; Chief Deputy to Councilman David Cunningham, 1973-76; Elected rep. of 48th Dist. Calif. State Assembly, 1976---. Apptd. by Pres. Carter to Nat. Advisory Com. for Women, 1978; Chmn. for Black Caucus at Internat. Women's Year Conf., 1977; Apptd. by Assem. Speaker, Leo T. McCarthy to Commn. on the Status of Women, 1977; co-chmn., Affirmative Action Task Force and Party Task Force on Recruitment and Devel. of Women Candidates. Office: 7900 S. Central Ave., Los Angeles, CA 90001.

WATROUS, HOWARD RALPH
Lecturer — Business Executive
b. Apr. 3, 1930, Akron, Ohio; s. Darwin E. and Lora Oreta Watrous; B.S., Ohio State Univ., 1953; M.S., Univ. of Oregon, 1958; Ph.D., Ohio State Univ., 1969; m. Mavis Elaine Swanson, June 24, 1957, Las Vegas, Nev. Career: mem. University staff, The Ohio State Univ., Fresno State College and Portland State Univ., 8½ years; presently chmn. bd., Living Dynamics International, owner ranches, businesses; pvt. syndicator, 1963---; public syndicator, 1977---; author (w/Dr. Fred Case of UCLA), Real Estate Casses II, pub. by Calif. Real Estate Dept., 1963 (used throughout state, required text at Portland State Univ.); creator Real Estate Program, courses and texts for Ore. Div. Higher Edn., community colls.; author: A New Experience in the Art of Living, (book and 30 hour tape series), 1969; lectr. on mgmt. and sales, real estate bds. and companies. Served USAF, cost acct., 4 years. Hobby: photog. Rec.: Horseback riding; Office: 3250 Wilshire Blvd, Suite 2200, L.A., CA 90010.

WATSON, NORMAN ERNEST
College Chancellor
b. Sept. 27, 1915, Santa Ana, Calif.; s. Ernest A. and
M. Gladys (Dofflemyer) Watson; A.B., Pomona Coll.
1938; M.A., USC 1940; Ed.D., Stanford Univ. 1951;
m. Gwenda E. Aitchison, Pasadena, Calif., July 12,
1941; chil.: Sandra Gordon, Kevin, Katherine. Career:
Radio prodn., Hollywood, 1939-42; teacher, Calif. H.S.
1942-43; rancher, San Juan Capistrano, 1943-46;
Teacher, Capistrano Union H.S. 1946-48; supt.
1948-52; dean, Orange Coast Eve. Coll., Costa Mesa,
Calif. 1952-54; dean, stu. personnel, Orange Coast
Coll. 1954-55, asst. supt. 1955-57, v.p. 1957-63; supt.
Orange Coast Jr. Coll. Dist., Chancellor, Coast
Community Coll. Dist., Costa Mesa, 1963---. Pres.
KOCE-TV, Huntington Beach. Listed, various biog.
publs., USA; Royal Blue Book and Dictionary of
Internat. Biog., London, Eng.; Mem.: Amer., Calif.
Assns. of Sch. Admrs.; bd. dirs., Orange Co. Coast
Assn.; bd. dirs., Calif. Jr. Coll. Assn.; pres. Orange Co.
Ind.-Edn. Council; pres. Costa Mesa Unified Fund;
NEA, Calif. Teachers Assn., Natl. Soc. Stu. Edn.,
Comm. on Higher Edn., Calif. Assn. Secondary Sch.
Admrs., Amer. Assn. Jr. Colls., Phi Delta Kappa. Res.:
2401 Buckeye Rd., Newport Beach, CA 92660; Office:
1370 Adams Ave., Costa Mesa, CA 92626.

WATSON, RAYMOND LEE
Development Company President
b. Oct. 4, 1926, Seattle, Wash.; s. Leslie and Olive
Watson; A.B., Arch., Univ. Calif., Berkeley, 1951;
M.A., 1953; m. Elsa C. Coito, Sept. 18, 1954,
Stockton; children: Kathy Ann, b. 1956; Bryan, b.
1958; Lisa, b. 1961; David, b. 1969. Career: Architect
Assoc., Donald F. Haines & Assoc., 1955-60; Mgr.
Planning, The Irvine Co., 1960-64, vice president,
1964-67, sr. vice pres., 1967-70, exec. vice pres.,
1970-73, pres., The Newport Development Co.,
1973-77, partner, pres., 1977---. Dir.: The Irvine Co.,
1970-77, Disney Prodns., 1974---; Pacific Mutual Life
Insurance, 1975---; New Communities Group, 1973-77.
AUS Air Corps, 1944-45. Fellow, AIA. Named Build
of Year 1973, Builder Mag. Protestant. Hobbies:
skiing, tennis. Res.: 2501 Alta Vista Dr., Newport
Beach, CA; Office: 500 Newport Center Dr., Suite
345, Newport Beach, CA 92660.

WATTS, JOYCE LANNOM
University Administrator
b. June 1, 1942, Los Angeles; d. Kenneth L. and Elsie M.
(Weston) Lannom; B.A. English (honors), 1976; m. Dr.
John Ransford Watts, Dec. 20, 1975, Long Beach, Calif.
Career: adminstrv. asst., Pres. at California State Univ.
Long Beach, 1976---; research asst., U.S. Commn. on Civil
Rights', 1975-76. Life mem., Calif. Scholarship Fedn., So.
Calif. Award for Distinguished Speaking; panelist,
Internat. Edn., 1978; bd. dir. as cultural rep., AAUW;
Outstanding young women in America for 1977; mem.:
Council for Advancement and Support of Edn. (CASE);
Fine Arts affiliates, alumni assn. Cal. State Univ., L.B.;
L.A. Co. Mus. of Art; L.A. Co. Natural Hist. Museum;
Long Beach mayor's com. on the clean community;
statewide alumni Council. Hobbies: swimming, travel.
Home: 3701 Country Club Dr., L.B., CA 90807; Office:
CSULB, 1250 Bellflower Blvd., Long Beach, CA 90840.

WATTS, VAN
Producer — Writer
b. Aug. 26, 1920, Mooers, N.Y.; s. Bert Watts and
Margaret Baker; m. Lilie Remoreras, Hollywood, Calif.
Jan. 11, 1971. Editor: Watts Family Bicentennial
Encyclopedia; Father of the Navy's Sailor of the
Week, Month and Year Programs, An important part
of today's people-oriented Navy. Created Navy's
Original Sailior of the Week in Norfolk, 1952. Press
editorialized Norfolk's New Look. Awarded thanks of
the City. Navy Department gave program Navy-wide
coverage with press releases to 2000 ship, station and
overseas commands. Norfolk's famous Big Ship
Homecoming Ceremony was another idea which found
fruition in his attack on the old Norfolk-Navy
problem. Navy career 1937-62. Naval travels incl.
Europe, Africa, Asia, Aus. and No. and So. America.
Productions incl.: Norfolk Sailor of the Week's
Welcome to Town WTAR-TV, 1952-53; WTOV-TV
1954; Sailor of the Week's Bon Voyage WCAV, 1952;
WGH 1953-54; Sailor of the Year, WTOV-TV 1954;
WGH 1954; Navy Guide Cover Girls, WLOW 1952-54;
Portsmouth Sailor of the Week, WSAP, 1953-54;
Campaign ribbons and medals: National Defense
Service, Amer. Defense Service, American Campaign
Service, Asiatic-Pacific Campaign, WW II Victory
Medal, Navy Occupation Service Medal (Europe);
Armed Forces Expeditionary Medal (Lebanon); Battle

Star Guadalcanal (Solomons); Battle Star New Guinea.
Sponsor Michigan's USS MacKinac Memorial Navy
Bicentennial 1975. Created only nationwide family
celebration of America's Bincentennial 1973-79.
Wide-ranging Bicen. Projects incl. Oregon's Watts
House, Mexico's Watts Castle, Missouri's Foghorn Watts
Memorial and Watts Family's Beverly Hills Exhibit.
Mem.: Naval Historical Foundation, Supply Corps
Alumni Assn. and Hollywood Council Navy League.
Res.: 12401 Burton St., N. Hollywood, CA 91605.

WAXMAN, HENRY ARNOLD
United States Congressman
b. Sept. 12, 1939, Los Angeles, Calif.; s. R. Louis
and Esther Waxman; A.B. (polit. sci.), UCLA 1961;
LL.B., UCLA Sch. of Law, 1964; m. Janet Kessler,
Los Angeles, Calif.; Children: Carol, Michael, David.
Career: Atty. at law, 1964-69; elected to Calif. State
Assembly, 1969-74; U.S. House of Reps., 24th Dist.
1975---. Jewish (mem. Tiffereth Israel, Wash., D.C.).
Office: 8425 W. Third St., No. 400, Los Angeles, CA
90048; U.S. House Ofc. Bldg., Wash., D.C. 20515.

WAYNE, HUGH A.
Mayor
b. Jan. 27, 1914, San Diego, Calif.; s. Hugh A., and
Lyda Wayne; ed. E.E., Douglas Sch.; Calif. Sch. of
Fine Arts; m. Bernice I. Bartlett, San Mateo, Calif.,
May 22, 1938; dau. Suzanne Maffei. Career:
Propr.-pres. Wayne Adv. and Pub. Rels. Agcy. 1951---;
publ. S.F. Peninsula Visitor's Guide, and author,
Alphabet Zoo. Councilman, San Mateo (12 yrs.);
Mayor, San Mateo (5 terms). Mem.: pres. San Mateo
C. of C. 1948; pres. San Mateo Co. Chamber of
Comm. 1951; Mason, Kiwanis, Elks Club. Republican
(Co. Central Com., 5 yrs.). Hobbies: guitar, wood
carving. Rec.: hiking, swim. Res.: 115 Elm St., San
Mateo, CA; Office: City Hall, and 72 Third Ave., San
Mateo, CA.

WEAVER, JOHN DOWNING
Author — Editor
b. Feb. 4, 1912, Wash., D.C.; s. Henry B. and Beatrice
(Petty) Weaver; A.B., Coll. of William and Mary, 1932;
M.A., George Washington Univ., 1933; m. Harriett
Sherwood, May 28, 1937, Kansas City, Mo. Career:
Reporter and feature writer Kansas City Star, 1936-40;
freelance writer, 1940---: Articles and short stories in
Atlantic Monthly, Harpers, Saturday Evening Post,
Colliers, American Mercury, Liberty, American
Magazine, Esquire, Holiday, Redbook, McCalls, Travel
and Leisure, etc. Books: Wind Before Rain (Macmillan,
1942); Another Such Victory (Viking Press, 1948); As
I Live and Breathe (Rinehart & Co., 1959); Tad
Lincoln, Mischief Maker in the White House (Dodd,
Mead, 1963); The Great Experiment (Little, Brown &
Co., 1965); Warren: The Man, The Court, The Era
(Little, Brown & Co., 1967); The Brownsville Raid
(W.W. Norton, 1970); L.A. — El Pueblo Grande (Ward
Ritchie Press, 1973). Two motion pictures (Holiday
Affair and The Love Man) based on novelettes. West
Coast editor, Holiday Mag., 1964; West Coast Editor,
Travel and Leisure Mag., 1971---. Address: 3893
Deervale Dr., Sherman Oaks, CA 91403.

WEBB, JAMES SIDNEY, JR.
Corporate Executive
b. Oct. 14, 1919, Salt Lake City, Utah; s. James Sidney,
Sr. and Josephine Isabel (Hornung) Webb; B.S. bus.
admin., San Jose State Univ., 1941; m. Lucille Marian
Gardner, June 28, 1941, San Jose, Calif.; chil.: Janet
Webb (Sippl), b. Aug. 9, 1946; James Sidney III, b. Feb.
18, 1953. Career: with TRW, Inc., 1954---, gen. mgr.
Electronics Group, Corp. v.p. 1963-66; exec. v.p., 1966;
director, 1967---; vice chairman, 1978---; with Shell
Chemical Co., 1945-48; U.S. Steel Corp., 1948-52; Varian
Associates, 1952-54; Dir.: DeSoto, Inc.; Bertea Corp.; the
May Department Stores Company; TRW Foundation;
pres., TRWE International Services; pres., TRW Datacom
Internat., Inc.; former dir., Electronic Memories, Inc.
(now Electronic Memories & Magnetics Corp.) and UMF
Systems Inc.; former chmn. bd., Design Line, Inc.;
founder, Gateway Bank; Founder, former chmn. bd.,
Independence Bank. Served to Lt., USNR, 1942-45. Dir.:
L.A. Philharmonic Assn.; Independent Colleges of
Southern Calif.; Estelle Doheny Eye Found.; bd. trustees,
City of Hope; bd. govs., Hugh O'Brian Youth Found.;
past dir., Merchants & Mfgs. Assn. of L.A.; past bd.
regents, Calif. Lutheran Coll.; past bd. govs., Electronic
Industries Assn.; past dir. Western Electronic Mfgs. Assn.
Office: 10880 Wilshire Blvd., Suite 1700, Los Angeles,
CA 90024.

WEBB, STEPHEN RICHARD
Scientist
b. July 3, 1938, Franklin, Ind.; s. Harold D. and M. Margaret (Hougham) Webb; B.S., Math, Univ. Ill., 1959; M.S. Statistics, Univ. Chicago, 1969; Ph.D., 1962; children: J. Douglas, b. 1960; Jennifer S., b. 1962; Timothy R., b. 1966. Career: with Westinghouse Research Labs, Pittsburgh, summers 1955-59; Am. Oil Research Lab., Whiting, Ind., summers, 1960, 61; principal scientist, statistics, Rocketdyne, Canoga Park, 1962-68; Chief Scientist, mathematics, McDonnell Douglas Astronautics Co., 1968-75; Independent cons. to industry, 1975-77; Sr. Systems Analyst, Teledyne Brown Engineering, Costa Mesa, 1977---. Contbr. articles in Technometrics 1971, Naval Research Logistics Quarterly 1969. Pres., So. Calif. Chpt., Am. Statistical Assn., 1973-74. Hobbies: writing, music. Res.: 6401 Warner, No. 335, Huntington Beach, CA 92647; Office: 125 Baker, Suite 205, Costa Mesa, CA 92626.

WEBSTER, MARJORIE ELLEN
Artist — Lecturer
b. Aug. 23, Cleveland, Oh.; d. William Holcomb and Edna (Robb) Webster (noted author, lecturer, explorer); direct desc. of Noah Webster; ed. Cleveland Inst. of Art; pvt. art stu.; UCLA Ext. course; (life) Credentials, arts and culture of Mayas and in design; m. Robert B. Stacy-Judd, 1949 (div. 1957). Career: photographers' model; freelance commerical artist, copywriter, photog. (spec. in third-dimension color); assoc. ed., Who's Who in L.A. County and Who's Who in Calif. 1949-58; proofreader, secret and confidential material for space, missile and defense; est. own art studio; designer-mfr., Margette ceramics and jewelry; cond. tours to Mayan areas, Mex. and Hawaii; teacher, Hawaiian Dancing; first teacher, Mayan art and archaeology in adult edn., L.A. City Schs. 1965---; lecturer, Ancient Mayas, Hawaii, Mex., Europe, Arts and Flowers of the World, Our Great Southwest. Pilot's license (at 18 yrs.). Author: (book poems), Double Reflections, (with mother); articles, poems publ. in books, newspapers, mags.; newspaper columnist. Awards: oil painting, ceramics, photog.; prize winner, many radio and TV shows. Protestant. Hobbies: cooking, astrology, Rec.: music, swimming, dancing. Res.-Studio: 12848 Milbank St., North Hollywood, CA 91604.

WEDBUSH, EDWARD WILLIAM
President, Wedbush, Noble, Cooke, Inc.
b. Sept. 14, 1932, St. Louis, Mo.; s. William H. and Edith Marie (Herman) Wedbush; B.A., Mech. engring., Univ. Cincinnati, 1955; M.B.A., UCLA, 1957; m. Jean A. Lawrence, Dec. 18, 1960, Los Angeles; children: Gary Lance, b. 1964; Eric Dean, b. 1967; Leigh Ann, b. 1969. Career: Student Engr., Wagner Electric 1949-55; Engr., Hughes Aircraft, 1955-58; assoc. in Engring., UCLA 1957-59; pres., Chief exec. ofcr., Wedbush, Noble, Cooke, Inc. and predecessors, 1958---; chmn., Pacific Stock Exchange, 1976-77. Dir.: Pacific Securities Depository Trust Co., 1976, 78, Pacific Clearing Corp., 1975, PC Service Corp., 1964. Mem.: Los Angeles Stock Exchange Club, Triangle frat. Lutheran, treas. 1967-69. Rec.: tennis. Res.: 5441 Senford Ave., Los Angeles, CA 90056; Office: P.O.B. 30014 T.A., Los Angeles, CA 90030.

WEIBEL, LAUREL A.
Physician and Surgeon
b. Sept. 10, 1923, Hollister, Calif.; d. Dare Edward and Alice M. (Summers) Weibel; B.S., La Sierra Coll. 1946; M.D., Loma Linda Univ. 1947; m. Rolland A. Truman, Bellflower, Calif., Sept. 15, 1953; chil.: Tracy Norton, b. May 31, 1962; Tamara Ann, b. Apr. 30, 1963; Trina Maureen, b. Oct. 3, 1964; Trent Martin, b. Feb. 24, 1966; Tricia Lynn, b. Oct. 24, 1968. Career: Intern, L.A. Co. Hosp. 1946-48, res. gen. surg. 1948-52; diplomate, Calif., Natl. Bds. Med. Examiners, 1947, 48; Certified Amer. Bd. Surgs. 1953; fellow, Amer. Coll. Surgs. 1956; est. pvt. practice gen. surg., Lakewood, Calif. 1952---. Instr.-asst. clin. prof. surg. Loma Linda Univ. 1956---; asst. clin. prof. surg. USC Med. Sch. 1965---. Mem.: AMA; Calif., L.A. Co. Med. Assns.; br. past pres. Amer. Med. Women's Assn. 1952---; Soc. Grad. Surgs. L.A. Co. Hosp. 1952---; Bus. and Profl. Women's Club, 1952-62; Zonta Club, 1954-63; Long Beach Surgical Soc. 1956---; pres. L.A. Phys. Art Soc. 1968. Seventh-Day Adventists. Hobbies: oil painting, sewing. Rec.: hiking, camping. Res.: 4522 Green Meadow Rd., Long Beach, CA 90808; Office: 3650 E. South St., Lakewood, CA.

WEIDE, WILLIAM WOLFE
Manufactured Housing Company President
b. Aug. 19, 1923, Toledo, Oh.; s. Samuel and Pearl Weide; cousin, Joseph Weider, founder: Weider publ. (body bldg.), health foods and weight hardware equipment, U.S.-Can.; ed. Univ. of Toledo; Marquette Univ., Milwaukee, Wis.; B.S., USC 1948; m. Beatrice Weide, 1950; sons: Brian S., Bruce M., Robert B. Career: Dir., Fleetwood Enterprises, Inc. 1959--- (controller, asst. secty., asst. v.p., adm. v.p., sr. v.p.), exec. com. 1969---, pres. 1973---. Mobile Home and Rec. Vehicle Assn. (co-founder, chmn., dir., chmn. legialative coms.); chmn. Ind. Legislative Coord. Council; treas.-bd. dirs. S.E. Mfg. Housing Inst., Atlanta, Ga.; Wash. Affairs Com. 1972---; (Task Forces: Wash., Kan;, Ariz., Ala., Ind., N.Y., Pa. 1959---. Chmn. Mfg. Housing Inst. 1975-76. Ofcr., USN, PTO 1941-46. Awards: Pac. Theatre with 3 clusters. Mem.: Beta Alpha Psi, 1949---. Hobby: coin collecting. Rec.: tennis, golf. Res.: 2341 Terraza Pl., Fullerton, CA 92635; Office: 3125 Myers St., Riverside, CA 92503.

WEINBERGER, CASPAR WILLARD
Attorney at Law
b. Aug. 18, 1917, San Francisco, Calif.; s. Herman and Cerise Carpenter (Hampson) Weinberger; ed. A.B., Harvard Coll. 1938; LL.B., Harvard Law Sch. 1941; m. Jane Dalton, Aug. 16, 1942; chil.: Arlin Cerise, b. Apr. 27, 1944; Caspar Willard, Jr., b. Jan. 9, 1947. Career: Law clerk, U.S. Circuit Judge William E. Orr, 1946-47; partner, firm of Heller, Ehrman, White & McAuliffe, San Francisco, 1947-69; counsel, Repub. Co. Central Com., S.F. 1951, chmn. 1963; elected to Assembly, Calif. Legislature, 1952-58; Director of Finance, State of California, 1968-70; chmn. Federal Trade Comm. 1970; dep. dir. U.S. Ofc. of Mgmt. and Budget, Wash., D.C. 1970-72, dir. 1972-73; Counsellor to the Pres. 1973; secty., U.S. Dept. HEW 1973-74. Staff book reviewer, S.F. Chronicle. Pvt., U.S. Army Infantry, 1941; Capt., overseas, 41st Div. and with Gen. MacArthur's Hdqrs., Australia, New Guinea, Philippines (1941-45), WW II. Mem.: American Legion; Veterans of Foreign Wars; bd. trustees, Bay Area Edn. TV Assn.; bd. trustees, Golden Gate Coll., S.F.; bd. trustees, Mechanic's Inst.; gov. YMCA, S.F.; exec. bd., S.F. Council, BSA; Calif., Amer. Bar Assns.; Clubs: Century, N.Y.; Harvard, Bohemian, S.F.; Georgetown, Wash. D.C.; S.F. Press-Union Leag.

WEINER, STEPHEN S.
University Dean
b. June 11, 1939, Morristown, N.J.; B.S., UCLA, 1961, M.S., 1963; Ph.D., Stanford Univ., 1973; m. Patricia Shields, Aug. 23, 1964, Los Angeles; daughters: Alisa, b. 1967; Wendy, b. 1969. Career: Adminstrv. asst. to Rep. James C. Corman (Demo., Calif.) 1964-67; special asst. Nat. Advisory Commn. on Civil Disorders, 1967-68; v.p., Monarch Fin. Corp., 1968-70; cons., Rand Corp., 1972-73; asst. prof. of edn., Stanford Univ., 1973-77; currently v.p., bd. of govs., Calif. Community Colls. and Assoc. Dean, Grad. Sch. of Public Policy, Univ. Calif., Berkeley ---. Calif. Assoc., Inst. for Ednl. Leadership, 1974---. Co-author: Organizing an Anarchy, Univ. Chicago Press, 1978. Office: 2607 Hearst Ave., Berkeley, CA 94720.

WEINER, TED
Oil Properties Company Owner
b. Mar. 9, 1911, Ft. Worth, Tex.; s. Samuel and Lillian (Blanc) Weiner; ed. N.Mex. Mil. Inst.; m. Lucile Clements, Cisco, Tex., Sept. 15, 1938; dau. Gwendolyn Patricia, b. Dec. 31, 1941. Career: partner, Tex. Crude Oil Co., Houston, 1951-76; independent oil opr. owner, Ted Weiner Oil Properties, Tex.; mem.: Ind. Petrol. Assn. of Amer.; Tex. Mid-Continent Oil and Gas Assn.; Ind. Royalty Owners Assn.; dir. Van Cliburn Internat. Competition, Ft. Worth, Tex.; dir. Palm Springs Desert Museum; (charter) Library of Presidential Papers; Pres.' Adv. Com. on Art; inspector gen. (hon.) Scottish rite; Blue Lodge Commandery Shrine, K.C.C.H. (33). Clubs: Racquet, Tamarisk Country, Palm Springs; Sleepy Hollow Country, Tarrytown, N.Y. Hobby: art. Rec.: golf. Res.: 991 Driver Way, Incline Village, Nev.; 4 Citadel Ct., The Springs, Rancho Mirage, CA 92270; Office: 2601 Ridgmar Plaza, Ft. Worth, TX 76116.

WEINSTEIN, IRWIN M.
Physician
b. Mar. 5, 1926; Denver, Colo.; s. Max and Esther

Katherine (Bershof) Weinstein; student, Dartmouth Coll., 1943-44; Williams Coll., 1944-45; M.D., Univ. of Colo., 1949; internship, Montefiore Hosp., N.Y.C., 1949-50; Jr. asst. resident in med., 1950-51; sr. asst. and resident in med. Univ. of Chicago, 1951-53; m. Judith Braun, 1951; chil.: James; David. Career: pvt. practice, Hematology and Internal Medicine, 1959---; clin. prof. of med., Center for Health Sciences, UCLA, 1970---; instr., asst. prof. of med., Univ. of Chicago, 1953-55; assoc. clin. prof., UCLA, 1961-70; chief, hematology sect. an; dir., Hematology Training Program, Cedars-Sinai Med. Center, L.A., 1960-72. Attending physician: Cedars-Sinai Med. Center; UCLA Center for Health Sci.; spec. Hematology, Wadsworth Gen. Hosp. Honors: Splenectomy, an exhibition, Am. Coll. of Surgeons, 1967; visiting prof., Hadassah Med. Center, 1967; cons. to N.I.H. on Leukemogenesis, 1967-68; hon. fellow, Israel Med. Assn., 1970; Health Affairs advisor to Hon. Alan Cranston, 1971---; bd. govs., Cedars-Sinai Med. Center, 1974-78; exec. Com., Am. Soc. of Hematology; chmn. ad hoc com. on practice, Am. Soc. of Hematology, 1978---. Diplomates: Am. Bd. of Internal Med., 1956, 1974; Am. Bd. of Hematology, 1972. Contbr. articles to med. journs.; author: Mechanisms of Anemia, McGraw-Hill, 1962; Trisophosphate Isomerase Deficiency in Hereditary Disorder of Erythrocyte Metabolism, McGraw-Hill, 1968; Diagnosis of Hematological and Splenic Disorders in Nuclear Medicine, McGraw-Hill, 1965, 2d ed. 1970; Lymphadenopathy and Splenomegaly: Lymphorecticular Disorders — Self-Limited Proliferative Responses in Hematology, McGraw-Hill, 1972, 2d ed. 1977; Polycythemia: Clinical Manifestations in Polycythemia, Charles C. Thomas Co., 1974. Mem.: Alpha Omega Alpha; AAAS; Am. Fedn. for Clin. Research; Am. Soc. of Hematology; Am. Soc. of Internal Med.; Assn. of Am. Med. Colleges; Fellow, Am. Coll. of Physicians; Internat. Soc. of Hematology; Internat. Soc. of Internal Med.; L.A. Acad. of Med.; L.A. Soc. of Nuclear Med.; N.Y. Acad. of Sci.; Reticulo-Endothelial Soc.; Royal Soc. of Med.; Western Soc. for Clin. Research; UCLA Comprehensive Cancer Center. Home: 9505 Heather Rd., Beverly Hills, CA 90210; Office: 465 N. Roxbury Dr., Beverly Hills, CA 90210.

WEINSTOCK, HERBERT FRANK
Public Relations Executive
b. July 26, 1913, Los Angeles; s. Frank and Sarah (Mantel) Weinstock; A.A. in Bus. Adm., Los Angeles City Coll., 1933; m. Evelyn June Hanson, July 27, 1940; children: Allan Herbert, William Jay, Joan Louise. Career: with copy desk, financial desk Los Angeles Post-Record, Los Angeles Daily News, 1935-42; financial editor Daily News, 1942-54; pub. relations exec. H.F. Weinstock & Assocs., 1954-64; Burton, Booth & Weinstock, Inc., 1964-66; v.p. charge corporate and financial pub. relations Kennett Pub. Relations Assocs., 1966-71; pres. Conway/Weinstock/Assocs., Inc., 1971---. Pres. Intercommunity Care Centers, Inc. Served wtih AUS, 1943-45; with 3d. Army, Eng., France, Luxembourg, Belgium and Germany, 1944-45. Clubs: Greater Los Angeles Press (charter mem.), Publicity (Los Angeles); Res.: 533 21st St., Manhattan Beach, CA 90266; Office: 550 N. Larchmont Blvd., Los Angeles, CA 90004.

WEISBERG, JACOB
Educator
b. Dec. 3, 1928, NYC; s. Joseph and Dorothy Weisberg; B.S., M.A.; Career: (past) Clin. Research Assoc., Dist. Sales Mgr., Regional Sales Mgr., Nat. Accts. Mgr. (current) Mem. of Faculty, West Caldwell Adult Sch., Livingston Communications Skills Workshop; Dir. of Tng., West Chemical Products, Inc., Los Angeles; with Ayerst Labs. Bd. mem. Creative Consultants. AUS, WW II. Mem. Am. Medical Writers Assn., National Speakers Assn.; contbr. writer, Sales and Marketing Mgmt. Mag. Hobby: duplicate bridge director. Rec.: tennis, table tennis. Res.: P.O.B. 3972, Torrance, CA 90510; Office: 4425 Bandini Blvd., Los Angeles, CA 90023.

WEISMAN, MARCIA SIMON
Art Collector — Patron
b. Aug. 22, 1918, Portland, Ore.; d. Myer and Lillian (Glickman) Simon; student, Mills Coll., Oakland; m. Frederick R. Weisman, Aug. 20, 1938, Los Angeles; children: Richard L., b. 1940; Nancy, b. 1943; Daniel, b. 1945. Career: Art Consultant: Mayo Clin. Found., Didi Hirsh Community Mental Health Center, Wight Inst., Devereux Sch. Goleta, initiator current Art Program at Cedars-Sinai Med. Center (over 6,000 paintings, sculptures, photographs, drawings, prints and posters grace the center's 9 flrs., 1.6 million sq. ft.), firms of Weisman and Dreisen, attys., Hitt and Murray, attys., Ball, Hunt, Hart, Brown & Baerwitz, attys., Mr. Richard Keating, Dr. Milton Gotlib, Siedman & Siedman, CPA, Mid-Atlantic Toyota Distributors, Inc., others; Tchr.: UCLA Ext., Arts and Humanities Program, 1972---; Lectr.: L.A. Co. Mus. of Art, La Jolla Mus. of Contemporary Art, Cal. State Univ., Long Beach, Detroit Mus., Cedars-Sinai Med. Center; Curator: Barnett Newman Memorial Exhibition, Mus. of Modern Art, 1970; 20th Century Prints, InterFaith Center, Columbia, Md., 1972; Calif. Artists in Wash., Wash. D.C., 1974; Collectors Choice, L.A. Inst. of Contemporary Art, 1975; Los Angeles Artists, State Capitol, Sacto., 1977. Pesonal collection one of most comprehensive Modern and Contemporary Art collections in U.S.; featured in "Connaissance des Arts," 1976, Vogue Mag., May 1974; helped acquire Japanese art from Edo Period for permanent collect. L.A. Co. Museum. Adj. Prof. of Art, Cal. State Univ., L.B., 1977-78; advis. bd., Univ. Art Mus., Berkeley, 1977-78; trustee, S.F. Art Inst., 1977-78; chmn. Advisory Council for Art, Cedars-Sinai Med. Center, 1976---; mem. Collectors Com., Nat. Gallery of Art, Wash. D.C.; mem. Friends, Whitney Mus., N.Y.; founding mem.: Fellow of Contemporary Art, Pasadena, Contemporary Art Council, L.A. Co. Mus. of Art, Friends of Pacificulture-Asia Mus., Pasadena; mem. Far Eastern Art Council, L.A. Co. Mus. Art. Res.: 1140 Angelo Dr., Beverly Hills, CA 90210.

WEISS, LIONEL EDWARD
Professor of Geology
b. Dec. 11, 1927, London, England; s. S. and E.M. (Carney) Weiss; B.Sc. (1st class), Univ. Birmingham, 1949, Ph.D., 1953; Sc.D., Univ. Edinburgh, 1956; m. Liv. Nissen-Sollie, Dec. 27, 1964, Oslo, Norway; children: Nicholas Erling, b. Sept. 3, 1966; Elin Katrina, b. Aug. 23, 1970. Career: Harkness Fellow, Univ. Calif., Berkeley, 1951-53; Sr. Research Fellow, Univ. Edinberg, Scotland, 1953-56; Prof. of Geology, Univ. Calif., Berkeley, 1956---; Guggenheim Fellow 1962, 1970; Fulbright Scholar 1974-75; Miller Research Prof., U.C., 1965-66. Co-author: Structural Analysis of Metamorphic Tectonites, 1963; The Earth, 1970; Minor Structures of Deformed Rocks, 1972; contbr. articles in sci. journs. Hobbies: photog., writing, sailing. Res.: 784 Euclid Ave., Berkeley, CA 94708; Office: Dept. Geology & Geophysics, Univ. Calif., Berkeley, CA 94720.

WELD, JOHN
Movie Producer — Writer
b. Feb. 24, 1905, Birmingham, Ala.; s. Harry S. and Nelle (Farrow) Weld; student, Auburn Univ., 1921-22; m. Gertrude Katherine McElroy, Feb. 12, 1937, Phoenix, Ariz. Career: Newspaper reporter, N.Y. American, 1926-29, N.Y. World, 1930-32, Paris (France) Herald, 1932-35; Scenario writer, Columbia Pictures, 1935-36, Universal Studios, 1936-38; Novelist, 1938-41; Pub. Rels. Dir., Ford Motor Co., 1942-49; Pub., Laguna Beach Post, 1950-68. Author: Don't You Cry For Me, Sabaath Has No End, The Pardners, Mark Pfeiffer, M.D. (pub. Charles Scribner's Sons). Prod.: documentary films, Beirut to Baghdad, Freightboat 'Round The World, Ireland From A Gypsy Caravan, The Basque Sheepherder. Dir.: So. Coast Community Hosp., So. Laguna, 1954-71; Scripps Mem. Hosp. Found., 1977---. Mem.: Kappa Sigma, Players, N.Y.; Pauma Valley CC. Res.: 140 Womsi Rd., Pauma Valley, CA 92061.

WELLS, JAMES THOMAS
Real Estate Management Company Executive
b. Mar. 24, 1939, Salt Lake City; s. Calvin Y. and Arvilla (Thomas) Wells; B.A. in Econs., Univ. Utah, 1964, M.B.A. in Finance and Accounting, 1966; grad. Calif. Assn. Realtors Inst., 1976; m. Luana Pearl Sharp, July 7, 1967; children: Rebecca, Elizabeth, Rachel, Jamie. Financial analyst corp. staff, budget adminstr. RCA, NYC, 1966-67, Los Angeles 1967-68; mgr. third-party leasing and finance Xerox Data Systems, Inc., El Segundo, Calif., 1968-70; v.p. finance and adminstrn. Holstein Industries, Inc., Costa Mesa, Calif., 1971-72; pres. J.T. Wells & Assocs., real estate cons. Costa Mesa, 1973---; dir. Investors Realty, Inc., Salt Lake City; cons. Boise Cascade Bldg. Co., Los Angeles, 1970; Am. Mobilehome Co., Los Angeles, 1970-71; Mem. Financial Execs. Inst., Nat., Calif. realtors assns., Interstate Bus. and Profl. Assn., Lambda Delta Sigma, Alpha Kappa Psi. Mem.: Ch. of Jesus Christ of Latter-day Saints. Author: Recent Real Estate Activity. Address: 1797 Oriole Dr., Costa Mesa, CA 92626.

WELLS, RICHARD LESLIE
Superior Court Judge
b. Aug. 6, 1921, Columbus, Oh.; s. Leslie R. and Ona (Menefee) Wells; ed. B.A., Stanford Univ., 1942; LL.B., Harvard Law Sch. 1950. Career: Assoc. with Gibson, Dunn and Crutcher law firm, L.A. 1950-61; Superior Ct. Judge, 1961---. Presbyterian (elder, Beverly Hills Community Ch.). Res.: 1423 Tanager Way, Los Angeles, CA 90069; Office: Los Angeles Superior Ct., Courthouse, Los Angeles, CA 90012.

WELPTON, SHERMAN SEYMOUR, JR.
Attorney at Law
b. Mar. 21, 1908, Omaha, Nebr.; LL.B., J.D., Univ. Nebr., 1931; Hon. LL.D., Pepperdine Univ. 1977, Univ. of Nebr. 1978; m. Dorothy Felber; children: Sherman S., III; Dr. Douglas F.; Mrs. William D. Ferguson, Jr. Career: Admitted to Nebr. bar, 1931, partner law firm Ramsey & Welpton, Omaha, 1931-41; assoc. firm Gibson, Dunn & Crutcher, Los Angeles, 1942-47, partner 1948, sr. partner, 1958---. Mem.: American Bar Assn.; Internat. Bar Assn.; Am. Coll. of Trial Lawyers (former Com. Chmn.); Am. Bar Found.; World Peace Through Law; Am. Judicature Soc.; Phi Delta Phi. Clubs: Los Angeles Country, Chancery, Stock Exchange, California. Res.: 407 Robert Lane, Beverly Hills, CA 90210; Office: 515 So. Flower St., Los Angeles, CA 90071.

WENCK, FREDERICK, JR.
Dentist
b. July 8, 1939, Evanston, Ill.; s. Frederick and Virginia (Hart) Wenck; B.S., St. Bonaventure Univ., 1961; D.D.S., Northwestern Univ. Dental Sch., 1966; m. Karen Leone Anne Simonini, Sept. 17, 1966, Algonquin, Ill.; children: Kelary Anne, b. 1968; Frederick Gilbert, b. 1970; Brennan Phillip, b. 1975; Brooke Elizabeth, b. 1977. Career: Navy Dental Corps, 1966-70; pvt. practice of dentistry, So. Lake Tahoe, 1966---. Comdr., USNR, 21st Dental Co., Sacto., 1977---. Elected Bd. Trustees, Lake Tahoe Community Coll., 1974---, pres. 1976-77; program chmn., Am. Soc. for Preventive Dentistry, Calif. chpt., 1975-78; pres., Calif. Soc. for Preventive Dentistry, 1978-79; Children's Dental Health Week Chmn., 1976. Mem. So. Tahoe Optimists Club, 1970---. Roman Catholic, Eucharistic Minister, 1977---. Hobbies: backpacking, photog. Res.: 2241 Inverness Dr., So. Lake Tahoe, CA 95731; Office: 950 Lake Tahoe Blvd., S. Lake Tahoe, CA 95731.

WENKE, ROBERT A.
Superior Court Judge
b. Sept. 6, 1926, Stanton, Nebr.; s. Adolph E. (Assoc. Justice, Supreme Ct. of Nebr. 1943-61) and Gertrude B. Wenke; A.B., Univ. of Nebr. 1948, LL.B. 1950; Ohio Wesleyan Univ., Univ. of Va.; m. Suzanne Samuelson, Long Beach, Calif., June 17, 1950; chil.: Cynthia, b. Apr. 14, 1952; Thomas R., b. Oct. 31, 1956. Career: admitted to practice law, Calif. 1951; assoc. with Samuelson & Buck, Long Beach, 1951-54; pvt. practice, L.B. 1954-57, 1960-65; partner, Wenke & Phelan law firm, 1957-59; legislative asst. to U.S. Senator Thomas N. Kuchel, 1959-60; Judge, L.B. Municipal Ct. 1965-66; Judge, L.A. Superior Ct. (Criminal, Family Law, Juvenile Civ., Discovery, Law & Motion, Writs & Receivers), 1966---; presiding judge, Juvenile Ct. 1969-70; supv. judge, Law Dept. 1972; asst. presiding judge, 1973-75; presiding judge, 1975---. Author: Making and Meeting Objections, and articles, Law Review. USN Seaman, 1944-46, WW II. Mem.: Order of the Coif; Anglo-Amer. Law Exch. 1973; Judicial Council of Calif. 1975---; various community serv. orgns. Democrat. Protestant. Rec.: tennis, bicycling, skiing, reading. Res.: 4216 E. 2nd St., Long Beach, CA; Office: 111 N. Hill St., Los Angeles, CA 90012.

WENRICH, JOHN WILLIAM
College President
b. June 8, 1937, York, Pa.; s. Ralph C. and Helen (McCollam) Wenrich; B.A., Princeton Univ., 1959; M.A., Univ. of Mich., 1961; Ph.D., 1968; San Francisco Theological Seminary 1961-62; m. Martha Lofberg, Sept. 1967, Ann Arbor, Mich.; chil.: Thomas Allen, b. 1966; Margaret Ann, b. 1968. Career: U.S. Foreign Service Officer, Bolivia and Wash., D.C., 1962-65; country rep. in Dominican Republic for Internat. Devel. Found., 1965-66; project director, Inst. for Social Research, Univ. of Mich., 1966-69; asst. to pres., Coll. of San Mateo, 1969-71; v.p., Ferris State Coll., Big Rapids, Mich., 1971-75; president, Canada College, Redwood City, 1975---. Co-author (w/father) Leadership in

Administration of Vocational and Technical Education, 1974. Mem. advisory bd., National Energy Extension Service; Rotary, bd. dir. 1976-78; YMCA bd. mem., treas. 1979-80; Redwood City C. of C., bd. mem. 1976-78. Protestant. Rec.: tennis, bridge, jogging; Home: 73 Wessex Way, San Carlos, CA 94070; Office: 4200 Farm Hill Blvd., Redwood City, CA 94061.

WEST, BARRY GEORGE
Attorney at Law
b. Feb. 3, 1943, New York City; s. Irven M. and Edith (Eisner) West; B.A., Queens Coll., City Univ., N.Y., 1959-63; LL.B., St. John's Univ., 1966; LL.M., Harvard, 1967; m. Sheila Blank, Aug. 6, 1966; Children: Stephen Todd, Karen Elyse. Career: admitted to N.Y. bar, 1967, Calif. bar, 1073; assoc. mem. firm Paul, Weiss, Rifkind, Wharton & Garrison, NYC, 1967-69; asst. compliance dir. Smith, Barney & Co. investment bankers, NYC, 1969-70; assoc. mem. firm, Paul, Weiss, Rifkind, Wharton & Garrison, NYC, v.p., gen. counsel Technicolor, Inc., Hollywood, 1972-73; assoc. mem. firm Greenberg & Glusker, Los Angeles, 1973-74; partner, 1975---. Mem. Beverly Hills, Los Angeles County bar assns. Res.: 4285 Pasadero Pl., Tarzana, CA 91356; Office: 1900 Ave. of Stars, Suite 2000, Los Angeles, CA 90067.

WEST, HOWARD NORTON
Corporate Executive
b. May 3, 1919, New York, N.Y.; s. Abraham D. and Flora (Simpson) West; B.A., Columbia Univ. 1940; m. Caroline E. Dawley, Portland, Me., Dec. 15, 1945; son, Andrew D., b. June 23, 1954. Career: Price Waterhouse and Co., San Francisco, 1945-52; Carter Hawley Hale Stores, Inc., Los Angeles 1952---; treas. 1963-72, v.p. & treas., 1973-76, sr. v.p., finance, 1976---. Trustee, Palos Verdes Peninsula Unified Sch. Dist. 1961-67, pres. 1964-65; trustee-treas. Chadwick Sch. (Roessler-Chadwick Found.) 1967-69; trustee-pres. So. Calif. Reg. Occupation Center, 1967-69; commr. Edn. Research Comm. of Calif. Legislature, 1970---. Lt., USN, destroyers, USS Bush, USS Kenneth D. Bailey, 1942-46, WW II. Res.: 527 17th St., Santa Monica, CA 90402; Office: 550 S. Flower St., L.A., CA 90071.

WEST, JOHN BURNARD
Bioengineer
b. Dec. 27, 1928, Adelaide, Australia; s. Esmond Frank and Meta Pauline (Spehr) West; M.B.B.S., Adelaide Univ., 1952; M.D., 1958; Ph.D., London Univ., 1960; m. Penelope Hall Banks, Oct. 28, 1967, London; children: Robert Burnard, b. 1969; Joanna Ruth, b. 1971. Career: Intern, Royal Adelaide Hosp., 1952; resident, Hammersmith Hosp., London, England, 1953-55; physiologist, Sir Edmund Hillary's Himalayan Expedition, 1960-61; dir., Respiratory Research Group Postgrad. Med. Sch., London, 1962-67; Prof. of Medicine and Bioengineering, Univ. Calif. San Diego, 1969---. Author: Ventilation/Blood Flow and Gas Exchange, 1965; Respiratory Physiology — The Essentials, 1974; Pulmonary Pathophysiology — The Essentials, 1977; also numerous articles in profl. journs. Mem.: AAAS; Am. Physiol. Soc.; Am. Soc. Clin. Investigation; British Physiol. Soc.; British Thoracic Soc.; Royal Coll. Physicians (London); Assn. Am. Physicians; Western Assn. Physicians; Western Soc. Clin. Res. Res.: 9626 Blackgold Rd., La Jolla, CA 92037; Office: Dept. of Medicine M-023, Sch. of Medicine, Univ. Calif., San Diego, La Jolla, CA 92093.

WEST, JULIAN RALPH
Certified Public Accountant
b. Dec. 12, 1915, Hot Springs, S. Dak.; s. Joseph C. and Helen E. (Nason) West; B.A., Univ. Okla.; CPA; Certified Internal Auditor; Certified Profl. Contracts Mgr.; m. Marvel E. Knorr, May 1, 1937, Alliance, Nebr.; children: Stuart J., b. 1938; R. Bruce, b. 1940; Judy (Mrs. Jerome H. Hagedorn), b. 1943. Career: Engaged in public acctg. 1946-49; with Office of Auditor Gen., USAF, 1949-62; Audit Policy Div., Office of Secty. of Defense, Wash. D.C. 1962-67; Chief, Procurement Audit Div., Office of the Secty. of Defense, 1967-73; lectr., UCLA-Extension, 1977---. Dir., Nat. Contract Mgmt. Assn., 1973-74. Club: Los Angeles Athletic. Presbyterian, Deacon. Hobby: photog. Res.: 1955 N. Tamarind Ave., Apt. 14, Hollywood, CA 90068.

WEST, PEARL S.
Director, California Youth Authority
b. Oct. 19, 1922, Linden, N.J.; d. Henry Joseph and

Gertrude (Davis) Steiner; B.A., Coll. of Pacific, 1944; M.A., Univ. of Pacific, 1969; m. Weldon West, M.D., June 15, 1945, Boston, Mass.; chil.: Donald Wells, b. Nov. 4, 1949; William Eric, b. Apr. 29, 1951; James Lowell, b. Jan. 19, 1953; Robert McCoy, b. Feb. 23, 1963. Career: tchr., Univ. of Calif., Berkeley, 1956-59; Moderator KVIE, Programs on Redevel., First Offenders, Women's orgns., medicare, 1960; tchr. Delta Coll. Model Un Delegation, 1963; coordinator of community edn., San Joaquin Delta Coll., 1969-72; cont. edn. spec., Univ. of Calif., Davis, 1973-74; apptd. to California Youth Authority Board, 1975---, apptd. vice-chmn, 1976, chairman and director, 1976---. Honors: Lincoln Dist. Sch. Employees Assn., 1975; Professional Tchrs. Assn., Lincoln Unified Sch. Dist., 1975; San Joaquin Co. Sch. Bd. Assn., 1972; 1st woman recipient of Mr. Stockton Award, San Joaquin Co. Bd. of Supervisors, 1971; Stockton Woman of the Year Award, 1966; commendation, Mayor of Stockton, 1960; 1977 Woman of the Year, Stockton Bus. & Profl. Women's Club, 1977; Alumna of the Year, Univ. of Pacific, 1977. Past pres., (or chmn.): League of Women Voters, Stockton; AAUW; Am. Assn. for the U.N., Stockton; World Affairs Council, Stockton; Citizens Com. for New Library; Delta Coll. Bonds com.; San Joaquin Co. Sch. Bds. Assn.; Lincoln Unified Sch. Dist. Trustee; Mem.: Am. Soc. for Pub. Adminstrn.; Am. Acad. Polit. Sci.; Am. Correctional Assn.; Am. Judicature Soc.; Calif. Juvenile Officers Assn.; Calif. Parole, Probation and Correctional Assn.; Calif. Peace Officers Assn.; Common Cause; State Juvenile Delinquency Program Adminstrs. Nat. Assn.; Nat. Council on Crime and Delinquency; Nat. Assn. of Prevention Professionals, Inc.; Nat. Orgn. for Women; Nat. Wildlife Fedn.; Planned Parenthood Assn.; Seventh Step Found.; U.N. Assn. Democrat; 1st pres., San Joaquin Co. Demo. Women's Club. Unitarian. Home: 7315 Parkwood Dr., Stockton, CA 95207; Office: 4241 Williamsbourgh Dr., Sacramento, CA 95823.

WESTMORELAND, DONALD R.
Headmaster, Castilleja School
b. Jan. 15, 1937, Durham, N.C.; s. Otis Kidd and Thelma Alford (Yates) Westmoreland; cousin, Gen. Westmoreland; A.B., Duke Univ. 1959; M.A., Univ. of Alabama, 1961; m. Leta Smith, June 11, 1960, Birmingham, Ala.; chil.: Leigh Donelle, b. Apr. 14, 1961; Donna Ellen, b. Jul. 7, 1963; Donald R. Jr. (Wes.), b. Sept. 30, 1968. Career: headmaster: Birmingham U. Sch., Ala., 1960-63; the Westminster Schools, Atlanta, Ga., 1963-71; Castilleja School, Palo Alto, 1971---. Mem.: Phi Kappa Sigma, 1956-59. Presbyterian. Hobbies: gardening, antiques, music. Rec.: jogging, tennis. Home: 461 Nevada Ave., Palo Alto, CA; Office: 1310 Bryant St., Palo Alto, CA 94301.

WESTOVER, HARRY CLAY
Judge, U.S. District Court
b. May 19, 1894, Williamstown, Ky.; s. John Homer and Anna (Musselman) Westover; LL.B., Univ. of Ariz. 1918; m. Helen Louise Equen, Columbus, Mississippi, Oct. 3, 1919; chil.: Dorothy E., Harry E. Career: Pvt. practice law, 1919-37; state senator, Orange Co. 1937-39; judge, Superior Ct., Orange Co. 1939-41; apptd. Collector of Internal Revenue, 6th Calif. Dist. 1943; judge, U.S. Dist. Ct., So. Dist. of Calif. 1949---. 2nd Lt., WW I. Mem.: Amer. Leg., L.A. Bar Assn., BPOE (Santa Ana), Sigma Chi, L.A. Breakfast Club. Democrat. Methodist. Res.: 203-D Avenida Majorca, Laguna Hills, CA 92653; Office: U.S. Courthouse and Post Ofc. Bldg., Los Angeles, CA 90012.

WHEAT, FRANCIS MILLSPAUGH
Attorney at Law
b. Feb. 4, 1921, Los Angeles; s. Carl I and Helen (Millspaugh) Wheat; A.B., Pomona Coll., 1942; LL.B., Harvard Law Sch., 1948; m. Nancy L. Warner, 1944, Chevy Chase, Md.; sons: Douglas Loring, b. 1947; Carl Irving, b. 1949; Gordon Warner, b. 1953. Career: Assoc. and partner, law firm Gibson, Dunn & Crutcher, Los Angeles, 1948-64, partner, 1969---; commnr., U.S. Securities & Exchange Commn., Wash. D.C. 1964-69. Dir., Phillips Petroleum Co., 1976---; vice chairman, Bd. Trustees, Pomona Coll., 1974---. Publs.: numerous articles, speeches and chpts. in profl. journs. USN, 1942-46, Lt., USNR. Pres., L.A. Co. Bar Assn, 1975-76. Mem.: Phi Beta Kappa. Democrat. Unitarian, pres. Neighborhood Ch. Pasadena 1962. Res.: 2130 Lombardy Rd., San Marino, CA 91108; Office: 515 S. Flower St., Los Angeles, CA 90071.

WHEELER, BEATRICE GERALDINE H.
Civic and Club Leader
b. Feb. 5, 1919, Pomona, Calif.; d. Albion True and

Beatrice Osa (Barnes) Hartshorn; A.A., Santa Barbara City Coll.; m. Lloyd Franklyn Wheeler, Pomona, Calif., Dec. 2, 1938; sons: Russell Lloyd, b. Dec. 6, 1939; Robert Gerald, b. July 28, 1944. Career: Co-owner, Atheling's (publ.-investments), 1971---, ed.-author, Atheling's Journ. 1971. Lectr., PTA, Am. Red Cross, Cub Scouts, 1943-60; coord. volunteer servs., Ofc. of Civil Def., City of Santa Barbara, 1965-76; bd. dirs. Calif. Central Coast Area, USO Council, 1968, treas. 1970-76; coord. TV series, Sta. KEYT, 1968; exec. secty. 1960 Nixon for Pres. Campaign Com.; Speakers' Bur., Nixon for Gov. Campaign, 1962; Repub. State Central Com., Calif. 1962-64; Blitz chmn. Santa Barbara Co. Rockefeller for Pres. Com. 1964; co-publ.-ed. Athelings (mag. of Noblesse Oblige), 1974-75; Listed: The Heredity Register, 1st edition, 1972---; featured other publs. Mem.: Jr. Ebell, Pomona, 1935-38; Claremont, Fontana Jr. Women's Clubs, 1947-52; Santa Barbara Choral Soc. 1956-59; Natl. Soc. DAR, hist., chpt. regent, 1967-69; chmn. 1970-71; Daus. of Amer. Colonists; Huguenot Soc. of Calif., state chaplain, 1970-75; Soc. of Mayflower Descs. of Calif., orgn. gov. Santa Barbara Colony; coms. Calif. Ct., Women Descs. of Ancient and Hon. Artillery Co.; state coms. Daus. of Founders and Patriots of Amer. 1970-72; state registrar, 1972-74, state v.p. 1974-76; orgn. pres., So. Calif. Chpt. 1976-78; Hereditary Order of Descs. of Colonial Govs., dep. gov. gen. 1973---; Soc., Daus. of Colonial Wars in Calif., state registrar, 1971-73, orgn.-com. chmn. Royal Spanish Visit, Santa Barbara, Nov. 1, 1973; cert. of Merit, 1973; Mil. and Hospitaller Order of St. Lazarus of Jerusalem, ofcr. companion, 1971---, found. v.p. Hereditary Soc. of Santa Barbara, 1973-76; Soc. of Descs. of Most Noble Order of Garter, Sovereign Colonial Soc., Amers. of Royal Descent; regent, So. Calif. Div., Nat. Soc. Magna Charta Dames, 1971---; ofcr. Augustan Soc. 1971-75; Colonial Dames of Amer., Pasa. Aux. div. chmn. 1972---. Hist. Soc. of Pomona Valley, Pilgrims Soc., Natl. Genealogical Soc., New Eng. Historic and Genealogical Soc. Protestant (bd. Spiritual Welfare; bd. Chr. Edn., soprano soloist, Ch. Choir). Hobbies: books, reading, genealogy, music, dress designing, garden, travel. Res.: 1047 Baseline Rd., Claremont, CA 91711.

WHEELER, LLOYD FRANKLYN
Public Utilities Administrator (Retired)
b. June 23, 1916, Pomona, Calif.; s. Arnold Franklin and Mary Elizabeth (Adair) Wheeler; A.A., Santa Barbara City Coll.; m. Beatrice Geraldine Hartshorn, Pomona, Calif., Dec. 2, 1938; sons: Russell Lloyd, b. Dec. 6, 1939; Robert Gerald, b. July 28, 1944. Career: Asosc. with So. Calif. Edison Co., 1942-76; supv.-admr. Santa Barbara Dist. 1952-76; propr. Atheling's (publ.-investments), publ. Atheling's Journ., 1971; co-owner-publ. Athelings, mag. of Noblesse Oblige, 1974-75; co-ed. Newsletter of Grand Priory of Amer., cert. of Merit, 1973. Mem.: Hist. Soc. of Pomona Valley, dir. 1977---; Pomona Valley Pioneer Soc., founder mem. & dir., 1977---; Order of Patricians, 1977, Patron; Pilgrim Soc.; Santa Barbara Choral Soc. 1956-59; Santa Barbara Repub. Central Com. 1959-65; bd. dirs. English Speaking Union, 1969-71; Calif. v.p. The Augustan Soc. 1971-75; Mil. and Hospitaller Order of St. Lazarus of Jerusalem, ofcr. companion, 1973---; Host, Royal Spanish Visit Com., Nov. 1, 1973; Protestant (trustee, chmn. mus.; chmn. bd. of Spiritual Welfare; baritone soloist, ch. choir). Hobbies: music, garden, travel, sports. Res.: 1047 Baseline Rd., Claremont, CA 91711; Office: P.O.B. 501, Claremont, CA 91711.

WHIPPLE, ROBERT P.
Company President
b. July 15, 1919, Oil City, Pa.; s. Ernest Alfred and Blanche S. Whipple; B.S., Lehigh Univ. 1943; LL.B., Akron Univ. 1951; m. Elinor R. Fitch, Oil City, Pa., Dec. 24, 1943; chil.: Cindy Ann, James Robert, Gregg Alan, Terri. Career: admitted: Oh. Bar, Patent Bar 1951; U.S. Supreme Ct., Fed. Dist. Ct., Ct. Customs and Patent Appeals; patent-dev. dept. Firestone Tire and Rubber Co., Akron, 1946-60, asst. patent counsel, 1955-60; orgn.-mgr. Patent Dept., Rexall Drug & Chem. Co. (Dart), 1960, worldwide dept. v.p. 1968, patent counsel, Dart Inds. 1960-69, v.p. 1969-73; founder-pres. Whipple Internat. Equip. Corp. 1973---; chmn. Derr Devel. Corp. 1975---. USNR, PTO 1944-46; Naval Air Res. 1946-60; Lt. Comdr. ret. 1965; Mem.: Chpt. pres., Delta Tau Delta, 1943; v.p. Akron Jr. C. of C. 1955; v.p. Licensing Exec. Soc. 1968, pres. 1971; Amer. Patent Law Assn.; L.A. Patent Law Assn.; Ohio Bar Assn. Episcopalian. Hobbies: history, stamps. Rec.: fishing, hunting, golf. Res.: 5212 Lubao Ave., Woodland Hills, CA 91364; Office: 10100 Santa Monica Blvd., Suite 940, Los Angeles, CA 90067.

WHIPPS, GILBERT FREDERICK
Physician — Surgeon — Banker
b. Nov. 13, 1917, Mead (Peone Township), Wash.; s. William Washington, Sr. and Amelia (Olsen) Whipps; ed. grad. (valedictorian-student body pres.) Mead (Wash.) Union H.S., 1936; B.S. (cum laude), Washington State Coll., June 1941; postgrad. UCLA 1946-47; M.D., Univ. of Ore. Sch. of Med. 1951; m. La Vay Lawrence, Las Vegas, Nev., Sept. 4, 1960; son: Craig Douglas, b. Sept. 22, 1951. Career: Licensed registered pharmacist, Wash. 1941; intern, Swedish Hosp., Seattle, Wash. 1951-52; res. (obstets.-gynecology), 1952-53; M.D., Wash. 1952; est. res. and med. practice, Calif. 1953; sr. staff, Santa Monica Hosp. 1959; staff, the Mem. Hosp. of So. Calif., Culver City, Calif. Co-Founder-dir., Wilshire Natl. Bank, L.A. 1962; adv. bd., Heritage-Wilshire Natl. Bank, 1965-66; co-founder, Gateway Natl. Bank, El Segundo, Calif. 1963-64; dir.-v.p., Marcraig, Inc. (real estate and allied interests), L.A. 2nd Lt., U.S. Army Inf. 1941; S.W. Pac. Theater of War, 1942-45; USAF 1943-46; disch. as Capt., WW II. Awards: Pres. Unit Cit. with 2 oak leaf clusters; Asiatic-Pac. Ribbon with 3 battle stars. Mem.: pres. Wash. State Coll. Br., Amer. Pharmaceutical Assn. 1940; L.A. Co. del., Calif. Med. Assn. 1963; legislative com., L.A. Co. Med. Assn. 1963, chmn. 1964-65; pres. Bay Dist. br. 1966, dir. 1967---; Calif. del., Assn. of Amer. Phys. and Surgs. 1963, 64, 65, 66, 67; exec. com., Calif. Com., Amer. Med. Polit. Action Comm. 1965-66; World Med. Assn., AMA, Amer. Phys. Assn., Acad. of Med. and Parapsychology, Amer. Acad. Family Practice, Town Hall of Calif.; Sports Car Club of America (race car driver). Republican. Rec.: golf, swimming, reading. Res.: Brentwood Heights, CA; Office: 12121 Wilshire Blvd., Los Angeles, CA 90025.

WHITCOMB, KAY
Artist — Craftsman
b. May 20, 1921, Arlington, Mass.; d. Herbert Hartwell and Mildred (Carr) Whitcomb; father and grandfather bred world record cattle; desc. James & Mary Howe, pilgrims last voyage of Mayflower; student, R.I. Sch. of Design, 1939-40, 1941-42; scholarship student, Cambridge Sch. of Art, 1940-41; m. Dr. Michael John Deith (dec.), NYC, July 11, 1951; children: Richard Y., b. 1952; Deborah Nickerson, b. 1953. Career: Apprenticed to Doris Hall in enameling, Cleveland, 1947-48; first studio of own, Winchester, Mass., 1948---; rec. Award of Merit, Young American Show, N.Y., 1950; rep. USA at German Internat. Kunsthandwerk Exhib., Stuttgart, 1969; exhib. at 1975 Limoges, France Internationale Biennale (arranged for 23 other Americans to also exhib.); organized 1976 Internat. Festival of Enamel at Laguna Beach Mus. of Art (involving 10 countries). Exhib. nationally and internat., Germ., France, Belgium, Japan, Italy, etc. Many major commissions incl. enamel on steel mural for Univ. Calif., San Diego Med. Center Auxiliary in hosp. lobby; currently tchr., Enameling, ELC, San Diego. Contr. line of needlepoint, other craft designs, Better Homes and Gardens mag. and Needlepoint Book (1948); lectrs. on enameling. Founder, 1st pres., Enamel Guild: West, 1976-78. USMC Women's Reserve, 1944-46. Mem.: Lz Jolla Civic Orch., treas., pres. women's com. 1961-63; San Diego Art Guild, bd. mem. 5 yrs.; pres. 1968-69; Allied Craftsmen of San Diego, v.p. Christian Sci. Hobbies: quilt designer, neeldepoint designer. Rec.: swimming. Address: 1631 Mimulus Way, La Jolla, CA 92037.

WHITE, CHARLES WILBERT
Artist
b. Apr. 2, 1918, Chicago; s. Charles and Ethel (Gary) White; stu. (Inst. Scholar), Art. Inst., Chicago, 1937; Art Student's League, NYC, 1942; Taller de Grafica and Esmeralda Sch. Painting and Sculpture, Mexico City, 1947; Dr. Art (hon.), Columbia Coll., Chicago, 1969; L.H.D., 1969; m. Frances Barrett, May 31, 1950; children: Jessica, Ian. Career: Instr. Southside Art Center, Chicago, 1939-40; artist-in-residence Howard Univ., 1945; instr. Workshop Sch. Art, NYC, 1950-53; Otis Art Inst., Los Angeles, 1965; exhibited in one-man shows incl. Heritage Gallery, Los Angeles; Forum Gallery, NYC; Krannert Art Mus., High Mus. Art, Montgomery Mus. Art, Hunter Mus. Art, Palm Beach Art Inst., exhibited in group shows U.S. and abroad, incl. Library of Congress, 1941; San Francisco Mus. Art, 1946; Whitney Mus. 1951; Am. Acad. Arts and Letters, 1952; Met. Mus. Art, 1952; Smithsonian Inst., 1954; Internat. Exhibit Art, Germany, 1959; Scripps Coll., 1966; Assn. pour la Racontre des Cultures, Paris, 1966; Fine Arts Gallery, San Diego, 1966; Dayton Art Inst., 1968; Boston Mus. Fine Arts,

1968; Nat. Center Afro-Am. Mus. Art, 1971; Los Angeles County Mus., 1976; Dallas Mus. Art, 1977; Brooklyn Mus. Art, 1977; Municipal Art Mus. Los Angeles, 1977; El Museo de Arte Moderne, Colombia, 1977; represented in permanent collections, incl. Wichita (Kans.) Art Mus.; executed murals Hampton (Va.) Inst., Los Angeles Pub. Library, 1976. Exec. bd. Black Acad. Arts and Letters, Nat. Center Afro-Am. Artists, Los Angeles City Commn. on Art. Recipient numerous awards. Mem. NAD. Contbr. to art books, publs. Agent: Heritage Gallery, 718 N. La Cienega Blvd., Los Angeles, CA 90069.

WHITE, EDWARD M.
Professor of English
b. Aug. 16, 1933, Brooklyn, N.Y.; s. Joseph and Ida (Eisen) White; B.A., NYU, 1955; M.A., Harvard Univ., 1956, Ph.D., 1960; m. 2d. Volney Douglas, Dec. 11, 1976, San Bernardino; children: Katherine, b. 1959; Elizabeth, b. 1963; stepchildren: Douglas, b. 1961; Dina, b. 1964; Frank, b. 1965. Career: Teaching Fellow in Gen. Edn., Harvard Univ., 1958-60; Instr., Asst. Prof. of English, Wellesley Coll., 1960-65; Prof. of English, Cal. State Coll., San Bernardino, 1965---, English Dept. Chmn. 1966-75; Coordinator of English Testing Programs and Dir., English Equivalence Exam. for California State University and Colleges, 1973---. Lectr. confs. and workshops; cons. various ednl. instns. in testing and evaluating; contbr. articles and revs. in scholarly journs., chpts. in English textbooks, monographs in field of testing and evaluating; author: (fiction) The Presence of Pain, Carleton Miscellary, Fall 1961. Bd. Dir., Calif. Assn. of Teachers of English, 1973-75; pres., English Council of Calif. State Colls., 1973-75; mem. exec. com., Coll. Conf. on Composition & Communication, 1976-78. Mem. Soc. for Values in Higher Education. Presbyterian, Elder. Hobbies: chess, tennis, gardening. Res.: 933 W. Edgehill Rd., San Bernardino, CA 92405; Office: Cal State Coll., San Bernardino, CA 92407.

WHITE, HARVEY ELLIOTT
Physicist
b. Jan. 28, 1902, Parkersburg, W. Va.; s. Elliott Adam and Elizabeth White; bro. Dr. Charles White, dentist; ed. A.B., Occidental Coll. 1925, Sc.D. 1961; Ph.D., Cornell Univ. 1929; m. Adeline Dally, Pasadena, Calif., Aug. 10, 1928; chil.: Donald H., b. Apr. 30, 1931 (physicist); Jerald P., b. Feb. 9, 1934; Vernita L., b. Mar. 23, 1937. Career: teaching asst., Cornell Univ. 1925-26; instr. 1926-29; internat. research fellow, Physikalische Technische Reichsanstalt, Berlin, Ger. 1929-30; asst. prof., Univ. of Calif., Berkeley, 1930-36, assoc. prof. 1936-42, prof. 1942---; Guggenheim fellow, Hawaii, 1948; dir. Lawrence Hall of Sci. 1960---. Teacher, Nationwide NBC-TV Broadcast, physics course for H.S. Teachers (first natl. edn. TV pgm.), 1958-59. Author: (textbooks) Introduction to Atomic Spectra (452 pages), Optics (682 pgs.), Classical and Modern Physics (760 pgs.), Descriptive College Physics (2 edits.), Modern College Physics (5 edits., 765 pgs.), Atomic and Nuclear Physics (560 pgs.), Atomic Age Physics, publs. USA and translated langs. foreign countries; author-lecturer, first complete introductory physics course on color film (162 half-hr. films). Civ. AEC, OSRD (1942-45), WW II. Awards: War Dept. Cit. 1946; Hans Christian Oersted Medal; Thomas Alva Edison TV Award; Peabody TV Award; Sylvania TV Award; Parents Mag. Medal; U.S. Sci. Exhib. Award, others. Mem.: Amer. Phys. Soc., Optical Soc. of Amer., Amer. Assn. of Physics Teachers, Sigma Xi, Phi Beta Kappa, Phi Kappa Phi, Sigma Pi Sigma. Presbyterian. Hobby: amateur radio. Rec.: golf. Res.: 543 Spruce St., Berkeley 94707. Office: Lawrence Hall of Science, University of Calif., Berkeley, CA.

WHITE, HOWARD ASHLEY
University President
B.A., M.A., Ph.D., Tulane University; m. Maxcine Feltman (dec.), Nashville, Tenn.; chil.: Ashley Feltman, b. Feb. 3, 1954; Howard Elliott, b. Aug. 6, 1957. Minister, Carrollton Avenue Church of Christ, New Orleans, 1941-53; prof. of history, chmn. of dept., David Lipscomb Coll., Nashville, Tenn. 1953-58; chmn. of Social Sci. Dept., Pepperdine Univ., L.A. 1958-63, Dean of Graduate Studies, Dean of Undergrad. studies, 1963-71, exec. v.p., 1971-78, president, 1978---. Author: The Freedmen's Bureau in Louisiana, Louisiana State University Press, 1970. Ch. of Christ. Office: 24255 Pacific Coast Highway, Malibu, CA 90265.

WHITE, IAN McKIBBIN
Museum Director
b. 1929, Honolulu, Hawaii; ed. Cate Sch., Carpinteria, Calif.; B.A. (arch.), Harvard Univ., 1951; Harvard Grad. Sch. of Design; UCLA (hon. D.F.A., Bowdoin Coll., 1977; m. Florence Hildreth, Cape Elizabeth, Maine; chil.: Peter, Daniel, Susanna. Career: Adm. and exhib. design spec. Brooklyn Museum, 1961-67; designer, Frieda Shiff Warburg Sculpture Garden; designer, Peary-MacMillan Arctic Museum, Bowdoin Coll., Brunswick, Me. 1967; assoc. dir. Calif. Palace Legion of Honor, 1967-70, dir. S.F. Fine Arts Museums, M.H. de Young Mem. Mus. and Calif. Palace Legion of Honor, 1970---. Art adv. Cate Sch., Carpinteria. Lt., USNR exec. ofcr. (3 yrs.). Mem.: secty. Rembrandt Club of Brooklyn, 1965-66; bd. dirs. Municipal Art Soc. of NYC 1966; adv. com. Victorian Soc. of Amer.; trustee; Loiise A. Boyd Natural Sci. Mus., Marin Co.; trustee, Corning Museum of Glass, 1977; council, Amer. Assn. of Museums, 1970; Amer. Assn. of Mus. Directors; U.S. Com. Internat. Council of Museums, 1972; trustee, Amer. Fed. of Arts 1972; Mus. Adv. Panel, Natl. Endowment for the Arts, 1973; Bohemian Club, 1973. Res.: Ross, CA; Office: Calif. Palace of the Legion of Honor, Lincoln Park, San Francisco, CA 94121.

WHITE, LELIA CAYNE
Library Director
b. Feb. 22, 1921, Berkeley; d. James Lloyd and Eulalia (Douglass) Cayne; B.A., Univ. Calif., Berkeley, 1943, M.L.S., 1969; div.; chil.: Douglass Fulton White; Cameron Jane White. Career: Bibliographer, lectr., assoc., Sch. of Library & Information Studies, 1969-72; supervising librarian, Oakland Pub. Lib., 1973-76; ref. librarian, Berkeley-Oakland Service System, 1970-73; director, Oakland Public Library, 1976---. Chmn., Pub. Lib. Execs. of Central Calif. 1978-79. Mem.: Soroptimist; League of Women Voters. Home: 1927 Napa Ave., Berkeley, CA 94707; Office: 125 14th St., Oakland, CA 94612.

WHITE, LYNN TOWNSEND, JR.
Professor of History
b. Apr. 29, 1907, San Francisco, Calif.; s. Rev. Dr. Lynn Townsend, Sr. (prof. San Francisco Theol. Sem. of Presb. Ch., San Anselmo, Calif.) and Mary (Tarrant) White; B.A., Stanford Univ. 1928; M.A., Union Theol. Sem. 1929; M.A., Harvard Univ. 1930; Ph.D. 1934; LL.D.: MacMurray Coll. 1946, Lake Erie Coll. 1957, Mills Coll. 1958; m. Maude Catherine McArthur, San Francisco, Calif., Sept. 10, 1940; chil.: Lynn Townsend III, b. Sept. 16, 1941; Catherine McArthur, b. Nov. 8, 1944; Ethel Ferguson and Mary Tarrant (twins), b. Jan. 28, 1946. Career: Instr. in hist., Princeton Univ. 1937-40; prof. 1940-43; pres. Mills Coll. 1943-58; prof. of hist., UCLA 1958-75; prof. emer. 1975---. Author: Latin Monasticism in Norman Sicily, publ. Cambridge, Mass. 1938; Educating Our Daughters, publ. Harper & Bros. 1950; Frontiers of Knowledge in the Study of Man, publ. Harper & Bros. 1956; Medevial Technology and Social Change, publ. Clarendon Press, 1962; Medieval Religion and Technology, publ. Univ. of Calif. Press, 1978. Awards: Officier d'Academie, 1948; Guggenheim Fellowship, 1958-59; listed, Directory of Amer. Scholars. Mem.: councillor, Hist. of Sci. Soc. 1955-58, 1961-63; fellow, Amer. Acad. of Arts and Scis. 1956; Amer. Hist. Assn., Calif. Hist. Soc., Medieval Acad. of Amer, Renaissance Soc. of Amer; pres. Soc. for the Host. of Tech. 1960-62; Phi Beta Kappa, Bohemian Club. Presbyterian. Hobby: cooking. Res.: 207 N. Saltair, Los Angeles, CA 90049.

WHITE, RUTH BENNETT
Educator — Author
b. Aug. 18, 1906, Howe, Okla.; d. A.L. and Sarah (Blevins) Bennett; desc. of Roger Williams, founder, Colony of R.I.; Oliver Cromwell, Lord Protector of Eng.; ed. B.A. (cum laude), Okla. Bapt. Univ. 1928; M.S., Univ. of Ia. 1930; postgrad. Cornell Univ. 1930-34; Columbia Univ. 1956-57; m. Dr. Carl Milton White, Heavener, Okla., Aug. 5, 1928; daus.: Sherril Spencner, Caroline Buchanan. Career: Prin., Jr. H.S., Heavener, Okla. 1926-27; Fellow in research nutrition, Univ. Ia., Cornell Univ.; instr. nutrition, Univs.; research spec. 4-H Clubs, 1931-34; Home Econs. teacher: NYC schs., Ft. Lee, N.J. 1955-60; lecturer, U.S. 1934---, Turkey 1960-61; Nigeria and Egypt, 1962-64; TV, radio; writer, speaker: Natl. League Amer. Pen Women Conf. 1974; Biennial Conv. Calif. Home Econs. Assn., Oakland, 1975. Author: If Food Could Talk, Cornel Univ. 1932; You and Your Food, 1961 (4th ed.), 1975 (only H.S. textbook on AMA

recommended list, 1966); Food and Your Future, publ. Prentice-Hall, Inc. 1972; contrib. to Journ. of Home Econs., Home Econs. Research Journ., Soc. for Proceedings of Exp. Biol.-Med.; Richard's Topical Ency., others. Awards: many 4-H Club hons.; Ambassador of Goodwill, Gov. David Hall, Okla. 1972; one of 16 Women of Achievement, S.D. 1973; Woman of Achievement, Calif. Home Econ. Assn., S.D' 1973, Woman of the Year, 1974. Mem.: Bd. Edn., Leonia, N.J. 1950-54; Friends of Univ. of Calif. Lib.; Nigerian Home Sci. Assn. 1962-64; Ad Hoc Com. 1969; publ. com. Calif. Home Econ. Assn. 1967-70; chmn. 1969, internat. rels. chmn. 1970-75; Lake Placid Conf. on Home Econs. 1973-74; del. to Internat. Fed. of Home Econs., Univ. Bristol, Eng. 1968, Ger. 1970, Cong. Helsinki Tech. Univ., Finalnd 1972; AAUW, Pi Lambda Theta, Pi Kappa Delta. Presbyterian. Res.: 935 Genter St., No. 3A, La Jolla, CA 92037.

WHITEHOUSE, JAMES MAX
Clinical Psychologist
b. Nov. 2, 1939, Los Angeles; s. James M. and Joan Lynn (Foss) Whitehouse; A.A., American River Coll., B.A., M.A., Sacramento State Univ.; Ph.D., California Sch. of Professional Psychology; m. Sharon Saunders, June 1968, Sacramento; son, Cale Joseph, b. Oct. 17, 1978. Career: instr. psychol., Sacramento State Univ. 1969-70; research asst., Dept. Motor Vehicles, 1969-70; dir. personnel, Kassis Enterprises, 1968-70; asst. prof. psychol., Bakersfield Coll. 1970-72, chemn. psychol. dept. 1972-75; clin. psychol., Kernview Hosp. ---; adjunct lectr. in grad. studies, Calif. State Coll., Bakersfield ---; prof. of psychology, Bakersfield Coll. ---; lectr., UCSB, 1971-76; postdoctoral fellowship with Joseph Wolpe, Temple Univ. Med. Sch. and E. Penn. Psychiat. Inst. 1977-78. Mem.: Western Assn. of Schs. and Colls. accreditation team ---; AAU track and field official ---. Dir., Palm Mutual Water Co. ---. Author: Guide to Giving Psychology Away, Canfield Press, 1973; The Behavioral Eating Manual; A guide to eating habit change, 1975. Served USN, 1960-63; flight crew. Pres. Psi Chi, Sacramento chpt. 1968-69; mem.: Kern Co. Psychol. Assn.; Calif. State Psychol. Assn.; Am. Psychol. Assn. Hobby: avocado farming. Rec.: tennis. Home: 3006 Harmony Dr., Bakersfield, CA 93306; Office: 1801 Panorama, Bakersfield, CA 93305.

WHITEHURST, DANIEL KEENAN
Mayor of Fresno
b. Oct. 4, 1948, Los Banos, Calif.; s. William S. and Tarie M. (James) Whitehurst; B.A., St. Mary's Coll., 1969; J.D., Univ. Calif., Hastings Coll. of Law, 1972; M.A., Occidental Coll., 1973; m. Kathleen McCann, July 5, 1969; chil.: Keenan, b. Jan. 11, 1976; Jamie, b. Oct. 8, 1977. Career: law practice, Fresno, 1973-75; v.p., Whitehurst Funeral Chapel, Fresno, 1975---; elected to City Council, Apr. 15, 1975; elected to office of Mayor, 1977---. Mem.: U.S. Conference Mayors Coms.: spec. com. on Urban Police, Energy & Environment Standing Com., Faculty, Mayor's Leadership Inst.; Nat. League of Cities effective government steering com. Mem.: State Bar of Calif.; Rotary Club of Fresno. Office: City Hall, 2326 Fresno St., Fresno, CA 93721.

WHITENACK, JANET LUCILLE
Realtor
b. Utica, Nebr.; d. Raymond F. and Ferne (Bishop) Hougland; B.S., Univ. of Nebr. (fellow student w/dau. Sandra), 1961; postgrad., Calif. State Univ., Fullerton (fellow student w/dau. Leslie); Graduate Realtors Inst. (G.R.I.) (fellow student w/son Dee); Life cert. elem. sch. tchr.; m. Lee W. Whitenack, Utica, Nebr.; chil.: Sandra (Nolte); Leslie (Welch); Dee. Career: tchr., elementary schs., Seward, Nebr., Lincoln, Nebr., Anaheim, Calif. 1943-63; life insurance correspondent, 1959-61; real estate agent, 1973---; broker, 1975---; owner Jan Whitenack, Herbert Hawkins Realtors, Orange, 1974---. Pres., Toastmasters Smedley Club No. 1, 1979; AAUW, 1963---; Calif. Assn. of Real Estate Teachers; East Orange Co. Bd. of Realtors, 1973---; Sun. Sch. tchr. 1949-63. Hobbies: dancing, swimming. Rec.: jogging, camping, travel. Home: 331 N. Wayfield, Orange, CA; Office: 817 S. Tustin Ave., Orange, CA 92667.

WHITMORE, SHARP
Attorney at Law
b. Apr. 26, 1918, Price, Ut.; s. Leland E. and Anne (Sharp) Whitmore; ed. A.B., Stanford Univ. 1939; J.D., Univ. of Calif., Berkeley, 1942; m. Frances Boswell Dorr, Pasadena, Calif., Aug. 14, 1940; chil.: Richard Sharp, b. Oct. 21, 1942; William Leland, b. Jan. 29, 1947; Ann Hartley, b. June 29, 1954. Career: Assoc., Gibson, Dunn & Crutcher, 1946-51, partner, 1951---.

Lecturer, USC Law Sch. 1959-64. USNR (1942-46), WW II, Lt. Comdr. (ret.) Mem.: pres. Calif. State Jr. Bar, 1952; Com. of Bar Examiners, State Bar of Calif. 1953-58, chmn. 1956-58, bd. govs. 1962-65, v.p.-treas. 1964-65; chmn. Natl. Conf. of Bar Examiners .1957-58; House of Dels., Amer. Bar Assn. 1957-58, 1968---, pres. 1970-71; pres. Chancery Club, 1961-62; bd. govs., Beverly Hills Bar Assn. 1964-67; bd. dirs., Calif. Repub. League, 1965-67; Commr. L.A. Bd. of Municipal Auditorium, 1973---; L.A. Country Club, Bohemian Club, Sunset Club, 100 Club, Calif. Club. Res.: 826 S. Napoli Dr., Pacific Palisades, CA; Office: 9601 Wilshire Blvd., Beverly Hills, CA.

WHITNEY, GEORGE HARRISON
Attorney at Law
b. Mar. 3, 1914, Chicago, Ill.; ed. Eighteenth St. Sch., Fannie D. Noe Sch., Upland, Calif.; prep. sch., Le Rosey, Switz (3 yrs.); grad. Webb Sch. of Claremont, Calif. 1931; A.B., Williams Coll., Williamstown, Mass 1946; LL.B., Stanford Univ. 1939; m. Isabel Chernoski; daus.: Mary Catherine and Olive Therese. Career: lawyer, partner, Gibson, Dunn & Crutcher, L.A. Dir. Liberty Groves Operating Corp., Upland; v.p-dir., San Antonio Water Co., Upland; secty. Trona Ry. Co., Trona. Lt. Comdr. USNR (1942-46), WW II. Mem.: Amer. Bar Assn.; L.A. Co. Bar Assn.; Calif. State Bar Assn., 1940---; Amer. Judicature Soc.; Amer. Acad. of Polit. and Soc. Sci.; pres. Friends of the Huntington Lib., San Marino; dir. Hosp. of the Good Samaritan, L.A.; pres., Stanford Law Soc. of So. Calif.; trustee, Webb Sch. of Calif., Claremont; secty. Zamarano Club, L.A.; chmn. Planning Comm., City of Upland; pres. Chancery Club, L.A. 1977; Pac. R.R. Soc., L.A. Co. Museum Assn., Southwest Mus., The Chaffey Community Art Assn., So. Calif. Hist. Soc., 'Calif. Hist. Soc.; Mo. Hist. Soc., St. Louis; Honnold Lib. Soc., Claremont; Pierpont Morgan Lib., N.Y.; Book Club of Calif.; St. Anthony's Club; Lions Club, Upland; Selden Soc., Cambridge, Mass.; Town Hall, L.A.; Sierra Soc., E. Clampus Vitus, Phi Alpha Delta, Phi Beta Kappa, Delta Psi; Calif., Bond, Univ., Stock Exch. Clubs, L.A. Res.: 805 W. Sixteenth St., Upland, CA; Office: Gibson, Dunn & Crutcher, Richfield Tower, Los Angeles, CA 90071.

WHITNEY, STEPHEN LOUIS
City Librarian
b. July 18, 1943, Chicago, Ill.; s. Walter Robert and Emma Agnes (Murray) Whitney; A.B., Rockurst Coll., Kansas City, Mo., 1965; M.L.S., Case-Western Reserve Univ. Sch. of Lib. and Info. Scis., 1966; m. Gloria Jean Lujan, June 5, 1965, Kansas City, Mo.; chil.: Laura Ann, b. 1966; Stephen Christopher, b. 1970; Mark Andrew, b. 1972. Career: Adult Servs. Librn., St. Louis (Mo.) Pub. Lib. 1966-67; coord., Municipal Lib. Coop. of St. Louis Co., Kirkwood, 1967-70; adminstrv. asst. to the Dir., St. Louis Co. Lib., Ladue, 1970-74; dir., Broward Co. Lib., Ft. Lauderdale, Fla., 1974-77; City Librn., San Bernardino Pub. Lib. 1977---. Publs.: Library System Trustees, Lib. Journ. 1970; Model for a State Public Relations Network, Wyoming Lib. Round-Up, 1973. Chmn., tchr. edn. com., White House Conf. on Edn., St. Louis, Mo., 1972; chmn. parent adv. council, Larkdale Elem. Sch., Ft. Lauderdale, 1975-77; pres. Parent Teacher Group, St. Anne's Elem. Sch., San Bernardino, 1978---; chmn. ALA Constitution & Bylaws Com. 1972-74; chmn. Mo. Lib. Assn., Pub. Lib. Div., 1971-73, pub. rels. com. chmn. 1970-74; dir., Fla. Lib. Assn. 1975-77; recording secty., San Bernardino Hist. Soc., 1977---; dir., Lung Assn. of San Bernardino, 1978---; dir., San Bernardino Symphony Assn., 1978---; dir., San Bernardino Pageant, Inc., 1978---; chmn. Fed. Com., San Bernardino C. of C. Govt. Affairs Div., 1978---; dir. & program chmn., Rotary Club, 1978-79. Res.: 5589 Newbury Ave., San Bernardino, CA 92404; Office: 401 N. Arrowhead Ave., San Bernardino, CA 92401.

WHITTIER, EDWARD JAMES
Life Insurance Company Executive
b. Aug. 12, 1928, Superior, Wis.; B.Sc., Univ. of Wis.; m. Marilyn Diane Growell, June 27, 1959; children: Michael James, b. 1962; Mary Diane, b. 1964. Career: entirely with Pacific Mutual Life Insurance Co., v.p., Agency Mgmt. Devel., 1971---. Sgt., AUS. Res.: 1301 Seacrest Dr., Corona del Mar, CA 92625; Office: 700 Newport Center Drive, Newport Beach, CA 92660.

WHYTE, JAMES G.
Superior Court Judge
b. Sept. 12, 1906, Ontario, Calif.; s. Frederick E. and

Charlotte (Leach) Whyte; A.B., Pomona Coll. 1928; LL.B., Univ. of Calif., Berkeley, 1932; m. Eleanor Crookshank, Santa Ana, Calif., June 24, 1937 (dec. Nov. 27, 1958); m. Marie E. Kinsey, Nov. 24, 1965; chil.: Fredrick Edwin, b. June 12, 1939; Ronald MacLeod, b. Oct. 29, 1942. Career: atty. at law, pvt. practice, Pomona, 1932-45; Claremont, 1945; city atty., Claremont, 1946-50, city judge, 1950; justice of peace, San Jose Township, 1951; judge, Superior Ct., L.A. Co. Presbyterian. Hobby: gardening. Res.: 302 N. McCadden Pl., Los Angeles, CA 90004; Office: Courthouse, Los Angeles, CA 90012.

WHYTE, JOHN
Attorney at Law
b. Mar. 11, 1911, Duluth, Minn.; s. Elmer Norman and Elizabeth (Morris) Whyte; grandson of Judge Page Morris, U.S. Dist. Ct., Minn. 1902-24; desc.: Mann Page, Speaker House of Burgesses, Va.; Gen. Hugh Mercer, Rev. War hero; B.A., Carleton Coll. 1932; LL.B., Univ. of Minn. Law Sch. 1939; Career: admitted to Bar, Minn. 1939, Calif. 1941; lawyer, L.A. 1941---; assoc. with O'Melveny & Myers law firm, 1943-53. Mem.: Annandale Golf Club, California Club, L.A. Ath. Club. Republican. Presbyterian. Hobbies: golf, fishing, canoeing, swim. Res.: 1155 E. Del Mar Blvd., Pasadena, CA 91106; Office: 811 West Seventh St., Los Angeles, CA 90017.

WIDENER, WARREN HAMILTON
Mayor
b. Mar. 25, 1938, Oroville, Calif.; s. Arnold and Ruby Widener; B.A., Speech, Univ. of Calif., 1960, J.D., Boalt Hall Sch. of Law, 1967; m. Mary Lee Thomas, Apr. 4, 1959, Oroville; sons: Warren, Jr., b. 1968; Michael and Stephen (twins), b. 1970. Career: Elected Councilmember, Berkeley City Council, 1969-71, Mayor, City of Berkeley, 1971---. Past pres., Nat. Black Caucus of local elected officials, 1974-75; pres., Calif. Black Caucus of local elected officials; past pres., Alameda Co. Mayor's Conf., 1977-78; Advisory Bd. mem., U.S. Conf. of Mayors, USAF, 1960-64; Capt., USAFR, 1964-75. Res.: 2309 Browning St., Berkeley, CA 94702; Office: 2180 Milvia St., Berkeley, CA 94704.

WIEDMANN, ELEANORE AGNES
Business Executive — Civic Leader
b. Apr, 17, 1923, Los Angeles, Calif.; d. Robert E. and Ann E. (Thornton) Ibbetson (father and twin bro. Edwin, listed Who's Who in Calif.); B.A., Mt. Holyoke Coll. 1944; m. Clark Vroman Wiedmann (check Capt. Pan Am. World Airways; honored by Queen Wilhelmina, 1943), Long Beach, Calif., Apr. 14, 1946; children: Louise Monroe (Mrs. Fred Koch), b. 1947, now hd. language dept. Miraleste H.S.; Clark Allen, b. 1948, now mem. faculty Univ. Mass. and author of two books; Cheryl Ann (Mrs. Ron Slyter), b. 1950, artist in clay, ceramics, porcelain; Darryl Lee, b. 1965. Career: Naval Intelligence Wave ofcr., USNR, Wash., D.C. 1944-46; jr. exec. Union Dev. Corp., Inc. 1952-61, treas.-dir. 1961---; treas.-dir. Dutch Village Bowling Center, Inc. 1965---; dir. Valley Properties, Inc. and Union Farms, Inc. 1966---. Pres., Portuguese Bend Nursey Sch. 1955-56; Palos Verdes Unified Sch. Dist. Bd. of Edn. 1961-69; v.p. 1964-66, pres. 1966-67; PTA Council rep. to Community Center Com., 1979; Awards: Palos Verdes Peninsula League of Women Voters Hon. Award for serv. 1964; Status of Women Award, AAUW, Palos Verdes-Rolling Hills, 1969; Palos Verdes Faculty Assn. Hon. Award, 1969; Palos Verdes Peninsula PTA Council Distinguished Serv. Award, 1969; Palos Verdes Unified Sch. Dist. Serv. Award, 1969. Mem.: pres. Lunada Bay PTA 1957-58; Cub Scout Den Mother, 1957-58; chmn. Palos Verdes Peninsula Multiple Sclerosis Fund, 1958; com. chmn. Palos Verdes Peninsula Coord. Council, 1959; Peninsula Planning Council, 1960; (hon. life) v.p. PTA Council, 1960-61; coms. League of Women Voters, 1960; Harbor Coll. Adv. Bd. 1961-65; Harbor Welfare Planning Council, 1962; luncheon chmn. Mt. Holyoke Alumnae, 1964; div. com., L.A. Reg. Planning Comm. 1968-69; Steering Com. for Save Our Coastline, 1969-70; Palos Verdes Peninsula Repub. Women's Club, Fed.; AAUW; Palos Verdes Tennis Club, King Harbor Yacht Club. Catholic. Rec.: tennis, boating, travel (own airplane world travel). Res.: 30032 Palos Verdes Dr. W., Palos Verdes Peninsula, CA 90274; Office: 8555 Artesia Ave., Bellflower, CA.

WIEGAND, JANE SHUTTLEWORTH
Attorney at Law
b. Cincinnati, Oh.; d. Washburn and Catherine

(Geygan) Shuttleworth; B.A., Univ. Calif., Berkeley; J.D. cum laude, Univ. San Diego Sch. of Law; m. Dr. Jeffery Wiegand, Cali, Colombia; children: Thomas J. and Gregory S. Career: Instr., Univ. del Valle, Cali, Colombia, Univ. Mayor de San Dimon, Cochabanba, Bolivia; Deputy City Atty., City of San Diego; Corporate Counsel, Solar Div., International Harvester; City Atty., City of Escondido, 1977-78; currently assoc., firm McDonald, Hecht & Worley, San Diego, ---. Editor, San Diego Law Rev.; named Distinguished Alumnus, Univ. San Diego Sch. of Law, 1977. Pres., Republican Assocs. of S.D. County; mem. Planning Commn., Rancho Santa Fe; Bd. dir., Mexican-Am. Found. of San Diego; charter mem., bd. dir., World Trade Assn. San Diego Co. Mem. Republican State Central Com. Res.: P.O.B. 961, Rancho Santa Fe, CA; Office: 600 B St., Suite 617, San Diego, CA 92101.

WIENPAHL, PAUL
Professor of Philosophy
b. Mar. 6, 1916, Rock Springs, Wyo.; s. Paul and Constance (DeVelin) Wienpahl; B.A., UCLA, 1937, M.A. 1939, Ph.D. 1946; m. Janet Ward, June 9, 1942, Ft. McLellan, Ala.; children: Mark, b. 1951; Jan, b. 1953. Career: Instr. of Philosophy, UCLA 1946, NYU 1947; Asst. Prof. of Philosophy, Univ. Calif., Santa Barbara, 1948, Assoc. Prof., 1954, Prof. 1962---, Dept. Chmn. 1962-66. Author: The Matter of Zen, NYU Press, 1964; Zen Diary, Harper & Row, 1970; The Radical Spinoza, NYU Press, 1979; contbr. to profl. journs., 1948---. Capt., AUS, 1942-46, ETO. Mem. Phi Beta Kappa, 1937. Rec.: sailing. Res.: 1489 Tunnel Rd., Santa Barbara, CA 93105; Office: Dept. of Philosophy, Univ. of California, Santa Barbara, CA 93106.

WILBUR, DWIGHT LOCKE
Physician
b. Sept. 18, 1903, Harrow-on-the-Hill, Eng.; s. Ray Lyman (secty. of the Interior, U.S., and Pres.-Chancellor of Stanford Univ.) and Marguerite (Blake) Wilbur; nephew of Judge Curtis D. Wilbur, Secty. of Navy and Presiding Judge, 9th Circuit Ct. of Appeals; A.B., Stanford Univ. 1923; M.D., Univ. of Pa. 1926; M.S., Univ. of Minn. 1933; m. Ruth Esther Jordan, Stanford Univ., Calif., Oct. 20, 1928; chil.: Dwight Locke III, Jordan Rockwood, Gregory Fiske. Career: Res. phys., Univ. of Pa. Hosp. 1926-28; 1st asst., sect. Pathological Anatomy, Mayo Clinic, Rochester, Minn. 1929-30; med. fellow, Mayo Found. 1929-31, 1st asst. 1931-33, assoc. in sect. 1933-37, cons. phys., Mayo Clinic, 1931-37, instr.-asst. prof. med. 1933-37; asst. and assoc. clin prof. med., Stanford Univ. Sch. of Med. 1937-49, clin. prof. 1949-69, emeritus prof. 1969---; asst. visiting physician, Stanford Serv., San Francisco Hosp. 1937---; br. sect. chief in gastroenterology, Vets. Adm. 1946-49, area sect. chief, 1949-53; chief, med. serv., French Hosp. 1946; expert cons., Letterman Army Hosp., Dept. of Army, 1946---; Civ. Adv. Council, Dept. of Def. 1953-59; Natl. Adv. Comm. Health Manpower, 1966-67; cons. phys. So. Pac. Hosp.; cons. USN Hosp., Oakland; cons. VA Hosp., Oakland, 1958-64; Martinez, 1964---; assoc. clin. prof. med., Coll. Phys. and Surgs., Sch. of Dentistry, 1948-52; Editor, Calif. Medicine, 1946-67; assoc. ed. Gastroenterology, 1943-51, chmn. ed. bd. 1958-63; ed. bd. Modern Med.; ed. bd. Post Grad. Med. 1950-69, ed.-in-chief, 1966---. Lt. Comdr., Comdr., M.C., USNR 1942-47, chief, Med. Serv., USN Hosp., Oakland, Calif. (1945-46), WW II. Awards: Frederick A. Packard Prize in clin. med., Univ. of Pa. 1926; Commendation, Surg. Gen., U.S. Army, 1950; Outstanding Civilian Serv. Medal, AUS, 1966; Julius Friedenwald Medal for Distinguished Achievement by Amer. Gastroenterological Assn.; Alfred Stengel Mem. Award, Amer. Coll. of Phys. 1970. Mem.: chmn. San Francisco Nutrition Council, 1941-42; bd. dirs., S.F. YMCA, 1941-48; council, Am. Soc. Clin. Investigation, 1942-45; House of Dels., AMA 1942-46, 1948-63; bd. trustees, 1963-70, pres. 1968-69, chmn. Council on Health Man Power, 1968---, World Med. Assn. Council, 1968---, secty. sect. exp. med. and therapeutics, 1942-47, v.-chmn. 1948, chmn. 1949; bd. dirs., Hosp. Serv. of Calif. 1946-52; council, Calif. Med. Assn. 1946-67; S.F. Co. Med. Soc.; Amer. Diabetes Assn.; secty. Amer. Gastroenterol. Assn. 1947---; pres. 1954-55; emeritus, Central Soc. Clin. Research; Calif. Acad. of Sci.; fellow-regent-gov., No. Calif. area, Amer. Coll. Phys. 1947-62, pres. 1958-59; bd. med. Inst. of Med. 1967-71, Natl. Acad. of Sci. 1971; Health Council, Comm. Chest of S.F.; bd. dirs., S.F. Tuberculosis Assn. 1948-53; trustee, Lux Coll. 1949-55; Miranda Lux Found. 1955---, pres. bd. 1964-68; Natl. Research Council; Amer. Gastroscopic

Soc.; bd. trustees, Mayo Found. 1951---, pres. Alumni Assocs. of Mayo Grad. Sch. of Med. 1967; pres. Assoc. Amer. Phys., Calif. Acad. of Med. 1954; Western Assn. of Phys.; Phi Beta Kappa, Sigma Xi, Alpha Omega Alpha; Calif. Nutrition Council; Bohemian Club, Commonwealth Club. Christian. Hobby: fishing, hunting. Rec.: gardening. Res.: 140 Sea Cliff Ave., San Francisco, CA 94121; Office: 655 Sutter St., San Francisco, CA 94102.

WILBURNE, MORRIS
Physician — Internist — Cardiologist
b. May 1, 1913, Chicago, Ill.; s. Jack and Gussie (Greene) Wilburne; B.A., Univ. of W.Va. 1933; M.D., Med. Coll. of Va. 1937; m. Shirley L. Winters, Oct. 14, 1941; daus.: Barbara, Harriet and Corinne. Career: Intern, Caledonian Hosp., Brooklyn, N.Y. 1937-38; asst. res. (chest div.). Kingston Ave. Hosp., Brooklyn, 1939; asst. res. med., Goldwater Mem. Hosp., Welfare Is., NYC 1939-40; Cardiovascular Dept. (under Dr. Louis N. Katz, dir.), Research Inst., Michael Reese Hosp., Chicago, Ill. 1941-42, research assoc. 1946-47; assoc. clin. prof. of med. (Cardiology), USC Sch. of Med.; co.-chief (chil's. cardiology), L.A. Co. Gen. Hosp., L.A., Calif.; staff: L.A. Co. Gen. Hosp., Cedars of Lebanon Hosp., Mt. Sinai Hosp., Temple Hosp., Beverly Hills Doctors Hosp., Midway Hosp. and Westside Hosp., L.A., Calif. Author: numerous sci. publs. contrib. to profl. journs. U.S. Army (1942-46), WW II. Awards: listed, various biog. works incl. Amer. Men of Med. Mem.: v.-chmn., Western region council, L.A. Heart Assn., chmn. profl. edn. com.; med. adv. com., Family Counseling Serv.; aviation com., Thomas A. Dooley Found.; diplomate, Amer. Bd. of Internal Med.; fellow, ACP; fellow, Amer. Coll. of Cardiology; Amer., Calif. and L.A. Co. Med. Assns., Calif. Soc. of Internal Med., Amer. Soc. of Internal Med., Calif. Heart Assn.; profl. edn. com., L.A. Co. Heart Assn., counseling serv.-chmn. profl. edn. com.v.-chmn., Western Region Council. Hobby: horseback riding. Res.: 604 N. Maple Dr., Beverly Hills, CA; Office: 9735 Wilshire Blvd., Beverly Hills, CA 90212.

WILCOX, COLLIN M.
Novelist
b. Sept. 21, 1924, Detroit, Mich.; s. Harlan and Lucille Wilcox; B.A., Antioch Coll., 1948; div.; sons: Christopher, Jeffrey. Career: Lamp mfr., 1955-70; novelist, mystery and suspense, first novel pub. 1967---: The Black Door, 1967; The Third Figure, 1968; The Lonely Hunter, 1969; The Disappearance, 1970; Dead Him, 1971; Hidin Place, 1972; Long Way Down, 1973; Aftershock, 1974; The Faceless Man, 1975; The Third Victim, 1976; Doctor, Lawyer, 1977; The Watcher, 1978; Twospot, 1978; Power Plays, 1979. Dir., Mystery Writers of America. Pvt., USAAF, 1943. Mem. Sierra Club. Address: 7174 26th St., San Francisco, CA 94131.

WILCOX, HOWARD ALBERT
Scientist
b. Nov. 9, 1920, Minneapolis; s. Hugh Brown (Prof., Univ. Minn.) and Jean (McGilvra) Wilcox (mother co-founder Birth Control League, Mnpls., early 1930s w/Margaret Sanger); B.A., physics, Univ. Minn., 1943, student, Harvard Univ., 1944; M.A., Univ. Chicago, Ph.D., physics, 1948; m. Evelyn Agnes Johnson, June 15, 1943, Chicago, Ill.; children: Carol Marilyn, b. 1946; Bruce McGilvra, b. 1948; Brian Howard, b. 1951. Career: Jr. Scientist, Los Alamos Sci. Labs., Los Alamos, N.M. 1944-46; Proj. Dir., Sidewinder Guided Missile, Naval Weapons Center, China Lake, 1951-55; Deputy Dir. of Def. Research & Engring., Office of Secty. of Def., Wash. D.C. 1959-60; Dir. of Research & Engring., GM Def. Research Labs, Santa Barbara, 1960-66; dir., Advanced Power Systems, GM Research Labs, Warren, Mich., 1966-67; v.p. & dir., Minicars Inc., Santa Barbara, 1967-74; mgr., USN Ocean Food & Energy Farm Project, 1972-77; staff scientist, Naval Ocean Systems Center, San Diego, 1974---. Author: Hothouse Earth, Praeger, 1975; contbr. 90+ sci. articles in tech. journs. Recipient Outstanding Technical Achievement Award, IEEE, 1977. Mem. Cosmos Club, Wash. D.C., 1959-72. Unitarian. Hobbies: table tennis, tennis, chess. Res.: 882 Golden Park Ave., San Diego, CA 92106; Office: Naval Ocean Systems Center, Code 5304, San Diego, CA 92152.

WILCOX, RAY ADNA
Realtor — Civic Leader
b. Dec. 6, 1903, Quinlan, Okla.; s. William Homer and Dessie Gertrude Wilcox; ed. grad. pub. schs., bus.

adm., Woodward, Okla.; night sch., Wichita, Kan.; m. Dora Irene Kullman, Oceanside, Calif., July 19, 1927; chil.: Roberta Virginia Thill, b. June 20, 1928; Marianna Bender, b. Aug. 24, 1930. Career: Salesman, Wilcox Investment Co. 1929-32; broker-owner, Ray A. Wilcox Co. 1932---; Mayor, City of Oceanside, 1946-47; partner, Wilcox-Veteto 1956-57. Lecturer, many civic, edn. and polit. groups, L.A. Mem.: Kappa Sigma, Phi Delta Phi, Phi Beta Kappa, Order of the Coif, Mason; clubs: Harvard of Assn. 1948, pres. 1948-52, dir. 1952---; Riverside, Calif. 1958---; dir. Oceanside Natl. Bank, 1963---. Chmn., USO, pres.-chmn. bd., Crestlawn Mem. Park, Ins. 1948---; est. Eternal Hills Cemetery, Oceanside (1943-45), WW II. Mem.: pres. Oceanside-Carlsbad Realty Bd. 1936, 40, 49; pres. Oceanside C. of C. 1938-39; bd. trustees, Oceanside-Carlsbad H.S. and Jr. Coll. 1940-46; exalted ruler, Oceanside BPOE, 1944-45; Calif. State Dem. Central Com. 1946-47; v.p. El Camino Country Club, 1959---; eligible: Mayflower Soc., SAR, Order of Cincinnatis. Presbyterian (chmn. bd. trustees, 1952-53). Hobbies: hist. research, photog. Rec.: golf, music. Res.: 120 Citadel Lane, Oceanside, CA; Office: 818 Mission Ave., P.O.B. 29, Oceanside, CA.

WILCOX, THOMAS ROBERT
Chairman, Crocker National Bank
b. Aug. 23, 1916, NYC; s. Thomas W. and Louise (Latimer) Wilcox; ed. NYU 1934-38; B.A., Princeton Univ. 1940; m. Jane Collette, Mar. 28, 1943; sons: Thomas R., Kirby C., Andrew M. Career: First Natl. Bank, 1934-71, v. chmn. 1967-71; v. chmn. Blyth Eastman Dillon, 1971-73; chmn. bd.-dir.-chief exec. ofcr., Crocker Natl. Corp. and Crocker Natl. Bank, 1974---. Dir.: Colgate Palmolive Co., Hilton Hotels Corp., dir., Internat. Exec. Serv. Corps; trustee, Scripps Clinic & Research Found.; mem., Paficic Union Club (S.F.), The Conference Bd., Pan American Internat. Advis. Bd.; dir., Bay Area Council; Calif. C. of C.; mem. Stanford Univ. Advis. Council, Grad. Sch. of Bus.; A Gov. of the Los Angeles Music Center's Performing Arts Council; Marine Hist. Assn., Mystic, Conn.; trustee, Mutual Life Ins. Co. of N.Y. Mem.: Univ. Club, The Links, Bond Club, N.Y.; Bohemian Club, S.F.; Natl. Golf Links of Amer.; Office: One Montgomery St., San Francisco, CA 94104; 611 West Sixth St., Los Angeles, CA 90017.

WILEY, BOB
Sheriff-Coroner
b. Nov. 18, 1936, Kingsburg, Calif.; s. Wayne and Esther Wiley; grad. Kingsburg H.S., 1954, Porterville Coll., 1956, Nat. FBI Acad., 1972; m. Sonja Tucker, Mar. 8, 1958, Kingsburg; children: Andrea, b. June 19, 1959; Acia, b. Sept. 3, 1962; Robert, b. Apr. 29, 1967. Career: with Tulare Co. Road Dept., 1956-59; profl, rodeo competitor, participant in seven nat. finals with the top ten claf ropers, was Reserve World Champion calf roper, 1963; reserve deputy sheriff, 1962-65; elected Tulare Co. Sheriff Coroner, 1966---. Partner on high sch. sporting teams with Rafer Johnson (Olympic Decathlon winner), setting records in the 880 Relay. Mem. Porterville Elks; Visalia Moose; Woodlake Masons. Protestant. Rec.: hunting. Res.: 22894 Road 140, Tulare, CA 93274; Office: County Civic Center, Visalia, CA 93277.

WILKEY, LUCILLE VIVIEN
Pianist — Composer
b. Apr. 5, Yeddo, Ind.; d. Elmer Sylvester and Madge (Dunn) Wilkey; desc. Amer. Rev. ancestors; A.B., Univ. of Ill. 1919; Brenau Coll. Cons.; DePauw Univ.; Ind. Univ. (varsity debate). Career: Teacher (French-Spanish): Ohio Univ. 1920-21, Ariz. State Coll. 1921-22; est. Calif. res. 1922; teacher, adult edn., Long Beach, 1926-35; real estate broker, L.B., 1943---. Composer, 15 ballads. Exhibits: Long Beach Art Assn. Awards: Medalist, L.A. Eisteddfod, piano open, 1925; L.B. Eisteddfod piano open, 1926; Red Cross Award, 1957; City of Hope Award, 1960; certificate of appreciation, 1961; Community Chest Award, 1960, certificate of appreciation, 1961; Woman of Yr., Amer. Bus. Women's Assn. 1966, Natl. cit. 1966; certificate, American Achievement, DAR, Calif. State Soc. 1967; Vip Award, mus. arts, 1967. Mem.: pres., Musical Arts Club, 1943-44, bd. dirs. 1959-65, pres. 1963-66; treas. President's Club, 1943-44; L.A. Women's Committee, Met. Opera Guild, 1944; bd. dirs., L.B. Art Assn. 1946-47; Community Chest, Capt. 1957-58; Susan B. Anthony Chapter, DAR 1961---; chmn. Heart Assn.; Sym. Assn. and Guild; Founder Club, Univ. Ill.; (life) L.B. Reg. Arts Council; AAUW; IPA; Opera Guild of So. Calif.; L.B. Civic Light Opera Assn.; L.B. Bd. of Realtors; S.W. Youth Music Festival, Judge, chmn.

1966-71; Alpha Chi Omega. Republican (L.B. Council of Repub. Women So. Conv., 1960-61; del. Calif. Republic. Women's Conv. 1967). Methodist (bd. dir. 1947-51). Hobbies: oil painting, landscapes. Res.: 2330 Pasadena Ave., Long Beach, CA 90806.

WILKINSON, ROSEMARY REGINA
Poet — Author
b. Feb. 21, 1924, New Orleans, La.; d. William Lindsay, Jr. and Julia (Sellen) Challoner; gr.dau. William Lindsay Challoner, Sr., ship's captain and artist; student, San Francisco State Univ. (life Calif. poetry tching. cred.); (hon.) Doctorate humane letters, Free Univ. of Pakistan; m. Henry Bertram Wilkinson, Oct. 15, 1949 (World Poetry Day), Hayward, Calif.; chil.: Denis James, b. Jan. 17, 1952; Marian Regina (Garcia), b. Dec. 8, 1954; Paul Francis, b. Aug. 11, 1959; Richard Challoner, b. Dec. 29, 1967. Career: hospital administration, 4 years as supr., 1945-55. Publs.: A Girl's Will, 1973 (Chinese trans.) 1974-75; New Lit., Repub. of China; Calif. Poet, 1976; Earth's Compromise, 1977; It Happened To Me, 1978; 2 prose epics, An Historical Epic (Chinese trans.), 1975; Epic of the Ship's Captain/Artist, 1978; music & lyrics: Alabama March of 1965; 200 Years USA, 1976; Something's Happening, 1977. Honored by Am. Poets Fellowship Soc., 1973; Dr. Amado Yuzon, Pres., UPLI, Phillipines; World Congress of Poets, 1973, 1976; internat. woman of 1975 with laureate honors, Philippines, 1975. Pres., World Congress of Poets, 1981 (1st woman pres. in Calif.); bd. mem., World Congress of Poets, Baltimore, 1976; pres., Friends of Library, 1976-77; charter bd. mem., Burlingame Civic Arts Council, 1975-76; mem. Calif. Fedn. of Chaparral Poets, pres. Toyon Chpt. Palo Alto, 1973, 1974; mem.: Nat. League Am. Pen Women, Berkeley chpt.; bd. mem. Ina Coolbrith Circle, S.F., 1977-79; Poetry Soc. London, Eng.; Calif. Writers Club; World Poetry Soc., India; Internat. Acad. of Poets, England. Democrat. Catholic, Confrat. Christian Doctrine chpt. pres. Hobby: painting. Rec.: gardening, tennis. Home: 1239 Bernal Ave., Burlingame, CA 94010.

WILKINSON, RUTH EVANGELINE
School District Administrator
b. Dec. 6, 1925, Michigan; d. James Jr. and Ruth E. (Bauhahn) Boyce; gr.niece, Dorothea Brandt, author; B.A., Western Mich. Univ., 1963; M.S., Cal. State, Fullerton, 1974; m. Francis A. Wilkinson, June 21, 1947, Mich.; chil.: James Lee, b. Mar. 20, 1948; Gerald Wayne, b. June 7, 1949; Steven Jay, b. Aug. 23, 1950. Career: tchr., elementary schs., Michigan, California, 1942-68; spec. in reading, Corona-Norco Unified Sch. Dist., 1968-71, sch. principal, Garretson Elem. Sch., 1971---. Author: Reading Levels Program; Dear Parents. Dir., Reading Specialists of Calif. 1971-75, pres. 1973-74; v.p., Corona-Norco Adminstrs. Assn. 1976-77; pres., Hadaway Sch. PTA 1959-60. Mem.: Zonta Internat., dir. Corona chpt. 1975-77; Internat. Reading Assn.; Nat. Assn. Elem. Sch. Principals; Assn. Calif. Sch. Adminstrs.; Calif. Reading Assn.; Nat. Assn. of Sch. Curriculum Devel.; Nat., Local PTA (hon, service award, 1977); Phi Kappa Phi. Republican. Protestant; organist 1950-62. Hobby: gardening. Home: 406 E. Monterey Rd., Corona, CA 91720; Office: 1650 Garretson Ave., Corona, CA.

WILLARD, DALLAS ALBERT
Philosopher — Educator
b. Sept. 4, 1935, Buffalo, Mo.; s. Albert Alexander and Mami (Lindasmith) Willard; B.A., psychol., Tenn. Temple Coll., 1956; B.A., philosophy and rel., Baylor Univ., 1957; Ph.D. philos. Hist. of Sci., Univ. of Wis. 1964; m. Jane Lakes, Aug. 26, 1955, Water Robins, Ga.; children: John Samuel, b. 1957; Rebecca, b. 1962. Career: Knapp Fellow, research and teaching asst., Univ. Wis., 1960-64; instr. in Philosophy Dept., 1964-65; Asst. Prof. of Philosophy, USC, 1965-69, Assoc. Prof., 1969-79. Ordained minister, Southern Baptist Convention, 1956---. Publs.: many articles and translations from German in tech. journals in philosophy, incl.: A Crucial Error in Epistemology, Mind, 1967; The Paradox of Logical Psychology, Am. Phil. Quarterly 1973; Husserl's Critique of Extensionalist' Logic, Idealistic Studies, 1979. Hobbies: woodworking, carpentry. Res.: 23535 Lake Manor Dr., Chatsworth, CA 91311; Office: Philosophy Dept., USC, University Park, Los Angeles, CA 90007.

WILLARD, ROBERT EDGAR
Attorney at Law
b. Dec. 13, 1929, Bronxville, N.Y.; s. William Edgar and Ethel Marie (Van Ness) Willard; B.A., economics, Washington State Univ., 1954; J.D., Harvard Law Sch., 1958; m. Shirley Fay Cooper, May 29, 1954, Pullman,

Wash.; chil.: Laura Marie, b. June 3, 1962; Linda Ann, b. June 21, 1963; John Judson, b. Oct. 3, 1967. Career: admitted to Calif. Bar. 1959; law clerk to U.S. Dist. Judge, 1958-59; assoc. firm Flint & Mackay 1959-61; individual practice 1962-64; member firm Willard & Baltaxe, 1964-65; Baird, Holley, Baird & Galen 1966-69; Baird, Holley, Galen & Willard 1970-74; Holley, Galen Willard, 1975---. Dir., various corporations. Served with AUS 1946-48, 1950-51. Mem.: Acacia Frat., Calcutta Saddle & Cycle Club. Democrat. Congregationalist. Rec.: sports. Home: 8434 Enramada, Whittier, CA 90605; Office: 611 W. Sixth St., Suite 2400, Los Angeles, CA 90017.

WILLIAMS, JOHN H.
Property Management Executive
b. Nov. 16, 1905, Los Angeles, Calif.; s. George (pres. L.A. City Council) and Jennie Frances (Potter) Williams; ed. L.A. schs.; USC; grad. McKay Bus. Sch. 1924; m. Jennie Mae Doak, Ch. of Our Savior, San Gabriel, Calif., July 2, 1930; dau. Mrs. Wayne A. (Diane Marie) Martin, b. Mar. 16, 1941. Career: Assoc. with R.A. Rowan & Co., L.A. 1924-38; formed J.H. Williams Co., Inc. (property mgmt.-real estate ins.), So. Calif., Ore., Wash. (located 47 stores in Gallenkamp Shoe Co., Mode O'Day, See's Candy, others), 1938-42; v.p.-dir. (in chg. sales and leasing dept., property mgmt), R.A. Rowan and Co. 1942---. Pres., R.A. Rowan Mgmt. Co. Mem.: dir.-secty.-treas., L.A. Bldg. Owners and Mgrs. Assn., pres. 1953; pres., Natl. Assn. of Bldg. Owners and Mgrs. 1960; dir.-asst. secty., Merchants Fireproof Bldg. Co.; v.p. dir., Braille Inst. for the Blind; pres.-dir., L.A. Realty Bd. 1963; dir. Calif. Real Estate Assn.; dir. Natl. Assn. of Real Estate Bds.; Masonic Lodge, San Gabriel Country Club, Calif. Club. Republican. Episcopalian. Hobby: travel (USA, Mex., Honolulu, Can. and Orient). Rec.: golf, swimming. Res.: 614 Twin Palms Dr., San Gabriel, CA; Office: 180 S. Lake Ave., Pasadena, CA 91101.

WILLIAMS, JOHN HAVILAND
California Auditor General
b. Oct. 4, 1939, Omaha, Nebr.; s. Walker (v.p., Ford Motor Co., ret.) and Evelyn F. Williams; B.B.A., 1964; M.B.A., 1966; CPA, 1971; m. Gail Frances Maginnis, Sept. 15, 1973, Carmel, Calif.; children: John Walker, b. 1964; Elizabeth Buchanan, b. 1968. Career: Instr. in Accounting and Fin., Armstrong Coll., 1965-67; Supervising Auditor, U.S. General Accounting Office, 1967-71; CPA, 1971-76; Cons. to U.S. Civil Service Commn., 1970-76; Auditor Gen. of the State of Calif., 1976---. Author: three textbooks on Govtl. Acctg. and Fin. Mgmt., 1973-75. Rec.: flying, fishing, hiking. Res.: General Delivery, Shingle Springs, CA 95682; Office: 925 L. St., Suite 750, Sacramento, CA 95814.

WILLIAMS, NICK BODDIE
Editorial Consultant, Times Mirror Co.
b. Aug. 23, 1906, Onancock, Va.; s. John F. and Anne (McKown) Williams; Univ. of the South, 1922-24; A.B., Univ. of Tex. 1929; m. Elizabeth Rickenbacker (dec. Jan. 11, 1973); m. Barbara Steele Troy, June 27, 1973; chil.: Susan Fairfield, b. Jan. 14, 1935; Nick Van Boddie, b. Feb. 11, 1937; Elliott Urban, b. Jan. 2, 1946; Elizabeth M., b. Aug. 23, 1948. Career: Copy ed., Ft. Worth Star Telegram, 1927-29; telegraph ed., Nashville, Tennessean, 1929-31; staff, Los Angeles Times, 1931---, copy ed., telegraph ed., picture ed., news ed., 1931-51; asst. mng. ed. 1951-58; mng. ed. 1958-59; editor 1959-72. Mem.: Kappa Alpha, Dr. of Civil Laws, Univ. of South; Knight Order of Leopold; Dutch Treat West, Twilight Club. Episcopalian. Hobby: gardening. Res.: 23 Lagunita, Laguna Beach; and Trinidad, CA.

WILLIAMS, PHILLIP L.
Publishing Company Executive
b. Aug. 30, 1922, St. Louis, Mo.; s. Eugene J. and Blanche W. (Becker) Williams; M.B.A., Harvard Univ. Grad. Sch. of Bus. Adm. 1948; A.B. (cum laude), Harvard Voll. 1943; m. Margaret Jane Hoebee, Wellesly, Mass., June 26, 1954; chil.: Margaret Beal, b. Oct. 19, 1947; Fred Johannes, b. July 14, 1949; James Thomas, b. Mar. 3, 1956; Diane Elizabeth, b. Jan. 23, 1958. Career: Sales and mgmt., mgr. marketing development, reinforced plastics div., Owens-Corning Fiberglas Corp., NY 1948-51, 1953-60; pres.-treas.-dir., Westland Capital Corp., L.A. 1962-64; chmn.-treas.-dir., Grove Mortgage Corp., L.A. 1964-65; v.p.-asst. to the pres., Beneficial Standard Life Ins. Co., L.A. 1965---, v.p. Beneficial Standard Corp. 1967-69; v.p. Times-Mirror Co. 1969---. U.S. Pacific Fleet, gunnery ofcr.-exec. ofcr., Carrier Task Forces and Amphibious Operations, USN (1943-46), WW II;

Korean War, 1951-53; Lt. Comdr., USNR (ret.) Mem.: Harvard Club, NYC; Harvard Bus. Sch. Club, Harvard Club, So. Calif.; Calif. Yacht Club. Presbyterian (ruling elder, chmn. Chr. Edn. Com.). Hobby: reading. Rec.: swimming, travel, family activities. Res.: 1156 Amalfi Dr., Pacific Palisades, CA 90272; Office: Times-Mirror Sq., Los Angeles, CA 90053.

WILLIAMS, SPENCER M.
U.S. District Judge
b. Feb. 24, 1922, Reading Mass.; s. Theodore Ryder and Anabel (Hutchison) Williams; A.B., UCLA 1943, LL.B. 1948; m. Kathryn Bramlage, Aug. 20, 1943; chil.: Carol, Peter, Spencer, Clark, Janice and Diane. Career: admitted to Calif. Bar 1948; pvt. practice, law San Jose, 1948-49, Sacramento, 1970-71; ofc. of County Counsel, Santa Clara Co. 1949-50, 1952-55; Co. Counsel, 1955-67; apptd. admr. Calif. Health Agcy., Sacramento (by Gov. Ronald Reagan), 1967-69; secty. Human Rels. Agcy., 1969-70; U.S. Dist. Judge, No. Dist. Calif. 1971---. Fire control ofcr., USS Chaster, PTO, USNR (1943-46), WW II; Lt. Judge Advocate Gens. Ofc., USN 1950-52. Awards: San Jose Man of Year, 1954. Mem.: dir. Kiwanis Club, Willow Glen, 1954-55, pres. 1958; pres. Natl. Assn. County Civil Attys. 1963-64; pres. Calif. Dist. Atty's. Assn. 1963-64; Calif., Santa Clara Co. Bar Assns., Theta Delta Chi. Hobby: sports fan. Rec.: golf. Res.: Menlo Park; Office: U.S. Courthouse, 450 Golden Gate Ave., San Francisco, CA 94102.

WILLIAMS, THEODORE
Metal Products Company President
b. May 9, 1920; Cleveland, Oh.; s. Stanley and Blanche (Albaum) Williams; B.S., mech. engring., Univ. Mich., 1942; grad. studies in indsl. engring., bus. admin.; m. Rita Cohen, Aug. 28, 1952, Los Angeles; children: Lezlie Atlas, b. 1944; Shelley Atlas, b. 1948; Wayne, b. 1953; Patti, b. 1962. Career: pres., Wayne Products, Detroit, 1942-43, Los Angeles 1947-49; Pres., Williams Metal Products, Inglewood, 1950-59; pres., chief exec. ofcr., Bell Industries, L.A., 1970---; instr., Univ. Mich. 1942. Holder two patents in machine tool indus. 1st Lt., AUS, 1943-46, Army Ord., Saipan. V.P., Leo Baeck Temple. Hobby: photog. Res.: 435 N. Layton Way, L.A., CA; Office: 1880 Century Park E., Los Angeles, CA 90067.

WILLIAMSON, RICHARD LAVERNE
University Administrator
b. Apr. 15, 1916, Corning, N.Y.; s. Linn Robert and Ellen Anis (Church) Williamson; ed. E. H.S., Buffalo, N.Y. 1930-35; A.B., Cornell Univ. 1938; Univ. of Buffalo, 1944-46; Northwestern Univ. 1947-48, M.B.A., 1951; Ind. Univ. 1953-55 (D.B.A., econ., bus. mgmt., 1956); m. Edith Julia Cunningham, West Danby, N.Y., Oct. 23, 1938; chil.: Richard L. Jr., b. Sept. 19, 1943; Linn Douglas, b. Apr. 22, 1947; Keith Allen, b. Aug. 28, 1957; Lee Ann, b. Nov. 27, 1959. Career: Asst. instr. acct., Cornell Univ., Ithaca, N.Y. 1938-39; acct. clerk, bldg. dept. 1940-42; real estate salesman, Erma D. Perkins, Realtor, Ithaca, 1939-40; acct. clerk-traveling auditor, dept. leader, Bell Aircraft Corp., Buffalo, N.Y. 1942-45; acct. trainee, Wickwire-Spencer Steel Div., Colo. Fuel and Iron Co., Buffalo, N.Y. 1945-46; instr.-asst. prof.-dir. dept. bus. adm. and econs., Wheaton (Ill.) Coll. 1946-53; teaching assoc., Ind. Univ., Bloomington, 1953-55; asst. prof. acct., Bowling Green State Univ., Ohio, 1955-56; assoc. prof. acct., USC 1956-62, prof. 1962-67; asst. dean, Grad. Sch. of Bus. Adm. 1969-60; assoc. dean, 1960-67; dean Coll. Bus. Adm., Loyola-Marymount Univ. 1967---. Author: Salesmanship in the Christian Bookstore, 1954. Drill Sgt.-pilot, Civil Air Patrol, WW II. Mem.: com. colls.-univs. rels., L.A. Chpt., Calif. Soc. of CPAs, 1958-61, profl. development council, 1964-66; bd. dirs. 1967---; chmn. USC com., Computer Scis. Lab. 1959-66; Amer. Acct. Assn.; Amer. Inst. of CPAs; Natl. Assn. of CPAs; Pi Gamma Mu, Phi Kappa Phi, Beta Alpha Psi; pres. Beta Chpt., Beta Gamma Sigma 1963---. Pres. Hobbies: music, photog. Rec.: camping, Res.: 961 Westchester Pl., Los Angeles, CA 90019; Office: St. Roberts Hall, Loyola University, 7101 W. 80th St., Los Angeles, CA 90045.

WILLIS, BEVERLY A.
Architect
b. Feb. 17, 1928, Tulsa, Okla.; d. Ralph William and Margaret (Porter) Willis; Granddau. Charles Wm. Willis, Nebr. pioneer; B.A., Univ. Hawaii, 1954; student Univ. of So. Calif., 1956; Ore. State Univ., 1956-58. Exhibited in one man show at Maxwell Art Gallery, San Francisco, 1952; owner Willis Workshop, Honolulu, 1954-56; executed murals Palama Music

Settlement, 1955, United Chinese Soc., 1956; pres. Willis & Assoc., Inc., San Francisco, 1956. Developer The Computerized Approach to Residential Land Analysis (CARLA). Mem.: bldg. research adv. bd. Nat. Acad. Scis.; chmn., Fed. Constrn. Council; bd. dirs. San Francisco chpt. Multiple Sclerosis Soc.; N. Calif. American Inst. of Architects; (pres. designate) Cal. Heritage Council. Recipient Excellence in Design award Honolulu Art and Artist Club, 1958; Nat. award for remodeling of Campbell-Ewald Bldg., San Francisco, 1965; Significant Achievement in Beautification citation Bldgs. Mag., 1966; AIA Bay Area award for Union St. Store Devel., 1967; award of exceptional distinction for environmental design for work on Union St., Gov. Cal., 1967; named Outstanding Woman in San Francisco Bay Area, Bay Area Bus. and Profl. Women's Club, 1958, One of San Francisco Distinguished Citizens, Hearst Newspapers, 1969, Award of Merit AIA, 1976; Mem. AIA, Lambda Alpha. Important works incl. rehab. Union St. stores, Campbell-Ewald Bldg., Vine Terrace. Former contbg. editor Archtl. Forum and Columnist Condominium World; contbr. articles profl. journs.; speeches, indus. confs. and seminars. Guest lectr. Univ. Ore., 1978, Rice Univ., Stanford Univ., Women in Arch. Wash. D.C., Univ. Ill., 1977, others. Res.: 3977 Clay St., San Francisco, CA 94118; Office: 545 Mission St., San Francisco, CA 94105.

WILLIS, FRANCES ELIZABETH
  U.S. Ambassador
b. May 20, 1899, Metropolis, Ill.; d. John Gilbert and Belle Whitfield (James) Willis; A.B., Stanford Univ. 1920, Ph.D. 1923; stu. Universite Libre de Bruxelles, 1920-21; Career: instr. hist., Goucher Coll. 1923-24; instr., asst. prof. polit. sci., Vassar, 1924-27; Internat. Grenfell Assn., Labrador, 1926; foreign serv. officer, unclassified, v.-consul of career, 1927; v.-consul, Valparaiso, Chile, 1928-31; Santiago, 1931, secty. in diplomatic serv., Dec. 17, 1931; 3rd. secty., Stockholm, Brussels, Luxembourg, 1931-37; 2nd secty. and consul, Madrid, 1940-43; 1st secty. 1943-44; ofc. of the secty., Dept. of State 1944; ofc. of Under-Secty. 1944-46, div. Western European Affairs, 1946-47; 1st secty. and consul, London, 1947; U.S. Ambassador to Switz., 1947-57; Norway, 1957-61; Ceylon, 1961-64. Mem.: Phi Beta Kappa; Sulgrave Club, Wash. D.C. Episcopalian. Hobby: organized living conditions. Rec.: theater, bridge, sym. concerts. Res.: 503 W. Highland Ave., Redlands, CA.

WILLRODT, MARVIN JAMES
  Electronic Engineer
Feb. 17, 1920, Chamberlain, S.D.; s. L. Henry and Christiana (Bergner) Willrodt; student, S.D. State Univ., 1939-42; B.S. Elec. Engring., 1949; postgrad. Univ. Ill.; 1949-51; m. Alice Elizabeth Washer, Dec. 28, 1957, Cleveland, Oh.; children: Christina H., Marvin James, Donald W.; Career: with Hewlett-Packard Co., Palo Alto and Santa Clara, Calif. 1951---, applications engr. electronic measuring equipment, 1962---; Active Menlo Park (Calif.) Elementary sch., 1968---. Served with AUS, 1942-45; ETO; decorated Purple Heart. Awards: Marvin J. Willrodt Measurements Lab. dedicated at the Coll. of Engring., S.Dak. State Univ., Brooking, 1977. Named mem. S. Dak. Beta Chpt. Tau Beta Pi (hon. engring. soc.), recipient Distinguished Engr. award, SDSC, Apr. 1978. Mem. IEEE, Sigma Tau. Club: Palo Alto Hills Golf and Country. Contbg. author: Basic Electronic Instrument Handbook, 1972. Contbr. articles to tech. journs. Patentee elec. delay generation circuit, 1956. Res.: 114 University Dr., Menlo Park, CA 94025; Office: 5301 Stevens Creek, Blvd., Santa Clara, CA 95050.

WILLSON, MEREDITH
  Composer — Conductor
b. May 18, 1902, Mason City, Ia.; s. John David and Rosalie (Reiniger) Willson; ed. Damrosch Inst. of Mus. Art; m. Elizabeth Wilson, Albert Lea, Minn., Aug. 29, 1920 (div. 1948); m. Ralina Zarova, Palos Verdes, Calif., Mar. 13, 1948 (dec. Dec. 6, 1966); m. Rosemary Sullivan, Los Angeles, Calif. Feb. 14, 1968. Career: Flutist with John Philip Sousa and N.Y. Philharmonic; mus. dir., Western Div., NBC; (Broadway mus. comedies) Libretto and Score for The Music Man; Scores for The Unsinkable Molly Brown; and Here's Love. Author: (books) The Music Man; And There I Stood With My Piccolo; But He Doesn't Know the Territory; Who Did What To Fedalia?; Eggs I Have Laid; composer: You And I; May The Good Lord Bless And Keep You; others; symphonic: Symphony of San Francisco; Missions of California Suite; The Fervis Bay; O.O. MacIntyre Suite; mot. pic. scores:

The Great Dictator; The Little Foxes. Maj. U.S. Army, 1942-46, WW II. Awards: The Music Man won N.Y. Critics Award and Perry Award for best musical of 1958: First Grammy Award in history of Natl Acad. of Recording Arts & Sciences, May 4, 1959 (The Music Man album); Big Brother of the Year Award, 1961 (by John F. Kennedy, Pres. of the United States in the WhityHouse, Apr. 19, 1962; The Edwin Frank Goldman Citation (by Amer. Bandmasters Assn., Mar. 7, 1964); Proclamation The Music Man Week by City of Grand Rapids, Mich. 1961; The Music Man won Golden Globe, Best Mot. Pic. Mus., and Seventeen Mag. Best Pic. of Mo. 1962. Hon. Doctorates: Regis Coll., Denver, Colo 1973; Parson Coll., Fairfield, Ia.; Coe Coll., Cedar Rapids, Ia. Mem.: Alpha Tau Chpt., Kappa Kappa Psi; ASCAP, Amer. Comps. and Conds., Calif. Comps.; Family Club, S.F. Westwood Hills Congl. Res.: 1750 Westridge Road, Los Angeles, CA 90049.

WILSON, HOLLY SKODOL
  Nursing School Dean — University Dean
b. Mar. 24, 1943, McKeesport, Pa.; d. C.H. and Mary Skodol; B.S.N., Duke Univ., 1964; M.S. Case Western Reserve Univ., 1966; Ph.D., Univ. Calif., Berkeley; children: Hillary Mary, b. 1970; Emily Kate, b. 1974; Molly Claire, b. 1977. Career: Asst. and Assoc. Prof., Sch. of Nursing, State Univ. N.Y., Buffalo, 1966-69; Lectr. & Research Assoc., Sch. of Nursing, Univ. Calif., S.F., 1970-71, Assoc. Prof., 1978---, also Assoc. Dean, Academic Programs, 1978---; Assoc. Prof., Dept. of Nursing, Sonoma State Coll., 1974-78; prin., Inst. of Nursing Consultants, Woodside, 1976---. Co-author, Current Perspectives in Psychiatric Nursing, Vols. I & II, 1976, 1978; Psychiatric Nursing, 1979; numerous articles in nursing and trade publs. Mem.: Am. Nurses' Assn., Calif. Nurses' Assn., Western Soc. for Research in Nursing, Sigma Theta Tau, Pi Lambda Theta, Research Steering Com. mem., Western Interstate Commn. on Higher Edn.; Nat. League for Nursing, Council on Baccalaureate and Higher Degrees. Res.: 523 Hillside Ave., Mill Valley, CA 94941; Office: School of Nursing, UCSF, 3rd & Parnassus Aves., San Francisco, CA 94143.

WILSON, LEWIS KENNETH
  City Librarian
b. Mar. 15, 1925, Lamar, Colo.; s. Ben R. and Effie B. (Kenner) Wilson; A.A., Colo. Coll., 1947; B.A., UCLA, 1949; M.L.S., USC, 1952; m. Wilma Fledderman, Sept. 6, 1956, El Monte, Calif.; dau. Heidi C., b. Oct. 3, 1958. Career: Geol. Librarian, Asst. Head, Circulation Dept., UCLA, 1947-55; Bus. & Tech. Librarian, Acting City-County Librarian, Santa Barbara Pub. Lib., 1957-59; City Librn., Palo Alto City Library, 1959-68; Mgr. Dir., Dept. of Community Services, City of Palo Alto, 1968-73; City Librn., Burbank Pub. Lib., 1973=78; City Librn., San Diego Pub. Lib., 1978---. Editor: California Librn., 1968; Ed. & Compiler: Know Your Geology Library, 1954; Know Your Geologic Literature, 1955. AUS, 1943-46. Mem.: Bd. dirs., San Diego-Tema Sister City Soc., 1978---; Burbank chpt., ARC, pres. 1972-73; Burbank Advisory Com., Salvation Army, 1970-73; bd. dirs., secty. Burbank YMCA, 1972-73; bd. dirs. Burbank Historical Soc., 1970-73; Burbank Sister City Com., pres. 1972; Palo Alto YMCA, secty. bd. dirs. 1963-73; Palo Alto Sister City Com., City Liaison, 1964-73; Palo Alto/Stanford United Way, bd. dirs. 1968-73. Mem. Kiwanis Club, Beta Theta Pi frat. Democrat. Protestant. Hobby: printing. Res.: 5415 Mantua Ct., San Diego, CA 92124; Office: 202 C St., San Diego, CA 92101.

WILSON, PETER BARTON
  Mayor
b. Aug. 23, 1933, Lake Forest, Ill.; s. James Boone and Margaret (Callaghan) Wilson; B.A., Yale Univ. 1955; LL.B., J.D., Univ. Calif. Law Sch. 1962; m. Dorothea Weedn Robertson, Sacramento, Calif., July 14, 1967. Career: asst. dir. Repub. Assocs. of San Diego Co. 1963; exec. dir. Repub. Central Com. of San Diego Co. 1964; gen. practice law, Davies & Burch, S.D. 1965-66; elected to Calif. State Assembly, 1966-71; elected Mayor, City of San Diego, Nov. 1971 & 1975. USMC Inf. ofcr. 1955-58. Awards: Outstanding Young Man of Yr., San Diego, 1968; Top Perf. Award, House & Home Mag. 1969; Outstanding Environmentalist of 1971 by Calif. Council of Landscape Archs., Calif. Mus. of Sci. and Indus. Fellowship, Honorary mem. Amer. Inst. of Architects, Anti-Defamation League of B'nai B'rith, S.D. C. oc C., YMCA, P. Leag. of Calif. Cities, Coastal Zone Mgmt. Adv. Com., Conservation Found., Natl. Assn. Reg.

Councils, Calif. Center for Research & Edn. in Govt., Calif. Manpower Plan. Council, Council for Urban Econ. Dev., City of Hope Pilot Med. Center, Natl. Conf. Chrs. and Jews, Inst. for Burn Med., Big Brothers, Inc., San Diego Kiwanis Club, Century Club, v.p. Muscular Dystrophy Assoc., Rose Institute. Office: City Adm. Bldg., 202 C St., San Diego, CA 92101.

WILSON, ROBERT CHARLES
Electronics Company President
b. Jan. 9, 1920, Hazelton, Idaho; s. John Willard and Daisy Irene (Sothern) Wilson; B.S., mech. engring., Univ. of Calif., Berkeley, 1941; m. Frances Miller, Feb. 1, 1947, Nutley, N.J.; children: Eleanor S., b. 1949; Kathleen S., b. 1951; Deborah B., b. 1955. Career: With General Electric Co., 1941-43, 1946-49; v.p. 1966-69, corp. v.p., then pres., Comml. Products Group, No. American Rockwell, 1969-71, exec. v.p., Indsl. Products and Electronics, 1971, also dir., mem. exec. com.; pres. and CEO, Collins Radio Co., 1971-74, also dir., mem. exec. com.; pres., chmn., CEO, Memorex Corp., Santa Clara, 1974---. Co-author: Capacitors for Industry, 1950. Lt., USN 1943-46. Hobbies: fishing, boating. Rec.: jogging, golf. Office: Memorex Corp., 12-40, San Tomas at Central Expy., Santa Clara, CA 95052.

WILSON, ROBERT C.
United States Congressman
b. Apr. 5, 1916, Calexico, Calif.; s. George Wellington and Olive Blanche Wilson; ed. S.D. State Coll.; Otis Art Inst.; chil.: Mrs. James S. Wilson, b. Jan. 1, 1939; Mrs. Michael Chapple, b. Feb. 15, 1942; Bryant, b. Nov. 24, 1949; m. 2d. Shirley Haughey Sarret, May 16, 1974. Career: Adv. and pub. rels.; v.p. The Tolle Co. 1946-63; elected to 83rd Congress, 36th Dist. of Calif. 1952, re-elected, 1954-78. Inf., operated Conship Commissary, WW II. Mem.: past pres., S.D. Jr. C. of C.; Amer. Legion Post 434; Advertising and Sales Club; Chula Vista Rotary Club; past pres. 20-30 Club; BPOE No. 168, Aztec Alumni Assn., Repub. Assembly; chmn. Natl. Repub. Cong. Com. 1961-69. Office: 2307 Rayburn House Office Bldg., Wash. D.C. 20515; 880 Front St., San Diego, CA.

WILSON, STANLEY THOMAS
Publisher
b. Feb. 1, 1911, Los Angeles, Calif.; s. Lawrence G. and Lessie (Worrall) Wilson; ed. Univ. of Redlands, 1930-31; m. Billie Ross, Long Beach, Calif., Nov. 19, 1932; chil.: Roy, b. May 24, 1935; Jim, b. Nov. 25, 1939. Career: Apprentice, printing bus. Casa Grande Dispatch, Ariz. (age 12 yrs.), 1923-25; writer, Casa Grande News for: Ariz. Daily Star, Tucson; Ariz. Gazette, Phoenix; Tucson Citizen; sports writer, San Bernardino Sun, 1930-31; reporter, Orange Daily News, 1931-38; circulation mgr., San Rafael Independent, 1938-45; purchased Mill Valley Record, 1945, publ. 1945-53; co-owner-publ., Turlock Daily Journal, 1953-65 (ret.). Mem.: pres. Calif. Circulation Mgrs. Assn. 1944; pres. Mill Valley Rotary Club, 1949; Calif. State Repub. Central Com. 1950; dir. Natl. Adv. Serv., Chicago, 1951; pres. Calif. Newspaper Publs. Assn. 1952; pres. Turlock Rotary Club, 1956; Palm Springs Rotary, Seven Lakes Country Club, Kappa Sigma Sigma, Sigma Delta Chi. Hobbies: fishing, golf. Res.: 309 Westlake Terrace, Seven Lakes Country Club, Palm Springs, CA 92262.

WILSON, STEVE D.
Research Director
b. May 9, 1928, Frackville, Pa.; s. Menes and Jennie Wilson; B.S., 1954; M.A., 1955; Ph.D., 1962: studied radiation biology, Univ. of Hawaii; biology, Cal. Tech Summer Inst.; physics scholarship, Univ. Calif., Berkeley; m. Nora Naur, Sept. 1, 1957, Solvang, Calif. Career: (past) asst. prof. of Nuclear Sci., Louisiana State Univ., asst. prof. of Zoology and Histology, Orange Coast Coll.; pres. and research dir., Solar Research Industries, Inc., 1976---; solar cons. ---; director of research, W.R.I. Inc. 1967---. Research and devel.: work on nine microscopic systems, pub. Applied and Experimental Microscopy, Buegess Pres 1967; ion generator; (for W.R.I. Inc.): highly efficient gas burner, centrifugal gas separator, new propane pressure-liquid device; absorption-transmission solar collector for greenhouse application and coiled flat plate solar collector (patents applied for); Publs.: Investigations Into Optical Contrast and High Resolution of Highly Refractile Living Organisms, Univ. Athens Press 1962; article in Applied Optics, 1966; Poetry Zodiac, London Lit. Editions Ltd. 1971. Served AUS, Corps Engrs. Pres., California Taxpayers Assn. Home: 101 Lily Way, Manresa Beach, CA 95076; Office: 8017 Soquel Dr., Aptos, CA 95003.

WIMMER, ELIZABETH JANE
Media Relations Executive
b. Duluth, Minn.; d. Thomas E. and Mercedes (Cashin) Wimmer; A.A., Univ. Wis.; B.J., Univ. Mo. Career: news editor, South Bay Daily Breeze, Torrance, 1958-63; copy editor, San Diego Union, 1963-67; correspondent Copley News Service, L.A. Bureau, 1967-68; mgr. of Media Relations, Los Angeles Dept. Water & Power, 1968---. Served USMC, Women's Reserve. Mem.: Women in Communication, past v.p. L.A. Chpt.; mem. Exec. Com., Women's Council, L.A. Area C. of C.; Calif. Press Women, Inc., past pres. L.A. Dist.; Greater Los Angeles Press Club; Marines Mem. Union; Catholic Press Council; Radio and TV News Assn. of So. Calif.; Nuclear Energy, Women. Res.: 1505 Laurel St., So. Pasadena, CA 91030; Office: 111 N. Hope St., Los Angeles, CA 90051.

WIMMER, GLEN ELBERT
Engineer — Management Consultant
b. Feb. 16, 1903, Creston, Iowa; s. Frank E. and Carrie Elizabeth Wimmer; B.S.M.E., Iowa State Univ., 1925, M.S.M.E., 1933; M.B.A., Northwestern Univ., 1935; m. Mildred G. McCullough, May 18, 1938, Chicago, Ill.; son Frank Thomas. Career: appointments include: instr. Mech. Engring., Mich. Coll. of Mining and Technology, 1936-67; Machine Designer, Firestone Tire and Rubber Co., Ohio, 1937-38; Engineer in Charge of Design, Chicago, Ill., 1938-39; Asst. to Chief Engr., Victograph Corporation, 1939-40; Designer, Tools and Machinery, Pioneer Engineering and Mfg., Detroit, 1940-41; Designer and cHecker, Engring. Service Corp., Detroit, 1942; Checker and Asst. Supt. of Design, Norman E. Miller and Assoc., Detroit, 1942; Engring. Checker, Lee Engring. Co., Detroit, 1942-43; Head of Design and Devel. Dept., Cummins Perforator Co., Chicago, 1943-45; Instr., Cost Analysis, Evenings, Illinois Institute of Technology, 1946-47; Staff Engr., in Charge of Design and Devel. Tammen and Denison Inc., Chicago, 1945-58; Engr., Barnes and Reinecke Inc., Chicago, 1958-60; Devel. Engr., B.H. Bunn and Co., Chicago, 1960-61; Engr., Barnes and Reinecke Inc., Chicago, 1961-68; Private practice, 1968---. Mem.: Ill Soc. Profl. Engrs.; Nat. Soc. Profl. Engrs.; Am. Ordnance Assn.; Soc. of Automotive Engrs.; Soc. Mfg. Engrs.; Delta Chi; Internat. Platform Assn.; dir., Ill. Engring. Council, 1958-66. Home: 3839-48 Vista Campana So., Oceanside, CA 92054.

WINANS, ALLAN D.
Poet
b. Jan. 12, 1936, San Francisco; s. Allan Davis, Sr. and Claire (Grierson) Winans; A.B., San Francisco State Univ., 1962. Career: Juvenile Probation Ofcr., Modesto, 1964; Special Agent, Alcoholic Beverage Control, State of Calif., 1965; Special Agent, Office of Naval Intelligence, 1965-72; Special Agent, Def. Investigative Service, 1973; freelance writer, 1973-75; editor-writer, San Francisco Art Commn., Neighborhood Arts Program-CETA, 1975---. Author of 7 books of poetry; poetry, prose, essays have appeared in over 300 lit. journs. and anthologies in U.S., Canada, New Zealand, Australia, England, Germany, Latin Am., etc. Grantee P.E.N. Writers, 1973; founder: Second Coming Mag. and Second Coming Press, 1970s, Nat. Endowment for the Arts grantee. Mem. Bd. dirs., COSMEP (Com. Small Mag. Editors and Pubs.) 1972-75; founder, WIP (Western Independent Pubs.), 1978---. USAF, 1954-58. Mem.: P.E.N. Writers Assn., CCLM (Coord. Council of Lit. Mags.). Hobby: photog. Res.: P.O.B. 31249, San Francisco, CA 94131; Office: Bldg. 312, Fort Mason, San Francisco, CA.

WINKLER, MARIANNE
Realtor
b. May 29, 1926, Detroit, Mich.; d. Philip and Charlott (Hoff) Osborne; student, real estate law, Santa Ana Coll., 1968-69; m. "Wink" Winkler, May 24, 1945, Detroit, Mich.; dau. Linda (Daly), b. Jan. 17, 1972. Career: with Denver Abstract Co. (pioneering micro-film records), 1946; with Title Insurance Co., L.A. (program, data computer), 1960; with Empire Title Co. 1963; real estate agent, Stephens Investment Co., 1965; mgr. Abbot Realty, Garden Grove, 1966; with Star Realty, 1968-70; licensed real estate broker, 1968; with United Properties — Investments, Inc., 1971---; started Villa Realty, Chino, 1969-71. Recipient: Good Citizenship award; commendations from cities of Garden Grove and Stanton; top sales agent with United 4 times since 1973. Active, leader, Girl Scouts of Am. Roman Catholic; tchr. certificate C.C.C. Hobby: bridge. Rec.: travel. Home: 8902 Lola, Anaheim, CA; Office: 9919 Walker, Cypress, CA 90630.

WINSOR, TRAVIS
Physician
b. Dec. 1, 1914, San Francisco, Calif.; s. Wiley and Mabel (McCarthy) Winsor; desc. Bishop Wiley, Meth. med. missionary to China; ed. Univ. of Calif. 1936; M.D., Stanford Univ. 1941; Tulane Univ. 1945; m. Elizabeth Adams, Alameda, Calif., Sept. 1, 1939; chil.: David Wiley, b. Mar. 1, 1942, New Orleans, La.; Susan Elizabeth, b. July 7, 1945, Los Angeles, Calif. Career: Intern, Alameda Co. Hosp. 1941; instr. in med., Tulane Med. Sch. New Orleans, La. 1941-45; visiting phys., Charity Hosp. New Orleans, 1941-45; clin. instr. USC Med. Sch. 1942-47; asst. clin. prof. 1947---: certified, cardiovascular diseases; dir. Heart Research Found., Los Angeles, 1954---. Lecturer, Army postgrad., basic sci. course, Walter Reed Hosp., Wash., D.C. 1948-49. Author: The Heart in Patients with Sickle Cell Anemia; Phlebostatis Axis Reference Level for Venous Pressure in Man, 1945; The Influence of Sodium Tetrathionate on the Raty of Blood Flow to the Digits, 1948; co-author: Syphilitic Coronary Stenosis with Nyocardial Infarction; Tuberculous Pericarditis with Effusion, 1942; The Phlebomanometer: A New Apparatus for Direct Measurement of Venous Pressure in Large and Small Veins, 1943; A Study of the Rate of Sedimentation of Erythrocytes in Sickle Cell Anemia; The Rate of Insensible Perspiration, 1945; Venous Pressures in Children in Health and Disease, 1947; A Primer of Electrocardiography, publ. Lea & Febiger (in 3 langs), 3rd edit. 1955; (textbook) Peripheral Vascular Diseases, publ. by Chas. Thomas; editor, EKG Test Book, publ. by Amer. Heart Assn. Mem.: ACP 1947; fellow, Periphral-Vascular Sect., Amer. Heart Assn. 1949---; AMA, Soc. for Experimental Biology and Med., Amer. Fed. for Clin. Research, Western Soc. for Clin. Research, Calif. Soc. for Internal Med., L.A. Soc. of Internal Med., Calif. Heart Assn., Med. Symposium Soc. of L.A.; fellow, Amer. Coll. of Chest Phys. 1955; fellow, Amer. Assn. for Advancement of Sci.; Internat. Cardiovascular Soc., Lake Arrowhead Yacht Club, Sigma Phi, Alpha Kappa Kappa, (hon.) Sigma Xi. Episcopalian. Hobby: magic. Rec.: swimming, boating, skiing, hiking. Res.: 541 S. Lorraine Blvd., Los Angeles, CA; Office: 4041 Wilshire Blvd., Los Angeles, CA 90005.

WISHON, JOHN ALBERT
Attorney at Law
b. Jan. 17, 1945, Los Angeles; s. Frank Rowntree and Dorothy (Woodhouse) Wishon; A.B. acctg., psychol., San Diego State Univ., 1968; J.D., Univ. San Diego, 1971. Career: private law practice, sr. partner (real estate law), Lieb, Wishon, Catterlin, Gay, 1972-76; vice. pres., gen. counsel, Hotel del Coronado, 1976---. Awarded certificate, Outstanding service, Phi Delta Phi law frat. 1970; selected from over 3,000 candidates as gen. counsel, Hotel del Coronado, constrd. 1887, designated both state, national historic landmark. Mem.: bd. dir., Coronado C. of C.; advisory com., S.D. Convention and Visitors Bureau; San Diego C. of C., pres. council 1978; San Diego and Am. Bar Assns.; Navy League; Coronado Hist. Assn.; Coronado Residential Assn.; S.D. Marlin Club, 1958---; judge adv. 1976; West Atwood Yacht Club, vice admiral 1972; Rotary Internat. 1976---; Sigma Alpha Epsilon; Phi Delta Phi law frat., pres. 1970; bd. dir., Sigma Alpha Epsilon Alumni, 1976---. Home: 412 Palm Ave., Coronado, CA 92118; Office: Hotel del Coronado, Coronado, CA 92118.

WITT, JOHN WILLIAM
City Attorney
b. Aug. 30, 1932, Los Angeles; A.B., USC, 1953; J.D., 1960; grad. studies in fin., San Diego State Univ.; m. Lenora J. Ticknor, Sept. 1, 1961, San Diego; children: John David, b. 1962; Stephanie Anne, b. 1965; William Westervelt, b. 1973. Career: admitted State Bar of Calif., U.S. Supreme Ct. Bar (on motion of late rep. Hale Boggs); Deputy City Atty., San Diego, 1961-64; Chief Criminal Dep. City Atty. 1964-67; Chief Dep. City Atty., 1967-69; Elected City Atty., City of San Diego, 1969, re-elected 1973, 77---. Pres., City Atty's. Dept., League of Calif. Cities, 1976-77; trustee, Nat. Inst. of Municipal Law Officers, 1976---; chmn. Municipal Labor Rels. Com., 1970-76; Bd. of Visitors, Sch. of Law, Univ. San Diego, 1974---; Advis. Com. to FCC on Fed., State, Local Regulation of Cable TV, 1972-74. USMC, 1955-57; Col., USMCR, 1975---. Contbr. articles to law revs. and journs. Mem.: Am. and San Diego Co. Bar Assn.; Calif. Conf. of Pub. Utility Counsel Phi Alpha Delta; BSA, exec. bd., 1970---, Distinguished Eagle Scout Award recipient 1975; bd. trsutee, Boys' Clubs of S.D., 1976---; Pt.

Loma Optimist Club of S.D., pres. 1975-76. Episcopalian, Vestryman, Parish Chancellor. Office: City Adminstrn. Bldg., 202 C St., San Diego, CA 92101.

WITTER, WENDELL WINSHIP
Consultant, Dean Witter Reynolds, Inc.
b. Oct. 16, 1910, Berkeley, Calif.; s. George Franklin and Mary Ann (Carter) Witter; ed. A.B., Univ. of Calif. 1932; m; Florence Corder, Oct. 18, 19355 (div. 1973); m. 2d. Janet Hutchinson Alexander (dec. 1977), Dec. 11, 1973; dau. Mrs. J. Philip (Wendelyn) Kistler; m. 3d. Evelyn Gooding, Mar. 26, 1978. Career: Assoc. with Dean Witter & Co. 1933---, partner 1950-68, exec. v.p. 1968-75, consultant 1975-78; cons., Dean Witter Reynolds Inc., 1978---. USAAF 1941-46; Lt. Col., AUS; chief, Price Adjustment Sect. AAF, Western Procurement Dist., WW II. Mem.: pres., Assn. of Stock Exchange Firms, 1961; chmn. Calif. Group, Investment Bankers Assn., 1963; past dir.: United Community Fund, S.F. Sales Execs. Assn., S.F. YMCA; dir. Sarah Dix Hamlin School; pres. Univ. of Calif. Alumni Assn. 1968-70; ex. off., regent, Univ. of Calif. 1969-70; Pac. Coast Stock Exch.; trustee, S.F. Bay Area Council; trustee, Calif. State Univ. and Colls. 1971-79; dir. S.F. Better Bus. Bur. 1972-76; dir.-treas. Golden Gate Chpt., Amer. Natl. Red Cross, 1972-78; bd. govs. S.F. Symphony, 1972-81; Zeta Psi; clubs: The Pac.-Union, Bohemian, S.F. Golf, Commonwelath Club of Calif. Episcopalian (bd, Diocese of Calif. 1969---; Grace Cath., S.F.). Hobby: golf. Res.: 303 Deer Hollow, Napa, CA 94558; Office: 45 Montgomery St., San Francisco, CA 94106.

WOELLNER, FREDRIC PHILIP
University Professor — Lecturer
b. Feb. 18, 1890, Cincinnati, Oh.; s. George Jacob and Katherine (Hamer) Woellner; ed. Woodward H.S., Cincinnati, 1908; A.B., Univ. of Cincinnati, 1912; diploma, Cincinnati Teachers Coll., 1912; M.A., Columbia Univ. 1915; Ph.D. 1923; LL.D., Coll. of Osteopathic Phys. and Surgs., L.A.; Litt. D., USC 1960; LL.D., Sch. of Med. Univ. of Calif., Irvine, 1966; m. Alice Lamont Dunkman, Nov. 22, 1915. Career: Teacher, elem. schs., Cincinnati, 1912-14; hist. critic, pvt. schs. of Teachers Coll. (Columbia), 1914-15; teacher-head of dept., Buffalo State Teachers Coll. 1915-21; research scholar, Columbia, 1921-23; lecturer, Univ. of Calif. 1923-25; assoc. prof.-prof. of edn., UCLA 1925-57, prof. emeritus, 1957---, extension lectr., Univ. of Calif., Berkeley and L.A.; lectr., Sun. Morning Club of Pasa. Presbyterian Ch. 1928---; lectr., Univ. of Hawaii, Univ. of Pa., Columbia (summers), others; broadcast lecturer, radio pgms. Author: Type Studies in Amer. Hist. (Vol. IV), 1921; Education for Citizenship, 1923; How We Govern, 1926; Highlands of the Mind, 1930; Life of Carrie Chapman Catt, 1941; The Key to Corinth, 1942; The Elements of Human Engineering, 1943; My Fifty Year Love In at UCLA, publ. 1969; contrib. many articles to mags. Mem. Civil Serv. Comm., City of L.A. 93 terms of 5 yrs.); adv. bd., Bank of Amer., 1934-46. Awards: Hon. Mem. Calif. State Legislature, 1936; Calif. Teacher of Yr., 1960; Professor of the Century, Alumni Assn. of UCLA (class 1952); Mem.: The Order of the Golden Star, Theta Xi, for 50 years of service membership; (hon. life) L.A. C. of C., Theta Xi, Alpha Phi Omega, Phi Delta Kappa, Mason (32° K.C.C.H.—, Amer. Acad. of Politics; Amer. Acad. of Political Soc. Sciences; (hon.) Lions Club; Jonathan Club, San Diego. Repub. Presbyterian (ruling elder; comr. to Gen. Assem., 1936). Res.: 432 S. Curson Ave., Los Angeles, CA 90036.

WOLFE, BURTON H.
Writer
b. Sept. 2, 1932, Washington, D.C.; s. Simon and Gertrude (Hinkle) Wolfe; B.A., spl. honors in journalism, George Washington Univ., 1954. Career: H.S. sports reporter, Wash. Daily News, 1950; Copyboy, cub reporter, Wash. Post, 1954; Reporter, columnist, Stars & Stripes/European Edit. 1955-56; Reporter, Burlington (Vt.) Free Press, 1957, International News Service, 1958; Freelance, 1959. Editor-pub. The Californian magazine, 1960-62; Public relations, B'nai B'rith, 1963; Publs. ed., Am. Fedn. of State, County & Municipal Employees, AFL-CIO, 1964; Editor-writer, Civic Education Service, 1965; Freelance writer, 1966---. Contbg. editor, Resident Physician, 1963-66; Stringer, Playboy, 1966, Ramparts, 1967; contbg. editor, City of San Francisco Weekly,

1975; contbg. writer, San Francisco Bay Guardian, 1968---. Publs.: 9000+ articles in various newspapers worldwide; 300+ articles in nat. mags., anthologies, encys., govt. publs.; Books: The Hippies (New American Library/Signet, 1968); Hitler and the Nazis (Putnam, 1970), selection of Child Study Association List; The Devil and Dr. Noxin (Wild West Publishing House, 1973); Pileup on Death Row (Doubleday, 1973); The Devil's Avenger: A Biography of Anton Szandor LaVey (Pyramid, 1974). Awards: AP Newswriting Award, 1957; Beta Phi Gamma Nat. Hon. Journalisn Frat. Award, 1962; Catholic Press Assn. Journalism Award for Best Non-Fiction, 1960, for Spirit of Ecumenism, 1970; Jane A. Harrah Mem. Media Bar Award, 1975 (bar assn. award). Sgt., AUS, 1954-56. Mem. Marines Mem. Club, Phi Beta Kappa. Hobbies: programming music tapes, handicapping horse races. Address: P.O.B. 1199, San Francisco, CA 94101.

WOLFE, HARVEY GWYNNE
Lecturer — Consultant
b. May 15, 1916; LL.B., Univ. Chicago, 1937, J.D., 1942; LL.M., 1945; LL.D (hon.); grad., Industrial Coll.; U.S. Army Command and Gen. Staff Coll. Career: adminstrv. asst., Wolfe Labs., 1937-39, vice pres., 1939-42; served to Col., U.S. Army (ret.), 1942-71; served as Deputy Dir. of Spec. Investigations in Great Britain, Liaison Officer to Scotland Yard, M.I.-5, The French Surete and Deuxieme Bureau; as spec. agent headed intelligence opn. for iron curtain penetration. Currently security cons., bus. & indus.; lecturer on espionage ---. Represented by Jack Blue Agency, Denver, Co.; Assoc. Clubs, Topeka, Kan.; Nat. Artist & Lecture Service, Studio City, Ca.; Ty Jurras Agency, Encino, Ca. Author: Not in Vain, 1940; Spies & Secret Agents, 1940; Fifth Columns Aren't New, 1941. Mem.: Rotary, Shrine; Fellow, Am. Assn. of Criminologists; So. Calif. Counter-Intelligence Corps Assn., past pres.; Delta Kappa Epsilon. Address: P.O.B. 3514, Grand Central Sta., Glendale, CA 91201.

WOLFE, THOMAS
Investment Company President
b. June 12, 1901, David City, Nebr.; s. Thomas and Modessa (Gueist) Wolfe; B.S., Northwestern Univ. 1924; m. Ehtel Ashley, Chicago, Ill, Apr. 16, 1925; son: Thomas, Jr., b. July 30, 1927. Career: Dist. mgr., United Airlines, 1926=36; v.p. Western Airlines, Inland Air Lines, 1936-46; exec. v.p., Pan Amer. World Airways, 1946-48; pres. Wolfe Enterprises, Consultants, 1948-50; pres.-chmn. bd., Pac. Air Motive Co. 1950-56; dir. procurement, Dept. of Def., Wash. D.C. 1956-58; pres. Wolfe Investment Company and Wolfe Property Company, 1958---. Dir.: Rexall Drug Co., Interstate Engraving Co., Adjustize Co., Drewry Photo Color Corporation, Copaltronics Corp.; pres. Aircraft Serv. Assn., Wash. D.C.; Air Calif.; Wyo. Air Serv.; pres. So. Calif. Aviation Council, 1969---; com. pres.-chmn. USC Aviation Council, Inc. Calif. State Atty's. Adv. Council, and others. Author: Air Transportation and Management, publ. McGraw-Hill, 1951. Construction operator, U.S. to Russia Air Route, WW II. Mem.: dir. S.F. C. of C.; L.A. Co. Museum, Harvey Mudd Coll. Forward Com., Aircraft Serv. Assn., Ontario Airport Friends; Clubs: Saddle & Sirloin, Rancheros Visitadores, Calif., Bohemian, Valley Hunt, Newport Harbor Yacht. Episcopalian. Hobby: photog., flying, horses. Res.: 1195 Rancheros Rd., Pasadena, CA; Office: 1191 Rancheros Rd., Pasa., CA; and 380 E. Green St., Pasadena, CA 91101.

WOLFE, THOMAS III
Business Executive
b. July 30, 1927, Evanston, Ill.; s. Thomas (aviation pioneer, author and bus. exec.) and Ethel (Ashley) Wolfe; B.A., Univ. of Calif. 1950; M.B.A., USC; chil.: James Ashley, b. July 10, 1953; Ann Ashley, b. Apr. 4, 1956; Patricia, b. Apr. 17, 1960. Career: Inspector, Mission Elec. Mfg. Co., Pasadena, Calif. 1950-51; research dir.-v.p., Pac. Viking Corp. (subsidiary), Wham-O Mfg. Co., San Gabriel, 1951-54; dir. Wolfe Enterprises, 1951---; v.p.-dir., Nay-Wolfe Engring. asst to pres., Trust Deed & Mortgage Exch. of L.A. 1958-60; pres.-dir., Wolfe Property Co., 1960---. Author: So. Calif. Management Consulting Survey, USC Lib. Naval Amphibious Corps., S. Pac. (1945-46), WW II; 1st Lt., USAF Reserve, 1951-60. Mem.: Beta Beta, Psi Upsilon, Skull & Keys, BPOE, Newport Harbor Yacht Club, Peninsula Point Racquet Club; Rancheros Visitadores. Episcopalian. Hobby: skiing, sailing, sailing, tennis. Res.: 205 7th St., Balboa, CA 92661; Office: Wolfe Property Co., Cabin 18, Cannery Village, 425 30th St., Newport Beach, CA 92663.

WOLFF, VICTORIA
Freelance Writer
b. Dec. 10, 1910, Heilbronn, Germany; d. Jacob I. and Truia Victor; B.S. chem., Univ. Heidelberg, Munich; m. Dr. Erich Wolff, Sept. 9, 1949, Los Angeles; chil.: Julie (Amador); Frank. Career: author seventeen publ. books: novels, geographies, incl. Fabulous City, hist. of old L.A.; four films; correspondent of European mags. and newspapers. Mem. Hollywood Foreign Press; Press Club. Rec.: sports. Address: Los Angeles, CA, (213) 939-1828.

WOLFORD, HELEN MOORE
Civic Leader
b. Sept. 30, 1922, Indio, Calif.; d. John C. and Margaret (McGregor) Moore; student, Univ. Calif., Berkeley, 1941-43; Harvard Coll., 1945; UCLA, 1955; m. Richard H. Wolford, Feb. 13, 1943, Cambridge, Mass.; children: Richard George, b. 1944; Mrs. Daniel Morrow, b. 1949; Peter Arlington, b. 1951. Career: Exec. Pres. of Blue Ribbon 400, Music Center of Los Angeles, 1979; v.p., Performing Arts Council, Music Center, 1979; trustee, Calif. Inst. of the Arts, 1979---, trustee, UCLA Found., 1979---, Hon. Mem. of Bd., UCLA Art Council, 1979---; Creator, Hollywood Bowl Open House (serves over 60,000 children annually). Chmn. 1st children's concert at Hollywood Bowl for 10,000+ children, past chmn. Hollywood Bowl Vols.; past: dir. Harvard Law Sch. Nursery Sch., Cambridge, Mass.; pres., Jr. Programs of Calif.; v.p., Children's Hosp. of L.A. Doll Fair; pres. UCLA Art Council; chmn. Thieves Mkt. for UCLA Art Council; Co-chmn. Special Gifts for Marlborough Sch. Awards: Los Angeles Times Woman of the Year, 1970; Distinguished Service Award for Community Service from UCLA; Friend to the Children from Calif. Jr. Programs. Rec.: golf, sailing. Res.: 2201 La Mesa Dr., Santa Monica, CA 90402; Office: Music Center, 135 N. Grand, Los Angeles, CA 90012.

WOLFORD, RICHARD HOWARD
Attorney at Law
b. Aug. 12, 1922, Chicago, Ill.; s. Darwin H. and Lila F. Wolford; ed. A.B., Harvard Univ. 1943, LL.B. 1948; m. Helen Moore, Cambridge, Mass., Feb. 13, 1943; chil.: Richard George, b. Sept. 27, 1944; Felicia Jane (Wolford) Morrow, b. May 23, 1949; Peter Arlington, b. Nov. 14, 1951. Career: Law Clerk, U.S. Ct. of Appeals, 9th Circuit, 1948; atty. Gibson, Dunn & Crutcher law firm, 1949---, sr. partner, 1966---. Dir. Ludlow Corp. 1970---. 1st Lt., Field Artillery, U.S. Army. Mem.: trustee, L.A. Co. Bar Assn. 1957-58; bd. dirs. Visiting Nurses Assn. of L.A. 1963-69; Commr. Calif. Law Rev. Comm. 1968-70; pres. Salt Air Club, 1970-72; California Club, Los Angeles Country Club. Episcopalian. Rec.: golf, tennis, sailing. Res.: 2201 La Mesa Dr., Santa Monica, 90402; Office: 515 S. Flower St., Los Angeles, CA 90071; and 2020 Century Park East, 40th Flr., Los Angeles, CA 90067.

WOOD, CLARA CHALOUPKA
Educator
b. Aug. 10, 1917, Yale, Iowa; d. Frank and Mary Elizabeth (Greenawalt) Wood; B.A., Manchester Coll. 1940; B.D., Yale Univ., 1945, M.A. 1946; Th.D., Pacific Sch. of Religion, 1959; m. Bruce K. Wood, June 13, 1940, Arlington, Va.; children: Loretta Jean (McNulty), b. 1950; Roger Bruce, b. 1951; Carol Rebecca, b. 1953; Marvin Chaloupka, b. 1955. Career: Tchr., secondary schs., Iowa and Ind.; Assoc. Dir., Prof., Mont. Sch. Rel., Montana State Univ. 1951-54; mission work (ch. of Brethren) Poland, 1946-49; pastor, Oakland Ch. of the Brethren, 1956-58; instr., Lewis and Clark Coll., Portland, Ore. 1960-61; instr., Diablo Valley Coll., 1964---. Pres., Am. Assn. of Women Ministers, 1953-55; dir., Brethren Service in Poland, 1946-49; mem. bd. dirs. and exec. com., Nat. Assn. for Humanities Edn., 1972-77, bd. dir., Nat. Humanities Faculty, 1977---. Co-author: Readings in the Humanities. Mem.: Nat. Orgn. of Women; Nat. Edn. Assn.; Calif. Humanities Assn.; Classical League. Hobbies: opera, Languages. Res.: 1011 Villa Nueva, El Cerrito, CA; Office: Diablo Valley College, Pleasant Hill, CA.

WOOD, MARYLAIRD LARRY
Journalist — Writer — Educator
b. Sandpoint, Ida.; d. Edward and Alice (McNeel) Small; B.A. (magna cum laude), Univ. Wash. 1938, M.A. (hons.), 1940; postgard. Stanford Univ. and Univ. Calif., Berkeley; m. Byron Wood (dec. 1975), Seattle, Wash., Jan. 30, 1942; chil.: Marylaird, Marcia, Barry. Carre: Newspaper columnist and freelance writer, approx, 2,500 articles publ. natl. mags. (subjs.: homes

and gardens, interior decoration, family and community, health, adoptions, chil., sports, sci., conservation, parks and rec., West Coast travel) incl. Parents', Sports' Illus., Mechanix Illus., Better Homes and Gardens, Amer. Home, House and Home, 1942---; feat. writer, Seattle Times, 1942-46; by-lined columnist, Oakland Tribune and San Francisco Chronicle, 1946---; Seattle Times Mag.; CSM News Syn. feat. series, 1975; 1500 publ. articles-features. Asst. Prof. of Journalism, Calif. State Univs. and Colls., 1974---, with appointments at San Diego State Univ., San Jose State Univ., Calif. State Univ., Hayward. Faculty mem., journalism, Univ. of Calif., Berkeley, Ext. Div., 1978---. Public relations dir.: YWCA and USO, Seattle, 1942-46; Oakland YWCA, No. Calif. Children's Home Soc. of Calif., and Eastbay Reg. Park Dist. 1946-56; Eastbay Girl Scouts, Eastbay Camp Fire Girls, Amer. Cancer Soc., Eastbay Hosp. Conf., Chil's. Med. Center of No. Calif., Oakland Park Dept., Amer. Assn. Park Execs. and Calif. Garden Show. Lecturer: Profl. and edn. orgns., incl. No. Calif. Writers' Conf., Calif. Writers' Club and Oakland Tribune; speakers' bur. Oakland Pub. Schs. Awards: Spec. Serv. Award for writing, U.S. Inf. Serv.; Woman of Yr. for Eastbay, Theta Sigma Phi, 1952; feat. Foremost Women in Publs., USA, 1970, others; award winner from Natl. Park Serv. and Natl. Forest Serv. for conservation features, 1976, 77, 78; nominee, 1978, Scripps-Howard conservation awards. Mem.: Oakland Ad. Club; Eastbay Women's Press Club; S.F. Press Club; Calif. Writers' Club; pub. chmn. No. Calif. Assn. Phi Beta Kappa, 1970-71; No. Calif. Mortar Bd. Theta Sigma Phi, No. Calif. coord. 1970-71; Sigma Delta Chi; Amer. Assn. for Edn. in Journ. 1972; Natl. Council of Environmental Cons. 1972; Natl. Assn. of Sci. Writers, Soc. of Amer. Travel Writers; Soc. of Prof. Journalists; Women in Communications; Natl. Press Photogs. Assn.; S.F. Press Club; Chi Omega; (charter) Jr. Center of Arts and Sci., Oakland; Mills Coll. Mothers Club; Natl. PTA; Audubon Soc.; Internat. Oceanographic Found. and Ocean Scis. Alumni Assn., Univ. of Wash.; dir. bldg. campaign, Montclair Presbyterian Ch. Hobby: oceanography, photog. Rec.: hiking, skiing, horseback riding, swim. Res.: 6161 Castle Dr., Oakland, CA 94611.

WOOD, RICHARD COKE
Author — Historian — Educator
b. Dec. 20, 1905, Cement, Okla.; s. Nathan Alexander and Lenora (Gilmore) Wood; B.A., Univ. of Pac. 1932; M.A. 1934; Ph.D., USC 1950; m. Ethelyn Edson, Lynwood, Calif., Aug. 28, 1936; dau. Colynn Lambert, b. Nov. 20, 1942. Career: H.S. teacher, 1932; Stockton Coll., 1951; Univ. of Pac. 1952; chmn. Div. Soc. Sci., San Joaquin Delta Coll. 1962; dir. Pac. Center for Western Studies, Univ. of Pac. 1968; exec. secty. Conf. of Calif. Hist. Socs.; propr. and co-dir. Old Timers Hist. Museum (in Mother Lode), Murphys, Calif.; Calif. Hist. on TV Stas. 1958, 68, 70, 71. Author: (10 books) incl.: The Calif. Story, (co-author, textbook in H.S. Calif. His.), publ. 1958, 3rd ed. 1969. Mem.: Phi Beta Kappa, 1950---; Phi Delta Kappa; Amer. Rev. Bicentennial of Calif. Comm.; Calif. Hist Landmarks Adv. Com. 1955---; chmn. 1969-71; Sheriff, Stockton Corral of Westerners, 1969. Congregationalist. Res.: 120 W. Elm St., Stockton, CA; Office: Univ. of the Pacific, Stockton, CA 95204.

WOOD, SARA-FAYE
Savings and Loan Company Executive
b. Mar. 9, 1935, Buffalo, N.Y.; d. Barney S. and Reta (Tyser) Gross; Music Maj., UCLA, 1952-54; profl. licenses; Nat. Assn. of Securities Dealer, 1964, Insurance License for State of Calif., 1964; m. Leonard Wood (dec.); children: Beth Loreen Palter, b. 1955; Harry Alan Palter, b. 1959. Career: owner, jewelry bus., 1963-65; stock broker and insurance sales agent, 1965-70; dir. of customer rels., Surety Savings and Loan Assn., 1970-73, asst. v.p., adminstrv. asst. to sr. v.p., 1973-74, v.p., 1974, currently v.p., So. Calif. Savings, br. mgr., Newhall --- (Surety Savings merged with So. Calif. Savings). Pres., Newhall-Saugus-Valencia C. of C., 1978 (1st Woman Pres., in its 55-yr. hist.), dir. 1975---. Bd. dir., Henry Mayo Newhall Hosp. Guild; dir., Canyon Country C. of C.; ofcr., Zonta Internat.; bd. dir., City of Hope Com. on Aging; bd. dir., Sponsor and 1st Advisor, Z Club and Zonta Internat. (H.S. service clubs, founder 1st club in Santa Clarita Valley); m. Interact Club, Rotary Internat. (founder 1st club in Valley); Sigma Alpha Iota, music sor., 1953---. Named Woman of the Year, Santa Clarita Valley, 1977. Hobbies: jewelry designing, poetry. Res.: 16133 Gledhill St., Sepulveda, CA 91343; Office: 26425 Sierra Hwy., Newhall, CA 91321.

WOOD, WAYNE BARRY
Photojournalist
b. June 23, 1958, Oakland; s. Byron and Marylaird "Larry" (Small) Wood; Cert. of Photog., Univ. Calif., 1975; student, Econ. and Bus. Admin., Cal. State Univ., Haywward and Transportation, Calif. State Univ., San Francisco. Career: Bylined Photojournalist, 1971---: with CSM News SYndicate 1973--- (work syndicated worldwide to 25 million readers), specializing in travel, sci., transportation, urban renewal, people profiles, edn. (Work for CSM syndicated in U.S. and Canada on 200 radio stations). Contbg. photojournalist for oceanographic mags.: Sea Frontiers, Internat. Oceanographic Soc., Miami, Fla.; Oceans, Oceanic Soc., Internat., Stamford, Conn.; also for Popular Mechanics, Passenger Train Journ., Mechanix Illustrated, Off Duty (internat. mil. pub.), other popular nat. mags.; Photog. (stringer) for Seattle Times (covers 14 Western States). Awards: Close Scholarship for outstanding junior in econ. and bus.; RR Soc. Awards for R.R. photos, (Calif.) series in CSM and adaptation for TV, 1978. Mem.: Soc. of Profl. Journalists, Nat. Press Photogs. Assn. Presbyterian. Hobbies: natural sci., magic. Res.: 6161 Castle Dr., Oakland, CA 94611.

WOODARD, CLARENCE JAMES
Consultant
b. May 8, 1923, Conde, S. Dak.; s. Wayne H. and Sarah (Halley) Woodard; B.S.M.E., Calif. Inst. of Tech. 1944; m. Patricia Ann Roberts, Jan. 12, 1946; chil.: Charles D., Sarah H., Scott D., Thomas J. Career: Div. gen. mgr. Baldwin-Lima-Hamilton, L.A. 1946-53; v.p.-gen. mgr. The Rucker Co., Oakland, 1953-63, pres. 1963-66, chmn. bd.-chief exec. ofcr. 1965-77. Currently consultant to the bd. and dir. of NL Industries, Inc. (plants in No. Calif., So. Calif., Tex., Okla., Scot., Iran, Singapore). Reg. Professional Mech. Engr., Calif. Lt. (j.g.) USN, PTO and ATO, WW II. Mem.: Chil's Hosp. Found., Oakland, 1967---; Adv. Council Schs. of Bus. Adm., Univ. of Calif., Berkeley, 1969---; natl. dir. Boys Clubs of Amer., chmn. Bay Area Council, 1969---; dir. Oakland Boys' Clubs, past pres.; adv. bd. Met. YMCA, Alameda Co.; gov. S.F. Bay Area Council; Natl. Council of Salk Inst.; A.S.M.E.; Amer. Soc. Tool and Mfg. Engrs.; Inst. Environ. Scis.; Pres.'s Assn. of Amer. Mgmt. Assn.; past chmn. West Coast Exec. Council of Conf. Bd.; Tau Beta Pi; Clubs: Athenian Nile, Oakland; World Trade, St. Francis Yacht, Commonwealth of Calif. Office: P.O.B. 23230, Oakland, CA 94623.

WOODFORD, LEWIS EARL
Bank Official
b. Aug. 16, 1907, Vienna Township, Oh.; s. Wade and Vina M. Woodford; ed. Youngstown Univ. 1929-33; LL.B., Salmon P. Chase Coll.; m. Isabel May Diven, Warren, Oh., July 29, 1933; chil.: Carol Ann, b. 1938; Donald Earl, b. 1942. Career: acct.-auditor, Trumbull Savings and Loan Co. 1928-33; examiner, Div. of Savings and Loan, State of Ohio, 1933-34; exam. div., Fed. Home Loan Bank Bd., Cincinnati, Oh. and L.A., Calif. 1934-55; chief examiner, L.A. ofc. 1953-55; v.p. Home Savings and Loan Co., Youngstown, Oh. 1955-56; v.p.-secty., Fed. Home Loan Bank, S.F. 1956-65; pres. 1965---. Mem.: Ohio State Bar Assn. Presbyterian. Hobby: travel, reading, woodcrafts. Res.: 700 Magnolia St., Menlo Park, CA; Office: 1 Bush St., San Francisco, CA 94104.

WOODS, GURDON
Museum Executive
b. Apr. 15, 1915, Savannah, Ga.; s. Frederick L. and Marian S. Woods; ed. Art Students Leag., N.Y. 1935-39; Brooklyn Mus. Sch., N.Y. 1945-46; (hon.) Dr. of Art, Coll. of S.F. Art Inst. Career: Teacher: Riverdale Country Sch., N.Y.; Town Sch., Lick-Wilmerding Sch., S.F. 1947-55; exec. dir. S.F. Art Inst. 1955-64; dir. Coll. of S.F. Art Inst. 1955-65; prof. Univ. of Calif., Santa Cruz, 1966-74, chmn. Bd. of Stus. in Art, 1966-70; acad. preceptor, Stevenson Coll. 1972-74; dir.-pres. Otis Art Inst. of L.A. Co. 1974-77; asst. dir. L.A. Co. Museum of Natural Hist. 1977---. Sculptor (travel stu., Eng., France, Netherlands, Denmark, Sweden, Portugal, Morocco, Italy, Lebanon, Palestine, Egypt, Cuba, Jamaica, Haiti, Mex., USA 1935-39; Eng., Belgium, France, Ger., Spain, 1970-71); commissions: arch. sculpture (plaster, bronze, marble), 1937-41; landscape-seascape sculptures, 1949-55; large-scale sculpture for IBM Bldg., San Jose, 1956; fountain for Paul Masson Winery, Saratoga, 1958; mural-sized ceramic panels in concrete, IBM 1961; 7 lg-scale concrete reliefs, McGraw-Hill publs., Novato, 1965. 1st Lt., USAF, WW

II. Awards: grants: Chapelbrook Found. 1965-66; Creative Art Inst., Univ. of Calif. 1968; Carnegie Corp. of N.Y. 1968; Medal Cit., NYC 1947; Helen Foster Barnett Prize, Natl. Acad. of Design, 1949; purchase awards, S.F. Art Festival for Aquarium, 1950, 1961; sculpture awards: S.F. Art Inst. Annual, 1952, 54, Richmond Art Center, 1953. Exhibitions: Continuing through 1978. Mem.: dir. No. Calif. Artists Equity Assn. 1949-60; S.F. Art Comm. 1954-56; acq. coms. S.F. Mus. of Art, 1958-61; artists adv. bd. Golden Gateawy Dev., S.F. 1961-65; Santa Cruz Co. Art Comm. 1970-74; College Art Assn., Bohemian Club. Office: 900 Exposition Blvd., Los Angeles, CA 90007.

WOODS, MARION J.
State Official
b. Nov. 28, 1931, Marietta, Ga.; s. Marion J., Sr. and Kathryn Lucille (Robinson) Woods; ed. A.B., Morehouse Coll. 1952; M.A., Atlanta Univ. 1952; m. Bertha Virginia Scott, Griffen, Ga., Oct. 22, 1955; chil.: Lynnis La Verne, b. June 3, 1957; Lisa Virginia, b. June 19, 1961; Leslie Beatrice, b. Mar. 19, 1971. Career: research analyst, California Hwy. Patrol, 1956-57; Dept. of Soc. Welfare, Co. of Sacramento, 1957-58; Dept. of Human Resources, State of Calif. 1958-71; dir. Natl. Cons. Servs., Computing and Software, Inc. 1970-74; pres. Marion J. Woods & Assocs., 1974-75; dir. Calif. Dept. of Benefit Payments, 1975---. Navigator, USAF, Korean War, 1952-56; Maj., USAF Res. Author: professional publs. 1963---. Mem.: NAACP, 1949---; Natl. Statistical Assn. 1957; bd. dirs. Women's Civic Improvement Club, Sacramento, 1964-66; Natl. Head Start Adv. Com. 1965; (charter) bd. dirs. Urban League, Sacramento, 1965; bd. dirs. Natl. Community Del. Council, 1965-66; med. coms. Univ. of Calif. Med. Sch., Davis, 1966; Adult Edn. Adv. Comm., State of Calif. 1968; chmn. Civil Serv. Comm., City of Sacramento, 1969-75; Vocational Edn. Adv. Comm., Calif. 1969; Adv. comm. on Affirmative Action, Calif. State Dept. of Edn. 1975; Basileus, Alpha Rho Chpt.; Omega Phi Phi. Deacon, United Ch. of Christ. Rec.: golf, swim. Res.: 1234 Silver Ridge Way, Sacramento, CA 95831; Office: 744 P St., Sacramento, CA 95814.

WOODS-JONES, DEZIE D.
College Administrator
b. Nov. 11, 1941, Ruston, La.; d. Roy M. and Tena Woods; student, Fresno City Coll., 1957-61; Fresno State Univ., 1961-64; Univ. of Calif., Berkeley, 1971; Cal. State Univ., Hayward, 1976; son Robert E. Jones, Jr., b. Nov. 14, 1971. Career: Asst. dir. Community Affairs, Camp Parks, 1966-67; dir. No. Oakland Devel. Center, Merritt Coll., 1968-71; dir., community serv., No. Peralta Comm. Coll., 1971-74; dir., community serv., Coll. of Alameda, 1974-75; dir., student affairs, 1975---. Recipient: Best Actress Award, Fresno, 1962; Nat. Speaking Champion, 1961, 1962; Outstanding Achievement Award, Howard Univ., 1974; New Oakland Com. Unity Award, 1978. Mem. Alameda Co. Grand Jury, 1976-77. Chmn., legislative com., Western Region Council on Black Am. Affairs; pres., Black Women Organized for Polit. Action; v.p., Oakland Black Caucus; bd. dir., Oakland Citizens Com. for Urban Renewal (OCCUR). Mem. Calif. Comm. & Jr. Coll. Assn. (CCJCA) commn. on community serv. Active mem. Student non-violent coordinating comm. (SNCC), NAACP and CURE, 1955-68. Hobbies: theatre, dance. Home: 10966 Cliffland Ave., Oakland, CA 94605; Office: 555 Atlantic Ave., Alameda, CA 94501.

WOODWARD, ALBERT FLETCHER
Petroleum Consultant
b. Jan. 3, 1913, Whittier, Calif.; s. Ray R. and Ruth (Fletcher) Woodward (prominent civic leader, Whittier; noted artist, Laguna Beach); ed. B.A., Stanford Univ. 1934; M.A., 1936; B.E., USC 1942; m. Margaret Virginia Fulenwider, Yuma, Ariz., Sept. 21, 1940; chil.: John A., b. June 18, 1942. Career: Jr. geologist, Tidewater Assoc. Oil Co. 1936; field geologist-party chief, Venezuela Gulf Oil Co. 1936-39; petroleum engr-geologist, Bush Oil Co., Long Beach, 1940-42; petroleum engineer, manager, exploration and production, Pacific Coast Division, Union Oil Company of Calif. 1949-62; staff engr. 1952-57, chief exploitation engr. 1957-60; cons. Petroleum engr. 1962---. Author: Sansinena Oil Field, Calif. 1958; (co-author) West Montebello Oil Field, 1940. 2nd Lt. through ranks to Maj., U.S. Army Corps of Engrs. (European Theatre 30 mos.), 1942-46, WW II. Awards: Campaign Stars, Normandy, No. Fr., Rhineland, Central Europe. Mem.: Delta Tau Delta, 1932---; Rotary Internat. 1951---; San Marino City Club, 1952---; Petroleum Club, 1960---; Balboa Bay Club. Episcopalian. Res.: 1660 Bedford Rd., San Marino

Calif. 91108; 139 Sierra Vista, Solvang, CA 93463; Office: 712 Fair Oaks Ave., So. Pasadena, CA 91030.

WOODWARD, DANIEL HOLT
Librarian
b. Oct. 17, 1931, Ft. Worth, Tex.; s. Enos Paul and Jessie (Butts) Woodward; B.A., Univ. Colo., 1951, M.A., 1955; Ph.D., Yale Univ., 1958; M.L.S., Catholic Univ. of America, 1969; m. Mary Jane Gessa, 1954, Boulder, Colo.; sons: Jeffrey, b. 1958; Peter, b. 1960. Career: asst., assoc., prof., Mary Washington Coll. and Univ. Va., 1957-72, Librn. 1969-72; Librn., Huntington Library, 1972---. AUS, 1952-54. Mem.: Phi Beta Kappa, Grolier Club, Zamorano Club. Res.: 1540 San Pasqual St., Pasadena, CA 91106; Office: 1151 Oxford Rd., San Marino, CA 91108.

WOOLDRIDGE, DEAN EVERETT
Co-Founder, TRW
b. May 30, 1913, Chickasha, Okla.; s. Auttie Noonan and Irene Amanda (Kerr) Wooldridge; A.B., Univ. of Okla. 1932, M.S. 1933; Ph.D., Calif. Inst. of Tech. 1936; m. Helene Detweiler, Los Angeles, Calif., Sept. 5, 1936; chil.: Dean Edgar, b. Dec. 6, 1939; Anna Lou, b. Oct. 9, 1942; James Allan, b. Dec. 1, 1949; Career: Tech. staff-head, Physical Electronics Research, Bell Tel. Labs., NYC, 1936-46; co-dir., dir., Research and Development Labs., v.p. research and development, Hughes Aircraft Co., Culver City, Calif. 1946-53; pres.-dir., The Ramo-Wooldridge Corp., Los Angeles, Calif. 1953-58; pres.-dir., Thompson Ramo Wooldridge, Inc., L.A. and Cleveland, Oh. 1958-62 (ret.), dir. 1962---; research assoc., Calif. Inst. of Tech. 1962---. Dir. Pac. Semiconductors, Inc.; trustee: Harvey Mudd Coll., John Thomas Dye Sch., City of Hope. Author: The Machinery of the Brain, 1963; The Machinery of Life, 1966; contrib. tech. publs. AAAS-Westinghouse Award for Sci. Writing, 1963. Awards: Cit. of Hon. for outstanding achievements in field of electronic research and development, by Air Force Assn. 1950; Raymond E. Hackett Award for outstanding achievement in field of electronic sci. 1955; Distinguished Serv. Cit., Univ. of Okla., 1960. Mem.: So, Calif. Stanford Parents Com., Orthopaedic Hosp. Bldg. Fund. Com., Univ. of Okla. Research Inst. Alumni Councilor Group, Amer. Assn. for the Advancement of Sci.; fellow, Amer. Physical Soc.; Inst. of Radio Engrs., Amer. Inst. of Physics, Inst. of Aerospace Scis., Amer. Inst. Aeronautics and Astronatuics, Stanford Assocs., So. Calif. Stanford Parents Com., Phi Beta Kappa, Tau Beta Pi, Sigma Xi, Phi Eta Sigma, Eta Kappa Nu, Bel-Air Assn., Bel-Air Country Club, and Cosmos Club, Wash. D.C. Res.: 4545 Via Esperanza, Santa Barbara, CA 93105.

WOOLEY, MARY ALICE
Civic Leader
b. Salt Lake City, Ut.; d. Roland Rich (noted L.A. lawyer) and Mary Alice (Spry) Woolley; granddau. of Gov. William Spry, Ut. 1909-17; great-granddau. of Charles Coulson Rich, early colonizer of San Bernardino, Calif.; ed. B.A., Occidental Coll. 1940; postgard. Univ. of Chicago. Career: Volunteer, Travel Aid Soc., Los Angeles Internat. Airport, 1964---; bd. dirs.-exec. com. 1969---; oil investments exec., 1946---. Mem.: pres., Daus. of Ut. Pioneers, L.A. Co., 1953-56; pres. Toluca Lake Garden Club, 1960; dir. San Fernando Valley Dist., Calif. Garden Clubs, Inc., 1972-74. State Bd. dirs., Calif. Fed. Repub. Women, 1951, 1957-63; del. Repub. Natl. Conv. 1952, alternate 1956; Repub. State Central Com. of Calif. 1952-66; pres. No. Hollywood Repub. Women's Club, 1953-55, 1957-59; Central Co. Rep. for So. Calif. Daus. of Utah Pioneers; secty. L.A. Co. Fed. of Repub. Women. Ch. of Jesus Christ of L.D.S. (Mormon, class teacher, dance dir., speech dir.); mem. State Bd. Calif. Garden Clubs, Inc. Hobby: horse races. Rec.: dancing. Res.: 10315 Woodbridge St., No. Hollywood, CA 91602; Office: 10850 Riverside Dr., No. Hollywood, CA 91602.

WOOTTON, DEVERE GARETH
Plastic Surgeon
b. Feb. 22, 1937, Lehi, Utah; s. Devere and Nora Wootton; B.S., Brigham Young Univ., 1959; M.D., George Washington Univ., 1963; m. Barbara Kadell, Las Vegas, Nev., 1963; children: Tony, b. 1969; Nicky, b. 1972. Career: Pvt. practice in partnership Santa Monica, 1971-76; solo pvt. practice, plastic and reconstructive surgery, Santa Monica, 1976---. Author, one published novel. USAR, 1964-70. Hobby: writing. Rec.: skiing. Res.: 59 Latimer Rd., Santa Monica, CA 90404; Office: 2001 Santa Monica Blvd., Suite 790-W, Santa Monica, CA 90404.

WORTHINGTON, LEONARD ALBERT
Attorney at Law

b. Feb. 4, 1908, San Francisco; s. William Frank and Caroline (Schmelz) Worthington; A.B., Univ. Calif., 1929; LL.B., J.D., Hastings Coll. of the Law, 1932; m. Doris Brown, Apr. 8, 1938, San Francisco. Career: Admitted to Calif. Bar, 1932, admitted to practice before all Calif. Cts., Fed. Cts., U.S. Supreme Ct.; Asst. Atty., State of Calif., Dept. of Pub. Works, 1934; pvt. practice, 1932--- (formerly partner in Worthington, Park, Fields, & Worthington), now Worthington & Worthington, San Francisco. Bd. Dir.: Valley Med. Convalescent Hosp., Hasting's Coll. of the Law (also exec. com.), St. Francis Convalescent Hosp. (pres.) Psychic Research, Inc., Acad. of Parapsychology and Med. (v.p.), Aletheia Psych-Phys. Found., Am. Acad. of Asian Studies, Great Western Univ., A.U.M. Found. (pres.), San Andreas Health Council (1976-77), Transpersonal Inst. Mil.: extensive mil. svc. Presidio of S.F., liaison ofcr. for Gov. Earl Warren. Past Comdr.: Blackstone Post Am. Legion, Mil. Order of World Wars, Legion of Guardsmen. Past Pres.: Gr. Western Univ., Young Voters League of S.F., S.F. Demo. Club, Castro Parlor Native Son of Golden West (past Dist. Dep. Grand Pres.), Demo. Confederation of Calif., Golden Gate Tennis Club, Lawyer's Club of S.F. Mem. San Francisco Bar Assn., serving on Legal Ethics Com. and Medico-Legal Interprofl. Com. Mem.: Alpha Chi Rho, Phi Alpha Delta Am. Trial Lawyer's Assn., Am. Judicature Soc., S.F. Bar Assn., Am. Bar Assn., Lawyer's Club of S.F. Office: 256 Montgomery St., San Francisco, CA 94104.

WRATHER, JACK D., JR.
Business Executive

b. May 24, 1918, Amarillo, Tex.; s. John D. and Mazie (Cogdell) Wrather; B.A., Univ. of Tex. 1939; m. Bonita Granville, Los Angeles, Calif., Feb. 5, 1947; chil.: Molly, Linda, Jack, Christopher. Career: Pres. Evansville Refining Co. 1938-40; pres. Overton Refining Co. 1940-46; pres. Jack Wrather Prodns. (mot. pics.), 1947---; pres. Freedom Prodns., Inc. 1948---; propr. L'Horizon Hotel, Palm Springs, Calif.; co-owner, Twin Lakes Lodge, Las Vegas, Nev. 1950---; pres. Wrather-Alvarez, Inc. and owner, KOTV, Tulsa, Okla. 1951-54; pres. Wrather-Alvarez Broadcasting, Inc.; owner, KFMB, KFMB-TV, San Diego, Calif. 1953; pres. Wrather-Alvarez Hotels, Inc. 1955---; co-owner, Disneyland Hotel; chmn. bd., Muzak Corp.; dir. Transcontinent Television Corp.; pres.-chmn. bd., Wrather Corp.; chmn. bd., Independent television Corp.; pres. Kona Kai Inc.; pres. Balboa Bay Club Inc.; Dir.: Continental Airlines, Neotec Corp., TelePROMOTer Corp.; Corp. for Pub. Broadcasting and Natl. Petroleum Council (apptd. by Pres. Nixon); A.C. Gilbert Co., New Haven, Conn. Maj., USMC, 1942-45, WW II. Mem.: Pres.'s Council, Loyola Univ.; exec. com. Chancellor's Council, Univ. of Texas; bd. dirs. Big Brothers; The Players (N.Y.), Balboa Bay, The Beverly Hills, Racquet, Kona Kai, Dallas Ath., Cipango (Dallas), Cat Key (Bahamas). Res.: 172 Delfern Dr., Los Angeles, CA; Office: 270 N. Canon Dr., Beverly Hills, CA.

WRIGHT, HOWARD WALTER, JR.
Business Executive

b. May 6, 1922, Pasadena, Calif.; s. Howard Walter and Ruth (Shelton) Wright; ed. Henry E. Huntington Grammar Sch. 1936; S. Pasa. H.S. 1940; A.B., Stanford Univ. 1947; m. Jane Miller, San Gabriel, Calif., June 28, 1947; chil.: Howard Candler, b. May 3, 1949; William Grandfield, b. Aug. 8, 1951; Richard Shelton, b. Feb. 28, 1954. Career: Credit mgr., Republic Supply Co. of Calif. 1949-52; plant mgr., Rheem Mfg. Co. 1953, dir. of pub. rels. 1954-56; v.p. Southwestern Engin. Co. 1956-62; pres. SWECO, Inc. 1963---. Dir. Natl. Engin. Sci. Co., Pasadena, 1958-65; dir. Empire Gen. 1965---. Lt. (j.g.) USN and Navigator, USS Thompson, Atlantic and Pac. Theaters (1946), WW II. Mem.: Calif. Club; dir. TransPac. Yacht Club, 1957-59; commodore, L.A. Yacht Club, 1962; Delta Tau Delta (Stanford Univ.). Episcopalian. Hobby: yachting. Res.: 1415 Lomita Dr., Pasadena, CA 91106; Office: 6033 E. Bandini Blvd., Los Angeles, CA 90051.

WRIGHT, WILLIAM ODIE
College and Schools Administrator

b. Apr. 15, 1913, Megargel, Tex.; s. William Odie and Harper E. (Dennis) Wright; A.B., Univ. of Calif. 1934; M.A., USC 1941; m. Lois G. Griffin, Palos Verdes, Calif., Aug. 5, 1939; chil.: Virginia Wilky, Jerry, Barbara. Career: Teacher, Long Beach Polytech. H.S. 1937-42, prin. 1952-55, dep. supt. and dir. personnel,

1955-62; dean, L.B. City Coll. 1946-52; supt. L.B. Unified Sch. Dist. 1962---; supt. Long Beach Community Coll. Dist. 1970---. USAF 1942-46, WW II. Mem.: Calif. Teachers Assn.; NEA; Calif. Edn. Admrs. Assn.; Petroleum Club; Rotary Club of L.B.; Protestant. Hobbies: orchid culture, photog. Res.: 5567 Lonna Linda Dr., Long Beach, CA 90815.

WRIGHT, WILLIAM T.
Architect and Engineer

b. May 9, 1905, San Diego, Calif.; s. William S. and Lucy S. Wright; B.S. (civ. engring.), Univ. of Wash. 1928, M.S. 1929, C.E. 1932; m. Amy Theresa Allsop, Los Angeles, Calif.; son, William David, b. June 21, 1953. Career: Chief structural engr., Kistner, Curtis & Wright, 1933; partner chief engr, Kistner, Wright & Wright arch. and engring. firm 1946---, exec. v.p.-gen. mgr. 1962---. Lt. USN, Civ. Engrs. Corps. Res. 1936, Cap. 1945-46; exec. ofcr., 3rd U.S. Naval Constr. Battalion, Philippine Campaign (1941-46), WW II. Mem.: Tau Beta Pi. Sigma Xi, Phi Beta Kappa, Theta Delta Chi; Jonathan Club, 1946---, treas. 1959-61, pres. 1964-65; L.A. Co. Bldg. Dept. Bd. of Appeals, 1951---; Calif. State Bd. of Registration and Civ. and Profl. Engrs. 1953-61; dir.-v.p.-pres., Structural Engrs. Assn. of So. Calif. 1955-57; dir. Cons. Engrs. Assn. of Calif. 1961-62; adv. com. So. Calif. Chpt., Amer. Concrete Inst.; dir. Downtown Bus. Men's Assn., L.A. 1963; const. Ind. Com., L.A. C. of C.; Fellow, Amer. Soc. of Civ. Engrs.; Amer. Soc. for Testing Materials, Navy League; Seabee Vets of Amer., Town Hall, L.A. Civic Light Opera Assn. Hobby: gardening, music. Rec.: spectator sports, soc. functions. Res.: 4435 Encinas Dr., La Canada, CA; Office: 500 Shatto Pl., Suite 500, Los Angeles, CA 90020.

WRIGLEY, ELIZABETH SPRINGER
Foundation President

b. Oct. 4, 1915, Pittsburgh, Pa.; d. Charles Woodward and Sarah Maria (Roberts) Springer; A.B., Univ. of Pittsburgh, 1935; B.S., Carnegie Inst. of Tech. 1936; m. Oliver Kenneth Wrigley (teacher, author), Wellsburg, W. Va., June 16, 1936. Career: Procedure analyst, U.S. Steel Corp. 1941-43; asst. personnel dir., Vanadium Corp. of Amer. 1943; research asst., The Francis Bacon Found., Inc. 1944-50; exec. secty.-trustee, 1950-53, dir. of research, 1953-54, pres. 1954---; contrib. to bibliographical and lib. journs.; ed. The Skeleton Text of the Shakespeare Plays, publ. by The Francis Bacon Found. 1952. Mem.: The Shakespeare Fellowship, The Renaissance Soc. of Amer.; Chpt. 448, OES, Pa.; White Shrine of Jerusalem, Damascus No. 1, Pa.; Alpha Delta Pi. Presbyterian. Hobby: modern art. Rec.: reading, gardening. Res.: 4805 N. Pal Mal, Temple City, CA; Office: The Francis Bacon Found., Inc., Claremont, CA.

WU, JULIA LI
Educator — Librarian

b. July 2, 1936, Nanking, China (U.S. Cit. 1968); B.A. Natl. Normal Univ., Taiwan, China, 1936; M.A., Grad. Sch. Library Sci., Immaculate Heart Coll., Hollywood, Calif. 1958; M.A. in Edn., 1976, Cal. State Univ. at L.A.; (life) diploma, secondary, community coll. teaching; m. Alfred Yung-Hsiang Wu, 1963; children: Alexander Alfred, Kelly King, Julius Joy. Career: English secty. to Minister of Edn., Taiwan, China, 1957-59; Mandarin Chinese corr., Voice of Amer, USIA 1961---; asst. insts lib., L.A. Co. Library, 1961-63, chil's. dept. dir. Montebello Lib 1963-68, govt. publ. 1968-69, Virgil Jr. H.S., L.A. Unified Sch. Dist. 1969---; commr. Bd. Edn. L.A. City Schs. 1973---; apptd. to Natl. Comm. on Library and Inf. Sci. by Pres. Nixon, 1973; coms. Calif. Assn. Sch. Libraries, 1970-72; faculty, English Dept., L.A. City Coll., 1972---. Mem.: Amer. Lib. Assn.; Amer., Calif., L.A. Assns. Sch. Libs. Res.: 2383 W. Silver Lake Dr., Los Angeles, CA 90039; Office: 1717 K St., N.W., Wash. D.C. 20036.

WUNDERMAN, IRWIN
Inventor

b. Apr. 24, 1931, Brooklyn, N.Y.; s. Leo and Ethel (Rosen) Wunderman; B.E.E., City Coll. of N.Y. 1952; M.S. (E.E.), USC 1956; E.E., Stanford Univ. 1961; Ph.D. (E.E.), 1964; m. Gilda Shirley Margulies, Rye, N.Y., Feb. 9, 1951; chil.: Richard Lloyd, b. Jan. 12, 1952; Lorna Ellen, b. Mar. 23, 1954; Alan Lee, b. Oct. 26, 1960; Career: Research engr., Lockheed Aircraft Corp., Burbank, Calif. 1952-56; lab. sect. leader, Hewlett-Packard Co. 1956-61; mgr. optoelectronic applicators, Hewlett-Packard Assocs. 1961-65, dept. dir., optical instrumentation,

Hewlett-Packard Laboratories, 1965-67; pres., Cintra, Inc. Inventor: 9 patents in solid state or optoelectronic devices and 6 patents pending. Author: (books) Mind Over Mexico, Radiometric and Photometric Measurements; approx. 25 publications on technology and society. Mem.: Chmn. S.F. (subsect.), Inst. Elec. and Electronic Engrs. 1964; del. Santa Clara Co. Confederation Homeowners Assn.; Sigma Xi. Hobbies: art collecting, painting, music. Rec.: swimming, boating, dancing, tennis, touring. Res.: 655 Eunice Ave., Mt. View, CA 94040.

WYCKOFF, CHARLOTTE
School Administrator
b. Oct. 8, 1934, Wichita, Kan.; d. Ray L. and Charlotte Ruth (McLain) Murphy; B.A., Psychol., LaVerne Coll., 1974; M.A., Edn., Cal. State Coll., San Bernardino; Doctorate Student, U.S. Internat. Univ., Special Tng. Workshops and Seminars, San Diego, 1978---; m. Bill Wyckoff, Oct. 15, 1954, Upland; children: Robert, Shirley, Paul, Brandy, Joseph. Career: Collection clerk, West Texas Utilities, Abilene, 1952-59; exec. payroll secty., Van De Kamps Bakeries, 1959-67; founder and dir., Calif. Learning Centers, Cucamonga, 1967---; faculty, Chaffey Community Coll. (mgmt., interpersonal rels., parent-child interaction), 1973---; adminstr., Claremont Collegiate Sch. (coll. prep. grades 7-12), Claremont ---. Lectr., parent groups, service clubs, State Dept. of Welfare. Mem. Chaffey Coll. Advisory Bds.: Mgmt. Dept., Early Childhood Devel., Plan Constrn., Children's Center; mem. advisory bds. Pomona and Bonita High Schs. Mem.: Pre-Sch. Assn.; Nat. Soc. of Autistic Children; Nat. Assn. for Edn. of Young Chil.; Calif. Assn. Neurologically Handicapped Chil.; Assn. Humanistic Psychols.; Am. Personnel and Guidance Assn.; Calif. Assn. of Spec. Schs.; Calif. State Psychol. Assn.; Calif. Assn. Sch. Psychols. & Psychometrists. Rec.: biking, boating, fishing, motorcycling. Office: 8736 Baker Ave., Cucamonga, CA 91730.

WYMAN, WILLARD GORDON
Headmaster, The Thacher School
b. Nov. 12, 1930, Peking, China; s. Gen. Willard Gordon (four-star Gen., U.S. Army) and Ethel (Megginson) Wyman; B.A. English, Colby Coll., 1956; M.A., English, Stanford Univ., 1961, Ph.D., English, 1969; m. Jane Fowler, May 1, 1964, San Francisco; chil.: Willard Gordon, III; Jedediah Fowler. Career: packer, Bar-33 Ranch, 1956; writer, Union Carbide, 1956-58; tchr., Menlo Sch., 1958-60; teaching asst., lectr., asst. desn. spec. asst. to pres., Stanford Univ., 1961-70; writer (Ford Found. Grant), 1970-71; dean of students, asst. prof., Colby Coll., 1971-75; headmaster, The Thacher School, 1976---. Contbr.: edn. newsletters, Change mag. Served USMC, 1948-50; student, Military Acad., West Point, 1950-52. Mem.: Cum Laude Soc., 1977. Hobbies: packing horses, mules, burros; summer packtrips into the high Sierra. Office: The Thacher School, 5025 Thacher Rd., Ojai, CA 93023.

WYNECOOP, JOSEPH A.
Information Manager, Jet Propulsion Lab.
b. Mar. 22, 1919, Reardan, Washington; s. Joseph Roger and Charlotte Louise (Plews) Wynecoop; B.A., Eastern Wash. Univ., 1946; B.S.L., Glendale Univ. Coll. of Law, 1971; m. Clarice Meigs, Oct. 31, 1944, Oakland; chil.: Madeleine (Blowers), b. Nov. 25, 1946; Gertrude Louise, b. Mar. 30, 1949. Career: tchr., Oakland, 1946-47; with Calif. Inst. of Tech., Jet Propulsion Lab., 1968---: training director, 1968-71; advisory com. for minority affairs, 1970-76; affirmative action program rep., 1970-78; adminstrv. spec., 1971-74; mgr., TIDD Support, 1974-76; mgr., Information Support, 1976---. V.P., dir., All Am. Indian Celebration Corp., 1969-70; Gov.'s Calif. Indian Assistance Project, rep. 1969-74; Am. Indian Enterprise, v.p., 1969-75; United Indian Devel. Assn., v.p., 1969-75; Am. Indian Scholarship Fund (TRY), dir., v.p., 1969-75; Nat. Am. Indian Council, 1971; Pacific Northwest Indian Center, fin. commissioner, 1971-73; Pasadena Child Health Found., dir. 1976, secty. 1977; Nat. Congress of Am. Indians, bd. dir., Indian Scholarship Com., 1977---. Served to Lt. Col., USAF (ret.), 1942-68; decorated: Outstanding Unit Award; medal for Humane Action; Jt. Chiefs of Staff Commend. Medal; AF commendation medal; Alexander the Great Medal (Greece). Mem.: Ret. Officers Assn.; Disabled Am. Vets.; Officers Benefit Assn.; Air Force Assn.; Spec. Libraries Assn.; Assn. for Computing Machinery; So. Calif. Am. Indian Aerospace Assn., charter mem. 1977---; Assn. Information Mgrs., charter mem., 1978---; Theta Alpha Phi, 1942; Lynn Athletic Club, London (hon.), 1950---; Masonic Lodge No. 13, Colo. Springs, 1956---; Scottish Rite, Pasadena; Al Malaikah Temple, L.A.; Sumola Shrine Club, dir. 1978;

Descanso Gardens Guild, 1979---. Democrat; state organizing com., 24th Congressional Dist. Rep. for Pres. elec. 1972; U.S. Senatorial Club, 1979---. Congregational. Hobbies: antique coll., photog. Rec.: pvt. pilot, equestrian, golf. Home: 3832 Hillway Dr., Glendale, CA 91208; Office: 4800 Oak Grove Dr., Pasadena, CA 91103.

WYNNE, HEYWOOD HUGH
Architect
b. Dec. 15, 1921, Atlanta, Ga.; s. Heywood Hughes and Grace (Lancaster) Wynne; grandson of Heywood Hughes Wynne, Justice of the Peace, Pulaski Co., Ga. and mem. Ga. House of Reprs. 1898-1900; B.Arch., USC 1951; m. Leila Lenardson, Burbank, Calif., Aug. 1952. (div. 1964); chil.: Jeffrey Heywood, b. Apr. 18, 1954; Debra Leila, b. Feb. 25, 1959. Career: Job capt., H.L. Gogerty firm (F.A.I.A.), Los Angeles 1951-54; proj. arch. A.C. Martin and Assocs. (F.A.I.A.), Los Angeles, 1954-58; staff arch., Greschner Investment Corp., Santa Ana, 1959-64; est. own arch. firm, Santa Ana, 1964---. Cits. Com. on City Planning, Santa Ana, 1963. Pres., Cross & Cockade, Soc. of WW I Aero Historians, editor of Cross & Cockade Journal, 1960-62. Staff Sgt., USAAF, 1942-46, WW II. Mem.: A.I.A., Sons of Confederate Vets., Orange Co. Pipe Band; pres. Soc. of WW I Aero Historians, 1959-60, 1964-65; Alpha Rho Chi. Republican. Baptist. Hobbies: music, photog. Rec.: swimming, reading, travel. Res.: 14601 Berkshire Pl., Tustin, CA 92680; Office: 1230 N. Bluegum St., Anaheim, CA 92805.

WYSHAK, LILLIAN WORTHING
Attorney at Law
b. July 19, 1928, NYC; d. Emil Michael and Stefanie (Dvorak) Worthing; ed. Alhambra H.S., 1945; B.S. (hons.), UCLA 1948; J.D., USC 1956; m. Robert H. Wyshak, So. Pasadena, Calif., July 16, 1961; chil.: Karen Roberta Stanley, b. Sept. 4, 1948; Robin Marie, b. Aug. 20, 1962; Susan Elizabeth, b. Jan. 13, 1964; Jeanne Grace, b. Feb. 28, 1965; Patricia Lynn, b. May 19, 1966. Career: Assoc. with Ira N. Frisbee and Co., PACs, 1948-52; partner, Worthing and Stanley, pub. acts. 1952-56; atty. at law: Boyle, Bissell and Atwill firm, 1956-57; Parker, Milliken and Kohlmeier firm, 1957-58; tax div., U.S. Atty., So. Dist. of Calif., L.A. 1958-62; tax atty.-partner, Wyshak and Wyshak, attys. at law, 1963---; admitted to practice, U.S. Supreme Ct., Wash. D.C. 1967---. Mem.: (Life) Calif. Scholarship Fed., Beta Gamma Sigma. Beverly Hills Community Presbyterian Ch. Res.: Beverly Hills, CA; Office: 9255 Sunset Blvd., Los Angeles, CA 90069.

WYSHAK, ROBERT HABEEB
Attorney at Law
b. Dec. 23, 1923, Boston, Mass.; s. Habeeb and Hafiza (Ameer) Wyshak; ed. Boston Latin Sch.; B.A. (hons.), Harvard Coll. 1945; LL.B., Harvard Law Sch. 1947; m. Lillian Worthing, So. Pasadena, Calif., July 16, 1961; chil.: Robin Marine, b. Aug. 20, 1962; Susan Elizabeth, b. Jan. 13, 1964; Jeanne Grace, B. Feb. 28, 1965; Patricia Lynn, b. May 19, 1966. Career: Tax atty.; asst. U.S. Atty., Chief, tax div., So. Dist. of Calif., L.A.; partner, Wyshak and Wyshak law firm, spec. in tax law, 1963---; admitted to practice, Supreme Ct. of U.S., Wash. D.C., 1967---. Mem.: pres. Lions Club, Boston, 1950; pres. Exch. Club of Boston, 1952; pres. Westwood Village Bar Assn. 1966-67. Beverly Hills Community Presbyterian Ch. Res.: Beverly Hills, CA; Office: Suite 720, 9255 Sunset Blvd., Los Angeles, CA 90069.

Y

YANCEY, LEONARD MARION
Electronics Engineer
b. Mar. 5, 1933, DeLeon Springs, Fla.; s. Leon and Ola (Wade) Yancey; student DeVry Tech. Ins., B.S., Univ. Ala., 1961; m. Ruth Bishop, May 23, 1953, Montreal, Quebec, Can.; children: Celia Ruth, b. 1954; Peter, b. 1961; Leonard, Jr., b. 1963. Career: Design engr. Lockheed Aircraft Co., 1961-62; Douglas Aircraft Co., Santa Monica, 1962-63, ITT Gilfillian Corp., 1963-64, Chrysler Corp., Space Div., Huntsville, Ala., 1964-66, Lockheed Missile & Space Co., Sunnyvale, Calif. 1966-68; electronics engr. Naval Ocean Systems Center, San Diego, 1968---. Patentee in field. USAF, 1951-55. Mem.: IEEE, Toastmasters Club. Res.: 6415 Salizar Ct., San Diego, CA 92111; Office: Naval Ocean Systems Center, San Diego, CA 92152.

YANG, HSUN-TIAO
Engineering Consultant — Lecturer
b. May 19, 1924, Hangchow, China; s. Kuang-Hang and Sue-Hsia (Huang) Yang; M.D., Univ. of Wash., 1950; Ph.D., Calif. Inst. of Tech., 1955; m. Jieh-Tze Shen, June 8, 1965, Taipei, China; chil.: C. Terrence, b. Mar. 29, 1966; C. Anders, b. Oct. 26, 1969; C. Jennifer, b. Nov. 28, 1970. Career: dept. of Aeronautics, Cal. Tech., 1955-56; Inst. for Fluid Dynamics, Univ. Maryland, 1956-68; dept. Applied Mechanics, summer 1957; Engnring. Center, USC, 1958-63; dept. mechan. engring., 1963-64, dept. aerospace engring., 1964---; Fulbright-Hays lectr., 1964-65; Nat. Sci. Found. Grant Prof. applied math., 1970-71; depts. of Aerospace and Mech. Engring., Univ. of Texas at Arlington, 1977-78; Consultant: Nat. Advisory Com. for Aeronautics, Langley Aeronautical Lab., 1957; Hughes Aircraft Co., 1962; 1966-68; Aero-jet, Litton System, 1964; Jet Propulsion Lab., Calif. Inst. of Tech., 1968-69; General Dynamics, 1969; Naval Weapon Center, 1972-74; R & D Associates, 1975; Mobil Oil Corp., 1976-78; Dir., Univ. Consults., Inc., 1972---. Frequent contbr. tech journs. Faculty advisor Am. Inst. Aeronautics and Astronautics, 1972-75; mem., Soc. Sigma Xi. Home: 8262 Seaport Dr., Huntington Beach, CA 92646; Office: USC, L.A., CA 90007.

YANKE, ELIZA BELLE
Physician
b. July 4, 1939, Collins, Ky.; B.A., Pikeville, Ky., 1961; M.D., Univ. Louisville, 1965; m. August Frank Yanke, July 2, 1966, Oakland; children: Christopher, b. 1967; Elizabeth, b. 1969; Patrick, b. 1970. Career: Intern, Highland Alameda County Hosp., Oakland, 1965-66; Assoc., Kaiser Permanente Med. Group, Hayward, 1966-70; partner, Kaiser Permanente Med. Group, Walnut Creek, 1970---, staff, Kaiser Permanente Hosp., Walnut Creek. Mem. Am. Coll. of Emergency Physicians. Catholic. Rec.: travel. Office: 1425 S. Main St., Walnut Creek, CA 94596.

YAP, ARLIENE O.
Pediatrician
b. Aug. 6, 1938, Philippines; d. Dr. Miguel and Adoracion (Oquendo) Yap; M.D., Far Eastern Univ., 1964; m. Hugo Rosas, July 24, 1971, Los Angeles; dau. Grace, b. 1972. Career: internship, Calif. Hosp. Med. Center, 1965-66, Children's Hosp. of L.A., 1967; Queen of Angels Hosp., 1967-69; pvt. practice, pediatrics, L.A., ---; consulting staff: Hollywood Presbyterian Med. Center, Queen of Angels Hosp., Calif. Med. Center; Mem.: AMA, CMA; L.A. Co. Med. Assn.; L.A. Co. Women's Assn.; L.A. Pediatric Soc.; bd. dir., Philippine Med. Soc.; secty.-treas., Far Eastern Alumni Found.; mem. Filipino-Am. Soc. Hobby: piano. Rec.: travel. Home: 3056 Arrowhead Dr., Lake Hollywood Estate, Hollywood, CA 90068; Office: Yap Medical Clinic, 1737 W. Beverly Blvd., Los Angeles, CA 90026.

YEEND, NANCY NEAL
Realtor
b. Mar. 18. 1943, Gloversville, N.Y.; B.S., Univ. of Wis., 1965; m. Warren Yeend, June 6, 1964, Madison, Wis.; dau. Erica, b. 1972. Career: Geologist, U.S. Geol. Survey, 1965-66; real estate agent, 1968---, opened own real estate bus., Nancy Yeend Realtor, Palo Alto, 1975---. Mem. Calif. Assn. of Realtors, dir. 1976, 77; Palo Alto Bd. of Realtors, pres. 1977, named 1975 Realtor of the Year. Office: 210 California Ave., Palo Alto, CA 94306.

YORTY, SAMUEL WILLIAM
Former Mayor, City of Los Angeles
b. Oct. 1, 1909, Lincoln, Nebr.; s. Frank Patrick and Johanna (Egan) Yorty; ed. Southwestern Univ.; USC; LL.B., La Salle Univ.; m. Betty Hensel, Los Angeles, Calif., Dec. 1, 1938; son: William Egan, b. July 6, 1946; Career: atty. at law, pvt. practice, L.A.; elected to Calif. Legislature, 1936, re-elected, 1938; elected to State Legislature, 1949; elected to Congress of U.S. 1950, re-elected, 1952. Dem. nominee, U.S. Senate 1954; elected Mayor of Los Angeles, 1961-73. Capt., 5th A.F., 6th Army, New Guinea, and Philippines (1942-45), WW II. Christ Ch. Unity. Hobby: tennis, swimming. Res.: Studio City, CA.

YOUNG, CHARLES EDWARD
University Chancellor
b. Dec. 30, 1931, San Bernardino, Calif.; s. Clayton Charles and Eula May (Walters) Young; A.B. (hons.), Univ. of Calif., Riverside, 1955; M.A., UCLA 1957; Ph.D. 1960; m. Sue Daugherty, 1950; chil.: Charles E. Jr., b. Sept. 7, 1955; Elizabeth Susan, b. Feb. 2,

1961. Career: Amer. Polit. Sci. Assn. Cong. Fellowship in U.S. Senate, 1958-59; adm. analyst, ofc. of the pres., Univ. of Calif., 1959-60; asst. prof. polit. sci., Univ. of Calif., Davis, 1960; asst. to chancellor, UCLA 1960-62; asst. prof. polit. sci. 1960-66, asst. chancellor, 1962-63, v-chancellor, adm. 1963-68, assoc. prof. 1966-69, chancellor, UCLA 1968---, prof. polit. sci. 1969---. Cons.: Peace Corps, 1961-62; NBC on Election Coverage, 1964; Ford Found. on Latin Amer. Activities, 1964-66. Sgt., Personnel Servs. supv., USAF in U.S. and Japan, 1951-52. Contrib. to professional, edn. and polit. journs., 1958---. Awards: Haynes Found. Scholarship, 1954-55; Charles Fletcher Scott Fellowship, 1958-59; Westwood Jr. Chamber of Comm. Young Man of Yr. Award, 1962; (hon.) Dr. of Humane Letters, Univ. of Judaism, L.A. 1969. Mem.: v.p. Young Musicians Found.; ITT Internat. Fellowship Adv. Comm.; Nat. Com. on United States-China Rels., Inc.; dir.: L.A. World Affairs Council; Greek Theatre/Huntington Hartford Assoc.; UMF Systems, Inc.; Directors Capital Fund, Inc.; Intel Corp.; Century Bank; Carlsberg Capital Corp.; Financial Corp. of Amer.; Bel-Air Country Club. Res.: 10570 Sunset Blvd., Los Angeles, 90024. Office: 405 Hilgard Ave., Los Angeles, CA 90024.

YOUNG, DOROTHY ANNE SMITH
Psychologist
b. July 16, 1937, NYC; d. John W. and Ann G. Smith; B.S., (Leopold Schepp Scholar) Columbia Univ. Coll. of Physicians & Surgs., 1959; M.A., USC, 1961; Ph.D., (HEW trainee) Calif. Sch. of Profl. Psychol., 1976; children: Catherine, b. 1963; John and Patricia, b. 1964; Joanne, b. 1966. Career: Intern in psychol., Child Guidance Clinic, Counseling Center for Handicapped, Crisis Services of Fresno Co. Mental Health Dept., Central Valley Regional Center, Fresno, 1974-76; Intern in occupational therapy, Rehabilitation Center, Stamford, Conn., Children's Hosp., Buffalo, N.Y. VA Hosp., Bronx, N.Y., 1959-60; Occ. Therapist, Kings Park State Hosp., N.Y., 1959-60; Hd. Occ. Therapist, Queen of Angels Hosp., L.A. 1960-62; Asst. Prof., Cal. State Univ., San Jose, 1961-62; Dir. Psychiatric O.T. Fresno Community Hosp., 1965-68; Instr., Cal. State Univ., Fresno, 1970-72; Chief O.T., VA Hosp., Fresno, 1972-73; pvt. practice, Cons., Psych. O.T. 1969---; instr., Fresno City Coll., 1970-76; Psychologist, Central Valley Regional Center, Fresno, 1976---. Mem.: Am., Calif. State Psychol. Assns.; Am., Central Calif. (founding pres.) Occ. Therapy Assns.; Fresno Community Council, apptd. mem. San Joaquin Valley Health Consortium; Cal State Univ. Fresno Newman Center; AAUW; Fresno City Coll. Faculty Wives, past pres. Res.: 2608 E. Fedora Ave., Fresno, CA 93726; Office: 4747 No. First St., Suite 195, Fresno, CA 93726.

YOUNG, JOHN ALAN
President, Hewlett-Packard Company
b. Apr. 24, 1932, Nampa, Idaho; B.S.E.E., Ore. State Univ., 1953; M.B.A., Stanford Univ., 1958; m. Rosemary Murray, Aug. 1, 1954, Klamath Falls, Ore.; children: Gregory, b. 1957; Peter, b. 1959; Diana, b. 1960. Career: Ofcr., AF Research & Devel. Command, Holloman Air Devel. Center, N.M., 1954-56; mktg. planner, Hewlett-Packard Co., Palo Alto, 1958, gen. mgr., Microwave Div., 1963, co. vice pres. in charge Electronic Products Group, 1968, exec. v.p. and dir., 1974, pres. and chief operating officer, 1977---. Dir.: Wells Fargo Bank, Wells Fargo & Co., Dillingham Corp. Trustee, Stanford Univ., mem. Advisory Coms. on Computer Sci. and Grad. Sch. of Bus., fund-raising chmn., nat. corps. for Stanford, mem. advisory council, SRI Internat.; co-chmn., Stanford Mid-Penin. Urban Coalition. Mem.: Am. Mgmt. Assn., WEMA (Western Electronics Mfrs. Assn.). Hobby: fishing. Res.: 526 Center Dr., Palo Alto, CA 94301; Office: 1501 Page Mill Rd., Palo Alto, CA 94304.

YOUNG, JOHN PARKE
Economist
b. Oct. 24, 1895, Los Angeles; s. William Stewart and Adele (Nichols) Young; A.B., Occidental Coll., Hon. LL.D., 1967, M.A., Columbia Univ., 1919; Ph.D., Princeton Univ., 1922; m. Florence Hunsel (dec. 1949); children: Richard Parke, Roger Hursel, Catherine (Selleck); m. 2d. Marie Louise Smith, 1952, Valparaiso, Chile. Career: Instr. Princeton Univ., 1922-23; dir. U.S. Senate Foreign Currency and Exchange Investigation 1923-25; chmn. Dept. of Economics, Occidental Coll. 1926-42; mem. Commn. Fin. Experts to Govt. of China, (in China), 1928-29; Econ. Adviser to Govt. of Chile 1952; adviser and chief, Div. of Internat. Fin., U.S. Dept. of State,

1942-64; Adviser Central American Common Mkt. on Monetary Union 1964-65; mem. U.S. Del. (to San Francisco Conf.) creating the UN, 1945, and to Bretton Woods Conf. creating Internat. Monteary Fund and World Bank, 1944; pres. Investment Counsel firm and Mutual Fund, 1933-42. Author several books incl. widely used text, The International Economy, numerous articles. Mem.: Phi Beta Kappa, Cosmos Club (Wash. D.C.), Twilight Club (Pasadena), Phi Gamma Delta. Res.: 1303 Wentworth Ave., Pasadena, CA 91106.

YOUNG, JOSEPH LOUIS
Artist
b. Nov. 27, 1919, Pittsburg; s. Louis and Jennie (Eger) Young; grad. Westminster Coll., New Wilmington, Pa., 1941; D.Litt., 1960; Edwin Austin Abbey mural painting scholar, 1949; grad. Boston Mus. Sch. Fine Arts, 1951; Albert H. Whitin traveling fellow, 1951; Am. Acad. in Rome, 1951-52; m. Millicant Goldstein, June 19, 1949; children: Leslie Sybil, Cecily Julie. Newspaperman, Pitts. and NYC, 1941-43; lectr. Tufts Coll., 1949; painting instr., Boston Mus. Sch., 1950; Idylwild Arts Found., 1959; Brandeis Camp Inst., 1962---; founder, dir. Joseph Young Mosaic Workshop, 1953---; founding chmn. dept. archtl arts Brooks Santa Barbara (Calif.) Sch. Fine Arts, 19569-75; head mus. exhibits Bowers Mus., Santa Ana, Calif., 1977; head visual arts CETA program City of Los Angeles, 1978---; true fresco, oil and mosaic mural commns. in Boston, Chicago, Pitts., Los Angeles; survey govt. sponsored mural painting programs, 1951; one man show Pitts. Arts and Crafts Center, 1950, Falk-Raboff Gallery (Los Angeles) 1953; ten year retrospective exhbn. archtl. art work Desert Mus., Palm Springs, Calif., 1963; Calif. council AIA Fine Arts Architecture Exhibn., 1964; Nat. Gold Medal Exhbn. of N.Y. Archtl. League, 1951; work reproduced in numerous books, mags., newspapers throughout the world; invited to submit designs for Nebr. State Capitol murals; paintings and mosaics in numerous pvt. collections; executed mosaic murals Los Angeles Police Facilities Bldg., 1955; Don Bosco Tech. High Sch., 1956; Temple Emanuel, 1957; Southland Shopping Center, 1958; Out Lady of Lourdes Ch., 1969; Cameo residence, Beverly Hills, Calif., 1961; Santa Barbara Stock Exchange, 1960; St. Martins Ch., La Mesa, Calif., 1966; stained glass windows, liturgical art program Congregation Beth Sholom, San Francisco, 1966; West Apse of Nat. Shrine of Immaculate Conception, Washington, 1966; mosaic arch. Eden Meml. Park, San Fernando, Calif., 1960; commd. to execute mural Los Angeles County Hall of Records, Shalom Meml. Park, Chicago, B.V.M. Presentation Ch., Midland, Pa., 1961; Hollenbeck Police Sta., Los Angeles, 1963; Beth Emet Temple, Anaheim, Calif., 1963; Temple Sinai, Glendale, Calif., 1963; Sinai Temple, Los Angeles, 1963; Valley Beth Israel, Sun Valley, Calif., 1964; Beth Tikvah, Westchester, Calif., 1964; Belmont High Sch., Los Angeles, 1972; commd. to design and execute 14 bas-relief concrete-mosaic murals for exterior of Math. Scis. Bldg. at UCLA; did liturgical art rpograms for Congreation B'nai B'rith, Santa Barbara, Temple Beth Torah, Alhambra; Temple Beth Ami, West Covina; Temple Menorah, Redondo Beach; and Temple Solael in Canoga Park (all Calif.), 1969; concrete bas reliefs South Gate County Pub. Library, 1973; mosaics for St. Mary of Angels, Hollywood, Calif., 1973; Triforium polyphonoptic, kinetic tower Los Angeles Mall, 1969-75; organized internat. sculpture competition for city of Huntington Beach, Calif., 1974; multimedia presentations for 400th anniversary Michelangelo, Italian Trade Commn., Casa de Maria, Santa Barbara, Hancock Coll., Santa Maria, Los Angeles County Mus. Art, Univ. Calif. at Los Angeles and Irvine; art cons. Allied Arts Commn., City of Huntington Beach, 1973-74; restoration of mosaics from Greek and Roman periods and Della Robbia sculpture, 1972-73. Huntington Hartford Found. fellow, 1952-53. Served with USAAF, 1943-46. Recipient Nat. Army Arts contest award, 1945. Fellow Internat. Inst. Arts and Letters (life); mem. Nat. Soc. Mural Painters (nat. v.p. 1969---); Artsits Equity Assn. (pres. So. Calif. chpt. 1956, nat. v.p. 1960); Calif. Confedn. Arts (founding pres. 1975-76). Author: A Course in Making Mosaics, 1957; Mosaics, Principles and Practice, 1963; also articles in profl. journs. Pub. mural painting bibliography, 1946. Assoc. founding editor Creative Crafts mag., 1960-64. Work featured 16mm documentary film, The World of Mosaic. Invited prin. speaker at nat. convs. AIA, Am. Craftsmen Council, 4th Congress, IAPA, 7th Nat. Sculpture Conf., Council of Am., Univ. Kans.; lectr. Rome, Venice, Florence (as guest Italian Govt. 1959). Res.: 7917½ W. Norton Ave., Los Angeles, CA 90046; Studio: 1434 S. Spaulding Ave., Los Angeles, CA 90019.

YOUNG, MATT NORVEL, JR.
Chancellor, Pepperdine University
b. Oct. 5, 1915, Nashville, Tenn.; s. Matt Norvel and Ruby (Morrow) Young; B.A., Abilene Christian Coll., 1936; M.A., Vanderbilt Univ., 1937; Ph.D., George Peabody Coll., 1943; L.H.D., Calif. Coll. Med., 1964; m. Helen Mattox, Aug. 31, 1939; children: Emily (Lemley), Matt III, Marilyn, Sara (Jackson). Career: Minister, College Ch. of Christ, David Lipscomb Coll., 1941-43; Broadway Ch. of Chrst, Lubbock, Tex., 1944-57; pres., Pepperdine Univ., 1957-71, Chancellor, 1971---. Regent, Pepperdine Univ.; dir.: Forest Lawn Mem. Park, Pub. Savins Life Insurance Co., U.S. Life Savings & Loan; Bd. Govs. L.A. County Mus. Natural Hist.; bd. dir. Alcoholism Council L.A. Co-founder 20th Century Christian mag., 1938, ed. & pub. 1945-76; editor: Power for Today mag., 1955---; author: History of Christian Colleges, 1949; The Church is Building, 1956; co-ed.: Preachers of Today, 1952, Vol. II, 1959, Vol. III 1964, Vol. IV 1970; Churches of Today, Vol. I 1960, Vol. II 1969; Poison Stress Is a Killer, 1978. Co-founder: Lubbock Christian Coll., 1955, Lubbock Children's Home, 1953. Recipient George Washington medal, Freedoms Found., 1962. Mem.: L.A. C. of C.; Phi Delta Kappa; Rotarian; Bohemian Club; California Club. Res.: 23200 Pacific Coast Hwy., Malibu, CA 90265; Office: Pepperdine Univ., Malibu, CA 90265.

YOUNG, ROBERT EARL
Company President
b. Oct. 14, 1930, Stockton, Calif.; s. Vincent Arlo and Margaret Louise Young; ed. B.S. (civil engring) Coll. of Pac., Stockton, 1954; m. Mary Mayotte, Sacramento, Calif., July 11, 1959; chil.: Sydney Elizabeth, b. Apr. 8, 1963; Julie Katherine, b. Apr. 7, 1966. Career: Calif. Div. of Hwy. 1952-55; Fiberboard Paper Prod. Co. 1955-56; Wilsey, Ham & Blair, 1956-57; H.C. Holman Cons. Engrs. 1957-60; pres. The Spink Corp. 1960---. Calif. Natl. Guard, 1952-58. Mem.: exec. bd. BSA; bd. dirs. Sacramento C. of C.; pres.-bd. dirs. Sacramento Engrs. Club; pres. Omega Phi Alpha, Coll. of Pacific. Hobby: photog. Rec.: golf, skiing. Res.: 2840 Latham Dr., Sacramento, CA; Office: 720 F St., Sacramento, CA 95811.

YOUNG, WILLIAM GOULD
Professor of Chemistry
b. July 30, 1902, Colorado Springs, Colo.; s. Henry A. and Mary Ella (Salisbury) Young; A.B., Colo. Coll. 1924, M.A. 1925, D.Sc. 1962, Ph.D., Calif. Inst. of Tech. 1929; (hon.) LL'D., Univ. of Pacific 1966; m. Helen Graybeal, June 4, 1926. Career: Research asst., Coastal Lab., Carnegie Inst. of Wash. 1925-27; fellow, Natl. ncil, Stanford Univ. 1929-30; instr. UCLA 1930-31, asst. prof. 1931-38, assoc. prof. 1938-43; chmn. Dept. of Chem. 1940-48, prof. of chem. 1943---, dean, Div. of Physical Scis. 1946-57, faculty research lecturer, 1947, v-chancellor of the univ. 1957-70. Lecturer, Welch Found. (chem.), 1962. Civ. cons., Natl. Def. Research Com. (1941-45), WW II. Awards: receipeint, Richard C. Tolman Medal, Amer. Chem. Soc. 1961, Award in Chm. Edn. 1962. Mem.: councilor, Amer. Chem. Soc. 1939-60, dist. dir. 1952-60; chmn. Ad Hoc. Com. to Study Tech. Training, 1964-66; Natl. Acad. of Scis., Sigma Xi, Kappa Sigma, Alpha Chi Sigma, Delta Upsilon, Phi Lambda Upsilon. Res.: 5036 Avenida Dell Sol, Laguna Hills, CA 92653.

YOUNGER, EVELLE J.
Former Attorney General of California
b. June 19, 1918, Nebr.; s. Harry C. Younger, Pasa.; ed. Midwest, Nebr. pub. schs.; A.B., LL.B., Nebr. Univ.; grad. work in criminology, Northwestern Law Sch., Chicago, Ill.; m. Mildred Eberhard (noted lecturer, radio and TV commentator), July 3, 1942; son: Eric, b. Aug. 8, 1943. Career: Spec. agt., FBI, permanent assignments, NYC Field Ofc. and supv., dep. city atty., trial dept., Criminal Div., L.A. 1946-47; city prosecutor, Pasa. 1947-50; est. pvt. law practice (gen.), Aug. 1, 1950-Oct. 1, 1953; judge, Municipal Ct., L.A. Judicial Dist., Sept. 28, 1953-58; elected judge, Superior Court, 1958-64; District Attorney, L.A. County, 1964-70; elected Atty. Gen. of Calif. 1970-78; partner, Buchalter, Nemer, Fields & Christie, 1978---. Chmn. Pres. Nixon's Task Force on Crime and Law Enforcement, 1968-69. Instr. (criminal law), Southwestern Univ. Law Sch., L.A. Author: Criminal Law Handbook (for police ofcr. training), publ. by Calif. State Dept. of Edn.; Criminal Practice in the Municipal Court, publ. L.A. Bar Bulletin, Oct. 1953; co-author: Judge and Prosecutor in Traffic Court, publ. by Amer. Bar Assn. and

Northwestern Univ. 1951; Capital Punishment, a Sharp Medicine, publ. Amer. Bar Assn. Journ., Feb. 1956; McNaughton Must Go, publ Calif. State Bar Journ. 1956; Mil. Intelligence, U.S. Army 4th Army, Presidio of S.F. and Wash., D.C.; chief, Far East and S.E. Asia sect., Counter Intelligence br., OSS; serv. overseas in CBI Theatre; Intelligence Sect., Brit. 15th Indian Army Corps for Burma Campaign, participated in landing Akyab and Ramree Is. (1942-46), WW II; recalled to active duty, USAF, Feb. 1951-July 1952; acting chief, Plans and Inspection br.-chief, Counter Intelligence Div., 18th Dist. Ofc. Spec. Investigators, Hdqrs., USAF; Col., USAF Res. 1962; Brig. Gen., USAFR 1966; Maj. Gen. 1971. Mem.: Amer. Legion, (past) chmn. Soc. of Former FBI Agents; exec. com., L.A. Peace Ofcrs. Assn.; fellow, Amer. Coll. of Trial Lawyers, 1950; President:s Hwy Safety Conf. 1950, 52; Calif. State and L.A. Bar Assns.; L.A. Lawyers Club; LAAC; (past) bd. dirs., Greater L.A. Chpt., Natl. Safety Council, State Bar Com. on Criminal Law and Procedure; (past) chmn. Traffic and Magistrate Cts. Com.-Council, Criminal Law Sect., Amer. Bar Assn.; chmn. Pasa. Com. for Edn. on Alcoholism; bd. dirs.: Red Cross Home Serv. Com., Family Servs., Camp Fire Girls, Inc. and Legal Aid; Masonic Lodge, Pasa. Consistory, Al Malaikah Shrine; pres. Peace Ofcrs. Shrine Club; Elks No. 99; past pres., Alpha Tau Omega Alumni Assn.; dir. Trojan Club. Republican. Episcopalian. Res.: 2461 Chislehurst Dr., Los Angeles, CA 90027; Office: State Bldg., Los Angeles, CA 90012.

YORK, HERBERT FRANK
  Physicist
b. Nov. 24, 1921, Rochester, N.Y.; s. Herbert F. and Nellie (Lang) York; ed. A.B., Univ. of Rochester, 1942; M.S. 1943; Ph.D., Univ. of Calif., Berkeley, 1949; m. Sybil Dunford, Berkeley, Calif., Sept. 28, 1947; chil.: Cynthia, Ranchel, David Winters. Career: Physicist, Univ. of Calif. Radiation Lab. 1943-44; dir. Lawrence Radiation Lab., Livermore, 1954-58; dir. def. research and engring., U.S. Dept. of Def. 1958-61; chancellor, Univ. of Calif., San Diego, 1961-64; prof. of physics, 1965-69, dean of grad. studies, 1969-70; acting chancellor, 1970---; Pres. Science Advisory Com. 1957-58, 1964-67; trustee, Aerospace Corp. 1962---; gen. adv. com., U.S. Arms Control & Disarmament Agcy. 1963-69; trustee, Inst. for Def. Analysis, 1965, 1967---. Author: (books) Race to Oblivion, 1969; Arms Control Readings, 1943; articles in professional journs. Awards: E.O. Lawrence Award, Atomic Energy Comm. 1962. Res.: 6110 Camino de la Costa, La Jolla, CA; Office: University of Calif. San Diego, La Jolla, CA 92037.

Z

ZACHRISSON, CARL UDDO, JR.
  Professor
b. Dec. 4, 1940, San Francisco; s. Carl U. and Erma (Luce) Zachrisson; B.A., Stanford Univ., 1962; Grad., Inst. of Internat. Studies, Univ. of Geneva, 1965; D.Phil., Oxford Univ., 1972; m. Adele Hall, 1971, NYC; sons: Carl Frederick, b. 1975; Christopher Dawes, b. 1977. Career: Dir. of Edn. Abroad, Pomona Coll. and Scripps Coll., 1973---; asst. prof. govt. and internat. rels., Claremont Grad. Sch., 1972---; asst. prof., internat. studies, Pomona Coll., 1974---; asst. prof. polit. studies, Pitzer Coll., 1970-74; instr. 1967-70; lectr., U.S. Information Serv., West & Equatorial Africa, 1972. Dir., Council on Internat. Ednl. Exchange, N.Y., 1978---. V.P. edn., So. Calif. Div., UN Assn. 1976---; pres., UN Assn., Pomona Valley chpt., 1974-76; v-chmn. Western Reg. Leadership Conf. on Emerging World Order, 1977; Dir. Calif. Council for UN Univ., 1975---. Mem.: University Club of S.F.; Oxford Union Soc.; Am. Soc. of Internat. Law; Am. Polit. Sci. Assn.; ACLU; AAUP. Episcopal. Rec.: sailing, skiing. Res.: 4047 Olive Point Pl., Claremont, CA 91711; Office: Pomona Coll., Claremont, CA 91711.

ZAHM, ELLSWORTH EDWARD
  Newspaper Editor
b. Dec. 15, 1930, Waco, Tex.; s. Ellsworth L.E. and Eugenia Mullens Zahm; B.S., Journalism, Univ. Kan., 1952. Career: Trainee, Copley Newspapers, the San Diego Union, 1956-57: Copy editor, asst. telegraph editor, asst. news ed., 1957-69; News Editor, 1969-71; asst. mng. editor, 1971-72; asst. to the Editor, 1972-75; News Editor, 1976---. AUS, 1954-56. Mem.:

AP Mng. Editors Assn. Res.: 232 Rosemont St., La Jolla, CA 92037; Office: 350 Camino de la Reina, San Diego, CA 92112.

ZAISER, SALLY SOLEMMA VANN
  Book Company Executive
b. Jan. 18, 1917, Birmingham, Ala.; d. Carl Waldo and Einnan (Herndon) Vann; student, Birmingham Southern Coll., 1933-36; B.A. bus. Admn., Akron Coll. of Business, 1937; m. Foster E. Zaiser, Nov. 11, 1939, Akron, Ohio. Career: accountant, A Simionato, S.F., 1956-55; head acctg. dept., Richard T. Clarke Co., S.F., 1965-66; acct., John Howell-Books, S.F., 1966-72; corporate secty.-treas., 1972---. Secty., Great Eastern Mines, Inc., Albuquerque, 1969---. Braille transcriber, Kansas City, Mo., 1941-45; vol. ARC hospital program, Sao Paulo, Brazil, 1952. Mem.: Book Club of Calif.; Soc. Lit. & the Arts; Calif. Hist. Soc.; Theta Upsilon. Republican. Episcopalian. Home: 355 Serrano Dr., Apt. 4-C, S.F., CA 94132; Office: 434 Post St., S.F., CA 94102.

ZAPATA, CARMEN
  Actress — Producer — Educator
b. July 15, 1927, NYC, dau. Julio and Ramona; ed. Washington Irvine H.S. Career: On Broadway Stage in Oklahoma, 1946, and Bloomer Girl, Carnival, Bells Are Ringing, Bye,Bye Birdie, Guys and Dolls, No Strings, Showboat, Can Can, Take Me Along, Stop the World I Wanna Get Off, many others; road company in Annie; films, Calif., 1967--- incl. Sol Madrid, Hail Hero, The Boatniks, Pete and Tillie, A Home Of Our Own, I Will! For Now!, Billie Jack Goes to Washington, Rabbit Test; TV appearances, 1967--- incl. Marcus Welby, Owen Marshall, Medical Center, Adam 12, Mod Squad, The Rookies, The Bold Ones, Bonanza, Treasury Agent, Streets of S.F., Jig Saw, Love American Style, MacMillan and Wife, Switch, Charlie's Angels, Baretta, Chico and the Man, etc.; starred own series, Viva Valdez, ABC-TV, 1976; many appearances in TV movies, commls., star of PBS children's TV show VIIIa Alegre, 4th Season; Emmy nominee, 1970 (for Storefront Lawyer), 1974 (for Med. Center), recnt. Nosotros Award for Best Actress, 1971; Drama-Logue Critics Award as best actress (Blood Wedding) 1977. Dir. Bilingual Arts Proj., Mex.-Am. Opportunity Found., L.A. Co., 1978---; tchr. drama, Acad. of Stage and Cinema Arts and East L.A. Coll.; founder-pres., Bilingual Found. of the Arts, 1976--- (brings the Hispanic culture to Hispanic audience in L.A. area). Bd. dir., Screen Actors Guild, 1972-77, chmn. Minorities Com. 1974-76; bd. dir. The Neighborhood Youth Assn.; trustee, Nat. Repertory Theatre Found., 1976---. Awardee: E.L.A. Coll. Pres. 1974, Latin Am. Civic Assn. 1975; Chicana Serv. Action Center 1977; L.A. Human Rels. Commn., 1977; Latin Businessmen's Assn. 1977; Mexican Am. Found. 1978. Roman Catholic. Hobby: community involvement. Office: Bilingual Found. of the Arts, 427 N. Ave. 19, Los Angeles, CA 90031.

ZAPHIROPOULOS, RENN
  Company President
b. Sept. 20, 1926, Port Said, Egypt; s. Leonidas and Galatea Zaphiropoulos; B.S., eng. physics, LeHigh Univ., 1947; M.S. physics, 1949; m. Marie Kaufmann, Oct. 14, 1970, San Jose; children: Eve, b. 1956; Gale, b. 1959. Career: with Phico Corp., Phila., 1949-51; Chromatic Lab., N.Y. and Calif. 1951-56; Varian Assocs., Palo Alto, 1956-69; pres., Versatec (subs. Xerox Corp.), Santa Clara, 1969---. Able Seaman Interpreter, Greek Navy, 1943-45. Mem. St. Francis Yacht Club, S.F. Hobbies: cooking, painting, music. Res.: 14474 Sobey Rd., Saratoga, CA 95040; Office: 2805 Bowers Ave., Santa Clara, CA 95051.

ZAREM, ABE M.
  Inventor
b. Mar. 7, 1917, Chicago, Ill.; s. I.H. and Lea (Kaufman) Zarem; B.S., (E.E.), Calif. Inst. Tech. 1939; M.S. 1940; Ph.D., 1944 (hon.) LL.D. 1967; m. Esther Meriam Moskovitz, Chicago, Ill., Oct. 4, 1941; chil.: Janet Ruth, b. 1945; David Michael, b. 1948; Mark Charles, b. 1951. Career: cons. engr. 1938---; instr., Calif. Inst. of Tech. 1939-44; civ. with Manhattan Dist. 1944; R&D engr., Allis Chalmers Mfg. Co., Wis. 1944-45; chief, elec. sect., Research Dept., U.S. Naval Ord. Test Sta 1945-48; mgr. L.A. Div., Stanford Research Inst. 1948-55; visiting prof. 1955---; pres. Electro-Optical Systems, Inc. 1955-67; chmn. bd. 1967-69; sr. v.p., Xerox Corp. 1967-69; dir. corporate development, 1958-69, mgmt.-engring. cons. 1969---. Inventor: Automatic Oscillograph with a Memory, Navy's Zarem Camera; Author: numerous technical and semi-technical publications, subjs. ranging from physics,

elec. engin. to atmospheric pollution, area development, and impact of technology. Awards: The Outstanding Young Elec. Engr. of U.S. by Eta Kappa Nu, 1948; one of America's Ten Outstanding Young Men by U.S. Chamber of Comm. for civic and professional achievements, 1950. Mem.: Amer. Chem. Soc., Amer. Inst. of Aerons. and Astronautics, Amer. Inst. of Physics, Amer. Ord. Assn., Amer. Phys. Soc., Instrument Soc. of Amer., Optical Soc. of Amer., Armed Forces Communications and Electronics Assn., (Assoc.) Assn. of U.S. Army, N.Y. Acad. of Scis., Soc. for INformation Display, Soc. of Photo-Optical Instrumentation Engrs.; (Assoc.) Soc. of Mot. Pic. and TV Engrs. (sci.) Solar Energy Soc.; fellow, Inst. of Elec. and Electronics Engrs; Delta Chpt., Eta Kappa Nu, 1937. Office: P.O.B. 525, Beverly Hills, CA 90213.

ZATHAS, JAMES
Real Estate Appraiser
b. July 2, 1927, Tripolis, Greece; s. Speros and Stavroula Zathas; B.S., acctg.; M.S. acctg., economics; Univ. of Athens, San Diego State Univ.; m. Kiki Skoubis, Oct. 1958, Chicago, Ill.; chil.: Voula, b. Feb. 1966; John, b. Feb. 1967. Career: with S.D. Federal Svgs. & Loan, S.D., 1964---: sr. auditor, 1964-71, appraisal dept. 1971, presently sr. commercial appraiser, asst. v.p. ---. Calif. licensed real estate broker, 1969---; MAI, Inst. of Real Estate Appraisers, 1978---; SRPA, Soc. of Real Estate Appraisers, 1974---, past pres. Greek Orthodox ch.; treas., exec. officer, parish council; co-founder, annual Greek charity bazaar. Hobby: racquetball. Home: 4150 Rochester Rd., San Diego, CA 92116; Office: 600 "B" St., San Diego, CA 92183.

ZAVARIN, EUGENE
Forest Products Chemist
b. Feb. 21, 1924, Sombor, Yugoslavia; s. Alexey and Iya (Shepkin) Zavarin; GG Grandson, M.S. Shepkin, founder of Russian realistic theatre; B.S. (equiv.) Univ. Gottingen, Germany, 1950; Ph.D. orgn. chem., Univ. Calif. Berkeley, 1954; m. Valentina Kusubov, July 15, San Francisco; children: Xenia, b. 1959; Sergei, b. 1962; Michael, b. 1965; Nina, b. 1968; Mavrikiy, b. 1970. Career: with Univ. of Calif., Berkeley and U.C. Forest Products Lab., 1952---: tchg. asst. 1952-53, sr. lab. technician 1952-54, asst. specialist 1954-56, asst. forest products chemist 1956-62, assoc. forest products chemist & lectr. 1968-75, Forest Products Chemist & Lecturer, 1968-75, Forest Prod. Chem. & Prof. of Forestry, 1975---. Contbr. articles to profl. publs. Christian Orthodox. Hobbies: Photog., collecting edible mushrooms. Res.: 280 Edgehill Way, San Francisco, CA; Office: 1301 South 46th St., Richmond, CA 94804.

ZEITLIN, HERBERT
College President
b. New York, N.Y.; s. Leonard and Martha Soff Zeitlin; B.S., N.Y. Univ., 1947; M.A., 1949; Ed.D., Stanford Univ., 1956; m. Eugenia Pawlik, July 3, 1949; Bellmore, N.Y.; chil.: Mark Clyde, b. Aug. 22, 1950; Joyce Therese (Harris), b. Aug. 23, 1954; Ann Victoria, b. Jan. 17, 1958; Clare Katherine, b. June 21, 1959. Career: tchr., counselor, dir. of testing. Phoenix Union H.S. and Coll. Dist., 1949-59; Dean of Evening Div., Antelope Valley Coll., 1957-59; prin., Antelope Valley Hi. Sch., 1959-62; dean of instrn., Southwestern Coll., 1962-64; pres., supt., Triton Coll., 1964-76; pres., West L.A. Coll., 1976---. Pres., Ariz. Vocational Assn., 1953; pres., Ariz. Vocational Guidance Assn., 1952. Served USAF, 1943-46, Mem.: Phi Delta Pi, treas., 1943; Maywood Rotary Club, pres. 1971-72. Hobbies: home movies. Rec.: swimming. Home: 20124 Phaeton Dr., Woodland Hills, CA 91364; Office: West L.A. Coll., 4800 Freshman Dr., Culver City, CA 90230.

ZEITLIN, JACOB ISRAEL
Bookseller
b. Nov. 4, 1902, Racine, Wis.; s. Louis and Bessie Fanny (Hurwitz) Zeitlin; m. Josephine Adriana Ver Brugge, Oct. 28, 1939, Los Angeles; children: Judith (Armstrong), David John, Adriana Brower, Joel Loeb. Career: Began bookselling, 1925---; founder with wife, firm Zeitlin & Ver Brugge, Los Angeles, 1928---; Lectr. many universities; contbr. articles in Reader's Digest, Saturday Review, others. Mem.: American Antiquarian Soc.; Am. Antiquarian Booksellers Assn., past pres. So. Calif. chpt.; Calif. Historical Assn., Award recipient. Democrat. Hobby: engravings of Peter Brueghel. Res.: 907 N. Alazed St., Los Angeles, CA 90069; Office: 815 N. La Cienega Blvd., Los Angeles, CA 90069.

ZELDITCH, MORRIS, JR.
Sociologist
b. Feb. 29, 1928, Pittsburgh, Pa.; s. Morris and Anne Hankin Zelditch; B.A., Oberlin Coll., 1951; Ph.D., Harvard Univ., 1955; m. Bernice Osmola, June 12, 1950, Oberlin, Oh.; children: Miriam Lea, b. 1952; Steven Morris, b. 1953. Career: Sociologist, N.Y. State Psychiatric Inst., 1958-61; instr./asst. prof. of Sociology, Columbia Univ., 1955-60; assoc./prof. of Sociology, Stanford Univ., 1960---, chmn. dept. 1964-68; fellow, Inst. for Advanced Study in the Behavioral Sciences, 1968-69. Editor, American Sociological Rev., 1975-78. Coauthor: Basic Course in Statistics, 1959, 3d ed. 1975; Types of Formalization in Small-Group Research, 1962; Sociological Theories in Progress, vol. 1, 1966, vol. 2, 1972; Status Characteristics and Social Interaction, 1977. AUS, 1945-47. Res.: 936 Lathrop Pl., Stanford, CA 94305; Office: Dept. of Sociology, Stanford University, Stanford, CA 94305.

ZENTMYER, GEORGE AUBREY, JR.
Plant Pathologist
b. Aug. 9, 1913, North Platte, Nebr.; s. George and Mary (Strahorn) Zentmyer; A.B., UCLA, 1935, M.S., 1936, Ph.D., 1938; m. Dorothy Dudley, May 24, 1941, New Haven, Conn.; children: Elizabeth (Mrs. Alfred C. Dossa), b. 1943; Jane (Mrs. Castle G.E. Fernald), b. 1946; Susan Dudley, b. 1954. Career: Asst. forest pathologist U.S. Dept. Agr., San Francisco, 1937-40; asst. pathologist Conn. Agrl. Expt. Sta., New Haven, 1940-44; asst. plant pathologist UC Riverside, 1944-62, prof. plant pathology, 1962---, chmn. dept. 1968-73. Cons. NSF, Trust Ty. of Pacific Islands, 1964, 66, Commonwealth of Australia Forest and Timber Bur., 1968, AID, Ghana and Nigeria, 1969; Dir. Riverside YMCA, 1949-58; pres. Town and Gown Orgn., Riverside, 1964; mem. NRC, 1968-73. Guggenheim fellow, Australia, 1964-65; NATO sr. sci. fellow, Eng., 1971; recipient award of honor Calif. Avocado Soc., 1954. NSF research grantee 1963, 68, 71, 74. Fellow Am. Phytopathol. Soc. (pres. 1966, pres. Pacific div. 1955), AAAS (pres. Pacific div. 1974-75); mem. Mycol. Soc. Am.; Am. Inst. Biol. Scis.; Bot. Soc. Am., Brit. Mycol. Soc., Australian Plant Pathology Soc., Philippine Phytopath. Soc., Indian Phytopath. Soc., Assn. Tropical Biology, Internat. Soc. Plant Pathology (councilor 1973---), Sigma Xi. Author: Plant Disease Development and Control, 1968; Recent Advances in Pest Control, 1957; Plant Pathology, an Advanced Treatise, 1977; Assoc. editor Annual Rev. of Phytopathology, 1971---, Journ. Phytopathology, 1951-54. Major Research Interest: The genus Phytophthora — biology, physiology, pathogenicity; diseases of avocado, macadamia, cacao, other tropical and subtropical crops; root diseases, soil fungicides. Congregationalist, Deacon, Moderator. Hobbies: photog., stamps. Rec.: fishing. Res.: 3892 Chapman Pl., Riverside, CA 92506; Office: Univ. of Calif., Riverside, CA 92521.

ZIFERSTEIN, ISIDORE
Psychiatrist
b. Aug. 10, 1909, Russia; s. Samuel David and Anna (Russler) Ziferstein; cousins, Joseph Shprintzak, First Speaker of Israeli Knesset (Parliament) and Moses, Yig'al, Amos, Deborah Mosenson, noted Israeli writers; A.B., Columbia Coll., NYC, 1931; M.D., Coll. of Physicians & Surgeons, Columbia Univ., 1935; Ph.D., So. Calif. Psychoanalytic Inst., 1977; m. Barbara Shapiro, June 20, 1935, Dutchess Co., N.Y.; children: D. Gail, b. 1938; J. Dan, b. 1940. Career: internship, Jewish Hosp., Brooklyn, 1935-37; staff psychiat., Mt. Pleasant State Hosp., Iowa, and Psychiat. Cons., Iowa State Pen., Ft. Madison, 1937-41; Chief Psychiat. Resident, Psychiat. Inst. of Grasslands Hosp., N.Y., 1941-44; Pvt. practice psychiat. and psychoanal. 1944---. Staff Psychiat., Community Med. Center, L.A. 1947-51; att. Psychiat.: Los Angeles Psychiat. Servs. 1954-63, UCLA Hosp. 1970---, Cedars-Sinai Med. Center 1975---; mem. faculty: So. Calif. Psychoanalytic Inst. 1951, USC 1960-64, Assoc. Clin. Prof. of Psychiat. Emeritus, UCLA, 1970-77; tng. inst., L.A. Group Psychotherapy Soc. 1970; Research Projects: Mt. Sinai Hosp. 1955-65, postgrad. Center for Metnal Health, N.Y. 1962, New Haven 1963-65, transcultural psychiat. NIMH, 1969-71. Dir.: Viewer sponsored TV found., 1967-72, ACLU 1962-78, Nat. Assn. for Better Broadcasting 1962; Trustee, So. Calif. Psychoanalytic Inst. 1957-61; bd. mem. SANE, 1955-74; pres. L.A. Group Psychotherapy Soc. 1962-63. Contbr. numerous articles on group dynamics, group psychotherapy, transcultural and social psychiatry, in med. and non-medical journals. Recipient Pulitzer Scholarship 1927; Phi Beta Kappa 1930, Peace Award, Women for Legislative Action 1962, Pawlowski Peace Prize 1974.

Life fellow, Am. Psychiatric Assn., fellow, Acad. of Psychoanalysis; Life fellow, AAAS; fellow, Internat. Assn. of Social psychiat.; mem. Am. and Internat. Psychoan. Assns.; Fedn. Am. Scientists; AMA; Assn. for Advance. of Psychotherapy; World Fedn. Mental Health; N.Y. Acad. of Sci.; Am. Acad. Polit. and Social Sci. Rel. Judaism. Hobbies: Pets, peace edn. Res.: 1819 N. Curson Ave., L.A., CA 90046.

ZONKER, PATRICIA
Writer
b. Huntington Park, Calif.; d. Alfred and Mildred (Niquette) Mathewson; sister of Fr. Robert Mathewson, S.J., pres. and principal, Bellarmine Coll. Prep.; sister of Charles M., stock broker, N.Y. Stock Exchange; cousin to Christy Mathewson, Baseball Hall of Fame; student, L.A. City Coll.; m. Thomas Zonker, Oct. 14, 1950; chil.: Laurie (Pevytoe); Jenny (Ashcroft); Daniel; Gregory. Career: secty. and asst. to editorial dir., Trade Journal, 1947-48; co-owner, Aladdin Employment Agency, South Gate, Calif., 1948-55; writer, 1966---; also co-owner w/husband, butane equip. distributorship. Author: Murdercycles, Nelson-Hall, 1979 (inspired by a hitch in a hosp. orthopedic ward); publs. incl.: Good Housekeeping, Teen, The Rotarian, Lady's Circle, The Christian Home (Prot.), St. Anthony Messenger (Cath.), The National

Jewish Monthly. Mem.: Internat. P.E.N.; Writers Workshop West (past secty.-treas.); Writers Club of Whittier (past secty.). Hobby: travels. Home: 11532 Samoline Ave., Downey, CA 90241.

ZUMBRUN, RONALD A.
President, Pacific Legal Foundation
b. Dec. 12, 1934, Oak Park, Ill.; s. Arthur Raymond and Jean (Crandall) Zumbrun; B.A., Pomona Coll. 1957; LL.B. Univ. Calif. Berkeley, Boalt Sch. of Law, 1961; m. Mary Ann Hartley, July 14, 1957, Riverside; children: Kevin Ronald, b. 1960; Richard Douglas, b. 1962; Heidi Ann, b. 1965. Career: Sr. Trial Atty., Calif. State Dept. of Public Works, 1961-71; Dep. Dir. Legal Affairs, Calif. State Dept. of Social Welfare, 1971-73; Spl. Counsel U.S. Dept. of HEW, 1973; legal arch. of Calif. welfare reform 1972-73; founding Legal Dir., Pacific Legal Found., Sacramento, 1973, pres., 1976---. Awarded formal recognition for achievements in legislative representation and handling of major State of Calif. litigation, Calif. Legis. 1968. Capt. USAR. Mem.: Rotary Club of Sacto., Phi Alpha Delta, Episcopalian, Vestryman. Hobbies: boating, photog. Office: 455 Capitol Mall, Suite 465, Sacramento, CA 95814.

Addendum To 12th Edition

THESE LATEST BIOGRAPHICAL PROFILES BECAUSE OF PRODUCTION SCHEDULES COULD NOT BE INCLUDED UNDER THE ALPHABETICAL HEADINGS:

GLOVER, ALAN HILARY
Locomotive Engineer
b. Sept. 20, 1946, San Francisco; s. Howard Raymond and Marie Josephine (Markham) Glover; grad., Alameda H.S., So. Pacific Co. Engine Service Tng. Center; m. Bonnie Ann McSharry, Feb. 14, 1971, Alameda, Calif.; children: Valerie Ann, b. Feb. 4, 1974; Stephanie Marie, b. July 18, 1976. Career: Locomotive Fireman, AT&SF Ry., 1964; Pacific Tel. & Tel. Co., 1965-66; Crash crew firefighter, Alameda Naval Air Sta., 1966; Freight Car Insp., Western Pacific RR, 1967-69; Locomotive Engr., So. Pacific Co., 1969---. Special interest: restoration of personal residence (one of the finest examples of Italianate style homes in Alameda) to its original decor, circa 1871; articles featuring the house have appeared in several publs. Electronics Technician, USNR, 1966-72. Hobbies: antique autos, photog., model railroading. Rec.: tennis, weight lifting. Res.: 1630 Central Ave., Alameda, CA 94501.

GOGARTY, HENRY A.
Tourist Board Executive
b. July 24, 1924, Castlegregory, Co. Kerry, Ireland; s. James and Ellen (Crowley) Gogarty; nephew, His Excellency Most Rev. Henry A. Gogarty, Bishop of Kilimanjaro (dec.); student, Rockwell Coll., Ireland, 1938-45, Boston Sch. of Accountancy, 1949-51; m. Winifred Flynn, Oct. 12, 1954, St. Patrick's Cathedral, NY; children: James Gerard, b. Aug. 12, 1955; Sean Patrick, b. Mar. 5, 1958; Mary Patricia, b. Jan. 20, 1959; Donal Joseph, b. Mar. 24, 1960; Catherine Ann, b. June 15, 1963. Career: Research Asst., Jonathan Marsh Co., 1949-50; Asst., KLM Royal Dutch Airlines, 1951-53; with Irish Tourist Bd., 1953---: Regional Dir., NY, Chicago, San Francisco, now Regional Mgr. West Coast ---. Mem.: Foreign Govt. Tourist Office Assn. pres. 1979; SKAL; Soc. of Am. Travel Writers; Irish Literary and Historical Soc.; Irish Cultural Center of S.F.; Hibernian Newman Club; Foreign Travel Club of S.F.; Foreign Travel Club of L.A.; Bon Vivants; United Irish Socs.; Am. Soc. of Travel Agents; S.F. Press Club; S.F. Publ. Rels. Round Table; Green Hills Country Club; Irish Center of S.F.; Commonwealth Club of No. Calif. Hobby: bridge. Res.: 1457 Bernal Ave., Burlingame, CA 94010; Office: 681 Market St., San Francisco, CA 94105.

GUALTIERI, VINCENT
Urologist
b. Jan. 5, 1934, Reggio Calabria, Italy; s. Joseph and Victoria Gualtieri; A.B., UCLA, 1955; M.D., Calif. Coll. of Med., 1962; m. Gina Coggi, May 19, 1963, Berkeley; children: Lisa, b. Aug. 13, 1964; Joseph, b. Feb. 12, 1967; Stephen, b. Nov. 22, 1968. Career: Urologist, Ross-Loos, 1966-68; pvt. practice of Urology, Sherman Oaks, 1968---; Clin. Instr., Urology, Calif. Coll. Med., UCI, 1966-68. Fellow, Am. Coll. of Surgeons, 1973---; mem. Los Angeles Urological Soc., 1966---; mem. Am. Urological Assn., 1975---. USAFR, 1953-61. Res.: 16444 Garvin Dr., Encino, CA; Office: 4955 Van Nuys Blvd., Sherman Oaks, CA 91403.

HAMMOND, GEORGE DENMAN
Associate Dean, USC School of Medicine
b. Feb. 5, 1923, Atlanta, Ga.; s. Percy and Elizabeth (Denman) Hammond; B.A., Univ. N.C., student Univ. N.C. Sch. of Med. 1944-46; M.D., Univ. Penna. Sch. of Med., 1947-48; m. Florence Williams, Mar. 30, 1946, Wash. D.C.; children: Lane Elizabeth (Clark), b. 1949; Christopher Scott, b. 1951; Bruce Benedict, b. 1953; Kirk Denman, b. 1955. Career: Pediatric Residency, Children's Hosp. of Phila., 1950, 1952-53; Flight Surgeon, USN, 1950-52; Pediatric Residency, Univ. Calif., San Francisco, 1953-54, Research Fellow, Research Assoc., Instr. of Pediatrics, 1954-56; Asst. Prof. of Pediatrics, UC, San Francisco Sch. of Med., 1956-57; Asst. Prof. of Ped., USC Sch. of Med. and Assoc. Hematologist, Children's Hosp., L.A., 1957-60; Assoc. Prof. of Ped., USC Sch. of Med., 1960-65; Head Div. of Hematology/Oncology and Dir., Hematology Res. Labs., Childrens Hosp. L.A., 1960-71; Assoc. Dean, USC Sch. of Med., 1971---; also Dir., Los Angeles Co.-USC Comprehensive Cancer Center and Kenneth Norris, Jr. Cancer Research Inst. of USC, 1971---. Chmn., Children's Cancer Study Group, 1968---; editorial bd.: The American Journal of Physiology, 1970, The Journal of Applied Physiology, 1970; mem. National Cancer Advisory Bd., 1974---. Publs. incl. numerous manuscripts, abstracts, books and book chpts. Active duty, USNR, 1944-45, 1950-52; U.S. Naval Flight Surgeon, 1950; Comdr., M.C. USNR (ret.). Protestant. Hobby: photog. Rec.: skiing, tennis, swimming. Res.: 851 S. El Molino, Pasadena, CA 91106; Office: 2025 Zonal Ave., L.A., CA 90033.